Politics in America

2012

112th Congress

By CQ Roll Call Staff • John Bicknell and David Meyers, Editors

CQ
ROLL
CALL

Keith White, Executive Vice President and Managing Director, CQ/Capitol Advantage
Mike Mills, Editorial Director and Senior Vice President
Mark Walters, Senior Vice President, Advertising
John A. Jenkins, President and Publisher, CQ Press, a division of SAGE

Published by CQ-Roll Call, Inc.
77 K Street N.E.
8th Floor
Washington, DC 20002
202-650-6500; toll-free, 1-800-432-2250
www.cqrollcall.com

The paper used in this publication exceeds the requirements of the American National Standard for Information Sciences — Permanence of Paper for Printed Library Materials, ANSI Z39.48-1992.

Printed and bound in the United States of America

11 10 09 08 07 5 4 3 2 1

ISBN 978-1-60871-799-6 (cloth)   ISBN 978-1-60871-800-9 (paper)

ISSN 1064-6809

The Library of Congress catalogued an earlier edition of this title as follows:

Congressional Quarterly's Politics in America: 1994, the 103rd
Congress / by CQ's political staff: Phil Duncan, Editor

p.   cm.

Includes index.

1. United States. Congress — Biography. 2. United States. Congress — Committees. 3. United States. Congress — Election districts — Handbooks, manuals, etc. I. Duncan, Phil. II. Congressional Quarterly Inc. III. Title: Politics in America.
JK1010.C67 1993   328.73'073'45'0202

EDITORS
John Bicknell, David Meyers

DEPUTY EDITOR
Amanda H. Allen

MANAGING EDITOR
Amanda Grace Johnson

CONTRIBUTING EDITORS
George Cahlink, Chris White

SENIOR WRITERS
Stacey Skotzko, Shawn Zeller

POLITICAL ANALYSIS
John Cranford (vote studies), Ryan Kelly (vote studies), Bob Benenson (redistricting)

CONTRIBUTING WRITERS
Kate Ackley, Rebecca Adams, Ambreen Ali, Joanna Anderson, Melissa Attias,
Rachael Bade, Jennifer Bendery, Susan Benkelman, Clea Benson, Nik Bonovich,
Jessica Brady, Jonathan Broder, Elizabeth Brotherton, Matthew Burch, Emily Cadei,
Charlene Carter, David Clarke, Doug Clendenin, Chuck Conlon, Kristin Coyner,
Steven T. Dennis, John M. Donnelly, David M. Drucker, Emma Dumain, Theo Emery,
Edward Epstein, Jessica Estepa, Emily Ethridge, Sam Feldman, Ellyn Ferguson,
Brian Friel, Matt Fuller, Lauren Gardner, Clayton Hanson, David Hawkings, Emily Heil,
Kathleen Hunter, Elham Khatami, Anne L. Kim, Matt Korade, Geof Koss, Paul M. Krawzak,
Jackie Kucinich, Mike LePage, Niels Lesniewski, Adam Levin, Jacqueline Linnane,
Rob Margetta, Will Matthews, John McArdle, Alison McSherry, Tait Militana, Tricia Miller,
Mike Mills, Scott Montgomery, Eugene Mulero, Matthew Murray, Eric Naing,
Daniel Newhauser, Jane Norman, Frank Oliveri, Alan K. Ota, Anna Palmer,
Christina Parisi, Daniel Peake, Steve Peoples, Keith Perine, Emily Pierce, Emily Poe,
John Reichard, Daphne Retter, Benett Roth, Richard Rubin, Joseph J. Schatz,
Jennifer Scholtes, Annie Shuppy, Paul Singer, Steven Sloan, Lauren Smith,
Megan Sowder-Staley, John Stanton, Melanie Starkey, Tim Starks, Gabe Starosta,
Seth Stern, Frances Symes, Michael Teitelbaum, Robert Tomkin, Neda Toloui-Semnani,
Kyle Trygstad, Greg Vadala, Ilyse Veron, Ben Weyl, Chris Wright, Kathryn A. Wolfe,
Jennifer Yachnin, Emily Yehle, Kerry Young, Melanie Zanona

SENIOR RESEARCHER
Ryan Kelly

RESEARCHERS
Reniqua Allen, Nell Benton, Rachel Bloom, Kris Broughton, Debra Bruno,
Alecia Burke, Mengfei Chen, Sam Feldman, Matt Fuller, Alex Knott, Kaitlin Kovach,
Sarah Lawrence, Kailyn McGillicuddy, Christina Parisi, Brandon Payne,
Peter Rocco, Dan Rogers, Michael Ruhl, Gail Sullivan, Frances Symes,
Michael Teitelbaum, Sarah Vanderbilt, Carolyn West, Tim Yoder

SENIOR COPY EDITORS
Arwen Bicknell, Victoria Forlini, Aleksandra Robinson

COPY EDITORS
Keith Barnes, Leah Carliner, Neal J. Conway, Christina Kapler, Julie Klavens,
Matt Korade, Melinda W. Nahmias, Adrienne Owens, Jamisha Purdy,
Jennifer Rubio, Sara Smith, Charlie Southwell, Joe Warminsky, Chris Wright

PHOTOGRAPHY
Bill Clark, Scott J. Ferrell, Douglas Graham, Tom Williams

LAYOUT AND DESIGN
Jamey Fry (cover), John Irons,
Kimberly Hallock and SpatiaLogic Mapping – Charlottesville, Va. (district maps)

INDEX
Nell Benton

PUBLISHING SOFTWARE
Mark Logic – San Carlos, Calif., Erin Miller

IT SUPPORT
Ron Brodmann, John Hanna, David Harris

PIA ONLINE EDITION
CQ Press, a division of SAGE – Thousand Oaks, Calif., Andrew Boney, Jerry Orvedahl

PRODUCTION MANAGER
CQ Press, a division of SAGE, Paul Pressau

BUSINESS MANAGER
Barkley Kern

MARKETING MANAGER
Deidre Miller

Politics in America
2012
112th Congress

Politics in America

America

16th Edition

If you're like many recipients of this edition of Politics in America for the 112th Congress, you'll keep it close by for the next two years and retire the previous volume to your bookshelf, where it will join PIAs from past sessions. This is the 16th volume of Politics in America, marking the 30th anniversary of a biennial series that began in 1981 with the 97th Congress.

Of all the election years chronicled by PIA volumes, few have been as seismic as 2010. Since the last edition of PIA, we've gone from President Obama's inaugural message of "hope and change," with Democrats controlling both chambers, to a Republican takeover of the House of Representatives fueled by the idealism of candidates who identify with the tea party's message of ultra-patriotism and smaller government.

When the polls closed in November, the largest House freshman class in decades was swept into power, adding 87 Republicans and nine Democrats. The GOP earned a decided advantage, with a net gain of 63 seats from the previous Congress. In the Senate, still controlled by Democrats, 13 new lawmakers were sworn in.

The lame-duck 111th hinted at the prospect of bipartisanship, racking up remarkable legislative achievements, including extensions of the Bush-era tax cuts and the repeal of the ban on gays serving openly in the military. In January, the tragic shooting in Arizona that took the lives of six and injured 13, including Rep. Gabrielle Giffords, sparked a dialogue on civility in public discourse. Both Obama and Speaker John A. Boehner of Ohio urged colleagues to disagree without being disagreeable.

But the makeup of the 112th has been a recipe for political stalemate. Pressured by emboldened tea party Republicans on the right, the House leadership has had little room to maneuver. A vote to repeal Obama's signature legislative achievement, the health care law, did not mollify the freshmen: They also pushed leadership much further on budget cuts than it had planned on going, raising the specter of a government shutdown. Meanwhile, Obama moved toward the center in search of compromise, but risked alienating the liberal base Democrats will need in 2012.

Inaction has its costs. The nation remained saddled with slow job and productivity growth, and a soaring federal budget deficit put more pressure than ever on lawmakers to confront the biggest source of spending: federal entitlement programs such as Social Security and Medicare.

Thus began the 112th Congress, and this edition of PIA, written and produced by the talented staff at CQ and Roll Call. Together, the newly merged CQ Roll Call newsroom has written or updated profiles for every member of the new Congress. Inside these pages you'll find the most thorough portraits of the 112th freshman class available anywhere.

"This book is concerned with influence," former CQ editor Alan Ehrenhalt wrote in the preface to the first PIA. "Its most important purpose is to assess members of Congress in a way that official biographies and interest group ratings never do. We are interested in what each individual member has tried to accomplish in his career, the approach he uses, the allies he has on the inside and the interests he works with on the outside."

That mission continues today. Editors John Bicknell and David Meyers assembled this year's impressive volume, with critical support from Amanda Allen and Amanda Johnson. But it is the breadth and depth of the combined editorial staff — reporters, editors, database editors, photographers, graphic designers — that make this book as rich and informative as it has been for the past three decades. We trust you'll turn to it often as you seek to know the politics and personalities of the 112th Congress.

Mike Mills
Editorial Director and Senior Vice President
CQ Roll Call

www.cqpress.com

Party Unity Being Put to the Test

When Robert Borosage and Stanley Greenberg wrote of "The Emerging Center-Left Majority" in the liberal American Prospect magazine after the 2008 election, they envisioned Democratic predominance as far as the eye could see, a liberal majority "far more durable than the fanciful 'permanent majority' that Karl Rove thought was within reach for Republicans after 2000."

One election later, the "durable" Democratic majority in the House was out on its ear, resoundingly rejected by voters — if not from sea to shining sea then certainly from the Appalachians to the Rockies. The once "veto-proof" Senate majority was barely more than a rump, giving Republicans in that chamber more than enough votes to work the rules and the room to their advantage. Outside Washington, Republicans captured a majority of governorships and state legislatures — crucial with redistricting imminent.

What happened?

In fact, Borosage and Greenberg's article made note of what would prove to be the cause, but swiftly moved past it as largely irrelevant. After detailing the many ways in which polling revealed that the swing voters of 2008 were increasingly liberal, they noted an exception: "Moderates remain far more skeptical about government — and government spending — than liberals do."

Those moderate voters swung to Republicans in 2010. They leaned right largely because, when President Obama and his congressional allies were confronted with rising unemployment and a nervous electorate, they doubled down on government activism.

A $787 billion economic stimulus, a $1 trillion health care overhaul, a cap-and-trade system intended to alleviate climate change (only passed in the House) and financial support for over-extended state governments all added to concerns about the budget deficit. As voters observed country after country falling into debt crisis, and saw their own personal economies foundering, they had to wonder: Could it happen here?

What they witnessed from unified Democratic government had to make them nervous on that score. In their four years in the majority under House Speaker Nancy Pelosi of California, the historically fractious Democratic Caucus was remarkably cohesive.

CQ's "party unity" scores measure the percentage of votes in which a member sides with his or her own party when a majority of Republicans votes one way and a majority of Democrats votes the other. Those scores jumped dramatically — 15-20 points in some cases — from 2007 to 2010 for many Democrats who had relatively low party-unity scores when they were in the minority. That is partly a reflection of the change in agendas — differences between what Democratic leaders offered members to vote on and what Republican leaders brought to the floor during their previous dozen years in control. But it is also a testament to the ability of Pelosi and her leadership team to hold the caucus together (some might say drive it off a cliff) on one tough vote after another.

Many of the self-styled moderate Democrats lost in 2010 — the fiscally conservative Blue Dog Coalition lost about half its members. You'll find examples of those party unity jumps in the profiles of the survivors

Moderate votes swung to the Republicans in 2010, largely because when President Obama and his congressional allies were confronted with rising unemployment and a nervous electorate, they doubled down on government activism.

About the Editors

John Bicknell has been an editor for more than 25 years, including almost a dozen years at Congressional Quarterly and its successor, CQ Roll Call. At CQ, he has led teams covering social policy, legal affairs, defense, foreign policy and intelligence. He also served as editor of CQ Homeland Security. Before coming to CQ, he held various editing positions for the Bradenton Herald, a Knight-Ridder (now McClatchy) newspaper in Florida, including assistant city editor and features editor. He has a bachelor's degree in political science from Indiana State University and lives in Haymarket, Va., with his wife, Arwen (also an editor at CQ), son, Thomas, and cats Jane and Gilda.

David Meyers joined the Roll Call staff in 1996 as editorial assistant, providing research assistance to Executive Editor Morton Kondracke. After serving as copy editor and news editor, he was named managing editor of Roll Call Daily in 2001, helping grow the newspaper's online presence. In 2003 he became managing editor for the entire newsroom, responsible for the copy desk, production process and online operations. Following Roll Call's acquisition of CQ, he was named managing editor of Member Information and Research, overseeing print and online products related to federal, state and local officeholders and staffs. He holds a bachelor's degree in English and political science from Tufts University and lives in Fairfax, Va., with his wife, Jennifer, and their two daughters, Samantha and Sophie.

throughout the book. One Democrat fairly typical of the phenomenon was Rep. David Scott of Georgia. A member of the Blue Dogs and the centrist New Democrat Coalition, he is also in the liberal Congressional Black Caucus. On party unity votes in 2010, he sided with Democrats 98 percent of the time, more than 20 percentage points higher than his first year in the chamber, 2003, when Republicans were in charge.

All of this presents several interesting scenarios — and raises several interesting questions — for the 112th Congress (2011-12).

How will the party unity scores of the remaining moderate Democrats develop now that they are back in the minority? History and common sense tell us they will go down, at least among those in somewhat competitive districts. Having witnessed what happened to their colleagues in 2010, many will cast votes with at least one eye on the folks back home.

As newly empowered Republicans move to keep their campaign promises of reduced federal spending, how will voters react when those cuts evolve from popular "smaller government" rhetoric to less-popular actual reductions in specific programs? For lawmakers, it might depend on where they are from. Expect Republicans in safer districts to take more chances — and tougher stands — than those elected from swing districts.

Internally, how will Congress work with more than 100 freshmen, some of whom are chairing key subcommittees? For example, reduction in the size of the federal workforce is a key element of tea-party Republicanism. The chairman of the House subcommittee with oversight of federal workers is Republican Dennis A. Ross of Florida, but he and his fellow GOP freshmen might not acquiesce to direction from above as readily as their predecessors.

What impact will all those tea-party-inspired freshmen have? Can they really change the institution of Congress, as many hoped and promised? As they gather seniority and power, their policy notions will certainly exert an influence. But changing the culture is a much more difficult task.

Can Senate Majority Leader Harry Reid of Nevada, who had enough trouble getting his agenda through the chamber when he had 59 Democratic votes, get anything accomplished now that his caucus has dwindled to 53?

The answer to that question might depend on the answer to another: How will Senate Republicans balance their desire to block the Obama agenda while trying to make a positive case to be returned to the majority themselves in 2012?

And what does all this mean for the presidential election in 2012? Presidents' parties usually lose seats in midterm elections. Almost all of them (in the past century) followed that loss with a re-election victory. The recent one who didn't — Jimmy Carter — is the Oval Office occupant who Republicans most like to compare with Obama.

Clearly, 2008 was not the "potential realignment election" Borosage and Greenberg (and others) imagined. What 2012 holds is a mystery, although what we learned in 2010 is that actions have consequences: What Congress and the president do matters to voters, who will react accordingly.

John Bicknell
May 2011

GOP Controls Redistricting, but Lacks Guarantees

The saying "timing is everything" is well-worn and applies to many aspects of life. Seldom, though, has it been more applicable to congressional redistricting, a process that takes place in most states after the national population census that kicks off each decade — and thus was under way as this edition of CQ Roll Call's Politics in America was published.

The Republican Party had suffered huge setbacks nationally in the 2006 and 2008 elections, in large part because of George W. Bush's unpopularity during his second term as president. But the GOP made a roaring comeback in the 2010 midterm elections, a rebound fueled in part by enduring economic distress stemming from the near-collapse of the nation's financial sector in the fall of 2008. Also contributing to the party's recovery was a backlash against the agenda pursued by President Obama and his fellow Democrats, who controlled both chambers of Congress and pushed through measures that included a major spending increase to stimulate the economy and a controversial overhaul of the nation's health insurance system.

The impact of the 2010 GOP surge on the balance of power in Congress drew tremendous national attention, as Republicans captured control of the House with a 63-seat gain (the biggest for either party since a 75-seat Democratic leap in the 1948 elections) and cut the size of the majority Democratic caucus in the Senate from 59 seats to 53. Less remarked upon were major GOP advances at the state level. The GOP saw a net gain of six governors' offices, putting the party in charge in 29 of the 50 statehouses, and a net gain of nearly 700 state legislative seats, giving the party new control in 21 legislative chambers. A February 2011 state Senate special election victory in Louisiana then pushed one more chamber into the Republican column.

As a result, Republicans entered this decade's redistricting arena dominating the process in 18 states with a combined 202 House seats, just short of half of the total 435. Democrats controlled the governorship and both chambers in just six states where congressional redistricting follows the "how a bill becomes law" model (47 House seats). Control of redistricting was split between the parties in 13 states with 91 total seats. Six states, with 88 seats, take redistricting out of the hands of the legislators and give it to bipartisan commissions; among them is California, which has by far the biggest House delegation with 53 seats and where voters in November 2010 opted to create a commission — thus depriving the Democrats of the full control they otherwise would have had over redistricting in the nation's most populous state. (The seven least-populous states have only one seat each and thus do not participate in redistricting.)

And yet . . . the advantages that the Republicans gained in the redistricting process with their strong 2010 showing do not ensure that the party, in the short run, will be able to maintain or grow its 242-seat House majority. And it is even less certain whether the lines will ensure a decade's worth of dominance for the GOP in congressional politics.

While the traditional "redistricting pen" has been replaced with high-tech tools that enable political mapmakers to draw lines with near-surgical precision, the ability of either party to achieve all of its strategic goals is limited by the volatile mood swings that have marked the electorate's voting behavior over a series of recent election cycles.

Republican partisans certainly hope their 2010 upswing indicates that their conservative agenda will have lasting appeal among voters and cement their House majority. But as they draw the lines in many states in

Biggest population gains since 2000		
District	Population change	% change
Nevada 03	377,773	56.7
Arizona 02	331,510	51.7
Arizona 06	330,404	51.5
Texas 10	329,747	50.6
Florida 05	290,238	45.4
California 45	275,121	43.0
Georgia 07	273,464	43.4
Texas 26	263,518	40.4
Texas 22	259,258	39.8
Texas 31	250,482	38.4
N.Carolina 09	233,199	37.7
Virginia 10	225,925	35.1
Utah 03	221,842	29.8
Florida 14	219,661	34.4
Arizona 07	214,440	33.4
N.Carolina 04	207,700	33.5
California 44	205,668	32.2
Texas 21	205,339	31.5
California 25	205,233	32.1
Florida 12	202,903	31.7
Texas 28	200,197	30.7
Texas 23	196,039	30.1
Texas 04	194,523	29.9
Georgia 09	193,855	30.8
Idaho 01	193,156	29.8

Biggest population losses since 2000		
District	Population change	% change
Louisiana 02	-145,210	-22.7
Michigan 13	-142,993	-21.6
Michigan 14	-112,098	-16.9
Ohio 11	-90,298	-14.3
Illinois 01	-66,051	-10.1
Pennsylvania 14	-61,520	-9.5
Illinois 04	-52,491	-8.0
Illinois 02	-50,889	-7.8
Mississippi 02	-42,901	-6.0
New York 28	-42,522	-6.5
Missouri 01	-34,621	-5.6
Pennsylvania 12	-33,865	-5.2
Ohio 01	-32,031	-5.1
Alabama 07	-31,948	-5.0
Ohio 10	-31,525	-5.0
Ohio 17	-30,619	-4.9
California 31	-27,752	-4.3
Michigan 05	-27,434	-4.1
Michigan 12	-25,962	-3.9
New York 27	-25,090	-3.8
Illinois 09	-24,788	-3.8
New York 11	-21,953	-3.4
Tennessee 09	-21,320	-3.4
Illinois 17	-18,855	-2.9
Kansas 01	-16,781	-2.5

hopes of boosting their candidates' prospects, they have to be cognizant that a growing portion of the voting public is made up of people who are dissatisfied with both major political parties — many of them registered or self-declared independents. The voters could give the political pendulum a big push back in the Democrats' direction in 2012, when Obama will be seeking re-election, if they dislike how the GOP has used its renascent clout in Congress.

"You can't, in the end, keep the waves from crashing over you when politics change," said E. Mark Braden, a veteran Republican redistricting attorney, as the remapping process was just beginning in January 2011. "In the end, the voters vote, and the votes are more important than the districts."

By the same token, Democratic redistricting mavens would be taking a big risk if they presume that 2010 was simply an aberration, a mere interruption in the momentum their party built through the 2006 and 2008 election cycles.

Redistricting is "predicting the future, which most people aren't too successful at," said Jeffrey M. Wice, a longtime Democratic redistricting lawyer.

In fact, the 2010 House elections, in which the Republicans greatly exceeded even their own ambitious expectations, may have been too much of a good thing in some states, limiting any further gains that the party might extract from redistricting. For example, a five-seat gain gave them a 13-5 advantage in Ohio, which is losing two of its 18 seats in the congressional reapportionment that accompanies redistricting. An identical five-seat gain in neighboring Pennsylvania, a state that is losing one of its 19 seats, flipped the state's House delegation from 12-7 Democratic to 12-7 Republican.

This is, as Braden put it, "one of those good problems" for his party. Yet it also means it would be almost impossible for Republicans to improve on the result without spreading their voting margins of safety too thinly in individual districts. That's why top Republican strategists, at the onset of this round of redistricting, described their goals for redistricting as securing as many of the 242 seats they won in 2010 as they can, rather than high-balling predictions of additional gains.

Republicans were chastened over the past decade when maps that initially appeared masterful examples of the art of gerrymandering — a two-century-old epithet for partisan redistricting — were undone by the Democratic wave that rose in 2006 and carried through the 2008 elections.

Although the GOP is in a much better position for this current round of redistricting than even party optimists could have anticipated after the 2008 elections, the political landscape in the states is not that different than it was 10 years ago: The 2000 elections occurred during a period of Republican strength, and many of the states where the party reclaimed control in 2010 were also Republican-dominated when the maps were drawn a decade ago.

One of these was the aforementioned Pennsylvania, where the delegation went from an 11-10 Republican edge after the 2000 elections to a 12-7 GOP advantage (the state lost two seats in reapportionment) after the 2002 elections that were run under a map drawn by the Republican-controlled legislature and signed by the Republican governor. Democrats sued to try to overturn the map, charging in the case of *Veith v. Jubeliler* that it amounted to an egregious partisan gerrymander that virtually precluded them from taking over any of the Republican-held seats for the duration of the decade. They only narrowly missed winning that claim, as the U.S. Supreme Court in 2004 upheld the map by a 5-4 vote.

Yet the Democrats' argument that they had no chance of picking up seats in Pennsylvania and the Republicans' hopes that their map would provide a resilient majority in the state both proved exaggerated. Democratic gains in 2006 and 2008 gave them 12 of Pennsylvania's seats to seven for the Republicans, exactly flipping the GOP's intended split. Similarly, in Ohio, a gerrymander that produced a 12-6 Republican advantage after the 2002 elections was converted to a 10-8 Democratic edge after 2008.

It is true that all of these states sprang back during the Republican rebound of 2010, suggesting that the GOP's gerrymandering efforts were not fatally flawed. But it underscored the fact that the farther a party reaches for gains through redistricting, the more risks it takes. Had Republicans settled for a seat or two fewer in Pennsylvania and Ohio, they could have packed more Republican voters into other districts and built up margins that might have held up more sturdily against the mid-decade Democratic wave.

Another factor mitigating against major Republican gains is that reapportionment, under which 12 seats are shifting from slower-growing to faster-growing states, does not appear the boon that it has been for the GOP's national prospects over recent decades.

It is true that this reapportionment is continuing the most dominant trend in American demographics since World War II. Most of the seats that are changing hands are moving from the traditional industrial population centers of the Northeast and Midwest, from which the Democrats derived much of their political base, to the Sunbelt states of the South, where a majority of voters hold conservative views that have turned the region into the foundation of the Republican Party's national strength.

Texas was the biggest winner in the 2010 reapportionment, adding four seats to its current 32. Florida, now at 25 seats, picked up two more. The states gaining one seat each — Arizona, Georgia, Nevada, South Carolina, Utah and Washington — are mainly in the South or Republican-leaning areas. On the other side of the scale were New York and Ohio, which are losing two seats apiece, and one-seat losers Illinois, Iowa, Louisiana, Massachusetts, Missouri, New Jersey, Ohio and Pennsylvania.

But three major factors mitigate against major GOP gains primarily from reapportionment. First, the pace of population and House seat shifts have slowed over the past generation. Following the 1990 census, 19 seats shifted among states. In 2000 and 2010 both, the number dropped to 12.

Second, while internal migrations from the North to the South and West accounted for much of the population shift over previous decades, the biggest storyline over the past 10 years was the fast-growing Hispanic populations in states such as Texas, Arizona and Florida, significantly made up of new immigrants. While the voting clout of this constituency lags behind its total numbers because many Hispanic residents are not naturalized citizens or are too young to vote, most Hispanics who do vote favor the Democratic Party.

Finally, while much of the population tilt has occurred in the South, the other big long-term growth area has been on the Pacific Coast. California, Oregon and Washington have long been hotbeds of partisan competition but most recently have leaned strongly Democratic. Led by the dominant 34-19 edge that Democrats have built in California, their party currently holds 43 of the 67 seats in the region, or nearly two-thirds.

The saving grace for Republicans is that the population boom in the far West has slowed. Washington's one-seat gain is the only one among the three states. And this decade marks the first time in California's 160-plus years as a state that it has not gained at least one seat in reapportionment.

Bob Benenson
Senior Political Analyst, Congressional Quarterly
May 2011

Most Populous Districts		
District	**Population**	**Member**
Nevada 03	1,043,855	Heck, R
Montana AL	989,415	Rehberg, R
Texas 10	981,367	McCaul, R
Arizona 02	972,839	Franks, R
Arizona 06	971,733	Flake, R
Utah 03	966,232	Chaffetz, R
Florida 05	929,533	Nugent, R
Texas 26	915,137	Burgess, R
California 45	914,209	Bono Mack, R
Texas 22	910,877	Olson, R
Utah 01	906,660	Bishop, R
Georgia 07	903,191	Woodall, R
Texas 31	902,101	Carter, R
Delaware AL	897,934	Carney, D
Utah 02	890,993	Matheson, D
Virginia 10	869,437	Wolf, R
Florida 14	858,956	Mack, R
S. Carolina 01	856,956	Scott, R
Texas 21	856,954	Smith, R
Arizona 07	855,769	Grijalva, D
N. Carolina 09	852,377	Myrick, R
Texas 28	851,824	Cuellar, D
Texas 23	847,651	Canseco, R
Texas 04	846,142	Hall, R
California 44	844,756	Calvert, R

Least Populous Districts		
District	**Population**	**Member**
Pennsylvania 12	612,384	Critz, D
New York 28	611,838	Slaughter, D
California 31	611,336	Becerra, D
Tennessee 09	610,823	Cohen, D
Iowa 04	609,487	Latham, R
Alabama 07	603,352	Sewell, D
Illinois 02	602,758	Jackson, D
Illinois 04	601,156	Guiterrez, D
Ohio 17	600,111	Ryan, D
Ohio 10	599,205	Kucinich, D
Ohio 01	598,699	Chabot, R
Iowa 01	596,443	Braley, D
West Virginia 03	588,817	Rahall, D
Illinois 01	587,596	Rush, D
Missouri 01	587,069	Clay, D
Pennsylvania 14	584,493	Doyle, D
Iowa 05	577,453	King, R
Wyoming AL	563,626	Lummis, R
Nebraska 03	561,378	Smith, R
Michigan 14	550,465	Conyers, D
Ohio 11	540,432	Fudge, D
Rhode Island 02	533,546	Langevin, D
Michigan 13	519,570	Clarke, D
Rhode Island 01	519,021	Cicilline, D
Louisiana 02	493,352	Richmond, D

2010 Census and Congressional Apportionment

STATE	2010 POPULATION	2000 POPULATION	PERCENT CHANGE	SEATS IN HOUSE 2013-2023	GAIN/ LOSS
California	37,253,956	33,871,648	10.0	53	0
Texas	25,145,561	20,851,820	20.6	36	4
Florida	18,801,310	15,982,378	17.6	27	2
New York	19,378,102	18,976,457	2.1	27	-2
Illinois	12,830,632	12,419,293	3.3	18	-1
Pennsylvania	12,702,379	12,281,054	3.4	18	-1
Ohio	11,536,504	11,353,140	1.6	16	-2
Georgia	9,687,653	8,186,453	18.3	14	1
Michigan	9,883,640	9,938,444	-0.6	14	-1
North Carolina	9,535,483	8,049,313	18.5	13	0
New Jersey	8,791,894	8,414,350	4.5	12	-1
Virginia	8,001,024	7,078,515	13.0	11	0
Washington	6,724,540	5,894,121	14.1	10	1
Arizona	6,392,017	5,130,632	24.6	9	1
Indiana	6,483,802	6,080,485	6.6	9	0
Massachusetts	6,547,629	6,349,097	3.1	9	-1
Tennessee	6,346,105	5,689,283	11.5	9	0
Maryland	5,773,552	5,296,486	9.0	8	0
Minnesota	5,303,925	4,919,479	7.8	8	0
Missouri	5,988,927	5,595,211	7.0	8	-1
Wisconsin	5,686,986	5,363,675	6.0	8	0
Alabama	4,779,736	4,447,100	7.5	7	0
Colorado	5,029,196	4,301,261	16.9	7	0
South Carolina	4,625,364	4,012,012	15.3	7	1
Kentucky	4,339,367	4,041,769	7.4	6	0
Louisiana	4,533,372	4,468,976	1.4	6	-1
Connecticut	3,574,097	3,405,565	4.9	5	0
Oklahoma	3,751,351	3,450,654	8.7	5	0
Oregon	3,831,074	3,421,399	12.0	5	0
Arkansas	2,915,918	2,673,400	9.1	4	0
Iowa	3,046,355	2,926,324	4.1	4	-1
Kansas	2,853,118	2,688,418	6.1	4	0
Mississippi	2,967,297	2,844,658	4.3	4	0
Nevada	2,700,551	1,998,257	35.1	4	1
Utah	2,763,885	2,233,169	23.8	4	1
Nebraska	1,826,341	1,711,263	6.7	3	0
New Mexico	2,059,179	1,819,046	13.2	3	0
West Virginia	1,852,994	1,808,344	2.5	3	0
Hawaii	1,360,301	1,211,537	12.3	2	0
Idaho	1,567,582	1,293,953	21.1	2	0
Maine	1,328,361	1,274,923	4.2	2	0
New Hampshire	1,316,470	1,235,786	6.5	2	0
Rhode Island	1,052,567	1,048,319	0.4	2	0
Alaska	710,231	626,932	13.3	1	0
Delaware	897,934	783,600	14.6	1	0
Montana	989,415	902,195	9.7	1	0
North Dakota	672,591	642,200	4.7	1	0
South Dakota	814,180	754,844	7.9	1	0
Vermont	625,741	608,827	2.8	1	0
Wyoming	563,626	493,782	14.1	1	0
Total	**308,143,815**	**280,849,847**	**9.7**	**435**	

www.cqpress.com

Official 2010 Population Count by District

Population figures are from the U.S. Census Bureau.
Democrats are listed in italics.

	2000	2010	PERCENT CHANGE
UNITED STATES	281,421,906	308,745,536	13.2
ALABAMA			
1 Bonner	635,300	687,841	8.3
2 Roby	635,300	673,877	6.1
3 Rogers	635,300	681,298	7.2
4 Aderholt	635,300	660,162	3.9
5 Brooks	635,300	718,724	13.1
6 Bachus	635,300	754,482	18.8
7 *Sewell*	635,300	603,352	-5.0
ALASKA			
(AL) Young	626,932	710,231	13.3
ARIZONA			
1 Gosar	641,329	774,310	20.7
2 Franks	641,329	972,839	51.7
3 Quayle	641,329	707,919	10.4
4 *Pastor*	641,329	698,314	8.9
5 Schweikert	641,329	656,833	2.4
6 Flake	641,329	971,733	51.5
7 *Grijalva*	641,329	855,769	33.4
8 *Giffords*	641,329	754,300	17.6
ARKANSAS			
1 Crawford	668,360	687,694	2.9
2 Griffin	666,058	751,377	12.8
3 Womack	672,756	822,564	22.3
4 *Ross*	666,226	654,283	-1.8
CALIFORNIA			
1 *Thompson*	639,087	704,012	10.2
2 Herger	639,087	708,596	10.9
3 Lungren	639,088	783,317	22.6
4 McClintock	639,088	774,261	21.2
5 *Matsui*	639,088	700,443	9.6
6 *Woolsey*	639,087	664,168	4.0
7 *Miller*	639,088	655,708	2.6
8 *Pelosi*	639,088	666,827	4.3
9 *Lee*	639,088	648,766	1.5
10 *Garamendi*	639,088	714,750	11.8
11 *McNerney*	639,088	796,753	24.7
12 *Speier*	639,088	651,322	1.9
13 *Stark*	639,088	665,318	4.1
14 *Eshoo*	639,088	653,935	2.3
15 *Honda*	639,088	677,605	6.0
16 *Lofgren*	639,088	676,880	5.9
17 *Farr*	639,088	664,240	3.9
18 *Cardoza*	639,088	723,607	13.2
19 Denham	639,088	757,337	18.5
20 *Costa*	639,088	744,350	16.5
21 Nunes	639,088	784,176	22.7
22 McCarthy	639,088	797,084	24.7
23 *Capps*	639,088	695,404	8.8
24 Gallegly	639,088	681,622	6.7
25 McKeon	639,087	844,320	32.1
26 Dreier	639,088	691,452	8.2
27 *Sherman*	639,088	684,496	7.1
28 *Berman*	639,087	660,194	3.3
29 *Schiff*	639,088	642,138	0.5
30 *Waxman*	639,088	662,319	3.6
31 *Becerra*	639,088	611,336	-4.3
32 *Chu*	639,087	642,236	0.5
33 *Bass*	639,088	637,122	-0.3
34 *Roybal-Allard*	639,088	654,303	2.4
35 *Waters*	639,088	662,413	3.6
36 VACANT	639,087	659,385	3.2
37 *Richardson*	639,088	648,847	1.5
38 *Napolitano*	639,088	641,410	0.4
39 *Sánchez*	639,088	643,115	0.6
40 Royce	639,088	665,653	4.2
41 Lewis	639,087	797,133	24.7
42 Miller	639,088	667,638	4.5
43 *Baca*	639,087	735,581	15.1
44 Calvert	639,088	844,756	32.2
45 Bono Mack	639,088	914,209	43.0
46 Rohrabacher	639,088	648,663	1.5
47 *Sanchez*	639,087	631,422	-1.2
48 Campbell	639,087	727,833	13.9
49 Issa	639,087	797,428	24.8
50 Bilbray	639,087	753,135	17.8
51 *Filner*	639,087	757,891	18.6
52 Hunter	639,087	673,893	5.4
53 *Davis*	639,087	662,854	3.7
COLORADO			
1 *DeGette*	614,465	662,039	7.7
2 *Polis*	614,465	733,805	19.4
3 Tipton	614,467	706,186	14.9
4 Gardner	614,466	725,041	18.0
5 Lamborn	614,467	725,902	18.1
6 Coffman	614,466	797,813	29.8
7 *Perlmutter*	614,465	678,410	10.4
CONNECTICUT			
1 *Larson*	681,113	710,951	4.4
2 *Courtney*	681,113	729,771	7.1
3 *DeLauro*	681,113	712,339	4.6
4 *Himes*	681,113	706,740	3.8
5 *Murphy*	681,113	714,296	4.9
DELAWARE			
(AL) *Carney*	783,600	897,934	14.6
FLORIDA			
1 Miller	639,295	694,158	8.6
2 Southerland	639,295	737,519	15.4
3 *Brown*	639,295	659,055	3.1
4 Crenshaw	639,295	744,418	16.4
5 Nugent	639,295	929,533	45.4
6 Stearns	639,295	812,727	27.1
7 Mica	639,295	812,442	27.1
8 Webster	639,295	805,608	26.0
9 Bilirakis	639,296	753,549	17.9
10 Young	639,295	633,889	-0.8
11 *Castor*	639,295	673,799	5.4
12 Ross	639,296	842,199	31.7
13 Buchanan	639,295	757,805	18.5
14 Mack	639,295	858,956	34.4
15 Posey	639,295	813,570	27.3
16 Rooney	639,295	797,711	24.8
17 *Wilson*	639,296	655,160	2.5
18 Ros-Lehtinen	639,295	712,790	11.5
19 *Deutch*	639,295	736,419	15.2
20 *Wasserman Schultz*	639,295	691,727	8.2
21 Diaz-Balart	639,295	693,501	8.5

	2000	2010	PERCENT CHANGE
22 West	639,295	694,259	8.6
23 *Hastings*	639,295	684,107	7.0
24 Adams	639,295	799,233	25.0
25 Rivera	639,295	807,176	26.3
GEORGIA			
1 Kingston	629,727	722,068	14.7
2 *Bishop*	629,727	631,973	0.4
3 Westmoreland	629,727	817,247	29.8
4 *Johnson*	629,726	665,541	5.7
5 *Lewis*	629,728	630,462	0.1
6 Price	629,726	767,798	21.9
7 Woodall	629,727	903,191	43.4
8 Scott	629,728	715,599	13.6
9 Graves	629,728	823,583	30.8
10 Broun	629,728	738,248	17.2
11 Gingrey	629,727	794,969	26.2
12 *Barrow*	629,727	692,529	10.0
13 *Scott*	629,727	784,445	24.6
HAWAII			
1 *Hanabusa*	606,718	658,672	8.6
2 *Hirono*	604,819	701,629	16.0
IDAHO			
1 Labrador	648,774	841,930	29.8
2 Simpson	645,179	725,652	12.5
ILLINOIS			
1 *Rush*	653,647	587,596	-10.1
2 *Jackson*	653,647	602,758	-7.8
3 *Lipinski*	653,647	663,381	1.5
4 *Gutierrez*	653,647	601,156	-8.0
5 *Quigley*	653,647	648,610	-0.8
6 Roskam	653,647	657,131	0.5
7 *Davis*	653,647	638,105	-2.4
8 Walsh	653,647	738,840	13.0
9 *Schakowsky*	653,647	628,859	-3.8
10 Dold	653,647	650,425	-0.5
11 Kinzinger	653,647	759,445	16.2
12 *Costello*	653,647	666,459	2.0
13 Biggert	653,647	773,095	18.3
14 Hultgren	653,647	840,956	28.7
15 Johnson	653,647	681,580	4.3
16 Manzullo	653,647	718,791	10.0
17 Schilling	653,647	634,792	-2.9
18 Schock	653,647	665,723	1.8
19 Shimkus	653,647	672,930	3.0
INDIANA			
1 *Visclosky*	675,562	705,600	4.4
2 *Donnelly*	675,766	679,254	0.5
3 Stutzman	675,457	723,633	7.1
4 Rokita	675,617	789,835	16.9
5 Burton	675,577	809,107	19.8
6 Pence	675,669	676,548	0.1
7 *Carson*	675,674	676,351	0.1
8 Bucshon	675,564	694,398	2.8
9 Young	675,599	729,076	7.9
IOWA			
1 *Braley*	585,302	596,443	1.9
2 *Loebsack*	585,241	620,856	6.1
3 *Boswell*	585,305	642,116	9.7
4 Latham	585,305	609,487	4.1
5 King	585,171	577,453	-1.3
KANSAS			
1 Huelskamp	672,091	655,310	-2.5
2 Jenkins	672,102	710,047	5.6

	2000	2010	PERCENT CHANGE
3 Yoder	672,124	767,569	14.2
4 Pompeo	672,101	720,192	7.2
KENTUCKY			
1 Whitfield	673,629	686,989	2.0
2 Guthrie	673,224	760,032	12.9
3 *Yarmuth*	674,032	721,626	7.1
4 Davis	673,588	741,464	10.1
5 Rogers	673,670	670,051	-0.5
6 *Chandler*	673,626	759,205	12.7
LOUISIANA			
1 Scalise	638,355	686,961	7.6
2 *Richmond*	638,562	493,352	-22.7
3 Landry	638,322	637,371	-0.1
4 Fleming	638,466	667,109	4.5
5 Alexander	638,517	644,296	0.9
6 Cassidy	638,324	727,498	14.0
7 Boustany	638,430	676,785	6.0
MAINE			
1 *Pingree*	637,450	668,515	4.9
2 *Michaud*	637,473	659,846	3.5
MARYLAND			
1 Harris	662,062	744,275	12.4
2 *Ruppersberger*	662,060	700,893	5.9
3 *Sarbanes*	662,062	719,856	8.7
4 *Edwards*	662,062	714,316	7.9
5 *Hoyer*	662,060	767,369	15.9
6 Bartlett	662,060	738,943	11.6
7 *Cummings*	662,060	659,776	-0.3
8 *Van Hollen*	662,060	728,124	10.0
MASSACHUSETTS			
1 *Olver*	634,479	644,956	1.7
2 *Neal*	634,444	661,045	4.2
3 *McGovern*	634,585	664,919	4.8
4 *Frank*	634,624	656,083	3.4
5 *Tsongas*	635,326	662,269	4.2
6 *Tierney*	636,554	650,161	2.1
7 *Markey*	634,287	648,162	2.2
8 *Capuano*	634,835	660,414	4.0
9 *Lynch*	634,062	650,381	2.6
10 *Keating*	635,901	649,239	2.1
MICHIGAN			
1 Benishek	662,563	650,222	-1.9
2 Huizenga	662,563	698,831	5.5
3 Amash	662,563	694,695	4.8
4 Camp	662,563	686,378	3.6
5 *Kildee*	662,563	635,129	-4.1
6 Upton	662,563	671,883	1.4
7 Walberg	662,563	676,899	2.2
8 Rogers	662,563	707,572	6.8
9 *Peters*	662,563	657,590	-0.8
10 Miller	662,562	719,712	8.6
11 McCotter	662,563	695,888	5.0
12 *Levin*	662,563	636,601	-3.9
13 *Clarke*	662,563	519,570	-21.6
14 *Conyers*	662,563	550,465	-16.9
15 *Dingell*	662,563	682,205	3.0
MINNESOTA			
1 *Walz*	614,935	644,787	4.9
2 Kline	614,934	732,515	19.1
3 Paulsen	614,935	650,185	5.7
4 *McCollum*	614,935	614,624	-0.1
5 *Ellison*	614,935	616,482	0.3
6 Bachmann	614,935	759,478	23.5

	2000	2010	PERCENT CHANGE
7 *Peterson*	614,935	625,512	1.7
8 Cravaack	614,935	660,342	7.4
MISSISSIPPI			
1 Nunnelee	711,160	788,095	10.8
2 *Thompson*	711,164	668,263	-6.0
3 Harper	711,115	756,924	6.4
4 Palazzo	711,219	754,015	6.0
MISSOURI			
1 *Clay*	621,690	587,069	-5.6
2 Akin	621,690	706,622	13.7
3 *Carnahan*	621,690	625,251	0.6
4 Hartzler	621,690	679,375	9.3
5 *Cleaver*	621,691	633,887	2.0
6 Graves	621,690	693,974	11.6
7 Long	621,690	721,754	16.1
8 Emerson	621,690	656,894	5.7
9 Luetkemeyer	621,690	684,101	10.0
MONTANA			
(AL) Rehberg	902,195	989,415	9.7
NEBRASKA			
1 Fortenberry	570,325	626,092	9.8
2 Terry	570,421	638,871	12.0
3 Smith	570,517	561,378	-1.6
NEVADA			
1 *Berkley*	666,088	820,134	23.1
2 VACANT	666,087	836,562	25.6
3 Heck	666,082	1,043,855	56.7
NEW HAMPSHIRE			
1 Guinta	617,575	657,984	6.5
2 Bass	618,211	658,486	6.5
NEW JERSEY			
1 *Andrews*	647,258	669,169	3.4
2 LoBiondo	647,258	692,205	6.9
3 Runyan	647,257	680,341	5.1
4 Smith	647,258	724,596	11.9
5 Garrett	647,258	666,551	3.0
6 *Pallone*	647,257	668,806	3.3
7 Lance	647,257	672,885	4.0
8 *Pascrell*	647,258	660,424	2.0
9 *Rothman*	647,257	661,379	2.2
10 *Payne*	647,258	634,343	-2.0
11 Frelinghuysen	647,258	674,349	4.2
12 *Holt*	647,258	701,881	8.4
13 *Sires*	647,258	684,965	5.8
NEW MEXICO			
1 *Heinrich*	606,400	701,939	15.8
2 Pearce	606,406	663,956	9.5
3 *Luján*	606,240	693,284	14.4
NEW YORK			
1 Bishop	654,360	705,559	7.8
2 Israel	654,360	679,893	3.9
3 King	654,361	645,508	-1.4
4 McCarthy	654,360	663,407	1.4
5 Ackerman	654,361	670,130	2.4
6 Meeks	654,361	651,764	-0.4
7 Crowley	654,360	667,632	2.0
8 Nadler	654,360	713,512	9.0
9 Weiner	654,360	660,306	0.9
10 Towns	654,361	677,721	3.6
11 Clarke	654,361	632,408	-3.4
12 Velázquez	654,360	672,358	2.8
13 Grimm	654,361	686,525	4.9

	2000	2010	PERCENT CHANGE
14 Maloney	654,361	652,681	-0.3
15 Rangel	654,361	639,873	-2.2
16 Serrano	654,360	693,819	6.0
17 Engel	654,360	678,558	3.7
18 Lowey	654,360	674,825	3.1
19 Hayworth	654,361	699,959	7.0
20 Gibson	654,360	683,198	4.4
21 Tonko	654,361	679,193	3.8
22 Hinchey	654,361	679,297	3.8
23 Owens	654,361	664,245	1.5
24 Hanna	654,361	657,222	0.4
25 Buerkle	654,361	668,869	2.2
26 Hochul	654,361	674,804	3.1
27 Higgins	654,361	629,271	-3.8
28 Slaughter	654,360	611,838	-6.5
29 Reed	654,361	663,727	1.4
NORTH CAROLINA			
1 *Butterfield*	619,178	635,936	2.7
2 Ellmers	619,178	741,576	19.8
3 Jones	619,178	735,979	18.9
4 *Price*	619,178	826,878	33.5
5 Foxx	619,178	693,414	12.0
6 Coble	619,178	714,412	15.4
7 *McIntyre*	619,178	742,938	20.0
8 *Kissell*	619,178	709,449	14.6
9 Myrick	619,178	852,377	37.7
10 McHenry	619,178	689,468	11.4
11 *Shuler*	619,177	703,606	13.6
12 *Watt*	619,178	736,346	18.9
13 *Miller*	619,178	753,104	21.6
NORTH DAKOTA			
(AL) Berg	642,200	672,591	4.7
OHIO			
1 Chabot	630,730	598,699	-5.1
2 Schmidt	630,730	673,873	6.8
3 Turner	630,730	640,899	1.6
4 Jordan	630,730	632,771	0.3
5 Latta	630,730	627,799	-0.5
6 Johnson	630,730	623,742	-1.1
7 Austria	630,730	683,371	8.3
8 Boehner	630,730	663,644	5.2
9 *Kaptur*	630,730	619,010	-1.9
10 *Kucinich*	630,730	599,205	-5.0
11 *Fudge*	630,730	540,432	-14.3
12 Tiberi	630,730	756,303	19.9
13 *Sutton*	630,730	649,102	2.9
14 LaTourette	630,730	648,128	2.8
15 Stivers	630,730	681,557	8.1
16 Renacci	630,730	644,691	2.2
17 *Ryan*	630,730	600,111	-4.9
18 Gibbs	630,730	653,167	3.6
OKLAHOMA			
1 Sullivan	690,131	754,310	9.3
2 *Boren*	690,130	729,887	5.8
3 Lucas	690,131	732,394	6.1
4 Cole	690,131	785,424	13.8
5 Lankford	690,131	749,336	8.6
OREGON			
1 *Wu*	684,280	802,570	17.3
2 Walden	684,280	769,987	12.5
3 *Blumenauer*	684,279	762,155	11.4
4 DeFazio	684,280	739,234	8.0
5 Schrader	684,280	757,128	10.6

	2000	2010	PERCENT CHANGE
PENNSYLVANIA			
1 *Brady*	646,357	655,146	1.4
2 *Fattah*	646,355	630,277	-2.5
3 Kelly	646,311	640,356	-0.9
4 *Altmire*	646,609	647,418	0.1
5 Thompson	646,397	651,762	0.8
6 Gerlach	646,221	726,465	12.4
7 Meehan	646,522	673,623	4.2
8 Fitzpatrick	645,403	672,685	4.2
9 Shuster	646,628	666,810	3.1
10 Marino	646,534	669,257	3.5
11 Barletta	646,209	687,860	6.4
12 *Critz*	646,249	612,384	-5.2
13 *Schwartz*	647,435	674,188	4.1
14 *Doyle*	646,013	584,493	-9.5
15 Dent	646,300	721,828	11.7
16 Pitts	646,328	723,977	12.0
17 *Holden*	646,420	681,835	5.5
18 Murphy	646,374	653,385	1.1
19 Platts	646,389	728,630	12.7
RHODE ISLAND			
1 *Cicilline*	524,157	519,021	-1.0
2 *Langevin*	524,162	533,546	1.8
SOUTH CAROLINA			
1 Scott	668,668	856,956	28.2
2 Wilson	668,668	825,324	23.4
3 Duncan	668,669	722,675	8.1
4 Gowdy	668,669	770,226	15.2
5 Mulvaney	668,668	767,773	14.8
6 *Clyburn*	668,670	682,410	2.1
SOUTH DAKOTA			
(AL) Noem	754,844	814,180	7.9
TENNESSEE			
1 Roe	632,143	684,093	8.2
2 Duncan	632,144	723,798	14.5
3 Fleischmann	632,143	692,346	9.5
4 DesJarlais	632,143	688,008	8.8
5 *Cooper*	632,143	707,420	11.9
6 Black	632,143	788,754	24.8
7 Blackburn	632,139	792,605	25.4
8 Fincher	632,142	658,258	4.1
9 *Cohen*	632,143	610,823	-3.4
TEXAS			
1 Gohmert	651,619	723,464	11.0
2 Poe	651,620	782,375	20.1
3 Johnson	651,619	842,449	29.3
4 Hall	651,619	846,142	29.9
5 Hensarling	651,619	725,642	11.4
6 Barton	651,619	809,095	24.2
7 Culberson	651,620	780,611	19.8
8 Brady	651,620	833,770	28.0
9 *Green*	651,619	733,796	12.6
10 McCaul	651,620	981,367	50.6
11 Conaway	651,620	710,682	9.1
12 Granger	651,619	831,100	27.5
13 Thornberry	651,620	672,781	3.2
14 Paul	651,619	779,704	19.7
15 *Hinojosa*	651,625	787,124	20.8
16 *Reyes*	651,619	757,427	16.2
17 Flores	651,620	760,042	16.6
18 *Jackson Lee*	651,619	720,991	10.6
19 Neugebauer	651,619	698,137	7.1
20 *Gonzalez*	651,619	711,705	9.2

	2000	2010	PERCENT CHANGE
21 Smith	651,615	856,954	31.5
22 Olson	651,619	910,877	39.8
23 Canseco	651,612	847,651	30.1
24 Marchant	651,620	792,319	21.6
25 *Doggett*	651,618	814,381	25.0
26 Burgess	651,619	915,137	40.4
27 Farenthold	651,619	741,993	13.9
28 *Cuellar*	651,627	851,824	30.7
29 *Green*	651,619	677,032	3.9
30 *Johnson*	651,620	706,469	8.4
31 Carter	651,619	902,101	38.4
32 Sessions	651,620	640,419	-1.7
UTAH			
1 Bishop	744,389	906,660	21.8
2 *Matheson*	744,390	890,993	19.7
3 Chaffetz	744,390	966,232	29.8
VERMONT			
(AL) *Welch*	608,827	625,741	2.8
VIRGINIA			
1 Wittman	643,514	786,237	22.2
2 Rigell	643,510	646,184	0.4
3 *Scott*	643,476	663,390	3.1
4 Forbes	643,477	738,639	14.8
5 Hurt	643,497	685,859	6.6
6 Goodlatte	643,504	704,056	9.4
7 Cantor	643,499	757,917	17.8
8 *Moran*	643,503	701,010	8.9
9 Griffith	643,514	656,200	2.0
10 Wolf	643,512	869,437	35.1
11 *Connolly*	643,509	792,095	23.1
WASHINGTON			
1 *Inslee*	654,904	739,455	12.9
2 *Larsen*	654,903	760,041	16.1
3 Herrera Beutler	654,898	779,348	19.0
4 Hastings	654,901	774,409	18.2
5 McMorris Rodgers	654,904	723,609	10.5
6 *Dicks*	654,902	709,570	8.3
7 *McDermott*	654,902	704,225	7.5
8 Reichert	654,905	810,754	23.8
9 *Smith*	654,902	723,129	10.4
WEST VIRGINIA			
1 McKinley	602,545	615,991	2.2
2 Capito	602,243	648,186	7.6
3 *Rahall*	603,556	588,817	-2.4
WISCONSIN			
1 Ryan	670,458	728,042	8.6
2 *Baldwin*	670,457	751,169	12.0
3 *Kind*	670,462	729,957	8.9
4 *Moore*	670,458	669,015	-0.2
5 Sensenbrenner	670,458	707,580	5.5
6 Petri	670,440	705,102	5.2
7 Duffy	670,462	689,279	2.8
8 Ribble	670,480	706,840	5.4
WYOMING			
(AL) Lummis	493,782	563,626	14.1

Table of Contents

Explanation of Statistics

State Profiles

State profile pages contain information on governors, compositions of state legislatures and information about major cities. Details about the makeup of the state legislatures, elected officials' salaries, the legislative schedule, registered voters and state term limits were obtained from state officials and reflect their status as of May 2011.

• POPULATION AND URBAN STATISTICS

Statistical information was obtained from the U.S. Census Bureau, the Defense Department and the FBI. Place of origin statistics, violent crime rates, poverty rates, and federal worker and military personnel statistics are from 2009.

• STATISTICS BY DISTRICT

Demographic information relates to current congressional district lines. The figures for racial composition, Hispanic origin, median household income, types of employment, age, education, urban versus rural residence and size of each congressional district are from the Census Bureau.

The racial composition figures reflect census respondents who described themselves as of one race. The white population figure is for non-Hispanic whites. The median household income figure is for 2009.

The occupational breakdown combines figures from the Census Bureau's management, professional and related occupations category and its sales and office occupations category to make up the white-collar category. The blue-collar category includes three bureau categories: farming, fishing and forestry; construction, extraction and maintenance; and production, transportation and material moving occupations.

The college education table shows the percentage of people age 25 and older who have earned at least a bachelor's degree. The district's area is presented in square miles of land area.

District Descriptions

In most states, congressional district lines were redrawn in 2001 or 2002 to reflect reapportionment and changes in population patterns revealed in the 2000 census. Maine's constitution calls for redistricting in the third year of each decade, and so new lines were drawn in 2003 for the 2004 election. Other mid-decade changes were in response to legal challenges.

A second set of Pennsylvania district lines drawn in 2002 was not effective until the 2004 election. Georgia districts were reconfigured in 2005 for the 2006 election. Texas had five districts — the 15th, 21st, 23rd, 25th and 28th — redrawn by a federal court for the 2006 election. No congressional district lines changed for the 2008 and 2010 elections.

The district description briefly sets forth the economic, sociological, demographic and political forces that are the keys to elections and that influence the legislative agenda of the district's member of Congress. City population figures are from the U.S. Census Bureau.

Military base figures are compiled by CQ Roll Call from information provided by each base and from annual Defense Department reports. The military base listings do not include Coast Guard, National Guard or reserve bases, and do not include all depots and arsenals due to space limitations.

Presidential Vote by District

CQ determined the 2008 presidential vote in each House district by acquiring and calculating vote returns from state and county election offices in the 43 states that have more than one House district. In seven of those states — Connecticut, Kentucky, Maine, Minnesota, Nebraska, North Carolina and Virginia — CQ used the presidential district vote calculations produced by state election officials. Seven states — Alaska, Delaware, Montana, North Dakota, South Dakota, Vermont and Wyoming — have only one House district.

Party Abbreviations

AC	American Constitution
AKI	Alaskan Independence
ALP	American Labor Party
AMI	American Independent
ANO	Action No Talk Party
ARM	American Renaissance Movement
BLU	Blue Enigma
CFL	Connecticut for Lieberman
C	Conservative*
CNSTP	Constitution
D	Democratic
DAC	Defend American Constitution
FE	Free Energy
GBS	Gravity Buoyancy Solution
GREEN	Green
GRP	Green Populist
GTP	Green Tea Patriots
I	Independent

(continued on p. xxii)

(continued from p. xxi)

IA	Independent American
IGREEN	Independent Green
INDC	Independence*
IRFM	Independent Reform
LIBERT	Libertarian
MDE	Moderate
MOUNT	Mountain
NL	Natural Law
PFP	Peace and Freedom
PRO	Progressive
PTF	Party Free
R	Republican
REF	Reform
RTH	Rent Is Too High
S	Socialist
TEA	Tea Party
TFC	Time For Change
TVH	Truth Vision Hope
UC	United Citizens
USTAX	U.S. Taxpayers
WFM	Working Families*
YCA	Your Country Again
X	Not Applicable

* In the New York election results, last names only were used for lawmakers to accommodate multiple party designations.

Member Profiles

Committees

Committee assignments are as of June 2011, and a complete roster for each panel begins on page 1128.

Career and Political Highlights

The member's principal occupations before becoming a full-time public official are given, with the most recent occupation listed first. Often, lawmakers' prior political offices were part-time jobs, and the member continued working at his or her "career" job. Political highlights listed include elected positions in government, high party posts, posts requiring legislative confirmation and unsuccessful candidacies for public office. Dates given cover years of service, not election dates.

Elections

Results for 2008 and 2010 are listed for House members, with primary results for 2010. For senators and governors, the most recent election results are listed. Because candidates who received less than 1 percent of the vote are not listed and percentages have been rounded, election results do not always add up to 100 percent.

Earlier election victories are noted for members of the House and Senate, with the member's percentage of the vote given. If no percentage is given for a year, the member either did not run or lost the election.

For special elections and primaries where a candidate would have won outright if he or she had received a majority of the votes, two election tallies are given, one for the initial election and one for the subsequent runoff.

• PRIMARY ELECTIONS

Prior to 2009 Louisiana held its primary on Election Day. It was an open primary, with candidates from all parties on the ballot. Any candidate who received more than half the votes, or who was unopposed, was elected. If no candidate received an outright majority, the top two vote-getters, regardless of party, advanced to a runoff election to decide the winner.

In March 2008, the Washington state Supreme Court upheld the "top two" primary system in which voters are able to vote for one candidate from among all candidates running for each office without having to declare a party affiliation or select a party ballot. The two candidates in each race who receive the most votes qualify for the general election, provided the candidate received at least 1 percent of the total votes cast for that office. Candidates for partisan office have the opportunity to state a political party preference on the primary ballot, but that preference is not an indication of approval, support, nomination, endorsement or association by the party that is listed.

Key Votes

Profiles of members who served in the 111th Congress (2009-10) are accompanied by key votes chosen by CQ editors from that Congress. Following is a description of those votes, including President Obama's position on that particular vote, if he unambiguously took one beforehand.

• Key Senate Votes

2010

Health Care Reconciliation/Passage (Senate Vote 105): Passage of the bill (HR 4872) that would make changes to the 2010 health care overhaul law, revise student loan programs and include revenue-raising provisions. It would increase federal subsidies to help low- and moderate-income families purchase coverage through new health insurance exchanges established by the overhaul measure, phase out the coverage gap for Medicare prescription drug enrollees and adjust the federal matching funds for Medicaid. It would increase penalties levied on employers that do not offer health benefits and change the formula used to calculate penalties on employers with workers who use subsidies to obtain health insurance through the exchanges. It would freeze Medicare Advantage payments in 2011 and then re-formulate payments according to local costs. It also would specify that in all states, the federal government would cover 100 percent of the cost of coverage to newly eligible Medicaid recipients from 2014 to 2016. It would delay for five years, until 2018, the effective date of a tax on high-cost health plans and adjust the dollar amounts used to determine who would be affected by the tax. It would repeal a provision to allow the cellulosic biofuels producer credit to be claimed by producers of certain paper products. It also would make the federal government the sole originator of federal student loans and direct the savings generated to education programs, including Pell grants. It would shift all new federal student lending to the Direct Loan Program beginning July 1, 2010. It would increase the maximum annual Pell Grant scholarship to $5,975 in 2017 and provide $2.6 billion for minority-serving institutions. Passed 56-43: D 54-3, R 0-40, I 2-0. A "yea" was a vote in support of the president's position. March 25, 2010.

Greenhouse Gas Regulation/Motion to Proceed (Senate Vote 184): Murkowski, R-Alaska, motion to proceed to consideration of a joint resolution (SJ Res 26) that would provide for congressional disapproval of an endangerment finding by the EPA that greenhouse gases qualify as dangerous pollutants under the Clean Air Act. That finding, which stemmed from a 2007 Supreme Court decision, triggered a requirement for the EPA to regulate emissions. Motion rejected 47-53: D 6-51; R 41-0; I 0-2. A "nay" was a vote in support of the president's position. June 10, 2010.

Financial Regulatory Overhaul/Conference Report (Senate Vote 208): Adoption of the conference report on the bill (HR 4173) that would overhaul the regulation of the financial services industry. The measure would create new regulatory mechanisms to assess risks posed by very large financial institutions and facilitate the orderly dissolution of failing firms that pose a threat to the economy. It would create a new federal agency to oversee consumer financial products, bring the derivatives market under significant federal regulation for the first time and give company

CQ editors selected key votes from roll-call votes taken during the 111th Congress. The following symbols are used:

Yes voted for

No voted against

paired for

+ announced for

X paired against

– announced against

P voted "present"

C voted "present" to avoid possible conflict of interest

? did not vote or otherwise make a position known

I ineligible

S Speaker exercised her discretion to not vote

Key Votes Symbols

Yes voted for

No voted against

paired for

+ announced for

X paired against

− announced against

P voted "present"

C voted "present" to avoid possible conflict of interest

? did not vote or otherwise make a position known

I ineligible

S Speaker exercised her discretion to not vote

Key Senate Votes cont.

shareholders and regulators greater say on executive pay packages. The costs would be offset by terminating the Troubled Asset Relief Program and increasing deposit insurance premiums paid by some banks. Adopted (thus cleared for the president) 60-39: D 55-1; R 3-38; I 2-0. A "yea" was a vote in support of the president's position. July 15, 2010.

Campaign Finance Disclosure/Cloture (Senate Vote 240): Motion to invoke cloture (thus limiting debate) on the motion to proceed to the bill (S 3628) that would require corporations and unions to disclose in their campaign advertising the chief donors who paid for the ad. Motion rejected 59-39: D 57-0; R 0-39; I 2-0. Three-fifths of the total Senate (60) is required to invoke cloture. (Previously, a Reid, D-Nev., motion to reconsider was adopted by unanimous consent.) A "yea" was a vote in support of the president's position. Sept. 23, 2010.

Tax Rates Extensions/Cloture (Senate Vote 272): Motion to invoke cloture (thus limiting debate) on the Reid, D-Nev., motion to concur in the House amendment to the Senate amendment with a further Reid and McConnell, R-Ky., substitute amendment to the bill (HR 4853) that would extend the 2001 and 2003 tax cuts for all taxpayers for two years, as well as reinstate the estate tax at a 35 percent rate on the value of estates in excess of $5 million. It also would continue expanded unemployment insurance benefits for 13 months. Motion agreed to 83-15: D 45-9; R 37-5; I 1-1. Three-fifths of the total Senate (60) is required to invoke cloture. Dec. 13, 2010.

Immigration Policy Revisions/Cloture (Senate Vote 278): Motion to invoke cloture (thus limiting debate) on the Reid, D-Nev., motion to concur in the House amendment to the third Senate amendment to the bill (HR 5281). The House amendment would allow the Homeland Security Department to grant conditional non-immigrant status to the undocumented children of illegal immigrants if they meet certain requirements, including having been in the United States continuously for more than five years, having been younger than 16 when they entered the country and having been admitted to a U.S. college or university or enlisted in the military. The individual would have to pay a $525 application surcharge and a subsequent fee and could be eligible to apply for legal permanent status after 10 years. Motion rejected 55-41: D 50-5; R 3-36; I 2-0. Three-fifths of the total Senate (60) is required to invoke cloture. A "yea" was a vote in support of the president's position. Dec. 18, 2010.

'Don't Ask, Don't Tell' Policy Repeal/Motion to Concur (Senate Vote 281): Reid, D-Nev., motion to concur in the Senate amendment to the bill (HR 2965) with a House amendment that would allow for the repeal of the "don't ask, don't tell" policy, which prohibits military service by openly gay men and women, after certain requirements are met, including the submission of a written certification, signed by the president, the secretary of Defense and the chairman of the Joint Chiefs of Staff, that the repeal is consistent with military readiness and effectiveness and that they have considered the recommendations of the Comprehensive Review Working Group and prepared the necessary policies and regulations to implement the repeal. Motion agreed to, thus clearing the bill for the president, 65-31: D 55-0; R 8-31; I 2-0. A "yea" was a vote in support of the president's position. Dec. 18, 2010.

Key Senate Votes cont.

New START Agreement/Adoption (Senate Vote 298): Adoption of the resolution of ratification for the New Strategic Arms Reduction Treaty (Treaty Doc 111-5) with Russia. The treaty would restrict each country to a maximum of 1,550 deployed nuclear warheads, a cut of about 30 percent. The resolution of ratification would state that the April 2010 unilateral statement by Russia on missile defense does not impose any legal obligation on the United States. Adopted (thus consenting to ratification) 71-26: D 56-0; R 13-26; I 2-0. A two-thirds majority of those present and voting (65 in this case) is required for adoption of resolutions of ratification. A "yea" was a vote in support of the president's position. Dec. 22, 2010.

2009

Troubled Asset Relief Program Disapproval/Passage (Senate Vote 5): Passage of the joint resolution (S J Res 5) that would prevent the release of the second half of the $700 billion provided under the 2008 financial industry bailout law. Rejected 42-52: R 33-6; D 8-45; I 1-1. Jan. 15, 2009.

Wage Discrimination/Passage (Senate Vote 14): Passage of the bill (S 181) that would amend the 1964 Civil Rights Act to clarify time limits for workers to file employment discrimination lawsuits. The bill would allow workers who allege discrimination based on race, gender, national origin, religion, age or disability to file charges of pay discrimination within 180 days of the last received paycheck affected by the alleged discriminatory decision. The bill would renew the statute of limitations with each act of discrimination. Passed 61-36: R 5-36; D 54-0; I 2-0. (By unanimous consent, the Senate agreed to raise the majority requirement for passage of the bill to 59 votes.) Jan. 22, 2009.

Children's Health Insurance/Passage (Senate Vote 31): Passage of the bill (HR 2) that would reauthorize the State Children's Health Insurance Program for four and a half years and increase funding by $32.8 billion. To offset the cost of the expansion, the bill would increase the federal tax on cigarettes to 62 cents per pack and raise taxes on other tobacco products. It would remove a five-year waiting period for new legal immigrants, including pregnant women, to be enrolled in the program, and loosen citizenship and eligibility documentation requirements. The bill would limit program eligibility to families earning three times the federal poverty level or less and would require states to phase out coverage of childless adults. Passed 66-32: R 9-32; D 55-0; I 2-0. Jan. 29, 2009.

Economic Stimulus/Cloture (Senate Vote 59): Motion to invoke cloture (thus limiting debate) on the Reid, D-Nev. (for Nelson, D-Neb., and Collins, R-Maine), substitute amendment that would provide approximately $838 billion in tax cuts and additional spending to stimulate the economy, including a provision to exempt additional taxpayers from paying the alternative minimum tax in 2009. The amendment to the bill (HR 1) would provide funds for a state fiscal stabilization fund and a one-time payment to seniors, disabled veterans and those who receive disability payments. The amendment would expand bonus depreciation for 2009, increase weekly unemployment benefits and provide an additional 20 weeks of unemployment benefits (an additional 33 weeks in states with high unemployment rates). It would suspend federal income tax on the first $2,400 of unemployment benefits for 2009. It would also expand the homeownership tax

Key Votes Symbols

Yes voted for

No voted against

paired for

+ announced for

X paired against

– announced against

P voted "present"

C voted "present" to avoid possible conflict of interest

? did not vote or otherwise make a position known

I ineligible

S Speaker exercised her discretion to not vote

Key Senate Votes cont.

credit by up to $15,000 and allow use of the credit for purchases of a primary residence. It would temporarily increase federal Medicaid matching payments for states by an estimated $87 billion. Motion agreed to 61-36: R 3-36; D 56-0; I 2-0. Three-fifths of the total Senate (60) is required to invoke cloture. Feb. 9, 2009.

District of Columbia Voting Rights/District Gun Laws (Senate Vote 72): Ensign, R-Nev., amendment that would ban the District of Columbia from prohibiting an individual to possess firearms and repeal District laws barring possession of semiautomatic firearms. The amendment to the bill (S 160) would repeal the District's mandates for firearm registration and the requirement that firearms be disassembled or secured with a trigger lock in the home. District residents would be allowed to purchase firearms in Maryland and Virginia. Adopted 62-36: R 40-1; D 22-33; I 0-2. Feb. 26, 2009.

Fiscal 2010 Defense Authorization/Cloture (Senate Vote 233): Motion to invoke cloture (thus limiting debate) on the Leahy, D-Vt., amendment that would expand federal hate crimes law to cover crimes based on sexual orientation, gender identity or disability. Motion agreed to 63-28: R 5-28; D 56-0; I 2-0. Three-fifths of the total Senate (60) is required to invoke cloture. (Subsequently, the Leahy amendment was adopted by voice vote.) July 16, 2009.

Fiscal 2010 Defense Authorization/F-22 Aircraft (Senate Vote 235): Levin, D-Mich., amendment that would strike $1.75 billion from the bill (S 1390) for the procurement of F-22A aircraft. It would increase the authorization for operations and maintenance by $350 million for the Army, $100 million for the Navy, $250 million for the Air Force and $150 million across the Defense Department. It would increase the authorization for military personnel by $400 million and general Defense Department activities by $500 million. Adopted 58-40: R 15-25; D 42-14; I 1-1. A "yea" was a vote in support of the president's position. July 21, 2009.

• Key House Votes

2010

Health Care Overhaul/Motion to Concur (House Vote 165):
Spratt, D-S.C., motion to concur in the Senate amendment to the bill (HR 3590) that would overhaul the nation's health insurance system and would require most individuals to buy health insurance by 2014. It would create a system of private insurance plans supervised by the Office of Personnel Management and create state-run marketplaces for purchasing health insurance. Those who do not obtain coverage would be subject to an excise tax, with exceptions. Employers with more than 50 workers would have to provide coverage or pay a fine if any employee gets a subsidized plan on the exchange. Certain small businesses would get tax credits for providing coverage, and people with low incomes, excluding illegal immigrants, could get subsidies. It would bar the use of federal funds to pay for abortions in the new programs, except in the cases of rape or incest or if the woman's life is in danger. Insurance companies could not deny coverage based on pre-existing medical conditions beginning in 2014 and could not drop coverage of people who become ill. It would expand eligibility for Medicaid and would shrink Medicare's so-called doughnut hole. Motion agreed to, thus clearing the bill for the president, 219-212: D 219-34; R 0-178. A "yea" was a vote in support of the president's position. March 21, 2010.

Fiscal 2011 Defense Authorization/'Don't Ask, Don't Tell' Policy Repeal (House Vote 317): Murphy, D-Pa., amendment that would repeal the "don't ask, don't tell" policy on military service by openly gay men and women after receipt of Pentagon recommendations on how to implement a repeal. It would take effect 60 days after certification by the Defense secretary, chairman of the Joint Chiefs and the president that the repeal is consistent with the standards of military readiness, military effectiveness, unit cohesion and recruiting. Adopted in Committee of the Whole 234-194: D 229-26; R 5-168. A "yea" was a vote in support of the president's position. May 27, 2010.

Financial Regulatory Overhaul/Conference Report (House Vote 413): Adoption of the conference report on the bill (HR 4173) that would overhaul the regulation of the financial services industry. The measure would create a new regulatory mechanism to assess risks posed by very large financial institutions and facilitate the orderly dissolution of failing firms that pose a threat to the economy. It would create a new federal agency to oversee consumer financial products, bring the derivatives market under significant federal regulation for the first time and give company shareholders and regulators greater say on executive pay packages. The costs would be offset by terminating the Troubled Asset Relief Program and increasing deposit insurance premiums paid by some banks. Adopted (thus sent to the Senate) 237-192: D 234-19; R 3-173. A "yea" was a vote in support of the president's position. June 30, 2010.

Supplemental Appropriations/Passage (House Vote 432): Fourth portion of the divided question on the Obey, D-Wis., motion to concur in the Senate amendments to the bill (HR 4899) with House amendments. The fourth portion consists of a Lee, D-Calif., amendment that would limit the use of military funding for Afghanistan to activities relating to the safe with-

Yes voted for

No voted against

paired for

+ announced for

X paired against

– announced against

P voted "present"

C voted "present" to avoid possible conflict of interest

? did not vote or otherwise make a position known

I ineligible

S Speaker exercised her discretion to not vote

Key Votes Symbols

Yes voted for

No voted against

paired for

+ announced for

X paired against

− announced against

P voted "present"

C voted "present" to avoid possible conflict of interest

? did not vote or otherwise make a position known

I ineligible

S Speaker exercised her discretion to not vote

Key House Votes cont.

drawal of U.S. troops and the protection of civilian and military personnel in the country. Motion rejected 100-321: D 93-157; R 7-164. A "nay" was a vote in support of the president's position. July 1, 2010.

Offshore Drilling Regulation Overhaul/Passage (House Vote 513): Passage of the bill (HR 3534) that would repeal the $75 million cap on liability for offshore oil spills. It also would abolish the agency formerly known as the Minerals Management Service in the Interior Department and assign its responsibilities to three new agencies in the department. It would create numerous new safety regulations for leases for offshore oil and gas development, including features designed to prevent well blowouts, and it would require some holders of leases to renegotiate royalty payments disputed by industry. As amended, it would prevent oil companies from shifting oil spill cleanup costs to taxpayers in the event one of its subsidiaries goes bankrupt. Passed 209-193: D 207-39; R 2-154. July 30, 2010.

Immigration Policy Revisions/Motion to Concur (House Vote 625): Conyers, D-Mich., motion to concur in Senate amendments to the bill (HR 5281) with a House amendment that would add language to allow the Homeland Security Department to grant conditional non-immigrant status to the undocumented children of illegal immigrants if they meet certain requirements, including having been in the United States continuously for more than five years, been younger than 16 when they entered the country and been admitted to a U.S. college or university or enlisted in the military. The individuals would have to pay a $525 application surcharge and a subsequent fee and could be eligible to apply for legal permanent status after 10 years. Motion agreed to, thus sent to the Senate, 216-198: D 208-38; R 8-160. A "yea" was a vote in support of the president's position. Dec. 8, 2010.

Tax Rates Extensions/Motion to Concur (House Vote 647): Levin, D-Mich., motion to concur in the Senate amendment to the House amendment to the Senate amendment to the bill (HR 4853) that would extend the 2001- and 2003-enacted tax cuts for all taxpayers for two years and revive the lapsed estate tax, setting the tax rate at 35 percent on the value of estates in excess of $5 million for 2011 and 2012. It would also continue expanded unemployment insurance benefits for 13 months and cut the employee portion of the Social Security tax by 2 percentage points. Motion agreed to, thus clearing the bill for the president, 277-148: D 139-112; R 138-36. A "yea" was a vote in support of the president's position. Dec. 17, 2010 (in the session that began in the Congressional Record dated Dec. 16, 2010).

2009

Children's Health Insurance/Motion to Concur (House Vote 50): Waxman, D-Calif., motion to concur in the Senate amendment to the bill (HR 2) that would reauthorize the Children's Health Insurance Program over four and a half years and increase funding by $32.8 billion. To offset the cost of the expansion, the bill would increase the federal tax on cigarettes by 62 cents per pack and raise taxes on other tobacco products. It would remove a five-year waiting period for new, legal immigrants,

including pregnant women, to be enrolled in the program, and loosen citizenship and eligibility documentation requirements. The bill would limit program eligibility to families earning three times the federal poverty level or less and would require states to phase out coverage of childless adults. Motion agreed to (thus clearing the bill for the president), 290-135: R 40-133; D 250-2. Feb. 4, 2009.

Economic Stimulus/Conference Report (House Vote 70): Adoption of the conference report on the bill (HR 1) that would provide an estimated $787.2 billion in tax cuts and spending increases to stimulate the economy. It would prevent the alternative minimum tax from applying to millions of additional taxpayers in 2009 and increase the ceiling on federal borrowing by $789 billion to $12.104 trillion. The tax provisions, estimated to cost $211.8 billion through 2019, include extending current accelerated depreciation allowances for businesses, suspending taxes on the first $2,400 of unemployment benefits for 2009 and expanding a number of individual tax credits. Mandatory spending increases, expected to cost $267 billion through 2019, include an extension of unemployment and welfare benefits, Medicaid payments to states and grants for health information technology. Discretionary spending, estimated at $308.3 billion through 2019, includes grants for state and local schools and funds for public housing, transportation and nutrition assistance. Adopted (thus sent to the Senate) 246-183: R 0-176; D 246-7. A "yea" was a vote in support of the president's position. Feb. 13, 2009.

Mortgage Loans Modification/Passage (House Vote 104) Passage of the bill that would allow bankruptcy judges to write down the principal and interest rates of loans issued before the bill's (HR 1106) enactment to a home's current market value, for individuals whose mortgages are larger than the value of their homes or who meet other requirements. It would allow the government to reimburse mortgage lenders for reduced principal, interest rates or fees if the mortgage was guaranteed by the Federal Housing Administration, the Veterans Affairs Department or other federal mortgage guarantors. It also would modify the Hope for Homeowners program and would permanently increase, to $250,000, Federal Deposit Insurance Corporation and National Credit Union Administration deposit insurance coverage on individual bank accounts. The amount would be indexed to inflation from 2015 on. Passed 234-191: R 7-167; D 227-24. March 5, 2009.

Greenhouse Gas Emissions/Passage (House Vote 477): Passage of the bill (HR 2454) that would create a cap-and-trade system to limit greenhouse gas emissions and set new requirements for electric utilities. Emission allowances would permit buyers to emit a certain amount of greenhouse gases. Most of the allowances initially would be provided free of charge. By 2030, most would be auctioned to polluters. The bill would set emissions limits at 17 percent below current levels in 2020, expanding to 83 percent in 2050. It would require utilities to produce 15 percent of the nation's electricity from renewable sources by 2020. It would establish programs to assist consumers with higher utility bills resulting from the new system. Passed 219-212: R 8-168; D 211-44. A "yea" was a vote in support of the president's position. June 26, 2009.

Key Votes Symbols

Yes voted for

No voted against

\# paired for

\+ announced for

X paired against

– announced against

P voted "present"

C voted "present" to avoid possible conflict of interest

? did not vote or otherwise make a position known

I ineligible

S Speaker exercised her discretion to not vote

Key House Votes cont.

Car Voucher Program Funding/Passage (House Vote 682): Obey, D-Wis., motion to suspend the rules and pass the bill (HR 3435) that would provide $2 billion for the "cash for clunkers" vehicle trade-in program, which offers vouchers worth up to $4,500 toward the purchase of new vehicles to consumers who trade in their older, less-efficient models. The funds would be transferred from the Energy Department's innovative technologies loan-guarantee program. Motion agreed to 316-109: R 77-95; D 239-14. A two-thirds majority of those present and voting (284 in this case) is required for passage under suspension of the rules. A "yea" was a vote in support of the president's position. July 31, 2009.

Student Loan Overhaul/Passage (House Vote 719): Passage of the bill (HR 3221) that would end the role of private lenders in providing government-subsidized loans to students after June 30, 2010. The bill would make the government the sole source of federally backed loans for higher education. Most of the savings would be used to increase funding for education programs, including Pell grants, early-childhood education and community colleges. As amended, it would bar federal agreements from being entered into with certain organizations, including the Association of Community Organizations for Reform Now (ACORN). Passed 253-171: R 6-167; D 247-4. A "yea" was a vote in support of the president's position. Sept. 17, 2009.

Health Care Overhaul/Abortion Funding Ban (House Vote 884): Stupak, D-Mich., amendment that would bar the use of federal funds authorized in the bill (HR 3962) to pay for abortion or to cover any part of the costs of any health plan that includes abortion coverage, unless the pregnancy is the result of rape or incest or would endanger the woman's life. Individuals with subsidized policies who also want abortion coverage would have to purchase it separately, using their own money. The amendment would prohibit individuals from using affordability credits to purchase a plan that provides for elective abortions. Adopted 240-194: D 64-194; R 176-0. Nov. 7, 2009.

Vote Studies

Each year, CQ studies the frequency with which each member of Congress supports or opposes the position of their own party's majority and the position of the president. Scores are based only on votes cast; not voting does not alter a member's score. All votes have equal statistical weight in the analysis. Scores are rounded to the nearest whole percentage point, although rounding is not used to increase any score to 100 percent or to reduce any score to zero.

• PARTY UNITY

Party unity votes are defined as all votes in the Senate and House that split the two parties — a majority of voting Democrats opposing a majority of voting Republicans. Votes on which the parties agree, or on which one party divides evenly, are excluded. In recent years, more than half of all votes in the Senate and at least 40 percent of all votes in the House — sometimes more than half — have been designated as party unity votes.

Support scores represent the percentage of party unity votes on which a member voted yes or no in agreement with a majority of the member's party. Opposition scores represent the percentage of party unity votes on which a member voted yes or no in disagreement with a majority of the member's party.

• PRESIDENTIAL SUPPORT

CQ tries to determine what the president personally, as distinct from other administration officials, wants or does not want in the way of legislative action. This is done by reviewing messages to Congress, news conference remarks and other public statements and documents. Every roll call vote in the House and Senate is reviewed in that context, and those votes where the editors of CQ decide that the president had a clear stake in the outcome carry presidential positions. Occasionally, important bills are so extensively amended that it is impossible to characterize votes on final passage as a victory or a defeat for the president. At the same time, procedural votes on motions to recommit, to reconsider or to table (kill) sometimes govern the outcome and these are included in the presidential support tabulations. In the House in recent years, fewer than 10 percent of all votes have been judged to carry presidential positions. In the Senate, 20 percent or more of all votes typically meet the definition.

Support scores represent the percentage of votes on which a member voted yes or no in agreement with the president's position. Opposition scores represent the percentage of votes on which a member voted yes or no in disagreement with president's position.

Interest Group Ratings

Ratings for members by four advocacy groups are chosen to reflect labor, liberal, business and conservative viewpoints.

• AFL-CIO

The AFL-CIO was formed when the American Federation of Labor and the Congress of Industrial Organizations merged in 1955. For senators, ratings are based on 15 votes in 2006, 19 in 2007, 11 in 2008, 18 in 2009 and 16 in 2010. For House members, ratings are based on 14 votes in 2006, 24 in 2007, 18 in 2008, 21 in 2009 and 14 in 2010. (www.aflcio.org)

Congress by its Numbers

A new Congress is elected in each even-numbered year and convenes at the beginning of each odd-numbered year. As a shorthand, this book frequently refers to the actions of a particular Congress by its number. The sequence began with the 1st Congress, which was elected in 1788.

Congress	Year elected	Years in session
112th	2010	2011 and 2012
111th	2008	2009 and 2010
110th	2006	2007 and 2008
109th	2004	2005 and 2006
108th	2002	2003 and 2004
107th	2000	2001 and 2002
106th	1998	1999 and 2000
105th	1996	1997 and 1998
104th	1994	1995 and 1996
103rd	1992	1993 and 1994
102nd	1990	1991 and 1992
101st	1988	1989 and 1990
100th	1986	1987 and 1988

• ADA

Americans for Democratic Action was founded in 1947 by a group of liberal Democrats that included Minnesota Sen. Hubert H. Humphrey and Eleanor Roosevelt. The ADA ratings are based on 20 votes each year in each chamber of Congress. (www.adaction.org)

• CCUS

The Chamber of Commerce of the United States represents local, regional and state chambers as well as trade and professional groups. It was founded in 1912 to be "a voice for organized business." For senators, ratings are based on 12 votes in 2006, 11 in 2007, 8 in 2008, seven in 2009 and 11 in 2010. For House members, ratings are based on 15 votes in 2006, 20 in 2007, 18 in 2008, 15 in 2009 and nine in 2010. (www.uschamber.com)

• ACU

The American Conservative Union was founded in 1964 "to mobilize resources of responsible conservative thought across the country and further the general cause of conservatism." The organization intends to provide education in: political activity; "prejudice in the press;" foreign and military policy; domestic economic policy; the arts; professions and sciences. For senators, ratings are based on 25 votes in each of the last five years. For House members, the ratings are based on 25 votes in each year from 2006 to 2009 and 24 votes in 2010. (www.conservative.org)

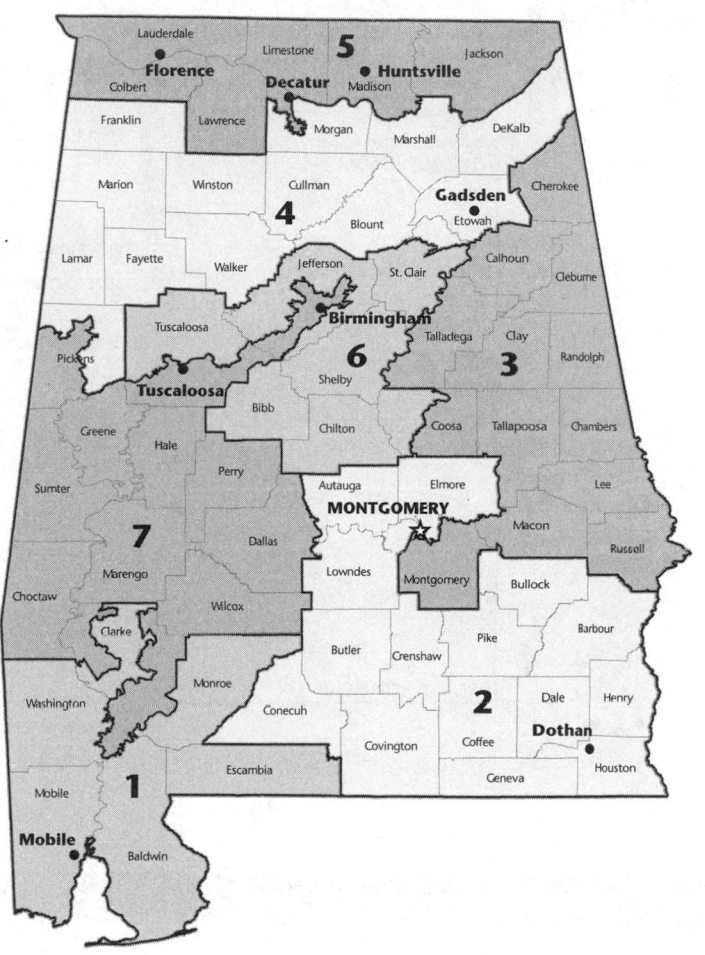

Gov. Robert Bentley (R)

First elected: 2010

Length of term: 4 years

Term expires: 1/15

Salary: $112,895

Phone: (334) 242-7100

Residence: Tuscaloosa

Born: Feb. 3, 1943; Columbiana, Ala.

Religion: Baptist

Family: Wife, Dianne Bentley; four children

Education: U. of Alabama, B.S. 1964 (chemistry), M.D. 1968

Career: Physician

Political highlights: Ala. House, 2002-10

ELECTION RESULTS

2010 GENERAL

Robert Bentley (R)	860,052	57.9%
Ron Sparks (D)	625,052	42.1%

Lt. Gov. Kay Ivey (R)

First elected: 2010

Length of term: 4 years

Term expires: 1/15

Salary: $75,556

Phone: (334) 242-7900

LEGISLATURE

Legislature: Annually, limit of 30 legislative days within 105 calendar days

Senate: 35 members, 4-year terms

2011 ratios: 22 R, 12 D, 1 independent; 30 men, 5 women.

Salary: $10/day; $50/day per diem; $4,108/month expenses.

Phone: (334) 242-7800

House: 105 members, 4-year terms

2011 ratios: 65 R, 40 D; 91 men, 14 women

Salary: $10/day; $50/day per diem; $4,108/month expenses.

Phone: (334) 242-7600

TERM LIMITS

Governor: 2 consecutive terms

Senate: No

House: No

URBAN STATISTICS

CITY	POPULATION
Birmingham	212,237
Montgomery	205,764
Mobile	195,111
Huntsville	180,105
Tuscaloosa	90,468

REGISTERED VOTERS

Voters do not register by party.

POPULATION

2010 population	4,779,736
2000 population	4,447,100
1990 population	4,040,587
Percent change (2000-2010)	+7.5%
Rank among states (2010)	23
Median age	37.2
Born in state	70.9%
Foreign born	2.8%
Violent crime rate	450/100,000
Poverty level	17.5%
Federal workers	64,817
Military	11,896

ELECTIONS

STATE ELECTION OFFICIAL

(334) 242-7210

DEMOCRATIC PARTY

(334) 262-2221

REPUBLICAN PARTY

(205) 212-5900

MISCELLANEOUS

Web: www.alabama.gov

Capital: Montgomery

U.S. CONGRESS

Senate: 2 Republicans

House: 6 Republicans, 1 Democrat

2010 Census Statistics by District

District	2008 Vote for President Obama	McCain	White	Black	Asian	Hispanic	Median Income	White Collar	Blue Collar	Service Industry	Over 64	Under 18	College Education	Rural	Sq. Miles
1	38%	61%	66%	28%	1%	3%	$41,627	56%	27%	17%	14%	25%	20%	36%	6,317
2	37	63	63	31	1	3	39,538	55	29	16	14	25	19	50	10,502
3	43	56	63	32	1	3	37,304	54	30	16	13	23	19	47	7,834
4	22	76	86	5	<1	6	37,379	48	38	15	15	24	13	73	8,372
5	38	61	73	18	1	5	45,832	60	26	14	13	24	26	41	4,486
6	25	74	80	13	2	4	57,328	68	21	12	12	24	33	38	4,564
7	71	29	33	63	1	3	31,021	53	28	20	13	25	17	28	8,669
STATE	39	60	67	26	1	4	41,216	57	28	15	14	24	22	45	50,744
U.S.	53	46	64	12	5	16	51,425	60	23	17	13	25	28	21	3,537,438

Sen. Richard C. Shelby (R)

Capitol Office
224-5744
shelby.senate.gov
304 Russell Bldg. 20510 0103; fax 224-3416

Committees
Appropriations
Banking, Housing & Urban Affairs - Ranking Member
Rules & Administration
Special Aging

Residence
Tuscaloosa

Born
May 6, 1934; Birmingham, Ala.

Religion
Presbyterian

Family
Wife, Annette Nevin Shelby; two children

Education
U. of Alabama, A.B. 1957, LL.B. 1963

Career
Lawyer; city prosecutor

Political Highlights
Ala. Senate, 1971-79 (served as a Democrat); U.S. House, 1979-87 (served as a Democrat)

ELECTION RESULTS

2010 GENERAL

Richard C. Shelby (R)	968,181	65.2%
William G. Barnes (D)	515,619	34.7%

2010 PRIMARY

Richard C. Shelby (R)	405,398	84.4%
N.C. "Clint" Moser (R)	75,190	15.6%

2004 GENERAL

Richard C. Shelby (R)	1,242,200	67.6%
Wayne Sowell (D)	595,018	32.4%

Previous Winning Percentages
1998 (63%); 1992 (65%); 1986 (50%); 1984 House Election (97%); 1982 House Election (97%); 1980 House Election (73%); 1978 House Election (94%)

Elected 1986; 5th term

Shelby is a cagey legislator who often goes his own way. Long known for holding his political cards close to his vest, he regularly asserts his independence as the Banking, Housing and Urban Affairs Committee's ranking member and has opposed major financial services legislation under both Republican and Democratic administrations.

He has also been critical of the Federal Reserve Board and voted against confirming Fed Chairman Ben S. Bernanke to another term in early 2010. Later in the year, he opposed President Obama's nomination of Nobel Prize-winning economist Peter Diamond to a seat on the board.

"Professor Peter Diamond is certainly a skilled economist; it's just not a matter, however, that every skilled economist is the best-qualified individual to serve on the Federal Reserve Board," Shelby said.

Shelby helped block confirmation in December 2010 of Joseph A. Smith Jr. to head the agency that oversees mortgage giants Fannie Mae and Freddie Mac, arguing he would be beholden to the Obama administration. "We need a watchdog, not a lapdog," Shelby said.

One of Congress' first party switchers in the 1990s, Shelby is a frequent skeptic of what he sees as over-regulation — as well as over-legislating. During the 111th Congress (2009-10) he played a critical role in curbing the most sweeping overhaul of the financial services industry since the Great Depression. Although Shelby, a chief Republican negotiator on the regulatory package, was unsuccessful in getting the legislation to end government support of Fannie Mae and Freddie Mac, he continued to prove a formidable opponent of the legislation that would severely curtail market activity.

Shelby struck a deal with Banking Chairman Christopher J. Dodd, a Connecticut Democrat, to remove a $50 billion industry-financed "too big to fail" fund from the package. Still, he opposed the final legislation: "I cannot support legislation that threatens business conditions and threatens job creation."

Shelby also said Congress was acting too swiftly and there needed to be more time to work on the legislation — a concern he has often voiced on the committee. He prefers to conduct exhaustive hearings and offstage reviews before drafting legislation. And as the top Republican on the panel overseeing the industry, he refused to be involved with the Bush administration's plans to help ailing financial firms in 2008.

His deliberate approach avoids roiling the financial markets with quick fixes to problems, but it can also slow the legislative response to abuses. It took Congress more than two years to crack down on unscrupulous financial services and insurance companies that prey on members of the military, in large part because Shelby insisted on waiting for a series of reports on the abuses from government agencies. "He may be slow, he may be cautious, he may be frustrating," the now retired Dodd told The New York Times in May 2008. "But once he makes the deal, it happens."

Shelby also opposed 2010's other major overhaul of a large swath of the economy, the Democrats' health care legislation. He told Chris Wallace on "Fox News Sunday" that the bill "will be the first steps in . . . destroying the best health care system the world has ever known."

Before taking the helm of the Banking panel when the GOP controlled the Senate in 2003, Shelby had served as chairman and then vice chairman of the Intelligence Committee. He called the Sept. 11, 2001, terrorist attacks "an intelligence failure of unprecedented magnitude" and singled out the CIA for relying too much on technological tools and not enough on agents in the field. He regularly called for the resignation of then-CIA Director George J. Tenet.

Fallout from that period in his career continued into the 109th Congress (2005-06), with a Senate Ethics Committee investigation into allegations that Shelby leaked secret government information to the media. The Ethics panel cleared him of any wrongdoing in 2005.

In 2010, Shelby opposed Senate approval of ratification of a strategic arms reduction treaty with Russia and cuffed the Obama White House in the process. "It should not be a surprise that the administration lacks commitment to a robust missile defense system, but that does not mean the Senate needs to support it," he said.

Shelby, a longtime Appropriations Committee member, steers vast sums of federal money to Alabama.

In May 2010, he successfully added an amendment to the fiscal 2010 supplemental spending bill to provide assistance to Gulf Coast fishermen harmed by the BP oil spill, allocating $15 million to the fisheries disaster declaration in the Gulf of Mexico, $10 million for an expanded stock assessment of the gulf fisheries and $1 million to study long-term ecosystem service effects of the spill on the gulf.

Shelby helped foster the space and defense economy in Huntsville, home to NASA's Marshall Space Flight Center and the Army's Redstone Arsenal. A Shelby provision included in the fiscal 2010 budget helped protect NASA spending on the Ares rocket, part of which is built in Alabama, even after the program was effectively canceled.

In the new Congress, he switched from top Republican on the committee that handles the NASA budget to lead the minority on the Labor-Health and Human Services-Education panel.

He is willing to play hardball when money for Alabama interests is harder to secure. In early 2010, Shelby put holds on dozens of Obama's nominees awaiting Senate confirmation in an effort to get the administration to release funds appropriated for an FBI center in Huntsville, and to protest how the Air Force was proceeding on a tanker contract that could mean jobs for Alabama.

Shelby got his Appropriations seat after switching parties less than 24 hours after Republicans learned they had won control of Congress in 1994. Shelby, like many other Southern Democrats, said he made the move because of what he described as the demise of the pro-defense, conservative wing of their party. It also followed an attempt by the Clinton administration to move some space programs out of Alabama after Shelby had criticized President Bill Clinton's budget while standing next to Vice President Al Gore in front of TV cameras. Prior to the switch, Shelby never voted with a majority of Democrats against a majority of Republicans more than 54 percent in a given year. Since, his party unity score has never been below 80 percent.

Shelby spent most of the 1960s as a municipal prosecutor in Tuscaloosa. He served eight years in the state Senate, where he was often at odds with Gov. George C. Wallace Jr. Though he was initially interested in running for lieutenant governor in 1978, more than a dozen other Democrats had the same idea. When one of his former law partners, Democrat Walter Flowers, gave up his House seat that year to run for the Senate, Shelby was easily persuaded to change course and run for Congress.

Shelby operated largely behind the scenes in the House for eight years, working on federal projects for his district and often siding with Republicans. His election to the Senate as a Democrat in 1986 was a slim victory over one-term incumbent Jeremiah Denton, a celebrated Vietnam prisoner of war. His re-elections have been by comfortable margins. In 2010, he won 65 percent of the vote against Democrat William Barnes.

Key Votes	
2010	
Pass budget reconciliation bill to modify overhauls of health care and federal student loan programs	NO
Proceed to disapproval resolution on EPA authority to regulate greenhouse gases	YES
Overhaul financial services industry regulation	NO
Limit debate to proceed to a bill to broaden campaign finance disclosure and reporting rules	NO
Limit debate on an extension of Bush-era income tax cuts for two years	YES
Limit debate on a bill to provide a path to legal status for some children of illegal immigrants	NO
Allow for a repeal of "don't ask, don't tell"	NO
Consent to ratification of a strategic arms reduction treaty with Russia	NO
2009	
Prevent release of remaining financial industry bailout funds	YES
Make it easier for victims to sue for wage discrimination remedies	NO
Expand the Children's Health Insurance Program	NO
Limit debate on the economic stimulus measure	NO
Repeal District of Columbia firearms prohibitions and gun registration laws	YES
Limit debate on expansion of federal hate crimes law	NO
Strike funding for F-22 Raptor fighter jets	YES

CQ Vote Studies				
	PARTY UNITY		PRESIDENTIAL SUPPORT	
	SUPPORT	OPPOSE	SUPPORT	OPPOSE
2010	96%	4%	41%	59%
2009	83%	17%	58%	42%
2008	95%	5%	74%	26%
2007	88%	12%	80%	20%
2006	88%	12%	86%	14%
2005	94%	6%	89%	11%
2004	94%	6%	86%	14%
2003	96%	4%	95%	5%
2002	80%	20%	87%	13%
2001	88%	12%	97%	3%

Interest Groups				
	AFL-CIO	ADA	CCUS	ACU
2010	13%	0%	100%	96%
2009	22%	10%	86%	88%
2008	20%	15%	75%	84%
2007	21%	20%	73%	88%
2006	7%	10%	83%	74%
2005	23%	10%	89%	88%
2004	25%	20%	88%	84%
2003	15%	10%	82%	90%
2002	38%	10%	85%	80%
2001	19%	5%	93%	100%

Sen. Jeff Sessions (R)

Capitol Office
224-4124
sessions.senate.gov
326 Russell Bldg. 20510-0104; fax 224-3149

Committees
Armed Services
Budget - Ranking Member
Environment & Public Works
Judiciary

Residence
Mobile

Born
Dec. 24, 1946; Hybart, Ala.

Religion
Methodist

Family
Wife, Mary Sessions; three children

Education
Huntingdon College, B.A. 1969 (history);
U. of Alabama, J.D. 1973

Military Service
Army Reserve, 1973-86

Career
Lawyer; teacher

Political Highlights
Assistant U.S. attorney, 1975-77; U.S. attorney, 1981-93; Ala. attorney general, 1995-97

ELECTION RESULTS

2008 GENERAL

Jeff Sessions (R)	1,305,383	63.4%
Vivian Davis Figures (D)	752,391	36.5%

2008 PRIMARY

Jeff Sessions (R)	199,690	92.3%
Earl Mack Gavin (R)	16,718	7.7%

2002 GENERAL

Jeff Sessions (R)	792,561	58.6%
Susan Parker (D)	538,878	39.8%
Jeff Allen (LIBERT)	20,234	1.5%

Previous Winning Percentages
1996 (52%)

Elected 1996; 3rd term

Reliably conservative on fiscal issues, Sessions has long championed smaller government and tax cuts. He earned praise from ideological compatriots for his work on immigration issues and judicial nominations as a senior member of the Judiciary Committee. As the GOP's new point man on the Budget Committee, he is well positioned to push his small-government philosophy.

A member of the Budget panel since 2003, Sessions has backed pared-down entitlement spending and a cap on non-defense discretionary spending. In his first appearance as ranking member, he stressed the need to combine budget discipline with economic growth.

"Our goal is not an era of austerity, but an era of prosperity," he said during the panel's first hearing in the 112th Congress (2011-12).

He called President Obama's fiscal 2012 budget "a blueprint for losing the future. It puts us on the road to decline. It simply spends, taxes, and borrows too much."

Equally conservative on social issues, the mild-mannered but tenacious Sessions led Republicans on the Judiciary Committee from May 2009 through the end of the 111th Congress (2009-10). He relinquished that spot to Charles E. Grassley of Iowa — GOP term limits ended Grassley's tenure as the top GOP member on the Finance Committee — to take the ranking spot on Budget. The swap stems from a deal reached after Judiciary's then-ranking Republican, Arlen Specter of Pennsylvania, switched parties in April 2009.

On Judiciary, Sessions consistently cast himself as a foil to Obama and the committee's Democratic chairman, Patrick J. Leahy of Vermont, particularly on the topic of judicial nominees. At a glance, Sessions doesn't cut an imposing figure; he is slight in stature, courtly and unpretentious. But he does not back down from a fight. "Sen. Sessions is a scrapper," said John Cornyn of Texas, a like-minded GOP colleague on the committee.

During the 111th Congress, a number of lower court nominees faced fierce opposition from GOP panel members, including Sessions, who has been sharply critical of the president's "flawed philosophy" of nominating what he calls judicial activists. But Sessions garnered the most attention for his role in the confirmation battles of Obama's nominees to the U.S. Supreme Court.

Less than a month after assuming the Judiciary ranking member post, Sessions was handed the task of leading the scrutiny of Judge Sonia Sotomayor, Obama's first nominee to the Supreme Court. While Sessions conceded that Sotomayor had a "well-rounded resume" and "a wonderful personal story," he voiced concerns that she had exhibited a pattern of activism in her speeches and writings. However, he refused to go along with conservative activists who had pushed to block a vote on her confirmation — which appeared likely to fail, in any case — and acquiesced to holding a vote before the August 2009 recess.

Sessions also led GOP opposition to Obama's second Supreme Court pick, Elena Kagan, questioning her qualifications and judicial philosophy. "I believe she does not have the gifts and the qualities of mind or temperament that one must have to be a justice," he said. "And worse still, she possesses a judicial philosophy that does not properly value discipline, restraint and rigorous intellectual honesty."

A former Alabama attorney general and U.S. attorney, Sessions has been on familiar turf dealing with the Judiciary Committee's other issues. He has been an ardent advocate of broad executive authority in the war on terrorism, but he worked with Democrats to narrow a disparity in federal sentences for offenses involving crack and powdered cocaine.

Sessions has also displayed an unyielding stance against illegal immigration. When the Senate passed a bill in 2006 offering guest worker permits and a path to citizenship for those in the country illegally, he called it "the worst piece of legislation to come before the Senate since I've been here." After the bill died in a standoff with the House, he was among those who pushed through legislation, signed into law, authorizing construction of a 700-mile fence along the U.S.-Mexican border.

In March 2008, he led a dozen GOP senators in introducing a package of enforcement-oriented measures, even as Republican presidential candidate Sen. John McCain of Arizona supported a more comprehensive overhaul of the system with a less stringent approach toward illegal immigrants. And in 2010, Sessions opposed legislation to create a path to conditional legal status for some illegal immigrant children who go to college or join the military.

Sessions' emergence as a leader on immigration developed late. "But as I watched and studied and looked around and saw nobody else willing to pick up the issue and run with it, I felt like I was doing the right thing," he told The Birmingham News.

On Armed Services, Sessions is an advocate for a missile-defense system and seeks more development of space-based devices, which could help his state's aerospace industry. He was a leading GOP critic of a strategic arms reduction treaty with Russia that the Senate approved in late 2010. "I disagree with my colleagues who are overly confident that this is going to make the world safer," he said on the Senate floor.

He has been a firm supporter of the war on terrorism, and he opposed Obama's nomination of James Cole to the No. 2 spot at the Justice Department, citing Cole's testimony in favor of civilian trials for accused terrorists.

From his seat on the Environment and Public Works Committee, Sessions wants to clear away regulatory hurdles for new construction of nuclear power plants. He unsuccessfully sought in May 2009 to kill a provision in a broad energy bill that mandated greater use of renewable energy, a priority of Obama's. But subsequently he became one of four committee Republicans to support the measure, which also expanded offshore oil and gas drilling.

Sessions grew up in the towns of Hybart and Camden, southwest of Montgomery. His father owned a general store and then a farm equipment dealership, and Sessions worked in both. At Huntingdon College in Alabama, Sessions joined the Young Republicans and served as student body president. After earning a law degree, he joined a law firm in Russellville, becoming assistant U.S. attorney in 1975 and U.S. attorney for the Southern District of Alabama in 1981.

The top GOP Judiciary post put Sessions in the unusual position of being at the forefront of a committee that rejected him for a federal judgeship in 1986; Leahy was among those voting against him. President Ronald Reagan nominated Sessions, the region's chief federal prosecutor, but critics accused Sessions of "gross insensitivity" on racial issues. Justice Department lawyers said he called the NAACP and the American Civil Liberties Union "communist-inspired" and said they tried to "force civil rights down the throats of people." Sessions said his words were misrepresented.

In 1994, he ran for state attorney general. With a corruption scandal raging in Montgomery, he rode to victory on a vow to clean up the mess. Two years later, Sessions entered the Senate race to succeed retiring Democrat Howell Heflin. He won a seven-way primary, then defeated Democrat Roger Bedford, giving Alabama two Republican senators for the first time since Reconstruction. Sessions easily won his next two Senate contests in 2002 and 2008.

Key Votes

2010

Pass budget reconciliation bill to modify overhauls of health care and federal student loan programs	NO
Proceed to disapproval resolution on EPA authority to regulate greenhouse gases	YES
Overhaul financial services industry regulation	NO
Limit debate to proceed to a bill to broaden campaign finance disclosure and reporting rules	NO
Limit debate on an extension of Bush-era income tax cuts for two years	NO
Limit debate on a bill to provide a path to legal status for some children of illegal immigrants	NO
Allow for a repeal of "don't ask, don't tell"	NO
Consent to ratification of a strategic arms reduction treaty with Russia	NO

2009

Prevent release of remaining financial industry bailout funds	YES
Make it easier for victims to sue for wage discrimination remedies	NO
Expand the Children's Health Insurance Program	NO
Limit debate on the economic stimulus measure	NO
Repeal District of Columbia firearms prohibitions and gun registration laws	YES
Limit debate on expansion of federal hate crimes law	NO
Strike funding for F-22 Raptor fighter jets	NO

CQ Vote Studies

	PARTY UNITY		PRESIDENTIAL SUPPORT	
	SUPPORT	OPPOSE	SUPPORT	OPPOSE
2010	98%	2%	40%	60%
2009	96%	4%	41%	59%
2008	98%	2%	74%	26%
2007	92%	8%	85%	15%
2006	96%	4%	91%	9%
2005	97%	3%	90%	10%
2004	97%	3%	96%	4%
2003	98%	2%	99%	1%
2002	87%	13%	88%	12%
2001	95%	5%	97%	3%

Interest Groups

	AFL-CIO	ADA	CCUS	ACU
2010	7%	5%	82%	100%
2009	13%	5%	60%	96%
2008	10%	20%	50%	84%
2007	16%	10%	40%	83%
2006	20%	0%	92%	92%
2005	14%	0%	78%	100%
2004	8%	10%	88%	96%
2003	0%	0%	100%	75%
2002	25%	10%	84%	90%
2001	20%	5%	86%	96%

Rep. Jo Bonner (R)

Capitol Office
225-4931
bonner.house.gov
2236 Rayburn Bldg. 20515-0101; fax 225-0562

Committees
Appropriations
Ethics - Chairman

Residence
Mobile

Born
Nov. 19, 1959; Selma, Ala.

Religion
Episcopalian

Family
Wife, Janee Bonner; two children

Education
U. of Alabama, B.A. 1982 (journalism), attended 1998 (law)

Career
Congressional and campaign aide

Political Highlights
No previous office

ELECTION RESULTS

2010 GENERAL

Jo Bonner (R)	129,063	82.6%
David Walter (CNSTP)	26,357	16.9%

2010 PRIMARY

Jo Bonner (R)	56,937	75.2%
Peter Gounares (R)	18,725	24.7%

2008 GENERAL

Jo Bonner (R)	210,652	98.3%
write-ins	3,707	1.7%

Previous Winning Percentages
2006 (68%); 2004 (63%); 2002 (61%)

Elected 2002; 5th term

One of Bonner's assignments in the 112th Congress probably has some colleagues envious of his posting: the Appropriations Committee. But they are probably not so jealous of his other position of authority. With Republicans back in control of the House, he is chairman of the Ethics Committee.

Riding herd on the ethical missteps of fellow lawmakers is not a task for someone in search of favorable publicity, and Bonner, a Republican loyalist and one-time congressional aide, prefers to follow the key tenets of staffer survival: Let others get the attention and lend a hand to the leaders when they need it.

As the top Republican on what was known in the 111th Congress (2009-10) as the Committee on Standards of Official Conduct, Bonner helped lead a subcommittee investigating allegations that lawmakers, House officers or aides might have been aware of improper conduct by Eric Massa, a New York Democrat who faced accusations that he had sexually harassed his own staffers before resigning in March 2010. That probe continued into the new Congress.

He also confronted Charles B. Rangel during his ethics trial for multiple financial misdeeds. "Mr. Rangel should only look into the mirror if he wants to know who to blame," Bonner said, prior to the House voting to censure the New York Democrat.

As chairman in the 112th (2011-12), Bonner will be tasked with resuming the investigation of California Democrat Maxine Waters, accused of breaking House rules in seeking federal help for a Los Angeles bank where her husband was a board member and shareholder.

Bonner's ability to get along with members from both parties — and his desire to shun the limelight — should serve him well in his new job.

"Bonner has demonstrated repeatedly that he has the diplomatic skills needed to build productive relationships with almost anyone, regardless of party affiliation," the Mobile Press-Register editorialized in early 2011.

Bonner, who served as the top aide to Republican Sonny Callahan before succeeding him in 2003, also sits on the Appropriations Committee, where he hopes to provide funding to aid his Gulf Coast district's recovery from the April 2010 oil spill. "This is something that has national and perhaps global implications. It's a multifaceted problem," he said, pointing to concerns ranging from environmental damage to ruined livelihoods to lost tax revenue.

Backing up an annoyed GOP leadership, Bonner garnered attention when he demanded that Texas Republican Joe L. Barton step down from the top Republican seat on the House Energy and Commerce Committee after Barton apologized to BP CEO Tony Hayward at a congressional hearing. Barton characterized the $20 billion escrow fund that BP agreed to in a meeting at the White House as a "shakedown."

But even with all the added attention and the need to address the spill, Bonner notes that the day-to-day demands of his office have not diminished.

"If you're not good at multitasking, you better get good at it," Bonner said. "The impact of this is so much broader and far-reaching than anything I've had to deal with to date. I've really had to re-acclimate."

As the spill threatened to stall economic revival in the district, one of the highest-priority items on Bonner's agenda grew even more important.

Although the Air Force granted a contract for new aerial refueling tankers to the European Aeronautic Defence and Space Co. (EADS), it rescinded the award after the Government Accountability Office determined the Pentagon had erred in its initial decision. In the new contest, EADS, which would build the tankers in Mobile, faces competition from Boeing Co. The subject dominated Bonner's attention on Appropriations in the 110th Congress (2007-08), and he fought hard for EADS in the new round. The rebid contract went to Boeing.

He also successfully pushed for a nearly $5 billion shipbuilding deal in the fiscal 2011 defense policy bill that would bring 1,800 jobs to the Mobile shipyard.

Bonner's family is among the most prominent in southern Alabama. His grandfather was a banker in Wilcox County, and his great-uncles were a doctor, a lawyer and a local newspaper publisher. Bonner, whose given name is Josiah Robins Bonner Jr., is named for his father, a Georgetown-trained attorney who was a county judge — a powerful local post.

At one time, Bonner thought he'd be a journalist. As a kid in Camden, he launched a community newspaper with a press loaned by the local newspaper editor, whose son was a playmate. In high school, Bonner was student council president and a broadcast announcer at basketball games.

He earned a degree in journalism, then followed his interest in politics to the 1982 gubernatorial campaign of George McMillan, who was challenging incumbent George C. Wallace Jr. in the Democratic primary. McMillan lost, but Bonner met Callahan, who was a candidate for lieutenant governor. Callahan also lost, but two years later he was elected to the House and hired Bonner to be his press secretary. Bonner eventually rose to chief of staff.

Callahan quietly encouraged his aide to prepare himself to run for the seat. In 1997, Bonner moved from Washington to the district, a rarity for a chief of staff, most of whom work on Capitol Hill. He paid close attention to constituent service, joining the local Rotary Club and board of the local Junior League. When Callahan announced his retirement in 2002, Bonner was ready.

His toughest competition came from Tom Young, a Mobile native and a fellow Republican who, like Bonner, was a career congressional aide. Young was chief of staff for another Alabama Republican, Sen. Richard C. Shelby. It was one of the most expensive and hotly contested races of the season. Bonner led in a seven-way June primary but fell short of a majority, forcing a runoff that he won with 62 percent of the vote. In November, Bonner easily defeated Democratic businesswoman Judy McCain Belk.

He won easily in his next three contests. In 2010, Bonner drew primary competition from developer Peter Gounares, who was motivated by Bonner's fall 2008 vote in favor of the George W. Bush administration's financial services industry rescue. Bonner defended his decision as an economic necessity and defeated Gounares with more than 75 percent of the vote. Democrats didn't field a candidate against him in November.

Key Votes

2010

Overhaul the nation's health insurance system	NO
Allow for repeal of "don't ask, don't tell"	NO
Overhaul financial services industry regulation	NO
Limit use of new Afghanistan War funds to troop withdrawal activities	NO
Change oversight of offshore drilling and lift oil spill liability cap	NO
Provide a path to legal status for some children of illegal immigrants	NO
Extend Bush-era income tax cuts for two years	YES

2009

Expand the Children's Health Insurance Program	NO
Provide $787 billion in tax cuts and spending increases to stimulate the economy	NO
Allow bankruptcy judges to modify certain primary-residence mortgages	NO
Create a cap-and-trade system to limit greenhouse gas emissions	NO
Provide $2 billion for the "cash for clunkers" program	NO
Establish the government as the sole provider of student loans	NO
Restrict federally funded insurance coverage for abortions in health care overhaul	YES

CQ Vote Studies

	PARTY UNITY		PRESIDENTIAL SUPPORT	
	SUPPORT	OPPOSE	SUPPORT	OPPOSE
2010	94%	6%	29%	71%
2009	87%	13%	22%	78%
2008	97%	3%	76%	24%
2007	93%	7%	83%	17%
2006	96%	4%	93%	7%

Interest Groups

	AFL-CIO	ADA	CCUS	ACU
2010	7%	0%	88%	95%
2009	5%	0%	87%	92%
2008	13%	15%	94%	83%
2007	13%	15%	85%	83%
2006	7%	0%	100%	88%

Alabama 1

Southwest—Mobile

Mobile anchors the solidly GOP 1st, Alabama's only Gulf Coast district. The beaches of southern Mobile County and resorts in Baldwin County give way to pine forests and cotton and soybean fields to the north. The coastal counties suffered environmental and economic loss as a result of the Deepwater Horizon oil spill in 2010 — oil and tar polluted the beaches, and the gulf's recreational and commercial fishing industries shut down for months.

The shipping and manufacturing industries in Mobile remain strong. ST Mobile Aerospace Engineering converts planes for FedEx at its Mobile facility. International Shipholding relocated from New Orleans in 2007, and the city's port capacity continues to expand. Austal USA — the county's largest industrial employer — is building naval combat ships at its Mobile shipyard.

Other industrial expansion in the district includes a new ThyssenKrupp steel manufacturing plant in Calvert 30 miles north of Mobile. Following the oil-spill-based hit to Baldwin County's tourism sector, the coastal county continues to rely on farming — sod, peanut and wheat

dominate its agricultural economy.

Development in the district's eastern reaches includes a gaming and entertainment establishment in Escambia County, where Wind Creek Casino and Hotel opened in January 2009.

Rural Monroe County relies on timber production and manufacturing, while Washington County, west of the Tombigbee River, is home to several major chemical plants.

The shift to GOP voting seen in much of the South took root early in Alabama's 1st. Republicans have held the U.S. House seat since 1965, and the district has overwhelmingly favored Republican presidential candidates for decades. In 2010, Gov. Robert Bentley won every county that falls wholly or partly within the 1st.

Major Industry
Commercial shipping, aerospace, timber, distribution, agriculture

Cities
Mobile, 195,111; Prichard, 22,659; Daphne, 21,570

Notable
Author Harper Lee based the fictional setting of "To Kill a Mockingbird" on her hometown of Monroeville.

Rep. Martha Roby (R)

Capitol Office
225-8913
roby.house.gov
414 Cannon Bldg. 20515-0102; fax 225-8913

Committees
Agriculture
Armed Services
Education & the Workforce

Residence
Montgomery

Born
July 26, 1976; Montgomery, Ala.

Religion
Presbyterian

Family
Husband, Riley Roby; two children

Education
New York U., B.M. 1998 (music, business and technology); Samford U., J.D. 2001

Career
Lawyer

Political Highlights
Montgomery City Council, 2004-11

ELECTION RESULTS

2010 GENERAL

Martha Roby (R)	111,645	51.0%
Bobby Bright (D)	106,865	48.8%

2010 PRIMARY RUNOFF

Martha Roby (R)	39,169	60.0%
Rick Barber (R)	26,091	40.0%

Elected 2010; 1st term

Roby arrived in Congress planning to balance her fiscal conservatism with her desire to protect the interests of large military installations in her district. She hopes to rein in federal domestic spending — but wants to keep robust military expenditures to support "the tip of the spear."

Her top goal as a member of the Armed Services Committee is to maintain and expand the missions of the Maxwell-Gunter Air Force Base, headquarters of the Air University and the 42nd Air Base Wing, and Fort Rucker, the Army's primary air training base, which includes two aviation brigades.

Roby also won a seat on the Agriculture Committee. Her district is home to many family farms, producing soybeans, cotton and peanuts — the 2nd is the nation's No. 2 peanut-producing district.

Her other committee assignment is Education and the Workforce.

Born in Montgomery, she received her bachelor's degree in music, specializing in music business and technology, from New York University and a law degree in 2001 from Samford University's Cumberland School of Law, where she met her husband. She practiced law for two years, a choice that pleased her father, a U.S. Circuit Court of Appeals judge.

Roby served on the Montgomery City Council for seven years.

She was the GOP establishment's candidate for the House in 2010, but fell just short of a majority in the primary and was forced into a second round against businessman and former Marine Rick Barber. He had the support of local tea party activists, but Roby coasted to a 20-percentage-point victory in the run-off.

In the general election she faced one-term lawmaker Bobby Bright, the first Democrat to hold the 2nd District seat since 1965.

Bright opposed the Democrats' health care overhaul and President Obama's $787 billion economic stimulus. Time magazine described him as "sprinting away from his party's legislative achievements." But it wasn't enough to save him in a district that went 63-37 for GOP presidential candidate John McCain in 2008. In one of the closest House races of the year, she defeated Bright with 51 percent of the vote.

Alabama 2

Southeast — part of Montgomery, Dothan

The 2nd takes in a chunk of Montgomery, the growing city of Dothan, and small towns that dot the southern Alabama coastal plain. Agriculture, still vital to the economy in rural areas here, includes peanut, cotton and soybean farming. Tourists visit the antebellum homes in Eufaula and fish on Lake Eufaula, on the border with Georgia.

Defense and state government still provide many jobs in the Montgomery area, and Maxwell Air Force Base and its Gunter Annex host many of the Air Force's computer systems and training centers. Dothan, in the southeast, relies on manufacturing and retail development and is a regional distribution hub. Fort Rucker, 20 miles to the northwest, is an Army aviation training center and supports activities at the Dothan Regional Airport.

A large military retiree population underscores the district's conservative bent overall — of the 15 counties wholly in the 2nd, only black-majority Bullock and Lowndes voted for Democrat Barack Obama in the 2008 presidential election. In 2010, the GOP regained its nearly four-decade hold on the district, unseating conservative Democrat Bobby Bright after one term.

Major Industry
Agriculture, defense, manufacturing, government

Military Bases
Fort Rucker (Army), 4,460 military, 2,402 civilian; Maxwell-Gunter Air Force Base, 3,089 military, 3,914 civilian (2009)

Cities
Montgomery (pt.), 122,409; Dothan, 65,496; Prattville, 33,960

Notable
The Boll Weevil Monument in Enterprise honors the insect, whose taste for cotton compelled local farmers to grow peanuts.

Rep. Mike D. Rogers (R)

Capitol Office
225-3261
www.house.gov/mike-rogers
324 Cannon Bldg. 20515-0103; fax 226-8485

Committees
Armed Services
Homeland Security
   (Transportation Security - Chairman)

Residence
Anniston

Born
July 16, 1958; Hammond, Ind.

Religion
Baptist

Family
Wife, Donna Elizabeth "Beth" Rogers; three children

Education
Jacksonville State U., B.A. 1981 (political science & psychology), M.P.A. 1985; Birmingham School of Law, J.D. 1991

Career
Lawyer; laid-off worker assistance program director; psychiatric counselor

Political Highlights
Calhoun County Commission, 1987-91; candidate for Ala. House, 1990; Ala. House, 1995-2002 (minority leader, 1998-2000)

ELECTION RESULTS

2010 GENERAL

Mike D. Rogers (R)	117,736	59.4%
Steve Segrest (D)	80,204	40.5%

2010 PRIMARY

Mike D. Rogers (R)	unopposed

2008 GENERAL

Mike D. Rogers (R)	150,819	53.4%
Joshua Segall (D)	131,299	46.5%

Previous Winning Percentages
2006 (59%); 2004 (61%); 2002 (50%)

Elected 2002; 5th term

Conservative and outspoken, Rogers harbors ambitions for a leadership role even though he employs his sharp tongue in a bipartisan fashion. Now that he possesses the gavel for a key Homeland Security subcommittee, he will be one of the party's point men on the touchy subject of transportation security in the 112th Congress.

Rogers serves as chairman of the Transportation Security panel, where controversial airport screening procedures are likely to be a hot topic.

On the full committee, Rogers has pushed for consolidation of oversight into one panel. Currently, that task is spread over dozens of committees and subcommittees, despite a 2004 recommendation from the 9/11 Commission to create a centralized point of congressional oversight. Rogers said he knows that shifting jurisdiction — and power — out of other committees would be a "tough political lift, to do that to all of these old bulls," but he remains hopeful that his argument that the move would make the nation safer will eventually win out.

Rogers feels border security is not getting the attention — or funding — it deserves from either party. He called President George W. Bush an "open borders president" and said Obama is "even worse."

On the legislative front, Rogers won a rare Republican victory in 2010 when President Obama signed into law his bill allowing the Center for Domestic Preparedness in Anniston to accept donated items such as emergency-response equipment to be used for training of first-responders.

His relations with those on the other side of the aisle are not always so accommodating.

Rogers threw caution to the wind in 2009 when, in a speech at Auburn University-Montgomery, he described House Speaker Nancy Pelosi of California as "mean as a snake," "crazy" and "Tom DeLay in a skirt" — a reference to the former GOP majority leader known as "The Hammer."

When his comments made national news, Rogers refused to apologize. Asked if he worried that an attack on such a powerful person could come back to hurt him later, Rogers said, "she can't do anything to me. . . . She probably considers it a compliment."

Rogers, who is generally affable and chatty, has been known to get tough with his own leaders as well. When top Republicans announced that they expected their members to participate in a moratorium on earmark requests, Rogers bristled. He said he believes strongly that members of Congress have a responsibility to direct spending to deserving projects in their districts, and he doesn't feel that the relatively small percentage of federal spending going toward those projects is a threat to his fiscal conservatism. Rogers said he took his complaints to the top and told every member of the GOP leadership that "this is not going to go past this year, or I am off the team."

Rogers hopes that one day he will be in a position to help make such decisions for his party — he makes no secret of his desire for a leadership post. He said those ambitions helped spur his contribution of more than $76,000 to fellow candidates in fiscal 2010 through his campaign committee and leadership political action committee.

The former state legislator is a reliable GOP vote — he sided with his party on 95 percent of the votes that pitted a majority of Republicans against a majority of Democrats in 2010 — and he said he rarely hears complaints from constituents. When he opposed the extension of unemployment benefits in 2010 because the legislation did not include any way to pay for them,

Rogers said that Alabama voters understood. "You can't just keep charging more on the credit card, and they know that," he said.

He was the only member of the Alabama House delegation to oppose legislation in late 2010 that extended the Bush-era tax rates. He didn't oppose the tax cuts — in fact, he wants the rates to be made permanent for all income levels. It was the spending provisions in the measure — including another jobless benefits extension — that were not offset that led Rogers to vote no.

In 2009, Rogers went the other way, bucking the majority of his party to support an expansion of the Children's Health Insurance Program, which covers children from low-income families that make too much money to qualify for Medicaid. He explained the vote by saying that families seemed to be "really hurting the most" when that bill came up. "That was just my way to show some sympathy for people," he said.

A member of the Armed Services Committee, Rogers looks out for the interests of Anniston Army Depot, which is located in his hometown and refers to itself as the "Pit Crew of the American Warfighter." He also protects nearby Maxwell-Gunter Air Force Base, northwest of Montgomery, and Fort Benning, across the state line in Georgia.

Rogers is the son of a textile worker. He defends that diminished industry in his state. He opposes free trade with China and is wary of any trade pacts that might hurt the domestic textile industry. He voted for the 2005 Central America Free Trade Agreement after he and fellow Alabama Republican Spencer Bachus secured protections for their state's textile firms.

He traces his ancestry back five generations in eastern Alabama. His father was a firefighter at the Anniston Depot, while his mother worked in a textile factory. Neither graduated from high school. While working for the United Way as a career counselor, he met his wife, who worked for a local power company. They attended law school at night, and after graduating she stayed at the power company while he started his own law practice in Anniston.

At 28, Rogers became the first Republican elected to the Calhoun County Commission. In 1994 he was elected to the Alabama House, where he eventually became minority leader.

When Republican Bob Riley ran successfully for governor in 2002, Rogers jumped into the race for his House seat. He faced Joe Turnham, a businessman aided by national Democratic Party organizations that saw an opportunity to take away a GOP seat. Rogers won by a slim 2 percentage points.

He cruised to re-election in 2004 and 2006, then was held to 53 percent of the vote in 2008 against Joshua Segall, a Montgomery attorney. He returned to form in 2010, winning with 59 percent.

Key Votes

2010

Overhaul the nation's health insurance system	NO
Allow for repeal of "don't ask, don't tell"	NO
Overhaul financial services industry regulation	NO
Limit use of new Afghanistan War funds to troop withdrawal activities	NO
Change oversight of offshore drilling and lift oil spill liability cap	NO
Provide a path to legal status for some children of illegal immigrants	NO
Extend Bush-era income tax cuts for two years	NO

2009

Expand the Children's Health Insurance Program	YES
Provide $787 billion in tax cuts and spending increases to stimulate the economy	NO
Allow bankruptcy judges to modify certain primary-residence mortgages	NO
Create a cap-and-trade system to limit greenhouse gas emissions	NO
Provide $2 billion for the "cash for clunkers" program	YES
Establish the government as the sole provider of student loans	NO
Restrict federally funded insurance coverage for abortions in health care overhaul	YES

CQ Vote Studies

	PARTY UNITY		PRESIDENTIAL SUPPORT	
	SUPPORT	OPPOSE	SUPPORT	OPPOSE
2010	95%	5%	26%	74%
2009	80%	20%	42%	58%
2008	88%	12%	53%	47%
2007	90%	10%	74%	26%
2006	96%	4%	83%	17%

Interest Groups

	AFL-CIO	ADA	CCUS	ACU
2010	7%	5%	75%	96%
2009	29%	15%	93%	adu1
2008	40%	50%	89%	50%
2007	21%	20%	90%	80%
2006	36%	10%	87%	84%

Alabama 3

East — part of Montgomery, Anniston, Auburn

From the capital city to rural Appalachia, the 3rd enjoys a diversified economy that includes technology, manufacturing, government and universities. Among the district's many significant historical sites and tourist attractions, its section of Montgomery hosts the State Capitol Complex, the first White House of the Confederacy and the Dexter Avenue Baptist Church, where the 1955 bus boycott was launched.

To the north, Anniston, the Calhoun County seat, relies heavily on federal government jobs. FEMA operates a training site for first-responders to chemical, biological and nuclear terrorist attacks at the former Fort McClellan Army base. The Anniston Army Depot has hosted a chemical weapons incinerator and combat vehicle maintenance facilities.

Auburn University, one of the state's largest employers and a national leader in agricultural research, has partnered with the city of Auburn and the state of Alabama to develop a research park that has begun to attract major firms. The city also has had some success diversifying beyond its economic reliance on the university. The district's industrial sector includes a Honda plant in Lincoln and Hyundai's first U.S. plant, south of Montgomery. The collapse of the once-thriving textile and construction industries has hit Chambers County particularly hard.

The Republican-leaning 3rd is home to many conservative voters who generally favor GOP presidential and gubernatorial candidates, and also to a substantial black population and small pockets of university liberals. Although John McCain took 56 percent of the district's 2008 presidential vote, Macon County gave Barack Obama his highest percentage of any county in the state (87 percent).

Major Industry
Higher education, technology, manufacturing, defense

Military Bases
Anniston Army Depot, 37 military, 5,033 civilian (2009)

Cities
Montgomery (pt.), 83,355; Auburn, 53,380; Phenix City, 32,822; Opelika, 26,477; Anniston, 23,106

Notable
Tuskegee University, founded in 1881, was the first historically black college to be recognized as a National Historic Landmark..

Rep. Robert B. Aderholt (R)

Capitol Office
225-4876
aderholt.house.gov
2264 Rayburn Bldg. 20515-0104; fax 225-5587

Committees
Appropriations
(Homeland Security - Chairman)

Residence
Haleyville

Born
July 22, 1965; Haleyville, Ala.

Religion
Congregationalist Baptist

Family
Wife, Caroline Aderholt; two children

Education
Birmingham-Southern College, B.A. 1987 (history & political science); Samford U., J.D. 1990

Career
Lawyer; gubernatorial aide

Political Highlights
Republican nominee for Ala. House, 1990; Haleyville municipal judge, 1992-96

ELECTION RESULTS

2010 GENERAL

Robert B. Aderholt (R)	167,714	98.8%
write-ins (WRI)	2,007	1.2%

2010 PRIMARY

Robert B. Aderholt (R)	unopposed

2008 GENERAL

Robert B. Aderholt (R)	196,741	74.8%
Nicholas B. Sparks (D)	66,077	25.1%

Previous Winning Percentages
2006 (70%); 2004 (75%); 2002 (87%); 2000 (61%); 1998 (56%); 1996 (50%)

Elected 1996; 8th term

Aderholt sees himself as an old-school economic conservative, fighting for lower taxes and smaller government. But as a senior member of the Appropriations Committee, he also sees himself as an advocate for his district, unabashedly seeking government help that will send money or jobs to his rural swath of Alabama.

Even with a moratorium on earmarks, which Aderholt has said he hopes is not permanent, his chairmanship of the subcommittee handling Homeland Security spending in the 112th Congress (2011-12) adds to his ability to deliver for his district.

"Since we'll be in this position, we'll have the ability to stress to the leaders in the departments what we feel like are important aspects of the work they're doing," Aderholt told the Birmingham News. "They certainly pay attention to or try to take note of the issues you're interested in."

Aderholt told the News that in collaboration with fellow Alabama Republican Mike D. Rogers, who will lead the Homeland Security Subcommittee on Transportation Security, he would like to see the Heart of Dixie become a bigger player in homeland security. "We can try to maybe make Alabama more focused on homeland security, make it more of something that we can look at the resources we have in Alabama and see how we can guide that toward helping the nation," Aderholt said.

His defense of Congress' power of the purse puts him at odds with fellow members of the Republican Study Committee (RSC) who have worked to eliminate earmarks, the funding set-asides for projects in members' districts.

Many in the RSC, a group of the House's most conservative members, pressed for an end to earmarking in the 110th Congress (2007-08). But Aderholt joined a small band of GOP appropriators led by Frank R. Wolf of Virginia in proposing an alternative: a temporary moratorium on earmarks and the creation of a bipartisan, bicameral select committee to study the issue. Neither plan went anywhere then, but the GOP unilaterally adopted a one-year moratorium for fiscal 2011.

While defending his own earmarking record, he went along with the moratorium, calling the earmark process "a symbol of why Washington is broken." He points out that if Congress could not direct funding to local projects, that task would fall to agency workers and administration officials who have never set foot in Alabama.

Aderholt had a fight on his hands in the 111th Congress (2009-10) as he opposed the Democratic administration's efforts to eliminate the Constellation program for human spaceflight. The program employs about 2,600 people spread between Aderholt's district and the neighboring 5th District. Aderholt used his seat on the Commerce-Justice-Science Appropriations Subcommittee to try to keep the program alive, and he introduced a bill intended to block NASA from terminating Constellation-related contracts.

Aderholt became the top Republican on the Legislative Branch Appropriations Subcommittee at the beginning of the 111th. The year before, he had praised the panel's chairwoman, Florida Democrat Debbie Wasserman Schultz, for crafting the fiscal 2010 Legislative Branch bill, but he voted against the conference report when House leaders attached a stopgap spending measure to it.

The son of a judge who was also a Baptist pastor, Aderholt was raised in a deeply conservative community, and he believes in bringing religious values into the public sphere. He has fought to permit public displays of the Ten Commandments. In 2003, when a federal judge ordered the removal of a stone display of the Ten Commandments from the state judicial complex in Montgomery, Aderholt said it was a "scene one would expect to see in the former Soviet Union, not the United States of America."

As a member of the Helsinki Commission monitoring human rights in Europe and the countries of the former Soviet Union, Aderholt has extended his campaign for freedom of religious expression overseas, particularly in Georgia and Turkmenistan. In 2008, he supported Georgia in its struggle to repel a Russian invasion and backed U.S. aid to help the country rebuild.

Aderholt regards most trade deals with a wary eye. After a Gulf States Steel plant in Gadsden closed in 2000, eliminating 1,700 jobs, he backed legislation providing loan guarantees for steel companies hurt by foreign imports.

The next year, when VF Corp., manufacturer of Lee and Wrangler jeans, closed four factories in and around the 4th District, Aderholt voted against granting the president fast-track authority to negotiate trade deals. Seven months later, he voted for the final version of the bill after House leaders promised to fight against lifting tariffs on socks made in the Caribbean — of importance because of the role textile mills play in the local economy.

He voted for the 2005 Central America Free Trade Agreement, but only after receiving written assurances from top administration officials — and a personal phone call from President George W. Bush — that they would help protect domestic sockmakers from import surges. The trade pact passed the House by two votes. When a local sock manufacturer closed its doors in 2008, Aderholt blamed what he said was the Bush administration's failure to live up to the deal.

Aderholt grew up with politics. When he was 5, he wrote a campaign letter touting his father in a local election, and he recalls meeting Republican Sen. Bob Dole of Kansas when he was about 11. A month after his law school graduation, he was nominated for a state House seat but lost the general election. He was appointed a municipal judge in 1992 and went to work for Republican Gov. Fob James Jr. in 1995.

When Democrat Tom Bevill retired in 1996 after 15 terms, Aderholt made a run for the seat. He took 49 percent of the primary vote against four rivals; he won the nomination when the second-place finisher conceded without a runoff. Democrats backed former state Sen. Robert T. "Bob" Wilson Jr., who was nearly as conservative as Aderholt on social issues. Aderholt prevailed by 2 percentage points and has won handily since.

Key Votes

2010

Overhaul the nation's health insurance system	NO
Allow for repeal of "don't ask, don't tell"	NO
Overhaul financial services industry regulation	NO
Limit use of new Afghanistan War funds to troop withdrawal activities	NO
Change oversight of offshore drilling and lift oil spill liability cap	NO
Provide a path to legal status for some children of illegal immigrants	NO
Extend Bush-era income tax cuts for two years	YES

2009

Expand the Children's Health Insurance Program	?
Provide $787 billion in tax cuts and spending increases to stimulate the economy	NO
Allow bankruptcy judges to modify certain primary-residence mortgages	NO
Create a cap-and-trade system to limit greenhouse gas emissions	NO
Provide $2 billion for the "cash for clunkers" program	YES
Establish the government as the sole provider of student loans	NO
Restrict federally funded insurance coverage for abortions in health care overhaul	YES

CQ Vote Studies

	PARTY UNITY		PRESIDENTIAL SUPPORT	
	SUPPORT	OPPOSE	SUPPORT	OPPOSE
2010	95%	5%	29%	71%
2009	84%	16%	28%	72%
2008	96%	4%	67%	33%
2007	89%	11%	75%	25%
2006	95%	5%	87%	13%

Interest Groups

	AFL-CIO	ADA	CCUS	ACU
2010	7%	92%	88%	0%
2009	10%	5%	92%	92%
2008	21%	25%	82%	92%
2007	17%	20%	79%	84%
2006	21%	10%	87%	84%

Alabama 4

North central – Gadsden, part of Decatur

Taking in mountains, foothills, flatlands and large waterways, the rural 4th runs the width of the state, bordering both Mississippi and Georgia. A small black population and the absence of a major city distinguish the relatively poor district from the rest of Alabama.

The 4th relies on assistance from the Appalachian Regional Commission, a decades-old federal-state partnership to aid development and reduce poverty in the area. Completion of "Corridor X," an interstate route following U.S. 78 across the 4th from Mississippi, is a priority of the commission and of local officials, who hope the route will attract new midsize businesses. Many local residents work in nearby metropolitan areas, such as Huntsville (in the 5th) and Birmingham (in the 6th and 7th).

Textiles, mining and rubber, and other manufacturing are still major job sources here despite volatility in the coal market and the loss of some manufacturing and textile jobs abroad.

The industrial sector has diversified beyond steel and textiles to include food processing and wood products. The Tennessee Valley Authority's Guntersville Reservoir, shared with the 5th, supports a shipping-based economy in Guntersville. Gadsden, the district's only sizable city, has had some success with economic diversification efforts following manufacturing plant closures.

Agri-businesses, especially cattle and poultry enterprises, form a significant sector of the local economy. The mountainous landscape provides opportunities for outdoor recreation. Smith Lake — a 21,000-acre man-made body of water shared by Cullman, Walker and Winston counties — lures visitors to the 4th.

Once a Democratic stronghold, the 4th's conservative population now supports the GOP at all levels. In 1996, voters sent a Republican to Congress for just the second time since Reconstruction, and GOP Rep. Robert B. Aderholt has won re-election easily since. In 2010, Republican Gov. Robert Bentley took every county wholly or partly in the 4th.

Major Industry
Manufacturing, textiles, mining, agriculture, tourism

Cities
Gadsden, 36,856; Albertville, 21,160; Cullman, 14,775; Jasper, 14,352

Notable
Formerly dry Cullman County serves non-alcoholic beverages, including one called "Oktoberzest," at its annual Oktoberfest celebration.

Rep. Mo Brooks (R)

Capitol Office
225-4801
brooks.house.gov
1641 Longworth Bldg. 20515-0105; fax 225-4392

Committees
Armed Services
Homeland Security
Science, Space & Technology
    (Investigations & Oversight - Chairman)

Residence
Huntsville

Born
April 29, 1954; Charleston, S.C.

Religion
Christian

Family
Wife, Martha Brooks; four children

Education
Duke U., B.A. 1975 (economics & political science);
U. of Alabama, J.D. 1978

Career
Special assistant state attorney general; lawyer;
county prosecutor

Political Highlights
Ala. House, 1983-91; Madison County district at-
torney, 1991-93; defeated for election as Madison
County district attorney, 1992; Madison County
Commission, 1996-2011; sought Republican nomi-
nation for lieutenant governor, 2006

ELECTION RESULTS

2010 GENERAL

Mo Brooks (R)	131,109	57.9%
Steve Raby (D)	95,192	42.1%

2010 PRIMARY

Mo Brooks (R)	35,746	50.8%
Parker Griffith (R)	23,525	33.4%
Les Phillip (R)	11,085	15.8%

Elected 2010; 1st term

The conservative newcomer's top priority is pushing for a constitutional amendment requiring a balanced budget. Brooks also wants aggressive changes to U.S. tax policy.

"I'm not talking about the dog-and-pony shows going on in Congress
right now, where Congress pretends to address the issue to fool voters
into believing something substantive is being done," he said prior to taking
office. "I'm talking about real reform with teeth in it."

Brooks won a seat on the Armed Services Committee, and his district
is home to the Army's Redstone Arsenal for rocket and missile programs.
He also sits on the Science, Space and Technology Committee, from which
he can tend to the district's Marshall Space Flight Center, a NASA facility
that develops rocket propulsion technology and spaceflight vehicles.

An attorney and former state legislator, Brooks is the first Republican
elected from Alabama's 5th since Reconstruction — his predecessor,
Parker Griffith, was elected as a Democrat before switching to the GOP
in December 2009.

One of his priorities entering Congress was to repeal the health care
overhaul enacted in 2010, and he voted to do just that in January 2011.
"The president has his view. He thinks socialized medicine is a good thing.
We disagree," Brooks told the Huntsville Times in January 2011.

Born in South Carolina, Brooks moved to Huntsville when he was a boy,
where he now resides. He attended Duke University, double-majoring in
political science and economics, graduating in three years. He received a
law degree from the University of Alabama in 1978.

After serving in the Alabama House from 1983 to 1991, and working in
a private law practice, he was briefly a special assistant attorney general
under GOP Sen. Jeff Sessions, who was then Alabama attorney general.

In 2006, Brooks launched an unsuccessful bid for the Republican nomination for lieutenant governor. In 2010, he handily beat Griffith in the
primary and then defeated Democrat Steve Raby in the general election
with almost 58 percent of the vote.

Alabama 5

North — Huntsville

The Tennessee River winds through the
5th, which stretches across the state's
northern tier and borders Mississippi, Tennessee and Georgia. The Tennessee Valley
Authority maintains a strong presence
along the river, and the government and
industrial facilities lining its famous shores
are vital to the 5th.

Huntsville relies on federal government, defense and contracting jobs. NASA's Marshall
Space Flight Center develops rocket propulsion technology and spaceflight vehicles,
and the Army's Redstone Arsenal is home to
rocket and missile programs.

Strong technology, manufacturing and
research sectors bolster the 5th's economy.
Huntsville's Cummings Research Park has
25,000 employees, and a Toyota engine plant
employs almost 800.

Decatur's industrial economy boasts a 3M
chemical plant, a United Launch Alliance
satellite rocket booster plant and a Nucor
steel mill. Agriculture represents a healthy
portion of the 5th's rural economy, and crops
include corn, cotton and soybeans.

The generally conservative voters in the 5th
favor GOP presidential candidates but historically elected Democrats to state and local
offices. The district had not been represented
by a Republican since 1869 until Rep. Parker
Griffith switched to the GOP in 2009.

Major Industry
Defense, government, manufacturing, technology, agriculture

Military Bases
Redstone Arsenal (Army), 1,930 military,
16,932 civilian (2011)

Cities
Huntsville, 180,105; Decatur (pt.), 46,485;
Madison, 42,938; Florence, 39,319

Notable
Muscle Shoals' Fame Recording Studios
merged rhythm and blues, country and gospel to create the "Muscle Shoals Sound."

Rep. Spencer Bachus (R)

Elected 1992; 10th term

The conservative Bachus, chairman of the Financial Services Committee, won't let the fact that Democrats recently rewrote the rules governing Wall Street deter him from his appointed mission. He sees his job as keeping a close watch on the newly empowered watchdogs, and perhaps rolling back some of the new regulations.

"In Washington, the view is that the banks are to be regulated, and my view is that Washington and the regulators are there to serve the banks," he told the Birmingham News before the 112th Congress (2011-12) convened. That means, Bachus said, regulators should set broad outlines and then get out of the way to let bankers run banks.

Bachus (BACK-us) applies much the same standard to other financial activities. He opposed the regulatory overhaul enacted in 2010 and would prefer that some of its provisions be revisited. He wants the Federal Reserve to go slow on writing rules that would reduce debit transaction fees paid by retailers because of worries that cuts could hurt competition. And he warned other regulators against requiring companies that use derivatives to hedge risk to set aside large amounts to cover potential losses, arguing that such a requirement would immobilize too much capital.

A member of the Republican Study Committee, a group of the most conservative Republicans in the House, Bachus is typically in step with his party on everything from abortion rights to tax cuts. But after taking over as top Republican on the Financial Services Committee at the start of the 110th Congress (2007-08), he saw his inside-the-Beltway fortunes rise and dip along with the national economy.

As markets tumbled and the GOP divided on solutions, he found himself alone among party leaders in negotiating a financial services industry rescue plan. In fall 2008, his decision to work with Democratic leaders on the $700 billion proposal to stabilize the economy led conservatives to accuse him of "drinking the Kool-Aid." He went so far as to suggest, along with Treasury Secretary Henry M. Paulson Jr., that the plan could be a revenue-raiser.

Such positions were often maddening to many conservatives, and Minority Leader John A. Boehner of Ohio eventually stripped him of his power to speak for the GOP at the deliberations. Bachus eventually had to turn back a bid by Californian Ed Royce for the committee gavel after Republicans gained control of the House in the 2010 elections.

He was more in sync with Republicans as President Obama took office; in February 2009, he dismissed a proposal by Treasury Secretary Timothy F. Geithner to bolster the rescue law, saying it was "just a broad outline" needing more work. He criticized its extensions, reminding lawmakers that the rescue law was supposed to be a "temporary plan" that instead created a "permanent bailout agency and petty cash drawer for politically favored interests."

Like all but three Republicans, he opposed the final version of the financial services regulatory overhaul in 2010. "Instead of enacting real reform to modernize our financial regulatory structure and protect taxpayers, the Democrats have delivered a bill that enshrines 'too big to fail,' hurts our Main Street companies, kills jobs and places taxpayers at risk for trillions of dollars in bailouts authorized under this bill," he said.

Bachus frequently stands against government intervention and regulation, but the growth of subprime mortgage lending had him investigating action long before the troubles came. He ordered studies on the lending, drafted bills to tighten regulation and ultimately supported a plan by his

Capitol Office
225-4921
bachus.house.gov
2246 Rayburn Bldg. 20515-0106; fax 225-2082

Committees
Financial Services - Chairman

Residence
Vestavia Hills

Born
Dec. 28, 1947; Birmingham, Ala.

Religion
Baptist

Family
Wife, Linda Bachus; five children

Education
Auburn U., B.A. 1969; U. of Alabama, J.D. 1972

Military
Ala. National Guard, 1969-71

Career
Lawyer; sawmill owner

Political Highlights
Ala. Senate, 1983; Ala. House, 1983-87; Ala. Board of Education, 1987-91; candidate for Ala. attorney general, 1990; Ala. Republican Party chairman, 1991-92

ELECTION RESULTS

2010 GENERAL

Spencer Bachus (R)	205,288	98.0%
write-ins (WRI)	4,076	1.9%

2010 PRIMARY

Spencer Bachus (R)	80,725	75.6%
Stan Cooke (R)	25,997	24.4%

2008 GENERAL

Spencer Bachus (R)	280,902	97.8%
write-ins	6,335	2.2%

Previous Winning Percentages
2006 (98%); 2004 (99%); 2002 (90%); 2000 (88%); 1998 (72%); 1996 (71%); 1994 (79%); 1992 (52%)

predecessor as Financial Services chairman, Democrat Barney Frank of Massachusetts, to keep more bad mortgages from being issued. Late in 2008, he said more-stringent rules might be needed.

But often he and Frank took opposite stands on issues. In 2008, Bachus successfully fought Frank's plan to dismantle an online gambling bill. He carried that fight into 2010 citing concerns about Frank's new effort to license online gambling organizations, and continues to argue that keeping the ban in place is a high priority.

A devout Baptist, Bachus' religious beliefs have led to his support of Third World debt relief and education, and to unusual alliances with the likes of U2 frontman Bono and liberal California Democrat Maxine Waters. Bachus, whose son served in the Marines, said canceling the debt of poorer countries can help stabilize their governments, combat poverty and prevent terrorism.

He has supported economic sanctions on Sudan in the hopes of halting the killings of Christians in the southern region, and he sponsored legislation in 2004 to prevent foreign oil companies from raising capital through American financial markets if the companies continue to do business in Sudan.

Bachus takes pride in pointing out that the American Civil Liberties Union rates him as one of the worst Alabama congressmen.

Back home, he helped secure a new national veterans' center in Birmingham and won a provision setting aside 30,000 acres for a wildlife refuge along a stretch of the Cahaba River. He and the Alabama delegation successfully lobbied the Base Realignment and Closure Commission to retain the Birmingham International Airport Air Guard Station, home to the 117th Air Refueling Wing.

Early in his career, Bachus owned a sawmill, but for the most part he earned a living as a trial lawyer. He began his career in elective office in 1983, serving first in the state legislature, then on the state board of education and then as chairman of the Alabama GOP.

In his first House bid, Bachus benefited from the post-1990 census remapping of Alabama's congressional districts that transformed the district held for five terms by Democrat Ben Erdreich into a Republican bastion. Bachus took 52 percent of the vote in 1992 and always has been re-elected with at least 70 percent. He was unopposed in 2010.

In an unfortunate bit of irony for the chairman of the Financial Services Committee, Bachus suffered bigger investment losses in his campaign account than any other House member during the 2010 election cycle — more than $168,000.

Key Votes

2010

Overhaul the nation's health insurance system	NO
Allow for repeal of "don't ask, don't tell"	NO
Overhaul financial services industry regulation	NO
Limit use of new Afghanistan War funds to troop withdrawal activities	NO
Change oversight of offshore drilling and lift oil spill liability cap	NO
Provide a path to legal status for some children of illegal immigrants	NO
Extend Bush-era income tax cuts for two years	YES

2009

Expand the Children's Health Insurance Program	NO
Provide $787 billion in tax cuts and spending increases to stimulate the economy	NO
Allow bankruptcy judges to modify certain primary-residence mortgages	NO
Create a cap-and-trade system to limit greenhouse gas emissions	NO
Provide $2 billion for the "cash for clunkers" program	YES
Establish the government as the sole provider of student loans	NO
Restrict federally funded insurance coverage for abortions in health care overhaul	YES

CQ Vote Studies

	PARTY UNITY		PRESIDENTIAL SUPPORT	
	SUPPORT	OPPOSE	SUPPORT	OPPOSE
2010	95%	5%	32%	68%
2009	86%	14%	29%	71%
2008	94%	6%	68%	32%
2007	93%	7%	83%	17%
2006	97%	3%	97%	3%

Interest Groups

	AFL-CIO	ADA	CCUS	ACU
2010	7%	0%	88%	96%
2009	11%	5%	80%	92%
2008	20%	20%	94%	84%
2007	14%	10%	79%	92%
2006	21%	0%	93%	88%

Alabama 6

Central — suburban Birmingham and Tuscaloosa

Some of the sweetest homes in Alabama are found in the 6th District, a mix of white and wealthy suburbs of Birmingham and Tuscaloosa, parts of the cities themselves and nearby rural areas in central Alabama. The U-shaped 6th surrounds a thin peninsula of land in the adjacent 7th that stretches southwest from downtown Birmingham to Tuscaloosa. Decades of population decline in Birmingham contrast with the overall growth of the metropolitan area. The 6th takes in much of the area's suburbs, while most of the city is in the 7th. Many commuters reside in historically wealthy areas in southern Jefferson County, particularly Mountain Brook and Homewood. Shelby County, mainly south of Birmingham, has seen significant suburban growth over the past three decades and has the highest median household income of any county in the state.

The 6th includes a section of Tuscaloosa north of the Black Warrior River, which bisects the city and separates the district from the county's biggest employer, the University of Alabama in the 7th. On autumn Saturdays,

more than 101,000 fans from across the state wind up just south of the river at the University of Alabama's Bryant-Denny Stadium to watch Crimson Tide football.

Birmingham's suburbs are encroaching on the district's rural areas, but agriculture, manufacturing and mining remain important to the economic health in some areas. Agricultural production in the area has slowed, but peaches remain a point of pride in Chilton County. Mercedes-Benz vehicles are produced in Vance, within the strip of the 7th bordered on both sides by the 6th.

The growing conservative, white-collar Birmingham suburbs that account for much of the district's population have kept the 6th reliably Republican. Democrats have not fielded a candidate to face Rep. Spencer Bachus since 1998.

Major Industry
Manufacturing, higher education, mining, agriculture

Cities
Hoover, 81,619; Vestavia Hills, 34,033; Alabaster, 30,352; Birmingham (pt.), 28,108; Pelham, 21,352

Notable
The Cahaba River National Wildlife Refuge is a natural habitat for longleaf pine and hosts the largest known stand of endangered shoals lily.

Rep. Terri A. Sewell (D)

Capitol Office
225-2665
sewell.house.gov
1133 Longworth Bldg. 20515-0107; fax 226-9567

Committees
Agriculture
Science, Space & Technology

Residence
Birmingham

Born
Jan. 1, 1965; Huntsville, Ala.

Religion
Christian

Family
Single

Education
Princeton U., A.B. 1986 (Woodrow Wilson School);
Oxford U., M.A. 1988 (politics; Marshall Scholar);
Harvard, J.D. 1992

Career
Lawyer

Political Highlights
No previous office

ELECTION RESULTS

2010 GENERAL

Terri A. Sewell (D)	136,696	72.4%
Don Chamberlain (R)	51,890	27.5%

2010 PRIMARY RUNOFF

Terri A. Sewell (D)	32,366	55.0%
Sheila Smoot (D)	26,481	45.0%

Elected 2010; 1st term

Sewell is the first African-American woman to serve in Congress from Alabama and joined Republican Martha Roby as the first Alabama women of any race to be elected, rather than appointed, to a full congressional term.

A self-described "daughter of the Black Belt," she represents the poorest district in the state. That makes her top priority creating jobs, Sewell said.

"Part of my job is being a cheerleader for my district," the former high school cheerleader told the Tuscaloosa News in December 2010.

To accomplish that goal, Sewell wants to secure funding for infrastructure projects — including roads, bridges, sewers and broadband Internet.

She says training and development will make workers in her district more attractive to companies such as Mercedes-Benz, which operates a plant in Vance, and she will be able to promote competitiveness initiatives as a member of the Science, Space and Technology Committee.

Her other committee assignment is Agriculture, where she can look after west Alabama's burgeoning catfish industry.

Sewell had no previous elective experience before winning her House seat. Her mother, Nancy Gardner Sewell, was the first black woman elected to the Selma City Council. During her college summers, Sewell worked for Richard C. Shelby, now a Republican senator who was then serving in the House as a Democrat. She graduated from Princeton in 1986 and received her master's degree in politics from Oxford University in 1988. She then received her law degree from Harvard in 1992. She clerked for a federal judge, then worked at a New York law firm before returning to Alabama, where she became a partner in a Birmingham firm.

A well-funded but relatively unknown Sewell faced a crowded Democratic field in the 2010 race, which included state Rep. Earl Hilliard Jr., whose father held the seat for a decade, and Jefferson County Commissioner Sheila Smoot. She finished first in the primary, taking 37 percent of the vote, then bested Smoot six weeks later in the runoff, 55 percent to 45 percent. That was tantamount to election in the heavily Democratic district. In November, she took 72 percent of the vote against Republican Don Chamberlain, a former Marine.

Alabama 7

West central – parts of Birmingham and Tuscaloosa

Marked by stark regional contrasts, the 7th District includes chunks of Birmingham and Tuscaloosa, as well as struggling rural areas in west central Alabama. Health care and banking sectors have taken root, but the 7th remains Alabama's poorest district overall. Economic growth in the 7th's part of Birmingham, the densely populated downtown area that includes a Civil Rights District, has trailed the rest of the city. Decades of redevelopment efforts have yielded some success, and the sprawling University of Alabama at Birmingham continues to expand.

To the west, manufacturing, medical services and the University of Alabama's flagship campus anchor Tuscaloosa's economy. Nearby Vance is home to a Mercedes-Benz plant.

Almost all of the rest of the 7th falls into the state's portion of the Black Belt, a historically poverty-filled region of rich soil that stretches from Texas to Virginia. Agricultural diversification has been modestly successful, but jobs remain scarce and the population has been declining for decades.

In contrast to its white, well-to-do neighbor — the Republican 6th — the bulk of the 7th's residents are poor to middle class blacks who overwhelmingly back Democrats. The district, as redrawn after the 1990 census, has been held by three African-American representatives, including Alabama's first black female U.S. House member.

Major Industry
Agriculture, manufacturing, higher education

Cities
Birmingham (pt.), 184,129; Tuscaloosa (pt.), 78,408; Bessemer (pt.), 25,216

Notable
Selma's Edmund Pettus Bridge was the site of "Bloody Sunday," when state troopers assaulted peaceful civil rights activists on their way to Montgomery in 1965.

ALASKA

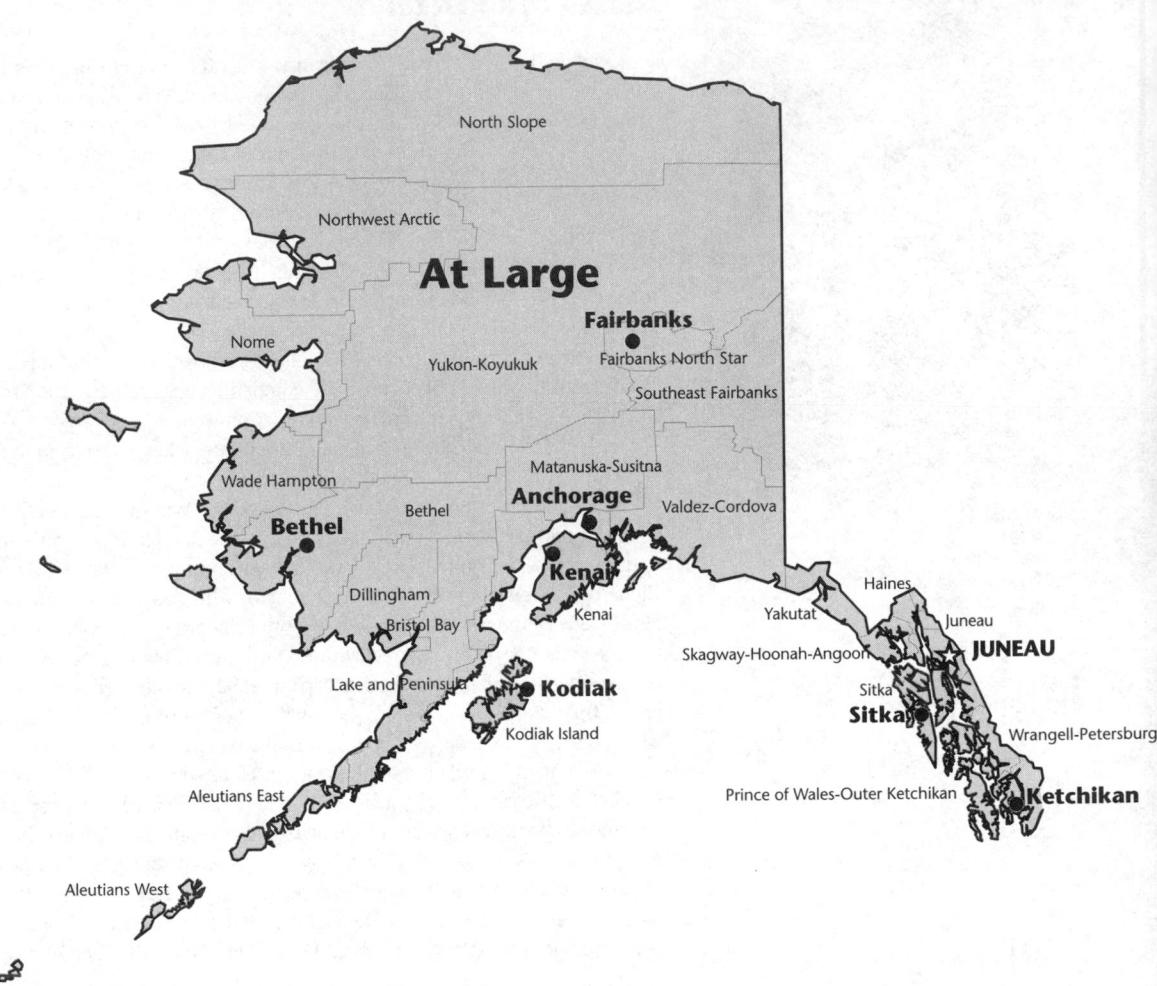

Gov. Sean Parnell (R)

First elected: 2010
Took office July 26, 2009, due to the resignation of Sarah Palin, R.

Length of term: 4 years

Term expires: 12/14

Salary: $125,000

Phone: (907) 465-3500

Residence: Anchorage

Born: Nov. 19, 1962; Hanford, Calif.

Religion: Christian

Family: Wife, Sandy Parnell; two children

Education: Pacific Lutheran U., B.B.A. 1984; U. of Puget Sound, J.D. 1987

Career: Lawyer; state natural resources official; lobbyist

Political highlights: Alaska House, 1993-97; Alaska Senate, 1997-2001; lieutenant governor, 2006-09; sought Republican nomination for U.S. House 2008

ELECTION RESULTS

2010 GENERAL

Sean Parnell (R)	151,318	59.1%
Ethan Berkowitz (D)	96,519	37.7%
Don R. Wright (AKI)	4,775	1.9%
William S. Toien (LIBERT)	2,682	1.0%

Lt. Gov. Mead Treadwell (R)

First elected: 2010

Length of term: 4 years

Term expires: 12/10

Salary: $100,000

Phone: (907) 465-3520

LEGISLATURE

Legislature: January to April

Senate: 20 members, 4-year terms

2011 ratios: 10 R, 10 D; 16 men, 4 women

Salary: $50,400

Phone: (907) 465-3701

House: 40 members, 2-year terms

2011 ratios: 24 R, 16 D; 30 men, 10 women

Salary: $50,400

Phone: (907) 465-3725

TERM LIMITS

Governor: 2 consecutive terms

Senate: No

House: No

URBAN STATISTICS

CITY	POPULATION
Anchorage	291,826
Fairbanks	31,535
Juneau	31,275
Sitka	8,881
Ketchikan	8,050

REGISTERED VOTERS

Unaffiliated	53%
Republican	26%
Democrat	15%
Others	5%

POPULATION

2010 population	710,231
2000 population	626,932
1990 population	550,043
Percent change (2000-2010)	+13.3%
Rank among states (2010)	47
Median age	32.7
Born in state	39.5%
Foreign born	6.3%
Violent crime rate	633/100,000
Poverty level	9.0%
Federal workers	22,244
Military	23,178

ELECTIONS

STATE DIVISION OF ELECTIONS
(907) 465-4611

DEMOCRATIC PARTY
(907) 258-3050

REPUBLICAN PARTY
(907) 276-4467

MISCELLANEOUS

Web: www.alaska.gov

Capital: Juneau

U.S. CONGRESS

Senate: 1 Democrat, 1 Republican

House: 1 Republican

2010 Census Statistics by District

District	2008 Vote for President Obama	McCain	White	Black	Asian	Hispanic	Median Income	White Collar	Blue Collar	Service Industry	Over 64	Under 18	College Education	Rural	Sq. Miles
AL	38%	59%	64%	3%	5%	6%	$64,635	59%	24%	17%	7%	27%	27%	34%	571,951
STATE	38	59	64	3	5	6	64,635	59	24	17	7	27	27	34	571,951
U.S.	53	46	64	12	5	16	51,425	60	23	17	13	25	28	21	3,537,438

Sen. Lisa Murkowski (R)

Capitol Office
224-6665
murkowski.senate.gov
709 Hart Bldg. 20510; fax 224-5301

Committees
Appropriations
Energy & Natural Resources - Ranking Member
Health, Education, Labor & Pensions
Indian Affairs

Residence
Girdwood

Born
May 22, 1957; Ketchikan, Alaska

Religion
Roman Catholic

Family
Husband, Verne Martell; two children

Education
Willamette U., attended 1977; Georgetown U., B.A.
1980 (economics); Willamette U., J.D. 1985

Career
Lawyer; state legislative aide

Political Highlights
Anchorage district attorney, 1987-89; Alaska House,
1999-2002

ELECTION RESULTS

2010 GENERAL

Lisa Murkowski — write-in	101,091	39.2%
Joe Miller (R)	90,839	35.3%
Scott T. McAdams (D)	60,045	23.3%
write-ins	2,719	1.1%

2010 PRIMARY

Joe Miller (R)	55,878	50.9%
Lisa Murkowski (R)	53,872	49.1%

Previous Winning Percentages
2004 (47%)

Elected 2004; 2nd full term

Appointed 2002

Murkowski has risen rapidly, fallen suddenly and enjoyed the rarest of political rebirths since her 2002 appointment to the Senate. She is an appropriator, a moderate in a conservative party and heir to her father's political legacy.

Few elected officials could legitimately claim to have had as eventful a year as Murkowski in 2010.

As her quest for a second full term began, she appeared to be a shoo-in. But the tea party movement that swept other moderates of both parties out of office appeared to claim Murkowski, too, when she lost the August GOP primary to attorney Joe Miller, who had been endorsed by former Alaska Gov. Sarah Palin, by 2,006 votes.

About three weeks later, Murkowski re-entered the race as a write-in candidate. Because she was challenging the nominated Republican, she resigned her position as GOP Conference vice chairwoman, although party leaders allowed her to keep her designation as ranking member of the Energy and Natural Resources Committee.

Murkowski went to great lengths to educate voters about how to write in her name, and Miller made a number of campaign missteps. In the most drawn-out election contest of the year, Murkowski claimed victory two weeks after Election Day, but had to wait until the final day of the year before Miller threw in the towel on his legal challenges. Winning 39 percent of the vote, she became the first write-in candidate to win a Senate race since Strom Thurmond of South Carolina in 1954.

Murkowski first came to office in controversy — she was appointed by her father, Frank H. Murkowski, to take his seat after he was elected governor — but she has subsequently avoided the negative publicity that has afflicted some of her fellow Alaskans. The late Ted Stevens, a longtime GOP force on the Senate Appropriations Committee, lost his 2008 bid for a seventh term after being convicted on corruption charges. (The conviction was later vacated.) The state's only House member, Republican Don Young, yielded his top-ranking slot on the Natural Resources Committee in December 2008 amid ethics questions, of which he was subsequently cleared.

She succeeded Pete V. Domenici as the top Republican on the Energy and Natural Resources Committee for the 111th Congress (2009-10) after the veteran senator from New Mexico retired. She also received a coveted seat on the Appropriations Committee at the outset of the 111th and was named a counsel to Minority Leader Mitch McConnell of Kentucky. Murkowski subsequently became an official member of the Senate GOP leadership in June 2009 when she succeeded South Dakota's John Thune as Republican Conference vice chairwoman, the spot she subsequently gave up after her defeat in the 2010 primary.

Legislatively, Murkowski has been at the center of efforts to enact comprehensive energy legislation, and her focus is broader than oil and gas drilling — mainstays of Alaska's economy. "How have we gotten to this point where Republicans are just for drilling and Democrats are just for conserving or locking everything up? That's not the way things should be," she said.

Murkowski has a good relationship with her Democratic counterpart on Energy and Natural Resources, Chairman Jeff Bingaman of New Mexico. She signed on as a cosponsor to his legislation in the 110th Congress (2007-08) to set up a cap-and-trade system to limit carbon emissions that was more industry-friendly than the version the Senate considered in 2008. But she led opposition to the EPA plan to impose regulations to limit such emissions — her resolution to block that authority was defeated in the Senate in June 2010 and is likely to reappear in the 112th Congress (2011-12). In the new Congress, she is the ranking Republican on the Interior-Environment Appropriations Subcommittee, with jurisdiction over EPA funding.

"The sweeping powers being pursued by the EPA are the worst possible option for reducing greenhouse gas emissions," she said on the Senate floor. "It would amount to an unprecedented power grab, ceding Congress' responsibilities to unelected bureaucrats, and move an important debate from our open halls to behind an agency's closed doors."

While energy issues are paramount in Alaska, Murkowski's priorities extend well beyond that theme. She has introduced or cosponsored several health-related bills, including one to combat fetal alcohol syndrome, a major problem in her state. A member of the Health, Education, Labor and Pensions Committee, she has frequently teamed with Democrats to push proposals to improve prevention and treatment of cardiovascular disease in women and to get junk food out of schools.

On the Indian Affairs panel, where she was the top Republican in the 110th Congress, she teamed with Chairman Byron L. Dorgan of North Dakota on efforts to improve American Indian housing and health care. She also worked with Barack Obama when he was in the Senate on a bill to ban exports of mercury, which can make fish, a staple food of Alaska's native peoples, unsafe to eat. That bill was signed into law in 2008.

After serving two years as an appointed senator, Murkowski began her first full term in 2005 in a strengthened position politically after winning the seat in her own right. The election helped lift the nepotism cloud, as did her ability to chalk up several legislative victories with the help of Stevens, who called Murkowski "a hell of a lot better senator than her dad ever was."

But Murkowski doesn't have Stevens' seniority and is operating in a different political and fiscal reality.

"It is a very dramatically different environment in Washington, D.C., when it comes to earmarks specifically," she said. "I will argue that at the federal level, we must do more to contain our spending. We've got to work to reduce that pie. But once that pie is determined, I'm going to do my darnedest to make sure that Alaska gets its fair share of that pie."

Aside from being compared with Stevens, she also contends with comparisons to her father. Her voting record is more moderate — she sided with the GOP only 70 percent of the time in 2009 and 83 percent in 2010 on votes that divided the two parties. She supports abortion rights and backed legislation in late 2010 that repealed the military's ban on homosexuals serving openly.

The second of six children, Murkowski grew up in Ketchikan in the Alaskan Panhandle and attended high school in Fairbanks. She interned for Stevens in her senior year, then went to Georgetown University. Her father was launching his first Senate campaign, and she and her siblings joined the effort. Later, with a law degree from Willamette University in Oregon, she spent two years as Anchorage's district attorney before opening a solo law practice.

She ran successfully for the state House in 1998, was re-elected twice and was chosen by her peers late in 2002 as majority leader, a post she never filled because of her appointment to the U.S. Senate.

During her 2004 campaign, she faced Democrat Tony Knowles, a former two-term governor. Murkowski tried to distance herself politically from her father, who was proving to be an unpopular governor. Under the banner "Team Alaska," Murkowski played up her working relationships with Stevens and Young, who chaired the Transportation and Infrastructure Committee. While Republican George W. Bush swept 61 percent of Alaska's vote for president, Murkowski squeaked past Knowles by 3 percentage points.

Key Votes

2010

Pass budget reconciliation bill to modify overhauls of health care and federal student loan programs	NO
Proceed to disapproval resolution on EPA authority to regulate greenhouse gases	YES
Overhaul financial services industry regulation	NO
Limit debate to proceed to a bill to broaden campaign finance disclosure and reporting rules	?
Limit debate on an extension of Bush-era income tax cuts for two years	YES
Limit debate on a bill to provide a path to legal status for some children of illegal immigrants	YES
Allow for a repeal of "don't ask, don't tell"	YES
Consent to ratification of a strategic arms reduction treaty with Russia	YES

2009

Prevent release of remaining financial industry bailout funds	YES
Make it easier for victims to sue for wage discrimination remedies	YES
Expand the Children's Health Insurance Program	YES
Limit debate on the economic stimulus measure	NO
Repeal District of Columbia firearms prohibitions and gun registration laws	YES
Limit debate on expansion of federal hate crimes law	YES
Strike funding for F-22 Raptor fighter jets	NO

CQ Vote Studies

	PARTY UNITY		PRESIDENTIAL SUPPORT	
	Support	Oppose	Support	Oppose
2010	83%	17%	60%	40%
2009	70%	30%	66%	34%
2008	72%	28%	72%	28%
2007	71%	29%	77%	23%
2006	82%	18%	89%	11%
2005	93%	7%	87%	13%
2004	92%	8%	87%	13%
2003	94%	6%	93%	7%

Interest Groups

	AFL-CIO	ADA	CCUS	ACU
2010	21%	20%	100%	73%
2009	56%	35%	71%	68%
2008	40%	25%	86%	58%
2007	32%	30%	91%	67%
2006	13%	5%	100%	71%
2005	14%	20%	100%	83%
2004	50%	35%	94%	74%
2003	15%	20%	86%	70%

Sen. Mark Begich (D)

Capitol Office
224-3004
begich.senate.gov
111 Russell Bldg 20510; fax 224-2354

Committees
Armed Services
Budget
Commerce, Science & Transportation
Homeland Security & Governmental Affairs
Veterans' Affairs

Residence
Anchorage

Born
March 30, 1962; Anchorage, Alaska

Religion
Roman Catholic

Family
Wife, Deborah Bonito; one child

Education
U. of Alaska, Anchorage, attended 1981-88

Career
Property development company owner; city
government employee

Political Highlights
Anchorage Assembly, 1988-98 (chairman, 1993,
1996-98); candidate for mayor of Anchorage, 1994,
2000; mayor of Anchorage, 2003-09

ELECTION RESULTS

2008 GENERAL

Mark Begich (D)	151,767	47.8%
Ted Stevens (R)	147,814	46.5%
Bob Bird (AKI)	13,197	4.2%

2008 PRIMARY

Mark Begich (D)	63,747	90.8%
Ray Metcalfe (D)	5,480	7.8%
Frank Vondersaar (D)	965	1.4%

Elected 2008; 1st term

A freshman senator with a political pedigree, Begich cultivates a moderate image and touts "consensus-building" skills developed in local and state politics. He joined the leadership team in 2010 as chairman of the Democratic Steering and Outreach Committee, the party's No. 5 post.

Begich says the idea of moving quickly into leadership came from others.

"I didn't ask for it," he told Roll Call in December 2010. "They're asking me to be part of a team because I bring a different perspective that, I think, they recognize was missing."

Begich has not been shy about pushing Senate Democrats to be more assertive in their messaging efforts. He has taken a particularly strong stand on shaking up Senate procedures and rules. Among the changes Begich and others pushed at the start of the 112th Congress (2011-12) were forcing around-the-clock sessions that would require the minority to repeatedly renew holds and adjusting rules to make it easier to overcome filibusters.

At the end of January, the Senate voted to eliminate secret holds but proposals to overhaul the filibuster rules were rejected.

"We're a little more aggressive about these things," he said in December 2010. "We're not concerned with tradition as much as 'let's do the business and let the public see what it is,' and you're seeing that."

One stylistic tactic Begich and other first-term Democratic senators have suggested is to have more made-for-TV conference committee meetings, as lawmakers did in 2010 for the financial regulatory overhaul legislation.

In what turned out to be a prelude to his entry into the leadership, Begich occasionally met with a group including Democrats Sheldon Whitehouse of Rhode Island, Patty Murray of Washington, Mark Pryor of Arkansas and Debbie Stabenow of Michigan to keep tabs on leadership transparency efforts. Begich also sought compromise with GOP colleagues, believing that approach more effective than tactics employed by his abrasive 40-year predecessor, the late Ted Stevens. One area in which he hopes to emulate Stevens' skill is sending federal dollars to Alaska. He has released scores of press releases touting funding for home-state projects, often with Alaska GOP Sen. Lisa Murkowski.

When Democrats were unable to pass an omnibus spending bill at the end of 2010, Begich wrote constituency groups in Alaska apologizing. "I am disappointed, plain and simple, since we have worked in a bipartisan manner to create a bill that contains projects as requested by nearly every senator," he wrote in a letter reported by the Anchorage Daily News.

Begich was displeased when Appropriations Chairman Daniel K. Inouye of Hawaii, announced a two-year earmark moratorium in February 2011.

"While I agree we need to look at every possible step to cut the deficit, I don't agree with the decision to impose a two-year ban on earmarks. As I have said many times before, Alaska is a young state with many needs, and we deserve our fair share of federal funding to develop our resources and our infrastructure," said Begich, who continued to accept constituent earmark requests.

Begich sits on the Commerce, Science and Transportation Committee, where Stevens served and from where the Democrat hopes to make his mark on climate change legislation as chairman of the Subcommittee on Oceans, Atmosphere, Fisheries and Coast Guard. When he was mayor of Anchorage, Begich implemented policies to reduce carbon emissions and save energy.

Begich favors both an expansion of energy development and increased federal spending on energy-efficient practices. Like Stevens, Begich favors opening more of Alaska to energy development and drilling for oil in the Arctic National

Wildlife Refuge. He also believes energy exploration should be complemented by an expansion of renewable energy.

The Commerce panel will, at some point, write a reauthorization of the 2005 surface transportation bill, a measure that traditionally is a vehicle for funding local projects. Begich favors building a light rail system to ease the commute for workers traveling between Anchorage and the Palmer-Wasilla region.

From his seat on the Armed Services Committee, Begich looks out for his state's numerous military bases and robust defense industry. He backed the bill, which became law, that ended the military's "don't ask, don't tell" policy that bars openly gay individuals from military service.

Begich sided with his party 93 percent of the time in the 111th Congress (2009-10) on votes that divided a majority of Democrats from a majority of Republicans, and he backed the Democratic health care overhaul in 2010. After the bill became law, Begich, who sits on the Veterans' Affairs Committee, introduced legislation that would allow military dependents to receive health care coverage up to age 26, mirroring a provision in the overhaul requiring private insurers to extend health care coverage to dependents up to that age.

Begich has said small businesses should get more assistance in offering employees health care. He supports a buy-in program for the uninsured similar to the Federal Employees Health Benefits Program, which serves members of Congress as well as federal employees and retirees. Begich often talks about his former career as a small-businessman, which began at 16 when he and his brother started several businesses, including a nightclub for teens and vending machine ventures. He later managed apartment buildings that catered to low-income renters and became a real estate agent in the 1990s.

On social issues, Begich has aligned with Democrats to support abortion rights, and he favors allowing same-sex couples to receive benefits through their partners. But as a lifetime member of the National Rifle Association, he has routinely bucked party leaders on gun owners' rights.

Begich is the third of six children born to schoolteachers who moved from Minnesota to Alaska in the late 1950s. His father, Nick Begich, was elected to the House as a Democrat in 1970. The senior Begich disappeared in 1972 with House Democratic leader Hale Boggs of Louisiana aboard a plane that was never found. (Republican Don Young, who had lost to Begich in the 1972 election, won the seat in a special election in early 1973 and has held it since.)

Begich never graduated from college, instead getting a business license at the age of 16. His political career started in the 1980s, when he worked for then-Anchorage Mayor Tony Knowles, a Democrat who later served two terms as governor. At 26, Begich was elected to the Anchorage Assembly and served 10 years, including three years as chairman and two as vice chairman. He lost 1994 and 2000 mayoral races before being elected in 2003, becoming the first Alaskan-born citizen to serve as Anchorage's top elected official.

The boyish Begich barely outran 85-year-old Stevens in a heated race that was too close to call weeks after Election Day 2008. During the campaign, Begich highlighted his respect for the Alaska institution, but said the state would benefit from a changing of the guard. "I just saw Alaska moving and shifting and changing, and he was not in touch [with] what was going on," he said.

Just days before the election, Stevens was found guilty on seven corruption charges of making false statements on financial disclosure forms. The Justice Department decided in April 2009 to drop the case and asked that the conviction be vacated after the judge criticized prosecutors for failing to turn over documents to defense lawyers, a decision Begich called "reasonable."

Stevens led by more than 3,000 votes at election's end, but the race wasn't called until late November. Absentee ballots allowed Begich to defeat the incumbent by fewer than 4,000 votes in a state that favored GOP presidential nominee John McCain over Barack Obama with almost 60 percent of the vote.

Key Votes

2010

Pass budget reconciliation bill to modify overhauls of health care and federal student loan programs	YES
Proceed to disapproval resolution on EPA authority to regulate greenhouse gases	NO
Overhaul financial services industry regulation	YES
Limit debate to proceed to a bill to broaden campaign finance disclosure and reporting rules	YES
Limit debate on an extension of Bush-era income tax cuts for two years	YES
Limit debate on a bill to provide a path to legal status for some children of illegal immigrants	YES
Allow for a repeal of "don't ask, don't tell"	YES
Consent to ratification of a strategic arms reduction treaty with Russia	YES

2009

Prevent release of remaining financial industry bailout funds	NO
Make it easier for victims to sue for wage discrimination remedies	YES
Expand the Children's Health Insurance Program	YES
Limit debate on the economic stimulus measure	YES
Repeal District of Columbia firearms prohibitions and gun registration laws	YES
Limit debate on expansion of federal hate crimes law	YES
Strike funding for F-22 Raptor fighter jets	NO

CQ Vote Studies

	PARTY UNITY		PRESIDENTIAL SUPPORT	
	Support	Oppose	Support	Oppose
2010	93%	7%	97%	3%
2009	93%	7%	93%	7%

Interest Groups

	AFL-CIO	ADA	CCUS	ACU
2010	100%	85%	27%	4%
2009	100%	100%	57%	12%

Rep. Don Young (R)

Capitol Office
225-5765
donyoung.house.gov
2314 Rayburn Bldg. 20515-0201; fax 225-0425

Committees
Natural Resources
  (Indian & Alaska Native Affairs - Chairman)
Transportation & Infrastructure

Residence
Fort Yukon

Born
June 9, 1933; Meridian, Calif.

Religion
Episcopalian

Family
Widowed; two children

Education
Yuba Junior College, A.A. 1952; California State U.,
Chico, B.A. 1958

Military Service
Army 1955-57

Career
Elementary school teacher; riverboat captain

Political Highlights
Fort Yukon City Council, 1960-64; mayor of Fort Yukon, 1964-68; Alaska House, 1967-70; Alaska Senate, 1971-73; Republican nominee for U.S. House, 1972

ELECTION RESULTS

2010 GENERAL
Don Young (R)	175,384	69.0%
Harry T. Crawford (D)	77,606	30.5%

2010 PRIMARY
Don Young (R)	74,310	70.4%
Sheldon Fisher (R)	24,709	23.4%
John R. Cox (R)	6,605	6.2%

2008 GENERAL
Don Young (R)	158,939	50.1%
Ethan Berkowitz (D)	142,560	45.0%
Don R. Wright (AKI)	14,274	4.5%

Previous Winning Percentages
2006 (56%); 2004 (71%); 2002 (70%); 2000 (70%);
1998 (63%); 1996 (59%); 1994 (57%); 1992 (47%);
1990 (52%); 1988 (63%); 1986 (56%); 1984 (55%);
1982 (71%); 1980 (74%); 1978 (55%); 1976 (71%);
1974 (54%); 1973 Special Election (51%)

Elected 1973; 19th full term

The self-described "alpha wolf" of Alaska politics has lost some of the bite that usually comes with seniority, but his bark remains intact. The acerbic Young no longer wields a full committee gavel, but his post as chairman of the newly created Natural Resources Subcommittee on Indian and Alaska Native Affairs allows him to continue focusing his energy on delivering funding for his home state and keeping a vigilant eye on public-lands issues.

"I asked the chairman to resurrect the subcommittee, because I'm actively involved in the whole Native American area," Young told CQ Weekly in January 2011. "I need a platform. I need the ability to be heard to a greater extent on issues that affect Alaska."

The appointment marks a rebirth of sorts for Young. Heading into the 111th Congress (2009-10), he dropped his bid for a second term as the Natural Resources Committee's top Republican amid questions about possible ethics problems and vowed to reclaim the position from Washington's Doc Hastings. "For the good of the Republican Party, the right thing for me to do is to temporarily step down from my post as ranking member on the House Committee on Natural Resources while my name is cleared," Young said in December 2008.

During the 2008 campaign, news reports indicated that Young was the subject of a Justice Department probe for his ties to VECO Corp., an oil services company at the center of the public-corruption probe of his Alaska GOP colleague, Sen. Ted Stevens. Young denied accepting personal gifts and doing favors for the company. His campaign spent more than $1 million on his legal expenses and tried to reimburse a VECO executive for $37,626 in expenses for annual pig roasts the executive had sponsored for Young over 10 years. The company never cashed the check and Young's campaign eventually sent the money to the Treasury. In the summer of 2010 Young was cleared of any wrongdoing by the Public Integrity Section of the Department of Justice, but he failed to win back the ranking member post.

(Stevens was defeated for re-election soon after being convicted of failing to report gifts from VECO and other business interests, but his conviction was subsequently vacated after the Justice Department dropped all charges, alleging prosecutorial misconduct.)

Young is also a senior member of the Transportation and Infrastructure Committee, a panel he chaired in the 109th Congress (2005-06). He played a role in promoting a $10 million design study for the "Coconut Road" highway interchange off Interstate 75 in Florida in the six-year, $286.5 billion highway law he steered to passage in 2005. In 2008 the Senate included a provision in a technical corrections law that directed the Justice Department to examine the earmark's origin. Young denied that the funding set-aside, which was revised after the bill had cleared both chambers, was intended to aid a developer and other interests that donated to his campaign. Even after the Justice Department dropped its probe, political opponents continued to press Young to release details about the earmark.

Young has long made clear that despite the scrutiny he has received, he does not intend to end his pursuit of funding for his state, and he rejected the Republicans' one-year moratorium on fiscal 2011 earmarks. "I believe that to do that would be turning my back on the state that I love while handing over control to President Obama and his appointed government officials," Young wrote in March 2010 in the Anchorage Daily News.

Young sometimes joins with Democrats in promoting routine measures such as public land swaps and funding to fight forest fires, but he typically takes the opposing side on broad land management and environmental issues. He has pushed in vain to open a portion of Alaska's Arctic National Wildlife Refuge to oil drilling and to provide tax incentives for property owners who implement plans to aid the recovery of animals listed under the Endangered Species Act.

He sponsored legislation that would allow Sealaska Corp., one of 12 regional corporations Congress created through the Alaska Native Claims Settlement Act, to select its final allotment of land outside the areas the government originally designated for such use in the Tongass National Forest. When 58 lawmakers wrote to colleagues in opposition to the proposal, Young responded that their position "embodies the act of holding native people and their native land entitlement hostage to the agenda of national conservation groups."

Raised on a farm in California, Young got an introduction to Alaska through his favorite book, Jack London's "The Call of the Wild." After completing college and military service, he headed for Alaska in 1959 and settled in as a 5th-grade teacher for Alaska Native students at a school in Fort Yukon, seven miles above the Arctic Circle. He taught school in the winter and captained his own tug and barge operation, ferrying supplies to villages along the Yukon River, in the summer. He is the only licensed mariner in Congress.

He served as mayor of Fort Yukon and as a state House member before moving to a state Senate seat in 1970. The only election he ever lost was his first U.S. House race, in 1972. His opponent, freshman Democrat Nick Begich, disappeared without a trace, along with House Majority Leader Hale Boggs, during an October flight from Anchorage to Juneau. But Begich still beat Young by almost 12,000 votes in November. After Begich's seat was declared vacant, Young edged out Emil Notti, the former state Democratic chairman, in a 1973 special election. (Begich's son Mark defeated Stevens in 2008.)

On the campaign trail in 2008, Young made the case that Alaskans needed him to take care of the state's interests with Democrats gaining clout in Washington. He survived a 2008 primary challenge by Lt. Gov. Sean Parnell, who was backed by Gov. Sarah Palin, by just 304 votes and edged Democrat Ethan Berkowitz, a former state legislator, in the general election with 50 percent of the vote. In 2010, he took 69 percent against Democrat Harry Crawford.

Key Votes

2010

Overhaul the nation's health insurance system	NO
Allow for repeal of "don't ask, don't tell"	NO
Overhaul financial services industry regulation	?
Limit use of new Afghanistan War funds to troop withdrawal activities	?
Change oversight of offshore drilling and lift oil spill liability cap	NO
Provide a path to legal status for some children of illegal immigrants	NO
Extend Bush-era income tax cuts for two years	YES

2009

Expand the Children's Health Insurance Program	YES
Provide $787 billion in tax cuts and spending increases to stimulate the economy	NO
Allow bankruptcy judges to modify certain primary-residence mortgages	NO
Create a cap-and-trade system to limit greenhouse gas emissions	NO
Provide $2 billion for the "cash for clunkers" program	NO
Establish the government as the sole provider of student loans	NO
Restrict federally funded insurance coverage for abortions in health care overhaul	YES

CQ Vote Studies

	PARTY UNITY		PRESIDENTIAL SUPPORT	
	SUPPORT	OPPOSE	SUPPORT	OPPOSE
2010	81%	19%	38%	62%
2009	71%	29%	42%	58%
2008	88%	12%	54%	46%
2007	83%	17%	65%	35%
2006	92%	8%	90%	10%

Interest Groups

	AFL-CIO	ADA	CCUS	ACU
2010	30%	10%	100%	75%
2009	40%	10%	90%	75%
2008	77%	55%	73%	71%
2007	64%	30%	88%	65%
2006	36%	25%	100%	72%

Alaska

At Large

Alaska's remoteness belies its dependence on Washington, D.C., from which it receives billions of dollars in annual federal spending. Nevertheless, state and local governments — which together provide the largest number of jobs in the state — are waging a never-ending battle against federal control of the local economy that has made voters hostile to Washington.

The state's proximity to Russia and the Far East makes it a military stronghold, and its vulnerable economic boosters — oil and gas, minerals and timber — lie mostly on federally owned land. Most Alaskans and local lawmakers view opening land to oil and gas exploration as the best way to independence and heavily favor drilling in the Arctic National Wildlife Refuge. But economic turmoil has delayed construction of a natural gas pipeline from Prudhoe Bay through Canada to the lower 48 states.

The state continues to build a privatized economy in the health care, retail and tourism sectors. Alaska has not had state sales and income taxes since black gold was discovered near Prudhoe Bay in the 1970s.

Alaska tends to support Republicans at the federal level and overwhelmingly backed the 2008 GOP presidential ticket, which included then-Gov. Sarah Palin.

But voters in some cities, the panhandle and the isolated tundra are more Democratic, and moderates dominate the state legislature. Most residents in this cold, conservative frontier state pay more attention to personality than to party affiliation, and register as either third-party or unaffiliated voters. A sense of loyalty to elected officials led many voters here to support incumbent Sen. Lisa Murkowski as a write-in candidate after she lost the Republican primary in 2010.

Major Industry
Oil and gas, defense, government, tourism, fishing, timber, mining

Military Bases
Joint Base Elmendorf-Richardson, 12,200 military, 3,000 civilian (2011); Fort Wainwright (Army), 6,400 military, 1,100 civilian (2010); Eielson Air Force Base, 2,573 military, 574 civilian; Fort Greely (Army), 1 military, 271 civilian (2009)

Cities
Anchorage, 291,826; Fairbanks, 31,535; Juneau, 31,275

Notable
Mt. McKinley is the highest point in North America, at 20,320 feet.

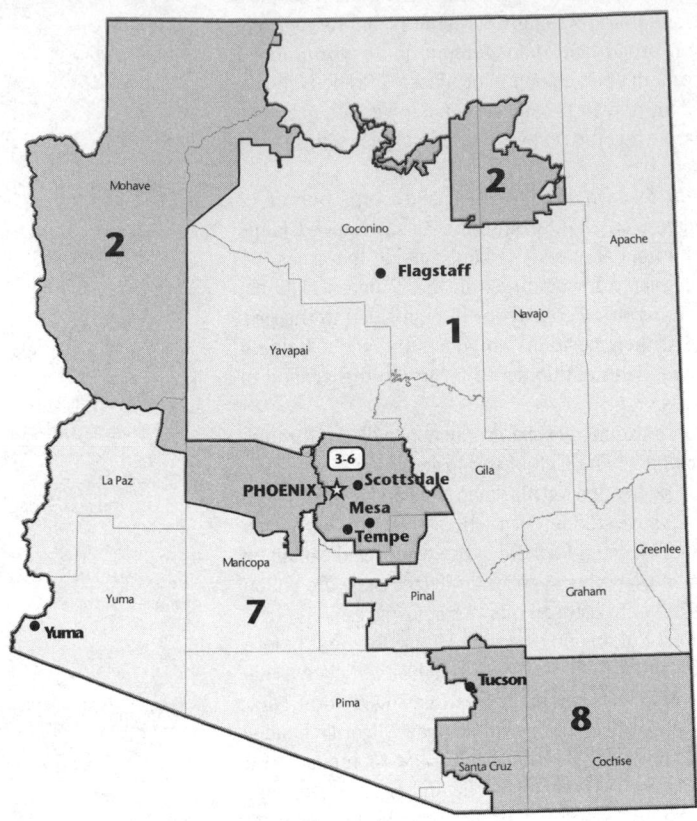

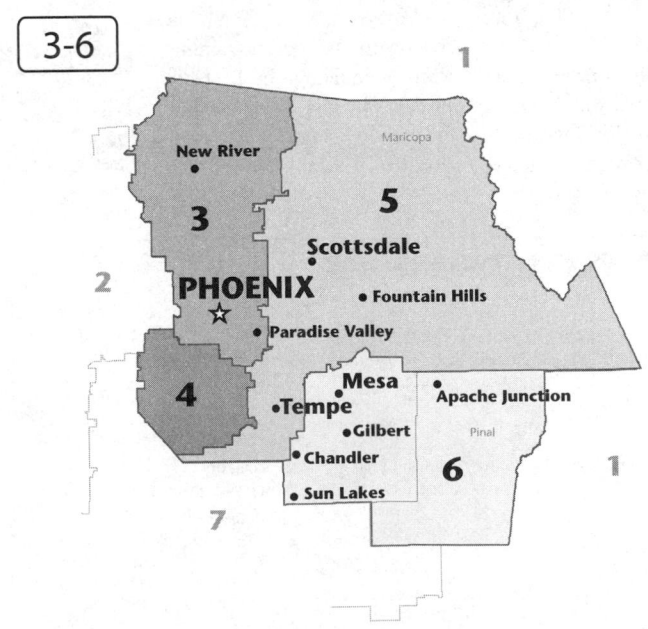

Gov. Jan Brewer (R)

First elected: 2010
Took office Jan. 21, 2009,
due to the resignation of
Janet Napolitano, D.

Length of term: 4 years

Term expires: 1/15

Salary: $95,000

Phone: (602) 542-4331

Residence: Glendale

Born: Sept. 26, 1944;
Los Angeles, Calif.

Religion: Lutheran — Missouri Synod

Family: Husband, John Brewer; three children (one deceased)

Education: Verdugo Hills H.S., graduated 1962

Career: Homemaker, office manager

Political highlights: Ariz. House, 1983-87; Ariz. Senate, 1987-96 (minority whip, 1993-96); Maricopa County Board of Supervisors, 1997-2002; Ariz. Secretary of State, 2003-09

ELECTION RESULTS

2010 GENERAL

Jan Brewer (R)	938,934	54.3%
Terry Goddard (D)	733,935	42.5%
Barry Hess (LIBERT)	38,722	2.2%

Secretary of State
Ken Bennet (R)

(no lieutenant governor)

Assumed office: 2009

Length of term: 4 years

Term expires: 1/15

Salary: $70,000

Phone: (602) 542-4285

LEGISLATURE

Legislature: 100 days January-April

Senate: 30 members, 2-year terms

2011 ratios: 21R, 9 D; 20 men, 10 women

Salary: $24,000

Phone: (602) 926-3559

House: 60 members, 2-year terms

2011 ratios: 40 R, 20 D; 40 men, 20 women

Salary: $24,000

Phone: (602) 926-42211

TERM LIMITS

Governor: 2 consecutive terms

Senate: 4 consecutive terms

House: 4 consecutive terms

URBAN STATISTICS

CITY	POPULATION
Phoenix	1,445,632
Tucson	520,116
Mesa	439,041
Chandler	236,123
Glendale	226,721

REGISTERED VOTERS

Republican	1,142,605
Democrat	1,008,689
Independent/others	1,010,725

POPULATION

2010 population (est.)	6,392,017
2000 population	5,130,632
1990 population	3,665,228
Percent change (2000-2010)	+24.6%
Rank among states (2010)	16
Median age	34.8
Born in state	36.2%
Foreign born	14.6%
Violent crime rate	408/100,000
Poverty level	16.5%
Federal workers	69,533
Military	21,343

ELECTIONS

STATE ELECTION OFFICIAL
(602) 542-4285

DEMOCRATIC PARTY
(602) 298-4200

REPUBLICAN PARTY
(602) 957-7770

MISCELLANEOUS

Web: www.az.gov

Capital: Phoenix

U.S. CONGRESS

Senate: 2 Republicans

House: 5 Republicans, 3 Democrats

2010 Census Statistics by District

District	2008 Vote for President Obama	McCain	White	Black	Asian	Hispanic	Median Income	White Collar	Blue Collar	Service Industry	Over 64	Under 18	College Education	Rural	Sq. Miles
1	44%	54%	57%	2%	1%	19%	$41,483	54%	25%	21%	15%	25%	19%	45%	58,608
2	38	61	69	4	3	21	53,568	61	21	18	17	25	21	11	20,220
3	42	56	71	3	3	19	57,034	67	17	16	11	25	32	4	598
4	66	33	22	9	2	64	37,573	42	36	22	6	33	13	0	199
5	47	52	70	4	4	17	61,175	71	13	16	12	22	42	3	1,406
6	38	61	69	3	4	21	60,414	65	20	16	13	29	28	3	724
7	57	42	33	4	2	56	40,025	51	28	21	11	30	15	16	22,873
8	46	52	68	3	3	23	50,893	66	16	18	18	22	34	13	9,007
STATE	45	54	58	4	3	30	50,296	60	22	18	13	26	26	12	113,635
U.S.	53	46	64	12	5	16	51,425	60	23	17	13	25	28	21	3,537,438

Sen. John McCain (R)

Capitol Office
224-2235
mccain.senate.gov
241 Russell Bldg. 20510-0303; fax 228-2862

Committees
Armed Services - Ranking Member
Energy & Natural Resources
Health, Education, Labor & Pensions
Homeland Security & Governmental Affairs
Indian Affairs

Residence
Phoenix

Born
Aug. 29, 1936; Panama Canal Zone, Panama

Religion
Episcopalian

Family
Wife, Cindy McCain; seven children

Education
U.S. Naval Academy, B.S. 1958; National War College, attended 1974

Career
Navy officer; Navy Senate liaison; beer distributor

Military Service
Navy, 1958-81

Political Highlights
U.S. House, 1983-87; sought Republican nomination for president, 2000; Republican nominee for president, 2008

ELECTION RESULTS

2010 GENERAL

John McCain (R)	1,005,615	58.9%
Rodney Glassman (D)	592,011	34.6%
David F. Nolan (LIBERT)	80,097	4.7%

2010 PRIMARY

John McCain (R)	333,744	56.2%
J.D. Hayworth (R)	190,229	32.1%
Jimmie Lee Deakin (R)	69,328	11.7%

Previous Winning Percentages
2004 (77%); 1998 (69%); 1992 (56%); 1986 (61%)

Elected 1986; 5th term

Many of the issues that have come to define McCain in his nearly three decades in Congress have begun to backfire politically, and the 2008 GOP presidential nominee has adjusted to the new reality. He still sees himself as a maverick conservative, but now he emphasizes the second part of that construction more often than the first.

His bipartisan ways became an issue for McCain both in the 2008 presidential election and in the 2010 GOP Senate primary, during which former Rep. J.D. Hayworth waged an aggressive — though ultimately unsuccessful — challenge from the right. Hayworth campaigned with a message that he would be more consistently conservative than McCain, who over the years has sided with Democrats on a broad range of issues including campaign finance, tax policy and immigration.

As members of his own party have increasingly criticized McCain for working too often with lawmakers across the aisle, Democrats have begun to complain that he let political considerations dilute his commitment to overhauling immigration policy.

After Congress enacted a $600 million border security law in August 2010 that McCain cosponsored, Illinois Democratic Rep. Luis V. Gutierrez said he hoped McCain would return from defeating his opponent recommitted to comprehensive immigration legislation. It's a charge McCain tends to dismiss, admitting to little more than a change in emphasis and a bow to legislative reality. It is not politically possible to enact broad immigration changes without first securing the border, he says, a lesson he learned after two failed attempts in the 2000s.

McCain can be hard to categorize, despite more than a quarter of a century's experience in national politics. He is conservative on fundamental issues, including national security and government spending. He has been a committed supporter of the Iraq War and was a lonely voice in Congress in ardently supporting the troop surge that eventually proved effective. He is admired and reviled for using Senate floor time to read lengthy lists of "pork barrel" spending in appropriations bills. But McCain racks up enough exceptions to the party line to often be viewed as a moderate.

He is the top Republican on the Armed Services Committee, a role befitting his history: son and grandson of admirals, Naval aviator and prisoner of war who suffered cruel treatment at the hands of his Vietnamese captors.

That history gave him virtually unquestioned credibility when he stood against harsh interrogation of terrorist detainees. He pushed Congress to bar such tactics, and President George W. Bush eventually signed a ban into law.

When, as one of his first acts in office, President Obama signed an order to close the detention camp at Guantánamo Bay, Cuba, McCain applauded the move. But he also said it was a mistake to put the process in motion before deciding what to do with the prisoners, and he has been proven prescient — Obama hasn't been able to figure out what to do with many of the prisoners, and the facility remains open.

McCain opposed repeal of the military's ban on openly gay servicemembers, but said he would work to see the new policy is effectively implemented.

Not surprisingly, McCain's party unity score — tracking how often he votes with a majority of his party against a majority of Democrats — has been all over the map. He matched a career low in 2001 with 67 percent and hit a high of 98 percent in 2010.

His voting record often perturbs colleagues, but probably not as much as his attitude does. In a chamber where members are expected to treat one another with deference, McCain can be quick to discard courtesies and sometimes comes off as self-righteous.

Perhaps nowhere has that sense been more evident than when McCain talks about campaign finance, a signature issue for him. He was one of the authors of the 2002 campaign finance overhaul that many conservative groups deplore.

McCain can be blunt, funny and testy — often in the same sitting. Several of his colleagues have been subjected to his aggressive, obscenity-laced tirades. He is also famously self-deprecating; a favorite campaign line of his was, "I am older than dirt and have more scars than Frankenstein."

Besides his role as the ranking Republican on the Armed Services Committee, McCain serves on Energy and Natural Resources; Homeland Security and Governmental Affairs; Health, Education, Labor and Pensions; and Indian Affairs. On the Energy and Natural Resources Committee, he made his stand as the Senate's leading supporter of the development of nuclear energy, calling Obama's attempt to close the Yucca Mountain nuclear-waste repository "a political decision devoid of scientific guidance." He has worked with one of his closest friends, independent Joseph I. Lieberman of Connecticut, on climate change legislation that many Republicans consider a job killer.

McCain has marched in line with his party in the shaping of economic issues, working with a group of Republicans to propose an alternative to Obama's stimulus plan and voting against releasing the second half of the $700 billion in financial sector rescue funds approved in 2008. On the HELP Committee, he opposed the Democrats' health care overhaul, saying their math did not add up.

McCain was born in the Panama Canal Zone. His mother, in her mid-90s, campaigned with him for president in 2007 and 2008.

McCain attended the Naval Academy in Annapolis to follow in the footsteps of his father and grandfather. Although McCain never made it to admiral, he is widely admired for his bravery as a prisoner of war. During the Vietnam War, McCain's fighter plane was shot down, and he was captured by the North Vietnamese. He spent five and a half years in solitary confinement, often being subjected to physical abuse and torture.

Transitioning from his position as the Navy's Senate liaison, McCain ran for Congress in 1982. After two terms in the House, he won the Senate seat that opened when conservative icon Barry Goldwater retired, drawing 61 percent of the vote. Shortly thereafter, McCain was accused of interceding with federal regulators on behalf of a wealthy savings and loan operator and was given a mild rebuke in 1991 after a protracted Ethics Committee investigation. He has pointed to that incident as his inspiration for becoming a crusader for changes in the campaign finance system. Following the scandal, he was held to 56 percent in his 1992 re-election win, but bounced back to take 69 percent of the vote six years later.

In 2000 he sought the GOP presidential nomination, but lost to Bush.

He was easily re-elected to the Senate in 2004, then made another run for the White House in 2008. He trailed in early polls and lost in the Iowa caucuses, but recovered to win the nomination.

His choice of Alaska Gov. Sarah Palin as his vice presidential candidate was a typically maverick move for McCain, though results were mixed. She sparked interest in his campaign among conservative voters, who were generally unenthusiastic about his nomination, but she was not popular among the independent voters McCain himself tended to attract. Unable to compete with Obama's fundraising and mantra of change in a tough year for Republicans across the board, McCain lost the election and returned to his job in the Senate.

After dispatching Hayworth in the GOP primary in 2010, he cruised to a 24-point victory over Democrat Rodney Glassman in November.

Key Votes

2010

Pass budget reconciliation bill to modify overhauls of health care and federal student loan programs	NO
Proceed to disapproval resolution on EPA authority to regulate greenhouse gases	YES
Overhaul financial services industry regulation	NO
Limit debate to proceed to a bill to broaden campaign finance disclosure and reporting rules	NO
Limit debate on an extension of Bush-era income tax cuts for two years	YES
Limit debate on a bill to provide a path to legal status for some children of illegal immigrants	NO
Allow for a repeal of "don't ask, don't tell"	NO
Consent to ratification of a strategic arms reduction treaty with Russia	NO

2009

Prevent release of remaining financial industry bailout funds	YES
Make it easier for victims to sue for wage discrimination remedies	NO
Expand the Children's Health Insurance Program	NO
Limit debate on the economic stimulus measure	NO
Repeal District of Columbia firearms prohibitions and gun registration laws	YES
Limit debate on expansion of federal hate crimes law	NO
Strike funding for F-22 Raptor fighter jets	YES

CQ Vote Studies

	PARTY UNITY		PRESIDENTIAL SUPPORT	
	SUPPORT	OPPOSE	SUPPORT	OPPOSE
2010	98%	2%	39%	61%
2009	96%	4%	43%	57%
2008	93%	7%	89%	11%
2007	90%	10%	95%	5%
2006	76%	24%	89%	11%
2005	84%	16%	77%	23%
2004	79%	21%	92%	8%
2003	86%	14%	91%	9%
2002	80%	20%	90%	10%
2001	67%	33%	91%	9%

Interest Groups

	AFL-CIO	ADA	CCUS	ACU
2010	6%	0%	100%	100%
2009	17%	15%	71%	96%
2008	0%	5%	100%	63%
2007	0%	10%	100%	80%
2006	7%	15%	100%	65%
2005	7%	10%	72%	80%
2004	33%	35%	67%	72%
2003	15%	35%	61%	75%
2002	33%	20%	79%	78%
2001	27%	40%	50%	68%

Sen. Jon Kyl (R)

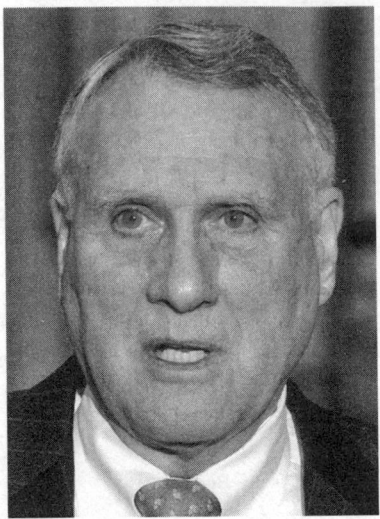

Capitol Office
224-4521
kyl.senate.gov
730 Hart Bldg. 20510-0304; fax 224-2207

Committees
Finance
Judiciary

Residence
Phoenix

Born
April 25, 1942; Oakland, Neb.

Religion
Presbyterian

Family
Wife, Caryll Kyl; two children

Education
U. of Arizona, B.A. 1964 (political science),
LL.B. 1966

Career
Lawyer

Political Highlights
U.S. House, 1987-95

ELECTION RESULTS

2006 GENERAL

Jon Kyl (R)	814,398	53.3%
Jim Pederson (D)	664,141	43.5%
Richard Mack (LIBERT)	297,636	3.2%

2006 PRIMARY

Jon Kyl (R)	297,636	100%

Previous Winning Percentages
2000 (79%); 1994 (54%); 1992 House Election (59%);
1990 House Election (61%); 1988 House Election
(87%); 1986 House Election (65%)

Elected 1994; 3rd term

Kyl is a brainy and influential member of the Senate Republican leadership whose positions on foreign policy, taxes and legal matters often become the de facto positions of his GOP colleagues.

He has built solid relationships with members of all factions of his caucus, from the conservative Jim DeMint of South Carolina to the moderate Olympia J. Snowe of Maine to fellow Arizonan John McCain. His early 2011 announcement that he would not seek re-election will open up the No. 2 spot in the Senate GOP leadership following the 2012 elections.

With his lawyerly focus on policy and an ability to avoid making controversial statements, Kyl is a regular spokesman for the party on cable news and Sunday talk shows. He was one of only two senators to make Time Magazine's list of the world's 100 most influential people.

But his defining role in the Senate plays out in behind-the-scenes negotiations over legislation. "I have made an effort not to be partisan in an in-your-face sense," he once said. "Ordinarily, I don't talk about Republicans and Democrats. I talk about ideas."

In the 111th Congress (2009-10), Kyl became the GOP point man on negotiations over a nuclear arms agreement with Russia. Although he does not sit on the Foreign Relations Committee, fellow Republicans made it clear they believed the fate of President Obama's New START treaty rested with Kyl. To help win his support, Senate Democrats in September 2010 included in a stopgap funding measure $624 million for modernization of the nuclear stockpile. Democrats knew from experience to take him seriously, since he can claim credit for derailing the 1999 Comprehensive Nuclear Test Ban Treaty. But this time Kyl's opposition did not prevail, and 13 Republicans joined with the Democrats in approving the treaty in late December 2010.

His history as one of the GOP's pre-eminent advocates of a robust national security posture includes an ongoing push for a tough stance against Iran and stalwart opposition to Obama's plans to close the Guantánamo Bay detention facility for terrorism suspects. On some issues, Kyl crosses the aisle; he has joined hands with New Yorker Charles E. Schumer, a member of the Democratic leadership, on pushing for sanctions against Iran.

As a member of the Judiciary Committee and a junior senator from a state that shares a 370-mile border with Mexico, Kyl is a key player on immigration issues. In the 110th Congress (2007-08), he took the lead in an unsuccessful attempt to broker comprehensive immigration legislation with Democrats and the George W. Bush administration. His willingness to back creation of a pathway to citizenship for illegal immigrants drove a rare wedge between Kyl and conservative activists. But since that legislation fell apart in June 2007, resurrecting broad immigration legislation is impossible until the federal government largely eliminates illegal border crossings, Kyl says. "When that is accomplished, I think there will be more of an open mind to readdressing comprehensive reform," Kyl said. In the meantime, he has criticized the Obama administration for suing Arizona over the state's 2010 law pushing for local and state enforcement of immigration restrictions.

Kyl frequently blocked legislation the Bush administration opposed and he proved a thorn in the side of Judiciary Chairman Patrick J. Leahy, a Vermont Democrat, opposing a patent law overhaul and an effort to broaden the Freedom of Information Act.

But Kyl also had repeatedly thwarted the panel's previous chairman, Arlen Specter, when the GOP controlled the Senate and the party-switching

Pennsylvanian was a Republican. Operating in the shadows, Kyl helped block the Supreme Court nomination of Harriet Miers, Bush's White House counsel, whom conservatives considered under-qualified and unreliably conservative. He also torpedoed Specter's efforts to oversee the president's domestic surveillance programs.

Kyl's roles in the leadership and as a senior member of the Finance Committee give him an authoritative voice on tax policy. "Every time Democrats try to raise taxes, we'll have a chance to vote on that so that they're on record as voting for tax increases and our members get an opportunity to vote against those tax increases," he said. He has taken the lead for Republicans on the estate tax, pushing a provision with moderate Democrats to reduce the federal levy on wealthy estates. He has also pushed back against Democratic deficit reduction proposals to couple tax cuts with offsetting tax increases, arguing that such moves negate the economic benefits of reducing taxes. He does support offsetting spending cuts for any spending increases.

The White House criticized Kyl for making those arguments, with Press Secretary Robert Gibbs saying Kyl was essentially arguing that "you can't get your unemployment benefits extended unless they're paid for, but if you were a recipient of the Bush tax cuts above $250,000, that doesn't need to be paid for." Those remarks note the significant adjustment for Kyl in dealing with a Democratic administration after eight years of enjoying close ties to Vice President Dick Cheney, his political mentor from their days together in the House. "My father said you should find somebody you can trust," Kyl recalled. "So I went to Dick Cheney."

Kyl's voting record has been uniformly conservative. He voted against both of Obama's Supreme Court nominees, Elena Kagan and Sonia Sotomayor. In September 2010, Kyl led conservative opposition to an appeals court nominee supported by fellow Republican leader Lamar Alexander of Tennessee, arguing that the nominee was willing to consider foreign laws, not just the U.S. Constitution, in deciding cases. He also voted against a payroll tax cut for firms that hire unemployed workers, which was cosponsored by fellow Republican Orrin G. Hatch of Utah because of a variety of spending add-ons.

Kyl was born in northeastern Nebraska near the small college town of Wayne, where his father, John H. Kyl, was a school principal and led the local Chamber of Commerce. In the 1950s, the family moved to Iowa, where the elder Kyl joined his brother in a clothing business; he later was elected to the U.S. House and served 11 years. He helped prepare his son for a life in politics by coaching him in public speaking, and he brought young Kyl to spend the summer of 1963 with him in Washington.

Kyl went to college and law school at the University of Arizona, inspired by the state's GOP icon, Sen. Barry Goldwater. He read and reread Goldwater's "Conscience of a Conservative" and William F. Buckley's "Up from Liberalism."

After law school, he joined a Phoenix law firm. In 1985 he became president of the Phoenix Chamber of Commerce, building strong business ties that helped him win a 1986 GOP primary over John Conlon, a former House member trying for a comeback. Kyl handily won the general election.

Kyl won three easy re-elections to the House and launched a Senate bid in 1994 even before incumbent Democrat Dennis DeConcini announced his retirement. He breezed to the GOP nomination as first-term Rep. Sam Coppersmith struggled to secure the Democratic nomination. Voters in Arizona liked the themes Kyl stressed: smaller government, lower taxes and reduced regulation. He prevailed by 14 percentage points. Six years later, the Democrats did not even field a candidate. In 2006, Kyl bucked the year's strong Democratic tide to win a third term by almost 10 percentage points over millionaire shopping-mall developer Jim Pederson, a former state Democratic Party chairman.

Key Votes

2010

Pass budget reconciliation bill to modify overhauls of health care and federal student loan programs	NO
Proceed to disapproval resolution on EPA authority to regulate greenhouse gases	YES
Overhaul financial services industry regulation	NO
Limit debate to proceed to a bill to broaden campaign finance disclosure and reporting rules	NO
Limit debate on an extension of Bush-era income tax cuts for two years	YES
Limit debate on a bill to provide a path to legal status for some children of illegal immigrants	NO
Allow for a repeal of "don't ask, don't tell"	NO
Consent to ratification of a strategic arms reduction treaty with Russia	NO

2009

Prevent release of remaining financial industry bailout funds	NO
Make it easier for victims to sue for wage discrimination remedies	NO
Expand the Children's Health Insurance Program	NO
Limit debate on the economic stimulus measure	NO
Repeal District of Columbia firearms prohibitions and gun registration laws	YES
Limit debate on expansion of federal hate crimes law	NO
Strike funding for F-22 Raptor fighter jets	YES

CQ Vote Studies

	PARTY UNITY		PRESIDENTIAL SUPPORT	
	SUPPORT	OPPOSE	SUPPORT	OPPOSE
2010	97%	3%	40%	60%
2009	95%	5%	45%	55%
2008	100%	0%	83%	17%
2007	93%	7%	89%	11%
2006	95%	5%	90%	10%
2005	98%	2%	89%	11%
2004	98%	2%	100%	0%
2003	99%	1%	99%	1%
2002	96%	4%	96%	4%
2001	98%	2%	99%	1%

Interest Groups

	AFL-CIO	ADA	CCUS	ACU
2010	6%	0%	100%	96%
2009	6%	5%	71%	92%
2008	0%	0%	63%	96%
2007	0%	5%	60%	100%
2006	13%	0%	92%	92%
2005	0%	5%	83%	100%
2004	0%	5%	88%	100%
2003	0%	10%	96%	90%
2002	15%	0%	90%	100%
2001	6%	5%	100%	100%

Rep. Paul Gosar (R)

Capitol Office
225-2315
gosar.house.gov
504 Cannon Bldg. 20515-0301; fax 226-9739

Committees
Natural Resources
Oversight & Government Reform

Residence
Flagstaff

Born
Nov. 27, 1958; Rock Springs, Wyo.

Religion
Roman Catholic

Family
Wife, Maude Gosar; three children

Education
Creighton U., B.S. 1981 (biology), D.D.S. 1985

Career
Dentist

Political Highlights
No previous office

ELECTION RESULTS

2010 GENERAL

Paul Gosar (R)	112,816	49.7%
Ann Kirkpatrick (D)	99,233	43.7%
Nicole Patti (LIBERT)	14,869	6.6%

2010 PRIMARY

Paul Gosar (R)	21,941	30.7%
Sydney Hay (R)	16,328	22.9%
Bradley Beauchamp (R)	11,356	15.9%
Russell "Rusty" Bowers (R)	10,552	14.8%
Steve Mehta (R)	5,846	8.2%
Thomas J. Zaleski (R)	2,105	2.9%
Jon Jensen (R)	1,736	2.4%
Joe Jaraczewski (R)	1,530	2.1%

Elected 2010; 1st term

Though he aligns with conservatives and tea party activists, Gosar emphasizes his independence by saying he is a "Paul Gosar Republican."

Gosar has focused mostly on efforts to limit federal bureaucracy. He said Democrats have "built levels upon levels of bureaucracy" that are choking off job creation and must be stripped away. A member of the Natural Resources Committee, he cites environmental regulation as a case in point. Businesses not only must deal with the EPA, but also with state and local regulators, he explained.

He also can keep an eye on the regulators as a member of the Oversight and Government Reform Committee.

Gosar said his 25 years as a dentist have given him a unique perspective on the health care system and small businesses. He joined with the rest of the Republican Conference in voting to repeal the health care overhaul enacted in 2010.

He would like to cut federal spending and the federal workforce to help make the government "lean and mean." But he said government spending has a role to play in fostering economic activity by building roads, bridges and other infrastructure and by spending on agriculture.

With a degree from the Creighton Boyne School of Dentistry and his own practice, Gosar has been active in the dental community, holding various chairmanships and association posts, but had never held an elected office before his 2010 election.

First-term Democrat Ann Kirkpatrick was a target for Republicans in 2010. Gosar won a crowded GOP primary, with help from an endorsement by former Alaska Gov. Sarah Palin.

He bested Kirkpatrick with just under 50 percent of the vote in a district where GOP presidential candidate and Arizona favorite son John McCain won by 10 percentage points in 2008.

Gosar hired Palin's family attorney as his legislative director and deputy chief of staff, and for the chief of staff post he tapped the Wasilla, Alaska, dentist who brought Gosar and Palin together.

Arizona 1

North and east — Flagstaff, Prescott, Navajo reservation

A population that includes artistic liberals, rural conservatives and a large American Indian population makes the immense 1st appear ripe for unpredictable elections. Sprawling across much of northern and eastern Arizona, the 58,608-square-mile swath is larger than 30 states.

Democrats have a slight voter registration advantage, and many locals call themselves environmentalists in a district that includes both sides of the Grand Canyon. Despite the Democrats' edge, however, residents of the 1st gave Arizona Sen. John McCain 54 percent of the district's 2008 presidential vote and went for the GOP in the 2010 U.S. House race when freshman Ann Kirkpatrick lost her re-election bid.

Sedona, a tourist destination renowned for its natural beauty, is home to art galleries and luxury resorts. The 1st also features mining and timber operations, but droughts and fires, which hit the area hard in the last decade, worry residents and officials. The district has the nation's largest American Indian population (19 percent), and high rates of poverty and unemployment continue to be problems in American Indian communities. Because of longstanding land disputes, the 1st is missing a chunk of land in its northern section to avoid placing the Hopi Nation in the same district as the Navajo Nation.

Major Industry
Tourism, agriculture, timber, mining

Cities
Flagstaff, 65,870; Casa Grande (pt.), 48,540; Prescott, 39,843; Prescott Valley, 38,822

Notable
Sedona claims the only place in the world where you can find non-golden McDonald's arches — the city's artistically inclined residents painted them turquoise.

Rep. Trent Franks (R)

Capitol Office
225-4576
www.house.gov/franks
2435 Rayburn Bldg. 20515-0302; fax 225-6328

Committees
Armed Services
Judiciary
   (Constitution - Chairman)

Residence
Peoria

Born
June 19, 1957; Uravan, Colo.

Religion
Baptist

Family
Wife, Josephine Franks; two children

Education
Ottawa U. (Ariz.), attended 1989-90

Career
Oil company executive; conservative think tank
president; state children's programs director

Political Highlights
Ariz. House, 1985-87; defeated for re-election to Ariz.
House, 1986; sought Republican nomination for
U.S. House, 1994

ELECTION RESULTS

2010 GENERAL

Trent Franks (R)	173,173	64.9%
John Thrasher (D)	82,891	31.1%
Powell Gammill (LIBERT)	10,820	4.0%

2010 PRIMARY

Trent Franks (R)	81,252	80.9%
Charles Black (R)	19,220	19.1%

2008 GENERAL

Trent Franks (R)	200,914	59.4%
John Thrasher (D)	125,611	37.2%
Powell Gammill (LIBERT)	7,882	2.3%
William Crum (GREEN)	3,616	1.1%

Previous Winning Percentages
2006 (59%); 2004 (59%); 2002 (60%)

Elected 2002; 5th term

Franks is consistently ranked as one of the most conservative members of the House, and he has staked out a position as a hard-line supporter of missile defense and a robust U.S. stance in the world. He vigorously confronts Democrats, both on cultural issues at home and on threats from abroad.

"We fight on fronts that are moving," he said. "I've just gotten louder, is all."

His spots on the Armed Services and Judiciary committees give him ample opportunity to sound a hawkish note on a broad range of national security issues, and to look out for the interests in his district, notably Luke Air Force Base. In April 2010, he also was named to a GOP National Security Solutions Group.

Franks' ongoing missile defense efforts played a role in his sharp criticism of the strategic arms treaty that the Senate approved in December 2010.

"The Obama administration's urgent insistence to ratify the New START treaty with Russia during a lame-duck session — notwithstanding that Russia and the United States fundamentally disagree on whether it permits further development of U.S. missile defense and that Russia is redeploying battlefield nuclear weapons to the borders of our allies in the North Atlantic Treaty Organization — reveals the same weakness that characterized U.S. foreign policy under President Jimmy Carter in the 1970s," Franks wrote in Politico in advance of the Senate vote.

Arguing that it could help deter Iran from building and deploying ballistic missiles, he backed deployment of an anti-missile system in Eastern Europe, but it was canceled by Obama.

"Iran now has missile technology superior to North Korea even though early technology came from North Korea," Franks told The Hill newspaper in late 2010. "There is a coincidence of jihadist terrorism and nuclear proliferation, but this administration by and large seems to be asleep at the wheel."

Franks sees the Iranian threat through the lens of the war on terror and as a devoted supporter of Israel, and he calls Obama's policy of engagement a "slow-motion train wreck." He is a co-founder of the congressional Israel Allies Caucus, and wrote in an April 2010 opinion piece in the Washington Examiner that enemies of Israel and the United States see Obama administration policies as "an opportunity to boldly advance violence against Israel."

That sort of tough rhetoric is a staple of Franks' arsenal.

He suggested that terrorists would be "dancing in the streets" after Obama's election. A vigorous defender of tough interrogation tactics used on enemy combatants during the George W. Bush administration, he argues that giving suspects the right to challenge their detention would be "a disaster waiting to happen."

Franks, a member of the Republican Study Committee, is equally devoted to conservative economic policies and voted against all the legislative efforts aimed at boosting federal spending to stimulate the economy.

His devotion to the Republican Party — he sided with the GOP 99 percent of the time on votes that divided Republicans from Democrats in the 111th Congress (2009-10) — allowed him few legislative victories while Democrats were in charge. He can expect a friendlier audience in the 112th (2011-12) for ideas such as his repeated efforts to replicate a program he promoted in Arizona: tax credits for charitable contributions to groups that provide tuition vouchers for children enrolled in private or parochial schools.

"Children's issues have been my political life," Franks said, and he supports overturning the Supreme Court's *Roe v. Wade* decision legalizing abortion. In keeping with the tough rhetoric he delivers on national security issues, Franks has called legalized abortion "the greatest genocide in the history of mankind" and Planned Parenthood "a death-dealing organization."

During his first term in Congress, he initially opposed the Bush administration's Medicare prescription-drug benefit program until, during dramatic balloting that lasted through the night, he switched his vote and a key measure was passed. He explained that without his vote the House bill would have died and the Senate bill — "twice as big without market reforms" — would have passed. "It was the only way we had to stop the Senate version," he said. "It was a choice between bad and worse."

Franks grew up in the uranium- and vanadium-mining town of Uravan, Colo., (now a ghost town), the son of a geologist and a nurse. The eldest of five children, he was born with severe lip and palate deformities that took nine surgeries to correct. He is an active booster of Operation Smile, which in 25 countries provides free surgeries to babies with birth defects.

When he was just out of high school, he and a brother went looking for oil in Texas. Starting with a truck-mounted rig, the two were so young they had to hire an 18-year-old friend to get a drilling permit. They drilled a lot of dry holes and lived out of a trailer, but eventually struck oil, a modest well that produced a few barrels and earnings of $100 a day.

Busy with the growing oil-drilling business, Franks never finished college. He settled in the Phoenix suburbs after getting married in 1980.

In 1984, he made a successful bid for a state House seat, but was defeated for re-election. He then founded a think tank, the Arizona Family Research Institute (now the Center for Arizona Policy). In 1987, he was appointed director of the Arizona Governor's Office for Children by Republican Evan Mecham.

He lost the 1994 GOP primary for the open 4th District seat to now-retired Rep. John Shadegg. Franks tried another congressional run in 2002, this time in the 2nd District, and edged past Lisa Atkins, former chief of staff for retiring GOP Rep. Bob Stump of Arizona's 3rd District, by just 797 votes. He handily won the November election.

Early in his first re-election cycle, Franks looked like he might be in trouble. He was held to 64 percent in the GOP primary against radio station owner Rick L. Murphy, who came at Franks from the right for his vote on the Medicare prescription drug law. He went on to win in November with 59 percent — a vote-share he matched in his 2006 and 2008 re-elections, and surpassed, with 65 percent, in 2010.

Key Votes

2010

Overhaul the nation's health insurance system	NO
Allow for repeal of "don't ask, don't tell"	NO
Overhaul financial services industry regulation	NO
Limit use of new Afghanistan War funds to troop withdrawal activities	NO
Change oversight of offshore drilling and lift oil spill liability cap	NO
Provide a path to legal status for some children of illegal immigrants	NO
Extend Bush-era income tax cuts for two years	NO

2009

Expand the Children's Health Insurance Program	NO
Provide $787 billion in tax cuts and spending increases to stimulate the economy	NO
Allow bankruptcy judges to modify certain primary-residence mortgages	NO
Create a cap-and-trade system to limit greenhouse gas emissions	NO
Provide $2 billion for the "cash for clunkers" program	NO
Establish the government as the sole provider of student loans	NO
Restrict federally funded insurance coverage for abortions in health care overhaul	YES

CQ Vote Studies

	PARTY UNITY		PRESIDENTIAL SUPPORT	
	Support	Oppose	Support	Oppose
2010	99%	1%	21%	79%
2009	99%	1%	10%	90%
2008	99%	1%	87%	13%
2007	99%	1%	95%	5%
2006	96%	4%	90%	10%

Interest Groups

	AFL-CIO	ADA	CCUS	ACU
2010	0%	5%	75%	100%
2009	0%	0%	73%	100%
2008	0%	0%	76%	100%
2007	4%	0%	70%	100%
2006	7%	10%	93%	100%

Arizona 2

Northwest and central – most of Glendale, Peoria, Lake Havasu City; Hopi reservation

The 2nd spans the northwest corner of Arizona, but Republicans living in the western Phoenix suburbs to the southeast dominate its politics. Home to the vast majority of the 2nd's residents, this area takes in a corner of the city and suburbs such as rapidly growing Peoria and Surprise, most of Glendale and the retirement community of Sun City. Although the district is mostly white, its Hispanic population has grown rapidly.

A diverse economy here includes manufacturing jobs in the aerospace, electronics, communications and chemical industries. A Glendale-based Honeywell Aerospace division provides many of these jobs. Luke Air Force Base is the 2nd's largest employer and contributes more than $2 billion to the local economy annually. Successful zoning restrictions have kept the expanding metropolitan area from encroaching on the base nearly 20 miles west of downtown Phoenix. Currently a training center for F-16 pilots, the base is in line to host the F-35 Joint Strike Fighter training program once the Air Force phases out the F-16 fleet.

Most of the district's land is in Mohave County, where Lake Havasu City, Bullhead City and Kingman are located. The Democratic Party maintains some isolated areas of influence among American Indians in the northwest region, where younger, lower-income and larger minority populations live.

The 2nd also includes the Hopi reservation, an appendage separated from the surrounding Navajo reservation (located in the 1st). Redistricting following the 2000 census kept the tribes in different districts due to historical tensions between them. To reach the Hopi land in northeastern Arizona, the 2nd follows the Colorado River through the Grand Canyon, both sides of which are in the 1st.

Major Industry
Retail, manufacturing

Military Bases
Luke Air Force Base, 5,000 military, 1,500 civilian (2011)

Cities
Peoria, 154,065; Glendale (pt.), 151,014; Surprise, 117,517; Goodyear (pt.), 65,194; Lake Havasu City, 52,527; Phoenix (pt.), 48,418

Notable
The Hopi have used "dry farming" to grow crops in the rough terrain.

Rep. Ben Quayle (R)

Capitol Office
225-3361
quayle.house.gov
1419 Longworth Bldg. 20515-0303; fax 225-3462

Committees
Homeland Security
Judiciary
Science, Space & Technology
(Technology & Innovation - Chairman)

Residence
Phoenix

Born
Nov. 5, 1976; Fort Wayne, Ind.

Religion
Christian

Family
Wife, Tiffany Quayle

Education
Duke U., B.A. 1998 (history); Vanderbilt U., J.D. 2002

Career
Business investment company owner; lawyer

Political Highlights
No previous office

ELECTION RESULTS

2010 GENERAL

Ben Quayle (R)	108,689	52.2%
Jon Hulburd (D)	85,601	41.1%
Michael Shoen (LIBERT)	10,478	5.0%
Leonard Clark (GREEN)	3,294	1.6%

2010 PRIMARY

Ben Quayle (R)	17,400	22.0%
Steve Moak (R)	14,211	18.0%
Jim Waring (R)	13,850	17.6%
Vernon B. Parker (R)	13,411	17.0%
Pamela Gorman (R)	6,473	8.2%
Paulina Morris (R)	6,138	7.8%
Sam Crump (R)	3,886	4.9%
Ed Winkler (R)	1,353	1.7%
Bob Branch (R)	1,141	1.4%
LeAnn Hull (R)	1,044	1.3%

Elected 2010; 1st term

Quayle was born three days after his father, Dan Quayle — who would cap his political career as vice president — was first elected to the House. The younger Quayle hadn't even been elected to his Arizona seat when speculation began as to whether he would follow in his father's footsteps to the Senate and beyond.

Quayle's immediate ambitions do not extend beyond the boundaries of the 3rd District. "I'll solely be focused on the job at hand," he said prior to his win.

An attorney and owner of an investment firm, Quayle put cutting government spending at the top of his priorities. He has proposed freezing staff, member and executive branch pay — and has said that if there isn't a 20 percent cut in the federal budget deficit each year until it is balanced, then those federal employees should have their pay cut by 15 percent.

Another priority is boosting security on the border with Mexico. Quayle won seats on the two committees that handle most immigration legislation: Homeland Security and Judiciary. He also sits on the Science, Space and Technology Committee.

Quayle spent a chunk of his childhood in the Washington, D.C. area, attending Gonzaga College High School and serving as a congressional page. He would, his mother has told reporters, travel to his grandmother's farm in Wickenburg during some August recesses.

He graduated from Duke University, where as a freshman he was a walk-on on the lacrosse team, and then from Vanderbilt University law school.

Moving throughout the country, working in law and specializing in mergers and acquisitions with real estate, he moved to Arizona in the early 2000s.

The family name and fundraising connections helped him win a 10-way primary to replace retiring Republican John Shadegg in the heavily GOP district.

During his campaign, Quayle made headlines with some caustic rhetoric, labeling Barack Obama "the worst president in history" and running an ad promising to "knock the hell out of" Washington.

Quayle's general election contest proved closer than expected, in part because of questions raised by postings he made on a racy website in 2007. He took more than 52 percent of the vote against Democrat Jon Hulburd.

Arizona 3

Northern Phoenix; Paradise Valley

The 3rd District takes in a large chunk of northern Phoenix and the hills and suburbs north of the city. The 3rd remains predominately white, but a booming Hispanic population in the district has cut into that majority.

Northern Phoenix is home to many large planned communities. Significant population growth has caused the political dynamics of the northern part of the district to fluctuate. Young professionals moving into communities such as New River are mixed with conservative residents in such areas as the large community of Anthem.

Many of the state's most affluent and politically active residents live east of Phoenix in the posh community of Paradise Valley. The town is exclusively zoned for single-family residences and collects no property taxes. The local economy relies on electronics and aerospace equipment manufacturing. Aerospace manufacturer Honeywell, which has locations throughout the area, is one of the district's largest employers. The 3rd also is home to the Mayo Clinic Hospital, and health care accounts for a significant portion of the district's economy.

District voters tend to support economically and socially conservative candidates at both the local and federal levels. Democrats are concentrated in the southern part of the 3rd, where the district extends to downtown Phoenix.

Major Industry
Technology, manufacturing, electronics, health care

Cities
Phoenix (pt.), 642,533; Anthem, 21,700; New River, 14,952; Paradise Valley, 12,820

Notable
Locally brewed Cave Creek Chili Beer has a pepper in every bottle.

Rep. Ed Pastor (D)

Capitol Office
225-4065
www.house.gov/pastor
2465 Rayburn Bldg. 20515-0304; fax 225-1655

Committees
Appropriations

Residence
Phoenix

Born
June 28, 1943; Claypool, Ariz.

Religion
Roman Catholic

Family
Wife, Verma Mendez Pastor; two children

Education
Arizona State U., B.A. 1966 (chemistry), J.D. 1974

Career
Teacher; gubernatorial aide; public policy consultant

Political Highlights
Maricopa County Board of Supervisors, 1977-91

ELECTION RESULTS

2010 GENERAL

Ed Pastor (D)	61,524	66.9%
Janet Contreras (R)	25,300	27.5%
Joe Cobb (LIBERT)	2,718	3.0%
Rebecca DeWitt (GREEN)	2,365	2.6%

2010 PRIMARY

Ed Pastor (D)	24,613	100%

2008 GENERAL

Ed Pastor (D)	89,721	72.1%
Don Karg (R)	26,435	21.2%
Rebecca DeWitt (GREEN)	4,464	3.6%
Joe Cobb (LIBERT)	3,807	3.1%

Previous Winning Percentages
2006 (73%); 2004 (70%); 2002 (67%); 2000 (69%);
1998 (68%); 1996 (65%); 1994 (62%); 1992 (66%);
1991 Special Election (56%)

Elected 1991; 10th full term

The senior member of Arizona's House delegation and an appropriator, Pastor looks out for the interests of more than just his Phoenix-based district because some of his home-state colleagues share an anti-earmark philosophy.

Republican Sen. John McCain has spent years attacking the funding set-asides that most lawmakers pursue, while Rep. Jeff Flake — Pastor's new colleague on the Appropriations Committee — is a leader of the anti-earmark movement among House Republicans.

Pastor (pas-TORE), on the other hand, has steered hundreds of millions of dollars to his district and state over the years, especially for transportation and water projects. Phoenix's rapid population growth is creating serious strains, he said. "When I was a county supervisor, the biggest scare was that Phoenix was going to one day wake up and be like L.A.," Pastor said. "We looked like L.A. in size, but we didn't in freeways."

From the Appropriations subcommittees dealing with transportation, energy and water funding, he has kept a steady stream of grants and contracts flowing to his district. He helped get a federal commitment of $587 million for a light rail project for the city that began operating in late 2008. And Pastor has helped direct funds to several local water programs, including $9.6 million for a project designed to reclaim and reuse wastewater. He also sits on the Financial Services Subcommittee.

He drew some unflattering attention in 2007 when The Arizona Republic reported he had funneled $1 million in earmarks to a local community college scholarship program just months before his daughter was hired to direct it.

Pastor is a trusted insider in the Democratic leadership. He has been one of his party's chief deputy whips since 1999 and helps assign members to committees and advises leadership on policy. He voted for all of President Obama's major economic initiatives during the 111th Congress (2009-10), including the health care and financial regulatory overhauls and the stimulus.

He has always been a reliable vote for Democrats, but took that support to new heights when Democrats took control of the House in 2007. During the ensuing four years, he sided with his party on 98 percent of votes in which a majority of Democrats opposed a majority of Republicans.

He pushed unsuccessfully for comprehensive changes in the immigration system during the 110th (2007-08) and 111th Congresses. Nowhere are tensions higher over illegal immigration than in Arizona, especially after the state enacted a tough anti-illegal immigration measure in April 2010. The first Hispanic elected to Congress from Arizona, Pastor has long held naturalization workshops in his district and staffed them with volunteers, including local lawyers who help legal immigrants apply for citizenship. Pastor harshly criticized the state law, which empowers police to check the immigration status of people detained for some other reason. But he did not join fellow Arizona Democrat Raúl M. Grijalva in calling for an economic boycott of the state. Instead, Pastor called on the Justice Department to challenge the law in court, which it did.

Pastor roundly criticized the House Republican majority's immigration proposal in the 109th Congress (2005-06). That plan would have made it a felony to be in the United States illegally or to hire undocumented workers. He backed a bill by two Arizona GOP colleagues, Jim Kolbe and Flake, that was similar to an approach taken by McCain and Senate Democrats, combining enhanced border security and worksite enforcement with a guest worker program and a path to citizenship for most illegal immigrants.

Pastor chaired the Congressional Hispanic Caucus in 1995 and 1996. He opposed GOP efforts to roll back bilingual education and make English the official language of the federal government. His wife, Verma, was the longtime director of bilingual programs for the Arizona Department of Education.

The oldest son of a copper miner, Pastor grew up in a working-class household about 85 miles east of Phoenix. Many of his peers were destined for jobs in the mines, but Pastor's parents wanted him to go to college, so they saved their money and bought him encyclopedias. His father pushed him to deliver newspapers for The Arizona Republic so he could qualify for a college scholarship the newspaper was sponsoring. From sixth grade through high school, Pastor delivered papers, while also lettering in football and baseball, and winning election as senior class president. He went to Arizona State University on a scholarship — the first member of his family to attend college — and worked in the mines during the summers to help pay expenses.

After graduating with a degree in chemistry and a teaching certificate, Pastor taught high school and worked nights helping adults learn to read and write. He got involved with a nonprofit group, The Guadalupe Organization Inc., and eventually became its deputy director.

During that time, Pastor got interested in the Chicano movement and its charismatic leader, Cesar Chavez. Believing Mexican-Americans needed more decisive political leadership, he started volunteering for Mexican-American candidates in south Phoenix. He also went to law school.

After working for the successful gubernatorial campaign of Democrat Raúl Castro in 1974, he became one of the governor's aides. Pastor was elected to the Maricopa County Board of Supervisors in 1976.

He had been eyeing a run for Congress since the 2nd District was drawn in 1982 as the state's most heavily Hispanic. Democratic Rep. Morris K. Udall, who suffered from Parkinson's disease, resigned in May 1991. Two days later, Pastor quit his post on the board to campaign for the seat. He was the establishment's choice, having built up a healthy war chest and solid name recognition as a supervisor. In the five-person special primary, he prevailed by 5 percentage points over Tucson Mayor Tom Volgy. His 11-percentage-point victory in the special election over Republican Pat Conner, a Yuma County supervisor, remains his closest House election.

Reapportionment after the 2000 census gave Arizona two additional House seats, and Pastor chose to run in the newly drawn 4th District nestled in the suburbs of Phoenix. Its population was slightly less Hispanic than his old one, but that caused him no difficulty. He has been re-elected with more than 65 percent of the vote since.

Key Votes

2010

Overhaul the nation's health insurance system	YES
Allow for repeal of "don't ask, don't tell"	YES
Overhaul financial services industry regulation	YES
Limit use of new Afghanistan War funds to troop withdrawal activities	YES
Change oversight of offshore drilling and lift oil spill liability cap	YES
Provide a path to legal status for some children of illegal immigrants	YES
Extend Bush-era income tax cuts for two years	YES

2009

Expand the Children's Health Insurance Program	YES
Provide $787 billion in tax cuts and spending increases to stimulate the economy	YES
Allow bankruptcy judges to modify certain primary-residence mortgages	YES
Create a cap-and-trade system to limit greenhouse gas emissions	YES
Provide $2 billion for the "cash for clunkers" program	YES
Establish the government as the sole provider of student loans	YES
Restrict federally funded insurance coverage for abortions in health care overhaul	NO

CQ Vote Studies

	PARTY UNITY		PRESIDENTIAL SUPPORT	
	SUPPORT	OPPOSE	SUPPORT	OPPOSE
2010	98%	2%	90%	10%
2009	99%	1%	96%	4%
2008	99%	1%	13%	87%
2007	98%	2%	2%	98%
2006	90%	10%	20%	80%

Interest Groups

	AFL-CIO	ADA	CCUS	ACU
2010	93%	85%	14%	0%
2009	100%	100%	33%	0%
2008	100%	100%	50%	4%
2007	96%	95%	47%	0%
2006	93%	100%	33%	8%

Arizona 4

Downtown and southern Phoenix; part of Glendale

The 4th District, located solely within Maricopa County in Arizona's "Valley of the Sun," includes southern and central Phoenix, as well as Guadalupe and part of Glendale. Overall, the 4th, a Democratic stronghold, has the state's highest percentage of both Hispanic and black residents. Much of the recent growth in the Hispanic-majority district has been among the Latino population.

Trying to rebound from the collapse of the real estate economy, local officials may turn toward urban redevelopment of downtown areas hosting mostly vacant commercial and residential buildings — the city has been sprawling outward for decades. A long-awaited pedestrian- and light rail-friendly mixed-use development opened in late 2010, and construction at the downtown campus for Arizona State University continues, but community groups worry that there isn't enough support for the struggling retail sector to draw visitors from the wider metropolitan area.

An initial 20-mile segment of the Valley Metro light-rail line that connects Tempe and Mesa to downtown Phoenix opened in late 2008, but further extension of the transit system is uncertain. Phoenix Sky Harbor International Airport postponed some planned terminal and infrastructure expansion, including a rail link to the Valley Metro line.

Glendale (shared with the 2nd) is a growing white-collar, conservative community. Few agricultural areas remain in the 4th as a decade of development in Phoenix has encroached on the district's southwestern edge.

Arizona's Hispanic voters tend to support Democratic candidates on immigration but break from the party on some social issues, opposing abortion rights and favoring some traditionally Republican "family values"-type legislation.

Major Industry
Manufacturing, retail, education

Cities
Phoenix, 610,722; Glendale (pt.), 75,707; Guadalupe (pt.), 5,523

Notable
The 4th's portion of Phoenix includes City Hall, the state Capitol, Chase Field, US Airways Center and Mystery Castle.

Rep. David Schweikert (R)

Capitol Office
225-2190
schweikert.house.gov
1205 Longworth Bldg. 20515-0305; fax 225-0096

Committees
Financial Services

Residence
Fountain Hills

Born
March 3, 1962; Los Angeles, Calif.

Religion
Roman Catholic

Family
Wife, Joyce Schweikert

Education
Scottsdale Community College, A.A. 1985; Arizona State U., B.S. 1987 (real estate); Arizona State U., M.B.A. 2005

Career
Real estate company owner; county deputy treasurer; financial consultant; Realtor

Political Highlights
Sought Republican nomination for Ariz. House, 1988; Ariz. House, 1991-95 (majority whip, 1993-94); sought Republican nomination for U.S. House, 1994; Ariz. State Board of Equalization chairman, 1995-2003; Maricopa County treasurer, 2004-06; Republican nominee for U.S. House, 2008

ELECTION RESULTS

2010 GENERAL

David Schweikert (R)	110,374	52.0%
Harry E. Mitchell (D)	91,749	43.2%
Nick Coons (LIBERT)	10,127	4.8%

2010 PRIMARY

David Schweikert (R)	26,678	37.2%
Jim Ward (R)	18,480	25.8%
Susan Bitter Smith (R)	17,297	24.1%
Chris Salvino (R)	7,156	10.0%
Lee Gentry (R)	1,157	1.6%
Mark Spinks (R)	884	1.2%

Elected 2010; 1st term

Schweikert plans to use a calculator to hack away at the federal budget. "People around here seem to make decisions by folklore instead of facts," he said. "What I'd love to do is budgeting based on what the numbers really are."

The former state legislator and county treasurer who won a seat on the Financial Services Committee said the Republican Party lost the majority in Congress in 2006 because it "ceased being the party of fiscal responsibility."

He also will devote much of his energy to immigration, a key issue in the 5th District. Schweikert backs cracking down on companies that hire illegal immigrants, continuing construction of border fencing, and beefing up other aspects of border security — including additional use of the unmanned Predator-B aircraft.

He criticized the major initiatives of the 111th Congress (2009-10), calling the health care law enacted in 2010 "devastating fiscally." He said changes made to the financial regulatory regime were a missed opportunity to increase transparency and called the $787 billion stimulus package enacted in early 2009 as ineffective. He told Fox News in January 2011 that the way to bring the budget into balance is to "flatline the crazy spending."

Born in California, Schweikert was adopted after birth — a circumstance he says inspired his anti-abortion views.

Schweikert received a bachelor's degree from Arizona State University in real estate and an MBA in 2005. He has worked in real estate, running a consulting business with his wife.

He was a frequent candidate for public office before winning election to the House in 2010. He ran for the Arizona House in 1988, lost, then ran again and won in 1990. Schweikert made his first congressional run in 1994, but lost the Republican nod. He tried again in 2008 and won the party's nomination, but lost to incumbent Democrat Harry E. Mitchell by about 10 percentage points.

In 2010, he beat out five other Republicans in the primary, then rode the GOP wave to a 9-percentage-point win over Mitchell.

"Two years ago, the voters were harsh," Schweikert told an Arizona paper before the 2010 election. "Some people said: 'I'm not ever voting for a Republican again. You seem like a nice guy, but get out of here.' Now, some of those same people are putting my campaign signs in their yards."

Arizona 5

Scottsdale; Tempe; parts of Phoenix and Mesa

Wealth, beautiful sunsets and conservative politics abound in the 5th, which takes in a sliver of Phoenix and spreads east to Tempe, Scottsdale and the western parts of Chandler and Mesa. The 5th also encompasses smaller towns that highlight the area's trademarks: nature and leisure.

With luxury resorts, golf courses, museums, art galleries and spring training baseball, the district relies on the success of its hospitality and tourism industries and caters to both business travelers and vacationers. The 5th's part of Phoenix includes the zoo and the Desert Botanical Garden.

American Indians comprise less than 3 percent of the majority-white district, but casinos and resorts at Salt River and Fort Mc-Dowell Indian reservations lure guests to the district. Salt River also boats the Scottsdale

Pavilions shopping mall.

Health care is a steady employer in the 5th, and Mayo Clinic research facilities employ many district residents.

Scottsdale and Fountain Hills draw retirees and their bank accounts to the state's wealthiest district.

To the south, Tempe hosts Arizona State University.

Tempe's younger and more liberal voters can offset some of the 5th's GOP bent, but there are more independents registered to vote here than Democrats. John McCain won the district by almost 5 percentage points in the 2008 presidential election.

Major Industry
Tourism, education, health care

Cities
Scottsdale (pt.), 217,219; Tempe (pt.), 161,719; Mesa (pt.), 89,530; Phoenix (pt.), 86,824

Notable
Taliesin West in Scottsdale was Frank Lloyd Wright's winter home, and the Taliesin Fellowship seeks to continue his work.

Rep. Jeff Flake (R)

Capitol Office
225-2635
www.house.gov/flake
240 Cannon Bldg. 20515-0306; fax 226-4386

Committees
Appropriations

Residence
Mesa

Born
Dec. 31, 1962; Snowflake, Ariz.

Religion
Mormon

Family
Wife, Cheryl Flake; five children

Education
Brigham Young U., B.A. 1986 (international relations),
M.A. 1987 (political science)

Career
Public policy think tank director; African business
trade representative; lobbyist

Political Highlights
No previous office

ELECTION RESULTS

2010 GENERAL

Jeff Flake (R)	165,649	66.4%
Rebecca Schneider (D)	72,615	29.1%
Darell Tapp (LIBERT)	7,712	3.1%
Richard Grayson (GREEN)	3,407	1.4%

2010 PRIMARY

Jeff Flake (R)	62,285	64.6%
Jeff Smith (R)	34,137	35.4%

2008 GENERAL

Jeff Flake (R)	208,582	62.4%
Rebecca Schneider (D)	115,457	34.6%
Rick Biondi (LIBERT)	10,137	3%

Previous Winning Percentages
2006 (75%); 2004 (79%); 2002 (66%); 2000 (54%)

Elected 2000; 6th term

Flake's congressional career takes a new path in the 112th Congress, and it has a bit of an Old Testament flavor to it: "And they brought Daniel, and cast him into the den of lions," says Daniel 6:16. The Arizonan might find that familiar as he serves his first term on the Appropriations Committee.

Flake's legislative identity is inextricably linked to his battle against earmarks. After a decade in Congress filled mostly with failure on that score, he has been joined by a multitude of others in what had been a lonely crusade.

One of the enduring images of the annual appropriations process is that of Flake, standing at his desk or in the well of the House, railing — if his quiet manner could be considered railing — against what he sees as congressional profligacy. But until recently, victories were rare. Most often, his amendments to spending bills were defeated by wide margins.

His consistent opposition to earmarks — funding set-asides for projects in lawmakers' districts — has won him few friends. "I'm sick and tired of phony amendments that act like they are going to save money," Republican John Culberson of Texas complained in 2007 after Flake tried to eliminate a $300,000 Culberson earmark for the Houston Zoo. In a representative outcome, he failed on a vote of 77-347.

But with increased scrutiny of earmarks and a ballooning federal deficit, leaders who once ignored Flake have begun to co opt his position. Dozens of Republican freshmen in the 112th Congress are echoing his themes.

In March 2010, House Democrats announced a ban on earmarks benefiting for-profit entities. Shortly afterward, House Republicans declared a fiscal 2011 moratorium on all earmarks.

Aside from earmarks, Flake's broader philosophy reflects one of his political heroes, the late Republican Sen. Barry Goldwater of Arizona, icon of the conservative movement.

In early 2009, Flake joined his party in opposing President Obama's economic stimulus plan. In late 2008, he opposed two $700 billion measures — the second of which became law — intended to shore up the ailing financial services industry, and he voted against a $14 billion loan, which later stalled in the Senate, to bail out the auto industry.

Flake said his fellow Republicans have too often trampled on the principle of federalism, overriding states on everything from social policy to regulatory matters. And on some issues, he lines up with Democrats. He was one of 15 Republicans to support repeal of the military's "don't ask, don't tell" policy barring openly gay servicemembers. Flake antagonized his leadership with his support for an immigration overhaul that would have allowed millions of illegal immigrants in the country to gain legal status. In 2006, Flake told the San Antonio Express-News he was stripped of his assignment to the Judiciary Committee because he supported the immigration legislation.

He has tweaked his party's orthodoxy on other scores. He argued that the George W. Bush administration "overstepped" with its policy of warrantless wiretapping of terrorism suspects, although he supported the 2008 law that included retroactive liability immunity for telecommunications companies that participated in the program. A former member of the Foreign Affairs Committee, he has praised Obama's efforts to ease restrictions on travel to Cuba by U.S. citizens.

Flake's road to the Appropriations panel was a rocky one. When a committee seat came open in 2008, he asked Minority Leader John A. Boehner for the spot. An array of budget watchdog groups lined up behind Flake, but he was passed over — an outcome probably not helped by his call after the 2008 elections to replace the Republican leadership. Instead, those leaders put him on the Oversight and Government Reform Committee, and Flake used that forum to push for earmark changes. He also sat on the Natural Resources Committee, where he fought against what he calls "a new vehicle for earmarks," the National Heritage Areas, which he says siphon money away from the National Park system.

Despite his legislative confrontations with colleagues, Flake is easygoing and personable, although he's not afraid to spend some time on his own. He engaged in his own private "Survivor" episode in the fall of 2009 by spending a week by himself on an uninhabited island in the Pacific Ocean. "No food, just mask, fins and a pole-spear to obtain it," he told The Washington Post.

Married with five children, he's a regular on the basketball court in the House gym and is a star of the GOP's team in the Annual Roll Call Congressional Baseball Game.

Flake and his 10 siblings grew up on the family ranch near Snowflake, about 100 miles northeast of Phoenix. Established in 1878, the town is named after its Mormon founders, Erastus Snow and William Flake, the lawmaker's great-great-grandfather. In 1982, Flake began a two-year church mission to Zimbabwe and South Africa. He majored in international relations at Brigham Young University and moved to Namibia in 1989 as director of the Foundation for Democracy, a group helping the country develop a constitution after its break from South Africa. He returned to Arizona in 1992 to lead the Goldwater Institute, a conservative public policy think tank.

Flake first ran for public office in 2000, when he got in the race to succeed retiring GOP Rep. Matt Salmon. With Salmon's endorsement, Flake won a five-way primary. In the general election, Flake bested Democratic labor lobbyist David Mendoza with 54 percent of the vote, and he has not been seriously challenged by a Democrat since then. In 2004, Flake briefly considered taking on John McCain in the GOP Senate primary. In the end, "after much soul-searching, I came to the conclusion I'd get whipped," he said at the time. That year he faced a primary challenge from an opponent who took issue with his resistance to taking earmarks, saying Flake's ideological purity was hurting the district. State Sen. Stan Barnes held Flake to 59 percent.

Flake was the first candidate to announce a bid to succeed retiring GOP Sen. Jon Kyl, throwing his hat into the ring in February 2011, just days after Kyl announced he would not seek another term in 2012.

Key Votes

2010

Overhaul the nation's health insurance system	NO
Allow for repeal of "don't ask, don't tell"	NO
Overhaul financial services industry regulation	NO
Limit use of new Afghanistan War funds to troop withdrawal activities	NO
Change oversight of offshore drilling and lift oil spill liability cap	NO
Provide a path to legal status for some children of illegal immigrants	NO
Extend Bush-era income tax cuts for two years	NO

2009

Expand the Children's Health Insurance Program	?
Provide $787 billion in tax cuts and spending increases to stimulate the economy	NO
Allow bankruptcy judges to modify certain primary-residence mortgages	NO
Create a cap-and-trade system to limit greenhouse gas emissions	?
Provide $2 billion for the "cash for clunkers" program	NO
Establish the government as the sole provider of student loans	NO
Restrict federally funded insurance coverage for abortions in health care overhaul	YES

CQ Vote Studies

	PARTY UNITY		PRESIDENTIAL SUPPORT	
	SUPPORT	OPPOSE	SUPPORT	OPPOSE
2010	97%	3%	20%	80%
2009	97%	3%	8%	92%
2008	99%	1%	85%	15%
2007	95%	5%	89%	11%
2006	86%	14%	72%	28%

Interest Groups

	AFL-CIO	ADA	CCUS	ACU
2010	0%	10%	75%	96%
2009	0%	0%	71%	100%
2008	0%	0%	61%	100%
2007	4%	5%	68%	100%
2006	0%	20%	79%	100%

Arizona 6

Southeast Phoenix suburbs – most of Mesa and Chandler, Gilbert, Apache Junction

Rooted in the conservative leanings of an affluent, historically Mormon population, the suburban 6th favors Republican candidates. The district still has a significant population of Mormons, as well as a mix of young couples who commute to Phoenix. The area's warm sunny days have helped draw an established population of retirees from other states.

East of Phoenix, the district takes in all but the westernmost segments of Mesa and Chandler. Adjacent to the two cities is Gilbert, and the district spreads east to take in part of still largely rural Pinal County, including Apache Junction near the county's northern border. The southeastern Phoenix suburbs experienced decades of population growth that is characteristic of the area, but collapsing real estate markets hurt home prices and local governments still face budget shortfalls. A newly opened public transportation line that connects community colleges and a local airport through Gilbert may alleviate some congestion and spur commercial growth. The retail sector is important to the district's economy, and Wal-Mart is a

major employer in the 6th.

Manufacturing aids the economy in Mesa, and the city hosts a large Boeing facility that builds the new A160T Hummingbird unmanned helicopter. Technology manufacturing plays a role here as well: Intel has two locations in Chandler that employ roughly 10,000 people and has plans to upgrade its two facilities in the district. Agriculture, especially alfalfa and dairy operations, once figured strongly in the district's economy but has mostly been replaced due to sprawling development.

Republicans hold a nearly 20-percentage-point edge in party registration here, and the 6th gave John McCain 61 percent of its 2008 presidential vote, his highest percentage in the state.

Major Industry
Manufacturing, technology, retail, construction

Cities
Mesa (pt.), 349,511; Gilbert, 208,453; Chandler (pt.), 171,230; San Tan Valley, 81,321; Apache Junction, 35,840

Notable
Chandler's Ostrich Festival, held each March, features ostrich races and a parade.

Rep. Raúl M. Grijalva (D)

Capitol Office
225-2435
www.house.gov/grijalva
1440 Longworth Bldg. 20515-0307; fax 225-1541

Committees
Education & Labor
Natural Resources

Residence
Tucson

Born
Feb. 19, 1948; Tucson, Ariz.

Religion
Roman Catholic

Family
Wife, Mona Grijalva; three children

Education
U. of Arizona, B.A. 1987 (sociology)

Career
University dean; community center director

Political Highlights
Candidate for Tucson Unified School District
Governing Board, 1972; Tucson Unified School
District Governing Board, 1974-86; Pima County
Board of Supervisors, 1989-2002 (chairman, 1997,
2001-02)

ELECTION RESULTS

2010 GENERAL

Raúl M. Grijalva (D)	79,935	50.2%
Ruth McClung (R)	70,385	44.2%
Harley Meyer (I)	4,506	2.8%
George Keane (LIBERT)	4,318	2.7%

2010 PRIMARY

Raúl M. Grijalva (D)	33,931	100.0%

2008 GENERAL

Raúl M. Grijalva (D)	124,304	63.3%
Joseph Sweeney (R)	64,425	32.8%
Raymond Petrulsky (LIBERT)	80,354	3.9%

Previous Winning Percentages
2006 (61%); 2004 (62%); 2002 (59%)

Elected 2002; 5th term

A vocal opponent of immigration laws, which he views as racially tinged, and an advocate of codifying a path to citizenship for individuals who entered the U.S. illegally, Grijalva has taken a leading role in pushing for an overhaul of the system. He still lives in the working-class, heavily Latino section of south Tucson where he was born and raised, and his background as a social worker and community center director lends itself to his work on education, health care and worker rights.

In April 2010, Grijalva (gree-HAHL-va) called for an economic boycott of his own state after Republican Gov. Jan Brewer signed into law a measure that empowers law enforcement officers to check the immigration status of those they have detained for some other suspected offense, such as a traffic stop. He later acknowledged that might not have been the best political strategy, but was undeterred by the narrowness of his re-election victory and the Republican sweep in the 2010 elections.

"I'm not coming back to Congress with a new sense of caution," he told The Arizona Republic. "I haven't changed."

Grijalva's southwestern Arizona district shares 300 miles of border with Mexico. He opposes what he considers punitive immigration policies and guest worker programs that do not lead to a path to legalization because, he says, they are reminiscent of the "bracero" Program, under which migrant Mexican workers flocked to low-wage U.S. farm jobs created by World War II labor shortages. Grijalva's father, a Mexican cowboy, was a bracero and later married a U.S. citizen.

During the immigration debate in the 109th Congress (2005-06), Grijalva backed legislation sponsored by Republican Sen. John McCain, a fellow Arizonan, to create a guest worker program that included a path to U.S. citizenship. GOP-led opposition eventually killed the measure, and Congress instead voted to authorize a 700-mile fence along the border with Mexico, a plan Grijalva opposed.

A co-chairman of the Congressional Progressive Caucus, Grijalva supported all of the top Democratic legislative priorities in the 111th Congress (2009-10) and has long been one of the chamber's most staunch liberals.

Grijalva opposed the 2005 bill to implement the Central America Free Trade Agreement, as well as a 2007 free-trade pact with Peru. He assailed "this destructive process of corporate globalization that has done so much harm to this nation and our neighbors."

He also vigorously opposes the war in Iraq and refuses to vote for war funding bills.

Grijalva is a favorite among environmentalists, and he served as chairman of the Natural Resources subcommittee that oversaw public lands in the 111th Congress. His colleagues on the committee and in the Congressional Hispanic Caucus strongly urged President Obama to select Grijalva to be his Interior secretary, but Obama opted for Democratic Sen. Ken Salazar of Colorado instead.

He turned down a spot on the powerful Ways and Means Committee in the 111th Congress, a seat he once sought and one that would have given him a larger role in tax and health policy. But he was unwilling to give up his chairmanship of the Natural Resources subcommittee, where top priorities have been a rewrite of the 1872 Mining Law that governs hard-rock mining on public lands and a permanent ban on mining near the Grand Canyon. He serves as ranking member of the subcommittee in the 112th Congress (2011-12).

In 2005, President George W. Bush signed into law Grijalva's bill returning 16,000 acres of land to four Colorado River Indian tribes who lost the property to the government in 1915 after they refused to lease it for mining. Grijalva also steered to passage a bill to spur economic growth on Gila River Indian lands. Grijalva's district has seven tribes; on his office wall he displays a carved mask from the Yaquis.

He also uses his committee slot to push back against public-lands policies that he says favor oil and gas drilling, mining and other resource-use activities over other uses. "We're talking about creating a balance between the extraction that's available on public lands and the protection that's necessary of those resources," he said.

Following the April 2010 explosion of BP's Deepwater Horizon oil rig, Grijalva led a group of Democrats in urging the Interior Department to shut down a second BP rig in the Gulf of Mexico. Grijalva had been concerned about possible safety lapses and had sent a letter to Interior's Minerals Management Service in February.

Grijalva has served on the Education and Labor Committee since he arrived in Congress and has pushed to boost funding for the education overhaul program known as No Child Left Behind. In 2003, he fought GOP-inspired changes to Head Start aimed at giving states more control over the preschool program. When Congress reauthorized the program in 2007, he worked to ensure funding to help children with limited English proficiency and those of American Indian and migrant worker families.

Grijalva says he dislikes the nonstop fundraising of modern campaigns, and his staff has to badger him to keep at it. Advised to hold a golf tournament to raise money, he instead threw a bowl-a-thon.

He attended the University of Arizona, but quit to get married. Grijalva became a social worker and community activist, then ran for the Tucson school board in 1972 and was "embarrassingly" defeated. In his second attempt in 1974, he followed through with voter ID work and door-to-door mailings. He served 12 years on the board, then won election to the Pima County Board of Supervisors. While in local government, he frequently advised young people to stay in school. To set an example, he finished nine credit hours left on his sociology degree, graduating from the U of A at 39.

When redistricting created a new seat in southern Arizona, Grijalva jumped into the crowded 2002 primary race. In the general election, the Hispanic-majority makeup of the district ensured Grijalva's victory, and he won re-election easily until Republican Ruth McClung, a physicist, held Grijalva under 50 percent of the vote in 2010. He won by 4 percentage points.

Key Votes

2010

Overhaul the nation's health insurance system	YES
Allow for repeal of "don't ask, don't tell"	YES
Overhaul financial services industry regulation	YES
Limit use of new Afghanistan War funds to troop withdrawal activities	YES
Change oversight of offshore drilling and lift oil spill liability cap	YES
Provide a path to legal status for some children of illegal immigrants	YES
Extend Bush-era income tax cuts for two years	NO

2009

Expand the Children's Health Insurance Program	YES
Provide $787 billion in tax cuts and spending increases to stimulate the economy	YES
Allow bankruptcy judges to modify certain primary-residence mortgages	YES
Create a cap-and-trade system to limit greenhouse gas emissions	YES
Provide $2 billion for the "cash for clunkers" program	YES
Establish the government as the sole provider of student loans	YES
Restrict federally funded insurance coverage for abortions in health care overhaul	NO

CQ Vote Studies

	PARTY UNITY		PRESIDENTIAL SUPPORT	
	SUPPORT	OPPOSE	SUPPORT	OPPOSE
2010	96%	4%	80%	20%
2009	99%	1%	93%	7%
2008	99%	1%	10%	90%
2007	99%	1%	4%	96%
2006	99%	1%	10%	90%

Interest Groups

	AFL-CIO	ADA	CCUS	ACU
2010	92%	90%	13%	0%
2009	100%	100%	33%	0%
2008	100%	100%	44%	8%
2007	96%	100%	50%	0%
2006	93%	100%	27%	4%

Arizona 7

Southwest — part of Tucson, Yuma, Avondale

Stretching mainly to the south and west from Phoenix, the strongly Democratic 7th is Hispanic-majority. It crosses large reservations and rural areas to take in Yuma, downtown Tucson and most of Arizona's borders with California and Mexico, including the border town Nogales. The district's chunk of Tucson is home to the University of Arizona, one of southern Arizona's top employers.

A large population of seasonal immigrant workers — particularly in vegetable farming — supports the local agriculture and service industries but also boosts the district's poverty statistics. The 7th has more blue-collar workers and fewer college graduates than most Arizona districts.

Illegal immigration is a political flash point and a major problem here. Crossing the border in the vast desert region is especially dangerous due to the extreme heat and lack of water, and those who attempt the crossing hamper military training activities on the Barry M. Goldwater Range, which covers more than 100 miles of the border.

The Tohono O'odham and Gila River reservations are the 7th's largest, and American Indians make up roughly 6 percent of the population here. Gila River, south of Phoenix, and Tohono O'odham, at the district's southern edge, host resorts and casinos, but also have invested in commercial and industrial parks to diversify economically.

Republicans are competitive in most of the 7th's counties. Pima County, the district's most populous, includes the 7th's portion of Tucson and many American Indian residents. Barack Obama took 57 percent of the district's vote for president in 2008.

Major Industry
Agriculture, tourism, education

Military Bases
Marine Corps Air Station Yuma, 4,098 military, 904 civilian (2011); Yuma Proving Ground (Army), 175 military, 800 civilian (2011)

Cities
Tucson (pt.), 247,473; Yuma, 93,064; Avondale (pt.), 76,231

Notable
Yuma Territorial Prison — a late-19th-century penitentiary — was once a high school, and then a shelter for railroad vagrants, and now is a state historic park.

Rep. Gabrielle Giffords (D)

Capitol Office
225-2542
giffords.house.gov
1728 Longworth Bldg. 20515-0308; fax 225-0378

Committees
Armed Services
Foreign Affairs
Science, Space & Technology

Residence
Tucson

Born
June 8, 1970; Tucson, Ariz.

Religion
Jewish

Family
Husband, Mark Kelly

Education
Scripps College, B.A. 1993 (sociology & Latin
American history); Cornell U., M.R.P. 1997
(regional planning)

Career
Property management company owner; retail
tire company president; regional economic and
employment analyst

Political Highlights
Ariz. House, 2001-03; Ariz. Senate, 2003-05

ELECTION RESULTS

2010 GENERAL

Gabrielle Giffords (D)	138,280	48.8%
Jesse Kelly (R)	134,124	47.3%
Steven Stoltz (LIBERT)	11,174	3.9%

2010 PRIMARY

Gabrielle Giffords (D)	55,530	100%

2008 GENERAL

Gabrielle Giffords (D)	179,629	54.7%
Timothy S. Bee (R)	140,553	42.8%
Paul Davis (LIBERT)	8,081	2.5%

Previous Winning Percentages
2006 (54%)

Elected 2006; 3rd term

Giffords' substantive accomplishments in the 112th Congress might not reach her prior levels of achievement. But her emotional and spiritual contributions are beyond question.

The Jan. 8, 2011, shooting that left Giffords seriously wounded and six others dead, including a member of her staff and a federal judge, brought on a moment of reflection on Capitol Hill and in other political precincts.

The attack sparked a national debate about the civility of political discourse, even though there was no evidence that the tone of debate had anything to do with motivating the shooter. It brought members together, literally, in a bipartisan seating arrangement for President Obama's State of the Union speech. And it put a sympathetic human face on Congress, which has been sorely lacking in public approval.

Before the attack, Giffords was well-liked and respected inside the halls of Congress. After, a wider audience came to know a bit more about her, and they liked what they saw.

"That is why on the left and the right in her district, Republicans and Democrats alike embrace her," said Florida Democratic Rep. Debbie Wasserman Schultz, a close friend. "And I'll tell you, you just look at the results of this election from 2010, not a great climate for Democrats by any means. The fact that she was able to be re-elected in a climate like that in Arizona is indicative of how special people think she is."

She narrowly hung on to her seat in 2010, as some of her fellow Arizona Democrats fell in the GOP sweep of 2010.

Part of her appeal is that Giffords is no ideologue. On votes that split a majority of Democrats from a majority of Republicans in 2010, she sided with her party only 60 percent of the time. Only seven Democrats broke more often from the party line. Only one of those — Heath Shuler of North Carolina — was re-elected

Giffords allies herself with the fiscally conservative Blue Dog Coalition, but she supported the major economic initiatives of the Obama administration. Her legislative focus has been on immigration issues, alternative energy policy and relations with Latin America.

The 100-mile border that her district shares with Mexico influences Giffords' views on immigration. She called the state law that targeted illegal immigrants "divisive" and "extreme" and said it does "nothing to make the communities I represent safer from smugglers and the dangerous spillover effects of border violence." She supports a federal immigration overhaul that would stiffen border security, impose tougher penalties against employers who hire illegal immigrants and create a guest worker program allowing foreign citizens to work seasonally in the United States.

But Giffords, who speaks Spanish and owns a home in Mexico, took issue with a boycott of local businesses that was supported by home-state colleague Raúl M. Grijalva, the Democrat who represents the district adjacent to hers. Instead, she called for the deployment of the National Guard and more Border Patrol agents to the region. Giffords claimed victory when the Obama administration allotted 1,200 National Guard troops to the U.S.-Mexico border and dedicated about $600 million to add technology and border agents.

The wife of astronaut Mark Kelly, she has a seat on the Science, Space and Technology Committee, where she is the ranking Democrat on the Space and Aeronautics Subcommittee, which she chaired in the 111th Congress (2009-10).

She is particularly interested in developing solar power and other renewable energy sources in Arizona. "We have the land, the technology, the concentrated sunshine," Giffords said. "I want to see south Arizona be the 'Solarcon Valley' of the United States."

She votes with her party on most social issues. In 2007, she voted to override President George W. Bush's veto on a bill to expand the Children's Health Insurance Program, which covers children from low-income families that make too much money to qualify for Medicaid, and voted against allowing faith-based Head Start preschool program providers to take religion into account when hiring. She supports abortion rights. But in 2008, she backed a measure to roll back District of Columbia gun laws.

Giffords is a third-generation Arizonan who grew up in Tucson. Her father owned a tire business and served on the school board. Her mother is an art conservator, specializing in Latin American art. Giffords grew up riding horses and racing motorcycles competitively and loves working on old cars.

At 18, she was inspired by Supreme Court Justice Sandra Day O'Connor — also of Arizona — to register as a Republican. She attended Scripps College in California, and after graduation was awarded a Fulbright grant to study in Chihuahua, Mexico. Giffords also spent a year in San Diego studying a border control program.

After earning a master's degree in regional planning and completing a consulting stint in New York, Giffords returned to Tucson to take over the family tire and automotive business when her father became ill.

In 1999, she changed her party affiliation because she viewed herself as more moderate on social issues than most Arizona Republicans. She was elected to the Arizona House in 2000 and to the state Senate two years later.

When GOP Rep. Jim Kolbe decided to retire, Giffords beat out five primary challengers and in the general election faced former GOP state Rep. Randy Graf, who touted a tough enforcement-first approach to immigration. Graf's primary victory split local Republicans, and Giffords prevailed with 54 percent of the vote. In 2008, she beat GOP state Senate President Timothy S. Bee by 12 percentage points.

Her party-line votes for major Democratic priorities in the 111th Congress cost her some of her centrist bona fides in 2010, but she eked out a win by barely more than 1 percentage point over retired Marine Jesse Kelly.

Giffords, who was moved to Houston's Institute for Rehabilitation and Research at Memorial Hermann Hospital System in late January, has made steady progress in her recovery from the shooting, but it was not clear when she might return to her legislative duties.

Key Votes

2010

Overhaul the nation's health insurance system	YES
Allow for repeal of "don't ask, don't tell"	YES
Overhaul financial services industry regulation	YES
Limit use of new Afghanistan War funds to troop withdrawal activities	NO
Change oversight of offshore drilling and lift oil spill liability cap	YES
Provide a path to legal status for some children of illegal immigrants	YES
Extend Bush-era income tax cuts for two years	YES

2009

Expand the Children's Health Insurance Program	YES
Provide $787 billion in tax cuts and spending increases to stimulate the economy	YES
Allow bankruptcy judges to modify certain primary-residence mortgages	YES
Create a cap-and-trade system to limit greenhouse gas emissions	YES
Provide $2 billion for the "cash for clunkers" program	NO
Establish the government as the sole provider of student loans	YES
Restrict federally funded insurance coverage for abortions in health care overhaul	NO

CQ Vote Studies

	PARTY UNITY		PRESIDENTIAL SUPPORT	
	SUPPORT	OPPOSE	SUPPORT	OPPOSE
2010	60%	40%	88%	12%
2009	82%	18%	90%	10%
2008	86%	14%	19%	81%
2007	87%	13%	6%	94%

Interest Groups

	AFL-CIO	ADA	CCUS	ACU
2010	86%	75%	38%	13%
2009	90%	95%	40%	20%
2008	87%	80%	67%	20%
2007	96%	80%	61%	4%

Arizona 8

Southeast — part of Tucson and northern suburbs

Nestled in the state's southeastern corner, the 8th District is home to swing voters and independents. Cochise County accounts for most of the 8th's land area, but most district residents live in Pima County in the Tucson area. The district runs along more than 100 miles of Arizona's border with Mexico, and immigration and border security are major issues here.

Tucson is surrounded by several mountain ranges and "sky islands" towering over the desert, but the majestic Santa Catalinas north of the city are the local landmark.

Decades of population growth in Tucson and north of the city led to new home construction and put a strain on water resources and water services in this arid region. Recovery from and high unemployment rates and a housing market collapse continues slowly. South of the city, Green Valley is known for retirement communities, and more than 70 percent of the population is older than 65.

Military jets flying past Tucson on their way to or from Davis-Monthan Air Force Base, southeast of the city, reveal one the area's economic engines:

the military. Defense and aerospace contractor Raytheon Missile Systems is a major district employer, and local officials hope to lure biotechnology and other high-technology companies to the area.

In Sierra Vista to the south, Fort Huachuca — home to the U.S. Army Intelligence Center of Excellence — employs thousands of contractors. Although its flagship campus is in the neighboring 7th, the University of Arizona has a campus in Sierra Vista and it is one of the largest employers in the district, supporting research and development interests across the region.

Major Industry

Military, aerospace, technology

Military Bases

Davis-Monthan Air Force Base, 6,361 military, 1,487 civilian (2009); Fort Huachuca (Army), 4,729 military, 3,004 civilian (2009)

Cities

Tucson (pt.), 272,643; Casas Adobes (unincorporated), 66,795; Catalina Foothills (unincorporated), 50,796; Sierra Vista, 43,888

Notable

Tombstone, notorious for its mining-boomtown lawlessness in the late 1800s, has been a popular setting for outlaw fiction and Westerns.

Gov. Mike Beebe (D)

Pronounced: BEE-bee
First elected: 2006
Length of term: 4 years
Term expires: 1/15
Salary: $87,352
Phone: (501) 682-2345
Residence: Searcy
Born: Dec. 28, 1946; Amagon, Ark.
Religion: Episcopalian
Family: Wife, Ginger Beebe; three children
Education: Arkansas State U., B.A. 1968 (political science); U. of Arkansas, J.D. 1972
Military service: Army Reserve, 1968-74
Career: Lawyer
Political highlights: Ark. Senate, 1983-2003 (president pro tempore, 2001-03); Ark. attorney general, 2003-07

ELECTION RESULTS

2010 GENERAL

Mike Beebe (D)	503,336	64.4%
Jim Keet (R)	262,784	33.6%
Jim Lendall (GREEN)	14,513	1.9%

Lt. Gov. Mark A. Darr (R)

First elected: 2010
Length of term: 4 years
Term expires: 1/15
Salary: $41,896
Phone: (501) 682-2144

LEGISLATURE

General Assembly: At least 60 days, even-numbered years beginning in February
Senate: 35 members, 4-year terms
2011 ratios: 20 D, 15 R; 27 men, 8 women
Salary: $15,869
Phone: (501) 682-6107
House: 100 members, 2-year terms
2011 ratios: 54 D, 45 R, 1 vacancy; 77 men, 22 women
Salary: $15,869
Phone: (501) 682-7771

TERM LIMITS

Governor: 2 terms
Senate: 2 terms
House: 3 terms

URBAN STATISTICS

CITY	POPULATION
Little Rock	193,524
Fort Smith	86,209
Fayetteville	73,580
Springdale	69,797
Jonesboro	67,263

REGISTERED VOTERS

Voters do not register by party.

POPULATION

2010 population (est.)	2,915,918
2000 population	2,673,400
1990 population	2,350,725
Percent change (2000-2010)	+9.1%
Rank among states (2010)	32
Median age	36.9
Born in state	61.1%
Foreign born	3.8%
Violent crime rate	518/100,000
Poverty level	18.8%
Federal workers	28,860
Military	6,717

ELECTIONS

STATE ELECTION OFFICIAL
(501) 682-5070
DEMOCRATIC PARTY
(501) 374-2386
REPUBLICAN PARTY
(501) 372-7301

MISCELLANEOUS

Web: www.arkansas.gov
Capital: Little Rock

U.S. CONGRESS

Senate: 1 Democrat, 1 Republican
House: 3 Republicans, 1 Democrat

2010 Census Statistics by District

District	2008 Vote for President Obama	McCain	White	Black	Asian	Hispanic	Median Income	White Collar	Blue Collar	Service Industry	Over 64	Under 18	College Education	Rural	Sq. Miles
1	38%	59%	79%	17%	1%	3%	$34,266	51%	33%	17%	15%	25%	13%	56%	17,151
2	44	54	71	21	1	5	43,741	61	23	16	13	25	26	34	5,922
3	33	64	80	2	2	12	41,543	55	29	15	13	26	21	46	8,490
4	39	58	69	24	1	5	34,464	49	34	17	16	24	15	55	20,505
STATE	39	59	75	15	1	6	38,542	55	29	16	14	25	19	47	52,068
U.S.	53	46	64	12	5	16	51,425	60	23	17	13	25	28	21	3,537,438

Sen. Mark Pryor (D)

Capitol Office
224-2353
pryor.senate.gov
255 Dirksen Bldg. 20510; fax 228-0908

Committees
Appropriations
Commerce, Science & Transportation
(Consumer Protection, Product Safety & Insurance
- Chairman)
Homeland Security & Governmental Affairs
(Disaster Recovery & Intergovernmental Affairs
- Chairman)
Rules & Administration
Small Business & Entrepreneurship
Select Ethics

Residence
Little Rock

Born
Jan. 10, 1963; Fayetteville, Ark.

Religion
Christian

Family
Wife, Jill Pryor; two children

Education
U. of Arkansas, B.A. 1985 (history), J.D. 1988

Career
Lawyer

Political Highlights
Ark. House, 1991-95; sought Democratic nomination
for Ark. attorney general, 1994; Ark. attorney general,
1999-2003; U.S. Senate, 2009

ELECTION RESULTS

2008 GENERAL

Mark Pryor (D)	804,678	79.5%
Rebekah Kennedy (GREEN)	207,076	20.5%

2008 PRIMARY

Mark Pryor (D)		unopposed

2002 GENERAL

Mark Pryor (D)	433,386	53.9%
Tim Hutchinson (R)	370,735	46.1%

Elected 2002; 2nd term

Pryor sees the middle ground as the best place from which to govern, despite Democrats and Republicans becoming increasingly polarized. The approach has paid off politically for the son of former Arkansas governor and three-term senator David Pryor. "The center is where things get done," he said.

But there are occupational hazards to being a political centrist. Mark Pryor took heat from Arkansas liberals and conservatives over the health care overhaul legislation in 2009 and 2010. He voted for the Senate version of the bill in December 2009; it became law in March 2010. That month, he objected to a follow-up bill designed to adjust the overhaul. Pryor opposed the $65 billion price tag, a payroll tax on unearned income and fines on employers who do not offer employee health insurance. He was one of three Democrats to vote against the bill, which passed 56-43.

Over the years, Pryor has emerged as a leader of his party's centrist faction, often serving as a hub for ad hoc coalitions to pressure leaders of both parties to resolve stalemates. He made his first big mark in 2005 as part of the "Gang of 14" — seven Democrats and seven Republicans — formed to end Democratic filibusters of President George W. Bush's judicial nominees, while blocking GOP leaders from using a parliamentary "nuclear option" to abolish such filibusters.

Pryor's highlight of the 111th Congress (2009-10) was his partnership with Democrat John Kerry of Massachusetts and Republican John Ensign of Nevada that produced a law requiring software makers, smart-phone manufacturers and Internet service companies to provide user-friendly features for blind and deaf consumers.

That bill and others were the outgrowth of his work as chairman of the Commerce, Science and Transportation Subcommittee on Consumer Protection, Product Safety and Insurance. During the 110th Congress (2007-08), he steered to enactment a law to ban lead in children's products, protect whistleblowers and outlaw the use of certain plastic softeners, called phthalates, in toys. His work stemmed from a series of 2007 recalls of Chinese-made toys. He also won permanent extension of the Do Not Call Registry that limits telemarketing calls to consumers, and enactment of a law that established new safety standards for swimming-pool drain covers.

Pryor gained a seat on the Appropriations Committee for the 111th, but he had to leave the Armed Services panel, where he had immersed himself in defense issues. His consensus-building helped gain approval for a measure extending military leave five days (to 20 days from 15) following a 15-month tour of duty. He also worked to ensure that soldiers receiving combat pay could still qualify for the earned-income tax credit.

A seat on the Appropriations Committee has generally been considered a plum assignment because it allows members to direct federal money to their home states. Pryor said the growing federal deficit means leaner times for committee members. "We're going to have to cut some spending," he said.

Pryor's focus on finding middle ground often takes him well outside his party's liberal mainstream.

In the 111th, he focused on tracking economic stimulus money to make sure it was spent effectively. He talked with agency leaders and sent letters to inspectors general inquiring about their watchdog activities.

Pryor, who also sits on the Select Ethics Committee and the Rules and Administration Committee, said he is not trying to make his Democratic colleagues nervous, but that his belief is that Congress should conduct nonpartisan oversight.

"One of the problems in Washington is that Republicans tend to be too easy on their fellow Republicans. Democrats tend to be too easy on their fellow Democrats. We're really elected by the people to keep each other accountable," he said.

During the 110th (2007-08), he supported Bush's position more often than did all but two other Democrats. In the 111th, he stuck with his party on several Democratic priorities, including President Obama's push for an economic stimulus. The Senate measure, which passed in February 2009, was a product of negotiations led by the chamber's moderates.

He also voted for an expansion of a children's health insurance program and a bill making it easier for workers to sue for wage discrimination.

At the end of the 111th, he backed repeal of the military's "don't ask, don't tell" policy that bars homosexuals from serving openly. And he joined every other Senate Democrat in voting to approve a strategic arms reduction treaty with Russia.

But Pryor still ranked among the Democrats least supportive of Obama's positions on legislation. He differed with Senate Democrats over the administration's efforts to regulate greenhouse gas emissions. Pryor was among six Democrats who backed an unsuccessful attempt by Alaska Republican Lisa Murkowski to strip the EPA of the authority to regulate such emissions. A member of the Homeland Security and Governmental Affairs Committee, in late 2010 he was one of five Senate Democrats to oppose a measure to grant conditional legal status to certain illegal immigrant children.

Pryor, who also serves on the Small Business and Entrepreneurship Committee, voted to preserve the Bush-era tax cuts for all income levels after initially opposing extension of the lower rates for the highest income levels.

Gun control and abortion rights are other areas where he differs with most members of his party. In 2006, he was among six Democrats to support a bill making it a crime to take a minor across state lines to obtain an abortion, which was a way to circumvent state parental consent laws. In another vote, Pryor, who says neither the "pro-choice" or "pro-life" label fits him, declined to affirm the principles of Roe v. Wade, the Supreme Court case that legalized abortion.

Pryor was 15 when his family moved to the Washington area after his father's 1978 election to the Senate. He got an early start in politics as class president at Walt Whitman High School in Bethesda. He was a congressional page, as had been his father.

Pryor, hoping for a political career, returned to his hometown of Fayetteville and earned undergraduate and law degrees from the University of Arkansas.

Elected to the state House in 1990 at age 27, Pryor lost the Democratic primary for attorney general in 1994. Shortly thereafter, he was diagnosed with sarcoma, a rare cancer, and, for a year following surgery, was unable to walk unassisted. After the cancer went into remission, Pryor restarted his career. He was elected attorney general in 1998.

Pryor defeated conservative Republican Sen. Tim Hutchinson by 8 percentage points in 2002. Hutchinson, a Baptist minister who had campaigned as a "traditional values" Republican, had divorced his wife of 29 years and married a former Senate aide. Pryor never spoke directly about the divorce but touted his own commitment to his religion and his family.

In 2008, after former Arkansas Gov. Mike Huckabee had run unsuccessfully for the GOP presidential nomination and had decided not to run for the Senate, Pryor found himself to be the only incumbent senator without major-party opposition.

Key Votes

2010

Pass budget reconciliation bill to modify overhauls of health care and federal student loan programs	NO
Proceed to disapproval resolution on EPA authority to regulate greenhouse gases	YES
Overhaul financial services industry regulation	YES
Limit debate to proceed to a bill to broaden campaign finance disclosure and reporting rules	YES
Limit debate on an extension of Bush-era income tax cuts for two years	YES
Limit debate on a bill to provide a path to legal status for some children of illegal immigrants	NO
Allow for a repeal of "don't ask, don't tell"	YES
Consent to ratification of a strategic arms reduction treaty with Russia	YES

2009

Prevent release of remaining financial industry bailout funds	NO
Make it easier for victims to sue for wage discrimination remedies	YES
Expand the Children's Health Insurance Program	YES
Limit debate on the economic stimulus measure	YES
Repeal District of Columbia firearms prohibitions and gun registration laws	YES
Limit debate on expansion of federal hate crimes law	YES
Strike funding for F-22 Raptor fighter jets	YES

CQ Vote Studies

	PARTY UNITY		PRESIDENTIAL SUPPORT	
	SUPPORT	OPPOSE	SUPPORT	OPPOSE
2010	85%	15%	92%	8%
2009	91%	9%	95%	5%
2008	79%	21%	46%	54%
2007	81%	19%	46%	54%
2006	76%	24%	64%	36%
2005	80%	20%	58%	42%
2004	81%	19%	68%	32%
2003	84%	16%	60%	40%

Interest Groups

	AFL-CIO	ADA	CCUS	ACU
2010	80%	65%	60%	29%
2009	94%	90%	57%	8%
2008	100%	85%	75%	4%
2007	84%	70%	45%	12%
2006	73%	75%	75%	20%
2005	79%	90%	78%	24%
2004	92%	85%	71%	20%
2003	85%	70%	61%	30%

Sen. John Boozman (R)

Capitol Office
224-4843
boozman.senate.gov
320 Hart Bldg. 20510-0404; fax 228-1371

Committees
Agriculture, Nutrition & Forestry
Commerce, Science & Transportation
Environment & Public Works
Veterans' Affairs

Residence
Rogers

Born
Dec. 10, 1950; Shreveport, La.

Religion
Baptist

Family
Wife, Cathy Boozman; three children

Education
U. of Arkansas, attended 1969-72; Southern College
of Optometry, O.D. 1977

Career
Optometrist; cattle farm owner

Political Highlights
Rogers Public Schools Board of Education,
1994-2001; U.S. House, 2001-11

ELECTION RESULTS

2010 GENERAL

John Boozman (R)	451,618	57.9%
Blanche Lincoln (D)	288,156	36.9%
Trevor Drown (I)	25,234	3.2%
John Laney Gray III (GREEN)	14,430	1.8%

2010 PRIMARY

John Boozman (R)	75,010	52.7%
Jim Holt (R)	24,826	17.4%
Gilbert Baker (R)	16,540	11.6%
Conrad Reynolds (R)	7,128	5.0%
Curtis Coleman (R)	6,928	4.9%
Kim Hendren (R)	5,551	3.9%
Randy Alexander (R)	4,389	3.1%
Fred Ramey (R)	1,888	1.3%

Previous Winning Percentages
2008 House Election (79%); 2006 House Election
(62%); 2004 House Election (59%); 2002 House
Election (99%); 2001 Special Election (56%)

Elected 2010; 1st term

Although a social and fiscal conservative in tune with the national GOP, Boozman's decade in the House showed that he can work comfortably with Democrats on issues of concern to his constituents while remaining a loyal party man.

Boozman's party unity score — the annual percentage of votes on which he sided with a majority of his party against a majority of Democrats — never fell below 91 during his House tenure. More typically, it was in the mid- to high-90s.

In the 112th Congress (2011-12), his focus is likely to be on economic issues and agriculture.

When Boozman (BOZE-man) defeated Democratic incumbent Blanche Lincoln in 2010, Arkansas lost its home-state Agriculture, Nutrition and Forestry chairwoman. But the nation's top rice producer will still have a member on the panel because Republican leader Mitch McConnell of Kentucky fulfilled a promise to seat Boozman on the Agriculture Committee.

In a stance at odds with most other conservative Republicans, Boozman has advocated ending the U.S. trade embargo against Cuba, a priority for the state's rice and poultry farmers who see a potentially lucrative market. In the House, he sat on the Foreign Affairs Committee, where he focused on trade issues and ways to combat drug smuggling.

In addition to his work on agricultural issues, Boozman said he will make "getting people back to work [by] giving businesses incentives" a top priority, while remaining active on veterans' issues and public works. He served on the Veterans' Affairs and Transportation and Infrastructure committees in the House and has won seats on their parallel panels in the Senate.

Also while in the House, Boozman championed local interests, including retail giant Wal-Mart Stores Inc., which is headquartered in Bentonville, and the Springdale-based poultry and meat processor Tyson Foods Inc. He will be able to continue those efforts from his posting to the Commerce, Science and Transportation Committee in the 112th. He also serves as ranking Republican on the panel's Science and Space Subcommittee.

Because he sees lower taxes as a way to revive the economy, Boozman not only supported extending the income tax cuts Congress approved in 2001 and 2003 under President George W. Bush, but talks about the necessity of additional cuts.

"Right now the industrialized world is cutting its taxes," Boozman has said. "I think I would be in favor, in order to get the economy back on track, to cut taxes on business to create jobs."

The emphasis on business reflects on Boozman's experience as a cattle rancher and co-founder with his brother, Fay, of an eye-care clinic.

He says Congress could cut taxes, spend wisely on priority needs and still chip away at the federal deficit.

"We're going to have to be very, very careful where we spend our dollars and make sure they are for projects that will not only create jobs when they're being done, but create tremendous economic opportunity after that," Boozman said.

After initially expressing some reservations, Boozman endorsed the GOP earmark moratorium in the Senate, days after saying he was worried about what such a restriction would mean for some projects under way in Arkansas.

"While not all earmarks are bad, it is clear that the system is broken and in need of reform," Boozman said in November 2010.

He also favors withholding funding of the health care overhaul enacted in 2010. "I think the best thing we can do is defund it. Try to take away the dollars so that it can't go forward," Boozman told KHBS and KHOG in Fort Smith and Fayetteville.

From the Commerce Committee, Boozman will be able to monitor the Interstate 49 extension project, another carryover item from his House tenure.

In his first House term, GOP leaders gave him a seat on the Transportation panel, and in 2007 he became the top Republican on its Water Resources and Environment Subcommittee. Boozman used his committee post to secure politically popular funding for the interstate. Planned to be a north-south artery between Kansas City, Mo., and port cities in Louisiana, it would cut through western Arkansas. He is now serving on the Environment and Public Works Committee in the Senate.

On the House Veterans' Affairs Committee, Boozman was the senior Republican on the Economic Opportunity panel. He wants the federal government to do more to help recent veterans apply the professional training they have picked up in the military — working as medics, truck drivers, office managers and the like — to the private sector.

Boozman is the second of three children of an Air Force master sergeant. The family moved around with his father's service assignments, and Boozman spent his early childhood in London, attending a British all-boys school. Eventually, the family returned to Fort Smith, where it had roots dating to the late 19th century. The 6-foot-3-inch Boozman was a standout football player at Northside High School in Fort Smith and then an offensive tackle for the University of Arkansas.

He was going to be a dentist until his brother, Fay, who was studying ophthalmology, persuaded him to go to optometry school so they could practice together. They co-founded Boozman-Hof Regional Eye Clinic in 1977 in their hometown of Rogers.

Fay Boozman, who died in March 2005 in an accident while working on his farm, was always the higher-profile politician. He had served in the state Senate and eventually ran, unsuccessfully, against Lincoln in the 1998 open-seat U.S. Senate race.

John Boozman grew up among Southern Democrats, but was drawn to the GOP by President Ronald Reagan in the 1980s. He began his political career on the Rogers school board, where he served for six years.

When Bush appointed GOP Rep. Asa Hutchinson to head the Drug Enforcement Administration, Fay Boozman passed on a chance to seek the seat. John, who had never been to Washington, jumped in. He finished first in the four-candidate GOP primary but was forced into a runoff by state Sen. Gunner DeLay, a distant cousin of then-House Majority Leader Tom DeLay, a Texas Republican.

Endorsed by GOP Gov. Mike Huckabee, Boozman won both the primary runoff and the 2001 special election. He had little trouble getting re-elected in the following years. As his state's lone Republican House member, Boozman modeled himself after John Paul Hammerschmidt, a member of the GOP who represented the 3rd District from 1967 until 1993.

As the 2010 elections neared, Boozman emerged as the early clear-cut favorite to take on Lincoln, who faced a challenge from the left in her own party and barely fended off Lt. Gov. Bill Halter. During the general election campaign, Boozman showed sizable leads in virtually every poll, then coasted to a 21-percentage-point victory.

Boozman's campaign manager was Sarah Huckabee Sanders, daughter of the former governor and 2008 GOP presidential hopeful. As a teenager she had worked as a page in the Arkansas legislature for Boozman's brother.

Key Votes (while House member)

2010

Overhaul the nation's health insurance system	NO
Allow for repeal of "don't ask, don't tell"	NO
Overhaul financial services industry regulation	NO
Limit use of new Afghanistan War funds to troop withdrawal activities	NO
Change oversight of offshore drilling and lift oil spill liability cap	NO
Provide a path to legal status for some children of illegal immigrants	NO
Extend Bush-era income tax cuts for two years	YES

2009

Expand the Children's Health Insurance Program	NO
Provide $787 billion in tax cuts and spending increases to stimulate the economy	NO
Allow bankruptcy judges to modify certain primary-residence mortgages	NO
Create a cap-and-trade system to limit greenhouse gas emissions	NO
Provide $2 billion for the "cash for clunkers" program	NO
Establish the government as the sole provider of student loans	NO
Restrict federally funded insurance coverage for abortions in health care overhaul	YES

CQ Vote Studies (while House member)

	PARTY UNITY		PRESIDENTIAL SUPPORT	
	Support	Oppose	Support	Oppose
2010	96%	4%	30%	70%
2009	96%	4%	22%	78%
2008	95%	5%	71%	29%
2007	91%	9%	74%	26%
2006	97%	3%	92%	8%
2005	96%	4%	77%	23%
2004	96%	4%	82%	18%
2003	97%	3%	93%	7%
2002	95%	5%	85%	15%
2001	100%	0%	100%	0%

Interest Groups (while House member)

	AFL-CIO	ADA	CCUS	ACU
2010	7%	0%	88%	100%
2009	10%	0%	80%	96%
2008	13%	25%	94%	84%
2007	13%	15%	90%	92%
2006	21%	5%	100%	92%
2005	15%	0%	93%	96%
2004	13%	10%	100%	96%
2003	7%	10%	97%	84%
2002	11%	0%	95%	96%
2001	25%		100%	100%

Rep. Rick Crawford (R)

Capitol Office
225-4076
crawford.house.gov
1408 Longworth Bldg. 20515-0401; fax 225-5602

Committees
Agriculture
Transportation & Infrastructure

Residence
Jonesboro

Born
Jan. 22, 1966; Homestead Air Force Base, Fla.

Religion
Southern Baptist

Family
Wife, Stacy Crawford; two children

Education
Southwest Missouri State U., attended 1991-93;
Arkansas State U., B.S. 1996 (agriculture business
economics)

Military Service
Army, 1985-89

Career
Agricultural news service owner; radio and
television broadcaster; rodeo announcer;
automotive decal and sign shop employee

Political Highlights
No previous office

ELECTION RESULTS

2010 GENERAL

Rick Crawford (R)	93,224	51.8%
Chad Causey (D)	78,267	43.5%
Ken Adler (GREEN)	8,320	4.6%

2010 PRIMARY

Rick Crawford (R)	14,461	71.8%
Princella D. Smith (R)	5,682	28.2%

Elected 2010; 1st term

A former rodeo announcer and news broadcaster, Crawford brings an eclectic mix of professional experience to the House.

His eastern Arkansas district is the poorest in the state, and heavily dependent on agriculture. That's a field in which he has extensive experience, making him a natural fit for the Agriculture Committee.

An Army veteran who grew up in a military family, he spent most of his working life in agriculture-related news services, including stints as an agriculture reporter for TV and radio stations. He also owns AgWatch, a farm news radio and TV network that is broadcast in multiple Southern states. In 2006, former Republican Rep. Asa Hutchinson of Arkansas enlisted Crawford as an adviser to his gubernatorial campaign with a focus on agriculture issues.

"Agriculture is the No. 1 industry hands-down in this district," Crawford said.

Crawford also sits on the Transportation and Infrastructure Committee, where he can address another key local issue as vice chairman of the Subcommittee on Economic Development, Public Buildings and Emergency Management, which has jurisdiction over the Federal Emergency Management Agency (FEMA). "FEMA flood zone re-mapping is going to be front and center," he told KAIT-TV in Jonesboro. "That's going to be an issue we want to get our hands on quickly."

Outside the district, the self-described deficit hawk calls the national debt the "single greatest threat facing the United States."

Institutionally, Crawford has said he feels there is too much power centralized in House leadership at the expense of committee work.

"Let the committees hammer out the legislation, bring it to the floor and let the debate take place," he told an Arkansas TV station.

Crawford won the GOP nomination with almost 72 percent of the vote, then faced retiring Democratic incumbent Marion Berry's former chief of staff, Chad Causey, in the general election. Crawford won with almost 52 percent of the vote. In his first elective office, Crawford represents a district that had been in Democratic hands for more than a century.

Arkansas 1
Northeast — Jonesboro, West Memphis

Settled in the state's northeastern corner, the 1st stretches from the Mississippi Delta through fertile plains and into the hilly north near the Ozark Mountains. The district, the state's poorest, borders Missouri to the north and Tennessee and Mississippi to the east. Large- and small-scale farming operations rise out of the 1st's alluvial cotton delta and fertile rice lands. Jonesboro, the most populous city here, is the hub for northeast Arkansas' agricultural production. Riceland Foods, one of the world's leading rice millers, is based in Stuttgart, and cattle and poultry farms prosper in the north. A volatile market may endanger steel production plants near Blytheville.

Poverty is most notably present in the largely white, older populations in the northwest and within the former sharecropping communities in the Democratic Delta. These communities struggle, with many residents undereducated and unemployed.

The White River National Wildlife Refuge, located in the southeastern portion of the 1st and shared with the 4th, routinely attracts tourists. Each year, thousands of enthusiasts travel to the migratory bird preserve.

Despite a history of electing few Republicans at either the state or federal level, the socially conservative and heavily Christian 1st elected Rep. Rick Crawford in 2010, sending a Republican to the U.S. House for the first time since 1875.

Major Industry
Agriculture, manufacturing, steel production

Cities
Jonesboro, 67,263; West Memphis, 26,245; Paragould, 26,113; Cabot, 23,776

Notable
Hattie Caraway, who in 1932 became the first woman elected to the U.S. Senate, lived in Jonesboro.

Rep. Tim Griffin (R)

Capitol Office
225-2506
griffin.house.gov
1232 Longworth Bldg. 20515-0402; fax 225-5903

Committees
Armed Services
Foreign Affairs
Judiciary

Residence
Little Rock

Born
Aug. 21, 1968; Charlotte, N.C.

Religion
Baptist

Family
Wife, Elizabeth Griffin; two children

Education
Hendrix College, B.A. 1990 (economics and business); Oxford U., attended 1991 (history); Tulane U., J.D. 1994

Military
Army Reserve, 1996-present

Career
Lawyer; political consultant; White House aide; federal prosecutor; party official; congressional aide; associate investigative counsel

Political Highlights
Assistant U.S. attorney, 2006-07

ELECTION RESULTS

2010 GENERAL

Tim Griffin (R)	122,091	57.9%
Joyce Elliott (D)	80,687	38.3%
Lance Levi (I)	4,421	2.1%
Lewis Kennedy (GREEN)	3,599	1.7%

2010 PRIMARY

Tim Griffin (R)	24,610	61.7%
Scott Wallace (R)	15,285	38.3%

Elected 2010; 1st term

A former aide to President George W. Bush, congressional staff member, federal prosecutor and military lawyer, Griffin has been immersed in politics for much of his professional life — but the 2nd District seat is his first elected office.

Griffin brings his military and legal experience to a House committee portfolio focused on national security issues — Armed Services, Foreign Affairs and Judiciary. He also serves as an assistant whip.

Griffin, who was deployed to Iraq in 2006, said the United States has an obligation to leave Afghanistan stable, and he counts the 2007 surge in Iraq as a military and political success. He supports continued aid and security assistance to Israel and said that under "no circumstances" should Iran obtain a nuclear weapons.

He traveled to the Guantánamo Bay detention facility in January 2011 and argues that it should remain open. "The detainees are on the end of an island in the Caribbean. I'd rather have them there than in Jacksonville, Ark.," Griffin told The Times Record.

Long considered a protege of Bush adviser Karl Rove, Griffin worked for the Republican National Committee during the 2000 and 2004 presidential campaigns, and moved over to the White House in 2005.

He was in the national spotlight in 2006 when he was appointed U.S. attorney for the Eastern District of Arkansas, part of a midterm house cleaning of federal prosecutors by the Bush administration that sparked Democratic complaints. Griffin resigned after six months.

Griffin announced in September 2009 that he would challenge Democratic Rep. Vic Snyder. But Snyder announced in January 2010 that he was retiring, making the seat a prime target for a Republican takeover. Griffin won the GOP nomination with 62 percent of the vote over restaurateur Scott Wallace, who had been endorsed by former governor and 2008 GOP presidential hopeful Mike Huckabee. Democrat Joyce Elliott tried to make hay with Griffin's ties to Rove and the U.S. attorney firings, but voters sided with Griffin, giving him 58 percent of the vote in November.

Arkansas 2

Central — Little Rock

An urban hub in a relatively rural state, the state capital, Little Rock, is the focal point of the 2nd — more than half of the district's population lives in the Little Rock area. The district has the state's largest white-collar population and its highest median household income. To the west, the 2nd climbs the Ouachita Mountains. In the eastern reaches, White County hosts Church of Christ-affiliated Harding University.

In Little Rock, a University of Arkansas campus and the system's medical school lead a regional health care, education and research hub, employing thousands of district residents. The River Market District lures partygoers looking for club and bar venues, and the Quapaw Quarter's Victorian buildings draw history buffs to downtown. The nearby Clinton Presidential Center also sits along the Arkansas River, and the entertainment district spills across the Big Dam

Bridge to North Little Rock, which hosts the 18,000-seat multipurpose Verizon Arena. Little Rock's Pulaski County, poor and working-class neighborhoods, and strong union and university populations account for any Democratic votes here. The 2nd twice supported favorite-son Bill Clinton in presidential elections, but residents now support GOP candidates in federal races. There has been population growth outside of Pulaski in more-conservative Saline, Perry and Faulkner counties.

Major Industry
Government, higher education, health care

Military Bases
Little Rock Air Force Base, 5,257 military, 432 civilian (2009)

Cities
Little Rock, 193,524; North Little Rock, 62,304; Conway, 58,908

Notable
Little Rock Air Force Base has the largest C-130 training and airlift facility in the world.

Rep. Steve Womack (R)

Capitol Office
225-4301
womack.house.gov
1508 Longworth Bldg. 20515; fax 225-5713

Committees
Appropriations

Residence
Rogers

Born
Feb. 18, 1957; Russellville, Ark.

Religion
Baptist

Family
Wife, Terri Womack; three children

Education
Arkansas Tech, B.A. 1979 (speech)

Military
Ark. National Guard, 1979-2009

Career
Securities broker; college ROTC program director;
radio station manager

Political Highlights
Rogers City Council, 1983-84, 1997-98; mayor of
Rogers, 1999-2010

ELECTION RESULTS

2010 GENERAL

Steve Womack (R)	148,581	72.4%
David Whitaker (D)	56,542	27.6%

2010 PRIMARY RUNOFF

Steve Womack (R)	18,334	51.8%
Cecile Bledsoe (R)	17,080	48.2%

Elected 2010; 1st term

Womack is a former mayor who parlayed his assistance to fellow Republican candidates into a plum assignment on the Appropriations Committee and a first step onto the leadership ladder as a deputy whip.

Running in an overwhelmingly Republican district, Womack was free to turn part of his campaign funds into $50,000 for the National Republican Congressional Committee and make donations directly to 14 GOP House candidates, eight of whom were elected.

Womack "helped bring people across the line," House Majority Whip Kevin McCarthy of California told Politico. "It definitely did not hurt one iota."

The Arkansan was one of three members of the GOP class of 2010 to be named to the Appropriations panel. But, rather than seeing the posting primarily as an opportunity to funnel federal funds back home, Womack told a Fort Smith crowd a month after the election that his main task is to "shrink government and cut spending."

As mayor of Rogers, Womack earned a reputation as straightforward and strong-willed. He was among the first to sign up his city's police officers for so-called 287(g) training, allowing them to serve as U.S. immigration agents in the field or at jails.

He served in the Arkansas National Guard from 1979 until 2009 and was deployed to Egypt after the Sept. 11, 2001, attacks on the Pentagon and the World Trade Center.

Womack also has experience in other professions: He briefly worked as a broker for Merrill Lynch, a broadcaster and a radio station manager.

Republican John Boozman vacated the 3rd District seat for a successful Senate run, and Womack finished first in the June primary, outdistancing his nearest competitor by about 18 percentage points, then hung on to win the subsequent runoff by 4.

That all but assured him a seat in Congress. Womack cruised to victory in the general election, taking 72 percent of the vote against Democrat David Whitaker, a Fayetteville attorney.

Arkansas 3

Northwest — Fort Smith, Fayetteville

Arkansas' hilly northwest subscribes to a blend of rugged and religious conservatism rooted in both mountain ranges and suburbia. Rough terrain gives way to retail outlets, interstates and the Arkansas River valley at the southern edge of the district.

Bentonville, Rogers, Springdale and Fayetteville form the commercial hub of the district. Hometown giants Wal-Mart Stores in Bentonville and Tyson Foods in Springdale provide jobs, as does the University of Arkansas' flagship campus in Fayetteville, but this fast-growing metropolitan corridor is not immune to economic instability. Further south, Fort Smith — the state's manufacturing hub, focusing on appliances and home improvement products — is the site of a new Mitsubishi wind turbine plant. Anchored by the Ozark National Forest to the south and Beaver Lake in the north, the area lures tens of thousands of visitors each year. Outdoor enthusiasts take in the scenery and history buffs visit Civil War sites such as Pea Ridge National Military Park, as well as the museums and landmarks in Fort Smith, which cover everything from the founding of the namesake fort to the Belle Grove Historic District. Religion-oriented tourism in Carroll County conveys the local conservative, Bible Belt character.

The 3rd, a solidly GOP district, has sent Republicans to Congress since the 1966 election. John Boozman took 68 percent of his former district's U.S. Senate vote in 2010.

Major Industry
Retail, tourism, agriculture, manufacturing

Cities
Fort Smith, 86,209; Fayetteville, 73,580; Springdale, 69,797; Rogers, 55,964

Notable
Eureka Springs boasts the 67-foot-tall Christ of the Ozarks statue.

Rep. Mike Ross (D)

Capitol Office
225-3772
www.ross.house.gov
2436 Rayburn Bldg. 20515-0404; fax 225-1314

Committees
Energy & Commerce

Residence
Prescott

Born
Aug. 2, 1961; Texarkana, Ark.

Religion
Methodist

Family
Wife, Holly Ross; two children

Education
Texarkana Community College, attended 1979-81;
U. of Arkansas, Little Rock, B.A. 1987 (political science)

Career
Pharmacy owner; wholesale drug and medical supply company field representative; aide to lieutenant governor

Political Highlights
Nevada County Quorum Court, 1983-85; Ark. Senate, 1991-2001

ELECTION RESULTS

2010 GENERAL

Mike Ross (D)	102,479	57.5%
Beth Anne Rankin (R)	71,526	40.2%
Josh Drake (GREEN)	4,129	2.3%

2010 PRIMARY

Mike Ross (D)	unopposed

2008 GENERAL

Mike Ross (D)	203,178	86.2%
Josh Drake (GREEN)	32,603	13.8%

Previous Winning Percentages
2006 (75%); 2004 (100%); 2002 (61%); 2000 (51%)

Elected 2000; 6th term

Ross' moderate instincts and conservative district often puts him at odds with his own party. The former small-town pharmacist won a national audience, if no liberal fans, for his role as a fiscal watchdog during the health care debate in the 111th Congress. In the 112th, he wants to see fiscally conservative Democrats help forge a deficit-reduction deal.

As co-chairman of the Blue Dog Coalition, Ross bemoans his party leadership's liberal tendencies.

"We would welcome an opportunity to work with this new majority and the White House on developing a responsible plan to put us on a path toward restoring fiscal discipline and accountability to our government," Ross told Roll Call early in 2011. "We think we're the perfect group to do that."

Ross expressed his displeasure in a more public, if symbolic, way when he voted for North Carolina's Heath Shuler for Speaker, one of 19 Democrats who did not support Minority Leader Nancy Pelosi of California.

"If our leadership had listened to us a little bit more, perhaps we'd be in the majority today," he told Roll Call.

After leading negotiations for the Blue Dogs as the health care overhaul bill made its way through the Energy and Commerce Committee in 2009, he voted against the measure on the House floor later that year, and again in March 2010. And he was one of three Democrats to vote in January 2011 to repeal the law.

He was no more enthusiastic about some of the other major initiatives of the 111th Congress (2009-10). He voted for the $787 billion economic stimulus, but complained that it didn't include enough money for infrastructure projects and too much money for other programs and tax cuts that didn't stimulate the economy.

Ross voted against legislation to establish a cap-and-trade system designed to regulate carbon emissions based on merits, and also criticized the tactics, saying Democratic leaders should not have brought it to the floor when they knew the Senate would never pass the bill.

In 2010, Ross was one of 19 Democrats to vote against the final version of a financial services overhaul. He said the measure was too broad and would "punish small town, community banks that have played by the rules all along." That year he sided with his party on 84 percent of the votes in which a majority of Republicans opposed a majority of Democrats, his lowest score during the Democratic Caucus' four-year run controlling the House.

In December 2007, he was one of 64 Democrats who opposed a bill to provide a one-year "patch" exempting an additional 21 million people from the alternative minimum tax, which was originally intended to target the highest-earning taxpayers but was not indexed for inflation. Ross criticized the exemption, which was signed into law, for violating pay-as-you-go rules. But he voted for a similar bill in 2008.

His fiscal conservatism is not without limits, however, particularly when it comes to economic help for his district. "I am committed to providing a helping hand, but not a handout," he said. "It's about helping those who want to help themselves."

In 2009 Ross joined the Foreign Affairs Committee, where he backed President Obama's troop surge in Afghanistan, but cautioned that U.S. involvement in Iraq should end soon. "Iraqis must want a democracy in order for it to happen and work in the long-term. America cannot continue to fight their civil war for them," Ross said.

On certain social issues, Ross aligns with the Republican Party. He opposes same-sex marriage and abortion rights, though he voted to lift restrictions on federally funded embryonic stem cell research. He was one of 15 Democrats who voted against repealing the military's "don't ask, don't tell" policy that bars homosexuals from serving openly. In 2007, he was one of 25 Democrats to oppose a bill to prohibit job discrimination based on sexual orientation.

Ross also is a fierce opponent of gun control legislation. He gathered signatures in 2008 and 2010 for amicus briefs encouraging the Supreme Court to overturn gun control laws in the District of Columbia and Chicago.

Ross has said that he believes his conservatism has made him a target. In September 2009, ProPublica, a nonprofit organization that produces investigative articles, published a story suggesting that Ross and his wife were paid well over market prices when a pharmaceutical company purchased their pharmacy in 2007. The watchdog group Citizens for Responsibility and Ethics in Washington filed a complaint about the transaction with the Justice Department, prompting Ross to release detailed records on the sale to his local newspaper. He dismissed the accusations as a "political witch hunt."

Ross was born in Texarkana, the son of schoolteachers who encouraged him to get involved in public service. At the age of 21, he ran for a term on Nevada County's legislative body, the Quorum Court, and drove Bill Clinton around during Clinton's campaign for governor. Both of them won. "It was me and him in a Chevy Citation," Ross recalls.

Working his way through college as a radio announcer, Ross graduated at 25, while working as a top aide to Arkansas Lt. Gov. Winston Bryant. In 1988, he was a regional coordinator for Democrat Michael S. Dukakis' presidential campaign. He worked as a field representative for a wholesale drug and medical supply company and, later, he and his pharmacist wife, Holly, opened their own pharmacy in the small town of Prescott.

He stayed active in politics, winning a 1990 election to the state Senate. In 2000, he challenged four-term GOP Rep. Jay Dickey. Ross was widely regarded as the front-runner for the Democratic nomination, but faced three opponents in a bitter primary. Two of his foes later endorsed Dickey. Ross' win, by 2 percentage points, was the Democrats' only congressional victory over an incumbent outside California that year.

Some Republicans explained away Dickey's defeat as the revenge of Clinton, whose impeachment Dickey had supported in 1998. But Ross handily defeated Dickey again in 2002 with 61 percent of the vote, and he has easily won re-election since.

Key Votes

2010

Overhaul the nation's health insurance system	NO
Allow for repeal of "don't ask, don't tell"	NO
Overhaul financial services industry regulation	NO
Limit use of new Afghanistan War funds to troop withdrawal activities	NO
Change oversight of offshore drilling and lift oil spill liability cap	NO
Provide a path to legal status for some children of illegal immigrants	NO
Extend Bush-era income tax cuts for two years	YES

2009

Expand the Children's Health Insurance Program	YES
Provide $787 billion in tax cuts and spending increases to stimulate the economy	YES
Allow bankruptcy judges to modify certain primary-residence mortgages	YES
Create a cap-and-trade system to limit greenhouse gas emissions	NO
Provide $2 billion for the "cash for clunkers" program	YES
Establish the government as the sole provider of student loans	YES
Restrict federally funded insurance coverage for abortions in health care overhaul	YES

CQ Vote Studies

	PARTY UNITY		PRESIDENTIAL SUPPORT	
	SUPPORT	OPPOSE	SUPPORT	OPPOSE
2010	84%	16%	74%	26%
2009	90%	10%	87%	13%
2008	95%	5%	24%	76%
2007	89%	11%	11%	89%
2006	74%	26%	53%	47%

Interest Groups

	AFL-CIO	ADA	CCUS	ACU
2010	64%	45%	88%	25%
2009	76%	60%	80%	20%
2008	93%	85%	67%	12%
2007	96%	85%	70%	28%
2006	86%	50%	67%	60%

...uff, Hot Springs

Planted across most of Arkansas' southern half, the 4th is the state's largest district in area and features an abundant timber industry, small farming communities and one of the state's most lucrative tourist areas.

Tourism revolves around Hot Springs and the nearby Ouachita Mountains. Hot Springs, heralded as America's first resort, attracts tourists to its national park, and visitors hope the warm waters that were once used to treat illness will still promote relaxation.

The timber industry, located mostly in the district's western portion in and around the Ouachita Mountains, employs thousands of district residents. East of Hot Springs, the Pine Bluff Arsenal once produced the nation's supply of biological weapons. The arsenal completed scheduled destruction of its chemical weapons stockpile but still operates a center for toxicological research.

Rice, soybeans, cotton and rural poverty characterize the eastern edge of the 4th, where many Mississippi River communities have black-majority populations.

Most of Arkansas' catfish production — a prime aquaculture product of the state — is in Chicot County.

Democrats receive their most faithful support from the Delta region. Republicans can fare better in the oil- and chemical-producing south, as well as in the western tier of counties along the Oklahoma and Texas borders.

The socially conservative 4th elected its first GOP representative of the 20th century in 1992, but overwhelmingly supported Hope-born and Hot Springs-raised Bill Clinton in both of his presidential bids. The district gave former 3rd District Rep. John Boozman nearly 70 percent of its vote in the 2010 U.S. Senate race.

Major Industry
Timber, agriculture, livestock, tourism

Military Bases
Pine Bluff Arsenal (Army), 18 military, 1,360 civilian (2009)

Cities
Pine Bluff, 49,083; Hot Springs, 35,193; Texarkana, 29,919

Notable
Hot Springs, once a getaway for mobsters such as Charles "Lucky" Luciano and Al Capone in the 1930s, now hosts the Gangster Museum of America.

CALIFORNIA

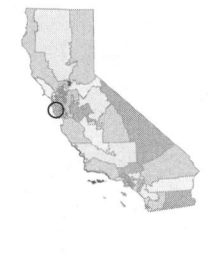

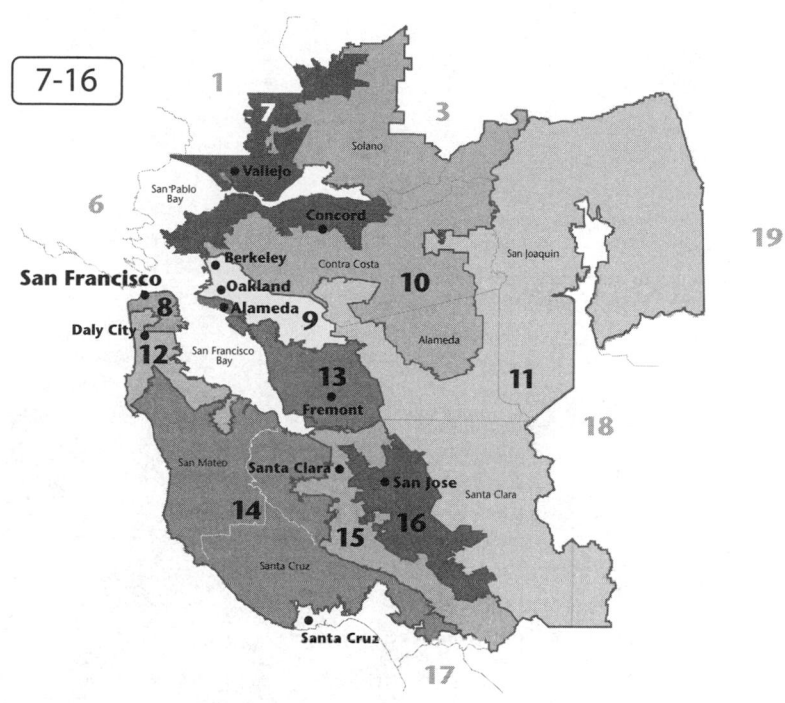

7-16

2010 CENSUS STATISTICS BY DISTRICT

District	2008 VOTE FOR PRESIDENT Obama	McCain	White	Black	Asian	Hispanic	Median Income	White Collar	Blue Collar	Service Industry	Over 64	Under 18	College Education	Rural	Sq. Miles
1	66%	32%	63%	2%	6%	24%	$51,036	58%	22%	19%	13%	23%	28%	24%	11,006
2	43	55	70	1	4	19	43,959	56	25	19	14	24	20	32	21,758
3	49	49	62	6	11	16	66,231	67	17	16	12	26	29	14	3,374
4	44	54	78	1	4	12	64,980	64	18	17	14	23	30	33	16,453
5	70	28	36	14	16	27	47,964	61	20	19	11	26	25	0	147
6	76	22	69	2	4	21	70,878	66	17	17	14	22	40	10	1,625
7	72	26	35	15	15	30	64,539	59	22	19	11	25	25	1	349
8	85	12	42	6	31	17	66,895	73	11	17	14	14	50	0	35
9	88	10	35	20	18	22	54,960	68	17	16	11	21	42	0	132
10	65	33	53	7	13	21	81,132	68	17	15	12	26	39	3	1,013
11	54	44	50	5	14	26	78,111	66	21	13	10	29	31	10	2,277
12	74	24	41	2	33	18	85,609	72	14	15	14	20	46	0	117
13	74	24	26	7	36	25	75,976	66	20	14	11	25	36	1	221
14	73	25	51	2	22	21	93,328	75	12	13	12	23	56	6	826
15	68	30	37	2	36	21	86,378	72	15	13	11	24	45	1	286

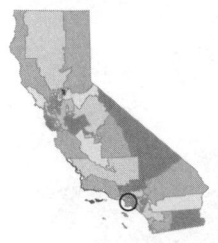

26-40, 42-44, 46-48

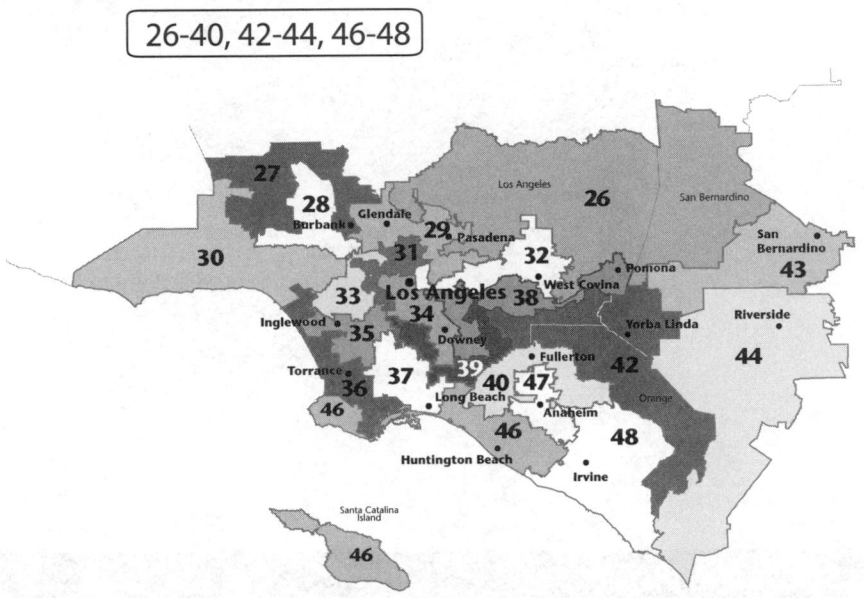

2010 CENSUS STATISTICS BY DISTRICT

District	2008 VOTE FOR PRESIDENT		White	Black	Asian	Hispanic	Median Income	White Collar	Blue Collar	Service Industry	Over 64	Under 18	College Education	Rural	Sq. Miles
	Obama	McCain													
16	70%	29%	26%	3%	28%	40%	$76,397	61%	22%	17%	9%	26%	31%	1%	230
17	72	26	39	2	5	50	59,508	53	28	19	10	26	27	10	4,820
18	59	39	29	6	9	53	43,031	45	37	18	9	32	11	9	3,052
19	46	52	50	4	5	37	53,900	57	25	17	11	27	21	19	6,692
20	60	39	17	6	5	70	34,641	35	45	20	7	33	7	9	4,982
21	42	56	37	2	7	51	47,796	51	31	17	10	31	18	20	8,026
22	38	60	54	6	4	32	54,351	57	24	19	11	28	20	18	10,417
23	66	32	41	2	5	49	55,583	56	25	19	12	24	27	2	1,042
24	51	48	60	2	6	29	78,978	67	17	16	12	26	34	6	3,883
25	49	48	42	10	6	39	61,882	58	23	19	8	31	21	12	21,484
26	51	47	43	5	19	31	76,321	71	16	13	11	25	36	1	752
27	66	32	38	4	12	42	59,118	63	20	17	11	24	29	0	151
28	76	22	30	3	7	58	51,878	54	26	20	9	26	27	0	77
29	68	30	40	5	28	25	58,345	70	15	15	14	21	38	1	101
30	70	28	72	3	11	10	79,917	85	5	10	15	18	58	2	286

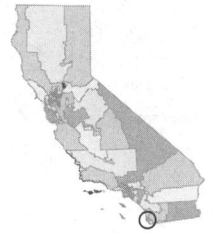

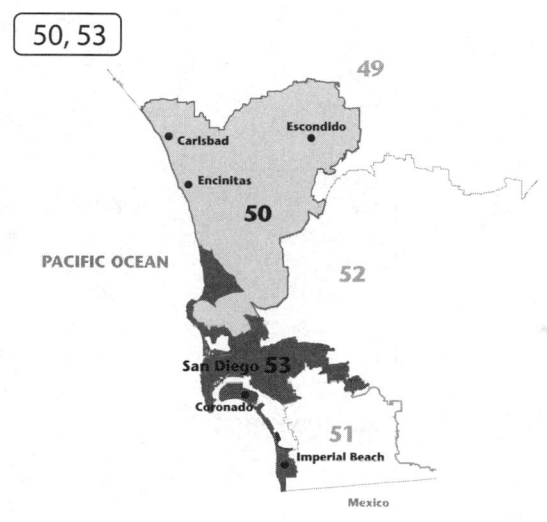

50, 53

49

Carlsbad
Escondido

Encinitas

50

PACIFIC OCEAN

52

San Diego 53

Coronado

51

Imperial Beach

Mexico

2010 CENSUS STATISTICS BY DISTRICT

District	2008 VOTE FOR PRESIDENT Obama	McCain	White	Black	Asian	Hispanic	Median Income	White Collar	Blue Collar	Service Industry	Over 64	Under 18	College Education	Rural	Sq. Miles
31	80%	18%	11%	4%	15%	68%	$35,701	45%	29%	25%	8%	26%	19%	0%	39
32	68	30	10	2	22	64	51,591	51	31	19	10	28	16	0	92
33	87	12	22	25	13	37	42,563	61	17	22	10	22	33	0	48
34	75	23	9	5	6	79	37,210	44	38	19	8	31	11	0	58
35	84	14	9	28	6	54	41,710	49	29	22	8	30	16	0	55
36	64	34	44	4	16	32	68,297	71	15	15	11	23	42	0	75
37	80	19	14	21	12	49	45,848	53	26	20	8	31	19	0	75
38	71	27	9	3	11	75	53,742	50	32	18	10	29	15	0	104
39	65	32	16	5	10	66	55,943	54	31	16	9	30	17	0	65
40	47	51	39	2	20	35	68,912	64	21	15	11	26	30	0	100
41	44	54	51	6	5	35	50,518	56	24	19	13	28	20	11	13,314
42	45	53	45	2	20	29	88,450	74	14	12	10	26	38	1	314
43	68	30	15	10	4	69	49,490	46	36	18	6	34	11	1	191
44	50	49	41	5	8	43	70,397	60	24	15	8	29	26	2	522
45	52	47	41	6	4	45	54,180	54	24	22	14	29	21	10	5,980

Gov. Jerry Brown (D)

First elected: 2010

Length of term: 4 years

Term expires: 1/15

Salary: $173,987

Phone: (916) 445-2841

Residence: Oakland

Born: April 7, 1938; San Francisco, Calif.

Religion: Roman Catholic

Family: Wife, Anne Gust

Education: Santa Clara U., attended 1955-56; U. of California, B.A. 1961 (classics); Yale U., J.D. 1964

Career: Lawyer; international relations think tank chairman

Political highlights: Los Angeles Community College Board of Trustees, 1969-71; Calif. secretary of state, 1971-75; governor, 1975-83; sought Democratic nomination for president, 1976, 1980; Democratic nominee for U.S. Senate, 1982; Calif. Democratic Party chairman, 1989-91; sought Democratic nomination for president, 1992; mayor of Oakland, 1999-2007; Calif. attorney general, 2007-11

ELECTION RESULTS

2010 GENERAL

Jerry Brown (D)	5,428,149	53.8%
Meg Whitman (R)	4,127,391	40.9%
Chelene Nightingale (AMI)	166,312	1.7%
Laura Wells (GREEN)	129,224	1.2%
Dale F. Ogden (LIBERT)	150,895	1.5%

Lt. Gov. Gavin Newsom (D)

First elected: 2010

Length of term: 4 years

Term expires: 1/15

Salary: $130,490

Phone: (916) 445-8994

LEGISLATURE

Legislature: Year-round with recess

Senate: 40 members, 4-year terms

2011 ratios: 25 D, 15 R; 28 men, 12 women

Salary: $95,291

Phone: (916) 651-4181

Assembly: 80 members, 2-year terms

2011 ratios: 52 D, 28 R; 58 men, 22 women

Salary: $95,291

Phone: (916) 445-3614

TERM LIMITS

Governor: 2 terms

Senate: 2 terms

Assembly: 3 terms

URBAN STATISTICS

CITY	POPULATION
Los Angeles	3,792,621
San Diego	1,307,402
San Jose	945,942
San Francisco	805,235
Fresno	494,66

REGISTERED VOTERS

Democrat	44%
Republican	31%
Unaffiliated/others	25%

POPULATION

2010 population	37,253,956
2000 population	33,871,648
1990 population	29,760,021
Percent change (2000-2010)	+10.0%
Rank among states (2010)	1
Median age	34.6
Born in state	52.9%
Foreign born	26.1%
Violent crime rate	472/100,000
Poverty level	14.2%
Federal workers	335,024
Military	117,806

ELECTIONS

STATE ELECTION OFFICIAL

(916) 657-2166

DEMOCRATIC PARTY

(916) 442-5707

REPUBLICAN PARTY

(916) 841-5210

MISCELLANEOUS

Web: www.ca.gov

Capital: Sacramento

U.S. CONGRESS

Senate: 2 Democrats

House: 33 Democrats, 19 Republicans

The 36th District seat is vacant.

2010 Census Statistics by District

District	2008 Vote for President Obama	McCain	White	Black	Asian	Hispanic	Median Income	White Collar	Blue Collar	Service Industry	Over 64	Under 18	College Education	Rural	Sq. Miles
46	48%	50%	56%	2%	19%	20%	$75,732	71%	14%	14%	15%	21%	40%	0%	264
47	60	38	12	1	17	68	51,802	40	36	24	7	31	13	0	55
48	49	49	58	1	19	18	87,229	80	9	11	13	22	52	0	212
49	45	53	48	4	5	39	61,908	57	24	18	11	28	23	10	1,690
50	51	47	59	2	14	22	79,999	71	14	15	12	25	46	2	300
51	63	35	15	7	12	62	50,615	55	23	22	10	29	18	4	4,582
52	45	53	64	4	7	19	70,315	67	17	16	12	25	32	6	2,113
53	68	30	48	6	10	32	50,377	66	15	19	10	19	39	0	95
STATE	61	37	40	6	13	38	60,392	61	22	17	11	26	30	6	155,959
U.S.	53	46	64	12	5	16	51,425	60	23	17	13	25	28	21	3,537,438

Sen. Dianne Feinstein (D)

Capitol Office
224-3841
feinstein.senate.gov
331 Hart Bldg. 20510-0504; fax 228-3954

Committees
Appropriations
 (Energy-Water - Chairwoman)
Judiciary
Rules & Administration
Select Intelligence - Chairwoman

Residence
San Francisco

Born
June 22, 1933; San Francisco, Calif.

Religion
Jewish

Family
Husband, Richard Blum; one child, three stepchildren

Education
Stanford U., A.B. 1955 (history)

Career
Civic board official

Political Highlights
San Francisco Board of Supervisors, 1970-78 (president, 1970-71, 1974-75, 1978); candidate for mayor of San Francisco, 1971, 1975; mayor of San Francisco, 1978-89; Democratic nominee for governor, 1990

ELECTION RESULTS

2006 GENERAL

Dianne Feinstein (D)	5,076,289	59.4%
Richard "Dick" Mountjoy (R)	2,990,822	35.0%
Todd Chretien (GREEN)	147,074	1.7%
Michael S. Metti (LIBERT)	133,851	1.6%
Marsha Feinland (PFP)	117,764	1.4%

2006 PRIMARY

Dianne Feinstein (D)	2,176,888	87.0%
Colleen Fernald (D)	199,180	8.0%
Martin Luther Church (D)	127,301	5.1%

Previous Winning Percentages
2000 (56%); 1994 (47%); 1992 Special Election (54%)

Elected 1992; 3rd full term

Staunchly liberal on some issues and moderate on others, Feinstein often bucks orthodoxies in favor of pragmatism. She also burrows deeply on the topics about which she is most passionate.

"I'm probably less an ideologue than I am one for solving the problem of the day, whatever it might be," she said. "Most problems around here require bipartisan solutions; therefore, I think working across partisan lines is very important where one can."

Despite holding many positions that put her solidly in the left wing of her party, Feinstein has never been a cookie-cutter "San Francisco liberal," even as a former mayor of that city. She is known for often-protracted deliberations before making up her mind — a trait that makes her seem less overtly partisan than many of her colleagues.

That style has helped Feinstein become one of the most popular politicians in her state. In February 2010, Feinstein announced that she would not run for governor, although polls showed that she would hold double-digit leads over the next most popular candidate.

Exhibiting a calm demeanor even when on the attack, Feinstein's philosophical duality also has led her into confrontations with powerful forces, including former House Speaker and fellow California Democrat Nancy Pelosi, as well as advocates of gun rights, supporters of Israel and President Obama.

In the Senate, her top concern is with her gavel as chairwoman of the Select Intelligence Committee.

Writing in the Wall Street Journal in December 2010, Feinstein argued that WikiLeaks founder Julian Assange's leaking of sensitive U.S. intelligence and foreign policy information "damages our national interests and puts innocent lives at risk. He should be vigorously prosecuted for espionage."

She began 2009 with a determination to outlaw the use of harsh interrogation tactics employed on terrorism suspects by the Bush administration. Shortly after taking office, Obama issued an executive order that banned such practices. Feinstein has not always been in harmony with Obama's White House on intelligence matters, however. She challenged several of the administration's picks for spy posts, and after Yemen emerged as a prominent terrorist haven following a failed Christmas 2009 terror attack on a U.S.-bound airliner, she voiced strong sentiment against sending any more Guantánamo Bay detainees to that country.

Her chief priority on the panel in the 111th Congress (2009-10) was to restore annual passage of legislation that would reauthorize spy activities, and she succeeded, following a dry spell of more than five years. Overcoming a veto threat and Pelosi's desire for stricter notification requirements, Feinstein helped fashion a compromise that would enhance the information Congress receives from the executive branch on intelligence operations.

A senior member of the Judiciary Committee, Feinstein struck a compromise with Chairman Patrick J. Leahy, a Vermont Democrat, in 2009 on legislation to overhaul expiring provisions of the 2001 anti-terror law known as the Patriot Act. Her proposals dragged the bill to the right, earning her criticism from civil liberties advocates.

When it comes to gun control, a topic dear to party liberals, Feinstein is a fierce proponent. In 2009, she was dismayed with an amendment added to the District of Columbia voting rights measure that rewrote D.C.'s gun laws to allow semi-automatic weapon ownership and to drop criminal penalties for owning an unregistered firearm. "If successful, it will be the first new step in a march to remove all common-sense gun regulations all over this land," she said, although she ultimately voted for the bill.

Feinstein, the author of a long-expired federal ban on certain semi-automatic weapons, vowed to seek its renewal, although she acknowledged that the issue divided her own party and that it would be an "uphill battle."

Feinstein came to support gun control in part through tragic firsthand experience. In November 1978, while president of San Francisco's Board of Supervisors, Feinstein discovered the body of Mayor George Moscone in his office after he and Harvey Milk, the city's first openly gay supervisor, were gunned down by Dan White, a former supervisor. To evade the building's security force, White had sneaked into City Hall through an unlocked window.

Besides chairing the Intelligence Committee, Feinstein holds the gavel of the Appropriations Energy-Water Subcommittee, giving her a leading voice on nuclear weapons, research laboratories and water projects, all critical components of California's economy. Following the end of the 111th Congress, she gave up the chair of the Interior-Environment Subcommittee, where she had crusaded against the use of chemicals viewed as public health threats. Her measure to ban phthalates — chemicals used to make plastics softer — in children's toys was included in a Consumer Product Safety Commission bill enacted in August 2008. Phthalates have been tied to possible reproductive problems, especially in males. Next on her radar is a ban of bisphenol A from food bottles, cans and jars. Food and Drug Administration officials have said the widely used chemical has not been proven unsafe, but have suggested that parents take "reasonable" steps to limit children's exposure.

Long a supporter of Israel, Feinstein, began to seriously question the nation's actions in 2010. She voiced "grave concerns" about Israel's continued expansion of settlements in East Jerusalem and the West Bank. Feinstein is the only senator to have demanded an "impartial inquiry" into the May 2010 deadly Israeli commando raid on a flotilla trying to break the blockade of Gaza.

She also sits on the Rules and Administration Committee, which she chaired in the 110th Congress (2007-08).

Feinstein's mother was once a model; her father was a surgeon. Her marriage to investment banker Richard Blum has made her one of the wealthiest members of Congress, but has also resulted in her being a frequent target of criticism that his government contracts and other business dealings present a conflict of interest. Feinstein has uniformly denied any connection between her legislative positions and her husband's interests.

Her affinity for politics began in college, where she built on her volunteer work to become Stanford's student body vice president. In 1960, Gov. Pat Brown appointed her to the women's parole board.

"I found that I believe we should work to our strong suit, and I think my strong suit is working in this sector — making government work for people," she said.

As San Francisco board president, Feinstein succeeded Moscone as mayor, a job she had sought unsuccessfully at the ballot box. As mayor, she defeated a recall effort that gun rights advocates had helped put on the ballot. After leaving City Hall in 1989, she prepared for her 1990 gubernatorial race against GOP Sen. Pete Wilson, a race that she lost.

In 1992, she ran for the Senate and defeated John Seymour, whom Wilson had appointed as his successor. Two years later, Feinstein got a scare from Rep. Michael Huffington, an oil family scion, who spent millions of his own money on the race. But she prevailed, as she did in 2000 against Rep. Tom Campbell, a moderate Republican. In 2006, she coasted to victory over former state Sen. Richard "Dick" Mountjoy.

Feinstein underwent knee replacement surgery at the beginning of the 112th Congress, which delayed her return to work for several weeks.

Key Votes

2010

Pass budget reconciliation bill to modify overhauls of health care and federal student loan programs	YES
Proceed to disapproval resolution on EPA authority to regulate greenhouse gases	NO
Overhaul financial services industry regulation	YES
Limit debate to proceed to a bill to broaden campaign finance disclosure and reporting rules	YES
Limit debate on an extension of Bush-era income tax cuts for two years	YES
Limit debate on a bill to provide a path to legal status for some children of illegal immigrants	YES
Allow for a repeal of "don't ask, don't tell"	YES
Consent to ratification of a strategic arms reduction treaty with Russia	YES

2009

Prevent release of remaining financial industry bailout funds	NO
Make it easier for victims to sue for wage discrimination remedies	YES
Expand the Children's Health Insurance Program	YES
Limit debate on the economic stimulus measure	YES
Repeal District of Columbia firearms prohibitions and gun registration laws	NO
Limit debate on expansion of federal hate crimes law	YES
Strike funding for F-22 Raptor fighter jets	NO

CQ Vote Studies

	PARTY UNITY		PRESIDENTIAL SUPPORT	
	Support	Oppose	Support	Oppose
2010	97%	3%	98%	2%
2009	96%	4%	96%	4%
2008	91%	9%	38%	62%
2007	93%	7%	39%	61%
2006	90%	10%	54%	46%
2005	92%	8%	40%	60%
2004	95%	5%	62%	38%
2003	91%	9%	49%	51%
2002	83%	17%	76%	24%
2001	85%	15%	71%	29%

Interest Groups

	AFL-CIO	ADA	CCUS	ACU
2010	94%	90%	27%	8%
2009	100%	100%	43%	0%
2008	100%	100%	63%	4%
2007	89%	90%	45%	0%
2006	100%	90%	50%	0%
2005	62%	95%	50%	12%
2004	100%	100%	65%	4%
2003	92%	90%	39%	5%
2002	92%	80%	55%	20%
2001	94%	85%	71%	12%

Sen. Barbara Boxer (D)

Capitol Office
224-3553
boxer.senate.gov
112 Hart Bldg. 20510-0505; fax 228-3972

Committees
Commerce, Science & Transportation
Environment & Public Works - Chairwoman
Foreign Relations
(International Operations & Organizations
- Chairwoman)
Select Ethics - Chairwoman

Residence
Rancho Mirage

Born
Nov. 11, 1940; Brooklyn, N.Y.

Religion
Jewish

Family
Husband, Stewart Boxer; two children

Education
Brooklyn College, B.A. 1962 (economics)

Career
Congressional aide; journalist; stockbroker

Political Highlights
Candidate for Marin County Board of Supervisors,
1972; Marin County Board of Supervisors, 1977-83
(president, 1980); U.S. House, 1983-93

ELECTION RESULTS

2010 GENERAL

Barbara Boxer (D)	5,218,441	52.2%
Carly Fiorina (R)	4,217,366	42.2%
Gail K. Lightfoot (LIBERT)	175,242	1.8%
Marsha Feinland (PFP)	135,093	1.4%
Duane Roberts (GREEN)	128,510	1.3%
Edward C. Noonan (AMI)	125,441	1.2%

2010 PRIMARY

Barbara Boxer (D)	1,957,920	80.9%
Brian Quintana (D)	338,442	14.0%
Robert M. "Mickey" Kaus (D)	123,573	5.1%

Previous Winning Percentages
1998 (53%); 1992 (48%); 1990 House Election (68%);
1988 House Election (73%); 1986 House Election
(74%); 1984 House Election (68%); 1982 House
Election (52%)

Elected 1992; 4th term

Re-elected to a fourth term in November 2010 — perhaps the most inhospitable year for Democrats in a generation — Boxer has firmly established herself as a fixture of the Senate and of California politics. She chairs the Environment and Public Works Committee, where she champions climate change legislation and irritates conservatives — and occasionally, fellow Democrats.

Boxer enjoys close working and personal relationships with President Obama and the Senate Democratic leadership — she is the chief deputy whip — and is the only senator to currently hold the gavel on two committees. Boxer also chairs the Select Ethics Committee.

Those closest to Boxer say her sometimes-newsworthy quotes have long obscured an individual who is a pragmatist at heart and who works hard to build consensus in a legislative chamber that demands it. Her voting record is down-the-line liberal, and she voted with a majority of fellow Democrats against a majority or Republicans 97 percent of the time in the 111th Congress (2009-10).

Her public persona is defined by incidents such as telling U.S. Army Corps of Engineers Brig. Gen. Michael Walsh during a 2010 hearing to refer to her as "Senator," rather than "ma'am," which he did. "Ma'am" is customary for military officials and considered a designation of respect.

"Do me a favor," Boxer told Walsh during testimony on post-Hurricane Katrina coastal restoration. "Could [you] say senator instead of ma'am? It's just a thing, I worked so hard to get that title, so I'd appreciate it, thank you."

For all of the negative attention she received for that incident and her periodic policy squabbles with Oklahoma Sen. James M. Inhofe, the ranking Republican on Environment and Public Works, over the scientific legitimacy of global climate change, Boxer has been active legislatively in engineering compromises with the GOP and moderate Democrats. She even received a call from the U.S. Chamber of Commerce following the November 2010 elections. The business advocacy group told Boxer that it hoped to work with her during the 112th Congress (2011-12) on infrastructure spending.

In the lame-duck session at the end of the 111th, she backed a two-year extension of the Bush-era tax cuts for all income levels after being a vociferous critic of the tax cuts when they were enacted. During the health care overhaul debate, Boxer was brought in by Democratic leaders at the 11th hour to help engineer a compromise on abortion funding that was suitable to the abortion rights Democrats she represented and anti-abortion Democrats led by Sen. Ben Nelson of Nebraska.

The Environment and Public Works Committee was one of the few Senate panels to report out climate change legislation, although the overall effort stalled because of Republican opposition and the inability of the other committees of jurisdiction to deliver their parts of the package. She said in January 2011 that she would vigorously oppose GOP efforts to rein in EPA efforts to regulate carbon emissions by rule rather than legislation.

Prior to Obama taking office, Boxer occasionally found her agenda thwarted — either by a Republican Senate majority, or, in 2007 and 2008, President George W. Bush. Boxer was long among the Republican chief executive's most ardent critics. She tangled with the Bush administration over its refusal to list polar bears as an endangered species and its decision to end the ban on offshore drilling, a significant environmental concern in California. And she was a consistent and vocal critic of the Iraq War.

A key legislative victory for Boxer came in November 2007, when the Senate voted to override Bush's veto of the $23.2 billion Water Resources Development Act, a popular piece of legislation authorizing water projects that Bush criticized as too expensive. His veto prompted a rare legislative moment in which Boxer and Inhofe worked together to reverse the president.

As chairwoman of the Ethics Committee, Boxer oversaw appointment of a special counsel in early 2011 to lead the investigation of Nevada Republican Sen. John Ensign, who faced allegations that he tried to cover up an affair with the spouse of his former top aide.

Boxer also serves on the Foreign Relations Committee, where she helped block Senate confirmation of Obama's nominee as ambassador to Azerbaijan, citing "a pattern of unwillingness to speak out forcefully in the face of increasing Azerbaijani aggression against Nagorno Karabakh," a region in dispute between Azerbaijan and Armenia. Armenian-Americans are a small but influential voting bloc in California. She holds the gavel of the International Operations and Organizations, Human Rights, Democracy, and Global Women's Issues Subcommittee.

Boxer's other committee assignment is Commerce, Science and Transportation. During a 2008 debate on consumer product safety legislation, she responded to GOP resistance about a ban on certain phthalates — compounds commonly used to make plastics more flexible — by putting 90 scientific studies on the dangers of phthalates into the record. House and Senate conferees eventually reached a deal in which several of the compounds were banned.

Boxer, a Brooklyn-born stockbroker, got her political start in Marin County, just across the Golden Gate Bridge from San Francisco, after she moved there at age 27 with her husband, Stewart, an Oakland labor attorney. She won a county board of supervisors seat in 1976, on her second try, and won a House seat in 1982, taking over from her longtime friend and mentor, Rep. John L. Burton, after he decided to retire. Although still often thought of as a Bay Area politician, Boxer and her husband moved to Southern California in 2000, purchasing a home in Republican-leaning Riverside County, in the upscale community of Rancho Mirage, adjacent to Palm Springs.

Boxer is a friend of House Minority Leader Nancy Pelosi, and their relationship dates back to a time in the 1980s when they represented adjoining House districts. Boxer also is close with former President Bill Clinton and his wife, Secretary of State Hillary Rodham Clinton. Boxer's daughter, Nicole, married Tony Rodham, the former first lady's brother. The couple had a son, Zachary, in 1996, but divorced in 2000.

Boxer hasn't limited her energies to politics. She has published three books, the writing of which she does while flying back and forth between California and Washington, D.C. Among her books: "A Time to Run," written with Mary-Rose Hayes, about a female senator whose former lover attempts to sabotage her career; "Blind Trust," also a novel; and "Strangers in the Senate," a nonfiction book about women and politics that she wrote shortly after winning her first Senate race in 1992 by 5 percentage points over TV commentator Bruce Herschensohn.

She won re-election over state Treasurer Matt Fong by 10 percentage points, then won a third term in 2004 by a 20-percentage-point margin over former California Secretary of State Bill Jones.

Republicans targeted her in 2010, and former Hewlett Packard CEO Carly Fiorina won a contested GOP primary. While fellow GOP candidate and former eBay CEO Meg Whitman spent tens of millions of her own money on her unsuccessful gubernatorial campaign, Fiorina stuck mostly to conventional fundraising and lost the money race to Boxer. The contest polled tightly for most of the year, but Boxer won going away, 52 percent to 42 percent.

Key Votes

2010

Pass budget reconciliation bill to modify overhauls of health care and federal student loan programs	YES
Proceed to disapproval resolution on EPA authority to regulate greenhouse gases	NO
Overhaul financial services industry regulation	YES
Limit debate to proceed to a bill to broaden campaign finance disclosure and reporting rules	YES
Limit debate on an extension of Bush-era income tax cuts for two years	YES
Limit debate on a bill to provide a path to legal status for some children of illegal immigrants	YES
Allow for a repeal of "don't ask, don't tell"	YES
Consent to ratification of a strategic arms reduction treaty with Russia	YES

2009

Prevent release of remaining financial industry bailout funds	NO
Make it easier for victims to sue for wage discrimination remedies	YES
Expand the Children's Health Insurance Program	YES
Limit debate on the economic stimulus measure	YES
Repeal District of Columbia firearms prohibitions and gun registration laws	NO
Limit debate on expansion of federal hate crimes law	YES
Strike funding for F-22 Raptor fighter jets	NO

CQ Vote Studies

	PARTY UNITY		PRESIDENTIAL SUPPORT	
	SUPPORT	OPPOSE	SUPPORT	OPPOSE
2010	97%	3%	98%	2%
2009	97%	3%	96%	4%
2008	99%	1%	30%	70%
2007	97%	3%	34%	66%
2006	97%	3%	47%	53%
2005	99%	1%	30%	70%
2004	96%	4%	65%	35%
2003	99%	1%	44%	56%
2002	95%	5%	65%	35%
2001	98%	2%	64%	36%

Interest Groups

	AFL-CIO	ADA	CCUS	ACU
2010	100%	95%	18%	0%
2009	100%	100%	43%	0%
2008	100%	95%	57%	4%
2007	100%	80%	33%	4%
2006	100%	95%	25%	8%
2005	92%	100%	24%	12%
2004	100%	95%	56%	4%
2003	100%	95%	22%	10%
2002	100%	90%	40%	5%
2001	100%	95%	42%	0%

Rep. Mike Thompson (D)

Capitol Office
225-3311
mikethompson.house.gov
231 Cannon Bldg. 20515-0501; fax 225-4335

Committees
Ways & Means
Select Intelligence

Residence
St. Helena

Born
Jan. 24, 1951; St. Helena, Calif.

Religion
Roman Catholic

Family
Wife, Janet Thompson; two children

Education
California State U., Chico, B.A. 1982 (political science),
M.A. 1996 (public administration)

Military
Army, 1969-73

Career
Grape farmer; winery maintenance supervisor; state
legislative aide; college instructor

Political Highlights
Calif. Senate, 1990-98

ELECTION RESULTS

2010 GENERAL

Mike Thompson (D)	147,307	62.8%
Loren Hanks (R)	72,803	31.0%
Carol Wolman (GREEN)	8,486	3.6%
Mike Rodrigues (LIBERT)	5,996	2.6%

2010 PRIMARY

Mike Thompson (D)	unopposed

2008 GENERAL

Mike Thompson (D)	197,812	68.1%
Zane Starkewolf (R)	67,853	23.4%
Carol Wolman (GREEN)	24,793	8.5%

Previous Winning Percentages
2006 (66%); 2004 (67%); 2002 (64%); 2000 (65%);
1998 (62%)

Elected 1998; 7th term

Thompson is a longstanding member of the Blue Dog Coalition of fiscally conservative Democrats, but he supported virtually all of the Obama administration's legislative proposals for government action to address the faltering economy.

He justified his support for the spending initiatives in purely Keynesian terms. "I'm willing to borrow and spend a little money now to get the things we need," he said. The time to cut spending is "when we have the money."

Thompson said Congress failed to rein in spending and pay down debt when the economy was in good shape, leaving members to make emergency decisions to prevent disaster when markets began to fail and unemployment shot up.

A member of the Ways and Means Committee since 2005, Thompson argues that taxes, not just spending, need to be figured into the equation. He backs the general notion of overhauling the tax system — particularly the estate tax — but argues that any changes should be revenue neutral.

At a Ways and Means hearing in early 2011, Thompson questioned the wisdom of GOP suggestions that an overhaul could result in a decrease in overall tax receipts.

"I just don't think you can put that off the table or take care of it later on," Thompson said. "This is a real, real important issue."

Thompson backed both the $700 billion measure to shore up the ailing financial services industry in fall 2008, in the waning days of the George W. Bush administration, and the $787 billion economic stimulus measure that cleared Congress in February 2009. "Had we not done the bailout and the stimulus, I'm convinced that we would be deep in a recession," he said more than a year after the stimulus vote.

He also backed the health care overhaul measure, which several Blue Dog colleagues opposed in the 111th Congress (2009-10) and three voted to repeal early in the 112th (2011-12).

Closer to Thompson's comfort zone was his February 2010 vote to reinstate pay-as-you-go rules, requiring offsets for tax cuts and spending increases. "That was worth something," Thompson said.

Although he considered that vote a victory for fiscal conservatism, Thompson said he has been disappointed that the Obama administration and Congress continued the practice of using emergency supplemental appropriations bills to pay for the wars in Iraq and Afghanistan. Thompson noted that although the war in Iraq started almost a decade ago, it is still treated like an unforeseen expense. "If we don't know what we we're doing by now, we've got bigger problems," he said.

Thompson is a Vietnam combat veteran and Intelligence Committee member who opposed both the Iraq War's authorization in 2002 and Bush's proposal in early 2007 to send in more than 20,000 additional U.S. combat troops. In 2006 and 2007, he offered unsuccessful bills calling for troop withdrawals. In Afghanistan, he said, he fears that increases in troop levels have little chance of turning around the conflict. "Counterinsurgency plans don't work unless you have a strong partner government, which we do not have," Thompson said.

Thompson comes from a family of grape growers, and he owns a vineyard where he grows organic sauvignon blanc grapes. He's a founder and co-chairman of the Congressional Wine Caucus. Thompson is usually willing to expend effort and money to benefit the vineyards in his district. He has worked to expand trade markets for California's wine and produce, and pressed for federal dollars to fight insect-borne crop diseases.

He also fought back in 2009 when GOP Sen. John McCain of Arizona made an example of congressional spending on the "wine train" in Thompson's district as a frivolous earmark. The money was going to a flood control project that involved moving some of the train's tracks. Thompson told the Vallejo Times Herald that McCain's missive was "intellectually dishonest."

Thompson has argued for measures to improve rural health care, including legislation to create programs that offer health care advice and doctor consultations via computer and telephone. He succeeded in getting those "tele-health" provisions added to the House version of the health care overhaul in 2009, but they were left on the cutting room floor after the House passed the Senate version instead.

Thompson grew up in his district before the wine boom, picking walnuts and prunes to make extra money. During his lifetime, winemaking turned from a sleepy profession into a tourist attraction and a major industry.

As a young man, he worked as a maintenance supervisor at the Beringer Vineyard in Napa Valley. "I was the guy the Hispanic field laborers would come to with their problems," he said. When he once sought to intervene on behalf of a Hispanic worker who had been cheated by a mechanic, Thompson recalled, "The guy in the repair shop said: 'What do you care? The guy's just a Mexican.'"

Outraged by the incident, Thompson said, he realized that to be able to help people effectively, he would have to complete his education. He had dropped out of high school and joined the Army, serving as a staff sergeant and platoon leader with the 173rd Airborne Brigade in Vietnam, where he was wounded and received a Purple Heart. In his late 20s and early 30s, he earned his high school diploma and a college degree.

He followed the advice of a political science professor who suggested he apply for a fellowship working with the state legislature. He later served as chief of staff for Assemblyman Lou Papan. When Papan left, Thompson packed up his office and prepared to leave the legislature, agreeing only to help Papan's successor, Jackie Speier, find a replacement. Speier ultimately persuaded him to stay. (Thompson supported Speier's successful bid for Congress in a special election in 2008.)

Thompson first ran for elective office in 1990, winning a seat in the state Senate. Term limited, he set his sights on Congress in 1998. He easily defeated Napa County Supervisor Mark Luce, a Republican, and has since won re-election handily.

Key Votes

2010	
Overhaul the nation's health insurance system	YES
Allow for repeal of "don't ask, don't tell"	YES
Overhaul financial services industry regulation	YES
Limit use of new Afghanistan War funds to troop withdrawal activities	NO
Change oversight of offshore drilling and lift oil spill liability cap	YES
Provide a path to legal status for some children of illegal immigrants	YES
Extend Bush-era income tax cuts for two years	NO
2009	
Expand the Children's Health Insurance Program	YES
Provide $787 billion in tax cuts and spending increases to stimulate the economy	YES
Allow bankruptcy judges to modify certain primary-residence mortgages	YES
Create a cap-and-trade system to limit greenhouse gas emissions	YES
Provide $2 billion for the "cash for clunkers" program	YES
Establish the government as the sole provider of student loans	YES
Restrict federally funded insurance coverage for abortions in health care overhaul	NO

CQ Vote Studies

	PARTY UNITY		PRESIDENTIAL SUPPORT	
	SUPPORT	OPPOSE	SUPPORT	OPPOSE
2010	97%	3%	88%	12%
2009	98%	2%	96%	4%
2008	95%	5%	15%	85%
2007	96%	4%	4%	96%
2006	93%	7%	23%	77%

Interest Groups

	AFL-CIO	ADA	CCUS	ACU
2010	100%	100%	13%	0%
2009	100%	100%	40%	0%
2008	100%	90%	56%	8%
2007	96%	90%	55%	0%
2006	86%	90%	47%	20%

California 1

Northern Coast — Eureka; Napa, Davis

The 1st District is notable for its breadth and diversity. Even the weather patterns vary across the district, with a rainy north and arid farmland in the south. It takes about nine hours to travel the length of the district, a journey that starts in Yolo County, across the river from Sacramento, moves through Napa Valley's famous wineries and the northern coast's towering redwood forests, and ends at the Oregon border in Del Norte County, one of the district's three coastal counties.

In the north, Mendocino, Humboldt and Del Norte counties were a battleground for environmentalists and the timber industry two decades ago, but debates about sustainability policy and carbon credits have largely replaced protests. East of Mendocino, Lake County has a mix of ranching, farming and tourism. Once attractive to retirees for its relatively low cost of living compared with Bay Area cities, the county is trying to rebound from high unemployment and home foreclosure rates.

South of Mendocino, the 1st takes in part of wine-producing Sonoma County and all of Napa County. More than 300 wineries are in the 1st, a large segment of the state's total. In addition to wine sales, winery tours

also bring revenue. Napa is the second-most popular tourist destination in California after Disneyland.

Apart from wine, timber and tourism, the 1st's economy extends to commercial fishing in Crescent City, Eureka and Fort Bragg. The University of California, Davis, in Yolo County is a major employer, although just one-quarter of district residents have a college degree.

Politically, the district can show an independent streak, but it remains predominately liberal.

Democrats have a substantial lead in voter registration overall, and every county except Del Norte registers more Democrats than Republicans. Barack Obama took 66 percent of the 1st's vote in the 2008 presidential election, and in the 2010 gubernatorial race Democrat Jerry Brown won every county wholly or partly in the 1st.

Major Industry
Agriculture, timber, tourism

Cities
Napa, 76,915; Davis, 65,622; West Sacramento, 48,744

Notable
At more than 5,000 acres, the campus in Davis is the largest in the University of California system.

Rep. Wally Herger (R)

Capitol Office
225-3076
www.house.gov/herger
242 Cannon Bldg. 20515-0502; fax 226-8852

Committees
Ways & Means
  (Health - Chairman)
Joint Taxation

Residence
Chico

Born
May 20, 1945; Sutter County, Calif.

Religion
Mormon

Family
Wife, Pamela Herger; nine children (one deceased)

Education
American River College, A.A. 1967; California State U.,
Sacramento, attended 1969

Career
Rancher; gas company executive

Political Highlights
Calif. Assembly, 1980-86

ELECTION RESULTS

2010 GENERAL

Wally Herger (R)	130,837	57.1%
Jim Reed (D)	98,092	42.8%

2010 PRIMARY

Wally Herger (R)	57,272	65.3%
Pete Stiglich (R)	30,487	34.7%

2008 GENERAL

Wally Herger (R)	163,459	57.9%
Jeff Morris (D)	118,878	42.1%

Previous Winning Percentages
2006 (64%); 2004 (67%); 2002 (66%); 2000 (66%);
1998 (63%); 1996 (61%); 1994 (64%); 1992 (65%);
1990 (64%); 1988 (59%); 1986 (58%)

Elected 1986; 13th term

Mild-mannered and easygoing, Herger is rarely one to stir controversy or grab headlines. He represents a reliably Republican district that is one of the least affluent and most rural in the state, generally flying under the media radar while building seniority and developing solid conservative credentials as a member of the Ways and Means Committee.

With Republicans trying to counteract the health care overhaul pushed through by Democrats in 2010, Herger may develop a higher profile as chairman of the panel's Health Subcommittee in the 112th Congress (2011-12).

To date, though, arguably the most attention Herger has received in his career came in 2009, when, at a town hall meeting, he said, "Amen. God bless you. There is a great American," to a constituent who stood and proclaimed he was a "proud right-wing terrorist." The line quickly spread across cable TV and left-wing blogs. But Herger stood by his statement, saying his constituent was "rightfully fed up with being called 'un-American' or 'extremist' or a 'political terrorist' by liberals in Washington, for simply exercising his First Amendment rights." The incident had a short shelf life, and Herger quickly returned to his status as a low-profile lawmaker best known for his advocacy of free trade and a simpler tax code.

After slowly ascending the Ways and Means seniority list, Herger was named the top Republican on the Health Subcommittee at the beginning of the 111th Congress (2009-10) — after being edged out for the full committee's ranking member post by Dave Camp of Michigan, now the chairman.

Herger was named to a group to develop a GOP alternative to the health care overhaul plan in February 2009. He became a severe critic of the overhaul enacted in 2010 and voted to repeal it in January 2011.

"This government takeover of health care and implementation of an unconstitutional mandate flies in the face of the principles that have made America great — individual freedom, competition and open markets," Herger, a member of the conservative Republican Study Committee, wrote in Roll Call.

Herger rarely takes to the House floor for debate, but when he does, his high-pitched voice can often be heard discussing Medicare. In September 2009, before voting for a bill that would prevent about 11 million Medicare Part B recipients from having to shoulder more than their usual share of an annual premium increase, Herger reiterated the argument that the larger health care overhaul legislation would take a chunk out of Medicare benefits.

"This will help some seniors, and I intend to vote for it," Herger said. "But seniors shouldn't sleep well tonight, for they're facing massive cuts in Medicare [under] legislation proposed by the president."

Herger also is a strong supporter of a bill he worked on with a fellow Californian and ideological opposite, Democrat Pete Stark, that would bar executives of companies convicted of Medicare fraud from participating in the program again, even if they go to work for a different firm.

Beyond health care, Herger's legislative focus has long been on trade and taxes. In March 2010, he derided a Democratic proposal to stimulate the economy with modest tax cuts, saying, "It's hard to see how a collection of minor tax relief measures will spur job creation when small businesses are staring down the barrel of unprecedented tax increases in the year ahead."

Herger has faced some criticism for not maintaining a focus on Northern California. During the 2008 wildfires that tore through the dry Northern Valley that lies in his district, constituents protested that the congressman did not do enough to respond to the disaster. At the start of the 2009 fire season, Herger introduced a bill that required the departments of Agriculture and Interior to expedite forest management projects related to the clearing of timber and brush that fuel fires. He has also taken an interest in what he calls the "government-caused disaster" in the Klamath River basin of Northern California and southern Oregon, in which water needed by farmers for irrigation was withheld to protect two species of fish. And in February 2010, Herger introduced a bill that would prohibit the extension or establishment of national monuments in California without congressional authorization.

During the 110th Congress (2007-08), Herger was the Republicans' standard-bearer on free trade as the top GOP member of the Ways and Means Subcommittee on Trade. He fought for free-trade deals with Colombia, Peru, South Korea and Panama — only Peru's has became law — while trying unsuccessfully to preserve fast-track authority, which allows the president to send Congress trade deals for simple up-or-down votes.

A convert to Mormonism with a large family, Herger takes particular interest in children's programs. In 2001, he sponsored legislation, which became law, to increase funding for adoption, foster care and post-adoption services. In 2006, Herger chaired another Ways and Means subcommittee that produced a bill renewing several programs to combat child abuse and neglect. It gave the states $345 million annually, including $40 million that Herger insisted be set aside to pay for once-a-month visits by social workers.

Herger grew up on his family's 200-acre cattle ranch and plum farm in the Northern California town of Rio Oso. His grandparents purchased the land after their arrival from Switzerland in 1907. Financially well-to-do, Herger made his money in ranching and running Herger Gas, a propane company in Rio Oso, with his father. He married young and had two children, but the marriage broke up. He remarried months after meeting his present wife, Pamela. She was a nurse who, like him, was divorced with a child and had converted to the Mormon faith. They both wanted a big family and eventually had six more children, one of whom died of a stroke at age 2.

In the late 1970s, high inflation and interest rates spurred him to volunteer for local GOP candidates. "The next thing I knew, I was running for the state Assembly," he said. "And then once I got in, I thought, 'What am I doing?'"

Herger won his Assembly seat in 1980 and was in his third term when Republican Gene Chappie announced his retirement from the U.S. House in 1986. Herger won the general election with 58 percent of the vote. He has had little electoral difficulty since. Redistricting in 2001 shifted his district to the west but left him with his two major population centers, Redding and Chico, and presented him with no re-election worries.

Key Votes

2010

Overhaul the nation's health insurance system	NO
Allow for repeal of "don't ask, don't tell"	NO
Overhaul financial services industry regulation	NO
Limit use of new Afghanistan War funds to troop withdrawal activities	NO
Change oversight of offshore drilling and lift oil spill liability cap	NO
Provide a path to legal status for some children of illegal immigrants	NO
Extend Bush-era income tax cuts for two years	YES

2009

Expand the Children's Health Insurance Program	NO
Provide $787 billion in tax cuts and spending increases to stimulate the economy	NO
Allow bankruptcy judges to modify certain primary-residence mortgages	NO
Create a cap-and-trade system to limit greenhouse gas emissions	NO
Provide $2 billion for the "cash for clunkers" program	NO
Establish the government as the sole provider of student loans	NO
Restrict federally funded insurance coverage for abortions in health care overhaul	YES

CQ Vote Studies

	PARTY UNITY		PRESIDENTIAL SUPPORT	
	Support	Oppose	Support	Oppose
2010	99%	1%	29%	71%
2009	98%	2%	16%	84%
2008	97%	3%	78%	22%
2007	95%	5%	85%	15%
2006	100%	0%	95%	5%

Interest Groups

	AFL-CIO	ADA	CCUS	ACU
2010	0%	0%	88%	100%
2009	5%	0%	73%	100%
2008	0%	10%	89%	88%
2007	4%	5%	80%	96%
2006	14%	0%	93%	92%

California 2
North central — Redding, Chico

The mountainous 2nd forms a north-south strip down the center of northern California, from the Oregon border through the Sacramento Valley. It includes the Sutter Buttes mountain range west of Yuba City.

Agriculture dominates the sprawling 2nd, the largest district in California at almost 22,000 square miles. Almost one-third of the district is rural, with rice farms and orchards that produce walnuts, almonds and plums. Sunsweet Growers, headquartered in Yuba City, operates the world's largest dried-fruit packing plant.

The 2nd endures harsh weather, and conditions cause major fires every year, especially in the northern counties of Shasta, Trinity and Siskiyou, and in the valley county of Butte.

Much of the district is extremely dry and temperatures soar during the summer. Water also is a perennial issue: Two-thirds of the state's supply comes from the upper third of the state, which has caused tension between northern and southern California.

Much of the 2nd's economic activity is centered in Shasta County despite high unemployment rates there. Redding is about 160 miles north of

Sacramento in Shasta County and attracts tourists who visit nearby Shasta Lake, the state's largest man-made reservoir. In Butte County, health care and higher education are major employers in Chico. More than 17,000 students attend California State University, Chico.

The 2nd is largely white, Republican and relatively poor. The district has seen a steady influx of Sikhs in the Yuba City area, as well as an infusion of Democratic-leaning Hispanic farm workers. Chico has a large Democratic presence, but 2010 GOP gubernatorial candidate Meg Whitman won in every county in the district and by 18 percentage points here overall.

Major Industry
Agriculture, timber, tourism, health care

Military Bases
Beale Air Force Base, 4,000 military, 1,200 civilian (2009)

Cities
Redding, 89,861; Chico, 86,187; Yuba City, 64,925

Notable
Redding's Sundial Bridge at Turtle Bay, a pedestrian bridge that spans the Sacramento River, functions as a working sundial but only gives the accurate time one day a year — on the summer solstice in June.

Rep. Dan Lungren (R)

Capitol Office
225-5716
lungren.house.gov
2313 Rayburn Bldg. 20515-0503; fax 226-1298

Committees
Homeland Security
 (Cybersecurity, Infrastructure Protection & Security
Technologies - Chairman)
House Administration - Chairman
Judiciary

Residence
Gold River

Born
Sept. 22, 1946; Long Beach, Calif.

Religion
Roman Catholic

Family
Wife, Bobbi Lungren; three children

Education
U. of Notre Dame, B.A. 1968 (English); Georgetown
U., J.D. 1971

Career
Lawyer

Political Highlights
Republican nominee for U.S. House, 1976; U.S. House,
1979-89; Calif. attorney general, 1991-99; Republican
nominee for governor, 1998

ELECTION RESULTS

2010 GENERAL

Dan Lungren (R)	131,169	50.1%
Ami Bera (D)	113,128	43.2%
Jerry L. Leidecker (AMI)	6,577	2.5%
Douglas Tuma (LIBERT)	6,275	2.4%
Michael Roskey (PFP)	4,789	1.8%

2010 PRIMARY

Dan Lungren (R)	unopposed

2008 GENERAL

Dan Lungren (R)	155,424	49.5%
Bill Durston (D)	137,971	43.9%
Dina J. Padilla (PFP)	13,378	4.3%
Douglas Tuma (LIBERT)	7,273	2.3%

Previous Winning Percentages
2006 (56%); 2004 (62%); 1986 (73%); 1984 (73%);
1982 (69%); 1980 (72%); 1978 (54%)

Elected 2004; 9th term

Also served 1979-89

Lungren combines an easygoing manner with a solidly conservative outlook on the national security issues that have dominated his second tour of duty in Congress.

In hearings, Lungren can go from jocular to serious on the topics he is most focused on. The native Californian, who left Congress in 1989 and returned in 2005, says he can't help it. "My passion, and the real reason I came back to Congress was in response to 9/11, so I have a continued interest in our vigilance when it comes to terrorism," he said.

But Lungren said he has an additional priority in the 112th Congress (2011-12) — reducing federal spending — along with a new responsibility — chairing the House Administration Committee, which oversees federal elections and the day-to-day operations of the House.

Those priorities clashed early on, when Lungren opposed an amendment to a catchall spending bill early in 2011 that would have cut legislative branch spending — including funding for the Capitol Police — by 11 percent. The amendment, rejected by the House, was offered by Lungren's fellow Republican Study Comittee member Jim Jordan of Ohio, the group's chairman. The Capitol Police were the only congressional agency spared from cuts in the original version of the spending bill.

Lungren has been a solid conservative, siding with Republicans on about 94 percent of votes in the 111th Congress (2009-10) that divided majorities of the two parties. His office walls are adorned with photos of President Ronald Reagan, and he says his conservative thinking is based on the 40th president.

Still, Lungren has said he worries that the partisan divide on Capitol Hill has become too deep and personal, and that lawmakers have increasingly disregarded decorum, such as showing up to votes without wearing a tie. After the shooting of Arizona Democratic Rep. Gabrielle Giffords in January 2011, Lungren said that the House Administration Committee would examine the issue of civility in public debate, as well as how members can protect themselves from attack. He abolished the Subcommittee on Capitol Security, shifting security matters to the full committee level.

Lungren often has worked in concert with Democrats. He helped to forge a compromise on the rewrite of the Foreign Intelligence Surveillance Act that became law in 2008 and joined with liberal Democrat Jim McGovern of Massachusetts to promote efforts to reduce nuclear weapons in the United States and Russia. During the 109th Congress (2005-06), he worked with California Democrat Jane Harman to pass a port security bill, which became law in 2006.

Early in 2011, he introduced a bill to criminalize the aiming of laser pointers at airplanes, saying that thousands of pilots are distracted, or even hurt, every year. The laser pointer proposal made its way into a Federal Aviation Administration reauthorization bill.

Lungren's national security concerns have evolved since the Sept. 11, 2001, terrorist attacks. He now says that two of his top legislative priorities will be to push for action on cybersecurity and a finalized regulatory scheme for facilities that handle hazardous chemicals. As chairman of the Homeland Security Subcommittee on Cybersecurity, Infrastructure Protection and Security Technologies, Lungren is in a position of leadership on both of those issues.

Lungren argues that one of the most significant challenges is connecting federal security agencies with the private companies that control the vast majority of America's banks, power plants, communications networks and other critical infrastructure. Lungren thinks the federal government also needs a way to reach out to the general public on the issue. "How do we find a Smokey the Bear for cybersecurity?" he said.

Lungren has advocated tightening chemical plant security for years, including sponsoring legislation for that purpose in the 109th Congress that didn't move but served as a basis for provisions added to a 2007 spending bill.

Now, he says he wants to see legislation to modify and extend the Chemical Facility Anti-Terrorism Standards adopted in 2007. Lungren is among the Republicans who oppose such an extension including language covering "inherently safer technologies," which would give the government the power to order facilities to use chemicals judged as less hazardous.

On the Judiciary Committee, Lungren favors restricting terrorist trials to military tribunals, and holding an open discussion on the Guantánamo Bay, Cuba, detention facility. "I happen to believe that Guantánamo is not only defensible, but it's what we ought to be using," he said.

The second of seven children, Lungren remembers walking precincts for Republican candidates at age 6, when his father was President Richard Nixon's personal physician. Lungren originally wanted to follow his dad into medicine, but discovered early in college that he wasn't academically suited for medical school.

He made an unsuccessful bid for the House in 1976, and two years later won a rematch and served in Congress for 10 years representing a Southern California district before leaving to serve as California's treasurer. But Lungren was accused of being overly partisan and didn't win state Senate confirmation. He bounced back, winning election twice as state attorney general.

In 1998, he made a failed bid for the governorship. He stayed in the Sacramento area and jumped into the 2004 House race when three-term Republican Doug Ose announced his retirement. In the primary, Lungren defeated two well-financed candidates, including Mary Ose, the incumbent's sister. He cruised to a general election victory. In the 2006 race against Democrat Bill Durston, a physician and Vietnam veteran, he garnered 60 percent of the vote. He again held off Durston in a 2008 rematch.

In the wake of the Republican defeat in 2008, Lungren launched a largely symbolic challenge to John A. Boehner of Ohio for minority leader. The attempt was seen mostly as a means for the Republican Study Committee — the House GOP's conservative wing — to pressure Boehner to embrace more of its priorities.

In 2010, Lungren defended one of the few vulnerable GOP seats, facing a tight race against Democratic nominee Ami Bera, a physician and political novice. He took 51 percent of the vote, beating Bera by 8 percentage points.

Key Votes

2010

Overhaul the nation's health insurance system	NO
Allow for repeal of "don't ask, don't tell"	NO
Overhaul financial services industry regulation	NO
Limit use of new Afghanistan War funds to troop withdrawal activities	NO
Change oversight of offshore drilling and lift oil spill liability cap	NO
Provide a path to legal status for some children of illegal immigrants	NO
Extend Bush-era income tax cuts for two years	YES

2009

Expand the Children's Health Insurance Program	NO
Provide $787 billion in tax cuts and spending increases to stimulate the economy	NO
Allow bankruptcy judges to modify certain primary-residence mortgages	NO
Create a cap-and-trade system to limit greenhouse gas emissions	NO
Provide $2 billion for the "cash for clunkers" program	NO
Establish the government as the sole provider of student loans	NO
Restrict federally funded insurance coverage for abortions in health care overhaul	YES

CQ Vote Studies

	PARTY UNITY		PRESIDENTIAL SUPPORT	
	Support	Oppose	Support	Oppose
2010	93%	7%	27%	73%
2009	95%	5%	26%	74%
2008	95%	5%	86%	14%
2007	96%	4%	87%	13%
2006	94%	6%	93%	7%

Interest Groups

	AFL-CIO	ADA	CCUS	ACU
2010	8%	0%	88%	96%
2009	10%	5%	80%	100%
2008	7%	5%	94%	88%
2007	4%	0%	83%	96%
2006	21%	10%	80%	84%

California 3

Central — Sacramento suburbs

The 3rd stretches west from Alpine County on the Nevada border, bends around Sacramento and reaches Solano County, near Napa. It experiences periodic flooding from the Sacramento and American rivers, making water and flood control important local issues. The politically competitive district is predominately white and white-collar.

More than 80 percent of the 3rd's population comes from a chunk of Sacramento County that includes the Sacramento suburbs of Citrus Heights and Rio Linda. Many residents here moved to the 3rd to work in state government or to escape the state's more crowded urban areas while still working in the technology industries.

Folsom, to Sacramento's northeast, is home to an Intel campus partially powered by a nearly 6-acre solar field, but the Sacramento suburbs are looking to rebound from falling home values and high unemployment rates.

Wineries and agriculture dominate the 3rd's economy. Amador County, southeast of Sacramento, is home to several large wineries.

Elsewhere, growers rely on grape, almond and prune production, except in forestry-heavy Alpine County, where mountains and skiing are prevalent. McClellan Air Force Base closed in 2001 and was converted into a business park north of Sacramento (shared with the 5th) that has successfully attracted high-tech and manufacturing businesses.

Sacramento County in the district's western arm is the politically competitive heart of the 3rd, while neighboring Amador and Calaveras counties tend to be largely rural and Republican.

Entirely rural and sparsely populated Alpine County bucks that trend, though, and its voters increasingly support Democrats at the federal level. The 3rd was the only district statewide to back Demcorat Jerry Brown in 2010 while re-electing a Republican to the U.S. House.

Major Industry
Agriculture, timber, technology

Cities
Elk Grove (pt.), 151,433; Citrus Heights, 83,301; Folsom, 72,203; Carmichael (unincorporated) 61,762

Notable
Folsom Powerhouse, which was completed in 1895 and is now the site of a state park, was the nation's first long-distance hydroelectric power plant.

Rep. Tom McClintock (R)

Capitol Office
225-2511
mcclintock.house.gov
428 Cannon Bldg. 20515-0504; fax 225-5444

Committees
Budget
Natural Resources
  (Water & Power - Chairman)

Residence
Elk Grove

Born
July 10, 1956; Bronxville, N.Y.

Religion
Baptist

Family
Wife, Lori McClintock; two children

Education
U. of California, Los Angeles, B.A. 1978 (political
science)

Career
Conservative public policy group director; state
legislative aide; newspaper columnist

Political Highlights
Ventura County Republican Central Committee
chairman, 1979-81; Calif. Assembly, 1982-92; Republican nominee for U.S. House, 1992; Republican
nominee for Calif. controller, 1994; Calif. Assembly,
1996-00; Calif. Senate, 2000-2008; Republican nominee for Calif. controller, 2002; candidate for governor
(recall election), 2003; Republican nominee for
lieutenant governor, 2006

ELECTION RESULTS

2010 GENERAL

Tom McClintock (R)	186,397	61.3%
Clint Curtis (D)	95,653	31.4%
Benjamin Emery (GREEN)	22,179	7.3%

2010 PRIMARY

Tom McClintock (R)	89,443	78.5%
Michael Babich (R)	24,528	21.5%

2008 GENERAL

Tom McClintock (R)	185,790	50.2%
Charlie Brown (D)	183,990	49.8%

Elected 2008; 2nd term

McClintock's three decades in California politics and his devotion to the ideal of smaller government have made him an ideological touchstone in his state, as GOP candidates use his endorsement to demonstrate their own conservative bona fides. But in many ways he remains a lone reed often blown over by the liberal winds that prevail in Golden State politics.

Now though, for the first time in his career, McClintock finds himself in the majority. That allowed him to claim the chairmanship of the Natural Resources Subcommittee on Water and Power, a plum for his northern California agricultural constituency and a platform for his vocal criticism of a program that diverts Sacramento River water from Central Valley farms to protect the endangered delta smelt.

"At the same time this administration is denying California Central Valley agriculture 1.1 million acre feet of their rightfully contracted water in one of the wettest years on record, it is dumping 1.4 million acre feet of additional water into the Pacific Ocean," he said on the House floor in January 2011, calling the policy "insane."

McClintock's consistent conservatism has endeared him to a generation of California GOP activists. But, after winning a state Assembly seat in 1982, McClintock faced years of political and policy defeat as the state and legis-lature grew increasingly Democratic. In ensuing years, while winning re-election to the Assembly and winning a state Senate seat, he lost one U.S. House race, two races for state controller, one for lieutenant governor and one for governor. The Los Angeles Times wrote in 2008: "No politician in modern California history has lost as many statewide races as McClintock."

That record has not deterred McClintock, who kept a picture of Winston Churchill — who endured his own long political exile before emerging victorious — on the wall of his state legislative office.

A member of the Budget Committee, he urges House colleagues to ana-lyze California's mistakes when considering legislation on taxes, energy, health care and the economy. His speeches on the House floor and through-out his district contain blunt, partisan and often dramatic quotes. "Sadly, California has reached the terminal stage of a bureaucratic state, where government has become so large and so tangled that it can no longer per-form even basic functions, a warning to all of us here in this House," he said in June 2009. Anticipating a vote on a debt limit increase, he introduced legislation in January 2010 that would require the government to pay off debt held by the public before covering other obligations.

He once told The Sacramento Bee that, as a state legislator, he refused to "beg for table scraps" on GOP legislation in exchange for "supporting the majority party's agenda."

"Table scraps" are not on his menu in Washington any more than they were in Sacramento. In February 2009, he joined all House Republicans in opposing President Obama's $787 billion economic stimulus bill, then balked at a subse-quent $410 billion catchall spending bill. "We do not need to stimulate govern-ment. Government continues to grow just fine," he said on the floor.

He opposed the Democratic health care overhaul from his seat on the Educa-tion and Labor Committee, a panel he did not return to for the 112th Congress (2011-12). When the House cleared the measure in March 2010, McClintock called its individual mandate "contrary to the fundamental concept of individu-al liberty," and he warned that more like it would follow. "Nor is this brave new doctrine limited to health care. Once the precedent is established that government may usurp individual decisions in the marketplace, what limitation remains on its power to order any other of our decisions as consumers?"

McClintock was born in Bronxville, N.Y., where he spent his early childhood. His father studied political science in college but then became an accountant; his mother worked in real estate.

His father helped campaign for a local school board candidate in White Plains in 1964, but it was McClintock who took the more active role at an early age. As a third-grader, having saved enough money in his piggy bank, he rode a bus to Republican presidential candidate Barry Goldwater's campaign office near the family home in White Plains.

By the time he was 14, and the family had moved to Southern California, he was writing letters to the editor. In high school, he volunteered for President Richard Nixon's 1972 re-election campaign. He became involved in civic work and continued his letter-writing, which led to a column in the now-defunct Thousand Oaks Chronicle. When he graduated from UCLA in 1978, he started a syndicated column that ran in 10 newspapers.

McClintock worked for former Los Angeles Police Chief Ed Davis as chief of staff in the state Senate before winning his own seat in the Assembly in 1982, representing a suburban Los Angeles district. He served a total of 14 years in two stints before term limits forced him out, followed by another eight years in the state Senate. In the Assembly, he took great pride in authoring the state's "death by lethal injection" law and for co-writing a 1987 law that returned more than $1 billion in tax overpayments to state residents.

In the state Senate, he was well known for helping lead the charge to roll back the motor vehicle registration fee and for voting against nearly every state budget. The Bee said he "sounded alarms that fellow Republican Gov. Arnold Schwarzenegger was papering over a crisis of deficit spending."

He had a tough time in his 2008 bid to replace John T. Doolittle, who was under federal scrutiny for his ties to convicted lobbyist Jack Abramoff. Both his primary opponent, former Rep. Doug Ose, and his general-election opponent, Democrat Charlie Brown, accused McClintock of being a "carpetbagger." McClintock had moved his family to the Sacramento area in the mid-1990s so they could be together during the legislative session. California law required him to retain his legal residence in Thousand Oaks, 400 miles south.

McClintock was also criticized for writing only two laws during his eight years in the Senate. But he touted his ideological leadership and raised nearly $3.7 million — to Brown's $2.6 million — and eked out a 2,000-vote victory in a race that wasn't called until weeks after Election Day. He had an easier time of it in 2010, defeating Democrat Clint Curtis by 29 percentage points.

Key Votes

2010

Overhaul the nation's health insurance system	NO
Allow for repeal of "don't ask, don't tell"	NO
Overhaul financial services industry regulation	NO
Limit use of new Afghanistan War funds to troop withdrawal activities	NO
Change oversight of offshore drilling and lift oil spill liability cap	NO
Provide a path to legal status for some children of illegal immigrants	NO
Extend Bush-era income tax cuts for two years	YES

2009

Expand the Children's Health Insurance Program	NO
Provide $787 billion in tax cuts and spending increases to stimulate the economy	NO
Allow bankruptcy judges to modify certain primary-residence mortgages	NO
Create a cap-and-trade system to limit greenhouse gas emissions	NO
Provide $2 billion for the "cash for clunkers" program	NO
Establish the government as the sole provider of student loans	NO
Restrict federally funded insurance coverage for abortions in health care overhaul	YES

CQ Vote Studies

	PARTY UNITY		PRESIDENTIAL SUPPORT	
	SUPPORT	OPPOSE	SUPPORT	OPPOSE
2010	95%	5%	29%	71%
2009	97%	3%	13%	87%

Interest Groups

	AFL-CIO	ADA	CCUS	ACU
2010	0%	0%	88%	100%
2009	0%	0%	73%	100%

Northeast — Roseville, Rocklin

The 4th District, featuring lakes, rivers and mountains, starts at the Oregon border and drops down the Nevada line to Lake Tahoe. The district's southwestern corner also takes in areas near Sacramento.

The mining counties of El Dorado and Placer give the 4th a Gold Rush feel, but the modern industry here is based in technology. Placer, El Dorado and Nevada counties host more than three-fourths of the district's population and facilities for big technology firms like Hewlett-Packard and Oracle. These areas draw residents who want to leave crowded cities but still work in technology fields.

Timber and farming also play important roles in the economy, and the 4th is a popular vacation destination.

Ski resorts dot the Sierra Nevada mountain range, and Lake Tahoe in eastern El Dorado and Placer counties offers skiing, hiking, shopping and golf. Placer's abundant natural beauty is a draw for retirees.

Economic uncertainty leaves the local technology, tourism and retail markets vulnerable, and some former agricultural areas have sought new sources of economic stability.

Susanville, in Lassen County near the rural center of the 4th, is home to only 17,000 residents but hosts more than 9,000 inmates in two prisons — the High Desert State Prison and the California Corrections Center. The 4th is predominately white and is safe GOP territory. Republican John McCain won easily here in the 2008 presidential election, and his two highest percentages statewide were in Modoc and Lassen counties. Every county in the 4th, including the district's portion of Democratic Sacramento, backed GOP gubernatorial candidate Meg Whitman in 2010, and she won her highest percentage statewide in Modoc.

Major Industry
Technology, agriculture, mining, tourism

Military bases
Sierra Army Depot, 1 military, 881 civilian (2009)

Cities
Roseville, 118,788; Rocklin, 56,974

Notable
Lake Tahoe is the second-deepest lake in the nation and 10th-deepest in the world.

Rep. Doris Matsui (D)

Capitol Office
225-7163
matsui.house.gov
222 Cannon Bldg. 20515-0505; fax 225-0566

Committees
Energy & Commerce

Residence
Sacramento

Born
Sept. 25, 1944; Poston, Ariz.

Religion
Methodist

Family
Widowed; one child

Education
U. of California, Berkeley, B.A. 1966 (psychology)

Career
Lobbyist; White House aide; homemaker; state computer systems analyst

Political Highlights
No previous office

ELECTION RESULTS

2010 GENERAL

Doris Matsui (D)	124,220	72.0%
Paul A. Smith (R)	43,577	25.3%
Gerald Allen Frink (PFP)	4,594	2.7%

2010 PRIMARY

Doris Matsui (D)	unopposed

2008 GENERAL

Doris Matsui (D)	164,242	74.3%
Paul A. Smith (R)	46,002	20.8%
L. R. Roberts (PFP)	10,731	4.8%

Previous Winning Percentages
2006 (71%); 2005 Special Election (68%)

Elected 2005; 3rd full term

Though she is only in her third full term, Matsui is a Washington insider with decades of Beltway experience. A longstanding relationship with the Democratic leader in the House helped the party loyalist claim spots on powerful committees early in her tenure.

Matsui arrived on Capitol Hill after winning a special election for the seat once occupied by her late husband, Robert T. Matsui, who died just days before he was to be sworn in for his 14th term. She had more than "congressional spouse" on her résumé: Her credentials included having served as a member of President Bill Clinton's staff and working as a lobbyist.

The Washington connections certainly have helped. Matsui has known Minority Leader Nancy Pelosi, a fellow California Democrat, since the 1970s, when Pelosi was active in the state party and Robert Matsui was campaigning for a congressional seat. Following Robert Matsui's death in 2005, Pelosi helped drum up Democratic Party support for his widow's run, and since her first election Matsui has continued to advocate for a number of her late husband's legislative causes.

After Matsui won the special election in March 2005, Pelosi gave her a seat on the Rules Committee, which shapes the debate on major bills. In June 2008, she won a plum spot on the Energy and Commerce Committee. Democratic losses in the 2010 election meant Matsui had to choose between the two, and she opted for policy over process, leaving Rules and remaining on Energy and Commerce.

Matsui is a loyal Democrat — she sided with her party on every vote she cast in the 111th Congress (2009-10) that pitted a majority of Democrats against a majority of Republicans. She strongly supported the health care overhaul, using her position as a member of both the Rules and Energy and Commerce panels to help usher the legislation through Congress.

"I have heard so many personal stories from my constituents who are struggling to make ends meet and who are being burdened by the current health insurance market," Matsui said during the debate. "The status quo is not working."

Matsui also was a major supporter of the Democrats' effort to overhaul the financial regulatory system and won adoption of a pair of amendments to the House version of the bill. The first would preserve the Federal Trade Commission's authority to conduct rule-making on unfair practices. The second would require mortgage lenders who take part in the Making Home Affordable Program, which provides federal support to help borrowers reduce their monthly mortgage payments, to publicly report their progress in reducing foreclosures.

Matsui's insider reputation might help her in Washington, but it has occasionally generated criticism from more ideologically driven Democrats in her district. And she has displayed a willingness to break from the Sacramento establishment at times.

In 2008, despite opposition from local developers and the mayor, she refused to challenge the Federal Emergency Management Agency's designation of parts of northern Sacramento as a floodplain. Critics said the decision would limit development and the resulting tax revenue.

As part of her husband's legacy, Matsui promotes legislation to preserve as historic sites the World War II Japanese-American internment camps, in which both of them spent part of their childhoods. She was born in the Poston camp in Arizona, but was too young to remember the experience;

her family moved out when she was 3 months old. Her parents tried to shield her from their painful memories. "They never lost hope in the idea that this country is the best country in the world," she said.

Matsui drew on that background in 2006 when speaking against legislation to codify rules governing the interrogation of detainees in the war on terror. "I know something about what can happen to the rights of Americans when the executive branch overreaches in a time of war," she said.

Matsui, who helped push through the North American Free Trade Agreement when she was part of the Clinton White House, voted against the Central America Free Trade Agreement in 2005. She said it lacked adequate labor and environmental protection, and she suggested her husband, an ardent supporter of free trade, had similar reservations. She voted for the Peru Free Trade Agreement in November 2007.

Matsui serves on the Smithsonian Institution's Board of Regents, another fruit born of her relationship with Pelosi, who appointed her to the board. In that role, she helped oversee an intense internal review after the head of the museum complex stepped down amid criticism of his expense account spending.

But not everything Matsui does with the Smithsonian is so serious. In May 2009, she attended the premiere of the film "Night at the Museum: Battle of the Smithsonian" at the Air and Space Museum. Matsui sat next to actor Hank Azaria and got to meet Robin Williams, she told Roll Call.

Matsui met her husband at a college dance and they married in 1966. While her husband pursued a political career, Matsui raised their son and worked with Sacramento-area nonprofit organizations before they moved to Washington.

In 1992, Clinton rewarded her for her early support of his campaign with a spot on his eight-member presidential transition committee. She became a deputy assistant to the president and the highest-ranking Asian-American official in the White House. After leaving the Clinton administration in 1998, she went to work as a lobbyist and as government relations director at the Washington law firm Collier Shannon Scott, a job she held until running for Congress.

Though he had been diagnosed with a rare bone disease, Robert Matsui was re-elected in November 2004. But he was admitted to the hospital shortly afterward and died on New Year's Day 2005.

As he lay dying in the hospital, he encouraged his wife to run for the seat. She won 68 percent of the vote in the special election to replace him and took more than 70 percent in each of the following three elections.

Key Votes

2010

Overhaul the nation's health insurance system	YES
Allow for repeal of "don't ask, don't tell"	YES
Overhaul financial services industry regulation	YES
Limit use of new Afghanistan War funds to troop withdrawal activities	YES
Change oversight of offshore drilling and lift oil spill liability cap	YES
Provide a path to legal status for some children of illegal immigrants	YES
Extend Bush-era income tax cuts for two years	NO

2009

Expand the Children's Health Insurance Program	YES
Provide $787 billion in tax cuts and spending increases to stimulate the economy	YES
Allow bankruptcy judges to modify certain primary-residence mortgages	YES
Create a cap-and-trade system to limit greenhouse gas emissions	YES
Provide $2 billion for the "cash for clunkers" program	YES
Establish the government as the sole provider of student loans	YES
Restrict federally funded insurance coverage for abortions in health care overhaul	NO

CQ Vote Studies

	PARTY UNITY		PRESIDENTIAL SUPPORT	
	SUPPORT	OPPOSE	SUPPORT	OPPOSE
2010	100%	0%	90%	10%
2009	100%	0%	96%	4%
2008	99%	1%	13%	87%
2007	99%	1%	5%	95%
2006	97%	3%	25%	75%

Interest Groups

	AFL-CIO	ADA	CCUS	ACU
2010	100%	100%	0%	13%
2009	100%	100%	40%	0%
2008	100%	100%	56%	0%
2007	96%	95%	55%	0%
2006	93%	95%	33%	4%

California 5

Sacramento

State politics and triple-digit temperatures dominate the 5th District, located in California's Central Valley. The 5th is home to the state capital, Sacramento, and reaches east and south to include a few upper-middle-class suburbs such as Arden-Arcade and Elk Grove (both of which are shared with the 3rd District).

Sacramento first attracted fortune hunters after gold was found on the banks of the nearby Sacramento River in 1848. In recent decades, the presence of cheaper land kept local housing prices below those of San Francisco and elsewhere in the area, and the cost of living was only slightly above the national average. A national housing market crisis, however, forced foreclosure on many district residents.

State government has provided the lion's share of the district's employment, but state and city budget shortfalls have led to layoffs and an unstable economic environment.

Sacramento is home to a California State University campus, and, outside of government, the city's largest employer is the University of California, Davis, medical center.

Other key employers include large technology firms such as Intel and Hewlett-Packard, but high-tech sectors have struggled with high unemployment rates.

The nearby Port of Sacramento (located in the 1st), which handles more than 1 million tons of cargo each year and is linked to the San Francisco Bay and Pacific Ocean, is another economic driver.

The city works to lure tourists to the Old Sacramento neighborhood on the waterfront, home to museums, restaurants, shopping and an annual jazz festival. The California State Fair also attracts visitors.

The 5th is racially diverse, with Hispanic, Asian and black residents accounting for roughly half of the district's total population. Democratic Gov. Jerry Brown won 68 percent of the 5th's vote in 2010.

Major Industry
State government, technology, health care

Cities
Sacramento, 466,488; Florin (unincorporated), 47,513; Arden-Arcade (unincorporated) (pt.), 41,485

Notable
The Crocker Art Museum, located in downtown Sacramento, was founded in 1885 and is the oldest public art museum west of the Mississippi River.

Rep. Lynn Woolsey (D)

Capitol Office
225-5161
woolsey.house.gov
2263 Rayburn Bldg. 20515-0506; fax 225-5163

Committees
Education & the Workforce
Science, Space & Technology

Residence
Petaluma

Born
Nov. 3, 1937; Seattle, Wash.

Religion
Presbyterian

Family
Divorced; four children

Education
U. of Washington, attended 1955-57 (business);
U. of San Francisco, B.S. 1980 (human resources &
organizational behavior)

Career
Employment placement company owner; human
resources manager

Political Highlights
Petaluma City Council, 1985-93

ELECTION RESULTS

2010 GENERAL

Lynn Woolsey (D)	172,216	65.9%
Jim Judd (R)	77,361	29.6%
Eugene E. Ruyle (PFP)	5,915	2.3%
Joel Smolen (LIBERT)	5,660	2.2%

2010 PRIMARY

Lynn Woolsey (D)	66,006	100.0%

2008 GENERAL

Lynn Woolsey (D)	229,672	71.7%
Mike Halliwell (R)	77,073	24.1%
Joel Smolen (LIBERT)	13,617	4.2%

Previous Winning Percentages
2006 (70%); 2004 (73%); 2002 (67%); 2000 (64%);
1998 (68%); 1996 (62%); 1994 (58%); 1992 (65%)

Elected 1992; 10th term

Woolsey is an impassioned voice against U.S. military action and a persistent advocate for women and children. As a former welfare recipient, she believes in the value of public assistance and that government has a role to play in balancing work and family life. But for all her dedication and agitation, some friends on the left have questioned her effectiveness, and she has publicly voiced the possibility of retiring at the end of the current Congress.

For three terms Woolsey (WOOL-zee) shared leadership of the Congressional Progressive Caucus, a collection of the House's most liberal members. She championed the group's alternative budgets with flamboyant rhetoric, and in 2009 she said anything less than a $1 trillion stimulus package "would be like trying to put out a forest fire with a squirt gun." Ultimately, she supported the lower-cost compromise.

Woolsey has followed that pattern — dramatic stands followed by acquiescence in a compromise — in other cases, and it sometimes results in scorching criticism from less malleable allies.

During the health care overhaul debate in the 111th Congress (2009-10), Woolsey helped lead a group of Democratic lawmakers who threatened to oppose any final bill that did not include a government-run "public option."

"We have put our party's leadership on notice that . . . a majority of the Progressive Caucus will only support health care legislation which includes a public option that will expand access, cut costs, and provide all consumers with a choice of plans," she wrote in The Huffington Post in June 2009.

After it became clear the votes were not there to include such a provision, Woolsey — like every other member of the group — supported the version that became law. That brought down a cascade of criticism from liberal bloggers, including a demand that she resign as co-chairwoman of the Progressive Caucus (she later said she would not seek another term). Woolsey defended her vote as in the best interests of her constituents. She said they told her, "'Don't be stubborn, we have to have something on health reform.'" She argued that this "meaningful first step" would expand coverage and correct "injustices" in the system.

At the end of the 111th Congress, though, she stood firm in her opposition to extending the George W. Bush-era tax cuts for the top tax brackets, voting against a bill that extended the rates for all income levels for two years.

Woolsey, who chaired the Education and Labor Subcommittee on Workforce Protections in the 111th Congress and serves as ranking member in the 112th (2011-12), focuses on workplace issues. She sponsored legislation that would expand protections provided by the Occupational Safety and Health Act of 1970. She also has offered in multiple Congresses a measure she calls the Balancing Act, which would authorize a menu of expanded leave options and in-school and after-school assistance intended to help people with children and other dependents cope with busy work schedules.

Woolsey secured provisions in the fiscal 2008 defense authorization bill allowing for six months of job-protected leave for family members who need time off to care for injured soldiers. The following year Congress extended leave to injured veterans' families.

On the Science and Technology Committee (renamed Science, Space and Technology in 2011), she pushed legislation to create a federal research program on oil spills, an issue important to many Californians. Combining her Science responsibilities with her egalitarian instincts, she offered a successful amendment requiring agencies' strategic plans to detail efforts to attract more women and minorities to pursue postsecondary degrees in networking and information technology to a bill that would boost research in those fields.

Woolsey has demonstrated a flair for the dramatic, most famously when she and California Democratic colleague Nancy Pelosi were expelled from a 1999 Senate hearing by Foreign Relations Chairman Jesse Helms, a North Carolina Republican. They were trying to publicize Helms' decision not to take up an international treaty against the discrimination of women.

But it is on the wars in Iraq and Afghanistan where she has made the biggest public impression. She was a strident opponent of the Iraq War and opposed President Obama's troop buildup in Afghanistan. She argues that the Afghan Taliban "aren't a particular threat to us anyway."

In 2007 Woolsey joined California Democratic Reps. Barbara Lee and Maxine Waters in taking anti-war rhetoric to states holding early presidential primaries. She told activists to "go after the Democrats" for not being tough enough about ending the war, even if it cost them their majority.

Woolsey grew up in Seattle in a Republican family. Her stepfather, a veterinarian, ran a small-animal clinic with her mother. In the 1950s she dropped out of college to get married and moved with her husband to the San Francisco suburbs. But the marriage fractured, and at 29 she was divorced with three preschool-age children.

She became a secretary, supplementing her income for three years with Aid to Families with Dependent Children. "I know firsthand what a difference it makes," Woolsey said. At 42 she graduated from the University of San Francisco while working a personnel management job. She also started her own human resources consulting company.

Woolsey says she was influenced by the election of President John F. Kennedy and drawn to the Democratic Party, but her entry into politics came decades later. In 1981, she joined a local effort to control development in Petaluma. She had been on the city council for several years when, in 1992, Democrat Barbara Boxer opened the district seat with a run for Senate. Woolsey beat a crowded field of nine candidates in the primary and faced a tough race against Republican Bill Filante, a liberal assemblyman. Filante had to end his campaign for health reasons, but it was too late to take his name off the ballot, and Woolsey coasted to a 31-percentage-point victory.

She typically has had easy re-elections, though in 2004 Woolsey had to deal with news reports that she tried to persuade a Marin County judge to reduce the sentence for an aide's son convicted of rape. She apologized and ended up taking 73 percent of the vote.

Key Votes

2010

Overhaul the nation's health insurance system	YES
Allow for repeal of "don't ask, don't tell"	YES
Overhaul financial services industry regulation	+
Limit use of new Afghanistan War funds to troop withdrawal activities	+
Change oversight of offshore drilling and lift oil spill liability cap	YES
Provide a path to legal status for some children of illegal immigrants	YES
Extend Bush-era income tax cuts for two years	NO

2009

Expand the Children's Health Insurance Program	YES
Provide $787 billion in tax cuts and spending increases to stimulate the economy	YES
Allow bankruptcy judges to modify certain primary-residence mortgages	YES
Create a cap-and-trade system to limit greenhouse gas emissions	YES
Provide $2 billion for the "cash for clunkers" program	YES
Establish the government as the sole provider of student loans	YES
Restrict federally funded insurance coverage for abortions in health care overhaul	NO

CQ Vote Studies

	PARTY UNITY		PRESIDENTIAL SUPPORT	
	SUPPORT	OPPOSE	SUPPORT	OPPOSE
2010	98%	2%	89%	11%
2009	98%	2%	92%	8%
2008	98%	2%	16%	84%
2007	99%	1%	6%	94%
2006	98%	2%	7%	93%

Interest Groups

	AFL-CIO	ADA	CCUS	ACU
2010	100%	100%	14%	0%
2009	100%	100%	33%	0%
2008	100%	80%	56%	4%
2007	96%	80%	40%	0%
2006	93%	100%	20%	4%

California 6

Northern Bay Area — Sonoma and Marin counties

Travel north across the Golden Gate Bridge and the scenery changes from the cityscape of San Francisco to the Pacific coastline and inland hills that make up the 6th District.

The 6th takes in all of Marin County, a very affluent area filled with highly educated residents, many of whom are self-employed or commute to San Francisco for high-tech or other white-collar jobs. Marin's suburban population is mainly divided between towns in the foothills of Mt. Tamalpais and waterfront locales like tony Sausalito, Tiburon and Stinson Beach. Home prices here have begun to recover after a housing market collapse, and unemployment rates remain lower than many regions of the state. Marin also is home to San Quentin State Prison — the state's oldest correctional facility — as well as San Rafael and popular getaway spots such as Point Reyes National Seashore and Muir Woods.

Wine and dairy ranching are key to the district's economy, and Sonoma County is one of the nation's leading producers of wine. Sonoma (shared with the 1st) has hundreds of wineries and is home to a California State

University campus and Santa Rosa, the district's largest city. Vineyard tours, tastings and sales form the bedrock of the local tourism industry. Some technology companies have made inroads in the district — Marin County hosts biomedical and software engineering firms — but the high cost of housing, commercial real estate prices and lack of developable land for expansion may continue to limit high-tech growth. Although Lucasfilm's Skywalker Ranch retreat is tucked among the hills in a remote area of Marin, the production company has followed many video game and software developers to San Francisco.

Solidly Democratic, the district's affluent residents, despite their wealth, tend to have progressive views. Democrats outnumber Republicans more than 2 to 1 in voter registration, and Democrat Jerry Brown took 68 percent of the district's 2010 gubernatorial vote.

Major Industry
Agriculture, telecommunications, tourism

Cities
Santa Rosa (pt.), 167,779; Petaluma, 57,941; San Rafael, 57,713

Notable
The Charles M. Schulz Museum in Santa Rosa celebrates the work of the "Peanuts" creator.

Rep. George Miller (D)

Capitol Office
225-2095
www.house.gov/georgemiller
2205 Rayburn Bldg. 20515-0507; fax 225-5609

Committees
Education & the Workforce - Ranking Member

Residence
Martinez

Born
May 17, 1945; Richmond, Calif.

Religion
Roman Catholic

Family
Wife, Cynthia Miller; two children

Education
San Francisco State U., B.A. 1968; U. of California,
Davis, J.D. 1972

Career
Lawyer; state legislative aide

Political Highlights
Democratic nominee for Calif. Senate, 1969

ELECTION RESULTS

2010 GENERAL

George Miller (D)	122,435	68.3%
Rick Tubbs (R)	56,764	31.7%

2010 PRIMARY

George Miller (D)	52,210	68.1%
John Fitzgerald (D)	9,188	12.0%

2008 GENERAL

George Miller (D)	170,962	72.8%
Roger Allen Petersen (R)	51,166	21.8%
Bill Callison (PFP)	6,695	2.8%
Camden McConnell (LIBERT)	5,950	2.5%

Previous Winning Percentages
2006 (84%); 2004 (76%); 2002 (71%); 2000 (76%);
1998 (77%); 1996 (72%); 1994 (70%); 1992 (70%);
1990 (61%); 1988 (68%); 1986 (67%); 1984 (66%);
1982 (67%); 1980 (63%); 1978 (63%); 1976 (75%);
1974 (56%)

Elected 1974; 19th term

A close ally of Minority Leader Nancy Pelosi, Miller has accumulated the institutional power and political connections to set his priorities in motion. While his abilities to push more funding for public education, stronger workers' rights and tougher consumer safety and environmental regulation are lessened by losing his chairmanship, he has been a force at the negotiating table whether in the majority or under Republicans with a vastly different agenda.

A founder of the Congressional Progressive Caucus, he encouraged Pelosi to run for a party leadership post in 2001 that set up her eventual run for Speaker. He benefited when she succeeded. Pelosi named him co-chairman of the Democratic Steering and Policy Committee, and he has headed the policy side of the operation since 2003.

As chairman of the Education and Labor Committee in the 110th and 111th Congresses (2007-10), Miller was a central player in obtaining more than $100 billion for education in the $787 billion economic stimulus bill. In final negotiations, he helped restore funds for some education programs that had been removed from the bill in the Senate. In the end, the legislation included dollars to shore up local school budgets and Pell grants, as well as money for school modernization and construction. The education program known as No Child Left Behind also received its full authorized funding for the first time — a matter that had been high on Miller's agenda since the law was enacted in 2002.

In a symbolic display of bipartisanship, Miller sat with the new GOP committee chairman, John Kline of Minnesota, at the 2011 State of the Union address and said he doesn't want to prejudge GOP ideas about reauthorizing the George W. Bush-era law.

Despite his longstanding efforts to boost education funding, Miller took some tough treatment from teachers unions when he proposed a major expansion in pay-for-performance funding in 2008. When Miller unveiled his proposal on his website, he ran into what he called a "mindless assault" from teachers unions. "Come on! This is about the future of this country," Miller later said of his proposal.

Miller's committee was the first to approve the health care overhaul in 2009. The overall measure, which included his proposal to make the government the sole provider of student loans, changed considerably before making it to President Obama's desk, but Miller was a constant presence at the negotiating table.

He saw success early in the 111th on the labor front as well, shepherding to enactment legislation dealing with wage discrimination against women. The House had previously passed the bill in 2007 before it stalled in the Senate.

On the other hand, he and Democratic Sen. Tom Harkin of Iowa unsuccessfully pushed politically charged legislation to make it easier to unionize workplaces without a secret ballot.

Miller has been exuberant in his support of Obama's secretary of Education, Arne Duncan. "To watch this secretary speak with this passion and this knowledge — I've been here 35 years, and this is about as good as it gets, and as exciting as things could possibly get," Miller said.

When Democrats took control of the House in 2007, he brought to fruition two items on the Democrats' "Six for '06" agenda: student loan interest rate cuts and a minimum wage increase. He also made good on promises for ramped-up labor protections, bolstering mine safety legislation and working to gain passage of a bill to ban job discrimination against gays and lesbians. Some of Miller's successes have stemmed from his willingness to bring in other leaders and GOP members when drafting legislation. Working on an overhaul of the Higher Education Act in 2007, he allowed subcommittee chairmen and influential GOP committee members to take the lead on substantial portions of the rewrite. House-Senate negotiations on the final version were a self-described "love fest."

Miller has also been around long enough to know how to exact revenge when he believes the occasion warrants it. He has frequently warned opponents that if they want to go head to head with him, "they better bring lunch." In the fall of 2009, a $32 million Miller-sponsored water bill designed to expand the Bay Area Regional Water Recycling Program did not win passage under a fast-track procedure that requires a two-thirds majority vote. Miller was especially irked by the "no" vote of California Republican John Campbell. Two weeks later, Miller used his gavel to pull from the schedule a Campbell resolution that would have congratulated the University of California-Irvine Anteaters men's volleyball champs, who are based in Campbell's district. Campbell told Roll Call that Miller was happy to explain why the bill didn't get a vote. "You voted against my water bill. . . . There has to be a penalty for that, and this is the penalty," Campbell recalled Miller saying. Miller's bill passed the following day; the Anteaters never got their day in the sun.

Democratic losses in 2010 pushed Miller off the Natural Resources Committee, where he had battled GOP attempts to revise environmental laws. He opposes drilling for oil off California's coast and in Alaska's Arctic National Wildlife Refuge.

Miller developed an interest in politics when he was growing up and watching his father, George Jr., broker legislative deals on water issues and education during a 20-year career in the state Senate. The Bay Area is home to a physical testament to the father and son's complementary — though decades apart — work: A bridge named for the younger Miller that opened in 2007 sits alongside an older bridge named for his father. His grandfather, George Miller Sr., was the assistant civil engineer in Richmond, Calif.

Miller was a law student in 1969 when his father died. He went to work as a legislative aide to state Sen. George Moscone, the Democratic floor leader and later San Francisco mayor. He was 29 in 1974 when he was elected to succeed Democratic Rep. Jerome Waldie, who ran unsuccessfully for governor. Miller won his seat in part by capitalizing on the Watergate scandal, which was fresh in voters' minds. He took 56 percent of the vote and has won re-election easily since.

Key Votes

2010

Overhaul the nation's health insurance system	YES
Allow for repeal of "don't ask, don't tell"	YES
Overhaul financial services industry regulation	YES
Limit use of new Afghanistan War funds to troop withdrawal activities	YES
Change oversight of offshore drilling and lift oil spill liability cap	YES
Provide a path to legal status for some children of illegal immigrants	YES
Extend Bush-era income tax cuts for two years	NO

2009

Expand the Children's Health Insurance Program	YES
Provide $787 billion in tax cuts and spending increases to stimulate the economy	YES
Allow bankruptcy judges to modify certain primary-residence mortgages	YES
Create a cap-and-trade system to limit greenhouse gas emissions	YES
Provide $2 billion for the "cash for clunkers" program	YES
Establish the government as the sole provider of student loans	YES
Restrict federally funded insurance coverage for abortions in health care overhaul	NO

CQ Vote Studies

	PARTY UNITY		PRESIDENTIAL SUPPORT	
	SUPPORT	OPPOSE	SUPPORT	OPPOSE
2010	99%	1%	88%	12%
2009	99%	1%	97%	3%
2008	99%	1%	13%	87%
2007	99%	1%	5%	95%
2006	98%	2%	13%	87%

Interest Groups

	AFL-CIO	ADA	CCUS	ACU
2010	100%	100%	13%	0%
2009	100%	95%	33%	0%
2008	100%	95%	50%	0%
2007	96%	100%	42%	0%
2006	92%	90%	29%	4%

California 7

Northeastern Bay Area — Vallejo, Richmond

Situated along the San Pablo Bay and the marshes and deltas where the Sacramento and San Joaquin rivers merge, the 7th combines industrial and suburban areas of northern Contra Costa County with the western end of more rural Solano County.

In Contra Costa County, the district takes in residential Concord (shared with the 10th) and the industrial cities of Richmond and Martinez along San Pablo Bay, home to oil, steel and biotech interests. Chevron facilities in Richmond are major employers, and Shell Oil operates a petroleum refinery in Martinez, the Contra Costa County seat. Cities in Contra Costa are recovering from high unemployment and foreclosure rates.

The 7th's military footprint, stamped down during World War II, is almost gone. Some of Richmond's former Kaiser Shipyards — one of the largest World War II shipbuilding operations — has been redeveloped. The inland half of Concord Naval Weapons Station closed in 1999, and its port, transferred in 2008 to the Army as Military Ocean Terminal, Concord, is the only remaining active military installation in the district.

Health care also is important to the district's economy. The medical system implemented during World War II at the Kaiser Shipyards was the foundation for the modern Kaiser Permanente health organization. Although it is still a key employer, the company has had to cut some jobs in the region. Pittsburg was once known for a thriving steel industry, but local officials hope to encourage economic diversification through redevelopment efforts.

The 7th is safe Democratic territory, as just 20 percent of its voters are registered Republicans. The district gave 67 percent of its vote to Democratic Gov. Jerry Brown in 2010.

Major Industry
Petrochemicals, steel, biotech, agriculture, health care

Military Bases
Military Ocean Terminal, Concord, 11 military, 91 civilian (2009)

Cities
Vallejo, 115,942; Richmond, 103,701; Vacaville (pt.), 92,412

Notable
The Rosie the Riveter World War II Home Front National Historical Park in Richmond commemorates the contributions of women who held industrial jobs in support of the war effort.

Rep. Nancy Pelosi (D)

Capitol Office
225-4965
www.house.gov/pelosi
235 Cannon Bldg. 20515-0508; fax 225-4188

Committees
No committee assignments

Residence
San Francisco

Born
March 26, 1940; Baltimore, Md.

Religion
Roman Catholic

Family
Husband, Paul Pelosi; five children

Education
Trinity College (D.C.), A.B. 1962

Career
Public relations consultant; senatorial campaign committee finance chairwoman; homemaker

Political Highlights
Calif. Democratic Party chairwoman, 1981-83

ELECTION RESULTS

2010 GENERAL

Nancy Pelosi (D)	167,957	80.1%
John Dennis (R)	31,711	15.1%
Gloria E. La Riva (PFP)	5,161	2.5%
Philip Berg (LIBERT)	4,843	2.3%

2010 PRIMARY

Nancy Pelosi (D)	unopposed

2008 GENERAL

Nancy Pelosi (D)	204,996	71.9%
Cindy Sheehan (I)	46,118	16.2%
Dana Walsh (R)	27,614	9.7%
Philip Berg (LIBERT)	6,504	2.3%

Previous Winning Percentages
2006 (80%); 2004 (83%); 2002 (80%); 2000 (84%); 1998 (86%); 1996 (84%); 1994 (82%); 1992 (82%); 1990 (77%); 1988 (76%); 1987 Special Runoff Election (63%)

Elected 1987; 12th full term

Pelosi, the first female Speaker of the House, established herself as a unique historical figure by breaking through what she calls the "marble ceiling" — in 2002 she became the first woman to lead a party caucus, and in 2007, the first to lead the House.

Beyond that, she was able to lead the typically tough-to-rein-in Democrats with an iron determination, in the face of scornful Republican opposition, to accomplish far-reaching legislative goals that she, President Obama and other congressional leaders laid out.

And, even after a crushing electoral rejection of her party in which her leadership was a central campaign theme, Pelosi's Democratic colleagues voted to keep her as minority leader in the 112th Congress (2011-12).

Still, 18 Democrats voted for someone other than Pelosi for Speaker. "Most great leaders step down after their troops get massacred," Oregon Democrat Kurt Schrader told Roll Call. "That didn't happen. I think someone has to take responsibility for that. At the end of the day, regardless of how you feel about the Speaker, she was the symbol."

That symbolic show of defiance seemed not to have phased Pelosi in the least. She kept her leadership team intact and said in a welcome-back speech to the Congressional Black Caucus that "two years from now when we come together, things will be different."

Whether that prediction comes to pass or not, Pelosi has cemented her legacy. In shepherding the $787 billion economic stimulus bill to enactment in the first month of Obama's presidency, passing the health care overhaul, rewriting Wall Street regulations and getting a cap-and-trade plan through the House, Pelosi was involved in the intimate details of big legislation. When it came time to cut the make-or-break deals to push bills forward, it was Pelosi — not the relevant committee chairmen — who made the final decisions. That's exactly what happened on health care: Pelosi negotiated with Michigan's Bart Stupak, leader of Democratic anti-abortion forces in the House, on language that Stupak and his allies found acceptable, providing the winning margin for the House version of the legislative package.

The concentration of such power in the hands of Pelosi, who is widely admired by Democrats and regularly used as a campaign foil by Republicans to mobilize their conservative base, is something that hasn't been seen in the Speaker's office in decades.

But even as she expanded her office's power, Pelosi kept the loyalty of her leadership team and committee chairmen. This is particularly notable because she has had a long and at times contentious relationship with Minority Whip Steny H. Hoyer of Maryland. The two first met in the early 1960s when they both worked in the offices of then-Maryland Democratic Sen. Daniel B. Brewster. After the Democratic victory in the 2006 elections, Pelosi backed her close friend, John P. Murtha of Pennsylvania, as he competed with Hoyer for the majority leader's post. But Hoyer easily defeated him when the caucus voted.

Pelosi admits her biggest disappointment in the 110th (2007-08) and 111th (2009-10) Congresses was the failure to end the war in Iraq, which she had opposed from the outset. The Democratic House voted again and again for a timetable to withdraw, but the idea was either blocked in the Senate or vetoed by Bush. And after Obama was elected, she said she was forced to make the toughest appeal of her career to her fellow anti-war Democrats by asking them to vote for the money to continue operations in Iraq as a way of giving

Obama time to implement his plan to draw down the number of troops. By September 2010, the military had pulled the last combat troops out of Iraq; that summer, she was among those in a divided caucus who voted for a plan to impose a withdrawal timetable for U.S. forces in Afghanistan.

All this political and policy wheeling and dealing seems to come naturally to Pelosi. Her father was Thomas D'Alesandro Jr., a New Deal Democratic congressman from Baltimore who also served three terms as that city's mayor. Growing up in a corner row house in crowded Little Italy, politics was a family affair for Pelosi and her five brothers. They took turns staffing a desk in the D'Alesandro home, where constituents would come by to ask for help finding a job or a doctor, getting food or making the rent. It was a lesson in retail politics, where favors and constituent services could translate into votes and loyalty. And she recalled that her mother, Anunciata (for whom she is named), played a major behind-the-scenes role in D'Alesandro's long political success.

Pelosi attended Catholic schools in Baltimore, then went to Trinity College in Washington. It was while attending Trinity that she met San Franciscan Paul Pelosi, who was a student at Georgetown University. They married in 1963 and Pelosi gave birth to her five children over the next six years while the couple lived in New York City.

The Pelosis moved back to Paul's hometown and she became increasingly active in Democratic Party politics in a city that was refashioning itself into a bastion of Democratic liberalism. She rose to become state party chairwoman and played a role in hosting the 1984 Democratic National Convention.

She became a close ally of Rep. Philip Burton, the firebrand Democratic liberal from San Francisco who had narrowly lost a race for majority leader and whose brother, former Rep. John Burton, remains a close Pelosi friend.

When Burton died in 1983, he was succeeded by his widow, Sala Burton, another of Pelosi's friends who had a reputation as a tough, focused politician. Pelosi's career in elective politics began in 1987, when Sala Burton was stricken with cancer and personally summoned Pelosi to her hospital room to ask her to run for the seat. With her youngest child in high school, Pelosi took the plunge, winning a wild Democratic primary and runoff to score a victory in her first run for public office.

Since her first election, Pelosi has been re-elected overwhelmingly in a district that covers about three-quarters of the city's 47 square miles. Her 2008 victory, with 72 percent of the vote, was unusually low because she faced a strong challenger from the left: anti-Iraq War activist Cindy Sheehan, who ran as an independent. Pelosi won with 80 percent of the vote in 2010.

Key Votes

2010

Overhaul the nation's health insurance system	YES
Allow for repeal of "don't ask, don't tell"	YES
Overhaul financial services industry regulation	YES
Limit use of new Afghanistan War funds to troop withdrawal activities	S
Change oversight of offshore drilling and lift oil spill liability cap	YES
Provide a path to legal status for some children of illegal immigrants	YES
Extend Bush-era income tax cuts for two years	S

2009

Expand the Children's Health Insurance Program	YES
Provide $787 billion in tax cuts and spending increases to stimulate the economy	YES
Allow bankruptcy judges to modify certain primary-residence mortgages	YES
Create a cap-and-trade system to limit greenhouse gas emissions	YES
Provide $2 billion for the "cash for clunkers" program	S
Establish the government as the sole provider of student loans	YES
Restrict federally funded insurance coverage for abortions in health care overhaul	NO

CQ Vote Studies

	PARTY UNITY		PRESIDENTIAL SUPPORT	
	SUPPORT	OPPOSE	SUPPORT	OPPOSE
2010	100%	0%	95%	5%
2009	100%	0%	100%	0%
2008	98%	2%	25%	75%
2007	99%	1%	5%	95%
2006	98%	2%	25%	75%

Interest Groups

	AFL-CIO	ADA	CCUS	ACU
2010	100%		0%	0%
2009	100%		17%	0%
2008	100%	50%	38%	0%
2007	100%		22%	0%
2006	93%	95%	40%	8%

California 8

Most of San Francisco

San Francisco is famous for its landmarks, food and diverse collection of neighborhoods, from the Italian and Hispanic centers of North Beach and the Mission District to Chinatown, hippie haven Haight-Ashbury and the gay mecca of Castro.

More than 80 percent of the city's residents live in the 8th, which takes in the city's north and east and at 35 square miles is the state's smallest district. The 8th's sizable Asian population is the sixth-largest in the country. The Chinatown neighborhood is one of the largest Chinese communities in North America.

The city boasts many tourist destinations. Alcatraz prison — used as a federal maximum-security facility from 1934 to 1963 and where Al Capone, George "Machine Gun" Kelly and Robert "Birdman" Stroud were once jailed — receives more than 1 million visitors annually.

Other popular attractions include: Fisherman's Wharf, on the city's northern waterfront; the Golden Gate Bridge, which connects San Francisco to Marin County; and the Bay Bridge, which traverses the neck of the bay over Treasure Island to Oakland. The city's part of the Golden Gate National Recreation Area hosts a Lucasfilm facility that opened in 2005 on the site of the former Letterman Army Medical Center at the Presidio.

The 8th also is home to San Francisco's financial district along Montgomery Street, known as the "Wall Street of the West."

The Federal Reserve Bank of San Francisco is there, as is the Transamerica Pyramid and the headquarters of brokerage firm Charles Schwab.

The city also has a biomedical industry led by the University of California at San Francisco, the city's second-largest employer after local government. The Democratic Party dominates the 8th.

In the 2008 presidential election, Barack Obama sailed to victory here with 85 percent of the district's vote. In 2010, Democrat Jerry Brown took 80 percent of the district's gubernatorial vote.

Major Industry
Tourism, financial services, health care

Cities
San Francisco (pt.), 666,827

Notable
The city's famous cable cars were developed by Andrew Smith Hallidie after he witnessed an accident involving a horse-drawn streetcar.

Rep. Barbara Lee (D)

Capitol Office
225-2661
www.house.gov/lee
2267 Rayburn Bldg. 20515-0509; fax 225-9817

Committees
Appropriations

Residence
Oakland

Born
July 16, 1946; El Paso, Texas

Religion
Baptist

Family
Divorced; two children

Education
Mills College, B.A. 1973 (psychology); U. of California, Berkeley, M.S.W. 1975

Career
Congressional aide

Political Highlights
Calif. Assembly, 1990-96; Calif. Senate, 1996-98

ELECTION RESULTS

2010 GENERAL

Barbara Lee (D)	180,400	84.3%
Gerald Hashimoto (R)	23,054	10.8%
Dave Heller (GREEN)	4,848	2.3%
James Eyer (LIBERT)	4,113	1.9%

2010 PRIMARY

Barbara Lee (D)	unopposed

2008 GENERAL

Barbara Lee (D)	238,915	86.1%
Charles Hargrave (R)	26,917	9.7%
James Eyer (LIBERT)	11,704	4.2%

Previous Winning Percentages
2006 (86%); 2004 (85%); 2002 (81%); 2000 (85%); 1998 (83%); 1998 Special Election (67%)

Elected 1998; 7th full term

Lee's status as the embodiment of the far left wing of her party has been enhanced by her ascension to the powerful Appropriations Committee. As a passionate supporter of liberal causes and a sometimes lonely foe of U.S. military action, she is often regarded as outside the mainstream even of her own party. But her politics are a perfect fit for her northern California constituency.

Representing some of the most liberal communities in her state and the nation, Lee is generally unfazed by the fact that her politics are more radical than those of most elected officials.

"What I've tried to do over the years is help the Democratic Party become more Democratic . . . to push the party to be what I think the true Democratic Party should be," she said.

In 2001, she was the only member of Congress to vote against authorizing President George W. Bush to use force in response to the Sept. 11, 2001, terrorist attacks. It was a vote roundly criticized in many quarters, but her fans endorsed it: In Santa Cruz, they declared the following July 2 "Barbara Lee Day."

Since her first election to Congress, Lee has been an outspoken advocate for abortion rights, environmentalism and using the powers of the federal government to improve the lot of the less fortunate.

She won a coveted spot on the Appropriations Committee in the 110th Congress (2007-09). In the 112th (2011-12), she will have a hand in writing the spending bills for the departments of Labor, Health and Human Services, Education and the Treasury.

Formerly a member of the Foreign Affairs Committee, she has been a leader in the fight against AIDS at home and abroad as an original cosponsor of a five-year, $19 billion international AIDS measure Bush signed into law in 2003. She also cosponsored an expansion of the program in 2008. Another law she spearheaded bars foreign companies from receiving U.S. government contracts if they invest in Sudan, where the Sudanese government is accused of carrying out genocide in the Darfur region.

Most recently, Lee offered an amendment to the fiscal 2010 supplemental war appropriations package that would have required the withdrawal of U.S. troops and military contractors from Afghanistan. Though the amendment was not adopted by the House, she was heartened by the 100 votes it garnered. "This is coming from having cast the only vote in 2001 against it," she said.

Lee also carved out a niche for herself as chairwoman of the Congressional Black Caucus in the 111th Congress (2009-10). From that perch, she helped shape the final health care overhaul bill President Obama signed into law in 2010. She pushed successfully for the expansion of health clinics in minority communities to be included in the law, though she failed in her efforts to include a government-run insurance program in the legislation.

She called the January 2011 House vote to repeal the law "a sham and a shame."

Lee's focus on social justice was born out of her own early memories of inequality and discrimination. In 1946 in El Paso, Texas, her mother, in labor with Lee, was initially refused treatment at the hospital because she was black.

"My grandmother, who looked like she was white, had to convince the hospital that this was her daughter so they would admit her," Lee said.

But she was left unattended for so long that she became delirious with pain. Lee was ultimately delivered at the last minute with forceps, which left a mark on her forehead for years to come. "My birth put me on the path" of progressive politics, Lee said. "You look at the fact that I almost didn't get into this world, almost died — almost was not born — because of racism. My whole life has been about trying to make life better for people who were discriminated against, shut out and disenfranchised."

Lee spent her early years in El Paso, where the public school system was segregated. She and her sister attended a Catholic school where, Lee said, they were the only black students.

Her family moved to Southern California in 1960. Her public high school had never chosen a black cheerleader, so she set about to become the first. With the help of the NAACP, she put pressure on the selection committee to make the audition process more transparent and inclusive, and was ulti-mately awarded a spot on the team.

Lee first registered to vote in 1972, when a course at Mills College in Oakland required her to work for a political campaign. She was, at first, prepared to flunk the class: "I didn't feel the two-party system, or politics, was a way to make change," she recalled.

But her outlook shifted when Democratic Rep. Shirley Chisholm of New York came to Mills to speak before the Black Student Union, which Lee headed. Chisholm, after becoming the first African-American woman to be elected to Congress, was also readying herself to become the first black female candidate for president.

"I went up to her and talked to her about this class I was getting ready to flunk," Lee said, "and she took me to task and said, she's running for presi-dent, so why didn't I help her?"

Lee was inspired by Chisholm's progressive agenda and social conscious-ness. She registered to vote and went on to run the Chisholm for President Northern California campaign. In the end, she got an "A" in the course, a passion for politics and a new belief in the potential of enacting change within the two-party system, further reinforced after working for another liberal Democrat, Ronald V. Dellums of California.

In 1975, after earning a master's degree in social work, Lee went to work for Dellums in California and Washington. She then ran for the state legislature and served for six terms in the Assembly and 17 months in the Senate.

When Dellums decided to leave Congress in 1998, he endorsed Lee to succeed him. She easily won the special election and has coasted to re-election since.

Key Votes

2010

Overhaul the nation's health insurance system	YES
Allow for repeal of "don't ask, don't tell"	YES
Overhaul financial services industry regulation	YES
Limit use of new Afghanistan War funds to troop withdrawal activities	YES
Change oversight of offshore drilling and lift oil spill liability cap	YES
Provide a path to legal status for some children of illegal immigrants	YES
Extend Bush-era income tax cuts for two years	NO

2009

Expand the Children's Health Insurance Program	YES
Provide $787 billion in tax cuts and spend-ing increases to stimulate the economy	YES
Allow bankruptcy judges to modify certain primary-residence mortgages	YES
Create a cap-and-trade system to limit greenhouse gas emissions	YES
Provide $2 billion for the "cash for clunkers" program	YES
Establish the government as the sole provider of student loans	YES
Restrict federally funded insurance cover-age for abortions in health care overhaul	NO

CQ Vote Studies

	PARTY UNITY		PRESIDENTIAL SUPPORT	
	SUPPORT	OPPOSE	SUPPORT	OPPOSE
2010	98%	2%	85%	15%
2009	99%	1%	93%	7%
2008	99%	1%	14%	86%
2007	98%	2%	9%	91%
2006	99%	1%	7%	93%

Interest Groups

	AFL-CIO	ADA	CCUS	ACU
2010	93%	95%	0%	0%
2009	100%	100%	33%	0%
2008	100%	100%	41%	4%
2007	96%	90%	45%	0%
2006	93%	100%	20%	4%

California 9

Northwest Alameda County — Oakland, Berkeley

Across the bay from San Francisco, the 9th District is anchored by Oakland and Berkeley, two racially diverse, liberal communities.

A majority of district residents live in Oakland, which is more than one-fourth black. Oakland's unemployment rate is above the national average and crime is a major concern, while areas in the city's eastern hills tend to be wealthy and less diverse. Urban revitalization efforts and downtown de-velopment lured new residents and businesses into the area and bolstered the local economy, but statewide budget shortfalls have hampered contin-ued growth. The city may struggle to finance a new stadium and keep the Athletics baseball team in Oakland.

The 9th also includes the fast-growing bayside city of Emeryville, which is home to commercial development and biotech firms. Other high-tech companies include animation studio Pixar, educational technology devel-oper LeapFrog, and software and wireless technology firms.

Just north of Oakland, Berkeley is home to the flagship campus of the Uni-versity of California system and looks out over the bay from the Berkeley Hills.

The rest of the district includes smaller communities such as Albany, a liberal suburb at the north end of the district; Piedmont, a residential city entirely surrounded by Oakland's hills; and unincorporated sections of Alameda County southeast of Oakland: Ashland, Castro Valley, Cherryland and Fairview. With a core constituency in left-leaning Oakland and Berkeley, the 9th is a Democratic stronghold where Republicans account for less than 10 percent of registered voters. Barack Obama had his best showing in the state here in the 2008 presidential election, capturing 88 percent of the district's vote, and former Oakland mayor Jerry Brown took his statewide highest percentage (85 percent) and total number of votes here in the 2010 gubernatorial election.

Major Industry
Biotech, shipping

Cities
Oakland (pt.), 390,687; Berkeley, 112,580; Castro Valley (unincorporated) (pt.), 61,284; Ashland (unincorporated), 21,925

Notable
Wham-O Toys, based in Emeryville, has marketed many famous toys, including the Frisbee, Hula Hoop, Hacky Sack and Slip 'n Slide; the synthetic element Berkelium was created at UC-Berkeley.

Rep. John Garamendi (D)

Capitol Office
225-1880
garamendi.house.gov/
228 Cannon Bldg. 20515-0510; fax 225-5914

Committees
Armed Services
Natural Resources

Residence
Walnut Grove

Born
Jan. 24, 1945; Camp Blanding, Fla.

Religion
Christian

Family
Wife, Patricia Wilkinson Garamendi; six children

Education
U. of California, Berkeley, B.S. 1966 (business administration); Harvard U., M.B.A. 1970

Career
Rancher; Peace Corps volunteer

Political Highlights
Calif. Assembly, 1974-76; Calif. Senate, 1976-90 (majority leader, 1982-84); sought Democratic nomination for governor, 1982; sought Democratic nomination for Calif. controller, 1986; Calif. insurance commissioner, 1991-95; sought Democratic nomination for governor, 1994; deputy Interior secretary, 1995-98; Calif. insurance commissioner, 2003-07; lieutenant governor, 2007-09

ELECTION RESULTS

2010 GENERAL

John Garamendi (D)	137,578	58.8%
Gary Clift (R)	88,512	37.9%
Jeremy Cloward (GREEN)	7,716	3.3%

2010 PRIMARY

John Garamendi (D)	unopposed

2009 SPECIAL

John Garamendi (D)	72,817	52.8%
David Harmer (R)	59,017	42.8%
Jeremy Cloward (GREEN)	2,515	1.8%
Mary C. McIlroy (PFP)	1,846	1.3%
Jerry Denham (AMI)	1,591	1.2%

Elected 2009; 1st full term

Garamendi's previous work as deputy Interior secretary and California insurance commissioner quickly made him a player in congressional policy debates during his first term. Known for a self-confidence that some say borders on arrogance, the outspoken liberal's familiarity with health care and offshore oil drilling — honed during three decades in elective and appointive office before arriving in the House — has served him well.

"My years of experience in different places continues to play out here," said the tall, handsome Garamendi, who was a heavyweight wrestler and football player at the University of California at Berkeley.

Garamendi's career in the House — he was elected in 2009 to fill out the term of fellow Democrat Ellen O. Tauscher after she became undersecretary of State for arms control and international disarmament — started with a bang. Just a few days after he was sworn in, he voted for the House version of a health care overhaul bill. "It was so satisfying to arrive here and one or two days later to vote on the reform and then work on improving the insurance reform element" in the legislation that eventually was enacted, he said.

But, Garamendi said, the overhaul won't be complete until the health insurance industry's antitrust exemption is abolished. Such a change was included in the House's original package, but was dropped by the Senate and then not included in the final bill signed by President Obama in March 2010.

He capped his first term by opposing the extension of the Bush-era tax cuts enacted in December 2010, arguing that the measure's partial payroll tax holiday would endanger Social Security.

"For the first time ever in the history of Social Security, we are now going to fund Social Security from the general fund," he said on the Fox News Channel. "That is extremely risky."

The first bill Garamendi introduced in Congress drew on his experience at Interior and his long years as a California environmentalist. The legislation, written in response to the spring 2010 Gulf of Mexico oil spill, would make permanent the ban on offshore drilling in federal waters off California, Oregon and Washington. Garamendi contends the Gulf spill reinforced what he learned as deputy to Interior Secretary Bruce Babbitt from 1995 to 1998: that the Minerals Management Service, the agency responsible for overseeing offshore drilling safety, has been ineffective and resistant to change for a long time. "It's the handmaiden of the industry," he said, noting that the Obama administration has begun to redirect the agency. The administration announced plans in January 2011 to split the agency into two new organizations.

His support of gay and lesbian rights, a government-run health care program, gun control and climate change legislation make him a favorite among liberal voters in the strongly Democratic 10th District. In the November 2009 special election to replace Tauscher, he enjoyed strong name recognition, already having served 14 years as a state legislator (including two as Senate majority leader), two terms as the state's insurance commissioner, three years at Interior and two years as lieutenant governor under Republican Arnold Schwarzenegger.

California's governor and lieutenant governor are elected separately, and the Schwarzenegger-Garamendi relationship was uneasy at best. After he called Schwarzenegger the "worst governor in California history" early in 2009, the governor stripped Garamendi of most of his office budget.

In the House, Garamendi moved quickly to get committee assignments matching his district's interests and biggest employers. He won a seat on the

Armed Services Committee, where Tauscher also served, to look out for Travis Air Force Base, which has a total of 15,000 military and civilian employees. From the Science and Technology Committee, he kept an eye out for the Livermore and Sandia National Laboratories, two of the nation's main nuclear weapons research facilities. Together, the labs have about 8,000 employees. He left the Science panel in the 112th in favor of the Natural Resources Committee, where he can champion his environmental causes.

Garamendi's career has had its share of disappointments, as his aspirations for California's top elected offices have been thwarted.

He entered the state Assembly at age 29, soon after completing Harvard Business School, and two years later jumped to the state Senate. In the middle of his Senate tenure, in 1982, he unsuccessfully sought the Democratic nomination for governor. Four years later, he made another failed bid, but for the Democratic nomination for controller.

But he won a race to become California's first elected insurance commissioner, serving from 1991 to 1995 and developing enemies in the industry for forcing rate rollbacks.

His colleagues in the state Senate dumped him from the majority leader's job after just two years, saying he was too focused on his own political ambitions, according to the Los Angeles Times.

Garamendi lost the 1994 Democratic nomination for governor to state Treasurer Kathleen Brown, sister of Gov. Jerry Brown. President Bill Clinton then hired him as deputy secretary of the Interior. Garamendi later returned to California and reclaimed his job as insurance commissioner after a successor, Chuck Quackenbush, was forced to resign amid a campaign finance scandal. Garamendi then won the race for lieutenant governor in 2006.

He had initially planned to run for governor in 2010 but abandoned that effort when he was down in the polls and Tauscher was nominated for the State Department position.

Garamendi owns a cattle ranch in Mokelumne Hill, in the Sierra foothills, and grew up on a ranch nearby. He married his wife, Patti, while a senior at Berkeley; strongly affected by the assassination of President John F. Kennedy, the pair joined the Peace Corps and spent two years in Ethiopia.

During the 2009 special election campaign, Garamendi topped the 15-candidate primary field with 26 percent of the vote — far short of the majority he needed to win the seat without proceeding to a general election. He defeated Republican businessman David Harmer in the general by 10 percentage points. In 2010, he defeated GOP candidate Gary Clift by 20 percentage points.

Key Votes

2010

Overhaul the nation's health insurance system	YES
Allow for repeal of "don't ask, don't tell"	YES
Overhaul financial services industry regulation	YES
Limit use of new Afghanistan War funds to troop withdrawal activities	YES
Change oversight of offshore drilling and lift oil spill liability cap	YES
Provide a path to legal status for some children of illegal immigrants	YES
Extend Bush-era income tax cuts for two years	NO

2009

Restrict federally funded insurance coverage for abortions in health care overhaul	NO

CQ Vote Studies

	PARTY UNITY		PRESIDENTIAL SUPPORT	
	SUPPORT	OPPOSE	SUPPORT	OPPOSE
2010	99%	1%	83%	17%
2009	100%	0%	100%	0%

Interest Groups

	AFL-CIO	ADA	CCUS	ACU
2010	100%	100%	0%	0%
2009	100%		14%	0%

California 10

East Bay suburbs — Fairfield, Antioch, Livermore

Travel through the Caldecott Tunnel across the Alameda-Contra Costa county line or on Interstate 680 during rush hour and you will likely be surrounded by 10th District residents commuting to and from San Francisco or San Jose. Separated from the rest of the Bay Area by the hills east of Oakland, the 10th's residents are mainly well-educated, wealthy professionals who work outside the district.

Residents here are a mix of an older generation that moved in from Oakland and newer, younger commuters who identify more with San Francisco or Berkeley. Almost two-thirds of residents live in the 10th's portion of Contra Costa County, including Antioch and most of Concord (shared with the 7th). Housing market concerns and job losses have affected the East Bay. The district's Solano County portion, which includes Fairfield, is a growing but still largely agricultural area where commuters may head south to the Bay Area or northeast to Sacramento. Travis Air Force Base also provides a significant source of jobs in the county.

The 10th is home to two Energy Department defense program laboratories that form the hub of the district's high-tech sector. Lawrence Livermore National Laboratory is one of the country's leading centers of experimental physics research and defense analysis, and the California branch of the Sandia National Laboratory provides engineering support and systems integration for nuclear weapons.

The 10th has a relatively moderate political character — residents tend to be more fiscally conservative but share their Bay Area neighbors' views on the environment and other quality-of-life issues. The combination of the working-class agricultural sector and more moderate, but still largely liberal, suburbanites helps tilt the 10th Democratic. Barack Obama won 65 percent of the district's 2008 presidential vote.

Major Industry
Research, health care, agriculture, service

Military bases
Travis Air Force Base, 7,393 military, 3,692 civilian (2011)

Cities
Fairfield (pt.), 104,969; Antioch (pt.), 102,309; Livermore, 80,968

Notable
The world's oldest-known working light bulb, first installed in 1901, is housed by the Livermore-Pleasanton Fire Department.

Rep. Jerry McNerney (D)

Capitol Office
225-1947
mcnerney.house.gov
1210 Longworth Bldg. 20515-0511; fax 225-4060

Committees
Science, Space & Technology
Veterans' Affairs

Residence
Pleasanton

Born
June 18, 1951; Albuquerque, N.M.

Religion
Roman Catholic

Family
Wife, Mary McNerney; three children

Education
U.S. Military Academy, attended 1969-71; U. of New Mexico, B.S. 1973 (mathematics), M.S. 1975 (mathematics), Ph.D. 1981 (mathematics)

Career
Wind engineering company owner; wind engineer; renewable energy consultant and researcher

Political Highlights
Democratic nominee for U.S. House, 2004

ELECTION RESULTS

2010 GENERAL

Jerry McNerney (D)	115,361	48.0%
David Harmer (R)	112,703	46.9%
David Christensen (AMI)	12,439	5.2%

2010 PRIMARY

Jerry McNerney (D)	unopposed

2008 GENERAL

Jerry McNerney (D)	164,500	55.3%
Dean Andal (R)	133,104	44.7%

Previous Winning Percentages
2006 (53%)

Elected 2006; 3rd term

A loyal Democrat, McNerney focuses on parochial issues in the formerly Republican-leaning district, where his experience as a wind turbine executive gives him an edge on energy issues. He advocates greater usage of electric vehicles, ethanol, biodiesel and other renewable-energy sources, and is skeptical of expanding drilling for oil and natural gas.

His professional experience in the renewable-energy field and a kinship with a pair of influential fellow California Democrats, then-Speaker Nancy Pelosi and Energy and Commerce Chairman Henry A. Waxman, helped him secure a spot on the powerful panel in the 111th Congress (2009-10). But, with Democrats back in the minority in the 112th (2011-12), Pelosi and Waxman lost their gavels and McNerney lost his prized committee assignment.

He supported the Democrats' doomed 2009 plan to restrict carbon emissions by creating a cap-and-trade program, a bill that played a role in ending the careers of many of his Democratic colleagues. After casting his vote, McNerney said, "We are one step closer to revitalizing our nation's economy and cutting our dependence on foreign oil" and said it will "lay the foundation for our country's long-term economic prosperity."

McNerney represents a district with a narrow partisan divide, but his voting record is solidly liberal.

In the 111th Congress, McNerney backed the Democrats' health care overhaul, financial industry regulatory changes and $787 billion stimulus package. He called the health care bill "a critical step toward making health care more affordable for American families and helping to guarantee our nation's long-term economic prosperity."

He also has backed an increase in the minimum wage; an expansion of the Children's Health Insurance Program, which covers children from low-income families that make too much money to qualify for Medicaid; and a ban on job discrimination based on sexual orientation.

Among the issues that spurred McNerney's decision to run for Congress was his frustration with the Iraq War. Throughout his 2006 campaign, which was fueled by donations from anti-war activists and environmentalists, McNerney touted his opposition to the war and advocated for withdrawal. Yet he angered those supporters in late 2007, when, after returning from his sole visit to Iraq, he said he was willing to negotiate the details of a phased withdrawal.

When McNerney strays from Democratic leadership, it's usually on an issue that unites his typically divided constituency, which includes Silicon Valley executives and multigenerational farm owners.

In December 2010, he backed a two-year extension of the Bush-era tax cuts for all income levels. "On the whole, I believe this bill will create jobs and help the economy recover," McNerney told the Lodi News-Sentinel. In 2007, he supported a Republican-sponsored bill to repeal the estate tax.

In his first term, McNerney sat on the Science and Technology Committee, and he returned to the panel, renamed Science, Space and Technology, in the 112th. In his first go-round, he pushed through a bill in 2007 to authorize $80 million annually through fiscal 2012 to support the development and use of geothermal energy technologies. Despite bipartisan committee support, Democratic leaders didn't move it to the floor. In March 2007, he obtained bipartisan support in the House for a bill to authorize $125 million to extend a pilot program aimed at developing alternative water source projects. But the measure stalled in the Senate.

McNerney said he did not get discouraged by the failure of those measures to advance. "It was always fun to speak up on these issues," he said. "And I could show up a little bit, even though I was this little freshman back here in the very last chair of the committee."

He also sits on the Veterans Affairs Committee, where he supported a 2008 bill that called for a new 10-year veterans' education plan at a cost of almost $62 billion. He also pushed through the committee a bill to create a special panel within the Department of Veterans Affairs to assess the ability of the federal government to treat veterans with traumatic brain injury.

McNerney was born in Albuquerque, N.M., the youngest of five children. His father was a civil engineer; his mother was a secretary at a local high school. His political roots stem from his dad, who was a San Francisco union organizer before serving in the Philippines during World War II and eventually earning his engineering degree.

McNerney and his twin brother, John, attended St. Joseph's Military Academy in Hays, Kan. He won appointment to the U.S. Military Academy in 1969 but left West Point two years later because he opposed the Vietnam War. He registered for the draft but was not called. Subsequently, he enrolled at the University of New Mexico, eventually earning a Ph.D. in mathematics — he is the only member of Congress to earn a doctorate in that field.

He worked several years for Sandia National Laboratories in New Mexico before moving to Massachusetts, then to California for a senior engineering position with U.S. Windpower, later called Kenetech Corp. Just prior to his election to Congress, he was an energy consultant and CEO of a startup company that manufactures wind turbines.

A quiet frustration with national politics probably would have remained masked had McNerney's son not urged him to challenge Republican Richard W. Pombo in the 2004 election. An Air Force reservist, McNerney's son had received an absentee ballot and was furious to see Pombo — a blunt-talking conservative who frequently clashed with environmentalists — running unopposed. McNerney lost to Pombo in the general election by 23 percentage points.

But in 2006, with strong backing from environmental groups, he defeated Pombo, the Resources Committee chairman, by 7 percentage points. McNerney was the first candidate in more than a decade to oust a sitting chairman. In 2008, he bested Republican Dean Andal by 10 percentage points. In 2010, he ran one of the closest House races in the country. In a contest not decided until three weeks after Election Day, McNerney defeated Republican lawyer David Harmer by 2,658 votes.

Key Votes

2010

Overhaul the nation's health insurance system	YES
Allow for repeal of "don't ask, don't tell"	YES
Overhaul financial services industry regulation	YES
Limit use of new Afghanistan war funds to troop withdrawal activities	NO
Change oversight of offshore drilling and lift oil spill liability cap	YES
Provide a path to legal status for some children of illegal immigrants	YES
Extend Bush-era income tax cuts for two years	YES

2009

Expand the Children's Health Insurance Program	YES
Provide $787 billion in tax cuts and spending increases to stimulate the economy	YES
Allow bankruptcy judges to modify certain primary-residence mortgages	YES
Create a cap-and-trade system to limit greenhouse gas emissions	YES
Provide $2 billion for the "cash for clunkers" program	YES
Establish the government as the sole provider of student loans	YES
Restrict federally funded insurance coverage for abortions in health care overhaul	NO

CQ Vote Studies

	PARTY UNITY		PRESIDENTIAL SUPPORT	
	SUPPORT	OPPOSE	SUPPORT	OPPOSE
2010	91%	9%	86%	14%
2009	90%	10%	93%	7%
2008	93%	7%	17%	83%
2007	91%	9%	4%	96%

Interest Groups

	AFL-CIO	ADA	CCUS	ACU
2010	93%	85%	25%	8%
2009	100%	100%	40%	12%
2008	100%	85%	61%	13%
2007	96%	95%	50%	4%

California 11

San Joaquin Valley; inland East Bay; part of Stockton

A mix of commuter bedroom communities east of the San Francisco Bay and inland agricultural country, the wrench-shaped 11th runs along Interstate 680 and south past San Jose, while the north end surrounds Stockton on three sides (central Stockton is in the 18th District).

The 11th includes nearly half of Stockton's residents and almost all of surrounding San Joaquin County, where high-end development is overtaking farmland. Gridlock plagued Stockton during the technology boom, as Bay Area commuters were pushed to the city.

Traffic remains a concern, and hourlong trips to San Jose or San Francisco can take twice as long during rush hour. The high-tech bust a decade ago and the more recent housing market collapse left the Stockton area vulnerable.

Dairy products and wine grapes are the primary agricultural goods here. Lodi leads the state in production of several premium wine grapes, many of which are shipped to the Napa Valley for bottling.

The agriculture sector in San Joaquin County has come under scrutiny because of local air pollution resulting from the raising of livestock and transportation of farm products. Agricultural exports travel through the trucking centers of Lodi and Tracy on their way out of the 11th. The port of Stockton on the San Joaquin River specializes in bulk cargo, and cement is the main import.

Friendly to some GOP candidates, the moderate 11th gave George W. Bush 54 percent of its 2004 presidential vote, but Democrat Barack Obama won the district with the same percentage in 2008. In 2010, the 11th was the only district represented by a Democrat to back Republican gubernatorial candidate Meg Whitman.

Major Industry
Agriculture, technology, service

Military Bases
Defense Distribution Depot San Joaquin, 27 military, 2,677 civilian (2007)

Cities
Stockton (pt.), 137,118; Tracy, 82,922; Manteca, 67,096

Notable
The museum operated by the San Joaquin County Historical Society, in Lodi, boasts a working blacksmith's shop.

Rep. Jackie Speier (D)

Capitol Office
225-3531
speier.house.gov
211 Cannon Bldg. 20515-0512; fax 226-4183

Committees
Homeland Security
Oversight & Government Reform

Residence
Hillsborough

Born
May 14, 1950; San Francisco, Calif.

Religion
Roman Catholic

Family
Husband, Barry Dennis; two children

Education
U. of California, Davis, B.A. 1972 (political science); U. of California, Hastings, J.D. 1976

Career
Lawyer; game software company executive; disability services nonprofit officer; congressional aide

Political Highlights
Candidate for U.S. House (special election), 1979; San Mateo County Board of Supervisors, 1981-86; Calif. Assembly, 1986-96; Calif. Senate, 1998-2006; sought Democratic nomination for lieutenant governor, 2006

ELECTION RESULTS

2010 GENERAL

Jackie Speier (D)	152,044	75.6%
Mike Moloney (R)	44,475	22.1%
Mark Williams (LIBERT)	4,611	2.3%

2010 PRIMARY

Jackie Speier (D)	unopposed

2008 GENERAL

Jackie Speier (D)	200,442	75.1%
Greg Conlon (R)	49,258	18.5%
Nathalie Hrizi (PFP)	5,793	2.2%
Barry Hermanson (GREEN)	5,776	2.2%
Kevin Peterson (LIBERT)	5,584	2.1%

Previous Winning Percentages
2008 Special Election (78%)

Elected 2008; 2nd full term

Speier has shown the same traits in Washington that she demonstrated as a member of the California Legislature for 18 years. She combines a liberal voting record, a knack for latching onto newsworthy issues and a willingness to work with conservative Republicans.

Speier (pronounced SPEAR) represents part of San Mateo County and shares representation of the city and county of San Francisco with Democratic leader Nancy Pelosi, and she is a reliable supporter of Democratic leadership; in 2010 she voted with her party 99 percent of the time on measures that split a majority of Democrats from a majority of Republicans.

But on some issues she has struck out on her own. A particular focus has been revamping earmarking, the practice of getting funds for hand-picked projects through the appropriations process. Speier, who supports members' power to seek earmarks as a constitutional prerogative, says she has become the first House member to completely remove herself from the process of selecting projects for her district. Instead, she has turned it over to a panel of former local elected officials and business and education leaders who screen applications from local governments and nonprofits. They give Speier a final, much-shortened list that she then pushes into the appropriations process.

The Oversight and Government Reform Committee member said her goal is complete transparency. "Our choice," she said, "is either to ban earmarks or create a system where there is not the appearance of a quid pro quo for getting an earmark."

She went further, introducing legislation in the 111th Congress (2009-10) with Republican Bill Cassidy of Louisiana that would establish a single database where all members' earmark requests would be detailed for easy reference. Another of her proposals would require all members to hold a meeting in their districts or via Web or teleconference to justify earmark requests to their constituents.

Speier has a new outlet in her fight for increasing transparency in the 112th Congress (2011-12) as the ranking member of the Homeland Security Subcommittee on Oversight, Investigations & Management. "We must make certain the Department is operating as efficiently as possible so it can meet its mission of keeping the American people safe," she said.

She also plans to use her Homeland Security seat to improve pipeline security and safety, a major focus for her since a natural-gas pipeline exploded in San Bruno in September 2010, killing eight people. She introduced legislation is the early days of the 112th Congress to address safety issues.

Her desire for transparency was also apparent in her work on the Financial Services Committee, on which she served in the 111th. A supporter of the financial services overhaul enacted in 2010, she sponsored legislation to require public disclosure of the terms of lawmakers' home mortgages.

Speier adopted as a cause honoring the role of the Buffalo Soldiers in establishing the National Park System. The African-American regiment marched from San Francisco's Presidio along the historic El Camino Real through San Mateo County to assume duties in Yosemite and Sequoia National Parks.

Speier's life of hard-to-believe twists and turns reads like the screenplay for a melodrama. In November 1978, while working for her mentor, Democratic Rep. Leo Ryan of California, she was shot five times and left for dead on an airstrip in Guyana by gunmen associated with Peoples Temple cult leader Jim Jones. Years later, her first husband, physician Steve Sierra, was killed by a drunken driver, leaving Speier a widow pregnant with her second child after suffering two miscarriages. Before he was killed, Sierra and Speier had also adopted a baby whom Speier introduced to her colleagues on the state Assembly floor. But a short while later, the birth mother changed her mind. Early in 2011, she took to the House floor during a debate on funding for Planned Parenthood to tell her colleagues that she had undergone an abortion procedure nearly two decades earlier.

With two co-authors, she drew on her life experiences in writing a book in 2007, "This Is Not the Life I Ordered: 50 Ways to Keep Your Head Above Water When Life Keeps Dragging You Down."

Speier is a San Francisco native whose working-class parents moved south to San Mateo County when she was a child. She took the name Jackie for her Catholic confirmation in honor of former first lady Jacqueline Kennedy. She met Ryan when she was 16, working as a volunteer in his 1966 re-election campaign for the state Assembly. She went on to study at the University of California at Davis. During her freshman year, Ryan offered her an academic internship. That led to a full-time job working for him in Sacramento, and she followed him to Washington after he won the House seat in 1972.

When Speier was serving as his legal counsel, Ryan launched an investigation of Jones, founder of a San Francisco church that he moved to the South American country of Guyana with hundreds of his followers. Speier was among a group of aides and reporters who accompanied Ryan to Guyana. When gunfire broke out, Speier and nine others were wounded, and Ryan was among five who were killed. Speier was flown to Washington for treatment. Later that day, Jones and more than 900 people died in a mass suicide.

After recovering from serious wounds and a bacterial infection, she entered the crowded 1979 special election race to succeed Ryan. She lost to Republican Bill Royer, who lost to Democrat Tom Lantos the following year.

In 1981, Speier successfully ran for the San Mateo County Board of Supervisors, where she served five years. In 1986, she sought a state Assembly seat, winning the Democratic nomination by just 500 votes.

In 2006, Speier lost a hotly contested primary for lieutenant governor. When Lantos died in February 2008, just a few months after he was diagnosed with cancer of the esophagus, she took another run for the seat in a special election. She romped to victory in April with 78 percent of the vote. In November, she won with 75 percent, a figure she matched in 2010.

In January 2010, Speier caused a brief sensation in California politics when she indicated she might give up the House seat she had sought for so long in order to run for state attorney general. After a few days that included a family meeting, she said she had decided to stay in the House.

Key Votes

2010

Overhaul the nation's health insurance system	YES
Allow for repeal of "don't ask, don't tell"	YES
Overhaul financial services industry regulation	YES
Limit use of new Afghanistan War funds to troop withdrawal activities	YES
Change oversight of offshore drilling and lift oil spill liability cap	YES
Provide a path to legal status for some children of illegal immigrants	YES
Extend Bush-era income tax cuts for two years	NO

2009

Expand the Children's Health Insurance Program	YES
Provide $787 billion in tax cuts and spending increases to stimulate the economy	YES
Allow bankruptcy judges to modify certain primary-residence mortgages	YES
Create a cap-and-trade system to limit greenhouse gas emissions	YES
Provide $2 billion for the "cash for clunkers" program	YES
Establish the government as the sole provider of student loans	YES
Restrict federally funded insurance coverage for abortions in health care overhaul	NO

CQ Vote Studies

	PARTY UNITY		PRESIDENTIAL SUPPORT	
	SUPPORT	OPPOSE	SUPPORT	OPPOSE
2010	99%	1%	87%	13%
2009	95%	5%	92%	8%
2008	99%	1%	10%	90%

Interest Groups

	AFL-CIO	ADA	CCUS	ACU
2010	100%	95%	13%	0%
2009	95%	95%	33%	4%
2008	100%	60%	43%	0%

California 12
Part of San Mateo County; most of western San Francisco

A mix of scenic coastal mountains and bayside commuter traffic jams, California's 12th District lies between its two well-known neighbors, downtown San Francisco and the Silicon Valley. To the west of the district is the Pacific Ocean and to the east lies the San Francisco Bay.

The wishbone-shaped district includes southwestern San Francisco and the heavily populated San Mateo County suburbs: Daly City and locales found between two main commuter routes — the Junipero Serra and U.S. Route 101. The 12th's western spur runs south along the Pacific coastline from the Great Highway in San Francisco through Pacifica to Moss Beach, while the eastern spur stretches along the bay to San Carlos and part of Redwood City, about halfway to San Jose.

After an early-2000s downturn in the district's technology economy and in Silicon Valley to the south, the region has begun to rebound. The planned community Redwood Shores is home to software giants Oracle and Electronic Arts, and the popular Internet video site YouTube was founded in

San Mateo. South San Francisco, home to several biotech firms, anchors the northern part of the district. San Francisco Airport remains a key employer and cargo traffic hub.

The 12th has the one of the nation's largest Asian populations, and Daly City, where more than half of the population is Asian, has a significant Filipino community. The Farallon Islands — a national wildlife refuge 28 miles west of San Francisco and a popular destination for whale watchers and shark divers — also belong to the district.

Democrats hold an overwhelming voter registration edge here, as less than 20 percent of voters have registered Republican. The district gave 74 percent of its vote to Barack Obama in the 2008 presidential election and 68 percent to Jerry Brown in the 2010 gubernatorial race.

Major Industry
Biotech, airport, software

Cities
San Francisco (pt.), 138,408; Daly City, 101,123; San Mateo, 97,207

Notable
The most lucrative big-wave surfing competition in the world is held at a wave break called Maverick's, off Half Moon Bay.

Rep. Pete Stark (D)

Capitol Office
225-5065
www.house.gov/stark
239 Cannon Bldg. 20515-0513; fax 226-3805

Committees
Ways & Means

Residence
Fremont

Born
Nov. 11, 1931; Milwaukee, Wis.

Religion
Atheist

Family
Wife, Deborah Roderick Stark; seven children

Education
Massachusetts Institute of Technology, B.S. 1953
(engineering); U. of California, Berkeley, M.B.A. 1960

Military
Air Force, 1955-57

Career
Banker

Political Highlights
Sought Democratic nomination for Calif. Senate,
1969

ELECTION RESULTS

2010 GENERAL

Pete Stark (D)	118,278	72.0%
Forest Baker (R)	45,575	27.7%

2010 PRIMARY

Pete Stark (D)	48,603	84.3%
Justin Jelincic (D)	9,021	15.6%

2008 GENERAL

Pete Stark (D)	166,829	76.4%
Raymond Chui (R)	51,447	23.6%

Previous Winning Percentages
2006 (75%); 2004 (72%); 2002 (71%); 2000 (70%);
1998 (71%); 1996 (65%); 1994 (65%); 1992 (60%);
1990 (58%); 1988 (73%); 1986 (70%); 1984 (70%);
1982 (61%); 1980 (55%); 1978 (65%); 1976 (71%);
1974 (71%); 1972 (53%)

Elected 1972; 20th term

Stark is one of Congress' most colorful characters, a liberal lawmaker who stands out as fearlessly — often heedlessly — unfiltered among his more cautious and polite colleagues. And, although Stark's blue-collar constituents seem to admire his fierce attacks on those who don't agree with his views, his ever-growing list of angry barbs and off-handed quips has cost him dearly within the clubby confines of Congress.

The 111th Congress (2009-10) could be remembered as a high point for Stark, when a lifetime of advocating for universal health care culminated in a law that took strides in that direction. As chairman of the Ways and Means Subcommittee on Health, Stark had a seat at the table as Congress worked on the largest expansion of health insurance coverage in more than 40 years. And Stark's idea to temporarily provide subsidies to laid-off workers to lower the cost of their premiums caught on in the midst of a weakened economy. Written into the 2009 economic stimulus bill, Stark's subsidy has been extended multiple times.

But the 111th also saw Stark pay his highest price yet for his inability to play nice with others. When Ways and Means Chairman Charles B. Rangel of New York was forced to give up his gavel following accusations of ethical lapses, House Democrats made clear that they did not believe Stark could be trusted to fill the position, even temporarily. Despite a record 37 years on the committee, Stark agreed to forgo the chairmanship.

Back in the minority for the 112th Congress (2011-12), Stark is ranking member on the Health Subcommittee and appears fated to return to the role of caustic critic.

When a federal judge ruled in December that part of the health care overhaul was unconstitutional, Stark said, "apparently Republicans are now for judicial activism after they were against it."

He blasted the Republican repeal legislation in January 2011, saying, "the Republicans' NoCare plan would raise the number of uninsured by 32 million, balloon the deficit, raise health care costs for seniors, and raise taxes on small businesses that provide health care for their employees."

Those reactions were pale imitations of some of Stark's most memorable diatribes.

In October 2007, a Stark broadside against President George W. Bush nearly led to his censure on the House floor. Amid debate over Democrats' failed effort to override Bush's veto of legislation to expand a health care program for children, Stark lashed out: "You don't have money to fund the war or children. But you're going to spend it to blow up innocent people if we can get enough kids to grow old enough for you to send to Iraq to get their heads blown off for the president's amusement."

Republicans demanded an apology. Stark initially refused, despite pressure from then-Speaker Nancy Pelosi of California. But after the effort to censure him failed, Stark backed down and apologized.

He once called Republican Bill Thomas of California a "fascist," Republican Scott McInnis of Colorado a "little wimp" and "fruitcake," and Republican Nancy L. Johnson of Connecticut a "whore for the insurance industry." Of former White House chief of staff and one-time House Democratic colleague Rahm Emanuel of Illinois, Stark said "he's never had an honest job in his life."

When a constituent at a 2009 town hall meeting said, "Congressman, don't pee on my leg and tell me it's raining," Stark quickly struck back with, "It wouldn't be worth wasting the urine."

Despite his proclivity for offense, Stark has achieved several major legislative successes over the years. A leading critic of private Medicare plans, he claimed victory in July 2007 when the House passed legislation to cut funding for them. He also helped shepherd legislation, enacted in 2008, that protects patients against discrimination by health insurance providers and employers based on their genetic predisposition to disease or chronic conditions.

He might be best known for two laws enacted in 1989 and 1993 known as Stark I and Stark II. They strictly regulate physician referrals of Medicare patients to medical facilities in which the doctors have a financial interest, such as laboratories and physical therapy clinics.

The last time the GOP held the House majority, he showed a willingness to work across party lines on occasion, helping to win new preventive care benefits for Medicare beneficiaries and push Congress to reduce out-of-pocket costs for hospital outpatient services. In the 112th, he will work with California Republican Wally Herger to move a bill the House passed in the 111th Congress that would bar executives of companies convicted of Medicare fraud from working for another Medicare provider.

Stark often makes news simply by breaking the mold. Early in his career, the Congressional Black Caucus rejected his request to join the group. Stark said his constituency and personal views should make him eligible. In 2007 he acknowledged — after the Secular Coalition of America sponsored a contest to find the highest-ranking atheist in elected office — that he doesn't believe in a supreme being.

Stark grew up in Wisconsin and graduated from the Massachusetts Institute of Technology. After serving in the Air Force in the 1950s, he moved West and got a master's degree in business from the University of California at Berkeley. At age 31, he had already founded two banks.

Even as a banker, Stark made sure the public knew where he stood on issues. He created an uproar when he registered his opposition to the Vietnam War by posting a large peace sign on the bank's headquarters and small peace symbols on the bank's checks.

In 1969, he made his first bid for public office, losing a primary for a state legislative seat to George Miller, then a young law school student and now a House colleague. Three years later, Stark took on another George Miller, who had represented Oakland in Congress as a Democrat for 28 years.

Stark spent his own money and made Miller's support of the Vietnam War a major issue on the way to a primary victory, followed by an election win with 53 percent of the vote. He has won his past seven elections with at least 70 percent of the vote.

Key Votes

2010

Overhaul the nation's health insurance system	YES
Allow for repeal of "don't ask, don't tell"	YES
Overhaul financial services industry regulation	YES
Limit use of new Afghanistan War funds to troop withdrawal activities	YES
Change oversight of offshore drilling and lift oil spill liability cap	YES
Provide a path to legal status for some children of illegal immigrants	YES
Extend Bush-era income tax cuts for two years	NO

2009

Expand the Children's Health Insurance Program	?
Provide $787 billion in tax cuts and spending increases to stimulate the economy	YES
Allow bankruptcy judges to modify certain primary-residence mortgages	?
Create a cap-and-trade system to limit greenhouse gas emissions	NO
Provide $2 billion for the "cash for clunkers" program	YES
Establish the government as the sole provider of student loans	YES
Restrict federally funded insurance coverage for abortions in health care overhaul	NO

CQ Vote Studies

	PARTY UNITY		PRESIDENTIAL SUPPORT	
	SUPPORT	OPPOSE	SUPPORT	OPPOSE
2010	97%	3%	85%	15%
2009	96%	4%	87%	13%
2008	94%	6%	13%	87%
2007	97%	3%	12%	88%
2006	99%	1%	5%	95%

Interest Groups

	AFL-CIO	ADA	CCUS	ACU
2010	93%	90%	0%	0%
2009	93%	70%	43%	10%
2008	93%	90%	47%	13%
2007	95%	80%	47%	4%
2006	92%	95%	8%	4%

California 13

East Bay — Fremont, Hayward, Alameda

Tucked between the San Francisco Bay to the west, Silicon Valley to the south and Oakland to the north, the 13th is an industrially and culturally diverse suburban area. The district is dotted with working-class communities, and although it is described as the less glamorous side of the bay, its large Hispanic and Asian populations — including immigrants from India, China, Afghanistan and the Philippines — have flourished culturally. Asians, concentrated in Fremont, account for 36 percent of the population and the third-highest districtwide percentage in the nation.

Fremont's joint General Motors-Toyota auto plant closed in 2010 when GM declared bankruptcy, but Tesla Motors bought the factory for large-scale production of its electric car. Although Tesla's workforce is considerably smaller than the joint venture's, the new production line will provide some jobs. Both Fremont and Hayward have become more oriented toward high-tech industries as Silicon Valley has extended its influence to the East Bay. Corsair and Lexar, manufacturers of computer memory devices, are based in Fremont. Hayward also is home to a California State University campus.

San Leandro, just south of Oakland, is home to Ghirardelli Chocolate, Otis Spunkmeyer's cookie empire, and The North Face, which produces outdoor equipment.

Cargill Salt has a refinery and production facility in Newark. The 13th also includes Oakland International Airport — although Oakland itself is located in the neighboring 9th District — and cargo and passenger traffic has rebounded following several years of nationwide declines.

Two-thirds of the district's workers are considered white collar, but the area's blue-collar industry historically has given Democrats solid support. Jerry Brown took 69 percent of the district's vote in the 2010 gubernatorial election.

Major Industry
Electronics, manufacturing, food product processing

Cities
Fremont, 214,089; Hayward, 144,186; San Leandro (pt.), 84,948

Notable
Ghirardelli Chocolate is the nation's longest continually operating chocolate manufacturer.

Rep. Anna G. Eshoo (D)

Capitol Office
225-8104
eshoo.house.gov
205 Cannon Bldg. 20515-0514; fax 225-8890

Committees
Energy & Commerce

Residence
Menlo Park

Born
Dec. 13, 1942; New Britain, Conn.

Religion
Roman Catholic

Family
Divorced; two children

Education
Canada College, A.A. 1975 (English literature)

Career
State legislative aide; homemaker

Political Highlights
Candidate for San Mateo County Community College Board of Trustees, 1977; Democratic National Committee, 1980-92; San Mateo County Board of Supervisors, 1982-92 (president, 1986); Democratic nominee for U.S. House, 1988

ELECTION RESULTS

2010 GENERAL

Anna G. Eshoo (D)	151,217	69.1%
Dave Chapman (R)	60,917	27.8%
Paul Lazaga (LIBERT)	6,735	3.1%

2010 PRIMARY

Anna G. Eshoo (D)	unopposed

2008 GENERAL

Anna G. Eshoo (D)	190,301	69.8%
Ronny Santana (R)	60,610	22.2%
Brian Holtz (LIBERT)	11,929	4.4%
Carol Brouillet (GREEN)	9,926	3.6%

Previous Winning Percentages
2006 (71%); 2004 (70%); 2002 (68%); 2000 (70%); 1998 (69%); 1996 (65%); 1994 (61%); 1992 (57%)

Elected 1992; 10th term

Part of Minority Leader Nancy Pelosi's inner circle, Eshoo is a liberal who usually promotes the interests of the technology businesses that have made her Silicon Valley district an international economic powerhouse.

She describes herself as a lawmaker who "will work with anyone and everyone who really wants to push the edges of the envelope out and create new opportunities." But she is a reliable supporter of the Democratic leadership, siding with her party 99 percent of the time in the 111th Congress (2009-10) on votes that divided majorities of the two parties.

Eshoo fended off a challenge from Rep. Bobby L. Rush of Illinois to be named top Democrat on the Energy and Commerce Subcommittee on Communications and Technology, positioning her to influence policy central to the district's economic well-being. During the 111th, she introduced legislation to require states to set up broadband infrastructure as part of highway projects. As co-chairwoman of the E911 Caucus, she backed a bill to give grants to help 911 services move to IP-enabled networks. She introduced another measure that would extend indefinitely a ban on Internet access taxes. She also pushed that idea in the 110th Congress (2007-08), but won only a temporary extension of the current ban.

In past years, she supported a law to authorize using "electronic signatures" to seal some contracts and has repeatedly tried to push through legislation requiring doctors, hospitals and other health care providers to adopt electronic medical records — a cause boosted in the 2009 economic stimulus law.

She has also taken up more populist causes, such as a bill signed into law in December 2010 to prohibit television commercials from being louder than television programs.

Eshoo's pro-business side emerges when the interests of her district are at stake. She was active in unsuccessful efforts to block a proposed accounting rule that requires companies to treat employee stock options — popular with technology firms — as an expense they have to deduct from earnings.

In 2009, when she was still a member of Energy and Commerce's Health Subcommittee, she led efforts to allow for "biosimilars" — essentially generic versions of biologic drugs — after a 12-year exclusivity period, which was eventually included in the health care overhaul enacted in 2010. That put her at odds with fellow Californian Henry A. Waxman, who was then chairman of the Energy and Commerce Committee. He wanted fewer years. Eshoo's district is home to many biotechnology firms.

Eshoo was a driving force behind House Democrats' adoption of an "innovation agenda" that Pelosi touted when the party successfully campaigned to retake control of the chamber in 2006. That agenda also helped Democrats raise campaign cash in Silicon Valley. In 2005, Eshoo arranged a private meeting at Stanford University for Pelosi and other lawmakers to discuss ideas for legislation with such high-tech powerhouses as Cisco Systems CEO John Chambers. The meeting resulted in proposals to create incentives for broadband development, to get the federal government to foster new nanotechnology industries and to make the research and development tax credit permanent.

One instance in which Eshoo departs from a major technology company in her district is on "network neutrality," the idea that broadband providers should be barred from blocking certain traffic or establishing tiered pathways for Internet content. She opposed a 2010 proposal by Google — based in Mountain View — and Verizon that included provisions to exclude wireless broadband providers from Federal Communications Commission enforcement of net neutrality, arguing that doing so would favor their view on wireless and leave out the interests of consumers. If the plan that the companies proposed was in place in 1997 or 1998, Google would not have become the company it is today, Eshoo said.

A subcommittee chairwoman on the House Intelligence panel in the 111th Congress — she no longer sits on the committee following the Democratic losses in 2010 — Eshoo pushed for more integration and oversight of intelligence agencies. She pushed to include in the fiscal 2010 intelligence authorization bill a provision that would give the Government Accountability Office the ability to audit intelligence agencies, language the Obama administration opposed strongly enough to threaten a veto. The bill signed into law in fall 2010 included language that would require the director of national intelligence to work with GAO and issue a directive governing its access to intelligence information.

Eshoo was a fierce critic of President George W. Bush's policies regarding the treatment of suspected terrorist detainees and his interpretation of executive authority on national security matters. She also opposed the Obama administration's 2009 plan to send an additional 30,000 troops to Afghanistan.

Eshoo and Pelosi have known each other for more than 30 years. Eshoo performed the rites for the wedding of one of Pelosi's daughters in 2008. In her 2008 autobiography, Pelosi described Eshoo as "one of my dearest friends in the world."

The daughter of immigrants of Armenian and Assyrian descent, Eshoo was drawn to politics in her native New Britain, Conn. Her father was a New Deal Democrat who named his daughter after Franklin D. Roosevelt's wife, whose full name was Anna Eleanor Roosevelt.

The family eventually moved west to California. Eshoo married (she has been divorced since the 1980s) and devoted herself to motherhood while earning an associate's degree in English literature from a local college. Yet she continued her political activity, taking an internship with California Assembly Speaker Leo T. McCarthy, who was also a close Pelosi friend, and later serving as his chief of staff.

In 1982, McCarthy urged her to run for the San Mateo County Board of Supervisors, where she served for a decade.

In 1988, Eshoo lost a House race to Republican Tom Campbell. She was successful four years later, when Campbell was running for the U.S. Senate. She has won easily since.

Key Votes

2010

Overhaul the nation's health insurance system	YES
Allow for repeal of "don't ask, don't tell"	YES
Overhaul financial services industry regulation	YES
Limit use of new Afghanistan War funds to troop withdrawal activities	NO
Change oversight of offshore drilling and lift oil spill liability cap	YES
Provide a path to legal status for some children of illegal immigrants	YES
Extend Bush-era income tax cuts for two years	NO

2009

Expand the Children's Health Insurance Program	YES
Provide $787 billion in tax cuts and spending increases to stimulate the economy	YES
Allow bankruptcy judges to modify certain primary-residence mortgages	YES
Create a cap-and-trade system to limit greenhouse gas emissions	YES
Provide $2 billion for the "cash for clunkers" program	YES
Establish the government as the sole provider of student loans	YES
Restrict federally funded insurance coverage for abortions in health care overhaul	NO

CQ Vote Studies

	PARTY UNITY		PRESIDENTIAL SUPPORT	
	SUPPORT	OPPOSE	SUPPORT	OPPOSE
2010	99%	1%	93%	7%
2009	99%	1%	97%	3%
2008	99%	1%	14%	86%
2007	98%	2%	5%	95%
2006	96%	4%	23%	77%

Interest Groups

	AFL-CIO	ADA	CCUS	ACU
2010	100%	95%	0%	13%
2009	100%	100%	33%	0%
2008	100%	90%	61%	0%
2007	96%	95%	55%	0%
2006	93%	95%	40%	4%

California 14

Southern San Mateo and northwestern Santa Clara counties; most of Santa Cruz County

The 14th District stretches south from northern San Mateo County on the Pacific coast, taking in the majority of Santa Cruz County and a C-shaped arc of northwestern Santa Clara County just south of the San Francisco Bay. The district is home to Stanford University, technology firms and fruit orchards.

Workers in the 14th are largely wealthy, educated and professional. More than half of residents here have earned a college degree, and more than three-quarters of the local workforce hold white-collar jobs. The region is not immune to layoffs during nationwide economic downturns, but very high incomes and relatively stable job and housing markets have helped insulate the district's economy.

Technology is a dominant industry here. Corporate headquarters in the 14th include Google in Mountain View, Hewlett-Packard in Palo Alto, and Yahoo, Palm and AMD in Sunnyvale. Facebook plans to boost its

workforce following a move from Palo Alto to a 57-acre campus in Menlo Park, where local development continues to be a hot issue. NASA's Ames Research Center near Mountain View collaborates with technology firms and colleges on high-tech computing and space-related research and development projects.

Voters in the 14th are liberal on social and environmental issues, particularly in Santa Cruz County. Many residents are more conservative economically, however, and some GOP voting blocs exist in wealthy areas in Santa Clara County. Democrats hold an overall 24-percentage-point edge in voter registration, and the district gave Democrat Jerry Brown 64 percent of its vote in the 2010 gubernatorial election.

Major Industry
Computers, biotechnology, defense, agriculture

Cities
Sunnyvale, 140,081; Mountain View, 74,066; Palo Alto, 64,403; Redwood City (part), 53,702; Menlo Park, 32,026

Notable
Stanford University's Cantor Arts Center has the nation's largest concentration of bronze sculptures by Auguste Rodin; Stanford's Linear Accelerator Center claims to be the "world's straightest object."

Rep. Michael M. Honda (D)

Capitol Office
225-2631
www.honda.house.gov
1713 Longworth Bldg. 20515-0515; fax 225-2699

Committees
Appropriations
Budget

Residence
San Jose

Born
June 27, 1941; Stockton, Calif.

Religion
Protestant

Family
Widowed; two children

Education
San Jose State U., B.S. 1969 (biological sciences), B.A. 1970 (Spanish), M.A. 1973 (education)

Career
Teacher; principal; Peace Corps volunteer

Political Highlights
San Jose School Board, 1981-90; Santa Clara County Board of Supervisors, 1990-96; Calif. Assembly, 1996-00

ELECTION RESULTS

2010 GENERAL

Michael M. Honda (D)	126,147	67.6%
Scott Kirkland (R)	60,468	32.4%

2010 PRIMARY

Michael M. Honda (D)	unopposed

2008 GENERAL

Michael M. Honda (D)	170,977	71.7%
Joyce Stoer Cordi (R)	55,489	23.3%
Peter Myers (GREEN)	12,123	5.1%

Previous Winning Percentages
2006 (72%); 2004 (72%); 2002 (66%); 2000 (54%)

Elected 2000; 6th term

Honda's life experiences inspire his philosophy and political accomplishments in a way few others who have served in Congress can claim. Born in California to Japanese-American farm workers less than six months before the Japanese bombed Pearl Harbor, Honda and his family were shipped to an internment camp in Colorado after the attack. They spent two and a half years there before being allowed to move to Chicago when his father joined Navy intelligence. And Honda's late wife, Jeanne, whom he married in 1967 and who died in 2004, survived the atomic bombing of Hiroshima.

The Honda family moved back to California in 1953, and his parents became strawberry sharecroppers. Honda took janitorial and delivery jobs to pay his way through San Jose State University. He was one credit shy of graduation when he joined the Peace Corps in 1965. After two years in El Salvador, where he helped build schools and medical clinics, he returned to California to finish college. He took a job as a science teacher, later serving as a principal.

His family's internment and his own Peace Corps experience profoundly influenced Honda. "I think since I came back from the Peace Corps in '67, I saw the niche that I needed to fill. . . . I had to teach myself to learn from others, then try to figure out through the political process or educational process to seek change, reconciliation," he said.

Honda remembers little of his internment as an infant and toddler. But he was a key participant in the Japanese-American lobbying campaign that culminated in a 1988 law providing a formal apology and compensation to interned Japanese-Americans. That effort inspired Honda, once he reached Congress, to work for reparations for Americans who were prisoners of the Japanese during World War II. He also was a leading supporter of legislation signed into law by President George W. Bush in late 2006 that authorized $38 million to preserve the remnants of the internment camps.

In 2007, Honda introduced and won House adoption of a resolution calling on the Japanese government to acknowledge and apologize for the use of sex slaves, known as "comfort women," during World War II.

In March 2010, when South Carolina Republican Sen. Lindsey Graham compared the Democrats' effort to pass health care legislation to a Japanese kamikaze attack and said then-Speaker Nancy Pelosi, Honda's fellow California Democrat, had her caucus "liquored up on sake," Honda took him to task. Honda said he was "disheartened that Sen. Graham chose to use racially tinged rhetoric to express his opposition to health care reform."

Honda is a member of the Congressional Progressive Caucus, a group of the House's most liberal members, and he chairs its Afghanistan Task Force. Like many other members of the caucus, he broke ranks with President Obama on his decision to boost troop strength in Afghanistan. "My serious concerns about U.S. strategy have led me to oppose the war funding supplemental bill in 2009, oppose increased funding for the 30,000-troop surge, support a war tax and call for an about-face in funding priorities," he wrote in a blog post on his congressional website in March 2010.

During the 110th Congress (2007-08), Honda was a prime mover in pushing for congressional hearings into the 2004 death in Afghanistan of Army Cpl. Pat Tillman and the Bush administration's handling of the announcement of his death. Tillman, hailed for giving up a lucrative National Football League career to enlist just months after the Sept. 11 attacks, was initially reported killed in an engagement with the enemy. It was weeks before the Pentagon notified his family, which lives in Honda's district, that he was the victim of friendly fire.

Honda gained a coveted seat on the Appropriations Committee in 2007 and joined the Budget Committee in 2011. From his spot on the Appropriations Legislative Branch Subcommittee, where he is the top Democrat in the 112th Congress (2011-12), Honda said he will push for increased funding for member security in the wake of the shooting of Arizona Democrat Gabrielle Giffords in January 2011. He also serves on the subcommittee that provides funding for science and space programs, where he looks out for the NASA-Ames Research Center near his district.

He combined his role as outgoing chairman of the Congressional Asian Pacific American Caucus with his seat on the subcommittee that oversees the census by doing a public service announcement for asianamericancensus.org urging participation in the decennial count. And he cites census statistics on growing U.S. diversity as justification for a measure he introduced in March 2010 that would require federal employees who use more than one language in their official duties to be paid a 5 percent salary premium above their basic pay rate.

Representing a district with a healthy slice of Silicon Valley, Honda looks out for the technology industry. He favors the repeal of export controls on high-performance computers and permanent renewal of the research and development tax credit. In 2008, he introduced legislation to coordinate various initiatives to boost funding for science, mathematics, engineering and technology education.

Honda got his start in public service more than three decades ago. He went to Norman Y. Mineta — another Japanese-American who spent time in an internment camp as a child and was then a San Jose city councilman — to volunteer. After being elected mayor, Mineta named Honda to the city planning commission in 1971. In 1981, Honda won election to the local school board, and later to the county board of supervisors and the California Assembly.

When moderate Republican Rep. Tom Campbell left the 15th District seat open in 2000 to pursue a run for the Senate, Honda entered the race. A phone call from President Bill Clinton convinced him the national party would back his bid, and Honda won the race by 12 percentage points.

Bolstered by redistricting and his ties to the Asian and Hispanic communities in a district where almost half the residents are from those constituencies, Honda has easily won re-election since.

Key Votes

2010

Overhaul the nation's health insurance system	YES
Allow for repeal of "don't ask, don't tell"	YES
Overhaul financial services industry regulation	YES
Limit use of new Afghanistan War funds to troop withdrawal activities	YES
Change oversight of offshore drilling and lift oil spill liability cap	YES
Provide a path to legal status for some children of illegal immigrants	YES
Extend Bush-era income tax cuts for two years	NO

2009

Expand the Children's Health Insurance Program	YES
Provide $787 billion in tax cuts and spending increases to stimulate the economy	YES
Allow bankruptcy judges to modify certain primary-residence mortgages	YES
Create a cap-and-trade system to limit greenhouse gas emissions	YES
Provide $2 billion for the "cash for clunkers" program	YES
Establish the government as the sole provider of student loans	YES
Restrict federally funded insurance coverage for abortions in health care overhaul	NO

CQ Vote Studies

	PARTY UNITY		PRESIDENTIAL SUPPORT	
	Support	Oppose	Support	Oppose
2010	97%	3%	90%	10%
2009	99%	1%	94%	6%
2008	100%	0%	15%	85%
2007	99%	1%	5%	95%
2006	97%	3%	23%	77%

Interest Groups

	AFL-CIO	ADA	CCUS	ACU
2010	100%	95%	0%	0%
2009	100%	100%	33%	0%
2008	100%	95%	50%	0%
2007	100%	95%	58%	0%
2006	93%	95%	33%	4%

California 15

Santa Clara County — part of San Jose

Home to one-third of San Jose's residents, the 15th touches the southern tip of the San Francisco Bay in the north, then descends inland through Silicon Valley to still-rural but fast-growing farm towns and the San Benito County border. Fruit orchards that once covered much of the district were converted into housing and businesses after World War II.

The population is predominately affluent, although wealth here is vulnerable to economic uncertainty. It also has a high percentage of white-collar workers and has one of the state's lowest percentages of service industry workers.

Lying in the heart of Silicon Valley, the 15th is home to several prominent technology firms — Apple in Cupertino and Intel in Santa Clara — and Internet ventures like online auction house eBay in San Jose and Netflix in Los Gatos. Recent job growth at some high-tech employers has boosted the local economy, but periodic downturns in the technology industry, particularly within smaller companies, can affect the wealthy suburbs west of San Jose. The software and semiconductor sectors have benefited from

federal funding and relationships with research universities.

Agriculture also is important here. Gilroy, located in the southern part of the district and known as the "Garlic Capital of the World," is home to several food processing plants. Singapore-based Olam International bought the ConAgra plant that produces vegetables.

The diverse 15th, which is home to many foreign-born residents, includes the nation's second-highest percentage of Asian residents (36 percent) and a sizable Hispanic population (21 percent). Illegal immigration is a key policy issue, but voters in the 15th tend to be liberal on social and environmental issues. Registered Democrats outnumber Republicans by a wide margin, and Jerry Brown won 60 percent of the district's 2010 gubernatorial vote.

Major Industry
Computers, biotechnology, health care, agriculture

Cities
San Jose (pt.), 303,958; Santa Clara (pt.), 116,450; Milpitas, 66,790

Notable
Two tons of garlic are consumed during Gilroy's annual Garlic Festival, which features garlic french fries, garlic ice cream — and free gum.

Rep. Zoe Lofgren (D)

Capitol Office
225-3072
www.house.gov/lofgren
1401 Longworth Bldg. 20515-0516; fax 225-3336

Committees
House Administration
Judiciary
Science, Space & Technology

Residence
San Jose

Born
Dec. 21, 1947; San Mateo, Calif.

Religion
Lutheran

Family
Husband, John Marshall Collins; two children

Education
Stanford U., A.B. 1970 (political science); U. of Santa Clara, J.D. 1975

Career
Lawyer; nonprofit housing development director; professor; congressional aide

Political Highlights
San Jose-Evergreen Community College District Board of Trustees, 1979-81; Santa Clara County Board of Supervisors, 1981-95

ELECTION RESULTS

2010 GENERAL

Zoe Lofgren (D)	105,841	67.8%
Daniel Sahagun (R)	37,913	24.3%
Edward Gonzalez (LIBERT)	12,304	7.9%

2010 PRIMARY

Zoe Lofgren (D)	unopposed

2008 GENERAL

Zoe Lofgren (D)	146,481	71.3%
Charel Winston (R)	49,399	24.1%
Steven Wells (LIBERT)	9,447	4.6%

Previous Winning Percentages
2006 (73%); 2004 (71%); 2002 (67%); 2000 (72%);
1998 (73%); 1996 (66%); 1994 (65%)

Elected 1994; 9th term

A liberal veteran of 16 years in the House, Lofgren rose to leadership roles on the Ethics Committee and subcommittees dealing with immigration and elections. As the representative for a large chunk of Silicon Valley, she also has taken an interest in telecommunications and technology issues.

Lofgren took on the unenviable task of chairing what was then called the Committee on Standards of Official Conduct in the 111th Congress, a chore that consumed a good deal of her time and left her looking elsewhere in the 112th Congress (2011-12). In early January 2011, she agreed to stay on the panel temporarily. Less than three weeks later, she vacated the top Democratic spot in favor of fellow Californian Linda T. Sánchez.

Her tenure leading the committee was a busy one. Beginning in early 2009 and dragging on well into 2010, the panel conducted a total of 111 inquiries, including a probe of financial impropriety involving Ways and Means Chairman Charles B. Rangel, a New York Democrat. Rangel was eventually censured by the House. The panel's investigation of California Democrat Maxine Waters, accused of breaking House rules by seeking federal help for OneUnited Bank, a Los Angeles institution where her husband was a board member, dragged on into the new Congress.

This marked Lofgren's second go-round on the Ethics Committee. Earlier in her career, she participated in the investigation that led to the July 2002 expulsion of Democrat James A. Traficant Jr. of Ohio following his conviction on bribery, racketeering and tax fraud charges.

She chaired the Judiciary Subcommittee on Immigration in the last Congress and is the top Democrat on the panel in the 112th. A former immigration lawyer, Lofgren's inside view of the system is not a positive one. "Americans don't realize how bulky and inefficient and counterintuitive it is until someone they know gets involved, and then people are stunned at how ridiculous the rules are," she said.

She backs an approach to immigration overhaul that combines enhanced border security, tighter workplace enforcement and a path to citizenship for illegal immigrants already in the United States.

When Republican leaders pushed a border-security-first bill in 2006, she led the opposition. At the start of the 110th Congress (2007-08), with Democrats newly in charge, expectations were high that progress could be made on a broader bill. But after a Senate measure bogged down in June 2007, Lofgren and fellow House Democrats shifted to a piecemeal strategy, introducing a series of more-limited measures. Only one of Lofgren's proposals, to help foreign medical students stay after graduation, became law.

In December 2010, she backed legislation passed by the House that would have created a path to legalization for certain illegal immigrant children. The measure died in the Senate in the waning days of the 111th Congress (2009-10).

The Judiciary Committee acted quickly in January 2011 to approve her bill to ease the filing requirements for active-duty military members serving abroad who sponsor a non-U.S. spouse for permanent residency.

Lofgren's district has one of the largest concentrations of Vietnamese-Americans, and she advocates using economic pressure on Vietnam to pursue human rights issues. In 2009, in her capacity as co-chairwoman of the Congressional Caucus on Vietnam, Lofgren urged U.N. Ambassador Susan E. Rice to ask tough questions during a Human Rights Council review of Vietnam. She played a part in the 2008 release of Nguyen Quoc Quan, a democracy activist from California who was detained in Vietnam for six months.

She served as chairwoman of the Elections Subcommittee of the House Administration Committee during the 110th, sponsoring legislation to reimburse state and local governments for the cost of providing backup paper ballots, and to limit robocalls. In the 111th, she used the post to press for online voter registration. She is the ranking Democrat on the panel's Oversight Subcommittee in the 112th.

As the representative for San Jose, the capital of Silicon Valley, Lofgren keeps a close eye on the evolution of technology-related policy. She receives a lot of financial support from telecommunications groups and joined the Science, Space and Technology Committee in the 112th Congress. In July 2010, she sponsored a bill that would create a federal task force to track foreign governments' restrictions on trade that might interfere with open use of the Internet, and provide an annual report to Congress.

Lofgren grew up in a blue-collar neighborhood in south Palo Alto. Her father was a truck driver and her mother was a secretary and a school cafeteria cook. While other mothers went door-to-door collecting for the March of Dimes, Lofgren's mother went after "dollars for Democrats."

After completing her undergraduate studies at Stanford University on a scholarship, she headed to Washington, D.C., landing an internship with Democratic Rep. Don Edwards of California. She stayed on as a staffer through the 1970s, and was inspired to go to law school when a draft bill of her's was "ripped to shreds" by the House legislative counsel. She practiced immigration law as a partner in the firm of Webber & Lofgren, and taught the subject at the University of Santa Clara. Lofgren's husband is a lawyer in San Jose whom she met one election night while working for Edwards.

She was the first executive director of the nonprofit San Jose's Community Housing Developers. In 1979, a colleague urged her to run for the local community college board of trustees, and she won.

In 1980, she was elected to the Santa Clara County Board of Supervisors, where she stayed for 14 years and was often in conflict with San Jose Mayor Tom McEnery, a Democrat, who pushed downtown redevelopment while Lofgren argued for more money for education and human services.

When Edwards retired from the House after 32 years, the 1994 Democratic primary featured a face-off between Lofgren and McEnery. She benefited from an uproar that ensued when state election officials barred her from describing herself as "county supervisor/mother" on the ballot. The flap drew national attention to her candidacy, and she went on to win the primary. She won handily that November and has coasted to re-election since in the heavily Democratic district.

Key Votes

2010

Overhaul the nation's health insurance system	YES
Allow for repeal of "don't ask, don't tell"	YES
Overhaul financial services industry regulation	YES
Limit use of new Afghanistan War funds to troop withdrawal activities	YES
Change oversight of offshore drilling and lift oil spill liability cap	YES
Provide a path to legal status for some children of illegal immigrants	YES
Extend Bush-era income tax cuts for two years	NO

2009

Expand the Children's Health Insurance Program	YES
Provide $787 billion in tax cuts and spending increases to stimulate the economy	YES
Allow bankruptcy judges to modify certain primary-residence mortgages	YES
Create a cap-and-trade system to limit greenhouse gas emissions	YES
Provide $2 billion for the "cash for clunkers" program	YES
Establish the government as the sole provider of student loans	YES
Restrict federally funded insurance coverage for abortions in health care overhaul	NO

CQ Vote Studies

	PARTY UNITY		PRESIDENTIAL SUPPORT	
	Support	Oppose	Support	Oppose
2010	98%	2%	90%	10%
2009	99%	1%	93%	7%
2008	99%	1%	14%	86%
2007	99%	1%	6%	94%
2006	97%	3%	23%	77%

Interest Groups

	AFL-CIO	ADA	CCUS	ACU
2010	93%	95%	0%	4%
2009	100%	95%	40%	0%
2008	100%	100%	56%	0%
2007	96%	95%	55%	0%
2006	93%	100%	33%	4%

California 16
Most of San Jose

The 16th includes two-thirds of San Jose, California's third-largest city, where almost all district residents live. The remainder are scattered among unincorporated areas of Santa Clara County.

The tremendous growth during the technology boom of the 1990s — which earned San Jose the reputation as "the capital of Silicon Valley" — created a largely white-collar workforce and helped to establish the region as a leading exporter of high-tech goods. Unemployment levels had rebounded after a downturn in the industry a decade ago before more recent economic uncertainty struck the district again, but San Jose's economy has fared slightly better than the rest of the Bay Area and other regions of the state. Although Santa Clara County has the area's highest median household income, homeowners still struggle with high foreclosure rates.

Major technology firms in the 16th include Cisco Systems, Adobe, IBM's Almaden Research Center and a Hitachi division. San Jose also has several large medical centers, including Good Samaritan Hospital, and is home to

financial management software company Intacct. Local government and San Jose State University are key sources of jobs in the public sector, but budget shortfalls will affect employment rates.

The 16th is one of the most ethnically diverse districts in the Bay Area. Its Asian population includes the nation's second-largest Vietnamese community. Hispanics constitute a plurality of district residents, and whites make up roughly one-fourth of the population. The district's growth has resulted in one of the state's lowest percentages of population over the age of 64. The 16th is solidly Democratic. Barack Obama took 70 percent of the district's vote in the 2008 presidential election, and Gov. Jerry Brown won 62 percent here in 2010.

Major Industry
Technology, health care, finance

Cities
San Jose (pt.), 632,415; Alum Rock (unincorporated), 15,536

Notable
The Tech Museum of Innovation, a mango-colored building in downtown San Jose, welcomes hundreds of thousands of visitors to its exhibits, galleries and educational center.

Rep. Sam Farr (D)

Capitol Office
225-2861
www.farr.house.gov
1126 Longworth Bldg. 20515-0517; fax 225-6791

Committees
Appropriations

Residence
Carmel

Born
July 4, 1941; San Francisco, Calif.

Religion
Episcopalian

Family
Wife, Shary Baldwin Farr; one child

Education
Willamette U., B.S. 1963 (biology)

Career
State legislative aide; Peace Corps volunteer

Political Highlights
Monterey County Board of Supervisors, 1975-80;
Calif. Assembly, 1980-93

ELECTION RESULTS

2010 GENERAL

Sam Farr (D)	118,734	66.6%
Jeff Taylor (R)	53,176	29.8%
Eric Petersen (GREEN)	3,397	1.9%
Mary V. Larkin (LIBERT)	2,742	1.5%

2010 PRIMARY

Sam Farr (D)	52,689	88.8%
Art Dunn (D)	6,653	11.2%

2008 GENERAL

Sam Farr (D)	168,907	73.9%
Jeff Taylor (R)	59,037	25.8%

Previous Winning Percentages
2006 (76%); 2004 (67%); 2002 (68%); 2000 (69%);
1998 (65%); 1996 (59%); 1994 (52%); 1993 Special
Runoff Election (54%)

Elected 1993; 9th full term

Farr is a party loyalist and supporter of liberal causes who uses his post on the powerful Appropriations Committee to steer funding to his geographically diverse district.

He sees his role in Congress as that of a low-key auto mechanic. "I fix things that are broken," he said. Among the items Farr feels are in need of repair is America's reputation abroad, and he wants to help fix it by bolstering Peace Corps funding and participating in the House Democracy Partnership, which helps countries such as Afghanistan and Indonesia develop and maintain strong legislative bodies. The effort, combined with foreign aid and other development programs, projects an image of "smart Americans, rather than ugly Americans," Farr said.

Farr credits his time in the Peace Corps, spent in Colombia in the mid-1960s, for leading him to public service. His goal to double the agency's budget ranks among his top priorities in the 112th Congress (2011-12), a potentially tough task with Republicans in charge of the House.

An outspoken advocate for agribusiness in the Salinas Valley, Farr represents America's nearly $4 billion a year "salad bowl" — some 85 crops grown year-round that include strawberries, lettuce, spinach and peppers. As the top Democrat on the Agriculture Subcommittee, Farr is in a good position to ensure that his district, which hosts a particularly high number of government projects and houses 10 military facilities that have a total annual budget of about $1 billion, is not forgotten when Congress sets its spending priorities.

Farr, who also sits on the Military Construction spending panel, has also worked for the successful conversion to civilian use of the Army's once-vast Fort Ord, north of Monterey. Part of the base now houses a California State University campus and below-market housing. And he has assisted with efforts to establish a veterans' cemetery at the former base.

Farr has also worked to send money to his district through earmarks, member-directed funding requests that many budget hawks and ethical watchdogs would like to see banned. Earmarks are a necessary avenue for a district like his to get what it needs from the federal government because, he argues, agency formulas that dole out federal funds favor more urban areas.

A fifth-generation Californian, Farr has long advocated protection of the Big Sur coastline and the second-largest national marine sanctuary outside Hawaii. As co-chairman of the House Oceans Caucus, he has sought funding for the dozen research institutions located near the Monterey Bay coastline.

With fellow California Democratic Rep. John Garamendi, he backed legislation to ban new offshore oil drilling on the Pacific Coast. "Our ability to extract has exceeded our ability to anticipate and prevent disaster," the pair wrote in Roll Call in July 2010 in the wake of the Gulf of Mexico spill earlier that year. "It will happen again if we allow new offshore oil drilling to continue."

In the last two Congresses, Farr introduced bipartisan legislation to implement the top recommendations of the 16-member U.S. Commission on Ocean Policy, which he helped create in the late 1990s. The panel recommended creating a stronger ocean agency that would use an ecosystem-based approach to improving protection for oceans and coasts. The legislation never moved, but President Obama signed an executive order in the summer of 2010 that included many of the bill's provisions.

Farr, whose district's growers are dependent on migrant laborers, was widely criticized for remarks he made at a Homeland Security Appropriations hearing in February 2008 comparing the Immigration and Customs Enforcement component of the Homeland Security Department to Nazi Germany's brutal secret police. "What happens is, the public image of you becomes one of not this compassionate law enforcement agency but essentially a Gestapo-type agency that is knocking on doors," he said.

He also has used his Appropriations seat to try to eliminate a Food and Drug Administration rule that bars any man who engaged in homosexual sex after 1977 from donating blood. Farr was able to get a provision written into law that required the FDA to hold public meetings on the issue.

Farr has cosponsored legislation to reclassify medical marijuana under federal law so it can be legally prescribed. And he has cosponsored legislation to allow people accused of violating federal marijuana laws to introduce evidence that they followed state law allowing them to use marijuana.

Farr is a staunch party loyalist and no fan of gestures toward bipartisanship. "Every new president begins by reaching out to the opposition party. It isn't too long before they realize the role of the opposition party is to kick you in the teeth," he said in January 2009. Two years later, he derided Republican plans to open the new Congress with a bipartisan reading of the government's founding document. "I don't see what benefit will come from the reading of the Constitution," Farr said. "It's going to require a lot of work by clerks and recorders taking all of this down, wasting taxpayer dollars."

Farr was born in San Francisco on the Fourth of July. His father was a long-time state senator and the first national director of highway beautification under President Lyndon B. Johnson. He grew up surrounded by people who influenced his path in life, including liberal California Gov. Edmund G. "Pat" Brown and photographer Ansel Adams, a family friend. Farr is an avid photographer known for snapping pictures of his colleagues at work and play.

Farr graduated from Willamette University in 1963, then joined the Peace Corps. His mother died of cancer while he was serving. After that, his family visited him in Colombia and, while on an outing, his younger sister was thrown from a horse and injured her head. She died on the operating table.

After leaving the Peace Corps, Farr got a staff job in the California Assembly. He later won election to the Monterey County Board of Supervisors, followed by more than a dozen years in the Assembly.

In 1993, he won a special election to replace veteran Democratic Rep. Leon E. Panetta, who had become President Bill Clinton's budget director. Farr took 54 percent of the vote in a runoff against the GOP nominee, Pebble Beach lawyer Bill McCampbell. He hung on in their 1994 rematch and has been re-elected easily since.

Key Votes

2010

Overhaul the nation's health insurance system	YES
Allow for repeal of "don't ask, don't tell"	YES
Overhaul financial services industry regulation	YES
Limit use of new Afghanistan War funds to troop withdrawal activities	YES
Change oversight of offshore drilling and lift oil spill liability cap	YES
Provide a path to legal status for some children of illegal immigrants	YES
Extend Bush-era income tax cuts for two years	NO

2009

Expand the Children's Health Insurance Program	YES
Provide $787 billion in tax cuts and spending increases to stimulate the economy	YES
Allow bankruptcy judges to modify certain primary-residence mortgages	YES
Create a cap-and-trade system to limit greenhouse gas emissions	YES
Provide $2 billion for the "cash for clunkers" program	YES
Establish the government as the sole provider of student loans	YES
Restrict federally funded insurance coverage for abortions in health care overhaul	NO

CQ Vote Studies

	PARTY UNITY		PRESIDENTIAL SUPPORT	
	SUPPORT	OPPOSE	SUPPORT	OPPOSE
2010	99%	1%	86%	14%
2009	99%	1%	94%	6%
2008	99%	1%	13%	87%
2007	98%	2%	4%	96%
2006	97%	3%	13%	87%

Interest Groups

	AFL-CIO	ADA	CCUS	ACU
2010	100%	90%	13%	0%
2009	100%	100%	33%	0%
2008	100%	100%	61%	0%
2007	100%	95%	55%	0%
2006	93%	95%	27%	4%

California 17

Monterey, San Benito and Santa Cruz counties — Salinas, Santa Cruz

The 17th takes in the most populated part of Santa Cruz County, with its namesake city and several sizable seaside communities, and stretches south to include San Benito and Monterey counties, where Monterey attracts tourists and exclusive Pebble Beach is home to celebrities and Silicon Valley executives.

South of Santa Cruz County, agriculture drives the economy. The Salinas Valley, where farmers and local officials have fought over water quality regulations, supplies nearly 80 percent of America's artichokes, as well as lettuce, spinach, cauliflower, cut flowers and other crops. Major wineries and vineyards also dot the landscape. The valley is home to most of the district's Hispanic population.

More than 60 percent of district residents live in Monterey County. The region has developed as a center for marine sciences, with more than a dozen major research institutions located near the Monterey Bay coastline. The county also attracts tourists to its coastline, wineries and Cannery Row,

once a fishing and canning hub and now a shopping center. The 17th hosts several colleges, including the University of California, Santa Cruz, and California State University Monterey Bay.

Santa Cruz County is a Democratic stronghold, and the party has a strong voter registration edge in Monterey and San Benito counties. Jerry Brown took 64 percent of the district's 2010 gubernatorial vote.

Major Industry
Agriculture, tourism, higher education

Military Bases
Fort Hunter Liggett (Army), 3,793 military, 2,160 civilian (2009); Defense Language Institute Foreign Language Center/Presidio of Monterey (Army), 5,419 military, 2,481 civilian (2007); Naval Postgraduate School, 1,557 military, 149 civilian (2010); Fleet Numerical Meteorology and Oceanography Center, 40 military, 133 civilian (2011)

Cities
Salinas, 150,441; Santa Cruz, 59,946; Watsonville city (pt.), 51,073

Notable
Monterey Canyon is the deepest submarine canyon off the North American coast of the Pacific Ocean.

Rep. Dennis Cardoza (D)

Capitol Office
225-6131
www.house.gov/cardoza
2437 Rayburn Bldg. 20515-0518; fax 225-0819

Committees
Agriculture
Foreign Affairs

Residence
Atwater

Born
March 31, 1959; Merced, Calif.

Religion
Roman Catholic

Family
Wife, Kathleen McLoughlin; three children

Education
U. of Maryland, B.A. 1982 (government & politics)

Career
Bowling alley executive; Realtor; state legislative aide; congressional aide

Political Highlights
Atwater City Council, 1984-87; Merced City Council, 1994-95; Calif. Assembly, 1996-2002

ELECTION RESULTS

2010 GENERAL

Dennis Cardoza (D)	72,853	58.5%
Michael Clare Berryhill Sr. (R)	51,716	41.5%

2010 PRIMARY

Dennis Cardoza (D)	unopposed

2008 GENERAL

Dennis Cardoza (D)	unopposed

Previous Winning Percentages
2006 (66%); 2004 (67%); 2002 (51%)

Elected 2002; 5th term

Cardoza served as a link between his party's liberal leadership and the fiscally conservative Blue Dog Coalition when the Democrats were in charge of the House. But after he cast a vote against Minority Leader Nancy Pelosi of California for Speaker at the start of the 112th Congress, he lost his seat at the leadership table, as well as his post on the Rules Committee, which translates leadership's wishes into the parameters for floor debates on major legislation.

"I assumed when I didn't vote for her that that may happen, but I am a little disappointed that she has not called me and told me that we've been disinvited," he told Roll Call in a February 2011 interview.

During his time as the Blue Dog liaison, Cardoza was much more a party man than when he first arrived in Congress. Now he faces new dilemmas and reduced clout with Republicans back in control of the House.

His party-loyalty scores — the percentage of votes in which he sided with a majority of Democrats against a majority of Republicans — rose from about 80 percent under Republican rule to the mid-90s under Democrats. He might have tipped his hand about where he's headed on that score by voting for Central Valley colleague Jim Costa for Speaker at the start of the 112th Congress (2011-12), rather than for Pelosi. (Costa voted for Cardoza.)

Despite his connections to leadership, though, he remained ready to clash with the Obama administration, and Housing and Urban Development Secretary Shaun Donovan in particular: "I think he's done a horrible job advocating for American homeowners," Cardoza said.

Cardoza also criticized HUD officials for traveling to Rio de Janeiro in 2010 and proposed an amendment to the fiscal 2011 spending bill for HUD to strip the department's $21 million travel budget. The measure, which Cardoza once called the "keep his ass in Washington" amendment, was included in the House version of the spending legislation. In the meantime, Cardoza succeeded in netting his district $19 million in federal funds from the Neighborhood Stabilization Program in 2010 to redevelop foreclosed and abandoned properties.

As a conduit between the Blue Dogs and the Democratic leadership, Cardoza walked a fine line between loyalty to Pelosi and loyalty to his district.

In December 2010, he voted with bipartisan majorities — but against 112 other Democrats — in support of legislation to extend for two years the George W. Bush-era tax cuts for all income levels.

He split with the majority of his party in December 2008 and voted against the proposed $14 billion package to assist the U.S. auto industry; the bill ultimately died in the Senate. But he supported the $787 billion stimulus package that cleared Congress in February 2009.

He objected to a proposal that the House pass the health care overhaul bill without taking a separate vote, then supported the legislation when the House sent it to Obama.

At the start of the 110th Congress (2007-08), Cardoza and the Blue Dogs successfully pushed for adoption of pay-as-you-go budget rules requiring Congress to find offsets for new tax cuts or spending increases.

Although he had to give up other committee assignments to serve on the Rules panel, Cardoza was allowed to stay on Agriculture and became chairman of its Subcommittee on Horticulture and Organic Agriculture. He zealously promoted the interests of his state during the drafting of a five-year reauthorization of agriculture and nutrition programs. When it was enacted in 2008, he hailed its "historic investments" in specialty crops, conservation and nutrition programs. "California agriculture is finally getting the respect and treatment it deserves," he said. In the new Congress, he is the top Democrat on the Subcommittee on Livestock, Dairy and Poultry — a key spot for a member from the nation's No. 1 dairy-producing state — and also joined the Foreign Affairs Committee.

Cardoza has an personal interest in the foster care system. In 2000, he and his wife, Kathleen McLoughlin, a physician, adopted a sibling pair, Joey and Elaina, when the children were 6 and 3. In 2008, the Child Welfare League of America awarded Cardoza its annual Congressional Voice for Youth Award in recognition of his efforts to improve the foster care system.

Cardoza grew up in the small town of Atwater, the grandson of immigrants who came from Portugal's Azores Islands in the 1920s.

His parents were dairy and sweet-potato farmers who later opened bowling alleys in Atwater and Merced. Interested in politics as a youth, he earned a degree in government and politics from the University of Maryland and then interned for Democratic Rep. Martin Frost of Texas.

After college, Cardoza went home to manage the family's bowling business. In 1984, he was elected to the Atwater City Council. He volunteered in the campaign of California Assemblyman Gary A. Condit, who became a political mentor.

Cardoza made it to the Assembly himself in 1996, serving six years. Foreshadowing his role in the U.S. House, he was a leader of a moderate Democratic faction and chaired the Rules Committee.

Condit moved up to the U.S. House but saw his career cut short after he admitted to an extramarital affair with intern Chandra Levy. The young woman from Modesto disappeared in 2002 and was later found slain in a Washington, D.C., park, the victim of an assault while she was jogging.

Condit refused to bow out of the 2002 Democratic primary, so Cardoza challenged him.

Both of Condit's grown children circulated letters in the district calling Cardoza a "traitor." But he had the Democratic establishment on his side. He won the primary, then prevailed over GOP state Sen. Dick Monteith by 8 percentage points that November.

Cardoza has had no primary opposition since, and in 2008 he faced no opposition in the general election.

In 2010, he defeated Republican Michael Berryhill with 58 percent of the vote.

Key Votes

2010

Overhaul the nation's health insurance system	YES
Allow for repeal of "don't ask, don't tell"	YES
Overhaul financial services industry regulation	YES
Limit use of new Afghanistan War funds to troop withdrawal activities	NO
Change oversight of offshore drilling and lift oil spill liability cap	YES
Provide a path to legal status for some children of illegal immigrants	YES
Extend Bush-era income tax cuts for two years	YES

2009

Expand the Children's Health Insurance Program	YES
Provide $787 billion in tax cuts and spending increases to stimulate the economy	YES
Allow bankruptcy judges to modify certain primary-residence mortgages	YES
Create a cap-and-trade system to limit greenhouse gas emissions	YES
Provide $2 billion for the "cash for clunkers" program	YES
Establish the government as the sole provider of student loans	YES
Restrict federally funded insurance coverage for abortions in health care overhaul	YES

CQ Vote Studies

	PARTY UNITY		PRESIDENTIAL SUPPORT	
	Support	Oppose	Support	Oppose
2010	93%	7%	95%	5%
2009	94%	6%	96%	4%
2008	97%	3%	16%	84%
2007	94%	6%	7%	93%
2006	79%	21%	50%	50%

Interest Groups

	AFL-CIO	ADA	CCUS	ACU
2010	100%	75%	25%	0%
2009	95%	90%	43%	8%
2008	93%	85%	65%	8%
2007	96%	90%	63%	4%
2006	85%	60%	79%	46%

California 18

Central Valley — Merced, part of Stockton and Modesto

The 18th takes in most of Stockton in San Joaquin County, then dives south to pick up half of Stanislaus County and Merced County, which make up the district's agricultural base.

A narrow strip stretches through Madera and Fresno counties to almost reach the city of Fresno. Modesto, the Stanislaus County seat, experienced years of growth as businesses fled California's congested coastal cities. The Central Valley's successful agriculture industry also supported a stable economy that has been beset by rising unemployment and foreclosure rates.

Many of the district's blue-collar workers — the 18th has the third-highest percentage in the state — work in the canning and food-processing industry. The district's portion of Modesto includes the headquarters of Foster Farms Dairy, the largest privately owned dairy in California, as well as a full-service plant. National companies such as Del Monte and Frito-Lay also have facilities here. Hometown Gallo Winery is the nation's second-largest wine producer.

Although dominated by agriculture, the district also takes in the diverse and Democratic central portion of the port city of Stockton (shared with the 11th), which is a transportation hub on the San Joaquin River. More than half of Stockton's residents live in the 18th. In 2005, the University of California opened a Merced campus, the system's 10th and the first U.S. public research university to be built in the 21st century.

The area has a long history of sending Democrats to Congress, having done so for decades, and Democrat Jerry Brown carried the 18th by more than 11 percentage points in the 2010 gubernatorial election. Hispanics now enjoy a majority of the district's population, and more than 15 percent of voting-age residents are naturalized citizens. Stockton has one of the largest Sikh populations in the United States.

Major Industry
Agriculture, wine, food processing

Cities
Stockton (pt.), 154,589; Modesto (pt.), 128,394; Merced, 78,958; Ceres (pt.), 42,591; Los Banos, 35,972

Notable
Stockton hosts an annual asparagus festival, during which more than 40,000 pounds of asparagus are consumed.

Rep. Jeff Denham (R)

Capitol Office
225-4540
denham.house.gov
1605 Longworth Bldg. 20515-0519; fax 225-3402

Committees
Natural Resources
Transportation & Infrastructure
(Economic Development, Public Buildings &
Emergency Management - Chairman)
Veterans' Affairs

Residence
Atwater

Born
July 29, 1967; Hawthorne, Calif.

Religion
Presbyterian

Family
Wife, Sonia Denham; two children

Education
Victor Valley Junior College, A.A. 1989 (liberal arts);
California Polytechnic State U., San Luis Obispo, B.A.
1992 (political science)

Military
Air Force, 1984-88; Air Force Reserve, 1988-00

Career
Agricultural packaging company owner; almond
orchard owner

Political Highlights
Republican nominee for Calif. Assembly, 2000; Calif.
Senate, 2002-10

ELECTION RESULTS

2010 GENERAL

Jeff Denham (R)	128,394	64.6%
Loraine Goodwin (D)	69,912	35.1%

2010 PRIMARY

Jeff Denham (R)	26,594	36.3%
Jim Patterson (R)	22,355	30.5%
Richard W. Pombo (R)	15,196	20.7%
Larry Westerlund (R)	9,126	12.5%

Elected 2010; 1st term

When Denham talks about running his congressional offices, he sounds less like a veteran politician and more like the businessman he has been.

And, as a former state senator who represented a district more populous than his current U.S. House district, he is no stranger to the necessity of taking care of the folks back home. "Customer service is not something that's talked about in politics very much," Denham said.

In addition to a 16-year active-duty and reserve career in the Air Force — he served in both Operation Desert Storm in Iraq and Operation Restore Hope in Somalia — Denham's résumé shows ownership of an almond orchard in California's Central Valley and a plastic-container company.

He is particularly interested in addressing issues facing recent Iraq and Afghanistan combat veterans from his seat on the Veterans' Affairs Committee.

Water supply issues are a priority to his Central Valley constituency, and he can tackle them from both his spots on the Natural Resources Committee and Transportation and Infrastructure, where he chairs the economic development panel.

Denham, a self-described fiscal conservative, also said that one of his priorities will be to find ways to reduce the national debt. "I think it is hurting us on a worldwide scale," he said. The debt has led to a "lack of confidence from consumers and from businesses." He wants to make current tax rates on capital gains and dividends permanent.

Denham was an unsuccessful Republican nominee for the California Assembly in 2000; two years later he won a state Senate seat. He was the target of a recall campaign in 2008, but held his seat with 75 percent of the vote.

He had considered running for lieutenant governor or a state Assembly seat before he was contacted by Republican Rep. George Radanovich, who was retiring after eight terms. Radanovich reportedly called Denham on Dec. 24, asking if he would consider running in the reliably Republican 19th District.

He won a crowded GOP primary with 36 percent of the vote, then cruised to victory against Democrat Loraine Goodwin with just less than two-thirds of the vote.

California 19

Central Valley — part of Fresno and Modesto, Turlock, Madera

A fertile farm district, the 19th includes the heart of the San Joaquin Valley. It takes in about half of Stanislaus County, grabbing a portion of Modesto. East of Stanislaus, it moves south from Tuolumne to Mariposa County into almost all of Madera County and part of the city of Fresno, home to large Hispanic, Hmong and Armenian populations. The district's portion of Stanislaus County includes just more than one-third of Modesto's population and the city of Turlock. Some tracts of farmland north of Modesto may give way to highway routes as local officials address smart growth issues and business development.

Along with Madera County to the south, sparsely populated Tuolumne and Mariposa counties host Yosemite National Park. These counties feature ski slopes and forests of the Sierra Nevada range in the east and former Gold Rush towns in the west.

This agricultural district — boasting the nation's third-highest orchard acreage and about 10 percent of California's milk cows — has a Foster Farms Dairy milk and juice processing plant in Fresno. A ConAgra plant in Oakdale is the city's largest employer. Madera County has several notable wineries and their tasting tours attract tourists. The 19th is reliably Republican at both the statewide and federal levels, and GOP candidate Meg Whitman won 55 percent of the district's 2010 gubernatorial vote.

Major Industry
Agriculture, dairy, tourism

Cities
Fresno (pt.), 221,365; Modesto (pt.), 72,771; Turlock, 68,549; Madera, 61,416

Notable
Yosemite National Park was founded in 1890, and its El Capitan rock formation is the world's largest granite monolith.

Rep. Jim Costa (D)

Capitol Office
225-3341
www.house.gov/costa
1314 Longworth Bldg. 20515-0520; fax 225-9308

Committees
Agriculture
Natural Resources

Residence
Fresno

Born
April 13, 1952; Fresno, Calif.

Religion
Roman Catholic

Family
Single

Education
California State U., Fresno, B.A. 1974 (political science)

Career
Lobbyist; state legislative aide; congressional district aide; almond orchard owner

Political Highlights
Calif. Assembly, 1978-94; Democratic nominee for Calif. Senate, 1993; Calif. Senate, 1994-2002

ELECTION RESULTS

2010 GENERAL

Jim Costa (D)	46,247	51.7%
Andy Vidak (R)	43,197	48.3%

2010 PRIMARY

Jim Costa (D)	19,599	79.3%
Steven Haze (D)	5,122	20.7%

2008 GENERAL

Jim Costa (D)	93,023	74.3%
Jim Lopez (R)	32,118	25.7%

Previous Winning Percentages
2006 (100%); 2004 (53%)

Elected 2004; 4th term

Costa, who earned his legislative credibility during 24 years in Sacramento, has built up a specialty in agricultural and natural resource issues that are critical in the San Joaquin Valley.

A member of the Blue Dog Coalition of fiscally conservative Democrats, Costa once said, "I don't like being labeled." In his first congressional term, he displayed something of a moderate voting record but he was a more reliable Democratic vote under Democratic leadership of the House than he was under Republican leadership. The new political and fiscal realities following the 2010 elections will test Costa's party loyalties anew.

He made an early bid to re-assert his independence by voting for someone other than Minority Leader Nancy Pelosi, a fellow California Democrat, for Speaker at the start of the 112th Congress (2011-12).

Costa sits on the Natural Resources Committee, where he chaired the Energy and Minerals Resources panel in the 111th Congress (2009-10). In 2010 he led the first subcommittee hearings on BP and the Minerals Management Service following the company's oil spill in the Gulf of Mexico, noting that he and then-committee Chairman Nick J. Rahall II of West Virginia had chaired about 20 oversight hearings on the agency since 2007.

While chastising BP, Costa defended offshore drilling. "I am a strong supporter of offshore drilling — I believe it is one of the tools in our energy toolbox that we will continue to depend on for decades to come," he said.

Costa managed to anger the oil and gas industries soon after taking over the chairmanship in the 110th Congress (2007-08) by pushing to require mining companies to pay royalties on mines near national parks. He told McClatchy Newspapers that Congress "needs to bring a 135-year-old law into the 21st century." The House passed the measure in 2007, but it stalled in the Senate with the threat of a White House veto.

In April 2010 he picked a fight with neighboring Democrat George Miller over water allocated for the San Joaquin Valley. "George Miller is a poster boy for polluters whose toxic waste creates stress factors that kill fish upstream while he pushes for water restrictions that solely blame and punish us for dwindling fish populations," Costa said. Later that month Costa and California Democrat Dennis Cardoza — Costa's choice for Speaker over Pelosi — announced that nearly $21 million of California's stimulus funds would be set aside for a water project in the valley.

When Republicans contended that Costa and Cardoza agreed to support Obama's health care overhaul in 2010 in exchange for getting more water for the valley, Costa called the charge "absolutely false and almost laughable" on Bakersfield.com.

He also proposed to fund the restoration of the San Joaquin River with a fee on outer continental shelf leases that are not producing oil or gas. The restoration would return salmon to the river. Obama signed into law a catch-all public-lands bill that includes $88 million for the work necessary to restore water flows and the salmon population.

Costa worked on the 2008 reauthorization of farm programs on the Agriculture Committee, keeping an eye on how it deals with the specialty crops that are abundant in California's Central Valley. In the 112th, he serves as ranking member on the Rural Development, Research, Biotechnology and Foreign Agriculture Subcommittee, where he can push for agricultural research funding at Fresno State and for increased access to foreign markets for the district's crops.

Costa's agricultural roots run deep. His immigrant grandfather started milking cows on the day he arrived in the Central Valley a century ago from the Portuguese Azores island of Terceira. Costa's father and uncle later ran the roughly 500-acre farm, and he started helping out at age 7. The family sold its dairy herd in the 1970s, and the farm was divided after his father and uncle died. Costa still owns 240 acres of the property, now an almond orchard.

Costa comes from a politically active family. His father served as treasurer for a friend running for the county board of supervisors. His mother, who died in 2006 at 90, served on a county social services board and as a school trustee. She belonged to Democratic clubs and thought President Harry S. Truman was "a heck of a guy," Costa told the Fresno Bee when his mother died.

Despite his parents' civic involvement, farming and skiing occupied most of Costa's attention in high school and college. It wasn't until he interned in the office of California Democratic Rep. B.F. Sisk in the summer of 1973 and attended the Senate Watergate hearings that Costa caught the political bug.

He worked on the winning 1974 House campaign of California Democrat John Krebs, then was an aide in his Washington office before returning to California to help on a state legislative race. After 18 months as the legislator's administrative assistant, Costa decided to run for the Assembly himself in 1978, when the incumbent in his hometown district made a run for governor.

When term limits forced him out of the state Senate in 2002, Costa opened his own lobbying firm. Having flirted with a House run three previous times, Costa quickly declared his candidacy after six-term Democrat Cal Dooley announced he would not run again. Getting to know the electorate was not a problem; The state Senate district Costa represented for eight years included the entire congressional district. "I'm like an old shoe who's been working with those folks for a long time," Costa said.

Costa trounced former Dooley chief of staff Lisa Quigley in the 2004 primary, which featured a TV ad citing Costa's 1986 arrest in a prostitution sting, for which he had earlier apologized, and a 1994 incident in which police found marijuana in his apartment. (The drug was never linked to him and no charges were filed.) He faced a tough challenge in November from well-funded Republican state Sen. Roy Ashburn. But Costa won by 7 percentage points and was re-elected without opposition in 2006. He easily won re-election in 2008, then won one of the closest House races of 2010, nipping Republican Andy Vidak by just more than 3,000 votes in a contest that was not decided until three weeks after election day.

Key Votes

2010

Overhaul the nation's health insurance system	YES
Allow for repeal of "don't ask, don't tell"	YES
Overhaul financial services industry regulation	YES
Limit use of new Afghanistan War funds to troop withdrawal activities	NO
Change oversight of offshore drilling and lift oil spill liability cap	NO
Provide a path to legal status for some children of illegal immigrants	YES
Extend Bush-era income tax cuts for two years	YES

2009

Expand the Children's Health Insurance Program	YES
Provide $787 billion in tax cuts and spending increases to stimulate the economy	YES
Allow bankruptcy judges to modify certain primary-residence mortgages	YES
Create a cap-and-trade system to limit greenhouse gas emissions	NO
Provide $2 billion for the "cash for clunkers" program	YES
Establish the government as the sole provider of student loans	?
Restrict federally funded insurance coverage for abortions in health care overhaul	YES

CQ Vote Studies

	PARTY UNITY		PRESIDENTIAL SUPPORT	
	Support	Oppose	Support	Oppose
2010	86%	14%	93%	7%
2009	91%	9%	93%	7%
2008	94%	6%	26%	74%
2007	92%	8%	8%	92%
2006	76%	24%	47%	53%

Interest Groups

	AFL-CIO	ADA	CCUS	ACU
2010	86%	70%	50%	8%
2009	90%	85%	67%	12%
2008	100%	80%	67%	9%
2007	96%	90%	65%	4%
2006	86%	70%	93%	56%

California 20

Central Valley — Kings County, parts of Fresno and Bakersfield

The Hispanic-majority and largely blue-collar 20th District reaches from Fresno to Bakersfield, through rural portions of Fresno, Kings and Kern counties. Nearly one-third of Fresno's residents live in the 20th, which takes in much of downtown and Hispanic areas in the southern section of the city.

Federal water projects in the Westlands spawned vast farms with battalions of workers growing a variety of crops, including alfalfa, cotton, fruits, sugar beets, wheat and nuts.

Years of over-irrigation damaged some of the once-fertile land, and a public-private partnership hopes to repurpose tens of thousands of acres as solar energy fields. Fresno's agricultural contribution is more industrial, with fruit and other food processing plants, a Foster Farms poultry farm and several dairy farms. Overall, the district has the nation's fourth-largest orchard acreage.

California's 20th District bears much of the heavy burden created by the fast-growing San Joaquin Valley's urban and rural poor population, and it is beset by unemployment and crime. Its residents struggle with the lowest median household incomes in the state and among the lowest rates of formal education nationally.

Many district workers are Hispanic and Hmong immigrants who work in the local farming communities that are vulnerable to economic uncertainty during prolonged drought conditions.

Democrats enjoy a distinct voter registration advantage in the 20th overall. Although Democrat Jerry Brown won the district's gubernatorial vote in 2010 with 56 percent, GOP candidate Meg Whitman won by more than 12 percentage points in Republican-leaning Kings County.

Major Industry
Agriculture, dairy, prisons

Military Bases
Naval Air Station Lemoore, 6,008 military, 724 civilian (2011)

Cities
Fresno (pt.), 159,688; Bakersfield (pt.), 62,235; Hanford, 53,967; Delano, 53,041

Notable
The Fresno Sanitary Landfill is the country's oldest.

Rep. Devin Nunes (R)

Capitol Office
225-2523
nunes.house.gov
1013 Longworth Bldg. 20515-0521; fax 225-3404

Committees
Ways & Means
Select Intelligence

Residence
Tulare

Born
Oct. 1, 1973; Tulare, Calif.

Religion
Roman Catholic

Family
Wife, Elizabeth Nunes; two children

Education
College of the Sequoias, A.A. 1993 (agriculture);
California Polytechnic State U., San Luis Obispo,
B.S. 1995 (agricultural business), M.S. 1996 (agriculture)

Career
Farmer; U.S. Agriculture Department program
administrator

Political Highlights
College of the Sequoias Board of Trustees, 1996-
2002; sought Republican nomination for U.S. House,
1998

ELECTION RESULTS

2010 GENERAL

Devin Nunes (R)		unopposed

2010 PRIMARY

Devin Nunes (R)		unopposed

2008 GENERAL

Devin Nunes (R)	143,498	68.4%
Larry Johnson (D)	66,317	31.6%

Previous Winning Percentages
2006 (67%); 2004 (73%); 2002 (70%)

Elected 2002; 5th term

Nunes applies his conservative principles as a member of the Ways and Means Committee, which gives him a forum to address "big picture" ideas like overhauling entitlement programs. He wrote a book published in 2010 that details his plan to change the economic course of the country.

"It's a policy book," Nunes said. "I offer real legislative proposals that I think would fix and change the country today." The book, "Restoring the Republic," focuses on programs such as Social Security and Medicare as well as tax law and energy policy, Nunes said. "Entitlement reform, tax reform and energy — those are the three most important issues at the highest level."

He has a history of controversial positions on topics where some colleagues try to tread lightly. In early 2010, Nunes became one of the first supporters of Wisconsin Republican Paul D. Ryan's "Roadmap for America's Future," a long-term plan to balance the budget that includes specific recommendations for trimming entitlement programs.

"If anyone wants to have an adult conversation about Ryan's reforms, they are good reforms," Nunes said. "We are the only ones trying to save Social Security. We are the only plan out there that tries to save the program. No one else has it."

Nunes has built strategic alliances within the Republican leadership — he backed Speaker John A. Boehner of Ohio in his initial 2006 contest for GOP leader — although he evinces no interest in joining their ranks. Instead, he focuses on moving up on Ways and Means, where he is sixth in seniority among Republicans. He was also named by Boehner to the Select Committee on Intelligence in the 112th Congress (2011-12), joining what he described to The Fresno Bee as "arguably the most important committee in Congress for national security issues." He is the youngest member of the committee.

Republican leaders can almost always rely on Nunes — he voted with his party 99 percent of the time in 2010 when a majority of Republicans differed from a majority of Democrats. (His annual rating has never been below 95 percent.) He voted against an expansion of a children's health insurance program that was one of first measures to clear Congress and be signed by President Obama in 2009. He also opposed Obama's $787 billion economic stimulus package, signed into law in February 2009, stating: "It is little more than a magician's grab-bag, loaded with tricks and treats but totally lacking in substance."

When Nunes gained a seat on Ways and Means, he had to give up the top GOP slot on the Natural Resources subcommittee on national parks, where he typically sided with landowners in their frequent disputes with environmentalists. A descendant of dairy farmers from the middle of California, Nunes has battled environmentalists, Democrats and even Republicans to protect the water and agricultural interests of his constituents.

Nunes spent much of the 110th Congress (2007-08) embroiled in a dispute with other members of the California delegation on water allocations from the San Joaquin River. The issue stems from a court settlement reached by environmentalists and some local officials to restore water to a 60-mile dry stretch of the river in the hope of returning Chinook salmon to the area. Nunes in 2006 had joined with many of his California colleagues in announcing legislation to implement the settlement. But he soon turned against the deal. He complained that under the court settlement "my district will provide the bulk of water used to restore the river. Perhaps this is the reason so many other valley legislators were willing to move forward without finding ways to offset water losses."

In 2006, Nunes won passage of a measure requiring dairy producers to operate in a federally regulated system. The bill was aimed at an Arizona-based dairy, Sarah Farms, which was operating outside the system and selling milk for a lower price in California. Nunes' district is the top milk producer.

Nunes' family hails from the Azores, the nine-island chain off the coast of Portugal, where several hundred years ago everyone "had three cows, fished and made wine," he said. His immigrant grandfather established the 640-acre family farm, where his grandmother still runs a dairy operation with the help of two of Nunes' uncles. Nunes and his brother, Anthony, once ran an alfalfa hay harvesting business. Nunes' only involvement in agriculture today is in wine; he is part-owner of the Alpha Omega winery.

The district is home to a concentration of Portuguese-Americans, many of them related by blood or marriage, and most are Roman Catholic. They share food traditions, festivals and other cultural elements. In 2003, Nunes married Elizabeth Tamariz, a Portuguese-American who teaches elementary school and whom he's known since childhood. His office wall features a soccer jersey from Portuguese star Luis Figo.

After graduating from California Polytechnic State University with a master's degree in 1996, Nunes volunteered to help a candidate for the board of the two-year College of the Sequoias, which he had attended. The candidate unexpectedly quit, and Nunes, then 22, decided to run. He wound up ousting a seasoned incumbent. The next day Nunes, wearing work clothes and fixing his grandmother's water heater, was surprised when a local television crew drove out to interview him. He was hooked on politics.

While on the school board, he met Bill Thomas, the local congressman. In 1998, he agreed to an all-but-hopeless challenge to Democratic incumbent Cal Dooley in the 20th District and lost. In 2000, Nunes campaigned for GOP presidential candidate George W. Bush and was rewarded when Thomas helped him get appointed state director for the Agriculture Department's rural development program when Bush became president in 2001.

Reapportionment gave California an additional seat, and the 21st District was created. In 2002, Nunes beat two better-known Republicans in the primary, Fresno Mayor Jim Patterson and state Rep. Mike Briggs. The two competitors split the GOP vote in the Fresno area, to Nunes' advantage. He also benefited from the solid support of Portuguese-American voters in Tulare County. He cruised to victory in the general election and has easily won re-election since.

Key Votes

2010

Overhaul the nation's health insurance system	NO
Allow for repeal of "don't ask, don't tell"	NO
Overhaul financial services industry regulation	NO
Limit use of new Afghanistan War funds to troop withdrawal activities	NO
Change oversight of offshore drilling and lift oil spill liability cap	?
Provide a path to legal status for some children of illegal immigrants	NO
Extend Bush-era income tax cuts for two years	YES

2009

Expand the Children's Health Insurance Program	NO
Provide $787 billion in tax cuts and spending increases to stimulate the economy	NO
Allow bankruptcy judges to modify certain primary-residence mortgages	NO
Create a cap-and-trade system to limit greenhouse gas emissions	NO
Provide $2 billion for the "cash for clunkers" program	NO
Establish the government as the sole provider of student loans	-
Restrict federally funded insurance coverage for abortions in health care overhaul	YES

CQ Vote Studies

	PARTY UNITY		PRESIDENTIAL SUPPORT	
	SUPPORT	OPPOSE	SUPPORT	OPPOSE
2010	99%	1%	27%	73%
2009	97%	3%	18%	82%
2008	97%	3%	83%	17%
2007	97%	3%	81%	19%
2006	98%	2%	95%	5%

Interest Groups

	AFL-CIO	ADA	CCUS	ACU
2010	0%	0%	100%	100%
2009	0%	0%	73%	96%
2008	7%	0%	94%	100%
2007	5%	5%	79%	100%
2006	8%	0%	100%	84%

California 21

Central Valley — Tulare County, part of Fresno

The agriculture-dominated 21st is home to all of Tulare County and part of Fresno County, which vie each year for the title of top farm-goods-producing county in the nation. The 21st ranks first in the country in both orchard acreage and total number of milk cows. In addition to more than one-fifth of the city of Fresno, the district takes in some of the mountains and forests of the Sierra Nevada chain on its eastern edge.

Tulare County is the world's largest dairy-producing area and the nation's second-largest agricultural county. The county produces more than 250 agricultural goods, including oranges, grapes, nuts and cotton. But a large Land O'Lakes cheese processing plant in Tulare closed in 2010, and extended drought conditions can hurt production. Tulare's economy has been hit hard by high unemployment rates in recent years.

The city of Tulare hosts the annual World Ag Expo, the world's largest agricultural exposition, which draws an annual attendance of more than 100,000 people from more than 60 countries. Visalia is the site of a Provisions Food Company cheese manufacturing plant.

The 21st includes the eastern portion of Fresno, including Fresno Yosemite International Airport. The city also is home to a solar-powered Gap clothing distribution center and the Foster Farms turkey hatchery. Tourists are attracted to the district's location in the Sequoia Valley: The Giant Sequoia National Monument and the Sequoia National Forest are located east of Porterville and offer camping, hiking, kayaking or mountain biking either in the forest or in the nearby Sierra Nevada range.

The district's share of Fresno is the more conservative area of the city, and the rest of the 21st is reliably Republican. Republicans hold a solid edge in voter registration in the district's portion of Fresno County and in Tulare, and the district gave GOP candidate Meg Whitman 58 percent of its 2010 gubernatorial vote, her third-best showing in the state.

Major Industry
Agriculture, dairy, transportation, tourism

Cities
Visalia, 124,442; Fresno (pt.), 113,612; Clovis, 95,631; Tulare, 59,278; Porterville, 54,165

Notable
The Porterville High School marching band is said to be the oldest high school band in California.

Rep. Kevin McCarthy (R)

Capitol Office
225-2915
kevinmccarthy.house.gov
326 Cannon Bldg. 20515-0522; fax 225-8798

Committees
Financial Services

Residence
Bakersfield

Born
Jan. 26, 1965; Bakersfield, Calif.

Religion
Baptist

Family
Wife, Judy McCarthy; two children

Education
Bakersfield College, attended 1984-85; California
State U., Bakersfield, B.S. 1989 (business administration), M.B.A. 1994

Career
Congressional district director; sandwich shop
owner

Political Highlights
Kern County Republican Central Committee, 1992-
2002; Kern County Community College District
Board of Trustees, 2000-02; Calif. Assembly, 2002-06
(minority leader, 2004-06)

ELECTION RESULTS

2010 GENERAL

Kevin McCarthy (R)	173,490	98.8%
John Uebersax (WRI)	2,173	1.2%

2010 PRIMARY

Kevin McCarthy (R)	unopposed

2008 GENERAL

Kevin McCarthy (R)	unopposed

Previous Winning Percentages
2006 (71%)

Elected 2006; 3rd term

McCarthy's ascent to majority whip — the No. 3 spot in the House GOP leadership — in only his third term is a testament to his political savvy and pleasant personality as well as his devotion to unglamorous behind-the-scenes work. It's also a by-product of his ability to raise money — and his willingness to share it.

As Republicans worked to regain their footing after the 2008 elections, McCarthy began to emerge as a secret weapon of sorts. Young, telegenic and devoted to the cause, he impressed the right people in the party leadership and was rewarded in short order.

After only one term in the House, McCarthy was appointed chief deputy whip for the 111th Congress (2009-10), charged with helping then-Minority Whip Eric Cantor of Virginia count votes and bring the party's disparate factions to consensus. He also served on the executive committee of the National Republican Congressional Committee, where he had spectacular success recruiting House candidates for 2010. And he sits on the Republican Steering Committee, which helps guide committee assignments.

Once he had persuaded a candidate to run, he stuck close by for the hand-holding that can be needed in tough races.

"He just makes you feel like you've known him your whole life," freshman Stephen Fincher, R-Tenn., said to the San Luis Obispo Tribune.

His efforts to get Republicans elected are not restricted to his own recruits. He contributed more than a half-million dollars to GOP candidates in the 2010 election cycle. McCarthy uses his weekly five-hour plane ride from Washington to Bakersfield to study the economic and political characteristics of his colleagues' districts, looking for ways to market his policy ideas. "Hopefully, I can get to where I understand their districts better than them," McCarthy said. "They may be able to be part of some legislation and not know it."

In his mid-40s, McCarthy has spent nearly his entire adult life in politics, serving as an aide to his predecessor, Republican Bill Thomas, and as a state legislator before easily winning the seat following Thomas' retirement in 2006. Like Thomas, McCarthy is a fiscal conservative who tends to be only marginally engaged on the issues that preoccupy social conservatives. And like Thomas, he immerses himself in the policy details of legislation as well as in the politics. As Republican Devin Nunes, a longtime friend who represents the adjoining 21st District, told the Los Angeles Times in January 2009, "Kevin lives and breathes politics."

But McCarthy's personality is the polar opposite of that of the abrasive Thomas, who as chairman and ranking member of the Ways and Means Committee was often condescending to his colleagues and hostile to the press. McCarthy is congenial and approachable; whether it is a staff member or a stranger, he greets a visitor with a pat on the back, and it is not unusual for him to conduct a meeting with his feet propped on the desk.

At the start of 2009, he joined the Financial Services Committee. The previous fall, he voted against two $700 billion measures — the second of which became law — aimed at shoring up the nation's financial sector. "I cannot support a bailout using tax dollars to throw our hard-earned money at bad decisions with just the hope that the problem gets fixed," he said. He also opposed a subsequent $14 billion package for the auto industry, which did not become law. And he opposed the Democrats' economic stimulus bill at the start of the 111th Congress, helping craft alternative legislation as a member of a GOP working group.

McCarthy was an enthusiastic supporter of the 2010 decision by House GOP leadership to place a moratorium on the practice of congressional earmarking, or making appropriations requests for projects that affect members' districts. The issue made trouble for McCarthy a year earlier, when Democrats noted that he had requested millions of dollars in earmarks during his first term. McCarthy argued that he voluntarily listed earmark requests on his website before the rules required it and that his feelings about the practice have evolved over the years.

In moving up the leadership ladder, McCarthy surrendered his seat on the House Administration Committee, where his 2009 bill to help ensure that absentee ballots of overseas military personnel are delivered promptly to their proper polling places and swiftly counted was signed into law as part of the Defense authorization measure.

McCarthy's mother was a dental assistant, who then stayed home to raise her three children. His father was a full-time firefighter who also worked as a furniture mover. After turning 18, the younger McCarthy earned a certification and worked three summers as a firefighter.

In high school, McCarthy was class president. He supported President Ronald Reagan's re-election in 1984, which meant going against the strong pro-union sentiment in his family. His father belonged to the firefighters union, and his grandfather was a railroad worker.

To help pay for college, McCarthy bought cars at auctions in Los Angeles and resold them in Bakersfield. On the second day of the California lottery, McCarthy, then 19, won $5,000 from a scratch-off ticket. He invested part of his winnings in the stock market and part to open Kevin O's Deli. Before finishing college, he sold the deli at a profit, after which he worked as an unpaid intern in Thomas' district office. The internship turned into a full-time position; he eventually filled almost every role in that office, from clipping newspapers to handling casework to serving as district director.

In 2000, McCarthy won election to the Kern County Community College board of trustees. Two years later, voters sent him to the state Assembly, where he was the first freshman to be elected Republican leader. As leader, he was included in California's "Big 5," an informal decision-making group that also counted as members GOP Gov. Arnold Schwarzenegger, the Senate president pro tempore, the GOP Senate leader and the Speaker of the Assembly.

In the race to succeed Thomas in 2006, McCarthy defeated two lesser-known candidates in the GOP primary, then breezed past Democrat Sharon M. Beery in the general election with 71 percent of the vote. McCarthy raised $1.2 million to Beery's $27,000. He was unopposed in 2008 and took almost 99 percent of the vote against a write-in candidate in 2010.

Key Votes

2010

Overhaul the nation's health insurance system	NO
Allow for repeal of "don't ask, don't tell"	NO
Overhaul financial services industry regulation	NO
Limit use of new Afghanistan War funds to troop withdrawal activities	NO
Change oversight of offshore drilling and lift oil spill liability cap	?
Provide a path to legal status for some children of illegal immigrants	NO
Extend Bush-era income tax cuts for two years	YES

2009

Expand the Children's Health Insurance Program	NO
Provide $787 billion in tax cuts and spending increases to stimulate the economy	NO
Allow bankruptcy judges to modify certain primary-residence mortgages	NO
Create a cap-and-trade system to limit greenhouse gas emissions	NO
Provide $2 billion for the "cash for clunkers" program	NO
Establish the government as the sole provider of student loans	NO
Restrict federally funded insurance coverage for abortions in health care overhaul	YES

CQ Vote Studies

	PARTY UNITY		PRESIDENTIAL SUPPORT	
	SUPPORT	OPPOSE	SUPPORT	OPPOSE
2010	97%	3%	30%	70%
2009	96%	4%	24%	76%
2008	97%	3%	73%	27%
2007	97%	3%	85%	15%

Interest Groups

	AFL-CIO	ADA	CCUS	ACU
2010	0%	0%	95%	100%
2009	5%	0%	80%	100%
2008	13%	10%	94%	100%
2007	8%	5%	85%	100%

California 22

Kern and San Luis Obispo counties — most of Bakersfield

The 22nd District stretches inland from San Luis Obispo County near the coast to Ridgecrest in Kern County before dipping south into northwest Los Angeles County. It then turns north again to take in most of Bakersfield and most of the remaining parts of Kern. More than 70 percent of district residents live in fast-growing Kern County.

Kern is known for oil production and a strong agricultural base. Along with vineyards and cattle in the San Luis Obispo area (the city itself is in the coastal 23rd), the two counties annually produce billions of dollars' worth of crops such as grapes, citrus, cotton and nuts. Kern County is expanding its energy industry with solar, wind, natural gas, geothermal and biomass facilities.

Kern is also home to the Hyundai-Kia California Proving Ground testing facility in the Mojave Desert area north of Edwards Air Force Base.

Bakersfield (shared with the 20th) is Kern County's largest city and sits in the southern end of the San Joaquin Valley. The city, as well as Lancaster (shared with the 25th) in Los Angeles County, continues to grow. Oil and agriculture dominate, but Bakersfield hopes technology jobs will improve economic diversity.

The 22nd is thoroughly GOP territory with Republican voter registration ahead of Democratic registration throughout the district's communities. GOP candidate John McCain took 60 percent of the district's 2008 vote for president, his highest percentage statewide. And Republican Meg Whitman took her second-highest percentage and highest vote total statewide here in the 2010 gubernatorial race.

Major Industry
Agriculture, oil, military

Military Bases
Edwards Air Force Base, 1,851 military, 5,592 civilian (2010) (shared with the 25th); Naval Air Warfare Center Weapons Division, China Lake, 640 military, 4,204 civilian (2011) (shared with the 25th)

Cities
Bakersfield (pt.), 285,248; Lancaster (pt.), 84,263; Oildale (unincorporated), 32,684; Paso Robles, 29,793; Atascadero, 28,310

Notable
Edwards Air Force Base was the site of Chuck Yeager's 1947 flight that broke the sound barrier.

Rep. Lois Capps (D)

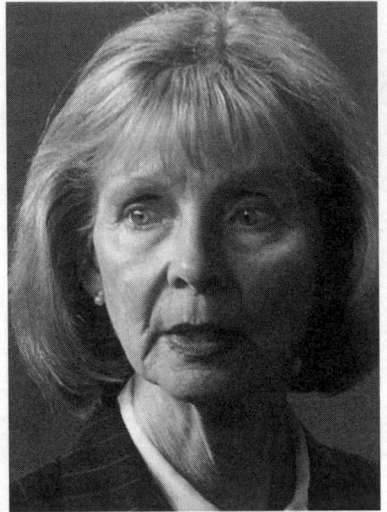

Capitol Office
225-3601
www.house.gov/capps
2231 Rayburn Bldg. 20515-0523; fax 225-5632

Committees
Energy & Commerce

Residence
Santa Barbara

Born
Jan. 10, 1938; Ladysmith, Wis.

Religion
Lutheran

Family
Widowed; three children (one deceased)

Education
Pacific Lutheran U., B.S. 1959 (nursing); Yale U., M.A. 1964 (religion); U. of California, Santa Barbara, M.A. 1990 (education)

Career
Elementary school nurse; college instructor

Political Highlights
No previous office

ELECTION RESULTS

2010 GENERAL

Lois Capps (D)	111,768	57.8%
Tom Watson (R)	72,744	37.6%
John V. Hager (I)	5,625	2.9%
Darrell M. Stafford (LIBERT)	3,326	1.7%

2010 PRIMARY

Lois Capps (D)	unopposed

2008 GENERAL

Lois Capps (D)	171,403	68.1%
Matt T. Kokkonen (R)	80,385	31.9%

Previous Winning Percentages
2006 (65%); 2004 (63%); 2002 (59%); 2000 (53%); 1998 (55%); 1998 Special Election Runoff (54%)

Elected 1998; 7th full term

Capps' legislative passions — health care and the environment — reflect training and geography: She's a registered nurse who represents a district with some of the most spectacular coastal scenery in the country.

Capps keeps her nurse's license current — studying and taking an exam every two years, even though it is no longer her primary occupation — because she believes it enhances her credibility on health care issues. "My long life as a nurse and being able to, as I frame it, continue to be a nurse through advocacy for health in Congress" is important, she said. And she has been busy. In 2003 she founded the Congressional Nursing Caucus. She praised President Obama's early action to expand a children's health insurance program to include families that make too much money to qualify for Medicaid, and she was a decisive voice in the debate over the 2010 health care overhaul legislation.

Capps, a member of the Energy and Commerce Subcommittee on Health, wrote a provision intended to ensure that federal dollars would be kept in separate accounts when flowing into insurance plans, and that accounts funded by federal money could not be used to pay for abortions. Some anti-abortion activists said the proposed firewall was weak and derided the plan as "money laundering." More restrictive language by Michigan Democrat Bart Stupak eventually was adopted by the House. But a variation on Capps' language written by Pennsylvania Democratic Sen. Bob Casey made it into law.

After many analysts blamed the Democratic losses in the 2010 elections on the health care overhaul, Capps remained sanguine about the law.

"It is about to make a difference in people's lives and in our economy, too, as folks gain the confidence they are going to have health care insurance, and we'll see the fear tactics melt away," she told the Ventura County Star.

The loss of her 35-year-old daughter, Lisa, to lung cancer in 2000 inspired Capps to become a tenacious advocate for better awareness of health issues and for improvements in treatment. In the 110th Congress (2007-08), she pushed legislation to provide more information on stroke prevention and treatment; to ease the transition from cancer patient to cancer survivor; and to educate health care professionals about female cardiovascular disease and how treatment for women might differ from that for men.

Capps brings a quiet intensity to environmental issues. Her district, a strip of Southern California coast that includes Santa Barbara, is considered one of the birthplaces of the modern environmental movement. A 1969 oil-well rupture that fouled beaches made her a determined foe of offshore drilling, and when President George W. Bush announced in June 2008 that he would seek to allow more offshore oil production, she called the proposal "half-baked." A co-chairwoman of the National Marine Sanctuary Caucus and of the Congressional Coastal Caucus, Capps said she is encouraged by Obama's decision to exclude California from plans for new offshore leases. Her own proposal would go a step further by ending drilling off the California coast and barring new ventures.

She was a supporter of the House Democrats' cap-and-trade bill to reduce carbon emissions, calling it a good beginning. "In order for this to work, everybody has to be on board," Capps said in March 2009, when the Energy and Commerce Committee was beginning work on the bill. "It doesn't have to start with perfection." A measure she introduced to boost the public health response to climate change was added to the cap-and-trade bill, which the House passed in June 2009 but the Senate never considered.

Even though she once was named the nicest member of Congress, Capps can display a steely resolve. In 2005, she nearly outmaneuvered Republican Majority Leader Tom DeLay of Texas over the potential liability for costs of cleaning up water contaminated by a fuel additive made mostly in Texas. When the GOP's energy policy bill was on the House floor, Capps ambushed DeLay by challenging a provision exempting U.S. producers of the fuel additive methyl tertiary butyl ether (MTBE), from lawsuits over water contamination. Democrats, led by Capps, said a liability shield could shift billions of dollars in cleanup costs to local governments, violating a 1995 law barring the federal government from imposing new costs on states and localities without providing federal money to help meet the mandates. Though her challenge failed on a close vote, the debate called new attention to allegations of MTBE contamination.

Capps had more luck in a showdown with California Republican Duncan Hunter (the father of the current congressman bearing the same name) over public access to Santa Rosa Island, part of Channel Islands National Park. In the fiscal 2008 Interior-Environment spending bill, Capps fought successfully for repeal of Hunter's provision that removed a deadline for ending big game hunting on Santa Rosa Island. The provision, which Hunter said benefited military veterans, would have kept the island closed to the public for the annual five-month hunting season.

The daughter and granddaughter of Lutheran ministers, Capps grew up in small towns in Wisconsin and Montana. She earned a master's degree in religion from Yale and worked as a nurse for many years in Santa Barbara schools. She also ran the county's teen pregnancy counseling project.

When her husband, Walter Capps, ran for the House in 1996, she stood in for him at campaign events while he recovered from injuries suffered in a car accident caused by a drunken driver. When he had a fatal heart attack less than a year into his first term, she ran for his seat in a special election to represent what was then the 22nd District. She benefited from his political organization as well as disunity among Republicans, whose race pitted conservative state Rep. Tom Bordonaro Jr. against moderate state Rep. Brooks Firestone in a bitter struggle won by Bordonaro.

Capps stayed focused on local issues and stressed Democratic themes of protecting the environment and improving education and health care. She won by 9 percentage points over Bordonaro in a runoff. She won a full term in November 1998, again besting Bordonaro, but by 12 percentage points. Republicans targeted her district in 2000, but she held on. Redistricting gave her a boost, peeling away some Republican areas, and she has won easily since 2002.

Key Votes

2010

Overhaul the nation's health insurance system	YES
Allow for repeal of "don't ask, don't tell"	YES
Overhaul financial services industry regulation	YES
Limit use of new Afghanistan War funds to troop withdrawal activities	NO
Change oversight of offshore drilling and lift oil spill liability cap	YES
Provide a path to legal status for some children of illegal immigrants	YES
Extend Bush-era income tax cuts for two years	YES

2009

Expand the Children's Health Insurance Program	YES
Provide $787 billion in tax cuts and spending increases to stimulate the economy	YES
Allow bankruptcy judges to modify certain primary-residence mortgages	YES
Create a cap-and-trade system to limit greenhouse gas emissions	YES
Provide $2 billion for the "cash for clunkers" program	YES
Establish the government as the sole provider of student loans	YES
Restrict federally funded insurance coverage for abortions in health care overhaul	NO

CQ Vote Studies

	PARTY UNITY		PRESIDENTIAL SUPPORT	
	Support	Oppose	Support	Oppose
2010	100%	0%	98%	2%
2009	99%	1%	97%	3%
2008	99%	1%	14%	86%
2007	99%	1%	3%	97%
2006	98%	2%	15%	85%

Interest Groups

	AFL-CIO	ADA	CCUS	ACU
2010	100%	95%	25%	0%
2009	100%	100%	29%	0%
2008	100%	100%	61%	0%
2007	100%	95%	55%	0%
2006	93%	95%	27%	4%

California 23

Central Coast — Oxnard, Santa Barbara, Santa Maria, San Luis Obispo

The Democratic 23rd is a sliver of coastline stretching south from the Monterey County line through San Luis Obispo, Santa Barbara and Oxnard into Ventura County, which lies northwest of Los Angeles.

Agriculture is a mainstay in the San Luis Obispo area. Fast-growing Santa Maria in Santa Barbara County is known for its manufacturing sector as well as its impressive agricultural output of strawberries, broccoli and wine grapes. The Goleta Valley, just north of Santa Barbara, was once a farming region but is now attracting high-tech research.

Oxnard is home to the Port of Hueneme, the only international port on the central coast. It is responsible for importing the majority of California's bananas and cars, and handles more than $10 billion worth of cargo annually. The largest single employer in the county is the Naval Base Ventura County near the port. Tourism also bolsters this beachfront district's economy.

Strongly Democratic Oxnard, which has experienced consistent population growth for decades, is home to a significant portion of the 23rd's growing Hispanic population. The 23rd's college students, such as those at University of California, Santa Barbara, and California Polytechnic State University in San Luis Obispo, mix with the Hollywood elite to form a left-leaning district. Democrat Jerry Brown won the district by more than 17 percentage points in the 2010 gubernatorial race.

Major Industry
Agriculture, military, tourism

Military Bases
Naval Base Ventura County, 6,500 military, 4,400 civilian (2011) (shared with the 24th); Vandenberg Air Force Base, 2,798 military, 4,072 civilian (2010) (shared with the 24th)

Cities
Oxnard, 197,899; Santa Maria (pt.), 99,137; Santa Barbara, 88,410; San Luis Obispo (pt.), 45,113; Goleta, 29,888

Notable
Hearst Castle, a historic house museum at San Simeon, was home to William Randolph Hearst; Channel Islands National Park is home to 145 unique species of flora and fauna and 2,000 other species.

Rep. Elton Gallegly (R)

Capitol Office
225-5811
www.house.gov/gallegly
2309 Rayburn Bldg. 20515-0524; fax 225-1100

Committees
Foreign Affairs
Judiciary
    (Immigration Policy & Enforcement - Chairman)

Residence
Simi Valley

Born
March 7, 1944; Huntington Park, Calif.

Religion
Protestant

Family
Wife, Janice Gallegly; four children

Education
California State U., Los Angeles, attended 1962-63

Career
Real estate broker

Political Highlights
Simi Valley City Council, 1979-86; mayor of Simi
Valley, 1980-86

ELECTION RESULTS

2010 GENERAL
Elton Gallegly (R)	144,055	59.9%
Timothy J. Allison (D)	96,279	40.1%

2010 PRIMARY
Elton Gallegly (R)	unopposed

2008 GENERAL
Elton Gallegly (R)	174,492	58.2%
Marta Ann Jorgensen (D)	125,560	41.8%

Previous Winning Percentages
2006 (62%); 2004 (63%); 2002 (65%); 2000 (54%);
1998 (60%); 1996 (60%); 1994 (66%); 1992 (54%);
1990 (58%); 1988 (69%); 1986 (68%)

Elected 1986; 13th term

Throughout his congressional career, Gallegly has been a low-profile but loyal Republican — considerably more loyal than the GOP leadership has sometimes been to him. But he was finally rewarded when he was named chairman of the panel with jurisdiction over his signature issue: immigration.

One of the few non-lawyers on the Judiciary Committee, Gallegly (GAL-uh-glee) was given the gavel of the Immigration Policy and Enforcement Subcommittee over the more senior — perhaps even harder-line, certainly more rhetorically robust — Steve King of Iowa, who was the ranking Republican on the panel in the 111th Congress (2009-10).

Gallegly says expanding workplace enforcement and broadening the use of E-Verify, used to determine whether employees are eligible to work in the United States, are high on his priority list for the 112th Congress (2011-12). He took a first step in January 2011 by introducing two E-Verify bills, one requiring federal contractors to participate in the program and another banning legislative branch offices from hiring vendors to work in the Capitol if they do not use E-Verify.

Gallegly has also backed legislation that would end birthright citizenship for illegal immigrants, and he opposed efforts to create a path to citizenship for illegal immigrants already in the country.

"This whole term 'comprehensive,' that's spin at its best," Gallegly told the Ventura County Star in July 2010. "It is plain and simple amnesty."

In 2005, he helped win enactment of the Real ID Act, which set minimum security requirements that states must meet for their driver's licenses to be accepted as identification to board commercial flights or enter federal facilities. Full implementation of the law has been delayed multiple times.

Gallegly led an unsuccessful 1996 effort to allow local school districts to decide whether to provide a public school education to the children of illegal immigrants. He argued that states such as California could not afford public education for those children and that the promise of free schooling served as a magnet drawing illegal immigrants into the country.

After leading a 1995 task force on immigration laws, he proposed the pilot electronic employment eligibility verification program that became E-Verify.

Another of Gallegly's legislative passions is fighting animal cruelty. He is a founder and co-chairman of the Animal Protection Caucus.

He is the author of a 1999 law banning "crush videos" — films in which animals are tortured or killed — that was struck down by the Supreme Court in April 2010 on free speech grounds. In July, the House passed a narrower bill aimed at punishing those who sell or distribute such videos for money. President Obama signed it into law in December. "This bill will once again stop these violating, these revolting, videos," Gallegly said.

A former member of the Intelligence Committee, he also sits on the Foreign Affairs panel, where he has taken a tough stand against Iran's nuclear program. He backed sanctions legislation, but wrote in the Los Angeles Jewish Journal in July 2010 that "the United States needs a backup plan in place if Tehran is undeterred. A crucial element of U.S. policy must be to emphasize that all U.S. options are on the table to stop Iran from obtaining nuclear warheads."

A traditional Western conservative, Gallegly's party unity score — the percentage of votes on which he sides with a majority of the GOP against a majority of Democrats — has fallen below 90 percent only once, in the 106th Congress (1999-2000).

But he was twice passed over for the top GOP slot on the Natural Resources Committee. In late 2002, he waged an aggressive campaign to become chairman, but GOP leaders skipped over a number of more senior Republicans, including Gallegly, in favor of Richard W. Pombo of California, a protégé of Majority Leader Tom DeLay of Texas. In 2008, as the GOP organized for the 111th Congress, Gallegly pre-emptively announced he wouldn't be a candidate for top Republican seat on the panel, saying he didn't want to give up his assignment to the Intelligence Committee to take the post (he surrendered the Intelligence seat in the 112th).

Gallegly occasionally casts his lot with Democrats. As a former mayor of Simi Valley, a community close enough to Los Angeles that many of its residents are concerned about the spread of urban crime, Gallegly has voted for gun restrictions that are opposed by many Republicans.

When he was growing up in southeast Los Angeles, Gallegly followed the political persuasions of his father, a lifelong Democrat and poor Dust Bowl migrant from Oklahoma. He described his father in an interview with the Los Angeles Times as "an FDR Democrat, and they're much different from the Democrats of today. He believed in government helping people who couldn't help themselves, but not those who could."

After dropping out of college because he couldn't afford to continue, Gallegly went into the real estate business and built a successful brokerage. He also operated a couple of antique shops, specializing in coin-operated machines and brass cash registers. Frustrated in his dealings with local government, he decided to run for office in 1979.

Gallegly won a seat on the Simi Valley City Council and served concurrently as mayor for six years before running for Congress in 1986. Touting his record of boosting Simi Valley's economic development, Gallegly defeated Anthony J. Hope, comedian Bob Hope's son, in the GOP primary and won the general election by 40 percentage points.

The area he represented in the 1990s was competitive: Democrat Al Gore had carried the district in the 2000 presidential race, when Gallegly was held to 54 percent of the vote. District lines were redrawn in 2001 with incumbent protection in mind, and Gallegly easily won in 2002 and 2004.

Gallegly announced in early 2006 he would not run for an 11th term, citing an unspecified medical issue. But he changed his mind after receiving entreaties by California Republican leaders and President George W. Bush. He returned to the campaign trail and won easily. In 2008, saying he had passed his most recent physical exam with flying colors, Gallegly won re-election with 58 percent. He boosted his winning total to 60 percent in 2010.

Key Votes

2010

Overhaul the nation's health insurance system	NO
Allow for repeal of "don't ask, don't tell"	NO
Overhaul financial services industry regulation	NO
Limit use of new Afghanistan War funds to troop withdrawal activities	NO
Change oversight of offshore drilling and lift oil spill liability cap	NO
Provide a path to legal status for some children of illegal immigrants	NO
Extend Bush-era income tax cuts for two years	YES

2009

Expand the Children's Health Insurance Program	NO
Provide $787 billion in tax cuts and spending increases to stimulate the economy	NO
Allow bankruptcy judges to modify certain primary-residence mortgages	NO
Create a cap-and-trade system to limit greenhouse gas emissions	NO
Provide $2 billion for the "cash for clunkers" program	NO
Establish the government as the sole provider of student loans	NO
Restrict federally funded insurance coverage for abortions in health care overhaul	YES

CQ Vote Studies

	PARTY UNITY		PRESIDENTIAL SUPPORT	
	Support	Oppose	Support	Oppose
2010	97%	3%	29%	71%
2009	90%	10%	25%	75%
2008	96%	4%	63%	37%
2007	94%	6%	86%	14%
2006	96%	4%	94%	6%

Interest Groups

	AFL-CIO	ADA	CCUS	ACU
2010	7%	0%	88%	95%
2009	11%	5%	79%	96%
2008	13%	15%	89%	92%
2007	13%	5%	89%	92%
2006	14%	0%	100%	84%

California 24

Ventura and Santa Barbara counties — Thousand Oaks, Simi Valley

North and west of the close-in Los Angeles suburbs, the 24th includes ski-friendly mountains, fertile valleys and a slice of coastline with excellent surfing. The district takes in nearly all of Ventura County and inland Santa Barbara County.

Ventura County, where most district residents live, is a mix of lower-income farming communities — many workers in the local agricultural industry are immigrants — and more-upscale residential areas. But some cities, particularly Moorpark, Fillmore and Camarillo, have experienced high home-vacancy rates and slow economic growth. Ventura's biotech, insurance, finance and electronics sectors supported what had been a steady economy before the housing market began struggling and unemployment rates began rising.

Citrus fruit thrives in the sunshine and fertile soil of Ventura County, while the central and western portions of the 24th in Santa Barbara County produce grapes, broccoli and strawberries. Western Ventura includes most of the Los Padres National Forest. San Nicolas Island, the Anacapa Islands and part of the Santa Monica Mountains National Recreation Area also fall within the 24th's boundaries.

Interior areas of Santa Barbara County, military families and retirees, and southern Ventura cities such as Simi Valley and Thousand Oaks form a Republican base. Despite that GOP lean, Barack Obama eked out a slim 51 percent win here in the 2008 presidential race. GOP candidate Meg Whitman won 54 percent of the district's 2010 gubernatorial vote.

Major industry
Aeronautics, biotech, service, agriculture

Military bases
Naval Base Ventura County, 6,500 military, 4,400 civilian (2011) (shared with the 23rd); Vandenberg Air Force Base, 2,798 military, 4,072 civilian (2010) (shared with the 23rd)

Cities
Thousand Oaks, 126,683; Simi Valley, 124,237; Ventura (pt.), 85,226; Camarillo, 65,201; Lompoc, 42,434; Moorpark, 34,421

Notable
The Ronald Reagan Presidential Library is in Simi Valley.

Rep. Howard P. "Buck" McKeon (R)

Capitol Office
225-1956
mckeon.house.gov
2184 Rayburn Bldg. 20515-0525; fax 226-0683

Committees
Armed Services - Chairman
Education & the Workforce

Residence
Santa Clarita

Born
Sept. 9, 1938; Los Angeles, Calif.

Religion
Mormon

Family
Wife, Patricia McKeon; six children

Education
Brigham Young U., B.S. 1985

Career
Clothing store owner

Political Highlights
William S. Hart School Board, 1978-87; Santa Clarita
City Council, 1987-92 (mayor, 1987-88)

ELECTION RESULTS

2010 GENERAL

Howard P. "Buck" McKeon (R)	118,308	61.8%
Jackie Conaway (D)	73,028	38.2%

2010 PRIMARY

Howard P. "Buck" McKeon (R)	unopposed

2008 GENERAL

Howard P. "Buck" McKeon (R)	144,660	57.7%
Jackie Conaway (D)	105,929	42.3%

Previous Winning Percentages
2006 (60%); 2004 (64%); 2002 (65%); 2000 (62%);
1998 (75%); 1996 (62%); 1994 (65%); 1992 (52%)

Elected 1992; 10th term

McKeon saw the focus of his congressional career switch markedly from butter to guns in June 2009, when Republican leaders chose him to be the ranking member of the Armed Services Committee. As chairman in the 112th Congress, he offers a starkly different vision of the future of the U.S. military than the one preferred by the Obama administration.

"I cannot say it strongly enough: I will not support any measures that stress our forces and jeopardize the safety of our men and women in uniform," McKeon said at the first Armed Services hearing of the new Congress. He was reacting to a proposal from the Obama administration for a net $78 billion in defense cuts over five years. "I will also oppose any plans that have the potential to damage or endanger our national security."

McKeon's opportunity to lead Armed Services arose when President Obama picked Republican John M. McHugh of New York to become Army secretary in June 2009. The amiable McKeon had to fight for the ranking member job, beating out Roscoe G. Bartlett of Maryland — who had more seniority on Armed Services — and William M. "Mac" Thornberry of Texas. Being a close ally of House Republican leader John A. Boehner of Ohio and a solid fundraiser for GOP candidates did not hurt his cause.

McKeon has been an advocate of spending generously on defense — for the wars in Iraq and Afghanistan as well as for modernizing the military to face other kinds of challenges. He said the Obama administration does not pay enough attention to equipping for potential threats, notably an increasingly muscular China. "Choosing to win in Iraq and Afghanistan should not mean our country must also choose to assume greater risk in the conventional national defense challenges of today and tomorrow," he said in February 2010.

To fight wars against other nations will require more spending, particularly in naval and aerospace power, McKeon has contended. Missile defense has been a major concern, and McKeon has assailed the Pentagon for revising President George W. Bush's plans for an antimissile shield in Europe.

Prior to a GOP ban on earmarks, McKeon was known for ensuring that spending was funneled to California aerospace manufacturers and military bases in his district.

Also of paramount concern to McKeon are prospective transfers of detainees from the U.S. military prison at Guantánamo Bay, Cuba, either to the United States or to nations such as Yemen, where al Qaeda-affiliated groups are based and where there might be a risk of the prisoners' release. Starting the day he took the top Republican spot on Armed Services, he has repeatedly pushed legislation that would block such transfers.

McKeon has backed Obama's buildup of forces in Afghanistan but opposed the president's decision to set a date — July 2011 — to begin a drawdown. Likewise, McKeon supported the war in Iraq and during the 110th Congress (2007-08) rejected Democratic efforts to set a timeline for withdrawal of U.S. troops.

He opposed repealing the 1993 "don't ask, don't tell" law, which barred openly gay people from serving in the military. He said he will conduct strict oversight of implementation of the repeal, enacted in late 2010.

Part of his task as chairman will be in leading a new crop of panel members: 13 freshmen Republicans and a new Democratic leadership team. To help bring them all up to speed, McKeon scheduled a series of classified briefings on ongoing military operations and other issues.

To take the Armed Services slot, McKeon had to give up his ranking member spot on Education and Labor, though he still serves on the committee (now called Education and the Workforce), where he has had mixed success. He held that gavel for less than a year in 2006 after Boehner left the post to become Majority Leader and before Democrats took over the House in 2007. In the minority, he complained about "pretty much just playing defense."

With a Democratic White House, his frustrations only grew. McKeon and other Republicans on the Education panel raised questions about the inclusion of $100 billion in education spending in the $787 billion economic stimulus law in early 2009. During the 110th Congress (2007-08), he had to watch as California colleague George Miller guided bills to boost mine safety and raise the minimum wage over his objections. He could do little as Democrats made the government the sole provider of federal student loans in 2010.

But he won inclusion in the 2006 higher education bill a requirement that the Education Department assign an "affordability index" to every college that uses federal financial aid programs and compile reports on the tuition increases. That bill never made it in the Senate. But in the 110th, the new Democratic majority took a cue from the former chairman and included college cost provisions in the 2008 reauthorization of the Higher Education Act.

Before he became immersed in politics, McKeon worked in his family business, a chain of Western wear stores based in Santa Clarita that was founded by his parents in 1962. The business closed in 1999, though McKeon still has a soft spot for ostrich-skin cowboy boots.

Fears that his oldest daughter would be bused from their Santa Clarita home into a neighboring school district prompted his first foray into elected office in 1978. He won a 14-person race for the local school board.

Years later, after McKeon served as a city council member, the first mayor of Santa Clarita and a start-up bank chairman, naïveté drove his bid for a newly created congressional district in suburban Los Angeles. A mayor of a neighboring town called and asked for his support for the seat. Instead, McKeon decided in 1991 to launch his own campaign. "I thought, 'If he could do it, I could do it,'" McKeon said. "I didn't know what a congressman did. I'd only met two."

After a fierce campaign, McKeon narrowly defeated a 14-year state Assembly veteran, Phillip D. Wyman, in the primary. In November, McKeon easily defeated Democratic lawyer and rancher James H. "Gil" Gilmartin by 19 percentage points. His re-elections have usually been easy, but in 2008, a difficult year for many Republicans, he earned less than 60 percent of the vote for the first time since 1992. He was back up to 62 percent in 2010.

Key Votes

2010	
Overhaul the nation's health insurance system	NO
Allow for repeal of "don't ask, don't tell"	NO
Overhaul financial services industry regulation	NO
Limit use of new Afghanistan War funds to troop withdrawal activities	NO
Change oversight of offshore drilling and lift oil spill liability cap	?
Provide a path to legal status for some children of illegal immigrants	NO
Extend Bush-era income tax cuts for two years	YES
2009	
Expand the Children's Health Insurance Program	NO
Provide $787 billion in tax cuts and spending increases to stimulate the economy	NO
Allow bankruptcy judges to modify certain primary-residence mortgages	NO
Create a cap-and-trade system to limit greenhouse gas emissions	NO
Provide $2 billion for the "cash for clunkers" program	YES
Establish the government as the sole provider of student loans	NO
Restrict federally funded insurance coverage for abortions in health care overhaul	YES

CQ Vote Studies

	PARTY UNITY		PRESIDENTIAL SUPPORT	
	SUPPORT	OPPOSE	SUPPORT	OPPOSE
2010	96%	4%	26%	74%
2009	88%	12%	28%	72%
2008	97%	3%	78%	22%
2007	95%	5%	87%	13%
2006	96%	4%	95%	5%

Interest Groups

	AFL-CIO	ADA	CCUS	ACU
2010	7%	0%	86%	96%
2009	14%	15%	87%	96%
2008	7%	5%	100%	88%
2007	9%	10%	80%	96%
2006	14%	5%	100%	80%

California 25

Northern Los Angeles and San Bernardino counties; Inyo and Mono counties

The vast 25th stretches from east-central California on the Nevada border south along the mountains and through Death Valley before crossing the Mojave Desert and San Bernardino County into densely populated northern suburban Los Angeles County.

The Antelope Valley desert due north of Los Angeles experienced rapid growth for decades, but home foreclosures, high unemployment rates and an economic downturn have stalled growth. The valley includes Lancaster (shared with the 22nd) and Palmdale, the commercial and transportation center for the high desert. Palmdale also has been a research, development and flight testing site for the aerospace industry and is home to major Lockheed Martin and Boeing facilities.

Most of the land in Inyo and Mono counties is government-owned, and a few towns rely on mining, agriculture and tourism.

Suburban Santa Clarita Valley on the district's southwestern edge has manufacturing, aerospace and defense industries, but can struggle when there are fewer visitors to key regional employer Six Flags Magic Mountain in Valencia, which is expected to add three new roller coasters.

Historically Republican, a mix of upper-middle-class residents and more-conservative working-class whites supported Democrat Barack Obama by slightly more than 1 percentage point in the 2008 presidential election but backed GOP candidate Meg Whitman by nearly 10 percentage points in the 2010 gubernatorial race.

Major Industry
Tourism, aerospace, manufacturing, construction, military

Military Bases
Fort Irwin (Army), 4,572 military, 959 civilian (2010); Edwards Air Force Base, 1,851 military, 3,741 civilian (2010) (shared with the 22nd); Naval Air Warfare Center Weapons Division, China Lake, 640 military, 4,204 civilian (2011) (shared with the 22nd); Marine Corps Logistics Base Barstow, 142 military, 1,958 civilian (2010)

Cities
Santa Clarita, 176,320; Palmdale, 152,750; Victorville, 115,903; Lancaster (pt.), 72,370; Adelanto, 31,765

Notable
Badwater Basin in Death Valley is the lowest point in North America.

Rep. David Dreier (R)

Capitol Office
225-2305
dreier.house.gov
233 Cannon Bldg. 20515-0526; fax 225-7018

Committees
Rules - Chairman

Residence
San Dimas

Born
July 5, 1952; Kansas City, Mo.

Religion
Christian Scientist

Family
Single

Education
Claremont Men's College, B.A. 1975 (political science); Claremont U. Center, M.A. 1976 (American government)

Career
Real estate developer; university fundraiser

Political Highlights
Republican nominee for U.S. House, 1978

ELECTION RESULTS

2010 GENERAL

David Dreier (R)	112,774	54.1%
Russ Warner (D)	76,093	36.5%
David L. Miller (AMI)	12,784	6.1%
Randall Weissbuch (LIBERT)	6,696	3.2%

2010 PRIMARY

David Dreier (R)	42,400	72.3%
Mark Butler (R)	16,220	27.7%

2008 GENERAL

David Dreier (R)	140,615	52.6%
Russ Warner (D)	108,039	40.4%
Ted Brown (LIBERT)	18,476	6.9%

Previous Winning Percentages
2006 (57%); 2004 (54%); 2002 (64%); 2000 (57%); 1998 (58%); 1996 (61%); 1994 (67%); 1992 (58%); 1990 (64%); 1988 (69%); 1986 (72%); 1984 (71%); 1982 (65%); 1980 (52%)

Elected 1980; 16th term

The dapper Dreier is the House GOP's go-to guy on parliamentary procedure and legislative process, talents he puts to use in pursuit of his small-government ideals and Republican leadership strategy. He is in his second tour as chairman of the powerful Rules Committee, which serves GOP leaders by setting the procedural guidelines that govern floor action on legislation.

Those procedures often determine the outcome, as Republicans could attest from the many floor battles they lost while the Democrats were in charge of the House. They also can inspire rage and rebellion from the minority, as demonstrated during the health care overhaul debate in 2010. That's a situation the always-cordial Dreier says he hopes to avoid repeating.

His goal in winning back the gavel, he said, was to make the House "more transparent and accountable to the American people." Similar promises were made by the new Republican majority in 1995 and the restored Democratic majority in 2007. In both cases, political and legislative reality quickly trumped good intentions.

This time, Dreier took a quick step to live up to the promises, allowing regular television coverage of Rules Committee proceedings. He also hit an embarrassing speed bump when two Republican lawmakers, including Rules member Pete Sessions of Texas, voted on the floor before being officially sworn in. Their votes were quickly voided.

Rather than making rules intended to pass legislation and grease the wheels of democracy, Dreier spent much of the 111th Congress (2009-10) employing parliamentary tactics in an effort to defeat legislation and bring floor action to a standstill. He usually lost. One notable victory came when Republicans forced Democrats to vote on a motion to bar the use of funds to pay the salaries of government employees who were disciplined for viewing pornography on their work computers — and in the process made the majority jump through multiple legislative hoops to pass a bill to reauthorize science research and education programs.

His position on Rules and inclination for procedural battles led Republican leaders to put him in charge of highlighting the Democrats' alleged bending of the rules to pass health care overhaul legislation in 2010. Dreier led the charge against the "Slaughter Solution," which would have deemed the bill passed after the rule, which normally sets the terms for debate, was agreed to. Democrats eventually abandoned that strategy. Writing a closed rule for the Republican-sponsored repeal of the law was among his first tasks in the 112th Congress (2011-12).

As chairman of the Rules Committee, Dreier is an extension of the leadership team, though he sometimes strays from the fold. In 2009, he sided with a majority of the GOP against a majority of Democrats only 86 percent of the time. In almost three decades in Congress, he had a lower party unity score only once. In 2010, his score was back up to 97 percent.

In 2008, he successfully argued during a GOP leadership meeting to strike the term "Communist China" from a policy paper. He was one of just 35 Republicans who voted in 2007 to prohibit employment discrimination on the basis of sexual orientation, and he has twice broken with the majority of his party to vote against proposed constitutional amendments that would outlaw same-sex marriage. In 2006, he voted to override President George W. Bush's veto of legislation expanding federal funding for embryonic stem cell research.

On tax-and-spend issues, Dreier is a more traditional Republican. Among the first bills he introduced in 2011 were measures to simplify the tax code and cut tax rates and to create a two-year budget cycle.

Dreier is a strong backer of free trade. He fought to fast-track a trade accord with Colombia during the 110th Congress (2007-08). He teamed up with Senate Foreign Relations Chairman John Kerry, a Massachusetts Democrat, to encourage the administration to seek a trade agreement with the former Soviet republic of Georgia.

And he has worked with fellow lawmakers to spread the democratic process to other countries. He and Democrat David E. Price of North Carolina founded the House Democracy Partnership, which teaches government officials from developing countries about constituent services, the legislative process and government operations. Working with parliaments in 15 countries — including Georgia, East Timor, Kenya and Mongolia — Dreier has hosted visiting parliamentarians to help them learn from his congressional activities.

Dreier has never needed a lecture on civil debate, but he has held hearings on the topic. After Democrats regained control of the House in 2007, Dreier led weekly training sessions for his colleagues, dubbed "Parliamentary Bootcamp," that included a lecture on "Decorum and Civility in the House." His trademark of introducing members on the floor by announcing the names of their hometowns (if he doesn't know them by memory, he has staff look them up) often evokes smiles even during contentious debates with Democrats. The practice landed Dreier in procedural purgatory once. While presiding in the chair, he referred to a member on the floor by his hometown, rather than the state as is the custom, and was told by the parliamentarian that when in the chair, he was to use the state when addressing another member.

Dreier fell in love with congressional process in college, when he interned for GOP Rep. Barry Goldwater Jr. of California in the mid-1970s. He launched his first House bid in 1978 from a dorm at Claremont McKenna College, his alma mater, where he was working in the planning and development office.

Dreier's father, a Marine Corps drill instructor, figured his son would come home to Kansas City, Mo., to work in the family's real estate development business. But Dreier, whose stake in the company makes him one of the richest members of Congress, had been bitten by the political bug.

Two years after he lost to Rep. James F. Lloyd, he swamped the Democratic incumbent in fundraising and rode the 1980 Republican wave to victory. He generally has had little trouble since; he defeated Democrat Russ Warner in 2008 by 12 percentage points, then beat him again by 17 in 2010.

Key Votes

2010

Overhaul the nation's health insurance system	NO
Allow for repeal of "don't ask, don't tell"	NO
Overhaul financial services industry regulation	NO
Limit use of new Afghanistan War funds to troop withdrawal activities	NO
Change oversight of offshore drilling and lift oil spill liability cap	NO
Provide a path to legal status for some children of illegal immigrants	NO
Extend Bush-era income tax cuts for two years	YES

2009

Expand the Children's Health Insurance Program	NO
Provide $787 billion in tax cuts and spending increases to stimulate the economy	NO
Allow bankruptcy judges to modify certain primary-residence mortgages	NO
Create a cap-and-trade system to limit greenhouse gas emissions	NO
Provide $2 billion for the "cash for clunkers" program	YES
Establish the government as the sole provider of student loans	NO
Restrict federally funded insurance coverage for abortions in health care overhaul	YES

CQ Vote Studies

	PARTY UNITY		PRESIDENTIAL SUPPORT	
	SUPPORT	OPPOSE	SUPPORT	OPPOSE
2010	97%	3%	31%	69%
2009	86%	14%	28%	72%
2008	96%	4%	78%	22%
2007	95%	5%	87%	13%
2006	94%	6%	93%	7%

Interest Groups

	AFL-CIO	ADA	CCUS	ACU
2010	0%	5%	88%	96%
2009	10%	5%	86%	92%
2008	13%	10%	100%	86%
2007	4%	20%	85%	88%
2006	14%	10%	100%	72%

California 26

Northeastern Los Angeles suburbs

Set along the foothills of the San Gabriel Mountains, the 26th District is a mix of Los Angeles bedroom communities and the mountainous Angeles National Forest, which makes up its northern half. The commuter-heavy district takes in middle- to upper-class suburbs, many of which have retained their own identities and quaint downtowns.

In the far western part of the 26th, a high-tech flavor is set by La Cañada Flintridge and Pasadena (in the neighboring 29th), which is home to NASA's Jet Propulsion Laboratory and the California Institute of Technology. Monrovia boasts engineering firms and start-up technology companies that employ a highly educated workforce.

The Santa Anita racetrack in Arcadia draws visitors and continues to contribute tax revenue to the local economy, but the area's thoroughbred racing industry faces uncertainty.

Rancho Cucamonga, in the 26th's chunk of San Bernardino County, is a destination for young, middle-class families and a distribution hub. Technology firms dot the San Bernardino Inland Valley suburbs, and small defense subcontractors also provide jobs. Traffic congestion caused by

district residents who commute to Los Angeles or technology jobs in the areas surrounding the 26th continues to be a hot issue locally.

While not as diverse as most of its neighbors, the 26th has significant Hispanic and Asian communities, notably in Arcadia. Rapid development in communities surrounding Pasadena and in other Los Angeles County cities — particularly Arcadia, Glendora, Monrovia and San Dimas — brought young, wealthy, fiscally minded, socially moderate Republicans to the district, and the GOP carries a slight edge in party registration here. The 26th swung narrowly for Democrat Barack Obama in the 2008 presidential election (51 percent), but gave GOP candidate Meg Whitman a nearly 7 percentage point win in the 2010 gubernatorial race.

Major Industry

Service, manufacturing, health care, biotech

Cities

Rancho Cucamonga, 165,269; Upland, 73,732; Arcadia, 56,364; Glendora, 50,073; Montclair, 36,664; Monrovia, 36,590; Claremont, 34,926

Notable

The collection at the Huntington Library in San Marino includes Thomas Gainsborough's painting "The Blue Boy" and a Gutenberg Bible.

Rep. Brad Sherman (D)

Capitol Office
225-5911
www.house.gov/sherman
2242 Rayburn Bldg. 20515-0527; fax 225-5879

Committees
Financial Services
Foreign Affairs

Residence
Sherman Oaks

Born
Oct. 24, 1954; Los Angeles, Calif.

Religion
Jewish

Family
Wife, Lisa N. K. Sherman; two children

Education
U. of California, Los Angeles, B.A. 1974 (political communication); Harvard U., J.D. 1979

Career
Accountant; lawyer

Political Highlights
Calif. State Board of Equalization, 1991-97 (chairman, 1991-95)

ELECTION RESULTS

2010 GENERAL

Brad Sherman (D)	102,927	65.2%
Mark Reed (R)	55,056	34.8%

2010 PRIMARY

Brad Sherman (D)	unopposed

2008 GENERAL

Brad Sherman (D)	145,812	68.5%
Navraj Singh (R)	52,852	24.8%
Tim Denton (LIBERT)	14,171	6.7%

Previous Winning Percentages
2006 (69%); 2004 (62%); 2002 (62%); 2000 (66%); 1998 (57%); 1996 (50%)

Elected 1996; 8th term

Sherman doesn't take himself too seriously. But he is earnest about his job as a lawmaker and has taken on a decidedly unfunny topic — nuclear proliferation — as his signature issue.

The balding, self-deprecating Californian gives away plastic combs emblazoned with his name and phone number at town hall and campaign events. In his 2008 appearance on Comedy Central's "Colbert Report," he did an impersonation of a robot and pretended to be unaware that the adult film industry is centered in his district.

He's been known to start speeches by joking that he's drawn to jobs held in declining public esteem, which explains why he went from certified public accountant to lawyer, then to simultaneous stints as politician and tax collector.

But he turns serious when discussing his chief preoccupation in Congress. As a senior member of the Foreign Affairs Committee — he chaired the Subcommittee on Terrorism, Nonproliferation and Trade in the 111th Congress (2009-10) and is the ranking member in the 112th (2011-12) — Sherman sees Iran as the No. 1 security threat in the world. "The spread of nuclear weapons is perhaps the only thing that poses a national security threat to ordinary Americans and a threat to their safety and to our way of life," he said in February 2009. "We should be prioritizing non-proliferation at a higher level."

After badgering President George W. Bush about the threat posed by Iran, Sherman didn't hesitate to push just as hard with an administration from his own party. As Congress negotiated with the White House in 2010 over legislation to punish companies that sell refined petroleum products to Iran or help that country's oil industry, Sherman told the Los Angeles Times that he believed the Obama administration was working against the measure. "The administration doesn't carry out the laws that are on the books, and they want the new law to be as weak and loophole-ridden as possible," Sherman said.

Just weeks after Obama signed the sanctions bill into law, Sherman went back to the drawing board, drafting new legislation to close what he said were several loopholes in the measure.

During consideration of a supplemental war spending bill in 2009, Sherman urged colleagues to bar money from the International Monetary Fund from going to countries such as Iran. Republicans already were threatening to block the bill if it included any IMF funding, contending that such money could go to countries that support terrorism. The final bill included $5 billion for the IMF, and Sherman was among 32 Democrats who voted against it.

Sherman was concerned when the Obama administration submitted for ratification a civilian nuclear agreement between the United States and the United Arab Emirates. He, along with Florida Republican Ileana Ros-Lehtinen and Massachusetts Democrat Edward J. Markey, had called on the president to review the Bush-era agreement, which allows civilian nuclear commerce between the two countries.

Sherman also urged Obama to enlist China in pressuring North Korea to halt its nuclear program, and he has suggested that Beijing's access to U.S. markets be contingent on cooperation on the issue.

Sherman is particularly vocal about his belief in an aggressive U.S. foreign policy when it comes to Israel. In 2009, he spoke out strongly when the House passed a resolution condemning Hamas for its role in the conflict in Gaza and southern Israel. "While Israel seeks to lie aside a Palestinian state, Hamas seeks to kill or expel every Jew in the Middle East," he said.

Sherman also sits on the Financial Services Committee, where he has found his background as a CPA invaluable.

Sherman argued forcefully that the financial meltdown of 2008 was largely caused by decisions made by credit rating agencies driven by conflicts of interest. He successfully helped push for a provision in the financial sector regulatory overhaul bill that would prohibit compliance officers from working on ratings, methodologies or sales and to prevent other employees from selling ratings services and rating the securities.

A former member of the Budget Committee, Sherman opposed both versions — the second of which became law — of $700 billion legislation to aid the ailing financial services sector in fall 2008.

Sherman was a vocal critic of just about every proposal Treasury Secretary Timothy F. Geithner made to deal with the economic crisis in 2009. He unsuccessfully fought the creation of a new Consumer Financial Protection Agency to supervise banks and write rules for mortgages and credit cards, as well as a proposal to give regulators the authority to dismantle the largest firms if the government determines they are about to fail. Sherman called the plan "TARP on steroids," saying it would give the Treasury Department unlimited authority to use taxpayer funds if another financial crisis occurred. He also warned that Congress might be giving away some of its law-making power to the executive branch if it established the agency.

He voted for the two-year extension of the Bush-era tax cuts at the end of 2010, although he was no fan of keeping the lower rate in place for the highest earners. "We're going to have to swallow hard," Sherman told the Washington Times.

One of Sherman's pet projects is altering the order of presidential succession. He has introduced multiple bills seeking to ensure the presidency remains in the hands of the same political party by allowing the president to designate either the Speaker or the House minority leader as second in line after the vice president, followed by either the majority or minority leader of the Senate, rather than the Senate president pro tempore. He also wants to add someone who lives outside Washington to the succession list.

Sherman got his start in politics as a child, stuffing envelopes for Democratic Rep. George E. Brown Jr., a family friend. A tax law specialist, he was elected to the California State Board of Equalization in 1990 and 1994.

In 1996, he ran for the seat of retiring Democratic Rep. Anthony C. Beilenson, who endorsed him. He won the nomination with 54 percent of the vote, besting six other candidates, and carried the general election by 8 percentage points. Since then, he has won re-election comfortably.

Key Votes

2010

Overhaul the nation's health insurance system	YES
Allow for repeal of "don't ask, don't tell"	YES
Overhaul financial services industry regulation	YES
Limit use of new Afghanistan War funds to troop withdrawal activities	NO
Change oversight of offshore drilling and lift oil spill liability cap	YES
Provide a path to legal status for some children of illegal immigrants	YES
Extend Bush-era income tax cuts for two years	YES

2009

Expand the Children's Health Insurance Program	YES
Provide $787 billion in tax cuts and spending increases to stimulate the economy	YES
Allow bankruptcy judges to modify certain primary-residence mortgages	YES
Create a cap-and-trade system to limit greenhouse gas emissions	YES
Provide $2 billion for the "cash for clunkers" program	YES
Establish the government as the sole provider of student loans	YES
Restrict federally funded insurance coverage for abortions in health care overhaul	NO

CQ Vote Studies

	PARTY UNITY		PRESIDENTIAL SUPPORT	
	SUPPORT	OPPOSE	SUPPORT	OPPOSE
2010	97%	3%	98%	2%
2009	99%	1%	96%	4%
2008	98%	2%	14%	86%
2007	98%	2%	5%	95%
2006	94%	6%	28%	72%

Interest Groups

	AFL-CIO	ADA	CCUS	ACU
2010	100%	90%	25%	0%
2009	100%	100%	33%	0%
2008	100%	85%	61%	9%
2007	96%	100%	50%	0%
2006	100%	95%	33%	4%

California 27

Part of the San Fernando Valley; part of Burbank

While most of the 27th District is within Los Angeles, people who live here do not generally think of themselves as residents of the city. Instead, they view themselves as part of the Los Angeles communities of Van Nuys, Encino or Sherman Oaks in the San Fernando Valley north of central Los Angeles. The valley's portion of the city lies primarily in the 27th and 28th districts.

Biomedical firms and entertainment ventures located just outside Hollywood drive the economy here. Health testing company Quest Diagnostics has a clinical trials site in Northridge, and other firms are in Sylmar, Van Nuys and North Hollywood. Toymaker MGA Entertainment has its corporate office in Van Nuys, while the San Fernando Valley is home to much of the nation's adult entertainment industry.

The valley has a stable hospitality industry — particularly its hotels and small conference sites — because of its proximity to Hollywood and the local airports. The flat, grid-like streets of much of the 27th take in both the Bob Hope (Burbank) and Van Nuys airports. There are several colleges here

as well, including California State University, Northridge. Reservoirs and aqueducts in the northwest provide water to millions of Los Angeles County residents, and regional efforts continue to conserve water resources. The region is at risk for heavy wildfires that damage homes and endanger residents.

Asian immigrants, particularly from India and Pakistan, have made the mostly white and Hispanic district home. This rise of immigration increased demand for housing, which in turn led to higher housing rates. But some new developments and established areas have felt the sting of foreclosures.

A majority of the district's workers are employed in white-collar jobs, and the district is solidly Democratic. Residents here gave Jerry Brown a more than 20-percentage point win in the 2010 gubernatorial election.

Major Industry
Biotech, service

Cities
Los Angeles (pt.), 635,177; Burbank (pt.), 46,533

Notable
The Valley Performing Arts Center opened at California State University, Northridge, in 2011.

Rep. Howard L. Berman (D)

Capitol Office
225-4695
www.house.gov/berman
2221 Rayburn Bldg. 20515-0528; fax 225-3196

Committees
Foreign Affairs - Ranking Member
Judiciary

Residence
Valley Village

Born
April 15, 1941; Los Angeles, Calif.

Religion
Jewish

Family
Wife, Janis Berman; two children

Education
U. of California, Los Angeles, B.A. 1962 (international relations), LL.B. 1965

Career
Lawyer

Political Highlights
Calif. Assembly, 1972-82 (majority leader, 1973-79)

ELECTION RESULTS

2010 GENERAL

Howard L. Berman (D)	88,385	69.5%
Merlin Froyd (R)	28,493	22.4%
Carlos A. Rodriguez (LIBERT)	10,229	8.0%

2010 PRIMARY

Howard L. Berman (D)	26,092	83.4%
Richard A. Valdez (D)	5,203	16.6%

2008 GENERAL

Howard L. Berman (D)	137,471	99.9%

Previous Winning Percentages
2006 (74%); 2004 (71%); 2002 (71%); 2000 (84%); 1998 (82%); 1996 (66%); 1994 (63%); 1992 (61%); 1990 (61%); 1988 (70%); 1986 (65%); 1984 (63%); 1982 (60%)

Elected 1982; 15th term

Berman is the antithesis of the stereotypical smooth-talking, back-slapping politician, but his unassuming demeanor belies a savvy and tenacious operative who excels both at policy making and political maneuvering. In that sense, he has much in common with his close friend Henry A. Waxman, a fellow California Democrat he has known since their days at UCLA.

Berman, who took over the gavel of the Foreign Affairs Committee in 2008 and surrendered it three years later, pursues an ambitious agenda to shape U.S. foreign policy, successfully prodding action from the executive branch on a number of initiatives.

Perhaps the best example from the 111th Congress (2009-10) of Berman's legislative dexterity was his ability to push through a bill initiating a new round of sanctions aimed at Iran that threaded the needle between the desires of his colleagues to get tough and the Obama administration's pressure not to do anything to inhibit multilateral efforts. Berman cited that bill as a prime example of how Congress can insert itself into international affairs.

But he has had less success in getting the Senate to act on the legislative priorities he furthers in the Judiciary Committee, where he is a senior member and former subcommittee chairman.

Berman, now the ranking Democrat on Foreign Affairs, assumed the chairmanship in March 2008 after another California Democrat, Tom Lantos, died of cancer. Before long, he orchestrated a delicate compromise on President George W. Bush's global anti-AIDS program, increasing funding above what Republicans wanted but leaving in the legislation some restrictions on family planning that they favored.

According to Berman, his mission on the Foreign Affairs Committee is to "restore some of our legislative authority." To that end, in 2009 he pushed a State Department authorization bill through the House for the first time in four years — one hasn't been enacted since 2002. He also led committee efforts to rewrite the 1961 Foreign Assistance Act, which governs U.S. aid to foreign countries, as well as draft legislation reauthorizing and reforming the Export Administration Act.

Berman is an unswerving supporter of Israel and cites the U.S.-Israeli relationship as one of the leading issues that prompted his interest in joining Foreign Affairs as a freshman. He has not, however, joined other pro-Israel lawmakers who have criticized the Obama administration for its handling of its differences with the Israeli government. "Both sides have made some mistakes," Berman said of the series of spats that divided the two governments in 2010. "But I think they're getting rectified."

His support for Israel and hawkish attitude toward Iraq and Afghanistan is the one area where he shifts from an otherwise liberal orthodoxy. Berman voted for both wars and continues to support Obama's efforts on both fronts, although he remains unsure "whether this Afghan strategy is going to work."

From his seat on the Judiciary Committee, Berman looks out for the entertainment industry — an important constituency in his district — and is a leading expert on copyrights and patents. He served as chairman of what was then the Subcommittee on Courts, the Internet and Intellectual Property in the 110th Congress (2007-08) but gave up that gavel in 2009 after getting the top spot on Foreign Affairs.

Legislation to require radio stations to compensate performers for songs played over the airwaves remains high on Berman's agenda, although he acknowledged it is "a fight that has not been resolved" in the 111th Congress. In 2007, he was the lead House Democrat on bipartisan legislation to overhaul the patent system, which critics said fostered excessive infringement lawsuits and stifled innovation.

Berman notes that his Foreign Affairs post contributes to his fight to protect intellectual property. He said pushing other countries to combat piracy and defend intellectual property rights "has become a standard part" of his interactions with foreign governments.

Berman came up through the ranks of California Democratic politics with Waxman and Minority Leader Nancy Pelosi, and he is part of Pelosi's inner circle. He was Pelosi's choice when she needed someone in 2006 to step into the party's senior slot on what is now called the Ethics Committee, which had broken down amid partisan squabbling. Berman had served in the role from 1997 to 2003.

The son of a Polish immigrant who owned a textile business in Los Angeles, Berman credits a high school teacher with igniting his career in politics. "My parents weren't political, so she was the person who moved me to challenge assumptions and to debate issues," he said. His interest in foreign affairs started in high school and college, where he majored in international relations and toyed with the idea of going into the Foreign Service.

At UCLA, he had an internship with the California Assembly's Agriculture Committee, where he worked on labor issues with Cesar Chavez's United Farm Workers. He met Waxman in school and the two became fast friends and card-playing buddies. Berman helped Waxman win a seat in the state Assembly, marking the start of the Berman-Waxman political network that helped their handpicked candidates with money and organization. The alliance was a power in Los Angeles County for years.

In 1972, Berman won an Assembly seat by defeating an incumbent Republican. He rose to majority leader, but lost a bid for Speaker to Democrat Willie L. Brown Jr., who then approved a congressional map with an ideal district for Berman. Since his first win in 1982, he has won re-election easily. He contemplated runs for mayor of Los Angeles in 1993 and 1997 but decided against it both times.

In California's redistricting after 2000, House Democrats hired Berman's brother, Michael Berman, as a consultant to draft new post-census lines. The map that was eventually approved carved several Hispanic communities out of Berman's district, making it less likely that he would face a primary challenge by a Hispanic. Berman backed an unsuccessful effort in 2010 to repeal a California law that took responsibility for redistricting out of the hands of the legislature.

Key Votes

2010

Overhaul the nation's health insurance system	YES
Allow for repeal of "don't ask, don't tell"	YES
Overhaul financial services industry regulation	YES
Limit use of new Afghanistan War funds to troop withdrawal activities	NO
Change oversight of offshore drilling and lift oil spill liability cap	YES
Provide a path to legal status for some children of illegal immigrants	YES
Extend Bush-era income tax cuts for two years	YES

2009

Expand the Children's Health Insurance Program	YES
Provide $787 billion in tax cuts and spending increases to stimulate the economy	YES
Allow bankruptcy judges to modify certain primary-residence mortgages	YES
Create a cap-and-trade system to limit greenhouse gas emissions	YES
Provide $2 billion for the "cash for clunkers" program	YES
Establish the government as the sole provider of student loans	YES
Restrict federally funded insurance coverage for abortions in health care overhaul	NO

CQ Vote Studies

	PARTY UNITY		PRESIDENTIAL SUPPORT	
	SUPPORT	OPPOSE	SUPPORT	OPPOSE
2010	99%	1%	97%	3%
2009	99%	1%	97%	3%
2008	98%	2%	20%	80%
2007	98%	2%	7%	93%
2006	96%	4%	29%	71%

Interest Groups

	AFL-CIO	ADA	CCUS	ACU
2010	100%	90%	25%	0%
2009	100%	100%	33%	0%
2008	100%	85%	69%	4%
2007	100%	85%	53%	4%
2006	92%	90%	43%	8%

California 28

Part of the San Fernando Valley

The 28th is centered in the San Fernando Valley north of Los Angeles, where it takes in the small city of San Fernando and includes parts of the Los Angeles communities of Pacoima, Arleta, Panorama City, Van Nuys and North Hollywood.

The southern border follows in part iconic Mulholland Drive, taking in Encino, Sherman Oaks and Studio City, as well as the famed Hollywood Bowl, in the Hollywood Hills north of Beverly Hills.

Economic downturns have struck the 28th's commercial district. Centered on financial services along famed Ventura Boulevard, just south of Route 101, bank branches in office towers compete with miles of strip malls, fast-food outlets, restaurants and residential developments. Traffic congestion is a major concern, and Interstate 405, one of the nation's most congested routes, runs through the district's southwestern arm.

The technology and entertainment industries fueled the district's economy for the last decade. NBC Universal has plans for a $3 billion overhaul of the studio's property, including construction of filming studios, office space and a hotel.

The CBS Studio Center in Studio City is off Ventura Boulevard just south of the Los Angeles River.

Local officials and environmentalists have targeted the river for conservation and urban revitalization.

The manufacturing sector here declined in the 1990s after a General Motors plant closed, but the Pepsi Bottling Group still has a plant in San Fernando.

Among the district's biomedical and medical equipment firms, Kaiser Permanente opened a large hospital in Panorama City in 2008.

New immigrants are driving service industry growth here. Once mainly middle-class and white, suburban city communities have attracted many Hispanics, who make up more than half of the 28th's population. This influx keeps the 28th in the Democratic column, and the district gave Jerry Brown 69 percent of its gubernatorial vote in 2010.

Major Industry

Service, entertainment, health care, manufacturing

Cities

Los Angeles (pt.), 636,549; San Fernando, 23,645

Notable

The Academy of Television Arts and Sciences, which presents the annual Emmy Awards, is based in North Hollywood.

Rep. Adam B. Schiff (D)

Capitol Office
225-4176
schiff.house.gov
2411 Rayburn Bldg. 20515; fax 225-5828

Committees
Appropriations
Select Intelligence

Residence
Burbank

Born
June 22, 1960; Framingham, Mass.

Religion
Jewish

Family
Wife, Eve Schiff; two children

Education
Stanford U., A.B. 1982 (political science & pre-med);
Harvard U., J.D. 1985

Career
Federal prosecutor; lawyer

Political Highlights
Assistant U.S. attorney, 1987-93; Democratic
nominee for Calif. Assembly (special election), 1994;
Democratic nominee for Calif. Assembly, 1994; Calif.
Senate, 1996-2000

ELECTION RESULTS

2010 GENERAL

Adam B. Schiff (D)	104,374	64.8%
John P. Colbert (R)	51,534	32.0%
William P. Cushing (LIBERT)	5,218	3.2%

2010 PRIMARY

Adam B. Schiff (D)	unopposed

2008 GENERAL

Adam B. Schiff (D)	146,198	68.9%
Charles Hahn (R)	56,727	26.7%
Alan Pyeatt (LIBERT)	9,219	4.3%

Previous Winning Percentages
2006 (65%); 2004 (65%); 2002 (63%); 2000 (53%)

Elected 2000; 6th term

Schiff's committee assignments have allowed him to promote a broad view of national security. He sees nuclear proliferation as the gravest threat facing the United States, takes a tough line in the war on terror and backs efforts to promote economic stability and the rule of law in places where terrorism has taken root. As a lawmaker representing one of the largest Armenian communities in the world, he has been a key player in efforts to recognize as genocide the deaths of 1.5 million Armenians almost 100 years ago.

Schiff won a seat on the Appropriations Committee in 2007, the start of his fourth term. Although an assignment to the spending panel often requires members to leave others, he was granted a waiver to remain on the Judiciary Committee, then won appointment to the Intelligence Committee in the 111th Congress (2009-10). He left Judiciary in the 112th (2011-12), but still has a hand in related issues as a member of the Appropriations subcommittee that funds the Justice Department.

A former federal prosecutor, Schiff co-founded a group called the Democratic Study Group on National Security "to get Democrats to speak more knowledgeably, more forcefully" on those issues. He sometimes sides with Republicans. He backed a broad use of the state secrets privilege to keep intelligence information out of open court; favored a lower standard of cause for certain types of electronic surveillance of terrorist suspects; and voted for renewal of authority to conduct surveillance on "lone wolf" terrorists not connected to a larger organization.

A co-founder of the Congressional Caucus on Nuclear Security, Schiff was the sponsor of legislation signed into law by President Obama in February 2010 to make the Domestic Nuclear Detection Office responsible for developing a method for "fingerprinting" nuclear materials in order to trace them to their point of origin.

But Schiff wants to do more than play defense. He works to promote press freedom and economic development around the world. "We have seen in Afghanistan and elsewhere that the economic development, rule of law issues are intertwined with national security issues," he said. From the Appropriations panel that funds the State Department and foreign aid, he pushes for an increase in the number of Foreign Service officers and a boost in development spending.

He wrote the Daniel Pearl Freedom of the Press Act, named for a Wall Street Journal reporter murdered by terrorists in Pakistan in 2002. It requires the State Department to identify countries where press freedoms are violated and report whether the governments are taking action.

While he supports tough anti-terror laws, Schiff teamed with Republican Jeff Flake of Arizona in the 109th (2005-06) and 110th (2007-08) Congresses to curtail a National Security Agency warrantless surveillance program that targets terrorist suspects overseas in communication with people in the United States. They contended that surveillance involving anyone in the United States should be conducted under the eye of a special court; a provision making such review mandatory was part of the 2008 overhaul of the Foreign Intelligence Surveillance Act that President George W. Bush signed into law.

Winning U.S. recognition of the Armenian genocide has been central to Schiff's political life since he was first elected in 2000, when he ran campaign ads in Armenian. He is the sponsor of a resolution that would label as genocide the deaths of 1.5 million Armenians between 1915 and 1923 at the hands of the Ottoman Empire, now modern-day Turkey. He wants to use the Congressional Record to preserve oral histories of the genocide, asking people to send in their personal and family stories for him to include in the daily digest of congressional goings-on.

"I find that talking about 1.5 million people that were wiped out during the genocide is just too big a number for people to come to grips with," Schiff told public radio station KPCC in May 2010. "But when you talk about it in terms of a single life, someone who survived, someone who lost all their family, it's really much easier for members to get their minds around."

Although he considers himself a moderate, Schiff's voting record has moved closer to his party's liberal core. In his first year in office, he sided with Bush on about two of every five votes. In 2007, his support for Bush had fallen to 6 percent. His party unity score — the percentage of votes on which he sided with a majority of Democrats against a majority of Republicans — for the 111th Congress was 99.

In 2008 Schiff was named chairman of a Judiciary impeachment task force to investigate allegations that U.S. District Judge G. Thomas Porteous committed perjury by signing false financial disclosure forms under oath. The House impeached and the Senate convicted Porteous in 2010.

Schiff was born in Massachusetts; when he was 11, his family moved to northern California, where his father bought a lumber yard. He and his brother had to help out in the business. Schiff could not decide between medicine and law, so he majored in both pre-med and political science at Stanford University and was accepted to medical school and law school. Although his parents urged him to become a doctor, Schiff chose law. "All my doctor friends say I made the right decision, and all my lawyer friends say I messed up," Schiff said. "Now that I'm in politics, everyone says I messed up."

After getting his law degree from Harvard, he returned to California and clerked for a federal judge, then worked in the U.S. attorney's office. A colleague there, Tom Umberg, who was elected to the California Assembly, was the inspiration for his shift into politics. "I wanted to deal with the root causes of the problems I was dealing with as a U.S. attorney," Schiff said.

He was unsuccessful in his first attempt, losing to Republican James E. Rogan in a 1994 contest for an Assembly seat. He rebounded in 1996, winning a state Senate seat. In 2000, he again faced Rogan, by then a U.S. House member who had played a high-profile role in the GOP attempt to impeach President Bill Clinton. The race was viewed nationally as a referendum on the impeachment proceedings, although Schiff said the race actually turned on local concerns. He defeated Rogan by 9 percentage points and has been re-elected easily since.

Key Votes

2010

Overhaul the nation's health insurance system	YES
Allow for repeal of "don't ask, don't tell"	YES
Overhaul financial services industry regulation	YES
Limit use of new Afghanistan War funds to troop withdrawal activities	NO
Change oversight of offshore drilling and lift oil spill liability cap	YES
Provide a path to legal status for some children of illegal immigrants	?
Extend Bush-era income tax cuts for two years	YES

2009

Expand the Children's Health Insurance Program	YES
Provide $787 billion in tax cuts and spending increases to stimulate the economy	YES
Allow bankruptcy judges to modify certain primary-residence mortgages	YES
Create a cap-and-trade system to limit greenhouse gas emissions	YES
Provide $2 billion for the "cash for clunkers" program	YES
Establish the government as the sole provider of student loans	YES
Restrict federally funded insurance coverage for abortions in health care overhaul	NO

CQ Vote Studies

	PARTY UNITY		PRESIDENTIAL SUPPORT	
	SUPPORT	OPPOSE	SUPPORT	OPPOSE
2010	99%	1%	98%	2%
2009	99%	1%	97%	3%
2008	98%	2%	14%	86%
2007	98%	2%	6%	94%
2006	94%	6%	35%	65%

Interest Groups

	AFL-CIO	ADA	CCUS	ACU
2010	100%	90%	25%	0%
2009	100%	100%	33%	0%
2008	100%	90%	61%	4%
2007	96%	95%	60%	0%
2006	86%	85%	47%	12%

California 29

Glendale; Pasadena; Alhambra; part of Burbank

Set in the foothills of the San Gabriel Mountains, the 29th includes the largely residential Los Angeles suburbs of Glendale, Pasadena, Alhambra and part of Burbank. The district suffers from heavy traffic congestion, and although Glendale and Pasadena are part of the Los Angeles area, they have their own downtowns.

Television and movie production studios drive much of the economy in both Burbank, home to Walt Disney Studios, and Glendale, containing DreamWorks Animation SKG. NBC announced in late 2007 that it is moving from its 34-acre complex in Burbank to a complex near Universal Studios, which is in the adjacent 28th District. Glendale also is home to the corporate headquarters of Nestlé USA and the International House of Pancakes. A technology community has sprung up near a number of colleges and universities in the area, including the California Institute of Technology and NASA's Jet Propulsion Laboratory.

The region includes a wide mix of ethnicities. The 29th has one of the highest percentages of Asian residents in California and in the nation, and there is a sizable Hispanic population. Monterey Park (shared with the 32nd District) is known as "Little Taipei" for its Taiwanese and other Asian immigrants. Glendale is home to more than 80,000 Armenians, one of the largest such communities outside of Armenia, and Alhambra is heavily Asian and Hispanic.

Over the years, immigration and the nearby Hollywood economy have transformed once-WASPish neighborhoods, giving the district a strong Democratic lean. The 29th gave Barack Obama 68 percent of its 2008 presidential vote, and Pasadena and Alhambra both gave at least 65 percent to Democrats Jerry Brown and Barbara Boxer in their 2010 gubernatorial and Senate races, respectively.

Major Industry
Entertainment, technology, engineering

Cities
Glendale, 191,719; Pasadena, 137,122; Alhambra, 83,089; Burbank (pt.), 56,807; San Gabriel, 39,718; Altadena (unincorporated) (pt.), 38,546

Notable
More people have looked through the Zeiss Telescope at the Griffith Observatory than any other telescope in the world; Pasadena's annual Tournament of Roses Parade is never held on a Sunday.

Rep. Henry A. Waxman (D)

Capitol Office
225-3976
www.house.gov/waxman
2204 Rayburn Bldg. 20515-0530; fax 225-4099

Committees
Energy & Commerce - Ranking Member

Residence
Beverly Hills

Born
Sept. 12, 1939; Los Angeles, Calif.

Religion
Jewish

Family
Wife, Janet Waxman; two children

Education
U. of California, Los Angeles, B.A. 1961 (political science), J.D. 1964

Career
Lawyer

Political Highlights
Calif. Assembly, 1968-74

ELECTION RESULTS

2010 GENERAL

Henry A. Waxman (D)	153,663	64.6%
Charles E. Wilkerson (R)	75,948	31.9%
Erich D. Miller (LIBERT)	5,021	2.1%
Richard R. Castaldo (PFP)	3,115	1.3%

2010 PRIMARY

Henry A. Waxman (D)	unopposed

2008 GENERAL

Henry A. Waxman (D)	unopposed

Previous Winning Percentages
2006 (72%); 2004 (71%); 2002 (70%); 2000 (76%);
1998 (74%); 1996 (68%); 1994 (68%); 1992 (61%);
1990 (69%); 1988 (72%); 1986 (88%); 1984 (63%);
1982 (65%); 1980 (64%); 1978 (63%); 1976 (68%);
1974 (64%)

Elected 1974; 19th term

Waxman is one of Washington's shrewdest operators, a tenacious advocate and self-professed "unapologetic liberal" who has positioned himself to play a key role in executing, and now more often defending, Democratic policy initiatives he has spent much of his lengthy congressional career championing.

As chairman of the Energy and Commerce Committee in the 111th Congress (2009-10), Waxman was a major player on several of President Obama's chief priorities, most notably the health care overhaul that became law in 2010 and legislation designed to curb carbon emissions that didn't. As ranking Democrat on the panel in the 112th Congress (2011-12), his job will be to challenge Republican efforts to undo what the Democrats accomplished in the previous four years.

"Minorities get united when the majority oversteps its bounds," Waxman told Roll Call in early 2011.

In an Orange County Register op-ed, he warned Republicans against overreaching — a sin he has been accused of himself from time to time — saying the best check on congressional oversight power is "self-restraint and the power of public opinion."

Partisan purity and methodical patience have helped Waxman advance, as have his ties to top Democrats in Washington. He is a close ally of Minority Leader Nancy Pelosi, a fellow California Democrat. His longtime aide Philip Schiliro was Obama's first director of congressional relations.

The 5-foot-5-inch Waxman — with his mustache, wire-rimmed spectacles, thick black eyebrows and bald pate — is not physically intimidating; Time magazine described him as having "all the panache of your parents' dentist." But Republicans have learned to respect him: Former GOP Sen. Alan K. Simpson of Wyoming once griped that he was "tougher than a boiled owl."

Waxman is single-mindedly focused on his job; he has few hobbies, avoids socializing with colleagues and claims not to have much of an ego. "I don't care whether the world knows about me," he told The Washington Post in 2002. "I just want the world to care about some of these issues and care about some of these things that I care about."

Waxman's political chops were on display in 2008 when he took the Energy and Commerce gavel from Michigan's John D. Dingell — the House's longest-serving member and the panel's top Democrat since 1981 — by taking a page from Obama's playbook and portraying himself as an agent of change.

In a campaign that cast aside the House tradition of seniority, Waxman appealed to younger Democrats who wanted to push an aggressive agenda on environmental and energy issues. Many had criticized Dingell, an ardent defender of his state's auto industry, for moving too slowly on restricting carbon emissions.

Waxman's rivalry with Dingell dates to the 1980s, when the two clashed on environmental issues. An uneasy truce collapsed in 2008 when Dingell revived a proposal to bar Waxman's home state and others from setting tougher vehicle emissions standards than the federal government.

But after taking over the chairmanship, Waxman didn't relegate Dingell to the sidelines. Instead, he designated him "chairman emeritus" and allowed him to play a key role in the committee's consideration of health care legislation in 2009.

Not that he needed a lot of expert advice. Before besting Dingell, Waxman had made the committee's Health and Environment Subcommittee his main base of operations. He chaired the panel for 16 years before the GOP takeover of 1995.

In that post, Waxman — a former smoker who had a tough time quitting — became a crusader against tobacco. At a 1994 hearing, he grilled the chief executives of the seven largest tobacco companies, all of whom testified under oath that they did not believe nicotine was addictive. The hearing helped lay the groundwork for multibillion-dollar lawsuits against the industry as well as for Waxman's successful fight a decade and a half later to expand the Food and Drug Administration's power to regulate tobacco advertising and marketing.

His grilling foreshadowed his efforts in 2010 to hold oil industry executives' feet to the fire following the oil rig explosion that spurred a massive oil spill in the Gulf of Mexico. The Energy and Commerce panel launched an investigation into the circumstances surrounding the incident and called in top oil company executives to testify. During a nationally televised hearing in June, Waxman calmly but persistently bird-dogged BP chief executive officer Tony Hayward, questioning the company's commitment to safety and why "warnings fell on deaf ears" prior to the incident.

As chairman of the Oversight and Government Reform Committee in the 110th Congress (2007-08), he was a constant thorn in President George W. Bush's side, drawing praise from liberals and charges of partisan witch-hunting from conservatives.

Despite his reputation as a partisan, Waxman has shown he is willing to work with Republicans, in some cases even to take on the Obama administration. In January 2010, he joined Energy and Commerce Republicans in requesting information from the White House about deals it had negotiated with drug companies, labor unions and hospitals as part of its effort to garner support for the health care overhaul.

Waxman grew up in an apartment above a Los Angeles grocery store run by his father. The elder Waxman was the son of Russian immigrants and a New Deal Democrat. Waxman's political career began at the University of California, Los Angeles, in the 1960s, when he and fellow student — and now House colleague — Howard L. Berman became active in California's Federation of Young Democrats. In 1968, after a term as chairman of the state federation, Waxman, with Berman's support, challenged Democratic state Assemblyman Lester McMillan in a primary and beat him handily.

He entered Congress in the huge Democratic wave of 1974 and is one of just two "Watergate babies" still in the House (the other is fellow Californian George Miller). Waxman has never been seriously challenged for re-election.

Key Votes

2010	
Overhaul the nation's health insurance system	YES
Allow for repeal of "don't ask, don't tell"	YES
Overhaul financial services industry regulation	YES
Limit use of new Afghanistan War funds to troop withdrawal activities	YES
Change oversight of offshore drilling and lift oil spill liability cap	YES
Provide a path to legal status for some children of illegal immigrants	YES
Extend Bush-era income tax cuts for two years	YES
2009	
Expand the Children's Health Insurance Program	YES
Provide $787 billion in tax cuts and spending increases to stimulate the economy	YES
Allow bankruptcy judges to modify certain primary-residence mortgages	YES
Create a cap-and-trade system to limit greenhouse gas emissions	YES
Provide $2 billion for the "cash for clunkers" program	YES
Establish the government as the sole provider of student loans	YES
Restrict federally funded insurance coverage for abortions in health care overhaul	NO

CQ Vote Studies

	PARTY UNITY		PRESIDENTIAL SUPPORT	
	SUPPORT	OPPOSE	SUPPORT	OPPOSE
2010	99%	1%	95%	5%
2009	99%	1%	99%	1%
2008	99%	1%	16%	84%
2007	99%	1%	7%	93%
2006	98%	2%	8%	92%

Interest Groups

	AFL-CIO	ADA	CCUS	ACU
2010	100%	90%	25%	0%
2009	100%	100%	33%	0%
2008	100%	95%	61%	4%
2007	100%	90%	53%	0%
2006	100%	95%	33%	4%

California 30
West Los Angeles County — Santa Monica, West Hollywood, part of Los Angeles

With such glamorous locales as Beverly Hills, Malibu, Bel Air and Pacific Palisades, the 30th has few places that have not been immortalized by movies or television. The Democratic district stretches west from Santa Monica along the scenic Pacific Coast Highway, past Malibu to the Ventura County line. It also extends north across the Santa Monica Mountains to Calabasas and Hidden Hills on the north side of the range.

The entertainment industry drives the economy here. Many movie and television studios have facilities in the 30th, including MGM, Time Warner, Fox Broadcasting and CBS Studios. Tourism also brings revenue to the district. The 30th is home to attractions such as Grauman's Chinese Theater and several blocks of the Hollywood Walk of Fame.

Even during economic downturns, exclusive Rodeo Drive offers ample high-end shopping, and international tourism helps prop up the luxury retail sector on the posh street. Health care is another economic driver here. The 30th has several medical campuses, including the Cedars-Sinai

Medical Center and a Department of Veterans Affairs-run site that combined employ more than 15,000 people.

The district, more than 70 percent white, has an active gay community in West Hollywood and a large Jewish population. Its economy is overwhelmingly white-collar and has the nation's third-highest percentage of college-educated residents. Local colleges and universities, including Pepperdine University and UCLA, provide tens of thousands of jobs.

The district votes overwhelmingly Democratic in elections at all levels. Barack Obama won the district with more than 70 percent of its presidential vote in 2008, and Jerry Brown took a nearly 30-percentage-point win here in the 2010 gubernatorial race.

Major Industry
Entertainment, higher education, health care, tourism

Cities
Los Angeles (pt.), 415,188; Santa Monica, 89,736; West Hollywood, 34,399

Notable
The Page Museum at the La Brea Tar Pits boasts 3 million Ice Age fossils; Santa Monica Airport, formerly Clover Field, was the takeoff and landing point in 1924 for the first circumnavigation of the Earth by air.

Rep. Xavier Becerra (D)

Capitol Office
225-6235
becerra.house.gov
1226 Longworth Bldg. 20515-0531; fax 225-2202

Committees
Ways & Means

Residence
Los Angeles

Born
Jan. 26, 1958; Sacramento, Calif.

Religion
Roman Catholic

Family
Wife, Carolina Reyes; three children

Education
Stanford U., A.B. 1980 (economics), J.D. 1984

Career
State prosecutor; state legislative aide; lawyer

Political Highlights
Calif. Assembly, 1990-92; candidate for mayor of Los
Angeles, 2001

ELECTION RESULTS

2010 GENERAL

Xavier Becerra (D)	76,363	83.8%
Stephen C. Smith (R)	14,740	16.2%

2010 PRIMARY

Xavier Becerra (D)	20,550	88.0%
Sal Genovese (D)	2,795	12.0%

2008 GENERAL

Xavier Becerra (D)	unopposed

Previous Winning Percentages
2006 (100%); 2004 (80%); 2002 (81%); 2000 (83%);
1998 (81%); 1996 (72%); 1994 (66%); 1992 (58%)

Elected 1992; 10th term

Becerra is a loyal lieutenant in Minority Leader Nancy Pelosi's inner circle. He serves as vice chairman of the Democratic Caucus, the group of all House Democrats, where he represents the views of the party's liberal Progressive Caucus and the Hispanic Caucus, which he once led.

As part of the leadership team, Becerra (full name: HAH-vee-air beh-SEH-ra) says it will be easier to develop an effective message for the 2012 election cycle while playing defense rather than offense.

"Now that we get to compare and contrast with what Republicans do — not what they say they want to do, not what they say they would have done, but what they do," he told Roll Call in early 2011.

He sought the Caucus vice chairmanship in 2006 but dropped his bid when John B. Larson of Connecticut, another Pelosi ally, decided to keep the post. Pelosi responded by creating a position for Becerra (assistant to the Speaker), giving him a seat in leadership meetings. When Larson moved up to the Caucus chairmanship in late 2008, Becerra won the job over the more centrist Marcy Kaptur of Ohio.

The first Hispanic to serve on the tax-writing Ways and Means Committee, Becerra sees himself as a guardian of lower-income taxpayers. He kept his spot on the panel in the new Congress, even as some rank-and-file Democrats suggested the party's leaders should step aside to make room for other members. The Democratic roster on Ways and Means shrank from 26 in the 111th Congress (2009-10) to 15 in the 112th (2011-12).

Becerra is a reliable Democratic and liberal vote. He followed the party line 99 percent of the time during President George W. Bush's administration on votes that pitted a majority of Republicans against a majority of Democrats. That number didn't change much after President Obama moved into the White House.

He was an enthusiastic supporter of the Democrats' health care overhaul enacted in March 2010, saying the measure would "lay the groundwork for a more just and prosperous America." But he also supported a government-run "public option," which was not included in the final version of the bill, and he subsequently became a cosponsor of legislation to create one.

Becerra favors immigration legislation that would emphasize keeping families together and providing a route to permanent U.S. residency for illegal immigrants already in the country. As the issue simmered but no legislative action was forthcoming, he accused Republicans of holding the country's immigration system "hostage" for partisan gain.

"The reality is we've got to fix something that everyone in this country agrees is broken and doesn't make any sense," he told Roll Call.

An opponent of the Iraq War, he supports withdrawing U.S. troops immediately and votes — as he did in July 2010 — against supplemental funding for the wars in Iraq and Afghanistan.

He joined other liberals in opposing two $700 billion measures — the second of which became law — to assist the ailing financial services sector. A member of the Budget Committee at the time, he said the legislation didn't do enough for taxpayers or businesses. But he praised Obama's subsequent $787 billion economic stimulus law, signed in February 2009, for its emphasis on "jobs, jobs, jobs."

Becerra's rise through the House ranks has increasingly made it possible for him to get things done. He has long championed the idea of a Smithsonian museum honoring American Latinos. His persistence paid off in May

2008 when Bush signed legislation creating a 23-member commission to conduct a feasibility study for such a museum.

In March 2010, Pelosi named him to the National Commission on Fiscal Responsibility and Reform, charged with coming up with ways to reduce the soaring federal debt, but he voted against the group's final recommendations. "I do not believe this report significantly targeted for reform the principal drivers of our economic crisis," which he suggested were the wars in Iraq and Afghanistan, the Medicare prescription drug benefit enacted in 2003 and the Bush-era tax cuts.

With one of the nation's largest seaports in the Los Angeles area, Becerra generally has backed trade deals, including the 1993 North American Free Trade Agreement, and he decided in December 2008 to turn down an offer to become Obama's U.S. trade representative.

But in 2005, he opposed the Central America Free Trade Agreement, citing a lack of worker protections. Months later, he voted against the Oman Free Trade Agreement, again citing labor rights and port security concerns. But he backed the 2007 Peru trade deal after a compromise between the Bush administration and Democrats created additional protections for workers and the environment.

Becerra was born in Sacramento. His mother was born in Mexico, and his American-born father spent much of his early life moving across the border to earn money by shining shoes, canning tomatoes and working on highway construction crews. Becerra still wears his father's wedding ring as a reminder of his humble origins.

The first member of his family to obtain a degree from a four-year college, he earned a bachelor's in economics and a law degree from Stanford. He helped pay his way by working summers on road construction crews in Sacramento and tutoring students in the community during the school year. A state Senate fellowship cemented his interest in advocacy and policy work. He then worked with a legal services firm in Worcester, Mass., that specialized in helping mentally ill clients. After returning to California, Becerra was an aide for a state senator and worked for the state attorney general.

In 1990, he ran a successful race for a state Assembly seat. Two years later, his interest in the "bigger picture issues" of national and foreign policy led him to run for Congress.

He easily outdistanced nine other candidates in the 1992 primary, then bested a Republican and three minor-party candidates in November with 58 percent of the vote. He has been re-elected handily since. In 2001, he ran for mayor of Los Angeles, finishing fifth in a field of 14 candidates.

Key Votes

2010

Overhaul the nation's health insurance system	YES
Allow for repeal of "don't ask, don't tell"	YES
Overhaul financial services industry regulation	YES
Limit use of new Afghanistan War funds to troop withdrawal activities	YES
Change oversight of offshore drilling and lift oil spill liability cap	YES
Provide a path to legal status for some children of illegal immigrants	YES
Extend Bush-era income tax cuts for two years	NO

2009

Expand the Children's Health Insurance Program	YES
Provide $787 billion in tax cuts and spending increases to stimulate the economy	YES
Allow bankruptcy judges to modify certain primary-residence mortgages	YES
Create a cap-and-trade system to limit greenhouse gas emissions	YES
Provide $2 billion for the "cash for clunkers" program	YES
Establish the government as the sole provider of student loans	YES
Restrict federally funded insurance coverage for abortions in health care overhaul	NO

CQ Vote Studies

	PARTY UNITY		PRESIDENTIAL SUPPORT	
	SUPPORT	OPPOSE	SUPPORT	OPPOSE
2010	98%	2%	90%	10%
2009	99%	1%	100%	0%
2008	99%	1%	10%	90%
2007	99%	1%	4%	96%
2006	99%	1%	21%	79%

Interest Groups

	AFL-CIO	ADA	CCUS	ACU
2010	100%	95%	13%	0%
2009	100%	100%	33%	4%
2008	100%	100%	50%	8%
2007	96%	95%	58%	0%
2006	100%	95%	21%	4%

California 31

Northeast and South Los Angeles

The only district set entirely within the city of Los Angeles, the 31st is densely populated, heavily Hispanic and staunchly Democratic. The district wraps around west of downtown to extend south into South Los Angeles and northeast toward Pasadena. Most of the population is Hispanic, and Asian residents outnumber whites here.

Rapid immigration has changed many of the district's already diverse communities — a majority of residents were born abroad — and some newcomers are finding a mixed reception. Many Hispanics are among the new residents, and Pico Union and Westlake are dominated by Central American and Mexican immigrants.

Other heavily Hispanic areas include Glassell Park and Highland Park, which boasts numerous historic homes. The eastern side of the district includes Lincoln Heights and El Sereno — heavily Hispanic, blue-collar areas with a significant Mexican immigrant presence.

Filipinotown, between Echo Park and Westlake, also has a strong Mexican and Central American presence — the traditional Filipino presence in the neighborhood has dwindled.

Directly west of Elysian Park, where Dodger Stadium is located, is the artsy Echo Park.

In the northeast sits Eagle Rock, a hilly, middle-class pocket of relative affluence that votes Democratic but leans more toward the political center than other parts of the 31st. The still trendy neighborhood, home to Occidental College, has seen commercial slowdowns, and some residential units stand empty.

Despite economic contributions from Paramount Studios, a slew of area hospitals and white-collar businesses along the Wilshire Boulevard central business corridor, the 31st has one of the state's lowest median household incomes at $36,000 per year.

The 31st supports Democrats, although voter turnout is traditionally low. Barack Obama won 80 percent of the district's 2008 presidential vote, and Jerry Brown took the same percentage here in the 2010 gubernatorial election.

Major Industry
Service, entertainment, tourism, health care

Cities
Los Angeles (pt.), 611,336

Notable
Dedicated in 1886, 575-acre Elysian Park is the city's oldest public park.

Rep. Judy Chu (D)

Capitol Office
225-5464
chu.house.gov
1520 Longworth Bldg. 20515-0532; fax 225-5467

Committees
Judiciary
Small Business

Residence
Monterey Park

Born
July 7, 1953; Los Angeles, Calif.

Religion
Unspecified

Family
Husband, Mike Eng

Education
U. of California, Santa Barbara, attended 1970-73; U. of California, Los Angeles, B.A. 1974 (mathematics); California School of Professional Psychology, Los Angeles, Ph.D. 1979 (clinical psychology)

Career
Professor

Political Highlights
Garvey School District Board of Education, 1985-88; Monterey Park City Council, 1988-2001 (mayor, 1994-95, 1999); sought Democratic nomination for Calif. Assembly, 1994, 1998; Calif. Assembly, 2001-06; Calif. Board of Equalization, 2007-09 (chairwoman, 2008-09)

ELECTION RESULTS

2010 GENERAL

Judy Chu (D)	77,759	71.0%
Edward Schmerling (R)	31,697	29.0%

2010 PRIMARY

Judy Chu (D)	unopposed

2009 SPECIAL

Judy Chu (D)	16,194	61.8%
Betty Chu (R)	8,630	33.0%
Christopher Agrella (LIBERT)	1,356	5.2%

Elected 2009; 1st full term

The first Chinese-American woman to serve in Congress, Chu is a liberal Democrat sporting a résumé that aligns with her advocacy on education and immigration issues.

Chu spent much of the 20 years preceding her election to the House as a city council member and state legislator. But she points to an even earlier experience, when she was part of a group that opposed an English-only movement in Monterey Park during the 1980s, when she discusses events that shaped her approach to politics.

"That experience was my entrée into politics, and it deeply influences the way that I see my political life, which is to be a coalition builder and to work on quality-of-life issues from a grass-roots perspective," Chu said.

In her first year in Congress, Chu sided with her party on every vote in which a majority of Democrats opposed a majority of Republicans, and she sided with President Obama every time he had a clear preference on legislation.

Chu, whose largely Hispanic and Asian district is two-fifths foreign-born, said she arrived in Congress wanting to work on immigration overhaul legislation and successfully lobbied for a seat on the Judiciary Committee for that purpose.

She wants to see legislation that would penalize employers who hire illegal workers and establish a path toward citizenship for illegal immigrants already in the country. In late 2010, she backed House-passed legislation to grant legal status to certain illegal immigrant children. The bill died in the Senate.

In response to proposals to eliminate birthright citizenship for illegal immigrants, Chu said, "it is deeply disturbing to me that today, in the 21st century, there are those who would take us back to a time when our nation didn't fully live up to the ideals of equality and fairness upon which it was founded."

Chu, who taught psychology at community colleges for 20 years, sat on the Education and Labor Committee in the 111th Congress (2009-10). Labor unions are her biggest campaign contributors, and she was a member of the American Federation of Teachers.

In May 2010 she introduced legislation that would establish a grant program to provide support services for students who are pregnant or have children. She has criticized the Obama administration's approach to boosting the performance of the country's lowest-performing schools and has called for an overhaul of the program in the next reauthorization of the Elementary and Secondary Education Act.

"Instead of providing teachers and administrators with the tools necessary to build better schools, the models deprive schools of the flexibility necessary to respond to the specific needs of their students," Chu wrote about the administration's approach in a report she released of her own teachers union-backed plan.

At the district level, Chu said her focus is transportation infrastructure, which she described as a pressing concern in her working-class district, as well as water supply issues. Chu has also noted that some cities in her district have a high unemployment rate and that a focus on economic stimulus and job creation is needed. Efforts are under way to extend the Gold Line route of the Los Angeles mass transit rail system, and Chu said she hopes to gain additional funding for the project. "We are a district that's rather hard-hit by the foreclosures and the high unemployment rate," said Chu, who joined the Small Business Committee in the 112th Congress (2011-12) and predicted a fully funded Gold Line extension "would bring in 30,000 new jobs as well as $43 billion in stimulus to this area."

Chu grew up in south-central Los Angeles as a third-generation Chinese-American. Her grandfather ran a Chinese restaurant in the Watts neighborhood of Los Angeles. Her father was an electrician for the Pacific Telephone Company, while her mother was alternately a stay-at-home mother and cannery worker with a Teamsters card.

She entered college during the Vietnam War and initially planned to be a computer scientist. While walking on campus, she was handed a flier for an Asian-American studies course.

"I went to college going to be this quiet little math major, and I took ethnic and women's studies classes and was appalled at the disparities I discovered," she once recalled. "I was soon involved in the anti-war movement."

Chu received her undergraduate degree in mathematics and later obtained a doctorate in clinical psychology from the California School of Professional Psychology in Los Angeles.

She started down her political road in 1985 as a member of the school board in suburban Garvey. A resident of an area with many immigrants of varied ethnic backgrounds, she was a leader in a successful fight against an English-only movement in Monterey Park and in 1987 won a seat to that city's council.

Although thwarted in primary bids for the state Assembly in 1994 and 1998, she won a seat in that chamber in 2000 and brought with her a reputation as a champion of diversity. Rep. Hilda L. Solis, another California Democrat, endorsed Chu's successful Assembly campaign in a legislative district that, like the surrounding congressional district, was heavily Hispanic.

Chu steadily climbed rungs on the ladder until she become chairwoman of the Assembly's appropriations committee and later a member of the state's tax commission.

In 2009, Solis was nominated to be secretary of Labor and endorsed Chu as her successor in a special election. Other Hispanic leaders, including California Democratic Rep. Loretta Sanchez, also backed her, helping insulate Chu from the difficulties she might otherwise have faced in the May 2009 race, which included several Hispanic contenders.

Under California's rules for special-election primaries, all 12 candidates, including three Republicans and a Libertarian, ran on the same ballot. Chu comfortably defeated her closest Democratic rival, state Sen. Gil Cedillo, 33 percent to 23 percent, then bested Republican Betty Chu in the general election by almost 30 percentage points. She was re-elected easily in 2010.

Key Votes

2010

Overhaul the nation's health insurance system	YES
Allow for repeal of "don't ask, don't tell"	YES
Overhaul financial services industry regulation	YES
Limit use of new Afghanistan War funds to troop withdrawal activities	YES
Change oversight of offshore drilling and lift oil spill liability cap	YES
Provide a path to legal status for some children of illegal immigrants	YES
Extend Bush-era income tax cuts for two years	NO

2009

Provide $2 billion for the "cash for clunkers" program	YES
Establish the government as the sole provider of student loans	YES
Restrict federally funded insurance coverage for abortions in health care overhaul	NO

CQ Vote Studies

	PARTY UNITY		PRESIDENTIAL SUPPORT	
	SUPPORT	OPPOSE	SUPPORT	OPPOSE
2010	99%	1%	88%	12%
2009	100%	0%	100%	0%

Interest Groups

	AFL-CIO	ADA	CCUS	ACU
2010	100%	100%	0%	0%
2009	100%		40%	0%

California 32

East Los Angeles; El Monte; West Covina

The 32nd takes in a small chunk of the city of Los Angeles and extends east into largely Hispanic and Asian working-class suburbs. It includes the southern and central San Gabriel Valley, and reaches east to Azusa and Covina, capturing a few good-size cities.

The district lacks a dominant industry, although manufacturing is key in several areas. Many residents commute out of the 32nd for work, but cities in the San Gabriel Valley have suffered from higher unemployment rates than the rest of the nation despite consistent population growth. Once a small farming town, El Monte became home to some small aerospace factories and is now a light manufacturing area with a retail auto complex. Irwindale, dominated by rock quarries and landfills, is among the district's industrial centers.

Rosemead has a large ethnic Chinese population, and it is the headquarters for the Panda Express food chain. The 32nd's small piece of the city of Los Angeles hosts a California State University campus.

As city dwellers continue to leave Los Angeles, local officials in the 32nd have focused on residential and commercial development over the past decade. Two-fifths of the population here is foreign-born, and many residents speak a language other than English at home. Monterey Park (shared with the 29th) has strong Taiwanese and other Asian immigrant communities. Another large Asian population lives in wealthy, Democratic-leaning West Covina.

El Monte, in the heart of the San Gabriel Valley, and Baldwin Park, to the east, are blue-collar cities that form the 32nd's Democratic base. Although there had been pockets of Republicans and older white voters in Azusa, these groups are shrinking, and the city supported Democrat Jerry Brown in the 2010 gubernatorial election. He won here with 65 percent of the district's vote.

Major Industry
Service, light manufacturing, higher education

Cities
El Monte, 113,475; West Covina, 106,098; Baldwin Park, 75,390; Rosemead, 53,764; Covina, 47,796; Azusa (pt.), 46,248

Notable
The first In-N-Out Burger restaurant opened in 1948 in Baldwin Park.

Rep. Karen Bass (D)

Capitol Office
225-7084
karenbass.house.gov
408 Cannon Bldg. 20515-0533; fax 225-2422

Committees
Budget
Foreign Affairs

Residence
Los Angeles

Born
Oct. 3, 1953; Los Angeles, Calif.

Religion
Baptist

Family
Divorced; one child (deceased) and four stepchildren

Education
San Diego State U., attended 1971-73 (philosophy); California State U., Dominguez Hills, B.S. 1990 (health sciences)

Career
Nonprofit community activism organization founder; college instructor; physician's assistant; nurse

Political Highlights
Calif. Assembly, 2004-10 (majority floor leader, 2006-08; Speaker, 2008-10)

ELECTION RESULTS

2010 GENERAL
Karen Bass (D)	131,990	86.1%
James L. Andion (R)	21,342	13.9%

2010 PRIMARY
Karen Bass (D)	41,250	85.3%
Felton Newell (D)	3,096	6.4%
Morris F. Griffin (D)	2,075	4.3%
Nick Juan Mostert (D)	1,937	4.0%

Elected 2010; 1st term

Bass brings political savvy, legislative skills and leadership experience with her to Congress. Four years after her election to the California Assembly, she was chosen Speaker.

During her tenure, as the state's economy was crashing, she devoted considerable time and energy to legislation intended to create jobs. Now a member of the Budget Committee, she says jobs — specifically in the transportation and the entertainment industries — will continue to be her focus.

A former physician's assistant and clinical instructor, she voted against repealing the health care law in early 2011, tying it to her top priority.

"Health care reform is a job creator, producing made-in-America work that can never be outsourced," she said.

Bass also sits on the Foreign Affairs Committee, and said on MSNBC in January 2011 that one way to address spending cuts would be to "look at the area of defense. We should look at bases around the world that maybe aren't necessarily needed any longer."

But she wants to maintain social support programs even in the face of mounting debt. "Job training and unemployment support are reducing the crime and expensive incarceration associated with desperate economic times," she wrote in an op-ed in April 2010. "Keeping these and other safety net threads strong takes courage and investment up front, but pays great dividends down the road, both human and fiscal."

Bass, who has brown belts in tae kwon do and hapkido martial arts, was born and raised in Los Angeles. She graduated from California State University in 1990 with a degree in health sciences and went on to establish the nonprofit Community Coalition in 1990 to address crack cocaine use. She served as the organization's executive director for 14 years.

When Diane Watson announced her retirement in February 2010, Bass called on contacts from her years of community service and emerged as the overwhelming favorite, with Watson's blessing.

She took the primary with 85 percent of the vote and surpassed that total in November.

California 33

West Los Angeles; Culver City

The 33rd is a Democratic, ethnically diverse district that begins a mile inland from Venice Beach, runs east through Culver City and ends up in South Los Angeles. The northern part of the district includes a section of Wilshire Boulevard from the "Miracle Mile" district to Koreatown and hooks north and east through Hollywood.

Blacks, Hispanics and Asians account for most of the population, but the district has no single racial majority. The 33rd has a solid middle class, as well as some sharply contrasting areas such as wealthy Hancock Park and the city's poor South Los Angeles neighborhood.

The largest business sector is the service industry, with health care also providing many jobs. The University of Southern California is in the 33rd's portion of Los Angeles. Although the district is no longer the film production hub it used to be, it is home to the real Tinseltown — Hollywood — and entertainment continues to be a factor in its economy. Sony Pictures Studios (formerly MGM Studios) makes its home in Culver City, and the Kodak Theater is the site of the annual Academy Awards ceremony.

For recreation, residents and tourists flock to Exposition Park in downtown Los Angeles. In addition to the Los Angeles County Natural History Museum and the California Science Center, the park boasts the Los Angeles Memorial Coliseum.

Democrats have an overwhelming advantage here. Jerry Brown took 83 percent of the district's 2010 gubernatorial vote, his second-highest percentage in the state.

Major Industry
Service, entertainment, health care

Cities
Los Angeles (pt.), 580,666; Culver City, 38,883

Notable
Howard Hughes built his infamous wooden plane, the "Spruce Goose," in Culver City.

Rep. Lucille Roybal-Allard (D)

Capitol Office
225-1766
www.house.gov/roybal-allard
2330 Rayburn Bldg. 20515-0534; fax 226-0350

Committees
Appropriations

Residence
Los Angeles

Born
June 12, 1941; Boyle Heights, Calif.

Religion
Roman Catholic

Family
Husband, Edward Allard; four children

Education
California State U., Los Angeles, B.A. 1965 (speech)

Career
Nonprofit worker

Political Highlights
Calif. Assembly, 1987-92

ELECTION RESULTS

2010 GENERAL

Lucille Roybal-Allard (D)	69,382	77.2%
Wayne Miller (R)	20,457	22.8%

2010 PRIMARY

Lucille Roybal-Allard (D)	14,309	70.7%
David Sanchez (D)	5,917	29.2%

2008 GENERAL

Lucille Roybal-Allard (D)	98,503	77.1%
Christopher Balding (R)	29,266	22.9%

Previous Winning Percentages
2006 (77%); 2004 (74%); 2002 (74%); 2000 (85%);
1998 (87%); 1996 (82%); 1994 (81%); 1992 (63%)

Elected 1992; 10th term

The first Mexican-American woman elected to Congress, Roybal-Allard represents a Los Angeles district where more than three out of four residents are Hispanic and nearly half are immigrants. She is outspoken in defending their interests.

Success has come in fits and spurts, and not nearly as quickly as she would like: Even a large Democratic majority in Washington couldn't spur action on a long-awaited overhaul of U.S. immigration policy during the 111th Congress (2009-10). "The costs of inaction are rising," she said. And while she added that Congress could not "accept excuses or embrace half-measures that fall short of true comprehensive reform," she is a shrewd enough politician to accept compromise, which will be even more of an imperative with Republicans back in charge.

Even though she helped draft a major immigration overhaul bill backed by the Congressional Hispanic Caucus, Roybal-Allard has embraced incremental change as the larger effort languished. In January 2010, for instance, the Obama administration, at Roybal-Allard's urging, dropped a longstanding policy of detaining immigrants seeking asylum. In such cases, immigrants must prove they have a legitimate fear of persecution in their home countries. The administration said that asylum seekers could remain free pending a decision on their case, so long as they posed neither a flight risk nor a danger to the community. She backed stand-alone legislation at the end of 2010 to create a path to legal status for certain children of illegal immigrants, but the measure died in the Senate.

Likewise, as chairwoman of the Congressional Hispanic Caucus' Task Force on Health, Roybal-Allard embraced the health care overhaul enacted in March 2010 — even though it contained provisions barring illegal immigrants from receiving health coverage under Medicaid and preventing them from participating in the new government exchanges that will serve as marketplaces for people seeking insurance policies.

"Clearly it is not perfect," she said of the law. "But with an issue that impacts so many stakeholders and involves so many competing interests, it is doubtful that any single legislative effort could ever satisfy everyone."

Roybal-Allard has also pressed administration officials to handle illegal immigrants taken into custody more humanely and introduced legislation to restrict the use of child labor in agriculture.

Her sensitivity to the problems of immigrants stems not just from her roots but also from the discrimination and discouragement she faced growing up. She recalls being punished for speaking Spanish in school and her parents being questioned when they tried to enter hotels. Even when her father began serving on the Los Angeles City Council in the 1950s, he met with resistance. "The racial slurs and not-so-quiet whispers directed at him and our family when we attended events and dinners remain vivid in our minds even today," she said.

The discrimination didn't stop Roybal-Allard's father, Edward R. Roybal, from pursuing his political career. He was elected to Congress in 1962 to represent Los Angeles and went on to serve 15 terms, eventually becoming a subcommittee chairman on the powerful Appropriations Committee before retiring in 1992. Roybal founded the Congressional Hispanic Caucus, and in 1999 his daughter became the first woman to head the group.

And as her father did, Roybal-Allard serves on Appropriations, where she looks out for her district and the surrounding area. She can address some of her immigration concerns from her spot on the Homeland Security Sub-committee. And she takes a particular interest in the health care needs of the poor. In 2007 she sponsored a bill, which President George W. Bush signed into law in April 2008, to establish grant programs to expand health assessments of newborns.

Before entering politics, Roybal-Allard worked for the United Way and served as an assistant director on the Alcoholism Council of East Los Angeles. She now focuses considerable legislative energy on fighting underage drinking. A member of the Labor, Health and Human Services, and Education Subcommittee, Roybal-Allard won a $1 million provision in 2001 for the Health and Human Services Department to develop programs to curb the problem. She built on that over the years and in 2006 won enactment of legislation to coordinate all federal programs and research efforts on underage drinking and provide grants to colleges, states and nonprofits to combat the problem.

Roybal-Allard drew plaudits in the late 1990s for her role in awakening the power of the California congressional delegation, which had been divided and ineffective. As the first elected chairwoman of the state's Democratic delegation, she worked with her GOP counterpart, Jerry Lewis, to find issues on which the majority of Golden State lawmakers could agree.

Trade is not usually on that list. She is an ally of labor unions and voted against free-trade deals with Peru, the Dominican Republic and Central American countries in recent years. In 2010, she pressured the Obama administration to crack down on illegal steel imports from China that she said were hurting manufacturers in her district.

Roybal-Allard says her own family tried to dampen her ambitions when she was young. Her father's relatives ridiculed him for sending his daughters to college, saying all that was expected of daughters was marriage and children. Later, her siblings discouraged her from entering politics, citing the difficulties their father faced.

Roybal-Allard was undeterred. She easily won election to the California Assembly in a special election in 1987 and served nearly three terms before winning election to the House in 1992. Her father had hoped that as a result of redistricting she could serve beside him in Congress. But her mother's poor health and the strain of travel prompted him to retire. Democrat Xavier Becerra, now vice chairman of the House Democratic Caucus, won her father's old seat that year, while she captured a neighboring Hispanic district by a 2-to-1 margin. She has won with no less than 74 percent of the vote in subsequent elections in the heavily Democratic district.

Key Votes

2010

Overhaul the nation's health insurance system	YES
Allow for repeal of "don't ask, don't tell"	YES
Overhaul financial services industry regulation	YES
Limit use of new Afghanistan War funds to troop withdrawal activities	NO
Change oversight of offshore drilling and lift oil spill liability cap	YES
Provide a path to legal status for some children of illegal immigrants	YES
Extend Bush-era income tax cuts for two years	NO

2009

Expand the Children's Health Insurance Program	YES
Provide $787 billion in tax cuts and spending increases to stimulate the economy	YES
Allow bankruptcy judges to modify certain primary-residence mortgages	YES
Create a cap-and-trade system to limit greenhouse gas emissions	YES
Provide $2 billion for the "cash for clunkers" program	YES
Establish the government as the sole provider of student loans	YES
Restrict federally funded insurance coverage for abortions in health care overhaul	NO

CQ Vote Studies

	PARTY UNITY		PRESIDENTIAL SUPPORT	
	SUPPORT	OPPOSE	SUPPORT	OPPOSE
2010	98%	2%	93%	7%
2009	99%	1%	97%	3%
2008	99%	1%	11%	89%
2007	99%	1%	3%	97%
2006	93%	7%	27%	73%

Interest Groups

	AFL-CIO	ADA	CCUS	ACU
2010	100%	100%	13%	0%
2009	100%	100%	33%	0%
2008	100%	95%	44%	8%
2007	96%	100%	55%	0%
2006	100%	100%	33%	4%

California 34

East central Los Angeles; Downey; Bellflower

The Democratic 34th takes in the heart and southeastern part of Los Angeles and has an overwhelming Hispanic majority. The district has the largest concentration of Hispanics in California and the fourth-largest in the country. Forty-five percent of the adult population does not have a high school diploma.

The economy here relies on businesses in revitalized downtown areas and in nearby light industrial centers such as Vernon and Commerce. Downtown hosts toy, jewelry and garment manufacturers and retailers. Some space downtown is being converted into mixed-use units, creating residential loft space. Many of Los Angeles' civic buildings, including city hall, the county prison and courthouses, are in the 34th. Despite redevelopment and many small businesses, crime continues to be an issue.

Although crime and unemployment rates have increased in parts of the district and Los Angeles faces budget shortfalls, brighter spots include Walt Disney Concert Hall, home of the Los Angeles Philharmonic; the Dorothy Chandler Pavilion, home of the Los Angeles Opera; the Los Angeles Convention Center; and Staples Center, home to basketball's Lakers, Clippers and Sparks, and hockey's Kings.

Transportation hub Union Station and the terminus of the 20-mile Alameda Corridor rail link connecting the city to the ports of Los Angeles and Long Beach also are in the district.

Vernon's population explodes during the workday as people head to its manufacturing and food processing plants. Business-friendly zoning and utilities laws have long kept Vernon a haven for industry, but a potential disincorporation of the city could see it annexed by a neighbor.

The 34th averages some of California's youngest, poorest and least-educated residents and generally has low voter turnout. Even slightly more suburban and conservative Bellflower and Downey in the south supported Democrats. In 2010, Democrat Jerry Brown won 72 percent of the district's vote overall in the gubernatorial election.

Major Industry
Government, manufacturing, service, retail

Cities
Los Angeles (pt.), 202,335; Downey, 111,772; Bellflower, 76,616

Notable
The first Taco Bell opened in 1962 in Downey.

Rep. Maxine Waters (D)

Capitol Office
225-2201
www.house.gov/waters
2344 Rayburn Bldg. 20515-0535; fax 225-7854

Committees
Financial Services
Judiciary

Residence
Los Angeles

Born
Aug. 15, 1938; St. Louis, Mo.

Religion
Christian

Family
Husband, Sidney Williams; two children

Education
California State U., Los Angeles, B.A. 1970

Career
Head Start program coordinator; city council aide; public relations firm owner; telephone company service representative; clothing factory worker

Political Highlights
Calif. Assembly, 1976-90

ELECTION RESULTS

2010 GENERAL

Maxine Waters (D)	98,131	79.3%
K. Bruce Brown (R)	25,561	20.7%

2010 PRIMARY

Maxine Waters (D)	unopposed

2008 GENERAL

Maxine Waters (D)	150,778	82.6%
Ted Hayes (R)	24,169	13.2%
Herb Peters (LIBERT)	7,632	4.2%

Previous Winning Percentages
2006 (84%) 2004 (81%); 2002 (78%); 2000 (87%); 1998 (89%); 1996 (86%); 1994 (78%); 1992 (83%); 1990 (79%)

Elected 1990; 11th term

Waters stands out for her open disdain of the sometimes-delicate dance of congressional etiquette. Even within her own party, Waters is not afraid to criticize, arm-twist and attack to get what she wants — she says she has no time for nuances when her poor and mostly minority constituents are counting on her.

That abrasive style has won her some major legislative victories over the years, on issues from helping the poor to fighting for human rights in China. But it has left her with fewer allies as she faces serious ethics charges.

Waters' success in the House can be largely attributed to her position in one of Congress' most unified factions: the Congressional Black Caucus. She led the charge in 2009 to stall the financial regulatory overhaul — a top priority for the White House — to force the inclusion of $4 billion to help prevent home mortgage foreclosures. The negotiations weren't pretty, and they started weeks prior, when Waters led the 10 Black Caucus members on the Financial Services Committee in a boycott of a panel vote on the relevant portion of the regulation package.

Waters had no regrets about holding up a measure with which she was fundamentally in agreement. "In the Senate, one person can really negotiate and influence something. . . . Over here, you have to work together in groups that are aligned because of their common interest," she said.

Even when fighting battles close to home, Waters remained defiant. When the Ethics Committee, then known as the Committee on Standards of Official Conduct, announced in summer 2010 that Waters would face three charges that she violated House rules, she demanded that the detailed charges be released to the public and that her ethics trial be scheduled immediately.

The allegations against Waters, who chaired the Financial Services Subcommittee on Housing and Community Opportunity in the last Congress, focused on whether she broke House rules in seeking federal help for OneUnited Bank, a Los Angeles institution where her husband was a board member from 2004 to 2008 and owned a minimum of $500,000 in stock in 2007. Waters quickly developed a mantra declaring her innocence: "No improper action. No benefit. No failure to disclose. No one influenced. No case!"

She didn't get her wish for a speedy trial, and the investigation dragged on into the 112th Congress (2011-12), slowed by infighting among committee staff, according to a December 2010 story in The Washington Post.

The ethics allegations came on the heels of a string of successes for Waters. Her bill to encourage the cancellation of Haiti's foreign debt to aid in the nation's recovery from a devastating January 2010 earthquake became law three months after the quake. Later in the year, she oversaw passage of a bill to shore up the financial stability of the Federal Housing Administration.

In 2008, Waters was in a pivotal position as lawmakers tried to address the collapse of the residential housing sector and financial markets. Waters and Financial Services Chairman Barney Frank, a Massachusetts Democrat, ushered through bills to renew a variety of low-income housing programs. And they pushed through a massive bill that included a Federal Housing Administration overhaul, housing tax breaks, and authorization for the government to purchase stock in mortgage giants Fannie Mae and Freddie Mac.

The most important pieces for Waters were the creation of a federal housing trust fund and the inclusion of $3.9 billion in grants to states and localities to buy and rehabilitate foreclosed homes. President George W. Bush initially threatened to veto any measure that included either provision, but

Waters and Frank stared down the threat as financial markets and the foreclosure crisis worsened. "The president is attempting to get a lot in this bill," Waters said. "You don't give him all this and not get something else."

She felt the same way about giving Treasury Secretary Henry M. Paulson Jr. $700 billion to aid the failing financial industry in fall 2008. Although she voted to release the funding, she later said she was having second thoughts. "If there is one thing I regret," she said at a December 2008 hearing, "I regret attempting to be cooperative in providing to Treasury the flexibility to deal with our economic crisis."

Waters, who is part of the Democratic leadership team as one of nine chief deputy whips, has been frustrated with Democrats in conservative-leaning districts who have voted in favor of GOP procedural maneuvers to amend bills — frequently housing-related — on the floor. She penned a "Dear Colleague" letter eviscerating party leaders for allowing the votes, which she told Roll Call "are designed to divide our caucus and undermine our work."

From her seat on the Judiciary subcommittee with jurisdiction over antitrust matters, Waters weighed in against a proposed merger of Comcast and NBC, writing to the Federal Communications Commission in late 2010 that commitments to diversity made by the companies were "a series of vague goals and nominal gestures lacking specificity and binding authority on the applicants."

Waters has been a constant critic of the Iraq War and in June 2005 founded the Out of Iraq Caucus with a group of fellow liberals to press for withdrawal of U.S. troops.

Born in St. Louis as one of 13 children in a family on welfare, Waters bused tables in a segregated restaurant as a teenager and later landed a job as a clothing factory worker. She married just after high school and moved in 1961 with her first husband and two children to Los Angeles, where she worked at a telephone company.

Her public career began in 1965 when she took a job as a program coordinator in the Head Start early-childhood development program while attending college. She got involved in community organizing, which led her to politics. After working as a volunteer and a consultant to several candidates, she won an upset victory in 1976 for a seat in the California Assembly.

In 1990, Waters ran for Democratic Rep. Augustus F. Hawkins' seat; he was retiring after 14 terms. She had been preparing for the move for years. During redistricting debates in the Assembly in 1982, Waters maneuvered to remove from Hawkins' district a blue-collar, mainly white suburb she saw as unfriendly territory. She won the 1990 race with 79 percent of the vote, and has won every election since with at least 75 percent of the vote.

Key Votes

2010

Overhaul the nation's health insurance system	YES
Allow for repeal of "don't ask, don't tell"	YES
Overhaul financial services industry regulation	YES
Limit use of new Afghanistan War funds to troop withdrawal activities	YES
Change oversight of offshore drilling and lift oil spill liability cap	YES
Provide a path to legal status for some children of illegal immigrants	YES
Extend Bush-era income tax cuts for two years	NO

2009

Expand the Children's Health Insurance Program	YES
Provide $787 billion in tax cuts and spending increases to stimulate the economy	YES
Allow bankruptcy judges to modify certain primary-residence mortgages	YES
Create a cap-and-trade system to limit greenhouse gas emissions	YES
Provide $2 billion for the "cash for clunkers" program	YES
Establish the government as the sole provider of student loans	YES
Restrict federally funded insurance coverage for abortions in health care overhaul	NO

CQ Vote Studies

	PARTY UNITY		PRESIDENTIAL SUPPORT	
	SUPPORT	OPPOSE	SUPPORT	OPPOSE
2010	97%	3%	78%	22%
2009	98%	2%	93%	7%
2008	98%	2%	18%	82%
2007	97%	3%	10%	90%
2006	96%	4%	13%	87%

Interest Groups

	AFL-CIO	ADA	CCUS	ACU
2010	93%	90%	25%	4%
2009	100%	90%	36%	0%
2008	100%	95%	47%	0%
2007	95%	85%	42%	0%
2006	100%	90%	31%	4%

California 35

South and Southeast Los Angeles; Inglewood

The overwhelmingly Democratic 35th District is centered in South and Southeast Los Angeles and is bordered by downtown Los Angeles to the north, Los Angeles International Airport to the west, Torrance to the south and the industrial Alameda Corridor to the east.

Although the 35th is mostly poor, Inglewood and the South Bay cities of Hawthorne, Gardena and Lawndale have middle-class areas. Officials in Inglewood hope to lure commercial and residential developers to the Hollywood Park area, which also hosts a casino. West of Inglewood, Los Angeles International Airport is one of the region's largest employers. A precipitous decline in the district's manufacturing base has allowed poverty, crime and street gangs to dominate the area. A successful federal empowerment zone and local revitalization zone had helped increase the number of jobs in areas affected by riots that followed the 1992 acquittal of white police officers accused of beating black motorist Rodney King. But, in response to budget shortfalls, the state will likely halt funding to programs providing tax credits and incentives to employers. The region still struggles with infrastructure problems such as street maintenance and development of recreational space. Police-community relations, public safety and economic development continue to be central public policy concerns.

Once predominately African-American, and still hosting the state's highest percentage of black residents, the district now has a Hispanic-majority population. Gardena, which is 26 percent Asian, also has a large and politically influential Japanese community. The 35th leads the state in Democratic Party registration — 66 percent of voters have aligned themselves with the party — and Jerry Brown won 79 percent of the district's vote for governor in 2010.

Major Industry
Aerospace, service, manufacturing

Cities
Los Angeles (pt.), 302,188; Inglewood, 109,673; Hawthorne, 84,293

Notable
Central Avenue, on the district's eastern edge, was the West Coast hub of African-American entertainment during the jazz age; Hawthorne is the birthplace of The Beach Boys.

Vacant Seat

Rep. Jane Harman (D)
Resigned February 2011

Los Angeles City Councilwoman Janice Hahn is the overwhelming favorite in the race to succeed fellow Democrat Jane Harman, who retired from Congress at the end of February 2011 to become president of the Woodrow Wilson Center, a foreign policy think tank.

Hahn finished first in an all-candidate primary in May 2011 and faces Republican businessman Craig Huey in the July special election.

Huey finished ahead of California Secretary of State Debra Bowen, a Democrat who was re-elected in November and represented the area for six years in the state Assembly and eight in the state Senate before winning statewide office in 2006.

Hahn comes from a Democratic political dynasty in Los Angeles: Her father is former Los Angeles County Supervisor Kenneth Hahn; her uncle Gordon Hahn was a city councilman; and her brother, James K. Hahn, was mayor.

Hahn, who lost the Democratic primary for lieutenant governor in 2010, also lost a 1998 House race in a less Democratic 36th District.

The 36th was redrawn after the 2000 census to give it a stronger Democratic tilt, and the coastal district that stretches from Venice Beach south along the Los Angeles County coastline has grown increasingly Democratic in the ensuing decade. Before the district was redrawn, Democratic Vice President Al Gore topped Bush in the district in the 2000 election by only 51 percent to 44 percent. Democrat John Kerry bested President George W. Bush 59 percent to 40 percent in 2004. District voters gave Democrat Barack Obama 64 percent of the vote to Republican John McCain's 34 percent in the 2008 presidential election.

Hahn received no official endorsement from Harman but was her guest at President Obama's State of the Union address about two weeks before Harman announced her resignation.

When that announcement came, Hahn was ready to go. She quickly won endorsements from a series of high-profile Democratic leaders — Sen. Dianne Feinstein, Reps. Loretta Sanchez and Laura Richardson, and Los Angeles Mayor Antonio Villaraigosa — as well as several other prominent state and local officials.

Many analysts expected Bowen to make the general election an all-Democratic affair, but she finished third in the 16-candidate field, about 700 votes behind Huey.

Hahn led with 24.6 percent of the vote, followed by Huey with 22.2 percent and Bowen with 21.1 percent. All told, Democratic candidates won about 56 percent of the votes in the first round.

Hahn is a conventional liberal. She supports the 2010 health care overhaul, favors government subsidies for renewable-energy projects and calls herself "a strong supporter of organized labor and the rights of workers to organize."

One parochial concern she would be likely to carry from the city council to Congress is her strong support for modernizing Los Angeles International Airport.

Likewise, Huey espouses core Republican principles: balancing the budget, making the Bush-era tax cuts permanent, reducing federal regulation and boosting national defense.

California 36
Southwest Los Angeles County – Torrance, Redondo Beach, part of Los Angeles

The 36th is home to some of Los Angeles' most famous beaches and biggest aerospace firms. The district begins in the Venice area of the city, then runs along the Pacific coast south through El Segundo to Manhattan, Hermosa and Redondo beaches before hitting Torrance. It then skirts inland, picking up parts of the Wilmington and San Pedro neighborhoods.

Torrance, the district's largest whole city, is dotted with oil wells and derricks. The ExxonMobil refinery in the north end of the city, along with Chevron in El Segundo, help fuel Southern California. Torrance is also home to the sales headquarters of several major automakers, and its Del Amo Fashion Center is one of the largest malls in the country.

Economic slowdowns affected retail sectors, the auto industry, construction and manufacturing, and recent layoffs at Northrop Grumman have added uncertainty. The aerospace industry — based out of El Segundo, Redondo Beach and Torrance — long provided stability for the district's highly educated residents, and some firms have converted jobs to non-defense projects in order to diversify the economy. The posh, white-collar areas of the district are not immune to rising unemployment and home foreclosure rates.

Torrance is split politically: It is wealthier toward the coast, but inland sections include middle- and working-class areas that have conservative and labor-heavy pockets. Venice's eclectic beaches are considered the state's most liberal havens outside of Berkeley, while Manhattan Beach and Marina del Rey are ritzier. Overall, the 36th is trending more Democratic and gave Barack Obama 64 percent of its 2008 presidential vote.

Major Industry
Aerospace, technology, manufacturing

Military Bases
Los Angeles Air Force Base, 1,497 military, 869 civilian (2010)

Cities
Los Angeles (pt.), 300,582; Torrance, 145,438; Redondo Beach, 66,748; Manhattan Beach, 35,135

Notable
The Hyperion sewage treatment plant in Playa del Rey, the former focus of a lengthy lawsuit, is now one of the cleanest plants in the region.

Rep. Laura Richardson (D)

Capitol Office
225-7924
richardson.house.gov
1330 Longworth Bldg. 20515-0537; fax 225-7926

Committees
Homeland Security
Transportation & Infrastructure

Residence
Long Beach

Born
April 14, 1962; Los Angeles, Calif.

Religion
Christian non-denominational

Family
Divorced

Education
U. of California, Santa Barbara, attended 1980-81;
U. of California, Los Angeles, B.A. 1984 (political science); U. of Southern California, M.B.A. 1996

Career
Lieutenant gubernatorial aide; congressional district aide; document management company marketing director; customized clothing company owner; teacher

Political Highlights
Sought Democratic nomination for Calif. Assembly, 1996; Long Beach City Council, 2000-2006; Calif. Assembly, 2006-07

ELECTION RESULTS

2010 GENERAL

Laura Richardson (D)	85,799	68.4%
Star Parker (R)	29,159	23.2%
Nicholas Dibs (I)	10,560	8.4%

2010 PRIMARY

Laura Richardson (D)	22,574	67.3%
Peter Mathews (D)	6,144	18.3%
Lee Davis (D)	2,848	8.5%
Terrance Ponchak (D)	1,955	5.8%

2008 GENERAL

Laura Richardson (D)	131,342	75.0%
Nicholas Dibs (I)	42,774	24.4%

Previous Winning Percentages
2007 Special Election Runoff (67%)

Elected 2007; 2nd full term

A rocky start to her congressional career notwithstanding, Richardson has found solid footing as a senior member of a subcommittee key to her district's seaport-related industries and major highways carrying cargo inland.

In late 2010, she was elected to the House Democratic Steering and Policy Committee, giving her a step onto the leadership ladder.

Early on, revelations about her financial problems overshadowed her legislative work. Her seats on the Transportation and Infrastructure and Homeland Security committees could hardly be more advantageous assignments for her district, home to California freeway congestion and critical infrastructure around the Port of Long Beach. A member of the centrist New Democrat Coalition, she was named to lead the group's task force on infrastructure in the 112th Congress (2011-12).

Although she is a New Democrat, Richardson's voting record is in the liberal mold of her former employer, predecessor and mentor, Democrat Juanita Millender-McDonald, who died of cancer in April 2007. One of Richardson's first legislative successes was her bill passed by the House in 2008 — and subsequently signed into law — naming a portion of California State Route 91 in Millender-McDonald's honor.

She introduced a bill in 2008 to have cargo interests pay a national container fee, which would be used to improve freight transportation, protect shipped goods more carefully and lessen the environmental harm caused by freight transportation. It did not make it out of committee.

Richardson also is involved in cargo issues as a member of the Homeland Security Committee. As a witness at a Budget Committee hearing in March 2010, she stressed the importance of funding to protect port infrastructure, citing the Gerald Desmond Bridge in Long Beach, which she said carries 10 percent of the cargo that enters the United States.

She is the ranking Democrat on the Emergency Communications, Preparedness and Response Subcommittee, which she chaired in the 111th Congress (2009-10). She won full-committee approval in June 2010 of her legislation that would allow recipients of Federal Emergency Management Agency grants more leeway in how to spend the money, although the bill moved no further.

But she had a difficult first term after winning a special election to succeed Millender-McDonald in August 2007.

Richardson's difficulties began with news stories in May 2008 about her losing her Sacramento home to foreclosure. The property was sold at auction, but the action was reversed after Richardson said she hadn't received proper notice. Subsequent articles said she defaulted on loans on two other California homes and owed $9,000 in property taxes. And the Long Beach Press-Telegram reported that she failed to pay a mechanic for hundreds of dollars in car repairs and then abandoned the car at another shop — while leasing the most expensive car among House members, at taxpayer expense.

Richardson found herself fending off criticism from watchdog groups — Citizens for Responsibility and Ethics in Washington listed her on its "Most Corrupt" list two years running — as well as Republicans. But House Democratic leaders rallied to her side, and an ethics committee investigation eventually cleared her of wrongdoing in July 2010. That month, Roll Call reported she was renting out the home in Sacramento.

Richardson said her path toward politics was set at a young age. A child of an African-American father and Caucasian mother, she recalls when she was a child asking her divorced mother why strangers threw eggs at their car and cursed at them while they shopped at stores. "My mother tried to explain all those things to me, but eventually she just said to me, 'You should be a person who makes better laws,'" she said.

Richardson credits her mother, who worked as a teamster for a local trucking company and attended college while raising her two daughters, for instilling in her a strong work ethic.

She attended the University of California at Santa Barbara — where she earned a spot on the basketball team — thanks to California's Educational Opportunity Program, which is designed to improve access for and retention of historically low-income and educationally disadvantaged students. She eventually transferred to UCLA, earning a political science degree.

Over the next 15 years, she dabbled in a range of professions — as a marketing manager for Xerox, owner of a T-shirt design company and a teacher. She then worked as a field deputy for Millender-McDonald. While working for Democratic Lt. Gov. Cruz Bustamante, she entered her first successful political race in 2000 — for a seat on the Long Beach City Council — and defeated Dee Andrews, a well-known local sports hero, by six votes.

Six years later Richardson was elected to the state Assembly, and within a year decided to run for Congress to succeed Millender-McDonald. She was one of three favorites, along with her predecessor's daughter, Valerie McDonald, in a contest marked by racial divisiveness. Minorities make up almost 85 percent of the district's population, with Hispanics totaling 43 percent of residents. Black activists who wanted to maintain African-American representation in the district rallied around Richardson. Hispanics found a candidate to champion in Democratic state Sen. Jenny Oropeza, who was endorsed by the state party. Running in an all-parties election in June 2007, Richardson prevailed with 37 percent of the vote, not enough to avoid a runoff but tantamount to victory in the strongly Democratic district. She had little trouble in the runoff, easily winning with just over two-thirds of the vote.

The publicity about Richardson's foreclosure came on the eve of the 2008 Democratic primary, but Richardson trounced college professor Peter Mathews and community newspaper publisher Lee Davis with 74 percent of the vote. As more news emerged about her finances, Mathews and Davis both decided to run as write-in candidates in the general election. She also faced an Independent Party candidate, teacher Nicholas Dibs. But Richardson again cruised to victory with 75 percent of the vote. In 2010, she defeated conservative Republican Star Parker, a syndicated columnist and author known for her frequent television and radio appearances, with 68 percent.

Key Votes

2010

Overhaul the nation's health insurance system	YES
Allow for repeal of "don't ask, don't tell"	YES
Overhaul financial services industry regulation	YES
Limit use of new Afghanistan War funds to troop withdrawal activities	YES
Change oversight of offshore drilling and lift oil spill liability cap	YES
Provide a path to legal status for some children of illegal immigrants	YES
Extend Bush-era income tax cuts for two years	YES

2009

Expand the Children's Health Insurance Program	YES
Provide $787 billion in tax cuts and spending increases to stimulate the economy	YES
Allow bankruptcy judges to modify certain primary-residence mortgages	YES
Create a cap-and-trade system to limit greenhouse gas emissions	YES
Provide $2 billion for the "cash for clunkers" program	YES
Establish the government as the sole provider of student loans	YES
Restrict federally funded insurance coverage for abortions in health care overhaul	NO

CQ Vote Studies

	PARTY UNITY		PRESIDENTIAL SUPPORT	
	Support	Oppose	Support	Oppose
2010	96%	4%	83%	17%
2009	98%	2%	94%	6%
2008	99%	1%	16%	84%
2007	99%	1%	7%	93%

Interest Groups

	AFL-CIO	ADA	CCUS	ACU
2010	93%	95%	25%	0%
2009	100%	100%	31%	0%
2008	100%	100%	59%	0%
2007	100%		67%	0%

California 37
Southern Los Angeles County — most of Long Beach, Compton, Carson

The 37th combines some of the state's poorest and most Democratic areas with a large chunk of middle-class Long Beach. Minorities make up more than 85 percent of the population, with Hispanics as the dominant group, totaling 49 percent of residents. The district is more than one-fifth black and nearly 12 percent Asian.

The district contains a sliver of Los Angeles, as well as the lower- and middle-class suburbs of Compton and Carson to the south. These communities boost Democratic presidential candidates to high margins of victory in the 37th: in 2008, Compton gave Barack Obama 95 percent — his highest margin in Los Angeles County — and Carson gave him 76 percent. Compton has a multiracial and ethnic population, and its poverty, crime rate and ongoing gang activity often lead it to be labeled as an "inner-city" community. But, commercial and residential development in areas previously considered undevelopable, coupled with police action, has propped up the economy and brought down notoriously high murder rates. Facto-

ries, refineries and other industrial sites occupy a large portion of Carson. The non-coastal portion of Long Beach (the port is in the 46th) contains a more suburban, politically mixed community, and dozens of languages are spoken in local schools. The area has relied on high-tech and aerospace industries, although Boeing has cut jobs at its local facilities, including its C-17 production plant in Long Beach. The multibillion-dollar Alameda Corridor project — which runs through the district linking the ports of Long Beach and Los Angeles to the south with distribution areas in the city of Los Angeles to the north — created construction jobs. But prospects for robust growth in transportation and warehousing sectors, as well as continued economic development in the district, remain uncertain.

Major Industry
Service, manufacturing, oil

Cities
Long Beach (pt.), 365,708; Compton, 96,455; Carson, 91,714; Los Angeles city (pt.), 37,862

Notable
The Home Depot Center's multiuse sports complex in Carson is home to soccer's Chivas USA and LA Galaxy.

Rep. Grace F. Napolitano (D)

Capitol Office
225-5256
www.napolitano.house.gov
1610 Longworth Bldg. 20515-0538; fax 225-0027

Committees
Natural Resources
Transportation & Infrastructure

Residence
Norwalk

Born
Dec. 4, 1936; Brownsville, Texas

Religion
Roman Catholic

Family
Husband, Frank Napolitano; five children

Education
Brownsville H.S., graduated 1954

Career
Regional transportation claims agent

Political Highlights
Norwalk City Council, 1986-92 (mayor, 1989-90);
Calif. Assembly, 1992-98

ELECTION RESULTS

2010 GENERAL

Grace F. Napolitano (D)	85,459	73.4%
Robert Vaughn (R)	30,883	26.5%

2010 PRIMARY

Grace F. Napolitano (D)	unopposed

2008 GENERAL

Grace F. Napolitano (D)	130,211	81.7%
Christopher Agrella (LIBERT)	29,113	18.3%

Previous Winning Percentages
2006 (75%); 2004 (100%); 2002 (71%); 2000 (71%);
1998 (68%)

Elected 1998; 7th term

Napolitano's grandmotherly image — silvery hair and a fondness for making tacos and guacamole for her staff — belies the assertive lawmaker who is fiercely protective of her Hispanic-majority district. She is a powerful advocate for Southern California on questions of water resources and power generation, and dedicates considerable energy to mental health issues.

Napolitano is the ranking Democrat on the Natural Resources Subcommittee on Water and Power; she chaired the panel in the 111th Congress (2009-10).

In June 2010, the House passed her bill to set rules for how power generated by Hoover Dam would be distributed for the next five decades. The measure, never considered by the full Senate, would make American Indian organizations eligible to receive power allocations for the first time. She worked with California Republican David Dreier to pass legislation in 2007 authorizing $11.2 million for groundwater cleanup in the San Gabriel Basin — part of Southern California's strategy to generate its own supply of clean water and ease dependence on the Colorado River or the San Francisco Bay and Delta.

From her seat on the Transportation and Infrastructure Committee, Napolitano helped push through a railroad safety bill she wrote in response to five derailments that occurred in or near the 38th district. The language was signed into law in October 2008. In the fiscal 2011 transportation funding bill, she won inclusion of $1 million to study the expansion to 10 lanes of Interstate 5, which runs through her district.

But she has been less committal about a proposed $42 billion high-speed rail line running from San Diego to San Francisco that received about $1.8 billion from the 2009 economic stimulus legislation. "High-speed rail will have to earn the congressional funding it gets," Napolitano told the San Gabriel Valley Tribune in August 2010. "They have to work with the communities, respect their wishes, and let us know what their plans are."

Napolitano has a passion for mental health issues that stems from her work on the Norwalk City Council in the 1980s, when hospitals in her area began closing and sending mentally ill patients onto the streets. She co-chairs the Congressional Mental Health Caucus and has worked to help Iraq War veterans suffering from post-traumatic stress disorder. From her committee seats she pushed BP officials to take the post-trauma mental health of Gulf Coast residents into consideration when settling claims related to the spring 2010 oil spill in the Gulf of Mexico.

After the January 2011 shooting in Tucson of Arizona Democratic Rep. Gabrielle Giffords, Napolitano co-hosted a briefing for congressional staff on the resources available to them if they believed a constituent to be mentally ill. "I want to make sure some of our employees — those that are interested — are able to at least benefit from some kind of information that almost everybody else in law enforcement knows about," she told The Hill.

But she expressed disappointment at the lack of response to calls for more mental health funding. "You would think it would be an ideal time for everyone to jump on board. . . . Since it involved a member of Congress, now it's personal," Napolitano told the San Gabriel Valley Tribune.

Although an almost automatic Democratic vote — on votes that split a majority of Democrats and Republicans in 2010 she sided with her party 98 percent of the time — Napolitano has made her displeasure known on occasion.

She blasted a $700 billion financial sector rescue law in fall 2008, ignoring pleas from her party leadership. "We already bailed out several other entities," she said. "Who's next? At the taxpayers' expense? I don't think so."

She was an avid supporter of New York Sen. Hillary Rodham Clinton's 2008 presidential bid, and as late as June of that year was questioning Barack Obama's commitment to seeking common cause with Hispanic voters. "We were told that he was going to make some approach to us to join the fold," Napolitano said at the time. "I haven't heard from Mr. Obama."

Napolitano stood by Clinton during the Democratic convention in Denver, casting her ballot for the former first lady. But in a convention speech she proclaimed in Spanish, "Votemos por Obama para presidente." She subsequently campaigned for Obama, helping him court Latino voters who overwhelmingly supported Clinton during the primary elections.

The daughter of a Mexican immigrant who raised her two children on a shoestring budget, Napolitano has cultivated a strong connection to her mother's homeland. A former chairwoman of the Congressional Hispanic Caucus, Napolitano expressed disappointment to party leaders in 2006 that Democrats did not include immigration in their "Six for '06" campaign platform.

As a result, then-Speaker Nancy Pelosi asked her fellow Californian to help write a comprehensive immigration overhaul package in 2007. Later that year, Napolitano and others met with President George W. Bush to promote their bill, which would have created a guest-worker program and provided a pathway for illegal immigrants to gain legal status.

Napolitano married at 18 and had five children by 23. She caught the political bug as a volunteer in Norwalk's efforts to cultivate a sister-city relationship with Hermosillo, Mexico. She says she joined the effort to show her children and "other youngsters on this side how lucky they were."

She launched her first political campaign, for city council, with $35,000 she borrowed against her home, and won by just 28 votes. She served six years, two of them as mayor, before moving up to the California Legislature for six years.

In 1998, she ran for the House seat of retiring Democrat Esteban E. Torres, challenging his hand-picked successor — his son-in-law — for the Democratic nomination. She won the primary by just 618 votes, but sailed to victory in the general election and has easily won re-election since in the overwhelmingly Democratic district.

Napolitano drew some scrutiny in 2009 when Bloomberg News revealed that she had earned more than $200,000 in interest over the years on a $150,000 loan she had made to her initial 1998 campaign from money withdrawn from a retirement fund — and that her campaign still hadn't paid off the loan. The debt, according to Bloomberg, was the biggest asset listed on Napolitano's personal financial disclosure forms.

Key Votes

2010

Overhaul the nation's health insurance system	YES
Allow for repeal of "don't ask, don't tell"	YES
Overhaul financial services industry regulation	YES
Limit use of new Afghanistan War funds to troop withdrawal activities	YES
Change oversight of offshore drilling and lift oil spill liability cap	YES
Provide a path to legal status for some children of illegal immigrants	YES
Extend Bush-era income tax cuts for two years	NO

2009

Expand the Children's Health Insurance Program	YES
Provide $787 billion in tax cuts and spending increases to stimulate the economy	YES
Allow bankruptcy judges to modify certain primary-residence mortgages	YES
Create a cap-and-trade system to limit greenhouse gas emissions	YES
Provide $2 billion for the "cash for clunkers" program	YES
Establish the government as the sole provider of student loans	YES
Restrict federally funded insurance coverage for abortions in health care overhaul	NO

CQ Vote Studies

	PARTY UNITY		PRESIDENTIAL SUPPORT	
	Support	Oppose	Support	Oppose
2010	98%	2%	83%	17%
2009	99%	1%	93%	7%
2008	99%	1%	10%	90%
2007	99%	1%	3%	97%
2006	98%	2%	21%	79%

Interest Groups

	AFL-CIO	ADA	CCUS	ACU
2010	100%	100%	13%	0%
2009	100%	100%	33%	0%
2008	100%	95%	44%	8%
2007	96%	100%	45%	0%
2006	100%	100%	33%	8%

California 38

East Los Angeles County — Pomona, Norwalk

The Democratic 38th is a growing middle- and working-class Hispanic-majority district. A sideways "L" shape, the district takes in the city of Norwalk in southeastern Los Angeles County and stretches north along Interstate 5 to include nearly half of East Los Angeles. It then runs east through Montebello, Pico Rivera and La Puente, before extending a thin arm parallel to the California 60 freeway into the Inland Valley to take in Pomona, the district's largest city, at the county's eastern edge.

The 38th relies on its many small businesses in the district and includes the East Los Angeles business district. Economic downturns have hurt local retail operations, many of which are owned or operated by Hispanics. Unemployment-rate spikes in the city of Industry, an almost entirely industrial area in the center of the district, have hit the few thousand businesses that the city claims once provided more than 80,000 jobs. Like the commuter towns near Industry, Norwalk is mainly a bedroom community, but it received a publicity boost in 2006 when the multi-agency Joint Regional Intelligence Center opened.

Although it has a large blue-collar workforce, the district contains some affluent and conservative areas such as Hacienda Heights, Rowland Heights (shared with the 42nd) and a narrow sliver of Whittier. Montebello is a middle-class Hispanic area with an Armenian community. Southeast Pomona is densely populated and has experienced some crime problems in recent years. Efforts to revitalize the city's dilapidated downtown are ongoing.

The 38th's working-class residents ensure that the district votes reliably Democratic. Barack Obama received 71 percent of the vote here in the 2008 presidential election. California State Polytechnic University, Pomona, and Cerritos College (shared with the 39th) add students to the Democratic mix.

Major Industry
Manufacturing, oil

Cities
Pomona, 149,058; Norwalk, 105,549; Pico Rivera, 62,942; Montebello, 62,500; Hacienda Heights (unincorporated) (pt.), 53,602

Notable
The Pomona Swap Meet and Car Show is billed as the largest collection of antique cars, parts and accessories on the West Coast.

Rep. Linda T. Sánchez (D)

Capitol Office
225-6676
www.lindasanchez.house.gov
2423 Rayburn Bldg. 20515-0539; fax 226-1012

Committees
Ethics - Ranking Member
Judiciary
Veterans' Affairs

Residence
Lakewood

Born
Jan. 28, 1969; Orange, Calif.

Religion
Roman Catholic

Family
Husband, Jim Sullivan; one child, three stepchildren

Education
U. of California, Berkeley, B.A. 1991 (Spanish literature); U. of California, Los Angeles, J.D. 1995

Career
Union official; campaign aide; lawyer

Political Highlights
No previous office

ELECTION RESULTS

2010 GENERAL

Linda T. Sánchez (D)	81,590	63.3%
Larry S. Andre (R)	42,037	32.6%
John Smith (AMI)	5,334	4.1%

2010 PRIMARY

Linda T. Sánchez (D)	unopposed

2008 GENERAL

Linda T. Sánchez (D)	125,289	69.7%
Diane A. Lenning (R)	54,533	30.3%

Previous Winning Percentages
2006 (66%); 2004 (61%); 2002 (55%)

Elected 2002; 5th term

The younger of the two Sánchez sisters in Congress has taken on the mostly thankless task of serving as the top Democrat on the Ethics Committee. She was one of five Democrats who lost a spot on the powerful Ways and Means Committee following the party's losses in the 2010 elections. But she retained her seat on Judiciary, where she can continue her legislative work on immigration issues. She also joined the Veterans' Affairs panel.

Among her first tasks on Ethics will be deciding how to move forward on an investigation of fellow Southern California Democrat Maxine Waters, who was accused of intervening on behalf of a bank where her husband served on the board. Her case dragged on through the 111th Congress (2009-10) and spilled into the 112th (2011-12).

As Ethics chairwoman, Sánchez will be helping to lead a committee that once investigated her.

In 2009, the panel reviewed whether Sánchez and her sister, California Democratic Rep. Loretta Sanchez, violated House rules when Linda Sánchez put three of her sister's aides on her own payroll in 2006 because another aide embezzled money from Loretta Sanchez's office. No action was taken against either sister in the case.

Linda Sánchez has devoted much effort to immigration issues and spoke out against Arizona's 2010 law allowing police officers to question anyone stopped for another offense about their immigration status. Sánchez called the law, modeled on a 1995 federal law that authorizes state and local police agencies to perform immigration enforcement functions, the "most oppressive piece of legislation since the Jim Crow laws."

"It's a sad day for a country founded on freedom when one misguided state condones racial profiling into law to win a few more votes from the hate-monger wing of the Republican party," she said. She also said "there is a concerted effort behind promoting these kinds of laws on a state-by-state basis by people who have ties to white-supremacist groups."

Sánchez was the first Hispanic female to serve on both Judiciary and Ways and Means, where she focused on trade issues. She was an enthusiastic supporter of Barack Obama in the 2008 Democratic presidential primaries, and Obama named Sánchez to the President's Export Council in May 2010, a group that advises the White House on trade policy. She co-founded the Labor and Working Families Caucus and the House Trade Working Group, and she opposed free-trade agreements during President George W. Bush's administration, arguing they failed to protect workers' rights.

Before arriving in the House, Sánchez practiced civil rights and labor law; her sister was a businesswoman with an MBA. The sisters spell their last name differently: Linda Sánchez uses an accent, and Loretta Sanchez does not.

Although their voting records are similar, their personal styles are markedly different. Linda Sánchez is a night owl, while Loretta Sanchez is an early riser. Linda Sánchez is messy; Loretta Sanchez neat.

And Linda Sánchez is funnier. "I grew up in a family of seven, and my brothers teased me unmercifully, so I learned to be quick with a comeback," she said. A hit at charity fundraisers, she has a stand-up comedy routine that in 2006 won her the title of "Funniest Celebrity in Washington, D.C."

For all their differences, the sisters are fiercely loyal. When Loretta Sanchez quit the Congressional Hispanic Caucus in 2007, charging that its chairman, Democrat Joe Baca of California, had been demeaning to women, Linda Sánchez swiftly did the same. Linda Sánchez returned to the caucus in early

2009 when Nydia M. Velázquez of New York became chairwoman. The sisters also co-authored two books, including "Dream in Color: How the Sánchez Sisters Are Making History in Congress," a 2008 account of their childhoods that explains how their values and traditions helped them succeed.

Sánchez also made some personal news in November 2008 by announcing she was pregnant. She was not married to the father, Jim Sullivan, a government and public relations consultant, when she made the announcement. The two eventually wed, and Sánchez gave birth to Joaquin Sánchez Sullivan.

Sánchez's House colleagues got a sense of her views on gender equality when she joined the overwhelmingly male roster of players in the annual baseball game between Democrats and Republicans (sponsored by CQ Roll Call). The back of her shirt bore the Roman numerals IX, for Title IX, shorthand for the landmark 1972 law that mandated equal treatment for women in education programs and led to the dramatic growth of women's sports.

She had no experience in local or state government before her election in 2002. Her father, Ignacio, was a mechanic at a tire shop, where he met her mother, Maria Macias, who was working in its accounting office. Her mother began organizing for a union and met her father as she sought workers to sign up.

Sánchez often questioned why her traditional Latino family gave males special status. "There was a very clear distinction between what boys could do and what girls could do," she said. Her mother told Sánchez to either accept the way things were or try to change them. She once took Sánchez to hear farm labor organizer Cesar Chavez speak. Sánchez, who had worked her way through college as a nanny, security guard, bilingual teacher's aide and ESL instructor, was inspired by Chavez's words to go back to school for a law degree and get involved in organizing labor. She later became executive secretary-treasurer of the AFL CIO in Orange County.

Her political activism started in high school in Anaheim. Upset by her local congressman, conservative Republican Robert K. Dornan, Sánchez knocked on doors for Democratic challenger Dave Carter, who lost. But in 1996, Sánchez was the field organizer for sister Loretta Sanchez's successful campaign against Dornan.

After the 2000 census, the California Legislature drew a new district south of downtown Los Angeles that favored a Hispanic Democrat. In 2002, incumbent Republican Steve Horn declined to run for the seat. Sánchez jumped in, winning a six-way primary contest with help from Loretta Sanchez's fundraising network and vigorous campaigning by her family. She has had no trouble maintaining her grip on the seat.

Key Votes

2010

Overhaul the nation's health insurance system	YES
Allow for repeal of "don't ask, don't tell"	YES
Overhaul financial services industry regulation	YES
Limit use of new Afghanistan War funds to troop withdrawal activities	YES
Change oversight of offshore drilling and lift oil spill liability cap	YES
Provide a path to legal status for some children of illegal immigrants	YES
Extend Bush-era income tax cuts for two years	NO

2009

Expand the Children's Health Insurance Program	YES
Provide $787 billion in tax cuts and spending increases to stimulate the economy	YES
Allow bankruptcy judges to modify certain primary-residence mortgages	YES
Create a cap-and-trade system to limit greenhouse gas emissions	YES
Provide $2 billion for the "cash for clunkers" program	YES
Establish the government as the sole provider of student loans	YES
Restrict federally funded insurance coverage for abortions in health care overhaul	NO

CQ Vote Studies

	PARTY UNITY		PRESIDENTIAL SUPPORT	
	Support	Oppose	Support	Oppose
2010	99%	1%	85%	15%
2009	99%	1%	95%	5%
2008	99%	1%	10%	90%
2007	99%	1%	3%	97%
2006	98%	2%	15%	85%

Interest Groups

	AFL-CIO	ADA	CCUS	ACU
2010	100%	100%	13%	0%
2009	100%	85%	36%	5%
2008	100%	100%	50%	8%
2007	100%	100%	55%	0%
2006	93%	100%	33%	4%

California 39

Southeast Los Angeles County — South Gate, Lakewood, most of Whittier

The U-shaped 39th District starts in South Gate and Lynwood, just south of Los Angeles, before stretching south and east to take in Lakewood and Cerritos, then northeast through La Mirada to South Whittier and Whittier. Despite external similarities — ethnic populations and working-class economic bases — most of these communities have little interaction with one another. The district is two-thirds Hispanic.

Whittier (shared mainly with the 42nd) and South Whittier are home to many second- and third-generation Hispanic families, and pockets of wealth exist there. Growing La Mirada and the Asian-American-heavy Cerritos are more conservative communities that resemble cities in neighboring, wealthier Orange County — former farm areas now dependent on an array of aerospace and technology jobs. Lakewood is more blue-collar. South Gate, Lynwood and Paramount are heavily working-class and include many new immigrants, and those cities voted overwhelmingly for Democrat Barack Obama in the 2008 presidential election.

The district has a strong organized-labor movement. Towns like Whittier and Lakewood have a number of industrial and retail centers, and more residents work in the district or nearby rather than commuting to downtown Los Angeles, Orange County or Long Beach. Whittier, an area once dominated by car dealerships, looked to reorient its local economy following several years of nationwide declines in auto sales.

Democrats still control the 39th, but it is not as strongly Democratic as is most of Los Angeles County — only 52 percent of voters here are registered Democrats and the district has one of the highest rates of registered Republicans among the 13 districts contained entirely in the county. Jerry Brown won 60 percent of the 2010 gubernatorial vote here two years after Barack Obama took 65 percent in the presidential race.

Major Industry
Manufacturing, aerospace

Cities
South Gate, 94,396; Lakewood, 80,048; Lynwood, 69,772; South Whittier (unincorporated), 57,156; Whittier (pt.), 56,555; Paramount, 54,098

Notable
Paramount is home to Zamboni, maker of the ice resurfacing machines used at skating and hockey rinks.

Rep. Ed Royce (R)

Capitol Office
225-4111
royce.house.gov
2185 Rayburn Bldg. 20515-0540; fax 226-0335

Committees
Financial Services
Foreign Affairs
  (Terrorism, Nonproliferation & Trade - Chairman)

Residence
Fullerton

Born
Oct. 12, 1951; Los Angeles, Calif.

Religion
Roman Catholic

Family
Wife, Marie Royce

Education
California State U., Fullerton, B.A. 1977 (accounting
& finance)

Career
Tax manager

Political Highlights
Calif. Senate, 1982-92

ELECTION RESULTS

2010 GENERAL

Ed Royce (R)	119,455	66.8%
Christina Avalos (D)	59,400	33.2%

2010 PRIMARY

Ed Royce (R)	unopposed

2008 GENERAL

Ed Royce (R)	144,923	62.5%
Christina Avalos (D)	86,772	37.4%

Previous Winning Percentages
2006 (67%); 2004 (68%); 2002 (68%); 2000 (63%);
1998 (63%); 1996 (63%); 1994 (66%); 1992 (57%)

Elected 1992; 10th term

Royce's nearly two decades in Congress have been marked by a consistent approach to legislating: Limited government is better than bigger government, and free trade is better than foreign aid in helping developing countries prosper.

He lost his bid to chair the Financial Services Committee in the 112th Congress (2011-12) to Alabama Republican Spencer Bachus, but Royce remains a senior member of that panel and of Foreign Affairs. He also was named a vice chairman of the National Republican Congressional Committee.

Royce has been a severe critic of President Obama's economic policies and of the Democrats' financial regulatory overhaul.

A longtime advocate of bringing government-sponsored mortgage companies Fannie Mae and Freddie Mac under tighter rein, Royce asserts that their problems — and the ensuing economic displacement — could have been averted if Congress had enacted legislation he introduced as far back as 2003 to assign a government agency to oversee their lending practices.

It has mattered little to Royce whether the president pushing government-centric solutions is a Republican or a Democrat. During George W. Bush's administration, he voted against a 2008 housing bill that included a financial lifeline potentially worth hundreds of billions of dollars to the troubled mortgage giants. That same year, he opposed a $289 billion farm bill and legislation that stopped scheduled cuts in Medicare reimbursements for doctors. He was one of 28 Republicans to vote, early in 2008, against providing so-called tax rebates to help spur the economy, and one of 54 to vote against overriding Bush's veto of a bill authorizing billions in water resources projects in 2007.

He also opposed Bush's 2008 plan to shore up ailing banks with a $700 billion package. Royce called it "state socialism" and said he would have preferred that Congress lift regulatory caps limiting the investments private equity firms can make in banks.

At the end of 2010, he backed a two-year extension of the Bush-era tax cuts, writing in the Orange County Register that the measure was less a compromise than "a clear GOP victory."

Throughout the 1990s, Royce was co-chairman of the Congressional Porkbusters Coalition, which opposed appropriations earmarks — funding set-asides to specific projects in members' districts — and in 2005 was one of just eight House members, all Republicans, to vote against the surface transportation law stuffed with funding for such projects.

Royce chairs the Foreign Affairs panel on Terrorism, Nonproliferation and Trade, and he writes a blog on national security issues, called Foreign Intrigue, for his congressional website.

At the start of the 112th Congress, he introduced legislation that would bar Vietnamese officials complicit in human rights abuses from traveling to the United States and doing business with U.S. companies. "With the Communist government in Vietnam increasing its crackdown on human rights, Congress needs to respond. Those squashing freedom must pay a price," Royce said.

He has focused on the risk posed by Islamic extremism in Pakistan, a nuclear power and major recipient of U.S. foreign aid. Royce would make that aid conditional on steps taken by the Pakistani government to crack down on terrorism. After a foiled 2010 bomb plot in New York City was linked to the Pakistani Taliban, Royce wrote on his blog: "Would-be Times Square bomber Faisal Shahzad wasn't a 'lone-wolf' or 'one-off,' as we were originally led to believe by Homeland Security Secretary Janet Napolitano.

For a few days . . . the mainstream media was putting just as much emphasis on his foreclosed house as his extensive stays in Pakistan."

Royce also is co-chairman of the Congressional India Caucus. He takes pride in Congress' approval in 2008 of a trade deal permitting the sale of civilian nuclear materials to India; he had led the successful 2006 effort to pass legislation permitting the president to complete negotiations on the treaty. Another legislative victory came in 2002, when Congress created Radio Free Afghanistan, an idea Royce had been promoting for five years to counter the influence of the governing Taliban. It took the Sept. 11 attacks to inspire Congress to act on the proposal. Royce also has been a leading voice on Africa policy, having chaired the Foreign Affairs panel on Africa from 1997 to 2005 and fought for economic liberalization and free trade.

Royce grew up in a blue-collar Democratic household but developed a conservative viewpoint early on. In high school, he became intrigued by the free-market message in Henry Hazlitt's book "Economics in One Lesson." The author challenged prevailing economic thinking that gave the government a central role. That spurred Royce to read similar books, and he found himself defending the unorthodox viewpoints to fellow students and teachers, honing his debating skills as a result. At California State University in Fullerton, he went to the aid of a young woman staffing a College Republicans recruiting table after three men overturned it and caused a disturbance. "I stepped in and was explaining the concept of free speech and nonviolence on campus," he recalls. He wound up joining the CR.

Royce spent 10 years in the California Senate, where he was the guiding force behind a 1990 ballot proposition, approved by voters, setting forth rights for crime victims. He also wrote the nation's first law making it a felony to stalk or threaten someone with injury. In Washington, he won enactment of a similar bill, signed into law in 1996, that made it a crime to cross state lines with the intent to stalk or harass. In 1999, he helped win enactment of a bill expanding the definition of stalking.

Royce jumped at the chance to run for the House in 1992 when iconoclastic Republican William E. Dannemeyer gave up his seat to run for the Senate. Royce had represented a sizable slice of the House district in the state Senate, and he drew no primary opposition. His Democratic opponent, Molly McClanahan, proved too liberal for Orange County and Royce prevailed by almost 20 percentage points. In redistricting after the 2000 census, the Los Angeles County portion of Royce's old 39th District was removed and the district was renumbered the 40th, where Royce has continued to win with ease.

Key Votes

2010

Overhaul the nation's health insurance system	NO
Allow for repeal of "don't ask, don't tell"	NO
Overhaul financial services industry regulation	NO
Limit use of new Afghanistan War funds to troop withdrawal activities	NO
Change oversight of offshore drilling and lift oil spill liability cap	NO
Provide a path to legal status for some children of illegal immigrants	NO
Extend Bush-era income tax cuts for two years	YES

2009

Expand the Children's Health Insurance Program	NO
Provide $787 billion in tax cuts and spending increases to stimulate the economy	NO
Allow bankruptcy judges to modify certain primary-residence mortgages	NO
Create a cap-and-trade system to limit greenhouse gas emissions	NO
Provide $2 billion for the "cash for clunkers" program	NO
Establish the government as the sole provider of student loans	NO
Restrict federally funded insurance coverage for abortions in health care overhaul	YES

CQ Vote Studies

	PARTY UNITY		PRESIDENTIAL SUPPORT	
	SUPPORT	OPPOSE	SUPPORT	OPPOSE
2010	99%	1%	26%	74%
2009	98%	2%	11%	89%
2008	99%	1%	82%	18%
2007	97%	3%	90%	10%
2006	94%	6%	93%	7%

Interest Groups

	AFL-CIO	ADA	CCUS	ACU
2010	7%	0%	88%	100%
2009	5%	0%	80%	100%
2008	0%	0%	83%	100%
2007	8%	0%	70%	100%
2006	7%	5%	100%	96%

California 40

North central Orange County — Orange, Fullerton

Like most of Orange County, the 40th is historically wealthy and Republican, although these inland areas are less affluent than the coast. The district forms a half circle that contains Orange County's northern and western midsize cities. It extends north from Los Alamitos on the Los Angeles County border to take in most of Fullerton before turning southeast to reach Orange and Villa Park. It wraps around Anaheim and Garden Grove, taking in small chunks of each.

Before massive growth a generation ago, Orange County was largely agricultural and blanketed with orange and lemon groves, and many cities were dairy farm communities — there are no longer any orange juice processing plants in the county. Relying heavily on aerospace, defense and technology, the 40th's economy achieved more diversity in recent decades but remains vulnerable to job losses. Despite economic slowdowns, Knott's Berry Farm amusement park and other venues in Buena Park still lure tourists.

Fullerton is home to a Raytheon facility and a Kimberly-Clark paper mill, as well as a California State University campus that is one of the city's major employers. Adams Rite Aerospace in Fullerton makes airplane cockpit security doors, which Congress mandated on commercial airliners after the Sept. 11 terrorist attacks. Orange plays a major role as the district's health care center, home to four hospitals. Cypress is the headquarters of PacifiCare Health Systems.

Orange, the solidly suburban district's largest city, and Fullerton are both upper middle class and have seen modest growth in the last decade; Stanton is a more blue-collar community. Whites make up 39 percent of the district's population, and an influx of wealthier Hispanics and Asians has shifted the 40th's demographics. Republicans tend to dominate local, state and national elections here, but John McCain earned only 51 percent of the district's 2008 presidential vote.

Major Industry
Aerospace, defense, manufacturing, health care

Cities
Orange, 136,416; Fullerton (pt.), 117,680; Anaheim (pt.), 89,273; Buena Park, 80,530; Cypress, 47,802; Placentia (pt.), 40,053; Stanton, 38,186

Notable
Fullerton is the center of the influential Orange County punk rock scene.

Rep. Jerry Lewis (R)

Capitol Office
225-5861
www.house.gov/jerrylewis
2112 Rayburn Bldg. 20515-0541; fax 225-6498

Committees
Appropriations

Residence
Redlands

Born
Oct. 21, 1934; Seattle, Wash.

Religion
Presbyterian

Family
Wife, Arlene Willis; seven children

Education
U. of California, Los Angeles, B.A. 1956 (government)

Career
Insurance executive

Political Highlights
San Bernardino School Board, 1965-68; Calif. Assembly, 1968-78; Republican nominee for Calif. Senate, 1973

ELECTION RESULTS

2010 GENERAL

Jerry Lewis (R)	127,857	63.2%
Pat Meagher (D)	74,394	36.8%

2010 PRIMARY

Jerry Lewis (R)	42,462	66.3%
Eric R. Stone (R)	21,607	33.7%

2008 GENERAL

Jerry Lewis (R)	159,486	61.6%
Tim Prince (D)	99,214	38.4%

Previous Winning Percentages
2006 (67%); 2004 (83%); 2002 (67%); 2000 (80%);
1998 (65%); 1996 (65%); 1994 (71%); 1992 (63%);
1990 (61%); 1988 (70%); 1986 (77%); 1984 (85%);
1982 (68%); 1980 (72%); 1978 (61%)

Elected 1978; 17th term

Lewis has been a good fit as a member of the powerful Appropriations Committee, a panel once known for collegiality and a "to do" list loaded with vital legislation. Affable and armed with a 200-watt smile, his rise to the top of that committee in 2005 solidified his reputation as both a reliable Republican and someone who can get things done.

The 112th Congress (2011-12) marks the first time in more than a decade that Lewis has not held a leadership position on the spending panel, after his party's term limits forced him to relinquish his position as the top Republican. He was given the honorific title of "chairman emeritus," and something more substantial — seats on five of the 12 Appropriations subcommittees.

He would have enjoyed being chairman again, but serving as ranking Republican during four years under a Democratic majority wasn't all that much fun for Lewis. During the 110th Congress (2007-08), Democrats bypassed the committee on funding for the war in Iraq and other key legislation, causing Lewis to complain that the majority party was denying Republicans a voice and destroying the comity that had defined the spending panel. And as Democrats quickly pushed through large spending packages in early 2009, he voiced concern about them heading down a path with no direction.

The situation was much different for Lewis a few years ago, when he beat out a more senior Republican, Ralph Regula of Ohio, to become chairman. House GOP leaders chose Lewis for his track record of raising money for the party and his willingness to let them exert more control over appropriations.

His short tenure was marked by a career accomplishment: He coordinated with the Senate to get every spending bill through Congress in 2005, something appropriators have rarely achieved in recent years.

Within his own party, Lewis is viewed warily by conservatives, who were emboldened by a 2010 voter backlash against spending in general and earmarks, or congressionally directed spending on special projects, in particular. When Lewis sought a term limit waiver to keep his gavel, he found himself the target of nearly two dozen conservative groups. Lewis scrambled to remind his party of his cost-cutting bona fides and tried to downplay his prolific earmarking past, although a Taxpayers for Common Sense analysis found that he ranked second in steering millions of dollars toward his district in fiscal 2010 spending bills.

Lewis came under scrutiny in 2006 when the Justice Department opened a probe into whether he improperly directed tens of millions of dollars to the clients of a lobbyist friend. The inquiry was closed four years later without any charges filed.

Broadly, though, Lewis has pushed to limit government spending. From 1995 to 1999, when he was in charge of the subcommittee that funds housing and veterans' programs, he restrained the growth in spending more effectively than other "cardinals," as the subcommittee chairmen are known.

He called for caution early in the 111th Congress (2009-10), when the House passed a $410 billion catchall spending measure for fiscal 2009. "Even as the president talks about the need to put our economic house in order, this House continues to spend and spend and spend and spend. Clearly, this Congress has lost its way," he said. And when the House considered a $787 billion economic stimulus measure in early 2009, he warned against "creating an untenable situation down the line" through a dramatic increase in spending.

In late 2010, he introduced a bill to rescind unspent stimulus funds — the Congressional Budget Office estimated the amount at about $12 billion —

and Lewis said he would reintroduce the measure at the start of the 112th Congress.

In the past, Lewis has called on the Defense Department to modernize more quickly to meet post-Cold War threats to security, even if it means scrapping existing projects. In 1999, he waged a losing battle to deny $1.9 billion for the chronically over-budget F-22 jet fighter. Ultimately, lobbying by the Air Force and the plane's contractors led Congress to approve the money. A decade later, President Obama and the Democratic-led Congress were able to end funding for the plane.

Over the years, Lewis tried to move up the leadership ladder but was edged out by conservatives who were more confrontational in dealing with the Democrats. After Republicans took control of the House in 1995, Lewis strained his relations with Democratic appropriators by dutifully enforcing the new GOP leadership's cuts in domestic programs.

In recent years, Lewis has become a more reliable vote for his party. During most of his first two decades in the House, Lewis' party unity score — the percentage of votes in which he sided with a majority of Republicans against a majority of Democrats — fell in the '70s and '80s. But since 2001, he has only twice scored below 92 percent.

Lewis dates his interest in government to a trip he made to Washington in 1955. Some of his fellow University of California, Los Angeles, students were forced to ride on a separate tourist boat on the Potomac because they were black, and Lewis decided that public service was the best way to change things.

A successful insurance broker, Lewis entered GOP politics in the 1960s and won a seat on the San Bernardino School Board. After three years there, he sought a state Assembly seat in 1968 and won the first of five terms.

With an Assembly constituency that covered more than half a congressional district, he was an obvious choice for Republicans in 1978 when GOP Rep. Shirley N. Pettis retired. Earlier in his career, Lewis had worked as a field representative for Jerry Pettis, Shirley's husband, who represented the district for eight years before his death in a plane crash in 1975. Declaring himself a candidate in the "Pettis tradition," Lewis won the five-candidate GOP primary with 55 percent of the vote, then won the general election handily.

He had his pick of two districts after the 1982 redistricting and chose the one (then numbered the 35th) that, although less Republican, included his home. He soon established dominance, and his seat has remained generally safe since. His San Bernardino County-based district has given him at least 61 percent of the vote in 17 elections, including in 2010.

Key Votes

2010

Overhaul the nation's health insurance system	NO
Allow for repeal of "don't ask, don't tell"	NO
Overhaul financial services industry regulation	NO
Limit use of new Afghanistan War funds to troop withdrawal activities	NO
Change oversight of offshore drilling and lift oil spill liability cap	NO
Provide a path to legal status for some children of illegal immigrants	NO
Extend Bush-era income tax cuts for two years	YES

2009

Expand the Children's Health Insurance Program	NO
Provide $787 billion in tax cuts and spending increases to stimulate the economy	NO
Allow bankruptcy judges to modify certain primary-residence mortgages	NO
Create a cap-and-trade system to limit greenhouse gas emissions	NO
Provide $2 billion for the "cash for clunkers" program	NO
Establish the government as the sole provider of student loans	NO
Restrict federally funded insurance coverage for abortions in health care overhaul	YES

CQ Vote Studies

	PARTY UNITY		PRESIDENTIAL SUPPORT	
	SUPPORT	OPPOSE	SUPPORT	OPPOSE
2010	96%	4%	27%	73%
2009	85%	15%	25%	75%
2008	94%	6%	82%	18%
2007	84%	16%	80%	20%
2006	94%	6%	90%	10%

Interest Groups

	AFL-CIO	ADA	CCUS	ACU
2010	0%	0%	88%	96%
2009	19%	5%	80%	84%
2008	20%	20%	100%	84%
2007	13%	10%	80%	88%
2006	21%	15%	93%	67%

California 41

Most of San Bernardino County — Redlands

The 41st includes vast desert and mountain stretches and most of San Bernardino County, the nation's largest by area, although it is home to less than one-third of the county's residents. The western quarter of the 41st, where the district's Inland Empire, Victor Valley and Riverside County areas are located, contains the majority of its population. As the 41st moves east, development is difficult, as high desert, dry lakes and mountains dominate the landscape to the Arizona and Nevada borders. Local hospitals, government and the military are major employers.

The district starts in the San Jacinto Valley in a sliver of northwestern Riverside County — which includes San Jacinto, Banning, Beaumont and Calimesa — before crossing into San Bernardino County to pick up communities south of the San Bernardino Mountains. Redlands, Highland, Yucaipa and part of San Bernardino (shared with the 43rd) are here, and Highland's San Manuel Indian Reservation resort casino is a key employer. The 41st has a large population of day laborers, many of whom are Hispanic immigrants. An expanded border patrol presence has led to increased deportation efforts in the Inland Empire region.

On the north side of the mountains are the growing Victor Valley cities of Hesperia and Apple Valley, communities that are attractive to Los Angeles and Orange county commuters. The local housing market remains volatile following widespread foreclosures.

The district gave John McCain 54 percent of its 2008 presidential vote and Republicans still enjoy an 11-point edge in voter registration, but growing Hispanic populations may change the political lean.

Major Industry
Service, manufacturing, military

Military Bases
Marine Corps Air Ground Combat Center, Twentynine Palms, 13,214 military, 1,239 civilian (2010)

Cities
Hesperia, 90,173; Apple Valley, 69,135; Redlands, 68,747; San Bernardino city (pt.), 61,534; Highland (pt.), 53,022

Notable
The Mojave National Preserve features the Devils Playground dunes.

Rep. Gary G. Miller (R)

Capitol Office
225-3201
www.house.gov/garymiller
2349 Rayburn Bldg. 20515-0542; fax 226-6962

Committees
Financial Services
   (International Monetary Policy & Trade - Chairman)
Transportation & Infrastructure

Residence
Diamond Bar

Born
Oct. 16, 1948; Huntsville, Ark.

Religion
Protestant

Family
Wife, Cathy Miller; four children

Education
Mt. San Antonio Community College, attended
1968-70

Military
Army, 1967

Career
Real estate developer

Political Highlights
Diamond Bar Municipal Advisory Council, 1988-89;
Diamond Bar City Council, 1989-90; sought Repub-
lican nomination for Calif. Senate, 1990; Diamond
Bar City Council, 1991-95 (mayor, 1993-94); sought
Republican nomination for Calif. Senate (special
election), 1994; Calif. Assembly, 1995-98

ELECTION RESULTS

2010 GENERAL

Gary G. Miller (R)	127,161	62.2%
Michael Williamson (D)	65,122	31.9%
Mark Lambert (LIBERT)	12,115	5.9%

2010 PRIMARY

Gary G. Miller (R)	32,669	48.8%
Phil Liberatore (R)	25,181	37.6%
Lee McGroarty (R)	7,113	10.6%
David Su (R)	2,041	3.0%

Previous Winning Percentages
2008 (60%); 2006 (100%); 2004 (68%); 2002 (68%);
2000 (59%); 1998 (53%)

Elected 1998; 7th term

Miller's background as a business owner and family man with strong religious convictions shape his limited-government, pro-business attitude and views on social issues. His conservative, Southern California roots are reflected in his positions on illegal immigration and water issues.

Miller is an enthusiastic backer of legislation that would deny "birthright citizenship" to children born in the United States whose parents are illegal immigrants. "It is unfair to grant birthright citizenship to children of illegal immigrants because it undermines the intention of the Fourteenth Amendment, rewards those that have recklessly broken our nation's immigration laws and costs American taxpayers billions annually," Miller said in early 2011.

In March 2010 Miller co-founded the Reclaim American Jobs Caucus, aimed at bringing attention to the nexus of unemployment and illegal immigration. "How do you justify having 15 million people unemployed in this country and 8 million illegals in this country taking those jobs?" Miller said in an exchange with Democratic Rep. Luis V. Gutierrez of Illinois on Fox News in April 2010. Early in 2009, he cosponsored measures requiring that all official U.S. business be printed in English and another mandating that ballots for federal elections be printed only in English.

From his seat on the Transportation and Infrastructure Committee, Miller works on water issues, a matter of great consequence in thirsty Southern California. He has blasted restrictions on pumping water in the Sacramento-San Joaquin Delta intended to protect the Delta smelt, and he has cosponsored legislation to waive the Endangered Species Act provisions that are the basis for the restrictions. In November 2007 he supported an override of President George W. Bush's veto of a $23.2 billion bill authorizing water projects, including $35 million for his district.

Miller also sits on the Financial Services Committee, where he chairs the International Monetary Policy and Trade Subcommittee. Unlike some conservatives who are ready to dispense with mortgage backers Fannie Mae and Freddie Mac, Miller has defended continuing some forms of government backing for mortgages.

He opposed the financial industry regulatory overhaul enacted in 2010, saying it "will make Wall Street bailouts permanent and increase the intrusion of the federal government in the private sector."

Miller can claim some legislative successes, such as a 2008 mortgage rescue law he backed that included a provision he wrote to increase the size of home loans that government-sponsored mortgage giants Fannie Mae and Freddie Mac can purchase, while increasing the size of loans that the Federal Housing Administration can insure.

Miller is a Civil War buff and keeps in his office a large collection of history books, which he reads during his six-hour flights between California and Washington, D.C. His study of history has translated into legislative action: In 2002, he won enactment of a law to provide federal grants to states and localities to preserve battle sites. He pushed for the law's reauthorization in the 110th Congress (2007-08), achieving success in his chamber, but the bill failed to advance through the Senate. The House in March 2009 passed his measure to direct the Interior secretary to establish a program to provide grants for the preservation of Civil War battle sites.

Miller's district is home to the Richard Nixon Library in Yorba Linda (Miller grew up in Whittier, where Nixon spent some of his childhood years and attended college), and he secured $4 million in 2004 to house Nixon's presidential papers and tapes. The funds secured by Miller paid for the transfer of the papers from the National Archives facility in Maryland to California, and for a new building.

Miller's social conservatism was evident during the 2009 debate on the Democrats' health care overhaul, when he chastised the majority for writing a provision that he said would force taxpayers "to send part of their hard-earned dollars to Washington every year to end the life of an unborn child."

Miller was raised by his mother and grandparents. At an early age, his family moved from Arkansas to Whittier, where many other poor families from Oklahoma and Arkansas had settled. His mother worked as a checker at a grocery store; his grandfather was a custodian for the local school district. Miller, who plays the trumpet, aspired to be a musician as a child.

After attending community college but leaving without a degree, he formed a partnership with a building contractor and they bid on Department of Housing and Urban Development home-improvement contracts. He says he learned construction skills on the job and moved on to build single-family homes and, eventually, planned communities.

Miller began his political career on the Diamond Bar Municipal Advisory Council. He was a member of Diamond Bar's first council after the city was incorporated in 1989 and became mayor in 1993. He lost primary bids for the California Senate in 1990 and 1994. Early in 1995, when voters forced a recall election of state Assemblyman Paul Horcher, Miller ran for the seat and won.

In 1998, three-term Rep. Jay C. Kim was convicted of violating campaign finance laws, and Miller challenged him for the seat. He defeated Kim by 15 percentage points in the open primary and won the general election by nearly 13 points. In remapping after the 2000 census, Democratic and Latino portions of the district — renumbered the 42nd — were removed and the boundary was extended into Orange County to pick up more conservative voters.

Shortly after the 2006 election, Miller came under FBI scrutiny for a provision he added to a 2005 surface transportation bill that improved land a mile from property he owned. The bureau also looked into his deferral of capital gains taxes on land sales he made to the city of Monrovia in 2002 and to Fontana in 2005 and 2006. Miller contended he sold the land under threat of eminent domain; city officials disputed that account. Miller said he paid all necessary taxes and added that he had provided House Republican leaders with documents showing he did nothing wrong. He said in July 2008 that he had never been contacted by the FBI. Democrats sensed an opportunity, but Montebello School Board Member Edwin "Ed" Chau lost to Miller by 20 percentage points. He won by a more than 2-1 margin in 2010.

Key Votes

2010

Overhaul the nation's health insurance system	NO
Allow for repeal of "don't ask, don't tell"	NO
Overhaul financial services industry regulation	NO
Limit use of new Afghanistan War funds to troop withdrawal activities	NO
Change oversight of offshore drilling and lift oil spill liability cap	P
Provide a path to legal status for some children of illegal immigrants	NO
Extend Bush-era income tax cuts for two years	YES

2009

Expand the Children's Health Insurance Program	NO
Provide $787 billion in tax cuts and spending increases to stimulate the economy	NO
Allow bankruptcy judges to modify certain primary-residence mortgages	?
Create a cap-and-trade system to limit greenhouse gas emissions	NO
Provide $2 billion for the "cash for clunkers" program	YES
Establish the government as the sole provider of student loans	NO
Restrict federally funded insurance coverage for abortions in health care overhaul	YES

CQ Vote Studies

	PARTY UNITY		PRESIDENTIAL SUPPORT	
	Support	Oppose	Support	Oppose
2010	98%	2%	29%	71%
2009	87%	13%	27%	73%
2008	97%	3%	79%	21%
2007	96%	4%	86%	14%
2006	98%	2%	95%	5%

Interest Groups

	AFL-CIO	ADA	CCUS	ACU
2010	0%	0%	100%	96%
2009	13%	5%	77%	90%
2008	27%	5%	100%	81%
2007	10%	0%	89%	100%
2006	7%	0%	100%	88%

California 42

Parts of Orange, Los Angeles and San Bernardino counties — Mission Viejo, Chino

Although the bulk of its population lives in Orange County, the Republican-leaning 42nd is centered around the suburbs where Orange, Los Angeles and San Bernardino counties come together east of Los Angeles proper. From there, the 42nd has a long arm that stretches southeast and then southwest farther into Orange County to Mission Viejo and Rancho Santa Margarita. A chunk of eastern Anaheim also falls within the district's borders.

Chino and Chino Hills in San Bernardino County have an agricultural heritage, but the economic influence of dairy production is waning due to residential development and the increasing presence of manufacturing and service sectors. Retail and residential property growth has been volatile in the San Bernardino portions of the district, but home construction continues.

Diamond Bar and Rowland Heights (shared with the 38th) in Los Angeles County have large Asian populations. Hispanics and Asians also live in the northern Orange County cities of Brea (which has experienced downturns in the commercial and financial sectors), La Habra and Placentia (shared with the 40th), although this segment of Orange County is predominately white-collar and white. Overall, the district is mostly middle and upper class and dominated by residential communities. Many residents work in technology firms and commute to Los Angeles or Irvine (which is located in the 48th).

Conservatism persists here, and the district gave GOP candidate Meg Whitman her highest percentage statewide (59 percent) in the 2010 gubernatorial election, but the influx of Hispanic and Asian residents in the past decade may swing the political lean.

Major Industry
Service, light manufacturing, dairy

Cities
Mission Viejo, 93,305; Chino, 77,983; Chino Hills, 74,799; Yorba Linda, 64,234; La Habra, 60,239; Anaheim (pt.), 56,208; Diamond Bar, 55,544

Notable
Yorba Linda, the birthplace and burial site of President Richard Nixon, is the home of the Nixon Library; La Habra has hosted an annual Corn Festival since 1949; Chino is home to the Planes of Fame museum.

Rep. Joe Baca (D)

Capitol Office
225-6161
www.house.gov/baca
2366 Rayburn Bldg. 20515-0543; fax 225-8671

Committees
Agriculture
Financial Services

Residence
Rialto

Born
Jan. 23, 1947; Belen, N.M.

Religion
Roman Catholic

Family
Wife, Barbara Baca; four children

Education
California State U., Los Angeles, B.A. 1971 (sociology)

Military
Army, 1966-68

Career
Travel agency owner; corporate community relations executive

Political Highlights
San Bernardino Community College District Board of Trustees, 1979-93; sought Democratic nomination for Calif. Assembly, 1988, 1990; Calif. Assembly, 1992-98 (Speaker pro tempore, 1995); Calif. Senate, 1998-99

ELECTION RESULTS

2010 GENERAL

Joe Baca (D)	70,026	65.5%
Scott Folkens (R)	36,890	34.5%

2010 PRIMARY

Joe Baca (D)	unopposed

2008 GENERAL

Joe Baca (D)	108,259	69.1%
John Roberts (R)	48,312	30.9%

Previous Winning Percentages
2006 (65%); 2004 (66%); 2002 (66%); 2000 (60%); 1999 Special Election Runoff (51%)

Elected 1999; 6th full term

The first Hispanic elected to Congress from Southern California's Inland Empire, "working Joe Baca" styles himself as the champion of immigrants — legal and illegal — and organized labor. He is prone to ruffle the feathers of his colleagues and doesn't seem to mind much when he does.

Baca has kept the immigration issue before his colleagues via a series of speeches and inserts in the Congressional Record honoring the contributions of immigrants. His district is nearly 60 percent Hispanic, and he has often referred to "hardworking" immigrant mothers who "sometimes work three jobs" and fathers who "wake up at 4 a.m. to go to work, earn below minimum wages, and manage to provide for their families."

He holds no quarter for those who oppose his views on the subject. He called a federal judge's July 2010 ruling barring enforcement of an Arizona law targeting illegal immigrants "an important victory over fear and hatred."

Early in the 111th Congress (2009-10), he appeared on the House floor every few days to push for an immigration overhaul. Baca and other members of the Congressional Hispanic Caucus met with President Obama on the subject in summer 2010. "It is encouraging to know the president understands the very real consequences that America's broken immigration system has on families, our economy and our national security," he said after the meeting, although no major legislative proposal was forthcoming.

Instead, Obama signed a $600 million border security bill in August that Democrats touted as a preliminary step to a broader overhaul. He backed House passage of legislation later in the year that would have created a path to legal status for certain illegal immigrant children, but it died in the Senate.

Baca also led efforts for immigration changes as chairman of the Hispanic Caucus during the 110th Congress (2007-08). But the caucus spent more time fending off crackdowns on illegal immigrants and measures targeting non-English speakers than it did advancing legislation to help them.

And Baca had to deal with disruptions in the caucus after he alienated its female members in 2007, soon after taking the helm. Fellow California Democrat Loretta Sanchez complained he had referred to her as a "whore" in a conversation with a California state legislator. Sanchez and her sister, Linda T. Sánchez, both quit the caucus after the dispute. Baca denied Sanchez's accusation, although he acknowledged calling Hilda L. Solis, then a Democratic member of the House and now secretary of Labor, a "kiss-up" to Speaker Nancy Pelosi. He apologized to Solis, but the grumbling continued within the caucus. New York's Nydia M. Velázquez succeeded him as chair in 2009.

Baca has sought to help immigrant families and farmers from the Agriculture Committee, where he is the ranking Democrat on the subcommittee that handles nutrition issues, which he chaired in the 111th. He successfully included in the 2008 reauthorization of agriculture and nutrition programs provisions to boost food stamp aid and to expand a fruit and vegetable pilot program to all 50 states.

Baca is a member of both the Financial Services Committee and the fiscally conservative Blue Dog Coalition. After first voicing opposition to extending the Bush-era tax cuts, at the end of 2010 he reluctantly voted for a two-year extension for all income levels. Similarly, he first voted against a $700 billion measure to shore up the nation's financial sector in 2008, saying it didn't do enough to help homeowners facing foreclosure. He changed his mind three days later and voted for a second measure that included increased limits for federally insured bank deposits.

During July 2010 consideration of a measure that would effectively repeal an online gambling ban, the Financial Services panel rejected an amendment by Baca that would have required states and Indian tribes to opt in to a federal licensing program before a licensee could operate an Internet gambling facility in its territory. Committee Chairman Barney Frank, a Massachusetts Democrat, said Baca's proposal was a veiled attempt to kill the bill, and Baca was one of only four Democrats to oppose the measure.

He is a strong supporter of organized labor, which, in turn, has backed him. But Baca sides with Republicans on some issues, including supporting gun owners' rights. He also breaks with his party on oil drilling in Alaska's Arctic National Wildlife Refuge, aligning himself with the Teamsters, who value the jobs the drilling would create.

Formerly a member of the Natural Resources Committee, Baca won House passage in 2010 of a bill to require an Interior Department study of water quality in the Inland Empire. The bill did not make it to the Senate floor for a vote, but he reintroduced it in January 2011. In 2004, the House passed his bill authorizing $50 million to help clean up groundwater contaminated with perchlorate, a rocket-fuel additive, in the Santa Ana River watershed.

Baca was born in tiny Belen, N.M. The son of a railroad laborer and the youngest of 15 children in a house where little English was spoken, Baca as a boy moved with his family to Barstow, Calif. He shined shoes, delivered newspapers and worked as a janitor. He was a laborer for the Santa Fe Railroad between his high school graduation and getting drafted in 1966. He was a paratrooper with the 101st and 82nd Airborne divisions but was not sent to Vietnam. After the Army, Baca earned a degree in sociology, then worked as a community affairs representative for a local phone company.

His political career began in 1979 with election to the San Bernardino Community College District Board of Trustees, on which he served 14 years. After two failed attempts to oust a fellow Democrat from the state Assembly, he won the seat in 1992 when the incumbent retired. He was re-elected twice and then won a state Senate seat in 1998.

The following year, after Democratic Rep. George Brown died, Baca ran against his widow, Marta Macias Brown, in the special-election primary. He defeated her, then posted a 6-percentage-point win over GOP businessman Elia Pirozzi in the runoff. He has won handily ever since.

Baca aspired as a child to a career in baseball. Well into his 30s, he played catcher for the San Bernardino Stars, a semi-pro fast-pitch softball team. In the 2010 congressional baseball game sponsored by CQ Roll Call, he pitched a complete game victory over the GOP, earning co-MVP honors.

Key Votes

2010

Overhaul the nation's health insurance system	YES
Allow for repeal of "don't ask, don't tell"	YES
Overhaul financial services industry regulation	YES
Limit use of new Afghanistan War funds to troop withdrawal activities	NO
Change oversight of offshore drilling and lift oil spill liability cap	YES
Provide a path to legal status for some children of illegal immigrants	YES
Extend Bush-era income tax cuts for two years	YES

2009

Expand the Children's Health Insurance Program	YES
Provide $787 billion in tax cuts and spending increases to stimulate the economy	YES
Allow bankruptcy judges to modify certain primary-residence mortgages	YES
Create a cap-and-trade system to limit greenhouse gas emissions	YES
Provide $2 billion for the "cash for clunkers" program	YES
Establish the government as the sole provider of student loans	YES
Restrict federally funded insurance coverage for abortions in health care overhaul	YES

CQ Vote Studies

	PARTY UNITY		PRESIDENTIAL SUPPORT	
	SUPPORT	OPPOSE	SUPPORT	OPPOSE
2010	98%	2%	93%	7%
2009	98%	2%	97%	3%
2008	98%	2%	19%	81%
2007	97%	3%	6%	94%
2006	91%	9%	35%	65%

Interest Groups

	AFL-CIO	ADA	CCUS	ACU
2010	100%	90%	14%	0%
2009	100%	90%	40%	4%
2008	100%	90%	67%	8%
2007	96%	100%	55%	0%
2006	100%	95%	47%	20%

California 43

Southwest San Bernardino County — Ontario, Fontana, most of San Bernardino

The San Bernardino County communities of Ontario, Fontana and San Bernardino form the base of the 43rd, which lies in the heart of the Inland Empire east of Los Angeles. The district has retained a diverse and working-class feel despite decades of explosive growth that had resulted in years of economic prosperity similar to that of its neighbors in Orange and Los Angeles counties.

The area relied on a strong home construction sector to drive further growth and bolster the region's economy. But state and local government budget shortfalls and high foreclosure and unemployment rates affect the local workforce.

Some residents commute into Los Angeles along the Pomona and San Bernardino freeways, and technology, manufacturing and aerospace industries will play a large role in economic recovery here. Homeowners in Fontana have been hit particularly hard, although the widespread foreclosure crisis may result in a glut of lower-priced homes in these established suburbs.

The renovated Ontario airport is part of a transportation and container warehousing sector and serves as a hub for UPS, and demand for air travel through the airport has remained steady. Local officials hope expansion and new high-end stores at the large Ontario Mills mall will spur economic activity. The manufacturing sector supports companies such as Mag Instrument, the maker of the Maglite flashlight. Rialto, which is more than two-thirds Hispanic, is home to regional distribution centers for Staples and Toys "R" Us.

The district is now 69 percent Hispanic, and registered Democrats outnumber Republicans by nearly 20 percentage points. The 43rd favors Democrats on all levels and gave Jerry Brown 62 percent of its 2010 gubernatorial vote. Traffic congestion and illegal immigration are big issues among residents here.

Major Industry
Manufacturing, electronics, agriculture

Cities
Fontana, 196,069; Ontario, 163,924; San Bernardino (pt.), 148,390; Rialto, 99,171; Colton (pt.), 47,411

Notable
Fontana is the birthplace of the Hells Angels motorcycle club.

Rep. Ken Calvert (R)

Capitol Office
225-1986
calvert.house.gov
2269 Rayburn Bldg. 20515-0544; fax 225-2004

Committees
Appropriations
Budget

Residence
Corona

Born
June 8, 1953; Corona, Calif.

Religion
Protestant

Family
Divorced

Education
Chaffey College, A.A. 1973 (business); San Diego
State U., B.A. 1975 (economics)

Career
Real estate executive; restaurant executive

Political Highlights
Sought Republican nomination for U.S. House,
1982; Riverside County Republican Party chairman,
1984-88

ELECTION RESULTS

2010 GENERAL

Ken Calvert (R)	107,482	55.6%
Bill Hedrick (D)	85,784	44.4%

2010 PRIMARY

Ken Calvert (R)	37,327	66.3%
Chris Riggs (R)	18,994	33.7%

2008 GENERAL

Ken Calvert (R)	129,937	51.2%
Bill Hedrick (D)	123,890	48.8%

Previous Winning Percentages
2006 (60%); 2004 (62%); 2002 (64%); 2000 (74%);
1998 (56%); 1996 (55%); 1994 (55%); 1992 (47%)

Elected 1992; 10th term

Calvert is committed to the conservative principles of limited federal regulation of private property, stricter controls on immigration and less government spending. He also is an appropriator who seeks federal support for concerns vital to his Southern California district, particularly for water resources.

His congressional career has included narrow victories, primary challenges, an encounter with a prostitute and allegations — unproven — of financial misdealing. In the last two election cycles he faced serious threats, one from the left and one from the right, but managed to keep his job.

He did not, however, keep his job on the Select Intelligence Oversight Panel, which brought together appropriators and members of the Intelligence Committee to review the $80 billion budget for U.S. intelligence agencies. In the 111th Congress (2009-10), Calvert was the top GOP member of the panel, which was created by Democrats in 2007. Republicans decided to abolish it in the 112th Congress (2011-12), a proposal Calvert supported.

"I think it's a good idea, not that it didn't serve a function," Calvert said. "That function is just better served in other ways."

He has long focused on water issues, and the Appropriations Subcommittee on Interior-Environment gives him a venue to continue those efforts. As chairman of the Natural Resources Subcommittee on Water and Power in 2004, he worked with California's Democratic Sen. Dianne Feinstein to win enactment of a bill to reauthorize and restructure the California Federal Bay-Delta Program, or Calfed, which provides irrigation and drinking water for two-thirds of the state's population.

Calvert also owns a seat on the Budget Committee, one of three appropriators pulling double duty in the spending process.

Calvert occasionally sides with Democrats, but on the Obama administration's major economic initiatives he has solidly been with his party. He voted against the health care overhaul legislation, saying it "expands government spending, kills jobs, drives up our national debt and raises taxes."

He supported the GOP's one-year moratorium on earmarks and voted against President Obama's $787 billion economic stimulus plan, a supplemental spending bill to fund disaster relief and summer jobs and an extension of unemployment benefits that was not offset by cuts in other programs.

"We cannot continue down this road of fiscal insanity," Calvert said after his vote on the disaster relief and summer jobs bill.

Calvert backs measures to tighten immigration laws and is a longtime champion of the E-Verify program, which allows businesses to confirm the employment eligibility of new hires. He said the removal from the stimulus bill of his provision to reauthorize the program for four years contributed to his unhappiness with that measure.

Calvert also pointed to immigration concerns when voting against a bill, signed into law in early 2009, to expand the Children's Health Insurance Program. "I find it unconscionable that Speaker [Nancy] Pelosi has hijacked a successful program . . . in an effort to provide benefits to illegal immigrants and bring the U.S. one step closer to a nationalized system of health care," he said. CHIP covers children from low-income families that make too much money to qualify for Medicaid.

Calvert was born in Corona, just west of Riverside, making him a native son of the area he now represents — not all that common in the ever-changing Los Angeles megalopolis. His father, who changed parties to become a

Republican in the 1960s, won election to the city council and then served as Corona's mayor. The younger Calvert worked on Richard Nixon's 1968 presidential campaign and interned in the Capitol Hill office of Rep. Victor Veysey, a California Republican.

In 1982, at age 28, Calvert entered an open-seat House race in a district that contained most of Riverside County, losing the GOP primary by just 868 votes. But he stayed active in party affairs, helping run the gubernatorial campaigns of Republicans George Deukmejian and Pete Wilson.

When reapportionment created a new 43rd District for western Riverside County in 1992, Calvert ran again and won narrowly by relying on write-in ballots to reverse an apparent defeat. But tragedy marred his triumph: In September of that year, Calvert's father committed suicide.

Calvert had a rough start in his first term when a tryst with a prostitute drew widespread notice. He said his "inappropriate" behavior stemmed from depression over his recent divorce and his father's suicide. Calvert won the 1994 primary by just 2 percentage points, and the national surge that delivered the House to the GOP carried him to victory with 55 percent.

In 2000, he won with 74 percent. In 2002, in redistricted territory, numbered the 44th, Calvert took 70 percent in a three-way primary and cruised to a sixth term. He won easily in 2004 and 2006.

Before the 2008 campaign, Calvert had been under increasing criticism from bloggers, and watchdog groups questioned whether he used his seat on the Appropriations Committee to increase the value of some of his land deals.

They pointed to a 2006 Los Angeles Times story that reported he and a partner held numerous properties near transportation projects that Calvert had supported with federal earmarks, funding set-asides for special projects. Calvert denied wrongdoing, and an FBI review of public documents never led to any action.

But the Democratic tidal wave of 2008 combined with the questions raised about his financial activities held him to a 2-percentage-point victory over Democrat Bill Hedrick.

His votes against key components of the Obama economic agenda made him the target of radio ads sponsored by the Democratic Congressional Campaign Committee in early 2009. But before he even faced the Democratic candidate, he had to deal with a challenge from the right by real estate agent Chris Riggs, who had support from some tea party activists. In a tough primary race, Calvert defeated Riggs with 66 percent of the vote. He went on to once again defeat Hedrick by a margin considerably more comfortable than in 2008, winning by 11 percentage points.

Key Votes

2010

Overhaul the nation's health insurance system	NO
Allow for repeal of "don't ask, don't tell"	NO
Overhaul financial services industry regulation	NO
Limit use of new Afghanistan War funds to troop withdrawal activities	NO
Change oversight of offshore drilling and lift oil spill liability cap	NO
Provide a path to legal status for some children of illegal immigrants	NO
Extend Bush-era income tax cuts for two years	YES

2009

Expand the Children's Health Insurance Program	NO
Provide $787 billion in tax cuts and spending increases to stimulate the economy	NO
Allow bankruptcy judges to modify certain primary-residence mortgages	NO
Create a cap-and-trade system to limit greenhouse gas emissions	NO
Provide $2 billion for the "cash for clunkers" program	YES
Establish the government as the sole provider of student loans	NO
Restrict federally funded insurance coverage for abortions in health care overhaul	YES

CQ Vote Studies

	PARTY UNITY		PRESIDENTIAL SUPPORT	
	SUPPORT	OPPOSE	SUPPORT	OPPOSE
2010	96%	4%	27%	73%
2009	86%	14%	24%	76%
2008	96%	4%	76%	24%
2007	91%	9%	83%	17%
2006	95%	5%	95%	5%

Interest Groups

	AFL-CIO	ADA	CCUS	ACU
2010	7%	0%	100%	96%
2009	14%	10%	87%	92%
2008	13%	15%	100%	83%
2007	5%	15%	89%	88%
2006	14%	5%	100%	80%

California 44

Northwestern Riverside County — Riverside, Corona

A residential district that lies east of Los Angeles and north of San Diego, the 44th contains about one-third of Riverside County's residents and takes in the southeastern portion of Orange County that borders San Diego County. The Orange County areas include coastal San Clemente, a premier surfing spot, and Santa Ana Mountain forests.

The 44th is the 25th-largest district in the nation, according to the 2010 census. Much of the population growth in Riverside County, where more than four-fifths of the district's residents live, has been among the Latino population. Nearly half of the 44th's portion of the county is now Hispanic, and the district as a whole is 43 percent Hispanic.

Riverside County's traffic congestion, especially from white-collar workers who commute to Orange or Los Angeles counties, remains an issue despite a recent expansion of Route 91. The area's high levels of air pollution make it part of the greater-Los Angeles "smog belt."

The manufacturing sector still contributes to the local economy, but job losses have been widespread. In Riverside, farmland is being driven farther east and out of the district as the Los Angeles area continues to expand. Water issues threaten citrus, grape, date and avocado crops, and once-prevalent dairy farms are now scarce.

Registered Republicans outnumber Democrats here. The district's portion of Orange County is strongly Republican, but the more blue-collar Riverside communities and the areas around the University of California, Riverside, lean Democratic. Barack Obama edged John McCain here by less than 1 percentage point in the 2008 presidential election, but GOP gubernatorial candidate Meg Whitman took a 12-percentage-point win 2010.

Major Industry
Manufacturing, agriculture, health care

Military Bases
Naval Surface Warfare Center, Corona Division, 6 military, 990 civilian (2011)

Cities
Riverside, 303,871; Corona, 152,374; San Clemente, 63,522

Notable
Riverside's Mission Inn was the site of Richard and Pat Nixon's wedding, and Ronald and Nancy Reagan stopped there while honeymooning.

Rep. Mary Bono Mack (R)

Capitol Office
225-5330
bono.house.gov
104 Cannon Bldg. 20515-0545; fax 225-2961

Committees
Energy & Commerce
  (Commerce, Manufacturing & Trade
  - Chairwoman)

Residence
Palm Springs

Born
Oct. 24, 1961; Cleveland, Ohio

Religion
Protestant

Family
Husband, Rep. Connie Mack, R-Fla.; two children, three stepchildren

Education
U. of Southern California, B.F.A. 1984 (art history)

Career
Homemaker; restaurateur

Political Highlights
No previous office

ELECTION RESULTS

2010 GENERAL

Mary Bono Mack (R)	106,472	51.5%
Steve Pougnet (D)	87,141	42.1%
Bill Lussenheide (AMI)	13,188	6.4%

2010 PRIMARY

Mary Bono Mack (R)	42,981	70.6%
Clayton Thibodeau (R)	17,940	29.4%

2008 GENERAL

Mary Bono Mack (R)	155,166	58.3%
Julie Bornstein (D)	111,026	41.7%

Previous Winning Percentages
2006 (61%); 2004 (67%); 2002 (65%); 2000 (59%);
1998 (60%); 1998 Special Election (64%)

Elected 1998; 7th full term

Bono Mack has established an eclectic voting record by catering to the often conflicting interests of her ideologically divided district. She is not as conservative as most of her California GOP colleagues, but still manages to hang with her party on about nine of every 10 votes that split Republicans and Democrats.

A member of the powerful Energy and Commerce Committee, she supports expanding alternative energy sources, including nuclear power. Chairwoman of the Commerce, Manufacturing and Trade Subcommittee in the 112th Congress (2011-12), she said she wants to be a "reasoned voice" on efforts to curb global warming, warning of the need to protect businesses affected by legislation.

A top priority in her district has been obtaining funding to restore the Salton Sea, a Southern California lake threatened by pollution and increased salinity. In 2007, she voted to override President George W. Bush's veto of a $23.2 billion water projects bill, which included $30 million for the restoration project.

Bono Mack's district tends to lean Republican, featuring a fiscally conservative and socially liberal style. It also has a sizable gay population, leading the congresswoman to break from her party on issues related to gay rights. She was one of 35 Republicans to vote for a 2007 measure prohibiting job discrimination on the basis of an individual's actual or perceived sexual orientation, and also opposed the GOP's effort in 2004 to amend the Constitution to ban same-sex marriage. In the 109th Congress (2005-06), she sponsored a bill shifting some AIDS funding from urban centers to less-populated rural areas. Signed into law, the legislation helped districts like hers.

But in May 2010, she voted against an amendment to the annual defense authorization bill that would repeal the military's ban on gays serving openly, saying that the Pentagon should have been given more time to review the effects of a repeal. When the House voted in December on a stand-alone bill to repeal the policy, after the military's review was completed, Bono Mack supported the measure, which was signed into law by President Obama.

In the 111th Congress (2009-10), Bono Mack voted with her party against the health care overhaul legislation, calling it flawed and overly partisan. She also joined her party to vote against the $787 billion stimulus package and legislation to make the government the sole provider of student loans.

But she maintained her reputation for going her own way by joining 40 Republicans in February 2009 who favored an expansion of the Children's Health Insurance Program, which covers children from low-income families that make too much money to qualify for Medicaid. And a few weeks after voting against the stimulus package, she became the only California Republican to back a $410 billion catchall spending bill for 2009. "There are simply too many vitally important priorities contained in this bill not to support it during these difficult economic times," she said.

Bono Mack is passionate about mental health and substance abuse issues; she serves as vice chairwoman of the Congressional Addiction Treatment and Recovery Caucus. She also helped launch the Youth Drug Prevention Caucus and the Congressional Caucus on Prescription Drug Abuse, which was founded in June 2010.

President George W. Bush signed into law a bill sponsored by Bono Mack in 2008 that bans online pharmacies from selling controlled substances without valid prescriptions, and she's continued to work to combat prescription drug abuse, especially regarding OxyContin, a pain medication. The issue hits close to home for Bono Mack. In February 2009, she and her son Chesare gave a candid interview to People magazine about his addiction to OxyContin and heroin, and his subsequent recovery.

She supports federal funding for medical research using embryonic stem cells, which are harvested from surplus embryos at in vitro fertilization clinics, a practice that opponents liken to abortion. She says that her physician father and chemist mother influenced her thinking on the issue.

In her early years in the House, Bono Mack pursued legacy issues, matters important to her late first husband, entertainer-turned-politician Sonny Bono, who died in a 1998 skiing accident. She helped to pass a copyright extension bill first championed by and eventually named for Sonny. Since the 108th Congress (2003-04), she has often focused on intellectual property issues of interest to the entertainment industry. She continues to co-chair the Recording Arts and Sciences Congressional Caucus.

Bono Mack grew up in South Pasadena, Calif. She worked her way through college as a cocktail waitress, majoring in art history at the University of Southern California.

As she was celebrating her college graduation at Sonny Bono's West Hollywood restaurant, she met the owner. They married two years later, in 1986, when she was 24 — about half Sonny's age. She helped manage the restaurant, which he relocated to their new home in Palm Springs, and other companies associated with his entertainment interests. The first time she voted was for Sonny, who was elected mayor of Palm Springs in 1988.

She arrived in Washington after he was elected to the House in 1994 and was a stay-at-home mother to their two children. When he died in a skiing accident in January 1998, GOP leaders urged her to run for his seat. Her Democratic opponent, actor Ralph Waite, played the father in the 1970s television show "The Waltons" (whose CBS run coincided for a few years with that of "The Sonny and Cher Comedy Hour"). Bono Mack won the special election in April with almost two-thirds of the vote.

In 2008, while Barack Obama was winning her district by 5 percentage points, Bono Mack was re-elected by nearly 17 percentage points. But her margin was cut to 10 in 2010, making her an early 2012 target of the Democratic Congressional Campaign Committee.

Bono Mack and her second husband divorced in September 2005 after a little less than four years of marriage. About two years later, she married Rep. Connie Mack, a Florida Republican. Since they wed, the pair have split their time between the Sunshine and Golden states.

Key Votes

2010

Overhaul the nation's health insurance system	NO
Allow for repeal of "don't ask, don't tell"	NO
Overhaul financial services industry regulation	NO
Limit use of new Afghanistan War funds to troop withdrawal activities	NO
Change oversight of offshore drilling and lift oil spill liability cap	NO
Provide a path to legal status for some children of illegal immigrants	NO
Extend Bush-era income tax cuts for two years	YES

2009

Expand the Children's Health Insurance Program	YES
Provide $787 billion in tax cuts and spending increases to stimulate the economy	NO
Allow bankruptcy judges to modify certain primary-residence mortgages	NO
Create a cap-and-trade system to limit greenhouse gas emissions	YES
Provide $2 billion for the "cash for clunkers" program	YES
Establish the government as the sole provider of student loans	NO
Restrict federally funded insurance coverage for abortions in health care overhaul	YES

CQ Vote Studies

	PARTY UNITY		PRESIDENTIAL SUPPORT	
	Support	Oppose	Support	Oppose
2010	90%	10%	31%	69%
2009	88%	12%	31%	69%
2008	90%	10%	64%	36%
2007	85%	15%	58%	42%
2006	85%	15%	81%	19%

Interest Groups

	AFL-CIO	ADA	CCUS	ACU
2010	7%	20%	88%	91%
2009	38%	30%	80%	79%
2008	29%	40%	88%	74%
2007	25%	30%	89%	65%
2006	17%	25%	86%	68%

California 45

Riverside County — Moreno Valley, Palm Springs

Riverside County's booming population — in Inland Empire cities, such as Moreno Valley, Hemet and Murrieta, and the resort-filled Coachella Valley farther east — has made the 45th California's most populous district leading up to decennial remapping. Desert resorts, a service industry workforce and agriculture fuel the economy here. Air pollution in the Los Angeles exurbs are a concern for residents and officials.

In the Coachella Valley, every city except the already established Palm Springs experienced at least 17 percent growth in the last decade. Once known as a playground for the rich and retired, a younger, middle-class population began to move in when housing was inexpensive and have stayed despite high home foreclosure and unemployment rates. Beyond tourism and service sectors across the district, the resort region also relies on health care, shopping and gambling industries. Wind turbine generators, which have taken advantage of particularly breezy areas in the mountains for decades, are becoming more common.

Migrant farm laborers, the majority of whom are Hispanic, provide much of the agricultural workforce in the Temecula wine country and the Coachella and San Jacinto valleys, which produce citrus, dates, alfalfa and grapes. Immigration enforcement in the district's cities and farm worker conditions in rural areas remain divisive public policy issues.

Fiscally conservative and socially liberal, Palm Springs has sizable Jewish and Hispanic communities and a growing gay population — the city elected its first gay mayor in 2003. Palm Springs also ranks among the nation's most successful gay and lesbian tourism destinations.

Although Republicans have a slight registration edge in the 45th, areas in Rancho Mirage and Palm Springs vote Democratic. The district gave Democrat Barack Obama 52 percent of its 2008 presidential vote and GOP candidate Meg Whitman 50 percent in the 2010 gubernatorial race.

Major Industry
Service, tourism, agriculture

Cities
Moreno Valley (pt.), 193,326; Murrieta (pt.), 89,097; Hemet (pt.), 78,640; Indio, 76,036; Cathedral City, 51,200; Palm Desert, 48,445

Notable
The Palm Springs Aerial Tramway boasts the world's largest rotating tramcars.

Rep. Dana Rohrabacher (R)

Capitol Office
225-2415
rohrabacher.house.gov
2300 Rayburn Bldg. 20515-0546; fax 225-0145

Committees
Foreign Affairs
   (Oversight & Investigations - Chairman)
Science, Space & Technology

Residence
Costa Mesa

Born
June 21, 1947; Coronado, Calif.

Religion
Christian

Family
Wife, Rhonda Rohrabacher; three children

Education
Los Angeles Harbor College, attended 1965-67;
California State U., Long Beach, B.A. 1969 (history);
U. of Southern California, M.A. 1971 (American studies)

Career
White House speechwriter; newspaper reporter

Political Highlights
No previous office

ELECTION RESULTS

2010 GENERAL

Dana Rohrabacher (R)	139,822	62.2%
Ken Arnold (D)	84,940	37.8%

2010 PRIMARY

Dana Rohrabacher (R)	unopposed

2008 GENERAL

Dana Rohrabacher (R)	149,818	52.5%
Debbie Cook (D)	122,891	43.1%
Tom Lash (GREEN)	8,257	2.9%
Ernst P. Gasteiger (LIBERT)	4,311	1.5%

Previous Winning Percentages
2006 (60%); 2004 (62%); 2002 (62%); 2000 (62%);
1998 (59%); 1996 (61%); 1994 (69%); 1992 (55%);
1990 (59%); 1988 (64%)

Elected 1988; 12th term

An iconoclastic conservative with a libertarian lean, Rohrabacher's governing philosophy is embodied in a motto that hangs on his wall and decorates coffee cups: "Fighting for Freedom . . . and Having Fun."

Rohrabacher (ROAR-ah-BAH-ker) is well practiced in the art of the sound bite, and he can be equally withering to Democrats and Republicans.

Just days after President Obama took office, he said at a Republican retreat: "The president is a naïve man. He is naïve about what to expect from enemies of the United States overseas and about what to expect from the left wing of his party."

In 2008, he joined Democrats in criticizing the George W. Bush administration for being unwilling to seek congressional approval for an agreement on Iraq. "I am a Republican, and at times I am embarrassed by the lack of cooperation that this president and his appointees have had with the legislative branch," he said.

A senior member of the Foreign Affairs Committee — he chairs the Oversight and Investigations Subcommittee — he was one of seven GOP cosponsors of a bill to require the Pentagon to submit a report to Congress outlining the U.S. exit strategy from Afghanistan. He also defended Obama's months-long deliberation on a new strategy for the war in Afghanistan, a country central to Rohrabacher's not-your-typical-politician image: In 1988, after he was first elected to Congress but before he took his seat, he traveled with a mujahideen unit fighting the Soviet army.

Rohrabacher has long been a critic of China's Communist regime. He was a vigorous opponent of the law, enacted in 2000, permanently permitting Chinese goods to enter the United States under the same low tariffs afforded most countries. And he teamed with liberal Democrat Maxine Waters of California in cosponsoring a 2007 resolution calling for a boycott of the 2008 Olympic Games in Beijing.

In February 2009, a Beijing-based company lost a contract to provide scanning units to the Port of Los Angeles to screen incoming containers for dangerous cargo. Officials said the scanners didn't meet performance standards, and Rohrabacher said he didn't want that company or any other Chinese business to get another shot at the contract. That same year, he was so put off by the Taiwanese government's efforts at conciliation with the mainland that he resigned as a co-chairman of the Congressional Taiwan Caucus.

Rohrabacher is not limited to the legislative sphere in his quest for windmills to tilt at. He took up the cause of three Navy SEALs charged with abusing an al Qaeda suspect. "These Navy SEALs were apprehending a terrorist murderer, and they are being accused of roughing him up? Give me a break. These men should be given medals, not prosecuted. These men are heroes," Rohrabacher said. All three were eventually acquitted.

That was reminiscent of another legal case on which Rohrabacher took a public stand: a pair of Border Patrol agents sentenced to prison in October 2006 for the non-fatal shooting of a drug smuggler attempting to flee across the Mexican border from Texas. The trial showed the agents hid evidence of the shooting, and the suspect was given immunity from prosecution for his testimony against them. The case swiftly became a cause for conservatives. Rohrabacher denounced Bush for refusing to intervene and invited the wife of one of the imprisoned agents to be his guest at the president's 2007 State of the Union address. Just before leaving office, Bush commuted the agents' sentences.

Rohrabacher, who has called for aggressive steps to combat illegal immigration, called Bush "the lamest of lame ducks" for supporting a Senate immigration measure in 2007 that would have created a path to citizenship for millions of illegal immigrants already in the country.

A generally reliable Republican vote, Rohrabacher has split with his party on some high-profile issues. In 2005, he was one of 15 Republicans voting to protect states that chose to permit medical use of marijuana. He voted in 2006 to override Bush's veto of a bill expanding federal funding of embryonic stem cell research, which uses discarded embryos created for in vitro fertilization. And in February 2011 he joined with 26 other Republicans in opposing a three-month extension of the Patriot Act that expanded the FBI's authority on anti-terrorism investigations.

Science fascinates Rohrabacher. As entrepreneurs began building private aircraft capable of reaching altitudes previously seen only by government spacecraft, he decided to help. (Boeing Co.'s space division is one of the 46th District's largest employers.) As chairman of the Science and Technology Subcommittee on Space and Aeronautics from 1997 to 2005, he introduced several bills intended to foster private space flight, including one to offer a prize of up to $100 million for the first private spacecraft to make three orbits of the Earth. That one went nowhere, but he did push through a law supporting the development of commercial space projects and allowing the Federal Aviation Administration to regulate private spacecraft.

Rohrabacher represents Huntington Beach and is an avid surfer. Among his friends are writers, artists and musicians, including heavy metal vocalist Sammy Hagar and folk singer Joan Baez. During his younger days, he was a hard-drinking, banjo-playing wanderer who worked as a house painter. He says actor John Wayne showed him how to drink tequila — in a small glass with one ice cube and a squeeze of lime. The father of young triplets says, though, that he drinks less tequila than he used to.

He worked as a reporter for City News Service and an editorial writer for the Orange County Register. He served as assistant press secretary for Ronald Reagan's 1976 and 1980 presidential campaigns, then became a White House speech writer for Reagan.

In his first bid for elective office, in 1988, Rohrabacher ran for the House seat being vacated by GOP Rep. Dan Lungren. He won despite primary competitors who had name recognition and Lungren's support. He won re-election with no less than 54 percent of the vote until 2008, when he faced a tough challenge from Huntington Beach Mayor Debbie Cook, a Democrat, and was held to 53 percent. He was back up to 62 percent in 2010.

Key Votes

2010

Overhaul the nation's health insurance system	NO
Allow for repeal of "don't ask, don't tell"	NO
Overhaul financial services industry regulation	NO
Limit use of new Afghanistan War funds to troop withdrawal activities	YES
Change oversight of offshore drilling and lift oil spill liability cap	NO
Provide a path to legal status for some children of illegal immigrants	NO
Extend Bush-era income tax cuts for two years	YES

2009

Expand the Children's Health Insurance Program	NO
Provide $787 billion in tax cuts and spending increases to stimulate the economy	NO
Allow bankruptcy judges to modify certain primary-residence mortgages	NO
Create a cap-and-trade system to limit greenhouse gas emissions	NO
Provide $2 billion for the "cash for clunkers" program	NO
Establish the government as the sole provider of student loans	NO
Restrict federally funded insurance coverage for abortions in health care overhaul	YES

CQ Vote Studies

	PARTY UNITY		PRESIDENTIAL SUPPORT	
	SUPPORT	OPPOSE	SUPPORT	OPPOSE
2010	97%	3%	24%	76%
2009	91%	9%	23%	77%
2008	95%	5%	74%	26%
2007	95%	5%	83%	17%
2006	90%	10%	90%	10%

Interest Groups

	AFL-CIO	ADA	CCUS	ACU
2010	7%	5%	88%	96%
2009	10%	5%	73%	100%
2008	14%	10%	82%	96%
2007	13%	5%	75%	96%
2006	7%	15%	93%	88%

California 46

Coastal Los Angeles and Orange counties — Huntington Beach, Costa Mesa

The 46th runs along the coast south of Los Angeles with an eclectic mix of residents — including senior citizens, surfers and aerospace workers — who live in several different areas. The mountainous peninsula in the district's northwest is home to ultra-wealthy areas such as Rancho Palos Verdes. In the center is a more blue-collar community around Long Beach Harbor, home to one of the nation's largest port complexes. To the southeast, the district takes in Orange County communities such as Huntington Beach and Costa Mesa.

The housing construction sector had benefited from a residential real estate boom in Orange County but home values remain volatile, especially along the coast. Aerospace and technology once provided tens of thousands of jobs in the district, but cuts at Boeing's Huntington Beach campus and elsewhere in Southern California have hurt the local economy. Costa Mesa hosts pharmaceutical firms, and manufacturing remains in a diminished role. High-skilled aircraft assemblage and technology jobs had replaced textile factory positions here.

Following a statewide trend, Hispanic and Asian populations in the 46th have grown markedly — white residents now make up only 56 percent of the population.

Some areas in the district's interior, which includes most of Westminster — home to a large Vietnamese population and shared with the 40th District — tend to be less affluent than coastal cities.

The once comfortably conservative district backed GOP gubernatorial candidate Meg Whitman with 56 percent of its vote in 2010, but John McCain won here with less than 50 percent in the 2008 presidential race.

Major Industry
Aerospace, technology, manufacturing

Military Bases
Naval Weapons Station Seal Beach, 60 military, 344 civilian (2010)

Cities
Huntington Beach, 189,992; Costa Mesa, 109,960; Long Beach (pt.), 87,116; Westminster (pt.), 62,190; Fountain Valley, 55,313

Notable
Huntington Beach is home to the International Surfing Museum; the 46th includes two channel islands: Santa Catalina and San Clemente.

Rep. Loretta Sanchez (D)

Capitol Office
225-2965
lorettasanchez.house.gov
1114 Longworth Bldg. 20515-0547; fax 225-5859

Committees
Armed Services
Homeland Security
Joint Economic

Residence
Garden Grove

Born
Jan. 7, 1960; Lynwood, Calif.

Religion
Roman Catholic

Family
Engaged to Jack Einwechter

Education
Chapman College, B.S. 1982 (economics); American U., M.B.A. 1984 (finance)

Career
Financial adviser; strategic management associate

Political Highlights
Candidate for Anaheim City Council, 1994

ELECTION RESULTS

2010 GENERAL

Loretta Sanchez (D)	50,832	53.0%
Van Tran (R)	37,679	39.3%
Cecilia "Ceci" Iglesias (I)	7,443	7.8%

2010 PRIMARY

Loretta Sanchez (D)	unopposed

2008 GENERAL

Loretta Sanchez (D)	85,878	69.5%
Rosemarie "Rosie" Avila (R)	31,432	25.4%
Robert Lauten (AMI)	6,274	5.1%

2008 PRIMARY

Loretta Sanchez (D)	unopposed

Previous Winning Percentages
2006 (62%); 2004 (60%); 2002 (61%); 2000 (60%); 1998 (56%); 1996 (47%)

Elected 1996; 8th term

Sanchez is an influential figure on such high-profile issues as national security and immigration and a strong partisan voice on matters affecting women, Hispanics and organized labor. Her ascent over the past decade and a half was buoyed by her close relationship with Minority Leader Nancy Pelosi of California and her fundraising abilities, but she lost her bid to be the top Democrat on the Armed Services Committee in the new Congress.

Sanchez's background is in investment banking, but she has carved out a national security niche in Congress. Pelosi, one of the few national politicians to back her long-shot bid in 1996, granted Sanchez the Democrats' No. 2 position on the Homeland Security Committee when it was created in 2003. She served as chairwoman of the Armed Services Subcommittee on Terrorism, Unconventional Threats, and Capabilities in the 111th Congress (2009-10), but lost to Washington Democrat Adam Smith in a contest for the ranking minority spot on the full committee in the 112th Congress (2011-12). She is the top Democrat on the Strategic Forces Subcommittee.

On Homeland Security, she has helped chart the party's position on immigration, a three-pronged approach addressing border security, the demand for temporary workers and illegal immigrants already in the country. But it is her personality — gregarious, candid and opinionated — and her presence on the political talk show circuit that have most boosted her profile.

The 111th Congress was an active one for Sanchez. The House passed her bill to clarify existing stalking statutes and increase penalties for offenders. She also wrote legislation that would create and define guidelines for U.S. agents and any other Department of Homeland Security official authorized to search electronic devices during border searches. Neither bill became law, but the department changed its electronics search-and-seizure policies based on the measure. She also ensured language was included in the fiscal 2011 defense authorization bill that would guarantee military leaders play an active role in prosecuting and preventing sexual attacks. The provisions also would ensure that alleged victims have access to legal and counseling services.

The daughter of Mexican immigrants, Sanchez considers herself a spokesperson for women and America's growing population of Latinos. She and her sister, Democratic Rep. Linda T. Sánchez of California, are the first set of sisters elected to Congress, and they published a book in 2008 titled "Dream in Color: How the Sánchez Sisters Are Making History in Congress."

The sisters had a public split from Washington's Hispanic establishment in early 2007, owing to a feud with Congressional Hispanic Caucus Chairman Joe Baca, another California Democrat. Sanchez and her sister resigned their memberships in the caucus, charging that Baca had demeaned women, abused the group's political action committee and held improper elections. Baca denied the allegations, but the episode bitterly divided Hispanic Democrats just as they were about to assert greater power in the 110th Congress (2007-08). In early 2009, Linda Sánchez rejoined the caucus after Nydia M. Velázquez of New York became chairwoman, succeeding Baca. Loretta Sanchez did not follow suit, however.

The sisters have appeared on talk shows to discuss their efforts on behalf of women and Hispanics. Loretta was an early backer of New York Sen. Hillary Rodham Clinton for the Democratic presidential nomination, while her sister backed Barack Obama. "Our mother brought us up to be independent people," Loretta Sanchez said during a February 2008 appearance on NBC's "Today" show.

Sanchez is known for standing her ground, even when her behavior is viewed as unconventional. In 2000, she embarrassed some Democrats on the eve of their national convention in Los Angeles by at first refusing to cancel a fundraiser at the Playboy mansion, relenting only at the last minute. Her annual Christmas cards usually generate a buzz; one version featured her lounging in her bed with her pet cat.

Sanchez is a reliable vote for the House Democratic leadership, voting with a majority of her party on more than 90 percent of votes in which most Democrats oppose most Republicans. She is a member of the Blue Dog Coalition, a group of fiscally conservative Democrats, and backs pay-as-you-go budget rules that require offsets for new tax cuts or increased mandatory spending.

Her Orange County-based district is home to one of the largest Vietnamese communities in the nation, and Sanchez has been a vocal advocate of human rights in Vietnam. But she caused a bit of stir in September 2010 when she said in a Spanish-language interview that "the Vietnamese" were trying to take her seat. Her opponent, Republican state Assemblyman Van Tran, called her remarks offensive.

Sanchez, the second of seven children, said she grew up a "shy, quiet girl" who did not speak English. Her parents both worked at a manufacturing plant, where her father was a machinist and her mother was a secretary.

Sanchez credits government with her success. "I am a Head Start child, a public school kid, a Pell grant recipient," she said. She opposed the GOP's unsuccessful effort to restructure Head Start, an early-childhood development program for low-income preschoolers, in the 108th Congress (2003-04), invoking her experience growing up poor and challenged by a speech impediment.

She worked her way through college and earned a master's degree in business administration. Feeling isolated as a Hispanic woman in the investment world, she made her first foray into politics in 1994, losing a race for an Anaheim City Council seat. In 1996, she took on conservative GOP Rep. Robert K. Dornan. After winning a four-way primary with 35 percent of the vote, she drew attention from liberal groups. A backlash against a ballot initiative to end state affirmative action programs helped Sanchez score a 984-vote upset.

Dornan claimed he lost to illegal voting by non-citizens, but a House task force said it didn't find enough such instances to prove they altered the outcome. In a 1998 rematch, Sanchez defeated Dornan by 17 percentage points. Her subsequent re-elections were by larger margins until 2010, when she defeated Tran by 14 percentage points.

Key Votes

2010
Overhaul the nation's health insurance system	YES
Allow for repeal of "don't ask, don't tell"	YES
Overhaul financial services industry regulation	YES
Limit use of new Afghanistan War funds to troop withdrawal activities	YES
Change oversight of offshore drilling and lift oil spill liability cap	YES
Provide a path to legal status for some children of illegal immigrants	YES
Extend Bush-era income tax cuts for two years	NO

2009
Expand the Children's Health Insurance Program	YES
Provide $787 billion in tax cuts and spending increases to stimulate the economy	YES
Allow bankruptcy judges to modify certain primary-residence mortgages	YES
Create a cap-and-trade system to limit greenhouse gas emissions	YES
Provide $2 billion for the "cash for clunkers" program	YES
Establish the government as the sole provider of student loans	YES
Restrict federally funded insurance coverage for abortions in health care overhaul	NO

CQ Vote Studies

	PARTY UNITY		PRESIDENTIAL SUPPORT	
	Support	Oppose	Support	Oppose
2010	99%	1%	86%	14%
2009	97%	3%	94%	6%
2008	96%	4%	9%	91%
2007	99%	1%	5%	95%
2006	95%	5%	26%	74%

Interest Groups

	AFL-CIO	ADA	CCUS	ACU
2010	100%	95%	0%	0%
2009	100%	90%	36%	0%
2008	93%	80%	41%	8%
2007	100%	100%	60%	0%
2006	93%	100%	47%	12%

California 47

Orange County — most of Santa Ana, Anaheim and Garden Grove

An inland chunk of Orange County full of older suburban homes and younger families, the Hispanic-majority 47th is unlike its mostly affluent, Republican neighbors in the county. Located roughly 30 miles southeast of Los Angeles, it takes in parts of four cities: Santa Ana, Anaheim, Garden Grove and Fullerton. A growing number of Hispanics, Vietnamese and other ethnic minorities are changing the demographics here and creating a strong Democratic base.

More than 40 percent of the district's population is in Santa Ana (the Orange County seat), where the blue-collar workforce is more vulnerable to unemployment than surrounding areas. Aerospace subcontractors and small businesses are scattered throughout the district, but apart from Disneyland in Anaheim, no single employer drives the area's economy. The 47th's part of Anaheim is home to baseball's Angels and hockey's Ducks, and local officials have approved plans that would lure basketball's Sacramento Kings to the city. Biomedical and information technology jobs broaden the economic base in the 47th.

Three-fourths of Garden Grove's culturally diverse residents live in the 47th. Many years of refugees arriving from Southeast Asia caused concerns that increased demand for social services would lead to higher taxes. Santa Ana is one of only a few Orange County cities that trends Democratic, and the 47th also has some of Anaheim's most Democratic areas. The small part of Fullerton in the district's northern end is heavily Hispanic, although the city overall historically leans Republican. The Asian community, some of which is heavily Christian, also has a conservative side. Democrat Barack Obama won here easily in 2008, taking 60 percent of the district's presidential vote.

Major Industry
Small business, service, defense, tourism

Cities
Santa Ana (pt.), 283,250; Anaheim (pt.), 190,784; Garden Grove (pt.), 129,231; Fullerton (pt.), 17,481

Notable
The 10,000-member Crystal Cathedral Ministries mega-church is located in Garden Grove.

Rep. John Campbell (R)

Capitol Office
225-5611
www.house.gov/campbell
1507 Longworth Bldg. 20515; fax 225-9177

Committees
Budget
Financial Services
Joint Economic

Residence
Irvine

Born
July 19, 1955; Los Angeles, Calif.

Religion
Presbyterian

Family
Wife, Catherine Campbell; two children

Education
U. of California, Los Angeles, B.A. 1976 (economics); U. of Southern California, M.S. 1977 (business taxation)

Career
Car dealership president; accountant

Political Highlights
Calif. Assembly, 2000-04; Calif. Senate, 2004-05

ELECTION RESULTS

2010 GENERAL

John Campbell (R)	145,481	59.9%
Beth Krom (D)	88,465	36.4%
Mike Binkley (LIBERT)	8,773	3.6%

2010 PRIMARY

John Campbell (R)	unopposed

2008 GENERAL

John Campbell (R)	171,658	55.6%
Steve Young (D)	125,537	40.7%
Don Patterson (LIBERT)	11,507	3.7%

Previous Winning Percentages
2006 (60%); 2005 Special Election (44%)

Elected 2005; 3rd full term

For Campbell, a successful businessman and certified public accountant before coming to Congress, it's all about the numbers. He has taken as his mission a reduction in federal spending, with a particular emphasis on earmarks, funds set aside by lawmakers for home-state projects.

For a numbers guy, Campbell has the right assignments: the Financial Services, Budget and Joint Economic committees. Those spots give him the opportunity to dig deeply into fiscal and tax policy. "I try and fiddle around with other things, but I always wind up back with numbers," he said.

Campbell claimed a victory when House Republicans endorsed a one-year moratorium on earmarks in March 2010, one-upping the Democrats, who had earlier announced a moratorium on earmarks aimed at for-profit organizations. When they regained the majority, they barred earmarks for fiscal 2011 and 2012. For Campbell, the move was a long time coming.

In the Budget Committee, he tried and failed to add a moratorium to the House's fiscal 2009 spending plan. In 2007, he backed a 10-step earmark overhaul proposal advanced by Citizens Against Government Waste, a budget watchdog group, that included public disclosure of requests and disallowing earmarks that have not been the subject of a congressional hearing.

Campbell wants to drastically alter the entire process by abolishing the Appropriations committees and handing their tasks to the relevant authorizers.

Campbell, who writes his own Green Eyeshade blog in which he critiques federal spending, also targets federal largesse beyond earmarks. At a January 2011 hearing, he pointed to the double counting of Medicare cuts in the health care overhaul to show that it would not provide the budget savings Democrats claim. Before he came to Congress he was a supporter of the tax cuts enacted in 2001 and 2003, during President George W. Bush's first term. But he opposed legislation enacted in late 2010 that extended those rates for two years, saying the temporary extension created uncertainty and the bill included too much new spending.

Campbell is a member of the Republican Study Committee, a group of the most conservative House Republicans. In the 110th Congress (2007-08) he headed the group's budget and spending task force, making him a high-profile critic of the Democratic majority's spending policies, and he was regarded as a front-runner for the RSC chairmanship in fall 2008.

But then he backed the Bush administration's $700 billion proposal to shore up the financial services industry. Fellow RSC members opposed the measure as unwelcome and unworkable, and after voting in favor of the two bills — the second of which became law — he abandoned his candidacy. But Campbell, whose district had been hit hard by subprime mortgage problems, had no regrets. "During the course of the last 10 days, our financial trading markets have basically become dysfunctional," he told the Register in September 2008.

Campbell is a reliable Republican vote — his annual party unity score (the percentage of votes in which he sided with a majority of the GOP against a majority of Democrats) has never fallen below 95. His guiding philosophy is reflected in the gift he likes to give to some of his office help: " 'Atlas Shrugged' is the book I give to our interns after they spend a summer here, working for free. I consider it to be the authoritative work on the power of the individual," he said.

In line with other Southern California conservatives, he backs tougher enforcement of immigration laws and opposes a path to citizenship for illegal immigrants already in the country. He drew the wrath of left-wing commentators who accused him of feeding paranoia about President Obama's citizenship by cosponsoring a measure to require future presidential candidates to include proof of citizenship when filing papers to run.

Campbell spent almost 25 years in the automobile industry as a corporate officer and owner of franchises that sold Nissan, Mazda, Ford, Saturn, Porsche and Saab models. His Capitol Hill office is accented with photographs of cars and a model of a 1957 Corvette convertible, representing a boyhood passion of his that turned into a career.

He grew up in the Hancock Park area of Los Angeles, in a house built in 1922 by his maternal grandfather. An Irvine resident for more than 30 years and a fourth-generation Californian, Campbell lives in a house he designed and built with his wife and said he will "never, ever move to Washington. I'm a Californian through and through."

Campbell's great-grandfather on his father's side, Alexander, was elected to the California Assembly in 1860 on the same GOP ticket as Abraham Lincoln. Campbell is a member of the Sons of Union Veterans and has occasionally participated in Civil War re-enactments. The congressman's father, also named Alexander, ran unsuccessfully for the state Senate when John Campbell was 11. Campbell's father was a classic-car collector and dealership investor, spurring Campbell's own interest in cars.

In 1978, after receiving an economics degree from UCLA and a graduate degree in business taxation from the University of Southern California, Campbell moved to Orange County to be a corporate comptroller for car dealerships. He became a GOP volunteer and campaign donor, as well as a second tenor for the Irvine Presbyterian Church.

In 2000, Campbell was recruited to run for the Assembly and won. When term limits forced out the local GOP state senator in 2004, Campbell moved up. But he didn't stay in Sacramento long. Although he harbored aspirations for higher state office, the 48th District seat opened up in 2005 when Republican Rep. Christopher Cox left to become chairman of the Securities and Exchange Commission. In the 10-candidate open special primary to fill Cox's seat, Campbell got 45 percent of the vote. He prevailed in the special general election, taking 44 percent in a three-way race that included the independent candidacy of the founder of the anti-immigration Minuteman Project. He's won with relative ease since.

In January 2011, the House Ethics Committee announced that it would not pursue allegations that Campbell violated House rules in connection with his fundraising efforts in advance of a vote on the financial regulatory overhaul vote. He opposed the bill, which became law, and held two fundraisers with stakeholders in advance of the vote.

Key Votes

2010

Overhaul the nation's health insurance system	NO
Allow for repeal of "don't ask, don't tell"	NO
Overhaul financial services industry regulation	NO
Limit use of new Afghanistan War funds to troop withdrawal activities	YES
Change oversight of offshore drilling and lift oil spill liability cap	?
Provide a path to legal status for some children of illegal immigrants	NO
Extend Bush-era income tax cuts for two years	NO

2009

Expand the Children's Health Insurance Program	-
Provide $787 billion in tax cuts and spending increases to stimulate the economy	-
Allow bankruptcy judges to modify certain primary-residence mortgages	NO
Create a cap-and-trade system to limit greenhouse gas emissions	NO
Provide $2 billion for the "cash for clunkers" program	YES
Establish the government as the sole provider of student loans	NO
Restrict federally funded insurance coverage for abortions in health care overhaul	YES

CQ Vote Studies

	PARTY UNITY		PRESIDENTIAL SUPPORT	
	SUPPORT	OPPOSE	SUPPORT	OPPOSE
2010	95%	5%	18%	82%
2009	97%	3%	14%	86%
2008	97%	3%	89%	11%
2007	97%	3%	92%	8%
2006	95%	5%	90%	10%

Interest Groups

	AFL-CIO	ADA	CCUS	ACU
2010	0%	20%	83%	95%
2009	15%	10%	86%	92%
2008	0%	5%	76%	86%
2007	4%	10%	70%	92%
2005	0%	0%	50%	100%

California 48

Southern Orange County — Irvine, Newport Beach

The 48th covers the Orange County coast from Newport Beach south through Laguna Beach to Dana Point, and it takes in a chunk of the county inland from the coast through Irvine to the foothills of the Santa Ana mountains. The district is distinguished by its large white-collar labor force and its historically high median household income. Nearly 60 percent of district residents are white.

Newport Beach is known for its beautiful sandy beaches, luxurious housing and solid Republicanism. Picturesque Laguna Beach attracts tourists and scuba divers. Inland is Laguna Niguel, Laguna Hills and Laguna Woods, home to a significant number of senior citizens.

The engineering and biomedical research programs at the University of California, Irvine, have attracted a large number of high-tech and biotech firms to the area, and the university is the district's largest employer. The national housing market crisis affected the region's foreclosure rates, home prices and unemployment — a major mortgage lender based in Irvine collapsed, taking thousands of local jobs with it.

Smog, crime and other problems endemic to Los Angeles generally do not affect these areas. Irvine consistently rates as the nation's safest city with more than 100,000 people, based on the FBI's crime reporting statistics. But the sheer number of people who commute into the district from the north and east makes transportation among the toughest problems here, as traffic backs up and increases the threat of pollution. Toll roads in the area have helped, and more funding for road improvements aims to ease congestion. Rising gas prices have led to increased use of the expanding regional mass transit rail and bus system.

While registered Republicans outnumber Democrats by 15 percentage points, and GOP candidate Meg Whitman received her highest vote total statewide here in the 2010 gubernatorial election, some pockets of Democratic strength can be found in the district's inland sections and in the more liberal-leaning community surrounding the university.

Major Industry
Technology, research, tourism

Cities
Irvine, 212,375; Newport Beach (pt.), 82,169; Lake Forest, 77,264

Notable
The Ayn Rand Institute is located in Irvine.

Rep. Darrell Issa (R)

Capitol Office
225-3906
issa.house.gov
2347 Rayburn Bldg. 20515-0549; fax 225-3303

Committees
Judiciary
Oversight & Government Reform - Chairman

Residence
Vista

Born
Nov. 1, 1953; Cleveland, Ohio

Religion
Antioch Orthodox Christian Church

Family
Wife, Kathy Issa; one child

Education
Kent State U., A.A. 1976 (general studies); Siena
Heights College, B.A. 1976 (business administration
and management)

Military
Army, 1970-72; Army, 1976-80; Army Reserve,
1980-88

Career
Car alarm company owner; electronics manufacturing company executive

Political Highlights
Sought Republican nomination for U.S. Senate, 1998

ELECTION RESULTS

2010 GENERAL
Darrell Issa (R)	119,088	62.8%
Howard Katz (D)	59,714	31.5%
Dion Clark (AMI)	6,585	3.5%
Mike Paster (LIBERT)	4,290	2.3%

2010 PRIMARY
Darrell Issa (R)	unopposed

2008 GENERAL
Darrell Issa (R)	140,300	58.3%
Robert Hamilton (D)	90,138	37.4%
Lars Grossmith (LIBERT)	10,232	4.2%

Previous Winning Percentages
2006 (63%); 2004 (63%); 2002 (77%); 2000 (61%)

Elected 2000; 6th term

In Washington, Issa has prospered as "Obama's annoyer-in-chief" — as The New York Times dubbed him — even with the limited tools available to the top Republican when Democrats dominated the Oversight and Government Reform Committee. He is almost certain to be even more annoying to Obama as chairman of the panel in the 112th Congress.

Democrats worry that Issa (EYE-sah), armed with subpoena power, will launch high-profile investigations, much as former GOP Chairman Dan Burton of Indiana and Democratic Chairman Henry A. Waxman of California did when they ran the panel.

The annoyance might come in ways Democrats are not expecting, though. From the minority, he hounded the White House to provide more information about reports that officials sought to persuade Pennsylvania Democratic Rep. Joe Sestak to drop out of the Senate primary against incumbent Arlen Specter in return for a government job. As chairman, Issa said he won't pursue the matter. And he backed away quickly from remarks in which he called the administration corrupt.

Issa says he can use the Oversight panel to ferret out excessive government spending. He believes he can find $200 billion in waste, he said on CBS' "Face the Nation" in early 2011. Breaches of national security by WikiLeaks, alleged corruption in programs in Afghanistan and the genesis of the mortgage and housing crisis are also on the agenda. The first subpoena his committee issued in the 112th Congress (2011-12) sought documents related to Countrywide Financial's VIP loan program and whether members of Congress and staff members received special deals on mortgages and rental agreements.

Issa worked hard to win the oversight slot, leapfrogging more-senior members by throwing himself into his work and mastering mundane subjects such as government procurement; he won the favor of the committee's former top Republican, Thomas M. Davis III of Virginia, who retired at the end of 2008. Issa schmoozed GOP leaders and got a boost when another aspirant, Connecticut's Christopher Shays, lost his re-election bid.

With the job in hand, Issa set out to make the committee staff his own, replacing much of the panel's Republican staff with seasoned investigators. Issa said he stood "ready to proactively probe any critical failures of government neglected by the committee majority."

Issa has demonstrated his ability to frustrate Democrats. At a May 2008 hearing, tempers flared when he demanded that Waxman give panel Republicans equal time to question EPA Administrator Stephen L. Johnson about new ozone standards. Waxman threatened to throw Issa from the committee room; Issa said Waxman was "arrogant and unprofessional."

During the final year of the George W. Bush administration, as Waxman pressed for investigations of administration interference in the regulatory process, Issa charged Waxman with unfairness. When Waxman investigated whether Transportation Department officials lobbied EPA civil servants to decide against allowing California to enforce clean air rules more stringent than the federal government's, Issa pressed him to also determine whether EPA staff lobbied agency decision-makers to side with California.

But Issa didn't shy away from criticizing the Bush administration. He voted twice against giving the administration $700 billion to shore up the financial services sector; after Congress passed the bill, and again at the start of the 111th Congress (2009-10), he introduced legislation to create an independent panel to study how to address the financial crisis.

Issa has championed less partisan probes, such as investigating how the Interior Department can increase federal revenue via the sale of public lands and a review of retirement policies and business practices in the Postal Service.

Issa also sits on the Judiciary Committee, where during the 110th Congress (2007-08) he was a key player in an ill-fated bid to revamp the country's patent approval process to protect high-tech companies from infringement litigation. The House passed the bill, but the Senate didn't take it up.

The Lebanese-American Issa has spent much time condemning Middle East terrorists, but he also wants the United States to reach out to friendly Arab nations. His approach draws condemnations from pro-Israel advocates. At the same time, Arab commentators complain about his pro-Israel votes.

A major player in California politics, Issa bankrolled the recall effort in 2003 that ousted Democratic Gov. Gray Davis and led to the election of Republican Arnold Schwarzenegger in his place. Although Issa wanted to replace Davis, GOP House colleagues persuaded him to step aside for Schwarzenegger.

In 2007, Issa helped fund an effort to convince Californians to award their electoral votes in presidential elections by congressional district, a potential boon to GOP candidates. No Republican has won the state since George Bush in 1988. The initiative died when organizers failed to gather enough signatures.

Issa was born in Cleveland, where his father was a salesman and an X-ray technician. He quit high school at 17 and joined the Army. After Issa had served two years, the Army paid for his college education with the understanding that he would return to active duty upon graduation.

In 1972, he and his older brother, William, were arrested for allegedly stealing a Maserati from a car dealership. The charges were dropped. In 1980, the two were charged with faking the theft of Issa's Mercedes-Benz; again, the charges were dropped. In both cases, Issa blamed his brother.

After fulfilling his Army obligation, Issa returned to Cleveland and used $7,000 in savings to purchase assets from a struggling electronics business. He and his wife turned those into a highly profitable operation that gained renown as the maker of the popular Viper automobile anti-theft device. In 1985, they moved the business to Vista. In 1999 and 2000, Issa was chairman of the board of the Consumer Electronics Association. He sold the business at the end of 2000.

In 1998, Issa spent $11 million on a failed bid for the GOP Senate nomination. He hit the campaign trail again in 2000, when Republican Ron Packard announced his retirement from the 48th District, a reliably Republican district. Issa weathered a nine-candidate primary, sinking $2 million into the race, then won the general election with 61 percent of the vote. His re-elections have been easy in what is now the 49th District.

Key Votes

2010

Overhaul the nation's health insurance system	NO
Allow for repeal of "don't ask, don't tell"	NO
Overhaul financial services industry regulation	NO
Limit use of new Afghanistan War funds to troop withdrawal activities	NO
Change oversight of offshore drilling and lift oil spill liability cap	NO
Provide a path to legal status for some children of illegal immigrants	NO
Extend Bush-era income tax cuts for two years	YES

2009

Expand the Children's Health Insurance Program	NO
Provide $787 billion in tax cuts and spending increases to stimulate the economy	NO
Allow bankruptcy judges to modify certain primary-residence mortgages	NO
Create a cap-and-trade system to limit greenhouse gas emissions	NO
Provide $2 billion for the "cash for clunkers" program	YES
Establish the government as the sole provider of student loans	NO
Restrict federally funded insurance coverage for abortions in health care overhaul	YES

CQ Vote Studies

	PARTY UNITY		PRESIDENTIAL SUPPORT	
	SUPPORT	OPPOSE	SUPPORT	OPPOSE
2010	95%	5%	29%	71%
2009	98%	2%	19%	81%
2008	99%	1%	79%	21%
2007	96%	4%	86%	14%
2006	94%	6%	95%	5%

Interest Groups

	AFL-CIO	ADA	CCUS	ACU
2010	0%	0%	88%	100%
2009	14%	5%	73%	100%
2008	7%	10%	94%	100%
2007	8%	20%	74%	88%
2006	21%	5%	100%	80%

California 49

North San Diego County; West Riverside County

Based in northwestern San Diego County and western Riverside County, the heavily residential 49th is home to many bedroom communities, including Vista and Oceanside.

While some residents work in the district, others commute to jobs in San Diego (a sliver of which falls in the 49th) or, to a lesser extent, Orange County. The massive Camp Pendleton Marine Corps Base, which is now powered partially from a large solar energy field on base, sits on the largest undeveloped portion of coast in Southern California, but the district's economy relies less on military contracts than its San Diego or Orange County neighbors. In northeast San Diego County, Rancho Bernardo hosts manufacturing and defense employers, including Hewlett-Packard and Northrop Grumman. Visitors to Oceanside and the beaches along the coast also boost the local economy.

Most residents live in San Diego County, but more than a decade of prodigious growth in Riverside County established tourism and retail bases. Economic downturns, however, have hurt those sectors. Old Town Temecula

still welcomes tourists who visit the area's wineries, and the desert terrain of the Temecula Valley also has become known for balloon rides, skydiving and golf. The agricultural base in Riverside County has begun to contract. The Pechanga Resort and Casino near Temecula employs thousands and lures visitors to the area.

Some areas have large Hispanic populations; less than 50 percent of the district is white. The 49th supports Republicans, and John McCain took 53 percent of its 2008 presidential vote. Perris, with a large retirement community, is one of the few places in which Democrats hold an edge.

Major Industry
Medical devices, services, manufacturing, defense

Military Bases
Camp Pendleton Marine Corps Base, Air Station and Naval Hospital, 46,242 military, 2,872 civilian (2010); Naval Weapons Station Seal Beach, Detachment Fallbrook, 140 military, 530 civilian (2011)

Cities
Oceanside, 167,086; Temecula (pt.), 96,780; Vista, 93,834; Perris, 68,386

Notable
Oceanside's Mission San Luis Rey de Francia, dedicated in 1798, has been restored to its original design.

Rep. Brian P. Bilbray (R)

Capitol Office
225-0508
www.house.gov/bilbray
2410 Rayburn Bldg. 20515-0550; fax 225-2558

Committees
Energy & Commerce

Residence
Carlsbad

Born
Jan. 28, 1951; Coronado, Calif.

Religion
Roman Catholic

Family
Wife, Karen Bilbray; six children (one deceased)

Education
Southwestern College (Calif.), attended 1970-74
(history)

Career
Tax firm owner; lifeguard; lobbyist

Political Highlights
Imperial Beach City Council, 1976-78; mayor of
Imperial Beach, 1978-85; San Diego County Board
of Supervisors, 1985-95; U.S. House, 1995-2001;
defeated for re-election to U.S. House, 2000

ELECTION RESULTS

2010 GENERAL

Brian P. Bilbray (R)	142,247	56.6%
Francine Busby (D)	97,818	39.0%
Lars Grossmith (LIBERT)	5,546	2.2%
Miriam E. Clark (PFP)	5,470	2.2%

2010 PRIMARY

Brian P. Bilbray (R)	unopposed

2008 GENERAL

Brian P. Bilbray (R)	157,502	50.2%
Nick Leibham (D)	141,635	45.2%
Wayne Dunlap (LIBERT)	14,365	4.6%

Previous Winning Percentages
2006 (53%); 2006 Special Election (50%); 1998 (49%);
1996 (53%); 1994 (49%)

Elected 2006; 6th full term
Also served 1995-2001

On Bilbray's most visible issue — illegal immigration — he stands with the most conservative members of the House. But on some topics important to his Southern California district, particularly the environment, he evinces more moderate stripes. A seat on the powerful Energy and Commerce Committee gives him a chance to broaden his legislative portfolio.

"The liberal members of Congress who have had their way for the last two years have just got to learn that the system's designed for the ebb and flow of the political tide," Bilbray said in an interview with NBC's San Diego affiliate in early 2011. "Both parties have to accept that they've got to be talking to each other if they're going to do anything."

Born and raised in the San Diego area, Bilbray attributes his deep interest in immigration to growing up with a backyard "full of illegal immigrants hiding from Border Patrol agents." He also cites his time as a lifeguard as formative on the issue: "I'm probably the only member of Congress to have rescued illegals when they were drowning," he told MSNBC's Ed Schultz.

As chairman of the Immigration Reform Caucus, Bilbray backs tougher border enforcement, but likes to stress that better enforcement of laws barring businesses from hiring illegal immigrants would treat the cause rather than the "symptom" that is illegal border crossings. He is an enthusiastic cosponsor of legislation by North Carolina Democrat Heath Shuler that would expand use of E-Verify, an electronic employee eligibility verification system.

His remarks on immigration have sometimes generated controversy.

He cited the murders of 72 would-be illegal immigrants in northern Mexico in a September 2010 op-ed and laid partial responsibility at the feet of those who support legalization for those already in the country illegally. "When my colleagues talk about providing amnesty (or 'a pathway to citizenship') they become an accessory to these murders," he wrote. "When they support amnesty, introduce bills that provide a pathway to citizenship and, in the most irresponsible of cases, use amnesty to motivate voters, they tell people: 'work with the cartels and come across our border illegally, for we will eventually give you amnesty and citizenship.'"

When the head of Immigration and Customs Enforcement said his agency might not process illegal immigrants handed over by Arizona officials after Arizona enacted a law in 2010 empowering police officers to detain people on suspicion of immigration violations if stopped for another offense, Bilbray signed a letter urging Homeland Security Secretary Janet Napolitano, a former Arizona governor, to condemn the remarks.

Bilbray worked in 2007 to stop a bill backed by the Senate and the George W. Bush administration that would have offered the nation's estimated 12 million illegal immigrants a path to citizenship. As an alternative, he teamed with Shuler to introduce legislation to boost the ranks of Border Patrol agents, provide more technology to secure the borders and establish a program to recruit former military personnel to serve in Customs and Border Protection. The bill had more than 150 cosponsors but never came to a vote in either chamber.

His immigration stance makes Bilbray appear to be a down-the-line conservative, and, indeed, he opposed many of the Bush and Obama administrations' initiatives to shore up the financial sector and stimulate the economy. He voted against both versions of the $700 billion aid package for banks and other institutions, and he called on House leaders to bring the Financial Services Committee back into session in late 2008 to develop plans to rebuild the financial markets. He opposed President Obama's $787 billion stimulus in 2009 and called the 2010 health care overhaul measure "a massive failure of leadership in Washington."

But his politics are moderate on some social issues; he has supported some gun control measures and has generally voted for abortion rights. The same holds true on environmental issues. A staple of his political biography is the story of how, as the young mayor of Imperial Beach, he became so frustrated with the federal response to complaints that the Tijuana River was carrying pollution from Mexico onto U.S. beaches that he climbed aboard a bulldozer and dammed the offending stream.

Bilbray won inclusion of funding in the fiscal 2010 Energy-Water spending bill for a San Diego-based project to research and develop ways to produce gasoline, diesel and jet fuel from algae. Now a member of the Energy and Commerce Committee and its Energy and Power Subcommittee, he champions nuclear energy as a way to both meet future electricity demand and to reduce greenhouse gas emissions. But he opposed the Democrats' measure that would create a cap-and-trade system for such emissions. "I look at this bill . . . and come to the conclusion that the greatest threat to the environment seems to be all the smoke coming out of the backroom deals that appear to have been made to put this package together," he said on the House floor.

Bilbray sides with his party on supporting offshore drilling in many places, but opposes it in California, fearing it would harm the tourism industry.

Bilbray served as a city councilman and mayor from the mid-1970s to the mid-1980s. The attention devoted to the dam-building episode helped him win election in 1984 to the San Diego County Board of Supervisors, where he was serving when he won election to the House in 1994 — in the old 49th District — with less than half the vote. He never bested 53 percent in winning re-election, and finally lost the seat in 2000. He said he spent the next six years doing a lot of "sailing and surfing," and served as co-chairman of the National Board of Advisors for the Federation for American Immigration Reform, a group that advocates limiting immigration and beefing up border security.

In 2006, he returned in a special election to fill the 50th District seat of GOP Rep. Randy "Duke" Cunningham, who was sent to prison after admitting to taking bribes from defense contractors. The new district was more Republican than his old one, but Democrats hoped the taint from the Cunningham scandal would overcome that tilt. It didn't. Bilbray won by 5 percentage points, then defeated the same opponent by 10 points in the November general election. He won again in 2008 with a bit more than 50 percent of the vote, and more handily in 2010, with 57 percent.

Key Votes

2010

Overhaul the nation's health insurance system	NO
Allow for repeal of "don't ask, don't tell"	NO
Overhaul financial services industry regulation	NO
Limit use of new Afghanistan War funds to troop withdrawal activities	NO
Change oversight of offshore drilling and lift oil spill liability cap	NO
Provide a path to legal status for some children of illegal immigrants	?
Extend Bush-era income tax cuts for two years	YES

2009

Expand the Children's Health Insurance Program	NO
Provide $787 billion in tax cuts and spending increases to stimulate the economy	NO
Allow bankruptcy judges to modify certain primary-residence mortgages	NO
Create a cap-and-trade system to limit greenhouse gas emissions	NO
Provide $2 billion for the "cash for clunkers" program	YES
Establish the government as the sole provider of student loans	NO
Restrict federally funded insurance coverage for abortions in health care overhaul	YES

CQ Vote Studies

	PARTY UNITY		PRESIDENTIAL SUPPORT	
	SUPPORT	OPPOSE	SUPPORT	OPPOSE
2010	88%	12%	39%	61%
2009	87%	13%	35%	65%
2008	94%	6%	67%	33%
2007	95%	5%	85%	15%
2006	93%	7%	93%	7%

Interest Groups

	AFL-CIO	ADA	CCUS	ACU
2010	17%	15%	100%	85%
2009	19%	10%	93%	88%
2008	20%	15%	88%	92%
2007	8%	10%	80%	92%
2006	11%	5%	100%	94%

California 50

North San Diego; Escondido; Carlsbad

With its beach communities and upper-class neighborhoods, the San Diego-area 50th District combines affluent suburbs like Carlsbad, coastal areas such as Encinitas, the northern part of San Diego itself, and inland Escondido and San Marcos, which are tucked within the district's northeast curve.

The area's wealth is a testament to one of the state's top technology sectors. With national economic downturns, the technology industry in San Diego has suffered losses, and San Diego County has seen rising unemployment. But the area has weathered the recession better than other regions because of its diversified economy. The growth of technology companies and computer firms, combined with established military and defense contracting, has helped stabilize the area.

Northern San Diego hosts some of the city's renewable-energy firms. Home construction has long been profitable in the north San Diego region but has slowed recently. The mild climate of the coastal area is friendly to commercial production of flowers and fruits.

Unlike San Diego's south side, the 50th is mostly white, although there is a growing Hispanic population and illegal immigration is an issue here. The 50th's conservative corridor runs north and south along Interstate 15, including the Marine Corps base in Miramar (shared with the 52nd). Coastal cities such as Del Mar, Carlsbad and Encinitas, where beach pollution and the environment are issues, add liberals to the district.

In a district where registered Republicans outnumber Democrats by 10 percentage points, Democrat Barack Obama narrowly edged out John McCain in the 2008 presidential election.

Major Industry
Technology, defense, manufacturing, tourism, agriculture

Military Bases
Marine Corps Air Station Miramar, 7,785 military, 664 civilian (2010) (shared with the 52nd)

Cities
San Diego (pt.), 289,098; Escondido (pt.); Carlsbad, 105,328; San Marcos (pt.), 83,734; Encinitas, 59,518

Notable
Carlsbad is home to the Legoland theme park.

Rep. Bob Filner (D)

Capitol Office
225-8045
www.house.gov/filner
2428 Rayburn Bldg. 20515-0551; fax 225-9073

Committees
Transportation & Infrastructure
Veterans' Affairs - Ranking Member

Residence
San Diego

Born
Sept. 4, 1942; Pittsburgh, Pa.

Religion
Jewish

Family
Divorced; two children

Education
Cornell U., B.A. 1963 (chemistry); U. of Delaware,
M.A. 1969 (history); Cornell U., Ph.D. 1973 (history of science)

Career
Congressional aide; professor

Political Highlights
San Diego Unified School District Board of Education, 1979-83 (president, 1982); candidate for San Diego City Council, 1983; San Diego City Council, 1987-92 (deputy mayor, 1990-91)

ELECTION RESULTS

2010 GENERAL

Bob Filner (D)	86,423	60.0%
Nick Popaditch (R)	57,488	39.9%

2010 PRIMARY

Bob Filner (D)	unopposed

2008 GENERAL

Bob Filner (D)	148,281	72.7%
David Lee Joy (R)	49,345	24.2%
Dan "Frodo" Litwin (LIBERT)	6,199	3.0%

Previous Winning Percentages
2006 (67%); 2004 (62%); 2002 (58%); 2000 (68%); 1998 (99%); 1996 (62%); 1994 (57%); 1992 (57%)

Elected 1992; 10th term

Filner is a one-time aide to and liberal disciple of the late Minnesota senator and former Vice President Hubert H. Humphrey, but he is no Happy Warrior. His temper has drawn as much attention as his successful advocacy for veterans, though it seldom seems to get in the way of achieving his legislative goals.

When he was chairman of the Veterans' Affairs Committee, Filner — to a degree — suppressed his appetite for political theater. As ranking Democrat in the 112th Congress (2011-12), he is freer to return to the kind of partisan fireworks that earned him a reputation for volatility inside and outside the halls of Congress.

Filner made headlines in 2007 when he got into an altercation with an airline employee who claimed he screamed and pushed past her to find his luggage at Dulles International Airport outside of Washington, D.C. Local authorities eventually reduced assault and battery charges to trespassing and levied a $100 fine. The House Ethics Committee established a special investigative subcommittee to review the charge before concluding Filner was not guilty of wrongdoing.

Earlier that year, Filner launched a profanity-laced tirade outside the Veterans Affairs Department headquarters over the VA's failure to protect veterans' personal data from computer theft and other potential threats.

Filner sees himself as the guardian of both veterans and the employees of the department, so when then-Minority Leader John A. Boehner of Ohio proposed some cuts in the fiscal 2011 spending bill funding VA programs, Filner pounced.

"Going into an election, you want to be against veterans?" asked Filner. "This shows what they [Republicans] really mean when they say 'support the troops.' They don't support them once they come home."

After reports surfaced of elevated rates of suicide among Iraq and Afghanistan veterans, Filner called the numbers "staggering" and said they were "an indication that we are simply not doing the job of providing adequate mental health care for both our active-duty service people and our veterans." He said he would work on creating a pilot program to help service members reintegrate into society that would require psychological evaluations and screenings for brain trauma and provide for follow-up care.

He called President Obama's fiscal 2011 budget for veterans spending "robust," and he was the author of legislation that became law in 2009 to allow Congress to write VA appropriations for health programs two years in advance, to avoid the kind of shortfalls that had plagued the department in past years.

But he was critical of the VA's use of the "miscellaneous obligation" process, which allows it to allocate funds for undetermined future expenses. "In fiscal 2009, the VA spent almost $12 billion on miscellaneous obligations, which was doubled from the reported 2007 levels," he said at a July 2010 hearing of his committee.

During the 110th Congress (2007-08), Filner saw his agenda on veterans' care furthered by a series of news reports of unsatisfactory conditions, outpatient neglect and mismanagement at Washington's Walter Reed Army Medical Center. He helped secure record VA budgets in 2008 and 2009 spending bills in the wake of the scandals, then called for Congress to scrupulously monitor the sprawling department's activities.

Also in that Congress, he won House approval of a bill to grant compensation payments to Filipino veterans who served with U.S. forces in World War

II, continuing his years-long effort to secure full benefits for them. The $787 billion economic stimulus plan, signed into law in early 2009, included $198 million of already-appropriated money to make payments to about 18,000 surviving Filipino veterans.

A 1960s civil rights activist who by his own account avoided the draft with repeated student deferments, Filner landed on Veterans' Affairs almost by accident. Soon after he was elected in 1992, he ran into Democratic Sen. Alan Cranston of California, who had chaired the veterans' panel in the Senate. Cranston urged Filner to seek the House assignment, telling him it was good politics for a liberal to champion the cause of veterans.

He showed up at a reception hosted by Chairman G.V. Sonny Montgomery, a Mississippi Democrat and a legend in the veterans' community. Filner had never heard of him. "Mr. Chairman," he said, "I was once a tourist through your state. I took a Greyhound bus to your capital, Jackson. I got off and the police chief showed me around his jail. The sheriff in Hines County showed me around his jail, and then I spent a couple of months in your state penitentiary. I was one of the first Freedom Riders." Montgomery did not bat an eyelash. "I was the head of the National Guard that arrested you," he replied. The two men became close. Filner is also a longtime friend of California Republican Rep. Brian P. Bilbray, who jokingly — sort of — calls Filner "a pinko commie."

A member of the Transportation and Infrastructure Committee, Filner wants to see stricter rules on Mexican trucks crossing into the United States. His district runs the length of the California-Mexico border. And he is often in the middle of congressional debates over immigration controls and border security. At the start of the 111th Congress (2009-10), he introduced several immigration bills, including a measure to bar detention of legal immigrants for minor crimes.

A native Pennsylvanian, Filner is the son of a former union organizer and businessman who was an early fundraiser for the Rev. Dr. Martin Luther King Jr., whom Filner met as a teenager. He left college to join the Freedom Riders in 1961 and was arrested during a sit-in at a Mississippi lunch counter with John Lewis, now a Democratic House colleague from Georgia.

Filner taught history at San Diego State University starting in the 1970s. After working for Humphrey and Rep. Donald M. Fraser, both Minnesota Democrats, he spent four years on the San Diego school board and five on the city council. He then ran for a newly created 50th District seat in 1992, defeating five primary foes. The Democratic makeup of his district — now the 51st — has allowed him a string of easy general-election victories.

Key Votes

2010

Overhaul the nation's health insurance system	YES
Allow for repeal of "don't ask, don't tell"	YES
Overhaul financial services industry regulation	YES
Limit use of new Afghanistan War funds to troop withdrawal activities	YES
Change oversight of offshore drilling and lift oil spill liability cap	YES
Provide a path to legal status for some children of illegal immigrants	YES
Extend Bush-era income tax cuts for two years	NO

2009

Expand the Children's Health Insurance Program	YES
Provide $787 billion in tax cuts and spending increases to stimulate the economy	YES
Allow bankruptcy judges to modify certain primary-residence mortgages	YES
Create a cap-and-trade system to limit greenhouse gas emissions	YES
Provide $2 billion for the "cash for clunkers" program	YES
Establish the government as the sole provider of student loans	YES
Restrict federally funded insurance coverage for abortions in health care overhaul	NO

CQ Vote Studies

	PARTY UNITY		PRESIDENTIAL SUPPORT	
	Support	Oppose	Support	Oppose
2010	96%	4%	80%	20%
2009	98%	2%	93%	7%
2008	95%	5%	13%	87%
2007	99%	1%	4%	96%
2006	97%	3%	18%	82%

Interest Groups

	AFL-CIO	ADA	CCUS	ACU
2010	100%	100%	13%	0%
2009	100%	95%	33%	0%
2008	93%	100%	47%	12%
2007	100%	90%	45%	0%
2006	92%	95%	33%	12%

California 51

Central and southern San Diego; Imperial County

The part-urban, part-rural 51st runs along almost the entire length of California's border with Mexico, except for the western tip at the Pacific Ocean. In the east, it takes in all of Imperial County, and near the Pacific, it climbs north from the border to include part of central San Diego and some close-in suburbs. Rural Imperial County, which relies heavily on its agricultural yields and tends to have very high unemployment, is 80 percent Hispanic.

The 51st's part of San Diego, which starts south and east of downtown, is working-class, crime-ridden and heavily Hispanic. Local shopping centers are a draw for Mexican shoppers. Chula Vista attracted upscale housing developers in the last decade but recently has struggled with high foreclosure rates. South of Chula Vista and across the border from Tijuana, Otay Mesa is a busy port of entry — there are plans to expand facilities to the east of the existing border crossing — that is known for manufacturing plants that have twin sites in Mexico.

Water is a concern in the 51st. Both San Diego and Imperial counties are under pressure to reduce their dependency on the Colorado River, and a proposed solution — to lower the Salton Sea's high salinity and pesticide levels — has environmentalists concerned about the local ecosystem and migratory birds.

The Hispanic-majority district gave Democrat Barack Obama 63 percent of its 2008 presidential vote. Voters in Imperial are more conservative than their city cousins, but still lean heavily Democratic. Border issues, particularly illegal immigration — which fills many agricultural labor jobs — is a key issue here. Ranchers and growers see illegal immigration as a necessary source of labor, while others say it threatens the district's quality of life.

Major Industry
Service, manufacturing, agriculture, retail

Military Bases
Naval Station San Diego (shared with the 53rd), 23,205 military, 5,768 civilian (2011); El Centro Naval Air Facility, 95 military, 131 civilian (2010)

Cities
San Diego (pt.), 252,194; Chula Vista, 243,916; National City, 58,582

Notable
El Centro is the winter training home of the Navy's Blue Angels.

Rep. Duncan Hunter (R)

Capitol Office
225-5672
hunter.house.gov
223 Cannon Bldg. 20515-0552; fax 225-0235

Committees
Armed Services
Education & the Workforce
(Early Childhood, Elementary & Secondary
Education - Chairman)
Transportation & Infrastructure

Residence
Alpine

Born
Dec. 7, 1976; San Diego, Calif.

Religion
Baptist

Family
Wife, Margaret Hunter; three children

Education
San Diego State U., B.S. 2001 (business administration)

Military
Marine Corps, 2002-05; Marine Corps Reserve, 2005-08

Career
Business strategies analyst; residential real estate developer

Political Highlights
No previous office

ELECTION RESULTS

2010 GENERAL

Duncan Hunter (R)	139,460	63.1%
Ray Lutz (D)	70,870	32.1%
Michael Benoit (LIBERT)	10,732	4.8%

2010 PRIMARY

Duncan Hunter (R)	72,506	90.8%
Terri R. Linnell (R)	7,355	9.2%

2008 GENERAL

Duncan Hunter (R)	160,724	56.4%
Mike Lumpkin (D)	111,051	38.9%
Michael Benoit (LIBERT)	13,316	4.7%

Elected 2008; 2nd term

Like his father and predecessor in the House, a man whose name he shares, Hunter is a solid conservative who defines the core of his political mission in terms of national security.

And now the younger Hunter, a Marine combat veteran, is well positioned to emerge as a leading hawk in the Republican House.

Hunter enters his second term as one of the youngest members of the 112th Congress (2011-12) and one of only a handful to have served in Iraq and Afghanistan. He is expected to use his spot on the Armed Services Committee, a panel once led by his father, to raise questions about the Obama administration's war policies, particularly proposed timelines for withdrawing forces from Afghanistan.

"I think you'll see the House Armed Services Committee become more of a war committee than it has been in the last few years," Hunter told Stars and Stripes newspaper.

Hunter, who represents a Southern California district with a large defense industry and military workforce, will also likely join other Armed Services Republicans in opposing a proposal by the Pentagon to begin scaling back defense spending as the wars wind down.

When Defense Secretary Robert M. Gates announced that he wanted to cancel the Marines' Expeditionary Fighting Vehicle, Hunter leaped to the Corps' defense. "I personally think he's trying to destroy the Marine Corps," Hunter said in Politico. "If you take away their core competency, you're not going to have a Marine Corps anymore."

Aside from his military-related work, Hunter chairs the Education and the Workforce Subcommittee on Early Childhood, Elementary and Secondary Education. In that post, Hunter could emerge as a lead negotiator on bipartisan efforts to renew the federal Elementary and Secondary Education Act, known in its most recent iteration as No Child Left Behind.

The Obama administration has signaled it wants to overhaul the 2002 law aimed at improving failing schools by calling for greater accountability. Hunter told The Washington Post in January 2011 that there is "a lot of common ground" on the issue and it is "time to get it done."

Hunter's conservative views are most evident in his approach to handling illegal immigrants.

In the 111th Congress (2009-10), he introduced legislation that would have barred the Obama administration from pursuing a lawsuit to block Arizona from implementing a new state law aimed at cracking down on illegal immigrants. He's also backed an effort that would clarify the 14th Amendment's provision regarding citizenship to bar children of illegal immigrants born on U.S. soil from automatically becoming citizens.

He also strongly favors the security fence being constructed along the southwestern U.S. border, introducing a bill in July 2009 to speed completion of the project.

Combining his interest in military matters with a local concern, Hunter urged the Obama administration to protect a cross at the Mount Soledad war memorial in La Jolla after a federal court ruled that its presence violated the Constitution, and he introduced legislation in January 2011 to ensure religious symbols may be placed in military monuments. A cross has been at the site since 1913.

Hunter is a reliable Republican vote, and his loyalty earned him a position on the GOP leadership ladder as an assistant minority whip in the

111th Congress, a role that has carried over into the 112th. In 2010 he sided with his party on 98 percent of votes in which a majority of Republicans opposed a majority of Democrats.

Like most Republicans, Hunter opposed the Obama administration's health care and financial service overhauls. A member of the Transportation and Infrastructure Committee, he slammed Obama's $787 billion stimulus law in early 2009 as well as other Democratic policies aimed at dealing with the economic downturn.

Hunter was 4 when his father arrived in Washington; he attended schools in the District of Columbia and later earned a business administration degree from San Diego State University.

As a college sophomore, Hunter and a friend started a Web design firm called Jones Hunter Web Design. After graduation, they sold the company and Hunter accepted a position as an information technology analyst. Aides say he remains tech-savvy, often acting as the IT guy in his Capitol Hill office, staying abreast of the latest technology and collecting the latest cell phones and gadgets.

The day after the Sept. 11 terrorist attacks, Hunter quit his job and joined the Marine Corps. He served in Iraq twice — he was ambushed just five hours into his first tour and later fought in the first battle of Fallujah — and one tour in Afghanistan as a reservist before retiring from active duty.

His father made it known in early 2007 that he planned to leave the House, paving the way for his son's bid. In an unusual twist, the younger Hunter was absent for nearly eight months of the primary and general election campaign while he completed his final tour with the reserves. Election laws allow reservists to run for office, but not while deployed. The laws prohibit active-duty military personnel from taking partisan positions, making campaign speeches or fundraising, so Hunter turned his campaign over to his wife, Margaret, before heading to training for his deployment.

When Hunter returned from combat, he campaigned vigorously and cruised past three other primary candidates with more than 72 percent of the vote.

In the general election, he faced Democrat Mike Lumpkin, a retired Navy SEAL commander, who sought to make an issue of the Hunters trying to keep the seat in the family. Lumpkin derisively called his opponent "a congressman's kid." Hunter outraised Lumpkin by a 3-to-1 margin and the district's GOP tilt — it gave Arizona Sen. John McCain 53 percent of its 2008 presidential vote — enabled Hunter to win with 56 percent of the vote. He was re-elected in 2010 with 63 percent.

Key Votes

2010

Overhaul the nation's health insurance system	NO
Allow for repeal of "don't ask, don't tell"	NO
Overhaul financial services industry regulation	NO
Limit use of new Afghanistan War funds to troop withdrawal activities	NO
Change oversight of offshore drilling and lift oil spill liability cap	NO
Provide a path to legal status for some children of illegal immigrants	NO
Extend Bush-era income tax cuts for two years	YES

2009

Expand the Children's Health Insurance Program	NO
Provide $787 billion in tax cuts and spending increases to stimulate the economy	NO
Allow bankruptcy judges to modify certain primary-residence mortgages	NO
Create a cap-and-trade system to limit greenhouse gas emissions	NO
Provide $2 billion for the "cash for clunkers" program	NO
Establish the government as the sole provider of student loans	NO
Restrict federally funded insurance coverage for abortions in health care overhaul	YES

CQ Vote Studies

	PARTY UNITY		PRESIDENTIAL SUPPORT	
	Support	Oppose	Support	Oppose
2010	98%	2%	26%	74%
2009	95%	5%	21%	79%

Interest Groups

	AFL-CIO	ADA	CCUS	ACU
2010	7%	0%	88%	100%
2009	10%	5%	80%	100%

Eastern San Diego; inland San Diego County

The 52nd wraps around the east side of San Diego from Poway in the north to east of Otay Mesa in the south, and stretches about 100 miles further east and north through mountains and protected desert parks to reach San Diego County's borders with Riverside and Imperial counties. Most residents live in the predominately wealthy, conservative suburbs or the roughly 22 percent of San Diego that is in the district.

An economic downturn has affected suburban developments, where property values had been increasing for a decade. Poway, whose economic roots lie in agriculture, has a wealthier, more rural feel to it than the surrounding sprawl. Despite municipal budget uncertainty and some empty storefronts, the city has fared better than other areas in the region. Just outside of Poway is an expanse of evenly developed areas that includes part of Rancho Bernardo (shared with the 49th and 50th) and Scripps Ranch.

San Diego's large military- and defense-related workforce contributes to both the district's conservatism and its economy. Although most of the area's military bases are in the 53rd, many residents commute to nearby defense contracting jobs.

Changing demographics in the district over the past decade have resulted in a district that is now nearly one-fifth Hispanic. Blue- and white-collar workers alike tend to vote Republican and support GOP House members. Registered Republicans maintain a 12-percentage-point lead over Democrats here, and John McCain took 53 percent of the district's 2008 presidential vote.

Major Industry
Technology, manufacturing, defense

Military Bases
Marine Corps Air Station Miramar, 7,785 military, 664 civilian (2010) (shared with the 50th)

Cities
San Diego (pt.), 180,454; El Cajon, 99,478; La Mesa, 57,065; Santee, 53,413; Poway, 47,811

Notable
Members of the Unarius Academy of Science, based in El Cajon, believe UFOs will bring technologies that will rid human civilization of pollution and poverty.

Rep. Susan A. Davis (D)

Capitol Office
225-2040
www.house.gov/susandavis
1526 Longworth Bldg. 20515-0553; fax 225-2948

Committees
Armed Services
Education & the Workforce

Residence
San Diego

Born
April 13, 1944; Cambridge, Mass.

Religion
Jewish

Family
Husband, Steve Davis; two children

Education
U. of California, Berkeley, B.A. 1965 (sociology); U. of North Carolina, M.A. 1968 (social work)

Career
High school leadership program director; public television producer; social worker

Political Highlights
San Diego Unified School District Board of Education, 1983-92 (president, 1989-92); Calif. Assembly, 1994-2000

ELECTION RESULTS

2010 GENERAL

Susan A. Davis (D)	104,800	62.3%
Michael Crimmins (R)	57,230	34.0%
Paul Dekker (LIBERT)	6,298	3.7%

2010 PRIMARY

Susan A. Davis (D)	unopposed

2008 GENERAL

Susan A. Davis (D)	161,315	68.5%
Michael Crimmins (R)	64,658	27.4%
Edward M. Teyssier (LIBERT)	9,569	4.1%

Previous Winning Percentages
2006 (68%); 2004 (66%); 2002 (62%); 2000 (50%)

Elected 2000; 6th term

Davis' "consistent and quiet approach" to education and defense issues has yielded considerable legislative success. She chaired an Armed Services subcommittee in the previous Congress and has most of San Diego's military bases in her district, but she is happy to remain in the background if that helps move her agenda.

As chairwoman of the Armed Services Subcommittee on Military Personnel in the 111th Congress (2009-10) — she's the ranking Democrat in the 112th (2011-12) — Davis was a leading voice against the ban on gays serving openly in the military. The fiscal 2011 defense policy bill that passed the House included a provision to repeal the "don't ask, don't tell" policy once the military had completed a review on how to implement the change. Once that review was completed, on her motion the House passed and the president signed into law stand-alone legislation that repealed the ban. She said the move put Congress "on the right side of history."

Davis also was instrumental in the 111th Congress in bringing attention to the issue of sexual assault in the ranks. In the fiscal 2010 defense authorization law, Davis set forward comprehensive changes on how the military handles the problem, honing the military's strategic direction on the topic, improving prevention, training and response to victims, and increasing accountability.

Davis, who has a master's degree in social work, also focuses on improving troops' quality of life in housing and health care. She has pushed legislation to maintain military families' eligibility for such government programs as free or reduced-cost school lunches and Supplemental Security Income, which provides payments to the poor, elderly and disabled. In the fiscal 2010 defense authorization act, Davis helped put in place a requirement that certain servicemembers separating from the military be screened for traumatic brain injury and post-traumatic stress disorder.

As a member of the Veterans' Affairs Committee in the 108th Congress (2003-04), she was able to see enactment of legislation that contained her provisions dealing with veterans' home loans and disability benefits.

A member of the Education and the Workforce Committee, Davis is a strong proponent of federal education funding — her district is home to three universities. Like many Democrats, she argues that President George W. Bush's No Child Left Behind 2001 education law should be backed with more money. Similarly, she says the federal government should pick up more of the costs of educating students with disabilities.

Davis quietly won legislative victories during the health care overhaul debate. Three of her provisions made it into the final version of the measure that was signed into law in March 2010: a diabetes prevention provision, which offers grants to health and community organizations to help those with pre-diabetes prevent full onset of the type 2 form of the illness; a provision requiring insurance plans to allow women direct access to their OB/GYN without needing a referral from a primary care physician; and a provision that would permit matching funds for state Medicaid payments for freestanding birth center facility fees.

Davis expanded her portfolio in the 110th Congress (2007-08) to include election reform. She was appointed to the House Administration Committee, which oversees federal elections as well as the internal operations of the House. Davis won the committee's approval of a bill to prohibit states from requiring voters to declare an excuse in order to vote absentee. She no longer serves on the committee.

Davis is an ally of Minority Leader Nancy Pelosi, a fellow California liberal, who first urged her to run for Congress and helped her raise money. In 2010, Davis sided with the Democrats 98 percent of the time on votes that pitted the majorities of each party against each other.

But she sometimes breaks with her party on trade issues. In 2001, she was among 21 Democrats who voted in favor of giving the president authority to negotiate trade agreements that cannot be amended by Congress. Several of her pro-trade colleagues in the moderate New Democrat Coalition voted against it, saying the timing was wrong. She also broke with her party in 2003 to back trade agreements with Chile and Singapore, but in 2005 she opposed the Central America Free Trade Agreement.

Davis was raised in Richmond, Calif., the daughter of a pediatrician. She said a desire to help people led her to the mental health field. She was studying social work in graduate school in North Carolina when she met Steve Davis, who was studying to be a psychiatrist. They married and spent two years in Japan while he served in the Air Force.

When the family returned stateside and settled in San Diego, Davis became active in community affairs. She joined the League of Women Voters, serving as president of the San Diego chapter. She also worked at the local public TV station.

In 1983, when California Democrat Bob Filner, who now represents the neighboring 51st District, left the San Diego school board to run for the city council, Davis won the election to replace him. While still on the school board, she helped start a local fellowship program for preteens and teenagers to learn about how business and government work. She did not seek re-election to the board in 1992 and became the fellowship program's first executive director.

Two years later, Davis won the first of three terms in the California Assembly. Term limits barred her from running again for the Assembly in 2000, so Pelosi urged her to run for Congress.

The political vulnerability of the 49th District's GOP incumbent, Brian P. Bilbray, who had twice won with less than 50 percent of the vote, handed Davis an opportunity. She took advantage, capturing the seat by 3 percentage points. (Bilbray now represents the neighboring 50th.) In her first re-election bid in the new 53rd District, her vote in favor of Bush's trade legislation cost her the support of the AFL-CIO. But she benefited from the newly drawn district and won with 62 percent. She has been re-elected easily ever since.

Key Votes

2010

Overhaul the nation's health insurance system	YES
Allow for repeal of "don't ask, don't tell"	YES
Overhaul financial services industry regulation	YES
Limit use of new Afghanistan War funds to troop withdrawal activities	NO
Change oversight of offshore drilling and lift oil spill liability cap	YES
Provide a path to legal status for some children of illegal immigrants	YES
Extend Bush-era income tax cuts for two years	YES

2009

Expand the Children's Health Insurance Program	YES
Provide $787 billion in tax cuts and spending increases to stimulate the economy	YES
Allow bankruptcy judges to modify certain primary-residence mortgages	YES
Create a cap-and-trade system to limit greenhouse gas emissions	YES
Provide $2 billion for the "cash for clunkers" program	YES
Establish the government as the sole provider of student loans	YES
Restrict federally funded insurance coverage for abortions in health care overhaul	NO

CQ Vote Studies

	PARTY UNITY		PRESIDENTIAL SUPPORT	
	SUPPORT	OPPOSE	SUPPORT	OPPOSE
2010	98%	2%	95%	5%
2009	99%	1%	97%	3%
2008	99%	1%	15%	85%
2007	97%	3%	7%	93%
2006	94%	6%	26%	74%

Interest Groups

	AFL-CIO	ADA	CCUS	ACU
2010	100%	90%	25%	0%
2009	100%	100%	40%	0%
2008	100%	95%	56%	0%
2007	100%	90%	55%	0%
2006	86%	90%	33%	8%

California 53

Downtown San Diego; Imperial Beach

The coastal 53rd is the economic engine that drives surrounding districts. It includes San Diego's downtown and large employers as well as most of its military bases. The district also runs south along the Pacific Coast through Coronado and Imperial Beach to the Mexican border.

The defense industry, based around the military installations, is a major economic contributor.

The mild climate, wide beaches and attractions — such as SeaWorld, Balboa Park (including the San Diego Zoo) and PETCO Park, where baseball's Padres play — draw tourists, but environmentalists are split over long-term solutions to pollution and sewage that still cause occasional beach closures. Foreclosure rates and weakened employment rates have affected the city's downtown area.

Colleges in the district include the University of California, San Diego, in the north, San Diego State University and the University of San Diego. Some private companies have formed research agreements with the schools, and residents in the district hope local biotech and telecommunications firms will boost the economy.

The 53rd includes Hispanic Democratic sections east of the city in places such as Lemon Grove. It also contains blue-collar, central city areas like North Park, City Heights, Barrio Logan and Hillcrest, which is one of the area's most liberal and Democratic neighborhoods and the center of the city's gay community. Overall, the 53rd District is less than one-third Hispanic, and Democrat Barack Obama took 68 percent of the district's 2008 presidential vote.

Major Industry

Defense, tourism, biotech, telecommunications, higher education

Military Bases

Naval Station San Diego (shared with the 51st), 23,205 military, 5,768 civilian (2011); Naval Air Station North Island/Naval Amphibious Base Coronado, 27,000 military, 6,000 civilian; Naval Base Point Loma, 5,969 military, 6,159 civilian (2008); Naval Medical Center San Diego, 3,300 military, 2,500 civilian; Marine Corps Recruit Depot San Diego, 1,492 military, 1,201 civilian (2011)

Cities

San Diego (pt.), 570,664; Imperial Beach (pt.), 26,272

Notable

Imperial Beach is home to the U.S. Open Sandcastle Competition.

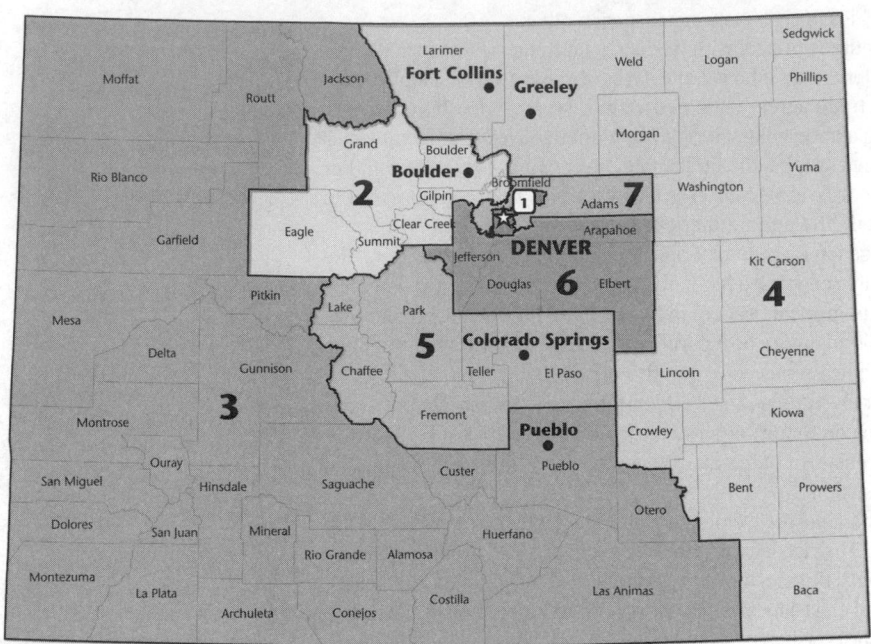

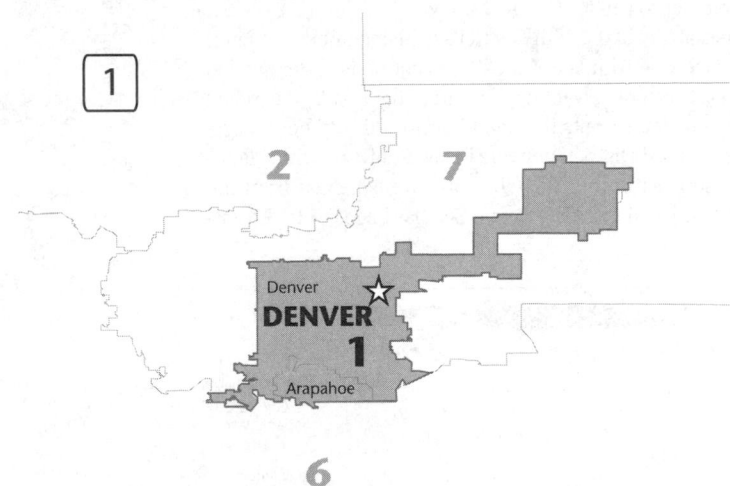

Gov. John W. Hickenlooper (D)

First elected: 2010
Length of term: 4 years
Term expires: 1/15
Salary: $90,000
Phone: (303) 866-2471
Residence: Denver
Born: Feb. 7, 1952; Narberth, Pa.
Religion: Episcopalian
Family: Wife, Helen Thorpe; one child
Education: Wesleyan U., B.A. 1974 (English), M.S. 1980 (earth and environmental science)
Career: Brewery owner and restaurateur; real estate developer; geologist
Political highlights: Mayor of Denver, 2003-11

ELECTION RESULTS

2010 GENERAL
John W. Hickenlooper (D)	912,005	51.0%
Tom Tancredo (AC)	651,232	36.4%
Dan Maes (R)	199,034	11.1%

Lt. Gov. Joseph Garcia (D)

First elected: 2010
Length of term: 4 years
Term expires: 1/15
Salary: $68,500
Phone: (303) 866-2087

LEGISLATURE

General Assembly: 120 days, January-May
Senate: 35 members, 5-year terms
2011 ratios: 20 D,15 R; 17 women, 18 men
Salary: $30,000
Phone: (303) 866-2316
House: 65 members, 2-year terms
2011 ratios: 33 R, 32 D; 24 women, 41 men
Salary: $30,000
Phone: (303) 866-2904

TERM LIMITS

Governor: 2 terms
Senate: 2 consecutive terms
House: 4 consecutive terms

URBAN STATISTICS

CITY	POPULATION
Denver	600,158
Colorado Springs	416,427
Aurora	325,078
Fort Collins	143,986
Lakewood	142,980

REGISTERED VOTERS

Republican	39%
Democrat	33%
Unaffiliated	28%

POPULATION

2010 population	5,029,196
2000 population	4,301,261
1990 population	3,294,394
Percent change (2000-2010)	+16.9%
Rank among states (2010)	22
Median age	35.5
Born in state	42.2%
Foreign born	9.5%
Violent crime rate	338/100,000
Povery level	12.9%
Federal workers	66,435
Military	35,404

ELECTIONS

STATE ELECTION OFFICIAL
(303) 894-2200
DEMOCRATIC PARTY
(303) 623-4762
REPUBLICAN PARTY
(303) 758-3333

MISCELLANEOUS

Web: www.colorado.gov
Capital: Denver

U.S. CONGRESS

Senate: 2 Democrats
House: 4 Republicans, 3 Democrats

2010 Census Statistics by District

District	2008 Vote for President Obama	McCain	White	Black	Asian	Hispanic	Median Income	White Collar	Blue Collar	Service Industry	Over 64	Under 18	College Education	Rural	Sq. Miles
1	74%	24%	54%	9%	3%	31%	$45,044	63%	19%	18%	11%	23%	39%	0%	171
2	64	34	72	1	4	20	64,851	65	19	16	8	24	41	13	5,615
3	48	50	72	1	1	24	46,744	56	26	18	14	24	26	39	53,963
4	49	50	75	1	2	20	51,454	59	24	17	11	25	32	25	30,898
5	40	59	74	5	2	15	54,322	64	19	18	10	25	33	14	7,708
6	46	52	82	3	4	9	85,500	75	12	12	9	27	48	15	4,104
7	59	39	59	7	3	28	51,369	59	24	17	11	25	27	2	1,258
STATE	54	45	70	4	3	21	56,222	63	20	16	10	25	35	16	103,718
U.S.	53	46	64	12	5	16	51,425	60	23	17	13	25	28	21	3,537,438

Sen. Mark Udall (D)

Capitol Office
224-5941
markudall.senate.gov
328 Hart Bldg. 20510; fax 224-6471

Committees
Armed Services
Energy & Natural Resources
    (National Parks - Chairman)
Select Intelligence
Special Aging

Residence
Eldorado Springs

Born
July 18, 1950; Tucson, Ariz.

Religion
Christian

Family
Wife, Maggie Fox; two children

Education
Williams College, B.A. 1972 (American civilization)

Career
Colo. Outward Bound School executive director

Political Highlights
Colo. House, 1997-99; U.S. House, 1999-2009

ELECTION RESULTS

2008 GENERAL

Mark Udall (D)	1,230,994	52.8%
Bob Schaffer (R)	990,755	42.5%
Douglas Campbell (AC)	59,733	2.6%
Bob Kinsey (GREEN)	50,004	2.2%

2008 PRIMARY

Mark Udall (D)	unopposed

Previous Winning Percentages
2006 House Election (68%); 2004 House Election (67%);
2002 House Election (60%); 2000 House Election (55%);
1998 House Election (50%)

Elected 2008; 1st term

Throughout a decade representing a district that includes the famously liberal haven of Boulder, Udall developed a reputation as a moderate willing to make a deal, although he sports a fairly party-line voting record. His first years in the Senate have worked out similarly.

"I'd like to believe that it's hard to pin me down, that I'm not beholden to any particular political philosophy," he said.

That ethos served Udall well during his first two years as a senator representing the quintessential "purple" state, which includes conservative bastions such as Colorado Springs in addition to Democratic-leaning Denver and its exurbs. To demonstrate his fiscal hawkishness, he endorsed a GOP-sponsored balanced budget constitutional amendment at the start of the 112th Congress (2011-12).

Tall and telegenic, Udall has benefited from being part of what can be considered the West's first family of politics. His father, Morris K. Udall, represented Arizona in the House and ran for president in 1976; his uncle, Stewart L. Udall, was Interior secretary under Presidents John F. Kennedy and Lyndon B. Johnson, and also served in the House. And Mark Udall was elected to the House — and later the Senate — at the same time as his cousin Tom, a Democrat from neighboring New Mexico.

Udall became Colorado's senior senator early in 2009, just months after his election, when Democrat Ken Salazar joined the Obama administration as Interior secretary.

In the 111th Congress (2009-10), Udall teamed with other first-term Democratic senators to flex their muscles on policy — particularly energy legislation — and process, with the goal of overhauling the Senate's filibuster rules. Early in 2011 they won elimination of secret holds, which had allowed members blocking legislation to remain anonymous, but no major changes to the filibuster.

Since moving over from the House, Udall has remained active on energy and environmental matters. He uses his position on the Energy and Natural Resources Committee to press for renewable energy and nuclear power, and works on on public lands issues affecting his state as chairman of the National Parks Subcommittee.

In the closing weeks of the 111th, Udall helped marshal support among Senate Democrats for legislation that would require 15 percent of electricity to be generated from renewable sources such as wind or solar energy by 2021.

The renewable-energy standard has been a goal of Udall's dating back to 2004, when he helped lead a successful ballot initiative imposing a similar mandate in Colorado. During the 110th Congress (2007-08), he and his cousin Tom played a key role in seeing similar legislation pass the House.

Udall has supported efforts to enact cap-and-trade legislation to reduce carbon emissions, although he has drawn criticism for seeking to ease the bill's expected impact on coal-dependent states. He acknowledged the dilemma of attempting to simultaneously protect the environment and the economy, noting that his last name creates an expectation that he "bleeds green."

He angered some Colorado environmentalists in 2006 by sponsoring a bill to ease reviews of tree-cutting in forests damaged by beetles. Local officials wanted to get rid of dying trees that could worsen forest fires, but environmentalists feared it would hasten timber harvests without adequate review of the impact on the environment. Udall cites that as an example of where he has "looked to be a problem-solver and not blindly embrace a philosophy."

In the Senate — as he did in the House — Udall serves on the Armed Services Committee, a position that allows him to look out for his state's military interests. He traveled to Iraq, Afghanistan and Pakistan in 2009 and was also an early proponent of lifting the military's "don't ask, don't tell" prohibitions on openly gay servicemembers.

He scored a legislative victory in the 2010 financial regulation overhaul, which contains his provision that requires credit card companies to provide consumers with free copies of their credit rating if they are rejected for credit.

Udall also sits on the Select Intelligence and Special Aging committees.

He waited until later in life to get into politics, saying he wanted to step in when he felt ready, not simply to follow his father, although he had served as a field director in New Hampshire during the elder Udall's run for president.

Udall was 10 when his father, "Mo," a legendary wit and energetic liberal, first won election to the House from Arizona in 1961. He remembers being roused from sleep to join his five pajama-clad siblings to celebrate. Although he has said that he didn't see his father much after age 13 (his parents divorced when he was 15), one of his proudest moments was witnessing his dad become the first prominent House Democrat to come out against Johnson's troop buildup in Vietnam in 1967.

He cited his father's 1964 vote in favor of the Gulf of Tonkin resolution when he announced in October 2002 that he would not support the resolution that gave President George W. Bush the authority to use military force against Iraq. The elder Udall, the son said, regretted that vote. "I fear that this Congress, a generation later, is poised to make a similar mistake," he said.

After graduating from Williams College in 1972 with a degree in American civilization, Udall didn't go home to Arizona, but rather moved to Colorado's Western Slope and launched a career with the Colorado Outward Bound School. He was a course director for 10 years and later served as executive director from 1985 to 1995.

He once was an avid mountain climber, scaling Kanchenjunga in the Himalayas, the world's third-highest peak; Aconcagua, the highest point in South America; and Alaska's Mount McKinley, the highest peak in North America. In 1994, Udall reached 26,000 feet on Mount Everest via a route that has been climbed only once. He says he gave up mountain climbing out of concern for his two young children.

In his first House race for the seat that Democrat David E. Skaggs gave up after a dozen years, Udall hammered hard when his GOP opponent, former Boulder Mayor Bob Greenlee, questioned the scientific validity of global warming. Udall also campaigned door-to-door to prove he was a "legitimate Coloradan" and was not trying to capitalize on a famous name. In one of the more costly House races of 1998, he prevailed by just 5,500 votes. A month after the election, his father died of Parkinson's disease.

In subsequent elections, Udall's victory margins steadily increased to comfortable levels. He briefly entered the 2004 Colorado Senate race when Republican Sen. Ben Nighthorse Campbell retired, but withdrew once Salazar, who was then state attorney general, decided to run. Udall announced early in 2005 that he would try in 2008 for the Senate seat then occupied by Republican Wayne Allard, who announced in 2007 that he would retire from the Senate.

Udall's GOP opponent was Bob Schaffer, a conservative former House member serving on the state board of education. Schaffer sought to paint Udall as a "Boulder liberal," an allusion to the left-leaning reputation of his political base, the home of the University of Colorado's main campus. But Schaffer was at a disadvantage because of the difficult national political environment for Republicans and Udall's superior fundraising. Udall won with about 53 percent of the vote.

Key Votes

2010

Pass budget reconciliation bill to modify overhauls of health care and federal student loan programs	YES
Proceed to disapproval resolution on EPA authority to regulate greenhouse gases	NO
Overhaul financial services industry regulation	YES
Limit debate to proceed to a bill to broaden campaign finance disclosure and reporting rules	YES
Limit debate on an extension of Bush-era income tax cuts for two years	NO
Limit debate on a bill to provide a path to legal status for some children of illegal immigrants	YES
Allow for a repeal of "don't ask, don't tell"	YES
Consent to ratification of a strategic arms reduction treaty with Russia	YES

2009

Prevent release of remaining financial industry bailout funds	NO
Make it easier for victims to sue for wage discrimination remedies	YES
Expand the Children's Health Insurance Program	YES
Limit debate on the economic stimulus measure	YES
Repeal District of Columbia firearms prohibitions and gun registration laws	YES
Limit debate on expansion of federal hate crimes law	YES
Strike funding for F-22 Raptor fighter jets	YES

CQ Vote Studies

	PARTY UNITY		PRESIDENTIAL SUPPORT	
	SUPPORT	OPPOSE	SUPPORT	OPPOSE
2010	90%	10%	95%	5%
2009	93%	7%	97%	3%
2008	94%	6%	21%	79%
2007	94%	6%	8%	92%
2006	92%	8%	30%	70%
2005	91%	9%	20%	80%
2004	94%	6%	32%	68%
2003	95%	5%	24%	76%
2002	93%	7%	33%	67%
2001	96%	4%	30%	70%

Interest Groups

	AFL-CIO	ADA	CCUS	ACU
2010	94%	90%	18%	8%
2009	94%	95%	43%	16%
2008	93%	80%	61%	13%
2007	96%	90%	60%	4%
2006	93%	85%	53%	16%
2005	87%	90%	37%	8%
2004	93%	100%	53%	8%
2003	83%	80%	32%	18%
2002	89%	95%	40%	4%
2001	100%	100%	35%	0%

Sen. Michael Bennet (D)

Capitol Office
224-5852
bennet.senate.gov
458 Russell Bldg. 20510-0605; fax 228-5036

Committees
Agriculture, Nutrition & Forestry
(Energy, Science & Technology - Chairman)
Banking, Housing & Urban Affairs
Health, Education, Labor & Pensions
Special Aging

Residence
Denver

Born
Nov. 28, 1964; New Delhi, India

Religion
Unspecified

Family
Wife, Susan Daggett; three children

Education
Wesleyan U., B.A. 1987 (history); Yale U., J.D. 1993

Career
School superintendent; investment company
executive; laywer; mayoral and gubernatorial aide

Political Highlights
No previous office

ELECTION RESULTS

2010 GENERAL

Michael Bennet (D)	851,590	48.0%
Ken Buck (R)	822,731	46.4%
Bob Kinsey (GREEN)	38,768	2.2%
Maclyn Stringer (LIBERT)	22,589	1.3%
Jason Napolitano (IRFM)	19,415	1.1%

2010 PRIMARY

Michael Bennet (D)	184,714	54.1%
Andrew Romanoff (D)	156,419	45.8%

Elected 2010; 1st full term

Appointed January 2009

Days before the 2010 election, Bennet was expected to lose in the GOP landslide. But he bucked the trend, and his moderate campaign, which relied heavily on support in the Hispanic community, became a prototype that Democrats hope to emulate in 2012.

Appointed to his seat in January 2009 after fellow Democrat Ken Salazar agreed to become President Obama's Interior secretary, Bennet had never won an election to public office before his 2010 victory.

He was aided by an impressive fundraising effort and the unwavering support of Obama. He raised more than $11 million, and outside groups spent millions more on his behalf. His Republican opponent, Weld County District Attorney Ken Buck, a tea party favorite, was also the recipient of generous aid from ideological groups, and the race ended up costing more than $45 million.

Bennet was given ample credit for helping Democrats preserve their Senate majority. And his display of political mettle indicated that then-Gov. Bill Ritter Jr., a Democrat, was on to something when he appointed the former Denver Public Schools superintendent to fill the last two years of Salazar's term, amid much skepticism back home.

That skepticism meant that Bennet — almost from the moment he arrived in Washington — found himself campaigning, first to prove himself worthy of the appointment, then to fend off a vigorous primary challenge by former Colorado House Speaker Andrew Romanoff, an old friend of Bill Clinton's who had the former president's endorsement.

Bennet immediately set out to establish his credentials as a reformer willing to challenge Senate leaders. He proposed changes to Senate rules that would limit filibusters and the secret holds that often delay legislation or stop it completely. (The Senate eventually changed the rules for holds at the start of the 112th Congress (2011-12), but filibusters remain intact.) He said Congress should forgo its annual pay raise and that retiring members of Congress should be barred from entering the lobbying profession.

He gained favor with the powerful gun lobby by voting in 2009 to repeal firearms regulations in the District of Columbia. A member of the Banking, Housing and Urban Affairs Committee, Bennet also helped Republicans defeat a Democratic proposal to allow bankruptcy court judges to alter the terms of mortgages to help struggling borrowers. Salazar had backed the proposal.

At the same time, he established some liberal bona fides by pushing hard for the creation of a government-run health insurance plan as part of the overhaul that became law in March 2010.

Taking on the touchy subject of immigration from his post on the Agriculture, Nutrition and Forestry Committee, he expressed support for a broad overhaul that includes a revamped guest worker program.

Bennet won his first election in August 2010, defeating Romanoff by 8 percentage points. And he may have caught a break when Lt. Gov. Jane Norton lost to the more conservative Buck in the GOP primary.

A month later, Bennet was the first Democratic senator to nix Obama's plan for a second stimulus law that would pour $50 billion into infrastructure improvements. With Republicans united in opposition, Bennet's announcement sealed the plan's defeat.

Still, Bennet's opponent, Buck, stressed during his campaign that on the key legislative debates of the 111th Congress (2009-10) — the economic stimulus, the health care law and the financial services regulatory overhaul — Bennet lined up with the Democrats.

The health care vote, in particular, became contentious back home. A few days before a crucial Senate vote on the bill, Bennet, a member of the Health, Education, Labor and Pensions Committee, railed against "backroom deals" that had been cut to secure support for the measure, but then voted for it. The Denver Post editorialized that it demonstrated how Bennet had yet to live up to expectations. "So much potential, yet not enough spine," the paper wrote.

Bennet said it was better to expand health insurance coverage now than to hold out for a perfect bill.

As if to confirm that contention, Bennet was among the Democratic backers of a Republican bill early in the 112th Congress that would repeal a widely lambasted provision of the law requiring businesses to file reports with the IRS for each vendor to whom they pay more than $600 per year.

Bennet's balancing act — combined with his relentless advertising attack painting Buck as too conservative — failed to persuade a majority of Coloradans to send him back to Washington, but it did secure enough support to win re-election. Bennet edged out Buck 48 percent to 46 percent, with minor party candidates taking the remainder.

Bennett also serves on the Special Aging Committee, alongside fellow Colorado Democrat Mark Udall.

Bennet was born into privilege. His father, Douglas Bennet, was a State Department official who went on to become president of National Public Radio and Wesleyan University. Raised in Washington, Bennet attended one of the city's boys schools, went to Wesleyan, then earned a law degree at Yale.

He left a prestigious law firm to become a counsel in the Clinton administration's Justice Department, where one of his responsibilities was to write speeches for Attorney General Janet Reno.

But Bennet grew weary of the law and followed his future wife, Susan Daggett, to Montana, where he spent his time repairing furniture for their cabin. When they contemplated where to settle and raise a family, he was adamant that it not be Washington.

They decided to move to Denver after Daggett was offered a position with the Sierra Club there in 1997. Looking for a job, Bennet reached out to some fellow Wesleyan alumni and was eventually referred by one to Phil Anschutz, the billionaire entrepreneur and donor of conservative causes. Though Bennet had no business experience, Anschutz hired him and tasked Bennet with refurbishing a chain of movie theaters he owned. Bennet's success eventually earned him a multimillion-dollar payday.

And there was surely more money to be made. But Bennet had also become friendly during his time on Anschutz's staff with John W. Hickenlooper, a fellow Wesleyan alumnus and Denver brew pub owner who is now Colorado governor. Bennet advised Hickenlooper in his 2003 run for mayor. After Hickenlooper was elected, he hired Bennet to be his chief of staff.

Two years later, despite the fact that Bennet had no experience in education, Hickenlooper offered him the job running Denver's public school system. As superintendent, Bennet promoted a merit pay system that increased teachers' starting salaries and linked teacher bonuses to student achievement. He closed low-performing and underperforming schools and won praise from African-American ministers and activists who initially had labeled him a "dictator" by working to reopen one high school serving a mostly minority student body. Enrollment grew to its highest levels in three decades and Bennet was praised as a "visionary."

His reputation took a hit during his 2010 campaign when The New York Times reported that an elaborate financing deal Bennet had persuaded the Denver Board of Education to accept to fill a hole in a city pension fund had blown up after the market collapse of 2008, costing Denver millions in interest and other fees.

Key Votes

2010

Pass budget reconciliation bill to modify overhauls of health care and federal student loan programs	YES
Proceed to disapproval resolution on EPA authority to regulate greenhouse gases	NO
Overhaul financial services industry regulation	YES
Limit debate to proceed to a bill to broaden campaign finance disclosure and reporting rules	YES
Limit debate on an extension of Bush-era income tax cuts for two years	YES
Limit debate on a bill to provide a path to legal status for some children of illegal immigrants	YES
Allow for a repeal of "don't ask, don't tell"	YES
Consent to ratification of a strategic arms reduction treaty with Russia	YES

2009

Make it easier for victims to sue for wage discrimination remedies	YES
Expand the Children's Health Insurance Program	YES
Limit debate on the economic stimulus measure	YES
Repeal District of Columbia firearms prohibitions and gun registration laws	YES
Limit debate on expansion of federal hate crimes law	YES
Strike funding for F-22 Raptor fighter jets	YES

CQ Vote Studies

	PARTY UNITY		PRESIDENTIAL SUPPORT	
	SUPPORT	OPPOSE	SUPPORT	OPPOSE
2010	87%	13%	98%	2%
2009	92%	8%	96%	4%

Interest Groups

	AFL CIO	ADA	CCUS	ACU
2010	88%	85%	36%	8%
2009	94%	95%	57%	8%

Rep. Diana DeGette (D)

Capitol Office
225-4431
www.house.gov/degette
2335 Rayburn Bldg. 20515-0601; fax 225-5657

Committees
Energy & Commerce

Residence
Denver

Born
July 29, 1957; Tachikawa, Japan

Religion
Presbyterian

Family
Husband, Lino Lipinsky; two children

Education
Colorado College, B.A. 1979 (political science); New York U., J.D. 1982

Career
Lawyer; state public defender

Political Highlights
Colo. House, 1993-96 (assistant minority leader, 1995-96)

ELECTION RESULTS

2010 GENERAL
Diana DeGette (D)	140,073	67.4%
Mike Fallon (R)	59,747	28.8%
Gary Swing (GREEN)	2,923	1.4%
Clint Jones (LIBERT)	2,867	1.4%
Chris Styskal (AC)	2,141	1.0%

2010 PRIMARY
Diana DeGette (D)	unopposed

2008 GENERAL
Diana DeGette (D)	203,756	71.9%
George C. Lilly (R)	67,346	23.8%
Martin L. Buchanan (LIBERT)	12,136	4.3%

Previous Winning Percentages
2006 (80%); 2004 (74%); 2002 (66%); 2000 (69%); 1998 (7%); 1996 (57%)

Elected 1996; 8th term

DeGette is relentless in her pursuit of legislative goals, often spending several years on particular issues. Her persistence has yielded victories on increased funding of stem cell research and expansion of a children's health insurance program.

DeGette backed her mentor, Michigan Democrat John D. Dingell, in his losing fight for chairman of the Energy and Commerce Committee in the 111th Congress (2009-10), but it hasn't cost her. In the minority in the 112th (2011-12), she serves as top Democrat on the committee's Oversight and Investigations panel.

DeGette was in the middle of the health care debate in the 111th. A fervent supporter of abortion rights, she opposed efforts by Democrat Bart Stupak of Michigan to prohibit federal funding of abortion coverage in the overhaul legislation. But when the time came for final passage, DeGette accepted the compromise worked out by Stupak with the Democratic leadership and the White House, saying it went no further than current law, the so-called Hyde amendment that bars federal funding of abortion.

"We think it's something we can fix later. We would like to overturn the Hyde amendment," said DeGette, who co-chairs the House Pro-Choice Caucus. "But we said we would compromise to current law in order to make this a health care bill, not an abortion bill." Abortion foes argue that the legislation and accompanying executive order go beyond current law in loosening restrictions on federal funding of abortions.

When Republicans revisited the issue at the beginning of 2011 with a bill to permanently ban federal funding and eliminate tax breaks for health insurance premiums on policies that cover abortion-related services, DeGette called it "the biggest intrusion on a woman's right to choose in our lifetime."

DeGette also been in the thick of debates on energy policy.

When Energy and Commerce considered in 2010 a bill that would authorize grants for drinking-water projects, she pushed an amendment based on legislation she sponsored to require disclosure of chemicals used in hydraulic fracturing, then withdrew it, saying a compromise was possible. (Hydraulic fracturing, or fracking, involves injecting water and chemicals under high pressure to fracture rock in which oil and gas are embedded.)

She pursued a similar line of questioning related to the spring 2010 Gulf of Mexico oil spill, raising questions about the safety of dispersants. At a May 2010 Energy and Commerce hearing on the spill, DeGette suggested it might be time to cease offshore drilling altogether. When a witness from the environmental advocacy group Oceana said, "We think it's time to get out of the offshore," DeGette responded, "You know, I agree with you."

Broadly, she defends government regulation. "The mantra that regulations are inherently bad and kill jobs is wrong and dangerous," she said at an Oversight and Investigations Subcommittee hearing in January 2011.

DeGette has persisted across multiple Congresses on stem cell research. For years, she battled President George W. Bush's restrictions on federally funded embryonic stem cell research, which uses discarded embryos created for in vitro fertilization. Bush twice vetoed bills to expand funding, but the election of Barack Obama made DeGette's goal a reality.

DeGette's activism on the subject was shaped in part by personal experience: One of her daughters has diabetes, and her hope is that stem cell research can someday provide an improved treatment or a cure. After her first defeat in 2006, DeGette helped campaign for a number of candidates who shared her position, picking up 14 votes when she pushed her bill through the House a second time in 2007. The final count was still short of the two-thirds majority required to override a veto, however. Her book on the saga, "Sex, Science and Stem Cells: Inside the Right Wing's Assault on Reason," was released just before the Democratic National Convention kicked off in her Denver district in August 2008.

One of the Democrats' nine chief deputy whips, DeGette counts her bipartisan whip effort on a renewable-energy standard in 2007 as one of her biggest successes, although the legislation fell one vote short in the Senate. She also helped steer through the House in the 110th Congress (2007-08) an expansion of the Children's Health Insurance Program, which covers children from low-income families that make too much money to qualify for Medicaid, only to see it fall to Bush's veto. But the legislation sailed through Congress in 2009 and was swiftly signed into law by Obama.

Born in Japan, where her father was stationed with the Air Force, DeGette spent most of her childhood in the Denver area. She was deeply affected, at age 10, by news coverage of the assassination of the Rev. Martin Luther King Jr. "It hit me, the whole idea of social justice and fighting for equality. I decided I was going to become a lawyer."

After earning a law degree at New York University, DeGette became a public defender in Denver and then went into private practice, specializing in cases about discrimination based on disability, sex and age. She volunteered in Federico Peña's mayoral campaign, spurring her interest in public service. "I can do these cases one at a time," she recalls thinking, "or I can get elected to office and I can affect many people by changing the laws."

She won a Colorado House seat in 1992. As a freshman member of the minority party, DeGette won enactment of a law — upheld by the Supreme Court in 2000 — requiring protesters to stay eight feet from anyone within 100 feet of entrances to clinics where abortions are performed.

DeGette moved up to the party leadership in the chamber but resigned from the legislature in early 1996 to concentrate on her bid to succeed Democrat Patricia Schroeder in the U.S. House.

DeGette defeated the Republican nominee, Joe Rogers, a lawyer and former aide to Colorado GOP Sen. Hank Brown, by 17 percentage points. Her seven re-elections have been with at least two-thirds of the vote.

When Obama named Colorado Sen. Ken Salazar as Interior secretary, DeGette figured in speculation about Salazar's successor. But she took herself out of the running, saying she could be more effective as Colorado's senior House member.

Key Votes

2010

Overhaul the nation's health insurance system	YES
Allow for repeal of "don't ask, don't tell"	YES
Overhaul financial services industry regulation	YES
Limit use of new Afghanistan War funds to troop withdrawal activities	YES
Change oversight of offshore drilling and lift oil spill liability cap	YES
Provide a path to legal status for some children of illegal immigrants	YES
Extend Bush-era income tax cuts for two years	NO

2009

Expand the Children's Health Insurance Program	YES
Provide $787 billion in tax cuts and spending increases to stimulate the economy	YES
Allow bankruptcy judges to modify certain primary-residence mortgages	YES
Create a cap-and-trade system to limit greenhouse gas emissions	YES
Provide $2 billion for the "cash for clunkers" program	YES
Establish the government as the sole provider of student loans	YES
Restrict federally funded insurance coverage for abortions in health care overhaul	NO

CQ Vote Studies

	PARTY UNITY		PRESIDENTIAL SUPPORT	
	SUPPORT	OPPOSE	SUPPORT	OPPOSE
2010	99%	1%	92%	8%
2009	99%	1%	97%	3%
2008	99%	1%	13%	87%
2007	99%	1%	5%	95%
2006	98%	2%	25%	75%

Interest Groups

	AFL-CIO	ADA	CCUS	ACU
2010	100%	95%	13%	0%
2009	100%	100%	33%	0%
2008	100%	80%	59%	0%
2007	100%	90%	55%	0%
2006	100%	95%	33%	4%

Colorado 1

Denver

The capital city of Denver takes up most of the 1st District, which stretches north and east following the city limits to reach the airport. The 1st, a bastion of liberalism in the once-conservative state, is Colorado's smallest district in size, but Denver's presence allows the district to set the tone for the Centennial State's economic future.

Denver was once dependent on the region's oil and gas industries, but the city boomed during the 1990s as its economy broadened to include technology and telecommunications. These industries now rival state government as the major employers here, although fossil fuel energy remains important. State and local officials are encouraging further diversification, working to attract renewable-energy firms to the area.

Health care is also important to Denver's economic well-being. There are several hospitals and service providers downtown or in surrounding areas, but the region's health industry is anchored by the University of Colorado Denver Health Sciences Center campus and bioscience research park at the former Fitzsimons Army Medical Center, located just outside the district's borders in Aurora (in the 7th). Concerns over foreclosures and job losses in several sectors trouble some residents.

Decades of revitalization efforts in the city's lower downtown district, known by locals as "LoDo," have created a pedestrian-friendly residential and commercial area with a vibrant nightlife. Tourists visit art galleries, restaurants and large entertainment venues. Denver International Airport, which opened in 1995, has become one of the nation's busiest.

Denver has the state's most diverse population — the district's growing Hispanic community makes up more than 30 percent of residents while blacks make up almost one-tenth of the population.

Ninety percent of the 1st's residents live in Denver, which has not sent a Republican to the U.S. House since 1970. Barack Obama won 74 percent of the 1st's 2008 presidential vote, easily his highest percentage in the state.

Major Industry
Telecommunications, computers, government, health care, tourism

Cities
Denver, 600,158; Englewood (pt.), 30,170

Notable
The Great American Beer Festival is the nation's largest and oldest annual brewing competition.

Rep. Jared Polis (D)

Capitol Office
225-2161
polis.house.gov
501 Cannon Bldg. 20515-0602; fax 226-7840

Committees
Rules

Residence
Boulder

Born
May 12, 1975; Boulder, Colo.

Religion
Jewish

Family
Partner, Marlon Reis

Education
Princeton U., A.B. 1996 (politics)

Career
Internet entrepreneur and venture capitalist; at-risk charter schools founder

Political Highlights
Colo. Board of Education, 2001-07 (chairman, 2004-05)

ELECTION RESULTS

2010 GENERAL

Jared Polis (D)	148,720	57.4%
Stephen Bailey (R)	98,171	37.9%
Jenna Goss (AC)	7,080	2.7%
Curtis Harris (LIBERT)	5,056	2.0%

2010 PRIMARY

Jared Polis (D)	unopposed

2008 GENERAL

Jared Polis (D)	215,571	62.6%
Scott Starin (R)	116,591	33.9%
J.A. Calhoun (GREEN)	10,026	2.9%

Elected 2008; 2nd term

Polis is one of the youngest, wealthiest and most tech-savvy members of Congress. He is a reliable liberal vote and has used his fundraising abilities to quickly make a mark as a Democratic insider and leadership ally.

An Internet entrepreneur turned education philanthropist, Polis launched an Internet access company as a college sophomore. He then helped spin his family's greeting card company into BlueMountain.com and founded one of the largest online floral companies. And he launched a chain of movie theaters that screen Hollywood films dubbed or subtitled in Spanish.

His Internet ventures, which netted him a place on Fortune's list of "40 Richest Under 40," helped him self-fund his first House campaign. Roll Call ranked him the seventh wealthiest member of Congress in 2010, with a net worth of $56.5 million.

Polis reaches out to his constituents, who he says are already net savvy, through Facebook and Twitter. He won a contest among members to see who could gain the most Facebook, Twitter and You Tube followers and is involved in the Democratic caucus' New Media Working Group.

Upon his arrival on Capitol Hill for the 111th Congress (2009-10), he was viewed as a dependable leadership ally and was one of two freshman Democrats put on the Rules Committee, which governs floor debate of bills. He also serves on the Democratic Steering Committee, which sets committee assignments.

Polis has voted to end funding for the wars in Iraq and Afghanistan. And he has expressed support for the idea of moving terrorist detainees from the detention facility at Guantánamo Bay, Cuba, to a federal maximum security prison in Colorado. "We want to keep them locked up with no chance of escape," Polis said. "If [Supermax] is the best facility for the purpose of the country, then that's where we should lock them up."

Polis was one of three Democrats to side with Republicans in voting "no" in the Education and Labor Committee on a provision to help fund the health care overhaul with a $544 billion surtax on people earning more than $280,000 a year. He organized a letter to Democratic leaders expressing concerns about the tax proposal. But he ended up voting for the final version of the legislation.

Similarly, he opposed extending the Bush-era tax cuts for the highest earners, but voted for the measure signed into law that extended the rates for two years for all income levels. "We can't let taxes go up for people making $60,000, $70,000, $80,000 a year on our watch," he said on MSNBC.

Although he left the Education panel because of Democratic losses in the 2010 elections, Polis remains interested in playing a part in rewriting the "No Child Left Behind" education law and pushing legislation to create more high-performing charter schools.

His desire to overhaul the nation's education system was hatched when he was elected to the Colorado State Board of Education in 2000. Since arriving in Congress, he has introduced bills that would award grants to public charter schools to expand and to enhance childhood nutrition and wellness education.

He also left the Judiciary Committee, where he backed efforts at broad immigration legislation. He laments the number of immigrants in detention being held "like criminals at taxpayer expense." He called for a requirement that illegal immigrants "register within a year, pay a fine and finally be able to lawfully work within our borders. Those with a criminal background would be kicked out and banned from re-entering."

Polis spends much of his time trying to raise awareness of equality issues. He is the first openly gay man elected to Congress as a non-incumbent. He investigated the treatment of gays in Iraq for months before touring the country in 2009. Along with the other two openly homosexual members of Congress — Democrats Barney Frank of Massachusetts and Tammy Baldwin of Wisconsin — he asked Secretary of State Hillary Rodham Clinton to work with the Iraqi government, United Nations and human rights organizations to end the execution of gay Iraqis.

He cosponsored a successful House measure to expand the definition of federal hate crimes to those based on a person's gender identity, sexual orientation or disability. Polis, Frank and Baldwin — who co-chair the LGBT Equality Caucus — encouraged the Democratic leadership to pave the way for the passage of other bills: Baldwin's measure to allow same-sex partners of federal employees to receive the same benefits as married spouses and Frank's employment non-discrimination bill that includes protections for gays and transgender people. He expressed satisfaction when the law barring openly gay and lesbian members from serving openly was repealed in late 2010. "Our government will no longer be an instrument of discrimination against us," he said on the House floor.

Polis also has spoken against hate crimes against Sikhs, warning in a May 2009 floor speech, "There is a danger that the gravity of the problem will escape the attention of lawmakers and law enforcement officials."

Polis was introduced to political activism at a young age. His journalist-turned-poet mother and physicist-turned-artist father, who had been antiwar activists during the 1960s, took their young son with them to demonstrations against nuclear proliferation. As a teenager he volunteered for Michael Dukakis' 1988 presidential campaign and Josie Heath's 1990 campaign for the Senate.

Polis spent summers in Colorado and the school year in San Diego, where he founded a Democratic Club. At 16, he entered Princeton University, where he was active in Jewish community activities, student government, the College Democrats and the ROTC.

Before running for office, Polis had a history of fundraising in Colorado; he had worked with three other wealthy activists to funnel millions into state races over the years.

When Democratic Rep. Mark Udall decided to run for the Senate, Polis self-funded his 2008 House campaign with almost $6 million of his own money. He rejected campaign donations from political action committees associated with industries, then accused his opponents of accepting money from oil and mining interests. He won the general election with nearly 63 percent of the vote, having spent more than $7.3 million. In 2010 he defeated Republican Stephen Bailey 57 percent to 38 percent.

Key Votes

2010

Overhaul the nation's health insurance system	YES
Allow for repeal of "don't ask, don't tell"	YES
Overhaul financial services industry regulation	YES
Limit use of new Afghanistan War funds to troop withdrawal activities	YES
Change oversight of offshore drilling and lift oil spill liability cap	YES
Provide a path to legal status for some children of illegal immigrants	YES
Extend Bush-era income tax cuts for two years	YES

2009

Expand the Children's Health Insurance Program	YES
Provide $787 billion in tax cuts and spending increases to stimulate the economy	YES
Allow bankruptcy judges to modify certain primary-residence mortgages	YES
Create a cap-and-trade system to limit greenhouse gas emissions	YES
Provide $2 billion for the "cash for clunkers" program	NO
Establish the government as the sole provider of student loans	YES
Restrict federally funded insurance coverage for abortions in health care overhaul	NO

CQ Vote Studies

	PARTY UNITY		PRESIDENTIAL SUPPORT	
	Support	Oppose	Support	Oppose
2010	97%	3%	81%	19%
2009	97%	3%	88%	12%

Interest Groups

	AFL-CIO	ADA	CCUS	ACU
2010	71%	90%	25%	4%
2009	90%	95%	47%	4%

Colorado 2

Northwest Denver suburbs; Boulder

The rapidly growing 2nd takes in suburbs north and west of Denver, along with Boulder, before heading into the mountains, crossing the Continental Divide and scooping up national forests, wilderness areas, reservoirs and part of ski country. Boulder's liberal culture pulls the generally moderate district to the left, and environmental issues play heavily here.

Boulder, at the foothills of the majestic Rocky Mountains, is home to the University of Colorado's flagship campus and a committed corps of environmentalists. Outdoor sports remain the city's most popular pastime, and bicycling is highly regarded in the snowy city, where plows clear 60 miles of bike paths for commuters. The city center also boasts a vibrant shopping and nightlife district.

Several federal research laboratories and biotechnology companies have facilities in the district in order to take advantage of the well-educated workforce. Scientists at the National Institute of Standards and Technology campus in Boulder perform physics, optics, statistics and computer science research, and NIST is the nation's official timekeeper. Renewable energy firms, particularly in wind and solar power, play a role in the economy.

The district also includes the northern part of Jefferson and western Adams counties, including nearly all of Westminster as well as growing suburbs between Boulder and Denver. Urban sprawl has gained attention here, and some local officials have urged reviews of zoning and planning regulations to accommodate mixed-use development.

Skiing is king in the mountain counties of Eagle, Grand and Summit, located in the western part of the district. Eagle is home to the resort city of Vail, and these skiing communities and other towns along Interstate 70 make the district a tourist magnet year-round. Scenic Rocky Mountain National Park (shared with the 4th) is another draw to the area.

Major Industry
Technology, research, higher education, tourism

Cities
Thornton (pt.), 117,713; Westminster (pt.), 105,986; Boulder, 97,385

Notable
Eisenhower Memorial Tunnel, which takes Interstate 70 across the Continental Divide, is the world's highest vehicular tunnel.

Rep. Scott Tipton (R)

Capitol Office
225-4761
tipton.house.gov
218 Cannon Bldg. 20515-0603; fax 226-9669

Committees
Agriculture
Natural Resources
Small Business
  (Agriculture, Energy & Trade - Chairman)

Residence
Cortez

Born
Nov. 9, 1956; Espanola, N.M.

Religion
Anglican

Family
Wife, Jean Tipton; two children

Education
Fort Lewis College, B.A. 1978 (political science)

Career
Pottery company owner

Political Highlights
Montezuma County Republican Party chairman,
1980-84; Republican nominee for U.S. House, 2006;
Colo. House, 2009-10

ELECTION RESULTS

2010 GENERAL

Scott Tipton (R)	129,257	50.1%
John Salazar (D)	118,048	45.8%
Gregory Gilman (LIBERT)	5,678	2.2%
Jake Segrest (UNA)	4,982	1.9%

2010 PRIMARY

Scott Tipton (R)	39,346	55.8%
Bob McConnell (R)	31,214	44.2%

Elected 2010; 1st term

Tipton's political views have been called "vintage Republican." He wants less government and lower taxes, and he holds conservative social values regarding issues such as abortion and gay marriage.

A small-business owner who served a single term in his state's General Assembly, Tipton calls agriculture the "backbone" of his large Colorado district, adding that it is important to protect the water supply from "downstream threats and from in-state water grabs."

In addition to holding a seat on the Agriculture Committee, he serves as chairman of the Small Business Committee's Agriculture, Energy and Trade panel. Tipton also won a spot on the Natural Resources Committee.

The husband of a retired teacher, Tipton also lists education among his priorities. He backs tougher graduation standards, stronger safety programs at schools and greater federal support for charter schools.

Tipton supports gun owners' rights, opposes a path to citizenship for illegal immigrants and says abortion should be limited to cases of "rape, incest or threat to the life of the mother." He says the definition of marriage should be left to states, "not co-opted by judges and the federal government."

Tipton graduated from Fort Lewis College in Durango with a degree in political science in 1978. He then co-founded Mesa Verde Pottery with his brother, selling handmade Navajo and Ute items.

Tipton first made a bid for the House in 2006 in the politically competitive 3rd district, but lost to incumbent Democrat John Salazar, taking 37 percent of the vote. Two years later Tipton won election to the Colorado House.

A victory over tea party favorite Bob McConnell in the 2010 GOP primary set up a rematch with Salazar. Riding the Republican wave, Tipton improved on his previous performance by 13 percentage points, topping the brother of Interior Secretary Ken Salazar 50 percent to 46 percent.

After the election, Roll Call reported that Tipton's personal cell phone number and e-mail address were among those released by one of the largest coalitions of tea party activists, listing him among the new GOP members in danger of being "co-opted" by Washington insiders.

Colorado 3
Western Slope; Pueblo

Spanning 29 counties, the 3rd includes more than half of Colorado's land area, moving from the Wyoming border in the north to the Ute Mountain Indian Reservation and Four Corners area in the southwest, before heading east to include all but one county on the state's southern edge. It displays some of the variety found outside the state's urban centers: rural poor, resort rich, old steel-mill towns and isolated Hispanic counties.

Most of Colorado's rivers flow down the Western Slope to Nevada and California, and residents here want more of the water stored for local use. Former robust mining areas have dwindled and manufacturing has declined, but the 3rd has added energy sector jobs. Pueblo's Colorado State University campus thrives, and local officials hope to diversify the 3rd's economy by creating a more educated workforce.

Pueblo, the district's most populous county, was once dependent on steel but is beginning to attract people back to its namesake city's downtown. In the north and west parts of the 3rd, national parks and ski resorts combine to support the economic mainstay: tourism. Visitors hike, bike or raft through the San Juan and Sawatch Mountains, the latter of which include Aspen's ski resort. Residential Colorado has spilled over the Continental Divide onto the Western Slope. Independent-minded baby boomers in this mountainous terrain tend to give the 3rd a Republican lean. But Pueblo County, heavily unionized and more than 40 percent Hispanic, keeps the district competitive.

Major Industry
Tourism, skiing, agriculture

Cities
Pueblo, 106,595; Grand Junction, 58,566; Pueblo West (unincorporated), 29,637

Notable
The Federal Citizen Information Center is in Pueblo.

Rep. Cory Gardner (R)

Capitol Office
225-4676
gardner.house.gov
213 Cannon Bldg. 20515-0604; fax 225-5870

Committees
Energy & Commerce

Residence
Yuma

Born
Aug. 22, 1974; Yuma, Colo.

Religion
Lutheran - Missouri Synod

Family
Wife, Jaime Gardner; one child

Education
Colorado State U., B.A. 1997 (political science);
U. of Colorado, J.D. 2001

Career
Lawyer; congressional aide; agricultural advocacy organization spokesman; farm equipment parts dealer

Political Highlights
Colo. House, 2005-10

ELECTION RESULTS

2010 GENERAL

Cory Gardner (R)	138,634	52.5%
Betsy Markey (D)	109,249	41.4%
Doug Aden (AC)	12,312	4.7%
Ken Waszkiewicz (UNA)	3,986	1.5%

2010 PRIMARY

Cory Gardner (R)	unopposed

Elected 2010; 1st term

Agriculture is central to Gardner's political ambitions and his district. The fifth-generation Coloradan is a one-time spokesman for a corn growers association, operator of a farm equipment parts dealership and former Senate aide who counted agriculture as part of his brief.

He was one of six GOP freshmen to win a coveted seat on the Energy and Commerce Committee, with jurisdiction over issues including energy, health care and telecommunications.

Gardner would like to further renewable-energy development and places an emphasis on advancements in crop technologies.

His experience in Denver and in Washington, where he was an aide to former GOP Sen. Wayne Allard, gives him some familiarity with the legislative process. He wants to draw on that background to reduce the federal government's regulatory burden on water storage projects, which are vital to both farming and residential development.

Gardner says disagreements over climate change could be eased by working together to produce more renewable sources such as wind energy and developing traditional sources, such as natural gas, "in an environmentally responsible manner."

He was no fan of legislation the Democratic House passed in 2009 designed to limit carbon emissions, and he is an even more vociferous critic of plans by the EPA to implement some of the proposals included in that measure, which died in the Senate.

"Whether you're Democratic or Republican," Gardner said, "you ought to be concerned that EPA is doing an end run around Congress and taking action that is the purview of Congress, not the executive branch."

Gardner's predecessor, one-term Rep. Betsy Markey, was the first Democrat elected to the seat in decades when she defeated incumbent Republican Marilyn Musgrave by 13 percentage points in 2008. Gardner turned the tables on her in 2010, winning an often-feisty campaign with 53 percent of the vote to Markey's 41 percent.

Colorado 4

North and east — Fort Collins; Greeley

The 4th, which covers Colorado's eastern plains and touches five other states, looks more like the Kansas prairies than the rugged Rockies of much of the rest of the state. Thanks to intensive irrigation, the 4th's southern and eastern portions include productive wheat and corn fields. Climate and market volatility can hurt yields and prices.

The southern part of the district is spread across mainly small, rural communities, and with roughly 7,000 residents, Lamar is the only town or city in the 4th's southern half with more than 3,000 people.

The northwestern part of the district, including Larimer and almost all of Weld counties, along with the 4th's small part of Boulder County, holds nearly 85 percent of the district's population while occupying less than a third of its land. In Larimer, Fort Col-

lins — which is the district's most populous city — is home to Colorado State University. The school's research facilities and the local workforce lure technology firms and stabilize the economy.

Taking in mostly rural GOP territory, the 4th has a history of sending Republicans to the House, but federal elections have become a bit more competitive. Republican John McCain won here in the 2008 presidential election — eight of his top 10 counties statewide were in rural parts of the 4th — by less than 1 percentage point, and the GOP took back the House seat after a one-term hiatus.

Major Industry
Agriculture, meatpacking, higher education

Cities
Fort Collins, 143,986; Greeley, 92,889; Longmont, 86,270; Loveland, 66,859

Notable
Greeley hosts the Greeley Stampede rodeo and music festival each year leading up to July Fourth.

Rep. Doug Lamborn (R)

Capitol Office
225-4422
lamborn.house.gov
437 Cannon Bldg. 20515-0605; fax 225-1942

Committees
Armed Services
Natural Resources
    (Energy & Mineral Resources - Chairman)
Veterans' Affairs

Residence
Colorado Springs

Born
May 24, 1954; Leavenworth, Kan.

Religion
Christian

Family
Wife, Jeanie Lamborn; five children

Education
U. of Kansas, B.S. 1978 (journalism), J.D. 1985

Career
Lawyer

Political Highlights
Republican nominee for Kan. House, 1982; Colo.
House, 1995-98; Colo. Senate, 1998-2007 (president
pro tempore, 1999-2000)

ELECTION RESULTS

2010 GENERAL

Doug Lamborn (R)	152,829	65.8%
Kevin Bradley (D)	68,039	29.3%
Brian "Barron X" Scott (AC)	5,886	2.5%
Jerell Klaver (LIBERT)	5,680	2.4%

2010 PRIMARY

Doug Lamborn (R)	unopposed

2008 GENERAL

Doug Lamborn (R)	183,178	60.0%
Hal Bidlack (D)	113,025	37.0%
Brian "Barron X" Scott (AC)	8,894	2.9%

Previous Winning Percentages
2006 (60%)

Elected 2006; 3rd term

It is hard to establish a legacy as a junior member of the minority party, but Lamborn managed this achievement: He is one of the most reliably conservative members of the House. Now in the majority, he chairs the Natural Resources Subcommittee on Energy and Mineral Resources, a plum assignment for a Coloradan.

He will be the point man for Republicans' "all of the above" energy proposals, which include pushing for development of renewable sources along with increased production of oil, natural gas and coal.

"America was built on abundant and affordable energy. President Obama's policy of locking-up energy goes against what makes America great," Lamborn wrote in a Washington Examiner op-ed in early 2011.

During his first four years in Congress, Lamborn sided with Republicans on 99 percent of the votes that pitted the majority of each party against each other. He received a perfect 100 rating in 2009 from the American Conservative Union and got a score of 90 percent or above from the National Taxpayers Union each year from 2007 to 2009.

"I am proud of that," Lamborn said. "I am standing up for and not compromising conservative values, which is very much the desire of at least a majority of my district." The 5th, site of the Air Force Academy, also is home to a number of evangelical groups, including Focus on the Family.

Lamborn is a reliable vote on social conservative agenda items, opposing abortion and defending gun owners' rights. A member of the Armed Services Committee, he opposed congressional action to repeal the armed forces' "don't ask, don't tell" policy that bars gays from serving openly.

He also has taken the lead on more esoteric areas of concern to the right. In 2009, Lamborn launched the Congressional Sovereignty Caucus with Republicans Thaddeus McCotter of Michigan and Scott Garrett of New Jersey to "protect and defend the rights of American citizens and the interests of American institutions from the increasing influence of international organizations and multilateral agreements."

Lamborn also joined nine of his colleagues in launching the 10th Amendment Task Force, a project of the Republican Study Committee (a group of the House GOP's most conservative lawmakers). The task force's goal is to "develop and promote proposals to disperse power, decision-making and money from Washington back to states, local governments and individuals."

He has been a leader in efforts to end federal funding for public broadcasting entities, a task being renewed with vigor in the 112th Congress (2011-12). "I have nothing against NPR, despite what appeared to be liberal bias in their mishandling of [the firing of journalist] Juan Williams," he wrote in The Hill newspaper. "What I oppose is subsidizing an organization that no longer provides, if it ever did, an essential government service." The House folded his proposal to eliminate public broadcasting funding into the fiscal 2011 spending bill the chamber passed in February 2011.

Lamborn is as committed to fiscal conservatism as he is the social variety. But, before the GOP instituted a moratorium, he differentiated himself from some conservatives by seeking funding for earmarks. He distinguished his requests by seeking funding only for defense-related items. Unlike local road or water projects, he says, defense projects deliver value to all taxpayers. Still, when House Republicans adopted their ban, Lamborn was on board. "I am going along wholeheartedly . . . because we have to reform the way things are done because of the abuses that other people do."

The 5th District is home to five major military installations and more than 100,000 veterans, and one of his primary legislative initiatives on the Veterans' Affairs Committee has been the establishment of a national veterans cemetery in southern Colorado. In April 2010, Lamborn announced that the Department of Veterans Affairs had confirmed it is reviewing sites there for a new cemetery.

Lamborn is an avid hiker and says one of his hobbies is climbing the dozens of 14,000-foot peaks in the state. A member of the Natural Resources Committee during the 110th Congress (2007-08), he led an effort to turn Colorado's famous Pikes Peak into a national monument. Local agencies criticized him for not telling them first, and some officials said it would have little effect on the mountain or protection of the land. He later abandoned the effort.

He grew up on a family farm near Leavenworth, Kan. His mother was a homemaker; his father was a farmer, who supplemented the family income by working at a federal penitentiary. He and his three brothers attended a three-room school near Fairmount before graduating from Lansing High School. Lamborn was class valedictorian and went to the University of Kansas as a National Merit Scholar. He graduated with a journalism degree and later earned a law degree, then worked for a law firm in Omaha. As a young lawyer, he once sneaked out in the middle of the night to reclaim a client's car from an ex-girl-friend, according to the Colorado Springs Gazette Telegraph.

Lamborn said he was inspired to enter politics when Ronald Reagan was elected president. In 1982, Lamborn ran unsuccessfully for a seat in the Kansas legislature. He moved to Colorado Springs with his wife in 1986 and won a seat in the Colorado House in 1994.

Republican Rep. Joel Hefley's retirement in 2006 sparked a free-for-all in the August GOP primary. With the backing of the conservative Club for Growth, Lamborn edged ex-Hefley aide Jeff Crank in the primary. That November, Lamborn defeated retired Air Force Lt. Col. Jay Fawcett by nearly 20 percentage points.

In September 2007, he attracted attention for leaving a message on a Colorado Springs couple's phone, saying there would be "consequences" if the couple didn't withdraw a letter criticizing him for accepting money from the Nevada-based International Gaming Technology. Lamborn, who had returned the $1,000 check, later apologized to the couple, saying he meant only that he would report the matter to the county GOP chairman.

In 2008, Crank again challenged Lamborn in the primary. Lamborn won by 14 percentage points, then took 60 percent in the general election. He won almost two-thirds of the vote against Democrat Kevin Bradley in 2010.

Key Votes

2010

Overhaul the nation's health insurance system	NO
Allow for repeal of "don't ask, don't tell"	NO
Overhaul financial services industry regulation	NO
Limit use of new Afghanistan War funds to troop withdrawal activities	NO
Change oversight of offshore drilling and lift oil spill liability cap	NO
Provide a path to legal status for some children of illegal immigrants	NO
Extend Bush-era income tax cuts for two years	NO

2009

Expand the Children's Health Insurance Program	NO
Provide $787 billion in tax cuts and spending increases to stimulate the economy	NO
Allow bankruptcy judges to modify certain primary-residence mortgages	NO
Create a cap-and-trade system to limit greenhouse gas emissions	NO
Provide $2 billion for the "cash for clunkers" program	NO
Establish the government as the sole provider of student loans	NO
Restrict federally funded insurance coverage for abortions in health care overhaul	YES

CQ Vote Studies

	PARTY UNITY		PRESIDENTIAL SUPPORT	
	SUPPORT	OPPOSE	SUPPORT	OPPOSE
2010	99%	1%	21%	79%
2009	99%	1%	13%	87%
2008	99%	1%	83%	17%
2007	99%	1%	95%	5%

Interest Groups

	AFL-CIO	ADA	CCUS	ACU
2010	0%	5%	75%	100%
2009	5%	0%	73%	100%
2008	0%	0%	83%	100%
2007	4%	0%	70%	100%

Colorado 5

South central — Colorado Springs

God and country dominate the 5th, an overwhelmingly conservative district in the shadows of the Rocky Mountains in central Colorado. Military bases employ tens of thousands in the Colorado Springs area, and James Dobson's Focus on the Family and other evangelical groups are based in the 5th.

The district has made itself an indispensable arm of the military. Colorado Springs in El Paso County houses the Air Force Space Command, the North American Aerospace Defense Command (NORAD) and the U.S. Northern Command at Peterson Air Force Base. The city has broadened its economic base beyond the military and satellite research —much of the 5th's industry, including superconductor and computer development, still depends on the defense sector — but new jobs are scarce.

The Colorado Springs area is a prime destination for tourists who stop at spots such as: the U.S. Air Force Academy; Pikes Peak, the most visited mountain in North America; Glen Eyrie, the 19th-century castle formerly owned by Colorado Springs founder Gen. William Jackson Palmer; and, the nearby Garden of the Gods. More than 85 percent of district residents live in El Paso County, and Colorado Springs consistently ranks as one of the nation's best big cities to live in.

El Paso, the largest county in the 5th, gave Republican John McCain 59 percent of its vote — the same percentage with which he took the district overall — in a state that Democrat Barack Obama carried in the 2008 presidential election. Democratic Sen. Mark Udall was held to less than 40 percent in El Paso, Teller and Fremont counties and, of districts wholly within the 5th, won only in Lake County.

Major Industry
Military, defense, tourism, technology

Military Bases
Fort Carson (Army), 30,700 military, 3,090 civilian (2011); U.S. Air Force Academy, 5,745 military, 1,582 civilian (2009); Peterson Air Force Base, 3,342 military, 2,466 civilian (2009); Schriever Air Force Base, 1,644 military, 802 civilian (2010)

Cities
Colorado Springs, 416,427; Security-Widefield (unincorporated), 32,882

Notable
The U.S. Olympic Committee headquarters are in Colorado Springs.

Rep. Mike Coffman (R)

Capitol Office
225-7882
coffman.house.gov
1222 Longworth Bldg. 20515-0606; fax 226-4623

Committees
Armed Services
Natural Resources
Small Business
   (Investigations, Oversight & Regulations -
   Chairman)

Residence
Aurora

Born
March 19, 1955; Fort Leonard Wood, Mo.

Religion
United Methodist

Family
Wife, Cynthia Coffman

Education
U. of Colorado, B.A. 1979 (political science)

Military
Army, 1972-74; Army Reserve, 1975-79; Marine Corps,
1979-83; Marine Corps Reserve, 1983-94; Marine
Corps Reserve, 2005-06

Career
Property management company owner

Political Highlights
Candidate for Aurora City Council, 1985; Colo. House,
1989-94; Colo. Senate, 1994-98; Colo. treasurer, 1999-
2007; Colo. secretary of state, 2007-08

ELECTION RESULTS

2010 GENERAL

Mike Coffman (R)	217,368	65.7%
John Flerlage (D)	104,104	31.5%
Rob McNealy (LIBERT)	9,466	2.9%

2010 PRIMARY

Mike Coffman (R)	unopposed

2008 GENERAL

Mike Coffman (R)	250,877	60.7%
Hank Eng (D)	162,639	39.3%

Elected 2008; 2nd term

Coffman is a veteran of both the Army and the Marine Corps, with a conservative vision of his role as a lawmaker that reflects his military ethos: Take care of national security and the troops, and make the government stay within its means.

Coffman led combat troops in the first Gulf War while a member of the state legislature, and his service turned him from a somewhat obscure lawmaker into "a celebrity in [state] House chambers just by not being there," the Rocky Mountain News reported in 2008. Coffman also helped organize local elections in Iraq in 2005 and 2006.

His military experience led to a seat on the Armed Services Committee. He has been supportive of the U.S. war effort in Iraq and Afghanistan, but is less sanguine about the follow-up.

"I think this nation made a terrible mistake in relying on nation-building as a principal tool for achieving our national security interests," he said on CNN in July 2010. "And I think what the [George W.] Bush administration did initially was great. We gave air logistical and advisory support to the anti-Taliban forces after we were attacked on 9/11. But after they achieved victory, instead of using our leverage to say you need to reach out to the anti-Taliban Pashtun elements of the country and form some governing coalition that fits the political culture of the country, we pushed them aside, superimposed a political process on them, gave them the government that we wanted them to have, and we are defending that government today."

On Iraq, he said, "I wish we had not gone in, in the manner that we did, but that's hindsight and it's always 20/20. Once in, we had to make it work and we did in fact make it work."

In March 2010, the House passed his bill to extend re-employment protections for National Guard members assigned to either a homeland security or overseas mission. He won inclusion in the fiscal 2011 defense policy bill of a provision that would provide combat benefits to the families and victims of the Fort Hood, Texas, shooting in 2009. His amendment to require the release of a Pentagon report on the attack, however, was defeated. "I'm deeply disappointed that the majority has chosen to be complicit in the Defense Department's willful concealment of the restricted portion of this report because it may be politically embarrassing," he said.

Tapping Coffman's reputation for frugality, House leaders named him to a special Panel on Defense Acquisition Reform, which led to legislation enacted in May 2009 to boost oversight of the Defense Department's procurement process to limit cost growth and improve delivery times.

He has proposed a 10 percent pay cut for lawmakers and a mandatory unpaid two-week furlough for all federal employees not involved in public safety or national security, which he says would save $5.5 billion a year.

Acting on behalf of his state, Coffman tried, unsuccessfully, to dissuade fellow lawmakers from blocking funds for the expansion of the Army's Piñon Canyon training area southeast of Colorado Springs. He's also a strong supporter of NASA's Constellation program, part of which is built in Colorado, and he objected to Obama administration proposals to kill it. "I feel as Neil Armstrong does, that this historic decision to end manned space flight by the U.S. government was 'poorly advised,'" Coffman wrote in a letter to the president in June 2010.

Coffman is a champion of boosting domestic production of rare-earth elements, important in the production of surveillance and weapons systems, as well as consumer electronics such as cell phones and batteries for hybrid cars. Most of the supply comes from China. He won inclusion in the fiscal 2011 defense policy measure of a provision requiring the Pentagon to study the issue. He also has sponsored legislation that would, among other things, require the establishment of a national stockpile of rare earth elements.

Coffman, who also sits on the Small Business Committee, is an advocate of smaller government as an instrument to aid economic growth. He was an enthusiastic supporter of the GOP moratorium on earmarks, and in March 2010 he co-founded the Balanced Budget Amendment Caucus. He also is a charter member of the Tea Party Caucus, founded by Minnesota Republican Michele Bachmann to be a conduit for the populist conservative movement.

On the Natural Resources Committee, Coffman seeks an "appropriate balance" between environmental and economic concerns. He voted against the Democrats' broad climate change bill in June 2009. At a committee hearing that September, he decried Interior Secretary Ken Salazar's announcement that the department would end its oil and gas royalty program: "So, we can't drill onshore, we can't drill offshore, we can't develop oil shale, we can't develop nuclear, and we can't develop solar? Mr. Secretary, why won't you let Americans develop American energy?"

Coffman was born at Fort Leonard Wood, Mo. His father was in the Army and the family lived there for about a year before bouncing between Alaska, Arkansas and Europe, settling in Colorado when Coffman was 9.

As a teenager Coffman volunteered at Fitzsimons Army Medical Center (now closed), where he saw wounded soldiers returning from Vietnam. He joined the Army when he was 17, completed his high school equivalency degree while in the Army and later joined the Marine Corps.

After active duty, he started a property management firm in the Denver area. He lost a race for the Aurora City Council in 1985 but three years later won a seat in the Colorado House, where he served six years, followed by four in the state Senate, where he chaired the Finance Committee. Elected state treasurer in 1998, he battled the governor and state senators, but earned praise from conservatives and the Colorado Union of Taxpayers.

Coffman was narrowly elected Colorado secretary of state in 2006. He easily defeated three opponents in the GOP House primary in 2008 in a heavily Republican district. He was then accused of purging voter lists in statewide races in a controversy that became the subject of a court challenge and led to a federal judge calling on Coffman to cease pulling voters from state registration rolls. In the end, he coasted with 61 percent of the vote. He was re-elected in 2010 over Democrat John Flerlage with 66 percent.

Key Votes

2010

Overhaul the nation's health insurance system	NO
Allow for repeal of "don't ask, don't tell"	NO
Overhaul financial services industry regulation	NO
Limit use of new Afghanistan War funds to troop withdrawal activities	NO
Change oversight of offshore drilling and lift oil spill liability cap	NO
Provide a path to legal status for some children of illegal immigrants	NO
Extend Bush-era income tax cuts for two years	YES

2009

Expand the Children's Health Insurance Program	NO
Provide $787 billion in tax cuts and spending increases to stimulate the economy	NO
Allow bankruptcy judges to modify certain primary-residence mortgages	-
Create a cap-and-trade system to limit greenhouse gas emissions	NO
Provide $2 billion for the "cash for clunkers" program	NO
Establish the government as the sole provider of student loans	NO
Restrict federally funded insurance coverage for abortions in health care overhaul	YES

CQ Vote Studies

	PARTY UNITY		PRESIDENTIAL SUPPORT	
	SUPPORT	OPPOSE	SUPPORT	OPPOSE
2010	95%	5%	29%	71%
2009	98%	2%	24%	76%

Interest Groups

	AFL-CIO	ADA	CCUS	ACU
2010	7%	0%	88%	100%
2009	15%	5%	73%	92%

Colorado 6

Denver suburbs — part of Aurora; Douglas County

White-collar suburbs south of Denver make up the heart of the 6th. Managing growth is a top priority for the affluent district, and commuters complain about traffic congestion in the densely populated counties around the Mile High City. An expansion of metropolitan light rail, as well as highway improvements, has eased some of the gridlock traveling to and from Denver.

Technology-sector manufacturing makes up the economic base for the district's well-educated residents. Employers include Raytheon and Lockheed Martin, which both rely heavily on federal funding. Although the financial transaction technology firm First Data relocated its corporate headquarters from Greenwood Village to Atlanta in 2009, the company still employs many area residents.

A plurality of district residents lives in Arapahoe County, which is mostly urbanized in the west near the Denver suburbs and exurbs and is more rural in the east. A small portion of Aurora, Colorado's third-most-populous city, is in the 6th's chunk of Arapahoe. Douglas County has experienced

overwhelming growth for decades. The county's population is more than three and half times larger than it was in 1990, and the GOP stronghold now accounts for 36 percent of the district's residents.

Largely due to the population growth in Douglas County, the 6th now is the most populous district in Colorado. It will have to shed tens of thousands of residents to a neighboring district during reapportionment and remapping, but its strong GOP lean will likely remain. Minorities total 18 percent of residents in the district, making the 6th the state's only district where minorities are less than 20 percent of the population. Democrats account for only one-fourth of registered voters in the district, and John McCain took 52 percent of the 6th's 2008 presidential vote.

Major Industry
Manufacturing, technology

Cities
Aurora (pt.), 112,113; Centennial, 100,377; Highlands Ranch (unincorporated), 96,713; Castle Rock, 48,231; Parker, 45,297; Littleton, 41,737

Notable
The Comanche Crossing Railroad Site near Strasburg marks the place where the last spike was driven in 1870 to create the first continuous transcontinental railroad.

Rep. Ed Perlmutter (D)

Capitol Office
225-2645
perlmutter.house.gov
1221 Longworth Bldg. 20515-0607; fax 225-5278

Committees
Financial Services

Residence
Golden

Born
May 1, 1953; Denver, Colo.

Religion
Protestant

Family
Wife, Nancy Perlmutter; three children

Education
U. of Colorado, B.A. 1975 (political science), J.D. 1978

Career
Lawyer

Political Highlights
Colo. Senate, 1995-2003 (president pro tempore, 2001-03)

ELECTION RESULTS

2010 GENERAL

Ed Perlmutter (D)	112,667	53.4%
Ryan Frazier (R)	88,026	41.8%
Buck Bailey (LIBERT)	10,117	4.8%

2010 PRIMARY

Ed Perlmutter (D)	unopposed

2008 GENERAL

Ed Perlmutter (D)	173,931	63.5%
John W. Lerew (R)	100,055	36.5%

Previous Winning Percentages
2006 (55%)

Elected 2006; 3rd term

Perlmutter arrived in Congress determined to have an impact on energy policy. Despite drawing assignments to committees that focus elsewhere, he has been successful in pushing to use federal leverage to enhance conservation efforts. He also has kept busy trying to protect government installations and contractors in his state.

Perlmutter developed a reputation for crossing party lines when he served in the Colorado General Assembly, and he is co-chairman of the centrist New Democrat Coalition's Energy Task Force. But he has been a party loyalist, siding with Democrats a career-high 98 percent of the time in 2010 on votes that split majorities of the two parties.

In his first term, Perlmutter was assigned to the Financial Services and Homeland Security committees, common stations for freshmen. He left Homeland Security after one term when he joined the leadership-dominated Rules Committee, which he exited in the 112th Congress (2011-12). While those panels have little to do with energy policy, Perlmutter has not hesitated to legislate on the topic.

On the Financial Services Committee in the 110th Congress (2007-08), he won adoption of an amendment to a bill tightening regulation of Fannie Mae and Freddie Mac that would encourage the two mortgage companies to support energy efficiency standards for low- and moderate-income housing. He chaired an energy efficiency task force, whose work resulted in a new directive to public-housing authorities: Institute energy efficient building standards in all new public housing built under the HOPE VI program, which is aimed at revitalizing the nation's public-housing stock. Both the Fannie-Freddie bill and the HOPE VI bill passed the House but stalled in the Senate.

He praised President Obama's $787 billion economic stimulus law, enacted in February 2009, for its investments in mass transit and energy efficient upgrades to public housing. He said it would help his state's burgeoning renewable-energy sector: "This bill gives Colorado's green businesses the shot in the arm they need to grow and expand."

Even when he looks to protect the interests of his district, Perlmutter often finds an energy-related connection. After years of stagnant budgets, the National Renewable Energy Laboratory, which employs about 1,200 people in Perlmutter's district, faced layoffs. But he and fellow Colorado Democrat, Sen. Mark Udall, then in the House, were able to persuade Democratic leaders to include another $300 million for the Energy Department's Office of Energy Efficiency and Renewable Energy — the lab's major sponsor — in a 2007 spending bill. From the funding, the department directed $100 million to the lab. "I felt like I could retire after that one," he said.

Perlmutter likens the goal of energy independence to President John F. Kennedy's challenge to land a man on the moon. He advocates the creation of a federal research program akin to the Apollo Project. One likely beneficiary of such a program would be his district's lab.

Space exploration is more than just a metaphor for Perlmutter, however. He joined other Colorado officials in a lobbying effort to save the Orion space vehicle, which is being built in their state, from the Obama administration's plans to cancel the broader Constellation program of manned space flight, of which Orion was a part. "The arguments for Orion were easy," Perlmutter said. "You could restructure the mission, but there was still a role for the capsule to play."

Away from the energy front, he backed the financial services regulatory overhaul signed into law by Obama in July 2010, saying it would end "the Wild West era on Wall Street."

At the end of the 111th Congress (2009-10), Perlmutter opposed legislation that extended for two years the Bush-era tax cuts for all income levels.

"I support and voted repeatedly to extend tax relief for middle-income earners, families and small businesses, as well as to extend unemployment benefits and extend estate tax relief," he said. "I simply believed extending tax cuts for millionaires and billionaires was too expensive for our country."

Perlmutter drew some unwelcome headlines in early 2009 when he and other Colorado lawmakers were a subject of news reports focused on a potential connection between campaign contributions from the now-defunct lobbying firm The PMA Group and earmarks — funding set-asides for special projects — it secured for clients. He denied wrongdoing in obtaining an earmark for IHS Inc., a defense consulting firm and PMA client. His spokeswoman said he did not receive money from IHS, but from PMA's political action committee. He gave the money to charity.

For decades, Perlmutter's grandfather and father ran a cement business in the Denver area, where Perlmutter was born and raised. His father was active in the Democratic Party, and Perlmutter's first taste of politics came by walking precincts with his family and handing out fliers.

He worked his way through law school as a laborer on the family business's construction projects, then spent nearly 30 years at a single law firm, mostly focusing on bankruptcy cases.

Perlmutter was elected to the Colorado Senate in 1994 in a district traditionally held by Republicans. He served two terms and eventually became president pro tempore. He considered a run for Congress in 2002 but demurred; in 2004, he co-chaired John Kerry's presidential campaign operation in Colorado.

He saw an opportunity to run for the House in 2006 when incumbent Republican Bob Beauprez launched an unsuccessful bid for governor. Perlmutter's GOP opponent was Rick O'Donnell, a former state education commissioner. What was originally viewed as a toss-up race turned into a resounding victory for Perlmutter.

He notched another easy win over Republican John W. Lerew, founder of a financial planning center, in his 2008 re-election race. He raised nearly $1.8 million, compared with Lerew's $37,100, and gave nearly $300,000 to other Democratic campaigns. In 2010, he won by 11 points over Republican businessman Ryan Frazier.

Key Votes

2010

Overhaul the nation's health insurance system	YES
Allow for repeal of "don't ask, don't tell"	YES
Overhaul financial services industry regulation	YES
Limit use of new Afghanistan War funds to troop withdrawal activities	NO
Change oversight of offshore drilling and lift oil spill liability cap	?
Provide a path to legal status for some children of illegal immigrants	YES
Extend Bush-era income tax cuts for two years	NO

2009

Expand the Children's Health Insurance Program	YES
Provide $787 billion in tax cuts and spending increases to stimulate the economy	YES
Allow bankruptcy judges to modify certain primary-residence mortgages	YES
Create a cap-and-trade system to limit greenhouse gas emissions	YES
Provide $2 billion for the "cash for clunkers" program	YES
Establish the government as the sole provider of student loans	YES
Restrict federally funded insurance coverage for abortions in health care overhaul	NO

CQ Vote Studies

	PARTY UNITY		PRESIDENTIAL SUPPORT	
	Support	Oppose	Support	Oppose
2010	98%	2%	95%	5%
2009	97%	3%	97%	3%
2008	97%	3%	16%	84%
2007	94%	6%	8%	92%

Interest Groups

	AFL-CIO	ADA	CCUS	ACU
2010	93%	95%	29%	4%
2009	100%	95%	40%	0%
2008	93%	95%	59%	0%
2007	96%	95%	60%	4%

Colorado 7

Denver suburbs — Lakewood, parts of Aurora and Arvada

Surrounding Denver (and the 1st District) on three sides, the suburban 7th includes parts of Adams, Arapahoe and Jefferson counties, with nearly half of its residents in Jefferson. Commerce City, north of Denver in Adams, and most of Aurora (shared with the 6th), in Arapahoe, are also in the 7th. Minorities account for more than two-fifths of the population, giving the district the second-highest percentage in the state.

The 7th's portion of Jefferson includes Golden, most of Arvada and Lakewood. The county relies on federal government jobs — Lakewood, a middle class area just west of Denver is home to the Denver Federal Center's 55 federal buildings and more than 6,000 employees, and Golden hosts the National Renewable Energy Laboratory.

The district's decommissioned military facilities have received new life, as the former Fitzsimons Army Medical Center has been revived by the University of Colorado Denver to serve as the region's health industry anchor with several hospital and research facilities.

Also, the former weapons-producing Rocky Mountain Arsenal is now a national wildlife refuge and the largest contiguous open space in the Denver area. Buckley Air Force Base remains a link in the Air Force Space Command satellite tracking system.

The 7th has been politically competitive for the decade since it was created following the 2000 census. Recent federal elections suggest that the district leans Democratic despite the close registration split between Democrats (38 percent) and Republicans (34 percent) and a large number of independents.

Major Industry
Health care, aerospace, manufacturing, telecommunications

Military Bases
Buckley Air Force Base, 3,157 military, 2,390 civilian (2011)

Cities
Aurora (pt.), 212,965; Lakewood (pt.), 142,871; Arvada (pt.), 98,107; Commerce City, 45,913; Brighton (pt.), 33,009

Notable
The MillerCoors brewery in Golden features free tours and tastings; Commerce City is home to the Colorado Rapids soccer stadium.

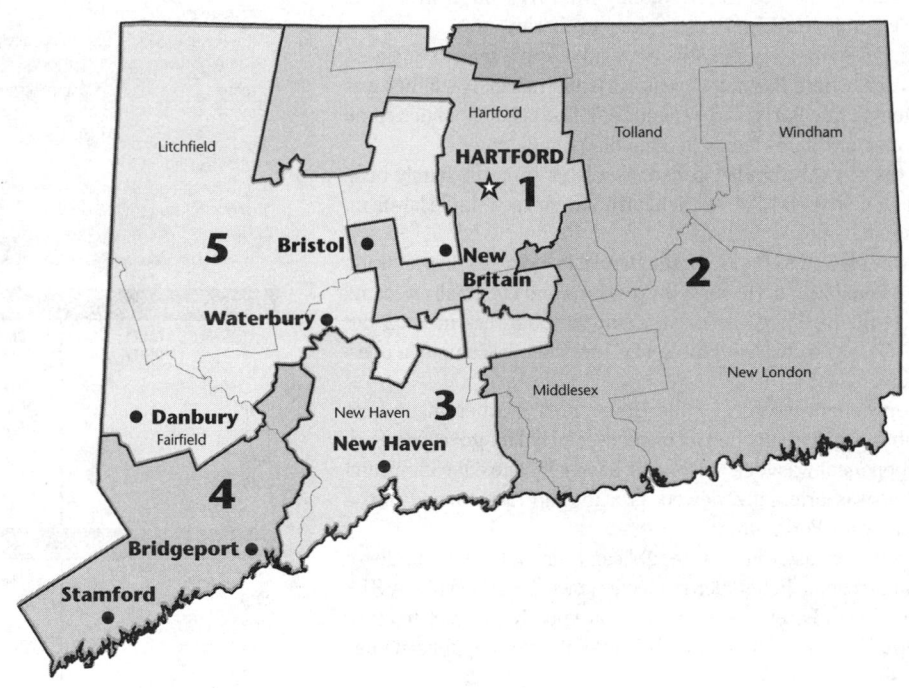

Gov. Dannel P. Malloy (D)

First elected: 2010
Length of term: 4 years
Term expires: 1/15
Salary: $150,000
Phone: (860) 566-4840
Residence: Stamford
Born: July 21, 1955; Stamford, Conn.
Religion: Roman Catholic
Family: Wife, Cathy Malloy; two children
Education: Boston College, B.A. 1977, J.D. 1980
Career: Lawyer; city prosecutor
Political highlights: Stamford Board of Finance, 1983-94; mayor of Stamford, 1995-2009; sought Democratic nomination for governor, 2006

ELECTION RESULTS

2010 GENERAL
Dannel P. Malloy (D)	567,278	49.5%
Tom Foley (R)	560,874	48.9%
Thomas Marsh (I)	17,629	1.5%

Lt. Gov. Nancy Wyman (D)

First elected: 2010
Length of term: 4 years
Term expires: 1/15
Salary: $110,000
Phone: (860) 524-7384

LEGISLATURE

General Assembly: January-June in odd-numbered years; February-June in even-numbered years
Senate: 36 members, 2-year terms
2011 ratios: 22 D, 14 R; 27 men, 9 women
Salary: $28,000
Phone: (860) 240-0500
House: 151 members, 2-year terms
2011 ratios: 99 D, 52 R; 104 men, 47 women
Salary: $28,000
Phone: (860) 240-0400

TERM LIMITS

Governor: No
Senate: No
House: No

URBAN STATISTICS

CITY	POPULATION
Bridgeport	144,229
New Haven	129,779
Hartford	124,775
Stamford	122,643
Waterbury	110,366

REGISTERED VOTERS

Others/unaffiliated	43%
Democrat	37%
Republican	20%

POPULATION

2010 population (est.)	3,574,097
2000 population	3,405,565
1990 population	3,287,116
Percent change (2000-2010)	+4.9%
Rank among states (2010)	29
Median age	39
Born in state	55.9%
Foreign born	12.5%
Violent crime rate	299/100,000
Poverty level	9.4%
Federal workers	24,973
Military	1,914

ELECTIONS

STATE ELECTION OFFICIAL
(860) 509-6200
DEMOCRATIC PARTY
(860) 560-1775
REPUBLICAN PARTY
(860) 826-7378

MISCELLANEOUS

Web: www.ct.gov
Capital: Hartford

U.S. CONGRESS

Senate: 1 independent, 1 Democrat
House: 5 Democrats

2010 Census Statistics by District

District	2008 Vote for President Obama	McCain	White	Black	Asian	Hispanic	Median Income	White Collar	Blue Collar	Service Industry	Over 64	Under 18	College Education	Rural	Sq. Miles
1	66%	33%	65%	14%	4%	15%	$61,841	65%	18%	17%	14%	23%	32%	7%	653
2	58	40	84	4	3	7	70,071	63	19	18	13	22	32	33	2,028
3	62	36	69	12	4	13	62,295	65	19	16	14	22	32	3	459
4	60	40	65	11	5	17	83,985	69	15	16	13	26	46	4	457
5	56	42	73	6	3	16	65,726	64	21	16	14	24	34	14	1,248
STATE	61	38	71	9	4	13	$67,721	65	19	16	14	24	35	12	4,845
U.S.	53	46	64	12	5	16	$51,425	60	23	17	13	25	28	21	3,537,438

Sen. Joseph I. Lieberman (I)

Capitol Office
224-4041
lieberman.senate.gov
706 Hart Bldg. 20510-0703; fax 224-9750

Committees
Armed Services
   (Airland - Chairman)
Homeland Security & Governmental Affairs -
   Chairman
Small Business & Entrepreneurship

Residence
Stamford

Born
Feb. 24, 1942; Stamford, Conn.

Religion
Jewish

Family
Wife, Hadassah Lieberman; four children

Education
Yale U., B.A. 1964 (politics & economics), LL.B. 1967

Career
Lawyer

Political Highlights
Conn. Senate, 1971-80 (served as a Democrat;
majority leader, 1975-80); Democratic nominee for
U.S. House, 1980; Conn. attorney general, 1983-89
(served as a Democrat); Democratic nominee for
vice president, 2000; sought Democratic nomination
for president, 2004; defeated in Democratic primary
for re-election to U.S. Senate, 2006

ELECTION RESULTS

2006 GENERAL

Joseph I. Lieberman (CFL)	564,095	49.7%
Ned Lamont (D)	450,844	39.7%
Alan Schlesinger (R)	109,198	9.6%

Previous Winning Percentages
2000 (63%); 1994 (67%); 1988 (50%)

Elected 1988; 4th term

Lieberman has carved out a niche for himself as a critical swing vote, and his propensity for deal-making — and raising Democratic loyalists' hackles — could be further enhanced in the divided 112th Congress.

But it will be his last chance to strike the compromises he treasures. In January 2011 he announced that he would not seek a fifth term in 2012.

In many ways, the Connecticut independent and former Democrat is a conventional Northeastern liberal — a supporter of organized labor, pro-abortion rights, in favor of governmental action to address climate change. But he also consistently serves as an in-house pain in the neck for Democrats on a handful of major policy issues.

In the lame-duck session of the 111th Congress (2009-10), Lieberman supported extending tax cuts for all income groups. The year before, Lieberman infuriated liberals by threatening to join a GOP filibuster of the health care overhaul, saying provisions to allow some uninsured to buy Medicare coverage and create a government-run insurance plan that would compete with the private sector were fiscally unsound and unnecessary. He eventually supported the overhaul, though.

But it is on foreign policy where he most often, and most profoundly, separates himself from the Democrats with whom he caucuses.

Lieberman is less a centrist than he is a throwback to an older, nearly vanished version of Democratic politics, one that combined a hawkish foreign policy with domestic liberalism, more President John F. Kennedy than Sen. Edward M. Kennedy.

Lieberman has said he believes, like others who admire the late Washington Democratic Sen. Henry M. "Scoop" Jackson, that evil must be confronted with power. And, in matters of national security, he echoes the words of Michigan Republican Sen. Arthur Vandenberg: Politics stops at the water's edge.

Those who recall his years prior to joining Vice President Al Gore's ticket in the 2000 presidential election know that Lieberman has never completely conformed to political expectations.

Lieberman's tone has often veered toward moralistic, which some credit for Gore's selection of him for the No. 2 spot — to distance the vice president from the personal excesses of President Bill Clinton. During Clinton's Senate impeachment trial in 1998, Lieberman took the floor to denounce the president's sexual affair with White House aide Monica Lewinsky. "Such behavior is not just inappropriate," he said. "It is immoral and it is harmful." But he never called for Clinton's resignation or voted to convict him in 1999. A year later, Gore tapped Lieberman, making him the first member of the Jewish faith on a major party's national ticket.

Despite Lieberman's conservatism on national security and foreign policy, his loyalties lie with Democratic presidents the bulk of the time. Studies of his voting record over 20 years show Lieberman's support for a president's policies averages 90 percent during Democratic administrations and only 54 percent during Republican reigns dating back to President George Bush in the late 1980s and early 1990s. In measures of party unity, or how often a senator votes with the majority of his or her party against the majority of the other, Lieberman shows significantly more like-mindedness with lawmakers of his former party during GOP administrations and less during Democratic ones.

The one-time leader of the now-defunct centrist Democratic Leadership Council was castigated, and then effectively cast out, of his party for his support of the Iraq War. After losing his 2006 re-election primary to anti-war candidate Ned Lamont, Lieberman re-emerged as a political independent to win the general election — a moment that would ultimately define him politically.

He continued to caucus with the Democrats and maintained his committee seniority. But within two years, he was not only campaigning for but giving an exuberant endorsement speech at the Republican National Convention in support of his close friend and ideological twin on national defense, Arizona Sen. John McCain. Post-election stories would later report that McCain had wanted Lieberman — not Alaska Gov. Sarah Palin — as his vice-presidential running mate, but the idea fell flat with GOP conservatives.

Lieberman's convention appearance set Washington abuzz with reports of repercussions from Senate Democrats. But in what was either a doubly ironic twist or a careful calculus, when Democrats took the majority in 2006 and kept it in 2008, he kept his gavel on the Homeland Security and Governmental Affairs Committee — a platform that could be used for stringent oversight of the executive branch — largely through the intervention of then-Sen. Obama.

Some Democrats had been critical of Lieberman for what they considered his softer approach to oversight of the Bush administration than was conducted by his Democratic House counterpart, former Oversight and Government Reform Chairman Henry A. Waxman of California. Lieberman tends to shy away from confrontation publicly and has said he prefers his panel be bipartisan and produce "legislation that matters" — a method Lieberman has continued during President Obama's tenure. In early 2011, he was named by Majority Leader Harry Reid of Nevada to a bipartisan working group charged with finding ways to streamline the process for confirming executive branch nominees.

Lieberman works closely with ranking Republican Susan Collins of Maine. Their collaboration has produced legislation to implement the Sept. 11 commission's recommendations, a reorganization of the intelligence community that includes the Office of the Director of National Intelligence (when Collins was chairwoman) and creation of the Department of Homeland Security.

The Homeland Security gavel and his spot on the Armed Services Committee — including chairmanship of its Airland Subcommittee — have provided Lieberman with an important platform for airing his concerns on homegrown radicalization, cybersecurity and a nuclear Iran. He has also leveled sharp criticism at the Defense Department for its investigation of the shootings at Fort Hood, Texas, in 2009, arguing the Pentagon paid insufficient attention to the shooter's links to terrorism. But he joined Democrats in supporting the nuclear arms reduction treaty with Russia approved by the Senate in late 2010.

And domestically, Lieberman has been a reliable liberal vote. He was one of the strongest advocates of doing away with the ban on openly gay service members, a goal he helped bring to fruition at the end of the 111th Congress. He worked with Massachusetts Democrat John Kerry on a measure to cap carbon emissions, but the legislation gained no headway. As a member of the Small Business and Entrepreneurship Committee, he supported creation of a fund to provide incentives to banks to boost lending to small-business owners.

Lieberman's religion has been a driving force in his political life, from his citation of "tikkun olam," or the Jewish belief in repairing the world, as a call to environmental stewardship to his fervent support for Israel.

He was first elected in 1970 to the Connecticut Senate — helped by Clinton, then a 24-year-old campaign aide and Yale Law School student — and soon rose to majority leader. After losing a race for the U.S. House in 1980, he rebounded in 1982 to become Connecticut attorney general. Six years later he narrowly upset Lowell P. Weicker Jr., a three-term liberal Republican, in the race for U.S. Senate, and he prevailed comfortably until the 2006 race. Representative of his maverick streak, before he announced his retirement there had been speculation that Lieberman could run as a Democrat, a Republican or an independent in 2012.

Key Votes

2010

Pass budget reconciliation bill to modify overhauls of health care and federal student loan programs	YES
Proceed to disapproval resolution on EPA authority to regulate greenhouse gases	NO
Overhaul financial services industry regulation	YES
Limit debate to proceed to a bill to broaden campaign finance disclosure and reporting rules	YES
Limit debate on an extension of Bush-era income tax cuts for two years	YES
Limit debate on a bill to provide a path to legal status for some children of illegal immigrants	YES
Allow for a repeal of "don't ask, don't tell"	YES
Consent to ratification of a strategic arms reduction treaty with Russia	YES

2009

Prevent release of remaining financial industry bailout funds	NO
Make it easier for victims to sue for wage discrimination remedies	YES
Expand the Children's Health Insurance Program	YES
Limit debate on the economic stimulus measure	YES
Repeal District of Columbia firearms prohibitions and gun registration laws	NO
Limit debate on expansion of federal hate crimes law	YES
Strike funding for F-22 Raptor fighter jets	NO

CQ Vote Studies

	PARTY UNITY		PRESIDENTIAL SUPPORT	
	SUPPORT	OPPOSE	SUPPORT	OPPOSE
2010	87%	13%	97%	3%
2009	90%	10%	96%	4%
2008	81%	19%	52%	48%
2007	81%	19%	62%	38%
2006	85%	15%	62%	38%
2005	90%	10%	46%	54%
2004	89%	11%	63%	37%
2003	95%	5%	32%	68%
2002	85%	15%	77%	23%
2001	93%	7%	69%	31%

Interest Groups

	AFL-CIO	ADA	CCUS	ACU
2010	88%	75%	30%	4%
2009	88%	95%	43%	20%
2008	100%	85%	75%	8%
2007	84%	70%	73%	8%
2006	77%	75%	44%	17%
2005	92%	80%	61%	8%
2004	83%	75%	79%	0%
2003	100%	70%	25%	0%
2002	92%	85%	60%	20%
2001	93%	95%	43%	28%

Sen. Richard Blumenthal (D)

Capitol Office
224-2823
blumenthal.senate.gov
706 Hart Bldg. 20510-0703; fax 224-9750

Committees
Armed Services
Health, Education, Labor & Pensions
Judiciary
Special Aging

Residence
Greenwich

Born
Feb. 13, 1946; Brooklyn, N.Y.

Religion
Jewish

Family
Wife, Cynthia Blumenthal; four children

Education
Harvard U., A.B. 1967 (political science); Cambridge
U., attended 1967-68; Yale U., J.D. 1973

Military Service
Marine Corps Reserve, 1970-75

Career
Lawyer; congressional aide; White House aide

Political Highlights
U.S. attorney, 1977-81; Conn. House, 1984-87; Conn.
Senate, 1987-91; Conn. attorney general, 1991-2011

ELECTION RESULTS

2010 GENERAL
Richard Blumenthal (D,WFM)	636,040	55.2%
Linda McMahon (R)	498,341	43.2%

2010 PRIMARY
Richard Blumenthal (D)	unopposed

Elected 2010; 1st term

Blumenthal brings to the Senate decades of experience in public life in Washington and Connecticut, as well as a list of high-powered friends including former Obama White House counsel Greg Craig, a Harvard classmate, and George W. Bush-era Defense Secretary Donald H. Rumsfeld.

A traditional Northeastern Democrat, Blumenthal is unlikely to depart significantly from the liberal voting pattern of Democrat Christopher J. Dodd, who held the seat for 30 years until retiring at the end of the 111th Congress (2009-10).

Blumenthal is that rarest of political animals — a popular politician who is not a natural back-slapper, a private person in a public profession. A 2004 Hartford Courant profile described him as "the ultimate carnival performer, hiding behind a public mask, trick mirrors and spotlights."

He took on important public-sector roles at an early age, working in the Nixon White House for future Democratic Sen. Daniel Patrick Moynihan of New York and becoming a U.S. attorney at 31 under President Jimmy Carter. He later became a state legislator and state attorney general, earning the appellation "the perennial golden boy of New England politics" because he always seemed to be the right candidate to move up. But he never found the next rung until Dodd retired.

Often accused of being too cautious to take on a tough electoral challenge, he certainly faced one in the 2010 Senate race, overcoming a self-financed opponent, his own missteps and an electoral wave that repudiated his party across the nation.

Like many Democrats who sought to distance themselves from Washington during the 2010 campaign, Blumenthal said he would be an independent voice. Most notably, he said he would have voted against the 2008 financial industry bailout — which Dodd helped draft — and the 2009 economic stimulus law — which no Senate Democrat opposed.

More parochially, Blumenthal, like Dodd, opposed President Obama's decision to cancel the F-22 fighter program — the engine is made in Connecticut — and said he would fight to restart production.

Blumenthal got a taste of the Senate when he worked as an administrative assistant to Connecticut Democrat Abraham A. Ribicoff early in his career. It was Ribicoff who recommended him for the U.S. attorney post.

He has promised to bring an attorney general's mind-set to the legislative branch, with a focus on consumer protection issues — particularly with regard to the pharmaceutical and energy industries. He was a harsh critic of BP after the 2010 oil spill in the Gulf of Mexico, and he recently called for an investigation into banks' handling of foreclosures.

Connecticut has sought to position itself as a leader in fuel cell technology, and Blumenthal wants to extend the federal "48c" tax credit, enacted as part of the 2009 stimulus, for clean-energy manufacturers. Utility costs are a major issue in Connecticut, and Blumenthal has promised to press for changes to the Federal Energy Regulatory Commission. He expressed support for the cap-and-trade bill passed in the House in 2009 aimed at reducing carbon emissions blamed for global warming.

Ironically, one of his first actions as a senator was to call for federal aid to help pay for snow removal after a series of severe storms struck the Nutmeg State.

His Senate career got off to a bit of a bumpy start after he showed up late one afternoon in the first weeks of the 112th Congress (2011-12), when he was supposed to be present to gavel the chamber to order. Majority Leader Harry

Reid of Nevada, who had to preside in Blumenthal's absence, gave him a bit of a lecture about senatorial courtesy that was reportedly audible to spectators in the gallery. Blumenthal's office blamed his tardiness on the senator being in a meeting with Carl Levin, a Michigan Democrat who chairs the Armed Services Committee, on which Blumenthal serves.

The former state attorney general also won a seat on the Judiciary Committee, as well as the Health, Education, Labor and Pensions panel. He'll use both seats to defend the health care overhaul enacted in 2010 — Republicans hope to repeal the law, and it also is threatened by legal challenges. Blumenthal said he believes the law "is not only constitutional, but that the provisions already in effect are providing real and important benefits."

Blumenthal was born in Brooklyn in the first wave of the baby boom, the son of a German Jewish immigrant who came to the United States in the 1930s to escape Nazi persecution and built a successful import-export business. He attended the private Riverdale Country School in the Bronx and graduated Phi Beta Kappa from Harvard, where he served as chairman of the Harvard Crimson newspaper. He followed that with a year spent as an intern at The Washington Post and had plans to become a journalist.

But he left journalism to take a job at the White House, where he worked under Moynihan and met Rumsfeld. He and the future Defense secretary, then head of the Office of Economic Opportunity, became tennis partners, according to the Courant profile, and remain in contact.

Blumenthal received multiple draft deferments during the Vietnam War. When they were exhausted, he enlisted in the Marine Corps Reserve.

Having left journalism behind, he attended Yale Law School, where he edited the law journal and won a clerkship with Supreme Court Justice Harry A. Blackmun. Stints as U.S. attorney and state legislator followed, and he was elected state attorney general in 1988 when the occupant of that office, Joseph I. Lieberman, ran successfully for the Senate.

A rapid rise was expected after that, but he remained attorney general. He might have been elected to the Senate in 2000 if Lieberman, running for vice president on the Democratic ticket with Al Gore, had not chosen to simultaneously seek re-election to the Senate. Instead, he turned the attorney general's job into a consumer protection division, winning popular fights against tobacco companies, banks and health insurers.

When Dodd announced he would retire in 2010, Blumenthal was the automatic choice of Connecticut Democrats.

Three Republicans entered the race — former Rep. Rob Simmons, investment adviser Peter Schiff and professional wrestling magnate Linda McMahon. McMahon spent millions of dollars of her own money to capture the primary, and she kept spending in the general election.

Blumenthal's military record became an issue when The New York Times reported that he had, as he put it, "misspoken" about his service.

"We have learned something important since the days that I served in Vietnam," the Times quoted Blumenthal as saying to a group in Norwalk in March 2008. But he never served in Vietnam, and he had made similar allusions to being in the theater of war on other occasions, as well.

He apologized, and although he took a temporary hit in some polls, he never came close to relinquishing the lead he had held all year.

McMahon outspent Blumenthal about 6-to-1, but the Democrat cruised to victory with 55 percent of the vote.

Blumenthal is the wealthiest member of the congressional class of 2010, and one of the richest members overall, with a minimum net worth of about $64 million, according to an analysis of financial disclosure forms performed by Roll Call. Blumenthal's wealth stems in part from his wife, Cynthia, daughter of New York real estate mogul Peter Malkin.

Rep. John B. Larson (D)

Capitol Office
225-2265
www.house.gov/larson
1501 Longworth Bldg. 20515-0701; fax 225-1031

Committees
Ways & Means

Residence
East Hartford

Born
July 22, 1948; Hartford, Conn.

Religion
Roman Catholic

Family
Wife, Leslie Larson; three children

Education
Central Connecticut State U., B.S. 1971 (history)

Career
High school teacher; insurance company owner

Political Highlights
East Hartford Board of Education, 1978-79; East
Hartford Town Council, 1979-83; Conn. Senate,
1983-95 (president pro tempore, 1987-95); sought
Democratic nomination for governor, 1994

ELECTION RESULTS

2010 GENERAL

John B. Larson (D)	138,440	61.2%
Ann Brickley (R)	84,076	37.2%
Kenneth Krayeske (GREEN)	2,564	1.1%

2010 PRIMARY

John B. Larson (D)	unopposed

2008 GENERAL

John B. Larson (D)	211,493	71.6%
Joe Visconti (R)	76,860	26.0%
Stephen Fournier (GREEN)	7,201	2.4%

Previous Winning Percentages
2006 (74%); 2004 (73%); 2002 (67%); 2000 (72%);
1998 (58%)

Elected 1998; 7th term

As Democratic Caucus chairman, Larson could adopt a high public profile by appearing frequently in the media. Instead, he prefers a lower-key and less public role as a behind-the-scenes conciliator and sounding board.

He stayed as the party's fourth-ranked House leader in the 112th Congress (2011-12) even as one of the leadership spots above him — Speaker of the House — switched to Republican control. Minority Leader Nancy Pelosi of California created a new post that allowed former Majority Whip James E. Clyburn of South Carolina to remain in the top tier and headed off his challenge to Minority Whip Steny H. Hoyer of Maryland for the No. 2 spot.

In addition to maintaining his spot in the party pecking order, Larson also kept his seat on the tax-writing Ways and Means Committee, to the consternation of some of his colleagues who felt leadership should make way for other members of the depleted caucus.

"I understand the concern of the members," Larson said. "However, Ways and Means is the only committee I will sit on and it is of vital importance to my district."

He has used that committee assignment to press the Democrats' plans for middle-class tax cuts, and he voted against the December 2010 compromise struck between President Obama and congressional Republicans to extend the Bush-era tax rates for two years.

Larson also raised a few eyebrows when he invited some of the Democrats defeated in the 2010 elections to attend a panel at the House Democratic retreat in the first weeks of the new Congress. Critics of the idea said looking back was not the best way to chart the party's path forward.

Generally, though, colleagues praise Larson and suggest he doesn't get the credit he deserves for his patient approach.

Top Democrats say Larson's willingness to turn the caucus into a non-stop seminar on the intricacies of Democratic health care proposals was vital in passing the legislation that President Obama signed into law in 2010. Seven out of every eight House Democrats voted for the final bill, and then-Energy and Commerce Chairman Henry A. Waxman, a California Democrat, said that was in part because Larson convened 61 caucus meetings on the complex legislation over a 12-month period. "He was insistent we have opportunities for members to learn the details," said Waxman, one of the bill's key drafters.

Larson ascended into the upper reaches of leadership in early 2006, besting Jan Schakowsky of Illinois and Joseph Crowley of New York in the race for the caucus vice chairmanship. He was aided in the race by his friend and mentor, the late John P. Murtha of Pennsylvania. But Larson's victory also showed how his behind-the-scenes role as top Democrat on the perks-dispensing House Administration Committee from 2003 to 2005 had helped him collect a long list of political IOUs. He was unopposed in his bid to succeed Illinois Democrat Rahm Emanuel as caucus chairman.

Larson has consciously adopted a strategy of staying in the background and letting other members get the credit for things he might have helped accomplish. But sometimes, especially if the issues involve the economic interests of his home state or his Hartford-based district, Larson will take a loud public stand. An example was the spring 2010 fight over engines for the F-35 Joint Strike Fighter. The plane's engines are made in Connecticut by Pratt & Whitney, a company whose fate has deep resonance for Larson, a native of East Hartford. His father was a Pratt & Whitney fireman who moonlighted as an auto mechanic and butcher to support his family. Larson has been a staunch defender of the hometown company's interests.

In the case of the F-35, General Electric and its allies in Congress wanted the government to also buy an alternative engine, an idea that Obama has attacked as wasteful.

In a losing effort to eliminate the GE engine from a defense authorization bill, Larson took to the House floor and made an impassioned plea. "I guess competition in this town means buying two of everything with taxpayers' money," said Larson, a former Armed Services Committee member. With regional interests trumping loyalty to leader, 115 Democrats voted against Larson as the amendment to eliminate funding for the alternative engine went down, 193-231.

But Larson finally found the support he needed in, of all the places, the Republican freshmen who pushed him into the minority. With affirmative votes from the class of 2010, many of whom campaigned on a platform that included fiscal austerity, the House voted in February 2011 to eliminate the alternative engine funding from the catchall fiscal 2011 spending bill.

Larson grew up in an East Hartford public housing project originally built for workers of United Aircraft, precursor to United Technologies Corp., the parent company of Pratt & Whitney. He got an early taste of politics through his mother, a state employee, who served on the town council and was active in Democratic Party organizing.

After graduating from Central Connecticut State University, Larson taught high school history and coached sports for about five years. He then joined an insurance company that he eventually bought. After stints on the school board and town council, he was elected in 1982 to the state Senate, where he served a dozen years, rising to Senate president.

Larson lost a bid for governor in 1994, gaining endorsements of party leaders but losing the primary to state Comptroller Bill Curry. In 1996, he led a statewide volunteer drive to wire schools and libraries to the Internet. Later, in Congress, he founded the Digital Divide Caucus, which aims to make technology available to all Americans.

When veteran 1st District Democratic Rep. Barbara B. Kennelly announced she was running for governor in 1998, Larson was the first Democrat to file for her seat. He edged past Connecticut Secretary of State Miles S. Rapoport in the primary, then rolled to a 17-percentage-point victory in the general election and has not been seriously threatened since.

Key Votes

2010

Overhaul the nation's health insurance system	YES
Allow for repeal of "don't ask, don't tell"	YES
Overhaul financial services industry regulation	YES
Limit use of new Afghanistan War funds to troop withdrawal activities	YES
Change oversight of offshore drilling and lift oil spill liability cap	YES
Provide a path to legal status for some children of illegal immigrants	YES
Extend Bush-era income tax cuts for two years	NO

2009

Expand the Children's Health Insurance Program	YES
Provide $787 billion in tax cuts and spending increases to stimulate the economy	YES
Allow bankruptcy judges to modify certain primary-residence mortgages	YES
Create a cap-and-trade system to limit greenhouse gas emissions	YES
Provide $2 billion for the "cash for clunkers" program	YES
Establish the government as the sole provider of student loans	YES
Restrict federally funded insurance coverage for abortions in health care overhaul	NO

CQ Vote Studies

	PARTY UNITY		PRESIDENTIAL SUPPORT	
	SUPPORT	OPPOSE	SUPPORT	OPPOSE
2010	99%	1%	88%	12%
2009	99%	1%	98%	2%
2008	99%	1%	13%	87%
2007	99%	1%	4%	96%
2006	97%	3%	24%	76%

Interest Groups

	AFL-CIO	ADA	CCUS	ACU
2010	100%	100%	13%	0%
2009	100%	100%	33%	0%
2008	100%	95%	65%	0%
2007	96%	95%	55%	0%
2006	100%	95%	43%	8%

Connecticut 1

Central — Hartford, Bristol

Resembling a backward "C," the 1st District carves a path from the state's sparsely populated northwestern towns along the Massachusetts border to the capital of Hartford before winding west to take in the central city of Bristol. Situated midway between Boston and New York — roughly 100 miles from each — the staunchly Democratic district is a commercial center for the Northeast Corridor.

Insurance, financial services and state government traditionally formed the backbone of the 1st's economy. Once recognized as the international insurance capital, Hartford still hosts the headquarters or offices of some firms, but layoffs in the financial sector have contributed to rising unemployment and emptying office buildings. Hometown company Colt firearms continues area operations, but the 1st's manufacturing base has contracted. Many city residents also struggle, and test scores in the city's school system still lag behind the rest of the region.

Commercial aerospace and defense firms long provided many area jobs, but continued cuts at industry giants such as United Technologies'

Pratt & Whitney, which builds aircraft engines, has hurt the district. Reflecting a state trend, the 1st's predominately white and wealthy suburbs thrive, while cities such as Hartford depopulate and decay. Local officials hope that efforts to renew the city's historic downtown and riverfront — and to continue construction of certified "green" residential and commercial buildings — will draw residents and retail investment. Hartford-area voters have not sent a Republican to the U.S. House since 1956, and the city's large minority population, mostly Hispanics of Puerto Rican descent, is firmly Democratic. In the 2008 presidential election, the 1st gave Democrat Barack Obama nearly 66 percent overall, his highest statewide vote percentage.

Major Industry
Insurance, banking, defense, government

Cities
Hartford, 124,775; West Hartford (unincorporated), 63,268; Bristol, 60,477; East Hartford (unincorporated), 51,252

Notable
Hartford's Wadsworth Atheneum is the nation's oldest public art museum; ESPN headquarters are in Bristol.

Rep. Joe Courtney (D)

Capitol Office
225-2076
courtney.house.gov
215 Cannon Bldg. 20515-0702; fax 225-4977

Committees
Agriculture
Armed Services

Residence
Vernon

Born
April 6, 1953; Hartford, Conn.

Religion
Roman Catholic

Family
Wife, Audrey Budarz Courtney; two children

Education
Tufts U., B.A. 1975 (history); U. of Connecticut, J.D. 1978

Career
Lawyer; public defender

Political Highlights
Conn. House, 1987-95; Democratic nominee for lieutenant governor, 1998; Democratic nominee for U.S. House, 2002

ELECTION RESULTS

2010 GENERAL

Joe Courtney (D)	147,748	59.9%
Janet Peckinpaugh (R)	95,671	38.8%
G. Scott Deshefy (GREEN)	3,344	1.4%

2010 PRIMARY

Joe Courtney (D)	unopposed

2008 GENERAL

Joe Courtney (D)	212,148	65.7%
Sean Sullivan (R)	104,574	32.4%
G. Scott Deshefy (GREEN)	6,300	2.0%

Previous Winning Percentages
2006 (50%)

Elected 2006; 3rd term

With a little help from some powerful friends, the liberal Courtney has taken a leading role in securing defense funding for his district and looking out for the interests of his allies in organized labor.

Leadership took a special interest in aiding Courtney after his 83-vote margin of victory in 2006, setting him up to claim a string of political successes rare for a newcomer.

He was given a seat on the Armed Services Committee, where he works to protect the New London Naval Submarine Base and the U.S. Coast Guard Academy, two major employers in his district. Senior committee members and Democratic appropriators helped the freshman secure $588 million in fiscal 2008 defense spending for advanced work on nuclear submarines for General Dynamics' Electric Boat facility in Groton. Electric Boat had cut 1,400 jobs, and another 2,000 of the 10,200 jobs were considered at risk before the spending boost.

Courtney, with the help of fellow Connecticut Democrat John B. Larson, a member of the party leadership, was credited with persuading the late Defense Appropriations Chairman John P. Murtha, a Pennsylvania Democrat, to visit the Electric Boat plant and then to include funding for the project in his spending bill.

Subsequent talk among some Democrats of cutting spending on military procurement left Courtney determined to protect submarines. In December 2008, he led more than a dozen House members in urging President-elect Obama to double production of two new *Virginia*-class subs starting in 2011, one year ahead of the Navy's schedule.

Courtney also butted heads with the Obama administration over the future of the Navy's ballistic-missile submarines. In April 2010, he blasted Defense Secretary Robert M. Gates, who threatened to cut the program as a cost-saving measure. Courtney, in whose district the subs are built, argued they are vital to the country's nuclear deterrent.

Courtney moved from parochial Connecticut concerns to a more national stage when he emerged as a leader of a group of Democrats opposing the excise tax on so-called Cadillac insurance plans designed to help pay for the Democrats' health care overhaul legislation.

The efforts of Courtney and other union allies eventually led the White House to cut a deal to delay the excise tax start date. He was among the last of the holdout liberal Democrats to declare his position in favor of the legislation.

Courtney was also active on health issues before the overhaul debate. He backed legislation that would have prohibited insurers from refusing to cover people with pre-existing conditions, and he supported the expansion of health benefits for unemployed veterans. He also joined Connecticut Democratic Sen. Christopher J. Dodd in December 2008 in urging drug manufacturer Pfizer Inc. to reconsider a decision to hire foreign workers to replace some local contractors in his district.

Courtney says he put his experience during a 1990s budget crisis in Connecticut to use during the health care debate. A state legislator at the time and the husband of a nurse practitioner, he helped tackle the complex long-term-care reimbursement process, a multi-year legislative effort. "About six of us understood it," he said. "It's not something that people are going to get their blood racing to hear about."

Courtney successfully fought in 2008 to have the Eightmile River, running through the towns of East Haddam, Lyme and Salem, recognized as a federal Wild and Scenic River, providing it with greater environmental protection. Most Republicans opposed the measure, arguing it included language that could allow the use of eminent domain to seize private property.

New to the Agriculture Committee in the 112th Congress (2011-12), Courtney counts a number of small dairy farmers as constituents. In 2009 he successfully lobbied Agriculture Secretary Tom Vilsack to increase government purchases of dairy products in an effort to support prices.

Courtney grew up as a "political junkie" in West Hartford in the 1960s. "I was an Irish Catholic kid who remembered John F. Kennedy — the nuns actually prayed for him during the election in second grade," he said.

He became a Democrat, even though his father was a moderate Republican. But he followed in his father's footsteps by pursuing a law degree at the University of Connecticut. His mother was a homemaker.

While in law school, Courtney worked as an aide to Democrat Sam Gejdenson when he was in the General Assembly. Courtney later ran for the state House, where he served from 1987 to 1995; he left after the birth of his second child.

He made an unsuccessful bid for lieutenant governor in 1998 and for the U.S. House in 2002, when Republican Rob Simmons bested him by 8 percentage points. But Courtney came back to knock off Simmons in 2006 by 83 votes out of more than 242,000 cast.

"It was a healthy way to come to Congress," Courtney said. "It's not something you should just count on."

Despite Courtney's narrow victory, Simmons decided not to challenge him in 2008. Courtney raised almost six times as much as his GOP opponent, Norwich attorney Sean Sullivan, and won with more than 65 percent of the vote. He took 60 percent in 2010 against Republican Janet Peckinpaugh, a former TV news anchor.

He said the prospect of running for a Senate seat in 2012 was tempting, but announced in February 2011 that he would pass on the race to replace the retiring Joseph I. Lieberman, an independent, and instead seek reelection to the House, citing a need to protect his district from Republicans' spending cuts affecting homeless veterans, firefighters and infrastructure investment.

"Their efforts highlight what is at stake for this district, and why it is critical that eastern Connecticut continue to have a strong voice defending its priorities over the next two years," Courtney said.

Key Votes

2010

Overhaul the nation's health insurance system	YES
Allow for repeal of "don't ask, don't tell"	YES
Overhaul financial services industry regulation	YES
Limit use of new Afghanistan War funds to troop withdrawal activities	NO
Change oversight of offshore drilling and lift oil spill liability cap	YES
Provide a path to legal status for some children of illegal immigrants	YES
Extend Bush-era income tax cuts for two years	YES

2009

Expand the Children's Health Insurance Program	YES
Provide $787 billion in tax cuts and spending increases to stimulate the economy	YES
Allow bankruptcy judges to modify certain primary-residence mortgages	YES
Create a cap-and-trade system to limit greenhouse gas emissions	YES
Provide $2 billion for the "cash for clunkers" program	YES
Establish the government as the sole provider of student loans	YES
Restrict federally funded insurance coverage for abortions in health care overhaul	NO

CQ Vote Studies

	PARTY UNITY		PRESIDENTIAL SUPPORT	
	SUPPORT	OPPOSE	SUPPORT	OPPOSE
2010	96%	4%	95%	5%
2009	99%	1%	96%	4%
2008	99%	1%	10%	90%
2007	97%	3%	3%	97%

Interest Groups

	AFL-CIO	ADA	CCUS	ACU
2010	100%	90%	25%	0%
2009	100%	95%	33%	0%
2008	100%	95%	50%	8%
2007	96%	100%	50%	0%

Connecticut 2
East — Norwich, New London, Storrs

The 2nd, the state's largest district, runs from coastal Middlesex and New London counties north to the Massachusetts border through small former mill towns and the main campus of the University of Connecticut in Storrs. Defense steers the 2nd's ship: General Dynamics' Electric Boat Corp. in Groton and the New London Naval Submarine Base are major employers. But the massive American Indian-owned casino resorts, once the engine in the 2nd's economy, are vulnerable to economic instability. Both Foxwoods and Mohegan Sun — the resort casino in Uncasville that hosts the state's only major league sports team, the WNBA's Connecticut Sun — have seen recent employment cuts. Pfizer, once a key employer in eastern Connecticut, plans to cut a quarter of its workforce.

Casinos and surrounding towns also have quarreled over taxes and the application of regulations to reservation land. A significant portion of Connecticut's state revenue comes from tax on casinos, and any declines in gaming hurt state funding.

Home foreclosures, job losses and pay freezes have stung the district's economy. Mainstays of local tourism, such as the attractions in historic Mystic Seaport, have been particularly hard hit. Officials hope to use federal funding to address chronic transportation issues in the region, some of which have been caused by years of heavy traffic to and from the casinos. The predominately middle-class 2nd is largely white, with growing black and Hispanic communities. There is a sizable military retiree community near Groton and New London. Barack Obama took 58 percent of the 2008 presidential vote here, winning by wide margins in areas such as New London and Mansfield, where registered Democrats easily outnumber Republicans.

Major Industry
Defense, casinos, tourism

Military Bases
New London Naval Submarine Base, 5,110 military, 834 civilian (2011)

Cities
Norwich, 40,493; New London, 27,620

Notable
New London is home to the U.S. Coast Guard Academy.

Rep. Rosa DeLauro (D)

Capitol Office
225-3661
www.house.gov/delauro
2413 Rayburn Bldg. 20515-0703; fax 225-4890

Committees
Appropriations

Residence
New Haven

Born
March 2, 1943; New Haven, Conn.

Religion
Roman Catholic

Family
Husband, Stanley Greenberg; three children

Education
London School of Economics, attended 1962-63;
Marymount College (N.Y.), B.A. 1964; Columbia U.,
M.A. 1966 (international politics)

Career
Political activist; congressional and mayoral aide

Political Highlights
No previous office

ELECTION RESULTS

2010 GENERAL

Rosa DeLauro (D)	143,565	65.1%
Jerry Labriola Jr. (R)	74,107	33.6%
Charles Pillsbury (GREEN)	2,984	1.4%

2010 PRIMARY

Rosa DeLauro (D)	unopposed

2008 GENERAL

Rosa DeLauro (D)	230,172	77.4%
Bo Itshaky (R)	58,583	19.7%
Ralph A. Ferrucci (GREEN)	8,613	2.9%

Previous Winning Percentages
2006 (76%); 2004 (72%); 2002 (66%); 2000 (72%);
1998 (71%); 1996 (71%); 1994 (63%); 1992 (66%);
1990 (52%)

Elected 1990; 11th term

Outspoken and liberal, DeLauro is a passionate advocate for women and children, focusing on equal pay, food safety and child nutrition. Typically brightly clad, scarved and bespectacled, DeLauro is difficult to miss on Capitol Hill, with her demeanor as energized as her attire.

In addition to her official and unofficial ties to leadership — she is co-chairwoman of the Democratic Steering Committee and an ally of Minority Leader Nancy Pelosi of California — DeLauro (da-LAUR-o) also wields considerable power as an appropriator. In the 112th Congress (2011-12), she is the top Democrat on the Labor-Health and Human Services-Education Subcommittee, where she looks to defend against Republican attempts to defund parts of the 2010 health care overhaul.

Her defense of the law is both political and personal.

In the fall of 2009, after heated debate about how to secure a majority from a caucus divided on abortion, Pelosi enlisted DeLauro, an abortion-rights-supporting Catholic like herself, to find common ground among Democrats and between the House and Senate. "There should be no gains and no losses. We wanted to make sure we maintained current law. That's what our goal was and that's what we accomplished," DeLauro said, a view not shared by anti-abortion lawmakers and activists.

When independent Connecticut Sen. Joseph. I. Lieberman raised the possibility of joining a Republican filibuster on the legislation, DeLauro said he should be recalled, even though the state they both call home has no provision for recalling elected officials and members of Congress are not subject to recall under the U.S. Constitution.

Even as chairwoman of the Agriculture Appropriations panel in the previous two congresses, DeLauro was front and center on health care issues.

DeLauro argues that trade should never trump public health. In 2007 and 2008, after a spate of tainted drug imports from China, several E. coli and salmonella scares and the biggest beef recall in U.S. history, she became a leading voice for food industry regulation.

She supported legislation signed into law in 2010 that strengthened the Food and Drug Administration's regulatory authority and allowed the agency to order mandatory recalls.

"You're not dealing with roads and bridges," she said of her FDA oversight in the wake of a 2010 recall of children's medication. "You are dealing with people's lives."

Not that she ignores roads and bridges. She assists her Connecticut colleagues in delivering funds to state-based aircraft manufacturers; Stratford-based Sikorsky Aircraft Corp., maker of the UH-60 Black Hawk helicopter; and East Hartford-based Pratt & Whitney, a maker of engines used in military aircraft.

In 2010 DeLauro, who then served on the Budget Committee, brought together economic luminaries to share ideas with Congress for boosting the economy and creating jobs. She has proposed that Congress emulate Europe in establishing a public-private partnership called the National Infrastructure Development Bank to attract private investors to critical building projects.

DeLauro, who tapped her political network on presidential candidate Barack Obama's behalf before a narrow Connecticut primary victory, emerged during the 2008 presidential transition as a contender for two Cabinet posts — secretary of Labor and secretary of Health and Human Services. She got neither, but has been a stalwart supporter of President

Obama's agenda and message. He signed into law a bill she championed that would give employees who believe they have suffered wage discrimination more time to sue.

In the last year of President George W. Bush's tenure, she pushed through the House a bill that would require employers to justify unequal pay for male and female workers and a bill that would enable women to get insurance coverage for longer stays in the hospital after breast-cancer-related surgery. DeLauro's interest in women's health issues stems in part from her own battle with ovarian cancer more than 20 years ago.

DeLauro grew up in Wooster Square, a tight-knit Italian neighborhood in New Haven. Her father, Ted, was an immigrant, and her mother, Luisa, was a factory worker; both served on the New Haven council, and their home was the hub of neighborhood meetings about issues related to the schools, jobs and immigration officials. When her father first ran for the city council, he kept a file box filled with voters' names and their concerns, then walked door-to-door to seek their votes.

In the 1960s, DeLauro was a community organizer in President Lyndon B. Johnson's War on Poverty, and then worked for the mayor of New Haven. In 1980 she ran Connecticut Democrat Christopher J. Dodd's first Senate campaign and then became his chief of staff for seven years. She also took the helm of EMILY's List, a fundraising group for women running for office who support abortion rights.

In 1990, DeLauro ran for the seat of Democratic Rep. Bruce Morrison, who was running for governor. Her political contacts enabled her to raise money quickly and shoo away intraparty competition. She went on to defeat GOP state Sen. Thomas Scott, an energetic conservative. In a 1992 rematch, she defeated him with 66 percent of the vote and she has been re-elected easily ever since.

In the 107th Congress (2001-02), she ran the party's communications arm as the assistant of Minority Leader Richard A. Gephardt of Missouri. When Democrats met late in 2002 to organize for the 108th Congress (2003-04), DeLauro lost a race for caucus chief by one vote. But new Minority Leader Pelosi appointed her co-chairwoman of the Democratic Steering Committee, which makes committee assignments.

DeLauro is married to Stanley Greenberg, a prominent Democratic pollster. In early 2009, tax experts and conservative bloggers questioned the living arrangement they had created for White House Chief of Staff Rahm Emanuel — rent-free in the basement of their Capitol Hill home. Emanuel, who served in the House with DeLauro, subsequently moved out.

Key Votes

2010	
Overhaul the nation's health insurance system	YES
Allow for repeal of "don't ask, don't tell"	YES
Overhaul financial services industry regulation	YES
Limit use of new Afghanistan War funds to troop withdrawal activities	YES
Change oversight of offshore drilling and lift oil spill liability cap	YES
Provide a path to legal status for some children of illegal immigrants	YES
Extend Bush-era income tax cuts for two years	NO

2009	
Expand the Children's Health Insurance Program	YES
Provide $787 billion in tax cuts and spending increases to stimulate the economy	YES
Allow bankruptcy judges to modify certain primary-residence mortgages	YES
Create a cap-and-trade system to limit greenhouse gas emissions	YES
Provide $2 billion for the "cash for clunkers" program	YES
Establish the government as the sole provider of student loans	YES
Restrict federally funded insurance coverage for abortions in health care overhaul	NO

CQ Vote Studies

	PARTY UNITY		PRESIDENTIAL SUPPORT	
	SUPPORT	OPPOSE	SUPPORT	OPPOSE
2010	99%	1%	90%	10%
2009	99%	1%	99%	1%
2008	99%	1%	13%	87%
2007	99%	1%	4%	96%
2006	98%	2%	13%	87%

Interest Groups

	AFL-CIO	ADA	CCUS	ACU
2010	100%	100%	13%	0%
2009	100%	100%	33%	0%
2008	100%	100%	56%	0%
2007	96%	100%	45%	0%
2006	100%	100%	27%	8%

Connecticut 3

South — New Haven, Milford

The 3rd includes coastal New Haven County towns, such as Guilford on Long Island Sound and the port city of New Haven, and takes in Stratford in Fairfield County and most of inland Middletown in Middlesex County. As with other cities in the state, New Haven is far poorer than its affluent suburbs. Yale University is the city's largest employer, but labor issues historically caused tension between the school and the city's blue-collar workers.

Tax issues further strain the relationship between the city and the school — in order to ease tension, Yale invested millions of dollars into development and infrastructure improvements. Construction of a research park attracted biotechnology firms to the area to collaborate with Yale's scientific research departments. The university in 2011 announced funding for a scholarship program aimed at supporting New Haven public school graduates. The city of New Haven has begun a revitalization of downtown, attempting to lure visitors to the waterfront and convention centers and continuing plans to develop mixed-used communities in the city's center.

Beyond Yale's influence, the economy relies on the defense industry, manufacturing and technology. Stratford-based Sikorsky Aircraft, which builds helicopters such as the Army's Black Hawk and Navy's Sea Hawk models, employs hundreds of district residents but depends on military contracts for continued viability. Professionals commute from the district's suburbs to jobs throughout the state and as far away as New York City.

The 3rd's working-class constituents and liberal elite, along with New Haven's Hispanic and black residents, combine to make the district strongly Democratic. Many Italian-Americans still reside in the district's suburbs. Overall, Barack Obama took nearly 63 percent of the district's 2008 presidential vote.

Major Industry

Higher education, defense, biotechnology, manufacturing

Cities

New Haven, 129,779; West Haven, 55,564; Stratford (unincorporated), 51,384; Milford, 51,271; Middletown (pt.), 37,765; Naugatuck, 31,862

Notable

New Haven, home to strong Italian communities, claims to be the birthplace of pizza in America.

Rep. Jim Himes (D)

Capitol Office
225-5541
himes.house.gov
119 Cannon Bldg. 20515-0704; fax 225-9629

Committees
Financial Services

Residence
Greenwich

Born
July 5, 1966; Lima, Peru

Religion
Presbyterian

Family
Wife, Mary Himes; two children

Education
Harvard U., A.B. 1988 (social studies); Oxford U.,
M.Phil. 1990 (Rhodes scholar)

Career
Affordable housing nonprofit executive; investment
banker

Political Highlights
Housing Authority of the Town of Greenwich, 2003-
06 (chairman, 2003-06); Greenwich Democratic
Town Committee chairman, 2004-08; Greenwich
Board of Estimate and Taxation, 2006-07

ELECTION RESULTS

2010 GENERAL

Jim Himes (D)	115,351	53.1%
Dan Debicella (R)	102,030	46.9%

2010 PRIMARY

Jim Himes (D)	unopposed

2008 GENERAL

Jim Himes (D)	158,475	51.3%
Christopher Shays (R)	146,854	47.6%

Elected 2008; 2nd term

A self-styled centrist who unabashedly supported President Obama's agenda after working for more than a decade at one of Wall Street's most embattled investment titans, Himes touts himself as "New England's most independent congressman."

Educated at Harvard and Oxford — on a Rhodes Scholarship — and a 12-year veteran of Goldman Sachs prior to winning his first House race, Himes is a member of the moderate New Democrat Coalition. But he largely stuck with his liberal leadership in the 111th Congress (2009-10) on the economy, health care and education. He was one of the few Democratic incumbents who actively courted electoral support from Obama, who attended an October 2010 rally in Bridgeport.

Sitting on the Financial Services Committee, Himes backed the financial industry regulatory overhaul enacted in 2010. His proposal for an ombudsman in the Consumer Financial Protection Bureau was included in the final version of the legislation.

"These reforms will put rules in place to monitor and clamp down on risky behavior that could endanger our financial system," he said in July 2010.

Congress must still rein in mortgage giants Fannie Mae and Freddie Mac, Himes told The Hour Newspapers in early 2011, so "they're not in sub-prime, they're not running foundations, they're not allowed to lobby."

In one divergence from Democratic orthodoxy, he was a staunch advocate for extending the Bush-era tax cuts. He said so in January 2010, almost a year before Obama struck a deal with Republicans to extend the rates for two years for all income levels. On including the highest earners in the extension, he told Fox News "there's fairness issues with that, there's deficit issues with that, but just from the standpoint of not raising taxes in a very weak recovery, there's a logic for doing it."

Those close to Himes regard him as determined and detailed, though he described his tendencies to The New York Times as "bullheaded stubbornness, mixed with a little bit of unhinged."

Himes, who left Goldman Sachs to focus on affordable-housing efforts, said job creation is his most important duty. "I take seriously my role in helping the employers in my district as well as the employees, and I've built very good relationships with companies and employers like GE and Pitney Bowes and all kinds of small businesses," he told the Fairfield Weekly in 2010.

In the 111th, Himes also sat on the Homeland Security Committee, where he worked to tighten port security and scrutinize the Homeland Security Department. During the late 2010 uproar over new airport screening procedures, he told GreenwichTime.com that the Transportation Security Administration "has been very heavy-handed in their roll-out of this thing."

He came to Congress vowing to clean up the way members operate. He was an early cosponsor of a bipartisan bill to ban lawmakers from accepting campaign money from beneficiaries of their earmarks, special funding set-asides in spending bills. And he was one of 11 freshmen who repeatedly bucked the leadership by supporting Arizona Republican Jeff Flake's unsuccessful resolution calling on the ethics committee to probe ties between Pennsylvania Democrat John P. Murtha, chairman of the Defense Appropriations Subcommittee, and the now-defunct lobbying firm PMA. Himes said he wasn't convinced Democratic leaders were doing enough to combat the perception of influence peddling. He also backed fellow Connecticut Democrat John B. Larson's bill to create a public financing system for House candidates.

Born in Lima, Peru, where his father worked for the Ford Foundation, Himes spent his early years there and in Bogota, Colombia. When he was 10, his parents divorced and he moved to New Jersey with his two sisters and his mother, who worked as an administrator for nonprofit groups such as the Aspen Institute and for the State Board of Higher Education. He volunteered as an emergency medical technician as a teenager, and he eventually earned a social studies degree at Harvard, where he was captain of the lightweight crew team.

Though he thought about working at the State Department, Himes took a job at Goldman Sachs, which was opening a Latin America group. He sold investors on the privatization of Telmex, the Mexican telephone company, until Goldman disbanded the group in 1994. Himes then worked in mergers and acquisitions and the technology group, but when the dot com boom ended, he decided he'd had enough. "I wanted to be part of something nonprofit, something that had business sensibility to it," he said.

Having developed an interest in Mexico in fighting poverty with business-oriented solutions, he landed at the Enterprise Foundation, a nonprofit that financed low-income housing. He eventually became director of the New York City branch. He also served as a commissioner of the Greenwich Housing Authority, later was elected to his town's finance board and served as the city's Democratic Town Committee chairman.

In 2008, he decided to run for the 4th District seat, undaunted by the fact that 10-term moderate Christopher Shays, who in the 110th Congress (2007-08) was the only House Republican to represent New England, had survived several previous tough challenges. Himes quickly became the leading Democratic candidate, raising more than $3.9 million.

In the midst of the recession, he pitched both his investment and nonprofit careers as giving him the kind of expertise needed to address the voters' economic concerns. Riding Obama's strong coattails in Connecticut, he bested Shays with 51 percent of the vote.

Republicans targeted the seat in 2010 and chose state Sen. Dan Debicella to challenge Himes. Debicella tried to tie Himes to the Democratic leadership, including then-Speaker Nancy Pelosi of California. Himes said Debicella represented a return to the policies of President George W. Bush. Bucking the Republican trend, Himes improved on his 2008 performance, winning 53 percent of the vote.

Key Votes

2010

Overhaul the nation's health insurance system	YES
Allow for repeal of "don't ask, don't tell"	YES
Overhaul financial services industry regulation	YES
Limit use of new Afghanistan War funds to troop withdrawal activities	NO
Change oversight of offshore drilling and lift oil spill liability cap	+
Provide a path to legal status for some children of illegal immigrants	YES
Extend Bush-era income tax cuts for two years	YES

2009

Expand the Children's Health Insurance Program	YES
Provide $787 billion in tax cuts and spending increases to stimulate the economy	YES
Allow bankruptcy judges to modify certain primary-residence mortgages	YES
Create a cap-and-trade system to limit greenhouse gas emissions	YES
Provide $2 billion for the "cash for clunkers" program	YES
Establish the government as the sole provider of student loans	YES
Restrict federally funded insurance coverage for abortions in health care overhaul	NO

CQ Vote Studies

	PARTY UNITY		PRESIDENTIAL SUPPORT	
	SUPPORT	OPPOSE	SUPPORT	OPPOSE
2010	88%	12%	97%	3%
2009	90%	10%	92%	8%

Interest Groups

	AFL-CIO	ADA	CCUS	ACU
2010	93%	90%	29%	13%
2009	95%	95%	40%	4%

Connecticut 4
Southwest — Bridgeport, Stamford

The 4th extends from the outskirts of New York City and runs along the wealthy "Gold Coast" towns on Long Island Sound. It also takes in the industrial city of Norwalk, white-collar Stamford, and, in stark contrast to the coastal affluence, Bridgeport, the state's most populous city.

Financial workers riding commuter trains and Interstate 95 long brought wealth from Wall Street to the district's tony suburbs. But Greenwich, home of the hedge fund industry, felt the effects of high-end housing and financial market collapses. Following a spate of foreclosures on multimillion-dollar homes and contraction of the local luxury goods market, Greenwich has begun to rebound.

Although Bridgeport's population increased over the past decade — the city's first decennial uptick since the 1950 census — it has suffered the fate of many post-industrial cities and frequently registers an unemployment rate above the national average. The South End has seen marked progress, as apartments and businesses take over abandoned factories, but crime and drugs have plagued the city, and development efforts have achieved only mixed success.

Bridgeport Harbor is the terminus for ferry service to central Long Island. The southwestern Connecticut district is growing, but municipal budget shortfalls and sluggish employment rates contribute to economic uncertainty.

The district's extremes create difficult terrain for politicians to navigate. Several affluent suburbs still elect GOP mayors, and Stamford has a Republican at the helm after Democrat Dannel P. Malloy, a 14-year incumbent, left the office to run for governor in 2010. But most of the district's urban poor vote Democratic, and the 4th has preferred the last four Democratic presidential candidates overall. Barack Obama — who took 84 percent of the vote in Bridgeport — won the district with 60 percent of its 2008 presidential vote.

Major Industry
Banking, manufacturing, health care

Cities
Bridgeport, 144,229; Stamford, 122,643; Norwalk, 85,603; Trumbull (unincorporated), 36,018; Shelton (pt.), 29,122

Notable
The headquarters for WWE, the wrestling entertainment franchise, is in Stamford.

Rep. Christopher S. Murphy (D)

Capitol Office
225-4476
chrismurphy.house.gov
412 Cannon Bldg. 20515-0705; fax 225-5933

Committees
Foreign Affairs
Oversight & Government Reform

Residence
Cheshire

Born
Aug. 3, 1973; White Plains, N.Y.

Religion
Protestant

Family
Wife, Cathy Holahan; one child

Education
Williams College, B.A. 1996 (history & political science); U. of Connecticut, J.D. 2002

Career
Lawyer; state legislative and campaign aide

Political Highlights
Southington Planning & Zoning Commission, 1997-99; Conn. House, 1999-2003; Conn. Senate, 2003-07

ELECTION RESULTS

2010 GENERAL

Christopher S. Murphy (D)	122,879	54.1%
Sam Caligiuri (R, I)	104,402	45.9%

2008 GENERAL

Christopher S. Murphy (D)	179,327	59.2%
David J. Cappiello (R)	117,914	39.0%
Thomas L. Winn (I)	3,082	1.0%

2008 PRIMARY

Christopher S. Murphy (D)	unopposed

Previous Winning Percentages
2006 (57%)

Elected 2006; 3rd term

Eager and ambitious, Murphy quickly won a seat on the powerful Energy and Commerce Committee — although he had to give up that assignment in the 112th Congress. He had moved quickly up the ladder in state politics and, after three terms in the House, announced early in 2011 that he would seek to succeed retiring independent Joseph I. Lieberman in the Senate in 2012.

Murphy won a third term in Congress in 2010 despite the Republican wave that ousted dozens of his Democratic colleagues. "They have a certain degree of Yankee independence to them, and sort of never follow the national trends," Murphy said of his constituents.

But Murphy also acknowledges his own independence as a lawmaker, one who is difficult to pinpoint along the ideological spectrum.

He is socially liberal and was a staunch advocate of including a government-run "public option" in the health care overhaul bill enacted in the 111th Congress (2009-10). At the same time, he is a member of the moderate New Democrat Coalition. "I don't have ideological rules," Murphy said. "My district doesn't worry too much about 'liberal,' 'moderate,' 'conservative,' so I don't worry about those labels. . . . I've always just focused more on pragmatism than on ideology."

One of Murphy's goals in the 112th Congress is to finesse relationships with freshman Republicans to push "buy American" initiatives for federal agencies. He sees it as an issue that does not break along party lines. Murphy said he also wants to strengthen the Buy American Caucus he founded with North Carolina Republican Walter B. Jones.

"If we continue down our current path, where America's national security is for sale to the lowest bidder, we will surely lose our edge as the world's largest and most vibrant economy," said Murphy. He will attempt to further the cause from his seat on the Oversight and Government Reform Committee.

He might reintroduce two relevant bills that did not gain much traction in the 111th. One measure would allow contracting officers in federal agencies to consider, before offering contracts, whether the requesting manufacturer or business owner would use the contracts to spur U.S. job growth; the other would require federal agencies to consider the long- and short-term impact of granting waivers allowing a foreign contract on domestic employment.

One of the House's youngest members, Murphy also is among its most driven. He arrived on Capitol Hill in his early 30s, having held several local and state government offices — though he never stayed in any longer than four years. Before that, he managed the congressional campaign of a virtual unknown who almost beat the incumbent Republican whom Murphy ousted a decade later.

Murphy has shown a knack for making friends among fellow Democrats in his state's increasingly influential delegation, including Democratic Caucus Chairman John B. Larson and Rosa DeLauro, co-chairwoman of the panel that makes Democratic committee assignments. With their help, he landed the seat on Energy and Commerce in the 111th Congress.

He helped get the health care overhaul package moving through that panel, the last of the three committees with jurisdiction over the legislation. With the bill moving slowly over several all-day markups in July 2009, Murphy helped secure revisions to trim $100 billion from the cost of the bill.

Murphy had less success in his fight to include a government-run "public option," but he voted for the bill anyway and says he wants to continue to be a champion of the legislation as the Republican majority moves to repeal or defund it.

"I came to Congress to pass health care reform," Murphy said. "I'm going to continue to be a proponent of health care reform and an opponent of efforts to roll back protections that my constituents need."

In 2007, he pushed, unsuccessfully, legislation to establish a government-run Medicare drug plan that would allow the federal government to use savings from negotiations with pharmaceutical companies to provide more coverage.

Murphy also stands with the Democratic orthodoxy on energy policy.

He supports a nationwide mandate for states to provide at least 15 percent of their electricity from wind, solar and other renewable resources and backs a cap-and-trade system aimed at reducing carbon emissions.

In 2006, he followed the example of fellow Democratic freshman Peter Welch of Vermont by spending out of his own pocket — congressional rules bar the use of government funds — to ensure his offices in Washington and Connecticut do not emit excess carbon.

Murphy, who has traveled to Iraq, Afghanistan, Israel, Egypt, Turkey, Qatar, Kuwait, and Pakistan since his election, joined the Foreign Affairs Committee in the 112th Congress and promised to be active on its Middle East and South Asia Subcommittee.

Murphy's mother grew up in public housing and his grandfather and great-grandfather worked at a New Britain ball bearing factory, which he said is why he supports organized labor.

He attended Williams College, where he earned a dual degree in history and political science. Shortly after graduating, he managed the congressional campaign of activist Charlotte Koskoff, who came within 1,600 votes of upsetting veteran Republican Nancy L. Johnson. Ten years later, Murphy finished the job, ousting Johnson by a solid margin in an election season that heavily favored his party.

In the decade in between, while attending law school, Murphy captured a seat in the state House, unseating a 14-year incumbent, and won election to the state Senate four years later.

In 2008, he beat GOP state Sen. David J. Capiello by a nearly 20-point margin after raising more than twice as much money. Two years later, Murphy won a third term in office, defeating state Sen. Sam Caligiuri by a narrower — but still substantial — 8-point margin.

Key Votes

2010

Overhaul the nation's health insurance system	YES
Allow for repeal of "don't ask, don't tell"	YES
Overhaul financial services industry regulation	YES
Limit use of new Afghanistan War funds to troop withdrawal activities	NO
Change oversight of offshore drilling and lift oil spill liability cap	YES
Provide a path to legal status for some children of illegal immigrants	YES
Extend Bush-era income tax cuts for two years	NO

2009

Expand the Children's Health Insurance Program	YES
Provide $787 billion in tax cuts and spending increases to stimulate the economy	YES
Allow bankruptcy judges to modify certain primary-residence mortgages	YES
Create a cap-and-trade system to limit greenhouse gas emissions	YES
Provide $2 billion for the "cash for clunkers" program	YES
Establish the government as the sole provider of student loans	YES
Restrict federally funded insurance coverage for abortions in health care overhaul	NO

CQ Vote Studies

	PARTY UNITY		PRESIDENTIAL SUPPORT	
	SUPPORT	OPPOSE	SUPPORT	OPPOSE
2010	97%	3%	90%	10%
2009	97%	3%	97%	3%
2008	98%	2%	17%	83%
2007	96%	4%	5%	95%

Interest Groups

	AFL-CIO	ADA	CCUS	ACU
2010	93%	95%	13%	4%
2009	100%	100%	40%	4%
2008	100%	95%	61%	0%
2007	96%	100%	50%	0%

Connecticut 5

West — Danbury, New Britain, most of Waterbury

Based in the bucolic western part of the state, the 5th is a mix of rolling farmland along the Housatonic River in the Litchfield Hills and midsize industrial cities. Its longstanding manufacturing cities are struggling through the transition into successful centers of technology and skilled manufacturing.

Waterbury is the district's most populous city, with more than 80 percent of its residents living in the 5th (the rest live in the 3rd). It is middle-class and diverse, with blacks and Hispanics together accounting for nearly half of the population. East of Waterbury, on the 5th's southeastern edge, are Cheshire, an upper-income, liberal-leaning but politically competitive area, and Meriden, a Democratic-voting area.

Growing Danbury, located in the 5th's southwestern corner, has experienced an influx of immigrants, resulting in both changes in municipal regulations and community development investment. Employers in the Danbury region include Praxair, which makes industrial gases, and pharmaceutical company Boehringer Ingelheim.

North and east of Waterbury, the district branches off to take in New Britain. Although the Hand Tools Division of Stanley Works still operates out of New Britain, continuing manufacturing job losses have hurt the area. New Britain votes overwhelmingly Democratic and is home to both a very large Polish community and a sizable Hispanic community.

The population of the 5th has grown over the past decade, and the district has grown increasingly likely to favor Democratic candidates for federal office. Although Democrat John Kerry barely won the 2004 presidential vote here, Barack Obama took a comfortable 56 percent in 2008. Kerry's 2004 Republican opponent, George W. Bush, carried several towns north and east of Danbury, including New Milford and Newtown, but both supported Obama in 2008.

Major Industry
Manufacturing, health care

Cities
Waterbury (pt.), 91,104; Danbury, 80,893; New Britain, 73,206; Meriden, 60,868; Torrington (pt.), 20,441

Notable
Cheshire was designated the "Bedding Plant Capital of Connecticut" by the state legislature.

DELAWARE

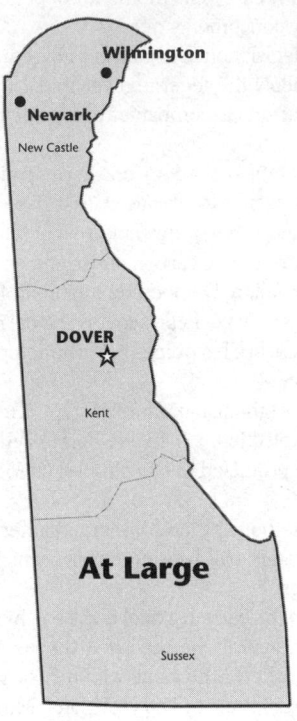

GOV. JACK MARKELL (D)

First elected: 2008

Length of term: 4 years

Term expires: 1/13

Salary: $171,000

Phone: (302) 739-4101

Residence: Wilmington

Born: Nov. 26, 1960; Newark, Del.

Religion: Jewish

Family: Wife, Carla Markell; two children

Education: Brown U., 1982 B.A. (development studies & economics); U. of Chicago, 1985 M.B.A.

Career: Telecommunications company executive; banker

Political highlights: Del. treasurer, 1999-2009

ELECTION RESULTS

2008 GENERAL
Jack Markell (D)	266,861	67.5%
William Swain Lee (R)	126,662	32.0%

LT. GOV. MATTHEW DENN (D)

First elected: 2008

Length of term: 4 years

Term expires: 1/13

Salary: $76,250

Phone: (302) 744-4333

LEGISLATURE

General Assembly: January-June

Senate: 21 members, 4-year terms

2011 ratios: 14 D, 7 R; 14 men, 7 women

Salary: $42,750

Phone: (302) 744-4129
(Note: To accommodate redistricting, all Senate seats are up in 2012, then terms return to 4 years.)

House: 41 members, 2-year terms

2011 ratios: 26 D, 15 R; 34 men, 7 women

Salary: $42,750

Phone: (302) 744-4087

TERM LIMITS

Governor: 2 terms

Senate: No

House: No

URBAN STATISTICS

CITY	POPULATION
Wilmington	70,851
Dover	36,047
Newark	31,454
Middletown	18,871
Smyrna	10,023

REGISTERED VOTERS

Democrat	50%
Republican	31%
Other	25%

POPULATION

2010 population	897,934
2000 population	783,600
1990 population	666,168
Percent change (2000-2010)	+14.6%
Rank among states (2010)	45
Median age	37.8
Born in state	46.1%
Foreign born	7.5%
Violent crime rate	637/100,000
Poverty level	10.8%
Federal workers	8,846
Military	3,870

ELECTIONS

STATE ELECTION OFFICIAL
(302) 739-4277

DEMOCRATIC PARTY
(302) 328-9036

REPUBLICAN PARTY
(302) 668-1954

MISCELLANEOUS

Web: www.delaware.gov

Capital: Dover

U.S. CONGRESS

Senate: 2 Democrats

House: 1 Democrat

2010 CENSUS STATISTICS BY DISTRICT

District	2008 VOTE FOR PRESIDENT Obama	McCain	White	Black	Asian	Hispanic	Median Income	White Collar	Blue Collar	Service Industry	Over 64	Under 18	College Education	Rural	Sq. Miles
AL	62%	37%	65%	21%	3%	8%	$57,618	63%	20%	17%	14%	24%	28%	20%	1,954
STATE	62	37	65	21	3	8	57,618	63	20	17	14	24	28	20	1,954
U.S.	53	46	64	12	5	16	51,425	60	23	17	13	25	28	21	3,537,438

Sen. Thomas R. Carper (D)

Capitol Office
224-2441
carper.senate.gov
513 Hart Bldg. 20510-0803; fax 228-2190

Committees
Environment & Public Works
(Clean Air & Nuclear Safety - Chairman)
Finance
Homeland Security & Governmental Affairs
(Federal Financial Management - Chairman)

Residence
Wilmington

Born
Jan. 23, 1947; Beckley, W.Va.

Religion
Presbyterian

Family
Wife, Martha Carper; two children

Education
Ohio State U., B.A. 1968 (economics); U. of Delaware,
M.B.A. 1975

Military Service
Navy, 1968-73; Naval Reserve, 1973-91

Career
State economic development official

Political Highlights
Del. treasurer, 1977-83; U.S. House, 1983-93; governor,
1993-2001

ELECTION RESULTS

2006 GENERAL

Thomas R. Carper (D)	170,567	67.1%
Jan Ting (R)	69,734	27.4%
Christine O'Donnell (WRI)	11,127	4.4%
William E. Morris (LIBERT)	2,671	1.0%

2006 PRIMARY

Thomas R. Carper (D)	unopposed

Previous Winning Percentages
2000 (56%); 1990 House Election (66%); 1988 House
Election (68%); 1986 House Election (66%); 1984
House Election (58%); 1982 House Election (52%)

Elected 2000; 2nd term

Carper takes a middle-of-the-road approach to governing that has endeared him to Delaware voters and Senate colleagues — and has frequently put him at the center of legislative negotiations. "When you're a centrist, you're in on every play," he said. That philosophy is evident in how he practices moderation in other aspects of his life.

On the Finance Committee he was a key player in a hallmark issue of the 111th Congress (2009-10), the health care overhaul, and he was a leading moderate voice for Democrats when the measure moved to the Senate floor. Although no Senate Republicans supported the legislation, Carper said the final product was more centrist than most people supposed. "We tacked to the middle," he said. "Our Republican friends sailed off in another direction."

He also is positioned to be a central figure in what will be a hallmark issue for the 112th Congress (2011-12): government spending. He joined with Arizona Republican John McCain to push "enhanced rescission authority," which would allow the president to force Congress to vote to either delete or protect portions of appropriations bills challenged by the White House. By giving Congress the final say, the plan is designed to overcome legal challenges that doomed a law giving the president line-item veto authority.

"What we need is a culture of thrift . . . to replace a culture of spendthrift," Carper said on CNBC in January 2011.

Throughout his Senate tenure, Carper has tried to ensure that politics isn't all about the extremes. In 2004, he was co-founder of Third Way, a think tank formed with the idea of giving moderates a higher profile and generating middle-of-the-road legislation. A former state treasurer, governor and House member, Carper said his consensus-building skills were sharpened by his work with the National Governors Association.

"I really think that we need more people in Congress who think like governors — who are results-oriented, who are not so ideologically driven, people who are impatient with gridlock, and maybe a little less partisan," he said.

In mid-2005, he was named vice chairman of the moderate (and now defunct) Democratic Leadership Council once headed by Bill Clinton, and party leaders later tapped him as a deputy whip. Carper also sits on the Democratic Policy Committee, and his name was floated as a potential choice to replace Byron L. Dorgan as chairman when the North Dakotan retired at the end of the 111th Congress. "I wouldn't rule it out, but I'm not campaigning for it," Carper said of the job, which eventually went to New York liberal Charles E. Schumer.

Carper's moderate approach extends beyond the legislative process. On Thursdays, he attends a bipartisan and nondenominational Bible study group — a practice he said "helps bridge the partisan divide." He also leads orientation sessions for freshman senators and their spouses, during which each new senator is provided with both a Republican and a Democratic mentor.

Carper also keeps a list of several hundred birthdays of current and former colleagues, staffers and others, calling each to wish them well. "It gives me a chance to talk to them outside the course of their normal business . . . and just to talk to them on a personal level," he told the Wilmington News Journal.

Carper is popular among colleagues for his quick wit. At a news conference, when aides removed the box that diminutive Environment and Public Works Chairwoman Barbara Boxer, a California Democrat, uses behind the lectern for such events, Carper quipped, "Actually, I'd like the box. I want people to say, 'He's a giant among the supporters of doing something about global warming.'"

But Carper is serious about the issue. He serves on the Environment panel and in 2009 was named to its just-launched Subcommittee on Green Jobs and the New Economy. He has been a proponent of a cap-and-trade system that would limit carbon dioxide emissions and establish a system for buying and selling emission allowances.

"I think there's a broad belief that one of the ways to [create more clean-energy jobs] . . . is to put a price on carbon," he said.

In 2009, Boxer chose Carper to oversee a working group on coal research and technology made up primarily of senators from states that are heavily reliant on coal mining or coal-fired power plants. He was an original cosponsor of a bill aimed at developing offshore wind power and has supported increased funding for more energy-efficient transportation initiatives.

Carper also serves on the Homeland Security and Governmental Affairs Committee, where as chairman of the subcommittee that oversees postal issues he has fought to give the Postal Service increased autonomy while criticizing its proposals to cut mail-delivery days. With the 2012 retirement of Connecticut independent Joseph I. Lieberman, Carper is a candidate to chair the committee in the next Congress if Democrats retain their majority.

A strong supporter of Amtrak, the federally subsidized passenger railroad service, Carper frequently commutes from his home in Wilmington to Washington on the train.

Carper was raised in Roanoke, Va., and later Columbus, Ohio. As a boy, he was active in the Civil Air Patrol and Boy Scouts and earned an ROTC scholarship to attend Ohio State University. Years later, he told the Columbus Dispatch that, until he became governor, the best job he ever had was washing dishes at an Ohio State sorority house.

In college, he underwent a political transformation. Carper said that at first he held the Republican views of his parents, campaigning in 1964 for GOP presidential candidate Barry Goldwater. But by 1968, his skepticism about the Vietnam War led him to volunteer in the anti-war presidential campaign of Democrat Eugene J. McCarthy.

Despite his anti-war sentiments, he joined the Navy that year and wore his uniform to his college graduation. He went on to serve for five years and for another 18 in the Naval Reserve, retiring as a captain in 1991. During his time in the Navy he was smitten by Delaware, flying into Dover aboard a military transport plane and later telling a friend he'd "like to move to a little state where you would not need a lot of money and fame, and maybe run for office."

After the Navy, Carper enrolled in the University of Delaware's business school, where he earned a master's degree in business administration. When Jim Soles, a favorite professor, ran for Congress in 1974, Carper worked on his campaign, which was unsuccessful.

One day in 1976, he was lying in the sand at Dewey Beach and listening to his transistor radio when he heard a news report that said Democrats could not find a candidate for state treasurer. He entered the race and, at age 29, beat a strongly favored Republican.

In 1982, Carper ran for the House after Democrats again had trouble lining up a candidate. Delaware's economic woes at the time — and revelations that Republican incumbent Thomas B. Evans was romantically involved with a lobbyist — boosted Carper's campaign, and the state's House seat went Democratic for the first time since 1966.

Carper ran successfully for governor in 1992, swapping jobs with moderate Republican Michael N. Castle. After two terms as governor, Carper in 2000 returned to Washington in a battle-of-the-titans challenge to five-term Republican Sen. William V. Roth Jr. that, as it ended up, was not even close. Carper defeated the Finance chairman, whose name is attached to a type of individual retirement account, by almost 12 percentage points. In 2006, Carper won two-thirds of the vote.

Key Votes

2010

Pass budget reconciliation bill to modify overhauls of health care and federal student loan programs	YES
Proceed to disapproval resolution on EPA authority to regulate greenhouse gases	NO
Overhaul financial services industry regulation	YES
Limit debate to proceed to a bill to broaden campaign finance disclosure and reporting rules	YES
Limit debate on an extension of Bush-era income tax cuts for two years	YES
Limit debate on a bill to provide a path to legal status for some children of illegal immigrants	YES
Allow for a repeal of "don't ask, don't tell"	YES
Consent to ratification of a strategic arms reduction treaty with Russia	YES

2009

Prevent release of remaining financial industry bailout funds	NO
Make it easier for victims to sue for wage discrimination remedies	YES
Expand the Children's Health Insurance Program	YES
Limit debate on the economic stimulus measure	YES
Repeal District of Columbia firearms prohibitions and gun registration laws	NO
Limit debate on expansion of federal hate crimes law	YES
Strike funding for F-22 Raptor fighter jets	YES

CQ Vote Studies

	PARTY UNITY		PRESIDENTIAL SUPPORT	
	Support	Oppose	Support	Oppose
2010	95%	5%	100%	0%
2009	93%	7%	97%	3%
2008	80%	20%	45%	55%
2007	88%	12%	46%	54%
2006	79%	21%	64%	36%
2005	77%	23%	38%	62%
2004	86%	14%	66%	34%
2003	81%	19%	53%	47%
2002	74%	26%	79%	21%
2001	80%	20%	72%	28%

Interest Groups

	AFL-CIO	ADA	CCUS	ACU
2010	94%	90%	27%	0%
2009	89%	90%	57%	4%
2008	100%	85%	63%	0%
2007	89%	85%	55%	8%
2006	87%	90%	58%	20%
2005	64%	90%	72%	8%
2004	100%	95%	71%	12%
2003	77%	75%	70%	10%
2002	85%	80%	50%	25%
2001	93%	90%	58%	24%

Sen. Chris Coons (D)

Capitol Office
224-5042
coons.senate.gov
127A Russell Bldg. 20510-0802; fax 228-3075

Committees
Budget
Energy & Natural Resources
Foreign Relations
   (African Affairs - Chairman)
Judiciary

Residence
Wilmington

Born
Sept. 9, 1963; Greenwich, Conn.

Religion
Presbyterian

Family
Wife, Annie Lingenfelter; three children

Education
Amherst College, A.B. 1985 (chemistry & political
science); Yale U., J.D. 1992, M.A.R. 1992 (ethics)

Career
Lawyer; education foundation aide; campaign aide

Political Highlights
New Castle County Council president, 2001-05; New
Castle County executive, 2005-10

ELECTION RESULTS

2010 SPECIAL

Chris Coons (D)	174,012	56.6%
Christine O'Donnell (R)	123,053	40.0%
Glenn A. Miller (I)	8,201	2.7%

2010 PRIMARY

Chris Coons (D)	unopposed

Elected 2010; 1st term

Cut from a decidedly progressive cloth, Coons is the rarest type of fresh-man to win a Senate seat in 2010 — an avowed liberal who believes government can and should do more.

While much of the freshman class serving in the 112th Congress (2011-12) was swept in on a wave of economic discontent and anti-Obama sentiments, Coons might end up being the sole new supporter the administration and Democratic leaders can consistently count on in the Senate.

Like Democratic predecessors Ted Kaufman and Vice President Joseph R. Biden Jr., Coons — a lawyer and former New Castle County executive — can be expected to bring a fairly traditional liberal approach to his work in the Senate.

He got a head start on the class of 2010 by being seated immediately because he replaced an appointed senator, Kaufman, and he quickly lined up with his fellow Democrats on a range of issues.

Like both Kaufman and Biden, Coons is expected to be a vigorous sup-porter of infrastructure spending. In particular, Coons will become one of the new standard bearers for Amtrak, the passenger train service that runs the length of Delaware and is an important employer in the state.

He also is a supporter of spending more on research to boost manufactur-ing, and he made his maiden Senate floor speech on the sector's role in job creation and economic growth.

"The formula for our economic success has long been the unstoppable combination of an innovative citizenry and investment in cutting-edge research," he said on the floor. "This is what generates companies that invent new products, often high-tech and research-driven products, and, along with these, create skilled jobs right here in the United States."

With the economy expected to dominate the political landscape for the foreseeable future, Coons, assigned to the Budget Committee, will likely line up behind Democratic leaders on issues such as Social Security, unemploy-ment benefits and efforts to boost the economy through government action.

In some areas, though, there are slight deviations.

On taxes, Coons was ahead of the curve. Before President Obama struck a deal with Republicans, Coons backed the idea of extending all of the Bush-era tax cuts — including those for people in the upper income brackets — as part of a bipartisan agreement that included other provisions backed by Democrats. That was similar to the compromise reached at the end of the 111th Congress (2009-10), which Coons supported.

He may prove to be more in conflict with the Obama administration on trade issues. While the White House will look to move a series of trade agree-ments in the 112th Congress, Coons sides with organized labor and other liberal constituencies in demanding protections for the environment and workers.

From his seat on the Foreign Relations Committee, where he chairs the African Affairs panel, Coons will be deeply involved in U.S. policy in Afghan-istan — and he has expressed some ambivalence about Obama's strategy.

"I support the president's commitment to continuing a very tough fight against al Qaeda, wherever they are," he said on MSNBC after the election. "There are elements affiliated with al Qaeda that are in Yemen, that are in Somalia, that are in Pakistan, that are in Afghanistan. . . . The real question is, are we going to be able to stand up a successful Afghan security force? Are we going to be able to get a good and effective partner in the Karzai government? Are we going to be able to persuade Pakistan under President Zardari to work with us to close down those parts in the border regions that the Taliban and al Qaeda are using?" He said he would reserve judgment on those questions pending further developments.

Coons backed the strategic arms reduction treaty between the United States and Russia that the Senate approved as one of the last acts of the 111th Congress, calling the agreement "a pressing security matter of the highest order."

A member of the Energy and Natural Resources Committee, he supports climate change legislation and alternative-energy projects. Coons praised a strategic plan unveiled by the Interior and Energy departments in early 2011 that would give Delaware's offshore wind energy projects expedited reviews.

On social issues, Coons will be a reliably liberal vote. A member of the Judiciary Committee, he opposes attempts to impose restrictions on abortion rights and supports same-sex marriage. He voted for stand-alone legislation, signed into law in December 2010, that repealed the ban on homosexuals serving openly in the military. "I'm convinced 'don't ask, don't tell' is discrimination, plain and simple, and doesn't have any place in our modern armed forces," he said on PBS in November 2010.

He also sided with most Democrats in supporting legislation, which died in the Senate after passing the House, that would have provided a path to legal status for certain illegal immigrant children.

Coons was born in Greenwich, Conn., but grew up in Hockessin, Del., and attended Tower Hill, a private school founded by the du Pont family. His mother taught elementary school and his father worked for a food-processing company and founded his own kitchen cabinet and counter-top manufacturing company.

In what became a famous bit of youthful writing, he described his path from young Republican to "bearded Marxist," tracing his journey away from his affluent parents' moderate Republicanism.

He says a period in which his parents' economic fortunes went south, followed by a divorce, caused him to re-evaluate his political outlook. He had helped found a College Republicans group at Amherst College, but within a year Coons switched sides.

He graduated from Amherst with a degree in chemistry and political science, then earned a law degree from Yale Law School and a master's in ethics from Yale Divinity School. He also studied at the University of Nairobi in Kenya, where he says up-close experience with poverty added to his altered ideological leanings.

Coons worked as an attorney for Delaware-based W.L. Gore & Associates, a fabric manufacturer owned by his step-father's family, as well as with several nonprofits, including the National Coalition for the Homeless, the education-oriented "I Have a Dream" Foundation and the Investor Responsibility Research Center.

Elected to the New Castle County Council in 2000, he served as its president for four years before becoming county executive in 2005.

Coon's path to the Senate involved several twists. The seat was vacated by Biden when he was elected vice president, and most observers assumed his son — state Attorney General Beau Biden — would be the Democratic nominee. Kaufman, a Biden aide, was appointed as a seat-warmer.

But when the younger Biden opted not to participate in the race, Coons jumped in. He was expected to face a difficult challenge from moderate Republican Michael N. Castle, a House veteran in his ninth term, but Castle was upset in his primary by tea party favorite Christine O'Donnell, a conservative with no electoral track record. Coons jumped to an early big lead in the polls and never relinquished it, defeating O'Donnell by 17 percentage points.

Key Votes

2010	
Limit debate on an extension of Bush-era income tax cuts for two years	YES
Limit debate on a bill to provide a path to legal status for some children of illegal immigrants	YES
Allow for a repeal of "don't ask, don't tell"	YES
Consent to ratification of a strategic arms reduction treaty with Russia	YES

CQ Vote Studies

	PARTY UNITY		PRESIDENTIAL SUPPORT	
	SUPPORT	OPPOSE	SUPPORT	OPPOSE
2010	100%	0%	100%	0%

Interest Groups

	AFL-CIO	ADA	CCUS	ACU
2010	100%		50%	0%

Rep. John Carney (D)

Capitol Office
225-4165
johncarney.house.gov
1429 Longworth Bldg. 20515-0801; fax 225-2291

Committees
Financial Services

Residence
Wilmington

Born
May 20, 1956; Wilmington, Del.

Religion
Roman Catholic

Family
Wife, Tracey Quillen; two children

Education
Dartmouth College, A.B. 1978 (English); U. of
Delaware, M.P.A. 1987

Career
Renewable energy company executive;
gubernatorial and congressional district aide;
county government official; religious youth
programs coordinator; high school and college
athletics coach

Political Highlights
Del. secretary of finance, 1997-2000; lieutenant
governor, 2001-09; sought Democratic nomination
for governor, 2008

ELECTION RESULTS

2010 GENERAL
John Carney (D)	173,543	56.8%
Glen Urquhart (R)	125,442	41.0%
Earl R. Lofland (I)	3,704	1.2%

2010 PRIMARY
John Carney (D)	unopposed

Elected 2010; 1st term

Carney brings experience in Delaware politics to the House, where he plans to focus on bipartisan legislative efforts — particularly on his top priority, energy.

In a Republican-controlled House, the freshman Democrat's style of governing might prove advantageous: He has not been reticent about criticizing his own party. "Even in the first couple of caucuses on my side, I was amazed that people were ready to go to battle," he told Politico. "That's going to be frustrating for me."

Energy security complements national security, he says, because fossil fuels are a potential source of conflict throughout the world. The renewable-energy business is an opportunity, Carney says, to boost manufacturing in the United States and create jobs. He was president and chief operating officer of a renewable-energy company prior to his election.

During the campaign, Carney outlined a six-point plan that included a payroll tax holiday and an extension of tax cuts for all income levels while Congress works on a long-term policy for reducing the national debt. Both proposals were part of legislation enacted in Congress's post-election session.

Carney won a seat on the Financial Services Committee, where he can tend to Delaware's myriad headquarters of major financial services companies.

An All-Ivy League football player who became a lacrosse and football coach, Carney went to graduate school in Delaware. While studying for his MPA and immediately after finishing it, he served as a staff assistant to Sen. Joseph R. Biden Jr. (now the vice president) and then as deputy chief of staff to Gov. Thomas R. Carper (now a senator).

Later Carney took a turn as the state's secretary of finance and was twice elected lieutenant governor. He also made an unsuccessful bid for the Democratic nomination for governor in 2008.

In October 2009, after nine terms in the House, Republican Michael N. Castle announced he was running for the Senate. Carney had a clear field in the primary, then defeated Republican Glen Urquhart with 57 percent of the vote.

Delaware

At Large

Delaware's coastal terrain and inland agricultural sector contrast with Wilmington and its suburbs. A string of beach resorts in the state's southeast corner, from Cape Henlopen State Park and Rehoboth Beach south to Fenwick Island on the Maryland border, draws hordes of visitors to the state.

Favorable tax rates and incorporation rules and a specialized business court attracted financial services companies for decades. Delaware has been the on-paper home to hundreds of Fortune 500 companies. Once known for a strong manufacturing sector, the state continues to lose factory jobs and unemployment hovers around the national average. Even the DuPont Company, the hometown chemical giant, has cut jobs. Three gambling and racing facilities are mainstays of the local tourism industry. Strongly Democratic New Castle County is the state's population center. The county's

largest city, Wilmington, is the state's economic engine, and there has been redevelopment there along the Delaware River. Immigration, legal and illegal, has resulted in some majority-minority communities across the state. Increasingly Democratic-leaning voters here supported Barack Obama and Delaware's favorite son, Joseph R. Biden Jr., in the 2008 presidential election, and Democrat Jack Markell won an overwhelming victory in the 2008 gubernatorial race. Democrats also control both chambers of the state legislature.

Major Industry
Financial services, health care, tourism

Military Bases
Dover Air Force Base, 3,491 military, 837 civilian (2011)

Cities
Wilmington, 70,851; Dover, 36,047

Notable
In 1787, Delaware became the first state to ratify the U.S. Constitution.

FLORIDA

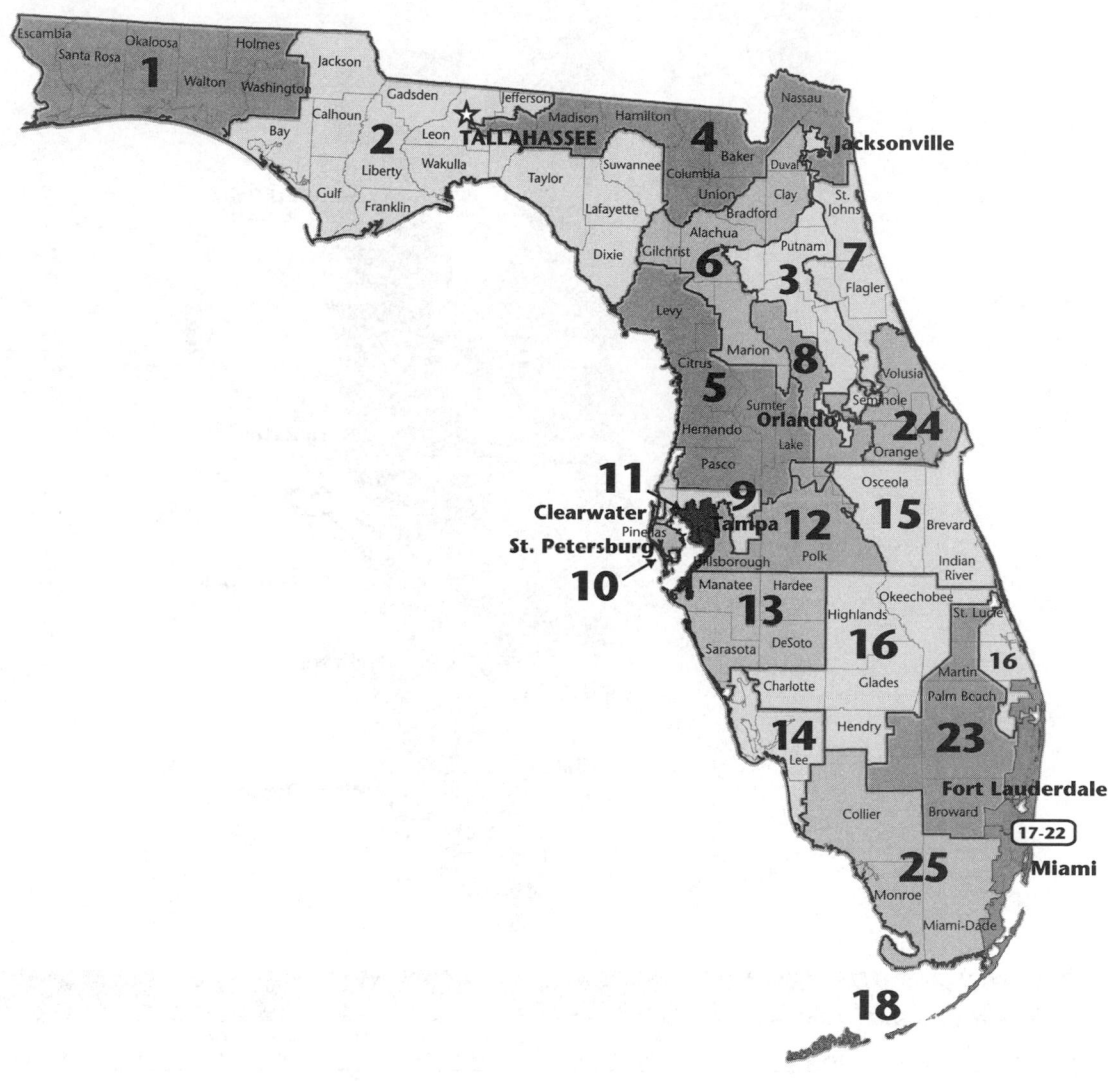

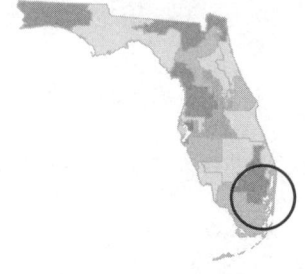

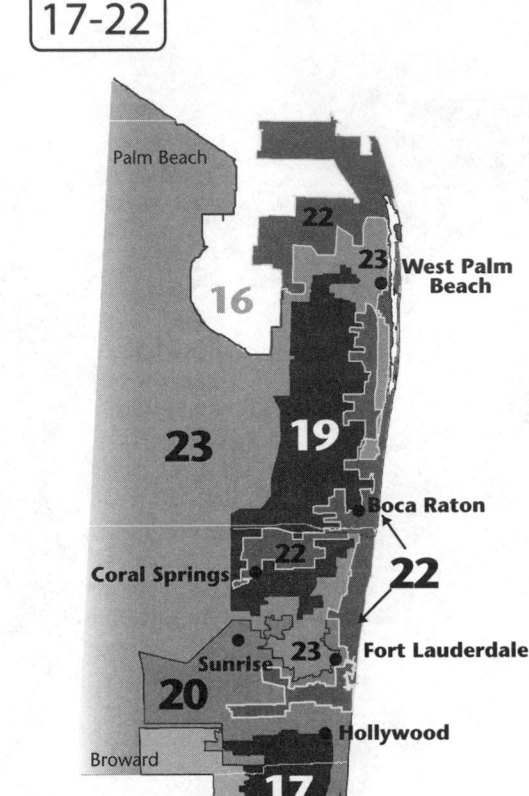

17-22

2010 CENSUS STATISTICS BY DISTRICT

| District | 2008 VOTE FOR PRESIDENT | | White | Black | Asian | Hispanic | Median Income | White Collar | Blue Collar | Service Industry | Over 64 | Under 18 | College Education | Rural | Sq. Miles |
	Obama	McCain													
1	32%	67%	75%	14%	2%	5%	$46,555	58%	22%	20%	13%	23%	23%	23%	4,642
2	45	54	68	22	2	5	42,957	61	19	20	13	21	25	38	9,425
3	71	28	33	51	2	11	34,213	50	26	24	11	26	15	10	1,796
4	37	62	72	15	4	7	54,429	64	20	15	12	23	27	22	4,118
5	43	56	80	6	2	11	44,845	58	23	19	23	20	19	36	4,044
6	43	56	71	14	3	9	46,068	61	21	18	17	22	23	31	2,912
7	46	53	75	10	2	11	50,103	64	19	17	17	22	28	13	1,797
8	52	47	57	10	5	26	50,693	64	19	18	13	24	29	8	987
9	47	52	76	5	3	14	51,497	69	16	15	17	22	29	6	634
10	52	47	81	5	3	8	45,035	66	18	16	21	18	27	0	175
11	66	33	41	27	3	28	39,382	59	21	20	12	24	24	0	244
12	49	50	59	15	2	21	46,188	58	25	17	16	25	20	16	1,956
13	47	52	80	5	1	12	48,336	59	23	18	26	18	27	11	2,599
14	42	57	74	7	1	17	52,389	59	22	19	25	19	28	9	1,057
15	48	51	66	9	2	20	47,699	58	22	20	19	22	25	10	2,545

Gov. Rick Scott (R)

First elected: 2010
Length of term: 4 years
Term expires: 1/15
Salary: $130,273
Phone: (850) 488-7146
Residence: Naples
Born: Dec. 1, 1952; Bloomington, Ill.
Religion: Christian
Family: Wife, Ann Scott; two children
Education: U. of Missouri, Kansas City (business administration)
Military service: Navy, 1971-73
Career: Venture capitalist; hospital CEO; lawyer
Political highlights: No previous office

ELECTION RESULTS

2010 GENERAL
Rick Scott (R)	2,619,335	48.9%
Alex Sink (D)	2,557,785	47.7%
Peter Allen (I)	123,831	2.3%

Lt. Gov. Jennifer Carroll (R)

First elected: 2010
Length of term: 4 years
Term expires: 1/15
Salary: $124,851
Phone: (850) 488-4711

LEGISLATURE

Legislature: 60 days, March-May
Senate: 40 members, 4-year terms
2011 ratios: 28 R, 12 D; 14 women, 26 men
Salary: $29,697
Phone: (850) 487-5270
House: 120 members, 2-year terms
2011 ratios: 80 R, 39 D, 1 vacancy; 92 men, 27 women
Salary: $29,697
Phone: (850) 488-1157

TERM LIMITS

Governor: 2 terms
Senate: 2 consecutive terms
House: 4 consecutive terms

URBAN STATISTICS

CITY	POPULATION
Jacksonville	821,784
Miami	399,457
Tampa	335,709
St. Petersburg	244,769
Orlando	238,300

REGISTERED VOTERS

Republican	43%
Democrat	36%
Unaffiliated/others	21%

POPULATION

2010 population	18,801,310
2000 population	15,982,378
1990 population	12,937,926
Percent change (2000-2010)	+17.6%
Rank among states (2010)	4
Median age	39.7
Born in state	34.2%
Foreign born	18.1%
Violent crime rate	613/100,000
Poverty level	14.9%
Federal workers	166,903
Military	42,642

ELECTIONS

STATE ELECTION OFFICIAL
(850) 245-6500
DEMOCRATIC PARTY
(580) 222-3411
REPUBLICAN PARTY
(850) 222-7920

MISCELLANEOUS

Web: www.myflorida.gov
Capital: Tallahassee

U.S. CONGRESS

Senate: 1 Republican, 1 Democrat
House: 19 Republicans, 6 Democrats

2010 Census Statistics by District

District	2008 Vote for President Obama	McCain	White	Black	Asian	Hispanic	Median Income	White Collar	Blue Collar	Service Industry	Over 64	Under 18	College Education	Rural	Sq. Miles
16	47%	52%	71%	9%	1%	16%	$47,885	57%	24%	19%	23%	21%	22%	15%	4,538
17	87	12	12	56	2	28	36,140	50	23	26	11	27	17	0	97
18	51	49	25	6	1	67	40,506	59	21	21	17	19	31	1	355
19	65	34	62	12	3	21	50,253	65	17	18	26	20	30	0	231
20	63	36	52	12	3	31	55,822	70	14	16	15	22	36	0	160
21	49	51	14	7	2	76	47,764	61	22	17	15	23	27	0	135
22	52	48	72	7	2	16	62,111	68	15	16	20	19	38	1	268
23	83	17	23	55	2	18	38,757	49	25	27	11	27	16	2	3,362
24	49	51	70	8	3	16	53,940	65	18	17	14	22	28	9	1,583
25	49	50	17	9	2	72	54,457	60	22	18	10	27	24	6	4,268
STATE	51	48	58	15	2	22	47,450	61	21	19	17	22	26	11	53,927
US	53	46	64	12	5	16	51,425	60	23	17	13	25	28	21	3,537,438

Sen. Bill Nelson (D)

Capitol Office
224-5274
billnelson.senate.gov
716 Hart Bldg. 20510-0905; fax 228-2183

Committees
Budget
Commerce, Science & Transportation
 (Science & Space - Chairman)
Finance
 (Fiscal Responsibility & Economic Growth -
 Chairman)
Select Intelligence
Special Aging

Residence
Orlando

Born
Sept. 29, 1942; Miami, Fla.

Religion
Presbyterian

Family
Wife, Grace C. Nelson; two children

Education
Yale U., B.A. 1965 (political science); U. of Virginia,
J.D. 1968

Military Service
Army Reserve, 1965-71; Army, 1968-70

Career
Lawyer

Political Highlights
Fla. House, 1972-78; U.S. House, 1979-91; sought
Democratic nomination for governor, 1990; Fla.
treasurer and insurance commissioner, 1995-2001

ELECTION RESULTS

2006 GENERAL

Bill Nelson (D)	2,890,548	60.3%
Katherine Harris (R)	1,826,127	38.1%

2006 PRIMARY

Bill Nelson (D)	unopposed

Previous Winning Percentages
2000 (51%); 1988 House Election (61%); 1986 House
Election (73%); 1984 House Election (61%); 1982
House Election (71%); 1980 House Election (70%);
1978 House Election (61%)

Elected 2000; 2nd term

Nelson generally takes a low-key, centrist approach to legislating. But in the middle of his second term he has had a higher profile on a pair of issues critical to his home state: offshore drilling and space exploration.

Nelson's seats on Finance and four other committees give him many angles from which to watch out for Florida. As a member of the Special Aging Committee, he keeps up on issues of concern to the state's large elderly population. His role as chairman of the Commerce, Science and Transportation Subcommittee on Science and Space enables him to look out for the jobs the space program provides. He also sits on the Budget and Select Intelligence committees.

A major concern for Nelson has been protecting areas off the Florida coast from oil drilling, an issue that took center stage after an oil rig explosion and subsequent spill in the Gulf of Mexico in the spring of 2010. He vehemently opposed White House-backed energy legislation that would allow new drilling in portions of the eastern gulf and negate a deal Nelson helped negotiate in 2006 that banned wells close to the Florida coast.

A Senate climate bill unveiled in May 2010 by John Kerry, a Massachusetts Democrat, and Joseph I. Lieberman, a Connecticut independent, incorporated Nelson's legislation establishing a moratorium on new drilling until an investigation of the spill had been conducted, as well as a concession to Nelson that would allow states to prohibit drilling within 75 miles of their shores and provide further protections for Florida. The measure went nowhere.

Nelson led the Senate crackdown on the Interior Department's Minerals Management Service, writing to the department's inspector general demanding an investigation into whether the oil and gas industry influenced a decision not to require remote-control shutoff switches as a backup to the standard emergency shut-off valves on drilling rigs.

He also is involved in space policy. As a member of the House in 1986, Nelson spent six days orbiting Earth aboard the space shuttle Columbia, two weeks before the Challenger explosion. He is a strong advocate of human spaceflight and funding increases for NASA and was one of the first in Congress to warn of the dangers of delaying upgrades to the space shuttles. His point was tragically driven home in 2003 when Columbia exploded while re-entering Earth's atmosphere.

In 2010, Nelson and other space-state senators anxiously awaited Obama's fiscal 2011 budget blueprint for NASA. With constituents' jobs on the line, U.S. leadership in spaceflight diminishing and commercial space companies yet to demonstrate capability, he made it clear he would not accept delaying development of a bigger rocket for human space exploration.

He criticized Obama's proposal to funnel billions of dollars from the canceled Constellation program, envisioned as the shuttle's replacement, into the commercial space industry to prompt development of private spacecraft. But Obama retreated slightly, suggesting that NASA develop a new heavy-lift rocket and a crew-rescue vehicle based on existing development designs in the Constellation program. The measure ultimately introduced by Nelson and passed by the Senate would direct NASA to retain its shuttle-related workforce through fiscal 2011 while authorizing the agency to foster development of commercial crew services.

He also has proposed creating regional enterprise zones to attract commercial space jobs to areas with an existing population of scientists and engineers, as well as allowing tax breaks for businesses in those zones.

Nelson was an active participant in shaping the health care overhaul enacted in 2010. Shoring up his moderate bona fides and drawing from his experience as a state insurance commissioner, he advocated a bipartisan approach to the legislation and the creation of state-based insurance pools. Nelson worked with Finance Chairman Max Baucus of Montana to refine Baucus' revenue-raising proposal that would have made it more difficult for taxpayers to deduct medical expenses — a provision that would have disproportionately affected senior citizens, Nelson complained. The panel ended up adopting a Nelson amendment to allow people 65 and older to continue taking an itemized deduction for medical expenses that exceed 7.5 percent of their adjusted gross income, at least through 2016.

"We should not raise taxes on the seniors to pay for health reform, particularly in this case, seniors suffering extreme medical hardship," he said.

But Nelson was unable to drum up support for an amendment that would have required the pharmaceutical industry to give the government price breaks on drugs sold to a group of Medicare patients who also qualify for Medicaid. A portion of the savings generated from the amendment would have gone to close the "doughnut hole" gap in Medicare prescription drug coverage.

After a federal judge in Florida declared the entire law unconstitutional in early 2011, Nelson introduced a resolution calling on the Supreme Court to take the case without further appeals "so we don't keep arguing over this for the next several years."

Nelson previously served on the Armed Services Committee, where he sought a middle ground on repealing the military's codified "don't ask, don't tell" policy. He was one of three Senate Democrats — along with Ben Nelson of Nebraska and Jim Webb of Virginia — on the committee who initially expressed reservations about legislating on the issue while the Pentagon was in the midst of a review of the law. He ultimately supported a compromise that allowed the policy to be repealed after the Pentagon finished its study of the implications of repeal. When the study was completed at the end of 2010, Nelson backed legislation repealing the policy that was signed into law by President Obama.

Nelson is a fifth-generation Floridian. His great-great-grandfather emigrated from Denmark in 1829, settling near Chipley in the Florida Panhandle, where much of Nelson's family still lives. Nelson's father was a lawyer; his mother was a schoolteacher.

Nelson majored in political science at Yale and wrote his senior thesis about the Kennedy Space Center. After law school and a brief stint in the Army, he won a seat in the state legislature that he held for six years.

In 1978, he won a bid for an open U.S. House seat. He was an early member of the moderate, and now defunct, Democratic Leadership Council that helped boost Bill Clinton to the national stage. Despite a string of re-elections and the publicity attending his adventure as an astronaut, Nelson lost the 1990 Democratic primary for governor, his only electoral defeat, to former Sen. Lawton Chiles.

Four years later he was elected state insurance commissioner, and he dealt with the aftermath of Hurricane Andrew, which ravaged southern Florida and the state's insurance market in 1992.

From the time he announced his run for the Senate, Nelson was the front-runner for the seat Republican Connie Mack was surrendering after two terms. Nelson portrayed his opponent, 10-term congressman Bill McCollum, as too conservative for Florida, and won with 51 percent of the vote. In 2006, he glided to a 22-percentage-point victory over Republican Rep. Katherine Harris.

Key Votes

2010

Pass budget reconciliation bill to modify overhauls of health care and federal student loan programs	YES
Proceed to disapproval resolution on EPA authority to regulate greenhouse gases	NO
Overhaul financial services industry regulation	YES
Limit debate to proceed to a bill to broaden campaign finance disclosure and reporting rules	YES
Limit debate on an extension of Bush-era income tax cuts for two years	YES
Limit debate on a bill to provide a path to legal status for some children of illegal immigrants	YES
Allow for a repeal of "don't ask, don't tell"	YES
Consent to ratification of a strategic arms reduction treaty with Russia	YES

2009

Prevent release of remaining financial industry bailout funds	NO
Make it easier for victims to sue for wage discrimination remedies	YES
Expand the Children's Health Insurance Program	YES
Limit debate on the economic stimulus measure	YES
Repeal District of Columbia firearms prohibitions and gun registration laws	NO
Limit debate on expansion of federal hate crimes law	YES
Strike funding for F-22 Raptor fighter jets	YES

CQ Vote Studies

	PARTY UNITY		PRESIDENTIAL SUPPORT	
	SUPPORT	OPPOSE	SUPPORT	OPPOSE
2010	89%	11%	98%	2%
2009	93%	7%	97%	3%
2008	89%	11%	42%	58%
2007	90%	10%	42%	58%
2006	76%	24%	60%	40%
2005	84%	16%	47%	53%
2004	92%	8%	62%	38%
2003	90%	10%	56%	44%
2002	77%	23%	78%	22%
2001	92%	8%	70%	30%

Interest Groups

	AFL-CIO	ADA	CCUS	ACU
2010	94%	90%	36%	8%
2009	100%	100%	43%	4%
2008	100%	95%	50%	8%
2007	95%	90%	45%	4%
2006	60%	60%	83%	40%
2005	71%	80%	50%	20%
2004	100%	80%	65%	4%
2003	77%	80%	48%	20%
2002	85%	70%	70%	30%
2001	100%	95%	43%	16%

Sen. Marco Rubio (R)

Capitol Office
224-3041
rubio.senate.gov
317 Hart Bldg. 20510-0903; fax 228-5171

Committees
Commerce, Science & Transportation
Foreign Relations
Small Business & Entrepreneurship
Select Intelligence

Residence
West Miami

Born
May 28, 1971; Miami, Fla.

Religion
Roman Catholic

Family
Wife, Jeanette Rubio; four children

Education
Tarkio College, attended 1989-90; Santa Fe Community College, attended 1990-91; U. of Florida, B.S. 1993 (political science); U. of Miami, J.D. 1996

Career
Lawyer; campaign aide

Political Highlights
West Miami City Commission, 1998-00; Fla. House, 2000-2008 (majority leader, 2003-06; Speaker, 2006-08)

ELECTION RESULTS

2010 GENERAL

Marco Rubio (R)	2,645,743	48.9%
Charlie Crist (I)	1,607,549	29.7%
Kendrick B. Meek (D)	1,092,936	20.2%

2010 PRIMARY

Marco Rubio (R)	1,069,936	84.6%
William "Billy" Kogut (R)	112,080	8.9%
William Escoffery III (R)	82,426	6.5%

Elected 2010; 1st term

The second-youngest U.S. senator and the only Hispanic Republican in the chamber, Rubio is a telegenic rising star in the GOP who is already being mentioned as a future presidential candidate, although he dismisses such talk as premature.

He got to the Senate by consolidating conservative support, which led his primary competitor, Gov. Charlie Crist, to abandon the Republican Party and run as an independent. Rubio rode the national Republican wave into office, promising to seek repeal of the Democrats' health care overhaul, block tax increases and cut federal spending.

"The past two years provided a frightening glimpse at what could become of our great nation if we continue down the current path," he said in the first post-election GOP response to the president's weekly radio address. "It is nothing short of a path to ruin, a path that threatens to diminish us as a nation and a people."

He says that part of any serious effort to cut federal spending will include overhauling entitlements. Rubio once backed the notion of allowing younger people to put some of their Social Security taxes into accounts they manage themselves, but now rejects such proposals. But he remains open to altering the formula for calculating cost-of-living increases and to raising the retirement age as a way to put the program on sounder fiscal footing.

On social issues, Rubio also strikes a conservative chord. He opposes abortion and says he would have voted against Elena Kagan's nomination to the Supreme Court.

During his campaign, Rubio tacked to the right of Crist on immigration, proclaiming his support for Arizona's right to pass a law toughening local law enforcement's role in combatting illegal immigration and promoting a focus on border security. A son of immigrants — his parents were refugees from Fidel Castro's Cuba — he supports efforts to bolster legal immigration.

A member of the Commerce, Science and Transportation Committee, Rubio favors offshore oil and gas drilling, despite opposition to drilling off the state's coasts by most Floridians.

Assigned to the Foreign Relations and Select Intelligence committees, Rubio is an implacable foe of the Castro dictatorship and serves as the ranking Republican on the Western Hemisphere, Peace Corps and Global Narcotics Affairs Subcommittee.

He also has questioned Obama's commitment to Israel.

"Support for Israel by the United States in a time of crisis has been a given for over 60 years," Rubio said in a June 2010 speech to the Florida branch of the Republican Jewish Coalition. "And yet, lately, there is the emerging sense that this longstanding relationship isn't what it used to be."

As Florida House speaker, Rubio developed an initiative called "100 Innovative Ideas for Florida's Future." He followed a similar strategy as a Senate candidate, proposing 80 "Ideas to Reclaim America." That kind of policy-centered thinking is likely to help him assume a role in the Senate Republican caucus as a policy and legislative strategist.

GOP leaders have also said Rubio could be a good national spokesman for the party and could help Republicans reach out to Hispanic and young voters. He also is tuned in to social media — his Facebook page was hailed by users as one of the best of 2010. And with Republicans holding their 2012 nominating convention in Tampa, Rubio is likely to play a very public role at the four-day, media-saturated gathering.

Rubio's Cuban-born parents settled in Miami before moving to Las Vegas when he was 8. His mother and father both worked at hotels: Mario as a bartender, Oria as a housekeeper. His father also worked as a street vendor and school crossing guard after the family returned to Miami in 1985. His mother was a Kmart stock clerk.

He spent one year at Tarkio College in Missouri on a football scholarship before transferring to a community college in Florida, then earning an undergraduate degree from the University of Florida and a law degree at the University of Miami.

His first foray into electoral politics came as a candidate for the West Miami City Commission in 1998. He served two years on the panel before being elected to the Florida House in 2000. He became majority leader in 2003 and speaker in 2006.

Highlights of his years in Tallahassee include his work chairing a select committee that wrote legislation aimed at safeguarding property rights in the wake of the U.S. Supreme Court's decision in Kelo v. City of New London that allowed local governments to cite opportunities for economic development as a "public use" under the Takings Clause of the Fifth Amendment.

When Rubio announced his Senate candidacy in May 2009, he was given no chance of winning. The GOP nominee would be Crist, whose moderate image, high approval ratings and backing from party circles all but guaranteed he would have no trouble with the upstart former state House speaker.

But Crist's lack of devotion to core Republican principles did not sit well with the party's base. Rubio was able to make especially good use of Crist's endorsement of Obama's economic stimulus. Crist had shared a stage — and a hug — with the president in February 2009 and effusively praised the legislation. Little by little, conservatives who were no fans of Crist but felt they had no other option began to feel that they did.

Rubio got a lift from the tea party movement, was endorsed by the Club for Growth and won added cachet from a glowing cover story in the conservative magazine National Review in August 2009. Crist's predecessor as governor, Republican Jeb Bush, began praising Rubio.

Within months the race had pivoted and Rubio held a commanding lead in the polls, and Crist was contemplating a bolt from the Republican Party. In April 2010 Crist officially dropped out of the GOP primary contest and declared he would run as an independent. Democratic Rep. Kendrick B. Meek drew billionaire businessman Jeff Greene as a primary opponent on the last day of filing, but held him off to win the nomination.

Less than two weeks after the primary, Rubio's father died and he briefly suspended his campaign. Once it resumed, polls showed a seesaw race between Rubio and Crist, with Meek mostly an afterthought.

Crist tried, with little success, to make hay out of Rubio's evolving position on personal Social Security accounts. Rubio stuck to his theme of lower taxes and a less intrusive government.

Days before the vote, the race took another turn. Crist reportedly asked Meek to withdraw from the race to give him a clear shot at Rubio. Questions were also raised about whether former President Bill Clinton lobbied Meek to drop out and endorse Crist. Meek said they talked about it but that Clinton never pushed him to quit.

On Election Day, Rubio prevailed easily, winning 49 percent of the vote to Crist's 30 percent and Meek's 20 percent.

But Rubio turned down "hundreds" of national media interview requests, Roll Call reported, in a deliberate strategy to keep his profile low and dampen the talk of national office. "If anyone who supported him thought that they were electing a showhorse they were wrong; he's a workhorse," Florida Republican Rep. Mario Diaz-Balart told the Capitol Hill newspaper.

Rep. Jeff Miller (R)

Capitol Office
225-4136
jeffmiller.house.gov
2416 Rayburn Bldg. 20515; fax 225-3414

Committees
Armed Services
Veterans' Affairs - Chairman
Select Intelligence

Residence
Chumuckla

Born
June 27, 1959; St. Petersburg, Fla.

Religion
Methodist

Family
Wife, Vicki Griswold Miller; two children

Education
U. of Florida, B.A. 1984 (journalism)

Career
State agriculture department official; real estate broker; deputy county sheriff

Political Highlights
Fla. House, 1998-2001

ELECTION RESULTS

2010 GENERAL

Jeff Miller (R)	170,821	80.0%
Joe Cantrell (NPA)	23,250	10.9%
John Krause (NPA)	18,253	8.5%

2010 PRIMARY

Jeff Miller (R)	unopposed

2008 GENERAL

Jeff Miller (R)	232,559	70.2%
Jim Bryan (D)	98,797	29.8%

Previous Winning Percentages
2006 (67%); 2004 (77%); 2002 (75%); 2001 Special Election (66%)

Elected 2001; 5th full term

Miller's Panhandle district is home to thousands of active-duty military personnel at Naval Air Station Pensacola and Eglin Air Force Base, as well as tens of thousands of military retirees. Their interests dominate his legislative agenda as chairman of the Veterans' Affairs Committee and as a member of the Armed Services and Select Intelligence panels.

A fiscal conservative, Miller is the man tasked with finding savings in a place where lawmakers have been reluctant to look — veterans' benefits.

"In the first bite of the apple, defense, homeland security and veterans will not be part of the cuts," Miller said. "But I believe that as we move forward, everything needs to be on the table."

He said he believes veterans are willing to "sacrifice again."

"It is very clear that they understand where this country is financially, and the last decade we've been able to provide record increases in veterans spending," Miller said. "But that would not be the case in the future as we try to rein in our deficit. And dealing with the vet community, they have all pledged, while continuing to serve their memberships and constituencies, to work with the committee to find ways to help deliver the services that many of them participate in."

Miller's years on the committee, in the majority and the minority, have yielded several legislative successes.

As the top Republican on the Veterans' Affairs Subcommittee on Health during the 110th Congress (2007-08), he backed quicker, more responsive treatment of veterans. A long backlog of service-connected disability claims led him to call for an overhaul of the Veterans Affairs Department.

He said improving the claims process at the department would be a priority in the 112th Congress (2011-12).

After The Washington Post disclosed in early 2007 widespread problems at Walter Reed Army Medical Center, Miller criticized the Pentagon's failure to address the shortcomings sooner. In a letter to Defense Secretary Robert M. Gates, he "strongly recommended" the firing of the Army's surgeon general and former commander at Walter Reed, Lt. Gen. Kevin Kiley. Miller, an ardent supporter of the Iraq War, was one of many calling for Kiley's head; he soon retired under pressure.

Miller successfully added an amendment to the annual defense authorization bill in 2004 that eliminated the "widows' tax" on surviving spouses of military retirees. Under the military's Survivor Benefit Plan, enacted in the 1970s, spouses of deceased career military retirees initially received 55 percent of the soldier's annual retirement pay, but that payment was cut to 35 percent when the spouse reached age 62, when individuals first become eligible for Social Security. But anyone starting Social Security at age 62 faces reduced benefits for life. Miller's provision allowed military spouses older than 62 to retain 55 percent of their deceased spouse's military retirement pay.

In 2003, Miller cosponsored a measure allowing disabled veterans to simultaneously receive both military pension checks and veterans' disability benefits. A version of the plan was rolled into that year's defense authorization bill.

A member of the Republican Study Committee, a group of the House's most conservative members, he voted against the fiscal 2011 defense authorization bill because it included a provision that would repeal the ban on openly gay individuals serving in the military, and opposed stand-alone legislation to do the same that was signed into law at the end of 2010.

The threat posed by the Iranian nuclear program has been a topic of interest for the Intelligence Committee. In 2010, Miller took a symbolic stand against the Iranian regime by voting against a resolution that recognized the Iranian new year, called Nowruz, and wished all Iranians a prosperous new year. "The language," he said, "fails to exclude terrorists and dictators like Mahmoud Ahmadinejad," the Iranian president who has called for wiping Israel off the map. "Even on non-binding resolutions with seemingly good intentions, our votes have consequences."

A former small-business owner, Miller is close to the business leaders in his community, many of whom rely on a robust tourism economy. He fought the George W. Bush administration's plan to open gas and oil drilling within 20 miles of the coast, complaining it would interfere with military training and weapons testing. He said he supports current policy that requires the Defense and Interior departments to coordinate on any oil and gas leases that might affect the military's training in the gulf.

After an oil rig explosion in the Gulf of Mexico caused a massive spill in April 2010, Miller sought relief through legislation similar to that enacted after Hurricane Katrina to allow affected states to issue tax-exempt bonds, increase the depreciation deduction for certain properties and create a low-income housing tax credit. When Joe L. Barton of Texas, top Republican on the Energy and Commerce Committee, said BP was the victim of a "shakedown" by the Obama administration and termed the $20 billion BP agreed to set aside for compensating spill victims a "slush fund," Miller said Barton should surrender his post.

Miller, a sixth-generation Floridian whose parents sold real estate and operated a cattle ranch near Clearwater, understands the needs of the culturally Southern 1st District, which is dotted with rural farm towns.

A former real estate broker and political aide, Miller has an eclectic résumé. While in high school, he was a disc jockey for the local radio station. Later, he had a stint as a deputy county sheriff and held part-time jobs as a stock car racer and auctioneer.

He studied journalism at the University of Florida, where he served as president of the university's education fraternity, Alpha Gamma Rho, and then president of the school's fraternity system. Subsequently he was elected president of college fraternities for southeast Florida.

After college, Miller joined the staff of Florida Agriculture Commissioner Doyle Connor. He later served as a state representative for the heavily Republican north Florida district he now represents in Congress.

Miller arrived in Congress in October 2001 after winning a special election to replace Republican Joe Scarborough, who had resigned. Miller garnered 66 percent of the vote. He has coasted to re-election since.

Key Votes

2010

Overhaul the nation's health insurance system	NO
Allow for repeal of "don't ask, don't tell"	NO
Overhaul financial services industry regulation	NO
Limit use of new Afghanistan War funds to troop withdrawal activities	NO
Change oversight of offshore drilling and lift oil spill liability cap	NO
Provide a path to legal status for some children of illegal immigrants	NO
Extend Bush-era income tax cuts for two years	YES

2009

Expand the Children's Health Insurance Program	NO
Provide $787 billion in tax cuts and spending increases to stimulate the economy	NO
Allow bankruptcy judges to modify certain primary-residence mortgages	NO
Create a cap-and-trade system to limit greenhouse gas emissions	NO
Provide $2 billion for the "cash for clunkers" program	NO
Establish the government as the sole provider of student loans	NO
Restrict federally funded insurance coverage for abortions in health care overhaul	YES

CQ Vote Studies

	PARTY UNITY		PRESIDENTIAL SUPPORT	
	SUPPORT	OPPOSE	SUPPORT	OPPOSE
2010	98%	2%	33%	67%
2009	98%	2%	11%	89%
2008	99%	1%	85%	15%
2007	97%	3%	88%	12%
2006	97%	3%	92%	8%

Interest Groups

	AFL-CIO	ADA	CCUS	ACU
2010	7%	0%	88%	96%
2009	5%	0%	73%	100%
2008	7%	5%	89%	100%
2007	13%	10%	58%	92%
2006	14%	5%	93%	92%

Florida 1

Panhandle — Pensacola, Fort Walton Beach

Occupying the western portion of the Panhandle — wedged between Alabama and the Gulf of Mexico — the 1st District stretches from Washington County north of Panama City to Pensacola and the Perdido River. Often dubbed "Lower Alabama," the 1st's Bible Belt culture is much closer to the Old South than to Florida's big cities.

A strong defense presence stabilizes the economy in the 1st, which is home to several large military bases. Eglin Air Force Base is the military's center for air-delivered weaponry. Eglin will be the training school for the contentious F-35 Joint Strike Fighter program, which could bring thousands of military, civilian and contractor jobs to the area. Naval Air Station Pensacola is the training base for all Navy, Marine Corps and Coast Guard aviators.

Tourism and the area's building boom created economic and population growth as condominiums and retirement communities popped up in previously rural areas. Big-ticket construction and military development have partially buoyed workers from collapses in the manufacturing and homebuilding sectors. Bucolic open spaces and the white-sand beaches of Emerald Coast towns such as Destin (a small part of which is in the 2nd) draw vacationers, and coastal tourism is recovering from a series of hurricanes and the 2010 Deepwater Horizon oil spill.

The 1st, even more conservative than its largest-in-the-state GOP registration edge would indicate, gave John McCain 67 percent of its 2008 presidential vote, his highest percentage statewide. The 1st's Democrats are more "Dixiecrat" than liberal, and the political ideology of the predominately white district is heavily influenced by the military.

Major Industry
Defense, tourism, health care

Military Bases
Naval Air Station Pensacola, 17,076 military, 4,067 civilian (2011); Hurlburt Field (Air Force), 7,404 military, 1,260 civilian (2009); Eglin Air Force Base, 7,283 military, 5,710 civilian (2011); Naval Air Station Whiting Field, 705 military, 2,078 civilian (2011)

Cities
Pensacola, 51,923; Navarre (unincorporated), 31,378

Notable
The Blue Angels flight group is housed at Naval Air Station Pensacola.

Rep. Steve Southerland II (R)

Capitol Office
225-5235
southerland.house.gov
1229 Longworth Bldg. 20515-0902; fax 225-5615

Committees
Agriculture
Natural Resources
Transportation & Infrastructure

Residence
Panama City

Born
Oct. 10, 1965; Nashville, Tenn.

Religion
Southern Baptist

Family
Wife, Susan Southerland; four children

Education
Troy State U., B.S. 1987 (business management);
Jefferson State Community College, A.A. 1989
(mortuary science)

Career
Funeral home owner

Political Highlights
Fla. Board of Funeral Directors and Embalmers,
1992-95

ELECTION RESULTS

2010 GENERAL

Steve Southerland II (R)	136,371	53.6%
Allen Boyd (D)	105,211	41.4%
Paul C. McKain (NPA)	7,135	2.8%
Dianne Berryhill (NPA)	5,705	2.2%

2010 PRIMARY

Steve Southerland II (R)	28,269	46.9%
David Scholl (R)	14,483	24.0%
Ron McNeil (R)	6,447	10.7%
Eddie Hendry (R)	6,164	10.2%
Barbara F. Olschner (R)	4,965	8.2%

Elected 2010; 1st term

Southerland, a small-business owner and co-founder of a Florida tea party group, says federal interference is the source of many of the country's problems.

The CEO of his family's funeral home business, Southerland said that small businesses like his are "battling senseless regulation."

He singled out the 2010 health care overhaul as an "egregious" example of the growth of government. He says repeal — which he supported in early 2011 — "realistically can't be done" in the 112th Congress (2011-12), but he has more confidence that efforts to limit the law's funding could work. On the Agriculture Committee, Southerland can look out for the Florida panhandle's abundant agricultural interests. His seat on Natural Resources gives him a platform from which to defend the region's timber industry.

He is one of 19 freshman Republicans assigned to the Transportation and Infrastructure Committee, which is expected to write a new surface transportation law in the 112th Congress.

Southerland graduated from Troy State University in 1987 with a degree in business management, then with an associate's in mortuary science from Jefferson State Community College in 1989.

The 2nd District race was in some ways a microcosm of the 2010 elections.

In seven previous races, incumbent Democratic Rep. Allen Boyd had never had a close call. But he supported the health care overhaul as he was fending off a primary challenge from the left by state Senate Minority Leader Al Lawson. That gave Republicans ammunition to go after Boyd, and the National Republican Congressional Committee poured money into Southerland's campaign.

Democrats answered, spending $338,000 — most of it after Oct. 15 — to assist Boyd, who had $2 million of his own to spend.

But Southerland — once a Democrat, like many Panhandle Republicans — was able to ride the GOP wave and parlayed support from his home area in the rural western part of the district into a relatively easy 12-percentage-point victory.

Florida 2
Panhandle — part of Tallahassee, Panama City

The 2nd skims around Florida's Big Bend, from the Panhandle and state capital of Tallahassee (a slice of which is in the 4th) to the north-central part of the state. Taking in all or part of 16 counties, the 2nd has tobacco and peanut farms, forests and small towns. The district's natural resources — from the Gulf Coast beaches where oysters are harvested to abundant farmland and forests — drive its economy, and there is a steady base of government employees working in the state capital. Panama City, in Bay County, relies on tourism and the economic contribution of Tyndall Air Force Base.

Registered Democrats outnumber Republicans here, but many of them, including farmers and retirees, hold conservative views on fiscal and social issues. The exception is the Tallahassee area (Leon County), home to Florida State University and Florida A&M University. Bay County has a stronger conservative element, as do the smaller communities that ring the Gulf Coast. The district's black residents — nearly two-thirds of whom live in Leon or neighboring Gadsden counties — make up more than one-fifth of the population. Barack Obama took 69 percent of Gadsden's 2008 presidential vote, but John McCain won 54 percent of the district's vote overall.

Major Industry
Agriculture, government, manufacturing

Military Bases
Tyndall Air Force Base, 4,930 military, 874 civilian (2010)

Cities
Tallahassee (pt.), 174,994; Panama City, 36,484; Lynn Haven, 18,493

Notable
Tallahassee's National High Magnetic Field Laboratory is home to the highest-powered magnet in the world.

Rep. Corrine Brown (D)

Capitol Office
225-0123
www.house.gov/corrinebrown
2336 Rayburn Bldg. 20515-0903; fax 225-2256

Committees
Transportation & Infrastructure
Veterans' Affairs

Residence
Jacksonville

Born
Nov. 11, 1946; Jacksonville, Fla.

Religion
Baptist

Family
Single; one child

Education
Florida A&M U., B.S. 1969 (sociology), M.A. 1971
(education); U. of Florida, Ed.S. 1974

Career
College guidance counselor; travel agency owner

Political Highlights
Candidate for Fla. House, 1980; Fla. House, 1982-92

ELECTION RESULTS

2010 GENERAL

Corrine Brown (D)	94,744	63.0%
Michael "Mike" Yost (R)	50,932	33.9%
Terry Martin-Back (NPA)	4,625	3.1%

2010 PRIMARY

Corrine Brown (D)	35,312	92.8%
Scott Fortune (D)	2,718	7.1%

2008 GENERAL

Corrine Brown (D)	unopposed

Previous Winning Percentages
2006 (100%); 2004 (99%); 2002 (59%); 2000 (58%);
1998 (55%); 1996 (61%); 1994 (58%); 1992 (59%)

Elected 1992; 10th term

Brown has an acid tongue and often courts controversy, but as a member of the Transportation and Infrastructure Committee she has been highly successful in procuring federal dollars for her district.

She takes credit for winning tens of millions of dollars worth of earmarks, funding for special projects in a member's district. In fact, she has generated more than many senior lawmakers and some who sit on the Appropriations Committee. Her clout is lessened in the Republican-led House in the 112th Congress (2011-12), where spending cuts are a priority and earmarks are banned, but that won't change her focus: "to continue what I have been doing every single day since my first election in 1992, specifically bringing home a fair share of the federal dollars."

Brown is a loyal Democrat. The percentage of votes on which she breaks ranks with a majority of her party has risen above 10 only once in her nearly two decades in Congress, and her hewing to the party line reached a crescendo in the 111th Congress (2009-10) when she sided with leadership more than 98 percent of the time. In early 2009, she initially claimed dissatisfaction with President Obama's economic stimulus bill for not including more for infrastructure projects, but she ultimately supported it.

As the top Democrat on the Transportation and Infrastructure Subcommittee on Railroads, Pipelines and Hazardous Materials, Brown is an advocate for increased funding for high-speed rail expansion. "My goal is to have high-speed, intercity passenger and commuter rail lines connecting nationwide," she wrote in a Roll Call op-ed. A June 2009 draft of legislation to reauthorize surface transportation programs — likely to be considered in the 112th Congress — included a proposal for $50 billion over six years for the development of high-speed rail. True to form, Brown said she will work to ensure that "Florida gets back even more money to invest in infrastructure and create jobs."

She has been a strong supporter of transportation giant CSX Corp., which is located in her district. Her subcommittee held a hearing on investment in railroads in March 2008, just as CSX faced hedge fund efforts to oust members of its board. Around the same time, CSX donated $25,000 and CSX chief executive Michael Ward donated $1 million to Edward Waters College in Brown's district, a school where she has taught and where she chaired the inaugural committee for a new president in 2008. Brown sided with CSX and harshly criticized the hedge funds.

Brown's acerbic talk is not reserved for the corporate boardroom.

She briefly lost her speaking privileges on the House floor in 2004 after accusing GOP lawmakers of participating in a "coup d'etat" — her description of the contested 2000 presidential election in Florida. Unapologetic after the incident, she said, "If they're going to take my words down for telling the truth, that's OK. . . . We had a coup d'etat. Straight out, they stole the election."

Brown has also stirred controversy in other ways. During Tropical Storm Fay in 2008, her staff called local officials to ask for sandbags for her Jacksonville home near the Trout River. That set off a furor about special treatment, and she repaid the city for the $886.04 in labor and sandbags. Brown's staff said she asked for the help in the belief that it was available to all citizens.

Brown also raised eyebrows in 2007 when Citizens for Responsibility and Ethics in Washington pointed out she had paid her son-in-law, Tyree Fields, $5,500 for political consulting during the 2006 election cycle. Fields is married to Brown's lobbyist daughter, Shantrel Brown Fields, who has been connected to controversy in the past because she accepted a car from an African businessman who sought help from Brown. Fields has worked for Alcalde and Fay, a suburban Washington law firm with numerous Florida clients, and has lobbied on transportation issues. Brown's staff has said the daughter does not lobby her mother. The House Committee on Standards of Official Conduct said it had "insufficient evidence" to pursue the case and dropped the investigation. In October 2010, the Florida Times-Union reported that Brown had sought millions of dollars in earmarks for projects represented by the firm.

Brown is the No. 2 Democrat on the Veterans' Affairs Committee. She joined other Florida lawmakers in successfully pushing for funding for a new Veterans Affairs Department hospital in Orlando and a new VA health clinic and cemetery in Jacksonville.

Brown earned two degrees from Florida A&M University and worked as a college teacher and guidance counselor. She was steered into politics by one of her sorority sisters at the university, Gwendolyn Sawyer Cherry, who went on to become Florida's first black state representative. Although Brown lost her first state House race in 1980, Cherry kept after her to try again, and Brown won a seat in 1982. She served in the state House for a decade.

When a majority-black 3rd District was created by redistricting for the 1990s, Brown was one of four candidates in the 1992 Democratic primary for the seat. She survived a runoff with 64 percent of the vote, then won 59 percent in November against Republican Don Weidner.

Until recent years, Brown had to work for most of her election victories. Republicans ran a black candidate against Brown in three of her re-election contests. Her fortunes have since improved: In 2004, Brown faced only a write-in opponent, and in 2006 and 2008 she was unopposed.

In late July 2009, Brown formed a Senate exploratory committee for the 2010 election, but ultimately decided she would seek re-election in the House. "I can use my position in the House to do even more to help my constituents," she said. Brown easily defeated Republican Michael Yost with more than 62 percent of the vote.

In November 2010, Brown filed a lawsuit to block implementation of a state constitutional amendment adopted by referendum that sets rules for drawing congressional districts in the state. Along with fellow Floridian Mario Diaz-Balart, a Republican, Brown argued that the new standards would threaten districts that currently have black- and Hispanic-majority populations. The pair had earlier filed, and lost, a lawsuit seeking to keep the amendment off the November ballot.

Key Votes

2010

Overhaul the nation's health insurance system	YES
Allow for repeal of "don't ask, don't tell"	YES
Overhaul financial services industry regulation	YES
Limit use of new Afghanistan War funds to troop withdrawal activities	NO
Change oversight of offshore drilling and lift oil spill liability cap	YES
Provide a path to legal status for some children of illegal immigrants	YES
Extend Bush-era income tax cuts for two years	NO

2009

Expand the Children's Health Insurance Program	YES
Provide $787 billion in tax cuts and spending increases to stimulate the economy	YES
Allow bankruptcy judges to modify certain primary-residence mortgages	YES
Create a cap-and-trade system to limit greenhouse gas emissions	YES
Provide $2 billion for the "cash for clunkers" program	YES
Establish the government as the sole provider of student loans	YES
Restrict federally funded insurance coverage for abortions in health care overhaul	NO

CQ Vote Studies

	PARTY UNITY		PRESIDENTIAL SUPPORT	
	Support	Oppose	Support	Oppose
2010	98%	2%	87%	13%
2009	99%	1%	99%	1%
2008	98%	2%	17%	83%
2007	97%	3%	6%	94%
2006	95%	5%	33%	67%

Interest Groups

	AFL-CIO	ADA	CCUS	ACU
2010	93%	100%	13%	0%
2009	100%	100%	40%	0%
2008	100%	95%	69%	0%
2007	100%	90%	60%	0%
2006	100%	100%	40%	20%

Florida 3

North — parts of Jacksonville, Orlando and Gainesville

The Democratic, blue-collar 3rd bounces among three of Florida's northern cities and includes both heavily urban areas and long stretches of swamps and lakes along the St. Johns River. It slithers south along the river into a large portion of working-class Putnam County, where bass fishing is prevalent, before taking in part of Gainesville, home to the University of Florida (in the 6th), and continuing southeast to Orlando (shared with the 8th and 24th). Most of the area in between the northern cities is dominated by agricultural land and lacks major private employers, hampering efforts at job and economic growth in the 3rd.

The district relies on Jacksonville's port, Naval Air Station Jacksonville (in the 4th District) and other area government facilities for jobs. Transportation company CSX Corp. is based in the 3rd's portion of Jacksonville. The local financial services sector held relatively steady amid recent economic slowdowns and high unemployment rates, and has buoyed the city's economy. At the district's southern end, many Orlando residents work in the volatile tourism industry at locations such as Walt Disney World (in the 8th). Renovations at the Florida Citrus Bowl stalled as city tax revenues dropped during the recent economic downturn, but construction of a new arena for basketball's Magic brought jobs to the area.

Blacks make up a majority (51 percent) of district residents, and the median household income is just more than $34,000. Democrats dominate the 3rd, outnumbering Republicans by more than 3-to-1 in party registration. Some rural areas in Clay County and in the Palatka area (shared with the 7th) on the St. Johns River are home to Republicans and old-line conservative Democrats, but not enough to counter the 3rd's strong proclivity toward Democrats in federal elections. Barack Obama won 71 percent of the district's 2008 presidential vote.

Major Industry
Defense, government, transportation, higher education

Cities
Jacksonville (pt.), 245,902; Orlando (pt.), 75,376; Pine Hills (unincorporated), 60,076; Gainesville (pt.), 36,710

Notable
The St. Johns River and its tributaries flow north to Jacksonville.

Rep. Ander Crenshaw (R)

Capitol Office
225-2501
crenshaw.house.gov
440 Cannon Bldg. 20515-0904; fax 225-2504

Committees
Appropriations
  (Legislative Branch - Chairman)

Residence
Jacksonville

Born
Sept. 1, 1944; Jacksonville, Fla.

Religion
Episcopalian

Family
Wife, Kitty Crenshaw; two children

Education
U. of Georgia, A.B. 1966 (political science); U. of
Florida, J.D. 1969

Career
Investment bank executive; lawyer

Political Highlights
Fla. House, 1972-78; candidate for Fla. secretary of
state, 1978; sought Republican nomination for U.S.
Senate, 1980; Fla. Senate, 1986-94 (president, 1992-93);
sought Republican nomination for governor, 1994

ELECTION RESULTS

2010 GENERAL
Ander Crenshaw (R)	178,238	77.2%
Troy Dwayne Stanley (NPA) 52,540		22.8%

2010 PRIMARY
Ander Crenshaw (R)	unopposed

2008 GENERAL
Ander Crenshaw (R)	224,112	65.2%
Jay McGovern (D)	119,330	34.7%

Previous Winning Percentages
2006 (70%); 2004 (100%); 2002 (100%); 2000 (67%)

Elected 2000; 6th term

Crenshaw is an appropriator who pursues the interests of his military-driven district while rarely compromising his conservative philosophy on fiscal and social issues. He leads the Appropriations subcommittee that provides the money for Congress, a tricky job in the current fiscal environment.

As chairman of the Legislative Branch spending panel, Crenshaw will have to keep his fellow lawmakers happy while putting in place the cuts to congressional spending that his party leaders promised — and dozens of new Republican lawmakers insisted on.

The subcommittee writes the bill that funds operations of the House and congressional agencies such as the Government Accountability Office and the Library of Congress. His role also includes being the fiscal overseer of the Capitol Police, a task that took on added significance in the aftermath of the January 2011 attack on Democratic Rep. Gabrielle Giffords in Tucson, Ariz., in which six people were killed and Giffords was seriously wounded.

Crenshaw said he plans to review security procedures and is willing to increase Capitol Police funding, if warranted.

"But it would be a sad day in America if we had to wall off our elected representatives from the people that elect them," he told Roll Call. "This is a reminder that if you have a form of government like ours that's based on freedom of assembly and openness and access, that's not without risk."

Before House Republicans imposed a moratorium on earmarks — member-requested money for special projects — Crenshaw was an avid seeker of such funding. He serves on the Homeland Security and Defense subcommittees, and most of his efforts have gone toward military spending.

He previously sat on the Military Construction-Veterans Affairs Subcommittee, and Crenshaw saw a longtime plan come to fruition in 2009 when Jacksonville VA National Cemetery began operations. He helped champion the effort to build the cemetery.

But Crenshaw largely focuses on Jacksonville's robust Navy sector. He applauded the Navy's reaffirmation in 2010 of plans first announced two years earlier for the Mayport naval station to be the new home of a nuclear aircraft carrier to be relocated from Virginia. The effort could be worth hundreds of millions of dollars for the 3,400-acre facility.

Crenshaw is careful to keep his footing with the party after a few slips. He secured a seat on the Budget Committee in his first term and Appropriations in his second. He was in line for the ranking Republican spot on Budget at the start of the 110th Congress (2007-08), but leaders passed him over for Paul D. Ryan of Wisconsin, a conservative favorite and now the committee's chairman. Crenshaw lost some favor among leaders after it became known he had accompanied Majority Leader Tom DeLay of Texas and others on an expenses-paid trip to South Korea in 2001 that was sponsored by a nonprofit Korean group later identified as a front for a foreign lobbying campaign. House rules prohibit lawmakers from taking trips financed by lobbyists or foreign agents. Crenshaw then picked the wrong horse in the race to succeed DeLay, backing the unsuccessful Roy Blunt of Missouri, now a senator, over John A. Boehner of Ohio, now Speaker of the House.

Still, Crenshaw has maintained his party loyalty. During his first four terms, he sided with Republicans 95 percent of the time on votes that pitted majorities of each party against each other. That number dipped a bit in

2009, to 84, but recovered to 92 in 2010. And he stood with his party against the major initiatives of the Obama administration, including the $787 billion economic stimulus and the health care overhaul. Highlighting his conservative bona fides, he was among the first group of lawmakers to join the new Congressional Tea Party Caucus when it formed in the summer of 2010.

An investment banker by trade and a member of the Republican Whip's Economic Recovery Solutions Group, Crenshaw voted against both the House version and the final version of the financial services regulatory overhaul enacted in 2010.

Crenshaw is a member of the Congressional Down Syndrome Caucus and has pushed legislation to provide tax-advantaged savings accounts for the care of family members with disabilities. His bill gained no traction during the 110th Congress, and he reintroduced it in 2009, one of only two bills he sponsored in the 111th Congress (2009-10). He has introduced fewer than 20 bills in his entire congressional career.

Crenshaw's family has been in the Jacksonville area since 1901. The son of a lawyer, he was senior class president at Robert E. Lee High School. A lanky 6 feet 4 inches, he went to the University of Georgia on a basketball scholarship and was the third member of his family, following his father and brother, to earn a letter in a sport for the Bulldogs. The first name he uses, Ander, is a shortened version of his given name, Alexander.

Of draft age during the Vietnam War, Crenshaw served in the ROTC but avoided combat through a student deferment and a high draft lottery number. While working on a law degree at the University of Florida, he formed a Campus Crusade for Christ chapter. He eventually found he wasn't interested in practicing law and turned to investment banking. He said he began thinking about running for political office after he started dating Kitty Kirk, daughter of former Florida Gov. Claude R. Kirk Jr. The two later married.

In 1972, Crenshaw won election to the state House, where he served six years, and then to the state Senate in 1986. In 1993 he became the first Republican to preside over the Florida Senate in 118 years.

Over time, Crenshaw lost three statewide elections — a bid for secretary of state in 1978, the Republican primary for Senate in 1980 and the GOP primary for governor in 1994.

After leaving the state Senate in 1994, he stayed out of politics until an opportunity to run for the House came in 2000, when Republican Tillie Fowler stuck to her term-limit pledge and retired. Crenshaw won the primary easily, ensuring victory in the solidly Republican district. He has won re-election easily since.

Key Votes

2010

Overhaul the nation's health insurance system	NO
Allow for repeal of "don't ask, don't tell"	NO
Overhaul financial services industry regulation	NO
Limit use of new Afghanistan War funds to troop withdrawal activities	NO
Change oversight of offshore drilling and lift oil spill liability cap	NO
Provide a path to legal status for some children of illegal immigrants	NO
Extend Bush-era income tax cuts for two years	YES

2009

Expand the Children's Health Insurance Program	NO
Provide $787 billion in tax cuts and spending increases to stimulate the economy	NO
Allow bankruptcy judges to modify certain primary-residence mortgages	NO
Create a cap-and-trade system to limit greenhouse gas emissions	NO
Provide $2 billion for the "cash for clunkers" program	NO
Establish the government as the sole provider of student loans	NO
Restrict federally funded insurance coverage for abortions in health care overhaul	YES

CQ Vote Studies

	PARTY UNITY		PRESIDENTIAL SUPPORT	
	SUPPORT	OPPOSE	SUPPORT	OPPOSE
2010	92%	8%	34%	66%
2009	84%	16%	37%	63%
2008	97%	3%	74%	26%
2007	90%	10%	79%	21%
2006	96%	4%	97%	3%

Interest Groups

	AFL-CIO	ADA	CCUS	ACU
2010	7%	5%	100%	88%
2009	10%	5%	87%	84%
2008	7%	10%	100%	90%
2007	18%	15%	87%	83%
2006	7%	0%	100%	84%

Florida 4

North — part of Jacksonville, sliver of Tallahassee

The Republican 4th is anchored in Jacksonville and the surrounding beach communities of Duval County. It wraps around the northeast corner of the state and then runs across the northern border counties as far west as Leon County, where it narrows to a finger to take in a small part of eastern Tallahassee, the state capital. Much of the 4th shadows Interstate 10, a highway that traverses the 150 miles of rural territory between Jacksonville and Tallahassee.

Defense, agriculture, inland water and coastal issues dominate the 4th's politics. Republicans hold a slight but growing edge in voter registration after decades of Democratic dominance. Many nominal Democrats in the more rural areas of the district are old-line conservatives who now side with GOP candidates. One such example is Baker County, where Democrats account for 53 percent of registered voters but gave John McCain 78 percent in the 2008 presidential election, his third-highest percentage in a county statewide. Overall, McCain took 62 percent of the 4th's vote.

Jacksonville is a major city, with health care and financial services sectors. The local economy is still partly supported by manufacturing. The Port of Jacksonville (located in the 3rd District) is the southern hub for international importers and exporters. The Navy's strong presence along the St. Johns River, which slashes through the center of Jacksonville, bolsters the city's economy and provides many jobs. This area depends on the tourism and hospitality industries — visitors have come to the district's plentiful beaches and golf courses for decades, and many residents work for hotels, resorts and other vacation spots.

Major Industry
Defense, financial services, tourism, health care

Military Bases
Naval Air Station Jacksonville, 9,995 military, 6,153 civilian (2011); Naval Station Mayport, 1,651 military, 931 civilian (2009)

Cities
Jacksonville (pt.), 462,018; Jacksonville Beach, 21,362

Notable
Fernandina Beach is the only part of the current United States to have existed under eight flags: France, Spain (twice), England, "Patriot," "Green Cross of Florida," Mexico, Confederate States and United States.

Rep. Rich Nugent (R)

Capitol Office
225-1002
nugent.house.gov
1517 Longworth Bldg. 20515-0905; fax 226-6559

Committees
House Administration
Rules

Residence
Spring Hill

Born
May 26, 1951; Evergreen Park, Ill.

Religion
United Methodist

Family
Wife, Wendy Nugent; three children

Education
Saint Leo College, B.A. 1991 (criminology); Troy State
U., MacDill Air Force Base, M.P.A 1995

Military
Ill. Air National Guard, 1969-75

Career
Deputy county sheriff

Political Highlights
Hernando County sheriff, 2001-10

ELECTION RESULTS

2010 GENERAL

Rich Nugent (R)	208,815	67.4%
James Jim Piccillo (D)	100,858	32.6%

2010 PRIMARY

Rich Nugent (R)	52,586	62.2%
Jason Sager (R)	31,969	37.8%

Elected 2010; 1st term

The first item in the navigation bar on Nugent's House website says "Meet the Sheriff." His no-nonsense manner leaves no doubt that you're talking to a lawman. He has spent his professional life in the military and law enforcement, and among his first tasks in Congress is overseeing security of the Capitol Hill campus and his fellow lawmakers as a member of the House Administration Committee.

He also serves as an enforcer of a different sort, for the GOP leadership as a member of the Rules Committee.

Nugent said he plans to use his investigative background — his most recent position prior to his election to the House was nearly 10 years as Hernando County sheriff — to hold the Obama administration accountable.

But his first priority is to "repeal Obamacare. It has absolutely nothing to do with health care. All it's going to do is create jobs for government workers, in the IRS or someplace else." Among his first votes in the House was one to repeal the health care overhaul enacted in 2010.

Nugent intends to follow in the footsteps of the four-term GOP congresswoman who retired and endorsed his candidacy, Ginny Brown-Waite. That means focusing on issues of importance to his district north of Tampa, home to vast numbers of retirees, many of them ex-military.

"With the number of vets that we have in this district, and my three kids in it, that's obviously close to my heart," said Nugent, who has three children currently serving in the military.

A member of the Tea Party Caucus, Nugent holds conservative social values: He is anti-abortion, opposes gay marriage and says he is a "staunch" defender of gun rights. He voted for a short-term extension of expiring provisions of the anti-terrorism law known as the Patriot Act.

Brown-Waite endorsed Nugent the same day she said she would not run again because of health reasons — the last day of qualifying to get on the ballot, limiting other Republicans from jumping into the race.

Nugent took 62 percent of the GOP primary vote and won more than two-thirds of the vote in November against Democrat James Piccillo.

Florida 5

Northern west coast — Pasco, Hernando counties

Located north of Tampa on Florida's west coast, the 5th includes Hernando, Citrus and Sumter counties, as well as portions of Pasco and four other counties. The district makes up the southern half of Florida's Nature Coast along the Gulf of Mexico, and the district's eastern edge, in Lake County, extends to the greater Orlando area.

Tourism, integral to the 5th's economy, is centered on the Nature Coast. Gated communities and golf courses clustered on the coast served as havens for retirees, while the area's beaches, snorkeling spots, preserves and parks, and historic towns attract visitors. Agriculture is a mainstay in the district's less developed areas. Levy County in the north depends on cattle, dairy and nuts, while the southeast part of the 5th relies on citrus. Controlled growth has been important here as the region expanded with a steady influx of retirees and young professionals. Over the past decade, the population grew by 45 percent, and the district is the fastest-growing and most populous in the state ahead of decennial remapping.

Social Security, prescription drugs and veterans' affairs dominate politics in the 5th, where more than one-fifth of residents are 65 or older. The 5th's electorate is largely conservative, especially on fiscal issues. Republicans outnumber Democrats in voter registration and 17 percent of voters are independents. John McCain took 56 percent of the 5th's 2008 presidential vote.

Major Industry
Tourism, service, agriculture, health care

Cities
Spring Hill (unincorporated), 98,621; Wesley Chapel (unincorporated), 44,092

Notable
Weeki Wachee Springs water park is known for its live "mermaid" performances.

Rep. Cliff Stearns (R)

Capitol Office
225-5744
www.house.gov/stearns
2306 Rayburn Bldg. 20515-0906; fax 225-3973

Committees
Energy & Commerce
   (Oversight & Investigations - Chairman)
Veterans' Affairs

Residence
Ocala

Born
April 16, 1941; Washington, D.C.

Religion
Presbyterian

Family
Wife, Joan Stearns; three children

Education
George Washington U., B.S. 1963 (electrical engineering)

Military
Air Force, 1963-67

Career
Hotel and restaurant executive; advertising account
executive

Political Highlights
No previous office

ELECTION RESULTS

2010 GENERAL

Cliff Stearns (R)	179,349	71.5%
Steve Schonberg (NPA)	71,632	28.5%

2010 PRIMARY

Cliff Stearns (R)	50,432	71.5%
Don Browning (R)	20,111	28.5%

2008 GENERAL

Cliff Stearns (R)	228,302	60.9%
Tim Cunha (D)	146,655	39.1%

2008 PRIMARY

Cliff Stearns (R)	unopposed

Previous Winning Percentages
2006 (60%); 2004 (64%); 2002 (65%); 2000 (100%);
1998 (100%); 1996 (67%); 1994 (99%); 1992 (65%);
1990 (59%); 1988 (53%)

Elected 1988; 12th term

During his more than two decades in Congress, Stearns has evolved from a crusading social conservative to a well-studied expert on technology and communications issues — his House website features him walking onto pages and offering brief introductions — with an eclectic legislative record.

He still holds to the same views on social issues. But his energies are now focused on topics related to his Energy and Commerce Committee seat, where he applies his inclusive, businesslike manner as chairman of the Oversight and Investigations Subcommittee.

His prime targets for oversight in the 112th Congress (2011-12) include implementation of the health care overhaul enacted in 2010 and EPA regulations aimed at reducing carbon emissions.

Stearns receives top ratings from conservative groups and credits President Ronald Reagan with his decision to join the GOP. He said that as a businessman in Florida, he took from Reagan "the belief in the importance of freedom and the opportunity to choose, free markets and owning your own property."

He applies those principles to the issues he deals with, making clear his distaste for burdensome regulation.

Stearns has been at the center of bipartisan efforts to bolster data security on the Internet. But he has found himself at odds with the Energy and Commerce's liberal Democrats on other issues, including so-called network neutrality, under which Internet service providers would be barred from imposing restrictions or conditions on subscribers' use. Stearns criticized a 2008 bill by Massachusetts Democrat Edward J. Markey that many said failed to reach a middle ground. Stearns said the measure would not allow for "legitimate network management."

He also takes a tough line against the Federal Communications Commission acting on the issue without Congress weighing in. Expanding the scope of the FCC's regulatory reach is "a matter best left to Congress," he and full committee ranking Republican Joe L. Barton of Texas wrote to FCC Commissioner Julius Genachowski in May 2010.

Stearns supported the House's major rewrite of the nation's telecommunications laws in the 104th Congress (1995-96), when he won adoption of an amendment to allow broadcast companies to own more stations within a given market. He argued new technologies made ownership restrictions outdated.

On some matters related to consumer protection, though, Stearns strays a bit from the anti-regulatory straight and narrow.

He backed an indefinite extension of the do-not-call registry, under which phone customers are shielded from unwanted solicitations, calling the program "one of the most popular laws we've ever enacted." Stearns won approval of his proposal — included in a bill President George W. Bush signed in 2008 — to scrap the original 2012 expiration of funding for the program.

To help car buyers, he re-introduced legislation in 2009 to require vehicle identification numbers of totaled vehicles to be sent immediately to car history databases to give consumers better data on salvaged or flooded cars.

He also advocates setting national standards for the protection and care of racehorses — the area around Ocala, located in his district, is thoroughbred country. Co-chairman of the Congressional Horse Caucus, Stearns developed concerns about the welfare of racehorses following the death of

Eight Belles at the 2008 Kentucky Derby and the death of Barbaro, the Derby winner in 2006. Both had sustained career-ending injuries and had to be put down.

As a member of the Veterans' Affairs Committee, Stearns in 2008 backed bills to expand GI educational benefits and provide a monthly housing stipend — provisions of which were included in the war spending bill that year. When he was chairman of the committee's Health panel from 1997 through 2000, he won passage of a bill to improve access to long-term care for disabled veterans and expanded the Veterans' Affairs Department's obligation to provide alternatives to nursing home care.

Stearns is a charter member of the Tea Party Caucus founded in 2010, but his conservative roots run deep. While these days he tends to let others take the lead on social issues, he remains a steadfast foe of abortion and has backed a number of proposals intended to restrict access to pornography. He was a leader in efforts during the 1990s to clip funding of the National Endowment for the Arts in response to grants that funded projects many found offensive. And he was chief sponsor of a bill enacted in 2005 that shields firearms manufacturers and dealers from liability lawsuits when their products are used in crimes.

The son of a Justice Department lawyer, Stearns was born and raised in Washington, D.C., where he was a basketball and track star at Woodrow Wilson High School. He attended George Washington University on an Air Force ROTC scholarship. After graduation, he was stationed at Vandenberg Air Force base in California, serving four years as a specialist in aerospace engineering and satellite reconnaissance.

When he got out of the service, Stearns worked in advertising before he took over a dilapidated motel in Massachusetts and renovated it. In the 1970s, spotting what he viewed as an undervalued Howard Johnson motel for sale in northern Florida, Stearns moved to the Sunshine State. He built a small motel and restaurant management business in Ocala that ultimately employed 120 people. He served on the board of the Monroe, Fla., regional hospital and was director of the local Chamber of Commerce.

In 1988, Stearns ran for an open House seat and, through his local alliances and political savvy, was able to win the Republican nomination. Though he was an underdog in the general election against Democratic state House Speaker Jon Mills, Stearns' limited political background gave him a salient, populist theme — he called himself "a citizen congressman" — and he out-hustled Mills for the seat. He has never fallen below 59 percent of the vote in winning re-election.

Key Votes

2010

Overhaul the nation's health insurance system	NO
Allow for repeal of "don't ask, don't tell"	NO
Overhaul financial services industry regulation	NO
Limit use of new Afghanistan War funds to troop withdrawal activities	NO
Change oversight of offshore drilling and lift oil spill liability cap	NO
Provide a path to legal status for some children of illegal immigrants	NO
Extend Bush-era income tax cuts for two years	YES

2009

Expand the Children's Health Insurance Program	NO
Provide $787 billion in tax cuts and spending increases to stimulate the economy	NO
Allow bankruptcy judges to modify certain primary-residence mortgages	NO
Create a cap-and-trade system to limit greenhouse gas emissions	NO
Provide $2 billion for the "cash for clunkers" program	YES
Establish the government as the sole provider of student loans	NO
Restrict federally funded insurance coverage for abortions in health care overhaul	YES

CQ Vote Studies

	PARTY UNITY		PRESIDENTIAL SUPPORT	
	SUPPORT	OPPOSE	SUPPORT	OPPOSE
2010	98%	2%	33%	67%
2009	95%	5%	26%	74%
2008	97%	3%	76%	24%
2007	94%	6%	81%	19%
2006	93%	7%	85%	15%

Interest Groups

	AFL-CIO	ADA	CCUS	ACU
2010	7%	0%	88%	96%
2009	14%	5%	80%	96%
2008	13%	15%	89%	100%
2007	13%	5%	80%	92%
2006	21%	10%	93%	96%

Florida 6

North central — parts of Jacksonville, Gainesville and Ocala

The landlocked and boomerang-shaped 6th District takes in large swaths of rural territory along with suburbs of northern cities. Stretching from western Duval County (Jacksonville), the district takes in portions of Gainesville before swinging southeast into Marion County. The 6th's southern tip runs along the western shore of Lake Harris in Leesburg, which is within Orlando's sphere in central Florida.

The 6th contains three regions with distinct interests. The northern end, centered in Jacksonville (shared with the 3rd and 4th districts), is heavily influenced by the military and the city's busy port. Gainesville, in the middle of the district and shared with the 3rd, is home to the University of Florida and the Malcom Randall VA Medical Center, a major veterans' hospital. The area south of Ocala, famed for its thoroughbred horse farms, is a haven for retirees and roughly an hour from either Florida coast. Gainesville mostly escaped the widespread unemployment and real estate market collapse that Ocala experienced.

The district includes all of two small counties — Gilchrist and Bradford —

and parts of six others, including Alachua (Gainesville) and Marion (Ocala), each of which contains about one-fourth of the 6th's population. Alachua is the biggest Democratic outpost in the district, while Republicans have their strongest registration edge in the Clay County Jacksonville suburbs and exurbs west of the St. Johns River. The district's political agenda is dominated by defense interests.

The 6th is firmly conservative, and although the GOP maintains a clear edge in most federal races, registered Republicans maintain only a slight advantage over Democrats.

Regardless of a voter's party affiliation, many are willing to support some moderate Democratic candidates. John McCain took 56 percent of the district's vote in the 2008 presidential election — 5 percentage points less than George W. Bush won in 2004.

Major Industry

Higher education, defense, health care, agriculture

Cities

Jacksonville (pt.), 113,864; Gainesville (pt.), 87,644; Ocala (pt.), 38,913; Lakeside (unincorporated), 30,943

Notable

The University of Florida hosts the Florida Museum of Natural History.

Rep. John L. Mica (R)

Capitol Office
225-4035
www.house.gov/mica
2187 Rayburn Bldg. 20515-0907; fax 226-0821

Committees
Oversight & Government Reform
Transportation & Infrastructure - Chairman

Residence
Winter Park

Born
Jan. 27, 1943; Binghamton, N.Y.

Religion
Episcopalian

Family
Wife, Pat Mica; two children

Education
Miami-Dade Community College, A.A. 1965; U. of
Florida, B.A. 1967 (political science & education)

Career
Congressional aide; real estate investor; trade
consultant; cellular telephone company executive;
lobbyist

Political Highlights
Fla. House, 1976-80; Republican nominee for Fla.
Senate, 1980

ELECTION RESULTS

2010 GENERAL

John L. Mica (R)	185,470	69.0%
Heather Beaven (D)	83,206	31.0%

2010 PRIMARY

John L. Mica (R)	unopposed

2008 GENERAL

John L. Mica (R)	238,721	62.0%
Faye Armitage (D)	146,292	38.0%

Previous Winning Percentages
2006 (63%); 2004 (100%); 2002 (60%); 2000 (63%);
1998 (100%); 1996 (62%); 1994 (73%); 1992 (56%)

Elected 1992; 10th term

In many ways, Mica is a GOP loyalist who votes reliably with his leadership on most issues. But he has always gotten along well with Democrats on the Transportation and Infrastructure Committee, which he chairs. A shift in priorities and a grim fiscal outlook will test that friendly relationship as his panel works to write a new surface transportation bill.

When he was the panel's ranking Republican, Mica (MY-cah) had a close working relationship with then-Chairman James L. Oberstar, a Minnesota Democrat. He said he was optimistic the same would be true with West Virginia Democrat Nick J. Rahall II, the new ranking member.

"Our committee has always been pretty bipartisan," Mica told Roll Call shortly after the 2010 elections handed the Republicans the majority. "I think he'll be very compatible to work with."

Mica has been a longtime Amtrak critic, and his parting of the ways with Democrats on transportation funding might best be represented by his response to President Obama's early 2011 proposals for high-speed rail. Mica has been generally supportive of high-speed rail projects in the past, but he compared the plan to spend $53 billion on such projects to giving money to disgraced financier Bernie Madoff, saying the Federal Railroad Administration was "neither a capable grant agency, nor should it be involved in the selection of projects." Mica also suggested, as he has in the past, that the selection process for high-speed rail stimulus grants were politically motivated.

In 2008, Mica worked with Democrats to advance a long-stalled five-year reauthorization of Amtrak that called for major new spending on the railroad. At the time he said he supported the spending because the bill also included a provision he had drafted to allow private companies to bid on a high-speed rail project to connect Washington, D.C., and New York City.

However, he was critical of the administration's selection criteria for high-speed rail projects funded with money from the $787 billion economic stimulus legislation, saying they were poorly chosen and implying they were more motivated by politics — including a line in his home state of Florida that he complained would not be able to achieve truly high speeds.

Despite his ability to work with Transportation Committee Democrats, Mica has frequently been at odds with Obama. His voting record in the 111th Congress (2009-10) reads like a point-by-point repudiation of Obama's priorities since taking office: He voted against the health care overhaul; the "cash for clunkers" program that gave subsidies for buying newer, more fuel-efficient cars; a food safety overhaul; a cap-and-trade climate change bill; and the economic stimulus, which provided billions of dollars for infrastructure spending. Mica argued that it didn't spend enough of the total price tag on transportation. However, the first year of the Obama administration also saw Mica deviate from his party more than in any other year. His party unity score — the percentage of votes in which he sides with a majority of his party against a majority of Democrats — dropped to a career low 90 percent.

Mica also wasn't afraid to disagree with his own party when it was in power, though he usually confined his disagreements to the transportation sphere. When President George W. Bush was in the White House, Mica frequently served as the committee's liaison to the administration, more often seeking to persuade Bush to see the committee's point of view rather than the other way around.

Most of Mica's legislative focus in the 111th Congress centered on the unsuccessful effort to write a new surface transportation bill. Oberstar wanted to raise the 18.4-cents-per-gallon federal tax on gasoline. Mica preferred a combination of federal tax revenue, public-private partnerships and bond financing. No consensus was reached and the debate will be joined again in the 112th Congress (2011-12).

Mica chaired the Aviation Subcommittee before the Democrats won control of Congress in 2006. After the Sept. 11 terrorist attacks, the panel became a hub of new security measures that have changed the way Americans travel. He championed the effort to arm airline pilots and helped write the law establishing the Transportation Security Administration under the Homeland Security Department. He has criticized the agency repeatedly for being unresponsive to local concerns and slow to utilize new technology. In early 2011, Mica blasted a White House plan to give collective bargaining rights to TSA screeners. "This turnover of airport screening to the administration's union cronies . . . will be President Obama's biggest gift to organized labor," he said.

Mica is also a senior member of the Oversight and Government Reform Committee, but his work on Transportation absorbs most of his time and energy. In the mid-1990s, though, as chairman of Government Reform's Civil Service Subcommittee, his eagerness to downsize the government and overhaul federal work rules led the president of a federal employees union to call Mica "the most dangerous man in history to chair" the subcommittee.

He says he has no particular recreational interests. "I'm a pretty dull guy," he said. "I don't have a lot of hobby activities. But I love politics."

Like a lot of Floridians, Mica grew up in New York. After years of trips back and forth, the family settled in Florida when Mica was in high school. His father's health was poor, and Mica and his brothers interrupted their schooling to help support the family.

Mica's other family members are largely Democrats, including his brother, Daniel A. Mica, who served in the House from 1979 to 1989. His other brother worked for Lawton Chiles, a former Democratic U.S. senator and Florida governor. But the first campaign Mica worked on was Republican Richard Nixon's 1960 presidential race against John F. Kennedy.

Mica served in the state Legislature from 1976 to 1980, then arrived in Washington as chief of staff for GOP Sen. Paula Hawkins. After Hawkins lost her re-election bid in 1986, Mica turned to business ventures, including international trade consulting and the cellular telephone business, becoming a millionaire. In 1992, GOP Rep. Craig T. James decided not to seek a third term, and Mica went after the seat. He won by 13 percentage points and has been re-elected easily ever since.

Key Votes

2010

Overhaul the nation's health insurance system	NO
Allow for repeal of "don't ask, don't tell"	NO
Overhaul financial services industry regulation	NO
Limit use of new Afghanistan War funds to troop withdrawal activities	NO
Change oversight of offshore drilling and lift oil spill liability cap	NO
Provide a path to legal status for some children of illegal immigrants	NO
Extend Bush-era income tax cuts for two years	YES

2009

Expand the Children's Health Insurance Program	NO
Provide $787 billion in tax cuts and spending increases to stimulate the economy	NO
Allow bankruptcy judges to modify certain primary-residence mortgages	NO
Create a cap-and-trade system to limit greenhouse gas emissions	NO
Provide $2 billion for the "cash for clunkers" program	NO
Establish the government as the sole provider of student loans	NO
Restrict federally funded insurance coverage for abortions in health care overhaul	YES

CQ Vote Studies

	PARTY UNITY		PRESIDENTIAL SUPPORT	
	SUPPORT	OPPOSE	SUPPORT	OPPOSE
2010	97%	3%	29%	71%
2009	90%	10%	19%	81%
2008	93%	7%	77%	23%
2007	97%	3%	83%	17%
2006	99%	1%	95%	5%

Interest Groups

	AFL-CIO	ADA	CCUS	ACU
2010	7%	0%	88%	96%
2009	10%	0%	80%	100%
2008	0%	10%	94%	100%
2007	4%	5%	89%	100%
2006	14%	0%	100%	92%

Florida 7

East — St. John's County, Daytona Beach

The 7th parallels Interstate 95 from southeast of Jacksonville to northern Daytona Beach, where it turns to follow Interstate 4 southwest into the Orlando area. It includes all of Flagler and St. Johns counties, as well as much of Volusia County, parts of Putnam and Seminole counties, and a tiny sliver of Orange County. More than one third of the population lives in Volusia, mostly from Ormond Beach to Daytona Beach.

A steady influx of people into the 7th spurred the district's economy in recent years and pushed growth-management issues to the top of the local agenda.

Retirees flocked to once-small towns near the ocean, drawing retail shops but not as many larger employers. A growing aerospace industry near Daytona Beach, helped by Embry-Riddle Aeronautical University, has broadened the tourism-based economy. But the district is just starting to rebound from a housing market collapse and years of layoffs and fewer visitors to area hotels and resorts.

Once a major agricultural area, Seminole County became the suburban home to middle- and upper-class Orlando commuters and their families.

But some inland portions retain their agrarian heritage, especially in bucolic Flagler County. The Daytona Beach area still attracts millions of visitors annually. Although gas prices and air travel fares can affect its popularity as a spring break destination for college students, it draws bikers and race car fans to its beaches and sporting events, including the Daytona 500 stock car race, which is held in the nearby 24th District.

Although Republicans hold a slight registration edge and have won the 7th's presidential vote since 1992, some moderate Democratic candidates also have success with voters here, and the district is home to many independent voters. Republican John McCain took 53 percent of the district's presidential vote here in 2008.

Major Industry
Tourism, aerospace, service

Cities
Palm Coast, 75,180; Deltona (pt.), 56,341; Daytona Beach (pt.), 49,175; Ormond Beach, 38,137

Notable
Daytona Beach hosts minor league Jackie Robinson Ballpark, the site of the first integrated professional baseball game — a spring training game in which Robinson featured.

Rep. Daniel Webster (R)

Capitol Office
225-2176
webster.house.gov
1039 Longworth Bldg. 20515-0908; fax 225-0999

Committees
Rules

Residence
Orlando

Born
April 27, 1949; Charleston, W.Va.

Religion
Baptist

Family
Wife, Sandy Webster; six children

Education
Georgia Institute of Technology, B.E.E. 1971

Career
Air conditioning and heating company owner

Political Highlights
Fla. House, 1980-98 (minority leader pro tempore, 1992-94; minority leader, 1994-96; Speaker, 1996-98); Fla. Senate, 1998-2008 (majority leader, 2006-08)

ELECTION RESULTS

2010 GENERAL

Daniel Webster (R)	123,586	56.1%
Alan Grayson (D)	84,167	38.2%
Peg Dunmire (TEA)	8,337	3.8%
George L. Metcalfe (NPA)	4,143	1.9%

2010 PRIMARY

Daniel Webster (R)	24,753	40.2%
Todd Long (R)	14,082	22.9%
Kurt Kelly (R)	8,311	13.5%
Patricia Sullivan (R)	6,507	10.6%
Bruce O'Donoghue (R)	4,394	7.1%
Dan Fanelli (R)	1,896	3.1%
Ross Bieling (R)	1,645	2.7%

Elected 2010; 1st term

The conservative Webster brings a wealth of legislative experience to Congress. He served in the Florida House for eight years, becoming the state's first Republican House speaker in more than 100 years. He then served in the state Senate for 10 years, eventually as majority leader.

Accordingly, GOP leaders enlisted him to join the Rules Committee, which serves the leadership by setting the parameters for floor debate of all legislation in the House. He joined the Republican Study Committee, a group of the most conservative House members that comprises about two-thirds of the GOP Conference, but not the more anti-establishment Tea Party Caucus.

As a longtime politician, Webster acknowledges the public's instinctive dislike of his profession, but says his years of political experience make a difference in his ability to get things done.

Webster's conservative values, which extend to the social side of the spectrum, are rooted in his devout Baptist faith — he and his wife, Sandy, home-schooled their six children. Before and after entering politics, Webster operated his family's air conditioning business, an experience that he says allows him to connect with other small-business owners.

While he was in the state Senate, Webster got a taste of national attention in 2005 for unsuccessfully moving legislation that would have kept alive Terri Schiavo, a brain-damaged Florida woman being sustained by a feeding tube. Schiavo eventually was at the center of a court battle and national debate over her estranged husband's desire to remove the tube against her parents' wishes.

Webster was briefly a candidate for the GOP nomination for senator in 2004. Six years later he joined a crowded GOP field seeking the right to challenge the liberal — and abrasive — Democratic Rep. Alan Grayson.

After Webster won the primary, Grayson ran an ad that compared Webster's religious faith to the Afghan Taliban, using edited video to try to show that Webster was saying the opposite of what he was actually saying. The ad, ripped by FactCheck.org and others, backfired and Webster cruised past the incumbent with 56 percent of the vote to Grayson's 38 percent.

Florida 8

Central — most of Orlando

One of Florida's few landlocked districts, the 8th is powered by the presence of Walt Disney World, Sea World and Universal Studios' resort in the Orlando area. The district surrounds western Orlando and includes upscale parts of the region, much of the city's downtown area, and the Walt Disney World complex. It then pushes north to take in parts of Lake and Marion counties.

Local tourism relies on out-of-state visitors and is vulnerable to economic slowdowns, but the industry is the 8th's undisputed economic leader. The local economy has broadened to include a technology sector headed by Oracle and defense and aerospace contractor Lockheed Martin. Health care and medical research facilities may help stabilize the 8th's economy.

Economic growth and redevelopment of downtown Orlando brought office parks and upscale condominiums to the city. A housing market collapse hurt the more well-to-do areas of the district, but a declining cost of living and plummeting home values made once out-of-reach areas available for some of the tourism-based workforce.

Both Orange County (Orlando) and the district as a whole have more registered Democrats than Republicans, but many residents back the GOP on social and economic issues. The 8th's population in Orange County is younger, wealthier and more educated than in most Florida districts, and the county's Hispanic population, which is mostly of Democratic-leaning Puerto Rican heritage, can put it within political reach of Democratic candidates.

Major Industry
Tourism, aerospace, technology

Cities
Orlando (pt.), 154,969; Ocoee (p.t), 34,896

Notable
There are more than 100 lakes in the Orlando metropolitan area.

Rep. Gus Bilirakis (R)

Capitol Office
225-5755
bilirakis.house.gov
407 Cannon Bldg. 20515-0909; fax 225-4085

Committees
Foreign Affairs
Homeland Security
(Emergency Preparedness, Response &
Communications - Chairman)
Veterans' Affairs

Residence
Palm Harbor

Born
Feb. 8, 1963; Gainesville, Fla.

Religion
Greek Orthodox

Family
Wife, Eva Bilirakis; four children

Education
St. Petersburg Junior College, attended 1981-83; U.
of Florida, B.A. 1986 (political science); Stetson U.,
J.D. 1989

Career
Lawyer; college instructor

Political Highlights
Fla. House, 1998-2006

ELECTION RESULTS

2010 GENERAL
Gus Bilirakis (R)	165,433	71.4%
Anita de Palma (D)	66,158	28.6%

2010 PRIMARY
Gus Bilirakis (R)	unopposed

2008 GENERAL
Gus Bilirakis (R)	216,591	62.2%
Bill Mitchell (D)	126,346	36.3%

Previous Winning Percentages
2006 (56%)

Elected 2006; 3rd term

Bilirakis has the same everyman quality as his father, former GOP Rep. Michael Bilirakis, who represented the Tampa-area district for 12 terms before stepping aside in 2006. The younger Bilirakis has continued his father's work on veterans' issues, important in a district where about 15 percent of the population served in the military.

As a member of the Veterans' Affairs Committee, Bilirakis has pressed for bills to boost veterans' benefits and to provide tax incentives for businesses that hire reservists or National Guard members. He serves as chairman of the Veterans' Affairs Task Force for the Republican Policy Committee.

Bilirakis (bil-uh-RACK-iss) also focuses on security concerns as a member of the Foreign Affairs and Homeland Security panels.

The only Floridian on Homeland Security, Bilirakis became chairman of its Emergency Preparedness, Response and Communications Subcommittee in the 112th Congress (2011-12). It's a good spot for a member representing a hurricane-prone coastal district.

In the 111th Congress (2009-10) Bilirakis was the top Republican on the Management, Investigations and Oversight Subcommittee. He told The Tampa Tribune that the assignment is "not flashy" but is important to the nation's battle against terrorism, and he remains on the panel, renamed Oversight, Investigations and Management in the 112th.

He introduced legislation in May 2010 that would strengthen background checks for student-visa applicants from high-risk areas. "Over the past several years there have been multiple instances which demonstrate shortcomings in our ability to properly screen and monitor foreign students," he said.

In 2008, the House passed his bill to authorize a Coast Guard pilot program to test mobile biometric screening systems to verify that people on boats are not attempting to enter the United States unlawfully. The Senate never took up the measure, and he tried and failed again in 2009.

Bilirakis also championed legislation to create a nationwide "Silver Alert" system to help find missing senior citizens, much like the Amber Alert for missing children. His proposal was incorporated into other legislation that twice passed the House but not the Senate.

On Foreign Affairs, Bilirakis has been supportive of closer ties between Greece and Israel. "With Turkey becoming increasingly antagonistic to the rule of law and moving eastward, it behooves both Greece and Israel to bond together and forge a strategic relationship that strengthens the security of each nation," he said in an October 2010 speech in Washington.

Like his father, he is a champion of Greek causes — his hometown, Tarpon Springs, was settled by Greek immigrants. Bilirakis, co-chairman of the Congressional Hellenic Caucus, periodically takes to the House floor to criticize the Turks who control northern Cyprus, and he introduced a measure in September 2010 calling for the protection of religious sites in the area.

Most of the time, though, Bilirakis avoids the spotlight, advancing his priorities by way of amendments to bills and by building friendships with lawmakers. Typically he finds the path well-paved for him; lawmakers warm to him quickly because of their affection for his father. "I think it's an advantage because people like my dad," Bilirakis said. "There's a lot of good will there. It gets you in the door, but you have to prove yourself."

Bilirakis is generally a loyal Republican vote. He joined many of his GOP colleagues in opposing two bills to aid the ailing financial services industry in fall 2008, the second of which became law. And he stuck with his party in voting against President Obama's $787 billion economic stimulus legislation in February 2009. He said the measure, which became law, "is simply a long wish list of big government spending" that "will hand a huge 'IOU' to our children and grandchildren." He called the health care overhaul enacted in March 2010 "a trillion-dollar expansion of the federal government marred with special deals, mandates, tax hikes and Medicare cuts."

But he has strayed from the GOP leadership on some issues. He supported the 2007 increase in the minimum wage and the following year's legislation to have insurers treat mental illness the same as physical ailments. He opposes oil drilling in Alaska's Arctic National Wildlife Refuge and supports a buffer on drilling around Florida's coast.

Though he is not a member of the Natural Resources Committee, he was allowed to participate in a subcommittee hearing in June 2010 on the effects of the oil spill in the Gulf of Mexico earlier that year. Bilirakis' district includes coastline in Pinellas and Pasco counties, and Tarpon Springs is a hub for commercial fishing.

Bilirakis' ancestors settled in Tarpon Springs a century ago. He says he always wanted to follow his father's example of a career in politics. He attended public schools, then studied at a community college in St. Petersburg before earning his undergraduate degree at the University of Florida with a major in political science. After getting a law degree from Stetson College of Law, he worked in his father's Palm Harbor practice.

Bilirakis' first foray into electoral politics on his own behalf was a successful run in 1998 for the state House seat representing Tampa. During his eight years in the state legislature, he chaired committees on crime prevention and public safety.

His opportunity to move up to the U.S. House came in 2006 with his father's retirement. Bilirakis breezed through the primary, but the general election was tougher. Democrats targeted the district as a potential takeover and put up Phyllis Busansky, a former Hillsborough County commissioner with a solid reputation for innovative local programs. Republicans sent in a bevy of blockbuster political names to boost Bilirakis, including President George W. Bush, Vice President Dick Cheney and Speaker J. Dennis Hastert of Illinois. Bilirakis also was helped by his name recognition and a political legacy from his father; he won by a convincing 12 percentage points.

Bilirakis easily topped his 2008 opponent, Navy veteran Bill Mitchell, taking 62 percent of the vote, and won by more than 40 points in 2010.

Key Votes

2010

Overhaul the nation's health insurance system	NO
Allow for repeal of "don't ask, don't tell"	NO
Overhaul financial services industry regulation	NO
Limit use of new Afghanistan War funds to troop withdrawal activities	NO
Change oversight of offshore drilling and lift oil spill liability cap	NO
Provide a path to legal status for some children of illegal immigrants	NO
Extend Bush-era income tax cuts for two years	NO

2009

Expand the Children's Health Insurance Program	NO
Provide $787 billion in tax cuts and spending increases to stimulate the economy	NO
Allow bankruptcy judges to modify certain primary-residence mortgages	NO
Create a cap-and-trade system to limit greenhouse gas emissions	NO
Provide $2 billion for the "cash for clunkers" program	NO
Establish the government as the sole provider of student loans	NO
Restrict federally funded insurance coverage for abortions in health care overhaul	YES

CQ Vote Studies

	PARTY UNITY		PRESIDENTIAL SUPPORT	
	SUPPORT	OPPOSE	SUPPORT	OPPOSE
2010	92%	8%	33%	67%
2009	87%	13%	31%	69%
2008	89%	11%	63%	37%
2007	90%	10%	71%	29%

Interest Groups

	AFL-CIO	ADA	CCUS	ACU
2010	14%	15%	75%	88%
2009	10%	5%	73%	100%
2008	13%	30%	83%	88%
2007	29%	20%	90%	80%

Florida 9
West — suburbs north of Tampa

Suburban and rural areas northwest of Tampa Bay and St. Petersburg form the bulk of Florida's mostly residential 9th District, which encompasses coastal areas of Pinellas and Pasco counties as well as a large chunk of mostly suburban Hillsborough County.

With a large number of retirees from the North, a significant portion of the population is 65 or older. Clearwater (shared with the 10th) is known as a beach resort and is the "spiritual headquarters" of the Church of Scientology, which has a large community here. Palm Harbor and Tarpon Springs have long-established Greek Orthodox populations.

For decades, the 9th's economy was driven by tourism, fueled by "snowbirds" who spend winters here and visitors to its beaches. Plant City is the exception, as families move in from out of state and settle in the mid-size city. Many year-round residents commute to nearby Tampa or St. Petersburg. Years of growth in the district encouraged a local real estate boom that has since collapsed. Real estate values continue to decline across the district — the double-digit drops have targeted both well-off enclaves as well as struggling communities — and neighborhoods full of foreclosed

homes dot the suburbs. Service-oriented industries had supplemented the construction and hospitality industries, but layoffs in retail sectors have hurt the economy.

The 9th long has been a home for mostly GOP retirees, and Republicans retain an edge here due to their dominance in the district's portion of Hillsborough. Many of Hillsborough's most heavily GOP precincts are in the 9th despite a strong lean in favor of Democratic candidates in the county overall.

The district's part of Pinellas also is decidedly Republican, while the two parties are nearly even in registration in its share of Pasco County. In 2008, Republican John McCain won the district with 52 percent of its presidential vote.

Major Industry
Tourism, service, health care, technology

Cities
Clearwater (pt.), 77,929; Tampa (pt.), 41,764

Notable
Tarpon Springs, still known as the "Sponge Capital of the World," was settled in the late 19th century by Greek immigrants who came to dive for the natural sponges.

Rep. C.W. Bill Young (R)

Capitol Office
225-5961
www.house.gov/young
2407 Rayburn Bldg. 20515-0910; fax 225-9764

Committees
Appropriations
  (Defense - Chairman)

Residence
Indian Shores

Born
Dec. 16, 1930; Harmarville, Pa.

Religion
Methodist

Family
Wife, Beverly Young; six children

Education
St. Petersburg H.S., graduated 1948

Military
Fla. National Guard, 1948-57

Career
Insurance executive; public official

Political Highlights
Fla. Senate, 1960-70 (minority leader, 1966-70)

ELECTION RESULTS

2010 GENERAL

C.W. Bill Young (R)	137,943	65.9%
Charlie Justice (D)	71,313	34.1%

2010 PRIMARY

C.W. Bill Young (R)	unopposed

2008 GENERAL

C.W. Bill Young (R)	182,781	60.7%
Bob Hackworth (D)	118,430	39.3%

Previous Winning Percentages
2006 (66%); 2004 (69%); 2002 (100%); 2000 (76%);
1998 (100%); 1996 (67%); 1994 (100%); 1992 (57%);
1990 (100%); 1988 (73%); 1986 (100%); 1984 (80%);
1982 (100%); 1980 (100%); 1978 (79%); 1976 (65%);
1974 (76%); 1972 (76%); 1970 (67%)

Elected 1970; 21st term

Young has been in Congress longer than 16 members of the freshman class of 2010 have been alive. He has been in elected office for more than half a century and is the House's longest-serving Republican, an appropriator well-schooled in the legislative legerdemain that has allowed him to prosper on the tight-knit spending committee.

Back in the majority in the 112th Congress (2010-11), but operating under tighter restrictions on earmarks — as well as greater scrutiny from the public and colleagues — will be a different experience for Young, who has specialized in funneling billions of dollars to the Defense Department and millions to his constituents.

Ever the friendly gentleman, Young has weighed retirement in the recent past, having grown weary of partisanship, ethics scandals and the political money chase. "I will admit to having given some serious thought to retiring," he said. "I had a serious debate with myself." But in February 2010, he announced his intention to seek a 21st term.

Young's non-confrontational style personifies the go-along, get-along culture of the Appropriations Committee, where there has been an unwritten agreement to accede to others' parochial spending projects in exchange for their approval of yours. That atmosphere is likely to change somewhat with the addition to the committee of Republican anti-earmark crusader Jeff Flake of Arizona and a sprinkling of other like-minded spending hawks.

When GOP leaders unveiled their plans in spring 2010 for a one-year moratorium on earmarks, Young was skeptical. "I don't think that members of the House are going to look with favor upon senators being able to deliver monies to their states when the members of the House can't," he told Roll Call in April 2010. But the moratorium was broadly adhered to, and it was renewed for fiscal 2011.

Young's manner is the product of 24 years spent in the House minority before the GOP victories of 1994. Those years taught him that working with Democrats was a prerequisite for getting legislation passed.

When Republicans won the majority, Speaker Newt Gingrich of Georgia skipped over Young and two other senior members for the Appropriations chairmanship. Young settled for chairing the Defense Subcommittee. When he finally got the full panel's gavel in 1999, he allowed conservatives to dominate the early stages of budget negotiations until legislative reality — the need to gain President Bill Clinton's signature — set in.

Term limits forced him back to the subcommittee chairmanship in 2005, a position he held until 2007, when Democrats gained control. With Republicans back in charge, he is once again at the helm the Defense panel.

Young shared a close working relationship with Democrat John P. Murtha of Pennsylvania, the late chairman of the Defense Subcommittee. Along with panel members from both parties, they gave a green light to the defense buildup that followed the Sept. 11 terrorist attacks, directing hundreds of billions of dollars to the Pentagon for its regular operations as well as for the wars in Iraq and Afghanistan.

The pair also teamed up with their Appropriations colleagues to obtain earmarks, spending targeted for special projects in a particular district or state. Murtha and Young far outpaced their House colleagues in this regard.

The practice of earmarking has brought Young unwanted attention. In 2009, the Office of Congressional Ethics opened an investigation involving seven members of the Defense Subcommittee. The Center for

Public Integrity reported that "Young requested earmarks for companies that hired three of his former staffers as lobbyists. The same companies . . . contributed $145,000 to Young's campaign that same year." The ethics office dropped its investigation in early 2010, with a statement that read, "Young and his chief of staff credibly articulated a process that separates the member's legislative activities and his campaign fundraising activities."

Young also sits on the Military Construction-Veterans Affairs Subcommittee, where he works to deliver aid to wounded veterans. He found himself on the defensive in 2007, when concerns arose about mismanagement and soldiers' poor living conditions at Walter Reed Army Medical Center in Washington, D.C., after he routinely visited soldiers without commenting on the center's conditions. Young said he knew of the problems as early as 2003, but that he preferred to privately confront the hospital commander rather than go public or wield his appropriator's clout.

Young is among the House Republicans most likely not to follow the party line. He opposed the Democrats' health care overhaul in 2010 and the economic stimulus in 2009, but overall he sided with his party less than 85 percent of the time on votes that divided a majority of Republicans from a majority of Democrats in the 111th Congress (2009-10).

He has supported a minimum wage increase, a ban on certain semiautomatic weapons, federal aid to help protect Florida's beaches from erosion, and opposed offshore oil and gas drilling. And when he chaired Appropriations, he resisted demands that chairmen raise large amounts of political cash for the party.

Young was born into hardscrabble poverty in Pennsylvania's coal country during the Great Depression. His father, an alcoholic, abandoned the family when Young was a boy. After his mother became ill, the family stayed with relatives in St. Petersburg. Young never went to college, but worked his way to success in the insurance business. He entered politics in 1960, when he was elected as the sole Republican in the Florida Senate, where he rose to minority leader.

In 1970 he won the state's most dependably Republican U.S. House seat, which opened up after William C. Cramer decided to run for the Senate. The 10th District has tilted Democratic in recent years — Barack Obama carried it by 5 percentage points in the 2008 presidential election — but Young has been re-elected with ease more often than not. Since 1982, Democrats have fielded a candidate only about half the time. In 2010, he beat Democratic state Sen. Charlie Justice with 66 percent of the vote.

Key Votes

2010

Overhaul the nation's health insurance system	NO
Allow for repeal of "don't ask, don't tell"	NO
Overhaul financial services industry regulation	NO
Limit use of new Afghanistan War funds to troop withdrawal activities	NO
Change oversight of offshore drilling and lift oil spill liability cap	?
Provide a path to legal status for some children of illegal immigrants	NO
Extend Bush-era income tax cuts for two years	?

2009

Expand the Children's Health Insurance Program	YES
Provide $787 billion in tax cuts and spending increases to stimulate the economy	NO
Allow bankruptcy judges to modify certain primary-residence mortgages	NO
Create a cap-and-trade system to limit greenhouse gas emissions	NO
Provide $2 billion for the "cash for clunkers" program	YES
Establish the government as the sole provider of student loans	NO
Restrict federally funded insurance coverage for abortions in health care overhaul	YES

CQ Vote Studies

	PARTY UNITY		PRESIDENTIAL SUPPORT	
	SUPPORT	OPPOSE	SUPPORT	OPPOSE
2010	90%	10%	32%	68%
2009	77%	23%	32%	68%
2008	92%	8%	64%	36%
2007	83%	17%	64%	36%
2006	90%	10%	87%	13%

Interest Groups

	AFL-CIO	ADA	CCUS	ACU
2010	9%	10%	100%	84%
2009	25%	15%	80%	92%
2008	33%	25%	83%	88%
2007	33%	30%	90%	72%
2006	43%	10%	87%	84%

Florida 10

West — most of Pinellas County, St. Petersburg

The 10th has sandy beaches, a modern urban center, moderate politics, and an economy reeling from a foreclosure crisis. The district takes in about 70 percent of Pinellas County's residents, including most of St. Petersburg and its upscale beachfront communities. It skirts most of Clearwater (shared with the 9th) in the central part of the county and grabs Dunedin and half of Palm Harbor at its northern tip.

Roughly one-fifth of the district's residents are 65 or older, and many retirees live in Largo and the Gulf Coast towns. Pinellas Park and St. Petersburg attract younger residents who want to live closer to major employers and Tampa.

A large part of the district's economy relies on tourism. Attractions such as The Pier and Sunken Gardens still lure visitors, but the sector has been vulnerable to nationwide economic downturns. Financial services and an emerging technology sector diversified the 10th's economy and brought more white-collar jobs to the area in the last decade but did not insulate Pinellas from rising unemployment rates.

Downtown St. Petersburg experienced a cultural revival with renovations to the Mahaffey Theater and the Ponce de Leon hotel, and locals flock to the area's museums, orchestra performances, theaters and nightclubs. Residents also take pride in the preservation of the area's white-sand beaches and wildlife areas.

Republicans hold a slight voter registration advantage over Democrats here, and the majority of locally elected officials are Republican: The Pinellas County Board of Commissioners, for example, has been controlled by the GOP since 1951. Twenty percent of district voters are registered as independent, however, and the 10th's loyalties can flip between parties in presidential elections. In 2008, Democrat Barack Obama carried the 10th with 52 percent of its presidential vote.

Major Industry
Tourism, health care, retail, technology

Cities
St. Petersburg (pt.), 179,045; Largo, 77,648; Pinellas Park, 49,079

Notable
The Salvador Dalí Museum — which moved to a new site on the St. Petersburg waterfront — houses the largest collection of art by the Spanish surrealist outside of Europe.

Rep. Kathy Castor (D)

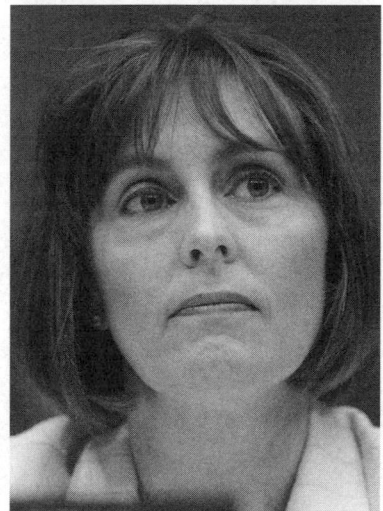

Capitol Office
225-3376
castor.house.gov
137 Cannon Bldg. 20515-0911; fax 225-5652

Committees
Armed Services
Budget

Residence
Tampa

Born
Aug. 20, 1966; Miami, Fla.

Religion
Presbyterian

Family
Husband, Bill Lewis; two children

Education
Emory U., B.A. 1988 (political science); Florida State
U., J.D. 1991

Career
Lawyer

Political Highlights
Democratic nominee for Fla. Senate, 2000;
Hillsborough County Board of Commissioners,
2002-06

ELECTION RESULTS

2010 GENERAL

Kathy Castor (D)	91,328	59.6%
Mike Prendergast (R)	61,817	40.4%

2010 PRIMARY

Kathy Castor (D)	29,556	85.3%
Tim Curtis (D)	5,097	14.7%

2008 GENERAL

Kathy Castor (D)	184,106	71.7%
Eddie Adams Jr. (R)	72,825	28.3%

Previous Winning Percentages
2006 (70%)

Elected 2006; 3rd term

Castor is a rising star in her party and a member of a prominent Florida political family. Minority Leader Nancy Pelosi of California has taken Castor under her wing, campaigning in her district and tapping her to serve on the Democratic Steering Committee, which makes committee assignments.

Castor had also been given plum assignments on the Energy and Commerce and Rules committees, but Democratic losses in 2010 forced her off those panels. One duty she might not miss: She'll no longer sit in judgment of her colleagues, having also left the Ethics Committee.

At the beginning of the 112th Congress (2011-12), she moved to Armed Services and Budget.

The Armed Services spot allows her to look out for MacDill Air Force Base in Tampa. She was an enthusiastic supporter of President Obama's economic agenda and will look to defend it against Republican attempts to curtail spending from her Budget Committee seat.

Castor also looks out for her constituents by trying to improve travel options between Florida and Cuba. She applauded when Congress approved language in the 2009 catchall spending bill that would allow Cuban-Americans to visit relatives on the island once a year rather than once every three years, which had been the policy under the Bush administration.

When the Obama administration further loosened restrictions to allow Cuban-Americans to visit relatives on the island and made it possible for more U.S. airports to offer charter service to the island, Castor said Tampa planned to be "first in line" when new airports are approved to offer service.

When she was on Energy and Commerce, Castor brought experience in environmental issues, concern for her district's coastline and an interest in renewable energy to the table. She practiced environmental law for a decade and served as chairwoman of the Environmental Protection Commission when she was a Hillsborough County commissioner. She opposes efforts to drill for oil and natural gas off the Florida coast.

When gasoline prices were rising in the fall of 2008, House Republicans pushed through legislation to lift a moratorium on drilling off the Atlantic and Pacific coasts. Castor and other coastal district members opposed the measure, saying they were worried about the impact of drilling on tourism, fishing and even military exercises.

Coastal drilling is one of the few areas in which she has disagreed with President Obama. In March 2010, he proposed studying areas in the eastern gulf for expanded leases. Castor countered that a 235-mile buffer zone off the west coast of Florida that was created in 2006 should be maintained. After the April 2010 Deepwater Horizon disaster spilled millions of barrels of oil into the gulf, Obama retreated on his call for more study, and Castor proposed permanently prohibiting oil drilling off the Gulf Coast and the straits of Florida.

As a member of the Energy and Commerce Subcommittee on Health, Castor was involved in another issue important to her constituents as she helped shape Democrats' health care legislation in the 111th Congress (2009-10). Those efforts built on her work on legislation to expand the Children's Health Insurance Program, which provides insurance to children in low-income families that make too much money to qualify for Medicaid. She had voted no on the original version in 2007 because it would have stripped provisions making it easier for parents to enroll their children. That bill also included a tax increase that would have hurt Tampa's cigar-making industry. But Castor eventually supported a failed override of President George W. Bush's veto. The expansion cleared in early 2009 and was one of the first measures signed into law by Obama.

She is as reliable a Democrat as there is in the House, siding with her party 99 percent of the time on votes that divided a majority of Democrats from a majority of Republicans in 2008, 2009 and 2010.

Castor's parents, who divorced when she was 11, were active in Florida politics. Her father, Don, was a Hillsborough County judge and helped found Bay Area Legal Services, a nonprofit group that serves low-income families. Castor's mother, Betty, was the first woman to serve on the Hillsborough County Board of Commissioners, one of the first women to sit in the Florida Senate and the first to serve in the state cabinet, where she was education commissioner.

From 1993 to 1999, Castor's mother served as president of the University of South Florida and in 2004 ran an unsuccessful campaign for the U.S. Senate, losing to Mel Martinez by 1 percentage point.

After graduating from Emory University in Atlanta and earning a law degree from Florida State, Castor worked in the Department of Community Affairs in Tallahassee as an attorney enforcing environmental laws. She returned to Tampa in the mid-1990s to work in a law firm representing the city on zoning and code enforcement issues.

She then tried her hand at politics, losing a 2000 bid for the state Senate but winning a 2002 election to the Hillsborough County board, where she was a liberal voice amid the conservative majority. She won support for greater disclosure of commissioners' meetings with lobbyists and board members' travel expenses. In 2005, she was the lone dissenting vote when the commission passed a measure forbidding the county government from recognizing gay pride displays or events.

Castor's path to the House opened when Democratic Rep. Jim Davis made an ultimately failed bid for governor in 2006. She became the early favorite for his seat by capitalizing on her name recognition and financial support from EMILY's List, a political committee that backs Democratic women who support abortion rights.

She won the five-way primary with 54 percent of the vote. Two months later she trounced GOP architect Eddie Adams Jr. in the general election with 70 percent of the vote. In 2008 she again ran against Adams and won with 72 percent. In 2010, she topped Republican Mike Prendergast, a retired Army colonel, with 60 percent.

Key Votes

2010

Overhaul the nation's health insurance system	YES
Allow for repeal of "don't ask, don't tell"	YES
Overhaul financial services industry regulation	YES
Limit use of new Afghanistan War funds to troop withdrawal activities	NO
Change oversight of offshore drilling and lift oil spill liability cap	YES
Provide a path to legal status for some children of illegal immigrants	YES
Extend Bush-era income tax cuts for two years	YES

2009

Expand the Children's Health Insurance Program	YES
Provide $787 billion in tax cuts and spending increases to stimulate the economy	YES
Allow bankruptcy judges to modify certain primary-residence mortgages	YES
Create a cap-and-trade system to limit greenhouse gas emissions	YES
Provide $2 billion for the "cash for clunkers" program	YES
Establish the government as the sole provider of student loans	YES
Restrict federally funded insurance coverage for abortions in health care overhaul	NO

CQ Vote Studies

	PARTY UNITY		PRESIDENTIAL SUPPORT	
	SUPPORT	OPPOSE	SUPPORT	OPPOSE
2010	99%	1%	93%	7%
2009	99%	1%	96%	4%
2008	99%	1%	14%	86%
2007	98%	2%	7%	93%

Interest Groups

	AFL-CIO	ADA	CCUS	ACU
2010	100%	95%	25%	0%
2009	100%	100%	33%	0%
2008	100%	95%	63%	9%
2007	96%	95%	55%	0%

Florida 11

West — Tampa, south St. Petersburg

The 11th, one of the state's younger and more racially diverse districts, ranges from Tampa's urban center and part of Bradenton across the bay to south St. Petersburg. The Tampa area's service and technology sectors helped make it the commercial, industrial and financial hub of Florida's west coast, and its skyline grew significantly during the last decade.

After nearly a decade of rapid growth in the 2000s, a nationwide economic downturn hit the area hard. Unemployment rates have begun to rebound, and some new construction projects are under way in Tampa. Although the city's airport and seaport make it a major shipping and transit hub, the hospitality industry centered around the major cruise lines hosted at the port depends on a high volume of visitors. The University of South Florida is one of the state's largest schools and still an economic engine for the city.

Tampa has a rich history as "Cigar City," one of the nation's biggest producers of cigars, and the Tampa Bay History Center in the Channel District has a permanent exhibit on the city's cigar industry — at its height, Tampa produced more than 400 million cigars annually. The influence of Cuban and Spanish culture is pronounced in Ybor City, a downtown Tampa neighborhood, and its success at reinventing itself as a nighttime hot spot has given the area new life.

Blacks and Hispanics make up more than half the population, with heavy concentrations of blacks in south St. Petersburg, east Tampa and parts of Bradenton, and Hispanics in west Tampa and the Egypt Lake-Leto and Town 'n' Country areas just northwest of the city. Democrats outnumber Republicans more than two to one in the 11th, where Barack Obama took 66 percent of the district's 2008 presidential vote.

Major Industry
Service, health care, finance, tourism

Military Bases
MacDill Air Force Base, 4,290 military, 1,837 civilian (2009)

Cities
Tampa (pt.), 293,945; Town 'n' Country (unincorporated), 78,442; St. Petersburg (pt.), 65,724; University (unincorporated), 41,163

Notable
The Sunshine Skyway Bridge is the world's longest cable-stayed concrete bridge.

Rep. Dennis A. Ross (R)

Capitol Office
225-1252
dennisross.house.gov
404 Cannon Bldg. 20515-0912; fax 226-0585

Committees
Education & the Workforce
Judiciary
Oversight & Government Reform
(Federal Workforce, U.S. Postal Service & Labor
Policy - Chairman)

Residence
Lakeland

Born
Oct. 18, 1959; Lakeland, Fla.

Religion
Presbyterian

Family
Wife, Cindy Ross; two children

Education
U. of Florida, attended 1977-78; Auburn U., B.S.B.A.
1981 (organization management); Samford U., J.D.
1987

Career
Lawyer; state legislative aide

Political Highlights
Polk County Republican Party chairman, 1992-95;
Fla. House, 2000-2008; Republican nominee for Fla.
Senate, 1996

ELECTION RESULTS

2010 GENERAL

Dennis A. Ross (R)	102,704	48.1%
Lori Edwards (D)	87,769	41.1%
Randy Wilkinson (TEA)	22,857	10.7%

2010 PRIMARY

Dennis A. Ross (R)	33,212	69.0%
John W. Lindsey Jr. (R)	14,936	31.0%

Elected 2010; 1st term

Ross says he hopes to follow in the footsteps of his predecessor, Adam H. Putnam — to a point. Putnam, one-time member of the House GOP leadership, left the seat open to run successfully for state agriculture commissioner.

"My goal is to hopefully be a part of leadership," Ross said. "That's going to allow me to make the necessary changes the country needs."

Ross was given a rare gift for a freshman: chairmanship of the Oversight and Government Reform Subcommittee on the Federal Workforce, U.S. Postal Service and Labor Policy. He backs a freeze in federal hiring and says there is plenty of savings to be had on the personnel front.

"With 2.65 million workers we know that there are some inefficiencies in there," he said on Fox Business Network in January 2011. "There is some waste in there. There is probably some fraud in there. And our first task is going to be to identify where all this money is going."

Ross, who also sits on the Education and the Workforce and Judiciary committees, says his primary legislative mission — job creation — will be informed by his two decades running a small law firm that he started after borrowing money from a neighbor.

"That means extending the Bush tax cuts and incentivizing economic development, whether it be ensuring corporate taxes aren't higher than European corporate taxes or eliminating the capital gains tax," Ross said. "I want to do whatever we can do to allow the infusion of private capital back into the economy so that people start creating jobs again."

He also supports adding a balanced budget amendment to the Constitution, abolishing the IRS and implementing a flat tax.

Ross spent four years in the Florida House; in addition to running his own firm, he counts a year as in-house counsel for Disney World among his legal experience. Early on, Democrats viewed the 12th District as a potential pickup and were further buoyed by a split in the Republican ranks. But Ross held off Polk County Supervisor of Elections Lori Edwards, a Democrat, winning 48 percent of the vote to her 41 percent. Tea Party candidate Randy Wilkinson picked up 11 percent.

Florida 12

West central — Polk and Hillsborough counties

Florida's 12th has plenty of land, but much of it is covered by citrus groves and natural lakes rather than beaches. Centered east of Tampa and southwest of Orlando, the fast-growing district includes almost all of Polk County, suburban and exurban areas of southern and eastern Hillsborough County, and a tiny slice of western Osceola County. Agriculture in Polk County, the state's top producer of citrus, drives the 12th's economy, while the Hillsborough County portion of the district grows tomatoes and strawberries. The district's central location makes it a distribution hub, as well as home to sizable finance and health care sectors.

Despite a thriving agriculture sector and steady growth for a decade in the area's secondary industries — both blue- and white-collar jobs — the Polk County economy was hit hard by high unemployment and foreclosure rates.

Democrats now outnumber Republicans in portions of all three counties in the 12th. The growing Democratic registration advantage belies the social and economic conservatism of most residents here, and traditional Southern Democratic voters make state and local elections here competitive. The district has backed GOP presidential candidates since 1992, but Republican John McCain edged out Barack Obama by fewer than 4,000 votes in the 2008 presidential election, winning the district with only 50 percent of its vote.

Major Industry
Agriculture, financial services

Cities
Brandon (unincorporated) (pt.), 101,076; Lakeland (pt.), 89,142

Notable
The largest LEGOLAND amusement park will open in Winter Haven in the fall of 2011.

Rep. Vern Buchanan (R)

Capitol Office
225-5015
buchanan.house.gov
221 Cannon Bldg. 20515-0913; fax 226-0828

Committees
Ways & Means

Residence
Longboat Key

Born
May 8, 1951; Detroit, Mich.

Religion
Baptist

Family
Wife, Sandy Buchanan; two children

Education
Cleary College, B.B.A. 1975 (business administration);
U. of Detroit, M.B.A. 1986

Military
Mich. Air National Guard, 1970-76

Career
Car dealership owner; copy and printing company
owner; marketing representative

Political Highlights
No previous office

ELECTION RESULTS

2010 GENERAL

Vern Buchanan (R)	183,811	68.9%
James T. Golden (D)	83,123	31.1%

2010 PRIMARY

Vern Buchanan (R)	61,517	83.4%
Don Baldauf (R)	12,197	16.5%

2008 GENERAL

Vern Buchanan (R)	204,382	55.5%
Christine Jennings (D)	137,967	37.5%
Jan Schneider (X)	20,289	5.5%
Don Baldauf (X)	5,358	1.5%

Previous Winning Percentages
2006 (50%)

Elected 2006; 3rd term

Buchanan is a pro-business fiscal conservative who sways from the Republican norm on a handful of issues important to his elderly, beach-loving constituency. Despite his policy deviations, he is a man on the move in his party, joining the powerful Ways and Means Committee and being named vice chairman of finance for the National Republican Congressional Committee.

Buchanan, who made a fortune in the auto dealership business, said his political philosophy is aligned with Reagan-era conservatism: small government, low taxes and a strong national defense. At the same time, he dislikes hewing to ideology. "I think it is a problem in our country when people are hard-core partisan," he said.

On Ways and Means, he will push for easing the tax burden on businesses and simplifying the process for everybody.

"Calling our tax code 'an anchor' around the neck of our people, our businesses and our economy doesn't do justice to the enormous dead weight it represents," he wrote in a Bradenton Herald op-ed in January 2011. "It's well past time for the Congress and president to put aside their respective political interests and work together on a major tax reform package. And, the guiding principle of this effort must be tax simplification."

Buchanan has made similar appeals for bipartisanship before, and he has walked the walk as well as talked the talk.

In the 110th Congress (2007-08), Buchanan was one of 19 Republicans to support five of the first six Democratic bills introduced, including a measure allowing the federal government to negotiate prescription drug prices on behalf of Medicare recipients. He subsequently voted with Democrats to override President George W. Bush's veto of a bill to expand the Children's Health Insurance Program, which covers children whose low-income families make too much money to qualify for Medicaid.

He supports Republican proposals to increase nuclear energy production and open Alaska's Arctic National Wildlife Refuge to oil drilling. But he opposes expanded drilling in the Gulf of Mexico, contending that the risk is too high to Gulf Coast beaches and the tourism industry they support. In 2008, he backed legislation by fellow Floridian Kathy Castor, a Democrat, calling for a permanent ban on drilling within 125 miles of the state's coast.

After a rig off the coast of Louisiana exploded in April 2010 and leaked tens of thousands of gallons of oil into the gulf, Buchanan told the Bradenton Herald: "I think that anybody who was seriously considering opening up Florida's coast for drilling is going to have to take a good look at what has happened. I think back to being assured that there is a 100 percent chance that something like this could never happen. Well, it has happened."

In the 112th Congress (2011-12), he proposed legislation intended to block drilling in Cuban waters, which reach within about 50 miles of the Florida coast. The bill would allow the secretary of the Interior to deny drilling leases to companies that do business with countries facing trade sanctions.

He opposed the Democrats' health care overhaul in the 111th Congress (2009-10), saying the bill "represents all that is wrong with Washington. Deficit spending, higher taxes, more government control and an arrogant dismissal of the will of the American people." In January 2010, he unsuccessfully attempted to force a floor vote on his proposal to require that all negotiations on the final health care bill be open to the public. A year later, at the start of the 112th Congress, he voted to repeal the law.

A former owner of Ford and Dodge dealerships, he opposed a failed effort in December 2008 to aid U.S. automakers. He said he favored an alternative by Senate Republicans to allow the car companies access to $25 billion in federally subsidized loans to help them retool plants to build fuel-efficient vehicles.

Buchanan, like many of the winter residents known as snowbirds who flock to the Gulf Coast, is a native Midwesterner. He was born into a blue-collar family with five siblings that lived in Inkster, a small city near Detroit. His father was a factory foreman for a computer company, married to a stay-at-home mom. Buchanan earned an MBA from the University of Detroit after working his way through college. He served six years in the Air National Guard.

In his early 20s, Buchanan started American Speedy Printing Centers, which grew to about 750 outlets nationwide. In 1992 he resigned his last duties at the company, which entered bankruptcy. He has since paid millions of dollars to settle allegations of fraud and taking excessive compensation.

In 1990, he moved from Michigan to Florida, where he built his auto dealership empire.

Buchanan had some background in politics prior to running for office: He gave nearly $100,000 to the Republican National Committee and served as fundraising chairman for Mel Martinez's successful 2004 Senate campaign and as chairman of the Florida Chamber of Commerce.

In the 2006 general election, he faced Democrat Christine Jennings, his former banker. Buchanan won by 369 votes in the third-closest race of the 2006 election cycle. Jennings contested the results, claiming widespread voting irregularities, including malfunctions of electronic voting machines. But in early 2008, the Government Accountability Office concluded that the touch-screen voting machines appeared to have worked properly.

Jennings challenged Buchanan again two years later. Despite the Democratic tide across the nation and in Florida, Buchanan cruised to an 18-percentage-point victory. He won by 38 percentage points in 2010.

After the election, the Federal Election Commission filed a suit against a company Buchanan owned and a business partner, accusing them of offering reimbursements for campaign donations and exceeding contribution limits in 2006 and 2008. Buchanan himself wasn't named as a defendant.

Buchanan has been mentioned as a possible Senate candidate in 2012. He has the ability to self-fund — he was worth more than $55 million in 2009, making him the eighth-richest member of Congress, according to Roll Call — and he had almost $1 million in his campaign account at the end of 2010.

Key Votes

2010

Overhaul the nation's health insurance system	NO
Allow for repeal of "don't ask, don't tell"	NO
Overhaul financial services industry regulation	NO
Limit use of new Afghanistan War funds to troop withdrawal activities	NO
Change oversight of offshore drilling and lift oil spill liability cap	NO
Provide a path to legal status for some children of illegal immigrants	NO
Extend Bush-era income tax cuts for two years	YES

2009

Expand the Children's Health Insurance Program	YES
Provide $787 billion in tax cuts and spending increases to stimulate the economy	NO
Allow bankruptcy judges to modify certain primary-residence mortgages	NO
Create a cap-and-trade system to limit greenhouse gas emissions	NO
Provide $2 billion for the "cash for clunkers" program	P
Establish the government as the sole provider of student loans	YES
Restrict federally funded insurance coverage for abortions in health care overhaul	YES

CQ Vote Studies

	PARTY UNITY		PRESIDENTIAL SUPPORT	
	SUPPORT	OPPOSE	SUPPORT	OPPOSE
2010	89%	11%	39%	61%
2009	82%	18%	41%	59%
2008	80%	20%	44%	56%
2007	90%	10%	66%	34%

Interest Groups

	AFL-CIO	ADA	CCUS	ACU
2010	0%	0%	88%	83%
2009	20%	15%	87%	88%
2008	40%	50%	83%	60%
2007	33%	35%	85%	84%

Florida 13

Southwest — Sarasota, most of Bradenton

Retirees from the North flock to the 13th District's Gulf Coast cities of Sarasota and Bradenton. Sarasota and Manatee counties make up nearly 90 percent of the district's population; the more affluent tend to live near Sarasota, with middle-class residents more prevalent around Bradenton. Coastal Sarasota County cultivates a refined image with its art museums, theater and symphony performances. Overall, the 13th has highest median age of any district in the nation.

Although most of the district's development is near the coast, with farmland and citrus groves inland, beach communities have experienced a decline in their permanent populations. The populations in Manatee and Sarasota counties overall have grown over the past decade, but there has been a shift inland to make room for vacation rentals near the water. A significant population increase in middle-class Hispanic communities in Sarasota and Manatee accounted for more than a quarter of the counties' overall growth since 2000.

Bradenton (shared with the 11th) is the retail center of Manatee County.

The city is partly a Tampa-St. Petersburg suburb and has a more noticeable mix of incomes and ethnic groups than Sarasota. It also is home to the IMG Academies — residential sports-training and academic facilities for top athletes in several sports.

Economic growth here has stalled as unemployment rates continue to hover above the national average and many commercial and office sites remain vacant. The district's agricultural industry remains strong, however, with large tomato and citrus crops.

The GOP holds a decided party registration advantage in the district, and voters here routinely favor Republicans in statewide races. Despite the strong GOP base, John McCain took only 52 percent of the district's 2008 presidential vote. The area's gulf beaches, barrier islands and state park make environmental policy a bipartisan concern here.

Major industry
Agriculture, tourism, health care, service

Cities
North Port, 57,357; Sarasota, 51,917; Bradenton (pt.), 39,752

Notable
The John and Mable Ringling Museum of Art, located on the Sarasota Bay, boasts the mansion once owned by John Ringling.

Rep. Connie Mack (R)

Capitol Office
225-2536
mack.house.gov
115 Cannon Bldg. 20515-0914; fax 226-0439

Committees
Foreign Affairs
  (Western Hemisphere - Chairman)
Oversight & Government Reform

Residence
Fort Myers

Born
Aug. 12, 1967; Fort Myers, Fla.

Religion
Roman Catholic

Family
Wife, Rep. Mary Bono Mack, R-Calif.; two children,
two stepchildren

Education
U. of Florida, B.S. 1993 (advertising)

Career
Marketing consultant; health products sales
representative

Political Highlights
Fla. House, 2000-03

ELECTION RESULTS

2010 GENERAL

Connie Mack (R)	188,341	68.6%
James Lloyd Roach (D)	74,525	27.1%
William St. Claire (NPA)	11,825	4.3%

2010 PRIMARY

Connie Mack (R)	unopposed

2008 GENERAL

Connie Mack (R)	224,602	59.4%
Robert M. Neeld (D)	93,590	24.8%
Burt Saunders (X)	54,750	14.5%
Jeff George (X)	4,949	1.3%

Previous Winning Percentages
2006 (64%); 2004 (68%)

Elected 2004; 4th term

Mack is a fiscal conservative with a libertarian streak, much like his father and namesake, who served 18 years in the House and Senate. He will enjoy increased visibility as chairman of the House panel overseeing relations with the Western Hemisphere, where he takes a tough line against U.S. adversaries in Latin America.

Mack reportedly declined slots on two of the most powerful House committees — Ways and Means, and Energy and Commerce — in favor of the chairmanship of the Foreign Affairs Subcommittee on the Western Hemisphere. He can use that spot to continue to castigate figures unpopular with much of Florida's diverse population, including Venezuelan President Hugo Chávez and Cuba's Castro brothers, Fidel and Raul. Many analysts thought that positioned him well for a 2012 Senate run. But Mack announced in March 2011 he wouldn't be a candidate.

In 2008, Mack introduced a resolution declaring Venezuela a state sponsor of terrorism. Again echoing his father, Mack is a defender of Israel, and he sounded the alarm in early 2009 when Chavez expelled the Israeli ambassador from Venezuela.

He also sponsored legislation to withhold U.S. contributions to the Organization of American States if the group granted Cuba full membership. He was among a group of House Republicans who asked the Government Accountability Office to investigate charges that the U.S. ambassador to Honduras overstepped his authority in trying to prevent the removal of exiled former President Manuel Zelaya.

A spending hawk, Mack opposed all the major economic recovery bills of late 2008 and early 2009. He voted against legislation aimed at rescuing ailing banks and automobile companies as well as President Obama's $787 billion economic stimulus, which he called "little more than a massive spending plan filled with earmarks and liberal social-planning programs." Within days of the enactment of the Democratic health care overhaul in 2010, he introduced legislation to repeal it.

Mack's libertarian instincts led him to oppose key provisions of the anti-terrorism law known as the Patriot Act because, he said, it "tramples on the civil liberties that are part of the foundation of this country." And he used harsher language than other GOP critics of a 2010 Arizona law that empowered police officers to inquire about the immigration status of people they have stopped for other offenses, saying it was "reminiscent of a time during World War II when the Gestapo in Germany stopped people on the street and asked for their papers."

During his first term, he cosponsored a bill to permanently prohibit offshore oil and gas drilling along Florida's coast. But when the issue moved atop the GOP agenda in 2008, he said he had second thoughts, "as long as the state of Florida has a say" in the decision-making and distribution of revenue. After a rig explosion caused a massive oil spill in the Gulf of Mexico in 2010, he said the oil company BP should be held responsible "for every dime" of the cost of the cleanup and recovery.

Aside from the libertarian deviations, Mack is a solid GOP vote. He sided with his party 97percent of the time on votes that split a majority of Republicans and Democrats in the 111th Congress (2009-10). But like his father, he differs from most conservatives on expanded federal funding for embryonic stem cell research, which abortion opponents such as Mack tend to oppose because it requires the destruction of human embryos. He has felt keenly the toll cancer has wreaked on his family and believes the research could help find a cure. Both of his grandparents on his father's side, as well as an uncle, died of cancer. His mother and sister nearly did as well.

Mack comes from a long line of politicians. His great-great-grandfather, John L. Sheppard, was a Democratic House member from Texas; his great-grandfather, Morris Sheppard, also served in the House, then moved on to a 28-year tenure in the Senate. His father, Connie Mack III, spent three terms in the House and two in the Senate. But it was another relative who provided Mack with enviable name recognition: Another great-grandfather was the original Connie Mack, the legendary owner and manager of the Philadelphia Athletics baseball team. And like him, Mack uses the familiar rather than the given version of his name: Cornelius McGillicuddy IV.

Mack grew up in southwestern Florida and was a student at Cape Coral High School when his father was elected to Congress. The Macks moved to the nation's capital, settling in McLean, Va. Mack graduated from Massanutten Military Academy in Woodstock, Va.

Mack "stuffed envelopes and walked precincts" for his father, but he hated the sometimes-critical appraisals of the elder Mack in the press. "I think that some of the shots taken at my father really had a negative impact on me," he said. "But as you get older, you realize that's just part of politics these days."

After the military academy, he attended the University of Florida and earned a degree in advertising. He was a health products salesman and marketing consultant, but he soon thought of following in his father's footsteps. In 2000, at age 33, he was elected to the Florida House from Fort Lauderdale. During three years as a state legislator, he organized a group of members opposed to all new taxes and government fees.

When Republican Porter J. Goss resigned just before the end of his eighth term to become CIA director, Mack moved from Fort Lauderdale to Fort Myers to run in the 2004 race in the overwhelmingly Republican 14th District. He eked out a primary victory in a four-way race marked by opponents' jabs about his lack of ties to the area. Voters didn't seem to mind. After winning the primary, he cruised to a lopsided general-election victory. He was re-elected by wide margins in 2008 and 2010.

His first term in Washington turned out to be difficult for his family. Mack split from Ann, his wife of nine years, in August 2005, and weeks later he was linked romantically to another member of Congress, Republican Mary Bono of California — the widow of Sonny Bono, a pop-star-turned-congressman — who was divorcing her second husband. Mack and Bono (who now goes by Mary Bono Mack) married in 2007.

Key Votes

2010

Overhaul the nation's health insurance system	NO
Allow for repeal of "don't ask, don't tell"	NO
Overhaul financial services industry regulation	NO
Limit use of new Afghanistan War funds to troop withdrawal activities	NO
Change oversight of offshore drilling and lift oil spill liability cap	NO
Provide a path to legal status for some children of illegal immigrants	NO
Extend Bush-era income tax cuts for two years	NO

2009

Expand the Children's Health Insurance Program	NO
Provide $787 billion in tax cuts and spending increases to stimulate the economy	NO
Allow bankruptcy judges to modify certain primary-residence mortgages	NO
Create a cap-and-trade system to limit greenhouse gas emissions	NO
Provide $2 billion for the "cash for clunkers" program	NO
Establish the government as the sole provider of student loans	NO
Restrict federally funded insurance coverage for abortions in health care overhaul	YES

CQ Vote Studies

	PARTY UNITY		PRESIDENTIAL SUPPORT	
	SUPPORT	OPPOSE	SUPPORT	OPPOSE
2010	97%	3%	29%	71%
2009	97%	3%	13%	87%
2008	98%	2%	77%	23%
2007	95%	5%	85%	15%
2006	93%	7%	87%	13%

Interest Groups

	AFL-CIO	ADA	CCUS	ACU
2010	0%	5%	75%	96%
2009	5%	0%	73%	100%
2008	7%	10%	88%	100%
2007	5%	5%	79%	88%
2006	8%	25%	93%	84%

Florida 14

Southwest — Cape Coral, Fort Myers, Naples

Traditionally a haven for retirees and tourists, the solidly Republican 14th features Gulf Coast beaches and golf courses. The district's population is centered in Lee County, where migration of families and young professionals from the North and from Florida's east coast have added to the mix. The 14th also takes in the coastal edge of Collier County and a small slice of Charlotte County.

The district's population boomed in the last decade and it is one of the nation's top 20 most-populous and fastest-growing congressional districts ahead of decennial remapping. Most residents live near the coast, between the shore and Interstate 75, which runs north and south through the district before turning east into the Everglades.

Originally a retirement community built on undeveloped rural land, Cape Coral began attracting young professionals with white-collar job opportunities, and many businesses relocated to the area. The city long relied on its service and home construction industries. Fort Myers' Florida Gulf Coast University, with its environmental and science programs, and

the nearby Everglades help promote marine biology and an eco-tourism industry. Wealthier retirees live around Naples in Collier, where golf courses and high-rise condominiums are plentiful, and a decade of construction helped raise the tax base for the area.

A collapse of the housing market in Lee and Collier counties caused property values to plummet. The supply of residential units was based on growth patterns that have now stalled, and many homes are still vacant even as continued foreclosures lead to some home sales.

Small Democratic pockets exist within Lee County, but the 14th has the second-largest GOP voter-registration advantage in the state, and residents here regularly give Republican candidates large vote percentages. John McCain won the 2008 presidential vote here with 57 percent.

Major Industry
Tourism, health care, service

Cities
Cape Coral, 154,305; Lehigh Acres (unincorporated), 86,784; Fort Myers, 62,298

Notable
The J.N. "Ding" Darling National Wildlife Refuge on Sanibel Island, an area barrier island, hosts migratory birds in its mangrove forests.

Rep. Bill Posey (R)

Capitol Office
225-3671
posey.house.gov
120 Cannon Bldg. 20515-0915; fax 225-3516

Committees
Financial Services

Residence
Rockledge

Born
Dec. 18, 1947; Washington, D.C.

Religion
Methodist

Family
Wife, Katie Posey; two children

Education
Brevard Junior College, A.A. 1969

Career
Realtor; insurance claims adjuster; space program engineering inspector

Political Highlights
Rockledge City Council, 1976-86; Fla. House, 1992-2000; Fla. Senate, 2000-08

ELECTION RESULTS

2010 GENERAL

Bill Posey (R)	157,079	64.7%
Shannon Roberts (D)	85,595	35.3%

2010 PRIMARY

Bill Posey (R)	unopposed

2008 GENERAL

Bill Posey (R)	192,151	53.1%
Stephen Blythe (D)	151,951	42.0%
Frank Zilaitis (X)	14,274	3.9%

Elected 2008; 2nd term

Easygoing and witty, Posey is a patron of government accountability. He earned the nickname "Mr. Accountability" during his 16 years in the Florida Legislature, and it's been his mission since he entered politics in 1976.

Posey applies his philosophy from his seat on the Financial Services Committee, which produced the overhaul of the financial regulatory regime enacted in 2010. As a freshman in the minority, Posey had little impact on the final legislative product, and he opposed the measure, saying it offered "zero accountability for government regulators who were asleep at the switch."

He gained considerably more notoriety for a measure he introduced that went nowhere.

Posey pursued his theme of accountability with a call for President Obama's birth certificate, making him the target of liberals and drawing accusations of catering to a fringe movement. But Posey said he had received calls daily from constituents concerned about Obama's place of birth. So he introduced a bill in March 2009 to require future presidential candidates (including Obama, if he runs for re-election) to provide copies of their birth certificates. He said he simply aimed to put the issue to rest and avoid similar problems for future candidates. "If he had filed that the very first day he filed for office, we wouldn't be having any problems right now," Posey told the St. Petersburg Times in 2009.

He immediately became the butt of jokes on late-night television and the scourge of liberal websites and commentators. The Orlando Sentinel called on Posey to withdraw the bill after he voted for a resolution that celebrated the 50th anniversary of Hawaiian statehood and recognized it as Obama's birthplace. But Posey refused, insisting the bill was in line with his broader efforts to promote transparency.

Posey, described by the St. Petersburg Times as vaguely resembling Mister Rogers, isn't accustomed to such criticism. He was known in Florida as a low-key legislator with a reputation for working across party lines. Party regulars back home think of him as "the nice guy."

He has had some success in other endeavors toward accountability. The Financial Services Committee unanimously approved his "accountability amendment," which requires the panel to post all votes on its website within two days, to its rules package in early 2009. He also has introduced a resolution to require a 72-hour waiting period before legislation can be brought to the House floor.

But Posey was wary of new regulations to combat the kind of lapses that led to the near-collapse of the financial system in 2008. "I think that it's not a matter of too few regulations. I think it's a matter of regulations we have not being enforced," he said at a 2009 Financial Services hearing.

Posey broke with his fellow panel Republicans in the early months of 2009 to support a bill to curb what consumer advocates called "unfair and abusive" practices by credit card companies. It was signed into law after gaining broader GOP support on the floor. But Posey, who received strong backing from business interests in the 2008 campaign, voted on the floor against a Democratic initiative to provide shareholders and regulators greater say on executive compensation packages at financial institutions.

Posey, a member of the conservative Republican Study Committee, also focuses on limiting spending. He opposed Obama's $787 billion economic stimulus law in early 2009. At the start of the 112th Congress (2011-12), he backed repeal of the 2010 health care overhaul and supported legislation to end taxpayer financing of presidential campaigns and party conventions.

He also has focused on bringing money back to his district, home to Cape Canaveral Air Force Station and neighbor of Kennedy Space Center. He has sought millions of dollars for dredging Port Canaveral. And with layoffs under way at NASA following the final trip of the space shuttle, Posey, a former space program engineering inspector, introduced a bill to extend the shuttle through 2015. But the measure didn't gain traction. Posey called moves to terminate the Constellation manned space program and not extend the life of the space shuttle "a series of ill-advised decisions."

In 2011 he called for making sure human spaceflight remains the focus of NASA as budget cuts are considered, and he derided Obama administration plans to have the agency ramp up research on climate change.

"NASA's primary purpose is human space exploration, and directing NASA funds to study global warming undermines our ability to maintain our competitive edge in human spaceflight," Posey said.

Born in Washington, D.C., Posey moved with his family to California when he was 2. In 1956, they moved to Orlando before settling in Brevard County. He still recalls the influence of two of his grade-school teachers, Vi Williams and Lucille Quillen, and sends them each Valentine's Day cards every year.

Growing up, Posey was active in Boy Scouts. He bonded with his father through an interest in stock car racing: They worked on cars, attended races and even raced. Later in life, Posey bought a racetrack with a friend and won an award for short-track driver achievement. Posey also adopted his father's interest in aerospace, working for Douglas after high school like his father. He worked on the Thor rocket, one of the first space launch vehicles, and later as a rocket inspector on the Apollo 11 project.

He married his high school sweetheart, Katie, and after his stint in the racetrack business he worked in insurance and real estate before developing an interest in politics. "I went to a city council meeting and . . . didn't like what I saw," Posey said. He won a seat on the Rockledge City Council in 1976. In 1992 he ran successfully for the Florida House, eight years later for the state Senate.

When Republican Dave Weldon decided to retire in 2008, Posey received the strong backing of business interests and had little trouble in the GOP primary. He took 53 percent of the vote in the general election against Democratic physician Stephen Blythe. In January 2009, he gave six tickets to the presidential inauguration to Blythe, who called the move "magnanimous." He was easily re-elected in 2010.

Key Votes

2010

Overhaul the nation's health insurance system	NO
Allow for repeal of "don't ask, don't tell"	NO
Overhaul financial services industry regulation	NO
Limit use of new Afghanistan War funds to troop withdrawal activities	NO
Change oversight of offshore drilling and lift oil spill liability cap	NO
Provide a path to legal status for some children of illegal immigrants	NO
Extend Bush-era income tax cuts for two years	YES

2009

Expand the Children's Health Insurance Program	NO
Provide $787 billion in tax cuts and spending increases to stimulate the economy	NO
Allow bankruptcy judges to modify certain primary-residence mortgages	NO
Create a cap-and-trade system to limit greenhouse gas emissions	NO
Provide $2 billion for the "cash for clunkers" program	NO
Establish the government as the sole provider of student loans	NO
Restrict federally funded insurance coverage for abortions in health care overhaul	YES

CQ Vote Studies

	PARTY UNITY		PRESIDENTIAL SUPPORT	
	SUPPORT	OPPOSE	SUPPORT	OPPOSE
2010	89%	11%	43%	57%
2009	89%	11%	22%	78%

Interest Groups

	AFL-CIO	ADA	CCUS	ACU
2010	14%	10%	88%	83%
2009	14%	0%	93%	100%

East central — Indian River County; parts of Brevard, Osceola and Polk counties

Most residents of the 15th live along the Atlantic Coast in Brevard and Indian River counties between Merritt Island and Vero Beach. In addition to all of Indian River and three-fourths of Brevard, the 15th contains regional agricultural hubs in inland Osceola County and in its slice of Polk County. Melbourne and Palm Bay are on the Treasure Coast along the district's central shore. A growing Hispanic population and a movement of residents from the coast to inland Brevard are changing the district's communities. The Cape Canaveral Air Force Station, Patrick Air Force Base and the Kennedy Space Center (located in the neighboring 24th) have long been the Space Coast's economic engines.

NASA's presence has provided high-paying jobs, lucrative federal contracts and tourist attractions, but much of the highly skilled aerospace workforce may leave following the 2011 end of the nation's space shuttle program. Local officials hope to lure new employers to take advantage of the aviation, technology, robotics and energy sectors that have built up around the region.

Even beyond the throngs of people who have come to the area for shuttle take-offs, tourism remains a key pillar of the economy. Port Canaveral launches cargo and cruise ships, and beach draws include prime Atlantic surfing spot Sebastian Inlet and Disney's Vero Beach Resort. Kissimmee depends on Orlando's rebounding tourism industry.

Registered Democrats outnumber Republicans in the 15th's portions of Osceola and Polk, but the GOP has a slight registration edge overall here. Voters have favored GOP presidential candidates since 1992, but John McCain won only 51 percent of the district's 2008 presidential vote.

Major Industry
Technology, defense, tourism, agriculture

Military Bases
Patrick Air Force Base, 1,824 military, 2,212 civilian (2010)

Cities
Palm Bay, 103,190; Melbourne, 76,068; Kissimmee, 59,682

Notable
An early name of Yeehaw Junction, at a crossroads of what is now the Florida turnpike, was "Jackass Crossing."

Rep. Tom Rooney (R)

Capitol Office
225-5792
rooney.house.gov
1529 Longworth Bldg. 20515-0916; fax 225-3132

Committees
Agriculture
  (Livestock, Dairy & Poultry - Chairman)
Armed Services
Select Intelligence

Residence
Tequesta

Born
Nov. 21, 1970; Philadelphia, Pa.

Religion
Roman Catholic

Family
Wife, Tara Rooney; three children

Education
Syracuse U., attended 1989; Washington & Jefferson
College, B.A. 1993 (English literature); U. of Florida,
M.A. 1996 (political science); U. of Miami, J.D. 1999

Military
Army, 2000-2004

Career
College instructor; lawyer; children's services
organization director; military and state prosecutor;
congressional aide

Political Highlights
No previous office

ELECTION RESULTS

2010 GENERAL

Tom Rooney (R)	162,285	66.8%
Jim Horn (D)	80,327	33.1%

2010 PRIMARY

Tom Rooney (R)		unopposed

2008 GENERAL

Tom Rooney (R)	209,874	60.1%
Tim Mahoney (D)	139,373	39.9%

Elected 2008; 2nd term

Rooney has a vision of where he would like to be a decade from now: Out of Congress and on the sidelines at one of his sons' sporting events. Until then, he'll push conservative causes and look out for his district's military retirees. He joined the GOP leadership team in 2011, the only second-term member to be named as a deputy whip.

"I've always sort of loosely said that when Tommy starts playing high school football, I'm done," Rooney said in 2010, when his son was a third-grader. "That's an age where they really need their father more. I always remember that my dad never missed a game of mine in football, basketball or baseball. And that's big. . . . That meant the world to me. So for when my kids get to be that age, I want to be full-time able to do those things."

Rooney said his commitment to his family also explains why he moved them from Florida to the Washington area after spending the first six months of his tenure sleeping on a cot in his office. "Anybody [that] has a perception . . . that if you move your family, your wife and kids to D.C., and that's a bad thing, has no idea what they are talking about when it comes to what's more important: politics or your marriage."

Family is a large part of Rooney's persona in part because he comes from a well-known family with a beloved patriarch. His grandfather, Art Rooney, founded the Pittsburgh Steelers in 1933 and the family still runs the football team, though the congressman and several other family members had to sell their shares in 2009 to meet a league requirement to consolidate ownership. Rooney says his children will inherit some shares from his father, but he holds none.

But he still carries the family name, and the sense of responsibility that goes with it. "It weighs heavily on me to make sure that I conduct myself in a way that my grandfather would be proud of and my dad would be proud of. If you do that, obviously his name speaks for itself," he said.

That's no small issue in a district where the past two representatives were tarred by scandal. Republican Mark Foley's lewd text messages to male congressional pages created a scandal just before the 2006 elections. His successor, Democrat Tim Mahoney, was a favorite to win re-election until late in 2008, until he admitted to having an affair with a former staffer and paying $121,000 to avoid a sexual harassment lawsuit. Rooney clobbered Mahoney at the polls a few weeks later. In 2010, he won by a more than 2-1 ratio.

Rooney's legislative focus is largely defined by his military background, and he serves on the Armed Services and Select Intelligence committees.

Rooney and his wife, Tara, worked in the Army Judge Advocate General's Corps, and he prosecuted crimes for two years at Fort Hood in Texas and taught for another two years at West Point. The former JAG prosecutor says all detainees held at Guantánamo Bay, Cuba, should be tried by military commissions in the court facility constructed at the base. His friends in Congress tend to be other veterans, regardless of party affiliation. Included in that circle was Pennsylvania Democrat Patrick J. Murphy. They are fellow veterans and former West Point instructors who served together on Armed Services, but Murphy lost his run for re-election in 2010.

From that panel, Rooney helped lead the fight early in 2011 against funding for an alternate engine for the F-35 Joint Strike Fighter.

His top agenda item has been improving medical care for veterans with traumatic brain injuries and mental health disorders, and he has pushed for increased funding for mental health programs for veterans.

He says he has been deeply frustrated by the inability of Congress to advance seemingly non-controversial measures — including a bill he worked on with Democrats Tom Perriello of Virginia and Michael E. McMahon of New York (both defeated in 2010) to require mental health screenings of soldiers — because the calendar is full of bigger, more complex legislation, such as the Democratic health care overhaul and President Obama's $787 billion economic stimulus, both of which he vehemently opposed in the 111th Congress (2009-10).

On those issues — and most others — Rooney lines up with his party. On votes that divided a majority of Republicans from a majority of Democrats in 2010, he cast his lot with his own 95 percent of the time. He is a strong defender of gun owners' rights and opposes creating a path to citizenship for illegal immigrants, though he has backed Democratic-sponsored bills to establish a national shield law for reporters. On the Agriculture Committee, Rooney keeps an eye on the interests of his district's cattle ranchers as chairman of the Livestock, Dairy and Poultry Subcommittee.

Rooney was born in Philadelphia and grew up in Pennsylvania, where his family owned a horse-racing track. They moved to Florida to operate a dog-racing track around the time Rooney began high school. He attended Syracuse University, then transferred to Washington & Jefferson College near Pittsburgh. After graduation, he spent a year on Capitol Hill working in the office of GOP Sen. Connie Mack of Florida, where he says he "got the political bug. I subscribed to National Review magazine and really bought into what William Buckley was talking about. I thought, hey, I agree with what he's saying . . . and I've been a subscriber ever since."

Rooney said he ran for office only after the assumed front runner, state Sen. Joe Negron, begged off. He was in private law practice at the time, head of the Northern Palm Beach County Republican Club and had been offered a job as a deputy to incoming Florida Attorney General Bill McCollum. Rooney says the day after he accepted the job, Negron announced he would not run. He called McCollum back, "and he said to me, 'These opportunities come up once in a lifetime, and that seat might not come up again for 20 years.'"

Though Rooney was the first in his family to run for office, two of his six siblings ventured into politics in 2010, also as Republicans. Brother Brian Rooney, a Marine who served in Iraq, ran for Congress in Michigan but lost in a primary to ex-Rep. Tim Walberg, who went on to retake the seat. Another brother, Pat Rooney Jr., was elected to a state House seat in Florida. But the Rooney family also crosses party lines: Steelers owner Dan Rooney, the congressman's uncle, endorsed Obama in 2008 and later was appointed ambassador to Ireland.

Key Votes

2010

Overhaul the nation's health insurance system	NO
Allow for repeal of "don't ask, don't tell"	NO
Overhaul financial services industry regulation	NO
Limit use of new Afghanistan War funds to troop withdrawal activities	NO
Change oversight of offshore drilling and lift oil spill liability cap	NO
Provide a path to legal status for some children of illegal immigrants	NO
Extend Bush-era income tax cuts for two years	YES

2009

Expand the Children's Health Insurance Program	NO
Provide $787 billion in tax cuts and spending increases to stimulate the economy	NO
Allow bankruptcy judges to modify certain primary-residence mortgages	NO
Create a cap-and-trade system to limit greenhouse gas emissions	NO
Provide $2 billion for the "cash for clunkers" program	NO
Establish the government as the sole provider of student loans	NO
Restrict federally funded insurance coverage for abortions in health care overhaul	YES

CQ Vote Studies

	PARTY UNITY		PRESIDENTIAL SUPPORT	
	SUPPORT	OPPOSE	SUPPORT	OPPOSE
2010	95%	5%	32%	68%
2009	90%	10%	30%	70%

Interest Groups

	AFL-CIO	ADA	CCUS	ACU
2010	8%	0%	88%	100%
2009	10%	5%	87%	96%

Florida 16

South central — Port St. Lucie, parts of Port Charlotte and Wellington

The 16th sprawls over south-central Florida, connecting wealthy east coast communities with Charlotte Harbor on the west coast. In between, rural Floridians raise cattle and grow citrus fruits and sugar cane, particularly around Lake Okeechobee. The 16th envelops the west side of the lake and also takes in most of St. Lucie County's population near the Atlantic Ocean. The district's coast-to-coast geography can prove to be more of a curse than a blessing — it is vulnerable to hurricanes and wildfires, either of which can cause billions of dollars in damage. With the lake, beaches and water needs for farming and ranching, the environment is a significant issue here.

Port St. Lucie is within commuting distance to major area cities, and it attracted some new residents fleeing skyrocketing housing prices during a since-collapsed housing boom in southern Florida. But the district has not been immune from high foreclosure rates.

A decade of population growth in the district has been driven by an influx of Hispanic residents, particularly in St. Lucie County.

The district's chunk of the still mostly white county — including Port St. Lucie and some of Fort Pierce and Lakewood Park — has seen significant population increases in both Hispanic and black communities. The district's slice of Palm Beach county also has added Hispanic residents since 2000.

Registered Republicans edge out Democrats in the district overall, but the 16th's share of St. Lucie County — the district's most populous jurisdiction, which accounts for 30 percent of its residents — has more Democrats than Republicans and many independent voters. The district's portion of Martin County is older and more Republican. John McCain won the district, taking 52 percent of its 2008 presidential vote.

Major Industry
Agriculture, government, health care

Cities
Port St. Lucie (pt.), 164,575; Port Charlotte (unincorporated) (pt.), 45,541; Wellington (pt.), 38,303

Notable
LaBelle hosts the Swamp Cabbage Festival at the end of each February.

Rep. Frederica S. Wilson (D)

Elected 2010; 1st term

It is hard to miss Wilson, well known in Florida for her flamboyant hats, although House rules bar them from the floor. An educator before she launched her political career, Wilson is a liberal who developed a reputation during her years in Florida politics for working across the aisle.

She teamed with Republican Gov. Jeb Bush on criminal justice issues and on removing the Confederate flag from the state Capitol. "I'm no stranger to working with Republicans," she said.

Wilson is one of a half-dozen Floridians on the Foreign Affairs Committee — her district is home to more Haitian Americans than any other, according to the Miami Herald, and also is home to significant immigrant populations from elsewhere in the Caribbean and Latin America.

Citing reports that deportations of Haitians had resumed for the first time since a devastating earthquake struck the country in 2010, Wilson urged the Obama administration to stop that practice. "Current political instability, widespread human rights abuses and the cholera outbreak make conditions on the ground too risky for Haitians to return safely," she told the South Florida Sun-Sentinel.

Having been an elementary school teacher, principal and school board member, Wilson hopes to play a role in revamping the Bush-era education law known as No Child Left Behind. She believes the law has hurt some students with its focus on testing and college preparedness.

A member of the Science, Space and Technology Committee, she wants the next version of the law to provide incentives for more vocational training, with the aim of teaching students how to become small-business owners and entrepreneurs.

Wilson followed Democrat Kendrick B. Meek into the Florida House and Senate, and she entered the 2010 House race after Meek announced his candidacy for the Senate seat eventually won by Republican Marco Rubio.

The Democratic primary was crowded, with a number of Haitian-American candidates splitting a sizable chunk of the ballots. Wilson won with 35 percent of the vote, tantamount to election in the overwhelmingly Democratic 17th.

Capitol Office
225-4506
wilson.house.gov
208 Cannon Bldg. 20515-0917; fax 226-0777

Committees
Foreign Affairs
Science, Space & Technology

Residence
Miami Gardens

Born
Nov. 5, 1942; Miami, Fla.

Religion
Episcopalian

Family
Widowed; three children

Education
Fisk U., B.A. 1963 (childhood education); U. of Miami, M.Ed. 1972 (elementary education)

Career
At-risk youth mentorship program founder; elementary school teacher and principal; homemaker

Political Highlights
Miami-Dade County School Board, 1992-98; Fla. House, 1998-2002; Fla. Senate, 2002-10 (minority leader pro tempore, 2006-08)

ELECTION RESULTS

2010 GENERAL

Frederica S. Wilson (D)	106,361	86.2%
Roderick D. Vereen (NPA)	17,009	13.8%

2010 PRIMARY

Frederica S. Wilson (D)	17,047	34.5%
Rudolph "Rudy" Moise (D)	7,986	16.1%
Shirley Gibson (D)	5,900	11.9%
Yolly Roberson (D)	5,080	10.3%
Phillip J. Brutus (D)	4,173	8.4%
Marleine Bastien (D)	2,967	6.0%
Scott Galvin (D)	2,750	5.6%
James Bush III (D)	2,693	5.4%
Andre L. Williams (D)	856	1.7%

Florida 17

Southeast — parts of Miami and Hollywood

The majority-black and solidly Democratic 17th is a compact district that takes in part of northeast Miami-Dade County and a slice of southeast Broward County. It stretches south from Hollywood and Pembroke Pines into Miami, taking in part of Miramar and North Miami, and it includes an array of ethnically and economically diverse neighborhoods. The district has the state's highest percentage of black residents (56 percent), and after a decade of growth, Hispanics now make up more than one-quarter of the residents. The 17th is home to Little Haiti, the cultural heart of southern Florida's Haitian community, but the Cuban-American population is not as large here as elsewhere in southern Florida. Many residents speak a language other than English at home, and a sizable cohort were born outside of the United States.

Infrastructure is important to the district, which is home to Opa-Locka Airport, a general aviation airport. Miami International Airport is located just outside the 17th. Interstate 95 — a major hurricane evacuation route — runs through the district. Health concerns are a major topic for residents, many of whom are uninsured. In addition, the HIV/AIDS epidemic has hit the 17th hard. Democrats win at all levels in the 17th. Seventy-one percent of voters are registered Democrats, and independent voters outnumber Republicans. Barack Obama won 87 percent of the district's 2008 presidential vote, his highest percentage statewide, and John McCain lost every precinct in the district.

Major Industry
Transportation, service, entertainment

Cities
Miami Gardens (pt.), 102,818; Miami (pt.), 77,377; Hollywood (pt.), 59,379

Notable
Opa-Locka's architecture is based on an Arabian theme.

Rep. Ileana Ros-Lehtinen (R)

Capitol Office
225-3931
www.house.gov/ros-lehtinen
2206 Rayburn Bldg. 20515; fax 225-5620

Committees
Foreign Affairs - Chairwoman

Residence
Miami

Born
July 15, 1952; Havana, Cuba

Religion
Episcopalian

Family
Husband, Dexter Lehtinen; two children, two stepchildren

Education
Miami-Dade Community College, A.A. 1972 (English); Florida International U., B.A. 1975 (English & education), M.S. 1986 (education); U. of Miami, Ph.D. 2004 (education)

Career
Teacher; private school administrator

Political Highlights
Fla. House, 1982-86; Fla. Senate, 1986-89

ELECTION RESULTS

2010 GENERAL

Ileana Ros-Lehtinen (R)	102,360	68.9%
Rolando A. Banciella (D)	46,235	31.1%

2010 PRIMARY

Ileana Ros-Lehtinen (R)	unopposed

2008 GENERAL

Ileana Ros-Lehtinen (R)	140,617	57.9%
Annette Taddeo (D)	102,372	42.1%

Previous Winning Percentages
2006 (62%); 2004 (65%); 2002 (69%); 2000 (100%); 1998 (100%); 1996 (100%); 1994 (100%); 1992 (67%); 1990 (60%); 1989 Special Election (53%)

Elected 1989; 11th full term

Ros-Lehtinen's ascension to chairwoman of the Foreign Affairs Committee gives her a prominent platform from which to serve as a conservative counterweight to much of the Obama administration's foreign policy agenda.

One of the strongest anti-Castro voices on Capitol Hill, Ros-Lehtinen (full name: il-ee-AH-na ross-LAY-tin-nen) also has sought to shape U.S. foreign policy in regions beyond Cuba. She has long advocated pro-Israel policies and seeks to penalize nations, particularly Iran, that tolerate terrorism, violate human rights and pose a nuclear threat.

The first Cuban-American and first Hispanic woman elected to Congress, she also looks out for the thousands of immigrants seeking to flee the Cuban Communist regime, as her family did when she was a young girl.

The most obvious effect of Ros-Lehtinen becoming Foreign Affairs chairwoman is expected to be her strong opposition to lifting or even relaxing the trade embargo against Cuba. She is a leading opponent of President Obama's proposals to lift travel restrictions to Cuba and remove limits on remittances sent by exiles to families and friends on the island.

Even before becoming chairwoman, she had an effect on other nations' relations with Cuba. In 2010, Castro said in an interview that Israel had a right to exist as a Jewish state, leading Israeli President Shimon Peres to thank him. Some analysts viewed the exchange as a possible opening to warmer relations. Ros-Lehtinen took exception to that view, and Prime Minister Benjamin Netanyahu called her to clarify that the remarks were not intended to imply any new diplomatic initiative between Israel and Cuba.

"I just said look, this guy has been an enemy of Israel, just because he said something that a normal person would say — after 50 years of anti-Israel incitement, it's one phrase from an old guy who doesn't even know where he's standing," Ros-Lehtinen told Politico.

Ros-Lehtinen will make inter-American relations a priority for the committee, and she plans to re-introduce legislation that would help coordinate anti-terrorism efforts in the region.

She also said that preventing Iran from obtaining nuclear weapons would be a high priority, while acknowledging that congressional options on such issues are limited by executive branch prerogatives. "The bills that we pass become interesting historical documents but not really bills that have been implemented," she told The Hill newspaper in early 2011. "But we hope to have oversight hearings that will ask the administration, 'Why aren't you sanctioning more banks and companies and countries? What are we doing and what are you waiting for?'"

She also wants to end U.S. participation in and funding of the U.N. Human Rights Council until the United Nations acts to "bar gross human rights abusers from hijacking the council agenda and from enjoying the legitimacy which membership on the Council affords them."

Outside the foreign policy realm, Ros-Lehtinen is a moderately reliable Republican vote, siding with her party on 85 percent of the votes in 2010 that separated majorities of the two parties, but only 70 percent in 2009. She has been an ardent supporter of equal rights for gays and lesbians, a reflection of her South Florida district that includes the Florida Keys, home to a large gay population. She backed a repeal — signed into law at the end of 2010 — of the statutory ban on openly gay people serving in the military. And she was one of 27 Republicans to vote against a 2006 proposal to ban same-sex marriage.

She also has opposed Republican leaders' hard line on immigration policy and was one of only six Republicans to vote against construction of a 700-mile fence across the U.S.-Mexico border. She backs proposals to combine enforcement with an expansion of visas and a path to legalization for illegal immigrants.

Ros-Lehtinen was a strong defender of President George W. Bush's conduct of the war in Iraq, where her stepson, a Marine, and his wife served in 2006. But she criticized the Bush administration's October 2008 decision to remove North Korea from a list of state sponsors of terrorism to keep alive a deal involving denuclearization by North Korea. Months earlier, Ros-Lehtinen had included in the legislation to overhaul the arms export control regime a requirement that North Korea take verifiable action to end its proliferation activities, such as its nuclear assistance to Syria and Iran, before it could be considered for removal from the list. And just days earlier, Bush had signed into law Ros-Lehtinen's measure advancing human rights in North Korea and speeding up resettlement of North Korean refugees in China.

On international trade, which is vital to Florida's economy, Ros-Lehtinen opposed granting President Bill Clinton the power to negotiate trade agreements that Congress could approve or reject but not amend; but in 2002, she backed such authority for Bush. In 2000, she voted against granting China normal trade status. After Bush was in office, she backed most of his trade proposals, including the 2005 Central America Free Trade Agreement.

Ros-Lehtinen's concern for Cuba and its treatment of political dissidents shaped her rise in politics. In 1999 and 2000, she led the forces arguing that 5-year-old Elián González, who was rescued at sea along with a disabled boat full of refugees, should be allowed to stay with his U.S. relatives. The boy's mother drowned in the crossing. The Clinton administration favored having him returned to his father in Cuba, which was the eventual outcome. The island's state-run newspaper, Granma, called Ros-Lehtinen a "ferocious wolf disguised as a woman." She took it as a compliment and had "loba feroz" (shortened to "loba frz") stamped on a personalized license plate.

She was 8 when her family fled Cuba for Florida. After growing up in Miami and graduating from college, she became a teacher and ran a bilingual private school in south Florida. In 2004 she completed a doctorate in education. Her dissertation studied House members' perspectives on educational testing.

In 1982, at age 30, she became the first Hispanic woman elected to the state legislature. In a 1989 special election to replace the late Democratic Rep. Claude Pepper, Ros-Lehtinen easily defeated three other candidates for the Republican nomination, then beat Democrat Gerald Richman, a Miami Beach lawyer, with 53 percent of the vote. She has not been seriously challenged since.

Key Votes

2010

Overhaul the nation's health insurance system	NO
Allow for repeal of "don't ask, don't tell"	YES
Overhaul financial services industry regulation	NO
Limit use of new Afghanistan War funds to troop withdrawal activities	NO
Change oversight of offshore drilling and lift oil spill liability cap	NO
Provide a path to legal status for some children of illegal immigrants	YES
Extend Bush-era income tax cuts for two years	YES

2009

Expand the Children's Health Insurance Program	YES
Provide $787 billion in tax cuts and spending increases to stimulate the economy	NO
Allow bankruptcy judges to modify certain primary-residence mortgages	YES
Create a cap-and-trade system to limit greenhouse gas emissions	NO
Provide $2 billion for the "cash for clunkers" program	YES
Establish the government as the sole provider of student loans	YES
Restrict federally funded insurance coverage for abortions in health care overhaul	YES

CQ Vote Studies

	PARTY UNITY		PRESIDENTIAL SUPPORT	
	Support	Oppose	Support	Oppose
2010	85%	15%	46%	54%
2009	70%	30%	53%	47%
2008	67%	33%	33%	67%
2007	79%	21%	63%	37%
2006	89%	11%	85%	15%

Interest Groups

	AFL-CIO	ADA	CCUS	ACU
2010	21%	30%	88%	70%
2009	57%	40%	73%	72%
2008	67%	65%	78%	32%
2007	46%	25%	90%	60%
2006	15%	15%	87%	63%

Florida 18

Southeast — most of Miami; Florida Keys

The 18th features the glitz of downtown Miami and the southern part of Miami Beach, but its political base comes from the Hispanic-dominated areas west of downtown.

The district winds its way south along the coast from Miami and follows U.S. 1 through the Florida Keys, taking in downtrodden sections of Little Havana, as well as wealthy Coral Gables (home to the University of Miami), Key Biscayne and Fisher Island.

The Keys — a 120-mile-long island chain between the Gulf of Mexico and the Atlantic Ocean — and in particular Key West, have a significant gay and lesbian population, in addition to older natives who adhere to the independence and environmentalism of the "Conch Republic." The Keys are vulnerable to hurricanes, and the economy depends on out-of-state visitors. Miami International Airport, which is nearby in the 21st, and the Port of Miami and are major transportation centers that feed the local trade and tourism industries.

Despite this bedrock industry, falling real estate values and rising foreclosure rates are having a deep impact on Miami-Dade County and Miami in particular. Local officials hope that redevelopment projects in midtown Miami and a new stadium in Little Havana for baseball's Marlins will give an economic boost to the area.

A majority of district residents were born outside the United States, and two-thirds of the population is Hispanic. While the older Cuban- American base in this district is reliably Republican and stridently anti-Fidel Castro, issues such as the economy are increasingly important to younger voters. Overall, residents tend to be conservative on foreign policy issues but more in line with Democrats on welfare and other social issues. Democrat Barack Obama won 51 percent of the district's 2008 presidential vote, although there are still pockets of GOP support in areas such as Little Havana and Coral Gables.

Major Industry
Trade, transportation, tourism

Cities
Miami (pt.), 312,331; Miami Beach (pt.), 75,056; Coral Gables, 46,780; Westchester (unincorporated), 29,862; Key West, 24,649

Notable
"Independence Day" celebrations in the Conch Republic honor the one-minute rebellion of Key West residents against a 1982 federal blockade.

Rep. Ted Deutch (D)

Capitol Office
225-3001
deutch.house.gov
1024 Longworth Bldg. 20515-0919; fax 225-5974

Committees
Foreign Affairs
Judiciary

Residence
Boca Raton

Born
May 7, 1966; Bethlehem, Pa.

Religion
Jewish

Family
Wife, Jill Deutch; three children

Education
U. of Michigan, B.A. 1988 (political science), J.D. 1990

Career
Lawyer

Political Highlights
Fla. Senate, 2006-10

ELECTION RESULTS

2010 GENERAL
Ted Deutch (D)	132,098	62.6%
Joe Budd (R)	78,733	37.3%

2010 PRIMARY
Ted Deutch (D)	unopposed

2010 SPECIAL
Ted Deutch (D)	43,269	62.1%
Edward J. Lynch (R)	24,549	35.2%
Jim McCormick	1,905	2.7%

Elected April 2010; 1st full term

Deutch got a late start in the 111th Congress but made good use of his time. He arrived in Washington in April 2010; by May he had already set up his own leadership political action committee, which he used to move money to the Democratic Congressional Campaign Committee, a sure way of getting in the good graces of his party leadership. And he staked out positions on issues of paramount importance to his Florida constituency: championing sanctions against Iran and defending Social Security.

Deutch represents a solidly Democratic region with a large number of condo communities that are home to one of the largest Jewish retiree populations of any district in the country.

Building on his work as a state senator to get Florida to divest from Iran, Deutch won a seat on the Foreign Affairs Committee and quickly became a leading voice on implementing the sanctions law enacted in 2010. That measure was enacted less than two months after he won a special election to succeed Democrat Robert Wexler, who resigned from Congress to become president of the S. Daniel Abraham Center for Middle East Peace.

Attempting to go further, Deutch introduced legislation that would require companies that do business in Iran to disclose that information in their SEC filings.

Deutch has been a vocal opponent of raising the eligibility age for Social Security. And, after a second consecutive year without a cost-of-living adjustment (COLA) for current recipients, he introduced legislation to adjust the formula for calculating the COLA to put more emphasis on price increases in goods and services. He also supported a one-time $250 payment to retirees. "The method by which cost-of-living adjustments are calculated is clearly broken, and seniors are right to be frustrated," he said. And he wants to phase in an elimination of the cap on wages subject to Social Security taxes.

He vigorously opposed the one-year "holiday" on 2 percentage points of the Social Security payroll tax that was enacted at the end of 2010 as part of legislation extending the George W. Bush-era tax rates for two years.

"The debate over the expiration of the Bush tax cuts has illustrated that taxes are easy to cut but hard to restore. So, one year of reduced employee contributions to Social Security could easily become two years, and some will surely argue they should even be made permanent," he wrote in The Huffington Post.

But he ended up voting for what he called "this deeply flawed bill," saying the package's extension of expanded unemployment benefits and the extension of the lower tax rates for the middle class were necessary.

Deutch also sits on the Judiciary Committee. Following the April 2010 oil spill in the Gulf of Mexico, he backed legislation to revise maritime liability law to allow the families of those killed in the explosion of the Deepwater Horizon oil rig to be compensated for non-monetary losses.

Where Wexler was, in his own words, a "fire-breathing liberal," Deutch projects a more civil tone while expressing many of the same sentiments. During a special-election candidate debate in West Boca Raton in February 2010, he answered a combustible question about the use of enhanced interrogation methods on enemy combatants by saying simply, "I'm not sure exactly what 'enhanced interrogation' methods are. If they are torture, no. That's not what we do in this country."

Deutch has been a reliable voice for his liberal constituency, as would be expected in a district that gave Barack Obama 65 percent of its presidential vote in 2008. That goes for social issues, as well. In the state Senate, he opposed a bill that mirrors the 2004 federal Unborn Victims of Violence Act, which established a separate offense for federal crimes against pregnant women that result in harm to the fetus. Deutch argued that, under the state legislation, doctors could potentially be prosecuted for performing abortions.

In Congress, looking to assist people in his district who might face the ravages of a hurricane, Deutch won adoption of an amendment to energy conservation legislation that extended rebates to families who choose energy efficient upgrades when repairing their homes after natural disasters.

Deutch was born in Bethlehem, Pa., and earned his undergraduate and law degrees at the University of Michigan. After a brief stop after college at the Washington, D.C., law firm known today as Dickstein Shapiro, Deutch moved to Cleveland before settling in South Florida in 1998. He began work at the firm Broad and Cassell, where his brother also practiced law.

Before he entered politics, Deutch became very active in the local Jewish community in Palm Beach County. That's where he first met Wexler, and the two worked together on issues affecting the local Jewish community.

"Ted was very active and still is in the South Palm Beach county Jewish federation, and we both share a passion for the American-Israeli relationship, which is also, of course, very important to the interests of a very significant number of our mutual constituents," Wexler told Roll Call.

Deutch's path from electoral novice to congressman representing a safe district has been surprisingly short. When he decided to jump into an open state Senate seat race, he went to Wexler for support.

Originally Wexler planned to stay neutral in the primary. But when the front-runner, a well-funded state representative, took issue with Wexler's endorsement policy, a war of words developed. By the spring of that year Wexler became Deutch's most prominent supporter.

When Wexler decided to retire from Congress, Deutch moved quickly, joining the race the next day. Top potential rivals began dropping out of the race and other party endorsements flowed in, including those of neighboring Reps. Ron Klein and Debbie Wasserman Schultz. Deutch also had the backing of former President Bill Clinton, who became a key fundraiser.

In the special-election primary, Deutch beat Ben Graber, a former Broward County commissioner and former state legislator. He went on to handily defeat Republican Edward Lynch in the special election. In the November general election, Deutch was able to increase his margin against Republican Joe Budd despite the GOP wave that swept four Florida Democratic incumbents from office, including Klein.

Key Votes

2010	
Allow for repeal of "don't ask, don't tell"	YES
Overhaul financial services industry regulation	YES
Limit use of new Afghanistan War funds to troop withdrawal activities	NO
Change oversight of offshore drilling and lift oil spill liability cap	YES
Provide a path to legal status for some children of illegal immigrants	YES
Extend Bush-era income tax cuts for two years	YES

CQ Vote Studies

	PARTY UNITY		PRESIDENTIAL SUPPORT	
	SUPPORT	OPPOSE	SUPPORT	OPPOSE
2010	98%	2%	97%	3%

Interest Groups

	AFL-CIO	ADA	CCUS	ACU
2010	100%	80%	20%	0%

Southeast — parts of Coral Springs, Margate and Boca Raton

Seventy percent of the heavily Democratic 19th's residents live in Palm Beach County and the rest live in Broward County, mostly west of Interstate 95, where subdivisions and gated communities dot the landscape. The 19th has no coastline in either county, and it stretches from a small part of West Palm Beach as far south as a sliver of Fort Lauderdale, taking in parts of Boca Raton, Margate and Deerfield Beach. In the last decade, the district's Hispanic population has grown to one-fifth of the 19th's residents, and the black population has more than doubled.

Despite a high percentage of residents age 65 or older and a history as a home to retirees — elderly voters still make up a significant portion of the electorate in the 19th's portion of Palm Beach County — the district has seen a shift toward a more middle-aged population.

Older residents make health care an important industry in the district, and federal assistance for the elderly dominates the political agenda. A large Jewish community, primarily in condominium communities that replaced previously rural land in the district, adds foreign policy concerns and U.S. relations with Israel to the political discussion.

Health care facilities in Palm Beach and Broward counties support the district's economy. The 19th's portion of Boca Raton has been home to corporate headquarters for several years and has an established business atmosphere. But the district has not escaped the high unemployment rates plaguing the state, with large-scale layoffs having an impact.

Retirees and the politically active Jewish community have traditionally provided a consistent base of Democratic support throughout much of the district. Registered Democrats outnumber Republicans by more than 2-to-1 here, and Barack Obama won 65 percent of the district's vote in the 2008 presidential election.

Major Industry
Health care, financial services

Cities
Coral Springs (pt.), 77,479; Margate (pt.), 42,477; Greenacres, 37,573; Tamarac (pt.), 28,253; Coconut Creek (pt.), 25,475

Notable
Coconut Creek is home to a butterfly and hummingbird aviary called Butterfly World.

Rep. Debbie Wasserman Schultz (D)

Capitol Office
225-7931
www.house.gov/wassermanschultz
118 Cannon Bldg. 20515-0920; fax 226-2052

Committees
Budget
Judiciary

Residence
Weston

Born
Sept. 27, 1966; Queens, N.Y.

Religion
Jewish

Family
Husband, Steve Schultz; three children

Education
U. of Florida, B.A. 1988 (political science), M.A. 1990 (political science)

Career
University program administrator; college instructor; state legislative aide

Political Highlights
Fla. House, 1992-2000 (Democratic leader pro tempore, 2000); Fla. Senate, 2000-04; Democratic National Committee chairwoman, 2011-present

ELECTION RESULTS

2010 GENERAL

Wasserman Schultz (D)	100,787	60.1%
Karen Harrington (R)	63,845	38.1%

2010 PRIMARY

Wasserman Schultz (D)	unopposed

2008 GENERAL

Wasserman Schultz (D)	202,832	77.5%
Margaret Hostetter (X)	58,958	22.5%

Previous Winning Percentages
2006 (100%); 2004 (70%)

Elected 2004; 4th term

Wasserman Schultz has established herself as a fast-rising star of the Democratic Party who has deft fundraising abilities and an assertive presence. Her popularity among peers led to a spot as chief deputy whip and as vice chairwoman of the Democratic Steering and Policy Committee, which makes committee assignments.

When Democratic National Committee (DNC) Chairman Tim Kaine announced in April 2011 that he would give up his post to run for the Senate, Wasserman Schultz was tapped by President Obama to take over. In that role, she'll be as much a creature of the White House as Congress, where she had to surrender her spot as the Democratic Congressional Campaign Committee's national chairwoman overseeing incumbent retention and redistricting in order to lead the DNC.

She had already been bumped from her seat on the Appropriations Committee when the new Republican majority reduced the size of the panel in the 112th Congress (2011-12).

In addition to her quick climb up the ranks, Wasserman Schultz has had some legislative victories — she secured almost $40 million in federal funds for South Florida for various community projects, helped provide funds for Everglades restoration and won enactment of a handful of child-safety measures. She'll be somewhat able to keep her eye on the fiscal cookie jar from her seat on the Budget Committee.

But she is best known for her no-nonsense personality and devotion to the Democratic leadership. She called a GOP-sponsored bill aimed at ensuring no tax money is used to pay for abortions "a violent act against women," in an interview with the website Raw Story.

Speaking as a former appropriator, she told Roll Call that "Republicans are going to have to own up — they're going to have to put their name next to those cuts. They're going to have to make sure that they explain why it is that their decisions on cuts are not going to strangle the recovery."

She defended Minority Leader Nancy Pelosi of California against charges from fiscally conservative "Blue Dog" Democrats that the leader had not reached beyond her liberal allies after the Democrats' stinging defeat in House elections in 2010.

"I have seen a very diverse array of members that previously — I don't think — would have been at the table," she said to Roll Call. "So I think she's making a significant effort."

In the 112th Congress she was back on the Judiciary Committee — where she served prior to becoming an appropriator — before taking a leave of absence because of her DNC duties. In her previous stint on the panel, Wasserman Schultz battled conservatives on several fronts. During committee debate in 2006 on a bill aimed at preserving the phrase "under God" in the Pledge of Allegiance, language that had been ruled unconstitutional by a federal court, she said Republicans supporting the measure were ignoring "the things that people actually have to deal with in their daily lives, like gas prices, health care costs, fiscal responsibility, a real debate on Iraq."

In 2005, when congressional Republicans sought to intervene in the high-profile court case concerning Terri Schiavo, a severely brain-damaged Florida woman kept alive by a feeding tube, Wasserman Schultz became a forceful opponent of intervention. She was well-versed in the long legal battle from her days in the Florida Legislature.

Wasserman Schultz has three young children, including a set of twins, and she often flies to Washington on Tuesday mornings, and back home on Thursday nights, to maximize time spent with her family. She occasionally gives her children a taste of Congress by bringing them to hearings. Her husband, banker Steve Schultz, stays with their children in Florida during the week.

In December 2007, President George W. Bush signed into law her bill providing federal grants to states that require fences around pools and devices that prevent children from becoming trapped in drains. The House in November 2007 passed her bill expanding investigations of computer-generated pornography, authorizing more than $1 billion over eight years to hire federal and state investigators and to establish a special counsel's office in the Justice Department. The measure was later wrapped into a broader Senate bill and signed into law.

Wasserman Schultz announced in March 2009 that she successfully had battled breast cancer and was going public to warn young women of its prevalence. "I'm a very focused, methodical person, and I wasn't going to let this beat me," she told The Miami Herald.

She introduced legislation that directs the Centers for Disease Control and Prevention to implement an education campaign on breast cancer's threat to young women. The measure became law as part of the health care overhaul legislation enacted in 2010. And in 2009, with Missouri Republican Jo Ann Emerson, she established a charity softball game featuring female members of Congress; the game raises money for the Young Survival Coalition, which deals with issues related to young women and breast cancer.

Wasserman Schultz grew up in New York, on the southern shore of Long Island. Her father was the chief financial officer for a girls' clothing company, Roanna Togs; her mother was a horticulturist. She attended the University of Florida, her father's alma mater, earning both undergraduate and graduate degrees in Gainesville.

She has said that she "never really wanted to do anything other than be a member of a legislative body." Wasserman Schultz made a foray into politics when she was an aide to Florida state Rep. Peter Deutsch, a Democrat. She followed in his footsteps, first winning Deutsch's seat when he ran successfully for Congress. Local party bosses dismissed her, but she prevailed in a six-way primary and became, at 26, the youngest woman ever to serve in the Florida House. Eight years later, she was elected to the state Senate.

After four years there, she won Deutsch's House seat, taking more than 70 percent of the vote in the heavily Democratic district when he waged an unsuccessful Senate campaign. Even before getting herself elected to the House, she donated $100,000 from her campaign to help other candidates in 2004, exceeding amounts given by many senior House Democrats.

She has had no trouble winning re-election.

Key Votes

2010

Overhaul the nation's health insurance system	YES
Allow for repeal of "don't ask, don't tell"	YES
Overhaul financial services industry regulation	YES
Limit use of new Afghanistan War funds to troop withdrawal activities	NO
Change oversight of offshore drilling and lift oil spill liability cap	YES
Provide a path to legal status for some children of illegal immigrants	YES
Extend Bush-era income tax cuts for two years	YES

2009

Expand the Children's Health Insurance Program	YES
Provide $787 billion in tax cuts and spending increases to stimulate the economy	YES
Allow bankruptcy judges to modify certain primary-residence mortgages	YES
Create a cap-and-trade system to limit greenhouse gas emissions	YES
Provide $2 billion for the "cash for clunkers" program	YES
Establish the government as the sole provider of student loans	YES
Restrict federally funded insurance coverage for abortions in health care overhaul	NO

CQ Vote Studies

	PARTY UNITY		PRESIDENTIAL SUPPORT	
	SUPPORT	OPPOSE	SUPPORT	OPPOSE
2010	99%	1%	95%	5%
2009	99%	1%	97%	3%
2008	99%	1%	13%	87%
2007	98%	2%	6%	94%
2006	94%	6%	33%	67%

Interest Groups

	AFL-CIO	ADA	CCUS	ACU
2010	100%	90%	14%	0%
2009	100%	100%	40%	0%
2008	100%	100%	59%	0%
2007	100%	90%	55%	0%
2006	100%	95%	40%	4%

Florida 20

Southeast — parts of Hollywood, Sunrise, Davie and Fort Lauderdale

Middle-class suburbs mix with beach communities as the 20th snakes through Broward and Miami-Dade counties as far north as Tamarac and as far south as Miami Beach. The district takes in part of Fort Lauderdale and accounts for about one-third of Broward's population.

In addition to western Broward suburbs, the 20th wraps around to reach some coastal northeastern Miami suburbs, with their golf courses and condominium developments. It twists through portions of Hollywood and Hallandale and moves south into Aventura and North Miami before jumping the Intracoastal Waterway to take in highly developed Bal Harbour and a chunk of northern Miami Beach.

Economic downturns have hit Broward hard. The collapse of the housing market in southern Florida resulted in high foreclosure rates, stagnating home sales and vacant residential units in the district. Residents and officials are concerned about widespread layoffs in the once-thriving financial services sector, and employment levels have not begun to rebound as

they have in other metropolitan areas.

Two-thirds white 10 years ago, the 20th now has a decidedly more Hispanic flavor. A 10-percentage-point increase in the Hispanic population — the biggest jump in the percentage of Hispanic residents of any district statewide — and significant growth in the district's black communities mean that the district is now only slightly majority-white.

The 20th's large Jewish population makes U.S.-Israel relations politically important. Wilton Manors has a significant gay and lesbian community, and Dania Beach is a prominent gay resort area. Davie, with cattle ranches and horse farms in the central part of the 20th, has retained some of its rural feel. Democrats tend to win elections here at all levels.

Major Industry
Tourism, business services, retail

Cities
Davie (pt.), 84,064; Hollywood (pt.), 81,206; Sunrise (pt.), 70,981; Plantation (pt.), 67,850; Weston (pt.), 65,333; Pembroke Pines (pt.), 42,721

Notable
The BankAtlantic Center, home to the National Hockey League's Florida Panthers, is located in Sunrise.

Rep. Mario Diaz-Balart (R)

Capitol Office
225-4211
diaz-balart.house.gov
436 Cannon Bldg. 20515; fax 225-8576

Committees
Appropriations

Residence
Miami

Born
Sept. 25, 1961; Fort Lauderdale, Fla.

Religion
Roman Catholic

Family
Wife, Tia Diaz-Balart; one child

Education
U. of South Florida, attended 1979-82

Career
Marketing firm executive; mayoral aide

Political Highlights
Fla. House, 1988-92; Fla. Senate, 1992-2000;
Fla. House, 2000-02

ELECTION RESULTS

2010 GENERAL

Mario Diaz-Balart (R)		unopposed

2010 PRIMARY

Mario Diaz-Balart (R)		unopposed

2008 GENERAL

Mario Diaz-Balart (R)	130,891	53.0%
Joe Garcia (D)	115,820	46.9%

Previous Winning Percentages
2006 (59%); 2004 (100%); 2002 (65%)

Elected 2002; 5th term

Diaz-Balart maintains an unwavering hard line against Cuba's Castro regime. But like his older brother Lincoln, whose 21st district he switched to in the 2010 elections, Diaz-Balart strives to cast a wider legislative net. He said his immediate focus is economic recovery and job creation. His new placement on the Appropriations Committee gives him a powerful seat from which to act on those issues.

"Priority No. 1, priority No. 10, is the unemployment situation and the economy," said Diaz-Balart (DEE-az ba-LART). "To me, that also entails the deficit, spending and debt. The last four years, particularly the last two, have brought us to the brink of bankruptcy."

Diaz-Balart says he wants "everything on the table" to address the country's fiscal problems — but "everything" means every spending program. "When I say everything, everything to help to lower the debt and to help economic growth, which means everything except for tax increases," he said.

To that end, he backed an extension of the Bush-era tax rates that was enacted at the end of the 111th Congress (2009-10). "I think if you want to destroy job creation, raise taxes on any American, particularly on businesses," he said.

But when it comes to spending, Diaz-Balart, formerly a member of the Budget Committee, hasn't always made austerity a hallmark. He supported the Democrats' "cash for clunkers" tax credit in the summer of 2009 that gave Americans money for trading in their cars for more fuel-efficient vehicles. He was also among a group of 40 Republicans who joined Democrats in early 2009 to pass an expansion of the Children's Health Insurance Program, which covers children whose low-income families make too much money to qualify for Medicaid.

Still, he is viewed as an ally of GOP deficit hawk and Budget Chairman Paul D. Ryan of Wisconsin and he is looked to as a cost-cutter on Appropriations.

Diaz-Balart ties repealing the health care law enacted in 2010 to any economic restoration — he voted to repeal it in early 2011 and suggested that further efforts at piecemeal dismantling and defunding would also gain his support. "We have to look at how we can reverse some of those job-killing aspects of the health care bill," he said.

Pending trade deals with Colombia and Panama have Diaz-Balart's strong backing. "That's thousands of jobs without spending a penny," he said.

Diaz-Balart sits on the State-Foreign Operations spending panel, where he has defended foreign aid against conservative assaults, arguing that such programs are "in the U.S. national security interest," while acknowledging that some cuts are likely in the offing.

Diaz-Balart wants a comprehensive energy policy that reduces the nation's reliance on foreign oil, even when gasoline is cheap. He wants to open up more areas for domestic energy production, including Alaska's Arctic National Wildlife Refuge and offshore areas. "I've never quite understood why Congress has basically outlawed a number of domestic sources of energy that are plentiful, abundant and that are safe and clean," he said.

One area where Diaz-Balart consistently sides with Democrats is on immigration.

In 2010 he backed a measure that would create a path to conditional legal status for some illegal immigrants who go to college or join the military. In 2005, he voted with Democrats against a bill that tightened rules for immigrants trying to obtain asylum, and he sharply criticized GOP immigration legislation that would have made being an illegal immigrant a felony. Diaz-Balart said the idea was "offensive, excessive and demonized hard-working immigrants."

Much of his congressional career has been spent in the shadow of his older brother — at one time critics dismissed him as "Lincoln Lite," and during the 111th Congress they both sided with their party in less than 82 percent of the votes that saw a majority of Republican oppose a majority of Democrats. But Mario differs from his Lincoln in several respects. While Lincoln was born in Cuba and lived there until Fidel Castro forced their family into exile, Mario was born in Fort Lauderdale. Mario is quick-talking and gregarious; Lincoln, who retired in 2010, is more an inside player.

Diaz-Balart's family is sometimes referred to as the "Cuban Kennedys." Florida International University's law school building was named in honor of Diaz-Balart's grandfather. His father, Rafael Diaz-Balart, was once majority leader of the Cuban House, and his aunt was Castro's first wife and mother of Castro's son. According to Ann Louise Bardach's book, "Cuba Confidential: Love and Vengeance in Miami and Havana," Castro used to jokingly boast to foreign guests about having two nephews serving in Congress, but he also has called the Diaz-Balarts his "most repulsive enemies." The Diaz-Balarts were a wealthy and politically prominent family under Cuban leader Fulgencio Batista, before Castro toppled Batista's government in 1959. Their home was looted and burned as the family vacationed in Paris.

The youngest of four brothers, Diaz-Balart dropped out of the University of South Florida to work on the campaign of Miami Mayor Xavier Suarez in 1985, the same year he and his brother switched to the Republican Party.

In 1988, he was elected to the Florida House, and four years later to the state Senate. Forced out of the Senate by term limits in 2000, he ran successfully to return to the state House. When Florida got two new seats in Congress as a result of the census, Diaz-Balart was appointed by Florida House Speaker Tom Feeney to head the panel drawing a new congressional map. Diaz-Balart drew a Hispanic-majority district, the 25th, for himself.

In his first federal election, Diaz-Balart outspent Annie Betancourt, a Cuban-American Democrat, 6-to-1 and won with 65 percent of the vote. He was unopposed in 2004 and won easily in 2006. In 2008, he faced a stronger challenger in Democrat Joe Garcia, the former head of the Cuban American National Foundation, winning with 53 percent of the vote.

In 2010, he switched out of the 25th District after four terms because of his brother's retirement from the less competitive 21st. Diaz-Balart had the easiest race of all of Florida's incumbent lawmakers by running unopposed. His old district was won by Republican David Rivera.

Key Votes

2010

Overhaul the nation's health insurance system	NO
Allow for repeal of "don't ask, don't tell"	NO
Overhaul financial services industry regulation	NO
Limit use of new Afghanistan War funds to troop withdrawal activities	NO
Change oversight of offshore drilling and lift oil spill liability cap	NO
Provide a path to legal status for some children of illegal immigrants	YES
Extend Bush-era income tax cuts for two years	YES

2009

Expand the Children's Health Insurance Program	YES
Provide $787 billion in tax cuts and spending increases to stimulate the economy	NO
Allow bankruptcy judges to modify certain primary-residence mortgages	YES
Create a cap-and-trade system to limit greenhouse gas emissions	NO
Provide $2 billion for the "cash for clunkers" program	YES
Establish the government as the sole provider of student loans	NO
Restrict federally funded insurance coverage for abortions in health care overhaul	YES

CQ Vote Studies

	PARTY UNITY		PRESIDENTIAL SUPPORT	
	SUPPORT	OPPOSE	SUPPORT	OPPOSE
2010	87%	13%	40%	60%
2009	74%	26%	44%	56%
2008	80%	20%	41%	59%
2007	84%	16%	68%	32%
2006	90%	10%	90%	10%

Interest Groups

	AFL-CIO	ADA	CCUS	ACU
2010	21%	20%	88%	79%
2009	52%	45%	80%	72%
2008	60%	55%	83%	52%
2007	42%	25%	89%	60%
2006	14%	15%	93%	64%

Florida 21

Southeast — most of Hialeah and Kendall

The Hispanic-majority 21st District is adjacent to the eastern edge of the Florida Everglades and includes middle-class suburbs in Miami-Dade County and a slice of Broward County, from parts of Pembroke Pines and Miramar in the north through most of Hialeah in its center and much of the Colombian-American area of Kendall to the south. It includes one-fourth of Miami-Dade's population.

Residents tend to commute from Hialeah, which has a significant Cuban-American community, to other parts of the Miami area for work. Miramar, where the population has skyrocketed in the last decade, and Pembroke Pines host young professionals from Latin America. The 21st has the highest percentage of foreign-born residents (56 percent) of any district in the nation.

Transportation-related businesses, including Carnival Cruise Lines, have headquarters and facilities close to Miami International Airport in Fountainbleau, but tourism-based industries can be volatile and the local economy is vulnerable to dips mirroring nationwide economic downturns. The airport — a major international hub that carries tens of millions of pas-

sengers annually, many of them to Latin America — is a key employment source and economic driver in southern Florida.

Traditionally, the 21st's politics center around immigration issues and opposition to Fidel Castro, but these political norms are shifting, and much of the local Cuban-American community no longer supports continuing the embargo against Cuba.

Residents also take moderate stances on labor and social policy matters, and nearly one-quarter of registered voters here are unaffiliated with a political party. Historically GOP-leaning in statewide and federal elections, the district now holds nearly as many registered Democrats as Republicans. Republican John McCain took 51 percent of the district's 2008 presidential vote.

Major Industry

Transportation, trade, small business

Cities

Hialeah (pt.), 204,437; Pembroke Pines (pt.), 63,021; Kendall (unincorporated) (pt.), 60,083; Miramar (part), 58,246

Notable

The Audubon Society has designated Hialeah Park Racetrack a sanctuary for the American flamingo.

Rep. Allen B. West (R)

Capitol Office
225-3026
west.house.gov
1708 Longworth Bldg. 20515-0922; fax 225-8398

Committees
Armed Services
Small Business

Residence
Plantation

Born
Feb. 7, 1961; Atlanta, Ga.

Religion
Christian

Family
Wife, Angela West; two children

Education
U. of Tennessee, B.A. 1983 (political science); Kansas
State U., M.A. 1996 (political science)

Military
Army, 1983-2004

Career
Army officer; military training and management
consultant; high school teacher

Political Highlights
Republican nominee for U.S. House, 2008

ELECTION RESULTS

2010 GENERAL
Allen B. West (R)	118,890	54.4%
Ron Klein (D)	99,804	45.6%

2010 PRIMARY
Allen B. West (R)	30,024	76.7%
David Brady (R)	9,137	23.3%

Elected 2010; 1st term

West, a retired Army officer who arrived on Capitol Hill for orientation carrying a camouflage helmet bag, is an assertive, outspoken conservative.

One of two black Republicans elected to the House in 2010, he quickly roiled the waters and left no reason to expect he will not continue to do so.

He criticized fellow Florida Rep. Debbie Wasserman Schultz, a Democrat known for her own tart tongue, for suggesting that lawmakers needed to tone down their rhetoric. And he criticized the work schedule created by Majority Leader Eric Cantor of Virginia for not being rigorous enough.

Unlike Tim Scott of South Carolina, the other African-American Republican in the House, West joined the Congressional Black Caucus. "You had 42 blacks that ran on the Republican ticket this cycle. Fourteen of them made it to the general election and two of us made it to the House of Representatives. So I think that there is a new movement that needs to have a voice in the Congressional Black Caucus," he said on Fox News in early 2011.

In addition to the Small Business Committee, West won a seat on the Armed Services Committee, where he can put to use his military experience, which includes service in several combat zones. After his discharge from the Army, he trained Afghan soldiers as a private contractor.

While in Iraq, he made headlines in 2003 for firing a pistol near the head of an Iraqi policeman believed to have information about an attack. The man admitted to a plot and named accomplices, but later recanted all of it. The incident — and the criticism it engendered from some quarters — made West a hero in conservative circle. He was found guilty of aggravated assault and fined $5,000, but the Army decided against a court-martial.

After his military service, West was briefly a high school social studies teacher.

He tried and failed to unseat Democratic Rep. Ron Klein in 2008, losing by 9 percentage points. The 2010 rematch was a hard-fought affair. At one point, a mailer from the Florida Democratic Party revealed West's Social Security number. West prevailed the second time around, winning 54 percent of the vote.

Florida 22

Southeast— coastal Broward and Palm Beach counties, part of Fort Lauderdale

The 22nd follows Route A1A down a sliver of Atlantic coastline from northern Palm Beach County to Fort Lauderdale in Broward County. Although it reaches inland in places to pick up middle-class suburbs and gated communities, the district is defined by its upscale beachfront areas, including parts of Boca Raton. Mostly white and well-off, the 22nd has a large Jewish population.

The district has a corporate presence and is home to Fort Lauderdale/Hollywood International Airport, Port Everglades and the Port of Palm Beach. It boasts ritzy hotels and shopping centers, and the ports lure cruise line and shipping business. Economic downturns stalled some development, and layoffs hit retail, construction and financial services sectors. The wealth of many district residents helps protect them from economic pressures, but the area relies on tourism. Large hospitals and the local health care industry, serving the elderly population and many military veterans, support the district's economy.

Social Security, the Middle East and port issues top the political agenda here. Residents also are concerned about roads, as urbanization and development have stretched aging infrastructure and exacerbated heavy traffic problems. Republicans no longer hold a voter registration edge in the 22nd, and the district is politically competitive. Barack Obama won here with 52 percent of the district's vote for president.

Major Industry
Health care, tourism, shipping

Cities
Boca Raton (pt.), 65,152; Fort Lauderdale (pt.), 62,122; Pompano Beach (pt.), 47,088

Notable
The International Swimming Hall of Fame Museum is in Fort Lauderdale.

Rep. Alcee L. Hastings (D)

Capitol Office
225-1313
alceehastings.house.gov
2353 Rayburn Bldg. 20515-0923; fax 225-1171

Committees
Rules

Residence
Miramar

Born
Sept. 5, 1936; Altamonte Springs, Fla.

Religion
African Methodist Episcopal

Family
Divorced; three children

Education
Fisk U., B.S. 1958 (zoology & botany); Howard U., attended 1958-60 (law); Florida A&M U., J.D. 1963

Career
Judge; lawyer

Political Highlights
Sought Democratic nomination for U.S. Senate, 1970; U.S. District Court judge, 1979-89; Democratic nominee for Fla. secretary of state, 1990

ELECTION RESULTS

2010 GENERAL

Alcee L. Hastings (D)	100,066	79.1%
Bernard Sansaricq (R)	26,414	20.9%

2010 PRIMARY

Alcee L. Hastings (D)		unopposed

2008 GENERAL

Alcee L. Hastings (D)	172,835	82.2%
Marion D. Thorpe Jr. (R)	37,431	17.8%

Previous Winning Percentages
2006 (100%); 2004 (100%); 2002 (77%); 2000 (76%);
1998 (100%); 1996 (73%); 1994 (100%); 1992 (59%)

Elected 1992; 10th term

Hastings' past continues to shadow his achievements despite his popularity back home and his loyalty to the Democratic Party. The 10-term congressman is influential in his state and party, and he is a national leader on human rights. But Hastings' impeachment as a federal judge has been a roadblock to his moving into House leadership roles.

The House impeached him in 1988 after he was hit with criminal charges related to a bribery conspiracy; the Senate removed him from office the following year. He had been cleared of the charges before being removed from his seat, but the issue still dogs him even as he has developed a track record in Congress.

Hastings was passed over for the chairmanship of the Select Intelligence Committee at the start of the 110th Congress (2007-08) after Republicans raised the issue of the bribery case and his impeachment. When he saw trouble looming, Hastings told incoming Speaker Nancy Pelosi of California he would bow out. She "thanked me, and she hugged me," he said. Still, he felt bitter about the outcome. "No one ever cared that I was found not guilty in a court of law, that I was innocent of what I was charged with," he said.

He then shifted much of his attention from intelligence matters to foreign affairs. Pelosi appointed him chairman of the U.S. Commission on Security and Cooperation in Europe, better known as the Helsinki Commission, an independent government agency that focuses on democracy and human rights. In 2009, he handed over the gavel to Sen. Benjamin L. Cardin, a Democrat from Maryland, assuming the role of co-chairman.

In 2006, he wrapped up a second one-year term as the first American president of the Parliamentary Assembly of the Organization for Security and Cooperation in Europe, a 56-nation organization of mostly European nations that focuses on security issues, ranging from arms control to human rights. In that position, he visited nearly three dozen countries, continuing his longtime interest in election monitoring in places such as Azerbaijan, Ukraine and Belarus, where he led a group of 400 election monitors in March 2006.

As chairman of the Helsinki Commission, he scolded European governments at a June 2007 hearing on the future of the U.S. military detention center on the U.S. naval base at Guantánamo Bay, Cuba, complaining that they criticized the U.S. government but refused to take custody of more terror suspects.

Despite being denied a gavel while the Democrats maintained their majority, Hastings remained a loyal party man, and he has not been completely locked out of the hierarchy: He sits on the leadership-dominated Rules Committee. When Republicans previously controlled the House, he used his Rules seat and his fiery oratorical style to protest the substance of Republican legislation as well as the floor procedures used by GOP leaders. That's a role he is likely to resume with Democrats back in the minority in the 112th Congress (2011-12).

He was a sharp critic of President George W. Bush's policies both at home and abroad. As a member of the Intelligence panel, Hastings regularly asked some of the most pointed questions in the House about the veracity of the administration's intelligence assessments of Iraq's possession of weapons of mass destruction.

Hastings sided with a majority of his party against a majority of Republicans 99 percent of the time while Democrats controlled Congress from 2007 through 2010. But he has sometimes been outspoken regarding the way Democrats in the other chamber have been unable to move all the legislation he supported. Hastings criticized the Senate for being "the place where things we pass in the House go to die."

At home, Hastings criticized local tea party activists and declined their invitation to debate his opponent during the 2010 campaign.

"I decline to participate in any tea party — arranged, touted, contrived or sponsored — event anywhere at anytime," Hastings wrote in a letter to Tea Party Fort Lauderdale. He said his constituents had shown no interest in seeing him subject himself to tea party "shenanigans."

His disdain extends to those on his own side who have a different vision of the Democratic Party agenda. He has long resisted what he sees as efforts by some white Florida Democrats to shift the state party to the right, diminishing the influence of black voters. He has several times urged African-Americans to consider voting for Republicans to send the Democratic Party a signal that it should not take their support for granted.

In 2007, Hastings and Florida Democratic Sen. Bill Nelson sued the Democratic National Committee (DNC) after it moved to strip Florida of its delegate votes at the August 2008 national convention. The committee said Florida violated party rules that set Feb. 5 as the first date on which most states could hold presidential nominating contests. The state legislature had moved up Florida's primary date to Jan. 29. A U.S. district judge ruled in favor of the DNC, but the party relented anyway and counted all delegate votes.

Hastings earned a degree in zoology and botany at Fisk University and was accepted to medical school. He chose to pursue a law career instead. In 1979, President Jimmy Carter nominated Hastings for a U.S. District Court seat in Miami, and he became the first black federal judge in Florida.

In 1983, a jury acquitted Hastings of charges that he solicited a $150,000 bribe in exchange for granting a lenient sentence, but a federal judicial panel later concluded he had lied and made up evidence to secure that verdict. The vote to impeach him was 413-3 in the House; the Senate voted 69-26 to remove him from office. After losing a bid for Florida secretary of state in 1990, Hastings in 1992 won a House seat representing the new 23rd District, drawn for the 1990s with a slight black majority. State Rep. Lois Frankel, a liberal white Democrat, took 35 percent of the primary vote to his 28 percent, but Hastings prevailed in a primary runoff with 58 percent. He won in November with 59 percent and has coasted to re-election since.

In early 2011, the Ethics Committee, citing "insufficient evidence," closed an investigation of whether Hastings and five other lawmakers had improperly kept excess per diem funds used for official travel.

Key Votes

2010

Overhaul the nation's health insurance system	YES
Allow for repeal of "don't ask, don't tell"	?
Overhaul financial services industry regulation	YES
Limit use of new Afghanistan War funds to troop withdrawal activities	YES
Change oversight of offshore drilling and lift oil spill liability cap	YES
Provide a path to legal status for some children of illegal immigrants	YES
Extend Bush-era income tax cuts for two years	NO

2009

Expand the Children's Health Insurance Program	YES
Provide $787 billion in tax cuts and spending increases to stimulate the economy	YES
Allow bankruptcy judges to modify certain primary-residence mortgages	YES
Create a cap-and-trade system to limit greenhouse gas emissions	?
Provide $2 billion for the "cash for clunkers" program	YES
Establish the government as the sole provider of student loans	YES
Restrict federally funded insurance coverage for abortions in health care overhaul	NO

CQ Vote Studies

	PARTY UNITY		PRESIDENTIAL SUPPORT	
	SUPPORT	OPPOSE	SUPPORT	OPPOSE
2010	99%	1%	83%	17%
2009	99%	1%	98%	2%
2008	99%	1%	13%	87%
2007	99%	1%	3%	97%
2006	94%	6%	31%	69%

Interest Groups

	AFL-CIO	ADA	CCUS	ACU
2010	92%	85%	25%	5%
2009	100%	95%	36%	0%
2008	100%	95%	65%	0%
2007	100%	90%	50%	0%
2006	100%	95%	33%	8%

Florida 23

Southeast — parts of Fort Lauderdale, West Palm Beach and Lauderhill

One of three black-majority districts in the state, the heavily Democratic 23rd stretches southwest from working-class Fort Pierce to the eastern shores of Lake Okeechobee and back east toward coastal hubs such as West Palm Beach and Fort Lauderdale. Most residents live in Broward County, and much of the area west of the Florida Turnpike, including a significant portion of the Everglades, is rural. The eastern borders of the 23rd tend to be several blocks off the coast, with the neighboring 22nd taking in much of the prime beachfront property.

Most urban areas in the 23rd — such as Lauderhill, Lauderdale Lakes, Riviera Beach and portions of West Palm Beach — contain largely black neighborhoods and attract local government employees, educators and other middle-class professionals.

The 23rd is growing more diverse, drawing in many Hispanic and Caribbean immigrants — the district's Hispanic population has grown by more than 40 percent in the last decade.

Citrus, sugar cane and rice growers work the large but sparsely populated rural portions of the district, some of which were recently converted to conservation land. The 23rd lacks a major employment sector, and the vulnerability of citrus crops to bad weather contributes to lagging income levels.

Democrats outnumber Republicans by a ratio of roughly 4-to-1, and voters routinely give Democratic candidates more than 75 percent of the vote in competitive statewide elections. Indeed, many heavily black precincts — including some in western Fort Lauderdale and Lauderdale Lakes — give Democratic candidates more than 90 percent of the vote. Overall, the district gave Barack Obama 83 percent of its presidential vote in 2008.

Major Industry
Agriculture, local government, service

Cities
West Palm Beach (pt.), 66,721; Fort Lauderdale (pt.), 63,838; Lauderhill (pt.), 54,985; Pompano Beach (pt.), 39,759; North Lauderdale (pt.), 39,507

Notable
Lake Okeechobee, part of which is in the 23rd, is the second-largest freshwater lake contained wholly within the United States.

Rep. Sandy Adams (R)

Capitol Office
225-2706
adams.house.gov
216 Cannon Bldg. 20515; fax 226-6299

Committees
Judiciary
Science, Space & Technology

Residence
Orlando

Born
Dec. 14, 1956; Wyandotte, Mich.

Religion
Episcopalian

Family
Husband, John H. Adams; three children

Education
Columbia College, Orlando, B.A. 2000 (criminal justice administration)

Military
Air Force, 1974-75

Career
Deputy county sheriff

Political Highlights
Fla. House, 2002-10

ELECTION RESULTS

2010 GENERAL
Sandy Adams (R)	146,129	59.6%
Suzanne M. Kosmas (D)	98,787	40.3%

2010 PRIMARY
Sandy Adams (R)	19,898	30.1%
Karen Diebel (R)	19,355	29.3%
Craig S. Miller (R)	18,282	27.7%
Tom Garcia (R)	6,446	9.8%
Deon Long (R)	2,079	3.1%

Elected 2010; 1st term

Adams is a high school dropout who joined the Air Force, became a deputy county sheriff and espouses a "tough, no-nonsense" style of governing.

The former single mother said her life experiences will guide her first term in Congress. She learned to balance her personal budget under difficult circumstances, Adams noted, so the government should do the same.

Adams said she will focus on reducing overall federal spending. But the needs of one particular program will be her priority as a member of the Science, Space and Technology Committee: NASA, which is a significant contributor to the economy of her central Florida district.

"They spent a lot of money over the last few years," she said of the Democratic-controlled Congress. "Some of that money could have been devoted to the space industry. We need to re-prioritize."

She sees the Kennedy Space Center as important to national security and keeping the United States at the forefront of developing new technologies. She wants to see the continuation of human spaceflight, including a manned mission to Mars.

She said in early 2011 that the agency's spending on climate change research "undercuts one of NASA's primary and most important objectives" — human spaceflight.

On the Judiciary Committee, Adams has a chance to work on another of her priorities, illegal immigration. "I don't believe in amnesty," she told a Daytona newspaper in October 2010. "There already is a pathway. Go back and come back legally."

Having grown up in a military family, she quit high school at 17 and joined the Air Force. An Orange County deputy sheriff for 17 years, Adams ran for the Florida House in 2002 to advocate for victims' rights. The cause was personal; her first husband, also a deputy, died in the line of duty in 1989.

In 2010, one-term incumbent Suzanne M. Kosmas was seen as a vulnerable Democrat in the competitive district. Adams beat four other Republicans in the primary, then swept to an easy victory against Kosmas, winning 60 percent of the vote.

Florida 24

East central — Orlando suburbs, part of Space Coast

The 24th includes nearly 60 miles of Atlantic coastline before it sweeps west to take in much of the area between the Space Coast and the Orlando suburbs. Orange County is the district's most populous jurisdiction, providing nearly 35 percent of the population. The 24th pulls equally from Seminole and Volusia counties, with just more than 15 percent of the population living in its portion of Brevard County. It picks up several suburban communities north or east of Orlando, including most of Altamonte Springs and all of Oviedo.

The Kennedy Space Center has been the region's economic engine. Residents are concerned about how the retirement of NASA's space shuttle program will impact the thousands of district jobs that rely on the aerospace and technology industries.

Tourism is another important piece of the local economy. The district's coastline and nature preserves attract eco-tourists and beach-seeking visitors. The 24th takes in one of Daytona Beach's jewels — Daytona International Speedway, home to NASCAR's Daytona 500 stock car race — as well as parts of the city of Daytona Beach, most of which is in the neighboring 7th, and popular beach communities.

The 24th has a slight Republican lean in voter registration but is politically competitive. The U.S. House seat has flipped party hands in each of the last two elections, and Republican John McCain took only 51 percent of the district's 2008 presidential vote.

Major Industry
Aerospace, tourism, technology

Cities
Alafaya (unincorporated) (pt.), 78,075; Port Orange, 56,048; Titusville, 43,761

Notable
One Space Coast-region area code is 321, chosen to mimic the countdown to liftoff.

Rep. David Rivera (R)

Capitol Office
225-2778
rivera.house.gov
417 Cannon Bldg. 20515-0925; fax 226 0346

Committees
Foreign Affairs
Natural Resources

Residence
Miami

Born
Sept. 16, 1965; Brooklyn, N.Y.

Religion
Roman Catholic

Family
Single

Education
Florida International U., B.A. 1986 (political science),
M.P.A. 1994

Career
State party Hispanic outreach director; U.S. broad-casting agency aide; human rights advocacy organi-zation aide; congressional aide; campaign aide

Political Highlights
Fla. House, 2002-10; Miami-Dade County Republican
Party chairman, 2008-10

ELECTION RESULTS

2010 GENERAL

David Rivera (R)	74,859	52.1%
Joe Garcia (D)	61,138	42.6%
Roly Arrojo (TEA)	4,312	3.0%
Craig Porter (FWP)	3,244	2.3%

2010 PRIMARY

David Rivera (R)	19,228	62.7%
Paul Crespo (R)	8,158	26.6%
Marili Cancio (R)	3,272	10.7%

Elected 2010; 1st term

Much of Rivera's life has focused on U.S. policy regarding Cuba. As a state lawmaker from a majority-Hispanic district — and a Cuban-American — he has worked for various federal agencies and advocacy organizations with a focus on Cuban policy. He'll continue that work as a member of the Foreign Affairs Committee.

Like his predecessor, Republican Mario Diaz-Balart (who won election to his brother's former seat in the neighboring 21st District), Rivera takes a strong stance against Cuban dictator Fidel Castro. "I do not believe we should give any unilateral concessions until all political prisoners are freed, civil liberties are restored and free elections are held," he said.

During his time in the state legislature, Rivera was the author of a 2006 law that banned state funding for educational research and travel to nations that are deemed "sponsors of terrorism," a designation that includes Cuba.

Regarding other aspects of Latin American policy, Rivera says Congress should move forward on the free-trade deal with Colombia, estimating that it could create jobs in his district and elsewhere.

His constituents can expect him to champion traditional Republican policies such as cutting spending and easing taxes on small businesses. He will play a role in setting policy for the nearby Everglades as a member of the Natural Resources Committee.

He received a degree in political science and an MPA from Florida International University. He peppered his professional experience with work on political campaigns, including for former Republican Sen. Connie Mack.

Questions arose during the 2010 campaign about his sources of income, but he bested Democrat Joe Garcia by nearly 10 percentage points. The allegations continued after he came to Congress, however. He faced a state criminal investigation of his finances, and The Associated Press reported in January 2011 that he paid himself more than $60,000 in campaign reimbursements during his years in the state legislature. Rivera said the payments covered campaign expenses such as travel, meals and supplies, and that "all information provided was accurate and all expenses properly reported."

Florida 25

South — western Miami-Dade County, the Everglades

The predominately Hispanic 25th takes in a broad swath of land covering the western portion of Miami-Dade County and almost all of Collier and Monroe counties' land area. Although geographically centered in Everglades National Park and Big Cypress National Preserve, more than 85 percent of the population lives in Miami-Dade County, mostly on the western edge of the Miami region and in areas south of the city.

The Hispanic community has grown mark-edly since 2000, and the 25th now has more Hispanic residents than any other Florida district, although overall population growth means the percentage of Hispanic residents remains lower than the 21st District's.

Many residents commute to Miami for work, but agriculture is a mainstay for the local economy.

Infrastructure development in Collier County might aid economic recovery in the area, after retail and construction downturns and housing market collapses hit Collier and Miami-Dade. National parks give the 25th an ecosystem and array of wildlife — from manatees to panthers — not commonly found in North America, and they are significant tourist draws. Restoration of the Everglades, oil drilling and the pace of development will remain conten-tious issues.

A shrinking party registration edge means that Republicans only slightly outnumber Democrats here. The 25th has the state's highest percentage of independent voters.

Major Industry
Agriculture, tourism

Cities
Homestead, 60,512; Kendale Lakes (unincor-porated), 56,148; Tamiami (unincorporated), 55,271

Notable
Everglades National Park covers 1.5 million acres, just a small portion of the Everglades.

GEORGIA

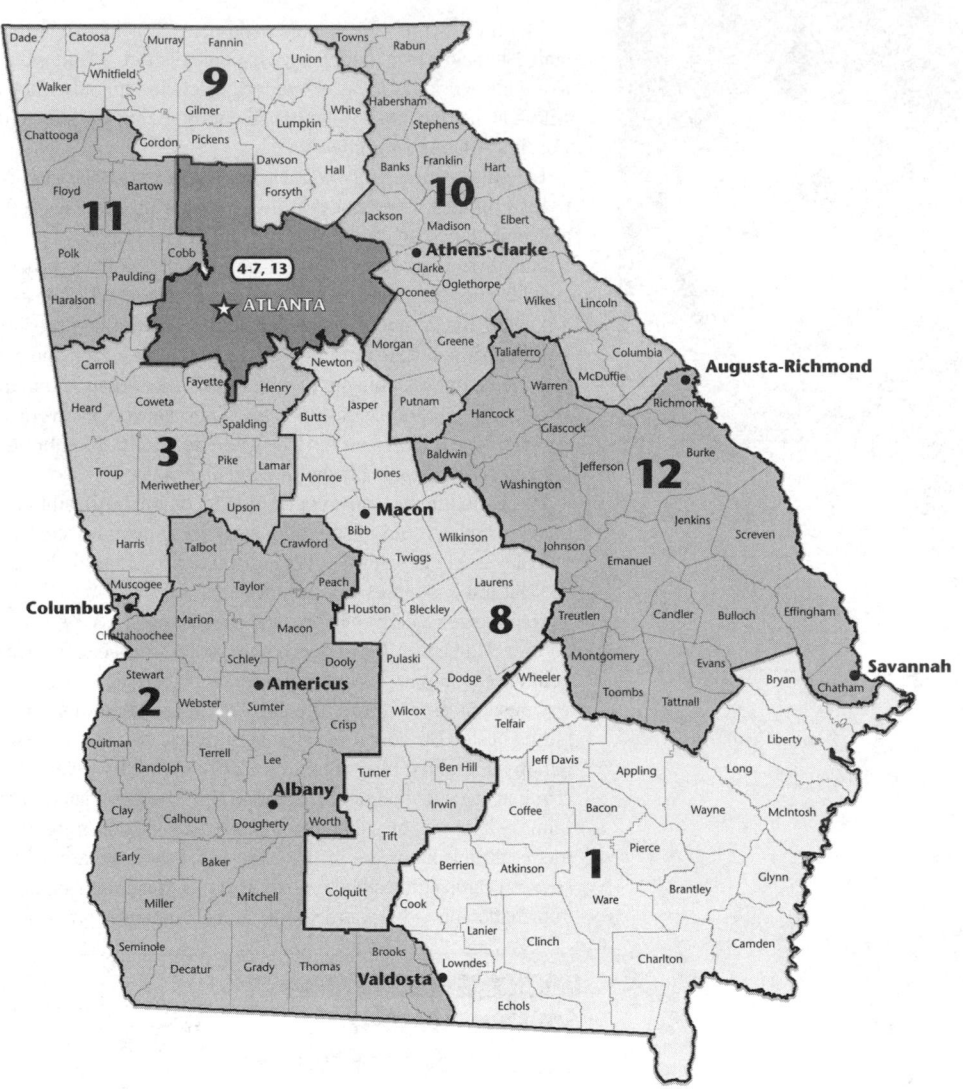

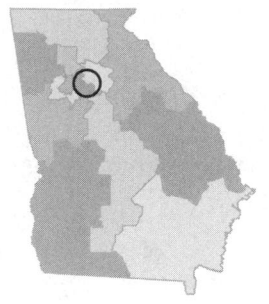

4-7, 13

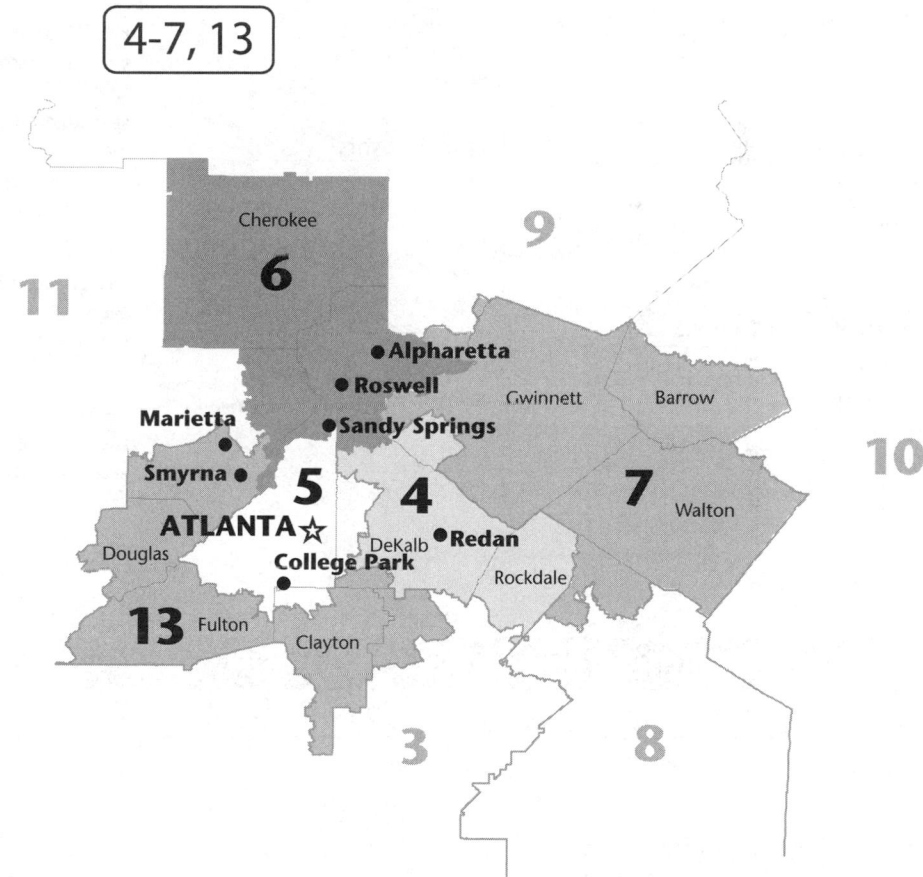

Gov. Nathan Deal (R)

First elected: 2010
Length of term: 4 years
Term expires: 1/15
Salary: $139,339
Phone: (404) 656-1776
Residence: Atlanta
Born: Aug. 25, 1942; Millen, Ga.
Religion: Baptist
Family: Wife, Sandra Dunagan Deal; four children
Education: Mercer U., B.A. 1964, J.D. 1966
Military Service: Army, 1966-68
Career: Lawyer; state prosecutor
Political highlights: Hall County Juvenile Court judge, 1971-72; Hall County attorney, 1977-79; Ga. Senate, 1981-93 (served as a Democrat; president pro tempore, 1991-93); U.S. House, 1993-2010

ELECTION RESULTS

2010 GENERAL

Nathan Deal (R)	1,365,832	53.0%
Roy E. Barnes (D)	1,107,011	43.0%
John H. Monds (LIBERT)	103,194	4.0%

Lt. Gov. Casey Cagle (R)

First elected: 2006
Length of term: 4 years
Term expires: 1/15
Salary: $91,609
Phone: (404) 656-5030

LEGISLATURE

General Assembly: January-April, limit of 40 days
Senate: 56 members, 2-year terms
2011 ratios: 36 R, 20 D; 48 men, 8 women
Salary: $16,200
Phone: (404) 656-0028
House: 180 members, 2-year terms
2011 ratios: 115 R, 63 D, 1 independent, 1 vacancy; 132 men, 47 women
Salary: $16,200
Phone: (404) 656-5015

TERM LIMITS

Governor: 2 terms
Senate: No
House: No

URBAN STATISTICS

CITY	POPULATION
Atlanta	420,003
Augusta	200,549
Columbus	189,885
Savannah	136,286
Athens-Clarke	116,714

REGISTERED VOTERS

Voters do not register by party.

POPULATION

2010 population (est.)	9,687,653
2000 population	8,186,453
1990 population	6,478,216
Percent change (2000-2010)	+18.3%
Rank among states (2010)	9
Median age	34.5
Born in state	55.9%
Foreign born	8.9%
Violent crime rate	426/100,000
Poverty level	16.5%
Federal workers	129,041
Military	73,988

ELECTIONS

STATE ELECTION OFFICIAL
(404) 656-2871
DEMOCRATIC PARTY
(678) 278-2010
REPUBLICAN PARTY
(404) 257-5559

MISCELLANEOUS

Web: www.georgia.gov
Capital: Atlanta

U.S. CONGRESS

Senate: 2 Republicans
House: 8 Republicans, 5 Democrats

2010 Census Statistics by District

District	2008 Vote for President Obama	McCain	White	Black	Asian	Hispanic	Median Income	White Collar	Blue Collar	Service Industry	Over 64	Under 18	College Education	Rural	Sq. Miles
1	37%	62%	65%	25%	1%	6%	$42,178	54%	28%	18%	11%	26%	19%	43%	11,406
2	54	45	45	48	1	5	34,480	51	30	19	12	26	15	42	10,841
3	35	64	67	24	2	5	56,019	60	25	14	11	28	24	44	4,112
4	79	20	21	55	5	16	48,126	59	24	16	7	26	29	2	330
5	79	20	37	50	3	8	50,704	70	14	16	9	21	45	0	246
6	35	63	71	10	8	9	79,973	76	12	12	8	28	51	7	681
7	39	60	54	22	9	13	65,441	67	20	13	7	30	34	13	972
8	43	56	58	35	1	5	42,529	55	29	17	12	27	18	43	7,171
9	23	75	80	3	2	14	48,234	54	32	14	12	27	20	53	4,334
10	37	62	71	19	2	6	42,406	57	26	17	13	24	25	50	5,892
11	33	66	72	15	2	9	52,833	60	26	14	10	27	25	30	2,693
12	54	45	50	43	1	5	35,825	51	30	20	11	25	16	40	8,657
13	72	27	26	56	3	13	50,764	59	25	16	7	29	25	4	572
STATE	47	52	56	30	3	9	49,466	60	24	16	10	26	27	28	57,906
US	53	46	64	12	5	16	51,425	60	23	17	13	25	28	21	3,537,438

Sen. Saxby Chambliss (R)

Capitol Office
224-3521
chambliss.senate.gov
416 Russell Bldg. 20510-1005; fax 224-0103

Committees
Agriculture, Nutrition & Forestry
Armed Services
Rules & Administration
Select Intelligence - Ranking Member
Special Aging
Joint Printing

Residence
Moultrie

Born
Nov. 10, 1943; Warrenton, N.C.

Religion
Episcopalian

Family
Wife, Julianne Chambliss; two children

Education
Louisiana Tech U., attended 1961-62; U. of Georgia,
B.B.A. 1966 (business administration); U. of Tennes-
see, J.D. 1968

Career
Lawyer; hotel owner; firefighter; construction worker

Political Highlights
Sought Republican nomination for U.S. House, 1992;
U.S. House, 1995-2003

ELECTION RESULTS

2008 GENERAL RUNOFF

Saxby Chambliss (R)	1,228,033	57.4%
Jim Martin (D)	909,923	42.6%

2008 PRIMARY

Saxby Chambliss (R)	unopposed

2002 GENERAL

Saxby Chambliss (R)	1,071,352	52.7%
Max Cleland (D)	932,422	45.9%
Claude Thomas (LIBERT)	27,830	1.4%

Previous Winning Percentages
2000 House Election (59%); 1998 House Election
(62%); 1996 House Election (53%); 1994 House
Election (63%)

Elected 2002; 2nd term

Chambliss is a loyal vote for his party and a member of the Senate Republicans' whip team, but his work on behalf of Georgia farmers and national security sometimes launches him into partnerships with the other party. His longtime interest in intelligence matters got a boost in the 112th Congress as he took on the role of top Republican on the Select Intelligence Committee.

The business-friendly Chambliss (full name: SAX-bee CHAM-bliss) is one of the Senate's most conservative members. His voting record has earned a 100 percent positive ranking from the U.S. Chamber of Commerce more than once, and he sided with Republicans almost 98 percent of the time on votes that divided majorities of the two parties in the 111th Congress (2009-10).

He is a budget hawk and says the intelligence community will have to brace for cuts like the rest of the government. "As the budget debate heats up in Washington, the days of bloated government budgets, including for the IC, must be behind us," he said. One of Chambliss' suggestions: The director of national intelligence could reduce the size of his office.

No one questions Chambliss' conservative bona fides, giving him considerable leeway to work across the aisle. Early in the 112th Congress (2011-12) he worked with Virginia Democrat Mark Warner on legislation to implement the recommendations of President Obama's fiscal commission.

Chambliss joined a fellow Intelligence Committee member, Democrat Ron Wyden of Oregon, in backing legislation in 2007 that would have required a National Intelligence Estimate on U.S. energy security.

Chambliss is able to maintain his conservative reputation while cooperating with Democrats partly because many of the issues in which he is involved are not rigidly partisan. In addition to Intelligence, he serves on Agriculture, Armed Services, Special Aging, Rules and Administration and Joint Printing. Each requires some routine work that calls upon its members to set aside partisanship and put national or regional interests above party loyalty.

Before taking over as ranking minority member on Intelligence, he was the top Republican on the Agriculture, Nutrition and Forestry Committee, where he worked in tandem with Chairwoman Blanche Lincoln of Arkansas on the 2008 farm bill, child nutrition programs, crop insurance and trade agreements.

Chambliss came by his agricultural expertise as a small-town lawyer in southern Georgia, representing peanut and cotton growers. "No one else in town wanted to take the time to read the regulations and study the law and figure out how the farm bill operates," he said.

From his Agriculture perch, Chambliss watches out for his farm-dependent state, a major producer of peanuts, cotton and tobacco, and he will have a leading role in the next rewrite of the farm bill in 2012.

During the last farm bill debate in 2008, Chambliss helped write a reauthorization that President George W. Bush vetoed on the grounds that it had too much unnecessary spending. Congress overwhelmingly voted to override the veto of the $289 billion measure.

Chambliss initially had hoped the 2008 farm legislation could benefit Georgia's peanut farmers, whom he said were wronged in the 2002 farm bill. The earlier measure ended the peanut subsidy program and guaranteed farmers no more than coverage of their losses for five years. But the 2008 law continued that policy with only modest changes. When a peanut processor failed to report tests showing salmonella-contaminated products at a Georgia plant in 2009, Chambliss defused demands for more aggressive oversight by calling for the creation of a central data bank for information on outbreaks.

In February 2009, he led a group of Republicans and moderate Democrats in demanding that Obama's Agriculture secretary, Tom Vilsack, follow the farm bill's liberalized intent regarding payment limit rules to farmers rather than more stringent proposals the Bush administration issued shortly before leaving office. Chambliss also joined members of both parties who balked at Obama's budget proposal to phase out direct payments to farmers with more than $500,000 in sales revenue and to cap commodity supports at $250,000.

On Armed Services, Chambliss continues a long line of guardians for his state's military installations, which have thrived since World War II, thanks partly to the nearly continuous presence of a Georgian on the committee. A proposal championed by Chambliss that reduced the age for receipt of retirement pay by three months for every 90 days that a National Guard or Reserve member spends on active duty was signed into law by Bush in 2008.

The son of an Episcopal priest, Chambliss said his family's frequent moves when he was young made him learn to make friends quickly and prepared him for politics. When he was 5, his father was the announcer for the Rock Hill Chicks, a minor league baseball club in North Carolina. Chambliss dreamed of becoming a baseball star and played second base on the University of Georgia baseball team. At college he met Johnny Isakson, now his home-state Senate colleague. In the years after college, Chambliss worked as a firefighter to pay for law school.

Chambliss and Isakson talk often, issue joint press releases and travel the state together. When their stay-at-home wives (who were in the same sorority) are in town, the couples frequently dine together. When they're not, Chambliss and Isakson are part of a group of Republican men who eat out together and gather at each other's homes. The pack has included Sens. Lindsey Graham of South Carolina, Tom Coburn of Oklahoma, John Thune of South Dakota and Richard M. Burr of North Carolina, and occasionally House Speaker John A. Boehner of Ohio.

Chambliss lost his first bid for public office in 1992 when he sought the Republican nomination to challenge Democratic Rep. J. Roy Rowland. But when Rowland retired in 1994, Chambliss defeated Democrat Craig Mathis, becoming the first Republican since Reconstruction to represent the rural Georgia district. He declined entreaties to run for the Senate against Democrat Zell Miller in 2000. Chambliss chose to stay in the House at the urging of GOP Speaker J. Dennis Hastert of Illinois and expected to be rewarded with the chairmanship of the Budget Committee. When that prize went instead to Jim Nussle of Iowa, Chambliss again began thinking about the other chamber.

Three days after the Sept. 11 terrorist attacks in 2001, Chambliss' nascent challenge to Democratic Sen. Max Cleland got a boost when Hastert picked Chambliss to chair a new Intelligence Subcommittee on Terrorism and Homeland Security. He caused a stir soon after when he said that one route to security would be for local sheriffs to "arrest every Muslim that comes across the state line." But Chambliss then went on the offensive against Cleland, a Vietnam veteran, for opposing portions of Bush's plans to create a Department of Homeland Security. Democrats charged him with impugning Cleland's patriotism, but Chambliss won by 7 percentage points.

In 2008, Democrats targeted Chambliss by nominating Jim Martin, a former state representative, Georgia commissioner of human resources and 2006 nominee for lieutenant governor. In November, Chambliss came two-tenths of a percentage point short of an outright majority, forcing a December runoff. With Democratic gains having pushed them close to a 60-vote super majority in the Senate, both parties focused intensely on the runoff. Chambliss brought in Alaska Gov. Sarah Palin — the party's vice presidential nominee and a favorite of conservatives — and other luminaries. He ended up prevailing by nearly 15 percentage points.

Key Votes

2010

Pass budget reconciliation bill to modify overhauls of health care and federal student loan programs	NO
Proceed to disapproval resolution on EPA authority to regulate greenhouse gases	YES
Overhaul financial services industry regulation	NO
Limit debate to proceed to a bill to broaden campaign finance disclosure and reporting rules	NO
Limit debate on an extension of Bush-era income tax cuts for two years	YES
Limit debate on a bill to provide a path to legal status for some children of illegal immigrants	NO
Allow for a repeal of "don't ask, don't tell"	NO
Consent to ratification of a strategic arms reduction treaty with Russia	NO

2009

Prevent release of remaining financial industry bailout funds	YES
Make it easier for victims to sue for wage discrimination remedies	NO
Expand the Children's Health Insurance Program	NO
Limit debate on the economic stimulus measure	NO
Repeal District of Columbia firearms prohibitions and gun registration laws	YES
Limit debate on expansion of federal hate crimes law	NO
Strike funding for F-22 Raptor fighter jets	NO

CQ Vote Studies

	PARTY UNITY		PRESIDENTIAL SUPPORT	
	SUPPORT	OPPOSE	SUPPORT	OPPOSE
2010	98%	2%	42%	58%
2009	97%	3%	42%	58%
2008	95%	5%	72%	28%
2007	96%	4%	83%	17%
2006	94%	6%	93%	7%
2005	95%	5%	91%	9%
2004	99%	1%	100%	0%
2003	97%	3%	97%	3%
2002	98%	2%	90%	10%
2001	98%	2%	93%	7%

Interest Groups

	AFL-CIO	ADA	CCUS	ACU
2010	6%	0%	100%	100%
2009	17%	10%	71%	92%
2008	30%	25%	100%	76%
2007	11%	10%	82%	92%
2006	13%	0%	92%	96%
2005	21%	5%	94%	96%
2004	0%	5%	93%	96%
2003	15%	5%	91%	90%
2002	0%	0%	90%	100%
2001	17%	0%	95%	100%

Sen. Johnny Isakson (R)

Capitol Office
224-3643
isakson.senate.gov
131 Russell Bldg. 20510-1006; fax 228-0724

Committees
Commerce, Science & Transportation
Foreign Relations
Health, Education, Labor & Pensions
Veterans' Affairs
Select Ethics - Vice Chairman

Residence
Marietta

Born
Dec. 28, 1944; Atlanta, Ga.

Religion
Methodist

Family
Wife, Dianne Isakson; three children

Education
U. of Georgia, B.B.A. 1966 (real estate)

Military Service
Ga. Air National Guard, 1966-72

Career
Real estate company president

Political Highlights
Candidate for Cobb County Commission, 1974; Ga.
House, 1977-90 (Republican leader, 1983-90); Republican nominee for governor, 1990; Ga. Senate, 1993-96; sought Republican nomination for U.S. Senate, 1996; Ga. Board of Education chairman, 1996-99; U.S. House, 1999-2005

ELECTION RESULTS

2010 GENERAL

Johnny Isakson (R)	1,489,904	58.3%
Michael Thurmond (D)	996,516	39.0%
Chuck Donovan (LIBERT)	68,750	2.7%

2010 PRIMARY

Johnny Isakson (R)	unopposed

Previous Winning Percentages
2004 (58%); 2002 House Election (80%); 2000 House Election (75%); 1999 Special House Election (65%)

Elected 2004; 2nd term

Isakson is known as a moderate in his home state and a conservative nationally. His business-friendly, small-government instincts are combined with an interest in tangible results. That approach has produced several efforts involving the folksy, gentlemanly Georgian bringing the parties together and yielding a few victories.

In early 2011, he lined up with a bipartisan group of senators in backing a budget plan that would cut spending more gradually than the proposal put forth by House Republicans.

Isakson also employed his consensus-building skills at the start of the 111th Congress (2009-10) to win Senate adoption of his amendment to the economic stimulus package that would have offered homebuyers a $15,000 tax credit in order to spur housing sales, an area of special interest to the former real estate company executive. But after Isakson and all but three other Republicans refused to vote for the bill itself, the tax credit was halved in the final version. Isakson later persuaded Democrats to vote to extend the deadline for the closing date of the tax credit to September 2010, but the version that passed also differed from his original proposal.

A financial fraud bill that President Obama signed in May 2009 included an amendment by Isakson and Budget Chairman Kent Conrad, a North Dakota Democrat, that created a Financial Crisis Inquiry Commission. Modeled after the bipartisan panel that investigated the Sept. 11 terrorist attacks, the commission was tasked with delving into the causes of the economic crisis and making recommendations for future action.

On other issues, Isakson has been a reliable Republican vote, winning high marks from the U.S. Chamber of Commerce and conservative interest groups. From the Health, Education, Labor and Pensions Committee, Isakson has sought to curtail union influence.

He readily voices praise for Democrats, but most of them are conservative Georgians who stray from the national party line such as former Sens. Zell Miller and Sam Nunn. Regarding Obama, Isakson said that the president's election was a historically significant event and an inspirational example "that anyone can rise to the highest office in the land." However, Isakson finds the administration to be "more political than practical sometimes," and he has "been disappointed with the president's approach to many of the problems we confront in the country, principally economically."

Isakson said he hopes to be around for years to address the rising problem of national debt, despite a health scare during his 2010 re-election campaign that landed him in the hospital with what he said was a staph bacteria infection. One of his biggest concerns is the level of government debt held by the United States and European countries. "It's something everyone has talked about for a long time, and now it's incumbent for Congress to do something to get the debt under control," he said.

Isakson's reputation as a moderate has grown from several successes during his Senate term and the nearly three House terms that preceded it. At one time, during a failed 1990 bid for governor, Isakson supported abortion rights, a position he later repudiated.

Isakson worked closely with the late Sen. Edward M. Kennedy, a Massachusetts Democrat, on an overhaul of the law governing private pension plans and a rewrite of mine safety standards. He labored successfully to ensure the final pension measure included provisions to give Atlanta-based Delta Air Lines and other financially strapped airlines extra time to fully fund their pension plans, which otherwise could have been dumped on the federal Pension Benefit Guaranty Corporation.

Earlier in 2006, Isakson, then chairman of HELP's Employment and Workplace Safety Subcommittee, went to West Virginia two days after an explosion at the Sago Mine killed a dozen coal miners. Isakson, Kennedy, West Virginia Democrat John D. Rockefeller IV and Wyoming Republican Michael B. Enzi talked to miners' families, the company and experts. Within months, they had steered a new mine safety law to enactment.

Education has always been a top priority for Isakson. He was chairman of the Georgia Board of Education from 1996 to 1999 after then-Gov. Miller tapped him for the position. As a member of the House he helped write the 2001 No Child Left Behind education law, working closely with Kennedy, among others. He is eager to revise and renew the law, which he considers a success, in the 112th Congress (2011-12), although he wants to allow greater flexibility in assessing and serving non-English-speaking children and those in special education.

Isakson credits his dad, a high school dropout, for instilling his passion for education. After his older sister died as a young child, his father repeatedly told Isakson he was destined to be the first in the family to attend college. The elder Isakson bought season tickets to Georgia Tech football games, then deliberately parked 2 miles away so he could walk his son across the campus to the stadium. Isakson's father would point to the buildings and say, "One day you're going to go to a school like this."

Isakson began his policy focus on education in his House career. Though he was the lowest-ranking Republican on the Education and the Workforce Committee in the 106th Congress (1999-2000), he was the driving force behind a proposal to help states pay for federally mandated school modernization costs. Committee Republicans were resisting Democratic plans for the federal government to pay for the school repairs, but Isakson saw the potential political impact of the construction issue and convinced GOP leaders they would lose the debate without their own proposal.

In the 110th Congress (2007-08), he landed a seat on the Foreign Relations Committee, where he has been a vocal advocate for human rights in Sudan. He is the ranking Republican on the African Affairs panel. Late in 2010, he joined with every Democrat and a dozen other Republicans to approve a strategic arms reduction treaty with Russia that was opposed by most of his GOP colleagues.

In the 111th, he traded a seat on the Environment and Public Works Committee for the Commerce, Science and Transportation Committee. He also drew a less welcome assignment, as vice chairman of the Select Ethics Committee, and he sits on the Veterans' Affairs Committee.

A fixture in Georgia politics, he was in the General Assembly for almost 17 years and was the GOP candidate for governor in 1990. He lost to Miller, the lieutenant governor at the time. In 1996, he sought the Republican nomination for the U.S. Senate but lost. "I pretty much figured my political career was over," he said. But Miller fired the state school board members and asked Isakson to take the chairman's job.

When House Speaker Newt Gingrich, a Georgia Republican, resigned in 1999, Isakson ran for his seat. Enjoying a huge advantage in name recognition and campaign funds, he took 65 percent of the vote against five opponents in the special election. He cruised to re-election in 2000 and 2002.

Miller, meanwhile, won appointment to the Senate in 2000 and retired in 2004. Isakson jumped into the Senate race, challenged by Republicans Herman Cain and Rep. Mac Collins. Isakson took 53 percent of the vote, avoiding a runoff, and defeated one-term Democratic Rep. Denise L. Majette with 58 percent. He cruised to re-election in 2010, again winning 58 percent of the vote.

Key Votes

2010

Pass budget reconciliation bill to modify overhauls of health care and federal student loan programs	?
Proceed to disapproval resolution on EPA authority to regulate greenhouse gases	YES
Overhaul financial services industry regulation	NO
Limit debate to proceed to a bill to broaden campaign finance disclosure and reporting rules	NO
Limit debate on an extension of Bush-era income tax cuts for two years	YES
Limit debate on a bill to provide a path to legal status for some children of illegal immigrants	NO
Allow for a repeal of "don't ask, don't tell"	NO
Consent to ratification of a strategic arms reduction treaty with Russia	YES

2009

Prevent release of remaining financial industry bailout funds	YES
Make it easier for victims to sue for wage discrimination remedies	NO
Expand the Children's Health Insurance Program	NO
Limit debate on the economic stimulus measure	NO
Repeal District of Columbia firearms prohibitions and gun registration laws	YES
Limit debate on expansion of federal hate crimes law	NO
Strike funding for F-22 Raptor fighter jets	NO

CQ Vote Studies

	PARTY UNITY		PRESIDENTIAL SUPPORT	
	SUPPORT	OPPOSE	SUPPORT	OPPOSE
2010	93%	7%	42%	58%
2009	97%	3%	45%	55%
2008	94%	6%	72%	28%
2007	97%	3%	85%	15%
2006	97%	3%	93%	7%
2005	95%	5%	91%	9%
2004	99%	1%	89%	11%
2003	99%	1%	96%	4%
2002	94%	6%	85%	15%
2001	97%	3%	90%	10%

Interest Groups

	AFL-CIO	ADA	CCUS	ACU
2010	0%	5%	100%	91%
2009	17%	5%	86%	96%
2008	20%	25%	88%	76%
2007	11%	10%	82%	96%
2006	13%	0%	92%	96%
2005	21%	5%	94%	100%
2004	8%	5%	100%	95%
2003	0%	5%	100%	84%
2002	0%	5%	100%	96%
2001	9%	5%	100%	88%

Rep. Jack Kingston (R)

Capitol Office
225-5831
kingston.house.gov
2372 Rayburn Bldg. 20515-1001; fax 226-2269

Committees
Appropriations
    (Agriculture - Chairman)

Residence
Savannah

Born
April 24, 1955; Bryan, Texas

Religion
Anglican

Family
Wife, Libby Kingston; four children

Education
U. of Georgia, B.A. 1978 (economics)

Career
Insurance broker

Political Highlights
Ga. House, 1984-92

ELECTION RESULTS

2010 GENERAL

Jack Kingston (R)	117,270	71.6%
Oscar L. Harris II (D)	46,449	28.4%

2010 PRIMARY

Jack Kingston (R)	unopposed

2008 GENERAL

Jack Kingston (R)	165,890	66.5%
Bill Gillespie (D)	83,444	33.5%

Previous Winning Percentages
2006 (67%); 2004 (100%); 2002 (72%); 2000 (69%);
1998 (100%); 1996 (68%); 1994 (77%); 1992 (58%)

Elected 1992; 10th term

Kingston is an appropriator with a reputation as an outspoken fiscal conservative — and as one of the Democrats' toughest critics. He's an effective and frequent guest on television news and commentary shows, where he displays a quick wit and easygoing manner that helps keep him on friendly terms with colleagues even as he denounces many of their proposals.

Since taking office one term ahead of the Republican Revolution of 1994, Kingston has focused on limiting the role of government. He made an unsuccessful bid for the chairmanship of the Appropriations Committee in the 112th Congress (2011-12), but came away with the gavel of its Agriculture Subcommittee.

He also sits on the Defense Subcommittee and the Labor, Health and Human Services, Education, and Related Agencies Subcommittee — the two panels that handle the biggest slices of the spending pie.

When House Republicans put together their spending plan for the remainder of 2011, Kingston said "not a single account has been spared."

A former chairman of the Appropriations Subcommittee on the Legislative Branch, Kingston said Capitol Hill itself is ripe with potential cuts. "If the public has elected you with the job of balancing the budget, solving Iraq and Middle East peace, perhaps you should have enough sense to know to look both ways before going through the stop sign," he said to Roll Call in suggesting parking lot attendants might not be necessary. He also questioned whether there was still a need for the Government Printing Office.

He voted against a measure at the end of 2010 that extended the Bush-era tax rates for two years because it included new spending that was not offset.

During the 111th Congress (2009-10), Kingston voted against President Obama on nearly 80 percent of the votes in which the president had a clear position, and he consistently opposed Obama's spending plans.

In the same Congress, Kingston opposed the Democratic health care overhaul, saying that "never has such a well-financed minority thrust such a burden on the American people against its own will."

Kingston also opposed measures aimed at aiding the ailing economy, both the major bills from President George W. Bush's last year in office and those introduced after President Obama took office: tax rebates, emergency loans to automakers and the $700 billion financial industry stabilization measures.

On the Agriculture spending panel, Kingston is sometimes at odds with fellow Republicans who view federal subsidy programs for crops such as peanuts and cotton — which help sustain his district's economy — as antithetical to free enterprise.

And, before House Republicans banned earmarks, Kingston wasn't afraid to request them for programs and facilities in his district, such as $7.6 million in 2010 for projects at a Georgia Air National Guard facility in Savannah.

But he has been supportive of the idea of a moratorium, in concert with hearings to "define and reform" earmarks.

While Kingston tends to focus on fiscal matters, he does weigh in on other issues. In spring 2010, the congressman called for hearings on the Obama administration's decision to disinvite the Rev. Franklin Graham from a National Day of Prayer event at the Pentagon after he made remarks critical of Islam.

In 2006, he was the only Georgia Republican to vote in favor of renewing the 1965 Voting Rights Act, siding with leaders of both political parties. He credits the law with opening up the political process to Southern Republicans in addition to African-Americans. "If not for the Voting Rights Act, I don't think I would be in Congress," he said. He was also a key Republican to sign on to Georgia Democratic Rep. John Lewis' proposal for an African-American museum on the National Mall, approved in 2003.

Kingston served as vice chairman of the House Republican Conference, which promotes the GOP's image, from 2003 to 2006. He lost the position in the 110th Congress (2007-08) after a failed bid for the conference chairmanship.

For more than a decade, Kingston has hosted salons for GOP members in a group called the "Theme Team." Launched two decades ago by Texas Republican Lamar Smith and taken over by Kingston in 1997, the team typically brings together 20 to 30 people to hear talks by speakers from across the political spectrum.

Kingston is a regular on the talk show circuit, frequently appearing on conservative mainstays such as "Hannity" and "Fox and Friends" on the Fox News Channel. But he also makes appearances on left-leaning programs such as "Real Time with Bill Maher," and he notably was the first member of Congress willing to appear on "Better Know a District," a recurring segment on "The Colbert Report," comedian Stephen Colbert's satirical take on political punditry on Comedy Central.

He's even been in the movies. Kingston snagged an $8-an-hour gig as an extra in the Miley Cyrus tearjerker "The Last Song," which was filmed in his southeast Georgia district. He made the final cut, appearing for a few frames in a funeral scene beside actress Kelly Preston.

Born in Texas, where his father was an art professor, Kingston and his family spent a few months in Ethiopia — his father was working with the Education Department to help set up schools — before settling in the Peach State when Kingston was a toddler. He claims Georgia as his native state, once joking, "If you're potty-trained in a state, I think that gives you native status."

After earning an undergraduate degree in economics, Kingston moved to Savannah to sell insurance. He won election in 1984 to the state House, where he served for eight years. When Democratic Rep. Lindsay Thomas retired in 1992, Kingston was well-positioned to woo voters into the GOP column; many of them already had been voting Republican for president. Kingston drew minor primary opposition, then dispatched Democrat Barbara Christmas, a school principal. His 58 percent share of the vote that year remains his lowest.

Redistricting after the census put Kingston and GOP colleague Saxby Chambliss in the same House district in the 2002 election, but Chambliss ran successfully for the Senate. The new 1st District had an even more Republican flavor, and Kingston has continued to win easily.

Key Votes

2010

Overhaul the nation's health insurance system	NO
Allow for repeal of "don't ask, don't tell"	NO
Overhaul financial services industry regulation	NO
Limit use of new Afghanistan War funds to troop withdrawal activities	NO
Change oversight of offshore drilling and lift oil spill liability cap	NO
Provide a path to legal status for some children of illegal immigrants	NO
Extend Bush-era income tax cuts for two years	NO

2009

Expand the Children's Health Insurance Program	NO
Provide $787 billion in tax cuts and spending increases to stimulate the economy	NO
Allow bankruptcy judges to modify certain primary-residence mortgages	NO
Create a cap-and-trade system to limit greenhouse gas emissions	NO
Provide $2 billion for the "cash for clunkers" program	YES
Establish the government as the sole provider of student loans	NO
Restrict federally funded insurance coverage for abortions in health care overhaul	YES

CQ Vote Studies

	PARTY UNITY		PRESIDENTIAL SUPPORT	
	SUPPORT	OPPOSE	SUPPORT	OPPOSE
2010	97%	3%	26%	74%
2009	95%	5%	17%	83%
2008	93%	7%	68%	32%
2007	95%	5%	90%	10%
2006	95%	5%	97%	3%

Interest Groups

	AFL-CIO	ADA	CCUS	ACU
2010	0%	5%	75%	100%
2009	15%	5%	73%	96%
2008	15%	10%	61%	96%
2007	8%	10%	65%	96%
2006	7%	5%	100%	92%

Georgia 1

Southeast — Valdosta, Savannah suburbs

As recently as two decades ago, the 1st was a Democratic stronghold of peanut and tobacco farmers. Today, the 1st still relies heavily on agriculture, but its voters now overwhelmingly favor Republicans. Spanning 25 counties in southeast Georgia, the 1st takes in all of the state's coastline, part of the border with Florida to the south, and primarily rural areas to the north and west.

The 1st's economy is wedded to agriculture — peanuts, cotton, carrots and blueberries are among the important crops here. Valdosta, almost all of which is in the 1st, is home to health care facilities, a state university and major retailers. Military influence is strong, with three of the state's major military bases in the 1st. The manufacturing sector retains a presence in the district despite layoffs by major employers.

Tourism is important here, as retirees and well-off visitors flock to a string of islands known for golf courses and resorts off the coast of Brunswick. Regional tourism hubs Savannah and Brunswick also have active ports (Savannah's is in the neighboring 12th). The district's ports and coastline make trade and coastal conservation dominant issues.

The 1st votes reliably Republican, with GOP strength in Camden and Glynn counties on the coast and Chatham and Bryan counties near Savannah. In 2010, Rep. Jack Kingston won every county wholly or partially in the 1st. Liberty County — which in 2008 backed Barack Obama even as Republican John McCain won 62 percent of the district's presidential vote — gave Democratic former Gov. Roy Barnes one of his largest vote margins in his unsuccessful 2010 gubernatorial race.

Major Industry
Agriculture, military, tourism

Military Bases
Fort Stewart (Army), 18,549 military, 2,986 civilian (shared with the 12th); Kings Bay Naval Submarine Base, 1,660 military, 1,888 civilian (2009); Moody Air Force Base, 5,272 military, 653 civilian (2011)

Cities
Valdosta (pt.), 54,516; Hinesville, 33,437; Savannah (pt.), 22,744

Notable
The Okefenokee Swamp — roughly 7,000 years old — covers more than 438,000 acres and is home to about 10,000 alligators and 233 species of birds.

Rep. Sanford D. Bishop Jr. (D)

Capitol Office
225-3631
www.house.gov/bishop
2429 Rayburn Bldg. 20515-1002; fax 225-2203

Committees
Appropriations

Residence
Albany

Born
Feb. 4, 1947; Mobile, Ala.

Religion
Baptist

Family
Wife, Vivian Creighton Bishop; one stepchild

Education
Morehouse College, B.A. 1968 (political science);
Emory U., J.D. 1971

Military
Army, 1971

Career
Lawyer

Political Highlights
Ga. House, 1977-91; Ga. Senate, 1991-93

ELECTION RESULTS

2010 GENERAL

Sanford D. Bishop Jr. (D)	86,520	51.4%
Mike Keown (R)	81,673	48.6%

2010 PRIMARY

Sanford D. Bishop Jr. (D)	unopposed

2008 GENERAL

Sanford D. Bishop Jr. (D)	158,435	68.9%
Lee Ferrell (R)	71,351	31.0%

Previous Winning Percentages
2006 (68%); 2004 (67%); 2002 (100%); 2000 (53%);
1998 (57%); 1996 (54%); 1994 (66%); 1992 (64%)

Elected 1992; 10th term

The soft-spoken Bishop has built a base of support by paying close attention to his district's agriculture and military interests through his post on the Appropriations Committee.

Bishop and fellow Georgian David Scott are the only African-American members of the fiscally conservative Blue Dog Coalition. Bishop calls himself a "fiscally responsible Democrat" who also supports "social programs and policies that empower families and working Americans."

Bishop supported President George W. Bush more often than any other member of the Congressional Black Caucus, and he has earned relatively high marks from both liberal and conservative groups, from unions and business organizations. He refused to back California Democrat Nancy Pelosi for Speaker in the 112th Congress (2011-12), voting "present" when the roll was called.

He has been a successful practitioner of earmarking, the practice of dedicating funds to special projects, and doesn't apologize for it, saying he is looking out for his district. He'll have to find other ways to do that now that the Republican majority has banned the practice.

In the past, earmarking has led to some unwelcome attention for Bishop.

He came under scrutiny by Georgia investigators in 2009 for earmarks he steered to the Muscogee County Junior Marshal program based in Columbus, a program where he once worked and that provides mentoring for children before they enter high school. (In fiscal 2008, he steered $117,500 to the program.) News reports indicated Bishop's stepdaughter and her husband were employed by the program, and that paychecks were deposited directly to the account of Bishop's wife, the clerk of the county municipal court. Bishop denied having prior knowledge of the employment situation. "I have tried to be above that kind of innuendo," he told The Associated Press.

Bishop's assignments on Appropriations are Agriculture and Legislative Branch, and Military Construction-VA, where he is the top Democrat. He looks out for the 2nd District's military bases, the largest of which is Fort Benning, the Army's huge infantry training base.

On the Iraq War, Bishop voted several times in favor of setting a timetable for withdrawing U.S. troops but never agreed with those who preferred to end the U.S. military deployment to Iraq by terminating its funding. "Every dollar, every dime and every penny that the president's asking for Iraq is going to be provided — plus some," he said in 2007, when public support for the war was near its nadir.

Agriculture is also central to Bishop's mission in Congress. More peanuts are grown in the 2nd than in any other congressional district, and it produces more than a quarter of the nation's output. Bishop served on the Agriculture Committee for his first decade in Congress, and there he played a crucial role in protecting peanut farmers when their subsidy program was overhauled in 2002.

His reputation for fiscal conservatism notwithstanding, Bishop voted with his party on all the major initiatives in the 111th Congress (2009-10). He backed President Obama's $787 billion economic stimulus, the Democrats' health care overhaul, the financial sector regulatory changes, and House-passed energy legislation that would have created a cap-and-trade system designed to limit carbon emissions. In December 2010, he voted to repeal of the statutory "don't ask, don't tell" policy that barred openly gay servicemembers after previously supporting the ban.

One area where he comes closer to Republicans is domestic energy production. In 2006 he was one of 27 Democrats voting to permit oil drilling in Alaska's Arctic National Wildlife Refuge.

On social issues, too, he is often conservative. He was one of 34 in his own party who voted in 2006 for a proposed constitutional amendment to ban same-sex marriage. He has backed other conservative campaigns for constitutional amendments to require balanced federal budgets, to ban desecration of the flag and to allow voluntary non-denominational prayer in schools. But he aligns with his fellow Democrats in supporting abortion rights.

Bishop also previously served on Select Intelligence and had been in line to be the top Democrat in both the 107th (2001-02) and the 108th (2003-04) Congresses. But that position went to other lawmakers.

He grew up in Mobile, Ala., where his father was the president of a community college that is now named for him — Bishop State Community College. His mother was the college librarian.

While he was at Emory University Law School, Bishop spent a summer interning with the NAACP's Legal Defense Fund in New York. After earning his law degree, he practiced civil rights law in Columbus, Ga., representing inmates at a state prison whose 1972 lawsuit resulted in a Supreme Court decision ordering changes at the facility.

Bishop was elected to the state legislature in 1976, serving for 16 years. He was on the reapportionment committee that, with stern urging from the Justice Department, in 1992 drew new congressional district maps that made the 2nd District the state's third black-majority district. Columbus business leaders helped finance his challenge to white Democratic Rep. Charles Hatcher. Bishop won the nomination with 53 percent of the vote; in November, he coasted past Republican physician Jim Dudley.

In 1995, a federal court found the new district lines to be an unconstitutional "racial gerrymander" and handed down a revised map that put Columbus in the 3rd District. The black share of the population in the redrawn 2nd dropped from 51 percent to 39 percent. Bishop moved about 90 miles southeast to Albany, in the center of the 2nd, and weathered some tough races in his next three elections.

But redistricting following the 2000 census put part of Muscogee County, his longtime home, back in the 2nd District and increased the black share of the population to 44 percent.

He was unopposed in 2002 and had little trouble until 2010, when he survived a tough re-election campaign against GOP state Rep. Mike Keown, whom he defeated 51 percent to 49 percent.

Key Votes

2010

Overhaul the nation's health insurance system	YES
Allow for repeal of "don't ask, don't tell"	NO
Overhaul financial services industry regulation	YES
Limit use of new Afghanistan War funds to troop withdrawal activities	NO
Change oversight of offshore drilling and lift oil spill liability cap	YES
Provide a path to legal status for some children of illegal immigrants	YES
Extend Bush-era income tax cuts for two years	YES

2009

Expand the Children's Health Insurance Program	YES
Provide $787 billion in tax cuts and spending increases to stimulate the economy	YES
Allow bankruptcy judges to modify certain primary-residence mortgages	YES
Create a cap-and-trade system to limit greenhouse gas emissions	YES
Provide $2 billion for the "cash for clunkers" program	YES
Establish the government as the sole provider of student loans	YES
Restrict federally funded insurance coverage for abortions in health care overhaul	YES

CQ Vote Studies

	PARTY UNITY		PRESIDENTIAL SUPPORT	
	SUPPORT	OPPOSE	SUPPORT	OPPOSE
2010	96%	4%	90%	10%
2009	96%	4%	94%	6%
2008	98%	2%	21%	79%
2007	95%	5%	10%	90%
2006	72%	28%	63%	37%

Interest Groups

	AFL-CIO	ADA	CCUS	ACU
2010	100%	75%	38%	4%
2009	100%	95%	53%	8%
2008	100%	90%	67%	4%
2007	96%	90%	70%	4%
2006	93%	65%	87%	64%

Georgia 2

Southwest — Albany, part of Columbus and Valdosta suburbs

The 2nd sits in southwestern Georgia, extending south from Talbot and Crawford counties and running along the Alabama border on the west before reaching the Florida line. Although mostly rural, the 2nd takes in the cities of Albany and Americus and more than half of Columbus. The Democratic-leaning district is racially diverse — it is now a black-plurality district, and 45 percent of the population is white.

The farming industry is still the economic lifeline of the 2nd — more than 25 percent of the nation's peanuts are grown in the district. Farmers here also grow wheat, cotton, soybeans and tobacco, and a locally owned ethanol plant in Mitchell County produces up to 100 million gallons of ethanol annually.

Big-name manufacturers and retailers had become key, although an economic downturn cost the district jobs, and unemployment rates have continued to rise. The district's two military bases play a vital role in buffering the local economy. Fort Benning (shared with the 3rd) and the Marine

Corps base in Albany have expanded operations to accommodate tens of thousands of new soldiers, contractors and family members arriving as a result of base realignment.

Pockets of GOP strength exist in centrally located Lee County, as well as in Thomasville and other southern parts of the district. Dougherty County, whose county seat is Albany, is the most populous county wholly in the district and is reliably Democratic.

In the 2010 gubernatorial election, Democratic candidate Roy Barnes won 19 of the counties in or shared by the district, including five of his top 10 counties statewide, in a losing effort.

Major Industry
Agriculture, military, manufacturing, health care

Military Bases
Fort Benning (Army), 22,123 military, 3,978 civilian (shared with the 3rd); Marine Corps Logistics Base, 453 military, 332 civilian (2009)

Cities
Columbus (pt.), 109,418; Albany, 77,434; Thomasville, 18,413

Notable
Sylvester hosts the annual Georgia Peanut Festival every October.

Rep. Lynn Westmoreland (R)

Capitol Office
225-5901
westmoreland.house.gov
2433 Rayburn Bldg. 20515-1008; fax 225-2515

Committees
Financial Services
Select Intelligence
(Oversight & Investigations - Chairman)

Residence
Grantville

Born
April 2, 1950; Atlanta, Ga.

Religion
Southern Baptist

Family
Wife, Joan Westmoreland; three children

Education
Georgia State U., attended 1969-70

Career
Construction company owner; real estate developer

Political Highlights
Sought Republican nomination for Ga. Senate, 1988;
Republican nominee for Ga. Senate, 1990; Ga. House,
1993-2005 (minority leader, 2001-03)

ELECTION RESULTS

2010 GENERAL

Lynn Westmoreland (R)	168,304	69.5%
Frank Saunders (D)	73,932	30.5%

2010 PRIMARY

Lynn Westmoreland (R)	unopposed

2008 GENERAL

Lynn Westmoreland (R)	225,055	65.7%
Stephen Camp (D)	117,522	34.3%

Previous Winning Percentages
2006 (68%); 2004 (76%)

Elected 2004; 4th term

Westmoreland has shown little inclination to hold his tongue or yield on his steadfast conservative views and combative approach to legislating, tendencies that at times have gotten him into trouble.

He compared Democrats to "a tick on a fat dog" in a 2010 op-ed criticizing excessive taxing and spending. And days before the 2010 elections, Westmoreland said a government shutdown might be necessary to win spending cuts from the Obama administration.

Westmoreland felt few regrets about his choice of words at a critical moment. "Could I have gotten my same point across and chosen my words a little more carefully? Probably," he later said. "But my message that tough choices are needed is still very real and in order to do that, we must keep our options open."

Westmoreland has risen in status in the Republican Conference, thanks to his campaign work. As one of the National Republican Congressional Committee's five vice chairmen, he helped recruit some of the GOP's victorious 2010 candidates and joined NRCC Recruitment Chairman Kevin McCarthy of California on a four-state road trip in August 2009.

As one of eight vice chairmen during the 112th Congress (2011-12), Westmoreland leads the NRCC's redistricting efforts, and he trumpeted victories in several state legislative chambers in 2010. "Winning these state Houses and state Senates is going to pay off for the next decade," he told Roll Call after Election Day.

After the elections, Westmoreland was appointed to the Republican Steering Committee, which determines GOP committee assignments, as well as the Financial Services Committee and the Select Committee on Intelligence.

His higher profile will mean an even brighter spotlight on his sometimes careless choice of words.

In September 2008, Westmoreland called President Obama and his wife, Michelle, "uppity," a racially loaded word. Westmoreland later said he considered the word akin to "elitism" and not a slur. "I think everyone knew I was being as sincere as I could be," he said of not knowing the word's connotation. "Sometimes it makes you look like a dumbass if you admit things like that. But if it makes me look like a dumbass, then I'm just a dumbass."

The incident cost Westmoreland back home in Georgia, where he considered entering the 2010 race for governor. He ultimately bowed out of consideration. "There was so much unfinished business in Congress, I just felt this was a better place for me to serve the state of Georgia," Westmoreland said.

That wasn't the first time a racial issue put Westmoreland on the spot. In 2006, he battled with the leadership over the extension of the Voting Rights Act. He and other conservatives insisted that requiring some states, mostly in the South, to receive pre-approval for changes in election laws was outmoded and should be dropped, or required of all states.

Westmoreland felt some measure of vindication for his views on the Voting Rights Act when Chief Justice John G. Roberts Jr. wrote a Supreme Court opinion in 2009 noting the severe "federalism costs" imposed by the law and that "things have changed in the South."

"Thanks for noticing, Mr. Chief Justice," Westmoreland wrote in a Washington Post op-ed. "We're proud of how far we've come in the South. Maybe one day Congress, too, will work up the courage to recognize the obvious."

In July 2007, Westmoreland was one of two House members to oppose a bill, later enacted, requiring federal investigations into unsolved murder cases from the civil rights era, calling it a waste of money. Later that year, Hawaii Democrat Neil Abercrombie accused Westmoreland of blindsiding him in protesting as wasteful several provisions in another bill that provided funds to Native Hawaiians living in the state. "I am confining my remarks to the chair, because if I was saying it directly to [Westmoreland], he would know it a lot more physically," Abercrombie said in a floor speech.

Westmoreland's strong views cost him his first leadership post in his own caucus. He was stripped of his position as deputy whip the second day on the job for not supporting a leadership-backed rule governing debate on a bill, a violation of a GOP Conference rule. GOP leaders restored the title to him in the 111th Congress (2009-10).

In the 109th Congress (2005-06), then-Appropriations Chairman Jerry Lewis went after Westmoreland when he and a small group of Republican conservatives called for an end to earmarks, funding set-asides for projects in members' districts. Staffers working for Lewis, a California Republican, leaked to the press a list of earmarks Westmoreland and his allies had quietly requested. Westmoreland got the last laugh, though. Republicans imposed a one-year ban on earmarks in 2010, and renewed it when they reclaimed the majority in the 112th Congress.

Westmoreland hails from a family of Atlanta mill workers. His father was a firefighter in the Atlanta suburbs who died on the job while responding to an early-morning alarm at a warehouse fire in freezing weather. Westmoreland spent one year at Georgia State University, but left to work full time. He was married at the time and his father-in-law hired him in his home-building business. After a few years, he started his own construction business and later expanded into real estate development and sales in the late 1980s.

Westmoreland grew up in a family of conservative Democrats, but had little interest in politics until the mid-1980s, when he was inspired by another Georgian: Newt Gingrich, the fiery conservative who was emerging as a leader and later helped Republicans win control of Congress.

Westmoreland tried but failed twice to win a seat in the state legislature before prevailing in 1992. He was helped by a reapportionment that gave him a more favorable Republican state House district. He rose through the leadership ranks and had the chance to become the first Republican Speaker of the Georgia House. But he decided instead to run for Congress in 2004.

Westmoreland won a GOP primary runoff against a Gingrich-backed candidate, Dylan Glenn, with 55 percent of the vote, then won the general election by a 3-1 margin. He has had no trouble since.

Key Votes

2010

Overhaul the nation's health insurance system	NO
Allow for repeal of "don't ask, don't tell"	NO
Overhaul financial services industry regulation	NO
Limit use of new Afghanistan War funds to troop withdrawal activities	NO
Change oversight of offshore drilling and lift oil spill liability cap	NO
Provide a path to legal status for some children of illegal immigrants	NO
Extend Bush-era income tax cuts for two years	YES

2009

Expand the Children's Health Insurance Program	NO
Provide $787 billion in tax cuts and spending increases to stimulate the economy	NO
Allow bankruptcy judges to modify certain primary-residence mortgages	NO
Create a cap-and-trade system to limit greenhouse gas emissions	NO
Provide $2 billion for the "cash for clunkers" program	NO
Establish the government as the sole provider of student loans	NO
Restrict federally funded insurance coverage for abortions in health care overhaul	YES

CQ Vote Studies

	PARTY UNITY		PRESIDENTIAL SUPPORT	
	SUPPORT	OPPOSE	SUPPORT	OPPOSE
2010	99%	1%	27%	73%
2009	99%	1%	13%	87%
2008	98%	2%	76%	24%
2007	99%	1%	91%	9%
2006	97%	3%	83%	17%

Interest Groups

	AFL-CIO	ADA	CCUS	ACU
2010	7%	0%	88%	100%
2009	5%	0%	71%	100%
2008	80%	0%	67%	100%
2007	4%	0%	72%	100%
2006	14%	5%	100%	92%

Georgia 3

West central — Atlanta and Columbus suburbs

Solidly Republican, the 3rd takes in all or part of 15 counties, beginning in overflow areas near Atlanta and ranging south and west through rural areas to reach the Alabama border and part of Columbus.

Atlanta suburbs in Fayette, Coweta and Henry counties accounted for growth in the northeastern part of the district, as new homes and subdivisions replaced previously rural areas. The population of Henry County (shared with the 13th) has grown by more than 70 percent since 2000, but as residents have left Atlanta to escape urban congestion, Henry has had to endure traffic problems of its own. Peachtree City in Fayette County is a planned community of more than 30,000 residents that is known for golf cart paths that snake through the city. Residents and officials in Henry and Fayette are concerned about high unemployment rates.

In the 3rd's more rural counties, agriculture is a mainstay. Textile and poultry plants dot the landscape, and the timber industry flourishes here. In Troup County, manufacturing is playing a larger role in LaGrange, which is nearly half black and was once famous for its textile industry, and in West

Point, home to a Kia Motors plant. To the south, the 3rd's portion of Muscogee County includes part of Columbus, Fort Benning (shared with the 2nd and expanding as a result of base realignment) and regional health care providers. The district's portion of Muscogee hosts many of Columbus' residential communities.

The 3rd is dependably Republican, despite being nearly one-quarter black. John McCain earned 64 percent of the 3rd's vote in the 2008 presidential election, and Republican Rep. Lynn Westmoreland carried the parts of each county wholly or partially in the 3rd in 2010.

Major Industry
Agriculture, service, timber, poultry processing, manufacturing

Military Bases
Fort Benning (Army), 22,123 military, 3,978 civilian (shared with the 2nd) (2011)

Cities
Columbus (pt.), 80,467; Peachtree City, 34,364; Newnan, 33,039

Notable
Franklin D. Roosevelt died on April 12, 1945, at his Little White House in Warm Springs while posing for the "Unfinished Portrait," which is now on display in the home's museum.

Rep. Hank Johnson (D)

Capitol Office
225-1605
hankjohnson.house.gov
1427 Longworth Bldg. 20515-1004; fax 226-0691

Committees
Armed Services
Judiciary

Residence
Lithonia

Born
Oct. 2, 1954; Washington, D.C.

Religion
Buddhist

Family
Wife, Mereda Davis Johnson; two children

Education
Clark College, B.A. 1976 (political science); Texas
Southern U., J.D. 1979

Career
Lawyer; county judge

Political Highlights
Sought Democratic nomination for Ga. House, 1986;
DeKalb County Board of Commissioners, 2001-06

ELECTION RESULTS

2010 GENERAL

Hank Johnson (D)	131,760	74.7%
Lisbeth "Liz" Carter (R)	44,707	25.3%

2010 PRIMARY

Hank Johnson (D)	28,095	55.2%
Vernon Jones (D)	13,407	26.3%
Connie Stokes (D)	9,411	18.5%

2008 GENERAL

Hank Johnson (D)	224,494	99.9%

Previous Winning Percentages
2006 (75%)

Elected 2006; 3rd term

A former county judge, Johnson focuses his energy on issues surrounding the courts, discrimination and antitrust law, and he has rapidly won friends and new responsibilities within the Democratic Caucus.

But in the 111th Congress (2009-10), he had a difficult second term; amid swirling questions about his health and declining weight, Johnson revealed for the first time in December 2009 that he had been diagnosed with hepatitis C in 1998. He was declared virus-free in 2009, but his battle with the blood-borne disease left him with liver and thyroid problems, as well as depression. He underwent treatment at Walter Reed Army Medical Center and, by the end of 2010, had gained back weight and was "feeling great."

Johnson is soft-spoken and calm, with a judicious temperament he developed on the bench. He and Democrat Mazie K. Hirono of Hawaii, another member of the Class of 2006, were the first two Buddhists to be elected to Congress. "My approach is not to jump out and make a big splash," he said, "but to get into the water like a crocodile — just kind of slide right in" and start swimming.

His fellow Democrats named him a regional whip, with responsibility for rounding up the votes of colleagues from Florida, Mississippi and Alabama in addition to his home state. He's a reliable vote for Democratic priorities. One of his few high-profile departures came in opposing two $700 billion measures — the second of which became law — to aid the ailing financial services industry in fall 2008.

Johnson put his legal training to use in the 111th, primarily as chairman of the Judiciary Subcommittee on the Courts and Competition Policy — he is the No. 2 Democrat on the Courts subcommittee in the 112th Congress (2011-12). He says the criminal justice system hurts minorities and the poor through such initiatives as mandatory minimum sentencing, which he calls "fundamentally unfair," and the death penalty, which he considers "immoral."

In December 2010, he led a group of lawmakers in writing to the U.S. Equal Employment Opportunity Commission asking for an investigation into possible discrimination against the long-term unemployed, arguing that the issue has a disproportionate impact on minorities.

Johnson has examined the role of antitrust law in the newspaper industry, airline mergers and the consolidation of the banking sector, as well as competition in the concert ticket business.

He scored a significant success in 2008 when Congress enacted his legislation to reauthorize the Byrne grant program, which supports state and local law enforcement. The George W. Bush administration repeatedly sought to consolidate or kill the program, but Congress refused.

Johnson has twice introduced legislation to ban pre-dispute mandatory arbitration clauses in consumer contracts, such as cell phone agreements and employee contracts, that can forbid people from filing lawsuits.

In addition to Judiciary, he serves on the Armed Services Committee. Johnson drew some ridicule after saying at a hearing that he feared the island of Guam might "tip over and capsize" because of the military buildup there. His office later explained to The Hill newspaper that he was worried that the island's infrastructure and ecosystem couldn't handle the growth.

For Johnson, serving in the House has been a homecoming. He was born and raised in Washington and still has many friends around town. Johnson's mother taught school in Arlington County, Va., just across the Potomac River. His father was a high-level official with the Federal Bureau of Prisons.

He went south for college, first to his mother's alma mater, Clark College (now Clark Atlanta University), and then to Texas Southern University for law school, where he met his wife, Mereda.

He attributes both his career choice and his political path to the influence of a much older cousin, Archibald "Tokey" Hill, who graduated from law school when Johnson was a young child. "When Tokey graduated from law school, I decided I wanted to be a lawyer," he said. His cousin moved to Oklahoma, eventually winning election to the state legislature.

Johnson, meanwhile, grew up reading The Washington Post aloud to his mother each day as she washed the dinner dishes. He also frequently passed the Capitol. "Since I wanted to be an attorney, since I wanted to be a public official like my cousin Tokey, the only legislature that I knew was the United States Congress," he said. "So it was always kind of planted in the back of my head that I would be a member of Congress one day."

First, he set about building a legal career in Georgia. For nearly three decades he practiced law with his wife in Decatur, focusing on criminal and civil litigation. Along the way he spent 10 years as an associate judge in DeKalb County. He made one unsuccessful foray into politics, seeking the Democratic nomination for the Georgia House in 1986, then in 2000 won a seat on the DeKalb County Board of Commissioners.

Johnson told the Atlanta Journal Constitution in 2009 that upon his diagnosis with hepatitis C, a doctor initially gave him only 20 years to live — and that the news had helped drive him into politics. "I determined that if I only had 20 years to live, I am going to do everything I wanted to do in life," he said.

Johnson decided to take on Democratic Rep. Cynthia A. McKinney, an often confrontational advocate for liberal causes, in the 2006 primary. Though once among her supporters, he said she became "ineffective and divisive." He held her to less than 50 percentage points of the vote in the July 2006 primary as a third Democrat in the race, John F. Coyne III, captured more than 8 percentage points of the vote. That pushed McKinney into a runoff with Johnson, who won the contest in August.

Winning the primary is tantamount to being elected in the strongly Democratic, majority-black 4th District. Johnson cruised in the general election, beating Republican Catherine Davis, a human resources manager, by more than 50 percentage points. He was unopposed in 2008 but was held to 55 percent in the Democratic primary in 2010, besting former DeKalb County CEO Vernon Jones (26.3 percent) and DeKalb County Commissioner Connie Stokes (18.5 percent). He won by 50 percentage points in November over Republican Lisbeth Carter.

Key Votes

2010

Overhaul the nation's health insurance system	YES
Allow for repeal of "don't ask, don't tell"	YES
Overhaul financial services industry regulation	YES
Limit use of new Afghanistan War funds to troop withdrawal activities	NO
Change oversight of offshore drilling and lift oil spill liability cap	YES
Provide a path to legal status for some children of illegal immigrants	YES
Extend Bush-era income tax cuts for two years	YES

2009

Expand the Children's Health Insurance Program	YES
Provide $787 billion in tax cuts and spending increases to stimulate the economy	YES
Allow bankruptcy judges to modify certain primary-residence mortgages	YES
Create a cap-and-trade system to limit greenhouse gas emissions	YES
Provide $2 billion for the "cash for clunkers" program	YES
Establish the government as the sole provider of student loans	YES
Restrict federally funded insurance coverage for abortions in health care overhaul	NO

CQ Vote Studies

	PARTY UNITY		PRESIDENTIAL SUPPORT	
	Support	Oppose	Support	Oppose
2010	98%	2%	90%	10%
2009	99%	1%	96%	4%
2008	99%	1%	12%	88%
2007	99%	1%	4%	96%

Interest Groups

	AFL-CIO	ADA	CCUS	ACU
2010	92%	90%	25%	0%
2009	100%	95%	33%	0%
2008	100%	100%	47%	8%
2007	96%	100%	47%	0%

Georgia 4
Atlanta suburbs — most of DeKalb County

The Democratic, suburban, DeKalb County-based 4th District grabs most of DeKalb and Rockdale counties and part of Gwinnett County. One of Georgia's two black-majority districts, the 4th houses a population that is 56 percent African-American.

Like the rest of the Atlanta area, southern DeKalb and northern Rockdale experienced nearly two decades of explosive growth. Decatur (shared with the 5th) is fighting to retain its small-town feel but has filled up with condos and commuters. Residential development transformed previously unpopulated land from Lithonia east through Conyers, in Rockdale County. But the collapse of the home construction sector and high unemployment rates in the metropolitan area have slowed growth and strained the local economy.

Many residents rely on jobs in Atlanta or work in service-oriented firms in the 4th. Emory University and the Centers for Disease Control and Prevention, both on the eastern edge of the 5th, employ many 4th District residents who commute in from the suburbs.

South DeKalb is home to some wealthy black communities. To the north, towns such as Chamblee and Doraville (split with the 6th) are increasingly home to large foreign-born populations, and dozens of languages are spoken in schools and at the cities' many ethnic restaurants and shops. Many of Clarkston's residents are refugees, and nearly half of the 4th's part of Gwinnett is Hispanic.

The 4th is Democratic at all levels, and Barack Obama took his highest statewide percentage in the district — his 79 percent here was slightly higher than what he received in the neighboring 5th District. DeKalb is heavily Democratic, but some voters in the portions of Rockdale and Gwinnett, and in DeKalb's more white, affluent areas, favor the GOP.

Major Industry
Service, health care, government

Cities
Redan (unincorporated), 33,015; Tucker (unincorporated), 27,581; North Atlanta (unincorporated) (pt.), 25,990

Notable
Stone Mountain Park has a huge granite rock face onto which a sculpture of Robert E. Lee and other Confederate leaders is carved.

Rep. John Lewis (D)

Capitol Office
225-3801
www.house.gov/johnlewis
343 Cannon Bldg. 20515-1005; fax 225-0351

Committees
Ways & Means

Residence
Atlanta

Born
Feb. 21, 1940; Troy, Ala.

Religion
Baptist

Family
Wife, Lillian Lewis; one child

Education
American Baptist Theological Seminary, B.A. 1961 (theology); Fisk U., B.A. 1963 (religion & philosophy)

Career
Civil rights activist

Political Highlights
Sought Democratic nomination for U.S. House (special election), 1977; Atlanta City Council, 1982-86

ELECTION RESULTS

2010 GENERAL

John Lewis (D)	130,782	73.7%
Fenn Little (R)	46,622	26.3%

2010 PRIMARY

John Lewis (D)	unopposed

2008 GENERAL

John Lewis (D)	231,368	100.0%

Previous Winning Percentages
2006 (100%); 2004 (100%); 2002 (100%); 2000 (77%); 1998 (79%); 1996 (100%); 1994 (69%); 1992 (72%); 1990 (76%); 1988 (78%); 1986 (75%)

Elected 1986; 13th term

For many admirers, Lewis is a symbol — the last surviving speaker from the 1963 march on Washington and a hero of the civil rights era. But he is also a senior member of the powerful Ways and Means Committee and an influential voice in the Democratic ranks.

Lewis holds the appointive leadership post of senior chief deputy whip and is ranking Democrat on the Ways and Means Oversight Subcommittee. As expected from someone in such leadership roles, he has been a loyal Democrat, backing his party on nearly every vote in which a majority of Democrats opposed a majority of Republicans in the 111th Congress (2009-10).

He has advanced legislation related to his civil rights background — his bill creating the National Museum of African-American History and Culture was signed into law by President George W. Bush in 2003 — but that is by no means his only focus.

From his post on Ways and Means, Lewis has promoted bills to reduce racial disparities in health care, provide medical services for the poor and the uninsured, and prevent the IRS from using private firms to collect back taxes. With a phone call to the IRS commissioner, Lewis in 2008 helped Atlanta's struggling Grady Memorial Hospital switch quickly from public to tax-exempt nonprofit status, allowing it to receive a $200 million grant from the city's largest foundation.

During the 2010 debate on the Democrats' health care overhaul, Lewis invoked a message from the civil rights era: "There are those who have told us to wait," he said on the House floor. "They have told us to be patient. We cannot wait, we cannot be patient. The American people need health care, and they need it now."

When Congress approved new surveillance powers for law enforcement after the Sept. 11 terrorist attacks in 2001, Lewis voted no, saying he feared a return to the days when the government spied on him and other civil rights leaders. Lewis has also said he doubts he could ever vote for war funding, as a matter of conscience.

In his 1998 autobiography, "Walking With the Wind," Lewis wrote, "I've never been the kind of person who naturally attracts the limelight. I'm not a handsome guy. I'm not flamboyant. I'm not what you would call elegant."

But he was in the limelight in 2010 when he and several other lawmakers alleged that they faced a barrage of racial epithets while walking to the Capitol from a House office building for votes on the health care overhaul. "People being downright mean," Lewis told Fox News.

In his younger days, Lewis sat at segregated lunch counters and joined the Freedom Riders seeking to integrate interstate bus travel in the segregated South. He gained national fame as a leader of a March 7, 1965, protest march from Selma, Ala., to the state capitol at Montgomery. State and local police attacked the peaceful marchers on the Edmund Pettus Bridge at the start of their journey in what became known as "Bloody Sunday." The outrage sparked by images of the event inspired enactment of the landmark Voting Rights Act, which President Lyndon B. Johnson signed into law in August that year. Lewis shows those who visit his office the poster-sized pictures of him being clubbed over the head by police, blows that left him with a severe concussion. He leads members of Congress on a pilgrimage each year to Selma and other major landmarks of the civil rights era.

Lewis speaks to groups of schoolchildren and voters, reminding his listeners that voting now is nearly as easy as getting a glass of water. He was overcome with emotion at President Obama's inauguration as he gazed across the Mall from the Capitol's West Front. "And then my mind started reflecting back to the suffering, the struggles, the arrests, the jailings, the beatings, to the people who stood in an unmovable line, to Dr. King, to Robert Kennedy, to John Kennedy and to Lyndon Johnson," Lewis told CNN. "And I wish — I wish so much so that they all were here to witness what we all witnessed today here on the West Front of the United States Capitol."

In November 2010, the White House announced that Lewis would receive the Presidential Medal of Freedom, the nation's highest civilian honor. Just before he was presented the medal in February 2011, Lewis announced that he had signed a deal with an Atlanta-based comic book company to write a graphic novel titled "March," about his life in the civil rights movement.

One of 10 children of sharecroppers, Lewis recalls being shy when attending segregated schools in rural Alabama. He was inspired by King's sermons on the radio and developed a sense of outrage at the 1955 lynching in Mississippi of Emmett Till, who was the same age as the then-15-year-old Lewis. Later, as a student at the American Baptist Theological Seminary in Nashville, he attended workshops on non-violent resistance. He joined the Student Nonviolent Coordinating Committee, a youthful fulcrum of the civil rights movement that focused on civil disobedience.

In 1963, with 24 arrests under his belt, he was chosen to be chairman of the SNCC. Over the next three years, he led the SNCC's effort for voting rights, including the Selma march. But a rift formed between Lewis' old guard, with its emphasis on non-violence, and the newer, more confrontational activists led by Stokely Carmichael. In 1966, Lewis was replaced by Carmichael as chairman, and the SNCC's philosophy changed.

Lewis first ran for Congress in 1977, for the seat Andrew Young left to become U.N. ambassador, but lost to Wyche Fowler. He went to Washington to head the federal volunteer agency ACTION. Returning to Atlanta, he won a seat on the city council in 1981. He made his next bid for the House in 1986, when Fowler ran for the Senate. He beat state Sen. Julian Bond for the Democratic nomination in a race that turned the longtime allies and civil rights icons into bitter rivals, then breezed to victory by a 3-to-1 margin in November.

Lewis' initial reluctance to endorse Obama in 2008 led to a rare primary challenge against him by two Democratic candidates. But he claimed victory with 69 percent of the vote and was unopposed in November for the fourth straight election. He drew a Republican opponent, attorney Fenn Little, in 2010, and won easily with 74 percent of the vote.

Key Votes

2010

Overhaul the nation's health insurance system	YES
Allow for repeal of "don't ask, don't tell"	YES
Overhaul financial services industry regulation	YES
Limit use of new Afghanistan War funds to troop withdrawal activities	YES
Change oversight of offshore drilling and lift oil spill liability cap	YES
Provide a path to legal status for some children of illegal immigrants	YES
Extend Bush-era income tax cuts for two years	NO

2009

Expand the Children's Health Insurance Program	YES
Provide $787 billion in tax cuts and spending increases to stimulate the economy	YES
Allow bankruptcy judges to modify certain primary-residence mortgages	YES
Create a cap-and-trade system to limit greenhouse gas emissions	YES
Provide $2 billion for the "cash for clunkers" program	YES
Establish the government as the sole provider of student loans	YES
Restrict federally funded insurance coverage for abortions in health care overhaul	NO

CQ Vote Studies

	PARTY UNITY		PRESIDENTIAL SUPPORT	
	SUPPORT	OPPOSE	SUPPORT	OPPOSE
2010	100%	0%	83%	17%
2009	99%	1%	93%	7%
2008	99%	1%	15%	85%
2007	98%	2%	9%	91%
2006	99%	1%	15%	85%

Interest Groups

	AFL-CIO	ADA	CCUS	ACU
2010	100%	100%	13%	0%
2009	100%	85%	43%	0%
2008	100%	95%	50%	4%
2007	95%	85%	55%	0%
2006	85%	80%	10%	4%

Georgia 5

Atlanta

The heart of the 5th lies in Atlanta, the symbolic capital of the New South and the commercial center of the Southeast. The black-plurality (49.7 percent) and reliably Democratic 5th takes in all of the city of Atlanta, much of surrounding Fulton County and slices of DeKalb and Clayton counties to the east and south.

Atlanta is a transportation hub for the area, and Hartsfield-Jackson Atlanta International Airport delivers tens of billions of dollars to the region annually. The threatened loss of Delta Air Lines operations at the airport, the airline's primary hub, would cause substantial layoffs and other economic effects. Coca-Cola and CNN also have headquarters in the 5th. Renovation of the city's business and downtown districts fueled recent growth, but high foreclosure rates have stalled the economy in some neighborhoods and falling real estate prices may not be sufficient to continue new construction.

Traffic congestion remains a problem, and officials are trying to expand mass transit lines.

Atlanta's cultural and entertainment sites — the Georgia World Congress Center, which includes Centennial Olympic Park and the Georgia Dome; Woodruff Arts Center; Turner Field, home of baseball's Braves; the World of Coca-Cola venue; and the Georgia Aquarium — are still popular tourist destinations. The 5th also hosts Emory University, Georgia State University and the Georgia Institute of Technology.

Under military base realignment rules, the Army's Fort McPherson is slated to close by late 2011, although the land could be redeveloped as a science and technology research center.

Republicans have some luck in Atlanta's affluent outlying areas such as Buckhead, a mostly old-money neighborhood with trendy shops. Democrat Barack Obama took 79 percent of the 5th's 2008 presidential vote.

Major Industry
Transportation, distribution, higher education

Cities
Atlanta, 420,003; East Point (pt.), 32,623; Sandy Springs (pt.), 30,878

Notable
The Rev. Martin Luther King Jr.'s childhood home and the Ebenezer Baptist Church, where he was a pastor, are in the Sweet Auburn neighborhood.

Rep. Tom Price (R)

Capitol Office
225-4501
tom.house.gov
403 Cannon Bldg. 20515-1006; fax 225-4656

Committees
Budget
Ways & Means

Residence
Roswell

Born
Oct. 8, 1954; Lansing, Mich.

Religion
Presbyterian

Family
Wife, Elizabeth Clark Price; one child

Education
U. of Michigan, B.A. 1976 (general studies), M.D. 1979

Career
Surgeon

Political Highlights
Ga. Senate, 1997-2005 (minority whip, 1999-2002; majority leader, 2003)

ELECTION RESULTS

2010 GENERAL

Tom Price (R)	198,100	99.9%

2010 PRIMARY

Tom Price (R)	unopposed

2008 GENERAL

Tom Price (R)	231,520	68.5%
Bill Jones (D)	106,551	31.5%

Previous Winning Percentages
2006 (72%); 2004 (100%)

Elected 2004; 4th term

Price is a highly visible champion of conservative causes and a persistent thorn in the side of congressional Democrats and the Obama administration. Chairman of the Republican Policy Committee and a former head of the Republican Study Committee, the influential group of the most conservative House members, Price is a regular on news and commentary shows, making the case for smaller government and against President Obama's economic agenda.

Price, who added a coveted seat on the Ways and Means Committee in the 112th Congress (2011-12), said one place to start would be returning to the Treasury hundreds of billions of dollars still unspent from the 2009 economic stimulus legislation and the 2008 financial industry rescue measure, both of which he opposed.

"You talk about a message that would send to the markets, that would send to folks who say, maybe Washington is actually going to be fiscally responsible for the first time in over three years," he said on Fox Business Network in June 2010. Price also sits on the Budget Committee.

Price's persona — which led The Washington Post to dub him a "Republican guerrilla warrior" — has earned him comparisons to former Speaker Newt Gingrich, a fellow Republican whose suburban-Atlanta district Price now represents. Like Price, Gingrich made a name for himself with his repeated challenges to the Democratic majority. But Price comes across more as a country-club Republican than a conservative firebrand. A medical doctor before coming to Congress, he told the Atlanta Journal-Constitution he has "a surgeon's mentality.... Instead of creating controversy, I get things done."

On Fox News in July 2010, he called supposed Democratic plans for a lame-duck session to pass bills the majority couldn't get through before the November elections "reckless" and "not truly representative." He helped organize fellow Republican members in August 2008 to prod then-Speaker Nancy Pelosi of California to call the House back into session to take up GOP energy legislation to expand oil and gas drilling. Price said Republicans were forced to take a stand against Pelosi, who "wouldn't allow the minority party to speak," and at one point he led the group in an acapella rendition of "God Bless America."

In June 2010, Price made remarks similar to those that caused trouble for Republican Joe L. Barton of Texas regarding the $20 billion fund created by BP to compensate businesses and individuals harmed by the Gulf of Mexico oil spill. Price called the fund's creation "a Chicago-style shakedown." But he took considerably less flak than Barton, who added an inflammatory apology to BP along with his own "shakedown" comment.

Price, who sat on the Financial Services Committee before joining Ways and Means, has a long record of fiscal and social conservatism.

He favors abolishing the IRS and replacing virtually all taxes — including income, corporate, dividend and capital gains — with a 23 percent national sales tax.

In his first term, he introduced a bill requiring more public disclosure for earmarks, funding for special projects in members' districts. In January 2008, he announced that he wouldn't request any new earmarks until the system is overhauled. And he was an enthusiastic supporter of the GOP's moratorium on earmarks imposed in 2010.

Formerly a member of the Education and Labor Committee (since renamed Education and the Workforce), he has introduced legislation that would protect an employer's right to require that English be spoken at its workplace.

Price was the only member of the Education panel to vote against a bill that would expand the definition of the word "disabled." He argued that the expanded definition was too broad. "If everyone is disabled, then nobody is actually disabled," he said. Price's fellow committee members, he said, were afraid to vote against the bill because of its title. "How can you vote against the Americans with Disabilities Act?" he said.

Price put his medical degree to good use as a critic of the Democrats' health care overhaul enacted in 2010. "As a physician for over 25 years, I cared for patients who bristled at the notion that the federal government ought to be involved in their health care," he said at an Education and Labor markup in July 2009. He wants the United States to adopt a system of health courts to cut down on the number of malpractice suits and wants to use tax policy to provide incentives to help families obtain health insurance.

Price grew up the son of a dairy farmer in Michigan who decided to attend medical school at age 36 to become an emergency room doctor. The younger Price recalled going on rounds as a child with his grandfather, who was also a doctor. Price moved to Atlanta for a residency in orthopedic surgery at Emory University and eventually settled in the area with his anesthesiologist wife.

He was drawn to politics because he felt lawmakers wielded too much power over his actions as a doctor. Price became increasingly involved in civic organizations such as the Rotary Club and in Republican politics as an organizer and fundraiser. When a friend in the state Senate decided to retire in 1996, she urged Price to run. In the General Assembly, he was known as a quick study on the details of policy and the rules and mechanics of passing bills. Within two years, he was chosen for a leadership position, and when Republicans took control of the state Senate in 2003, he became majority leader.

After Gingrich resigned from Congress, Republican Johnny Isakson held the seat for almost three terms. When Isakson successfully ran for the Senate in 2004, it created an opening for Price. He finished first in a seven-candidate primary, then went into a runoff against fellow GOP state Sen. Robert Lamutt. Lamutt got Gingrich's endorsement, but Price prevailed, 54 percent to 46 percent. He was unopposed in the general election and has been easily re-elected since.

In early 2011, the House Ethics Committee said it would not pursue allegations that Price and two other members violated House rules in connection with fundraising efforts in advance of a 2009 vote on a financial industry regulatory overhaul.

Key Votes

2010

Overhaul the nation's health insurance system	NO
Allow for repeal of "don't ask, don't tell"	NO
Overhaul financial services industry regulation	NO
Limit use of new Afghanistan War funds to troop withdrawal activities	NO
Change oversight of offshore drilling and lift oil spill liability cap	NO
Provide a path to legal status for some children of illegal immigrants	NO
Extend Bush-era income tax cuts for two years	YES

2009

Expand the Children's Health Insurance Program	NO
Provide $787 billion in tax cuts and spending increases to stimulate the economy	NO
Allow bankruptcy judges to modify certain primary-residence mortgages	NO
Create a cap-and-trade system to limit greenhouse gas emissions	NO
Provide $2 billion for the "cash for clunkers" program	NO
Establish the government as the sole provider of student loans	NO
Restrict federally funded insurance coverage for abortions in health care overhaul	YES

CQ Vote Studies

	PARTY UNITY		PRESIDENTIAL SUPPORT	
	Support	Oppose	Support	Oppose
2010	99%	1%	26%	74%
2009	98%	2%	11%	89%
2008	99%	1%	76%	24%
2007	98%	2%	91%	9%
2006	96%	4%	97%	3%

Interest Groups

	AFL-CIO	ADA	CCUS	ACU
2010	0%	0%	88%	100%
2009	0%	0%	73%	100%
2008	7%	10%	72%	100%
2007	4%	0%	80%	100%
2006	7%	0%	100%	92%

Georgia 6

North Atlanta suburbs — Roswell, part of Alpharetta

Set in Atlanta's northern suburbs, the 6th takes in all of Cherokee County and parts of three other counties. It is home to corporate headquarters and Republican voters. Residents in the largely white 6th are mainly affluent and well-educated. Office parks, malls, golf courses and housing subdivisions dominate most of the landscape, and the foothills of the Blue Ridge Mountains rise from northern Cherokee County.

Northern Fulton County forms the center of the 6th. It hosts UPS' corporate headquarters between Sandy Springs and Dunwoody, which is in adjacent DeKalb County. Alpharetta is a technology and telecommunications center, and is home to large offices for technology companies such as ADP. Roswell, formerly a cotton-milling center, is now a Fulton County bedroom community and home to the regional headquarters of the city's largest employer, Kimberly-Clark's biomedical manufacturing and marketing offices. Roswell's historic district lures visitors with landmarks, outdoor recreation, and shopping and dining venues.

While northern Cherokee County remains largely rural, the southern portion of the county is becoming increasingly suburban. Despite job losses across the Atlanta area, towns in Cherokee are continuing with commercial development projects. Eastern Cobb County serves as a bedroom community for downtown Atlanta, but high unemployment rates have affected the largely white-collar, highly educated suburban workforce. GE Energy has its headquarters in the southern tip of the district.

The 6th has many fiscally conservative Republican voters, although the longtime GOP stronghold is trending more to the center. Northern DeKalb County is home to Atlanta's older, more traditional suburbs, and voters include more minorities and residents who tend to be socially moderate. John McCain won 63 percent of the district's 2008 presidential vote.

Major Industry
Technology, distribution, finance, health care

Cities
Roswell, 88,346; Johns Creek, 76,728; Sandy Springs (pt.), 62,975; Alpharetta, 57,551; Dunwoody, 46,267

Notable
The city of Mountain Park (Fulton County) is home to Indian Spring — Cherokee Indians would venture from the hills to the spring, believing the waters had healing powers.

Rep. Rob Woodall (R)

Capitol Office
225-4272
woodall.house.gov
1725 Longworth Bldg. 20515-1007; fax 225-4696

Committees
Budget
Rules

Residence
Lawrenceville

Born
Feb. 11, 1970; Athens, Ga.

Religion
Methodist

Family
Single

Education
Furman U., B.A. 1992 (political science); U. of Georgia, J.D. 1997

Career
Congressional aide

Political Highlights
No previous office

ELECTION RESULTS

2010 GENERAL

Rob Woodall (R)	160,898	67.1%
Doug Heckman (D)	78,996	32.9%

2010 PRIMARY RUNOFF

Rob Woodall (R)	39,987	56.0%
Jody Hice (R)	31,426	44.0%

Elected 2010; 1st term

Though Woodall is a freshman, he is well versed in the intricacies of Capitol Hill. After 16 years as a legislative aide, he knows how to navigate the complicated tunnels of the Capitol — and brings complementary experience navigating legislative and political decisions.

All that experience won him a seat on the Rules Committee, which serves the GOP leadership by setting the parameters under which legislation is considered on the floor.

Woodall's familiarity with the ways of the House is evident in the government-speak he sometimes employs, tossing out references to HIPAA and ERISA without pausing to explain to listeners what he's talking about. (The Employee Retirement Income Security Act of 1974 sets minimum standards for pension and health plans. The Health Insurance Portability and Accountability Act of 1996 protects the privacy of individuals' health information.)

But his familiarity with such arcana will come in handy on the Budget Committee. That panel can serve as a platform for espousing his favorite idea: a national sales tax that would replace almost all existing income taxes. Woodall's former boss and predecessor, Republican John Linder, was a stalwart advocate of the plan and the author of a book on the idea, "The FairTax Book: Saying Goodbye to the Income Tax and the IRS."

His party, Woodall said, must guard against repeating the mistakes of Republicans who won in 1994 but abandoned their small-government principles. "If it's wrong when Nancy Pelosi does it, then it's also going to be wrong when John Boehner does it," he said.

Prior to working for Linder, Woodall received a political science degree from Furman University and a law degree from the University of Georgia.

After nine terms in the House, Linder announced his retirement in February 2010. He endorsed Woodall, who finished well ahead of an eight-candidate Republican primary field. He won a runoff with talk show host and Baptist minister Jody Hice to claim the nomination in the overwhelmingly GOP district.

In the general election, he faced Democrat Doug Heckman, a veteran of both Iraq and Afghanistan, and won by 34 percentage points.

Georgia 7

East of Atlanta — outer Atlanta suburbs

A mix of eastern Atlanta suburbs and less-populous areas west of Athens, the solidly Republican 7th is centered in Gwinnett County (shared with the 4th).

The rest of the 7th is split between suburban and rural areas, which include small parts of Newton and Forsyth counties and all of sparsely populated Barrow and Walton counties.

The 7th was Georgia's fastest-growing district in the last decade — its population has increased by 43 percent since 2000. Despite their historically rural composition, western Walton, Barrow and Newton counties have begun to fill up with bedroom communities. Some district residents still commute to Atlanta for work, but jobs in Gwinnett County keep many locals here during the day, with an emerging science corridor along

Interstate 85 that hosts several technology firms. Retail and service jobs have replaced manufacturing, but there have been employment cuts in county government and the white-collar private sector.

Gwinnett accounts for more than three-fourths of the 7th's population, and the county's Hispanic population more than doubled during the last decade. There are more Hispanic and Asian residents in Gwinnett than in any other Georgia county.

The 7th's small portion of Newton County is more friendly to Democrats, but Gwinnett's Republican support keeps the district safely in the GOP corner. Changing demographics in Gwinnett, however, may alter the 7th's political makeup in the coming years.

Major Industry
Service, retail, technology, construction

Cities
Lawrenceville, 28,546; Duluth, 26,600

Notable
The people of Duluth elected the state's first female mayor, Alice H. Strickland, in 1922.

Rep. Austin Scott (R)

Capitol Office
225-6531
austinscott.house.gov
516 Cannon Bldg. 20515-1003; fax 225-3013

Committees
Agriculture
Armed Services

Residence
Ashburn

Born
Dec. 10, 1969; Augusta, Ga.

Religion
Baptist

Family
Wife, Vivien Scott; one child

Education
U. of Georgia, B.B.A. 1993 (risk management and insurance)

Career
Insurance agency owner

Political Highlights
Ga. House, 1997-2011

ELECTION RESULTS

2010 GENERAL

Austin Scott (R)	102,770	52.7%
Jim Marshall (D)	92,250	47.3%

2010 PRIMARY

Austin Scott (R)	22,191	52.4%
Ken DeLoach (R)	13,228	31.2%
Diane Vann (R)	6,959	16.4%

Elected 2010; 1st term

During a brief campaign for governor in 2009, Scott walked across the state — totaling more than 1,000 miles in 64 days. The conservative Republican is following another, less literal, road in Congress, one guided by traditional GOP principles: limited government, tax cuts and support for small business.

He secured an early commitment from Republican leaders for a seat on the Armed Services Committee. From that perch, he will be able to support veterans and workers affiliated with Robins Air Force Base, a major employer and community institution in the 8th District.

Speaker John A. Boehner of Ohio, then the minority leader, made the committee seat pledge during a campaign swing through the district to give Scott a boost against Democratic incumbent and eight-year panel veteran Jim Marshall.

Scott also won a seat on the Agriculture Committee, where he can look out for the cotton, peanut, peach, pecan and timber growers in the district.

Scott, who owns an insurance brokerage firm, voted in early 2011 to repeal the Democrats' health care overhaul enacted in 2010. With Democrats controlling the Senate, that effort is likely to proceed no further in the 112th Congress (2011-12), but Scott said defunding the legislation is an option.

After abandoning his gubernatorial bid, Scott entered the 8th District race to oust Marshall. The incumbent, in a nod to the district's conservative leanings, announced he would not vote again for Nancy Pelosi for Speaker, after Scott reportedly called him a "Pelosicrat."

During the campaign, a Democratic activist filed a motion to have Scott's 10-year-old divorce records unsealed. Marshall denied involvement and a judge delayed a ruling until after the election. The records were ordered released in February 2011.

Scott unseated Marshall by about 5 percentage points in a district where Republican John McCain defeated Democrat Barack Obama 56 percent to 43 percent in the 2008 presidential election.

He was chosen to give the GOP's Thanksgiving Day radio address, and his colleagues elected him freshman class president.

Georgia 8
Middle Georgia — Macon

The 8th, a long strip of central Georgia, extends from outer Atlanta suburbs in Newton County south through Macon to Colquitt County near the Florida border. The district is politically, economically and racially diverse and includes urban, suburban and rural areas. About one-third of residents are black, and although the district is generally middle class, pockets of poverty dot the 8th.

Macon has a diverse economy with regional distribution centers, a university and a hospital system. South of Macon, Robins Air Force Base is the area's economic engine; the base employs more than 25,000 people, including military and civilian personnel and aerospace contractors and manufacturers.

In the 8th's north, growing Newton County serves as a bedroom community for Atlanta, and some of the rural counties to the south of Newton also now house commuters. The 8th relies heavily on agriculture, especially in the southern tier of the district where cotton and peanuts are grown. Timber, peaches and pecans also are harvested in the 8th, and every county here has some agricultural production.

Many residents will support Democrats at the local level but back the GOP in national races. Macon, more than 60 percent black, is a Democratic stronghold. Colquitt and Tift, in the southern tip, have become solidly GOP counties. Increases in black and younger residents in the 8th's part of Newton may shift it to the left.

Major Industry
Agriculture, aerospace, distribution, timber

Military Bases
Robins Air Force Base, 6,614 military, 14,324 civilian (2011)

Cities
Macon, 91,351; Warner Robins (pt.), 66,224

Notable
Macon's Wesleyan College began granting degrees to women in 1840.

Rep. Tom Graves (R)

Capitol Office
225-5211
tomgraves.house.gov
1113 Longworth Bldg. 20515-1010; fax 225-8272

Committees
Appropriations

Residence
Ranger

Born
Feb. 3, 1970; St. Petersburg, Fla.

Religion
Baptist

Family
Wife, Julie Graves; three children

Education
U. of Georgia, B.B.A. 1993 (finance)

Career
Commercial property developer; landscape company owner; retail repossessions agent

Political Highlights
Gordon Co. Board of Election and Voter Registration, 2001-02; Ga. House, 2003-10

ELECTION RESULTS

2010 GENERAL

Tom Graves (R)		unopposed

2010 PRIMARY RUNOFF

Tom Graves (R)	41,878	55.2%
Lee Hawkins (R)	33,975	44.8%

2010 SPECIAL RUNOFF

Tom Graves (R)	22,694	56.4%
Lee Hawkins (R)	17,509	43.6%

Elected June 2010; 1st full term

For Graves, who first won his House seat in a June 2010 special election, "the No. 1 issue is out-of-control spending." He is in position to exert some influence because he has a hand on the tiller as a member of the Appropriations Committee.

But even before he officially took his seat on the spending panel in the 112th Congress (2011-12), he struck a blow for his version of fiscal responsibility, voting against a measure in late 2010 that extended the George W. Bush-era tax rates for two years while providing funding for unemployment benefits and other programs that was not offset.

He had pushed to give House members the option to amend the tax deal to permanently extend the tax rates and pay for its spending provisions, but Democratic leaders allowed no votes on amendments.

"I could not support a bill that simply kicked our economic problems down the road," he said. "Approving more deficit spending and temporarily extending tax rates means we will continue the cycle of uncertainty and have another tax fight in two years."

When the Appropriations Committee approved a bill to fund the government for the remainder of fiscal 2011, he "reluctantly" supported it, while prodding the GOP leadership — successfully, as it turned out — to go beyond the $32 billion cuts approved by the spending panel.

His focus on taxes combines the "less spending, smaller government" mantra with a pro-business emphasis on incentives for hiring. He blames stunted job growth on "excessive taxation, insufficient liquidity, economic uncertainty, and red tape and government mandates."

The best way government can help, he says, is "not by government getting engaged, but by getting out of the way."

Graves also signed on to the anti-tax group Club for Growth's pledge to undo the Democrats' health care overhaul enacted in March 2010. Graves is in favor of offering tax breaks on insurance for individuals. "There are plenty of solutions out there that don't involve a government takeover," he said.

Just over a month into his first term he introduced his first and only bill in the 111th Congress (2009-10): a measure to block funds to implement the health care law. In January 2011, he reintroduced the bill and voted for House-passed legislation to repeal the law.

Graves has also called for constitutional amendments requiring a balanced budget and giving the president a line-item veto.

In his seven years in the Georgia House, Graves backed tax cuts, including a plan to eliminate the state's net worth tax. At the federal level, he supports replacing the income tax with a nationwide sales tax.

Conservative social policy formed a large portion of Graves' platform in the state House, with a particular emphasis on abortion. He and his wife, Julie, opposed plans to open an abortion clinic in their home county in 2001. The clinic never opened, and in 2010 Graves won an endorsement from the Georgia Right to Life PAC.

But Graves voted against a measure in early 2011 to extend expiring provisions of the anti-terrorism law known as the Patriot Act, arguing that the law is "in conflict with the Fourth Amendment."

During his tenure in the state legislature, Graves clashed with members of his own party more than once. He was stripped of his committee assignments following a divisive confirmation vote, and a conservative caucus Graves organized fell apart in 2008 after four years.

Born in St. Petersburg, Fla., Graves grew up in Bartow County, Ga. Church is a central feature of his personal life: Graves met his wife during a singles program at their Baptist church, where he is now a deacon.

Graves' political career began when local Republican Party leaders nominated him in 2001 for a post on the Gordon County Board of Election and Voter Registration, to which he was confirmed by the Board of Commissioners and where he served for nine months. He resigned in 2002 to run for an open seat in the Georgia House.

Formerly an owner of a landscaping company, Graves also operated as a commercial property developer, an enterprise that became a distraction at the tail end of his special election campaign when it was reported that a bank had sued his company for non-payment of a loan. Graves filed a counter-claim against the bank.

To get to Congress and stay there, Graves had to defeat former state Sen. Lee Hawkins four times in 2010.

Backed by a groundswell of support from tea party activists and socially conservative Republicans in an April special election, Graves and Hawkins emerged out of an eight-candidate, all-party field, but neither achieved the 50 percent mark needed to win the seat outright. Two members of the Georgia GOP delegation in the U.S. House weighed in during the runoff contest, with John Linder providing robo-calls on behalf of Hawkins and Lynn Westmoreland endorsing Graves. Graves, who had beaten Hawkins by 12 percentage points in the first round, also was endorsed by House Republican leaders including Mike Pence of Indiana and Eric Cantor of Virginia. He won the June runoff by 13 percentage points.

A month later, in the GOP primary for the full term in the 112th Congress, Graves just barely failed to top 50 percent of the vote, with Hawkins again coming in second with 27 percent. In the August runoff, Graves bested Hawkins 56 percent to 44 percent. He was unopposed in November.

Graves made an impression quickly upon his arrival.

A day after being sworn into office in June, he bumped against a House rule that bars the use of footage from the floor being used on campaign websites. Staff had posted video of the ceremony on the campaign's You-Tube account and Facebook page. The video was quickly taken down.

On the upside, after only six weeks in office his fellow GOP first-termers voted him freshman of the year, and he was praised as a "rising star." He was a charter member of the Tea Party Caucus and also joined the more established Republican Study Committee, a group of the most conservative House members.

Key Votes

2010

Overhaul financial services industry regulation	NO
Limit use of new Afghanistan War funds to troop withdrawal activities	NO
Change oversight of offshore drilling and lift oil spill liability cap	NO
Provide a path to legal status for some children of illegal immigrants	NO
Extend Bush-era income tax cuts for two years	NO

CQ Vote Studies

	PARTY UNITY		PRESIDENTIAL SUPPORT	
	SUPPORT	OPPOSE	SUPPORT	OPPOSE
2010	99%	1%	24%	76%

Interest Groups

	AFL-CIO	ADA	CCUS	ACU
2010	0%	5%	67%	100%

North — Dalton, Gainesville

Anchored by North Georgia's mountains, the 9th runs across most of the state's northern border. It includes Cloudland Canyon State Park, the man-made Lake Lanier, a chunk of the Chattahoochee National Forest and several Atlanta suburbs, as well as bedroom communities outside of Chattanooga, Tenn.

The 9th's economy long depended on poultry processing and carpet manufacturing industries rooted in Gainesville and Dalton. A once-robust manufacturing sector has bled jobs, and recent periods of extended high unemployment have put a strain on Dalton.

As Atlanta expanded northward, the surge of new residents in the district's south brought white-collar and service-sector jobs to the 9th and began to diversify the local economy — Forsyth County is the seventh-fastest growing county in the nation since 2000. Gainesville is home to the Northeast Georgia Medical Center, a regional health care hub. Near the state's northwestern corner, Catoosa and Walker counties grew steadily as residents who commute to Chattanooga moved into new communities. In the northeast, mountainous Fannin, Union and White counties are popular destinations for tourists and retirees.

The district has the state's smallest proportion of black residents (3 percent), although its Hispanic population expanded when jobs were available in the blue-collar manufacturing and food processing industries. As a whole, the 9th's population is overwhelmingly white.

The district votes strongly Republican at both the national and local levels. Republican John McCain received 75 percent of the district's vote in the 2008 presidential election, his highest percentage statewide. Dawson and Forsyth counties were Gov. Nathan Deal's best and third-best counties in the 2010 gubernatorial election — he represented the district in the U.S. House for more than 16 years.

Major Industry
Poultry processing, service, manufacturing

Cities
Gainesville, 33,804; Dalton, 33,128

Notable
Springer Mountain is the southern terminus of the 2,175-mile Appalachian National Scenic Trail.

Rep. Paul Broun (R)

Capitol Office
225-4101
broun.house.gov
325 Cannon Bldg. 20515-1009; fax 226-0776

Committees
Homeland Security
Natural Resources
Science, Space & Technology
  (Investigations & Oversight - Chairman)

Residence
Watkinsville

Born
May 14, 1946; Atlanta, Ga.

Religion
Southern Baptist

Family
Wife, Niki Broun; three children

Education
U. of Georgia, B.S. 1967 (chemistry); Medical College
of Georgia, M.D. 1971

Military
Marine Corps Reserve, 1964-67; Naval Reserve,
1967-72; Ga. Air National Guard, 1972-73

Career
Physician

Political Highlights
Republican nominee for U.S. House, 1990; sought
Republican nomination for U.S. House, 1992; sought
Republican nomination for U.S. Senate, 1996

ELECTION RESULTS

2010 GENERAL

Paul Broun (R)	138,062	67.4%
Russell Edwards (D)	66,905	32.6%

2010 PRIMARY

Paul Broun (R)	unopposed

2008 GENERAL

Paul Broun (R)	177,265	60.7%
Bobby Saxon (D)	114,638	39.3%

Previous Winning Percentages
2007 Special Election (50%)

Elected 2007; 2nd full term

Broun is a passionate conservative with an affinity for colorful sound bites and a deep belief in limiting the powers of the federal government. Following the rousing electoral victories of dozens of similarly minded Republicans in 2010, he says he is even more encouraged to fight for his vision.

Broun (BROWN) has drawn attention for his insistence that the health care overhaul enacted in 2010 constitutes a government takeover of the system, his vocal skepticism about human-induced global warming and his suggestions that President Obama is a socialist. In the past, he has attracted publicity for introducing a bill to ban sales of Playboy and Penthouse at military bases and for taking part in a religious ceremony to anoint with oil the Capitol passageway that Obama walked through to take the presidential oath of office.

By 2009, Broun had risen to his party's top spot on the Investigations and Oversight Subcommittee of what was then called the Science and Technology Committee, and to deputy ranking member of the Homeland Security Committee's Intelligence panel. In the 112th Congress (2011-12), he took over as chairman of the Oversight panel of Science, Space and Technology, and became vice chairman of Homeland's Counterterrorism and Intelligence Subcommittee. From the latter seat, he told Homeland Security Secretary Janet Napolitano in early 2011 that DHS should "focus on those entities that want to do us harm," meaning violent Islamic extremists, and said "we've got to profile these folks."

From his seat on Homeland Security, Broun is in a position to pull in federal dollars for biodefense research facilities back home. Just southeast of the district is South Carolina's Savannah River Site, a nuclear facility. He also takes a hard line on illegal immigration and opposes proposals to give legal status and a path to citizenship to the millions of illegal immigrants in the United States.

He also sits on the Natural Resources Committee. In July 2010, Broun unsuccessfully pushed an amendment to legislation intended to reorganize the federal government's oversight of energy drilling and leasing practice. His proposal sought to prevent government officials from blocking media access to areas of the Gulf Coast after the spring 2010 oil spill in the Gulf of Mexico.

Broun, who won his seat in a 2007 special election, said the most outstanding aspect of serving in the minority during his first two terms was "how little the Democratic leadership would listen to the American people." He argues that federal government authority should be limited to the 18 powers outlined under Article I, Section 8 of the U.S. Constitution.

"I'm going to work very hard to try to push powers back to states and the people, as they should be. I'm trying to stop government from intruding on our lives," Broun said.

He has historically been loyal to the GOP agenda. In 2008, Broun was the only House Republican to back his party on every issue in which a majority of Republicans voted against a majority of Democrats. In 2009, he supported his party on such votes 98 percent of the time; in 2010, 99 percent. He has said he employs a four-part test to judge bills, taking into account their affordability, morality and necessity in addition to constitutionality.

He has no regrets about past comments on Obama, saying his characterization is appropriate given the president's policies and closest advisers. During the 2011 State of the Union address, Broun posted on Twitter: "Mr. President, you don't believe in the Constitution. You believe in socialism."

Much of Broun's ire is directed at the health care overhaul legislation, which he said is "designed to fail." A family physician by trade, he said employers already are dropping health insurance for their employees and pushing more people onto the "public option-light" state exchanges and, eventually, a single-payer health care system. He argues that a provision in the 2009 stimulus law provided for a cost-effectiveness research panel that will lead to denied treatment for the chronically ill and elderly, while also squashing innovation.

Broun backed repeal early in 2011, having sponsored alternatives in the previous Congress that he said would "put in place market principles," including providing more health care tax credits, creating Medicare health savings accounts and expanding insurance pooling options.

Broun was critical of Obama's $787 billion economic stimulus package in early 2009, as well as the two $700 billion proposals — the second of which became law — in fall 2008 to aid the ailing financial services sector. In 2010, he introduced legislation to reduce corporate tax rates to 25 percent.

Broun, who had previously lost three bids for Congress, confounded conventional wisdom by winning the 2007 special election to succeed the late Republican Charlie Norwood, who died of cancer. Broun edged out former state Sen. Jim Whitehead, a friend of Norwood's. Trying to build a political base, Broun spent his first few months in Congress attempting to heal remaining wounds from his bruising fight with Whitehead, who had been the best-known candidate and the only officeholder in the 10-person special-election field. Since then, he has won re-election easily.

Instead of focusing on fundraising, as many freshmen do, Broun set up district offices, including one in Augusta, Norwood's hometown and a city where Whitehead enjoyed an overwhelming advantage. Broun traveled extensively throughout the nearly 6,000-square-mile district, touting his conservatism and support for George W. Bush's policies in Iraq.

The son of a tire dealership owner and stay-at-home mother, Broun was 16 when his father was elected to the Georgia Senate, where he served for nearly four decades. The same year, a peanut farmer from Plains named Jimmy Carter was elected to the same chamber. Broun's parents and the Carters became friends, and the future president would use Broun's bed for the night when visiting Athens.

In high school, Broun joined the ROTC. For much of the Vietnam War, he was in the Naval Reserve and the Georgia Air National Guard, while also attending medical school. Broun did not see active duty. He remained in Athens to attend college, earning a bachelor's degree from the University of Georgia in 1967 and, four years later, a medical degree from the Medical College of Georgia in Augusta. Broun eventually opened a practice in his hometown and ran it with a personal touch, routinely making house calls.

Key Votes

2010

Overhaul the nation's health insurance system	NO
Allow for repeal of "don't ask, don't tell"	NO
Overhaul financial services industry regulation	NO
Limit use of new Afghanistan War funds to troop withdrawal activities	NO
Change oversight of offshore drilling and lift oil spill liability cap	NO
Provide a path to legal status for some children of illegal immigrants	NO
Extend Bush-era income tax cuts for two years	NO

2009

Expand the Children's Health Insurance Program	NO
Provide $787 billion in tax cuts and spending increases to stimulate the economy	NO
Allow bankruptcy judges to modify certain primary-residence mortgages	NO
Create a cap-and-trade system to limit greenhouse gas emissions	NO
Provide $2 billion for the "cash for clunkers" program	NO
Establish the government as the sole provider of student loans	NO
Restrict federally funded insurance coverage for abortions in health care overhaul	YES

CQ Vote Studies

	PARTY UNITY		PRESIDENTIAL SUPPORT	
	SUPPORT	OPPOSE	SUPPORT	OPPOSE
2010	99%	1%	22%	78%
2009	98%	2%	10%	90%
2008	100%	0%	83%	17%
2007	99%	1%	93%	7%

Interest Groups

	AFL-CIO	ADA	CCUS	ACU
2010	0%	5%	75%	100%
2009	0%	0%	73%	100%
2008	0%	0%	67%	100%
2007	0%		64%	100%

Georgia 10

Northeast — Athens; part of Augusta

The Republican-leaning 10th takes in the state's mountainous northeastern corner and traces its eastern border to Augusta's GOP-heavy suburbs. In the west, Athens is home to the University of Georgia.

Higher-education jobs lend stability to the district's economy, which mainly has escaped the high levels of unemployment affecting the rest of the state. The University of Georgia provides service and health care jobs, and expansion of the Georgia Health Sciences University is expected to spur job growth. Agriculture remains an economic mainstay for many in the 10th: dairy, cattle, corn, soybeans and some cotton are produced in the district. The 10th's northern tier is largely rural, and the tourism-based economy near the Blue Ridge Mountains and a chain of lakes along the South Carolina border remains important.

The 10th's southeastern arm takes in Augusta's northern and western suburbs in the district's portion of Richmond County and includes all of Columbia County, home to many Augusta commuters. Fort Gordon, mostly in Richmond, is home to the Army Signal Center. The Savannah River Site, a nuclear research facility located across the river in South Carolina, is still a key employer here despite losing thousands of jobs since the mid-1990s. Augusta is also a manufacturing and retail hub.

The majority of the district's population lives in rural areas that support the GOP, and the suburbs in Columbia County are also overwhelmingly Republican. Rep. Paul Broun won every county in the district in 2010 except for Clarke County, home to Athens, a liberal college town. Richmond, which has a large African-American population, supported Broun but also voted for Democratic gubernatorial candidate and former Gov. Roy Barnes.

Major Industry
Higher education, service, agriculture, manufacturing

Military Bases
Fort Gordon (Army), 10,408 military, 3,072 civilian (2009) (shared with the 12th)

Cities
Athens-Clarke, 115,452; Augusta-Richmond (pt.), 83,804; Martinez (unincorporated), 35,795

Notable
The annual Masters golf tournament is held at Augusta National Golf Club.

Rep. Phil Gingrey (R)

Capitol Office
225-2931
www.house.gov/gingrey
442 Cannon Bldg. 20515-1011; fax 225-2944

Committees
Energy & Commerce
House Administration
(Oversight - Chairman)

Residence
Marietta

Born
July 10, 1942; Augusta, Ga.

Religion
Roman Catholic

Family
Wife, Billie Gingrey; four children

Education
Georgia Institute of Technology, B.S. 1965 (chemistry); Medical College of Georgia, M.D. 1969

Career
Physician

Political Highlights
Marietta Board of Education, 1993-97 (chairman, 1994-97); Ga. Senate, 1999-2003

ELECTION RESULTS

2010 GENERAL
Phil Gingrey (R)		unopposed

2010 PRIMARY
Phil Gingrey (R)		unopposed

2008 GENERAL
Phil Gingrey (R)	204,082	68.2%
Hugh "Bud" Gammon (D)	95,220	31.8%

Previous Winning Percentages
2006 (71%); 2004 (57%); 2002 (52%)

Elected 2002; 5th term

Gingrey counts himself among the most conservative lawmakers in the House — he belongs to the Republican Study Committee and is a charter member of the Tea Party Caucus. An obstetrician before arriving in Congress, his medical background has been a prominent part of his political life, and he was a leading critic of the Democratic overhaul of the health care system enacted in 2010.

At the beginning of the 111th Congress (2009-10), Gingrey was granted coveted seats on the Energy and Commerce Committee and its Health Subcommittee, giving him a platform for his views on health care legislation but forcing him to give up seats on Armed Services and Science and Technology. In early 2009, he was tapped to join 15 other House Republicans to craft a GOP alternative to the Democratic plan.

He has cited his desire to limit medical malpractice suits as one of his reasons for running for Congress. The House in 2005 approved his legislation to cap punitive damage awards at $250,000, but the bill, like similar measures before it, died in the Senate. He came back in 2010 with a broader measure that would set caps, encourage early settlements and establish a statute of limitations, among other provisions.

And he bemoaned the absence of major changes to that system in the overhaul. "Why did health care reform not include meaningful medical liability reform?" Gingrey wrote with another physician-lawmaker, Louisiana Republican John Fleming, in a Roll Call opinion piece in July 2010. "Unfortunately, we believe that former Democratic National Committee Chairman Howard Dean got it right when he said at a town hall meeting last year that 'the people who wrote it did not want to take on the trial lawyers.' "

Though he doesn't participate in the confirmation process, Gingrey took issue with the recess appointment of Donald M. Berwick to head the Centers for Medicare and Medicaid Services.

"I feel sorry for those seniors who maybe have a family history of Alzheimer's and they're . . . getting into their 70s, and what kind of care they're going to get," Gingrey said on the Fox Business Network in July 2010, referring to Berwick's previous statements in favor of rationing health care. "They're going to be thrown under the bus."

In early 2009, Gingrey opposed a bill to expand the Children's Health Insurance Program, which covers children whose low-income families make too much money to qualify for Medicaid. He and other Republicans worried the bill did not focus on a limited group of low-income people.

He is opposed to requiring young girls to be vaccinated against human papilloma virus as a condition of attending school and favors government help to widen the use of information technology in the medical sector. He sponsored bills on both issues in the 111th Congress. He is one of the House's staunchest opponents of abortion, including in cases of rape or incest.

Gingrey is generally a fiscal conservative. In fall 2008, he joined many conservatives in voting against a $700 billion package — which became law — to rescue the financial services industry. Likewise, he opposed President Obama's economic stimulus package in early 2009. Gingrey backed a Republican alternative that included, among other things, a repeal of the alternative minimum tax, a cut in the top corporate tax rate and spending cuts.

Subsequently, he opposed a $410 billion catchall spending bill for 2009. Yet Taxpayers for Common Sense noted he obtained the third most earmarks — funding set-asides for special projects — in the bill, in terms of dollar value, among House members; he netted $36.3 million, mostly for water and infrastructure projects.

During the 110th Congress (2007-08), Gingrey used his seat on the Armed Services Committee to support the F-22 Raptor fighter, which is largely made at a Lockheed Martin plant in Marietta, in his district. He pressed the Obama administration in early 2009 — unsuccessfully — to continue production of the F-22.

In the 112th Congress (2011-12), Gingrey sits on the House Administration Committee, which oversees federal elections and the internal operations of the House. As chairman of the newly created Subcommittee on Oversight, Gingrey has jurisdiction over congressional support agencies such as the Library of Congress and the Architect of the Capitol.

In early 2009, Gingrey was the subject of numerous blogs and opinion pieces after he criticized conservative radio commentator Rush Limbaugh. He rebuked Limbaugh for saying he wanted President Obama to fail, then subsequently apologized to the radio host for his comments.

Gingrey's mother was the daughter of Irish immigrants and grew up in New York City. His father, who grew up in South Carolina, owned a series of small businesses, including a drive-through restaurant, a liquor store and a motel in Augusta, Ga. Gingrey worked his way through the Georgia Institute of Technology with a factory job. He intended to become an engineer, but after visiting an operating room with a family friend who was a neurosurgeon, he decided to go to medical school. Gingrey served about four years as Marietta school board chairman when his children were in school, then went on to two terms in the Georgia Senate while continuing his medical practice. He became well-known for advocating tighter teen driving laws.

In 2001, he considered challenging Democratic incumbent Max Cleland in the Senate. But after redistricting gave Georgia two new House seats, he decided to run for that chamber. The new 11th District had a Democratic tilt, so Republican Bob Barr, who represented a portion of it, chose to run in the 7th District primary against John Linder. With Barr out, Gingrey jumped in and won the primary in the 11th. In November, he took 52 percent of the vote against Roger Kahn, a wholesale liquor distributor who lent his campaign $2.5 million. Gingrey appealed to the right, including religious conservatives, and got help from the American Medical Association, which paid for polling and radio ads.

Mid-decade redistricting in 2005 was favorable to the GOP, and Gingrey won with 71 percent of the vote in 2006 and 68 percent in 2008. He was unopposed in 2010.

Key Votes

2010

Overhaul the nation's health insurance system	NO
Allow for repeal of "don't ask, don't tell"	NO
Overhaul financial services industry regulation	NO
Limit use of new Afghanistan War funds to troop withdrawal activities	NO
Change oversight of offshore drilling and lift oil spill liability cap	NO
Provide a path to legal status for some children of illegal immigrants	?
Extend Bush-era income tax cuts for two years	NO

2009

Expand the Children's Health Insurance Program	NO
Provide $787 billion in tax cuts and spending increases to stimulate the economy	NO
Allow bankruptcy judges to modify certain primary-residence mortgages	NO
Create a cap-and-trade system to limit greenhouse gas emissions	NO
Provide $2 billion for the "cash for clunkers" program	YES
Establish the government as the sole provider of student loans	NO
Restrict federally funded insurance coverage for abortions in health care overhaul	YES

CQ Vote Studies

	PARTY UNITY		PRESIDENTIAL SUPPORT	
	SUPPORT	OPPOSE	SUPPORT	OPPOSE
2010	99%	1%	25%	75%
2009	95%	5%	20%	80%
2008	99%	1%	72%	28%
2007	98%	2%	92%	8%
2006	96%	4%	87%	13%

Interest Groups

	AFL-CIO	ADA	CCUS	ACU
2010	8%	5%	75%	100%
2009	10%	5%	73%	96%
2008	7%	10%	78%	96%
2007	4%	0%	75%	100%
2006	14%	5%	87%	92%

Georgia 11

Northwest — Rome, most of Marietta

Nestled against the Alabama border in northwest Georgia, the 11th runs south from Chattooga County into Carroll County and east into the western Atlanta suburbs in Cobb County. The conservative district takes in all of six counties and parts of three others, spanning rural areas in the west, small cities such as Rome and suburbs such as Marietta.

The 11th's chunk of Cobb hosts white-collar, middle-income suburbs and most of the city of Marietta (shared with the 13th and 6th districts), where the economy relies on aerospace and military jobs. The local Lockheed Martin plant in Marietta builds cargo and fighter planes. A naval air station next to Lockheed Martin closed in 2009 as a result of the base realignment process, but the site transferred to the state and now hosts the headquarters for the state national guard. Unemployment across non-defense-related jobs has hurt Cobb's economy.

Paulding, the ninth-fastest-growing county in the nation since 2000, has been filling up with residents who commute to Atlanta. To the west, the string of rural counties along the Alabama border still depend on hay, cotton, corn and soybean farming. Haralson County hosts Honda facilities, and

Rome, in Floyd County, is home to three colleges, several medical centers and manufacturing plants — Pirelli Tires plans continued expansion of its large Rome factory. Textiles and carpet manufacturing remain important in the 11th's northern counties despite layoffs, and several small towns have attracted mid-size manufacturing firms.

Safe territory for the GOP in federal and state elections, the district does play host to some conservative Southern Democrats in rural counties who still vote for Democrats locally. The 11th's portion of Cobb, which accounts for roughly one-third of the district's population, remains a GOP stronghold, as does adjacent Paulding. Republican Nathan Deal took at least 60 percent of the vote in every county wholly in the 11th in the 2010 gubernatorial election.

Major Industry
Defense, manufacturing, textiles, agriculture

Cities
Marietta (pt.), 45,632; Rome, 36,303; Kennesaw, 29,783

Notable
Like its Italian namesake, Rome is built on seven hills; a Kennesaw law requires each household to have a gun and the appropriate ammunition.

Rep. John Barrow (D)

Capitol Office
225-2823
barrow.house.gov
2202 Rayburn Bldg. 20515-1012; fax 225-3377

Committees
Energy & Commerce
Veterans' Affairs

Residence
Savannah

Born
Oct. 31, 1955; Athens, Ga.

Religion
Baptist

Family
Divorced; two children

Education
U. of Georgia, B.A. 1976 (history & political science);
Harvard U., J.D. 1979

Career
Lawyer

Political Highlights
Sought Democratic nomination for Ga. House, 1986;
Athens-Clarke County Commission, 1991-2005

ELECTION RESULTS

2010 GENERAL

John Barrow (D)	92,459	56.6%
Raymond McKinney (R)	70,938	43.4%

2010 PRIMARY

John Barrow (D)	19,505	57.9%
Regina D. Thomas (D)	14,201	42.1%

2008 GENERAL

John Barrow (D)	164,562	66.0%
John Stone (R)	84,773	34.0%

Previous Winning Percentages
2006 (50%); 2004 (52%)

Elected 2004; 4th term

Barrow can often infuriate liberals, but his moderate voting record and seat on the powerful Energy and Commerce Committee keep constituents happy — even in a year like 2010, when many of his fellow Blue Dogs went down to defeat.

Barrow (BEAR-oh) voted to extend all of the Bush-era tax cuts at the end of 2010, and he opposed legislation designed to address global warming in 2009. His vote against the Democratic health care overhaul briefly generated talk of a primary challenge from the left, though he voted against repealing the law in early 2011. Overall, he sided with his party on 89 percent of the votes in which most Republicans opposed most Democrats during the 111th Congress (2009-10).

Barrow says he's simply doing what he'd promised his constituents he would do. "I said I would listen to both sides . . . and vote for the one I thought was right," he told the Savannah Morning News. "I've kept that promise."

Just how fine a line Barrow treads was evident in the campaign literature he mailed to different voters in 2010. One claimed Barrow worked "hand in hand" with President Obama, while he boasted in another about the fact he "stood up to Nancy Pelosi and the Democrats in Washington."

Barrow continued to distance himself from the Democratic Caucus' leadership after the election. He opposed Pelosi's bid to be minority leader, after refusing during the campaign to say whether he would once again vote for the Californian to be Speaker. When the roll was called in early January 2011, he voted for fellow Georgian John Lewis for Speaker.

But, because of the nature of his district, the party leadership cuts him some slack — Barrow is the only Democrat in the Deep South who represents a white-majority district. In addition to his Energy and Commerce slot, Barrow is a member of the Democratic Steering and Policy Committee, which makes committee assignments and advises leaders on policy.

He stuck with his party to support Obama's $787 billion economic stimulus package, signed into law at the start of the 111th Congress. "This job-creation package will rebuild America, making us more globally competitive and energy independent, and transforming our economy for long-term growth," he said. He also lauded the law's provisions calling for greater transparency in how funds are spent.

Barrow says he supports offshore drilling as one solution to the energy crisis. But when his party responded to GOP pressure in September 2008 to pass a bill to expand offshore drilling, he voted against it.

He is tougher on the issue of immigration than many of his Democratic colleagues. In the 109th Congress (2005-06), he joined Republicans in voting to authorize a 700-mile fence along the border with Mexico and to make it a felony to be in the United States without legal papers. He was one of four Democrats who supported an end to bilingual voting assistance. In late 2010, Barrow voted against a bill that would provide a path to legal residency for hundreds of thousands of illegal immigrants first brought to the United States by their parents.

The son of two Army captains, Barrow is a big booster of the military and a strong supporter of the war in Iraq. He opposed a war spending bill that would have required the Pentagon to set deadlines for the withdrawal of troops from Iraq. But in late 2010, he voted with his party in support of repealing the "don't ask, don't tell" policy that barred gays and lesbians from serving openly in the armed forces.

Barrow also is a supporter of organized labor. In early 2009, he supported two bills designed to make it easier for workers to challenge alleged wage discrimination. In 2007, he backed an increase in the minimum wage and legislation that would allow unions to organize workplaces without a secret ballot.

A member of the Health Subcommittee in the 111th Congress, Barrow supported a bill that Obama signed into law to expand the Children's Health Insurance Program, which covers children whose families make too much money to qualify for Medicaid.

Early in 2008, Barrow's district was hit by tragedy when an Imperial Sugar Co. refinery exploded and burned, killing 12 people. He and Democrat George Miller of California pushed a bill to require greater regulation of combustible dust in factories. Investigators concluded that the blast at the Imperial plant was linked to sugar dust that had been allowed to accumulate. His bill passed in the House but stalled in the Senate. Barrow renewed the effort in 2009, but it did not advance in the 111th Congress, either.

Barrow, whose district is home to three large military installations, won a seat on the Veterans' Affairs Committee in the 112th Congress (2011-12). He has long sought to increase the amount veterans are reimbursed for their travel to Veterans Affairs hospitals for medical care.

Barrow is a native of Athens, Ga. His parents were civil rights advocates, serving in the 1960s as co-chairmen of the local chapter of Help Our Public Education, or HOPE, which fought for integration. After Harvard Law School, he returned to Athens to work as a trial lawyer. In 1986, he made a failed bid for the state House, losing by 30 votes in a special-election runoff. In 1990, he won a seat on the Athens-Clarke County Commission, where he served for 14 years.

In his first U.S. House race in 2004, he took 51 percent of the vote in a four-way primary and went on to oust Republican Max Burns by 4 percentage points in a district that had been drawn to favor Democrats. A 2005 redistricting by a GOP-controlled state legislature stripped away much of Barrow's Democratic base. Burns set out to retake the seat, but Barrow moved to Savannah, at the heart of his new district, raised $2.5 million and built a centrist voting record that helped him withstand the challenge. He won by 864 votes. In 2008, Barrow faced John Stone, who had been an aide to both Burns and former Georgia Republican Rep. Charlie Norwood. Stone was unable to raise much money and was trounced at the polls.

In 2010, Barrow defeated Republican challenger Raymond McKinney, a nuclear power plant manager, with 57 percent of the vote.

Key Votes

2010

Overhaul the nation's health insurance system	NO
Allow for repeal of "don't ask, don't tell"	YES
Overhaul financial services industry regulation	YES
Limit use of new Afghanistan War funds to troop withdrawal activities	NO
Change oversight of offshore drilling and lift oil spill liability cap	YES
Provide a path to legal status for some children of illegal immigrants	NO
Extend Bush-era income tax cuts for two years	YES

2009

Expand the Children's Health Insurance Program	YES
Provide $787 billion in tax cuts and spending increases to stimulate the economy	YES
Allow bankruptcy judges to modify certain primary-residence mortgages	YES
Create a cap-and-trade system to limit greenhouse gas emissions	NO
Provide $2 billion for the "cash for clunkers" program	YES
Establish the government as the sole provider of student loans	YES
Restrict federally funded insurance coverage for abortions in health care overhaul	YES

CQ Vote Studies

	PARTY UNITY		PRESIDENTIAL SUPPORT	
	SUPPORT	OPPOSE	SUPPORT	OPPOSE
2010	91%	9%	83%	17%
2009	87%	13%	85%	15%
2008	83%	17%	27%	73%
2007	70%	30%	24%	76%
2006	65%	35%	65%	35%

Interest Groups

	AFL-CIO	ADA	CCUS	ACU
2010	71%	65%	75%	17%
2009	86%	75%	64%	17%
2008	87%	75%	67%	24%
2007	88%	70%	80%	24%
2006	64%	45%	87%	76%

Georgia 12

East — most of Savannah and Augusta

The 12th reaches from Augusta to Savannah along the South Carolina border, taking in a string of sparsely populated counties on its western edge. The politically competitive district includes urban Democratic strongholds, socially conservative rural counties and GOP-friendly suburbs.

Savannah's port, which continues to grow, fuels the 12th's economy, and Fort Stewart (shared with the 1st) and Hunter Army Airfield together employ tens of thousands of people. Savannah's downtown still has a solid tourism industry. Many residents of Richmond County (Augusta) work at Fort Gordon (shared with the 10th) or at the Energy Department's Savannah River Site, across the river in South Carolina. Local leaders have focused on supporting General Dynamics' local Gulfstream facility following extensive layoffs in 2009.

Textile factories in the center of the district have shut down, and the rest of the 12th relies mainly on farming. Toombs County's Vidalia grows its famous sweet onion, and Bulloch and Emanuel counties produce timber. Effingham County, north of Savannah, now hosts many white residents

who have left urban areas of Chatham County (Savannah). GOP strength is rooted in Effingham and the southern counties of Toombs, Tattnall and Bulloch. The 12th's portions of Chatham and Richmond are reliably Democratic, as is Hancock County in the district's northwest. Hancock County has the highest percentage of black residents of any Georgia county and is one of the state's poorest counties. Democrat Barack Obama took 54 percent of the district's presidential vote in 2008, and Democrat John Barrow easily held the U.S. House seat in 2010.

Major Industry
Agriculture, manufacturing, timber

Military Bases
Fort Stewart (Army), 18,549 military, 2,986 civilian (shared with the 1st); Fort Gordon (Army), 10,408 military, 3,072 civilian (2009) (shared with the 10th); Hunter Army Airfield, 6,200 military, 769 civilian (2011)

Cities
Savannah (pt.), 113,542; Augusta-Richmond (pt.), 112,040; Statesboro, 28,422

Notable
Vidalia onions were named the official state vegetable in 1990.

Rep. David Scott (D)

Capitol Office
225-2939
davidscott.house.gov
225 Cannon Bldg. 20515-1013; fax 225-4628

Committees
Agriculture
Financial Services

Residence
Atlanta

Born
June 27, 1946; Aynor, S.C.

Religion
Baptist

Family
Wife, Alfredia Scott; two children

Education
Florida A&M U., B.A. 1967 (English & speech); U. of
Pennsylvania, M.B.A. 1969

Career
Advertising agency owner; recruiting firm executive;
defense contracting company manager

Political Highlights
Ga. House, 1975-83; Ga. Senate, 1983-2003

ELECTION RESULTS

2010 GENERAL

David Scott (D)	140,294	69.4%
Mike Crane (R)	61,771	30.6%

2010 PRIMARY

David Scott (D)	34,374	76.1%
Mike Murphy (D)	7,556	16.7%
Michael Frisbee (D)	3,229	7.2%

2008 GENERAL

David Scott (D)	205,919	69.0%
Deborah Honeycutt (R)	92,320	31.0%

Previous Winning Percentages
2006 (69%); 2004 (100%); 2002 (60%)

Elected 2002; 5th term

The product of nearly three decades in the Georgia legislature, Scott was something of a party rebel in his early years in the House. After Democrats took control in 2007, he became a much more reliable vote for the leadership. Back in the minority, he is ready to team up with Republicans on select issues.

One of two African-American members of the fiscally conservative Blue Dog Coalition and a member of the centrist New Democrat Coalition, Scott is also a member of the liberal Congressional Black Caucus. On votes that split a majority of Republicans and Democrats in 2010, Scott sided with his party 98 percent of the time, more than 20 percentage points higher than his first year in the chamber, 2003.

In the 111th Congress (2009-10), he was with his party and president on major initiatives: He voted for the health care overhaul, even though it did not include the government-run public option he endorsed; he backed the $787 billion economic stimulus; and he voted for the House version of a measure that would create a cap-and-trade system intended to reduce carbon emissions.

A member of the Financial Services Committee, he backed both the House version and the final version of legislation to overhaul the financial industry regulatory structure.

In the fall of 2008, he initially voted against President George W. Bush's $700 billion plan to help the ailing financial services industry, but helped secure the bill's passage when it came up a second time because, he said, the revised measure strengthened assistance to homeowners. That December, he supported a bill backed by President-elect Obama to provide loans to ailing automobile companies.

Given Scott's voting history, Democrats might have to work hard to maintain his loyalty now that power has again shifted to the GOP side of the chamber.

At the start of the 112th Congress (2011-12), he joined fellow Georgian Phil Gingrey, a conservative Republican, in backing legislation to impose a cap on non-economic damages and establish other restrictions on medical malpractice lawsuits. He was one of 14 Democrats to back similar legislation proposed by Gingrey in 2005.

He was one of seven Democrats to vote for Bush's 2003 tax cuts, and he backed a two-year extension in 2010.

Formerly a member of the Foreign Affairs Committee, Scott sometimes sounds a slightly different tone than the liberal orthodoxy that permeates his party in Congress. He is a co-founder of the Democrats' national security study group and says they can again be the party associated with a strong military by returning to the hawkish defense postures of presidents Franklin D. Roosevelt and John F. Kennedy. But he opposed the Iraq War from the beginning and has pushed for a quicker end to U.S. involvement.

Though Atlanta's sprawl affects much of his district, other parts are rural, and Scott keeps an eye on agricultural issues. A member of the Agriculture Committee, he has long supported the efforts of black farmers to win compensation from the Agriculture Department for past discrimination. And during the debate over the 2008 reauthorization of agriculture and nutrition programs, Scott fought for increased food stamp benefits and funding for school lunch programs.

When Financial Services approved a bill in April 2010 that would create a national risk pool for flood insurance, he won adoption of an amendment to give low-income homeowners who were required to buy flood insurance the option to pay in installments.

Born in impoverished Aynor, S.C., Scott attended elementary school in Pennsylvania. When he was in sixth grade, his family moved to Scarsdale, N.Y., where his parents worked for a wealthy family as a chauffeur and a maid. An only child, Scott was also the only black student in his school. His classmates had money, while he lived in an apartment over the garage on the estate owned by his parents' employer. Civil rights protests raged across the country, and though Scott says he encountered little overt bigotry among Scarsdale's upper crust, his racial isolation was stressful. "I learned at a very young age how to have confidence in myself and how to get along with people who don't look like me," he said.

Scott finished high school in Daytona Beach, Fla., then attended Florida A&M University. During an internship in Washington with the Labor Department, Scott met George W. Taylor, a noted labor management expert who suggested Scott apply to the University of Pennsylvania's Wharton School of Finance, where Taylor was on the faculty.

With a Wharton MBA in hand, in the early 1970s, Scott was attracted to Atlanta and its emerging crop of black leaders. He was a volunteer with Democrat Andrew Young's successful campaign for the U.S. House in 1972.

Two years later, Scott won his first election to the Georgia House, launching a 28-year career in the legislature. He chaired the state Senate Rules Committee.

When Scott ran for Congress in 2002, establishment Democrats in his suburban Atlanta district backed a rival in the primary. Scott won the nomination over state Sen. Greg Hecht with strong support from affluent suburbanites and business leaders, then easily defeated Republican Clay Cox in the general election. Some campaign ads featured his wife's brother, baseball great Hank Aaron.

Over the years, Scott was closely associated with Atlanta's black and liberal leaders — former mayors Young and Maynard Jackson as well as Jimmy Carter, the governor who became president — but he calculated correctly that only a centrist could win the district.

In recent years, he has come under fire from ethics groups for, among other things, failing to pay his taxes on time and putting family members on his campaign payroll. In 2007, the advertising company in which Scott was once a principal and which is now run by his wife and daughters was revealed to have about 40 tax liens, which Alfredia Scott said were her mistakes. In June 2008, the Atlanta Journal-Constitution reported he had paid off all his personal local and state tax liens. The controversies inspired primary opposition in 2008, but the voters of the 13th District have continued to give him overwhelming majorities. He won by nearly 40 percentage points in 2010.

Key Votes

2010

Overhaul the nation's health insurance system	YES
Allow for repeal of "don't ask, don't tell"	YES
Overhaul financial services industry regulation	YES
Limit use of new Afghanistan War funds to troop withdrawal activities	NO
Change oversight of offshore drilling and lift oil spill liability cap	YES
Provide a path to legal status for some children of illegal immigrants	YES
Extend Bush-era income tax cuts for two years	YES

2009

Expand the Children's Health Insurance Program	YES
Provide $787 billion in tax cuts and spending increases to stimulate the economy	YES
Allow bankruptcy judges to modify certain primary-residence mortgages	YES
Create a cap-and-trade system to limit greenhouse gas emissions	YES
Provide $2 billion for the "cash for clunkers" program	YES
Establish the government as the sole provider of student loans	YES
Restrict federally funded insurance coverage for abortions in health care overhaul	NO

CQ Vote Studies

	PARTY UNITY		PRESIDENTIAL SUPPORT	
	SUPPORT	OPPOSE	SUPPORT	OPPOSE
2010	98%	2%	95%	5%
2009	97%	3%	93%	7%
2008	98%	2%	18%	82%
2007	96%	4%	12%	88%
2006	85%	15%	45%	55%

Interest Groups

	AFL-CIO	ADA	CCUS	ACU
2010	100%	90%	25%	0%
2009	100%	95%	47%	0%
2008	100%	95%	67%	4%
2007	96%	90%	65%	4%
2006	86%	85%	60%	32%

Georgia 13

Atlanta suburbs — parts of Clayton, Cobb and Douglas counties

The 13th forms a crescent that cradles the southwest corner of Atlanta and takes in parts of six counties, including sizable chunks of Cobb and Douglas to the west and most of densely populated Clayton in the east.

The 13th includes a mix of middle-income urban, suburban and rural areas. A significant number of residents commute to Atlanta, where many district residents depend on jobs with major corporations. Regional health care providers are large employers in the 13th, as are universities nearby in the 5th (in Fulton County). The 13th experienced rapid growth over the past two decades, especially in southern Fulton and eastern Douglas counties, where working-class families and retirees poured into once less-populated areas. Residents and local officials are concerned about high unemployment rates and a stalled local economy.

Cobb County accounts for about one-third of the district's population and has a growing black population. Some residents in southern Cobb work in defense-related industries near Marietta. A national housing construction downturn forced layoffs at Home Depot, which has headquarters in the 13th and is a key employer here.

South of Atlanta, Clayton County, which also has one-third of the population, has suffered from job losses and difficulties in the local education sector. Many commuters from Clayton still rely on transportation and warehousing jobs around the busy Hartsfield-Jackson Atlanta International Airport (in the 5th).

Changing demographics have made the 13th one of only two black-majority districts in Georgia ahead of decennial remapping, and white residents account for only one-quarter of the population. The district overall is solidly Democratic, but Republicans have some success in eastern Douglas. Democrat Barack Obama easily won here in the 2008 presidential election, taking 72 percent of the district's vote.

Major Industry
Distribution, aerospace, health care, service

Cities
Smyrna (pt.), 48,603; Mableton (unincorporated), 37,115

Notable
Jonesboro was the setting for Tara, the plantation in Margaret Mitchell's novel "Gone With the Wind."

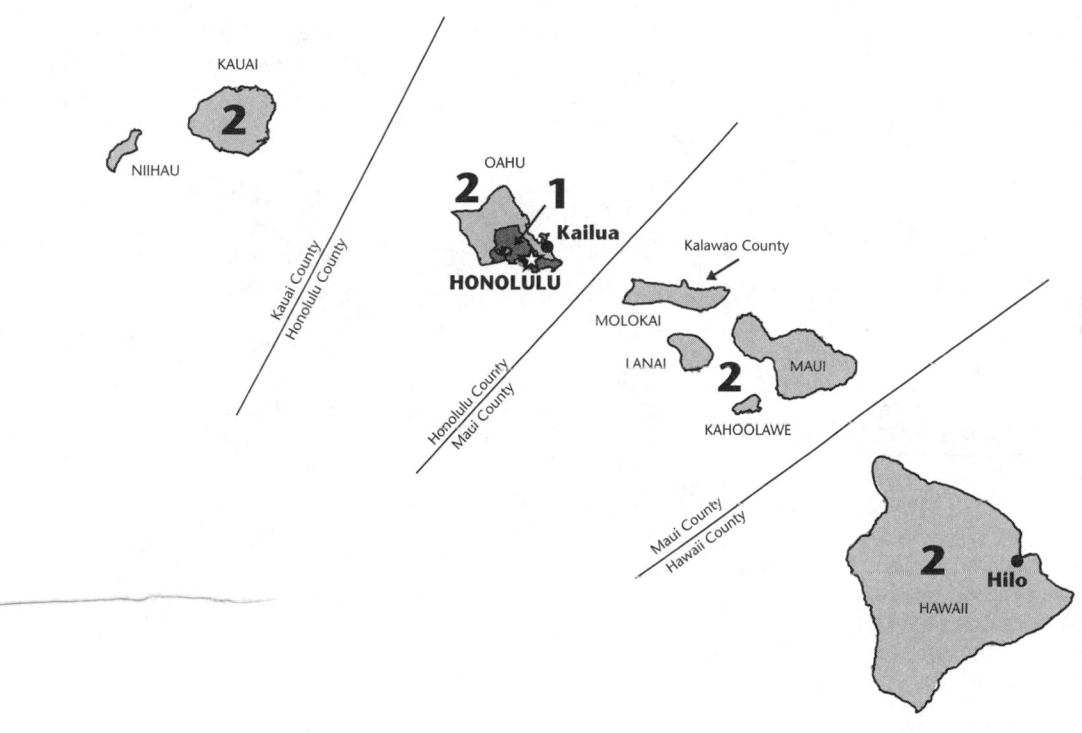

KAUAI

2

NIIHAU

Kauai County
Honolulu County

OAHU

2 **1**

Kailua

HONOLULU

Kalawao County

MOLOKAI

LANAI

KAHOOLAWE

2

MAUI

Honolulu County
Maui County

Maui County
Hawaii County

2

Hilo

HAWAII

Gov. Neil Abercrombie (D)

First elected: 2010
Length of term: 4 years
Term expires: 12/14
Salary: $129,660
Phone: (808) 586-0034
Residence: Honolulu
Born: June 26, 1938; Buffalo, N.Y.
Religion: Unspecified
Family: Wife, Nancie Caraway
Education: Union College (N.Y.), B.A. 1959; U. of Hawaii, M.A. 1964, Ph.D. 1974 (American studies)
Career: Educator
Political highlights: Sought Democratic nomination for U.S. Senate, 1970; Hawaii House, 1974-78; Hawaii Senate, 1978-86; U.S. House, 1986-87; defeated in primary for re-election to U.S. House, 1986; Honolulu City Council, 1988-90; U.S. House, 1991-2010

ELECTION RESULTS

2010 GENERAL
Neil Abercrombie (D)	222,724	57.8%
Duke Aiona (R)	157,311	40.8%

Lt. Gov. Brian Schatz (D)

First elected: 2010
Length of term: 4 years
Term expires: 12/14
Salary: $114,420
Phone: (808) 586-0255

LEGISLATURE

Legislature: 60 days January-April
Senate: 25 members, 4-year terms
2011 ratios: 24 D, 1 R; 16 men, 9 women
Salary: $46,272
Phone: (808) 586-6720
House: 51 members, 2-year terms
2011 ratios: 43 D, 8 R; 33 men, 18 women
Salary: $46,272
Phone: (808) 586-6400

TERM LIMITS

Governor: 2 consecutive terms
Senate: No
House: No

URBAN STATISTICS

CITY	POPULATION
Urban Honolulu	337,256
East Honolulu	49,914
Pearl City	47,698
Hilo	43,263
Kailua	38,635

REGISTERED VOTERS

Voters do not register by party.

POPULATION

2010 population (est.)	1,360,301
2000 population	1,211,537
1990 population	1,108,229
Percent change (2000-2010)	+12.3%
Rank among states (2010)	40
Median age	37.5
Born in state	54.0%
Foreign born	15.8%
Violent crime rate	275/100,000
Poverty level	10.4%
Federal workers	38,378
Military	40,874

ELECTIONS

STATE ELECTION OFFICIAL
(808) 453-868
DEMOCRATIC PARTY
(808) 596-2980
REPUBLICAN PARTY
(808) 593-8180

MISCELLANEOUS

Web: www.hawaii.gov
Capital: Honolulu

U.S. CONGRESS

Senate: 2 Democrats
House: 2 Democrats

2010 Census Statistics by District

District	2008 Vote for President Obama	McCain	White	Black	Asian	Hispanic	Median Income	White Collar	Blue Collar	Service Industry	Over 64	Under 18	College Education	Rural	Sq. Miles
1	70%	28%	17%	2%	51%	7%	$64,861	63%	16%	21%	16%	20%	32%	1%	191
2	73	25	29	1	25	11	64,463	56	21	23	12	25	26	16	6,232
STATE	72	27	23	1	38	9	64,661	60	19	22	14	23	29	9	6,423
U.S.	53	46	64	12	5	16	51,425	60	23	17	13	25	28	21	3,537,438

Sen. Daniel K. Inouye (D)

Capitol Office
224-3934
inouye.senate.gov
722 Hart Bldg. 20510-1102; fax 224-6747

Committees
Appropriations - Chairman
  (Defense - Chairman)
Commerce, Science & Transportation
Indian Affairs
Rules & Administration

Residence
Honolulu

Born
Sept. 7, 1924; Honolulu, Hawaii

Religion
Methodist

Family
Wife, Irene Hirano; one child

Education
U. of Hawaii, A.B. 1950 (government & economics);
George Washington U., J.D. 1952

Military Service
Army, 1943-47

Career
Lawyer; city prosecutor

Political Highlights
Hawaii Territorial House, 1954-58 (majority leader);
Hawaii Territorial Senate, 1958-59; U.S. House,
1959-63

ELECTION RESULTS

2010 GENERAL

Daniel K. Inouye (D)	277,228	74.8%
Cam Cavasso (R)	79,939	21.6%
Jim Brewer (NPA)	7,762	2.1%

2010 PRIMARY

Daniel K. Inouye (D)	198,711	88.3%
Andrew D. Woerner (D)	26,411	11.7%

Previous Winning Percentages
2004 (76%) 1998 (79%); 1992 (57%); 1986 (74%); 1980
(78%); 1974 (83%); 1968 (83%); 1962 (69%); 1960
House Election (74%); 1959 Special House Election
(68%)

Elected 1962; 9th term

Inouye's unfailingly polite and quiet manner might seem at odds with his powerful posting as chairman of the Appropriations Committee. Yet, it is perhaps key to his success as a legislator.

His public appearances in the Capitol are decidedly infrequent. Inouye (in-NO-ay) is rarely seen on the floor unless shepherding through a bill, and he doesn't hold news conferences. Instead, he spends much of his day in private talks with fellow senators, trying to iron out the inevitable conflicts involved in legislating. "I find that if you take the extra step to be friendly, considerate, most members reciprocate," Inouye said.

Driven by his notion of honor, Inouye is a throwback to an earlier political era, when collegiality was valued over partisan bombast and reverence for the Senate as an institution was the norm. The good will that Inouye has banked over nearly a half-century in the Senate serves him well as he leads the Appropriations Committee at a time of heightened concern about the national debt.

He reluctantly agreed that the catchall spending bill for fiscal 2011 and the regular appropriations bills for 2012 would include no earmarks after senators followed the lead of House Republicans in banning such funding for local projects. "Given the reality before us, it makes no sense to accept earmark requests that have no chance of being enacted into law," he said.

Defending the congressional prerogative to set spending levels, he opposed a proposal by a pair of senators, Delaware Democrat Thomas R. Carper and Arizona Republican John McCain, to create "enhanced rescission authority," which would give the president more power to challenge discretionary spending items. Inouye said ceding that much power to the White House would leave Congress as little more than a "rubber stamp" in the spending process.

The altered appropriations landscape will keep Inouye busy, but he also has other legislative duties.

He sits on the Indian Affairs Committee, chaired by fellow Hawaii Democrat Daniel K. Akaka. The pair can be expected to renew their push for legislation that would grant federal recognition to Native Hawaiians, allowing them to form their own sovereign entities similar to those created by American Indians and Alaska Natives. A similar measure made it through the House in the 111th Congress (2009-10) but died in the Senate.

He also serves on the Commerce, Science and Transportation Committee, as well as the Rules and Administration panel.

Inouye has been noted for being all but fanatical in his loyalty to colleagues.

He backed state Senate President Colleen Hanabusa in a three-way special election in May 2010 for the House seat previously held by Democrat Neil Abercrombie, who resigned to run for governor. Hawaii newspapers reported that Inouye resisted pressure from national Democrats to get Hanabusa to step aside in favor of former Rep. Ed Case, who had made an unsuccessful 2006 bid to replace Akaka, an upstart move that Inouye opposed. Republican Charles K. Djou prevailed in the three-way race; Hanabusa unseated him in November.

Inouye campaigned in 2008 for Alaska Republican Ted Stevens. Inouye and Stevens had long called each other "co-chairmen" while changes in control of Congress rotated which of the pair held the Appropriations gavel. The Los Angeles Times reported that at a campaign appearance on behalf of Stevens, Inouye said: "Our parties don't understand . . . but there are things that are more important than political considerations. And that's friendship."

In 2001, Inouye declined to cast a tie-breaking vote for a Democratic amendment to President George W. Bush's tax bill in order to keep his promise to "pair" his votes that day with Stevens, who would have voted the other way but was home in Alaska speaking at his granddaughter's high school graduation ceremony. And Stevens isn't the only Republican whom Inouye has helped. In 1990, Inouye taped a radio advertisement for another Republican colleague on Senate Appropriations, Oregon's Mark O. Hatfield.

Inouye's deeply personal approach to politics may have held him back in 1989, when he made a failed bid for majority leader, a post requiring fervent communication of the party's agenda outside of the Senate. Inouye attracted only 14 of the Senate's 55 Democratic votes.

Still, in his long years in the Senate, Inouye's colleagues have relied on him to handle delicate tasks that require the appearance of impartiality and unquestioned probity. His 1987 appointment to chair the committee investigating the Iran-Contra affair stemmed not only from his evenhanded manner but also from the esteem he won during the 1973 Watergate hearings that led to the resignation of President Richard Nixon.

On the rare occasions when Inouye speaks out publicly, his words command attention. During the 2002 debate on whether to grant Bush authority to go to war with Iraq, Inouye made headlines when he took exception to a Bush comment that Democrats were not sufficiently concerned about national security. Inouye, who was awarded the Medal of Honor in 2000 for his exploits during World War II, rose on the Senate floor to protest. "It grieves me when my president makes statements that would divide this nation," he said. "This is not a time for Democrats and Republicans to say, 'We got more medals than you, we've lost more limbs than you, we've shed more blood than you.'"

In 1943, as an 18-year-old pre-med student, he enlisted in the famed all-Nisei "Go for Broke" 442nd Regimental Combat Team and fought across Italy and France. When he advanced alone to take out a machine gunner who had pinned down his men, he lost his right arm and spent 20 months in military hospitals.

Inouye turned to a career in politics after that wartime injury ended his earlier plans to become a surgeon. While recovering in Michigan, he met another recuperating soldier — Bob Dole of Kansas, who later became a Republican Senate majority leader. Dole told Inouye he planned to be in Congress someday, and Inouye decided he, too, would try politics. The hospital where Dole, Inouye and another future senator, Democrat Phil Hart of Michigan, recovered was renamed in their honor in 2003. (There's also a Daniel K. Inouye building at another site dedicated to healing wounded veterans, at the Walter Reed Army Institute of Research in Silver Spring, Md.)

These are the rare examples of federal buildings carrying Inouye's name, and they are far from his home state. He says he turns down requests to name things after him, an unusual stance in his profession and one that makes a particularly sharp contrast between Inouye and his predecessor as Appropriations chairman, the late Robert C. Byrd, a Democrat whose name dots the landscape in West Virginia.

Inouye won his first election in 1954, to Hawaii's territorial House. He helped guide Hawaii to statehood in 1959 and was elected that year as its first U.S. House member. He won his Senate seat in 1962.

The first Japanese-American elected to Congress, Inouye is revered by Hawaii's large Japanese-American community.

Inouye in 2006 lost his wife of almost 57 years, Maggie, to cancer. Always faithful to his duties, he was back at his Senate desk the day after her death to vote on amendments to the annual budget resolution. In May 2008, he married Irene Hirano, the president and CEO of the Japanese American National Museum in Los Angeles.

Key Votes

2010

Pass budget reconciliation bill to modify overhauls of health care and federal student loan programs	YES
Proceed to disapproval resolution on EPA authority to regulate greenhouse gases	NO
Overhaul financial services industry regulation	YES
Limit debate to proceed to a bill to broaden campaign finance disclosure and reporting rules	YES
Limit debate on an extension of Bush-era income tax cuts for two years	YES
Limit debate on a bill to provide a path to legal status for some children of illegal immigrants	YES
Allow for a repeal of "don't ask, don't tell"	YES
Consent to ratification of a strategic arms reduction treaty with Russia	YES

2009

Prevent release of remaining financial industry bailout funds	NO
Make it easier for victims to sue for wage discrimination remedies	YES
Expand the Children's Health Insurance Program	YES
Limit debate on the economic stimulus measure	YES
Repeal District of Columbia firearms prohibitions and gun registration laws	NO
Limit debate on expansion of federal hate crimes law	YES
Strike funding for F-22 Raptor fighter jets	NO

CQ Vote Studies

	PARTY UNITY		PRESIDENTIAL SUPPORT	
	SUPPORT	OPPOSE	SUPPORT	OPPOSE
2010	98%	2%	98%	2%
2009	99%	1%	96%	4%
2008	83%	17%	46%	54%
2007	94%	6%	36%	64%
2006	90%	10%	56%	44%
2005	90%	10%	44%	56%
2004	95%	5%	59%	41%
2003	93%	7%	48%	52%
2002	90%	10%	76%	24%
2001	98%	2%	66%	34%

Interest Groups

	AFL-CIO	ADA	CCUS	ACU
2010	93%	80%	27%	0%
2009	94%	95%	43%	0%
2008	100%	85%	71%	0%
2007	94%	90%	45%	0%
2006	100%	95%	50%	8%
2005	100%	90%	44%	5%
2004	100%	100%	50%	8%
2003	100%	85%	40%	15%
2002	92%	80%	41%	0%
2001	100%	90%	43%	9%

Sen. Daniel K. Akaka (D)

Capitol Office
224-6361
akaka.senate.gov
141 Hart Bldg. 20510-1103; fax 224-2126

Committees
Armed Services
Banking, Housing & Urban Affairs
Homeland Security & Governmental Affairs
  (Oversight of Government Management - Chairman)
Indian Affairs - Chairman
Veterans' Affairs

Residence
Honolulu

Born
Sept. 11, 1924; Honolulu, Hawaii

Religion
Congregationalist

Family
Wife, Millie Akaka; five children

Education
U. of Hawaii, B.Ed. 1952, M.Ed. 1966

Military Service
Army Corps of Engineers, 1945-47

Career
Elementary school principal and teacher; state economic grants official; gubernatorial aide

Political Highlights
Sought Democratic nomination for lieutenant governor, 1974; U.S. House, 1977-90

ELECTION RESULTS

2006 GENERAL

Daniel K. Akaka (D)	210,330	61.3%
Cynthia Thielen (R)	126,097	36.8%
Lloyd Jeffrey Mallan (LIBERT)	6,415	1.9%

2006 PRIMARY

Daniel K. Akaka (D)	129,158	54.6%
Ed Case (D)	107,163	45.3%

Previous Winning Percentages
2000 (73%); 1994 (72%); 1990 Special Election (54%); 1988 House Election (89%); 1986 House Election (76%); 1984 House Election (82%); 1982 House Election (89%); 1980 House Election (90%); 1978 House Election (86%); 1976 House Election (80%)

Elected 1990; 3rd full term

Appointed 1990

In a chamber full of attention hounds and extroverts, Akaka tends to the other extreme: He is better known outside the Beltway for his name being called first in each roll call vote than anything else. Leaving the publicity to his colleagues has proved to be an effective style for the behind-the-scenes workhorse, who has logged several legislative victories.

But after more than three decades in the House and Senate, Akaka announced in early 2011 that he would retire at the end of his current term.

He is among the oldest senators and has worked in close partnership with Hawaii's senior senator, Democrat Daniel K. Inouye. Inouye, chairman of the Appropriations Committee, has long overshadowed Akaka, but in recent years Akaka has begun to amass a legislative record of his own, primarily on veterans' issues.

As the only ethnic Native Hawaiian ever to serve in the Senate — his mother was Hawaiian and his father was of Chinese and Hawaiian ancestry — Akaka's advocacy on behalf of his people is a central focus of his career.

In the 110th (2007-08) and 111th (2009-10) Congresses, he chaired the Veterans' Affairs Committee, a post he surrendered in the 112th Congress (2011-12) to take over as chairman of the Indian Affairs panel. There, he will lead the fight for legislation that would grant federal recognition to ethnic Native Hawaiians, allowing them to form their own sovereign entities similar to those created by American Indians and Alaska Natives. The House passed a similar measure early in 2010, but conservative Republicans have consistently blocked the legislation, arguing it could disrupt military operations and discriminate against Hawaiians of other ethnic backgrounds.

Hawaii's last monarch, Queen Liliuokalani, was dethroned in 1893 in a rebellion led by the U.S. minister to Hawaii and supported by U.S.-owned business interests on the islands and the U.S. military. A century later, President Bill Clinton signed a resolution sponsored by Akaka officially apologizing. An Akaka measure enacted in 1995 compensates Native Hawaiians by transferring federal land to a trust in return for lands seized by the United States during the state's territorial period.

Akaka also chairs the Homeland Security and Governmental Affairs Committee's oversight panel and sits on the Banking, Housing and Urban Affairs Committee. From the Banking panel, he put his stamp on several provisions that were included in the financial regulation overhaul enacted in 2010, including language to protect immigrants who use electronic funds transfers to send money back to their communities abroad. And on Armed Services, he looks out for the islands' myriad military installations.

Most of Akaka's legislative victories in the 111th Congress were on veterans' issues, and he is still on the Veterans' Affairs Committee despite relinquishing the top seat. After Democrats celebrated passage of the 2010 health care overhaul, he set to work making sure that veterans were not inadvertently harmed by the legislation. Just weeks after the measure became law, Obama signed a bill that Akaka helped draft to ensure that some children of Vietnam War and Korean War veterans who have spina bifida would not be adversely affected.

Akaka was quick to defend spending for veterans in 2009, when Oklahoma Republican Tom Coburn held up a package of benefits with a demand that the costs be offset. Akaka beat back Coburn's amendment that would have required Congress to come up with a way to pay for the programs, arguing that the cost did not need to be offset because "the price has already been paid, many times over, by the service of the brave men and women who wore our nation's uniform."

Akaka has pressed for improvements in the handling of post-traumatic stress disorder and traumatic brain injuries. He successfully pushed to enactment a bill to implement regulations for notifying veterans who claim medical benefits about the status of their requests in understandable language. He also saw enacted a catchall measure addressing other concerns of returning troops, including housing, employment and access to courts. And after years of effort, he and Inouye won authorization in 2009 of lump-sum payments to Filipino World War II veterans who fought with the United States.

Akaka, who often recalls witnessing as a boy the Japanese attack on Pearl Harbor in 1941, likens the plight of the Filipino veterans to that of veterans from his home state of Hawaii. "Both Hawaii and the Philippines were U.S. possessions. . . . Both were attacked that December," Akaka said. "For the duration of the Second World War, both Hawaii and the Philippines would send their children to battle under the command of the U.S. military."

One of only three remaining World War II veterans in the Senate, Akaka also serves on the Armed Services Committee, where he has pressed commanders in Afghanistan on whether enough Afghan troops are being trained and deployed to hasten the end of U.S. involvement.

As chairman of the Homeland Security Subcommittee on Oversight of Government Management, the Federal Workforce and the District of Columbia, he has sought to clear some of the red tape that can affect government personnel. He also joined efforts to restore some collective bargaining and appeals rights for federal workers. Those changes became law as part of the fiscal 2008 defense authorization bill.

Akaka's career is a study in quiet perseverance. After graduating from the Kamehameha School for Boys, he served in the Army Corps of Engineers during World War II.

Returning home, he got a degree in education from the University of Hawaii and became a teacher, then a principal. He rose through the Honolulu education bureaucracy and in 1976 prevailed in a tough primary contest for the 2nd District seat in the House. He rose to the middle tier of seniority on the House Appropriations Committee, where he concentrated almost entirely on parochial needs.

When Democratic Sen. Spark M. Matsunaga died in April 1990, Akaka was a logical choice to fill the vacancy. He won appointment to the seat because he was on good terms with Democratic Gov. John Waihee. He was also close to the state party leadership and had the support of Japanese-Americans.

But in the special election that fall to fill out Matsunaga's term, he faced a serious challenge from GOP Rep. Patricia F. Saiki. Akaka had been a sedate figure during his House career and was not readily identifiable to many Hawaiians. But he stressed his ability to deliver federal largess to Hawaii and prevailed with 54 percent of the vote. He won his next two Senate elections easily.

In 2006, Akaka drew his first serious political challenge in years when Democratic Rep. Ed Case, almost 30 years his junior, decided to take him on in the primary. While expressing respect and "the deepest aloha" for the incumbent, Case said it was time for "the next generation" of leadership. Akaka retorted that Hawaii benefited from his depth of experience, and his Senate colleagues rushed to his aid. So did the voters; he took almost 55 percent of the vote against Case in the primary and easily won re-election, although his 61 percent share of the general-election vote was his lowest since his initial Senate election.

Speculation about the octogenarian Akaka's possible retirement bloomed in early 2011 when his campaign finance report showed he had raised less than $2,000 in the fourth quarter of 2010 and had only $66,000 on hand at the end of the year. He confirmed the speculation in March when he announced he would not seek re-election in 2012.

Key Votes

2010

Pass budget reconciliation bill to modify overhauls of health care and federal student loan programs	YES
Proceed to disapproval resolution on EPA authority to regulate greenhouse gases	NO
Overhaul financial services industry regulation	YES
Limit debate to proceed to a bill to broaden campaign finance disclosure and reporting rules	YES
Limit debate on an extension of Bush-era income tax cuts for two years	YES
Limit debate on a bill to provide a path to legal status for some children of illegal immigrants	YES
Allow for a repeal of "don't ask, don't tell"	YES
Consent to ratification of a strategic arms reduction treaty with Russia	YES

2009

Prevent release of remaining financial industry bailout funds	NO
Make it easier for victims to sue for wage discrimination remedies	YES
Expand the Children's Health Insurance Program	YES
Limit debate on the economic stimulus measure	YES
Repeal District of Columbia firearms prohibitions and gun registration laws	NO
Limit debate on expansion of federal hate crimes law	YES
Strike funding for F-22 Raptor fighter jets	NO

CQ Vote Studies

	PARTY UNITY		PRESIDENTIAL SUPPORT	
	SUPPORT	OPPOSE	SUPPORT	OPPOSE
2010	98%	2%	98%	2%
2009	98%	2%	97%	3%
2008	99%	1%	30%	70%
2007	95%	5%	40%	60%
2006	96%	4%	48%	52%
2005	96%	4%	40%	60%
2004	97%	3%	56%	44%
2003	97%	3%	51%	49%
2002	91%	9%	63%	37%
2001	98%	2%	70%	30%

Interest Groups

	AFL-CIO	ADA	CCUS	ACU
2010	94%	85%	27%	0%
2009	94%	95%	43%	0%
2008	100%	100%	50%	0%
2007	89%	95%	36%	0%
2006	93%	95%	30%	0%
2005	100%	95%	39%	8%
2004	100%	95%	29%	5%
2003	100%	90%	30%	11%
2002	100%	80%	53%	0%
2001	100%	95%	50%	13%

Rep. Colleen Hanabusa (D)

Capitol Office
225-2726
hanabusa.house.gov
238 Cannon Bldg. 20515-1101; fax 225-0688

Committees
Armed Services
Natural Resources

Residence
Honolulu

Born
May 4, 1951; Honolulu, Hawaii

Religion
Buddhist

Family
Husband, John Souza

Education
U. of the Pacific, attended 1969-70; Colorado College, attended 1970-71; U. of Hawaii, B.A. 1973 (economics & sociology), M.A. 1975 (sociology), J.D. 1977

Career
Lawyer

Political Highlights
Hawaii Senate, 1999-2010 (majority leader, 2003-07; president, 2007-10); candidate for U.S. House (special election), 2003; sought Democratic nomination for U.S. House, 2006; candidate for U.S. House (special election), 2010

ELECTION RESULTS

2010 GENERAL

Colleen Hanabusa (D)	94,140	53.2%
Charles K. Djou (R)	82,723	46.8%

2010 PRIMARY

Colleen Hanabusa (D)	85,732	78.9%
Rafael Del Castillo (D)	22,874	21.1%

Elected 2010; 1st term

Hanabusa brings solid liberal credentials and legislative experience to the House. She served for more than a decade in the state Senate and was elected its president in 2006, the first woman to lead either chamber of the Hawaii legislature. Now that she is in Congress, her priorities remain Hawaii-centric.

On the Natural Resources Committee, where she sits on the Indian and Alaska Native Affairs Subcommittee, she plans to push for legislation that would grant federal recognition to Native Hawaiians, allowing them to form their own sovereign entities similar to those created by American Indians and Alaska Natives. A similar measure was passed by the House in the 111th Congress (2009-10) but died in the Senate.

Hanabusa also said she is eager to make Hawaii a leader in renewable energy production. "We have wind, we have sun, like no one else does," she said.

The only freshman Democrat named to the Armed Services Committee, Hanabusa has expressed support for President Obama's strategy in Afghanistan, despite what she has called grave concerns about the U.S. military presence there. She opposed the U.S. invasion of Iraq. That seat will give her a voice in looking out for the many and varied military installations on the islands.

After working as a labor attorney, Hanabusa won election to the state Senate in 1998. During her time in Honolulu, Hanabusa chaired a bicameral committee investigating the state's progress in providing educational services to students with mental and physical disabilities.

Her election to the 1st District seat was her second attempt at the post within a few months. Incumbent Democrat Neil Abercrombie resigned in February 2010 to run for governor. A three-way special election in May split the Democratic vote between Hanabusa and former Rep. Ed Case, handing victory to Republican Charles K. Djou.

Case opted not to enter the regular Democratic primary, and Hanabusa cruised to the nomination. In November she beat Djou with 53 percent of the vote, one of only two Republican seats that went Democratic in 2010.

A Buddhist, Hanabusa joins two other House members who share her faith, which she describes as "more of a philosophy than a religion" for her.

Hawaii 1
Oahu — Honolulu, Waipahu, Pearl City

On Oahu's southern coast, the compact 1st takes in a narrow plain that includes Honolulu — the engine that drives all of Hawaii — and Waipahu to the west. Rising above the plain to the north is part of the Koolau mountain range, and Keaiwa Heiau park's trails and campsites are north of Aiea. Honolulu, the state capital, hosts most of Hawaii's business and nearly 30 percent of its people, leading to pervasive traffic congestion throughout the city.

Waikiki to the east is the heart of tourism, the state's leading industry. The legacy of World War II remains etched in the 1st's consciousness — Pearl Harbor anchors a strong military presence.

Democrats are entrenched in the 1st and do very well in local races, although moderate Republican enclaves exist near Diamond Head and in Liliha and Ewa Beach. By far, the district has the highest percentage (51 percent) of Asian residents in the nation and a high percentage (16 percent) of multi-ethnic residents. Ethnic Native Hawaiians make up 7 percent of the population. In 2008, Honolulu-born Democrat Barack Obama took 70 percent of the district's presidential vote.

Major Industry
Tourism, military, construction

Military Bases
Joint Base Pearl Harbor-Hickam, 19,095 military, 11,986 civilian (shared with the 2nd); Fort Shafter (Army), 3,797 military, 3,186 civilian (2011); Tripler Army Medical Center, 1,427 military, 1,642 civilian (2007); Camp H.M. Smith Marine Corps installation, 1,655 military, 682 civilian (2011)

Cities
Urban Honolulu, 337,256; East Honolulu, 49,914; Pearl City, 47,698; Waipahu, 38,216

Notable
Iolani Palace is in downtown Honolulu.

Rep. Mazie K. Hirono (D)

Capitol Office
225-4906
hirono.house.gov
1410 Longworth Bldg. 20515-1102; fax 225-4987

Committees
Education & the Workforce
Ethics
Transportation & Infrastructure

Residence
Honolulu

Born
Nov. 3, 1947; Fukushima, Japan

Religion
Buddhist

Family
Husband, Leighton Kim Oshima; one stepchild

Education
U. of Hawaii, B.A. 1970 (psychology); Georgetown
U., J.D. 1978

Career
Lawyer; campaign and state legislative aide

Political Highlights
Hawaii House, 1981-94; lieutenant governor, 1994-
2002; Democratic nominee for governor, 2002

ELECTION RESULTS

2010 GENERAL

Mazie K. Hirono (D)	132,290	72.2%
John W. Willoughby (R)	46,404	25.3%
Pat Brock (LIBERT)	3,254	1.8%

2010 PRIMARY

Mazie K. Hirono (D)	unopposed

2008 GENERAL

Mazie K. Hirono (D)	165,748	76.1%
Roger B. Evans (R)	44,425	20.4%
Shaun Stenshol (I)	4,042	1.8%
Lloyd Mallan (LIBERT)	3,699	1.7%

Previous Winning Percentages
2006 (61%)

Elected 2006; 3rd term

Hirono is an experienced legislator who caught on quickly to the congressional art of earmarking. Learning from one of the masters, fellow Hawaii Democrat Daniel K. Inouye, she became a prolific funder of special projects in her home state. With an earmark moratorium in place, she'll have to look elsewhere for legislative victories. In 2012, she'll seek to join Inouye in the Senate.

The Japanese native sees herself as less a disciple of the Senate Appropriations chairman than a successor to the late Hawaii Democratic Rep. Patsy T. Mink, the first non-Caucasian woman elected to Congress. Though less fiery than the famously temperamental Mink, Hirono shares her predecessor's liberal views. "Patsy fought for working men and women, and she fought for education," she said. "Those are the issues that are really important to me."

Hirono (full name: may-ZEE hee-RO-no) isn't an appropriator, but her connections to Inouye have helped her secure earmarks — funding set-asides requested by lawmakers — as though she were.

A member of the Education and the Workforce Committee, Hirono was a cosponsor of the single largest earmark in the fiscal 2010 spending bill that funds the Education Department: $40.1 million for arts education in schools through the federal Arts in Education program. Also a member of the Transportation and Infrastructure Committee, she claimed one of the largest earmarks in the Transportation funding bill that year: $4 million for the Honolulu High-Capacity Transit Corridor Project, which she sponsored with one-time House colleague Democrat Neil Abercrombie, now Hawaii's governor.

And she got one of the biggest earmarks in the Agriculture spending bill, also in tandem with Abercrombie: $6.7 million for the National Institute of Food and Agriculture Tropical and Subtropical Research/T-Star program.

She joined the Transportation Committee's Water Resources and Environment panel in the 112th Congress (2011-12), giving her some added leverage on issues of critical importance to her state. She'll also have a role in writing the new surface transportation law, expected to be considered in the new Congress. She also won election to the Democratic Steering and Policy Committee, which recommends committee assignments and committee leaders.

She is a vocal advocate for early-childhood education. In the 111th Congress (2009-10) she reintroduced a bill to provide grants to the neediest states to hire teachers, buy supplies and improve nutrition services in preschools. The Education panel approved her bill during the 110th Congress (2007-08), but it didn't reach the House floor. The May 2007 reauthorization of the Head Start program included her provision ensuring preschool teacher training is conducted by people with expertise in infant and toddler development.

She was a strong supporter of the Democrats' health care overhaul in the 111th Congress. During what was then the Education and Labor Committee's consideration of the measure, she won adoption of an amendment that provided a waiver for Hawaii's state-based health care system from some of the law's requirements. She argued that the state program exceeds the standard likely to be set for the plans operating in the health insurance exchange created by the law. Hirono called the GOP-backed repeal passed by the House in early 2011 a "resounding failure."

A loyal Democrat, Hirono sided with her party on 99 percent of the votes in the 111th Congress in which a majority of Democrats split with a majority of Republicans. And she has been a loyal foot soldier for President Obama. Hirono supported Obama's $787 billion economic stimulus bill in

January 2009 and lauded the 2009 omnibus spending bill's funding for educational, agricultural and infrastructure projects and programs in Hawaii.

Hirono was born in 1947 in Fukushima, Japan. She said she never really knew her father, an alcoholic and compulsive gambler. In 1955, her mother, Laura Chie Hirono, decided that life in rural Japan with an abusive husband was "no life for her family." The move to Hawaii took covert plotting, but her mother managed to leave with Hirono and her oldest son. A year later, another son and Hirono's grandparents joined them.

Her mother worked various jobs to support the family and relied on the children to help her learn English. Her mother's struggle inspired Hirono's political career. "I know what it feels like to be discriminated against, to feel powerless, to have landlords who threaten to kick you out, and not having a place to go," she told the Honolulu Advertiser in 2002. To succeed, she immersed herself in school and books, and worked hard to learn the language. She eventually graduated Phi Beta Kappa from the University of Hawaii.

She majored in psychology, thinking she might want to be a social worker to "help people one by one." In college she met anti-war protester David Hagino, who asked Hirono to run his 1970 campaign for the state House. He lost, but two years later Hirono helped in the successful state House campaign of Democrat Anson Chong. She then went to work in Chong's legislative office.

After earning a law degree from Georgetown University, Hirono returned to Hawaii and served as a deputy attorney general before winning a state House seat.

She served 14 years in the state legislature. "I think that I truly exemplify the American dream as an immigrant who came here with nothing, not speaking the language," she said.

She was elected lieutenant governor in 1994 and served eight years. In 2002, she was thwarted in her effort to move up by Republican Linda Lingle, whose victory ended 40 years of Democratic control of the governorship.

In 2006, Hirono leveraged her name recognition to run for the 2nd District seat, which opened when Democrat Ed Case mounted an unsuccessful primary challenge to Sen. Daniel K. Akaka. Hirono faced nine other Democrats in the primary, gaining an edge with support from EMILY's List, a national fundraising group for Democratic women who support abortion rights. She placed first in the primary, beating out the next highest contender by 844 votes. She won the general election easily over GOP state Sen. Bob Hogue, with 61 percent. That year, Hirono and Democrat Hank Johnson of Georgia became the first Buddhists elected to Congress. She won re-election in 2008 with 76 percent of the vote and took 72 percent in 2010.

Key Votes

2010

Overhaul the nation's health insurance system	YES
Allow for repeal of "don't ask, don't tell"	YES
Overhaul financial services industry regulation	YES
Limit use of new Afghanistan War funds to troop withdrawal activities	YES
Change oversight of offshore drilling and lift oil spill liability cap	YES
Provide a path to legal status for some children of illegal immigrants	YES
Extend Bush-era income tax cuts for two years	NO

2009

Expand the Children's Health Insurance Program	YES
Provide $787 billion in tax cuts and spending increases to stimulate the economy	YES
Allow bankruptcy judges to modify certain primary-residence mortgages	YES
Create a cap-and-trade system to limit greenhouse gas emissions	YES
Provide $2 billion for the "cash for clunkers" program	YES
Establish the government as the sole provider of student loans	YES
Restrict federally funded insurance coverage for abortions in health care overhaul	NO

CQ Vote Studies

	PARTY UNITY		PRESIDENTIAL SUPPORT	
	SUPPORT	OPPOSE	SUPPORT	OPPOSE
2010	99%	1%	93%	7%
2009	99%	1%	97%	3%
2008	99%	1%	13%	87%
2007	99%	1%	4%	96%

Interest Groups

	AFL-CIO	ADA	CCUS	ACU
2010	100%	95%	13%	0%
2009	100%	100%	33%	0%
2008	100%	100%	56%	4%
2007	96%	100%	45%	0%

Hawaii 2

Suburban and Outer Oahu; 'Neighbor Islands'

The 2nd is amazing in its geographic diversity, with sandy beaches, volcanoes, mountains, tropical rain forests and deserts, all inhabited by indigenous plants and animals unique to the district's islands. The district includes part of Oahu and all of Hawaii's seven other major islands, as well as the Papahanaumokuakea Marine National Monument, which is larger than all U.S. national parks combined. The southernmost point of the 50 states is located in the district at Ka Lae on the island of Hawaii, also called the Big Island.

Tourism and agriculture, two of the 2nd's leading industries for decades, remain key, as the closure of all but one of Hawaii's sugar plantations forced growers to turn to macadamia nuts and coffee. Some farmers are working to bring pineapples back to a leading position in the industry, and the district's aquaculture sector also is growing.

The tourism industry is vulnerable both to American and Asian economic downturns, and the islands' economies rely on revenue generated from out-of-state visitors. Oahu, the Big Island and Maui are the most-visited islands and have been able to rebound better than Kauai, Molokai and Lanai from several years of hospitality sector struggles.

The 2nd has the highest percentage of a multi-ethnic population in the nation (23 percent), a large Asian population (25 percent) and Native Hawaiians (11 percent). Economic problems offered the GOP an opening at the local level, but the 2nd has kept Democrats in office. Hawaii-born Barack Obama won more than 73 percent of the 2nd's 2008 presidential vote, and all but two state legislative races in the district went to the Democratic candidate in 2010.

Major Industry
Tourism, agriculture, military

Military Bases
Schofield Barracks (Army), 19,362 military, 4,228 civilian; Joint Base Pearl Harbor-Hickam, 19,095 military, 11,986 civilian (shared with the 1st) (2011); Marine Corps Base Hawaii, 5,729 military, 694 civilian (2009)

Cities
Hilo, 43,263; Kailua, 38,635; Kaneohe, 34,597

Notable
The world's largest active volcano, Mauna Loa, is located on the island of Hawaii.

IDAHO

Gov. C.L. "Butch" Otter (R)

First elected: 2006
Length of term: 4 years
Term expires: 1/15
Salary: $115,348
Phone: (208) 334-2100
Residence: Star
Born: May 3, 1942; Caldwell, Idaho
Religion: Roman Catholic
Family: Wife, Lori Otter; four children
Education: College of Idaho, B.A. 1967 (political science)
Military Service: Idaho National Guard, 1968-73
Career: Agribusiness company executive; oil company partner
Political highlights: Idaho House, 1972-76; sought Republican nomination for governor, 1978; lieutenant governor, 1987-2001; U.S. House, 2001-07

ELECTION RESULTS

2010 GENERAL
C.L. Butch Otter (R)	267,483	59.1%
Keith Allred (D)	148,680	32.9%
Jana M. Kemp (I)	26,655	5.9%
Ted Dunlap (LIBERT)	5,867	1.3%
Pro-Life (I)	3,850	0.9%

Lt. Gov. Brad Little (R)

Assumed Office: 2009
Length of term: 4 years
Term expires: 1/15
Salary: $29,184
Phone: (208) 334-2200

LEGISLATURE

Legislature: January-March or April
Senate: 35 members, 2-year terms
2011 ratios: 28 R, 7 D; 26 men, 9 women
Salary: $16,116
Phone: (208) 334-2475
House: 70 members; 2-year terms
2011 ratios: 57 R, 13 D; 51 men, 19 women
Salary: $16,116
Phone: (208) 334-2475

TERM LIMITS

Governor: No
Senate: No
House: No

URBAN STATISTICS

CITY	POPULATION
Boise	205,671
Nampa	81,557
Meridian	75,092
Idaho Falls	56,813
Pocatello	54,255

REGISTERED VOTERS

Voters do not register by party.

POPULATION

2010 population (est.)	1,567,582
2000 population	1,293,953
1990 population	1,006,749
Percent change (2000-2010)	+21.1%
Rank among states (2010)	39
Median age	34.0
Born in state	46.0%
Foreign born	5.5%
Violent crime rate	228/100,000
Poverty level	14.3%
Federal workers	20,044
Military	4,967

ELECTIONS

STATE ELECTION OFFICIAL
(208) 334-2852
DEMOCRATIC PARTY
(208) 336-1815
REPUBLICAN PARTY
(208) 343-6405

MISCELLANEOUS

Web: www.idaho.gov
Capital: Boise

U.S. CONGRESS

Senate: 2 Republicans
House: 2 Republicans

2010 Census Statistics by District

District	2008 Vote for President Obama	McCain	White	Black	Asian	Hispanic	Median Income	White Collar	Blue Collar	Service Industry	Over 64	Under 18	College Education	Rural	Sq. Miles
1	36%	62%	85%	<1%	1%	10%	$47,666	58%	26%	16%	12%	27%	23%	34%	39,525
2	36	61	82	1	1	13	44,675	56	27	17	11	28	25	33	43,222
STATE	36	62	84	1	1	11	46,183	57	26	17	12	27	24	34	82,747
U.S.	53	46	64	12	5	16	51,425	60	23	17	13	25	28	21	3,537,438

Sen. Michael D. Crapo (R)

Capitol Office
224-6142
crapo.senate.gov
239 Dirksen Bldg. 20510-1205; fax 228-1375

Committees
Banking, Housing & Urban Affairs
Budget
Environment & Public Works
Finance
Indian Affairs

Residence
Idaho Falls

Born
May 20, 1951; Idaho Falls, Idaho

Religion
Mormon

Family
Wife, Susan Crapo; five children

Education
Brigham Young U., B.A. 1973 (political science);
Harvard U., J.D. 1977

Career
Lawyer

Political Highlights
Idaho Senate, 1984-92 (president pro tempore,
1988-92); U.S. House, 1993-99

ELECTION RESULTS

2010 GENERAL
Michael D. Crapo (R)	319,953	71.2%
P. Tom Sullivan (D)	112,057	24.9%
Randy Bergquist (CNSTP)	17,429	3.9%

2010 PRIMARY
Michael D. Crapo (R)	127,332	79.3%
Claude M. "Skip" Davis III (R)	33,150	20.7%

2004 GENERAL
Michael D. Crapo (R)	499,796	99.2%

Previous Winning Percentages
1998 (70%); 1996 House Election (69%); 1994 House
Election (75%); 1992 House Election (61%)

Elected 1998; 3rd term

Crapo's knack for finding bipartisan solutions has not stopped him from taking a tough stand against Democratic initiatives he views as wasteful or misguided. Conservative in philosophy, he is moderate in demeanor and does not have much thirst for attention. But he is likely to play an increasingly visible role as a GOP spokesman on fiscal issues.

Unassuming and well-liked by colleagues, Crapo (CRAY-poe) says his view of his own role has changed as the nation has been beset by a financial and economic meltdown, increasing debt and government policies that he believes are only making things worse. Criticizing the stimulus as more likely to hurt the economy than help it, Crapo also opposed the fiscal 2010 omnibus spending bill and the Senate's fiscal 2011 budget resolution, saying both were too costly.

"The reality is this," he said on Fox Business Network after President Obama released his fiscal 2012 budget. "If we do nothing, if we continue to simply spend ourselves, try to spend ourselves through this, then we are going to see an economic collapse that will be far more difficult and far more damaging to every American in every walk of life than any kind of reductions in spending or physical restraint that we're debating here on the Hill."

He has taken on a variety of behind-the-scenes tasks on behalf of Senate Republican leaders, rallying support for their priorities as a deputy whip. He also is serving his fourth term as chairman of the party's Committee on Committees, helping Minority Leader Mitch McConnell of Kentucky make Republican committee assignments.

Crapo was among three GOP senators named by McConnell to serve on the president's National Commission on Fiscal Responsibility and Reform. A member of the Budget Committee, he had cosponsored legislation to create a statutory deficit reduction panel whose recommendations would have had more teeth. Early in the 112th Congress (2011-12), Crapo was part of a bipartisan effort to bring the commission's recommendations to the floor for a vote.

Another bipartisan effort yielded what he considers one of his proudest moments: Inclusion of the Owyhee initiative in a public lands bill signed by Obama in early 2009. The initiative was the culmination of an eight-year effort to settle a long running turf battle among conservationists, American Indians, the Air Force, ranchers and off-road-vehicle groups in southwest Idaho. The resulting legislation protects more than 700,000 acres. Crapo, who sits on the Indian Affairs Committee, calls it a "model for how we should approach decision-making with regard to land management issues."

In 2010, he and Minnesota Democratic Sen. Amy Klobuchar succeeded in passing legislation to prohibit composite wood products from containing potentially hazardous levels of formaldehyde. "In order to build consensus you often have to find alternative routes to a better solution and a better outcome," he said. "And that involves working with a lot of different points of view."

From his seat on the Finance Committee, Crapo took a leading role in the GOP effort to defeat the health care overhaul during the 111th Congress (2009-10), including offering a motion to prevent the legislation from increasing taxes on upper-income earners. He predicted the law will result in higher costs and an "unprecedented expansion of governmental control over health care." He has pledged to work for its repeal in the 112th Congress.

He also serves on the Banking, Housing and Urban Affairs Committee, an unusual choice for a senator from a sparsely populated Western state. But, he said, his committees deal with issues critical to farmers.

Crapo took the lead in 2006 on a wide-ranging banking regulation bill aimed at easing restrictions on banks, credit unions and other financial institutions. He opposed a measure in October 2008 to aid the ailing financial services sector, contending it didn't do enough to protect taxpayers. In 2010 he joined other Republicans in voting against the financial regulatory overhaul bill, saying it would make credit more expensive, discourage capital formation and unreasonably extend government control over the economy.

In 2009, Crapo rejoined the Environment and Public Works Committee, where he had served in his first term. He is a co-chairman of the Senate Renewable Energy and Energy Efficiency Caucus and seeks ways to advance nuclear energy as well as new technologies being developed at the Idaho National Laboratory.

Crapo frequently goes to bat for home-state interests. He joined other senators in objecting to cuts in farm programs proposed by Obama in 2009, and a year later he called on the administration to make sure there was a level playing field for Idaho dairy producers in trade agreements.

Wary of Canadian policies toward timber and agricultural trade, as a House member he opposed legislation to implement both the 1993 North American Free Trade Agreement and the 1994 General Agreement on Tariffs and Trade. Since then, he voted to enact the 2000 law making permanent the normalized U.S.-China trade relationship and supported a 2007 trade deal with Peru. But he opposed the 2005 Central America Free Trade Agreement out of concern over its potential impact on Idaho sugar beet producers.

Crapo grew up in Idaho Falls, the youngest of six children of the local postmaster and his homemaker wife. His father also farmed 200 acres of potatoes, grain and pasture for cattle-grazing, and the children pitched in to help. The family farm expanded over the years and today is run by Crapo's uncles and cousins. He served as his high school's student body president.

At Brigham Young University, he earned a degree in political science and indulged a passion for dirt-bike racing. He then worked as a Washington intern for Idaho GOP Rep. Orval Hansen. He considered a career in medicine, but changed his mind after gaining admission to Harvard Law School.

A cum laude graduate, Crapo spent a year clerking in San Diego before returning to his hometown to practice law. He is a devout Mormon and said his experiences with the church, which gives its lay leaders considerable responsibilities in dealing with personal and community issues, helped prepare him for public office.

Crapo was elected to the Idaho Senate at age 33 and chosen as its president pro tempore four years later. In 1992 he ran for the U.S. House seat being vacated by Democrat Richard Stallings, who ran unsuccessfully for the Senate. He defeated Democrat J.D. Williams by nearly 26 percentage points. In his first term he landed a sought-after seat on the Energy and Commerce Committee.

Crapo has never faced a tough election. When Republican Sen. Dirk Kempthorne ran for governor in 1998, Crapo quickly became the ordained frontrunner to succeed him. Crapo's popularity and a strong Republican tide enabled him to crush Bill Mauk, a former Democratic state chairman, by more than 40 percentage points. He had token opposition in 2004 and easily defeated businessman Tom Sullivan in 2010.

Crapo's sunny demeanor belies an ambition that is fueled in part by his dedication to his oldest brother. An Idaho state legislator who was his mentor and law partner, Terry Crapo died just two weeks after being diagnosed with leukemia in 1982. Crapo faced his own health trial when doctors diagnosed him with prostate cancer in 2000 and operated. Early in 2005, the cancer returned and Crapo underwent radiation treatments while still working in the Senate. As of early 2011, he remains cancer free.

Key Votes

2010

Pass budget reconciliation bill to modify overhauls of health care and federal student loan programs	NO
Proceed to disapproval resolution on EPA authority to regulate greenhouse gases	YES
Overhaul financial services industry regulation	NO
Limit debate to proceed to a bill to broaden campaign finance disclosure and reporting rules	NO
Limit debate on an extension of Bush-era income tax cuts for two years	YES
Limit debate on a bill to provide a path to legal status for some children of illegal immigrants	NO
Allow for a repeal of "don't ask, don't tell"	NO
Consent to ratification of a strategic arms reduction treaty with Russia	NO

2009

Prevent release of remaining financial industry bailout funds	YES
Make it easier for victims to sue for wage discrimination remedies	NO
Expand the Children's Health Insurance Program	NO
Limit debate on the economic stimulus measure	NO
Repeal District of Columbia firearms prohibitions and gun registration laws	YES
Limit debate on expansion of federal hate crimes law	NO
Strike funding for F-22 Raptor fighter jets	NO

CQ Vote Studies

	PARTY UNITY		PRESIDENTIAL SUPPORT	
	SUPPORT	OPPOSE	SUPPORT	OPPOSE
2010	98%	2%	36%	64%
2009	94%	6%	48%	52%
2008	94%	6%	76%	24%
2007	92%	8%	81%	19%
2006	95%	5%	88%	12%
2005	95%	5%	84%	16%
2004	96%	4%	90%	10%
2003	98%	2%	97%	3%
2002	92%	8%	96%	4%
2001	94%	6%	96%	4%

Interest Groups

	AFL-CIO	ADA	CCUS	ACU
2010	6%	0%	100%	100%
2009	17%	10%	71%	92%
2008	20%	15%	75%	88%
2007	5%	15%	82%	88%
2006	7%	0%	83%	88%
2005	21%	10%	94%	100%
2004	8%	10%	94%	92%
2003	15%	5%	91%	89%
2002	9%	10%	94%	94%
2001	19%	10%	100%	92%

Sen. Jim Risch (R)

Capitol Office
224-2752
risch.senate.gov
483 Russell Bldg. 20510; fax 224-2573

Committees
Energy & Natural Resources
Foreign Relations
Small Business & Entrepreneurship
Select Ethics
Select Intelligence

Residence
Boise

Born
May 3, 1943; Milwaukee, Wis.

Religion
Roman Catholic

Family
Wife, Vicki Risch; three children

Education
U. of Wisconsin, Milwaukee, attended 1961-63; U.
of Idaho, B.S. 1965 (forest resources management),
J.D. 1968

Career
Lawyer; rancher; trailer company owner; property
management company owner; college instructor

Political Highlights
Ada County prosecuting attorney, 1970-74; Idaho
Senate, 1974-89 (majority leader, 1976-82; president
pro tempore, 1982-89); defeated for re-election to
Idaho Senate, 1988; sought Republican nomination
for Idaho Senate, 1994; Idaho Senate, 1995-2003 (majority leader, 1997-2003); lieutenant governor, 2003-06;
governor, 2006; lieutenant governor, 2007-09

ELECTION RESULTS

2008 GENERAL

Jim Risch (R)	371,744	57.6%
Larry LaRocco (D)	219,903	34.1%
Rex Rammell (I)	34,510	5.4%
Kent A. Marmon (LIBERT)	9,958	1.5%

Elected 2008; 1st term

While many Senate Republicans resist the "party of no" moniker given them by the Democratic majority, Risch seems happy to embody it.

He has sponsored a limited number of bills since joining the Senate in 2009, and cites as his biggest accomplishment "just being part" of the GOP minority "that's been able to stop a lot of these things."

In particular, Risch is interested in stopping increases in government spending. "It's really hard to come" to Washington, Risch said, "when you have a background that understands debt. I've owned and operated lots of businesses. I was head of the state Senate for all of the 22 years I was there except my freshman years. And we did things so differently."

"You figured out how much money you had and then you spent that amount of money and when it was gone it was gone," he said.

Risch is equally plain-spoken when it comes to offering solutions for other problems facing the country.

The ranking member of the Energy and Natural Resources Subcommittee on Energy heartily opposed a cap-and-trade energy bill proposed in the Senate in 2010. "If you want to clean up the air in this country, clean up the air in this country. Don't construct a complicated, politically charged, easily manipulable formula that does social engineering attempting to clean up the air," Risch said.

He backs nuclear energy as the main solution to the country's energy needs, though he advocates a comprehensive approach that takes advantage of every option available, including drilling in Alaska's Arctic National Wildlife Refuge and federal spending on clean coal technology. Risch laments the fact that the administration is instead focused on just bolstering solar and wind energy production, which he paints as "wonderful and warm and fuzzy to talk about, but they don't solve the energy problems in this country."

Natural resources form one of the top issues of concern to Idahoans, and Risch has cosponsored a number of bills addressing water use, land preservation and rural infrastructure. He has significant experience in the stewardship of public lands — he negotiated a high-profile lands deal during his brief guber-natorial tenure and spearheaded a deal on a proposal to protect millions of roadless acres in the state.

The hot-button issue on the natural resources front, Risch says, is the status of gray wolves, which have been classified as endangered since 1973.

The Interior Department announced in early 2009 that the wolves would be taken off the endangered-species list, but a federal judge ordered the wolves reinstated in August. Risch and his Idaho partner in the Senate, Republican Michael D. Crapo, pushed a bill to de-list the wolf, and a bipartisan provision to do that was included in the final version of the catchall spending bill for fiscal 2011.

Risch sits on the Select Intelligence and Foreign Relations committees. He is the first senator from Idaho on the latter panel in three decades, he notes, and he is the ranking Republican on the Near East and South Central Asian Affairs Subcommittee. He helped lead GOP opposition to the strategic arms reduction treaty the Senate approved in the waning days of the 111th Congress (2009-10).

Risch is a fiscal conservative who favors a balanced-budget amendment and making the 2001 and 2003 tax cuts permanent, although he went along with legislation in late 2010 that extended the rates for two years.

He opposed virtually all of President Obama's economic initiatives, and his views on social issues also regularly put him at odds with the administration. He is anti-abortion and pro-gun rights. He opposed the confirmation of Eric H.

Holder Jr. for attorney general in 2009 based on a disagreement over the interpretation of the Second Amendment. He also voted against confirming Obama's two Supreme Court nominees — Sonia Sotomayor and Elena Kagan.

Risch has been an outspoken opponent of earmarks, the funding set-asides for special projects. While his predecessor, Republican Larry E. Craig, steered millions of federal dollars to Idaho and its national laboratory, Risch has made a practice of requesting earmarks only in conjunction with Crapo, part of Risch's promise to "operate as a team" in Washington. "We are probably closer than any delegation in the United States Senate," Risch said.

The two men have been friends since the 1980s, beginning with Risch's decision to recruit Crapo for a slot in the state Senate leadership, and Crapo encouraged Risch to run for the U.S. Senate seat when Craig announced he would not seek re-election. Craig pleaded guilty to a misdemeanor disorderly conduct charge after an undercover police officer in 2007 interpreted some of the senator's actions in a restroom as a solicitation for sex and arrested him.

Risch hails from Milwaukee, where his father climbed telephone poles for Wisconsin Bell. The nuns at the Catholic high school he attended thought he "needed some direction," so they gave him a career aptitude test. Risch was thrilled to learn he would make a fine forest ranger. After two years attending college in his hometown, Risch headed west to study forestry at the University of Idaho.

He fell in love with Idaho's mountains, but his interest in being a forest ranger faded. After marrying his wife, Vicki, and graduating from law school, Risch was first elected to office in 1970, as prosecutor for Ada County. After seeing a murderer he convicted go free after serving only 18 months of a life sentence, Risch decided to run for the state Senate.

"The only way you could control the parole board was to get into the state Senate," Risch said. "I started rejecting all the appointments to the parole board real quick, and then the rest of them got mad and quit, and that was just fine by me."

Risch opened a private law practice that would make him wealthy. At the same time, he flourished in the state Senate, beating Craig for majority leader in 1976 and 1978. Risch wasn't afraid to make enemies as he mastered the inside political game.

He carried an index card in his back pocket — one side listing the bills he wanted to pass and on the other those he wanted to kill. He lost his seat in 1988 after frequent clashes with the governor, but he returned to the state Senate in 1995 with a less aggressive style.

In 2002, Risch spent $360,000 of his own money on a successful run for lieutenant governor, a part-time job that paid $26,750 a year. He won another term and became Idaho's shortest-tenured governor when he filled out the seven-month term of Gov. Dirk Kempthorne, who had left the state in 2006 to be President George W. Bush's Interior secretary.

In his brief but popular tenure, Risch overhauled the state's tax structure and made major inroads in the environmental community as an unexpected ally in the fight to keep Idaho's wild places pristine.

Risch, with Crapo as his campaign co-chairman, took on former Democratic state Rep. Larry LaRocco in the 2008 Senate campaign. It was a rematch of sorts, as Risch had beat LaRocco 58 percent to 39 percent in the 2006 race for lieutenant governor. Risch won easily, again taking 58 percent of the vote.

As a member of the Ethics Committee, Risch participated in a rare event in 2010: the Senate conviction of District Judge G. Thomas Porteous Jr., only the eighth federal judge ever to be removed from office by impeachment.

Risch is the 15th richest member of Congress, according to Roll Call's analysis of financial disclosure reports filed by members, with a net worth of at least $19.69 million in 2009.

Key Votes

2010

Pass budget reconciliation bill to modify overhauls of health care and federal student loan programs	NO
Proceed to disapproval resolution on EPA authority to regulate greenhouse gases	YES
Overhaul financial services industry regulation	NO
Limit debate to proceed to a bill to broaden campaign finance disclosure and reporting rules	NO
Limit debate on an extension of Bush-era income tax cuts for two years	YES
Limit debate on a bill to provide a path to legal status for some children of illegal immigrants	NO
Allow for a repeal of "don't ask, don't tell"	NO
Consent to ratification of a strategic arms reduction treaty with Russia	NO

2009

Prevent release of remaining financial industry bailout funds	YES
Make it easier for victims to sue for wage discrimination remedies	NO
Expand the Children's Health Insurance Program	NO
Limit debate on the economic stimulus measure	NO
Repeal District of Columbia firearms prohibitions and gun registration laws	YES
Limit debate on expansion of federal hate crimes law	NO
Strike funding for F-22 Raptor fighter jets	NO

CQ Vote Studies

	PARTY UNITY		PRESIDENTIAL SUPPORT	
	SUPPORT	OPPOSE	SUPPORT	OPPOSE
2010	98%	2%	37%	63%
2009	95%	5%	47%	53%

Interest Groups

	AFL-CIO	ADA	CCUS	ACU
2010	6%	0%	100%	100%
2009	17%	10%	71%	96%

Rep. Raúl R. Labrador (R)

Capitol Office
225-6611
labrador.house.gov
1523 Longworth Bldg. 20515-1201; fax 225-3029

Committees
Natural Resources
Oversight & Government Reform

Residence
Eagle

Born
Dec. 8, 1967; Carolina, P.R.

Religion
Mormon

Family
Wife, Rebecca Johnson Labrador; five children

Education
Brigham Young U., B.A. 1992 (Spanish); U. of Washington, J.D. 1995

Career
Lawyer

Political Highlights
Idaho House, 2006-10

ELECTION RESULTS

2010 GENERAL

Raúl R. Labrador (R)	126,231	51.0%
Walt Minnick (D)	102,135	41.3%
Dave Olson (D)	14,365	5.8%
Mike Washburn (LIBERT)	4,696	1.9%

2010 PRIMARY

Raúl R. Labrador (R)	38,711	47.6%
Vaughn Ward (R)	31,582	38.8%
Michael L. Chadwick (R)	5,356	6.6%
Harley D. Brown (R)	3,168	3.9%
Allan M. Salzberg (R)	2,471	3.0%

Elected 2010; 1st term

Labrador says he gets unnecessary attention in Washington for being a Hispanic Republican. He would rather focus on preventing the Republicans from repeating what he sees as the mistakes of the Democrats.

"If we ignore the American people for the next two years, and we are not humble about our victory, we don't do the things that we were asked to do, I think we're going to be fired as well," he said in a Fox News Channel interview in November 2010.

Labrador knows that he represents a fresh face for the GOP, despite his protestations. Along with fellow House freshmen Kristi Noem of South Dakota and Allen B. West of Florida, Labrador made a splash early in 2011 at the Conservative Political Action Conference in Washington when he pointed to himself, the woman from South Dakota and the black man from Florida and said "you can see the great diversity this election brought."

"We represent the three shades of the Republican Party," he said.

With more than 15 years as an immigration lawyer, Labrador hopes to make a splash in the immigration debate, although his committee assignments — Natural Resources and Oversight and Government Reform — don't lend themselves naturally to that issue.

Labrador advocates sending the U.S. military to the Mexican border "to battle the drug terrorists just like they are battling Islamic terrorists in Afghanistan and Iraq." He opposes a path to citizenship for illegal immigrants, while supporting development of a program that would offer those here illegally an incentive to come forward — such as guaranteeing them first consideration to return legally after going back to their countries.

He also urges streamlining the guest worker program — particularly for agricultural workers, who play an important role in his state's economy.

Labrador was carried into office on a wave of tea party support. He upended the National Republican Congressional Committee's preferred candidate, Vaughn Ward, in the primary, then defeated perhaps the most conservative member of the Democratic Caucus, one-term lawmaker Walt Minnick, by 9 percentage points.

Idaho 1
West — Nampa, Panhandle, part of Boise

From its smokestack-shaped panhandle that opens into British Columbia in the north, the 1st District stretches 500 miles south to the Nevada state line, bordering both Washington and Oregon to the west. Rural and rugged, the 1st features rivers, canyons and the trails that Lewis and Clark traveled as they sought a route to the Pacific Ocean.

The most populated region of the rapidly growing district includes part of Boise, as well as suburban Meridian and Nampa, located in Ada and Canyon counties. The Boise area has a diverse economy that includes technology, agriculture, manufacturing, construction and health services. Urbanization has brought the traffic congestion and environmental concerns common to other cities to this once undeveloped landscape. Higher-education jobs and the timber sector drive the midsize cities and heavily forested counties in the center of the district. In the northern part of the district, Coeur d'Alene and Sandpoint rely on tourism and recreation.

The traditionally Republican district's Democratic core has shifted south from its former base near Coeur d'Alene to Latah and Nez Perce counties, near Lewiston and the University of Idaho's main campus in Moscow. But only two Democrats have held the U.S. House seat since 1967, and Republican John McCain took 62 percent of the district's presidential vote in 2008, winning every county in the 1st except Latah.

Major Industry
Technology, manufacturing, timber

Cities
Nampa, 81,557; Meridian, 75,092; Boise City (pt.), 73,796; Caldwell, 46,237

Notable
Hells Canyon, near Riggins in Idaho County, is the nation's deepest river gorge.

Rep. Mike Simpson (R)

Capitol Office
225-5531
www.house.gov/simpson
2312 Rayburn Bldg. 20515-1202; fax 225-8216

Committees
Appropriations
  (Interior-Environment - Chairman)
Budget

Residence
Idaho Falls

Born
Sept. 8, 1950; Burley, Idaho

Religion
Mormon

Family
Wife, Kathy Simpson

Education
Utah State U., attended 1968-72 (pre-dentistry);
Washington U. (Mo.), D.M.D. 1977; Utah State U., B.S.
2002 (pre-dentistry)

Career
Dentist

Political Highlights
Blackfoot City Council, 1980-84; Idaho House, 1984-
98 (Speaker, 1992-98)

ELECTION RESULTS

2010 GENERAL

Mike Simpson (R)	137,468	68.8%
Mike Crawford (D)	48,749	24.4%
Brian Schad (I)	13,500	6.8%

2010 PRIMARY

Mike Simpson (R)	45,148	58.3%
Chick Heileson (R)	18,644	24.1%
Russ Mathews (R)	7,452	9.6%
Katherine Burton (R)	6,214	8.0%

2008 GENERAL

Mike Simpson (R)	205,777	71.0%
Deborah Holmes (D)	83,878	29.0%

Previous Winning Percentages
2006 (62%); 2004 (71%); 2002 (68%); 2000 (71%);
1998 (53%)

Elected 1998; 7th term

Simpson is becoming an increasingly important voice on fiscal matters. He is the No. 3 Republican on the Budget Committee and, more importantly, is now chairman of the Interior-Environment Appropriations Subcommittee.

As soon as Simpson settled into his new role on the spending panel, he set his sights on a favorite target of conservatives, especially Western ones: the Environmental Protection Agency.

The catchall fiscal 2011 spending bill the House passed in February 2011 included $4.5 billion in spending reductions for federal environmental and energy regulators, including a ban on using any funds for imposing EPA rules targeting carbon emissions. Overall, the EPA absorbed 69 percent of the cuts in programs under Simpson's jurisdiction.

"There are areas where we can find reductions, which we've done," Simpson told the New York Times. "Are all of those acceptable to everybody? I don't know."

That statement sums up Simpson's legislative philosophy. His political instincts are conservative — he is anti-abortion, anti-regulation, anti-tax and pro-gun rights — but his voting record reflects another instinct: to listen to the arguments of the other side, and to seek agreement when possible.

Since his days in the Idaho House, Simpson has kept in his office a 12-point set of "Simpson's Rules," which include "hear both sides before judging" and "never, never make an enemy needlessly." As a demonstration of his desire to hear other viewpoints, he once joined the American Civil Liberties Union and the Idaho Conservation League.

"I can sometimes work better with some of the Democrats than I could with some of the Republicans," Simpson said.

Simpson was one of 48 Republicans to vote for pay-as-you-go spending rules that Democrats set in 2007. Later that year, he joined Democrats in an unsuccessful effort to override President George W. Bush's vetoes of the fiscal 2008 Labor, Health and Human Services, and Education spending bill and a bill to expand the Children's Health Insurance Program, which covers children from families that make too much money to qualify for Medicaid — a measure he backed again in early 2009 when it became law. Both of those years he sided with his party on just 79 percent of votes in which a majority of Republicans opposed a majority of Democrats. In no other year has his score fallen below 90 percent.

At the start of the 110th Congress (2007-08), while many Republicans complained loudly about the Democrats' unamendable package of fiscal 2007 spending bills left unfinished from the year before, Simpson refused to join in the criticism. He was the only Republican to vote for the rule governing debate on the legislation and one of a handful opposing procedural protest votes that Republicans forced. "I have a really hard time criticizing the Democrats in general when it's a result of our inability to pass the budget," he said.

Simpson won his seat on Appropriations in the 108th Congress (2003-04). In addition to holding the Interior-Environment gavel, he sits on the Energy-Water panel, another prime spot for a Westerner. He advocates expanding nuclear energy and developing a new generation of nuclear reactors.

Rare is the hearing when Simpson doesn't let out a loud and deep laugh, either while talking to colleagues before getting started or in response to a remark during the meeting. Simpson will need all his affability and consensus-building skills as he tries again to win enactment of legislation overhauling how public lands in central Idaho can be used.

For years, he has tried to push through a bill that would create three new wilderness areas while releasing other federal land for development. The House passed his measure in July 2006, but it was removed at the last minute from a catchall tax bill as outgoing Speaker J. Dennis Hastert, an Illinois Republican, substituted provisions aimed at helping his own state. Simpson introduced another version in May 2010, with revisions intended to make it more palatable to environmentalists, but it went nowhere.

Simpson grew up in the eastern Idaho town of Blackfoot, where his father and uncle had a dental practice. He met his wife, Kathy, in high school; he was on the football team and she was a cheerleader. They both attended Utah State University. He received a dentistry degree from Washington University in St. Louis, but had left Utah State a few credits shy of his degree. Simpson finally collected his degree there in 2002 when a professor suggested he have some dental school credits transferred.

Returning to Blackfoot to join the family business, Simpson decided to run for a city council seat, a nonpartisan job. He says his interest in politics was sparked by a high school teacher who was a Democrat, but when he decided to run for the state legislature four years later, Simpson had to choose a party affiliation and concluded he was more comfortable with the GOP.

Simpson started out with a reputation as an occasionally angry maverick, but mellowed and made a name for himself in Boise, rising through the ranks in the state House and serving as Speaker during his last six years there. He gave thought to seeking the governorship in 1998 but decided against it when Republican Sen. Dirk Kempthorne chose to run. Republican Rep. Michael D. Crapo made a bid for Kempthorne's Senate seat, which created an opening for Simpson in the 2nd District. He won a four-way GOP primary despite criticism from social conservatives that he was insufficiently ardent on their issues.

During the campaign, Simpson was more worried about voters learning of his memberships in the ACLU and the Idaho Conservation League than of his use of marijuana in college. He made no effort to hide that he is a lapsed Mormon who once smoked and still drinks occasionally, but these personal details seemed to have little effect on the heavily Mormon and Republican electorate. He went on to defeat Democrat Richard Stallings, who had held the seat from 1985 to 1993, and has easily won re-election since.

Three opponents, who focused on Simpson's votes in favor of the $700 billion financial industry rescue enacted in late 2008, held him under 60 percent in the 2010 GOP primary. He won by 45 percentage points in November.

Key Votes

2010

Overhaul the nation's health insurance system	NO
Allow for repeal of "don't ask, don't tell"	NO
Overhaul financial services industry regulation	NO
Limit use of new Afghanistan War funds to troop withdrawal activities	NO
Change oversight of offshore drilling and lift oil spill liability cap	NO
Provide a path to legal status for some children of illegal immigrants	NO
Extend Bush-era income tax cuts for two years	NO

2009

Expand the Children's Health Insurance Program	YES
Provide $787 billion in tax cuts and spending increases to stimulate the economy	NO
Allow bankruptcy judges to modify certain primary-residence mortgages	NO
Create a cap-and-trade system to limit greenhouse gas emissions	NO
Provide $2 billion for the "cash for clunkers" program	YES
Establish the government as the sole provider of student loans	NO
Restrict federally funded insurance coverage for abortions in health care overhaul	YES

CQ Vote Studies

	PARTY UNITY		PRESIDENTIAL SUPPORT	
	SUPPORT	OPPOSE	SUPPORT	OPPOSE
2010	90%	10%	29%	71%
2009	79%	21%	32%	68%
2008	92%	8%	62%	38%
2007	79%	21%	73%	27%
2006	95%	5%	89%	11%

Interest Groups

	AFL-CIO	ADA	CCUS	ACU
2010	7%	5%	75%	96%
2009	19%	10%	80%	84%
2008	27%	35%	94%	80%
2007	29%	20%	84%	72%
2006	21%	5%	93%	80%

Idaho 2

East — Pocatello, Idaho Falls, part of Boise

Covering the Gem State's eastern and central portions, the 2nd includes most of Boise, a few midsize cities and a vast swath of agricultural land fed by the Snake River. The central and northern parts of the district are full of mountain ranges, rivers and fishing sites. Idaho's Sun Valley ski resort is located in the 2nd, and with natural wonders such as Shoshone Falls, the district attracts tourists. Waterfalls, snowmobile trails and spectacular views leave visitors with Idaho's motto, "Esto Perpetua" ("Let it be perpetual"), in mind.

Elmore County, in the district's west, contains Mountain Home Air Force Base, but most of the district's livelihoods rely on agriculture, mainly potatoes, sugar beets and grain. Blackfoot, in Bingham County, is known as the potato-producing capital of the world — eastern Idaho supplies about one-third of the nation's potato crop — while the district's southern tier produces most of the nation's trout. Technology firms played a key role in the last decade, but layoffs at major firms, including Micron Technology, hurt the local economy.

Members of The Church of Jesus Christ of Latter-day Saints make up the district's largest religious group, and like most Mormon areas, the district is strongly conservative — eastern Idaho has been represented by a Mormon in the U.S. House since 1951. The district consistently supports Republicans in federal elections but elects Democrats to the state legislature in the Boise area and can support them in Blaine and Bannock counties in the center of the 2nd. Blaine County, home to Sun Valley, is the only county to vote reliably for Democratic candidates in presidential elections. In 2008, Republican John McCain won the district with 61 percent of its presidential vote.

Major Industry
Agriculture, food processing, tourism, technology

Military Bases
Mountain Home Air Force Base, 4,131 military, 315 civilian (2011)

Cities
Boise City (pt.), 131,875; Idaho Falls, 56,813; Pocatello, 54,255; Twin Falls, 44,125; Rexburg, 25,484

Notable
The Idaho National Laboratory near Idaho Falls is the Department of Energy nuclear research site.

ILLINOIS

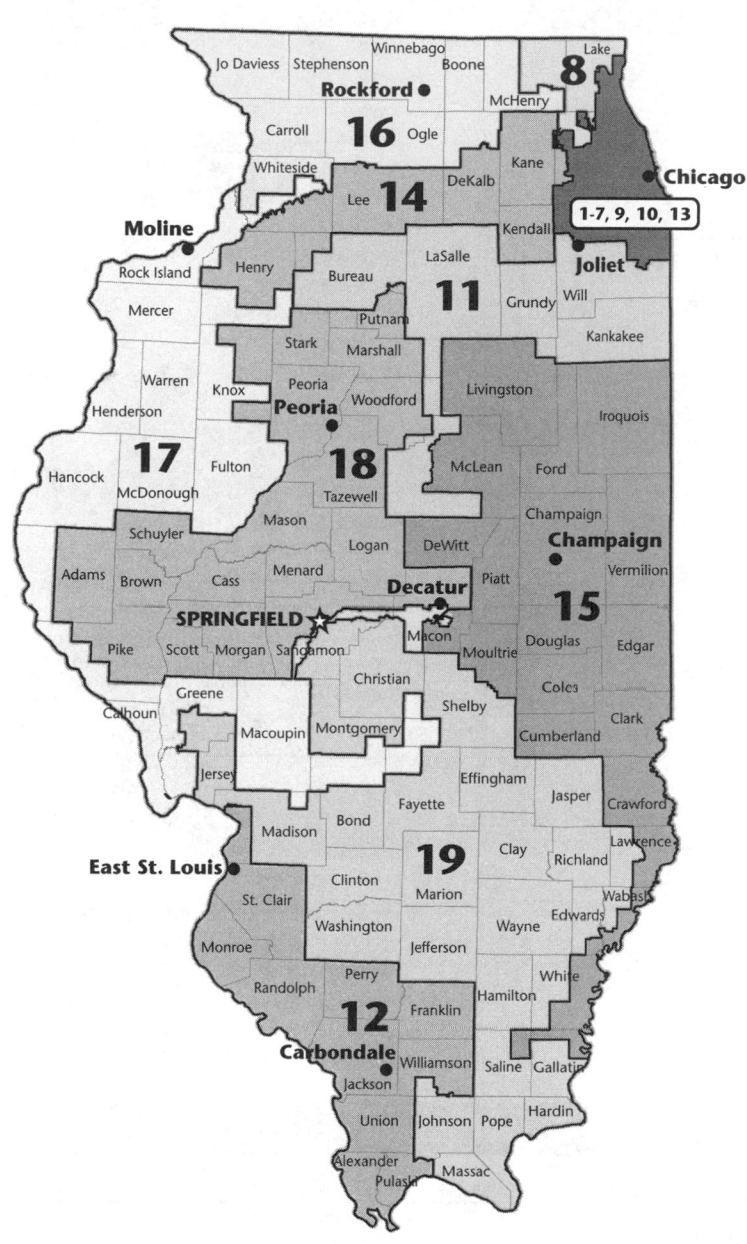

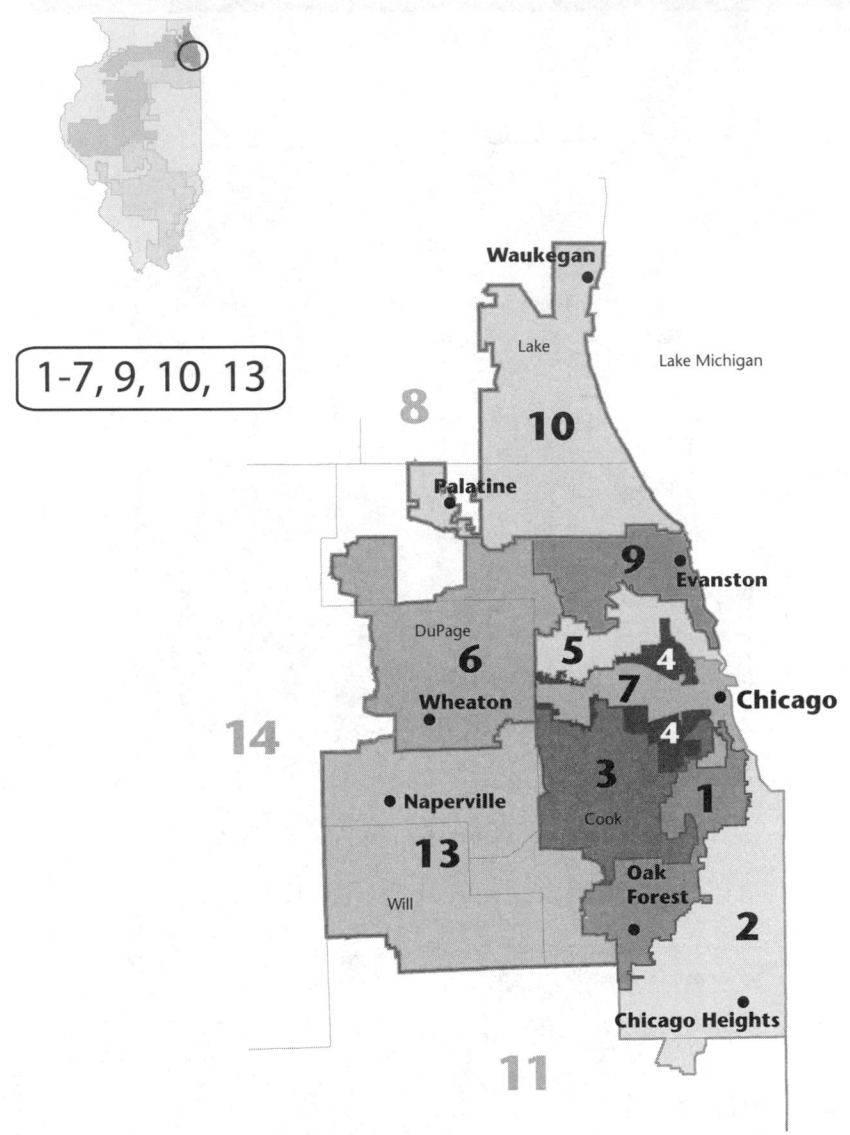

1-7, 9, 10, 13

2010 CENSUS STATISTICS BY DISTRICT

District	2008 VOTE FOR PRESIDENT Obama	McCain	White	Black	Asian	Hispanic	Median Income	White Collar	Blue Collar	Service Industry	Over 64	Under 18	College Education	Rural	Sq. Miles
1	87%	13%	26%	62%	2%	9%	$41,177	59%	20%	21%	13%	26%	21%	0%	98
2	90	10	16	69	1	13	45,710	58	23	19	12	28	21	0	185
3	64	35	55	7	4	34	55,884	55	27	18	13	26	23	0	124
4	85	13	19	4	2	74	42,837	45	34	21	6	29	21	0	39
5	73	26	60	3	7	29	59,685	64	19	17	11	20	40	0	57
6	56	43	66	4	10	18	71,147	67	20	13	11	25	37	0	213
7	88	12	32	51	7	9	51,026	72	13	15	10	23	39	0	56
8	56	43	69	4	8	17	73,943	67	20	13	9	27	36	4	608
9	72	26	60	10	14	13	55,973	69	15	16	15	20	44	0	75
10	61	38	69	5	8	16	83,225	73	15	12	13	27	51	0	250

GOV. PAT QUINN (D)

First elected: 2010
Took office Jan. 29, 2009, due to the impeachment and removal from office of Rod R. Blagojevich.

Length of term: 4 years

Term expires: 1/15

Salary: $177,500

Phone: (217) 782-0244

Residence: Chicago

Born: Dec. 16, 1948; Hinsdale, Ill.

Religion: Roman Catholic

Family: Divorced; two children

Education: Geogetown U., 1971 B.S. (international economics); Northwestern U., 1980 J.D.

Career: Lawyer, college instructor; city government official, political activist, campaign and gubernatorial aide

Political highlights: Cook County Board of Tax Appeals, 1982-86; sought Democratic nomination for Ill. treasurer, 1986; Ill. treasurer, 1991-95; Democratic nominee for Ill. secretary of State, 1994; sought Democratic nomination for U.S. Senate, 1996; lieutenant governor, 2002-09

ELECTION RESULTS

2010 GENERAL

Pat Quinn (D)	1,745,219	46.8%
Bill Brady (R)	1,713,385	45.9%
Scott Lee Cohen (I)	135,705	3.6%
Rich Whitney (GREEN)	100,756	2.7%

LT. GOV. SHEILA SIMON (D)

First elected: 2010

Length of term: 4 years

Term expires: 1/15

Salary: $135,669

Phone: (217) 558-3085

LEGISLATURE

General Assembly: January-May; meets in October or November to consider vetoes

Senate: 59 members, rotates between 2- and 4-year terms

2011 ratios: 35 D, 24 R; 43 men, 16 women

Salary: $67,836

Phone: (217) 782-5715

House: 118 members, 2-year terms

2011 ratios: 64 D, 54 R; 81 men, 37 women

Salary: $67,836

Phone: (217) 782-8223

TERM LIMITS

Governor: No

Senate: No

House: No

URBAN STATISTICS

CITY	POPULATION
Chicago	2,695,598
Aurora	197,899
Rockford	152,871
Joliet	147,433
Naperville	141,853

REGISTERED VOTERS

Voters do not register by party.

POPULATION

2010 population	12,830,632
2000 population	12,419,293
1990 population	11,430,602
Percent change (2000-2010)	+3.3%
Rank among states (2010)	5
Median age	35.9
Born in state	66.9%
Foreign born	13.3%
Violent crime rate	497/100,000
Poverty level	13.3%
Federal workers	111,692
Military	10,111

ELECTIONS

STATE ELECTION OFFICIAL

(217) 782-4141

DEMOCRATIC PARTY

(217) 546-7404

REPUBLICAN PARTY

(217) 525-0011

MISCELLANEOUS

Web: www.illinois.gov

Capital: Springfield

U.S. CONGRESS

Senate: 1 Republican, 1 Democrat

House: 11 Republicans, 8 Democrats

2010 CENSUS STATISTICS BY DISTRICT

District	2008 Vote for President Obama	McCain	White	Black	Asian	Hispanic	Median Income	White Collar	Blue Collar	Service Industry	Over 64	Under 18	College Education	Rural	Sq. Miles
11	53%	45%	78%	8%	1%	11%	$58,246	55%	28%	17%	11%	26%	21%	22%	4,241
12	56	43	76	18	1	3	41,975	56	24	20	14	24	20	23	4,425
13	54	44	71	7	9	11	81,730	73	15	12	10	27	45	1	355
14	55	44	66	5	3	25	66,319	60	26	15	9	28	30	14	2,852
15	48	50	84	7	4	4	45,393	58	25	17	14	22	26	36	10,072
16	53	46	80	6	2	10	56,323	57	27	16	13	26	24	46	4,098
17	56	42	83	8	1	5	40,454	53	28	19	16	22	18	42	8,120
18	48	50	86	7	1	3	50,782	60	24	17	15	23	24	50	8,186
19	44	54	92	4	1	2	47,650	56	27	17	16	23	20	54	11,519
STATE	62	37	64	14	5	16	55,222	61	23	16	12	25	30	12	55,584
U.S.	53	46	64	12	5	16	51,425	60	23	17	13	25	28	21	3,537,438

Sen. Richard J. Durbin (D)

Capitol Office
224-2152
durbin.senate.gov
711 Hart Bldg. 20510-1304; fax 228-0400

Committees
Appropriations
   (Financial Services - Chairman)
Foreign Relations
Judiciary
   (Constitution, Civil Rights & Human Rights - Chairman)
Rules & Administration
Joint Library

Residence
Springfield

Born
Nov. 21, 1944; East St. Louis, Ill.

Religion
Roman Catholic

Family
Wife, Loretta Durbin; three children (one deceased)

Education
Georgetown U., B.S.F.S. 1966 (international affairs & economics), J.D. 1969

Career
Lawyer; gubernatorial and state legislative aide

Political Highlights
Democratic nominee for Ill. Senate, 1976; Democratic nominee for lieutenant governor, 1978; U.S. House, 1983-97

ELECTION RESULTS

2008 GENERAL

Richard J. Durbin (D)	3,615,844	67.8%
Steve Sauerberg (R)	1,520,621	28.5%
Kathy Cummings (GREEN)	119,135	2.2%

2008 PRIMARY

Richard J. Durbin (D)	unopposed

Previous Winning Percentages
2002 (60%); 1996 (56%); 1994 House Election (55%); 1992 House Election (57%); 1990 House Election (66%); 1988 House Election (69%); 1986 House Election (68%); 1984 House Election (61%); 1982 House Election (50%)

Elected 1996; 3rd term

It might not seem possible for the second-ranking member of the U.S. Senate to simultaneously fly above and below the radar, but Durbin has managed just that. He can remain out of sight partly because his boss, Majority Leader Harry Reid of Nevada, is a lightning rod who draws much of the fire from the news media and Republican critics.

Sometimes fiery, and almost always liberal, Durbin is the point man in the Democratic leadership team's outreach to the party's left wing. When Senate Democrats unveiled their "Winning the Future" budget blueprint early in the 112th Congress (2011-12) to counter GOP spending plans, Durbin dismissed the other chamber's majority by saying "the House Republican approach is to cut everything," Roll Call reported.

Durbin's ties to party liberals make him a good complement to Reid, who has stronger connections to Democratic moderates.

Durbin's friendship with Reid dates back to their early days as House freshmen in 1983. Durbin said he has an open invitation to attend meetings Reid has with other Democratic senators; Reid called his handpicked sidekick "one of the nicest and kindest members of the Senate."

Of course, nice guys don't always finish first on Capitol Hill or anywhere else, but Durbin's earnest, attentive style serves him well as a party leader, and his reputation for solving problems has helped make him a front-runner to eventually succeed Reid.

As majority whip, Durbin played key roles in the passage of three signature pieces of legislation pushed by President Obama during his first 18 months in office: the $787 billion economic stimulus package enacted in February 2009, the health care overhaul enacted in March 2010 and the financial regulatory reform package enacted in July 2010.

Lesser known was the extent to which Durbin acted as a conduit between the Senate and the Obama administration since Illinois' one-time junior senator assumed control of the White House in 2009. Durbin is in frequent contact with Obama, either in person or via telephone, and Obama's chief of staff, Pete Rouse, is Durbin's former chief of staff.

Like Reid, Durbin can be combative, but he has a friendly Midwestern demeanor off the floor and often uses humor to disarm colleagues and reporters. He jokes about the "added burden" he endures living and working with Democratic Conference Vice Chairman Charles E. Schumer of New York, who is a potential future rival for party leader. They share a Capitol Hill row house.

Durbin was the natural choice for whip when Reid moved up to replace Minority Leader Tom Daschle after the South Dakotan was defeated by Republican John Thune in 2004. Liberals who dominate the Democratic caucus were initially wary of Reid, who sometimes sided with Republicans on social and gun issues. But they trusted Durbin as one of their own. He had honed his leadership skills under Daschle, heading a group of senators who met weekly to set the party's message.

Durbin's people skills were tested by the furor surrounding Obama's replacement in the Senate. Illinois Democratic Gov. Rod R. Blagojevich appointed Roland W. Burris to succeed the president in late 2008 after the governor was accused of trying to sell the seat but before he was impeached and removed from office over the scandal. The Senate Ethics Committee investigated whether Burris lied under oath about his contacts with Blagojevich before his appointment. Durbin initially said that no one was likely to accept Blagojevich's appointment given the hint of scandal that would accompany it, but was forced to backtrack when Burris not only accepted the assignment but rebuffed the efforts of Democratic leaders to block him from being seated.

Durbin looks out for Illinois' interests from his perch on the Appropriations Committee, where he chairs the Financial Services Subcommittee.

He is well positioned to weigh in on proposals to merge the Commodity Futures Trading Commission with the Securities and Exchange Commission. The CFTC has been criticized for being a weak regulator of traders for the CME Group, an important constituent formed in the 2007 merger of the Chicago Mercantile Exchange and Chicago Board of Trade.

Throughout his career, but particularly during the battle over the financial regulatory overhaul during the 111th Congress (2009-10), Durbin focused on strengthening consumer protection laws. Durbin, teaming with moderate Democratic Sen. Mark Pryor of Arkansas, had previously succeeded in doubling the budget of the Consumer Product Safety Commission. Within the financial overhaul bill, there was a confluence of his dogged work on behalf of his constituents and his concern for consumer protection. In 2010, Durbin used his leadership position to include a provision to toughen regulation of the credit card industry. Large banks fought the measure, but Durbin succeeded in getting Democrat Christopher J. Dodd of Connecticut, chairman of the Banking, Housing and Urban Affairs Committee, to include it.

From his seat on the Judiciary Committee, Durbin has pushed for tighter oversight of temporary work visas and for a path to citizenship for certain children of illegal immigrants. That effort failed once again at the tail end of 2010 when the latest iteration of the legislation won 55 votes, five short of the 60 needed to overcome a filibuster threat in the Senate.

In the wake of protests that toppled Egyptian President Hosni Mubarak in early 2011, Durbin, a new member of the Foreign Relations Committee, spoke out against other despots and in favor of U.S. backing for democratic forces. "There are battles going on all over the world, and our support for that effort can make a difference," he told The Hill newspaper.

In the late 1980s, he led the successful effort to ban smoking on domestic airline flights. And in the 110th Congress (2007-08), he helped persuade the Rules and Administration Committee, on which he serves, to ban the sale of tobacco products in the Senate and to close two designated smoking rooms in the Senate office buildings. The youngest of three brothers raised in East St. Louis, Ill., by an Irish-American father who was a railroad night watchman and a Lithuanian-born mother who was a switchboard operator, Durbin was 14 when his chain-smoking father died of lung cancer.

Durbin caught the politics bug in college when he was an intern for Democrat Paul Douglas, whose seat he now holds. He held long conversations with Douglas, who used to tell Durbin stories as the young intern handed him letters to sign. One of Durbin's sons is named after Douglas. After law school, Durbin returned home. For about five years in the 1970s, he was co-owner of a bar in Springfield. His early political career included stints as Illinois Senate parliamentarian and aide to Lt. Gov. Paul Simon, later a U.S. senator and presidential candidate. In 1982, Durbin unseated 11-term GOP Rep. Paul N. Findley by 1,410 votes in a Springfield-based House district.

When Simon announced he would not seek re-election in 1996, Durbin got into the race and won by 15 percentage points against conservative state Rep. Al Salvi. Durbin coasted to a second term in 2002 and a third six years later. The 2008 election marked a high-water mark for Durbin, as Obama, Illinois' junior senator, won the White House and Democrats increased their Senate majority by eight seats. The period, however, was marked by personal tragedy when Durbin's adult daughter, Christine, died three days before Election Day from complications related to a congenital heart condition.

Key Votes

2010

Pass budget reconciliation bill to modify overhauls of health care and federal student loan programs	YES
Proceed to disapproval resolution on EPA authority to regulate greenhouse gases	NO
Overhaul financial services industry regulation	YES
Limit debate to proceed to a bill to broaden campaign finance disclosure and reporting rules	YES
Limit debate on an extension of Bush-era income tax cuts for two years	YES
Limit debate on a bill to provide a path to legal status for some children of illegal immigrants	YES
Allow for a repeal of "don't ask, don't tell"	YES
Consent to ratification of a strategic arms reduction treaty with Russia	YES

2009

Prevent release of remaining financial industry bailout funds	NO
Make it easier for victims to sue for wage discrimination remedies	YES
Expand the Children's Health Insurance Program	YES
Limit debate on the economic stimulus measure	YES
Repeal District of Columbia firearms prohibitions and gun registration laws	NO
Limit debate on expansion of federal hate crimes law	YES
Strike funding for F-22 Raptor fighter jets	YES

CQ Vote Studies

	PARTY UNITY		PRESIDENTIAL SUPPORT	
	SUPPORT	OPPOSE	SUPPORT	OPPOSE
2010	99%	1%	100%	0%
2009	100%	0%	100%	0%
2008	98%	2%	31%	69%
2007	98%	2%	36%	64%
2006	98%	2%	47%	53%
2005	99%	1%	33%	67%
2004	96%	4%	54%	46%
2003	97%	3%	46%	54%
2002	97%	3%	67%	33%
2001	95%	5%	62%	38%

Interest Groups

	AFL-CIO	ADA	CCUS	ACU
2010	100%	95%	18%	0%
2009	94%	95%	43%	0%
2008	100%	100%	63%	4%
2007	100%	95%	45%	0%
2006	100%	100%	45%	4%
2005	100%	100%	28%	0%
2004	92%	95%	47%	4%
2003	85%	95%	35%	10%
2002	100%	95%	50%	0%
2001	94%	95%	31%	0%

Sen. Mark Steven Kirk (R)

Capitol Office
224-2854
kirk.senate.gov
524 Hart Bldg. 20510-1305; fax 228-4260

Committees
Appropriations
Banking, Housing & Urban Affairs
Health, Education, Labor & Pensions
Special Aging

Residence
Highland Park

Born
Sept. 15, 1959; Champaign, Ill.

Religion
Congregationalist

Family
Divorced

Education
Cornell U., B.A. 1981 (history); London School of
Economics, M.S. 1982; Georgetown U., J.D. 1992

Military Service
Navy Reserve, 1989-present

Career
Lawyer; U.S. State Department aide; World Bank
officer; congressional aide

Political Highlights
U.S. House, 2001-10

ELECTION RESULTS

2010 GENERAL

Mark Steven Kirk (R)	1,778,698	48.0%
Alexi Giannoulias (D)	1,719,478	46.4%
LeAlan M. Jones (GREEN)	117,914	3.2%
Mike Labno (LIBERT)	87,247	2.4%

2010 SPECIAL

Mark Steven Kirk (R)	1,677,729	47.3%
Alexi Giannoulias (D)	1,641,486	46.3%

Previous Winning Percentages
2008 House Election (53%); 2006 House Election
(53%); 2004 House Election (64%); 2002 House Election (69%) 2000 House Election (51%)

Elected 2010; 1st term

Kirk, who charted a path of fiscal conservatism and social moderation during his five terms in the House, says he plans to continue in that vein as the junior senator occupying the seat once held by President Obama.

But despite his concerns about the deficit, he wants to expand the Small Business Administration, the Agriculture Department and the U.S. Trade Development Agency to help Illinois farmers and small businesses boost exports into growing markets.

Kirk pledged to be an advocate for heavy manufacturing and agriculture — both major drivers of the Illinois economy — and he won a coveted seat on the Appropriations Committee, where he is well-positioned to boost his state's fortunes. He sits on five spending subcommittees: Financial Services, Labor-Health and Human Services-Education, State-Foreign Operations, Transportation-Housing and Urban Development and Military Construction-Veterans Affairs, where he is the ranking Republican.

The Transportation panel provides a perch from which he can help update the state's rail, aviation and highway systems, which Kirk said would boost the Illinois economy by making it easier to get goods to markets. Kirk has also said he wants to improve airport security and continue his work on Transportation Security Administration measures. He had served on the Homeland Security spending panel in the House.

As the top Republican on the Military Construction subcommittee, Kirk can look out for the state's military installations and veterans' hospitals.

The self-described "national security hawk" hopes to be an asset on broader defense issues as well. He took part in two weeks of training missions in Afghanistan as a Navy reservist in 2008 and said his background could be useful in both military policy and homeland security issues. He has pushed to boost the rewards for information on international terrorists, including Osama bin Laden, and opposes moving prisoners from Guantánamo Bay, Cuba, to detention facilities in the United States.

He voted against ratification of the strategic arms reduction treaty the Senate approved in late 2010, saying it would damage U.S. national security. But he was among a handful of Republicans who sided with Democrats in supporting repeal of the statutory ban on gays and lesbians serving openly in the military.

In 2009, he led opposition to the nomination of Charles "Chas" Freeman to lead the National Intelligence Council; Freeman eventually withdrew from consideration. Critics complained that Freeman served on the board of directors of the China-owned Chinese National Offshore Oil Corp. and was president of the Middle East Policy Council, a think tank funded by the Saudi government. Many also were concerned about remarks he had made on China's actions during the 1989 Tiananmen Square protests and some of Israel's policies toward Palestinians. "There comes a point where somebody is mortally wounded and can't carry out their job," Kirk said of Freeman.

Kirk has backed gun control measures but supported the Supreme Court decision negating the Washington, D.C., handgun ban. He supports an energy policy that includes nuclear energy, offshore oil exploration, and a tax credit for renewable hydro, wind, solar and biomass energy production.

At the same time, he pushes for fiscal restraint, an end to earmarking and a balanced budget. Kirk signed onto legislation introduced in early 2011 by Republican Bob Corker of Tennessee and Democrat Claire McCaskill of Missouri that would place caps on future spending, starting in fiscal 2013. Under the bill, outlays would be cut each year over the next 10 years, until spending fell to less than 21 percent of gross domestic product. Current spending equals about 25 percent of GDP.

He said lawmakers were in "a collective state of shock" over the size of the deficit.

When a catchall $1.1 trillion spending bill was defeated near the end of the 111th Congress (2009-10), Kirk drew the ire of more senior senators when he celebrated a bit more than Senate decorum tends to call for.

"As the most junior people, for those who don't understand what just happened, did we just win?" Kirk asked disingenuously on the floor.

He supports making the George W. Bush-era tax cuts permanent, but acquiesced in legislation enacted late in 2010 that extended the rates for two years.

Kirk's slot on three other committees — Banking, Housing and Urban Affairs; Health, Education, Labor and Pensions; and Special Aging — should help him pursue some of his goals on economic social policies.

Kirk grew up in Kenilworth, a wealthy suburb of Chicago. His near-drowning at age 16, when he almost died in a boating accident on Lake Michigan, convinced him to do something positive with his life. "To be given a second chance means it has to mean something," he told the Chicago Tribune. "For me, that means making a difference through public service."

He graduated from New Trier High School, long one of Illinois' top public high schools, and followed up with three university degrees, a stint in Mexico to learn Spanish, and a career in military intelligence. He has traveled in more than 40 countries. One of his earliest jobs was as a legislative counsel for the House International Relations Committee. He also worked for several years on the staff of his predecessor in the House, fellow GOP centrist John Edward Porter, and worked at the State Department and the World Bank.

When Porter announced his retirement before the 2000 election, Kirk ran in a primary field jammed with 10 other Republicans. With Porter's backing, Kirk defeated his nearest rival by 16 percentage points. In the general election, he prevailed over Democratic state Rep. Lauren Beth Gash by 2 percentage points. He won with ease in 2002 and 2004 before facing tough battles with Democrat Dan Seals in his last two House elections, when he was a top target of the Democrats. In 2008, he won an endorsement from Planned Parenthood and was one of only six Republican congressional candidates endorsed by the Sierra Club. He raised more than $5 million, more than any other House member seeking reelection that year, and took 53 percent of the vote.

When Obama was elected president, embattled Democratic Gov. Rod R. Blagojevich appointed longtime party stalwart Roland W. Burris to fill the seat until the next election. Blagojevich was subsequently removed from office, and Burris faced a potential rebellion among Senate Democrats. He survived but decided against seeking election in 2010. When other top Democrats in the state, including Attorney General Lisa Madigan, passed on the race, the nomination was won by state Treasurer Alexi Giannoulias. Kirk won the GOP nod easily over a collection of lesser-known opponents.

In a seesaw general election campaign, Giannoulias tried to make hay out of exaggerations Kirk had made in his military record; Kirk highlighted work Giannoulias' family bank did with mobsters before federal regulators seized the institution.

The president and first lady Michelle Obama campaigned hard for Giannoulias, but Kirk prevailed by 2 percentage points, winning 48 percent of the vote.

Kirk was seated before most of the rest of the freshman senators elected in 2010 because he was replacing the appointed Burris, which allowed him to participate in Senate debates during the lame-duck session of the 111th Congress.

Key Votes

2010 (while House member)

Overhaul the nation's health insurance system	NO
Allow for repeal of "don't ask, don't tell"	NO
Overhaul financial services industry regulation	NO
Limit use of new Afghanistan War funds to troop withdrawal activities	NO

2010 (while Senate member)

Change oversight of offshore drilling and lift oil spill liability cap	NO
Limit debate on an extension of Bush-era income tax cuts for two years	YES
Limit debate on a bill to provide a path to legal status for some children of illegal immigrants	NO
Allow for a repeal of "don't ask, don't tell"	YES
Consent to ratification of a strategic arms reduction treaty with Russia	NO

2009

Expand the Children's Health Insurance Program	YES
Provide $787 billion in tax cuts and spending increases to stimulate the economy	NO
Allow bankruptcy judges to modify certain primary-residence mortgages	NO
Create a cap-and-trade system to limit greenhouse gas emissions	YES
Provide $2 billion for the "cash for clunkers" program	YES
Establish the government as the sole provider of student loans	NO
Restrict federally funded insurance coverage for abortions in health care overhaul	YES

CQ Vote Studies (while House member)

	PARTY UNITY		PRESIDENTIAL SUPPORT	
	Support	Oppose	Support	Oppose
2010	76%	24%	45%	55%
2009	78%	22%	50%	50%
2008	73%	27%	53%	47%
2007	70%	30%	41%	59%
2006	79%	21%	80%	20%
2005	80%	20%	67%	33%
2004	84%	16%	63%	37%
2003	87%	13%	81%	19%
2002	85%	15%	85%	15%
2001	85%	15%	74%	26%

Interest Groups (while House member)

	AFL-CIO	ADA	CCUS	ACU
2010	0%	10%	100%	63%
2009	48%	35%	87%	72%
2008	47%	55%	83%	48%
2007	52%	40%	84%	40%
2006	36%	45%	80%	54%
2005	20%	30%	81%	36%
2004	29%	45%	90%	63%
2003	7%	10%	89%	58%
2002	11%	20%	95%	76%
2001	25%	25%	83%	48%

Rep. Bobby L. Rush (D)

Capitol Office
225-4372
www.house.gov/rush
2268 Rayburn Bldg. 20515-1301; fax 226-0333

Committees
Energy & Commerce

Residence
Chicago

Born
Nov. 23, 1946; Albany, Ga.

Religion
Protestant

Family
Wife, Carolyn Rush; six children (one deceased)

Education
Roosevelt U., B.A. 1973 (political science); U. of Illinois,
Chicago, attended 1975-77 (political science), M.A.
1994 (political science); McCormick Theological
Seminary, M.A. 1998 (theological studies)

Military
Army, 1963-68

Career
Insurance broker; political activist

Political Highlights
Candidate for Chicago City Council, 1975; sought
Democratic nomination for Ill. House, 1978; Chicago
City Council, 1983-93; candidate for mayor of
Chicago, 1999

ELECTION RESULTS

2010 GENERAL

Bobby L. Rush (D)	148,170	80.4%
Raymond Wardingley (R)	29,253	15.9%
Jeff Adams (D)	6,963	3.8%

2010 PRIMARY

Bobby L. Rush (D)	68,585	79.7%
JoAnne Guillemette (D)	8,035	9.3%
Fred Smith (D)	5,203	6.0%
Harold L. Bailey (D)	4,232	4.9%

Previous Winning Percentages
2008 (86%); 2006 (84%); 2004 (85%); 2002 (81%);
2000 (88%); 1998 (87%); 1996 (86%); 1994 (76%);
1992 (83%)

Elected 1992; 10th term

Rush's life has taken him from the rural South to a congressional chairmanship, from the Boy Scouts to the Black Panthers, from defeat at the hands of Richard M. Daley to victory over a future president of the United States. It has been quite a journey for the man who has been an inspirational voice for liberal causes, a consumer advocate and a target for critics who decry his injection of race into politics.

Rush is among the most liberal House members, active in both the Progressive Caucus and the Congressional Black Caucus.

He worked assiduously on consumer issues when Democrats were in charge and he was chairman of the Energy and Commerce Subcommittee on Commerce, Trade and Consumer Protection. His focus shifted at the start of the 112th Congress (2011-12) when he took over as ranking member of the Energy and Power Subcommittee.

He echoes Democratic orthodoxy on energy policy, criticizing increased drilling for oil and gas and pushing government subsidies for renewable energy. "We need to get about the task of transforming the world's energy system into a low-carbon, low-emissions system," he said at a subcommittee hearing in February 2011.

He said he was "very deeply disappointed and disturbed" by proposed cuts in the Low-Income Home Energy Assistance Program included in the Obama administration budget for fiscal 2012. That concern is in line with what he calls his main goal in Congress: to better the lives of his South Side Chicago constituents, among the city's poorest residents.

In March 2010 he introduced a bill intended to, among other things, create summer jobs for at-risk youth — perhaps a bit surprising considering that in his successful 1992 race to unseat Charles A. Hayes, Rush had derided the incumbent for the election-year introduction of jobs bills that never moved.

But he opposed the Democratic jobs bill the House passed that month, even after House leaders added a provision that would direct some transportation funding to small businesses determined to be "controlled by socially and economically disadvantaged individuals."

"At a time when the African-American community's unemployment rate hovers in the range of 17 percent, I cannot go back to them, look them in the eye and tell them 'I got big business a tax cut today' and simply walk away in the hopes that they'll be hired," Rush said.

Rush, who once served six months in prison for illegal possession of weapons, has been an advocate of strict controls on firearms — a position that was further strengthened when his son Huey (named after Black Panther leader Huey Newton) was shot and killed in a Chicago sidewalk robbery in 1999. Shortly before the assailants were convicted in 2002, Rush's nephew was charged with murder in what police said was a drug deal gone bad.

In February 2008 Rush learned he had a cancerous tumor on his salivary gland. The cancer was localized, and the tumor was surgically removed the next month. Subsequent radiation treatment and recovery kept him away from Capitol Hill for about five months. During his absence, Rush directed his staff to prepare brief tributes to gun victims that were inserted in the Congressional Record every few days.

In March 2010 he took up the cause of state regulation of alcohol distribution, tying it to the protection of poor communities. Stepping over to the other side of the witness table, he testified at a House Judiciary subcommittee hearing on the issue.

Rush stoked a good deal of controversy following Barack Obama's election to the presidency. Illinois Democratic Gov. Rod R. Blagojevich was subsequently impeached and removed from office for a series of alleged crimes that included trying to sell Obama's Senate seat, but not before the governor appointed former Illinois Attorney General Roland W. Burris. Other Illinois lawmakers immediately called on Burris to refuse the appointment. But Rush became Burris' most outspoken defender, asking reporters not to "hang or lynch" the man who would be the Senate's only African-American. He later suggested senators would be akin to George C. Wallace, the one-time segregationist Democratic governor of Alabama, if they barred Burris.

Senate Democrats backed away from challenging Burris' appointment, but Rush's comments provoked an outpouring of criticism: Even Illinois Democrat Richard J. Durbin, the Senate majority whip, said Rush's comments "were painful and hurtful."

Born in southern Georgia, Rush grew up in Chicago, where his mother moved when he was 7 and her marriage ended. She worked as a GOP activist because whites dominated the city's Democratic machine. Rush was a Boy Scout in an integrated troop and later volunteered for the Army. When he became disillusioned by a commanding officer he viewed as racist, he joined the Student Non-Violent Coordinating Committee, then went AWOL after the assassination of Martin Luther King Jr. (He was later honorably discharged.)

He joined the Black Panthers and soon founded the Illinois chapter. He coordinated a Panthers-run program that provided free breakfasts for children and a clinic that developed a mass screening effort for sickle cell anemia. By 1974 Rush had quit the Panthers and earned a political science degree from Chicago's Roosevelt University. After graduation he sold insurance and entered politics. He won a 1983 election to the city council on the coattails of 1st District Democratic Rep. Harold Washington, who was elected Chicago's first black mayor in an upset.

Rush ousted Hayes in 1992. Since then, he has won every general election with ease. But he had a poor showing when he sought to oust Daley as mayor in 1999, receiving 28 percent in the primary.

Following that defeat, Rush faced an emboldened field of primary challengers in 2000 but still took 61 percent of the vote. Among the aspirants was Obama, then a state senator, who said at the time that Rush "exemplifies a politics that is reactive, that waits for crises to happen then holds a press conference, and hasn't been particularly effective at building broad-based coalitions." Rush dismissed Obama as an "educated fool" with an "ivory tower" outlook. Even though President Bill Clinton had supported Rush in the 2000 race, Rush endorsed Obama over Hillary Rodham Clinton in the 2008 presidential contest.

Key Votes

2010
Overhaul the nation's health insurance system	YES
Allow for repeal of "don't ask, don't tell"	YES
Overhaul financial services industry regulation	YES
Limit use of new Afghanistan War funds to troop withdrawal activities	YES
Change oversight of offshore drilling and lift oil spill liability cap	YES
Provide a path to legal status for some children of illegal immigrants	YES
Extend Bush-era income tax cuts for two years	NO

2009
Expand the Children's Health Insurance Program	YES
Provide $787 billion in tax cuts and spending increases to stimulate the economy	YES
Allow bankruptcy judges to modify certain primary-residence mortgages	YES
Create a cap-and-trade system to limit greenhouse gas emissions	YES
Provide $2 billion for the "cash for clunkers" program	YES
Establish the government as the sole provider of student loans	YES
Restrict federally funded insurance coverage for abortions in health care overhaul	NO

CQ Vote Studies

	PARTY UNITY		PRESIDENTIAL SUPPORT	
	SUPPORT	OPPOSE	SUPPORT	OPPOSE
2010	96%	4%	83%	17%
2009	97%	3%	97%	3%
2008	99%	1%	29%	71%
2007	98%	2%	5%	95%
2006	93%	7%	32%	68%

Interest Groups

	AFL-CIO	ADA	CCUS	ACU
2010	93%	85%	14%	9%
2009	100%	100%	47%	0%
2008	100%	30%	67%	13%
2007	100%	100%	60%	0%
2006	92%	80%	46%	9%

Illinois 1

Chicago — South Side and southwest

The nation's first majority-black district, the 1st covers much of Chicago's South Side. Starting at 26th Street in the historic black hub, the district spreads out to the south and west through residential areas. It narrows through the southwestern neighborhoods of Washington Heights, Beverly and Morgan Park, then expands outside the city to scoop up close-in suburbs as it extends south to Cook County's border with Will County. Sixty-five percent of the 1st's residents live in Chicago.

The 1st is home to several of the city's subsidized housing projects, and a significant portion of the population lives in poverty — the median household income in the district is one of the lowest in Illinois. Many people work in the service industry, and residents endure long commutes. Despite the presence of the University of Chicago in the Hyde Park neighborhood, only about one-fifth of residents have a college degree.

The district has several solidly middle-class black neighborhoods, including Chatham and Avalon Park. Bronzeville, in the district's north end, has worked to attract black-owned businesses and young black professionals, encouraging residents to rehabilitate old houses. Local leaders are trying to use its rich

history to attract tourism by renovating buildings, investing in heritage sites and promoting its jazz and blues tradition.

The 1st, represented by black congressmen since 1929, is 62 percent African-American. A decade of migration from the city of Chicago to its suburbs cost the district 10 percent of its population since 2000. Despite the overall loss of residents, the Hispanic population here has swelled in the same time period.

In the 2008 presidential election, the strongly Democratic parts of the district within Chicago gave hometown candidate Barack Obama 98 percent of the vote, but he won relatively less support in parts of the 1st outside of the city. Obama took 87 percent of the district's vote in 2008.

Major Industry
Hospitals, higher education, manufacturing

Cities
Chicago (pt.), 384,879; Oak Forest (pt.), 27,832; Orland Park (pt.), 26,722; Tinley Park (pt.), 25,362; Blue Island (pt.), 23,652

Notable
The first self-sustaining nuclear reaction took place at the University of Chicago under the stands at Stagg Field in 1942, and the location is marked by a Henry Moore statue.

Rep. Jesse L. Jackson Jr. (D)

Capitol Office
225-0773
www.house.gov/jackson
2419 Rayburn Bldg. 20515-1302; fax 225-0899

Committees
Appropriations

Residence
Chicago

Born
March 11, 1965; Greenville, S.C.

Religion
Baptist

Family
Wife, Sandi Jackson; two children

Education
North Carolina A&T State U., B.S. 1987 (business management); Chicago Theological Seminary, M.A. 1990 (theology); U. of Illinois, J.D. 1993

Career
Political activist

Political Highlights
No previous office

ELECTION RESULTS

2010 GENERAL

Jesse L. Jackson Jr. (D)	150,666	80.5%
Isaac C. Hayes (R)	25,883	13.8%
Anthony Williams (GREEN)	10,564	5.6%

2010 PRIMARY

Jesse L. Jackson Jr. (D)	unopposed

2008 GENERAL

Jesse L. Jackson Jr. (D)	251,052	89.4%
Anthony W. Williams (R)	29,721	10.6%

Previous Winning Percentages
2006 (85%); 2004 (88%); 2002 (82%); 2000 (90%);
1998 (89%); 1996 (94%); 1995 Special Election (76%)

Elected 1995; 8th full term

Jackson's once-meteoric rise up the political ladder has been slowed amid personal and legal scandals, despite his position as the son of a famous civil rights leader and friend and political confidante of President Obama. In Washington, where he continues to hold considerable power via his seat on the Appropriations Committee, he has been a strong supporter of liberal causes.

Once considered a possible successor to appointed Democratic Sen. Roland W. Burris or Chicago Mayor Richard M. Daley, Jackson has faced a spate of recent scandals, including revelations by his wife that he cheated on her with a Washington waitress and bribery allegations involving former Illinois Gov. Rod R. Blagojevich, a fellow Democrat.

The Justice Department's indictment of Blagojevich mentioned a candidate No. 5 whom Blagojevich, in wiretapped conversations, had said was willing to raise money for him in exchange for appointment to the Senate seat vacated by Barack Obama. Federal authorities later told reporters that Jackson was that candidate.

Jackson immediately denied that he offered Blagojevich anything and said he received assurances from federal investigators that he wasn't a target of the probe. But it continues to cloud his future. "I'm fighting now for my character, and I'm also fighting for my life," Jackson told CNN in the midst of the uproar. "When the process is over, I profoundly hope that the people will give me my name back."

In August 2010, Blagojevich was found guilty of one count of lying to federal agents. In October, Jackson announced he would not be a candidate to succeed Daley as mayor.

But Jackson appears likely to survive the tempest, at least electorally. His father, Jesse Jackson Sr., told the Associated Press: "It's temporary. You're going to feel the impact of the wind even if you're not directly in the storm."

The Jackson family remains popular in the South Side of Chicago. Chicagoans refer to Jackson and his wife, Sandi, as "The Jackson Two" since she was elected alderman in Chicago's 7th Ward in 2007, defeating Darcel Beavers, the daughter of a local powerhouse, Cook County Board member William Beavers.

In February 2008, Sandi Jackson ousted Beavers himself in the race for Democratic committeeman, a job that gives her a seat inside the councils of the vaunted Cook County party organization.

On Capitol Hill, Jackson uses his seat on the Appropriations Committee to help fund a variety of projects in his South Side and suburban Chicago district. "If it doesn't immediately impact the people of the 2nd District, it's not what I wake up thinking about," he has said.

Over several years, he helped direct more than $148 million in federal funds to the Deep Tunnel Project, which is designed to improve flood protection and water quality across Chicagoland.

But his efforts to boost construction of a third airport for the region, which he says will provide economic expansion for his district as well as relieve overcrowding at Chicago's O'Hare International Airport, have met with little success. Jackson and others want the new airport built on rural land outside of Peotone, just south of his district. It would aim to attract discount air carriers. But Daley had backed a rival plan to expand O'Hare and moved ahead with construction of a new runway and control tower.

A member of the Congressional Progressive Caucus, Jackson is a predictable vote on liberal issues, backing Obama's $787 billion stimulus package, the health care overhaul enacted in 2010, a "cram-down" proposal that would allow bankruptcy judges to modify underwater mortgages and an energy bill that would establish a cap-and-trade system designed to limit carbon emissions.

At the end of the 111th Congress (2009-10), he voted against legislation, signed into law by Obama, that extended the Bush-era tax cuts for two years for all income groups.

Jackson sits on the State-Foreign Operations Appropriations Subcommittee, where he has pushed aid for African nations, especially Liberia and Sudan.

He is a fitness buff who holds a black belt in tae kwon do. Jackson also frequently gets around Capitol Hill on his own Segway.

Although his family has Chicago roots, Jackson graduated from Washington's elite St. Albans School, and earned degrees in both theology and law. He followed in his father's footsteps, serving as vice president at-large of Operation PUSH (People United to Serve Humanity) and as national field director for the Rainbow Coalition.

But he rebuked his father in July 2008 after an open microphone picked up the elder Jackson whispering a crude criticism of Obama. Jackson said his father was wrong to use "divisive and demeaning" language and "ugly rhetoric."

Reflecting his family's civil rights heritage and his interest in history, Jackson has been active in promoting recognition of the contributions of African-Americans. In the 110th Congress (2007-08), he joined Republican Rep. Zach Wamp of Tennessee to pass legislation that named the main venue in the new Capitol Visitor Center "Emancipation Hall" in honor of the black slaves who played a major role in building the Capitol. He also shepherded through legislation to commission a $370,000 statue in the Capitol of civil rights pioneer Rosa Parks.

Jackson was first elected to Congress in a 1995 special election to replace Democrat Mel Reynolds, who resigned after being convicted of sexual misconduct. Jackson countered criticism that he was too young for the job by arguing that being the son of Jesse Jackson gave him a wealth of political experience.

After winning a hard-fought primary against state Sen. Emil Jones Jr., who later became Obama's political mentor in the state legislature, Jackson easily won the general election. He has sailed to re-election, taking more than 80 percent of the vote in 2010.

Key Votes

2010

Overhaul the nation's health insurance system	YES
Allow for repeal of "don't ask, don't tell"	YES
Overhaul financial services industry regulation	YES
Limit use of new Afghanistan War funds to troop withdrawal activities	YES
Change oversight of offshore drilling and lift oil spill liability cap	YES
Provide a path to legal status for some children of illegal immigrants	YES
Extend Bush-era income tax cuts for two years	NO

2009

Expand the Children's Health Insurance Program	YES
Provide $787 billion in tax cuts and spending increases to stimulate the economy	YES
Allow bankruptcy judges to modify certain primary-residence mortgages	YES
Create a cap-and-trade system to limit greenhouse gas emissions	YES
Provide $2 billion for the "cash for clunkers" program	YES
Establish the government as the sole provider of student loans	YES
Restrict federally funded insurance coverage for abortions in health care overhaul	NO

CQ Vote Studies

	PARTY UNITY		PRESIDENTIAL SUPPORT	
	SUPPORT	OPPOSE	SUPPORT	OPPOSE
2010	98%	2%	79%	21%
2009	99%	1%	99%	1%
2008	99%	1%	14%	86%
2007	99%	1%	3%	97%
2006	98%	2%	23%	77%

Interest Groups

	AFL-CIO	ADA	CCUS	ACU
2010	93%	100%	13%	0%
2009	100%	90%	36%	0%
2008	100%	100%	61%	4%
2007	96%	100%	50%	0%
2006	100%	100%	27%	4%

Illinois 2

Chicago — far South Side; Chicago Heights

The 2nd begins on Chicago's South Side along Lake Michigan and extends south along the Indiana border, as well as southwest, to take in Chicago Heights and other Cook County suburbs before reaching into Will County. The Chicago part of the district starts in the Hyde Park area near the University of Chicago (in the 1st) and takes in the South Shore, South Chicago, Roseland, Pullman and heavily Hispanic East Side neighborhoods. A decade of migration of city residents to the suburbs has left the district with only 37 percent of residents in Chicago and one of the nation's smallest populations overall ahead of decennial remapping.

The district once was built on the steel business, but the industry's collapse in the late 1970s devastated the local economy. Ford Motor Co. is one of the few large manufacturing interests remaining here, with a stamping plant in Chicago Heights and an assembly plant north of Calumet City — the company's oldest operating facility in the world. A planned commuter line from Crete (in the 11th) to Chicago could encourage growth and ease transportation difficulties.

A long-term plan to redevelop almost 500 acres at the former U.S. Steel South Works industrial site along the lakefront will include parkland, commercial and residential development and a high school. Construction has not begun, but the Chicago government has approved initial funding. A proposed third Chicago-area airport in the neighboring 11th District near University Park could channel jobs to the 2nd District.

The district's working-class suburbs are a mix of heavily black areas such as Harvey, Dolton and Ford Heights, and largely white areas like Homewood, Flossmoor and Thornton. Overall, the 2nd has the nation's highest percentage of black residents (69 percent). A staunchly Democratic base helped the district give Barack Obama his highest 2008 presidential vote percentage (90 percent) in the state and the sixth-highest in the nation.

Major Industry

Automotive manufacturing, health care

Cities

Chicago (pt.), 224,161; Calumet City, 37,042; Chicago Heights, 30,276

Notable

Pullman, now part of Chicago, was built by the Pullman Palace Car Co. in the 1880s and was the nation's first company-planned industrial town.

Rep. Daniel Lipinski (D)

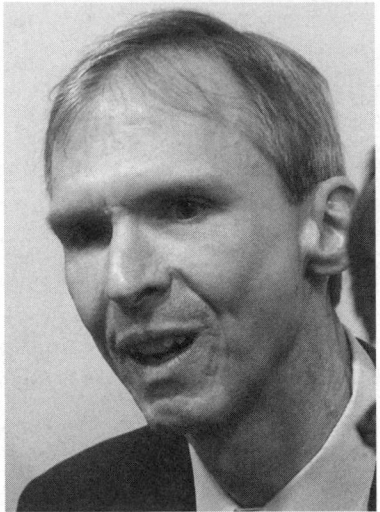

Capitol Office
225-5701
www.house.gov/lipinski
1717 Longworth Bldg. 20515-1303; fax 225-1012

Committees
Science, Space & Technology
Transportation & Infrastructure

Residence
Western Springs

Born
July 15, 1966; Chicago, Ill.

Religion
Roman Catholic

Family
Wife, Judy Lipinski

Education
Northwestern U., B.S. 1988 (mechanical engineering); Stanford U., M.S. 1989 (engineering-economic systems); Duke U., Ph.D. 1998 (political science)

Career
Professor; congressional and campaign aide

Political Highlights
No previous office

ELECTION RESULTS

2010 GENERAL

Daniel Lipinski (D)	116,120	69.7%
Michael A. Bendas (R)	40,479	24.3%
Laurel Schmidt (GREEN)	10,028	6.0%

2010 PRIMARY

Daniel Lipinski (D)	57,684	77.9%
Jorge Mujica (D)	16,372	22.1%

2008 GENERAL

Daniel Lipinski (D)	172,581	73.3%
Michael Hawkins (R)	50,336	21.4%
Jerome Pohlen (GREEN)	12,607	5.4%

Previous Winning Percentages
2006 (77%); 2004 (73%)

Elected 2004; 4th term

Through an open window in Lipinski's Washington office, train whistles can be heard across Capitol Hill. It's a fitting soundtrack for a lawmaker who represents an area that has been the rail hub of America for almost as long as there have been railroads. He assiduously focuses on securing funds for rail projects in the Chicagoland area and broadens his perspective to include other transportation issues.

Lipinski espouses the same economic populist, socially conservative views that helped keep his predecessor, William O. Lipinski, in office for more than two decades — but there are clear differences between father and son. The elder Lipinski was an old-style urban pol who dropped out of college. His more analytically minded son earned engineering degrees from Northwestern and Stanford — plus a doctorate in political science from Duke. Neither has been afraid to buck the Democratic Caucus when voting to protect the interests of their working-class district, where the younger Lipinski was born and raised.

One of Lipinski's most notable divergences from his party was his vote in March 2010 against the final version of the health care overhaul — he was the only Illinois Democrat to defy his home-state president. Although the bill's abortion language formed his "stumbling block," he outlined other "serious flaws," including Medicare cuts and a lack of cost controls. Regarding abortion, Lipinski said, "I do not believe the last-minute effort to address these concerns through an executive order is sufficient because there is every indication that the federal courts would strike down this order, and the order could be repealed at any time in the future." But when Republicans moved early in the 112th Congress (2011-12) to repeal the law, Lipinski sided with all but three Democrats in voting to keep it in place.

He stuck to his guns on abortion, though, cosponsoring a bill early in the new Congress that would prohibit federal funds from being used to cover any costs of any health insurance plan that includes coverage of abortion services.

Lipinski sits on the Transportation and Infrastructure Committee, where he is persistent in seeking funding for local transportation projects. He voted "present" in 2009 on a $787 billion economic stimulus bill, which became law, arguing it didn't include enough money for transportation. He pushes for grants for the Chicago Region Environmental and Transportation Efficiency Program, a partnership among the federal, state and city governments, a regional commuter rail agency, Amtrak and freight railroads. A high priority is funding for a bypass project for Central Avenue in his district, a traffic clog that he says has plagued residents for nearly 40 years.

He also seeks additional consumer protections for travelers. Lipinski authored a provision in the 2009 Federal Aviation Administration reauthorization bill that would require the Government Accountability Office to study compensation for delayed baggage on flights — inspired, he said, after an hourlong wait for a bag at Chicago's O'Hare airport.

Lipinski puts his engineering education to work as the top Democrat on the Science, Space and Technology Committee's Research and Science Education panel. He chaired the subcommittee in the 111th Congress (2009-10). He is a firm advocate of creating incentives for inventors and innovators, and he sponsored legislation to award cash prizes in areas of research funded by the National Science Foundation.

He teamed with then-Rep. Bob Inglis, a South Carolina Republican, to win enactment in 2007 of their bill to authorize $52 million over nine years to establish a national prize in hydrogen energy technology research.

Lipinski sides with Democrats on labor issues, opposing the 2005 Central America Free Trade Agreement and backing an increase in the minimum wage in 2007. Lipinski has introduced "buy American" legislation to increase the requirement for American-made content in federal projects. He seeks the creation of a quadrennial National Manufacturing Strategy, akin to the Quadrennial Defense Review conducted by the Pentagon.

Lipinski's family connections have been both a help and a hindrance. The senior Lipinski all but assured that his son would succeed him. He first filed to run for re-election in 2004 and was unopposed in the March Democratic primary. Then he announced during the August recess that he would retire after 11 terms. A committee of 3rd District Democrats, which included the senior Lipinski and several of his allies, unanimously selected Daniel Lipinski to fill the vacated ballot slot. In November, the younger Lipinski defeated Republican political unknown Ryan Chlada by a ratio of almost 3-to-1. Some Democratic activists were annoyed by what they viewed as nepotistic shenanigans, and they remind Lipinski of it each time he faces re-election by backing other candidates. But he won a solid majority in the 2010 primary, with 78 percent of the Democratic vote, and has had no problems getting re-elected.

Lipinski has received criticism on other family-related fronts. His father works as a lobbyist for the Association of American Railroads and other transit organizations. A Chicago Loop federal building, the national headquarters for the U.S. Railroad Retirement Board, was named in the senior Lipinski's honor, and a Washington Post story in 2007 raised questions as to whether he was hired to influence his son. But Lipinski denied that his father lobbies him or has acted improperly.

Lipinski worked as an associate professor at the University of Tennessee in Knoxville. When he moved back to the Chicago area after 15 years away for his first run for public office, he wasn't a total novice, although he committed the greenhorn's error of admitting to being a fan of the North Side's Cubs, not a popular position in a district situated in the southwestern portion of the city. He had worked on numerous Illinois campaigns, served as a congressional aide to another Illinois Democrat, Rep. Rod R. Blagojevich, and earned a fellowship in the office of House Minority Leader Richard A. Gephardt of Missouri.

His career in academia was devoted to politics as well. He has published several papers on how politicians communicate with constituents, including their increasing use of the Internet. At Duke, the judge of his doctoral thesis was Democratic Rep. David E. Price of North Carolina, who was between congressional stints.

Key Votes

2010

Overhaul the nation's health insurance system	NO
Allow for repeal of "don't ask, don't tell"	NO
Overhaul financial services industry regulation	YES
Limit use of new Afghanistan War funds to troop withdrawal activities	NO
Change oversight of offshore drilling and lift oil spill liability cap	YES
Provide a path to legal status for some children of illegal immigrants	NO
Extend Bush-era income tax cuts for two years	YES

2009

Expand the Children's Health Insurance Program	YES
Provide $787 billion in tax cuts and spending increases to stimulate the economy	P
Allow bankruptcy judges to modify certain primary-residence mortgages	YES
Create a cap-and-trade system to limit greenhouse gas emissions	YES
Provide $2 billion for the "cash for clunkers" program	YES
Establish the government as the sole provider of student loans	YES
Restrict federally funded insurance coverage for abortions In health care overhaul	YES

CQ Vote Studies

	PARTY UNITY		PRESIDENTIAL SUPPORT	
	SUPPORT	OPPOSE	SUPPORT	OPPOSE
2010	88%	12%	86%	14%
2009	94%	6%	90%	10%
2008	97%	3%	16%	84%
2007	93%	7%	14%	86%
2006	86%	14%	49%	51%

Interest Groups

	AFL-CIO	ADA	CCUS	ACU
2010	86%	65%	25%	8%
2009	100%	90%	43%	8%
2008	100%	90%	59%	8%
2007	96%	85%	55%	20%
2006	100%	70%	47%	33%

Illinois 3

Chicago — southwest side; south and west suburbs

The 3rd covers the southwest corner of Chicago and adjacent suburbs, part of a working-class region known as the Bungalow Belt that has been stocked with voters of Eastern European, Italian and Irish descent. Even as the district's population grew only modestly since 2000, the Hispanic population here surged from one-fifth of residents to 34 percent. Chicago residents make up about 40 percent of the district population. The 3rd includes the historically Irish neighborhood of Bridgeport, which is the political base of the powerful Daley family, and southwest Chicago neighborhoods such as Beverly, West Lawn, Clearing and Garfield Ridge, where Midway Airport is located. The largely Hispanic West Lawn and West Elsdon neighborhoods experienced rapid growth overall despite losing thousands of white residents in the last decade.

Crisscrossed by highways, railroads and the Chicago Sanitary and Ship Canal, the 3rd has historically served as a manufacturing and distribution center. A significant amount of rail traffic has shifted from the 3rd's congested lines to other suburban areas in recent years. The district also has relied on food processing and distribution. Midway drives the district's retail and service base. Southwest Airlines continues to expand operations at the airport, filling the void left by departures of other major carriers. Bridgeview, just southwest of the airport, has shifted away from its industrial past, centering commercial growth around Toyota Park, home to soccer's Fire and a concert venue.

In national elections, the 3rd typically votes Democratic, but not by the same wide margins as other Chicago-based districts — Barack Obama won 64 percent of the 2008 presidential vote here. Many working- and middle-class voters lean to the right on social issues, and there are GOP pockets in the district's more affluent western Cook County suburbs.

Major Industry
Transportation, warehouses, manufacturing

Cities
Chicago (pt.), 266,118; Oak Lawn, 56,690; Berwyn (pt.), 53,959

Notable
Berwyn is home to the World's Largest Laundromat, with roughly 300 washers and dryers combined, which runs on solar power.

Rep. Luis V. Gutierrez (D)

Capitol Office
225-8203
luisgutierrez.house.gov
2266 Rayburn Bldg. 20515-1304; fax 225-7810

Committees
Financial Services
Select Intelligence

Residence
Chicago

Born
Dec. 10, 1953; Chicago, Ill.

Religion
Roman Catholic

Family
Wife, Soraida Arocho Gutierrez; two children

Education
Northeastern Illinois U., B.A. 1975 (liberal arts)

Career
Teacher; social worker; mayoral aide

Political Highlights
Chicago City Council, 1986-93

ELECTION RESULTS

2010 GENERAL

Luis V. Gutierrez (D)	63,273	77.4%
Israel Vasquez (R)	11,711	14.3%
Robert J. Burns (GREEN)	6,808	8.3%

2010 PRIMARY

Luis V. Gutierrez (D)	unopposed

2008 GENERAL

Luis V. Gutierrez (D)	112,529	80.6%
Daniel Cunningham (R)	16,024	11.5%
Omar Lopez (GREEN)	11,053	7.9%

Previous Winning Percentages
2006 (86%); 2004 (84%); 2002 (80%); 2000 (89%);
1998 (82%); 1996 (94%); 1994 (75%); 1992 (78%)

Elected 1992; 10th term

Gutierrez has for years made no secret that he has grown restless in Congress. But he keeps pledging to return for the same reason: his desire to see passage of an immigration overhaul, a passion that has turned him into Congress' most outspoken advocate on the issue.

When Chicago Mayor Richard M. Daley announced in September 2010 that he would not run again, Gutierrez began collecting signatures for a possible mayoral run and mused about his interest in returning to the city where he learned to feint and dodge in the world of bare-knuckled politics.

He finally announced his decision to a crowd at the University of Illinois-Chicago, where his daughter was a graduate student: "I have unfinished business to complete" in Congress, he said, referring to his signature issue. "History is not written by those who change battles in the middle of the fight."

It was an apt analogy for the combative Gutierrez, whose gusto in political fights earned him the nickname "El Gallito" — or little fighting rooster — when he was on the Chicago City Council. He's taken knocks for wavering about staying in Congress, but his unwillingness to abandon the immigration fight has also earned him a reputation for tenacity.

The 10-term lawmaker rarely pulls his punches, even with allies. Gutierrez had said that candidate Barack Obama's decision to run for president and push through immigration legislation in his first year helped convince him to stay in Congress. So he didn't hide his disappointment with President Obama when immigration failed to gain traction, deriding his announcement that he was sending guardsmen to the border as "sound-bite driven politics." He was arrested in spring 2010 at a White House sit-in, along with about three dozen other demonstrators. He was released and paid a $100 fine.

During the 111th Congress (2009-10), Gutierrez was the most outspoken House advocate for a broad immigration overhaul that would include a path to legal residency and citizenship for illegal immigrants already in the country, beefed up border security, changes to the foreign guest worker program and workplace enforcement. House legislation never advanced, because no bill materialized in the deadlocked Senate until the last day of the regular session. In the session's waning days, he put his support behind a less ambitious bill aimed at legalizing certain children of illegal immigrants. The House passed it, but it died in the Senate.

Following that defeat — and Democratic losses in the 2010 elections — Gutierrez suggested it might be time to forget about trying to pass legislation and instead turn to executive orders and the courts, since he can't win in Congress. "You have to ask yourself, if you cannot obtain through a legislative process fairness and justice, then you have to ask yourself, where can you? In America, there's two other branches of government: You go to court or you seek relief from the executive branch of government. I think we need to look at those areas," he said.

With Democrats out of the majority, the prospects for immigration legislation that Gutierrez would support are even dimmer. He also lost his primary legislative perch for debating the issue, having left the Judiciary Committee and moved to the Intelligence Committee in the 112th Congress (2011-12). But he remains chairman of the Congressional Hispanic Caucus' Immigration Task Force.

The fight to overhaul immigration laws has heightened Gutierrez's reputation and made him one of the nation's most prominent Hispanic elected officials, so much so that one advocate called him "the closest thing we have to an Al Sharpton figure" in the immigration fight.

Not all the attention has been positive. The Chicago Tribune reported that Gutierrez had received a loan from a real estate developer who was convicted of bribery charges, and had written a letter to city officials and advocated on the developer's behalf. Gutierrez has denied any wrongdoing and said his decision not to run for mayor had no connection to his links with the developer. After the election, the Chicago Sun-Times reported that Tony Rezko, a Democratic fundraiser convicted of fraud, had provided free work on Gutierrez's home. A spokesman said the claim was "completely false."

Though considered a scrappy outsider, Gutierrez chaired the Financial Services Subcommittee on Financial Institutions and Consumer Credit in the last Congress and is the top Democrat on the Insurance, Housing and Community Opportunity panel in the new Congress.

He backed the financial services regulatory overhaul enacted in 2010 and used even that occasion to make a pitch for immigration changes, calling the law "an example of what this president and this Congress can achieve when we roll up our sleeves and get to work. I hope we are able to put the same level of effort into other matters of critical importance . . . not the least of which is comprehensive immigration reform."

Born in Chicago, he attended high school in his parents' native Puerto Rico. His political leanings developed early — he was nearly expelled from school for promoting Puerto Rican independence. He attended Northeastern Illinois University, where he was part of a takeover of the president's office over English classes for incoming students.

He has worked as a teacher, social worker and community activist. In 1983, he worked on the mayoral campaign of Harold Washington, who defeated then-Cook County State Attorney Richard M. Daley to become Chicago's first black mayor.

Gutierrez went to work for Washington after trying and failing to unseat Rep. Dan Rostenkowski, the Democratic chairman of the House Ways and Means Committee, for ward boss of the 32nd Ward. Gutierrez won a city council seat three years later.

After Washington died in office in 1987, Gutierrez mended relations with Daley, who became mayor in 1989. When the legislature created the downtown Chicago Hispanic-majority 4th District for the 1992 election, Daley backed Gutierrez for the seat, cementing white support for Gutierrez.

He handily won the heavily Democratic district that year and every election since.

Key Votes

2010

Overhaul the nation's health insurance system	YES
Allow for repeal of "don't ask, don't tell"	YES
Overhaul financial services industry regulation	YES
Limit use of new Afghanistan War funds to troop withdrawal activities	YES
Change oversight of offshore drilling and lift oil spill liability cap	YES
Provide a path to legal status for some children of illegal immigrants	YES
Extend Bush-era income tax cuts for two years	YES

2009

Expand the Children's Health Insurance Program	YES
Provide $787 billion in tax cuts and spending increases to stimulate the economy	YES
Allow bankruptcy judges to modify certain primary-residence mortgages	YES
Create a cap-and-trade system to limit greenhouse gas emissions	YES
Provide $2 billion for the "cash for clunkers" program	YES
Establish the government as the sole provider of student loans	YES
Restrict federally funded insurance coverage for abortions in health care overhaul	NO

CQ Vote Studies

	PARTY UNITY		PRESIDENTIAL SUPPORT	
	Support	Oppose	Support	Oppose
2010	95%	5%	82%	18%
2009	98%	2%	93%	7%
2008	99%	1%	16%	84%
2007	98%	2%	3%	97%
2006	97%	3%	23%	77%

Interest Groups

	AFL-CIO	ADA	CCUS	ACU
2010	100%	90%	14%	0%
2009	100%	100%	33%	0%
2008	100%	90%	56%	0%
2007	100%	100%	44%	0%
2006	100%	80%	31%	4%

Illinois 4

Chicago — parts of North Side, southwest side

Surrounding the black-majority 7th District in the center of Chicago, the small, horseshoe-shaped 4th was drawn to unite the city's Hispanic neighborhoods into one voting bloc. Eighty-five percent of district residents live in Chicago.

A narrow strip of land about 10 miles in length — running along railroad tracks, highways and cemeteries — attaches the Puerto Rican neighborhood of Logan Square in the northern part of the 4th to Mexican-American populations in Little Village and Pilsen in the southern portion. There are large Hispanic majorities in these parts of the South Lawndale and Lower West Side communities around Cermak Road in the southern arm of the district. Close-in Chicago suburbs such as Cicero and Stone Park, formerly home to Slavic and Italian populations, respectively, also have seen significant Hispanic growth.

The 4th's primarily blue-collar workforce, which is made up of a significant population of immigrants, tend to live in the district's Hispanic, Ukrainian and Polish neighborhoods. Most jobs in the district are in the transportation and manufacturing sectors, and the warehousing industry is strong. The district contains the state's largest Hispanic population, and the nation's eighth-largest, at 74 percent. The 4th is largely young, poor and with low levels of formal education. The district suffered the second-most population loss between 2000 and 2010 of all Illinois districts, shedding 8 percent of its residents.

The district is plagued by low voter turnout, but is solidly Democratic and takes in left-leaning areas of Cicero as well as the gentrifying Wicker Park and Bucktown neighborhoods in Chicago. Barack Obama took 85 percent of the district's vote in the 2008 presidential election.

Major Industry
Light manufacturing, transportation

Cities
Chicago (pt.), 510,423; Cicero (pt.), 70,624; Melrose Park (pt.), 6,414

Notable
Cermak Road is named for former Chicago Mayor Anton Cermak, who was killed in 1933 by a bullet meant for President-elect Franklin D. Roosevelt; the Back of the Yards neighborhood in Chicago was the subject of Upton Sinclair's 1906 novel "The Jungle."

Rep. Mike Quigley (D)

Capitol Office
225-4061
quigley.house.gov
1124 Longworth Bldg. 20515-1305; fax 225-5603

Committees
Judiciary
Oversight & Government Reform

Residence
Chicago

Born
Oct. 17, 1958; Indianapolis, Ind.

Religion
Roman Catholic

Family
Wife, Barbara Quigley; two children

Education
Roosevelt U., B.A. 1981 (political science); U. of Chicago, M.P.P 1985; Loyola U. (Chicago), J.D. 1989

Career
College instructor; lawyer; legislative aide

Political Highlights
Candidate for Chicago City Council, 1991; Cook County Board of Commissioners, 1998-2009

ELECTION RESULTS

2010 GENERAL

Mike Quigley (D)	108,360	70.6%
David Ratowitz (R)	38,935	25.4%
Matt Reichel (GREEN)	6,140	4.0%

2010 PRIMARY

Mike Quigley (D)	unopposed

2009 SPECIAL

Mike Quigley (D)	30,561	69.2%
Rosanna Pulido (R)	10,662	24.2%
Matt Reichel (GREEN)	2,911	6.6%

Elected April 2009; 1st full term

Quigley's Washington office has a motto: "We live in the weeds." The self-described policy wonk says he will dig into the nitty-gritty of an issue, particularly a less visible one, and push for action — even if that means occasionally lining up against his fellow Democrats in Congress.

The avid hockey fan and player — he has talked about getting into brawls in his youth in old Chicago Stadium during Blackhawk games — has been called "scrappy" by numerous media outlets.

"If you get here on your own, you can stay here on your own," Quigley said. "You can vote no, you can introduce stuff that they don't necessarily want you to. You can push issues that aren't a priority. ... The bottom line: I've been with the Republicans when I thought they were right and they weren't exploiting the situation."

Quigley arrived in the House following an April 2009 special election after his predecessor, Rahm Emanuel, resigned to become President Obama's chief of staff. During his 10 years as a Cook County commissioner, Quigley staked out a position as a maverick, often ruffling the feathers of Chicago Mayor Richard M. Daley's administration.

On the Oversight and Government Reform Committee, Quigley has chosen to sometimes stand apart from his party on earmarked spending and transparency issues. He won plaudits from open-government advocates for introducing a bill to tighten lobbying rules, create a searchable database for earmarks and make it easier to find information on lawmakers' finances, travel, gifts and earmarks.

In 2010, Quigley joined with Republican Darrell Issa of California, now the committee chairman, in founding the Congressional Transparency Caucus.

Quigley claims as one of his first victories the House Democratic leadership's declaration in March 2010 of a one-year moratorium on earmarks going to for-profit entities — Quigley had introduced a resolution in July 2009, with Republicans Jeff Flake of Arizona and Mark Steven Kirk of Illinois, to require such a prohibition.

But, across the broad spectrum of policy, Quigley is a reliable Democratic vote, siding with his party 96 percent of the time in the 111th Congress (2009-10) on votes that divided a majority of Republicans and Democrats. He voted for the health care overhaul legislation enacted in 2010 and against repealing it in 2011, while noting that his "single biggest frustration" was the bill's failure to address cost containment. He voted for the House climate change legislation and called critics of the bill members of the Flat Earth Society, even as revelations about malfeasance in climate change research appeared to call into question some of the conclusions on which the legislation was based.

On the environment, Quigley votes globally but acts personally — he bikes across Washington, is a member of the Congressional Bike Caucus and his D.C. office, like many others, has numerous recycling bins, including one for compost. Its contents are "pulped" each night in the Longworth basement, then transported to a private facility in Maryland where it is held for 90 days until it turns into commercial-grade topsoil to be packaged and sold.

Quigley's eight years as a criminal defense attorney primed him for his spot on the Judiciary Committee. In a nod to his district's Polish-American constituency, he introduced a bill to extend visa waiver authority in the hope that the program, which allows citizens of certain countries to enter the

United States without a visa, would eventually include Poland.

Quigley's north Chicago district includes the gay community Boystown. He told the Windy City Times, Chicago's gay newspaper, in June 2009 that he believes the "administration has to do better" regarding gay rights and that Democrats "absolutely" take gay constituents' votes for granted. He supported the decision to recognize same-sex married couples in the 2010 Census, wrote the Food and Drug Administration urging it to rescind its policy barring blood donations by gay men, and supported repeal of the statutory "don't ask, don't tell" policy that barred openly gay people from serving in the military.

Quigley was born in Indianapolis and moved to the Chicago suburbs in second grade. His mother was a schoolteacher and his father worked for a telephone company. He earned a political science degree from Roosevelt University and worked as an aide to Chicago Alderman Bernard Hansen while attending graduate school at the University of Chicago. Quigley obtained a law degree from Loyola University in Chicago in 1989 and eventually became an adjunct professor of political science at both Loyola and Roosevelt, lecturing on the environment, politics and local government.

In the 1980s Quigley was one of the leaders of Citizens United for Baseball in Sunshine, a neighborhood group that unsuccessfully fought the Chicago Cubs over installing lights at Wrigley Field. Quigley's 5th District includes the Friendly Confines, and he considers himself a fan of the luckless team.

Quigley took his first foray into electoral politics in 1991 when he unsuccessfully ran for alderman in Chicago's 46th Ward. Seven years later he was elected to the Cook County Board of Commissioners, where he was an occasional thorn in the side of Daley, particularly on the issue of tax increment financing. He briefly sought the presidency of the Cook County Board in 2005 but withdrew to ensure anti-incumbent unity.

In the special election for Emanuel's vacated House seat in 2009, he defeated 11 opponents by winning 22 percent of the primary vote, then took 69 percent against Republican Rosanna Pulido, a Mexican-American and a founder of the Illinois Minutemen, an anti-immigration group.

Quigley's district has been represented by lawmakers who have not exactly covered themselves in glory — Democrat Dan Rostenkowski, who went to prison on federal charges, and impeached Democratic Gov. Rod R. Blagojevich — but Quigley maintains an optimism about the political process.

"I tell people: Save the world, change the world," he said. "And I was in Chicago politics since 1982, so if anyone should be cynical by now, it should be me."

Key Votes

2010

Overhaul the nation's health insurance system	YES
Allow for repeal of "don't ask, don't tell"	YES
Overhaul financial services industry regulation	YES
Limit use of new Afghanistan War funds to troop withdrawal activities	YES
Change oversight of offshore drilling and lift oil spill liability cap	YES
Provide a path to legal status for some children of illegal immigrants	YES
Extend Bush-era income tax cuts for two years	YES

2009

Create a cap-and-trade system to limit greenhouse gas emissions	YES
Provide $2 billion for the "cash for clunkers" program	YES
Establish the government as the sole provider of student loans	YES
Restrict federally funded insurance coverage for abortions in health care overhaul	NO

CQ Vote Studies

	PARTY UNITY		PRESIDENTIAL SUPPORT	
	SUPPORT	OPPOSE	SUPPORT	OPPOSE
2010	95%	5%	88%	12%
2009	96%	4%	97%	3%

Interest Groups

	AFL-CIO	ADA	CCUS	ACU
2010	100%	95%	29%	4%
2009	93%		42%	0%

Chicago — North Side

The 5th spans Chicago's North Side, stretching from Lake Michigan in the east to near O'Hare International Airport (located in the 6th) in the west. The district is home to one of the city's few remaining active industrial sectors, running through the middle of the 5th along the Chicago River's north branch. It continues west of the city to pick up parts of Northlake and Schiller Park.

DePaul University students and "lakefront liberals" inhabit wealthy east-side communities such as Lincoln Park. Areas such as Roscoe Village and Lakeview, which includes the gay community Boystown, have seen an influx of younger residents. Overdevelopment, especially in the Wrigleyville area, is a concern for residents hoping to keep neighborhoods' identities intact. Ethnic restaurants and entertainment spots in eastern parts of the district provide weekend and evening destinations for residents from other parts of the north side, the west side and suburbs.

The district's west covers part of the Bungalow Belt, a stretch of 1930s brick homes separating the suburbs from downtown Chicago. The west's working-class base routinely supports populist-style Democrats, but far west-side areas and portions of the Bungalow Belt can support Republicans in local elections. Middle- and working-class neighborhoods and second- and third-generation German and Polish residents still dominate this part of town.

Although the district's population overall has decreased since 2000, the Hispanic population boomed — the 5th, two-thirds white a decade ago, now is 29 percent Hispanic, a lower percentage than only the majority-Hispanic 4th and southwest-side 3rd districts.

The combination of minority, ethnic and liberal-leaning groups makes for a largely Democratic constituency here. The 5th supports Democrats in federal races, and Democratic statewide candidates also do well here. Barack Obama won 73 percent of the district's vote in the 2008 presidential election.

Major Industry
Manufacturing, warehousing and storage, electronics, health care

Cities
Chicago (pt.), 544,937; Elmwood Park (pt.), 23,259

Notable
Wrigley Field hosts baseball's Chicago Cubs.

Rep. Peter Roskam (R)

Capitol Office
225-4561
roskam.house.gov
227 Cannon Bldg. 20515-1306; fax 225-1166

Committees
Ways & Means

Residence
Wheaton

Born
Sept. 13, 1961; Hinsdale, Ill.

Religion
Anglican

Family
Wife, Elizabeth Roskam; four children

Education
U. of Illinois, B.A. 1983 (political science); Illinois
Institute of Technology, J.D. 1989

Career
Lawyer; nonprofit education scholarship executive
director; congressional aide; teacher

Political Highlights
Ill. House, 1993-99; sought Republican nomination
for U.S. House, 1998; Ill. Senate, 2000-07

ELECTION RESULTS

2010 GENERAL

Peter Roskam (R)	114,456	63.6%
Benjamin S. Lowe (D)	65,379	36.4%

2010 PRIMARY

Peter Roskam (R)	unopposed

2008 GENERAL

Peter Roskam (R)	147,906	57.6%
Jill Morgenthaler (D)	109,007	42.4%

Previous Winning Percentages
2006 (51%)

Elected 2006; 3rd term

Roskam has risen quickly in the House, winning a coveted seat on the tax-writing Ways and Means Committee in his second term and being named chief deputy whip in his third. Party elders also entrusted him with leadership of a group commissioned to fashion a successor document to 1994's Contract With America that helped lay the intellectual groundwork for the GOP electoral victories in 2010.

As he steps up the leadership ladder, it will be his first time in the majority — and that's not necessarily a bad thing, he said.

"There's benefits to that," Roskam told Roll Call in a post-election interview. "We also need to be listening to a lot of folks on what the majority is like, the level of scrutiny and all those sorts of things that come with it." He and Majority Whip Kevin McCarthy of California were both first elected to the House in 2006.

Roskam arrived in Congress with a firm philosophical viewpoint and some inside knowledge of the institution. He attributes his vision of "less government is better" to his experience working as a legislative aide for the late Republican Henry J. Hyde, who represented the same suburban Chicago district as Roskam for 16 terms, and on the staff of former GOP Rep. Tom DeLay of Texas in the mid-1980s.

In April 2010, Roskam was tasked with helping create the GOP's "Pledge to America," a 2010 version of the 1994 Contract with America that many Republicans credit with helping the party end 40 years of Democratic control of Congress. Part of the process, with Roskam as vice chairman, involved soliciting input via social media networks, which played to one of his enthusiasms: He is fond of using Twitter to comment on everything from health care policy to "Lost" plot lines.

He has been a consistent critic of President Obama's economic and regulatory agenda. He opposed the Democrats' financial industry overhaul enacted in 2010 because, Roskam argued, it ignored the biggest part of the problem. "No true financial reform bill will be complete until it deals with reform of Fannie Mae and Freddie Mac and their $5.4 trillion in liabilities," Roskam wrote of the ailing mortgage giants in May 2010 on the conservative Heritage Foundation's Foundry blog.

As a member of Ways and Means, Roskam aims to use the tax code to make a statement about the government's deep involvement in the mortgage industry. In early 2010 he introduced legislation that would effectively cap the salary of Fannie and Freddie officers and employees during any conservatorship or receivership at the same level as the chairman of the Joint Chiefs of Staff of the armed forces.

At the end of the 111th Congress (2009-10), he voted for a measure that Obama signed into law extending the Bush-era tax rates for two years. He wants to see the rates made permanent.

A member of the Financial Services Committee during the 110th Congress (2007-08), Roskam voted in the fall of 2008 against two versions of a $700 billion measure — the second of which became law — to shore up the struggling financial industry. He said it would place too great a burden on taxpayers, while providing no guarantee of success.

Roskam also follows in the conservative footsteps of his predecessor on social policy and foreign policy. Like Hyde, whose name is attached to a law that long barred federal funding of most abortions, Roskam opposes abortion. He has been an unwavering supporter of the Iraq War. During the

110th Congress, he repeatedly denounced Democratic proposals to tie war funding to a time line for withdrawal of U.S. troops from Iraq.

Roskam vehemently opposed Obama's plan to relocate the terrorist detainees at Guantánamo Bay, Cuba, to Thomson Correctional Center west of his district, saying the move would put Americans in danger.

As co-chairman of the House Republican Israel Caucus, Roskam was critical of the Obama administration's "attempt to suppress Israel's right to natural growth in its capital of Jerusalem. . . . Let us all be clear: Jerusalem is not a settlement."

Roskam was born into a middle-class family from Glen Ellyn. His mother was a homemaker and later opened a nursery school; his father was a sales manager.

The elder Roskam dropped out of college because he was unable to afford it, but a gift from wealthy farmers enabled him to return. Years later, as a successful businessman, he started a nonprofit scholarship program, Education Assistance. During much of the 1990s, the son served as executive director of the program, which collects extra inventory from corporations and donates it to colleges. The colleges then grant scholarships in the amounts of the merchandise.

Roskam was a varsity gymnast in high school. His first foray into politics was a successful campaign for student senate president. He went on to earn a bachelor's degree in political science from the University of Illinois, then taught history and government in the U.S. Virgin Islands for a year. He moved to Washington in 1985 and worked for DeLay, who was then a freshman representative. Roskam worked for Hyde before graduating law school in 1989.

Roskam won a state House seat in 1992 and served three terms before losing his first bid for the U.S. House. In that 1998 race in the 13th District, he lost the Republican primary to Judy Biggert, who still holds the seat. He was appointed in 2000 to a state Senate seat, where he served until his successful 2006 bid for Congress.

The race drew national attention because many saw it as a referendum on the Iraq War. His opponent, Democrat Tammy Duckworth, was a member of the Illinois Army National Guard who lost her legs when a rocket-propelled grenade hit her helicopter in Iraq. In the heyday of Hyde's long House career, GOP victory was a sure thing. But Roskam eked out a 3-percentage-point win. He faced another Iraq War veteran, retired Army Col. Jill Morgenthaler, in 2008, defeating her by a more comfortable 15 percentage points. He topped Democrat Benjamin S. Lowe by 28 points in 2010.

Key Votes

2010

Overhaul the nation's health insurance system	NO
Allow for repeal of "don't ask, don't tell"	NO
Overhaul financial services industry regulation	NO
Limit use of new Afghanistan War funds to troop withdrawal activities	NO
Change oversight of offshore drilling and lift oil spill liability cap	NO
Provide a path to legal status for some children of illegal immigrants	NO
Extend Bush-era income tax cuts for two years	YES

2009

Expand the Children's Health Insurance Program	NO
Provide $787 billion in tax cuts and spending increases to stimulate the economy	NO
Allow bankruptcy judges to modify certain primary-residence mortgages	NO
Create a cap-and-trade system to limit greenhouse gas emissions	NO
Provide $2 billion for the "cash for clunkers" program	NO
Establish the government as the sole provider of student loans	NO
Restrict federally funded insurance coverage for abortions in health care overhaul	YES

CQ Vote Studies

	PARTY UNITY		PRESIDENTIAL SUPPORT	
	SUPPORT	OPPOSE	SUPPORT	OPPOSE
2010	98%	2%	29%	71%
2009	94%	6%	26%	74%
2008	95%	5%	71%	29%
2007	95%	5%	77%	23%

Interest Groups

	AFL-CIO	ADA	CCUS	ACU
2010	8%	5%	86%	100%
2009	10%	0%	80%	100%
2008	13%	10%	94%	96%
2007	29%	10%	84%	96%

Illinois 6

Northwest and west Chicago suburbs

Just west of Chicago, the 6th includes northern DuPage County and northwestern Cook County. Residents are mostly wealthy, white-collar workers who live in the older, mostly built-out suburbs along commuter rail lines that run into the city.

Residents here, most of whom are professionals, commute both to Chicago and to the booming northwest satellite cities. O'Hare International Airport (an extension of the city of Chicago and the district's eastern border) is one of the busiest airports in the world and is the center of the 6th District's commercial neighborhood. Hotels and other businesses related to the travel industry, and firms seeking close airport access, are located nearby.

Plans to modernize O'Hare have been met with mixed results: Construction is expected to generate local jobs, but expansion of the airport and surrounding expressways has been met with opposition from residents in Bensenville and Elk Grove Village, as Chicago acquires land west of the airport.

After a decade of population shifts in Illinois, the 6th is now nearly one-fifth

Hispanic. More than one-quarter of the Cook County residents in the 6th are Hispanic, and suburban communities in DuPage County — such as Addison, Bensenville and Glendale Heights — are becoming more racially diverse as their populations expand.

The district has a reputation as a Republican bastion, historically working in opposition to Chicago's Democrats. This is particularly true of DuPage, which accounts for nearly three-fourths of the district's population, but the Cook County portions of the district traditionally also have a conservative lean.

Despite supporting Illinois Democrat Barack Obama with 56 percent of its vote in the 2008 presidential election, the district's brand of conservatism remains.

Major Industry
Airport, light manufacturing, health care

Cities
Wheaton (pt.), 52,890; Elmhurst (pt.), 44,121; Lombard, 43,165; Carol Stream, 39,711; Streamwood (pt.), 38,389; Addison, 36,942

Notable
Barnes & Noble traces its beginnings to 1873, when Charles M. Barnes sold books from his home in Wheaton.

Rep. Danny K. Davis (D)

Capitol Office
225-5006
www.house.gov/davis
2159 Rayburn Bldg. 20515-1307; fax 225-5641

Committees
Homeland Security
Oversight & Government Reform

Residence
Chicago

Born
Sept. 6, 1941; Parkdale, Ark.

Religion
Baptist

Family
Wife, Vera G. Davis; two children

Education
Arkansas AM&N College, B.A. 1961 (history & education); Chicago State U., M.A. 1968 (guidance); Union Institute, Ph.D. 1977 (public administration)

Career
Health care association executive; teacher; postal clerk

Political Highlights
Chicago City Council, 1979-90; sought Democratic nomination for U.S. House, 1984, 1986; Cook County Commission, 1990-97; sought Democratic nomination for mayor of Chicago, 1991

ELECTION RESULTS

2010 GENERAL

Danny K. Davis (D)	149,846	81.5%
Mark M. Weiman (R)	29,575	16.1%
Clarence Clemons (I)	4,428	2.4%

2010 PRIMARY

Danny K. Davis (D)	52,728	66.8%
Sharon Denise Dixon (D)	10,851	13.7%
Darlena Williams-Burnett (D)	10,173	12.9%
Jim Ascot (D)	5,221	6.6%

2008 GENERAL

Danny K. Davis (D)	235,343	85.0%
Steve Miller (R)	41,474	15.0%

Previous Winning Percentages
2006 (87%); 2004 (86%); 2002 (83%); 2000 (86%); 1998 (93%); 1996 (82%)

Elected 1996; 8th term

Davis, an advocate for anti-poverty programs and increased access to health care, briefly occupied a position of legislative influence in the form of a Ways and Means Committee seat. He has cast a wandering political eye on a number of other offices, but he keeps coming back to the House.

Although his district takes in tonier parts of Chicago, including trendy new developments near the Loop and the downtown office core, it is marked by poor, drug-ravaged neighborhoods. "I'm very conscious of the taxpayers' money, but I'm also conscious of the fact that if there is no investment, there is no return," said Davis, who is given to impassioned speeches about poverty in his distinctive deep baritone.

Democratic losses in 2010 led to Davis losing the Ways and Means Committee seat he had won in 2009, and longtime friend Charles B. Rangel, a New York Democrat, had already lost the chairmanship. But Davis can call in some chits with President Obama, whom he has supported since Obama served in the Illinois Senate. Davis found much to applaud in the president's economic measures, and he was an enthusiastic supporter of the health care overhaul law enacted in 2010. Davis, once the president of the National Association of Community Health Centers, is the facilities' greatest advocate in Congress, and he helped secure a sharp funding increase in the legislation.

In the 112th Congress (2011-12), Davis serves as top Democrat on the Oversight and Government Reform Committee's panel with jurisdiction over health care issues. He also has oversight responsibility as a new member of the Homeland Security Committee's Oversight, Investigations and Management panel.

A former postal clerk, he previously held the gavel of Oversight and Government Reform's Postal Service subcommittee. Congress passed his bill in 2008 awarding back pay to Government Accountability Office analysts denied raises after the agency overhauled its pay system. In June 2008, the House passed his bill ordering the Office of Personnel Management to set in motion a plan to boost minority representation in the senior executive ranks, but the bill stalled in the Senate.

Davis also has tried to boost minority college attendance by pushing legislation to increase federal grants to low-income blacks. He is encouraging a focus on African-American boys, who, he says, sometimes don't fit the "rising-tide-lifts-all-boats" theory. "Some of those boats are kind of stuck and anchored," Davis said, "so when the tide comes along, they're still at the bottom."

He is also an advocate for released criminals. Congress passed his bill in 2008 reauthorizing a grant program to help former prisoners re-enter society, although he wants more money dedicated to the program. In 2009, he sponsored a bill that would reduce sentences for criminals who maintain a good record of conduct while in prison. A member of the Congressional Black Caucus, Davis also has pushed for a federal review of police brutality and racial profiling. He had found himself a victim of what he called driving while being black when given a ticket in Chicago in 2007 for allegedly crossing over the center line. Davis fought the charge and was ultimately acquitted.

Davis and his 10 siblings were born to sharecroppers in southeastern Arkansas. The children went to a segregated school four or five months of the year, spending the rest of the time doing farm work.

After graduating college, he accepted $50 from his father and left Arkansas with the intention of heading for California — but he was in Chicago when his money ran out. He stayed with an older sister and got a job teaching language arts and social studies at a high school while moonlighting at the post office. Davis got involved in the community and eventually ran the health centers association. In 1979, he led a committee of neighborhood leaders looking for a candidate to challenge the Democratic machine in a Chicago City Council race, but failed to turn up anyone. "So I said, 'What the hell,' and decided to run myself," he said.

On the council in the early 1980s, he was a close associate of Harold Washington, a former House member and the city's first black mayor. He made two unsuccessful attempts — in 1984 and 1986 — to unseat Democratic Rep. Cardiss Collins in the 7th District. In 1991, he ran a losing race in a Democratic primary for mayor against incumbent Richard M. Daley. He made another bid for the House when Collins announced plans to retire in 1996. Davis emerged from a crowded primary field and coasted to victory in the general election in the heavily Democratic district. He has had decisive wins since, though he has occasionally flirted with other opportunities.

When Cook County Board President John Stroger suffered a stroke prior to the Democrats winning the House in November 2006, Davis let it be known he was interested in the post, one of the most powerful jobs in Chicago politics. But the party regulars chose the former board president's son, Todd Stroger. Davis pondered another run for the job in 2010, going so far as to file for the race. But he pulled out in November 2009 and ran for re-election instead.

In December 2008, Davis turned down a chance to take Obama's Senate seat — a post he would have loved to accept, but the offer came from Democratic Gov. Rod R. Blagojevich, who had just been indicted (and was later impeached) for allegedly trying to sell the vacant seat. In August 2010, Davis said he had been approached about a potential mayoral campaign.

"I've been very pleased with my political career as such," he said. "I'm not really looking to do anything else at this juncture except trying to be the best member of Congress that I can be." He officially announced on New Year's Eve 2010 that he would not be a candidate to succeed longtime Mayor Richard M. Daley.

Davis' hopes of advancing often have been undermined by his 2004 appearance at an event in Washington honoring Sun Myung Moon, head of the Unification Church. Davis carried one of the crowns placed on Moon and his wife during a ceremony in a Senate office building. Moon went on to tell the crowd he was the Messiah. Davis told the Chicago Tribune his involvement in the ceremony was intended as a "promotion of peace."

Key Votes

2010	
Overhaul the nation's health insurance system	YES
Allow for repeal of "don't ask, don't tell"	YES
Overhaul financial services industry regulation	YES
Limit use of new Afghanistan War funds to troop withdrawal activities	YES
Change oversight of offshore drilling and lift oil spill liability cap	YES
Provide a path to legal status for some children of illegal immigrants	YES
Extend Bush-era income tax cuts for two years	YES
2009	
Expand the Children's Health Insurance Program	YES
Provide $787 billion in tax cuts and spending increases to stimulate the economy	YES
Allow bankruptcy judges to modify certain primary-residence mortgages	YES
Create a cap-and-trade system to limit greenhouse gas emissions	YES
Provide $2 billion for the "cash for clunkers" program	YES
Establish the government as the sole provider of student loans	YES
Restrict federally funded insurance coverage for abortions in health care overhaul	NO

CQ Vote Studies

	PARTY UNITY		PRESIDENTIAL SUPPORT	
	Support	Oppose	Support	Oppose
2010	96%	4%	83%	17%
2009	99%	1%	97%	3%
2008	99%	1%	16%	84%
2007	99%	1%	3%	97%
2006	97%	3%	25%	75%

Interest Groups

	AFL-CIO	ADA	CCUS	ACU
2010	93%	85%	29%	4%
2009	100%	95%	40%	0%
2008	100%	80%	56%	0%
2007	100%	90%	55%	0%
2006	100%	90%	40%	8%

Illinois 7

Chicago — downtown, West Side; west suburbs

East to west, the 7th stretches from the Loop, Chicago's downtown business district, almost to the DuPage County line, taking in the well-to-do western suburbs of River Forest and Oak Park. North to south, the district runs from the upscale Lincoln Park neighborhood (shared with the 5th) to 57th Street on the South Side.

The eastern end of the 7th hosts some of Chicago's gems, including the Willis Tower (formerly known as the Sears Tower), newer skyscrapers and the plush high-rises of River North, several museums, and about a dozen colleges and universities. Chicago's "Magnificent Mile" includes high-end shops and first-rate hotels, but economic slowdowns hurt revenue and occupancy rates along the famous stretch of Michigan Avenue. Most people employed in the 7th commute from nearby suburbs to the downtown headquarters of companies such as Boeing, United Airlines, Quaker and Hyatt, as well as to Chicago's financial center. The district also is home to most of Chicago's professional sports teams.

Once home to Chicago's most notorious public housing projects, some dilapidated areas have seen a transition to lofts and galleries, while former residents found homes in communities on the west and south sides of the city. But many residents have begun leaving the poverty-stricken neighborhoods that stretch from the western Loop to the edge of the county. Except for a few communities of middle-class blacks, the West Side has had problems with gang violence, unemployment and crumbling infrastructure.

The 7th fills with white commuters during the day, but the district is still black-majority. A reliably Democratic district at all levels, the only genuine political contests in the 7th are the Democratic primaries. Barack Obama won 88 percent of the 7th's vote in the 2008 presidential election — his second-highest percentage in the state.

Major Industry
Insurance, financial services, health care

Cities
Chicago (pt.), 493,676; Oak Park, 51,878; Maywood (pt.), 22,081

Notable
The Home Insurance Building, built in 1885 and demolished in 1931, is considered the nation's first skyscraper; the Grant Park Music Festival, held annually outdoors in Millennium Park, offers free classical music.

Rep. Joe Walsh (R)

Capitol Office
225-3711
walsh.house.gov
432 Cannon Bldg. 20515-1308; fax 225-7830

Committees
Homeland Security
Oversight & Government Reform
Small Business
(Economic Growth, Tax & Capital Access - Chairman)

Residence
McHenry

Born
Dec. 27, 1961; Evanston, Ill.

Religion
Roman Catholic

Family
Wife, Helene Walsh; three children, two stepchildren

Education
U. of Iowa, B.A. 1985 (English); U. of Chicago, A.M. 1991 (public policy)

Career
Investment banker; international humanitarian organization fundraiser; college instructor; nonprofit education organization director; think tank analyst; job training program teacher

Political Highlights
Republican nominee for U.S. House, 1996; Republican nominee for Ill. House, 1998

ELECTION RESULTS

2010 GENERAL

Joe Walsh (R)	98,115	48.5%
Melissa Bean (D)	97,825	48.3%
Bill Scheurer (GREEN)	6,495	3.2%

2010 PRIMARY

Joe Walsh (R)	16,162	34.2%
Dirk W. Beveridge (R)	11,708	24.8%
Maria Rodriguez (R)	9,803	20.7%
Christopher Geissler (R)	4,267	9.0%
John Dawson (R)	3,921	8.3%
Gregory S. Jacobs (R)	1,445	3.0%

Elected 2010; 1st term

Calling himself a Reagan Republican, Walsh pledges to serve only three terms in the House, to eschew earmarking and to vote against bills that increase the size of government.

He also said he would not participate in the congressional health plan, even though his wife has a pre-existing condition. Coverage for pre-existing conditions has been one of the main selling points used by Democrats to promote the health care law enacted in 2010. One of Walsh's first votes was to repeal the law.

"We said a lot of things in the campaign," he told Roll Call on his first day in office. "And I'm not going to back out on it."

Walsh, who has worked as an investment banker and sits on the Small Business Committee, is a fierce defender of free-market solutions, saying he would like to help find private-sector, market-based answers to questions on health care, taxation, education and entitlement programs.

Walsh has said that beyond budgeting issues, he wants to focus on transportation — namely, improving congestion and roads in his district. He was named vice chairman of the Homeland Security Committee's Transportation Security panel. His also sits on the Oversight and Government Reform Committee.

A former think-tanker who advocates school choice, Walsh supports charter schools and merit pay for teachers, and argues that responsibility for education should be left to the states and local communities.

Walsh twice sought other electoral posts. In 1996, he waged a spirited, but unsuccessful, campaign to unseat longtime Democratic Rep. Sidney Yates. He also ran an unsuccessful race for the Illinois House in 1998.

For Walsh, his third bid for office was the charm, although he had to explain losing a home to foreclosure while running on a platform of fiscal discipline.

He won a six-way GOP primary with tea party help and took on three-term Democrat Melissa Bean, who had been a GOP target since she toppled longtime Republican Rep. Philip M. Crane in 2004. The race was too close to call on election night and for days after. Bean didn't concede until Nov. 16. The final tally gave Walsh the victory by 290 votes, the closest House election of 2010.

Illinois 8

Northwest Cook County — Schaumburg; part of Lake and McHenry counties

The 8th, in the northeast corner of the state, takes in northwestern Cook County and parts of Lake and McHenry counties. Most residents live in the affluent, well-established suburbs just northwest of Chicago or farther north through western Lake County and toward the Chain O' Lakes vacation communities near the Wisconsin border.

The district is home to many white-collar employers, including sales and health care companies. Some of the 8th's cities, such as Palatine (shared with the 10th) and Schaumburg (a small part of which is in the 6th and 10th districts), have lured corporate headquarters. A major shopping mall in Schaumburg draws business from across the northwest

and west exurbs. Cook County benefits from its access to interstates and proximity to O'Hare International Airport (in the 6th).

The 8th includes most of Lake County, where a slight majority of district residents live. This area is largely upscale and well-educated, particularly in the southwest Lake villages of North Barrington and Kildeer. The northeastern part of McHenry County is home to sparsely populated, affluent towns.

After more than a half-century of sending Republicans to the U.S. House followed by three terms electing a Democrat, the state's northeast corner has developed a swing character. Democrat Barack Obama won 56 percent of the 8th's 2008 presidential vote.

Major Industry
Health care, insurance, retail, government

Cities
Schaumburg (pt.), 70,380; Palatine (pt.), 48,255; Hoffman Estates (pt.), 42,559

Notable
The Volo Auto Museum features classic and celebrity cars.

Rep. Jan Schakowsky (D)

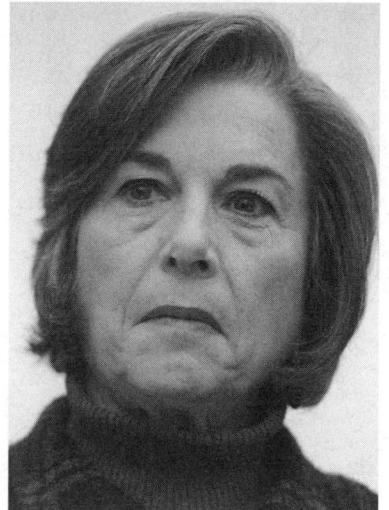

Capitol Office
225-2111
www.house.gov/schakowsky
2367 Rayburn Bldg. 20515-1309; fax 226-6890

Committees
Energy & Commerce
Select Intelligence

Residence
Evanston

Born
May 26, 1944; Chicago, Ill.

Religion
Jewish

Family
Husband, Robert Creamer; three children

Education
U. of Illinois, B.S. 1965 (elementary education)

Career
Senior citizens group director; consumer advocate; teacher; homemaker

Political Highlights
Candidate for Cook County Commission, 1986; Ill. House, 1991-99 (floor leader, 1994-99)

ELECTION RESULTS

2010 GENERAL

Jan Schakowsky (D)	117,553	66.3%
Joel Barry Pollak (R)	55,182	31.1%
Simon Ribeiro (GREEN)	4,472	2.5%

2010 PRIMARY

Jan Schakowsky (D)	unopposed

2008 GENERAL

Jan Schakowsky (D)	181,948	74.7%
Michael Younan (R)	53,593	22.0%
Morris Shanfield (GREEN)	8,140	3.3%

Previous Winning Percentages
2006 (75%); 2004 (76%); 2002 (70%); 2000 (76%); 1998 (75%)

Elected 1998; 7th term

A consumer activist before her election to Congress, Schakowsky has focused on health and safety issues during her seven terms in the House, viewing herself as a protector of average Americans against corporations that she suggests don't have the public's best interests in mind.

But she's also a practical politician who's been willing to compromise some of her liberal beliefs to get legislation passed. In the spring of 2010, for example, Schakowsky (shuh-KOW-ski) voted for a health care overhaul containing language she opposed that requires plans that cover abortion and receive federal funds to keep those funds segregated. It also did not include the government-run health insurance program that she'd once said was a prerequisite for her support. The stakes, she said, were too high to vote no.

Her "yes" vote didn't mean, however, that Schakowsky was done pushing for the so-called public option. Later that summer, she joined with other liberals in introducing a bill to create one. Ever a consumer activist, Schakowsky also sponsored legislation that would allow the secretary of Health and Human Services to block rate increases sought by private insurers and repeatedly blasted insurers that raised rates while reducing their spending on benefits.

A close ally of Minority Leader Nancy Pelosi of California, Schakowsky serves as a chief deputy whip, helping to enforce impressive discipline among House Democrats. During Pelosi's four-year tenure as Speaker, the notoriously restive Democratic Caucus defied its reputation, setting records for voting together on bills that divide majorities of the two parties.

Pelosi also named Schakowsky one of three House Democrats to serve on President Obama's National Commission on Fiscal Responsibility, but she opposed the group's final recommendations, saying they threatened both the middle class and lower-income Americans. Her alternative included more tax increases, additional cuts in defense and no changes to Social Security.

She co-chairs, with California Democrat Doris Matsui, the Congressional Task Force on Seniors, a Democratic initiative to shore up party support among the elderly.

Schakowsky's post on the Energy and Commerce Committee enables her to continue the work she began more than three decades ago on behalf of consumers. In 2008, she won enactment of legislation requiring automakers to adopt safety measures to decrease the number of deaths and injuries resulting from children being backed over, strangled by power windows or killed when cars are inadvertently shifted into gear. During the 111th Congress (2009-10), she pursued legislation to require heightened regulation of cosmetics, mercury and long-term-care facilities for senior citizens.

In the 112th Congress (2011-12), she is defending the health care law against Republican attempts to repeal and block funds for it.

Like other members of the Progressive Caucus, Schakowsky is restive about the U.S. military involvement in Iraq and Afghanistan. A member of the Select Committee on Intelligence, she sent Pelosi a letter in the summer of 2010 asking for assurances about withdrawal plans, and later she voted against a $58.8 billion spending bill to pay for the wars.

It was clear in that instance that Pelosi had the votes to approve the funding sought by President Obama. Schakowsky hasn't been so steadfast in her anti-war position when her vote really mattered. In April 2007, for example, when a $124.2 billion emergency spending bill for the Iraq War and other purposes came to a vote, some liberals decided to buck Pelosi and voted against it because it did not set tough enough benchmarks leading to a withdrawal of U.S. troops. But when it came time to vote, Schakowsky's loyalty was to Pelosi: She voted for the bill, which passed narrowly.

A community activist for more than 25 years before entering Congress, Schakowsky and her husband, Robert Creamer, created a training program for political advocates that has been replicated nationwide. The program brought volunteers to a "campaign school" in Chicago where they were given instruction and political tools and then put to work on several House races.

Her husband was sentenced to prison for five months in 2006 for writing bad checks to generate cash for his failing nonprofit group, Illinois Public Action, and for failing to withhold taxes from employees' paychecks.

Schakowsky was a stay-at-home mother in the early 1970s when she helped launch a successful nationwide campaign to require freshness dates on food products. She said six women got together and decided they wanted to know how old the food was in their local grocery. She continued as a community activist and was elected to the Illinois House in 1990. She rose to become chairwoman of the Labor and Commerce Committee and Democratic floor leader.

When liberal Democrat Sidney R. Yates, who had held the 9th District seat for 48 years, decided to retired in 1998, Schakowsky entered the race. She bested state Sen. Howard W. Carroll and Hyatt hotel heir Jay "J.B." Pritzker in the primary and easily won the general election in the heavily Democratic district. She won each election since with more than 70 percent of the vote, until 2010.

Schakowsky had hoped to be appointed to Obama's Senate seat after he was elected president; after Roland W. Burris won the appointment, she considered running for the Senate in 2010. Ultimately she decided against it, saying she wanted to focus her attention on helping Pelosi in the House instead of raising the money necessary to run for the Senate.

In 2010, her support for the health care overhaul prompted Republican Joel Pollak, a recent Harvard Law School graduate and political novice, to challenge her. Pollak also played up Schakowsky's decision in October 2009 to speak to the members of J Street, a dovish Jewish group that is often critical of the Israeli government. Several other members of Congress had backed out of speaking to the group's annual conference at the last minute, pressured by more traditional pro-Israel advocates. The critique seemed to resonate. Schakowsky had to fend off angry constituents at a town hall meeting in Skokie in May 2010, and Harvard Law School Professor Alan M. Dershowitz endorsed her opponent. Schakowsky won with 66 percent of the vote, while working conspicuously to bolster her support among Jewish voters in the district.

Key Votes

2010

Overhaul the nation's health insurance system	YES
Allow for repeal of "don't ask, don't tell"	YES
Overhaul financial services industry regulation	YES
Limit use of new Afghanistan War funds to troop withdrawal activities	YES
Change oversight of offshore drilling and lift oil spill liability cap	YES
Provide a path to legal status for some children of illegal immigrants	YES
Extend Bush-era income tax cuts for two years	YES

2009

Expand the Children's Health Insurance Program	YES
Provide $787 billion in tax cuts and spending increases to stimulate the economy	YES
Allow bankruptcy judges to modify certain primary-residence mortgages	YES
Create a cap-and-trade system to limit greenhouse gas emissions	YES
Provide $2 billion for the "cash for clunkers" program	YES
Establish the government as the sole provider of student loans	YES
Restrict federally funded insurance coverage for abortions in health care overhaul	NO

CQ Vote Studies

	PARTY UNITY		PRESIDENTIAL SUPPORT	
	SUPPORT	OPPOSE	SUPPORT	OPPOSE
2010	98%	2%	88%	12%
2009	99%	1%	96%	4%
2008	99%	1%	16%	84%
2007	99%	1%	3%	97%
2006	99%	1%	15%	85%

Interest Groups

	AFL-CIO	ADA	CCUS	ACU
2010	100%	95%	25%	0%
2009	100%	100%	33%	0%
2008	100%	100%	61%	0%
2007	100%	100%	50%	0%
2006	100%	95%	20%	0%

Illinois 9

Chicago — North Side lakefront; Evanston

The 9th starts in upscale Wilmette (shared with the 10th), runs south through the liberal suburbs of Evanston and Skokie and Chicago's multiethnic North Side, and then drops into one of the city's most prosperous lakefront neighborhoods. It also extends west to blue-collar Des Plaines (shared with the 6th and 10th districts) and Rosemont (shared with the 6th), which is crisscrossed by expressways and has numerous hotels, entertainment venues and convention sites.

After a decade of population loss in the city, Chicago now accounts for only 43 percent of the district's residents. The neighborhoods of Uptown, Edgewater and Rogers Park — home to Loyola University Chicago — once housed Eastern European and Irish immigrants, but are now an eclectic mix of Asian, European and African immigrants. Uptown in particular has seen rapid gentrification, and residents are divided over redevelopment of what had been a working-class area. The 9th also has the state's largest percentage of Asian residents, and the district's suburbs, namely Skokie, contain a sizable Jewish population. The district includes a significant elderly population as well.

Young professionals have moved into the area near Wrigley Field (in the adjacent 5th), and most of the other Chicagoans in the 9th live in the far northwestern part of the city, near O'Hare International Airport (in the neighboring 6th). Some Park Ridge residents have opposed plans for the modernization of O'Hare because of expected air traffic noise increases.

Most jobs are concentrated in a few major industries. Northwestern University provides the bulk of jobs in Evanston, and health care also is a major employer as many residents work at several area hospitals.

Ranging from the very wealthy to the very poor, the mix of immigrants, affluent urbanites and college students make the 9th solidly Democratic. Barack Obama took 72 percent of the district's 2008 presidential vote.

Major Industry
Health care, higher education, insurance, light manufacturing

Cities
Chicago (pt.), 271,403; Evanston, 74,486; Skokie, 64,784; Des Plaines (pt.), 41,569; Park Ridge, 37,480; Niles, 29,803

Notable
Tinkertoy sets were invented by an Evanston stonemason in 1913.

Rep. Robert Dold (R)

Capitol Office
225-4835
dold.house.gov
212 Cannon Bldg. 20515-1310; fax 940-7143

Committees
Financial Services

Residence
Kenilworth

Born
June 23, 1969; Evanston, Ill.

Religion
Christian

Family
Wife, Danielle Dold; three children

Education
Denison U., B.A. 1991 (political science); Indiana U., J.D. 1996; Northwestern U., M.B.A. 2000

Career
Pest control company owner; Internet data storage company manager; congressional aide; White House aide

Political Highlights
No previous office

ELECTION RESULTS

2010 GENERAL

Robert Dold (R)	109,941	51.1%
Dan Seals (D)	105,290	48.9%

2010 PRIMARY

Robert Dold (R)	19,605	38.0%
Elizabeth Coulson (R)	16,084	31.2%
Dick Green (R)	7,566	14.7%
Arie Friedman (R)	7,223	14.0%
Paul Hamann (R)	1,073	2.1%

Elected 2010; 1st term

Dold is a small-business owner who was born and raised in Chicago's north suburbs. A self-described fiscal conservative and social moderate, Dold follows in the path trod by his predecessor, Republican Mark Steven Kirk, who was elected to the Senate in 2010.

Even with his longtime residence in Chicagoland, Dold is no stranger to Washington. During the 1990s, he was a member of the White House staff in President George Bush's administration, then worked as a counsel for the House Oversight and Government Reform Committee.

As the owner of a small pest control business, he says he understands the pressures small-business owners face.

"I meet a payroll. I hire people. I understand what regulations do to small businesses. I live it each and every day," he said.

Dold, who serves on the Financial Services Committee, wants to lower the corporate tax rate. He also supports an indefinite extension of the 2001 and 2003 tax cuts for all income levels.

He opposes the 2010 health care law and wants to see major changes in medical liability litigation to cut the costs of defensive medicine. He also backs greater transparency in medical pricing and outcomes.

When Kirk announced in 2009 that he was running for the Senate seat previously occupied by Barack Obama, several Republicans jumped into the race for the 10th District. Dold captured the crowded Republican primary with 38 percent of the vote.

His Democratic opponent, Dan Seals, was well-known in the district, having twice before run and lost to Kirk. Dold stressed his ties to the district — his family has lived in the area for three generations — and his business experience.

Polls seesawed through the late summer and fall. Seals, who had lost to Kirk by 7 percentage points in 2006 and 5 points in 2008, fared slightly better in 2010, but Dold still prevailed 51 percent to 49 percent.

He quickly became a Democratic target for 2012 in a district where President Obama won 61 percent of the vote in the 2008 presidential race.

Illinois 10

North and northwest Chicago suburbs — Waukegan

The mostly upscale 10th hugs Lake Michigan, taking in southeast Lake County and northeast Cook County. Along the lakefront, Chicagoland's old-money elite live in tony areas such as Wilmette (shared with the 9th), Kenilworth and Winnetka.

The 10th is home to well-educated, white-collar workers. The wealth of the workforce mirrors the wealth of local industry. The 10th is home to several Fortune 500 companies, including Allstate Insurance in Northbrook and Walgreens in Deerfield, but a nationwide economic downturn has led to layoffs at Abbott Laboratories in North Chicago.

Most of the 10th's minorities live in the northern area between Highwood and Waukegan (a small part of which is in the 8th). That area also is home to the Great

Lakes naval base, the nation's only naval recruit training command. Waukegan is majority Hispanic and nearly 20 percent black, and North Chicago, just south of Waukegan, also has a minority majority. The 10th also has a large Jewish constituency.

Suburban white-collar workers and the more working-class residents of Waukegan mix to make the 10th fiscally conservative but socially liberal. Area residents have sent a Republican to the U.S. House for decades but generally support Democratic presidential candidates.

Major Industry
Pharmaceutical research, insurance, military

Military Bases
Naval Station Great Lakes, 3,922 military, 2,562 civilian (2011)

Cities
Waukegan (pt.), 78,405; Arlington Heights (pt.), 68,428; Buffalo Grove, 41,496

Notable
Highland Park's Ravinia Festival is the oldest outdoor music festival in North America.

Rep. Adam Kinzinger (R)

Capitol Office
225-3635
kinzinger.house.gov
1218 Longworth Bldg. 20515; fax 225-3521

Committees
Energy & Commerce

Residence
Manteno

Born
Feb. 27, 1978; Kankakee, Ill.

Religion
Protestant

Family
Single

Education
Illinois State U., B.A. 2000 (political science)

Military
Ill. Air National Guard, 2001-03; Wis. Air National
Guard, 2003-present

Career
Information technology services company account
representative

Political Highlights
McLean County Board, 1998-2003

ELECTION RESULTS

2010 GENERAL

Adam Kinzinger (R)	129,108	57.3%
Debbie Halvorson (D)	96,019	42.6%

2010 PRIMARY

Adam Kinzinger (R)	32,233	63.7%
Dave White (R)	5,257	10.4%
David McAloon (R)	4,880	9.6%
Henry W. Meers Jr. (R)	4,555	9.0%
Darrel Miller (R)	3,701	7.3%

Elected 2010; 1st term

Kinzinger's House career, like his wider political life, got off to a fast start.

He was one of four freshmen recruited by party leaders to serve on the GOP transition team preparing for the 112th Congress (2011-12), then was named a deputy whip, the first step on the leadership ladder. Most significantly, he is one of five freshman Republicans to win a coveted seat on the Energy and Commerce Committee.

He hopes to play a leading role in developing new energy sources, particularly nuclear. His district has three nuclear power plants, and Illinois leads the country in nuclear power generation. "I'm very passionate about energy security," he said. "My district is very energy-intensive. We've got nuke power plants, oil refineries, ethanol, wind, everything."

First elected to public office at age 20, Kinzinger also served five tours in Iraq and Afghanistan as a pilot with Wisconsin and Illinois Air National Guard units. He opposes setting a timetable for U.S. withdrawal from Afghanistan, and backs both a military and political surge — more troops to fight the enemy, and more aid for infrastructure and educational training.

Like many Republicans in the 112th Congress, he says restoring economic growth is the first priority, and "you don't do it with more programs and spending. You do that with a promise to start fiscal restraint."

Kinzinger's five-pronged approach for turning around the economy would limit the federal government's role in the private sector, provide business tax incentives, limit new spending to national security and infrastructure, explore new energy resources, and make the 2001 and 2003 tax cuts permanent.

Kinzinger was raised in Bloomington and graduated from nearby Illinois State University. He signed up for the Air National Guard shortly after the Sept. 11, 2001, attacks. He won an Air Force Airman's Medal in Milwaukee for his actions saving a woman whose boyfriend was trying to stab her.

While a sophomore at ISU, Kinzinger made his first bid for office, defeating an incumbent for the McLean County Board.

Challenging one-term Democrat Debbie Halvorson, Kinzinger won going away, with 57 percent of the vote.

Illinois 11

South Chicago exurbs — Joliet; part of Bloomington-Normal

Beginning south of Chicago in suburban Will County, the 11th heads west through the old industrial city of Joliet and into farm country, with a sliver making a southward turn in LaSalle County to run parallel to Interstate 39 as it heads to Bloomington-Normal.

Will County (shared mainly with the 13th) has seen an influx of families, and fast-growing Joliet's proximity to the Chicago metropolitan area has helped alleviate past economic troubles here. Many visitors to Joliet come to the Harrah's Casino and Hotel and the Rialto Square Theatre.

Ongoing debate over construction of a third Chicago metro-area airport in Peotone, southeast of Joliet, pits residents in the 11th's northern areas, who say a new airport would bring an economic boost to the suburbs, against rural residents, who worry it would disrupt their way of life.

South of Will, the 11th includes Kankakee County, still in the ambit of Chicagoland, before assuming a more rural posture as it takes in a small corner of Livingston County, all of Grundy and LaSalle counties, and most of Bureau County. A jaunt south takes it to Bloomington-Normal (shared with the 15th), home of Illinois State University. The politically competitive 11th gave Democrat Barack Obama 53 percent of its 2008 presidential vote but the U.S. House seat has switched party control in two consecutive elections.

Major Industry
Farm equipment manufacturing, agriculture

Cities
Joliet (pt.), 133,173; Bloomington (pt.), 33,339; Normal (pt.), 32,056; Kankakee, 27,537

Notable
The notoriously tough and now-closed Joliet Prison, immortalized in "The Blues Brothers," inspired the name of a new minor-league independent baseball team, the Slammers.

Rep. Jerry F. Costello (D)

Capitol Office
225-5661
www.house.gov/costello
2408 Rayburn Bldg. 20515-1312; fax 225-0285

Committees
Science, Space & Technology
Transportation & Infrastructure

Residence
Belleville

Born
Sept. 25, 1949; East St. Louis, Ill.

Religion
Roman Catholic

Family
Wife, Georgia Cockrum Costello; three children

Education
Belleville Area College, A.A. 1971; Maryville College
of the Sacred Heart, B.A. 1973

Career
Law enforcement official

Political Highlights
St. Clair County Board chairman, 1980-88

ELECTION RESULTS

2010 GENERAL

Jerry F. Costello (D)	121,272	59.8%
Teri Newman (R)	74,046	36.5%
Rodger Jennings (GREEN)	7,387	3.6%

2010 PRIMARY

Jerry F. Costello (D)	unopposed

2008 GENERAL

Jerry F. Costello (D)	213,270	71.4%
Timmy Richardson Jr. (R)	74,634	25.0%
Rodger Jennings (GREEN)	10,931	3.7%

Previous Winning Percentages
2006 (100%); 2004 (69%); 2002 (69%); 2000 (100%);
1998 (60%); 1996 (72%); 1994 (66%); 1992 (71%);
1990 (66%); 1988 (53%); 1988 Special Election (51%)

Elected 1988; 12th full term

Costello isn't flashy, and he keeps a low profile in Washington. But he has spent more than two decades building up seniority and quietly steering millions of dollars to his southern Illinois district and his hometown of East St. Louis for light rail, bridges, housing and Scott Air Force Base.

From his senior spot on the Transportation and Infrastructure Committee's Aviation panel, he has helped push through a raft of changes to the airline industry, many of them far-reaching. He also is a senior member of the Science, Space and Technology Committee.

Although the Science committee's legislative jurisdiction is relatively narrow, its oversight jurisdiction is broad, allowing it to examine issues ranging from space policy to children's health to toxic substances. That plays into Costello's penchant for oversight hearings. He stepped in as acting ranking Democrat on the Space and Aeronautics Subcommittee in the absence of Arizona Democrat Gabrielle Giffords, who was seriously wounded in an assassination attempt at the start of the 112th Congress (2011-12).

Among his policy accomplishments, Costello has helped shepherd through bills on aviation safety, including one to significantly increase the number of flight hours a pilot must have to fly for a commercial airline. He also advocated requiring airlines to let passengers get off the plane after idling on the tarmac for three hours, and pressed the Federal Aviation Administration (FAA) to wrap up a decades-long effort to revise its rules on pilot fatigue and flight time.

When Republicans at the start of the 112th Congress included a provision in an FAA authorization bill that would make it tougher for labor unions to organize rail and aviation workers, Costello balked. He called the provision a "poison pill" and said "if we are serious about passing a long-term FAA bill, this provision must come out."

Although Costello has become concerned with issues important to the entire nation, his background is rooted in working behind the scenes to boost economic prospects in East St. Louis, a struggling urban area that was once a thriving steel industry town.

When his former colleague in the state delegation, Barack Obama, moved to the White House, he saw promise for some of his priorities that had been blocked by President George W. Bush. He immediately set out to include a range of infrastructure funds in President Obama's economic stimulus package in early 2009. He won some, but failed to get approval for his request to include $1 billion for the construction of a clean-coal research facility known as FutureGen — a project he and Republican John Shimkus of the adjacent 19th District argue would help revive the area's sagging coal industry.

Nevertheless, Costello supported the final $787 billion stimulus, making a traditional Democratic argument: "For the last six years, we have spent over $860 billion in Iraq and Afghanistan, billions of which have gone to rebuilding those countries, and it is time we made similar investments here at home."

Over the years, Costello has had considerable success looking out for the folks back home. He won approval of legislation in 1999 to set aside federal land for a visitor center devoted to the journey of explorers Meriwether Lewis and William Clark, near where the expedition departed on its westward journey in 1804. He helped protect Scott Air Force Base from the 2005 round of military base closings, and it subsequently was awarded new missions producing 800 jobs.

Despite his propensity for sending dollars home and his support for the expensive economic initiatives of the Obama administration, Costello calls himself a fiscal conservative. He usually votes with his party — he sided with Democrats about 92 percent of the time in the 111th Congress (2009-10) on votes that divided a majority of Republicans from a majority of Democrats. But in line with the cultural conservatism found downstate, he opposes abortion and supports gun owners' rights.

For a lawmaker who prefers to stay out of the limelight, Costello has on occasion garnered publicity he'd rather not have. Media reports in 2002 revealed Illinois Secretary of State Jesse White hired Costello's 26-year-old son for a $50,000-a-year job over a more experienced candidate after Costello called on his son's behalf. Costello described it as a routine reference call and attributed the flap, in part, to a feud with his hometown newspaper, the Belleville News-Democrat.

In 1997, he was named an "unindicted co-conspirator" in the trial of childhood friend and former business partner Amiel Cueto, who was convicted of trying to block the federal investigation of a convicted racketeer. Witnesses testified that Costello was a silent partner in two casino deals and that he helped pass a bill to aid an American Indian tribe that owned the land where one of the casinos was to be built. Costello denied wrongdoing, and the prosecutor later said he was not the target of the investigation.

Costello grew up in East St. Louis, and the family moved to nearby Belleville when he was in high school after his father was elected county sheriff. While attending a local community college, Costello took a job as a bailiff. He eventually became administrator of the local court system.

He entered local politics after he was frustrated in his efforts to push for expanding a juvenile-detention facility. In 1980, he was elected chairman of the St. Clair County Board, a job he held for eight years. Costello ran his first race for the House in 1988, after Democrat Melvin Price decided against seeking re-election. In the primary, Madison County Auditor Pete Fields portrayed Costello as an old-style, hardball "boss" in the county Democratic Party. Costello had a sizable financial advantage and prevailed with 46 percent of the vote.

When Price died in April, Costello squared off against Republican college official Robert H. Gaffner in a special election. Costello barely won the special election, then went on to win in November with 53 percent. In 1998, he faced Price's son, Bill, an orthopedic surgeon. Costello overcame questions about his connections with Cueto and took 60 percent of the vote. He had not dipped below 69 percent until 2010, when he won with 60 percent of the vote.

Key Votes

2010

Overhaul the nation's health insurance system	YES
Allow for repeal of "don't ask, don't tell"	NO
Overhaul financial services industry regulation	YES
Limit use of new Afghanistan War funds to troop withdrawal activities	YES
Change oversight of offshore drilling and lift oil spill liability cap	YES
Provide a path to legal status for some children of illegal immigrants	NO
Extend Bush-era income tax cuts for two years	NO

2009

Expand the Children's Health Insurance Program	YES
Provide $787 billion in tax cuts and spending increases to stimulate the economy	YES
Allow bankruptcy judges to modify certain primary-residence mortgages	YES
Create a cap-and-trade system to limit greenhouse gas emissions	NO
Provide $2 billion for the "cash for clunkers" program	YES
Establish the government as the sole provider of student loans	YES
Restrict federally funded insurance coverage for abortions in health care overhaul	YES

CQ Vote Studies

	PARTY UNITY		PRESIDENTIAL SUPPORT	
	SUPPORT	OPPOSE	SUPPORT	OPPOSE
2010	90%	10%	79%	21%
2009	94%	6%	87%	13%
2008	96%	4%	15%	85%
2007	93%	7%	10%	90%
2006	87%	13%	37%	63%

Interest Groups

	AFL-CIO	ADA	CCUS	ACU
2010	93%	70%	0%	13%
2009	95%	85%	50%	12%
2008	100%	85%	50%	13%
2007	96%	95%	47%	16%
2006	93%	70%	40%	48%

Illinois 12

Southwest — Belleville, East St. Louis, Carbondale

The 12th begins in the St. Louis suburbs along the Mississippi River and extends south along the river to Cairo at the southern tip of Illinois, where the Mississippi and Ohio rivers converge.

East St. Louis, an overwhelmingly black city in St. Clair County, has experienced declining population and some of the state's worst urban blight for years, and crime rates remain high. Federal and state aid, along with revenue from casino gambling, provide income for the city, but residents still face high unemployment and poverty rates.

Other cities in the 12th also are attempting to overcome difficult economic situations. Alton is in the midst of a major revitalization aimed at providing jobs, growing industry and creating new tourism. The city, along with Clark Properties, converted the long-vacant Owens-Illinois Glass factory into usable office, warehouse and light industrial space. Belleville, largely dependent upon defense industry jobs, relies heavily on Scott Air Force Base, the area's major employer.

Higher education remains one of the area's few steadfast employers, with

Carbondale's Southern Illinois University, and its 20,000 students, bolstering Jackson County's economy.

The district's economic anxiety and minority population (blacks make up 18 percent) make it solid Democratic turf. St. Clair County has voted Democratic in the past nine presidential elections and gave Democrat Barack Obama his third-highest percentage statewide in the 2008 election. Despite only carrying St. Clair, Pulaski, Jackson and Alexander counties among the nine entirely in the 12th, Obama still captured 56 percent of the 12th's presidential vote that year.

Major Industry
Manufacturing, higher education, casinos, agriculture

Military Bases
Scott Air Force Base, 5,533 military, 5,085 civilian (2011)

Cities
Belleville, 44,478; Granite City, 29,849; O'Fallon, 28,281; Alton (pt.), 27,850; East St. Louis, 27,006; Carbondale, 25,902

Notable
Cahokia Mounds, a prehistoric civilization, was designated by the United Nations as a World Heritage Site in 1982; the Gateway Geyser, which stands at 600 feet, is a man-made fountain in East St. Louis.

Rep. Judy Biggert (R)

Capitol Office
225-3515
www.house.gov/biggert
2113 Rayburn Bldg. 20515-1313; fax 225-9420

Committees
Education & the Workforce
Financial Services
   (Insurance, Housing & Community Opportunity
   - Chairwoman)
Science, Space & Technology

Residence
Hinsdale

Born
Aug. 15, 1937; Chicago, Ill.

Religion
Episcopalian

Family
Husband, Rody Biggert; four children

Education
Stanford U., A.B. 1959 (international relations);
Northwestern U., J.D. 1963

Career
Lawyer

Political Highlights
Hinsdale Board of Education, 1982-85 (president,
1983-85); Village of Hinsdale Plan Commission,
1989-93; Ill. House, 1993-99

ELECTION RESULTS

2010 GENERAL

Judy Biggert (R)	152,132	63.8%
Scott Harper (D)	86,281	36.2%

2010 PRIMARY

Judy Biggert (R)	unopposed

2008 GENERAL

Judy Biggert (R)	180,888	53.6%
Scott Harper (D)	147,430	43.6%
Steve Alesch (GREEN)	9,402	2.8%

Previous Winning Percentages
2006 (58%); 2004 (65%); 2002 (70%); 2000 (66%);
1998 (61%)

Elected 1998; 7th term

Biggert unabashedly describes herself as a consensus builder. Her views on the federal role in education, housing and health care sometimes leave the moderate Republican on the outskirts of her own party but in prime position to negotiate with Democrats — a comfortable place for her.

"I am proud of that," she said. "I think we really need to be able to work together and not have so much of the political bickering that is going on. . . . I see myself as trusted by both sides of the aisle."

Her moderate bona fides make her feel at home in the House GOP's Tuesday Group and the Republican Main Street Partnership, both middle-of-the-road organizations, and she prides herself on cosponsoring Democrats' bills. She was one of only five Republicans to vote for an amendment to the fiscal 2011 defense authorization bill that would end the statutory "don't ask, don't tell" policy barring gays from serving openly in the military, and she voted to repeal it again in stand-alone legislation enacted at the end of the 111th Congress (2009-10).

But Biggert generally sides with her party on labor and economic issues, and she values fiscal restraint.

Biggert's consensus seeking is evident in her committee work, which reflects interests important to her suburban Chicago district and her experiences before arriving in Congress.

On the Education and the Workforce Committee, the former school board president has some notions about how to rewrite the Bush-era education law known as No Child Left Behind, which she helped draft in 2001. She says the law, which ties federal aid for elementary and secondary education to improvement in student test scores, has brought about greater accountability, but she wants a broader model for judging schools' performances.

Biggert was part of the team drafted by Minority Leader John A. Boehner of Ohio to create a Republican health care alternative. She later grew frustrated at the lack of GOP participation during the process. "That was unfortunate, because it was such a major, major piece of legislation that you need to work together," she said. "But you can't start with, 'OK, this is what we're going to do' in 2,000 pages, and then, 'What do you want to add to it?'"

On a more bipartisan note, Biggert worked with New York Democratic Rep. Louise M. Slaughter in the 110th Congress (2007-08) on enacting a long-sought measure that bars employers and health insurers from basing enrollment or premium decisions on the results of genetic testing.

She ran a home-based law practice specializing in real estate and estate planning before winning election to Congress, and the government response to the bursting of the real estate bubble occupied a considerable amount of her time and effort on the Financial Services Committee, where she chairs the Insurance, Housing and Community Opportunity Subcommittee.

Biggert, one of 25 Republicans to oppose the first version of a proposal by President George W. Bush to spend $700 billion to shore up the financial services sector, voted for a second version in late 2008. "With the clock ticking, credit markets seizing up, and the market swinging wildly, it is clear that the time for seeking better options has run out," she said at the time. "I'm glad we held out for the taxpayer protections that we got, but if we don't act now, those who are least to blame for this mess will suffer the most."

In February 2005 she helped found the Financial and Economic Literacy Caucus. "I used to say that I started this caucus because I used to think some of our members needed Econ 101," she said with a laugh.

She has been a tough critic of President Obama's economic agenda. She voted against the rewrite of the nation's financial regulations, and said of the $787 billion stimulus legislation: "Our economy needs a shot of adrenaline, not a load of long-term pet projects."

She also opposed Democrats' effort to institute a cap-and-trade system for carbon credits, aimed at reducing global warming, saying it wouldn't do enough to support nuclear energy. As a member of the Science, Space and Technology Committee, alternative energy research has been a priority for Biggert. Argonne National Laboratory, one of the Energy Department's largest facilities, is located in her district.

In the 110th Congress, Bush signed into law her bill to create energy research extension centers modeled on agricultural extension programs — an idea, she said, that came from an energy conservation program used by Home Run Inn Pizza in her district.

Biggert came of age in the 1950s, a time when career choices for women were considerably more restricted than they are today. After earning her undergraduate degree at Stanford, Biggert inquired about a master's degree program in business. She received a letter saying women weren't accepted, but that she was welcome to take a few night classes.

Instead, she enrolled at Northwestern to study law and later clerked for a federal appeals court judge. She worked at home for 20 years while raising four children.

Elected to the Illinois House in 1992, Biggert was picked by her peers to be assistant Republican leader after just one term. She was endorsed for Congress by her predecessor, Republican Harris W. Fawell, after he announced his retirement in 1998. She defeated five men vying for the GOP nomination and went on to win the seat with 61 percent of the vote.

When Biggert arrived in Washington, Fortune magazine identified her as one of the newcomers most likely to be a star. She was a prolific fundraiser for the GOP, but her efforts to enter the leadership ranks were twice thwarted by more conservative candidates. She lost a race for Republican Conference secretary in 2001 and withdrew in 2002 after concluding she couldn't win.

In 2004, party leaders were beating the bushes for a Senate candidate to replace a primary winner who withdrew amid a sex scandal. She refused the entreaties, and the seat was won easily by a Democratic newcomer named Barack Obama. She was held under 60 percent for the first time in her 2006 re-election bid, and in 2008 Biggert defeated a well-funded challenger with about 54 percent of the vote. She took almost 64 percent in 2010.

Key Votes

2010

Overhaul the nation's health insurance system	NO
Allow for repeal of "don't ask, don't tell"	YES
Overhaul financial services industry regulation	NO
Limit use of new Afghanistan War funds to troop withdrawal activities	NO
Change oversight of offshore drilling and lift oil spill liability cap	NO
Provide a path to legal status for some children of illegal immigrants	NO
Extend Bush-era income tax cuts for two years	YES

2009

Expand the Children's Health Insurance Program	NO
Provide $787 billion in tax cuts and spending increases to stimulate the economy	NO
Allow bankruptcy judges to modify certain primary-residence mortgages	NO
Create a cap-and-trade system to limit greenhouse gas emissions	NO
Provide $2 billion for the "cash for clunkers" program	YES
Establish the government as the sole provider of student loans	NO
Restrict federally funded insurance coverage for abortions in health care overhaul	YES

CQ Vote Studies

	PARTY UNITY		PRESIDENTIAL SUPPORT	
	SUPPORT	OPPOSE	SUPPORT	OPPOSE
2010	87%	13%	38%	62%
2009	76%	24%	45%	55%
2008	89%	11%	69%	31%
2007	83%	17%	66%	34%
2006	88%	12%	80%	20%

Interest Groups

	AFL-CIO	ADA	CCUS	ACU
2010	7%	20%	100%	71%
2009	29%	20%	93%	80%
2008	20%	35%	94%	84%
2007	42%	30%	85%	68%
2006	21%	30%	93%	64%

Illinois 13

Southwest Chicago suburbs — Naperville

More than half of the suburban Chicago-based 13th's population lives in the district's southern part of DuPage County, an area that includes Naperville. Nearly 40 percent of district residents live in fast-growing northern Will County communities such as Bolingbrook and Romeoville, with the rest living in the southwestern edge of Cook County.

Naperville, Downers Grove (a small part of which is in the 6th) and Oak Brook (shared with the 6th) have become leading suburban Chicago business centers, and companies such as OfficeMax, Sara Lee and McDonald's have corporate headquarters here. These large corporations and other high-paying employers have been attracted to the district by Chicago's busy O'Hare International Airport (nearby in the 6th), as well as by a mostly white-collar workforce. The presence of these corporations has helped the 13th achieve one of the highest median household incomes in the state and the nation.

The Argonne National Laboratory, in southeast DuPage, and the Fermi National Accelerator Laboratory, in the neighboring 14th, have made the

area into a scientific research and technology hub. DePaul University also has a campus in Naperville.

Even as suburban communities here grow, some cities in the district are experiencing rising unemployment rates and municipal budget shortfalls. The growth in the district has been in minority populations, while the white population has decreased overall. The district's growth over the past decade also has created serious traffic problems for its suburban residents. Voters in the 13th tend to be fiscally conservative and have a history of voting Republican in federal elections. But many residents here hold moderate views on social and environmental issues, and home-state Democrat Barack Obama won the 13th with 54 percent of the vote in the 2008 presidential election.

Major Industry
Scientific research, health care, insurance

Cities
Naperville (pt.), 141,838; Bolingbrook, 73,366; Aurora (pt.), 59,075

Notable
The Millennium Carillon in Naperville is among the four largest in the world, with a system of 72 bronze bells weighing up to 6 tons each.

Rep. Randy Hultgren (R)

Capitol Office
225-2976
hultgren.house.gov
427 Cannon Bldg. 20515-1314; fax 225-0697

Committees
Agriculture
Science, Space & Technology
Transportation & Infrastructure

Residence
Winfield

Born
March 1, 1966; Park Ridge, Ill.

Religion
Protestant

Family
Wife, Christy Hultgren; four children

Education
Bethel College, B.A. 1988 (communications & political science); Illinois Institute of Technology, J.D. 1993

Career
Securities company executive; financial planning consultant; lawyer; congressional aide

Political Highlights
DuPage County Board, 1994-98; DuPage County Forest Preserve District Board of Commissioners, 1994-98; Ill. House, 1999-2007; Ill. Senate, 2007-11

ELECTION RESULTS

2010 GENERAL

Randy Hultgren (R)	112,369	51.3%
Bill Foster (D)	98,645	45.0%
Daniel J. Kairis (GREEN)	7,949	3.6%

2010 PRIMARY

Randy Hultgren (R)	34,833	54.7%
Ethan A. Hastert (R)	28,840	45.3%

Elected 2010; 1st term

Hultgren has been involved in Illinois politics for more than two decades, starting with his work in the office of former House Speaker J. Dennis Hastert, to precinct committeeman, to county board member, to state legislator.

He can be expected to practice mainline, Midwestern conservatism. But he will not be an automatic vote for the Republican leadership.

He displayed his independent streak early on, voting against an extension of expiring provisions of the anti-terrorism law known as the Patriot Act. Hultgren said he had substantive objections to the bill, opposing a provision that allows investigators access to materials such as library records, as well as procedural objections.

"I was also disappointed by the fact that this important measure was brought to the floor with such limited opportunity for debate and no opportunity for any amendments to be offered," he said.

He won a seat on the Agriculture Committee, where he'll look out for the district's soybean and corn growers as well as farm machinery manufacturer Caterpillar Inc., based in Peoria. He also sits on the Transportation and Infrastructure and Science, Space and Technology committees.

Hultgren grew up in suburban Wheaton, upstairs from his family's funeral home. He graduated from Bethel College and earned a law degree from the Illinois Institute of Technology's Chicago-Kent College of Law. Beyond his political experience, he has worked as an attorney and as vice president for investment and financial management organizations.

To win the Republican nomination, Hultgren defeated the son of his former boss, topping Ethan Hastert 55 percent to 45 percent. He then faced Democratic incumbent Bill Foster, who had won a March 2008 special election to replace the elder Hastert, who resigned, and then won again in November 2008.

Hultgren was able to paint Foster, who backed almost all of President Obama's economic initiatives, as too liberal for the district. He won with just more than 51 percent of the vote.

Illinois 14

North central — Aurora, Elgin, DeKalb

The majority of the 14th's residents live in Kane County on the district's eastern side, in established towns along the Fox River Valley. West of the river, prairies and farms stretch to Henry County, nearly to the Mississippi River. Rich in soybeans and corn, the flat landscape is interrupted only by Northern Illinois University in DeKalb.

The district's population center can be found in Kane County on the outskirts of Chicago. Aurora (shared with the 13th) and neighboring cities in Kane are experiencing sprawl across the county line into Kendall, the fastest-growing county in the nation since 2000. Despite the city's increasingly residential feel, Aurora has a long history of manufacturing, although heavy-equipment maker Caterpillar, its key employer, has been forced into widespread layoffs.

Aurora and Elgin (small parts of which are in the 8th and 6th) have benefited from job growth in nearby Naperville and Schaumburg, suburban cities that have emerged as Chicagoland business centers. Aurora and Elgin also each host riverboat casinos. The two cities are more than 40 percent Hispanic, and many of these residents are in the local blue-collar workforce.

Areas in Kane, Kendall and DuPage counties backed Republicans for decades. But Republican John McCain won only Lee County and the 14th's portions of Bureau and Henry counties here in the 2008 presidential race, and Barack Obama won the district overall with 55 percent of the vote.

Major Industry
Manufacturing, casinos, agriculture

Cities
Aurora (pt.), 138,824; Elgin (pt.), 84,156; DeKalb, 43,862; Carpentersville, 37,691

Notable
President Ronald Reagan's birthplace in Tampico and boyhood home in Dixon are museums.

Rep. Timothy V. Johnson (R)

Capitol Office
225-2371
www.house.gov/timjohnson
1207 Longworth Bldg. 20515-1315; fax 226-0791

Committees
Agriculture
  (Rural Development, Research, Biotechnology &
  Foreign Agriculture - Chairman)
Transportation & Infrastructure

Residence
Urbana

Born
July 23, 1946; Champaign, Ill.

Religion
Christian

Family
Divorced; ten children (one deceased)

Education
U.S. Military Academy, attended 1964; U. of Illinois,
B.A. 1969, J.D. 1972

Career
Lawyer; Realtor

Political Highlights
Urbana City Council, 1971-75; Ill. House, 1977-2000

ELECTION RESULTS

2010 GENERAL

Timothy V. Johnson (R)	136,915	64.3%
David Gill (D)	75,948	35.7%

2010 PRIMARY

Timothy V. Johnson (R)	unopposed

2008 GENERAL

Timothy V. Johnson (R)	187,121	64.2%
Steve Cox (D)	104,393	35.8%

Previous Winning Percentages
2006 (58%); 2004 (61%); 2002 (65%); 2000 (53%)

Elected 2000; 6th term

Johnson accepts the mantle of unconventional Republican. Throughout his decade in the House, he has been among the lawmakers most likely to buck his party's leadership. But he argues that he doesn't break from the GOP just to be irksome. "I have a consistent philosophy, but it's not always conventional," he said.

In 2010, his party unity score — the percentage of votes on which he sided with a majority of the GOP against a majority of Democrats — was 80 percent, up from a career low of 69 percent in 2007.

He broke with the Republican leadership early in the 112th Congress (2011-12) on extending the anti-terrorism law known as the Patriot Act.

"You're seeing an emerging belief among conservative Republicans that we need to embrace a commitment to individual liberties," said Johnson, who also opposed the extension enacted in early 2010.

In 2007, he was one of 17 GOP House members to vote against President George W. Bush's plan to send additional U.S. troops into Iraq, although he opposed Democratic efforts to set a timetable for withdrawal. And he was one of 10 Republicans to back a January 2009 bill aimed at reversing a Supreme Court decision that limited the time frame for filing gender discrimination suits.

Johnson doesn't make headlines often and rarely speaks on the House floor. According to archived video from C-SPAN, he was among the members who spoke least during the 111th Congress (2009-10).

But he is very vocal through another medium: the telephone. Johnson says he calls 75 to 300 constituents a day, seven days a week. He is a familiar figure when the House is in session, walking purposefully through corridors with a cell phone held to his ear. "It is part of our responsibility as legislators to make sure we personally know and personally care about the people we represent," he said.

He says talking with constituents keeps him grounded, and it has given footing to his top legislative priorities, including his plans to overhaul the spending and oversight of the rules governing congressional travel. "There are tremendous abuses within that area," he said. "There's no indication on how much money we're spending."

He introduced legislation in early 2011 that would impose a moratorium on travel outside the country by lawmakers and staff until a comptroller general report is issued.

Another major frustration for Johnson has been the handling of the FutureGen project — a proposal to build the world's first coal-fueled, near-zero-emissions power plant in Mattoon, located in his district. Expected to funnel jobs into the area, the project received a setback in January 2008 when the Energy Department announced the government was pulling out, citing rising costs. In October 2010, the Energy Department announced it would use a Meredosia plant — in the western portion of the neighboring 18th District — for the carbon dioxide storage facility. Johnson said both the Bush and Obama administrations "completely misled" his district about the project.

"Now the DOE has turned its back on us," he said after the 2008 announcement. "We played by their rules. This was the DOE's initiative, undertaken at the president's directive in 2003, with the goal of clean-coal energy that was underscored . . . in the president's State of the Union address. Mattoon responded with all the right answers, every step of the way."

Johnson chairs the Agriculture Subcommittee on Rural Development, Research, Biotechnology and Foreign Agriculture. His 10,000 square-mile district is home to thousands of farms that concentrate on corn, soybeans and hogs. Johnson wants to see a strengthening of alternative fuels, the maintaining of a "safety net" for farmers and a strong school nutrition program in a 2012 farm bill.

He supported the successful override of Bush's veto of a $289 billion farm programs reauthorization, saying the legislation preserved a farmer's ability to produce, compete and contribute to "nutritional independence and energy independence."

From his seat on the Transportation and Infrastructure Committee, Johnson was disappointed in the lack of progress on advancing a surface transportation reauthorization in the 111th Congress and will be involved in writing the bill in the 112th Congress.

Johnson is an advocate of wellness initiatives, introducing a bill that would provide tax incentives for employer-provided wellness programs. The rail-thin, former Illinois state assemblyman eats the same foods every day: fruit, rice cakes, granola, vitamin supplements, juice and farmer cheese. He's also a fitness buff, devoting a chunk of every day to his House gym regimen, swimming laps or pounding out miles on a treadmill while catching up on reading or calling constituents.

His voting behavior blends with his interest in building comity in the House. Johnson and New York Democrat Steve Israel formed the Center Aisle Caucus in 2005 to encourage members to respect others' points of view.

Johnson's mother and her parents were active in McLean County GOP politics. His father, originally a Democrat, became a Republican and served on the Urbana City Council. Johnson, who began passing out campaign literature when he was 3 or 4 years old, became a GOP precinct committee member at age 21 while still in college. By 24, he was on the Urbana City Council, and at 30 he was elected to the Illinois House, where he stayed for nearly two dozen years. Johnson also worked in real estate and practiced law.

In 2000, he ran for the House when GOP Rep. Thomas W. Ewing retired. Johnson won 44 percent of the vote in a four-man primary and beat Democratic university instructor Mike Kelleher with 53 percent.

Johnson promised to limit himself to three two-year terms, but revoked that pledge right before the 2002 election. Redistricting that year put Democratic Rep. David Phelps' home in the 15th District, but Phelps ran in the 19th instead. Johnson cruised to a 2-to-1 victory over political novice Joshua T. Hartke. He has been easily re-elected since.

Key Votes

2010

Vote	
Overhaul the nation's health insurance system	NO
Allow for repeal of "don't ask, don't tell"	NO
Overhaul financial services industry regulation	NO
Limit use of new Afghanistan War funds to troop withdrawal activities	YES
Change oversight of offshore drilling and lift oil spill liability cap	YES
Provide a path to legal status for some children of illegal immigrants	NO
Extend Bush-era income tax cuts for two years	YES

2009

Vote	
Expand the Children's Health Insurance Program	NO
Provide $787 billion in tax cuts and spending increases to stimulate the economy	NO
Allow bankruptcy judges to modify certain primary-residence mortgages	NO
Create a cap-and-trade system to limit greenhouse gas emissions	NO
Provide $2 billion for the "cash for clunkers" program	NO
Establish the government as the sole provider of student loans	YES
Restrict federally funded insurance coverage for abortions in health care overhaul	YES

CQ Vote Studies

	PARTY UNITY		PRESIDENTIAL SUPPORT	
	SUPPORT	OPPOSE	SUPPORT	OPPOSE
2010	80%	20%	29%	71%
2009	80%	20%	27%	73%
2008	72%	28%	43%	57%
2007	69%	31%	43%	57%
2006	79%	21%	74%	26%

Interest Groups

	AFL-CIO	ADA	CCUS	ACU
2010	21%	25%	88%	79%
2009	33%	15%	87%	80%
2008	36%	50%	67%	68%
2007	68%	35%	84%	60%
2006	50%	20%	86%	76%

Illinois 15

East central — Champaign, Bloomington, Danville

Agriculture is the dominant industry in the 15th, which takes in all or part of 22 counties, including the county and city of Champaign. The 15th runs nearly 250 miles north to south, with a long, narrow appendage that hugs the Indiana border on the western bank of the Wabash River down to Gallatin County. The district's roughly 10,000 square miles encompass several population centers separated by expansive farmland.

Corn and soybean fields cover much of the territory, and the land both around Bloomington-Normal and in counties south of Champaign produces high crop yields. Both the district's family and commercial farms produce feed and raw material for food products manufactured just over the district border at Decatur-based worldwide distributor Archer Daniels Midland (in the 17th). The area food-processing industry served by the district has remained steady despite several years of a nationwide economic downturn and rising transportation costs.

Scattered amid the farms are several midsize towns, including Danville, that center around agribusiness and manufacturing. Higher education is big business in the 15th, with more than 40,000 students at the University of Illinois' flagship campus in Urbana-Champaign. Bloomington-Normal's Illinois State and Illinois Wesleyan universities are just outside the district (in the 11th). Bloomington, home to State Farm Insurance, leads downstate Illinois in insurance and finance.

The district has a GOP lean, and Republicans typically run strongest in counties north of Champaign, including Iroquois and Ford. Both gave Republican John McCain almost 65 percent of their vote in the 2008 presidential election. Champaign County's academic community keeps Democrats competitive in the county, and it gave Barack Obama 58 percent of the vote in 2008, his highest percentage in the district. Overall, McCain won the 15th with 50 percent of the vote.

Major Industry
Agriculture, higher education, food processing, insurance

Cities
Champaign, 81,055; Bloomington (pt.), 43,271; Urbana, 41,250; Danville, 33,027; Charleston, 21,838; Normal (pt.), 20,441; Mattoon, 18,555

Notable
The Lincoln Log Cabin State Historic Site in Coles County preserves the last home of President Abraham Lincoln's father and stepmother.

Rep. Donald Manzullo (R)

Elected 1992; 10th term

The socially and fiscally conservative Manzullo champions manufacturing and small business, and he has effectively courted Democrats and confronted Republicans on issues he sees as critical to the mixed agricultural and industrial economy of his district.

Manzullo (man-ZOO-low) does not give many floor speeches, nor does he introduce stacks of bills. Instead, he attaches himself to lower-profile issues — the majority of which affect U.S. manufacturers — and digs in to implement changes. "Success is not necessarily measured in terms of legislation," he said. He ranks sixth among Republicans in seniority on both the Foreign Affairs and Financial Services committees and was the longest-serving Republican chairman of the Small Business Committee, from 2001 to 2006.

Working across the aisle, Manzullo has advanced a number of his priorities. In 2008, he worked with Democrats Brad Sherman of California and Joseph Crowley of New York to push through the House a bill to streamline licensing procedures for defense-related exports. The Senate did not take up the measure.

Unlike some other friends of manufacturing in Congress, Manzullo defends free trade. As chairman of the Foreign Affairs Committee's Asia panel, he hopes to pressure China to revalue its currency. Manzullo, chairman of the U.S.-China Interparliamentary Exchange from 1999 to 2006, has made policy recommendations that include influencing China to tighten its intellectual property laws and prohibiting China from competing for federal contracts.

"As experience has shown, China's unfair trade practices, including currency manipulation, illegal subsidies and lax enforcement of intellectual property law, make it very difficult for the hardworking people of America to compete on a level playing field and benefit from this relationship," he said at a committee briefing in early 2011.

His northern Illinois district drew national attention when the Obama administration sought to purchase Thomson Correctional Center and move detainees kept in Guantánamo Bay, Cuba, to the unused facility. The plan drew some local support, but congressional opposition blocked funding. Manzullo suggested reopening the facility, sans detainees, to create jobs in the district.

The 16th is home to a Chrysler assembly plant, and Manzullo was one of 32 Republicans to support a proposed $14 billion loan to the domestic auto industry in December 2008, although he complained the measure lacked provisions "to get people back in the showrooms to buy cars."

He sought to remedy that in 2009, when he proposed that President Obama's $787 billion economic stimulus should be replaced with a tax credit for the purchase of certain new and used cars.

Manzullo has a well-earned reputation for combativeness. As chairman of the Small Business Committee, he fought over provisions in a corporate tax bill with Ways and Means Chairman Bill Thomas, a California Republican not exactly known as a shrinking violet. "One day [Thomas] stood up in conference," Manzullo said. "He said, 'Manzullo, I've given you four out of five things that you want. What more do you want?' 'I want it all,' I said."

In the summer of 2005, Manzullo led a highly unusual floor revolt against legislation by Henry J. Hyde, a fellow Illinois Republican who headed the International Relations Committee. Hyde's bill would have imposed sanctions on foreign companies that sell military technology to China. Manzullo said the bill would have hurt U.S. businesses that unknowingly sold goods to companies linked to the Chinese military. More than 60 lawmakers

Capitol Office
225-5676
www.house.gov/manzullo
2228 Rayburn Bldg. 20515-1316; fax 225-5284

Committees
Financial Services
Foreign Affairs
   (Asia & the Pacific - Chairman)

Residence
Egan

Born
March 24, 1944; Rockford, Ill.

Religion
Christian

Family
Wife, Freda Manzullo; three children

Education
American U., B.A. 1967 (political science); Marquette U., J.D. 1970

Career
Lawyer

Political Highlights
Sought Republican nomination for U.S. House, 1990

ELECTION RESULTS

2010 GENERAL

Donald Manzullo (R)	138,299	65.0%
George W. Gaulrapp (D)	66,037	31.0%
Terry G. Campbell (GREEN)	8,425	4.0%

2010 PRIMARY

Donald Manzullo (R)	unopposed

2008 GENERAL

Donald Manzullo (R)	190,039	60.9%
Robert G. Abboud (D)	112,648	36.1%
Scott Summers (GREEN)	9,533	3.0%

Previous Winning Percentages
2006 (64%); 2004 (69%); 2002 (71%); 2000 (67%); 1998 (100%); 1996 (60%); 1994 (71%); 1992 (56%)

switched their votes on the bill, embarrassing GOP leaders. The measure later passed, with a revision that companies had to knowingly break U.S. law to be sanctioned.

Despite the handful of high-profile examples of bucking his party, Manzullo is a reliable Republican vote. He has never had a party unity score — the percentage of votes on which he sided with a majority of the GOP against a majority of Democrats — lower than 92.

Manzullo says his views on helping small business stem from his boyhood, when he lived in a one-room apartment above the family's struggling grocery store in Rockford in the late 1940s. Manzullo's father, Frank, extended store credit to newly arrived immigrants from Poland, Latvia and Lithuania. In 1964, Manzullo's father started an Italian eatery and later brought Manzullo's brother into the business. The restaurant remained in operation for nearly four decades but closed, Manzullo said, because they could no longer afford to pay for the employees' health insurance. "He had to sell $70,000 of spaghetti in a year just to afford it for himself and his wife," said Manzullo, who has pushed several bills to help small businesses with the cost of health insurance — including one the House passed in 2005 allowing trade groups to sponsor plans for their members.

As an ardent social conservative, Manzullo early in his law career helped start pregnancy crisis centers in Rockford and picketed clinics that performed abortions. His wife, Freda, a microbiologist, taught their three children at home until eighth grade, when they went to a small Christian high school in suburban Washington. When the House was in recess, the family used to work a small beef cattle farm in Illinois.

In his spare time Manzullo attends Bible study and visits factories. "I live for machine oil," he said. "Sometimes if I get a little bit depressed and I'm back home, our district rep will say, 'Get Don into a factory because he needs the smell of machine oil. It does something to him. It gets him all excited.'"

Manzullo recalls deciding at age 4 he wanted to be a lawyer — and at 10 he decided he wanted to be in Congress. He spent 20 years practicing in Oregon, Ill., handling family cases, writing deeds and wills, and advising small companies.

When Republican Rep. Lynn Martin decided to try for the Senate in 1990, Manzullo ran for her seat. He got a respectable 46 percent of the vote in the GOP primary, but Democrat John W. Cox Jr. won the general election. Two years later, Manzullo tried again, winning the primary with 56 percent. In November, the district reverted to its traditional GOP form; Manzullo beat Cox by 12 percentage points. He has not had a serious challenge since.

Key Votes

2010

Vote	
Overhaul the nation's health insurance system	NO
Allow for repeal of "don't ask, don't tell"	NO
Overhaul financial services industry regulation	NO
Limit use of new Afghanistan War funds to troop withdrawal activities	NO
Change oversight of offshore drilling and lift oil spill liability cap	NO
Provide a path to legal status for some children of illegal immigrants	NO
Extend Bush-era income tax cuts for two years	YES

2009

Vote	
Expand the Children's Health Insurance Program	NO
Provide $787 billion in tax cuts and spending increases to stimulate the economy	NO
Allow bankruptcy judges to modify certain primary-residence mortgages	NO
Create a cap-and-trade system to limit greenhouse gas emissions	NO
Provide $2 billion for the "cash for clunkers" program	YES
Establish the government as the sole provider of student loans	NO
Restrict federally funded insurance coverage for abortions in health care overhaul	YES

CQ Vote Studies

	PARTY UNITY		PRESIDENTIAL SUPPORT	
	SUPPORT	OPPOSE	SUPPORT	OPPOSE
2010	95%	5%	36%	64%
2009	94%	6%	22%	78%
2008	92%	8%	73%	27%
2007	95%	5%	81%	19%
2006	95%	5%	94%	6%

Interest Groups

	AFL-CIO	ADA	CCUS	ACU
2010	14%	10%	88%	92%
2009	10%	5%	73%	96%
2008	13%	20%	83%	92%
2007	13%	0%	80%	100%
2006	9%	10%	100%	91%

Illinois 16

North — Rockford, part of McHenry County

The 16th spans most of the Illinois-Wisconsin border, taking in Rockford and covering the rolling northern prairie where family farmers grow corn and raise dairy cows. It includes all of six counties and parts of three others, including all of Winnebago and the majority of McHenry counties.

McHenry County (shared with the 8th) contains large expanses of farmland, and its proximity to Chicago draws many residents to the county's suburban enclaves. McHenry experienced several decades of growth, as did Boone County, to its west. Both counties were largely white GOP strongholds a decade ago, but growing Hispanic and black populations have brought diversity.

Roughly one-fifth of the 16th's voters live in the industrial hub of Rockford in Winnebago County. At one time a major machine-tool manufacturing center, Rockford suffered a typical Rust Belt decline. Although the transition from traditional manufacturing was difficult, the city upgraded to technology manufacturing. It is still one of the most densely populated manufac-

turing communities in the United States. An upswing in unemployment rates hurt the city, but construction of new manufacturing facilities has provided some jobs.

The 16th includes Illinois' leading dairy producers, and Jo Daviess County, in the northwest corner, is a state leader in raising beef cattle and producing hay. Galena, in the rolling hills of Jo Daviess near the Mississippi River, has a tourist-based economy.

About 70 percent of the district's black residents live in Rockford, giving the city a base of loyal Democrats. But the 16th overall covers historically conservative, GOP territory, and only once in the 20th century did voters here elect a Democrat to the House. Democrat Barack Obama won 53 percent of the district's vote in the 2008 presidential election.

Major Industry
Manufacturing, aircraft and machine parts, agriculture, trade

Cities
Rockford, 152,871; Crystal Lake (pt.), 40,320; Lake in the Hills, 28,965

Notable
The Rockford Peaches, three-time champions of the All-American Girls Professional Baseball League, were one of only two teams to play every season of the league's existence (1943-54).

Rep. Bobby Schilling (R)

Capitol Office
225-5905
schilling.house.gov
507 Cannon Bldg. 20515-1317; fax 225-5396

Committees
Agriculture
Armed Services

Residence
Colona

Born
Jan. 23, 1964; Rock Island, Ill.

Religion
Roman Catholic

Family
Wife, Christie Schilling; ten children

Education
Black Hawk College, attended 1982-83

Career
Restaurateur; financial services agent; factory worker

Political Highlights
No previous office

ELECTION RESULTS

2010 GENERAL

Bobby Schilling (R)	104,583	52.6%
Phil Hare (D)	85,454	43.0%
Roger K. Davis (GREEN)	8,861	4.5%

2010 PRIMARY

Bobby Schilling (R)	unopposed

Elected 2010; 1st term

Elected with tea party backing, Schilling gave an early indication of his political philosophy when he joined both the Republican Study Committee, home to the most conservative members of the House, and the Tuesday Group, made up of House GOP moderates.

Schilling certainly lines up with most of his fellow Republicans in his desire to trim federal spending and reduce taxes. And he said it was unrealistic to think the GOP could repeal the health care law enacted in 2010, so he wants to go after it piecemeal and through the appropriations process.

The owner of St. Giuseppe's Heavenly Pizza in Moline, Schilling seized on President Obama's offer made during the State of the Union address to listen to ideas about changing the law by offering to have a "Pizza Summit" with his fellow Illinoisan.

But, as a former union steward, Schilling also has some ties to organized labor and says he wants to bring labor and business interests together. Farm equipment manufacturing is a critical component of his area's economy. So is farming, and he won a seat on the Agriculture Committee.

He also sits on the Armed Services Committee. Early in the 112th Congress (2011-12), Schilling voted against a short-term extension of the anti-terrorism law known as the Patriot Act.

"During my campaign, I stated that we need increased national security, but not without a thorough and complete look at the Patriot Act and its scope," Schilling said.

In the 2010 election, Schilling took on what appeared early in the process to be the hopeless task of challenging two-term Democrat Phil Hare. Republicans hadn't even fielded a candidate against Hare in 2008. But Schilling was able to ride the Republican wave and some Hare missteps — the incumbent famously said he was "not worried about the Constitution" when supporting the health care overhaul — to a narrow victory.

Democrats, looking forward to a favorable outcome in redistricting with their majority in the state legislature redrawing the lines, quickly made Schilling a target in 2012.

Illinois 17

West — Moline, Rock Island; parts of Decatur and Springfield

The 17th is one of the state's most expansive districts. Winding over nine full counties and parts of 14 others, it hugs much of the border along the Mississippi River and reaches its tentacle-like arms past Springfield as far inland as Decatur. The 17th includes rich farmland along the Mississippi, as well as Rock Island and Moline — Illinois' half of the industrial Quad Cities that straddle the river across from Iowa.

Moline, whose overall population has decreased since 2000 even as its Hispanic population has grown, is a retail hub. The John Deere Commons — with historical exhibits, shopping, dining and lodging — revitalized the city's downtown.

Corn, soybeans and hogs fuel most of the rest of the 17th's economy, and even the industrial sector here, which is dominated by John Deere and Archer Daniels Midland, depends on agriculture. Economic downturns have hurt agriculture-dependent economies and family farm profits, but the Rock Island Arsenal remains a major area employer.

A longtime Democratic tilt has given way to highly competitive national and statewide races. Springfield and Decatur no longer overcome GOP tendencies in rural areas and new Republican strength is in Rock Island.

Major Industry
Farm equipment manufacturing, agriculture, defense, food processing

Military Bases
Rock Island Arsenal (Army), 374 military, 4,868 civilian (2011)

Cities
Decatur (pt.), 53,454; Moline, 43,483; Quincy, 40,633; Rock Island, 39,018

Notable
Moline is known as the "Farm Implement Capital of the World."

Rep. Aaron Schock (R)

Capitol Office
225-6201
schock.house.gov
328 Cannon Bldg. 20515-1318; fax 225-9249

Committees
House Administration
Ways & Means
Joint Printing

Residence
Peoria

Born
May 28, 1981; Morris, Minn.

Religion
Baptist

Family
Single

Education
Illinois Central College, attended 1999-2002; Bradley
U., B.S. 2002 (finance)

Career
Real estate developer; home improvement company owner

Political Highlights
Board of Education of the City of Peoria, 2001-05
(president, 2004-05); Ill. House, 2005-09

ELECTION RESULTS

2010 GENERAL

Aaron Schock (R)	152,868	69.1%
Deirdre "DK" Hirner (D)	57,046	25.8%
Sheldon Schafer (GREEN)	11,256	5.1%

2010 PRIMARY

Aaron Schock (R)	unopposed

2008 GENERAL

Aaron Schock (R)	182,589	58.9%
Colleen Callahan (D)	117,642	37.9%
Sheldon Schafer (GREEN)	9,857	3.2%

Elected 2008; 2nd term

As the youngest member of Congress — and the first to be born during Ronald Reagan's presidency — Schock has already proven himself
to be ambitious. While he is eager to push his ideas for a "traditional"
conservative agenda that can strengthen the Republican Party, Schock's
methods of connecting with his constituency tout the technological
savvy of his generation.

Tagged as a future leader and the new face of the GOP, Schock won a seat
on the Ways and Means Committee in the 112th Congress (2011-12).

His priorities include tax code simplification and reducing marginal rates.
"I believe reducing the tax burden on individual Americans and businesses
is the best way to spur job creation in the private sector, Schock said.

Schock also sponsored bipartisan legislation to create a commission
made up of former lawmakers and outside experts to eliminate duplicative
and wasteful programs.

In early 2011 he voted to repeal the health care law enacted in 2010 and
signed onto a letter to Illinois Attorney General Lisa Madigan, a Democrat,
urging her to join a lawsuit challenging its constitutionality.

In the new Congress, Schock also joined the House Administration Committee, which oversees the internal operations of the chamber and federal
elections. Schock criticized the Justice Department's handling of problems
with military voting during the 2010 elections, which resulted in ballots
being mailed late and meant "thousands of Illinois men and women in our
armed forces were unable to have their votes counted."

Shortly after his 2008 primary victory, Schock started a "GOP Generation
Y Fund," which donated thousands of dollars to fellow incoming freshmen.
He did so hoping to win a slot on the GOP Steering Committee, which
makes committee assignments. While he failed in that bid, Schock attracted
the attention of party leaders, who invited him to speak at the Republican
National Convention. After his speech, Schock began popping up frequently on TV news shows and GOP leaders designated him a deputy whip once
he arrived in Congress.

Republican leaders view Schock as emblematic of the future of the party.
House Majority Leader Eric Cantor of Virginia told the Chicago Tribune
that Schock "has already established himself as a leader." Speaker John A.
Boehner of Ohio told the Journal Star of Peoria that Schock was one of the
stars of the class of 2008. Transportation Secretary Ray LaHood, Schock's
predecessor in the House, told Chicago Business that Schock was "the new
face of the Republican Party."

Schock draws coverage from sources not typically seen around the Capitol, including the celebrity gossip site TMZ.com and GQ, which featured
him in a September 2009 fashion layout. He has used the pop culture attention to his advantage, telling Details magazine, "I've had Republicans come
to me and say, 'Tell me how I should talk to young people!' as if it's some
foreign language or something." Schock operates two Twitter accounts, a
YouTube channel and a Facebook page.

He opposed President Obama's $787 billion economic stimulus package,
even after being lobbied by the president. "I think all the president's men
thought that the youngest member of Congress was the most impression-
able member of Congress," he told an audience in East Peoria. When Caterpillar, Peoria's largest employer, subsequently laid off about 900 employees, he said it was proof the stimulus wasn't working.

But he backed Democratic bills to expand national service programs, to allow the Food and Drug Administration to regulate tobacco, and to impose restrictions and set standards for mortgage lenders .

He had success working across the dais when he served on the Small Business Committee in his first term. Chairwoman Nydia M. Velázquez, a New York Democrat, embraced his bill to help small-business development centers by setting up new grant programs dealing with access to credit, capital and procurement training. The House in May 2009 included provisions of Schock's bill in legislation to overhaul entrepreneurial assistance programs for small businesses.

Although not a member of the Financial Services Committee, Schock also persuaded then-Chairman Barney Frank, a Massachusetts Democrat, to add language to a measure that would create stipulations for the release of the second portion of the funds from the $700 billion financial services bailout law of 2008. Schock's amendment required the creation of a database to track how money is spent under the Troubled Asset Relief Program — something Schock compared to "a Google for TARP."

Schock was born in Morris, Minn., but his family later moved to Peoria. The move away from his family's farm led to him becoming "a bit of an entrepreneur," he said. In junior high school, he started doing database management for a local bookstore. He worked for an online ticket brokerage firm and in a gravel pit throughout high school. Schock started an individual retirement account at age 14, bought his first piece of real estate on his 18th birthday and, after graduating from Bradley University in two years, opened a local franchise of a home-improvement company.

After the school board wouldn't let him graduate high school early, he ran for the Peoria board of education at age 19. After being taken off the ballot on a technicality, Schock won as a write-in candidate. He served on the board for four years and was the youngest school board president in history.

He then served in the Illinois House for four years and developed a reputation for being responsive to constituents. In 2007, he shared an award with then-Sen. Obama from a watchdog group, the Illinois Committee for Honest Government, for outstanding legislative and constituent service.

When LaHood announced his retirement after seven terms, Schock jumped into the race. He cruised through a three-person primary and took nearly 59 percent of the vote in November 2008, 9 points ahead of Arizona GOP Sen. John McCain's showing in the district's presidential vote. He took 69 percent in 2010.

Key Votes

2010

Overhaul the nation's health insurance system	NO
Allow for repeal of "don't ask, don't tell"	NO
Overhaul financial services industry regulation	NO
Limit use of new Afghanistan War funds to troop withdrawal activities	NO
Change oversight of offshore drilling and lift oil spill liability cap	NO
Provide a path to legal status for some children of illegal immigrants	NO
Extend Bush-era income tax cuts for two years	YES

2009

Expand the Children's Health Insurance Program	NO
Provide $787 billion in tax cuts and spending increases to stimulate the economy	NO
Allow bankruptcy judges to modify certain primary-residence mortgages	NO
Create a cap-and-trade system to limit greenhouse gas emissions	NO
Provide $2 billion for the "cash for clunkers" program	NO
Establish the government as the sole provider of student loans	NO
Restrict federally funded insurance coverage for abortions in health care overhaul	YES

CQ Vote Studies

	PARTY UNITY		PRESIDENTIAL SUPPORT	
	SUPPORT	OPPOSE	SUPPORT	OPPOSE
2010	93%	7%	33%	67%
2009	84%	16%	36%	64%

Interest Groups

	AFL-CIO	ADA	CCUS	ACU
2010	7%	0%	100%	88%
2009	15%	5%	93%	92%

Central — Peoria, parts of Springfield and Decatur

The 18th takes in all or part of 20 counties in central and western Illinois, with Peoria County making up nearly 30 percent of the population. In the south, it takes in the northern part of Springfield (the state capital), some Republican-leaning suburbs north and west of the city, and rural turf that stretches west of the capital almost to the Mississippi River. In the southeast, it runs to northern Decatur.

The middle-class city of Peoria is the 18th's population center and hosts five hospitals, a University of Illinois College of Medicine campus and Bradley University. Peoria's population as a whole increased slightly over the last decade, and the minority populations now account for a larger share of the still largely white city's populace.

The downtown area works to remain vibrant, with continuing development of corporate, government, medical, convention and educational sites. Many of the city's residents live in high-rise condominiums, riverfront lofts or converted office and warehouse apartments. Local leaders have been pursuing funding for passenger rail connections, either to Bloomington-Normal or to Chicago.

In much of this predominately agricultural district, voters worry about crop prices, ethanol, free trade and estate taxes. The district's economic health still depends on Peoria-based manufacturer Caterpillar, which makes earth-moving and other heavy machinery. The manufacturer is still the largest employer in the county, and any layoffs by the company can unsettle residents.

Peoria, with its strong manufacturing base, tends to vote Democratic, but the Republican lean of rural areas north of Springfield and in the district's west tips the 18th to the GOP. In the 2008 presidential election, Democrat Barack Obama won 60 percent of Peoria's vote, but Republican John McCain won the district overall with 50 percent.

Major Industry
Manufacturing, ethanol and grain products, agriculture, health care

Cities
Peoria, 115,007; Springfield (pt.), 59,545; Pekin, 34,094; East Peoria, 23,402

Notable
Abraham Lincoln's tomb in Springfield is a state historic site.

Rep. John Shimkus (R)

Capitol Office
225-5271
www.house.gov/shimkus
2452 Rayburn Bldg. 20515-1319; fax 225-5880

Committees
Energy & Commerce
   (Environment & the Economy - Chairman)

Residence
Collinsville

Born
Feb. 21, 1958; Collinsville, Ill.

Religion
Lutheran

Family
Wife, Karen Muth Shimkus; three children

Education
U.S. Military Academy, B.S. 1980; Southern Illinois U.,
M.B.A. 1997

Military
Army, 1980-86; Army Reserve, 1986-2008

Career
Teacher

Political Highlights
Candidate for Madison County Board, 1988; Collins-
ville Township Board of Trustees, 1989-93; Madison
County treasurer, 1990-97; Republican nominee for
U.S. House, 1992

ELECTION RESULTS

2010 GENERAL

John Shimkus (R)	166,166	71.2%
Tim Bagwell (D)	67,132	28.8%

2010 PRIMARY

John Shimkus (R)	48,680	85.3%
Michael Firsching (R)	8,363	14.7%

2008 GENERAL

John Shimkus (R)	203,434	64.5%
Daniel Davis (D)	105,338	33.4%
Troy Dennis (GREEN)	6,817	2.2%

Previous Winning Percentages
2006 (61%); 2004 (69%); 2002 (55%); 2000 (63%);
1998 (61%); 1996 (50%)

Elected 1996; 8th term

Shimkus doesn't shrink from arguing with colleagues, either in Energy and Commerce Committee meetings or on the House floor. As a pitcher for the Republicans in the annual charity baseball game against the Democrats (which CQ Roll Call sponsors), he doesn't mind throwing the occasional high hard one.

"I am one who doesn't apologize for strong disagreements based upon ideology," he said. "And I also think that colleagues respect that. As long as you don't get mean and nasty, and lose control. If it's on policy, you can be emotional, you can be strong."

Shimkus (SHIM-kus) has been a member of Energy and Commerce since 1997 and was an unsuccessful contender for the chairmanship in the 112th Congress (2011-12). Instead, he chairs its Environment and Economy Subcommittee, a crucial spot as the new Republican majority duels with the Obama administration on climate change.

Shimkus says his biggest legislative victory in the 111th Congress (2009-10) actually happened in the Senate: stopping a Democratic climate change bill from advancing. It passed the House, but was never brought up in the other chamber. Shimkus and other opponents argue that the bill would have increased costs to consumers and, more broadly, he contends Democratic attempts to deal with global warming by capping industrial emissions could be "deadly" to the oil, gas and coal industries.

With climate change legislation dead for the immediate future, Shimkus has turned his sights on EPA regulations that would achieve what the Democrats could not get legislatively: caps on carbon emissions.

He backed an amendment added to a catchall spending bill the House passed early in 2011 that would bar the EPA from using funds provided by the legislation to implement or enforce any regulations pertaining to the emission of greenhouse gases from stationary sources, such as power plants.

Shimkus supports opening Alaska's Arctic National Wildlife Refuge and the outer continental shelf to energy exploration. In mid-2008, when gas prices averaged $4 a gallon across the nation, Shimkus spoke on the issue almost daily on the House floor. "Let's explore for oil and gas, wind and solar," he said in June that year. "The great thing about the Republican policy is that we want everything, more of everything."

He is a backer of nuclear energy, and favors easing environmental restrictions on refineries and power plants. In the 109th Congress (2005-06), he pushed legislation to provide incentives for coal-to-liquid refineries that would benefit coal-producing areas. Shimkus said it was a "slap in the face" to Illinoisans when plans for a virtually emissions-free, state-of-the-art coal-fueled power plant were pulled by the Energy Department in 2008, citing rising costs. Called FutureGen, the plant would have been in Mattoon, in the neighboring 15th District, and Shimkus and other lawmakers have urged the Obama administration to make a renewed commitment. New plans announced in August 2010 proposed an amended version, coined FutureGen 2.0, that would create a clean-coal repowering program and carbon dioxide storage network, retrofitting an established plant in Meredosia, in the 18th. Shimkus, co-chairman of the Congressional Coal Caucus, wasn't impressed. "I don't mind what they are doing now, but they cannot label it as FutureGen," he said.

Shimkus is a West Point graduate and retired Army Reserve lieutenant colonel who was an unwavering supporter of President George W. Bush's conduct of the Iraq War. Representing a chunk of southern Illinois, he considers himself a "pro-life Christian" and typically backs his party, siding with Republicans 96 percent of the time on votes in which a majority of the two parties diverged in 2010.

He called the Democrats' health care overhaul an "unmitigated disaster" and walked out during President Obama's September 2009 address to Congress on the issue, frustrated at the lack of bipartisanship. From his senior position on Energy and Commerce, he hopes to work to repeal or defund the law, or at least team up with disgruntled Democrats on amending it.

He co-chairs the 50-member E911 Caucus, which seeks to strengthen the nation's 911 emergency system and in 2007 helped secure first-time funding of $5 million for a Commerce Department agency to make matching grants to ensure that 911 call centers can locate emergency calls from mobile phones.

Shimkus is of Lithuanian ancestry — he co-founded the House Baltic Caucus — and grew up in Collinsville. His father worked at a local telephone company for 50 years while his mother was at home rearing seven children. In college, Shimkus played junior varsity baseball at West Point. He is still active, playing paddleball and basketball in the House gym, in addition to pitching for the GOP baseball team.

He served in the Army from 1980 to 1986, then returned to Collinsville to teach high school history and government.

Shimkus won his first election to the Collinsville Township Board of Trustees in 1989 and went on to be Madison County treasurer. In 1992, he challenged Democratic Rep. Richard J. Durbin, who had represented the 20th District for 10 years, and lost. When Durbin was elected to the Senate in 1996, Shimkus was ready to try again. In the general election, he faced state Rep. Jay C. Hoffman and won by 1,238 votes.

In 2002, reapportionment cost Illinois one of its House seats, and Shimkus and Democrat David Phelps ran against each other in the new 19th District. District demographics favored Shimkus, and he won the incumbent-vs.-incumbent match by almost 10 percentage points. He was re-elected in 2004 with more than two-thirds of the vote.

As chairman of the three-member board that oversees the House's high school page program, he found himself in the middle of a 2006 uproar over sexually oriented "instant messages" sent to former male pages by Republican Rep. Mark Foley of Florida. The incident embarrassed Shimkus and forced Foley to resign, but Shimkus was re-elected in 2008 with 65 percent of the vote and took 71 percent in 2010.

Key Votes

2010

Vote	
Overhaul the nation's health insurance system	NO
Allow for repeal of "don't ask, don't tell"	NO
Overhaul financial services industry regulation	NO
Limit use of new Afghanistan War funds to troop withdrawal activities	NO
Change oversight of offshore drilling and lift oil spill liability cap	NO
Provide a path to legal status for some children of illegal immigrants	NO
Extend Bush-era income tax cuts for two years	YES

2009

Vote	
Expand the Children's Health Insurance Program	NO
Provide $787 billion in tax cuts and spending increases to stimulate the economy	NO
Allow bankruptcy judges to modify certain primary-residence mortgages	NO
Create a cap-and-trade system to limit greenhouse gas emissions	NO
Provide $2 billion for the "cash for clunkers" program	YES
Establish the government as the sole provider of student loans	NO
Restrict federally funded insurance coverage for abortions in health care overhaul	YES

CQ Vote Studies

	PARTY UNITY		PRESIDENTIAL SUPPORT	
	SUPPORT	OPPOSE	SUPPORT	OPPOSE
2010	96%	4%	31%	69%
2009	92%	8%	35%	65%
2008	94%	6%	71%	29%
2007	89%	11%	70%	30%
2006	93%	7%	92%	8%

Interest Groups

	AFL-CIO	ADA	CCUS	ACU
2010	7%	0%	88%	96%
2009	24%	5%	73%	92%
2008	8%	20%	88%	91%
2007	38%	15%	85%	84%
2006	29%	0%	93%	83%

Illinois 19

South — southern rural counties; part of Springfield

The 19th sprawls across southern Illinois, meandering over all or part of 30 counties to create the largest congressional district in the state. The district reaches from Springfield, in central Illinois, south to Metropolis, which borders Kentucky. In the east, it reaches from the Ohio River in Gallatin, Hardin, Pope and Massac counties across the state to the Mississippi River in Jersey and Madison counties.

The 19th's part of Madison County contains more than 20 percent of the district's population, and its piece of Sangamon County (Springfield) holds 11 percent.

The rest of the population is spread widely across the remaining counties. Pope County, the state's second-least populous, is partly within the Shawnee National Forest.

The northern counties cover typical Midwestern country — acres of corn and soybean fields dotted by small towns. The southern half, however, looks more like Appalachia than Midwestern prairie. The hilly, forested counties here hold rich deposits of coal and once were one of the nation's chief coal mining regions. Despite periodic upticks in mining, the economy is driven by manufacturing and agriculture.

Factory jobs account for most employment in Madison County's Edwardsville, Collinsville, Glen Carbon and Godfrey, but job losses have hurt the county. Edwardsville hosts a Southern Illinois University campus, while state government, the University of Illinois-Springfield and the Southern Illinois University Medical School (in the nearby 17th) sustain the state capital of Springfield in Sangamon County.

The 19th has a historically conservative past and has voted for the GOP candidate in the last three presidential elections. In 2008, Republican John McCain won a statewide-high 54 percent in the district, and only the 19th's portion of Gallatin County supported Barack Obama.

Major Industry
Agriculture, manufacturing, food products

Cities
Springfield (pt.), 28,853; Edwardsville (pt.), 24,280; Collinsville (pt.), 22,534

Notable
Metropolis was declared the official hometown of Superman in 1972.

INDIANA

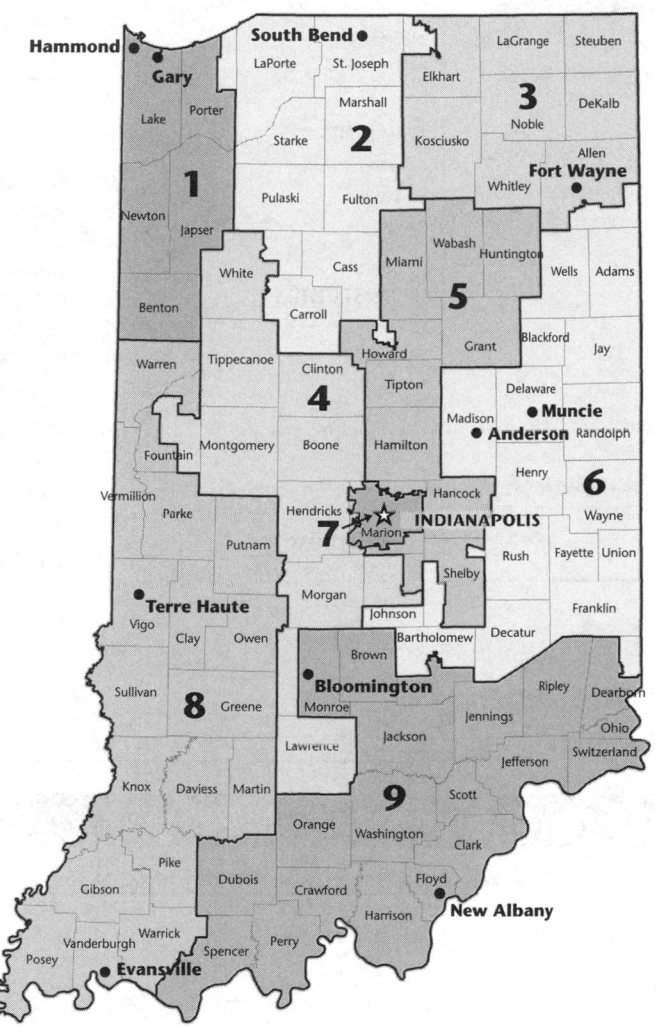

Gov. Mitch Daniels (R)

First elected: 2004

Length of term: 4 years

Term expires: 1/13

Salary: $95,000

Phone: (317) 232-4567

Residence: Indianapolis

Born: April 7, 1949; Monongahela, Pa.

Religion: Presbyterian

Family: Wife, Cheri Daniels; four children

Education: Princeton U., A.B. 1971 (urban studies); Indiana U., attended 1975-76 (law); Georgetown U., J.D. 1979

Career: Pharmaceutical company executive; public policy institute executive; lawyer; White House aide; congressional and campaign aide; mayoral aide

Political highlights: U.S. Office of Management and Budget director, 2001-03

ELECTION RESULTS

2008 GENERAL

Mitch Daniels (R)	1,563,885	57.8%
Jill Long Thompson (D)	1,082,463	40.0%
Andy Horning (LIBERT)	57,376	2.1%

Lt. Gov. Rebecca Skillman (R)

First elected: 2004

Length of term: 4 years

Term expires: 1/13

Salary: $79,192

Phone: (317) 232-4545

LEGISLATURE

General Assembly: January-April in odd-numbered years; January-March in even-numbered years

Senate: 50 members, 4-year terms

2011 ratios: 37 R, 13 D; 39 men, 11 women

Salary: $22,616

Phone: (317) 232-9400

House: 100 members, 2-year terms

2011 ratios: 60 R, 40 D; 80 men, 20 women

Salary: $22,616

Phone: (317) 232-9600

TERM LIMITS

Governor: 2 terms

Senate: No

House: No

URBAN STATISTICS

CITY	POPULATION
Indianapolis	829,718
Fort Wayne	253,691
Evansville	117,429
South Bend	101,168
Hammond	80,830

REGISTERED VOTERS

Voters do not register by party.

POPULATION

2010 population	6,483,802
2000 population	6,080,485
1990 population	5,544,159
Percent change (2000-2010)	+6.6%
Rank among states (2010)	15
Median age	36.4
Born in state	68.5%
Foreign born	4.0%
Violent crime	333/100,000
Poverty level	14.4%
Federal workers	46,627
Military	3,108

ELECTIONS

STATE ELECTION OFFICIAL

(317) 232-3939

DEMOCRATIC PARTY

(317) 231-7100

REPUBLICAN PARTY

(317) 635-7561

MISCELLANEOUS

Web: www.indiana.gov

Capital: Indianapolis

U.S. CONGRESS

Senate: 2 Republicans

House: 6 Republicans, 3 Democrats

2010 Census Statistics by District

District	2008 Vote for President Obama	McCain	White	Black	Asian	Hispanic	Median Income	White Collar	Blue Collar	Service Industry	Over 64	Under 18	College Education	Rural	Sq. Miles
1	62%	37%	65%	18%	1%	14%	$50,736	54%	29%	17%	13%	26%	19%	13%	2,209
2	54	45	80	9	1	8	44,438	51	33	16	13	25	19	27	3,679
3	43	56	84	6	2	7	48,729	53	33	14	12	27	21	35	3,240
4	43	56	88	3	2	5	53,944	58	26	15	12	25	25	32	4,016
5	40	59	88	4	3	3	61,207	66	21	14	12	26	35	26	3,266
6	46	52	91	4	1	2	43,754	51	31	17	15	24	17	41	5,550
7	71	28	53	32	2	11	38,654	57	24	19	11	26	23	0	262
8	47	51	91	4	1	2	43,599	51	31	17	14	23	17	42	7,042
9	48	50	91	3	2	3	44,735	52	32	16	13	23	19	48	6,603
STATE	50	49	82	9	2	6	47,465	55	29	16	13	25	22	29	35,867
U.S.	53	46	64	12	5	16	51,425	60	23	17	13	25	28	21	3,537,438

Sen. Richard G. Lugar (R)

Capitol Office
224-4814
lugar.senate.gov
306 Hart Bldg. 20510-1401; fax 228-0360

Committees
Agriculture, Nutrition & Forestry
Foreign Relations - Ranking Member

Residence
Indianapolis

Born
April 4, 1932; Indianapolis, Ind.

Religion
Methodist

Family
Wife, Charlene Lugar; four children

Education
Denison U., B.A. 1954; Oxford U., M.A. 1956 (Rhodes scholar)

Military Service
Navy, 1957-60

Career
Manufacturing company executive; farm manager

Political Highlights
Indianapolis School Board, 1964-67; mayor of Indianapolis, 1968-75; Republican nominee for U.S. Senate, 1974; sought Republican nomination for president, 1996

ELECTION RESULTS

2006 GENERAL
Richard G. Lugar (R)	1,171,553	87.4%
Steve Osborne (LIBERT)	168,820	12.6%

2006 PRIMARY
Richard G. Lugar (R)	unopposed

Previous Winning Percentages
2000 (67%); 1994 (67%); 1988 (68%); 1982 (54%); 1976 (59%)

Elected 1976; 6th term

The serious and scholarly Lugar is the Senate's most senior Republican, commanding a level of respect accorded few lawmakers. Party polarization in the Senate, however, has left this pragmatic policy wonk in a lonely position in the center, and he has found working with the Democratic majority easier than bringing fellow Republicans on board.

Lugar, the chamber's elder statesman on diplomatic and national security issues, is often the sole Republican cosponsor of "bipartisan" legislation. He is close to the White House, thanks to longstanding relationships with both President Obama and Vice President Joseph R. Biden Jr. And as ranking member on the Foreign Relations Committee, he has also formed a close partnership with its chairman, John Kerry of Massachusetts.

"I've learned how to work in the Senate to bring about as broad a consensus on issues that I think are extremely important for our national security or for world security," Lugar told Gannett News Service in 2008. But his willingness to work across the aisle — reflecting both his practical ideology and his dogged desire to get things done — has increasingly distanced him from his own party's leadership, leaving him with less influence in the caucus.

One example: Lugar was the only Republican senator who came out immediately in support of a new strategic arms reduction treaty with Russia when it was signed in spring 2010, defying GOP leaders who preferred to hold out in an attempt to wring concessions from the administration. Although he is an undisputed expert on arms control, his siding with Democrats led many Republicans to turn to Jon Kyl of Arizona to head up their negotiations on the treaty, which replaces the START I treaty that expired in December 2009. With Lugar in the lead, the new treaty was ratified by the Senate in late December 2010.

Nuclear nonproliferation has long been Lugar's signature issue. He teamed in 1991 with Democrat Sam Nunn of Georgia to create a program to help countries of the former Soviet Union secure and dispose of weapons of mass destruction. Under the Nunn-Lugar program, 13,300 warheads have been deactivated. Starting in 2004, the program extended its reach beyond the former Soviet Union, helping destroy chemical weapons in Albania.

Thanks in large part to that landmark legislation, the Indiana Republican was nominated for the Nobel Peace Prize in 2000, and in 2008 the nonprofit Council for Excellence in Government named him one of the 25 great public servants of the past 25 years.

An arms-control-related trip to Russia in 2005 helped foster the relationship between Lugar and Obama, then a freshman senator. Obama subsequently worked with Lugar on nuclear weapons security, touting their efforts in a July 2008 presidential campaign ad.

In recent years, Lugar has also worked across the aisle to help pass a $7.5 billion aid package for Pakistan; a landmark civilian nuclear cooperation agreement with India; and a significant expansion in the efforts to fight AIDS, tuberculosis and malaria overseas. In the 110th Congress (2007-08), he partnered with then-Foreign Relations Chairman Biden to hold dozens of oversight hearings on Iraq, probing the U.S. effort there even as Lugar backed Bush's refusal to set a timetable for troop withdrawal.

Lugar signaled his independence in his early years in the Senate, pushing for faster moves toward democracy in South Africa and the Philippines in the 1980s, putting him at odds with President Ronald Reagan.

In 2010, he sided with Democrats in backing a failed measure to provide a path to legal status for certain illegal immigrant children.

He is a more reliable conservative when it comes to domestic and particularly fiscal issues. Lugar opposed Obama's $787 billion economic stimulus law. And although he supports expanding use of renewable energy, he opposed a cap-and-trade bill sponsored by Kerry and Connecticut independent Joseph I. Lieberman in 2010 because it "could add significant and perhaps debilitating expense to our already-fragile economy," he said.

Lugar instead introduced an energy bill that focused on creating incentives for states to generate electricity from "low carbon" sources. His bill quickly won support from fellow centrist Republicans Lisa Murkowski of Alaska and Lindsey Graham of South Carolina. Energy, to Lugar, is a top national security issue, given the geopolitical nature of oil-supply issues.

The six-term senator looks out for the interests of his home state as a member of the Agriculture, Nutrition and Forestry Committee, where he has tapped his own experience to shape policy. For more than half a century, he has run a 604-acre corn, soybean and walnut farm that belonged to his father.

Lugar was Agriculture chairman from 1995 to 2001, during which time he helped steer to enactment a sweeping 1996 reauthorization of agriculture programs that replaced New Deal-era crop subsidies and moved farmers toward a free-market system. But pressure from farmers prompted Congress in 2002 to undo most of the changes. Six years later, he was the only Senate conferee who did not sign the conference report reauthorizing the measure, agreeing with Bush that there was too much unneeded spending.

Food security and hunger are important priorities for Lugar, who has cited the crop subsidies paid to U.S. and European farmers as a major contributor to the global food crisis. In a floor statement in February 2009, he said that "a more focused effort on our part to join with other nations to increase yields, create economic opportunities for the rural poor and broaden agricultural knowledge could begin a new era in U.S. diplomacy."

The senator's constituent outreach is enhanced by a dedicated local staff, many of whom have been with him for much of his 30-plus years in office, a sign of the loyalty he has engendered in Indiana, where he is a virtual icon.

Lugar was sick often as a child, plagued by allergies and ear infections. He passed the time reading biographies and publishing a family newspaper on a toy printing press. He learned piano and cello at his mother's urging, and showed a flair for improvisation and composition. He was first in his class in high school and at Denison University, where he was student body co-president with his wife-to-be, Charlene Smeltzer. He later attended Oxford University as a Rhodes Scholar and served as a naval intelligence officer.

He first ran for office in 1963, winning a school board seat. He was elected mayor of Indianapolis in 1968 and went on to merge the city and surrounding Marion County into a single governmental unit. In 1974, a Watergate-dominated year, while running for the Senate with a reputation as "Richard Nixon's favorite mayor," Lugar came within a respectable 75,000 votes of Democratic incumbent Birch Bayh. In 1976, he handily defeated Democratic incumbent Vance Hartke, and he has been re-elected five times since. In 2006, he was the only senator granted a free ride to re-election, facing token opposition.

While some political observers speculated that may have been his final race, Lugar sounded like a candidate early in 2011, although he is not likely to have another cakewalk. Tea party and other conservative activists have targeted Lugar, and they have a high-profile challenger in state Treasurer Richard Mourdock.

Briefly considered as a vice presidential prospect in 1980, Lugar was stung again eight years later when the No. 2 spot on the GOP ticket went to the less-experienced junior senator from Indiana, Dan Quayle. Lugar made an abbreviated presidential run in 1996. Analysts said that it was doomed by a stiff campaign style and his complex policy speeches on international affairs.

Key Votes

2010

Pass budget reconciliation bill to modify overhauls of health care and federal student loan programs	NO
Proceed to disapproval resolution on EPA authority to regulate greenhouse gases	YES
Overhaul financial services industry regulation	NO
Limit debate to proceed to a bill to broaden campaign finance disclosure and reporting rules	NO
Limit debate on an extension of Bush-era income tax cuts for two years	YES
Limit debate on a bill to provide a path to legal status for some children of illegal immigrants	YES
Allow for a repeal of "don't ask, don't tell"	NO
Consent to ratification of a strategic arms reduction treaty with Russia	YES

2009

Prevent release of remaining financial industry bailout funds	NO
Make it easier for victims to sue for wage discrimination remedies	NO
Expand the Children's Health Insurance Program	YES
Limit debate on the economic stimulus measure	NO
Repeal District of Columbia firearms prohibitions and gun registration laws	NO
Limit debate on expansion of federal hate crimes law	YES
Strike funding for F-22 Raptor fighter jets	YES

CQ Vote Studies

	PARTY UNITY		PRESIDENTIAL SUPPORT	
	SUPPORT	OPPOSE	SUPPORT	OPPOSE
2010	84%	16%	55%	45%
2009	73%	27%	68%	32%
2008	81%	19%	87%	13%
2007	67%	33%	78%	22%
2006	82%	18%	91%	9%
2005	84%	16%	84%	16%
2004	94%	6%	93%	7%
2003	97%	3%	98%	2%
2002	91%	9%	100%	0%
2001	92%	8%	100%	0%

Interest Groups

	AFL-CIO	ADA	CCUS	ACU
2010	20%	25%	100%	71%
2009	33%	35%	86%	68%
2008	20%	25%	100%	63%
2007	32%	45%	91%	60%
2006	20%	15%	100%	64%
2005	21%	10%	100%	88%
2004	8%	20%	100%	84%
2003	0%	10%	96%	80%
2002	31%	5%	95%	90%
2001	13%	15%	100%	92%

Sen. Dan Coats (R)

Capitol Office
224-5623
coats.senate.gov
493 Russell Bldg. 20510-1404; fax 228-1377

Committees
Appropriations
Energy & Natural Resources
Select Intelligence
Joint Economic

Residence
Indianapolis

Born
May 16, 1943; Jackson, Mich.

Religion
Presbyterian

Family
Wife, Marsha Coats; three children

Education
Wheaton College, B.A. 1965 (political science);
Indiana U., Indianapolis, J.D. 1972

Military Service
Army Corps of Engineers, 1966-68

Career
Lobbyist; congressional district aide; lawyer

Political Highlights
U.S. House, 1981-89; U.S. Senate, 1989-99; U.S. ambassador to Germany, 2001-05

ELECTION RESULTS

2010 GENERAL

Dan Coats (R)	952,116	54.6%
Brad Ellsworth (D)	697,775	40.0%
Rebecca Sink-Burris (LIBERT)	94,330	5.4%

2010 PRIMARY

Dan Coats (R)	217,225	39.5%
Marlin Stutzman (R)	160,981	29.2%
John Hostettler (R)	124,494	22.6%
Don Bates Jr. (R)	24,664	4.5%
Richard Behney (R)	23,005	4.2%

Previous Winning Percentages
1992 (57%); 1990 (54%); 1988 House Election (62%); 1986 House Election (70%); 1984 House Election (61%); 1984 House Election (61%); 1982 House Election (64%); 1980 House Election (61%)

Elected 2010; 2nd full term

Also served 1989-99

Coats has been a fixture in Indiana politics for much of the past three decades. Starting as a congressional aide, he went on to the House, the Senate and a stint as an elder statesman. Returning to the Senate in 2011, he brings to the job a conservative outlook and a wealth of experience on national security matters.

Coats served on the Armed Services and Intelligence committees during his 1990s tenure in the Senate. Since then he has served as U.S. ambassador to Germany and spent time as a lobbyist. That experience is "something I'll be able to employ to address the critical national security issues we face from day one," he said.

He returns to the Intelligence panel in the 112th Congress (2011-12), and also serves on three Appropriations subcommittees: Defense, Military Construction-Veterans Affairs and Homeland Security. He is ranking Republican on the Homeland panel.

Coats opposes what he refers to as the Obama administration's "nice diplomacy" approach in the Middle East and says he will pursue sanctions to prevent Iran from developing nuclear weapons. If such sanctions fail to persuade the leaders in Tehran to abandon their nuclear weapons program, Coats says, the White House should consider a military strike against Iranian nuclear facilities.

Coats' conservatism is evident on most other issues, as well. He wants to halt the funding of any new federal programs as a starting point to bringing the budget into balance. He says that at current levels, federal spending is adding to the growing number of problems that future generations must address.

"I want to be a central part of the effort to change the culture of that committee from a spending committee to a spending-reduction committee," he told the Fort Wayne Journal Gazette about his Appropriations assignment.

Coats was a co-author of the Clinton-era line item veto law that was declared unconstitutional by the Supreme Court. He joined an effort early in 2011 to revisit the issue, backing so-called enhanced rescission authority for the president that would give Congress the final say on spending items and thus get around the constitutional objections to a presidential line-item veto.

"This is people from both parties, individuals from both parties, that have said, 'We are in serious fiscal straits and we need to look at those tools which will help us work through this process of getting our house back and on a fiscally-sound setting,'" Coats said.

He voted to repeal the Democrats' health care overhaul and favors replacing it with market-based changes, including overhauling the medical liability system. "I think this package is unmanageable and fatally flawed," he said during a campaign stop in Terre Haute in July 2010.

Coats used the occasion of an Energy and Natural Resources Committee hearing in February 2011 to tell Energy Secretary Steven Chu that his department's budget is a prime candidate as lawmakers look for ways to cut spending.

"I think the handwriting's on the wall that there are a lot of things we would like to do but we're not able to afford to do them," Coats said.

The son of a legal immigrant, Coats favors expedited deportation of people found to be in the country illegally, reimbursing states for the costs of incarcerating violators and prohibiting the payment of federal benefits to illegal immigrants. Coats also favors hiring additional immigration officers, increasing penalties for individuals who smuggle undocumented workers into the country and bolstering programs for worker verification.

Throughout his career, Coats has been a champion of the anti-abortion movement. One of the most memorable moments in his previous congressional tenure came in 1993, during Senate committee consideration of a measure that would provide a federal statutory guarantee of the right to an abortion.

When Iowa Democrat Tom Harkin said, "We wouldn't be here if women represented half the Supreme Court. Abortions do not happen to men, they happen to women," Coats replied, "And children."

But Coats was the first Republican to express interest in some of the changes in Senate rules proposed by Democrats at the start of the 112th Congress. "I'm just trying to get a more transparent process in place that keeps minority rights but also allows the majority to move," Coats told Roll Call shortly after Election Day.

Coats was born in Jackson, Mich., where his father was a salesman and his mother, a Swedish immigrant, stayed at home with her only child. After a stint in the Vietnam-era Army — he served in the Corps of Engineers — he studied law at the Indianapolis campus of the Indiana University School of Law. He then went to work for an insurance company in Fort Wayne, where he met GOP Rep. Dan Quayle.

He went to work for Quayle as a district aide, then took the House seat when Quayle was elected to the Senate in 1980. When Quayle was elected vice president in 1988, Republican Gov. Robert D. Orr named Coats to take the Senate position.

In the special election held two years later, running to fill the remainder of Quayle's term, Coats faced state Rep. Baron P. Hill, at that time best known in the Hoosier State as a former high school basketball star. Hill proved to be an effective campaigner, but Coats was more in tune with the state's Republican leanings and triumphed with 54 percent of the vote. Hill eventually won election to the House in 1998; he was ousted in 2010.

In 1992, Coats bested Indiana Secretary of State Joseph H. Hogsett, a Democrat and close associate of Gov. Evan Bayh, by an even larger spread, taking 57 percent of the vote. Coats retired from the Senate in 1998 citing a self-imposed term limit — leaving the field to Bayh, who captured the seat that had been held by his father, Birch, until the elder Bayh's defeat by Quayle in 1980.

Coats was named ambassador to Germany by President George W. Bush in 2001, serving in that role until 2005. Bush also tapped him to shepherd — briefly — the quixotic Supreme Court nomination of White House counsel Harriet Miers in 2005. After that, Coats worked as a lobbyist, with a client list that included General Electric and Google.

Coats' entry into the Senate race in February 2010 was a surprise to many observers. Days after Coats joined the race, Bayh announced he would not seek re-election, withdrawing from the race too late to add a name to the primary ballot.

Democratic Party leaders selected Rep. Brad Ellsworth, a member of the fiscally conservative Blue Dog Coalition, from the southwest part of the state.

Coats' wide name recognition and conservative bona fides quickly made him the front-runner on the GOP side. State Sen. Marlin Stutzman — now a member of the House — became a favorite of tea party activists, but Coats' financial advantage and name recognition helped him top Stutzman and former Rep. John Hostettler in the GOP primary, taking 40 percent of the vote.

Coats led Ellsworth all year in polls, and on Election Day he decisively defeated the former Vanderburgh County sheriff by 15 percentage points, winning 84 of the state's 92 counties, including Vanderburgh.

Rep. Peter J. Visclosky (D)

Capitol Office
225-2461
www.house.gov/visclosky
2256 Rayburn Bldg. 20515-1401; fax 225-2493

Committees
Appropriations
Financial Services

Residence
Merrillville

Born
Aug. 13, 1949; Gary, Ind.

Religion
Roman Catholic

Family
Wife, Joanne Royce; two children

Education
Indiana U., Northwest, B.S. 1970 (accounting); U. of
Notre Dame, J.D. 1973; Georgetown U., LL.M. 1982

Career
Congressional aide; lawyer

Political Highlights
No previous office

ELECTION RESULTS

2010 GENERAL

Peter J. Visclosky (D)	99,387	58.6%
Mark Leyva (R)	65,558	38.6%
Jon Morris (LIBERT)	4,762	2.8%

2010 PRIMARY

Peter J. Visclosky (D)	unopposed

2008 GENERAL

Peter J. Visclosky (D)	199,954	70.9%
Mark Leyva (R)	76,647	27.2%
Jeff Duensing (LIBERT)	5,421	1.9%

Previous Winning Percentages
2006 (70%); 2004 (68%); 2002 (67%); 2000 (72%);
1998 (73%); 1996 (69%); 1994 (56%); 1992 (69%);
1990 (66%); 1988 (77%); 1986 (73%); 1984 (71%)

Elected 1984; 14th term

Visclosky relishes his nearly two-decade run on the Appropriations Committee, where he has been a roaring success at steering federal dollars to his northwest Indiana district. But his success in that role landed him at the center of an ethics investigation of earmarking practices, at least temporarily curbing his power.

Two other factors will weigh on his ability to deliver for the district: Democrats moving into the minority and a moratorium on earmarks.

When Democrats gained control of the House in 2007, Visclosky (vis-KLOSS-key) became a "cardinal," as the panel's subcommittee chairmen are called. He headed the Energy and Water Development Subcommittee, which funds the Energy Department and politically popular water projects undertaken by the Army Corps of Engineers. He is now the Energy-Water panel's ranking member and also sits on the Defense and Financial Services subcommittees.

Visclosky has capitalized on his Appropriations Committee post to set aside tens of millions of dollars for projects and programs in his district and state. But his proclivity for earmarking drew him unwelcome attention in early 2009 when news reports revealed he was the top recipient of contributions from the family of Paul Magliocchetti, founder of The PMA Group. The now-defunct lobbying group specialized in earning its clients defense contracts but came under investigation for its campaign contributions. Magliocchetti and nine of his relatives gave $138,500 to Visclosky's campaign committee and his leadership political action committee, Calumet PAC, between 2000 and 2008. Magliocchetti is a former Appropriations aide who, when assembling his business, hired former top aides to Visclosky and Virginia Democrat James P. Moran.

Visclosky stayed quiet during the probe, although he did push back against Republican efforts to force the House Ethics Committee to conduct a probe into an alleged connection between PMA's campaign contributions and the earmarking process. He also said he would return the contributions. After a federal grand jury subpoenaed records from Visclosky's congressional and campaign offices, he announced he would step aside temporarily and allow the congressman next in line, Arizona Democrat Ed Pastor, to manage the fiscal 2010 Energy-Water spending bill. He did not even attend the panel's consideration of the legislation in July 2010. With Democrats in the minority in the 112th Congress (2011-12), Visclosky reclaimed the top Democratic spot, albeit as ranking member.

Magliocchetti was indicted in August 2010 for allegedly coordinating illegal campaign contributions and making false statements. His son, Mark, pleaded guilty to making illegal corporate campaign contributions at his father's behest. Visclosky was cleared by the Ethics Committee of charges that he exchanged earmarks for campaign contributions.

The controversy threw Visclosky into the national spotlight he had worked assiduously to avoid. His floor speeches are typically brief tributes to individuals or groups in his district, and his name seldom appears in the national news media. Visclosky's low-key approach should not be confused with a lack of determination. He showed early on in his chairmanship that the Energy Department could expect a focused watchdog as its funding overseer. "Since the history of cost estimates is so incredibly rotten, how would you suggest Congress evaluate major projects?" he asked Energy Secretary Samuel W. Bodman at a hearing in March 2007.

As chairman, he worked to direct funds in the fiscal 2009 Energy-Water spending bill toward renewable-energy and water infrastructure programs, while pushing to sharply cut various nuclear weapons initiatives. He didn't play a public role in writing the fiscal 2010 or 2011 measures.

Visclosky has battled with presidents — both Democratic and Republican — who he believes haven't done enough to protect the domestic steel industry from unfair foreign competition. As the son of an ironworker and as chairman of the Congressional Steel Caucus, he fights to revive the flagging domestic steel industry, still a major economic engine of his northwestern Indiana district. He supported efforts to include "buy American" provisions in President Obama's $787 billion economic stimulus.

Visclosky is generally a reliable vote for his party, but he breaks with leadership on some budgetary matters. In fall 2008, he opposed both versions of the $700 billion legislation to aid the nation's ailing financial sector, saying it was "in essence a blank check" with no concrete plan for how the money would be used. (He did back a subsequent failed proposal to rescue domestic automakers.)

And he was one of 44 House Democrats to oppose legislation in 2009 that would create a cap-and-trade system for limiting greenhouse gas emissions. "Climate change is real," Visclosky said, calling it "a serious problem that threatens our way of life." But he voted no because the legislation "leaves no margin of error as it relates to jobs in the domestic steel industry."

As a teenager, Visclosky aspired to the priesthood. But he dropped out of a Roman Catholic seminary at age 15 and earned degrees at two Catholic institutions, the University of Notre Dame and Georgetown University. Despite a passion for history, he made the practical decision to pursue an accounting degree. After graduating from Notre Dame law school in 1973, he linked his fortunes to those of Adam Benjamin Jr., then a state senator and rising political star in Indiana. Visclosky coordinated Benjamin's successful campaign for Congress in 1976 and served as one of his top aides in Washington for nearly six years. When Benjamin died in September 1982, Democrats were without a candidate for the November election. First District Democratic Party Chairman Richard G. Hatcher chose Katie Hall, a state senator and loyal ally, as the nominee. She won the seat easily.

In 1984, Visclosky challenged Hall in the primary, putting on dozens of $2 "dog and bean" dinners to attract the young, the elderly and the unemployed. His "Slovak kid" background helped, as did the memory that older voters had of his father, John Visclosky, who had served as Gary's comptroller in the 1950s and its mayor in 1962 and 1963. Visclosky bested Hall by 2 percentage points, then swamped Republican Joseph B. Grenchik, the mayor of Whiting, in November. He has won handily since.

Key Votes

2010

Overhaul the nation's health insurance system	YES
Allow for repeal of "don't ask, don't tell"	YES
Overhaul financial services industry regulation	YES
Limit use of new Afghanistan War funds to troop withdrawal activities	NO
Change oversight of offshore drilling and lift oil spill liability cap	YES
Provide a path to legal status for some children of illegal immigrants	NO
Extend Bush-era income tax cuts for two years	NO

2009

Expand the Children's Health Insurance Program	YES
Provide $787 billion in tax cuts and spending increases to stimulate the economy	YES
Allow bankruptcy judges to modify certain primary-residence mortgages	YES
Create a cap-and-trade system to limit greenhouse gas emissions	NO
Provide $2 billion for the "cash for clunkers" program	YES
Establish the government as the sole provider of student loans	YES
Restrict federally funded insurance coverage for abortions in health care overhaul	NO

CQ Vote Studies

	PARTY UNITY		PRESIDENTIAL SUPPORT	
	SUPPORT	OPPOSE	SUPPORT	OPPOSE
2010	95%	5%	83%	17%
2009	97%	3%	93%	7%
2008	99%	1%	12%	88%
2007	98%	2%	4%	96%
2006	90%	10%	20%	80%

Interest Groups

	AFL-CIO	ADA	CCUS	ACU
2010	79%	95%	14%	4%
2009	90%	90%	47%	8%
2008	100%	80%	53%	8%
2007	96%	100%	50%	4%
2006	100%	100%	27%	12%

Indiana 1

Northwest — Gary, Hammond

A Rust Belt district bordered by Lake Michigan to the north and Illinois to the west, the Democratic 1st is home to steelworkers, a large union presence and some large minority populations in Lake County. Most of the 1st's population is in Lake County, which includes Gary, where more than 80 percent of residents are black, and East Chicago, where more than half of the population is Hispanic. The 1st also is home to many Eastern European ethnic neighborhoods.

In contrast to the farming that dominates other Indiana districts, the steel industry has been a mainstay in the 1st for decades. But decades of job losses in steel production and the heavy manufacturing that relies on steel continue despite some investment by giants U.S. Steel and ArcelorMittal. There are still thousands of steelworkers residing in Gary, Hammond and East Chicago, and more steel is produced here than in any other district in the nation, but local officials hope to lure non-industry employment.

Residents in and around Gary still struggle with the effects of unemployment, high crime rates and a rapidly shrinking population, and local lead-

ers now count on Lake Michigan-based tourism to lure people to the 1st. The region's lake boat gambling has brought in some jobs and attracted tourists, but has not countered the cutbacks and lower production in the steel industry and manufacturing. A stable health care sector may help prop up the region's economy as widespread job losses continue and the economy stalls.

The 1st generally supports Democratic candidates by large margins. There are GOP pockets in Lake County suburbs, but the northern cities are mostly Democratic. Lake County gave Democrat Barack Obama 67 percent of its 2008 presidential vote — his best county statewide — and despite some Republican support in growing Porter County and in farming communities farther south, the 1st overall gave Obama 62 percent.

Major Industry
Steel, health care, manufacturing, gambling

Cities
Hammond, 80,830; Gary, 80,294; Portage, 36,828; Merrillville, 35,246; Valparaiso (pt.), 31,145; East Chicago, 29,698; Schererville, 29,243

Notable
"A Christmas Story" is based on life in Hammond in the early 1940s.

Rep. Joe Donnelly (D)

Capitol Office
225-3915
donnelly.house.gov
1530 Longworth Bldg. 20515-1402; fax 225-6798

Committees
Financial Services
Veterans' Affairs

Residence
Granger

Born
Sept. 29, 1955; Queens, N.Y.

Religion
Roman Catholic

Family
Wife, Jill Donnelly; two children

Education
U. of Notre Dame, B.A. 1977 (government), J.D. 1981

Career
Customized office products company owner; lawyer

Political Highlights
Democratic nominee for Ind. Senate, 1990; Democratic nominee for U.S. House, 2004

ELECTION RESULTS

2010 GENERAL

Joe Donnelly (D)	91,341	48.2%
Jackie Walorski (R)	88,803	46.8%
Mark Vogel (D)	9,447	5.0%

2010 PRIMARY

Joe Donnelly (D)	unopposed

2008 GENERAL

Joe Donnelly (D)	187,416	67.1%
Luke Puckett (R)	84,455	30.2%
Mark Vogel (LIBERT)	7,475	2.7%

Previous Winning Percentages
2006 (54%)

Elected 2006; 3rd term

Donnelly is one of the most conservative Democrats in the House. But while considered a fiscal hawk, he also is a strong ally of organized labor, a combination born of his manufacturing-oriented district.

He has long prided himself on being an independent voter. "Since coming to Congress, I've pledged to put the needs of north central Indiana first," Donnelly said. He will have the entire state in his sights in 2012 as he runs for the Senate seat now held by Republican Richard G. Lugar.

In his first week in the House in 2007, Donnelly was one of four freshman Democrats to vote against a measure to lift restrictions on federally funded embryonic stem cell research, which uses discarded embryos created for in vitro fertilization. He also opposes gun control, abortion rights, same-sex marriage and a path to citizenship for illegal immigrants.

During the health care debate in the 111th Congress (2009-10), Donnelly was among the anti-abortion Democrats who at first stood firm in their insistence on tougher abortion funding restrictions. But he signed onto the bill after President Obama promised to sign an executive order that ensured no tax credits or cost-sharing reduction payments would be used for abortion-related services in the insurance exchange. It also ensured that federal community health center funding is subject to the Hyde Amendment, which bars federal funding of abortions. Critics called the executive order a fig leaf.

Donnelly is a member of the Blue Dog Coalition, a group of fiscally conservative Democrats who saw their number dwindle by two dozen in the 2010 midterm elections. With some of that group joining him, he opposed the bid by Speaker Nancy Pelosi of California to serve as minority leader in the 112th Congress (2011-12). He also voted for Democrat Heath Shuler of North Carolina, rather than Pelosi, for Speaker.

Early in 2011, he joined a dozen other Democrats in voting for an amendment added to a catchall spending bill for fiscal 2011 that would bar the EPA from using funds provided by the bill to implement or enforce regulations related to carbon emissions.

But when Pelosi needed him most, as in the health care vote, Donnelly was usually there in the 111th Congress.

A member of the Financial Services Committee, he backed the financial regulatory overhaul and won inclusion of three of his amendments in the final bill: a provision intended to ensure that an office created within the Securities Exchange Commission to regulate credit rating agencies is given enough staff and rulemaking authority to perform its duties, to prevent the FDIC from being used to purchase equity shares of troubled banks during a rescue attempt and to clarify that manufactured housing retailers are not subject to the proposed Consumer Financial Protection Agency's authority.

Donnelly is usually in step with his party on labor issues. He cosponsored a 2007 measure that increased the federal minimum wage from $5.15 an hour to $7.25. He opposed that year's Peru free-trade agreement and wants labor and environmental standards to be included in future trade agreements.

Also a member of the Veterans' Affairs Committee, he took over as the ranking Democrat on the panel's Oversight and Investigations Subcommittee in the 112th Congress. In 2010, a benefits bill signed into law by Obama included Donnelly's provision to increase supplemental coverage for veterans with 100 percent service-connected disabilities.

Donnelly grew up in Massapequa, N.Y., on Long Island, with one brother and three sisters. His mother died when he was 10, leaving his father, the manager of a printing shop in New York City, to raise five children. "My dad, for probably 50 years, got up in the morning, got on the train — hour and a half into work, hour and a half back from work — he worked like a dog every day. He set a wonderful example for his family and how a person should conduct themselves, and he let us know that we have an obligation to give back as well," he said.

He graduated from a Catholic high school, then went on to the University of Notre Dame for his undergraduate and law degrees. In college, he met his wife, Jill, and the two eventually settled in South Bend, where she grew up. Donnelly practiced law and became a member of the board of Mishawaka Marian High School.

His first stab at politics came in 1986, when he worked on the unsuccessful campaign of Democrat Thomas W. Ward, a candidate for what was then Indiana's 3rd District. He made an unsuccessful bid for state attorney general in 1988 before becoming a member of the State Election Board for a year. In 1990, he lost a bid for the state Senate.

Discouraged, Donnelly retreated from politics. He coached his kids' baseball and softball teams, and later opened an office supply business, splitting his time between his work as an attorney and developing his new business.

In 2004, Donnelly decided to try again. He challenged Rep. Chris Chocola, a conservative Republican in a district roughly split between the two parties. He lost again, by 10 percentage points.

In a rematch two years later, the political atmosphere was strikingly different. President George W. Bush's job approval ratings had plunged, and Donnelly dwelled on Chocola's frequent support for the president on House votes. Donnelly also was able to raise about twice as much money as he had two years earlier, and won the seat with 54 percent of the vote.

He had little trouble winning re-election in 2008, besting GOP businessman Luke Puckett with 67 percent of the vote.

In 2010, Donnelly faced an electorate that was in many ways the mirror image of the one that had elected him over Chocola in 2006 — unhappy with the incumbent president and ready to take it out on their representative. But unlike Chocola, Donnelly hung on, topping GOP state Rep. Jackie Walorski, who received an endorsement from former Alaska Gov. Sarah Palin, 48 percent to 47 percent. Libertarian Mark Vogel won 5 percent and might have saved Donnelly's seat.

His victory, in a year in which Hoosier Democrats suffered major losses, gave rise to speculation that Donnelly could mount a statewide race for governor or senator in 2012. He chose the Senate race.

Key Votes

2010

Overhaul the nation's health insurance system	YES
Allow for repeal of "don't ask, don't tell"	NO
Overhaul financial services industry regulation	YES
Limit use of new Afghanistan War funds to troop withdrawal activities	NO
Change oversight of offshore drilling and lift oil spill liability cap	NO
Provide a path to legal status for some children of illegal immigrants	NO
Extend Bush-era income tax cuts for two years	YES

2009

Expand the Children's Health Insurance Program	YES
Provide $787 billion in tax cuts and spending increases to stimulate the economy	YES
Allow bankruptcy judges to modify certain primary-residence mortgages	YES
Create a cap-and-trade system to limit greenhouse gas emissions	NO
Provide $2 billion for the "cash for clunkers" program	YES
Establish the government as the sole provider of student loans	YES
Restrict federally funded insurance coverage for abortions in health care overhaul	YES

CQ Vote Studies

	PARTY UNITY		PRESIDENTIAL SUPPORT	
	SUPPORT	OPPOSE	SUPPORT	OPPOSE
2010	73%	27%	76%	24%
2009	77%	23%	85%	15%
2008	79%	21%	25%	75%
2007	77%	23%	19%	81%

Interest Groups

	AFL-CIO	ADA	CCUS	ACU
2010	79%	60%	63%	25%
2009	81%	70%	53%	24%
2008	87%	70%	72%	28%
2007	88%	85%	60%	44%

Indiana 2

North central — South Bend, parts of Elkhart and Kokomo

The 2nd begins in Kokomo and moves north through small farming communities before reaching counties on the state's northern border, which include the cities of South Bend, Mishawaka and Elkhart and are home to nearly 30 percent of district residents.

South Bend, in St. Joseph County, is home to an ideologically and economically diverse population. The wealthy, white-collar, Catholic Notre Dame community that hosts faculty and professionals is joined by low-income, minority residents downtown, as well as blue-collar areas east of the city. The city has shed thousands of residents over the last decade even as neighboring Mishawaka experienced modest population growth. Michigan City's steel manufacturers along the shores of Lake Michigan in the district's northwest have led to a strong northern Democratic-leaning region.

East of Mishawaka, communities in Elkhart County (shared with the 3rd) round out the 2nd's heavily populated northeast. Farming and business in Elkhart create a faithfully conservative constituency. But Elkhart, a national center for the manufactured housing industry, was rocked by high unemployment rates, the collapse of local manufacturing industry and reduced demand for the recreational vehicles produced in the county. Kokomo (shared with the 5th) is another mainly white, blue-collar area; it relies on the struggling auto industry, and volatile markets cause concern for key local employers Delphi and Chrysler.

The once Republican-leaning U.S. House seat flipped to Democratic control in 2006, although the district remains competitive. LaPorte County gave Democrat Barack Obama his fifth-highest statewide percentage in the 2008 presidential election, and Obama won the district with 54 percent overall.

Major Industry
Manufacturing, higher education, agriculture

Cities
South Bend, 101,168; Mishawaka, 48,252; Elkhart (pt.), 47,025; Michigan City, 31,479

Notable
The World Whiffleball Championship is played every year in Mishawaka.

Rep. Marlin Stutzman (R)

Capitol Office
225-4436
stutzman.house.gov
1728 Longworth Bldg. 20515-1403; fax 225-3479

Committees
Agriculture
Budget
Veterans' Affairs
(Economic Opportunity - Chairman)

Residence
Howe

Born
Aug. 31, 1976; Sturgis, Mich.

Religion
Baptist

Family
Wife, Christy Stutzman; two children

Education
Glen Oaks Community College, attended 1999; Tri-State U., attended 2005-07

Career
Farmer; commercial trucking company owner

Political Highlights
Ind. House, 2003-09; Ind. Senate, 2009-10

ELECTION RESULTS

2010 GENERAL

Marlin Stutzman (R)	116,140	62.8%
Thomas Hayhurst (D)	61,267	33.1%
Scott Wise (D)	7,631	4.1%

Elected November 2010; 1st full term

Stutzman brings political experience and a bit of tea-party zeitgeist to Washington after almost eight years as a state legislator. A fourth-generation farmer and owner of a farm-trucking company, Stutzman's focus primarily lies with small business and agriculture, coupled with socially conservative values.

That's a good match with his northeast Indiana district, home to conservative farmers and medical device manufacturing companies.

"We will not take it from Washington anymore, and this adversity is causing us to wake up and take back our country," he told supporters on election night.

Stutzman's experience as a farmer and owner of a farm-trucking company made him a natural fit for the Agriculture Committee, which he called his No. 1 choice.

He has been critical of farm subsidies, while participating in the subsidy program. His family's operations have received just under $1 million in agricultural subsidies since 1995. Stutzman said he would prefer a system of crop insurance to protect farmers against losses. He got into a bit of trouble during the 2010 campaign when he said he had no choice but to accept the payments; the Department of Agriculture said that was not necessarily the case.

Stutzman describes many of Washington's problems — and, in turn, his solutions — as "full spectrum."

From his seat on the Budget Committee, he was highly critical of President Obama's fiscal 2012 spending blueprint.

"A budget that increases taxes on small businesses and job creators and runs a $1.6 trillion deficit will kill job growth and put America on the fast track to bankruptcy," he said.

He was among the 93 Republicans who backed an amendment to a catchall spending bill for fiscal 2011 that would have cut spending to fiscal 2006 levels.

The first bill he introduced would require the federal government to give priority to debt payments, Social Security benefits and military funding in the event that the debt limit is reached.

Stutzman's economic platform reflects his membership in the Republican Study Committee, the group of the most conservative House Republicans that comprises about two-thirds of the GOP Conference. Although he won considerable tea party support, he did not join the Tea Party Caucus.

To spur job creation Stutzman wants to lower taxes on businesses, eliminate taxes on capital gains, spend money on infrastructure and halt what he calls "market-killing schemes," such as cap-and-trade legislation aimed at restricting carbon emissions and the health care overhaul enacted in 2010. Ultimately, he would prefer to replace the income tax with a national sales tax.

Late in the 111th Congress (2009-10), he backed the compromise struck between President Obama and congressional Republican leaders that extended the Bush-era tax rates for two years for all income levels, although he would have preferred they be made permanent.

Early in the 112th Congress (2011-12), Stutzman voted to repeal the health care law and to bar the EPA from being able to spend money to enforce regulations pertaining to the emission of greenhouse gases.

During the campaign, he called the $787 billion economic stimulus enacted in early 2009 a "disaster," because it added to the debt, did little to revive the economy and allowed the government, rather than markets, to pick winners and losers.

Stutzman also stands to the right on social issues: He is anti-abortion and voted to bar federal funding for Planned Parenthood in the catchall spending bill the House passed in early 2011.

A member of the Veterans' Affairs Committee, he voted against legislation, signed into law by President Obama in late 2010, that repealed the statutory ban on gays and lesbians serving openly in the military. When he was in the Indiana General Assembly, he pushed for a measure banning same-sex marriage. He supports gun owners' rights; in the state House he won enactment of a 2006 law creating handgun permits that last for a gun owner's lifetime.

A Baptist, Stutzman has traveled extensively on mission trips, including to Russia, Haiti, Guatemala and Mexico.

Stutzman is one of the younger members of the House, but is not wanting in legislative experience. He was first elected to the Indiana House at the age of 26 and was the youngest member of the legislature until 2006.

He also worked for Republican Rep. Mark Souder's district office while serving in the legislature.

He was in the state House from 2003 to 2009, and then the Indiana Senate from 2009 until he was elected to Congress.

Stutzman's ascent to Congress was quick but less than straightforward, as he had two congressional campaigns for what were technically three races in 2009 and 2010.

He first sought to replace retiring Sen. Evan Bayh, a Democrat. He ran a respectable campaign against the much better known and party-backed former Sen. Dan Coats and former Rep. John Hostettler in the GOP primary, finishing second behind Coats. Some activists dubbed him the next "conservative rock star."

When Republican Rep. Mark Souder resigned in May 2010 after confessing to an extramarital affair, Stutzman joined the special election contest to succeed him. He won the party's nod through a crowded field of 15 contenders — party leaders chose the nominee because Souder's resignation came after the primary — and gathered tea party backing. He was helped by name recognition gained from his Senate race, and by being one of the few GOP candidates not from Fort Wayne or Allen County.

Stutzman simultaneously won both the special election and the race for a full term in the 112th Congress with almost 63 percent of the vote against Democrat Tom Hayhurst, a former Fort Wayne city councilman.

Winning the special election allowed Stutzman to be seated immediately, and he served out the remainder of Souder's term in the lame-duck session of the 111th Congress.

Key Votes

2010

Provide a path to legal status for some children of illegal immigrants	•
Extend Bush-era income tax cuts for two years	YES

CQ Vote Studies

	PARTY UNITY		PRESIDENTIAL SUPPORT	
	SUPPORT	OPPOSE	SUPPORT	OPPOSE
2010	100%	0%	25%	75%

Interest Groups

	AFL-CIO	ADA	CCUS	ACU
2010	0%		67%	100%

Northeast — Fort Wayne

While the manufacturing center located around Fort Wayne may drive the 3rd's economy, it is conservative farmers living across the vast agricultural land who influence local politics and make the district Republican.

Allen County (Fort Wayne) is the 3rd's population center, and both Fort Wayne and the district as a whole have experienced moderate growth in the last decade — nearly half of the district's population lives in the county.

Like other Midwestern cities, Fort Wayne has suffered from a downturn in the manufacturing industry, especially in the production of recreational vehicles and manufactured homes. Nevertheless, the 3rd remains a leading producer of orthopedic products, such as knee and hip replacement devices. Medical device manufacturing, health care technology and white-collar businesses, including financial services, have prevented the 3rd's economy from crumbling.

Fort Wayne has a rich entertainment history and attracts musical and theater performers to venues in the city. Educators and students visit Fort Wayne's Science Central, an interactive educational station that is recognized statewide and designed to help Indiana become a leader in science and math.

In the 3rd's northwest, particularly near Shipshewana, Indiana's Amish Country draws tourists each year. Various lakes throughout the district, including the state's deepest in Kosciusko County, become summer hotspots.

Despite union ties, social conservatism tends to have more influence over voters in the 3rd, and many district residents hold deep-rooted religious beliefs driven by traditional values. Rural voters, especially in Kosciusko County — which gave John McCain a statewide high of 68 percent in the 2008 presidential election — bolster the state's Republican leanings. McCain won the district as a whole with 56 percent.

Major Industry

Manufacturing, agriculture, health care

Cities

Fort Wayne (pt.), 250,606; Goshen (pt.), 28,777

Notable

Warsaw, which calls itself the Orthopedic Manufacturing Capital of the World, was home to the first orthopedic device manufacturer, established in 1895.

Rep. Todd Rokita (R)

Capitol Office
225-5037
rokita.house.gov
236 Cannon Bldg. 20515-1404; fax 226-0544

Committees
Budget
Education & the Workforce
House Administration

Residence
Indianapolis

Born
Feb. 9, 1970; Chicago, Ill.

Religion
Roman Catholic

Family
Wife, Kathy Rokita; two children

Education
Wabash College, B.A. 1992 (political science); Indiana
U., Indianapolis, J.D. 1995

Career
State government official; lawyer

Political Highlights
Ind. secretary of state, 2003-10

ELECTION RESULTS

2010 GENERAL

Todd Rokita (R)	138,732	68.6%
David Sanders (D)	53,167	26.3%
John Duncan (LIBERT)	10,423	5.2%

2010 PRIMARY

Todd Rokita (R)	36,411	42.4%
Brandt Hershman (R)	14,712	17.1%
R. Michael Young (R)	6,991	8.1%
Eric L. Wathen (R)	5,493	6.4%
Firefighter LaRon Keith (R)	3,549	4.1%
Charles E. Henderson (R)	3,531	4.1%
Jon Acton (R)	3,444	4.0%
Cheryl Denise Allen (R)	2,972	3.5%
Mike Campbell (R)	2,407	2.8%
James T. "Jim" Hass (R)	2,161	2.5%
Phillip J. "PJ" Steffen (R)	1,737	2.0%
Mark Seitz (R)	1,562	1.8%
Daniel L. Dunham (R)	981	1.1%

Elected 2010; 1st term

Rokita won a seat on the Budget Committee, where he can participate in what he calls the "adult conversation" needed to address the growing U.S. debt and overhaul the tax system.

His to-do list includes making the 2001 and 2003 tax cuts permanent, reducing the number of tax brackets, curbing debt-limit increases, and establishing presidential line-item veto authority.

A member of the Republican Study Committee, the caucus of the most conservative House GOP members, Rokita (ro-KEE-ta) was one of 93 Republicans who backed an amendment to a catchall spending bill for fiscal 2011 that would have cut spending to fiscal 2006 levels. His own amendments, to eliminate federal workers' pay raises and bar federal workers from performing union activities on the job, did not come up for a vote.

A veteran of state government — he served as Indiana's secretary of state from 2003 to 2010 and was deputy before that — Rokita oversaw implementation of Indiana's requirement that voters show a photo identification at polling places. He can put that experience to use on the House Administration Committee, which has jurisdiction over federal elections.

As secretary of state, he also pushed for changes in redistricting that would have made the highly partisan practice slightly less partisan.

Rokita parlayed his experience into a leadership role in the huge GOP freshman class. His peers elected him to the Republican Steering Committee, which handles committee assignments. He also serves on the Education and the Workforce Committee.

Rokita briefly flirted with a Senate candidacy in 2010, but when 4th District Republican Rep. Steve Buyer announced in January of that year that he was retiring, Rokita jumped into the race. Riding name recognition gained from having won statewide twice, he easily outdistanced a 13-candidate primary field that included state Sen. Brandt Hershman, an aide to Buyer, who had his former boss' support.

That all but settled the matter in the Republican stronghold. Rokita cruised to victory in November with almost 69 percent of the vote.

Indiana 4

West central — Indianapolis suburbs, Lafayette

The nearly 175-mile-long slender district takes in a mixture of farmland, small towns and suburbs. It spans from White County, which is roughly halfway between Chicago and Indianapolis, south to Lawrence County, which is about halfway between Indianapolis and Louisville.

Tippecanoe County takes in the 4th's largest metropolitan area — Lafayette and West Lafayette. The latter is home to the main campus of Purdue University, and its enrollment of more than 39,000 students. Known for its engineering school, Purdue grooms students to lead the district's influential manufacturing industry. The area's signature architecture and its historic neighborhoods make West Lafayette much more than a college town in the middle of expansive cornfields.

Montgomery, White (shared with the 2nd) and Boone counties, arrayed across the district's north near Tippecanoe, grow soybeans and corn. Moving south and east, the 4th cuts into a western sliver of Marion County (Indianapolis) and takes in Hendricks County suburbs west of the city and Johnson County suburbs as it curves south of the city. Johnson is filling up with young, well-educated families.

The remaining southern counties of the 4th consist of smaller farming communities similar to those found elsewhere across the state. The 4th's agriculture industry and rural areas make it Republican territory.

Major Industry
Higher education, agriculture, manufacturing

Cities
Lafayette, 67,140; Indianapolis (pt.), 50,988; Greenwood (pt.), 49,444

Notable
Then-governor, and later president, William Henry Harrison led troops against an American Indian force at Tippecanoe in 1811.

Rep. Dan Burton (R)

Capitol Office
225-2276
www.house.gov/burton
2308 Rayburn Bldg. 20515-1405; fax 225-0016

Committees
Foreign Affairs
(Europe & Eurasia - Chairman)
Oversight & Government Reform

Residence
Indianapolis

Born
June 21, 1938; Indianapolis, Ind.

Religion
Christian

Family
Wife, Samia Burton; four children

Education
Indiana U., attended 1958-59; Cincinnati Bible
Seminary, attended 1959-60

Military
Army, 1956-57; Army Reserve, 1957-62

Career
Real estate and insurance agent

Political Highlights
Ind. House, 1967-69; Ind. Senate, 1969-71; Republican
nominee for U.S. House, 1970; sought Republican
nomination for U.S. House, 1972; Ind. House, 1977-81;
Ind. Senate, 1981-83

ELECTION RESULTS

2010 GENERAL

Dan Burton (R)	146,899	62.1%
Tim Crawford (D)	60,024	25.4%
Richard Reid (LIBERT)	18,266	7.7%
Jesse C. Trueblood (I)	11,218	4.7%

2010 PRIMARY

Dan Burton (R)	32,769	29.7%
Luke Messer (R)	30,502	27.6%
Others	47,172	42.7%

2008 GENERAL

Dan Burton (R)	234,705	65.5%
Mary Etta Ruley (D)	123,357	34.4%

Previous Winning Percentages
2006 (65%); 2004 (72%); 2002 (72%); 2000 (70%); 1998
(72%); 1996 (75%); 1994 (77%); 1992 (72%); 1990 (63%);
1988 (73%); 1986 (68%); 1984 (73%); 1982 (65%)

Elected 1982; 15th term

A conservative with humble roots, Burton has often been accused of getting too accustomed to the trappings of power during his nearly three decades in the House. But he doesn't care much about what the media or even his colleagues think, even those who share his ideological perspective. In his two most recent re-election campaigns, he faced stiff primary challenges but eked out victories.

When he eventually leaves the House, voluntarily or not, Burton will leave a strong conservative legacy. He was a co-founder in 1995 of the Conservative Action Team, now known as the Republican Study Committee, a group of the House's most conservative members. A year later, with North Carolina GOP Sen. Jesse Helms, he authored the law that codified the U.S. embargo against Cuba.

But Burton's career took a turn soon thereafter when he used his position at the time, chairman of the Government Reform Committee, to launch repeated investigations of President Bill Clinton. (He's now the No. 2 Republican on the Oversight and Government Reform panel, as it is currently known.) Burton tested the patience of colleagues by suggesting that Clinton presidential counsel Vincent W. Foster Jr., who committed suicide in 1994, was murdered. He raised eyebrows again when he decided to conduct his own investigation, literally in his own back yard. Assisted by a homicide detective, he fired a gun into what he would describe only as "a head-like object" — reportedly a pumpkin or watermelon — to see whether the sound could be heard at a distance. Winning no friends among Democrats (and few among Republicans), Burton called critics in the other party "squealing pigs."

Even so, Burton's seat was safe until a news report in 2007 revealed that he had consistently skipped House votes when they coincided with an annual celebrity golf tournament in Palm Springs, Calif. Burton says now that the story was overblown, that he no longer golfs and that he's consistently made more than 90 percent of House votes. Still, it was a key point of contention during his most recent primary campaign.

Days before the primary vote, The Indianapolis Star editorial board pleaded with Republican voters to defeat him, accusing Burton of "feasting on the perks that come with his status as a Washington insider."

Burton has long had a strained relationship with the media. The Star was among the outlets to report in 1998 that he had fathered a son out of wedlock in the early 1980s. But Burton broke with normal practice during his 2010 primary campaign by granting interviews and talking to reporters on the campaign trail. Questioned about his eroding support among local GOP officials, Burton told a Star reporter: "I wear this badge with great pride. I do what I believe is right for my constituents, and to the rest of 'em, good luck. The political bosses don't like me much."

In Washington, that would also be a fair assessment of Burton's standing with Republican leaders. He usually aligns himself with them on contentious votes — in the 111th Congress (2009-10) he sided with a majority of his party against a majority of Democrats 98 percent of the time — but he has gone his own way on certain issues.

Although thousands of employees of pharmaceutical giant Eli Lilly live in his district, Burton has sided with Democrats in their efforts to force down prescription drug prices. His stance stems from the days when his first wife was battling breast cancer (she died in 2002), and he met similarly afflicted patients who could not afford cancer-fighting drugs.

In a similar vein, since hearing of the 2009 suicide in Iraq of Army Specialist Chancellor Keesling, one of his constituents, Burton led an effort to persuade President Obama to drop a policy denying White House condolence letters to the families of soldiers who die by suicide. The president "ought to understand that the grieving families like the Keeslings deserve a letter," said Burton, who is chairman of the Foreign Affairs Subcommittee on Europe and Eurasia.

He has also helped direct millions of dollars in funding to the Indiana University Medical Center-based Christian Sarkine Autism Treatment Center, which is named after his autistic grandson.

Burton endured a difficult childhood. He says that his father regularly beat both him and his mother, and was eventually jailed for abuse. His family lived in hotels and trailer parks, and by the time he was 12, Burton had lived in 38 states, Mexico and Canada. "I never stopped worrying that Dad would come back after he got out of jail," he told People magazine in 1994.

After a stint in the Army and a couple years of college, Burton worked as an insurance agent. At the time, he considered himself an independent, but he often voted Democratic. In 1964, though, he read an interview with Norman Thomas, a socialist presidential candidate, who said that the Democratic Party was moving toward socialism. Burton says he looked at the Congressional Record and studied the legislation that Democrats were supporting. This led him to conclude that Thomas was correct: Burton called the local GOP and joined.

Two years later, at age 28, he won a seat in the state legislature. He served a total of 10 years there, with stints interrupted where he made unsuccessful congressional bids in 1970 and 1972. In 1982, he won the House seat he had been seeking and coasted to re-election each time until 2008.

That year, after the reports of his golf outings appeared, Marion County coroner John McGoff challenged Burton in the GOP primary. McGoff's strong showing — he lost by just 7 percentage points — inspired six primary opponents to join the 2010 race, including McGoff, who was eager for another crack at Burton.

Burton struggled in 2010 to secure votes in the Indianapolis area, picking up just 22 percent in Marion County, but was stronger in the counties north of the city. He garnered just 30 percent of the vote in the May 2010 primary, but the rest of the field split the remainder, with former state Rep. Luke Messer falling 2,263 votes short of toppling Burton.

Burton won easily in November, with 62 percent of the vote, but it was his lowest share of the general election total of his career.

Key Votes

2010

Overhaul the nation's health insurance system	NO
Allow for repeal of "don't ask, don't tell"	NO
Overhaul financial services industry regulation	NO
Limit use of new Afghanistan War funds to troop withdrawal activities	NO
Change oversight of offshore drilling and lift oil spill liability cap	NO
Provide a path to legal status for some children of illegal immigrants	NO
Extend Bush-era income tax cuts for two years	YES

2009

Expand the Children's Health Insurance Program	NO
Provide $787 billion in tax cuts and spending increases to stimulate the economy	NO
Allow bankruptcy judges to modify certain primary-residence mortgages	NO
Create a cap-and-trade system to limit greenhouse gas emissions	NO
Provide $2 billion for the "cash for clunkers" program	YES
Establish the government as the sole provider of student loans	NO
Restrict federally funded insurance coverage for abortions in health care overhaul	YES

CQ Vote Studies

	PARTY UNITY		PRESIDENTIAL SUPPORT	
	Support	Oppose	Support	Oppose
2010	98%	2%	26%	74%
2009	98%	2%	18%	82%
2008	99%	1%	77%	23%
2007	98%	2%	85%	15%
2006	96%	4%	91%	9%

Interest Groups

	AFL-CIO	ADA	CCUS	ACU
2010	7%	0%	100%	100%
2009	14%	5%	73%	96%
2008	7%	10%	89%	100%
2007	17%	10%	75%	96%
2006	21%	0%	92%	88%

Indiana 5

East central — part of Indianapolis and suburbs

Dominated by Indianapolis suburbanites and rural farmers, the 5th is Indiana's wealthiest district and is staunchly Republican turf. Although Hamilton, Hancock and the district's portion of Marion counties, which surround the state capital on three sides, make up a small percentage of the land area, nearly two-thirds of the 5th's population lives there.

The district's most affluent residents live in northern Indianapolis (Marion County) and in the Hamilton County suburbs of Carmel, Fishers and Noblesville.

Here, growing populations of white-collar workers bring median household incomes well above state and national averages. Hamilton and Hancock in particular have used a growing base of white-collar residents to boost income levels. Southeast of Indianapolis, the district takes in most of Shelby County and a chunk of northeastern Johnson County.

The northern part of the 5th includes small cities that are closer to Fort Wayne than Indianapolis and are much different from the district's sub-urban southern portion. These residents earn modest incomes from the area's stable farming industry, based mostly in corn, and from operating small businesses. Residents have been leaving the counties north of Hamilton for decades, however, and Grant and Wabash counties have been hit hard by sharp population declines. The 5th also takes in most of Howard County, including part of working-class Kokomo (shared with the 2nd) and all of Tipton County, where the manufacturing industry has struggled. Suburban Indianapolis residents have made the 5th into a solidly Republican district. While the rural communities are not as affluent as their suburban counterparts, they too support GOP candidates. Republican John McCain captured 59 percent of the district's 2008 presidential vote — his best showing in the state.

Major industry
Financial services, electronics, agriculture

Cities
Indianapolis (pt.), 159,952; Carmel, 79,191; Fishers, 76,794

Notable
Kokomo's Elwood Haynes Museum honors the local inventor who was among the first to build a gasoline-powered car; Fairmount hosts an annual James Dean Festival to honor their beloved rebel without a cause.

Rep. Mike Pence (R)

Capitol Office
225-3021
mikepence.house.gov
100 Cannon Bldg. 20515-1406; fax 225-3382

Committees
Foreign Affairs
Judiciary

Residence
Columbus

Born
June 7, 1959; Columbus, Ind.

Religion
Christian

Family
Wife, Karen Pence; three children

Education
Hanover College, B.A. 1981 (history); Indiana U., J.D. 1986

Career
Think tank president; lawyer; radio and television broadcaster

Political Highlights
Republican nominee for U.S. House, 1988, 1990

ELECTION RESULTS

2010 GENERAL

Mike Pence (R)	126,027	66.6%
Barry A. Welsh (D)	56,647	29.9%
T.J. Thompson (LIBERT)	6,635	3.5%

2010 PRIMARY

Mike Pence (R)	unopposed

2008 GENERAL

Mike Pence (R)	180,608	64.0%
Barry A. Welsh (D)	94,265	33.4%
George Holland (LIBERT)	7,539	2.7%

Previous Winning Percentages
2006 (60%); 2004 (67%); 2002 (64%); 2000 (51%)

Elected 2000; 6th term

A favorite of conservative activists, Pence has long wielded considerable ideological influence outside the Beltway. But just as he had begun to match that popularity with real power inside the halls of Congress, he gave it up and cast his gaze elsewhere.

In the 111th Congress (2009-10), Pence served as chairman of the Republican Study Committee, the influential caucus of GOP conservatives, and chairman of the House Republican Conference, the No. 3 position in the party leadership. He gave up both posts in the 112th Congress (2011-12), reportedly telling colleagues that he could not commit to serving a full term. Often mentioned as a potential 2012 presidential candidate, he announced early in 2011 that he would not seek the White House, and soon declared he would run for governor.

Pence has been an articulate spokesman in opposition to the policies of President Obama, just as he was when he believed President George W. Bush and his fellow Republicans had strayed from conservative principles.

"America is changing, and she is not changing for the better," he told a National Rifle Association convention in May 2010. "A nation conceived in liberty has come of age in bondage to big government."

Pence calls himself "a Christian, a conservative and a Republican, in that order." Putting conservative in front of Republican has caused him a few headaches during his House tenure.

Pence captured the conference chairman's job without opposition after the 2008 elections with the backing of Minority Leader John A. Boehner of Ohio — a reversal of their earlier relationship. Pence had challenged Boehner, now Speaker of the House, for the top GOP position in late 2006, losing by a whopping 168-27 tally. He failed to garner support even from most of the membership of the Republican Study Committee, despite coming off a two-year stint as chairman. Some groused he had made the party look bad before the elections with his focus on the GOP majority's lack of restraint on spending — "we did not just lose our majority, we lost our way," Pence said often.

But following that defeat, Pence maintained a cordial relationship with Boehner. Once ensconced in leadership, the former radio talk show host and media savvy communicator wasted little time outlining a communications strategy. He dispatched "tiger teams" to offer daily takes on issues on television and radio talk shows. He has pushed for increased use of blogs and other new media, a strategy that has proved effective in helping Republicans get their messages out on YouTube, Twitter and Facebook.

Pence can claim some credit for the earmark moratoriums Republicans declared for fiscal 2011 and 2012. He had sought in 2008 to persuade his colleagues to fight for a one-year moratorium on earmarks, the special projects appropriators tuck into bills for their home districts. When Republicans rejected Pence's plan, he took a pledge not to request any earmarks.

Just as he had with government expansion under Bush — the $400 billion-plus Medicare prescription drug bill, the No Child Left Behind education overhaul and both versions of $700 billion legislation aimed at rescuing ailing banks and automobile companies — Pence opposed Obama's major initiatives: the $787 billion stimulus bill, legislation aimed at reducing carbon emissions and the health care overhaul.

In early 2011 he voted to repeal the health care law and to defund it. A fervent foe of abortion, he also won adoption of his amendment to a catchall spending bill for fiscal 2011 that barred funding for Planned Parenthood.

But Pence has at times bewildered some conservatives. Now vice chairman of the Judiciary Subcommittee on the Constitution, he is a longtime backer of a so-called shield law that would bar reporters from being required to disclose the identity of confidential sources. Perhaps his furthest stray from orthodoxy came in 2006 when he proposed a comprehensive immigration bill that would have required illegal immigrants to leave the country but would have allowed them to eventually return and become eligible for U.S. citizenship.

Vice chairman of the Foreign Affairs Subcommittee on the Middle East and South Asia, he is a strong defender of Israel and has questioned the direction of Obama's Middle East policy. "I never thought I would live to see the day that an American administration would denounce the state of Israel for rebuilding Jerusalem," Pence said on the House floor in March 2010.

Pence grew up in Columbus, where his father ran a group of gas stations. The family was Irish Catholic and Democratic, and President John F. Kennedy was practically an icon. But Pence's political views changed after he joined an evangelical fellowship group at Hanover College. He met his wife, Karen, at an evangelical church service, where she was playing the guitar.

In 1988, at age 29, Pence challenged veteran Democratic Rep. Philip R. Sharp and lost by 6 percentage points. Two years later, Sharp won again, by almost 19 points. In the latter race, Pence ran a harshly negative campaign. He later repented with an article called "Confessions of a Negative Campaigner," in which he wrote, "It is wrong, quite simply, to squander a candidate's priceless moment in history, a moment in which he or she could have brought critical issues before the citizenry, on partisan bickering."

It was during that period that conservative commentator Rush Limbaugh captured Pence's imagination. Pence's first radio show aired in 1989 in Rushville. He eventually built up a syndicated talk show that was heard on 18 stations across Indiana, sometimes as Limbaugh's "warm-up act."

His years as a radio broadcaster and host of a public affairs television show in Indianapolis kept his name before the public. When he decided in 2000 to run for the seat of GOP Rep. David M. McIntosh, who ran unsuccessfully for governor, Pence easily beat five opponents in the primary. He then topped Democratic lawyer Bob Rock by 12 percentage points in November.

Democrats who controlled the remapping process after the 2000 census sought to bolster vulnerable Democratic Rep. Baron P. Hill in the neighboring 9th District. In shaping the new 6th, the Democrats gave Pence some of Hill's Republican-leaning rural territory. Pence won easily in 2002 and in every election since.

Key Votes

2010

Overhaul the nation's health insurance system	NO
Allow for repeal of "don't ask, don't tell"	NO
Overhaul financial services industry regulation	NO
Limit use of new Afghanistan War funds to troop withdrawal activities	NO
Change oversight of offshore drilling and lift oil spill liability cap	NO
Provide a path to legal status for some children of illegal immigrants	NO
Extend Bush-era income tax cuts for two years	NO

2009

Expand the Children's Health Insurance Program	NO
Provide $787 billion in tax cuts and spending increases to stimulate the economy	NO
Allow bankruptcy judges to modify certain primary-residence mortgages	NO
Create a cap-and-trade system to limit greenhouse gas emissions	NO
Provide $2 billion for the "cash for clunkers" program	NO
Establish the government as the sole provider of student loans	NO
Restrict federally funded insurance coverage for abortions in health care overhaul	YES

CQ Vote Studies

	PARTY UNITY		PRESIDENTIAL SUPPORT	
	SUPPORT	OPPOSE	SUPPORT	OPPOSE
2010	99%	1%	25%	75%
2009	99%	1%	12%	88%
2008	99%	1%	88%	12%
2007	98%	2%	92%	8%
2006	96%	4%	90%	10%

Interest Groups

	AFL-CIO	ADA	CCUS	ACU
2010	0%	5%	71%	100%
2009	5%	0%	73%	100%
2008	0%	5%	81%	100%
2007	8%	5%	74%	96%
2006	8%	15%	100%	100%

Indiana 6

East — Muncie, Anderson, Richmond

Covering most of Indiana's eastern border with Ohio, the 6th District combines a mix of farmland, midsize cities and suburban populations. The district's economy, anchored in Muncie, is driven by manufacturing, education and health care industries.

The auto industry has declined in the 6th, and widespread layoffs at other manufacturing interests have in turn hurt the economies of the district's most populous cities (Muncie and Anderson). But there has been some positive news, as Honda opened a new automobile plant in Decatur County in Greensburg in late 2008 and international gear maker Brevini opened its headquarters in Delaware County. Brevini, which makes parts for wind turbines, fits well in a region that has seen a recent surge of wind-power projects.

The 6th's largest cities also are its educational hubs. Muncie is home to Ball State University, and Anderson University is in nearby Anderson. The centerpiece of Anderson's revitalized downtown arts and culture center is the Paramount Theatre.

South and east of Muncie and Anderson, the 6th takes in Wayne and

Henry counties, which are still home to many older residents. This fertile land also hosts rich corn and soybean farms, as well as dairy silos and hog barns.

The 6th has a Democratic past that was fueled by its union population, but like most of rural Indiana, its residents now lean conservative. The district's overall percentage of residents over the age of 65 is the highest in the state at 15 percent. Democrat Barack Obama won Delaware (57 percent) and Madison (53 percent) counties, but Republican John McCain carried the other 17 counties wholly or partly in the 6th, earning 52 percent of the district's vote overall in 2008. Franklin County, in the district's south, and Wells County, near Fort Wayne, were among McCain's highest percentages statewide.

Major Industry
Auto manufacturing, agriculture, light manufacturing

Cities
Muncie, 70,085; Anderson, 56,129; Richmond, 36,812

Notable
The Wilbur Wright Birthplace and Museum is in Millville; the Academy of Model Aeronautics is located in Muncie; the Indiana Basketball Hall of Fame is in New Castle.

Rep. André Carson (D)

Capitol Office
225-4011
carson.house.gov
425 Cannon Bldg. 20515-1407; fax 225-5633

Committees
Financial Services

Residence
Indianapolis

Born
Oct. 16, 1974; Indianapolis, Ind.

Religion
Muslim

Family
Wife, Mariama Shaheed-Carson; one child

Education
Concordia U. Wisconsin, Indianapolis, B.A. 2003
(management of criminal justice); Indiana Wesleyan
U., M.S. 2005 (management)

Career
Marketing representative; state investigative agency
officer

Political Highlights
Indianapolis and Marion County City-County
Council, 2007-08

ELECTION RESULTS

2010 GENERAL

André Carson (D)	86,011	58.9%
Marvin B. Scott (R)	55,213	37.8%
Dav Wilson (LIBERT)	4,815	3.3%

2010 PRIMARY

André Carson (D)	26,364	89.0%
Bob Kern (D)	2,150	7.3%
Carl Kakasuleff (D)	737	2.5%
Pierre Quincy Pullins (D)	354	1.2%

2008 GENERAL

André Carson (D)	172,650	65.1%
Gabrielle Campo (R)	92,645	34.9%

Previous Winning Percentages
2008 Special Election (54%)

Elected 2008; 2nd full term

Like his district — which is home to major corporations and some of Indiana's most entrenched poverty — Carson has led a life of extremes. Neglected by his mother, he spent part of his pre-school days in a homeless shelter, only to be rescued by his maternal grandmother. Julia Carson, his grandmother, was a pioneering African-American politician who would go on to serve in the House and blaze the path her grandson would follow in succeeding her.

An outspoken liberal with a populist bent, Carson looks out for the working-class and poor minority residents of his urban district. But during his first full term, Carson devoted much of his time to defending President Obama's policies in a GOP-leaning state.

The 7th District was Obama's strongest in Indiana in 2008; he took 71 percent of the district vote but only narrowly won the state en route to defeating Arizona Republican Sen. John McCain for the presidency. But with the health care overhaul enacted by the Democrats in 2010 under heavy fire from the new Republican majority in the House, Republican Gov. Mitch Daniels and state Attorney General Greg Zoeller — who joined a lawsuit challenging the law — Carson has been its leading defender in the Hoosier State.

Carson became the subject of national attention when he said protestors had shouted racial slurs at him and two other black representatives amid the House debate on the measure in March 2010. And when the House voted in early 2011 to repeal the law, Carson called it "political theater at a time when the American people want progress."

Although he has defended the law, Carson doesn't see it as perfect. He was an early proponent of a government-run health insurance option, which would have competed with private sector insurers and — in Carson's view — kept the cost of insurance in check. In pushing the idea, Carson said he was standing up for the 18 percent of residents in his district without health insurance. He was also bucking WellPoint Inc., the nation's largest insurer, as well as drugmaker Eli Lilly and Co., both of which are headquartered in his district and opposed a public option.

Carson is no more sympathetic to big business when it comes to issues related to his seat on the Financial Services Committee.

In fall 2008, Carson defied his party and voted against a $700 billion plan to rescue the financial sector. Under heavy pressure from party leaders, he relented when the bill came up a second time.

But Carson got his way when the committee considered legislation to increase shareholder oversight of corporate spending on politics in July 2010. The panel adopted a Carson amendment that would hit company officers and directors with steep fines for failing to disclose the spending to shareholders. The panel approved the measure, but it never came up for a vote on the House floor.

Carson joined with colleagues in the Congressional Black Caucus, where he serves as whip, to include foreclosure prevention funding in a law revamping regulation of Wall Street that was enacted in the summer of 2010. And later in the year, Carson persuaded the committee to include an amendment to a proposed small-business lending fund that would require banks participating in the program to advertise the loans to women and minorities. He has proposed legislation that would allow ex-convicts to access federal disability and Medicaid benefits more quickly after their release than allowed under current law.

Carson's liberal political philosophy mirrors that of his grandmother, who took him in as a child when it became clear his mother could not care for him. Julia Carson died of lung cancer in December 2007, halfway through her sixth term.

Raised a Baptist, Carson considered entering the Catholic priesthood while attending parochial school, but was encouraged by a priest to study different faiths to be sure. He did so, reading "The Autobiography of Malcolm X" among other things, and eventually converted to Islam in the mid-1990s. He is one of two Muslims in Congress, along with Minnesota Democrat Keith Ellison. And he is one of the few members of Congress to express strong sympathy for the Palestinians in their conflict with Israel.

As a young man, Carson immersed himself in poetry, music and breakdancing to escape the crack cocaine culture sweeping across his Indianapolis neighborhood. He performed at local variety shows, rapping under the stage name "Juggernaut," with dreams of becoming a professional singer after graduating from Arsenal Technical High School.

His musical career didn't result in a major record deal. Carson eventually returned to school to study criminal justice while working as a state excise police officer, enforcing alcohol, tobacco and gambling laws. He graduated from the Indianapolis center of Concordia University Wisconsin in 2003. Three years later, he was named a liaison to the state's homeland security agency, working on such concerns as supremacist groups and terrorism threats.

His political career began in late 2007, when he was chosen to fill an open seat on the Indianapolis City-County Council. Less than seven months later, he ran to succeed his grandmother.

Carson spent the first few months of 2008 campaigning against Republican state Rep. Jon Elrod. Carson raised more than five times as much money as Elrod and won by 11 percentage points in the March special election.

With fewer than two months under his belt, he faced the regular Democratic primary for the next term. He ran against a large field that included state Reps. David Orentlicher and Carolene Mays, and Woodrow A. "Woody" Myers Jr., a former Indiana health commissioner. Myers, who also held private sector positions as a health director for Ford Motor Co. and chief medical officer for WellPoint, loaned his own campaign more than $1.6 million.

But Carson benefited from his popular last name and an endorsement from Obama. He won with 47 percent of the vote, nearly double that of any challenger. He crushed a little-known Republican, Gabrielle Campo, to hold the seat in November, taking more than 65 percent of the vote. He was re-elected in 2010 with 59 percent.

Key Votes

2010

Overhaul the nation's health insurance system	YES
Allow for repeal of "don't ask, don't tell"	YES
Overhaul financial services industry regulation	YES
Limit use of new Afghanistan War funds to troop withdrawal activities	NO
Change oversight of offshore drilling and lift oil spill liability cap	YES
Provide a path to legal status for some children of illegal immigrants	YES
Extend Bush-era income tax cuts for two years	YES

2009

Expand the Children's Health Insurance Program	YES
Provide $787 billion in tax cuts and spending increases to stimulate the economy	YES
Allow bankruptcy judges to modify certain primary-residence mortgages	YES
Create a cap-and-trade system to limit greenhouse gas emissions	YES
Provide $2 billion for the "cash for clunkers" program	YES
Establish the government as the sole provider of student loans	YES
Restrict federally funded insurance coverage for abortions in health care overhaul	NO

CQ Vote Studies

	PARTY UNITY		PRESIDENTIAL SUPPORT	
	SUPPORT	OPPOSE	SUPPORT	OPPOSE
2010	99%	1%	93%	7%
2009	99%	1%	97%	3%
2008	99%	1%	12%	88%

Interest Groups

	AFL-CIO	ADA	CCUS	ACU
2010	100%	90%	25%	0%
2009	100%	100%	33%	0%
2008	100%	75%	53%	4%

Indiana 7

Most of Indianapolis

The 7th, Indiana's smallest district in size, is the only one without a rural, farming identity. Despite the district's largely white-collar workforce, it has the state's lowest median household income and is overwhelmingly Democratic. The 7th has the state's highest percentage of black residents and the second-highest percentage of Hispanic residents.

More than three times bigger than Fort Wayne, the state's next-most-populous city, Indianapolis is Indiana's banking and commercial center. Manufacturing plays a role in the city's economy, with a few automotive plants hanging on despite industry downturns. The joint Indiana University-Purdue University at Indianapolis campus and Butler University make it a hub for higher education. Several large pharmaceutical and health care companies are located in Indianapolis, including Eli Lilly & Co., the district's largest employer.

Indianapolis also is home to the state's major professional sports teams: football's Colts and basketball's Pacers and Fever. Despite the teams' local support, the 7th's biggest pro sport is auto racing — the Indianapolis Motor Speedway hosts the annual Indianapolis 500 race.

Indianapolis also is home to the national headquarters of The American Legion, the largest veterans' organization in the world. The Soldiers' and Sailors' Monument, located in Monument Circle, complements a skyline graced by the state Capitol. The city has undergone considerable revitalization, particularly in the Fountain Square area.

Large minority populations in central Indianapolis form the 7th's core and the base of its strong Democratic support. In the city's northern tier, white-collar residents are some of the wealthiest in the state and are more receptive to Republican candidates. Democrat Barack Obama won the state in the 2008 presidential election despite capturing only two districts: The 7th gave him 71 percent of its presidential vote, 9 percentage points higher than he took in the 1st District.

Major Industry
Manufacturing, health care, higher education

Cities
Indianapolis (pt.), 609,505; Lawrence (pt.), 34,088

Notable
President Benjamin Harrison, poet James Whitcomb Riley, three vice presidents and 11 governors are buried in the Crown Hill cemetery.

Rep. Larry Bucshon (R)

Capitol Office
225-4636
bucshon.house.gov
1123 Longworth Bldg. 20515-1408; fax 225-3284

Committees
Education & the Workforce
Science, Space & Technology
Transportation & Infrastructure

Residence
Newburgh

Born
May 31, 1962; Taylorville, Ill.

Religion
Lutheran

Family
Wife, Kathryn Bucshon; four children

Education
U. of Illinois, B.S. 1984 (chemistry); U. of Illinois, Chicago, M.D. 1988

Military
Naval Reserve, 1989-98

Career
Surgeon

Political Highlights
No previous office

ELECTION RESULTS

2010 GENERAL

Larry Bucshon (R)	117,259	57.5%
Trent Van Haaften (D)	76,265	37.4%
John Cunningham (LIBERT)	10,240	5.0%

2010 PRIMARY

Larry Bucshon (R)	16,262	32.7%
Kristi Risk (R)	14,273	28.7%
John Lee Smith (R)	4,715	9.5%
Dan Stockton (R)	4,697	9.5%
Steve Westell (R)	4,324	8.7%
John K. Snyder (R)	2,523	5.1%
Bud Bernitt (R)	1,469	3.0%
Billy J. Mahoney (R)	1,410	2.8%

Elected 2010; 1st term

Bucshon, a heart surgeon and former lieutenant commander in the Naval Reserve, says he can put his training to good use in Congress, and not just on health care issues.

"Physicians are trained to evaluate data and come to good conclusions about what [solutions] we think are best for our patients," he told Roll Call in a pre-election interview.

His political philosophy reflects the meat and potatoes of the GOP platform.

"I'm a person that always believes in limited government, low taxation by government on business, and I'm a strong believer in the private sector and free-market economy," he said.

He voted to repeal the health care law enacted in 2010, an effort that is unlikely to get beyond the House. But, as a member of the Education and the Workforce Committee, he'll play a role in GOP efforts to withhold funding for the law and dismantle it piecemeal.

A member of the Science, Space and Technology Committee, he opposes Democratic efforts to create a cap-and-trade system designed to reduce carbon emissions. Bucshon backed an amendment to a catchall spending bill for fiscal 2011 that would bar the EPA from implementing or enforcing regulations related to such emissions. The coal industry is a major employer in the district.

On the Transportation and Infrastructure Committee, Bucshon will have a hand in writing a new surface transportation law. One of his priorities is likely to be securing funding for a bridge over the Ohio River that would link the proposed Indiana and Kentucky portions of Interstate 69.

By the time Rep. Brad Ellsworth announced in February 2010 that he was seeking the seat of retiring Democratic Sen. Evan Bayh, Bucshon was already in the House race.

He won an eight-way GOP primary with almost 33 percent of the vote, then had little trouble topping Democratic state Rep. Trent Van Haaften, winning by almost 20 percentage points.

Indiana 8
West — Evansville, Terre Haute

Indiana's southwest corner, formed by the converging Wabash and Ohio rivers, is home to the 8th, a district characterized by laborers and social conservatives. Evansville, an Ohio River port and the state's third-largest city, is southern Indiana's industrial center. It is located in Democratic-leaning Vanderburgh County, the district's most populous, and is home to the 8th's only substantial minority and liberal populations.

North of Evansville, the 8th takes on a more rural and culturally conservative flavor. Gibson and Knox counties are among Indiana's top corn-producing areas. This region also grows soybeans, wheat and various fruits and vegetables. Daviess County has a large Amish population.

Terre Haute, farther north in generally Democratic Vigo County, is the district's other manufacturing center. Terre Haute provides some Democratic votes from Indiana

State University's faculty and students, and Evansville is home to Southern Indiana and Evansville universities. Having refurbished its downtown, Evansville is trying to establish tourism revenue, and the Casino Aztar is docked on the Ohio River.

The district's manufacturing base and history as a mining center long gave Democrats an edge. Cultural issues moved the district to the right, but the two parties can split local elections. McCain won 51 percent of the 8th's 2008 presidential vote overall and took his second-highest percentage in the state in Daviess County.

Major Industry
Manufacturing, agriculture, higher education

Military Bases
Naval Surface Warfare Center, Crane Division, 26 military, 4,000 civilian (2009)

Cites
Evansville, 117,429; Terre Haute, 60,785

Notable
Vincennes is the oldest city in Indiana.

Rep. Todd Young (R)

Capitol Office
225-5315
toddyoung.house.gov
1721 Longworth Bldg. 20515-1409; fax 226-6866

Committees
Armed Services
Budget

Residence
Bloomington

Born
Aug. 24, 1972; Lancaster, Pa.

Religion
Christian

Family
Wife, Jennifer Young; four children

Education
U.S. Naval Academy, B.S. 1995 (political science);
U. of London, M.A. 2001 (United States studies); U. of
Chicago, M.B.A. 2002; Indiana U., Indianapolis, J.D. 2006

Military
Marine Corps, 1995-2000

Career
Lawyer; congressional aide; conservative think tank
aide

Political Highlights
No previous office

ELECTION RESULTS

2010 GENERAL

Todd Young (R)	118,040	52.3%
Baron P. Hill (D)	95,353	42.3%
Greg Knott (LIBERT)	12,070	5.4%

2010 PRIMARY

Todd Young (R)	19,141	34.6%
Travis Hankins (R)	17,909	32.3%
Mike Sodrel (R)	16,868	30.5%
Rick Warren (R)	1,453	2.6%

Elected 2010; 1st term

Young describes himself as a libertarian conservative in the manner of Ronald Reagan, and says that he has one goal as a legislator: to "get our balance sheet back in order as a country."

Young, a member of the Budget Committee, says that until Congress shrinks the federal government, the budget will remain his primary concern. "I think we need to very quickly embrace this issue and solve it as opposed to dancing around it and doing the Potomac two-step," Young said at a hearing on President Obama's budget early in the 112th Congress (2011-12).

Young is a Navy and Marine Corps veteran who sits on the Armed Services Committee, but says he is ready to look at defense spending in his quest to balance the books. "I'm not one of these legislators who, without pause, thinks we ought to ramp up our spending in the military," he said.

Young received a degree in political science from the Naval Academy, where he also played soccer. He went on to receive three more degrees: a master's from the University of London, an MBA from the University of Chicago and then a law degree from Indiana University-Indianapolis.

Young also has experience working on Capitol Hill; he was an energy and economic policy aide for Republican Sen. Richard G. Lugar, and counts the longtime Hoosier lawmaker as one of his political idols, citing particularly his ability to work with members of the other party. His other role model is former British Prime Minister Margaret Thatcher.

In 2010, Democrat Baron P. Hill sought a sixth term in Congress. Although known as a centrist, Hill had cast a number of votes in support of Obama's economic initiatives that made him a prime GOP target.

The primary could have given Hill what would have been a fifth consecutive match-up with former Republican Rep. Mike Sodrel, but Young narrowly won the four-candidate GOP primary.

The general election proved to be a battle, and included a Young advertisement featuring a nationally noted incident in which Hill scolded a college student who was trying to shoot a video during a town hall event. Young prevailed by 10 percentage points.

Indiana 9

Southeast — Bloomington, New Albany

Bordering the Ohio River to the south, the 9th shares a socially conservative lean with Indiana's other river valley district (the 8th). Manufacturing forms the economic foundation, although agriculture and retail trade also are prevalent. The district extends as far north as Monroe County to take in almost all of Bloomington.

Residents from Cincinnati and Ohio suburbs moved into the 9th's northeastern counties, creating a slightly more suburban feel to the largely rural area. To the southwest, Clark and Floyd counties grow in parallel to growth in the Louisville metropolitan area — more of the 9th's residents live in Clark than in any of the district's other 19 counties. Manufacturing, retail jobs and the health care sector in these areas have helped these counties. Elizabeth, in Harrison County west and south of Louisville, hosts a riverboat casino and resort that is a key employer in the region. Factories also provide jobs for residents of the small and midsize cities of the district, while corn and soybean fields occupy most of the rural landscape.

Bloomington is home to Indiana University, which gives Monroe County a Democratic lean. While the university helps make Monroe one of Indiana's best-educated counties, the 9th as a whole is more blue-collar with a lower percentage of college graduates. Despite the district's Democratic heritage, the area's social conservatism has propelled Republican candidates to victory.

Major Industry
Manufacturing, agriculture, retail

Cities
Bloomington (pt.), 78,306; Jeffersonville, 44,953; New Albany, 36,372

Notable
The 1954 Milan High School basketball team inspired the movie "Hoosiers."

IOWA

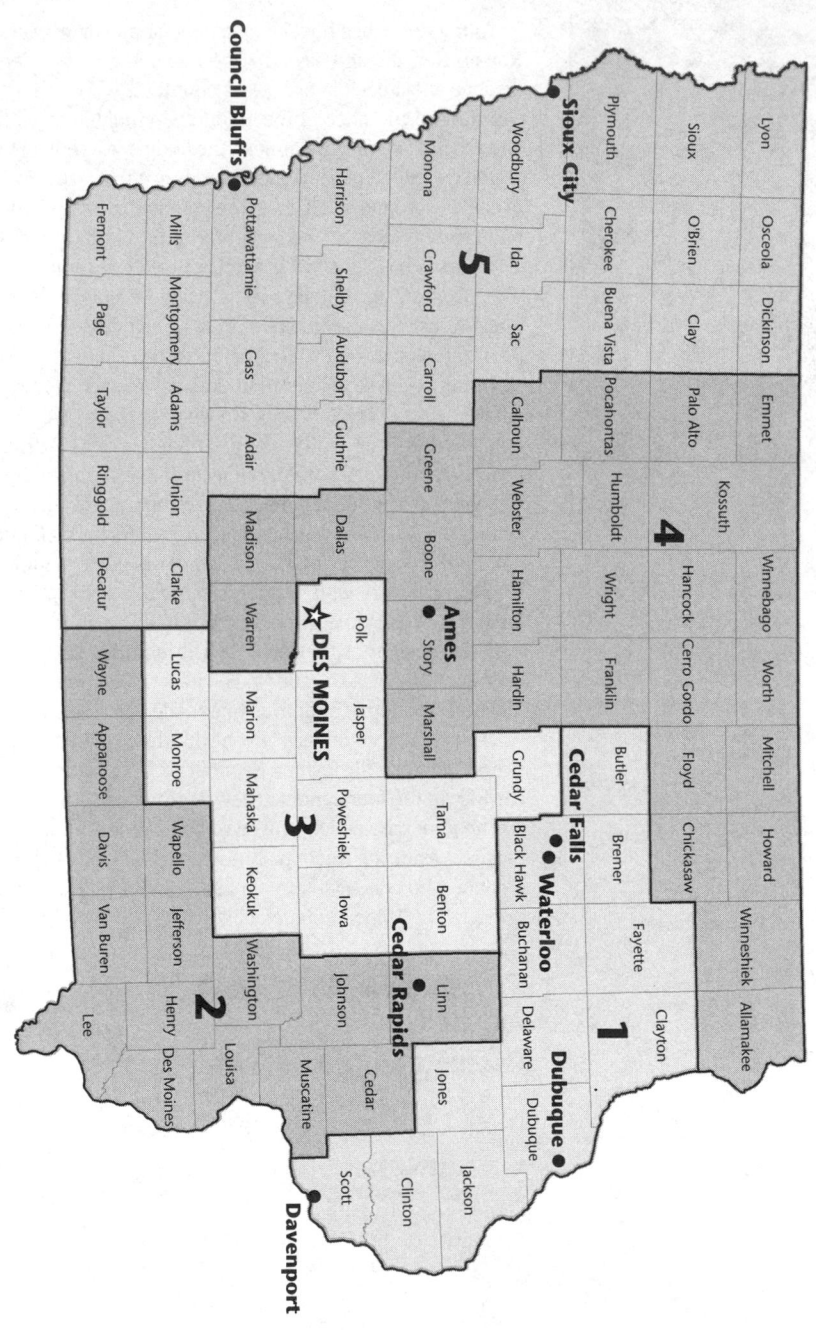

Gov. Terry E. Branstad (R)

First elected: 2010
Length of term: 4 years
Term expires: 1/15
Salary: $130,000
Phone: (515) 281-5211
Residence: Boone
Born: November 17, 1946; Leland, Iowa
Religion: Roman Catholic
Family: Wife, Chris Branstad; three children
Education: U. of Iowa, B.A. 1969 (political science & sociology); Drake U., J.D. 1974
Military service: Army, 1969-71
Career: University president; business consultant; farm owner
Political highlights: Iowa House, 1973-79; lieutenant governor, 1979-83; governor, 1983-99

ELECTION RESULTS

2010 GENERAL

Terry E. Branstad (R)	592,494	52.9%
Chet Culver (D)	484,798	43.3%
Jonathan Narcisse (I)	20,859	1.8%
Eric Cooper (LIBERT)	14,398	1.3%

Lt. Gov. Kim Reynolds (R)

First elected: 2010
Length of term: 4 years
Term expires: 1/15
Salary: $108,000
Phone: (515) 281-5211

LEGISLATURE

General Assembly: January-April
Senate: 50 members, 4-year terms
2011 ratios: 26 D, 24 R; 41 men, 9 women
Salary: $25,000
Phone: (515) 281-3371
House: 100 members, 2-year terms
2011 ratios: 60 R, 40 D; 74 men, 26 women
Salary: $25,000
Phone: (515) 281-3221

TERM LIMITS

Governor: No
Senate: No
House: No

URBAN STATISTICS

CITY	POPULATION
Des Moines	203,433
Cedar Rapids	126,326
Davenport	99,685
Sioux City	82,684
Waterloo	68,406

REGISTERED VOTERS

Others/unaffiliated	37%
Democrat	33%
Republican	30%

POPULATION

2010 population	3,046,355
2000 population	2,926,324
1990 population	2,776,755
Percent change (2000-2010)	+4.1%
Rank among states (2010)	30
Median age	37.9
Born in state	72.7%
Foreign born	3.7%
Violent crime rate	279/100,000
Poverty level	11.8%
Federal workers	25,821
Military	1,296

ELECTIONS

STATE ELECTION OFFICIAL
(515) 281-0145
DEMOCRATIC PARTY
(515) 244-7292
REPUBLICAN PARTY
(515) 282-8105

MISCELLANEOUS

Web: www.iowa.gov
Capital: Des Moines

U.S. CONGRESS

Senate: 1 Democrat, 1 Republican
House: 3 Democrats, 2 Republicans

2010 Census Statistics by District

District	2008 Vote for President Obama	McCain	White	Black	Asian	Hispanic	Median Income	White Collar	Blue Collar	Service Industry	Over 64	Under 18	College Education	Rural	Sq. Miles
1	58%	41%	89%	5%	1%	3%	$46,902	55%	28%	17%	15%	24%	23%	34%	7,217
2	60	39	88	3	2	5	47,371	59	25	16	13	23	28	34	7,566
3	54	45	85	4	3	6	53,241	63	22	15	13	25	28	27	6,979
4	53	46	91	1	2	4	47,496	57	27	16	16	23	23	49	15,760
5	44	55	90	1	1	7	45,287	54	30	16	17	24	18	51	18,348
STATE	54	45	89	3	2	5	48,052	58	26	16	15	24	24	39	55,869
U.S.	53	46	64	12	5	16	51,425	60	23	17	13	25	28	21	3,537,438

Sen. Charles E. Grassley (R)

Capitol Office
224-3744
grassley.senate.gov
135 Hart Bldg. 20510; fax 224-6020

Committees
Agriculture, Nutrition & Forestry
Budget
Finance
Judiciary - Ranking Member
Joint Taxation

Residence
New Hartford

Born
Sept. 17, 1933; New Hartford, Iowa

Religion
Baptist

Family
Wife, Barbara Grassley; five children

Education
U. of Northern Iowa, B.A. 1955, M.A. 1956 (political science); U. of Iowa, attended 1957-58 (graduate studies)

Career
Farmer

Political Highlights
Republican nominee for Iowa House, 1956; Iowa House, 1959-75; U.S. House, 1975-81

ELECTION RESULTS

2010 GENERAL

Charles E. Grassley (R)	718,215	64.4%
Roxanne Conlin (D)	371,686	33.3%
John Heiderscheit (LIBERT)	25,290	2.3%

2010 PRIMARY

Charles E. Grassley (R)	197,194	98.0%
write-in	3,926	2.0%

2004 GENERAL

Charles E. Grassley (R)	1,038,175	70.2%
Arthur Small (D)	412,365	27.9%
Christy Welty (LIBERT)	15,218	1.0%

Previous Winning Percentages
1998 (68%); 1992 (70%); 1986 (66%); 1980 (54%); 1978 House Election (75%); 1976 House Election (57%); 1974 House Election (51%)

Elected 1980; 6th term

Grassley's longstanding independent streak often took a backseat to his conservative leanings during the 111th Congress as his party pitched to the right and a Democratic president pushed health and spending legislation that was too liberal for his taste.

Still, with more than 35 years in Congress, Grassley remains a conservative who happily collaborates with Democrats to pass legislation, sometimes flustering his Republican colleagues. But he regards his legislative work as secondary to his oversight efforts: He has made a career of needling administrations both Republican and Democratic with investigations into their bureaucratic blunders.

In the 112th Congress (2011-12), Grassley surrendered the top Republican spot on the Finance Committee, which he had held for the past decade, in favor of becoming the ranking Republican on the Judiciary Committee, giving him a perch from which to weigh in on President Obama's judicial nominees and work with Chairman Patrick J. Leahy of Vermont on a long-stalled patent overhaul, which the Senate passed in March 2011.

On Finance, where he continues to serve, Grassley has been key to advancing initiatives on taxes, health care, Social Security, trade and welfare, often working hand-in-glove with Democrat Max Baucus of Montana, who took over the panel's chairmanship from Grassley when Democrats gained control in the 110th Congress (2007-08). The two men have swapped roles three times since 2001, and agreements between them helped clear the way for some of President George W. Bush's biggest victories, beginning with 2001's 10-year, $1.35 trillion tax cut. They also were central to passage of 2002's fast-track trade authority, which allowed quick up-or-down votes on trade deals in Congress, and the 2003 Medicare prescription drug benefit.

Grassley and Baucus much prefer deal-cutting to partisan purity. When they have parted ways on major bills, it's usually been because their respective party leaders insisted they toe the line. But neither blames the other when that happens. "Not as much gets done out of the Finance Committee that would get done if the leadership would leave us to our own pursuits," Grassley said.

The dynamic didn't work in 2009, as Baucus courted Grassley's support for Obama's signature priority, an overhaul of the health care system. Baucus struggled to keep a Republican trio — Grassley, Olympia J. Snowe of Maine and Michael B. Enzi of Wyoming — at the negotiating table for months as he tried to hammer out a bipartisan deal. But Grassley, facing the threat of a primary challenge from his right, took flak from GOP conservatives who questioned his authority to speak for them in the negotiations, and he started criticizing the Democratic plan in town hall meetings with constituents. In the end, he opposed the bill, as he did most other Democratic fiscal initiatives throughout the 111th Congress (2009-10).

Grassley, who sits on the Budget Committee, expects results from the programs Congress creates and compliance with the tax benefits that the Finance Committee hands out. His investigations have targeted the Food and Drug Administration, the Defense Department, nonprofits like the Nature Conservancy and the Smithsonian Institution, and televangelists, which has displeased some in the Christian conservative movement. Oversight, Grassley says, is Congress' highest responsibility. And it is necessary, he said, because "Congress has delegated so much power over the last 50 years to the executive branch of government."

Grassley is the leading congressional champion of whistleblowers, both inside and outside government. His proudest legislative achievement is a 1986 update of the Civil War-era False Claims Act that allows private citizens to sue government contractors for fraud, and share in any money recovered for the government. He said the law has recouped more than $20 billion for taxpayers. He and Senate Majority Whip Richard J. Durbin, an Illinois Democrat, advanced legislation in early 2009 to broaden the law's reach and counter court decisions that Grassley said have weakened the powerful tool.

Grassley has kept pressure on the Treasury Department to be transparent in its handling of the taxpayer-financed General Motors Corp. bankruptcy.

Perhaps no agency has received more scrutiny from Grassley than the FBI. A longtime member of the Judiciary Committee, he has criticized what he regards as the FBI's heavy-handed tactics and bureaucratic shortcomings and is known for sending letter after letter to its directors demanding they explain themselves.

His rebellious streak is cushioned by a disarming candor, the product of a lifetime in small-town Iowa. He grows corn and soybeans on 720 acres near New Hartford with his son and grandson, and, to keep in touch with his staff, he tucks a cell phone set to vibrate under his cap while on a tractor. Grassley has also embraced Twitter, using the social media service to share his some-times-ornery thoughts on legislation and politics. A veteran member of the Agriculture, Nutrition and Forestry Committee, he looks out for his state's many pork producers and corn growers with a farmer's eye for policy.

Grassley holds public hearings in all of Iowa's 99 counties every year. His devotion hasn't kept him away from Washington, however. He has the Senate's longest-running perfect attendance record; as of the end of the 111th Congress, the last time he missed a roll call was in July 1993.

Grassley delivers scathing speeches from the Senate floor against his opponents when crossed. After then-Ways and Means Chairman Charles B. Rangel, a New York Democrat, told him a relief package for Midwest flood victims would have to be offset by spending cuts or tax increases, Grassley took to the floor to note that similar relief programs for victims of Hurricane Katrina were not subject to the same requirement. "Why the double standard?" Grassley asked. "Is it because people aren't on rooftops complaining for helicopters to revive them and you see it on television for two months? We aren't doing that in Iowa; we're trying to help ourselves in Iowa. We have a can-do attitude." For Grassley, the matter was personal: New Hartford was struck by both a massive tornado and the worst floods of his lifetime.

Grassley is a social conservative who opposes abortion and gun control. He opposed both of Obama's Supreme Court nominees, Elena Kagan and Sonia Sotomayor.

On fiscal matters, he's not as conservative as some Republicans would like, but they can't argue with his personal thrift. He refuses to buy the lunch offered at the party's weekly policy lunches — "I think they want $23 for it; that's ridiculous," he said. And a pet peeve of late is the SUVs and sedans that idle around the Capitol, waiting to ferry high-ranking bureaucrats around Washington. In his late 70s, Grassley runs four times a week, usually three miles, a habit he adopted in 1999 as a New Year's resolution.

Grassley had dreamed of a career in politics since high school. After graduating from the University of Northern Iowa, he continued with graduate work there and at another Iowa university while working in a factory, where he was a Machinists union member. A few years later, he and his wife, Barbara, took over his family's grain and livestock operation. He spent 16 years in the Iowa House and was elected to the U.S. House in 1974, succeeding the retired H.R. Gross, a revered Republican figure in the state. Six years later, he unseated liberal Democratic Sen. John C. Culver. He has won with ease since. In 2010, he defeated Democrat Roxanne Conlin by a nearly 2-to-1 ratio.

Key Votes

2010

Pass budget reconciliation bill to modify overhauls of health care and federal student loan programs	NO
Proceed to disapproval resolution on EPA authority to regulate greenhouse gases	YES
Overhaul financial services industry regulation	NO
Limit debate to proceed to a bill to broaden campaign finance disclosure and reporting rules	NO
Limit debate on an extension of Bush-era income tax cuts for two years	YES
Limit debate on a bill to provide a path to legal status for some children of illegal immigrants	NO
Allow for a repeal of "don't ask, don't tell"	NO
Consent to ratification of a strategic arms reduction treaty with Russia	NO

2009

Prevent release of remaining financial industry bailout funds	YES
Make it easier for victims to sue for wage discrimination remedies	NO
Expand the Children's Health Insurance Program	NO
Limit debate on the economic stimulus measure	NO
Repeal District of Columbia firearms prohibitions and gun registration laws	YES
Limit debate on expansion of federal hate crimes law	NO
Strike funding for F-22 Raptor fighter jets	NO

CQ Vote Studies

	PARTY UNITY		PRESIDENTIAL SUPPORT	
	SUPPORT	OPPOSE	SUPPORT	OPPOSE
2010	93%	7%	42%	58%
2009	92%	8%	47%	53%
2008	93%	7%	72%	28%
2007	79%	21%	79%	21%
2006	93%	7%	87%	13%
2005	96%	4%	89%	11%
2004	97%	3%	94%	6%
2003	96%	4%	99%	1%
2002	88%	12%	95%	5%
2001	93%	7%	99%	1%

Interest Groups

	AFL-CIO	ADA	CCUS	ACU
2010	13%	10%	91%	88%
2009	22%	20%	71%	96%
2008	30%	25%	100%	76%
2007	32%	30%	64%	84%
2006	20%	5%	92%	88%
2005	14%	5%	100%	96%
2004	17%	20%	100%	96%
2003	0%	5%	100%	80%
2002	15%	10%	95%	95%
2001	13%	5%	100%	92%

Sen. Tom Harkin (D)

Capitol Office
224-3254
harkin.senate.gov
731 Hart Bldg. 20510-1502; fax 224-9369

Committees
Agriculture, Nutrition & Forestry
Appropriations
  (Labor-HHS-Education - Chairman)
Health, Education, Labor & Pensions - Chairman
Small Business & Entrepreneurship

Residence
Cumming

Born
Nov. 19, 1939; Cumming, Iowa

Religion
Roman Catholic

Family
Wife, Ruth Harkin; two children

Education
Iowa State U., B.S. 1962 (government & economics);
Catholic U. of America, J.D. 1972

Military Service
Navy, 1962-67; Naval Reserve, 1968-74

Career
Lawyer; congressional aide

Political Highlights
Democratic nominee for U.S. House, 1972; U.S.
House, 1975-85; sought Democratic nomination for
president, 1992

ELECTION RESULTS

2008 GENERAL
Tom Harkin (D)	941,665	62.7%
Christopher Reed (R)	560,006	37.3%

2008 PRIMARY
Tom Harkin (D)	unopposed

2002 GENERAL
Tom Harkin (D)	554,278	54.2%
Greg Ganske (R)	447,892	43.8%
Timothy Harthan (GREEN)	11,340	1.1%

Previous Winning Percentages
1996 (52%); 1990 (54%); 1984 (56%); 1982 House
Election (59%); 1980 House Election (60%); 1978
House Election (59%); 1976 House Election (65%);
1974 House Election (51%)

Elected 1984; 5th term

The longest-serving Democratic senator in Iowa history, Harkin has survived on a populist streak accompanied by a good dose of pragmatism. He believes government should intervene to help the poor, the disabled and family farmers, and he has been relentless in pushing to fulfill his liberal vision.

He takes a dim view of Republican proposals to cut federal spending and stirred a bit of controversy early in the 112th Congress (2011-12) when he met with about 400 lobbyists and advocates looking for help in keeping the dollars flowing to their programs. Harkin referred to House Republican spending cuts as "savage."

He has effective platforms from which to promulgate his style of old-fashioned liberalism.

In September 2009, he became chairman of the Health, Education, Labor and Pensions Committee, succeeding the late Democratic Sen. Edward M. Kennedy of Massachusetts just as the Senate was putting the final touches on its version of the Democrats' health care overhaul legislation.

In November 2008, Kennedy assigned Harkin to draft the prevention and public health provisions of the committee's health care bill. Harkin, also chairman of the Labor-Health and Human Services-Education Appropriations Subcommittee, pushed for the creation of a new federal council to develop a national health strategy, increased doctor training and coverage of preventive services. He also helped broker a compromise to include mandatory disclosure of calories on menus and menu boards.

Harkin leveraged his higher-profile role to be a voice for liberals in the latter stages of the debate. Although he did not win inclusion of a government-run insurance plan, he still cheered enactment of the law as a major moment of his legislative life. "Today I cast one of the defining votes of my Senate career — a vote that will bring the promise of comprehensive health reform closer to every American," Harkin said in December 2009.

Harkin pledged to uphold Kennedy's legacy in "ensuring that our economy works for all Americans, guaranteeing every child the opportunity to pursue a quality education and, of course, the cause of his life: access to quality, affordable health care for all Americans."

In the 112th Congress, a high priority will be rewriting the Bush-era education law known as No Child Left Behind. The HELP Committee held 11 hearings on the law in 2010.

Harkin is proud of his old-school progressivism; during his 1992 presidential run, he proclaimed he was the "only Democrat in the race," tacking to the left of eventual winner Bill Clinton. His signature legislative achievement remains the 1990 Americans With Disabilities Act, which extended broad civil rights protections to an estimated 54 million Americans with mental and physical disabilities. Harkin said he was inspired by his deaf brother, Frank, at the time of its passage and again in 2008, when President George W. Bush signed his bill expanding the number of people who qualify for the law's protections.

Organized labor has long been a big backer of Harkin. He led a small group of senators who met for months in 2009 to woo reluctant Democrats who aligned with Republicans on "card check" legislation that would allow unions to organize workplaces without a secret ballot. He acknowledged in July of that year that his party lacked the 60 votes needed to move the bill.

Harkin's Appropriations panel oversees the largest of the 12 annual spending bills and he brings large sums of federal funding back home. During debate on a $410 billion catchall spending bill in March 2009, he vehemently defended a $1.7 million provision for swine odor and manure management research.

He challenged Republican Tom Coburn of Oklahoma, who criticized the provision, to visit pig farms to witness the importance of odor control.

Harkin joined forces with Sen. Arlen Specter of Pennsylvania, a Republican at that point, on legislation to lift Bush's restrictions on federal funding of embryonic stem cell research, which uses discarded embryos created for in vitro fertilization.

After years of fruitless attempts, the pair saw the legislation pass in 2006 and draw the first veto of Bush's presidency. An override attempt failed. President Obama overturned the restrictions in 2009.

In taking over the HELP panel, Harkin had to give up the top job on the Agriculture, Nutrition and Forestry Committee, although he still serves on the panel. As its chairman, Harkin oversaw the 2008 passage of a $289 billion bill reauthorizing agriculture and nutrition programs for five years. The law boosted funding for ethanol production, a major priority for Iowa's corn farmers.

He also sits on the Small Business and Entrepreneurship Committee.

Harkin was among the senators pushing to change the chamber's filibuster rules in the 112th Congress. He had to settle for a ban on anonymous holds on nominations, which allowed senators to block nominees without revealing they were doing it.

The son of a coal miner, Harkin grew up in a small, crowded house in Cumming. His life took a tragic turn at age 10 when he lost his mother, a Slovenian immigrant. After working his way through college and law school, Harkin spent five years as a Navy pilot during the Vietnam War.

Though interested in politics since college — he was president of the Young Democrats at Iowa State — he stumbled into the field as a career. In 1968, out of the Navy and out of work, he was watching TV at a diner when President Lyndon B. Johnson startled him by announcing he would not seek another term. The next morning, a friend working for the Iowa Democratic Party offered him a job. "I thought, 'I'm going broke, I've got no prospects for the future. Why not?' " Harkin recalled.

In 1969, he was hired by Iowa Democratic Rep. Neal Smith as an aide on the House select committee investigating the U.S. military's progress in Vietnam. He made a name for himself with his discovery of South Vietnam's "tiger cages." Outwitting a government official on a guided tour of a prison camp, Harkin found, behind a hidden door, hundreds of men, women and children crammed into underground cells, with open grates on top through which guards poured skin-searing doses of the chemical lime. His photographs and story in Life magazine energized the anti-war movement. The move cost the 30-year-old Harkin his Capitol Hill job.

Harkin ran for the House in 1972 against GOP incumbent William Scherle. He lost, but tried again and toppled Scherle by a slim margin in 1974. In each of four re-election campaigns, he captured about 60 percent of the vote.

His Senate campaigns have been tougher. He won his seat in 1984 by ousting Republican Roger W. Jepsen with 56 percent of the vote. In 1990, his GOP challenger, Rep. Tom Tauke, accused Harkin of abusing congressional mailing privileges and voting for excessive spending. Harkin eventually won by 9 percentage points. He won a third term in 1996 by defeating GOP Rep. Jim Ross Lightfoot by 5 percentage points.

Enactment of the 2002 reauthorization of the farm bill just before the elections helped him stave off a tough challenge from Republican Rep. Greg Ganske.

In 2008, Harkin eclipsed 60 percent for the first time as a senator.

Key Votes

2010

Pass budget reconciliation bill to modify overhauls of health care and federal student loan programs	YES
Proceed to disapproval resolution on EPA authority to regulate greenhouse gases	NO
Overhaul financial services industry regulation	YES
Limit debate to proceed to a bill to broaden campaign finance disclosure and reporting rules	YES
Limit debate on an extension of Bush-era income tax cuts for two years	YES
Limit debate on a bill to provide a path to legal status for some children of illegal immigrants	YES
Allow for a repeal of "don't ask, don't tell"	YES
Consent to ratification of a strategic arms reduction treaty with Russia	YES

2009

Prevent release of remaining financial industry bailout funds	NO
Make it easier for victims to sue for wage discrimination remedies	YES
Expand the Children's Health Insurance Program	YES
Limit debate on the economic stimulus measure	YES
Repeal District of Columbia firearms prohibitions and gun registration laws	NO
Limit debate on expansion of federal hate crimes law	YES
Strike funding for F-22 Raptor fighter jets	YES

CQ Vote Studies

	PARTY UNITY		PRESIDENTIAL SUPPORT	
	SUPPORT	OPPOSE	SUPPORT	OPPOSE
2010	98%	2%	95%	5%
2009	99%	1%	97%	3%
2008	97%	3%	25%	75%
2007	96%	4%	35%	65%
2006	95%	5%	46%	54%
2005	98%	2%	27%	73%
2004	94%	6%	52%	48%
2003	98%	2%	46%	54%
2002	92%	8%	69%	31%
2001	97%	3%	63%	37%

Interest Groups

	AFL-CIO	ADA	CCUS	ACU
2010	100%	100%	9%	0%
2009	100%	100%	43%	0%
2008	100%	95%	50%	4%
2007	100%	95%	36%	8%
2006	100%	100%	36%	8%
2005	100%	100%	33%	4%
2004	100%	100%	59%	8%
2003	100%	95%	32%	15%
2002	100%	80%	45%	15%
2001	100%	100%	38%	8%

Rep. Bruce Braley (D)

Capitol Office
225-2911
braley.house.gov
1727 Longworth Bldg. 20515-1501; fax 226-5051

Committees
Oversight & Government Reform
Veterans' Affairs

Residence
Waterloo

Born
Oct. 30, 1957; Grinnell, Iowa

Religion
Presbyterian

Family
Wife, Carolyn Braley; three children

Education
Iowa State U., B.A. 1980 (political science); U. of Iowa,
J.D. 1983

Career
Lawyer

Political Highlights
No previous office

ELECTION RESULTS

2010 GENERAL

Bruce Braley (D)	104,428	49.5%
Benjamin Lange (R)	100,219	47.5%
Rob J. Petsche (LIBERT)	4,087	1.9%

2010 PRIMARY

Bruce Braley (D)	12,316	99.4%

2008 GENERAL

Bruce Braley (D)	186,991	64.6%
David Hartsuch (R)	102,439	35.4%

Previous Winning Percentages
2006 (55%)

Elected 2006; 3rd term

Like William Jennings Bryan, another Midwestern lawyer with a reputation for full-throated eloquence, Braley can command a courtroom or a hearing room. And, like the three-time Democratic presidential standard-bearer of a century ago, Braley has become a spokesman for populist causes.

Braley, a longtime trial lawyer who had no electoral experience before winning his first race for Congress, is the founding chairman of the House Populist Caucus. The group of two dozen or so Democrats is pro-union and advocates a liberal stance on social policy.

"One of the things we've tried to do is try to bring more of a laser focus to these middle-class economic issues," he said.

For Braley, that means more government programs intended to "create good-paying jobs."

That runs directly counter to the Republican majority's mantra of smaller government, and Braley called the GOP's catchall spending measure passed by the House early in 2011 "a reckless, job killing bill."

Having given up his seat on the Energy and Commerce Committee following the Democratic losses in 2010, he will put his oratorical skills to use as a foil to the Republican majority on the Oversight and Government Reform Committee. He also joined the Veterans' Affairs panel, where he is the ranking member of the Economic Opportunity Subcommittee. He quickly introduced legislation in the 112th Congress (2011-12) that would require private employers to give Veterans Day off to employees who served in the military.

Braley is a loyal Democratic vote. He sided with his party 99 percent of the time in the 111th Congress (2009-10) on votes that divided majorities of the two parties, and he supported all of President Obama's major economic initiatives: the health care overhaul, the economic stimulus and an energy bill that would create a cap-and-trade system for carbon emissions. Although Braley initially opposed a $700 billion plan to shore up the financial services industry in fall 2008, he voted for a second version, which became law.

After the 2010 elections, Braley was tapped by Minority Leader Nancy Pelosi of California to serve on the Democratic Steering and Policy Committee, which makes committee assignments. In 2009 he was given responsibility for recruitment, fundraising and training as a vice chairman of the Democratic Congressional Campaign Committee. DCCC Chairman Chris Van Hollen of Maryland had entrusted Braley in 2008 with Democrats' "Red to Blue" program, which targeted seats held by Republicans.

During his first term, Braley won plaudits from liberals after a March 2007 Oversight and Government Reform Committee hearing in which he was asked to lead Democratic debate and question Lurita Doan, administrator of the General Services Administration, during an investigation of alleged improper political activity by government employees during the George W. Bush administration. Both Braley and then-Chairman Henry A. Waxman, a California Democrat, asked Doan if she recalled discussing 2008 Republican goals during a meeting between the GSA and White House officials. Democrats claimed there was a violation of the Hatch Act, which bars partisan activity in government offices; Doan said she could not recall exactly what was said.

"One of the difficult challenges that any committee member faces in any type of hearing is how you get meaningful information from a witness in five minutes," Braley said. "And I have the benefit of asking questions of people in all matter of circumstances and learning techniques that can encourage them to give you truthful answers and do it without wasting time." Doan resigned at the end of April 2008. By that time, an Internet video of Braley relentlessly questioning Doan had attracted more than 100,000 viewers.

Sometimes Braley will part from liberal orthodoxy when it benefits his district. Despite his pro-union bona fides, he protested to Treasury Secretary Timothy F. Geithner in 2009 after Geithner pulled the plug on a program, despised by federal employee unions, that enlisted private collection companies in going after back taxes. One of the private firms was in Braley's district.

Braley's family roots in Iowa date back 150 years, when his great-great-grandfather walked from Vermont and staked out a farm. The son of a grain elevator worker and a fourth-grade teacher, Braley says his blue-collar upbringing in the town of Brooklyn made him a natural advocate for the Democratic Party. His interest in politics began during his adolescent years, when his father, a moderate Republican, and his mother, a Democrat, routinely talked about the daily news around the dinner table with their four children. Two of the major topics were the Vietnam War and the Watergate scandal.

Braley's grandmother and great-grandmother also were teachers. When he was a child, his mother drove back and forth from their home to the University of Iowa in Iowa City to earn her degree. His wife, Carolyn, teaches at Waterloo West High School, which all three of their children attended.

As a third-grader, Braley landed his first job: paperboy for the Des Moines Tribune. Later he tackled some of the more labor-intensive jobs well-known to sweaty Midwestern teens — baling hay, detasseling corn, working at a grain elevator and driving dump trucks. In high school he earned varsity letters in football, baseball, basketball, golf and track and field.

Braley graduated in 1980 with a degree in political science from Iowa State University, where he also met his wife. After he earned a law degree from the University of Iowa, they settled in Waterloo, where Braley made a career as a plaintiffs' lawyer.

Braley made a bid for Congress in 2006 when GOP Rep. Jim Nussle made an unsuccessful run for governor. In the primary, Braley edged Rick Dickinson, a longtime Dubuque economic development official, 36 percent to 34 percent. Braley faced restaurant and hotel entrepreneur Mike Whalen in the general election. The two political novices spent a combined $4.8 million on the race, with Braley defeating Whalen by 12 percentage points. He handily defeated Iowa state Sen. David Hartsuch in 2008 for a second term.

He nearly got caught by the Republican wave in 2010, but held on to defeat lawyer and former congressional aide Benjamin Lange, 49 percent to 47 percent.

Key Votes

2010	
Overhaul the nation's health insurance system	YES
Allow for repeal of "don't ask, don't tell"	YES
Overhaul financial services industry regulation	YES
Limit use of new Afghanistan War funds to troop withdrawal activities	NO
Change oversight of offshore drilling and lift oil spill liability cap	YES
Provide a path to legal status for some children of illegal immigrants	YES
Extend Bush-era income tax cuts for two years	NO
2009	
Expand the Children's Health Insurance Program	YES
Provide $787 billion in tax cuts and spending increases to stimulate the economy	YES
Allow bankruptcy judges to modify certain primary-residence mortgages	YES
Create a cap-and-trade system to limit greenhouse gas emissions	YES
Provide $2 billion for the "cash for clunkers" program	YES
Establish the government as the sole provider of student loans	YES
Restrict federally funded insurance coverage for abortions in health care overhaul	NO

CQ Vote Studies

	PARTY UNITY		PRESIDENTIAL SUPPORT	
	SUPPORT	OPPOSE	SUPPORT	OPPOSE
2010	98%	2%	93%	7%
2009	99%	1%	97%	3%
2008	98%	2%	13%	87%
2007	96%	4%	6%	94%

Interest Groups

	AFL-CIO	ADA	CCUS	ACU
2010	100%	100%	13%	0%
2009	100%	95%	40%	0%
2008	100%	90%	56%	4%
2007	96%	90%	63%	0%

Iowa 1

East — Davenport, Waterloo, Dubuque

The 1st takes in half of Iowa's Mississippi River counties as well as farmland to the west. It is dominated by three midsize industrial cities: Dubuque and Davenport on the river, and Waterloo in inland Black Hawk County. A decade of population loss has left the 1st one of the nation's least populous districts ahead of decennial remapping.

Located at the 1st's southern tip, Davenport and Bettendorf make up Iowa's half of the Quad Cities that straddle the Mississippi River into Illinois. Davenport is a district health care hub, and riverfront redevelopment projects are ongoing. Downtown boasts the area's minor league baseball team — the Quad Cities River Bandits — and a five-story-high pedestrian sky bridge that offers visitors a sweeping view of the Mississippi River. North of the Quad Cities and built against the bluffs facing the Mississippi River, Dubuque is Iowa's oldest city.

Meatpacking no longer dominates the economy here, and manufacturing has struggled even with key employers such as heavy-equipment manufacturer John Deere, in the area. Overall job growth, particularly in finance, insurance, health care and information technology sectors, has buffered the economy.

West along Route 20, Waterloo diversified its traditional meatpacking and farm implement industries to include finance and insurance businesses. Black Hawk County, which also includes Cedar Falls and the University of Northern Iowa, has a strong Democratic base from its academic and labor workforce.

There are many GOP voters in the rural farmland between the three main cities, and Democratic Gov. Chet Culver won only two counties here — Black Hawk and Dubuque — in his unsuccessful 2010 re-election bid.

Major Industry
Health care, agriculture, farm machinery, meatpacking

Cities
Davenport, 99,685; Waterloo, 68,406; Dubuque, 57,637; Cedar Falls, 39,260

Notable
Modern Woodmen Park, home of the River Bandits, has a cornfield in left field — players' entrances through the cornstalks during pre-game introductions resemble a scene from "Field of Dreams," which was filmed in Dyersville, 25 miles west of Dubuque.

Rep. Dave Loebsack (D)

Capitol Office
225-6576
loebsack.house.gov
1527 Longworth Bldg. 20515-1502; fax 226-0757

Committees
Armed Services
Education & the Workforce

Residence
Mount Vernon

Born
Dec. 23, 1952; Sioux City, Iowa

Religion
Methodist

Family
Wife, Teresa Loebsack; four children

Education
Iowa State U., B.S. 1974 (political science), M.A. 1976 (political science); U. of California, Davis, Ph.D. 1985 (political science)

Career
Professor

Political Highlights
No previous office

ELECTION RESULTS

2010 GENERAL

Dave Loebsack (D)	115,839	51.0%
Mariannette Miller-Meeks (R)	104,319	45.9%
Gary Sicard (LIBERT)	4,356	1.9%
Jon Tack (CNSTP)	2,463	1.1%

2010 PRIMARY

Dave Loebsack (D)	13,324	99.1%

2008 GENERAL

Dave Loebsack (D)	175,218	57.2%
Mariannette Miller-Meeks (R)	118,778	38.8%
Wendy Barth (GREEN)	6,664	2.2%
Brian White (X)	5,437	1.8%

Previous Winning Percentages
2006 (51%)

Elected 2006; 3rd term

Loebsack credits much of his drive to growing up in poverty with a single parent and working to help put himself through school. A college professor before winning election to Congress, he says he doesn't believe in "big government," but he has voted a solid liberal line since arriving in the Capitol.

He focuses his legislative energy on three main issues: jobs, the Iowa National Guard and helping his state recover from a series of devastating floods.

Loebsack (LOBE-sack) tends to keep a low profile and doesn't speak on the floor much. He jokes that he had his time grandstanding while he was a college professor. But he will speak up when he thinks it will yield results — such as advancing his bill in July 2010 that was aimed at promoting worker training and connecting educators and industries.

He backed an increase in the minimum wage, supported expanded federal funding of embryonic stem cell research and worked for a measure banning job discrimination on the basis of sexual orientation. His party unity vote — the percentage of votes on which he sided with a majority of Democrats against a majority of Republicans — has never fallen below 97 percent.

Loebsack is a member of the Education and the Workforce Committee and is eager to help rewrite the Bush-era No Child Left Behind education law, up for reauthorization in the 112th Congress (2011-12). The law, which requires annual testing of public school students to assess progress, has come under fire for lacking flexibility. "I'm not sure at all that I would have voted for it if I would have been here at the time," said Loebsack, who taught international relations at Cornell College in the small town of Mount Vernon, Iowa. His wife is a retired elementary school teacher.

He has introduced bills aimed at expanding the school lunch program and getting kids to eat more nutritious meals at school. Loebsack is also a believer in expanding federal student financial aid, voting with other Democrats in 2010 for a government takeover of the student loan program.

From his position on the Armed Services Committee, he introduced a bill that would expand certain National Guard missions to qualify for post-9/11 educational benefits. He supports the Iowa National Guard deployment of Agri-Business Development Teams in Afghanistan to assist in agricultural education.

Loebsack, who taught college-level foreign policy courses for 24 years and traveled extensively overseas, was a vocal critic of the Iraq War even though his stepson served in both Iraq and Afghanistan. He voted in favor of U.S. troop withdrawal deadlines and benchmarks. After President George W. Bush vetoed a war-funding bill in 2007 that would have set a withdrawal goal of March 31, 2008, Loebsack voted against the second version, which lacked a time line. He says he is now "satisfied" with the drawdown of forces in Iraq.

At an Armed Services hearing days after Obama announced a troop surge and new strategy for Afghanistan, Loebsack called for "clearly laid-out goals, a well-defined mission and a rubric for measuring progress."

He opposed the Republicans' catchall spending bill passed by the House in early 2011, calling its spending cuts "devastating" and "indiscriminate," but backed amendments to eliminate some Pentagon boards and commissions.

Loebsack says recovery from the 2008 floods in Iowa — during which 85 out of 99 counties were declared disaster areas — is a continuing legislative priority. More flooding in the summer of 2010 created other hardships in the region. He joined the rest of the Iowa delegation in seeking federal aid to help the state recover and worked with Iowa's Charles E. Grassley, the top Republican on the Senate Finance Committee, to win tax relief for flood victims. In the 112th Congress he wants to see changes to national flood insurance and FEMA's flood map modernization effort.

In 2009, he backed Obama's $787 billion economic stimulus package and from his seat on what was then called the Education and Labor Committee helped draft an expansion of national service programs that Obama sought.

Loebsack also wants his constituents to have an enjoyable experience when they visit the Capitol. In 2009, he joined Republican Rep. Mark Steven Kirk of Illinois, now a senator, in protesting restrictions on tours led by lawmakers' staff, instituted when the Capitol Visitor Center opened. In response, visitor center officials opened more slots for staff tours and said they would work to improve the process.

That kind of low-key, bipartisan work comes naturally to Loebsack, who is a member of the Center Aisle Caucus, a group of about 40 House members who look for ways to find common ground across the ideological spectrum. Caucus member Jeff Flake, an Arizona conservative, calls it a "civility caucus."

The son of a single mother who struggled with mental illness, Loebsack and his three siblings moved into his maternal grandmother's Sioux City home when he was in the fourth grade. At 16, he started working at the Sioux City Waste Treatment Control Plant under a federally funded program providing employment opportunities for poor students.

To help pay for college he used student loans and Social Security survivor benefits from a father he hardly knew who died while he was in high school. He also worked during the summers as a janitor at his high school, Sioux City East. Loebsack said the principal offered him a job there so he would have money for college.

He entered Iowa State University thinking he would study meteorology, but eventually earned undergraduate and master's degrees in political science. He earned a doctorate from the University of California at Davis, then moved back to Iowa in 1982 to teach political science at Cornell College.

Loebsack decided to challenge 15-term Republican Jim Leach for his House seat in 2006. He failed to meet the petition requirements to qualify for the primary, but since no other Democrat filed to run, state law allowed the party to appoint Loebsack as the nominee.

Despite Leach's image as a GOP iconoclast, Loebsack convinced enough voters that a vote for Leach was tantamount to endorsing continued Republican control of Congress. Loebsack won with 51 percent of the vote. In 2008, he took 57 percent against ophthalmologist and Army veteran Mariannette Miller-Meeks, who cut Loebsack's winning total to 51 percent in a 2010 rematch.

Key Votes

2010	
Overhaul the nation's health insurance system	YES
Allow for repeal of "don't ask, don't tell"	YES
Overhaul financial services industry regulation	YES
Limit use of new Afghanistan War funds to troop withdrawal activities	NO
Change oversight of offshore drilling and lift oil spill liability cap	YES
Provide a path to legal status for some children of illegal immigrants	YES
Extend Bush-era income tax cuts for two years	YES

2009	
Expand the Children's Health Insurance Program	YES
Provide $787 billion in tax cuts and spending increases to stimulate the economy	YES
Allow bankruptcy judges to modify certain primary-residence mortgages	YES
Create a cap-and-trade system to limit greenhouse gas emissions	YES
Provide $2 billion for the "cash for clunkers" program	YES
Establish the government as the sole provider of student loans	YES
Restrict federally funded insurance coverage for abortions in health care overhaul	NO

CQ Vote Studies

	PARTY UNITY		PRESIDENTIAL SUPPORT	
	SUPPORT	OPPOSE	SUPPORT	OPPOSE
2010	97%	3%	95%	5%
2009	97%	3%	97%	3%
2008	97%	3%	13%	87%
2007	97%	3%	3%	97%

Interest Groups

	AFL-CIO	ADA	CCUS	ACU
2010	100%	95%	25%	4%
2009	100%	95%	36%	0%
2008	100%	90%	56%	0%
2007	96%	95%	58%	0%

Iowa 2

Southeast — Cedar Rapids, Iowa City

Shaped like a backward-facing L, the Democratic-leaning 2nd spreads across cornfields to take in 15 southeastern Iowa counties, bending from Cedar Rapids in its north to Wayne County in its southwest.

Cedar Rapids, in Linn County, is the state's second-most-populous city. Long a grain-processing center, the city now is home to a large Quaker Oats cereal plant. The city was ravaged by a 500-year flood in 2008, but long-term economic recovery has shown signs of success and many key employers have stayed. A diversified local economy insulated Cedar Rapids from the worst of nationwide economic downturns. The largest area employer is now a defense contractor, and technology, telecommunications equipment and energy are important sectors here.

About 25 miles south of Cedar Rapids is Iowa City, home to the University of Iowa. The university is by far the city's dominant employer while its hospital system is the second-largest job source. Technology companies and a strong health care industry support the local economy, and the academic community gives the city a strong liberal tilt.

The 2nd's other population center runs along the Mississippi River in the southeast, in Des Moines and Lee counties.

Unions retain some influence in Burlington, a manufacturing hub, and riverboat-casino-based tourism also contributes to the economy. The land in the 2nd's southwestern arm is mostly rural, depending mainly on corn and soybeans.

The 2nd has a decidedly Democratic tilt, anchored by strongholds in Linn (Cedar Rapids), Johnson (Iowa City), Lee, Des Moines (Burlington) and Jefferson counties — those counties accounted for five of Gov. Chet Culver's nine wins statewide in his unsuccessful 2010 re-election race. Democrat Barack Obama took 60 percent of the 2nd's presidential vote in 2008, his highest percentage statewide.

Major Industry
Technology, telecommunications, health care, grain processing, higher education

Cities
Cedar Rapids, 126,326; Iowa City, 67,862; Marion, 34,768; Burlington, 25,663; Ottumwa, 25,023; Muscatine, 22,886

Notable
The Cedar Rapids Museum of Art hosts the largest collection of art by "American Gothic" painter Grant Wood.

Rep. Leonard L. Boswell (D)

Capitol Office
225-3806
boswell.house.gov
1026 Longworth Bldg. 20515-1503; fax 225-5608

Committees
Agriculture
Transportation & Infrastructure

Residence
Des Moines

Born
Jan. 10, 1934; Harrison County, Mo.

Religion
Community of Christ

Family
Wife, Dody Boswell; three children

Education
Graceland College, B.A. 1969 (business administration)

Military
Army, 1956-76

Career
Farmer; Army officer

Political Highlights
Iowa Senate, 1985-97 (president, 1992-97); sought Democratic nomination for U.S. House, 1986; Iowa Democratic Central Committee, 1992-96; Democratic nominee for lieutenant governor, 1994

ELECTION RESULTS

2010 GENERAL

Leonard L. Boswell (D)	122,147	50.7%
Brad Zaun (R)	111,925	46.5%
Rebecca Williamson (SW)	6,258	2.6%

2010 PRIMARY

Leonard L. Boswell (D)	13,107	97.5%
write-in (D)	338	2.5%

2008 GENERAL

Leonard L. Boswell (D)	176,904	56.3%
Kim Schmett (R)	132,136	42.1%
Frank V. Forrestal (SW)	4,599	1.5%

Previous Winning Percentages
2006 (52%); 2004 (55%); 2002 (53%); 2000 (63%); 1998 (57%); 1996 (49%)

Elected 1996; 8th term

Boswell, a livestock farmer, Vietnam veteran and longtime politician, has long held the respect of his colleagues for his calm demeanor and life experience. He represents a swing district and has survived several rounds of tough challenges.

Boswell came to Washington with a reputation built in the Iowa General Assembly for seeking bipartisan solutions, and during his first few terms in Congress he was considered a moderate-to-conservative Democrat. A Republican majority and his loyalty to the Blue Dog Coalition, a group of fiscally conservative Democrats, fueled his independence from party leaders. He voted for several GOP spending and tax proposals and bills to ban flag desecration and to outlaw a procedure opponents call "partial birth" abortion. But after he rebuffed an overture to join the Republican Party during the 107th Congress (2001-02) — and after redistricting shifted him to a more liberal constituency — he moved closer to the Democratic party line.

Boswell was not among the Blue Dogs who called for new leadership after the party lost its majority in the 2010 elections. He backed outgoing Speaker Nancy Pelosi of California for minority leader, although he said he would like her to steer a more moderate course. "We need a new message," Boswell said.

Boswell enthusiastically supported the Democrats' health care law enacted in 2010, joining liberals in calling for a government-run program that did not make it into the final version of the legislation.

He also voted for energy legislation that would create a cap-and-trade system intended to reduce carbon emissions, President Obama's $787 billion economic stimulus and an expansion of the Children's Health Insurance Program, which covers children whose low-income families make too much money to qualify for Medicaid.

A member of the Agriculture Committee since he entered Congress in 1997, Boswell is the top Democrat on its General Farm Commodities and Risk Management Subcommittee, which he chaired in the 111th Congress (2009-10). He helped write a portion of the Democrats' five-year farm bill reauthorization in 2008, including changes to the federal milk-marketing order system and an extension of a program that helps dairy farmers pay for losses when the price of milk dips below a government target.

Concerned about the arbitration system designed to settle disputes between producers and meatpackers, Boswell inserted an amendment into the farm bill that limits mandatory arbitration agreements in livestock contracts and allows producers to settle disputes locally rather than in the jurisdiction of the company's headquarters. He had voted against the House farm bill in 2001 because it didn't include similar language, although he ultimately supported the final version negotiated with the Senate.

He also uses his seat on Agriculture to advocate the use of ethanol. Even before alternative fuels were part of the everyday vernacular, he championed research efforts in his home state to develop them from various crops, including Iowa's ubiquitous corn.

Concerned about the federal debt, he warned that the 2012 farm bill might cut some programs. "There's going to be a major effort to get our arms around reducing the debt and starting to draw back on it," he told the Cedar Rapids Gazette.

As a member of the Transportation and Infrastructure Committee, Boswell will take part in a renewal of the 2005 surface transportation law.

He said he will try to steer funds to Hawkeye State areas devastated by flooding and tornadoes in early 2008. "There is no way a community can pick up after something like that. But in a country like ours, they don't have to. We help," Boswell said after flying over the hard-hit areas in his personal plane. In June 2008, he supported a supplemental spending bill that included $2.7 billion for flood and tornado relief. From his Transportation seat, he has also sought to boost passenger aviation service to Des Moines.

Boswell in 2002 crossed party lines to support a resolution authorizing President George W. Bush to use force against Iraq. It is a vote Boswell later said he regretted. In early 2007, he opposed Bush's plan to send more than 21,000 additional U.S. combat troops to Iraq and supported an emergency war spending bill that set a goal for withdrawal of troops from Iraq by March 2008.

Raised in a farming family in southern Iowa, Boswell was destined to work in the state's rolling cornfields. But that path was derailed when he was drafted into the Army shortly after getting married in 1956. He would later go to Officer Candidate School and achieve the rank of lieutenant colonel. He served two one-year stints as an assault helicopter pilot in Vietnam.

Boswell eventually returned home to raise cattle on 475 acres in his native Decatur County, where he still raises about 140 cows a year. He also earned a degree in business administration and became involved in local politics, spending 12 years in the Iowa Senate and rising to become its president.

In 1996, he ran for the U.S. House, seeking the seat of Republican Jim Ross Lightfoot, who was running for the Senate. He won the primary easily. In the general election, he won the endorsement of the Iowa Farm Bureau and eked out a win against Mike Mahaffey, a county prosecutor and former state GOP chairman. At 63, he was the oldest House freshman in 1997.

Redistricting in 2002 compelled him to move to Des Moines, and he had to show his more liberal constituents he could serve their interests, too. He has since prevailed, albeit with margins less impressive than most incumbents. In 2004, he broke a pledge to serve only four terms by running for — and winning — a fifth, with 55 percent of the vote.

In 2005, he spent 11 weeks recovering from treatment for a non-cancerous tumor in his stomach and lost 70 pounds, but was re-elected with 52 percent in 2006. In 2008, he underwent surgery that "made some corrections" to the earlier procedure, and won again with 56 percent of the vote over Republican Kim Schmett, a former congressional aide. In 2010, Boswell defeated Republican state Sen. Brad Zaun with 51 percent of the vote, to 47 percent for Zaun.

Key Votes

2010	
Overhaul the nation's health insurance system	YES
Allow for repeal of "don't ask, don't tell"	YES
Overhaul financial services industry regulation	YES
Limit use of new Afghanistan War funds to troop withdrawal activities	NO
Change oversight of offshore drilling and lift oil spill liability cap	YES
Provide a path to legal status for some children of illegal immigrants	YES
Extend Bush-era income tax cuts for two years	YES
2009	
Expand the Children's Health Insurance Program	YES
Provide $787 billion in tax cuts and spending increases to stimulate the economy	YES
Allow bankruptcy judges to modify certain primary-residence mortgages	YES
Create a cap-and-trade system to limit greenhouse gas emissions	YES
Provide $2 billion for the "cash for clunkers" program	YES
Establish the government as the sole provider of student loans	YES
Restrict federally funded insurance coverage for abortions in health care overhaul	NO

CQ Vote Studies

	PARTY UNITY		PRESIDENTIAL SUPPORT	
	SUPPORT	OPPOSE	SUPPORT	OPPOSE
2010	97%	3%	93%	7%
2009	96%	4%	97%	3%
2008	98%	2%	17%	83%
2007	93%	7%	6%	94%
2006	78%	22%	47%	53%

Interest Groups

	AFL-CIO	ADA	CCUS	ACU
2010	100%	90%	25%	0%
2009	100%	95%	47%	0%
2008	100%	95%	61%	4%
2007	96%	90%	60%	8%
2006	86%	70%	67%	44%

Iowa 3

Central and east central — Des Moines

Squeezed between the state's other four districts, the 3rd is Iowa's only district not to border another state and is in some ways a microcosm of the Hawkeye State. It includes relatively well-off urban and suburban areas, as well as rural counties, industrial cities and scattered towns.

Most of the district's residents live in Des Moines or surrounding Polk County. Unlike the rest of Iowa's urban centers, the capital city is not dependent on agriculture, and the economy is stable without it. Des Moines' economy experienced decades of growth, and the city is an anchor for insurance and financial companies. Some firms, such as Wells Fargo Insurance Services, have headquarters in the city, and others have regional offices in the metropolitan area. A bustling health care industry and a smaller but significant manufacturing industry provides jobs despite nationwide economic downturns. The city's economy also is the hub of state government.

Des Moines' modern skyline includes the Iowa Events Center — a four-venue, multipurpose complex under one interconnected roof and home to the city's sports teams — which bolsters the city's economy. The city's 4 miles of skywalk allows residents to move quickly among downtown developments, commercial centers and historical areas, such as East Village, where the state Capitol is located.

The rest of the 3rd takes on a more rural flavor, and no county outside of Polk has more than 40,000 residents. Des Moines' black and Hispanic residents help make the 3rd Iowa's most minority-populated district, although whites still make up 85 percent of the population here. Democrat Barack Obama took 54 percent of the district's 2008 presidential vote, but although the Democratic lean of Des Moines kept Polk County competitive in the 2010 gubernatorial election, no county in the 3rd supported Democratic Gov. Chet Culver in his unsuccessful re-election bid.

Major Industry

Insurance, health care, government, agriculture, manufacturing

Cities

Des Moines (pt.), 203,419; Ankeny, 45,582; West Des Moines (pt.), 44,999; Urbandale (pt.), 33,126; Johnston, 17,278; Newton, 15,254

Notable

The Amana Colonies, seven villages originally settled in 1855 by the Community of True Inspiration, are a tourist draw for Iowa County.

Rep. Tom Latham (R)

Capitol Office
225-5476
www.house.gov/latham
2217 Rayburn Bldg. 20515-1504; fax 225-3301

Committees
Appropriations
  (Transportation-HUD - Chairman)

Residence
Ames

Born
July 14, 1948; Hampton, Iowa

Religion
Lutheran

Family
Wife, Kathy Latham; three children

Education
Wartburg College, attended 1967; Iowa State U.,
attended 1967-70 (agriculture & business)

Career
Seed company executive; insurance agency marketing representative; insurance agent; bank teller

Political Highlights
Franklin County Republican Party chairman, 1984-91

ELECTION RESULTS

2010 GENERAL

Tom Latham (R)	152,588	65.6%
Bill Maske (D)	74,300	32.0%
Dan Lensing (I)	5,499	2.4%

2010 PRIMARY

Tom Latham (R)	42,605	99.4%

2008 GENERAL

Tom Latham (R)	185,458	60.5%
Becky Greenwald (D)	120,746	39.4%

Previous Winning Percentages
2006 (57%); 2004 (61%); 2002 (55%); 2000 (69%);
1998 (99%); 1996 (65%); 1994 (61%)

Elected 1994; 9th term

Latham is a fiscal conservative who uses his seat on the Appropriations Committee to look out for his fellow farmers as well as his state and district. Latham's roots are deeply planted in the rich soil of Iowa, where he farmed and at one time co-owned a seed company with his brothers. He typically supports the Republican agenda on national policy, but strays on occasion when he thinks that agenda clashes with the needs of his constituents.

The dean of Iowa's five-member House delegation, Latham is a close friend of House Speaker John A. Boehner, an Ohio Republican. Since the 1990s, the two have met regularly in an informal dinner club that includes two former GOP House members now in the Senate, Richard M. Burr of North Carolina and Saxby Chambliss of Georgia.

Latham voted for some of the cuts proposed by conservative Republicans to the catchall spending bill the House passed early in the 112th Congress (2011-12), while voting against others. As an appropriator, he thought it made more sense to move quickly on the bill the spending panel wrote than to spend a lot of time trying to hash out a deal with the Democratic-led Senate.

"There could have been agreement with the Senate about where we were before," Latham said.

But he voted for the final product, and wrote in an op-ed that he and his GOP colleagues "chose the path of fiscal sanity, restraint and job growth rather than driving the country further down the road toward financial ruin and driving our children's and grandchildren's hope of the American Dream off a cliff."

He ridiculed President Obama's fiscal 2012 budget. "Only in Washington can running a $1.6 trillion deficit in a single year be considered living within our means," he said.

Now chairman of the Transportation-Housing and Urban Development Appropriations Subcommittee, he voted with his party to oppose Obama's 2009 economic stimulus package, which the then-Democratic majority sold as providing billions in funding for "shovel-ready" transportation and infrastructure projects. He told attendees at a town hall meeting in Jefferson in July 2009 that such transportation projects accounted for less than 4 percent of the bill's spending.

He also resisted the speed with which the bill was enacted, and he opposed a "use it or lose it" provision to require that half the money for highway, aviation, transit and rail projects be obligated within 90 days. Months after the bill was enacted, Latham decried its ineffectiveness. "I cautioned that forcing through such massive spending with so little accountability would expose American taxpayers to government waste and unwieldy bureaucracy," he said. "It's now evident that those predictions have come true."

A good portion of his district is dependent on agriculture, and Latham is the No. 2 Republican on the Agriculture spending panel.

He voted to override President George W. Bush's veto of a five-year farm bill in 2008, even though he disliked some of the legislation's provisions. And unlike many in the Republican Party, he has been an ardent advocate of earmarks, using his Appropriations Committee seat to promote funding for projects not just in his district, but other portions of his state as well. As the only Iowan on House Appropriations, Latham said he has "a tremendous amount of pressure from all five districts ... to help out with their projects." Prior to the Republicans placing a moratorium on earmarks for fiscal 2011 and 2012 — actions he endorsed — Latham was able to direct millions of dollars to the National Animal Disease Center, a livestock health research facility in Ames.

He has gone out of his way to honor Nobel laureate Norman Borlaug, who grew up in Latham's district. Borlaug's high-yield seeds increased global food supplies and he is credited with saving hundreds of millions of people worldwide from starvation. Following Borlaug's death in 2009, Latham led the Iowa delegation's effort to put a statue of him in Statuary Hall.

Latham grew up doing farm chores and helping in the family seed business. He attended Wartburg College about 50 miles east of his hometown of Alexander, then went to Iowa State University, about 60 miles south in Ames.

In his early 20s he headed to Colorado, spurred in large part by his father's admonition that his children had to do something on their own before they could take their place in the family business. There, Latham worked as a bank teller, a bookkeeper and an insurance agent. The insurance firm transferred him to Des Moines; two years later, Latham moved back to Alexander, where he remained until moving to Ames in late 2006.

His interest in politics was sparked by a trip he took to Russia and Poland in 1990 as a member of a farm delegation. He was appalled at the primitive agricultural methods and machinery in the former communist countries.

Latham chaired the Franklin County Republican Party for seven years but rebuffed entreaties to run for the state legislature because the seasonal nature of the seed business conflicted with legislative sessions. In 1994, however, when GOP Rep. Fred Grandy gave up the 5th District seat in an unsuccessful try for the governorship, Latham decided to run. He breezed to election.

He was returned to the House easily in three subsequent elections, but in 2002 new district lines drafted by a nonpartisan state agency made the district more competitive. The new map put Latham's home in the 4th District, while more than half his constituents lived in the 5th.

Latham decided to run in the 4th anyway. He was well known to many of its residents, owing to his days as a traveling farm-seed salesman. He won by almost 12 percentage points against Democrat John Norris, a former state party chairman. Latham cruised to re-election in 2004 and 2006. He was mentioned as a possible 2008 challenger to veteran Democratic Sen. Tom Harkin, but he opted to stay where he was in a year that did not look bright for Republicans. He sailed to an eighth term, taking nearly 61 percent of the vote against Becky Greenwald, a Democratic activist who had worked in sales and marketing for seed companies and had support from EMILY's List and the national Democratic Party. He won with almost two-thirds of the vote in 2010.

Key Votes

2010

Overhaul the nation's health insurance system	NO
Allow for repeal of "don't ask, don't tell"	NO
Overhaul financial services industry regulation	NO
Limit use of new Afghanistan War funds to troop withdrawal activities	NO
Change oversight of offshore drilling and lift oil spill liability cap	NO
Provide a path to legal status for some children of illegal immigrants	NO
Extend Bush-era income tax cuts for two years	YES

2009

Expand the Children's Health Insurance Program	NO
Provide $787 billion in tax cuts and spending increases to stimulate the economy	NO
Allow bankruptcy judges to modify certain primary-residence mortgages	NO
Create a cap-and-trade system to limit greenhouse gas emissions	NO
Provide $2 billion for the "cash for clunkers" program	YES
Establish the government as the sole provider of student loans	NO
Restrict federally funded insurance coverage for abortions in health care overhaul	YES

CQ Vote Studies

	PARTY UNITY		PRESIDENTIAL SUPPORT	
	SUPPORT	OPPOSE	SUPPORT	OPPOSE
2010	90%	10%	29%	71%
2009	81%	19%	35%	65%
2008	90%	10%	63%	37%
2007	86%	14%	71%	29%
2006	95%	5%	97%	3%

Interest Groups

	AFL-CIO	ADA	CCUS	ACU
2010	0%	0%	88%	91%
2009	14%	5%	80%	80%
2008	20%	30%	89%	88%
2007	25%	20%	95%	84%
2006	21%	5%	100%	84%

Iowa 4

North and central — Ames, Mason City

The vast 4th takes up most of the state's northern border and dips deeply south, hooking around the state capital of Des Moines (in the 3rd District), to reach Dallas, Madison and Warren counties.

Ames, nestled along Squaw Creek and the Skunk River, is about 30 miles north of the capital city and represents the district's largest population center. It is home to Iowa State University, and the university has become a renowned agricultural engineering institution. The university's influence gives Story County a Democratic lean.

Rural farming communities and smaller cities make up the rest of the 4th. Marshalltown, east of Ames, is home to a large meatpacking industry, which has brought Hispanic immigrants. The immigrant workforce has divided officials over immigration enforcement policy. Mason City, still the 4th's second-most-populous city despite losing residents over the last decade, depends on manufacturing. Fort Dodge in Webster County is home to trucking firms, gypsum factories, veterinary pharmaceuticals and a state prison, but has lost population in recent years.

Southwest of Ames, Dallas County is a big exception to Iowa's generally sluggish population growth. Suburban growth west of Des Moines fueled Dallas' sustained population increase since the 1990s, and the county has a median household income well above district and state averages.

The 4th's support for the Republican presidential candidate dipped recently — Democrat Barack Obama took 53 percent of the district's vote in the 2008 presidential election four years after Republican George W. Bush won 51 percent of the presidential vote — but Democratic Gov. Chet Culver won only Story and Floyd counties here in his unsuccessful 2010 gubernatorial re-election campaign. Registered Republicans now outnumber Democrats in 17 of the district's 28 counties.

Major Industry
Meatpacking, health care, veterinary pharmaceuticals, agriculture

Cities
Ames, 58,965; Mason City, 28,079; Marshalltown, 27,552

Notable
In 1959, after playing a last concert, Buddy Holly, Ritchie Valens and J.P. "The Big Bopper" Richardson died in a plane crash near Clear Lake; Madison County's covered bridges were popularized in Robert James Waller's book.

Rep. Steve King (R)

Capitol Office
225-4426
www.house.gov/steveking
1131 Longworth Bldg. 20515-1505; fax 225-3193

Committees
Agriculture
Judiciary
Small Business

Residence
Kiron

Born
May 28, 1949; Storm Lake, Iowa

Religion
Roman Catholic

Family
Wife, Marilyn King; three children

Education
Northwest Missouri State U., attended 1967-70

Career
Construction company owner

Political Highlights
Iowa Senate, 1997-2002

ELECTION RESULTS

2010 GENERAL

Steve King (R)	128,363	65.7%
Matthew Campbell (D)	63,160	32.4%
Martin James Monroe (I)	3,622	1.9%

2010 PRIMARY

Steve King (R)	47,117	99.2%

2008 GENERAL

Steve King (R)	159,430	59.8%
Rob Hubler (D)	99,601	37.4%
Victor Vara (I)	7,406	2.8%

Previous Winning Percentages
2006 (58%); 2004 (63%); 2002 (62%)

Elected 2002; 5th term

King's flights of rhetorical excess are not a bug, they're a feature. He endeavors to spark controversy and get under the skin of the opposition — and has been successful at both. He has fought a long rear-guard action on his most visible topic, immigration, but lost out in his bid to lead the Judiciary Committee panel handling the issue in the 112th Congress.

The Immigration Policy and Enforcement Subcommittee gavel went instead to Elton Gallegly of California, who holds views on illegal immigration similar to King's but has kept a considerably lower profile.

That doesn't mean King won't be heard on the topic.

"I have renewed my resolve to drive it even harder, and I'll use all the tools at my disposal to do the right thing for America," he said.

He also has resolved to increase his visibility on other issues, in an effort to become more of a force among national conservatives, emulating the role played by South Carolina Republican Sen. Jim DeMint. "What Steve and I are trying to do is encourage people, as we look at our presidential candidates, not to just look at personalities or how well they speak, but decide really what they stand for," DeMint told Roll Call in early 2011.

King's rhetorical edginess contrasts with his avuncular demeanor; in individual encounters, he is unfailingly polite, with a self-deprecating sense of humor. But in political combat, he often unleashes scathing commentary.

He has characterized the immigration debate as being between "amnesty mercenaries" sporting "a big, bright, scarlet letter 'A' branded on their robes" and "the patriotic passengers and crew of Lifeboat America." King suggested Arizona Democratic Rep. Raúl M. Grijalva is more of an advocate "for Mexico rather than the United States."

King was the top Republican on the immigration panel in the 111th Congress (2009-10), serving as a front man in the battle over whether to offer a path to citizenship for the millions of illegal immigrants already in the country. He has backed numerous measures intended to address the issue and opposed others he sees as exacerbating it. A bill he introduced in 2009 would have prohibited employers from deducting as a business expense wages paid to illegal immigrants, aimed at cracking down on employers who hire people not authorized to work in the United States. He opposed a bill in May 2008 that would have created a new visa category for fashion models. "This bill should be called the Ugly American Act. It's based on the premise that there aren't enough attractive people in the United States," he said. Later that year, he opposed a measure designed to make it easier for foreign nationals to obtain legal residency when their U.S. citizen spouse or parent dies before their applications are cleared. King said he was concerned about writing "blanket legislation" based on a few sympathetic cases.

King supported a 2006 law calling for construction of a 700-mile fence along the U.S. border with Mexico. In urging support, he built a small model out of wood and cardboard to demonstrate how it could be done. King also has pushed for English to be the nation's official language. As a state senator he sponsored a bill making English the official language of Iowa. In 2007, he successfully sued Democratic Gov. Chet Culver and Secretary of State Michael Mauro for providing voter registration forms in other languages.

King has shown a tendency toward the attention-grabbing quote on other issues as well. He said terrorists would be "dancing in the streets" if Barack Obama won the White House, and he likened President Obama's economic policies to those of Venezuela's anti-American leader, Hugo Chavez.

California Democratic Rep. Barbara Lee once likened King to liberal bogeyman Joseph R. McCarthy. King responded by praising the late senator from Wisconsin, known for his pursuit of communists in government in the 1950s, as a "hero for America."

King has been a consistent vote against Obama's legislative agenda, opposing the Democratic health care overhaul — he called it "a toxic stew" — and backing legislation to repeal and defund it.

King has had some success with district-focused legislation, particularly from his seat on the Agriculture Committee. In his first term he inserted into an energy bill a provision granting a tax credit for small ethanol producers. It was aimed at making the half-dozen producers in his district more competitive with ethanol giants Archer Daniels Midland and Cargill. King backed the successful override of Bush's 2008 veto of the reauthorization of farm programs.

A former small-business owner himself, his seat on the Small Business Committee provides a forum to continue working on the issue he says drove him into politics in the first place: frustration with federal regulations imposed on his mom-and-pop operation.

King has deep roots in the district, a jumping-off place for migration to Oregon, California and Utah in the middle of the 19th century. His maternal great-grandparents were among the original homesteaders in the region after the Civil War. In 1975, he started the King Construction Co., a small earth-moving firm that specialized in soil erosion solutions for farmers. His annual sales were about $700,000. His son now runs the business. King said he became increasingly angry at rising federal taxes, government regulations and IRS audits of his business. "After they picked my pocket, I went to work and sat there every day, thinking about how to get rid of them," he said.

In 1996, he won a seat in the Iowa Senate and became known for a culturally conservative agenda. His "God and Country" law requires Iowa public schools to teach that the United States has "derived its strength from Biblical values." King fought an executive order in 2000 by Democratic Gov. Tom Vilsack banning discrimination against gays and lesbians in state jobs, arguing it gave preferential treatment to certain groups of people. He took the fight to the Iowa Supreme Court and won, overturning Vilsack's order.

Redistricting put 5th District Rep. Tom Latham's home in another district in 2002, and Latham chose to run in the redrawn 4th. King faced primary competition for the vacated 5th district, but when no candidate won the required 35 percent of the vote, the race was decided by a nominating convention. King prevailed, then won the general with 62 percent. He has been re-elected with relative ease since.

Key Votes

2010

Overhaul the nation's health insurance system	NO
Allow for repeal of "don't ask, don't tell"	NO
Overhaul financial services industry regulation	NO
Limit use of new Afghanistan War funds to troop withdrawal activities	NO
Change oversight of offshore drilling and lift oil spill liability cap	NO
Provide a path to legal status for some children of illegal immigrants	NO
Extend Bush-era income tax cuts for two years	NO

2009

Expand the Children's Health Insurance Program	NO
Provide $787 billion in tax cuts and spending increases to stimulate the economy	NO
Allow bankruptcy judges to modify certain primary-residence mortgages	NO
Create a cap-and-trade system to limit greenhouse gas emissions	NO
Provide $2 billion for the "cash for clunkers" program	NO
Establish the government as the sole provider of student loans	NO
Restrict federally funded insurance coverage for abortions in health care overhaul	YES

CQ Vote Studies

	PARTY UNITY		PRESIDENTIAL SUPPORT	
	SUPPORT	OPPOSE	SUPPORT	OPPOSE
2010	98%	2%	22%	78%
2009	99%	1%	13%	87%
2008	97%	3%	77%	23%
2007	99%	1%	89%	11%
2006	96%	4%	83%	17%

Interest Groups

	AFL-CIO	ADA	CCUS	ACU
2010	0%	5%	75%	96%
2009	5%	0%	73%	96%
2008	0%	5%	83%	96%
2007	4%	0%	75%	100%
2006	21%	15%	93%	100%

Iowa 5

West — Sioux City, Council Bluffs

The 32-county 5th takes in miles of fertile soil and gently undulating hills across the western part of the state. This bountiful land has enabled the region to remain more like the Iowa of old than has any other part of the state. The 5th has the most farmland in Iowa and grows the most corn and soybeans in the state, but it has the fewest residents of any Iowa district, as of the 2010 census.

Sioux City is the district's largest metropolitan center and has a rich link to America's history: Lewis and Clark passed through it on their way to the Pacific Northwest. With South Dakota and Nebraska to its west, Sioux City has become a major trading center for the tristate area. Home of the original annual "Corn Palaces" in the late 19th century, Sioux City is now a distribution center for the state's primary crop. The growth of alternative-fuel production was a boon for the area, and dozens of ethanol plants operate within 90 miles of the city. Rising costs in the corn-based-fuel industry, nationwide economic downturns and federal regulations can cause uncertainty for the industry.

Council Bluffs, nicknamed "Iowa's Leading Edge," also is located on the state's western border, farther south along the Missouri River, which divides it from Omaha, Neb. Public improvement projects under way since the mid-1990s attracted companies to the city, but layoffs have affected all economic sectors. City officials plan to continue investment in infrastructure and riverfront development. Gaming became big business: The city is Iowa's largest casino market, and three of the city's major employers are casinos. Other residents commute across the river to work for Omaha businesses.

The Corn Belt farmland found in the rest of the 5th gives it a strong GOP feel. Republican John McCain took 55 percent of the 2008 presidential vote in the 5th — the only Iowa district he won — and Republican Gov. Terry Branstad won every county here in the 2010 election.

Major Industry
Agriculture, distribution, gaming

Cities
Sioux City, 82,684; Council Bluffs, 62,230; Spencer, 11,233

Notable
The Lewis and Clark Interpretive Center is located in Sioux City; the Union Pacific Railroad Museum is located in Council Bluffs.

KANSAS

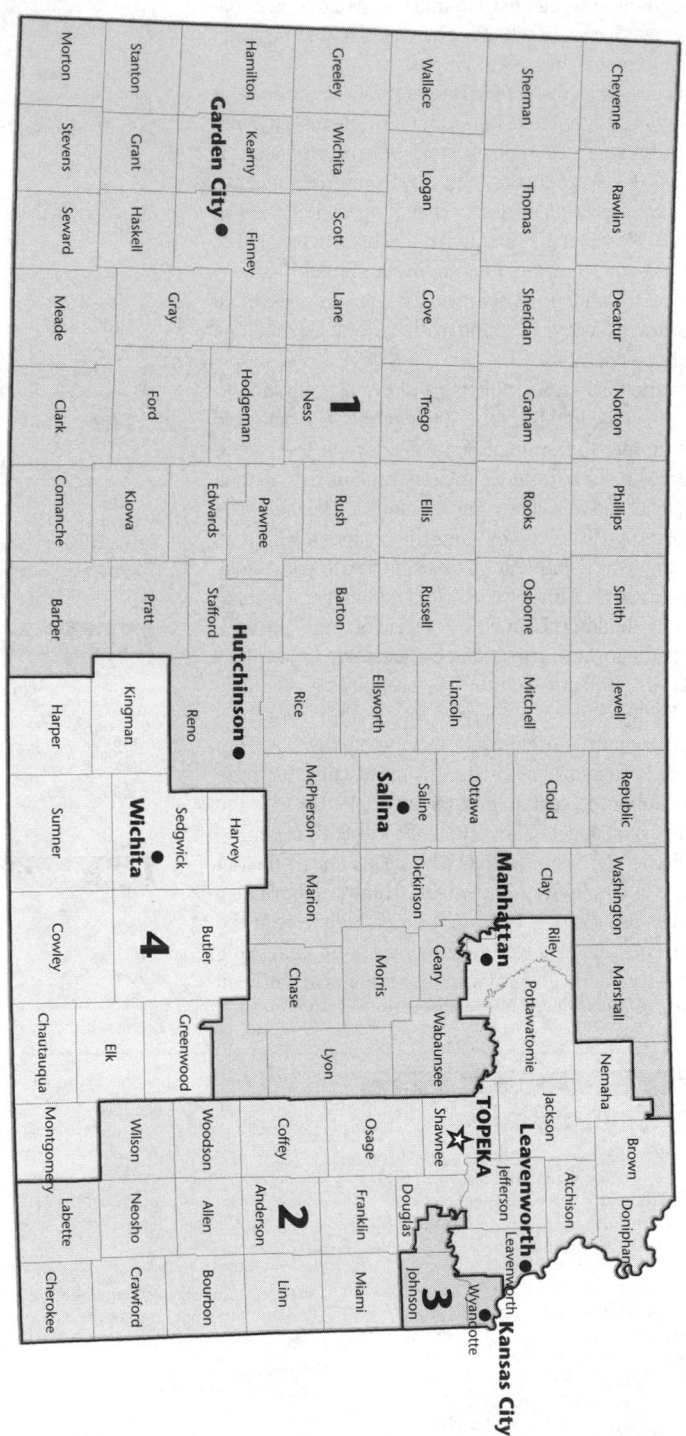

GOV. SAM BROWNBACK (R)

First elected: 2010
Length of term: 4 years
Term expires: 1/15
Salary: $110,707
Phone: (785) 296-3232
Residence: Topeka
Born: Sept. 12, 1956; Garnett, Kan.
Religion: Roman Catholic
Family: Wife, Mary Brownback; five children
Education: Kansas State U., B.S. 1979 (agricultural economics); U. of Kansas, J.D. 1982
Career: College instructor; lawyer; White House fellow
Political highlights: Kan. secretary of Agriculture, 1986-93; U.S. House, 1995-96; U.S. Senate, 1996-2011

ELECTION RESULTS

2010 GENERAL
Sam Brownback (R)	530,760	63.2%
Tom Holland (D)	270,166	32.2%
Andrew P. Grey (LIBERT)	22,460	2.6%
Kenneth W. Cannon (REF)	15,397	1.8%

LT. GOV. JEFF COLYER (R)

First elected: 2010
Length of term: 4 years
Term expires: 1/15
Salary: $31,313
Phone: (785) 296-2213

LEGISLATURE

Legislature: January to spring, limit of 90 days in even-numbered years
Senate: 40 members, 4-year terms
2011 ratios: 32 R, 8 D; 28 men, 12 women
Salary: $89/day in session; $123/day expenses
Phone: (785) 296-7633
House: 125 members, 2-year terms
2011 ratios: 92 R, 33 D; 92 men, 33 women
Salary: $89/day in session; $123/day expenses
Phone: (785) 296-7633

TERM LIMITS

Governor: 2 terms
Senate: No
House: No

URBAN STATISTICS

CITY	POPULATION
Wichita	382,368
Overland Park	173,372
Kansas City	145,786
Topeka	127,473
Olathe	125,872

REGISTERED VOTERS

Republican	44%
Unaffiliated/others	29%
Democrat	27%

POPULATION

2010 population	2,853,118
2000 population	2,688,418
1990 population	2,477,574
Percent change (2000-2010)	+6.1%
Rank among states (2010)	33
Median age	35.9
Born in state	59.1%
Foreign born	5.8%
Violent crime rate	400/100,000
Poverty level	13.4%
Federal workers	35,148
Military	25,482

ELECTIONS

STATE ELECTION OFFICIAL
(785) 296-4561
DEMOCRATIC PARTY
(785) 234-0425
REPUBLICAN PARTY
(785) 234-3456

MISCELLANEOUS

Web: www.kansas.gov
Capital: Topeka

U.S. CONGRESS

Senate: 2 Republicans
House: 4 Republicans

2010 CENSUS STATISTICS BY DISTRICT

District	2008 VOTE FOR PRESIDENT Obama	McCain	White	Black	Asian	Hispanic	Median Income	White Collar	Blue Collar	Service Industry	Over 64	Under 18	College Education	Rural	Sq. Miles
1	30%	69%	80%	2%	1%	15%	$42,403	53%	30%	17%	16%	25%	20%	48%	57,373
2	43	55	84	5	1	6	44,994	58	25	17	13	24	26	40	14,134
3	51	48	74	8	4	11	61,927	69	16	15	10	25	43	5	778
4	40	58	75	7	3	11	47,076	57	27	16	13	27	25	21	9,531
STATE	42	57	78	6	2	11	48,394	60	24	16	13	25	29	29	81,815
U.S.	53	46	64	12	5	16	51,425	60	23	17	13	25	28	21	3,537,438

Sen. Pat Roberts (R)

Capitol Office
224-4774
roberts.senate.gov
109 Hart Bldg. 20510-1605; fax 224-3514

Committees
Agriculture, Nutrition & Forestry - Ranking Member
Finance
Health, Education, Labor & Pensions
Rules & Administration
Select Ethics

Residence
Dodge City

Born
April 20, 1936; Topeka, Kan.

Religion
Methodist

Family
Wife, Franki Roberts; three children

Education
Kansas State U., B.A. 1958 (journalism)

Military Service
Marine Corps, 1958-62

Career
Newspaper owner; reporter; congressional aide

Political Highlights
U.S. House, 1981-97

ELECTION RESULTS

2008 GENERAL

Pat Roberts (R)	727,121	60.1%
Jim Slattery (D)	441,399	36.5%
Randall Hodgkinson (LIBERT)	25,727	2.1%
Joseph L. Martin (REF)	16,443	1.4%

2008 PRIMARY

Pat Roberts (R)	unopposed

2002 GENERAL

Pat Roberts (R)	641,075	82.5%
Steven A. Rosile (LIBERT)	70,725	9.1%
George Cook (REF)	65,050	8.4%

Previous Winning Percentages
1996 (62%); 1994 House Election (77%); 1992 House
Election (68%); 1990 House Election (63%); 1988 House
Election (100%); 1986 House Election (77%); 1984
House Election (76%); 1982 House Election (68%)

Elected 1996; 3rd term

Although he has bucked his party in the past, Roberts is a conservative who uses his strong voice to promote the party line as well as his own opinions. That ability to blaze his own path, combined with a homespun and pithy style, has served him well during his three decades in Congress.

Roberts is a reliable GOP vote on most issues, although he has reached across the aisle at times in defiance of party leaders. On votes that pitted a majority of Republicans against a majority of Democrats, Roberts went with Republicans 90 percent of the time in 2009 and 99 percent the following year, up from 84 percent in 2007.

Rep. Barney Frank, a liberal Massachusetts Democrat, once told the Kansas City Star that Roberts was "not one of the impossible ideologues." In 2007, Roberts was one of 18 Republicans to defy President George W. Bush and vote to more than double spending over five years for the Children's Health Insurance Program, which provides insurance for children from low-income families that make too much money to qualify for Medicaid. In 2008, he was one of nearly two dozen Republican senators who opposed cutting fees for physicians who participate in the Medicare program. And he voted against Bush's $700 billion financial rescue plan in October 2008, saying it did not protect taxpayers and contained no meaningful oversight.

But Roberts spent much of 2010 becoming one of the GOP's loudest voices against the Democrats' health care overhaul and leading the fight against Donald M. Berwick, President Obama's pick to lead the Centers for Medicare and Medicaid Services. He repeatedly called on Berwick to testify before the Finance Committee, on which Roberts sits, and warned that Berwick had made statements in favor of government rationing of health care.

After Obama gave Berwick a recess appointment and renominated him at the start of the 112th Congress (2011-12), Roberts expressed disappointment that "despite Dr. Berwick's six months on the job as head of CMS, he has appeared before the Finance Committee exactly once." The Democratic chairman of the panel, Max Baucus of Montana, never scheduled a confirmation hearing.

Roberts, who also sits on the Health, Education, Labor and Pensions Committee, voted in early 2011 to repeal the health care law.

His involvement in health care issues increased when he took a spot on Finance after leaving the Select Intelligence Committee in 2007. He was chairman of that panel for four years. Drama from Intelligence panel followed him when documents released in early 2010 claimed that Roberts had raised no objection to the CIA's plan to destroy videotapes that allegedly showed agents waterboarding terror suspects. Roberts denied approving the plan.

Although he does not tout the fact, few members have as good a claim as Roberts to foreseeing the threat of a terrorist attack before Sept. 11, 2001. As the first chairman of the Armed Services Subcommittee on Emerging Threats and Capabilities, which focuses on terrorism threats, Roberts in 1999 began pressing the Pentagon and Congress to get beyond a Cold War mentality and prepare for attacks that would use unconventional weapons. He urged preparedness for a gamut of possible terrorist assaults — attacks on civilian populations with nuclear, chemical or biological weapons and cyberattacks on critical computer networks.

Roberts also gave up his slot on Armed Services, although he has remained an outspoken defender of Kansas military installations and Boeing Co.'s ultimately successful efforts to secure a contract for U.S. military refueling planes, which will be built largely in Wichita. He also joined the Senate Aerospace Caucus when it was established in 2010.

Another issue that has always been high on Roberts' agenda is agriculture. A former House Agriculture chairman, Roberts was a prime architect of the 1996 farm law, which replaced traditional crop subsidies with a system of fixed but declining payments to farmers. He voted against the 2002 farm bill, which undid a number of the changes he and other Republicans had earlier written into law. He had the seniority to claim the top GOP slot on the Senate Agriculture, Nutrition and Forestry Committee in the 110th Congress (2007-08), when the panel drafted an overhaul of the nation's farm policy, but deferred to Saxby Chambliss of Georgia. At the start of the 112th Congress, with another farm bill to be written, Roberts took over the lead GOP chair.

He wrote in a Wichita Eagle op-ed that his priorities would be "maintaining the production agriculture safety net, expanding trade opportunities for farmers and ranchers, conducting oversight of regulations that threaten to destroy the competitiveness of America's farmers, and maintaining the security of our food and agriculture sectors." He is the first person ever to have served as chairman and ranking member of the House Agriculture Committee and ranking member of the Senate's complementary panel.

Roberts scored a coup for his state in December 2008, when the Homeland Security Department recommended that Manhattan, Kan., become the home of the National Bio- and Agro-Defense Facility, a federal site for animal disease research and bioterrorism defense. Roberts had lobbied for the recommendation since 2005.

Since 1999, Roberts has been on the Select Ethics Committee, where he was the chairman from late 1999 to mid-2001. He also sits on the Senate Rules and Administration Committee.

Roberts is not all business, however. More than once, Washingtonian magazine's annual survey of congressional staff found him the "funniest senator." Lamenting his lack of input on the 2004 intelligence overhaul, Roberts said, "I'm like a one-legged chicken." In 2003, he said asking the federal agency that administers Medicare and Medicaid for help would be akin to "asking the Boston Strangler for a necklace."

A fourth-generation Kansan, Roberts earned a journalism degree from Kansas State University, intending to follow a family tradition in the news business. His great-grandfather, J.W. Roberts, founded the Oskaloosa Independent, the second-oldest newspaper in Kansas, after moving to the Kansas Territory from Ohio with "a Bible, a six-shooter and printing press in tow," according to a 1996 profile of Roberts in the Kansas City Star. Politics ran in the family, too; Roberts' father, Wes, was chairman of the Republican National Committee under President Dwight D. Eisenhower.

After graduation, Roberts was drafted, so he joined the Marines, as his father had, and his office is decorated with Corps regalia. Returning home in 1962, he worked as a reporter and then co-owned a weekly newspaper.

He first arrived in Washington to work as a Senate aide and later ran the office of Republican Rep. Keith G. Sebelius of Kansas. When Sebelius announced his retirement in 1980, Roberts was ready. He cruised to victory in the general election, capitalizing on Sebelius' popularity and referring to "our record" so frequently that he sounded like an incumbent.

Roberts initially balked at making a Senate bid in 1996 when Republican Nancy Landon Kassebaum retired, saying he wanted to focus on shepherding the farm bill into law. But he eventually entered the race and handily won the GOP nod. Facing Democratic state Treasurer Sally Thompson in the fall, he won with 62 percent of the vote. In 2002, Democrats didn't field a candidate. Despite a Democratic tide nationally in 2008, he won again handily, with 60 percent, over former Democratic Rep. Jim Slattery.

Key Votes

2010

Pass budget reconciliation bill to modify overhauls of health care and federal student loan programs	NO
Proceed to disapproval resolution on EPA authority to regulate greenhouse gases	YES
Overhaul financial services industry regulation	NO
Limit debate to proceed to a bill to broaden campaign finance disclosure and reporting rules	NO
Limit debate on an extension of Bush-era income tax cuts for two years	YES
Limit debate on a bill to provide a path to legal status for some children of illegal immigrants	NO
Allow for a repeal of "don't ask, don't tell"	NO
Consent to ratification of a strategic arms reduction treaty with Russia	NO

2009

Prevent release of remaining financial industry bailout funds	YES
Make it easier for victims to sue for wage discrimination remedies	NO
Expand the Children's Health Insurance Program	NO
Limit debate on the economic stimulus measure	NO
Repeal District of Columbia firearms prohibitions and gun registration laws	YES
Limit debate on expansion of federal hate crimes law	NO
Strike funding for F-22 Raptor fighter jets	NO

CQ Vote Studies

	PARTY UNITY		PRESIDENTIAL SUPPORT	
	SUPPORT	OPPOSE	SUPPORT	OPPOSE
2010	99%	1%	29%	71%
2009	90%	10%	51%	49%
2008	87%	13%	65%	35%
2007	84%	16%	81%	19%
2006	94%	6%	88%	12%
2005	94%	6%	93%	7%
2004	99%	1%	92%	8%
2003	96%	4%	97%	3%
2002	96%	4%	96%	4%
2001	95%	5%	99%	1%

Interest Groups

	AFL-CIO	ADA	CCUS	ACU
2010	7%	0%	100%	96%
2009	11%	5%	67%	96%
2008	30%	20%	88%	72%
2007	26%	20%	73%	92%
2006	27%	5%	92%	84%
2005	8%	0%	100%	88%
2004	17%	15%	100%	92%
2003	0%	15%	100%	90%
2002	15%	0%	100%	100%
2001	13%	0%	93%	100%

Sen. Jerry Moran (R)

Capitol Office
224-6521
moran.senate.gov
354 Russell Bldg. 20510-1604; fax 228-6966

Committees
Appropriations
Banking, Housing & Urban Affairs
Small Business & Entrepreneurship
Veterans' Affairs
Special Aging

Residence
Hays

Born
May 29, 1954; Great Bend, Kan.

Religion
Methodist

Family
Wife, Robba Moran; two children

Education
Fort Hays Kansas State College, attended 1972-73; U. of Kansas, B.S. 1976 (economics), J.D. 1981

Career
Lawyer; banker

Political Highlights
Kan. Senate, 1989-97 (vice president, 1993-95; majority leader, 1995-97); U.S. House, 1997-2011

ELECTION RESULTS

2010 GENERAL

Jerry Moran (R)	587,175	70.1%
Lisa Johnston (D)	220,971	26.4%
Michael Dann (LIBERT)	17,922	2.1%
Joe Bellis (D)	11,624	1.4%

2010 PRIMARY

Jerry Moran (R)	163,483	49.7%
Todd Tiahrt (R)	146,702	44.6%
Tom Little (R)	10,256	3.1%
Robert Londerholm (R)	8,278	2.5%

Previous Winning Percentages
2008 House Election (82%); 2006 House Election (79%); 2004 House Election (91%); 2002 House Election (91%); 2000 House Election (89%); 1998 House Election (81%); 1996 House Election (73%)

Elected 2010; 1st term

Moran entered the Senate prepared to reach across the aisle just as he often tried to do in the House, where his legislative focus was on the needs of his mostly rural constituency.

"I'm a conservative, but I am not an overly partisan member," he said, emphasizing his ability to work with lawmakers of both parties and bridge the gap between conservatives and moderates. "I respect other people's points of view."

His independent streak can run in either ideological direction.

In early 2011, he was one of 15 Republicans siding with Democrats against an amendment to the Federal Aviation Administration reauthorization legislation that would have eliminated the Essential Air Service, which provides subsidized flights to rural airports. In 2003, he voted against the Republican-sponsored Medicare prescription drug program because he considered it a budget buster. He has often sided with many Democrats in supporting an easing of restrictions on trade with Cuba. In each instance, he saw the measures as bad deals for rural Kansans.

He sounded a bipartisan tone after President Obama took office in 2009, telling a Wichita audience that the new president appeared to want to find "some level of common ground we can agree upon."

He was soon disappointed, though, and said Democrats "got off track by making health care first and foremost" in the 111th Congress (2009-10). When Moran crossed to the other side of the Capitol in 2011, he became a founding member of the Senate Tea Party Caucus.

While acknowledging the need for changes to the health care system, Moran has been frustrated with the Democrats' overhaul enacted in 2010. Immediately after Congress cleared the bill, he introduced legislation to repeal the law, but recognized a repeal will not happen while Obama is in office. As a member of the Appropriations Committee, he plans to take part in efforts to reduce the law's "effects and burdens" by altering or refusing to fund portions of it. As a former co-chairman of the House Rural Health Care Coalition, he is particularly concerned about the law's effect on health care delivery in rural areas.

"Employment, jobs, economy need to remain the top priority," he said. In setting goals for the 112th Congress (2011-12), lawmakers should get spending under control, overhaul the earmarking process, balance the budget and promote "the opportunity for business to succeed," he said.

In Moran's view, that generally means lower taxes and less government intrusion.

He opposed Obama's economic stimulus plan in 2009, a vote in keeping with his opposition in fall 2008 to two $700 billion measures — the second of which President George W. Bush signed into law — aimed at helping the ailing financial industry. "I did not see the benefit to Kansans and was not convinced the administration had any concrete plan of how to turn the economy around despite being given $700 billion," said Moran, who is the ranking Republican on the Financial Services and General Government Appropriations panel and also won a seat on the Banking, Housing and Urban Affairs Committee.

Moran had a hand in writing two farm bills during his time in the House, and he sees himself as an important voice for farmers when lawmakers consider a new farm bill in the 112th, which he calls a "very urban and suburban Congress."

During debate in the 110th Congress (2007-08) on the rewrite of the 2002 farm law, Moran said, he attended every field hearing the committee held, listening to testimony from everyone from "rice growers in California to catfish growers in Mississippi." When debate bogged down, he introduced a bill to extend the previous law for one year. Moran opposed the final bill, saying it failed to protect direct payments to farmers and maintain support for crop insurance.

Moran hopes to work on energy policy as well, and he strongly supports expanding the use of nuclear power and developing renewable energy.

He served on the House Veterans' Affairs Committee and continues that work on the Senate panel.

In 2008 he saw Bush sign into law his bill aimed at improving health care for veterans who live in rural areas. The law established a pilot program under which the Veterans Affairs Department must contract with local providers if a veteran lives a significant distance from a VA hospital.

When the Bush administration, in response to the terrorism threat, stopped a program that gave visas to foreign doctors who promised to work in rural outposts, Moran rallied opposition among rural lawmakers. The administration ultimately agreed to resume processing applications and in 2004 Moran helped win a two-year extension of the program.

He also sits on the Homeland Security and Governmental Affairs, Small Business and Entrepreneurship and Special Aging committees.

Moran is a native of western Kansas' 1st District, which at 57,373 square miles is among the nation's largest. He was the first in his family to attend college; his father was a laborer in the oil fields and his mother worked as a secretary at an electric utility.

As a high school student government officer, Moran was in charge of inviting the local congressman, Republican Keith G. Sebelius, to speak at a fundraising dinner. In the summer of 1974, Moran went to Washington to work as an intern for Sebelius (father-in-law of Obama's secretary of Health and Human Services, former Kansas Gov. Kathleen Sebelius). That was at the height of the Watergate scandal, and Moran attended almost every House Judiciary Committee hearing on President Richard Nixon's impeachment.

After graduating from college with a degree in economics in 1976, Moran took a job as a banker. He earned his law degree five years later and opened his own practice in Hays.

He made a long-shot race for the state Senate in 1988 against an 18-year incumbent and won by a couple hundred votes as a Republican in a historically Democratic district. Moran went on to become chairman of the chamber's Judiciary Committee, then ascended to majority leader in 1995.

He ran for Congress in 1996 when Republican Pat Roberts left the House to succeed Republican Nancy Landon Kassebaum in the Senate. Moran rolled to an easy victory with 73 percent of the vote against Democrat John Divine, a former Salina mayor. In redistricting following the 2000 census, the Big First got even larger to make up for population losses in many of the western and central counties. Moran continued racking up decisive wins.

When Republican Sam Brownback announced he was leaving the Senate to run for governor, Moran jumped into the 2010 race. He faced House colleague and conservative stalwart Todd Tiahrt in the GOP primary. Tiahrt attacked Moran as not dependably conservative enough on a range of issues. Moran countered that he has been "a conservative even when Republicans are in charge and are doing things we can't afford," pointing to his vote against the prescription drug benefit. Moran slipped past Tiahrt by 4 percentage points in the August primary.

That all but decided who would succeed Brownback. Kansas hasn't elected a Democrat to the Senate since 1932, and Moran easily defeated Lisa Johnston, a college administrator, with 70 percent of the vote.

Key Votes (while House member)

2010

Overhaul the nation's health insurance system	NO
Allow for repeal of "don't ask, don't tell"	NO
Overhaul financial services industry regulation	NO
Limit use of new Afghanistan War funds to troop withdrawal activities	NO
Change oversight of offshore drilling and lift oil spill liability cap	?
Provide a path to legal status for some children of illegal immigrants	NO
Extend Bush-era income tax cuts for two years	NO

2009

Expand the Children's Health Insurance Program	YES
Provide $787 billion in tax cuts and spending increases to stimulate the economy	NO
Allow bankruptcy judges to modify certain primary-residence mortgages	NO
Create a cap-and-trade system to limit greenhouse gas emissions	NO
Provide $2 billion for the "cash for clunkers" program	NO
Establish the government as the sole provider of student loans	NO
Restrict federally funded insurance coverage for abortions in health care overhaul	YES

CQ Vote Studies (while House member)

	PARTY UNITY		PRESIDENTIAL SUPPORT	
	SUPPORT	OPPOSE	SUPPORT	OPPOSE
2010	99%	1%	18%	82%
2009	96%	4%	21%	79%
2008	90%	10%	69%	31%
2007	87%	13%	71%	29%
2006	87%	13%	70%	30%
2005	92%	8%	76%	24%
2004	92%	8%	68%	32%
2003	92%	8%	82%	18%
2002	89%	11%	72%	28%
2001	90%	10%	77%	23%

Interest Groups (while House member)

	AFL-CIO	ADA	CCUS	ACU
2010	8%	5%	71%	100%
2009	19%	5%	80%	96%
2008	14%	15%	89%	92%
2007	21%	30%	80%	88%
2006	29%	5%	93%	84%
2005	29%	15%	93%	96%
2004	21%	10%	95%	92%
2003	27%	25%	90%	92%
2002	0%	5%	90%	96%
2001	25%	5%	96%	88%

Rep. Tim Huelskamp (R)

Capitol Office
225-2715
huelskamp.house.gov
126 Cannon Bldg. 20515-1601; fax 225-5124

Committees
Agriculture
Budget
Veterans' Affairs

Residence
Fowler

Born
Nov. 11, 1968; Fowler, Kan.

Religion
Roman Catholic

Family
Wife, Angela Huelskamp; four children

Education
College of Santa Fe, B.A. 1991 (education); American U., Ph.D. 1995 (political science)

Career
Farmer

Political Highlights
Kan. Senate, 1997-2011

ELECTION RESULTS

2010 GENERAL

Tim Huelskamp (R)	142,281	73.8%
Alan Jilka (D)	44,068	22.8%
Jack Warner (D)	6,537	3.4%

2010 PRIMARY

Tim Huelskamp (R)	34,819	34.8%
Jim Barnett (R)	25,047	25.0%
Tracey Mann (R)	21,161	21.2%
Rob Wasinger (R)	9,296	9.3%
Sue Boldra (R)	7,892	7.9%
Marck Cobb (R)	1,768	1.8%

Elected 2010; 1st term

Huelskamp says he will be a "reliable conservative vote" in Congress, and he has a record in the Kansas Senate to back that up.

During his 14-year tenure in the legislature, he sponsored an amendment to strip Planned Parenthood of state funding and pushed for amendments to the state constitution to ban gay marriage and guarantee individual gun rights. Early in the 112th Congress (2011-12) he reprised his vote against funding Planned Parenthood on a catchall spending bill for fiscal 2011. Huelskamp, a member of the Budget Committee, also won inclusion of an amendment to bar funding for nine so-called czar positions, including the director of the White House Office of Health Reform.

Huelskamp also has a familiarity with immigration: Two of his four adopted children are from Haiti. He says the international adoption process could be streamlined, and he advocates a hard-line approach to illegal immigration. "I've been through Immigration and Customs Enforcement [and] the paperwork," he said. "And it was a difficult situation, going through all that paper. But when I look at that situation, I see that citizenship should be a privilege, not a right. It should be difficult."

A farmer, Huelskamp will play a role in the crafting of a new farm bill on the Agriculture Committee. Among his priorities for the legislation, he has said, is to boost exports. He also serves on the Veterans' Affairs Committee.

Huelskamp was born in Fowler and resides there today. He attended Catholic seminary in Santa Fe and received degrees from both the College of Santa Fe and American University.

Huelskamp opened a federal campaign account in 2006 when then-Rep. Jerry Moran was mulling a gubernatorial bid. When Moran announced in 2008 that he would make a bid two years later for Republican Sen. Sam Brownback's to-be vacated Senate seat, Huelskamp jumped in.

He won the endorsement of the anti-tax Club for Growth and raised the most money in taking 35 percent of the vote in a six-way primary that included former Brownback chief of staff Rob Wasinger. He took almost 74 percent against the Democratic nominee, former Salina Mayor Alan Jilka.

Kansas 1

West — Salina, Hutchinson, Garden City, Emporia

In the 1960s, Truman Capote described western Kansas as a "lonesome area that other Kansans call 'out there.'" The conservative Big 1st takes in all of western Kansas and stretches as far east as Nemaha County in the north and the city of Emporia farther south, covering most of rural Kansas in the process. The district covers 70 percent of the state and has more land area than most U.S. states.

The 1st's economy depends on agriculture, but several years of drought have hurt local wheat, sorghum and corn yields. The departure of young people from rural areas, plus an aging population, have stalled growth; many counties here have smaller populations now than they did a century ago. The largest population center, Salina, is in the district's eastern portion and relies on agriculture and manufacturing. Food-related industry, manufacturing and health care jobs dominate Hutchinson, the site of the annual Kansas State Fair. The return of the Army's Big Red One brigade to Fort Riley (in the 2nd) sparked a population boom in Junction City and the surrounding counties. In the west, towns such as Garden City and Dodge City rely on meatpacking and tourism; the cattle industry in Kansas remains relatively stable and has drawn large numbers of Mexican immigrants.

The 1st is comfortably Republican, and the GOP dominates local offices. Many counties have no Democratic Party organizations.

Major Industry
Agriculture, manufacturing, oil and gas

Cities
Salina, 47,707; Hutchinson, 42,080

Notable
Dwight D. Eisenhower's burial place and presidential library are in Abilene.

Rep. Lynn Jenkins (R)

Capitol Office
225-6601
lynnjenkins.house.gov
1122 Longworth Bldg. 20515-1602; fax 225-7986

Committees
Ways & Means

Residence
Topeka

Born
June 10, 1963; Topeka, Kan.

Religion
United Methodist

Family
Divorced; two children

Education
Kansas State U., A.A. 1985 (business administration);
Weber State College, B.S. 1985 (accounting)

Career
Homemaker; accountant

Political Highlights
Kan. House, 1999-2001; Kan. Senate, 2001-03; Kan.
treasurer, 2003-09

ELECTION RESULTS

2010 GENERAL

Lynn Jenkins (R)	130,034	63.1%
Cheryl Hudspeth (D)	66,588	32.3%
Robert Garrard (D)	9,353	4.5%

2010 PRIMARY

Lynn Jenkins (R)	41,458	57.2%
Dennis Pyle (R)	31,085	42.8%

2008 GENERAL

Lynn Jenkins (R)	155,532	50.6%
Nancy Boyda (D)	142,013	46.2%
Leslie S. Martin (REF)	5,080	1.6%
Robert Garrard (LIBERT)	4,683	1.5%

Elected 2008; 2nd term

Jenkins, a certified public accountant and former Kansas treasurer and legislator, carved out a niche in her first term as a watchdog of fiscal responsibility and congressional transparency. At the start of her second, she moved to the powerful Ways and Means Committee, where she can broaden her portfolio to include taxes, health care and trade.

She serves on the panel's Oversight Subcommittee, which fits in nicely with her efforts to bird dog not just of the executive branch but the legislative branch as well.

Jenkins introduced legislation in 2010 and again in 2011 intended to bar lame-duck sessions of Congress. "We should never, ever allow folks who are no longer accountable to wreak havoc with our country," she said on Fox News after the extended lame-duck session of the 111th Congress (2009-10) had come to an end.

The nameplate outside Jenkins House office reads "Lynn Jenkins, C.P.A." It's a designation she takes seriously in advocating more-careful money management by government. In February 2009, she criticized a Democratic mortgage assistance bill that included language, known as the "cramdown" provision, to allow bankruptcy courts to modify the terms of residential mortgages. "Congress should not be in the business of rewarding bad actors," she said in a House floor speech.

Jenkins introduced legislation in July 2009 to enable any House member to force a vote specifically to recognize how any piece of pending legislation would affect the budget deficit or national debt, based on a Congressional Budget Office review.

Jenkins is a consistent GOP vote. She sided with her party 96 percent of the time in her first term on votes in which majorities of the two parties diverged.

In her second week in office, she voted against an expansion of a children's health insurance program, arguing that allowing families with higher incomes to participate would put at risk "valuable health coverage ... for America's neediest children."

In February 2009 she was the only freshman named to a group of 16 Republicans to draft a GOP alternative to the Democratic health care overhaul. The group released an outline that included some provisions that made it into law, such as allowing dependents to remain on their parents' health policies into their 20s. But it focused on ideas eventually rejected by Democrats, such as allowing small businesses and other organizations to join forces to cut the cost of health insurance. After the overhaul was enacted, Jenkins urged Kansas' attorney general to join other states in challenging the law's constitutionality. In 2011, she voted to repeal the law.

Jenkins favors making permanent the George W. Bush-era tax cuts that were extended for two years near the end of 2010. And she wants to abolish the federal estate tax, which she says places burdens on Kansans who want to pass family farms to subsequent generations. She sponsored legislation to provide a tax credit to small businesses that hire members of the National Guard and Reserves.

Jenkins sought earmarks — member-requested provisions added to spending and sometimes authorization bills — in 2009 to upgrade highways, conduct research into plastics engineering at Pittsburg State University and expand a cancer center at the University of Kansas. She also supports a proposed national facility at Kansas State University to research ways to prevent and cope with terrorist attacks on the nation's food supply. She endorsed the GOP's earmark moratorium, but broke with other fiscal conservatives in supporting the fiscal 2010 Agriculture spending bill, which contained funding important to her state's farmers.

Alarmed by President Obama's plans in early 2009 to shut down the military detention facility on the U.S. naval base at Guantánamo Bay, Cuba, Jenkins worked to ensure that detainees held there were not sent to a federal prison at Fort Leavenworth in her district. "It will be over my dead body that those detainees are sent to Leavenworth," she said. On her first day as a new member of Congress, she introduced a bill to block any such transfer.

The energetic Jenkins puts a premium on constituent service, traveling back to Kansas every week. Jenkins' devotion to keeping in touch landed her in a bit of hot water when it was revealed that she spent $422,000 on taxpayer-funded mailings in 2009, three times as much as the other three members of the Kansas House delegation combined. In a guest column in the Topeka Capital-Journal in April 2010, she wrote that "compared to my predecessor in Congress, I spent approximately the same amount on mailings. Any difference in constituent communications expense is largely attributable to telephone conferences with constituents, which my predecessor did not fully utilize."

Jenkins grew up on a dairy farm north of Topeka, where she helped her parents milk cattle before and after school each day. The attitude in her family was that government should "get out of the way," save for when it comes to national defense. As a child, she marched in the Jackson County 4-H Club State Parade wearing sandwich boards for Republican candidates. She served as student body president at her high school; went on to receive a degree in accounting from Weber State College in Ogden, Utah; and worked as a CPA for more than a decade.

She got involved in the local Republican Women's Club, and when a state House vacancy opened in 1997, she ran in a special election decided by party officials, losing by a single vote. But she ran again the following year and won. After two years in the Kansas House and two in the state Senate, she ran for state treasurer in 2002 and won with 56 percent of the vote.

After easily winning a second term as treasurer, Jenkins set her sights on the seat held by first-term Democrat Nancy Boyda, who had upset Republican Jim Ryun in 2006. But Jenkins first had to get past Ryun, who sought to recapture his seat. She edged the former track star with 51 percent of the vote.

Jenkins' race against Boyda was an acrimonious campaign to which both national parties devoted serious attention, with Jenkins winning by 4 percentage points. Three days after the election, Jenkins' husband filed for divorce.

She was re-elected in 2010 with 63 percent of the vote.

Key Votes

2010

Overhaul the nation's health insurance system	NO
Allow for repeal of "don't ask, don't tell"	NO
Overhaul financial services industry regulation	NO
Limit use of new Afghanistan War funds to troop withdrawal activities	NO
Change oversight of offshore drilling and lift oil spill liability cap	NO
Provide a path to legal status for some children of illegal immigrants	NO
Extend Bush-era income tax cuts for two years	YES

2009

Expand the Children's Health Insurance Program	NO
Provide $787 billion in tax cuts and spending increases to stimulate the economy	NO
Allow bankruptcy judges to modify certain primary-residence mortgages	NO
Create a cap-and-trade system to limit greenhouse gas emissions	NO
Provide $2 billion for the "cash for clunkers" program	NO
Establish the government as the sole provider of student loans	NO
Restrict federally funded insurance coverage for abortions in health care overhaul	YES

CQ Vote Studies

	PARTY UNITY		PRESIDENTIAL SUPPORT	
	SUPPORT	OPPOSE	SUPPORT	OPPOSE
2010	97%	3%	26%	74%
2009	95%	5%	22%	78%

Interest Groups

	AFL-CIO	ADA	CCUS	ACU
2010	0%	0%	88%	100%
2009	10%	5%	87%	92%

Kansas 2

East — Topeka, Manhattan, Leavenworth

The 2nd District runs the length of east Kansas from Nebraska to Oklahoma, passing west of Kansas City. This district combines rural farm communities and urbanized areas, including the state capital of Topeka. One-fourth of the 2nd's residents live in Topeka or surrounding Shawnee County, where state government is the largest employer.

The 2nd has enjoyed steady economic growth for decades, and construction of a new federal biodefense facility in Manhattan has brought new jobs. The $725 million National Bio and Agro-Defense Facility will open in 2015 and focus on research relating to the introduction of animal disease threatening crops, livestock and human populations.

Fort Riley and Fort Leavenworth are integral to the local economy. Revenue and new residents arrived in the district with the return of the Army's famed Big Red One infantry division to Fort Riley, in Manhattan, and many servicemembers from Fort Riley retire in the district. Rural areas rely on cattle, corn, soybeans and wheat, but farming, especially in the district's southeast, is vulnerable to droughts.

Rural areas in the district are mainly Republican, while Democrats can find more success in Topeka, western Lawrence (the liberal University of Kansas is in the 3rd's portion of the city), the blue-collar southeast corner, and Manhattan, home to Kansas State University.

The 2nd overall has become more solidly conservative in the last decade, however, and gave John McCain 55 percent of its vote in the 2008 presidential election. In 2010, Rep. Lynn Jenkins won every county in the district, and Republican Sen. Jerry Moran won every county wholly contained in the district.

Major Industry
Agriculture, defense, higher education, government

Military Bases
Fort Riley (Army), 18,553 military, 8,337 civilian; Fort Leavenworth (Army), 2,077 military, 2,377 civilian (2011)

Cities
Topeka, 127,473; Manhattan, 52,281; Leavenworth, 35,251; Lawrence (pt.), 32,550

Notable
The Kansas Museum of History is in Topeka; Mine Creek Battlefield in Pleasanton was the site of Kansas' only major Civil War battle.

Rep. Kevin Yoder (R)

Capitol Office
225-2865
yoder.house.gov
214 Cannon Bldg. 20515-1603; fax 225-2807

Committees
Appropriations

Residence
Overland Park

Born
Jan. 8, 1976; Hutchinson, Kan.

Religion
Christian

Family
Wife, Brooke Robinson Yoder

Education
U. of Kansas, B.A. 1999 (political science & English),
J.D. 2002

Career
Lawyer

Political Highlights
Kan. House, 2003-11

ELECTION RESULTS

2010 GENERAL

Kevin Yoder (R)	136,246	58.4%
Stephene Moore (D)	90,193	38.7%
Jasmin Talbert (LIBERT)	6,846	2.9%

2010 PRIMARY

Kevin Yoder (R)	32,210	44.4%
Patricia Lightner (R)	26,695	36.8%
Craig McPherson (R)	2,664	3.7%
Dan Gilyeat (R)	2,581	3.6%
Jerry M. Malone (R)	2,099	2.9%
Jean Ann Uvodich (R)	1,934	2.7%
Garry R. Klotz (R)	1,873	2.6%
John Timothy Rysavy (R)	1,633	2.2%
Dave King (R)	820	1.1%

Elected 2010; 1st term

A fifth-generation Kansan who grew up on a grain and livestock farm near the community that carries his family name, Yoder is one of three freshman Republicans named to the Appropriations Committee in the 112th Congress. It's a rare honor for a first-term lawmaker, even one who served as chairman of the Appropriations Committee in the state legislature.

Yoder showed early on that he takes a different view of the role of appropriator than some of his elders. "I am committed to the historic challenge of dramatically reducing the size of our government and getting our economy on a sustainable and responsible path," he said upon joining the committee.

He was one of seven appropriators who unsuccessfully backed a plan to cut $22 billion from a catchall spending bill for fiscal 2011.

But Yoder cast a more traditional appropriator's vote — one in support of a local interest — against an amendment to eliminate funding for the National Bio and Agro-Defense Facility in Manhattan, Kan., pointing out that money for the NBAF has been included in the White House budget for several years and is not an earmark.

His agricultural background informs his position on several issues, including the estate tax, which he wants to eliminate because it affects families that want to pass farms on to their descendants.

Yoder campaigned against the health care overhaul enacted in 2010, and he voted to repeal and defund it in the first few weeks of his House tenure.

Yoder has been involved in politics since college, when he was student body president at the University of Kansas. He was a Democrat then, but switched parties before running for the Kansas House. He said the move to the right was a natural progression in political ideology. He got his law degree in 2002, the same year he first ran for the state House, where he served eight years.

Six-term Democratic Rep. Dennis Moore announced in November 2009 that he was retiring. Moore's wife, Stephene, an obstetric nurse, sought to succeed her husband in what is generally considered the only swing district in Kansas.

Yoder won 44 percent of the vote in a nine-candidate primary, then had a fairly easy time defeating Moore, winning with 58 percent of the vote.

Kansas 3

Kansas City region — Overland Park, eastern Lawrence

Eastern Kansas' 3rd differs markedly from the state's other districts. Compact, it is almost entirely within the sphere of Kansas City, Mo., and more than 90 percent of residents live in Kansas City, Kan., or in its Johnson County suburbs. The district hosts Overland Park, Kansas City and Olathe, three of the state's most populous cities. To the west, the 3rd takes in eastern Douglas County and most of Lawrence, Kansas' liberal bastion and home to the University of Kansas. The district contains both the state's richest and poorest counties, and poverty and unemployment abound in the Kansas City, Kan., area. But Kansas City, an industrial town that has had its share of Rust Belt blues, will benefit from a Google pilot program installing super-high-speed Internet lines throughout the city in 2011.

Johnson County is Kansas' economic engine — it is the state's richest county, with telecommunications company headquarters, suburban developments and a stable service sector. While Kansas City has lost population over the past decade, Johnson has grown, and its largest city, Overland Park, is now the second-largest in the state.

Populous, wealthy Johnson County tends to be strongly Republican, but there are areas of Democratic strength in Wyandotte and parts of Douglas counties. Democrat Barack Obama took 51 percent of the 2008 presidential vote in the 3rd, the only district in Kansas that he won.

Major Industry
Telecommunications, manufacturing

Cities
Overland Park, 173,372; Kansas City, 145,786; Olathe, 125,872; Shawnee, 62,209

Notable
The Mahaffie Stagecoach Stop in Olathe is the last remaining Santa Fe Trail stagecoach stop that is still open to the public.

Rep. Mike Pompeo (R)

Capitol Office
225-6216
pompeo.house.gov
107 Cannon Bldg. 20515; fax 225-3489

Committees
Energy & Commerce

Residence
Wichita

Born
Dec. 30, 1963; Orange, Calif.

Religion
Presbyterian

Family
Wife, Susan Pompeo; one child

Education
U.S. Military Academy, B.S. 1986 (engineering management); Harvard U., J.D. 1994

Military
Army, 1986-91

Career
Oilfield equipment company president; aerospace parts manufacturing company president; lawyer

Political Highlights
Republican National Committee, 2008-present

ELECTION RESULTS

2010 GENERAL

Mike Pompeo (R)	119,575	58.8%
Raj Goyle (D)	74,143	36.4%
Susan G. Ducey (REF)	5,041	2.5%
Shawn Smith (LIBERT)	4,624	2.3%

2010 PRIMARY

Mike Pompeo (R)	31,180	38.7%
Jean Kurtis Schodorf (R)	19,099	23.7%
Wink Hartman (R)	18,365	22.8%
Jim Anderson (R)	10,294	12.8%
Paij Rutschman (R)	1,596	2.0%

Elected 2010; 1st term

Pompeo is expected to fit comfortably with his fellow Republican conservatives on both social and fiscal issues.

With experience as chief executive of an aerospace parts manufacturing company and an oil field equipment firm, Pompeo won a coveted seat on the Energy and Commerce Committee, one of five freshman Republicans on the panel.

He wants to reduce the size of government, which he says is destroying jobs and creating uncertainty for private-sector job creators. And he believes the Republican Party needs to return to its core ideals: that "freedom, combined with rewards for risk taking, drives prosperity."

Beyond aligning with much of the Republican platform for the 112th Congress (2011-12), Pompeo will be looking out for particular interests of his 4th District, which includes Wichita, known as the "Air Capital of the World."

Outside of aviation, Pompeo has other military-related experience. He graduated first in his class at West Point and served as a cavalry officer in the Army. He seeks a more concrete strategy in Afghanistan and laments what he sees as months of wavering from the Obama administration on war strategy. He said he supports a "peace through strength" policy toward national defense, wanting to focus on supplying and fully training the U.S. military for 21st century threats.

Pompeo was born in California, and after West Point, he earned a law degree from Harvard, where he was editor of the law review. He began his business career in Wichita in the 1990s.

Republican Rep. Todd Tiahrt left the 4th District seat open for an unsuccessful 2010 Senate bid, opening the door for a newcomer.

In a sometimes nasty GOP primary, Pompeo topped businessman Wink Hartman and state Sen. Jean Schodorf. The general election proved less competitive. Pompeo defeated the Democratic candidate, state Rep. Raj Goyle, with 59 percent of the vote.

Pompeo is the only member of Congress who is also a member of the Republican National Committee.

Kansas 4

South central — Wichita

Wichita, the state's largest city, has long been known as the "Air Capital of the World" because general aviation aircraft production powered the district's economy. The moderately conservative 4th District is centered on Wichita and much of the rest of the district is farmland.

Cessna Aircraft, Hawker Beechcraft, Bombardier Leerjet, Boeing and other airplane manufacturers have operations in the area. Aerostructures manufacturer Spirit Aero-Systems also is headquartered in Wichita. New Boeing defense contracts will bring stability to aerospace and commercial airline sectors that have faced uncertainty in recent years.

City leaders hope that health care facilities and the area's universities can bolster the local economy. Regional agricultural production has fed food manufacturing here. Sumner County, on the Oklahoma border,

leads Kansas in wheat yields, and Harper and Kingman counties to the west also rely heavily on the crop. Sustained drought conditions, however, have hurt agricultural output.

Cattle graze in sparsely populated Greenwood, Elk and Chautauqua counties. Republicans won the 4th's U.S. House seat in 1994 and have kept control of the GOP-leaning district since. Despite higher Republican voter registration, Democrats — aided by a strong union presence in Wichita — do capture some local offices.

Major Industry
Aviation, defense, agriculture, health care

Military Bases
McConnell Air Force Base, 2,850 military, 468 civilian (2011)

Cities
Wichita, 382,368; Derby, 22,158

Notable
Pizza Hut was founded in Wichita in 1958 by students at the University of Wichita (now called Wichita State University).

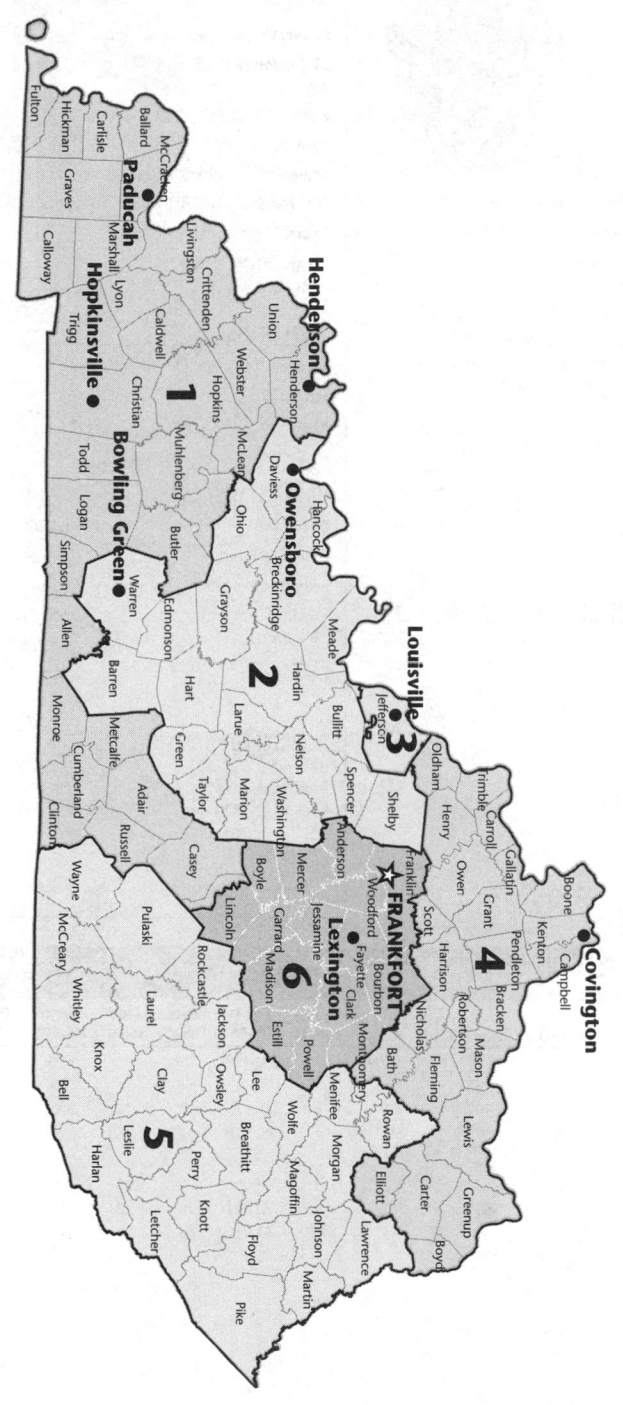

Gov. Steven L. Beshear (D)

First elected: 2007
Length of term: 4 years
Term expires: 1/12
Salary: $145,885
Phone: (502) 564-2611
Residence: Lexington
Born: Sept. 21, 1944; Dawson Springs, Ky.
Religion: Disciples of Christ
Family: Wife, Jane Beshear; two children
Education: U. of Kentucky, B.A. 1966 (history), J.D. 1968
Military service: Army Reserve, 1969-75
Career: Lawyer
Political highlights: Ky. House, 1975-79; attorney general, 1979-83; lieutenant governor, 1983-87; sought Democratic nomination for governor, 1987; Democratic nominee for U.S. Senate, 1996

ELECTION RESULTS

2007 GENERAL

Steven L. Beshear (D)	619,552	58.7%
Ernie Fletcher (R)	435,773	41.3%

Lt. Gov. Daniel Mongiardo (D)

First elected: 2007
Length of term: 4 years
Term expires: 1/12
Salary: $99,312
Phone: (502) 564-2611

LEGISLATURE

General Assembly: January-April in even-numbered years, limit of 60 days; January-March in odd-numbered years, limit of 30 days
Senate: 38 members, 4-year terms
2011 ratios: 22 R, 15 D, 1 I; 32 men, 6 women
Salary: $188 per day in session
Phone: (502) 564-8100
House: 100 members, 2-year terms
2011 ratios: 58 D, 42 R; 81 men, 19 women
Salary: $188 per day in session
Phone: (502) 564-8100

TERM LIMITS

Governor: 2 terms
Senate: No
House: No

URBAN STATISTICS

CITY	POPULATION
Louisville Metro	741,096
Lexington-Fayette	295,803
Bowling Green	58,067
Owensboro	57,265
Covington	40,640

REGISTERED VOTERS

Democrat	56%
Republican	37%
Unaffiliated/Other	7%

POPULATION

2010 population	4,339,367
2000 population	4,041,769
1990 population	3,685,296
Percent change (2000-2010)	+7.4%
Rank among states (2010)	26
Median age	37.3
Born in state	71.1%
Foreign born	2.7%
Violent crime rate	259/100,000
Poverty level	18.6%
Federal workers	42,823
Military	43,138

ELECTIONS

STATE ELECTION OFFICIAL
(502) 573-7100
DEMOCRATIC PARTY
(502) 695-4828
REPUBLICAN PARTY
(502) 875-5130

MISCELLANEOUS

Web: www.kentucky.gov
Capital: Frankfort

U.S. CONGRESS

Senate: 2 Republicans
House: 4 Republicans, 2 Democrats

2010 Census Statistics by District

District	2008 Vote for President Obama	McCain	White	Black	Asian	Hispanic	Median Income	White Collar	Blue Collar	Service Industry	Over 64	Under 18	College Education	Rural	Sq. Miles
1	37%	62%	88%	7%	<1%	3%	$36,608	49%	34%	17%	15%	23%	14%	63%	11,683
2	38	61	88	6	1	3	43,545	51	33	16	12	25	16	53	7,567
3	56	43	70	21	2	4	45,577	63	21	16	13	24	29	2	367
4	38	60	92	3	1	2	49,549	59	26	15	12	25	21	40	5,679
5	31	67	96	1	<1	1	27,884	50	33	17	13	23	11	79	10,676
6	43	55	83	8	2	4	44,646	60	24	16	12	23	28	29	3,757
STATE	41	57	86	8	1	3	41,197	56	28	16	13	24	20	44	39,728
U.S.	53	46	64	12	5	16	51,425	60	23	17	13	25	28	21	3,537,438

Sen. Mitch McConnell (R)

Capitol Office
224-2541
mcconnell.senate.gov
317 Russell Bldg. 20510-1702; fax 224-2499

Committees
Agriculture, Nutrition & Forestry
Appropriations
Rules & Administration

Residence
Louisville

Born
Feb. 20, 1942; Sheffield, Ala.

Religion
Baptist

Family
Wife, Elaine L. Chao; three children

Education
U. of Louisville, B.A. 1964; U. of Kentucky, J.D. 1967

Career
Lawyer; congressional aide; U.S. Justice Department official

Political Highlights
Jefferson County judge-executive, 1978-85

ELECTION RESULTS

2008 GENERAL

Mitch McConnell (R)	953,816	53.0%
Bruce Lunsford (D)	847,005	47.0%

2008 PRIMARY

Mitch McConnell (R)	168,127	86.1%
Daniel Essek (R)	27,170	13.9%

2002 GENERAL

Mitch McConnell (R)	731,679	64.7%
Lois Combs Weinberg (D)	399,634	35.3%

2002 PRIMARY

Mitch McConnell (R)	unopposed

Previous Winning Percentages
1996 (55%); 1990 (52%); 1984 (50%)

Elected 1984; 5th term

McConnell is a canny conservative, formidable backroom dealer and skilled parliamentarian. He believes his job as minority leader is to keep his party tightly unified to counter Democratic initiatives while angling to reclaim the majority in the next election.

In the 112th Congress (2011-12), he faces a difficult balancing act: The House Republican majority is freer to act than his Senate minority, which still dances to the tune set by Democratic Leader Harry Reid of Nevada. But he still must maintain discipline in his increasingly conservative caucus as he attempts to stymie Obama administration initiatives while keeping both the Senate and the federal government operating.

He won a few early procedural battles in 2011, beating back attempts by some Democrats to weaken the filibuster and other minority rights while striking a gentlemen's agreement with Reid for a more open amendment process than the Senate saw in the 111th Congress (2009-10).

McConnell is also in a stronger position than in the 111th on legislative matters, a point made clear by the budget battles fought early in the new Congress. "Don't they realize that current levels of spending are the reason we just had the biggest wave election in a generation?" he said on the Senate floor in February 2011.

Under less favorable circumstances — 41 votes rather than the 47 he now leads — McConnell made a compelling case to moderates to close ranks in an effort to preserve the rights of the minority party during the 111th Congress. He portrayed the victory of Republican Scott P. Brown of Massachusetts in a January 2010 special election to succeed the late Democrat Edward M. Kennedy as a signal that voters wanted Congress to "go in a different direction." Although several moderate Republicans defected on the financial regulation overhaul in 2010 and the $787 billion economic stimulus in 2009, all of them heeded their leader's call to oppose the 2010 health care overhaul, and every member of the larger Republican Conference voted in early 2011 to repeal the law.

At the same time, to conservatives he defended traditional prerogatives, ranging from filibusters to earmarks, as essential tools of legislators while emphasizing traditional themes of fiscal discipline and lower taxes. He portrayed Democratic proposals to allow tax cuts for higher income earners to expire at the end of 2010 as the "worst thing we could do to small business" in a weak economy.

More often than not, he is able to bridge the gaps between the two wings effectively, partly because he sits astride the two philosophically — he's a conservative but not a fire breather, devoted to baseline Republican principles but not a movement conservative.

Bridging the gap with the Obama White House has been more problematic.

Obama had been president for seven months before he invited McConnell to their first one-on-one meeting at the White House. "The president's a very smart guy, and I think he figures he'll be seeing a lot more of me in the future," McConnell said the day after the meeting.

McConnell knows how to block and barter. He helped stymie Democratic climate change initiatives in 2010 but clinched a deal on a bipartisan $58.8 billion fiscal 2010 supplemental war spending bill. "I'm a conservative Republican. On most issues, I would like to see a right-of-center result," he has said. "But I've also been in legislative politics long enough to know that rarely do you get exactly what you want. Our whole process is about accepting less than what you want in order to advance the ball."

In his push to expand his party's clout, McConnell has also taken a pragmatic approach. He helped prod contentious colleague Jim Bunning, a fellow Kentucky Republican, to drop out of his Senate re-election race, clearing the way for younger candidates. In a rare moment of political vulnerability, McConnell watched his hand-picked candidate and home-state ally, Kentucky Secretary of State Trey Grayson, lose to tea party champion Rand Paul in a May 2010 Senate primary. But McConnell quieted speculation about his future by staging a post-election "party unity" meeting in Kentucky, and Paul was elected in November.

While opposing Obama's fiscal priorities and his proposals to try terrorism suspects in civilian courts and close the U.S. military detention facility at Cuba's Guantánamo Bay, McConnell backed his approach to the wars in Iraq and Afghanistan.

McConnell was intensely loyal to President George W. Bush, who named McConnell's wife, Elaine L. Chao, Labor secretary. When Bush backed an immigration overhaul that conservatives abhorred, McConnell stayed out of the floor debate.

On the Appropriations and Agriculture, Nutrition and Forestry committees, McConnell protects Kentucky's tobacco growers and other farming interests.

He also serves on the Rules and Administration Committee, which handles Senate housekeeping matters as well as campaign finance and election legislation. McConnell blocked a rewrite of campaign finance rules for 15 years, mounting more than 20 filibusters against various iterations of the legislation. When the measure finally was enacted in 2002, he took the battle to the Supreme Court, which narrowly upheld the law in 2003. And he led opposition to a Democratic push to impose new disclosure mandates for corporate campaign donations in 2010 as a violation of free speech.

McConnell has served in a variety of insider roles, some more pleasant than others. From 1999 to 2002, he chaired the Rules panel. He also chaired the Select Ethics Committee in 1995 when it voted to expel Oregon Republican Bob Packwood over charges of sexual misconduct. (Packwood subsequently resigned.) During the 1998 and 2000 election cycles, he chaired the National Republican Senatorial Committee, the party's Senate campaign arm.

An only child, McConnell was born in Alabama, lived in Georgia for part of his childhood and moved to Kentucky at age 13. His father, an Army officer who fought in World War II, became a civilian Army employee after the war and then a human resources director for DuPont in Louisville.

While the family was living in Alabama, McConnell, at age 2, was stricken with polio. His mother administered a physical therapy regimen and took him to specialists in Warm Springs, Ga. At their urging, she kept the child from walking until he was 4, a seemingly impossible task that saved him from permanent damage to his afflicted left leg. "She was a true saint," he said.

McConnell showed an early taste for politics. He was student body president in high school and college, and president of his law school class. After law school, he worked for GOP Sen. Marlow W. Cook of Kentucky, then as a deputy assistant attorney general in the Ford administration. He served two terms as the chief executive of Jefferson County before ousting two-term Democratic Sen. Walter D. Huddleston in a close race in 1984.

In 1990, McConnell was re-elected with 52 percent of the vote. His margin of victory got more comfortable in his next two races. In 2008, he faced wealthy Democratic businessman Bruce Lunsford amid a hostile national political climate for the GOP. Lunsford spent millions of his personal fortune on attack ads, though not enough to keep up with McConnell, who outspent Lunsford by a 2-1 margin and captured 53 percent of the vote.

Key Votes

2010

Pass budget reconciliation bill to modify overhauls of health care and federal student loan programs	NO
Proceed to disapproval resolution on EPA authority to regulate greenhouse gases	YES
Overhaul financial services industry regulation	NO
Limit debate to proceed to a bill to broaden campaign finance disclosure and reporting rules	NO
Limit debate on an extension of Bush-era income tax cuts for two years	YES
Limit debate on a bill to provide a path to legal status for some children of illegal immigrants	NO
Allow for a repeal of "don't ask, don't tell"	NO
Consent to ratification of a strategic arms reduction treaty with Russia	NO

2009

Prevent release of remaining financial industry bailout funds	YES
Make it easier for victims to sue for wage discrimination remedies	NO
Expand the Children's Health Insurance Program	NO
Limit debate on the economic stimulus measure	NO
Repeal District of Columbia firearms prohibitions and gun registration laws	YES
Limit debate on expansion of federal hate crimes law	NO
Strike funding for F-22 Raptor fighter jets	NO

CQ Vote Studies

	PARTY UNITY		PRESIDENTIAL SUPPORT	
	SUPPORT	OPPOSE	SUPPORT	OPPOSE
2010	98%	2%	41%	59%
2009	95%	5%	46%	54%
2008	97%	3%	76%	24%
2007	95%	5%	86%	14%
2006	96%	4%	91%	9%
2005	99%	1%	93%	7%
2004	99%	1%	98%	2%
2003	99%	1%	100%	0%
2002	97%	3%	96%	4%
2001	98%	2%	97%	3%

Interest Groups

	AFL-CIO	ADA	CCUS	ACU
2010	6%	0%	100%	96%
2009	22%	10%	71%	96%
2008	20%	20%	100%	80%
2007	11%	10%	82%	92%
2006	13%	5%	100%	84%
2005	14%	5%	94%	100%
2004	8%	15%	94%	96%
2003	0%	10%	100%	84%
2002	23%	0%	95%	100%
2001	6%	5%	93%	96%

Sen. Rand Paul (R)

Capitol Office
224-4343
paul.senate.gov
208 Russell Bldg. 20510-1703; fax 228-6917

Committees
Energy & Natural Resources
Health, Education, Labor & Pensions
Homeland Security & Governmental Affairs
Small Business & Entrepreneurship

Residence
Bowling Green

Born
Jan. 7, 1963; Pittsburgh, Pa.

Religion
Presbyterian

Family
Wife, Kelley Paul; three children

Education
Baylor U., attended 1981-84; Duke U., M.D. 1988

Career
Ophthalmologist

Political Highlights
No previous office

ELECTION RESULTS

2010 GENERAL

Rand Paul (R)	755,411	55.7%
Jack Conway (D)	599,843	44.2%

2010 PRIMARY

Rand Paul (R)	206,986	58.8%
Trey Grayson (R)	124,864	35.4%
Bill Johnson (R)	7,861	2.2%
John Stephenson (R)	6,885	2.0%

Elected 2010; 1st term

Paul arrived in the Senate as perhaps the best-known of the new conservative firebrands. The son of Rep. Ron Paul, a Texan who sought the presidency as a Libertarian in 1988 and as a Republican in 2008, he helped to found a tea party caucus in the Senate and made clear he would not be a 'go along to get along' lawmaker.

He suggested $500 billion in spending cuts for fiscal 2011 at a time when other conservatives were being called "extreme" for proposing $100 billion in cuts, the House passed a catchall spending bill with $58 billion in reductions and Senate Republicans proposed $50 billion.

"My proposal, not surprisingly, has been greeted skeptically in Washington, where serious spending cuts are a rarity. But it is a modest proposal when measured against the size of our mounting debt," he wrote in The Wall Street Journal.

He has vigorously pushed a plan to overhaul Social Security that includes raising the retirement age and means testing.

"I think we need to find common ground, but I think both sides haven't woken up to the enormity of the problem," Paul said on PBS's "Newshour."

He called for an end to all foreign aid — including the $3 billion given annually to Israel, a budget line item sometimes viewed as sacrosanct as Social Security.

A member of the Homeland Security and Governmental Affairs Committee, he also opposed extension of expiring provisions of the anti-terrorism law known as the Patriot Act.

"I firmly believe it is a primary duty of our government to do what it can to protect the lives of its citizens," Paul said. "But I also believe it must in equal measure protect our liberty, and in this our government has failed us."

Paul rejects any notion that he will alter his methods or be co-opted by Washington, and he does not shy away from applying his libertarian outlook to any legislative controversy.

His priorities include term limits for lawmakers, a balanced-budget amendment to the Constitution and a requirement that members of Congress cite the specific parts of the Constitution that allow for the measures they introduce. "These are not radical ideas," he told National Review. "They are reform-minded, good-government ideas."

Paul, who sits on the Health, Education, Labor and Pensions Committee, calls the 2010 health care overhaul unconstitutional, supports efforts by several state attorneys general to challenge the law in court and voted to repeal the measure early in the 112th Congress (2011-12).

More conventionally — as a conservative and a Kentuckian — Paul is "absolutely opposed to cap-and-trade, absolutely opposed to any carbon tax." On the Energy and Natural Resources Committee he says he will be "a great friend of coal."

Paul called earmarks — funding for special projects in members' districts or states — a symbol of government spending run amok and said he supports the GOP's one-year moratorium. But he also told The Wall Street Journal he "will advocate for Kentucky's interests."

"I will argue within the committee process for things that are good for Kentucky that they want and also within the context of a balanced budget," he said on ABC's "This Week." "Here's what happens. You go to the Transportation Committee and they say, 'What do you want?' But it should be, 'How much do we have?' No one asks, 'How much do we have?' So we just spend it."

Paul is likely to diverge from most Senate Republicans on some national security and foreign policy matters. Aside from the Patriot Act, which he views as an infringement on civil liberties, he has expressed skepticism about the war in Afghanistan. "How long is long enough? It's too simplistic to say there is never a time to come home, or that it's unpatriotic to debate," he told National Review. "There are reasonable people, conservatives like me, who believe that defense is the primary role of the federal government, but do not believe that you can make Afghanistan into a nation. It never has been one."

He says the biggest threat to national security comes from a leaky border, and he backs a moratorium on visas from certain "rogue states" until there are improvements in managing the visa process. He also opposes a path to citizenship for illegal immigrants already in the country.

He calls U.S. participation in organizations such as the United Nations a threat to the nation's sovereignty. And, although he backs free trade, he includes the World Trade Organization in that category.

Paul, who sits on the Small Business and Entrepreneurship Committee, has been very critical of the Federal Reserve and supports his father's proposal to audit the central bank's books.

Growing up in the Texas home of a libertarian, Paul was not given an allowance, which his parents viewed as equivalent to being on the dole, according to a New York Times profile.

He attended Baylor University and later received a degree from Duke Medical School, following his doctor father — an obstetrician — into medicine, as an ophthalmologist.

He moved to Kentucky in 1993 to open his practice and quickly got involved in political activism as well, founding Kentucky Taxpayers United, a watchdog group.

When Paul entered the Senate race to succeed retiring Republican Jim Bunning, he was considered the underdog. Kentucky Secretary of State Trey Grayson had the backing of most party officials in the state and, most important, was considered the protégé of Senate Minority Leader Mitch McConnell.

But Paul rallied conservative activists and was among the earliest candidates to get a boost from the tea party movement. He easily defeated Grayson, 59 percent to 35 percent, in the May primary.

The general election contest, in which he faced state Attorney General Jack Conway, was bitterly contested.

The Democrat cast aspersions on Paul's religious faith in what came to be known as the Aqua Buddha ad; a Paul supporter was charged with assault for stepping on a liberal activist outside a debate. And the two disagreed on almost every issue.

Paul got into hot water during the campaign when he cited some aspects of the Civil Rights Act of 1964 as an example of government overreach. In an interview on MSNBC, Paul questioned the constitutional foundation of provisions in the law that barred discrimination by private companies.

After receiving severe criticism from political opponents and only lukewarm support from GOP allies, none of which came on the substance of his argument, he clarified his remarks by saying "there was a need for federal intervention to say that you can't have segregation, that we shouldn't be doing that."

A month before the election, he credited his campaign successes to his father. "I couldn't have done this two years ago, but the reason why I'll tell you it's winnable now is, and I'm honest about this, my father's fame helps me quite a bit," the Lexington Herald-Leader quoted Paul as saying. "It helps me in raising money, it helps me get started, it helps the media pay attention to me. Without that, I couldn't do it."

On Election Day, Paul took 56 percent of the vote to Conway's 44 percent.

Rep. Edward Whitfield (R)

Capitol Office
225-3115
www.house.gov/whitfield
2368 Rayburn Bldg. 20515-1701; fax 225-3547

Committees
Energy & Commerce
  (Energy & Power - Chairman)

Residence
Hopkinsville

Born
May 25, 1943; Hopkinsville, Ky.

Religion
Methodist

Family
Wife, Constance Harriman Whitfield; one child

Education
U. of Kentucky, B.S. 1965 (business); Wesley Theological Seminary, attended 1966; U. of Kentucky, J.D. 1969

Military
Army Reserve, 1967-73

Career
Lawyer; oil distributor; railroad executive

Political Highlights
Ky. House, 1974-75 (served as a Democrat)

ELECTION RESULTS

2010 GENERAL

Edward Whitfield (R)	153,519	71.2%
Charles Kendall Hatchett (D)	61,960	28.8%

2010 PRIMARY

Edward Whitfield (R)	unopposed

2008 GENERAL

Edward Whitfield (R)	178,107	64.3%
Heather A. Ryan (D)	98,674	35.6%

Previous Winning Percentages
2006 (69%); 2004 (67%); 2002 (65%); 2000 (58%); 1998 (55%); 1996 (54%); 1994 (51%)

Elected 1994; 9th term

The soft-spoken Whitfield is a guardian of his region's coal and tobacco interests and staunch defender of another of Kentucky's great resources — horses. He has been an effective behind-the-scenes advocate on health, energy and other issues as a senior member of the Energy and Commerce Committee, and has taken on a more public role in the 112th Congress as chairman of the Energy and Power Subcommittee.

Whitfield has been an ardent supporter of the coal industry, a leading employer in his district, and is a proponent of clean-coal technology, saying its widespread use would reduce energy costs. He was a vocal opponent of Democrats' plan to enact a cap-and-trade system for carbon emissions and in a February 2010 opinion piece he called the Obama administration "no friend of coal."

He sponsored a successful amendment to a House-passed catchall spending bill early in 2011 aimed at ending the Green the Capitol Initiative, launched in 2007 by then-Speaker Nancy Pelosi, a California Democrat. Whitfield has been no fan of the program since Democratic leaders moved in 2009 to switch from coal to natural gas at the Capitol Power Plant. And Whitfield joined a "friend of the court" brief with two other lawmakers opposing efforts by eight states to force electric companies to reduce carbon emissions. That is Washington's responsibility, Whitfield and the others argued, a position supported by the Obama administration.

But Whitfield and the White House diverge on who in Washington should be making those decisions. He backs legislation to block the EPA from regulating carbon emissions under the Clean Air Act without congressional approval, and he voted to bar funding for such regulations in the spending bill.

Whitfield sides with Republicans on about 9 of every 10 votes that divide majorities of the two parties, though he was slightly more inclined to go his own way when Democrats were in the majority than when Republicans were in charge during his first six terms.

He was among a minority of Republicans to vote for an increase in the minimum wage in 2007, as well as for new pay-as-you-go budget rules and transparency in the process of approving earmarks — funds designated to specific projects in members' districts.

But he stuck with his party on the health care overhaul enacted in 2010, opposing the bill as it worked its way through Congress in 2009 and 2010 and voting to repeal it in 2011. He also opposed a measure, signed into law by President Obama in 2009, that expanded a program that provides health insurance for children in lower-income families that make too much money to qualify for Medicaid.

Whitfield made a campaign pledge several years ago to work to ban the slaughter of horses. It has become his defining national issue in recent years. He and his wife, Constance Whitfield (a senior adviser to the Humane Society of the United States), are horse lovers who have rescued several animals. The couple began working on the issue after being at a 2004 horse auction in Pennsylvania and witnessing a feeble and very sick horse being loaded onto a trailer for a 1,500-mile trip to Texas for slaughter. The Whitfields felt euthanasia would have been the humane approach, and he subsequently sponsored a bill in the 109th Congress (2005-06) to make it a crime to transport, sell or buy horses with the intent of killing them for human consumption. It passed the House overwhelmingly in 2006, but the Senate never took it up.

With the last horse slaughter plants shuttered in 2007, Whitfield now is pushing legislation to bar the shipping of horses abroad for slaughter. Whitfield in 2008 added the care of race horses to his agenda after a second Kentucky Derby contender in a space of three years had to be euthanized following a racing injury. He said he is planning to back legislation to ban the use of steroids in the sport.

He was brought onto Energy and Commerce in his first term, when the GOP took control of the House following the 1994 elections. An influential Republican from another tobacco state, Thomas J. Bliley Jr. of Virginia, became chairman and sought to bring friends of the industry onto the panel. Whitfield fought Clinton administration attempts in the latter half of the 1990s to sue tobacco companies for selling hazardous products. In 2004, he pushed for provisions in a comprehensive corporate tax bill giving tobacco farmers a 10-year, $10 billion buyout. Congress passed the measure and Bush signed it.

Born in Hopkinsville, near the Tennessee border, Whitfield is the son of a railroad conductor. His mother worked in finance at a local hospital. Whitfield spent a year at Wesley Theological Seminary in Washington, D.C., before switching to law school. He was a Democrat in those days, and served for two years in the state House shortly after law school. Like many other Southern Democrats, he switched parties during the Reagan presidency.

He spent much of his early career doing regulatory and legislative work for major railroads. He lived many of those years in Washington and in the early 1990s was a lawyer for the Interstate Commerce Commission.

In 1994, Kentucky Republican Sen. Mitch McConnell recruited Whitfield to challenge Democratic Rep. Tom Barlow. Whitfield had not lived in the state for a dozen years (to be eligible for the race, he moved from CSX Corp. headquarters in Jacksonville, Fla.), but efforts to paint him as a carpetbagger were offset by the strength of his roots in the 1st District, where his extended family had been farming since 1799.

Whitfield won with 51 percent of the vote, becoming the first Republican to represent the district. He easily survived the anti-Republican tide of 2006, taking 60 percent of the vote in a rematch with Barlow, and won handily in 2008 and 2010.

He was a speaker at a Paducah tea party event in April 2009, but later was critical of the movement's penchant for targeting Republicans who don't adhere to its ideals. "We'd like to say that the tea parties are supporting Republicans. But from what I hear, some of them are just as likely to go after us as a Democrat," Whitfield said.

Key Votes

2010

Overhaul the nation's health insurance system	NO
Allow for repeal of "don't ask, don't tell"	NO
Overhaul financial services industry regulation	NO
Limit use of new Afghanistan War funds to troop withdrawal activities	NO
Change oversight of offshore drilling and lift oil spill liability cap	NO
Provide a path to legal status for some children of illegal immigrants	NO
Extend Bush-era income tax cuts for two years	YES

2009

Expand the Children's Health Insurance Program	NO
Provide $787 billion in tax cuts and spending increases to stimulate the economy	NO
Allow bankruptcy judges to modify certain primary-residence mortgages	NO
Create a cap-and-trade system to limit greenhouse gas emissions	NO
Provide $2 billion for the "cash for clunkers" program	NO
Establish the government as the sole provider of student loans	NO
Restrict federally funded insurance coverage for abortions in health care overhaul	YES

CQ Vote Studies

	PARTY UNITY		PRESIDENTIAL SUPPORT	
	SUPPORT	OPPOSE	SUPPORT	OPPOSE
2010	90%	10%	39%	61%
2009	81%	19%	30%	70%
2008	89%	11%	56%	44%
2007	84%	16%	69%	31%
2006	90%	10%	87%	13%

Interest Groups

	AFL-CIO	ADA	CCUS	ACU
2010	14%	15%	88%	77%
2009	19%	0%	93%	88%
2008	29%	35%	72%	78%
2007	26%	25%	90%	83%
2006	21%	0%	93%	76%

Kentucky 1

West — Hopkinsville, Henderson, Paducah

Located in the western part of the Bluegrass State, Kentucky's rural 1st is a hub of agricultural activity. Tobacco remains a major economic force, and the coal mining industry still contributes to the regional economy despite decades of decline. Volatility in agricultural and mining markets makes the district susceptible to high unemployment rates.

The Ohio River port of Paducah (McCracken County) traditionally has been western Kentucky's political and population center, although its population has been surpassed by both Henderson and Hopkinsville. Hopkinsville is an agricultural market center and has an ethanol plant that uses locally grown corn and produces 33 million gallons of fuel ethanol annually. The city also is heavily dependent on nearby Fort Campbell, much of which is in Tennessee.

Tobacco yields have decreased throughout much of the 1st — the industry here was hit hard after the federal government buyout of local tobacco farmers ending long-standing production quotas and price controls. The 1st also has an abundance of coal, and the mining industry provides many

jobs in the region, especially in Webster and Henderson counties. Tourism and recreation also play a role in the economy, especially near the 170,000-acre forested Land Between the Lakes area.

The 1st is no longer the Democratic stronghold that it once was, and the 1994 GOP wave sent the district's first Republican to Congress. There are nearly twice as many Democrats as Republicans registered in the 1st, and the district has the largest Democratic Party registration edge in the state, but John McCain took 62 percent of the district's presidential vote in 2008 and only lost one county (Henderson) here.

Major Industry
Tobacco, agriculture, manufacturing, coal

Military Bases
Fort Campbell, 30,438 military, 8,058 civilian (2011) (shared with Tennessee's 7th District)

Cities
Hopkinsville, 31,577; Henderson, 28,757; Paducah, 25,024

Notable
The Jefferson Davis Monument, located at his birthplace in Fairview, is a 351-foot obelisk; the nation's only plant that turns uranium into nuclear fuel is operated in Paducah by USEC, an energy company.

Rep. Brett Guthrie (R)

Capitol Office
225-3501
guthrie.house.gov
308 Cannon Bldg. 20515; fax 226-2019

Committees
Energy & Commerce

Residence
Bowling Green

Born
Feb. 18, 1964; Florence, Ala.

Religion
Church of Christ

Family
Wife, Beth Guthrie; three children

Education
U.S. Military Academy, B.S. 1987 (mathematical economics); Yale U., M.P.P.M 1997

Military
Army, 1987-90; Army Reserve, 1990-2002

Career
Automotive supply company executive

Political Highlights
Ky. Senate, 1999-2009

ELECTION RESULTS

2010 GENERAL

Brett Guthrie (R)	155,906	67.9%
Ed Marksberry (D)	73,749	32.1%

2010 PRIMARY

Brett Guthrie (R)	unopposed

2008 GENERAL

Brett Guthrie (R)	158,936	52.6%
David E. Boswell (D)	143,379	47.4%

Elected 2008; 2nd term

Guthrie's experiences as a small-business executive and state senator helped shape his small-government approach, while his background as a West Point graduate and veteran of the 101st Airborne has made him strongly pro-defense.

In his second term, he won a spot on the powerful Energy and Commerce Committee and serves on the Health Subcommittee, where he can build on his work on the Education and Labor Committee in the 111th Congress (2009-10).

Guthrie opposed the Democratic health care overhaul approved by his old panel in part because the legislation included a government-run insurance program. He eventually voted against the measure on the floor, by which time the "public option" had been deleted. He also voted to repeal the law early in the 112th Congress (2011-12).

With a master's degree in management from Yale University, the soft-spoken Southerner says he trusts markets far more than government. Guthrie opposed President Obama's early economic initiatives, including the $787 billion economic stimulus law of early 2009, which he called a "partisan bill" that wouldn't stimulate the economy or create jobs. He said the rising national debt is partly what motivated him to run for Congress.

A member of the Republican Study Committee, the most conservative faction of House members, Guthrie broke with his wing of the party on providing federal aid to the ailing automobile industry. He supported the creation of the "cash for clunkers" vehicle trade-in program and voted to pour an additional $2 billion into it after the initial $1 billion in rebates were snapped up in a week's time. Guthrie's interest in the faltering industry has a personal element: His father worked for Ford — before his plant shut down — and then founded an automobile die-casting company, where Guthrie worked as a vice president.

Watching the local plant close in the early 1980s made a lasting impression. "I still remember coming in one day and a guy came up to me literally with tears in his eyes, saying, 'What are we gonna do, what are we gonna do?'" Guthrie said. "I remember thinking then, having people have opportunities to get skills, or something they can sell personally, is important because that gives them so many more options if something like this happens."

For the most part, though, Guthrie is with his party. He sided with Republicans on about 9 of every 10 votes in the 111th Congress on which a majority of the GOP voted differently than a majority of Democrats.

In particular, he was highly critical of President Obama's fiscal 2012 budget. "Continuing the spending binge and imposing massive tax hikes on families and small businesses is not a viable option," he said.

When the Education and Labor Committee (now called Education and the Workforce) in 2009 approved Obama's plan to convert all federally subsidized student loans into direct government loans, Guthrie joined other Republicans in resisting the idea of creating a government monopoly. He offered an unsuccessful alternative that would have let companies continue to offer student loans, which they would then sell to the government. When the bill came to the House floor two months later, he offered — again unsuccessfully — an amendment to preserve existing subsidies for private lenders through 2014 and create a commission to develop a new private-sector model for student lending.

Late in 2010, he signed a bipartisan letter to the comptroller general challenging a Government Accountability Office report that was critical of recruiting practices at for-profit colleges and universities.

Although he lacks the relevant committee assignments, Guthrie is interested in military and veterans' issues. Fort Knox is in his district, and the first bill he introduced would have ensured that family members of soldiers who die in combat do not lose their health care coverage. He opposes Obama's plans to shutter the detention facility at Guantánamo Bay, Cuba; after visiting the prison, he called it "an immense resource to U.S. military and intelligence operations."

Guthrie grew up in Florence, Ala., where his mother looked after him and his three brothers while his father worked. He dreamed of playing professional football, but became captivated as a teenager by Ronald Reagan's 1980 campaign and the early years of Reagan's presidency. Guthrie decided to pursue a military career, and while completing an obstacle course as a student at the U.S. Military Academy at West Point, he was knocked down by a swinging log; trying to catch his breath, he let out a "Goll-ly!" An upperclassman, now an Army general, promptly christened him "Huck," after Huckleberry Hound, the blue cartoon dog with a Southern drawl.

After West Point, Guthrie served as a field artillery officer in the 101st Airborne Division until 1990, when he went into the Army Reserve; he did not see combat. Guthrie recalls his decision to leave active duty as "an emotional day." But he had recently married; he and his wife, Beth, concluded that a military career, with lots of travel, was not the life they wanted for their family, so he joined his father's nascent business in Bowling Green, Ky.

Before running for Congress, Guthrie spent 10 years in the Kentucky Senate, where he focused on education initiatives. One of his proudest accomplishments, he said, was writing a law that would lead to more black students enrolling in Advanced Placement courses.

In his race to succeed seven-term Republican Ron Lewis, who had announced his retirement on the last filing day for the May 2008 primary, Guthrie was set for a primary battle against Lewis' chief of staff, Daniel London, but London later withdrew. In the general election he faced Democratic state Sen. David E. Boswell. Both national parties funded ads in the district, and first lady Laura Bush and former President Bill Clinton made appearances.

Guthrie touted his business and military background and his conservative credentials in the Republican-leaning district, which proved to be enough in the end. He won with 53 percent of the vote. He swept to an easy victory over Democrat Ed Marksberry in 2010.

Key Votes

2010

Overhaul the nation's health insurance system	NO
Allow for repeal of "don't ask, don't tell"	NO
Overhaul financial services industry regulation	NO
Limit use of new Afghanistan War funds to troop withdrawal activities	NO
Change oversight of offshore drilling and lift oil spill liability cap	NO
Provide a path to legal status for some children of illegal immigrants	NO
Extend Bush-era income tax cuts for two years	YES

2009

Expand the Children's Health Insurance Program	NO
Provide $787 billion in tax cuts and spending increases to stimulate the economy	NO
Allow bankruptcy judges to modify certain primary-residence mortgages	NO
Create a cap-and-trade system to limit greenhouse gas emissions	NO
Provide $2 billion for the "cash for clunkers" program	YES
Establish the government as the sole provider of student loans	NO
Restrict federally funded insurance coverage for abortions in health care overhaul	YES

CQ Vote Studies

	PARTY UNITY		PRESIDENTIAL SUPPORT	
	SUPPORT	OPPOSE	SUPPORT	OPPOSE
2010	96%	4%	29%	71%
2009	85%	15%	32%	68%

Interest Groups

	AFL-CIO	ADA	CCUS	ACU
2010	8%	0%	88%	95%
2009	14%	10%	80%	88%

West central — Owensboro, Bowling Green

The mostly rural 2nd District, anchored in Kentucky's west-central heartland, takes in some suburban areas near Louisville and the city of Owensboro, and runs through rolling tobacco country, ending in the river country to the west.

Bowling Green's population growth in the last decade, fueled by Western Kentucky University and access to Interstate 65, propelled it past Owensboro as the state's third-most populous city. Officials in Owensboro, however, plan a major redevelopment of downtown that will include residential and mixed-use buildings as well as a riverfront park.

Tobacco remains a dominant crop in the 2nd, despite the federal buyout of tobacco farms and the end of the production quota system. Coal and oil also provide some jobs throughout the district. An Amazon.com distribution center in Campbellsville has brought stability to an otherwise grim economy in the 2nd's rural areas, which have been subject to volatility in the coal industry. Earlier layoffs at the Bowling Green General Motors

Corvette plant may be offset by plans for expanding the facility, but the district's manufacturing tradition is dwindling.

Tourism is a growing sector of the economy, and visitors tour the Mammoth Cave National Park in the southern part of the district, the barbecue joints of Daviess County in the northwest, and several of the distilleries on Kentucky's "Bourbon Trail" — the 2nd produces famous brands such as Jim Beam and Maker's Mark — to the east.

After a long period of Democratic dominance and a sizable Democratic edge in voter registration, 2nd District voters now side with the GOP in federal elections. In the 2008 presidential election, John McCain took 61 percent of the district's vote.

Major Industry
Tobacco, coal, oil, tourism, manufacturing

Military Bases
Fort Knox, 11,500 military, 5,200 civilian (2011)

Cities
Bowling Green, 58,067; Owensboro, 57,265; Elizabethtown, 28,531

Notable
The U.S. Bullion Depository, or "Gold Vault," at Fort Knox houses the largest portion of the U.S. gold reserve.

Rep. John Yarmuth (D)

Capitol Office
225-5401
yarmuth.house.gov
435 Cannon Bldg. 20515-1703; fax 225-5776

Committees
Budget
Ethics
Oversight & Government Reform

Residence
Louisville

Born
Nov. 4, 1947; Louisville, Ky.

Religion
Jewish

Family
Wife, Cathy Yarmuth; one child

Education
Yale U., B.A. 1969 (American studies); Georgetown U.
Law School, attended 1971-72

Career
Periodical publisher and columnist; television commentator; public relations executive; congressional aide; stockbroker

Political Highlights
Republican nominee for Louisville Board of Alderman, 1975; Republican nominee for Jefferson County Board of Commissioners, 1981

ELECTION RESULTS

2010 GENERAL

John Yarmuth (D)	139,940	54.7%
Todd Lally (R)	112,627	44.0%

2010 PRIMARY

John Yarmuth (D)	unopposed

2008 GENERAL

John Yarmuth (D)	203,843	59.4%
Anne M. Northup (R)	139,527	40.6%

Previous Winning Percentages
2006 (51%)

Elected 2006; 3rd term

A former columnist and talk radio host, Yarmuth built a career espousing liberal views. In Congress he is a dependable party man and a sharp-tongued critic of Republicans.

He lost his seat on the powerful Ways and Means Committee, where he had served one term, following the Democratic electoral losses in 2010. In the 112th Congress (2011-12), he brings his confrontational style of politics back to the Oversight and Government Reform Committee, where he served in his first term and where partisan confrontations are the norm, and to the Ethics Committee, where partisanship is supposed to give way to consensus.

"I don't back away or get cowed by shifting winds," Yarmuth says, and he demonstrated that by voting for the Democrats' health care overhaul, then continuing to support the law as public opinion solidified in opposition to it. He was among the few Democrats who continued to tout the measure during their re-election campaigns. He expressed faith that voters would come to support the law as they find out more about it, though most opinion polls suggested otherwise. "There are those people who may want to lynch you, and you take the time to explain what the health care reform package means to their lives. Invariably they feel much better about it," he said.

Yarmuth backed his leadership on 99 percent of the votes in the 111th Congress (2009-10) on which a majority of Republicans and Democrats diverged.

He has become a vocal advocate for restoring the nation's manufacturing base, sponsoring legislation to provide tax incentives for energy-efficient appliances that are made in the United States. In December 2009, Yarmuth and Democrat Michael H. Michaud of Maine founded the Congressional Task Force on Competitiveness.

Yarmuth, who also sits on the Budget Committee, said that companies such as General Electric, which has a consumer appliances division in his Louisville-area district, will bring work back to the United States from overseas if given even small government incentives. Yarmuth argues that when competing economically across the world, U.S. companies are rarely competing solely against private enterprise.

"If you take a purist ideological position that the government can't be involved, the market will determine it, you're going to lose," he said.

He has joined environmental groups in criticizing the practice — used in Kentucky and elsewhere — of mountaintop coal mining, in which the tops of mountains are leveled off to extract the coal and valleys are filled with the rubble. He applauded the Obama administration when it announced plans in 2009 to rein in the technique and said he supported forcing mine operators to find less harmful ways to dispose of byproducts of mountaintop removal.

Yarmuth also supported Democratic energy legislation to create a cap-and-trade system aimed at reducing greenhouse gas emissions — a position that brought some criticism from coal country.

"It's very complicated. It's not very easy to explain in 9.8 seconds, which is the average sound bite," said the radio veteran. "So it's much easier to say cap-and-tax in 9.8 seconds."

That sort of confrontational rhetoric is second nature to Yarmuth, who has a history of making clear — sometimes colorfully — his distaste for Republicans. In 2004, before running for Congress, he financed his own TV ad attacking tax cuts enacted in 2001 and 2003 under President George W. Bush.

At an October 2008 hearing on the financial crisis, Yarmuth described the three GOP panelists — former Federal Reserve Chairman Alan Greenspan, former Treasury Secretary John W. Snow and Christopher Cox, chairman of the Securities and Exchange Commission — as "three Bill Buckners," a reference to the Boston Red Sox first baseman whose infamous fielding error helped cost his team the 1986 World Series.

In October 2007, he began distributing tan lapel buttons emblazoned with "Article 1" — a reference the portion of the Constitution that invests legislative powers in Congress — to House colleagues as a way to display their displeasure with what he called Bush's "imperial presidency." The House parliamentarian told him the buttons couldn't be worn while speaking on the floor because they violate rules against badges designed to convey a message. After unsuccessfully arguing they were no different than flag pins, he continued to distribute the buttons — just when he wasn't holding the floor.

The product of a wealthy Kentucky family, Yarmuth's father founded National Industries, which at one time was Kentucky's second-largest public company, with holdings in retail business, manufacturing, transportation, oil and services. His maternal grandfather was a prominent Louisville banker.

Yarmuth's initial foray into politics came as a legislative aide to Kentucky Republican Sen. Marlow W. Cook from 1971 to 1974. He ran unsuccessfully for office twice as a Republican, first for the Louisville Board of Aldermen in 1975 at age 27 and then for the Jefferson County Board of Commissioners at the suggestion of a county judge named Mitch McConnell, who would go on to become a Kentucky senator and GOP leader.

Yarmuth's family fortune helped him begin a career in publishing. In 1976, he founded Louisville Today magazine, publishing it until 1982, along with an alternative newspaper, City Paper. After a stint in public relations in the 1980s, he founded and edited the weekly Louisville Eccentric Observer in the 1990s and appeared as a radio and TV commentator.

It was not until 1985 that he became a Democrat, deciding the party more closely reflected his views.

Yarmuth was a late entrant into the 2006 House race. Some of his more extreme suggestions as a columnist — such as removing "under God" from the Pledge of Allegiance — provided fodder for attack ads. But he won the primary handily and went on to edge out Republican Rep. Anne M. Northup by 2 percentage points.

Northup came back for a rematch in 2008, but the Democratic tide — locally, the 3rd District was the only one Obama carried in Kentucky — swamped her, and Yarmuth won with 59 percent of the vote. He won with 55 percent in 2010 against the GOP candidate, tea party-backed commercial pilot Todd Lally.

Key Votes

2010

Overhaul the nation's health insurance system	YES
Allow for repeal of "don't ask, don't tell"	YES
Overhaul financial services industry regulation	YES
Limit use of new Afghanistan War funds to troop withdrawal activities	YES
Change oversight of offshore drilling and lift oil spill liability cap	YES
Provide a path to legal status for some children of illegal immigrants	YES
Extend Bush-era income tax cuts for two years	NO

2009

Expand the Children's Health Insurance Program	YES
Provide $787 billion in tax cuts and spending increases to stimulate the economy	YES
Allow bankruptcy judges to modify certain primary-residence mortgages	YES
Create a cap-and-trade system to limit greenhouse gas emissions	YES
Provide $2 billion for the "cash for clunkers" program	YES
Establish the government as the sole provider of student loans	YES
Restrict federally funded insurance coverage for abortions in health care overhaul	NO

CQ Vote Studies

	PARTY UNITY		PRESIDENTIAL SUPPORT	
	SUPPORT	OPPOSE	SUPPORT	OPPOSE
2010	99%	1%	90%	10%
2009	99%	1%	97%	3%
2008	98%	2%	13%	87%
2007	97%	3%	3%	97%

Interest Groups

	AFL-CIO	ADA	CCUS	ACU
2010	100%	100%	13%	0%
2009	100%	100%	40%	0%
2008	100%	95%	61%	4%
2007	96%	100%	53%	0%

Louisville Metro

With the Ohio River forming its western border, the 3rd sprawls across ethnically and economically diverse neighborhoods of Louisville Metro. Compared to the rest of the state, Louisville has a sizable black population — nearly 40 percent of Kentucky's black residents live here.

Although tobacco, a statewide agricultural staple, still aids the 3rd's economy, other sectors now rival it. Local officials have focused on attracting new businesses to the area, and Louisville now hosts health care, financial services and insurance firms. Louisville's airport is an international hub for United Parcel Service, one of the area's largest private employers. UPS has completed an expansion of its sorting facilities at the airport, one of the busiest cargo airports in the nation.

Although the 3rd has Kentucky's highest percentage of white-collar workers, manufacturing retains a local presence. Two Ford assembly plants provide thousands of jobs, and the company has upgraded its manufacturing facilities here. Despite some layoffs, General Electric Consumer & Industrial still employs roughly 5,000 at its Louisville plant and may add jobs making appliances. Tourism — centered around horse racing and downtown

cultural sites — is another contributor to the local economy.

The only district in the state won by Barack Obama in the 2008 presidential election, the 3rd is Kentucky's most Democratic district. Obama took only 56 percent of the district's presidential vote that year, but the party runs well at the local level, especially downtown. Labor strength runs deep among the blue-collar residents of the city's South End, despite job losses from industrial decline.

Blacks living in the West End also back Democrats. Republicans near the river in the affluent East End, coupled with the growing number of white-collar suburbanites east of downtown, balance some of the left-leaning areas of the district.

Major Industry
Service, trade, manufacturing, health care

Cities
Louisville Metro (pt.), 578,087

Notable
The Kentucky Derby, called "the greatest two minutes in sports," is held at Churchill Downs in south Louisville; the Louisville Slugger Museum & Factory is in downtown Louisville.

Rep. Geoff Davis (R)

Capitol Office
225-3465
www.house.gov/geoffdavis
1119 Longworth Bldg. 20515-1704; fax 225-0003

Committees
Ways & Means
(Human Resources - Chairman)

Residence
Hebron

Born
Oct. 26, 1958; Montreal, Canada

Religion
Christian

Family
Wife, Pat Davis; six children

Education
U.S. Military Academy, B.S. 1981

Military
Army, 1976-87

Career
Manufacturing productivity consulting firm owner; aerospace technology consultant

Political Highlights
Republican nominee for U.S. House, 2002

ELECTION RESULTS

2010 GENERAL

Geoff Davis (R)	151,774	69.5%
John William Waltz (D)	66,675	30.5%

2010 PRIMARY

Geoff Davis (R)	unopposed

2008 GENERAL

Geoff Davis (R)	190,210	63.0%
Michael Kelley (D)	111,549	37.0%

Previous Winning Percentages
2006 (52%); 2004 (54%)

Elected 2004; 4th term

A fiscal and social conservative with an Army background, Davis focuses on assisting veterans and members of the military. He is also making himself a visible champion of limited government by leading House Republicans' efforts to curtail federal regulations.

Despite the occasional impolitic comment, he has solidified his control of a district that was once considered highly competitive. Although new to the Ways and Means Committee in the 112th Congress (2011-12), Davis is in sync with other Republicans on fiscal issues, favoring spending cuts to reduce the deficit while supporting extensions of the tax cuts enacted in 2001 and 2003. He sharply opposed the Democrats' health care overhaul, arguing in a committee markup that the bill did not do enough to limit medical malpractice lawsuits. Fear of such suits, Davis said during a tense debate, led to unnecessary procedures being performed on his dying mother.

As chairman of the Subcommittee on Human Resources, Davis says his major task is to balance the need for "streamlining" government assistance with ensuring that those most in need "do not fall through the cracks."

Davis has said that limited government is desirable. But personal experiences have sensitized him to the help government can provide: Social Security survivor benefits enabled his family to make ends meet after his stepfather died, and a government-subsidized loan made it possible for his mother to buy a house.

In 2010, Republican leaders pushed him to the forefront to talk about his attempt to rein in government regulation. Davis introduced legislation at the start of the 112th Congress to require congressional approval of all federal regulations with an annual economic impact exceeding $100 million, similar to a bill he had also proposed in the previous Congress. "When Congress forces through controversial legislation by purposefully leaving blanks for executive agencies to fill in, unelected bureaucrats end up writing laws with no accountability whatsoever," he said in the party's weekly radio address in September 2010. "This has to stop."

He scored a legislative victory in early 2009 when President Obama signed his bill to reauthorize and enhance programs to combat homelessness as part of larger legislation. He started his work on homelessness by pairing with Julia Carson, a Democrat from Indiana — a typical move for Davis on less controversial issues. In the 111th Congress (2009-10) he worked with Armed Services Chairman Ike Skelton of Missouri on improving coordination by national security agencies and with Ways and Means Chairman Sander M. Levin of Michigan on tax incentives for charitable contributions of food. He has remained generally supportive of the Obama administration's efforts in Afghanistan, although he is wary of the planned summer 2011 deadline to begin a withdrawal.

And, on occasion, he will stray from the party line on more contentious topics. In July 2009, Davis was one of 77 Republicans who backed a $2 billion infusion for the "cash for clunkers" program to purchase used automobiles. He joined Democrats to support a 2007 increase in the minimum wage. Earlier in his career, he split with most House Republicans to support a 2005 ban on cruel or degrading treatment of U.S. detainees, requiring that interrogators stick to standards set forth in the Army Field Manual.

Davis, a West Point graduate and former flight commander with the 82nd Airborne, has a history of occasional gaffes. He strongly backed President George W. Bush's policy in the Iraq War, but in the run-up to his 2006 re-election he faced stinging criticism for his answer in an October debate in which he badly underestimated the number of casualties in Iraq that month, one of the deadliest since the war began in March 2003. Davis said 17 U.S. military personnel had died, while the number was 71 on the day of the debate. Davis' campaign said he misspoke as a result of nervousness. But his Democratic opponent, former Rep. Ken Lucas, used the incident to paint Davis as out of touch and beholden to the Bush administration.

Davis survived it, but he put his foot in his mouth again in April 2008 when he called Democratic presidential nominee Barack Obama a "boy" during a fundraising dinner in Hebron. Davis said he had taken part in a "highly classified, national security simulation" with Obama and come away unimpressed. "That boy's finger does not need to be on the button," Davis said. He hand-delivered a written apology to Obama's office shortly thereafter.

Davis was successful in amending the 2009 defense authorization bill to equalize disability payments to members of the reserves injured in combat with payments made to active-duty military. From his seat on the Financial Services panel in the 109th Congress (2005-06), he sponsored a bill aimed at protecting members of the military from abusive or misleading sales practices by financial services companies. The legislation, enacted in 2006, gives state insurance regulators jurisdiction on military bases and prohibits the sale of certain products to members of the military.

Davis opposes abortion and efforts to restrict gun ownership. He believes schools should be allowed to search students and sponsored a bill, which the House passed in September 2006, to require local school systems to create policies that allow searches of students on "reasonable suspicion" that they might be carrying drugs or weapons. School systems that didn't create such policies would lose federal money for programs preventing drug use and violence, a provision that angered local school administrators and school boards. The measure died in the Senate.

Davis worked as a janitor while in high school to help his family pay the bills. After leaving the Army, he worked as an aerospace consultant before starting his own manufacturing and technology consulting firm.

Davis first tried for the 4th District seat in 2002, losing to Lucas by 3.5 percentage points. Lucas retired two years later, and Davis defeated actor George Clooney's father, longtime local newscaster and columnist Nick Clooney, to capture the seat in the 2004 general election. When Lucas tried for a comeback in 2006, Davis beat him by more than 8 percentage points. He won by wider margins in 2008 and 2010.

Key Votes

2010

Overhaul the nation's health insurance system	NO
Allow for repeal of "don't ask, don't tell"	-
Overhaul financial services industry regulation	NO
Limit use of new Afghanistan War funds to troop withdrawal activities	NO
Change oversight of offshore drilling and lift oil spill liability cap	-
Provide a path to legal status for some children of illegal immigrants	NO
Extend Bush-era income tax cuts for two years	YES

2009

Expand the Children's Health Insurance Program	NO
Provide $787 billion in tax cuts and spending increases to stimulate the economy	NO
Allow bankruptcy judges to modify certain primary-residence mortgages	NO
Create a cap-and-trade system to limit greenhouse gas emissions	NO
Provide $2 billion for the "cash for clunkers" program	YES
Establish the government as the sole provider of student loans	NO
Restrict federally funded insurance coverage for abortions in health care overhaul	YES

CQ Vote Studies

	PARTY UNITY		PRESIDENTIAL SUPPORT	
	SUPPORT	OPPOSE	SUPPORT	OPPOSE
2010	99%	1%	31%	69%
2009	90%	10%	21%	79%
2008	95%	5%	73%	27%
2007	94%	6%	83%	17%
2006	94%	6%	95%	5%

Interest Groups

	AFL-CIO	ADA	CCUS	ACU
2010	8%	0%	86%	96%
2009	10%	5%	87%	92%
2008	13%	15%	89%	96%
2007	17%	10%	83%	96%
2006	29%	5%	93%	84%

Kentucky 4

North — Covington, Florence, Ashland

The 4th travels across northern Kentucky, from the industrial city of Ashland along the Ohio River, past tobacco farms and small towns, and through the Ohio commuters' region before reaching the Oldham County suburbs northeast of Louisville Metro. Nearly half of district residents live in the Cincinnati suburbs.

Despite steady economic growth for more than a decade, the cities of northern Kentucky in Boone, Campbell and Kenton counties — which include Cincinnati suburbs — can struggle with high unemployment. Located in Boone County, the Cincinnati-Northern Kentucky International Airport is the region's largest economic force.

The international shipping company DHL, which provides more than 1,000 jobs, has plans to expand its hub at the airport. Covington also serves as a regional processing center for the IRS, and federal government jobs provide economic stability.

The economy in the eastern part of the district has struggled for years, although Elliott County's population has grown significantly since 2000. Ashland struggled to cope after businesses relocated and downsized in

the late 1980s, and the city has declined as an industrial hub. Boyd County, which includes Ashland, has been losing population since the 1990s. Other regional jurisdictions, including those across the Ohio and Big Sandy rivers in Ohio and West Virginia, respectively, are cooperating to try to attract more industrial firms to this tri-state area, and Ashland officials are planning new development.

The 4th backs GOP presidential candidates, and Oldham joins counties in the Cincinnati area in voting reliably Republican. John McCain took 60 percent of the 4th's 2008 presidential vote and won every county wholly or partially in the district except for one. Elliott County, where Democratic Party voter registration routinely tops 90 percent, has voted Democratic for president for nearly a century, and Barack Obama won 61 percent of the county's vote, his highest percentage statewide.

Major Industry
Transportation, manufacturing, health care, service

Cities
Covington, 40,640; Florence, 29,951; Independence, 24,757

Notable
The Kentucky Speedway racetrack is located near Sparta.

Rep. Harold Rogers (R)

Capitol Office
225-4601
halrogers.house.gov
2406 Rayburn Bldg. 20515-1705; fax 225-0940

Committees
Appropriations - Chairman

Residence
Somerset

Born
Dec. 31, 1937; Barrier, Ky.

Religion
Baptist

Family
Wife, Cynthia Doyle Rogers; three children

Education
Western Kentucky U., attended 1956-57;
U. of Kentucky, B.A. 1962, LL.B. 1964

Military
Ky. National Guard, 1956-57; N.C. National Guard,
1957-58; Ky. National Guard, 1958-63

Career
Lawyer

Political Highlights
Pulaski and Rockcastle counties commonwealth attorney, 1969-80; Republican nominee for lieutenant governor, 1979

ELECTION RESULTS

2010 GENERAL

Harold Rogers (R)	151,019	77.4%
Jim Holbert (D)	44,034	22.6%

2010 PRIMARY

Harold Rogers (R)	unopposed

2008 GENERAL

Harold Rogers (R)	177,024	84.1%
Jim Holbert (I)	33,444	15.9%

Previous Winning Percentages
2006 (74%); 2004 (100%); 2002 (78%); 2000 (74%);
1998 (78%); 1996 (100%); 1994 (79%); 1992 (55%);
1990 (100%); 1988 (100%); 1986 (100%); 1984 (76%);
1982 (65%); 1980 (68%)

Elected 1980; 16th term

Wielding the power that comes with being an appropriator is second nature to Rogers after three decades in the House. The man once dubbed "the prince of pork" has become chairman of the powerful spending panel and now casts himself as a born-again budget cutter.

After missing out on the top spot in 2005 to the less senior Jerry Lewis of California, the Kentuckian won the gavel in the 112th Congress (2011-12) despite concerns from many conservatives that his history of funding pet projects through earmarks made him the wrong man to lead the Appropriations Committee at this moment in history.

But the GOP leadership went with Rogers over Lewis, who tried and failed to get a waiver to the party's committee leadership term limits, and Jack Kingston of Georgia, who ranks fifth in GOP seniority on the committee.

Early reviews were favorable.

"He has the toughest job in town, and I think he's handling it well," Lewis told Roll Call early in 2011.

Rogers created a good first impression when he offered to cut his committee's own budget by 9 percent for the rest of fiscal 2011, almost twice the cut experienced by his legislative branch colleagues.

He hit a bump when conservatives balked at his committee's original version of a catchall spending bill that would have trimmed $32 billion in spending. So Rogers went back to the drawing board and rewrote the bill, coming up with $26 billion in additional cuts. He then presided over a vigorous floor debate that tacked on a few more reductions.

Rogers faces the delicate task of maintaining the momentum for reduced spending desired by much of his caucus while striking deals with the Democrats who run the Senate and the White House.

Just getting beyond the appropriations stalemate that has marked the past few Congresses would be a signal achievement.

Rogers would like to see a return to "regular order," where annual spending bills move through Appropriations subcommittees and the full committee before reaching the House floor. The House passed only two of its fiscal 2011 spending bills in 2010. It brought all 12 to the floor in 2009 but did so with closed rules that limited debate. In the previous year, only one spending bill — the one funding the Department of Veterans Affairs and military construction — reached the floor as a stand-alone measure.

"I would try to go back to the way we used to be, listening to all sides, encouraging debate and amendments," Rogers said.

Until his ascent to the chairmanship, Rogers was very much an old-school appropriator who strongly defended the practice of sending money back home. In June 2009, Rogers congratulated fellow GOP appropriator John Culberson of Texas on the floor for his ultimately successful effort to thwart a bid by GOP spending hawk Jeff Flake of Arizona — now a member of Rogers' committee — to strip a $1 million earmark for flood control in Culberson's district. Flake had argued that certain grant funding was being unfairly distributed unless "Mother Nature somehow finds those districts represented by appropriators and sends more floods, more earthquakes, more natural disasters."

Rogers countered that Culberson "would be derelict in his duties to the Congress and to the people of his district and the country if he didn't make these efforts to help the people that he represents . . . and I salute the gentleman."

When the House Republican leadership instituted a ban on fiscal 2011 earmarks, Rogers at first opposed the plan. He argued that the ban would not reduce overall spending but simply shift power over spending decisions away from Congress to executive branch agencies.

Rogers has taken flak for some of his own earmarks. "No one man, not even a powerful congressman in his 15th term in office, could change the economy of a region, much less a state or the country," the Lexington-Herald Leader stated in a July 2010 editorial critical of his earmarks. "But it's no coincidence that Rogers' district has remained mired in an economic nowhere land while a favored few have benefited from the congressman's position." The editorial pointed out that one of Rogers' donors, J.C. Egnew, serves on the board of the National Institute for Hometown Security, a Somerset-based nonprofit that has benefited from earmarks orchestrated by the congressman. It also noted Rogers' support for a wildlife bill that the congressman joined a Democratic majority in passing in April 2009. Rogers' daughter works as the grants administrator for the Cheetah Conservation Fund, which would benefit from the bill. Rogers' office noted that many organizations would be able to apply for funds under the measure and that Rogers' daughter's position wouldn't influence allocation of funding.

Rogers takes particular pride in having steered money home to fight the drug problem in southern and eastern Kentucky. According to his website, Rogers has directed more than $50 million in the past eight years to Operation UNITE (Unlawful Narcotics Investigations, Treatment and Education), which serves 29 Kentucky counties. For years, Rogers has been aggressively seeking federal help in fighting abuse of painkillers, such as OxyContin.

The congressman also is noted for keeping a particularly sharp eye on the Department of Homeland Security. While serving as chairman of the Appropriations Subcommittee on Homeland Security, Rogers threatened to slash fiscal 2006 funding for the Coast Guard's troubled Deepwater program by almost half, to $500 million, before relenting and allowing $933 million to be appropriated. At a 2010 hearing, Rogers told Homeland Security Secretary Janet Napolitano that he would seek to freeze certain funds for Deepwater and other programs unless the program improved its response to the committee's requests for reports.

After graduating from high school in rural Kentucky in 1955, Rogers left home in search of work in Cincinnati. He returned to earn undergraduate and law degrees at the University of Kentucky and made a name for himself in the southeastern part of the state as a civic activist, promoting industrial development.

Having earlier served as a prosecutor, Rogers lost a 1979 campaign for lieutenant governor. The name recognition he earned helped when he ran for the House in 1980 to succeed retiring Republican Tim Lee Carter. He won a 10-person GOP primary, then took 68 percent of the vote in November. It was the first in a long series of decisive victories.

Key Votes

2010

Vote	
Overhaul the nation's health insurance system	NO
Allow for repeal of "don't ask, don't tell"	NO
Overhaul financial services industry regulation	NO
Limit use of new Afghanistan War funds to troop withdrawal activities	NO
Change oversight of offshore drilling and lift oil spill liability cap	NO
Provide a path to legal status for some children of illegal immigrants	NO
Extend Bush-era income tax cuts for two years	YES

2009

Vote	
Expand the Children's Health Insurance Program	NO
Provide $787 billion in tax cuts and spending increases to stimulate the economy	NO
Allow bankruptcy judges to modify certain primary-residence mortgages	NO
Create a cap-and-trade system to limit greenhouse gas emissions	NO
Provide $2 billion for the "cash for clunkers" program	NO
Establish the government as the sole provider of student loans	NO
Restrict federally funded insurance coverage for abortions in health care overhaul	YES

CQ Vote Studies

	PARTY UNITY		PRESIDENTIAL SUPPORT	
	SUPPORT	OPPOSE	SUPPORT	OPPOSE
2010	97%	3%	26%	74%
2009	82%	18%	35%	65%
2008	96%	4%	69%	31%
2007	91%	9%	77%	23%
2006	96%	4%	93%	7%

Interest Groups

	AFL-CIO	ADA	CCUS	ACU
2010	7%	0%	88%	96%
2009	14%	0%	87%	88%
2008	13%	20%	94%	84%
2007	17%	10%	90%	96%
2006	29%	10%	87%	80%

Kentucky 5

East and southeast — Somerset, Middlesboro

The rural 5th, which takes in eastern Kentucky's hardscrabble coal country, has struggled with poverty, undereducation and a lack of economic diversity. The district has the nation's highest percentage of white residents (96 percent) and its second-lowest median household income.

Mining provides thousands of jobs in this sparsely populated Appalachian region, particularly in places such as Pike, Perry, Harlan and Knott counties. The region's coal industry has come under increased federal scrutiny regarding safety measures and the environmental impact of mountaintop removal, and these eastern counties are trying to diversify their economies and increase the number of residents active in the workforce. Some community leaders are trying to attract tourists by highlighting the area's country music heritage, building new arts centers and showcasing the area's coal history.

Population in the western portion of the district is concentrated in Pulaski and Laurel counties. Somerset, in Pulaski, relies heavily on tourism and recreation. Lake Cumberland is nearby, as is the Big South Fork National River and Recreation Area. The Daniel Boone National Forest extends from Rowan County in the north to the Tennessee border.

Methamphetamine abuse, a major problem in surrounding states, has become an issue in the 5th, but groups are attempting to improve local public awareness and drug enforcement efforts. Education also is a concern, as the 5th has the state's lowest percentage (11 percent) of residents with at least a bachelor's degree.

The 5th is secure GOP territory — no Democrat has represented the southeast Kentucky district since 1889. Republicans run particularly well in the more populous central and western areas. In 2008, John McCain carried the 5th with 67 percent of the presidential vote, his highest percentage statewide, and Jackson County was his best in the state. Democrat Barack Obama won three counties in the district's north.

Major Industry
Coal, service, tourism

Cities
Somerset, 11,196; Middlesborough, 10,334

Notable
Colonel Harland Sanders began making what would later be known as Kentucky Fried Chicken at his service station in Corbin.

Rep. Ben Chandler (D)

Capitol Office
225-4706
chandler.house.gov
1504 Longworth Bldg. 20515; fax 225-2122

Committees
Foreign Affairs
Select Intelligence

Residence
Versailles

Born
Sept. 12, 1959; Versailles, Ky.

Religion
Presbyterian

Family
Wife, Jennifer Chandler; three children

Education
U. of Kentucky, B.A. 1983 (history), J.D. 1986

Career
Lawyer

Political Highlights
Ky. auditor, 1992-96; Ky. attorney general, 1996-2004; Democratic nominee for governor, 2003

ELECTION RESULTS

2010 GENERAL

Ben Chandler (D)	119,812	50.1%
Andy Barr (R)	119,165	49.8%

2010 PRIMARY

Ben Chandler (D)	unopposed

2008 GENERAL

Ben Chandler (D)	203,764	64.7%
Jon Larson (R)	111,378	35.3%

Previous Winning Percentages
2006 (86%); 2004 (59%); 2004 Special Election (55%)

Elected 2004; 4th full term

Chandler paid a steep price for his party's defeat in the 2010 elections, losing his seat on the Appropriations Committee and about half his colleagues in the fiscally conservative Blue Dog Coalition. And, after three easy re-election wins, he barely managed to hang on to his own seat.

When the 112th Congress (2011-12) began, he returned to the Foreign Affairs Committee, where he served in his first full term (when it was called International Relations), and joined the Intelligence Committee. Both give him a chance to indulge his longtime interest in foreign policy. As a college student, he served as an intern in the British Parliament. Chandler said he hopes to use his assignments to bring to Kentucky foreign investment and the jobs that come with it.

As an appropriator, he had served on the subcommittee that funded the State Department and foreign aid programs.

Chandler stands a bit to the right on certain social and economic issues, leans left on environmental protection and keeps his eye centered on ways to bring funds to his district. He opposed the catchall spending bill the House passed early in 2011 that included $62 billion in spending cuts.

For the most part in the 111th Congress (2009-10), Chandler was a dependable vote on Democratic initiatives. His party loyalty numbers were markedly lower when Republicans were in the majority.

He had been an early supporter of Barack Obama in the 2008 presidential race, acknowledging he knew his decision would "go against the tide" in his district, which ultimately backed Republican John McCain with 55 percent of the vote.

He supported Obama's economic stimulus plan, legislation to make the federal government the sole provider of student loans and a measure to provide $2 billion for the "cash for clunkers" vehicle trade-in program. He also backed expansion of the Children's Health Insurance Program, which covers children from families that make too much money to qualify for Medicaid.

But on the highest-profile vote of the 111th Congress, Chandler went his own way, joining 33 other Democrats in voting "no" on the final version of the health care overhaul enacted in March 2010, citing "concerns I had about its effect on our seniors, rural hospitals and the overall cost to taxpayers." But he sided with Democrats when Republicans pushed repeal legislation through the House early in 2011. He said he favors repealing "many parts" of the law, but "will not vote to repeal parts of the law that protect Central Kentuckians by preventing insurance companies from dropping people if they get sick, ending lifetime caps on coverage, and eliminating pre-existing condition exclusions."

On another hot-button issue, Chandler wavered. As late as August 2010, he said he was undecided on extending the Bush-era tax cuts for the highest earners. When 31 Democratic colleagues wrote to their party leadership in September in support of extending all of the cuts, Chandler did not join in. But as his re-election race tightened, he told the Lexington Herald-Leader that he was "inclined to support all the tax cuts, at least temporarily, until the economy gets back on its feet." In the end, he voted for the two-year extension that was signed into law in late 2010.

Chandler considers environmental protection a priority and stood out in coal-rich Kentucky for his support of legislation to create a cap-and-trade system to limit greenhouse gas emissions, citing what he said was the bill's "$60 billion investment in clean coal."

While his old Appropriations seat was a plum, he also was given a seat in the 111th Congress that many members consider a prune: a spot on the ethics committee, which immediately faced the task of deciding how to proceed with an investigation of New York Democrat Charles B. Rangel's fundraising and personal finances. Chandler was one of three Democrats assigned to the Committee on Standards of Official Conduct, as the panel was then known, who had received campaign funds from the Ways and Means chairman's leadership PAC; he got $10,000 in 2004.

Chandler lives in Woodford County on land that has been in his family since 1784, eight years before Kentucky became a state. He was born in Versailles and said he can trace ancestors on his mother's side back to the second boat that arrived at Jamestown in 1609.

He also has deep political roots in Kentucky. His grandfather and namesake, A.B. "Happy" Chandler, was a two-time governor and a U.S. senator and may be best remembered for his five-year stint as commissioner of Major League Baseball.

Chandler was elected Kentucky auditor in 1991. He then won elections for attorney general in 1995 and 1999. As Kentucky's top law enforcement officer, he oversaw the establishment of the state's "do not call" telemarketing list.

He ran for governor in 2003 but was defeated by Republican Ernie Fletcher. After his loss, Chandler ran in the special election for the House seat vacated by Fletcher. His race against GOP state Sen. Alice Forgy Kerr drew widespread attention. Both national parties recognized that the contest would be perceived as a bellwether and spent heavily. Chandler won by 12 percentage points. A little more than eight months later he won election to a full term.

He took more than 85 percent of the vote in 2006 and declared himself so happy with his work that he declined to take another stab at the governorship. He won easily again in 2008 and considered a 2010 run for the Senate seat held by retiring Republican Jim Bunning.

He passed on that contest and ended up in a tough race against Lexington attorney Andy Barr, who ran a vigorous campaign aided by independent groups attacking Chandler as a tool of the Democratic leadership. Three days after Election Day, Barr conceded defeat. Chandler squeaked by with a 600-vote margin.

With an early eye on 2012, the independent conservative group Crossroads GPS was already back on the air in mid-February with an ad targeting Chandler's vote against the GOP-backed catchall spending bill for fiscal 2011.

Key Votes

2010

Overhaul the nation's health insurance system	NO
Allow for repeal of "don't ask, don't tell"	YES
Overhaul financial services industry regulation	NO
Limit use of new Afghanistan War funds to troop withdrawal activities	NO
Change oversight of offshore drilling and lift oil spill liability cap	YES
Provide a path to legal status for some children of illegal immigrants	NO
Extend Bush-era income tax cuts for two years	YES

2009

Expand the Children's Health Insurance Program	YES
Provide $787 billion in tax cuts and spending increases to stimulate the economy	YES
Allow bankruptcy judges to modify certain primary-residence mortgages	YES
Create a cap-and-trade system to limit greenhouse gas emissions	YES
Provide $2 billion for the "cash for clunkers" program	YES
Establish the government as the sole provider of student loans	YES
Restrict federally funded insurance coverage for abortions in health care overhaul	YES

CQ Vote Studies

	PARTY UNITY		PRESIDENTIAL SUPPORT	
	Support	Oppose	Support	Oppose
2010	89%	11%	78%	22%
2009	93%	7%	92%	8%
2008	93%	7%	19%	81%
2007	93%	7%	9%	91%
2006	83%	17%	56%	44%

Interest Groups

	AFL-CIO	ADA	CCUS	ACU
2010	71%	65%	63%	17%
2009	90%	80%	69%	20%
2008	100%	85%	61%	12%
2007	96%	95%	47%	8%
2006	86%	60%	57%	50%

Kentucky 6

East central — Lexington, Frankfort

The 6th embodies the culture and economic pursuits that most outsiders associate with Kentucky. This is the heart of the Bluegrass region, which spawns Kentucky Derby champions and is host to considerable tobacco and liquor interests. The 6th is a patchwork of urban, suburban and rural communities.

Lexington, known as the thoroughbred capital of the world, has a strong equine industry. The city is home to the University of Kentucky, central Kentucky's largest employer. Just north of Lexington is Georgetown, where Toyota's first hybrid vehicle produced in the United States rolled off the line in 2006. There have been no layoffs, but hits to domestic auto manufacturing forced operating changes at the plant. The state capital, Frankfort, is located about 30 miles northwest of Lexington.

Tobacco, always a highly charged subject in this region, continues to be a strong economic force. The end of the quota system — which controlled the supply and price of tobacco — and the government's tobacco buyout have made the industry more competitive. Production also has generally shifted away from the 6th in favor of the state's western regions, although increasing demand for smokeless tobacco has benefitted local dark-tobacco growers.

The 6th is a politically competitive district, and voters here, who tend to be socially conservative, will support candidates from either party and will back incumbents — Rep. Ben Chandler's solid base of support in Fayette (Lexington) and Franklin counties allowed him to eke out a slim victory in his 2010 re-election race. Despite the primarily Democratic government workers of Frankfort, Republican presidential candidate John McCain took Franklin County in 2008. The GOP runs up big margins in the farmland south of Lexington, especially in Garrard and Jessamine counties and the 6th's portion of Lincoln County.

Major Industry
Manufacturing, service, tobacco, retail

Military Bases
Blue Grass Army Depot, 139 military, 1,114 civilian (2009)

Cities
Lexington-Fayette, 295,803; Richmond, 31,364; Georgetown, 29,098

Notable
Bourbon whiskey was named after Bourbon County.

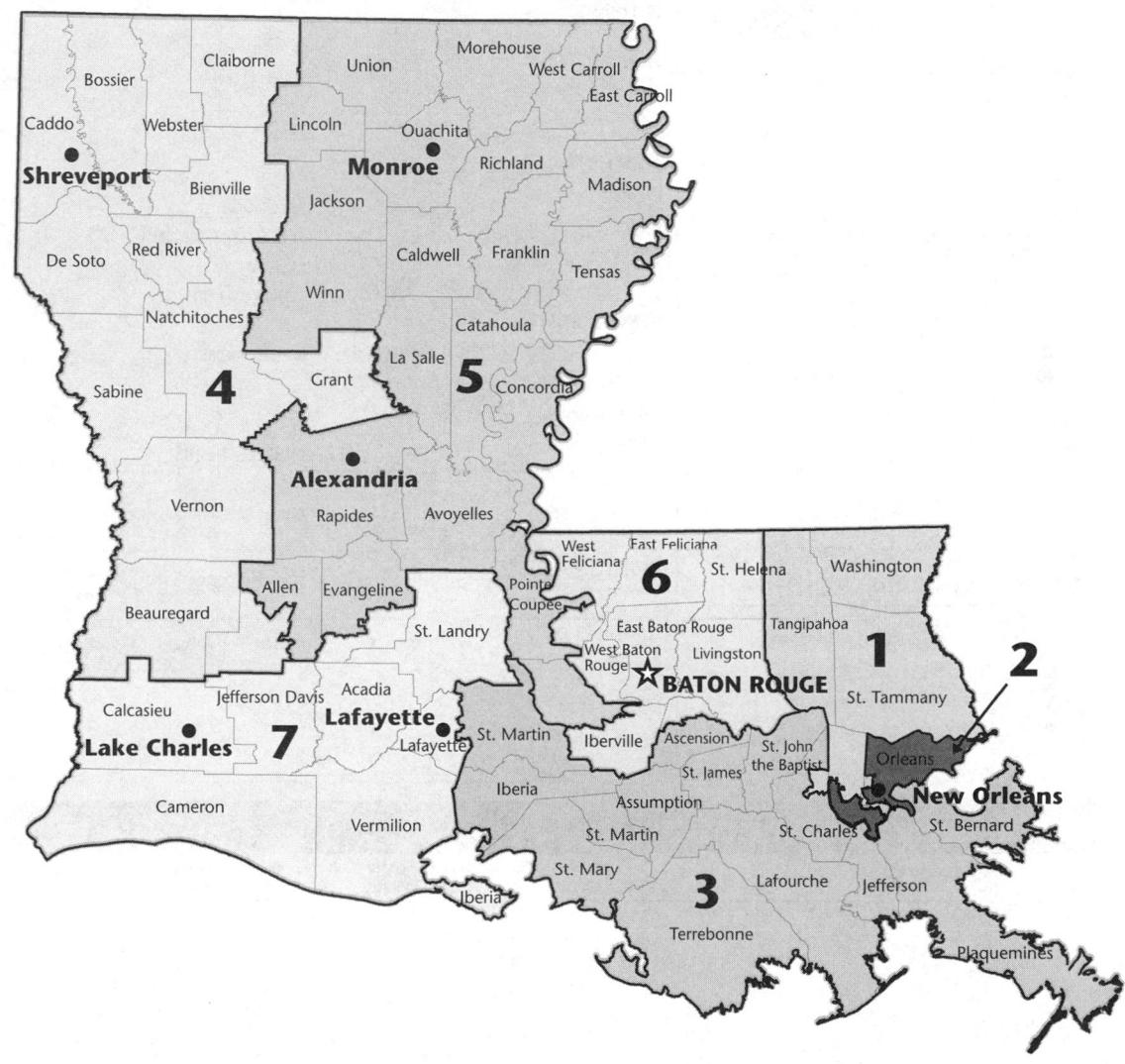

Gov. Bobby Jindal (R)

Pronounced: JIN-dle

First elected: 2007

Length of term: 4 years

Term expires: 1/12

Salary: $130,000

Phone: (225) 342-7015

Residence: Kenner

Born: June 10, 1971; Baton Rouge, La

Religion: Roman Catholic

Family: Wife, Supriya Jindal; three children

Education: Brown U., Sc.B. 1991 (biology & public policy); Oxford U., M.Litt. 1994 (Rhodes scholar)

Career: State university system president; management consultant

Political highlights: La. Health and Hospitals Department secretary, 1996-98; U.S. Health and Human Services assistant secretary for planning and evaluation, 2001-03; candidate for governor, 2003; U.S. House, 2005-08

ELECTION RESULTS

2007 GENERAL

Bobby Jindal (R)	699,275	53.9%
Walter J. Boasso (D)	226,476	17.5%
John Georges (X)	186,682	14.4%
Foster Campbell (D)	161,665	12.5%

Lt. Gov. Jay Dardenne (R)

First elected: 2010

Length of term: 4 years

Term expires: 1/12

Salary: $115,000

Phone: (225) 342-7009

LEGISLATURE

Legislature: March-June in odd-numbered years; April-June in even-numbered years

Senate: 39 members, 4-year terms

2011 ratios: 22 R, 17 D; 31 men, 8 women

Salary: $16,800

Phone: (225) 342-2040

House: 105 members, 4-year terms

2011 ratios: 55 R, 46 D, 4 I; 91 men, 14 women

Salary: $16,800

Phone: (225) 342-6945

TERM LIMITS

Governor: 2 terms

Senate: No

House: No

URBAN STATISTICS

CITY	POPULATION
New Orleans	343,829
Baton Rouge	229,493
Shreveport	199,311
Lafayette	120,623
Lake Charles	71,993

REGISTERED VOTERS

Democrat	50%
Republican	27%
Unaffiliated/Other	23%

POPULATION

2010 population	4,533,372
2000 population	4,468,976
1990 population	4,219,973
Percent change (2000-2010)	+1.4%
Rank among states (2010)	25
Median age	35.5
Born in state	79.2%
Foreign born	3.0%
Violent crime rate	620/100,000
Poverty level	17.3%
Federal workers	44,533
Military	17,398

ELECTIONS

STATE ELECTION OFFICIAL
(225) 922-0900

DEMOCRATIC PARTY
(225) 336-4155

REPUBLICAN PARTY
(225) 928-2998

MISCELLANEOUS

Web: www.louisiana.gov

Capital: Baton Rouge

U.S. CONGRESS

Senate: 1 Democrat, 1 Republican

House: 6 Republicans, 1 Democrat

2010 CENSUS STATISTICS BY DISTRICT

District	2008 Vote for President Obama	McCain	White	Black	Asian	Hispanic	Median Income	White Collar	Blue Collar	Service Industry	Over 64	Under 18	College Education	Rural	Sq. Miles
1	26%	72%	73%	16%	2%	8%	$51,240	64%	21%	15%	13%	24%	29%	20%	2,402
2	75	23	29	58	4	7	36,947	55	23	22	11	24	21	1	266
3	37	61	64	27	1	4	44,717	51	34	16	11	27	13	27	7,010
4	40	59	59	34	1	3	38,653	53	27	20	13	25	19	41	10,765
5	37	62	61	35	1	2	35,459	54	26	20	13	25	17	47	13,775
6	41	57	58	35	2	3	47,158	60	23	17	10	25	26	24	3,076
7	35	63	69	25	1	3	40,892	55	27	17	12	26	19	31	6,268
STATE	40	59	60	32	2	4	42,167	56	26	18	12	25	21	27	43,562
U.S.	53	46	64	12	5	16	51,425	60	23	17	13	25	28	21	3,537,438

Sen. Mary L. Landrieu (D)

Elected 1996; 3rd term

Landrieu chairs a committee and sits on three other panels of importance to her home state, making her the most powerful member of Louisiana's congressional delegation. Though her moderate leanings — along with her dogged pursuit of funds for her hurricane-ravaged state — occasionally put her at odds with her caucus, they make her an active player on energy and economic issues.

Since Hurricane Katrina hit in 2005, Landrieu (LAN-drew) has sought help for the Gulf Coast from any and all sources. She makes her case by using her seat on the Appropriations Committee, where she chairs the Homeland Security spending panel, and her seat on the Homeland Security and Governmental Affairs Subcommittee on Disaster Recovery, which she used to chair.

And as chairwoman of the Small Business and Entrepreneurship Committee, Landrieu plans to try to help Gulf Coast companies still reeling from Katrina. She also hopes to boost federal contracting for female-owned businesses and elevate the Small Business Administration to Cabinet-level status and increase its funding.

Landrieu and Olympia J. Snowe of Maine, the top-ranking Republican on the Small Business panel, are the first female duo to lead a committee in either chamber. They previously teamed together to lead a bipartisan organization of senators that sprang from the "Gang of 14," an informal coalition that resolved a contentious impasse over judicial nominations in 2005. The Gang of 14 combined with members of the old Centrist Coalition to form a new Common Ground Coalition in January 2007.

On the Energy and Natural Resources Committee, Landrieu has long been a strong critic of the Obama administration's regulations on oil drilling. She blasted an announcement from the Interior Department in December 2010 that it would not expand offshore oil exploration into the eastern Gulf of Mexico and along the Atlantic Coast, a move Landrieu called a "major step backwards for our nation's energy security." A fierce advocate on behalf of her state's oil and gas industries, Landrieu has opposed rolling back tax breaks for oil companies and imposing a "windfall profits" tax on the largest of them. She also wants more investment in a new electrical grid and a greater focus on nuclear power.

Energy isn't the only issue that sets Landrieu apart from her caucus. During the George W. Bush administration, she broke ranks with her party on roughly one-quarter of the votes in which the majority of Democrats diverged from a majority of Republicans. She has supported a constitutional amendment that would allow Congress to ban desecration of the American flag. And she was one of nine in her party to oppose a $700 billion rescue plan for the financial services industry that became law in fall 2008.

Landrieu can, by turns, be bipartisan and highly partisan. In both cases, she can be pugnacious. She is known to place legislative "holds" on nominations and bills as a means of seeking leverage. For two months in 2010 Landrieu held up President Obama's nominee to lead the Office of Management and Budget, Jacob J. Lew, to protest a deep-water drilling moratorium imposed after the explosion of an oil rig in the Gulf of Mexico in April. Landrieu lifted her hold in November, clearing the way for Lew's confirmation, saying "notable progress has been made, permits have been issued."

Likewise when the Senate considered a bill to overhaul the nation's flood insurance program in May 2008, Democrat Christopher J. Dodd of Connecticut sought to block an amendment package Landrieu and other Gulf Coast lawmakers had assembled. She threatened to delay the bill by reading aloud a litany of e-mail messages from constituents whose homes were destroyed by Katrina. Majority Leader Harry Reid of Nevada dissuaded her from doing so.

Capitol Office
224-5824
landrieu.senate.gov
431 Dirksen Bldg. 20510-1804; fax 224-9735

Committees
Appropriations
   (Homeland Security - Chairwoman)
Energy & Natural Resources
Homeland Security & Governmental Affairs
Small Business & Entrepreneurship - Chairwoman

Residence
New Orleans

Born
Nov. 23, 1955; Arlington, Va.

Religion
Roman Catholic

Family
Husband, Frank Snellings; two children

Education
Louisiana State U., B.A. 1977 (sociology)

Career
Realtor

Political Highlights
La. House, 1980-88; La. treasurer, 1988-96; candidate for governor, 1995

ELECTION RESULTS

2008 GENERAL
Mary L. Landrieu (D)	988,298	52.1%
John Kennedy (R)	867,177	45.7%

2008 PRIMARY
Mary L. Landrieu (D)	unopposed

2002 GENERAL RUNOFF
Mary L. Landrieu (D)	638,654	51.7%
Suzanne Haik Terrell (R)	596,642	48.3%

Previous Winning Percentages
1996 (50%)

As Senate GOP leaders struggled in March 2006 to push through a budget, Landrieu cut a deal with them. She provided the final vote needed to pass the budget resolution, which called for subsequent legislation to open Alaska's Arctic National Wildlife Refuge (ANWR) to oil drilling, a cause she has long supported. But she delivered her vote only after winning a provision to create a $10 billion Gulf Coast recovery fund that would draw some of the revenue from ANWR leases and offshore drilling. She was the only Democrat to vote for the resolution.

Later that year, Landrieu helped shepherd into law a measure to open new areas of the Gulf of Mexico to offshore drilling. The law could provide Louisiana with at least $13 billion in royalties over the next three decades.

She stuck with her party to support a $787 billion economic stimulus plan, signed into law in 2009, and the health care overhaul enacted in 2010, and she voted against repealing the overhaul in 2011. She defended the inclusion in the health care law of a $300 million Medicaid provision for her state. Critics dubbed the provision the "Louisiana Purchase" and suggested it was carved out to win her vote. Landrieu defended the provision on the Senate floor by explaining that her state's Medicaid funding needed to be changed after Hurricane Katrina.

Landrieu shares a strong bond with her female colleagues in the Senate. In 2000, she collaborated on a book about their rise, "Nine and Counting." She announced afterward she would not campaign against any of those women — Democrat or Republican.

Her relationship with her home-state colleague, Republican David Vitter, is far less cordial. The two have openly feuded over the size and specifics of hurricane relief bills, and Vitter held up a public housing bill she sponsored in 2007.

With two adopted children at home, she has fought tirelessly to increase the adoption tax credit, revamp the foster care system and ease international adoptions. She is co-chairwoman of the Congressional Coalition on Adoption.

She is the daughter of Moon Landrieu, who was mayor of New Orleans for eight years and secretary of Housing and Urban Development in the Carter administration. Her brother Mitch served as lieutenant governor and is now mayor of the Crescent City. That lineage aided Landrieu's swift political rise. She was elected to the Louisiana House at age 23, went on to become state treasurer, then made an unsuccessful run for governor in 1995. A year later, in a contest to fill the seat of retiring Democrat J. Bennett Johnston, she won by the slimmest margin ever in a Louisiana Senate race — 5,788 votes out of 1.7 million cast. The loser, conservative Louis "Woody" Jenkins, alleged voter fraud. Landrieu was seated, but the Senate Rules Committee, controlled by Republicans, conducted a probe that lasted months. In the end, the panel ruled there was no "quantum level of fraud" that would warrant unseating her.

She ran again in 2002 and was forced into a runoff after falling short of the 50 percent needed to claim victory. She had finished first with 46 percent in the nine-candidate field, which included three well-known Republicans: state Elections Commissioner Suzanne Haik Terrell, Rep. John Cooksey and state Rep. Tony Perkins. In the runoff, she increased the margin of her 1996 victory sevenfold, to 42,012 votes.

Republican strategists had been confident they could thwart her quest for a third term in 2008, given her previous tight races and the overall difficulty Democrats face in the Deep South. But Landrieu had little trouble winning in a state where Republican John McCain easily prevailed over Barack Obama.

Republicans recruited State Treasurer John Kennedy, who switched parties from Democrat to Republican. But national Democrats ran ads labeling Kennedy a flip-flopper for campaigning as a conservative after running, and losing, a 2004 Senate race as a liberal Democrat and supporting Massachusetts Sen. John Kerry's presidential bid. Landrieu also received the backing of the U.S. Chamber of Commerce and some of the state's elected Republicans. She captured 52 percent of the vote.

Key Votes

2010

Vote	
Pass budget reconciliation bill to modify overhauls of health care and federal student loan programs	YES
Proceed to disapproval resolution on EPA authority to regulate greenhouse gases	YES
Overhaul financial services industry regulation	YES
Limit debate to proceed to a bill to broaden campaign finance disclosure and reporting rules	YES
Limit debate on an extension of Bush-era income tax cuts for two years	YES
Limit debate on a bill to provide a path to legal status for some children of illegal immigrants	YES
Allow for a repeal of "don't ask, don't tell"	YES
Consent to ratification of a strategic arms reduction treaty with Russia	YES

2009

Vote	
Prevent release of remaining financial industry bailout funds	NO
Make it easier for victims to sue for wage discrimination remedies	YES
Expand the Children's Health Insurance Program	YES
Limit debate on the economic stimulus measure	YES
Repeal District of Columbia firearms prohibitions and gun registration laws	YES
Limit debate on expansion of federal hate crimes law	YES
Strike funding for F-22 Raptor fighter jets	YES

CQ Vote Studies

	PARTY UNITY		PRESIDENTIAL SUPPORT	
	Support	Oppose	Support	Oppose
2010	93%	7%	98%	2%
2009	90%	10%	97%	3%
2008	69%	31%	53%	47%
2007	78%	22%	47%	53%
2006	75%	25%	71%	29%
2005	76%	24%	64%	36%
2004	81%	19%	68%	32%
2003	78%	22%	58%	42%
2002	65%	35%	84%	16%
2001	81%	19%	74%	26%

Interest Groups

	AFL-CIO	ADA	CCUS	ACU
2010	93%	75%	36%	8%
2009	89%	90%	60%	16%
2008	100%	65%	75%	32%
2007	95%	80%	73%	40%
2006	73%	65%	75%	24%
2005	86%	95%	76%	44%
2004	100%	85%	71%	32%
2003	77%	60%	78%	20%
2002	83%	70%	84%	35%
2001	88%	85%	69%	28%

Sen. David Vitter (R)

Capitol Office
224-4623
vitter.senate.gov
516 Hart Bldg. 20510-1803; fax 228-5061

Committees
Armed Services
Banking, Housing & Urban Affairs
Environment & Public Works
Small Business & Entrepreneurship

Residence
Metairie

Born
May 3, 1961; New Orleans, La.

Religion
Roman Catholic

Family
Wife, Wendy Baldwin Vitter; four children

Education
Harvard U., A.B. 1983; Oxford U., B.A. 1985 (Rhodes scholar); Tulane U., J.D. 1988

Career
Lawyer; professor

Political Highlights
La. House, 1992-99; U.S. House, 1999-2005

ELECTION RESULTS

2010 GENERAL

David Vitter (R)	715,415	56.6%
Charlie Melancon (D)	476,572	37.7%
Randall Hayes (LIBERT)	13,957	1.1%

2010 PRIMARY

David Vitter (R)	85,225	87.6%
Chet D. Traylor (R)	6,841	7.0%
Nick J. Accardo (R)	5,232	5.4%

2004 GENERAL

David Vitter (R)	943,014	51.0%
Chris John (D)	542,150	29.3%
John Kennedy (D)	275,821	14.9%
Arthur A. Morrell (D)	47,222	2.6%

Previous Winning Percentages
2002 House Election (82%); 2000 House Election (80%)

Elected 2004; 2nd term

Vitter has worked diligently to establish himself as one of the Senate's most unyielding conservatives in the wake of a sex scandal that came to light in mid-2007. He has stood fast against President Obama's economic agenda and pushed legislation favored by social conservatives on abortion, public prayer, home schooling, drugs, the death penalty and illegal immigration.

Stung by the 2007 revelations that he was a client of a Washington, D.C., escort service, Vitter responded in earnest, filing 34 bills and resolutions on the first day of the 111th Congress (2009-10) in a package the New Orleans Times-Picayune said "amounts to a political manifesto."

And he joined forces with fellow conservatives in opposing most of Obama's spending proposals and by casting votes against or placing holds on key nominees. He opposed Supreme Court Justice Sonia Sotomayor's confirmation and joined GOP colleague Jim DeMint of South Carolina as the only "no" votes against Hillary Rodham Clinton's nomination as secretary of State; Vitter cited concerns about President Bill Clinton's overseas business and foundation dealings.

Vitter and DeMint teamed up numerous times in the 111th Congress to advance the conservative agenda. The pair, along with South Dakota Republican John Thune, have made a common practice of introducing amendments to require that funds from the $700 billion financial industry assistance package be used to pay down the national debt, holding up several major bills in the process. A member of the Banking, Housing and Urban Affairs Committee, Vitter also held up the confirmation of Ben S. Bernanke for Federal Reserve chairman to try to force the full Senate to vote on legislation to audit the Fed; he voted against Bernanke's confirmation in early 2010.

Vitter relishes being a thorn in the Democratic majority's side. He was largely responsible for blocking Iowa Democrat Tom Harkin's attempt to move up the vote for final passage of the health care overhaul in 2009 — first to the evening of Dec. 23, then to 12:15 a.m. Christmas Eve — resulting in a 7 a.m. Dec. 24 vote. After the measure became law in March 2010, Vitter was among the first to press for its repeal, and he voted to repeal the law early in the 112th Congress (2011-12).

"What is wrong with Obamacare is not one detail here and one comma there, it is not at the periphery of the plan; it is at the heart of the plan, it is the essentials, it is the core of the plan," Vitter said on the Senate floor in February 2011. "We can and should and must pass significant reforms such as protection for individuals with pre-existing conditions. That is why we have introduced those measures. We have advocated those measures in a targeted way. That does not mean we can or should or must preserve the whole of Obamacare, which has significant problems at the core of that gargantuan bill."

Vitter, the son of a petroleum engineer and member of the Environment and Public Works Committee, railed against the administration's moratorium on deep-water drilling in the Gulf of Mexico, instituted after the spring 2010 explosion of an offshore rig and subsequent spill. Instead of a ban on drilling, he called for immediate rig safety inspections.

"The moratorium is estimated to kill up to 10,000 Louisiana jobs and possibly 20,000 jobs throughout the course of the year," Vitter wrote in a blog post.

Vitter has a cool personal relationship with his senior Louisiana colleague, Democrat Mary L. Landrieu, and the two don't always work well together. After Hurricane Katrina devastated New Orleans and other Louisiana coastal areas in 2005, Vitter and Landrieu offered competing measures aimed at helping cash-strapped local governments pay workers. The conflict led to a confrontation on the Senate floor that ended only when Vitter walked out of the chamber. In 2007, Vitter blocked a bill backed by Landrieu and many local and state officials to reconstruct subsidized housing in New Orleans. Vitter claimed it would re-create the social problems, including high crime, that had plagued the housing developments before the hurricane.

A member of the Armed Services Committee, he has been highly critical of the Army Corps of Engineers, complaining the Corps did not move quickly enough to repair New Orleans' levees after Katrina.

Vitter also serves on the Small Business and Entrepreneurship Committee, from which he advocates for business-related tax cuts and a health care alternative that would lower costs for small businesses.

Vitter's use of an escort service was exposed when publisher Larry Flynt's Hustler magazine identified Vitter's telephone number in the records of "D.C. Madam" Deborah Jeane Palfrey after her arrest on charges of running a prostitution ring. His phone number appeared five times between 1999 and 2001, when he was serving in the U.S. House.

With his wife, Wendy, at his side, Vitter held a news conference July 16, 2007, in Metairie to offer "deep, sincere apologies to all of those I let down and disappointed with these actions from my past." The Senate Select Ethics Committee dismissed the matter in May 2008 without reprimanding Vitter because the liaisons occurred before he was elected to the Senate.

In the fall of 2007, Vitter's campaign committee had to pay $25,000 in fines for failing to include disclaimers on telephone bank calls in 2004.

The ethical and moral lapses were a stark turnabout for Vitter, who had modeled himself as a squeaky-clean foe of Louisiana's notoriously corrupt politics. Vitter wrote in a Rhodes scholarship application that he aspired to change the reputation of cronyism and corruption typified by Huey Long, Louisiana's legendary former governor. He won the scholarship.

He was elected to the Louisiana House in 1992. When Republican Robert L. Livingston announced in late 1998 that he would leave the U.S. House in six months, Vitter was one of nine candidates who jumped into the special-election campaign to replace him. After a second-place finish in the first round of voting, he defeated former Rep. and Gov. David C. Treen by 2 percentage points.

In 2004, Vitter ran for the Senate seat held by the retiring John B. Breaux against the incumbent's protégé, Democratic Rep. Chris John. Vitter won a rare outright victory by taking 51 percent of the vote, making him Louisiana's first Republican senator since Reconstruction.

The 2007 prostitution incident proved not to be a major factor in his 2010 re-election race. Vitter said the only people who continued to bring it up were reporters and "political hacks."

He had faced some trouble earlier in the campaign after a news report disclosed that an aide had pleaded guilty to three misdemeanor charges stemming from a domestic violence episode. The aide, who also had a history of drug and drunken-driving arrests, was reportedly tasked with handling women's issues, among others. The senator disputed that claim to reporters while formally filing his re-election papers in July, and later said the aide worked on abortion issues. Legislative directories over the past few years and the executive director of the Louisiana Coalition Against Domestic Violence have identified the aide as Vitter's designated point man on women's issues.

Vitter concentrated on tying his challenger, Democratic Rep. Charlie Melancon, to some of the policies that have defined Obama's two years in office — the health care overhaul, the $787 billion stimulus package and the drilling moratorium. That strategy worked: Vitter defeated Melancon with more than 56 percent of the vote.

Key Votes

2010

Vote	
Pass budget reconciliation bill to modify overhauls of health care and federal student loan programs	NO
Proceed to disapproval resolution on EPA authority to regulate greenhouse gases	YES
Overhaul financial services industry regulation	NO
Limit debate to proceed to a bill to broaden campaign finance disclosure and reporting rules	NO
Limit debate on an extension of Bush-era income tax cuts for two years	YES
Limit debate on a bill to provide a path to legal status for some children of illegal immigrants	NO
Allow for a repeal of "don't ask, don't tell"	NO
Consent to ratification of a strategic arms reduction treaty with Russia	NO

2009

Vote	
Prevent release of remaining financial industry bailout funds	YES
Make it easier for victims to sue for wage discrimination remedies	NO
Expand the Children's Health Insurance Program	NO
Limit debate on the economic stimulus measure	NO
Repeal District of Columbia firearms prohibitions and gun registration laws	YES
Limit debate on expansion of federal hate crimes law	NO
Strike funding for F-22 Raptor fighter jets	NO

CQ Vote Studies

	PARTY UNITY		PRESIDENTIAL SUPPORT	
	Support	Oppose	Support	Oppose
2010	94%	6%	37%	63%
2009	96%	4%	42%	58%
2008	98%	2%	76%	24%
2007	93%	7%	85%	15%
2006	94%	6%	87%	13%
2005	94%	6%	89%	11%
2004	98%	2%	94%	6%
2003	99%	1%	96%	4%
2002	99%	1%	85%	15%
2001	98%	2%	93%	7%

Interest Groups

	AFL-CIO	ADA	CCUS	ACU
2010	8%	5%	100%	95%
2009	17%	10%	86%	100%
2008	20%	5%	88%	84%
2007	21%	10%	73%	96%
2006	20%	0%	92%	92%
2005	29%	15%	83%	96%
2004	7%	5%	100%	96%
2003	0%	10%	97%	88%
2002	11%	0%	95%	100%
2001	8%	0%	100%	100%

Rep. Steve Scalise (R)

Capitol Office
225-3015
scalise.house.gov
429 Cannon Bldg. 20515-1801; fax 226-0386

Committees
Energy & Commerce

Residence
Jefferson

Born
Oct. 6, 1965; Baton Rouge, La.

Religion
Roman Catholic

Family
Wife, Jennifer Scalise; two children

Education
Louisiana State U., B.S. 1989 (computer science)

Career
Software engineer; technology company marketing executive

Political Highlights
La. House, 1996-2008; La. Senate, 2008

ELECTION RESULTS

2010 GENERAL

Steve Scalise (R)	157,182	78.5%
Myron Katz (D)	38,416	19.2%
Arden Wells (I)	4,578	2.3%

2010 PRIMARY

Steve Scalise (R)	unopposed

2008 GENERAL

Steve Scalise (R)	189,168	65.7%
Jim Harlan (D)	98,839	34.3%

Previous Winning Percentages
2008 Special Election (75%)

Elected 2008; 2nd full term

Whether discussing oil drilling, health care or fiscal policy, Scalise professes conservative principles that he likens to those of President Ronald Reagan, his "political idol." A seat on the powerful Energy and Commerce Committee gives him a forum from which to boost his state's multiple energy interests.

Much of his legislative energy in 2010 was spent on responding to the largest oil spill in U.S. history. After an oil rig exploded in the Gulf of Mexico that spring, Scalise was highly critical of the response by both the oil company and the Obama administration.

"Right now, unfortunately, you have the president trying to exploit this disaster to pass his national energy tax instead of actually meeting his obligation under the law to lead," Scalise said. "Instead, he's ceded much of that responsibility to BP, allowing BP to make decisions on the ground." He said the administration's attempt to impose a ban on deep-water offshore drilling was "causing more problems right now than the oil, long term."

He opposed legislation the House passed in July 2010 to lift the $75 million cap on liability for offshore spills. "BP has testified under oath that they will not be limited by any liability caps, and we will continue holding them accountable to pay for all oil-related damages," Scalise told the New Orleans Times-Picayune in June 2010. "While we are conducting investigations into this BP disaster, we need to be careful not to punish those who play by the rules, and avoid turning this environmental disaster into a worse economic disaster for our state."

With fellow Louisianan Mary L. Landrieu, a Democratic senator, he backed legislation to require that 80 percent of all money collected from BP for violations of the Clean Water Act be used for coastal restoration.

"We need to make it clear very early on — before the amount of money is known, before the money ends up in Washington in a big grab bag — we want to make it clear that that money ought to stay here among the Gulf Coast states that have been impacted by the disaster," Scalise told the Times-Picayune in September 2010.

More broadly, he wants to let Louisiana and other coastal states tap into offshore drilling lease revenues for such projects.

He struck another blow at Obama administration energy policy early in the 112th Congress (2011-12), winning adoption of his amendment to a catchall spending measure for fiscal 2011 that would bar the use of funds in the bill to pay the salaries and expenses of nine executive branch "czars," including the assistant to the president for energy and climate change.

Scalise loves the intricate details of policy and legislation, as well as the rigorous debate central to promoting his ideas.

On one of his first votes after winning a 2008 special election to succeed Republican Bobby Jindal, who had been elected governor, Scalise came out strongly against passage of a $289 billion law to reauthorize farm programs.

He voted in fall 2008 against a $700 billion package to shore up the financial services industry, advocating instead "a market-based approach that does not put taxpayer money at risk." While two other Louisianans changed their votes and supported a modified version that was signed into law, he remained firm.

He opposed Obama's early legislative measures, including a $787 billion economic stimulus measure in 2009. He said exchanging some new spending for tax cuts would "give us a better chance of turning around this economy."

He voted against a 2009 bill to expand the Children's Health Insurance

Program, which provides coverage to children whose low-income families make too much money to qualify for Medicaid, after failing to get support for a provision to bar illegal immigrants from obtaining coverage.

He is a supporter of gun owners' rights and a member of the National Rifle Association. As a state legislator he led a fight in 1999 against former New Orleans Mayor Marc Morial, a Democrat who sued a group of gun manufacturers to reimburse the city for expenses related to its efforts to stem violent crime. Scalise drafted a bill that prohibited municipalities from suing companies for what customers did with their products. The Supreme Court upheld the legislation in 2000.

He is an opponent of abortion and the original sponsor of Louisiana's constitutional amendment, approved by voters in 2004, that defines marriage as a union between a man and a woman.

Bringing in more funds to help his area recover from hurricanes Katrina and Rita was one of his campaign pledges. And when Hurricane Gustav was bearing down on the central Louisiana coast in August 2008, Scalise remained near the Mississippi River's southern end to monitor its effects rather than head north to St. Paul where the Republican National Convention was getting under way. He said he wanted to ensure the safety of his wife and young daughter and make sure other people were able to take care of their families.

The middle of three children, Scalise grew up in Metairie, a suburb of New Orleans. His father sold real estate while his mother was a homemaker and a volunteer in senior citizens' programs. As a child, Scalise roamed his local streets on a bicycle decked out in patriotic bunting, speaking into a battery-powered microphone and encouraging his neighbors to visit the polls at election time. He became a registered Republican the day he turned 18.

After college, he worked in computer engineering while volunteering for several campaigns, including Vice President George Bush's successful 1988 run for president. Scalise was elected to the state House in 1995 and served 11 years before being elected to the state Senate in 2007.

He first considered running for the U.S. House in 1999, when a special election was held to replace Republican Robert L. Livingston. He changed his mind after party leaders favored David Vitter. When Vitter left the House for the Senate in 2004, Scalise was overlooked again, this time in favor of Jindal.

In the May 2008 special election to succeed Jindal, Scalise outran Democrat Gilda Reed, a psychologist, and only one other listed in the vote tally. He took more than 65 percent of the vote that November for a full term. He crushed Democrat Myron Katz in 2010, taking 79 percent of the vote.

Heading into the 2011-12 election cycle, Scalise was named vice chairman of recruitment for the National Republican Congressional Committee.

Key Votes

2010

Overhaul the nation's health insurance system	NO
Allow for repeal of "don't ask, don't tell"	NO
Overhaul financial services industry regulation	NO
Limit use of new Afghanistan War funds to troop withdrawal activities	NO
Change oversight of offshore drilling and lift oil spill liability cap	NO
Provide a path to legal status for some children of illegal immigrants	NO
Extend Bush-era income tax cuts for two years	YES

2009

Expand the Children's Health Insurance Program	NO
Provide $787 billion in tax cuts and spending increases to stimulate the economy	NO
Allow bankruptcy judges to modify certain primary-residence mortgages	NO
Create a cap-and-trade system to limit greenhouse gas emissions	NO
Provide $2 billion for the "cash for clunkers" program	NO
Establish the government as the sole provider of student loans	NO
Restrict federally funded insurance coverage for abortions in health care overhaul	YES

CQ Vote Studies

	PARTY UNITY		PRESIDENTIAL SUPPORT	
	SUPPORT	OPPOSE	SUPPORT	OPPOSE
2010	97%	3%	31%	69%
2009	98%	2%	23%	77%
2008	99%	1%	79%	21%

Interest Groups

	AFL-CIO	ADA	CCUS	ACU
2010	0%	0%	88%	96%
2009	0%	0%	80%	100%
2008	0%	5%	94%	100%

Louisiana 1

East — Metairie, part of Florida Parishes

A short distance from downtown New Orleans, the conservative 1st skims the edges of the city, heads north across the Lake Pontchartrain Causeway and reaches the Mississippi border. North of Lake Pontchartrain, the 1st includes three of the "Florida Parishes," so named because they were part of Spanish Florida until 1810.

Since Hurricane Katrina in 2005, a significant portion of the population has spread from New Orleans and Jefferson Parish to neighborhoods on the lake's northern shore.

Once a community of seasonal homes, the north shore is now a booming bedroom community, having experienced a population influx as residents from the rest of the state flocked to the relatively stable residential area. As with much of the Greater New Orleans area, local officials and residents north of the lake, as well as in Lakeview in western Orleans Parish and parts of historic Old Metairie in Jefferson Parish to the south, hope that neighborhoods rebuilt since 2005 will retain their unique character.

Rebuilding and infrastructure redevelopment boosted tax-based revenues in the middle of the last decade, but budget woes in recent years have created uncertainty. Retail centers and residential development, particularly in St. Tammany and Tangipahoa parishes, have boosted the local economy.

The petrochemicals and oil and gas industries here are stable. Northrop Grumman spinoff Huntington Ingalls Industries still provides thousands of jobs to district residents at its shipbuilding operations, based at the Avondale Shipyard in the 2nd District and high-tech facilities in the 1st, but plans to close Avondale in 2013.

Residents warmly welcome the GOP on all levels, and John McCain won his highest percentage statewide here (72 percent) in the 2008 presidential election.

Major Industry
Petrochemicals, oil

Cities
Metairie (unincorporated) (pt.), 134,005; Kenner (pt.), 44,368; New Orleans (pt.), 31,001; Slidell, 27,068

Notable
The Lake Pontchartrain Causeway is the world's longest highway bridge over water.

Rep. Cedric L. Richmond (D)

Capitol Office
225-6636
richmond.house.gov
415 Cannon Bldg. 20515-1802; fax 288-4090

Committees
Homeland Security
Small Business

Residence
New Orleans

Born
Sept. 13, 1973; New Orleans, La.

Religion
Baptist

Family
Single

Education
Morehouse College, B.A. 1995 (business administration); Tulane U., J.D. 1998

Career
Lawyer

Political Highlights
La. House, 2000-11; sought Democratic nomination for U.S. House, 2008

ELECTION RESULTS

2010 GENERAL

Cedric L. Richmond (D)	83,705	64.6%
Anh "Joseph" Cao (R)	43,378	33.5%
Anthony Marquize (NPA)	1,876	1.4%

2010 PRIMARY

Cedric L. Richmond (D)	14,678	60.5%
Juan LaFonta (D)	5,171	21.3%
Eugene Green (D)	2,500	10.3%
Gary Johnson (D)	1,914	7.9%

Elected 2010; 1st term

Richmond is the sole Democrat in Louisiana's U.S. House delegation, a member of the minority party and a liberal. His policy proposals read like they come straight from the Democratic playbook — of 2008.

Among his priorities for the 112th Congress (2011-12), the former state representative lists protecting the health care law enacted in 2010, broadening eligibility for the earned-income tax credit, providing a federal match of up to $1,000 for new retirement plans, lowering interest rates charged to student loans, increasing Pell grants and cracking down on so-called predatory lending.

Richmond represents New Orleans, which is still suffering from Hurricane Katrina's devastation. A member of the Homeland Security Committee, he says "we will not get full recovery without more federal help."

His other committee assignment is Small Business.

Born and raised in New Orleans, Richmond spent 10 years in the Louisiana House, where he served as chairman of the Judiciary Committee. He successfully pushed for a tax credit for developers who invest in port construction.

Richmond, a graduate of Tulane University law school, has also worked as an attorney.

The largely Democratic 2nd District flipped to the GOP in 2008 when Anh "Joseph" Cao unseated incumbent Democrat William J. Jefferson, who was later convicted on bribery charges.

Richmond had sought the Democratic nomination in 2008, losing to Jefferson, and Democrats targeted the seat in 2010.

Running with the backing of much of the party power structure, he cruised to a primary victory over state Rep. Juan LaFonta, former Jefferson chief of staff Eugene Green and activist Gary Johnson.

Cao tried to portray himself as an independent voice looking out for his district. Richmond, though, sought to tie him to the national GOP, an effective strategy in a majority-black district that gave Barack Obama three-quarters of its presidential vote in 2008. Richmond defeated Cao, taking almost 65 percent of the vote.

Louisiana 2

New Orleans

New Orleans' population had already declined from its 1960 peak, but drastic population loss after Hurricane Katrina in 2005 devastated the below-sea-level city has left fewer than 350,000 residents. The black-majority district as a whole had the largest population loss of any district in the nation since 2000 and is now the least-populous district ahead of decennial remapping. The economy was fueled for years by post-hurricane construction and infrastructure redevelopment as locals attempted to restore the buildings and character of the Big Easy. The 9th Ward, Gentilly and other low-lying areas have yet to see full recovery, but higher-ground areas like the French Quarter and Uptown escaped most of the water. Famed for its food and jazz, the city still draws tourists to iconic events such as Mardi Gras and the Jazz & Heritage Festival.

The shipbuilding and petroleum sectors have held steady recently, and the port's cargo and cruise facilities have seen bursts of activity. But thousands of jobs may disappear when Huntington Ingalls Industries closes its Avondale Shipyard in 2013.

Republicans' one-term U.S. House victory in 2008 was merely a blip as the district retains a strongly Democratic tilt. The 2nd was the only district in the state won by Barack Obama in the 2008 presidential election, and he took 75 percent of the district's vote.

Major Industry
Shipping, oil and gas, tourism, shipbuilding

Military Bases
Naval Support Activity New Orleans, 1,073 military, 371 civilian (2011)

Cities
New Orleans (pt.), 312,828; Marrero (unincorporated) (pt.), 32,706

Notable
The National Shrine of Our Lady of Prompt Succor hosts a statue of the state's patron saint, who hears prayers in times of disaster.

Rep. Jeff Landry (R)

Capitol Office
225-4031
landry.house.gov
206 Cannon Bldg. 20515-1803; fax 226-3944

Committees
Natural Resources
Small Business
Transportation & Infrastructure

Residence
New Iberia

Born
Dec. 23, 1970; St. Martinville, La.

Religion
Roman Catholic

Family
Wife, Sharon Landry; one child

Education
U. of Southwestern Louisiana, B.S. 1999 (environmental and sustainable resources); Southern U. Law School, attended 2001-03; Loyola U. New Orleans, J.D. 2004

Military
La. National Guard, 1987-98

Career
Lawyer; oil and gas contamination cleanup company owner

Political Highlights
Republican nominee for La. Senate, 2007

ELECTION RESULTS

2010 GENERAL

Jeff Landry (R)	108,963	63.8%
Ravi Sangisetty (D)	61,914	36.2%

2010 PRIMARY RUNOFF

Jeff Landry (R)	19,657	65.1%
Hunt Downer (R)	10,549	34.9%

Elected 2010; 1st term

One topic has permeated Landry's professional and personal life, and now it will saturate his political life as well: energy and natural resources. The conservative Republican is expected to be a key voice on energy policy debates as a member of the Natural Resources and Transportation and Infrastructure committees.

His district serves as a hub for the oil industry in the Gulf of Mexico. And prior to his election to the House, Landry, who also sits on the Small Business Committee, formed an oil and gas contamination cleanup company in Louisiana.

Landry says he will be an ally of the petroleum industry. He opposes a cap-and-trade system designed to limit carbon emissions because, he says, it would devastate economies that depend on oil and gas. Although President Obama has lifted a drilling moratorium, Landry has criticized the slow pace of new permits.

"We must deal with a de facto moratorium placed on the shelf that is killing independent drillers that are the backbone of the oil and gas industry in Louisiana," said Landry.

He opposes abortion rights and gun control measures and is likely to be a reliably conservative vote across the board. He joined the Republican Study Committee, a group of the most conservative members of the House.

Landry said a good Republican is "one who follows the fundamentals of the party: less government, fiscally conservative, a strict adherence to constitutional principles."

Landry, who served more than a decade in the Louisiana National Guard, made an unsuccessful bid for the state Senate in 2007. He saw an opening for the U.S. House seat when Democratic Rep. Charlie Melancon announced in August 2009 that he would run for the U.S. Senate seat held by Republican David Vitter. Landry finished at the top in the first round of voting, then defeated former state House Speaker Hunt Downer in the GOP runoff. He had little trouble dispatching Democratic attorney Ravi Sangisetty, winning just under 64 percent of the vote.

Louisiana 3
South central — New Iberia, Houma, Chalmette

A maze of interconnected bayous, swamps and marshes, the 3rd runs along the coast of the Gulf of Mexico and takes in the Mississippi River delta and the eastern half of Acadiana, or Cajun country.

The same geography that attracts commercial fishermen and sportsmen also leaves the area susceptible to significant damage from hurricanes. In 2005, Katrina and Rita destroyed or severely damaged towns and cities across the district, submerging the mostly middle-class Plaquemines and St. Bernard parishes. In 2008, flooding and high winds from Gustav and Ike affected agriculture, fishing and infrastructure. Crop production in parishes west of Plaquemines has suffered and ranchers have lost cattle.

The 3rd long supported fishing, oystering and shrimping, and many small operations in Plaquemines and west along the coast had begun to get back on the water after last decade's storms. However, the 2010 Deepwater Horizon oil spill closed the Gulf to fishing, halted offshore drilling, and decimated wildlife populations and oyster yields. Democrats dominated the region for most of a century, but the Catholic 3rd now trends Republican. The ability to bring federal and state aid to the district may largely determine future political success here.

Major Industry
Oil and gas, petrochemicals, shipbuilding, agriculture

Military Bases
Naval Air Station Joint Reserve Base New Orleans, 250 military, 170 civilian (2009)

Cities
Houma, 33,727; New Iberia, 30,617; Laplace (unincorporated), 29,872

Notable
St. John the Baptist Parish holds its annual Andouille Festival in October.

Rep. John Fleming (R)

Capitol Office
225-2777
fleming.house.gov
416 Cannon Bldg. 20515-1804; fax 225-8039

Committees
Armed Services
Natural Resources
(Fisheries, Wildlife, Oceans & Insular Affairs - Chairman)

Residence
Minden

Born
July 5, 1951; Meridian, Miss.

Religion
Southern Baptist

Family
Wife, Cindy Fleming; four children

Education
U. of Mississippi, B.S. 1973 (medicine), M.D. 1976

Military
Navy Medical Corps, 1976-82

Career
Physician; sandwich store owner

Political Highlights
Webster Parish coroner, 1996-2000

ELECTION RESULTS

2010 GENERAL

John Fleming (R)	105,223	62.3%
David Melville (D)	54,609	32.4%
Artis "Doc" Cash (I)	8,962	5.3%

2010 PRIMARY

John Fleming (R)	unopposed

2008 GENERAL

John Fleming (R)	44,501	48.1%
Paul J. Carmouche (D)	44,151	47.7%
Chester T. "Catfish" Kelley (X)	3,245	3.5%

Elected 2008; 2nd term

Fleming is a self-described Reagan Republican who draws on his background as a physician and business owner to espouse a small-government philosophy. As chairman of a Natural Resources subcommittee, he backs development of domestic energy, including drilling for oil and gas off his state's coastline.

Fleming promotes developing the Haynesville Shale, a source of natural gas in his district, and supports expanded drilling for oil and natural gas on the outer continental shelf, which falls under his jurisdiction as chairman of the Subcommittee on Fisheries, Wildlife, Oceans and Insular Affairs. He would like to see tax credits for the production of natural gas, wind, solar and biomass energy along with an expansion of nuclear power.

He took the Obama administration to task for its response to the spring 2010 oil spill in the Gulf of Mexico, sharply criticizing attempts to institute a ban on deep-water drilling. "There's an uncertainty that the federal government won't back off and allow drilling to go forward as it should, and it's killing thousands of jobs and is having a devastating impact on the state of Louisiana," he told conservative publication Human Events in July 2010.

He strongly opposed Democrats' House-passed bill in 2009 to combat climate change through a cap-and-trade system of emissions credits, saying the bill would increase energy costs and drive businesses overseas while disproportionately affecting low-income people.

As a member of the Republican Study Committee and the Tea Party Caucus, he extends his conservative philosophy to social issues. An opponent of abortion and a supporter of gun rights, Fleming backs school prayer and the display of the Ten Commandments in public places. He takes a hard line against illegal immigration, advocating an end to automatic citizenship for children born in the U.S. to illegal immigrants. And he has cosponsored bills to bar federal family planning grants to organizations that perform abortions and to legally define marriage in the District of Columbia as a union between one man and one woman.

He opposed all of President Obama's economic initiatives during the 111th Congress (2009-10) and was a persistent opponent of the health care overhaul enacted in March 2010. Fleming's medical credentials — he was a Navy medical officer before going into private practice — made him a favorite of cable news shows, and he wrote on the topic for newspapers and websites.

Fleming backs a private insurance system in which people would have health savings accounts and government would help pay premiums on a sliding scale. "A system is the healthiest when you have people competing in an open and free market for dollars and for delivering goods and services that are going to meet the expectation of consumers," he told the Shreveport Times in May 2009. He drew attention two months later when he introduced a resolution calling on lawmakers who support a government-run insurance option to enroll themselves in such a health plan.

He voted to repeal the law in 2011, and called Democratic claims that the legislation would cut the budget deficit "a Disney fantasy of accounting" in a Fox News Channel interview.

Fleming sits on the Armed Services Committee, where he watches out for his district's Barksdale Air Force Base and the Army's Fort Polk while taking a hawkish view of national security.

In an April 2010 opinion piece in the Daily Caller, a conservative website, Fleming wrote that "President Obama is disadvantaging the United States one step at a time and undermining this country's national defense on purpose. Whether he is catering to the anti-war leftists or truly doing what he thinks is best for our security, the president is leading this nation down a very dangerous path."

He complained in May 2009 that Obama's proposed cuts to a national missile defense are "exactly the wrong thing to do," given the threats posed by Iran and North Korea. Worried about the aging U.S. bomber fleet, in 2009 he co-founded the Long Range Strike Caucus.

Fleming grew up in a working-class home in Meridian, Miss. His mother was a telephone operator. His father, a World War II veteran and a power substation operator, died of a heart attack when Fleming was a teenager. To help pay for college, Fleming received financial aid and worked manual-labor jobs. He had an early interest in medicine — his grandmother worked as a nurse, and he often heard stories about the hospital in which she worked.

Halfway through his first year of medical school, though, "I ran out of money," he said. He signed up for the Navy's Health Professions Scholarship Program to help pay for his education and eventually served six years in the Medical Corps. He started a private family practice in Minden, La., in 1982.

He wrote the 2006 book "Preventing Addiction: What Parents Must Know to Immunize Their Kids Against Drug and Alcohol Addiction," an extension of his work as a medical resident at a drug and alcohol treatment unit.

Fleming also is an entrepreneur: He owns 30 Subway restaurant franchises as well as Fleming Expansions, a sub-franchisor of The UPS Store.

He served four years as Webster Parish's coroner, was active in local and state medical groups, and served on Republican Gov. Bobby Jindal's transition team for social services.

GOP Rep. Jim McCrery announced in December 2007 that he would retire after the 110th Congress (2007-08), and Fleming began to eye a run in 2008. A September hurricane forced postponement of the primary, pushing both that contest and the general election back a month. Fleming took more than 35 percent of the vote in the GOP primary and bested trucking executive Chris Gorman in a runoff with nearly 56 percent.

In the December general election he faced Democrat Paul J. Carmouche, the former Caddo Parish district attorney. Fleming had workers at his Subways stuff sandwich bags with campaign literature and he said he paid his corporation for the advertising effort to comply with election laws. Fleming also loaned himself more than $1 million. His 350-vote margin of victory was the narrowest in any House race that year. He won re-election by 30 percentage points in 2010.

Key Votes

2010

Overhaul the nation's health insurance system	NO
Allow for repeal of "don't ask, don't tell"	NO
Overhaul financial services industry regulation	NO
Limit use of new Afghanistan War funds to troop withdrawal activities	NO
Change oversight of offshore drilling and lift oil spill liability cap	NO
Provide a path to legal status for some children of illegal immigrants	NO
Extend Bush-era income tax cuts for two years	NO

2009

Expand the Children's Health Insurance Program	NO
Provide $787 billion in tax cuts and spending increases to stimulate the economy	NO
Allow bankruptcy judges to modify certain primary-residence mortgages	NO
Create a cap-and-trade system to limit greenhouse gas emissions	NO
Provide $2 billion for the "cash for clunkers" program	NO
Establish the government as the sole provider of student loans	NO
Restrict federally funded insurance coverage for abortions in health care overhaul	YES

CQ Vote Studies

	PARTY UNITY		PRESIDENTIAL SUPPORT	
	SUPPORT	OPPOSE	SUPPORT	OPPOSE
2010	98%	2%	24%	76%
2009	97%	3%	26%	74%

Interest Groups

	AFL-CIO	ADA	CCUS	ACU
2010	0%	5%	75%	96%
2009	10%	0%	80%	100%

Louisiana 4

Northwest and west — Shreveport, Bossier City

Covering most of western Louisiana, the conservative 4th takes in Shreveport in the north and wanders into timber country in Beauregard and Allen parishes in the south.

The Red River divides Shreveport and Bossier City geographically, but unites them economically. Riverboat casinos dock on the river, and gambling sites dot the shores. But a major riverfront renewal project completed in 2005 is in danger of collapsing — the Louisiana Boardwalk shopping and entertainment complex, which helped support the economy in Bossier City, is in foreclosure. Empty storefronts on the property have meant the loss of important retail jobs, and the city's investment in the development has left its revenue base vulnerable.

Shreveport is a health care hub for northern Louisiana, eastern Texas and southern Arkansas, and nursing jobs will be in demand in local communities with older populations. The city's General Motors plant, which produces several pickup truck models, will shut down by 2012 and has already shed thousands of jobs.

Barksdale Air Force Base near Bossier City is a key employer for both cities, and base expansion is expected to bring construction, military and high-tech jobs.

Outside of the district's primary population hub, Natchitoches is the oldest permanent settlement in the former Louisiana Purchase territory and markets its history to lure tourists. The rest of the 4th, except for Fort Polk in Vernon Parish, relies on cotton and forestry.

Although registered Democrats outnumber Republicans here, Shreveport and Bossier City suburbs can back the GOP and the 4th overall typically prefers Republican candidates in federal elections. John McCain received 59 percent of the district's 2008 presidential vote.

Major Industry
Military, riverboat gambling, health care

Military Bases
Fort Polk (Army), 9,297 military, 1,929 civilian; Barksdale Air Force Base, 5,331 military, 1,177 civilian (2009)

Cities
Shreveport, 199,311; Bossier City, 61,315; Natchitoches, 18,323

Notable
Natchitoches has an annual Meat Pie Festival.

Rep. Rodney Alexander (R)

Capitol Office
225-8490
www.house.gov/alexander
316 Cannon Bldg. 20515-1805; fax 225-5639

Committees
Appropriations

Residence
Quitman

Born
Dec. 5, 1946; Quitman, La.

Religion
Baptist

Family
Wife, Nancy Alexander; three children

Education
Louisiana Tech U., attended 1965; U. of Louisiana, Monroe, B.A. 2009 (general studies)

Military
Air Force Reserve, 1965-71

Career
Road construction contractor; insurance agent

Political Highlights
Jackson Parish Police Jury, 1972-87 (president, 1980-87); La. House, 1988-2002 (served as a Democrat)

ELECTION RESULTS

2010 GENERAL

Rodney Alexander (R)	122,033	78.6%
Tom Gibbs (NPA)	33,279	21.4%

2010 PRIMARY

Rodney Alexander (R)	14,031	88.9%
Todd Slavant (R)	1,744	11.1%

2008 GENERAL

Rodney Alexander (R)		unopposed

Previous Winning Percentages
2006 (68%); 2004 (59%); 2002 (50%)
* Elected as a Democrat in 2002

Elected 2002; 5th term

Alexander is the dean of Louisiana's House delegation, but the role is an odd fit for the folksy conservative who prefers the constituent service side of his job to the backroom dealmaking usually associated with powerful leaders in the capital.

Alexander's seat on the Appropriations Committee would seem to lend itself to leadership among his fellow Louisianans in Congress. Those with seats on the spending panel tend to be popular among their colleagues because they can direct federal funds back to members' districts. Alexander has long embraced the role of earmark distributor, but in the aftermath of scandals related to the practice, even Alexander has cut back on doling out the dollars.

When House Republicans agreed to a one-year ban on earmarking for fiscal 2011 (re-upped for 2012), Alexander said he was on board, if reluctantly. "If someone abuses the system, they should be punished," he said. "But I don't think we need to abolish it." In 2009 and 2010, he dropped from fifth to 30th on a list of the most prolific recipients of earmarks in the House, according to the watchdog group Taxpayers for Common Sense.

Alexander says he doesn't see his senior status in the delegation as conferring any particular power, but he's hoping to start winning earmarks again soon, not just for his own district, but for all of Louisiana. "I don't think we should leave all federal spending to bureaucrats who don't even know where Louisiana is," he says.

But he backed the GOP's catchall spending bill passed in early 2011 that would cut spending by $62 billion and eliminate fiscal 2010 earmarks from continuing appropriations.

One of the last conservative Dixiecrats to defect to the Republican Party, Alexander sees eye to eye with fellow Republicans on most issues. Since his 2004 party switch, he's sided with the GOP more than 90 percent of the time on votes that split majorities of the two parties. And like most of his Republican colleagues, he opposed most of President Obama's agenda, voting "no" on bills to revamp the health care system and overhaul financial regulations. As a former small-business owner, he says he understands more than most how government regulation can make it difficult to run a company.

Alexander does not consider himself partisan. He reached across the aisle after Hurricane Katrina devastated the Gulf Coast in 2005, asking the federal government to contribute funding. More recently, he joined with Louisiana Democrats to press the Obama administration to lift a ban on deep-water drilling in the Gulf. Obama suspended much offshore drilling there in May 2010 following an oil spill caused by the explosion of a BP rig. Five months later, the administration nominally ended the ban. Alexander says the blanket moratorium went too far.

At the same time, Alexander parted ways with the rest of the Louisiana delegation — as well as the Obama administration — over the issue of flood insurance. Alexander worries that many of his poor, rural constituents are ill-equipped to pay for it and he has tried to delay the remapping of flood zones in the region that could force more of them to buy insurance. He also founded the Congressional Levee Caucus in 2010, arguing that the federal government should hold off on remapping flood zones until levees, designed to protect homes, are repaired.

Alexander was the only Louisiana House member to oppose legislation passed by the House in the summer of 2010 that would have given homeowners, told for the first time that they are living in flood zones, a five-year grace period before they would have to buy insurance. Alexander said he did so because the bill did nothing to forestall the remapping and also would have allowed premiums to rise more quickly than is permitted under current law. "I have constituents who've lived in areas for 30 years and haven't had to buy insurance, and now the government is saying: 'You have to buy it from us, and we are going to set premiums at whatever we want to set them.'" The bill did not advance in the Senate.

In the new Congress, Alexander introduced legislation that would require the Federal Emergency Management Agency to take into consideration the actual level of protection a levee or other flood-control structure would provide in a 100-year storm. Under current law, FEMA can redraw flood maps as if unaccredited levees don't exist.

Alexander's 2004 party switch, which infuriated Democrats, came just minutes before the filing deadline for re-election, preventing Democrats from recruiting a strong challenger. Alexander sailed to victory and Republicans rewarded him with a coveted seat on Appropriations in the 109th Congress (2005-06). He also served on the Budget Committee during the 110th Congress (2007-08) but had to relinquish that post after the Republicans lost seats in the 2008 election. But Alexander said he didn't switch parties to win perks. "I'm pro-life, pro-family, pro-gun," he said. "That's why I was uncomfortable being a Democrat."

Alexander's family has been in Louisiana for generations. His father ran a construction business and also sat on the Jackson Parish Police Jury, the Louisiana equivalent of a county board of supervisors. His mother was a preacher. Alexander dropped out of Louisiana Tech University to join his father's business and ultimately decided to follow him into politics, winning a seat on the police jury at age 25, the year after he left the Air Force Reserve. He served there for 15 years — eight of those with his father — then went on to serve 14 years in the state House before running for Congress.

In December 2009, after taking online courses through the University of Louisiana at Monroe, Alexander earned his bachelor's degree in general studies. "I was a self-employed contractor working in my father's business. I went into the service, got married, had kids. This is a long time in coming. It's just something I've always wanted to do."

Alexander won his first congressional race in 2002 by 974 votes but has had no trouble winning re-election since then. He took 59 percent of the vote after his 2004 party switch and garnered 68 percent in 2006. In 2008, he ran unopposed and faced only token opposition in 2010.

Key Votes

2010

Overhaul the nation's health insurance system	NO
Allow for repeal of "don't ask, don't tell"	NO
Overhaul financial services industry regulation	NO
Limit use of new Afghanistan War funds to troop withdrawal activities	NO
Change oversight of offshore drilling and lift oil spill liability cap	NO
Provide a path to legal status for some children of illegal immigrants	NO
Extend Bush-era income tax cuts for two years	YES

2009

Expand the Children's Health Insurance Program	NO
Provide $787 billion in tax cuts and spending increases to stimulate the economy	NO
Allow bankruptcy judges to modify certain primary-residence mortgages	NO
Create a cap-and-trade system to limit greenhouse gas emissions	NO
Provide $2 billion for the "cash for clunkers" program	NO
Establish the government as the sole provider of student loans	NO
Restrict federally funded insurance coverage for abortions in health care overhaul	YES

CQ Vote Studies

	PARTY UNITY		PRESIDENTIAL SUPPORT	
	Support	Oppose	Support	Oppose
2010	97%	3%	26%	74%
2009	87%	13%	27%	73%
2008	95%	5%	70%	30%
2007	87%	13%	74%	26%
2006	97%	3%	93%	7%

Interest Groups

	AFL-CIO	ADA	CCUS	ACU
2010	0%	5%	88%	100%
2009	19%	0%	80%	88%
2008	20%	25%	94%	84%
2007	29%	10%	90%	92%
2006	21%	5%	100%	80%

Louisiana 5

Northeast and central — Monroe, Alexandria

The 5th stretches south from the Arkansas border, with the Mississippi River delta parishes in its east and the national forests and midsize cities of central Louisiana in its west. It is conservative throughout and is plagued by pockets of poverty and unemployment despite numerous efforts to bring more economic opportunities to the area.

Although the rich, black soil along the Mississippi River produces much of the state's cotton and soybeans, poor education and transportation systems still hinder significant economic growth. The outlook is not entirely bleak, however — although the district still ranks last in the state for median household income at less than $36,000, it has risen markedly since 2000.

Monroe depends increasingly on health care, service and retail industries, and it is home to a University of Louisiana campus and CenturyLink, a telecommunications company. Development projects — including improvements to a Ouachita River port in West Monroe — brought some jobs, tourism and revenue to the district.

The 5th's portion of central Louisiana is fueled by Alexandria in Rapides Parish, which is home to a Procter & Gamble detergent manufacturing plant. In the district's northwest, Lincoln Parish hosts Louisiana Tech University in Ruston and the historically black Grambling State University in Grambling.

This once-Democratic district now leans Republican, but the 5th's voters will support conservatives of either party. More than one-third of the district's residents are black, and Democrats hold many local offices, although residents of Baptist- and Pentecostal-dominated northern Louisiana are more likely than the Catholics in the south to vote for Republicans. John McCain took 62 percent of the district's vote in the 2008 presidential election.

Major Industry
Agriculture, health care, higher education

Cities
Monroe, 48,815; Alexandria, 47,723; Ruston, 21,859

Notable
Grambling State became the first Louisiana college or university to receive a visit from a sitting president when Bill Clinton gave the 1999 commencement address.

Rep. Bill Cassidy (R)

Capitol Office
225-3901
cassidy.house.gov
1535 Longworth Bldg. 20515; fax 225-7313

Committees
Energy & Commerce

Residence
Baton Rouge

Born
Sept. 28, 1957; Highland Park, Ill.

Religion
Christian

Family
Wife, Laura Layden Cassidy; three children

Education
Louisiana State U., B.S. 1979 (biochemistry), M.D. 1983

Career
Physician

Political Highlights
La. Senate, 2006-08

ELECTION RESULTS

2010 GENERAL

Bill Cassidy (R)	138,607	65.6%
Merritt McDonald Sr. (D)	72,577	34.4%

2010 PRIMARY

Bill Cassidy (R)	unopposed

2008 GENERAL

Bill Cassidy (R)	150,332	48.1%
Don Cazayoux (D)	125,886	40.3%
Michael Jackson (X)	36,198	11.6%

Elected 2008; 2nd term

A proponent of smaller government, lower taxes and increased domestic energy production, Cassidy is a rising star in the Republican Party. He is a leader in the effort to repeal the health care overhaul enacted in 2010 and won a coveted spot on the Energy and Commerce Committee in the 112th Congress.

Cassidy was named an assistant to the party's whip team and a member of the House Republican Policy Committee when he entered Congress in 2009; he also joined the Republican Study Committee, a group of the chamber's most conservative members that now comprises about two-thirds of the GOP caucus.

Cassidy makes frequent calls for limiting federal purview over education and tightening spending, but it is his role as a vocal opponent of Democratic health care efforts that has garnered the most attention, and his background in the medical field gives him credibility. A gastroenterologist who taught medical students at Louisiana State University, he worked with uninsured patients as a physician at the Earl K. Long Hospital and helped found the Greater Baton Rouge Community Clinic, which provides free dental and health care to uninsured workers.

He opposed the Democratic-led health care overhaul in the 111th Congress (2009-10), arguing it would not control costs and ultimately will not work. Instead, Cassidy stepped forward during the introduction of the GOP's "Pledge to America" agenda to outline the Republican health care effort, which he said would " 'de-fund,' repeal and replace" the Democratic version.

He backed repeal when the House passed legislation early in the 112th Congress (2011-12) to do away with the overhaul, and he supported efforts to block funding for the law in a catchall spending bill for fiscal 2011. He applauded a pair of federal district court rulings that found the law to be unconstitutional. "If the Supreme Court agrees, we can implement real health reform that preserves liberty and lowers costs by empowering patients," he said.

Cassidy was among a group of medical professionals in the GOP Doctors Caucus who wrote to the American Medical Association in July 2009 criticizing the group for backing the overhaul bill.

And in February 2009, he opposed an expansion of the Children's Health Insurance Program, which covers children whose low-income families make too much money to qualify for Medicaid and was twice vetoed by President George W. Bush before being signed into law by President Obama. He cosponsored an alternative to enable states to provide assistance for private insurance with money saved by cutting certain Medicaid payments.

Even on issues unrelated to health care, the doctor in Cassidy comes out. In February 2009, he opposed a $787 million economic stimulus law, saying passage of the legislation was "as if a patient came to [him] with heart trouble and [he] treated her for a broken leg."

A member of the Natural Resources Committee in his first term, Cassidy aims to protect jobs in Louisiana's energy sector and increase alternative-energy production. He lobbied the White House to lift what he called the "ongoing de facto moratorium" on drilling in the Gulf of Mexico.

He called President Obama's original deep-water drilling moratorium — put in place after the 2010 BP oil spill — "a political reaction to a situation that demands rational solutions."

Cassidy said he feared that the 2009 House-passed bill to reduce carbon emissions through a system of trading industrial credits would result in lost jobs in his district's petrochemical industry, as well as higher energy prices.

He cosponsored an alternative bill to remove prohibitions on offshore drilling, bring new nuclear reactors online and provide tax credits for the production of renewable energy.

Cassidy is an enthusiastic advocate of the GOP moratorium on earmarks, funding for special projects in a member's district or state. Before the ban was in place, he partnered with California Democratic Rep. Jackie Speier to introduce legislation to make the process more transparent and pledged not to seek earmarks until significant changes are made to the system.

"Putting all earmarks in a searchable website gives taxpayers, the press and congressional watchdog groups real-time access to the information they need to hold Congress accountable," he said.

Cassidy was born in Highland Park, Ill., but raised in Baton Rouge, where his father sold life insurance. His interest in medicine was sparked during his senior year in high school, when doctors thought he had cancer but eventually diagnosed him with swollen lymph nodes. "I saw all these doctors and said, 'Wow, this is a fulfilling field,' " he said.

He holds a bachelor's degree in biochemistry from Louisiana State University and earned a medical degree in 1983 from the university's medical school, where he met his wife, Laura, also a physician. After Hurricane Katrina, he directed the conversion of an empty Kmart into an emergency medical facility for hurricane evacuees.

He served as chairman of the East Baton Rouge Parish Medical Society's health care overhaul committee until 1998 and raised concerns then about the future of the Medicaid program.

As a special-election candidate to fill a state Senate seat in 2006, he advocated using surplus state funds to improve health care. He suggested a redesign of the health care system to make it more affordable and accessible, and he called for the creation of a statewide electronic medical records system.

After starting his second term in the state Senate, he challenged U.S. Rep. Don Cazayoux, a Democrat, in 2008 and took back what had previously been a reliably Republican seat with 48 percent of the vote. A third candidate in the general election, Michael Jackson, ran as an independent after losing the Democratic primary and is credited with taking away some of Cazayoux's support, winning 11 percent of the vote.

When he ran for re-election in 2010, Cassidy captured 66 percent of the vote, easily defeating his Democratic opponent, a retired engineer who raised little money and didn't do much campaigning.

Cassidy was one of four House members who took on a supercomputer dubbed "Watson" in a non-televised Jeopardy competition in February 2011.

Key Votes

2010

Overhaul the nation's health insurance system	NO
Allow for repeal of "don't ask, don't tell"	NO
Overhaul financial services industry regulation	NO
Limit use of new Afghanistan War funds to troop withdrawal activities	NO
Change oversight of offshore drilling and lift oil spill liability cap	NO
Provide a path to legal status for some children of illegal immigrants	NO
Extend Bush-era income tax cuts for two years	YES

2009

Expand the Children's Health Insurance Program	NO
Provide $787 billion in tax cuts and spending increases to stimulate the economy	NO
Allow bankruptcy judges to modify certain primary-residence mortgages	NO
Create a cap-and-trade system to limit greenhouse gas emissions	NO
Provide $2 billion for the "cash for clunkers" program	YES
Establish the government as the sole provider of student loans	NO
Restrict federally funded insurance coverage for abortions in health care overhaul	YES

CQ Vote Studies

	PARTY UNITY		PRESIDENTIAL SUPPORT	
	SUPPORT	OPPOSE	SUPPORT	OPPOSE
2010	92%	8%	35%	65%
2009	92%	8%	37%	63%

Interest Groups

	AFL-CIO	ADA	CCUS	ACU
2010	14%	5%	100%	91%
2009	20%	20%	87%	88%

Louisiana 6

East central — Baton Rouge

Centered around Baton Rouge, the socially conservative 6th takes in a slew of petrochemical plants along the Mississippi River as well as rural parishes along the Mississippi border. Baton Rouge's economic stability has spurred population growth in neighboring parishes — Livingston and Ascension (shared with the 3rd District) parishes each experienced nearly 40 percent growth in the last decade.

Population growth in the area surrounding the state capital of Baton Rouge was fueled in part by new residents moving in after hurricanes Katrina and Rita in 2005, and a robust construction sector accommodating redevelopment across the state supported the local economy. Infrastructure and transportation issues are hot topics as communities cope with the need for improvements.

Government remains the primary employer in Baton Rouge. Higher education also drives the economy, as Louisiana State University and Southern University are here. Casinos and other ventures, such as the Shaw Center for the Arts, have helped Baton Rouge promote tourism, and the city has lured several new firms to the region. A proposed light rail system connecting Baton Rouge to New Orleans might help spur further growth, but implementation of those plans is still considered a long-term goal.

The Port of Greater Baton Rouge gives the area a boost, but there have been periodic job cuts in the vulnerable petrochemical industry. Agriculture fuels the 6th's rural parishes, with sugar cane in the west and paper mills and sweet potato farms in the northeast.

Socially conservative suburban and rural voters have shifted toward the GOP, but Baton Rouge's minority and blue-collar residents can support Democratic candidates. Republican John McCain won 57 percent of the 6th's 2008 presidential vote.

Major Industry
Government, higher education, petrochemicals

Cities
Baton Rouge, 229,493; Prairieville (unincorporated), 26,895

Notable
The state Capitol, completed in 1932, is the tallest in the United States; Gov. Huey Long, who led the fight for a new state Capitol, was assassinated there in 1935 and is buried on the Capitol grounds.

Rep. Charles Boustany Jr. (R)

Capitol Office
225-2031
boustany.house.gov
1431 Longworth Bldg. 20515-1807; fax 225-5724

Committees
Ways & Means
 (Oversight - Chairman)

Residence
Lafayette

Born
Feb. 21, 1956; Lafayette, La.

Religion
Episcopalian

Family
Wife, Bridget Boustany; two children

Education
U. of Southwestern Louisiana, B.S. 1978 (biology);
Louisiana State U., M.D. 1982

Career
Surgeon

Political Highlights
No previous office

ELECTION RESULTS

2010 GENERAL

Charles Boustany Jr. (R)		unopposed

2010 PRIMARY

Charles Boustany Jr. (R)		unopposed

2008 GENERAL

Charles Boustany Jr. (R)	177,173	61.9%
Donald "Don" Cravins Jr. (D)	98,280	34.3%
Peter Vidrine (X)	10,846	3.8%

Previous Winning Percentages
2006 (71%); 2004 (55%)

Elected 2004; 4th term

Boustany brings his surgeon's attention to detail to the Ways and Means Committee, where he chairs the Subcommittee on Oversight and looks to become a more prominent voice on international taxation and trade policy.

He spent much of the 111th Congress (2009-10) using his medical expertise to criticize the Democrats' health care legislation and develop alternative GOP proposals that would promote more competition among insurers and providers and focus less on expanding insurance coverage.

Now Boustany (boo-STAN-nee) wants to continue his work on that issue by scrutinizing the implementation of the health care overhaul law and analyzing ways to change it. He is particularly concerned about employers dropping insurance coverage and about how information from comparative effectiveness research might lead to a "cookbook approach" that could undermine the doctor-patient relationship.

But Boustany, who joined Ways and Means in 2009, is also thinking more broadly about the committee's role as he begins delving into areas of jurisdiction that didn't occupy his pre-congressional life. He wants to increase the number of oversight hearings, and he ticks off a list of possible topics, including the impact of the "Buy American" provisions of the 2009 stimulus legislation, the economic effects of trade policy and the IRS.

"Some of us guys in Congress who are relatively new — in our second, third, fourth terms — recognize that we're going to have to do some things differently," he said. "We need to be robust in oversight and ask the right questions. Otherwise, policy gets driven off in a direction that oftentimes is filled with flaws."

On taxes, he calls the "very complicated tax code" one of the major problems facing the country. His goals in international tax policy include a simplified system and changes designed to make it easier for U.S. companies to compete.

Boustany calls international trade a key to energizing the economy, and he typically supports free-trade agreements. The one exception came in 2005, when he voted against the Central America Free Trade Agreement to fulfill a campaign promise. In 2010, he took over the top GOP spot on the U.S.-China Working Group from Mark Steven Kirk of Illinois, with the goal of strengthening ties between the two countries and improving their long-term strategic relationship. China is an important market for Louisiana's agricultural products, farm machinery and chemicals.

Boustany also has pushed colleagues to allow more seasonal immigrants to enter the country legally. He cited concerns about rice and sugar farmers and shrimp-peeling facilities in his district that depend on seasonal workers.

Constituent service and disaster response were particularly important for Boustany during his first three terms, as his district along the Louisiana coast felt the impacts of major hurricanes in 2005 and 2008 as well as the Deepwater Horizon oil spill in 2010.

Just nine months into his first term, Boustany in 2005 won enactment of a bill giving the Labor Department more flexibility in providing temporary work and training in disaster areas. After the oil spill, Boustany warned about the economic consequences of the Obama administration's deepwater drilling moratorium, which has been causing layoffs in his district in the oil services industry and among the ancillary jobs that support it. "It's a jobs moratorium, and I have deep concerns about the lasting impact of that," he said in July 2010.

On social issues Boustany is almost always a doctrinaire conservative, and on most issues he is a reliable vote for Republican leaders. But he sided with Democrats — and President George W. Bush — in 2008 in moving a law expanding U.S. funding for global AIDS programs. And he joined with Democrats that July in voting for a new law aimed at helping homeowners struggling to pay their mortgages. He also supported the 2009 "cash for clunkers" program, which most House Republicans opposed.

In 2008, Boustany was one of 25 Republicans to switch his vote from "no" to "yes" on the financial industry rescue legislation, helping Bush and Democratic leaders pass the $700 billion package. Although other Republicans have since regretted that vote or suffered political consequences, Boustany said he stands by his decision.

Boustany grew up in Lafayette, the son of a longtime coroner for Lafayette Parish. His mother, a homemaker with 10 children, did charitable work in the community. He is of Lebanese descent; he led a 2007 effort to increase aid to the Palestinian Authority to combat the anti-American influence of the Islamist group Hamas.

His family was staunchly Democratic, but Boustany as a young man was influenced by columnist George Will and other conservative thinkers. "It created friction," Boustany said of his political split with his father. Boustany's wife, Bridget, is also a former Democrat, in addition to being the niece of former Louisiana Democratic Gov. Edwin Edwards.

In 2001, Boustany developed severe arthritis in his neck and hands, forcing him to close his Lafayette medical practice. "It was devastating, because I was at the peak of my career," he said.

As he pondered what to do with the rest of his life, Boustany began paying more attention to state politics. "That was an awakening," he said. "The common denominator here was a lack of good political leadership for the state." In 2004, after Democratic Rep. Chris John launched a bid for the Senate, Boustany talked it over with his wife and decided to run for John's seat.

After finishing first with 39 percent of the vote in the Nov. 2 all-party primary, Boustany cruised to a comfortable 10-percentage-point win in the runoff with state Sen. Willie Landry Mount, a Democrat who'd run afoul of the area's sizable black community in defeating Democratic state Sen. Don Cravins to make the runoff. Boustany made history as the first Republican to be elected from the area since 1884.

He was handily re-elected in 2006 and again in 2008, when he defeated Cravins' son, then-state Sen. Donald "Don" Cravins Jr. He ran unopposed in 2010.

Key Votes

2010

Overhaul the nation's health insurance system	NO
Allow for repeal of "don't ask, don't tell"	NO
Overhaul financial services industry regulation	NO
Limit use of new Afghanistan War funds to troop withdrawal activities	NO
Change oversight of offshore drilling and lift oil spill liability cap	NO
Provide a path to legal status for some children of illegal immigrants	NO
Extend Bush-era income tax cuts for two years	YES

2009

Expand the Children's Health Insurance Program	NO
Provide $787 billion in tax cuts and spending increases to stimulate the economy	NO
Allow bankruptcy judges to modify certain primary-residence mortgages	NO
Create a cap-and-trade system to limit greenhouse gas emissions	NO
Provide $2 billion for the "cash for clunkers" program	YES
Establish the government as the sole provider of student loans	NO
Restrict federally funded insurance coverage for abortions in health care overhaul	YES

CQ Vote Studies

	PARTY UNITY		PRESIDENTIAL SUPPORT	
	SUPPORT	OPPOSE	SUPPORT	OPPOSE
2010	96%	4%	33%	67%
2009	97%	3%	23%	77%
2008	94%	6%	68%	32%
2007	87%	13%	80%	20%
2006	95%	5%	95%	5%

Interest Groups

	AFL-CIO	ADA	CCUS	ACU
2010	0%	0%	88%	100%
2009	14%	5%	80%	96%
2008	8%	20%	94%	83%
2007	13%	5%	84%	100%
2006	21%	0%	100%	80%

Southwest — Lafayette, Lake Charles

Anchored by blue-collar Lake Charles in the west, white-collar Lafayette in the east and the Gulf of Mexico to the south, the 7th District contains both coastal and city communities.

Agriculture, along with oil and gas production, directs the local economy in the 7th. A new Halliburton manufacturing plant in Lafayette will produce oil field facility parts and provide hundreds of jobs. But the effects of the 2010 Deepwater Horizon oil spill in the Gulf of Mexico will be lasting.

In particular, increased marsh salinity has damaged important oyster ecosystems, compounding problems resulting from flooding during hurricanes Gustav and Ike that destroyed soybean, sugar and hay crops, rice fields, and thousands of cattle in 2008. Commercial fishing has also struggled, as the spill closed the gulf for months.

Before Gustav, Ike and Deepwater Horizon, the 2005 hurricane season battered Cameron and Calcasieu parishes. Cameron, once a key port for the nation's commercial fishing industry, has not recovered from years of population loss following the widespread devastation caused by Hurricane

Rita's landfall. Entire towns in the parish were demolished, and many of the residents who stayed or returned moved further inland, leaving long-inhabited homesteads near the coast.

Concerns about the age and effectiveness of waterway infrastructure worries local officials and Port of Lake Charles-based employers. Some officials in Lake Charles hope to build on the city's lakefront, but resistance to the development has kept the project from taking shape.

The 7th's sizable Catholic population bolsters its socially conservative leanings. Despite this bent, the area sent a Democrat to Congress in every election from 1884 until 2004. The GOP solidified its hold on the district's vote for president — John McCain won 63 percent of the district's vote in 2008, 3 percentage points more than George W. Bush won here in 2004 — and Republican candidates find support in every parish.

Major Industry
Oil and gas, petrochemicals, agriculture, fishing

Cities
Lafayette, 120,623; Lake Charles, 71,993; Sulphur, 20,410

Notable
Southwest Louisiana Institute (now University of Louisiana at Lafayette) in 1954 was the first all-white state college in the South to desegregate.

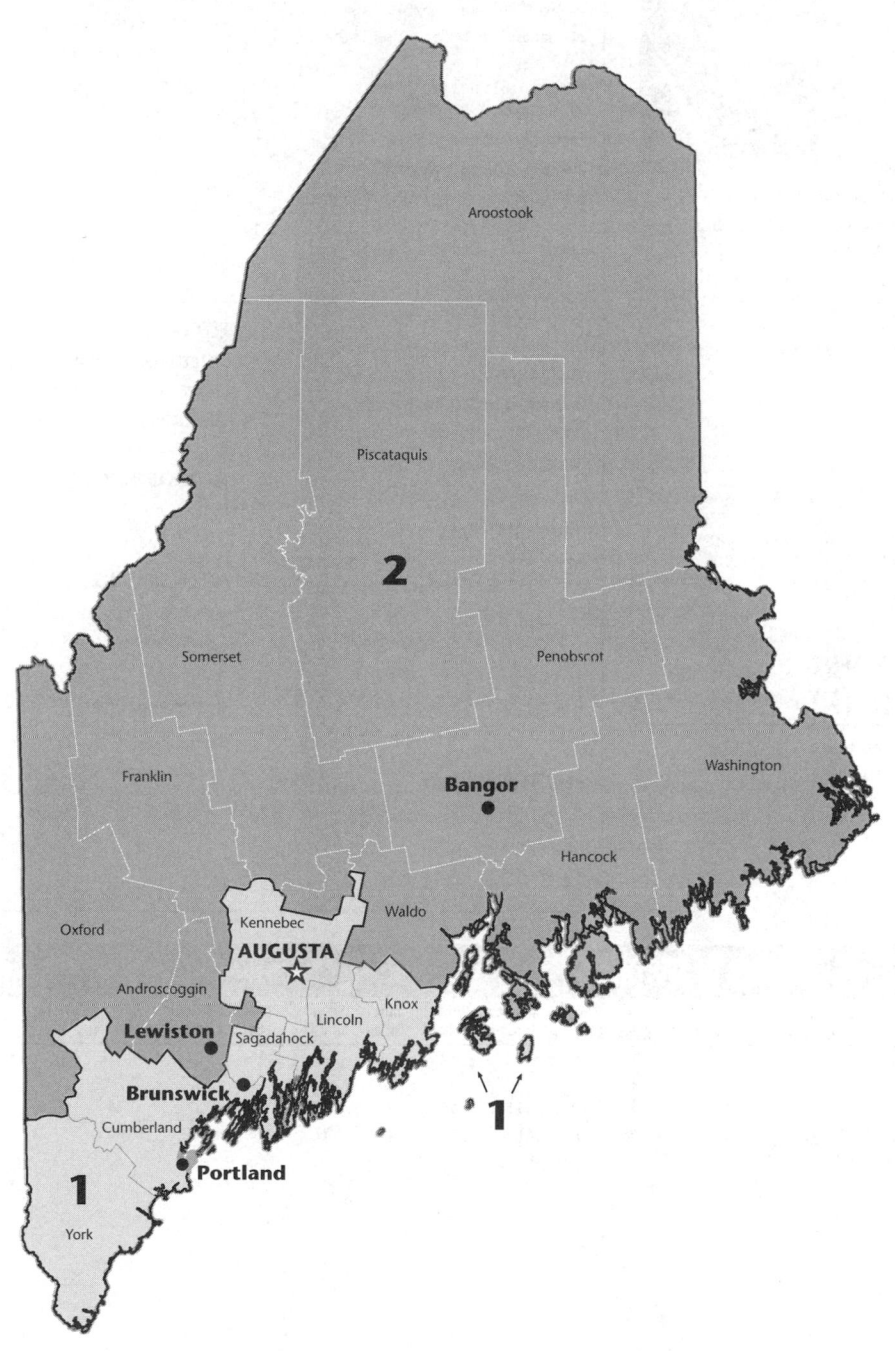

Gov. Paul R. LePage (R)

First elected: 2010

Length of term: 4 years

Term expires: 1/15

Salary: $70,000

Phone: (207) 287-3531

Residence: Waterville

Born: Oct. 9, 1948; Lewiston, Maine

Religion: Roman Catholic

Family: Wife, Ann LePage; five children

Education: Husson College, B.S. 1971 (business administration); U. of Maine, M.B.A. 1975

Career: Store manager; business consultant; forestry products company executive; state housing department officer

Political highlights: Waterville City Council, 1999-2003; mayor of Waterville, 2002-11

ELECTION RESULTS

2010 GENERAL

Paul LePage (R)	218,065	37.6%
Eliot R. Cutler (I)	208,270	35.9%
Libby Mitchell (D)	109,387	18.8%
Shawn H. Moody (I)	28,756	5.0%
Kevin L. Scott (I)	5,664	1.0%

SENATE PRESIDENT KEVIN L. RAYE (R)

(no lieutenant governor)

Phone: (207) 287-1500

LEGISLATURE

Legislature: January-May in odd-numbered years; January-April in even-numbered years.

Senate: 35 members, 2-year terms

2011 ratios: 20 R, 14 D, 1 other; 28 men, 7 women

Salary: $10,815 first year of term; $7,725 second year of term

Phone: (207) 287-1540

House: 151 members, 2-year terms

2011 ratios: 78 R, 72 D, 1 other; 105 men, 46 women

Salary: $10,815 first year of term; $7,725 second year of term

Phone: (207) 287-1400

TERM LIMITS

Governor: 2 consecutive terms

Senate: 4 consecutive terms

House: 4 consecutive terms

URBAN STATISTICS

CITY	POPULATION
Portland	66,194
Lewiston	36,592
Bangor	33,039
South Portland	25,002
Auburn	23,055

REGISTERED VOTERS

Unaffiliated/others	39%
Democrat	33%
Republican	28%

POPULATION

2010 population	1,328,361
2000 population	1,274,923
1990 population	1,227,928
Percent change (2000-2010)	+4.2%
Rank among states (2010)	41
Median age	41.4
Born in state	64.0%
Foreign born	3.3%
Violent crime rate	120/100,000
Poverty level	12.3%
Federal workers	16,159
Military	730

ELECTIONS

STATE ELECTION OFFICIAL

(207) 626-8400

DEMOCRATIC PARTY

(207) 622-6233

REPUBLICAN PARTY

(207) 622-6247

MISCELLANEOUS

Web: www.maine.gov

Capital: Augusta

U.S. CONGRESS

Senate: 2 Republicans

House: 2 Democrats

2010 CENSUS STATISTICS BY DISTRICT

District	2008 Vote for President Obama	2008 Vote for President McCain	White	Black	Asian	Hispanic	Median Income	White Collar	Blue Collar	Service Industry	Over 64	Under 18	College Education	Rural	Sq. Miles
1	61%	38%	94	1	1	1	$52,862	62	21	17	15	21	32%	51%	3,535
2	55	43	95	1	1	1	40,678	54	28	18	15	21	20	71	27,244
STATE	58	40	94	1	1	1	46,541	58	24	18	15	21	26	60	30,862
U.S.	53	46	64	12	5	16	51,425	60	23	17	13	25	28	21	3,537,438

Sen. Olympia J. Snowe (R)

Capitol Office
224-5344
snowe.senate.gov
154 Russell Bldg. 20510-1903; fax 224-1946

Committees
Commerce, Science & Transportation
Finance
Small Business & Entrepreneurship
  - Ranking Member
Select Intelligence

Residence
Falmouth

Born
Feb. 21, 1947; Augusta, Maine

Religion
Greek Orthodox

Family
Husband, John R. McKernan Jr.

Education
U. of Maine, B.A. 1969 (political science)

Career
City employee; congressional district aide

Political Highlights
Maine House, 1973-77; Maine Senate, 1977-79; U.S. House, 1979-95

ELECTION RESULTS

2006 GENERAL

Olympia J. Snowe (R)	402,598	74.0%
Jean M. Hay Bright (D)	111,984	20.6%
William H. Slavick (I)	29,220	5.4%

2006 PRIMARY

Olympia J. Snowe (R)	58,979	98.9%
write-ins	673	1.1%

Previous Winning Percentages
2000 (69%); 1994 (60%); 1992 House Election (49%); 1990 House Election (51%); 1988 House Election (66%); 1986 House Election (77%); 1984 House Election (76%); 1982 House Election (67%); 1980 House Election (79%); 1978 House Election (51%)

Elected 1994; 3rd term

Democratic leaders regularly turn to Snowe when they need a Republican vote to move legislation. Sometimes Snowe is with them — usually after protracted negotiations and dealmaking — and sometimes she isn't. As with Maine's other moderate GOP senator, Susan Collins, neither party can count on Snowe's tally ending up in its ledger. While her practice of crossing party lines occasionally inflames conservatives, it keeps her popular among her state's stubbornly independent constituents and makes her a central player in Senate deliberations.

The health care debate during the 111th Congress (2009-10) provided a prime example. Snowe was the only GOP senator to vote for the health care overhaul legislation at any step of the lengthy process when she supported the Finance Committee's version in the summer of 2009. But, even after much pleading on the part of the Democratic leadership, she refused to support the final version. Snowe took particular issue with the employer mandate provisions, which she said could "annihilate the job growth potential that is so vital to our economic recovery," as well as the increase in Medicare payroll taxes.

"Having been fully immersed in this issue for this entire year and as the only Republican to vote for health reform in the Finance Committee, I deeply regret that I cannot support the pending Senate legislation as it currently stands, given my continued concerns with the measure and an artificial and arbitrary deadline of completing the bill before Christmas that is shortchanging the process on this monumental and trans-generational effort," she said before the final vote.

When Republicans attempted to repeal the law at the beginning of the 112th Congress (2011-12), she voted "yes" along with every other member of the GOP. No Democrat voted "yes."

In Democrats' 2010 efforts to pass a campaign finance disclosure bill, the legislation was modified several times to defuse GOP arguments that it gave unions an unfair advantage, with the intent of winning over either Collins or Snowe. But Snowe, a longtime supporter of full disclosure in campaign advertising, was unmoved.

"No one wants to get this legislation right more than I do," she said. "That is why I am deeply disappointed that the legislation currently before the Senate . . . does not apply equally to everyone who is engaged in campaign advertising, contains provisions that are clearly unconstitutional, and has never benefited from full public review and vetting at even a single committee hearing."

When she gets the changes she wants — or is presented with something she likes — Snowe's vote can be had. Democrats wooed her successfully on an unemployment benefits extension by paring extraneous provisions, and she voted for a $26.1 billion package of aid to states in August 2010. In addition, she was one of five Republicans to back the nomination of Elena Kagan for Supreme Court justice.

Snowe also lined up with the other side on key elements of President Obama's economic agenda — the 2009 economic stimulus, which she supported after persuading Democrats to shrink the cost a bit, and the 2010 financial services regulatory overhaul. Among Senate Republicans, only Collins sided more often with Obama in 2010.

While serving as a power broker in the Senate, Snowe keeps a close watch on state issues, such as home heating assistance for low-income families. She blocked action in 2006 on a flood insurance bill until she was able to win $1 billion for the Low Income Home Energy Assistance Program.

Another priority is protection of Bath Iron Works, the builder of Navy ships that is one of the state's largest employers. One of the reasons for Snowe's initial hesitation to support the state aid package was its offset, which would have taken $107 million from Bath and $3 billion overall from the Department of Defense. During the 2005 round of military base closings, she successfully fought a proposal to shut down the Portsmouth Naval Shipyard.

Another local issue she watches closely as a member of the Commerce, Science and Transportation Committee, is the reauthorization of the Magnuson-Stevens fisheries conservation law, important to Maine and its 3,500 miles of coastline and robust fishing industry.

Snowe took the lead on legislation enacted in 2008 banning discrimination in jobs and health insurance based on the results of genetic testing. She and Democratic Rep. Louise M. Slaughter of New York had pressed for the legislation for a decade. She calls its passage one of the "major satisfactions of my career here."

Snowe likes being a role model for younger generations entering politics. As the top Republican on the Small Business and Entrepreneurship Committee, she encourages female entrepreneurs and is a close ally of the panel's chairwoman, Democratic moderate Mary L. Landrieu of Louisiana; they are the first female duo to lead a Senate committee. Snowe has pressed Obama to elevate the Small Business Administration to Cabinet-level status.

Snowe also serves on the Select Intelligence Committee. Her calls for a "cyber czar" in the White House to coordinate computer activities across spy and civilian agencies bore fruit with Obama in the White House.

Snowe's father, Greek immigrant George Bouchles, and her mother, Georgia, operated the State Street Diner in Augusta, down the street from the statehouse. Georgia Bouchles loved politics, and the diner was a magnet for politicians, business people and journalists. In 1955, when Snowe was 8, her mother died of breast cancer. The next year, her father died of heart disease.

She was sent to St. Basil's Academy, a school for girls run by the Greek Orthodox Church in Garrison, N.Y. She spent summers in Auburn, Maine, with an uncle, his wife and their five children. Snowe got through the University of Maine on student loans and with summer jobs at a Christmas ornament factory. After graduation, she married Peter Snowe, who, like her, was deeply interested in politics.

Her husband was elected to the Maine House, and she went to work as a district aide for GOP Rep. William S. Cohen, who later became a senator and secretary of Defense. In 1973, Peter Snowe was killed in an automobile accident and his wife was elected to succeed him.

Three years later, in 1976, she won a seat in the Maine Senate. When Cohen made a successful run for the U.S. Senate in 1978, she captured his 2nd District seat. She later fell in love for the second time — with former GOP Rep. John R. McKernan Jr., who represented the adjacent 1st District. They married in 1989, while he was serving the first of two terms as governor of Maine.

Snowe easily won re-election until 1990, when a deepening recession led to voter restlessness. She barely edged Democratic state Rep. Patrick K. McGowan, 51 percent to 49 percent. A 1992 rematch was even closer; she won with a 49 percent plurality.

When Senate Democratic leader George J. Mitchell retired in 1994, she ran for the seat and prevailed with 60 percent of the vote. In 2000 and 2006, she overwhelmed her Democratic opponents.

In 2012, she is likely to be targeted from two directions. Democrats view the seat as a potential pickup, and the Tea Party Express has announced it will seek a more conservative candidate to oppose her in the Republican primary.

Key Votes

2010

Pass budget reconciliation bill to modify overhauls of health care and federal student loan programs	NO
Proceed to disapproval resolution on EPA authority to regulate greenhouse gases	YES
Overhaul financial services industry regulation	YES
Limit debate to proceed to a bill to broaden campaign finance disclosure and reporting rules	NO
Limit debate on an extension of Bush-era income tax cuts for two years	YES
Limit debate on a bill to provide a path to legal status for some children of illegal immigrants	NO
Allow for a repeal of "don't ask, don't tell"	YES
Consent to ratification of a strategic arms reduction treaty with Russia	YES

2009

Prevent release of remaining financial industry bailout funds	NO
Make it easier for victims to sue for wage discrimination remedies	YES
Expand the Children's Health Insurance Program	YES
Limit debate on the economic stimulus measure	YES
Repeal District of Columbia firearms prohibitions and gun registration laws	YES
Limit debate on expansion of federal hate crimes law	YES
Strike funding for F-22 Raptor fighter jets	NO

CQ Vote Studies

	PARTY UNITY		PRESIDENTIAL SUPPORT	
	SUPPORT	OPPOSE	SUPPORT	OPPOSE
2010	73%	27%	66%	34%
2009	49%	51%	81%	19%
2008	39%	61%	48%	52%
2007	44%	56%	57%	43%
2006	56%	44%	75%	25%
2005	56%	44%	67%	33%
2004	71%	29%	74%	26%
2003	75%	25%	82%	18%
2002	57%	43%	90%	10%
2001	64%	36%	84%	16%

Interest Groups

	AFL-CIO	ADA	CCUS	ACU
2010	44%	40%	82%	64%
2009	72%	65%	86%	48%
2008	100%	80%	71%	12%
2007	68%	60%	64%	28%
2006	47%	45%	75%	36%
2005	64%	65%	78%	32%
2004	67%	65%	71%	60%
2003	0%	55%	65%	45%
2002	31%	30%	85%	65%
2001	50%	40%	79%	60%

Sen. Susan Collins (R)

Capitol Office
224-2523
collins.senate.gov
413 Dirksen Bldg. 20510-1904; fax 224-2693

Committees
Appropriations
Armed Services
Homeland Security & Governmental Affairs
- Ranking Member
Special Aging

Residence
Bangor

Born
Dec. 7, 1952; Caribou, Maine

Religion
Roman Catholic

Family
Single

Education
St. Lawrence U., B.A. 1975 (government)

Career
Business center director; congressional aide

Political Highlights
Maine Department of Professional and Financial
Regulation commissioner, 1987-91; Small Business
Administration official, 1992-93; Maine deputy trea-
surer, 1993; Republican nominee for governor, 1994

ELECTION RESULTS

2008 GENERAL
Susan Collins (R)	444,300	61.3%
Tom Allen (D)	279,510	38.6%

2008 PRIMARY
Susan Collins (R)	unopposed

2002 GENERAL
Susan Collins (R)	295,041	58.4%
Chellie Pingree (D)	209,858	41.6%

Previous Winning Percentages
1996 (49%)

Elected 1996; 3rd term

Over the past two years, Collins' status as a potential swing vote gave her an outsized voice on policy, a role she shared with fellow Maine Republican Olympia J. Snowe. Senate Democrats frequently court the votes of both — sometimes they get them, sometimes they don't.

Collins' role as a power broker is not happenstance — she has cultivated her centrist role, making a conscious effort to ensure that the bills she push-es have bipartisan support. Her role as ranking Republican on the Homeland Security and Governmental Affairs Committee has allowed her to foster a close working relationship with another New England centrist, Connecticut independent Joseph I. Lieberman, the committee chairman who caucuses with Democrats.

"I feel strongly that my constituents sent me to Washington to solve prob-lems," Collins said, "and not to stand on the sidelines and score political points."

In 2010, no Republican sided more often with President Obama than Col-lins, who backed the Democratic White House's position almost 69 percent of the time when the president had a clearly stated position.

Collins said her moderate position has enhanced her ability to shape leg-islation, such as the 2010 financial overhaul measure that created the Trea-sury Department's Consumer Financial Protection Bureau. Only three Sen-ate Republicans joined Democrats in passing the bill, all from New England: Collins, Snowe and Scott P. Brown of Massachusetts.

But that influence comes at a cost, she said, in the form of increased scrutiny from lawmakers and the media. "The negative side of that is that there's a great deal of pressure attendant to virtually every single vote," she said. "I'm well used to that, but it can be a difficult situation at times."

Throughout her Senate career, Collins has joined many of the bipartisan working groups and "gangs" created to strike deals on legislation.

In 2009, Collins joined Snowe and Pennsylvania's Arlen Specter as the only Republicans to support Obama's $787 billion economic stimulus law, agreeing to the measure only after its cost was sliced to less than $800 billion. She also supported an expansion of the Children's Health Insurance Program, which covers children from low-income families that make too much money to qual-ify for Medicaid, and congressional representation for the District of Columbia.

She voted to confirm both Sonia Sotomayor and Elena Kagan to the Supreme Court.

A member of the Armed Services Committee, Collins was one of three Republicans who voiced support early in the debate over a new strategic arms reduction treaty with Russia, a position that encouraged Democrats to push for approval of the treaty, which came in the 2010 lame-duck session.

Despite the grumbling such behavior elicits from some conservatives, Senate Republicans are often happy to have Collins around.

She joined in keeping the Democrats from garnering a single GOP vote on the health care overhaul in 2010. Though she favored repeal of the "don't ask, don't tell" law that banned openly gay people from the armed services, she sided with her party on a related procedural vote. When the Senate was considering a defense authorization bill with the repeal language built in two months before the 2010 elections, she refused to provide the vote that would have broken a Republican filibuster, accusing the Democrats of trying to limit GOP amendments. When stand-alone legislation to repeal the ban moved late in 2010, she backed it.

She also uses her spots on Armed Services and Appropriations, where she is the top Republican on the Transportation-Housing and Urban Development spending panel, to protect one of Maine's largest industrial employers, Bath Iron Works. The shipyard builds destroyers that face perennial funding threats among defense priorities. She worked with Mississippi lawmakers in 2006 to block a proposed Navy strategy to build the ships in only one of the two states.

But she does her highest-profile work on the Homeland Security and Governmental Affairs Committee, a panel she led until the Democratic take-over of 2007.

She and Lieberman describe their relationship as cooperative and friend-ly, and they frequently sponsor legislation together. Both have pushed to expand the committee's authority, complaining that the current arrangement for homeland security issues — which requires their committee to share oversight with dozens of other committees and subcommittees — stymies their ability to bring legislation to the floor and outline clear congressional priorities for the Department of Homeland Security.

The problem became apparent in 2010 when cybersecurity legislation that Collins and Lieberman introduced was up against competing measures from the Commerce, Science and Transportation Committee and the Intelligence Committee. Competing bills are expected again in 2011, although Collins has voiced confidence that a compromise can be reached.

She counts among her achievements with the committee her work with Lieberman in the 108th Congress (2003-04) to rewrite the nation's intelligence laws to create a more centralized spy infrastructure — a key recommendation of the independent commission that investigated the Sept. 11 attacks.

In the decade since Sept. 11, 2001, Collins said, some in the homeland security world worried that the issue had faded from public and congres-sional concern. But a series of high-profile threats in 2009 and 2010 — including the shooting at Fort Hood in Texas, a plot to attack New York City's transit system, the Christmas Day attempt to blow up a Northwest Airlines flight and the failed Times Square car bombing — brought terror-ism back to the forefront.

The incidents also highlighted a growing problem that Collins said she wants to focus on in the 112th Congress (2011-12): "homegrown" terrorism, involving U.S. citizens and residents.

She was highly critical of two DHS documents meant to shape the depart-ment's strategy in the years to come, saying they downplayed the home-grown threat. She was also highly critical of the FBI and the Defense Depart-ment for their handling of the 2009 Fort Hood shooting, saying they had ample evidence of the growing radicalization of suspect Army Maj. Nidal Malik Hasan, but failed to curb it. The incident, which resulted in 13 deaths and 30 injuries, could have been prevented if investigators had linked all of the information they had on Hasan, Collins said.

Collins hails from a political family; each of her parents served as Cari-bou's mayor. After graduating from St. Lawrence University in 1975, she moved to Washington to work as an aide to William S. Cohen, a moderate GOP senator from Maine who became her mentor. She then returned to Maine to serve as commissioner of the state's Department of Professional and Financial Regulation. In 1994, Collins won the Republican nomination for governor but finished a disappointing third behind Democratic nominee Joseph E. Brennan and independent Angus King, who won the contest. In 1996, when Cohen announced his retirement, Collins regrouped and took the race by 5 percentage points. She won handily in 2002, beating Demo-cratic challenger Chellie Pingree, who was elected to a House seat in 2008. That year, Collins faced an experienced opponent in Democratic Rep. Tom Allen, who had the backing of national Democrats. But she cruised to vic-tory with 61 percent of the vote.

Key Votes

2010

Pass budget reconciliation bill to modify overhauls of health care and federal student loan programs	NO
Proceed to disapproval resolution on EPA authority to regulate greenhouse gases	YES
Overhaul financial services industry regulation	YES
Limit debate to proceed to a bill to broaden campaign finance disclosure and reporting rules	NO
Limit debate on an extension of Bush-era income tax cuts for two years	YES
Limit debate on a bill to provide a path to legal status for some children of illegal immigrants	NO
Allow for a repeal of "don't ask, don't tell"	YES
Consent to ratification of a strategic arms reduction treaty with Russia	YES

2009

Prevent release of remaining financial industry bailout funds	YES
Make it easier for victims to sue for wage discrimination remedies	YES
Expand the Children's Health Insurance Program	YES
Limit debate on the economic stimulus measure	YES
Repeal District of Columbia firearms prohibitions and gun registration laws	YES
Limit debate on expansion of federal hate crimes law	YES
Strike funding for F-22 Raptor fighter jets	NO

CQ Vote Studies

	PARTY UNITY		PRESIDENTIAL SUPPORT	
	Support	Oppose	Support	Oppose
2010	69%	31%	69%	31%
2009	48%	52%	85%	15%
2008	46%	54%	59%	41%
2007	50%	50%	61%	39%
2006	66%	34%	79%	21%
2005	59%	41%	62%	38%
2004	78%	22%	82%	18%
2003	78%	22%	87%	13%
2002	57%	43%	88%	12%
2001	67%	33%	88%	12%

Interest Groups

	AFL-CIO	ADA	CCUS	ACU
2010	44%	40%	82%	64%
2009	61%	65%	86%	48%
2008	100%	75%	75%	20%
2007	68%	55%	64%	36%
2006	47%	45%	92%	48%
2005	64%	65%	78%	32%
2004	50%	45%	94%	68%
2003	31%	45%	78%	35%
2002	31%	35%	85%	55%
2001	50%	35%	79%	64%

Rep. Chellie Pingree (D)

Capitol Office
225-6116
pingree.house.gov
1318 Longworth Bldg. 20515; fax 225-5590

Committees
Agriculture
Armed Services

Residence
North Haven

Born
April 2, 1955; Minneapolis, Minn.

Religion
Lutheran

Family
Divorced; three children

Education
U. of Southern Maine, attended 1973; College of the
Atlantic, B.A. 1979 (human ecology)

Career
Inn owner; Common Cause president; knitting
company owner; farmer

Political Highlights
North Haven Board of Assessors, 1981-87
(chairwoman, 1982-83, 1984-87); North Haven
Planning Board, 1981-91; Maine School Administrative
District #7 Board of Directors, 1990-93 (chairwoman,
1991-93); Maine Senate, 1992-2000 (majority leader,
1996-2000); Democratic nominee for U.S. Senate,
2002

ELECTION RESULTS

2010 GENERAL

Chellie Pingree (D)	169,114	56.8%
Dean Scontras (R)	128,501	43.2%

2010 PRIMARY

Chellie Pingree (D)	unopposed

2008 GENERAL

Chellie Pingree (D)	205,629	54.9%
Charlie Summers (R)	168,930	45.1%

Elected 2008; 2nd term

From her political beginnings as a teenage anti-war protester to state legislative leader to president of a campaign watchdog group to her current role in the U.S. House, Pingree has pursued liberal causes with an activist's bent, unafraid of getting her hands dirty "either in politics or on the farm."

Pingree (her first name is pronounced "Shelley") is known to locals in North Haven for her former knitting and yarn business and as the owner of an inn and restaurant supplied with locally grown vegetables. But in Maine's political circles she is better known for working across the aisle, particularly to enact a prescription drug pricing law.

Pingree first garnered national attention as the state Senate majority leader who shepherded to passage Maine Rx, a 2000 law that allows the state to negotiate with drug companies and offer lower prices to the uninsured.

She now puts those experiences to use as a member of the Armed Services Committee, where she opposes U.S. military involvement in Iraq and Afghanistan and works to cut defense spending while aiding military contractors in her own district. Pingree sought a spot on Armed Services because the Portsmouth Naval Shipyard and military-related companies are significant economic drivers back home.

She took some flak for voting in July 2009 to block funding for the F-22 fighter jet program; a component of the aircraft was built in her district. She said she is working to see that it is replaced with other programs that will keep her constituents employed. But in May 2010, in defense of her district's shipyard, Pingree pushed back against Defense Secretary Robert M. Gates' calls for tighter shipbuilding budgets, suggesting that ending the wars in Iraq and Afghanistan would be a better way to reduce costs.

She backed a successful amendment to a House-passed catchall spending bill for fiscal 2011 that would block funding for a second engine for the new F-35 Joint Strike Fighter plane.

"Democrats and Republicans alike can see that spending money for a second F-35 engine is a waste of money," she said. "The Bush administration did not want this engine. The Obama administration doesn't want this engine. And the Pentagon tells us it's unnecessary."

Pingree was the first member to ask constituents to request earmarks on camera — one recipient that chose not to participate was the shipyard. She posted the videos of fiscal 2011 earmark requests on her website and allowed visitors to comment before she sent them on to the Appropriations Committee.

A member of the Congressional Progressive Caucus, she supported all the major economic initiatives of the Obama administration, including the health care overhaul, which she supported after joining the failed push to include a government-run insurance plan in the final version of the law.

As the former head of Common Cause, campaign finance is a central concern for Pingree. She cosponsored legislation in 2009 to create a public financing system for House candidates and sharply criticized a 2010 Supreme Court decision overturning restrictions on corporate and union political spending.

During a House Administration Committee hearing in July 2009, Pingree compared how she ran her first federal campaign — a 2002 Senate race — and how her daughter, Maine House Speaker Hannah Pingree, campaigned in a state that offers public financing for candidates. Pingree said she spent hours in a little room calling potential donors, while her daughter "went to grocery stores, to fish piers; she knocked on the doors of every person in that district that she wanted to represent."

Pingree grew up in a Republican family in Minnesota, where her mother was a nurse and her father was an accountant. After high school, Pingree moved to Maine, where she and her husband — they're now divorced — lived for a few years in a cabin without running water or electricity on North Haven, an island in Penobscot Bay.

Pingree picked up the agriculture interests of her grandfather, a dairy farmer, and earned a degree in human ecology from the College of the Atlantic in Bar Harbor. She then returned to North Haven, where she grew vegetables and raised cows, chickens and sheep. She now serves on the Agriculture Committee.

She also won some local, nonpartisan races for tax assessor and school board. When she decided to run for the state Senate in 1992, she didn't take long to decide she was a Democrat.

Her role as owner of North Island Designs — a mail-order knitting company that sold pattern books and yarn from her sheep — helped get her campaign off the ground. When she knocked on doors, women would announce, "Oh, my gosh, you're the knitting lady!" Pingree won that race and four years later became majority leader.

Term-limited at the state level, Pingree initially considered a 2002 gubernatorial bid, but stepped aside for the ultimately successful campaign of Democratic Rep. John Baldacci. She instead challenged Republican Sen. Susan Collins. Pingree raised almost as much money as Collins, but won only 42 percent of the vote.

She ended up with a Washington job anyway: president of Common Cause.

When six-term Democrat Tom Allen decided to give up his House seat to run against Collins in 2008, Pingree entered and won a six-way primary. The Republicans nominated former state Sen. Charlie Summers, a Navy Reserve lieutenant commander who had deployed to Iraq during the campaign. Pingree won with 55 percent of the vote.

In an ironic twist for a former Common Cause president and supporter of public financing of campaigns, Pingree is among the Democrats' most successful fundraisers. In 2002, she and the Democratic Senatorial Campaign Committee established a joint fundraising committee and received several large donations from a handful of individuals. Pingree later became engaged to one of those donors, S. Donald Sussman. Her activities sparked criticism, and Pingree swore off the practice of joint fundraising committees.

Key Votes

2010

Overhaul the nation's health insurance system	YES
Allow for repeal of "don't ask, don't tell"	YES
Overhaul financial services industry regulation	YES
Limit use of new Afghanistan War funds to troop withdrawal activities	YES
Change oversight of offshore drilling and lift oil spill liability cap	YES
Provide a path to legal status for some children of illegal immigrants	YES
Extend Bush-era income tax cuts for two years	NO

2009

Expand the Children's Health Insurance Program	YES
Provide $787 billion in tax cuts and spending increases to stimulate the economy	YES
Allow bankruptcy judges to modify certain primary-residence mortgages	YES
Create a cap-and-trade system to limit greenhouse gas emissions	YES
Provide $2 billion for the "cash for clunkers" program	YES
Establish the government as the sole provider of student loans	YES
Restrict federally funded insurance coverage for abortions in health care overhaul	NO

CQ Vote Studies

	PARTY UNITY		PRESIDENTIAL SUPPORT	
	SUPPORT	OPPOSE	SUPPORT	OPPOSE
2010	99%	1%	83%	17%
2009	99%	1%	90%	10%

Interest Groups

	AFL-CIO	ADA	CCUS	ACU
2010	100%	100%	13%	0%
2009	100%	100%	33%	0%

Maine 1

South — Portland, Augusta

Covering Maine's southern tip, the 1st boasts both rural oceanfront property and high-paying jobs. Residents of the state's largest city, Portland, continue to move into outlying areas, bringing single-family homes to once-uninterrupted forests and farmland.

The technology boom that spread north from Boston during the 1990s slowed, but software jobs still offset manufacturing and textile plant closures. Health care, financial services and insurance firms are here, and Interstate 95 offers a straight shot between the district and Boston for both commuters and seasonal residents, who tend to live on the coast. Tourism is important in the lower part of the state, as residents from across New England and Canada head to popular beaches and shopping areas, including the L.L. Bean flagship store in Freeport.

The 1st has had a longtime military influence, and Portsmouth Naval Shipyard is slated to receive federal funds for expansion of its nuclear-powered submarine repair operations. The 2011 closure of Brunswick Naval Air Station as a result of the base realignment process has cost the district thousands of jobs, but the former military site will transition into a general aviation airport. Local officials hope to use the redeveloped facilities to lure more businesses to the region.

Residents of the district tend to be white, wealthy and older, but the district's traditional Yankee Republican tendencies have given way to a Democratic voting preference in federal elections. Republicans still find some support at the state and local levels, especially in York County towns. In 2010, Kennebec County (shared with the 2nd District), gave Republican Gov. Paul R. LePage his second-highest percentage in the state, but the 1st overall favored Barack Obama by 23 percentage points in the 2008 presidential election.

Major Industry
Military shipbuilding, financial services, technology, tourism

Military Bases
Portsmouth Naval Shipyard, 80 military, 2,042 civilian (2011)

Cities
Portland, 66,194; South Portland, 25,002; Biddeford, 21,277

Notable
The Wadsworth-Longfellow House museum is the oldest standing structure on the Portland peninsula.

Rep. Michael H. Michaud (D)

Capitol Office
225-6306
michaud.house.gov
1724 Longworth Bldg. 20515-1902; fax 225-2943

Committees
Transportation & Infrastructure
Veterans' Affairs

Residence
East Millinocket

Born
Jan. 18, 1955; Millinocket, Maine

Religion
Roman Catholic

Family
Single

Education
Schenck H.S., graduated 1973

Career
Paper mill worker

Political Highlights
Maine House, 1981-94; Maine Senate, 1995-2002
(president, 2001)

ELECTION RESULTS

2010 GENERAL

Michael H. Michaud (D)	147,042	55.1%
Jason J. Levesque (R)	119,669	44.9%

2010 PRIMARY

Michael H. Michaud (D)	unopposed

2008 GENERAL

Michael H. Michaud (D)	226,274	67.4%
John N. Frary (R)	109,268	32.6%

Previous Winning Percentages
2006 (71%); 2004 (58%); 2002 (52%)

Elected 2002; 5th term

Michaud portrays himself as firmly on the side of the working man, a position for which he is unusually qualified — he actually was a blue-collar worker, unlike many of his House colleagues. For nearly three decades he punched a clock at a Great Northern Paper Co. mill.

Now Michaud (ME-shoo), who never went to college and still carries a union card, works to promote economic development in his district, taking aim at trade deals he says have hurt manufacturers such as his former employer.

He remains affiliated with what is now United Steelworkers Local 4-00037 and enjoys electoral and financial support from organized labor. Michaud's criticism of free-trade deals only intensified after he entered Congress in 2003: Three days after he was sworn in, Great Northern filed for bankruptcy and closed its two paper mills, including the one in East Millinocket where Michaud, his father and grandfather had worked. Michaud blamed the 1993 North American Free Trade Agreement, which he says has put U.S. manufacturers "at a competitive disadvantage."

Among his earliest legislative efforts were his cosponsorship of a bill to extend the length of federal unemployment assistance and to boost the tax deductibility of health care costs. Michaud also helped get $900,000 for the Millinocket Regional Hospital to treat uninsured workers.

In the 110th Congress (2007-08) and again in the 111th (2009-10), Michaud introduced legislation that would radically alter current and future U.S. trade deals. The legislation called for a review and renegotiation of major trade agreements, including NAFTA, and would have established labor, environmental, food and product safety standards that he says should be a part of all U.S. trade pacts.

Meanwhile, Michaud fights to secure federal aid for workers in his district who are displaced by trade deals. He won enactment, as part of the 2008 farm programs reauthorization, of his proposal to create a Northern Border Regional Commission to spend federal funds on economic development and job creation projects in the most economically distressed areas along the northeastern border. The commission was awarded $1.5 million in appropriations for its first year in operation.

Michaud expressed reservations about the health care overhaul bill enacted in 2010. Although he is the only New Englander affiliated with the fiscally conservative Blue Dog Coalition, his concerns reflected those of liberal critics — particularly the non-inclusion of a government-run "public option." He also backed an amendment to the health care overhaul that would have ensured that no federal funds were used to pay for abortion coverage. In the end, he supported the final version of the measure, which did not include the abortion or public option provisions.

Though he is a reliable Democratic vote — he sided with his party 91 percent of the time on votes that divided majorities of the parties in 2010 — Michaud has expressed frustration with what he considers the high level of partisanship in Washington. He blames "the leadership on both sides" for not working to find common ground.

Along with some other Blue Dogs, Michaud registered his unhappiness with Minority Leader Nancy Pelosi of California by casting a vote for North Carolina Rep. Heath Shuler for Speaker at the start of the 112th Congress (2011-12).

Michaud serves on the Transportation and Infrastructure Committee, where he will have a chance to steer highway funding to Maine as the panel continues work on a new multi-year surface transportation law. In the last highway reauthorization in 2005, Michaud helped secure a 30 percent increase in annual spending for Maine's highways. He sees the new highway bill as a chance to not only create jobs in the short term but also improve the transportation system that links Maine's rural economy to larger urban areas.

Michaud is also an active voice on the Veterans' Affairs Committee, where he is the ranking member on the Health panel. He has championed measures to improve medical care and to ensure its accessibility in rural areas. He helped pass legislation in 2009 that allows the Department of Veterans Affairs to receive appropriations for medical care a year in advance and avoid budget shortfalls when Congress fails to pass appropriations before the start of the fiscal year. He has also secured funding for new medical facilities for veterans in rural areas of Maine.

He has long been an opponent of the Iraq War and also opposed President Obama's decision to increase troop levels in Afghanistan. He was one of 26 House Democrats to oppose the fiscal 2011 defense policy bill, which authorized more than $159 billion for the Iraq and Afghanistan wars.

Michaud grew up in Medway, close to the Great Northern mill. Like his father and grandfather, he went to work at the mill after high school.

Michaud says he decided to run for the state House because he was concerned about pollution in the Penobscot River. Elected in 1980, he took advantage of a clause in his union contract that allowed workers to keep their jobs while serving in the legislature. He worked at the mill when the legislature was not in session; when it was, he chaired the Environment Committee and wrote bills to clean up the river. Sometimes he would put in a long day in Augusta, the state capital, then hurry to work a midnight shift at Great Northern.

Michaud served seven terms in the state House, then was elected to the Maine Senate in 1994. Two years later, he became chairman of the Appropriations Committee and in 2000 was elected state Senate president. At that point, he took a leave of absence from the mill.

In the 2002 race for the seat of Democratic Rep. John Baldacci, who was running for governor, support from organized labor helped Michaud eke out a narrow victory over Republican Kevin L. Raye, former chief of staff for GOP Sen. Olympia J. Snowe. Michaud won his next three terms by wide margins.

As Baldacci neared the end of his second term, there was speculation that Michaud would again follow in his footsteps. But Michaud demurred on a run for governor and was re-elected in 2010 with 55 percent of the vote over the Republican candidate, businessman and Army veteran Jason J. Levesque.

Key Votes

2010

Overhaul the nation's health insurance system	YES
Allow for repeal of "don't ask, don't tell"	YES
Overhaul financial services industry regulation	YES
Limit use of new Afghanistan War funds to troop withdrawal activities	YES
Change oversight of offshore drilling and lift oil spill liability cap	YES
Provide a path to legal status for some children of illegal immigrants	YES
Extend Bush-era income tax cuts for two years	NO

2009

Expand the Children's Health Insurance Program	YES
Provide $787 billion in tax cuts and spending increases to stimulate the economy	YES
Allow bankruptcy judges to modify certain primary-residence mortgages	YES
Create a cap-and-trade system to limit greenhouse gas emissions	YES
Provide $2 billion for the "cash for clunkers" program	YES
Establish the government as the sole provider of student loans	YES
Restrict federally funded insurance coverage for abortions in health care overhaul	YES

CQ Vote Studies

	PARTY UNITY		PRESIDENTIAL SUPPORT	
	SUPPORT	OPPOSE	SUPPORT	OPPOSE
2010	91%	9%	88%	12%
2009	92%	8%	92%	8%
2008	94%	6%	13%	87%
2007	96%	4%	8%	92%
2006	92%	8%	30%	70%

Interest Groups

	AFL-CIO	ADA	CCUS	ACU
2010	93%	90%	13%	0%
2009	100%	90%	40%	8%
2008	100%	90%	50%	12%
2007	92%	85%	55%	0%
2006	100%	90%	40%	12%

Maine 2

North — Lewiston, Bangor, Presque Isle

Millions of acres of trees surround the small towns of northern Maine's 2nd. The largest district in a state east of the Mississippi, the 2nd attracts millions of visitors "from away" — local lingo for out of state — to Acadia National Park, Baxter State Park and Maine's many lakes and ski slopes. Development of the privately owned timber forests of the North Woods is a major issue, as resorts, single-family homes and immigration of residents from other states could permanently alter the landscape.

Lobstering dominates the coast, and the timber industry reigns inland. Farming is in decline in parts of the district, although the 2nd remains one of the nation's largest producers of potatoes and blueberries. Sparsely populated in parts, the region is less wealthy than the 1st, which has benefited from a more diverse employment base.

As the national economy has become more service-based, the 2nd has suffered. Manufacturing jobs, especially in shoes and textiles, have gone abroad, and some residents have headed south to find work. Some residents have pushed for an east-west highway to promote economic growth, citing the district's easy access to Boston via Interstate 95. A weak party system throughout the state and a higher proportion of rural voters have helped make the 2nd the more competitive of Maine's two congressional districts. Voters here gave 55 percent of the vote to Barack Obama in the 2008 presidential election — 6 percentage points less than he enjoyed in the 1st District. The 2nd's voters will support candidates from either major party or independent candidates. In the 2010 gubernatorial election, Republican Paul R. LePage won every county in the district except Hancock, and Somerset gave him his highest winning percentage statewide.

Major Industry
Logging, agriculture, fishing, tourism, textiles

Cities
Lewiston, 36,592; Bangor, 33,039; Auburn, 23,055; Waterville, 15,722

Notable
Established in 1919, Acadia National Park was the first national park east of the Mississippi River; since 1992, Harrington-based Worcester Wreath has decorated, donated and delivered 5,000 wreaths every December for graveside ceremonies at Arlington National Cemetery.

MARYLAND

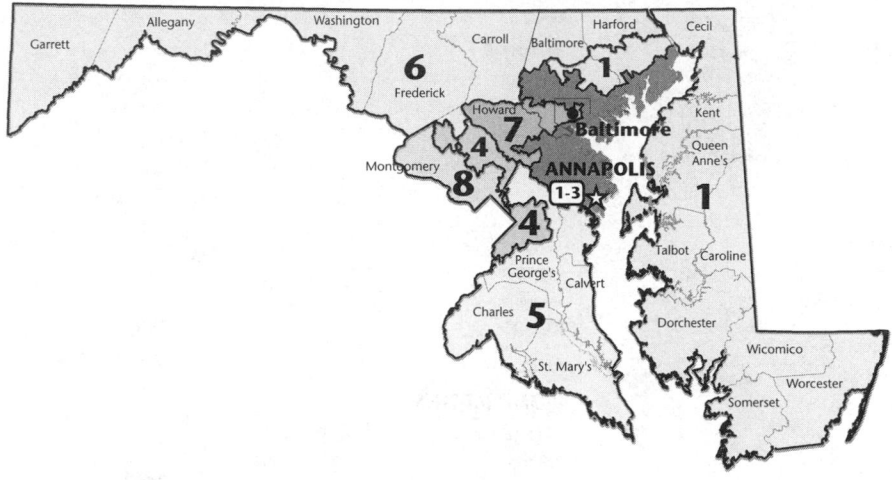

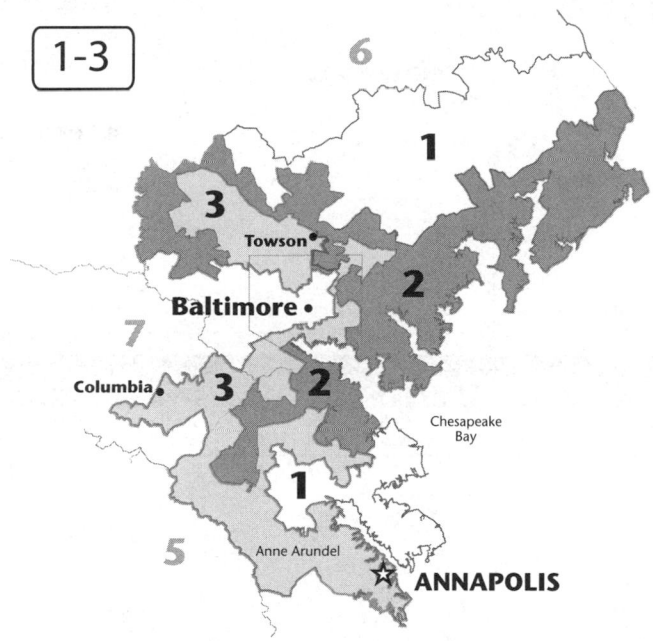

Gov. Martin O'Malley (D)

First elected: 2006
Length of term: 4 years
Term expires: 1/15
Salary: $150,000
Phone: (410) 974-3901
Residence: Baltimore
Born: Jan. 18, 1963; Washington, D.C.
Religion: Roman Catholic
Family: Wife, Catherine Curran O'Malley; four children
Education: Catholic U., B.A. 1985 (political science); U. of Maryland, Baltimore, J.D. 1988
Career: Lawyer; city prosecutor; campaign aide
Political highlights: Democratic nominee for Md. Senate, 1990; Baltimore City Council, 1991-99; mayor of Baltimore, 1999-2007

ELECTION RESULTS

2010 GENERAL

Martin O'Malley (D)	1,044,961	56.2%
Robert Ehrlich (R)	776,319	41.8%

Lt. Gov. Anthony G. Brown (D)

First elected: 2006
Length of term: 4 years
Term expires: 1/15
Salary: $125,000
Phone: (410) 974-2804

LEGISLATURE

General Assembly: 90 days January-April
Senate: 47 members, 4-year terms
2011 ratios: 35 D, 12 R; 36 men, 11 women
Salary: $43,500
Phone: (410) 841-3700
House: 141 members, 4-year terms
2011 ratios: 98 D, 43 R; 94 men; 47 women
Salary: $43,500
Phone: (410) 841-3800

TERM LIMITS

Governor: 2 consecutive terms
Senate: No
House: No

URBAN STATISTICS

CITY	POPULATION
Baltimore	620,961
Frederick	65,239
Rockville	61,209
Gaithersburg	59,933
Bowie	54,727

REGISTERED VOTERS

Democrat	56%
Republican	27%
Unaffiliated/others	17%

POPULATION

2010 population	5,773,552
2000 population	5,296,486
1990 population	4,781,468
Percent change (2000-2010)	+9.0%
Rank among states (2010)	19
Median age	37.3
Born in state	48.0%
Foreign born	12.0%
Violent crime rate	590/100,000
Poverty level	9.1%
Federal workers	280,658
Military	29,160

ELECTIONS

STATE ELECTION OFFICIAL
(410) 269-2840
DEMOCRATIC PARTY
(410) 269-8818
REPUBLICAN PARTY
(410) 263-2125

MISCELLANEOUS

Web: www.maryland.gov
Capital: Annapolis

U.S. CONGRESS

Senate: 2 Democrats
House: 6 Democrats, 2 Republicans

2010 Census Statistics by District

District	2008 Vote for President Obama	McCain	White	Black	Asian	Hispanic	Median Income	White Collar	Blue Collar	Service Industry	Over 64	Under 18	College Education	Rural	Sq. Miles
1	40%	58%	81%	11%	2%	3%	$68,336	64%	21%	15%	14%	23%	31%	36%	3,653
2	60	38	55	33	4	5	56,229	63	20	17	12	24	24	2	355
3	59	39	65	20	5	7	70,646	71	15	14	12	22	42	1	293
4	85	14	21	56	7	14	72,795	67	15	17	9	26	36	2	315
5	65	33	48	37	4	8	83,948	67	18	15	10	26	32	25	1,504
6	40	58	85	6	2	4	68,042	64	21	15	13	25	28	39	3,062
7	79	20	32	56	7	3	51,712	67	14	19	12	24	33	5	294
8	74	25	47	16	13	20	88,291	74	11	15	13	24	55	1	297
STATE	62	37	55	29	5	8	69,475	67	17	16	12	24	35	14	9,774
U.S.	53	46	64	12	5	16	51,425	60	23	17	13	25	28	21	3,537,438

Sen. Barbara A. Mikulski (D)

Capitol Office
224-4654
mikulski.senate.gov
503 Hart Bldg. 20510-2003; fax 224-8858

Committees
Appropriations
 (Commerce-Justice-Science - Chairwoman)
Health, Education, Labor & Pensions
 (Children & Families - Chairwoman)
Select Intelligence

Residence
Baltimore

Born
July 20, 1936; Baltimore, Md.

Religion
Roman Catholic

Family
Single

Education
Mount Saint Agnes College, B.A. 1958 (sociology); U. of Maryland, M.S.W. 1965

Career
Social worker

Political Highlights
Baltimore City Council, 1971-77; Democratic nominee for U.S. Senate, 1974; U.S. House, 1977-87

ELECTION RESULTS

2010 GENERAL

Barbara A. Mikulski (D)	1,140,531	62.2%
Eric Wargotz (R)	655,666	35.8%
Kenniss Henry (GREEN)	20,717	1.1%

2010 PRIMARY

Barbara A. Mikulski (D)	396,252	82.3%
Christopher J. Garner (D)	36,194	7.5%
Anthony Jaworski (D)	15,335	3.2%
Blaine Taylor (D)	11,049	2.3%
Theresa C. Scaldaferri (D)	8,092	1.7%
Sanquetta Taylor (D)	7,684	1.6%
Lih Young (D)	6,911	1.4%

Previous Winning Percentages
2004 (65%); 1998 (71%); 1992 (71%); 1986 (61%); 1984 House Election (68%); 1982 House Election (74%); 1980 House Election (76%); 1978 House Election (100%); 1976 House Election (75%)

Elected 1986; 5th term

The liberal Mikulski doesn't shy from a fight, whether it's battling to bolster NASA or protecting intelligence assets in her home state. She has also been willing to take on a president of her own party.

Mikulski is chairwoman of the Senate Appropriations subcommittee that oversees funding of the Commerce and Justice departments as well as space and science programs. She criticized the Obama administration's 2010 proposal to end the moon-bound Constellation program while favoring a plan to work with companies to ferry astronauts into space.

"Today, NASA is immediately associated with success in spite of insurmountable odds," Mikulski said. "If this proposal is the best that we can do as a nation, then we do not deserve, I believe, the rich heritage of human spaceflight which previous generations sacrificed to make this country's space program what it is: great."

Mikulski's ardent defense of the sciences over the years earned her a spot in Discover magazine's 2008 list of the "10 Most Influential People in Science." That put Mikulski, a former social worker, in a group with the founders of Microsoft and Google, Nobel-winning scientist Harold Varmus, and J. Craig Venter, who bested rivals in a race to sequence the human genome.

The 112th Congress (2011-12) has put Mikulski at the top of another class of lawmaker, as she became the longest-serving female senator, passing the late Margaret Chase Smith of Maine, who served 24 years.

Mikulski revels in her status as dean of Senate women. She has offered the newcomers introductory seminars and dispensed advice on everything from organizing their offices to setting long-range goals.

"The political bosses would still have me making pierogies in the basement of the church," she said, referring to her roots in Baltimore politics.

She served for a decade as Democratic caucus secretary, the No. 3 leadership post, before stepping down in 2004 to give another woman, Michigan's Debbie Stabenow, a boost onto the leadership ladder.

Mikulski in 2009 won a battle to bar insurers from charging co-payments for many preventive services for women, requiring insurers to provide full coverage for screenings and other such care.

"We organized the women of the Senate. We suited up in our pink jackets. The good men joined us," Mikulski said after her win. "You can get your preventive tests without a deductible and without a co-pay. Without hesitation, you will be able to get it."

Mikulski also holds the gavel on the Health, Education, Labor and Pensions Subcommittee on Children and Families, having previously chaired the Retirement and Aging panel. She says that one of her proudest accomplishments is having changed Medicaid law in the 1980s to allow people to protect certain assets while getting assistance in paying for a spouse's nursing home care.

As a member of the Select Intelligence Committee, Mikulski looks out for the National Security Agency, the eavesdropping arm of the spy community whose headquarters are in her state. Mikulski was one of 19 Democrats to side with a majority of Republicans in clearing a measure updating the warrantless surveillance laws for President George W. Bush in a 68-29 vote. Mikulski said the revisions to the Foreign Intelligence Surveillance Act would help law enforcement officials keep up with increasingly sophisticated terrorists.

"Terrorists remain on the hunt for U.S. vulnerabilities, using disposable phone cards, laptop computers and hundreds of different e-mail addresses — all in efforts to evade detection by our intelligence professionals," Mikulski said. The older version of the FISA law "made it nearly impossible for the U.S. to engage in 'techno-hot pursuit' of terrorists overseas."

She also looks out for her state in other ways. When Florida's Republican governor said in early 2011 that he didn't want federal funds for a high-speed rail project in his state, Mikulski was one of 10 senators who asked the Transportation Department to redirect the money to Maryland and other states in the Northeast Corridor.

Mikulski is a dependable Democratic vote, but she can display a certain stubbornness about making up her own mind on issues. When asked in 2010 how Democrats viewed a change in tax policy, she replied that she didn't know what her party as a group was thinking at the moment.

Responding to calls to more closely question government spending, Mikulski has increased the involvement of inspectors general in the appropriations process and she says she plans to take a tough stance on programs that report chronic cost overruns. She is considering a "three strikes" approach to programs funded by her appropriations bill, in which two warnings will be given, and then she might push to cancel those programs.

A 2007 report from the inspector general of the Justice Department infuriated Mikulski, with its revelations of the department paying high prices for food served at conferences, such as a widely reported $4 per Swedish meatball. While stressing that conferences can help law enforcement officials share information, she said that she will be watching to prevent that kind of extravagance in the future. She referred to this as a topic where "it sounds like Sen. Barb Mikulski meets Sen. Tom Coburn," referring to the Republican budget hawk from Oklahoma. "That's where we get a bad rap," Mikulski said. "You know, that's where, quite frankly, some of the folks who are cranky with government have every right to be cranky."

Mikulski's roots are in working-class east Baltimore. Her parents ran a grocery store called Willy's Market, across the street from their row house, opening early every morning so steel workers could buy lunch before their morning shift. Nearby, her Polish immigrant grandmother operated a bakery legendary for its jelly doughnuts and raisin bread.

She earned a master's degree in social work at the University of Maryland in 1965. When parts of her neighborhood were set ablaze after the 1968 assassination of Martin Luther King Jr., Mikulski delivered food to families, sometimes by riding atop a tank.

In the early 1970s, she jumped into a neighborhood battle to stop a highway project that would have leveled some Baltimore neighborhoods. At one point, she recalls, she jumped on a table and gave a fiery speech, saying, "The British couldn't take Fells Point, the termites couldn't take Fells Point and goddamn if we'll let the State Roads Commission take Fells Point!" to wild cheers from her audience. The battle against the highway project was successful, and Mikulski went on to win a city council seat in 1971.

Mikulski seized on the public backlash against Republicans in the post-Watergate election of 1974 by challenging Sen. Charles McC. Mathias Jr. She lost but positioned herself for 1976, when Democrat Paul S. Sarbanes gave up his seat as Baltimore's representative in the House to run for the Senate.

Mikulski won and went on to serve five terms in the House, becoming a champion of consumer causes. When Mathias retired in 1986, Mikulski won the race to succeed him, besting Republican Linda Chavez by 22 percentage points. She has not been seriously challenged since.

For years, Mikulski lived in a two-story Fells Point row house in Baltimore, commuting to the Capitol. In 1995, she was mugged as she walked from her car to her house, and the next year she moved to a "maintenance free" condo near Johns Hopkins University. "I am changing my address, not changing my roots," she told constituents.

Key Votes

2010

Pass budget reconciliation bill to modify overhauls of health care and federal student loan programs	YES
Proceed to disapproval resolution on EPA authority to regulate greenhouse gases	NO
Overhaul financial services industry regulation	YES
Limit debate to proceed to a bill to broaden campaign finance disclosure and reporting rules	YES
Limit debate on an extension of Bush-era income tax cuts for two years	YES
Limit debate on a bill to provide a path to legal status for some children of illegal immigrants	YES
Allow for a repeal of "don't ask, don't tell"	YES
Consent to ratification of a strategic arms reduction treaty with Russia	YES

2009

Prevent release of remaining financial industry bailout funds	NO
Make it easier for victims to sue for wage discrimination remedies	YES
Expand the Children's Health Insurance Program	YES
Limit debate on the economic stimulus measure	YES
Repeal District of Columbia firearms prohibitions and gun registration laws	NO
Limit debate on expansion of federal hate crimes law	YES
Strike funding for F-22 Raptor fighter jets	?

CQ Vote Studies

	PARTY UNITY		PRESIDENTIAL SUPPORT	
	SUPPORT	OPPOSE	SUPPORT	OPPOSE
2010	99%	1%	98%	2%
2009	99%	1%	99%	1%
2008	88%	12%	42%	58%
2007	94%	6%	42%	58%
2006	96%	4%	49%	51%
2005	98%	2%	35%	65%
2004	96%	4%	61%	39%
2003	97%	3%	44%	56%
2002	96%	4%	68%	32%
2001	98%	2%	66%	34%

Interest Groups

	AFL-CIO	ADA	CCUS	ACU
2010	100%	90%	27%	0%
2009	94%	95%	43%	0%
2008	100%	90%	63%	0%
2007	94%	85%	55%	0%
2006	93%	100%	42%	0%
2005	100%	90%	41%	5%
2004	100%	100%	56%	8%
2003	100%	90%	39%	15%
2002	100%	100%	47%	0%
2001	100%	95%	43%	12%

Sen. Benjamin L. Cardin (D)

Capitol Office
224-4524
cardin.senate.gov
509 Hart Bldg. 20510-2002; fax 224-1651

Committees
Budget
Environment & Public Works
    (Water & Wildlife - Chairman)
Finance
Foreign Relations
    (International Development - Chairman)
Small Business & Entrepreneurship

Residence
Baltimore

Born
Oct. 5, 1943; Baltimore, Md.

Religion
Jewish

Family
Wife, Myrna Edelman Cardin; two children (one deceased)

Education
U. of Pittsburgh, B.A. 1964 (economics); U. of Maryland, Baltimore, LL.B. 1967

Career
Lawyer

Political Highlights
Md. House, 1967-87 (Speaker, 1979-87); U.S. House, 1987-2007

ELECTION RESULTS

2006 GENERAL

Benjamin L. Cardin (D)	965,477	54.2%
Michael S. Steele (R)	787,182	44.2%
Kevin Zeese (GREEN)	27,564	1.5%

2006 PRIMARY

Benjamin L. Cardin (D)	257,545	43.7%
Kweisi Mfume (D)	238,957	40.5%
Josh Rales (D)	30,737	5.2%
Dennis F. Rasmussen (D)	10,997	1.9%

Previous Winning Percentages
2004 House Election (63%); 2000 House Election (76%); 1998 House Election (78%); 1996 House Election (67%); 1994 House Election (71%); 1992 House Election (74%); 1990 House Election (70%); 1988 House Election (73%); 1986 House Election (79%)

Elected 2006; 1st term

Cardin's regular-guy persona fits his wonky approach to public policy and helped him be named one of the "nicest senators" in Washingtonian magazine's survey of congressional staff. Cardin, who brought two decades of House experience to the Senate, sits on five committees and has been active on issues such as the environment and health care.

For the 112th Congress (2011-12) he added the Finance Committee to his portfolio.

His other committee assignments are varied: Foreign Relations, Budget, Small Business and Entrepreneurship, and Environment and Public Works. He dropped off the Judiciary Committee.

As chairman of the Environment panel's subcommittee on Water and Wildlife, Cardin led a congressional delegation in June 2010 to examine the damage caused by the spring 2010 Gulf of Mexico oil spill. "Oil was pretty much everywhere," he said at the time. "You truly can't comprehend the scale of the disaster until you see it firsthand." Cardin later cosponsored a bill to eliminate the $75 million cap on liability for damages from oil spills, which won committee approval but was not taken up on the Senate floor.

During Senate debate on global warming legislation in the 110th Congress (2007-08), Cardin added $171 million for public transportation, including funds for new rail transit systems, with the intent of curbing automobiles' greenhouse gas emissions and providing relief to the car-choked Washington suburbs. He also added an amendment authorizing more money to implement climate change policies. But the bill was pulled from the floor before a final vote, and the version of the legislation offered in the 111th Congress (2009-10) did not even make it to the Senate after winning House passage.

Cardin pays special attention to the Chesapeake Bay, working with home-state colleague Barbara A. Mikulski, a fellow Democrat, to include funding in the 2008 multi-year rewrite of farm policy to improve water quality and farm viability in the region. In 2010, he won unanimous approval from the Environment and Public Works Committee of a bill to authorize $1.5 billion in grants to restore the bay.

From his seat on the Budget Committee, Cardin supported President Obama's early legislative priorities, including the $787 billion economic stimulus bill, which he called "the greatest investment in America's future in over half a century." He called Obama's fiscal 2012 budget "a very credible plan on the spending side," but suggested at a Budget panel hearing in early 2011 that changes are necessary to the "outdated income tax structure we have."

When Florida's Republican governor announced that he would reject federal funds for a high-speed rail project in his state, Cardin joined other Northeast Corridor senators in asking the Transportation Department to redirect the money to their states.

Cardin was a vocal supporter of including a government-run program, or public option, in the health care overhaul enacted in 2010. He lost that fight but won inclusion of funding for oral health care and an amendment establishing the National Institute on Minority Health and Health Disparities within the National Institutes of Health.

As a Foreign Relations member, he says he has tried to be more skeptical about what the executive branch tells lawmakers. "I think prior to Iraq, the assumption always was that the piece of evidence we were receiving was substantiated," he said. "Now we're more likely to suggest that a specific piece of information may not lead to the conclusion that's in the document."

Cardin also co-chairs the U.S. arm of the Commission on Security and Cooperation in Europe, known as the Helsinki Commission, the world's largest regional security organization. In that capacity, Cardin led a congressional delegation in June 2009 to Belarus, where he urged President Alexander Lukashenka to release an imprisoned U.S. citizen on humanitarian grounds. "The president said he could make it happen, and it happened at the end of the day," Cardin recounts.

During the 110th Congress, Democrats on the Judiciary Committee gave Cardin responsibility for keeping tabs on voting rights and the Justice Department's Civil Rights Division. In 2009, he took over as chairman of the Terrorism and Homeland Security Subcommittee, which approved the reauthorization of intelligence-gathering provisions in the anti-terrorism law known as the Patriot Act and held hearings on closing the detention facility at Guantánamo Bay, Cuba.

Though a dependable Democratic vote, Cardin takes pride in being a lawmaker willing to work across party lines to develop consensus. In 2008, he teamed with Maine Republican Sen. Olympia J. Snowe on a proposal to create a group of "master teachers" who would get a break on their federal income taxes in exchange for working in substandard schools.

And as a member of the Ways and Means Committee when he served in the House, he developed a close relationship with Ohio Republican Rob Portman — the main conduit between the White House and GOP leaders during President George W. Bush's first term — who later became Bush's budget director and is now Cardin's Senate colleague. In the 108th Congress (2003-04), the two lawmakers developed an alternative to the president's plan to restructure Social Security and allow younger workers to divert a share of their payroll tax payments into personal retirement accounts.

Such endeavors didn't always sit well with House Democratic leaders. In 2006, Cardin was passed over for the top Democratic spot on the Ways and Means Subcommittee on Social Security after he said he was open to compromise on some GOP proposals for overhauling the program.

Cardin is a former "boy wonder" who entered the Maryland House of Delegates at age 23, before he had even graduated from the University of Maryland Law School. He was elected to a seat that had been held by his father and his uncle. Cardin went on to become the youngest House Speaker in Maryland in 100 years before being elected to a Baltimore-area U.S. House seat in 1986. His political hero is Theodore R. McKeldin, a GOP mayor of Baltimore and Maryland governor who helped build the city's urban and transportation infrastructure and who was among the first politicians to court the state's Jewish voters.

In 2006, after liberal longtime Sen. Paul S. Sarbanes announced his retirement, Cardin ran in a primary that included more than a dozen candidates. His chief competition was former Democratic Rep. Kweisi Mfume, a past NAACP president and longtime friend. Cardin narrowly won the September primary, 44 percent to 41 percent.

In the general election, he was up against another tough competitor — Lt. Gov. Michael S. Steele, Maryland's first black statewide elected official. The Republican tailored his TV and radio ads to black voters and brought in endorsements from several prominent black Democrats. But Cardin succeeded in tying Steele to Bush and won with 54 percent of the vote.

Cardin's family is close-knit and shares his interests — Myrna, his wife of more than 40 years, is among his most trusted advisers. The couple endured a tragedy in 1998 when their son Michael, 30, who worked as a volunteer with low-income Baltimoreans, committed suicide. "I look at what he was able to accomplish in a few years as a challenge to all of us to make the most of what we have," he said.

Key Votes

2010

Pass budget reconciliation bill to modify overhauls of health care and federal student loan programs	YES
Proceed to disapproval resolution on EPA authority to regulate greenhouse gases	NO
Overhaul financial services industry regulation	YES
Limit debate to proceed to a bill to broaden campaign finance disclosure and reporting rules	YES
Limit debate on an extension of Bush-era income tax cuts for two years	YES
Limit debate on a bill to provide a path to legal status for some children of illegal immigrants	YES
Allow for a repeal of "don't ask, don't tell"	YES
Consent to ratification of a strategic arms reduction treaty with Russia	YES

2009

Prevent release of remaining financial industry bailout funds	NO
Make it easier for victims to sue for wage discrimination remedies	YES
Expand the Children's Health Insurance Program	YES
Limit debate on the economic stimulus measure	YES
Repeal District of Columbia firearms prohibitions and gun registration laws	NO
Limit debate on expansion of federal hate crimes law	YES
Strike funding for F-22 Raptor fighter jets	YES

CQ Vote Studies

	PARTY UNITY		PRESIDENTIAL SUPPORT	
	SUPPORT	OPPOSE	SUPPORT	OPPOSE
2010	99%	1%	98%	2%
2009	99%	1%	99%	1%
2008	97%	3%	31%	69%
2007	97%	3%	37%	63%
2006	95%	5%	25%	75%
2005	95%	5%	22%	78%
2004	94%	6%	35%	65%
2003	93%	7%	24%	76%
2002	90%	10%	35%	65%
2001	89%	11%	35%	65%

Interest Groups

	AFL-CIO	ADA	CCUS	ACU
2010	100%	90%	27%	0%
2009	94%	95%	43%	0%
2008	100%	100%	63%	8%
2007	95%	95%	45%	0%
2006	100%	90%	40%	8%
2005	92%	95%	40%	0%
2004	100%	95%	43%	0%
2003	87%	90%	37%	20%
2002	100%	95%	55%	0%
2001	100%	100%	35%	4%

Rep. Andy Harris (R)

Capitol Office
225-5311
harris.house.gov
506 Cannon Bldg. 20515-2001; fax 225-0254

Committees
Natural Resources
Science, Space & Technology
   (Energy & Environment - Chairman)
Transportation & Infrastructure

Residence
Cockeysville

Born
Jan. 25, 1957; Brooklyn, N.Y.

Religion
Roman Catholic

Family
Wife, Sylvia "Cookie" Harris; five children

Education
U. of Pennsylvania, attended 1973-75; Johns Hopkins
U., B.A. 1977 (human biology), M.D. 1980, M.H.S. 1995
(health finance & management)

Military
Navy Reserve, 1988-2005

Career
Physician

Political Highlights
Md. Senate, 1999-2010 (Republican whip, 2003-06);
Republican nominee for U.S. House, 2008

ELECTION RESULTS

2010 GENERAL

Andy Harris (R)	155,118	54.1%
Frank Kratovil Jr. (D)	120,400	42.0%
Richard Davis (LIBERT)	10,876	3.8%

2010 PRIMARY

Andy Harris (R)	46,227	67.4%
Rob Fisher (R)	22,409	32.6%

Elected 2010; 1st term

As the first person from the Chesapeake Bay's western shore to win the 1st District in two decades and the first ever from Baltimore County, Harris doesn't fit the mold of the moderate Marylander.

The former state senator opposes abortion and gun control and favors opening the Arctic National Wildlife Refuge and the outer continental shelf to oil and gas production. He wants to make the Bush-era tax cuts permanent and eliminate earmarks. He favors cutting the size of government by, among other things, eliminating the Education Department.

A study by the conservative Heritage Action for America showed Harris voted for 90 percent of the non-security spending cuts offered during floor debate on a catchall spending bill for fiscal 2011.

A physician and former commander in the Navy Reserve, Harris attributes his concepts of governing to his family's story of immigration. Fleeing communism, his parents came to America from Eastern Europe after World War II and after his father spent time in a concentration camp in Siberia.

With a seat on the Natural Resources Committee, Harris wants to increase collaboration between state and federal agencies and make a priority of protecting Chesapeake Bay while preserving the Eastern Shore economy — poultry, fishing, agriculture and tourism — through private-sector job creation and cutting taxes. He could also have an impact as chairman of the Science, Space and Technology Subcommittee on Energy and Environment. He also sits on the Transportation and Infrastructure Committee.

Harris first faced Democratic Rep. Frank Kratovil Jr. in 2008, losing by less than 1 percentage point after winning a bruising primary against incumbent Republican Wayne Gilchrest. In the 2010 rematch, Harris topped Kratovil with 54 percent of the vote.

The new lawmaker, who voted early in the 112th Congress (2011-12) to repeal the health care overhaul enacted in 2010, caused a bit of stir when he complained that his health plan would not kick in for a month. Democrats were quick to yell hypocrisy; Harris said the episode was proof of the inefficiency of government-run health care.

Maryland 1

East — Eastern Shore, part of Anne Arundel County

The 1st includes the mostly rural Eastern Shore and some Anne Arundel County suburbs across the Chesapeake Bay. It crosses the Susquehanna River in northeastern Maryland and grabs chunks of Harford and Baltimore counties. The Eastern Shore, which holds about three-fifths of the district's population, has a steady agricultural base, relying mainly on vegetables, fruit and chicken breeding. Ocean City is a popular beach town on the Atlantic shore.

The central, more rural part of the Eastern Shore is solidly Republican. The northern counties, closer to Baltimore and Philadelphia, and the southern counties have larger working-class populations but do not factor as heavily in elections. Across the bay, the 1st includes some GOP-leaning parts of Anne Arundel, including the predominately

white, educated, upper-middle-class areas of Arnold, Severna Park and Millersville. Part of Baltimore's conservative northern suburbs also are included in the 1st.

Despite regional differences, all of the 1st's areas share a conservative bent that traditionally benefits Republicans. Every county wholly in the 1st supported Republican Robert L. Ehrlich Jr. in the 2010 gubernatorial race, and incumbent Democratic Sen. Barbara A. Mikulski lost in four counties here.

Major Industry
Agriculture, manufacturing, tourism

Military Bases
U.S. Naval Academy/Naval Station Annapolis, 592 military, 1,574 civilian (2011) (shared with the 3rd)

Cities
Bel Air South (unincorporated) (pt.), 43,284; Severna Park (unincorporated) (pt.), 32,736; Salisbury (pt.), 30,343

Notable
Wild ponies roam Assateague Island, a barrier island on the Atlantic Ocean.

Rep. C.A. Dutch Ruppersberger (D)

Capitol Office
225-3061
dutch.house.gov
2453 Rayburn Bldg. 20515; fax 225-3094

Committees
Armed Services
Select Intelligence - Ranking Member

Residence
Cockeysville

Born
Jan. 31, 1946; Baltimore, Md.

Religion
Methodist

Family
Wife, Kay Ruppersberger; two children

Education
U. of Maryland, attended 1963-67; U. of Baltimore,
J.D. 1970

Career
Lawyer; county prosecutor; collection agency owner

Political Highlights
Democratic nominee for Md. Senate, 1978; Baltimore
County Council, 1985-94; Baltimore County execu-
tive, 1994-2002

ELECTION RESULTS

2010 GENERAL

C.A. Dutch Ruppersberger (D)	134,133	64.2%
Marcelo Cardarelli (R)	69,523	33.3%
Lorenzo Gaztanaga (LIBERT)	5,090	2.4%

2010 PRIMARY

C.A. Dutch Ruppersberger (D)	42,262	74.0%
Raymond Atkins (D)	7,405	13.0%
Jeff Morris (D)	3,841	6.7%
Christopher C. Boardman (D)	3,575	6.3%

2008 GENERAL

C.A. Dutch Ruppersberger (D)	198,578	71.9%
Richard Pryce Matthews (R)	68,561	24.8%
Lorenzo Gaztanaga (LIBERT)	8,786	3.2%

Previous Winning Percentages
2006 (69%); 2004 (67%); 2002 (54%)

Elected 2002; 5th term

An affable former prosecutor and Baltimore County executive, Ruppersberger concentrates on what he calls the "operations" side of government,
with a focus on national security as a member of the Armed Services Committee and as top Democrat on the Select Committee on Intelligence.

Before Democrats lost the majority in the 2010 elections, he served as
chairman of the Select Intelligence Subcommittee on Technical and Tactical
Intelligence, which oversees the National Security Agency (NSA) as well as
the intelligence community's efforts to defend cyberspace.

A former appropriator — he lost that seat because of the Democratic
losses — Ruppersberger looks out for the intelligence and military assets
in his district, including the NSA, Fort George G. Meade and the Aberdeen
Proving Ground.

He also helped steer homeland security, defense and intelligence-related
funds to his district and has championed more spending for first-responders
(local fire, police and rescue squads).

Ruppersberger said he is looking forward to working with Republicans on
efforts to rein in federal spending. "We need to change directions, put the
economy first and balance the federal checkbook like all Americans do at
home," he said. But a study by the conservative Heritage Action for America
showed that Ruppersberger voted against every non-defense spending cut
offered during floor debate on a catchall spending bill for fiscal 2011.

"I agreed with some of the cuts contained in the spending bill that passed
the House . . . but we can't throw out the baby with the bathwater," he said.

He also has said he is open to cuts in intelligence and other national
security programs, including space programs and the Office of the Director
of National Intelligence.

Ruppersberger considers himself a practical politician who doesn't spend
a lot of time discussing ideology, preferring a results-oriented approach.

If he is on the House floor, chances are good that he is either congratulat-
ing a Marylander for an accomplishment or mourning the loss of a soldier
— and not debating for the benefit of C-SPAN's cameras.

Ruppersberger has been long willing to cross party lines to get things
done. Republican Peter Hoekstra of Michigan, who chaired the Intelligence
Committee when Ruppersberger joined it as a freshman, called him a "real
consensus-builder."

But he votes with his party on most issues — 97 percent of the time in
the 111th Congress (2009-10) when majorities of the two parties in the
House differed — and backed all the major initiatives of President Obama's
first years in office.

He criticized President George W. Bush's handling of the Iraq War, but
consistently supported funding legislation, saying "you must always support
your troops." He also split with a majority of his party to support a 2008 overhaul of the Foreign Intelligence Surveillance Act, although he had opposed
earlier FISA bills that contained fewer constraints on electronic spying.

"The NSA employees in my district need a clear law with a bright line
between legal and illegal surveillance activities, and this bill provides that,"
he said.

Ruppersberger, a grandfather, won a "Best of Congress" award in 2010
from Working Mother magazine. His office is noted for its family-friendly
policies, such as three months of paid maternity or paternity leave, com-
pressed workweeks, part-time schedules and telecommuting options.

He was born Charles Albert Ruppersberger III, but goes by Dutch. The son of a Baltimore manufacturing salesman and a schoolteacher, he said the doctor who delivered him described him as a "big, blond Dutchman." (His hair has since turned black.) As practical a politician as they come, Ruppersberger later adopted the nickname legally when he realized his last name was too long for a bumper sticker.

A good athlete as a youth, he played lacrosse at the University of Maryland and made the U.S. national team in 1967. During college summers, he was a lifeguard in Ocean City, Md., then worked his way through law school as an insurance claims adjuster.

Ruppersberger began his government career as a Baltimore County assistant state's attorney. While investigating a drug trafficking case in 1975, he was in a near-fatal car crash. He has said he devoted himself to public service thereafter at the urging of the doctor who saved his life at the University of Maryland's renowned Shock Trauma Center. He remains an avid supporter of the hospital, serving on the trauma center's board of visitors.

He lost a state Senate bid in 1978, but in 1985 he was appointed to finish a term on the Baltimore County Council, and was elected to the seat the following year.

In 1994, he was elected county executive and steered the county to triple-A bond ratings while building new schools, roads and parks.

Ruppersberger planned to run for governor in 2002 but was dogged by events that took place two years earlier. In 2000, he had aggressively pushed a bill to allow the county to condemn private property for urban revitalization. People in the affected areas fought back with a referendum that passed by a 2-to-1 ratio, an embarrassing setback for the county executive.

Then in November 2000, The Baltimore Sun reported he had steered government grants to an apartment rental firm with which he had personal business dealings. Ruppersberger called the report flawed and said he had broken no laws.

But he was too weakened politically to take on a primary fight against the well-financed Kathleen Kennedy Townsend, daughter of the late Sen. Robert F. Kennedy. House Democratic leader Steny H. Hoyer urged him to run instead in the newly redrawn 2nd District. Republicans put up former Rep. Helen Delich Bentley, who had represented the 2nd from 1985 to 1995. The new district lines, which brought in more Democratic voters, helped boost Ruppersberger to an almost 9 percentage point victory, while Townsend was losing the governor's race to Republican Rep. Robert L. Ehrlich Jr. Ruppersberger hasn't been seriously challenged since.

Key Votes

2010	
Overhaul the nation's health insurance system	YES
Allow for repeal of "don't ask, don't tell"	YES
Overhaul financial services industry regulation	YES
Limit use of new Afghanistan War funds to troop withdrawal activities	NO
Change oversight of offshore drilling and lift oil spill liability cap	YES
Provide a path to legal status for some children of illegal immigrants	YES
Extend Bush-era income tax cuts for two years	YES
2009	
Expand the Children's Health Insurance Program	YES
Provide $787 billion in tax cuts and spending increases to stimulate the economy	YES
Allow bankruptcy judges to modify certain primary-residence mortgages	YES
Create a cap-and-trade system to limit greenhouse gas emissions	YES
Provide $2 billion for the "cash for clunkers" program	YES
Establish the government as the sole provider of student loans	YES
Restrict federally funded insurance coverage for abortions in health care overhaul	NO

CQ Vote Studies

	PARTY UNITY		PRESIDENTIAL SUPPORT	
	SUPPORT	OPPOSE	SUPPORT	OPPOSE
2010	97%	3%	93%	7%
2009	97%	3%	96%	4%
2008	97%	3%	21%	79%
2007	96%	4%	10%	90%
2006	85%	15%	46%	54%

Interest Groups

	AFL-CIO	ADA	CCUS	ACU
2010	100%	80%	25%	0%
2009	100%	90%	40%	4%
2008	100%	90%	67%	4%
2007	96%	90%	63%	8%
2006	93%	85%	67%	24%

Maryland 2

Part of Baltimore and suburbs — Dundalk, Essex

The 2nd includes parts of northern and eastern Baltimore, suburbs on most sides of the city and most of the land east of Interstate 95 between Baltimore and the Susquehanna River, along the Chesapeake Bay coastline of Baltimore and Harford counties.

The district's Anne Arundel County portion, south of Baltimore, includes the Baltimore/Washington International Thurgood Marshall Airport and Fort George G. Meade, home of the National Security Agency and the U.S. Cyber Command. Fort Meade was assigned thousands of jobs following the 2005 round of the Base Realignment and Closure process and has completed construction projects to accommodate the arriving divisions. In eastern Baltimore County, the blue-collar industrial sector, including Dundalk, has struggled. The Sparrows Point steel plant is still a key employer, but steelworkers and local officials worry about the impact of sustained plant idling. Multiple recent sales of the plant, possible further consolidations, job losses, and health care and pension cuts are also concerns.

The district's northwest arm heads through the GOP-heavy northern suburbs but hooks west of Baltimore into largely African-American areas, including Randallstown, which has a core commercial center along state Route 26. Blacks overall make up one-third of the 2nd's population. Solidly Democratic voters in Baltimore County and Baltimore city, which together make up 70 percent of the district's population, push the 2nd into the Democratic column. Former Baltimore mayor Martin O'Malley, a Democrat, won more than 80 percent of the city's vote in his 2010 gubernatorial re-election run.

Major Industry
Defense, manufacturing, product distribution

Military Bases
Fort George G. Meade (Army), 11,961 military, 24,108 civilian; Aberdeen Proving Ground (Army), 2,600 military, 10,250 civilian (2007)

Cities
Baltimore (pt.), 111,499; Dundalk (unincorporated), 63,597; Essex (unincorporated), 39,262; Randallstown (unincorporated) (pt.), 30,151

Notable
Aberdeen is home to Cal Ripken Baseball, a youth division of the amateur Babe Ruth League.

Rep. John Sarbanes (D)

Capitol Office
225-4016
sarbanes.house.gov
2444 Rayburn Bldg. 20515-2003; fax 225-9219

Committees
Natural Resources
Science, Space & Technology

Residence
Towson

Born
May 22, 1962; Baltimore, Md.

Religion
Greek Orthodox

Family
Wife, Dina Sarbanes; three children

Education
Princeton U., A.B. 1984 (public & international affairs);
Harvard U., J.D. 1988

Career
Lawyer; state education consultant

Political Highlights
No previous office

ELECTION RESULTS

2010 GENERAL

John Sarbanes (D)	147,448	61.1%
Jim Wilhelm (R)	86,947	36.0%
Jerry McKinley (LIBERT)	5,212	2.2%

2010 PRIMARY

John Sarbanes (D)	54,710	83.0%
Michael Miller (D)	5,456	8.3%
John Kibler (D)	2,989	4.5%
Ryan Ludick (D)	1,425	2.2%
John M. Rea (D)	1,307	2.0%

2008 GENERAL

John Sarbanes (D)	203,711	69.7%
Thomas E. Harris (R)	87,971	30.1%

Previous Winning Percentages
2006 (64%)

Elected 2006; 3rd term

Like his father, who represented Maryland in the House and Senate for 36 years, Sarbanes has shown himself to be a loyal Democrat who sides with his party 99 percent of the time. But while Paul S. Sarbanes made his most lasting mark in financial regulation, his son has used a background in health care and education to begin carving his own niche in Congress.

Sarbanes said his approach to legislating is to engage citizens as full partners so they take ownership of an initiative. "By doing that, I think you open up a huge resource that's untapped right now," he said. "Government's responsibility is to create a structural framework that allows people, businesses, entrepreneurs to fully explore their potential."

That philosophy has manifested itself in support for initiatives that aid government employees and promote the idea of people working for the government or nonprofit organizations.

His student loan forgiveness bill, enacted in 2007 as part of a broader student aid measure, forgives debt for graduates who become government or nonprofit group employees for 10 years and make regular loan payments. President Obama highlighted the program in his 2010 State of the Union address; Sarbanes considers it his greatest legislative accomplishment.

Sarbanes also co-authored two bills promoting civic participation that were signed into law in 2009 as part of a measure that overhauled national service programs. One, which he introduced with Illinois Democrat Phil Hare, established a service corps of veterans to aid other veterans and the public; the second, introduced with Washington Democrat Jay Inslee, created a clean-energy corps to operate sustainable energy and housing projects.

Sarbanes brought his enthusiasm for civic engagement to the health care overhaul debate in 2009 and 2010 by advocating stronger preventive and primary care provisions. "I think when you do that you give ordinary citizens an opportunity to participate in their own care," he said. "That leads to more healthy living over time." He pushed for inclusion of a provision that authorizes a grant program for school-based health clinics to provide primary care to medically underserved children and families. He also wrote a provision creating a national commission to identify health care workforce shortages and backed others to expand investments in community health centers and redistribute residency positions to train primary care physicians.

Sarbanes won a seat on the Energy and Commerce Committee at the start of the 111th Congress (2009-10), but had to surrender it following Democrat losses in 2010. He'll still have a platform to promote his ideas on alternative energy and conservation as a member of the Science, Space and Technology Committee. He led House efforts to expand opportunities for the many federal employees in his area to "telework," or work remotely, to reduce automobile pollution and traffic congestion.

Sarbanes authored a measure to make interest on bonds that help homeowners and businesses install energy efficiency upgrades tax-free; that legislation was included on the U.S. Green Building Council's list of top 10 bills of the 111th Congress.

And he introduced legislation in each of the 110th (2007-08) and 111th Congresses to establish grant programs for environmental education at all grade levels; the measure passed the House in his first term, but was never taken up by the Senate. "The only way you can save the environment is by developing habits that millions of people exercise every day," he said.

Sarbanes further hopes to promote science and humanities education by incorporating new mandates into the reauthorization of the George W. Bush-era education law known as No Child Left Behind.

On the Natural Resources Committee, Sarbanes is an advocate for citizen — and government — stewardship of Chesapeake Bay. He introduced legislation, passed by the House in 2009, to reauthorize and boost funding for the Chesapeake Bay Gateways Network, which educates communities about their impact on the bay through a system of parks, refuges, museums, historic sites and trails.

Sarbanes is a purebred Baltimorean. Some of his earliest memories are of attending Orioles games at Memorial Stadium, just a few blocks from his childhood home in the Guilford-Waverly neighborhood, a comfortable middle-class enclave. His father was elected to the state legislature when John was 4 and entered Congress when he was 8.

Like his father, whose House seat he now occupies, Sarbanes was educated at Princeton University and Harvard Law School. He served as president of the Princeton University Democrats and co-chairman of the Harvard Law School Democrats. His father was a Rhodes scholar at Oxford; Sarbanes studied law and politics in Greece on a Fulbright scholarship.

After graduating from Harvard, where he met his wife, Dina, Sarbanes returned to Baltimore to clerk for U.S. District Judge J. Frederick Motz. He then spent 18 years representing hospitals and other medical providers at Baltimore's Venable LLP law firm, serving as the health care practice chairman during his final six years there. He also served as a board member for the Public Justice Center, a Baltimore organization providing legal assistance to the poor, for 15 years, and as a liaison to Baltimore City public schools for Maryland's superintendent for seven years.

Sarbanes got his shot at a House seat in 2006 when Democratic Rep. Benjamin L. Cardin launched his successful bid to succeed the senior Sarbanes, who was retiring from the Senate. There was intense interest in the seat, which has been the springboard for Maryland's three most recent senators — Sarbanes, Cardin and Democrat Barbara A. Mikulski. Eight candidates contested the primary, but the Sarbanes name trumped all; Sarbanes appeared alongside his father in ads and used his father's longtime motto of "fairness and opportunity" on his campaign literature.

In the November election, Sarbanes easily defeated Republican John White, an Annapolis marketing executive, with 64 percent of the vote. In 2008, he defeated Republican Thomas E. "Pinkston" Harris, a teacher from Baltimore, taking almost 70 percent.

Key Votes

2010

Overhaul the nation's health insurance system	YES
Allow for repeal of "don't ask, don't tell"	YES
Overhaul financial services industry regulation	YES
Limit use of new Afghanistan War funds to troop withdrawal activities	NO
Change oversight of offshore drilling and lift oil spill liability cap	YES
Provide a path to legal status for some children of illegal immigrants	YES
Extend Bush-era income tax cuts for two years	YES

2009

Expand the Children's Health Insurance Program	YES
Provide $787 billion in tax cuts and spending increases to stimulate the economy	YES
Allow bankruptcy judges to modify certain primary-residence mortgages	YES
Create a cap-and-trade system to limit greenhouse gas emissions	YES
Provide $2 billion for the "cash for clunkers" program	YES
Establish the government as the sole provider of student loans	YES
Restrict federally funded insurance coverage for abortions in health care overhaul	NO

CQ Vote Studies

	PARTY UNITY		PRESIDENTIAL SUPPORT	
	SUPPORT	OPPOSE	SUPPORT	OPPOSE
2010	99%	1%	95%	5%
2009	99%	1%	99%	1%
2008	99%	1%	16%	84%
2007	99%	1%	4%	96%

Interest Groups

	AFL CIO	ADA	CCUS	ACU
2010	100%	95%	25%	0%
2009	100%	100%	33%	0%
2008	100%	100%	61%	0%
2007	96%	100%	50%	0%

Maryland 3

Part of Baltimore; eastern Columbia; Annapolis

Like a Z-shaped lightning bolt, the 3rd District flashes through three of Maryland's large urban hubs — Baltimore, Columbia and Annapolis. Starting in traditionally Jewish suburbs northwest of Baltimore, the 3rd snakes east and south, grabbing northeastern suburbs and part of downtown by Fells Point and the stadiums for baseball's Orioles and football's Ravens. Many ethnic areas of eastern Baltimore are included in the district. The 3rd then twists south and west through suburban Arbutus, Linthicum Heights and Elkridge on its way to the eastern part of Columbia. Finally, the district moves southeast through Odenton and Crofton to Annapolis.

State and local governments provide jobs in Annapolis, which is both the state capital and the Anne Arundel County seat. Technology, financial services and health care push the economy of the Columbia area. Two key employers located in the neighboring 2nd District — Fort George G. Meade, near the 3rd's southwestern edge, and the Baltimore/Washington International Thurgood Marshall Airport, in the Linthicum area — lure defense-related firms to the region and employ many residents of the 3rd. Despite financial trouble for the Pimlico Race Course in northwestern Baltimore, its role as host of the Preakness Stakes, the second leg of horse racing's Triple Crown, has been secured by state legislation and new ownership.

The district has some GOP-leaning areas in Anne Arundel and Baltimore counties, but overall the 3rd supports Democrats for federal office. Barack Obama won 59 percent of the district's 2008 presidential vote.

Major Industry
Government, technology, defense

Military Bases
U.S. Naval Academy/Naval Station Annapolis, 592 military, 1,574 civilian (2011) (shared with the 1st)

Cities
Baltimore (pt.), 174,628; Glen Burnie (unincorporated) (pt.), 56,093; Columbia (unincorporated) (pt.), 47,173; Annapolis, 38,394

Notable
The Annapolis Historic District takes in more than 100 buildings from the 18th century — including the campus of St. John's College, itself a National Historic Landmark — and the City Dock.

Rep. Donna Edwards (D)

Capitol Office
225-8699
donnaedwards.house.gov
318 Cannon Bldg. 20515-2004; fax 225-8714

Committees
Ethics
Science, Space & Technology
Transportation & Infrastructure

Residence
Oxon Hill

Born
June 28, 1958; Yanceyville, N.C.

Religion
Baptist

Family
Divorced; one child

Education
Wake Forest U., B.A. 1980 (English); Franklin Pierce
Law Center, J.D. 1989

Career
Nonprofit executive director; lobbyist; lawyer; United
Nations publication editor; aeronautical company
project manager

Political Highlights
Sought Democratic nomination for U.S. House, 2006

ELECTION RESULTS

2010 GENERAL

Donna Edwards (D)	160,228	83.4%
Robert Broadus (R)	31,467	16.4%

2010 PRIMARY

Donna Edwards (D)	56,737	83.6%
Herman Taylor (D)	5,972	8.8%
George McDermott (D)	2,833	4.2%
Kwame Gyamfi (D)	2,355	3.5%

2008 GENERAL

Donna Edwards (D)	258,704	85.8%
Peter James (R)	38,739	12.8%
Thibeaux Lincecum (LIBERT)	3,384	1.1%

Previous Winning Percentages
2008 Special Election (81%)

Elected 2008; 2nd full term

Edwards is a liberal stalwart who arrived in Congress as a staunch critic of the Iraq and Afghanistan wars. She hasn't relented in her opposition to U.S. involvement in those conflicts, but has expanded her portfolio to focus on aiding transportation projects in her district.

Esquire Magazine named her one of the 10 best members of Congress in 2010, saying she possessed "an uncommon intelligence and legislative savvy." Edwards, the first African-American woman elected to the House from Maryland, made a bid to co-chair the Progressive Caucus in the 112th Congress (2011-12), losing out to Keith Ellison of Minnesota and Raúl M. Grijalva of Arizona.

She voted against the 2010 war funding bill, and when President Obama announced that his drawdown of U.S. forces in Iraq by August 2010 would leave behind as many as 50,000 troops, she questioned the strategy.

Edwards criticized Obama on another front in late 2010 over his plan for a two-year wage freeze for federal workers, many of whom live in her district.

But she has been a dependable Democratic vote on most issues; she sided with her party 99 percent of the time when majorities of Democrats and Republicans split during the 111th Congress (2009-10).

She backed the Democrats' health care overhaul, though not before losing out on her preference for inclusion of a government-run "public option." She called the law "a historic victory for the American people," and won inclusion of her provision that would bar insurers that institute "excessive" rate increases from the state exchanges created by the measure. "I was once one of those uninsured," she said on the House floor. "As a young mother, I became so sick I collapsed in a grocery store and was taken to an emergency room. Without health care [insurance] I was treated. I was one of those uncompensated, and now it's time for me to pay the American people back with a vote for comprehensive health care reform."

She was an enthusiastic supporter of the economic stimulus package enacted in 2009 and touts what she considers its many benefits for her district.

When she does break with her party's leaders, it is because she feels they are being too much like Republicans. In late 2008 she joined other liberals in opposing a $700 billion measure to assist the ailing financial services sector. She told The Baltimore Sun that lawmakers were given "a false set of choices" and that the legislation needed more protections for taxpayers. Though she remained critical of a reworked version, which became law, she said she decided to switch her vote after receiving assurances from Obama that he would address her concerns if elected president.

As a lawmaker, Edwards draws from her experience as a single mother and lawyer struggling to get by. "After I would go to work, I would drive around, maybe once, twice, three, four times a month to the various food pantries in the region," she said. "I'd be as embarrassed as all get-out because here I was college-educated, presumably a lawyer, not really practicing but trying to work, and a mom. And I had to go to a food pantry," she said.

She sits on the Transportation and Infrastructure Committee and has been able to push mass transit funding for two of her priorities: the Purple Line, a proposed 16-mile rapid-transit line extending from Bethesda, in Montgomery County, to New Carrollton, in Prince George's County; and a potential rail line across the Potomac River at the Woodrow Wilson Bridge.

On the Science, Space and Technology Committee she draws on her background as a project manager for Lockheed Martin Corp. at Goddard

Space Flight Center, located in the neighboring 5th District. She is the ranking member on the Investigations and Oversight Subcommittee.

She is a member of the Tom Lantos Human Rights Commission, a panel of lawmakers named for the late chairman of the House Foreign Affairs Committee. At a January 2009 hearing on human rights in China, she said, "I've been deeply concerned about the high rate of suicide among women in China, forced labor conditions and the inability to organize in factories where a lot of U.S. products are made."

She took on another, less enviable task in the 112th Congress as one of five Democrats — all new to the panel — serving on the Ethics Committee, which is called on to sit in judgment of fellow lawmakers accused of going astray of House rules.

Edwards is the second of six children raised by an Air Force officer and a stay-at-home mom. The family moved frequently before settling in the Washington suburbs for her senior year in high school.

She was elected class president when she attended high school in New Mexico and campaigned for Janet Napolitano, who was running for governor of Girls State, a weeklong program about government. Napolitano went on to be elected governor of Arizona and is now Homeland Security secretary.

Edwards volunteered on Jimmy Carter's 1976 presidential campaign and later Jesse Jackson's 1984 and 1988 presidential runs. On the campaign trail, she often talked about being a resident adviser in college and aiding a woman who had been battered by her boyfriend. She later became a volunteer in domestic violence shelters and helped found the National Network to End Domestic Violence.

She graduated from Wake Forest University with a degree in English, then worked for a U.N. publication and Lockheed Martin before attending Franklin Pierce Law Center in New Hampshire.

Edwards worked for Albert R. Wynn, a Democratic state senator in Maryland, after her second year in law school. Edwards later also campaigned for one of Wynn's early congressional races.

After completing law school in 1989 and a clerkship for D.C. Superior Court Judge Stephen Eilperin, Edwards worked at Public Citizen, a nonprofit organization that advocates changes in the campaign finance system. For the next 15 years, she worked for several nonprofit organizations.

She challenged Wynn in the 2006 primary, losing in a close race. She tried again in 2008, defeating him in the primary, then handily winning a special election called in June of that year after Wynn resigned from Congress to join a lobbying firm. She took 83 percent of the vote in winning re-election in 2010.

Key Votes

2010

Overhaul the nation's health insurance system	YES
Allow for repeal of "don't ask, don't tell"	YES
Overhaul financial services industry regulation	YES
Limit use of new Afghanistan War funds to troop withdrawal activities	YES
Change oversight of offshore drilling and lift oil spill liability cap	YES
Provide a path to legal status for some children of illegal immigrants	YES
Extend Bush-era income tax cuts for two years	NO

2009

Expand the Children's Health Insurance Program	YES
Provide $787 billion in tax cuts and spending increases to stimulate the economy	YES
Allow bankruptcy judges to modify certain primary-residence mortgages	YES
Create a cap-and-trade system to limit greenhouse gas emissions	YES
Provide $2 billion for the "cash for clunkers" program	YES
Establish the government as the sole provider of student loans	YES
Restrict federally funded insurance coverage for abortions in health care overhaul	NO

CQ Vote Studies

	PARTY UNITY		PRESIDENTIAL SUPPORT	
	SUPPORT	OPPOSE	SUPPORT	OPPOSE
2010	98%	2%	77%	23%
2009	99%	1%	94%	6%
2008	99%	1%	17%	83%

Interest Groups

	AFL-CIO	ADA	CCUS	ACU
2010	93%	95%	25%	5%
2009	100%	100%	33%	0%
2008	100%		58%	7%

Maryland 4

Inner Prince George's County; part of Montgomery County

The first suburban district in the nation with a black majority, the 4th includes Washington's eastern suburbs in Prince George's County and a sizable swath of northern Montgomery County. Democrats have a strong hold on the district's largely middle-class, black population.

The 4th's economy is built on small business and the spillover of technology companies from Montgomery County and the Northern Virginia suburbs. With a mostly white-collar workforce, the district includes major Prince George's County aerospace engineering, biotech and nanotech employers. The 4th's technology industries are bolstered by the University of Maryland and NASA's Goddard Space Flight Center (both nearby in the 5th).

Prince George's County is a national leader in black business formation, homeownership and education, but foreclosure rates in the county have remained high. Many county residents are federal employees who have moved out of Washington — more than 15 percent of the workforce here is employed by the federal government.

Public safety in Prince George's County has improved, but some areas of the county inside the Capital Beltway share Washington's problems of drug trafficking and violent crime.

Nearly 40 percent of the district's residents live in outer suburbs and exurbs found in Montgomery County, such as Burtonsville, Olney and Sandy Spring. The 4th's solid Democratic tendencies led voters to give Barack Obama 85 percent of the 2008 presidential vote there, his highest percentage in the state.

Major Industry
Retail, computers, technology, recreation

Military Bases
Andrews Air Force Base, 6,888 military, 1,079 civilian (2011); Adelphi Army Research Laboratory, 30 military, 1,912 civilian (2008)

Cities
Silver Spring (unincorporated) (pt.), 47,487; Germantown (unincorporated) (pt.), 43,009; Olney (unincorporated), 33,844

Notable
Air Force One is kept at Andrews Air Force Base.

Rep. Steny H. Hoyer (D)

Capitol Office
225-4131
hoyer.house.gov
1705 Longworth Bldg. 20515-2005; fax 225-4300

Committees
No committee assignments

Residence
Mechanicsville

Born
June 14, 1939; Manhattan, N.Y.

Religion
Baptist

Family
Widowed; three children

Education
U. of Maryland, B.S. 1963 (political science);
Georgetown U., J.D. 1966

Career
Lawyer

Political Highlights
Md. Senate, 1967-79 (president, 1975-79); sought
Democratic nomination for lieutenant governor,
1978; Md. Board of Higher Education, 1978-81

ELECTION RESULTS

2010 GENERAL

Steny H. Hoyer (D)	155,110	64.3%
Charles J. Lollar (R)	83,575	34.6%
H. Gavin Shickle (LIBERT)	2,578	1.1%

2010 PRIMARY

Steny H. Hoyer (D)	58,717	85.7%
Andrew Gall (D)	6,682	9.7%
Sylvanus G. Bent (D)	3,147	4.6%

2008 GENERAL

Steny H. Hoyer (D)	253,854	73.6%
Collins Bailey (R)	82,631	24.0%
Darlene H. Nicholas (LIBERT)	7,829	2.3%

Previous Winning Percentages
2006 (83%); 2004 (69%); 2002 (69%); 2000 (65%);
1998 (65%); 1996 (57%); 1994 (59%); 1992 (53%);
1990 (81%); 1988 (79%); 1986 (82%); 1984 (72%);
1982 (80%); 1981 Special Election (55%)

Elected 1981; 15th full term

Within the House Democratic leadership, the silver-haired Hoyer serves as a master tactician and a unifying force for the caucus. He prods the party toward the center on some issues, but on bigger items he typically presents a united front with his boss and former rival, Minority Leader Nancy Pelosi of California.

Even as the Democratic electoral disaster of 2010 claimed the party's majority and inspired a rump rebellion against Pelosi, Hoyer deflected suggestions that he nudge aside his boss. Settling in as minority whip, he said his ties to the fiscally conservative Blue Dog Coalition of House Democrats and Pelosi's deep roots in the liberal wing make for a balanced team. "We do complement one another," he said.

In trademark fashion, Hoyer helped prod the health care overhaul along by brokering a 2009 accord among three committee chairmen. In early 2010, Hoyer called for pragmatism: "You know me: If you can't do a whole, doing part is also good." He later joined Pelosi and President Obama to push for a comprehensive law.

On the Afghanistan War, Hoyer rallied support for a temporary increase in troops, while fending off antiwar initiatives such as a nonbinding resolution calling for a quick troop withdrawal that was defeated in March 2010. Hoyer said he backed the "limited strategy of counterinsurgency with withdrawals set to begin in 2011."

Hoyer's independent streak surfaces in some caucus races and budget debates. After the 2008 elections, he backed the unsuccessful bid of John D. Dingell of Michigan to retain the Energy and Commerce gavel when challenged by Henry A. Waxman of California, a Pelosi ally. In 2010 he opposed his party's planned across-the-board Medicare premium freeze, preferring one targeted at lower-income recipients. Despite such dissents, Hoyer helped Pelosi move key priorities in the 111th Congress (2009-10) such as the $787 billion economic stimulus law and the House-passed cap-and-trade system for carbon emissions allowances.

For his party's base, Hoyer serves as a champion of the poor and for civil rights initiatives, including a measure to allow openly gay people to serve in the military, which was enacted in late 2010. For moderates, Hoyer pushed for pay-as-you-go mandates and Obama's National Commission on Fiscal Responsibility and Reform, vowing to back House votes on the panel's recommendations — if they first pass the Senate. The recommendations never reached the floor of either chamber.

Hoyer's success as a dealmaker and largesse as a Democratic rainmaker — with one of the House's biggest leadership political action committees — have cemented his status in the caucus. He has also helped empower his fellow Marylanders — three hold the title of ranking Democrat on committees, and one of those three, Chris Van Hollen, twice led the Democratic Congressional Campaign Committee, the party's campaign arm in the House.

As majority leader in 2009, Hoyer helped achieve a high level of voting unity among Democrats, just shy of the high marks in each of the two prior years, and the figure dipped only slightly in 2010.

At the start of the 112th Congress (2011-12), he showed unity with much of the caucus in opposing every non-defense spending cut offered during floor debate on a catchall spending bill for fiscal 2011, according to a study by the conservative Heritage Action for America. Of the 192 Democrats in the chamber, 142 voted for none or only one of the 21 non-security spending cuts.

After Democrats captured the House in the 2006 elections, Hoyer won the majority leader post. Pelosi, then Speaker, vigorously supported John P. Murtha of Pennsylvania, whose 2005 conversion to the anti-Iraq War cause helped ignite legislative efforts to end U.S. involvement. But Hoyer, who has raised millions of dollars for colleagues' campaigns and built a loyal following during his rise, trounced Murtha.

That vote was just one episode in a long-running Pelosi-Hoyer relationship that veers between cooperation and rivalry. The two are almost the same age and have held a succession of similar jobs as congressional aides, appropriators and caucus leaders. Pelosi, a Maryland native, first met Hoyer in the early 1960s when they both worked for their state's Democratic senator, Daniel B. Brewster.

Almost 40 years later, in 2001, the San Francisco liberal defeated Hoyer for the Democratic whip post in his second try for the position. After the first loss, to David E. Bonior of Michigan, Hoyer was elected in 1989 as caucus chairman, at the time the fourth-highest job among House Democrats. When Pelosi was elected minority leader after the 2002 elections, Hoyer won the minority whip's post.

Hoyer, a graduate of the University of Maryland who was selected "outstanding male graduate" in 1963, said he was moved toward politics by hearing President John F. Kennedy tell a college crowd that public service is a noble calling. But while other Kennedy acolytes, including Pelosi, moved to the left, Hoyer remained a centrist with a more muscular approach to foreign policy.

Hoyer was born in New York City, the son of a Danish immigrant who abandoned his family when Hoyer was 9. His stepfather was in the Air Force and his mother worked at the Navy Federal Credit Union. He spent much of his childhood in Florida, but his stepfather's transfer to Andrews Air Force Base brought the family to Maryland when Hoyer was in high school.

In 1959, Hoyer was a public relations major when he heard then-Sen. Kennedy speak. He switched to political science, went to law school and landed the job with Brewster. In 1966, at age 27, he was elected to the Maryland Senate. Two terms later he became its youngest president.

Hoyer lost a 1978 primary race for lieutenant governor. Three years later, he revived his career by claiming the 5th District seat in a special election after Democratic Rep. Gladys Noon Spellman fell ill. He held the seat easily until redistricting in the 1990s added a conservative swath of southern Maryland. He got 53 percent of the vote in 1992, but has not fallen below 64 percent since 1996.

Key Votes

2010

Overhaul the nation's health insurance system	YES
Allow for repeal of "don't ask, don't tell"	YES
Overhaul financial services industry regulation	YES
Limit use of new Afghanistan War funds to troop withdrawal activities	NO
Change oversight of offshore drilling and lift oil spill liability cap	YES
Provide a path to legal status for some children of illegal immigrants	YES
Extend Bush-era income tax cuts for two years	YES

2009

Expand the Children's Health Insurance Program	YES
Provide $787 billion in tax cuts and spending increases to stimulate the economy	YES
Allow bankruptcy judges to modify certain primary-residence mortgages	YES
Create a cap-and-trade system to limit greenhouse gas emissions	YES
Provide $2 billion for the "cash for clunkers" program	YES
Establish the government as the sole provider of student loans	YES
Restrict federally funded insurance coverage for abortions in health care overhaul	NO

CQ Vote Studies

	PARTY UNITY		PRESIDENTIAL SUPPORT	
	SUPPORT	OPPOSE	SUPPORT	OPPOSE
2010	99%	1%	98%	2%
2009	99%	1%	97%	3%
2008	99%	1%	18%	82%
2007	98%	2%	8%	92%
2006	92%	8%	27%	73%

Interest Groups

	AFL CIO	ADA	CCUS	ACU
2010	100%	90%	14%	0%
2009	100%	100%	40%	0%
2008	100%	90%	67%	0%
2007	100%	90%	55%	4%
2006	100%	90%	40%	4%

Maryland 5

Outer Prince George's County; southern Maryland

The 5th includes part of Prince George's County, southern Anne Arundel County and all of the southern counties of Charles, Calvert and St. Mary's. The mix of liberals in Prince George's County and conservative Democrats and Republicans throughout much of the rest of the district gives the 5th a broad array of political interests. The tri-county's Southern rural character has begun to erode as traditional tobacco farming interests have given way to empty barns and subdivisions.

High-tech and government jobs, both in Prince George's County and in Southern Maryland, keep the economy stable. The district's proximity to Washington, and jobs near Annapolis (the state capital), gives the 5th the nation's highest percentage of residents who are government workers (29 percent). Many residents and companies have migrated from the Washington metropolitan area to the southern counties, attracted by the abundance of land and the military presence. St. Mary's, Charles and Calvert rank first, second and fourth among Maryland's 23 counties for population growth since 2000, and the new density has led to traffic problems as portions of the

workforce commute north to Washington.

Prince George's County, which accounts for nearly half the district's population and almost 60 percent of its registered Democrats, includes many liberal black communities as well as College Park, home of the University of Maryland's main campus. Republicans hold a slight registration edge among the 5th's Anne Arundel residents, but Democrats have the advantage elsewhere, and their statewide and federal candidates do well in the district. In the 2008 presidential election, Barack Obama won the district handily, taking 65 percent of the vote.

Major Industry
Defense, agriculture, technology

Military Bases
Naval Air Station Patuxent River, 1,300 military, 6,214 civilian; Naval Support Facility Indian Head, 558 military, 2,392 civilian (2011)

Cities
Waldorf (unincorporated), 67,752; Bowie (pt.), 51,002; Clinton (unincorporated) (pt.), 35,968; College Park, 30,413

Notable
NASA Goddard Space Flight Center is based in Greenbelt; the College Park Airport, established in 1909, is the world's oldest continuously operating airport.

Rep. Roscoe G. Bartlett (R)

Capitol Office
225-2721
bartlett.house.gov
2412 Rayburn Bldg. 20515-2006; fax 225-2193

Committees
Armed Services
  (Tactical Air & Land Forces - Chairman)
Science, Space & Technology
Small Business

Residence
Frederick

Born
June 3, 1926; Moreland, Ky.

Religion
Seventh-Day Adventist

Family
Wife, Ellen Bartlett; 10 children (one deceased)

Education
Columbia Union College, B.S. 1947 (theology &
biology); U. of Maryland, M.S. 1948 (physiology), Ph.D.
1952 (physiology)

Career
Farmer; biomedical engineer; scientific research
company owner; real estate developer; professor

Political Highlights
Sought Republican nomination for U.S. Senate, 1980;
Republican nominee for U.S. House, 1982

ELECTION RESULTS

2010 GENERAL

Roscoe G. Bartlett (R)	148,820	61.4%
Andrew James Duck (D)	80,455	33.2%
Dan Massey (LIBERT)	6,816	2.8%
Michael Reed (CNSTP)	5,907	2.4%

2010 PRIMARY

Roscoe G. Bartlett (R)	49,056	69.8%
Joseph T. Krysztoforski (R)	11,124	15.8%
Steve Taylor (R)	4,822	6.9%
Seth Edward Wilson (R)	3,860	5.5%

2008 GENERAL

Roscoe G. Bartlett (R)	190,926	57.8%
Jennifer P. Dougherty (D)	128,207	38.8%
Gary W. Hoover Sr. (LIBERT)	11,060	3.3%

Previous Winning Percentages
2006 (59%); 2004 (67%); 2002 (66%); 2000 (61%);
1998 (63%); 1996 (57%); 1994 (66%); 1992 (54%)

Elected 1992; 10th term

Bartlett's libertarian streak can make him a bit hard to pin down. A member of both the conservative Republican Study Committee and the Tea Party Caucus, he has often opposed his party's leadership, especially on energy policy and anti-terrorism measures. He points to his strong religious beliefs and a strict reading of the Constitution as the basis for his political views.

Bartlett was 66 when first elected to the House in 1992. His résumé shows a background as a scientist, inventor, teacher, businessman and farmer. He exudes a laid-back, folksy manner and styles himself a citizen-legislator.

Bartlett's doctorate in physiology makes him one of the few scientists in Congress, and he applies his background assiduously as a member of the Science, Space and Technology Committee. He wants to see more students specialize in math and science, and he donates scholarship money for residents of his district who major in math, science or engineering at colleges there.

His background in science informs his views on energy policy. Bartlett became a crusader on behalf of energy alternatives to petroleum long before oil prices soared and being "green" became fashionable. He was the first in Congress to drive a hybrid car, in which he commutes the 50 miles from his farmhouse in Frederick, which is heated by solar energy and a wood stove.

Bartlett is often the first to mention reducing consumption as a policy goal. He gives frequent after-hours speeches on the House floor explaining "peak oil," an idea to which he subscribes; it suggests the world is nearing a point at which global demand for oil will exceed production.

A former small-business owner, Bartlett also sits on the Small Business Committee. He opposed President Obama's $787 billion economic stimulus bill in early 2009, saying tax breaks would be more effective in boosting economic growth. He also voted against President George W. Bush's $700 billion financial industry rescue package in fall 2008, the only member of the Maryland delegation to oppose the second version of the plan, which became law.

Critics claimed the plan rewards bad behavior with help from the federal government. "We don't have the kind of money to do that, and now it's a debt we have passed on to our kids," he told the Washington Examiner in 2008.

A member of the Armed Services Committee, he was the top Republican on its Tactical Air and Land Forces panel in the 111th Congress (2009-10) and chairs the subcommittee in the 112th (2011-12).

He has taken up as a cause developing defenses against a potential electromagnetic pulse attack, and he helped establish a commission to study the threat in 2006.

Bartlett has also been a proponent of building an alternative engine for the F-35 Joint Strike Fighter jet, going so far as to suggest at a February 2011 hearing that the Pentagon was spreading misinformation about the program. The Pentagon has long said it did not want the second engine, and the House voted in early 2011 to cut off funding for it.

Showing his libertarian side, he has said he regrets his 2001 vote for the anti-terrorism law known as the Patriot Act, which gave the government new powers to track, arrest and prosecute suspected terrorists. "Probably the least patriotic thing I've done since I got here," he lamented in an interview several months later. In 2011, he voted against extending expiring provisions of the law.

Bartlett was also an early GOP critic of Bush's decision to detain alleged enemy combatants at the U.S. prison at Guantánamo Bay, Cuba. He said the facility has hurt America's image abroad.

Bartlett used his perch on the Armed Forces Committee to chastise supporters of the Democrats' health care overhaul, enacted in 2010, over changes it made to coverage for members of the military. He voted against the initial and final versions of the bill, and to repeal the law in early 2011.

Earlier in his career, Bartlett made headlines with his defense initiatives. He fought a 1994 Pentagon move to integrate men and women in housing and basic training, vowing to prevent a "powder puff" military. In 2010, he opposed a House measure to reverse the military's "don't ask, don't tell" policy, citing opposition from current members of the armed services. In 1996, he authored a provision to ban sale of "lascivious" materials, such as pornographic magazines, on military bases — a measure the courts later found unconstitutional.

Bartlett was born on his grandfather's farm in Kentucky. His father worked as a tenant farmer in western Pennsylvania during the Great Depression, but refused to take any assistance from the government during those hard times, fostering Bartlett's own devotion to self-sufficiency. He originally intended to become a minister but instead pursued physiology at the University of Maryland.

Bartlett is a Seventh-day Adventist, a group with roots in the apocalyptic Millerite movement of the mid-19th century's Second Great Awakening. He holds strong religious beliefs and displays the Ten Commandments in his office beside a mural of the first prayer held in Congress.

Bartlett taught in California and Washington, D.C., and did research for the National Institutes of Health and the Navy's School of Aviation Medicine, where his mechanical skill led him into engineering. He holds 20 patents, including those for components found in breathing equipment used by pilots, astronauts and rescue workers.

Bartlett was honored in 1999 for his lifetime achievements by the American Institute of Aeronautics and Astronautics.

In 1961, Bartlett moved to a dairy farm in Frederick County, which he operated while working at the Johns Hopkins Applied Physics Laboratory in Howard County. He later entered the homebuilding business.

He made an unsuccessful House bid in 1982, then a decade later narrowly won a three-way GOP primary. He expected to face conservative Democrat Beverly B. Byron, a seven-term incumbent who had defeated him almost 3-to-1 in that first bid.

But Byron lost the Democratic primary to former state delegate Thomas H. Hattery, whom Bartlett then beat by 8 percentage points. His subsequent victories have been relatively easy.

Key Votes

2010

Overhaul the nation's health insurance system	NO
Allow for repeal of "don't ask, don't tell"	NO
Overhaul financial services industry regulation	NO
Limit use of new Afghanistan War funds to troop withdrawal activities	NO
Change oversight of offshore drilling and lift oil spill liability cap	NO
Provide a path to legal status for some children of illegal immigrants	NO
Extend Bush-era income tax cuts for two years	YES

2009

Expand the Children's Health Insurance Program	NO
Provide $787 billion in tax cuts and spending increases to stimulate the economy	NO
Allow bankruptcy judges to modify certain primary-residence mortgages	NO
Create a cap-and-trade system to limit greenhouse gas emissions	NO
Provide $2 billion for the "cash for clunkers" program	NO
Establish the government as the sole provider of student loans	NO
Restrict federally funded insurance coverage for abortions in health care overhaul	YES

CQ Vote Studies

	PARTY UNITY		PRESIDENTIAL SUPPORT	
	SUPPORT	OPPOSE	SUPPORT	OPPOSE
2010	95%	5%	27%	73%
2009	90%	10%	18%	82%
2008	94%	6%	65%	35%
2007	90%	10%	75%	25%
2006	85%	15%	77%	23%

Interest Groups

	AFL-CIO	ADA	CCUS	ACU
2010	0%	0%	100%	92%
2009	10%	5%	93%	96%
2008	0%	15%	78%	96%
2007	8%	15%	80%	88%
2006	14%	25%	80%	84%

Maryland 6

North and west — Frederick, Hagerstown

The 6th reaches across the northern tier of the state from Western Maryland to the Susquehanna River. It takes in all of Garrett, Allegany, Washington, Frederick and Carroll counties, as well as large portions of Baltimore and Harford counties and a small, exurban corner of Montgomery County. The 6th's rural tradition and conservative lean benefits the GOP.

Frederick and Carroll counties grew economically over the last decade, as new residents fled urban and inner suburban areas in Baltimore and Washington, D.C. Frederick County has military, government, education and manufacturing industries, but lost hundreds of jobs in 2010 when a major BP Solar facility closed. Carroll retains an agricultural feel, and low unemployment and only moderate rates of new homebuilding insulated the county from recent economic downturns.

The three western counties are less populous and have a strong conservative bent. The decades-long demise of the old-line manufacturing industry hurt much of the Appalachian Mountain area, but the region still helps the 6th have the state's highest percentage of blue-collar workers.

Hagerstown, the largest city in Washington County, serves as a junction of several highways, acting as a hub between the Appalachians and the highly populated Mid-Atlantic region. Nestled in the mountains, Allegany County is slightly more than two hours from Baltimore, Washington or Pittsburgh. Allegany and Garrett counties struggle and have become dependent on tourism as companies have closed their operations here. Several business parks remain largely vacant.

The 6th also includes northern portions of Baltimore and Harford counties, where Republicans and conservative Democrats reign. The 6th gave John McCain 58 percent of its presidential vote in 2008.

Major Industry
Technology, manufacturing, agriculture, tourism

Military Bases
Fort Detrick (Army), 1,459 military, 3,800 civilian (2011)

Cities
Frederick, 65,239; Hagerstown, 39,662; Eldersburg (unincorporated), 30,531; Cumberland, 20,859; Westminster, 18,590

Notable
Camp David, the president's retreat, is located in Frederick County.

Rep. Elijah E. Cummings (D)

Capitol Office
225-4741
www.house.gov/cummings
2235 Rayburn Bldg. 20515-2007; fax 225-3178

Committees
Oversight & Government Reform - Ranking Member
Transportation & Infrastructure
Joint Economic

Residence
Baltimore

Born
Jan. 18, 1951; Baltimore, Md.

Religion
Baptist

Family
Wife, Maya Rockeymoore Cummings; three children

Education
Howard U., B.A. 1973 (political science); U. of Maryland, J.D. 1976

Career
Lawyer

Political Highlights
Md. House, 1983-96 (Speaker pro tempore, 1995)

ELECTION RESULTS

2010 GENERAL

Elijah E. Cummings (D)	152,669	75.2%
Frank Mirabile Jr. (R)	46,375	22.8%
Scott Spencer (LIBERT)	3,814	1.9%

2010 PRIMARY

Elijah E. Cummings (D)	59,649	91.0%
Charles U. Smith (D)	5,884	9.0%

2008 GENERAL

Elijah E. Cummings (D)	227,379	79.5%
Michael T. Hargadon (R)	53,147	18.6%
Ronald Owens-Bey (LIBERT)	5,214	1.8%

Previous Winning Percentages
2006 (98%); 2004 (73%); 2002 (74%); 2000 (87%);
1998 (86%); 1996 (83%); 1996 Special Election (81%)

Elected 1996; 8th full term

A trailblazing black politician in Maryland government turned determined legislator in Congress, Cummings has become a powerful force on Capitol Hill. He is a player in major legislative debates and a willing spokesman for the Democrats in even the most hostile forums.

One of those forums is the Oversight and Government Reform Committee, where Cummings is the ranking Democrat. He beat out New Yorker Carolyn Maloney for the spot in the 112th Congress (2011-12) after former Chairman Edolphus Towns of New York announced he would not take another turn at the top of the panel. Cummings was the choice of the party leadership for the spot, reflecting his growing influence. He is viewed as a prime contender for a future leadership post.

Cummings quickly made it clear that he is more than willing to butt heads with California Republican Darrell Issa, chairman of the typically contentious committee.

When Issa laid out his agenda for the new Congress, Cummings said he wouldn't stand for any "witch hunts" or "fishing expeditions." That was before lawmakers had even convened. Once they got into the same hearing room, the pair sparred over whether Democrats would have to be consulted on issuing subpoenas, on witness lists — even on opening statements.

He was no less persistent over the plight of ailing homeowners after the credit crisis struck in 2008. His efforts led to the inclusion, in a new financial regulatory overhaul law enacted in 2010, of a $1 billion fund from which struggling homeowners could apply for low-interest bridge loans to help them stay current on their mortgage payments.

"America has gained a large amount of its reputation by the fact that we come to the rescue of those who are going through difficulties. That's our moral authority," he said.

Cummings also authored three other provisions of the law. They require lenders to notify borrowers of the consequences of refinancing or purchasing a home equity loan, creditors to disclose their policies regarding the acceptance of partial payments for a residential mortgage loan and the Treasury Department to provide state-by-state breakdowns of the conditions banks are asking of struggling borrowers when borrowers seek to modify their existing loans.

His success there gave Cummings some peace of mind following the events of late 2008, when the George W. Bush administration asked Congress to support a $700 billion plan to rescue the faltering financial system. Cummings initially balked, saying the bill offered little to help his constituents. He changed his position after receiving a plea from the Democratic presidential nominee, Sen. Barack Obama of Illinois, and voted for the bill when it was brought up a second time.

Cummings clearly wasn't happy about it. He spent much of the next two years grilling corporate executives and federal regulators at Oversight and Government Reform Committee hearings about why the financial markets had veered off a cliff, as well as Obama administration officials about how they allowed some of the rescued firms to hand out generous bonuses. His dismay grew as he hosted seminars in his district on helping homeowners avoid foreclosure — they repeatedly drew large crowds.

Cummings' behind-the-scenes role wasn't so integral in the health care debate, which ultimately yielded another major overhaul in the spring of 2010. But in each case, Cummings was visible. He appeared repeatedly on television, often taking his case to Fox News. In every case, he was an adamant defender of the Democratic Party's position.

Cummings also oversees Baltimore's bustling port, having served as chairman of the Transportation and Infrastructure Subcommittee on Coast Guard and Maritime Transportation in the 111th Congress (2009-10). In 2010, Congress passed and President Obama signed into law a measure — much of it Cummings' handiwork — that reauthorized Coast Guard programs and overhauled the service's procurement practices in light of continuing problems with the effort to modernize its fleet.

To his disappointment, Cummings failed to persuade senators to require applicants to the Coast Guard Academy to have a nomination from their congressman, as is the case with other military service academies. Cummings had included such a provision in the House version of the bill, arguing that it would increase minority enrollment at the academy.

Though an opponent of U.S. involvement in Iraq and Afghanistan — Cummings took a rare vote in defiance of his caucus and President Obama in July 2010 when he opposed a $37 billion bill to pay for the wars — he is nonetheless well-known in his district for promoting military service. He sends staffers to local schools every year to encourage high school students to seek his nomination to the academies.

Born in Baltimore, Cummings was one of seven children of former sharecroppers who had migrated from South Carolina. "We did not have many opportunities. . . . We did not play on grass. We played on asphalt," he recalled of his childhood. But he was set on a productive course by "two very strong parents," who scrimped and saved to buy their own home in a city neighborhood that was integrating.

He graduated Phi Beta Kappa from Howard University in Washington, D.C., where he was also student government president. He said his mother was hesitant about attending his graduation ceremony because she did not want to embarrass her son in front of "all those sophisticated people" at Howard. Cummings told her he would be honored to have her there.

He then earned a law degree from the University of Maryland and six years later was elected to the Maryland House. In 13 years there, he rose to the chamber's second-ranking position, at the time the highest Maryland office ever held by an African-American.

In 1996, he outpaced 26 other Democrats and five Republicans to replace Democrat Kweisi Mfume, who resigned his House seat early to become president of the NAACP. Since then, Cummings has won re-election easily.

Key Votes

2010

Overhaul the nation's health insurance system	YES
Allow for repeal of "don't ask, don't tell"	YES
Overhaul financial services industry regulation	YES
Limit use of new Afghanistan War funds to troop withdrawal activities	YES
Change oversight of offshore drilling and lift oil spill liability cap	YES
Provide a path to legal status for some children of illegal immigrants	YES
Extend Bush-era income tax cuts for two years	NO

2009

Expand the Children's Health Insurance Program	YES
Provide $787 billion in tax cuts and spending increases to stimulate the economy	YES
Allow bankruptcy judges to modify certain primary-residence mortgages	YES
Create a cap-and-trade system to limit greenhouse gas emissions	YES
Provide $2 billion for the "cash for clunkers" program	YES
Establish the government as the sole provider of student loans	YES
Restrict federally funded insurance coverage for abortions in health care overhaul	NO

CQ Vote Studies

	PARTY UNITY		PRESIDENTIAL SUPPORT	
	SUPPORT	OPPOSE	SUPPORT	OPPOSE
2010	99%	1%	90%	10%
2009	98%	2%	97%	3%
2008	99%	1%	12%	88%
2007	98%	2%	3%	97%
2006	96%	4%	23%	77%

Interest Groups

	AFL-CIO	ADA	CCUS	ACU
2010	100%	95%	13%	0%
2009	100%	100%	40%	0%
2008	100%	100%	50%	5%
2007	96%	100%	50%	0%
2006	100%	100%	33%	8%

Maryland 7

Downtown Baltimore; part of Columbia

The 7th takes in both the largely poor neighborhoods of West Baltimore and much of downtown, with the bustling retail center of the Inner Harbor. The district then heads west to include Baltimore County's middle-class southwestern suburbs and the bulk of Howard County, including the western portion of Columbia, a liberal-leaning planned community between Baltimore and Washington.

Efforts to improve Baltimore's poor neighborhoods have been slow, and urban problems — such as crime, drug abuse, teen pregnancy and unemployment — prompted many of the city's middle-class residents to head to the suburbs. The 7th is the only district in Maryland to have shed population since 2000.

But the picture within the city is not all bleak. Many of Baltimore's most identifiable landmarks and businesses are in the 7th, and there are middle-class black communities along Liberty Heights Avenue in West Baltimore.

The 7th takes in the Mount Vernon area, home of the Walters Art Museum and the Peabody Institute, which is affiliated with Johns Hopkins University and is one of the nation's major music academies. Farther north are Johns Hopkins University and the Baltimore Museum of Art.

West of the downtown hub, the old retail section around Lexington Market and the 1st Mariner Arena still survives. Just southwest of the city, the University of Maryland, Baltimore County campus and its adjacent research area are attracting technology companies. West of Baltimore County are sprawling suburbs in racially diverse and mainly wealthy, well-educated Howard County.

The 7th, which has a slight edge over the 4th for the state's highest percentage of black residents, supports Democratic candidates in national and local contests throughout most of the district, but the GOP can win locally in parts of Howard County.

Major Industry
Health care, technology

Cities
Baltimore (pt.), 334,834; Ellicott City (unincorporated) (pt.), 65,834; Columbia (unincorporated) (pt.), 52,442; Catonsville (unincorporated), 41,567

Notable
The 7th's portion of Baltimore is home to NAACP national headquarters, author Edgar Allan Poe's grave site and the National Aquarium.

Rep. Chris Van Hollen (D)

Capitol Office
225-5341
vanhollen.house.gov
1707 Longworth Bldg. 20515-2008; fax 225-0375

Committees
Budget - Ranking Member

Residence
Kensington

Born
Jan. 10, 1959; Karachi, Pakistan

Religion
Episcopalian

Family
Wife, Katherine Wilkens Van Hollen; three children

Education
Swarthmore College, B.A. 1983 (philosophy); Harvard U., M.P.P. 1985; Georgetown U., J.D. 1990

Career
Lawyer; gubernatorial aide; congressional aide

Political Highlights
Md. House, 1991-95; Md. Senate, 1995-2003

ELECTION RESULTS

2010 GENERAL
Chris Van Hollen (D)	153,613	73.3%
Michael Lee Philips (R)	52,421	25.0%
Mark Grannis (LIBERT)	2,713	1.3%

2010 PRIMARY
Chris Van Hollen (D)	57,847	92.9%
Robert Long (D)	4,392	7.1%

2008 GENERAL
Chris Van Hollen (D)	229,740	75.1%
Steve Hudson (R)	66,351	21.7%
Gordon Clark (GREEN)	6,828	2.2%

Previous Winning Percentages
2006 (77%); 2004 (75%); 2002 (52%)

Elected 2002; 5th term

Van Hollen's swift rise to the House leadership's upper ranks has been fueled by a wonkish devotion to policy combined with an acumen for recruiting Democratic candidates and raising money for them. His nice-guy demeanor has led colleagues to describe him as a future Speaker, senator or president.

It's no secret that Van Hollen hopes to move up — the only question is where. He very nearly ran for the Senate in 2006, when five-term Democrat Paul S. Sarbanes retired. But with the party establishment favoring veteran Rep. Benjamin L. Cardin, Van Hollen took a hard look at the situation and stood down. Cardin won the seat.

Van Hollen served as chairman of the Democratic Congressional Campaign Committee, the House Democratic campaign unit, in both the 2008 and 2010 election cycles. He was given that post by party leaders after his success in leading candidate recruitment for the 2006 election, in which Democrats won control of the House. During the 2008 cycle, Van Hollen helped build on his party's success, strengthening a majority that gave President Obama a more sympathetic legislative partner.

Van Hollen had considered running for Democratic Caucus chairman in 2009, but he decided against it. That's when then-Speaker Nancy Pelosi of California asked him to stay on as DCCC chairman through 2010, for what proved to be a far more difficult challenge. With the economic recovery anemic, Obama's popularity tumbling and voters telling pollsters they don't like the party's agenda, the national mood swung sharply against Democrats. But few in the party seemed to blame Van Hollen for their losses. In the 112th Congress (2011-12), he traded in his DCCC post for the top Democratic spot on the Budget Committee.

In the 111th Congress (2009-10), Van Hollen also served as an assistant to then-Speaker Nancy Pelosi of California, with special responsibility as liaison to the Obama White House. He said the expanded responsibilities give him a hand in both politics and policy. "From my perspective, marrying the policy role and the political role is the best of both worlds," he said.

He is a liberal on most big social issues, favoring abortion rights and restrictions on gun owners' rights. He fought in vain to stop a bill shielding gun dealers and manufacturers from lawsuits by gun crime victims and another measure exempting gun sales statistics from public disclosure under the Freedom of Information Act.

He negotiated a controversial exemption for the National Rifle Association in 2010 as he wrote and sponsored legislation that would impose strict disclosure rules on campaign advertising by corporations, unions and other independent groups. The bill was a response to the Supreme Court's decision in Citizens United v. Federal Election Commission, which eased restrictions on how corporations and unions can spend their funds on efforts to sway elections, and Van Hollen played the lead role in getting the bill through the House, though it did not become law.

Well-educated and well-traveled, Van Hollen is a good match for his district, a swath of demographically elite suburbs located just outside Washington, D.C. Many of his constituents work for the federal government, contractors or lobbyists; many others are engaged in biomedical research and technology.

He has pressed for increased education funding, including for President George W. Bush's education law known as the "No Child Left Behind Act," which set testing standards for public schools. He also has sought to give mandatory status to federal aid for special-needs students in order to boost it to the 40 percent level envisioned under the Individuals with Disabilities Education Act.

He played a key role in drafting the Democrats' health care overhaul as a member of the Ways and Means Committee in the 111th Congress, a spot he no longer holds. Van Hollen regularly pushes tax breaks for advanced biofuel producers, and as part of the health care law he helped eliminate a tax code provision benefiting paper companies that generate a byproduct called "black liquor." He seeks to help his constituents by addressing the alternative minimum tax, which was originally intended to target the highest-earning taxpayers but was not indexed for inflation. And he strongly advocated revoking the IRS' authority to hire private debt-collection companies to collect back taxes — a major concern of federal workers and unions.

He has teamed up with other local lawmakers to press for parity between military personnel and civilian workers. He called President Obama's fiscal 2012 budget "a responsible place to start," but criticized his plan to freeze the pay of federal workers.

The son of a Foreign Service officer, Van Hollen was born in Karachi, Pakistan, and lived in Turkey, India and Sri Lanka, where his father was ambassador. His mother was an expert on Russia. He earned a graduate degree in public policy and national security studies from Harvard's Kennedy School of Government, where he met his wife, Katherine. He then joined the staff of Maryland Sen. Charles McC. Mathias Jr., a Republican moderate, as a legislative assistant for defense and foreign policy.

When Mathias retired in 1986, Van Hollen went to work for the Senate Foreign Relations Committee as an arms control and NATO specialist, while Katherine worked for the House Foreign Affairs Committee.

He won election to the Maryland House in 1990, and four years later went after a state Senate seat, taking on the incumbent Democrat in the primary, even though she had helped him win his House seat. He won and went on to serve eight years.

He saw his chance to move up to Congress when redistricting after the 2000 census packed more Democrats into Maryland's 8th District, where liberal Republican Constance A. Morella regularly won re-election. First, he had to survive a four-way primary, narrowly edging out state Rep. Mark K. Shriver, a nephew of President John F. Kennedy.

He and Morella then waged one of the costliest and most-watched contests of the 2002 election. Each spent about $3 million. Van Hollen eked out a 4-percentage-point win and has sailed to re-election since.

Key Votes

2010

Overhaul the nation's health insurance system	YES
Allow for repeal of "don't ask, don't tell"	YES
Overhaul financial services industry regulation	YES
Limit use of new Afghanistan War funds to troop withdrawal activities	NO
Change oversight of offshore drilling and lift oil spill liability cap	YES
Provide a path to legal status for some children of illegal immigrants	YES
Extend Bush-era income tax cuts for two years	NO

2009

Expand the Children's Health Insurance Program	YES
Provide $787 billion in tax cuts and spending increases to stimulate the economy	YES
Allow bankruptcy judges to modify certain primary-residence mortgages	YES
Create a cap-and-trade system to limit greenhouse gas emissions	YES
Provide $2 billion for the "cash for clunkers" program	YES
Establish the government as the sole provider of student loans	YES
Restrict federally funded insurance coverage for abortions in health care overhaul	NO

CQ Vote Studies

	PARTY UNITY		PRESIDENTIAL SUPPORT	
	SUPPORT	OPPOSE	SUPPORT	OPPOSE
2010	100%	0%	95%	5%
2009	99%	1%	97%	3%
2008	99%	1%	14%	86%
2007	98%	2%	6%	94%
2006	95%	5%	30%	70%

Interest Groups

	AFL-CIO	ADA	CCUS	ACU
2010	100%	100%	13%	0%
2009	100%	100%	33%	0%
2008	100%	100%	61%	0%
2007	96%	90%	55%	0%
2006	93%	90%	40%	4%

Maryland 8

Part of Montgomery County — Bethesda, Gaithersburg, Rockville

The 8th contains wealthy Montgomery County suburbs northwest of Washington, such as Bethesda, Chevy Chase and Potomac, along with less-affluent suburbs in eastern Montgomery and western Prince George's counties. It also includes the Interstate 270 technology corridor, a hotbed for high-tech and biotech companies that runs through Rockville and Gaithersburg, and traffic congestion plagues commuter routes and commercial centers throughout the 8th. In the western part of the district, officials struggle to preserve an agricultural heritage.

Government dominates the 8th, where federal agencies, such as the National Institutes of Health and the Nuclear Regulatory Commission, abound and where federal employees who work in Washington reside. County and state government also provide jobs in Rockville, the Montgomery County seat. The large contingent of highly educated professionals supports an economy that is bolstered by a wide array of big-name business interests, including Lockheed Martin and Marriott.

The district has a strong Democratic lean, helped by liberal Takoma Park

and heavily black and Hispanic neighborhoods in western Prince George's County. The 8th has the highest percentage of Asians (13 percent) and Hispanics (20 percent) of any Maryland district — population growth across Montgomery County since 2000 has had a particular impact on its minority communities, and white residents now account for less than half of the district's population. The district also has the state's highest median household income ($88,000) and percentage of residents with a college degree (55 percent).

Major Industry
Government, technology, service, retail

Military Bases
National Naval Medical Center, 3,175 military, 2,250 civilian (2009); Naval Surface Warfare Center, Carderock Division, 2 military, 3,521 civilian (2011)

Cities
Rockville (pt.), 61,209; Bethesda (unincorporated), 60,858; Gaithersburg (pt.), 59,861; Wheaton (unincorporated), 48,284

Notable
Glen Echo Park has a working Dentzel Carousel in the menagerie style with an original Wurlitzer band organ, one of only 11 that still exist.

MASSACHUSETTS

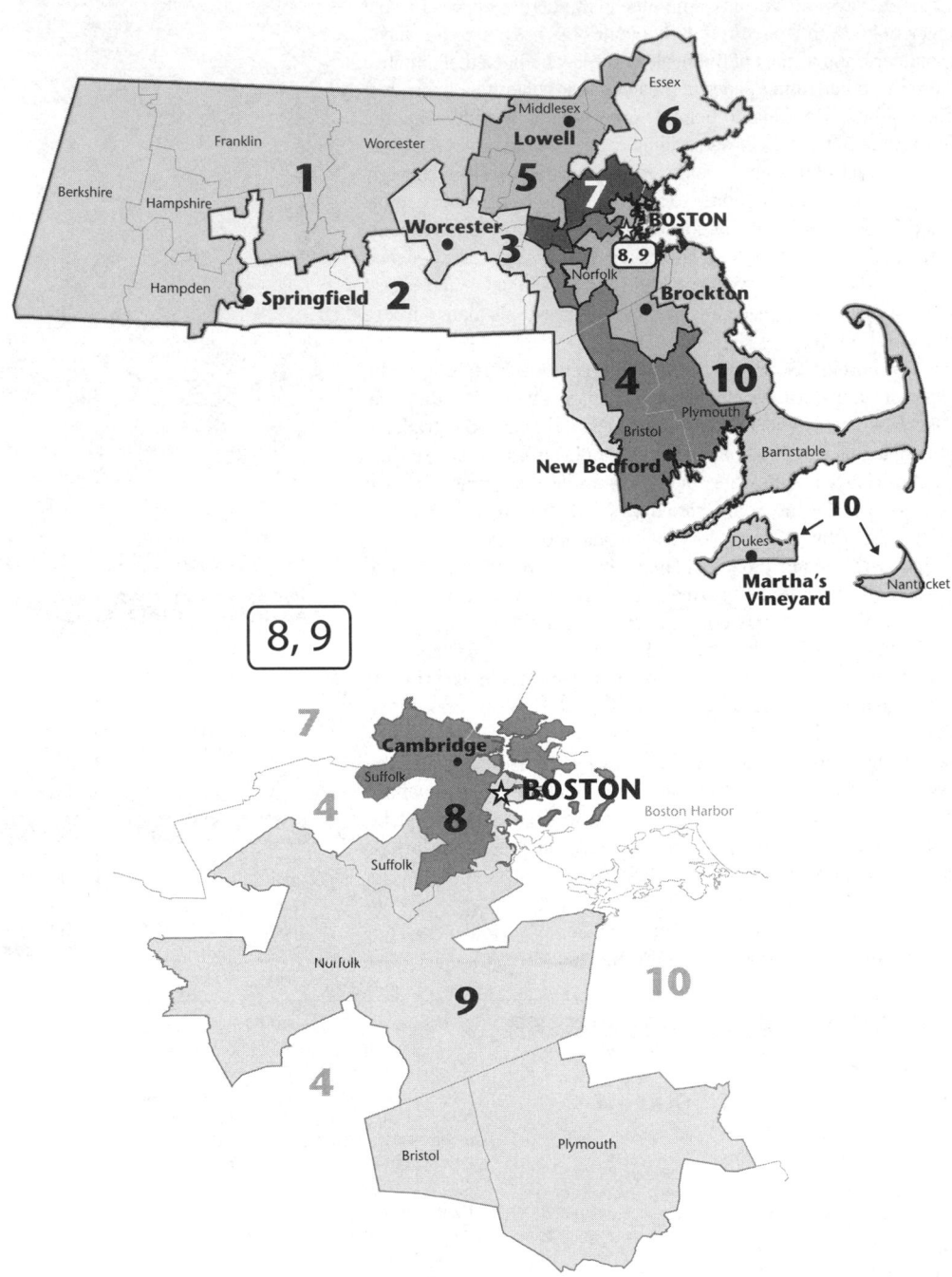

Gov. Deval Patrick (D)

First elected: 2006
Length of term: 4 years
Term expires: 1/15
Salary: $140,535
Phone: (617) 725-4000
Residence: Milton
Born: July 31, 1956; Chicago
Religion: Presbyterian
Family: Wife, Diane Patrick; two children
Education: Harvard U., A.B. 1978 (English & American Literature), J.D. 1982
Career: Lawyer; beverage company executive
Political highlights: Assistant attorney general, Civil Rights Division, 1994-97

ELECTION RESULTS

2010 GENERAL

Deval Patrick (D)	1,112,283	47.9%
Charles Baker (R)	964,866	41.6%
Tim Cahill (I)	184,395	7.9%
Jill Stein (GREEN)	32,895	1.4%

Lt. Gov. Timothy P. Murray (D)

First elected: 2006
Length of term: 4 years
Term expires: 1/15
Salary: $124,920
Phone: (617) 725-4005

LEGISLATURE

General Court: Usually year-round, but meeting times vary.
Senate: 40 members, 2-year terms
2011 ratios: 36 D, 4 R; 30 men, 10 women
Salary: $61,132.99
Phone: (617) 722-1276
House: 160 members, 2-year terms
2011 ratios: 129 D, 31 R; 124 men, 36 women
Salary: $61,132.99
Phone: (617) 722-2356

TERM LIMITS

Governor: 2 terms
Senate: No
House: No

URBAN STATISTICS

CITY	POPULATION
Boston	617,594
Worcester	181,045
Springfield	153,060
Lowell	106,519
Cambridge	105,162

REGISTERED VOTERS

Unenrolled/others	52%
Democrat	36%
Republican	11%

POPULATION

2010 population	6,547,629
2000 population	6,349,097
1990 population	6,016,425
Percent change (2000-2010)	+3.1%
Rank among states (2010)	14
Median age	38.5
Born in state	63.8%
Foreign born	14.1%
Violent crime rate	457/100,000
Poverty level	10.3%
Federal workers	60,027
Military	3,205

ELECTIONS

STATE ELECTION OFFICIAL
(617) 727-2828
DEMOCRATIC PARTY
(617) 776-2676
REPUBLICAN PARTY
(617) 523-5005

MISCELLANEOUS

Web: www.mass.gov
Capital: Boston

U.S. CONGRESS

Senate: 1 Democrat, 1 Republican
House: 10 Democrats

2010 Census Statistics by Districts

District	2008 Vote for President Obama	McCain	White	Black	Asian	Hispanic	Median Income	White Collar	Blue Collar	Service Industry	Over 64	Under 18	College Education	Rural	Sq. Miles
1	64%	33%	85%	2%	2%	9%	$54,241	60%	22%	18%	14%	22%	29%	31%	3,101
2	59	39	77	6	2	13	56,940	61	21	17	13	24	27	15	922
3	58	39	79	4	5	9	64,860	66	18	16	12	24	36	7	581
4	63	24	84	3	5	5	68,656	68	18	15	13	23	39	12	732
5	59	39	72	3	8	16	71,415	66	19	15	12	26	37	7	566
6	57	40	84	3	3	8	72,047	69	16	14	15	23	40	5	480
7	65	33	73	5	9	9	70,888	71	14	15	15	21	44	0	170
8	84	14	47	20	10	19	51,757	69	11	20	9	16	47	0	41
9	60	38	71	13	5	7	71,086	69	15	16	13	23	39	2	313
10	55	43	88	2	4	2	68,295	66	18	17	17	21	39	8	934
STATE	62	36	76	6	5	10	64,496	67	17	16	13	22	38	9	7,840
U.S.	53	46	64	12	5	16	51,425	60	23	17	13	25	28	21	3,537,438

Sen. John Kerry (D)

Capitol Office
224-2742
kerry.senate.gov
218 Russell Bldg. 20510-2102; fax 224-8525

Committees
Commerce, Science & Transportation
(Communications, Technology & the Internet -
Chairman)
Finance
Foreign Relations - Chairman
Small Business & Entrepreneurship

Residence
Boston

Born
Dec. 11, 1943; Denver, Colo.

Religion
Roman Catholic

Family
Wife, Teresa Heinz Kerry; two children, three
stepchildren

Education
Yale U., B.A. 1966 (political science); Boston College,
J.D. 1976

Military Service
Naval Reserve, 1966; Navy, 1966-70

Career
Lawyer; county prosecutor

Political Highlights
Democratic nominee for U.S. House, 1972; lieutenant governor, 1983-85; Democratic nominee for
president, 2004

ELECTION RESULTS

2008 GENERAL
John Kerry (D)	1,971,974	65.9%
Jeffrey K. Beatty (R)	926,044	31.0%
Robert Underwood (LIBERT)	93,713	3.1%

2008 PRIMARY
John Kerry (D)	342,446	68.9%
Edward J. O'Reilly (D)	154,395	31.1%

Previous Winning Percentages
2002 (80%); 1996 (52%); 1990 (57%); 1984 (55%)

Elected 1984; 5th term

Kerry has enjoyed perhaps the most productive phase of his long Senate career since resuming his work in the chamber after losing the 2004 presidential race. He not only has become one of the most recognizable and active U.S. officials on foreign policy, serving as a government emissary in some of the country's most delicate overseas relationships, but also has taken the lead on high-profile domestic policy debates, particularly climate change.

In some ways, Kerry is following the path of his mentor and longtime partner in the Massachusetts Senate delegation, the late Edward M. Kennedy. Like Kerry, Kennedy lost a presidential race, only to roar back and become one of the most influential lawmakers of his time.

Kerry said that Kennedy helped remind him that given his stature and seniority, he could "really do a lot as United States senator."

"And I've enjoyed it," Kerry said of his work since 2004. "I've really had a very rewarding time over the course of the last few years being deeply engaged in the Senate with a way to be able to get things done."

Kerry still has a ways to go to match Kennedy's legacy. He does not have the larger-than-life persona that Kennedy had — Kerry is knocked, rather, for being aloof and patrician — and he is not quite the same sort of liberal agitator. While he is certainly liberal on social issues, he has assumed a more pragmatic legislative approach as a senior senator, trying to build consensus to move bills through the chamber.

Kerry was stymied, however, in such efforts to move a climate change bill through the Senate in 2010.

Energy and the environment have long been a focus — dating back to his efforts to combat acid rain as lieutenant governor in the early 1980s — and he devoted the bulk of his time in the 111th Congress (2009-10) working to draft and pass climate change legislation. Kerry tallied more than 400 meetings with fellow lawmakers, the Obama administration and international leaders on the subject and won the backing of a diverse array of stakeholders.

But the coalition he built was dealt a setback when South Carolina Republican Lindsey Graham walked away from the legislation over a political beef with the Democratic Senate leadership. In June, the bill failed to garner the 60 votes necessary to move forward.

Thanks to Democrats' success in winning back the Senate in 2006 and Joseph R. Biden Jr.'s departure to become vice president in 2008, Kerry took over as chairman of the Foreign Relations Committee in 2009.

In that role, he has become increasingly visible on issues surrounding the war in Afghanistan and the interrelationships with neighboring Pakistan. Kerry has made several trips to Afghanistan as chairman, including a four-day visit in the wake of the contested presidential election there in October 2009. Kerry was widely credited with helping convince Afghan President Hamid Karzai to participate in a runoff, ending a tense political standoff in the country.

Kerry was also the first member of Congress to visit Pakistan after the August 2010 floods. While there he announced that the United States was prepared to commit additional aid. Some of that funding has come from a $7.5 billion economic assistance package Kerry, Foreign Relations ranking Republican Richard G. Lugar of Indiana and House Foreign Affairs Chairman Howard L. Berman, a California Democrat, co-authored in 2009.

Kerry has remained broadly supportive of President Obama's goals in Afghanistan, though he has not hesitated to question both the efficacy and implementation of Obama's strategy. One area where he firmly agrees with the administration is the notion that, as he said in a July 2010 committee hearing, "Pakistan is central to the resolution."

Along with Lugar, Kerry took the lead in shepherding through the Senate a new strategic arms control treaty with Russia signed in 2010, one of Obama's top foreign policy priorities. Republican misgivings about how the treaty would affect the U.S. nuclear deterrent slowed the process, but the Senate approved the treaty in late December 2010.

Kerry is quick to emphasize his independence from the Obama administration on foreign policy, despite their collaboration of many issues. "I'm pleased to work with them, but I don't work for them," he said. Kerry also has a good working relationship with Lugar, a former chairman of the committee.

As a member of the Finance Committee, Kerry was active in the drafting of Democrats' 2010 health care overhaul and fought to ensure the law did not undermine his home state's 2006 health care initiative.

On the Commerce, Science and Transportation Committee, Kerry chairs the panel on Communications, Technology and the Internet. In that post he is a fierce backer of so-called network neutrality, opposing attempts by some telecommunications companies to prioritize certain types of Internet traffic.

Kerry is a member and former chairman of the Small Business and Entrepreneurship Committee. Several of the legislative initiatives he proposed during his time as chairman to encourage small businesses to invest and expand found their way into Democrats' stimulus bill in 2009.

Kerry's father was a Foreign Service officer and attorney. His mother was a nurse and a member of the wealthy Forbes family. Largely because of the inherited wealth of his wife, Teresa Heinz Kerry, he is Congress' richest member, according to a study conducted by Roll Call in 2010.

A relative paid for Kerry's education at elite prep schools in Switzerland and New England, and he subsequently attended Yale. He joined the Naval Reserve in college and entered active duty in 1966.

After rising to the rank of lieutenant in the Navy, Kerry became one of the nation's most prominent demonstrators against the Vietnam War. He got front-page coverage in 1971 when he asked the Foreign Relations Committee, "How do you ask a man to be the last man to die for a mistake?"

He later chaired the Senate Select Committee on POW/MIA Affairs in the 102nd Congress (1991-92), joining forces with Republican Sen. John McCain of Arizona on a report that found no evidence that missing soldiers in Vietnam were still alive, helping pave the way for President Bill Clinton to normalize diplomatic relations.

Kerry tried to capitalize on the publicity from his Vietnam protests in a run for an open Massachusetts House seat in 1972. He won the primary, but lost in the fall to Republican Paul Cronin.

After his defeat, he went to law school, then worked as an assistant district attorney in Middlesex County. He was elected lieutenant governor in a 1982 challenge to the Democratic establishment. Two years later, he beat Democratic Rep. James M. Shannon for the nomination to replace retiring Sen. Paul E. Tsongas. He won the general election over GOP businessman Raymond Shamie with 55 percent of the vote.

In 1996 he faced his toughest challenge — from William F. Weld, the state's GOP governor. But Kerry's late spending and solid performance in a series of debates carried him to victory. The GOP did not run a candidate against him in 2002, and six years later he easily dispatched Republican Jeffrey K. Beatty.

Kerry lost his chance to topple President George W. Bush in a 2004 campaign marked by their frequent sparring over the Iraq War and the direction of U.S. foreign policy. Kerry ended up losing by 2.5 percentage points, winning 252 electoral votes to Bush's 286.

Key Votes

2010

Pass budget reconciliation bill to modify overhauls of health care and federal student loan programs	YES
Proceed to disapproval resolution on EPA authority to regulate greenhouse gases	NO
Overhaul financial services industry regulation	YES
Limit debate to proceed to a bill to broaden campaign finance disclosure and reporting rules	YES
Limit debate on an extension of Bush-era income tax cuts for two years	YES
Limit debate on a bill to provide a path to legal status for some children of illegal immigrants	YES
Allow for a repeal of "don't ask, don't tell"	YES
Consent to ratification of a strategic arms reduction treaty with Russia	YES

2009

Prevent release of remaining financial industry bailout funds	NO
Make it easier for victims to sue for wage discrimination remedies	YES
Expand the Children's Health Insurance Program	YES
Limit debate on the economic stimulus measure	YES
Repeal District of Columbia firearms prohibitions and gun registration laws	NO
Limit debate on expansion of federal hate crimes law	YES
Strike funding for F-22 Raptor fighter jets	YES

CQ Vote Studies

	PARTY UNITY		PRESIDENTIAL SUPPORT	
	SUPPORT	OPPOSE	SUPPORT	OPPOSE
2010	97%	3%	100%	0%
2009	99%	1%	97%	3%
2008	98%	2%	30%	70%
2007	95%	5%	40%	60%
2006	95%	5%	51%	49%
2005	97%	3%	34%	66%
2004	100%	0%	50%	50%
2003	100%	0%	30%	70%
2002	92%	8%	72%	28%
2001	98%	2%	65%	35%

Interest Groups

	AFL-CIO	ADA	CCUS	ACU
2010	94%	85%	27%	0%
2009	94%	95%	33%	0%
2008	100%	95%	63%	4%
2007	95%	90%	50%	4%
2006	87%	95%	55%	12%
2005	93%	100%	33%	8%
2004	100%	25%	0%	0%
2003	100%	85%	0%	13%
2002	92%	85%	55%	20%
2001	100%	95%	38%	4%

Sen. Scott P. Brown (R)

Capitol Office
224-4543
scottbrown.senate.gov
359 Dirksen Bldg. 20510-2101; fax 224-2417

Committees
Armed Services
Homeland Security & Governmental Affairs
Small Business & Entrepreneurship
Veterans' Affairs

Residence
Wrentham

Born
Sept. 12, 1959; Kittery, Maine

Religion
Protestant

Family
Wife, Gail Huff; two children

Education
Tufts U., B.A. 1981 (history); Boston College, J.D. 1985

Military Service
Mass. National Guard, 1979-present

Career
Lawyer

Political Highlights
Wrentham Board of Assessors, 1987-89; Wrentham
Board of Selectmen, 1996-99; Mass. House, 1999-
2004; Mass. Senate, 2004-10

ELECTION RESULTS

2010 SPECIAL

Scott P. Brown (R)	1,168,178	51.9%
Martha Coakley (D)	1,060,861	47.1%

2009 PRIMARY SPECIAL

Scott P. Brown (R)	146,057	88.8%
Jack E. Robinson III (R)	17,344	10.5%

Elected January 2010; 1st term

The first Massachusetts Republican to serve in the Senate in more than 30 years, Brown received a warm welcome from his party after capturing the late Edward M. Kennedy's seat in a January 2010 special election. His surprising victory thrust him into the national spotlight and gave him the self-proclaimed position as the "41st Republican" in a 100-member institution that requires 60 votes to get things done. But he has provided a key vote for Democrats on some high-priority legislation.

Brown developed his perspective on politics while serving on town boards and in both chambers of the Massachusetts General Court. But given the small size of the GOP contingent in Massachusetts — Republicans make up about 10 percent of both chambers — the party's lawmakers lack power. As a result, Brown could be having a greater influence in Washington than he did in either the state House or state Senate. He has the power to stop or at least slow down any piece of legislation, with his influence already being felt on health care, financial regulation and a small-business tax measure.

His election stripped the Democrats of their 60-vote supermajority and ultimately required the party's leadership to use alternative procedures to navigate the health care bill through the 111th Congress (2009-10). Following the bill's passage, Brown said, "My election in January deprived the Democrats of their 60th vote, and forced them to resort to a parliamentary maneuver known as reconciliation to ram this bill through Congress. While we all support improving our health care system, today's vote proves that the majority party will stop at nothing to force their disastrous health care plan onto a nation that doesn't want it, can't afford it and that is not good for my state."

Although Brown voiced strong opposition to the health care bill and several other Democratic initiatives, including extension of unemployment benefits without offsetting the costs and a tightening of campaign finance regulations, the fact that he comes from a traditionally blue state means he needs to demonstrate a strong bipartisan streak.

His willingness to work with Democrats on legislation opposed by most Senate Republicans was evident on the small-business tax bill and a sweeping overhaul of financial regulations. One of his earliest votes was for a $15 billion, Democratic-sponsored bill that would give companies a payroll tax break for hiring unemployed workers. A deal with Majority Leader Harry Reid of Nevada to narrow the bill's focus brought Brown, a member of the Small Business and Entrepreneurship Committee, on board. "I came to Washington to be an independent voice, to put politics aside and to do everything in my power to help create jobs for Massachusetts families," he said. "This Senate jobs bill is not perfect. I wish the tax cuts were deeper and broader, but I voted for it because it contains measures that will help put people back to work."

His influence on the financial regulatory bill was most apparent when Brown threatened to withdraw his support unless a $19 billion bank fee was removed from the measure. "I appreciate the efforts to improve the bill, especially the removal of the $19 billion bank tax," Brown said. "As a result, it is a better bill than it was when this whole process started. While it isn't perfect, I expect to support the bill when it comes up for a vote. It includes safeguards to help prevent another financial meltdown, ensures that consumers are protected and it is paid for without new taxes."

Brown's views on social issues, while moderate compared with many other Republicans, can land him in hot water with liberal voters. His support for abortion rights comes with caveats, including calls for strong parental consent laws for minors and opposition to a procedure opponents call "partial-birth" abortion. He voted against confirmation of Elena Kagan to the Supreme Court. He favors civil unions and previously advocated a ballot initiative to overturn Massachusetts' same-sex marriage laws. But he voted to repeal the "don't ask, don't tell" law banning openly gay servicemembers.

Brown is open to developing alternative energy sources, but he says he would vote against a cap-and-trade emissions program as currently envisioned by Democrats. He opposes a path to citizenship for illegal immigrants and supports military trials for suspected terrorists.

Brown, a three-decade member of the Massachusetts National Guard, won appointment to a trio of committees with jurisdiction over aspects of national security: Armed Services (where he is the ranking Republican on the Airland Subcommittee), Veterans' Affairs, and Homeland Security and Governmental Affairs (where he is top Republican on the Federal Financial Management, Government Information, Federal Services and International Security Subcommittee).

He disappointed conservatives when he backed ratification of a strategic arms reduction treaty with Russia during the lame-duck session at the end of the 111th Congress.

On fiscal matters, Brown stays firmly on conservative ground. During his Senate campaign, he spoke out against the $787 billion economic stimulus law that Congress passed in 2009 and railed against high taxes, calling his Democratic opponent, Massachusetts Attorney General Martha Coakley, a "tax-and-spend liberal."

Brown arrived in the Senate after a shocking special election victory. He replaced Democrat Paul G. Kirk Jr., a lawyer and one-time political staffer who had served as a short-term successor to Kennedy, who died in August 2009.

Coakley had been expected to sail to victory in the general election, and Brown remained a relative unknown even after his primary win. But Brown took advantage of voter unrest and a troubled Coakley campaign to seize the Senate seat for the last three years of Kennedy's term. He will face what will likely be a fierce challenge from Democrats in 2012.

Following his victory, Brown said his election could indicate "a new breed of Republican coming to Washington . . . who is not beholden to the special interests of the party and will look just to solve problems."

"If people are expecting an ideologue to come down from Massachusetts, that's not what they're going to get," said state Senate Minority Leader Richard Tisei, a Republican who has known Brown for 25 years.

Still, Brown tends to receive high ratings from gun owners' groups, business organizations and groups advocating lower taxes. He has scored low marks from the Massachusetts chapter of the National Organization for Women and labor groups.

Brown joined the Guard while a history student at Tufts University, where he was also a guard on the varsity basketball team. After graduating, he enrolled in law school at Boston College but took a year to try modeling and acting in New York while attending the Benjamin N. Cardozo School of Law at Yeshiva University as a part-time student. He finished law school at Boston College in 1985 and went into private practice while beginning to a build a record of public service by winning election to local offices.

In addition to his own newfound celebrity, Brown's family is accustomed to the limelight: His wife, Gail Huff, is a local television news reporter, and their daughter Ayla reached the semifinals on "American Idol" in 2006. Brown, as a 22-year-old law student, was named "America's Sexiest Man" by Cosmopolitan magazine in 1982. With the title came a photo display that included a shot of him nude, where only a strategically placed arm saved his modesty — and perhaps his future political aspirations.

Key Votes

2010

Pass budget reconciliation bill to modify overhauls of health care and federal student loan programs	NO
Proceed to disapproval resolution on EPA authority to regulate greenhouse gases	YES
Overhaul financial services industry regulation	YES
Limit debate to proceed to a bill to broaden campaign finance disclosure and reporting rules	NO
Limit debate on an extension of Bush-era income tax cuts for two years	YES
Limit debate on a bill to provide a path to legal status for some children of illegal immigrants	NO
Allow for a repeal of "don't ask, don't tell"	YES
Consent to ratification of a strategic arms reduction treaty with Russia	YES

CQ Vote Studies

	PARTY UNITY		PRESIDENTIAL SUPPORT	
	SUPPORT	OPPOSE	SUPPORT	OPPOSE
2010	78%	22%	61%	39%

Interest Groups

	AFL-CIO	ADA	CCUS	ACU
2010	25%	20%	82%	74%

Rep. John W. Olver (D)

Capitol Office
225-5335
www.house.gov/olver/index.shtml
1111 Longworth Bldg. 20515-2101; fax 226-1224

Committees
Appropriations

Residence
Amherst

Born
Sept. 3, 1936; Honesdale, Pa.

Religion
Unspecified

Family
Wife, Rose Olver; one child

Education
Rensselaer Polytechnic Institute, B.S. 1955 (chemistry); Tufts U., M.S. 1956 (chemistry); Massachusetts Institute of Technology, Ph.D. 1961 (chemistry)

Career
Professor

Political Highlights
Mass. House, 1969-73; Mass. Senate, 1973-91

ELECTION RESULTS

2010 GENERAL

John W. Olver (D)	128,011	60.0%
William J. Gunn (R)	74,418	34.9%
Michael Engel (I)	10,880	5.1%

2010 PRIMARY

John W. Olver (D)	unopposed

2008 GENERAL

John W. Olver (D)	215,696	72.8%
Nathan A. Bech (R)	80,067	27.0%

Previous Winning Percentages
2006 (76%); 2004 (99%); 2002 (68%); 2000 (68%); 1998 (72%); 1996 (53%); 1994 (99%); 1992 (52%); 1991 Special Election (50%)

Elected 1991; 10th full term

A bookish liberal with a professorial air, Olver is an unusual breed on Capitol Hill: a politician who dislikes the spotlight. During his first eight House terms, he shepherded just two bills into law, one during his first term naming a federal building for his predecessor, Silvio O. Conte, another a decade later ordering a study on whether to designate three trails in his Western Massachusetts district and Connecticut as national scenic trails.

Olver's profile rose during the 111th Congress (2009-10), when he served as chairman of the Appropriations Committee panel overseeing transportation and housing funding. He is the ranking Democrat on the panel in the 112th (2011-12).

Olver played his biggest role in the transportation portions of the fiscal 2010 omnibus spending bill. The final version gave a significant infusion of funds — $2.5 billion — toward the creation of a national high-speed rail network, a longtime Olver priority. Earlier in the year, Massachusetts put some of the first federal funding it received from the 2009 economic stimulus law toward a commuter rail project that runs through Olver's district. The fiscal 2011 spending bill, which passed the House but never made it into law, included $1.4 billion for high-speed rail grants.

But just as Olver has reached the pinnacle of his power on Capitol Hill, there are indications he might retire soon. Massachusetts lost a House seat in the congressional reapportionment following the 2010 census, and many remapping forecasts predict a merger of Olver's district with another in the western part of the state, where the population has declined.

Meanwhile, a former Massachusetts state senator and a fellow Democrat, Andrea F. Nuciforo Jr., filed papers indicating he plans to run for the 1st District seat in 2012. Olver has indicated he expects to seek re-election.

A solitary man, Olver enjoys perusing the details of spending bills. He says he believes it is the government's responsibility to solve society's problems and to play a part in economic development. "Better roads, bridges, airports, commuter rail systems and other public transit options are needed to connect people to educational centers, health and social services and, perhaps most importantly, good jobs," he said.

Securing earmarks is a common practice among appropriators, and Olver ranked among the most successful in 2009, directing nearly $100 million toward projects in his district and state. Some of the projects — including a $1 million grant for a three-person company in Pittsfield that's trying to develop new body armor for troops — became the subject of a Boston Globe investigation in late 2009.

But Olver brushes off critics who call such parochial projects wasteful, noting earmarks are a tiny part of the overall budget and have their place in the process, especially in helping rural and less-well-to-do regions. "We are closer to our people," he said, comparing members' earmarks to grants given by federal agencies on a competitive basis, a process he said favors wealthier regions that can hire good grant writers. He is the only House member from Massachusetts on Appropriations.

Olver wants to increase federal funding for Amtrak, the national passenger rail system, and for public housing. He has consistently opposed efforts to end subsidies to the railroad.

A member of the Progressive Caucus, the most liberal faction of House Democrats, he's usually loyal to his party leaders, supporting President Obama on nearly every vote where the president expresses a view, and the

Democratic Caucus nearly every time a vote splits majorities of the two parties.

But Olver did raise a rare criticism of Obama at a 2009 hearing of the transportation spending panel, telling Transportation Secretary Ray LaHood that the administration needed to "exert greater leadership" in moving an updated version of legislation that funds federal highway programs. Nonetheless, an overdue reauthorization of highway programs remained stalled in 2010 over how to pay for it, and the new Congress is expected to have another go at it.

Olver was a passionate supporter of the health care overhaul that congressional Democrats and Obama pushed through to enactment in 2010 and is also outspoken on the issue of climate change, saying the nation must do more to reduce carbon emissions and to increase automobile fuel economy.

Olver was a founder of the House's Climate Change Caucus. In the 110th Congress (2007-08), he pushed legislation to set caps on the amount of carbon dioxide emitted from the burning of fossil fuels and to create a market-based system that rewards companies for developing new technologies needed to combat climate change.

Olver has a quiet personality and enjoys a challenge. Fit and trim in his 70s, the 6-foot-4-inch Olver is an avid outdoorsman who still spends much of his free time hiking, rock climbing, wind surfing and cross-country skiing.

He grew up on a farm in the Poconos in Pennsylvania. His father ran the farm, which had a couple dozen milking cows, and his mother tended their boardinghouse that welcomed young families who traveled by train from Philadelphia or New York. The Olver house fronted on a lake and had its own beach.

Olver attended a three-room schoolhouse, graduating at age 15. He finished college when he was 18 and earned a doctorate from the Massachusetts Institute of Technology at age 24. He taught chemistry at the University of Massachusetts' Amherst campus for eight years before making his first foray into politics, winning a state House race in 1968.

Four years later he unseated an incumbent Republican state senator. He stayed in the state Senate until 1991, when Conte, the 17-term liberal Republican, died in February. Olver won the special election by fewer than 2,000 votes, marking the first time since 1892 that the area had sent a Democrat to the House.

He alternated close races in 1992 and 1996 (when he defeated Jane Swift, who would later serve as governor) with re-election romps in 1994 and 1998. His subsequent re-elections have been easy, including a 25-percentage-point win in 2010 over Republican William J. Gunn, who was arrested protesting the health care law at the Capitol in March 2010.

Key Votes

2010	
Overhaul the nation's health insurance system	YES
Allow for repeal of "don't ask, don't tell"	YES
Overhaul financial services industry regulation	YES
Limit use of new Afghanistan War funds to troop withdrawal activities	YES
Change oversight of offshore drilling and lift oil spill liability cap	YES
Provide a path to legal status for some children of illegal immigrants	YES
Extend Bush-era income tax cuts for two years	NO
2009	
Expand the Children's Health Insurance Program	YES
Provide $787 billion in tax cuts and spending increases to stimulate the economy	YES
Allow bankruptcy judges to modify certain primary-residence mortgages	YES
Create a cap-and-trade system to limit greenhouse gas emissions	YES
Provide $2 billion for the "cash for clunkers" program	YES
Establish the government as the sole provider of student loans	YES
Restrict federally funded insurance coverage for abortions in health care overhaul	NO

CQ Vote Studies

	PARTY UNITY		PRESIDENTIAL SUPPORT	
	SUPPORT	OPPOSE	SUPPORT	OPPOSE
2010	99%	1%	90%	10%
2009	99%	1%	99%	1%
2008	100%	0%	14%	86%
2007	99%	1%	4%	96%
2006	96%	4%	15%	85%

Interest Groups

	AFL-CIO	ADA	CCUS	ACU
2010	100%	100%	13%	0%
2009	100%	100%	33%	0%
2008	100%	100%	56%	0%
2007	96%	90%	50%	0%
2006	100%	95%	40%	4%

Massachusetts 1

West — Pittsfield, Leominster, Westfield, Amherst

The oranges of autumn, the whites of winter, and the greens of spring and summer attract vacationers to the 1st, which spans the western portion of the state. With three distinct geographical regions — the Berkshires, the Connecticut River Valley and the larger commuter towns to the northeast — the district embodies three vastly different population centers that rarely interact with one another.

Tourist areas include the kind of serene New England towns depicted in Norman Rockwell paintings. Tanglewood, the summer home of the Boston Symphony Orchestra, also attracts music fans to its outdoor theater in Lenox. The Yankee Candle Company, a large manufacturer of scented candles and a popular tourist attraction, is based in South Deerfield.

The region suffered heavy downsizing of its once-dominant textile mills, furniture manufacturing and plastics factories during a decades-long industry recession, with Pittsfield and Fitchburg suffering the most. Although Pittsfield lost residents over the last decade, the town's economy has gotten a boost from software and engineering jobs with military contrac-

tor General Dynamics. Holyoke, which has added Hispanic residents since 2000, hosts several printing firms. A developed retail industry and an influx of Boston commuters have kept the economy stable in Leominster, a western outgrowth of the Boston suburbs that sits at the junction of two major highways at the eastern edge of the district.

Once a Republican stronghold, the 1st still has some GOP-supporting sparsely populated rural areas along the Connecticut border, but these last toeholds of Rockefeller Republicanism are overwhelmed by large numbers of Democratic union voters in the northeast, retirees in Berkshire County and university liberals around Amherst, where the state's flagship university is located. Barack Obama took 64 percent of the 2008 presidential vote here.

Major Industry
Paper, tourism, higher education, plastics

Cities
Pittsfield, 44,737; Westfield, 41,094; Leominster, 40,759; Fitchburg, 40,318; Holyoke, 39,880; West Springfield Town, 28,391

Notable
William G. Morgan invented volleyball in 1895 in Holyoke, where the Volleyball Hall of Fame is currently located.

Rep. Richard E. Neal (D)

Capitol Office
225-5601
www.house.gov/neal
2208 Rayburn Bldg. 20515; fax 225-8112

Committees
Ways & Means

Residence
Springfield

Born
Feb. 14, 1949; Worcester, Mass.

Religion
Roman Catholic

Family
Wife, Maureen Neal; four children

Education
American International College, B.A. 1972 (political science); U. of Hartford, M.P.A. 1976

Career
College lecturer; teacher; mayoral aide

Political Highlights
Springfield City Council, 1978-84 (president, 1979); mayor of Springfield, 1984-89

ELECTION RESULTS

2010 GENERAL

Richard E. Neal (D)	122,751	57.3%
Tom Wesley (R)	91,209	42.6%

2010 PRIMARY

Richard E. Neal (D)	unopposed

2008 GENERAL

Richard E. Neal (D)	234,369	98.5%
write-ins	3,631	1.5%

Previous Winning Percentages
2006 (99%); 2004 (99%); 2002 (99%); 2000 (99%); 1998 (99%); 1996 (72%); 1994 (59%); 1992 (53%); 1990 (100%); 1988 (80%)

Elected 1988; 12th term

Neal, known for his in-depth knowledge of tax policy and ability to work with others, has advice for colleagues who want be spared a negative spotlight: Be a serious, sensible lawmaker.

"What you want to do, more than anything, is establish a reputation for thoughtful analysis. Immerse yourself with facts, reject demagoguery, try to find other men and women of common purpose and good will," he said. "Avoiding hypercharged terms is always good. Stay away from incendiary remarks."

Neal says those are the tenets that have guided him through his two-plus decades in Congress. He is a Democratic loyalist whose party unity score — the percentage of votes on which he sided with a majority of his party against a majority of Republicans — has never fallen below 91 and has touched 100. But he is a serious, intellectually driven, even-tempered politician who strives to make those around him understand not only the issues at stake, but also what solutions might already exist to address them.

As the sixth most senior Democrat on the Ways and Means Committee, his brief includes taxes, trade, health care and Social Security. He has served on the committee since 1993, a tenure that has included two terms as chairman of the Subcommittee on Select Revenue Measures.

When Ways and Means Chairman Charles B. Rangel, a New York Democrat, was forced to step aside amid ethics investigations in early 2010, Michigan's Sander M. Levin claimed the gavel for the remainder of the session. Levin and Neal then squared off for the post of ranking Democrat on the full committee after the party lost its majority in the November elections.

Levin positioned himself as the liberal choice. Neal won the backing of the Democratic Steering and Policy Committee by one vote, but the full Democratic Caucus selected Levin. Neal had to settle for ranking Democrat on the Select Revenue Measures panel.

Neal's main passion is overhauling the tax code. With exploding deficits, he says, Congress could be approaching a ripe opportunity to make the case for going forward with what is bound to be an ambitious and controversial undertaking. "This is a chance to reassess tax policy fundamentally," he said.

In late 2010, he voted against a two-year extension of the Bush-era tax rates, expressing concern about the inclusion of a partial Social Security tax holiday and the extension's effect on the deficit.

In 2007, the year he became chairman of the Select Revenue Measures Subcommittee, Neal began developing a plan to eliminate the alternative minimum tax, the levy intended to ensure that the highest earners pay some tax. It was never indexed for inflation, and many taxpayers who consider themselves middle-class are caught in its web. The effort ultimately fizzled as Democrats could not figure out a way to pay for the adjustment.

Many of Neal's other efforts on the tax front, like those of many fellow Democrats, have largely been thwarted by the broader conflict over pay-as-you-go rules, which stipulate that any tax cuts or spending increases must be balanced by revenue increases or spending cuts.

Neal is an Irish Catholic who represents a like-minded, blue-collar constituency that is less liberal than other voters in Democrat-leaning Massachusetts. He has said that "health care is a central theme in the teaching of Catholic social justice," and he played a role in writing the overhaul bill that dominated much of the work of the 111th Congress (2009-10) and set the tone for President Obama's first year in office.

He also was one of 64 Democrats to support a provision in the health care bill that would have prohibited the use of federal funds to pay for abortion, or cover any costs of the health care plan that would include coverage of abortion. But after the provision was weakened in the final version of the legislation, Neal supported the bill anyway.

Though he does not support the overturn of *Roe v. Wade*, the 1973 Supreme Court decision that struck down state abortion laws, Neal has opposed federal funding of abortions and voted in favor of the 2003 ban on a procedure opponents call "partial birth" abortion.

Like many of his generation, Neal, a former high school history and government teacher, attributes his initial interest in politics to President John F. Kennedy. His first foray in the world of electoral politics came when he served as co-chairman of Democrat George McGovern's 1972 presidential campaign in western Massachusetts. McGovern lost 49 states to incumbent Richard Nixon, winning only Massachusetts and the District of Columbia. Neal still calls the opportunity to work on the race his "big break."

That was also the year Neal graduated from American International College in the 2nd District's largest city of Springfield, with a bachelor's degree in political science. A year later he became an aide to the mayor of Springfield. In 1978, he was elected to serve on the city council and the next year became council president.

In 1983, Neal won the first of three elections to be Springfield mayor, drawing praise for stimulating downtown rehabilitation. He still directs legislative efforts toward the city, which falls within his district: He secured the funds for a new federal courthouse and more than $100 million in improvements for the Westover Air Reserve Base.

When Democrat Edward P. Boland announced his retirement in 1988 after 36 years in the House, Neal hit the ground running, winning the nomination unopposed and handily defeating his Republican opponent.

He faced a few serious challenges in the early 1990s, especially in the big Republican year of 1994, when he faced criticism for 87 overdrafts at the now-defunct House bank. Republicans again put forth a candidate in 1996, but that was the last time until 2010. He won easily, taking 57 percent of the vote against the GOP candidate, Navy veteran Tom Wesley.

"I'm visible in that district and have been forever. I accept speaking opportunities, I accept parade invitations, I visit classrooms regularly. . . . I think I've spent, in 22 years, maybe three or four weekends in Washington," Neal said. "Elections are won in off years."

Key Votes

2010

Overhaul the nation's health insurance system	YES
Allow for repeal of "don't ask, don't tell"	YES
Overhaul financial services industry regulation	YES
Limit use of new Afghanistan War funds to troop withdrawal activities	YES
Change oversight of offshore drilling and lift oil spill liability cap	YES
Provide a path to legal status for some children of illegal immigrants	YES
Extend Bush-era income tax cuts for two years	NO

2009

Expand the Children's Health Insurance Program	YES
Provide $787 billion in tax cuts and spending increases to stimulate the economy	YES
Allow bankruptcy judges to modify certain primary-residence mortgages	YES
Create a cap-and-trade system to limit greenhouse gas emissions	YES
Provide $2 billion for the "cash for clunkers" program	YES
Establish the government as the sole provider of student loans	YES
Restrict federally funded insurance coverage for abortions in health care overhaul	YES

CQ Vote Studies

	PARTY UNITY		PRESIDENTIAL SUPPORT	
	SUPPORT	OPPOSE	SUPPORT	OPPOSE
2010	99%	1%	88%	12%
2009	99%	1%	96%	4%
2008	100%	0%	14%	86%
2007	99%	1%	4%	96%
2006	96%	4%	18%	82%

Interest Groups

	AFL-CIO	ADA	CCUS	ACU
2010	100%	95%	0%	0%
2009	100%	95%	40%	4%
2008	100%	100%	61%	0%
2007	96%	95%	55%	0%
2006	100%	95%	36%	4%

Massachusetts 2

South central — Springfield, Chicopee, Northampton

The rolling hills and thick forests of the 2nd extend along the state's southern border from Springfield and Northampton in the west to Bellingham in the east. Springfield dwarfs all other communities in the 2nd; small, rural towns and intermittent farms fill out the rest of south-central Massachusetts.

The region's future rests with the insurance and health care industries — most notably MassMutual and Baystate Health System — which replaced some of Springfield's shrinking manufacturing base. Business parks are increasing commercial and industrial space, and service jobs and employment at Chicopee's Westover Air Reserve Base are also important to the area's economy. The Basketball Hall of Fame and the restored MassMutual Center arena have brought more visitors to Springfield — a needed boost, as the city has experienced a sustained period of high unemployment rates. New city programs may prop up areas such as Old Hill, which have been hit hard by foreclosures.

Hispanics once gravitated to Springfield's North End but are now more dispersed through the city. Most blacks, although significantly fewer in number than Hispanics, live near the city's center. These two populations account for more than half of the city's total population, making Springfield the district's multicultural region.

Residents in and around Springfield, many of whom are blue-collar and Irish Catholic, vote Democratic and dominate the district's elections. Smith and Mount Holyoke, liberal arts colleges for women, produce a strongly liberal vote in Northampton and South Hadley. Despite this strong Democratic lean, some Republicans have been competitive, particularly among small-town and rural voters. In 2008, the 2nd gave Barack Obama 59 percent of its presidential vote.

Major Industry
Insurance, health care, higher education, tourism

Cities
Springfield, 153,060; Chicopee, 55,298; Northampton, 28,549

Notable
Theodor Geisel, better known as Dr. Seuss, was born in Springfield, where the Dr. Seuss National Memorial Sculpture Garden now sits at the Springfield Museums.

Rep. Jim McGovern (D)

Capitol Office
225-6101
mcgovern.house.gov
438 Cannon Bldg. 20515-2103; fax 225-5759

Committees
Agriculture
Rules

Residence
Worcester

Born
Nov. 20, 1959; Worcester, Mass.

Religion
Roman Catholic

Family
Wife, Lisa McGovern; two children

Education
American U., B.A. 1981 (history), M.P.A. 1984

Career
Congressional aide; campaign aide

Political Highlights
Sought Democratic nomination for U.S. House, 1994

ELECTION RESULTS

2010 GENERAL

Jim McGovern (D)	122,708	56.5%
Marty Lamb (R)	85,124	39.2%
Patrick Barron (I)	9,388	4.3%

2010 PRIMARY

Jim McGovern (D)	unopposed

2008 GENERAL

Jim McGovern (D)	227,619	98.5%
write-ins	3,488	1.5%

Previous Winning Percentages
2006 (99%); 2004 (71%); 2002 (99%); 2000 (99%);
1998 (57%); 1996 (53%)

Elected 1996; 8th term

McGovern is a devoted liberal with a pragmatic political mind, allowing him to ably push his priorities in Congress. He is a party loyalist with a deep commitment to using an activist government to achieve social and economic ends at home and abroad, and has become a leader of the movement to end U.S. involvement in Afghanistan.

Before his 1996 election, McGovern spent nearly two decades in national politics, first as an intern and campaign aide to presidential candidate and former South Dakota Sen. George McGovern (no relation), and later working for Joe Moakley, the former Rules Committee chairman and dean of the Massachusetts House delegation until his death in 2001. "McGovern taught me it was OK to be an idealist," he told The Boston Globe. "Moakley taught me how to get things done."

McGovern recalls fondly his days working for the colorful Moakley, an old-fashioned, back-slapping pol who mentored him in politics. Before Moakley died, he helped engineer McGovern's move to Rules, where he is now the No. 2 Democrat behind Louise M. Slaughter of New York. McGovern is also a senior whip for the party.

He is a gifted bare-knuckle fighter in the Rules Committee's tartly partisan negotiations, which set the parameters for floor debate in the House. McGovern said eventually becoming chairman would be "kind of a dream come true," even though the powerful committee can sometimes put him in an uncomfortable position.

"Being on the Rules Committee is about not just what Jim McGovern wants. You've got to think of everybody else, and sometimes it's tough," he said. "It means oftentimes I don't get everything I want. But sometimes it means I get probably more than I would normally get if I were on another committee."

The co-chairman of the House Hunger Caucus, McGovern has long fought against domestic and global hunger. In part at McGovern's behest, President Bill Clinton created a pilot program that became the McGovern-Dole International Food for Education and Child Nutrition Program (named for George McGovern and Bob Dole), which has fed millions of children in the developing world. In his office hangs a picture of the McGoverns and Clinton commemorating the occasion.

"There are a lot of problems you can't solve, but hunger isn't one of them," McGovern said.

Central Massachusetts is not home to a lot of farming, but McGovern sees his appointment to the Agriculture Committee in the 112th Congress (2011-12) as an opportunity to pursue his interests in improving nutrition and fighting hunger as part of the 2012 farm bill the committee will produce. He also said he plans to be a voice for consumers on a panel historically dominated by farm interests.

McGovern led efforts in the 111th Congress (2009-10) to make changes to a Senate child nutrition bill because it used money intended for food stamp benefits as an offset to help pay for expanding programs in the legislation. He didn't get the changes he wanted, but got a promise from the Obama administration to find another way to protect food stamp recipients from the reduction.

McGovern was named co-chairman of the Congressional Human Rights Caucus in 2008, after the death of longtime Chairman Tom Lantos, a California Democrat. Later that year, McGovern helped persuade colleagues to pass a resolution creating a Tom Lantos Human Rights Commission, and he became its first chairman.

McGovern has been known to take his commitment to human rights to the street. He was one of five House members arrested during a 2006 protest outside the Sudanese embassy in Washington to speak out against the killing of civilians in that country's Darfur region.

McGovern has long held a keen interest in Latin America. He said the United States should pay greater attention to alleged human rights abuses in Colombia and should end its "stupid" policy toward Cuba.

He also has worked for years to shut down the School of the Americas, now named the Western Hemisphere Institute for Security Cooperation, which provides U.S. training to Latin American militaries. When he was a Moakley aide, he investigated the November 1989 murders of six Jesuit priests and two women in El Salvador by a number of SOA graduates. He won a victory when his amendment to the fiscal 2010 defense authorization bill was adopted, requiring the Defense Department to release information about the school's students.

McGovern was a strong voice against the Iraq War and has led the opposition to Obama's boosting of troop levels in Afghanistan. A McGovern amendment to a 2010 supplemental war spending bill, requiring the president to present a plan for a withdrawal by April 2011, was defeated. But it garnered votes from 60 percent of House Democrats.

During his childhood in working-class Worcester — his father ran a liquor store and his mother taught dance — the McGoverns were not politically active but were "devoted to the Kennedys as long as I can remember." He said that when Sen. Robert F. Kennedy of New York was assassinated in 1968, "My father gathered us around the kitchen table and we wrote sympathy cards to Ethel," Kennedy's wife.

McGovern had his first brush with politics as a junior high school student in 1972 when he became involved in George McGovern's presidential campaign and later worked in his Senate office. In 1984, he served as the Massachusetts campaign manager when the South Dakotan made another presidential bid and delivered a nominating speech at the Democratic National Convention.

He had made an unsuccessful bid in 1994 for the 3rd District seat, but in 1996 he upset two-term Republican Peter I. Blute, in part with an advertisement referring to then-House Speaker Newt Gingrich of Georgia that said, "You wouldn't vote for Newt, why would you vote for Blute?" He has won easily since.

Key Votes

2010

Overhaul the nation's health insurance system	YES
Allow for repeal of "don't ask, don't tell"	YES
Overhaul financial services industry regulation	YES
Limit use of new Afghanistan War funds to troop withdrawal activities	YES
Change oversight of offshore drilling and lift oil spill liability cap	YES
Provide a path to legal status for some children of illegal immigrants	YES
Extend Bush-era income tax cuts for two years	NO

2009

Expand the Children's Health Insurance Program	YES
Provide $787 billion in tax cuts and spending increases to stimulate the economy	YES
Allow bankruptcy judges to modify certain primary-residence mortgages	YES
Create a cap-and-trade system to limit greenhouse gas emissions	YES
Provide $2 billion for the "cash for clunkers" program	YES
Establish the government as the sole provider of student loans	YES
Restrict federally funded insurance coverage for abortions in health care overhaul	NO

CQ Vote Studies

	PARTY UNITY		PRESIDENTIAL SUPPORT	
	SUPPORT	OPPOSE	SUPPORT	OPPOSE
2010	99%	1%	85%	15%
2009	99%	1%	94%	6%
2008	99%	1%	13%	87%
2007	99%	1%	4%	96%
2006	98%	2%	23%	77%

Interest Groups

	AFL-CIO	ADA	CCUS	ACU
2010	100%	100%	13%	0%
2009	100%	100%	33%	0%
2008	100%	100%	50%	0%
2007	100%	95%	50%	0%
2006	100%	95%	40%	4%

Massachusetts 3

Central and south — Worcester, Attleboro, part of Fall River

The 3rd cuts a diagonal sliver from the mountains of Princeton to the fishing community of Fall River, winding its way from areas north of Worcester almost to the Atlantic Ocean far south of Boston.

Worcester, with its working-class roots, is the 3rd's population center. The city, which is the second-largest in the state after Boston, has a strong biotech industry and centralized its health care and research facilities into a medical center, spurring economic development and job growth. Worcester's emphasis on economic expansion and the presence of low housing costs relative to those in Boston were expected to draw residents to the area, but Worcester endured years of high foreclosure rates following a nationwide housing market collapse. Local officials hope that planned revitalization projects for downtown will support continued development. Suburban communities outside of Worcester are home to commuters who work in Boston as well as Providence, R.I.

At the district's southern tip, Fall River (shared with the 4th District) has long been a bastion of white, blue-collar, ethnic Democrats. The one-time textile hub has struggled for most of the past century during periods of high unemployment and shortages of affordable housing. Fall River had one of the state's highest unemployment rates in the 1990s before increased employment lowered the figure to roughly 5 percent in 2000. Early in 2011, however, the unemployment rate in Fall River again exceeded 18 percent, roughly twice the state average.

Democratic dominance in Worcester and Fall River allows Democrats to overcome Republican support in the towns surrounding Worcester. Barack Obama took 67 percent of the 2008 presidential vote in Worcester, and he won in the district as a whole with 58 percent.

Major Industry
Biotech, health care, heavy manufacturing, retail

Cities
Worcester, 181,045; Fall River (pt.), 51,975; Attleboro, 43,593

Notable
The Worcester Art Museum, home to an internationally recognized collection of paintings, sculptures, decorative arts, textiles and photography, boasts the nation's largest collection of Antiochian mosaics.

Rep. Barney Frank (D)

Capitol Office
225-5931
www.house.gov/frank
2252 Rayburn Bldg. 20515-2104; fax 225-0182

Committees
Financial Services - Ranking Member

Residence
Newton

Born
March 31, 1940; Bayonne, N.J.

Religion
Jewish

Family
Single

Education
Harvard U., A.B. 1962 (government), J.D. 1977

Career
Lawyer; mayoral and congressional aide

Political Highlights
Mass. House, 1973-81

ELECTION RESULTS

2010 GENERAL

Barney Frank (D)	126,194	53.9%
Sean Bielat (R)	101,517	43.4%
Susan Allen (D)	3,445	1.5%
Donald M. Jordan (I)	2,873	1.2%

2010 PRIMARY

Barney Frank (D)	39,974	79.5%
Rachel Brown (D)	10,289	20.5%

2008 GENERAL

Barney Frank (D)	203,032	68.0%
Earl Henry Sholley (R)	75,571	25.3%
Susan Allen (I)	19,848	6.6%

Previous Winning Percentages
2006 (99%); 2004 (78%); 2002 (99%); 2000 (75%);
1998 (98%); 1996 (72%); 1994 (99%); 1992 (68%);
1990 (66%); 1988 (70%); 1986 (89%); 1984 (74%);
1982 (60%); 1980 (52%)

Elected 1980; 16th term

Known for his verbal agility, tart tongue, legislative maneuvering and legendary impatience, Frank cemented his reputation as the House master of the intricacies of financial industry regulation after presiding over marathon negotiations on overhaul legislation in 2010.

Frank is a passionate liberal who has an abiding faith in the ability of government to solve problems. He also has amassed an encyclopedic knowledge of public policy and parliamentary rules during his three decades in Congress, and he employs it with precision as one of the House's most adept debaters.

His legislative victory on the Wall Street regulatory overhaul came on the heels of Frank flexing his influence in 2008 by guiding into law the $700 billion package of assistance for the financial services sector and a government rescue of troubled mortgage giants Fannie Mae and Freddie Mac.

As chairman of the Financial Services Committee in the 110th and 111th Congresses (2007-10), Frank worked closely with Republicans behind the scenes and regularly appeared before reporters to explain why the rescue effort needed quick approval. Speaker Nancy Pelosi of California labeled him a "maestro" when the House passed the measure in October 2008, four days after it had rejected an earlier version.

Several Democrats attributed their decision to support the bill the second time around to Frank's powers of persuasion. Fellow Massachusetts Democrat Stephen F. Lynch called the Bush administration's original plan "a nonstarter" and said "the only reason it got consideration was because of Barney Frank."

Frank's alliance with Treasury Secretary Henry M. Paulson Jr. helped make the effort a reality. Several months earlier, the two combined forces on legislation to help 400,000 homeowners facing foreclosure and prevent Fannie Mae and Freddie Mac from collapsing. "I thought it was remarkable when I came down here to find someone who had not been in the private sector and the capital markets who understood the capital markets as well as Barney Frank did," Paulson told The Washington Post.

Not everyone was so enamored, of course.

Conservatives were mistrustful of Frank's approach. "Barney has a great deal of faith in government's ability to solve people's problems," New Jersey Republican Scott Garrett, a frequent opponent on the Financial Services Committee, told The New Yorker in January 2009. "The question is whether that faith is justified."

When the new Republican leaders of Financial Services announced in early 2011 that they were targeting for elimination four of the Obama administration's foreclosure mitigation programs, Frank, now the panel's ranking member, defended the programs.

"As we continue to respond to the victims of the foreclosure crisis in a responsible way," he said, "we will make the case that there are better ways for the federal government to cut spending than by attacking these programs."

Frank delights in exploiting divisions in the Republican ranks. "The right hand doesn't know what the far right hand is doing," he once observed. When the first financial rescue bill failed to pass, GOP leaders said a dozen Republicans had been ready to support the legislation but were turned off by a partisan Pelosi floor speech. Frank pounced. "Give me those 12 people's names," he said, "and I will go talk uncharacteristically nicely to them and tell them what wonderful people they are, and maybe they'll now think about the country."

In the 111th Congress, Frank set out to tackle the regulatory overhaul of the financial services industry. "It has taken over my life in a way nothing ever has before," he told Newsweek.

In June 2010 Frank presided over negotiations for the legislation in a televised session. The final bill expanded the regulatory purview of the Federal Reserve and the Securities and Exchange Commission and created the new consumer protection agency.

Frank has not always been such an ardent advocate of regulation. Before the market collapse of 2008, he displayed a hands-off approach toward Fannie and Freddie that drew considerable criticism.

On the issue closest to his heart — affordable housing — Frank was the most potent critic of attempts to cut spending on rent assistance for low-income families. He won inclusion of provisions in 2008 housing legislation to establish an affordable-housing trust fund.

Frank was the first House member to acknowledge his homosexuality and does not shy away from allusions to his personal life. He quipped to The New York Times in May 2008 that asking the Republican White House to support more government intervention was "like asking me to judge the Miss America contest — if your heart's not in it, you don't do a very good job."

He has been on the front line opposing GOP-led attempts to ban same-sex marriage and backed the 2010 repeal of the "don't ask, don't tell" law that barred homosexuals from serving openly in the military.

Frank's honesty about his homosexuality since he came out in 1987 helped him survive politically three years later when the House reprimanded him after a male prostitute revealed he'd had an affair with Frank and had run his business out of the lawmaker's Washington apartment. His constituents barely noticed: They re-elected him with 66 percent of the vote that year.

He grew up in Bayonne, N.J., the son of a New Jersey Turnpike truck stop operator. The Franks loved to discuss politics, and all four of the children went on to careers tied to government service. Frank's sister Ann Lewis is a longtime Democratic operative.

Frank graduated from Harvard and considered a life in academia. But he went to work instead as an aide to Boston Mayor Kevin White in 1967. He was elected to the Massachusetts House in 1972 and stayed for eight years.

When Democratic Rep. Robert F. Drinan, a liberal Catholic priest, bowed to a papal prohibition on clergymen holding public office, Frank ran for his seat, winning in 1980 with 52 percent of the vote. He hadn't dropped below 60 percent until 2010, when Republican Sean Bielat held him to 54 percent of the vote.

Key Votes

2010

Overhaul the nation's health insurance system	YES
Allow for repeal of "don't ask, don't tell"	YES
Overhaul financial services industry regulation	YES
Limit use of new Afghanistan War funds to troop withdrawal activities	YES
Change oversight of offshore drilling and lift oil spill liability cap	YES
Provide a path to legal status for some children of illegal immigrants	YES
Extend Bush-era income tax cuts for two years	NO

2009

Expand the Children's Health Insurance Program	YES
Provide $787 billion in tax cuts and spending increases to stimulate the economy	YES
Allow bankruptcy judges to modify certain primary-residence mortgages	YES
Create a cap-and-trade system to limit greenhouse gas emissions	YES
Provide $2 billion for the "cash for clunkers" program	YES
Establish the government as the sole provider of student loans	?
Restrict federally funded insurance coverage for abortions in health care overhaul	NO

CQ Vote Studies

	PARTY UNITY		PRESIDENTIAL SUPPORT	
	SUPPORT	OPPOSE	SUPPORT	OPPOSE
2010	98%	2%	85%	15%
2009	99%	1%	97%	3%
2008	99%	1%	14%	86%
2007	99%	1%	4%	96%
2006	96%	4%	15%	85%

Interest Groups

	AFL-CIO	ADA	CCUS	ACU
2010	100%	100%	13%	0%
2009	100%	100%	33%	0%
2008	100%	100%	61%	0%
2007	96%	95%	60%	0%
2006	100%	95%	29%	12%

Massachusetts 4

New Bedford; Boston suburbs — Newton; Taunton; part of Fall River

Downtowns replete with 18th- and 19th-century town hall buildings dot the Yankee communities in the 4th, several of which have celebrated their 300th or 350th anniversaries. The district skips from thickly settled Boston suburbs south through rural cranberry bogs and encompasses urban New Bedford and parts of Fall River (shared with the 3rd District).

The economic environment of the 4th reflects a split between the northern and southern tiers of the district. The economies of the northern well-to-do towns and Boston's commuter-settled suburbs benefited from access to the Route 128 technology corridor, although some high-tech jobs have moved closer in to Boston and Cambridge. The southern fishing and former textile mill communities, including Fall River and New Bedford, struggle with double-digit unemployment rates, though fishing remains an important industry and way of life here. Cranberry bogs in Middleborough in the center of the district and biotech firms farther north provide a strong economic base. Other communities hit by sustained periods of unemployment rates higher than the state average, such as Taunton, hope that expansion of industrial parks and job creation programs will boost the local economy.

The blue-collar, immigrant-laden southern section of the district gives the 4th a strong Democratic lean. New Bedford, which has one of the lowest median household incomes in the state, and Fall River are heavily Portuguese and vote solidly Democratic. Westport, located south of Fall River and west of New Bedford, adds Democratic votes. The wealthy northwestern towns of Wellesley, Dover and Sherborn are more competitive, but the well-to-do and densely populated Newton and Brookline opt for liberal Democrats and supported Democratic state Attorney General Martha Coakley in the 2010 Senate special election.

Major Industry
Fishing, cranberries, health care

Cities
New Bedford, 95,072; Newton, 85,146; Brookline (unincorp.), 58,732; Taunton, 55,874; Fall River (pt.), 36,882; Wellesley (unincorp.), 27,982

Notable
Ocean Spray, the first producer of cranberry juice drinks, is headquartered in Lakeville-Middleborough.

Rep. Niki Tsongas (D)

Capitol Office
225-3411
tsongas.house.gov
1607 Longworth Bldg. 20515-2105; fax 226-0771

Committees
Armed Services
Natural Resources

Residence
Lowell

Born
April 26, 1946; Chico, Calif.

Religion
Episcopalian

Family
Widowed; three children

Education
Michigan State U., attended 1964-65; Smith College, B.A. 1968 (religion); Boston U., J.D. 1988

Career
College public affairs official; lawyer; homemaker; paralegal; social worker

Political Highlights
No previous office

ELECTION RESULTS

2010 GENERAL

Niki Tsongas (D)	122,858	54.8%
Jon Golnik (R)	94,646	42.2%
Dale E. Brown (I)	4,387	2.0%

2010 PRIMARY

Niki Tsongas (D)	unopposed

2008 GENERAL

Niki Tsongas (D)	225,947	98.7%
write-ins	2,960	1.3%

Previous Winning Percentages
2007 Special Election (51%)

Elected 2007; 2nd full term

A staunch liberal and party loyalist, Tsongas has sided with the Democratic leadership on virtually every vote since arriving in Congress. The widow of a prominent national politician — the late Sen. Paul E. Tsongas of Massachusetts — she keeps a relatively low profile on Capitol Hill.

Since she came to Congress, Tsongas (SONG-us) has sided with a majority of Democrats against a majority of Republicans more than 99 percent of the time. She was there for President Obama on all of his major initiatives, supporting the economic stimulus early on, the health care overhaul, the Wall Street regulatory changes and the House version of energy legislation designed to address climate change. Her loyalty helped her win selection as one of 12 regional whips for the 112th Congress (2011-12).

After the health care law was enacted in 2010, she told the Lawrence Eagle-Tribune that she had "heard strong opinions on all sides. Most people want to give it time to be put into effect. The reality is much of it won't be in place for another three years." More than a year after its enactment, she said the stimulus was "definitely supporting private sector growth." Along with all but three Democrats, she opposed a GOP measure to repeal the law early in 2011.

No amendments were allowed when the House voted on the repeal measure, but Tsongas made a pitch to the Rules Committee to allow consideration of an alternative that would have preserved some of the insurance protections provided by the law.

"Some of the most egregious insurance industry practices disproportionately impact women," she told the panel. "And repeal of health care reform would again allow the insurance companies to unfairly discriminate against women."

As the sole Massachusetts member on the Armed Services Committee, Tsongas looks out for the fate of the next generation of Navy destroyers. Raytheon Co., which is building electronic and combat systems for the Zumwalt-class destroyer, is an employer in the district, and Tsongas has intensely questioned Navy officials about their future building plans.

She also took up the withdraw-from-Iraq mantle on Armed Services from her Democratic predecessor, Martin T. Meehan. The first bill she introduced as a member of the House would have set deadlines for a withdrawal.

After traveling to Afghanistan in May 2010, she stressed the need for women to play a greater role in that country's future. "For us to achieve our goals there and for the Afghanistan government to achieve its goals, Afghan women have to be part of the process," she told the Boston Globe.

The daughter of an Air Force engineer, Tsongas takes particular interest in her seat on the panel's Military Personnel Subcommittee. In early 2009, she pushed for passage of two bills aimed at improving mental health care for veterans. One would require the Department of Veterans Affairs to report vacancies in mental health professional positions at facilities on a quarterly basis. The other would create a pilot program to train counselors at higher education facilities to recognize the signs of post-traumatic stress disorder.

Tsongas also is a member of the Natural Resources Committee, where she takes a liberal stance on environmental issues. She voted for Democratic legislation to create a cap-and-trade system for limiting carbon emissions, calling the measure "one of the most important pieces of legislation we have considered to safeguard the future of our children and grandchildren."

Legislation the House passed in July 2010 in response to that spring's Gulf of Mexico oil spill included language by Tsongas that would require oil companies to submit plans on containing and cleaning up worst-case spills. She said the spill "represents a failure by the oil industry, a failure of government to oversee that industry, and also a simple failure of imagination."

Her views on social issues are uniformly liberal. One of her first official actions was to join her party in an unsuccessful attempt to override President George W. Bush's veto of legislation expanding the Children's Health Insurance Program, which covers children from families that make too much money to qualify for Medicaid. She supported a nearly identical measure in early 2009 that Obama signed into law. She supports gay marriage and backed the 2010 repeal of the ban on homosexuals serving openly in the military.

Tsongas was born in the foothills of California's Cascade Range, but after five years in Chico she rarely stayed any place for long. Her father, who survived the attack on Pearl Harbor, moved frequently in his military job with stops in Germany, Japan, Texas and Virginia. Her mother was a painter and also worked as a copywriter.

Tsongas was 14 when she became interested in politics, inspired by Democrat John F. Kennedy's presidential candidacy.

During the summer between her junior and senior years at Smith College, she interned at an investment banking company in Washington, D.C., where she met her future husband, who was interning for former Republican Rep. F. Bradford Morse of Massachusetts.

In 1968, Tsongas volunteered in the presidential campaign of Minnesota Sen. Eugene McCarthy, who opposed the Vietnam War policies of President Lyndon B. Johnson, his fellow Democrat. Tsongas helped her husband get elected in 1974 to the U.S. House, where he served two terms before winning a Senate seat. She was a stay-at-home mother until Paul was diagnosed with cancer and retired from Congress in 1985. For years she had attended law school at night and earned a degree from Boston University in 1988. She then co-founded the first all-female law firm in Lowell.

Her husband made a brief return to politics in 1991, losing a bid for the Democratic presidential nomination. Suffering complications from his earlier cancer treatment, he died in 1997 at age 55.

Tsongas' name recognition helped in the race to succeed Meehan, an eight-term Democrat who resigned to become chancellor of the University of Massachusetts at Lowell. Her Republican opponent, retired Air Force officer Jim Ogonowski, drew attention for his connection to the Sept. 11 attacks. His brother was the pilot of the first airplane to be hijacked and flown into the World Trade Center. Tsongas prevailed, 51 percent to 45 percent, and ran unopposed in 2008. She won by 13 points in 2010 over Republican Jon Golnik.

Key Votes

2010

Overhaul the nation's health insurance system	YES
Allow for repeal of "don't ask, don't tell"	YES
Overhaul financial services industry regulation	YES
Limit use of new Afghanistan War funds to troop withdrawal activities	YES
Change oversight of offshore drilling and lift oil spill liability cap	YES
Provide a path to legal status for some children of illegal immigrants	YES
Extend Bush-era income tax cuts for two years	YES

2009

Expand the Children's Health Insurance Program	YES
Provide $787 billion in tax cuts and spending increases to stimulate the economy	YES
Allow bankruptcy judges to modify certain primary-residence mortgages	YES
Create a cap-and-trade system to limit greenhouse gas emissions	YES
Provide $2 billion for the "cash for clunkers" program	YES
Establish the government as the sole provider of student loans	YES
Restrict federally funded insurance coverage for abortions in health care overhaul	NO

CQ Vote Studies

	PARTY UNITY		PRESIDENTIAL SUPPORT	
	SUPPORT	OPPOSE	SUPPORT	OPPOSE
2010	99%	1%	88%	12%
2009	99%	1%	94%	6%
2008	99%	1%	15%	85%
2007	100%	0%	11%	89%

Interest Groups

	AFL-CIO	ADA	CCUS	ACU
2010	100%	95%	25%	0%
2009	100%	95%	29%	0%
2008	100%	100%	56%	0%
2007	100%		60%	0%

Massachusetts 5

North central — Lowell, Lawrence, Haverhill

More than a generation ago, billowing smokestacks put Lawrence and Lowell among the nation's leading industrial centers. Today, the cities remain blue-collar, strongly Democratic population hubs for the 5th, but the wealthy suburbs and rural communities — home to technology workers and some of the nation's most prestigious preparatory schools — give the district a more upscale flavor.

Manufacturing-based jobs are still vital to struggling Lawrence, where unemployment rates have risen past double the statewide average. The town is no stranger to high unemployment: Rates spiked in the early 1990s and again recently. Immigration has pushed Lawrence's growing Hispanic population, composed mostly of Dominicans and Puerto Ricans, into a wide majority and given Lawrence a Latin flavor, confirmed by the city's many ethnic restaurants.

Lowell and its surrounding suburbs largely succeeded in reinventing themselves following declines at once-major area employers. The retooled economic base attracted software firms and other technology companies, and previous economic upswings spurred growth in small towns where aging buildings that once housed textile mills and then defense contractors became homes for start-ups and financial services firms. But the area is now experiencing further economic struggles. Lowell — increasingly more diverse with a significant Cambodian population — has sought to become a cultural hub and now boasts the nation's largest free folk festival. The southern part of the 5th is generally wealthy, with Carlisle, Sudbury, Harvard and Bolton all registering six-figure median household incomes. Republican candidates can be competitive in these areas, but the district overall supports Democrats at the state and federal level. Barack Obama took the district with 59 percent of the vote in the 2008 presidential race.

Major Industry

Computer software, defense manufacturing, light manufacturing

Cities

Lowell, 106,519; Lawrence (pt.), 76,377; Haverhill, 60,879

Notable

Concord was the site of the first day of fighting in the Revolutionary War on April 19, 1775 (now celebrated each year as Patriots Day).

Rep. John F. Tierney (D)

Capitol Office
225-8020
www.house.gov/tierney
2238 Rayburn Bldg. 20515; fax 225-5915

Committees
Education & the Workforce
Oversight & Government Reform

Residence
Salem

Born
Sept. 18, 1951; Salem, Mass.

Religion
Unspecified

Family
Wife, Patrice Tierney

Education
Salem State College, B.A. 1973 (political science);
Suffolk U., J.D. 1976

Career
Lawyer; chamber of commerce official

Political Highlights
Democratic nominee for U.S. House, 1994

ELECTION RESULTS

2010 GENERAL

John F. Tierney (D)	142,732	56.8%
Bill John Hudak Jr. (R)	107,930	43.0%

2010 PRIMARY

John F. Tierney (D)	unopposed

2008 GENERAL

John F. Tierney (D)	226,216	70.4%
Richard A. Baker (R)	94,845	29.5%

Previous Winning Percentages
2006 (70%); 2004 (70%); 2002 (68%); 2000 (71%);
1998 (55%); 1996 (48%)

Elected 1996; 8th term

An unwavering liberal on matters foreign and domestic, Tierney built a close relationship with Minority Leader Nancy Pelosi of California — her daughter Christine was his chief of staff from 2001 to 2005 — and he has slowly emerged from among the crowd of Massachusetts' powerful all-Democratic House delegation.

His legislative focus has been on national security issues. He is the ranking Democrat on the Oversight and Government Reform Committee's National Security, Homeland Defense and Foreign Operations panel, which he chaired in the 110th (2007-08) and 111th (2009-10) Congresses. He previously served on the Select Intelligence Committee.

Tierney used his subcommittee's investigative power to lead a tenacious and rigorous oversight of U.S. operations in Afghanistan and Pakistan. His aggressive, take-no-prisoners style has differed little whether his party is in control. The difference was that as chairman he had a platform to garner media attention. That will be a bit tougher to come by in the 112th Congress (2011-12).

Tierney was in the spotlight when his subcommittee released a report in June 2010 titled "Warlord Inc.," which investigated the Host Nation Trucking contracts in Afghanistan. The report examined the flow of taxpayer dollars to warlords, corrupt officials and possibly insurgents, who were being paid to protect military supply convoys in Afghanistan. Tierney says the Defense Department's outsourcing of responsibility to private contractors has resulted in a system where "U.S. taxpayer dollars are feeding a protection racket in Afghanistan that would make Tony Soprano proud."

He shares President Obama's commitment to engaging a wider number of nations and has pledged to help the administration define its goals abroad. But he is an opponent of Obama's counterinsurgency strategy in Afghanistan. Tierney suggested that the problems identified in his subcommittee's report and elsewhere might "require reconsideration of the overall strategic approach to our mission in Afghanistan." He was one of 60 House Democrats who supported a non-binding resolution calling for a quick withdrawal of forces from the country.

Tierney says a better option would be a "more focused and sustainable counterterrorism effort" that targets the al Qaeda terrorist network in the countries where it operates, such as Pakistan. Tierney has supported development and military aid to that country. He worked with California Democrat Howard L. Berman, then chairman of the Foreign Affairs Committee, to add a provision to a Pakistan foreign aid bill that would make the military funds conditional on Pakistan's cooperation in fighting terrorist organizations within its own borders and dismantling nuclear supply networks.

He called Republicans' proposal to cut the State Department budget in fiscal 2012 "penny-wise and pound-foolish."

"After investing so much blood and nearly a trillion dollars in Iraq, we must give the State Department the basic resources they need to successfully relieve the military of their mission there and help ensure Iraq's stability and future prosperity," Tierney said at an Oversight subcommittee hearing in March 2011.

The issue of defense contracting has been a frequent topic for Tierney. He successfully amended the 2008 defense authorization legislation to create a Wartime Contracting Commission to audit contracts, and he blasted the Bush administration for resisting its implementation.

Tierney also gained attention in 2007, when his subcommittee investigated media reports of inadequate patient care at Walter Reed Army Medical Center, where injured soldiers from Iraq and Afghanistan are treated. He called a field hearing in March 2007 at Walter Reed and lambasted senior Army commanders who suggested they had been unaware of the problems: "I have to tell you, the first thing that pops into my mind is: Where've you been? Where has all the brass been?"

Tierney also sits on the Education and the Workforce Committee, where he was part of a successful effort to make the federal government the sole provider of student loans. Democratic supporters said the student loan takeover, enacted as part of the health care overhaul legislation in 2010, would save $61 billion over 10 years, money they want to use to expand other education programs.

A longtime advocate of universal health care coverage, Tierney was among the group pushing for the government-run option in the health care bill. But he supported the final package, which did not include the "public option." He likened GOP efforts at repeal in early 2011 to political theater.

His connections to Pelosi helped earn Tierney a spot on the Democratic Steering and Policy Committee, which sets committee assignments. He remains at the liberal end of his caucus and often tries to push party moderates in that direction.

A case in point is Tierney's longtime focus on a bill he calls "Clean Money, Clean Elections," which he first introduced in 1997. It includes public financing of elections, free broadcast time for candidates and limits on expenditures by political parties. A few provisions were included in the campaign finance law enacted in 2002, but the proposal has languished.

Tierney became interested in politics as a boy growing up in Salem. His uncle served as a ward councilor in Peabody, and Tierney campaigned with him. He worked to put himself through Salem State College, where he majored in political science. He obtained a law degree from Suffolk University and was a partner in the law firm of Tierney, Kalis and Lucas for more than 20 years, until his election to the House. Throughout his legal career, he was active in civic affairs in Salem, where he continues to reside.

Tierney launched his first campaign in 1994 and came within 4 percentage points of defeating freshman GOP Rep. Peter G. Torkildsen, who was aided by that year's Republican tide. They faced off again in 1996, and with President Bill Clinton sweeping the district by 28 percentage points, Tierney managed a 371-vote win. Torkildsen was back for another rematch in 1998, but Tierney won by 12 points. His re-elections have been a breeze since.

Key Votes

2010

Overhaul the nation's health insurance system	YES
Allow for repeal of "don't ask, don't tell"	YES
Overhaul financial services industry regulation	YES
Limit use of new Afghanistan War funds to troop withdrawal activities	YES
Change oversight of offshore drilling and lift oil spill liability cap	YES
Provide a path to legal status for some children of illegal immigrants	YES
Extend Bush-era income tax cuts for two years	NO

2009

Expand the Children's Health Insurance Program	YES
Provide $787 billion in tax cuts and spending increases to stimulate the economy	YES
Allow bankruptcy judges to modify certain primary-residence mortgages	YES
Create a cap-and-trade system to limit greenhouse gas emissions	YES
Provide $2 billion for the "cash for clunkers" program	NO
Establish the government as the sole provider of student loans	YES
Restrict federally funded insurance coverage for abortions in health care overhaul	NO

CQ Vote Studies

	PARTY UNITY		PRESIDENTIAL SUPPORT	
	Support	Oppose	Support	Oppose
2010	99%	1%	83%	17%
2009	98%	2%	94%	6%
2008	98%	2%	12%	88%
2007	99%	1%	4%	96%
2006	96%	4%	13%	87%

Interest Groups

	AFL-CIO	ADA	CCUS	ACU
2010	100%	95%	13%	0%
2009	95%	95%	33%	0%
2008	100%	95%	59%	4%
2007	92%	100%	50%	0%
2006	100%	100%	33%	8%

Massachusetts 6

North Shore — Lynn, Peabody

Pristine beaches line the cool ocean of Boston's North Shore, home to some of the state's largest homes. Country clubs, fox hunting and polo are popular diversions for residents of the northern inland, where the population is sparse but wealthy.

The population, and traffic, is denser along Route 128 in the southern part of the 6th, a high-tech center that developed when towns began to shift from manufacturing to an information-based economy in the 1990s. Lured in part by Boston's universities, computer and biotech firms line the corridor from Burlington to Gloucester, which hosts headquarters of semiconductor manufacturers and software companies. Gloucester's traditional fishing industry has declined, struggling to compensate for smaller catches and increasingly stringent federal regulations.

Urban dwellers are concentrated mostly in Lynn and Peabody and provide minority and blue-collar votes for Democrats. Lynn is home to aerospace and defense contractors; a General Electric jet engine plant is a key employer. Other population centers include the coastal cities of Beverly — which locals describe as the birthplace of the Navy because the first

ship commissioned by the Continental Congress sailed from its harbor in 1775 — and major tourist destination Salem, with its rich history as the site of the 1692 witch trials. Salem is middle-class and has a Democratic slant, while Beverly is more politically independent.

The 6th's Democratic past has begun to shift to support for some Republican candidates. The GOP can win by attracting independent-minded "unenrolled" voters in the wealthiest district in the state, and Republican Sen. Scott P. Brown did well in upscale towns such as Boxford, Lynnfield, Topsfield and Wenham in his 2010 special election.

Major Industry
Technology, defense, fishing

Military Bases
Hanscom Air Force Base, 1,400 military, 1,567 civilian (2008)

Cities
Lynn, 90,329; Peabody, 51,251; Salem, 41,340; Beverly, 39,502; Gloucester, 28,789; Saugus (unincorporated), 26,628

Notable
The 6th includes territory that spawned the original "gerrymander," a state legislative district named for Gov. Elbridge Gerry in 1812.

Rep. Edward J. Markey (D)

Capitol Office
225-2836
markey.house.gov
2108 Rayburn Bldg. 20515-2107; fax 226-0092

Committees
Energy & Commerce
Natural Resources - Ranking Member

Residence
Malden

Born
July 11, 1946; Malden, Mass.

Religion
Roman Catholic

Family
Wife, Susan Blumenthal

Education
Boston College, B.A. 1968, J.D. 1972

Military
Army Reserve, 1968-73

Career
Lawyer

Political Highlights
Mass. House, 1973-77

ELECTION RESULTS

2010 GENERAL

Edward J. Markey (D)	145,696	66.4%
Gerry Dembrowski (R)	73,467	33.5%

2010 PRIMARY

Edward J. Markey (D)	unopposed

2008 GENERAL

Edward J. Markey (D)	212,304	75.6%
John Cunningham (R)	67,978	24.2%

Previous Winning Percentages
2006 (98%); 2004 (74%); 2002 (98%); 2000 (99%);
1998 (71%); 1996 (70%); 1994 (64%); 1992 (62%);
1990 (100%); 1988 (100%); 1986 (100%); 1984 (71%);
1982 (78%); 1980 (100%); 1978 (85%); 1976 (77%)

Elected 1976; 18th full term

Markey is a liberal party loyalist with a gift for making the sort of deft, well-timed quips that journalists love to quote. Although early in his House career Markey struggled against the impression that he was fonder of one-liners than the patient pursuit of legislative goals, he has dispelled that notion by compiling a record of accomplishments.

He has also been loyal. Markey backed his leadership on 99 percent of the votes that pitted most Democrats against most Republicans during the 110th (2007-08) and 111th (2009-10) Congresses.

An advocate for fuel-efficient cars and against nuclear energy, with a portfolio of innovative technology ideas, Markey has become a power player on climate change, an issue he addresses as a member of the Energy and Commerce Committee and as the ranking member of the Natural Resources Committee in the 112th Congress (2011-12).

He also had two venues from which to make his mark on that topic in the 111th Congress. One, chairmanship of the Energy and Commerce panel on Energy and the Environment, was taken away when Democrats lost the majority in the 2010 elections, although he still sits on the renamed Energy and Power Subcommittee.

The other disappeared entirely. Then-Speaker Nancy Pelosi of California had tapped him to lead the Select Committee on Energy Independence and Global Warming, which she created at the start of the 110th Congress. Republicans dispensed with the panel after reclaiming the majority, saying it duplicated the work of other committees.

But while he had the leverage, Markey made the most of it.

He was one of the architects of sweeping energy and climate change legislation the House narrowly passed in 2009 that would have created a cap-and-trade system designed to limit carbon emissions.

The legislation stalled in the Senate, even as Democrats tried to change the calculus by tying the spring 2010 oil spill at an offshore drilling site in the Gulf of Mexico to the climate change issue. Markey became a regular on cable television talk shows, castigating BP, owner of the offshore well. At a high-profile hearing of his Energy and Commerce subcommittee, Markey brandished the contingency plans for such spills developed by BP and several other major companies, acidly noting that "the covers of the five response plans are different colors, but the content is 90 percent identical."

In 2011, he opposed a provision added to the House-passed catchall spending bill for fiscal 2011 to bar the EPA from implementing regulations that would put in place a system similar to the one Congress rejected.

Energy and Commerce also is a forum for Markey's interest in communications technology. During the 111th Congress, he wrote a provision into the $787 billion economic stimulus bill that required the Federal Communications Commission to develop a strategy for fostering broadband Internet access.

Markey also is active on consumer and electronic privacy issues as co-chairman of the Congressional Privacy Caucus; from that perch, he routinely queries big technology companies and federal regulators on the issue.

His signature achievement remains the 1996 telecommunications overhaul that opened local phone markets to competition, set conditions for the powerful Bell companies to enter new markets and regulated competition between telephone and cable companies. He is active in what is likely to be another multi-year effort to update communications law that Democrats began in 2010.

In 1992, Markey engineered the only override of a veto by President George Bush, leading the House to enact a bill he helped write that regulated the booming cable industry. But more recently Markey said government policies — or lack thereof — have undercut the 1996 act, leading to the country's loss of its pre-eminence in broadband Internet services.

"We just can't have a national plan put together alone by a small handful of communications colossi," said Markey, a leading advocate of "net neutrality," which would bar companies from putting what he considers undue restrictions on access to Internet services.

There was a time when Markey's biggest career frustration was his inability to move to the Senate. When Democratic Sen. Paul E. Tsongas decided against running for re-election in 1984, Markey quickly announced his candidacy, but dropped out after it became clear he was at best an even bet against his chief competitors, including the eventual winner, Democratic Lt. Gov. John Kerry. But when longtime Democratic Sen. Edward M. Kennedy died in 2009, Markey decided not to make a bid for the open seat. He reasoned that his state would be better off if he kept wielding his clout as one of the most senior Democrats in the House.

The son of a milk truck driver, Markey was greatly influenced in his early years by another Irish Catholic from Massachusetts: President John F. Kennedy. As a student at Malden Catholic High School, he listened to interviews with the Rev. Martin Luther King Jr. and Malcolm X on a night-time radio talk show. At the time, Massachusetts "was alive with the potential of the Kennedy vision of what our country could be," Markey recalls, although in 1968 he campaigned for anti-war Democratic Sen. Eugene J. McCarthy of Minnesota rather than the slain president's brother Robert, a Democratic senator from New York.

After earning a law degree, Markey won a race for a state House seat and quickly became a thorn in the side of establishment Democrats. He picked a fight in 1976 with party leaders over judicial reform, successfully pushing legislation to force judges to give up their law practices while in office. The Massachusetts bar endorsed the bill, but the Speaker kicked him off the Judiciary Committee. When he showed up for work the next day, his office was cleaned out.

That notoriety helped Markey prevail in a Democratic primary for an open House seat involving a dozen aspirants, employing the slogan, "The bosses can tell me where to sit, no one can tell me where to stand." He was elected to the seat with a substantial margin against his Republican opponent and has cruised to re-election in the ensuing decades.

Key Votes

2010

Overhaul the nation's health insurance system	YES
Allow for repeal of "don't ask, don't tell"	YES
Overhaul financial services industry regulation	YES
Limit use of new Afghanistan War funds to troop withdrawal activities	YES
Change oversight of offshore drilling and lift oil spill liability cap	YES
Provide a path to legal status for some children of illegal immigrants	YES
Extend Bush-era income tax cuts for two years	NO

2009

Expand the Children's Health Insurance Program	YES
Provide $787 billion in tax cuts and spending increases to stimulate the economy	YES
Allow bankruptcy judges to modify certain primary-residence mortgages	YES
Create a cap-and-trade system to limit greenhouse gas emissions	YES
Provide $2 billion for the "cash for clunkers" program	YES
Establish the government as the sole provider of student loans	YES
Restrict federally funded insurance coverage for abortions in health care overhaul	NO

CQ Vote Studies

	PARTY UNITY		PRESIDENTIAL SUPPORT	
	SUPPORT	OPPOSE	SUPPORT	OPPOSE
2010	99%	1%	86%	14%
2009	99%	1%	97%	3%
2008	99%	1%	14%	86%
2007	99%	1%	3%	97%
2006	98%	2%	7%	93%

Interest Groups

	AFL-CIO	ADA	CCUS	ACU
2010	100%	100%	13%	0%
2009	100%	100%	33%	0%
2008	100%	100%	56%	0%
2007	96%	100%	58%	4%
2006	100%	100%	20%	4%

Massachusetts 7

Northwest Boston suburbs — Framingham

The affluent strip along eastern Massachusetts' technology corridor has shaped the 7th District's character, although some are looking to rebrand the industry's image with the rise of local biotech employers. The district includes some of the state's most well-to-do communities as it jumps east from an urban retail center near Framingham to Route 128, which rings Boston, then through Medford and Malden to the middle-class coastal town of Revere.

The area takes pride in its history: Each year, Lexington re-enacts Paul Revere's ride and the first Revolutionary War battles (which took place in towns in the 7th and 5th districts) on Patriot's Day in April.

For decades, Revere has attracted vacationers to its beaches, but a stable software and Internet industry drives the 7th's economy. Many Medford and Malden residents commute to blue-collar jobs in Boston. Malden's Asian population has tripled in the past two decades, and the 7th is home to the second-largest Asian population in the state as well as numerous advocacy organizations for Asian-Americans.

The 7th's political roots are a mix of Protestant Yankee Republicans and Irish Democrats. The wealthy sections of the 7th vary from the moderate Weston to the liberal Lincoln. Democrats also draw votes from a blue-collar, middle-class base in Framingham and in the eastern part of the district, including Revere, Everett and Malden. Despite the presence of Republican voters, like all Massachusetts districts the 7th backs Democrats in federal races. Barack Obama won 65 percent of the district's 2008 presidential vote, and most of the district's towns backed Democratic state Attorney General Martha Coakley in her unsuccessful 2010 special-election bid for the Senate.

Major Industry
Technology, telecommunications, defense

Military Bases
Army Soldier Systems Center (Natick), 1,230 military, 2,050 civilian (2011)

Cities
Framingham (unincorporated), 68,318; Waltham, 60,632; Malden, 59,450; Medford, 56,173; Revere, 51,755; Arlington (unincorporated), 42,844

Notable
The New England Confectionery Company (NECCO), the oldest multiline candy company in the United States, is located in Revere.

Rep. Michael E. Capuano (D)

Capitol Office
225-5111
www.house.gov/capuano
1414 Longworth Bldg. 20515-2108; fax 225-9322

Committees
Financial Services
Transportation & Infrastructure

Residence
Somerville

Born
Jan. 9, 1952; Somerville, Mass.

Religion
Roman Catholic

Family
Wife, Barbara Teebagy Capuano; two children

Education
Dartmouth College, B.A. 1973 (psychology); Boston College, J.D. 1977

Career
Lawyer; state legislative aide

Political Highlights
Somerville Board of Aldermen, 1977-79; candidate for mayor of Somerville, 1979, 1981; Somerville Board of Aldermen, 1985-89; mayor of Somerville, 1990-99; sought Democratic nomination for Mass. secretary of state, 1994; sought Democratic nomination for U.S. Senate in special election, 2009

ELECTION RESULTS

2010 GENERAL

Michael E. Capuano (D)	134,974	98.0%
write-ins (WRI)	2,686	2.0%

2010 PRIMARY

Michael E. Capuano (D)	unopposed

2008 GENERAL

Michael E. Capuano (D)	185,530	98.6%
write-ins	2,722	1.4%

Previous Winning Percentages
2006 (91%); 2004 (99%); 2002 (100%); 2000 (99%); 1998 (82%)

Elected 1998; 7th term

A former alderman and mayor of the traditionally blue-collar — though increasingly upscale — Boston suburb of Somerville, Capuano fits the image of an old-time city pol. He has an affable public demeanor while being well attuned to the insider's game, and he believes strongly in the efficacy of activist government. He works closely with leadership and sits on key House committees, but he has eyed a run for governor, taken a shot at the Senate and might give that chamber another go.

He represents the historic Boston district that produced the dynasty of Kennedy Democrats and former House Speaker Thomas P. O'Neill Jr. Capuano's views are at least as liberal as his better-known predecessors': On votes that divided a majority of Democrats against a majority of Republicans in the 111th Congress (2009-10), he voted with his party 99 percent of the time. A Bay State blogger wrote that Capuano (KAP-you-AH-no) is "the bluest congressman from the bluest district of the bluest state in the Union."

His view of the role of government might have been best summed up when he suggested that government created the American middle class. "I will tell you that, for me, subjecting homeowners, or potential homeowners, to nothing but the private market has been tried in this country for 150 years and failed to create a middle class," he said at a Financial Services Committee hearing that addressed the role of mortgage giants Fannie Mae and Freddie Mac. "Since government got involved, indirectly, through Fannie and Freddie, we created the middle class and we sustained the middle class."

A tax attorney, Capuano voted for the $700 billion legislation to aid the financial services sector, which was signed into law in the fall of 2008, but he has been a critic of its implementation. When the House passed legislation in 2009 aimed at ensuring more congressional oversight of the program — he currently serves as ranking Democrat on the Financial Services Subcommittee on Oversight and Investigations — Capuano got language included to protect renters living in foreclosed properties from quick evictions.

He is a leading voice on human rights issues and serves as co-chairman of the Congressional Caucus on Sudan. He has said the situation in the African nation is grave enough that he would support U.S. military intervention in Darfur, the region where the Sudanese government has been accused of genocide. He had expressed "strong reservations" about the independence movement in Southern Sudan, but after a 2011 referendum there showed overwhelming support for breaking away from Khartoum, he said the United States should help the people there "chart their new course."

Yet his signature achievement as far as Bostonians are concerned has more to do with roads and bridges than with war and peace. As a member of the Transportation and Infrastructure Committee, he is credited with reversing the decline in grants to Massachusetts in reaction to the "Big Dig," the over-budget, scandal-ridden Boston tunnel project that had made many in Congress leery of the state's management of transportation funds.

When a concrete slab in a Big Dig tunnel fell, killing a motorist in 2006, Capuano led the state's congressional delegation in demanding a federal probe.

Capuano proved adept at the horse trading that goes on behind the scenes in the stiff competition for earmarked federal grants, and he ultimately secured hundreds of millions of dollars for the state in 2005 as part of a reauthorization of the surface transportation law. "We all have certain skills," he said. "I get along with these guys. I'm a compromiser when I need to be."

A member of the Progressive Caucus, a group of left-leaning House Democrats, he earned the trust of Democratic Leader Nancy Pelosi of California, who asked him to head the transition team after their party won control of the House in the 2006 election.

At the start of the 110th Congress (2007-08), then-Speaker Pelosi also asked Capuano to shoulder a task few lawmakers would relish: pushing for a rules change to allow outsiders to judge the ethical lapses of House members. His task force's report was first delayed and then widely criticized, but a hard push by Pelosi in March 2008 secured passage of its key recommendation: the creation of an independent Office of Congressional Ethics.

Pelosi endorsed Capuano in the Democratic primary for the special election to succeed the late Sen. Edward M. Kennedy in 2009. He lost by almost 20 percentage points to state Attorney General Martha Coakley, who subsequently lost to Republican state Sen. Scott P. Brown.

Although he has an Ivy League education (a degree in psychology from Dartmouth College), Capuano likes to stress his roots in working-class Somerville, where he launched his political career in the 1970s as a city alderman. Capuano won the 8th District seat after Joseph P. Kennedy II, the son of Robert F. Kennedy and the nephew of President John F. Kennedy, gave it up after six terms. The House seat still includes much of the territory it did when the late president represented it from 1947 to 1953.

Capuano hails from a more modest political dynasty. His father was the first Italian-American elected to local office in Somerville.

The district includes few Republicans, but political tensions among Democratic factions often bubble to the surface. When he was mayor of Somerville, detractors called him "tyrannical" and said he managed the city like a ward boss, hiring friends and relatives and running enemies out of public agencies — not necessarily an insult in the place where James Michael Curley, the legendary mid-century rogue who served as congressman, mayor and governor, once held sway.

Capuano triumphed in a 10-Democrat donnybrook created by Joseph Kennedy's 1998 retirement. The presumed front-runner was Raymond L. Flynn, a former Boston mayor and ambassador to the Vatican who had abandoned a flagging run for governor. But Capuano and others ganged up on Flynn; although greatly outspent by two other candidates, Capuano was lifted to victory by a strong turnout in Somerville. He breezed by a Republican opponent that November, and the GOP has not fielded a candidate since.

He briefly considered running for governor in 2006 but decided against it, and is considered a possible opponent for Brown in 2012.

Key Votes

2010

Overhaul the nation's health insurance system	YES
Allow for repeal of "don't ask, don't tell"	YES
Overhaul financial services industry regulation	YES
Limit use of new Afghanistan War funds to troop withdrawal activities	YES
Change oversight of offshore drilling and lift oil spill liability cap	YES
Provide a path to legal status for some children of illegal immigrants	YES
Extend Bush-era income tax cuts for two years	NO

2009

Expand the Children's Health Insurance Program	YES
Provide $787 billion in tax cuts and spending increases to stimulate the economy	YES
Allow bankruptcy judges to modify certain primary-residence mortgages	YES
Create a cap-and-trade system to limit greenhouse gas emissions	YES
Provide $2 billion for the "cash for clunkers" program	YES
Establish the government as the sole provider of student loans	YES
Restrict federally funded insurance coverage for abortions in health care overhaul	NO

CQ Vote Studies

	PARTY UNITY		PRESIDENTIAL SUPPORT	
	Support	Oppose	Support	Oppose
2010	98%	2%	85%	15%
2009	99%	1%	96%	4%
2008	99%	1%	22%	78%
2007	98%	2%	6%	94%
2006	96%	4%	25%	75%

Interest Groups

	AFL-CIO	ADA	CCUS	ACU
2010	93%	95%	13%	0%
2009	100%	95%	29%	0%
2008	100%	95%	67%	4%
2007	96%	95%	50%	0%
2006	100%	90%	40%	8%

Massachusetts 8

Part of Boston and suburbs — Cambridge, Somerville

The 8th combines Boston's historic Revolutionary War sites with neighborhoods that reflect its evolving future. It grabs roughly 70 percent of the city's population, almost all west of Interstate 93, picking up the Back Bay area, Chinatown and many largely black and Hispanic communities in areas like Roxbury, Dorchester and Jamaica Plain. Among the 8th's many oft-visited Beantown sights are Bunker Hill, the Old North Church, the USS Constitution and Logan International Airport (shared with the 7th).

The 8th is the state's only district where a majority of residents are minorities, and Boston's expanding Hispanic population led to faster population growth for the city than for the state as a whole over the last decade. Two of the world's most respected universities — Harvard and the Massachusetts Institute of Technology — lie across the Charles River from Boston in Cambridge. The district also takes in dozens of other colleges, which drive much of the economy, whether through blue-collar service employees who work at the schools and teaching hospitals or through

biotech software firms that employ local talent. The 8th is home to the highest percentage of college graduates in the state — almost half of all residents have at least an undergraduate degree.

Somerville, just north of Cambridge, has a thriving arts community, while Chelsea, with more-affordable housing and blue-collar jobs, has seen its Hispanic population expand to make up more than 60 percent of the city's residents.

Typifying the district's monolithically liberal politics, Cambridge gave Republican George W. Bush just 13 percent of the vote in the 2000 and 2004 presidential elections, and Democrat Barack Obama received 84 percent of the district's presidential vote in 2008, his statewide high.

Major Industry
Biotech, higher education, health care, tourism

Cities
Boston (pt.), 444,321; Cambridge, 105,162; Somerville, 75,754

Notable
The 8th is the descendant of the district once represented by John F. Kennedy (1947-53) and Thomas P. "Tip" O'Neill Jr. (1953-87); Fenway Park is home to baseball's Boston Red Sox.

Rep. Stephen F. Lynch (D)

Capitol Office
225-8273
www.house.gov/lynch
2348 Rayburn Bldg. 20515-2109; fax 225-3984

Committees
Financial Services
Oversight & Government Reform

Residence
Boston

Born
March 31, 1955; Boston, Mass.

Religion
Roman Catholic

Family
Wife, Margaret Lynch; two children

Education
Wentworth Institute of Technology, B.S. 1988 (construction management); Boston College, J.D. 1991; Harvard U., M.A. 1998 (public administration)

Career
Lawyer; ironworker

Political Highlights
Mass. House, 1995-96; Mass. Senate, 1996-2001

ELECTION RESULTS

2010 GENERAL
Stephen F. Lynch (D)	157,071	68.3%
Vernon Harrison (R)	59,965	26.1%
Phil Dunkelbarger (I)	12,572	5.5%

2010 PRIMARY
Stephen F. Lynch (D)	42,527	64.8%
Mac D'Alessandro (D)	23,109	35.2%

2008 GENERAL
Stephen F. Lynch (D)	242,166	98.7%
write-ins	3,128	1.3%

Previous Winning Percentages
2006 (78%); 2004 (99%); 2002 (99%); 2001 Special Election (65%)

Elected 2001; 5th full term

Lynch arrived in Congress in 2001 on the strength of his support among labor unions and his socially conservative views, which are still prevalent in South Boston, the city's historically Irish section. A former ironworker, Lynch has rock-solid union credentials, and he has made it clear he opposes both abortion and same-sex marriage, consistent with many of his fellow Roman Catholics in Southie.

But during a tumultuous 111th Congress (2009-10), Lynch demonstrated that his views have changed during his time in office.

While making a short-lived bid to replace the late Democratic Sen. Edward M. Kennedy in 2009, Lynch alienated his longtime labor allies by refusing to endorse key union-backed priorities for health care legislation, principally a government-run insurance option and a mandate that employers provide health insurance for their workers. Lynch was hoping to set himself up as the conservative Democrat in a race dominated by liberals, most notably his congressional colleague Michael E. Capuano of Somerville and the eventual nominee, Attorney General Martha Coakley.

But after that move, Lynch's labor support abandoned him for Coakley, even refusing to allow Lynch to speak at the Labor Day Breakfast, a key annual event for politicians looking to schmooze with Boston labor leaders.

Unable to raise enough money to make a competitive bid, Lynch dropped out of the race, but he wasn't done burning bridges to the state's labor movement. Though Lynch ultimately supported a House health care bill passed in the fall of 2009, he refused to back the final version enacted the following March. Despite entreaties from fellow Democrats desperate to line up votes, he said he couldn't back a bill without the government-run public option he had previously wavered on or one that taxed higher-cost union health insurance plans. Former labor supporters viewed his position as disingenuous. He was the only member of Massachusetts' House delegation to vote no.

Lynch announced in early 2010 that he'd switched his position on same-sex marriage. This was a particularly salient development because late in 2009 the District of Columbia's city council had approved an ordinance granting same-sex partners living in Washington the right to marry. Conservative activists asked Lynch, then chairman of the Oversight and Government Reform panel that oversees the District, to intervene. Lynch declined. "I'm trying to respect the local government here," Lynch told a Boston Globe reporter.

But it was clear that Lynch's views on the issue had changed. At the same time, he was also supporting legislation in the House that would grant same-sex partners of federal employees access to federal health care benefits.

The District subcommittee's chairmanship has often been seen as a millstone, a thankless job that rarely interests constituents back home. But Lynch took it seriously. Lynch has also been involved in examining how to get the Postal Service back on sound financial footing. In addition, he has sought to provide paid parental leave for federal workers.

Lynch is also a member of the Financial Services Committee, where he helped home-state Democratic colleague Barney Frank, who chaired the panel in the 111th Congress, move legislation in 2010 to overhaul the way the government regulates financial services companies to prevent the need for the type of assistance packages for big firms that occurred in 2008 and 2009, and which Lynch opposed.

Despite his turnaround on gay marriage, Lynch continues to oppose abortion. And he was one of 47 Democrats to vote with conservatives in 2005 in favor of congressional intervention in the case of Terri Schiavo, a severely brain-damaged Florida woman who was the subject of a major court battle.

He's also more hawkish on foreign policy than many Democrats. He voted to authorize the Iraq War in 2002 and later backed a 2006 Republican resolution supporting President George W. Bush's policies there.

"Calling me the least liberal member from Massachusetts is like calling me the slowest Kenyan in the Boston Marathon," he told the Globe amid the health care debate. "It's all relative." Indeed, his party unity score — the percentage of votes on which he sides with a majority of Democrats against a majority of Republicans — has never been out of the 90s and reached a career high of 98 in 2008 and 2009.

Lynch says he's most proud of his work on a local project, the construction of Cushing House, now a 30-bed facility for adolescents with drug problems. Inspired by a spate of drug-related teen suicides in his district, Lynch secured federal funding for the facility, which was completed in 2005. He talked old union pals into donating labor and a factory owner into donating space.

Lynch's father was an ironworker for 40 years, and his mother was a World War II welder who worked as a post office clerk. Lynch was an ironworker for 18 years, and at age 30 he was the youngest president ever elected of Ironworkers Local 7. He earned a law degree from Boston College and later a master's degree from Harvard. He joined a law firm and continued a practice he had begun in law school of representing housing-project residents for free.

In 1994, he unseated incumbent Paul Gannon in the Massachusetts House; two years later, he won a special election for a state Senate seat.

Lynch made his first run for the U.S. House in a special election in 2001 to replace longtime Rep. Joe Moakley, a Democrat who died of leukemia. He was up against six other Democrats, several of whom criticized his opposition to abortion. Two of them raised questions about an incident from Lynch's attorney days, when he defended 14 white teenagers accused of harassing a white girl and her Hispanic boyfriend. But Lynch benefited from his up-by-the-bootstraps personal story, as well as from publicity over his decision to donate 60 percent of his liver to his brother-in-law, who had liver cancer.

Lynch won the primary with 39 percent of the vote and went on to defeat Republican state Sen. Jo Ann Sprague with 65 percent. He faced a Republican opponent in 2006, and took more than three-quarters of the vote, but in 2002, 2004 and 2008, no Republican challenged him for re-election. Vernon Harrison stepped up in 2010, but Lynch won easily with 68 percent of the vote.

Key Votes

2010	
Overhaul the nation's health insurance system	NO
Allow for repeal of "don't ask, don't tell"	YES
Overhaul financial services industry regulation	YES
Limit use of new Afghanistan War funds to troop withdrawal activities	NO
Change oversight of offshore drilling and lift oil spill liability cap	YES
Provide a path to legal status for some children of illegal immigrants	YES
Extend Bush-era income tax cuts for two years	NO

2009	
Expand the Children's Health Insurance Program	YES
Provide $787 billion in tax cuts and spending increases to stimulate the economy	YES
Allow bankruptcy judges to modify certain primary-residence mortgages	YES
Create a cap-and-trade system to limit greenhouse gas emissions	YES
Provide $2 billion for the "cash for clunkers" program	YES
Establish the government as the sole provider of student loans	YES
Restrict federally funded insurance coverage for abortions in health care overhaul	YES

CQ Vote Studies

	PARTY UNITY		PRESIDENTIAL SUPPORT	
	SUPPORT	OPPOSE	SUPPORT	OPPOSE
2010	95%	5%	88%	12%
2009	98%	2%	96%	4%
2008	98%	2%	10%	90%
2007	96%	4%	5%	95%
2006	90%	10%	30%	70%

Interest Groups

	AFL-CIO	ADA	CCUS	ACU
2010	93%	95%	13%	0%
2009	100%	90%	36%	4%
2008	100%	95%	53%	8%
2007	96%	90%	60%	0%
2006	100%	90%	27%	20%

Massachusetts 9

Part of Boston; southern suburbs — Brockton, Braintree

The 9th begins with a central swath of downtown Boston, covering Beacon Hill, the West End and the financial district. The statehouse and brokerage houses — the 9th is home to one of the world's largest centers for mutual fund investing — dominate this part of Boston and share the area with sprawling Boston Common park and several of New England's major tourist attractions. Faneuil Hall Marketplace anchors a stable retail industry.

From central Boston the district hops the Fort Point Channel into South Boston, referred to as "Southie," and closely hugs Interstate 93 on its way into Milton. It connects through Dedham to West Roxbury, a rapidly diversifying but still mostly white suburban enclave in the southwestern part of Boston.

Some of the wealthiest neighborhoods in the state are along the Charles River, and the "Brahmin" homes of Beacon Hill are counterbalanced by the poor and working-class neighborhoods of traditionally Irish Southie and middle-class suburban communities south and west of the city. Although solidly Democratic, Southie's political tradition is one of supporting pro-labor Democrats who are more socially conservative.

The 9th's areas outside of Boston are relatively conservative for Massachusetts. The district's mostly blue-collar base in Boston and Brockton keeps it solidly Democratic in most federal elections — Barack Obama won 60 percent of the district's 2008 presidential vote — but Republican Sen. Scott P. Brown picked up wins in Dedham and Braintree during his 2010 special election.

Major Industry
Financial services, government, tourism

Cities
Boston (pt.), 173,273; Brockton, 93,810; Braintree Town, 35,744; Randolph (unincorporated), 32,112; Needham (unincorporated), 28,886

Notable
Patriots tossed boxes of tea into the Boston Harbor during the Boston Tea Party in 1773, a catalyst for the Revolutionary War; in the 1640s, Dedham authorized the nation's first solely taxpayer-funded school; the John F. Kennedy Library and Museum is in the 9th's portion of Boston.

Rep. William Keating (D)

Capitol Office
225-3111
keating.house.gov
315 Cannon Bldg. 20515-2110; fax 225-5658

Committees
Foreign Affairs
Homeland Security
Small Business

Residence
Quincy

Born
Sept. 6, 1952; Norwood, Mass.

Religion
Roman Catholic

Family
Wife, Tevis Keating; two children

Education
Boston College, B.A. 1974 (political science), M.B.A. 1982; Suffolk U., J.D. 1985

Career
Lawyer

Political Highlights
Mass. House, 1977-85; Mass. Senate, 1985-99; Norfolk County district attorney, 1999-2011

ELECTION RESULTS

2010 GENERAL

William Keating (D)	132,743	46.9%
Jeff Perry (R)	120,029	42.4%
Maryanne Lewis (I)	16,705	5.9%
James Sheets (I)	10,445	3.7%
Joe Van Nes (I)	3,084	1.1%

2010 PRIMARY

William Keating (D)	29,953	51.1%
Robert A. O'Leary (D)	28,656	48.9%

Elected 2010; 1st term

Keating — a former district attorney, state representative and state senator — represents a district carried by Republican Scott P. Brown in his 2010 special-election Senate victory. Keating's own tough election battle suggests that in his first term he might take a centrist approach on some issues.

"It's an electorate right now that has lost some trust in our institution, so I think they're frustrated with the inability of government trying to deal with issues," he said.

One area where Keating sees the possibility of bipartisan cooperation is human rights and democracy abroad. A member of the Foreign Affairs Committee, he wants to promote legislation to prevent U.S. companies from selling Internet censoring software to repressive regimes.

"The Internet is going to be a terrific tool for democracy. We cannot have American companies be part of . . . repressing human rights," he said on Bloomberg News in early 2011.

Keating, ranking Democrat on the Homeland Security Subcommittee on Oversight, Investigations, and Management, was among the lawmakers seeking a probe of security lapses in the case of a North Carolina teenager who died after stowing away on a plane bound for Boston's Logan International Airport. Keating was still Norfolk County district attorney when the incident occurred and oversaw the local investigation.

He also serves on the Small Business Committee.

Seeking to succeed the retiring seven-term Democrat Bill Delahunt, Keating won a close primary contest over state Sen. Robert A. O'Leary, then faced GOP former state Rep. Jeff Perry in the general election. Republicans charged Keating with being soft on rapists as district attorney. Democrats dredged up a two-decade-old case in which the victim of an illegal strip search accused Perry, then a policeman, of failing to protect her from his partner.

The congressional campaign committees of the two parties spent more than $2.1 million on the race, for the only open seat in Massachusetts.

On election night, Keating prevailed with 47 percent of the vote to Perry's 42 percent. Three independent candidates claimed 11 percent.

Massachusetts 10

South Shore — Quincy, Cape Cod, islands

Cool coastal breezes in the summer and warm ocean air in the winter lure retirees and tourists to the 10th, where most towns border the ocean. The region that spawned the nation's puritanical streak and Thanksgiving holiday still retains a Yankee flavor. Unlike the coastal communities, the northern part of the 10th has attracted residents from Boston and now boasts a strong ethnic flavor. Quincy officials hope that a downtown development project will bring jobs.

Outside of a few thriving cranberry bogs, the mainland coastal towns of the 10th, referred to as the South Shore, consist mostly of bedroom communities for Boston's professionals or Quincy's blue-collar workers. The software industry and health care are now key economic contributors.

On the Cape, tourism is dominant, but maritime technology and research are growing industries, especially in Woods Hole, home to world-renowned scientific institutions specializing in marine biology. Nantucket was hit harder than Martha's Vineyard by recent economic downturns.

The 10th is more evenly split politically than any other district in Massachusetts. While the state's most liberal population lives on the far end of Cape Cod, where Provincetown, a predominately gay artists' colony and resort area, thrives, the district also includes one of the highest concentrations of Republicans in the state on the South Shore and in the wealthier towns on the Cape.

Major Industry
Marine technology, biotech, tourism

Cities
Quincy, 92,271; Weymouth Town, 53,743; Barnstable Town, 45,193

Notable
The John Alden House in Duxbury is named for a Pilgrim who sailed on the Mayflower.

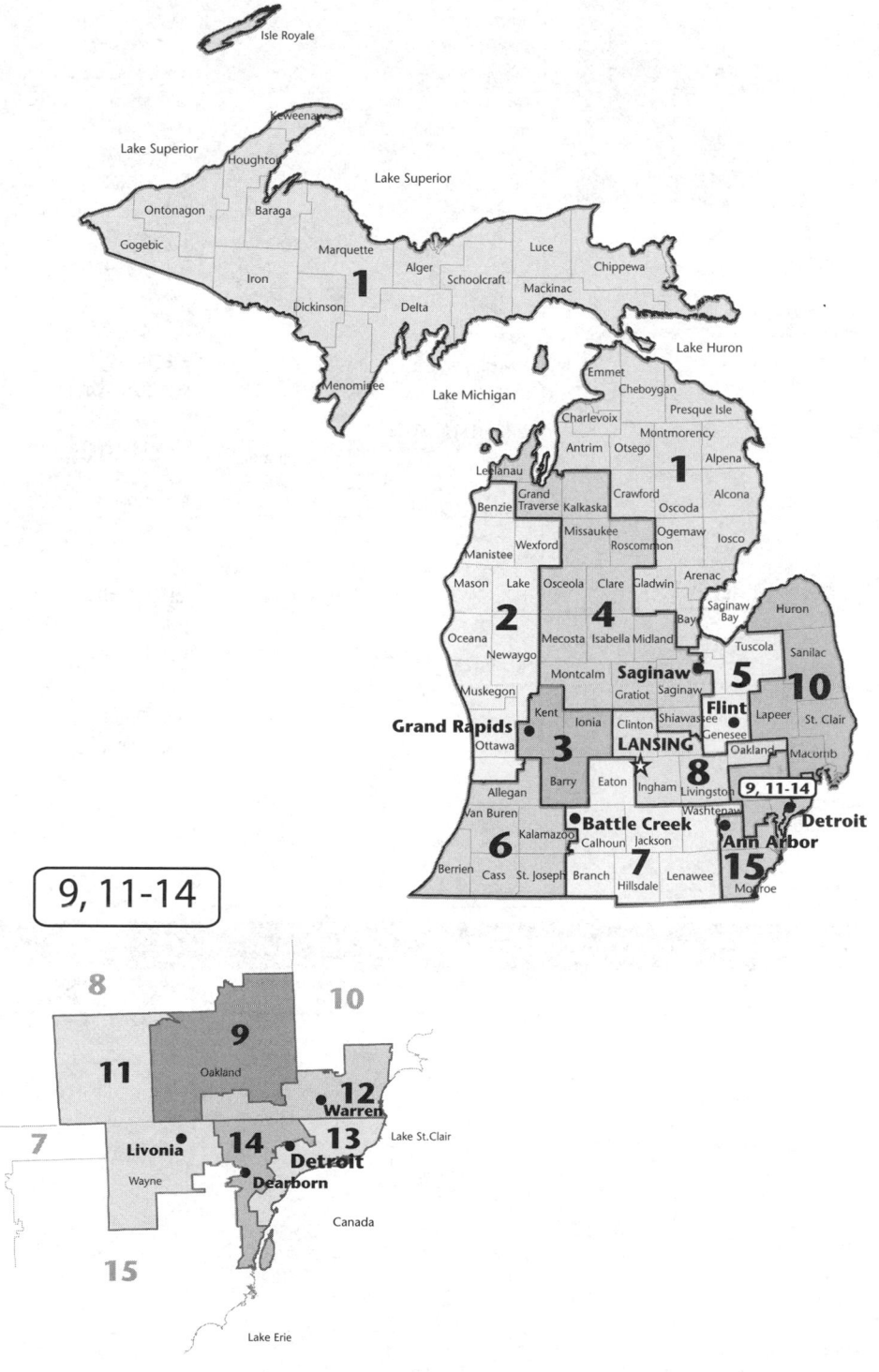

9, 11-14

Gov. Rick Snyder (R)

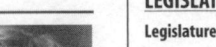

First elected: 2010
Length of term: 4 years
Term expires: 1/15
Salary: $159,300
Phone: (517) 373-3400
Residence: Ann Arbor
Born: Aug. 19, 1958; Battle Creek, Mich.
Religion: Presbyterian
Family: Wife, Sue Snyder; three children
Education: U. of Michigan, B.A. 1977 (general studies), M.B.A. 1979, J.D. 1982
Career: Venture capitalist; computer company executive; tax and acquisitions firm manager
Political highlights: No previous office

ELECTION RESULTS

2010 GENERAL

Rick Snyder (R)	1,874,834	58.1%
Virg Bernero (D)	1,287,320	39.9%
Others	63,907	2.0%

Lt. Gov. Brian Calley (R)

First elected: 2010
Length of term: 4 years
Term expires: 1/15
Salary: $111,510
Phone: (517) 373-3400

LEGISLATURE

Legislature: Year-round with recess
Senate: 38 members, 4-year terms
2011 ratios: 26 R, 12 D; 34 men, 4 women
Salary: $71,685
Phone: (517) 373-2400
House: 110 members, 2-year terms
2011 ratios: 63 R, 47 D; 84 men, 26 women
Salary: $71,685
Phone: (517) 373-0135

TERM LIMITS

Governor: 2 terms
Senate: 2 terms
House: 3 terms

URBAN STATISTICS

CITY	POPULATION
Detroit	713,777
Grand Rapids	188,040
Warren	134,056
Sterling Heights	129,699
Lansing	114,297

REGISTERED VOTERS

Voters do not register by party.

POPULATION

2010 population	9,883,640
2000 population	9,938,444
1990 population	9,295,297
Percent change (2000-2010)	-0.6%
Rank among states (2010)	8
Median age	37.7
Born in state	76.0%
Foreign born	6.1%
Violent crime rate	497/100,000
Poverty level	16.2%
Federal workers	65,360
Military	2,858

ELECTIONS

STATE ELECTION OFFICIAL
(517) 373-2540
DEMOCRATIC PARTY
(517) 371-5410
REPUBLICAN PARTY
(517) 487-5413

MISCELLANEOUS

Web: www.michigan.gov
Capital: Lansing

U.S. CONGRESS

Senate: 2 Democrats
House: 9 Republicans, 6 Democrats

2010 Census Statistics by District

District	2008 Vote for President Obama	McCain	White	Black	Asian	Hispanic	Median Income	White Collar	Blue Collar	Service Industry	Over 64	Under 18	College Education	Rural	Sq. Miles
1	50%	48%	93%	1%	1%	1%	$39,941	52%	26%	21%	18%	20%	18%	67%	24,887
2	47	51	85	5	1	7	47,396	53	31	16	13	25	21	44	5,365
3	49	49	78	8	2	9	50,231	58	26	16	11	26	27	23	1,854
4	50	48	91	3	1	3	43,427	55	26	20	15	22	21	59	7,451
5	64	35	74	19	1	4	42,297	54	26	20	13	25	17	21	1,754
6	54	44	82	9	1	5	44,487	55	28	17	13	24	24	42	3,331
7	52	46	86	6	1	4	50,065	56	28	17	13	24	22	46	4,295
8	53	46	85	5	3	5	59,414	64	20	16	10	24	32	30	2,254
9	56	43	75	11	8	4	70,551	74	13	13	13	23	47	1	311
10	48	50	91	3	2	3	57,757	58	27	15	13	25	21	34	3,549
11	54	45	80	9	5	3	66,505	66	19	15	12	24	33	3	399
12	65	33	71	21	3	2	48,929	59	23	18	15	22	22	0	160
13	85	14	28	58	1	10	31,489	50	25	25	11	28	15	0	108
14	86	13	34	59	2	3	36,141	52	24	24	12	27	15	27	123
15	66	33	75	14	4	4	53,471	60	22	17	11	23	29	23	961
STATE	57	41	77	14	2	4	48,700	58	24	18	13	24	24	25	56,804
U.S.	53	46	64	12	5	16	51,425	60	23	17	13	25	28	21	3,537,438

Sen. Carl Levin (D)

Capitol Office
224-6221
levin.senate.gov
269 Russell Bldg. 20510-2202; fax 224-1388

Committees
Armed Services - Chairman
Homeland Security & Governmental Affairs
   (Permanent Investigations - Chairman)
Small Business & Entrepreneurship

Residence
Detroit

Born
June 28, 1934; Detroit, Mich.

Religion
Jewish

Family
Wife, Barbara Levin; three children

Education
Swarthmore College, B.A. 1956 (political science);
Harvard U., LL.B. 1959

Career
Lawyer

Political Highlights
Michigan Civil Rights Commission general counsel,
1964-67; Detroit chief appellate defender, 1968-69;
Detroit City Council, 1970-77 (president, 1974-77)

ELECTION RESULTS

2008 GENERAL

Carl Levin (D)	3,038,386	62.7%
Jack Hoogendyk Jr. (R)	1,641,070	33.8%
Scotty Boman (LIBERT)	76,347	1.6%

2008 PRIMARY

Carl Levin (D)	unopposed

2002 GENERAL

Carl Levin (D)	1,896,614	60.6%
Rocky Raczkowski (R)	1,185,545	37.9%

Previous Winning Percentages
1996 (58%); 1990 (57%); 1984 (52%); 1978 (52%)

Elected 1978; 6th term

As his party's leading congressional voice on national security issues, Levin asserts that the wars in Afghanistan and Iraq are his first priority. But he says investigation and oversight "are what I'm all about."

The chairman of the Armed Services Committee was deeply skeptical of President Obama's decision in December 2009 to temporarily boost U.S. troop levels in Afghanistan by 30,000. While ultimately supporting the decision, Levin insisted that the surge emphasize the training and equipping of Afghanistan security forces.

And he argued, as he has for the Iraq War, for deadlines to be set for withdrawal of U.S. troops. Levin has consistently asserted that Obama should adhere to his deadline of July 2011 to begin the withdrawal.

"I strongly believe it is essential for success in Afghanistan that everyone understand the urgency with which the Afghans need to take responsibility for their own security," Levin said.

He pushed to include in the fiscal 2011 defense authorization bill a conditional repeal of the statutory ban on gays and lesbians serving openly in the military, after Obama announced that the Pentagon would launch a study to determine how the military would go about lifting the restriction. The language was added to the committee's version of the measure and was also included in the House-passed version of the bill. But it took stand-alone legislation passed by both chambers late in 2010 and signed by Obama to enact the change.

"I believe that allowing gay and lesbian service members to serve openly will open the ranks to patriotic men and women who wish to serve their country," Levin said. He is no Johnny-come-lately to the cause: Levin was quick to support President Bill Clinton's January 1993 proposal to end the ban on homosexuals serving in the military.

After regaining the Armed Services chairmanship in 2007 (he had served as chairman from June 2001 to January 2003), Levin was determined to assert a stronger congressional hand in war policy. He led hearings on issues ranging from interrogation techniques to detainee treatment to the conduct of U.S. contractors in Iraq.

Levin reacted to Obama's decision in early 2009 to reduce the U.S. commitment in Iraq — keeping as many as 50,000 troops stationed there in late 2010 — by declaring that his own calculations showed a far smaller residual presence was feasible.

In early 2011, he went along with a Senate resolution endorsing the creation of a "no fly" zone over Libya to support anti-government forces rebelling against Muammar el-Qaddafi, but said he wanted Congress to be kept fully informed.

"Are they attacking sites which are attacking civilians, or attacking troops that are attacking civilians?" Levin said. "Are they deterring something? Are they rescuing something? And what are the risks to those pilots flying in the no-fly zone? I need to see all of that, and I haven't seen that yet."

Levin has been critical, although ultimately supportive, of many weapons systems. He made the case during debate on the fiscal 2011 authorization bill for slowing down production purchases for the F-35 Joint Strike Fighter program even more than the administration proposed, although he ultimately supported the president's request for the plane.

He has shown a willingness to challenge the White House on particular issues. He called for the inclusion of funds in the defense authorization bill for an alternative engine for the F-35, as he did in fiscal 2010, despite a veto threat from Obama, even though he says he has "no back-home interest" in the program.

With his rumpled suits and reading glasses, Levin combines a professorial appearance with a prosecutorial demeanor. His investigative tenacity was on display in April 2010 during hearings before the Homeland Security and Governmental Affairs Subcommittee on Permanent Investigations, which he chairs, regarding the role of investment banks in the financial meltdown. His panel examined millions of pages of documents, interviewed hundreds of witnesses and conducted four hearings with more than 30 hours of testimony.

In a particularly bruising cross-examination, Levin excoriated Lloyd Blankfein, chairman and chief executive officer of Goldman Sachs, for selling securities to people and then not telling them that the firm was betting against those securities. In typically blunt questioning, Levin repeatedly challenged Blankfein to justify selling "junk" and then betting against the very product being sold. "You're picking up the phone. You're calling all these people. You don't tell them that you think it's a piece of junk. . . . And you want people to trust you?" Some of the problems Levin's investigation exposed were addressed in the Senate's financial regulatory overhaul bill.

Despite his high profile on a number of national issues, Levin devotes plenty of time and effort to his state's interests. He worked with Michigan Democratic Senate colleague Debbie Stabenow to reach an agreement with Canadian officials to reduce the amount of trash entering Michigan landfills from Canada. The two lawmakers cosponsored a provision requiring security inspections of trash at the border. Under their proposal, the trash trucks would be turned back if they appeared to pose a security risk.

On the Small Business and Entrepreneurship Committee, Levin called for expanding loan programs to small businesses and worked to provide such businesses with disaster relief when they are affected by drought conditions in the Great Lakes and elsewhere.

He was one of 13 Senate Democrats who opposed a two-year extension of the Bush-era tax cuts enacted in late 2010 because the measure extended the lower rates for the highest earners.

Levin and his older brother, Sander M. Levin, who represents Michigan's 12th District in the House, have collaborated on trade issues, focusing particularly on relations with China. Although Carl made it to the Senate four years before Sander won his House seat, he says he has always looked up to his older brother. Both absorbed a passion for politics from their father, a lawyer active in liberal causes in Detroit.

As a teenager, Levin worked the assembly line at a Chrysler DeSoto plant, and he still carries a fading United Auto Workers membership card in his wallet. Later, while in law school, Levin drove a taxi, an experience he said helped him deal with people of all backgrounds.

In the 1960s, he was general counsel to the Michigan Civil Rights Commission. He had no plans to run for office until riots destroyed parts of Detroit in 1967. Three years later, he was elected to the Detroit City Council and worked to rebuild the city. He butted heads with federal housing officials and said he decided to run for the Senate in 1978 in part to try to make federal agents "more responsive to local communities."

Levin has an avuncular manner, but he can play political hardball. In 1984, he aired an ad showing his GOP opponent, former astronaut Jack Lousma, telling an audience about the Toyota he owned — a faux pas in a state where the phrase "Japanese car" translates as joblessness. President Ronald Reagan carried Michigan with 59 percent of the vote that year, but Levin held on to win with 52 percent. In his four succeeding re-election efforts, Levin's margin of victory steadily increased. In 2008 he took 63 percent of the vote, nearly double that of his opponent, state Rep. Jack Hoogendyk Jr.

Key Votes

2010

Pass budget reconciliation bill to modify overhauls of health care and federal student loan programs	YES
Proceed to disapproval resolution on EPA authority to regulate greenhouse gases	NO
Overhaul financial services industry regulation	YES
Limit debate to proceed to a bill to broaden campaign finance disclosure and reporting rules	YES
Limit debate on an extension of Bush-era income tax cuts for two years	NO
Limit debate on a bill to provide a path to legal status for some children of illegal immigrants	YES
Allow for a repeal of "don't ask, don't tell"	YES
Consent to ratification of a strategic arms reduction treaty with Russia	YES

2009

Prevent release of remaining financial industry bailout funds	NO
Make it easier for victims to sue for wage discrimination remedies	YES
Expand the Children's Health Insurance Program	YES
Limit debate on the economic stimulus measure	YES
Repeal District of Columbia firearms prohibitions and gun registration laws	NO
Limit debate on expansion of federal hate crimes law	YES
Strike funding for F-22 Raptor fighter jets	YES

CQ Vote Studies

	PARTY UNITY		PRESIDENTIAL SUPPORT	
	SUPPORT	OPPOSE	SUPPORT	OPPOSE
2010	99%	1%	98%	2%
2009	99%	1%	99%	1%
2008	97%	3%	31%	69%
2007	95%	5%	39%	61%
2006	94%	6%	56%	44%
2005	97%	3%	41%	59%
2004	96%	4%	60%	40%
2003	98%	2%	50%	50%
2002	95%	5%	66%	34%
2001	98%	2%	65%	35%

Interest Groups

	AFL-CIO	ADA	CCUS	ACU
2010	100%	95%	9%	0%
2009	94%	95%	43%	0%
2008	100%	100%	63%	0%
2007	100%	95%	45%	4%
2006	100%	100%	50%	8%
2005	93%	100%	39%	17%
2004	100%	100%	41%	0%
2003	85%	100%	39%	25%
2002	100%	95%	40%	0%
2001	100%	100%	36%	8%

Sen. Debbie Stabenow (D)

Capitol Office
224-4822
stabenow.senate.gov
133 Hart Bldg. 20510-2204; fax 228-0325

Committees
Agriculture, Nutrition & Forestry - Chairwoman
Budget
Energy & Natural Resources
Finance
(Social Security, Pensions & Family Policy - Chairwoman)

Residence
Lansing

Born
April 29, 1950; Clare, Mich.

Religion
United Methodist

Family
Divorced; two children

Education
Michigan State U., B.A. 1972, M.S.W. 1975

Career
Leadership training consultant

Political Highlights
Ingham County Commission, 1975-78 (chair-woman, 1977-1978); Mich. House, 1979-91; Mich. Senate, 1991-94; sought Democratic nomination for governor, 1994; Democratic nominee for lieutenant governor, 1994

ELECTION RESULTS

2006 GENERAL

Debbie Stabenow (D)	2,151,278	57.0%
Mike Bouchard (R)	1,559,597	41.4%

2006 PRIMARY

Debbie Stabenow (D)	513,438	100.0%

Previous Winning Percentages
2000 (49%); 1998 House Election (57%); 1996 House Election (54%)

Elected 2000; 2nd term

Stabenow maintains her maternal demeanor through even the grittiest of political battles. She has spent more than 30 years in politics at the local, state and federal levels, including a stint as Senate Democratic Conference secretary — the fourth-ranking leadership job. Outside a few select energy issues important to her state, she is a conventional liberal.

In the 111th Congress (2009-10), she chaired the Senate Democratic Steering and Outreach Committee, which helps make committee assignments, and was named vice chairwoman of the new Senate Democratic Policy and Communications Center, which is driving the party's messaging in the 112th Congress (2011-12).

Stabenow also won the gavel of the Agriculture, Nutrition and Forestry Committee in the new Congress.

Leading the Agriculture panel gives Stabenow an opportunity to work on a reauthorization of the farm law, with an eye toward protecting her state's diverse agricultural interests.

But much of her legislative energy over the past few years has been spent in trying to protect another of Michigan's economic engines — the automobile industry — as the state's unemployment and foreclosure rates soared.

The daughter of an Oldsmobile dealer, Stabenow has worked with her Michigan Democratic colleague Carl Levin to try to rescue the state's Big Three auto companies, which pleaded that millions of industry-related jobs would be lost without federal help. "Do we care about 3 million people who have helped create the middle class of this country by making things for us in this country?" she asked the Banking, Housing and Urban Affairs Committee in November 2008. After a vote for federal aid fell short in the Senate, she joined her state's delegation in successfully persuading White House officials to use funds from the $700 billion financial services sector rescue package on a short-term loan for the auto industry.

When President Obama announced a series of steps in March 2009 aimed at saving General Motors and Chrysler, she hailed it as "further evidence that the administration is taking seriously the need for a viable domestic auto industry to save the manufacturing base of this country and preserve jobs here at home."

She blames Michigan's job losses on free-trade agreements. She opposed the Central America Free Trade Agreement in 2005, as well as the trade agreements with Panama, Peru and South Korea in 2007, despite Democratic leaders' efforts to secure long-sought labor and environmental standards.

Stabenow joined the Energy and Natural Resources Committee in 2009. While she is typically a faithful Democrat — she voted with a majority of her party against a majority of Republicans about 98 percent of the time in the 111th Congress — she stands apart on some energy issues, like other Democrats in the Michigan delegation.

She led a "Gang of 15" Democrats who raised concerns in early 2009 about Obama's plan for a "cap and trade" program. Many Rust Belt Democrats argue that such a system would increase the price of energy, hurt coal and place a heavy burden on their states' industries.

But she has championed a ban on oil and gas drilling in the Great Lakes, and she said in August 2009 that she believes climate change is a real problem. "Global warming creates volatility. I feel it when I'm flying. The storms are more volatile. We are paying the price in more hurricanes and tornadoes," Stabenow told the Detroit News in 2009.

On other issues, she toes the Democratic line.

On the Budget Committee, she backed Obama's early economic initiatives, including a $787 billion stimulus bill.

She has long been an advocate of government action to expand health coverage for the uninsured, and as a member of the Finance Committee she was an enthusiastic supporter of the health care overhaul enacted in 2010.

Stabenow has spent her congressional career promoting generic drugs over more costly brand-name prescription medicines and has battled in vain to allow imports of cheaper drugs from Canada. In her first Senate campaign, she ushered busloads of Michigan senior citizens across the Canadian border to illustrate the plight of the elderly taking extreme measures to find affordable medicines.

In December 2010, Stabenow spoke out against the extension of the Bush-era tax cuts for the highest earners. "The least way to create jobs is to put another bonus round of tax cuts in the hands of millionaires and billionaires who, if they invest it — we don't know if it will be overseas, taking jobs overseas," Stabenow said. "We don't know where it will be, but we know it hasn't trickled down to the people that I represent in Michigan."

In the end, she voted for legislation to extend the tax rates for two years for all income levels. It also provided a 13-month extension of unemployment benefits.

Stabenow's Agriculture gavel is important in a state that produces a number of specialty crops and has millions of acres of forest, which also falls under the panel's jurisdiction.

She backed a successful 2008 override of Bush's veto of the bill reauthorizing agriculture and nutrition programs for five years, because it increased payments to specialty crop growers and included a provision of hers to require schools to purchase fruits and vegetables from local farmers when available. In the 2002 renewal, she won a provision that helped Michigan farmers by mandating a $200 million annual increase in expenditures on blueberries, cherries and other specialty crops for food programs for the poor.

Stabenow was born and raised in the small town of Clare, known as the gateway to Michigan's "Up North." The eldest of three children, she credits her parents with urging her to aim high. "In high school, I would hear 'nurse' or 'teacher' as career options," she told the Detroit News in 2005. "But dad would say, 'No, doctor or engineer.' He gave me confidence to take risks, to push limits."

She chose neither path.

After graduating from Michigan State University, she got involved in politics. A social worker, she was angered by the closing of a local nursing home. She successfully challenged an incumbent to win a seat on the Ingham County Commission in 1975 and went on to serve 12 years in the Michigan House and a term in the state Senate.

In 1994, she lost the Democratic gubernatorial primary to veteran Democratic Rep. Howard Wolpe and subsequently lost in the general election as Wolpe's running mate for lieutenant governor. But she made a comeback in 1996, ending Republican Rep. Dick Chrysler's one-term tenure in the politically competitive 8th District. She was easily re-elected to the seat in 1998.

That set up Stabenow's 2000 challenge to Sen. Spencer Abraham, a long-time GOP operative and one-term senator. Stabenow had a campaign war chest of $8 million and was the top recipient of funds from EMILY's List, a political action committee that backs Democratic female candidates who support abortion rights. She won by less than 2 percentage points.

With a strong Democratic wind at her back in 2006, Stabenow handily defeated Oakland County Sheriff Mike Bouchard, winning 57 percent of the vote. Republicans, fresh off across-the-board wins in Michigan in 2010 (the party picked up House seats, won control of both chambers of the state Legislature and elected a governor), targeted Stabenow early in the 2012 cycle.

Key Votes

2010

Pass budget reconciliation bill to modify overhauls of health care and federal student loan programs	YES
Proceed to disapproval resolution on EPA authority to regulate greenhouse gases	NO
Overhaul financial services industry regulation	YES
Limit debate to proceed to a bill to broaden campaign finance disclosure and reporting rules	YES
Limit debate on an extension of Bush-era income tax cuts for two years	YES
Limit debate on a bill to provide a path to legal status for some children of illegal immigrants	YES
Allow for a repeal of "don't ask, don't tell"	YES
Consent to ratification of a strategic arms reduction treaty with Russia	YES

2009

Prevent release of remaining financial industry bailout funds	NO
Make it easier for victims to sue for wage discrimination remedies	YES
Expand the Children's Health Insurance Program	YES
Limit debate on the economic stimulus measure	YES
Repeal District of Columbia firearms prohibitions and gun registration laws	NO
Limit debate on expansion of federal hate crimes law	YES
Strike funding for F-22 Raptor fighter jets	YES

CQ Vote Studies

	PARTY UNITY		PRESIDENTIAL SUPPORT	
	Support	Oppose	Support	Oppose
2010	99%	1%	98%	2%
2009	97%	3%	96%	4%
2008	98%	2%	31%	69%
2007	94%	6%	32%	68%
2006	88%	12%	51%	49%
2005	95%	5%	33%	67%
2004	96%	4%	58%	42%
2003	97%	3%	49%	51%
2002	95%	5%	66%	34%
2001	96%	4%	64%	36%

Interest Groups

	AFL-CIO	ADA	CCUS	ACU
2010	100%	90%	36%	0%
2009	100%	100%	43%	0%
2008	100%	100%	50%	4%
2007	100%	100%	27%	8%
2006	100%	90%	50%	16%
2005	93%	100%	44%	12%
2004	100%	100%	65%	8%
2003	85%	95%	39%	20%
2002	100%	95%	45%	0%
2001	100%	100%	43%	8%

Rep. Dan Benishek (R)

Capitol Office
225-4735
benishek.house.gov
514 Cannon Bldg. 20515-2201; fax 225-4710

Committees
Natural Resources
Science, Space & Technology
Veterans' Affairs

Residence
Crystal Falls

Born
April 20, 1952; Iron River, Mich.

Religion
Roman Catholic

Family
Wife, Judy Benishek; five children

Education
U. of Michigan, B.S. 1974 (biology); Wayne State U., M.D. 1978

Career
Surgeon

Political Highlights
No previous office

ELECTION RESULTS

2010 GENERAL

Dan Benishek (R)	120,523	51.9%
Gary McDowell (D)	94,824	40.9%
Glenn Wilson (I)	7,847	3.4%
Patrick Lambert (USTAX)	4,200	1.8%
Keith Shelton (LIBERT)	2,571	1.1%

2010 PRIMARY

Dan Benishek (R)	27,077	38.1%
Jason Allen (R)	27,062	38.1%
Tom Stillings (R)	5,418	7.6%
Linda Goldthorpe (R)	4,980	7.0%
Don Hooper (R)	3,969	5.6%
Patrick Donlon (R)	2,490	3.5%

Elected 2010; 1st term

In case anyone was unsure about where Benishek stands on cutting spending, he hung a large banner in his Capitol Hill office that reads: "Welcome / If you are here to ask for more money, you're in the wrong office! / Congressman Dan Benishek M.D."

Benishek, a surgeon who had never held elected office before winning a seat in the House, said he decided to get into politics after Congress passed the $787 billion economic stimulus legislation in early 2009.

"I just couldn't believe they would spend nearly a trillion dollars without reading the legislation," he said. "This just put me over the top."

Benishek joins a number of newly elected physicians in the GOP caucus, all taking dead aim at the health care overhaul enacted in 2010. He voted to repeal it early in the 112th Congress (2011-12) and wants to see it replaced with legislation allowing insurance to be sold across state lines, a tax deduction for insurance costs and an overhaul of the medical liability system.

He won a spot on the Veterans' Affairs Subcommittee on Health and also serves on the Natural Resources and Science, Space and Technology committees.

When Benishek was 5, his father died while working in the mines of Iron County, Mich., leaving Benishek's mother to raise the family. "I didn't really get too much handed to me. I had to work my entire life," he said. "I think that's all Americans want — an opportunity to work."

He graduated from the University of Michigan and received his medical degree from Wayne State University.

The 1st District race became a priority for both parties after nine-term Democrat Bart Stupak announced he would not seek re-election.

In the Republican primary, Benishek finished one vote ahead of state Sen. Jason Allen on election night, and his margin grew to only 15 when the state certified the results soon after. Allen decided to forgo a recount, freeing Benishek to focus on Democratic state Rep. Gary McDowell.

Benishek took 52 percent of the vote to 41 percent for McDowell. A handful of minor party candidates took the rest.

Michigan 1

Upper Peninsula; northern Lower Michigan

Beginning along the Saginaw Bay shore, the 1st stretches 25,000 square miles from Michigan's northern Lower Peninsula to take in the entire Upper Peninsula (U.P.). Full of rolling, forested hills, the rural 1st encompasses 44 percent of Michigan's land mass, but does not contain a single city with more than 22,000 residents.

Tourism is a key economic engine in the 1st. Touching three of the Great Lakes, the 1st has more freshwater shoreline than any other district in the continental United States. Mackinac Island, known for its prohibition on cars, its Victorian-style lake houses and its fudge, is a popular destination. Isle Royale, the state's northernmost outpost, hosts wolves, elk and backpackers. Self-proclaimed "Yoopers" from the U.P. are connected to the rest of the district in

Northern Michigan only by the Mackinac Bridge. Isolated from the rest of their state, Yoopers tend to identify culturally with nearby Wisconsinites or Canadians. Logging is important here, but dwindling mining resources provide only modest incomes. The district has suffered from recent national economic downturns, the continuing auto industry decline and steady population loss. Housing markets crashed in Lower Peninsula lakefront towns, established beach resort and second-home havens for residents of the state and visitors from across the upper Midwest.

There is a strong current of GOP support and social conservatism in the 1st, particularly with regard to gun rights.

Major Industry
Tourism, logging, mining, auto parts

Cities
Marquette, 21,355; Sault Ste. Marie, 14,144

Notable
The National Ski Hall of Fame is in Ishpeming.

Rep. Bill Huizenga (R)

Capitol Office
225-4401
huizenga.house.gov
1217 Longworth Bldg. 20515-2202; fax 226-0779

Committees
Financial Services

Residence
Zeeland

Born
Jan. 31, 1969; Zeeland, Mich.

Religion
Christian Reformed

Family
Wife, Natalie Huizenga; five children

Education
Calvin College, B.A. 1992 (political science)

Career
Private school fundraiser; congressional district aide; Realtor

Political Highlights
Mich. House, 2003-09

ELECTION RESULTS

2010 GENERAL

Bill Huizenga (R)	148,864	65.3%
Fred Johnson (D)	72,118	31.6%
Joseph Gillotte (LIBERT)	2,701	1.2%
Ronald E. Graeser (USTAX)	2,379	1.0%

2010 PRIMARY

Bill Huizenga (R)	27,041	25.4%
Jay Riemersma (R)	26,378	24.8%
Wayne D. Kuipers (R)	23,226	21.8%
Bill Cooper (R)	20,584	19.3%
Field Reichardt (R)	4,517	4.2%
Ted Schendel (R)	2,401	2.2%
Chris Larson (R)	2,332	2.2%

Elected 2010; 1st term

Huizenga says he plans to be a voice of fiscal restraint — a member of Congress who "rages against the spending machine."

When the House passed a catchall spending bill that would have trimmed fiscal 2011 spending by $62 billion, Huizenga voted for every one of the non-security spending cut amendments offered.

As another means to the end, the former state lawmaker supports a constitutional amendment to require a balanced federal budget.

Huizenga also supports amending the Constitution in another manner: He wants a "Parental Rights" amendment, which, he says, would guarantee that parents could educate their children without being "threatened" by the state.

The issue is of personal interest to Huizenga, who home schooled some of his five children.

Across a broad spectrum of public policy, Huizenga brings a consistently conservative outlook to the economic issues considered by the Financial Services Committee, on which he sits.

Huizenga was a Realtor and co-owner of a gravel company before going to work for his predecessor, Republican Peter Hoekstra, as director of public policy. The job allowed him to stay in Michigan rather than move to Washington. He also served in the Michigan House from 2003 to 2008.

When Hoekstra decided to run for governor, seven Republicans entered the contest to succeed him. Huizenga was an upset winner in the primary, besting former NFL player Jay Riemersma by fewer than 700 votes.

In the strongly Republican district, Huizenga defeated Democrat Fred Johnson, who had lost to Hoekstra in 2008 by a better than 2-to-1 margin.

Huizenga was able to spread his campaign wealth to a number of other Republican candidates running in more closely contested races.

"I want to be in the majority, and if there are men and women that I've met that I've clicked with that we're starting to see a common vision and those kinds of things, whether it's through the [National Republican Congressional Committee] or giving them money directly, I want to do that," he told Roll Call.

Michigan 2

West — Muskegon, Holland

Stretching 160 miles along Lake Michigan on the western edge of the state's Lower Peninsula, the 2nd is full of cherry trees, asparagus farms and sandy beaches that fill up every summer with vacationers hoping for at least one completely sunny day. Most of the 2nd's land north of Muskegon, the district's largest city, consists of sparsely populated, smaller rural communities. Those small towns, once magnets for outdoor enthusiasts, are struggling as high unemployment rates and energy costs keep many would-be tourists at home.

Manufacturing, mostly based in the district's south, has replaced traditional logging jobs. South of Muskegon, a transition in the auto industry may lead to jobs making parts for hybrid cars. The southern part of the district still hosts several of the nation's top office furniture makers.

The 2nd has a large concentration of Dutch-Americans, and Holland is a conservative Dutch-settled port town that relies on tourism. Early 20th-century lifestyle is re-created in the Dutch Village Theme Park, and Holland's annual May tulip festival draws hundreds of thousands of visitors.

The 2nd is still one of Michigan's most Republican districts. Republican presidential candidates have won their highest percentages statewide in the district in the last two elections: George W. Bush won 60 percent in 2004 and John McCain took 51 percent here in 2008.

Major Industry
Furniture, tourism, agriculture, manufacturing

Cities
Muskegon, 38,401; Holland, 33,051; Norton Shores, 23,994

Notable
Grand Haven, known as Coast Guard City USA, honors the men and women of the U.S. Coast Guard during its annual festival.

Rep. Justin Amash (R)

Capitol Office
225-3831
amash.house.gov
114 Cannon Bldg. 20515-2203; fax 225-5144

Committees
Budget
Oversight & Government Reform
Joint Economic

Residence
Cascade Township

Born
April 18, 1980; Grand Rapids, Mich

Religion
Eastern Orthodox

Family
Wife, Kara Amash; three children

Education
U. of Michigan, B.A. 2002 (economics), J.D. 2005

Career
Lawyer; marketing consultant

Political Highlights
Mich. House, 2009-10

ELECTION RESULTS

2010 GENERAL

Justin Amash (R)	133,714	59.7%
Pat Miles (D)	83,953	37.5%
James Rogers (LIBERT)	2,677	1.2%

2010 PRIMARY

Justin Amash (R)	38,569	40.3%
Steve Heacock (R)	25,157	26.3%
Bill Hardiman (R)	22,715	23.8%
Bob Overbeek (R)	5,133	5.4%
Louise E. Johnson (R)	4,020	4.2%

Elected 2010; 1st term

Amash, a tea party favorite and the second-youngest member of the House, doesn't shy away from the libertarian label. He displays a careful conservatism and won't be rushed into making a decision on legislation he feels he hasn't had time to study.

Amash has said that if he receives the final text minutes before a vote, he wouldn't be comfortable approving legislation. In early 2011, he refused to cast a "yea" or "nay" vote on amendments to a catchall spending bill to cut off funding for Planned Parenthood and Obama administration policy "czars," arguing that he did not have enough time to fully consider the provisions.

A member of the Budget Committee, he voted against the final version of the catchall spending bill for 2011, arguing the $40 billion in cuts were not enough. He also serves on the Oversight and Government Reform panel, where one of his priorities will be to increase government transparency.

Amash was nationally noted for his use of online tools, such as Facebook and Twitter, during his one term in the Michigan House and on the campaign trail for Congress. He earned a spot on Time magazine's "40 Under 40" list of rising political stars in October 2010.

"One of the things that I [did] as a state legislator is to explain every single vote that I take in real time on the Internet, and I'd like to carry the practice forth to Congress," he said.

Amash is the son of immigrants. His mother is Syrian and his father is a Palestinian who lived in a refugee camp near Bethlehem before emigrating to the United States with his parents in the 1950s.

Amash supports a two-state solution and says he respects Israel's sovereignty and its special relationship with the United States. "I'm an American, and I look it at from that perspective," Amash told the Grand Rapids Press.

He graduated from law school in 2005 and was elected to the state House in 2008. Amash launched his run for Congress in February 2010, and incumbent Republican Vernon J. Ehlers announced the next day that he would retire. He beat four other candidates in the primary and defeated Democrat Pat Miles in November with almost 60 percent of the vote.

Michigan 3

West central — Grand Rapids

Nestled along the Grand River, Grand Rapids teems with auto plants and metals manufacturing, but Michigan's second-most-populous city is a world away from Detroit. Conservative Dutch Republicans, not auto union Democrats, control the 3rd.

Also unlike Detroit, residents in the 3rd escaped complete dependence on the auto industry, and a majority of jobs in the metropolitan area are downtown and not in sprawling suburbs. Grand Rapids' health care industry prompted Michigan State University to build a new medical school here, and the city still produces metal office furniture, avionics systems, tools and home appliances. Footwear manufacturer Wolverine World Wide has headquarters in Rockford, north of Grand Rapids. One of the largest employers here, direct-sales company Alticor, is based in Ada.

Major efforts to revitalize downtown Grand Rapids have attracted young professionals. New residential lofts, a convention center and numerous museums fuel rejuvenated business and entertainment districts. More than 80 percent of residents live in Kent County, which has experienced significant growth outside of Grand Rapids. The rest live in Ionia and Barry counties, east and southeast of Kent, respectively.

Gerald R. Ford made his way to the U.S. House and then the Oval Office from Grand Rapids — area roads, buildings and an airport are named for the 38th president — and his brand of small-government Republicanism and fiscal restraint still holds sway in the 3rd.

Major Industry
Health care, manufacturing

Cities
Grand Rapids, 188,040; Wyoming, 72,125

Notable
Grand Rapids is home to the Norton Mound Group, a Hopewell culture burial center.

Rep. Dave Camp (R)

Capitol Office
225-3561
camp.house.gov
341 Cannon Bldg. 20515-2204; fax 225-9679

Committees
Ways & Means - Chairman
Joint Taxation - Chairman

Residence
Midland

Born
July 9, 1953; Midland, Mich.

Religion
Roman Catholic

Family
Wife, Nancy Camp; three children

Education
Albion College, B.A. 1975 (economics); U. of San Diego, J.D. 1978

Career
Lawyer; congressional aide

Political Highlights
Mich. House, 1989-91

ELECTION RESULTS

2010 GENERAL

Dave Camp (R)	148,531	66.2%
Jerry M. Campbell (D)	68,458	30.5%
John Emerick (USTAX)	3,861	1.7%
Clint Foster (LIBERT)	3,504	1.6%

2010 PRIMARY

Dave Camp (R)	unopposed

2008 GENERAL

Dave Camp (R)	204,259	61.9%
Andrew Concannon (D)	117,665	35.7%
John Emerick (USTAX)	4,055	1.2%
Allitta Hren (LIBERT)	3,785	1.1%

Previous Winning Percentages
2006 (61%); 2004 (64%); 2002 (68%); 2000 (68%);
1998 (91%); 1996 (65%); 1994 (73%); 1992 (63%);
1990 (65%)

Elected 1990; 11th term

Although Camp has developed a reputation in recent years as an unassuming policy wonk with a penchant for compromise, he emerged as a vocal critic of Democratic fiscal and economic policies in the 111th Congress. While he is not as recognizable as his party's top leaders, his policy expertise has often helped shape Republican opposition on key pieces of legislation.

Camp possesses a deep understanding of tax law, and he succeeded retiring Republican Jim McCrery of Louisiana as ranking member of the Ways and Means Committee in late 2008. He assumed the committee's chairmanship in the 112th Congress (2011-12) with an eye on spending cuts, not tax increases, as the tool for dealing with the budget deficit.

He has served on the influential committee for close to two decades and credits his appointment to Ways and Means to the late President Gerald R. Ford, a fellow Michigander who contacted key legislators in 1992 to help Camp secure the spot. He also chairs the Joint Taxation Committee during the first session of the 112th.

When he arrived in the House in 1991, Camp was on the leading edge of the wave of Republican conservatives who now populate the chamber. While some of those lawmakers still try to maintain their images as political outsiders, Camp has made his mark the old-fashioned way — landing a choice committee assignment, digging into complex legislative issues and, for the most part, being a loyal party man.

Camp endorses the GOP criticism of much of the Democratic legislation aimed at creating jobs and spurring economic growth. He opposed a nearly $134 billion measure in May 2010 that included tax and social program extensions on the grounds that it amounted to "more spending on the same failed policies, and no net tax relief." He also criticized President Obama's $787 billion economic stimulus plan, saying it would "do more harm than good" and that he would have preferred a plan with less spending and more tax cuts.

Camp also voted against a bill to authorize $30 billion for a new small-business lending fund and legislation to provide small businesses with tax incentives to help them create jobs. In March 2010, he broke with his party, however, to support a fully offset $17 billion jobs measure that included tax incentives for businesses that hire unemployed workers.

A leader in the Republican Party's quest to make permanent the package of tax cuts enacted in 2001 and 2003, he backed the compromise Obama struck with Republicans in late 2010 that extended the rates for two years. But he called Obama's fiscal 2012 budget a "missed opportunity" to address the deficit.

Camp is a member of both the conservative Republican Study Committee and the moderate Republican Main Street Partnership. He sided with Republicans on 96 percent of the votes in 2010 on which a majority of the GOP opposed a majority of Democrats. "I'm a conservative on fiscal policy, but a moderate on some other issues," he has said.

He was one of 12 Republicans to vote for legislation authorizing a $6 billion "cash for caulkers" rebate program for energy-efficient home renovations. But Camp was a solid opponent of other major Democratic initiatives: He voted no on the financial regulatory overhaul, new campaign-finance disclosure requirements, and a government takeover of the student loan program.

The dire state of Michigan's economy — including his district, which had several counties mired in double-digit unemployment during the recession — occasionally spurs him to support Democratic responses that involve government action. He has previously backed Democratic measures to extend benefits for the nation's unemployed, including voting for two such extensions in the past year. In June 2010, however, he opposed an unemployment benefits extension, arguing that its spending was not offset.

Reflecting his commitment to the Big Three automakers in his state, Camp voted in support of an additional $2 billion in funding for the "cash for clunkers" program, which provided rebates to people who traded in lower-mileage vehicles to buy newer, more fuel-efficient models. He also backed a research and development program studying ways to reduce petroleum use and emissions from passenger and commercial vehicles. In 2008, he was one of 32 Republicans — including eight from Michigan — to back a measure allowing up to $14 billion in loans to domestic automakers.

He was the sponsor of an alternative to the health care overhaul enacted in 2010, with top party leaders cosponsoring, that would have allowed Americans to buy insurance across state lines, prevented insurance companies from canceling coverage or instituting lifetime spending caps, and overhauled the medical malpractice system. Camp supported repeal of the law in early 2011, saying "when you take a 'Washington knows best' approach to legislation, you usually end up with a bill that only works for Washington."

Camp has backed a number of bills aimed at limiting the federal deficit, requiring full offsets of program extensions, and repealing or making significant modifications to the health care law. He opposed a bill providing for a debt limit increase and has long promoted legislation to apply any lawmaker's unused office and staff funds to paying down the national debt. During his tenure he has returned to the Treasury more than $1 million in unused office money.

Aside from fiscal issues, he has sponsored legislation addressing the invasive Asian carp population in the Great Lakes and other waterways.

Camp's interest in politics began during law school, when he volunteered on the local judicial campaign of a lawyer for whom he was interning. He then got involved in GOP campaigns at the local and state levels. After practicing law for five years, Camp became chief of staff for Republican Rep. Bill Schuette, a childhood friend. He returned to Michigan in 1986 to manage Schuette's re-election campaign, and two years later Camp won an open state House seat based in Midland, his hometown.

When Schuette ran for the Senate against Democrat Carl Levin in 1990, Camp went after his mentor's House seat. With Schuette's endorsement, Camp eked out a primary victory. He went on to win the general election with 65 percent of the vote and has won re-election easily since.

Key Votes

2010	
Overhaul the nation's health insurance system	NO
Allow for repeal of "don't ask, don't tell"	NO
Overhaul financial services industry regulation	NO
Limit use of new Afghanistan War funds to troop withdrawal activities	NO
Change oversight of offshore drilling and lift oil spill liability cap	NO
Provide a path to legal status for some children of illegal immigrants	NO
Extend Bush-era income tax cuts for two years	YES

2009	
Expand the Children's Health Insurance Program	NO
Provide $787 billion in tax cuts and spending increases to stimulate the economy	NO
Allow bankruptcy judges to modify certain primary-residence mortgages	NO
Create a cap-and-trade system to limit greenhouse gas emissions	NO
Provide $2 billion for the "cash for clunkers" program	YES
Establish the government as the sole provider of student loans	NO
Restrict federally funded insurance coverage for abortions in health care overhaul	YES

CQ Vote Studies

	PARTY UNITY		PRESIDENTIAL SUPPORT	
	SUPPORT	OPPOSE	SUPPORT	OPPOSE
2010	96%	4%	37%	63%
2009	85%	15%	36%	64%
2008	95%	5%	72%	28%
2007	95%	5%	77%	23%
2006	95%	5%	100%	0%

Interest Groups

	AFL-CIO	ADA	CCUS	ACU
2010	14%	0%	100%	92%
2009	15%	15%	93%	88%
2008	20%	20%	94%	83%
2007	17%	5%	90%	96%
2006	14%	0%	100%	84%

Michigan 4

North central — Midland, Traverse City

Stretching from just west of Saginaw northwest to Leelanau Peninsula's lakeshore at the mouth of Grand Traverse Bay, bountiful forests, farms, vineyards and inland lakes cover much of the 14 central Michigan counties in the 4th, the state's second-largest district in land area. The sparsely populated white pine forests northwest of Midland were once logging lands but now host summer cottages for vacationers and homes for retirees.

On the district's eastern border, Midland, the 4th's largest city, is home to Dow Chemical and Dow Corning, makers of chemicals, plastics and silicone products. The city benefits from the company's philanthropy, with churches, schools, libraries and a local minor league baseball stadium built by its fortune. But like other major employers in the state, Dow has cut jobs. A bright spot for the region is an expansion of Hemlock Semiconductor, a Dow subsidiary, which makes components for solar panels and computer chips at its plant in Hemlock.

Thirty miles west of Midland, Mount Pleasant hosts Central Michigan University's nearly 30,000 students. The area's education sector growth — which

includes a new medical school expected to open in 2012 — has helped insulate it from economic downturns. Another key employer in Mount Pleasant is the Soaring Eagle Casino and Resort, although rising energy costs are keeping some potential visitors off the road.

West and south of Midland and Mount Pleasant, the district turns agricultural. Farmers — who till fields of sugar beets, dry beans, corn, wheat and oats — worry about free trade, price supports and crop insurance. The number of farms and small towns throughout the 4th traditionally gives an edge to local and statewide Republican candidates, but a slim 2-percentage-point majority of voters in the district supported Democrat Barack Obama in the 2008 presidential election.

Major Industry
Agriculture, chemical and plastics manufacturing, tourism

Cities
Midland (pt.), 41,706; Mount Pleasant, 26,016

Notable
Chesaning's Showboat Music Festival, which began during the Depression with hopes of aiding an ailing economy, has pumped millions of dollars into the community.

Rep. Dale E. Kildee (D)

Capitol Office
225-3611
www.house.gov/kildee
2107 Rayburn Bldg. 20515-2205; fax 225-6393

Committees
Education & the Workforce
Natural Resources

Residence
Flint

Born
Sept. 16, 1929; Flint, Mich.

Religion
Roman Catholic

Family
Wife, Gayle Kildee; three children

Education
Sacred Heart Seminary, B.A. 1952; U. of Detroit,
attended 1954 (teaching certificate); U. of Peshawar
(Pakistan), attended 1958-59 (Rotary fellowship); U.
of Michigan, M.A. 1961 (history)

Career
Teacher

Political Highlights
Mich. House, 1965-75; Mich. Senate, 1975-77

ELECTION RESULTS

2010 GENERAL

Dale E. Kildee (D)	107,286	53.0%
John Kupiec (R)	89,680	44.3%
Matthew de Heus (GREEN)	2,649	1.3%
Michael J. Moon (LIBERT)	2,648	1.3%

2010 PRIMARY

Dale E. Kildee (D)	34,902	78.4%
Scott Withers (D)	9,596	21.6%

2008 GENERAL

Dale E. Kildee (D)	221,841	70.4%
Matt Sawicki (R)	85,017	27.0%
Leonard Schwartz (LIBERT)	4,293	1.4%
Ken Mathenia (GREEN)	4,144	1.3%

Previous Winning Percentages
2006 (73%); 2004 (67%); 2002 (92%); 2000 (61%);
1998 (56%); 1996 (59%); 1994 (51%); 1992 (54%);
1990 (68%); 1988 (76%); 1986 (80%); 1984 (93%);
1982 (75%); 1980 (93%); 1978 (77%); 1976 (70%)

Elected 1976; 18th term

Colleagues call Kildee the "Cal Ripken of Congress," referencing the retired Baltimore Oriole who holds the record for playing the most consecutive Major League Baseball games. It's a testament to Kildee's commitment to the institution of the House. He so prides himself on his attendance record at votes that he scheduled knee replacement surgery in 2009 to coincide with a two-week break Congress takes in the spring. When the House returned to session, Kildee was ready.

In late February 2010 he cast his 20,000th vote, in favor of a resolution honoring Black History Month. Now in his 80s and in his 18th term, Kildee shows no signs of slowing down, telling the Flint Journal he would continue to run for re-election "as long as God and the voters are willing." And he added that he plans on missing no votes. He keeps in one of his suit pockets a laminated sheet — routinely updated by his staff — that details how many consecutive votes he has cast.

Kildee also prides himself on being frugal with taxpayer money. As of 2010, he'd given back to the U.S. Treasury nearly $1.5 million in office funds, which are used to pay for staff salaries, district office space and other office expenses. Conversely, the Detroit Free Press reported in March 2011 that Kildee spent more on salaries in 2010 than all but three other members.

He rarely draws the kind of attention that puts members on the front page of newspapers or gets them mentioned in political blogs. An exception came during the House debate on the 2010 health care overhaul. Kildee, a devout Catholic who studied to become a priest before entering politics, had broken with most of his Democratic colleagues late in 2009 to support an amendment barring the use of federal funding for insurance plans that cover abortion. When the provision was removed by the Senate, Kildee was faced with a tough choice: support the bill and help ensure its enactment, or anger many of his anti-abortion supporters. Kildee prayed with his priest, who told him that despite the official church position, he would be doing the right thing in voting yes. Kildee did so, prompting headlines back home.

It wasn't the type of publicity Kildee enjoys. He prefers to work quietly to protect the auto industry and labor unions, and to improve public schools through his seniority on the Education and the Workforce Committee, where he is ranking Democrat on the Early Childhood, Elementary and Secondary Education panel.

In 2009, he played a key role in drafting legislation, ultimately enacted as part of the health care overhaul, that expanded the federal government's role in providing loans and grants to college students while eliminating government subsidies to private lenders.

In 2001, Kildee helped negotiate the No Child Left Behind education law, which increased federal funding for education while setting strict accountability standards for states. With the law up for renewal, Kildee has joined Democrats in pushing to loosen some of those strictures while providing even more funding.

Kildee entered politics in the 1960s, the heyday of the civil rights movement and the Great Society, and his philosophy remains firmly rooted in that era. Though he was not a firebrand, he said he had a strong belief that "the government's role is to promote, protect, defend and enhance human dignity."

Kildee's concern for the auto industry and labor unions stems from his childhood, watching his father walk the 12 blocks from their Flint home to work on the assembly line at General Motors' Buick "40 plant." His father could not afford one of the cars when he started working at the plant, Kildee said, but thanks to the union's efforts on wages and pensions, he was able to buy a brand-new Buick when he retired in 1950.

Kildee supported efforts to prop up the ailing automobile industry during the 2009 recession, voting for government loans and a government-subsidized trade-in program aimed at getting older cars off the road and incentivizing new sales.

Kildee strongly opposes free-trade agreements, saying they are responsible for a huge drop-off in automobile industry jobs in his district. Kildee still lives in Flint, which has one of the highest unemployment rates in the country. Auto industry jobs there have dropped from 80,000 at their peak to about 6,000.

Kildee practices what he preaches. He requires his congressional employees who drive to work to do so in a car manufactured by members of the United Auto Workers.

As the second-ranking Democrat on the Natural Resources Committee and its Indian and Alaska Native Affairs panel, Kildee is also in a good position from which to press his other cause: protections for American Indians. His grandparents, immigrants from Ireland, had frequent contact with Indians on the reservation near Traverse City and he recalled hearing his father say Indians were treated unfairly. He carries a copy not only of the Constitution but also of the 1832 Supreme Court decision that gave the federal government exclusive jurisdiction over Indian affairs.

Kildee was a teacher at Flint Central High School when his political career began in 1964 with a successful bid for the state House. He won a state Senate seat in 1974, and two years later won election to an open U.S. House seat. He coasted through his re-election bids until 1992 and 1994, when Republican Megan O'Neill, who had worked in the White House under President George Bush, ran strong campaigns. In 1992, Kildee had become vulnerable following publication of reports that he had 100 overdrafts at the private bank for House members. But he pulled out narrow victories.

Kildee faced another challenge 10 years later after Michigan lost a seat in the House following the 2000 census. The GOP-dominated state legislature redrew district lines to force Kildee to face five-term incumbent Democrat James A. Barcia in the redrawn 5th District. But Barcia ran for the state Senate rather than take on Kildee in a 2002 primary, and Kildee locked up his seat once again. He took 53 percent of the vote in 2010 against Republican John Kupiec.

Key Votes

2010	
Overhaul the nation's health insurance system	YES
Allow for repeal of "don't ask, don't tell"	YES
Overhaul financial services industry regulation	YES
Limit use of new Afghanistan War funds to troop withdrawal activities	NO
Change oversight of offshore drilling and lift oil spill liability cap	YES
Provide a path to legal status for some children of illegal immigrants	YES
Extend Bush-era income tax cuts for two years	YES

2009	
Expand the Children's Health Insurance Program	YES
Provide $787 billion in tax cuts and spending increases to stimulate the economy	YES
Allow bankruptcy judges to modify certain primary-residence mortgages	YES
Create a cap-and-trade system to limit greenhouse gas emissions	YES
Provide $2 billion for the "cash for clunkers" program	YES
Establish the government as the sole provider of student loans	YES
Restrict federally funded insurance coverage for abortions in health care overhaul	YES

CQ Vote Studies

	PARTY UNITY		PRESIDENTIAL SUPPORT	
	SUPPORT	OPPOSE	SUPPORT	OPPOSE
2010	99%	1%	95%	5%
2009	98%	2%	96%	4%
2008	99%	1%	15%	85%
2007	97%	3%	7%	93%
2006	96%	4%	33%	67%

Interest Groups

	AFL-CIO	ADA	CCUS	ACU
2010	100%	95%	25%	0%
2009	100%	90%	33%	4%
2008	100%	100%	61%	0%
2007	96%	100%	50%	4%
2006	100%	80%	27%	20%

Michigan 5

East — Flint, Saginaw, Bay City

A thriving blue-collar tradition in the 5th has given way to Rust Belt deterioration and a workforce exodus. The vulnerable U.S. auto industry remains key to any economic stability here. The 5th's other staple is agriculture — in the northeastern part of the district that stretches across Tuscola County on Michigan's "Thumb" to Saginaw Bay, small towns rely on family-owned farms and the sugar beet industry.

A recent rebound in General Motors sales has led to increased production at its Flint truck plant, and engines for the Chevy Volt are built in another plant in the city while the auto parts manufacturing sector draws suppliers and distributors to the 5th. The auto industry in Flint and Saginaw, the district's most populous cities, at one time employed well more than 100,000 people, but years of widespread layoffs drained the population. Flint has lost 18 percent of its residents since 2000 and is no longer one of the state's five most-populous cities. Municipal budget shortfalls in Flint have made it difficult for the local government to provide public services. Vacant homes in crumbling neighborhoods illustrate the distress in some residential areas of Saginaw.

Despite new factory jobs, local officials hope to move away from the region's manufacturing past and develop education and health care hubs — Flint hosts a University of Michigan campus and engineering-focused Kettering University, and the aging population has required expansions to local hospitals.

The 5th's blue-collar voters adhere to fiscal populism and social conservatism, and they tend to identify strongly with the Democratic Party. Genesee County (Flint), which accounts for two-thirds of the district's population and is one-fifth black, is strongly influenced by the United Auto Workers union. Genesee gave Barack Obama 66 percent of its presidential vote in 2008 and was one of only four counties statewide to support Democrat Virg Bernero in the 2010 gubernatorial election.

Major Industry
Auto parts manufacturing, agriculture, sugar processing, health care

Cities
Flint, 102,434; Saginaw, 51,508; Bay City, 34,932; Burton, 29,999

Notable
Michael Moore's 1989 documentary "Roger & Me" chronicled the impact of GM's layoffs in the 1980s on Flint.

Rep. Fred Upton (R)

Capitol Office
225-3761
www.house.gov/upton
2183 Rayburn Bldg. 20515-2206; fax 225-4986

Committees
Energy & Commerce - Chairman

Residence
St. Joseph

Born
April 23, 1953; St. Joseph, Mich.

Religion
Protestant

Family
Wife, Amey Upton; two children

Education
U. of Michigan, B.A. 1975 (journalism)

Career
Congressional aide; White House budget analyst

Political Highlights
No previous office

ELECTION RESULTS

2010 GENERAL

Fred Upton (R)	123,142	62.0%
Don Cooney (D)	66,729	33.6%
Melvin D. Valkner (USTAX)	3,672	1.8%
Fred Strand (LIBERT)	3,369	1.7%

2010 PRIMARY

Fred Upton (R)	42,182	57.1%
Jack Hoogendyk Jr. (R)	31,660	42.9%

2008 GENERAL

Fred Upton (R)	188,157	58.9%
Don Cooney (D)	123,257	38.6%
Greg Merle (LIBERT)	4,720	1.5%
Edward Pinkney (GREEN)	3,512	1.1%

Previous Winning Percentages
2006 (61%); 2004 (65%); 2002 (69%); 2000 (68%);
1998 (70%); 1996 (68%); 1994 (73%); 1992 (62%);
1990 (58%); 1988 (71%); 1986 (62%)

Elected 1986; 13th term

With his hand on the gavel of one of the most powerful committees in Congress, Upton is at the apex of his House career. Though a moderate known for his willingness to seek common ground with Democrats, he made commitments to the GOP leaders who backed him for the Energy and Commerce chairmanship that he would pursue the party's conservative agenda.

With ties to the moderate wing of the House GOP caucus, Upton has long shown a willingness to depart from his party on such issues as the Iraq War, gun rights and the environment. During President George W. Bush's two terms, Upton declined to support the president roughly one-third of the time. Among the issues on which he split from fellow Republicans were a 2005 overhaul of the Endangered Species Act, the expanded use of federal funds for stem cell research and a 2007 resolution opposing Bush's plan to boost the number of troops in Iraq. Only 22 House Republicans serving in Congress at the end of the Bush administration broke with the president more frequently.

Upton has said in the past that it's the merits of a particular issue, rather than ideology, that drives his decision-making. "I'm not a rubber stamp and people know that," he once said. "If you can convince me of the merits, you will have my vote every time."

But his moderate voting record became an issue in late 2010, during the post-election fight for the Energy and Commerce chairmanship with Texas Republican Joe L. Barton, who chaired the panel in the 109th Congress (2005-06) and served as ranking member for the two succeeding Congresses. Hamstrung by GOP rules limiting members to three terms atop committees, Barton nonetheless launched a spirited battle to thwart his rival's ascension. Many conservative activists opposed Upton as too liberal for the job. Some backed Barton, while others favored John Shimkus of Illinois or Cliff Stearns of Florida.

In response, Upton issued a flurry of press releases and op-eds attacking Obama administration policies and promising to repeal the Democrats' 2010 health care overhaul, rein in the Environmental Protection Agency and expand oil drilling on public lands and offshore. He frequently dropped the name of his "old boss, President Ronald Reagan" — a reference to his stint as congressional liaison at the Office of Management and Budget during the 1980s — racking up endorsements from prominent elected conservatives along the way.

The counterattack worked; Upton was elevated to the chairman's seat in December, after defining an agenda for the panel "that focuses on cutting spending, removing the regulatory burden, restoring freedom, keeping government accountable through rigorous oversight, and jobs."

Despite his independent streak, Upton has generally been a reliable conservative vote on such social issues as federal recognition of same-sex marriage and abortion. After singer Janet Jackson's "wardrobe malfunction" during the 2004 Super Bowl halftime show, Upton sought to stiffen the fines the Federal Communications Commission could levy for broadcast indecency. He also has a long history of pushing to reduce the deficit, which stems from the nearly 10 years he spent working for former Rep. David A. Stockman, a Michigan Republican, both on his congressional staff and at OMB, where Stockman was Reagan's budget director.

At the start of the Obama administration, Upton indicated he wouldn't bend to Democrats' desires easily: He stuck with the 33-member, moderate Republican Main Street Partnership in opposing Obama's $787 billion stimulus, despite heavy lobbying by the president. In a statement following his vote, Upton commended Obama for trying to open the process but blamed then-Speaker Nancy Pelosi of California for closing the door to Republicans. He also complained Democrats stripped out $10 billion that would have allowed taxpayers to deduct state sales taxes and car loan interest.

As the top Republican on the Energy and Commerce Subcommittee on Energy and Environment, Upton was a key GOP voice in opposition to the Democrats' energy and climate measure that passed the House in June 2009. He introduced legislation in the 112th Congress (2011-12) that would strip the EPA of its regulatory authority over carbon emissions under the Clean Air Act. In a Wall Street Journal op-ed, he called the EPA's actions on that score "an unconstitutional power grab that will kill millions of jobs."

But he's shown a willingness to work with Democrats on other energy issues. With Democrat Edward J. Markey of Massachusetts, Upton in 2005 worked on a proposal to extend daylight saving time for eight weeks. Congress ultimately cleared a version providing a one-month extension, beginning in 2007, which the pair said could help conserve energy used for lighting. Upton also teamed up with California Democrat Jane Harman on a plan to phase out incandescent light bulbs in favor of more efficient compact fluorescent bulbs. The provision – signed into law in 2007 as part of a larger energy package — was widely hailed by efficiency advocates, but it was a sore point for many conservatives and Upton has said he plans to revisit it as chairman in the 112th Congress.

In a clear sign he intends to run the committee his way, one of Upton's early moves after being named chairman was to announce a revamp of the subcommittee structure. And in an effort to put the chairman's race behind him, he bestowed the honorary title of "chairman emeritus" on Barton.

Upton comes from one of Michigan's wealthier families; his grandfather helped found Whirlpool Corp., which is based in his district. After college, Upton began his alliance with Stockman by working on his 1976 congressional campaign. In 1986, Upton ousted conservative incumbent Rep. Mark D. Siljander in a Republican primary. He won that November with 62 percent of the vote. His subsequent re-elections were relatively easy, except in 1990 when he garnered less than 60 percent of the vote.

Upton became a deputy to Rep. Newt Gingrich when the Georgia Republican was elected GOP whip in 1989, and the next year joined Gingrich in castigating President George Bush for agreeing to raise taxes as part of a deal to reduce the deficit. But Upton resigned as a deputy whip in 1993 because he said he disliked Gingrich's confrontational style.

Key Votes

2010

Overhaul the nation's health insurance system	NO
Allow for repeal of "don't ask, don't tell"	NO
Overhaul financial services industry regulation	NO
Limit use of new Afghanistan War funds to troop withdrawal activities	NO
Change oversight of offshore drilling and lift oil spill liability cap	NO
Provide a path to legal status for some children of illegal immigrants	NO
Extend Bush-era income tax cuts for two years	YES

2009

Expand the Children's Health Insurance Program	YES
Provide $787 billion in tax cuts and spending increases to stimulate the economy	NO
Allow bankruptcy judges to modify certain primary-residence mortgages	NO
Create a cap-and-trade system to limit greenhouse gas emissions	NO
Provide $2 billion for the "cash for clunkers" program	YES
Establish the government as the sole provider of student loans	NO
Restrict federally funded insurance coverage for abortions in health care overhaul	YES

CQ Vote Studies

	PARTY UNITY		PRESIDENTIAL SUPPORT	
	SUPPORT	OPPOSE	SUPPORT	OPPOSE
2010	94%	6%	36%	64%
2009	80%	20%	53%	47%
2008	84%	16%	47%	53%
2007	86%	14%	54%	46%
2006	81%	19%	80%	20%

Interest Groups

	AFL-CIO	ADA	CCUS	ACU
2010	14%	10%	88%	92%
2009	38%	30%	93%	72%
2008	73%	60%	89%	44%
2007	50%	40%	100%	56%
2006	36%	10%	100%	80%

Michigan 6

Southwest — Kalamazoo, Portage, Benton Harbor

Forests, fertile soil and front-row seats to Lake Michigan in the state's southwestern corner make the 6th a prime spot for tourists in every season. Apples, blueberries and peaches grow in a fruit belt that extends north from St. Joseph and Benton Harbor through Van Buren County. The wooded shoreline north of the Indiana border boasts miles of sandy beaches where affluent Chicagoans have kept second homes. Local vineyards produce a strong crop of juice grapes, and area wineries account for a significant percentage of the state's wine grapes.

Appliance manufacturer Whirlpool Corp., based in Benton Harbor, and orthopedic company Stryker, in Kalamazoo, make their headquarters in the 6th, although overall job losses in manufacturing have hurt the district. Pharmaceutical giant Pfizer has turned the district into a regional hub for the state's booming health care industry — local officials have encouraged growth of pharmaceutical start-ups, which provide some jobs for the science-based workforce.

Education is another pillar of the local economy. Western Michigan University is home, at least for most of the year, to roughly 25,000 students. The "Kalamazoo Promise," a scholarship program aimed at supporting Kalamazoo Public Schools graduates by offering to sponsor up to 100 percent of tuition to attend an in-state public college, has attracted some new families to the city, helping prop up home values in the area.

The 6th's conservative Dutch heritage, white-collar corporate managers and rural conservatives have made it a Republican-leaning district in the past. The district's Democratic centers are in working-class Kalamazoo and predominately black Benton Harbor, balanced by conservative-leaning St. Joseph and Allegan counties. Democrat Barack Obama took 54 percent of the district's 2008 presidential vote, but Republican Rick Snyder easily won every county here in the 2010 gubernatorial election.

Major Industry

Manufacturing, agriculture, higher education, health care, tourism

Cities

Kalamazoo, 74,262; Portage, 46,292; Niles, 11,600; Sturgis, 10,994

Notable

The Berrien Springs courthouse, built in 1839 and now a museum, is the state's oldest courthouse; Colon, home to magic-trick manufacturers and an annual exposition, calls itself the "Magic Capital of the World."

Rep. Tim Walberg (R)

Capitol Office
225-6276
walberg.house.gov
418 Longworth Bldg. 20515-2207; fax 225-6281

Committees
Education & the Workforce
(Workforce Protections - Chairman)
Homeland Security
Oversight & Government Reform

Residence
Tipton

Born
April 12, 1951; Chicago, Ill.

Religion
Christian

Family
Wife, Sue Walberg; three children

Education
Western Illinois U., attended 1969-70 (forestry); Fort
Wayne Bible College, B.S. 1975 (Christian education);
Wheaton College (Ill.), M.A. 1978 (communications)

Career
Religious school fundraiser; education think tank
president; minister

Political Highlights
Candidate for Onsted Community Schools Board
of Education, 1981; Mich. House, 1983-98; sought
Republican nomination for U.S. House, 2004; U.S.
House, 2007-09; defeated for re-election to U.S.
House, 2008

ELECTION RESULTS

2010 GENERAL

Tim Walberg (R)	113,185	50.2%
Mark Schauer (D)	102,402	45.4%
Scott Aughney (USTAX)	3,705	1.6%
Greg Merle (LIBERT)	3,239	1.4%
Richard Wunsch (GREEN)	3,117	1.4%

2010 PRIMARY

Tim Walberg (R)	41,784	57.5%
Brian Rooney (R)	23,505	32.3%
Marvin Carlson (R)	7,413	10.2%

Previous Winning Percentages
2006 (50%)

Elected 2006; 2nd term

Did not serve 2009-11

Walberg picks up in the 112th Congress where he left off after losing his re-election race in 2008: staunchly advocating for conservative causes. A minister and former state representative, he has said that his Protestant faith defines him.

As a member of the Republican Study Committee, a group comprising the most conservative members of the House, Walberg opposes abortion, gay marriage and allowing illegal immigrants to obtain driver's licenses. He supports making English the nation's official language.

His stances on economic issues are just as consistently conservative and put him strongly at odds with the priorities of congressional Democrats and the Obama White House. "The trillion-dollar stimulus, government takeover of health care, and … trillion-dollar deficits are placing America on an unsustainable financial course," he said.

He voted to repeal the health care overhaul enacted in 2010, saying that getting rid of the law "is a crucial step in getting our economy growing again."

He backed a catchall fiscal 2011 spending bill that would cut spending by $62 billion. The measure included his amendment to trim $20.6 million from the National Endowment for the Arts.

"As a patron and former finance chair of a local arts organization, I appreciate and support the arts," Walberg said. "This funding cut would return the NEA to a funding level that it has previously operated from and yet allow it to remain an active participant in supporting the arts."

In 2007 he authored legislation that would have made the 2001 and 2003 tax cuts permanent and hopes to revisit the issue in the 112th Congress (2011-12) after a two-year extension was signed into law by President Obama late in 2010.

He also supports line-item veto authority and a balanced-budget amendment to the Constitution, and favors creating personal investment accounts in Social Security, saying that younger workers should have "the option to save their own money in their own name in their own account."

Walberg lines up with the GOP's "all of the above" energy policy, supporting increased exploration for and utilization of domestic oil and natural gas, along with development of wind, solar and other alternative sources. He represents a corn-growing region and authored two bills in the 110th Congress (2007-08) to boost ethanol and biodiesel, although neither bill advanced.

In 2011, he introduced legislation to prevent the EPA from regulating greenhouse gas emissions under the Clean Air Act.

Michigan's jobless rate still remains well above the national average, and Walberg sees his spot on the Education and the Workforce Committee as a way to address job creation. He served on the panel in his previous stint, when it was known as Education and Labor, and now serves as chairman of the Subcommittee on Workforce Protections, where he hopes to strike a balance between worker safety rules and regulatory overkill.

"Worker safety is a priority and so, too, is promoting policies that will allow businesses to grow and hire new workers," he said at a subcommittee hearing in early 2011. "Needless rules and onerous regulations are often roadblocks to economic growth and job creation, which we all want."

Walberg sits on the Homeland Security Committee, where he took the lead on the issue of flood insurance. He introduced legislation in February 2011 that would force the Federal Emergency Management Agency to delay for five years a requirement for homeowners inside the boundaries of newly drawn floodplain maps to purchase flood insurance through FEMA's National Flood Insurance Program. "The federal government is again over-reaching beyond what is appropriate, and this time it's to the detriment of hard-working families during tough economic times," he said.

He sees his spot on the Oversight and Government Reform Committee as an opportunity to "hold the federal bureaucracy accountable to the people."

Walberg grew up on Chicago's South Side. He worked in a steel mill before attending Western Illinois University, Moody Bible Institute, Taylor University and Wheaton College, earning bachelor's and master's degrees.

He served as a pastor for a decade before being elected to the state House in 1982. He stayed for 16 years, compiling a robustly conservative record that included a lifetime A+ rating from the National Rifle Association.

After leaving the legislature, Walberg served as president of the Warren Reuther Center for Education and Community Impact and as a division manager for the Moody Bible Institute of Chicago.

He made his first bid for a U.S. House seat in 2004, losing the GOP primary to a moderate, Joe Schwarz, in the race to succeed retiring six-term incumbent Republican Nick Smith.

Walberg challenged Schwarz again in the primary in 2006, labeling him a "RINO" — Republican in Name Only — and winning the endorsement and financial support of the anti-tax Club for Growth. Schwarz had the backing of most of the party establishment, but Walberg toppled him, winning 53 percent of the vote to Schwarz's 47 percent. Schwarz refused to endorse the victor, but Walberg outraised his Democratic opponent, organic farmer Sharon Marie Renier, by 20-to-1 and won the race by about 4 percentage points.

Two years later, while Democratic presidential candidate Barack Obama was carrying the district by 6 percentage points, Walberg lost to Democratic state Sen. Mark Schauer by a little more than 2 percentage points.

Walberg wasted no time trying to reclaim the seat, announcing in 2009 that he would be back for his fourth run in six years. He had primary opposition again, this time from Iraq War veteran Brian Rooney, brother of GOP Rep. Tom Rooney of Florida, and businessman Marvin Carlson. Walberg won 57 percent of the vote and got his rematch with Schauer.

The party campaign committees and independent groups poured money into the race: the Service Employees International Union and the American Federation of State, County and Municipal Employees for Schauer, the American Future Fund and Americans for Prosperity for Walberg.

For the fourth time in four elections the seat changed hands, with Walberg winning just a tad more than half the votes.

CQ Vote Studies				
	PARTY UNITY		PRESIDENTIAL SUPPORT	
	Support	Oppose	Support	Oppose
2008	92%	8%	68%	32%
2007	96%	4%	84%	16%

Interest Groups				
	AFL-CIO	ADA	CCUS	ACU
2008	21%	20%	88%	96%
2007	13%	0%	90%	100%

South central — Battle Creek, Jackson

The southern Michigan counties that make up the 7th take in small towns, farming communities and a few midsize cities. Kellogg's Tony the Tiger makes his home in Battle Creek, the district's largest city. The cereal giant is the city's largest employer, and its philanthropic arm donates generously to the Battle Creek area.

Kellogg moved into downtown headquarters in 2011 and is funding the conversion of a former museum into a new building for a regional math and sciences center. Auto parts manufacturing still drives many small-town economies here. Some auto workers had been able to return to work after sagging auto sales nationwide forced several years of salary buyouts and layoffs, but uncertainty in the industry remains.

Outside the cities and towns, expansive soybean and corn fields dominate the rest of the 7th, which is the state's leading producer of both crops. Lenawee County is at the forefront for both corn and soybeans and contains the most farms of any county in the state. Farm payments and insurance are key issues, as is the potential for using agricultural products and land for alternative energy.

A Quaker tradition shaped the district's political and social culture. In 1854, Jackson's abolitionists selected anti-slavery candidates in a state convention that has become known as "Under the Oaks" and as the birth of the Republican Party.

The farming counties of Eaton, Jackson, Branch, Hillsdale and Lenawee are fertile ground for the GOP, but there is Democratic support in more liberal Battle Creek to the west and the outskirts of heavily Democratic Ann Arbor (in the neighboring 15th) in Washtenaw County to the east.

Independent voters can swing the 7th in federal races — George W. Bush won the district twice while losing the state, Barack Obama took 52 percent of the 7th's presidential vote in 2008, and the U.S. House seat has changed hands four times, and party control three times, in the last four elections.

Major Industry
Agriculture, food processing, auto parts manufacturing, health care

Cities
Battle Creek, 52,347; Jackson, 33,534

Notable
Sojourner Truth lived in Battle Creek.

Rep. Mike Rogers (R)

Capitol Office
225-4872
www.mikerogers.house.gov
133 Cannon Bldg. 20515-2208; fax 225-5820

Committees
Energy & Commerce
Select Intelligence - Chairman

Residence
Howell

Born
June 2, 1963; Livonia, Mich.

Religion
Methodist

Family
Kristi Clemens Rogers; two children

Education
Adrian College, B.A. 1985 (sociology & criminal justice)

Military
Army, 1985-88

Career
Home construction company owner; FBI agent

Political Highlights
Mich. Senate, 1995-2000 (majority floor leader, 1999-2000)

ELECTION RESULTS

2010 GENERAL

Mike Rogers (R)	156,931	64.1%
Lance Enderle (D)	84,069	34.3%
Bhagwan Dashairya (LIBERT)	3,881	1.6%

2010 PRIMARY

Mike Rogers (R)	78,047	100.0%

2008 GENERAL

Mike Rogers (R)	204,408	56.5%
Robert D. Alexander (D)	145,491	40.2%
Will Tyler White (LIBERT)	4,373	1.2%
Aaron Stuttman (GREEN)	3,836	1.1%

Previous Winning Percentages
2006 (55%); 2004 (61%); 2002 (68%); 2000 (49%)

Elected 2000; 6th term

Rogers has been mentioned as a potential candidate for the Republican leadership almost from the day he arrived in Washington. The affable and well-liked former FBI agent has been a prolific fundraiser for his party and colleagues, while devoting his legislative attention to intelligence matters and aiding Michigan's sinking economy.

Rogers was tapped in December 2010 to lead the Select Intelligence Committee in the 112th Congress (2011-12) despite Texas Republican William M. "Mac" Thornberry owning one more year of seniority. Rogers also has a coveted seat on the Energy and Commerce Committee and was a member of the GOP transition team in late 2010.

After a series of scandals rocked the GOP in the 109th Congress (2005-06), Rogers announced in 2006 that he would run for Republican whip, the No. 3 post in the majority party, if Roy Blunt of Missouri moved up to majority leader, the No. 2 job. But John A. Boehner of Ohio prevailed over Blunt in the contest to succeed Tom DeLay of Texas, who resigned. That left Blunt in place and stymied Rogers' hopes of landing one of the top posts.

After only one term, Rogers had been considered by Blunt for chief deputy whip in 2002, but the job went to Eric Cantor of Virginia, now the majority leader. Rogers' consolation prize was appointment to Energy and Commerce and the deputy whip roster.

He has been a generous provider of campaign funds over the years — his leadership political action committee has handed out more than $1.3 million to Republican candidates since 2002. As finance chairman of the National Republican Congressional Committee for the 2004 elections, he raised $16 million to help fund the races of fellow GOP House members and candidates. In 2010, he headed the committee's successful incumbent retention effort.

Rogers, who served three years in the Army and six years in the FBI, joined the Intelligence Committee in 2005 and was the top Republican on the terrorism subcommittee in the 111th Congress (2009-10).

His priorities as chairman of the Intelligence panel include modernizing cybersecurity and wiretapping laws, boosting counterterrorism capabilities, addressing terrorist detention policy and taking a hard look at the budget for spy agencies. On the last point, he has suggested two ways to trim spending: reducing the size of the Office of the Director of National Intelligence and utilizing less expensive alternatives to satellite programs.

In response to the summer 2010 leak of thousands of pages of classified documents related to the Afghanistan war, Rogers blasted what he called the "culture of disclosure" and said the Army private suspected of leaking the material should face the death penalty if convicted. "In my mind, it's treason," Rogers said in an August interview on Michigan radio station WHMI.

When House Democrats proposed using biosecurity money to offset the cost of education provisions in a supplemental spending bill, Rogers circulated a letter to colleagues opposing the idea. "So they're going to take national security money and spend it on a throwaway program to try to get votes in the fall," he said. "I can't think of anything more unconscionable than that."

Even before he was assigned to the Intelligence panel, Rogers was a resource for colleagues as the Justice Department developed its legislative response to the Sept. 11, 2001, attacks that eventually became the anti-terrorism law known as the Patriot Act.

In the 110th Congress (2007-08), Rogers fought Democrats' efforts to increase restrictions on the National Security Agency's warrantless wiretapping of terrorist suspects as Congress rewrote the Foreign Intelligence Surveillance Act. After opposing one attempt to extend FISA that he argued included too many restraints on intelligence gathering, he voted for the final version, which permitted warrantless eavesdropping in certain cases.

When Democrats took control of the House after the 2006 elections, Rogers voted for two of their "Six for '06" priority measures: to cut interest rates on college student loans in half over five years, and to implement remaining recommendations of the independent Sept. 11 commission. But he opposed most of President Obama's economic initiatives during the 111th Congress, including the $787 billion economic stimulus plan in 2009 and the health care overhaul enacted in 2010. And he was vehement in his opposition to Democratic cap-and-trade legislation intended to combat global warming.

Rogers has spent considerable time focusing on Michigan's economy, repeatedly introducing a bill to give U.S. auto companies up to $20 billion in federally backed loan guarantees to develop new technologies. And he joined others in the Michigan delegation in successfully urging President George W. Bush to make an emergency loan to keep the auto industry afloat in late 2008 after the Senate defeated a loan bill the House had passed.

Rogers grew up in Livingston County, west of Detroit. His father was a high school vice principal, football coach and town supervisor. His mother ran the local Chamber of Commerce and served on the county commission.

Rogers knew as a teenager that he wanted to be an FBI agent. After graduating from college and leaving the Army, he attended the FBI Academy, finishing first in his class. He won a coveted assignment to the Chicago field office, where he unraveled a major case involving public officials in Cicero. Handcuffs and headlines from the case are framed in his Capitol Hill office.

In the 1990s, Rogers and his now ex-wife returned to Michigan to raise their family. With his father and brothers, he ran a modular home assembly company. He also entered state politics. When a longtime GOP incumbent retired from the state Senate, Rogers won the Republican district. Re-elected in 1998, he served as majority floor leader during his second, and last, term.

When Democrat Debbie Stabenow decided to give up her House seat to run for the Senate in 2000, Rogers made a bid and faced Democratic state Senate colleague Dianne Byrum in the general election. Rogers' 111-vote victory was not official until December. After redistricting added thousands of GOP voters to the district, he won re-election with 68 percent of the vote. He has been returned safely to office, but his victory margins were not overwhelming until 2010, when he won by 30 points. District voters backed Bush for president in 2000 and 2004 but supported Barack Obama in 2008.

Key Votes

2010

Overhaul the nation's health insurance system	NO
Allow for repeal of "don't ask, don't tell"	NO
Overhaul financial services industry regulation	NO
Limit use of new Afghanistan War funds to troop withdrawal activities	NO
Change oversight of offshore drilling and lift oil spill liability cap	?
Provide a path to legal status for some children of illegal immigrants	NO
Extend Bush-era income tax cuts for two years	YES

2009

Expand the Children's Health Insurance Program	NO
Provide $787 billion in tax cuts and spending increases to stimulate the economy	NO
Allow bankruptcy judges to modify certain primary-residence mortgages	NO
Create a cap-and-trade system to limit greenhouse gas emissions	NO
Provide $2 billion for the "cash for clunkers" program	YES
Establish the government as the sole provider of student loans	NO
Restrict federally funded insurance coverage for abortions in health care overhaul	YES

CQ Vote Studies

	PARTY UNITY		PRESIDENTIAL SUPPORT	
	SUPPORT	OPPOSE	SUPPORT	OPPOSE
2010	94%	6%	35%	65%
2009	90%	10%	31%	69%
2008	91%	9%	68%	32%
2007	93%	7%	77%	23%
2006	95%	5%	90%	10%

Interest Groups

	AFL-CIO	ADA	CCUS	ACU
2010	14%	10%	86%	91%
2009	11%	10%	93%	92%
2008	33%	25%	89%	84%
2007	25%	5%	90%	100%
2006	21%	5%	93%	88%

Michigan 8
Central — Lansing

Stamped with the state seal, the 8th — Michigan's capital district — used to be dominated by various manufacturing facilities for the influential auto industry. The district, once home to Olds Motor Vehicle Co., includes Lansing, East Lansing and various agricultural communities to the east, but it is emerging from its agrarian and industrial tradition toward a suburban future.

Auto industry cutbacks have hurt the 8th: General Motors' Oldsmobile line was eliminated in 2004, and GM plants and auto parts suppliers have shut down or been forced to cut shifts and lay off workers. GM is now only the third-largest employer in the Lansing area, behind the state government and Michigan State University. Parts of Lansing are beginning to show signs of rebirth after several years of economic contraction, especially around Cooley Law School Stadium, the home of the minor league Lansing Lugnuts, and in the north side's quirky Old Town neighborhood. Health care is an important field in the capital region, and the biotech sector is growing, too.

Just down the road from the capital, East Lansing caters to one of the most liberal constituencies in the state, the Michigan State community. The university, founded in 1855 as the nation's pioneer land grant college, is home to several top-ranked programs, including education and study abroad. The university is building an isotope accelerator that is expected to pump about $1 billion into the local economy and make the region a global hub for nuclear research.

Local support for Republican Rick Snyder in the 2010 gubernatorial race belied Ingham County's traditional Democratic lean — Snyder won there by a slim 220 votes. The 8th's powerful agricultural vote rests in Livingston and Shiawassee counties, which also are new commuter sanctuaries for residents who work in Lansing, Detroit and Flint. The remainder of the 8th's voters live in northern Oakland County.

Major Industry
State government, higher education, auto manufacturing

Cities
Lansing (pt.), 109,563; East Lansing, 48,579; Holt (unincorporated), 23,973

Notable
The unincorporated hamlet of Hell, in Putnam Township, is a tourist stop that plays to its devilish name.

Rep. Gary Peters (D)

Capitol Office
225-5802
peters.house.gov
1609 Longworth Bldg. 20515-2209; fax 226-2356

Committees
Financial Services
Small Business

Residence
Bloomfield Township

Born
Dec. 1, 1958; Pontiac, Mich.

Religion
Episcopalian

Family
Wife, Colleen Ochoa Peters; three children

Education
Alma College, B.A. 1980 (political science); U. of Detroit, M.B.A. 1984; Wayne State U., J.D. 1989; Michigan State U., M.A. 2007 (philosophy)

Military
Naval Reserve, 1993-2000; Navy Reserve, 2001-05

Career
College instructor; investment firm branch executive

Political Highlights
Democratic nominee for Mich. Senate, 1990; Rochester Hills City Council, 1991-93; Mich. Senate, 1995-2002; Democratic nominee for Mich. attorney general, 2002; Mich. Lottery Bureau commissioner, 2003-07

ELECTION RESULTS

2010 GENERAL

Gary Peters (D)	125,730	49.8%
Rocky Raczkowski (R)	119,325	47.2%
Adam Goodman (LIBERT)	2,601	1.0%

2010 PRIMARY

Gary Peters (D)	unopposed

2008 GENERAL

Gary Peters (D)	183,311	52.1%
Joe Knollenberg (R)	150,035	42.6%
Jack Kevorkian (X)	8,987	2.6%
Adam Goodman (LIBERT)	4,893	1.4%
Douglas Campbell (GREEN)	4,737	1.3%

Elected 2008; 2nd term

Peters touts himself as a fiscal conservative, but he voted for every major economic initiative the House Democratic leadership and President Obama pushed in the 111th Congress and sided with his party on nearly nine of every 10 votes that split majorities of the two parties.

A member of the moderate New Democrat Coalition, Peters voted for Obama's $787 billion economic stimulus package in early 2009, saying it would help local infrastructure and create jobs. He also supported the House leadership's bills aimed at reducing carbon emissions and overhauling the health care system.

His centrist bona fides were burnished by support for extending — temporarily — all of the expiring 2001 and 2003 tax cuts. And, at least rhetorically, he inveighs against the burgeoning federal debt.

"We are on an unsustainable path that threatens to bury our children in debt while not fulfilling promises to seniors for Social Security and Medicare," he said.

A former investment company executive, Peters sometimes takes a populist stand on the Financial Services Committee, where he is next to last in seniority among Democrats. Concerned about the use of funds approved as part of a $700 billion financial services rescue law cleared in 2008, he voted in January 2009 for an unsuccessful bill to impose significant restrictions on the Obama administration's use of the second half of those funds. He drew some attention two months later when he introduced a bill aimed at taxing bonuses distributed by insurance giant American International Group Inc., which had received some of the rescue funds. Peters estimated his proposed 60 percent surtax, when added to the applicable income tax rate, would allow the government to recoup nearly 100 percent of those bonuses. "Million-dollar bonuses for the very people who drove our economy into the ditch are simply unacceptable," he said. (Momentum instead carried another measure, which he supported, to bar recipients of rescue funds from paying compensation deemed "unreasonable or excessive.")

But Peters wasn't for giving all control to the government. When the Obama administration announced in October 2009 that it would order companies that received those same government funds to slash the base salaries of their top executives, Peters said the directive was "helpful" but not enough. He instead argued for a "democratic, market-based approach to solving this problem" by empowering shareholders — as outlined in legislation he had introduced in June with other Democrats.

Peters was among the moderate Democrats who called for a short-term extension of all 2001 and 2003 tax cuts in a letter to party leaders Nancy Pelosi of California and Steny H. Hoyer of Maryland, bucking the leadership's position that rates for the top tax brackets should return to pre-2001 levels in 2011.

A supporter of organized labor, Peters was a cosponsor of the so-called card check bill aimed at making it easier for unions to organize by not requiring a secret ballot election among workers to put a union in place.

Peters sits on the Small Business Committee, where he hopes to help his state develop the next generation of technology in the auto industry, saying Michigan is "uniquely situated" to benefit from advancements in technologies such as electric cars.

He backed the "cash for clunkers" vehicle trade-in program in 2009, and later laid some of the blame for the auto industry's problems at the feet of Wall Street.

"The reason the auto industry, one of reasons why it was in trouble was because of the disaster on Wall Street, because of the unbridled greed we saw there that brought down the capital markets," he said on MSNBC in early 2011.

The House passed in September 2009 his bill to authorize $2.9 billion to establish an Energy Department research program on vehicle technologies,; it focused on reducing petroleum use in cars. He also successfully included in a House-passed solar technology bill language requiring the Energy Department to give preference to research and development projects in states with high unemployment, such as Michigan.

Peters wavered until the last minute in June 2009 on whether to support the House bill aimed at reducing greenhouse gas emissions. But he ultimately voted for the measure, which would cap emissions and create a market for trading emissions credits.

Peters grew up in Rochester, where his family has lived since the 1840s. His father was a World War II veteran and taught in the public school system, and his mother worked as a nurse's aid.

Peters' interest in politics was sparked when, as a college student, he interned for a local union organizer. He worked for nine years at Merrill Lynch, becoming an assistant vice president while earning a master's in business administration and a law degree along the way. He later earned a master's in philosophy from Michigan State University, where he is also a doctoral candidate.

His tenure at Merrill Lynch was followed by 14 years at Paine Webber, where he became vice president of investments. And he served 12 years in the U.S. Naval Reserve, where he was a lieutenant commander and sharpshooter.

His political career began in 1991 with a two-year stint on the Rochester Hills City Council. That was followed by eight years in the state Senate.

Peters briefly entered the gubernatorial race in 2002 before focusing on an ultimately unsuccessful bid for state attorney general. Democratic Gov. Jennifer M. Granholm then appointed him lottery commissioner, a post he held until 2007.

In 2008 he challenged eight-term GOP Rep. Joe Knollenberg. Peters won by nearly 10 percentage points while Obama outran Republican Sen. John McCain of Arizona, 56 percent to 43 percent, in the presidential contest.

Republican Andrew "Rocky" Raczkowski, a former state representative, took Peters to the wire in 2010, but the incumbent squeaked by with 49.8 percent of the vote.

Key Votes

2010

Overhaul the nation's health insurance system	YES
Allow for repeal of "don't ask, don't tell"	YES
Overhaul financial services industry regulation	YES
Limit use of new Afghanistan War funds to troop withdrawal activities	NO
Change oversight of offshore drilling and lift oil spill liability cap	YES
Provide a path to legal status for some children of illegal immigrants	YES
Extend Bush-era income tax cuts for two years	YES

2009

Expand the Children's Health Insurance Program	YES
Provide $787 billion in tax cuts and spending increases to stimulate the economy	YES
Allow bankruptcy judges to modify certain primary-residence mortgages	YES
Create a cap-and-trade system to limit greenhouse gas emissions	YES
Provide $2 billion for the "cash for clunkers" program	YES
Establish the government as the sole provider of student loans	YES
Restrict federally funded insurance coverage for abortions in health care overhaul	NO

CQ Vote Studies

	PARTY UNITY		PRESIDENTIAL SUPPORT	
	SUPPORT	OPPOSE	SUPPORT	OPPOSE
2010	83%	17%	83%	17%
2009	91%	9%	87%	13%

Interest Groups

	AFL-CIO	ADA	CCUS	ACU
2010	100%	90%	25%	8%
2009	95%	95%	40%	8%

Suburban Detroit — eastern Oakland County

Michigan's heavily suburban 9th — the wealthiest and most educated district in the state — is wholly contained in Oakland County, home to the U.S. headquarters for Chrysler in Auburn Hills. Life in the district long revolved around the vulnerable auto industry, but unlike other suburban Detroit areas, the 9th has a more diverse economy.

Decades of whites' exodus from the city into Oakland County traced the corridor formed between Grand River Avenue and the Northwestern Highway north of the Detroit border (8 Mile Road). The county gained residents overall in the last decade even as people left the densely populated areas near Detroit. Once-rural expanses have been settled by white-collar workers, and the district's black and Hispanic populations have boomed while tens of thousands of white residents have left.

Troy, in the 9th's southeastern corner, is a major office center and home to Michigan's banking and high-tech automotive research and design industries. Several years of auto industry slowdowns caused local job cuts and municipal budget shortfalls, but the district still hosts several manufacturing plants and auto parts suppliers. North of Troy in Rochester, Oakland University is expanding; its William Beaumont School of Medicine has opened, and a new health care and research center is planned.

Traditionally Republican, upper-middle-class Bloomfield Township and Rochester Hills were politically competitive in the 2008 presidential election, and Democrats have always fared well in Pontiac, where blacks now account for a majority of residents. Barack Obama won 87 percent of the city's 2008 presidential vote while taking the 9th with 56 percent of the overall vote, 7 percentage points higher than John Kerry took in 2004.

Major Industry
Engineering, health care, auto manufacturing

Cities
Troy, 80,980; Farmington Hills, 79,740; Rochester Hills, 70,995; Waterford (pt.), 65,119; Pontiac, 59,515; Royal Oak (pt.), 51,824; Auburn Hills, 21,412

Notable
The Holocaust Memorial Center, the first Holocaust museum built in the United States, is in Farmington Hills.

Rep. Candice S. Miller (R)

Capitol Office
225-2106
candicemiller.house.gov
1034 Longworth Bldg. 20515-2210; fax 226-1169

Committees
Homeland Security
  (Border & Maritime Security - Chairwoman)
Transportation & Infrastructure

Residence
Harrison Township

Born
May 7, 1954; Detroit, Mich.

Religion
Presbyterian

Family
Husband, Donald Miller; one child

Education
Macomb Community College, attended 1973-74;
Northwood Institute, attended 1974

Career
Boat saleswoman

Political Highlights
Harrison Township Board of Trustees, 1979-80; Harrison Township supervisor, 1980-92; Republican nominee for U.S. House, 1986; Macomb County treasurer, 1993-95; Mich. secretary of state, 1995-2002

ELECTION RESULTS

2010 GENERAL

Candice S. Miller (R)	168,364	72.0%
Henry Yanez (D)	58,530	25.0%
Claude Beavers (LIBERT)	3,750	1.6%
Candace R. Caveny (GREEN)	3,286	1.4%

2010 PRIMARY

Candice S. Miller (R)	unopposed

2008 GENERAL

Candice S. Miller (R)	230,471	66.3%
Robert Denison (D)	108,354	31.2%
Neil Stephenson (LIBERT)	4,632	1.3%
Candace R. Caveny (GREEN)	4,146	1.2%

Previous Winning Percentages
2006 (66%); 2004 (69%); 2002 (63%)

Elected 2002; 5th term

Miller is a small-government Republican by instinct whose Michigan district and its reliance on the automobile industry sometimes steers her away from her nature. "I'm fiscally conservative, and I think my record reflects that," she said. "On the other hand, I play for the home team, too."

On a partisan level, that can cut both ways.

The soaring unemployment rate in her state and district led Republican leaders to turn to her to criticize the Democratic health care overhaul as a job-killer in the GOP weekly address in October 2009. It likewise led her to support an auto industry rescue and the "cash for clunkers" program.

Her district shares a border with Canada, which also gives her a focus on border security, albeit one that puts her more in tune with party leaders as chairwoman of the Homeland Security Subcommittee on Border and Maritime Security.

Although she has used the perch to highlight the border security needs to the north, she also has been an outspoken critic of Obama's policy to the south, such as the administration's decision to file suit against Arizona over the state's 2010 law targeting illegal immigrants.

She has been viewed as a trailblazer for women in politics since being elected Michigan's first female secretary of state in 1994. She has consistently won more than two-thirds of the vote in her House re-election bids.

Miller stands firmly behind Michigan's Big Three automakers; her daughter is a Ford assembly worker who belongs to the United Auto Workers. She backed a $14 billion loan to struggling domestic automakers in December 2008. When the bill failed in the Senate, she joined other members of Michigan's delegation in writing to President George W. Bush asking him to fund it. The Bush administration ultimately approved a loan through the $700 billion financial rescue law signed that fall. Miller had opposed that rescue bill.

When President Obama announced in March 2009 stringent conditions on further government aid to General Motors Corp. and Chrysler LLC, and forced the ouster of GM CEO Richard Wagoner, Miller said Obama and his Auto Task Force were now "accountable for the jobs, accountable for the livelihoods of the families which are at stake and accountable for the survival of American manufacturing."

Miller said she believes that the loans have paid off not only for Michigan but for the country as well. "It is unimaginable what would have happened to us" had the Big Three collapsed, she said.

When the Obama administration contemplated suspending the "cash for clunkers" program, which offered consumers money to trade in old cars and buy more energy-efficient models, Miller also backed extending it, writing a letter to the president touting it as an economic stimulus.

But she has bucked Obama on other economic initiatives, including the $787 billion economic stimulus law, which she voted against in part because it scaled down an incentive to spur auto sales. And she opposed the health care overhaul Obama signed into law in 2010. "We are going to have a complete government takeover of our health care system faster than you can say, 'This is making me sick,' " she said during floor debate.

Miller is a social conservative but on many issues tends to side with organized labor. She supported a 2007 bill to increase the minimum wage and in 2005 voted against a bill to implement the Central America Free Trade Agreement. But she backed a free-trade deal with Peru in 2007. And she was one of 35 Republicans who supported a bill that same year to prohibit job discrimination based on sexual orientation.

Miller had an early stumble in her House career. She received a rebuke from the ethics committee in 2004 for threatening political retaliation against a fellow Republican who refused to support Bush's Medicare prescription drug plan. The Committee on Standards of Official Conduct, as the ethics panel was known, said Miller went too far when she cornered fellow Michigan Republican Nick Smith on the House floor and threatened to use her influence in his son's House race unless Smith supported the bill. At the time, Brad Smith was seeking to take his retiring father's place, a race he ultimately lost. The elder Smith complained to the ethics panel of pressure from Miller and Republican leaders.

Miller, a member of the Transportation and Infrastructure Subcommittee on Water Resources and Environment, has supported a variety of water and boating causes, such as federal efforts in 2010 to halt the intrusion of Asian carp into Michigan waterways, something she traces not only to her district's Great Lakes interests but her own upbringing. She grew up in 1960s suburban Detroit, where her father owned a marina. Miller was a member of a high school boating crew. In 1970, she sailed as a member of the first all-woman crew to compete in a prestigious race across Lake Huron — after she and the other women beat back the local yacht club's effort to bar them.

Miller attended a community college but dropped out to sell boats for the family business. By 25, she was a divorced single mother with a toddler. (She later remarried.) When the local township board proposed a tax increase on marinas, she became a "noisy activist."

She was elected to Harrison Township board in 1979 and a year later unseated the supervisor, becoming the first woman to hold the job. In her two terms as secretary of state, she was recognized for making the office more efficient and for instituting fraud-proof driver's licenses. She made an unsuccessful bid to unseat Democratic Rep. David E. Bonior in 1986.

The Republican-controlled legislature redrew a congressional district in 2002 to include several GOP-leaning counties and Miller's base in Macomb County. She beat the county prosecutor, Carl J. Marlinga, with 63 percent of the vote. She has won easily since.

GOP leaders selected her for the 22-member transition team that guided the party as it assumed control of the House in the 112th Congress (2011-12). She was later named a regional director for the National Republican Congressional Committee. Miller also has been mentioned as a potential Senate candidate against Democrat Debbie Stabenow in 2012.

Key Votes

2010
Overhaul the nation's health insurance system	NO
Allow for repeal of "don't ask, don't tell"	NO
Overhaul financial services industry regulation	NO
Limit use of new Afghanistan War funds to troop withdrawal activities	NO
Change oversight of offshore drilling and lift oil spill liability cap	NO
Provide a path to legal status for some children of illegal immigrants	NO
Extend Bush-era income tax cuts for two years	YES

2009
Expand the Children's Health Insurance Program	YES
Provide $787 billion in tax cuts and spending increases to stimulate the economy	NO
Allow bankruptcy judges to modify certain primary-residence mortgages	NO
Create a cap-and-trade system to limit greenhouse gas emissions	NO
Provide $2 billion for the "cash for clunkers" program	YES
Establish the government as the sole provider of student loans	NO
Restrict federally funded insurance coverage for abortions in health care overhaul	YES

CQ Vote Studies
	PARTY UNITY		PRESIDENTIAL SUPPORT	
	Support	Oppose	Support	Oppose
2010	94%	6%	31%	69%
2009	77%	23%	56%	44%
2008	83%	17%	44%	56%
2007	84%	16%	52%	48%
2006	89%	11%	94%	6%

Interest Groups
	AFL-CIO	ADA	CCUS	ACU
2010	14%	5%	88%	88%
2009	38%	25%	93%	80%
2008	67%	50%	78%	63%
2007	67%	30%	100%	72%
2006	25%	10%	93%	84%

Michigan 10

Southeast — northern Macomb County, Port Huron, most of Michigan 'Thumb'

Stretching from Detroit's northern suburbs in Macomb County to the tip of Michigan's "Thumb," the 10th combines suburban, lakefront and rural communities. Like many parts of Michigan, the district has endured sustained high unemployment rates for several years. Unlike the state as a whole, however, the 10th has experienced modest population growth since 2000.

Macomb, where slightly more than half of the 10th's population resides, retains a traditionally blue-collar "Reagan Democrat" feel despite growth in suburbs such as Harrison Township, Shelby and Sterling Heights (shared with the 12th). Macomb has established its statewide bellwether status: in the 2008 presidential election, the county backed Democrat Barack Obama despite supporting Republican George W. Bush four years earlier — overall, Obama lost by fewer than 6,000 votes in the 10th — and Republican Rick Snyder won the county in the 2010 gubernatorial race. Lapeer County, northwest of Macomb, has become a landing spot for

upwardly mobile residents drifting farther away from urban centers in Flint (to the west) and Detroit (to the south). Northeast of Macomb is St. Clair County, a politically competitive region where roughly one-fourth of district residents live. St. Clair's Port Huron, a source of blue-collar Democratic votes, is the U.S. terminus of the Blue Water bridges, which cross into Ontario, Canada.

Water-quality issues are important to local residents along Lake Huron and near other bays and rivers, and many small businesses rely on the tourism industry.

Elsewhere in the 10th, rural communities depend on fruit, soybeans, corn and other crops. In particular, the fertile soil of the Thumb is known for its navy bean fields. Huron and Sanilac counties are leaders in Michigan dairy production.

Major Industry
Auto manufacturing, agriculture, recreation

Cities
Sterling Heights (pt.), 90,280; Shelby, 73,804; Port Huron, 30,184

Notable
The U.S. Senate's famous navy bean soup uses only Michigan navy beans.

Rep. Thaddeus McCotter (R)

Capitol Office
225-8171
mccotter.house.gov
2243 Rayburn Bldg. 20515-2211; fax 225-2667

Committees
Financial Services

Residence
Livonia

Born
Aug. 22, 1965; Detroit, Mich.

Religion
Roman Catholic

Family
Wife, Rita McCotter; three children

Education
U. of Detroit, B.A. 1987 (political science), J.D. 1990

Career
Lawyer

Political Highlights
Schoolcraft College Board of Trustees, 1989-92;
Wayne County Commission, 1993-98; Mich. Senate,
1999-2002

ELECTION RESULTS

2010 GENERAL

Thaddeus McCotter (R)	141,224	59.3%
Natalie Mosher (D)	91,710	38.5%
John Tatar (LIBERT)	5,353	2.2%

2010 PRIMARY

Thaddeus McCotter (R)	unopposed

2008 GENERAL

Thaddeus McCotter (R)	177,461	51.4%
Joseph W. Larkin (D)	156,625	45.4%
John Tatar (LIBERT)	6,001	1.7%
Erik Shelley (GREEN)	5,072	1.5%

Previous Winning Percentages
2006 (54%); 2004 (57%); 2002 (57%)

Elected 2002; 5th term

McCotter is quick-witted, quirky and conservative. After two terms as chairman of the House Republican Policy Committee, he suggested his job — and the entire operation — should be dissolved.

He argued in July 2010 that the committee's purpose — developing thoughtful position papers and crafting policy — had been co-opted by Republican solutions groups and other leadership offices. He proposed the committee's annual budget of $360,000 be used to pay down the debt.

Other Republican leaders pushed back against McCotter's idea, saying that it was up to the 112th Congress (2011-12) to decide whether the position should be cut from the rolls. After a brief dispute, McCotter yielded and agreed to let the next Congress decide the committee's fate. The new majority opted to keep the committee, under the leadership of Georgia's Tom Price.

During his tenure as the head of the committee, McCotter incorporated his eclectic turns of phrase and a love of rock 'n' roll into otherwise mundane policy statements. For example, the group issued position papers quoting Bob Dylan, and McCotter compared the 1994 GOP "Contract With America" to The Beatles' acclaimed "Sgt. Pepper's Lonely Hearts Club Band" album.

His affinity for The Beatles goes beyond working them into policy statements. On the 30th anniversary of John Lennon's murder in December 2010, McCotter paid tribute to him on the House floor: "I thank Mr. Lennon for striving through his enduring art to reveal the immutable human truths that eternally unite us in our mortality, our frailty and our beauty when we love."

The fracas over the policy panel is just one example of McCotter's independent streak. He was one of 36 Republicans to vote against the extension of the Bush-era tax rates that President Obama negotiated with Senate Republicans. McCotter said the temporary nature of the two-year extension would prolong the country's economic difficulties.

In September 2008, he denounced President George W. Bush's $700 billion financial sector rescue plan, making references to President Andrew Jackson and the battle over the Second Bank of the United States, along with "The Brothers Karamazov" and the 1917 Russian uprising. "In the Bolshevik Revolution, the slogan was 'peace, land and bread,'" said McCotter, a member of the Financial Services Committee. "Today you are being asked to choose between bread and freedom. I suggest the people on Main Street have said they prefer their freedom, and I am with them."

Two months later, McCotter supported $14 billion in loans to failing domestic automakers, a measure that died in the Senate. In 2009, he criticized the Obama administration for forcing out General Motors CEO Richard Wagoner, saying Wagoner was being scapegoated while Wall Street executives kept their jobs. He has further championed the auto industry by opposing higher fuel efficiency standards for vehicles, saying they are "unfunded mandates." The Detroit-centric portion of his agenda has also included signing on to numerous bills to clean up the Great Lakes and eliminate invasive species.

McCotter has also occasionally broken ranks with his party on economic issues. In 2007 he joined Democrats in supporting an increase in the minimum wage. He was critical of the GOP effort to eliminate spending earmarks — funding set-asides for projects in members' districts — although he announced in June 2008 that he would not seek any.

He also supported a Democratic measure in 2007 prohibiting job discrimination on the basis of a person's sexual orientation. But in late 2010, he opposed lifting the ban on homosexuals serving openly in the military.

Although most Republicans stayed mum as the Iraq War turned increasingly sour politically, McCotter in 2006 was one of six House Republicans to call for an independent, bipartisan commission to assess U.S. progress. In 2008, he said the 2007 "surge" of U.S. forces that sent more than 21,000 additional troops into Iraq "has fortunately been done in a manner that's allowed us to get closer to victory."

McCotter can be witheringly sarcastic in debate. He once took to the House floor with a series of charts on "speaking Democrat," with mock translations of "enhancing revenues" as raising taxes, "engage" as appease and "end the war" as lose it.

McCotter is seldom without a cigarette; he has been known to smoke while fielding fly balls during the Annual Roll Call Congressional Baseball Game, where he sports the uniform of the Detroit Tigers.

McCotter's parents were special-education teachers in the Detroit public schools. His mother, Joan, was elected to the Livonia City Council in 1985, a campaign he helped manage. In his youth, McCotter was a semi-professional musician playing guitar in several bands, including one called Sir Funk-a-Lot and the Knights of the Terrestrial Jam.

When stardom failed to materialize, McCotter attended the University of Detroit Law School and went into solo law practice. A friend persuaded him to get involved in the 1988 presidential campaign, and McCotter went to the Republican National Convention as a delegate pledged to George Bush.

In 1992, he won a seat on the Wayne County Commission, where he was the driving force behind a law requiring 60 percent voter approval for any tax increase. Elected to the state Senate in 1998, McCotter was vice chairman of the reapportionment committee that drew new congressional district maps after the 2000 census. That put him in position to draw the new 11th District, which included his entire state Senate district.

In 2002, McCotter beat businessman David C. Hagerty in the primary and Democrat Kevin Kelley in the general election. He has won re-election fairly easily since, although his margin shrank to 6 percentage points in the 2008 Democratic wave in which Obama carried the district by 9 percentage points. His margin rebounded to almost 21 points in 2010.

McCotter revived his musical dreams once elected to the House, teaming with four other lawmakers — Democrat Collin C. Peterson of Minnesota and Republicans Dave Weldon of Florida, Jon Porter of Nevada and Kenny Hulshof of Missouri — to form a bipartisan rock band, the Second Amendments. McCotter and Peterson are the only bandmates still in Congress.

Key Votes

2010

Overhaul the nation's health insurance system	NO
Allow for repeal of "don't ask, don't tell"	NO
Overhaul financial services industry regulation	NO
Limit use of new Afghanistan War funds to troop withdrawal activities	NO
Change oversight of offshore drilling and lift oil spill liability cap	NO
Provide a path to legal status for some children of illegal immigrants	NO
Extend Bush-era income tax cuts for two years	NO

2009

Expand the Children's Health Insurance Program	YES
Provide $787 billion in tax cuts and spending increases to stimulate the economy	NO
Allow bankruptcy judges to modify certain primary-residence mortgages	NO
Create a cap-and-trade system to limit greenhouse gas emissions	NO
Provide $2 billion for the "cash for clunkers" program	YES
Establish the government as the sole provider of student loans	NO
Restrict federally funded insurance coverage for abortions in health care overhaul	YES

CQ Vote Studies

	PARTY UNITY		PRESIDENTIAL SUPPORT	
	Support	Oppose	Support	Oppose
2010	91%	9%	34%	66%
2009	88%	12%	37%	63%
2008	86%	14%	58%	42%
2007	87%	13%	66%	34%
2006	87%	13%	82%	18%

Interest Groups

	AFL-CIO	ADA	CCUS	ACU
2010	14%	15%	75%	86%
2009	33%	20%	93%	84%
2008	60%	40%	82%	72%
2007	50%	20%	75%	84%
2006	50%	15%	93%	83%

Michigan 11

Southeast — Livonia, Westland, Novi

Carved from traditionally GOP-friendly suburbs north and west of Detroit, the 11th District has stood out in a region known for its support of pro-labor Democrats. But political and demographic shifts under way in the district led voters to support Democrat Barack Obama with 54 percent of the district's presidential vote — 2 percentage points higher than Republican George W. Bush won here in 2004.

As in other Michigan districts that surround the Motor City, auto and auto parts manufacturing — and the economic troubles plaguing those sectors — play a dominant role in the district despite efforts to diversify the area's economy.

While many areas were once almost entirely filled with auto workers, these communities have been affected by layoffs or factory closures. A refurbished Ford plant in Wixom, however, is projected to provide thousands of jobs as a solar energy equipment manufacturer.

The district's population center is in northwestern Wayne County, where nearly 70 percent of the 11th's residents live. This area is largely a collection of upper-middle-class communities such as Livonia and Redford Township, as well as Plymouth and growing Canton, which have seen success with downtown redevelopment efforts. Nearer to Detroit are Westland, Wayne and Garden City — Democratic strongholds that have held fast to their blue-collar union roots.

The 11th also covers the GOP-leaning southwestern portion of Oakland County. Revitalization efforts in the district's smaller communities in Oakland are attracting younger residents, and several townships have been growing quickly despite overall population loss throughout the state. Novi has seen steady population growth, including larger numbers of minority residents, for two decades. The city also boasts a convention center that draws more than a million visitors each year.

Major Industry
Auto manufacturing, engineering, health care

Cities
Livonia, 96,942; Canton, 90,173; Westland, 84,094; Novi, 55,224; Redford, 48,362; Garden City, 27,692

Notable
The Plymouth Ice Festival is North America's largest ice-carving festival.

Rep. Sander M. Levin (D)

Capitol Office
225-4961
www.house.gov/levin
1236 Longworth Bldg. 20515-2212; fax 226-1033

Committees
Ways & Means - Ranking Member
Joint Taxation

Residence
Royal Oak

Born
Sept. 6, 1931; Detroit, Mich.

Religion
Jewish

Family
Widowed; four children

Education
U. of Chicago, B.A. 1952; Columbia U., M.A. 1954
(international relations); Harvard U., LL.B. 1957

Career
Lawyer; U.S. Agency for International Development
official

Political Highlights
Oakland Board of Supervisors, 1961-64; Mich. Senate,
1965-71 (minority leader, 1969-70); Mich. Democratic Party chairman, 1968-69; Democratic nominee
for governor, 1970, 1974

ELECTION RESULTS

2010 GENERAL

Sander M. Levin (D)	124,671	61.1%
Don Voloric (R)	71,372	35.0%
Julia Williams (GREEN)	3,038	1.5%
Leonard Schwartz (LIBERT)	2,342	1.1%
Les Townsend (USTAX)	2,285	1.1%

2010 PRIMARY

Sander M. Levin (D)	42,732	76.0%
Michael Switalski (D)	13,480	24.0%

2008 GENERAL

Sander M. Levin (D)	225,094	72.1%
Bert Copple (R)	74,565	23.9%
John Vico (LIBERT)	4,767	1.5%
Les Townsend (USTAX)	4,076	1.3%

Previous Winning Percentages
2006 (70%); 2004 (69%); 2002 (68%); 2000 (64%); 1998
(56%); 1996 (57%); 1994 (52%); 1992 (53%); 1990 (70%);
1988 (70%); 1986 (76%); 1984 (100%); 1982 (67%)

Elected 1982; 15th term

The detail-oriented Levin ascended to the top of the Ways and Means Committee under unusual circumstances in 2010, and his rise gave the liberal
veteran new prominence and new influence over tax, trade and health policy.

Levin became chairman when Charles B. Rangel of New York stepped
aside amid ethics inquiries, and when a more senior Democrat, Pete Stark
of California, declined the top job. He surrendered the gavel after his party
lost its majority in the 2010 elections, then had to fend off a challenge for
the ranking Democratic spot in the 112th Congress (2011-12) from the
younger, more business-friendly Richard E. Neal of Massachusetts.

Neal won the backing of the Democratic Steering and Policy Committee
by one vote, but the full Democratic Caucus selected Levin, who made it
clear in the days before the caucus vote that he would continue to be a
partisan voice on economic issues in the new Congress.

Often rumpled and usually carrying a sheaf of papers under his arm, Levin
digs deeply into the weeds of complex legislation. He knows how to throw a
sharp partisan elbow, but he isn't a glib quote machine, and he never seems
quite comfortable in front of TV cameras, particularly in contrast with Rangel.

The beginning of Levin's tenure as chairman was difficult, because it came
amid a fast pivot on fiscal policy by moderates in both chambers, who shifted
their concern from economic stimulus to the budget deficit, even as Levin and
other leading liberal Democrats insisted that the government needed to continue pumping money into the economy. That tension showed up most prominently in the tax "extenders" bill, a grab-bag measure to extend unemployment insurance, revive expired tax breaks and plug state budget holes.

After weeks of talks, Levin and Senate Finance Chairman Max Baucus, a
Montana Democrat, released a proposal in mid-May that they hoped to move
swiftly through both chambers. The deal was the first major legislation crafted by Levin as chairman — and it cratered immediately. Fiscally conservative
Blue Dog Democrats in the House pressured Levin and House leaders to
scale the measure back before passage, and moderate Senate Republicans
prompted further reductions before preventing it from advancing.

The bill included one of Levin's top priorities from before his chairmanship — taxing the "carried interest" earned by private equity managers, real
estate investors, and venture capitalists as ordinary income instead of capital
gains. Because of concerns from Senate Democrats, Levin agreed to concessions that cut the revenue-raising impact of the provision nearly in half.

Despite the stalemate on the tax extenders bill, Levin can point to some
successes in his short tenure as chairman. He helped put the finishing touches on the Democrats' overhaul of the health care system after significantly
weakening an excise tax on high-cost health insurance that he worried would
harm middle-class workers and members of labor unions. Also, he moved a
bill through the committee and the House to provide tax breaks for small
businesses and infrastructure assistance to state and local governments.

At the end of the year, he backed a two-year extension of the Bush-era
income tax cuts with little enthusiasm. "I am not willing to put the fate of the
middle class and the unemployed in the hands of the Republican majority
next year," he said on the floor before the vote.

Before becoming chairman of the full committee, Levin focused largely
on trade and was known as his party's leading expert on the subject. As
chairman of the Trade Subcommittee, he said, he tried to craft a policy not
to stop globalization but to shape trade agreements to the benefit of workers.

But while in the majority during the 110th (2007-08) and 111th (2009-10) Congresses, Democrats did not move much trade legislation. They started on a positive note in 2007, when Levin and Rangel helped negotiate an agreement with the Bush administration on a framework for trade deals. The bargain required enforceable labor and environmental standards to be written into the pacts, which paved the way for the Peru free-trade agreement, which Levin supported despite opposition from a majority of House Democrats.

Since then, however, the "fast track" authority for the president to quickly negotiate trade deals — that Congress cannot amend — was allowed to lapse. Any new version must provide more opportunities for Congress to be involved in trade deals before the final vote, he argued. Levin showed little interest in moving stalled trade pacts with Colombia, Panama and South Korea.

Levin represents Macomb County outside Detroit, where the term "Reagan Democrat" was coined and where the sagging auto industry is a major employer. When Obama announced a series of tough steps aimed at rescuing the domestic auto industry in 2009, Levin expressed support but said the plan should include action to make technological advancements in new cars.

Levin, known as "Sandy," is the older half of a House-Senate sibling pair, but he was elected four years after Sen. Carl Levin, also a Michigan Democrat. They became just the second pair of brothers — and the first in nearly 200 years — to simultaneously hold committee gavels in the House and Senate. Both absorbed a passion for politics from their father, a lawyer active in liberal causes.

After four years as an appointed supervisor in Oakland County, Levin in 1964 won his first elective office, a state Senate seat. He was minority leader in Lansing, served as state Democratic Party chairman in the late 1960s and, as the party's gubernatorial nominee in 1970 and 1974, was seen as a rising star. But he lost both times.

He worked as an assistant administrator in the U.S. Agency for International Development, then ran for the House seat of retiring Democrat William M. Brodhead in 1982. With support from the party establishment, Levin overcame five primary opponents and went on to win the general election easily.

He had little trouble with re-election until redistricting after the 1990 census removed many Jewish voters from his district. In 1992, Republican John Pappageorge held him to 53 percent of the vote. Levin won two rematches, in 1994 and 1996, with 52 percent and 57 percent, respectively. The GOP-led state legislature subsequently redrew Levin's district to make it more Democratic, and in 2002 he easily prevailed with 68 percent. He has won re-election easily since.

Key Votes

2010

Overhaul the nation's health insurance system	YES
Allow for repeal of "don't ask, don't tell"	YES
Overhaul financial services industry regulation	YES
Limit use of new Afghanistan War funds to troop withdrawal activities	NO
Change oversight of offshore drilling and lift oil spill liability cap	YES
Provide a path to legal status for some children of illegal immigrants	YES
Extend Bush-era income tax cuts for two years	YES

2009

Expand the Children's Health Insurance Program	YES
Provide $787 billion in tax cuts and spending increases to stimulate the economy	YES
Allow bankruptcy judges to modify certain primary-residence mortgages	YES
Create a cap-and-trade system to limit greenhouse gas emissions	YES
Provide $2 billion for the "cash for clunkers" program	YES
Establish the government as the sole provider of student loans	YES
Restrict federally funded insurance coverage for abortions in health care overhaul	NO

CQ Vote Studies

	PARTY UNITY		PRESIDENTIAL SUPPORT	
	SUPPORT	OPPOSE	SUPPORT	OPPOSE
2010	99%	1%	98%	2%
2009	99%	1%	96%	4%
2008	99%	1%	16%	84%
2007	98%	2%	7%	93%
2006	93%	7%	25%	75%

Interest Groups

	AFL-CIO	ADA	CCUS	ACU
2010	100%	90%	25%	0%
2009	100%	90%	43%	0%
2008	100%	95%	59%	0%
2007	96%	90%	56%	0%
2006	100%	90%	40%	8%

Michigan 12

Suburban Detroit — Warren, Clinton, Southfield

Heavily Democratic and dependent on the vulnerable auto industry, the 12th includes well-settled suburbs in Macomb and Oakland counties above 8 Mile Road, Detroit's northern boundary. The shoe-shaped district borders Lake St. Clair at its heel and Detroit at its instep, before its toes extend to the city of Southfield.

Seventy percent of the 12th's residents live in Macomb in the district's eastern half. That county (shared with the 10th) supported Democrat Barack Obama with 53 percent of the vote in the 2008 presidential election. Warren, which is the district's most populous city, has been a traditional Democratic haven, and the city gave Obama 59 percent of its presidential vote in 2008. Clinton Township, at slightly less than 100,000 people, claims to be the most populous township in Michigan. St. Clair Shores, the self-proclaimed "boat capital of Michigan," has more than six miles of waterfront.

To the west, the 12th takes in several southern Oakland County communities near the Detroit boundary that are heavily Democratic and have large black populations: Southfield, which has become a haven for black urban professionals, as well as Lathrup Village and Oak Park. Other Oakland County communities in the 12th include Ferndale and Hazel Park, which also are solidly Democratic but are overwhelmingly white and have shed residents since 2000.

The district is lined with auto manufacturing facilities, including Sterling Heights' Chrysler stamping plant. Warren is home to the General Motors Technical Center design and engineering campus as well as the Army's Tank-automotive and Armaments Command.

But layoffs have caused concern in Detroit and across the district, and municipal budget shortfalls have resulted in local governments raising taxes and cutting programs.

Major Industry

Auto manufacturing, auto and tank research and design

Cities

Warren, 134,056; Clinton, 96,796; Southfield, 71,739; St. Clair Shores, 59,715; Roseville, 47,299; Sterling Heights (pt.), 39,419

Notable

The Detroit Zoo is in Royal Oak, which received its name in 1819 when Gov. Lewis Cass and his companions christened a large tree.

Rep. Hansen Clarke (D)

Capitol Office
225-2261
hansenclarke.house.gov
1319 Longworth Bldg. 20515-2213; fax 225-5730

Committees
Homeland Security
Science, Space & Technology

Residence
Detroit

Born
March 2, 1957; Detroit, Mich.

Religion
Roman Catholic

Family
Wife, Choi Palms-Cohen

Education
Cornell U., B.F.A. 1984 (painting); Georgetown U.,
J.D. 1987

Career
County government acquisitions administrator;
congressional district aide

Political Highlights
Mich. House, 1991-93; defeated for re-election
to Mich. House, 1992; Mich. House, 1999-2003;
Democratic nominee for Detroit City Council, 2001;
candidate for Detroit mayor, 2005; Mich. Senate,
2003-10

ELECTION RESULTS

2010 GENERAL

Hansen Clarke (D)	100,885	79.4%
John Hauler (R)	23,462	18.5%

2010 PRIMARY

Hansen Clarke (D)	22,573	47.3%
Carolyn Cheeks Kilpatrick (D)	19,507	40.9%
Glenn Plummer (D)	2,038	4.3%
John W. Broad (D)	1,872	3.9%
Vincent T. Brown (D)	893	1.9%
Stephen Hume (D)	820	1.7%

Elected 2010; 1st term

Clarke seeks to boost the economically hard-hit 13th District but, working in the minority, the former state legislator says he might have to look more to the executive branch than to the Republican majority in the House.

"I'll likely work a lot through the administrative agencies — a lot of times you can get more done that way," he said. "I'm looking more at the objective, the outcome. . . . That's putting more people back to work, helping them become more financially secure."

Education also will be a chief concern. He cites a shortage of nurses in his district as an example of how furloughed manufacturing workers can be retrained. "In Michigan, we're having to hire foreign workers on a temporary basis to meet that need," said Clarke, who can push for training and educational initiatives as the No. 2 Democrat on the Science, Space and Technology Subcommittee on Research and Science Education. He also sits on the Homeland Security Committee.

The son of an African-American mother and a Bangladeshi immigrant father, Clarke majored in painting at Cornell University. Born and raised in Detroit, at one point in his life he was homeless and living on food stamps. But he overcame those issues and has been in Michigan politics since 1990, when he was first elected to the state House. He moved to the state Senate in 2002.

He lost a bid for mayor to Kwame Kilpatrick in 2005. Kilpatrick went to jail in 2008 on corruption charges, the same year his mother, Rep. Carolyn Cheeks Kilpatrick, barely survived a Democratic primary challenge that year by winning a plurality in a three-candidate field.

Clarke made a second challenge to the family in 2010, taking on Rep. Kilpatrick in the primary.

Kilpatrick stressed her spot as Michigan's sole House appropriator and her leadership on minority issues as a former chairwoman of the Congressional Black Caucus. But the negative publicity surrounding her son's conviction lingered, and Clarke won 47 percent of the vote to Kilpatrick's 41 percent.

That assured Clarke a seat in Congress from the overwhelmingly Democratic district. He received almost 80 percent of the vote in November.

Michigan 13

Part of Detroit; Lincoln Park; Wyandotte

The auto industry and Motown Records kept Detroit humming for decades before economic problems overwhelmed the city, which remains among the most crime-ridden in the nation. Detroit still has a tough reputation, and many suburban regional office centers that have lured companies away from the city.

A slightly larger share of Detroit's population lives in the overwhelmingly Democratic 13th than in the adjacent 14th. The city's population overall has plummeted to less than half of what it was in 1950, and Detroit is now out of the top 10 most-populous U.S. cities for the first time since the late 19th century. The 13th suffered the second-largest population loss of any district in the nation between 2000 and 2010 — only Louisiana's New Orleans-based 2nd shed more —

dropping more than 140,000 residents in a decade. Wealthy areas to the northeast, such as Grosse Pointe, also are losing population, although not as drastically.

Revitalization plans, however, are attempting to bring the roar back into the city, and the resurgent downtown is showing signs of life. A massive downtown entertainment complex includes two cornerstone sports stadiums — Comerica Park for baseball's Tigers and Ford Field for football's Lions. Cobo Center hosts major cultural events and conventions, while Joe Louis Arena brings in the crowds for hockey's Red Wings. Downtown casinos are a draw, and General Motors' headquarters are in the Renaissance Center on the waterfront.

Major Industry
Auto manufacturing, government

Cities
Detroit (pt.), 378,375; Lincoln Park (pt.), 8,142

Notable
The Charles H. Wright Museum of African-American History is in the 13th.

Rep. John Conyers Jr. (D)

Capitol Office
225-5126
www.house.gov/conyers
2426 Rayburn Bldg. 20515-2214; fax 225-0072

Committees
Judiciary - Ranking Member

Residence
Detroit

Born
May 16, 1929; Detroit, Mich.

Religion
Baptist

Family
Wife, Monica Conyers; two children

Education
Wayne State U., B.A. 1957, LL.B. 1958

Military
Mich. National Guard, 1948-50; Army, 1950-54; Army Reserve, 1954-57

Career
Lawyer; congressional district aide

Political Highlights
Candidate for mayor of Detroit, 1989, 1993

ELECTION RESULTS

2010 GENERAL

John Conyers Jr. (D)	115,511	76.8%
Don Ukrainec (R)	29,902	19.9%
Marc J. Sosnowski (USTAX)	3,206	2.1%
Richard J. Secula (LIBERT)	1,859	1.2%

2010 PRIMARY

John Conyers Jr. (D)	unopposed

2008 GENERAL

John Conyers Jr. (D)	227,841	92.4%
Richard J. Secula (LIBERT)	10,732	4.4%
Clyde K. Shabazz (GREEN)	8,015	3.2%

Previous Winning Percentages
2006 (85%); 2004 (84%); 2002 (83%); 2000 (89%); 1998 (87%); 1996 (86%); 1994 (81%); 1992 (82%); 1990 (89%); 1988 (91%); 1986 (89%); 1984 (89%); 1982 (97%); 1980 (95%); 1978 (93%); 1976 (92%); 1974 (91%); 1972 (88%); 1970 (88%); 1968 (100%); 1966 (84%); 1964 (84%)

Elected 1964; 24th term

As dean of the Congressional Black Caucus, it seemed natural that the presidency of Barack Obama might be the pinnacle of Conyers' nearly half-century-long career in the House. Instead, he has found himself frustrated that Obama's health care overhaul didn't go far enough to suit him and disappointed about the administration's unwillingness to investigate and roll back President George W. Bush's anti-terrorism policies.

Conyers' personal life has been a source of even greater distress. His wife, Monica, a Detroit City Council member, was sentenced to three years in federal prison after pleading guilty to bribery charges in 2009. Her legal troubles put Conyers in a difficult position, given that he was chairman of the Judiciary Committee, which oversees the federal prison system. He maintained he had no knowledge of his wife's actions, but stayed away from her 2009 sentencing hearing to avoid any appearance of undue influence.

Asked by a Detroit News reporter in 2009 whether he was distancing himself from his wife, Conyers replied, "What would you do if you were in my position?" But Republicans on the notoriously partisan Judiciary Committee made no effort to exploit the issue, due in part to the respect his low-key demeanor has earned him on both sides of the aisle.

Few of Conyers' legislative priorities advanced as he had hoped in the 111th Congress (2009-10), and he can expect even less success with the Republicans back in the majority in the 112th (2011-12).

The rewrite of patent law he had worked with Republicans to advance remained stalled in the Senate. After pushing for years to equalize how crack and powdered cocaine are treated under federal sentencing laws, he had to settle for a more modest adjustment, which was all that could pass the Senate.

Nor could he get Senate Democrats to agree to his proposal to narrow or eliminate several counterterrorism programs under the anti-terrorism law known as the Patriot Act. He unsuccessfully sought to roll back the retroactive immunity granted to telecommunications companies that cooperated with warrantless surveillance of U.S. citizens' communications with suspected terrorists.

He unsuccessfully opposed an extension of expiring provisions of the Patriot Act early in 2011, calling the law "too flawed, too intrusive, and too overreaching."

Conyers, who got his start as a civil rights activist, remains an unabashed liberal willing to stand up to the nation's first African-American president. He picked a fight with Obama early in the 111th Congress over the president's plan to choose CNN correspondent Sanjay Gupta as surgeon general. Conyers called him unqualified; Gupta later avoided the confrontation by turning down the job offer.

Even as Obama sought to cut a deal to overhaul the nation's health care system, Conyers stuck to his longstanding plan to create a government-run single-payer system.

Conyers was at the center of partisan controversy when he pushed legislation through the House to allow bankruptcy court judges to rewrite mortgage terms to help struggling homeowners. Several moderate Democrats rejected the plan for fear it would encourage people to file for bankruptcy.

Conyers, who opposed legislation in 2008 aimed at rescuing ailing banks, said his bill was a better approach. "Unlike the hundreds of billions we have spent in recent months to bail out Wall Street banks, the mortgage modification provision in this legislation comes at no taxpayer expense," he said.

Despite his partisan rhetoric, Conyers worked closely with Judiciary Chairman F. James Sensenbrenner Jr., a Wisconsin Republican, when Democrats were in the minority prior to the 110th Congress (2007-08). And after assuming the chairmanship in 2007, Conyers forged a collegial relationship with ranking Republican Lamar Smith of Texas, who now holds the committee gavel with Conyers as top Democrat.

A co-founder of the Congressional Black Caucus, which celebrates its 40th anniversary in 2011, Conyers has championed the causes of civil rights, minorities and the poor. He introduced legislation to make the Rev. Martin Luther King Jr.'s birthday a national holiday just four days after the civil rights leader's assassination in 1968, and he pushed the bill until it was signed into law in 1983 by President Ronald Reagan. And he has long pursued legislation to establish a commission to study whether the government should pay reparations to descendants of slaves, reintroducing his bill in January 2011.

Conyers was a vociferous defender of President Bill Clinton during the 1998 impeachment debate. By that time, Conyers was the only remaining Judiciary Committee member from 1974, when the panel had voted to impeach President Richard Nixon for Watergate-related offenses.

Conyers argued that Bush's sins in Iraq were far graver when, in 2005, he called for impeachment proceedings. Conyers didn't press the issue, though, when House Democratic leaders made clear that they didn't want to move ahead.

In recent years, Conyers himself was under a cloud as the ethics committee investigated complaints he compelled his official staff to do campaign work and personal chores. The panel elicited a promise from Conyers in 2006 not to use his staff for campaign work.

After serving in the Army in Korea, Conyers went home to Detroit and became involved in the Democratic Party while in law school. The creation in 1964 of a second majority-black congressional district in the city provided an opening, and he won a primary race against accountant Richard H. Austin by 108 votes. Among the qualifications Conyers cited for holding office were three years as a district aide to Michigan Democrat John D. Dingell and service on a panel of lawyers picked by President John F. Kennedy to look for ways of easing racial tensions in the South. He won the Democratic district in a rout that November and has not been seriously challenged for re-election since.

Despite his popularity in his district, Conyers twice was unable to translate it into a successful bid for mayor of Detroit. He finished last in 1989 and again four years later. He has had no problems with re-election to the House.

Key Votes

2010

Overhaul the nation's health insurance system	YES
Allow for repeal of "don't ask, don't tell"	YES
Overhaul financial services industry regulation	YES
Limit use of new Afghanistan War funds to troop withdrawal activities	?
Change oversight of offshore drilling and lift oil spill liability cap	YES
Provide a path to legal status for some children of illegal immigrants	YES
Extend Bush-era income tax cuts for two years	NO

2009

Expand the Children's Health Insurance Program	YES
Provide $787 billion in tax cuts and spending increases to stimulate the economy	YES
Allow bankruptcy judges to modify certain primary-residence mortgages	YES
Create a cap-and-trade system to limit greenhouse gas emissions	YES
Provide $2 billion for the "cash for clunkers" program	YES
Establish the government as the sole provider of student loans	+
Restrict federally funded insurance coverage for abortions in health care overhaul	NO

CQ Vote Studies

	PARTY UNITY		PRESIDENTIAL SUPPORT	
	SUPPORT	OPPOSE	SUPPORT	OPPOSE
2010	99%	1%	92%	8%
2009	98%	2%	91%	9%
2008	98%	2%	12%	88%
2007	99%	1%	4%	96%
2006	98%	2%	8%	92%

Interest Groups

	AFL-CIO	ADA	CCUS	ACU
2010	92%	90%	13%	0%
2009	100%	85%	33%	0%
2008	100%	100%	50%	9%
2007	96%	95%	50%	0%
2006	93%	100%	20%	4%

Michigan 14
Parts of Detroit and Dearborn

The first half of the 20th century brought great prosperity to Detroit, as General Motors helped make it the "Motor City." But race riots during the summer of 1967 and the oil crisis of the early 1970s sparked an exodus that has not let up. In 1950, 1.85 million people lived in Detroit; in 2000, its population was 951,000; the most recent census counted fewer than 714,000 residents.

The 14th covers the residential neighborhoods that sprang up north of Detroit's auto plants. It includes slightly less than half of the city's residents (the rest are in the 13th), and Detroit accounts for 60 percent of the district's total population.

Redevelopment efforts in the district have stalled and the violent crime rates, while down in recent years, remain among the nation's highest. Vacant and abandoned properties are spread throughout neighborhoods in the city's east side, and local officials hope to demolish tens of thousands of blighted homes by 2013. The city's finances were in disarray for years — a problem in an area with a large public sector workforce.

The 14th includes two-thirds of Dearborn, which is home to Ford Motor Co. and its Rouge Center factory. Unlike other Detroit-area cities, Dearborn has not lost residents since 2000, a trend aided by a large Arab-American population that continued to grow in the last decade.

The district also includes two cities surrounded entirely by Detroit: Hamtramck, an ethnically diverse enclave originally settled by Polish immigrants, and Highland Park, an overwhelmingly black area plagued by high poverty rates.

The 14th has one of the country's highest percentages of black residents (59 percent) and is safely Democratic. In 2008, the 14th gave Barack Obama 86 percent of its presidential vote — his highest percentage in the state.

Major Industry
Auto and auto parts manufacturing, health care

Cities
Detroit (pt.), 335,402; Dearborn (pt.), 65,524; Southgate, 30,047; Allen Park city, 28,210; Hamtramck, 22,423

Notable
Woodward Avenue, between 6 Mile and 7 Mile roads, was the nation's first paved road (1909); the Henry Ford museum in Dearborn.

Rep. John D. Dingell (D)

Capitol Office
225-4071
www.house.gov/dingell
2328 Rayburn Bldg. 20515-2215; fax 226-0371

Committees
Energy & Commerce

Residence
Dearborn

Born
July 8, 1926; Colorado Springs, Colo.

Religion
Roman Catholic

Family
Wife, Debbie Dingell; four children

Education
Georgetown U., B.S. 1949 (chemistry), J.D. 1952

Military
Army, 1944-46

Career
County prosecutor

Political Highlights
No previous office

ELECTION RESULTS

2010 GENERAL

John D. Dingell (D)	118,336	56.8%
Rob Steele (R)	83,488	40.1%
Aimee Smith (GREEN)	2,686	1.3%

2010 PRIMARY

John D. Dingell (D)	unopposed

2008 GENERAL

John D. Dingell (D)	231,784	70.7%
John J. Lynch (R)	81,802	25.0%
Aimee Smith (GREEN)	7,082	2.2%
Gregory Stempfle (LIBERT)	4,002	1.2%

Previous Winning Percentages
2006 (88%); 2004 (71%); 2002 (72%); 2000 (71%);
1998 (67%); 1996 (62%); 1994 (59%); 1992 (65%);
1990 (67%); 1988 (97%); 1986 (78%); 1984 (64%);
1982 (74%); 1980 (70%); 1978 (77%); 1976 (76%);
1974 (78%); 1972 (68%); 1970 (79%); 1968 (74%);
1966 (63%); 1964 (73%); 1962 (83%); 1960 (79%);
1958 (79%); 1956 (74%); 1955 Special Election (76%)

Elected 1955; 28th full term

Dingell once called himself "just a simple Polish lawyer from Detroit," but he is assured a spot in history books. Legendary for his tenacity and toughness, his career has spanned more than a half-century and has given him a hand in transformational legislation, from the Civil Rights Act to the Endangered Species and Clean Air acts.

But the capstone to Dingell's legacy will likely be witnessing President Obama sign into law the health care overhaul in 2010. Dingell — who has proposed universal health care bills at the start of every Congress since he was elected in 1955 at age 29 to succeed his father, John Dingell Sr. — likened the achievement to the passage of Medicare and Social Security.

Dingell presided over the start of the debate on the health care legislation in the House on Nov. 7, 2009, and later lent then-Speaker Nancy Pelosi of California the gavel he used when the House passed Medicare in 1965. Throughout the day, his colleagues mobbed him for his autograph on the massive bill.

Dingell marked another achievement on Feb. 11, 2009, by becoming the longest-serving House member, surpassing Mississippi Democrat Jamie L. Whitten after 19,420 days of service. But he was unable to celebrate while serving in the position that earned him his formidable reputation. In November 2008, a longtime Democratic colleague and rival, Henry A. Waxman of California, ousted him from the chairmanship of the Energy and Commerce Committee in a 137-122 vote of House Democrats. Waxman is now ranking Democrat on the panel, where Dingell is No. 2.

In challenging Dingell, Waxman stressed his ties to Obama and his desire to implement an agenda for energy, climate and other issues unburdened by Dingell's uncompromising protection of his state's automobile industry. Dingell clashed with Pelosi in 2007 over an energy bill, urging her to let him craft a bipartisan measure.

"I'm going to get you a bill, not a Democratic bill, but a Democratic accomplishment," he said to Pelosi. But she kept a tight rein on the bill, and the dustup helped lead to Waxman's victory.

"I've had a good run," Dingell said in conceding defeat.

One of the last of the old bulls, Dingell served as Energy and Commerce chairman from 1981 to 1995 and then as top-ranking Democrat until 2007, when his party retook control of Congress and he regained the gavel. He built what scholars consider one of the most expansive congressional power centers of the post-World War II era, with jurisdiction on issues as diverse as energy, health care and telecommunications. "He will be remembered as one of the most influential members of Congress not to have served as president," said Texas Republican Joe L. Barton, who has served on the panel with Dingell for two decades.

Since losing his chairmanship, Dingell has repeatedly lamented the increased partisanship on both sides of the aisle. In an op-ed published in Roll Call the day he set the record for service in the House, Dingell recalled an earlier era when Republicans and Democrats socialized together and collaborated on legislation from the center. "We got along. We did good work. It wasn't perfect, and we certainly fought a lot, but we weren't paralyzed by partisanship either," Dingell wrote.

He retains a thorough grasp of House rules and legislative detail, so much so that Waxman and Pelosi kept Dingell front and center for the health care fight in recognition of the great influence and power he wields on the issue.

Waxman also let Dingell help draft food safety legislation in early 2009 that became the basis for what the panel considered, according to the chairman. And Dingell has remained active on energy and climate change. He was a central player in the 2007 debate on the energy bill, in which he reversed decades of opposition to tougher fuel efficiency standards for automobiles. The bill included the first statutory increase in such standards in 32 years. When Obama announced a tough series of steps for automakers in March 2009, Dingell vowed to do anything he could to help them avoid financial ruin. He also endorsed Waxman's cap-and-trade energy legislation, passed by the House in 2009, and opposed a GOP effort to bar the EPA from enforcing its rules on carbon emissions early in 2011.

Dingell stands with liberals on most issues but opposes abortion rights and gun control. He inherited his political philosophy from his father, who entered the House in 1933 with Franklin D. Roosevelt's New Deal generation. The younger Dingell grew up in Washington, first stepping onto the House floor at the age of 6. He became a House page when he turned 12 and was in the chamber with his father in 1941 when Roosevelt gave the "Day of Infamy" speech following the Japanese attack on Pearl Harbor that launched the United States into World War II. Less than three years later, Dingell was drafted into the Army, and his unit of 210 soldiers was decimated in the Battle of the Bulge. Dingell, who spent the battle in the hospital suffering from meningitis, was one of 10 survivors. He became a park ranger prior to his election, trapping bears, blowing up beaver dams and fighting forest fires. After earning a law degree from Georgetown University, he was an assistant county prosecutor in Dearborn, Mich., when his father died.

In 27 general elections, he drew less than 60 percent of the vote only twice — in 1994 and 2010, the last two times Republicans won control of the House. But in 2002, after the GOP-controlled state legislature redrew boundaries to reflect Michigan's post-census loss of a House seat, Dingell was pitted in the primary against another incumbent Democrat, eight-year veteran Lynn Rivers, whom he defeated with 59 percent of the vote.

Age has slowed Dingell. The tall, burly veteran walks slowly, leaning on a cane. In October 2008 he underwent knee replacement surgery, and a month later was hospitalized for what an aide called post-surgical complications.

But despite talk that he could soon be replaced by another Dingell — his wife, Debbie, or one of his four children — Dingell sounds like he wants to stick around and set a few more records.

"There's an old Polish saying, 'Before you sell the bear's hide, you first have to shoot the bear,'" he said in 2009. "This bear's doing pretty good."

Key Votes

2010	
Overhaul the nation's health insurance system	YES
Allow for repeal of "don't ask, don't tell"	YES
Overhaul financial services industry regulation	YES
Limit use of new Afghanistan War funds to troop withdrawal activities	NO
Change oversight of offshore drilling and lift oil spill liability cap	YES
Provide a path to legal status for some children of illegal immigrants	YES
Extend Bush-era income tax cuts for two years	YES

2009	
Expand the Children's Health Insurance Program	YES
Provide $787 billion in tax cuts and spending increases to stimulate the economy	YES
Allow bankruptcy judges to modify certain primary-residence mortgages	YES
Create a cap-and-trade system to limit greenhouse gas emissions	YES
Provide $2 billion for the "cash for clunkers" program	YES
Establish the government as the sole provider of student loans	YES
Restrict federally funded insurance coverage for abortions in health care overhaul	NO

CQ Vote Studies

	PARTY UNITY		PRESIDENTIAL SUPPORT	
	Support	Oppose	Support	Oppose
2010	99%	1%	95%	5%
2009	99%	1%	96%	4%
2008	99%	1%	15%	85%
2007	97%	3%	6%	94%
2006	90%	10%	23%	77%

Interest Groups

	AFL-CIO	ADA	CCUS	ACU
2010	100%	85%	25%	0%
2009	100%	95%	33%	0%
2008	100%	90%	56%	4%
2007	96%	95%	65%	0%
2006	100%	95%	33%	13%

Michigan 15

Southeast — Ann Arbor, Taylor, parts of Dearborn and Dearborn Heights, Ypsilanti

Situated in Michigan's southeast corner west and south of Detroit, the 15th's flat land contains a mix of academics, engineers and auto workers. GOP votes from the 15th's rural farming communities in the southwest are overshadowed by blue-collar strongholds in Wayne County's urban areas, as well as Ann Arbor, and Democrat Barack Obama carried the district with 66 percent of the 2008 presidential vote.

Home to the University of Michigan in the 15th's northwest corner in Washtenaw County, Ann Arbor is one of Michigan's most progressive cities and has remained stable in the face of significant economic pressure. A high standard of living, a strong medical research sector and a highly educated workforce make Ann Arbor a gem in an ailing state. Overall, the city gave Obama 82 percent of its presidential vote in 2008. Despite some plant closings, Ann Arbor has avoided widespread job losses by relying on expansions at the university and in the private sector at employers such as Google's AdWords, a company advertising vehicle.

Ypsilanti, the working-class town southeast of Ann Arbor, is home to

Eastern Michigan University and reliably backs Democrats. Engineering and robotics firms have emerged south and east of Ann Arbor, developing highly skilled and computerized auto manufacturing.

A little less than 40 percent of the 15th's residents live in the reliably Democratic Wayne County suburbs, including Taylor, located a few miles east of Detroit Metropolitan Wayne County Airport in Romulus. Local officials hope to spur job growth in developments between Metro Airport and nearby Willow Run Airport. Dearborn, the western third of which is in the 15th, Dearborn Heights (shared with the 11th) and Inkster form the district's northeast corner. Monroe County, south of Wayne and Washtenaw, abuts Lake Erie to the east and the Toledo area to the south.

Major Industry
Auto and auto parts manufacturing, higher education, medical research, steel

Cities
Ann Arbor (pt.), 113,929; Taylor, 63,131; Dearborn Heights (pt.), 44,151; Dearborn (pt.), 32,629; Inkster, 25,369; Romulus, 23,989; Monroe, 20,733

Notable
The National Oceanic and Atmospheric Administration's Great Lakes Environmental Research Laboratory is in Ann Arbor.

MINNESOTA

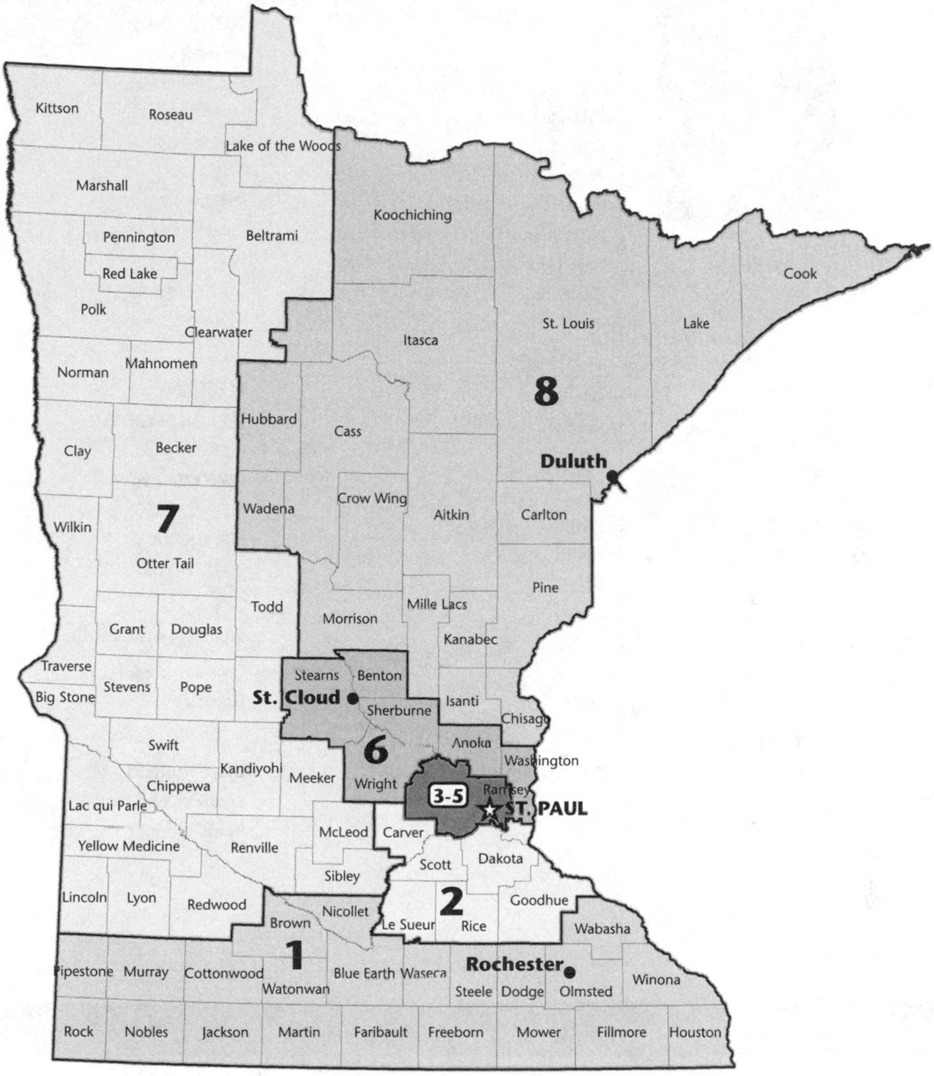

Gov. Mark Dayton (D)

First elected: 2010

Length of term: 4 years

Term expires: 1/15

Salary: $120,303

Phone: (651) 201-3400

Residence: St. Paul

Born: Jan. 26, 1947; Minneapolis, Minn.

Religion: Presbyterian

Family: Divorced; two children

Education: Yale U., B.A. 1969 (psychology)

Career: Investment company president; runaway youth home director; congressional and gubernatorial aide; social worker; teacher

Political highlights: Minn. commissioner of economic development, 1978; Democratic nominee for U.S. Senate, 1982; Minn. commissioner of energy and economic development, 1983-86; Minn. auditor, 1991-95; sought Democratic nomination for governor, 1998; U.S. Senate, 2001-07

ELECTION RESULTS

2010 GENERAL

Mark Dayton (D)	919,232	43.6%
Tom Emmer (R)	910,462	43.2%
Tom Horner (I)	251,487	11.9%

Lt. Gov. Yvonne Prettner Solon (D)

First elected: 2010

Length of term: 4 years

Term expires: 1/15

Salary: $90,227

Phone: (651) 201-3400

LEGISLATURE

Legislature: January-May in odd-numbered years; February-May in even-numbered years

Senate: 67 members, 4-year terms (2-year terms in redistricting years)

2011 ratios: 37 R, 30 D; 46 men, 21 women

Salary: $31,141

Phone: (651) 296-0504

House: 134 members, 2-year terms

2011 ratios: 72 R, 62 D; 90 men, 44 women

Salary: $31,141

Phone: (651) 296-2146

TERM LIMITS

Governor: No

Senate: No

House: No

URBAN STATISTICS

CITY	POPULATION
Minneapolis	382,578
St. Paul	285,068
Rochester	106,769
Duluth	86,265
Bloomington	82,893

REGISTERED VOTERS

Voters do not register by party.

POPULATION

2010 population	5,303,925
2000 population	4,919,479
1990 population	4,375,099
Percent change (2000-2010)	+7.8%
Rank among states (2010)	21
Median age	37
Born in state	69.0%
Foreign born	6.4%
Violent crime rate	244/100,000
Poverty level	11.0%
Federal workers	38,265
Military	1,897

ELECTIONS

STATE ELECTION OFFICIAL

(651) 215-1440

DEMOCRATIC PARTY

(651) 293-1200

REPUBLICAN PARTY

(651) 222-0022

MISCELLANEOUS

Web: www.state.mn.us

Capital: St. Paul

U.S. CONGRESS

Senate: 2 Democrats

House: 4 Republicans, 4 Democrats

2010 Census Statistics by District

District	2008 Vote for President Obama	McCain	White	Black	Asian	Hispanic	Median Income	White Collar	Blue Collar	Service Industry	Over 64	Under 18	College Education	Rural	Sq. Miles
1	51%	47%	89%	2%	2%	5%	$50,407	57%	27%	17%	15%	24%	25%	44%	13,322
2	48	50	86	3	4	5	73,800	66	20	14	8	28	35	20	3,035
3	52	46	79	8	7	4	74,313	72	15	12	11	25	43	4	468
4	64	34	69	10	10	8	54,055	67	17	16	13	24	37	0	202
5	74	24	65	15	5	10	49,627	67	16	17	11	21	41	0	124
6	45	53	90	2	3	2	69,386	62	24	14	9	27	29	36	3,081
7	47	50	90	1	1	4	45,690	54	29	17	17	24	19	66	31,796
8	53	44	93	1	1	1	46,335	54	27	19	16	22	20	63	27,583
STATE	54	44	83	5	4	5	57,007	62	22	16	12	24	31	29	79,610
U.S.	53	46	64	12	5	16	51,425	60	23	17	13	25	28	21	3,537,438

Sen. Amy Klobuchar (D)

Capitol Office
224-3244
klobuchar.senate.gov
302 Hart Bldg. 20510-2305; fax 228-2186

Committees
Agriculture, Nutrition & Forestry
Commerce, Science & Transportation
    (Competitiveness, Innovation & Export Promotion
    - Chairwoman)
Judiciary
    (Administrative Oversight & the Courts - Chairwoman)
Joint Economic

Residence
Minneapolis

Born
May 25, 1960; Plymouth, Minn.

Religion
Congregationalist

Family
Husband, John Bessler; one child

Education
Yale U., B.A. 1982 (political science); U. of Chicago,
J.D. 1985

Career
Lawyer; lobbyist

Political Highlights
Hennepin County attorney, 1999-2007

ELECTION RESULTS

2006 GENERAL

Amy Klobuchar (D)	1,278,849	58.1%
Mark Kennedy (R)	835,653	37.9%
Rob Fitzgerald (INDC)	71,194	3.2%

2006 PRIMARY

Amy Klobuchar (D)	294,671	92.5%
Darryl Stanton (D)	23,872	7.5%

Elected 2006; 1st term

Klobuchar has emerged as an influential center-left voice with close ties to party leaders and the White House. The former prosecutor portrays herself as "my own Democrat" and looks to forge bipartisan coalitions for her own bills, while lining up with President Obama on big issues.

With a disarming Midwestern monotone, Klobuchar (KLO-buh-shar) serves as a bridge from party leaders to younger members and is a linchpin of the 2006 class that will seek a second term with Obama in 2012.

A member of the whip team and a recruiter for the Democratic Senatorial Campaign Committee, Klobuchar has honed a reputation as a pragmatic dealmaker on topics such as her 2010 proposal to broaden anti-stalking laws (re-introduced in February 2011) as well as measures to expedite international adoptions and promote tourism. "It's just getting to know people, and treating them with respect, and seeing where you agree," she said of her consensus-forming style.

One of two women on the Judiciary Committee, Klobuchar has brushed aside speculation about her own prospects as a possible Supreme Court nominee by stressing how much she likes her present job, which includes chairing the subcommittee with jurisdiction over the federal courts in the 112th Congress (2011-12). A lawyer — unlike the other woman on the panel, Dianne Feinstein of California — Klobuchar helped the drive to confirm the nominations of Elena Kagan and Sonia Sotomayor to the Supreme Court in the 111th Congress (2009-10).

She served on the Senate Impeachment Trial Committee in the case of U.S. District Judge G. Thomas Porteous Jr., who was impeached and convicted on corruption charges in late 2010.

Klobuchar carried an extra load for much of 2009 until her home-state Democratic colleague, Al Franken, was declared the winner of a tightly contested race against incumbent Republican Norm Coleman. She has worked closely with the more liberal Franken on social issues, such as the fight to end workplace discrimination based on sexual orientation.

On the Agriculture, Nutrition and Forestry Committee, she urged final action in the summer of 2010 on a food safety bill to "protect the public from future harm" after an egg recall due to salmonella contamination. And she pressed for measures to promote alternative fuels such as cellulosic ethanol made from grasses and biomass crops, one of her top priorities in energy and farm legislation. She'll play a role in writing a new farm bill the 112th Congress and is newly installed as the co-chairwoman of the Congressional Farmer Cooperative Caucus, with Republican John Thune of neighboring South Dakota.

Klobuchar backed legislation in the 111th Congress to combat global warming. She applauded the EPA's March 2009 decision to establish a registry to track carbon emissions; the first bill she introduced in Congress made the same proposal. She supported renewable-fuel content standards for cars and trucks, and strong standards for renewable electricity generation that make greater use of wind, solar and other alternative sources.

In 2010 she opposed an effort to block the EPA from using its regulatory authority to regulate carbon emissions under the Clean Air Act.

She backed the 2010 financial regulation overhaul, after adding her language to retain the Federal Reserve's regional system for regulating community banks, to ban payments to lenders based on a mortgage's interest rate, and to mandate documentation of a homebuyer's income.

After joining six moderate Democrats to urge Finance Committee Chairman Max Baucus of Montana to focus on cost-cutting measures, she pushed for changes in the final health care overhaul enacted in 2010, such as a smaller increase in the tax on medical devices. She called the new law "a beginning, not an end."

She was among the Democrats pushing for repeal of an unpopular tax-reporting provision of the law that requires businesses to submit a 1099 form to the IRS for each vendor to whom they pay more than $600 each year. Small-business advocates have called the requirement a paperwork nightmare.

On the Commerce, Science and Transportation Committee she keeps an eye on regional priorities such as highway and bridge funding, while backing measures that capture public attention such as proposals to ban texting while driving and to increase protections for airline passengers and online privacy. Her home state borders the No. 1 trading partner of the United States, and Klobuchar chairs the Competitiveness, Innovation and Export Promotion Subcommittee.

She serves as Senate co-chairwoman, with North Carolina Republican Richard M. Burr, of the Congressional E-911 Caucus, which seeks to improve emergency communications.

In the 110th Congress (2007-08), she played a key role on a bipartisan consumer safety law that banned lead in all toys sold in the United States. And she is proud of her crusade against pool-drain accidents. After a wading-pool drain sucked out the intestines of a 6-year-old Minnesota girl — ultimately killing her — Klobuchar in 2007 quickly pushed through Congress a bill calling for tighter regulations.

Klobuchar grew up in the Minneapolis suburb of Plymouth; her mother taught second grade and her father was a longtime columnist for the Minneapolis Star Tribune. She attended Yale, where her senior thesis detailed the 10-year political debate over the building of the Hubert H. Humphrey Metrodome in Minneapolis. Published as a book, "Uncovering the Dome" has been used as a text in college courses.

After graduating from the University of Chicago's law school, Klobuchar returned to Minnesota to practice law and worked with Walter F. Mondale, who provided her first Washington experience through an internship in his office when he was the vice president.

She also helped her father, Jim Klobuchar, recover from alcoholism, a battle he subsequently chronicled in a book. The challenge gave her thick skin that came in handy during her Senate run. "Growing up with my dad being in the public eye was also very helpful," she said. His three DWI arrests "were all very prominent and well known."

She first caught the political bug on her high school student council, but the catalyst that drove her into big-league politics came in 1995, when her daughter Abigail was born with a frozen palate that prevented her from swallowing. While the baby stayed at the hospital, Klobuchar was discharged after 24 hours because it was all her health plan would cover. Outraged, she lobbied state lawmakers successfully for a law to guarantee new mothers 48 hours at the hospital.

Klobuchar entered the Hennepin County attorney's race in 1998 and defeated Sheryl Ramstad, sister of former Republican Rep. Jim Ramstad. Klobuchar was re-elected in 2002 without opposition.

When Democrat Mark Dayton announced his retirement from the Senate in early 2005, Klobuchar was recognized as an early favorite to secure the Democratic-Farmer-Labor Party nomination, and her three leading opponents dropped out of the race during the primary campaign.

In the general election, she topped Republican Rep. Mark Kennedy, with 58 percent of the vote to Kennedy's 38 percent. It was the largest margin of victory in a U.S. Senate race in the state since 1978.

Key Votes

2010

Pass budget reconciliation bill to modify overhauls of health care and federal student loan programs	YES
Proceed to disapproval resolution on EPA authority to regulate greenhouse gases	NO
Overhaul financial services industry regulation	YES
Limit debate to proceed to a bill to broaden campaign finance disclosure and reporting rules	YES
Limit debate on an extension of Bush-era income tax cuts for two years	YES
Limit debate on a bill to provide a path to legal status for some children of illegal immigrants	YES
Allow for a repeal of "don't ask, don't tell"	YES
Consent to ratification of a strategic arms reduction treaty with Russia	YES

2009

Prevent release of remaining financial industry bailout funds	NO
Make it easier for victims to sue for wage discrimination remedies	YES
Expand the Children's Health Insurance Program	YES
Limit debate on the economic stimulus measure	YES
Repeal District of Columbia firearms prohibitions and gun registration laws	NO
Limit debate on expansion of federal hate crimes law	YES
Strike funding for F-22 Raptor fighter jets	YES

CQ Vote Studies

	PARTY UNITY		PRESIDENTIAL SUPPORT	
	Support	Oppose	Support	Oppose
2010	90%	10%	100%	0%
2009	89%	11%	97%	3%
2008	94%	6%	31%	69%
2007	93%	7%	38%	62%

Interest Groups

	AFL-CIO	ADA	CCUS	ACU
2010	93%	90%	36%	4%
2009	100%	100%	43%	12%
2008	100%	100%	57%	16%
2007	95%	100%	45%	4%

Sen. Al Franken (D)

Capitol Office
224-5641
franken.senate.gov
309 Hart Bldg. 20510-2303; fax 224-0044

Committees
Energy & Natural Resources
Health, Education, Labor & Pensions
Indian Affairs
Judiciary
   (Privacy, Technology & the Law - Chairman)

Residence
Minneapolis

Born
May 21, 1951; Manhattan, N.Y.

Religion
Jewish

Family
Wife, Franni Franken; two children

Education
Harvard U., A.B. 1973 (general studies)

Career
Author; radio talk show host; screenwriter; comedian

Political Highlights
No previous office

ELECTION RESULTS

2008 GENERAL

Al Franken (D)	1,212,629	41.5%
Norm Coleman (R)	1,212,317	41.5%
Others	496,109	17.0%

2008 PRIMARY

Al Franken (D)	164,136	65.3%
Priscilla Lord Faris (D)	74,655	29.7%
Dick Franson (D)	3,923	1.6%
Bob Larson (D)	3,152	1.2%
Rob Fitzgerald (D)	3,095	1.2%

Elected 2008; 1st term

Franken wants to be seen as more than a partisan liberal capable of telling a good joke. With the controversy attached to his 312-vote margin of victory in the 2008 Senate race behind him, the former comedian, writer and actor is now trying to make the transition from showman to statesman. But his voting record is uniformly partisan, and his penchant for humor doesn't always sit well in the staid confines of the Senate.

He challenged Republican Sen. Norm Coleman in November 2008 in an election whose outcome was so close it became ensnared in legal challenges for the better part of a year. A trial court declared Franken the winner by 312 votes out of 2.9 million cast, but Coleman continued efforts to prevent Franken from being seated. The Minnesota Supreme Court subsequently agreed in June 2009 that Franken had won, prompting Coleman to concede.

Franken, meanwhile, stayed out of the spotlight, refusing most national media interview requests while preparing for the job he hoped to assume.

He was not always so restrained. As a writer and performer on NBC's "Saturday Night Live," he was known for pushing boundaries. His book "Rush Limbaugh is a Big Fat Idiot" not only attacked the popular talk-show host but took aim at then-House Speaker Newt Gingrich of Georgia and ex-United Nations ambassador Jeane Kirkpatrick.

In a subsequent book, "Lies and the Lying Liars Who Tell Them," Franken blasted President George W. Bush's administration and Fox News commentator Bill O'Reilly, among others.

In 2010 he got himself in a bit of hot water for making faces and gesticulating while presiding in the chair during a speech by Minority Leader Mitch McConnell of Kentucky, who was speaking on the nomination of Elena Kagan to the Supreme Court.

When McConnell was finished speaking, he approached Franken in the presiding officer's chair and reportedly told him "This is not 'Saturday Night Live,' Al." Franken later sent a note of apology.

But Franken has sought to be taken seriously as a senator. He portrays himself as a successor to the legacy of Minnesota Democratic Sen. Paul Wellstone, a champion of progressive causes who died in an October 2002 plane crash.

Franken is a dependable liberal and stalwart party man. In 2010, he sided with a majority of Democrats against a majority of Republicans 99 percent of the time.

At the same time, he has formed some cross-party alliances. He struck up a friendship with his ideological opposite, freshman Republican Rand Paul of Kentucky. And he worked with Georgia Republican Johnny Isakson on his first piece of legislation a couple of weeks after being sworn in: a measure to expand a pilot program that pairs service dogs with mentally and physically disabled veterans that was incorporated into the fiscal 2010 omnibus spending measure.

Not all of Franken's legislative initiatives are popular, bipartisan affairs, of course. In October 2009, he offered an amendment to the fiscal 2010 Defense appropriations bill that he hoped would prohibit the federal government from doing business with contractors that require employees to go through arbitration, rather than the legal system, in cases regarding sexual assault and rape.

The measure was inspired by Jamie Leigh Jones, an employee of defense contractor KBR Inc., who alleged that she was drugged and raped in 2005 by her co-workers in Baghdad. Jones was forced to sign a contract as a condition of her employment requiring her to settle work-related claims through private arbitration instead of a jury. Jones further alleged she was locked in a shipping container by the firm to prevent her from leaving Iraq and seeking medical treatment. Senate Republicans argued that Congress should not be involved in writing private contracts and cited opposition by the Defense Department, which said it would be difficult to enforce. The provision made it into the bill, which became law.

He also made waves during two of the biggest fights of the 111th Congress (2009-10): overhauls of the health care and financial regulatory systems.

A member of the Health, Education, Labor and Pensions Committee, he pushed an amendment to the Senate's health care bill that required 90 percent of premiums collected by insurers to be spent on clinical services and quality of care. Spurred by a suggestion from the Congressional Budget Office, the amendment was changed to 85 percent for large group plans and 80 percent for small group and individual plans. The amendment was included in the final version of the health care measure that was signed into law.

Franken also sought to end the practice of allowing banks to pick what credit rating agencies will judge the securities they issue. To accomplish this, he won adoption of an amendment to the Senate's financial regulation bill that would require an independent board to assign a rating agency to a bank. Facing opposition in conference from the Democratic chairmen of each chamber's relevant committee — House Financial Services Chairman Barney Frank of Massachusetts and Senate Banking, Housing and Urban Affairs Chairman Christopher J. Dodd of Connecticut — the provision was stripped from the bill before the final version was sent to the president. The Securities and Exchange Commission was instead directed to conduct a study on the feasibility of the proposal.

A member of the Judiciary Committee, where he chairs the subcommittee handling technology issues, he has been outspoken on "net neutrality" rules, which would limit providers' abilities to restrict the flow of information. He called net neutrality "the most important free speech issue of our time" in a Huffington Post opinion piece in 2010.

He combines his work on Judiciary and the Indian Affairs Committee to push for better crime data collection and more police officers on Indian reservations.

On Energy and Natural Resources, Franken backs legislation to cap carbon emissions and boost renewable energy sources, including ethanol made from Minnesota's corn crop.

Franken was born in New York City and raised in St. Louis Park, a Minneapolis suburb. His mother was a homemaker and sold real estate. His father owned a fabric factory and also worked as a printing agent.

After attending Harvard University, Franken and his high school friend and writing partner, Tom Davis, were hired in 1975 to write for the then-fledgling "Saturday Night Live." He won five Emmy Awards for his writing. Outside of "Saturday Night Live," he has also written for and appeared in movies and television shows such as "Stuart Saves His Family" and "Trading Places."

Franken appeared on CNN to provide commentary for the 1988 Democratic National Convention and anchored Comedy Central's 1992 and 1996 election coverage. As a comedian, he volunteered with the USO and has performed for military personnel in Kosovo, Iraq, and Afghanistan.

In 2004, Franken began broadcasting a daily radio show on the now-defunct Air America Radio. "The O'Franken Factor," later renamed "The Al Franken Show," tackled political issues from Franken's liberal perspective. The show remained on the air until 2007 when, at the end of the final episode, Franken announced that he would challenge Coleman.

Key Votes

2010

Pass budget reconciliation bill to modify overhauls of health care and federal student loan programs	YES
Proceed to disapproval resolution on EPA authority to regulate greenhouse gases	NO
Overhaul financial services industry regulation	YES
Limit debate to proceed to a bill to broaden campaign finance disclosure and reporting rules	YES
Limit debate on an extension of Bush-era income tax cuts for two years	YES
Limit debate on a bill to provide a path to legal status for some children of illegal immigrants	YES
Allow for a repeal of "don't ask, don't tell"	YES
Consent to ratification of a strategic arms reduction treaty with Russia	YES

2009

Limit debate on expansion of federal hate crimes law	YES
Strike funding for F-22 Raptor fighter jets	YES

CQ Vote Studies

	PARTY UNITY		PRESIDENTIAL SUPPORT	
	SUPPORT	OPPOSE	SUPPORT	OPPOSE
2010	99%	1%	98%	2%
2009	98%	2%	97%	3%

Interest Groups

	AFL-CIO	ADA	CCUS	ACU
2010	100%	90%	18%	0%
2009	100%		50%	0%

Rep. Tim Walz (D)

Capitol Office
225-2472
walz.house.gov
1722 Longworth Bldg. 20515-2301; fax 225-3433

Committees
Agriculture
Transportation & Infrastructure
Veterans' Affairs

Residence
Mankato

Born
April 6, 1964; West Point, Neb.

Religion
Lutheran

Family
Wife, Gwen Walz; two children

Education
Chadron State College, B.S. 1989 (social science education); Minnesota State U., Mankato, M.S. 2001 (educational leadership); Saint Mary's U. of Minnesota, attending

Military
Neb. National Guard, 1981-96; Minn. National Guard, 1996-2005

Career
Mortgage processor; teacher

Political Highlights
No previous office

ELECTION RESULTS

2010 GENERAL

Tim Walz (D)	122,365	49.3%
Randy Demmer (R)	109,242	44.0%
Steven Wilson (INDC)	13,242	5.3%
Lars Johnson (PTF)	3,054	1.2%

2010 PRIMARY

Tim Walz (D)	unopposed

2008 GENERAL

Tim Walz (D)	207,753	62.5%
Brian J. Davis (R)	109,453	32.9%
Gregory Mikkelson (INDC)	14,904	4.5%

Previous Winning Percentages
2006 (53%)

Elected 2006; 3rd term

Walz has made a name for himself as a lawmaker focused on constituent service and securing federal funds for his southern Minnesota district. The second of those tasks will be more difficult in the 112th Congress, with a Republican majority and the absence of fellow Minnesota Democrat James L. Oberstar at the helm of the Transportation and Infrastructure Committee, on which Walz sits.

Oberstar was defeated in the Republican wave of 2010, but Walz survived despite running 25 percentage points behind his 2008 victory total.

He has been a loyal Democrat throughout his career, siding with his party about 95 percent of the time when majorities of the two parties split.

During the 111th Congress (2009-10), Walz voted in favor of the $787 billion economic stimulus package, legislation to create a cap-and-trade system to limit carbon emissions and the health care overhaul that became law in 2010. On health care, Walz has highlighted payment structure changes that provide performance-based payments to providers. Rochester's world-renowned Mayo Clinic is in the 1st District.

But Walz breaks away from Democratic orthodoxy on some issues, such as gun rights. The National Rifle Association praised his voting record on gun legislation and endorsed him in 2010 over a similarly rated GOP challenger, who won the endorsement of the harder-line Gun Owners of America.

Mostly, though, he spends his legislative energies looking out for the folks back home.

In 2008, Walz helped another Minnesota Democrat, Agriculture Chairman Collin C. Peterson, move his bill updating federal farm programs through the House and eventually into law, saying the legislation would make it easier for southern Minnesota's farmers to enroll in conservation programs. Walz opposed an amendment to slash farm subsidies to the nation's richest farmers, although he has argued for revisions in the way such payments are doled out. With his district located in the Corn Belt, Walz is a champion of ethanol and supported a 2007 law that requires oil companies to double the amount of corn-based ethanol they blend with gasoline. He supports a combination of conservation, expansion of oil and gas drilling, and innovation for alternative fuels, including nuclear power. He'll have a hand in reauthorizing such programs as the committee tackles a new farm bill in the 112th Congress (2011-12).

Walz uses his seat on the Transportation panel to steer projects to his district — a role that could be diminished in the minority and without Oberstar — including $1 million for a rail rehabilitation initiative and money for road expansion in the fiscal 2010 omnibus spending bill.

A military veteran and member of the Veterans' Affairs Committee, Walz backs spending more on health care for veterans, although he has opposed the Iraq War. He has been among the Democrats continuing to support the war in Afghanistan, however.

He hailed the enactment of a war spending bill in 2008 that greatly expanded benefits under the GI Bill and granted equal veterans' education benefits to National Guard and reserve members who have served at least 20 months on active duty. "That is exactly why I ran for this job," Walz said in December 2008.

In early 2011, when new Veterans' Affairs Chairman Jeff Miller, a Florida Republican, proposed cuts in VA spending and said veterans were prepared to "sacrifice again" if the sacrifice were shared, Walz retorted with a familiar Democratic line of argument: "Attempting to balance the budget on the backs of veterans who have risked life and limb in service of our country is unacceptable."

Walz grew up in a middle-class family from the sand hills of north-central Nebraska. His mother was a homemaker; his father was a school superintendent. Walz was in high school when his father was diagnosed with cancer. His mother and 8-year-old brother soon found themselves living off his father's Social Security survivor benefits. "If there wouldn't have been a safety net, it would have been different," he said.

At 17, Walz joined the Nebraska National Guard to help pay for his studies at Chadron State College. After college, Walz was part of the first government-sanctioned group of American educators to teach in China. He speaks Mandarin and is one of nine House members on the Congressional-Executive Commission on China, which monitors human rights abuses there.

After a teaching stint in Nebraska, Walz moved to Minnesota in 1996 to take a position at Mankato West High School, where he taught geography and coached football. His wife, Gwen, is the assessment coordinator for Mankato Public Schools.

Walz retired from the military in 2005 after more than two decades in the Army National Guard, including a deployment to Italy to oversee supply shipments to troops serving in Afghanistan. He rose to the rank of command sergeant major, making him the highest-ranking enlisted soldier ever to serve in Congress.

Walz's only venture into politics before his 2006 campaign consisted of some community organizing for Massachusetts Sen. John Kerry's 2004 presidential campaign. That lack of political experience turned out to be an asset when he challenged Republican incumbent Gil Gutknecht in 2006. Walz won with 53 percent of the vote and went on to be elected president of the House Democrats' freshman class that year.

Early in his first term, GOP operatives dubbed Walz "Twinkle Toes" because they felt he danced around the issues. He dismissed such criticism and, benefitting from the national Democratic tide, cruised to victory over oncologist Brian J. Davis in 2008.

With the tide reversed two years later, Walz faced Republican state Rep. Randy Demmer, who tried to paint him as too liberal for the swing district. Walz defended the health care overhaul and pointed to Republican actions on the deficit and other issues when they were in the majority. He topped Demmer, 49 percent to 44 percent.

Key Votes

2010

Overhaul the nation's health insurance system	YES
Allow for repeal of "don't ask, don't tell"	YES
Overhaul financial services industry regulation	YES
Limit use of new Afghanistan War funds to troop withdrawal activities	NO
Change oversight of offshore drilling and lift oil spill liability cap	YES
Provide a path to legal status for some children of illegal immigrants	YES
Extend Bush-era income tax cuts for two years	YES

2009

Expand the Children's Health Insurance Program	YES
Provide $787 billion in tax cuts and spending increases to stimulate the economy	YES
Allow bankruptcy judges to modify certain primary-residence mortgages	YES
Create a cap-and-trade system to limit greenhouse gas emissions	YES
Provide $2 billion for the "cash for clunkers" program	YES
Establish the government as the sole provider of student loans	YES
Restrict federally funded insurance coverage for abortions in health care overhaul	NO

CQ Vote Studies

	PARTY UNITY		PRESIDENTIAL SUPPORT	
	SUPPORT	OPPOSE	SUPPORT	OPPOSE
2010	97%	3%	95%	5%
2009	94%	6%	96%	4%
2008	96%	4%	14%	86%
2007	94%	6%	5%	95%

Interest Groups

	AFL-CIO	ADA	CCUS	ACU
2010	100%	90%	25%	4%
2009	100%	100%	47%	4%
2008	93%	85%	50%	20%
2007	96%	100%	60%	0%

Minnesota 1

South — Rochester, Mankato

Stretching from the flat plains at the South Dakota border to the towering bluffs overlooking the Mississippi River, Minnesota's rural 1st District is cut horizontally by Interstate 90 and vertically by Interstate 35. Rural areas continue to lose population to the Twin Cities, but tens of thousands of residents have moved to Mankato and Rochester, home to an IBM facility and the Mayo Clinic.

Agriculture and food processing still drive the local economy. Corn, soybeans, sugar beets, hogs and dairy are staples here. The 1st has one of the highest agricultural market values of any district in the country, and more than 20,000 farms dot the 1st's landscape. Food processing, from fresh turkey to canned soup, is prevalent throughout the area west of Rochester. West of Mankato, no town has more than 15,000 residents.

Rochester, the district's largest city and the third-largest city in Minnesota, has a highly educated populace: 42 percent of the city's residents hold at least a bachelor's degree and 17 percent hold a graduate degree. Service and hospitality industries here depend on consistent patient and visitor

volumes at the Mayo Clinic, as well. Rochester hosts the newest University of Minnesota campus, and Winona and Mankato both have state universities.

Although the 1st is nearly 90 percent white, Hispanic, Asian and black immigrants have come to the district to work in processing plants, in agriculture and at Rochester's hospitals. Worthington in particular has a large immigrant population and a significant proportion of non-English-speaking children enrolled in its schools.

The 1st is politically moderate and will support Democratic candidates in federal elections. Barack Obama carried the district in 2008 with 51 percent of its presidential vote. Rep. Tim Walz was re-elected that year by a nearly 2-to-1 margin, although he only managed a plurality win in 2010.

Major Industry
Agriculture, food processing, health care

Cities
Rochester, 106,769; Mankato (pt.), 39,305; Winona, 27,592; Owatonna, 25,599; Austin, 24,718; Albert Lea, 18,016; New Ulm, 13,522

Notable
The birthplace of SPAM, Austin is home to the SPAM Museum.

Rep. John Kline (R)

Capitol Office
225-2271
kline.house.gov
2439 Rayburn Bldg. 20515-2302; fax 225-2595

Committees
Armed Services
Education & the Workforce - Chairman

Residence
Lakeville

Born
Sept. 6, 1947; Allentown, Pa.

Religion
Methodist

Family
Wife, Vicky Kline; two children

Education
Rice U., B.A. 1969 (biology); Shippensburg U., M.S.
1988 (public administration)

Military
Marine Corps, 1969-94

Career
Management consultant; farmer; think tank executive; Marine officer

Political Highlights
Republican nominee for U.S. House, 1998, 2000

ELECTION RESULTS

2010 GENERAL

John Kline (R)	181,341	63.3%
Shelley Madore (D)	104,809	36.6%

2010 PRIMARY

John Kline (R)	unopposed

2008 GENERAL

John Kline (R)	220,924	57.3%
Steve Sarvi (D)	164,093	42.5%

Previous Winning Percentages
2006 (56%); 2004 (56%); 2002 (53%)

Elected 2002; 5th term

Kline possesses the military bearing one would expect of a 25-year Marine Corps veteran, along with the easygoing charm of a man equally comfortable in the political arena. A solid conservative who focused on defense issues early in his career, he now spends the bulk of his time on education, health and labor issues as chairman of the Education and the Workforce Committee.

Kline ascended to the top GOP post on what was then called the Education and Labor Committee in June 2009 after California's Howard P. "Buck" McKeon left to take the ranking Republican slot on the Armed Services Committee. A sharp critic of President George W. Bush's education overhaul known as No Child Left Behind, Kline is the party's point man as Congress considers rewriting the 2002 law.

Another major focus in the 112th Congress (2011-12) is health care. Republican hopes of repeal are stymied by a Democratic Senate and president, but that doesn't mean they won't be putting the health care overhaul enacted in 2010 under a legislative microscope.

Kline wants to study the effect of the law's insurance mandate on hiring practices and look for ways to expand coverage that don't involve as much government participation as mandated by the 2010 law.

"We saw in November the American people flat-out rejected a Congress that jams through sweeping legislation without engaging the American people," Kline said at a January 2011 news conference. "We're starting on a process to engage our colleagues in Congress and the American people as we look at genuine, meaningful health care reform."

The focus on health care and education does not mean other issues under the committee's jurisdiction will get short shrift, he said.

"Just because we're going to be looking at the impact of this health care law on a lot of things including jobs, it doesn't mean the committees won't be actively engaged in other aspects of our responsibility," Kline said. "We don't have to limit ourselves to one subject at a time."

Kline was front and center during the health care debate in the 111th Congress (2009-10) and was one of the Republicans invited to the Blair House summit in February 2010 to discuss the bill with President Obama. He recommended starting over, with an emphasis on health insurance providers and businesses working together to reduce the cost of plans.

On education, Kline had kind words for some of the Obama administration's early ideas, but grew to worry about what he considered an overreach of federal power. He said his principles for a new bill include "restoring local control" and "protecting taxpayers," and he warned that an attempt to impose national standards on states would prompt a Republican rebellion.

In early 2011, he won inclusion in a catchall spending bill of his amendment to block the administration from implementing regulations aimed at curtailing allegedly deceptive marketing practices by for-profit colleges. "Make no mistake: this isn't just another regulation that will destroy jobs," Kline said. "It is an assault on students' ability to find an institution that best meets their needs."

As a Marine, Kline served in Vietnam and did stints carrying the "football" — a briefcase containing the nuclear attack codes — for Presidents Jimmy Carter and Ronald Reagan. His military skills contributed to his winning the as "Republican Top Gun" title at the Congressional Sportsmen's Foundation's annual shoot-out, where lawmakers compete on trap, skeet and sporting clay ranges.

He is one of the few members of Congress with a child who has served in the current conflicts. His son, John Daniel, is an Army Blackhawk helicopter pilot who served a yearlong tour in Iraq in 2006 and began his second tour in Afghanistan in 2010. "I'm worried about him," Kline said. "But I'm worried about them all."

When it comes to both war fronts, Kline insists that politicians need to listen to the judgments of the military leaders on the ground when deciding on a course of action. A member of the Armed Services Committee, he denounced Democratic efforts to set a timeline for withdrawal from Iraq, a place he has visited several times since arriving in Congress. He supports sending more troops to Afghanistan.

Kline belongs to the Republican Study Committee, the most conservative GOP bloc in the House, but split with many in the group when he backed a $700 billion financial-industry rescue bill in October 2008 and a bill in July 2009 to change food-safety laws and mandate inspections of food facilities.

Kline was born in Pennsylvania, but spent most of his childhood in Corpus Christi, Texas, near where his father had purchased a newspaper. His mother managed the Corpus Christi Symphony Orchestra for 40 years. He joined the ROTC at Rice University in Houston while pursuing a bachelor's degree in biology, and later earned a master's degree in public administration from Shippensburg University in Pennsylvania.

During his military career, Kline piloted helicopters in Vietnam, commanded aviation forces in Somalia, and flew the presidential helicopter, Marine One. He also worked at Marine Corps headquarters as a program development officer, responsible for developing a long-range spending plan. After retiring, in 1994 as a colonel, Kline settled in Lakeville, Minn., where he helped his father-in-law manage the family farm in Houston County, at the state's southeastern tip.

In 1998, he decided to run for the U.S. House and won the GOP nomination at an old-fashioned, Minnesota-style convention, only to lose the general election to Democratic incumbent Bill Luther. He tried again in 2000, getting help from national Republican groups the second time around. He lost by just 5,500 votes.

Redistricting paired Luther with GOP Rep. Mark Kennedy in the new 6th District in 2002. Luther moved to the redrawn 2nd District, which was far more Republican than before, and Kline challenged him again. Luther tried to portray Kline as an "extremist," but Kline's message of lower taxes, smaller government and a strong military prevailed with voters. He has won with at least 56 percent of the vote in the four elections since.

Key Votes

2010

Overhaul the nation's health insurance system	NO
Allow for repeal of "don't ask, don't tell"	NO
Overhaul financial services industry regulation	NO
Limit use of new Afghanistan War funds to troop withdrawal activities	NO
Change oversight of offshore drilling and lift oil spill liability cap	NO
Provide a path to legal status for some children of illegal immigrants	NO
Extend Bush-era income tax cuts for two years	YES

2009

Expand the Children's Health Insurance Program	NO
Provide $787 billion in tax cuts and spending increases to stimulate the economy	NO
Allow bankruptcy judges to modify certain primary-residence mortgages	NO
Create a cap-and-trade system to limit greenhouse gas emissions	NO
Provide $2 billion for the "cash for clunkers" program	YES
Establish the government as the sole provider of student loans	NO
Restrict federally funded insurance coverage for abortions in health care overhaul	YES

CQ Vote Studies

	PARTY UNITY		PRESIDENTIAL SUPPORT	
	SUPPORT	OPPOSE	SUPPORT	OPPOSE
2010	94%	6%	27%	73%
2009	98%	2%	17%	83%
2008	97%	3%	77%	23%
2007	98%	2%	86%	14%
2006	95%	5%	95%	5%

Interest Groups

	AFL-CIO	ADA	CCUS	ACU
2010	0%	0%	88%	96%
2009	10%	5%	80%	100%
2008	13%	15%	94%	88%
2007	8%	0%	80%	100%
2006	14%	0%	100%	88%

Minnesota 2

Southern Twin Cities suburbs

A blend of rural farmland in the south and an increasingly suburban north, the 2nd is tucked just south of the Minneapolis-St. Paul metropolitan area. The district includes all or part of seven counties and its population reflects two decades of influx to the Twin Cities region. Interstate 35 provides easy access to Minneapolis' cultural and entertainment centers for residents from Scott and Dakota counties.

The counties just south of the Twin Cities saw rapid growth starting in the 1990s, and expensive housing developments underscored the area's high incomes. Carver, Scott and particularly Dakota (shared with the 4th) have become younger and wealthier, but a national housing market slowdown left the local real estate market volatile.

Affordable housing in the southern counties of Le Sueur, Rice and Goodhue attracted new residents, but this area still has fertile farmland, producing corn and soybeans, among other crops. Development encroached on some of the smaller family farms, although agricultural success here tends to rely on larger, incorporated farms.

Northwest Airlines' headquarters in Eagan closed in 2009 following a merger with Delta Air Lines, but the Minneapolis-St. Paul International Airport (located in the 5th) remains an economic linchpin for the region and employs thousands of Dakota County residents.

Casinos are big business, and Mystic Lake Casino in Shakopee is one of the country's largest Indian-owned gaming centers. Other key employers include Blue Cross/Blue Shield in the 2nd's part of Dakota County; and 3M, headquartered in St. Paul (in the 4th).

The district leans slightly Republican, with GOP support in Scott and Carver counties, but many formerly Republican voters are trending left. Dakota County has some working-class Democratic-Farmer-Labor Party supporters, and the Rice County towns of Northfield — home to St. Olaf and Carleton colleges — and Faribault also provide Democratic votes.

Major Industry
Manufacturing, casinos, airport, agriculture

Cities
Eagan, 64,206; Burnsville, 60,306; Lakeville, 55,954; Apple Valley, 49,084

Notable
The late Sen. Paul Wellstone was a political science professor at Carleton College before beginning his political career.

Rep. Erik Paulsen (R)

Capitol Office
225-2871
paulsen.house.gov
127 Cannon Bldg. 20515-2303; fax 225-6351

Committees
Ways & Means

Residence
Eden Prairie

Born
May 14, 1965; Bakersfield, Calif.

Religion
Lutheran

Family
Wife, Kelly Paulsen; four children

Education
St. Olaf College, B.A. 1987 (mathematics)

Career
Business strategies analyst; congressional aide

Political Highlights
Minn. House, 1995-2009 (majority leader, 2003-07)

ELECTION RESULTS

2010 GENERAL

Erik Paulsen (R)	161,177	58.8%
Jim Meffert (D)	100,240	36.6%
Jon Oleson (INDC)	12,508	4.6%

2010 PRIMARY

Erik Paulsen (R)	unopposed

2008 GENERAL

Erik Paulsen (R)	178,932	48.5%
Ashwin Madia (D)	150,787	40.8%
David Dillon (INDC)	38,970	10.6%

Elected 2008; 2nd term

Paulsen is a serious-minded legislator not prone to grandstanding. He meshes business-friendly, free-market principles with a touch of Midwestern populism and a moderate stance on social issues. He won a coveted seat on the Ways and Means Committee in the 112th Congress.

The suburban Minneapolis district he represents is home to a number of companies that make medical devices, and Paulsen, who co-chairs the Medical Technology Caucus, leapt to their defense during debate on the Democrats' health care overhaul legislation in the 111th Congress (2009-10). He won a change in the bill that cut a tax on medical devices by half.

He introduced legislation to repeal the medical device tax, a goal that could be aided by his assignment to Ways and Means, but was the only Republican in the Minnesota delegation not to promise to seek a repeal of the entire bill. He did, however, vote for repeal legislation when it came to the floor early in the 112th Congress (2011-12).

Paulsen served on the Financial Services Committee in the 111th Congress, using that post to argue that the regulatory overhaul enacted in 2010 put up too many hurdles for community banks and didn't do enough to address the problems presented by institutions deemed "too big to fail."

"There's also nothing in the bill that would address eliminating the moral hazard to stop the 'too-big-to-fail mentality' for large corporations that get bailed out," Paulsen said at an October 2010 debate.

Paulsen has made similar arguments about the need for more oversight of the Troubled Asset Relief Program, the Treasury Department-run initiative that Congress approved in fall 2008 to strengthen the financial sector. And he has argued that more needs to be done through government-run programs to help small community banks and businesses.

He gained House passage of his bill in September 2009 to require the TARP special inspector general to include the effect of the program on small businesses in oversight, audits and reports. He introduced bills in 2009 and 2010 that would terminate the program.

Although an active participant at hearings, Paulsen is more likely to use his time to ask questions and get answers from the witnesses than make extended statements. One of three Republicans in the class of 2008 who won districts even as they went for President Obama, he has avoided harsh partisan rhetoric, although he hasn't hesitated to criticize the administration for what he characterizes as "misguided" economic policies.

Paulsen disliked much of the Democrats' economic agenda, including the stimulus package and auto industry rescue enacted in 2009, and the House-passed energy legislation that would have created a cap-and-trade system aimed at reducing greenhouse gas emissions.

Paulsen also pushed back against policies he feared would harm his constituents. He cosponsored a bipartisan bill that would protect the franchise agreements between auto dealers and General Motors Corp. and Chrysler LLC after the two carmakers began closing dealerships as part of bankruptcy proceedings during the summer of 2009. More than 50 dealerships in Minnesota were affected. He voted against adding funding to the "cash for clunkers" auto trade-in program, however, characterizing it as just a "short-term solution."

A firm believer in free trade, Paulsen has made a concerted effort to be engaged in international affairs, joining Congress' U.S.-China Working

Group and the Caucus on India and Indian Americans.

Despite his pro-business leanings, Paulsen was at the forefront of the populist wave that swept the country over bonuses paid out by insurance giant American International Group Inc., which had received money from the 2008 rescue package. Paulsen sponsored a bill that would have required the Treasury secretary to recoup the bonus payments.

While he sides with Republicans on most fiscal matters, Paulsen will cross the aisle on other issues. He sided with the majority of Democrats in early 2009 to pass a bill expanding the Children's Health Insurance Program, which covers children from low-income families that make too much money to qualify for Medicaid. He was the only Minnesota Republican to join his state's Democratic delegation in backing wilderness protection legislation and a measure that added sexual orientation and gender identity to the federal government's hate crimes statutes. But he opposed legislation enacted in late 2010 that repealed the statutory ban on gays and lesbians serving openly in the military.

Unlike his GOP colleague in the neighboring 6th District, Michele Bachmann, Paulsen can't afford to play up social issues. His district is far too moderate, sending centrist Republican Jim Ramstad to Congress nine times. He has said that he and Ramstad are "cut from the same cloth on many issues."

Paulsen was born in Bakersfield, Calif., and his family moved about a year later to Chanhassen, a western Minneapolis suburb. He said he grew up in a "regular" suburban Minnesota home before studying mathematics at St. Olaf College, a small Lutheran liberal arts school in Northfield, Minn.

After a stint in sales and marketing, Paulsen decided he wanted to do something more meaningful with his career and took an internship in the office of Sen. Rudy Boschwitz, a Minnesota Republican. From there he moved to Ramstad's office and then back to Minnesota as Ramstad's state director, before serving in the state House from 1995 to 2009, including four years as majority leader. He worked as a business analyst at Target Corp. while in the state legislature, which is a part-time job in Minnesota.

When Ramstad announced he was retiring in 2007, Paulsen was the consensus Republican choice to succeed him. Democrats saw the open seat in a swing district as an opportunity, but Paulsen resisted the Democratic tide to win by a relatively comfortable 8 percentage points against newcomer Ashwin Madia. In 2010, with the tide reversed, he defeated Democrat Jim Meffert by 22 percentage points.

Key Votes

2010

Overhaul the nation's health insurance system	NO
Allow for repeal of "don't ask, don't tell"	NO
Overhaul financial services industry regulation	NO
Limit use of new Afghanistan War funds to troop withdrawal activities	NO
Change oversight of offshore drilling and lift oil spill liability cap	NO
Provide a path to legal status for some children of illegal immigrants	NO
Extend Bush-era income tax cuts for two years	YES

2009

Expand the Children's Health Insurance Program	YES
Provide $787 billion in tax cuts and spending increases to stimulate the economy	NO
Allow bankruptcy judges to modify certain primary-residence mortgages	NO
Create a cap-and-trade system to limit greenhouse gas emissions	NO
Provide $2 billion for the "cash for clunkers" program	NO
Establish the government as the sole provider of student loans	NO
Restrict federally funded insurance coverage for abortions in health care overhaul	YES

CQ Vote Studies

	PARTY UNITY		PRESIDENTIAL SUPPORT	
	Support	Oppose	Support	Oppose
2010	89%	11%	33%	67%
2009	89%	11%	32%	68%

Interest Groups

	AFL-CIO	ADA	CCUS	ACU
2010	0%	0%	88%	92%
2009	14%	10%	87%	88%

Minnesota 3
Hennepin County suburbs — Bloomington, Brooklyn Park, Plymouth

Lakes, stores and office parks dot the affluent 3rd — at more than $74,000, the district's median household income is the highest in the state. The district takes in Hennepin County's major suburbs north, west and south of Minneapolis. The primarily white-collar population has a tradition of fiscal conservatism, adheres to moderate views on social issues and is known for its independent streak. As in much of the state, overall population growth has brought a more diverse mix to the 3rd — black, Hispanic and Asian communities here are all growing — although the district remains predominantly white.

A classic picture of suburban living, the 3rd boasts technology industries, white-collar workers in middle-class homes, excellent public schools, golf courses, and large indoor and outdoor shopping malls. The district has the most-educated residents in the state, with 43 percent holding at least a bachelor's degree. Several Fortune 500 corporations based in the district employ local residents, as do other large companies just outside the 3rd.

Although some built-out suburbs in the district shed residents in the last decade, traffic backups have become common for commuters heading east. Transportation policy and ongoing interstate highway upgrades from Maple Grove in the north to Bloomington in the south are important issues here.

Blue-collar Brooklyn Park, Coon Rapids (a small part of which is in the 6th) and Brooklyn Center host conservative Democratic-Farmer-Labor Party voters, but the affluent, GOP-backing south and west portions of the 3rd tend to have a greater impact on elections. Republican Tom Emmer won several jurisdictions in the district during his unsuccessful 2010 gubernatorial campaign, collecting support in Plymouth, Eden Prairie and parts of Minnetonka.

Major Industry
Electronics, manufacturing, transportation

Cities
Bloomington, 82,893; Brooklyn Park, 75,781; Plymouth, 70,576; Maple Grove, 61,567; Eden Prairie, 60,797; Coon Rapids (pt.), 58,525

Notable
Bloomington's Mall of America has 4.2 million square feet of retail and office space.

Rep. Betty McCollum (D)

Capitol Office
225-6631
www.mccollum.house.gov
1714 Longworth Bldg. 20515-2304; fax 225-1968

Committees
Appropriations
Budget

Residence
St. Paul

Born
July 12, 1954; Minneapolis, Minn.

Religion
Roman Catholic

Family
Divorced; two children

Education
Inver Hills Community College, A.A. 1980; College of St. Catherine, B.A. 1987 (education)

Career
Teacher; retail saleswoman

Political Highlights
Candidate for North St. Paul City Council, 1984; North St. Paul City Council, 1987-92; Minn. House, 1993-2001

ELECTION RESULTS

2010 GENERAL

Betty McCollum (D)	136,746	59.1%
Teresa Collett (R)	80,141	34.6%
Steve Carlson (INDC)	14,207	6.1%

2010 PRIMARY

Betty McCollum (D)	55,491	86.6%
Diana Longrie (D)	8,622	13.4%

2008 GENERAL

Betty McCollum (D)	216,267	68.4%
Ed Matthews (R)	98,936	31.3%

Previous Winning Percentages
2006 (70%); 2004 (57%); 2002 (62%); 2000 (48%)

Elected 2000; 6th term

McCollum is a firm liberal ally of Minority Leader Nancy Pelosi of California and a persistent voice for human rights abroad and broader access to health care at home. As a member of the House Democratic Steering and Policy Committee, she is positioned to help shape the caucus' response to the new Republican majority.

McCollum casts a dependable Democratic vote; she sided with her party almost 99 percent of the time during its reign in the 110th and 111th Congresses (2007-08; 2009-10) on votes in which majorities of the two parties were in opposition. On the rare occasions when she bucks party leaders, she usually thinks they aren't being liberal enough. She supports constitutional amendments to ban the death penalty and make health care a right for U.S. citizens.

As a member of the Budget and Appropriations committees, McCollum has been a defender of earmarks. "President Obama doesn't know my district as well as I do, and he'd be the first person to say that," she said. "I'm here to represent the needs, goals, wants, hopes, ambitions, investments in my district." McCollum points out that her constituents come to her to request funding, and there are several projects of which she is very proud: She helped obtain more than $39 million in a catchall spending bill, cleared in March 2009, for a range of local projects.

She termed GOP proposals for spending cuts in early 2011 "mean-spirited or just plain dumb."

McCollum said she is most proud of her work on the health care overhaul during the 111th Congress, particularly a hard-won compromise to ensure that geographic disparities in Medicare reimbursements were addressed in the law. She and three other House Democrats negotiated up to the final action on the health bills, resulting in the inclusion of money to address the disparities and written guarantees from Health and Human Services Secretary Kathleen Sebelius for further action to alter Medicare reimbursement rates.

McCollum's district includes more than 20 colleges and universities and she plans to work on education issues in the 112th Congress (2011-12). When she served on the Education and the Workforce Committee during the George W. Bush administration, McCollum criticized funding levels for the president's No Child Left Behind initiative, which overhauled federal education policy and tied financial support to students' performance on achievement tests. McCollum was one of six House Democrats to vote against the final bill in 2001. "As a former teacher, as a person who has really worked a lot in education, we were tracking the wrong things," she said. "When the bill left here, states were racing to the bottom." The law could be reauthorized in the 112th.

McCollum was an early and ardent critic of the war in Iraq. With that conflict winding down, she has turned her attention to Afghanistan.

She voted against final passage of a bill that provided supplemental funding for both wars in July 2010, while voting in favor of two amendments — one that would have limited the use of military funding for Afghanistan to activities relating to the withdrawal of troops and protection of civilian and military personnel in the country, and another that would have required the president to submit a plan for withdrawal. During a floor speech in December, McCollum pushed for an end to full-scale combat operations and "a shift to a long-term counterterrorism mission that will prevent al Qaeda from re-establishing safe havens from which to attack the United States."

She was one of 126 Democrats who opposed the 2002 resolution sanctioning Bush's decision to go to war.

McCollum supported the $700 billion financial sector rescue in late 2008, bringing a glossary of financial terms such as "warrants" and "asset managers" to a caucus meeting to help educate fellow members. "It troubled me to take some of the votes that I did," she said, but "I wasn't going to watch our seniors lose their entire pensions because the stock market was going to totally flip upside down." She expresses confidence that the financial regulation overhaul, which was signed into law in July 2010, will play an important part in guaranteeing that the financial sector is "required to behave responsibly."

McCollum is especially engaged in international health and women's rights issues. She sponsored legislation aimed at preventing child marriage and chairs the Congressional Global Health Caucus. "I look forward to working on issues that build sustainability for those countries to help them get themselves out of extreme poverty," she said. McCollum said her interest in international affairs is connected to the diversity of St. Paul and the large number of faith-based communities located in her district that are engaged in international issues. She also points to childhood family discussions, which often included world affairs and far-off places. "My father served in India and China during World War II, so we always had the atlas open at home, talking about countries and food and geography and culture and climate," she said.

McCollum was born and raised in the Twin Cities area in what she described as a frugal middle-class household. She studied at a community college and worked as a sales clerk at JC Penney and Sears department stores and as a substitute teacher while raising two children. She got her bachelor's degree at 32, about the time she was venturing into politics. After being rebuffed by the city of North St. Paul in her quest to get immediate repairs at a local playground, McCollum ran for the city council. She lost that bid but won in a second attempt. She moved to the state legislature six years later, beating two incumbents thrown into the same district by redistricting.

With 14 years in elected office under her belt, McCollum in 2000 jumped into the primary race for the House seat being vacated by Democrat Bruce M. Vento, who announced he had lung cancer and wouldn't run again. Six other Democrats ran, but McCollum gained an important edge when she was endorsed by the state Democratic Party. McCollum took 48 percent of the vote that November, outrunning Republican state Sen. Linda Runbeck and independent Tom Foley, and has been re-elected since by comfortable margins.

Key Votes

2010

Overhaul the nation's health insurance system	YES
Allow for repeal of "don't ask, don't tell"	YES
Overhaul financial services industry regulation	YES
Limit use of new Afghanistan War funds to troop withdrawal activities	YES
Change oversight of offshore drilling and lift oil spill liability cap	YES
Provide a path to legal status for some children of illegal immigrants	YES
Extend Bush-era income tax cuts for two years	NO

2009

Expand the Children's Health Insurance Program	YES
Provide $787 billion in tax cuts and spending increases to stimulate the economy	YES
Allow bankruptcy judges to modify certain primary-residence mortgages	YES
Create a cap-and-trade system to limit greenhouse gas emissions	YES
Provide $2 billion for the "cash for clunkers" program	YES
Establish the government as the sole provider of student loans	YES
Restrict federally funded insurance coverage for abortions in health care overhaul	NO

CQ Vote Studies

	PARTY UNITY		PRESIDENTIAL SUPPORT	
	SUPPORT	OPPOSE	SUPPORT	OPPOSE
2010	98%	2%	90%	10%
2009	99%	1%	96%	4%
2008	99%	1%	13%	87%
2007	99%	1%	4%	96%
2006	96%	4%	20%	80%

Interest Groups

	AFL-CIO	ADA	CCUS	ACU
2010	100%	100%	13%	0%
2009	100%	100%	33%	0%
2008	100%	100%	56%	0%
2007	96%	90%	58%	0%
2006	93%	95%	33%	4%

Minnesota 4

Ramsey County — St. Paul and suburbs

St. Paul, the state capital and the heart of the 4th, is a collection of distinct neighborhoods, which include residential areas, liberal university communities, labor populations and state government workers. St. Paul developed as a major port and railroading center and still has a strong labor tradition. For much of its history St. Paul was the upper Midwest's leading trade outpost, and the city had a strong manufacturing sector. For years, local leaders in St. Paul have aimed to fill the economic gaps caused by manufacturing downsizing with the growing renewable-energy and "green" building industries.

The 4th has a large percentage of white-collar workers who live in middle- and high-income neighborhoods and work at major companies based in the district or nearby in Minneapolis.

Dairy producer Land O'Lakes is the leader of agribusiness in the area. St. Paul and surrounding areas are home to many colleges and universities, including the University of Minnesota's agriculture school and Macalester College.

The downtown Xcel Energy Center, which hosted the 2008 Republican National Convention, draws major sports events and concerts and is home to the NHL's Minnesota Wild and the state high school hockey tournament. The St. Paul Saints minor league baseball team draws crowds to Midway Stadium, and the Minnesota State Fair attracts nearly 2 million visitors to St. Paul every August.

Represented in the U.S. House by a Democrat since 1949, voters in St. Paul, who still make up nearly half of the district's residents, consistently support the Democratic-Farmer-Labor Party at all levels. Today, blue-collar and growing black, Hispanic and Asian communities — the city has one of the nation's largest Hmong populations — contribute to the Democratic flavor. Asian residents now account for more than 10 percent of the population in the district.

Major Industry
State government, higher education, manufacturing

Cities
St. Paul, 285,068; Maplewood (pt.), 38,004; Roseville, 33,660

Notable
In 2002, the area elected Mee Moua to the state Senate, making her the first Hmong state legislator in the United States.

Rep. Keith Ellison (D)

Capitol Office
225-4755
ellison.house.gov
1027 Longworth Bldg. 20515-2305; fax 225-4886

Committees
Financial Services

Residence
Minneapolis

Born
Aug. 4, 1963; Detroit, Mich.

Religion
Muslim

Family
Separated; four children

Education
Wayne State U., B.A. 1986 (economics), attended
1986-87 (economics); U. of Minnesota, J.D. 1990

Career
Lawyer; nonprofit law firm executive director

Political Highlights
Minn. House, 2003-06

ELECTION RESULTS

2010 GENERAL

Keith Ellison (D)	154,833	67.7%
Joel Demos (R)	55,222	24.1%
Lynne Torgerson (I)	8,548	3.7%
Tom Schrunk (INDC)	7,446	3.3%
Michael Cavlan (IDP)	2,468	1.1%

2010 PRIMARY

Keith Ellison (D)	55,424	81.6%
Barb Davis White (D)	7,963	11.7%
Gregg A. Iverson (D)	4,575	6.7%

2008 GENERAL

Keith Ellison (D)	228,776	70.9%
Barb Davis White (R)	71,020	22.0%
Bill McGaughey (INDC)	22,318	6.9%

Previous Winning Percentages
2006 (56%)

Elected 2006; 3rd term

The first Muslim elected to Congress, Ellison is among the body's most liberal members and most loyal Democrats. In his first two terms he sided with his party 99 percent of the time on votes that pitted a majority of Republicans against a majority of Democrats.

He was rewarded with an appointment as a national chairman of the Democratic Congressional Campaign Committee, responsible for community partnerships. He also serves on the Democratic Steering and Policy Committee, which makes committee assignments.

Those may be low rungs on the party leadership ladder, but some observers see Ellison climbing higher in the future.

He's also a leader of the left. In the 112th Congress (2011-12), he serves as co-chairman of the Congressional Progressive Caucus, the group of the most liberal members of the House.

From his seat on the Financial Services Committee, he backed President Obama's $787 billion stimulus measure and President George W. Bush's 2008 proposal that allowed the administration to spend $700 billion to help the ailing financial services sector. But Ellison, a founding member of the House Populist Caucus, worries that such efforts aren't doing enough to help those in the lowest economic classes.

At the start of the 112th Congress, he opposed the committee's plans to eliminate a program that allocates funds to state and local governments to purchase and redevelop foreclosed and abandoned property.

"The Neighborhood Stabilization Program is one of the only tools that our districts have to fight the wave of foreclosures tearing communities apart," Ellison said.

On one high-profile issue, he stood apart from the vast majority of both Republicans and Democrats: Ellison — who ranks in the bottom 5 percent among House members in net worth — was one of 15 lawmakers to vote against legislation in April 2010 to freeze lawmakers' pay.

Because of Democratic losses in 2010, Ellison gave up the Foreign Affairs Committee seat he had won at the beginning of the 111th Congress (2009-10). He had pushed for closer ties between Islamic countries and the United States and a tougher line with Israel.

Ellison was one of 36 members who voted against a resolution calling on the president and secretary of State to oppose an official endorsement of the Goldstone Report, the fruit of a U.N.-sponsored investigation that was highly critical of Israel's response to the attacks from Gaza.

Ellison stirred controversy in a 2007 speech when he seemed to suggest that the Sept. 11, 2001, terrorist attacks were an inside job, comparing them to the Reichstag fire, an incident that helped consolidate the Nazi Party's hold on power in Germany.

"It's almost like the Reichstag fire, kind of reminds me of that," Ellison said in a speech before the organization Atheists for Human Rights, according to The Minneapolis Star Tribune. "After the Reichstag was burned, they blamed the communists for it and it put the leader of that country [Hitler] in a position where he could basically have authority to do whatever he wanted."

Afterward, Ellison sought to clarify that he did not mean to imply that the Bush administration was responsible for the attacks, as the Nazis were for setting the fire, but that "they have exploited the fears that grew from 9/11, in order to pass legislation and even start wars they could have never gotten away with but for that tragedy."

When the Homeland Security Committee held a hearing in early 2011 on radicalization among American Muslims, Ellison termed it "a scary proposition."

"This is a legitimate point to discuss violent radicalization, but you can't — not in America — go after a particular religious group. It's wrong," Ellison said on MSNBC.

Ellison is the third of five sons. His father was a psychiatrist, his mother a social worker. Ellison said the importance of education was impressed upon him early on: He and three brothers are lawyers, while the other is a doctor. After graduating from the University of Detroit High School, a Jesuit school on the city's northern edge, Ellison went to Wayne State University. It was there, while studying economics, that he converted to Islam at the age of 19. In the late 1980s, he moved to Minnesota for law school, graduating from the state's flagship public university in 1990.

Ellison remained in Minneapolis after law school, working on general commercial litigation before joining a nonprofit that specialized in the representation of indigent clients. He rose to become executive director of the Legal Rights Center.

He was elected to the Minnesota Legislature in 2002. His shot for a House seat arrived four years later, when Democrat Martin Olav Sabo retired after representing the strongly Democratic, Minneapolis-based 5th District for nearly three decades. Ellison won the party's primary, defeating longtime Sabo aide and former state Democratic-Farmer-Labor Party chairman Mike Erlandson and former state Sen. Ember Reichgott Junge. Ellison took 41 percent of the vote.

In the general election, Republican candidate Alan Fine, a Jewish business consultant, criticized Ellison for several articles he had written as a law student in which he defended Louis Farrakhan, the leader of the Nation of Islam, against allegations of anti-Semitism. In the end, Ellison received the endorsement of American Jewish World, Minnesota's Jewish newspaper, and took nearly 56 percent of the vote.

He used a Koran owned by Thomas Jefferson at a ceremonial swearing-in after he took the official oath in the House chamber in 2007. Republicans Bill Sali of Idaho and Virgil H. Goode Jr. of Virginia expressed misgivings, but Ellison responded by saying, "I just think it is a learning gap that we have to close."

Ellison faced no serious opposition in 2008, winning re-election by nearly 50 points. He took more than two-thirds of the vote in 2010.

Key Votes

2010

Overhaul the nation's health insurance system	YES
Allow for repeal of "don't ask, don't tell"	YES
Overhaul financial services industry regulation	YES
Limit use of new Afghanistan War funds to troop withdrawal activities	YES
Change oversight of offshore drilling and lift oil spill liability cap	YES
Provide a path to legal status for some children of illegal immigrants	YES
Extend Bush-era income tax cuts for two years	NO

2009

Expand the Children's Health Insurance Program	YES
Provide $787 billion in tax cuts and spending increases to stimulate the economy	YES
Allow bankruptcy judges to modify certain primary-residence mortgages	YES
Create a cap-and-trade system to limit greenhouse gas emissions	YES
Provide $2 billion for the "cash for clunkers" program	YES
Establish the government as the sole provider of student loans	YES
Restrict federally funded insurance coverage for abortions in health care overhaul	NO

CQ Vote Studies

	PARTY UNITY		PRESIDENTIAL SUPPORT	
	SUPPORT	OPPOSE	SUPPORT	OPPOSE
2010	97%	3%	83%	17%
2009	99%	1%	95%	5%
2008	99%	1%	13%	87%
2007	99%	1%	4%	96%

Interest Groups

	AFL-CIO	ADA	CCUS	ACU
2010	100%	100%	13%	0%
2009	100%	95%	40%	0%
2008	100%	100%	56%	0%
2007	91%	100%	50%	0%

Minnesota 5

Minneapolis and suburbs

Established at the northernmost navigable point on the Mississippi River, Minneapolis features skyscrapers, corporate headquarters and major sports venues. Minneapolis accounts for most of the 5th's residents, but the population growth of the 1990s slowed after 2000. The Hiawatha Line light rail, connecting southern suburbs to downtown, has eased the traffic congestion that had become a problem during a period of sustained population growth, and rail service will continue to expand both in the suburbs and downtown.

Minneapolis, which attracted well-educated, white-collar workers in the 1990s, is home to large corporations, including Target, U.S. Bancorp and General Mills, in addition to Best Buy in nearby Richfield. Widespread layoffs hit the economy hard, and local financial institutions and housing markets are still vulnerable.

The University of Minnesota, the Guthrie Theater and the Walker Art Center anchor the city's art and theater community — Minneapolis currently has the second-most theaters per capita, trailing only New York City. Downtown Minneapolis also hosts four professional sports teams: basketball's Timberwolves and Lynx, baseball's Twins, and football's Vikings. The Minnesota Twins' new baseball stadium, Target Field, has brought in full crowds since it opened in 2010. The University of Minnesota football team plays in the new TCF Bank Stadium on campus.

Although Minneapolis is known for its Scandinavian heritage, the 5th is the state's most racially diverse district. Hmong, Tibetans and blacks — including a sizable Somali population — add to the Democratic-Farmer-Labor Party voter rolls and help shape the district's traditionally liberal politics, as do large American Indian communities and many members of the white-collar workforce.

In the 2008 presidential election, Barack Obama carried the district with 74 percent of the vote, his highest percentage in the state.

Major Industry
Corporate offices, banking, higher education

Cities
Minneapolis, 382,578; St. Louis Park (pt.), 45,241; Richfield, 35,228

Notable
Minneapolis features the world's largest skyway system, which covers 80 blocks in an effort to protect pedestrians from harsh winter weather.

Rep. Michele Bachmann (R)

Capitol Office
225-2331
bachmann.house.gov
103 Cannon Bldg. 20515-2306; fax 225-6475

Committees
Financial Services
Select Intelligence

Residence
Stillwater

Born
April 6, 1956; Waterloo, Iowa

Religion
Evangelical Lutheran

Family
Husband, Marcus Bachmann; five children

Education
Winona State U., B.A. 1978 (political science & English); Oral Roberts U., J.D. 1986; College of William & Mary, LL.M. 1988 (tax law)

Career
Homemaker; U.S. Treasury Department lawyer

Political Highlights
Candidate for Stillwater Area School District Board, 1999; Minn. Senate, 2001-07

ELECTION RESULTS

2010 GENERAL

Michele Bachmann (R)	159,476	52.5%
Tarryl Clark (D)	120,846	39.8%
Bob Anderson (INDC)	17,698	5.8%
Aubrey Immelman (I)	5,490	1.8%

2010 PRIMARY

Michele Bachmann (R)	unopposed

2008 GENERAL

Michele Bachmann (R)	187,817	46.4%
El Tinklenberg (D)	175,786	43.4%
Bob Anderson (INDC)	40,643	10.0%

Previous Winning Percentages
2006 (50%)

Elected 2006; 3rd term

Bachmann's media savvy and penchant for tweaking liberals have made her a conservative favorite and enhanced her stature beyond the Beltway to the point that she is considering a statewide or national candidacy in 2012. Inside the halls of Congress, she has been less successful in advancing her legislative priorities and moving up the Republican ranks.

Bachmann (BOCK-man) said she wants to help fellow Republicans work on their ability to communicate and draw public notice. In her third term, she made a run at the No. 4 Republican leadership position against Jeb Hensarling of Texas. Bachmann announced her intentions on Facebook, then withdrew when it was clear she did not have the votes to become House Republican Conference chairwoman.

Bachmann said she had hoped to coach Republicans on outreach methods such as social media. "It's important to use these free avenues. It enhances our message," she said. "I wanted to work on members' communication skills and understanding of how to use different platforms and bring a voice to the table to reflect the results of the election."

Bachmann's position as activist icon was institutionalized by her creation of the House Tea Party Caucus in 2010, a group of about 50 Republicans dedicated to "fiscal responsibility, adherence to the Constitution and limited government."

The congresswoman's admirers laud her for speaking on behalf of like-minded Americans disenchanted with Democratic policies. Critics call her divisive and take her to task for what they say are her frequent factual distortions. Bachmann, who was in much the same position in her earlier stint as a state senator, takes the controversy she generates in stride.

In an appearance on MSNBC during the 2008 campaign, she suggested Barack Obama "may have anti-American views." She expressed regret in the days that followed for the term "anti-American." After he became president, she referred to Obama's administration as a "gangster government," and refused to retreat from that characterization.

She remained a visible figure in the months that followed. She charged that Democratic policies were driving the United States "down the lane of economic Marxism." She said on Fox News that she spurned earmarks, the member-generated spending requests to benefit their districts — only to have bloggers and pundits note she had sought $3.8 million for her district. She later clarified she had taken earmarks in the past.

She also contended that Obama's $787 billion economic stimulus law directed money away from GOP districts and included a "national rationing board" that would prevent doctors from making health care decisions. Her comments prompted Minnesota Democratic-Farmer-Labor Party Chairman Brian Melendez to respond that Bachmann "long ago showed that she'll say anything to anyone, even if it's totally untrue, so long as it grabs her a headline," although Senate Minority Leader Mitch McConnell of Kentucky and some health care analysts used the same phrase to describe the proposal.

Bachmann is a conservative across the board, on economic, social and national security matters and — for someone perceived as a lawmaker who bucks the traditional party apparatus — a loyal Republican. Her career party unity score — the percentage of votes on which she sides with a majority of Republicans against a majority of Democrats — is almost 98.

When GOP leaders selected Wisconsin Republican Paul D. Ryan, chairman of the Budget Committee, to deliver the official party response to

President Obama's 2011 State of the Union speech, Bachmann gave her own response through a webcast on the Tea Party Express website. Even though some of her allies called the speech a distraction, Bachmann downplayed the criticism.

A member of the Financial Services Committee, she sought to repeal the financial regulatory overhaul enacted in 2010 with the first piece of legislation she introduced in the 112th Congress (2011-12). She also added the Select Committee on Intelligence to her portfolio in the new Congress.

Bachmann was born in Waterloo, Iowa. Her mother worked in a factory before staying home to raise four children; her father was an engineer.

When Bachmann was a teenager, her father accepted a job with Honeywell in the Twin Cities. A few years later her parents divorced.

Bachmann met her husband, Marcus, at Winona State University. After working for Jimmy Carter's 1976 campaign, Bachmann made her first trek to Washington to attend Carter's inaugural. She says that while reading Gore Vidal's "Burr" during the train ride home, she realized she was no longer a Democrat. She said she thought the book — a novel about Aaron Burr, a Revolutionary War hero and suspected traitor — was mocking the founding fathers. Bachmann and Marcus, a clinical therapist, married in 1978. They later settled in St. Paul, where Bachmann was a federal tax litigation attorney.

She became a local activist after objecting to the state's performance-based Profile of Learning program; she favors local control of schools. Bachmann was encouraged to enter politics but lost a race in 1999 for the Stillwater Area School District Board. A year later, she won a campaign to unseat 28-year Republican incumbent Gary Laidig in the state Senate.

When Republican Rep. Mark Kennedy decided to run for the U.S. Senate, Bachmann entered the race and defeated two other well-known legislators in the primary. In the general election, Bachmann called herself a "woman on a mission" against Democrat Patty Wetterling, who gained prominence as a child-safety advocate after the 1989 abduction of her 11-year-old son, who never was found. Bachmann won by 8 percentage points. In 2008, she eked out a 3-percentage-point win over Democrat El Tinklenberg while Arizona GOP Sen. John McCain carried the district by 8 points in the presidential election.

In the 2010 contest, Bachmann was challenged by Democratic-Farmer-Labor nominee Tarryl Clark and independent candidate Bob Anderson. She spent $11.7 million on the race and won by more than 12 percentage points.

She said in early 2011 that she is weighing both Senate and presidential runs in 2012.

Key Votes

2010

Overhaul the nation's health insurance system	NO
Allow for repeal of "don't ask, don't tell"	NO
Overhaul financial services industry regulation	NO
Limit use of new Afghanistan War funds to troop withdrawal activities	NO
Change oversight of offshore drilling and lift oil spill liability cap	NO
Provide a path to legal status for some children of illegal immigrants	NO
Extend Bush-era income tax cuts for two years	NO

2009

Expand the Children's Health Insurance Program	NO
Provide $787 billion in tax cuts and spending increases to stimulate the economy	NO
Allow bankruptcy judges to modify certain primary-residence mortgages	NO
Create a cap-and-trade system to limit greenhouse gas emissions	NO
Provide $2 billion for the "cash for clunkers" program	NO
Establish the government as the sole provider of student loans	NO
Restrict federally funded insurance coverage for abortions in health care overhaul	YES

CQ Vote Studies

	PARTY UNITY		PRESIDENTIAL SUPPORT	
	SUPPORT	OPPOSE	SUPPORT	OPPOSE
2010	98%	2%	26%	74%
2009	98%	2%	14%	86%
2008	96%	4%	75%	25%
2007	98%	2%	89%	11%

Interest Groups

	AFL-CIO	ADA	CCUS	ACU
2010	0%	5%	75%	100%
2009	5%	0%	73%	100%
2008	7%	0%	94%	100%
2007	8%	0%	75%	100%

Minnesota 6

North and east Twin Cities suburbs; St. Cloud

One of Minnesota's three largely suburban districts, the 6th hooks counterclockwise from eastern Twin Cities suburbs through conservative areas northwest of Hennepin County to the former granite-quarrying city of St. Cloud, the 6th's only urban center. Overall, the 6th has welcomed more than 140,000 new residents since 2000 and has the largest population of any Minnesota district ahead of decennial remapping.

Home to the second-largest college in Minnesota — St. Cloud State University — St. Cloud has a strong college town atmosphere. Development has not yet made the city, in heavily Catholic Stearns County, a Twin Cities suburb. North Star Commuter Rail, a commuter train line linking Sherburne County with the Twin Cities, opened in late 2009 and has helped alleviate traffic problems along Interstate 94, although planned expansion has been delayed.

Anoka and Wright counties, to the north and west of Minneapolis and its first-ring suburbs, had boasted new, wealthy suburban developments to accommodate a growing population. But the effects of a nationwide housing market downturn are evident in Wright, which struggled with sinking property values and high foreclosure rates. Washington County, to the east and north of St. Paul, includes other towns, such as Woodbury (part of which is in the 2nd), that saw explosive population growth and now are vulnerable to economic slowdowns, and the small town of Stillwater on the St. Croix River, which marks the Wisconsin border.

The 6th has developed a strong GOP base — in 2008, the district gave Republican John McCain his largest victory in the state with 53 percent of its presidential vote. The young, high-income families that fueled the region's growth tend to favor fiscal conservatism, but are not uniformly conservative on social issues. Blue-collar communities in the suburbs of Anoka and Washington counties used to be faithful Democratic-Farmer-Labor Party supporters, but Republican gubernatorial candidate Tom Emmer picked up towns here in 2010.

Major Industry
Corporate offices, manufacturing

Cities
St. Cloud, 65,842; Woodbury (pt.), 60,481; Blaine, 57,186

Notable
Writer and radio show host Garrison Keillor was born in Anoka.

Rep. Collin C. Peterson (D)

Capitol Office
225-2165
collinpeterson.house.gov
2211 Rayburn Bldg. 20515-2307; fax 225-1593

Committees
Agriculture - Ranking Member

Residence
Detroit Lakes

Born
June 29, 1944; Fargo, N.D.

Religion
Lutheran

Family
Divorced; three children

Education
Moorhead State College, B.A. 1966 (accounting)

Military
Minn. National Guard, 1963-69

Career
Accountant

Political Highlights
Minn. Senate, 1977-87; sought Democratic nomination for U.S. House, 1982; Democratic nominee for U.S. House, 1984, 1986; sought Democratic nomination for U.S. House, 1988

ELECTION RESULTS

2010 GENERAL

Collin C. Peterson (D)	133,096	55.2%
Lee Byberg (R)	90,652	37.6%
Gene Waldorf (I)	9,317	3.9%
Glen Menze (INDC)	7,839	3.2%

2010 PRIMARY

Collin C. Peterson (D)	unopposed

2008 GENERAL

Collin C. Peterson (D)	227,187	72.2%
Glen Menze (R)	87,062	27.7%

Previous Winning Percentages
2006 (70%); 2004 (66%); 2002 (65%); 2000 (69%); 1998 (72%); 1996 (68%); 1994 (51%); 1992 (50%); 1990 (54%)

Elected 1990; 11th term

Peterson is a farm-focused lawmaker who is more conservative than most of his party colleagues. He sits on one standing committee, Agriculture, where he is the ranking Democrat. He chaired the panel while Democrats controlled the House, and his legislative single-mindedness allows him to be a specialist on what drives his district's economy.

His primary legislative concern in the 112th Congress (2011-12) will be writing a new farm bill, which he said might wait until the second session. The committee has 16 freshman members who will be writing their first agricultural policy legislation, so a full slate of hearings is likely needed to bring many of them up to speed.

As Agriculture chairman in the 110th Congress (2007-08) he shepherded the 2008 farm bill by juggling the competing agendas of disparate interest groups. Peterson's priority was to maintain subsidies for the major staple crops grown in the Midwest, such as wheat, corn and soybeans. But conservatives and President George W. Bush deemed such subsidies wasteful, while budget pressures required Peterson to find cuts or revenue for any new spending. Peterson also had his sights set on creating a new disaster fund to help farmers in the wake of severe droughts and floods.

Peterson undercut conservative opposition with language barring higher-income farmers from collecting subsidies. He appeased Southerners, many with larger farms, by lifting limits on short-term loans. His bill also included mandatory country-of-origin labeling, subsidies for California fruit and vegetable farmers, and his disaster fund, while maintaining most subsidies.

Much of his handiwork remained intact when the $289 billion measure cleared Congress. Bush vetoed it, saying its subsidies were too generous, but the House and Senate voted overwhelmingly to override the veto.

Peterson was in the thick of things when Congress tackled a regulatory overhaul for the financial services industry. He sat on the conference committee that produced the final bill, and negotiators accepted a key compromise from Peterson that required banks to set up firewalls between their deposit banking operations and their derivatives trading desks for commodities, energy, metals, agriculture, equities and below-investment-grade credit default swaps. Under the proposal, banks could keep trading desks for less risky derivatives such as foreign exchange swaps, gold and silver, investment-grade credit default swaps and any transaction used to hedge risk.

As complex as derivatives were, Peterson said the 2012 farm bill promises to be a bigger challenge. When President Obama proposed phasing out direct payments to farmers with more than $500,000 in sales revenue and capping commodity supports at $250,000, Peterson pushed back. "It's not clear what the situation will be, but given the deficit, it will be difficult," Peterson said during a hearing on issues likely to be addressed in the legislation.

Even without a farm bill to write, Peterson found himself in the middle of several big issues during the 111th Congress (2009-10), only one of which — regulating derivatives — actually fell under the jurisdiction of his panel. He was looking out for agricultural interests in other venues, negotiating deals to protect his constituents on climate change and food safety legislation.

"I think it looked to a lot of people like we were interjecting ourselves," Peterson said, referring to agricultural exemptions he negotiated with the House Energy and Commerce Committee on the two bills. "It's our responsibility to make sure that whatever we do here legislatively does not interfere with producing the food we need for the country."

On the food safety bill, he got provisions to keep most of agriculture under the Department of Agriculture inspection regime rather than the FDA. When it came to climate change, Peterson won exemptions for agriculture from greenhouse gas regulations. He voted for the House version of the climate change bill, which would create a cap-and-trade system for limiting carbon emissions. But he acknowledged that despite the changes he won, many of his constituents and farm trade associations still disliked the bill.

Peterson was one of three Democrats to sign on as a cosponsor of legislation in the new Congress that would block the EPA from regulating carbon emissions under the Clean Air Act without the approval of Congress.

A founder of the fiscally conservative Blue Dog Coalition and a member of the Democratic Steering and Policy Committee, Peterson was not on board with his party on health care overhaul legislation in 2009 and 2010. He voted against both the House version and the final version of the measure, faulting the legislation for not addressing regional imbalances in Medicare hospital and doctor reimbursements for areas, like his district, with high numbers of people covered by government health insurance programs.

But he was not one of the three Democrats who voted with every Republican to repeal the law early in 2011.

Peterson is a pilot and avid sportsman. He has earned high marks from the National Rifle Association — he once boasted that he has "more dead animals on my wall than anybody in this Congress, except for [Alaska Republican] Don Young."

Peterson gets along so well with the GOP opposition that he was long the lone Democrat in a five-lawmaker country rock band he fronted called the Second Amendments. Their gigs included performances for U.S. troops overseas.

Peterson grew up on his family's farm near the North Dakota border and learned self-sufficiency at an early age. He used money he earned on the farm to buy a guitar and at 16, he joined a touring band. He gave up his dream of stardom when it became clear he'd have to quit college to pursue it. He chose accounting as a career.

He got his start in politics with 10 years in the state Senate. In the 1980s, he made four unsuccessful bids for a U.S. House seat.

In 1990, Peterson ran against Republican incumbent Arlan Stangeland, who was weakened by revelations he had used his House credit card to charge several calls to or from the phone of a female Virginia lobbyist. Peterson prevailed with 54 percent of the vote. After scratching out close re-election victories in 1992 and 1994, he has since won relatively easily.

Key Votes

2010

Overhaul the nation's health insurance system	NO
Allow for repeal of "don't ask, don't tell"	NO
Overhaul financial services industry regulation	YES
Limit use of new Afghanistan War funds to troop withdrawal activities	NO
Change oversight of offshore drilling and lift oil spill liability cap	NO
Provide a path to legal status for some children of illegal immigrants	NO
Extend Bush-era income tax cuts for two years	YES

2009

Expand the Children's Health Insurance Program	YES
Provide $787 billion in tax cuts and spending increases to stimulate the economy	NO
Allow bankruptcy judges to modify certain primary-residence mortgages	YES
Create a cap-and-trade system to limit greenhouse gas emissions	YES
Provide $2 billion for the "cash for clunkers" program	NO
Establish the government as the sole provider of student loans	YES
Restrict federally funded insurance coverage for abortions in health care overhaul	YES

CQ Vote Studies

	PARTY UNITY		PRESIDENTIAL SUPPORT	
	Support	Oppose	Support	Oppose
2010	81%	19%	69%	31%
2009	87%	13%	83%	17%
2008	91%	9%	21%	79%
2007	87%	13%	14%	86%
2006	63%	37%	60%	40%

Interest Groups

	AFL-CIO	ADA	CCUS	ACU
2010	64%	40%	88%	21%
2009	71%	55%	40%	24%
2008	80%	80%	50%	20%
2007	96%	85%	60%	33%
2006	79%	35%	73%	72%

Minnesota 7

West — Moorhead, Willmar

Stretching 330 miles from north to south, the vast 7th spans almost the entire western third of Minnesota. The landscape varies from flat prairie in the west to hills, lakes and heavy forests in the middle of the state. Moorhead and East Grand Forks are population centers along the Red River, which forms the border between Minnesota and North Dakota. Both locales have much larger companion cities across the river.

The 7th's agricultural production includes sugar beets, soybeans, wheat, corn and sunflower seeds. The district also relies on poultry raising and processing. Willmar, in the district's southeast, is home to the headquarters of turkey processor Jennie-O Turkey Store, and Schwan Food is based in Marshall.

Floods and droughts are perpetual problems to the northwest, and recent major flooding of the Red River has threatened infrastructure as well as crop yields. Reductions in harvests have forced some farmers to supplement their livelihood with part-time work in other industries and have sent younger residents fleeing to the Twin Cities area or out of the state.

Western Minnesota's economy now includes renewable- and alterna-tive energy production. The 7th's manufacturing sector — producing winter-sports staples hockey sticks and snowmobiles — is vulnerable to economic difficulties, and the closure of Appleton's Prairie Correctional Facility, a private prison that housed out-of-state inmates, cost the district hundreds of jobs and tax revenue in 2010.

The district tends to be socially conservative and fiscally moderate, but has supported candidates from both parties. The 7th supported Republican John McCain in the 2008 presidential election, giving him 50 percent of its vote. Many of the more highly populated counties in the district's center and southeast provided Republican gubernatorial candidate Tom Emmer with solid support in 2010, but fast-growing Clay County (Moorhead) retains its Democratic lean.

Major Industry
Agriculture, poultry processing, light manufacturing, recreation

Cities
Moorhead, 38,065; Willmar, 19,610; Hutchinson, 14,178; Marshall, 13,680

Notable
Writer Sinclair Lewis, who was the first American to win the Nobel Prize in Literature, grew up in Sauk Centre.

Rep. Chip Cravaack (R)

Capitol Office
225-6211
cravaack.house.gov
508 Cannon Bldg. 20515-2308; fax 225-0699

Committees
Homeland Security
Science, Space & Technology
Transportation & Infrastructure

Residence
Lindstrom

Born
Jan. 29, 1959; Charleston, W.Va.

Religion
Roman Catholic

Family
Wife, Traci Cravaack; two children

Education
U.S. Naval Academy, B.S. 1981; U. of West Florida,
M.Ed. 1989 (educational leadership)

Military
Navy, 1981-90; Navy Reserve, 1990-2005

Career
Airline pilot

Political Highlights
No previous office

ELECTION RESULTS

2010 GENERAL

Chip Cravaack (R)	133,490	48.2%
James L. Oberstar (D)	129,091	46.6%
Tim Olson (INDC)	11,876	4.3%

2010 PRIMARY

Chip Cravaack (R)	unopposed

Elected 2010; 1st term

A Navy veteran and Northwest Airlines pilot, Cravaack sees reducing the government's role in business as the best way to promote economic growth and create jobs.

To boost employment in his district, he wants to ease regulatory restrictions and thus speed projects intended to aid nickel, copper and platinum mining.

Cravaack was once a union steward at Northwest and talked during the campaign about his days manning a picket line. He says Democrats have abandoned unionized workers like those in the Iron Range to curry favor with environmentalists. He opposes so-called card-check legislation that would allow unions to organize workplaces without a secret ballot.

His years as a commercial pilot give him a unique perspective among his fellow members of the Homeland Security Subcommittee on Transportation Security.

Cravaack called the 2009 economic stimulus "ludicrous" and said the rapid growth in government spending and debt threatens the country. He would make the 2001 and 2003 tax cuts permanent for all income levels and eliminate the deficit by limiting spending. One pot of funding that he calls unnecessary is for bike trails, which were championed by the Democrat ousted by Cravaack: former Transportation and Infrastructure Chairman James L. Oberstar. (The district is still represented on the panel: Cravaack is vice chairman of Aviation Subcommittee.)

"Our pockets are empty, and our credit's been tapped, so we've got to take a look at all these projects as best we can and do with what we've got," Cravaack told Roll Call in February 2010.

On social issues, Cravaack is just as conservative. He won the endorsement of Gun Owners of America, a group that argues the National Rifle Association is too prone to compromise.

Cravaack also serves on the Science, Space and Technology Committee.

Cravaack says he decided to run after visiting Oberstar's office in August 2009 to ask that the lawmaker hold a town hall meeting on the health care bill and being told Oberstar was too busy. The incumbent disputed the story, but Cravaack rode the Republican wave to a narrow victory.

Minnesota 8

Northeast — Duluth, Iron Range

The expansive 8th covers Minnesota's northeast quadrant, including Duluth and the Iron Range — taconite-mining communities that stretch across the middle of the state. The district has the most varied terrain in the state, from farms in the south and west through the Iron Range and a watery northern border near International Falls. Timber and mining, traditional economic mainstays here, still serve as a solid base for the region. Duluth, on Lake Superior, is the shipping point for much of the grain from the Plains states and is the westernmost deep-sea port to the Atlantic. The University of Minnesota has a regional campus in Duluth that serves more than 11,000 students. Resorts and casinos near the Canadian border traditionally draw both local and out-of-state tourists, supporting the local economy.

The district takes in the 61-mile Superior National Forest Scenic Byway, and winter sport tourism, fishing, canoeing and camping also draws visitors. Huge tracts of land in the 8th are designated as state and national forests, and the Boundary Waters Canoe Area Wilderness along the Canadian border is noted for its motor-free beauty.

Voters here favor a hands-off approach to federal land management and tend to oppose gun control and abortion. Blue-collar workers with strong ties to labor cemented a long affiliation with the Democratic-Farmer-Labor Party — until 2011, the district had not been represented by a Republican in the U.S. House since 1947.

Major Industry
Mining, timber, recreation

Cities
Duluth city, 86,265; Hibbing, 16,361; Brainerd, 13,590

Notable
The U.S. Hockey Hall of Fame is in Eveleth.

MISSISSIPPI

Gov. Haley Barbour (R)

First elected: 2003
Length of term: 4 years
Term expires: 1/12
Salary: $122,160
Phone: (601) 359-3150
Residence: Yazoo City
Born: Oct. 21, 1947; Yazoo City, Miss.
Religion: Presbyterian
Family: Wife, Marsha Barbour; two children
Education: U. of Mississippi, attended 1965-69 (political science), J.D. 1973
Career: Lobbyist; lawyer; White House aide; party official
Political highlights: Republican nominee for U.S. Senate, 1982; Republican National Committee chairman, 1993-97

ELECTION RESULTS

2007 GENERAL
Haley Barbour (R)	430,807	57.9%
John Eaves (D)	313,232	42.1%

Lt. Gov. Phil Bryant (R)

First elected: 2007
Length of term: 4 years
Term expires: 1/12
Salary: $60,000
Phone: (601) 359-3200

LEGISLATURE

Legislature: 90 days January-April
Senate: 52 members, 4-year terms
2011 ratios: 27 R, 24 D, 1 vacancy; 46 men, 5 women
Salary: $10,000
Phone: (601) 359-3202
House: 122 members, 4-year terms
2011 ratios: 69 D, 53 R; 102 men, 20 women
Salary: $10,000
Phone: (601) 359-3360

TERM LIMITS

Governor: 2 terms
Senate: No
House: No

URBAN STATISTICS

CITY	POPULATION
Jackson	173,514
Gulfport	67,793
Southaven	48,982
Hattiesburg	45,989
Biloxi	44,054

REGISTERED VOTERS

Voters do not register by party.

POPULATION

2010 population	2,967,297
2000 population	2,844,658
1990 population	2,573,216
Percent change (2000-2010)	+4.3%
Rank among states (2010)	31
Median age	35
Born in state	71.8%
Foreign born	1.9%
Violent crime rate	281/100,000
Poverty level	21.9%
Federal workers	37,510
Military	9,895

ELECTIONS

STATE ELECTION OFFICIAL
(601) 359-6357

DEMOCRATIC PARTY
(601) 969-2913

REPUBLICAN PARTY
(601) 948-5191

MISCELLANEOUS

Web: www.ms.gov
Capital: Jackson

U.S. CONGRESS

Senate: 2 Republicans
House: 3 Republicans, 1 Democrat

2010 CENSUS STATISTICS BY DISTRICT

District	2008 Vote for President Obama	McCain	White	Black	Asian	Hispanic	Median Income	White Collar	Blue Collar	Service Industry	Over 64	Under 18	College Education	Rural	Sq. Miles
1	37%	62%	68%	27%	1%	3%	$38,310	52%	34%	15%	13%	26%	17%	62%	11,413
2	66	33	30	66	1	2	30,107	52	28	20	11	28	18	37	13,625
3	39	61	60	35	1	2	37,960	58	27	16	13	26	23	60	13,168
4	32	67	70	23	1	4	40,786	53	29	18	12	25	18	46	8,701
STATE	43	56	58	37	1	3	36,796	54	29	17	12	26	19	51	46,907
U.S.	53	46	64	12	5	16	51,425	60	23	17	13	25	28	21	3,537,438

Sen. Thad Cochran (R)

Capitol Office
224-5054
cochran.senate.gov
113 Dirksen Bldg. 20510-2402; fax 224-9450

Committees
Agriculture, Nutrition & Forestry
Appropriations - Ranking Member
Rules & Administration
Joint Library

Residence
Oxford

Born
Dec. 7, 1937; Pontotoc, Miss.

Religion
Baptist

Family
Wife, Rose Cochran; two children

Education
U. of Mississippi, B.A. 1959 (psychology); Trinity
College (U. of Dublin, Ireland), attended 1963-64
(international law); U. of Mississippi, J.D. 1965

Military Service
Navy, 1959-61

Career
Lawyer

Political Highlights
U.S. House, 1973-78

ELECTION RESULTS

2008 GENERAL

Thad Cochran (R)	766,111	61.4%
Erik Fleming (D)	480,915	38.6%

2008 PRIMARY

Thad Cochran (R)	unopposed

2002 GENERAL

Thad Cochran (R)	533,269	84.6%
Shawn O'Hara (REF)	97,226	15.4%

Previous Winning Percentages
1996 (71%); 1990 (100%); 1984 (61%); 1978 (45%);
1976 House Election (76%); 1974 House Election
(70%); 1972 House Election (48%)

Elected 1978; 6th term

Cochran is one of what might be a vanishing breed of Washington power brokers. An archetypal appropriator, he is most comfortable operating behind the scenes to achieve his objectives, which center on sending prodigious sums of money to his state. He is a stickler for Senate procedure and works cordially with like-minded lawmakers regardless of their political beliefs.

But with the anti-earmark inclinations of the GOP in recent years, the man who bided his time for decades to ascend to the top Republican spot on the Appropriations Committee has been finding it more and more difficult to achieve his goals.

Though Taxpayers for Common Sense still counts him the most prolific earmarker in Congress for several years running, Cochran was hamstrung by his party's leadership from directing much federal largesse to his state during the 111th Congress (2009-10). Seeking to reclaim the mantle of fiscal conservatism that once defined Republicans, Minority Leader Mitch McConnell of Kentucky strong-armed Cochran and other earmark-friendly appropriators into writing a letter to their Democratic counterparts on the committee demanding a domestic spending freeze in mid-2010.

Cochran has consistently voted against several attempts by his fellow Republicans to implement earmark moratoriums on both the chamber and the GOP Conference, but his ardent defense of the practice was no match for an influx of tea party-inspired Republican winners following the 2010 elections. The party caucus adopted a non-binding moratorium on spending requests in November 2010, and though Cochran held out hope that the lame-duck Congress would pass an omnibus bill he helped write that included more than $560,000 of his earmark requests, those hopes were dashed when several appropriators who had promised to back the omnibus pulled their support in the face of a conservative uproar.

Still, Cochran and other old-school appropriators are betting the earmark practice will continue. "You know an earmark is an amendment that every senator ought to have the right to offer to bring up for consideration in committee or on the floor, on any subject," Cochran told Roll Call in December 2010. "That's what makes the Senate different from the House — you don't have to get permission from anybody to offer an amendment."

Cochran has maintained that his earmarks always receive his colleagues' blessings and greatly benefit his poor, rural state. Among the chief recipients of his earmarks have been universities conducting scientific research and communities ravaged by Hurricane Katrina and other storms. A member of the Agriculture, Nutrition and Forestry Committee, he has also made sure that Mississippi's cotton, peanut, rice and sugar farmers get emergency relief when they ask for it.

He even has helped defend others' earmarks and was one of only four Republicans in 2009 to vote to save the "cash for clunkers" program that, along with other non-emergency spending, was attached to a supplemental war spending bill.

An easygoing Southern gentleman who is seldom without a smile, Cochran generally refrains from criticizing others. Nevertheless, the most attention he drew in the 110th Congress (2007-08) came from an unusually blunt remark to a Boston Globe reporter about colleague John McCain of Arizona. "The thought of his being president sends a cold chill down my spine," Cochran said of his fellow Republican. "He is erratic. He is hotheaded. He loses his temper, and he worries me."

The comment became fodder for Democrats eager to build a case against McCain's presidential candidacy. The two senators eventually patched up their differences.

Cochran was Appropriations chairman in the 109th Congress (2005-06). An institutionalist at heart, he made a priority of getting all of the appropriations bills through the Senate in his first year at the helm, after several years in which the Republican majority had to rely on eleventh-hour omnibus bills to fund the government.

In mid-2008, Cochran took over for colleague Ted Stevens of Alaska as top-ranking Republican on the Defense Appropriations Subcommittee when Stevens became caught in an ethics controversy and was forced to relinquish the post. Cochran has long obtained money for Northrop Grumman Corp.'s naval shipyard in Pascagoula and the state's other military installations. He previously was top Republican on the Homeland Security Subcommittee, where he worked to bolster spending for the Federal Emergency Management Agency and the Coast Guard.

In late 2010, Cochran voted for a nuclear arms control treaty with Russia, known as New START, over the objections of some Republicans who were pushing for concessions on modernizing the U.S. nuclear weapons arsenal.

On the Agriculture Committee, he was a major player in the 2002 rewrite of the law that authorizes federal agriculture subsidies and conservation and nutrition programs. But his 2003-04 stint as Agriculture chairman was uneventful. He held few meetings to debate bills, in part to prevent Iowa Republican Charles E. Grassley, a panel member, from offering amendments to reduce the maximum federal payments a farmer could receive. Grassley wanted to free money for other farm programs, while Cochran opposed lower payment limits.

On the Rules and Administration Committee, where the jurisdiction includes election laws, Cochran played a pivotal role in the drive to curb the large individual donations to political parties known as soft money. His 2001 announcement that he would support a McCain-sponsored bill that GOP leaders opposed began an erosion of Republican opposition. The law was enacted 14 months later.

Cochran's father was a school principal and his mother, a math teacher. He was a standout in high school: valedictorian of his class, a Boy Scout leader, a member of the 4-H Club and an athlete, lettering in football, basketball, baseball and tennis.

At the University of Mississippi, Cochran was a fraternity president and cheerleader who was four years ahead of Trent Lott, later his congressional colleague and occasional rival. In his first year of law school, Cochran posted the highest scholastic average and later got a Rotary fellowship to study international law at Trinity College in Dublin. He joined a Jackson law firm after graduation and made partner in less than three years.

Cochran was active in local party politics during his law career and was a key state figure in Richard Nixon's 1968 presidential campaign. In 1972, when Democratic Rep. Charles H. Griffin retired, Cochran narrowly won the open seat. Lott was elected to the House the same year, and the two soon led warring factions within the state party. The pragmatists, led by Cochran, and the ideologues, led by Lott, feuded with increasing intensity for nearly two decades.

Cochran became Mississippi's first GOP senator in a century when longserving Democrat James O. Eastland retired in 1978. Cochran won with 45 percent of the vote, as an independent black candidate drew much of the black vote away from Democrat Maurice Dantin, a former Columbia mayor. All of Cochran's Senate re-elections have been cakewalks.

Cochran won election to the Senate a decade before Lott. But by 1995, Lott had zipped ahead of Cochran to become GOP whip. When Majority Leader Bob Dole resigned to focus on his 1996 presidential campaign, the two Mississippians battled each other for the job; Lott won easily, 44-8.

Key Votes

2010

Pass budget reconciliation bill to modify overhauls of health care and federal student loan programs	NO
Proceed to disapproval resolution on EPA authority to regulate greenhouse gases	YES
Overhaul financial services industry regulation	NO
Limit debate to proceed to a bill to broaden campaign finance disclosure and reporting rules	NO
Limit debate on an extension of Bush-era income tax cuts for two years	YES
Limit debate on a bill to provide a path to legal status for some children of illegal immigrants	NO
Allow for a repeal of "don't ask, don't tell"	NO
Consent to ratification of a strategic arms reduction treaty with Russia	YES

2009

Prevent release of remaining financial industry bailout funds	YES
Make it easier for victims to sue for wage discrimination remedies	NO
Expand the Children's Health Insurance Program	NO
Limit debate on the economic stimulus measure	NO
Repeal District of Columbia firearms prohibitions and gun registration laws	YES
Limit debate on expansion of federal hate crimes law	NO
Strike funding for F-22 Raptor fighter jets	NO

CQ Vote Studies

	PARTY UNITY		PRESIDENTIAL SUPPORT	
	SUPPORT	OPPOSE	SUPPORT	OPPOSE
2010	89%	11%	47%	53%
2009	75%	25%	62%	38%
2008	85%	15%	74%	26%
2007	85%	15%	82%	18%
2006	87%	13%	89%	11%
2005	97%	3%	96%	4%
2004	98%	2%	92%	8%
2003	98%	2%	98%	2%
2002	86%	14%	96%	4%
2001	84%	16%	96%	4%

Interest Groups

	AFL-CIO	ADA	CCUS	ACU
2010	6%	5%	100%	88%
2009	28%	10%	86%	84%
2008	10%	15%	88%	68%
2007	11%	15%	82%	83%
2006	15%	10%	92%	67%
2005	21%	0%	100%	88%
2004	8%	15%	100%	92%
2003	0%	5%	100%	85%
2002	23%	25%	100%	90%
2001	25%	15%	86%	88%

Sen. Roger Wicker (R)

Capitol Office
224-6253
wicker.senate.gov
555 Dirksen Bldg. 20510-2403; fax 228-0378

Committees
Armed Services
Banking, Housing & Urban Affairs
Commerce, Science & Transportation
Veterans' Affairs

Residence
Tupelo

Born
July 5, 1951; Pontotoc, Miss.

Religion
Southern Baptist

Family
Wife, Gayle Wicker; three children

Education
U. of Mississippi, B.A. 1973 (political science & journalism), J.D. 1975

Military Service
Air Force, 1976-80; Air Force Reserve, 1980-2004

Career
Lawyer; congressional aide; county public defender; military prosecutor

Political Highlights
Miss. Senate, 1988-94; U.S. House, 1995-2007

ELECTION RESULTS

2008 GENERAL

Roger Wicker (R)	683,409	55.0%
Ronnie Musgrove (D)	560,064	45.0%

Previous Winning Percentages
2006 House Election (66%); 2004 House Election (79%); 2002 House Election (71%); 2000 House Election (70%); 1998 House Election (67%); 1996 House Election (68%); 1994 House Election (63%)

Appointed December 2007; 1st term

Mississippi's junior senator speaks with a slow, rolling cadence and just the hint of an accent, and he has the unstinting courtesy of a Southern gentleman — but to equate Wicker's soft-spoken manner with a lack of fervency would be a grave mistake.

The native Mississippian is a dyed-in-the-wool Republican, politically active in the Grand Old Party since adolescence. He is willing to battle tooth and nail against any and all elements of the Democratic agenda that he views as contrary to his conservative standards. He fights just as hard to help his home state, both by bringing home federal funds and by pushing for relief for the Gulf of Mexico coastline, which has been ravaged by Hurricane Katrina and, later, the BP oil spill.

Mississippi, which has one of the highest poverty rates in the country, has long benefited from a Senate delegation that brings home the proverbial bacon. And Wicker quickly seized that role after being tapped to fill the seat vacated by former Republican leader Trent Lott in late 2007.

Wicker developed a knack for appropriations while in the House, where he grew to enjoy the often behind-the-scenes, but highly collaborative, work of the Appropriations Committee.

Despite his propensity for earmarking, Wicker says he is supportive of the earmark moratorium the Republican caucus established for the 112th Congress (2011-12), though he considers it more of a "pause" than a step toward elimination of the practice.

In other realms, Wicker has been a solid fiscal conservative. He opposed President Obama's $787 billion economic stimulus bill, which became law in early 2009, arguing that it called for too much spending. He also voted against President George W. Bush's $700 billion rescue of the financial sector, which became law in 2008, and helped sink a bill providing emergency loans for near-bankrupt automobile companies.

He called a bipartisan proposal made by Sens. Jeff Sessions, an Alabama Republican, and Claire McCaskill, a Missouri Democrat, to freeze non-defense appropriations "a good start."

A member of the Armed Services Committee, Wicker said he is also "supportive of the general principle" behind Defense Secretary Robert M. Gates' efforts to reduce Pentagon spending.

The first-term senator is not optimistic, however, about how much the divided 112th Congress will be able to get done from a legislative perspective. He blames the gridlock that has become common in the Senate squarely on the Democratic leadership. The way Majority Leader Harry Reid of Nevada has limited the minority's ability to bring up amendments "really reminds me more of the closed-rule practices I've seen from time to time on the House floor," Wicker said, referring to his 13 years on the other side of the Capitol.

He crossed over to the Senate on New Year's Eve 2007, when Mississippi Republican Gov. Haley Barbour appointed him to fill Lott's empty seat. He then secured the support of constituents in his state, with a 10-point win over former Democratic Gov. Ronnie Musgrove — who once roomed with Wicker when both were in the state Senate — in the 2008 election to complete the term. He faces the voters again in 2012.

Wicker's seats on the Armed Services, Veterans' Affairs, and Commerce, Science and Transportation panels have been essential to continuing the efforts he began on House Appropriations to turn his state into a magnet for defense jobs.

Another of Wicker's continuing priorities has been efforts to reconstruct areas of his state that were hard-hit by hurricanes in 2005 and then walloped again in 2010 by the oil spill, a task that will be aided by his new assignment on the Banking, Housing and Urban Affairs Committee.

He sponsored legislation to give $5,000 tax credits to hurricane victims; the bill went nowhere, but Wicker did manage to push through an extension of legislation, passed after Hurricane Katrina, that provides tax incentives to developers who build in the devastated regions of Mississippi and Louisiana. As member of the Commerce subcommittee with jurisdiction over insurance issues, he has also been working with others in the Mississippi delegation to add wind coverage to national flood insurance programs.

At the end of the 111th Congress (2009-10), he helped win extension of tax incentives for rebuilding in the Gulf Coast by getting a provision added to legislation that extended the Bush-era tax cuts for two years.

He also plans to keep a close eye on federal recovery programs for the oil spill, which he is far from satisfied with. Among the things the federal government needs to address, Wicker said, is "how we divide up the penalties . . . so that these funds don't go into the general treasury." They need to be used by the affected states, he argued.

"What this next Congress lacks in legislative accomplishments I hope we can make up for in oversight," Wicker said during the 111th. "And a good target for that is the entire response" to the oil spill.

Wicker is a social as well as fiscal conservative, and he is adamantly opposed to abortion. To that end, he has cosponsored a number of bills that seek to limit taxpayer dollars from even indirectly funding the procedure.

Wicker left the Foreign Relations Committee at the conclusion of the 111th Congress but intends to continue to fight for one international issue close to his heart — peace in Sudan.

"I do have a particular interest in preventing a huge outbreak of ethnic violence in that part of Africa," he said.

The grandson of sharecroppers from Benton, Wicker said his father's humble upbringing makes his ascension to Congress "a pretty powerful statement of the American dream." His father lived in a small farmhouse with his parents and four siblings before becoming a county attorney, a state senator and then a circuit judge for 20 years. Like virtually every officeholder in the South in those days, Wicker's father was a Democrat, but that didn't stop his son from organizing the local teenage Republican club in high school.

Wicker credits his early devotion to the GOP to his stint as a congressional page in 1967. "Although I was appointed by a Democrat [Rep. Jamie L. Whitten], I was assigned to the Republican page desk and got to observe up close people like Gerald Ford and Melvin Laird and the Republican leadership, so I guess I returned from my short stay as a Republican page a committed Republican," he said.

He was the first Republican ever to be elected student body president at the University of Mississippi and went on to serve as a delegate to the 1972 Republican National Convention. There he became acquainted with Lott, who was making his first run for Congress. After law school and four years on active duty in the Air Force, Wicker went to work for Lott in Washington in 1980. In 1987, he won a state Senate seat, using the post to help write Mississippi's strict abortion law and to push through an education overhaul that included a school choice provision.

When Whitten retired in 1994 after 53 years in the House — the longest service in the chamber's history at the time — the conservative-minded 1st District was ripe for GOP picking. Wicker emphasized his legislative experience and edged out Grant Fox, a former Senate aide, for the Republican nomination. In November, he won with 63 percent of the vote, and was never seriously challenged for his remaining House terms.

Key Votes

2010

Pass budget reconciliation bill to modify overhauls of health care and federal student loan programs	NO
Proceed to disapproval resolution on EPA authority to regulate greenhouse gases	YES
Overhaul financial services industry regulation	NO
Limit debate to proceed to a bill to broaden campaign finance disclosure and reporting rules	NO
Limit debate on an extension of Bush-era income tax cuts for two years	YES
Limit debate on a bill to provide a path to legal status for some children of illegal immigrants	NO
Allow for a repeal of "don't ask, don't tell"	NO
Consent to ratification of a strategic arms reduction treaty with Russia	NO

2009

Prevent release of remaining financial industry bailout funds	YES
Make it easier for victims to sue for wage discrimination remedies	NO
Expand the Children's Health Insurance Program	NO
Limit debate on the economic stimulus measure	NO
Repeal District of Columbia firearms prohibitions and gun registration laws	YES
Limit debate on expansion of federal hate crimes law	NO
Strike funding for F-22 Raptor fighter jets	NO

CQ Vote Studies

	PARTY UNITY		PRESIDENTIAL SUPPORT	
	SUPPORT	OPPOSE	SUPPORT	OPPOSE
2010	96%	4%	41%	59%
2009	88%	12%	49%	51%
2008	94%	6%	70%	30%
2007	89%	11%	81%	19%
2006	97%	3%	97%	3%
2005	97%	3%	84%	16%
2004	95%	5%	86%	14%
2003	97%	3%	96%	4%
2002	99%	1%	85%	15%
2001	99%	1%	95%	5%

Interest Groups

	AFL-CIO	ADA	CCUS	ACU
2010	0%	0%	100%	96%
2009	39%	15%	86%	88%
2008	20%	10%	88%	80%
2007	0%	5%	84%	96%
2006	7%	0%	100%	88%
2005	20%	5%	93%	96%
2004	8%	0%	100%	87%
2003	0%	10%	97%	88%
2002	11%	0%	90%	100%
2001	8%	0%	96%	96%

Rep. Alan Nunnelee (R)

Capitol Office
225-4306
nunnelee.house.gov
1432 Longworth Bldg. 20515-2401; fax 225-3549

Committees
Appropriations

Residence
Tupelo

Born
Oct. 9, 1958; Tupelo, Miss.

Religion
Baptist

Family
Wife, Tori Nunnelee; three children

Education
Mississippi State U., B.S. 1980 (marketing)

Career
Insurance company owner

Political Highlights
Miss. Senate, 1995-2010

ELECTION RESULTS

2010 GENERAL

Alan Nunnelee (R)	121,074	55.3%
Travis W. Childers (D)	89,388	40.8%
Wally Pang (I)	2,180	1.0%

2010 PRIMARY

Alan Nunnelee (R)	20,236	51.8%
Henry Ross (R)	12,894	33.0%
Angela McGlowan (R)	5,924	15.2%

Elected 2010; 1st term

Nunnelee brings to Congress a wealth of appropriations experience, a distaste for deficits and a reliably conservative outlook.

He won a rare opportunity to put that experience to work right away as one of three Republican freshmen named to the Appropriations Committee.

Nunnelee says his experience with making the "difficult decisions" involved in balancing state budgets as chairman of the Mississippi Senate Appropriations Committee will come in handy in Washington.

Representing a district that relies on manufacturing and agriculture, he sits on the Appropriations panel handling agriculture spending, as well as the Energy-Water and Military Construction-Veterans' Affairs panels.

But he says his main expertise is health policy. Prior to leaving the state Senate, he was the vice chairman of the Public Health and Welfare panel.

He voted early in 2011 to repeal the health care overhaul enacted in 2010. An insurance company owner, Nunnelee favors replacing the law with "patient-centered health care reform," which would include the ability to buy insurance across state lines and provide the same tax advantages to individuals and families that are given to employe-provided insurance.

Innovations in health care are of a personal interest to Nunnelee. A disease blinded him by the time he was a college senior, and doctors restored his vision with two cornea transplants. He says the knowledge that another person's death made it possible for him to see gives him "a very keen sense of responsibility."

Nunnelee won a three-way GOP primary, avoiding a runoff by taking 52 percent of the vote. The general election race against Democratic incumbent Travis W. Childers cast one of the most conservative Democrats in the House against an even more conservative Republican.

Childers was a member of the fiscally conservative Blue Dog Coalition, opposed abortion and same-sex marriage, and had the endorsement of the National Rifle Association. But Nunnelee was carried along by the national Republican wave and he won going away, with 55 percent of the vote to Childers' 41 percent.

Mississippi 1

North — Tupelo, Southaven, Columbus

The northeastern Hill Country and rich farmland on the edge of the Delta region in northwestern Mississippi support an agricultural economy in the 1st, while manufacturing dominates in Lee County (Tupelo) and surrounding areas. Tupelo is a major producer of upholstered furniture, Columbus has some steel manufacturing and Oxford is home to the University of Mississippi. The district includes Mississippi's entire portion of the planned Interstate 22 (currently Highway 78), which will connect Memphis and Birmingham through Tupelo. In addition to infrastructure development, the area received good news when Toyota announced a new Prius plant northwest of Tupelo. The city's status as the birthplace of Elvis Presley attracts hundreds of thousands of visitors each year.

Desoto County, the 1st's most populous and the state's fastest-growing, hosts residents who commute over the Tennessee border into Memphis. Southaven and Olive Branch, both in Desoto County, are distribution hubs for large manufacturing firms. To the east, Marshall and Benton counties are home to many of the district's African-American residents, a group that makes up more than one-fourth of the 1st's population. A history of backing Democrats for the U.S. House was broken in 1994, and voters now also support the GOP in presidential races.

Major Industry
Furniture, manufacturing, agriculture

Military Bases
Columbus Air Force Base, 1,494 military, 679 civilian (2011)

Cities
Southaven, 48,982; Tupelo, 34,546; Olive Branch, 33,484; Horn Lake, 26,066

Notable
Columbus lures visitors to its historic antebellum home tours.

Rep. Bennie Thompson (D)

Capitol Office
225-5876
benniethompson.house.gov
2466 Rayburn Bldg. 20515-2402; fax 225-5898

Committees
Homeland Security - Ranking Member

Residence
Bolton

Born
Jan. 28, 1948; Bolton, Miss.

Religion
United Methodist

Family
Wife, London Thompson; one child

Education
Tougaloo College, B.A. 1968 (political science);
Jackson State College, M.S. 1972 (educational
administration)

Career
Teacher

Political Highlights
Bolton Board of Aldermen, 1969-73; mayor of
Bolton, 1973-79; Hinds County Board of Supervisors,
1980-93

ELECTION RESULTS

2010 GENERAL
Bennie Thompson (D)	105,327	61.5%
William "Bill" Marcy (R)	64,499	37.6%

2010 PRIMARY
Bennie Thompson (D)	unopposed

2008 GENERAL
Bennie Thompson (D)	201,606	69.0%
Richard Cook (R)	90,364	31.0%

Previous Winning Percentages
2006 (64%); 2004 (58%); 2002 (55%); 2000 (65%);
1998 (71%); 1996 (60%); 1994 (54%); 1993 Special
Runoff Election (55%)

Elected 1993; 9th full term

Thompson's experiences as a black politician in Mississippi and the makeup of his constituency — largely black, rural and poor — helped him fashion a career as a champion of civil rights and rural development. Those experiences also made him an expert at maximizing opportunities.

When Hurricane Katrina struck the Gulf Coast, Thompson earned instant credibility on the topic of the Federal Emergency Management Agency and the Department of Homeland Security. He has since parlayed that opportunity to expand his influence across the entire portfolio of homeland issues.

Although his district might seem an unlikely terrorist target, he snared the senior Democratic slot on the Homeland Security Committee when it was created in 2005 and became chairman two years later. A staunch liberal with an even-keeled temperament and willingness to listen, he returned to the ranking minority spot in the 112th Congress (2011-12).

Throughout the 111th Congress (2009-10), Thompson honed in on persistent management issues that have dogged the Homeland Security Department for years, while addressing new threats, such as cybersecurity and growing worries about domestic extremism. In 2010, the committee examined incidents including a plot to bomb the New York Subway system, a failed car bombing in Times Square and a shooting attack at Fort Hood, Texas — all allegedly involving legal U.S. citizens or residents.

"There's no question that to some degree, we've succeeded from keeping people who would do us harm out of the country, and that's a work in progress," Thompson said. "But [those] who have been here and somehow have become radicalized, that is an ongoing problem."

Early in the 112th Congress, Thompson clashed with the committee's new chairman, New York Republican Peter T. King, over that issue.

When King called for hearings to examine the radicalization of American Muslims, Thompson argued that the focus was too narrow, saying the inquiry should have included other groups, such as neo-Nazis and extremist environmental groups.

"I cannot help but wonder how propaganda about this hearing focusing on the American Muslim community will be used by those who seek to find a new generation of suicide bombers," he said.

Thompson frequently disagrees with King, although the two have built a working relationship through three changes in control of the House.

In early 2011, the two cosponsored legislation to turn a valuable section of radio spectrum over to the public safety sector to build a nationwide communications network, a project both have identified as a priority for years. Thompson said that on other big-picture security issues, such as the need to protect the aviation sector, the two parties aren't far apart.

"The good part of the committee is, under Mr. King's chairmanship and under my chairmanship, we have tried to keep the broad issue of homeland security bipartisan," he said. "We've been able to work out the issues because we feel that the department's two primary missions — preventing terrorism and responding to natural disasters — transcend parties."

Thompson said he wants to reintroduce and push several measures in the 112th Congress, including a bill to modify and extend the 2007 Chemical Facility Anti-Terrorism Standards. "We have been discussing that for three or four years now," he said. "It's not going away."

Thompson is one of a group of Democrats in favor of building "inherently safer technologies" language into the legislation, which would give the government the power to order facilities such as water treatment plants to use chemicals deemed less risky to the public if misused. Republicans and interest groups such as the American Chemistry Council, however, have advocated a straight reauthorization, saying the proposed new requirements would be overly burdensome on industry with few real security benefits.

Thompson's other priorities for 2011 include his bill to enhance cybersecurity for federal computer networks, paying close attention to DHS resource allocation and pressing the Transportation Security Administration to balance its spending on land-based transit, including buses and trains, with the massive amounts of funding and attention aviation has received.

He also hopes to see an end to the years-long trend of the House passing homeland security authorization bills, only to have the Senate ignore them.

For years, Thompson has sought to gain more clout for his committee. More than 100 committees and subcommittees claim oversight jurisdiction for Homeland Security, a situation that Thompson said creates confusion for the department regarding congressional priorities. In 2009, he prevailed on his party's leadership to ensure that more legislation was referred to his committee. He was quick to criticize when Republican leadership opted not to act on jurisdiction at the start of 2011, saying that the beginning of a new session was the only time when Congress might be able to trim down the list of oversight panels.

Born in 1948, Thompson was educated in segregated elementary and secondary schools. His father, a mechanic, died when Thompson was in the 10th grade. At Tougaloo College, he met civil rights activist Fannie Lou Hamer, who inspired him to pursue politics. He graduated in 1968, the year he made his first run for public office and, at age 20, was elected alderman in his hometown of Bolton. The town's whites didn't want a black man on the board, so they barred him from City Hall. He got a court order forcing them to back down and let him claim his seat.

Four years later he was elected mayor. Then, at 32, he was elected to the board of supervisors for Hinds County, which includes the capital city, Jackson. President Bill Clinton named Thompson as one of 100 "unsung African-Americans" at the 2004 opening of his presidential library.

He ran for the House in a 1993 special election after Democrat Mike Espy resigned to become Clinton's Agriculture secretary. Thompson triumphed in a runoff, with 55 percent of the vote. One of the candidates he defeated was Clarksdale Mayor Henry Espy, Mike Espy's brother. In his 1994 bid for a full term, he won by 15 percentage points, and his subsequent re-elections have been by comfortable margins.

Key Votes

2010

Overhaul the nation's health insurance system	YES
Allow for repeal of "don't ask, don't tell"	YES
Overhaul financial services industry regulation	YES
Limit use of new Afghanistan War funds to troop withdrawal activities	YES
Change oversight of offshore drilling and lift oil spill liability cap	YES
Provide a path to legal status for some children of illegal immigrants	YES
Extend Bush-era income tax cuts for two years	NO

2009

Expand the Children's Health Insurance Program	YES
Provide $787 billion in tax cuts and spending increases to stimulate the economy	YES
Allow bankruptcy judges to modify certain primary-residence mortgages	YES
Create a cap-and-trade system to limit greenhouse gas emissions	YES
Provide $2 billion for the "cash for clunkers" program	YES
Establish the government as the sole provider of student loans	YES
Restrict federally funded insurance coverage for abortions in health care overhaul	NO

CQ Vote Studies

	PARTY UNITY		PRESIDENTIAL SUPPORT	
	SUPPORT	OPPOSE	SUPPORT	OPPOSE
2010	98%	2%	83%	17%
2009	99%	1%	97%	3%
2008	99%	1%	13%	87%
2007	98%	2%	5%	95%
2006	90%	10%	41%	59%

Interest Groups

	AFL-CIO	ADA	CCUS	ACU
2010	93%	95%	25%	4%
2009	100%	95%	43%	0%
2008	100%	90%	50%	8%
2007	88%	100%	50%	0%
2006	100%	90%	60%	30%

Mississippi 2

West central — Jackson, Mississippi Delta

Lying mostly west of Interstate 55 and north of Interstate 20, the 2nd combines most of Jackson — the state's capital and largest city — with Vicksburg and the nutrient-rich flatlands of the Mississippi Delta. North of Vicksburg, the road drops 15 feet in Issaquena County, marking the beginning of the Delta. In the last decade, the district has lost more than 40,000 residents, ranking among the fastest-contracting districts in the nation ahead of decennial remapping.

Agriculture is important both to the state and the district, and the 2nd supports catfish-raising and other aquaculture, cotton, rice, and soybeans. The Delta's agricultural economy has promoted landowner/tenant relationships that have made the 2nd one of the nation's poorest districts, with a median household income of slightly more than $30,000.

In Vicksburg, a mixture of tourism, casinos and a Mississippi River port have brought some local prosperity, as has a new ethanol plant that produces more than 50 million gallons annually, making it one of the largest plants in the South. Outside Canton, a Nissan assembly plant north of Jackson employs thousands of workers, and the company recently expanded the facility despite vulnerability in the auto industry.

Government, service and small-scale manufacturing jobs have long kept unemployment in check in Jackson, although nationwide economic downturns have hurt the capital. The city is working to revitalize its downtown area and opened a new convention center in 2009. Jackson also hosts the State Fair and annual rodeo.

Although some low-income white residents live in the 2nd, it is the only black-majority district in Mississippi, which has the highest percentage of black residents in the nation. Overall, the 2nd has the second-highest percentage of black residents of any district nationwide. Despite a Republican foothold in some areas near Jackson and to the northeast, the 2nd was the only Mississippi district to favor Barack Obama in the 2008 presidential election, giving him 66 percent of its vote.

Major Industry
Agriculture, government, casinos

Cities
Jackson (pt.), 141,565; Greenville, 34,400; Clinton, 25,216

Notable
Norris Bookbinding, based in Greenwood, is the largest Bible rebinding plant in the nation.

Rep. Gregg Harper (R)

Capitol Office
225-5031
harper.house.gov
307 Cannon Bldg. 20515-2403; fax 225-5797

Committees
Energy & Commerce
Ethics
House Administration
  (Elections - Chairman)
Joint Library
Joint Printing

Residence
Pearl

Born
June 1, 1956; Jackson, Miss.

Religion
Southern Baptist

Family
Wife, Sidney Harper; two children

Education
Mississippi College, B.S. 1978 (chemistry); U. of Mississippi, J.D. 1981

Career
City prosecutor; lawyer

Political Highlights
Rankin County Republican Party chairman, 2000-07

ELECTION RESULTS

2010 GENERAL
Gregg Harper (R)	132,393	68.0%
Joel L. Gill (D)	60,737	31.2%

2010 PRIMARY
Gregg Harper (R)	unopposed

2008 GENERAL
Gregg Harper (R)	213,171	62.5%
Joel L. Gill (D)	127,698	37.5%

2008 PRIMARY RUNOFF
Gregg Harper (R)	29,321	57.0%
Charlie Ross (R)	22,178	43.0%

Elected 2008; 2nd term

Harper is a committed conservative, but no one would call him a right-wing firebrand. He works to win legislative debates on the issues, but he also tries to be nice about it.

"I'm not an 'in your face' kind of a guy," Harper said. "I hope I'm more of a servant type than a screamer and a shouter."

But that doesn't mean Harper plans on being a quiet backbencher. The former Republican Party county chairman — who hadn't held elected office before arriving in Congress — has shown that he's a savvy political operator, a fact that hasn't escaped the notice of party leaders.

In his first term, he won a seat on the House Administration Committee. Though not well known off Capitol Hill, that panel is often viewed as a stepping stone for ambitious members — it has jurisdiction over everything from the distribution of office space on Capitol Hill to members' franking privileges. In his second term, he added a coveted spot on the Energy and Commerce Committee.

Although his district offered little in the way of a general election challenge, Harper still had to prove his political talent. In the spring of 2008, the little-known lawyer used his grass-roots organization to compete in a tough GOP primary against a wealthy opponent and a well-known state senator. After winning the nomination, he didn't wait around for the general election. That fall, Harper set up a political action committee, GreggPAC, and ended up distributing $42,000 to the National Republican Congressional Committee and more than 30 Republicans who were running that year, 19 of whom won.

The good will Harper earned from that effort probably didn't hurt when he beat out two other newly elected Republicans for the lone freshman spot on the Republican Steering Committee, which is charged with doling out committee assignments.

Harper immediately caught the eye of then-Minority Leader John A. Boehner of Ohio. Early in 2009 Boehner picked Harper to serve on a task force to ensure nonpartisanship in the 2010 census. In July of that year, Boehner tapped Harper for a less envious role when a seat came open on the Committee on Standards of Official Conduct, now the Ethics Committee.

Harper voted with his party against all the major legislative initiatives Democrats brought to the floor during the 111th Congress (2009-10), including the economic stimulus, the health care overhaul and climate change legislation. He called the cap-and-trade bill passed by the House in June 2009 a "fiasco" and has suggested that "even if [climate change] was man-made, and we could stop it, this is the worst time in the world to [do it] because of the current state of the economy."

Overall, he sided with a majority of Republicans against a majority of Democrats 94 percent of the time in his first term.

Though he prefers working behind the scenes, Harper isn't shy about his faith and his interest in helping children with special needs.

A Southern Baptist, he has said that one of his congressional mentors is Indiana Republican Mike Pence, who often describes himself as "a Christian, a conservative and a Republican, in that order."

"You can be a person up here hopefully that has some faith and be nice about it too," Harper said.

In July 2009, Harper was tapped to manage a bill on the House floor that directed the Architect of the Capitol to engrave the Pledge of Allegiance and the national motto "In God We Trust" in the underground Capitol

Visitor Center.

Harper's interest in special-needs children is a personal one. His son, Livingston, has Fragile X syndrome, a genetic disorder that causes behavioral, developmental and language disabilities and autistic-like behaviors. He has become a co-chairman in the Fragile X Caucus on Capitol Hill and has pushed several legislative priorities to aid those with mental disabilities.

Along with Sen. Thad Cochran, a fellow Mississippi Republican, Harper secured $11 million in funding for the Department of Education to develop a national postsecondary education program for intellectual disabilities. That program had been authorized in the 2008 Higher Education Opportunities Act but had not been appropriated. And he was instrumental in securing $1.9 million for the Centers for Disease Control for Fragile X programs.

He also created a pilot program with the House Administration Committee and George Mason University to offer congressional internships for adults with intellectual disabilities.

Harper was born in Jackson. His father was a petroleum engineer, his mother a homemaker. Because of the nature of his father's job Harper moved around the country during his school-age years. The family spent time in Texas, North Carolina and California before finally returning to Mississippi.

He didn't regularly attend church until a friend invited him to a Campus Life, Youth For Christ meeting during his sophomore year in high school. At age 17 he met his future wife, Sidney, in church and married her at age 23. Today, the Harpers are active members of Crossgates Baptist Church, where Harper serves as a deacon.

Harper graduated from Mississippi College in 1978 and went on to earn a law degree from the University of Mississippi Law School. In 2000, he served as an observer in the recount battle in Florida following the presidential election. In 2004, he was a legal volunteer for President George W. Bush's re-election effort in Ohio. From 2000 to 2007 he served as chairman of the Rankin County Republican Executive Committee.

In 2008, Harper put together a strong grass-roots campaign focusing on faith and family values. The seven-way GOP primary to replace a retiring Republican, Rep. Charles W. "Chip" Pickering Jr., turned into a wild and nasty contest. Of the four top contenders, Harper turned out to be the only candidate to avoid being caught up in the mudslinging. Connections developed during eight years as chairman of the most Republican county in the state helped him to slip, somewhat under the radar, into the runoff. He won the head-to-head contest against Charlie Ross, an 11-year veteran of the state legislature, then defeated Democrat Joel W. Gill by about 25 percentage points. Harper faced Gill again in 2010, winning by almost 37 points.

Key Votes

2010

Overhaul the nation's health insurance system	NO
Allow for repeal of "don't ask, don't tell"	NO
Overhaul financial services industry regulation	NO
Limit use of new Afghanistan War funds to troop withdrawal activities	NO
Change oversight of offshore drilling and lift oil spill liability cap	NO
Provide a path to legal status for some children of illegal immigrants	NO
Extend Bush-era income tax cuts for two years	YES

2009

Expand the Children's Health Insurance Program	NO
Provide $787 billion in tax cuts and spending increases to stimulate the economy	NO
Allow bankruptcy judges to modify certain primary-residence mortgages	NO
Create a cap-and-trade system to limit greenhouse gas emissions	NO
Provide $2 billion for the "cash for clunkers" program	?
Establish the government as the sole provider of student loans	NO
Restrict federally funded insurance coverage for abortions in health care overhaul	YES

CQ Vote Studies

	PARTY UNITY		PRESIDENTIAL SUPPORT	
	SUPPORT	OPPOSE	SUPPORT	OPPOSE
2010	97%	3%	26%	74%
2009	93%	7%	31%	69%

Interest Groups

	AFL-CIO	ADA	CCUS	ACU
2010	7%	0%	88%	96%
2009	6%	0%	80%	96%

Mississippi 3

East central to southwest — Jackson suburbs

The 3rd picks up Jackson's northeast corner and some of its mostly white northern and eastern suburbs as it sprawls across 28 counties, moving from Oktibbeha and Noxubee counties in the east central part of the state to the Mississippi River in the southwestern corner.

Rankin County's growth over the past two decades has been spurred by an influx of nearby Jackson residents moving out of the city. The district's white-collar and relatively well-educated workforce provides some economic stability — 23 percent of the district's residents have a four-year college degree, the highest percentage in the state — but unemployment rates have hovered above national averages in many counties outside Jackson's sphere.

Timber is dominant here, although prices depend on demand from construction sectors nationwide. Health care and defense also are important industries. Meridian is home to medical centers, a Naval Air Station, an Air National Guard base and Peavey Electronics, one of the world's largest guitar and amplifier manufacturers.

Elsewhere in the district poultry and dairy farms are prevalent. Pearl's minor league baseball stadium and a Bass Pro Shop outdoor store anchor an entertainment complex. Natchez, on the Mississippi River in Adams County, relies on tourism and attracts nearly 700,000 visitors annually to its antebellum homes and dockside casino. Mississippi State University, the state's largest university, is located in Starkville at the district's northeastern tip. Republicans now dominate the federal politics of the 3rd, as Democrats did for most of the 20th century. Black-majority and sparsely populated counties will still back Democratic candidates, but GOP Rep. Gregg Harper won convincing support in the district's population centers in 2010.

Major Industry
Timber, poultry, agriculture, defense

Military Bases
Naval Air Station Meridian, 412 military, 587 civilian (2011)

Cities
Meridian, 41,148; Jackson (pt.), 31,949; Pearl, 25,092

Notable
Mississippi State University is home to a large collection of papers from author and alumnus John Grisham.

Rep. Steven M. Palazzo (R)

Capitol Office
225-5772
palazzo.house.gov
331 Cannon Bldg. 20515-2404; fax 225-7074

Committees
Armed Services
Science, Space & Technology
(Space & Aeronautics - Chairman)

Residence
Biloxi

Born
Feb. 21, 1970; Gulfport, Miss.

Religion
Roman Catholic

Family
Wife, Lisa Palazzo; three children

Education
U. of Southern Mississippi, B.S.B.A. 1994 (accounting),
M.B.A. 1996

Military
Marine Corps Reserve, 1988-96; Miss. National Guard,
1997-present

Career
Accountant; defense contracting company financial
manager; oil rig inventory supervisor

Political Highlights
Miss. House, 2007-10

ELECTION RESULTS

2010 GENERAL

Steven M. Palazzo (R)	105,613	51.9%
Gene Taylor (D)	95,243	46.8%

2010 PRIMARY

Steven M. Palazzo (R)	15,556	57.2%
Joe Tegerdine (R)	11,663	42.8%

Elected 2010; 1st term

With his Gulf Coast district relying on defense-related employment, Palazzo focuses on military concerns. He served in the Marine Corps Reserve and the Mississippi National Guard — in which he is still active — and won a seat on the Armed Services Committee.

His district boasts military installations such as Keesler Air Force Base, the Naval Construction Training Center Gulfport, the Naval Oceanographic Office and a significant military shipbuilding industry.

His other committee assignment is Science, Space and Technology.

"We're in a global war on terror that will last through my children's lifetime," he said. "Equipping, training and preparing for future threats will be something I'll be focused on. We can't sacrifice that for any reason. That is why pruning the budget in other areas is extremely important."

Palazzo, who served in combat in the Persian Gulf War, says he will push for a significant expansion of the Navy. But with defense representing more than 50 percent of all discretionary spending, he says budget cutting will be "a long and arduous process."

Palazzo opposes virtually all of the Obama economic agenda, and he said on Fox Business Network that if the president "is serious about job creation, the first thing he will do is he will allow us to repeal the health care bill, give up on cap-and-trade, reduce spending and make the tax cuts permanents."

Palazzo has been a CPA, business owner and state legislator. He served four years in the Mississippi House, beginning in 2007.

Democratic Rep. Gene Taylor held the seat for more than 20 years, even as his district consistently backed Republican candidates for president. Arguably the most conservative Democrat in the House, Taylor fell below 60 percent of the vote in a re-election race only once until 2010.

But Palazzo, who topped businessman Joe Tegerdine for the Republican nomination, was able to tie Taylor to the Democratic leadership he so often opposed. Aided by a late financial boost from the National Republican Congressional Committee, Palazzo won with 52 percent of the vote to Taylor's 47 percent.

Mississippi 4

Southeast — Gulf Coast, Hattiesburg

Mississippi's only Gulf Coast district, the 4th relies on shipbuilding, casinos, petrochemicals and government jobs to fuel the economy in Hancock, Harrison and Jackson counties. The University of Southern Mississippi and Camp Shelby, a large military reserves training site, are in Hattiesburg. Rural areas to the north support poultry farms.

The coastal counties suffered catastrophic damage in 2005 when Hurricane Katrina displaced 100,000 residents, but populations there now surpass pre-Katrina levels. Harrison County again draws tourists to its 11 casinos, and Gulfport, the county's and district's largest city, has restored 80 downtown buildings since 2005. Tourism revenue, property values and wildlife populations along the district's coast took a hit following the 2010 Deepwater Horizon oil spill.

Huntington Ingalls Industries' shipbuilding facility employs more than 11,000 Jackson County residents, and the district has become a hub for the U.S. aerospace industry. NASA's John C. Stennis Space Center in Hancock hosts Lockheed Martin, Pratt & Whitney Rocketdyne and federal agency facilities.

Residents here are fiscally conservative and support the GOP. In the 2008 presidential election, John McCain took 67 percent of the vote, his best showing statewide.

Major Industry
Military, shipbuilding, casinos, tourism

Military Bases
Keesler Air Force Base, 5,353 military, 1,597 civilian (2009); Naval Construction Training Center Gulfport, 4,900 military, 900 civilian; Naval Oceanographic Office, 131 military, 898 civilian (2011)

Cities
Gulfport, 67,793; Hattiesburg, 45,989

Notable
Black Creek is the state's only National Scenic River.

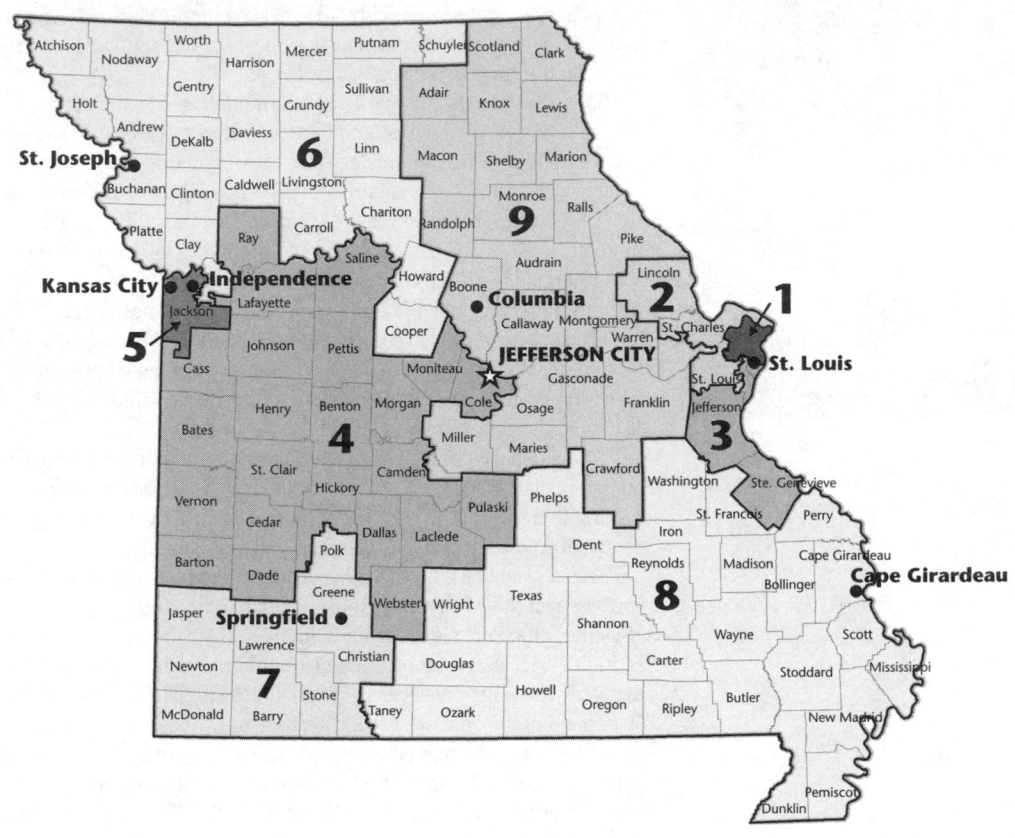

Gov. Jay Nixon (D)

First elected: 2008
Length of term: 4 years
Term expires: 1/13
Salary: $133,821
Phone: (573) 751-3222
Residence: Jefferson City
Born: Feb. 13, 1956; DeSoto, Mo.
Religion: Methodist
Family: Wife, Georganne Wheeler Nixon; two children
Education: U. of Missouri, B.A. 1978 (political science), J.D. 1981
Career: Lawyer
Political highlights: Mo. Senate, 1987-93; Democratic nominee for U.S. Senate, 1988; Mo. attorney general, 1993-2009; Democratic nominee for U.S. Senate, 1998

ELECTION RESULTS

2008 GENERAL
Jay Nixon (D)	1,680,611	58.4%
Kenny Hulshof (R)	1,136,364	39.5%
Andrew Finkenstadt (LIBERT)	31,850	1.1%
Gregory Thompson (CNSTP)	28,941	1.0%

Lt. Gov. Peter Kinder (R)

First elected: 2004
Length of term: 4 years
Term expires: 1/13
Salary: $86,484
Phone: (573) 751-4727

LEGISLATURE

General Assembly: January-May
Senate: 34 members, 4-year terms
2011 ratios: 26 R, 8 D; 28 men, 6 women
Salary: $35,915
Phone: (573) 751-3766
House: 163 members, 2-year terms
2011 ratios: 105 R, 55 D, 3 vacancies; 123 men, 37 women
Salary: $35,915
Phone: (573) 751-3659

TERM LIMITS

Governor: 2 terms
Senate: 2 terms
House: 4 terms

URBAN STATISTICS

CITY	POPULATION
Kansas City	459,787
St. Louis	319,294
Springfield	159,498
Independence	116,830
Columbia	108,500

REGISTERED VOTERS

Voters do not register by party.

POPULATION

2010 population	5,988,927
2000 population	5,595,211
1990 population	5,117,073
Percent change (2000-2010)	+7.0%
Rank among states (2010)	18
Median age	37.3
Born in state	66.4%
Foreign born	3.5%
Violent crime rate	492/100,000
Poverty level	14.6%
Federal workers	64,362
Military	17,925

ELECTIONS

STATE ELECTION OFFICIAL
(573) 751-2301
DEMOCRATIC PARTY
(573) 636-5241
REPUBLICAN PARTY
(573) 636-3146

MISCELLANEOUS

Web: www.mo.gov
Capital: Jefferson City

U.S. CONGRESS

Senate: 1 Republican, 1 Democrat
House: 6 Republicans, 3 Democrats

2010 Census Statistics by District

District	2008 Vote for President Obama	McCain	White	Black	Asian	Hispanic	Median Income	White Collar	Blue Collar	Service Industry	Over 64	Under 18	College Education	Rural	Sq. Miles
1	80%	19%	38%	55%	3%	2%	$41,228	60%	19%	21%	13%	25%	25%	1%	217
2	44	55	89	3	3	3	73,241	72	16	13	12	25	41	8	1,248
3	60	39	84	9	2	3	50,590	61	22	17	12	23	28	13	1,247
4	38	61	90	3	1	3	42,285	53	30	17	15	24	17	60	14,544
5	63	36	62	25	2	9	45,307	62	22	16	13	25	26	4	512
6	45	54	88	4	1	4	51,294	59	25	16	13	24	25	34	13,032
7	35	63	90	2	1	4	40,549	56	26	18	14	24	21	41	5,480
8	36	62	91	5	1	2	34,059	49	32	18	16	24	14	60	18,681
9	44	55	91	4	1	2	44,166	57	27	17	13	24	23	54	13,925
STATE	49.3	49.4	81	11	2	4	46,005	59	24	17	13	24	25	31	68,886
U.S.	53	46	64	12	5	16	51,425	60	23	17	13	25	28	21	3,537,438

Sen. Claire McCaskill (D)

Capitol Office
224-6154
mccaskill.senate.gov
506 Hart Bldg. 20510-2505; fax 228-6326

Committees
Armed Services
  (Readiness & Management Support -
  Chairwoman)
Commerce, Science & Transportation
Homeland Security & Governmental Affairs
  (Contracting Oversight - Chairwoman)
Special Aging

Residence
Kirkwood

Born
July 24, 1953; Rolla, Mo.

Religion
Roman Catholic

Family
Husband, Joseph Shepard; seven children

Education
U. of Missouri, B.A. 1975 (political science), J.D. 1978

Career
Lawyer; city prosecutor

Political Highlights
Mo. House, 1983-89; sought Democratic nomination for Jackson County prosecutor, 1988; Jackson
County Legislature, 1991-93; Jackson County prosecutor, 1993-99; Mo. auditor, 1999-2007; Democratic
nominee for governor, 2004

ELECTION RESULTS

2006 GENERAL

Claire McCaskill (D)	1,055,255	49.6%
Jim Talent (R)	1,006,941	47.3%
Frank Gilmour (LIBERT)	47,792	2.2%

2006 PRIMARY

Claire McCaskill (D)	282,767	80.8%
Bill Clinton Young (D)	67,173	19.2%

Elected 2006; 1st term

McCaskill's favorite adjective to describe herself is "independent," and she has certainly tried the patience of the Democratic leadership on issues from earmarks to legislative transparency to oversight of the executive branch.

"I've always gotten in trouble with my party's leaders — in the last legislative body I worked in, and sometimes in this," she said. "But I think we need to reform some things here where the train's kind of gone off the tracks."

Earmarks are one of the first things about the Senate that McCaskill would like to change by ending them. She acknowledges that Congress should be able to fund programs that presidents don't request — but she believes the vetting of unrequested projects should be open, competitive and fully autho-rized, not dropped into a spending bill without debate.

McCaskill persuaded the Armed Services Committee, on which she serves, to make its earmarks and their authors public in the reports that are published with the defense policy bill each year.

Sometimes her opposition to earmarks has put her in an awkward position. McCaskill, who chairs the Subcommittee on Readiness and Management Support, has tirelessly espoused construction of additional C-17 transport planes, made largely in Missouri, even though the Pentagon does not want more. Yet she has stopped short of signing any letters to appropriators explic-itly requesting an earmark for them — to avoid being "a hypocrite," she said.

Meanwhile, each year since she joined the committee, McCaskill has offered an amendment to make its markups open to the public, as they are in the comparable House panel, except when members are reviewing clas-sified or proprietary material.

McCaskill also has advocated limiting the practice of senators putting secret holds on nominations and bills, which blocks consideration without any public acknowledgement. She cosponsored legislation requiring that holds be made public within one legislative day, and the Senate changed the rules for the 112th Congress (2011-12) to require that members who place holds must be identified.

Oversight is second nature to the former auditor and prosecutor. In fact, McCaskill has been like a watchdog for U.S. watchdog agencies. In 2010, she advocated removal of the special inspector general for Afghanistan reconstruction after reports of his office lacking in experience and compe-tence. He resigned in early 2011. In 2009, she pushed for legislation that would strengthen oversight of the $700 billion rescue package for the finan-cial sector, which she had voted for the year before, saying: "This bill stinks, but the alternative is much worse."

McCaskill also serves on the Homeland Security Committee and chairs a panel created in 2009 that is charged with overseeing $500 billion a year in federal contracts.

In 2008, working with Susan Collins of Maine, the top Republican on the Homeland Security panel, McCaskill helped shepherd into law a measure designed to insulate the federal government's inspectors general from political influence. That same year, she helped pass a bill that would set up a database of unscrupulous or incompetent government contractors.

In her first year in the Senate, McCaskill teamed with fellow freshman Democrat Jim Webb of Virginia on an amendment to the fiscal 2008 defense authorization act that created a latter-day version of the Truman Committee, which uncovered profiteering during World War II.

She has emerged as a key centrist on economic issues, pushing her party and the president to compromise with Republicans. She has advocated capping government spending, except for authorized war expenses, at 1 percent growth per year from fiscal 2012 to 2014. She also espouses a pay-as-you-go policy, where new spending or tax cuts would have to be offset.

McCaskill also sits on the Commerce, Science and Transportation Committee, a post she uses to look out for consumer interests. And she serves on the Special Aging Committee — a good fit, as her state has a large elderly population. She works on improving hospital care for veterans and, in 2007, she supported a House-passed bill that would have allowed the government to negotiate prescription drug prices for seniors.

McCaskill has close ties to President Obama, who as a freshman senator in 2006 campaigned for McCaskill in her successful bid to unseat GOP incumbent Jim Talent. McCaskill and Obama worked together in the Senate on ethics rules and correcting problems at Walter Reed Army Medical Center.

She was the first Democratic woman in the Senate to back him in the 2008 primaries against then-New York Sen. Hillary Rodham Clinton.

On the other hand, McCaskill split with her party more often in the 110th Congress (2007-08) than all but three other Democrats on votes that divided the two parties. She continued that trend in the 111th (2009-10), and she isn't afraid to buck her friend the president. In his first year in White House, only one other Democratic senator — the retiring Evan Bayh of Indiana — broke with Obama more often than McCaskill. When the new president waived his own ethics rules to nominate William Lynn, a former lobbyist for defense contractor Raytheon Co., as deputy secretary of Defense, McCaskill cast the only Democratic vote against Lynn's confirmation.

McCaskill comes from a politically active family. Her father served as state insurance director, and her mother was the first woman to serve on the Columbia City Council. She recalls going to political events wearing sashes and "those obnoxious foam little bowler hats" to advertise candidates' campaigns. She caught the political bug, particularly after a teacher urged her to become a lawyer, noting she was better at arguing than she was in subjects that had obvious right and wrong answers.

After graduating from the University of Missouri and its law school, she clerked for the Missouri Court of Appeals and soon got a job as an assistant prosecutor in Kansas City. In 1982, she won a seat in the Missouri House, where she wrote the state's first minimum-sentencing law for repeat offenders. McCaskill was elected Jackson County prosecutor on her second try in 1992. Six years later, she was elected state auditor.

In 2004, McCaskill took on the Democratic Party establishment by defeating the incumbent governor, Bob Holden, in the primary. She lost the general election to Republican Matt Blunt, the son of then-House Majority Whip Roy Blunt, by 3 percentage points.

Party leaders urged McCaskill to make another run in 2006. She criticized Talent relentlessly for failing to ask tough questions of the George W. Bush administration on the Iraq War. She also was aided by the popularity of a ballot initiative to expand embryonic stem cell research, which she supported and Talent opposed. McCaskill won by a little more than 2 percentage points.

Her state will be a key battleground as Democrats try to retain their majority in 2012, and Republicans targeted McCaskill early in the cycle. The Missouri Republican Party filed two complaints with the Senate Ethics Committee in March 2011, asking the panel to investigate McCaskill's use of an airplane, owned by her family, for Senate- and campaign-related activities. McCaskill has since paid the U.S. Treasury $88,000 to cover her use of the plane for official business and she and her husband paid $287,000 in back taxes on the plane. They also announced their intention to sell the plane.

Key Votes

2010

Pass budget reconciliation bill to modify overhauls of health care and federal student loan programs	YES
Proceed to disapproval resolution on EPA authority to regulate greenhouse gases	NO
Overhaul financial services industry regulation	YES
Limit debate to proceed to a bill to broaden campaign finance disclosure and reporting rules	YES
Limit debate on an extension of Bush-era income tax cuts for two years	YES
Limit debate on a bill to provide a path to legal status for some children of illegal immigrants	YES
Allow for a repeal of "don't ask, don't tell"	YES
Consent to ratification of a strategic arms reduction treaty with Russia	YES

2009

Prevent release of remaining financial industry bailout funds	NO
Make it easier for victims to sue for wage discrimination remedies	YES
Expand the Children's Health Insurance Program	YES
Limit debate on the economic stimulus measure	YES
Repeal District of Columbia firearms prohibitions and gun registration laws	YES
Limit debate on expansion of federal hate crimes law	YES
Strike funding for F-22 Raptor fighter jets	YES

CQ Vote Studies

	PARTY UNITY		PRESIDENTIAL SUPPORT	
	SUPPORT	OPPOSE	SUPPORT	OPPOSE
2010	85%	15%	98%	2%
2009	72%	28%	80%	20%
2008	81%	19%	45%	55%
2007	81%	19%	41%	59%

Interest Groups

	AFL-CIO	ADA	CCUS	ACU
2010	94%	90%	27%	17%
2009	22%	95%	43%	28%
2008	90%	80%	75%	20%
2007	95%	90%	9%	8%

Sen. Roy Blunt (R)

Capitol Office
224-5721
blunt.senate.gov
260 Russell Bldg. 20510-2503; fax 224-8149

Committees
Appropriations
Commerce, Science & Transportation
Rules & Administration
Select Intelligence

Residence
Springfield

Born
Jan. 10, 1950; Niangua, Mo.

Religion
Baptist

Family
Wife, Abigail Blunt; four children

Education
Southwest Baptist U., B.A. 1970 (history); Southwest Missouri State U., M.A. 1972 (history & government)

Career
University president; teacher

Political Highlights
Greene County clerk, 1973-84; Republican nominee for lieutenant governor, 1980; Mo. secretary of state, 1985-93; sought Republican nomination for governor, 1992; U.S. House, 1997-2011

ELECTION RESULTS

2010 GENERAL

Roy Blunt (R)	1,054,160	54.2%
Robin Carnahan (D)	789,736	40.6%
Jonathan Dine (LIBERT)	58,663	3.0%
Jerry Beck (CNSTP)	41,309	2.1%

2010 PRIMARY

Roy Blunt (R)	411,040	70.9%
Chuck Purgason (R)	75,663	13.1%
Kristi Nichols (R)	40,744	7.0%
Deborah Solomon (R)	15,099	2.6%
Hector Maldonado (R)	8,731	1.5%
Others	22,881	4%

Previous Winning Percentages
2008 House Election (68%); (2006 House Election (67%); 2004 House Election (70%); 2002 House Election (75%); 2000 House Election (74%); 1998 House Election (73%); 1996 House Election (65%)

Elected 2010; 1st term

During his 14 years in the House, including nearly half of them in the leadership, Blunt earned a reputation as a business-friendly conservative and a deal-maker. It's safe to expect more of the same in the Senate.

Once spoken of as a potential future Speaker, he became one of his party's senior leaders thanks to his willingness to do favors for colleagues and his ability to stay cool under fire. An ally of former House Majority Leader Tom DeLay of Texas, Blunt rose quickly through the ranks. He became majority whip in 2003, six years after being elected and earlier in his congressional career than any lawmaker in the past eight decades. His leadership experience could come in handy on the Senate Rules and Administration Committee.

As majority whip, the No. 3 leadership post when Republicans control the House, Blunt was instrumental in ensuring that the George W. Bush administration and the House were in sync — which might have served the interests of Bush better than it did Blunt and other House Republicans.

"I think you can argue that our leadership was too close to President Bush," Blunt said in 2009. "One of our mistakes that harmed our majority and President Bush was not being willing to have more veto fights with him."

Republicans' poor electoral showings in November 2008 and shaky ties to conservatives led Blunt to step down from his whip post for the 111th Congress (2009-10). Out of the leadership, he set his sights on the Senate, "where the real battles will be fought," he said.

Foremost among those battles will be the follow-up to 2010's health care debate. Blunt, who sits on the Appropriations Committee, has vowed to repeal or block funding for the Democrats' health care overhaul, "replacing it with common-sense health care solutions that will create jobs and drive down health care costs."

While in the House he headed a group of 16 Republicans that wrote a GOP alternative and told President Obama it was possible to write legislation that could draw support from 70 percent to 80 percent of Congress. But he said a host of issues likely would cost his vote, starting with the proposed creation of a government-run plan to compete with private insurers. "I'm a big believer that a government-organized system would be much more effective than a government-operated system," he said in March 2009.

A member of the Commerce, Science and Transportation Committee, where he is the ranking Republican on the Competitiveness, Innovation and Export Promotion Subcommittee, he hopes to see final approval of pending trade agreements with Colombia, Panama and South Korea to bolster the exports from Missouri's farms and agribusinesses. As House majority whip in 2005, he helped push the Central America Free Trade Agreement to a narrow victory in the chamber.

In his first term, Blunt in 1997 voted against continuing China's most-favored-nation trade status, one of 79 House Republicans to do so. He expressed concern about China's record of religious persecution and other human rights violations. But three years later, he was part of the GOP whip team that helped win permanent normal trade relations for China.

Blunt has made energy policy one of his top priorities, and he is strongly opposed to cap-and-trade proposals for addressing greenhouse gas emissions. He urges an "all of the above" policy that encourages increased production of domestic oil, coal and natural gas. During the 110th Congress (2007-08), he chaired a GOP energy task force that led to a push for more oil and gas drilling and incentives for alternative energy.

As a House member, Blunt earned high grades from National Right to Life and the National Rifle Association, and he won solid high-80s to mid-90s scores from the American Conservative Union. He has blasted "record deficits and debts and out-of-control federal spending" by Democratic lawmakers, and he supports making the 2001 and 2003 tax cuts permanent.

But Blunt knows how to reach across the aisle. As minority whip in 2008, he teamed up with Majority Leader Steny H. Hoyer, a Maryland Democrat, on a clarification of the Americans with Disabilities Act and bipartisan legislation to reduce access to the chemicals that compose methamphetamines.

The two also worked together on an electronic surveillance overhaul that shielded telecommunications companies from liability suits when assisting the government. Blunt was named to the House Select Intelligence Committee in 2009, and he now serves on the Senate Select Intelligence panel.

Blunt once seemed a shoo-in to succeed DeLay as GOP leader. But he lost traction after the Texan left under an ethics cloud. In February 2006, Blunt fell shy of a majority needed to win a first-ballot caucus race and lost the second round to John A. Boehner of Ohio, who attracted backers of a third candidate, Arizona's John Shadegg. Instead of stepping aside as whip, Blunt kept that job. After the GOP lost its majority in the 2006 elections, Boehner and Blunt prevailed against conservative challengers.

A network of allies on both ends of Pennsylvania Avenue and on K Street helped Blunt win close votes, such as passage of CAFTA in 2005 and the Medicare prescription drug benefit in 2003. It also helped him to survive ethics questions about ties to lobbyists. In 2002, he tried to slip a provision benefiting Philip Morris USA into a homeland security bill at a time he was romantically involved with a Philip Morris lobbyist, Abigail Perlman, whom he later married after divorcing his first wife.

The son of a dairy farmer and a state legislator, Blunt was raised on a farm near Springfield. He still lives on a farm near there, and each summer he conducts an agricultural tour of the district, visiting farms and ranches and bringing in foreign trade representatives from Asia. He is the top Republican on the spending panel that handles agriculture.

After college, he became a high school government and history teacher. But he was active in politics at an early age, working in 1972 on an unsuccessful congressional bid by Republican John Ashcroft, who later became governor, senator and then U.S. attorney general. A year later, Blunt was appointed Greene County clerk by Missouri Gov. Christopher S. Bond, a Republican.

Blunt won the first of two terms as Missouri secretary of state in 1984. That set the stage for his campaign for governor in 1992. After losing the GOP primary, Blunt accepted the presidency of his alma mater, Southwest Baptist University. But he jumped back into public life when GOP Rep. Mel Hancock announced his retirement in 1996. Blunt cruised to victory with 65 percent of the vote and was easily re-elected in succeeding years.

When Bond, who had moved to the Senate, announced his retirement, Blunt entered the race as the favorite and cemented that spot when former state Treasurer Sarah Steelman passed on the contest.

Missouri Secretary of State Robin Carnahan, whose family has dominated state Democratic politics for decades, stayed within shouting distance in most polls. The seat was one of the very few Democrats thought, at least early in the 2010 cycle, they had a chance to take away from the Republicans.

Carnahan tried to tie Blunt to DeLay and Bush and paint him as a Washington insider — all of which accurately described Blunt. He just as accurately pointed to Carnahan's ties to the policies of congressional Democrats, highlighting her support for the 2009 economic stimulus and the health care overhaul.

Riding the Republican wave, Blunt grew his lead and won going away, 54 percent to 41 percent. He won every county in the state except for St. Louis.

Key Votes (while House member)

2010

Overhaul the nation's health insurance system	NO
Allow for repeal of "don't ask, don't tell"	NO
Overhaul financial services industry regulation	NO
Limit use of new Afghanistan War funds to troop withdrawal activities	NO
Change oversight of offshore drilling and lift oil spill liability cap	?
Provide a path to legal status for some children of illegal immigrants	?
Extend Bush-era income tax cuts for two years	YES

2009

Expand the Children's Health Insurance Program	NO
Provide $787 billion in tax cuts and spending increases to stimulate the economy	NO
Allow bankruptcy judges to modify certain primary-residence mortgages	NO
Create a cap-and-trade system to limit greenhouse gas emissions	NO
Provide $2 billion for the "cash for clunkers" program	YES
Establish the government as the sole provider of student loans	NO
Restrict federally funded insurance coverage for abortions in health care overhaul	YES

CQ Vote Studies (while House member)

	PARTY UNITY		PRESIDENTIAL SUPPORT	
	SUPPORT	OPPOSE	SUPPORT	OPPOSE
2010	96%	4%	29%	71%
2009	91%	9%	24%	76%
2008	97%	3%	80%	20%
2007	98%	2%	90%	10%
2006	98%	2%	97%	3%
2005	98%	2%	91%	9%
2004	97%	3%	100%	0%
2003	98%	2%	100%	0%
2002	98%	2%	91%	9%
2001	98%	2%	95%	5%

Interest Groups (while House member)

	AFL-CIO	ADA	CCUS	ACU
2010	0%	0%	80%	100%
2009	14%	5%	87%	92%
2008	7%	15%	83%	88%
2007	13%	10%	79%	96%
2006	7%	0%	100%	88%
2005	14%	0%	93%	96%
2004	7%	0%	100%	96%
2003	0%	5%	97%	88%
2002	14%	0%	100%	100%
2001	17%	5%	95%	96%

Rep. William Lacy Clay (D)

Capitol Office
225-2406
lacyclay.house.gov
2418 Rayburn Bldg. 20515-2501; fax 225-1725

Committees
Financial Services
Oversight & Government Reform

Residence
St. Louis

Born
July 27, 1956; St. Louis, Mo.

Religion
Roman Catholic

Family
Divorced; two children

Education
U. of Maryland, B.S. 1983 (government & politics)

Career
Congressional aide; paralegal; real estate agent

Political Highlights
Mo. House, 1983-91; Mo. Senate, 1991-2000

ELECTION RESULTS

2010 GENERAL

William Lacy Clay (D)	135,907	73.6%
Robyn Hamlin (R)	43,649	23.6%
Julie Stone (LIBERT)	5,223	2.8%

2010 PRIMARY

William Lacy Clay (D)	37,041	81.2%
Candice Britton (D)	8,546	18.7%

2008 GENERAL

William Lacy Clay (D)	242,570	86.9%
Robb Cunningham (LIBERT)	36,700	13.1%

Previous Winning Percentages
2006 (73%); 2004 (75%); 2002 (70%); 2000 (75%)

Elected 2000; 6th term

A second-generation congressman from St. Louis, Clay has become a spokesman for open government, including increasing the public's access to official documents. He is a senior member of both the Financial Services and Oversight and Government Reform panels, and he led the latter's subcommittee in charge of overseeing the 2010 census in the 111th Congress.

Clay shares the liberal views of his father, William L. Clay, an African-American political pioneer who served in the House for 32 years. In his sixth term, the younger Clay has never had an annual "party unity" score — the percentage of votes in which he sides with a majority of Democrats against a majority of Republicans — below 94.

As chairman of the Oversight and Government Reform Subcommittee on Information Policy, Census and National Archives in the 110th (2007-08) and 111th (2009-10) Congresses, Clay aggressively pushed the executive branch to adopt open-government policies, the issue on which he has done his most successful legislating.

Over the objections of the Bush administration, Clay won House passage in March 2007 of legislation to stop former presidents and vice presidents from shielding their records from the public. The legislation would have upended President George W. Bush's executive order of 2001 — aimed at protecting some of his father's White House records — that allowed former Oval Office occupants and their successors to keep certain documents secret.

Another House-passed bill that emerged from Clay's subcommittee would have required presidential libraries to disclose the identities of big donors. Both bills stalled in the Senate during the 110th Congress. Undeterred, Clay pushed them through the House again in early 2009. Though they both failed to win Senate passage the second time around, President Obama reversed the 2001 order one day into his administration.

Clay's persistence on open government paid off late in 2007 when Bush agreed to tighten the timeline by which executive branch agencies must respond to Freedom of Information Act requests. In the past, requesters from the public or media had sometimes waited years for responses. The law now requires agencies to respond to such requests within 20 business days and to establish a system for tracking the requests. "Nothing undermines public confidence as much as obstruction and obsessive secrecy," Clay said.

The census was Clay's foremost concern during the 111th Congress. He is among those who argue that the Census Bureau routinely leaves poor people and minorities out of its count, and he began the 111th with a series of hearings examining the bureau's strategy for getting the count right, while pressuring the agency to expand its outreach campaign to minority communities.

When GOP Sens. David Vitter of Louisiana and Robert F. Bennett of Utah suggested adding a question about immigration status to the form, Clay said they were playing politics with the census.

He helped lead an effort to have the postmaster general investigate whether an April 2010 mailing sent by the Republican National Committee violated a federal law aimed at preventing deceptive mailers about the census from reaching census recipients. He backed follow-up legislation by Republican Darrell Issa of California, now the Oversight and Government Reform chairman, that would prohibit use of the word "census" in any way that was visible through the envelope or on a wrapper. The bill was signed into law in May 2010. At the end of the process, he called the 2010 census "efficient and well oiled."

Clay also holds a leadership position on Financial Services, where he is the top Democrat on the Domestic Monetary Policy and Technology Subcommittee. In the fall of 2008 he turned aside a personal appeal from Obama and voted against a $700 billion financial rescue plan for Wall Street.

Clay also has occasionally deviated from Democratic orthodoxy on free trade, supporting a 2007 deal with Peru, even after he voted against a similar pact with Central American countries in 2005.

As Democrats took charge of the House in 2007, he was one of just 21 in his party to vote against their leaders' lobbying and ethics overhaul package. He said the bill, which became law, would "mandate unprecedented levels of record-keeping and disclosure that are more burdensome than productive."

He was among several Congressional Black Caucus members who supported a resolution sponsored by another caucus member, Ohio Democrat Marcia L. Fudge, that would block the independent Office of Congressional Ethics, created by the 2007 law, from making its investigations public and require a sworn complaint from a witness with direct knowledge of alleged wrongdoing before opening an investigation.

"Our own House committee does not need assistance," Clay said in August 2010. "Members who are under investigation don't know which one takes priority or who to respond to. There's a lot of confusion."

Clay is an avid cook and a golf fanatic, but his mother told a local newspaper that politics "has been his life." He was 12 when his father was elected to Congress, and he spent his teenage years in suburban Maryland, attending high school in Silver Spring and college at the University of Maryland. To pay for college, Clay was a House doorman for six years.

He was starting law school when an opening in the Missouri House led him back to St. Louis to run in a special election. He spent 18 years in the General Assembly, serving eight years in the House before winning a 1991 special election for a state Senate vacancy. He supplemented his part-time legislator's salary by working in real estate and as a paralegal.

When a judge ruled that the state had to allow the Ku Klux Klan to "adopt" a stretch of Interstate 55 to keep it clean, Clay orchestrated legislative action to name that segment of the road after civil rights icon Rosa Parks.

Clay was the presumed heir to the 1st District seat from the moment his father announced his retirement in 1999. The younger Clay both embraced his father and declared his independence when he entered the race to succeed him. He won easily in 2000 with 75 percent of the vote. The district was altered some after the 2000 census, but he has had no problems winning re-election over the ensuing decade.

Key Votes

2010

Overhaul the nation's health insurance system	YES
Allow for repeal of "don't ask, don't tell"	YES
Overhaul financial services industry regulation	YES
Limit use of new Afghanistan War funds to troop withdrawal activities	YES
Change oversight of offshore drilling and lift oil spill liability cap	YES
Provide a path to legal status for some children of illegal immigrants	YES
Extend Bush-era income tax cuts for two years	YES

2009

Expand the Children's Health Insurance Program	YES
Provide $787 billion in tax cuts and spending increases to stimulate the economy	YES
Allow bankruptcy judges to modify certain primary-residence mortgages	YES
Create a cap-and-trade system to limit greenhouse gas emissions	YES
Provide $2 billion for the "cash for clunkers" program	YES
Establish the government as the sole provider of student loans	YES
Restrict federally funded insurance coverage for abortions in health care overhaul	NO

CQ Vote Studies

	PARTY UNITY		PRESIDENTIAL SUPPORT	
	SUPPORT	OPPOSE	SUPPORT	OPPOSE
2010	97%	3%	80%	20%
2009	99%	1%	96%	4%
2008	97%	3%	11%	89%
2007	99%	1%	4%	96%
2006	94%	6%	28%	72%

Interest Groups

	AFL-CIO	ADA	CCUS	ACU
2010	92%	85%	25%	0%
2009	100%	100%	33%	4%
2008	100%	100%	47%	8%
2007	100%	95%	61%	4%
2006	93%	90%	67%	16%

Missouri 1

North St. Louis; northeast St. Louis County

Flanked by the Mississippi and Missouri rivers, the heavily Democratic, St. Louis-based 1st is a mixture of poor urban neighborhoods, middle-class suburbs and a business district that once was the center of one of the five largest cities in the United States. St. Louis has hemorrhaged more than 60 percent of its population since it peaked in 1950. Frustrated by failing schools and aging housing stock, residents were lured to suburbia, where seemingly endless acres were converted from farmland. The district as a whole has shed more than 5 percent of its population in the last 10 years, and the 1st is now one of the least-populous districts in the nation ahead of decennial remapping.

The 1st takes in the northern half of St. Louis, including popular attractions, such as the Gateway Arch and Forest Park, which attracts millions of visitors every year and is about 500 acres larger than New York's Central Park. Developers and lawmakers have poured billions of dollars into downtown projects, including a new stadium for baseball's St. Louis Cardinals, and have seen some success despite the exodus of residents. Key employers

Boeing, BJC HealthCare and Monsanto are scattered throughout the 1st, but cuts at Monsanto and the closure of several corporate headquarters in the city have hurt the workforce.

In the St. Louis County suburbs, Lambert International Airport serves as the region's main airport, and there are plans for major renovation of visitors' services there. A Ford SUV assembly plant in Hazelwood closed in 2006, eliminating nearly 1,500 local jobs, but officials hope to begin developing the land into a commercial and light-industrial business park.

By far the state's most heavily Democratic district, the 1st gave Barack Obama 80 percent of its vote in the 2008 presidential election. More than half of the district's population is black, and local and state contests almost always favor Democrats.

Major Industry

Aircraft and other manufacturing, health care, higher education

Cities

St. Louis (pt.), 150,682; Florissant, 52,158; Hazelwood, 25,703; University City (pt.), 22,012; Ferguson, 21,203; Spanish Lake (unincorp.), 19,650

Notable

The first suit filed by Dred Scott was tried in St. Louis' historic Old Courthouse, now part of Jefferson National Expansion Memorial Park.

Rep. Todd Akin (R)

Capitol Office
225-2561
www.house.gov/akin
117 Cannon Bldg. 20515-2502; fax 225-2563

Committees
Armed Services
(Seapower & Projection Forces - Chairman)
Budget
Science, Space & Technology

Residence
Town & Country

Born
July 5, 1947; Manhattan, N.Y.

Religion
Presbyterian

Family
Widowed; six children

Education
Worcester Polytechnic Institute, B.S. 1971 (engineering);
Covenant Theological Seminary, M.Div. 1985

Military
Army, 1972; Army Reserve, 1972-80

Career
Computer company marketing executive;
steel company manager; university lecturer

Political Highlights
Mo. House, 1989-2000

ELECTION RESULTS

2010 GENERAL

Todd Akin (R)	180,481	67.9%
Arthur Lieber (D)	77,467	29.2%
Steve Mosbacher (LIBERT)	7,677	2.9%

2010 PRIMARY

Todd Akin (R)	72,269	84.6%
William C. Haas (R)	9,494	11.1%
Jeffrey Lowe (R)	3,692	4.3%

2008 GENERAL

Todd Akin (R)	232,276	62.3%
William C. Haas (D)	132,068	35.4%
Thomas L. Knapp (LIBERT)	8,628	2.3%

Previous Winning Percentages
2006 (61%); 2004 (65%); 2002 (67%); 2000 (55%)

Elected 2000; 6th term

Akin's conservatism takes him to the far right of his party, and sometimes even further than that. But mostly he is a loyal Republican with no signs of giving an inch on fiscal, social or military issues.

A member of the Republican Study Committee, the coalition of the House's most conservative members, and a charter member of the Tea Party Caucus, Akin sides nearly all the time with his party on votes that split a majority of Democrats and Republicans — 97 percent or higher every year since first winning election in 2000. The Budget Committee member's departures come when he thinks party leaders aren't conservative enough.

The defense budget is the one area where Akin, chairman of the Armed Services Subcommittee on Seapower and Projection Forces and a former Army lieutenant, consistently supports higher spending. He won inclusion in the fiscal 2011 defense policy bill a multi-year authorization for eight F/A-18 fighters after criticizing the Navy for waffling on the need for the planes.

"What seems to be going on is they want to take the risk of being short on F/A-18s, hoping in five years the Joint Strike Fighter will come in," he told KMOX in May 2010. The planes are built by Boeing Co. in St. Louis.

Akin has backed the use of two engine manufacturers for the F-35 Joint Strike Fighter, arguing that the competition would save money and improve readiness. He opposed a provision added to the fiscal 2011 catchall spending bill early in the 112th Congress (2011-12) to eliminate funding for the program. He also opposes terminating the Marine Corps' Expeditionary Fighting Vehicle, a move Defense Secretary Robert M. Gates said would save about $12 billion.

He tried unsuccessfully in 2007 and 2008 to amend defense authorization bills that called for cuts to the Army's Future Combat Systems, the service's main modernization program. Boeing's Integrated Defense Systems, which is a prime contractor on the program, is headquartered in Akin's district.

Akin has been a staunch defender of the Iraq War, where his oldest son, Marine Lt. Perry Akin, served two stints as a combat engineer. "I pray every night for the troops," Akin told the St. Louis Post-Dispatch in July 2007. "But there's a little motivation to pray extra hard when it's your son."

But Akin, as the top Republican on Armed Services' Oversight and Investigations panel during the 110th Congress (2007-08), criticized his own party for not overseeing the war effectively. He also said the George W. Bush administration had conducted the war "on the cheap."

Despite that criticism, Akin thanked Bush in a January 2009 Washington Times opinion column for "outstanding decision-making on a number of essential issues," including a foreign policy that "blended the soft partnership of daring to dream of a better world with the muscular condemnation and opposition of evil."

Akin has found very little common ground with Bush's successor, and on occasion has used incendiary rhetoric to make his point.

When President Obama's fiscal 2012 budget called for a 9 percent increase for the IRS, he called the potential new agents to be hired "a goon squad." He voted against President Obama's economic stimulus, saying that "never before in history have so many owed so much because of so few."

Akin's opposition to what he considers outlandish government spending predates Obama, however. He also opposed Bush's $700 billion measure, which became law in the fall of 2008, aimed at helping the ailing financial services industry.

His positions on social policy are consistent: He favors restricting abortion and toughening enforcement of obscenity laws, and he steadfastly opposes same-sex marriage and gun control. His six children have been home-schooled and he wants to give parents more choice in the schools their children attend.

Akin is known for his efforts to protect the Pledge of Allegiance. In recent years he has pushed legislation to bar federal courts from hearing constitutional challenges to the pledge. Many conservatives were incensed by a 2002 U.S. Court of Appeals ruling that the phrase "under God" in the pledge was an unconstitutional endorsement of religion. The Supreme Court reversed the appeals court decision in June 2004 on technical, not constitutional, grounds, and Akin has pressed for legislation to prevent further rulings against the pledge. The House has twice passed his bill, but the Senate has never acted on it.

Akin also serves on the Science, Space and Technology Committee. He blasted Obama's decision in early 2009 to lift Bush's restrictions on federal funding of embryonic stem cell research, saying, "The fact that non-embryonic stem cell research is producing superior results makes the decision to issue such an executive order appear more politically than scientifically significant."

Akin's great-grandfather founded the Laclede Steel Co. of St. Louis, and his father worked there as well. Akin grew up in the St. Louis area and studied engineering at Massachusetts' Worcester Polytechnic Institute, where he joined the Army ROTC. After serving as an Army combat engineer, Akin sold computers for IBM in Massachusetts, where he met his wife, Lulli. After four years, he returned to Missouri and worked at Laclede Steel before entering state politics.

During 12 years in the Missouri House, he unsuccessfully sued the state after the legislature approved a schools bill with $310 million in tax increases. He also brought suit against the state's approval of riverboat casino licenses, which led to a state referendum that permitted the licenses yet resulted in stricter regulation of the industry.

Akin's reputation as a doctrinaire legislator spurred opponents to label him ideologically isolated when he launched his campaign for the House seat vacated by Republican Jim Talent, who ran for governor in 2000. But grassroots support enabled Akin to prevail narrowly in a five-way primary. He went on to defeat Democratic state Sen. Ted House by 13 percentage points and has won with more than 60 percent of the vote in every election since.

In May 2011, he announced he would challenge Democratic Sen. Claire McCaskill in 2012.

Key Votes

2010

Overhaul the nation's health insurance system	NO
Allow for repeal of "don't ask, don't tell"	NO
Overhaul financial services industry regulation	NO
Limit use of new Afghanistan War funds to troop withdrawal activities	NO
Change oversight of offshore drilling and lift oil spill liability cap	-
Provide a path to legal status for some children of illegal immigrants	NO
Extend Bush-era income tax cuts for two years	YES

2009

Expand the Children's Health Insurance Program	NO
Provide $787 billion in tax cuts and spending increases to stimulate the economy	NO
Allow bankruptcy judges to modify certain primary-residence mortgages	NO
Create a cap-and-trade system to limit greenhouse gas emissions	NO
Provide $2 billion for the "cash for clunkers" program	NO
Establish the government as the sole provider of student loans	NO
Restrict federally funded insurance coverage for abortions in health care overhaul	YES

CQ Vote Studies

	PARTY UNITY		PRESIDENTIAL SUPPORT	
	SUPPORT	OPPOSE	SUPPORT	OPPOSE
2010	99%	1%	20%	80%
2009	98%	2%	17%	83%
2008	99%	1%	81%	19%
2007	98%	2%	88%	12%
2006	97%	3%	95%	5%

Interest Groups

	AFL-CIO	ADA	CCUS	ACU
2010	8%	0%	86%	100%
2009	10%	0%	73%	100%
2008	0%	10%	89%	96%
2007	8%	0%	80%	100%
2006	14%	0%	100%	92%

Missouri 2

West St. Louis County; north and east St. Charles County — St. Charles

Composed mostly of upper-middle-class white suburbanites, the 2nd is the state's richest district. Its population swelled as a result of decades of residential and commercial migration out of St. Louis.

Economic downturns took a toll on neighborhoods in St. Charles County, one of Missouri's fastest-growing overall since the 2000 census, and subdivisions are dotted with foreclosed homes.

Commuter traffic into the St. Louis business district from St. Charles County remains heavy despite a $535 million reconstruction and improvement project to ease the congestion on Interstate 64 in St. Louis County (shared with the 1st).

Also, many local residents have solved their traffic problems by finding jobs away from downtown, and officials hope to mitigate rising unemployment rates by luring white-collar employers to the 2nd, which has the state's highest percentage of residents who have earned at least a bachelor's degree.

Boeing Co., with plants in the 2nd and on the outskirts of St. Louis (in the 1st) is a key employer, as are financial services and biotech companies. Production at a General Motors plant in Wentzville has picked up recently, but a Chrysler plant in Fenton closed after the automaker filed for bankruptcy in 2009.

The district's dwindling but diverse agricultural industry supports the northern fringes of the Mississippi-Missouri river junction. Lincoln County, located in the district's northwest, is still dependent on both manufacturing and agriculture.

The district's strong white-collar vote favors Republicans at nearly all levels. The 2nd gave John McCain 55 percent of its vote in the 2008 presidential election.

Major Industry
Manufacturing, biotechnology, agriculture

Cities
O'Fallon (pt.), 71,483; St. Charles, 65,794; St. Peters (pt.), 50,828; Chesterfield, 47,484; Wildwood, 35,517; Ballwin, 30,404; Wentzville (pt.), 28,940

Notable
St. Charles was the last established U.S. town that explorers Lewis and Clark visited as they embarked on their journey.

Rep. Russ Carnahan (D)

Capitol Office
225-2671
www.house.gov/carnahan
1710 Longworth Bldg. 20515-2503; fax 225-7452

Committees
Foreign Affairs
Transportation & Infrastructure
Veterans' Affairs

Residence
St. Louis

Born
July 10, 1958; Columbia, Mo.

Religion
Methodist

Family
Wife, Debra Carnahan; two children

Education
U. of Missouri, B.S. 1979 (public administration), J.D. 1983

Career
Lawyer; campaign aide; state legislative aide

Political Highlights
Democratic nominee for U.S. House, 1990; Mo. House, 2001-05

ELECTION RESULTS

2010 GENERAL

Russ Carnahan (D)	99,398	48.9%
Ed Martin (R)	94,757	46.7%
Steven R. Hedrick (LIBERT)	5,772	2.8%
Nicholas Ivanovich (CNSTP)	3,155	1.6%

2010 PRIMARY

Russ Carnahan (D)	36,976	80.1%
David Arnold (D)	6,467	14.0%
Edward Crim (D)	2,697	5.8%

2008 GENERAL

Russ Carnahan (D)	202,470	66.4%
Chris Sander (R)	92,759	30.4%
Kevin C. Babcock (LIBERT)	5,518	1.8%
Cynthia Redburn (CNSTP)	4,324	1.4%

Previous Winning Percentages
2006 (66%); 2004 (53%)

Elected 2004; 4th term

Carnahan has been in Congress since 2005, but he has been in politics all his life. The latest in a line of Carnahans who have represented Missouri in the House and Senate and held statewide offices, he is a dependable Democratic vote, a guardian of his district's transportation needs, and active on foreign policy, environmental and health care issues.

As is the case in other families with deep political roots, his famously recognizable surname is acknowledged as both a help and a hindrance. "It's a two-edged sword," Carnahan has said. "Some people will agree with you or disagree with you based on the name."

An early supporter of President Obama's White House run, Carnahan was an equally enthusiastic backer of the administration's economic agenda in the 111th Congress (2009-10).

He backed the $787 billion economic stimulus measure in 2009. During the months-long health care overhaul debate, Carnahan backed the Democratic measure, calling it "critically important to the continued economic well-being of America." He backed the government-run "public option" that was eventually removed from the House version of the legislation and voted against an amendment by Michigan Democratic Bart Stupak to bar the use of federal money to pay for abortion coverage. In the aftermath of the March 2010 vote, Carnahan made national headlines when his office suggested that an anti-abortion group's placement of a coffin outside his home was akin to a threat of violence. The coffin had been used earlier as a prop during a prayer vigil.

Carnahan has more than a family name to honor while building a solidly Democratic voting record: His political predecessor, Richard A. Gephardt, was the Democratic House leader for 13 and a half years. In 2010, Carnahan sided with fellow party members on 98 percent of the votes in which majorities of the two parties were divided.

International issues are also a priority for Carnahan, whose district includes many refugees, mainly Bosnians, who fled the former Yugoslavia. In late 2009 he was given the gavel of the Foreign Affairs Subcommittee on International Organizations, Human Rights and Oversight Subcommittee. He is now ranking Democrat on the successor Oversight and Investigations panel.

He also co-founded the American Engagement Caucus, a group created to "discuss best practices and lessons learned from international bodies like the United Nations and the African Union."

Energy and transportation issues are another priority for Carnahan. As a member of the Transportation and Infrastructure Committee, he has advocated the expansion and widening of several roads in the district, which is near or crossed by three major interstate highways, as well as construction of a light rail system in his district's fast-growing suburban areas.

Carnahan also promotes alternative-energy programs and supports legislative efforts to address climate change.

In 2009 he backed the Democrats' measure that would create a cap-and-trade system for limiting greenhouse gas emissions. And he introduced legislation in March 2010 that would require the president to develop a strategy to assist developing countries in preserving their environments.

In the 112th Congress (2011-12), Carnahan joined the Veterans' Affairs Committee, where he can tend to the health care issues that interest him as a member of the Health Subcommittee.

Before running for office, Carnahan was an attorney for nine years for the St. Louis-based health care provider BJC Healthcare. But it seems that he has always been in politics.

Carnahan remembers packing into the family's Pontiac station wagon in 1966 at age 8 for the "Caravan for Carnahan" as his father, Mel, campaigned for the state legislature. Led by a flatbed truck carrying a piano on the back, the caravan traveled to Missouri's small towns, where the family handed out campaign fliers while a musician belted out some tunes. Carnahan's first job after graduating in 1979 from the University of Missouri was driving an old Chevy van to take his father to every county as he campaigned for state treasurer.

His Washington office doubles as a museum for his family's history. One wall bears the congressional license plate used by his grandfather, A.S.J. Carnahan, who was named after Confederate Gen. Albert Sidney Johnson and who served in the House in the 1940s and 1950s. Also on display, under a glass-topped coffee table, are campaign buttons for his father, including some for his two successful campaigns for governor. Mel Carnahan died in a plane crash while campaigning for the Senate in 2000. When he posthumously won the race against Republican John Ashcroft, his widow, Jean, who is Russ Carnahan's mother, was appointed to the seat and served two years before losing her bid for a full term to Republican Jim Talent. Russ Carnahan's sister Robin is Missouri's secretary of state and lost a 2010 Senate race to Republican Roy Blunt.

Russ Carnahan attended law school, also at Missouri, where he met his wife, Debra. After earning his law degree, he worked as a legislative aide for the Missouri House speaker.

He worked at a St. Louis law firm before launching his first bid for elected office at age 31. In 1990 he posed an unsuccessful challenge to veteran Republican Rep. Bill Emerson but in 2000 he was elected to the Missouri House, where he served two terms.

Despite his name recognition and four years in the state legislature, Carnahan's election was hardly a sure thing when he ran to succeed Gephardt in 2004. He narrowly beat out a crowded field of nine other candidates in the primary, taking 23 percent of the vote. In the general election, he faced Republican Bill Federer, an author. Carnahan won with 53 percent of the vote. Despite concerns among Democrats that he might be vulnerable in 2006, he won re-election with 66 percent and matched that performance in 2008. He squeaked by Republican Ed Martin in 2010, winning 49 percent to Martin's 47 percent.

Key Votes

2010

Overhaul the nation's health insurance system	YES
Allow for repeal of "don't ask, don't tell"	YES
Overhaul financial services industry regulation	YES
Limit use of new Afghanistan War funds to troop withdrawal activities	NO
Change oversight of offshore drilling and lift oil spill liability cap	YES
Provide a path to legal status for some children of illegal immigrants	YES
Extend Bush-era income tax cuts for two years	YES

2009

Expand the Children's Health Insurance Program	YES
Provide $787 billion in tax cuts and spending increases to stimulate the economy	YES
Allow bankruptcy judges to modify certain primary-residence mortgages	YES
Create a cap-and-trade system to limit greenhouse gas emissions	YES
Provide $2 billion for the "cash for clunkers" program	YES
Establish the government as the sole provider of student loans	YES
Restrict federally funded insurance coverage for abortions in health care overhaul	NO

CQ Vote Studies

	PARTY UNITY		PRESIDENTIAL SUPPORT	
	SUPPORT	OPPOSE	SUPPORT	OPPOSE
2010	98%	2%	93%	7%
2009	99%	1%	99%	1%
2008	99%	1%	16%	84%
2007	97%	3%	4%	96%
2006	91%	9%	40%	60%

Interest Groups

	AFL-CIO	ADA	CCUS	ACU
2010	100%	95%	25%	0%
2009	100%	100%	40%	0%
2008	100%	90%	61%	0%
2007	96%	100%	55%	4%
2006	100%	90%	53%	12%

Missouri 3

South St. Louis; southeast St. Louis County; Jefferson and Ste. Genevieve counties

Bordered on the east by the Mississippi River, the 3rd includes the southern half of St. Louis, as well as older, established suburbs and newer, sprawling ones. Most of the district's suburban middle-class residents commute to St. Louis County's business district, although there are traces of small-scale farming, manufacturing and river trading.

Whereas St. Louis as a whole (shared with the 1st District) has declined in population, immigrant communities have swelled in south St. Louis' residential areas. Traditionally German, the Bevo and Tower Grove neighborhoods now host a large Vietnamese community, as well as one of the nation's largest Bosnian populations. To the south, Jefferson County has been one of the state's fastest-growing areas in the last decade.

Many suburban residents work outside the district, but Anheuser-Busch, headquartered in the 3rd's portion of St. Louis, is a major provider of jobs to the region. The brewery is a St. Louis icon, and thousands of tourists visit its historical center each year. The 2008 merger of Anheuser-Busch and Belgian InBev resulted in massive and continuous layoffs across the metropolitan area. The district's other large employers include a National Geospatial-Intelligence Agency facility and the St. Louis VA Medical Center-Jefferson Barracks Division, which provides medical assistance for veterans. Farther south, on the fringes of Ste. Genevieve County, small farming complements a sizable trading industry along the Mississippi River. The district's blue-collar base favors Democrats, although the GOP finds some support in middle-class communities. The 3rd gave Barack Obama 60 percent of its vote in the 2008 presidential election.

Major Industry
Beer manufacturing, defense, health care

Cities
St. Louis (pt.), 168,612; Oakville (unincorporated), 36,143

Notable
The 1904 Olympics — the first to award gold, silver and bronze medals for first, second and third places, respectively — were held at Washington University's Francis Field.

Rep. Vicky Hartzler (R)

Capitol Office
225-2876
hartzler.house.gov
1023 Longworth Bldg. 20515-2504; fax 225-0148

Committees
Agriculture
Armed Services

Residence
Harrisonville

Born
Oct. 13, 1960; Archie, Mo.

Religion
Evangelical Christian

Family
Husband, Lowell Hartzler; one child

Education
U. of Missouri, B.S. 1983 (home economics & education); Central Missouri State U., M.S. 1992 (education)

Career
Farmer; rancher; farm equipment dealership owner; homemaker; teacher

Political Highlights
Mo. House, 1995-2001

ELECTION RESULTS

2010 GENERAL

Vicky Hartzler (R)	113,489	50.4%
Ike Skelton (D)	101,532	45.1%
Jason Braun (LIBERT)	6,123	2.7%
Greg Cowan (CNSTP)	3,912	1.7%

2010 PRIMARY

Vicky Hartzler (R)	35,860	40.5%
Bill Stouffer (R)	26,573	30.0%
Jeff Parnell (R)	7,969	9.0%
James Scholz (R)	4,259	4.8%
Roy Viessman (R)	3,702	4.2%
Brian Riley (R)	3,197	3.6%
Brian Clark (R)	2,658	3.0%
Arthur John Madden (R)	2,484	2.8%
Eric James McElroy (R)	1,928	2.2%

Elected 2010; 1st term

Hartzler's conservative Christian views inform her political philosophy. She wrote the book on waging faith-based campaigns — it's called "Running God's Way" and is based on her election to the Missouri House.

Hartzler was also at the forefront of a 2004 campaign in favor of a state constitutional amendment banning gay marriage.

Improving the economy, creating jobs and balancing the budget will be her priorities. "We've got to make sure we've got a stable economy for our future and not bankrupt our country with the runaway spending that's under way," she said. Hartzler supports making the Bush-era tax cuts permanent for all income levels. She also calls estate taxes "highway robbery" and says she wants them kept low, if not eliminated.

Early in the 112th Congress (2011-12) she voted to repeal the 2010 health care overhaul. She has said she would prefer a revamp of the tort system and greater transparency in medical pricing.

Hartzler opposes climate-change legislation that would cap carbon emissions. "There's no reason to stifle our energy production here in America when our competitors aren't going to have to abide by the onerous regulations in that bill," she said.

Hartzler has platforms valuable to her district — which is largely agricultural and includes Fort Leonard Wood and Whiteman Air Force Base — on the Agriculture and Armed Services committees.

She said she will work to expand the missions of the military bases. And Hartzler, who with her husband owns an agricultural equipment business, will also have a hand in writing a new farm bill. She will have to balance her support for a safety net for farmers — her farm received subsidies from the government — with her pledge to cut federal spending.

Democratic Rep. Ike Skelton, who chaired the Armed Services Committee, had not faced a competitive election since 1982. But Hartzler was able to tap into voter discontent with Congress, the economy and the Democratic agenda to become one of three Republicans to unseat a committee chairman in 2010. She won with 50 percent of the vote to Skelton's 45 percent.

Missouri 4

West central — Kansas City suburbs, Jefferson City

With the exception of some southeast Kansas City suburbs, the state capital of Jefferson City and midsize Sedalia, the 4th District typifies rural and small-town Missouri. It is laden with lakes, rivers and farmland, and the 4th's northern border is formed in part by the Missouri River.

Agriculture has been an economic mainstay here for decades, and most residents work in small-scale farming. Others work for manufacturers of household goods, and tourism helps rural areas. With miles of shoreline, modern hotels and retail outlets, the Lake of the Ozarks region (shared with the 9th) attracts boaters and shoppers. The lake areas also draw retirees and professionals looking to set up second homes.

The 4th's piece of the Kansas City suburbs has not grown as fast as the area north of the city (in the 6th) and is not as affluent, but does provide some blue-collar manufacturing jobs. Moving east, the district picks up growing Warrensburg and Sedalia, where the Scott Joplin Ragtime Festival is held each June. State government employs more than 15,000 people in Jefferson City.

Voters in the 4th tend to be conservative, but sent a Democrat to the U.S. House for decades. John McCain took 61 percent of the district's 2008 presidential election vote, winning 24 of the 25 counties here.

Major Industry
Government, defense, agriculture, manufacturing

Military Bases
Fort Leonard Wood, 11,682 military, 3,896 civilian (2009); Whiteman Air Force Base, 3,500 military, 2,200 civilian (2011)

Cities
Jefferson City (pt.), 43,057; Sedalia, 21,387

Notable
President Harry S. Truman was born in Lamar.

Rep. Emanuel Cleaver II (D)

Capitol Office
225-4535
www.house.gov/cleaver
1433 Longworth Bldg. 20515-2505; fax 225-4403

Committees
Financial Services

Residence
Kansas City

Born
Oct. 26, 1944; Waxahachie, Texas

Religion
Methodist

Family
Wife, Dianne Cleaver; four children

Education
Murray State College (Okla.), attended 1963-64;
Prairie View A&M College, B.S. 1972 (sociology); Saint
Paul School of Theology, M.Div. 1974

Career
Minister; radio talk show host; civil rights group
chapter founder; charitable group manager; car
wash owner

Political Highlights
Sought Democratic nomination for Mo. House, 1970;
sought Democratic nomination for Kansas City
Council, 1975; Kansas City Council, 1979-91; mayor of
Kansas City, 1991-99

ELECTION RESULTS

2010 GENERAL

Emanuel Cleaver II (D)	102,076	53.3%
Jacob Turk (R)	84,578	44.2%
Randall Langkraehr (LIBERT)	3,077	1.6%

2010 PRIMARY

Emanuel Cleaver II (D)	unopposed

2008 GENERAL

Emanuel Cleaver II (D)	197,249	64.4%
Jacob Turk (R)	109,166	35.6%

Previous Winning Percentages
2006 (64%); 2004 (55%)

Elected 2004; 4th term

An ordained Methodist minister, Cleaver has often sought to minimize the role of race in politics. Merging that philosophy with his new role as chairman of the Congressional Black Caucus will test his noted determination to bring people together across racial lines.

After serving as the first vice chairman of the caucus in the 111th Congress (2009-10), he was elected to the top job for the 112th (2011-12). He says the group will find its own path — one that, at times, might be different than the path followed by President Obama.

That doesn't worry Cleaver.

"The CBC has had disagreement with every president that has come to office since it was created," Cleaver told The Washington Post after his election. "All of a sudden, it's like, 'Oh my goodness, black people are disagreeing with somebody black.' There is absolutely no way that we can function in a manner consistent with the wishes of our constituents and always be in lockstep with the president."

When Cleaver and Obama disagree, though, rest assured it will be a civil disagreement. In 2007, Cleaver formed the Civility Task Force with West Virginia Republican Shelley Moore Capito, and he has been dubbed "an avatar of agreeableness."

Cleaver found himself at the center of the civility debate in March 2010 when a protester yelling at lawmakers as they passed by on their way to debate the health care overhaul appeared to spit on Cleaver while shouting.

"I thought, when I first felt the moisture, that maybe it was an accident. That's why I said something to him, but with all the noise, and the crowd, and everybody's whipped up, he just continued to yell," Cleaver later told KSHB-TV in Kansas City.

Cleaver charged Republican lawmakers with encouraging the protesters and bemoaned what he describes as the increasing polarization of Congress.

"I think when members do that with impunity, it gives [others] license to go even further," he said. "We're up here fighting each other every day and polluting the nation."

Cleaver also disdains efforts by his colleagues to mix religion and politics. In his first term, he led a small group of House Democrats to vote against a resolution expressing support for Christmas.

On the other hand, in 2007 then-Speaker Nancy Pelosi of California appointed Cleaver to a panel on energy independence and global warming with the specific charge to reach out to his fellow ministers to get them engaged on the issue.

Cleaver parted ways with Pelosi in 2010 when the House voted to censure New York Democrat Charles B. Rangel, a member of the Black Caucus, for assorted financial misdeeds.

"I think most of us who really looked at all of the evidence of punishments meted out to others, we came to the conclusion that Charlie Rangel was put through an ordeal and not given a fair deal," he told Roll Call.

Cleaver's reputation for moderation is mostly a matter of style rather than legislative substance. On votes that split majorities of the two parties, he sided with Democrats almost 99 percent of the time during the Democrats' recent four years in the majority. But he can be unusually frank when discussing votes he regrets.

A member of the Financial Services Committee, he joined colleagues in March 2009 in supporting punitive taxes on bonuses to executives of American International Group Inc. The government had rescued AIG from bankruptcy, and many lawmakers were incensed about the bonuses. But shortly thereafter, Cleaver told a crowd of Missourians on Capitol Hill that he had erred. "I joined the cowards," Cleaver said, adding that his vote "was the only time since I've been in Congress that I was embarrassed to go home."

He is a passionate spokesman for energy independence — he uses a 1998 Ford Econoline van, converted to run on vegetable oil, as an office-on-wheels at home — and aims to transform his district into a model of sustainability. His "Green Impact Zone" is a 150-square-block area of urban Kansas City that will feature weatherized homes, a job-training program and an electric smart grid. The initiative was largely funded by the 2009 economic stimulus law. At Cleaver's insistence, a report detailing all expenditures is released every 45 days. He said "it might be the biggest and the best thing I've ever done."

The most prominent item in Cleaver's congressional office is a framed photo of the shack in which he grew up with his father, mother and three sisters in Waxahachie, Texas. Cleaver's description of the dwelling as a "slave shanty" is no exercise in rhetoric: It did in fact house slaves in the 1800s. Cleaver lived there until he was almost 8 years old, when the family moved to public housing. Eventually, Cleaver's father, a maître d' at an exclusive club, saved enough money to buy a home in a predominately white part of town. But racist neighbors soon forced them to move to the black district on the east side.

Cleaver has served as a pastor at St. James United Methodist Church in Kansas City since 1972 and still delivers occasional sermons. For years, he and the rabbi of a prominent Kansas City synagogue preached to each other's congregations. Cleaver also founded Harmony in a World of Difference, an organization that promotes interfaith dialogue.

Cleaver was elected to the Kansas City Council in 1979 and became the city's mayor in 1991. In eight years in office, he helped bring new firms to the region and oversaw the rejuvenation of the historic 18th and Vine jazz district as part of his frequently stated goal of making Kansas City a "world-class city." But he said he was most proud of averting strife at a time when racial disturbances occurred in other urban areas.

In 2004, Cleaver sought to succeed retiring Democratic Rep. Karen McCarthy. Emphasizing his mayoral record, he defeated Republican businesswoman Jeanne Patterson by a comfortable 13 percentage points.

In each of the next three elections, he faced Marine veteran Jacob Turk. Cleaver won 64 percent of the vote in 2006 and 2008. Amid the GOP wave of 2010, he was held to 53 percent.

Key Votes

2010

Overhaul the nation's health insurance system	YES
Allow for repeal of "don't ask, don't tell"	YES
Overhaul financial services industry regulation	YES
Limit use of new Afghanistan War funds to troop withdrawal activities	YES
Change oversight of offshore drilling and lift oil spill liability cap	YES
Provide a path to legal status for some children of illegal immigrants	YES
Extend Bush-era income tax cuts for two years	NO

2009

Expand the Children's Health Insurance Program	YES
Provide $787 billion in tax cuts and spending increases to stimulate the economy	YES
Allow bankruptcy judges to modify certain primary-residence mortgages	YES
Create a cap-and-trade system to limit greenhouse gas emissions	YES
Provide $2 billion for the "cash for clunkers" program	YES
Establish the government as the sole provider of student loans	YES
Restrict federally funded insurance coverage for abortions in health care overhaul	NO

CQ Vote Studies

	PARTY UNITY		PRESIDENTIAL SUPPORT	
	SUPPORT	OPPOSE	SUPPORT	OPPOSE
2010	98%	2%	81%	19%
2009	99%	1%	96%	4%
2008	99%	1%	13%	87%
2007	99%	1%	4%	96%
2006	93%	7%	32%	68%

Interest Groups

	AFL-CIO	ADA	CCUS	ACU
2010	92%	100%	13%	0%
2009	100%	95%	36%	0%
2008	100%	90%	61%	4%
2007	96%	95%	55%	0%
2006	100%	95%	50%	8%

Missouri 5

Kansas City and suburbs

Kansas City has long been known for its blues style of jazz and its barbecue grilling. The Democratic 5th takes in some of the city's minority, lower-income communities and some suburban middle-class areas in Jackson and Cass counties. Today, Kansas City is the nation's second-largest rail hub, and a resurgence in high-end loft communities has lured educated, younger, well-to-do residents to the city.

Most of the 5th's residents live in northern Jackson County cities, with two-thirds of the district's population either in Kansas City (shared with the 6th) or Independence (a small part of which is also in the 6th). A diverse economic base helped the district grow into a transportation and telecommunications hub, and the area is still home to a number of call centers and other electronic-based businesses. The 5th's workforce is mostly white-collar, and tax preparation and personal finance company H&R Block and Hallmark Cards both have headquarters in the district. Some residents still commute out of the 5th to companies in Kansas, but widespread layoffs at white-collar employers have strained the economy and municipal budgets.

Despite several years of uncertainty, the Kansas City area's steel and auto assembly plants still employ thousands of residents. The federal government is a key employer in Kansas City, although the city's Marine Corps Support Activity closed as part of the 2005 round of military base realignments. The southern communities depend on agriculture, and despite economic diversification, the 5th is still a viable market for winter wheat.

With nearly all of Kansas City's black neighborhoods — the 5th is one-fourth black — the district is reliably Democratic and socially moderate. Democrats have held the Kansas City seat since 1949, and Barack Obama took 63 percent of the district's vote in the 2008 presidential election.

Major Industry
Transportation, auto manufacturing, agriculture, telecommunications

Cities
Kansas City (pt.), 302,696; Independence (pt.), 113,245; Lee's Summit (pt.), 82,435; Raytown, 29,526; Grandview, 24,475; Belton, 23,116

Notable
The Harry S. Truman Library and Museum and the Negro Leagues Baseball Museum are in Kansas City.

Rep. Sam Graves (R)

Capitol Office
225-7041
www.house.gov/graves
1415 Longworth Bldg. 20515-2506; fax 225-8221

Committees
Small Business - Chairman
Transportation & Infrastructure

Residence
Tarkio

Born
Nov. 7, 1963; Fairfax, Mo.

Religion
Baptist

Family
Wife, Lesley Graves; three children

Education
U. of Missouri, B.S. 1986 (agronomy)

Career
Farmer

Political Highlights
Mo. House, 1993-95; Mo. Senate, 1995-2000

ELECTION RESULTS

2010 GENERAL

Sam Graves (R)	154,103	69.4%
Clint Hylton (D)	67,762	30.5%

2010 PRIMARY

Sam Graves (R)	54,566	82.5%
Christopher Ryan (R)	11,608	17.5%

2008 GENERAL

Sam Graves (R)	196,526	59.4%
Kay Barnes (D)	121,894	36.9%
Dave Browning (LIBERT)	12,279	3.7%

Previous Winning Percentages
2006 (62%); 2004 (64%); 2002 (63%); 2000 (51%)

Elected 2000; 6th term

Graves chairs the Small Business Committee in the 112th Congress, and his position there, coupled with his conservative views, colors most of what he does in the Capitol.

With gavel in hand, he passed on a 2012 Senate race against Democrat Claire McCaskill, saying "I can have a greater impact on federal policy in the next six years as a chairman in the House."

One of his priorities will be a long-term authorization for Small Business Administration programs "that will bring these programs into the 21st century." Another is oversight of government regulations that he says get in the way of small businesses expanding. "We will also be closely investigating federal policies that have the potential to adversely impact entrepreneurs and stifle job creation," Graves said.

Graves counts among that category the health care overhaul that became law in the spring of 2010 because "health care mandates and tax regulations" would place undue burdens on small businesses. He voted to repeal the law early in the 112th Congress (2011-12). He also opposed a 2010 bill revamping the regulation of the financial services industry, saying it would create "new hurdles" to the success of small companies.

As top Republican on the Small Business panel in the 111th Congress (2009-10), Graves voted against legislation ostensibly aimed at bolstering small businesses by providing them with greater access to credit. He said the bill offered few safeguards to ensure that small businesses would actually benefit and therefore risked wasting $30 billion in federal funds.

In each case, Graves proved a thorn in the side of the Democrats who supported the legislation, even as he failed to block them from enacting new laws. During the financial services debate, for instance, he forced a vote on an amendment to require a new consumer protection agency to consider the effect of the law's rules on small companies. During the health care debate, he offered alternative legislation to allow small-business owners and self-employed entrepreneurs the ability to deduct the full cost of health insurance premiums, saying such an approach was preferable to one that relied on more government intervention. Democrats rejected the amendment while ignoring Graves' health care bill.

On occasion, Graves is willing to see the government take a more active role in the economy, particularly when it will benefit his rural district. He's pushed the Obama administration to call for improved broadband Internet access in rural areas, for example, and supported increased federal appropriations for repairing bridges and helping farmers.

From his seat on the Transportation and Infrastructure Committee, Graves will have a hand in writing the next federal surface transportation bill. Graves says he will fight to ensure that the law continues to require states to spend some of the federal funds they're given to maintain bridges that aren't on major thoroughfares.

A sixth-generation farmer, Graves argues that farmers are at the mercy of factors beyond their control — including the imperative of providing low-cost food to consumers — so government involvement is essential. Formerly a member of the Agriculture Committee, Graves had a hand in a major rewrite of farm and nutrition programs in the 110th Congress (2007-08). The law is scheduled to be reauthorized in the 112th.

Graves' wife, Lesley, is an elementary school teacher, and he is active on education issues. He has pledged to work with Democrats on revamping the No Child Left Behind Act, which is also up for reauthorization. Graves agrees with many Democratic colleagues that the decade-old law — known for its testing and school accountability provisions — has proved too tough. He wants a new version to give schools more credit for success in lifting test scores in some areas, even if they are failing to boost students' scores in others. And he wants the federal evaluations of schools' success to measure the progress of each group of students as it advances through the grades, rather than comparing students with those that have come before.

A lifelong resident of tiny Tarkio, Graves returned to the family farm after graduating with a degree in agronomy from the University of Missouri in 1986. Now, his younger brother Danny and his father, Sam, run the farm, raising corn, soybeans and cattle. He still waxes rhapsodic about the many uses of baling wire and his memories of climbing up on the 1968 John Deere 4020 tractor that his grandfather bought new. When he's in his home district, Graves sometimes helps out.

Graves' involvement in politics was a natural fit, given his family's long history in northwest Missouri government. His great-grandfather, also named Sam, was a Democrat who served on the Atchison County Commission. And Graves' brother Todd was the U.S. attorney for western Missouri.

Graves became involved through the Missouri Farm Bureau, and he once was named the national organization's outstanding young farmer. He spent two years in the Missouri House and six in the state Senate.

Six months before the 2000 election, when Democratic Rep. Pat Danner unexpectedly announced her retirement after four terms, Graves jumped into the primary contest and quickly overshadowed several less-known Republican hopefuls.

The Democrats nominated the congresswoman's son, Steve Danner. But Graves' assertive campaign and conservative politics gave him momentum and the win. He has won re-election easily since, including in 2008, when he won a fifth term with 59 percent of the vote over Kay Barnes, former Democratic mayor of Kansas City. He did even better in 2010, taking 69 percent.

Graves was the subject of an anonymous ethics complaint in 2009 after he invited a business partner of his wife's to testify before the Small Business Committee during a hearing on renewable fuels. Both were investors in a renewable-fuels plant in Missouri. Neither Graves nor the witness acknowledged the relationship publicly at the hearing, but the Committee on Standards of Official Conduct (as the Ethics Committee was then known) exonerated Graves several months later, saying that no House rule prohibited such an invitation.

Key Votes

2010

Overhaul the nation's health insurance system	NO
Allow for repeal of "don't ask, don't tell"	-
Overhaul financial services industry regulation	NO
Limit use of new Afghanistan War funds to troop withdrawal activities	NO
Change oversight of offshore drilling and lift oil spill liability cap	NO
Provide a path to legal status for some children of illegal immigrants	NO
Extend Bush-era income tax cuts for two years	YES

2009

Expand the Children's Health Insurance Program	NO
Provide $787 billion in tax cuts and spending increases to stimulate the economy	NO
Allow bankruptcy judges to modify certain primary-residence mortgages	NO
Create a cap-and-trade system to limit greenhouse gas emissions	NO
Provide $2 billion for the "cash for clunkers" program	NO
Establish the government as the sole provider of student loans	NO
Restrict federally funded insurance coverage for abortions in health care overhaul	YES

CQ Vote Studies

	PARTY UNITY		PRESIDENTIAL SUPPORT	
	SUPPORT	OPPOSE	SUPPORT	OPPOSE
2010	95%	5%	28%	72%
2009	98%	2%	19%	81%
2008	89%	11%	54%	46%
2007	92%	8%	69%	31%
2006	98%	2%	95%	5%

Interest Groups

	AFL-CIO	ADA	CCUS	ACU
2010	8%	0%	88%	100%
2009	11%	0%	79%	96%
2008	47%	40%	83%	88%
2007	42%	15%	95%	82%
2006	15%	0%	100%	88%

Missouri 6
Northwest — St. Joseph, part of Kansas City

Set in Missouri's northwest sector, the 6th is bordered by Iowa to the north and the Missouri River to the west and much of the south. Rich farmland continues to fuel the district's economy, while suburban areas surrounding Kansas City and St. Joseph — both located on the Missouri River — provide a solid middle-class workforce for the area's shipping and manufacturing industries.

Platte, Clay and eastern Jackson counties surround Kansas City (shared with the 5th). Platte County's Kansas City International Airport, a major hub for Southwest Airlines, provides many district jobs. After a series of layoffs at a Ford assembly plant in Claycomo, production levels have risen and the company has invested hundreds of millions of dollars to retool the facility. But further cuts at the local Harley-Davidson plant have hurt the manufacturing workforce.

The state's largest city north of Kansas City — about an hour's drive — is St. Joseph, which was a Pony Express terminus for riders carrying mail to and from California in the early 1860s. It remains a distribution center and a district economic hub.

Outside of the two metropolitan areas, farmland spreads for miles. Corn and livestock are prevalent here, and processing plants have created a growing market for soybeans, as well, even as small, family farms are giving way to commercial outfits. Craig, in Holt County, is home to the Golden Triangle ethanol plant, and wind energy production is increasing as turbines pop up across the landscape. But several counties across the northern tier are losing population as younger residents move to urban centers or out of state.

The 6th has moved firmly into the GOP column over the last decade. John McCain won all but two of the 26 counties wholly or partly in the district — and lost in Buchanan County by fewer than 100 votes — in the 2008 presidential election. State-level Republican candidates also do well here, especially in the northern, rural areas.

Major Industry
Agriculture, international shipping, manufacturing

Cities
Kansas City (pt.), 157,091; St. Joseph, 76,780; Blue Springs (pt.), 43,598

Notable
The Jesse James Home in St. Joseph was where the outlaw was shot and killed in 1882.

Rep. Billy Long (R)

Capitol Office
225-6536
long.house.gov
1541 Longworth Bldg. 20515-2507; fax 225-5604

Committees
Homeland Security
Transportation & Infrastructure

Residence
Springfield

Born
Aug. 11, 1955; Springfield, Mo.

Religion
Presbyterian

Family
Wife, Barbara Long; two children

Education
U. of Missouri, attended 1973-74

Career
Auction company owner; Realtor; radio talk show
host

Political Highlights
No previous office

ELECTION RESULTS

2010 GENERAL

Billy Long (R)	141,010	63.4%
Scott Eckersley (D)	67,545	30.4%
Kevin Craig (LIBERT)	13,866	6.2%

2010 PRIMARY

Billy Long (R)	38,218	36.6%
Jack Goodman (R)	30,401	29.1%
Gary Nodler (R)	14,561	13.9%
Darrell L. Moore (R)	9,312	8.9%
Jeff Wisdom (R)	4,552	4.4%
Mike Moon (R)	4,473	4.3%
Steve Hunter (R)	2,173	2.1%

Elected 2010; 1st term

Long is a colorful Republican whose first campaign focused on being "fed up" with what he calls career politicians. An auctioneer, Realtor, avid bass fisherman, former radio host and wearer of cowboy hats, Long had never held office before arriving in Congress.

But Long isn't worried about not knowing his way around. He told the Joplin Globe that there is "enough experience in Washington to choke a horse."

Beyond his bold personality and dislike of the establishment, Long will mostly be a dependable vote for the GOP on both economic and social issues.

He says his first order of business is to repeal or defund the Democrats' 2010 health care overhaul, which he has termed an "unmitigated disaster." He voted to do both early in the 112th Congress (2011-12).

He backs giving small businesses more leeway to join together to buy coverage, health savings accounts and overhauling the medical liability system. Specific to his region, he favors loan forgiveness programs to encourage providers to serve rural areas.

He endorses a balanced-budget constitutional amendment coupled with an amendment to cap taxes at a specified percentage of personal income. His committee assignments — Transportation and Infrastructure and Homeland Security — will test his promise not to "seek, support, or enact earmarks."

Long also is a strong proponent of free trade, saying the opening up of new markets is essential to growing the economy of his southwest Missouri district. And he wants to eliminate "obsolete" agricultural subsidies, but is not specific on which ones qualify as obsolete.

Long grew up in his family's furniture business. He started selling real estate and left college for auction school. He opened his own auction company in 1983. He has described his six-year radio show in Springfield as "a poor man's cross between Paul Harvey and Rush Limbaugh."

Long emerged from a crowded and competitive GOP primary field with almost 37 percent of the vote. He then easily defeated Democrat Scott Eckersley in the solidly Republican district, where Roy Blunt, now a senator, had held sway since 1996.

Missouri 7

Southwest — Springfield, Joplin

The 7th District sits nestled in the southwest corner of Missouri. Springfield is the region's industrial and commercial center, while Branson leads the 7th's tourism sector. This part of the state, where unpredictable weather reigns, has a strong farming foundation. Springfield, in Greene County, is a manufacturing hub and also is home to a few large national retail chains.

Nearly 50 percent of district residents live in either Greene or neighboring Christian County. The other population center, Joplin, once a mining center, lies across the 7th in Jasper County.

A family-friendly entertainment destination, Branson is a magnet for country music fans. This town of 11,000 draws more than 7 million visitors a year, and Branson Airport, the first privately developed and operated commercial service airport in the country, helps bring in tourists. Overall, the area relies on the city's more than 50 theaters — including the Andy Williams Moon River, Mel Tillis and Dick Clark's American Bandstand theaters — and the resort industry around Taneycomo and Table Rock lakes.

The southwestern corner of the district supports beef and dairy cattle, along with poultry farming. Expansion of U.S. Highway 71, which runs from Kansas City into Arkansas and will become an interstate highway by 2012, has improved accessibility.

The 7th has long been a GOP bastion. The Assemblies of God, based in Springfield, is among the religious groups that reflect the area's devout, conservative population.

Major Industry
Agriculture, tourism, manufacturing

Cities
Springfield, 159,498; Joplin, 50,150

Notable
George Washington Carver's boyhood home in Diamond is a national monument.

Rep. Jo Ann Emerson (R)

Capitol Office
225-4404
www.house.gov/emerson
2230 Rayburn Bldg. 20515-2508; fax 226-0326

Committees
Appropriations
(Financial Services - Chairwoman)

Residence
Cape Girardeau

Born
Sept. 16, 1950; Washington, D.C.

Religion
Presbyterian

Family
Husband, Ron Gladney; two children, six stepchildren

Education
Ohio Wesleyan U., B.A. 1972 (political science)

Career
Public affairs executive; lobbyist

Political Highlights
No previous office

ELECTION RESULTS

2010 GENERAL

Jo Ann Emerson (R)	128,499	65.6%
Tommy Sowers (D)	56,377	28.8%
Larry Bill (I)	7,193	3.7%
Rick Vandeven (LIBERT)	3,930	2.0%

2010 PRIMARY

Jo Ann Emerson (R)	47,880	65.6%
Bob Parker (R)	25,118	34.4%

2008 GENERAL

Jo Ann Emerson (R)	198,798	71.4%
Joe Allen (D)	72,790	26.2%
Branden McCullough (LIBERT)	4,443	1.6%

Previous Winning Percentages
2006 (72%); 2004 (72%); 2002 (72%); 2000 (69%);
1998 (63%); 1996 (50%); 1996 Special Election (63%)

Elected 1996; 8th full term

Emerson could well be a case study in what went wrong for President Obama during the first two years of his presidency. A moderate who has long worked with Democrats, she looked like a rare Republican representative willing to help the president enact his agenda in 2009. Emerson signed off on a major spending bill and backed Democratic bills to expand health insurance for children and regulate tobacco products.

But that picture changed quickly. By 2010, Emerson was mostly in lockstep with her caucus, at least on the year's major legislative debates. She voted no on the health care overhaul that passed the House that spring, saying she could not support a law that required Americans to buy insurance. She was no more willing to compromise on the financial regulation bill — aimed at fixing the problems that led to the 2008 Wall Street meltdown — that Obama signed into law that summer.

Though she had frequently allied with Democrats on health care issues, she said the law Democrats pushed through "represents a huge intrusion of big government into our doctors' offices, pharmacies and hospitals." She backed repeal and defunding of the law early in the 112th Congress (2011-12).

Emerson also railed against illegal immigration, the budget deficit and EPA efforts to regulate greenhouse gases. Her shift was a clear indication that moderates in the Republican caucus were taking note of the political climate and moving right.

Her adjustment may have made it more difficult to advance her own policy priorities during the 112th Congress. She has typically made more headway with Democrats in charge than she has when her own party rules the House, a reflection of the skills she cultivated as a campaign staffer and lobbyist — and congressman's spouse — before she came to Congress.

But Emerson believes that moderates will still have plenty of cards to play. In June 2010, she became co-chairwoman of the Tuesday Group, a caucus of moderate House Republicans.

And her Appropriations Committee seat will likely keep her in good stead in her district by enabling her to direct federal dollars back home. A $100 million Mississippi River bridge linking Missouri and Illinois bears the name of her late husband, former Rep. Bill Emerson.

At the same time, as chairwoman of the committee's Financial Services panel, she has a voice in continued discussions on the economy and the financial services industry. In fall 2008, she supported a $700 billion measure aimed at rescuing ailing financial institutions, saying it would protect the "paychecks, jobs and retirement savings" of her constituents.

But she soured on those efforts soon after Obama became president. Late in 2009, she said the program had been badly misused. "The money has been spent and re-spent with little regard for the American taxpayer or the financial condition of our country." She demanded it be ended on the spot.

Emerson was steeped in politics from an early age. She grew up in suburban Washington, D.C., while her father, Ab Hermann, was executive director of the Republican National Committee. She says Hermann taught her to get along with Democrats, including family friend Hale Boggs, the powerful Louisiana representative who rose to majority leader before disappearing on a flight in Alaska in 1972.

Like Boggs' widow, Lindy, Emerson followed her husband to the House; Bill Emerson died of lung cancer in 1996 while seeking his ninth term. She has passionately taken up his cause of combating hunger. During the 110th

Congress (2007-08), she sponsored legislation — a version of which became law — to encourage federal agencies to donate leftover food to soup kitchens.

Emerson co-chairs the House Hunger Caucus, which carries on her husband's work by awarding fellowships in his name to individuals interested in receiving training to help fight hunger at home and abroad. "We're the richest country in the world, and we have the means by which to get every person in this country nutrition and food, but somehow there are people who are just falling through the cracks," she said.

Farming is a mainstay in Emerson's district, and she has become a self-taught expert on agriculture policy. Her first choice for an Appropriations subcommittee ranking member seat in January 2009 was the Agriculture panel, though she lost out to Jack Kingston of Georgia. She is among the proponents of creating an executive branch "food czar" to oversee food safety, though she voted to bar funding for nine other such executive branch positions in the fiscal 2011 catchall spending bill the House passed in early 2011.

Emerson is generally conservative on social issues. Although she supports federal funding of embryonic stem cell research, which uses discarded embryos created for in vitro fertilization, she opposes same-sex marriage and abortion. She voted to bar funding for Planned Parenthood Federation of America in the 2011 catchall spending bill.

She says her fear that the health care law enacted in the spring of 2010 would allow federal funds to subsidize abortions was one of the reasons she opposed it. She was also disappointed that the final law did not grant the Department of Health and Human Services the ability to negotiate with pharmaceutical companies over drug prices, which had long been one of her top priorities. She continues to work with Democratic colleagues on legislation that would grant that authority.

After graduating from Ohio Wesleyan, she worked for the National Republican Congressional Committee and then as a lobbyist. In Washington she met Bill Emerson, who was also a lobbyist, and they married. He was elected to the House in 1980. When he died, Emerson ran as an independent in the general election race to succeed him because the partisan filing deadline had passed. She won with 50 percent of the vote, finishing 13 percentage points ahead of Democrat Emily Firebaugh and 39 points ahead of the official GOP candidate, Richard A. Kline. She has not faced a serious challenge since.

In 2000, she married a Democrat, St. Louis labor lawyer Ron Gladney.

In early 2011, she announced she would take a pass on challenging Democratic Sen. Claire McCaskill in 2012, saying she could do more as a senior member of the House than as a junior member of the Senate.

Key Votes

2010

Overhaul the nation's health insurance system	NO
Allow for repeal of "don't ask, don't tell"	NO
Overhaul financial services industry regulation	NO
Limit use of new Afghanistan War funds to troop withdrawal activities	NO
Change oversight of offshore drilling and lift oil spill liability cap	NO
Provide a path to legal status for some children of illegal immigrants	NO
Extend Bush-era income tax cuts for two years	YES

2009

Expand the Children's Health Insurance Program	YES
Provide $787 billion in tax cuts and spending increases to stimulate the economy	NO
Allow bankruptcy judges to modify certain primary-residence mortgages	NO
Create a cap-and-trade system to limit greenhouse gas emissions	NO
Provide $2 billion for the "cash for clunkers" program	YES
Establish the government as the sole provider of student loans	NO
Restrict federally funded insurance coverage for abortions in health care overhaul	YES

CQ Vote Studies

	PARTY UNITY		PRESIDENTIAL SUPPORT	
	Support	Oppose	Support	Oppose
2010	94%	6%	33%	67%
2009	77%	23%	41%	59%
2008	86%	14%	53%	47%
2007	76%	24%	46%	54%
2006	89%	11%	74%	26%

Interest Groups

	AFL-CIO	ADA	CCUS	ACU
2010	14%	0%	88%	88%
2009	29%	10%	87%	72%
2008	60%	65%	83%	56%
2007	71%	50%	85%	60%
2006	50%	15%	93%	72%

Missouri 8

Southeast — Cape Girardeau, Ozark Plateau

The 8th is Missouri's largest district in size, and some of the state's most bountiful farmland can be found here alongside mountains, forests and Mississippi Valley towns. The district has the state's lowest median income (less than $35,000), and only 14 percent of the 8th's residents have at least a bachelor's degree — Missouri's smallest percentage.

Agriculture and lead mining fuel the central counties, while the southeast area, dubbed the "bootheel" because of its shape, is a former wheat-growing region that now produces soybeans, corn, cotton and rice. A slowdown in home construction across the country has put lumber jobs, which have featured heavily in the 8th, at risk. High unemployment rates across all sectors are straining the economy.

The northern counties of Phelps and St. Francois, which had relied on light manufacturing and defense subcontracting firms, hope to boost employment and revenue through infrastructure projects. Located on the Mississippi River, Cape Girardeau is the district's most populous city and is a regional hub for education, commerce and health care.

The district includes four-fifths of the 1.5 million-acre Mark Twain National Forest that dots the countryside of southern Missouri. Frequent flooding and earthquakes from the New Madrid fault line that runs through the eastern portion of the district make the 8th a disaster-prone region, and the strength of levees and highways concern local officials and residents. Preparation for smaller floods along the Mississippi is still an annual spring ritual in the border towns.

The 8th spans the political spectrum from solidly Republican counties in the west and in the northeast along the Mississippi River to territory in the bootheel where residents will back Democrats at the local and state level. Voters tend to be conservative on social issues such as abortion and gun control. John McCain carried the 8th with 62 percent of its 2008 presidential vote.

Major Industry

Agriculture, lead mining, lumber

Cities

Cape Girardeau, 37,941; Rolla, 19,559; Poplar Bluff, 17,023

Notable

The nation's mean center of population following the 2010 census remains in the 8th — it is now northeast of Plato in Texas County.

Rep. Blaine Luetkemeyer (R)

Capitol Office
225-2956
luetkemeyer.house.gov
1740 Longworth Bldg. 20515-2509; fax 225-5712

Committees
Financial Services

Residence
St. Elizabeth

Born
May 7, 1952; Jefferson City, Mo.

Religion
Roman Catholic

Family
Wife, Jackie Luetkemeyer; three children

Education
Lincoln U. (Mo.), B.A. 1974 (political science)

Career
Insurance agency owner; rancher; banker; state finance examiner

Political Highlights
Village of St. Elizabeth Board of Trustees, 1978-87; Mo. House, 1999-2005; sought Republican nomination for Mo. Treasurer, 2004; Mo. Tourism Commission director, 2006-08

ELECTION RESULTS

2010 GENERAL

Blaine Luetkemeyer (R)	162,724	77.4%
Christopher Dwyer (LIBERT)	46,817	22.3%

2010 PRIMARY

Blaine Luetkemeyer (R)	59,684	83.0%
James O. Baker (R)	12,248	17.0%

2008 GENERAL

Blaine Luetkemeyer (R)	161,031	50.0%
Judy Baker (D)	152,956	47.5%
Tamara A. Millay (LIBERT)	8,108	2.5%

Elected 2008; 2nd term

Luetkemeyer earned a reputation in the state legislature as a serious lawmaker and a social and fiscal conservative, and he has cemented that opinion among his House colleagues by standing fast against President Obama's agenda, arguing that it is not in the best interests of the constituents in his reliably GOP district.

Before arriving in Congress, Luetkemeyer (LUTE-ka-myer) served six years in the Missouri House, including a stint as chairman of the Financial Services Committee — he now serves on that panel in the U.S. House — and the Republican caucus. "He's not a grandstander," a former GOP colleague in the state once said of him.

He opposed Obama's economic stimulus package in 2009 and followed up in 2010 by voting for a measure to stop spending money on signs promoting stimulus projects. "Instead of creating the jobs that were promised from the stimulus, this government is throwing away people's hard-earned tax dollars on signs touting stimulus projects," Luetkemeyer said. "Like the majority of Americans, I opposed this stimulus bill, and this latest spending debacle is further evidence that the stimulus was a failure."

The sign legislation was part of the GOP's "YouCut" project, in which people cast votes online for projects they would like to see cut or eliminated. He was an enthusiastic supporter. "Clearly, the YouCut website has given our families an important voice in choosing what they want to see cut."

Luetkemeyer was an ardent opponent of House-passed legislation aimed at lowering carbon emissions through a cap-and-trade system. When Obama visited Missouri in April 2010, Luetkemeyer said "the president should take the time to speak to the folks along Main Street in the 9th District and address the inconsistencies between his support for disastrous cap-and-tax legislation and his stated goal of job creation."

Luetkemeyer is a member of the Republican Study Committee, made up of the House's most conservative Republicans, and cites as his mentor Missouri colleague Roy Blunt, the former House GOP whip and newly elected senator. He has also said he seeks to further the work of his predecessor, six-term Republican Kenny Hulshof. "Kenny and I are very much alike in our basic philosophy," Luetkemeyer said. During his first term in Congress, Luetkemeyer sided with his party on 97 percent of the votes in which a majority of Republicans opposed a majority of Democrats.

Luetkemeyer said his career as a state government official and a banking regulator gives him the experience to deal with economic matters. Language from the first bill he introduced was folded into another measure the House passed in 2009 that aimed to improve the Small Business Administration's entrepreneurial development programs by creating planning standards and a national task force to examine the programs. The Senate never considered the bill.

In a move to save jobs in his district, he co-wrote a letter to Obama in 2009 urging him to reverse his decision to force closure of General Motors and Chrysler dealerships across the country.

As a member of the Oversight and Government Reform Committee in the 111th Congress (2009-10), Luetkemeyer joined Missouri Democrat William Lacy Clay in successfully demanding an investigation in July 2010 of lax safety standards, including incidences of improperly cleaned dental equipment, that might have exposed thousands of veterans to bacteria and viruses at a VA medical facility in St. Louis.

His work in politics is also shaped by his religious views. Raised in a family with strong Catholic values, he taught Sunday school and served on the board of St. Lawrence Catholic Church. He was one of 180 lawmakers who signed a July 2010 letter to House and Senate leaders that urged rejection of a provision in the Senate's fiscal 2011 defense policy bill that would overturn a ban on abortions in Defense Department medical facilities.

Luetkemeyer grew up in St. Elizabeth, and his family raised cattle and hogs on his great-grandfather's nearby farm. He purchased his own cattle ranch after high school.

Luetkemeyer's mother was a teacher and his father an insurance agent. He and his wife, Jackie, now live two houses away from his family home. Luetkemeyer played baseball throughout high school and at Lincoln University; he tried out unsuccessfully for the Kansas City Royals and the Pittsburgh Pirates.

After college, he became a bank examiner for the state of Missouri in 1974 and followed in his father's footsteps to work for the family-owned Bank of St. Elizabeth, serving as a loan officer and vice president. In 1988, he started Luetkemeyer Insurance Agency LLP, which he sold after 20 years.

His foray into politics began with a seat on the Village of St. Elizabeth Board of Trustees, where he served for nine years. In 1998, he won election to the Missouri House. After Luetkemeyer ran unsuccessfully for the Republican nomination for state treasurer in 2004, Republican Gov. Matt Blunt appointed him director of the Missouri tourism division in 2006 to oversee a 10-member state commission.

When Hulshof gave up his House seat to wage an unsuccessful bid for governor, Luetkemeyer jumped in, campaigning as a social and fiscal conservative, voicing opposition to abortion, same-sex marriage and gun restrictions. In a five-way Republican primary, Luetkemeyer won with nearly 40 percent of the vote.

That November, he faced Democratic state Rep. Judy Baker, a former health care consultant. Luetkemeyer, citing Baker's support of abortion rights, said she was too liberal to represent the district. Using $1.8 million of his own money, he won by less than 3 percentage points — far short of the 11-point margin by which Republican Sen. John McCain of Arizona won the district's presidential vote.

Luetkemeyer's 27-year-old daughter-in-law, Amy, was killed in a car accident four days before the 2010 GOP primary, which he won with 83 percent of the vote. He faced no Democratic opponent in November.

Key Votes

2010

Overhaul the nation's health insurance system	NO
Allow for repeal of "don't ask, don't tell"	NO
Overhaul financial services industry regulation	NO
Limit use of new Afghanistan War funds to troop withdrawal activities	NO
Change oversight of offshore drilling and lift oil spill liability cap	NO
Provide a path to legal status for some children of illegal immigrants	NO
Extend Bush-era income tax cuts for two years	YES

2009

Expand the Children's Health Insurance Program	NO
Provide $787 billion in tax cuts and spending increases to stimulate the economy	NO
Allow bankruptcy judges to modify certain primary-residence mortgages	NO
Create a cap-and-trade system to limit greenhouse gas emissions	NO
Provide $2 billion for the "cash for clunkers" program	NO
Establish the government as the sole provider of student loans	NO
Restrict federally funded insurance coverage for abortions in health care overhaul	YES

CQ Vote Studies

	PARTY UNITY		PRESIDENTIAL SUPPORT	
	SUPPORT	OPPOSE	SUPPORT	OPPOSE
2010	96%	4%	29%	71%
2009	97%	3%	27%	73%

Interest Groups

	AFL-CIO	ADA	CCUS	ACU
2010	7%	0%	88%	100%
2009	10%	5%	80%	96%

Northeast — Columbia, St. Louis exurbs

Bordering Iowa and Illinois, as well as five other districts in Missouri, the 9th picks up small towns scattered across the farmland of northeastern and central Missouri. Columbia, the district's single large city, and some western St. Louis suburbs are the 9th's only population centers.

The 9th splits suburban St. Charles County with the neighboring 2nd and encompasses all of adjacent Warren and Franklin counties. General Motors has increased production at its plant in Wentzville, and many residents still work at Boeing plants in nearby districts. Small businesses, a source of economic growth for years, took a hit during the nationwide recession. Nestled along the district's portion of the Missouri River Valley, residents of Gasconade and surrounding counties boast a wine industry that dates back to the 19th century. In other rural areas, the district's economy still thrives on cattle, soybeans and corn.

About halfway between St. Louis and Kansas City, Columbia is a mostly middle-class city. The district's primary economic engine is the University of Missouri flagship campus in Columbia. The school is Missouri's largest public research university, but state revenue shortfalls have required tuition hikes and budget cuts. The city's health care facilities include the Harry S. Truman Memorial Veterans Hospital, and Columbia is a regional hub for companies in the insurance industry.

Historically Democratic, the 9th has become increasingly Republican over the past two decades as white-collar, GOP-friendly voters have replaced blue-collar and rural "Yellow Dog" Democrats in the district. In the 2008 presidential election, Republican John McCain won 55 percent of the district's vote.

Major Industry

Higher education, agriculture, health care

Cities

Columbia, 108,500; Hannibal, 17,916; Kirksville, 17,505

Notable

Samuel Clemens (Mark Twain) was born in the town of Florida in Monroe County and grew up in Hannibal, which attracts visitors to his boyhood home.

MONTANA

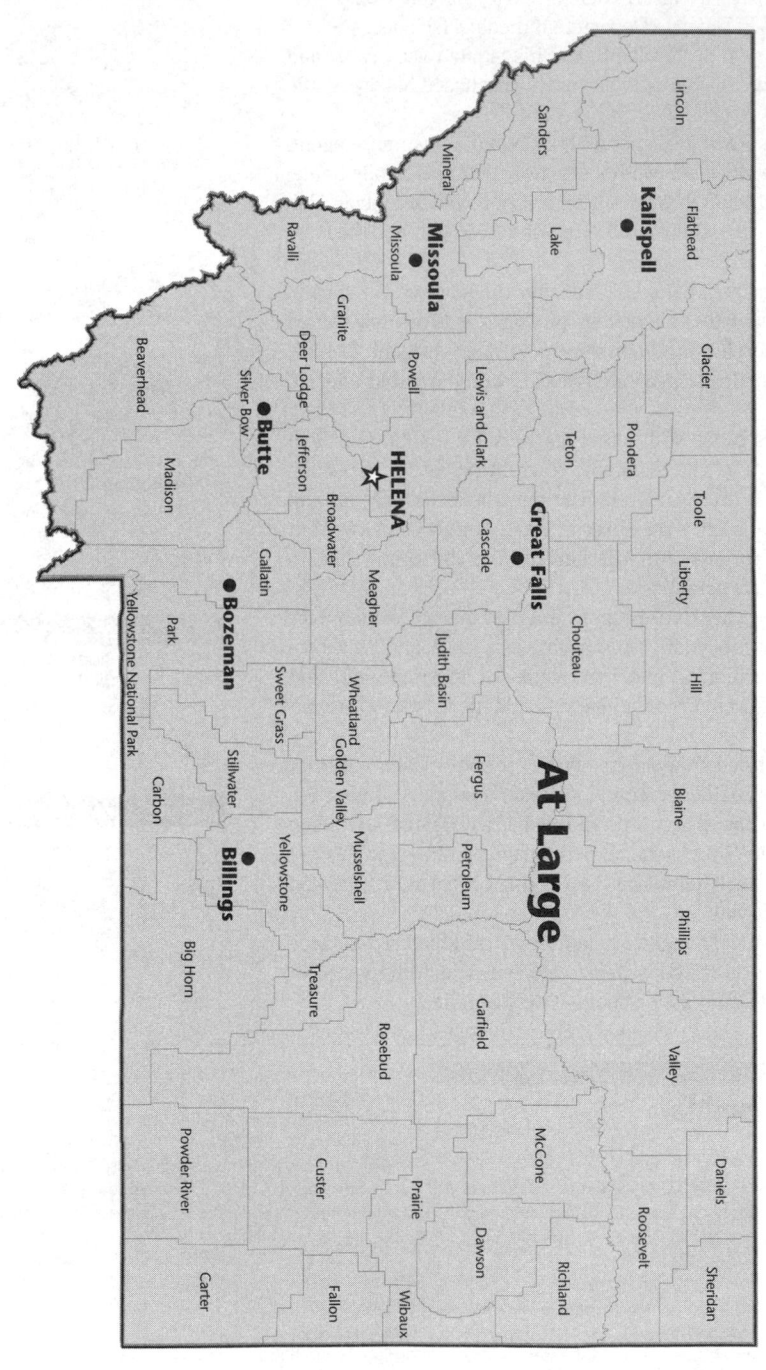

Gov. Brian Schweitzer (D)

First elected: 2004
Length of term: 4 years
Term expires: 1/13
Salary: $100,121
Phone: (406) 444-3111
Residence: Whitefish
Born: Sept. 4, 1955; Havre, Mont.
Religion: Roman Catholic
Family: Wife, Nancy Schweitzer; three children
Education: Colorado State U., B.S. 1978 (international agronomy); Montana State U., Bozeman, M.S. 1980 (soil science)
Career: Farmer; rancher; agronomist
Political highlights: Democratic nominee for U.S. Senate, 2000

ELECTION RESULTS

2008 GENERAL
Brian Schweitzer (D)	318,670	65.5%
Roy Brown (R)	58,268	32.5%
Stan Jones (LIBERT)	9,796	2.0%

Lt. Governor John Bohlinger (R)

First elected: 2004
Length of term: 4 years
Term expires: 1/13
Salary: $79,007
Phone: (406) 444-3111

LEGISLATURE

Legislature: January-April in odd-numbered years, limit of 90 days
Senate: 50 members, 4-year terms
2011 ratios: 28 R, 22 D; 42 men, 8 women
Salary: $85 per legislative day
Phone: (406) 444-4801
House: 100 members; 2-year terms
2011 ratios: 68 R, 32 D; 72 men, 28 women
Salary: $85 per legislative day
Phone: (406) 444-4819

TERM LIMITS

Governor: 8 years in a 16-year period
Senate: 8 years in a 16-year period
House: 8 years in a 16-year period

URBAN STATISTICS

CITY	POPULATION
Billings	104,170
Missoula	66,788
Great Falls	58,505
Bozeman	37,280
Butte-Silver Bow	34,200

REGISTERED VOTERS

Voters do not register by party.

POPULATION

2010 population	989,415
2000 population	902,195
1990 population	799,065
Percent change (2000-2010)	+9.7%
Rank among states (2010)	44
Median age	39
Born in state	54.4%
Foreign born	1.9%
Violent crime rate	254/100,000
Poverty level	15.1%
Federal workers	19,130
Military	3,623

ELECTIONS

STATE ELECTION OFFICIAL
(406) 444-4732
DEMOCRATIC PARTY
(406) 442-9520
REPUBLICAN PARTY
(406) 442-6469

MISCELLANEOUS

Web: www.mt.gov
Capital: Helena

U.S. CONGRESS

Senate: 2 Democrats
House: 1 Republican

2010 Census Statistics by District

District	2008 Vote for President Obama	McCain	White	Black	Asian	Hispanic	Median Income	White Collar	Blue Collar	Service Industry	Over 64	Under 18	College Education	Rural	Sq. Miles
AL	47%	50%	88%	<1%	1%	3%	$43,089	57%	24%	19%	14%	23%	27%	46%	145,552
STATE	47	50	88	<1	1	3	43,089	57	24	19	14	23	27	46	145,552
U.S.	53	46	64	12	5	16	51,425	60	23	17	13	25	28	21	3,537,438

Sen. Max Baucus (D)

Capitol Office
224-2651
baucus.senate.gov
511 Hart Bldg. 20510-2602; fax 224-9412

Committees
Agriculture, Nutrition & Forestry
Environment & Public Works
   (Transportation & Infrastructure - Chairman)
Finance - Chairman
Joint Taxation - Vice Chairman

Residence
Helena

Born
Dec. 11, 1941; Helena, Mont.

Religion
Protestant

Family
Engaged to Melodee Hanes; one child

Education
Stanford U., A.B. 1964 (economics), LL.B. 1967

Career
Lawyer

Political Highlights
Mont. House, 1973-75; U.S. House, 1975-78

ELECTION RESULTS

2008 GENERAL
Max Baucus (D)	348,289	72.9%
Bob Kelleher (R)	129,369	27.1%

2008 PRIMARY
Max Baucus (D)	unopposed

2002 GENERAL
Max Baucus (D)	204,853	62.7%
Mike Taylor (R)	103,611	31.7%
Stan Jones (LIBERT)	10,420	3.2%
Bob Kelleher (GR)	7,653	2.3%

Previous Winning Percentages
1996 (50%); 1990 (68%); 1984 (57%); 1978 (56%);
1976 House Election (66%); 1974 House Election
(55%)

Elected 1978; 6th term

The overhaul of the U.S. health care system signed into law by President Obama in 2010 has Baucus' fingerprints all over it, a testament to the central role the practical Montanan has carved out as chairman of the powerful Finance Committee.

After years of working on trade and tax policy, Baucus staked his claim to the health care debate early on, releasing his own blueprint just after Obama was elected in 2008. With Edward M. Kennedy, the Massachusetts Democrat who chaired the Health, Education, Labor and Pensions (HELP) Committee, absent — he later died of a brain tumor in August 2009 — Baucus and his committee took the lead role.

In many ways, the health care law was the culmination of Baucus' years on Finance. He can be a forceful advocate for the party line but has long been one of the centrist Democrats that Republicans look to on taxes, trade and even Medicare. He has served on the committee since 1979; if he completes his current term, he will have been on the panel longer than any senator in history.

Stylistically, Baucus stands in contrast to previous high-profile chairmen such as Republican Bob Dole of Kansas and Democrats Lloyd Bentsen of Texas and Daniel Patrick Moynihan of New York. Neither a glad-handing dealmaker nor a fixture on the TV talk show circuit, he can be standoffish.

But Baucus continues the committee's tradition of bipartisanship. He had an unusually strong working relationship — even by the clubby Senate's standards — with former ranking Republican Charles E. Grassley of Iowa, who also has taken turns as Finance chairman and still serves on the panel.

Utah's Orrin G. Hatch is the ranking Republican in the 112th Congress (2011-12). He and Baucus teamed up to pressure the Obama administration to move on trade deals with Panama and Colombia by linking approval of those agreements to a deal the administration wants with South Korea.

Baucus broke from his party to back President George W. Bush's 2001 tax cuts, although he voted against the 2003 follow-up that cut taxes on capital gains and dividends. He backed a two-year extension of the Bush-era rates as part of a deal struck in late 2010 between Obama and Senate Republicans.

Baucus was one of two Democrats Republicans allowed to participate in drafting the 2003 Medicare prescription drug law. The liberal Nation magazine dubbed him "K Street's favorite Democrat."

Baucus' tendency to go his own way was on display as he resisted efforts to fast-track the health care bill using special budget procedures and met behind the scenes for months with a health care "Gang of Six" that included Republicans Grassley, Olympia J. Snowe of Maine and Michael B. Enzi of Wyoming. Baucus left the government-run "public option" out of his plan, angering liberals. His gamble paid off only partially — it got only Snowe's vote in committee and no GOP support on the floor, where it was merged with the HELP Committee's version. But the bill signed into law was largely Baucus' handiwork, including an individual mandate initially opposed by Obama.

With Bush in the White House during the 110th Congress (2007-08), Baucus split with his party's majority more often than all but a half-dozen other Senate Democrats on votes that divided majorities of the two parties. But under Obama in 2009 and 2010, he was with his party 93 percent of the time on such votes, demonstrating that on most issues, he is a party loyalist. He helped kill Bush's 2005 push to create private investment accounts in Social Security and helped Obama win enactment of a $787 billion economic stimulus bill early in his presidency. He also dismayed Grassley by helping Democrats clear a 2009 expansion of the Children's Health Insurance Program that was broader than a 2008 version Grassley had helped negotiate. The program covers children from low-income families that make too much money to qualify for Medicaid.

An often-pugnacious negotiator, Baucus had a rocky relationship with his former House counterpart, Ways and Means Chairman Charles B. Rangel of New York, but he worked more closely throughout 2010 with Rangel's successor, Democrat Sander M. Levin of Michigan. But Baucus, who is vice chairman of the bicameral Joint Committee on Taxation with new Ways and Means Chairman Dave Camp, a Michigan Republican, struggled to deliver votes on deals he negotiated with Levin to extend jobless benefits and expired tax cuts.

A member of the Agriculture, Nutrition and Forestry Committee and champion of Montana beef producers, he wants Japan to open its markets to U.S. beef. As a negotiator on the 2008 law reauthorizing farm programs, he helped win inclusion of tighter country-of-origin meat-labeling requirements popular with Western ranchers.

On the Environment and Public Works Committee, where he chairs the Transportation and Infrastructure Subcommittee, he must balance competing interests in his state. As chairman of the full committee in the early 1990s, he was a key player on several major environmental laws. But over the years he has drawn the ire of environmentalists for seeking to protect miners and ranchers from tougher regulations.

Baucus faced conflict-of-interest accusations related to the revelation in late 2009 that he was having a romantic relationship with Melodee Hanes, his former state office director, when he recommended her to be U.S. attorney in Montana. Staff members said the relationship began after Baucus had separated from his wife, Wanda; the two divorced in April 2009. Hanes eventually withdrew from consideration, and the couple announced in late 2010 that they planned to marry.

Baucus attempts physical feats that most men half his age wouldn't contemplate. In recent years, he has suffered a motorcycle accident and major head injury when he fell during a 50-mile ultramarathon (the latter required an operation in which two small holes were drilled into his skull). He also had heart surgery to implant a pacemaker.

Baucus' ancestors emigrated from Germany in the late 1800s and settled in Montana. His great-grandfather Henry Sieben was named to the Hall of Great Westerners at the National Cowboy and Western Heritage Museum. Baucus' brother and sister-in-law now run the Sieben Ranch north of Helena.

He spent part of his junior year in college at an exchange program in France and then went to England, where he traveled with Gypsies before journeying across Europe, the Middle East and Africa. He was in the Congo, he said, when he had an "epiphany" that he should undertake a career in public service.

After finishing Stanford Law School in 1967, he was an attorney for the Securities and Exchange Commission for three years. He returned to Montana in 1971 to coordinate the state's constitutional convention, and in 1972 he won a seat in the state legislature. He captured a U.S. House seat in the post-Watergate election of 1974, ousting a two-term GOP incumbent. Four years later, he arrived in the Senate. Although he had just won a six-year term starting in January 1979, he was appointed to the seat in December 1978 after Democrat Paul G. Hatfield resigned. Hatfield had been appointed earlier in the year after the death of Sen. Lee Metcalf, who had served in Congress for 25 years, but Baucus defeated him in the Democratic primary.

His re-election contests have been routine except for 1996, when Baucus won by fewer than 20,000 votes over Republican Denny Rehberg, then the lieutenant governor and now Montana's sole House member and a Senate contender again in 2012.

Key Votes

2010

Pass budget reconciliation bill to modify overhauls of health care and federal student loan programs	YES
Proceed to disapproval resolution on EPA authority to regulate greenhouse gases	NO
Overhaul financial services industry regulation	YES
Limit debate to proceed to a bill to broaden campaign finance disclosure and reporting rules	YES
Limit debate on an extension of Bush-era income tax cuts for two years	YES
Limit debate on a bill to provide a path to legal status for some children of illegal immigrants	NO
Allow for a repeal of "don't ask, don't tell"	YES
Consent to ratification of a strategic arms reduction treaty with Russia	YES

2009

Prevent release of remaining financial industry bailout funds	NO
Make it easier for victims to sue for wage discrimination remedies	YES
Expand the Children's Health Insurance Program	YES
Limit debate on the economic stimulus measure	YES
Repeal District of Columbia firearms prohibitions and gun registration laws	YES
Limit debate on expansion of federal hate crimes law	YES
Strike funding for F-22 Raptor fighter jets	NO

CQ Vote Studies

	PARTY UNITY		PRESIDENTIAL SUPPORT	
	SUPPORT	OPPOSE	SUPPORT	OPPOSE
2010	93%	7%	97%	3%
2009	92%	8%	96%	4%
2008	89%	11%	35%	65%
2007	83%	17%	41%	59%
2006	79%	21%	61%	39%
2005	74%	26%	45%	55%
2004	72%	28%	57%	43%
2003	74%	26%	54%	46%
2002	67%	33%	88%	12%
2001	67%	33%	71%	29%

Interest Groups

	AFL-CIO	ADA	CCUS	ACU
2010	81%	85%	27%	12%
2009	83%	85%	57%	20%
2008	90%	80%	75%	8%
2007	89%	80%	55%	20%
2006	71%	70%	70%	8%
2005	85%	95%	71%	24%
2004	92%	85%	71%	29%
2003	62%	85%	74%	15%
2002	69%	75%	70%	37%
2001	81%	80%	71%	28%

Sen. Jon Tester (D)

Elected 2006; 1st term

On the campaign trail, Tester enjoyed saying that he wanted to make Washington a little bit more like Montana. That spirit animates his agenda on process issues, where he tries to increase government transparency, and on domestic policy, where he espouses a populist desire to aid rural America.

Tester posts his daily public schedule on his website, listing all appointments and activities. He also prohibits gifts, meals and travel from lobbyists to him or his staff, and bars any staff member who becomes a lobbyist from ever lobbying him or being rehired. Tester has introduced legislation to require federal agencies to post all public documents and records in a searchable online clearinghouse and cosponsored a bill to forbid members of Congress from ever working as lobbyists.

"Anytime you can shine sunlight and add more disclosure in government, the better the government works," he said.

Combining his focus on open government with his spot on the Appropriations Committee, Tester cosponsored legislation in the 111th Congress (2009-10) that would create an online, searchable database of all earmarks, the congressionally directed funding for special projects.

Tester projects an image of a Western moderate, but he generally votes with his party — more than 9 out of 10 times in the 111th on votes that divided a majority of Democrats from a majority of Republicans.

During debate on President Obama's $787 billion economic stimulus measure, Tester showed up with a photo of a Montanan holding a sign reading "Work Needed," and he blasted opposition to the package. "You're either for jobs or you're against jobs," he said. "Now some D.C. politicians say we don't need to pass a jobs bill because the current recession is only temporary. I ask you to tell that to this guy standing on the street in Whitefish, Montana."

Tester later introduced legislation intended to give small businesses in Montana a better shot at federal contracts and says his approach to government is based not on ideology but on how policies affect rural Americans.

"I look at it through the set of eyes that live on that farm," he said, pointing to the picture of his family farm that hangs prominently in his office. "I'm a Montana senator, but I also take into consideration policies as they impact America, but particularly rural America. That trumps everything."

In the closing days of the 110th Congress (2007-08), Tester opposed legislation that provided $700 billion in assistance to the financial services sector. He said it didn't "require the common-sense regulations needed to prevent this mess from happening again." He also balked at loans to struggling U.S. automakers, criticizing Detroit for not coming up with a credible business plan to escape bankruptcy.

In doing so, Tester — a burly third-generation Montana farmer who strides through the Capitol in cowboy boots and a 1950s-style flat-top haircut — helped further burnish his populist credentials.

Tester, who names President Theodore Roosevelt as a political role model, said Western Democrats, like Montana Gov. Brian Schweitzer and Colorado Sen. Mark Udall, have thrived in recent years "because we have a message that folks can believe in," which includes "making sure that we can have a health care system where you can afford to get sick, and you're not losing the farm that's been in the family for generations because you're unlucky enough to get a catastrophic illness."

Tester, chairman of the Banking, Housing and Urban Affairs Subcommittee on Economic Policy, won adoption of an amendment to the financial industry

Capitol Office
224-2644
tester.senate.gov
724 Hart Bldg. 20510-2603; fax 224-8594

Committees
Appropriations
Banking, Housing & Urban Affairs
  (Economic Policy - Chairman)
Homeland Security & Governmental Affairs
Indian Affairs
Veterans' Affairs

Residence
Big Sandy

Born
Aug. 21, 1956; Havre, Mont.

Religion
Church of God

Family
Wife, Sharla Tester; two children

Education
College of Great Falls, B.A. 1978 (music education & secondary education)

Career
Farmer; teacher

Political Highlights
Big Sandy School Board of Trustees, 1983-92 (chairman, 1986-91); Mont. Senate, 1999-2007 (minority whip, 2001-03; minority leader, 2003-05; president, 2005-07)

ELECTION RESULTS

2006 GENERAL

Jon Tester (D)	199,845	49.2%
Conrad Burns (R)	196,283	48.3%
Stan Jones (LIBERT)	10,377	2.6%

2006 PRIMARY

Jon Tester (D)	65,757	60.8%
John Morrison (D)	38,394	35.5%
Paul Richards (D)	1,636	1.5%
Robert Candee (D)	1,471	1.4%

overhaul to direct the Federal Deposit Insurance Corporation to charge banks premiums based on the risk of their activity. According to Tester, community banks currently pay 30 percent of all FDIC premiums while holding only 20 percent of the nation's banking assets. "These are the banks that make rural America run," Tester said on the Senate floor. "They don't deserve to be left holding the bag for risky behavior of the big banks."

He also won't budge on the issue of gun rights. He signed a brief in 2008 asking the Supreme Court to overturn the District of Columbia's ban on handguns, which the court eventually did, and partnered with Arizona Republican Sen. John McCain in 2010 on legislation backed by the National Rifle Association to repeal other firearm restrictions in Washington.

Tester uses his seat on the Veterans' Affairs Committee to help his state's relatively large veteran population (roughly one in nine Montanans). In 2007 he sponsored legislation, which was signed into law, to increase the mileage reimbursement rate for veterans traveling to Veterans Affairs Department health clinics, a big issue in a state as spread out as Montana. He also has worked to set up more VA clinics around the state and to establish a program where organizations operate "Vet Vans," which transport disabled veterans from their homes to VA facilities.

Another of Tester's priorities is overhauling forest management, something he says would reduce the risk of wildfires, create jobs, protect clean water and set aside land for recreation and hunting. He calls the bill "a Montana-made solution" because the state's different stakeholders, including loggers and conservationists, got together and worked out a compromise.

On the Homeland Security and Governmental Affairs Committee, Tester has called for a federal crackdown on the issuing of student visas by unaccredited universities. He says abuses in the system create an avenue for terrorists to enter the country.

Tester also sits on the Indian Affairs Committee. He introduced legislation in the 110th Congress (2007-08) to finalize a water rights agreement among the Crow Nation, Montana and the federal government; the bill stalled after clearing the committee.

Growing up on an 1,800-acre farm near Big Sandy, Tester and his brothers were put to work at an early age. The labor came at a price. Grinding meat as a child, he severed three fingers on his left hand. But Tester relishes farm work nonetheless, calling the long rides on his tractor during breaks back home ideal times to think through the issues facing Congress.

He had an early interest in politics and got involved in student government during high school. After graduating from college, he taught music for a couple of years at his hometown elementary school. He gave up teaching to concentrate on the farm, where the family also operated a custom butcher shop his parents had started in the 1960s. They went organic in 1987 and now grow wheat, barley, lentils, peas, millet, buckwheat, alfalfa and hay. In 2007, Tester's daughter and son-in-law moved back to the farm to run the place in his absence.

Tester served as chairman of the Big Sandy school board and of the local Soil Conservation Service Committee before winning election to the Montana Senate in 1998. He rose to minority whip and minority leader before becoming president of the state Senate in 2005.

Facing term limits, Tester entered the 2006 Senate race. He trounced state Auditor John Morrison, a better-known, better-funded candidate backed by the Democratic establishment. Morrison was leading in initial polls but lost support following revelations of an affair. In November, Tester beat the incumbent Republican, Conrad Burns, by less than 1 percentage point, taking just under 50 percent of the vote. Republicans have targeted the seat in 2012 and enlisted Montana's lone House member, Denny Rehberg, to challenge Tester.

Key Votes

2010

Pass budget reconciliation bill to modify overhauls of health care and federal student loan programs	YES
Proceed to disapproval resolution on EPA authority to regulate greenhouse gases	NO
Overhaul financial services industry regulation	YES
Limit debate to proceed to a bill to broaden campaign finance disclosure and reporting rules	YES
Limit debate on an extension of Bush-era income tax cuts for two years	YES
Limit debate on a bill to provide a path to legal status for some children of illegal immigrants	NO
Allow for a repeal of "don't ask, don't tell"	YES
Consent to ratification of a strategic arms reduction treaty with Russia	YES

2009

Prevent release of remaining financial industry bailout funds	#
Make it easier for victims to sue for wage discrimination remedies	YES
Expand the Children's Health Insurance Program	YES
Limit debate on the economic stimulus measure	YES
Repeal District of Columbia firearms prohibitions and gun registration laws	YES
Limit debate on expansion of federal hate crimes law	YES
Strike funding for F-22 Raptor fighter jets	NO

CQ Vote Studies

	PARTY UNITY		PRESIDENTIAL SUPPORT	
	SUPPORT	OPPOSE	SUPPORT	OPPOSE
2010	89%	11%	97%	3%
2009	92%	8%	97%	3%
2008	92%	8%	30%	70%
2007	84%	16%	37%	63%

Interest Groups

	AFL-CIO	ADA	CCUS	ACU
2010	81%	85%	36%	20%
2009	89%	90%	57%	16%
2008	90%	85%	63%	16%
2007	95%	95%	30%	16%

Rep. Denny Rehberg (R)

Capitol Office
225-3211
www.house.gov/rehberg
2448 Rayburn Bldg. 20515-2601; fax 225-5687

Committees
Appropriations
   (Labor-HHS-Education - Chairman)

Residence
Billings

Born
Oct. 5, 1955; Billings, Mont.

Religion
Episcopalian

Family
Wife, Janice Lenhardt Rehberg; three children

Education
Montana State U., attended 1973-74; Washington
State U., B.A. 1977 (political science)

Career
Congressional aide; rancher; Realtor

Political Highlights
Mont. House, 1985-91; lieutenant governor, 1991-97;
Republican nominee for U.S. Senate, 1996

ELECTION RESULTS

2010 GENERAL

Denny Rehberg (R)	217,696	60.4%
Dennis McDonald (D)	121,954	33.8%
Mike Fellows (LIBERT)	20,691	5.7%

2010 PRIMARY

Denny Rehberg (R)	96,796	74.7%
Mark T. French (R)	25,344	19.6%
A.J. Otjen (R)	7,461	5.8%

2008 GENERAL

Denny Rehberg (R)	308,470	64.1%
John Driscoll (D)	155,930	32.4%
Mike Fellows (LIBERT)	16,500	3.4%

Previous Winning Percentages
2006 (59%); 2004 (64%); 2002 (65%); 2000 (52%)

Elected 2000; 6th term

When the 112th Congress began, Rehberg took the gavel of the Appropriations panel with jurisdiction over the biggest chunk of spending in the budget. But within a month of assuming the chairmanship, he cast his eyes elsewhere, announcing he would be a Senate candidate in 2012.

"I'm willing to give that up to put my name on the ballot to create a contrast of philosophies between those that believe government is the solution and those of us who believe small business is the solution," Rehberg (REE-berg) told the Billings Gazette in early February 2011.

It will be Rehberg's second attempt. In 1996, he came within 5 percentage points of defeating Democrat Max Baucus, even as the incumbent was outspending him almost 3-to-1.

Money isn't likely to be a problem in 2012. Republicans and independent expenditure groups are sure to focus on the race. And Rehberg is one of the wealthiest members of Congress. His family ranch and other holdings were worth at least $11.5 million in 2009, according to Roll Call. Rehberg looks the part of the conservative Westerner — over the years his Capitol Hill office has been adorned with a mounted buffalo head, a stuffed black wolf and other specimens — and he sounds like one when discussing attempts by the federal government to dictate land use and resource development decisions to his state and region.

Rehberg argues that the federal government lays too heavy a hand on the region's land and resources. After a leaked memo revealed a proposal to designate as national monuments millions of acres in nine Western states, Rehberg signed a February 2010 letter to Interior Secretary Ken Salazar and cosponsored a resolution demanding the department release more information about the proposal. He also introduced legislation to bar the expansion or creation of any national monuments in Montana without congressional approval, an exception to the 1906 Antiquities Act added in 1950 for Wyoming.

"While Montanans would love to take Secretary Salazar's word that his agency isn't considering using the Antiquities Act to circumvent public opposition, I would feel more comfortable if the Interior Department didn't actively hide the facts," Rehberg said.

Rehberg chairs the Labor-Health and Human Services-Education spending panel, one of four Appropriations "cardinals" who also are members of the House Tea Party Caucus. He was the only one of the four to oppose the final version of a catchall spending bill enacted in April 2011 that trimmed about $40 billion from fiscal 2011 spending, saying it had too many budget "gimmicks" and not enough real spending reductions.

He was highly critical of the health care overhaul law enacted in 2010 and voted to repeal the law in 2011.

He also serves on the Energy-Water Appropriations Subcommittee, a spot he views as crucial to Montana's dams, which produce the state's hydroelectric power. At an April 2010 hearing, he pressed the Bureau of Reclamation about the agency's funding priorities for Montana water projects.

"Montana produces or provides $50 million a year to the Reclamation Fund," he said at the hearing, "and the president has seen fit to allow us back $3 million toward our two major projects that are both anticipated to cost between $200 million to $250 million apiece."

Coal is another energy source important to the state, which has the largest reserves in the country. Rehberg opposed the Democrats' cap-and-trade bill aimed at reducing carbon emissions, and he backs an "all of the above" energy policy that includes expanded domestic oil drilling, greater use of coal and nuclear power, and expanded research into alternative fuels.

Rehberg will cross party lines if he sees a threat to his state's agriculture sector. He was one of 27 Republicans who voted against the Central America Free Trade Agreement in 2005. He similarly opposed Australia trade legislation in the 108th Congress (2003-04), because he feared more beef imports would threaten the livelihood of Montana ranchers. In 2005, he sought to include language in the agricultural spending bill to speed up implementation of a country-of-origin labeling law that would distinguish U.S.-produced beef from imports. He has also pushed Japan to end its six-year ban on beef imports from the United States.

Rehberg grew up on his family's beef cattle and cashmere goat ranch, competing in gymnastics and playing the drums. His mother taught elementary school, and his father, Jack, ran the ranch and worked other jobs to help support the family. Jack Rehberg was a state legislator and an unsuccessful GOP nominee for a House seat in 1970.

After earning a degree in political science, Rehberg worked as an intern in the Montana Senate, sold real estate for two years, then moved to the nation's capital in 1979 to join the staff of GOP Rep. Ron Marlenee of Montana. He returned to the family ranch three years later and served six years in the state House. He managed political campaigns for Marlenee in 1986 and for Republican Conrad Burns in his successful 1988 Senate bid.

Rehberg was appointed lieutenant governor in 1991 when Allen Kolstad quit to join President George Bush's administration. Rehberg was elected to a four-year term in 1992.

In 2000, he was unopposed for the House nomination when GOP Rep. Rick Hill retired after two terms. He then beat Democratic state school superintendent Nancy Keenan by 5 percentage points. During that race, Rehberg removed himself from the management of the family ranch by arranging to move its 600 goats to the Baucus family ranch. The two families now share the profits from the operation. He has won easily since.

Rehberg was involved in a serious boat crash on Flathead Lake in August 2009 that left him with a broken ankle. Two aides were injured, including one who was in a coma for more than a week. GOP state Sen. Greg Barkus was driving the boat and pleaded guilty to charges of criminal endangerment. Barkus was fined and given a four-year deferred sentence.

Key Votes

2010
Overhaul the nation's health insurance system	NO
Allow for repeal of "don't ask, don't tell"	NO
Overhaul financial services industry regulation	NO
Limit use of new Afghanistan War funds to troop withdrawal activities	NO
Change oversight of offshore drilling and lift oil spill liability cap	NO
Provide a path to legal status for some children of illegal immigrants	NO
Extend Bush-era income tax cuts for two years	NO

2009
Expand the Children's Health Insurance Program	YES
Provide $787 billion in tax cuts and spending increases to stimulate the economy	NO
Allow bankruptcy judges to modify certain primary-residence mortgages	NO
Create a cap-and-trade system to limit greenhouse gas emissions	NO
Provide $2 billion for the "cash for clunkers" program	YES
Establish the government as the sole provider of student loans	NO
Restrict federally funded insurance coverage for abortions in health care overhaul	YES

CQ Vote Studies
	PARTY UNITY		PRESIDENTIAL SUPPORT	
	Support	Oppose	Support	Oppose
2010	95%	5%	26%	74%
2009	85%	15%	26%	74%
2008	93%	7%	65%	35%
2007	88%	12%	68%	32%
2006	97%	3%	95%	5%

Interest Groups
	AFL-CIO	ADA	CCUS	ACU
2010	7%	5%	75%	96%
2009	24%	15%	80%	92%
2008	33%	40%	89%	84%
2007	33%	20%	90%	88%
2006	29%	0%	100%	83%

Montana

At Large

Montana's Big Sky country was explored by fur trappers and miners and settled by farmers and ranchers who could outlast harsh winters. Now known as "The Last Best Place," Montana has become home to a vibrant community of writers, artists and celebrities in recent years.

The economy is supported by natural resources, forcing Montana to find a balance between exploiting its terrain and protecting it, especially in the face of increased global demand for energy resources. Wind, solar and biofuel industries are growing, and alternative energy companies are responsible for increasing numbers of jobs.

Unemployment rates in the northwestern counties have soared well above national and state averages, but the statewide economy remains stable. Butte, the site of decades of copper mining, is the site of a massive superfund toxic-runoff containment effort. The economy also relies on tourism, with three of the five entrances to Yellowstone National Park in southern Montana and Glacier National Park located in the northwestern part of the state.

Political ideology used to split the state geographically. The western,

mountainous half of the state, with an environmental base and a union tradition in mining and lumber mills, leaned Democratic, while the eastern half, a flat plain where wheat and cattle are raised, followed a tradition of rural Republicanism. Now, Democrats find support only in main population centers such as Billings, Great Falls and Butte, as well as state capital Helena and Missoula, which is home to a sizable university community. Voters here will split their tickets, though: In 2008, 13 of the state's 56 counties voted Democratic in the presidential election as John McCain narrowly won the state with 50 percent of the vote, but Democratic Sen. Max Baucus was re-elected easily that year.

Major Industry
Agriculture, tourism, forestry

Military Bases
Malmstrom Air Force Base, 3,142 military, 620 civilian (2009)

Cities
Billings, 104,170; Missoula, 66,788; Great Falls, 58,505; Bozeman, 37,280; Butte-Silver Bow, 33,525; Helena, 28,190

Notable
Montana elected Jeannette Rankin, the first woman in Congress, in 1916.

NEBRASKA

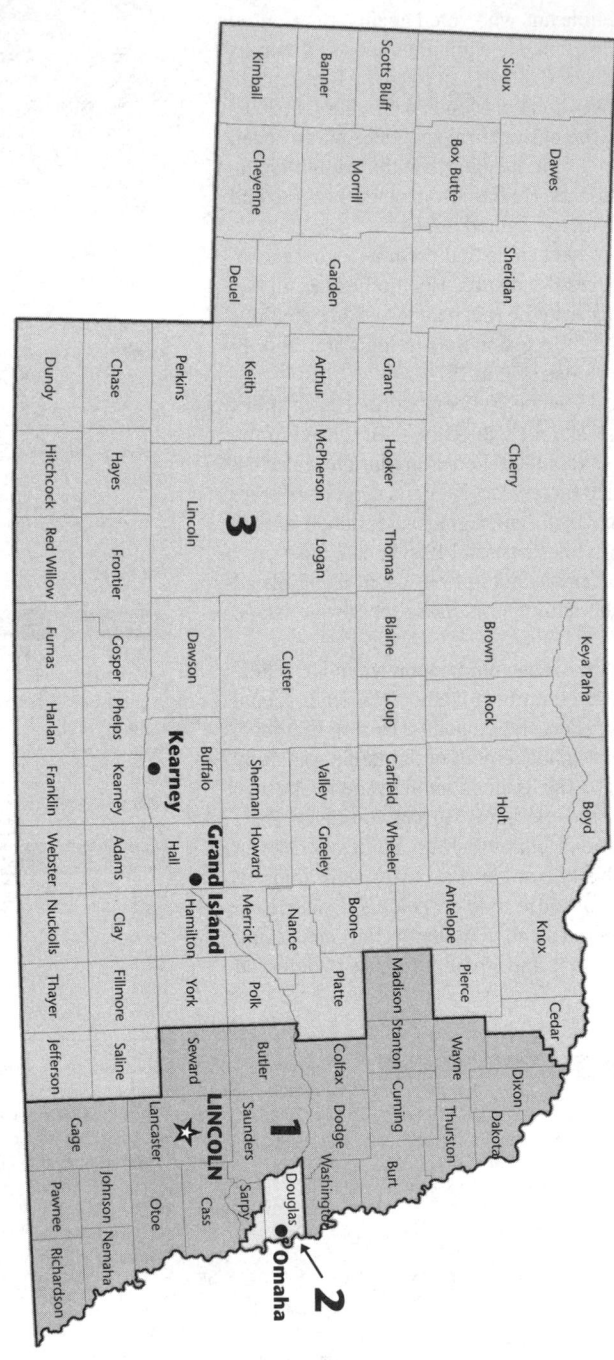

Gov. Dave Heineman (R)

First elected: 2006; assumed office Jan. 20, 2005, following appointment of Mike Johanns, R, to be Agriculture secretary

Length of term: 4 years

Term expires: 1/15

Salary: $105,000

Phone: (402) 471-2244

Residence: Lincoln

Born: May 12, 1948; Falls City, Neb.

Religion: Methodist

Family: Wife, Sally Ganem; one child

Education: U.S. Military Academy, B.S. 1970 (economics)

Military: Army, 1970-75

Career: Congressional aide; health and beauty products company salesman

Political highlights: Neb. Republican Party executive director, 1979-81; Fremont City Council, 1990-94; Neb. treasurer, 1995-2001; lieutenant governor, 2001-05

ELECTION RESULTS

2010 GENERAL

Dave Heineman (R)	360,645	73.9%
Mike Meister (D)	127,343	26.1%

Lt. Gov. Rick Sheehy (R)

First elected: 2006; assumed office Jan. 24, 2005, following Heineman's ascension to governor

Length of term: 4 years

Term expires: 1/15

Salary: $75,000

Phone: (402) 471-2256

LEGISLATURE

Unicameral Legislature: 90 days in odd-numbered years; 60 days in even-numbered years

Legislature: 49 nonpartisan members, 4-year terms

2011 ratios: 38 men, 11 women

Salary: $12,000

Phone: (402) 471-2271

TERM LIMITS

Governor: 2 consecutive terms

Legislature: 2 consecutive terms

URBAN STATISTICS

CITY	POPULATION
Omaha	408,958
Lincoln	258,379
Bellevue	50,137
Grand Island	48,520
Kearney	30,787

REGISTERED VOTERS

Republican	48%
Democrat	33%
Nonpartisan/others	19%

POPULATION

2010 population (est.)	1,826,341
2000 population	1,711,263
1990 population	1,578,385
Percent change (2000-2010)	+6.7%
Rank among states (2010)	38
Median age	35.9
Born in state	66.1%
Foreign born	5.4%
Violent crime rate	282/100,000
Poverty level	12.3%
Federal workers	18,284
Military	6,845

ELECTIONS

STATE ELECTION OFFICIAL
(402) 471-2555

DEMOCRATIC PARTY
(402) 434-2180

REPUBLICAN PARTY
(402) 475-2122

MISCELLANEOUS

Web: www.nebraska.gov

Capital: Lincoln

U.S. CONGRESS

Senate: 1 Democrat, 1 Republican

House: 3 Republicans

2010 Census Statistics by District

District	2008 Vote for President Obama	McCain	White	Black	Asian	Hispanic	Median Income	White Collar	Blue Collar	Service Industry	Over 64	Under 18	College Education	Rural	Sq. Miles
1	44%	54%	86%	2%	2%	7%	$49,827	59%	25%	16%	13%	24%	27%	35%	11,951
2	50	49	74	10	3	11	52,285	65	19	16	10	27	34	2	411
3	30	69	87	1	1	10	42,243	54	30	16	17	25	19	54	64,511
STATE	42	57	82	4	2	9	47,995	59	24	16	13	25	27	30	76,872
U.S.	53	46	64	12	5	16	51,425	60	23	17	13	25	28	21	3,537,438

Sen. Ben Nelson (D)

Capitol Office
224-6551
bennelson.senate.gov
720 Hart Bldg. 20510-2706; fax 228-0012

Committees
Agriculture, Nutrition & Forestry
(Commodities & Markets - Chairman)
Appropriations
(Legislative Branch - Chairman)
Armed Services
(Strategic Forces - Chairman)
Rules & Administration

Residence
Omaha

Born
May 17, 1941; McCook, Neb.

Religion
Methodist

Family
Wife, Diane Nelson; four children

Education
U. of Nebraska, B.A. 1963 (philosophy), M.A. 1965
(philosophy), J.D. 1970

Career
Lawyer; insurance company executive

Political Highlights
Neb. director of insurance, 1975-76; governor,
1991-99; Democratic nominee for U.S. Senate, 1996

ELECTION RESULTS

2006 GENERAL

Ben Nelson (D)	378,388	63.9%
Pete Ricketts (R)	213,928	36.1%

2006 PRIMARY

Ben Nelson (D)		unopposed

2000 GENERAL

Ben Nelson (D)	353,093	51.0%
Don Stenberg (R)	337,977	48.8%

Elected 2000; 2nd term

Nelson is the Senate's most conservative Democrat, but a Democrat nonetheless. He maintains he has no plans to switch parties, even as he sides with Republicans on close to half of Senate votes that divide the majority party and the GOP.

"I'm always running for support from Nebraskans," said the only Democrat in the state's five-person congressional delegation.

Emblematic of Nelson's legislative philosophy was the Senate debate on a pair of spending plans — one Democratic, one Republican — early in the 112th Congress (2011-12). The House-passed Republican plan would cut $61 billion in spending for the remainder of fiscal 2011; the Democratic plan called for about $10 billion in cuts. Nelson voted against both.

"Democrats did nothing to attract Republicans and Republicans did nothing to attract Democrats," Nelson said. "Who would pay attention to either one of these bills? Neither of them are serious."

He is used to finding himself in the middle.

Nelson was at the center of the Senate's consideration of health care overhaul legislation in the 111th Congress (2009-10). With 60 votes in the Democratic caucus at the time of the Senate debate, Majority Leader Harry Reid of Nevada could cut off a filibuster — if he could get Nelson on board. During those negotiations, Nelson won an increase in payments for Nebraska to help cover the cost of expanding Medicaid coverage, a proposal detractors called the "Cornhusker Kickback." Even Republican Gov. Dave Heineman roundly criticized the provision and the senator's role in securing it.

Nelson later voted against a health care and education reconciliation package that was designed, among other things, to remove the Nebraska provision. He indicated that much of his opposition stemmed from the inclusion of a student loan overhaul that made the federal government the sole originator of student loans.

Nelson often finds himself as the only Democrat — or one of a handful — joining Republicans.

He and Blanche Lincoln of Arkansas were the only Democrats to vote in support of a failed effort by South Carolina Republican Jim DeMint to add extensions of Bush-era income tax rates to a state-aid bill and require spending rescissions as offsets. The rates were later extended for two years, with Nelson's support.

Nelson also demonstrated his determination to keep a rein on federal spending by working with moderate Republican Susan Collins of Maine to pass a compromise economic stimulus bill that shaved more than $100 billion from the original proposal.

He learned his penny-pinching ways growing up in McCook, a small town in south-central Nebraska where his mother started a taxpayers' watchdog group. Her attention to the way tax revenue was spent wasn't lost on her son.

During debate on the fiscal 2010 budget resolution, Nelson repeatedly broke with his party to support GOP amendments aimed at cutting spending. He was one of two Democrats to vote against the final $3.56 trillion spending blueprint.

Nelson supported Obama's first nominee to the Supreme Court, Sonia Sotomayor, but cast the lone Democratic vote against the second, Elena Kagan, citing her lack of courtroom experience.

Nelson said he wouldn't support a filibuster of the nominee, though, and in the end no effort was made to block Kagan's confirmation.

In 2005, he helped lead a bipartisan group that wanted to avert a showdown over judicial nominees. An evenly split collection of Democrats and Republicans, known as the "Gang of 14," spent weeks hammering out a deal that stopped Tennessee Republican Bill Frist, the majority leader at the time, from using a parliamentary maneuver to do away with filibusters of nominees to the federal bench.

Nelson has been outspoken about the wars in Iraq and Afghanistan from his seat on the Armed Services Committee. In the 110th Congress (2007-08), he said Iraq needed to pay a greater share of its reconstruction costs. "The blank-check policy must end," Nelson said, "and the Iraqis need to invest — really invest — in their own future by repaying the United States for future reconstruction funds." In 2009, he called for clear benchmarks to measure U.S. progress in Afghanistan — a concept that Obama embraced.

Nelson opposes abortion in most cases. When he offered an amendment to the health care overhaul in 2009 to ensure that federal funds could not be used for abortion services, Nelson's fellow Democrats united to defeat the amendment, arguing that the underlying bill already barred such funding.

In 2010, Nelson showed his Democratic stripes only about half the time — he sided with his party on 54 percent of the votes in which a majority of Democrats opposed a majority of Republicans, the lowest in the Senate.

As a member of the Agriculture, Nutrition and Forestry Committee, he worked to override President George W. Bush's veto of a 2008 reauthorization of farm programs the president considered too costly.

On the Appropriations Committee, Nelson has unabashedly delivered earmarks to Nebraska, which he calls "just doing my job." When senators agreed to join the House in an earmark moratorium for fiscal 2012, Nelson insisted that the money be saved rather than simply redirected.

"We should earmark the earmarks for spending cuts and debt reduction, and make sure the money isn't just spent with little transparency by Washington bureaucrats," he said.

A slice of Nelson's work on the Appropriations Committee intersects with another committee assignment, giving him influence over the working of the Senate. He chairs the Legislative Branch spending panel and serves on the Rules and Administration Committee, which handles internal Senate matters and oversees election law.

Nelson yearned for statewide office since he was 17 and elected governor of a model Nebraska legislature. The election of his high school superintendent and debate coach, Ralph Brooks, as governor convinced Nelson "you didn't have to be from a big city to have an opportunity in politics."

He considered joining the ministry while at the University of Nebraska and would later serve as a lay minister in the Disciples of Christ. But Nelson eventually opted for law school and, upon graduation, began a long career in insurance. He ran an insurance company, headed a national association of insurance regulators and directed his state's insurance department. He launched his first statewide bid in 1990, surviving the Democratic primary for governor by just 42 votes. He went on to defeat the incumbent, Republican Kay Orr, by 4,000 votes.

After eight years as governor, he returned to his law firm, Kaufman-Nelson-Pattee. There he helped states develop Washington lobbying strategies, though he notes he was never a lobbyist himself. When Democratic Sen. Bob Kerrey announced in 1999 he would retire the next year, Nelson was a shoo-in for the party's nomination. He defeated Republican Attorney General Don Stenberg by 2 percentage points in the closest Senate election in Nebraska history. He won re-election — against a self-funded candidate who outspent Nelson almost 2-to-1 — by 28 percentage points.

Republican-leaning Nebraska will be a prime GOP target in 2012 as Nelson seeks re-election.

Key Votes

2010

Pass budget reconciliation bill to modify overhauls of health care and federal student loan programs	NO
Proceed to disapproval resolution on EPA authority to regulate greenhouse gases	YES
Overhaul financial services industry regulation	YES
Limit debate to proceed to a bill to broaden campaign finance disclosure and reporting rules	YES
Limit debate on an extension of Bush-era income tax cuts for two years	YES
Limit debate on a bill to provide a path to legal status for some children of illegal immigrants	NO
Allow for a repeal of "don't ask, don't tell"	YES
Consent to ratification of a strategic arms reduction treaty with Russia	YES

2009

Prevent release of remaining financial industry bailout funds	YES
Make it easier for victims to sue for wage discrimination remedies	YES
Expand the Children's Health Insurance Program	YES
Limit debate on the economic stimulus measure	YES
Repeal District of Columbia firearms prohibitions and gun registration laws	YES
Limit debate on expansion of federal hate crimes law	YES
Strike funding for F-22 Raptor fighter jets	YES

CQ Vote Studies

	PARTY UNITY		PRESIDENTIAL SUPPORT	
	SUPPORT	OPPOSE	SUPPORT	OPPOSE
2010	54%	46%	75%	25%
2009	63%	37%	90%	10%
2008	72%	28%	48%	52%
2007	70%	30%	49%	51%
2006	36%	64%	76%	24%
2005	46%	54%	76%	24%
2004	52%	48%	82%	18%
2003	57%	43%	80%	20%
2002	51%	49%	91%	9%
2001	58%	42%	74%	26%

Interest Groups

	AFL-CIO	ADA	CCUS	ACU
2010	31%	50%	73%	48%
2009	78%	70%	71%	44%
2008	100%	75%	71%	16%
2007	95%	75%	64%	32%
2006	47%	35%	83%	64%
2005	71%	55%	94%	60%
2004	82%	65%	81%	52%
2003	62%	45%	86%	42%
2002	62%	50%	63%	55%
2001	81%	70%	71%	56%

Sen. Mike Johanns (R)

Capitol Office
224-4224
johanns.senate.gov
404 Russell Bldg. 20510; fax 224-5213

Committees
Agriculture, Nutrition & Forestry
Banking, Housing & Urban Affairs
Environment & Public Works
Indian Affairs
Veterans' Affairs

Residence
Omaha

Born
June 18, 1950; Osage, Iowa

Religion
Roman Catholic

Family
Wife, Stephanie Johanns; two children

Education
St. Mary's College (Minn.), B.A. 1971 (communication arts); Creighton U., J.D. 1974

Career
Lawyer

Political Highlights
Lancaster County Board of Commissioners, 1983-87; Lincoln City Council, 1989-91; mayor of Lincoln, 1991-98; governor, 1999-2005; Agriculture secretary, 2005-07

ELECTION RESULTS

2008 GENERAL

Mike Johanns (R)	455,854	57.5%
Scott Kleeb (D)	317,456	40.1%
Kelly Renee Rosberg (NEB)	11,438	1.4%

2008 PRIMARY

Mike Johanns (R)	112,191	78.0%
Pat Flynn (R)	31,560	22.0%

Elected 2008; 1st term

A former mayor, governor and U.S. Agriculture secretary, Johanns approaches governing with an ironclad discipline that was instilled at age 4 when he began tending to the cows on his family's dairy farm. He has proved to be a tireless advocate for U.S. agricultural exports and a dependable Republican vote in the Senate, where he still starts every day at 5 a.m. nearly a half-century after relinquishing his boyhood chores.

"I always said, you know after growing up on a dairy farm with John and Adeline Johanns, everything in life has been easy after that," he said. "And I don't mean that in any kind of way except a very, very positive [way]."

During his nearly three-year tenure as Agriculture secretary, Johanns (JOE-hanns, rhymes with cans) was the George W. Bush administration's point man on a five-year reauthorization of farm programs, winning praise from congressional leaders for his directness and willingness to listen to all sides. He resigned in September 2007 to launch his candidacy for the Senate seat being vacated by Republican Chuck Hagel, drawing some criticism for leaving before the $289 billion bill was completed.

As senator of a state where an estimated one in three jobs is tied to agriculture, Johanns has continued to champion many of the same issues that occupied his time as Agriculture secretary. He sits on the Agriculture, Nutrition and Forestry Committee, where he can push efforts to reopen foreign markets to U.S. beef after cases of mad-cow disease. In 2010, he introduced a resolution with Blanche Lincoln, an Arkansas Democrat who was then chairwoman of the panel, pressing Japan to lift its partial ban on U.S. beef. He cosponsored another by Finance Chairman Max Baucus, a Democrat from the cattle state of Montana, urging seven countries to open their markets; the Senate adopted the measure in May 2010. According to the Nebraska Department of Agriculture, beef is the state's single largest industry.

When he was in the Cabinet, Johanns played an integral role in building congressional support for a 2005 free-trade agreement with five Central American countries and the Dominican Republic, and he has continued to advocate trade agreements. After the 2010 State of the Union address, he authored a letter to President Obama with 17 cosigners supporting the administration's goal of doubling U.S. exports over five years and urging implementation of pending trade agreements.

Johanns — in the Cabinet and as a member of the Environment and Public Works Committee — has promoted the development of alternative and renewable fuels. With his state ranked second in ethanol production according to the Nebraska Ethanol Board, he served as an original cosponsor of a 2010 bill to extend tax credits intended to boost ethanol production and a 2009 measure to create tax incentives that promote the development of biogas — a natural gas substitute created by the breakdown of organic wastes.

Johanns opposes cap-and-trade energy policies that he argues would drive up crop production costs. In 2009, he won adoption of language in the Senate version of the 2010 budget to bar the use of the filibuster-proof "reconciliation" process to advance such measures. House and Senate negotiators later dropped the language from the final version, which Johanns voted against. He also introduced a bill to establish a point of order against cap-and-trade legislation that is not debated and passed using normal Senate procedures.

Outside of the agricultural arena, Johanns is a fierce opponent of efforts to expand the breadth of the federal government with a belief that often "the federal government interferes more than it helps."

He was among a group of 11 conservative senators who urged House Speaker John A. Boehner of Ohio to push his chamber to cut at least $100 billion from a catchall spending bill for fiscal 2011. The original House bill had about $32 billion in cuts; the version that passed the House included $61 billion.

A member of the Banking, Housing and Urban Affairs Committee, he voted against the 2010 financial regulatory overhaul bill. "There's such a different story between the world you see from where you're at and those who are regulated," he told federal regulators at a March 2011 Agriculture Committee hearing on the law.

Johanns also voted against the 2010 health care overhaul legislation, which he called "one of the worst policy efforts ever by the United States Senate," and backed repeal of the law in early 2011.

On the Veterans' Affairs and Indian Affairs committees, Johanns has cosponsored measures to increase compensation for disabled veterans and to authorize grants for mental health care services for American Indian youth.

He opposes federal funding of abortion and led efforts to prohibit federal funding for the Association of Community Organizations for Reform Now (ACORN) in 2009 amid allegations that the group engaged in voter registration fraud; he introduced two stand-alone bills and won approval for amendments barring ACORN funding in several 2010 appropriations bills.

Johanns was raised on a dairy farm in Osage, Iowa, just south of the Minnesota border, where he inherited his parents' work ethic and devout Catholicism. Although his parents were not very interested in politics, their living room displayed pictures of the pope and President John F. Kennedy.

As teenagers, Johanns and his brother raised hogs. They began their small venture with a handshake agreement with a local minister who had some unused land and they kept it going throughout high school, making Johanns enough money to pay for some of his college education.

Johanns loved farming and considered making a career of it, but his parents encouraged him to continue his education and keep his options open. He graduated from college in 1971 and later earned a law degree from Creighton University in Omaha. He worked as a lawyer before starting his political career in 1983 on the Lancaster County Board of Commissioners.

On Christmas Eve 1986, Johanns married his wife, Stephanie, whom he met while the two served together on the county board. Soon after, he left politics, kicked a two- to three-pack-a-day smoking habit and switched his party affiliation from Democrat to Republican, inspired by President Ronald Reagan. In 1989, he returned to the political arena, winning election to the city council in Lincoln. He was elected mayor two years later and won re-election without opposition in 1995.

Johanns' low-key demeanor belies his strong campaign skills and competitiveness. During his 1998 run for governor, he visited each of Nebraska's 93 counties, racking up more than 140,000 miles on his Chevrolet Corsica. Four years later, he became the first Republican governor in Nebraska to win re-election since 1956. He resigned in January 2005, midway through his second four-year term, after Bush tapped him as Agriculture secretary.

Hagel's 2007 retirement announcement led Johanns to take a shot at the Senate. He faced Democrat Scott Kleeb, a Yale-educated rancher and educator who in 2006 took 45 percent of the vote against Republican Rep. Adrian Smith in the overwhelmingly Republican 3rd District. Though the Democrats surged nationwide, Johanns coasted past Kleeb with 58 percent of the vote.

After Minority Whip John Kyl of Arizona announced he would retire at the end of the 112th Congress (2011-12), Johanns announced he would seek the Republican Conference chairmanship, the No. 3 spot in the party's Senate leadership, in the 113th Congress (2013-14).

Key Votes

2010

Pass budget reconciliation bill to modify overhauls of health care and federal student loan programs	NO
Proceed to disapproval resolution on EPA authority to regulate greenhouse gases	YES
Overhaul financial services industry regulation	NO
Limit debate to proceed to a bill to broaden campaign finance disclosure and reporting rules	NO
Limit debate on an extension of Bush-era income tax cuts for two years	YES
Limit debate on a bill to provide a path to legal status for some children of illegal immigrants	NO
Allow for a repeal of "don't ask, don't tell"	NO
Consent to ratification of a strategic arms reduction treaty with Russia	YES

2009

Prevent release of remaining financial industry bailout funds	YES
Make it easier for victims to sue for wage discrimination remedies	NO
Expand the Children's Health Insurance Program	NO
Limit debate on the economic stimulus measure	NO
Repeal District of Columbia firearms prohibitions and gun registration laws	YES
Limit debate on expansion of federal hate crimes law	NO
Strike funding for F-22 Raptor fighter jets	NO

CQ Vote Studies

	PARTY UNITY		PRESIDENTIAL SUPPORT	
	Support	Oppose	Support	Oppose
2010	93%	7%	48%	52%
2009	94%	6%	52%	48%

Interest Groups

	AFL-CIO	ADA	CCUS	ACU
2010	13%	10%	100%	80%
2009	25%	15%	83%	95%

Rep. Jeff Fortenberry (R)

Capitol Office
225-4806
fortenberry.house.gov
1514 Longworth Bldg. 20515-2701; fax 225-5686

Committees
Agriculture
   (Department Operations, Oversight & Credit
   - Chairman)
Foreign Affairs

Residence
Lincoln

Born
Dec. 27, 1960; Baton Rouge, La.

Religion
Roman Catholic

Family
Wife, Celeste Fortenberry; five children

Education
Louisiana State U., B.A. 1982 (economics); George-
town U., M.P.P. 1986; Franciscan U. of Steubenville,
M.Div. 1996 (theology)

Career
Economist; congressional aide; publishing firm
public relations manager and sales representative

Political Highlights
Lincoln City Council, 1997-2001

ELECTION RESULTS

2010 GENERAL
Jeff Fortenberry (R)	116,871	71.3%
Ivy Harper (D)	47,106	28.7%

2010 PRIMARY
Jeff Fortenberry (R)	57,390	83.8%
David L. Hunt (R)	7,000	10.2%
Ralph M. Bodie (R)	4,053	5.9%

2008 GENERAL
Jeff Fortenberry (R)	184,923	70.4%
Max Yashirin (D)	77,897	29.6%

Previous Winning Percentages
2006 (58%); 2004 (54%)

Elected 2004; 4th term

Fortenberry is aligned with the most conservative lawmakers in the House as a member of the Republican Study Committee, but his voting record is among the group's least conservative. When addressing his sig-nature issues — agriculture and foreign policy — he can be found almost anywhere along the ideological spectrum.

When he succeeded 13-term Republican Doug Bereuter, long one of the leading Republican internationalists, Fortenberry won a seat on the Foreign Affairs Committee. To its Middle East and South Asia panel, he brings experiences as a college student traveling in Egypt, where he immersed himself in Arab history, culture and religion.

He also serves as vice chairman of the Africa, Global Health and Human Rights Subcommittee and has backed legislation aimed at spreading the benefits of scientific research to, among other places, the Muslim world.

"To the extent that the United States can better leverage its technical expertise through prudent public diplomacy, and engage others to join our commitment in the service of very worthy goals, we may actually help deprive twisted ideologies and corrupt institutions elsewhere of the resourc-es they might otherwise obtain by default to perpetrate misery and suffer-ing around the world," he said at a committee markup of the legislation. The bill was approved by the panel, but was never considered by the full House.

Fortenberry backed the war in Iraq while seeking to mitigate its effects. In 2007, he played a key role in promoting legislation (ultimately signed into law) to grant Iraqis who worked for the U.S. government as translators — and therefore were in danger of reprisals — access to more special immi-grant visas allowing them to move to the United States. "These translators and interpreters face mortal danger," he wrote in a column for local news-papers. "They are reviled and treated as traitors by the terrorist insurgents and are targets, often with bounties on their heads."

His humanitarian instincts surfaced again in sponsoring a bill to help speed the adoption of children left orphaned by the January earthquake in Haiti. He traveled to the country in November 2010 to observe the country's elections, the only Republican member of a 12-person delegation.

After meeting former child soldiers in Liberia, he sponsored a 2007 bill to prohibit U.S. assistance for governments whose armed forces use chil-dren as fighters, calling the practice "one of the most egregious human rights violations of our times." Provisions from Fortenberry's bill eventu-ally were signed into law by President George W. Bush.

A co-founder of the Congressional Nuclear Security Caucus, Fortenber-ry helped lead the charge in May 2010 against a civil nuclear cooperation agreement between the United States and Russia. Similarly, in September 2008 he was one of only 10 House Republicans to vote against a nuclear cooperation agreement with India.

Fortenberry's party unity score — the percentage of votes on which he sided with a majority of his party against a majority of Democrats — was 84 percent in the 111th Congress (2009-10), the lowest among Nebraska Republicans and near the bottom for Republican Study Committee members.

On economic and social issues, Fortenberry is a more reliable GOP vote. He stood with fellow Republicans late in 2008 and early in 2009 in voting against every major bill aimed at government intervention to boost the economy, including Bush's financial industry rescue and President Obama's $787 billion stimulus.

He signed onto a letter in May 2010 raising questions about Pentagon policy on distribution of the so-called morning-after pill, which many abortion foes oppose. Among other concerns, the letter sought to find out how the Defense Department would "integrate conscience protections" for medical workers with objections to the drug.

From his seat on the Agriculture Committee, where he chairs the Department Operations, Oversight and Credit Subcommittee, Fortenberry looks out for the small farmers who dot the landscape across eastern Nebraska. He added an amendment to the 2008 multi-year reauthorization of farm and nutrition programs to help schools purchase locally grown food. He'll have a hand in writing a new farm bill in the 112th Congress (2011-12).

He was the lone Agriculture Committee Republican to support a measure the House passed in July 2009 that would have created new traceability requirements for the food supply chain and strengthened facility inspections.

Fortenberry was born and raised in Baton Rouge, La. His father died in a car accident when Fortenberry was 12; he says that instilled in him a feeling of responsibility. He was interested in politics and international affairs from a young age — as a fifth-grader he wrote a letter to Richard Nixon about the president's 1972 trip to China.

At 17, Fortenberry served as a page to a Democratic state senator in Louisiana. He switched parties in 1982, citing the influence of President Ronald Reagan, whom he felt better reflected his conservative values.

After earning a master's degree in public policy at Georgetown University, Fortenberry interned for the Department of Agriculture, then worked for a Senate subcommittee, where he studied falling land prices in Nebraska.

But he felt something was missing. "I had a real deep nagging of the heart to really go into the deeper questions of life," Fortenberry told the Lincoln Journal Star in 2006.

He enrolled at Franciscan University in Steubenville, Ohio, where he earned a master's in theology and met his wife, Celeste. After graduation the couple headed west to Lincoln, where Fortenberry became public relations director for what is now Sandhills Publishing. He also won a seat on the Lincoln City Council, serving from 1997 to 2001.

After Bereuter announced his retirement, a free-for-all ensued in the 2004 Republican primary. In the seven-candidate field, Fortenberry ran as a social conservative and won with 39 percent of the vote. He went on to triumph that November by 11 percentage points in the solidly Republican 1st District, taking 54 percent of the vote. He pushed that up to more than 58 percent in 2006 and topped 70 percent in 2008 and 2010.

Key Votes

2010

Overhaul the nation's health insurance system	NO
Allow for repeal of "don't ask, don't tell"	NO
Overhaul financial services industry regulation	NO
Limit use of new Afghanistan War funds to troop withdrawal activities	NO
Change oversight of offshore drilling and lift oil spill liability cap	NO
Provide a path to legal status for some children of illegal immigrants	NO
Extend Bush-era income tax cuts for two years	NO

2009

Expand the Children's Health Insurance Program	NO
Provide $787 billion in tax cuts and spending increases to stimulate the economy	NO
Allow bankruptcy judges to modify certain primary-residence mortgages	NO
Create a cap-and-trade system to limit greenhouse gas emissions	NO
Provide $2 billion for the "cash for clunkers" program	NO
Establish the government as the sole provider of student loans	NO
Restrict federally funded insurance coverage for abortions in health care overhaul	YES

CQ Vote Studies

	PARTY UNITY		PRESIDENTIAL SUPPORT	
	SUPPORT	OPPOSE	SUPPORT	OPPOSE
2010	87%	13%	29%	71%
2009	81%	19%	46%	54%
2008	82%	18%	56%	44%
2007	81%	19%	65%	35%
2006	89%	11%	87%	13%

Interest Groups

	AFL-CIO	ADA	CCUS	ACU
2010	7%	15%	75%	96%
2009	14%	5%	87%	88%
2008	27%	40%	72%	84%
2007	21%	15%	90%	88%
2006	21%	5%	93%	84%

Nebraska 1

East — Lincoln, Fremont, Norfolk

The 1st takes in eastern Nebraska, excluding Omaha and its suburbs. The district includes the state's capital, Lincoln, and the University of Nebraska's Memorial Stadium, which could qualify as the state's third-largest city when filled to its 81,000-seat capacity. Despite the small-town, rural feel, economic diversification in Lincoln, Norfolk and South Sioux City is helping to make the eastern part of the state more urban.

Lincoln's economy — stabilized by state and city government jobs, health care and university sectors, and agricultural production — has remained relatively strong during economic slowdowns, but unemployment has affected many industries here.

The University of Nebraska Innovation Campus set to be completed in 2012 will add agricultural research jobs, and downtown development includes plans for a sports arena. Local officials hope that the campus, located on the former state fairgrounds, will complement growth at the university's technology park.

The region is still heavily dependent on agriculture, and traditional crop and hog farming is supplemented by other agribusiness, such as meat processing, food packaging and fertilizer production. Steadily improving agribusiness revenues support healthy retail growth in small and mid-size towns throughout the district. Polling and telemarketing call centers add white-collar jobs, but layoffs by small employers can hit residents in rural areas particularly hard.

Although the district was home to populist William Jennings Bryan and many of his supporters at the turn of the 20th century, the 1st now votes consistently Republican at all levels. Voter registration favors the GOP in both the city of Lincoln and surrounding Lancaster County, but Democrat Barack Obama won the county in the 2008 presidential election despite losing the district overall.

The 1st's strongest Democratic areas are in the northeast, especially in Thurston County, which is made up entirely of the Omaha and Winnebago American Indian reservations.

Major Industry

Agriculture, higher education, technology, health care, government

Cities

Lincoln, 258,379; Fremont, 26,397; Norfolk, 24,210

Notable

Johnny Carson, the late host of "The Tonight Show," grew up in Norfolk.

Rep. Lee Terry (R)

Capitol Office
225-4155
leeterry.house.gov
2331 Rayburn Bldg. 20515-2702; fax 226-5452

Committees
Energy & Commerce

Residence
Omaha

Born
Jan. 29, 1962; Omaha, Neb.

Religion
Protestant

Family
Wife, Robyn Terry; three children

Education
U. of Nebraska, B.S. 1984 (political science); Creighton U., J.D. 1987

Career
Lawyer

Political Highlights
Omaha City Council, 1991-99 (president, 1994-95)

ELECTION RESULTS

2010 GENERAL

Lee Terry (R)	93,840	60.8%
Tom White (D)	60,486	39.2%

2010 PRIMARY

Lee Terry (R)	18,478	63.1%
Matthew Sakalosky (R)	10,816	36.9%

2008 GENERAL

Lee Terry (R)	142,473	51.9%
Jim Esch (D)	131,901	48.1%

Previous Winning Percentages
2006 (55%); 2004 (61%); 2002 (63%); 2000 (66%); 1998 (66%)

Elected 1998; 7th term

Terry, like many of his fellow conservatives in the House, is no fan of President Obama. He has railed against what he sees as the "socialization of America," excessive spending and "draconian" regulation put in place since Obama teamed with Democrats in Congress to revamp the nation's health care and financial services sectors. But his constituents backed Obama in the 2008 presidential election.

A hard push by Obama that year yielded a Democratic registration advantage in Omaha for the first time in more than a decade. It's made Terry, a modest Midwesterner who prefers quiet dealmaking to overt salesmanship, into a prime Democratic target.

Terry's response was not a move to the middle, but to stress his conservative credentials. He voted against Obama's $787 billion economic stimulus package in 2009 on the grounds that it was too expensive, and he opposed health care and financial services overhauls in 2010 as expansions of the regulatory power of government. The same voters who gave Obama half the vote in 2008 re-elected Terry in 2010 with more than 60 percent of the vote.

And yet Terry also proved to be an ally to House Democratic leaders on more than a few occasions during the 111th Congress (2009-10) — although he hasn't stressed that fact. In 2009, for example, he voted to provide $2 billion to allow Americans to turn in their old gas guzzlers for new, more fuel-efficient cars, backed an overhaul of food safety laws and supported giving the Food and Drug Administration authority to regulate tobacco products. In 2010, he teamed with Democrat Rick Boucher of Virginia on legislation to expand telecommunications taxes to cover Internet phone services. The new revenues would help pay for the expansion of broadband Internet service in rural areas.

A member of the Energy and Commerce Committee, Terry has a good spot from which to advance his signature issue: promoting the use of ethanol. An increase in demand for the corn-based fuel would be a boon for both Nebraska's farmers, who are major producers of the fuel, and its small towns, home to ethanol processing plants. In 2010, Terry backed legislation with Iowa Democrat Leonard L. Boswell that would have authorized construction of a renewable fuel pipeline from the Midwest to the East Coast.

In early 2011, he resisted calls to address rising gasoline prices by opening up the Strategic Petroleum Reserve.

"That's when there's a severe disruption in the supply, not just high prices," he said on Fox Business Network.

Terry is a reliable social conservative. In February 2011 he backed an amendment to a fiscal 2011 catchall spending bill that would bar funding for Planned Parenthood, and in December 2010 he opposed repeal of the statutory ban on homosexuals serving openly in the military.

In a move inspired by many of the roughly 10,000 military retirees in the region near Offutt Air Force Base, just south of Omaha, Terry sponsored a resolution in the 107th Congress (2001-02) calling for Veterans Day to remain Nov. 11, the anniversary of the World War I armistice. A federal commission and others in Congress had suggested that Veterans Day be moved a week earlier to coincide with Election Day in a bid to boost voter turnout.

Omaha is also home to the headquarters of Union Pacific Railroad. Terry was a sponsor of the law enacted in 2001, at the behest of both labor and management, to restructure the federal railroad pension system to allow some of the funds to be invested in stocks and bonds.

He was the subject of media attention in 2003 as one of eight lawmakers who voted against creation of a federal "do not call" list for telemarketers. He explained that 39,000 people in his district are employed, directly or indirectly, by telemarketers. He also drew some attention for his temper in July 2007. During floor debate on an agriculture spending bill, he participated in a profanity-laced exchange with Illinois Democrat Jesse L. Jackson Jr. Terry said Jackson shouted at him, Terry shouted back, and other lawmakers separated the two men. Terry later apologized when he learned it was another Democrat — Anthony Weiner of New York — who instigated the shouting.

Terry was raised in Omaha, where his father was a news anchor with a political talk show. Terry sometimes went to work with his dad to watch interviews with House members, senators and other local celebrities. He had two autographs on his bedroom wall: one from Evel Knievel and the other from conservative Nebraska Sen. Roman Hruska. Talk around the Terry table was often about the wayward ways of a liberal Congress.

In 1976, when he was in eighth grade, Terry handed out pamphlets for his father's unsuccessful House run for the very seat Terry would win two decades later. In college, Terry planned a career in politics, and after getting his law degree he was elected to the Omaha City Council.

His eight years as a councilman made him the front-runner for the House seat given up by Republican Jon Christensen for an ultimately failed gubernatorial run in 1998. Terry won the five-way primary by 10 percentage points and then triumphed by 31 points in November over Democrat Michael Scott, a newscaster.

When he first ran for Congress, Terry pledged to serve no more than three terms, but later backed away from that promise. He said he quickly realized when he got to Washington the benefits that come with seniority. Voters didn't seem to mind, and Terry coasted to easy re-election wins until 2006. That year, with Republicans facing a nationwide backlash from voters upset over ethical scandals on Capitol Hill and the war in Iraq, Terry was forced to spend nearly $1 million to hold off Democrat Jim Esch, a lawyer and Chamber of Commerce official. Terry's tally fell to 55 percent of the vote. In an attempt to raise his profile, he put up pictures of himself on 17 large billboards in and around Omaha. The billboards said, "Thank you for your trust."

Esch tried again in 2008, questioning Terry's accomplishments on Capitol Hill while Terry argued that Esch was too liberal for the district, especially on social issues. Terry pulled out the win as Obama carried the district over Republican Arizona Sen. John McCain, but his margin tightened further, to 4 points.

Key Votes

2010

Overhaul the nation's health insurance system	NO
Allow for repeal of "don't ask, don't tell"	NO
Overhaul financial services industry regulation	NO
Limit use of new Afghanistan War funds to troop withdrawal activities	NO
Change oversight of offshore drilling and lift oil spill liability cap	NO
Provide a path to legal status for some children of illegal immigrants	NO
Extend Bush-era income tax cuts for two years	YES

2009

Expand the Children's Health Insurance Program	NO
Provide $787 billion in tax cuts and spending increases to stimulate the economy	NO
Allow bankruptcy judges to modify certain primary-residence mortgages	NO
Create a cap-and-trade system to limit greenhouse gas emissions	NO
Provide $2 billion for the "cash for clunkers" program	YES
Establish the government as the sole provider of student loans	NO
Restrict federally funded insurance coverage for abortions in health care overhaul	YES

CQ Vote Studies

	PARTY UNITY		PRESIDENTIAL SUPPORT	
	Support	Oppose	Support	Oppose
2010	92%	8%	29%	71%
2009	90%	10%	41%	59%
2008	90%	10%	68%	32%
2007	93%	7%	76%	24%
2006	97%	3%	97%	3%

Interest Groups

	AFL-CIO	ADA	CCUS	ACU
2010	7%	5%	88%	92%
2009	14%	15%	93%	88%
2008	13%	15%	100%	92%
2007	21%	10%	90%	88%
2006	14%	0%	100%	92%

Nebraska 2

East — Omaha and suburbs

Formerly the eastern terminus of the Union Pacific Railroad, Omaha is the heart of the 2nd District. It grew as a blue-collar city: a railroad junction, a Missouri River port and a place where cattle became steaks. To outsiders, this broad-shouldered, gritty image remains. But the city has become mainly a place of downtown office buildings and white-collar jobs in agriculture and insurance businesses. It also is known as the nation's 1-800 capital, thanks to its call centers for telemarketing, customer service and credit processing operations.

Omaha's population and economy grew steadily for the past decade, and residents still enjoy a relatively low cost of living. Local officials continue economic diversification efforts, and the city boasts the headquarters of five Fortune 500 companies — Berkshire Hathaway, Union Pacific Railroad, ConAgra Foods, Kiewit Corp., and Mutual of Omaha.

Building on the success of an earlier downtown redevelopment plan, the city has implemented a plan to guide revitalization of the northern section of downtown.

Omaha continues to expand outward, and officials from the city and parts of surrounding Douglas County have considered merging into a single municipality. Offutt Air Force Base, the district's largest employer, contributes billions of dollars to the local economy annually.

Traditionally a reliably Republican district, the 2nd supported Democrat Barack Obama by a 1-percentage-point margin in the 2008 presidential election. Omaha's dwindling blue-collar base and its university and African-American populations support Democrats. Obama became the first Democratic candidate to carry Douglas County, home to more than 80 percent of district residents, since Lyndon B. Johnson in 1964.

Major Industry
Phone service centers, military, agriculture, insurance

Military Bases
Offutt Air Force Base, 5,869 military, 2,450 civilian (2010)

Cities
Omaha, 408,958; Bellevue, 50,137; Papillion (pt.), 17,917

Notable
Billionaire investor Warren Buffett lives in Omaha — his father, Republican Howard Buffett, represented Omaha in the House from 1943-49 and 1951-53.

Rep. Adrian Smith (R)

Capitol Office
225-6435
adriansmith.house.gov
503 Cannon Bldg. 20515-2703; fax 225-0207

Committees
Ways & Means

Residence
Gering

Born
Dec. 19, 1970; Scottsbluff, Neb.

Religion
Christian

Family
Single

Education
U. of Nebraska, B.S. 1993 (secondary education);
Liberty U., attended 1989-90

Career
Storage company owner; Realtor; education workshop coordinator; substitute teacher

Political Highlights
Gering City Council, 1994-98; Neb. Legislature,
1999-2006

ELECTION RESULTS

2010 GENERAL

Adrian Smith (R)	117,275	70.1%
Rebekah Davis (D)	29,932	17.9%
Dan Hill (I)	20,036	12.0%

2010 PRIMARY

Adrian Smith (R)	65,664	88.0%
Dennis L. Parker (R)	8,979	12.0%

2008 GENERAL

Adrian Smith (R)	183,117	76.9%
Jay C. Stoddard (D)	55,087	23.1%

Previous Winning Percentages
2006 (55%)

Elected 2006; 3rd term

Smith represents the lonely plains of western Nebraska, which in the 19th century provided the pathway to the Pacific along the Oregon, California and Mormon trails — better known in those parts as the Great Platte River Road. The stark landscape has changed some over the ensuing century and a half, but not a lot. Smith is a social conservative who believes in smaller government, but he sees a role for Washington in aiding the rural residents of his expansive district.

In the 112th Congress (2011-12), he won a coveted seat on the tax-writing Ways and Means Committee, where he says his priorities will include repealing the estate tax and passing free trade agreements with Colombia, Panama and South Korea. Both would help his rural constituents, Smith argues.

"Nebraska and other rural states have seen a 'brain drain' in recent years. As the depletion occurs, we lose our most vital economic asset — the younger generation — to more populated areas," said Smith, who was born in 1970. "We want to reverse this trend by helping rural communities realize their potential."

To address a shortage of veterinarians in rural America, he authored a bill to create federal grants to pay for financial aid to veterinary students, equip veterinary offices and recruit faculty. He supported increased funding for the Essential Air Service program, which subsidizes low-traffic airports that "are integral to the economies of our small communities."

He is a co-chairman of the Congressional Rural Caucus and successfully sought exemptions for small, rural hospitals from Medicare regulations requiring the continuous presence of a physician with hospital privileges.

Smith also serves as a co-chairman of the Congressional Hydropower Caucus and has pushed for more production of U.S. energy sources by drilling offshore and in protected regions. He supports the GOP's "all of the above" approach, including the increased use of wind turbines, which make use of a resource western Nebraska has in abundance.

He opposed the Democrats' cap-and-trade legislation aimed at curbing greenhouse gases, calling it economically unrealistic. "We have to rely more on innovation rather than on the heavy hand of government," he told a citizens meeting in April 2010, the Chadron Record reported. Early in the new Congress he backed an amendment to a catchall spending bill for fiscal 2011 that would bar the EPA from enforcing its regulations on carbon emissions under the Clean Air Act.

Smith is one of the youngest Republicans in the House, but he has ample political experience. He served four years on the Gering City Council and nearly eight years in the Nebraska Legislature, where he was known as an anti-abortion, anti-bureaucracy, Christian conservative — a reputation he has cemented on Capitol Hill.

Party leaders have taken notice. In 2009 he won a slot on the Republican Steering Committee, which makes committee assignments. Leaders also gave him the top GOP seat on the Science and Technology Subcommittee on Technology and Innovation, a post he surrendered when he joined Ways and Means.

Smith almost always votes with his party, but is not hesitant about straying from the conservative line when it benefits his district. In 2007, he was one of 19 Republicans to vote for the Democrats' five-year rewrite of farm and nutrition policy. He also was among a narrow majority of his party that, a year later, voted to override President George W. Bush's veto of the bill.

A proud advocate for his state's cattle and meatpacking industries, Smith was successful early in 2009 in persuading the Food and Drug Administration to delay new rules aimed at preventing the spread of mad cow disease by limiting the use of cattle as feed for other animals. He argued that existing protections were working and that the rules would make disposing of dead cattle nearly impossible.

Reared in Nebraska's scenic west, Smith was an only child. His father still sells insurance, and his mother is a retired schoolteacher who owns a school supplies store. He attended a small grade school in Wildcat Hills, where he was one of just six students in his eighth-grade class. He was a percussion player for Gering High School and a member of the school's choir. He enjoys listening to contemporary Christian and country music, although he rented a luxury box at a Bruce Springsteen concert from aerospace contractor Alliant Techsystems Inc. for a 2009 fundraiser.

Smith's interest in politics stems from conversations with his maternal grandfather, a supporter of President Jimmy Carter, who lost to Ronald Reagan in 1980. "My parents told me the differences, and I figured I was for Reagan," Smith laughed. Almost three decades later, his Capitol Hill office is adorned with Reagan posters and memorabilia.

His father eventually served as the Scotts Bluff County GOP chairman, and his mother is the secretary of the Nebraska Republican Party. "I am probably more responsible for their political involvement than they are for mine," Smith said.

After high school, Smith attended Liberty University in Lynchburg, Va. But he became homesick and, after a year and a half, enrolled at the University of Nebraska, where he became active in the College Republicans.

After earning a degree in secondary education, he returned to western Nebraska and briefly worked as a substitute teacher. But envisioning a political future, Smith settled on a career in real estate, which gave him a more flexible schedule.

At age 23, he was elected to the Gering City Council, and four years later he captured a seat in the Nebraska Legislature. Smith's door to the U.S. House opened when Republican Rep. Tom Osborne made an unsuccessful bid for governor in 2006. Smith entered the race to replace Osborne, outpacing four rivals for the Republican nomination. Despite a difficult year for GOP candidates, Smith coasted to a 10-percentage-point win in the heavily Republican district that November. He trumped that in 2008 by crushing his Democratic opponent, Jay C. Stoddard, by nearly 54 points, and won by nearly as much in 2010.

Key Votes

2010

Overhaul the nation's health insurance system	NO
Allow for repeal of "don't ask, don't tell"	NO
Overhaul financial services industry regulation	NO
Limit use of new Afghanistan War funds to troop withdrawal activities	NO
Change oversight of offshore drilling and lift oil spill liability cap	NO
Provide a path to legal status for some children of illegal immigrants	NO
Extend Bush-era income tax cuts for two years	YES

2009

Expand the Children's Health Insurance Program	NO
Provide $787 billion in tax cuts and spending increases to stimulate the economy	NO
Allow bankruptcy judges to modify certain primary-residence mortgages	NO
Create a cap-and-trade system to limit greenhouse gas emissions	NO
Provide $2 billion for the "cash for clunkers" program	NO
Establish the government as the sole provider of student loans	NO
Restrict federally funded insurance coverage for abortions in health care overhaul	YES

CQ Vote Studies

	PARTY UNITY		PRESIDENTIAL SUPPORT	
	Support	Oppose	Support	Oppose
2010	97%	3%	26%	74%
2009	97%	3%	15%	85%
2008	98%	2%	74%	26%
2007	98%	2%	83%	17%

Interest Groups

	AFL-CIO	ADA	CCUS	ACU
2010	0%	0%	88%	100%
2009	5%	0%	80%	100%
2008	7%	15%	89%	96%
2007	4%	10%	95%	96%

Nebraska 3

West — Grand Island, North Platte, Scottsbluff

Scouting what would later become the Oregon Trail, early-19th-century explorers described this section of the country as the "Great American Desert." Most of the 3rd's land is arid, and most of the district's population lives along the Platte River.

Most of the land in the district's 69 counties is left to cattle ranchers and sugar beet, soybean and wheat farmers. Wind farms dot the landscape, and some areas have turned to the production of biofuels. The extensive Union Pacific railroad network, one of Nebraska's most prominent industries, brings crops from isolated areas to larger markets.

Although Grand Island, North Platte and Scottsbluff each serve as regional centers for the retail and health care needs of the surrounding counties, and Kearney, Columbus and Hastings cater to industry and manufacturing, agricultural production is the foundation of the district's economy. Monsanto recently refurbished its Kearney facility and built a new seed production plant in Waco. Small towns are prospering as regional farm and ranch revenues boost retail growth, and even relatively poor counties have experienced economic stability.

The 3rd's agrarian economy is susceptible to changes in the region's weather, and water is a precious commodity here. A decade of drought conditions hurt grazing operations and caused poor crop yields, but water regulations relieve some of the concern. Droughts remain a matter of particular urgency to residents in the 3rd, which contains several of the nation's poorest counties, many of which depend almost entirely on agricultural production.

Overall, the 3rd is conservative and strongly favors Republican candidates, but there are Democratic pockets in Greeley and Sherman counties. Democrat Barack Obama won Saline County in the 2008 presidential election, but Republican John McCain easily won the district with 69 percent of the vote.

Major Industry
Agriculture, food processing, transportation

Cities
Grand Island, 48,520; Kearney, 30,787; Hastings, 24,907

Notable
Union Pacific's Bailey Yard in North Platte is the world's largest railroad classification yard.

NEVADA

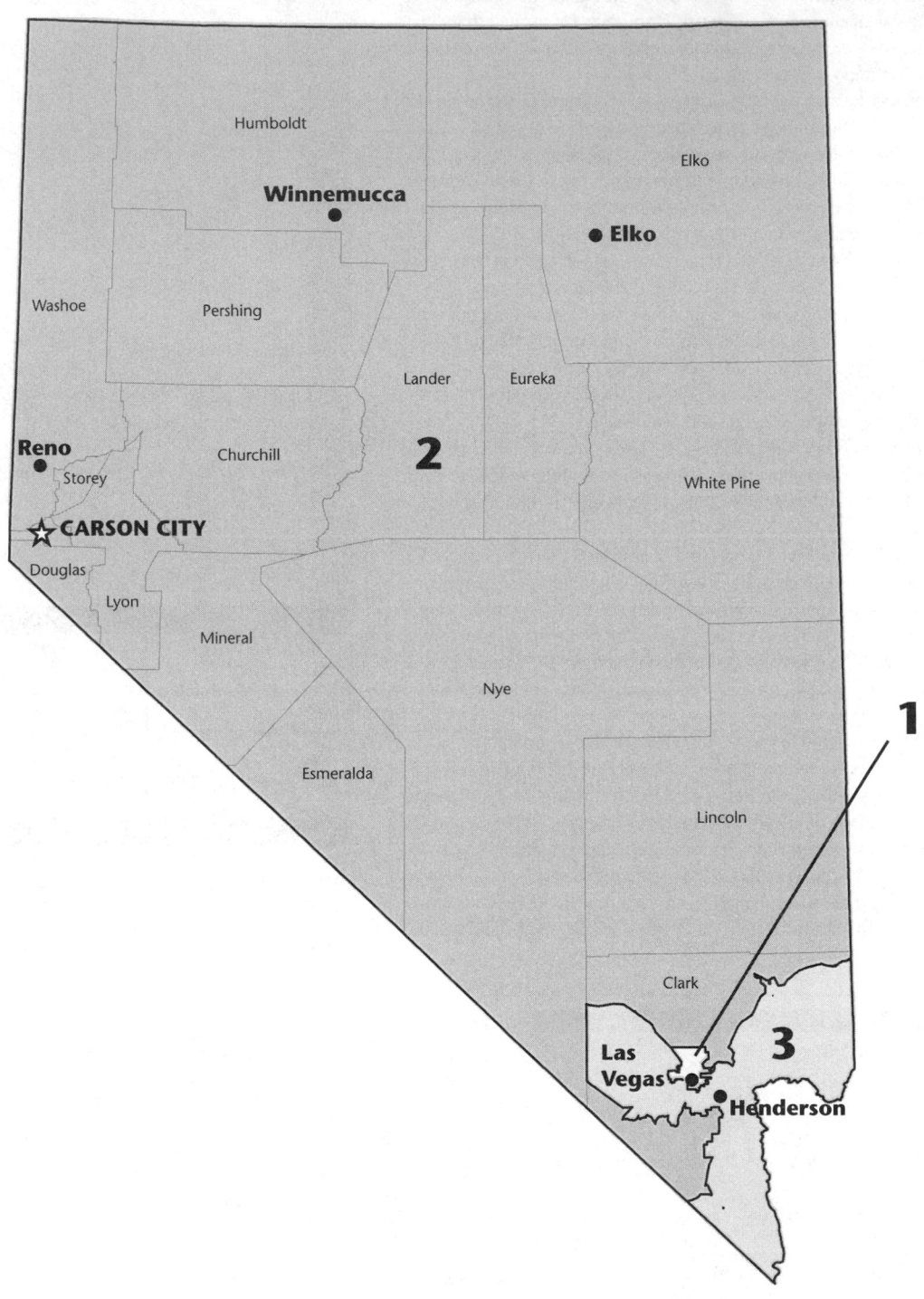

Humboldt

Elko

Winnemucca

● **Elko**

Washoe

Pershing

Lander

Eureka

Reno
●
Storey

Churchill

2

White Pine

☆ **CARSON CITY**

Douglas

Lyon

Mineral

Nye

Esmeralda

Lincoln

1

Clark

3

Las Vegas ●

● **Henderson**

Gov. Brian Sandoval (R)

First elected: 2010
Length of term: 4 years
Term expires: 1/15
Salary: $141,000
Phone: (775) 684-1402
Residence: Reno
Born: Aug. 5, 1963; Redding, Calif.
Religion: Roman Catholic
Family: Wife, Kathleen Sandoval; three children
Education: U. of Nevada, B.A. 1986 (English & economics); Ohio State U., J.D. 1989
Career: State gaming commission official; lawyer
Political highlights: Nev. House, 1994-97; Nev. attorney general, 2003-05; U.S. District Court judge, 2005-09

ELECTION RESULTS

2010 GENERAL

Brian Sandoval (R)	382,350	53.4%
Rory Reid (D)	298,171	41.6%
Other	23,777	3.3%
None of these candidates	12,231	1.7%

Lt. Gov. Brian R. Krolicki (R)

First elected: 2006
Length of term: 4 years
Term expires: 1/15
Salary: $60,000
Phone: (775) 684-5637

LEGISLATURE

Legislature: February-June in odd-numbered years, limit of 120 days
Senate: 21 members, 4-year terms
2011 ratios: 11 D, 10 R; 15 men, 6 women
Salary: $8,373
Phone: (775) 684-1402
Assembly: 42 members, 2-year terms
2011 ratios: 26 D, 16 R; 30 men, 12 women
Salary: $8,373
Phone: (775) 684-8555

TERM LIMITS

Governor: 2 terms
Senate: 3 terms
House: 6 terms

URBAN STATISTICS

CITY	POPULATION
Las Vegas	583,756
Henderson	257,729
Reno	225,221
North Las Vegas	216,961
Sparks	90,264

REGISTERED VOTERS

Democrat	43%
Republican	35%
Nonpartisan/others	22%

POPULATION

2010 population	2,700,551
2000 population	1,998,257
1990 population	1,201,833
Percent change (2000-2010)	+35.1%
Rank among states (2010)	35
Median age	35.3
Born in state	23.2%
Foreign born	17.6%
Violent crime rate	702/100,000
Poverty level	12.4%
Federal workers	24,586
Military	10,034

ELECTIONS

STATE ELECTION OFFICIAL
(775) 684-5705
DEMOCRATIC PARTY
(702) 737-8683
REPUBLICAN PARTY
(702) 258-9182

MISCELLANEOUS

Web: www.nv.gov
Capital: Carson City

U.S. CONGRESS

Senate: 1 Democrat, 1 Republican
House: 1 Republican, 1 Democrat
The 2nd District seat is vacant

2010 CENSUS STATISTICS BY DISTRICT

District	2008 Vote for President Obama	McCain	White	Black	Asian	Hispanic	Median Income	White Collar	Blue Collar	Service Industry	Over 64	Under 18	College Education	Rural	Sq. Miles
1	64%	34%	39%	13%	6%	37%	$49,700	47%	24%	29%	9%	28%	17%	0%	177
2	49	49	68	3	4	20	54,445	54	25	21	13	25	22	21	105,079
3	55	43	54	7	11	23	61,495	57	18	26	11	25	25	4	4,570
STATE	55	43	54	8	7	27	55,585	53	22	25	11	26	21	8	109,826
U.S.	53	46	64	12	5	16	51,425	60	23	17	13	25	28	21	3,537,438

Sen. Harry Reid (D)

Capitol Office
224-3542
reid.senate.gov
522 Hart Bldg. 20510-2803; fax 224-7327

Committees
No committee assignments

Residence
Searchlight

Born
Dec. 2, 1939; Searchlight, Nev.

Religion
Mormon

Family
Wife, Landra Reid; five children

Education
Southern Utah State College, A.S. 1959; Utah State U., B.A. 1961 (history & political science); George Washington U., J.D. 1964; U. of Nevada, Las Vegas, attended 1969-70

Career
Lawyer

Political Highlights
Nev. Legislature, 1969-71; lieutenant governor, 1971-75; Democratic nominee for U.S. Senate, 1974; candidate for mayor of Las Vegas, 1975; Nevada Gaming Commission chairman, 1977-81; U.S. House, 1983-87

ELECTION RESULTS

2010 GENERAL

Harry Reid (D)	362,785	50.3%
Sharron Angle (R)	321,361	44.5%

2010 PRIMARY

Harry Reid (D)	87,401	75.3%
None of these candidates	12,341	10.6%
Alex Miller (D)	9,717	8.4%
Eduardo Hamilton (D)	4,645	4.0%
Carlo Poliak (D)	1,938	1.7%

Previous Winning Percentages
2004 (61%); 1998 (48%); 1992 (51%); 1986 (50%); 1984 House Election (56%); 1982 House Election (58%)

Elected 1986; 5th term

The story of Reid's political rise is one of the great Horatio Alger tales of American politics. As a child he lived in a cabin without indoor plumbing in the tiny mining town of Searchlight on the edge of the Mojave Desert. His mother was a high school dropout who took in laundry to support the family; his father was an alcoholic miner who beat the boy's mother and killed himself at 58.

In high school, Reid's fortunes turned when he made a friend of history teacher and local Democratic Party chairman Donal "Mike" O'Callaghan, who helped Reid win a college scholarship that would get him out of Searchlight. O'Callaghan would later become Reid's political mentor as well. The two would serve side by side in Carson City in the early 1970s — O'Callaghan as governor, Reid as his lieutenant.

Reid has never forgotten his roots. New Deal-style liberalism aimed at lifting up the working man is core to his political philosophy. So he proved a willing partner to President Obama during the 111th Congress (2009-10) as Democrats took advantage of their large majorities in the House and Senate to move some of the most far-reaching liberal legislation since the 1960s, including revamping the nation's health care and financial regulatory systems.

Whatever Reid's deficiencies in the public eye — he's famously dour, rarely inspiring on the stump and sometimes shockingly uncharitable to his political opponents — he's shown that he can work his caucus in the Senate.

Those skills will be put to an even sterner test in the 112th Congress (2011-12), with a diminished Democratic majority and Republicans eyeing a potential takeover in 2012. The challenge was laid bare early in 2011, when Reid had difficulty moving even stop-gap spending bills to keep the government in operation.

But his ability to find just the right inducement to win over reluctant Democrats to his side on key votes is legendary. He is deferential to committee chairmen, as exemplified by his willingness to wait months in 2009 for Finance Chairman Max Baucus of Montana to try — unsuccessfully — to draft a bipartisan health care bill.

When that failed, Reid had to keep every Democrat in line to trump a GOP filibuster. The dealmaking that ensued wasn't pretty. Reid faced considerable criticism for cutting Democrat Ben Nelson of Nebraska a deal to ensure his state would not have to pay extra to support Medicaid patients. The provision, which became known as the "Cornhusker Kickback," was removed after Nelson cast his crucial vote.

Reid's problems winning over Republicans on key legislation extended beyond health care. He could get only four Republicans to support a financial regulatory overhaul in May 2010, and only three a year earlier in passing legislation aimed at reviving the flagging economy.

That didn't prove much of an impediment to Reid, so long as Democrats had 59 votes in their caucus, but it will be a bigger problem in the 112th Congress with their numbers are down to 53.

Reid has at times inflamed the partisan wars. In May 2005, he had to apologize for calling President George W. Bush a "loser" in remarks to Las Vegas high school students. Just before Bush left office, Reid told NBC News' David Gregory that "I really do believe President Bush is the worst president we've ever had."

Even so, Reid was able to move legislation during 2007 and 2008, the two years when he led the Senate and Bush was still president. During that time, Congress passed and Bush signed legislation increasing the minimum wage and funding veterans' programs as well as enacting new lobbying rules. Also enacted were an energy bill, a farm bill and economic recovery packages for the housing and financial services sectors.

That is a testament, perhaps, to the respectful relationship Reid has with Kentucky Republican Mitch McConnell, his savvy rival as minority leader. As longtime appropriators, Reid and McConnell became well acquainted early in their Senate careers and mastered the art of horse trading.

Liberals occasionally yearn for a more dynamic and dependably liberal figure at the Senate's helm. They chastise Reid for being overly cautious, using as an example the time he refused to insist that the health care overhaul create a new government-run health insurance plan, or later in 2010, when he decided not to pursue votes on legislation to combat global warming or to revamp immigration law in the face of almost-certain failure.

Reid doesn't focus solely on national issues; he also takes pains to tend to Nevada matters, especially when the two intersect. He has devoted most of his quarter-century in Congress to leading the opposition to the proposed Yucca Mountain nuclear waste repository in his state, an issue that unites Nevada politicians.

Before being elected leader, Reid was the party's second-in-command for six years under Tom Daschle of South Dakota. When Daschle was defeated for re-election in 2004, Reid, in a matter of hours, lined up the votes he needed to move up from whip. When Democrats won control in 2006, there was no question Reid would make the transition from minority to majority leader.

As a young man, Reid was an amateur middleweight boxer who sometimes sparred with pros in exhibition fights. But he wanted out of Searchlight and a boxer's hardscrabble life, so he applied himself to his studies, boarding with families 40 miles away in Henderson to attend Basic High School, where he became student body president. It was there that O'Callaghan took notice and helped arrange a scholarship for Reid at Utah State University. Reid later earned a law degree at George Washington University while moonlighting as a U.S. Capitol Police officer.

Reid returned to Henderson and won election to the Nevada Legislature. When O'Callaghan became governor in 1970, Reid was elected the youngest lieutenant governor in state history. He made a bid for the U.S. Senate in 1974 but lost to Republican Paul Laxalt. A few years later, O'Callaghan appointed Reid chairman of the Nevada Gaming Commission, giving him oversight of the state's top industry at a time it was tainted by organized crime.

In 1982, Reid won his first of two House terms. He tried again for the Senate in 1986 and won with 50 percent of the vote over Republican Rep. Jim Santini. He has had a few close calls since. In 1992, Democrat Charles Woods, a wealthy broadcast executive, held Reid to 53 percent in the primary. In the general election, Reid outspent GOP rancher Demar Dahl 5-to-1 to prevail with 51 percent of the vote. In his 1998 campaign, Reid won by only 428 votes over Republican John Ensign, then a House member from Las Vegas and later a Senate colleague who resigned in May 2011.

Hoping for a similar result in 2010, he ramped up his campaign operation early, attacking the GOP primary candidate who seemed the most likely threat, former state Republican Party Chairwoman Sue Lowden. Reid crippled her campaign by honing in on a comment she made at a campaign event that people could pay for health care on a barter system. Lowden's demise made way for former state assemblywoman Sharron Angle, a tea party favorite whom Reid thought he could easily caricature as a right-wing zealot. He tried, but Angle proved no pushover, raising more than $21 million to Reid's $17 million — independent groups spent millions more on behalf of both. In the end, Angle's army of enthusiasts was no match for Reid's get-out-the-vote operation, and he pulled out a surprisingly wide 6-point win.

Key Votes

2010

Pass budget reconciliation bill to modify overhauls of health care and federal student loan programs	YES
Proceed to disapproval resolution on EPA authority to regulate greenhouse gases	NO
Overhaul financial services industry regulation	YES
Limit debate to proceed to a bill to broaden campaign finance disclosure and reporting rules	YES
Limit debate on an extension of Bush-era income tax cuts for two years	YES
Limit debate on a bill to provide a path to legal status for some children of illegal immigrants	YES
Allow for a repeal of "don't ask, don't tell"	YES
Consent to ratification of a strategic arms reduction treaty with Russia	YES

2009

Prevent release of remaining financial industry bailout funds	NO
Make it easier for victims to sue for wage discrimination remedies	YES
Expand the Children's Health Insurance Program	YES
Limit debate on the economic stimulus measure	YES
Repeal District of Columbia firearms prohibitions and gun registration laws	YES
Limit debate on expansion of federal hate crimes law	YES
Strike funding for F-22 Raptor fighter jets	YES

CQ Vote Studies

	PARTY UNITY		PRESIDENTIAL SUPPORT	
	SUPPORT	OPPOSE	SUPPORT	OPPOSE
2010	95%	5%	97%	3%
2009	96%	4%	99%	1%
2008	84%	16%	43%	57%
2007	95%	5%	39%	61%
2006	93%	7%	57%	43%
2005	92%	8%	38%	62%
2004	83%	17%	61%	39%
2003	95%	5%	53%	47%
2002	94%	6%	71%	29%
2001	96%	4%	65%	35%

Interest Groups

	AFL-CIO	ADA	CCUS	ACU
2010	100%	75%	18%	0%
2009	94%	95%	43%	8%
2008	50%	70%	75%	16%
2007	89%	85%	45%	0%
2006	93%	90%	50%	12%
2005	93%	100%	50%	4%
2004	100%	90%	53%	21%
2003	100%	70%	35%	21%
2002	100%	85%	45%	10%
2001	100%	100%	43%	20%

Sen. Dean Heller (R)

Capitol Office
224-6244
heller.senate.gov
4 Russell Bldg. Courtyard 20510

Committees
Commerce, Science & Transportation
Energy & Natural Resources
Special Aging

Residence
Carson City

Born
May 10, 1960; Castro Valley, Calif.

Religion
Mormon

Family
Wife, Lynne Heller; four children

Education
U. of Southern California, B.S. 1985 (business administration)

Career
Commercial banker; chief deputy state treasurer; stockbroker

Political Highlights
Nev. Assembly, 1990-94; Nev. secretary of state, 1995-2007; U.S. House, 2007-11

ELECTION RESULTS

2010 HOUSE GENERAL
Dean Heller (R)	169,458	63.3%
Nancy Price (D)	87,421	32.7%
Russell Best (IA)	10,829	4.0%

2010 HOUSE PRIMARY
Dean Heller (R)	72,728	83.7%
Patrick J. Colletti (R)	14,162	16.3%

Previous Winning Percentages
2008 House Election (52%); 2006 House Election (50%)

Appointed April 2011; 1st term

When embattled Republican Sen. John Ensign announced in April 2011 that he would resign, the conservative Heller was the obvious choice to replace him.

Heller had already hinted at his intention to challenge Ensign in 2012 before the incumbent said in March that he would not seek re-election but planned to finish the remainder of his term.

Little more than a month later, though, Ensign announced his resignation, saying the "personal cost" of continued investigations was too high. Ensign had admitted to an extramarital affair with the spouse of his top aide and had faced Senate and federal investigations tied to the relationship.

Republican Gov. Brian Sandoval took little time to fill the vacancy. Getting the seat early gives Heller the advantage of incumbency and a head start on fundraising for the 2012 race.

Heller was four months into his third House term representing a GOP-leaning district that encompasses almost all of the state except for Las Vegas and its suburbs.

His commitment to conservative economic principles is reflected in his voting record. He has also displayed a propensity for speaking bluntly, sometimes to the annoyance of his Republican colleagues.

He credits a chance meeting with supply-side tax-cutting pioneer Jack F. Kemp of New York with helping shape his political beliefs. In the mid-1980s, Heller met the late Republican congressman and 1996 vice presidential nominee at a friend's wedding, and the two discussed economics. "It was part of developing my view of the world," Heller said.

Heller's House platform for his free-market agenda was the Ways and Means Committee. In the Senate, he won seats on the Commerce, Science and Transportation, Energy and Natural Resources, and Special Aging committees.

Heller doesn't often wander far from the party line. He sided with fellow Republicans on more than 92 percent of the votes splitting the parties during his first two terms. He strongly backs gun owners' rights and espouses a tough line on immigration-related issues. He opposed Democratic legislation to expand the Children's Health Insurance Program, which covers children whose low-income families make too much money to qualify for Medicaid. And in 2009 he voted against the $787 billion economic stimulus package.

"Clark County unemployment has gone up 40 percent, and that is undisputable, and that is failure," he said in a July 2010 back-and-forth debate on the House floor with Nevada Democrat and likely 2012 Senate candidate Shelley Berkley. "Since the stimulus . . . nearly 40,000 people have lost their jobs in Las Vegas. Tell me the stimulus is working in Las Vegas."

In response to the tough economic times in his home state, Heller was one of 31 Republicans who backed a measure that month to extend unemployment benefits, although he was denied an opportunity to offer an amendment that would have paid for the extension with unspent stimulus money.

He offered a bit of criticism for Senate Majority Leader Harry Reid's challenger in Nevada in 2010. Republican Sharron Angle had suggested that benefits such as unemployment insurance and entitlement programs had "spoiled our citizenry." "Three hundred dollars a week I don't think is spoiling my constituents or any constituents in the state of Nevada," Heller said on a local news program in July 2010.

That wasn't the first time he had taken a shot at his party.

Heller angered some in the GOP in 2008 when he told the Las Vegas

Review-Journal the Republican Party needed to "clean house. . . . The next couple of election cycles are going to do that." He said some of the Republicans who helped their party take control of Congress in 1994 "came to change Washington and Washington changed them."

He was among the 59 Republicans who opposed the final version of the catchall measure that trimmed about $40 billion from fiscal 2011 spending, arguing it did not cut spending enough.

But he backed the House-passed budget resolution calling for $4 trillion in cuts over 10 years, and appeared likely to have the unusual opportunity to vote for the same budget proposal a second time as a senator.

Before winning the Ways and Means seat, Heller was added to the Financial Services Committee halfway through his first term. He voted against both versions of the $700 billion effort to shore up the ailing financial services industry in fall 2008, the second of which became law. "That is Wall Street arrogance," he told the Las Vegas Review-Journal. "They created their problems and they want someone else to bail them out."

Instead of government intervention, he would like to see lower corporate tax rates and the elimination of deficit spending.

A member of the Natural Resources Committee at the start of the 110th Congress (2007-08), Heller opposed legislation that would have forced the hard-rock mining industry to pay royalties on minerals extracted from public lands, a favorite cause of Western conservatives. He warned that the measure "hurts, perhaps even kills, the domestic mining industry and with it the towns and communities in western Nevada and rural America." In the 111th Congress (2009-10), Heller sponsored legislation that would allow the government to lease federal land to be used for solar- and wind-energy projects, with the leaseholders paying royalties.

Heller is a product of the state capital of Carson City, and the son of an auto mechanic whose customers included a number of state legislators. As a boy, he rode his bike from his father's shop to play with the children of Paul Laxalt, the Nevada governor who went on to become a U.S. senator.

Heller was a star basketball player at Carson High School. As an adult, he played 17 consecutive years in the same recreational basketball league in Carson City. He also enjoys stock car racing, a hobby he shares with his father, and he competes in several races each year in Nevada and California.

At the University of Southern California, Heller studied business administration, specializing in finance and securities analysis. He put himself through college by working on the Pacific Stock Exchange. After graduation, he worked as a stockbroker and trader in Los Angeles.

In 1989, Heller returned to Carson City to become the deputy to Nevada Treasurer Ken Santor, a Republican. On Heller's first day on the job, Santor had a falling out with the state Assembly's powerful Ways and Means Committee chairman, and Heller was asked to substitute for his boss at committee meetings. The minority leader, a Republican, took notice and suggested Heller run for public office himself. The following year, he was elected to the Assembly with the help of his father and his father's reputation.

Heller was elected Nevada secretary of state in 1994. In his three terms, he became known for making Nevada the first state to implement an auditable paper trail for electronic voting machines. In 2006, as five-term Republican Rep. Jim Gibbons launched his successful campaign for governor, Heller was hitting his term limit. He went after the open House seat in a five-way GOP primary, edging out Angle, then a state assemblywoman, by 421 votes.

In the 2006 general election, Heller beat Democrat Jill Derby, a member of the Nevada System of Higher Education Board of Regents, by 5 percentage points in the GOP-leaning district. Heller prevailed again in a 2008 rematch. In 2010, he defeated Democrat Nancy Price by 30 percentage points.

Key Votes (while House member)

2010

Overhaul the nation's health insurance system	NO
Allow for repeal of "don't ask, don't tell"	NO
Overhaul financial services industry regulation	NO
Limit use of new Afghanistan War funds to troop withdrawal activities	NO
Change oversight of offshore drilling and lift oil spill liability cap	NO
Provide a path to legal status for some children of illegal immigrants	NO
Extend Bush-era income tax cuts for two years	YES

2009

Expand the Children's Health Insurance Program	NO
Provide $787 billion in tax cuts and spending increases to stimulate the economy	NO
Allow bankruptcy judges to modify certain primary-residence mortgages	NO
Create a cap-and-trade system to limit greenhouse gas emissions	NO
Provide $2 billion for the "cash for clunkers" program	NO
Establish the government as the sole provider of student loans	NO
Restrict federally funded insurance coverage for abortions in health care overhaul	YES

CQ Vote Studies (while House member)

	PARTY UNITY		PRESIDENTIAL SUPPORT	
	Support	Oppose	Support	Oppose
2010	92%	8%	33%	67%
2009	91%	9%	22%	78%
2008	92%	8%	68%	32%
2007	94%	6%	75%	25%

Interest Groups (while House member)

	AFL-CIO	ADA	CCUS	ACU
2010	7%	10%	100%	88%
2009	5%	5%	87%	92%
2008	36%	25%	89%	80%
2007	13%	15%	80%	96%

Rep. Shelley Berkley (D)

Capitol Office
225-5965
www.berkley.house.gov
405 Cannon Bldg. 20515-2801; fax 225-3119

Committees
Ways & Means

Residence
Las Vegas

Born
Jan. 20, 1951; Manhattan, N.Y.

Religion
Jewish

Family
Husband, Larry Lehrner; two children, two stepchildren

Education
U. of Nevada, Las Vegas, B.A. 1972 (political science); U. of San Diego, J.D. 1976

Career
Lawyer; casino executive

Political Highlights
Nev. Legislature, 1983-85; University and Community College System of Nevada Board of Regents, 1990-98

ELECTION RESULTS

2010 GENERAL

Shelley Berkley (D)	103,246	61.7%
Kenneth Wegner (R)	58,995	35.3%
Jonathan Hansen (IA)	2,847	1.7%
Edward Klapproth (LIBERT)	2,118	1.3%

2010 PRIMARY

Shelley Berkley (D)	unopposed

2008 GENERAL

Shelley Berkley (D)	154,860	67.6%
Kenneth Wegner (R)	64,837	28.3%
Caren Alexander (IA)	4,697	2.0%
Raymond Duensing Jr.(LIBERT)	4,528	2.0%

Previous Winning Percentages
2006 (65%); 2004 (66%); 2002 (54%); 2000 (52%); 1998 (49%)

Elected 1998; 7th term

Representing Nevada's 1st District, including the inimitable Las Vegas, Berkley stands out in the House just as her longtime home shines in the middle of the desert. The seven-term congresswoman, who plans to run for the Senate in 2012, has a reputation for living out loud while at the same time becoming an increasingly influential lawmaker.

Her Capitol Hill office is adorned with photos of the Vegas skyline and decorated with slot machines. In 1999, she was married at Bally's casino with 19 bridesmaids. In 2005, she cheerfully told her local newspaper she was still "black and blue" after cosmetic surgery.

But, lest the colorful images fool anyone into thinking Berkley is all flash and no substance, she sits on one of the most influential House committees, Ways and Means.

Berkley's fundraising skills — she has contributed hundreds of thousands of dollars to Democratic candidates and causes — helped her win a seat on Ways and Means in 2007 and a spot on its tax-writing subcommittee.

She backed the deal President Obama struck with Senate Republicans in late 2010 to extend the Bush-era tax rates for two years, and opposed efforts by party liberals to persuade the leadership not to allow a vote on the deal.

"We all have issues with this compromise, but I believe that it's a decent piece of tax legislation," she said. "It's got everything in it that my district needs."

One of her parochial causes is to revive the tax deduction for travel expenses of spouses who accompany a husband or wife on business travel — that's one more warm body for a Las Vegas hotel. The deduction was eliminated in the 1986 tax overhaul. Similarly, she wants to boost the deduction for business meals and entertainment.

Berkley also has pushed for an extension of tax credits for investments in renewable energy sources such as solar, wind and geothermal power.

She told her colleagues that construction of such projects takes years and their developers need certainty. Renewable-energy tax credits were added to a $700 billion proposal in fall 2008 aimed at shoring up the ailing financial services industry. After voting against the initial legislation, Berkley supported a second version that became law. In addition to the inclusion of the tax credits, she said the nation's fast-mounting financial troubles warranted her reconsideration. "I hate this like poison, but I think relief is necessary," she told the Las Vegas Sun.

Berkley was loyal to Obama's economic agenda during the 111th Congress (2009-10), backing legislation signed into law to expand a children's health insurance program that President George W. Bush had vetoed, as well as the $787 billion economic stimulus plan.

And she voted for the House version of the Democratic health care overhaul bill but was skeptical that changes backed by the leadership would be passed by the Senate. "I am not inclined to support the Senate version," she told the New York Times. "I would like something more concrete than a promise. The Senate cannot promise its way out of a brown paper bag." But she voted for the final version of the law, and the Senate passed the accompanying changes.

Representing Las Vegas necessarily means championing business and gambling causes, and Berkley has been an enthusiastic supporter of both. She co-chairs the Congressional Gaming Caucus and spent a quarter-century as a casino executive while leading the board of the Nevada Hotel and

Motel Association. Berkley's experiences in private industry make her a bit more sympathetic to business interests than the average Democrat, and she has fought to protect both brick-and-mortar and online gambling interests, the latter of which has become an increasingly hot topic in recent years.

Congress in 2006 barred online gambling businesses from accepting credit cards or electronic transfers for the purpose of betting, except for wagers made on horse races. Berkley fought that law, and in 2007 she introduced legislation calling for the National Academy of Sciences to study online gambling, hoping to lay the groundwork for future modifications. Berkley also cosponsored Massachusetts Democrat Barney Frank's 2009 legislation that seeks to repeal the ban on online gambling operations within the United States.

Berkley, who lost her Foreign Affairs Committee seat because of Democratic losses in 2010, has been an unwavering supporter of Israel. In March 2010, when the Israeli government announced the building of 1,600 housing units in Jewish neighborhoods in east Jerusalem during Vice President Joseph R. Biden Jr.'s visit to the city, Berkley called the State Department's criticism of Israel an "irresponsible overreaction."

Berkley's parents came to the United States from Eastern Europe and moved to Las Vegas when she was 6 years old. She attended the University of Nevada at Las Vegas, where she served as student body president before graduating with a political science degree. After earning a law degree from the University of San Diego, Berkley returned to Las Vegas to start a career. She did a stint as in-house counsel for Southwest Gas and served as vice president of government and legal affairs for the Sands Hotel. She served in the Nevada Legislature from 1983 to 1985 but became better-known as a state university regent. She was appointed to the board of regents in 1990 and served two four-year terms.

Berkley was first elected to the House in 1998 when the incumbent, Republican John Ensign, ran for the Senate. Following her easy primary victory, she defeated Republican Don Chairez by just 3 percentage points after battling ethics questions involving memos she had written several years earlier in which she advised a legal client to make campaign contributions to judges as a way to curry favor. In 2000, fending off the same questions, Berkley defeated state Sen. (later GOP Rep.) Jon Porter, by 8 percentage points. Redistricting following the 2000 census left her with a more urban, Democratic constituency, and Berkley has won since by wide margins. She announced in April 2011 that she would seek the Senate seat opened up in 2012 by Ensign's retirement.

Key Votes

2010

Overhaul the nation's health insurance system	YES
Allow for repeal of "don't ask, don't tell"	YES
Overhaul financial services industry regulation	YES
Limit use of new Afghanistan War funds to troop withdrawal activities	NO
Change oversight of offshore drilling and lift oil spill liability cap	YES
Provide a path to legal status for some children of illegal immigrants	YES
Extend Bush-era income tax cuts for two years	YES

2009

Expand the Children's Health Insurance Program	YES
Provide $787 billion in tax cuts and spending increases to stimulate the economy	YES
Allow bankruptcy judges to modify certain primary-residence mortgages	YES
Create a cap-and-trade system to limit greenhouse gas emissions	YES
Provide $2 billion for the "cash for clunkers" program	YES
Establish the government as the sole provider of student loans	YES
Restrict federally funded insurance coverage for abortions in health care overhaul	NO

CQ Vote Studies

	PARTY UNITY		PRESIDENTIAL SUPPORT	
	SUPPORT	OPPOSE	SUPPORT	OPPOSE
2010	98%	2%	95%	5%
2009	97%	3%	96%	4%
2008	97%	3%	18%	82%
2007	95%	5%	12%	88%
2006	90%	10%	32%	68%

Interest Groups

	AFL-CIO	ADA	CCUS	ACU
2010	93%	85%	38%	0%
2009	100%	100%	40%	0%
2008	100%	85%	67%	4%
2007	96%	85%	58%	8%
2006	100%	80%	54%	13%

Nevada 1

Las Vegas

Neon lights along the "Strip" and the chance of easy money still lure pleasure seekers to the 1st, which includes Las Vegas and its immediate environs. But a housing market collapse, declining gaming revenue and municipal budget shortfalls have led to layoffs and commercial construction stoppages.

The increasingly urbanized district experienced decades of explosive growth and skyrocketing home values, and it depends largely on its hospitality-based economy, which is starting to pick up after four years of the national economic downturn. Foreign visitors armed with an advantageous exchange rate picked up some of the slack as early signs of the recession appeared, but loss of major convention business from American companies prolonged some of the damage. Even as hotel-based revenues begin to rebound, recovery may be slow in service and construction sectors.

A few luxury resorts and casinos have continued planned development, and the most expensive casino ever built on the Strip opened in late 2010, but many projects have halted, slashing labor and service industry jobs. Loan defaults by large developers have extended the crisis into the financial sector. Local cultural centers have scaled back events, but cuts by health care providers are of much greater concern to residents.

Federal funding to support real estate market stabilization here — an area recognized as the hardest hit by the national foreclosure crisis — may keep some residential properties from falling into blight even as unemployment and foreclosure rates continue to rise.

Although pockets of Republicans live here, the 1st has a strong Democratic base in unionized service workers and does not include most of the GOP-leaning suburbs. In 2008, Democrat Barack Obama won the district with 64 percent of its presidential vote.

Major Industry
Tourism, gambling, conventions

Cities
Las Vegas (pt.), 416,551; North Las Vegas (pt.), 215,038; Paradise (unincorporated) (pt.), 74,970; Sunrise Manor (unincorporated) (pt.), 73,044

Notable
The Little White Wedding Chapel on Las Vegas Boulevard has a drive-through window for weddings.

Vacant Seat

Rep. Dean Heller (R)
Moved to Senate, May 2011

Republican Dean Heller's move to the Senate in May 2011 created a vacancy in the competitive but GOP-leaning 2nd District.

Heller won his third House term in 2010 by capturing 63 percent of the vote, but in 2006 and 2008 — stronger years for Democrats in Nevada as well as across the nation — he barely topped 50 percent. President Obama and Arizona Republican Sen. John McCain split the district's 2008 presidential vote almost evenly.

Heller's move to the Senate — he was appointed in April by GOP Gov. Brian Sandoval — necessitates the first special House election in Nevada's nearly century and a half as a state. That contest is scheduled for Sept. 13, 2011.

Democrats appeared to have prevailed in their desire to have a free-for-all contest when Democratic Secretary of State Ross Miller announced that the special election would be open to all qualified candidates. That would create a situation in which a multitude of GOP candidates could split the vote and send a Democrat to victory. Republicans would prefer the parties' central committees to nominate candidates, which would narrow the field and enhance the chances of a GOP win.

The final decision on how and when the election will be conducted rests with the courts. In May a judge in Carson City sided with Republicans, but that was unlikely to be the final word.

In three terms as secretary of state himself, Heller became known for making Nevada the first state to implement an auditable paper trail for electronic voting machines. In 2006, as five-term Republican Rep. Jim Gibbons launched his successful campaign for governor, Heller was hitting his term limit as secretary of state. He went after the open U.S. House seat in a five-way GOP primary, edging out Sharron Angle, then a state assemblywoman, by 421 votes.

In that year's general election, Heller beat Democrat Jill Derby, a member of the Nevada System of Higher Education Board of Regents, by 5 percentage points. Heller prevailed again in a 2008 rematch. In 2010, he defeated Democrat Nancy Price, an Air Force and Air National Guard veteran and former regent, by more than 30 percentage points. He was not coy about a 2012 Senate run, giving potential successors a heads-up.

Angle, who challenged Senate Majority Leader Harry Reid in 2010, has announced she will not run in 201. Lt. Gov. Brian Krolicki, viewed by many as the favorite of the state GOP establishment, announced in May that he would not be a candidate. Derby also took herself out of the running.

But Price is in. Among others who have expressed interest in the race are:

• State Republican Party Chairman Mark Amodei, who also is a former state senator;

• Greg Brower, an appointed GOP state senator and former U.S. attorney;

• Retired Navy Cmdr. Kirk Lippold, a Republican, who commanded the USS Cole when it was attacked by al Qaeda in 2000.

• Democratic state Treasurer Kate Marshall, who appeared to be the early favorite in her party.

Nevada 2
Reno, Carson City and the 'Cow Counties'

The 2nd takes in everything outside of Las Vegas and its suburbs, including almost all of the state's vast rural areas. Reno and the capital, Carson City, anchor the district in the west. In the "Cow Counties," agriculture, mining and ranching dominate. Nearly 90 percent of the district's land is federally owned. The 2nd also dips into two areas of Clark County in the southern part of the state, taking in Nellis Air Force Base and much of the northern part of Clark, as well as a few suburban communities in the county's southwest.

Several counties in the district were among the hardest hit by Nevada's housing market collapse. Lyon, Nye and Washoe counties saw high rates of mortgage defaults, and Clark — shared by the 1st and 3rd — will have to recover from oversupply in the condominium market. The gold rush attracted fortune hunters to Reno in the 1800s, and casinos drew them in for decades in the 20th century, making gambling and tourism big business here. But Washoe County has suffered prolonged declines in gambling revenue, and tourism revenue at Lake Tahoe resorts to the south depends on visitors from northern California. Diversification of the non-gaming economy through public and private development of other entertainment sectors and outdoor attractions may help prop up western Nevada, and government employment remains a key source of jobs in the district. The 2nd votes mostly Republican in local elections, and John McCain won handily in some of the district's rural counties in the 2008 presidential election. But left-leaning Carson City, Reno and Clark County residents favored Democrat Barack Obama, and McCain barely edged out a win in the district overall by fractions of a percentage point.

Major Industry
Gambling, mining, manufacturing

Military Bases
Nellis Air Force Base, 6,756 military, 1,105 civilian; Naval Air Station Fallon, 511 military, 287 civilian (2009)

Cities
Reno, 225,221; Sparks, 90,264; Carson City, 55,274; Pahrump (unincorporated), 36,441; Sunrise Manor (unincorporated), 27,616

Notable
Reno's National Bowling Stadium hosts championship tournaments.

Rep. Joe Heck (R)

Capitol Office
225-3252
heck.house.gov
132 Cannon Bldg. 20515-2803; fax 225-2185

Committees
Armed Services
Education & the Workforce
Select Intelligence
(Technical & Tactical Intelligence - Chairman)

Residence
Henderson

Born
Oct. 30, 1961; Queens, N.Y.

Religion
Roman Catholic

Family
Wife, Lisa Heck; three children

Education
Pennsylvania State U., B.S. 1984 (health education);
Philadelphia College of Osteopathic Medicine, D.O.
1988

Military
Army Reserve, 1991-present

Career
Physician; medical response training consultant;
Defense Department medical school administrator

Political Highlights
Nev. Senate, 2004-08; defeated for re-election to Nev.
Senate, 2008

ELECTION RESULTS

2010 GENERAL

Joe Heck (R)	128,916	48.1%
Dina Titus (D)	127,168	47.5%
Barry Michaels (I)	6,473	2.4%
Joseph P. Silvestri (LIBERT)	4,026	1.5%

2010 PRIMARY

Joe Heck (R)	36,911	80.6%
Steven P. Nohrden (R)	8,859	19.4%

Elected 2010; 1st term

Representing a district hurt more than most by the economic downturn and real estate crisis, Heck will look to help mold a fiscal policy aimed squarely at job creation.

His spot on the Education and the Workforce Committee will give him a platform to make his case.

There is no doubt that Heck's constituents have had a rough time lately. Comprising much of the Las Vegas suburbs, his district has seen home prices fall steeply while unemployment has risen steadily.

In the first months of the 112th Congress (2011-12), he was the only Republican to vote against a House-passed bill to terminate the Federal Housing Administration Refinance Program that was established to help homeowners refinance loans on homes that are worth less than they owe.

"A failed PR job should not be the reason a good program dies," Heck told the Las Vegas Sun. "The FHA refinancing program can be a good program, but it needs more attention, and perhaps reform, so homeowners know it's an option."

The health care system is also a central concern for Heck, a practicing physician.

"I think that we need to rely more on people who have real-world experience to craft changes to our health care system, as opposed to a 2,700-page behemoth," Heck said in reference to the health care overhaul enacted in 2010. He voted to repeal and defund it early in 2011.

Heck, a colonel in the Army Reserve who served in Operation Iraqi Freedom, won seats on the Armed Services and Select Intelligence committees. He was the only freshman to win a seat on the Intelligence panel.

Heck was also one of three freshman named to the Republican Steering Committee, responsible for making the party's House committee assignments.

A four-year veteran of the Nevada Senate, Heck nipped one-term Democrat Dina Titus in one of 2010's closest House races, prevailing by less than 1 percent of the vote.

Nevada 3

Las Vegas suburbs

The pinwheel-shaped 3rd is located in Clark County and saw explosive population growth, suburban expansion and an influx of white-collar workers in past decades. Despite prolonged double-digit unemployment, a housing crisis and declining gaming revenue recently hampering economic progress, the 3rd has gained nearly 380,000 residents since 2000. The fastest-growing district in the nation, it is also the most-populous district ahead of decennial remapping.

The district includes a chunk of Las Vegas but is mainly composed of the city's suburbs; most area casinos are in the urban 1st. The district is home to gaming industry union employees.

Most of the 3rd's population lives in suburbs such as Henderson, Spring Valley and Paradise. Summerlin, to the west, is a massive planned community along the western rim of Las Vegas Valley.

To the east, the population is largely Mormon. In the south, the 3rd takes in less-populous mining areas near Laughlin. Small ranching communities are in the district's western reaches. The demand on the Colorado River for fresh water, a valuable commodity in the 3rd's hot, desert communities, is a perennial issue here.

Taking in conservative-leaning new arrivals to the state, an elderly population and some blue-collar workers, the 3rd is politically competitive. Barack Obama won 55 percent of the district's 2008 presidential vote.

Major Industry
Gambling, mining, ranching

Cities
Henderson (pt.), 238,307; Spring Valley (unincorp.) (pt.), 177,756; Las Vegas (pt.), 167,205; Paradise (unincorp.) (pt.), 148,197

Notable
The Hoover Dam, about 30 miles southeast of Las Vegas, often is called one of the greatest engineering works in history.

Gov. John Lynch (D)

First elected: 2004

Length of term: 2 years

Term expires: 1/13

Salary: $113,833.98

Phone: (603) 271-2121

Residence: Hopkinton

Born: Nov. 25, 1952; Waltham, Mass.

Religion: Roman Catholic

Family: Wife, Susan Lynch; three children

Education: U. of New Hampshire, B.A. 1974 (English); Harvard U., M.B.A. 1979; Georgetown U., J.D. 1984

Career: Business consulting firm owner; furniture manufacturing company president; college admissions director; state party executive director

Political highlights: No previous office

ELECTION RESULTS

2010 GENERAL

John Lynch (D)	240,346	52.7%
John Stephen (R)	205,616	45.1%
John J. Babiarz (LIBERT)	10,089	2.2%

Senate President
Peter Bragdon (D)

(no lieutenant governor)

Phone: (603) 271-2675

LEGISLATURE

General Court: January-June

Senate: 24 members, 2-year terms

2011 ratios: 19 R, 5 D; 18 men, 6 women

Salary: $200/2-year term

Phone: (603) 271-2111

House: 400 members, 2-year terms

2011 ratios: 293 R, 101 D, 2 others, 1 I, 3 vacancies; 296 men, 101 women

Salary: $200/2-year term

Phone: (603) 271-3661

TERM LIMITS

Governor: No

Senate: No

House: No

URBAN STATISTICS

CITY	POPULATION
Manchester	109,565
Nashua	86,494
Concord	42,695
Derry	33,109
Dover	29,987

REGISTERED VOTERS

Unaffiliated	392,352
Republican	272,738
Democrat	264,110

POPULATION

2010 population	1,316,470
2000 population	1,235,786
1990 population	1,109,252
Percent change (2000-2010)	+9.7%
Rank among states (2010)	42
Median age	39.6
Born in state	41.9%
Foreign born	5.17%
Violent crime rate	160/100,000
Poverty level	7.5%
Federal workers	19,130
Military	675

ELECTIONS

STATE ELECTION OFFICIAL

(603) 271-3242

DEMOCRATIC PARTY

(603) 225-6899

REPUBLICAN PARTY

(603) 225-9341

MISCELLANEOUS

Web: www.nh.gov

Capital: Concord

U.S. CONGRESS

Senate: 1 Democrat, 1 Republican

House: 2 Republicans

2010 Census Statistics by District

District	2008 Vote for President Obama	McCain	White	Black	Asian	Hispanic	Median Income	White Collar	Blue Collar	Service Industry	Over 64	Under 18	College Education	Rural	Sq. Miles
1	53%	46%	92%	1%	2%	3%	$64,446	64	21	16	12	23	32%	33%	2,449
2	56	43	92	1	2	3	61,544	63	22	15	13	23	33	48	6,519
STATE	54	45	92	1	2	3	63,033	63	22	15	13	23	32	41	8,968
U.S.	53	46	64	12	5	16	51,425	60	23	17	13	25	28	21	3,537,438

Sen. Jeanne Shaheen (D)

Capitol Office
224-2841
shaheen.senate.gov
520 Hart Bldg. 20510; fax 228-4131

Committees
Armed Services
Energy & Natural Resources
    (Water & Power - Chairwoman)
Foreign Relations
    (European Affairs - Chairwoman)
Small Business & Entrepreneurship

Residence
Madbury

Born
Jan. 28, 1947; St. Charles, Mo.

Religion
Protestant

Family
Husband, Bill Shaheen; three children

Education
Shippensburg State College, B.A. 1969 (English);
U. of Mississippi, M.S.S. 1973 (political science)

Career
Teacher; campaign aide; jewelry store owner;
university public affairs institute director

Political Highlights
Democratic nominee for N.H. Senate, 1978; Madbury
Zoning Board of Adjustment, 1983-96 (chairwoman,
1987-96); N.H. Senate, 1990-96; governor, 1997-2003;
Democratic nominee for U.S. Senate, 2002

ELECTION RESULTS

2008 GENERAL

Jeanne Shaheen (D)	358,438	51.6%
John E. Sununu (R)	314,403	45.3%
Ken Blevens (LIBERT)	21,516	3.1%

2008 PRIMARY

Jeanne Shaheen (D)	42,968	88.3%
Raymond Stebbins (D)	5,281	10.8%

Elected 2008; 1st term

Shaheen is a seasoned politician with decades spent on the campaign trail and in state office developing the skills necessary to prosper in the Senate. Her legislative priorities are education, health care and energy, and she has been a faithful Democratic vote in her first years in office while playing stylistically to her state's iconoclastic image.

She quickly joined a group of 15 Democratic moderates who hoped to build bipartisan coalitions on key issues. She told MSNBC in a 2009 interview that issues such as health care and climate change often divide along geographic rather than partisan lines. "It's important for us to be able to build those bridges and relationships so we can bring everybody along," Shaheen said. She said she particularly admires Maine Republicans Olympia J. Snowe and Susan Collins, two of the Senate's most active moderates.

Shaheen is a supporter of a proposal — often made but never acted on — to shift Congress to biennial, rather than annual, budgeting, to address lawmakers' repeated failure to complete the appropriations process in a timely fashion. The plan, she and Republican cosponsor Johnny Isakson of Georgia wrote in Roll Call in March 2011, "would convert the federal budget process from an annual, chaotic spending event to a two-year, thoughtful process that would require Congress to conduct oversight."

Despite such cross-aisle efforts, in her first years in office Shaheen sided with her party on 95 percent of the votes that divided a majority of Democrats from a majority of Republicans.

Shaheen supported the health care overhaul in March 2010, saying it "is not a perfect fix to our health care problems, but it will put us on the path to a stable and secure health care system." She was able to include several of her own provisions, including one that would provide follow-up care to Medicare beneficiaries in order to reduce preventable hospital readmission.

Shaheen called President George W. Bush's restrictions on federally funded embryonic stem cell research "unconscionable" and applauded when President Obama lifted them. When a federal district court judge blocked such funding in August 2010, Shaheen said the decision "reaffirms that Congress should take swift action to lift the ban once and for all and ensure that this critical research can continue uninterrupted."

On the Energy and Natural Resources Committee, Shaheen joined other Democratic senators after the April 2010 Gulf of Mexico oil spill to push for elimination of the cap on how much money oil companies are responsible to pay for in the event of a spill. "Taxpayers should not shoulder the cost of this disaster," she said. "We must take the necessary steps to ensure that BP pays for its own negligence."

In June 2010, Shaheen introduced legislation with Colorado Democrat Mark Udall to increase funding for research and development to prevent future oil spills. Following reports of alleged corruption in the Minerals Management Service (MMS) and on the heels of the gulf oil spill, Shaheen sent a letter to Interior Secretary Ken Salazar calling for the dismantling of the agency. "MMS has had a culture of incompetence and corruption," she wrote. Although the administration proposed a reorganization of the MMS, Shaheen took a stronger stance. "I think we need to clean out that house. It is time to abolish MMS and start anew with a new agency and new people."

Shaheen introduced legislation in late 2010 to create a competitive grant program that focuses on science, technology, engineering and mathematics programs in public schools. A strong public education system has long been a key issue to Shaheen. Throughout her life, she attended public schools and universities; she taught language arts at a newly integrated high school in Mississippi to help put her husband through law school. In her 1996 gubernatorial race, Shaheen called for expanded access to kindergarten; as governor she instituted a kindergarten initiative and increased state assistance for public schools and the state's university system. She supports an overhaul of the 2001 education law known as No Child Left Behind and backed Democratic legislation — enacted as part of the health care overhaul — that makes the federal government the sole provider of student loans for college.

Shaheen chairs the Foreign Relations Subcommittee on European Affairs — the same panel Obama chaired when he served in the Senate — and joined the Armed Services Committee in the 112th Congress (2011-12). She was a vocal supporter of the New START agreement designed to limit the nuclear stockpiles in Russia and the United States that the Senate approved in late 2010. "The overwhelming and bipartisan consensus has been clear: the New START Treaty is squarely in the national security interests of the United States," she wrote in a Manchester Union Leader op-ed before the vote.

Shaheen, who ran a family jewelry business for eight years after she and her husband were first married, also serves on the Small Business and Entrepreneurship Committee, where she backed tax breaks for small businesses to encourage hiring.

Shaheen's father's family was solidly Republican, dating back to the Civil War, when they fed potatoes to Union troops in Missouri. After casting her first presidential vote for Richard Nixon, Shaheen said she migrated to the Democratic Party over opposition to the Vietnam War and inspiration from the civil rights movement, although many of the most staunch segregationists were Democrats.

Shaheen's future in New Hampshire politics began to take shape when she worked at a lobster pound in Maine the summer after graduating from college. It was there she met her husband, Bill Shaheen, a second-generation Lebanese-American who grew up in New Hampshire. After he completed law school and she finished her master's degree in political science, the couple settled in New Hampshire, where she signed up to be a regional organizer for Jimmy Carter's successful 1976 presidential campaign. She went on to serve as Gary Hart's state director in the 1984 presidential race, and followed that up with work on several state and local campaigns.

Building on the contacts made during those campaigns, in 1990 she was elected to the state Senate, and in 1997 became the state's first elected female governor. "When I first ran for governor, I was referred to in the newspaper as 'Betty Crocker,' " Shaheen said during a "Women, Power and Politics" PBS feature. "And that was a compliment!"

Shaheen first made a bid for the U.S. Senate seat in 2002, running against John E. Sununu, then a GOP House member. Sununu pulled out a 4-percentage-point victory.

After that defeat, she spent some time in academia. In 2003, she taught a university course on how to govern in a partisan environment, drawing on her experience as a Democratic governor with a Republican legislature.

But she couldn't stay away from politics. She served as national chairwoman for Massachusetts Sen. John Kerry's 2004 presidential campaign. In 2005, she became director of the Institute of Politics at Harvard's John F. Kennedy School of Government.

She entered the fray again in September 2007, after a University of New Hampshire poll showed Sununu trailing her by 16 points in a hypothetical rematch.

Shaheen benefited from a political environment that had shifted markedly toward the Democrats in the six years since her first Senate try, both nationally and in New Hampshire. She won by 6 percentage points.

Key Votes

2010

Pass budget reconciliation bill to modify overhauls of health care and federal student loan programs	YES
Proceed to disapproval resolution on EPA authority to regulate greenhouse gases	NO
Overhaul financial services industry regulation	YES
Limit debate to proceed to a bill to broaden campaign finance disclosure and reporting rules	YES
Limit debate on an extension of Bush-era income tax cuts for two years	YES
Limit debate on a bill to provide a path to legal status for some children of illegal immigrants	YES
Allow for a repeal of "don't ask, don't tell"	YES
Consent to ratification of a strategic arms reduction treaty with Russia	YES

2009

Prevent release of remaining financial industry bailout funds	YES
Make it easier for victims to sue for wage discrimination remedies	YES
Expand the Children's Health Insurance Program	YES
Limit debate on the economic stimulus measure	YES
Repeal District of Columbia firearms prohibitions and gun registration laws	NO
Limit debate on expansion of federal hate crimes law	YES
Strike funding for F-22 Raptor fighter jets	NO

CQ Vote Studies

	PARTY UNITY		PRESIDENTIAL SUPPORT	
	SUPPORT	OPPOSE	SUPPORT	OPPOSE
2010	94%	6%	100%	0%
2009	95%	5%	95%	5%

Interest Groups

	AFL-CIO	ADA	CCUS	ACU
2010	94%	90%	18%	0%
2009	100%	100%	43%	8%

Sen. Kelly Ayotte (R)

Capitol Office
224-3324
ayotte.senate.gov
144 Russell Bldg. 20510-2904; fax 224-4952

Committees
Armed Services
Commerce, Science & Transportation
Small Business & Entrepreneurship
Special Aging

Residence
Nashua

Born
June 27, 1968; Nashua, N.H.

Religion
Roman Catholic

Family
Husband, Joseph Daley; two children

Education
Pennsylvania State U., B.A. 1990 (political science);
Villanova U., J.D. 1993

Career
Gubernatorial aide; state prosecutor; lawyer; state
deputy attorney general

Political Highlights
N.H. attorney general, 2004-09

ELECTION RESULTS

2010 GENERAL
Kelly Ayotte (R)	273,218	60.0%
Paul W. Hodes (D)	167,545	36.8%
Chris Booth (I)	9,194	2.0%
Ken Blevens (LIBERT)	4,753	1.0%

2010 PRIMARY
Kelly Ayotte (R)	53,056	38.2%
Ovide M. Lamontagne (R)	51,397	37.0%
Bill Binnie (R)	19,508	14.0%
Jim Bender (R)	12,611	9.1%
Dennis Lamare (R)	1,388	1.0%

Elected 2010; 1st term

Ayotte's demographic characteristics immediately make her a potentially prominent face on the national scene for her party, and her conservative credentials have quickly won her allies inside the Senate.

Just a day after being sworn into office, she stood on a podium backed by a half-dozen of the most powerful Republicans in the Senate, part of the leadership's first Q&A of the year with the Washington press corps.

She was later tapped by National Republican Senatorial Committee Chairman John Cornyn of Texas to help lead a fundraising program that targets younger K Street types who might not have the means to contribute big money but can still afford to get involved.

And Ayotte (EYH-ott) has been mentioned as a potential candidate for a leadership spot in the 113th Congress (2013-14) as Republicans reshuffle their Senate hierarchy following the retirement of Arizonan Jon Kyl in 2012.

"What Kelly brings to our caucus is the diversity of being a mother of two young children, the wife of a small-businessman, she's a woman and she's from the Northeast," Lamar Alexander of Tennessee, the No. 3 Republican leader, told Roll Call.

She was chosen to deliver the first Republican response of 2011 to President Obama's weekly radio address. Presaging the debate that would consume much of the first few months of the 112th Congress (2011-12), she said "the American people sent us to Congress with clear instructions: make government smaller, not bigger. And stop spending money we don't have on programs that aren't working."

During the campaign, Ayotte demonstrated the ability to walk a careful political line, backing numerous positions favored by tea party activists and winning the endorsement of former Alaska Gov. Sarah Palin while running as the party favorite and appealing to the often more centrist sensibilities of New Hampshire's electorate.

She backed Arizona's law empowering police officers to check the immigration status of people they detain and espoused hawkish budgetary ideals while never tacking so far to the right that she alienated moderates and independents.

"I stand with [the tea party] on those issues, on protecting individual freedom," she told the conservative magazine National Review before her primary victory. "We need to stop the unprecedented expansion of government, appeasing our enemies, and creating an entitlement culture."

In March 2011, she joined other conservative senators in threatening to try to block all bills from advancing to the Senate floor unless Democratic leaders make time to debate proposals to cut spending and deal with broader budgetary problems. In May she won a seat on the Budget Committee.

She was one of a dozen senators and senators-elect who signed a letter to Alexander endorsing a constitutional amendment requiring a balanced budget. She also joined colleagues in backing a moratorium on earmarks, the spending set-asides for projects in a member's home state or district. She says earmarks vital to her state, such as projects at the Portsmouth Naval Shipyard, should go through the regular appropriations process.

"We are on the path to bankrupt the greatest nation in the world," she told the Portsmouth Herald editorial board in September 2010.

Ayotte is a member of the Armed Services Committee and a military spouse who takes a tough line on national security issues, saying Obama's "policies do not match his rhetoric." Her husband, Joseph Daley, flew combat missions over Iraq and still serves in the Air National Guard.

She ties the government's fiscal situation to U.S. security interests. "If we don't restore fiscal sanity to Washington and reduce our national debt, I'm concerned that rising debt payments will begin to significantly crowd out the finances we have to protect our nation and its interests," she said at an Armed Services hearing in March.

Ayotte also takes conservative stands on social issues, opposing abortion — she defended the state's parental notification law in court — and same-sex marriage, and strongly supporting gun owners' rights.

A member of the Commerce, Science and Transportation Committee, she backs the all-of-the-above approach to energy favored by many Republicans and opposes a cap-and-trade system to reduce carbon emissions. She told the Portsmouth Herald that "there is scientific evidence that demonstrates there is some impact from human activities. However, I don't think the evidence is conclusive."

Daley currently owns a landscaping business, giving Ayotte insight she can use during Small Business and Entrepreneurship Committee hearings. She also serves on the Special Aging Committee.

Ayotte was born and lives in Nashua, but she left the state to attend college and law school, earning a bachelor's degree in political science at Penn State, where she was a competitive skier, and a law degree from Villanova, where she served as executive editor of the Environmental Law Journal.

She spent a year clerking for a justice of the New Hampshire Supreme Court, then worked in private practice.

Ayotte then joined the state attorney general's office as a prosecutor, where she handled a number of gruesome murder cases. According to a profile in the Manchester Union Leader, "to read accounts of Ayotte's work over the next couple years is to descend the depths of human depravity."

She briefly served as legal counsel to GOP Gov. Craig Benson before returning to the attorney general's office as deputy. She was in the No. 2 spot for about a year when her boss resigned and she took over as attorney general.

In her most celebrated case, she defended the state's parental notification law, which required minors to inform their parents before obtaining an abortion. Having lost in two lower courts, she appealed to the Supreme Court, against the wishes of incoming Democratic Gov. John Lynch. The high court vacated the lower court's judgment but did not rule on the substance of the challenge to the law's constitutionality. The law was repealed in 2007.

Republican Sen. Judd Gregg announced in 2009 that he would not seek re-election — after deciding against joining the Obama administration as Commerce secretary — and Ayotte resigned as attorney general to run for the seat. She was backed by establishment Republicans, but also had support from some activists. Her primary opponent, Ovide M. Lamontagne, was the favorite among conservatives who feared Ayotte might be too moderate. But she was able to balance the wings of the party just enough, besting Lamontagne by less than 2 percentage points.

Her opponent in the general election was two-term Democratic Rep. Paul W. Hodes, who attacked Ayotte's pledge to support extension of the 2001 and 2003 tax cuts.

The candidates also sparred over spending on local transportation projects. Hodes called for extending commuter rail service from Boston through Nashua to Concord, the state capital. Ayotte said it made more sense to spend finite transportation dollars to widen Interstate 93.

Hodes gained little traction and he was swamped by a banner Republican year in New Hampshire — the GOP also captured both U.S. House seats and both chambers of the state legislature. Ayotte defeated Hodes with 60 percent of the vote.

Rep. Frank Guinta (R)

Capitol Office
225-5456
guinta.house.gov
1223 Longworth Bldg. 20515-2901; fax 225-5822

Committees
Budget
Oversight & Government Reform
Transportation & Infrastructure

Residence
Manchester

Born
Sept. 26, 1970; Edison, N.J.

Religion
Roman Catholic

Family
Wife, Morgan Guinta; two children

Education
Assumption College, B.A. 1993 (political science & philosophy); Franklin Pierce Law Center, M.I.P. 2000

Career
Campaign and congressional district aide; insurance and risk management consultant; insurance claims manager

Political Highlights
N.H. House, 2000-02; Manchester Board of Mayor and Aldermen, 2002-06; mayor of Manchester, 2006-10

ELECTION RESULTS

2010 GENERAL

Frank Guinta (R)	121,655	54.0%
Carol Shea-Porter (D)	95,503	42.4%
Philip Hodson (LIBERT)	7,966	3.5%

2010 PRIMARY

Frank Guinta (R)	22,237	31.9%
Sean Mahoney (R)	19,418	27.9%
Rich Ashooh (R)	19,376	27.8%
Robert Martin Bestani (R)	5,337	7.7%
Peter Bearse (R)	1,158	1.7%
Richard Charles Parent (R)	1,051	1.5%
Kevin Rondeau (R)	702	1.0%
Andrew P. Kohlhofer	397	0.6%

Elected 2010; 1st term

Guinta says he is "a small-government kind of guy" who wants to focus on tax policy, with an eye toward economic growth and job creation.

He takes credit for several fiscal moves made in Manchester while he was mayor, including a tax cut, budget cuts and a tax cap, and he'll have a hand in setting fiscal policy at the federal level as a member of the Budget Committee.

Guinta (GIN-ta, with hard G), who also sits on the Transportation and Infrastructure Committee, acknowledges that freshmen have limited influence. But he says that he learned a few things as a New Hampshire-based aide to Republican Jeb Bradley, who held the same seat from 2003 to 2007.

"Certainly having two years of experience understanding the needs of constituents and how the process works in Washington gives me a leg up," said Guinta, who was elected twice to the New Hampshire House.

He voted to repeal the 2010 health care law and says it should be replaced with measures that allow small businesses to pool employees together in larger groups and allow people to cross state lines to purchase insurance.

Guinta supports gun rights and opposes abortion, saying that society can do more to help women in "crisis pregnancies" to find alternatives to abortion. He backed an amendment to a fiscal 2011 catchall spending bill that would bar funding for Planned Parenthood.

He sits on the Oversight and Government Reform Committee and has suggested abolishing the departments of Education and Energy. His view of the tax code runs along the same lines.

"I favor scrapping the tax code, starting over, make it a flat tax and go from there, but I'm not sure that the Congress is ready for that, yet," he said on the Patriot Express Radio Show in February 2011.

After winning an eight-person GOP primary, Guinta held small but steady leads through most of the campaign season over two-term Democratic incumbent Carol Shea-Porter, who had won the seat in 2006 by upending Guinta's former boss.

Guinta was able to capitalize on Shea-Porter's solidly liberal voting record to post a nearly 12-percentage-point victory.

New Hampshire 1

East — Manchester, Rochester, Dover

The 1st covers about one-fourth of New Hampshire's land, mainly in the southeast, yet contains most of its larger communities, including the state's most populous, Manchester. Many residents of southeastern towns, especially Dover, Hampton and Exeter, still commute to work in Massachusetts. North along the Maine border, Carroll County relies on tourism and farming.

Manchester has hosted technology and manufacturing companies, and has a large health care sector. A decade of diversification helped stabilize the city after years of slow growth, but several years of job losses affected all areas of the economy.

The Portsmouth Naval Shipyard, across the state line in Kittery, Maine, employs many district residents and serves as an economic anchor in the eastern part of the district. Expansion of the shipyard's nuclear submarine repair facilities is expected to boost the local economy.

Despite strong GOP roots, the 1st elected a Democrat to the U.S. House twice in recent years. Throughout the district and the state, a plurality of voters identify as independents, and races can be competitive. Strafford County, which includes Dover and Durham (home to the University of New Hampshire), gives Democrats healthy margins at the polls. Republicans do well in midsize and smaller towns, but the GOP no longer dominates population centers such as Manchester.

The district overall backed Barack Obama with 53 percent of its vote in the 2008 presidential election.

Major Industry
Health care, computer manufacturing

Cities
Manchester, 109,565; Dover, 29,987

Notable
Robert Frost operated a farm in Derry that is now a state historic site.

Rep. Charles Bass (R)

Capitol Office
225-5206
bass.house.gov
2350 Rayburn Bldg. 20515-2902; fax 225-2946

Committees
Energy & Commerce

Residence
Peterborough

Born
Jan. 8, 1952; Boston, Mass.

Religion
Episcopalian

Family
Wife, Lisa L. Bass; two children

Education
Dartmouth College, A.B. 1974 (government)

Career
Congressional aide; architectural products executive; energy consultant

Political Highlights
Sought Republican nomination for U.S. House, 1980; N.H. House, 1982-88; N.H. Senate, 1988-92; defeated in primary for re-election to N.H. Senate, 1992; U.S. House, 1995-2007; defeated for re-election to U.S. House, 2006

ELECTION RESULTS

2010 GENERAL

Charles Bass (R)	108,610	48.3%
Ann McLane Kuster (D)	105,060	46.8%
Tim vanBlommesteyn (I)	6,197	2.8%
Howard L. Wilson (LIBERT)	4,796	2.1%

2010 PRIMARY

Charles Bass (R)	27,457	42.6%
Jennifer M. Horn (R)	22,868	35.5%
Robert J. Giuda (R)	11,145	17.3%
Joseph G. Reilly (R)	1,757	2.7%
Wesley Sonner (R)	1,192	1.8%

Previous Winning Percentages
2004 (58%); 2002 (57%); 2000 (56%); 1998 (53%); 1996 (50%); 1994 (51%)

Elected 2010; 7th term

Also served 1995-2007

Bass has been here before — he held the 2nd District seat during the 12 years of the previous Republican majority, winning election as part of the 1994 "Republican revolution" and losing in the Democratic takeover of 2006. That makes him something of a bellwether, but he is not altogether in tune with the full-spectrum conservatism displayed by so many of his freshman colleagues.

Bass is a fiscal conservative who stresses the need to cut government spending and reduce the debt. But in the tradition of New England Republicans, he tends to adopt a more moderate stance on social and environmental issues.

Early in the 112th Congress (2011-12), he backed the House-passed GOP bill to cut fiscal 2011 spending by $61 billion. But he was one of only seven Republicans who voted for a failed amendment to protect federal funding for Planned Parenthood in the catchall measure.

Bass also opposed the GOP effort in 2004 to amend the Constitution to prohibit same-sex marriage.

Bass had earlier angered his leadership by becoming one of the decisive final four lawmakers who forced a vote on the 2002 campaign finance overhaul bill opposed by most Republicans.

Still, Bass says his main motivation in seeking to reclaim his old seat was to counteract the "arrogance" Democrats have shown since gaining control of Congress in 2006. The Congressional Budget Office's prediction of $1 trillion annual federal deficits over the next decade was "the straw that broke the camel's back for me," he said.

Not only is he back in Congress, but also back on the powerful Energy and Commerce Committee, where he played a role in passing the 2005 energy bill and now can apply some real-world experience.

After leaving Congress, he worked as a consultant with companies that develop alternative-energy technologies, and he wants to form a biomass energy caucus in Congress to promote such technology, which uses plant material and animal waste to generate power.

In the past, he has deviated from the conservative position in his opposition to drilling in Alaska's Arctic National Wildlife Refuge. He also has long been a strong defender of the Low-Income Home Energy Assistance Program, known as LIHEAP. He tried and failed to add money for the program to the 2011 catchall spending bill.

Bass was once a supporter of an effort to establish a cap-and-trade system to reduce carbon emissions, but he said the Democratic plan the House passed in 2009 went too far and damaged the prospects for making progress on the issue.

"It's very disappointing. Now the environmental debate has been set back, rather than moved forward," he told Roll Call shortly after Election Day 2010. "And I believe we're going to have to think of a new approach."

On the broader questions of spending, regulation and the size of government, Bass is more of a traditional fiscal conservative.

Bass has said he would like to see the House establish a new standing committee dedicated to spending reduction. The panel would recommend cuts to the full House, giving members the opportunity to vote on them as resolutions.

He has applied the same strict standard of accountability to tax cuts, which at times put him at odds with party leaders.

In 2004 he was one of 11 Republicans to support a non-binding Democratic motion intended to put the House on record in favor of making both tax cuts and mandatory spending subject to pay-as-you-go rules.

Bass was born into a political family. From 1955 to 1963 his father, Perkins Bass, held the congressional seat he now occupies. His grandfather, Robert P. Bass, was the state's governor from 1911 to 1913.

After graduating from Dartmouth, Bass served two Republican House members from Maine: first as a field worker for William S. Cohen and then as chief of staff for David F. Emery. His first attempt to win a seat in Congress came in 1980, when Republican Rep. James C. Cleveland retired. But Bass was outmaneuvered by another of New Hampshire's political "blue bloods," Judd Gregg, whose father had been governor in the 1950s.

Two years later, while chairman of a company that fabricates architectural panel products for buildings, Bass won election to the state House and continued there for six years. In 1988, he won a seat in the state Senate, where he wrote the New Hampshire law on voluntary campaign spending limits.

In 1992, Bass lost his state Senate seat when a conservative beat him in the GOP primary. He tried for Congress again two years later, winning his party's nomination with 29 percent of the vote; two conservatives divided nearly half of the total. In November, the Republican takeover tide helped Bass oust the Democratic incumbent, Dick Swett, by 5 percentage points.

In both 1996 and 1998, Bass drew primary challenges from conservatives and went on to post narrow victories in the fall. In 2000, he avoided a primary challenge and took 56 percent against a well-funded Democratic newcomer, Barney Brannen.

In 2002, Bass was outspent by his opponent, Democrat Katrina Swett, the wife of the man he unseated in 1994 and a daughter of the late Rep. Tom Lantos of California, but he won with 57 percent. In 2004, he beat Paul Hodes, a former state assistant attorney general, by 20 points.

Hodes came back for a rematch in 2006, helping the Democrats win the House by defeating Bass by 7 points.

Hodes decided to make a run for the Senate in 2010, leaving the seat open in a strong Republican year.

Bass won a five-way Republican primary with relative ease, then slipped past Democrat Ann McLane Kuster by less than 2 percentage points, winning 48 percent of the vote.

Bass joined Steve Chabot of Ohio as the only members of the class of 1994 to have defeated Democratic incumbents that year, left Congress, then returned as part of the GOP wave of 2010.

CQ Vote Studies				
	PARTY UNITY		PRESIDENTIAL SUPPORT	
	SUPPORT	OPPOSE	SUPPORT	OPPOSE
2006	82%	18%	72%	28%
2005	87%	13%	67%	33%
2004	85%	15%	68%	32%
2003	91%	9%	78%	22%
2002	85%	15%	82%	18%
2001	85%	15%	79%	21%

Interest Groups				
	AFL-CIO	ADA	CCUS	ACU
2006	43%	40%	80%	56%
2005	13%	25%	85%	58%
2004	100%	100%	40%	0%
2003	100%	85%	67%	4%
2002	96%	85%	58%	8%
2001	100%	80%	54%	13%

West — Nashua, Concord

The 2nd District encompasses the entire western half of New Hampshire and most of the state's southern border with Massachusetts, extending from white-collar territory in the southern tier to the mountains and forests of the sparsely populated "North Country."

The district has an economy as varied as its population. Many former Massachusetts residents who fled higher tax rates live along the populous southern tier of the district in cities and towns such as Salem, Windham and Atkinson, but still work across the state line. Nashua, the 2nd's most populous city, remains deeply involved in the computer and defense electronics industries. A nascent green-technology sector is expected to bolster the local economy, and Nashua's housing market has remained stable.

The economy of the heavily forested North Country is closely tied to paper manufacturing and wood products. Local officials hope that diversification of the wood products manufacturing industry and developing renewable-energy interests in Coos County will boost the struggling economy here. In the far northern reaches of the state, about 20 miles from the border

with Quebec, is tiny Dixville Notch, where residents cast the nation's first votes at the stroke of midnight on Election Day.

Between the Massachusetts border and the North Country lie many smaller blue-collar towns that depend on tourism revenue from lake visitors and skiers.

In addition to its small towns, Grafton County hosts technology firms and Dartmouth College.

Once rock-ribbed Republican, the 2nd experienced a brief shift to the left, and Barack Obama won the district with 56 percent of its 2008 presidential vote. Nashua leans Democratic, and the liberalism of the college towns of Hanover and Keene, as well as of the state capital of Concord, add Democratic votes. Other population centers, such as Salem, Atkinson and Milford, are politically competitive.

Major Industry
High-tech, manufacturing

Cities
Nashua, 86,494; Concord, 42,695; Keene, 23,409; Claremont, 13,355

Notable
The State House in Concord is the oldest U.S. legislative building in which both houses continue to sit in their original chambers.

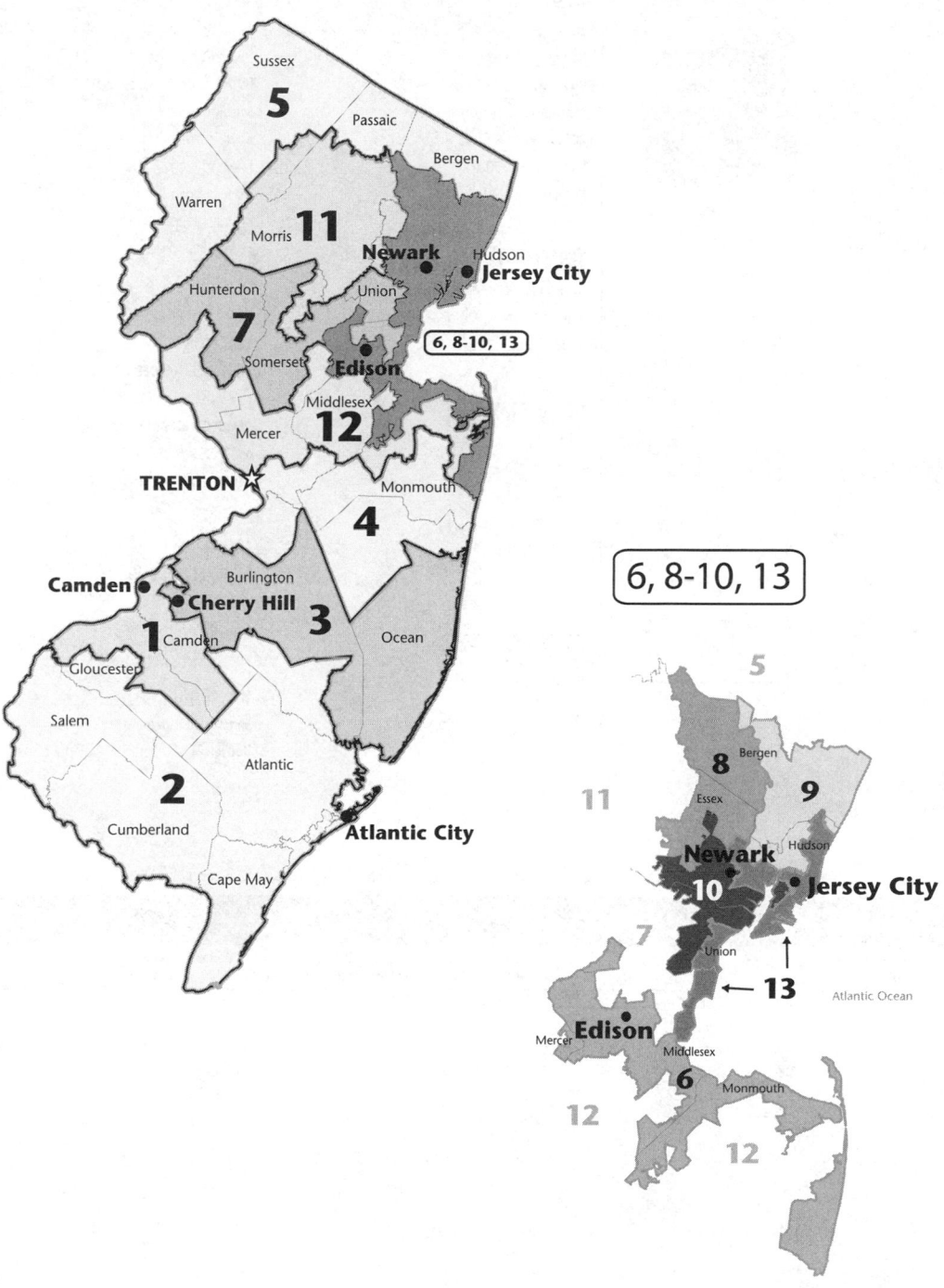

Gov. Chris Christie (R)

First elected: 2009
Length of term: 4 years
Term expires: 1/14
Salary: $175,000
Phone: (609) 292-6000
Residence: Mendham
Born: Sept. 6, 1962; Newark, N.J.
Religion: Roman Catholic
Family: Wife, Mary Pat Christie; four children
Education: U. of Delaware, B.A. 1984 (political science); Seton Hall U., J.D. 1987
Career: Lawyer; lobbyist
Political highlights: Morris County Board of Freeholders, 1995-97; sought Republican nomination for N.J. Assembly 1995; defeated in primary for re-election to Morris County Board of Freeholders, 1997; U.S. attorney, 2002-08

ELECTION RESULTS

2009 GENERAL
Chris Christie (R)	1,174,445	48.5%
Jon Corzine (D)	1,087,731	44.8%
Christopher J. Daggett (I)	139,579	5.8%

Lt. Governor
Kim Guadagno (R)

First elected: 2009
Length of term: 4 years
Term expires: 1/14
Salary: $141,000
Phone: (609) 292-6000

LEGISLATURE

Legislature: Year-round with recess
Senate: 40 members, 4-year terms
2011 ratios: 24 D, 16 R; 31 men, 9 women
Salary: $49,000
Phone: (609) 292-4840
Assembly: 80 members, 2-year terms
2011 ratios: 47 D, 33 R; 56 men, 24 women
Salary: $49,000
Phone: (609) 292-4840

TERM LIMITS

Governor: 2 consecutive terms
Senate: No
House: No

URBAN STATISTICS

CITY	POPULATIO
Newark	277,140
Jersey City	247,597
Paterson	146,199
Elizabeth	124,969
Edison	99,967

REGISTERED VOTERS

Unaffiliated/other	46%
Democrat	33%
Republican	20%

POPULATION

2010 population	8,791,894
2000 population	8,414,350
1990 population	7,730,188
Percent change (2000-2010)	+4.5%
Rank among states (2010)	11
Median age	38.3
Born in state	52.6%
Foreign born	19.3%
Violent crime rate	312/100,000
Poverty level	9.4%
Federal workers	83,107
Military	6,673

ELECTIONS

STATE ELECTION OFFICIAL
(609) 292-3760
DEMOCRATIC PARTY
(609) 392-3367
REPUBLICAN PARTY
(609) 989-7300

MISCELLANEOUS

Web: www.nj.gov
Capital: Trenton

U.S. CONGRESS

Senate: 2 Democrats
House: 7 Democrats, 6 Republicans

2010 Census Statistics by District

District	2008 Vote for President Obama	McCain	White	Black	Asian	Hispanic	Median Income	White Collar	Blue Collar	Service Industry	Over 64	Under 18	College Education	Rural	Sq. Miles
1	65%	34%	65%	17%	4%	12%	$60,014	63%	20%	16%	12%	24%	25%	1%	335
2	54	45	66	13	4	15	56,822	55	22	23	14	24	22	21	1,982
3	52	47	78	9	4	6	71,003	68	17	15	17	23	31	4	926
4	47	52	75	8	4	12	68,689	66	19	16	15	25	30	7	719
5	45	54	80	2	9	8	91,029	72	15	12	14	25	43	17	1,099
6	61	38	54	15	12	18	68,070	65	19	16	12	23	34	0	196
7	50	49	69	5	13	11	93,875	74	14	11	13	25	45	10	595
8	63	36	46	13	6	33	60,763	63	21	16	13	25	32	0	107
9	61	38	50	7	14	26	65,884	67	18	15	14	21	36	0	93
10	87	13	17	56	4	20	46,213	56	22	22	11	26	21	0	66
11	45	54	76	3	9	10	98,279	75	13	12	13	25	49	7	610
12	58	41	64	11	15	8	88,383	76	12	12	13	24	47	7	633
13	75	24	27	11	9	51	49,140	55	26	19	10	22	27	0	57
STATE	**57**	**42**	**59**	**13**	**8**	**18**	**68,981**	**66**	**18**	**16**	**13**	**24**	**34**	**6**	**7,417**
U.S.	**53**	**46**	**64**	**12**	**5**	**16**	**51,425**	**60**	**23**	**17**	**13**	**25**	**28**	**21**	**3,537,438**

Sen. Frank R. Lautenberg (D)

Capitol Office
224-3224
lautenberg.senate.gov
324 Hart Bldg. 20510-3003; fax 228-4054

Committees
Appropriations
Commerce, Science & Transportation
(Surface Transportation and Merchant Marine -
Chairman)
Environment & Public Works
(Superfund, Toxics & Environmental Health -
Chairman)

Residence
Cliffside Park

Born
Jan. 23, 1924; Paterson, N.J.

Religion
Jewish

Family
Wife, Bonnie Lautenberg; four children

Education
Columbia U., B.S. 1949 (economics)

Military Service
Army, 1942-46

Career
Paycheck processing firm founder

Political Highlights
No previous office

ELECTION RESULTS

2008 GENERAL

Frank R. Lautenberg (D)	1,951,218	56.0%
Dick Zimmer (R)	1,461,025	42.0%

2008 PRIMARY

Frank R. Lautenberg (D)	203,012	58.9%
Robert E. Andrews (D)	121,777	35.3%
Donald Cresitello (D)	19,743	5.7%

2002 GENERAL

Frank R. Lautenberg (D)	1,138,193	53.9%
Doug Forrester (R)	928,439	44.0%
Ted Glick (GREEN)	24,308	1.2%

Previous Winning Percentages
1994 (50%); 1988 (54%); 1982 (51%)

Elected 1982; 5th term

Did not serve 2001-03

Since starting his second Senate tour of duty in 2003, the unabashedly liberal Lautenberg has taken the lead on homeland security, environmental and transportation issues, while fending off critics who suggest that he make way for someone younger.

Diagnosed with a cancerous tumor in his stomach after falling in his home in February 2010, Lautenberg underwent chemotherapy treatments, losing weight and hair, before staging a rapid recovery. He offered his own testimonial in support of the health care overhaul enacted in 2010, telling the Star-Ledger he had learned the importance of "having a card to show when I went to the hospital."

In late June 2010, Lautenberg reported that his doctor said he was cancer-free. Several days later, he clinched a temporary coup by nudging aside Mary L. Landrieu of Louisiana to take over as interim chairman of the Appropriations Subcommittee on Homeland Security, succeeding the late Robert C. Byrd of West Virginia. He was the odd man out, though, in a shuffling of cardinals in the 112th Congress (2011-12) that ended with Landrieu taking over the Homeland Security panel.

But Lautenberg continues to influence the homeland security spending debate as vice chairman of the spending panel and holds two related subcommittee chairmanships.

Lautenberg uses his vice chairmanship to promote funding for the Coast Guard and for communities that are potential targets of terrorists. The Sept. 11 attacks remain a defining theme in his work: "Perhaps since the Civil War, nothing has changed our lives — life in America — like 9/11," Lautenberg said. He makes a passionate case for security upgrades along the "most dangerous two miles in America," a chain of refineries and tanks containing chlorine and other chemicals between Newark Liberty International Airport and Port Elizabeth, N.J. "We have an area of great susceptibility," he said.

The octogenarian stays fit with visits to the gym, takes casual strolls with hands in his pockets and animates speeches with sweeping gestures. With few political concerns until he faces possible re-election at age 90 in 2014, Lautenberg often takes the lead on liberal causes.

A longtime advocate of stricter gun laws, he pushed to ban higher-capacity ammunition magazines in the wake of the January 2011 attack that critically wounded Arizona Democratic Rep. Gabrielle Giffords and killed six others, including a staff member and a federal judge. "The only reason to have 33 bullets loaded in a handgun is to kill a lot of people very quickly," Lautenberg said. "These high-capacity clips simply should not be on the market."

He opposed a two-year extension of the Bush-era tax rates, one of 10 members of the Senate Democratic caucus to vote against the deal struck by President Obama in late 2010. "Windfalls for the wealthiest of us does not benefit our economy or create jobs — and they are what got us into this fiscal mess to begin with," he said on the Senate floor.

Although well-positioned to deliver projects to his state, Lautenberg faced an unexpected obstacle back home in GOP Gov. Chris Christie, who moved in October 2010 to kill one of the senator's trophies — a New Jersey-to-Manhattan rail tunnel — citing projected cost overruns and a desire to fund other projects. Lautenberg fought back by arguing the state should follow up on past commitments to the project.

He vowed to press in the 112th Congress for development of a national freight strategy as part of the surface transportation reauthorization debate, new disclosure requirements for chemical products and new mandates for the use of safer technology at some chemical plants to avert terrorist attacks.

Despite the lack of formal seniority rights from his first stint in the Senate, Lautenberg has the expertise and contacts of a senior member. As chairman of the Commerce, Science and Transportation Subcommittee on Surface Transportation and Merchant Marine Infrastructure, Safety and Security, he has led efforts to boost Amtrak. He shepherded into law in 2008 a bipartisan bill authorizing $14.4 billion over five years for the passenger railroad.

He chairs the Environment and Public Works panel on Superfund, Toxins and Environmental Health — a position that enables him to work closely with EPA Administrator Lisa P. Jackson, a former New Jersey environmental protection commissioner.

Born in Paterson, Lautenberg is the son of Polish and Russian immigrants. His parents moved their family a dozen times in their constant search for work. His father, Sam, worked in silk mills, sold coal and once ran a tavern. When his father died of cancer, Lautenberg, then a teenager, worked nights and weekends to help the family stay afloat.

After high school, Lautenberg enlisted and served in the Army Signal Corps in Europe during World War II. When he returned, he enrolled in Columbia University on the GI Bill, graduating with an economics degree in 1949. With two boyhood friends from his old neighborhood, he started a payroll services company, Automatic Data Processing, and turned it into one of the world's largest computing services companies.

Lautenberg also dabbled in politics as a Democratic activist and fundraiser. His $90,000 contribution to George McGovern's 1972 campaign earned him a place on President Richard Nixon's enemies list. In 1982, he ran for the Senate seat opened by the conviction of Democratic incumbent Harrison A. Williams Jr. in the Abscam corruption probe. Spending $4 million of his own money, Lautenberg took 51 percent of the vote to defeat GOP Rep. Millicent Fenwick.

In 1988, he beat back an aggressive challenge from Republican Peter M. Dawkins, once the Army's youngest brigadier general. Lautenberg survived the 1994 GOP tide with a 3-percentage-point victory over conservative state Assembly Speaker Garabed "Chuck" Haytaian.

Lautenberg retired from the Senate at the end of the 106th Congress (1999-2000) but was summoned back when Democrat Robert G. Torricelli abandoned his 2002 re-election bid amid revelations of improper dealings with a campaign donor. It was five weeks before the election. The party furiously courted replacement candidates, but they declined, and Democrats feared losing the seat to GOP businessman Doug Forrester.

Age 78 at the time, Lautenberg was perhaps an older candidate than party leaders would have preferred, but he was widely known. Lautenberg won by 10 percentage points. Democrats were grateful for his return but didn't restore the seniority he had accrued during his first stint in the Senate.

A Quinnipiac University poll in July 2007 found a narrow majority of respondents — and nearly half of the Democrats — felt Lautenberg was "too old to effectively serve another six-year term." He drew a Democratic opponent in 2008 — Rep. Robert E. Andrews, who had long been known to harbor ambitions for statewide office. But in the June primary, Lautenberg defeated Andrews with 59 percent of the vote and breezed past former GOP Rep. Dick Zimmer in the general election.

Lautenberg is one of the 10 wealthiest members of Congress, worth at least $49.7 million, according to his 2009 financial disclosure. His private family foundation had invested $7.3 million with financier Bernard Madoff, who confessed in 2008 to running a Ponzi scheme that lost investors more than $50 billion. In February 2009 the foundation sued Madoff's brother, Peter, who worked with Bernard.

Key Votes

2010

Pass budget reconciliation bill to modify overhauls of health care and federal student loan programs	YES
Proceed to disapproval resolution on EPA authority to regulate greenhouse gases	NO
Overhaul financial services industry regulation	YES
Limit debate to proceed to a bill to broaden campaign finance disclosure and reporting rules	YES
Limit debate on an extension of Bush-era income tax cuts for two years	NO
Limit debate on a bill to provide a path to legal status for some children of illegal immigrants	YES
Allow for a repeal of "don't ask, don't tell"	YES
Consent to ratification of a strategic arms reduction treaty with Russia	YES

2009

Prevent release of remaining financial industry bailout funds	NO
Make it easier for victims to sue for wage discrimination remedies	YES
Expand the Children's Health Insurance Program	YES
Limit debate on the economic stimulus measure	YES
Repeal District of Columbia firearms prohibitions and gun registration laws	NO
Limit debate on expansion of federal hate crimes law	YES
Strike funding for F-22 Raptor fighter jets	YES

CQ Vote Studies

	PARTY UNITY		PRESIDENTIAL SUPPORT	
	SUPPORT	OPPOSE	SUPPORT	OPPOSE
2010	99%	1%	97%	3%
2009	99%	1%	97%	3%
2008	99%	1%	30%	70%
2007	98%	2%	37%	63%
2006	97%	3%	46%	54%
2005	98%	2%	27%	73%
2004	96%	4%	57%	43%
2003	97%	3%	44%	56%

Interest Groups

	AFL-CIO	ADA	CCUS	ACU
2010	93%	95%	9%	0%
2009	94%	95%	43%	0%
2008	100%	100%	63%	4%
2007	100%	90%	55%	0%
2006	93%	100%	42%	0%
2005	93%	100%	29%	0%
2004	100%	100%	38%	0%
2003	100%	95%	26%	15%

Sen. Robert Menendez (D)

Capitol Office
224-4744
menendez.senate.gov
528 Hart Bldg. 20510-3004; fax 228-2197

Committees
Banking, Housing & Urban Affairs
(Housing, Transportation & Community
Development - Chairman)
Finance
Foreign Relations
(Western Hemisphere, Peace Corps & Global
Narcotics Affairs - Chairman)

Residence
Hoboken

Born
Jan. 1, 1954; Manhattan, N.Y.

Religion
Roman Catholic

Family
Divorced, two children

Education
Saint Peter's College, B.A. 1976 (political science &
urban studies); Rutgers U., J.D. 1979

Career
Lawyer

Political Highlights
Union City Board of Education, 1974-82; mayor of
Union City, 1986-92; N.J. Assembly, 1987-91; N.J. Sen-
ate, 1991-93; U.S. House, 1993-2006

ELECTION RESULTS

2006 GENERAL
Robert Menendez (D)	1,200,843	53.4%
Thomas H. Kean Jr. (R)	997,775	44.3%

2006 PRIMARY
Robert Menendez (D)	159,604	84.0%
James D. Kelly Jr. (D)	30,340	16.0%

Previous Winning Percentages
2004 House Election (76%); 2002 House Election
(78%); 2000 House Election (79%); 1998 House Election (80%); 1996 House Election (79%); 1994 House
Election (71%); 1992 House Election (64%)

Elected 2006; 1st full term

Appointed January 2006

Menendez is a fiercely partisan lawmaker and strategist who led Senate Democrats' campaign committee during the tough 2010 cycle. Ambitious and aggressive, he is likely to continue playing a leading role for his party on a variety of issues — most notably on immigration, as the only Hispanic Democrat in the Senate.

Quick to release a belly laugh at his own or his staff's jokes, Menendez has been a boisterous presence since his appointment to the Senate in 2006. He was given the reins of the Democratic Senatorial Campaign Committee (DSCC) for the 2010 cycle due to his political acumen and fundraising skills. He spent that election year hammering on the Republican Party in a success-ful effort to prevent a GOP takeover of the Senate. "They have stood with the special interests, with Wall Street, with the big banks, with Big Insurance, with Big Oil," Menendez said in September. "We have been fighting for the average person in this country."

He was the first Hispanic of either party elected to a top leadership post in Congress when he was chosen by his colleagues in 2003 as House Demo-cratic Caucus chairman, the No. 3 position. During his one term as DSCC in 2009-10, Menendez's committee out-raised its GOP counterpart despite the political environment favoring Republicans.

At the start of the 111th Congress (2009-10), Menendez gained a seat on the influential Finance Committee, where he helped Democrats push through a health care overhaul, President Obama's top legislative priority. The final legislation included a provision written by Menendez that increased consumers' ability to protest their health insurance companies' denial of claims.

On the Banking, Housing and Urban Affairs Committee — where he chairs the Housing, Transportation and Community Development panel — Menendez helped shape a major rewrite of financial regulations following the banking crisis in the fall of 2008. Recalling that time period, Menendez said he told Federal Reserve Chairman Ben S. Bernanke in a meeting with committee members that Congress needed to do such a rewrite. "You've got to have enough tools, Mr. Chairman, to take care of this at this time so we can think more proactively," Menendez told Bernanke. The Fed chairman answered: "Senator, if you and your colleagues don't respond in the next two to three weeks, we'll have a global economic meltdown." A $700 billion bank assistance bill followed.

With that history in mind, Menendez authored provisions in the 2010 financial regulatory overhaul requiring derivatives traders to disclose their actions and investment advisers to disclose potential conflicts of interests to their clients.

Formerly a member of the Energy and Natural Resources Committee, Menendez has opposed offshore drilling and railed against rising oil com-pany profits. In June 2009, Menendez voted in committee against compre-hensive legislation backed by Chairman Jeff Bingaman of New Mexico because it would allow expanded offshore drilling. Menendez urged the Senate to impose unlimited liability on oil companies for spills following the BP oil rig explosion in the Gulf of Mexico in April 2010.

Menendez takes a particularly strong stance via his post on the Foreign Relations Committee against easing U.S. relations with the Castro regime in Cuba. Menendez's parents moved to New York from Cuba in 1953 because of their opposition to the Batista government, but that has not made Menendez a friend of the Castro regime. As proponents of opening up American travel to Cuba pushed legislation in the House in 2010, Menendez made clear that he would use all his powers as a senator to block such action.

"I want to make it absolutely clear that I will oppose — and filibuster if need be — any effort to ease regulations that stand to enrich a regime that denies its own people basic human rights," he said on the Senate floor.

Menendez is sensitive to the concerns of all Hispanic immigrants. In 2009, he joined the ranks of senator-authors with his first book, "Growing American Roots: Why Our Nation Will Thrive as Our Largest Minority Flourishes."

During debate in 2007 on broad-based immigration legislation, Menendez was piqued by a proposed merit-based system for awarding green cards that valued highly skilled workers over applicants seeking family reunification. He pushed to give legal permanent-resident status to parents, spouses or children of active-duty military servicemembers. Underscoring his opposition to a fence along the Mexican border, Menendez suggested that some of the $3 billion for the project also be used to build a barrier along the Canadian border. In the end, he joined most Republicans in killing the legislation.

After efforts to resuscitate an immigration overhaul stalled repeatedly following that effort, Menendez unveiled his own sweeping immigration proposal in October 2010. It included a variety of provisions long sought by immigrant-rights groups, including a path to citizenship for illegal immigrants currently in the country and tougher border security enforcement measures that would have to be met before illegal immigrants could be granted legal status. Ever the political realist, Menendez couched his hopes for passing the legislation in 2011. "That's really our last chance," he said. "[If] we can't do it in early 2011, it ain't gonna happen in the course of the next two years."

Among his home-state pet projects is health aid for first-responders to the Sept. 11 terrorist attacks, many of whom live in New Jersey. He also spearheaded Foreign Relations Committee investigations into the 2009 release from a Scottish prison of a convicted Libyan terrorist involved in the 1988 bombing of Pan Am Flight 103 over Lockerbie. Thirty-four New Jerseyans died in that attack.

In early 2011 Menendez led the way in pushing the Obama administration to consider imposing a no-fly zone in Libya to aid rebels fighting the government of Muammar el-Qaddafi.

Menendez grew up in Union City, where his family lived in a tenement. When he was a high school senior, his teachers nominated him for the honors program. Menendez says he was a shy introvert then, but a public-speaking course that his teachers forced him to take taught him the skills that transformed him into an outspoken politician.

At 20, while attending St. Peter's College in Jersey City, Menendez was elected to the school board. He was elected mayor of Union City in 1986 and to the state legislature in 1987, serving in both offices simultaneously. In 1991, he was named to fill a vacancy in the state Senate, where he served until winning a U.S. House seat in 1992 in a district that saw its Hispanic population nearly double after redistricting that year.

Menendez outmaneuvered fellow New Jersey House Democrats to win appointment to the Senate in 2006 for the seat vacated by Democrat Jon Corzine, who was elected governor in November 2005. His campaign for a full six-year term that year was marked by a federal probe into charges by opponents that he steered federal funds to a nonprofit group that rented property from him. Menendez denied any wrongdoing and won by 9 percentage points. Facing re-election to a second full term in 2012, Menendez is not repeating his role as DSCC chairman, but his willingness to take that assignment in a tough year will keep him in good stead if he wins re-election and seeks a role in the Senate Democratic leadership in the years ahead.

Key Votes

2010

Pass budget reconciliation bill to modify overhauls of health care and federal student loan programs	YES
Proceed to disapproval resolution on EPA authority to regulate greenhouse gases	NO
Overhaul financial services industry regulation	YES
Limit debate to proceed to a bill to broaden campaign finance disclosure and reporting rules	YES
Limit debate on an extension of Bush-era income tax cuts for two years	YES
Limit debate on a bill to provide a path to legal status for some children of illegal immigrants	YES
Allow for a repeal of "don't ask, don't tell"	YES
Consent to ratification of a strategic arms reduction treaty with Russia	YES

2009

Prevent release of remaining financial industry bailout funds	NO
Make it easier for victims to sue for wage discrimination remedies	YES
Expand the Children's Health Insurance Program	YES
Limit debate on the economic stimulus measure	YES
Repeal District of Columbia firearms prohibitions and gun registration laws	NO
Limit debate on expansion of federal hate crimes law	YES
Strike funding for F-22 Raptor fighter jets	YES

CQ Vote Studies

	PARTY UNITY		PRESIDENTIAL SUPPORT	
	SUPPORT	OPPOSE	SUPPORT	OPPOSE
2010	97%	3%	100%	0%
2009	98%	2%	99%	1%
2008	98%	2%	28%	72%
2007	97%	3%	38%	62%
2006	95%	5%	50%	50%
2005	93%	7%	24%	76%
2004	93%	7%	34%	66%
2003	93%	7%	24%	76%
2002	87%	13%	28%	72%
2001	89%	11%	30%	70%

Interest Groups

	AFL-CIO	ADA	CCUS	ACU
2010	94%	90%	36%	0%
2009	94%	90%	43%	0%
2008	100%	100%	63%	4%
2007	95%	95%	55%	0%
2006	93%	90%	55%	4%
2005	93%	100%	40%	4%
2004	93%	85%	35%	8%
2003	93%	90%	37%	20%
2002	89%	95%	42%	8%
2001	100%	95%	35%	16%

Rep. Robert E. Andrews (D)

Capitol Office
225-6501
www.house.gov/andrews
2265 Rayburn Bldg. 20515-3001; fax 225-6583

Committees
Armed Services
Education & the Workforce

Residence
Haddon Heights

Born
Aug. 4, 1957; Camden, N.J.

Religion
Episcopalian

Family
Wife, Camille Spinello Andrews; two children

Education
Bucknell U., B.A. 1979 (political science); Cornell U., J.D. 1982

Career
Professor; lawyer

Political Highlights
Camden County Board of Freeholders, 1987-90 (director, 1988-90); sought Democratic nomination for governor, 1997; sought Democratic nomination for U.S. Senate, 2008

ELECTION RESULTS

2010 GENERAL

Robert E. Andrews (D)	106,334	63.2%
Dale M. Glading (R)	58,562	34.8%

2010 PRIMARY

Robert E. Andrews (D)	14,695	86.7%
John Caramanna (D)	2,262	13.3%

2008 GENERAL

Robert E. Andrews (D)	206,453	72.4%
Dale M. Glading (R)	74,001	26.0%

Previous Winning Percentages
2006 (100%); 2004 (75%); 2002 (93%); 2000 (76%); 1998 (73%); 1996 (76%); 1994 (72%); 1992 (67%); 1990 (54%); 1990 Special Election (55%)

Elected 1990; 11th full term

Andrews has worked to rehabilitate his reputation after infuriating many of his fellow Democrats by challenging Sen. Frank R. Lautenberg in a 2008 primary. He is a member of Minority Leader Nancy Pelosi's inner circle, and the Californian has entrusted him with several tasks that have helped bring him back into the party's good graces.

Andrews was one of two Democratic ambassadors to the Republicans' transition team following the GOP's takeover of the House in 2010. Pelosi also gave him a seat on the Democratic Steering and Policy Committee, which makes committee assignments and handles other leadership tasks.

Andrews now says he has laid his statewide ambitions to rest.

"Losing really hurts, but you learn a lot from it," Andrews told Roll Call in March 2011. "You learn what your weaknesses are and you look how to compensate for them, and I hope that I've become a better public servant by learning from defeat."

In the 111th Congress (2009-10), he took the lead on a major reorganization of defense acquisition procedure and offered vocal support of health care overhaul legislation. And Andrews has remained active in debates over the federal budget, pension programs and education policy.

Democrats on the Armed Services Committee relied heavily on Andrews during the overhaul of the Pentagon's purchasing process. He chaired that committee's Defense Acquisition Reform Panel, which was created in 2009 after the Government Accountability Office reported several hundred billion dollars in cost overruns for defense programs. Among other recommendations, the panel's report pushed for pay incentives for Pentagon employees whose acquisitions work keeps costs on budget. It also would require potential federal contractors to certify that they do not have "seriously delinquent" tax debts. "This was the culmination of our panel's work," Andrews said. "But in order for this to mean something, we need to make sure there's leadership at all levels to see it through."

The panel's report on spending and acquisition practices became the basis for legislation that passed the House and was then included in the annual defense authorization bill.

Hawkish on foreign policy early in his House tenure — he supported the U.S. invasion of Iraq — in early 2007 Andrews spoke out against President George W. Bush's plan to send more than 21,000 additional combat troops to Iraq, the "surge" that helped turn the tide in the war. He told The Star-Ledger of Newark in May 2008 that he considered the war a "fiasco" but he has since supported the Obama administration's increase in troop levels in Afghanistan.

When Democrats won control of the House in 2007, Andrews took the gavel of the Education and Labor Committee's Health, Employment, Labor and Pensions Subcommittee for the second time, and he has worked with the Obama administration on expanding and protecting retirement benefits and on the health care overhaul. He is now the subcommittee's ranking Democrat and will likely play a major role as the 112th Congress (2011-12) reauthorizes the Bush-era education law known as No Child Left Behind. (The full committee is now known as Education and the Workforce.)

Andrews was an outspoken voice in favor of the health care overhaul enacted in 2010 and was a member of a rapid-response team Democrats put in place during the August 2009 congressional recess, as the debate boiled over at several town hall meetings.

During the 109th Congress (2005-06), Andrews helped write legislation to rework federal regulation of the private pension system. He backed increased protections for older workers while giving corporations relief from excessive paperwork. In the end, however, House Republican leaders abandoned the negotiating process and brought another pension bill up for a vote. Andrews voted against that measure, objecting to the tactic and to the final bill's treatment of Continental Airlines, a major employer in New Jersey.

The son and grandson of shipyard workers, Andrews went to work at age 14 for the Suburban Newspaper Group, a local chain, hoping to cover basketball and football. Instead, he was assigned to report on local government, for $6 an article.

"The experience covering government and what went on in the local scene made me want to be a part of it," he said. The first in his family to go to college, Andrews was a teaching assistant in his senior year at Bucknell University and wrote this question to serve as the entire final exam for an introductory political science class: "Politics is everything. Explain."

After six years practicing law, Andrews, then 29, won a seat on the Camden County governing board. He was a protégé of liberal Democratic Rep. James J. Florio. After Florio was elected governor in 1989, Andrews won a 1990 special election to replace him in the House. Among his campaign staffers was a young opposition researcher by the name of Rahm Emanuel, who later would become a House colleague, White House chief of staff and mayor of Chicago.

Andrews has not faced significant opposition in any of his House primary races and has coasted in every general election since his first.

In 1997, Andrews ran for governor and narrowly lost in the Democratic primary to James E. McGreevey, who later resigned following a personal scandal. Andrews was again disappointed in 2005, when newly elected Gov. Jon Corzine chose Democratic Rep. Robert Menendez for the Senate seat vacated by Corzine.

In 2008, Andrews mounted an unsuccessful challenge to Lautenberg. Andrews won the endorsement of The Star-Ledger, but succeeded only in annoying the Democratic power structures in both New Jersey and Washington. Every Democratic member of the state's House delegation — Andrews' colleagues — endorsed Lautenberg.

Andrews' subsequent decision to seek re-election to the House — his wife, Camille, had won the Democratic primary to replace him, but then stepped aside for her husband — was met with criticism from several quarters. But the district's strong Democratic makeup ensured him an easy victory.

Key Votes

2010

Overhaul the nation's health insurance system	YES
Allow for repeal of "don't ask, don't tell"	YES
Overhaul financial services industry regulation	YES
Limit use of new Afghanistan War funds to troop withdrawal activities	NO
Change oversight of offshore drilling and lift oil spill liability cap	YES
Provide a path to legal status for some children of illegal immigrants	YES
Extend Bush-era income tax cuts for two years	YES

2009

Expand the Children's Health Insurance Program	YES
Provide $787 billion in tax cuts and spending increases to stimulate the economy	YES
Allow bankruptcy judges to modify certain primary-residence mortgages	YES
Create a cap-and-trade system to limit greenhouse gas emissions	YES
Provide $2 billion for the "cash for clunkers" program	YES
Establish the government as the sole provider of student loans	YES
Restrict federally funded insurance coverage for abortions in health care overhaul	NO

CQ Vote Studies

	PARTY UNITY		PRESIDENTIAL SUPPORT	
	SUPPORT	OPPOSE	SUPPORT	OPPOSE
2010	98%	2%	93%	7%
2009	99%	1%	96%	4%
2008	100%	0%	17%	83%
2007	97%	3%	6%	94%
2006	94%	6%	35%	65%

Interest Groups

	AFL-CIO	ADA	CCUS	ACU
2010	100%	90%	25%	0%
2009	100%	100%	33%	0%
2008	100%	85%	63%	0%
2007	96%	100%	50%	0%
2006	86%	85%	40%	16%

New Jersey 1

Southwest — Camden, Pennsauken

The 1st is a Democratic stronghold in southwestern New Jersey across the Delaware River from Philadelphia. Its largest concentration of residents lives in Camden, one of the poorest cities in the nation. Almost two-thirds of the district's population lives in Camden County, with most of the rest in Gloucester County and a handful on the western edge of Burlington County.

For decades, Camden has been plagued by the departure of residents and businesses, a shrinking tax base, surging unemployment and crime, particularly drug trafficking. Nearly a decade of state government control of the city's finances — including approval of a $175 million plan to redevelop and revitalize the area, as well as other construction and infrastructure improvements — ended in 2010. An aquarium and a 25,000-seat outdoor amphitheater have attracted more tourists to the waterfront, which is beginning to generate interest from corporations, thanks in part to tax incentives set up by the state. The city's port, a joint facility shared with Philadelphia, provides a revenue source for major projects, and EPA-funded industrial waste clean-up programs continue. Camden also is home to the

Campbell Soup Co., which donates money to the community for revitalization and health programs.

As distressed as the city is, some of its suburbs are developing, and Bridgeport, in northern Gloucester County, is home to a large industrial park, while a new cargo port is scheduled to open in Paulsboro, a refinery town on the Delaware River. The district also takes in the Rutgers University-Camden campus and Glassboro's Rowan University.

Blacks and Hispanics form an overwhelming majority of the population in Camden, while many whites live in the surrounding suburbs. Overall, blacks and Hispanics combined total nearly 30 percent of the district's population.

The 1st has a large working-class contingent, and Barack Obama took 65 percent of the 2008 presidential vote here. In Camden, which historically has low voter turnout, Obama received 94 percent.

Major Industry
Shipping, manufacturing, health care, education

Cities
Camden city, 77,344; Glassboro, 18,579; Lindenwold, 17,613

Notable
Poet Walt Whitman died in Camden in 1892.

Rep. Frank A. LoBiondo (R)

Capitol Office
225-6572
www.house.gov/lobiondo
2427 Rayburn Bldg. 20515-3002; fax 225-3318

Committees
Armed Services
Transportation & Infrastructure
(Coast Guard & Maritime Transportation - Chairman)
Select Intelligence

Residence
Ventnor

Born
May 12, 1946; Bridgeton, N.J.

Religion
Roman Catholic

Family
Wife, Tina Ercole; two children

Education
Saint Joseph's U., B.S. 1968 (business administration)

Career
Trucking company operations manager

Political Highlights
Cumberland County Board of Freeholders, 1985-87;
N.J. Assembly, 1988-94; Republican nominee for U.S.
House, 1992

ELECTION RESULTS

2010 GENERAL

Frank A. LoBiondo (R)	109,460	65.5%
Gary Stein (D)	51,690	30.9%
Peter F. Boyce (CNSTP)	4,120	2.5%

2010 PRIMARY

Frank A. LoBiondo (R)	19,337	78.1%
Linda Biamonte (R)	2,984	12.0%
Donna M. Ward (R)	2,451	9.9%

2008 GENERAL

Frank A. LoBiondo (R)	167,701	59.1%
David Kurkowski (D)	110,990	39.1%

Previous Winning Percentages
2006 (62%); 2004 (65%); 2002 (69%); 2000 (66%);
1998 (66%); 1996 (60%); 1994 (65%)

Elected 1994; 9th term

On Capitol Hill, where most lawmakers seek out publicity wherever they can find it, LoBiondo shuns the spotlight. He is rarely quoted or photographed in the national media, rarely seen before a bank of microphones. And he likes it that way.

"You need to make a decision . . . when you get here," the South Jersey Republican said. "Do you develop a Beltway agenda or a district agenda. Now, I don't think there is anything wrong with a Beltway agenda, but that has certain implications and realities that do not allow you to pursue a district agenda, at least the way I view it. It was clear to me from the beginning that I did not want a Beltway agenda."

LoBiondo (lo-bee-ON-dough) focuses on issues that directly affect his district, which is surrounded on three sides by water. He strongly opposes oil drilling off the state's coast, fearing spills that could despoil local beaches and fishing. He has introduced legislation to block any such exploration in every Congress of the past decade. "We want gambling in Atlantic City; we don't want gambling in our environment," he once said.

He introduced fewer than a dozen pieces of legislation in the 111th Congress (2009-10), most covering local priorities such as coastline protection, fishing and health benefits for New Jersey veterans. Asked about his proudest achievements, the Armed Services Committee member talks about supporting local military facilities and helping to establish a technical center in his district for the Federal Aviation Administration to develop the next-generation air traffic control system. He also serves on the Transportation and Infrastructure Committee and chairs its Coast Guard and Maritime Transportation Subcommittee.

LoBiondo's focus on local concerns has created an unusual profile on national issues. He is a Republican elected in the 1994 GOP sweep who carries broad support from casino interests, environmentalists and labor unions.

He led a group of GOP moderates in 2006 who pressured their leaders to permit a vote on increasing the minimum wage. In 2007, he joined House Democratic leaders in supporting the unionization of Government Accountability Office employees and worked to increase funding for the National Labor Relations Board. Political action committees affiliated with organized labor are his largest source of campaign contributions, giving more than two and a half times that of any other industry.

Some of his strongest critics are conservative Republicans, who savaged him in July 2009 for being one of eight GOP House members who voted for the Democrats' climate change bill. Conservative bloggers dubbed them the "Cap & Tax 8," a reference to the bill's provisions that would cap carbon emissions and allow facilities to trade emission permits.

But he banked enough goodwill with leadership to win a seat on the Select Intelligence Committee in the 112th Congress (2011-12), an appointment given by Speaker John A. Boehner of Ohio.

In keeping with his low-profile personality, LoBiondo has not been one to court a reputation as a party maverick, although his annual party unity score — the percentage of votes in which his sided with a majority of Republicans against a majority of Democrats — has been as low as 64 and never higher than 86. His departures from the conservative line, he says, are simply a response to his district's interests.

LoBiondo supported his party on some of the key votes of the 111th Congress, including the health care overhaul enacted in 2010. "This bill takes away the choice for patients and doctors to decide the best course of treatment, while empowering more than 100 new bureaucracies and an unelected, unaccountable 'health czar,'" he said before casting his vote against final passage of the bill in March 2010. "This bill takes away the choice of individuals to decide if they even want health insurance coverage, while empowering the IRS to penalize and prosecute those who refuse. This is the absolutely wrong approach to our nation's health care policy." He voted to repeal and defund the law early in 2011.

LoBiondo sees himself as a fiscal conservative, so much so that he is one of a handful of members who regularly spends less than he is allocated for official office expenses and returns the remainder to the U.S. Treasury. One way he saves money is his refusal to send out mass mailings. Constituents will hear from LoBiondo only if they contact him first, he said. And while coming in under budget in his office account doesn't get much attention, LoBiondo said, "I think it sends a message. Because while we have all these labels whether you are a moderate or this and that, the fiscal credentials are very important to me."

LoBiondo's grandparents arrived in southern New Jersey from Sicily and established a vegetable farm, where the congressman grew up. In the 1920s, when Atlantic City's hospitality industry was booming, his father bought a used truck to take his produce to market. Soon he was carrying his neighbors' produce as well, and the enterprise grew into LoBiondo Brothers Motor Express Inc., where the younger LoBiondo worked for 26 years. And he credits his father with kick-starting his political career. His father was mayor of rural Deerfield Township, president of the school board, an active member of the Kiwanis and founder of the local fire department.

LoBiondo was elected to a county office in 1984, not intending to go further. But his state assemblyman, who was retiring because he had cancer, urged LoBiondo to run for the seat. He won and served in the state House for almost seven years.

In 1992, he challenged Democratic Rep. William J. Hughes and lost. Two years later, Hughes retired and LoBiondo tried again, winning with 65 percent of the vote.

LoBiondo initially joined many fellow 1994 Republican candidates in vowing to serve no more than six terms. But as he reaped the benefits of congressional seniority, he backed off. Voters didn't mind — he has been re-elected with ease. He brushed aside a tea party challenger in the 2010 primary, then was re-elected with more than 65 percent of the vote.

Key Votes

2010

Overhaul the nation's health insurance system	NO
Allow for repeal of "don't ask, don't tell"	NO
Overhaul financial services industry regulation	NO
Limit use of new Afghanistan War funds to troop withdrawal activities	NO
Change oversight of offshore drilling and lift oil spill liability cap	NO
Provide a path to legal status for some children of illegal immigrants	NO
Extend Bush-era income tax cuts for two years	YES

2009

Expand the Children's Health Insurance Program	YES
Provide $787 billion in tax cuts and spending increases to stimulate the economy	NO
Allow bankruptcy judges to modify certain primary-residence mortgages	NO
Create a cap-and-trade system to limit greenhouse gas emissions	YES
Provide $2 billion for the "cash for clunkers" program	YES
Establish the government as the sole provider of student loans	NO
Restrict federally funded insurance coverage for abortions in health care overhaul	YES

CQ Vote Studies

	PARTY UNITY		PRESIDENTIAL SUPPORT	
	SUPPORT	OPPOSE	SUPPORT	OPPOSE
2010	86%	14%	40%	60%
2009	66%	34%	68%	32%
2008	73%	27%	39%	61%
2007	64%	36%	38%	62%
2006	73%	27%	73%	27%

Interest Groups

	AFL-CIO	ADA	CCUS	ACU
2010	29%	15%	88%	67%
2009	57%	35%	87%	60%
2008	67%	60%	72%	52%
2007	79%	50%	63%	44%
2006	50%	25%	73%	68%

New Jersey 2

South — Atlantic City, Vineland

One of the state's most politically and economically diverse districts, the 2nd stretches from the Philadelphia suburbs in Gloucester County to the beach communities of Ocean City and Cape May, taking in much of the southern tier of the state.

The western corner of the 2nd is largely rural Salem County, home to a nuclear energy plant run by PSEG. The district's center includes Cumberland and Atlantic counties, where farmers' markets and small agrarian communities grow peaches, blueberries, cranberries, tomatoes and soybeans. To the south, Cumberland County is the 2nd's most industrial area, although local officials hope to shift the economy from a reliance on glass and plastics manufacturing to service industries and construction. Cumberland County houses one federal prison and three state prisons.

The 2nd includes gambling resort destination Atlantic City. Hotels and casinos have created jobs, but the poorer parts of the city are ravaged by crime and urban blight. Fewer visitors are coming to the gambling mecca, and several casinos struggle with debt.

Tourism is the cash crop in shore communities on the eastern side of the

district. Boating and commercial and sport fishing do well on the Delaware Bay and on the Atlantic Ocean along the Cape May County coastline. The area is a leading producer of clams in the state, and the bay is the focus of a major oyster revitalization project.

Several areas expect to see offshore wind turbines start spinning along the Atlantic coast. The Delaware River's busy port also contributes to the economy.

This is a Republican-leaning district, and locals generally support smaller government and oppose gun control. Democrats do fare well in statewide elections in parts of Atlantic and Cumberland counties and in some of the district's more industrial towns. Democrat Barack Obama took 54 percent of the district's vote in the 2008 presidential election.

Major Industry
Gambling, tourism, agriculture, petroleum, manufacturing

Cities
Vineland, 60,724; Atlantic City, 39,558; Millville, 28,400; Bridgeton, 25,349

Notable
The main federal air marshal training facility is in Pomona at Atlantic City International Airport; the U.S. Coast Guard Training Center in Cape May is the only Coast Guard recruit training center.

Rep. Jon Runyan (R)

Capitol Office
225-4765
runyan.house.gov
1239 Longworth Bldg. 20515-3003; fax 225-0778

Committees
Armed Services
Natural Resources
Veterans' Affairs
  (Disability Assistance & Memorial Affairs -
  Chairman)

Residence
Mt. Laurel

Born
Nov. 27, 1973; Flint, Mich.

Religion
Roman Catholic

Family
Wife, Loretta Runyan; three children

Education
U. of Michigan, attended 1992-95 (movement science)

Career
Professional football player; professional arena football team owner

Political Highlights
No previous office

ELECTION RESULTS

2010 GENERAL

Jon Runyan (R)	110,215	50.0%
John Adler (D)	104,252	47.3%
Peter DeStefano (TEA)	3,284	1.5%

2010 PRIMARY

Jon Runyan (R)	17,250	60.4%
Justin Michael Murphy (R)	11,304	39.6%

Elected 2010; 1st term

Runyan, a hulking former professional football player, likely will stand out more for his 6-foot-7-inch frame than for his political views.

He expects to align closely with the positions of the most recent Republican to hold his seat: H. James Saxton, who retired in 2009.

Runyan won seats on two of the same committees occupied by Saxton: Natural Resources, where he can work to protect the pinelands and beaches of southern New Jersey; and Armed Services, where he can look out for one of his district's biggest employers — the huge military complex composed of McGuire Air Force Base, Fort Dix and the Lakehurst naval station. His other assignment is Veterans' Affairs, where he chairs the Subcommittee on Disability Assistance and Memorial Affairs.

He voted to repeal the health care law enacted in 2010, but Runyan says a full repeal is unrealistic in the 112th Congress (2011-12). Instead, lawmakers should "chip away at it" by eliminating its most costly provisions, a position he reinforced by supporting amendments to defund the law during debate on a catchall spending bill for fiscal 2011.

Although he's an economic conservative, Runyan veers toward the center on some social issues.

While believing marriage should be between a man and a woman, he backs civil unions for gay people. "Social issues are the only issues that really pull me back to be a moderate," Runyan said.

A Catholic, he supports abortion rights, except for late-term and partial-birth abortions.

Runyan, who spent most of his 13-year NFL career with the Philadelphia Eagles, said his charity work put him in touch with community leaders who urged him to run for Congress. He got 60 percent of the vote in the Republican primary, although late-September polls gave one-term Democrat John Adler a healthy lead, with tea party candidate Peter DeStefano drawing votes from Runyan. But Runyan was able to solidify conservatives behind him in the final weeks, and he upended Adler, winning 50 percent of the vote to Adler's 47 percent.

New Jersey 3

South central — Cherry Hill, Toms River

The 3rd District crosses the width of south-central New Jersey and takes in the entire political spectrum, from the solidly GOP shores of Ocean County to the traditionally Democratic Cherry Hill area in Camden County.

The environment is a perennial issue in Ocean County communities around Toms River, where the beach tourism industry is important. An expansion of the Garden State Parkway along much of the 3rd's coast has begun at the expense of hundreds of acres of trees that used to line the scenic drive — locals worry about the project's ecological impact. Burlington County, most of which is in the 3rd, is one of the largest cranberry-producing counties in the nation. Towns in the western portion of the county rely on white-collar jobs.

Integration of McGuire Air Force Base, Fort Dix and the Lakehurst naval station into a "mega-base" after the 2005 base realignment process brought thousands of new residents to the district. The presence of the joint base (shared with the 4th District) makes national defense a key issue here.

While Burlington leans Republican, the county's Democrats can combine with the 3rd's small share of Camden County to make elections here competitive. In 2008, Barack Obama took 52 percent of the district's presidential vote.

Major Industry
Retail, health care, agriculture, defense

Military Bases
Joint Base McGuire-Dix-Lakehurst (shared with the 4th), 8,950 military, 3,815 civilian (2011)

Cities
Toms River (unincorporated), 88,791; Ocean Acres (unincorporated), 16,142

Notable
NFL Films is based in Mt. Laurel.

Rep. Christopher H. Smith (R)

Capitol Office
225-3765
www.house.gov/chrissmith
2373 Rayburn Bldg. 20515-3004; fax 225-7768

Committees
Foreign Affairs
(Africa, Global Health & Human Rights - Chairman)

Residence
Robbinsville

Born
March 4, 1953; Rahway, N.J.

Religion
Roman Catholic

Family
Wife, Marie Smith; four children

Education
Trenton State College, B.A. 1975 (business)

Career
Sporting goods executive; state anti-abortion group director

Political Highlights
Republican nominee for U.S. House, 1978

ELECTION RESULTS

2010 GENERAL

Christopher H. Smith (R)	129,752	69.4%
Howard Kleinhendler (D)	52,118	27.9%
Joseph A. Siano (LIBERT)	2,912	1.6%

2010 PRIMARY

Christopher H. Smith (R)	21,723	68.8%
Alan R. Bateman (R)	9,839	31.2%

2008 GENERAL

Christopher H. Smith (R)	202,972	66.2%
Joshua M. Zeitz (D)	100,036	32.6%
Steven Welzer (GREEN)	3,543	1.2%

Previous Winning Percentages
2006 (66%); 2004 (67%); 2002 (66%); 2000 (63%);
1998 (62%); 1996 (64%); 1994 (68%); 1992 (62%);
1990 (63%); 1988 (66%); 1986 (61%); 1984 (61%);
1982 (53%); 1980 (57%)

Elected 1980; 16th term

Smith is tenacious, an attribute on full display whether he is stoking outrage about human rights violations around the world or opposing abortion at home and abroad. On the former, he sometimes finds common ground with Democrats, as he does on a few other issues, including veterans' health care and greater access to online information.

His willingness to devote long hours to his work, one of the House's most effective constituent-service operations and his reputation, untarnished by scandal, have kept him popular in a solidly Democratic state and Republican-leaning district. In 2008, when the GOP was drubbed at the polls in New Jersey and his district saw a surge in Democratic registration, Smith won by a 2-to-1 ratio. In 2010, he won almost 70 percent of the vote.

Smith prides himself on reaching across the aisle. His biggest contributors in the 2010 election cycle were unions. He was one of three Republicans (one of whom left Congress to join the Obama administration) to cosponsor legislation that would allow unions to organize workplaces without a secret ballot vote. "What my Republican colleagues often don't understand is that labor is a human-rights issue," Smith told The Star-Ledger.

His voting record reflects that bipartisan stance. On votes in which a majority of Republicans voted against a majority of Democrats, Smith has never sided with his party more than 89 percent of the time in a single year, with the high-water mark coming in 2002. In the 111th Congress (2009-10), he sided with his party 72 percent of the time.

Smith uses his platform as the No. 2 Republican on the Foreign Affairs Committee and chairman of its Africa, Global Health and Human Rights panel to further his causes. In March 2009, the House passed his bill demanding that Brazil's government return an 8-year-old New Jersey boy to his father under the Hague Convention, a treaty that provides for the recovery of a child from one nation to another. The boy's father, David Goldman, had been fighting for custody of his son since his Brazilian wife first took the boy out of the country in 2004, ignoring a court order to return. Smith traveled to Brazil with Goldman and helped reunite him with his son in February 2009.

In 2006 and 2009 he introduced measures to punish Internet companies that share users' personal information with foreign governments that restrict online access. He first introduced the legislation after learning that some companies were conforming to restrictions demanded by China. In 2010 he formed the Global Internet Freedom Caucus with Democrat David Wu of Oregon and condemned Microsoft for offering censored search engine results in China. "They [Microsoft] need to get on the right side of human rights rather than enabling tyranny, which they're doing right now," Smith said.

Smith is passionate about issues related to human trafficking. He was reappointed in 2009 as the special representative on human trafficking for the Commission on Security and Cooperation in Europe (better known as the Helsinki Commission), and he serves as co-chairman of the Congressional Caucus on Human Trafficking. In 2010 he pushed a bill that would require anyone convicted of a sex crime against a child to register with the U.S. government when traveling internationally. The measure is modeled on a similar domestic law named after a 7-year-old girl, Megan Kanka, who lived in Smith's district. In 2000, he won enactment of a law to combat trafficking in women and children, who are often forced into prostitution. In 2006, President George W. Bush signed Smith's bill toughening anti-trafficking measures and calling for $361 million in funding over two years.

Smith has long been among the vanguard of abortion opponents, pushing to prevent federal funds from paying for abortions, to stop foreign aid to agencies that counsel women about abortion and to protect the legal rights of abortion protesters.

Early in the 112th Congress (2011-12), the Judiciary Committee approved his bill to ban federal funding of abortions in almost all cases and prohibit the use of tax credits to pay for an abortion or to pay for health insurance that includes abortion coverage. Supporters said the measure would codify a series of policy riders that have long been attached to annual appropriation bills. Democrats said it would go beyond current law.

In the 108th Congress (2003-04), Smith spearheaded the drive that led to the enactment of a ban on a procedure that opponents call "partial birth" abortion.

In 2009 his endorsement of Republican gubernatorial candidate Chris Christie was seen as confirmation of Christie's anti-abortion bona fides.

Smith has said he first became interested in the issue of abortion when, as a 19-year-old student, he read a newspaper article about a child who had survived an abortion. "It got the wheels turning about where were those child's rights," he said.

Smith's dogged attention to his priorities has not always gone over well with party leaders. He was stripped of the Veterans' Affairs Committee chairmanship at the start of the 109th Congress (2005-06) and left the panel after serving on it for 24 years. Speaker J. Dennis Hastert, an Illinois Republican, took away the gavel after Smith stood firm in support of increased veterans' health care funding in the face of demands by Bush and GOP leaders for leaner budgets. Smith said the 2007 disclosures of severe problems at Walter Reed Army Medical Center in Washington and veterans' hospitals around the country vindicated his stance.

Smith, whose parents owned a New Jersey wholesale sporting goods business, studied business at Trenton State College. But after an internship with a state senator, he was hooked on politics. He ran the campaign of an unsuccessful Democratic Senate candidate in 1976, then lost his own race for the House two years later.

He was executive director of the New Jersey Right to Life Committee before winning election to Congress at age 27. He defeated 13-term Democrat Frank Thompson, who had been tainted by a bribery scandal. He faced a stiff challenge in his first re-election battle and was held to 53 percent of the vote, but he hasn't fallen below 60 percent since.

Key Votes

2010

Overhaul the nation's health insurance system	NO
Allow for repeal of "don't ask, don't tell"	NO
Overhaul financial services industry regulation	NO
Limit use of new Afghanistan War funds to troop withdrawal activities	NO
Change oversight of offshore drilling and lift oil spill liability cap	NO
Provide a path to legal status for some children of illegal immigrants	NO
Extend Bush-era income tax cuts for two years	YES

2009

Expand the Children's Health Insurance Program	YES
Provide $787 billion in tax cuts and spending increases to stimulate the economy	NO
Allow bankruptcy judges to modify certain primary-residence mortgages	NO
Create a cap-and-trade system to limit greenhouse gas emissions	YES
Provide $2 billion for the "cash for clunkers" program	YES
Establish the government as the sole provider of student loans	NO
Restrict federally funded insurance coverage for abortions in health care overhaul	YES

CQ Vote Studies

	PARTY UNITY		PRESIDENTIAL SUPPORT	
	SUPPORT	OPPOSE	SUPPORT	OPPOSE
2010	84%	16%	40%	60%
2009	65%	35%	65%	35%
2008	68%	32%	32%	68%
2007	62%	38%	37%	63%
2006	72%	28%	67%	33%

Interest Groups

	AFL-CIO	ADA	CCUS	ACU
2010	29%	15%	100%	67%
2009	57%	30%	80%	64%
2008	80%	65%	67%	28%
2007	79%	55%	70%	44%
2006	50%	30%	67%	68%

New Jersey 4

Central — part of Trenton, Lakewood

The 4th spreads across the center of the state, where the Garden State begins its transition from South to North Jersey, extending from Trenton and the Delaware River to the Jersey Shore and coastal communities such as Point Pleasant and Spring Lake. Lakewood Township, in Ocean County, is the state's fastest-growing municipality since 2000 and has a diverse mix: a well-established Orthodox Jewish community; seniors; and a growing Hispanic population.

The district includes much of the southern and eastern portions of Trenton, the state capital. While these areas vote Democratic, they do not lean quite as strongly as other parts of the city that are contained in the 12th District to the north. Most of Trenton's white residents live in the 4th, which includes the historically Italian neighborhood of Chambersburg. But the area is not without diversity — the district's portion of Trenton is more than 50 percent Hispanic and 30 percent black.

The area's major multi-branch military base is important to the economy, but the district does not rely solely on defense. Trenton and its suburbs have a diverse range of businesses, and the towns along the shore in

Ocean and Monmouth counties depend heavily on tourism. The 4th also includes rural territory dotted with horse and agricultural farms, in areas such as Colts Neck. Like much of central and southern New Jersey, the 4th is loaded with small towns, such as Hightstown and Manasquan in Mercer and Monmouth counties, and the district takes in a chunk of Burlington County, a suburban area outside of Philadelphia. Burlington Coat Factory, a clothing retail chain, is headquartered in Burlington.

Ocean and Monmouth counties dominate the 4th's geography and give the district its GOP lean. John McCain did 10 percentage points better here (52 percent) than he did statewide in the 2008 presidential election.

Major Industry
State government, tourism, manufacturing, defense

Military Bases
Joint Base McGuire-Dix-Lakehurst (shared with the 3rd), 8,950 military, 3,815 civilian (2011)

Cities
Lakewood (unincorporated), 53,805; Trenton (pt.), 41,096

Notable
Trenton, a Revolutionary War battle site, was temporarily the U.S. capital.

Rep. Scott Garrett (R)

Capitol Office
225-4465
garrett.house.gov
2244 Rayburn Bldg. 20515-3005; fax 225-9048

Committees
Budget
Financial Services
 (Capital Markets & Government Sponsored Enter-
 prises - Chairman)

Residence
Wantage

Born
July 9, 1959; Englewood, N.J.

Religion
Protestant

Family
Wife, Mary Ellen Garrett; two children

Education
Rutgers U., J.D. 1984; Montclair State College, B.A.
1981 (political science)

Career
Lawyer

Political Highlights
N.J. Assembly, 1990-2003; sought Republican nomination for U.S. House, 1998, 2000

ELECTION RESULTS

2010 GENERAL

Scott Garrett (R)	124,030	64.9%
Tod Theise (D)	62,634	32.8%
Ed Fanning (GREEN)	2,347	1.2%

2010 PRIMARY

Scott Garrett (R)	unopposed

2008 GENERAL

Scott Garrett (R)	172,653	55.9%
Dennis Shulman (D)	131,033	42.4%
Ed Fanning (GREEN)	5,321	1.7%

Previous Winning Percentages
2006 (55%); 2004 (58%); 2002 (59%)

Elected 2002; 5th term

Garrett defies the stereotype of the Northeastern liberal Republican. He is a solid conservative on fiscal and social issues and a stickler for "constitutional government." As chairman of the Financial Services Committee's Capital Markets and Government Sponsored Enterprises panel, he'll play a central role as Republicans oversee implementation of the financial regulatory overhaul enacted in 2010 and ponder ways to change the law.

When Republicans began the 112th Congress (2011-12) by putting in place a new rule to require lawmakers to defend the constitutionality of every bill they introduce, Garrett suggested going one step further. He offered a proposal to bar members from simply citing the "general welfare" or "necessary and proper" clauses.

"It is a gimmick if it has no teeth to it. If you do it right, then it compels Congress to actually have that debate on constitutionality," he told Roll Call.

As a founder of the Constitution Caucus, Garrett often refers to the reserve clause of the Constitution when arguing against funding for programs that weren't mentioned or envisioned by the framers. Garrett is also a founding member of the conservative 10th Amendment Task Force, which aims to restore to the states powers the Constitution reserved for the states that have been usurped by the federal government.

Garrett belongs to a cadre of vocal Republican Study Committee members on the Financial Services Committee who sometimes worked on routine bills with liberal Democrat Barney Frank of Massachusetts when he was chairman of the panel, but often took opposing sides on measures that would expand the scope of government programs.

He was a frequent critic of the Obama administration's approach to the financial crisis in general and of the regulatory overhaul in particular. He said on Fox Business Network that the law would maintain "the bail-out mentality that got us into this situation in the first place" and would not rein in the government-backed mortgage giants Fannie Mae and Freddie Mac, two entities that fall under Garrett's subcommittee's purview.

He helped lead committee efforts early in the 112th Congress to roll back some provisions of the law.

He offered an unsuccessful amendment to stand-alone legislation to create a financial services consumer protection agency — a bill later included in the broader overhaul package — that would have effectively barred outspoken advocate Elizabeth Warren from running it by requiring the director to have either a year of experience working in private-sector finance or be a current banking regulator. Warren met neither qualification. Obama eventually gave Warren an advisory post in his administration but did not nominate her as director of the new agency.

Garrett called for tough oversight of 2008's $700 billion financial rescue law, which he opposed, and attacked proposals to bail out troubled automakers. He told constituents in an open letter that lawmakers should "stand against this commitment of your money with little or no government oversight."

A member of the Budget Committee, he has occasionally taken a lead role in trying to curb the growth of domestic spending and, before Republicans imposed a moratorium, in killing earmarks. In one high-profile tussle in 2007, Garrett won applause from fellow conservatives for attempting to cut funding for an Alaska Native education program and weathering a tough rebuke by the program's champion, Republican Don Young of Alaska. "Too many members of Congress see the dollars that we appropriate here not as the taxpayers' dollar, but see it as their very own personal checking account." Garrett said in a thinly veiled slap at Young.

Garrett is consistently conservative on social issues. He opposes abortion and same-sex marriage, and he voted late in 2010 against repeal of the statutory ban on gays and lesbians serving openly in the military.

The son of a Uniroyal executive, Garrett represents a district that encompasses Wall Street commuters and family farm operators. As a youth, his family moved from Bergen County's suburbs to a 100-acre farm in Wantage, where they grew greenhouse tomatoes and Christmas trees, in addition to raising Yorkshire pigs. Garrett's farm roots attracted unwanted publicity in 2008, when his opponent accused him of omitting a 10-acre plot of land — on which his family claimed a tax break as farmland — from financial disclosure forms. Garrett argued the tax break was justified and said the property was exempt from disclosure because he lived there and had no stake in his brother's separate Christmas tree business.

Garrett is a lawyer with an interest in environmental law and occasionally tilts to the center on conservation-related themes. He pushed for the 2006 law that designated parts of the Musconetcong River for protection as a wild and scenic river. "One of the main reasons why I got involved in government was to try to preserve open space," he said.

He took an early interest in civics, publishing an alternative high school newspaper that questioned the school administration's spending practices and getting elected student government treasurer. After earning his law degree, he worked in insurance and jumped into politics. He served more than a decade in the New Jersey Legislature, where he belonged to a group of maverick, conservative Republicans called the "mountain men."

In 1998, Garrett launched a campaign to unseat moderate Republican Rep. Marge Roukema. Although he lost the primary, he captured the attention of national conservative groups including the Club for Growth, an influential anti-tax group that spent more than $250,000 on his behalf two years later. He lost again, but by only 2,000 votes. By 2002, Roukema had lost a bid to chair Financial Services and was ready to retire, paving the way for Garrett.

He won the 2006 primary against two moderate rivals and took 59 percent of the vote in defeating Democratic ophthalmologist Anne Sumers in the general election. Two years later, New York City Mayor Michael Bloomberg endorsed his Democratic rival, Dennis Shulman, a psychologist and rabbi. But Garrett had support from former New York City Mayor Rudolph Giuliani and won with 56 percent. He won by a nearly 2-to-1 ratio in 2010.

Key Votes

2010

Overhaul the nation's health insurance system	NO
Allow for repeal of "don't ask, don't tell"	NO
Overhaul financial services industry regulation	NO
Limit use of new Afghanistan War funds to troop withdrawal activities	NO
Change oversight of offshore drilling and lift oil spill liability cap	NO
Provide a path to legal status for some children of illegal immigrants	NO
Extend Bush-era income tax cuts for two years	NO

2009

Expand the Children's Health Insurance Program	NO
Provide $787 billion in tax cuts and spending increases to stimulate the economy	NO
Allow bankruptcy judges to modify certain primary-residence mortgages	NO
Create a cap-and-trade system to limit greenhouse gas emissions	NO
Provide $2 billion for the "cash for clunkers" program	NO
Establish the government as the sole provider of student loans	NO
Restrict federally funded insurance coverage for abortions in health care overhaul	YES

CQ Vote Studies

	PARTY UNITY		PRESIDENTIAL SUPPORT	
	Support	Oppose	Support	Oppose
2010	97%	3%	24%	76%
2009	98%	2%	18%	82%
2008	97%	3%	77%	23%
2007	97%	3%	86%	14%
2006	89%	11%	83%	17%

Interest Groups

	AFL-CIO	ADA	CCUS	ACU
2010	0%	5%	71%	100%
2009	0%	0%	73%	100%
2008	0%	5%	78%	100%
2007	4%	0%	70%	100%
2006	14%	20%	87%	100%

New Jersey 5

North and west — Bergenfield, Paramus

Although the 5th stretches across northern New Jersey, three-fifths of its population is packed into northern Bergen County, which is home to affluent voters, many of whom commute into New York City.

The rest of the district is scenic and hilly and includes the state's small portion of the Appalachian Trail. No municipality here has more than 30,000 residents. The 5th also has the smallest minority population of any New Jersey district.

Despite declining home prices, especially in the lower-priced neighborhoods that have been more vulnerable to downturns, the 5th's property values and income levels are still among the highest in the state — Saddle River, in wealthy Bergen County, is known for its multimillion-dollar homes. Bergen County's tony suburbs contrast with a more rural feel in the 5th's portion of Passaic County to the west, which includes the New Jersey Botanical Garden and colonial-era attractions.

The scenic back country of Sussex and Warren counties traditionally has been a mix of farmland and small towns, but both counties have started to change as young professionals from New York City move into the area.

Warren County's population boomed in the 2000s, and home construction accommodated the growth, but local officials and residents have remained committed to preserving an agricultural heritage across the county.

Although most voters register as independents, the 5th tends to vote Republican, particularly in Warren County, the only county to lie entirely within the district's boundaries. Democrats are successful in some areas, including Tenafly in Bergen County.

John McCain captured 54 percent of the 5th's vote in the 2008 presidential election. The Bergen County portion of the district favored McCain with a slim majority, but his margin was wider in the 5th's part of the three outlying counties.

Major Industry

Pharmaceuticals, electronics, shipping, agriculture

Cities

Bergenfield, 26,764; Paramus, 26,342; Ridgewood, 24,958; Dumont 17,479;

Notable

Hackettstown hosts the Mars Chocolate North America national office and an M&M's brand manufacturing plant.

Rep. Frank Pallone Jr. (D)

Capitol Office
225-4671
www.house.gov/pallone
237 Cannon Bldg. 20515-3006; fax 225-9665

Committees
Energy & Commerce
Natural Resources

Residence
Long Branch

Born
Oct. 30, 1951; Long Branch, N.J.

Religion
Roman Catholic

Family
Wife, Sarah Pallone; three children

Education
Middlebury College, B.A. 1973 (history & French);
Tufts U., M.A. 1974 (international relations); Rutgers
U., J.D. 1978

Career
Lawyer

Political Highlights
Long Branch City Council, 1982-88; N.J. Senate,
1984-88

ELECTION RESULTS

2010 GENERAL

Frank Pallone Jr. (D)	81,933	54.7%
Anna C. Little (R)	65,413	43.7%

2010 PRIMARY

Frank Pallone Jr. (D)	unopposed

2008 GENERAL

Frank Pallone Jr. (D)	164,077	66.9%
Robert McLeod (R)	77,469	31.6%
Herb Tarbous (I)	3,531	1.4%

Previous Winning Percentages
2006 (67%); 2004 (67%); 2002 (66%); 2000 (68%);
1998 (57%); 1996 (61%); 1994 (60%); 1992 (52%);
1990 (49%); 1988 (52%); 1988 Special Election (52%)

Elected 1988; 12th full term

Pallone has long been a prime purveyor of the Democratic message on the environment and energy. More recently, he devoted his considerable legislative energy to spreading the party's gospel on health care.

A member of the Progressive Caucus, Pallone is a dependably liberal Democrat, voting with his party on 99 percent of the votes that pitted a majority of Democrats against a majority of Republicans in the 111th Congress (2009-10). But he tempered his outspoken partisanship as he attempted to prove he could effectively legislate as chairman of the Energy and Commerce Subcommittee on Health. With Democrats back in the minority in the House in the 112th Congress (2011-12), Pallone appears ready once again wield the partisan cudgel.

Pallone was one of the party's major players in negotiating the health care overhaul enacted in 2010. Although he knew little of the details of health policy before the 110th Congress (2007-08), when his seniority status put him in position to take over the subcommittee, Pallone proved to be an effective crammer. He is now the subcommittee's ranking Democrat.

The months-long negotiations on the overhaul allowed Pallone to demonstrate his growing familiarity with the intricacies of health care as well as his skills in working with Republicans and the Senate. Early on, he reached out to Republicans, saying that Democrats would be willing to modify the bill to meet "legitimate concerns" and encouraging Republicans to talk with him about the draft bill. He also helped negotiate a deal with moderate Blue Dog Democrats, becoming a regular at private meetings between members of the group and leadership.

Pallone also made overtures to the GOP by bringing up Republican-supported legislation, especially after the rancorous health overhaul debate. For example, he shepherded through a bill to extend the Ryan White HIV/AIDS program, appeasing Republicans in part by moving the bill through regular order. When Republicans began moving to dismantle the health care overhaul early in 2011, though, Pallone began to revive the partisan rhetoric he once promulgated as communications chairman of the Democratic Steering and Policy Committee.

After his successor as Health Subcommittee chairman, Republican Joe Pitts of Pennsylvania, said the panel would consider a series of bills to convert mandatory spending in the law to discretionary and thus make it subject to the appropriations process, Pallone labeled it "simply an effort to dismantle the health care reform block by block, by cherry-picking the provisions."

His seats on Energy and Commerce and the Natural Resources Committee also allow him to continue his focus on environment and energy policies of interest to his coastline district. He speaks passionately about renewable energy and the cleanup of New Jersey's pollution sites.

A member of the Energy and Commerce Subcommittee on Environment and the Economy, Pallone opposes offshore drilling for oil and gas. The Deepwater Horizon oil spill in the Gulf of Mexico in April 2010 emboldened Pallone. "Advocates of offshore drilling will have a hard time convincing people along the East Coast that they have nothing to fear from drilling in our waters as they see the oil slick moving through the Gulf of Mexico towards the shorelines of three or four states," he said.

In May 2010 and again in January 2011, he introduced a bill that would ban all new drilling in U.S. waters. He also sponsored a bill to permanently ban drilling in all states from Maine to Virginia and held hearings on possible health effects associated with the Gulf spill. Pallone has opposed all major trade laws, in part because of his concerns about environmental damage from expanded global trade.

He watches out for the sizable Indian-American community in the 6th District; he is a founder of the House Caucus on India and Indian-Americans. He supported the 2006 U.S.-India nuclear pact allowing shipments of civilian nuclear fuel to India, saying it would help keep the country a strategic ally in the increasingly unstable region.

He also has taken a special interest in Armenian issues because of a large district presence and a longtime curiosity about the area. As co-chairman of the House Armenian Caucus, he cosponsored a resolution condemning as genocide the mass killings of Armenians in Ottoman Turkey in 1915. After backing off the idea amid administration warnings that it would damage U.S. relations with its ally, Pallone later renewed his call for the government to officially recognize the killings as genocide.

His father, who sparked his interest in politics, was a police officer in Long Branch and a longtime activist in local Democratic affairs, including the campaigns of former Rep. James J. Howard.

After graduating from Middlebury College in Vermont, Pallone enrolled at Tufts University's Fletcher School in Massachusetts to study international relations. He earned a degree and was accepted into an exchange program that would have allowed him to spend a year studying in Switzerland, a common track to a State Department job. But Pallone said he realized he preferred Jersey politics and chose to attend law school at Rutgers, where he later taught.

Howard urged Pallone to run for the Long Branch City Council in 1982. One year later, Pallone won a state Senate seat. In March 1988, Howard died of a heart attack and many Democratic insiders, including Howard's widow, lined up behind Pallone. In November, he won two elections on the same day: a special election to fill the vacancy and a full term in his own right, each by only 5 percentage points. He has faced several other electoral challenges since then, the closest of which came in 1990 when he squeaked by with a margin of just 4,258 votes.

New Jersey lost a House seat in reapportionment in the 1990s, and Pallone had to scramble to hold his redrawn district. But redistricting after the 2000 census made his subsequent re-elections easier. He defeated Republican Anna C. Little, mayor of the Borough of Highlands, by 11 points in 2010.

Pallone has been among the most eager of New Jersey's House Democrats considering a future Senate run.

Key Votes

2010

Overhaul the nation's health insurance system	YES
Allow for repeal of "don't ask, don't tell"	YES
Overhaul financial services industry regulation	YES
Limit use of new Afghanistan War funds to troop withdrawal activities	YES
Change oversight of offshore drilling and lift oil spill liability cap	YES
Provide a path to legal status for some children of illegal immigrants	YES
Extend Bush-era income tax cuts for two years	YES

2009

Expand the Children's Health Insurance Program	YES
Provide $787 billion in tax cuts and spending increases to stimulate the economy	YES
Allow bankruptcy judges to modify certain primary-residence mortgages	YES
Create a cap-and-trade system to limit greenhouse gas emissions	YES
Provide $2 billion for the "cash for clunkers" program	YES
Establish the government as the sole provider of student loans	YES
Restrict federally funded insurance coverage for abortions in health care overhaul	NO

CQ Vote Studies

	PARTY UNITY		PRESIDENTIAL SUPPORT	
	Support	Oppose	Support	Oppose
2010	99%	1%	93%	7%
2009	99%	1%	97%	3%
2008	99%	1%	17%	83%
2007	99%	1%	4%	96%
2006	97%	3%	23%	77%

Interest Groups

	AFL-CIO	ADA	CCUS	ACU
2010	100%	95%	25%	0%
2009	100%	95%	36%	0%
2008	100%	100%	67%	0%
2007	100%	100%	45%	0%
2006	100%	100%	27%	4%

New Jersey 6

East central — New Brunswick, Plainfield, part of Edison

Wedged in the heart of suburbs south of Newark and New York City, the 6th combines industrial communities in Middlesex County and a small corner of Somerset County with a long, thin stretch that grabs beach towns in Monmouth County.

The 6th includes residents with various ethnic backgrounds, ranging from the Irish and Polish who populate South Amboy in Middlesex County to the Italians who are prevalent in Long Branch in Monmouth County. Edison also has an established Indian community.

New Brunswick, in Middlesex, consolidates two Democratic voting blocs — students from Rutgers University (shared with the 12th) and minorities. Nearby Piscataway, Highland Park and Metuchen also favor Democrats. Upper-middle-class and independent-voting residents cluster around Edison (shared with the 7th), which is home to some corporate offices and manufacturing.

In Monmouth County, the problems of Asbury Park, a vacation site made famous by rocker Bruce Springsteen, are an exception to the area's generally sunny outlook — though a 10-year, $1.25 billion waterfront redevelopment plan that broke ground in 2004 and some reduction of the city's narcotics trade have helped. Other shore communities include Deal, a summer enclave for Syrian Jews, and Atlantic Highlands, where many area residents catch the ferry to jobs in New York City.

The 6th's former political competitiveness has shifted to Democratic support in federal elections. Heavily Democratic Plainfield in Union County has added to the leftward pull here. Barack Obama took 61 percent of the district's 2008 presidential vote, but Republican Gov. Chris Christie won Edison and Sayreville, among other towns, in 2009.

Major Industry
Higher education, technology, pharmaceuticals, manufacturing

Cities
New Brunswick, 55,181; Plainfield, 49,808; Sayreville, 42,704; Long Branch, 30,719; Asbury Park, 16,116; Highland Park, 13,982

Notable
The Sandy Hook Light, opened in 1764, is the nation's oldest standing lighthouse.

Rep. Leonard Lance (R)

Capitol Office
225-5361
lance.house.gov
426 Cannon Bldg. 20515-3007; fax 225-9460

Committees
Energy & Commerce

Residence
Lebanon

Born
June 25, 1952; Easton, Pa.

Religion
Roman Catholic

Family
Wife, Heidi A. Rohrbach; one stepchild

Education
Lehigh U., B.A. 1974 (American studies); Vanderbilt U., J.D. 1977; Princeton U., M.P.A. 1982

Career
Lawyer; gubernatorial aide

Political Highlights
N.J. Assembly, 1991-2002; sought Republican nomination for U.S. House, 1996; N.J. Senate, 2002-09 (minority leader, 2004-09)

ELECTION RESULTS

2010 GENERAL

Leonard Lance (R)	105,084	59.4%
Ed Potosnak (D)	71,902	40.6%

2010 PRIMARY

Leonard Lance (R)	17,200	56.1%
David Larsen (R)	9,475	30.9%
Lon Hosford (R)	2,534	8.3%
Bruce E. Baker (R)	1,448	4.7%

2008 GENERAL

Leonard Lance (R)	148,461	50.2%
Linda Stender (D)	124,818	42.2%
Michael P. Hsing (HFC)	16,419	5.6%
Dean Greco (ADBP)	3,259	1.1%

Elected 2008; 2nd term

A self-professed "Eisenhower Republican," Lance studied under presidential historian and Eisenhower scholar Fred Greenstein at Princeton University. Lance evinces a courtly manner by regularly referring to colleagues as "Mister," even off the House floor. And he shows his moderate stripes by hewing to the GOP line on economic matters while veering from it on most other legislation.

He sides with fiscal conservatives, pledging to oppose all tax increases and to fight for the repeal of estate and alternative minimum taxes. He has referred to a suggested value added tax as "precisely the wrong medicine for our ailing economy" and pronounced himself "quite disappointed" with President Obama's fiscal 2012 budget.

But in stark contrast to his socially conservative predecessor, Republican Mike Ferguson, he often aligns with Democrats — he supports abortion rights, backs expanded embryonic stem cell research funding and seeks to promote conservation by increasing incentives for hybrid vehicles and renewable energy.

For the 112th Congress (2011-12) he moved to the Energy and Commerce Committee, giving up a seat on Financial Services.

Lance, whose district is home to a number of pharmaceutical firms, sits on the Health Subcommittee. He opposed the health care overhaul enacted in 2010, and early in 2011 he backed repeal, saying on the House floor that the law used "sleights of hand used to mask the true cost of the measure."

But he bucked the majority of his party in supporting a number of House-passed Democratic bills in the early months of the 111th Congress (2009-10). They included an expansion of the Children's Health Insurance Program that was signed into law, a law making it easier for workers to challenge wage discrimination and a bill to expand federal hate crimes law to cover crimes based on sexual orientation.

None of those votes, however, brought him as much attention as his decision to become one of eight Republicans backing legislation to create a cap-and-trade system intended to reduce carbon emissions. He was castigated by conservative commentators, but Lance said no one should have been surprised. "I'm a strong environmentalist, and that was part of my campaign," he told the website PolitickerNJ. At the same time, he called for a "thorough and transparent investigation" of questions raised by leaked emails from the Climatic Research Unit of the University of East Anglia that suggested some of the scientists at the unit manipulated climate data and worked to suppress research that refuted their conclusions.

After first winning election in 2008, Lance lobbied to join the Financial Services Committee. He opposed the Democrats' regulatory overhaul of the financial industry, arguing that it would not do enough to ensure that another rescue would not be necessary.

He was joined by fellow freshman Gerald E. Connolly of Virginia, a Democrat also representing an affluent suburban district, in introducing a resolution in June 2009 opposing Obama's plans to limit the mortgage interest deduction for families making more than $250,000 a year.

Lance likes to describe himself as "a student of history." Among his political heroes is William H. Seward, President Abraham Lincoln's secretary of State, whom he calls one of the "underestimated figures" in American history. He acknowledges he's a reluctant convert to modern technology: He said he never used a cell phone until he was elected state Senate minority leader in 2004 and that his Capitol Hill staff "gently persuaded" him to begin using a BlackBerry.

That kind of thinking is rooted in tradition. Lance's family has lived in Hunterdon County since 1710; his home was built in 1780. His father helped shape the New Jersey constitution as state Senate president and his great-uncle also served in the state legislature. Lance said he grew up in "an adult-centered, not child-centered, household," where politics and policy were often discussed.

Lance was interested in a career in public service, but he wasn't sure if he would become a politician when he graduated Phi Beta Kappa from Lehigh University with a degree in American Studies in 1974. He went to law school at Vanderbilt University, where he met his wife, Heidi A. Rohrbach, a corporate lawyer. The couple married in 1996.

Lance worked as a court clerk and later received his master's degree in public administration at Princeton, where he concentrated on domestic policy. He worked as an assistant counsel on New Jersey Republican Gov. Thomas H. Kean's staff for seven years, then successfully ran for the state Assembly in 1991.

During his time in the state legislature, Lance became known as a fiscal conservative. He strenuously opposed former GOP Gov. Christine Todd Whitman's plan to fund a state pension system with borrowed money, a move that cost him the chairmanship of the Budget committee. In November 2008, voters approved an amendment to the state constitution requiring voter approval for the government to borrow funds. Lance considers the amendment, which was sponsored by and named after him, his proudest accomplishment.

Lance first sought a seat in Congress in 1996, when he ran in the GOP primary in the 12th District; he finished a distant third to the more conservative Michael Pappas, who went on to win the House seat. Once New Jersey's congressional districts were reconfigured after the 2000 census and Ferguson announced his retirement at the end of the 110th Congress (2007-08), Lance decided to run again. He emerged from a seven-candidate GOP primary with nearly 40 percent of the vote to face Democratic state Rep. Linda Stender, who had come within a percentage point of defeating Ferguson in 2006. Despite Stender's 4-to-1 spending advantage, Lance garnered endorsements from many of the district's major newspapers, and won by 8 percentage points even as Barack Obama narrowly carried the district.

Lance's moderation inspired a trio of conservative tea party activists to challenge him in the June 2010 primary, but he emerged victorious, with 56 percent of the vote. He was re-elected in November with 59 percent.

Key Votes

2010

Overhaul the nation's health insurance system	NO
Allow for repeal of "don't ask, don't tell"	NO
Overhaul financial services industry regulation	NO
Limit use of new Afghanistan War funds to troop withdrawal activities	NO
Change oversight of offshore drilling and lift oil spill liability cap	NO
Provide a path to legal status for some children of illegal immigrants	NO
Extend Bush-era income tax cuts for two years	YES

2009

Expand the Children's Health Insurance Program	YES
Provide $787 billion in tax cuts and spending increases to stimulate the economy	NO
Allow bankruptcy judges to modify certain primary-residence mortgages	NO
Create a cap-and-trade system to limit greenhouse gas emissions	YES
Provide $2 billion for the "cash for clunkers" program	YES
Establish the government as the sole provider of student loans	NO
Restrict federally funded insurance coverage for abortions in health care overhaul	YES

CQ Vote Studies

	PARTY UNITY		PRESIDENTIAL SUPPORT	
	SUPPORT	OPPOSE	SUPPORT	OPPOSE
2010	91%	9%	31%	69%
2009	78%	22%	47%	53%

Interest Groups

	AFL-CIO	ADA	CCUS	ACU
2010	7%	5%	88%	88%
2009	48%	40%	87%	68%

New Jersey 7

North central — Woodbridge Township

The 7th District, which is centered in bedroom communities for residents commuting to Newark and New York City, zigzags across north-central New Jersey from the Delaware River to Woodbridge. The wealthy, white-collar residents here drive the district's median household income, nearly $94,000, to the second-highest in the state.

Drug manufacturers fuel the economy, led by Whitehouse Station's Merck & Co., which merged with biotech firm Schering-Plough in 2009. A Roche Molecular Systems manufacturing plant in Branchburg is a key employer. Plummeting sales and revenue at international telecommunications company Alcatel-Lucent in Union County's Murray Hill led to major layoffs in the area, but the company has begun to rebound as demand for its equipment has skyrocketed. The company also plans to build a six-acre solar field on its campus.

The district has several of New Jersey's superfund toxic waste sites, and residents tend to be environmentally conscious. Other important local issues include aircraft noise from nearby Newark Liberty International Airport (in the adjacent 10th District) and money for infrastructure.

Amtrak's Metropark station, the only stop in the 7th for north-central New Jersey residents headed up or down the East Coast, is in Iselin.

The western areas of the district are less densely populated, but they have experienced some of the corporate and residential growth affecting the district overall. Parts of Somerset and Hunterdon counties once dotted by horse farms have been developed into office parks and shopping malls.

The 7th contains some heavily Republican areas in Somerset and Hunterdon counties, the northern tier of Middlesex County and a large chunk of Democratic Union County. Barack Obama narrowly won the district's vote in the 2008 presidential election, but Republicans have solidified their hold on the U.S. House seat.

Major Industry
Pharmaceuticals, manufacturing

Cities
Westfield, 30,316; South Plainfield, 23,385; North Plainfield (pt.), 21,924; Summit, 21,457; Woodbridge (unincorporated) (pt.), 19,097

Notable
The U.S. equestrian team's headquarters is in Gladstone.

Rep. Bill Pascrell Jr. (D)

Capitol Office
225-5751
pascrell.house.gov
2370 Rayburn Bldg. 20515-3008; fax 225-5782

Committees
Budget
Ways & Means

Residence
Paterson

Born
Jan. 25, 1937; Paterson, N.J.

Religion
Roman Catholic

Family
Wife, Elsie Marie Pascrell; three children

Education
Fordham U., B.A. 1959 (journalism), M.A. 1961 (philosophy)

Military
Army, 1961; Army Reserve, 1962-67

Career
City official; teacher

Political Highlights
Paterson Board of Education, 1977-81 (president, 1981); N.J. Assembly, 1988-97; mayor of Paterson, 1990-97

ELECTION RESULTS

2010 GENERAL

Bill Pascrell Jr. (D)	88,478	62.7%
Roland Straten (R)	51,023	36.1%
Raymond Giangrasso (I)	1,707	1.2%

2010 PRIMARY

Bill Pascrell Jr. (D)	unopposed

2008 GENERAL

Bill Pascrell Jr. (D)	159,279	71.1%
Roland Straten (R)	63,107	28.2%

Previous Winning Percentages
2006 (71%); 2004 (69%); 2002 (67%); 2000 (67%); 1998 (62%); 1996 (51%)

Elected 1996; 8th term

Pascrell, scrappy and forceful, stays true to his working-class roots by taking up both populist and popular causes.

In the 111th Congress (2009-10), he sponsored a bill designed to prevent concussions among school-aged athletes and called for investigations of the Ticketmaster-Live Nation merger and the business dealings of the new Russian owner of the New Jersey Nets.

That's all aside from his work on the Ways and Means Committee, where he uses his seat to push Democratic tax proposals. He's particularly proud of incentives he supported in 2008 and 2009 to encourage first-time homebuyers and to allow purchasers of cars to deduct their sales taxes.

More neighborhood politician than policy wonk, the voluble Pascrell rarely splits from other House Democrats and aims the occasional sharp barb across the aisle during floor debate.

In July 2010, though, Pascrell landed in the middle of an intraparty dustup when he criticized White House Press Secretary Robert Gibbs for saying the House majority was in jeopardy unless Democrats mounted strong campaigns. "What the hell do they think we've been doing the last 12 months? We're the ones who have been taking the tough votes," Pascrell said to The Washington Post after reportedly blasting Gibbs during a closed House Democratic Caucus meeting.

But he sided with President Obama and the Democratic leadership on all the major initiatives of the 111th Congress. He backed the deal the White House struck with Senate Republicans in late 2010 to extend for two years the Bush-era income tax rates, and called Obama's fiscal 2012 budget "a credible blueprint to begin with."

In 2008, Pascrell was one of 33 Democrats who ultimately supported the $700 billion rescue of the financial services industry after initially voting against it. To explain his switch, he cited tax provisions added in the Senate, along with "countless conversations" he had with constituents, fellow lawmakers and economists.

Pascrell got the coveted Ways and Means seat at the start of the 110th Congress (2007-08) in part because of his outspoken support of Pennsylvania Democrat John P. Murtha for majority leader. Murtha, who died in 2010, had been Nancy Pelosi's candidate, and the Speaker from California rewarded Pascrell even after Maryland Democrat Steny H. Hoyer defeated Murtha for the No. 2 leadership spot. Although Pascrell voted in 2002 to authorize the use of force in Iraq, he supported Murtha's 2005 resolution calling for the withdrawal of all U.S. forces. Afghanistan and Pakistan, not Iraq, "are really the epicenter of terrorism," said Pascrell, who did not return to the Homeland Security Committee in the 112th Congress (2011-12).

Ways and Means members typically are not allowed to serve on other committees, but Pelosi had granted a waiver to allow Pascrell to sit on Homeland Security, and he got another one to sit on the Budget Committee in the 112th. He champions more funding for firefighters and other emergency personnel, along with better coordination of planning efforts to protect against bioterrorism. He shepherded through Congress in 2000 — before the Homeland Security panel was created — a bill creating a federal program to direct hundreds of millions of dollars to hire, train and equip local firefighters.

Outside of his committee work, one longstanding cause has been research on and treatment of brain injuries. Inspired by the plight of a constituent, Pascrell was a co-founder in 2001 of the Congressional Brain Injury Task

Force. In April 2008, he helped steer into law the reauthorization of a traumatic brain injury treatment program that offers research and rehabilitation grants to states. In 2010, the House passed a Pascrell bill that would establish new guidelines for handling concussions among school-aged athletes.

In 2009 Pascrell won a bittersweet victory with the enactment, as part of an omnibus lands package, of legislation he had promoted for years to include the Great Falls in Paterson in the national park system. As a catcher on his high school baseball team, Pascrell always walked by the falls with his mother on their way home from games; it was a place they both cherished. His 95-year-old mother, Roffie, died two days before Obama signed the lands bill into law.

Paterson, the heart of the territory that he represents, is where his Italian immigrant grandparents settled. Pascrell, whose father worked for the railroad, was the first member of his family to go to high school, and his neighborhood pals razzed him when he went off to college. Despite his rise to prominence, he still lives in a modest house in a middle-class neighborhood in Paterson.

He worked his way through Fordham University, then embarked on a 12-year career as a high school teacher in neighboring Paramus. Along the way he also did a stint in the Army. In 1974, he became director of public works for the city of Paterson, then headed up the planning and development office. At the same time, he worked as a campaign volunteer for Democratic Rep. Robert A. Roe and others. He was appointed to the Paterson Board of Education and later was elected its president.

Pascrell won a seat in the state Assembly in 1987 and simultaneously served as mayor of Paterson beginning in 1990. As mayor, he promoted tough law enforcement measures, particularly in drug trafficking. To make it more difficult for dealers to communicate with their customers, he personally ripped out the lines and receivers of pay telephones that had not been issued a city permit.

Pascrell was his party's choice to take on Rep. Bill Martini in 1996, two years after the freshman Republican's narrow victory had ended 34 years of Democratic hegemony in the 8th District. The AFL-CIO targeted the race and the national party invited him to speak at the 1996 Democratic National Convention. Pascrell needed every bit of help he could get: He toppled Martini by just 6,200 votes. In acknowledgment of his tenuous hold on the seat, Pascrell immediately began amassing a war chest for 1998, which dissuaded Martini from running again. Since then, Pascrell's re-election contests have been routine.

Key Votes

2010

Overhaul the nation's health insurance system	YES
Allow for repeal of "don't ask, don't tell"	YES
Overhaul financial services industry regulation	YES
Limit use of new Afghanistan War funds to troop withdrawal activities	NO
Change oversight of offshore drilling and lift oil spill liability cap	YES
Provide a path to legal status for some children of illegal immigrants	YES
Extend Bush-era income tax cuts for two years	YES

2009

Expand the Children's Health Insurance Program	YES
Provide $787 billion in tax cuts and spending increases to stimulate the economy	YES
Allow bankruptcy judges to modify certain primary-residence mortgages	YES
Create a cap-and-trade system to limit greenhouse gas emissions	YES
Provide $2 billion for the "cash for clunkers" program	YES
Establish the government as the sole provider of student loans	YES
Restrict federally funded insurance coverage for abortions in health care overhaul	NO

CQ Vote Studies

	PARTY UNITY		PRESIDENTIAL SUPPORT	
	SUPPORT	OPPOSE	SUPPORT	OPPOSE
2010	99%	1%	95%	5%
2009	98%	2%	97%	3%
2008	99%	1%	13%	87%
2007	98%	2%	6%	94%
2006	95%	5%	25%	75%

Interest Groups

	AFL-CIO	ADA	CCUS	ACU
2010	100%	95%	25%	4%
2009	100%	90%	36%	0%
2008	100%	95%	56%	4%
2007	100%	95%	55%	0%
2006	100%	95%	27%	12%

New Jersey 8

Northeast — Paterson, Clifton, Passaic

The 8th is a mix of urban centers and suburban towns that begins in Pompton Lakes and moves south through the southern portion of Passaic County into northern Essex County, extending into parts of Livingston, West Orange and South Orange, just to the west of Newark. It includes Paterson, the state's third-largest city, as well as Clifton and Passaic. Paterson was once known for silk mills that made it a leading textile producer in the late 19th century. But after labor strife and the introduction of rayon and other materials, the city experienced a serious economic downturn from which it never fully recovered.

Despite a new development project downtown, city budget shortfalls have affected public services. The 8th also includes some less populated areas, which have more of a small-town feel but still battle the frequent nemesis of North Jersey residents — traffic.

Wayne is mostly residential, but is perhaps best known as the home of a retail power center: Willowbrook Mall. The district is a melting pot of cultures with dozens of ethnic groups, from a large Peruvian community in Paterson to an enclave of Italian and Polish residents in Clifton.

The 8th's slice of Passaic County has given Democrats a solid base in recent years — especially Paterson, with its deep-seated labor tradition. Overall, the district is one-third Hispanic and 13 percent black. Barack Obama received 63 percent of the district's presidential vote in 2008.

Republicans fare slightly better in the district's Essex County portion, which is mostly suburban and includes wealthy Livingston (shared with the 11th) and the middle-class towns of Nutley and Belleville. Many residents here commute to Newark or New York.

Major Industry

Pharmaceuticals, manufacturing, communications, education

Cities

Paterson, 146,199; Clifton, 84,136; Passaic, 69,781; Woodland Park, 11,819; Upper Montclair (unincorporated), 11,565; Pompton Lakes, 11,097

Notable

Lifestyle guru Martha Stewart and Sen. Frank R. Lautenberg graduated from Nutley High School.

Rep. Steven R. Rothman (D)

Capitol Office
225-5061
www.house.gov/rothman
2303 Rayburn Bldg. 20515; fax 225-5851

Committees
Appropriations

Residence
Fair Lawn

Born
Oct. 14, 1952; Englewood, N.J.

Religion
Jewish

Family
Divorced; two children

Education
Syracuse U., B.A. 1974 (political philosophy); Washington U., J.D. 1977

Career
Lawyer

Political Highlights
Mayor of Englewood, 1983-89; Democratic nominee for Bergen County Board of Freeholders, 1989; Bergen County Surrogate Court judge, 1993-96

ELECTION RESULTS

2010 GENERAL

Steven R. Rothman (D)	83,564	60.7%
Michael Agosta (R)	52,082	37.8%
Patricia Alessandrini (GREEN)	1,980	1.4%

2010 PRIMARY

Steven R. Rothman (D)	unopposed

2008 GENERAL

Steven R. Rothman (D)	151,182	67.5%
Vincent Micco (R)	69,503	31.0%
Michael Perrone Jr. (PRO)	3,200	1.4%

Previous Winning Percentages
2006 (72%); 2004 (68%); 2002 (70%); 2000 (68%);
1998 (65%); 1996 (56%)

Elected 1996; 8th term

Rothman chooses his words carefully and does not frequent the cable TV talk shows. Yet he quietly exerts his power as an appropriator to direct federal dollars to his densely populated district in the suburbs of New York City and to help shape U.S. foreign policy, particularly in the Middle East.

Rothman has snagged federal aid for rail service in the Northeast Corridor, highway improvements to ease congestion throughout the district, and downtown Newark revitalization projects. In January 2009, he jumped aboard Democratic efforts to stimulate the economy, ensuring that his district and other sections of New Jersey got at least their share of the $787 billion recovery package. According to his office, he has secured nearly $2 billion from the federal government since arriving in Congress.

Rothman cherishes his perches on the Appropriations panel's Defense and State-Foreign Operations subcommittees, where he has pushed to shore up the U.S. relationship with Israel and clamp down on Iran's drive for nuclear weapons. Following a report that companies doing business in Iran had received more than $100 billion in government contract payments and grants over the past decade, Rothman announced his intent to offer an amendment to each of the 12 fiscal 2011 appropriations bills to bar companies working in Iran from receiving federal funds.

Rothman calls the prospect of Iran obtaining nuclear weapons "extremely dangerous" and says he hopes the United States and its allies can prevent Iran from reaching nuclear weapons capability through diplomacy, including the use of sanctions. Military options, however, should remain on the table, he says. In March 2010, Rothman participated in a U.S.-Israel missile defense panel sponsored by the American Israel Public Affairs Committee; the following month, he penned an op-ed, widely circulated in the pro-Israel community, defending the roughly $3 billion in military aid Israel receives annually from the United States. "U.S. support for Israel is essential, not only for Israel's national security, but for America's," Rothman wrote. "Every bit of that support — and more — withstands all reasonable scrutiny." More broadly, he defends foreign aid spending as offering good value for the dollars spent.

While some other prominent Jewish politicians, such as Democratic Sen. Charles E. Schumer of New York, have castigated the Obama administration for its handling of the U.S.-Israel relationship, Rothman has refused to criticize the president directly. "There is no question that the relationship between Washington and Jerusalem is not perfect — but when has it ever been?" he wrote in a Roll Call op-ed in June 2010, arguing that those ties have never been stronger than they are now.

On domestic policy, Rothman is a virtually certain Democratic vote. In the 111th Congress (2009-10), he stuck with his party 99 percent of the time when the majority of Democrats and Republicans squared off on an issue.

The former Bergen County Surrogate Court judge occasionally strays into more conservative territory, sometimes siding with the GOP on tougher punishments for violent offenders, and he supports the death penalty.

Rothman believes one of his greatest legacies in the House is the Secure Our Schools Act, which he sponsored with the late Henry J. Hyde, an Illinois Republican, in 2000. Rothman said the bill was a response to letters he received from middle school pupils who felt unsafe because of fellow students who brought weapons to school. The law created a program to provide grants to schools for security devices such as cameras and metal detectors.

In 2006, while still a member of the Appropriations subcommittee handling transportation issues, he was the Washington point man for an intense local battle over noise and congestion at Teterboro Airport, a general-aviation facility convenient to Manhattan. Rothman brokered a deal to eliminate the loudest jets, impose a curfew on late-night flights, and keep heavy planes from operating there. And since entering Congress, he has fought to preserve the remaining 8,400 acres of undeveloped land in the Meadowlands, where a large sports complex is located. A newspaper clipping from The (Bergen County) Record hangs in his office praising his efforts as "a 'wild' idea."

Rothman keeps a tight connection with local party officials as he watches for a chance to run for the Senate upon the retirement of Democratic Sen. Frank R. Lautenberg, who will be 90 by the time of his next re-election contest and was recently treated for stomach cancer. In January 2009 — anticipating a future battle for that seat — Rothman secured the endorsement of Bergen County Democratic Party Chairman Michael Kasparian. "If an opening did arrive in the United States Senate, I would consider it," Rothman said.

Rothman was born in Englewood. His grandparents, Jewish immigrants from Russia, Poland and Austria, came through Ellis Island. His father was a tool-and-die maker until a moonlighting venture building houses with a friend evolved into an industrial real estate business. He credits nightly discussions at the family dinner table as a reason he became interested in politics.

After graduating from high school, Rothman landed a summer internship with a Democratic state senator, Matthew Feldman. As mayor of Teaneck in the early 1960s, Feldman had led that city's racial integration of neighborhoods and public schools, and in the 1940s he strongly supported the creation of the state of Israel. Feldman, who died in 1994, became Rothman's political role model.

Rothman majored in political philosophy at Syracuse University and then obtained a law degree from Washington University in St. Louis. He opened his practice in 1978 and got involved in local Democratic Party politics. In 1983, he was elected mayor of his hometown. "I was the candidate of the Black Clergy Council and the cops — it was the first time those groups had endorsed the same candidate for mayor," Rothman said. He later made an unsuccessful bid for Bergen County freeholder but won his next campaign, for the court judgeship, in 1993.

In 1996, he ran for the House when Democrat Robert G. Torricelli gave up his seat to run successfully for the Senate. Rothman took 80 percent of the primary vote and 56 percent in the general election. He has won re-election easily ever since.

Key Votes

2010

Overhaul the nation's health insurance system	YES
Allow for repeal of "don't ask, don't tell"	YES
Overhaul financial services industry regulation	YES
Limit use of new Afghanistan War funds to troop withdrawal activities	NO
Change oversight of offshore drilling and lift oil spill liability cap	YES
Provide a path to legal status for some children of illegal immigrants	YES
Extend Bush-era income tax cuts for two years	YES

2009

Expand the Children's Health Insurance Program	YES
Provide $787 billion in tax cuts and spending increases to stimulate the economy	YES
Allow bankruptcy judges to modify certain primary-residence mortgages	YES
Create a cap-and-trade system to limit greenhouse gas emissions	YES
Provide $2 billion for the "cash for clunkers" program	YES
Establish the government as the sole provider of student loans	YES
Restrict federally funded insurance coverage for abortions in health care overhaul	NO

CQ Vote Studies

	PARTY UNITY		PRESIDENTIAL SUPPORT	
	Support	Oppose	Support	Oppose
2010	99%	1%	95%	5%
2009	99%	1%	97%	3%
2008	98%	2%	14%	86%
2007	98%	2%	7%	93%
2006	98%	2%	9%	91%

Interest Groups

	AFL-CIO	ADA	CCUS	ACU
2010	100%	90%	29%	0%
2009	100%	100%	33%	0%
2008	100%	100%	56%	8%
2007	96%	95%	44%	0%
2006	100%	90%	27%	8%

New Jersey 9

Northeast — Hackensack, part of Jersey City

Across the Hudson River from northern Manhattan, the 9th is an overwhelmingly Democratic district that takes in southeast Bergen County before dipping into parts of Hudson County and suburbs adjacent to Newark. Prestigious areas lie in the north, including Englewood Cliffs and Fort Lee; the district becomes more blue-collar and middle-class as it runs south into Lyndhurst and parts of Jersey City.

The district is a mix of tightly packed neighborhoods in areas such as Leonia and Ridgefield and more-commercial parts such as Secaucus. As New York City apartment prices have climbed, many commuters have moved to the 9th's Hudson River towns, like Edgewater. In its northwestern sliver, the district's small section of Passaic County consists entirely of Hawthorne, an older bedroom community.

Anchored by East Rutherford's Meadowlands Sports Complex, the southern part of the 9th has seen new commercial and residential development. Football's Jets and Giants moved into their new joint stadium there in 2010, and light-rail connections to the stadium link East Rutherford to

Manhattan, Hoboken and Newark. But the news is not all good for the complex, as the loss of funders has delayed completion of the $2 billion shopping and entertainment portion of the Meadowlands Xanadu project. Hockey's Devils have moved south to Newark, and soccer's Red Bulls have a new stadium in Harrison (located in the 13th).

The 9th's part of Bergen is Democratic — Englewood, Hackensack and Teaneck all gave Barack Obama more than 70 percent of their 2008 presidential vote and backed Jon Corzine in the 2009 gubernatorial election. The Hispanic population around Jersey City (shared with the 10th and 13th) and sizable proportions of black, Jewish and Asian voters add to Democratic strength here. Obama won 61 percent of the 9th's vote overall in 2008.

Major Industry
Manufacturing, health care, shipping, stadium events

Cities
Jersey City (pt.), 55,975; Hackensack, 43,010; Kearny (pt.), 38,355; Fort Lee, 35,345; Fair Lawn, 32,457; Garfield, 30,487; Englewood, 27,147

Notable
Teterboro Airport is home to the Aviation Hall of Fame and Museum of New Jersey.

Rep. Donald M. Payne (D)

Capitol Office
225-3436
www.house.gov/payne
2310 Rayburn Bldg. 20515-3010; fax 225-4160

Committees
Education & the Workforce
Foreign Affairs

Residence
Newark

Born
July 16, 1934; Newark, N.J.

Religion
Baptist

Family
Widowed; three children

Education
Seton Hall U., B.A. 1957 (social studies)

Career
Teacher; company community affairs director; computer forms company executive

Political Highlights
Essex County Board of Freeholders, 1972-78; sought Democratic nomination for Essex County executive, 1978; sought Democratic nomination for U.S. House, 1980; Newark Municipal Council, 1982-88; sought Democratic nomination for U.S. House, 1986

ELECTION RESULTS

2010 GENERAL

Donald M. Payne (D)	95,299	85.2%
Michael J. Alonso (R)	14,357	12.8%
Robert Louis Toussaint (ANO)	1,141	1.0%

2010 PRIMARY

Donald M. Payne (D)	unopposed

2008 GENERAL

Donald M. Payne (D)	169,945	98.9%
Michael Taber (SW)	1,848	1.1%

Previous Winning Percentages
2006 (100%); 2004 (97%); 2002 (84%); 2000 (88%); 1998 (84%); 1996 (84%); 1994 (76%); 1992 (78%); 1990 (81%); 1988 (77%)

Elected 1988; 12th term

Payne is among the most liberal — and most low-key — members of the House, a quiet operator who defends traditional Democratic priorities and presses his concerns for human rights abroad and government assistance to the poor in his ethnically diverse, densely populated urban district.

In his role as chairman of the Congressional Black Caucus Foundation, he has combined those two interests, shining a spotlight on treating AIDS in the United States and elsewhere. "The epidemic continues to hurt us, not just here but on other continents, like Africa," Payne said.

The broader plight of many African nations is another issue important to Payne. The genocide in the Darfur region of Sudan, poverty in Zimbabwe and civil war in the Democratic Republic of the Congo topped the list of concerns he tackled while serving as chairman of the Foreign Affairs Subcommittee on Africa, Global Health and Human Rights, where he is now the ranking Democrat.

Payne first visited Africa more than 30 years ago, and since arriving in Congress in 1989 he has served on the panel. He travels regularly to the continent, and African sculptures, masks and artifacts adorn his office. The trips sometimes draw surprises: On an April 2009 visit to Somalia, insurgents fired mortar shells near Mogadishu's airport as his plane took off.

Payne is a member of the board of Discovery Channel's Global Education Partnership, which provides television and educational videos to Nigeria, Angola, South Africa and Venezuela. "The people back in Newark aren't always aware of what I'm doing in foreign affairs," he told The Star-Ledger in March 2009. "That's all right. I don't make an issue out of it."

The lawmaker has pushed successive administrations to provide more aid to Africa. In 1998 he helped persuade President Bill Clinton to travel there. Two years later he helped facilitate negotiations that led to enactment of a law expanding trade with sub-Saharan Africa. Payne enjoyed less clout with President George W. Bush's administration, although Bush did twice appoint Payne as a congressional delegate to the United Nations. And Payne was pleased with Bush's efforts to boost funding for AIDS relief. "He went beyond what any other president has done," Payne said of Bush.

Payne is equally committed to holding Africa's worst human rights abusers accountable. He says Ethiopia's role as a key ally in the volatile Horn of Africa and in the fight against terrorism shouldn't excuse its disregard for human rights. In 2007, he won House passage of a bill to condition U.S. military assistance to Ethiopia on the release of political prisoners, punishment of those involved in the killing of demonstrators and prisoners, and establishment of an independent judiciary. The White House could waive the restrictions, but it nevertheless opposed the bill, saying it would tie the administration's hands and could disturb negotiations for the release of prisoners.

Payne also led efforts to sanction Sudan for the murder, rape and plunder of black Africans in Darfur. The atrocities have been attributed to mostly Arab militias backed by the government. He was a founder of the Sudan Caucus, and in 2001 he took an uncharacteristically public step to push his case: He chained himself to the gates of the Sudanese Embassy and was arrested.

He has led lawmakers in pressuring the president of Ivory Coast, who clung to power after losing a November 2010 election, to concede defeat.

In the 111th Congress (2009-10), Payne guided legislation to provide financial relief to the residents of Haiti, who were devastated by a massive earthquake. "For the 22 years I have been a member of this Congress, Haiti was always No. 1 on the agenda," Payne said on the House floor.

On the domestic front, Payne pushes liberal solutions on a range of issues.

On the Education and the Workforce Committee, he wants more federal spending to aid low-income school districts. He has said it is time to "stop the apartheid we see in education — one side is black or Hispanic and poor, the other side is affluent and predominately white."

He backed all of the major economic initiatives of the Obama administration and sided with his party 98 percent of the time in the 111th Congress when a majority of Democrats split from a majority of Republicans.

In fall 2008, though, he voted against a $700 billion package to shore up the nation's struggling financial system, despite support for the plan from President-elect Obama. He said he would have preferred direct assistance to homeowners facing foreclosure, an economic stimulus package and provisions to prevent a future financial crisis.

Born in Newark, Payne's earliest years coincided with the Great Depression. His mother died when he was 7, and he lived with his grandmother because his father worked long hours on the docks. He took his first job at age 9, delivering The Newark Star-Ledger. He credits his rise in life to an organization called The Leaguers, which was founded by Reynold and Mary Burch, leaders of Newark's black community. Burch used her contacts with Seton Hall University to help Payne earn a four-year scholarship.

Payne was a high school history teacher and football coach after college, and he ran a storefront YMCA in Newark in the late 1950s. He became the first black president of the National Council of YMCAs in 1970, served as chairman of the YMCA's International Committee on Refugees and is still on the board of the Newark YMCA. In 1963, he became community affairs director for the Newark-based Prudential Insurance Co. and was vice president of a computer forms company founded by his brother. At the same time, the widowed Payne was raising his three children and establishing himself politically. He served six years as an Essex County freeholder, akin to a county councilman, and another six on the Newark Municipal Council.

He made unsuccessful attempts in 1980 and 1986 to win the U.S. House seat in the black-majority 10th District. Blocking his path was Democrat Peter W. Rodino Jr., who had held the seat since 1949 and led the 1974 impeachment proceedings against President Richard M. Nixon.

When Rodino decided to retire in 1988, party officials got behind Payne. He easily defeated city council colleague Ralph T. Grant Jr. in the primary, and his November victory was a formality in the overwhelmingly Democratic district. He became the first black representative from New Jersey and has won overwhelmingly since.

Key Votes

2010	
Overhaul the nation's health insurance system	YES
Allow for repeal of "don't ask, don't tell"	YES
Overhaul financial services industry regulation	YES
Limit use of new Afghanistan War funds to troop withdrawal activities	YES
Change oversight of offshore drilling and lift oil spill liability cap	YES
Provide a path to legal status for some children of illegal immigrants	YES
Extend Bush-era income tax cuts for two years	NO
2009	
Expand the Children's Health Insurance Program	YES
Provide $787 billion in tax cuts and spending increases to stimulate the economy	YES
Allow bankruptcy judges to modify certain primary-residence mortgages	YES
Create a cap-and-trade system to limit greenhouse gas emissions	YES
Provide $2 billion for the "cash for clunkers" program	YES
Establish the government as the sole provider of student loans	YES
Restrict federally funded insurance coverage for abortions in health care overhaul	NO

CQ Vote Studies

	PARTY UNITY		PRESIDENTIAL SUPPORT	
	SUPPORT	OPPOSE	SUPPORT	OPPOSE
2010	97%	3%	83%	17%
2009	99%	1%	94%	6%
2008	99%	1%	13%	87%
2007	99%	1%	4%	96%
2006	99%	1%	5%	95%

Interest Groups

	AFL-CIO	ADA	CCUS	ACU
2010	92%	95%	25%	5%
2009	100%	100%	33%	0%
2008	100%	95%	47%	8%
2007	100%	100%	42%	0%
2006	100%	85%	14%	4%

New Jersey 10

Northeast — parts of Newark and Jersey City

Covering a multiracial, urban region centered in Newark, the black-majority 10th provides a solid base for Democrats. Outside Newark (which is shared with the 13th), the district extends into Essex County's working-class suburbs of Irvington, East Orange and Orange. It also takes in portions of Jersey City (shared with the 9th and 13th) and Elizabeth (shared with the 13th).

The 10th's portion of Newark is made up of the largely black central, south and west wards of the city. Although deep poverty continues to be a problem in some spots, efforts to revitalize the area have had some success. A performing arts center in Newark that opened in 1997 engages in community outreach programs. The district's part of Newark also is home to University Heights Science Park, a collaboration between local universities and startup technology companies. The district hosts the University of Medicine and Dentistry of New Jersey, the New Jersey Institute of Technology, Essex County College and part of the Rutgers University,

Camden campus.

Newark Liberty International Airport is a transportation center for travelers to New York City. It is a hub for United Continental, and Southwest Airlines began service at the airport in 2011. Newark Penn Station is the state's busiest transit location, with connections to Amtrak, PATH and New Jersey Transit rail and bus service. Port Newark-Elizabeth (partly in the 13th) also provides jobs for the region.

The district votes consistently Democratic at all levels, although Millburn, a wealthy enclave shared with the 11th, hosts some Republicans. Barack Obama posted his highest percentage in the state here in the 2008 presidential election, winning 87 percent of the district's vote.

Major Industry
Aviation, shipping, insurance, higher education, pharmaceuticals

Cities
Newark (pt.), 154,695; Elizabeth (pt.), 75,422; East Orange, 64,270; Linden (pt.), 30,997; Rahway, 27,346

Notable
Economist Milton Friedman grew up in Rahway; the University of Medicine and Dentistry of New Jersey, headquartered in Newark, is the nation's largest public university of the health sciences.

Rep. Rodney Frelinghuysen (R)

Capitol Office
225-5034
frelinghuysen.house.gov
2369 Rayburn Bldg. 20515-3011; fax 225-3186

Committees
Appropriations
(Energy-Water - Chairman)

Residence
Harding

Born
April 29, 1946; Manhattan, N.Y.

Religion
Episcopalian

Family
Wife, Virginia T. Frelinghuysen; two children

Education
Hobart College, B.A. 1969; Trinity College (Conn.),
attended 1971 (American history)

Military
Army, 1969-71

Career
County board aide

Political Highlights
Morris County Board of Freeholders, 1974-83
(director, 1980); sought Republican nomination for
U.S. House, 1982; N.J. Assembly, 1983-94; sought
Republican nomination for U.S. House, 1990

ELECTION RESULTS

2010 GENERAL

Rodney Frelinghuysen (R)	122,149	67.2%
Douglas Herbert (D)	55,472	30.5%
Jim Gawron (LIBERT)	4,179	2.3%

2010 PRIMARY

Rodney Frelinghuysen (R)	32,631	76.4%
Richard T. Luzzi (R)	10,060	23.6%

2008 GENERAL

Rodney Frelinghuysen (R)	189,696	62.4%
Tom Wyka (D)	113,510	37.3%

Previous Winning Percentages
2006 (72%); 2004 (68%); 2002 (72%); 2000 (68%);
1998 (68%); 1996 (66%); 1994 (71%)

Elected 1994; 9th term

Frelinghuysen, the scion of perhaps the longest-running political dynasty in American history, is a low-key Republican described as "modest" and "conscientious" who quietly takes care of his upscale suburban district through his seat on the Appropriations Committee. While he splits with his party on social issues, he hews to conservative orthodoxy on taxes, immigration and national security.

Frelinghuysen (FREE-ling-high-zen) is the sixth member of his family to serve the state in Congress, and the family name dots the landscape across northern New Jersey. There's the Frelinghuysen Arboretum in Morris Township and the Frelinghuysen Middle School in Morristown, as well as Rutgers University's Frelinghuysen Hall. A Frelinghuysen served in the Continental Congress; another was a senator and secretary of State; a third was a senator and Henry Clay's vice presidential running mate on the losing Whig ticket in 1844. Rodney Frelinghuysen's father, Peter F. Frelinghuysen, served in the House for 22 years, until 1975. The family had a house in Georgetown, and the younger Frelinghuysen attended St. Albans prep school at the same time as future Vice President Al Gore.

Frelinghuysen has said he was aware of his family's singular role, and his place in it, from an early age, when his father first ran for Congress. "A lot of what you do in life is the direct result of those who bring you up. It either drives you toward this life or drives you away," he said.

Frelinghuysen was part of the 73-member Republican class of 1994, and he backed all the major items in the GOP's Contract With America. But he was less of an outraged outsider than many members of the first GOP House majority in decades. The difference is largely attributable to his family background and personal fortune: He is among the wealthiest lawmakers, ranking 14th in 2009 with a minimum net worth of $19.9 million, according to Roll Call.

Frelinghuysen accrued seniority on Appropriations in the years of GOP control, becoming chairman, or "cardinal," of the District of Columbia Subcommittee in 2003. But in 2005, he lost his gavel when Majority Leader Tom DeLay of Texas pushed through an Appropriations Committee reorganization that cut the number of subcommittees from 13 to 10. As the most junior cardinal, Frelinghuysen lost out.

He got a gavel back in the 112th Congress (2011-12), taking over the Energy-Water Subcommittee, where he had served as ranking Republican in the previous Congress. A moderate on environmental issues, he has long resisted the GOP push to allow oil drilling off the coast of his state. In the 109th Congress (2005-06), he voted against opening the Arctic National Wildlife Refuge in Alaska to drilling. But he joined with the vast majority of his party colleagues in opposing legislation in June 2009 that would create a cap-and-trade system for limiting greenhouse gas emissions. Only eight Republicans supported the bill, three of them from New Jersey.

He has worked to preserve scenic areas of his district. He pushed for expansion of the Morristown National Historic Park and the Great Swamp Wildlife Refuge, and he secured funds to clean up superfund sites, protect the state's coast and help protect against floods. He also has worked to preserve the Highland — mountainous and scenic watershed lands in northern New Jersey, New York, Pennsylvania and Connecticut. In 2004, he won enactment of a bill that authorized funds for land conservation partnerships in the four-state region. He also helped arrange for the federal purchase of lands in the Sterling Forest in 1996.

A Vietnam veteran, he also serves on the Defense Appropriations Sub-committee, where he was a consistent supporter of President George W. Bush's Iraq policy. In March 2010, he called efforts by liberal Democrats to set a timetable for withdrawal from Afghanistan "clearly the wrong resolution offered at precisely the wrong time." He also uses his spot to champion the Picatinny Arsenal, a 6,500-acre Defense Department armaments facility in Morris County.

Frelinghuysen tends to side with his party on taxes; he supported the 2001 and 2003 tax cuts pushed by George W. Bush's administration, voted to end the federal estate tax and backed a two-year extension of the Bush-era cuts in late 2010.

But he stands apart from most Republicans on some social issues. He was one of seven GOP House members who opposed an amendment to a catch-all spending bill the House passed early in 2011 that blocked funding for Planned Parenthood.

Over the years he has taken his share of earmarks, the funding set-asides for projects in members' districts. Even after Republicans instituted an ear-mark moratorium in 2010, Frelinghuysen defended the practice, telling Recorder Community Newspapers that "my duty is to look after my congres-sional district. It offends more people to the right of me in the Republican Party but I have to be responsible to look after New Jersey."

Frelinghuysen received a rare burst of attention in May 2007 when he was mugged in Georgetown and chased his perpetrators down the street, holding one of them until police arrived. Other lawmakers from New Jersey weren't surprised. Democratic Rep. Bill Pascrell Jr. said: "I want him on my side when I go into a fight."

Frelinghuysen entered politics after college and Army service in Viet-nam. He went to work for Dean A. Gallo, a Republican Morris County free-holder who later was elected to the House. Frelinghuysen became a free-holder, akin to a county councilman, in 1974. He lost a GOP primary for the 12th District House seat in 1982 but won a state Assembly seat the next year. In 1990 he lost again in a race for the 12th District nomination, running third in the primary.

He eventually won his House seat in 1994, but the victory was bittersweet because he took the seat of his mentor and friend Gallo, who had become ill. Gallo designated Frelinghuysen, who was managing the re-election effort, as his successor. Frelinghuysen won easily in one of the few remaining sol-idly Republican districts in New Jersey. He has been re-elected easily since, drawing 67 percent of the vote in 2010.

Key Votes

2010	
Overhaul the nation's health insurance system	NO
Allow for repeal of "don't ask, don't tell"	NO
Overhaul financial services industry regulation	NO
Limit use of new Afghanistan War funds to troop withdrawal activities	NO
Change oversight of offshore drilling and lift oil spill liability cap	NO
Provide a path to legal status for some children of illegal immigrants	NO
Extend Bush-era income tax cuts for two years	YES
2009	
Expand the Children's Health Insurance Program	YES
Provide $787 billion in tax cuts and spend-ing increases to stimulate the economy	NO
Allow bankruptcy judges to modify certain primary-residence mortgages	NO
Create a cap-and-trade system to limit greenhouse gas emissions	NO
Provide $2 billion for the "cash for clunkers" program	NO
Establish the government as the sole provider of student loans	NO
Restrict federally funded insurance cover-age for abortions in health care overhaul	YES

CQ Vote Studies

	PARTY UNITY		PRESIDENTIAL SUPPORT	
	SUPPORT	OPPOSE	SUPPORT	OPPOSE
2010	91%	9%	29%	71%
2009	77%	23%	42%	58%
2008	87%	13%	73%	27%
2007	79%	21%	63%	37%
2006	87%	13%	83%	17%

Interest Groups

	AFL-CIO	ADA	CCUS	ACU
2010	7%	5%	88%	88%
2009	19%	15%	93%	68%
2008	13%	15%	100%	80%
2007	25%	30%	80%	56%
2006	29%	25%	80%	60%

North central — Morris County

Exclusive, pastoral estates and Fortune 500 firms make the 11th one of the most privileged districts in the nation.

Located in northern New Jersey and centered in Morris County, the district has the nation's second-highest median household income ($98,000), and nearly half of all residents have earned at least a bachelor's degree.

Residents here live mainly in small to midsize bedroom communities con-nected by a number of interstate highways and state routes.

The district has experienced some population growth as couples and families move here to get away from large cities, and suburban sprawl has become a major issue.

In addition to all of Morris, the 11th takes in chunks of Essex County in the east, Somerset County in the south, Sussex County in the northwest and a sliver of Passaic County in the northeast.

While the 11th is loaded with commuters making trips to New York, it also hosts its own large, white-collar firms. The corporate presence in the district includes giants like Nabisco (Kraft Foods) in East Hanover and Honeywell's headquarters in Morristown.

Pharmaceuticals feed the district's economic growth. In 2009, Morris Plains-based Pfizer bought Wyeth, whose headquarters were in Madison, and Novartis is in East Hanover. But several years of widespread layoffs and corporate reorganization across the industry have hurt the district. Morris County officials also hope to lure tourists to historic parks, dwellings and other sites.

The area's voters have been economically conservative for some time, and the 11th is one of the most solidly Republican districts in the northeast. John McCain captured 54 percent of the vote here in the 2008 presidential election, his highest percentage in New Jersey.

Major Industry
Pharmaceuticals, finance, telecommunications, manufacturing

Military Bases
Picatinny Arsenal (Army), 93 military, 3,907 civilian (2011)

Cities
Morristown, 18,411; Dover, 18,157; Madison, 15,845

Notable
Morris County was considered the "Military Capital of the American Revo-lution" because of its repeated use by Gen. George Washington.

Rep. Rush D. Holt (D)

Capitol Office
225-5801
holt.house.gov
1214 Longworth Bldg. 20515-3012; fax 225-6025

Committees
Education & the Workforce
Natural Resources

Residence
Hopewell Township

Born
Oct. 15, 1948; Weston, W.Va.

Religion
Quaker

Family
Wife, Margaret Lancefield; three children

Education
Carleton College, B.A. 1970 (physics); New York U.,
M.S. 1980 (physics), Ph.D. 1981 (physics)

Career
University research assistant director; physics
professor

Political Highlights
Sought Democratic nomination for U.S. House, 1996

ELECTION RESULTS

2010 GENERAL

Rush D. Holt (D)	108,214	53.0%
Scott Sipprelle (R)	93,634	45.9%
Kenneth J. Cody (TVH)	2,154	1.1%

2010 PRIMARY

Rush D. Holt (D)	unopposed

2008 GENERAL

Rush D. Holt (D)	193,732	63.1%
Alan R. Bateman (R)	108,400	35.3%
David Corsi (CS)	4,802	1.6%

Previous Winning Percentages
2006 (66%); 2004 (59%); 2002 (61%); 2000 (49%);
1998 (50%)

Elected 1998; 7th term

In an age in which the political culture of Washington tends toward the confrontational, Holt seems to be of a different era. Although a staunch Democrat and unquestioned liberal, he does not display the trappings of an ideologue. Dressed in boat shoes and a sports jacket, he exudes the down-to-earth demeanor of a favorite professor, a persona somewhat out of place with the political caricature of his state.

Holt is a physicist, and he takes a scientist's approach to public policy, preferring to use empirical evidence when weighing issues such as the FBI's handling of the anthrax investigation — one of the anthrax-laden letters was mailed from his district in 2001 — or even electoral overhaul, a favorite issue.

After all that analysis, though, he almost always ends up siding with his party. On votes that divided a majority of Democrats from a majority of Republicans in the 111th Congress (2009-10), he voted with his leadership 99 percent of the time.

On the Natural Resources Committee, Holt has been at the forefront of trying to slow suburban sprawl and has worked to replenish the Land and Water Conservation Fund. He notes that his district is among the few in New Jersey that have retained some open space.

In the 112th Congress (2011-12) he is the ranking Democrat on the committee's Energy and Mineral Resources panel, which puts him in the center ring for the fight between Republicans and Democrats over expanding energy exploration on public lands.

He backed a bill early in 2011 that would require oil and gas companies to produce on the drilling leases they already own or risk losing their rights to drill. "If the House majority is going to continue to insist on 'drill, baby, drill' — including on public lands — then we should agree that oil companies should pay for the lands that they are leasing but not producing on," Holt said.

Holt has a 100 percent lifetime score from the League of Conservation Voters, a liberal environmental group.

On what has been renamed the Education and the Workforce Committee, Holt has actively promoted math and science education. A measure to reauthorize a higher education program, enacted in 2008, included several of his proposals, such as a program providing grants and loan forgiveness to math and science students committing to serve in a related field after graduation.

In the 111th Congress, Holt chaired an Appropriations panel charged with overseeing spending on intelligence programs, although he was not a member of the full Appropriations Committee. The subcommittee, which dovetailed with his work on the Select Intelligence Committee — on which he no longer serves — was established at the start of the 110th Congress (2007-08) in response to a recommendation from the independent commission that investigated the Sept. 11 attacks. Republicans eliminated the panel at the start of the 112th Congress, saying its functions were redundant.

He held several hearings following the release of a report that indicated the Office of the Director of National Intelligence needed to better manage problems such as reducing intelligence agency turf battles and establishing rules for protecting the privacy of U.S. citizens. He also pushed provisions to require the video recording of detainee interrogations and the preservation of those records, in light of charges of abuse and the destruction of tapes of the interrogations of terrorism suspects.

Holt's political career has been greatly influenced by his parents. When he left Princeton University's Plasma Physics Laboratory in 1997, he wanted to either write a biography of his father or run for Congress. Holt's father, Rush Dew Holt, was elected to the U.S. Senate from West Virginia at age 29, the youngest person ever elected to that chamber. He had to wait six months to take office because the U.S. Constitution requires that senators be at least 30 years old. At the time of his election in 1934, the elder Holt was an ardent New Dealer and supporter of President Franklin D. Roosevelt. However, beginning with his opposition to a 1935 law designed to set coal prices, Holt began to shift his political positions.

"He was an impetuous young firebrand in the '30s," the younger Holt said. "He was a New Dealer and always thought of himself as a friend of the workers. But he split with [United Mine Workers President] John L. Lewis and Roosevelt." The elder Holt became a critic of the New Deal and a staunch isolationist, appearing on stage with Charles Lindbergh and other members of the America First Committee in the run-up to World War II. Defeated for the Senate in 1940, Holt ran unsuccessfully for governor — as a Republican — in 1952. He died soon after.

Holt, who hands out bumper stickers proclaiming, "My congressman IS a rocket scientist!" said he developed his interest in science at an early age from his mother, who taught science at a junior college. She also was a West Virginia state legislator and secretary of state. When Holt's father died, he and his mother moved to Washington, D.C., where he went to high school and she worked for the Department of Housing and Urban Development.

Holt earned a Ph.D. in physics after completing a doctoral dissertation about the outer layer of the sun. He holds a patent for improving the efficiency of solar ponds, a source of thermal energy. After school, he worked at the State Department on arms control and space activities, before becoming assistant director of the Princeton laboratory.

He ran for Congress in 1996, losing in the Democratic primary to David M. Del Vecchio, who in turn lost a close race to Republican Michael Pappas. Two years later, Holt won by portraying Pappas as too conservative for the district. His 5,000-vote victory placed Holt high on the GOP's list of targeted incumbents in 2000. His campaign against moderate Republican Dick Zimmer, who had held the House seat for three terms ending in 1996, was bitter, and the outcome was in doubt for three weeks after Election Day. Holt was eventually declared the victor by 651 votes and has won easily ever since.

Holt says his greatest claim to fame might be his five wins on the TV quiz show "Jeopardy." Given the reaction he gets from journalists, he once joked, "It must be the most significant thing I've done." In 2011, he beat an IBM computer in a round of the game show.

Key Votes

2010

Overhaul the nation's health insurance system	YES
Allow for repeal of "don't ask, don't tell"	YES
Overhaul financial services industry regulation	YES
Limit use of new Afghanistan War funds to troop withdrawal activities	YES
Change oversight of offshore drilling and lift oil spill liability cap	YES
Provide a path to legal status for some children of illegal immigrants	YES
Extend Bush-era income tax cuts for two years	NO

2009

Expand the Children's Health Insurance Program	YES
Provide $787 billion in tax cuts and spending increases to stimulate the economy	YES
Allow bankruptcy judges to modify certain primary-residence mortgages	YES
Create a cap-and-trade system to limit greenhouse gas emissions	YES
Provide $2 billion for the "cash for clunkers" program	YES
Establish the government as the sole provider of student loans	YES
Restrict federally funded insurance coverage for abortions in health care overhaul	NO

CQ Vote Studies

	PARTY UNITY		PRESIDENTIAL SUPPORT	
	SUPPORT	OPPOSE	SUPPORT	OPPOSE
2010	99%	1%	90%	10%
2009	99%	1%	97%	3%
2008	98%	2%	15%	85%
2007	98%	2%	6%	94%
2006	97%	3%	15%	85%

Interest Groups

	AFL-CIO	ADA	CCUS	ACU
2010	100%	100%	13%	0%
2009	100%	100%	33%	0%
2008	100%	100%	61%	0%
2007	96%	90%	50%	0%
2006	100%	95%	20%	5%

New Jersey 12

Central — part of Trenton, East Brunswick, Princeton

Set in the middle of the state, the 12th District begins in Hunterdon County, slides south to hit ethnically diverse Trenton (shared with the 4th) and then picks up East Brunswick as it winds east to Monmouth County. It ends just short of the Atlantic Ocean in shore communities such as Rumson. Despite its jagged shape, many of the district's towns are similar. Office parks dominate the landscape in these affluent and still largely white communities.

But there are pockets of blue-collar diversity, such as in the state capital, Trenton, with its black-majority population. Plainsboro in Middlesex County is among the areas with large Asian populations.

The 12th has benefited from economic growth, although midsize communities such as Ewing in Mercer County contend with the effects of suburban sprawl. In addition to the Capitol, the district also boasts the governor's official residence, the stately and imposing Drumthwacket in Princeton. Delaware River towns, such as Frenchtown and Lambertville in Hunterdon County, offer quaint antiques shops and bed-and-breakfasts. The 2011 closure of Fort Monmouth dealt the 12th a blow, but the VA hospital on base will remain open.

A solidly Democratic constituency in Mercer County is anchored by Princeton's academic community, and an influx of independents and the northeast's rising Democratic wave in national elections have shifted the district's politics away from its historical old money and suburban-based Republican lean. Republican John McCain carried the district's portion of Monmouth County and eked out a plurality in the 12th's part of Hunterdon in the 2008 presidential election, but Barack Obama took 58 percent of the 12th's vote overall.

Major Industry
Higher education, pharmaceuticals

Cities
Trenton (pt.), 43,817; Old Bridge (unincorporated) (pt.), 20,576; Tinton Falls, 17,892; South River (unincorporated), 16,008

Notable
The New Jersey Vietnam Veterans' Memorial is on the grounds of the PNC Bank Arts Center, a 17,500-seat concert venue in Holmdel.

Rep. Albio Sires (D)

Capitol Office
225-7919
www.house.gov/sires
2342 Rayburn Bldg. 20515-3013; fax 226-0792

Committees
Foreign Affairs
Transportation & Infrastructure

Residence
West New York

Born
Jan. 26, 1951; Bejucal, Cuba

Religion
Roman Catholic

Family
Wife, Adrienne Sires; one stepchild

Education
Saint Peter's College, B.A. 1974 (Spanish & marketing); Middlebury College, M.A. 1985 (Spanish)

Career
Property title insurance firm owner; state community affairs agency aide; teacher

Political Highlights
Candidate for West New York Town Commission, 1983; Republican nominee for U.S. House, 1986; Republican nominee for Hudson County Board of Chosen Freeholders, 1987; candidate for West New York Town Commission, 1991; candidate for West New York Town Commission (recall election), 1993; West New York Town Commission, 1995-2006 (mayor, 1995-2006); N.J. Assembly, 2000-06 (Speaker, 2002-06)

ELECTION RESULTS

2010 GENERAL

Albio Sires (D)	62,840	74.1%
Henrietta Dwyer (R)	19,538	23.0%
Anthony Zanowic (IA)	1,508	1.8%
Maximo Nacer (GBS)	910	1.1%

2010 PRIMARY

Albio Sires (D)	16,022	86.9%
Jeffrey Boss (D)	2,409	13.1%

2008 GENERAL

Albio Sires (D)	120,382	75.4%
Joseph Turula (R)	34,735	21.7%
Julio A. Fernandez (X)	3,661	2.3%

Previous Winning Percentages
2006 (77.5%); 2006 Special Election (97%)

Elected 2006; 3rd full term

The burly, 6-foot-4-inch Sires is a loyal Democrat deeply invested in securing transportation funds for his district. He is also a Cuban-American determined to maintain a hard line against Cuba's Castro regime.

Sires (SEAR-eez — like "series") works on those tasks from his seats on the Foreign Affairs and Transportation and Infrastructure committees.

He supported his party in 98 percent of the votes in which a majority of Republicans and Democrats diverged in the 111th Congress (2009-10), and party leaders in early 2009 chose him as one of three vice chairmen for the Democratic Congressional Campaign Committee.

But he was among the first House Democrats after their defeat in the 2010 elections to call for then-Speaker Nancy Pelosi of California to make way for a new party leader.

"I think she's been a very strong leader, I support her, but the result of this election shows we need some new direction and I think the best way is for her to move on," Sires said days after the election.

He opposed her for minority leader, but was not among the 18 Democratic defectors who voted for someone besides Pelosi in the election for Speaker at the start of the 112th Congress (2011-12).

Sires, who used to be a member of the Republican Party, has shown a knack for connecting with people across political divides. In his first full year in the House, he forged an alliance with Cuban-born Republican brothers Lincoln and Mario Diaz-Balart of Florida. The brothers, like Sires, are fervent critics of Fidel Castro and his brother Raúl. In August 2007, Sires and the Diaz-Balarts traveled to the Czech Republic, Hungary and Poland to meet with former dissidents to discuss democratization for Cuba. (Lincoln Diaz-Balart is no longer in Congress.)

Since then, Sires — the No. 2 Democrat on the Foreign Affairs Subcommittee on Western Hemisphere — has joined a fellow New Jersey Democrat, Sen. Robert Menendez (who is also of Cuban heritage), in fighting colleagues' attempts to loosen travel and trade restrictions to the nation, citing its continued human-rights violations and jails holding multitudes of political prisoners. "We need to get some concessions from these people," Sires said of the Castros in April 2009. "We do from every other country, so why not Cuba?"

On the Transportation panel, Sires worked to include more than $56 million for his district's local projects in the fiscal 2009 catchall spending bill, including initiatives to ease traffic by building a new rail tunnel under the Hudson River from New Jersey to New York's Penn Station — a project cast into doubt by cost overruns.

He also hopes to use a multi-year surface transportation bill expected to be considered in the 112th Congress to increase light-rail service linking cities of the Hudson River waterfront.

Sires has been a political player in Hudson County for nearly three decades, with a reputation as a favorite son of the Cuban community in West New York. He was born in Bejucal, Cuba, and was not quite 8 when Castro's Communist regime seized power. When Sires and his schoolmates weren't marching in formation, they were being taught how to handle a Czechoslovakian machine gun.

In January 1962, Sires and his family fled Cuba and settled in what was then the predominately Italian town of West New York. Sires' father worked in a foam rubber factory making $1.39 an hour, and his mother was a seamstress. Little by little, the family saved enough money to move out of his aunt's house and into a $45-a-month cold-water flat.

Just 11 years old, Sires struggled to learn English and was left back following his first year in his new school. In time, playing basketball helped him make friends. As an all-state point guard for West New York's Memorial High School, he became a local celebrity and earned a scholarship to Saint Peter's College. After graduating from there, he decided to return to his high school to teach Spanish and coach basketball. By then, West New York had seen a dramatic influx of Cuban refugees.

Ethnic differences boiled over into the local politics, which were controlled in the 1980s by a Democratic political machine headed by Anthony DeFino, West New York's longtime mayor. DeFino worked to crush Sires' bid for the city commission.

Having been locked out of a future in the local Democratic Party, Sires switched his affiliation to Republican. In 1986, he ran as the GOP candidate for the House seat held by longtime incumbent and Hudson County Democrat Frank J. Guarini. Sires lost badly, getting less than 30 percent of the vote. (Once in office, though, Sires had a post office in Jersey City named in honor of Guarini, with whom he'd developed a friendship.)

No longer teaching and once again on the losing end of a campaign, Sires spent a year coordinating outreach to the Hispanic community for Republican Gov. Thomas H. Kean. Although Sires ultimately left the Republican Party, he still considers Kean a mentor.

Sires started a title insurance business and lost two bids for local office as an independent. When DeFino opted not to run for re-election in 1995, Sires jumped into the mayoral race and won. In 1999, he was overwhelmingly re-elected and rejoined the Democratic Party to run for the New Jersey Assembly.

He was two years into his career in the legislature when Governor-elect James E. McGreevey backed Sires to serve as Speaker, the third-highest position in New Jersey government. He spent almost four years as Speaker, then turned his attention to the U.S. House seat being vacated by Menendez, who was tapped by newly elected Gov. Jon Corzine in 2006 to fill his Senate seat.

Sires posted a landslide victory in the 2006 Democratic primary against state Rep. Joseph Vas. That win in the Democratic stronghold sewed up his election in November against Republican John J. Guarini, a second cousin to Frank J. Guarini. With Menendez having moved to the Senate, he was sworn in immediately. Sires breezed to re-election in 2008 and 2010.

Key Votes

2010

Overhaul the nation's health insurance system	YES
Allow for repeal of "don't ask, don't tell"	YES
Overhaul financial services industry regulation	YES
Limit use of new Afghanistan War funds to troop withdrawal activities	YES
Change oversight of offshore drilling and lift oil spill liability cap	YES
Provide a path to legal status for some children of illegal immigrants	YES
Extend Bush-era income tax cuts for two years	YES

2009

Expand the Children's Health Insurance Program	YES
Provide $787 billion in tax cuts and spending increases to stimulate the economy	YES
Allow bankruptcy judges to modify certain primary-residence mortgages	YES
Create a cap-and-trade system to limit greenhouse gas emissions	YES
Provide $2 billion for the "cash for clunkers" program	YES
Establish the government as the sole provider of student loans	YES
Restrict federally funded insurance coverage for abortions in health care overhaul	NO

CQ Vote Studies

	PARTY UNITY		PRESIDENTIAL SUPPORT	
	SUPPORT	OPPOSE	SUPPORT	OPPOSE
2010	98%	2%	86%	14%
2009	98%	2%	97%	3%
2008	99%	1%	16%	84%
2007	97%	3%	7%	93%
2006	100%	0%	40%	60%

Interest Groups

	AFL-CIO	ADA	CCUS	ACU
2010	100%	90%	14%	0%
2009	100%	100%	33%	0%
2008	100%	90%	71%	0%
2007	96%	95%	55%	0%
2006	0%	10%	0%	

New Jersey 13

Northeast — parts of Jersey City and Newark

Within sight of some of the nation's best-known landmarks, including the Statue of Liberty and Manhattan's skyscrapers, the 13th covers a long, thin swath from part of North Bergen to Perth Amboy along the Hudson River, Newark Bay and Arthur Kill. The 13th takes in parts of Jersey City and Newark, linking together several growing Hispanic areas to create a Hispanic majority (51 percent) in the district.

A transportation hub, the 13th includes parts of Port Newark-Elizabeth (shared with the 10th) and surrounds Newark Liberty International Airport (in the 10th). Several lines carry commuters across the district, and PATH trains, ferries and tunnels bring passengers to and from New York. There is a sizable manufacturing sector in areas such as Kearny (shared with 9th) and Carteret.

Young professionals and financial companies moved across the river from Manhattan to Hoboken as industrial sites were converted into condominiums and office space. Hoboken's retail sector is stable and new restaurants are popping up. A waterfront redevelopment initiative in Hoboken trans-

formed shipping piers into parks, but crumbling structures and budget shortfalls have put the future of the popular coast at risk. Hoboken is also home to Stevens Institute of Technology.

Officials spent decades turning long-suffering Jersey City, which is shared with the 9th and 10th districts, into "Wall Street West," but the worldwide financial market meltdowns caused uncertainty in the district's insurance and banking industries. Northwest of Jersey City, soccer's Red Bulls moved into a new 25,000-seat stadium in Harrison in 2010, part of a billion-dollar mixed-use redevelopment plan.

Portuguese, Indian, Irish and Puerto Rican communities add to the district's diversity and its overwhelming Democratic vote. A Middle Eastern community is growing, and much of the Cuban population is based in West New York and Union City. Barack Obama won 75 percent of the 13th's 2008 presidential vote.

Major Industry
Transportation, health care, retail, finance

Cities
Jersey City (pt.), 126,417; Newark (pt.), 122,445; Union City, 66,455

Notable
Frank Sinatra was born in Hoboken.

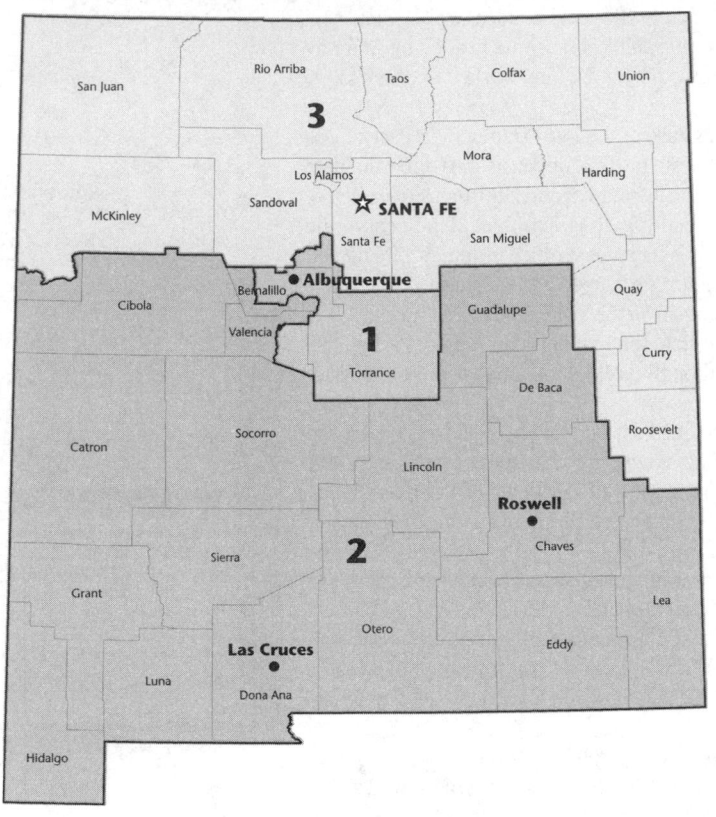

Gov. Susana Martinez (R)

First elected: 2010
Length of term: 4 years
Term expires: 1/15
Salary: $110,000
Phone: (505) 476-2200
Residence: Las Cruces
Born: July 14, 1959; El Paso, Texas
Religion: Roman Catholic
Family: Husband, Chuck Franco; one stepchild
Education: U. of Texas, El Paso, B.A. 1981 (criminal justice); U. of Oklahoma, J.D. 1986
Career: County prosecutor; state government agency lawyer
Political highlights: N.M. 3rd Judicial Circuit district attorney, 1996-2010

ELECTION RESULTS

2010 GENERAL
Susana Martinez (R)	321,219	53.3%
Diane D. Denish (D)	280,614	46.7%

Lt. Gov. John A. Sanchez (R)

First elected: 2010
Length of term: 4 years
Term expires: 1/15
Salary: $85,000
Phone: (505) 476-2250

LEGISLATURE

Legislature: 60 days January-March in odd-numbered years; 30 days January-February in even-numbered years
Senate: 42 members, 4-year terms
2011 ratios: 27 D, 15 R; 32 men, 10 women
Salary: $153/day
Phone: (509) 986-4714
House: 70 members, 2-year terms
2011 ratios: 36 D, 33 R, 1 other; 49 men, 21 women
Salary: $153/day
Phone: (505) 986-4751

TERM LIMITS

Governor: 2 consecutive terms
Senate: No
House: No

URBAN STATISTICS

CITY	POPULATION
Albuquerque	545,852
Las Cruces	97,618
Rio Rancho	87,521
Santa Fe	67,947
Roswell	48,366

REGISTERED VOTERS

Democrat	49%
Republican	32%
Unaffiliated/others	19%

POPULATION

2010 population	2,059,179
2000 population	1,819,046
1990 population	1,515,069
Percent change (2000-2010)	+13.2%
Rank among states (2010)	36
Median age	35.5
Born in state	51.7%
Foreign born	9.1%
Violent crime rate	619/100,000
Poverty level	18.0%
Federal workers	50,045
Military	11,038

ELECTIONS

STATE ELECTION OFFICIAL
(505) 827-3600
DEMOCRATIC PARTY
(505) 830-3650
REPUBLICAN PARTY
(505) 298-3662

MISCELLANEOUS

Web: www.newmexico.gov
Capital: Santa Fe

U.S. CONGRESS

Senate: 2 Democrats
House: 2 Democrats, 1 Republican

2010 CENSUS STATISTICS BY DISTRICT

District	2008 Vote for President Obama	McCain	White	Black	Asian	Hispanic	Median Income	White Collar	Blue Collar	Service Industry	Over 64	Under 18	College Education	Rural	Sq. Miles
1	60%	39%	42%	2%	2%	48%	$45,397	63%	20%	17%	12%	24%	30%	9%	4,717
2	49	50	40	2	1	52	37,093	53	26	21	14	26	19	29	69,493
3	61	38	40	1	1	39	46,140	58	23	19	12	26	26	37	47,146
STATE	57	42	40	2	1	46	42,742	58	23	19	13	26	25	25	121,356
U.S.	53	46	64	12	5	16	51,425	60	23	17	13	25	28	21	3,537,438

Sen. Jeff Bingaman (D)

Capitol Office
224-5521
bingaman.senate.gov
703 Hart Bldg. 20510-3102; fax 224-2852

Committees
Energy & Natural Resources - Chairman
Finance
  (Energy, Natural Resources & Infrastructure
  - Chairman)
Health, Education, Labor & Pensions
Joint Economic

Residence
Santa Fe

Born
Oct. 3, 1943; El Paso, Texas

Religion
Methodist

Family
Wife, Anne Bingaman; one child

Education
Harvard U., A.B. 1965 (government); Stanford U., J.D. 1968

Military Service
Army Reserve, 1968-74

Career
Lawyer

Political Highlights
N.M. attorney general, 1979-83

ELECTION RESULTS

2006 GENERAL

Jeff Bingaman (D)	394,365	70.6%
Allen W. McCulloch (R)	163,826	29.3%

2006 PRIMARY

Jeff Bingaman (D)	unopposed

Previous Winning Percentages
2000 (62%); 1994 (54%); 1988 (63%); 1982 (54%)

Elected 1982; 5th term

Bingaman's diligent work behind the scenes and as chairman of the Energy and Natural Resources Committee has made him one of the Senate's most respected Democrats. He deploys his legislative acumen and ability to cooperate with Republicans on issues including energy and public land use, as well as education and health care.

But after more than three decades in public office, Bingaman announced in early 2011 that he would not seek re-election in 2012.

The laconic New Mexican often defers to others — including, for many years, his more publicity-minded home-state colleague, Republican Pete V. Domenici — when it comes to taking credit for accomplishments. He tends to avoid the talk show circuit and seldom holds news conferences. His mastery of lackluster topics such as technology sharing between government and industry has furthered his obscurity.

But with energy still on the front burner for the Obama administration, Bingaman's work stirs plenty of interest. He's a centrist on energy, backing more domestic oil drilling along with increased conservation. He favors more widespread use of wind, solar and other renewable sources, and supports some expansion of nuclear power, a position from which he did not retreat after an earthquake and tsunami in Japan led to explosions and the release of radiation in several nuclear reactors in March 2011.

"I think nuclear power can be provided in a safe, reliable way and it is possible that we will learn some things from what's happened in Japan that will persuade us to put in place additional precautions," he said.

In the waning days of the 111th Congress (2009-10), Bingaman unsuccessfully set his sights on passing a stand-alone renewable-electricity standard, which would require utilities to produce a minimum percentage of their electricity from renewable sources. President Obama backs the idea, but it has drawn opposition from Southern lawmakers who argue their states lack enough wind power to make it economically feasible. Bingaman had championed it as part of a comprehensive energy bill in 2007, but Senate leaders jettisoned it along with a package of tax incentives for alternative energy to win passage of the bill and avoid a presidential veto.

His close relationship with Domenici (since retired) helped shape that bill, which set the first statutory increase in vehicle fuel efficiency standards in 32 years and mandated wider use of biofuels. Two years earlier, the two worked together on steering a separate energy bill to enactment.

Bingaman laid the groundwork in the last days of the 110th Congress (2007-08) to tee up a comprehensive energy bill in 2009. He solicited ideas for a bill tackling six challenges: making wider use of technology through renewable energy; improving energy efficiency; producing more oil and gas; increasing innovation; improving oversight of energy markets to prevent price spikes; and protecting the environment. He moved legislation out of committee that summer with the support of four Republicans, including Alaska's Lisa Murkowski, the top-ranking Republican on Energy and Natural Resources. In addition to a renewable-electricity standard, the legislation would have opened new areas in the Gulf of Mexico to oil and gas drilling and made it easier for the government to site new power transmission lines. Even though the bill didn't reach the Senate floor, Bingaman said it "laid the groundwork for legislative accomplishments in the future."

He's optimistic that bipartisan cooperation on a whole range of energy provisions will continue in the 112th Congress (2011-12). "Now that the Democratic majority is smaller in the Senate, that puts that much more importance on trying to find bipartisan agreement," he said.

Bingaman views the energy-related provisions in the 2009 economic stimulus law among his greatest successes in the 111th Congress. "There were a lot of provisions in there that we urged to be included and that were included," he said.

He was a central figure in the climate change debate in the 110th Congress, less so in the 111th. He supports legislation that would control carbon emissions, although jurisdiction over greenhouse gases lies largely with the Environment and Public Works Committee. He said previous bills have tried to accomplish too much apart from their original goal of limiting greenhouse gases.

He was one of 12 Democrats to oppose a U.S.-India nuclear agreement in October 2008, saying India's failure to sign the Nuclear Non-Proliferation Treaty alarmed him. Bingaman supported some of the Bush-era free-trade agreements that other Democrats assailed. Bingaman, who sits on the Health, Education, Labor and Pensions Committee, was one of 10 Democrats to support the 2005 Central America Free Trade Agreement and voted for a free-trade pact with Peru in 2007. He has met with Obama on the expected reauthorization of the "No Child Left Behind" education law in the 112th Congress.

As a member of the powerful Finance Committee — he's the only Democrat to sit on both Finance and HELP — Bingaman was a factor in the health care overhaul enacted in 2010 as one of the "Gang of Six" senators who unsuccessfully worked to find a bipartisan alternative. But he supported the final version and says he will work against the law's repeal, calling the overhaul "a significant step forward."

Bingaman has taken on a variety of unheralded assignments in the Senate. In the late 1990s he served on task forces studying Social Security and the settlement between tobacco companies and the states. At the request of Democratic leader Harry Reid of Nevada, Bingaman helped lead a 2005 effort to ensure that all the top-ranking Democrats on committees worked together smoothly. And he sits on the Democratic Steering and Outreach Committee, which helps make committee assignments.

Bingaman grew up in the mining town of Silver City. His father was a science professor at Western New Mexico University and his mother taught elementary school. As a boy, he had a paper route and was active in the Boy Scouts, earning the rank of Eagle Scout. His uncle John Bingaman was a confidant of Democratic Sen. Clinton P. Anderson, who represented the state for 24 years.

While at Stanford Law School, Bingaman worked for Democratic Sen. Robert F. Kennedy's 1968 presidential campaign. He also met and later married a fellow law student, Anne Kovacovich. Returning to New Mexico, he served as counsel to the 1969 state constitutional convention, joined a politically connected law firm and was elected attorney general in 1978. (Bingaman's wife served as assistant attorney general for antitrust law in the Clinton administration.)

When Bingaman ran for the Senate in 1982, he was little known outside the political and legal communities, but he also was politically unscarred. He won 54 percent of the vote to topple incumbent Republican Harrison "Jack" Schmitt, a former Apollo astronaut who was one of the last two men (and the only senator) to set foot on the moon.

Only one re-election race since has featured a serious challenger — Colin McMillan, a former Pentagon official who used much of his own money in 1994 to criticize Bingaman for his stance on fees for grazing on public lands and his support for President Bill Clinton's budget policy. Bingaman prevailed with 54 percent of the vote.

Key Votes

2010

Pass budget reconciliation bill to modify overhauls of health care and federal student loan programs	YES
Proceed to disapproval resolution on EPA authority to regulate greenhouse gases	NO
Overhaul financial services industry regulation	YES
Limit debate to proceed to a bill to broaden campaign finance disclosure and reporting rules	YES
Limit debate on an extension of Bush-era income tax cuts for two years	NO
Limit debate on a bill to provide a path to legal status for some children of illegal immigrants	YES
Allow for a repeal of "don't ask, don't tell"	YES
Consent to ratification of a strategic arms reduction treaty with Russia	YES

2009

Prevent release of remaining financial industry bailout funds	NO
Make it easier for victims to sue for wage discrimination remedies	YES
Expand the Children's Health Insurance Program	YES
Limit debate on the economic stimulus measure	YES
Repeal District of Columbia firearms prohibitions and gun registration laws	NO
Limit debate on expansion of federal hate crimes law	YES
Strike funding for F-22 Raptor fighter jets	NO

CQ Vote Studies

	PARTY UNITY		PRESIDENTIAL SUPPORT	
	SUPPORT	OPPOSE	SUPPORT	OPPOSE
2010	97%	3%	98%	2%
2009	95%	5%	96%	4%
2008	99%	1%	28%	72%
2007	95%	5%	40%	60%
2006	94%	6%	51%	49%
2005	85%	15%	43%	57%
2004	90%	10%	64%	36%
2003	91%	9%	50%	50%
2002	78%	22%	79%	21%
2001	91%	9%	68%	32%

Interest Groups

	AFL-CIO	ADA	CCUS	ACU
2010	100%	90%	18%	4%
2009	100%	100%	43%	4%
2008	100%	100%	50%	0%
2007	94%	90%	45%	4%
2006	93%	100%	36%	8%
2005	86%	95%	72%	13%
2004	92%	90%	71%	12%
2003	85%	95%	48%	10%
2002	92%	90%	60%	17%
2001	100%	90%	50%	29%

Sen. Tom Udall (D)

Capitol Office
224-6621
tomudall.senate.gov
110 Hart Bldg. 20510; fax 228-0900

Committees
Commerce, Science & Transportation
Environment & Public Works
 (Children's Health & Environmental Responsibility
 - Chairman)
Foreign Relations
Indian Affairs
Rules & Administration
Joint Printing

Residence
Santa Fe

Born
May 18, 1948; Tucson, Ariz.

Religion
Mormon

Family
Wife, Jill Z. Cooper; one child

Education
Prescott College, B.A. 1970 (government & political
science); Cambridge U., B.L.L. 1975; U. of New Mexico,
J.D. 1977

Career
Lawyer; congressional aide

Political Highlights
Assistant U.S. attorney, 1978-81; sought Democratic nomination for U.S. House, 1982; Democratic
nominee for U.S. House, 1988; N.M. attorney general,
1991-99; U.S. House, 1999-2009

ELECTION RESULTS

2008 GENERAL

Tom Udall (D)	505,128	61.3%
Steve Pearce (R)	318,522	38.7%

2008 PRIMARY

Tom Udall (D)	unopposed

Previous Winning Percentages
2006 House Election (75%); 2004 House Election
(69%); 2002 House Election (100%); 2000 House
Election (67%); 1998 House Election (53%)

Elected 2008; 1st term

Udall maintains the strong focus on energy and the environment that has given his family a reputation for stewardship of the West's natural resources. Affable and well-liked among his colleagues, he was a near-automatic vote for his party during 10 years in the House, and generally has remained so in the Senate.

Udall has a political bloodline longer than almost any other Democratic lawmaker whose last name isn't Kennedy. His father, Stewart L. Udall, who died in 2010, represented Arizona in the House and was secretary of Interior under presidents John F. Kennedy and Lyndon B. Johnson. His uncle, Morris K. Udall, succeeded Stewart in the House in 1961 and was a well-known leader on environmental protection for 30 years (he also made a presidential bid, in 1976). "From the time I was 6, I heard my father and uncle talk about public service," Tom Udall said.

Yet in his first two years as New Mexico's junior senator, Udall gained attention not for defending tradition but for trying to change the time-honored Senate filibuster tactic, which he contends has been abused by Republicans seeking to thwart President Obama's agenda. After he was elected in 2008, Udall re-read, at his father's suggestion, the autobiography of Clinton Anderson, a Democrat who held Udall's seat from 1949 to 1973 and tried for years to change the Senate's rules in order to abolish the filibuster.

A member of the Rules and Administration Committee, Udall played a leading role in a group of Democrats frustrated by the Senate's glacial pace. He backed proposed rules changes at the start of the 112th Congress (2011-12) that included reducing the 60-vote threshold needed to cut off debate. Udall and his allies had to settle for a ban on secret holds on nominations. "While I'm disappointed that ultimately this body lacked the necessary will to enact truly substantive reforms, we did achieve meaningful steps in the right direction," Udall wrote in a blog on his Senate website.

Udall was elected to the Senate at the same time as his cousin Mark, a Democrat from neighboring Colorado who also was completing five consecutive terms in the House. Tom Udall's voting record is a tad more liberal than his cousin's: He sided with his party 97 percent of the time in the 110th and 111th Congresses (2007-08; 2009-10) on votes that divided a majority of Republicans against a majority of Democrats, compared with Mark's 94 percent and 92 percent. But Tom said they share the same philosophy. "I don't know that there are that many differences between us," he said.

On the Environment and Public Works Committee, where he chairs the Subcommittee on Children's Health and Environmental Responsibility, Udall has sought an active role on climate change legislation. He was a regular attendee at meetings led by Sen. John Kerry, a Massachusetts Democrat, aimed at striking a deal on curbing carbon emissions that would win the support of lawmakers from states with energy-intensive industries. Udall also lent support to the idea that the Environmental Protection Agency could use regulations to achieve what the congressional Democrats could not.

Udall is a leading proponent of requiring states to obtain a certain portion of their electricity from renewable sources. In 2007, the House adopted — as part of an energy package — his language for a 15 percent national mandate for retail electricity production from renewable sources by 2020. But the proposal died in the Senate, as Southern lawmakers expressed concerns that their states lacked the wind capacity to meet the requirement. He resurrected the measure in slightly altered form soon after joining the Senate, where he has had the support of New Mexico colleague Jeff Bingaman, a Democrat who chairs the Energy and Natural Resources Committee.

Udall also shares Bingaman's desire to have New Mexico's two national laboratories, Los Alamos and Sandia, play a greater role in developing new energy technologies as they seek to diversify their missions beyond nuclear weapons research.

From his perch on the Commerce, Science and Transportation Committee, Udall wants to work on consumer protection issues, a specialty of his while serving as New Mexico's attorney general during the 1990s. He also wants to expand Internet and broadband access into rural areas and to help the U.S. railroad industry.

In the 112th Congress, Udall joined the Foreign Relations Committee. He has cited the war in Afghanistan, U.S.-China relations and "sustainable development" as areas of focus.

Udall's other priorities include universal health care coverage (he supported the 2010 overhaul). He wants to allow uninsured Americans age 55 and older to buy into Medicare at a fixed cost, a concept that met a quick demise in late 2009. And his request that Majority Leader Harry Reid, a Nevada Democrat, use a procedural maneuver to advance a "public option" provision for government-run insurance also fell on deaf ears. But he helped, from his seat on the Indian Affairs Committee, reauthorize the expired Indian Health Care Improvement Act, a key issue among New Mexico's large American Indian population.

When Udall strays from the party line, it's usually a concession to local sensibilities.

In early 2009, he was among 22 Senate Democrats — mostly from Western or conservative-leaning states — who backed an amendment by Nevada Republican John Ensign to codify a 2008 Supreme Court ruling striking down a District of Columbia gun ownership ban. The amendment was offered as part of legislation to grant District residents a House representative who would have full voting rights.

Udall was born in Arizona, the state where the Udall clan is centered. After earning degrees from both Prescott College and England's Cambridge University, he entered law school at the University of New Mexico, graduating in 1977. He stayed in the state as an appeals court law clerk, then worked as an assistant U.S. attorney and chief counsel to the state Department of Health and Environment before going into private practice.

Udall made two unsuccessful runs for the House: He lost the 1982 Democratic primary to Bill Richardson, who went on to serve as governor, and the 1988 election to Republican Steven H. Schiff. He became attorney general in 1991.

He made a third try for the House in 1998, winning an eight-candidate Democratic primary, then handily beating the incumbent, Republican Bill Redmond. He regularly won re-election with at least two-thirds of the vote and seemed a natural favorite to replace Pete V. Domenici when the veteran Republican senator announced in 2007 that he would not seek a seventh term.

But Udall initially turned down a chance to run, citing his seat on the Appropriations Committee as his best opportunity to serve his constituents. He eventually bowed to pressure from the national Democratic Party.

His opponent in the race was House colleague Steve Pearce, a conservative from the state's southeast corner. Pearce sought to portray Udall as too liberal for New Mexico, but it was an ill-timed message in a state that gave 57 percent of the vote to Obama after President George W. Bush had carried it four years earlier. Udall won easily, with 61 percent of the vote. Pearce returned to the House in 2010.

Key Votes

2010

Pass budget reconciliation bill to modify overhauls of health care and federal student loan programs	YES
Proceed to disapproval resolution on EPA authority to regulate greenhouse gases	NO
Overhaul financial services industry regulation	YES
Limit debate to proceed to a bill to broaden campaign finance disclosure and reporting rules	YES
Limit debate on an extension of Bush-era income tax cuts for two years	YES
Limit debate on a bill to provide a path to legal status for some children of illegal immigrants	YES
Allow for a repeal of "don't ask, don't tell"	YES
Consent to ratification of a strategic arms reduction treaty with Russia	YES

2009

Prevent release of remaining financial industry bailout funds	NO
Make it easier for victims to sue for wage discrimination remedies	YES
Expand the Children's Health Insurance Program	YES
Limit debate on the economic stimulus measure	YES
Repeal District of Columbia firearms prohibitions and gun registration laws	YES
Limit debate on expansion of federal hate crimes law	YES
Strike funding for F-22 Raptor fighter jets	NO

CQ Vote Studies

	PARTY UNITY		PRESIDENTIAL SUPPORT	
	SUPPORT	OPPOSE	SUPPORT	OPPOSE
2010	98%	2%	97%	3%
2009	96%	4%	96%	4%
2008	96%	4%	14%	86%
2007	98%	2%	3%	97%
2006	96%	4%	10%	90%
2005	97%	3%	11%	89%
2004	95%	5%	21%	79%
2003	97%	3%	18%	82%
2002	98%	2%	20%	80%
2001	96%	4%	23%	77%

Interest Groups

	AFL-CIO	ADA	CCUS	ACU
2010	100%	95%	18%	0%
2009	100%	100%	43%	8%
2008	100%	90%	47%	12%
2007	96%	100%	47%	0%
2006	100%	95%	29%	4%
2005	100%	95%	41%	0%
2004	93%	100%	29%	8%
2003	100%	100%	23%	12%
2002	89%	100%	35%	0%
2001	100%	100%	30%	4%

Rep. Martin Heinrich (D)

Capitol Office
225-6316
heinrich.house.gov
336 Longworth Bldg. 20515-3101; fax 225-4975

Committees
Armed Services
Natural Resources

Residence
Albuquerque

Born
Oct. 17, 1971; Fallon, Nev.

Religion
Lutheran

Family
Wife, Julie Heinrich; two children

Education
U. of Missouri, B.S. 1995 (mechanical engineering); U. of New Mexico, attended 2001-02

Career
State natural resources director; community advocacy consultant; outdoor education nonprofit director; mechanical engineering draftsman

Political Highlights
Albuquerque City Council, 2003-07 (president, 2005-06)

ELECTION RESULTS

2010 GENERAL

Martin Heinrich (D)	112,010	51.8%
Jon Barela (R)	104,215	48.2%

2010 PRIMARY

Martin Heinrich (D)	unopposed

2008 GENERAL

Martin Heinrich (D)	166,271	55.6%
Darren White (R)	132,485	44.3%

Elected 2008; 2nd term

Heinrich's experience as his state's natural resources trustee and executive director of a foundation dedicated to educating young people about wilderness has endeared him to environmental activists. But in representing one of the nation's most competitive swing districts and as an announced Senate candidate in 2012, he also seeks to appeal to moderate and independent voters concerned about federal spending.

His Albuquerque-based district boasts a strong technology industry in a state that has invested heavily in research on renewable and alternative energy. A member of the Natural Resources Committee, Heinrich (HINE-rick) proposes an "Apollo Project" for energy independence, reminiscent of President John F. Kennedy's 1960s space exploration initiative. Heinrich's plan rejects an incremental approach in favor of what he calls an "everything" agenda to utilize the collective energy of government, industry, labor, nonprofits and academics. He said a House-passed bill that would create a cap-and-trade system aimed at reducing carbon emissions was a step in that direction. The Senate never acted on the measure.

He introduced a bill in 2009 aimed at providing a dedicated funding stream for the Bureau of Land Management to process a backlog in alternative-energy project applications and to facilitate future projects. He also cosponsored legislation to require a percentage of electricity sold to be generated from renewable sources — a top priority for his state's Democratic senators, Jeff Bingaman and Tom Udall. He followed that up in May 2010 by introducing legislation that would direct the secretary of Defense to start a pilot program on collaborative energy security between military installations and national laboratories.

In July 2009, Heinrich introduced a bill, along with companion legislation from his state's senators, that would allow the federal government to use revenue from certain land sales to conserve other western lands.

But he takes some stands that are anathema to environmental groups, such as supporting an expansion of nuclear power. He prefers to call himself a "conservationist" rather than an environmentalist. "I'll be the first to fault some environmental organizations for not being good compromisers, for not getting what they want done by reaching out to people who are different," he told the Albuquerque Journal in October 2008.

On the Armed Services Committee, Heinrich looks to protect his district's Kirtland Air Force Base and Sandia National Laboratories, which conduct military- and energy-related research for the government. In his first term he helped secure $5.8 million for Kirtland in the House-passed Military Construction-VA spending bill and successfully added an amendment to the Energy-Water appropriations bill to increase the percentage of money spent on technology research and development at the laboratories. In February 2010, he added an amendment to a House-passed bill that would involve national laboratories like the one in his district in cybersecurity research and development.

Heinrich strongly backed President Obama's legislative efforts in early 2009 aimed at reviving the economy and said he was confident funds would trickle down to his chronically poor and federally dependent state.

In the months that followed, Heinrich at times broke ranks with his party in trying to show his fiscally moderate side. He supported unsuccessful Republican amendments to cut spending by 5 percent in the fiscal 2010 Transportation-HUD spending bill and by $803 million in the Labor-HHS-

Education spending bill. Heinrich opposed House-passed legislation to overhaul food safety laws in July 2010, contending it would hurt his state's small farmers and food processors. And he opposed virtually all of the GOP proposals to include additional cuts to fiscal 2011 spending in a catchall spending bill the House passed in the first weeks of the 112th Congress (2011-12).

Still, he was in the fold for the major priorities in the 111th Congress (2009-10), including the health care overhaul enacted in March 2010. "Unlike a lot of folks this year, I never shrank from the fact that I was proud to have voted for health care reform," Heinrich said at a political rally in November 2010.

Heinrich grew up on a ranch in central Missouri, along with two older sisters. His father, an FDR-era Democrat, had an early influence on his political philosophy. In high school, he participated in 4-H, math competitions, basketball and soccer. He earned a degree in mechanical engineering from the University of Missouri, where he met his wife, Julie.

Heinrich's political career began after he moved to New Mexico. He took a job as a mechanical engineering draftsman, but left after less than a year because he said he "wanted to spend more time in the outdoors." He eventually worked as executive director of the nonprofit Cottonwood Gulch Foundation and with environmental groups such as the Sierra Club and the New Mexico Wilderness Alliance.

He was elected in 2003 to Albuquerque's City Council, where he served four years. He helped establish a federal wilderness area northwest of the city and pushed for the city to acquire open-space land while supporting new green-building codes, curbside recycling and incentives for hybrid vehicles.

When Republican Heather A. Wilson decided to give up the 1st District to run for the Senate, Heinrich took a leave of absence in 2007 from his job as a state trustee overseeing the restoration of areas contaminated by hazardous materials and easily dispatched former New Mexico Secretary of State Rebecca D. Vigil-Giron in the 2008 Democratic primary. The Democratic tide and Barack Obama's coattails helped Heinrich win in November with almost 56 percent of the vote over Republican Darren White, the Bernalillo County sheriff and former secretary of New Mexico's Department of Public Safety.

The tide reversed in 2010, helping Republican businessman Jon Barela tie Heinrich to unpopular Democratic policies and Speaker Nancy Pelosi of California. But Heinrich struck back, attacking his opponent for favoring lax Wall Street regulation and President George W. Bush's policies, and he rode strong fundraising to victory with nearly 52 percent of the vote.

In April 2011, Heinrich announced he would seek to succeed Bingaman, who had earlier announced he would retire in 2012.

Key Votes

2010

Overhaul the nation's health insurance system	YES
Allow for repeal of "don't ask, don't tell"	YES
Overhaul financial services industry regulation	YES
Limit use of new Afghanistan War funds to troop withdrawal activities	NO
Change oversight of offshore drilling and lift oil spill liability cap	YES
Provide a path to legal status for some children of illegal immigrants	YES
Extend Bush-era income tax cuts for two years	NO

2009

Expand the Children's Health Insurance Program	YES
Provide $787 billion in tax cuts and spending increases to stimulate the economy	YES
Allow bankruptcy judges to modify certain primary-residence mortgages	YES
Create a cap-and-trade system to limit greenhouse gas emissions	YES
Provide $2 billion for the "cash for clunkers" program	YES
Establish the government as the sole provider of student loans	YES
Restrict federally funded insurance coverage for abortions in health care overhaul	NO

CQ Vote Studies

	PARTY UNITY		PRESIDENTIAL SUPPORT	
	SUPPORT	OPPOSE	SUPPORT	OPPOSE
2010	97%	3%	95%	5%
2009	94%	6%	87%	13%

Interest Groups

	AFL-CIO	ADA	CCUS	ACU
2010	100%	100%	13%	0%
2009	100%	100%	40%	4%

New Mexico 1

Central — Albuquerque

Built around Albuquerque, the 1st is the only urban district in a sparsely populated desert state. Since the Manhattan Project set the region on a technology-driven course in the 1940s, still-expanding Albuquerque has grown from 35,000 people before WWII to more than 545,000.

Sandia National Laboratories is the basis for steady defense and medical technology industries. Its success has contributed to a surge in computer, laser and research firms here, including Emcore and nearby Intel (located in the 3rd). Sandia coordinates with two other major employers in the district, the University of New Mexico and the Air Force Research Laboratory at Kirtland Air Force Base, to conduct energy and defense research. The local technology sector attracts Ph.D.s to Albuquerque, and 14 percent of district residents hold an advanced degree.

The 1st has the state's highest proportion of residents who have earned at least a bachelor's degree (30 percent) and smallest proportion of residents who have not earned a high school diploma (15 percent).

Statewide commitments to renewable- and alternative-energy research,

and state laws that require utilities to invest in alternative energy, have benefited local companies such as Sacred Power, a Native American-owned solar power company.

Democrats hold most local offices in the highly competitive 1st. Republicans controlled the U.S. House seat here from the district's creation in 1968 until Democratic Rep. Martin Heinrich won in 2008. Much of the GOP vote comes from the mainly white, upper-middle-class Northeast Heights section of Albuquerque, but the district's large government workforce and predominately Hispanic South Valley provide Democrats with an overall edge.

Major Industry
Higher education, scientific research, defense, government

Military Bases
Kirtland Air Force Base, 3,426 military, 2,385 civilian (2009)

Cities
Albuquerque (pt.), 522,261; South Valley (unincorporated), 40,976

Notable
The National Museum of Nuclear Science & History in Albuquerque features an aircraft collection and a replica fallout shelter.

Rep. Steve Pearce (R)

Capitol Office
225-2365
pearce.house.gov
2432 Longworth Bldg. 20515-3102

Committees
Financial Services

Residence
Hobbs

Born
Aug. 24, 1947; Lamesa, Texas

Religion
Baptist

Family
Wife, Cynthia Pearce; one child

Education
New Mexico State U., B.B.A. 1970 (economics);
Eastern New Mexico U., M.B.A. 1991

Military
Air Force, 1970-76

Career
Oil well services company owner; pilot

Political Highlights
N.M. House, 1997-2000; sought Republican nomina-
tion for U.S. Senate, 2000; Republican nominee for
U.S. Senate, 2008; U.S. House, 2003-09

ELECTION RESULTS

2010 GENERAL
Steve Pearce (R)	94,053	55.4%
Harry Teague (D)	75,708	44.6%

2010 PRIMARY
Steve Pearce (R)	33,021	84.8%
Cliff R. Pirtle (R)	5,913	15.2%

Previous Winning Percentages
2006 (59%); 2004 (60%); 2002 (56%)

Elected 2002; 4th term
Did not serve 2009-11

The self-described "very conservative" Pearce won his old job back in 2010. His resumption of congressional duties has included a return to the Financial Services Committee, where he served prior to his unwelcome two-year hiatus from Capitol Hill.

His slot on the panel in the 112th Congress (2011-12) gives him a platform for several of his priority issues, which include reducing taxes on invest-ments and capital gains. Pearce says such cuts would give the economy a boost. Another way to foster growth is to bring stability to the dollar, he says.

Along with other conservatives, he took a hard line on spending early in the 112th Congress. His backing of the catchall appropriations bill for fiscal 2011 included voting for almost all of the GOP amendments that added to the bills' $61 billion in cuts. Later, he voted against a short-term measure to keep the government in operation for three weeks, calling it "unacceptable."

"As a former small-business owner, I know that you can't run any organi-zation week-to-week," Pearce said.

Pearce, who left the Hill following an unsuccessful run for the Senate in 2008, is likely to reprise his role as a point person on the immigration debate. A former co-chairman of the Border Security Caucus, he has struck a tough but business-friendly tone on immigration, arguing for a guest worker pro-gram that would accompany stricter control of the border. He has called for adding border guards as well as putting money into advanced surveillance technologies. He voted in 2006 in favor of building a fence along the U.S.-Mexico border, which runs about half the length of his sprawling district.

In his previous congressional stint he sat on the Natural Resources Com-mittee and once chaired its Subcommittee on National Parks. Pearce had the panel examine whether too much emphasis was placed on preserving parks at the expense of recreation. "Too often," he said in December 2005, "parks have been managed as if a snapshot had been taken and nothing should change."

Pearce also introduced legislation aimed at resolving disputes over road rights of way, often a heated topic in rural areas with a large federal pres-ence. His bill would have enabled states and counties to claim ownership of roads across federal land that existed before 1986 and give them authority to act without seeking approval of federal agencies.

After Democrats won control of the House in the 2006 elections, the former oil field services company owner left the top spot on the parks panel and became ranking Republican on the Energy and Mineral Resources Subcommittee. Pearce says public lands should be open to more oil and gas exploration along with other commercial uses.

Pearce, an Air Force combat pilot in Vietnam, joined with others in the New Mexico delegation in fighting the Air Force's plans to retire F-117 Stealth fighters stationed at Holloman Air Force Base. To protect Holloman and other New Mexico bases, he introduced a bill in 2004 to force the Bureau of Land Management to turn over to the Pentagon millions of acres of land it owns on military bases. He said the bureau's ownership on military installations "puts us at a distinct disadvantage" when the Pentagon looks to close bases. That measure passed the House but did not make it through the Senate. He reintroduced it in 2005, and President George W. Bush signed it into law in January 2007.

In November 2006, Pearce challenged Texas Rep. Kay Granger for the vice chairmanship of the Republican Conference, the fourth-ranking position in the leadership. He said in a letter to colleagues that the elections had demonstrated that the public voted against Republicans rather than for Democrats and that his party "talked too much about things in the wrong way." Granger defeated him easily, 124-63.

Pearce shares with many in his party his conservative views on social issues. He opposes more gun control and expanded abortion rights, and he wants to amend the Constitution to prohibit same-sex marriage. He says he rises at 4:30 a.m. daily to read the Bible.

After two terms in the New Mexico House, Pearce jumped into the 2002 U.S. House race after incumbent Republican Joe Skeen's failing health led to his retirement announcement. Although conservative-leaning, the district has a large Hispanic population that helps yield a Democratic voter registration edge. And the socially conservative views of the Democratic nominee, state Sen. John Arthur Smith, gave the party hope that he might have crossover appeal. But Pearce had a money advantage and help from the Bush administration, and he won by 12 percentage points.

In 2004, Pearce squared off against an even better-known Democrat — Gary King, a businessman, lawyer and state legislator for 12 years who had deep New Mexico political roots. His father, Bruce King, was the longest-serving governor in state history. The year before the election, King moved into a rented house in Carlsbad and began putting what he said was more than 100,000 miles on his car traveling around the 69,493-square-mile district, which includes part of 18 New Mexico counties.

Pearce sought to portray King as a carpetbagger and a tax-and-spend liberal. King was unable to gain much traction in a swing state that Bush sought to add to the presidential victory column after barely losing it in 2000. With Bush and Vice President Dick Cheney making numerous campaign stops in New Mexico, Pearce won with 60 percent.

In 2006, he drew a far less politically seasoned opponent in Democrat Albert D. Kissling, a minister and activist for affordable housing. He again won easily, with 59 percent of the vote.

In 2008, he gave up the House seat to make an unsuccessful bid for the Senate. He defeated fellow Rep. Heather A. Wilson in the GOP primary, but was crushed in November by Democrat Tom Udall, 61 percent to 39 percent.

In 2010, with the national mood running more favorable to Republicans, Pearce attacked the Democrat who replaced him in the House, Harry Teague, for his support of President Obama's "big government" agenda. Outside groups and both party campaign committees targeted the district.

Pearce won a return ticket to Washington with 55 percent of the vote.

CQ Vote Studies				
	PARTY UNITY		PRESIDENTIAL SUPPORT	
	SUPPORT	OPPOSE	SUPPORT	OPPOSE
2008	94%	6%	70%	30%
2007	96%	4%	81%	19%
2006	98%	2%	97%	3%
2005	96%	4%	91%	9%
2004	94%	6%	98%	2%

Interest Groups				
	AFL-CIO	ADA	CCUS	ACU
2008	13%	20%	89%	92%
2007	13%	5%	80%	96%
2006	14%	5%	100%	92%
2005	27%	0%	96%	96%
2004	13%	0%	95%	96%

New Mexico 2
South — Las Cruces, Roswell, Little Texas

Before hosting the first atomic bomb explosion in 1945, the mostly rural 2nd, covering the southern half of the state, looked like the old American West. Since then, the area has attracted nuclear research and waste facilities to the remote Chihuahua Desert and its deep salt beds.

Towns in the 2nd have built a stable economy on traditional Western industries: copper and lead mining in the Mexican Highlands along the Arizona border; and oil and gas, as well as cattle and sheep ranching, in the southeastern corner of the state. Severe water shortages prevent large-scale industrial development and larger corporate farming, but the Tularosa Basin east of Las Cruces produces wine grapes and pistachios. New Mexico's strong military presence is evident in the 2nd, home of Holloman Air Force Base and White Sands Missile Range.

New Mexico State University, based in Las Cruces and known for agricultural research, uses a 64,000-acre section of its ranch as a proving ground for new border security technologies developed by government contractors.

The district has experienced only moderate growth since 2000, but the Hispanic community has now become a majority in the district, and American Indians account for nearly 5 percent of residents. The median household income here is the lowest in the state at just more than $37,000. Democrats hold the vast majority of local offices, although some voters still support GOP candidates at the federal level. Republican John McCain won 50 percent of the district's presidential vote in 2008, and Rep. Steve Pearce reclaimed a U.S. House seat in 2010, two years after an unsuccessful Senate run.

Major Industry
Agriculture, mining, oil and gas, defense

Military Bases
Holloman Air Force Base, 3,118 military, 870 civilian (2009); White Sands Missile Range, 850 military, 2,366 civilian (2011)

Cities
Las Cruces, 97,618; Roswell, 48,366; Hobbs, 34,122; Alamogordo, 30,403

Notable
Roswell hosts an annual UFO festival near the site where a UFO allegedly crashed in 1947; White Sands National Monument is the world's largest gypsum dune field.

Rep. Ben Ray Luján (D)

Capitol Office
225-6190
lujan.house.gov
330 Cannon Bldg. 20515-3103; fax 226-1331

Committees
Natural Resources
Science, Space & Technology

Residence
Nambe

Born
June 7, 1972; Santa Fe, N.M.

Religion
Roman Catholic

Family
Single

Education
U. of New Mexico, attended 1990-95; New Mexico
Highlands U., B.B.A. 2007 (business administration)

Career
Human resources manager; state government aide;
casino services supervisor; legislative publication
marketing director

Political Highlights
N.M. Public Regulation Commission, 2005-09 (chairman, 2005-07)

ELECTION RESULTS

2010 GENERAL

Ben Ray Luján (D)	120,048	57.0%
Tom Mullins (R)	90,617	43.0%

2010 PRIMARY

Ben Ray Luján (D)	unopposed

2008 GENERAL

Ben Ray Luján (D)	161,292	56.7%
Daniel K. East (R)	86,618	30.5%
Carol Miller (I)	36,348	12.8%

Elected 2008; 2nd term

An eighth-generation New Mexican, Luján's personal and political roots run deep, even if he is fairly new to both politics and Congress. The son of a powerful figure in state government, he is credited with having more savvy than many veteran lawmakers.

Luján's father, Ben Luján, is the longtime speaker of the New Mexico House of Representatives. In his campaign for the 3rd District seat, Ben Ray Luján often battled accusations that he was under-qualified, overly ambitious and riding his father's coattails. Since then, one of the state's newspapers has observed that the younger Luján "excels at old-fashioned retail politics" and is "adept at responding to questions with answers that sound as polished as those in his press releases."

Stepping into the breach left by predecessors, Luján — a member of the Science, Space and Technology Committee — works to direct more funding to Los Alamos National Laboratory in order to broaden its portfolio beyond nuclear weapons work into the renewable energy field.

Los Alamos can no longer look to Republican Sen. Pete V. Domenici — who until his retirement was a fierce protector as a member of the Appropriations Committee. Luján also points to "New Mexico's proud history of 'Science and Tech'" being exemplified by 10-term Republican House member and then Interior Secretary Manuel Luján Jr. (no relation).

Ben Ray Luján's legislative priorities include spurring U.S. competitiveness in innovation and technology. An $85.6 billion measure authorizing federal science research and education programs, which passed the House in May 2010, included several Luján-authored provisions, including one that would make funds available to help small businesses work in conjunction with national laboratories on innovative science and technology projects. Another would increase funding for an Energy Department program that focuses on collaborative efforts by national laboratories, universities, investors and private firms to develop new energy technologies.

In 2009, Luján joined a group of lawmakers in pushing the Energy and Commerce Committee to add provisions to an energy and climate bill to include almost $1 billion in funding for job training and education programs. He also worked to add language to the bill, which passed the House, directing that consideration be given to Hispanic and American Indian colleges in creating "energy innovation hubs" consisting of academic and private research groups. His legislative work in that area earned him recognition in Hispanic Business Magazine's 100 Most Influential Hispanics list.

Another of Luján's energy priorities is "net metering," in which electric utilities credit customers for power they generate at their homes and offices. More than 40 states have such policies in place, and Luján introduced a bill in 2009 with California Democrat Dennis Cardoza to bolster the practice.

In May 2010 Luján was assigned to the Natural Resources Committee, giving him a platform from which to help guide policy on the use of public lands, always a key issue in the West. He also sees it as a way to give voice on those issues to New Mexico's large Native American population, whose members he says "too often struggle to be heard." To that end, he earned a spot on the Indian and Alaska Native Affairs Subcommittee.

The 3rd District includes large swaths of rural areas, many of them public land. In July 2009, the House passed Luján's bill to designate six existing National Environmental Research Parks — one at Los Alamos — as protected outdoor research reserves. The parks are essentially outdoor labs that provide large tracts of federal land on which to perform ecological studies. In May 2010, Luján introduced a bill to preserve more than 200,000 acres of public land in northern New Mexico for grazing and the harvesting of piñon nuts, wild herbs and firewood.

Luján proved to be among the most reliable Democratic votes in his first term, siding with his party on 99 percent of votes that pitted a majority of Democrats against a majority of Republicans.

Luján grew up in the small farming community of Nambe, just north of Santa Fe. Throughout both his campaign and his work on Capitol Hill he has emphasized the importance of family.

With memories of wandering the halls of the New Mexico legislature and attending political events from an early age, he remembers watching his father deal with constituents.

"I was able to learn from Dad the importance of talking to people and treating everyone with respect," he said. His mother, Carmen, often accompanied him and has been involved in politics herself, most recently as a member of New Mexico's Human Rights Commission.

He speaks warmly of splitting firewood at his father's house, property that has been in the family for three generations. Luján's grandfather raised sheep for a living, a practice the family continues.

After high school, Luján took some classes at the University of New Mexico, although he did not receive a college degree until 2007, when he completed his course work at New Mexico Highlands University. In between he worked a series of jobs, including stints as a dealer at a casino and in human resources at a horse racetrack.

He entered government in 2002 as deputy state treasurer. Two years later, he was elected to the state's Public Regulation Commission, which oversees utilities, telecommunications, motor carriers and insurance companies, and he quickly became its chairman.

In the 2008 House race to succeed successful Democratic Senate candidate Tom Udall, Luján campaigned energetically while taking advantage of his family connections — the Albuquerque Journal reported in April 2008 that more than two dozen lobbyists and other campaign contributors who gave to the elder Luján also donated to his son — to beat five other primary candidates, with more than 41 percent of the vote.

That November, Luján beat Republican Daniel K. East and independent Carol Miller, taking 57 percent in the heavily Democratic district. He matched that figure in 2010.

Key Votes

2010

Overhaul the nation's health insurance system	YES
Allow for repeal of "don't ask, don't tell"	YES
Overhaul financial services industry regulation	YES
Limit use of new Afghanistan War funds to troop withdrawal activities	NO
Change oversight of offshore drilling and lift oil spill liability cap	YES
Provide a path to legal status for some children of illegal immigrants	YES
Extend Bush-era income tax cuts for two years	NO

2009

Expand the Children's Health Insurance Program	YES
Provide $787 billion in tax cuts and spending increases to stimulate the economy	YES
Allow bankruptcy judges to modify certain primary-residence mortgages	YES
Create a cap-and-trade system to limit greenhouse gas emissions	YES
Provide $2 billion for the "cash for clunkers" program	YES
Establish the government as the sole provider of student loans	YES
Restrict federally funded insurance coverage for abortions in health care overhaul	NO

CQ Vote Studies

	PARTY UNITY		PRESIDENTIAL SUPPORT	
	SUPPORT	OPPOSE	SUPPORT	OPPOSE
2010	99%	1%	95%	5%
2009	99%	1%	93%	7%

Interest Groups

	AFL-CIO	ADA	CCUS	ACU
2010	100%	100%	13%	0%
2009	100%	100%	40%	0%

North — Santa Fe, Rio Rancho, Farmington

Since Georgia O'Keeffe first painted northern New Mexico in 1929, the 3rd's breathtaking scenery and unique Spanish and American Indian heritage have attracted thousands of artists and tourists. Galleries and ski resorts still lure visitors from around the world, and nearly 90,000 more residents live here than in 2000. That growth has increased the proportion of Hispanic residents (39 percent) while the white (40 percent) and American Indian (17 percent) percentages have dropped in the last decade. Whites still account for a plurality of residents, and the district has the third-highest percentage of American Indian residents in the nation.

The district is marked by extremes. Luxury resorts and the bountiful art trade exist beside extraordinary poverty. Gallup, in McKinley County, boasts millionaires, while the county itself remains one of the nation's poorest. American Indian populations in the northwest struggle with modest farming and ranching ventures, while the same area provides lofty incomes for oil and gas producers.

Cannon Air Force Base, near Clovis, escaped closure after the 2005 BRAC round but lost its F-16 squadrons to other bases and required a complete overhaul of base activities. Cannon's new mission includes special operations units, and the base will expand activities at the nearby Melrose bombing range.

Santa Fe's wealthy, liberal base gives Democrats a nearly 2-to-1 edge in voter registration in the district, but conservative pockets exist in Los Alamos, where the atomic bomb was developed, and among energy producers in San Juan County in the state's northwest corner.

Major Industry
State government, ranching, defense

Military Bases
Cannon Air Force Base, 3,585 military, 501 civilian (2010)

Cities
Rio Rancho (pt.), 82,558; Santa Fe, 67,947; Farmington, 45,877; Clovis, 37,775; Albuquerque (pt.), 23,591; Gallup, 21,678

Notable
Santa Fe, the nation's second-oldest city, was founded in 1607; The Aztec Ruins National Monument in Aztec features structures and artifacts from the 1100s and 1200s.

NEW YORK

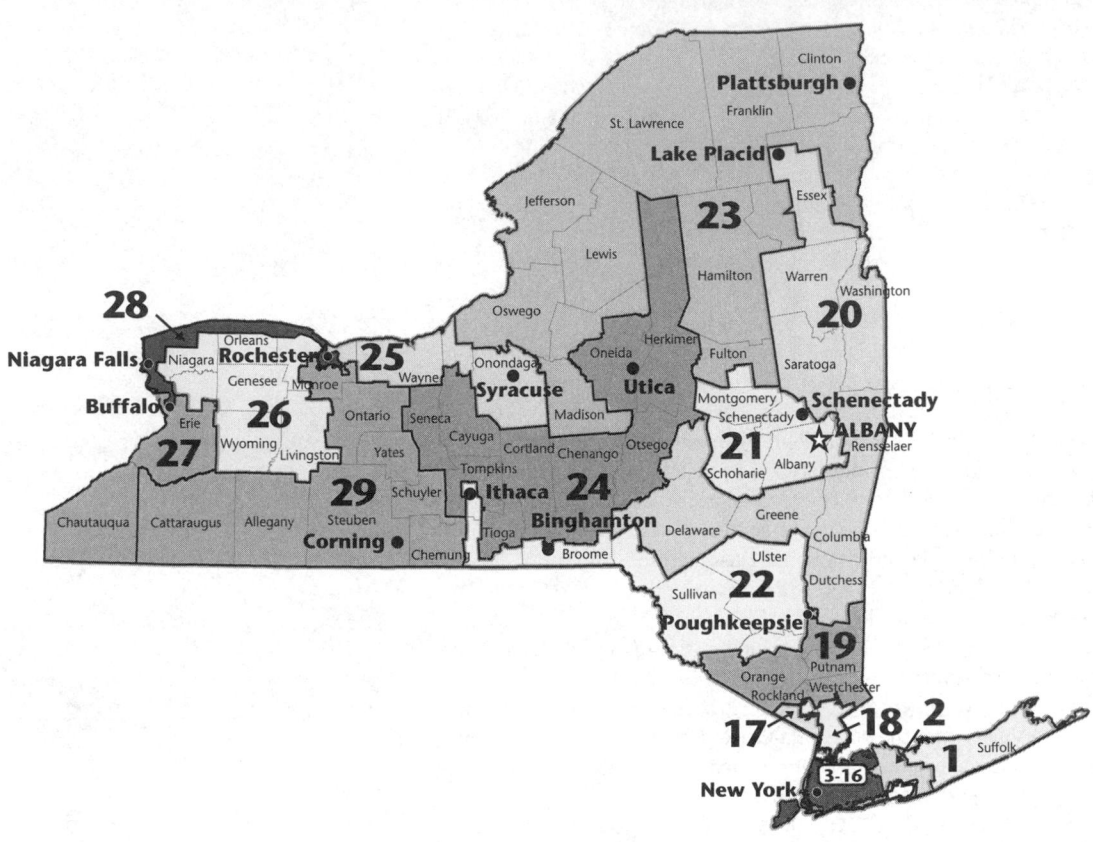

2010 Census Statistics by District

District	2008 Vote for President Obama	McCain	White	Black	Asian	Hispanic	Median Income	White Collar	Blue Collar	Service Industry	Over 64	Under 18	College Education	Rural	Sq. Miles
1	51%	48%	78%	5%	3%	13%	$82,297	66%	18%	16%	13%	24%	32%	6%	646
2	56	43	63	10	5	21	89,883	66	18	15	13	26	34	0	239
3	47	52	81	3	5	10	91,382	70	15	14	15	23	36	0	183
4	58	41	52	19	7	20	85,175	66	17	17	14	25	36	0	90
5	63	36	36	4	33	26	63,732	63	18	20	15	21	37	0	66
6	89	11	10	50	13	19	56,828	55	20	25	12	25	22	0	40
7	79	20	21	16	16	44	46,435	54	21	25	13	23	23	0	26
8	74	25	67	5	15	12	65,926	79	9	12	13	18	55	0	15
9	55	44	57	4	19	17	57,024	66	17	17	16	22	36	0	37
10	91	9	18	58	4	17	39,599	59	16	25	10	28	24	0	18
11	90	9	26	53	5	13	46,082	61	14	25	10	24	32	0	12
12	86	13	27	8	18	45	40,818	53	22	25	10	23	26	0	19
13	49	51	62	7	13	16	63,611	64	18	18	14	23	28	0	65
14	78	21	66	5	13	14	79,385	84	6	10	13	14	65	0	13
15	93	6	21	26	4	46	37,279	64	12	24	12	21	35	0	10

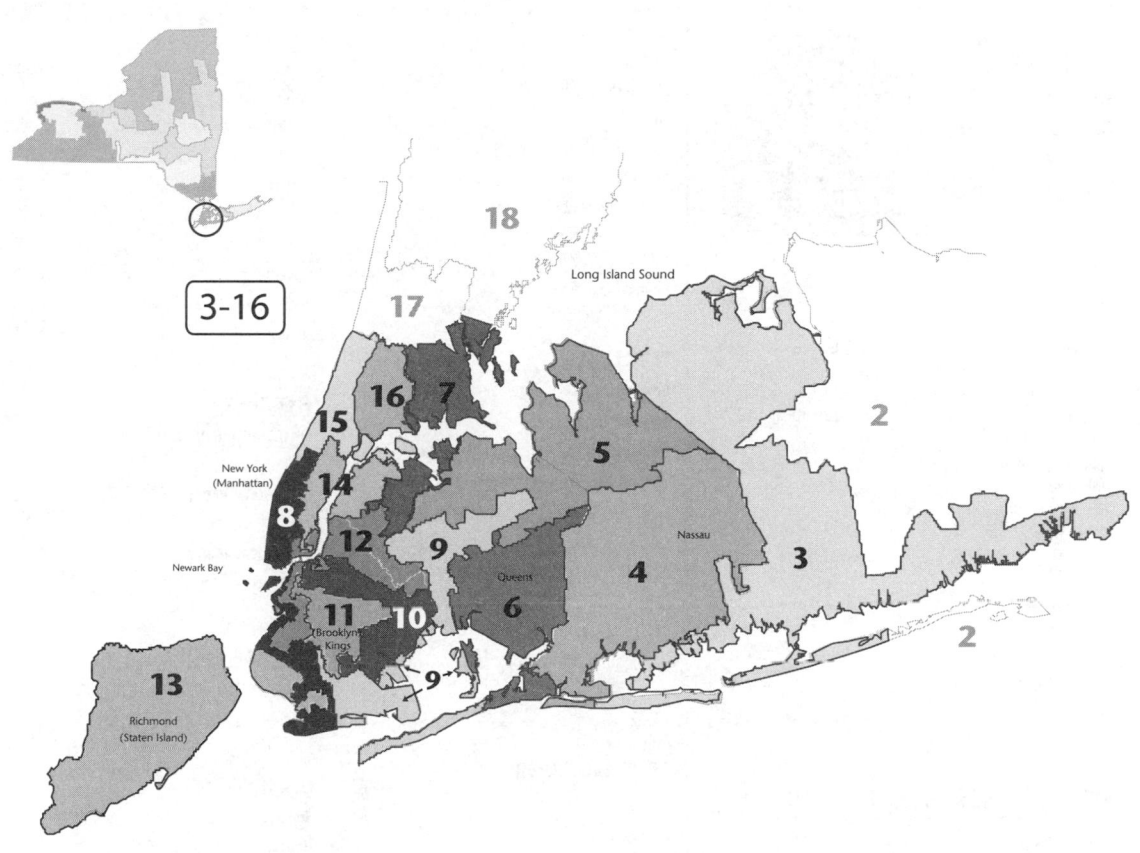

2010 CENSUS STATISTICS BY DISTRICT

District	2008 VOTE FOR PRESIDENT Obama	McCain	White	Black	Asian	Hispanic	Median Income	White Collar	Blue Collar	Service Industry	Over 64	Under 18	College Education	Rural	Sq. Miles
16	95%	5%	2%	28%	2%	67%	$23,073	40%	23%	37%	7%	32%	10%	0%	12
17	72	28	37	30	5	26	54,587	63	16	22	13	26	31	0	127
18	62	38	60	9	6	23	86,933	71	13	16	14	25	48	1	222
19	51	48	76	6	3	13	82,534	67	17	16	12	26	36	21	1,401
20	51	48	92	2	1	3	56,861	61	22	17	15	22	28	55	7,018
21	58	40	79	9	3	5	52,004	66	18	17	14	22	30	16	1,935
22	59	39	74	9	3	12	50,012	61	20	19	13	22	27	32	3,246
23	52	47	92	2	1	3	44,730	54	26	20	13	22	19	65	13,235
24	50	48	90	4	2	3	45,688	58	23	19	15	22	22	49	6,164
25	56	43	83	8	3	4	52,470	65	19	15	14	24	31	21	1,620
26	46	52	89	4	2	3	55,028	63	22	16	15	22	29	29	2,731
27	54	44	85	5	1	6	44,596	59	23	18	16	22	23	18	1,830
28	68	30	58	29	2	8	37,838	60	19	20	14	23	24	7	534
29	48	50	90	3	2	2	50,190	62	22	16	15	23	29	42	5,660
STATE	63	36	58	14	7	18	55,233	63	18	19	13	23	32	13	47,214
U.S.	53	46	64	12	5	16	51,425	60	23	17	13	25	28	21	3,537,438

Gov. Andrew M. Cuomo (D)

First elected: 2010
Length of term: 4 years
Term expires: 1/15
Salary: $179,000
Phone: (518) 474-7516
Residence: Queens
Born: Dec. 6, 1957; Queens, N.Y.
Religion: Roman Catholic
Family: Divorced; three children
Education: Fordham U., B.A. 1979; Albany Law School, J.D. 1982
Career: Real estate investor; U.S. Housing and Urban Development Department official; city homeless commission director; alternative housing nonprofit founder; lawyer; city prosecutor; gubernatorial and campaign aide
Political highlights: U.S. Department of Housing and Urban Development secretary, 1997-2001; Liberal Party candidate for governor, 2002; N.Y. attorney general, 2007-10

ELECTION RESULTS

2010 GENERAL

Andrew M. Cuomo (D)	2,911,721	62.6%
Carl Paladino (R)	1,548,184	33.3%
Howie Hawkins (GREEN)	59,929	1.3%
Others	134,518	2.8%

Lt. Gov. Robert Duffy (D)

First elected: 2010
Length of term: 4 years
Term expires: 1/15
Salary: $151,500
Phone: (518) 474-8390

LEGISLATURE

Legislature: Year-round; main session January-June
Senate: 62 members, 2-year terms
2011 ratios: 32 R, 30 D; 51 men, 11 women
Salary: $79,500
Phone: (518) 455-3216
Assembly: 150 members, 2-year terms
2011 ratios: 93 D, 52 R, 1 I, 4 vacancies; 112 men, 34 women
Salary: $79,500
Phone: (518) 455-4218

TERM LIMITS

Governor: No
Senate: No
House: No

URBAN STATISTICS

CITY	POPULATION
New York City	8,175,133
Buffalo	261,310
Rochester	210,565
Yonkers	195,976
Syracuse	145,170

REGISTERED VOTERS

Democrat	62%
Republican	31%
Unaffiliated/others	7%

POPULATION

2010 population	19,378,102
2000 population	18,976,457
1990 population	17,990,455
Percent change (2000-2010)	+2.1%
Rank among states (2010)	3
Median age	37.7
Born in state	64.5%
Foreign born	21.4%
Violent crime rate	385/100,000
Poverty level	14.2%
Federal workers	168,197
Military	29,553

ELECTIONS

STATE ELECTION OFFICIAL
(518) 474-6220
DEMOCRATIC PARTY
(212) 725-8825
REPUBLICAN PARTY
(518) 462-2601

MISCELLANEOUS

Web: www.ny.gov
Capital: Albany

U.S. CONGRESS

Senate: 2 Democrats
House: 22 Democrats, 7 Republicans

Sen. Charles E. Schumer (D)

Capitol Office
224-6542
schumer.senate.gov
322 Hart Bldg. 20510-3203; fax 228-1218

Committees
Banking, Housing & Urban Affairs
Finance
Judiciary
 (Immigration, Refugees & Border Security - Chairman)
Rules & Administration - Chairman
Joint Library - Vice Chairman
Joint Printing - Chairman

Residence
Brooklyn

Born
Nov. 23, 1950; Brooklyn, N.Y.

Religion
Jewish

Family
Wife, Iris Weinshall; two children

Education
Harvard U., A.B. 1971, J.D. 1974

Career
Lawyer

Political Highlights
N.Y. Assembly, 1975-81; U.S. House, 1981-99

ELECTION RESULTS

2010 GENERAL

Schumer (D)	3,047,775	66.3%
Jay Townsend (R)	1,480,337	32.2%

2010 PRIMARY

Schumer (D, INDC, WFM)	unopposed

2004 GENERAL

Schumer (D, INDC, WFM)	4,769,824	71.2%
Howard Mills (R)	1,625,069	24.2%
Marilyn F. O'Grady (C)	220,960	3.3%

Previous Winning Percentages
1998 (55%); 1996 House Election (75%); 1994 House
Election (73%); 1992 House Election (89%); 1990
House Election (80%); 1988 House Election (78%);
1986 House Election (93%); 1984 House Election
(72%); 1982 House Election (79%); 1980 House
Election (77%)

Elected 1998; 3rd term

The Senate's third-ranking Democrat, Schumer is a pivotal player with broad purview over strategy, fundraising and communications. The chairman of the Rules and Administration Committee, he is increasingly engaged in developing new parliamentary tactics to stifle the enlarged Republican minority.

As vice chairman of the Democratic Conference and chairman of the Democratic Policy Committee, Schumer remains high on the short list of potential successors to Majority Leader Harry Reid of Nevada. For now, he bides his time one rung below Majority Whip Richard J. Durbin of Illinois, with whom he shares a rented Capitol Hill house, along with Democratic Rep. George Miller of California. (Another roommate from the House side, Massachusetts Democrat Bill Delahunt, recently retired.)

Schumer was an architect of the Senate Democratic leadership's "Winning the Future" agenda for the 112th Congress (2011-12), which called for an overall spending freeze coupled with more spending on education, energy and highways, as well as targeted tax cuts. He called the House Republican spending plans for fiscal 2011 and beyond "a road map to disaster."

Schumer has been known to put in 17-hour workdays. "God has blessed me with a lot of energy," he said. With his Brooklyn accent and knowing grin, he is a familiar sight on the talking-head circuit, and he uses those TV appearances — as well as an incessant stream of news releases — to score political points and to promote legislation. He has cut a wide jurisdictional swath with seats on the Finance, Judiciary and Banking committees, and he jumps into any issue that strikes his fancy — such as banning text-messaging by motorists or fees for airline carry-on baggage.

Schumer has a knack for building coalitions on big issues. He prodded the Obama administration in early 2010 to drop plans for trying a suspected Sept. 11 terrorist in Manhattan, citing the costs and potential security risks. And from his seat on Finance, Schumer worked with Republican Orrin G. Hatch of Utah on an employer payroll tax break for new hires that became the centerpiece of a 2010 jobs bill. In the health care debate, Schumer helped woo support from moderates and led a short-lived effort to revive the so-called public option, or government-run health plan, by putting it on an even footing with private insurers.

On the Rules Committee, Schumer used hearings on filibusters to attack Republican obstacles to Obama's agenda, but he helped broker a deal at the start of the 112th Congress that fell far short of what some Democrats wanted. "I think that the basic view on both sides of the aisle was that the traditions of the Senate should not be undone with a snap of the fingers," he told Roll Call.

Sometimes his taste for the limelight draws controversy, as when champions for Wall Street such as New York Mayor Michael Bloomberg questioned Schumer's push to increase financial regulation rather than defend a home-state industry. But early in his Senate career, Schumer supported legislation that broke down barriers between commercial banks and investment banks. While still in the House, he backed liability protections for firms facing securities fraud charges.

From his seat on Banking, Housing and Urban Affairs, he pressed for inclusion of corporate governance provisions in the financial regulation overhaul enacted in 2010, allowing shareholders to take an advisory vote on executive pay and dividing the jobs of chairman and chief executive officer.

On Judiciary, Schumer weighs in on high-profile issues from abortion to the war on terrorism, and helps President Obama — a fellow Harvard Law School graduate — move Democratic judicial nominees. For Supreme Court Justice Sonia Sotomayor (likewise a New Yorker), he served as a guide, or "sherpa," during her Senate confirmation process. He was a leading critic of President George W. Bush's choices for the Supreme Court, voting against both Chief Justice John G. Roberts Jr. and Justice Samuel A. Alito Jr.

As chairman of the Judiciary subcommittee responsible for immigration issues, he replaced the late Democratic Sen. Edward M. Kennedy of Massachusetts as the point person on the issue. In April 2010 he unveiled, with Reid and Democrat Robert Menendez of New Jersey, an overhaul proposal that included a path to citizenship for millions of illegal immigrants already in the country.

In two terms as chairman of the Democratic Senatorial Campaign Committee, Schumer built close ties to lawmakers he helped recruit and elect in 2006 and 2008, and he continued to advise Menendez, his successor in the 2010 cycle. On the policy side of his vision of a durable Democratic majority, he argues for focusing on the middle class. His reference point is an imaginary Long Island couple, Joe and Eileen Bailey, whom he envisions when thinking about policy. The Baileys, he said, earn a combined $75,000 a year and believe politicians devote too much attention to either the very wealthy or the very poor. "Too often, the Democratic Party ignored them; I make it my mission not to," he wrote in his 2007 book, "Positively American."

As a House member, Schumer helped broker deals on several major bills, including the 1994 anti-crime law that helped fund 100,000 state and local police jobs, banned certain classes of semi-automatic weapons, and created a "three strikes" mandatory life sentence for repeat violent offenders. An ardent gun control advocate, he was the chief sponsor of the 1993 Brady law requiring background checks for handgun buyers, and of a 2006 bill requiring that stolen guns be reported in every state. When the National Rifle Association called him "the criminal's best friend," Schumer shot back, "I wear this like a badge of honor."

As one of the most prominent Jewish members of Congress, Schumer is a staunch defender of Israel. He was critical of Obama's efforts to publicly pressure Israel to stop expanding Jewish neighborhoods in east Jerusalem.

Schumer was born and raised in the Kings Highway section of Brooklyn. His father, Abe, owned a pest extermination business and his mother, Selma, stayed at home with Schumer and his two siblings. He said he "didn't have a political bone" in his body until he worked on Eugene McCarthy's presidential primary campaign during his freshman year at Harvard in 1968. Schumer decided to become a lawyer with the goal of getting into politics.

After law school, he declined a job at a prominent law firm to run for the state Assembly. His parents argued with him, but he was steadfast. Schumer won the seat at age 23. Six years later, Schumer easily won the Brooklyn-based House seat of Democrat Elizabeth Holtzman, who was running for the Senate.

In 1998, after 18 years in the House, Schumer took aim at Republican Sen. Alfonse M. D'Amato, winning the Democratic nomination with almost 51 percent of the vote against former Rep. Geraldine A. Ferraro, the Democrats' 1984 vice presidential nominee, and New York City Public Advocate Mark Green. Schumer, pointing to his anti-crime and gun control efforts in the House and recounting D'Amato's ethics problems, won with nearly 55 percent of the vote.

In 2004, he lost in only one New York county — Hamilton County in the Adirondacks. At times having been rumored to have an eye on the governorship, Schumer passed up the 2006 gubernatorial primary. He was re-elected to the Senate with almost two-thirds of the vote in 2010.

Key Votes

2010

Pass budget reconciliation bill to modify overhauls of health care and federal student loan programs	YES
Proceed to disapproval resolution on EPA authority to regulate greenhouse gases	NO
Overhaul financial services industry regulation	YES
Limit debate to proceed to a bill to broaden campaign finance disclosure and reporting rules	YES
Limit debate on an extension of Bush-era income tax cuts for two years	YES
Limit debate on a bill to provide a path to legal status for some children of illegal immigrants	YES
Allow for a repeal of "don't ask, don't tell"	YES
Consent to ratification of a strategic arms reduction treaty with Russia	YES

2009

Prevent release of remaining financial industry bailout funds	NO
Make it easier for victims to sue for wage discrimination remedies	YES
Expand the Children's Health Insurance Program	YES
Limit debate on the economic stimulus measure	YES
Repeal District of Columbia firearms prohibitions and gun registration laws	NO
Limit debate on expansion of federal hate crimes law	YES
Strike funding for F-22 Raptor fighter jets	YES

CQ Vote Studies

	PARTY UNITY		PRESIDENTIAL SUPPORT	
	SUPPORT	OPPOSE	SUPPORT	OPPOSE
2010	99%	1%	100%	0%
2009	99%	1%	99%	1%
2008	98%	2%	30%	70%
2007	97%	3%	35%	65%
2006	93%	7%	52%	48%
2005	93%	7%	31%	69%
2004	91%	9%	62%	38%
2003	96%	4%	47%	53%
2002	95%	5%	68%	32%
2001	92%	8%	65%	35%

Interest Groups

	AFL-CIO	ADA	CCUS	ACU
2010	94%	95%	27%	0%
2009	94%	95%	43%	0%
2008	100%	100%	63%	4%
2007	100%	90%	55%	0%
2006	100%	100%	64%	4%
2005	86%	100%	39%	8%
2004	100%	100%	65%	12%
2003	85%	95%	39%	10%
2002	92%	85%	50%	10%
2001	100%	95%	43%	16%

Sen. Kirsten Gillibrand (D)

Capitol Office
224-4451
gillibrand.senate.gov
478 Russell Bldg. 20510-3204; fax 228-0282

Committees
Agriculture, Nutrition & Forestry
(Livestock and Dairy - Chairwoman)
Armed Services
Environment & Public Works
Special Aging

Residence
Brunswick

Born
Dec. 9, 1966; Albany, N.Y.

Religion
Roman Catholic

Family
Husband, Jonathan Gillibrand; two children

Education
Dartmouth College, A.B. 1988 (Asian studies);
U. of California, Los Angeles, J.D. 1991

Career
Lawyer; U.S. Housing and Urban Development
Department aide

Political Highlights
U.S. House, 2007-09

ELECTION RESULTS

2010 SPECIAL

Gillibrand (D)	2,837,589	62.9%
Joseph J. DioGuardi (R)	1,582,603	35.1%

2010 PRIMARY

Gillibrand (D)	464,512	76.1%
Gail Goode (D)	145,491	23.8%

2008 HOUSE

Gillibrand (D, WFM)	193,651	62.1%
Sandy Treadwell (R, INDC, C)	118,031	37.9%

Previous Winning Percentages
2006 House Election (53%)

Appointed January 2009; 1st term

As a member of the House for a little more than one term before being appointed to the Senate, Gillibrand earned a reputation as someone willing to go her own way. She tended to have more conservative views than most Northeastern Democrats, particularly on gun owners' rights and economic issues. But her constituents in an expansive upstate district presented a different demographic than the state she now represents as a whole. In response, her issue priorities — and voting patterns — have changed.

Gillibrand (full name: KEER-sten JILL-uh-brand) had barely established herself in the House before New York Democratic Gov. David A. Paterson appointed her in January 2009 to fill the seat vacated by Hillary Rodham Clinton, who became secretary of State. "She is dynamic, she is articulate, she is perceptive, she is courageous, she is outspoken," Paterson said in announcing Gillibrand's appointment.

A lengthy profile of Gillibrand in New York magazine reported a request Paterson made of the senator-to-be hours before her appointment: He directed Gillibrand to contact Empire State Pride Agenda and inform the organization that she would support gay marriage. Her prior position seemed to indicate support only for civil unions. The organization issued a statement praising Gillibrand in advance of the Paterson announcement.

"After talking to Kirsten Gillibrand, I am very happy to say that New York is poised to have its first U.S. senator who supports marriage equality for same-sex couples," Executive Director Alan Van Capelle said.

After joining the Senate, Gillibrand became a leader in the successful effort to repeal the 1993 law that prohibits those who are openly gay from serving in the military, and she backed the Obama administration's 2011 decision not to defend the 1996 Defense of Marriage Act in court.

She calls the philosophical shifts a broadening of her views. Critics use harsher terms.

Gillibrand joined the Armed Services Committee in the 112th Congress (2011-12), and early on lined up behind a measure that would require President Obama to quickly develop a plan, with an end date, for withdrawing U.S. combat forces from Afghanistan.

"The reality is, we have to create a sense of urgency amongst the Afghan leadership and the Afghan people that they have to take security into their own hands," she said on MSNBC in March 2011.

Gillibrand grew up in a family of hunters and has opposed measures to curtail gun ownership — she supported legislation in 2008 to repeal the District of Columbia's gun laws and received a 100 percent score from the National Rifle Association. But in February 2009, she voted against a GOP amendment to repeal the District's restrictions on most semiautomatic weapons. She said her vote doesn't reflect a change in position: "I feel very strongly that I'm going to fight against gun violence in our communities and keep guns out of the hands of criminals, and I'm also going to protect the Second Amendment. I think those two views are not mutually exclusive."

As she was in the House, Gillibrand is very open with her constituents. She posts her daily schedule on the Internet so constituents can see which lobbyists she's meeting with and which fundraisers she's attending. "I can defend anything I spend congressional time doing," she said. "If an opponent uses it against me, so be it. This is what I do, this is whom I met with, and it's important that my constituents know." She was one of the first to post online a list of all earmarks — funding set-asides for special projects — she requested. Gillibrand said she wants to give everyone equal opportunity to solicit federal dollars.

Despite objections by her staff, Gillibrand allowed a New York Times reporter to sit in on a 2007 meeting where she sorted out which earmark requests to prioritize. During that budget cycle, she secured nearly $24 million in earmarks.

Gillibrand has a seat on the Environment and Public Works Committee, where she can take part in discussions on climate change legislation. She supports reducing carbon emissions by 80 percent by the year 2050 and calls for investments in renewable-energy production and energy-efficient technology. She was the author of a bill to create a grant program for businesses that develop clean-energy technologies.

She also sits on the Agriculture, Nutrition and Forestry Committee, where she continues work she started on the parallel committee in the House. As a senator, Gillibrand embarked on a "listening tour" of upstate New York to discuss needs for the 2012 farm bill. The region is a large producer of apples, dairy products and other farm goods.

She has sponsored bills aimed at boosting child nutrition, including one that would bar schools participating in federal school meal programs from serving foods that contain trans fats derived from partially hydrogenated oils. In addition, she has said a tax on junk food should be considered.

As a lawyer for Davis, Polk & Wardwell during the 1990s, Gillibrand spent five years representing tobacco giant Philip Morris USA as it endured civil lawsuits and criminal investigations. She told the Albany Times-Union that her work focused on assembling information sought by federal investigators checking out claims that the company was involved in crimes against consumers. When she ran for Congress, the company helped out: In the 2005-06 and 2007-08 campaign cycles, she received at least $26,500 from the company and its executives, according to Federal Election Commission records analyzed by CQ MoneyLine. She backed a measure in 2008 to allow the Food and Drug Administration to regulate tobacco. Philip Morris, which would prefer no regulation, nevertheless also supported the bill, which could give it a competitive edge against smaller companies.

Gillibrand was reared in Albany. Her father is a prominent Democratic lobbyist; her mother is a lawyer. As a young girl, she canvassed door to door with her grandmother, who founded the first women's Democratic club in Albany.

Gillibrand has a degree in Asian studies and is fluent in Chinese. She studied abroad in China and Taiwan, and while attending Dartmouth College she spent a month in India on a fellowship, during which she interviewed the Dalai Lama and Tibetan refugees for a senior project. She also worked for Republican Sen. Alfonse M. D'Amato of New York while in college.

She then attended law school and worked as an attorney, concentrating on securities litigation in addition to her work for Philip Morris. Near the end of the Clinton administration, she served as special counsel to Secretary of Housing and Urban Development Andrew M. Cuomo, who is now governor of New York.

In 2006, she challenged four-term Republican Rep. John E. Sweeney, winning with 53 percent of the vote as Democrats took control of Congress. Two years later, she faced Sandy Treadwell, a former state GOP chairman and secretary of State under former Republican Gov. George E. Pataki. Treadwell sought to tie Gillibrand to the liberal House Democratic leadership, but she answered by describing her voting record as "one of the most conservative in the state." In the end, she coasted to victory with 62 percent of the vote.

Gillibrand's 2010 Senate race to complete Clinton's term was a cakewalk after every potential high-profile Republican passed on the race. She defeated former Rep. Joseph DioGuardi with 63 percent of the vote; the Republican DioGuardi took 35 percent.

Key Votes

2010

Pass budget reconciliation bill to modify overhauls of health care and federal student loan programs	YES
Proceed to disapproval resolution on EPA authority to regulate greenhouse gases	NO
Overhaul financial services industry regulation	YES
Limit debate to proceed to a bill to broaden campaign finance disclosure and reporting rules	YES
Limit debate on an extension of Bush-era income tax cuts for two years	NO
Limit debate on a bill to provide a path to legal status for some children of illegal immigrants	YES
Allow for a repeal of "don't ask, don't tell"	YES
Consent to ratification of a strategic arms reduction treaty with Russia	YES

2009

Expand the Children's Health Insurance Program	YES
Limit debate on the economic stimulus measure	YES
Repeal District of Columbia firearms prohibitions and gun registration laws	NO
Limit debate on expansion of federal hate crimes law	YES
Strike funding for F-22 Raptor fighter jets	YES

CQ Vote Studies

	PARTY UNITY		PRESIDENTIAL SUPPORT	
	SUPPORT	OPPOSE	SUPPORT	OPPOSE
2010	99%	1%	98%	2%
2009	94%	6%	0%	100%
2008	91%	9%	22%	78%
2007	90%	10%	6%	94%

Interest Groups

	AFL-CIO	ADA	CCUS	ACU
2010	94%	100%	9%	0%
2009	93%	90%	50%	0%
2008	100%	70%	69%	23%
2007	96%	95%	60%	8%

Rep. Timothy H. Bishop (D)

ELECTION RESULTS

2010 GENERAL

Bishop (D)	98,316	50.1%
Randy Altschuler (R)	97,723	49.8%

2010 PRIMARY

Bishop (D, INDC, WFM)	unopposed

2008 GENERAL

Bishop (D, INDC, WFM)	162,083	58.4%
Lee M. Zeldin (R, C)	115,545	41.6%

Previous Winning Percentages
2006 (62%); 2004 (56%); 2002 (50%)

Elected 2002; 5th term

Bishop's self-described status as a "left-of-center guy" representing a politically divided district helps shape his approach to legislating. It also shapes his electoral prospects, and he barely won one of the most closely contested races of 2010.

Even as he remains a reliable vote for the Democratic leadership on big-picture issues, Bishop focuses on topics that resonate locally, such as shore-line preservation, cleaning up Long Island Sound and reopening local fishers' access to striped bass populations.

A member of the Education and the Workforce Committee, the former college administrator has also made higher education a legislative priority. In the 111th Congress (2009-10), he sponsored a bill intended to crack down on so-called diploma mill colleges and universities.

He supported President Obama's plan to make the federal government the sole provider of student loans, a proposal that became law as part of the health care overhaul enacted in 2010. He also was a forceful advocate in 2007 for a Democratic initiative that cut interest rates on college loans provided by private lenders.

"I am viewed as a go-to guy by various higher education groups," he has said. "I speak their language. I worked with these issues for close to 30 years."

He supports increasing federal funding to help schools adapt to the 2001 No Child Left Behind Law, due to be reauthorized in the 112th Congress (2011-12).

Some of Bishop's work addresses what might be considered quirks in the statute books.

In 2008, Bishop pushed a bill through the House to amend the 1993 federal family-leave law to cover airline flight crews, who currently cannot qualify because of the way their work hours are calculated. Although the bill did not advance in the Senate, Bishop started over in the 111th Congress, steering it through the House early in 2009, but it again stalled in the Senate.

After a low-cost airline announced in 2010 that it would charge up to $45 per bag for carry-on luggage, Bishop proposed changing a provision in the tax code that allows carriers to pocket the proceeds tax-free.

Despite the evenly divided district he represents, Democratic leaders can count on Bishop to support them — he voted with a majority of his party against a majority of Republicans 99 percent of the time in the 110th Congress (2007-08) and 96 percent of the time in the 111th.

During the 111th, he backed the Democrats' health care overhaul, President Obama's $787 billion economic stimulus measure, the $2 billion "cash for clunkers" vehicle trade-in program, and creation of a cap-and-trade system to limit carbon emissions.

At the end of 2010, he supported the compromise that temporarily extended the Bush-era tax rates for all income levels, while decrying inclusion of what he called "tax breaks for millionaires."

The son of a telephone lineman, Bishop is a friend of organized labor. In his first term in the House, he pushed a proposal to increase the minimum wage from $5.15 an hour to $7 an hour and another to require company pension boards to have employee representation. He actively opposed the Bush administration's plan to give workers the option to earn compensatory time instead of overtime pay. During debate, Bishop described how his father worked more than 80 hours a week and depended on overtime wages to put five children through college.

Bishop also sits on the Transportation and Infrastructure Committee, which is expected to take up a five-year reauthorization of the surface transportation law in the 112th Congress. He said he plans to work with Long Island's other four representatives to agree on a "game changer" project for the region, such as direct train access to Manhattan's east side or a track project that would allow for easier reverse commuting from New York City to Long Island.

He has been trying to strike a balance on proposed changes to the Plum Island Animal Disease Center in his district to prevent it from becoming home to more dangerous research, but also to prevent the facility from closing. Also close to home, Bishop, the ranking Democrat on Transportation's Water Resources and Environment Subcommittee, wants to build consensus around a long-delayed study of improvements to the Long Island shoreline.

Bishop has deep roots in the district. His father's family arrived in Southampton from Southampton, England, in 1643, and his great-great-grandfather was mayor of the town. He still lives a block from the house where he grew up. His mother's relatives were potato farmers, and Bishop has warm memories of weekends helping out during harvest time.

In 1973, Bishop took a job as an admissions counselor at Southampton College and worked his way up to dean of enrollment and director of financial aid. He eventually became provost of the school.

When he decided to take on incumbent Felix J. Grucci Jr. in 2002, Bishop's only political experience was a stint as chairman of the Southampton Town Board of Ethics. Grucci, former president of Fireworks by Grucci, was well-known, well-financed and a Republican in a district where the GOP enjoyed a registration edge over Democrats. But Bishop had some advantages, especially a 30-year friendship with entertainment mogul Robert F.X. Sillerman, who had a home in the Hamptons. Sillerman was Bishop's campaign chairman and tapped Hollywood and Hamptons money circles to help him. Bishop squeaked through with 50 percent of the vote.

His next three re-elections were relatively easy. But in 2010, he faced off against GOP businessman Randy Altschuler. The Republican spent more than $4 million of his own money on the campaign, and Bishop raised more than he ever had before, $2.9 million.

Bishop led by about 3,500 votes on election night, but Altschuler took a roughly 400-vote lead after a recanvass. Election officials spent more than a month sorting through absentee and challenged ballots to determine the outcome. The final results showed Bishop edging Altschuler by 593 votes, one of the closest House races of 2010 — and the last to be decided.

Key Votes

2010

Overhaul the nation's health insurance system	YES
Allow for repeal of "don't ask, don't tell"	YES
Overhaul financial services industry regulation	YES
Limit use of new Afghanistan War funds to troop withdrawal activities	NO
Change oversight of offshore drilling and lift oil spill liability cap	YES
Provide a path to legal status for some children of illegal immigrants	YES
Extend Bush-era income tax cuts for two years	YES

2009

Expand the Children's Health Insurance Program	YES
Provide $787 billion in tax cuts and spending increases to stimulate the economy	YES
Allow bankruptcy judges to modify certain primary-residence mortgages	YES
Create a cap-and-trade system to limit greenhouse gas emissions	YES
Provide $2 billion for the "cash for clunkers" program	YES
Establish the government as the sole provider of student loans	YES
Restrict federally funded insurance coverage for abortions in health care overhaul	NO

CQ Vote Studies

	PARTY UNITY		PRESIDENTIAL SUPPORT	
	SUPPORT	OPPOSE	SUPPORT	OPPOSE
2010	96%	4%	95%	5%
2009	96%	4%	97%	3%
2008	99%	1%	16%	84%
2007	99%	1%	4%	96%
2006	97%	3%	31%	69%

Interest Groups

	AFL-CIO	ADA	CCUS	ACU
2010	100%	95%	25%	0%
2009	100%	100%	33%	0%
2008	100%	85%	71%	0%
2007	96%	95%	55%	0%
2006	100%	85%	40%	16%

New York 1

Eastern Suffolk County — Hamptons, Smithtown, Brookhaven

Covering the eastern two-thirds of Long Island's Suffolk County, the 1st reaches out into the Atlantic Ocean. Its western edge is home to small communities that have grown alongside the district's research facilities, while its eastern end takes in second homes for some of New York's wealthiest residents in the Hamptons and Shelter Island. Villages and hamlets line Route 27 on the way to Montauk at the rural end of the island, which retains its pastoral character with scattered fishing villages and farms.

Scientific research, attracted by local colleges and Brookhaven National Laboratory, dominates the district's economy. The education and health care sectors have provided jobs in the region even as the economy struggled — Stony Brook University Medical Center is a renowned teaching hospital, and Brookhaven claims seven Nobel Prize projects. On a smaller economic scale, Suffolk County brings in the most agriculture money of any county in the state, and the 1st's portion of Long Island's wine industry also has a significant presence. In 35 years, the industry has grown from one vineyard to more than 30 wineries and 3,000 acres. Uncertainty in the retail and real estate sectors of the über-elite Hamptons has continued for several years.

The 1st takes in some blue-collar towns and areas that depend on fishing and tourism, where environmental issues rank high. The 1st's lingering rural temperament and small-town feel make it more likely to lean to the right than many other districts near New York City. As many liberal-leaning homeowners reside primarily in the Big Apple, voter registration favors the GOP. Republicans win at the local level, but Democrats make the 1st competitive at the federal level — Democrat Barack Obama secured a slim majority of 51 percent in the 2008 presidential election four years after Republican George W. Bush won a narrow plurality here.

Major Industry
Higher education, research, health care, tourism

Cities
Coram (unincorporated), 39,113; Centereach (unincorporated), 31,578; Shirley (unincorporated), 27,854; Medford (unincorporated), 24,142

Notable
The Montauk Point Lighthouse, built in 1796, was the first lighthouse in the state.

Rep. Steve Israel (D)

Capitol Office
225-3335
www.house.gov/israel
2457 Rayburn Bldg. 20515-3202, fax 225-4669

Committees
No committee assignments

Residence
Huntington

Born
May 30, 1958; Brooklyn, N.Y.

Religion
Jewish

Family
Wife, Marlene Budd; two children

Education
Nassau Community College, A.A. 1978 (liberal arts);
Syracuse U., attended 1978-79; George Washington
U., B.A. 1982 (political science)

Career
Public relations and marketing firm manager;
assistant county executive; university fundraising
director; Jewish advocacy group county director;
congressional aide

Political Highlights
Democratic nominee for Suffolk County Legislature,
1987; Huntington Town Board, 1993-2001 (majority
leader, 1997-2001)

ELECTION RESULTS

2010 GENERAL

Israel (D)	94,594	56.3%
John Gomez (R)	72,029	42.9%

2010 PRIMARY

Israel (D, INDC, WFM)	unopposed

2008 GENERAL

Israel (D, INDC, WFM)	161,279	66.9%
Frank J. Staltzer (R, C)	79,641	33.1%

Previous Winning Percentages
2006 (70%); 2004 (67%); 2002 (58%); 2000 (48%)

Elected 2000; 6th term

Israel has sought — sometimes in vain — to advance moderate views on issues such as energy policy and foreign affairs. Even as he has become a more reliable Democratic vote, he has generally shied away from the inter-party squabbles that largely defined the public perception of Congress in recent years.

But he will have a highly partisan role in the 112th Congress (2011-12), leading the Democratic Congressional Campaign Committee (DCCC) as the party attempts to stymie the Republican agenda and reclaim the majority in 2012.

In that role, his first major battle was an intraparty one, after Politico reported that Israel said Democrats could win the House without the Congressional Black Caucus (CBC).

In damage-control mode, Assistant Democratic Leader James E. Clyburn of South Carolina, a CBC member, was chosen to chair a new Member Advisory Board at the DCCC, which runs House Democrats' campaign recruitment and fundraising activities.

And Israel said he would alter the way the DCCC gives lawmakers cred-it for helping the party in ways other than giving money. Some CBC members had complained that the organization's dues structure doesn't account for the difficulty of raising money in lower-income districts.

When Israel turns his attention to fighting with the other party, the task he faces is a daunting one.

At the beginning of 2011, the DCCC was $20 million in debt and had $805,000 in cash on hand. In addition, the party was coming off an election year that turned its 256-seat majority into a 192-seat minority.

"There are 63 undefined, unvetted Republican freshmen, and we are introducing them to their constituents," he told Roll Call in February 2011. "And their constituents are getting buyer's remorse on many of them."

Israel joined the fiscally conservative Blue Dog Coalition upon arriving in the House in 2001 and created a bipartisan organization, the Center Aisle Caucus, in 2005. He started the group after a busy day, when he was racing to catch a flight home and flung open a House door with such force that it struck the man in front of him, Illinois Republican Timothy V. Johnson. The two had not met before, so Israel introduced himself. The two lawmakers are the caucus' co-founders.

Despite those efforts, his voting record has become increasingly loyal to Democratic leadership. In the first half of his decade in Congress, Israel's party-unity scores — the percentage of votes on which he sided with a majority of Democrats against a majority of Republicans — ranged from the low 80s to the low 90s. During the most recent four years in which Democrats held the majority, he almost never deviated from the party line.

While many Democrats seeking re-election in 2010 ran away from the health care overhaul enacted in 2010, Israel was one of the few to tout the law in his campaign advertisements. And he stoutly defended then-Speaker Nancy Pelosi of California against post-election criticism from party moderates.

Before taking over the DCCC, Israel sat on the Appropriations Committee, where he dedicated himself to becoming a leader on energy policy.

Inspired by President John F. Kennedy's 1962 call to put a man on the moon, Israel has developed a blueprint that includes expanded tax credits for families to offset the costs of alternative fuel and energy-efficient technologies. It also features a broad range of tax and investment incentives for businesses to encourage development of wind power, solar power and other renewable-energy sources. Israel joined Democrat Betty Sutton of Ohio in sponsoring a bill in 2009 to create a "cash for clunkers" program to encourage consumers to trade in older cars for more fuel-efficient models. Israel's bill was later replaced by a less stringent version that became law.

Middle East policy is high on Israel's priority list and he has not shied from expressing his desire for the Obama administration to use restraint in its criticism of the state of Israel, telling the Jerusalem Post that "to the extent that [the administration] has disagreements with Israel on policy matters, they should find a way to do so in private and do what they can to diffuse this situation."

A Brooklyn native, Israel became interested in politics at an early age. He started reading newspapers in elementary school, after hearing the news in school that Sen. Robert F. Kennedy, a New York Democrat and the late president's brother, had been assassinated.

In high school, he rode his bicycle after classes to the campaign headquarters of Democrat Franklin Ornstein, who in 1974 waged an unsuccessful challenge to GOP Rep. Norman F. Lent. As a political science student at George Washington University, Israel worked part-time for California Democratic Rep. Robert T. Matsui, then spent three years with Rep. Richard L. Ottinger, a New York Democrat. He returned to Long Island in 1983, where he worked as a fundraiser for Touro College, a Jewish-sponsored institution. In 1987, he lost a bid for the Suffolk County Legislature.

Israel formed his own fundraising and public relations firm and was director of the Institute on the Holocaust and the Law, which is affiliated with Touro and the American Jewish Congress. He stayed active in local politics, winning a seat on the Huntington Town Board in a 1993 special election.

During his years in Long Island politics, Israel said, he always had in mind a return to Washington. His chance came in 2000 when New York Mayor Rudolph Giuliani announced that he had prostate cancer and was giving up his bid for the Senate. The 2nd District's four-term congressman, Republican Rick A. Lazio, stepped in to take the GOP Senate nomination, and Israel immediately launched a campaign for the open seat. He narrowly beat out Suffolk County legislator David Bishop for the Democratic nod and went on to win in the general election by 13 points. His subsequent races have resulted in easy victories.

In 2009, Israel decided against challenging appointed Democratic Sen. Kirsten Gillibrand after Obama reportedly intervened to clear the primary field.

Key Votes

2010

Overhaul the nation's health insurance system	YES
Allow for repeal of "don't ask, don't tell"	YES
Overhaul financial services industry regulation	YES
Limit use of new Afghanistan War funds to troop withdrawal activities	NO
Change oversight of offshore drilling and lift oil spill liability cap	YES
Provide a path to legal status for some children of illegal immigrants	YES
Extend Bush-era income tax cuts for two years	YES

2009

Expand the Children's Health Insurance Program	YES
Provide $787 billion in tax cuts and spending increases to stimulate the economy	YES
Allow bankruptcy judges to modify certain primary-residence mortgages	YES
Create a cap-and-trade system to limit greenhouse gas emissions	YES
Provide $2 billion for the "cash for clunkers" program	YES
Establish the government as the sole provider of student loans	YES
Restrict federally funded insurance coverage for abortions in health care overhaul	NO

CQ Vote Studies

	PARTY UNITY		PRESIDENTIAL SUPPORT	
	SUPPORT	OPPOSE	SUPPORT	OPPOSE
2010	98%	2%	93%	7%
2009	99%	1%	97%	3%
2008	99%	1%	15%	85%
2007	98%	2%	4%	96%
2006	93%	7%	28%	72%

Interest Groups

	AFL-CIO	ADA	CCUS	ACU
2010	100%	90%	25%	0%
2009	100%	95%	33%	0%
2008	100%	95%	61%	0%
2007	95%	85%	58%	0%
2006	100%	90%	50%	12%

New York 2

Long Island — Brentwood, Commack

Covering most of western Suffolk County and a small part of east-central Nassau County on Long Island, the 2nd is full of upper-middle-class suburban communities that boost the district's median household income to almost $90,000. Many residents who do not commute to New York City also contribute to the district's large white-collar workforce by working at technology firms in the 2nd.

The district's portion of Nassau County includes Jericho, Old Bethpage, Plainview and Woodbury. The district, once dependent on the defense industry, now hosts computer and technology companies. Arrow Electronics and Audiovox both have headquarters in the district and are leaders in the district's key electronics sector.

The 2nd hosts an increasingly diverse population, mixing well-to-do communities such as the district's Nassau County portion and Dix Hills with solidly middle- and working-class neighborhoods. During the summer, many New Yorkers flock to the district's communities along the Atlantic Ocean in the south. Some residents in the coastal areas still make modest incomes in the fishing industry, but Fire Island (shared with the 3rd) relies on tourism.

The Hispanic and Asian populations in the 3rd have each increased by more than 50 percent since 2000. With a nearly 40 percent minority population, a significant Jewish community and a dwindling blue-collar base, the 2nd has a substantial, but not overwhelming, Democratic vote. Moderate Republicans can do well in local races, but the district favors Democratic candidates in federal elections. Registered Democrats outnumber Republicans here by 8 percentage points, and Barack Obama captured 56 percent of the district's vote in the 2008 presidential election.

Major Industry
Computers, electronics, service

Cities
Brentwood (unincorp.), 60,664; Commack (unincorp.), 36,124; Central Islip (unincorp.), 34,450; Huntington Station (unincorp.), 33,029

Notable
The Walt Whitman Birthplace State Historic Site and Interpretive Center is in West Hills (South Huntington); Ocean Beach, a village on the Fire Island National Seashore, prohibits eating and drinking on the beach.

Rep. Peter T. King (R)

Capitol Office
225-7896
www.house.gov/king
339 Cannon Bldg. 20515-3203; fax 226-2279

Committees
Financial Services
Homeland Security - Chairman
Select Intelligence

Residence
Seaford

Born
April 5, 1944; Manhattan, N.Y.

Religion
Roman Catholic

Family
Wife, Rosemary King; two children

Education
St. Francis College, B.A. 1965 (history); U. of Notre Dame, J.D. 1968

Military
N.Y. National Guard, 1968-73

Career
Lawyer

Political Highlights
Hempstead Town Council, 1978-81; Nassau County comptroller, 1981-93; Republican nominee for N.Y. attorney general, 1986

ELECTION RESULTS

2010 GENERAL

King (R)	131,674	71.9%
Howard A. Kudler (D)	51,346	28.0%

2010 PRIMARY

King (R)	21,915	90.8%
Robert Previdi (R)	2,231	9.2%

2008 GENERAL

King (R, INDC, C)	172,774	63.9%
Graham E. Long (D, WFM)	97,525	36.1%

Previous Winning Percentages
2006 (56%); 2004 (63%); 2002 (72%); 2000 (60%); 1998 (64%); 1996 (55%); 1994 (59%); 1992 (50%)

Elected 1992; 10th term

King is a GOP maverick and quote machine. In his second stint as chairman of the Homeland Security Committee, he seeks to prove he can engage Democrats to get things done, even as he shows he will not hesitate to court controversy on topics such as the radicalization of U.S. Muslims.

Outspoken and brusque, King once dismissed then-Speaker Newt Gingrich of Georgia, a fellow Republican, as "roadkill on the highway of American politics," and he has labeled France a "third-rate country."

But when King was made Homeland Security chairman in September 2005 after campaigning hard for the job, he was keen to show he could do more than just toss out lively sound bites. He guided the committee to a series of impressive accomplishments, including a $2 billion port-security law to improve the screening of the millions of containers that enter the United States each year. He also had a hand in restructuring the Federal Emergency Management Agency after its mishandling of relief efforts during the aftermath of Hurricane Katrina, which hit in late August 2005.

When he reclaimed the gavel following the 2010 elections, King set out an ambitious agenda that included hearings on homegrown Islamic radicals.

Democrats cried McCarthyism, and said that King was trying to smear all adherents of the religion. King said the hearings were necessary in light of multiple attacks by homegrown Muslim radicals over the past few years.

"Today we must be fully aware that homegrown radicalization is part of al Qaeda's strategy to continue attacking the United States," he said at the hearing. "Al Qaeda is actively targeting the American Muslim community for recruitment."

During his four years in the minority on the committee, King remained active in shaping legislation. He authored and piloted through the House a bill to set up an office within the Homeland Security Department to promote international cooperation in developing technology to fight terrorists. The legislation was rolled into a bill to adopt the recommendations of the Sept. 11 commission; the bill became law. He also guided through the House a separate proposal to create an office within the department to prevent terrorist bombing attacks; in 2009, he tried again to advance the proposal.

King, who added the Intelligence Committee to his portfolio in the 112th Congress (2011-12), is frustrated that despite the Sept. 11 commission's recommendations for consolidating oversight, Homeland still shares jurisdiction over the department with about 100 other panels. The son of a New York City police officer, King supports close coordination between the federal government and local police and firefighters in combating terrorism. He says Congress should try to make the public more vigilant about preventing terrorism.

Early in the 112th Congress, he introduced legislation designed to aid that cause, offering a measure that would provide legal protections to individuals who report suspicious activities to law enforcement.

King also sits on the Financial Services Committee, where he championed a bill that extended for seven years the Terrorism Risk Insurance Act, which obligates the government to help pay for financial losses from future attacks. The measure was signed into law in December 2007.

King is just enough of a GOP maverick to frequently get his name into the newspapers and on the air while at the same time being just enough of a conservative to keep himself in the good graces of the Republican leadership. He's one of the few members of Congress to be able to display pictures of himself with both President Bill Clinton and President George W. Bush.

King votes with his party on most fiscal and social issues, supporting expanded trade opportunities and private-school vouchers while opposing abortion. But he also supports labor unions' efforts to raise the minimum wage and expand worker protections.

King has had an important role in promoting peace efforts in Northern Ireland. He has made several trips there and has a close relationship with Gerry Adams, the leader of Sinn Fein, the political wing of the Irish Republican Army. Nevertheless, in 2005, frustrated with increasing criminal behavior in the IRA, King called for it to disband, a major step for one of Sinn Fein's biggest backers in Congress.

King draws on his experiences to fuel a favorite pastime: fiction writing. In his 2004 novel, "Vale of Tears," the protagonist, a congressman, faces radical Islamists in cahoots with the IRA. In the earlier "Deliver Us From Evil," another thinly disguised congressman character seeks an end to fighting in Northern Ireland. And in "Terrible Beauty," he chronicled a housewife's involvement with the IRA after her husband is wrongfully jailed for murder.

His interest in Irish affairs — three of his grandparents are from Ireland — brought King close to former Democratic Sen. Hillary Rodham Clinton of New York, now secretary of State. King worked closely with her husband's administration on a peace accord in 1998, and flew to Ireland on Air Force One for the celebration. The same year, King argued against impeaching the president and was one of four Republicans to vote against all four impeachment articles.

King grew up in a blue-collar Queens neighborhood, which proved good training for his future in neighboring Nassau County's rough-and-tumble politics. King also boxes for exercise.

He borrowed money to attend Notre Dame's law school. Afterward he interned (along with Rudolph Giuliani, who later became mayor of New York City) at Richard Nixon's New York law firm. He entered public life in 1972 as a deputy Nassau County attorney and eventually became the county comptroller, serving three terms. During his tenure, King lost a 1986 run for New York attorney general.

When veteran GOP Rep. Norman F. Lent stepped down in 1992, King moved quickly to claim the seat. After coasting through the primary, he edged the better-funded Democrat, Steve A. Orlins. He won re-election easily until 2006, when the anti-GOP tide held him to 56 percent of the vote.

King toyed with running for governor or senator in 2010, but decided against both races. He was re-elected to the House with 72 percent of the vote.

Key Votes

2010

Overhaul the nation's health insurance system	NO
Allow for repeal of "don't ask, don't tell"	NO
Overhaul financial services industry regulation	NO
Limit use of new Afghanistan War funds to troop withdrawal activities	NO
Change oversight of offshore drilling and lift oil spill liability cap	NO
Provide a path to legal status for some children of illegal immigrants	NO
Extend Bush-era income tax cuts for two years	YES

2009

Expand the Children's Health Insurance Program	YES
Provide $787 billion in tax cuts and spending increases to stimulate the economy	NO
Allow bankruptcy judges to modify certain primary-residence mortgages	NO
Create a cap-and-trade system to limit greenhouse gas emissions	NO
Provide $2 billion for the "cash for clunkers" program	YES
Establish the government as the sole provider of student loans	NO
Restrict federally funded insurance coverage for abortions in health care overhaul	YES

CQ Vote Studies

	PARTY UNITY		PRESIDENTIAL SUPPORT	
	SUPPORT	OPPOSE	SUPPORT	OPPOSE
2010	89%	11%	33%	67%
2009	74%	26%	54%	46%
2008	87%	13%	67%	33%
2007	80%	20%	63%	37%
2006	89%	11%	95%	5%

Interest Groups

	AFL-CIO	ADA	CCUS	ACU
2010	7%	10%	100%	92%
2009	38%	20%	93%	88%
2008	53%	45%	94%	50%
2007	57%	30%	90%	68%
2006	36%	5%	100%	76%

New York 3

Long Island — Levittown, Hicksville, Long Beach

Most of Long Island's eastern Nassau County and the south shore of western Suffolk County make up the 3rd, where extravagant estates mix with some of the nation's oldest middle-class suburbs. The district boasts New York's highest median household income — which is now more than $91,000 — and is still overwhelmingly white. The district has one of the lowest percentages of black residents (3 percent) in the state and the lowest percentage of Hispanics (10 percent) in the New York City area despite a decade of growth in minority populations.

Aircraft manufacturing giant Northrop Grumman, once a major local employer, still employs thousands but plays a reduced role in the 3rd's economy. Information technology companies have spread throughout the 3rd and neighboring Long Island districts, diversifying the local economy. Tourism helps the district's economy, as thousands of visitors flock to summer paradises like Freeport's "Nautical Mile" and to beautiful golf courses, including Bethpage State Park, which has joined the rotation of hosts of

the U.S. Open Championship. The 3rd boasts a variety of beautiful south shore beaches, including Long Beach and Jones Beach, which hosts an outdoor summer concert series. Other visitors travel to President Theodore Roosevelt's Sagamore Hill estate in Oyster Bay and his nearby grave in Youngs Memorial Cemetery.

The district, which has the state's highest median age, tends to favor Republican candidates, but a significant labor presence from construction and professional unions gives Democrats some areas of strength. Democrats also have made gains in Nassau County, which has been struggling with municipal budget shortfalls despite residents' high incomes and property values.

Major Industry
Higher education, information technology, service

Cities
Levittown (unincorporated), 51,881; Hicksville (unincorporated) (pt.), 39,902; Long Beach, 33,275; Glen Cove, 26,964; Lindenhurst (pt.), 26,696

Notable
The C.W. Post Campus of Long Island University, named for the breakfast cereal and food company founder, is located on the grounds of the former Brookville estate of the magnate's daughter.

Rep. Carolyn McCarthy (D)

Capitol Office
225-5516
carolynmccarthy.house.gov
2346 Rayburn Bldg. 20515-3204; fax 225-5758

Committees
Education & the Workforce
Financial Services

Residence
Mineola

Born
Jan. 5, 1944; Brooklyn, N.Y.

Religion
Roman Catholic

Family
Widowed; one child

Education
Glen Cove Nursing School, L.P.N. 1964

Career
Nurse

Political Highlights
No previous office

ELECTION RESULTS

2010 GENERAL

McCarthy (D)	94,483	53.6%
Fran Becker (R)	81,718	46.4%

2010 PRIMARY

McCarthy (D, WFM)	unopposed

2008 GENERAL

McCarthy (D, INDC, WFM)	164,028	64.0%
Jack M. Martins (R, C)	92,242	36.0%

Previous Winning Percentages
2006 (65%); 2004 (63%); 2002 (56%); 2000 (61%); 1998 (53%); 1996 (57%)

Elected 1996; 8th term

A series of tragedies in her life have shaped McCarthy's views, most strongly on gun control. But she brings the same determination to other issues on her plate, including education, health care and, more recently, financial matters.

She is a steady friend of organized labor and supports legislation to promote abortion rights and environmental regulation. She is a dependable Democratic vote, siding with a majority of her party against a majority of Republicans 96 percent of the time in 2010; her occasional outliers have included backing constitutional amendments to ban desecration of the U.S. flag, and to require a two-thirds congressional majority to raise federal taxes.

McCarthy first ran for Congress after a deranged gunman shot and killed her husband, Dennis, and seriously wounded her adult son, Kevin, on a Long Island commuter train in December 1993. She accepts that she will always be identified with the attack. "I've come to peace with the fact that that will be in my obituary," she told the Associated Press. And it has been the basis of much of her work in the House.

After a gunman in Tucson, Ariz., killed six and left Democratic Rep. Gabrielle Giffords and 13 others critically wounded in January 2011, McCarthy and Democratic Sen. Frank R. Lautenberg of New Jersey announced that they were working on legislation to prohibit the manufacture and sale of high-capacity ammunition magazines, such as the one used by the gunman. Such magazines had been illegal under the Clinton-era law that banned certain semi-automatic weapons, which expired in 2004. McCarthy had tried to extend the ban.

While acknowledging the unfavorable climate for gun control, McCarthy continues to work around the edges, promoting legislation to close what she calls gaps in the background-check system, and to prevent terrorism suspects from buying guns. McCarthy said she has never disputed whether people have the right to own guns, but says that people have "the right to have public safety." She points to polls that show that the majority of National Rifle Association members believe that people should go through a background check, and she stresses her continued work to build consensus for gun-safety measures.

"I will never give up on this issue," she said in January 2011. "That's why I came here, and I'll never forget."

McCarthy can point to some successes. The killing of 32 students and faculty members by a student at Virginia Tech University in 2007 provided the political momentum to strengthen laws aimed at keeping guns away from the mentally ill. A 1968 law prohibits people "adjudicated as a mental defective" from purchasing guns, but states had never systematically turned over records of mentally ill people for inclusion in the FBI's National Instant Criminal Background Check System. The Virginia Tech shooter, Seung-Hui Cho, had been treated for mental illness involuntarily in 2005 and, under the law, should have been on the list.

After the shootings, the NRA — despite opposition from other gun-rights advocates — backed McCarthy's legislation to require states to turn over mental health records to the FBI. The House passed it unanimously in June 2007, and it was signed by President George W. Bush the following January. Later in 2008, Bush signed legislation reauthorizing higher education programs; it included language drafted by McCarthy — a member of what is now known as the Education and the Workforce Committee — that requires universities to develop plans to inform students of on-campus emergencies.

Many criticized Virginia Tech for failing to notify students that two students had been killed by Cho hours before he massacred 30 more people.

Having struggled with dyslexia, McCarthy has a special interest in education. She served as chairwoman of the Subcommittee on Healthy Families and Communities in the 111th Congress (2009-10), where she led hearings on the effect of concussions on student achievement, cyber safety in schools, and bullying prevention.

McCarthy also sits on the Financial Services Committee, where she is the ranking Democrat on the International Monetary Policy and Trade Subcommittee. She helped put together the 2010 financial regulatory overhaul legislation. McCarthy said she preferred the House's version to the one eventually signed into law, and that she feels needs to be tweaked.

A 2008 housing law includes her provision directing funding to organizations that provide early outreach and counseling to people at risk of foreclosure. A 2007 law to reduce college costs includes her proposal to provide federal-loan forgiveness to people who go into nursing, teaching or certain other careers. She pushed through Congress in early 2009 a bill to expand national and community service programs.

McCarthy was born in Brooklyn, and her family moved about 20 miles to Mineola, on Long Island, when she was 8. She and her stockbroker husband later bought her childhood home from her parents. Twenty-seven years later, McCarthy held her husband's funeral reception there. Her kitchen is full of plates with Norman Rockwell paintings on them.

As a high school student, McCarthy planned on being a gym teacher. Then her boyfriend was involved in a serious car accident. She watched as a private-duty nurse cared for him during the few days before he died of his injuries. "I came home that day and applied to nursing school," she told Good Housekeeping magazine. She worked as a nurse for more than 30 years, caring for terminally ill patients. After the Long Island shootings, her son was paralyzed and not expected to have much of a chance to lead a normal life. But with McCarthy's care, he was able to resume his commute to work in Manhattan.

Since her initial race in 1996, McCarthy has won re-election with relative ease, with a couple of exceptions. In 1998, eight-term state Rep. Gregory R. Becker held her to a 6-percentage-point margin of victory. In 2010, she defeated Nassau County legislator Fran Becker by 8 points.

She briefly mulled a 2010 primary challenge to Democratic Sen. Kirsten Gillibrand, whose pro-gun-rights positions McCarthy had strongly criticized when Gillibrand was in the House. She chose not to run for the Senate, and Gillibrand has softened some of her positions on gun control since changing chambers.

Key Votes

2010

Overhaul the nation's health insurance system	YES
Allow for repeal of "don't ask, don't tell"	YES
Overhaul financial services industry regulation	YES
Limit use of new Afghanistan War funds to troop withdrawal activities	NO
Change oversight of offshore drilling and lift oil spill liability cap	YES
Provide a path to legal status for some children of illegal immigrants	YES
Extend Bush-era income tax cuts for two years	+

2009

Expand the Children's Health Insurance Program	YES
Provide $787 billion in tax cuts and spending increases to stimulate the economy	YES
Allow bankruptcy judges to modify certain primary-residence mortgages	YES
Create a cap-and-trade system to limit greenhouse gas emissions	YES
Provide $2 billion for the "cash for clunkers" program	+
Establish the government as the sole provider of student loans	YES
Restrict federally funded insurance coverage for abortions in health care overhaul	NO

CQ Vote Studies

	PARTY UNITY		PRESIDENTIAL SUPPORT	
	SUPPORT	OPPOSE	SUPPORT	OPPOSE
2010	96%	4%	93%	8%
2009	97%	3%	97%	3%
2008	99%	1%	16%	84%
2007	98%	2%	5%	95%
2006	92%	8%	30%	70%

Interest Groups

	AFL-CIO	ADA	CCUS	ACU
2010	100%	80%	17%	4%
2009	100%	95%	40%	0%
2008	100%	95%	65%	0%
2007	96%	90%	58%	0%
2006	100%	90%	47%	20%

New York 4

Southwest Nassau County — Hempstead

The Long Island-based 4th extends east from the Queens border to take in southwest and west-central Nassau County. The district combines wealthy white-collar suburbanites, some of whom still commute to Wall Street, with some low- and middle-income residents.

Bordered roughly by Interstate 495 in the north, the 4th picks up numerous midsize communities and includes a small portion of Long Island's Atlantic Ocean coastline in Atlantic Beach. Hempstead is home to Hofstra University's 240-acre campus, which continues to drive Hempstead's economy. Construction of a new medical school opening in 2011 has brought jobs and boosted the college's impact. Many local officials and residents hope that redevelopment of the area surrounding the Nassau Veterans Memorial Coliseum, home of hockey's New York Islanders, will bring jobs without exacerbating traffic issues.

Despite a decline in the defense industry that began two decades ago, defense technology companies still provide jobs here. A number of working-class residents are employed by John F. Kennedy International Airport (located nearby in the 6th District), Belmont Park race track or large shopping centers such as Garden City's Roosevelt Field Mall. Hospitals and health care facilities throughout the district also employ many area residents.

Several years of job losses affecting residents who commute to Manhattan's financial sector hurt the local economy.

The 4th has the largest minority population of Long Island's four congressional districts and has a Democratic base, particularly in Hempstead and Uniondale, which include large black and Hispanic communities. The largely Jewish "Five Towns" (Inwood, Lawrence, Cedarhurst, Woodmere and Hewlett), in the 4th's southwestern corner, also lean Democratic. In local elections, the 4th favors some moderate Republicans, but Democrats win in federal and statewide races. Barack Obama took 58 percent of the district's 2008 presidential vote.

Major Industry

Health care, technology, higher education

Cities

Hempstead, 53,891; East Meadow (unincorporated), 38,132; Valley Stream, 37,511; Freeport (pt.), 34,408; Elmont (unincorporated), 33,198

Notable

In 1957, Adelphi University hosted the first National Wheelchair Games.

Rep. Gary L. Ackerman (D)

Capitol Office
225-2601
www.house.gov/ackerman
2111 Rayburn Bldg. 20515-3205; fax 225-1589

Committees
Financial Services
Foreign Affairs

Residence
Roslyn Heights

Born
Nov. 19, 1942; Brooklyn, N.Y.

Religion
Jewish

Family
Wife, Rita Ackerman; three children

Education
Queens College, B.A. 1965

Career
Teacher; newspaper publisher and editor;
advertising executive

Political Highlights
Sought Democratic nomination for New York City
Council at large, 1977; N.Y. Senate, 1979-83

ELECTION RESULTS

2010 GENERAL

Ackerman (D)	72,239	63.0%
James Milano (R)	41,493	36.2%

2010 PRIMARY

Ackerman (D)	19,394	75.6%
Patricia M. Maher (D)	6,258	24.4%

2008 GENERAL

Ackerman (D, INDC, WFM)	112,724	71.0%
Elizabeth Berney (R)	43,039	27.1%
Jun Policarpio (C)	3,010	1.9%

Previous Winning Percentages
2006 (100%); 2004 (71%); 2002 (92%); 2000 (68%);
1998 (65%); 1996 (64%); 1994 (55%); 1992 (52%);
1990 (100%); 1988 (100%); 1986 (77%); 1984 (69%);
1983 Special Election (50%)

Elected 1983; 14th full term

Irreverent, witty and eminently quotable, Ackerman has become a darling of evening news coverage of congressional hearings, particularly because of his long-standing pet issues of financial services regulation, defense of Israel and national security.

While much of his attention is focused on those high-profile topics, Ackerman also finds time to tend to parochial concerns: He helped save the U.S. Coast Guard station at Eatons Neck, which was threatened with closure; he pushed for resolution of the 1994 Long Island Rail Road strike; and he lobbies relentlessly for funds to clean up Long Island Sound.

But it's when the spotlight is shining that Ackerman is in his element.

In a 2009 Financial Services subcommittee hearing, he hurled insults at Securities and Exchange Commission officials explaining why they failed to catch Bernard Madoff's investment scam before he ripped off thousands of investors. "You couldn't find your backside with two hands if the lights were on," said Ackerman, who had many constituents caught up in the Ponzi scheme. "We thought the enemy was Mr. Madoff. I think it's you."

In 2008, Ackerman showed a similar distaste for top executives of the Big Three U.S. automakers, each of whom had flown to Washington in a corporate jet for a hearing on their request for taxpayer funds. "It's almost like seeing a guy show up at the soup kitchen in high-hat and tuxedo. . . . I mean, couldn't you all have downgraded to first class or jet-pooled or something to get here?" Ackerman quipped to the disconcerted panelists.

Ackerman's outrage fit well with the anti-corporate tide, particularly among liberals, that swept the nation during the last years of the George W. Bush presidency and the first years of the Obama administration, but the former teacher from Queens' colorful, often acerbic, style is not reserved exclusively for populist causes.

As ranking Democrat (and chairman before that) on the Foreign Affairs Subcommittee on the Middle East and South Asia, Ackerman's hard-line national security positions have, at times, put him at odds with President Obama and the Democratic leadership.

He was ahead of others in calling for a cutoff of aid to Egypt during the protests that led to the resignation of President Hosni Mubarak. Ackerman said shutting off the flow of money if Mubarak didn't quit was the best way to show that the United States was not on the side of the Egyptian authorities.

When the Obama administration scrambled to persuade Pakistan that its 2009 aid package was not a threat to the nation's sovereignty, Ackerman released a statement that exhibited little patience for the debate.

"If Pakistan doesn't want us as a partner, that's up to them," he said. "But should they take such a decision, they should do so knowing full well that our military assistance, advanced technology and intelligence cooperation are not gifts, but the specific consequences of our cooperation."

Despite his fierce and historically uncompromising defense of Israel, Ackerman has tempered his comments on Obama's stern approach to dealing with the U.S. ally. In 2010, months after tensions with Israel spiked over the White House's public disapproval of the Netanyahu government's plan to expand Jewish neighborhoods in east Jerusalem, Ackerman acknowledged in an interview that he did not agree with Obama's strategy.

"Mistakes are easy to make in this situation, and I think the White House has made some," Ackerman said, adding that he had kept uncharacteristically quiet in an effort to work with the president behind the scenes.

Ackerman's tendency toward off-the-cuff commentary brought him national attention in 2008, when Caroline Kennedy, daughter of President John F. Kennedy, appeared to be the front-runner for the appointment to fill the New York Senate seat vacated by Secretary of State Hillary Rodham Clinton. While other lawmakers politely demurred on the question of Kennedy's suitability, Ackerman pounced.

"I don't know what Caroline Kennedy's qualifications are," Ackerman told a New York radio station. "Except that she has name recognition, but so does J. Lo."

In Washington, Ackerman lives on a Potomac River houseboat named the Unsinkable II (the first Unsinkable wasn't) and drives a vintage Plymouth Valiant. Every day, he sports a white carnation boutonniere, a habit he picked up more than 30 years ago as a New York public school teacher. One morning he stopped at a florist, added a flower to his lapel, and told his students, who assumed incorrectly that it was his birthday, "every day is special."

Ackerman was born in Brooklyn and grew up in a Queens housing project with his parents and a brother. His mother, like so many Queens residents, was an immigrant — in her case, from Poland. He trusted his cabbie father for a sense of what the people in New York were thinking, later calling him his "pollster" and someone who is "always right on the money."

After college, Ackerman became a social studies teacher. In 1969, as a new father, he successfully sued the New York City Board of Education for the right of a father to receive unpaid leave to care for newborns, a benefit then offered only to women. He left teaching to launch a community newspaper in Queens, which subsequently led to run-ins with the local Democratic machine. He is still on the board of managers of Tribco LLC, publisher of the Queens Tribune and other newspapers.

Ackerman was elected to the state Senate in 1978. After 7th District Democratic Rep. Benjamin S. Rosenthal died in 1983, Ackerman persuaded party leaders to support him in the special election. He won with 50 percent of the vote, then cruised through four re-elections.

In redistricting for the 1992 election, some of Ackerman's base in Queens was replaced with conservative, suburban areas in Nassau and Suffolk counties, throwing him into Long Island's 5th District. He was hurt by revelations he had 111 overdrafts at the House members' bank, but he prevailed by 7 percentage points. Further changes to the boundaries before the 2002 election made the 5th more Democratic, and he has since won re-election with ease.

Key Votes

2010

Overhaul the nation's health insurance system	YES
Allow for repeal of "don't ask, don't tell"	YES
Overhaul financial services industry regulation	YES
Limit use of new Afghanistan War funds to troop withdrawal activities	NO
Change oversight of offshore drilling and lift oil spill liability cap	YES
Provide a path to legal status for some children of illegal immigrants	YES
Extend Bush-era income tax cuts for two years	NO

2009

Expand the Children's Health Insurance Program	YES
Provide $787 billion in tax cuts and spending increases to stimulate the economy	YES
Allow bankruptcy judges to modify certain primary-residence mortgages	YES
Create a cap-and-trade system to limit greenhouse gas emissions	YES
Provide $2 billion for the "cash for clunkers" program	YES
Establish the government as the sole provider of student loans	YES
Restrict federally funded insurance coverage for abortions in health care overhaul	NO

CQ Vote Studies

	PARTY UNITY		PRESIDENTIAL SUPPORT	
	SUPPORT	OPPOSE	SUPPORT	OPPOSE
2010	99%	1%	93%	7%
2009	99%	1%	97%	3%
2008	99%	1%	15%	85%
2007	99%	1%	7%	93%
2006	95%	5%	33%	67%

Interest Groups

	AFL-CIO	ADA	CCUS	ACU
2010	100%	90%	13%	0%
2009	100%	100%	33%	0%
2008	100%	100%	67%	0%
2007	96%	90%	55%	0%
2006	93%	95%	47%	8%

New York 5

Northeast Queens; northwest Nassau County

The 5th stretches east from south of LaGuardia Airport in Queens into northwestern Nassau County, reaching Roslyn and East Hills. Almost 80 percent of the Democratic-leaning 5th's residents live in Queens.

Just under half of New York City's Asians live in Queens, especially in downtown Flushing, which has the second-largest Chinatown in New York. The district has the largest Asian population of any congressional district outside Hawaii or California. The neighborhoods in Corona have a strong Hispanic influence.

The 5th's economy, especially in Flushing, is supported both by small businesses and national chains. The economy here also is heavily driven by white-collar jobs located outside the district and is boosted by the U.S. Merchant Marine Academy at Kings Point. Sports fans and tourists visit major sporting venues Citi Field in Flushing, the home of baseball's Mets, and the USTA National Tennis Center in Flushing Meadows-Corona Park, where the U.S. Open tennis tournament is held each year. Continuing residential and retail development in Flushing aims to transform waterfront and former industrial sites.

Although pockets of low-income neighborhoods exist in the 5th, northeastern Queens has affluent areas such as Douglaston and Little Neck. Before fanning eastward into Nassau, the district buttonhooks to the south and west along the Grand Central Parkway to take in some communities in north Jamaica. Residents along Long Island's "Gold Coast" in Nassau County areas such as Roslyn Estates enjoy some of the nation's highest incomes and a generally rich lifestyle.

The district's portion of Nassau tends to be more politically competitive than its strongly Democratic section of Queens. Democrat Barack Obama won the parts of both counties that are in the district, and he took 63 percent overall in the district in the 2008 presidential election.

Major Industry
Higher education, health care, small business

Cities
New York (pt.), 531,615; Port Washington (unincorporated), 15,846

Notable
Trumpet virtuoso Louis Armstrong is buried at Flushing Cemetery; the Queens County Farm Museum is New York City's largest tract of farmland.

Rep. Gregory W. Meeks (D)

Capitol Office
225-3461
www.house.gov/meeks
2234 Rayburn Bldg. 20515-3206; fax 226-4169

Committees
Financial Services
Foreign Affairs

Residence
Queens

Born
Sept. 25, 1953; Harlem, N.Y.

Religion
African Methodist Episcopal

Family
Wife, Simone-Marie Meeks; three children

Education
Adelphi U., B.A. 1975; Howard U., J.D. 1978

Career
City prosecutor; workers' compensation board judge; lawyer

Political Highlights
N.Y. Assembly, 1993-98

ELECTION RESULTS

2010 GENERAL

Meeks (D)	85,096	87.7%
Asher Taub (R)	11,826	12.2%

2010 PRIMARY

Meeks (D)	unopposed

2008 GENERAL

Meeks (D)	141,180	100%

Previous Winning Percentages
2006 (100%); 2004 (100%); 2002 (97%); 2000 (100%);
1998 (100%); 1998 Special Election (56%)

Elected 1998; 7th full term

Though Meeks is a reliable Democrat who regularly votes with his party, he avoids the fiery rhetoric that permeated the major legislative debates of the past several years. A member of the New Democrat Coalition, Meeks often focuses on economic policies that could benefit his mostly middle-class, African-American district in Queens.

He is particularly interested in the banking and investment industry, which dominates the New York economy, and as a member of the Financial Services Committee was a key player in developing the 2010 Wall Street overhaul. While he enthusiastically supported the legislation, he opposed elements that might have posed a significant threat to the financial sector. He opposed a provision adopted by the panel that would have allowed regulators to break up firms that become so large and interconnected that their failure could threaten the broader economy.

He later sat on the conference committee that hashed out the different versions of the overhaul bill passed by the House and Senate. After several weeks of debate, he said he was "extremely pleased" with the final product, which included the provision he opposed on Financial Services.

When Democrats controlled the House, he chaired the committee's International Monetary Policy and Trade panel, where he held hearings on legislation that would penalize companies with ties to genocide in Sudan.

Meeks also used his subcommittee perch to stake centrist positions on trade issues. Although many Democrats are wary of free trade issues, Meeks' district is home to John F. Kennedy International Airport, and he has been an advocate for boosting cargo traffic there.

In 2008, he supported the U.S.-Colombia trade agreement, which had languished because of Democratic opposition. He also backed the 2005 Central America Free Trade Agreement, drawing the ire of labor groups. He pushes for debate over trade to also include consideration of poor nations, arguing that the so-called "global economy" ignores most of sub-Saharan Africa, as well as parts of Asia, the Pacific and the Middle East.

He applauded the deal President Obama reached with South Korea in December 2010. "Korea and New York have been strong allies with one another and this agreement will strengthen the relationship even further," Meeks said after the White House unveiled the deal. He urged the White House to finalize free trade agreements with Colombia and Panama.

Meeks, a co-founder of the Services Caucus, has also been a firm supporter of boosting trade in services such as banking, insurance, express delivery and information technology.

He extends his interest in international relations on the Foreign Affairs Committee, where he is ranking Democrat on the Europe and Eurasia panel.

He called proposed cuts in foreign assistance programs "more than just in my opinion penny-wise and pound-foolish. It is downright dangerous to our national interest."

Meeks is active in the civil rights realm. He was once arrested for protesting what he considered the under-representation of minority law clerks at the Supreme Court. And after four New York City police officers shot and killed Guinean immigrant Amadou Diallo in 1999, he joined other black leaders in protesting police violence against minorities.

Raised in public housing in East Harlem, Meeks traces his interest in public affairs to his mother, who resumed her education when her four children were in their teens, and frequently got her kids involved in community improvement projects. As a youth, his idol was civil rights attorney and Supreme Court

Justice Thurgood Marshall. "From the time that I could remember, I wanted to be a lawyer," Meeks told Newsday. "I always admired Thurgood Marshall, and I learned from my parents what he was doing to make life better for people of color."

After graduating from Howard University Law School, Meeks began his career as a Queens County assistant district attorney and narcotics crime prosecutor. After a brief stint on the state Commission of Investigation, which probes wrongdoing by state officials and organized crime, Meeks was appointed as a state workers' compensation judge. During those years, Meeks became involved in a variety of community projects — neighborhood cleanups, street repairs, traffic problems and street safety — in the working-class neighborhood of Far Rockaway, where his parents eventually moved.

Meeks said he always thought his involvement in politics would be behind the scenes, but in 1992 he ran for and won the first of three terms to the state Assembly. In his years in Albany, he had seats on committees that oversaw state codes, the judiciary, insurance, small business and government operations.

When six-term Democrat Floyd H. Flake resigned his 6th District House seat in late 1997 to lead an influential African Methodist Episcopal Church in Jamaica, Queens, he endorsed Meeks as his successor. Meeks also got the backing of local Democratic leaders in the February 1998 special election, which helped him capture 56 percent of the vote in a five-way contest. He was unopposed for a full term that November and has not been seriously challenged in subsequent elections.

But he has faced a series of questions about ethics.

Early in 2008, Meeks agreed to pay a $63,000 fine and to reimburse his campaign committee after the Federal Election Commission found that in 2006 he had illegally used campaign cash from the 2004 election for a personal trainer and had leased cars for personal use. Meeks blamed the problems on sloppy bookkeeping by his then-treasurer, who he said owned a gym. Meeks said he didn't know the treasurer was paying the trainer to work with him.

In 2010, The New York Times took him to task for buying a home built for him by a campaign contributor and for lavish expenditures on fundraising trips. Never charged with wrongdoing, he said that he had to travel to where the donors are.

"I do fundraisers where the people with the money are," he told the newspaper. "I am not going to raise the money in my district that I need to be a player here in Washington."

In January 2011, the New York Post reported that the Ethics Committee was investigating Meeks for alleged repeated omissions from his financial disclosure forms.

Key Votes

2010

Overhaul the nation's health insurance system	YES
Allow for repeal of "don't ask, don't tell"	YES
Overhaul financial services industry regulation	YES
Limit use of new Afghanistan War funds to troop withdrawal activities	NO
Change oversight of offshore drilling and lift oil spill liability cap	YES
Provide a path to legal status for some children of illegal immigrants	YES
Extend Bush-era income tax cuts for two years	YES

2009

Expand the Children's Health Insurance Program	YES
Provide $787 billion in tax cuts and spending increases to stimulate the economy	YES
Allow bankruptcy judges to modify certain primary-residence mortgages	YES
Create a cap-and-trade system to limit greenhouse gas emissions	YES
Provide $2 billion for the "cash for clunkers" program	YES
Establish the government as the sole provider of student loans	YES
Restrict federally funded insurance coverage for abortions in health care overhaul	NO

CQ Vote Studies

	PARTY UNITY		PRESIDENTIAL SUPPORT	
	SUPPORT	OPPOSE	SUPPORT	OPPOSE
2010	99%	1%	95%	5%
2009	98%	2%	97%	3%
2008	99%	1%	19%	81%
2007	98%	2%	6%	94%
2006	88%	12%	41%	59%

Interest Groups

	AFL-CIO	ADA	CCUS	ACU
2010	100%	90%	25%	0%
2009	100%	100%	40%	0%
2008	100%	90%	65%	0%
2007	96%	95%	58%	0%
2006	86%	90%	57%	8%

New York 6

Southeast Queens — Jamaica, St. Albans

The black-plurality, mostly middle-class 6th is economically focused around John F. Kennedy International Airport on Jamaica Bay in southeastern Queens. It is the only district wholly within the 2.2 million-resident borough of Queens.

The 6th is bound roughly by Cross Bay Boulevard to the west, Grand Central Parkway to the north and the Nassau County line to the east. South of the airport, across Jamaica Bay, the 6th takes in part of Rockaway, including Edgemere and Far Rockaway. Included in the 6th's boundaries are St. John's University, located in the far north, and Aqueduct Racetrack, in the far west. More than a generation ago, communities such as Springfield Gardens and St. Albans were settled by an Irish and Italian Catholic middle class.

After years of immigration, the demographics here have completely changed one of the nation's most economically sound black-majority districts into a highly diverse mix of overlapping Hispanic, Caribbean, Asian and African-American communities.

JFK Airport, the 6th's largest employer, provides a steady job base and is New York City's busiest and largest airport as well as the top international arrivals gateway into the United States. Airport-based jobs, complemented by employment in health care, municipal government and residential construction, give the 6th a strong union constituency. But residents here have to endure the longest average travel time to work — 46 minutes — of any district's workforce in the nation.

With sizable minority communities, the district is overwhelmingly Democratic — registered Democrats outnumber Republicans nearly 10-to-1 in the 6th. Barack Obama won 89 percent of the district's presidential vote in 2008.

Major Industry
Airport, health care, education

Cities
New York (pt.), 651,764

Notable
On Feb. 7, 1964, what would become known as "Beatlemania" began at JFK Airport as the Beatles held their first U.S. press conference; King Park in Jamaica was the farm of Rufus King, a delegate to the Constitutional Convention and later a Federalist senator from New York.

Rep. Joseph Crowley (D)

Capitol Office
225-3965
crowley.house.gov
2404 Rayburn Bldg. 20515-3207, fax 225-1909

Committees
Ways & Means

Residence
Queens

Born
March 16, 1962; Queens, N.Y.

Religion
Roman Catholic

Family
Wife, Kasey Crowley; three children

Education
Queens College, B.A. 1985 (communications & political science)

Career
State legislator

Political Highlights
N.Y. Assembly, 1987-99

ELECTION RESULTS

2010 GENERAL

Crowley (D)	71,247	80.5%
Ken Reynolds (R)	16,145	18.2%
Anthony Gronowicz (GREEN)	1,038	1.2%

2010 PRIMARY

Crowley (D, WFM)	unopposed

2008 GENERAL

Crowley (D, WFM)	118,459	84.6%
William E. Britt Jr. (R, C)	21,477	15.3%

Previous Winning Percentages
2006 (84%); 2004 (81%); 2002 (73%); 2000 (72%); 1998 (69%)

Elected 1998; 7th term

Crowley's outsized personality sometimes seems to be from another era in American politics. An Irishman with the gift of gab and an occasional fondness for singing in public, he at first glance might appear better suited to the 19th century than the 21st. But he is attuned to modern realities and uses his burly 6-foot-4-inch frame and New York City bluntness to advocate business-friendly policies and position himself for a future move into leadership.

Crowley (KRAU-lee) has been in politics for much of his life; he won a state Assembly seat at age 24 and served there until entering Congress in 1999 at age 37. The son of a police officer, he doesn't give up without a good fight — making him a suitable pick as one of the nine chief deputy whips who help round up votes and enforce party discipline.

Crowley was an avid supporter of government intervention during the economic downturn. He backed President Obama's economic stimulus bill in early 2009 and also helped rally support in fall 2008 for a $700 billion economic rescue package. As the first version of the bill failed in the House, Crowley screamed, "The Dow just dropped 600 points!" across the chamber at Republicans, in a last-ditch effort to sway votes.

More recently, Crowley has run into political turmoil over a December 2009 fundraiser and whether there were any links between the event and financial regulatory overhaul legislation passed by the House that month. The Office of Congressional Ethics recommended in August 2010 that the House Committee on Standards of Official Conduct further investigate Crowley, along with two other members. In January 2011, the Ethics Committee (as the panel was renamed) said it would not pursue the allegations.

While Crowley enjoys seniority among his Democratic counterparts, he has twice lost bids for a higher leadership post. Still, he cannot be counted out as a future contender. He is chairman of the business-friendly New Democrat Coalition and held onto his prized spot on the Ways and Means Committee as the party's ranks on the panel were thinned by losing the majority. He is an impressive fundraiser for the party, serving as the Democratic Congressional Campaign Committee's vice chairman of finance, and sits on the leadership-run Steering and Policy Committee, which makes committee assignments. Crowley holds significant power back home as head of the Queens Democratic Party, the most powerful political machine in New York.

On Ways and Means, Crowley often is in the thick of debate on tax issues. Although he supports the Democrats' overall approach to tilting the tax burden toward the highest earners, Crowley also tries to help certain industries, particularly the financial services sector that employs many New Yorkers.

He joined fellow New York Democrat Anthony Weiner in early 2009 in asking the IRS to clarify regulations concerning tax payments made on what turned out for thousands of investors to be "phantom income" derived from Ponzi schemes such as the one run by financier Bernard Madoff.

He voted for the two-year extension of the George W. Bush-era tax rates that was enacted in late 2010.

Crowley said he wants to be a voice "for reasonable, fair trade agreements" that incorporate labor and environmental standards. But he supported then-Speaker Nancy Pelosi of California's decision to delay a vote on a Colombia trade deal because of concerns about treatment of union organizers. In the 109th Congress (2005-06), he joined a bipartisan group of lawmakers who called on the Bush administration to renegotiate the Central America Free Trade Agreement.

Crowley is not categorically opposed to global trade deals, however. He split with his party to back free-trade pacts with Chile and Singapore in 2003, and in 2006 he cosponsored legislation to establish permanent normal trade relations with Vietnam. He also joined many Democrats in voting in 2007 for an agreement with Peru.

Crowley failed in his first two efforts to join the leadership. In February 2006, he made a bid for the vice chairmanship of the Democratic Caucus, the lowest rung on the elected leadership ladder, but lost to John B. Larson of Connecticut. Crowley was on the short list in 2005 to chair the Democratic Congressional Campaign Committee, an appointive post, but the job went to another rising star, Rahm Emanuel of Illinois, later White House chief of staff and now mayor of Chicago. In 2008, he thought about running for the vice chairmanship again, but deferred to Xavier Becerra of California.

Crowley comes from a close-knit family. Today he, his siblings and his mother all live within three miles of one another in Queens, where Crowley was born and raised. His mother emigrated from County Armagh in Northern Ireland as a young girl. His father, a first-generation Irish-American, was a city police officer who earned a law degree at night.

Crowley inherited his political thirst from his father as well as from his uncle, Walter Crowley, a well-known local politician who served on the New York City Council. But Crowley truly flourished under the mentoring of Democrat Thomas J. Manton, his predecessor in the House, whom he once considered an enemy.

In 1984, Manton beat Crowley's beloved uncle in a four-way primary for the House seat. Then in 1986, Manton tapped him on the shoulder at an Irish dinner dance and asked whether he'd thought about running for the local Assembly seat, which had opened up.

Crowley went on to win the seat, just a year out of college. During his 12 years in Albany he developed a close friendship with Manton. In 1998, Manton picked Crowley as his successor in the U.S. House by announcing his retirement several days after the filing deadline and then joining with other party officials in nominating him. Crowley swamped the Republican candidate, corporate security manager James J. Dillon, in the general election. Manton's tactics angered other Democrats, but Crowley successfully defended his seat in 2000. He has won since with ease.

A guitar player, Crowley does a decent imitation of rocker Van Morrison singing "Wild Night." In the great tradition of Irish pols, he occasionally sings in public, often for fundraising events, and once belted out the national anthem before a New York Knicks game.

Key Votes

2010

Overhaul the nation's health insurance system	YES
Allow for repeal of "don't ask, don't tell"	YES
Overhaul financial services industry regulation	YES
Limit use of new Afghanistan War funds to troop withdrawal activities	YES
Change oversight of offshore drilling and lift oil spill liability cap	YES
Provide a path to legal status for some children of illegal immigrants	YES
Extend Bush-era income tax cuts for two years	YES

2009

Expand the Children's Health Insurance Program	YES
Provide $787 billion in tax cuts and spending increases to stimulate the economy	YES
Allow bankruptcy judges to modify certain primary-residence mortgages	YES
Create a cap-and-trade system to limit greenhouse gas emissions	YES
Provide $2 billion for the "cash for clunkers" program	YES
Establish the government as the sole provider of student loans	YES
Restrict federally funded insurance coverage for abortions in health care overhaul	NO

CQ Vote Studies

	PARTY UNITY		PRESIDENTIAL SUPPORT	
	SUPPORT	OPPOSE	SUPPORT	OPPOSE
2010	99%	1%	87%	13%
2009	99%	1%	99%	1%
2008	98%	2%	19%	81%
2007	98%	2%	6%	94%
2006	89%	11%	35%	65%

Interest Groups

	AFL-CIO	ADA	CCUS	ACU
2010	100%	95%	25%	0%
2009	100%	100%	40%	0%
2008	100%	100%	67%	0%
2007	96%	95%	60%	0%
2006	93%	95%	57%	8%

New York 7

Parts of Queens and the Bronx

Few districts in the nation are as ethnically and racially diverse as the 7th, which takes in part of northern Queens and the eastern part of the Bronx. Blacks, Hispanics and Asians each make up more than 15 percent of the population, with Hispanics a clear plurality at 44 percent.

A majority of the 7th's residents live in the district's northern tier in the Bronx. This area reaches as far west as the Bronx Zoo and the New York Botanical Garden and as far north as Co-op City, which houses more than 15,000 apartments, and the Westchester County line. The Bronx portion also includes Morris Park, Pelham Bay and City Island, and the borough's half of the Throgs Neck Bridge. While portions of the Bronx struggle economically, the areas around Eastchester Bay have some of the borough's highest incomes. The health care industry and small retailers are major employers in the Bronx.

The district's southern portion climbs northeast from near the intersection of the Brooklyn-Queens and Long Island expressways (in the neighboring 12th) to take in Woodside, Jackson Heights, Elmhurst and LaGuardia Air-

port. This fast-growing area is heavily Hispanic and contributed to Queens' population boom during the 1990s. Jackson Heights and Woodside also have significant Indian populations. LaGuardia provides thousands of jobs here and, along with nearby John F. Kennedy International Airport (in the 6th), makes Queens a major transportation hub. East of the airport, the district also includes most of Flushing Bay, College Point and the Whitestone Bridge, and a small part of Flushing.

Like most New York City districts, the 7th strongly supports Democrats, although a bit less uniformly. It is generally middle-class with some lower-income sections. Barack Obama easily carried the district in the 2008 presidential election with 79 percent of the vote.

Major Industry
Airport, health care, service

Cities
New York (pt.), 667,632

Notable
The Maritime Industry Museum and SUNY Maritime College are at Fort Schuyler in Throgs Neck, where the East River hits Long Island Sound; the Bronx Zoo is the largest urban wildlife conservation facility in the nation.

Rep. Jerrold Nadler (D)

Capitol Office
225-5635
www.house.gov/nadler
2334 Rayburn Bldg. 20515-3208; fax 225-6923

Committees
Judiciary
Transportation & Infrastructure

Residence
Manhattan

Born
June 13, 1947; Brooklyn, N.Y.

Religion
Jewish

Family
Wife, Joyce L. Miller; one child

Education
Columbia U., A.B. 1969 (government); Fordham U.,
J.D. 1978

Career
State legislative aide; lawyer

Political Highlights
N.Y. Assembly, 1976-92; candidate for Manhattan
borough president, 1985; candidate for New York
City comptroller, 1989

ELECTION RESULTS

2010 GENERAL

Nadler (D)	88,758	73.4%
Susan Kone (R)	31,996	26.5%

2010 PRIMARY

Nadler (D, WFM)		unopposed

2008 GENERAL

Nadler (D, WFM)	160,730	80.4%
Grace Lin (R, C)	39,047	19.5%

Previous Winning Percentages
2006 (85%); 2004 (81%); 2002 (76%); 2000 (81%);
1998 (86%); 1996 (82%); 1994 (82%); 1992 (81%);
1992 Special Election (100%)

Elected 1992; 10th full term

Nadler is a consummate liberal who vehemently defends his view of civil liberties and the concerns of his constituents. His district, which stretches from Manhattan's Upper West Side through Greenwich Village and Wall Street into Brooklyn, is home to one of the largest concentrations of liberal Jewish voters and gay and lesbian political activists in the country.

Nadler (NAD-ler) is a long-time supporter of gay rights.

In late 2010, he helped lead the repeal of the statutory ban on homosexuals serving openly in the military. And after the Obama administration announced in February 2011 that it would no longer defend the provision of the Defense of Marriage Act that directs the federal government to recognize only marriages between one man and one woman, Nadler reintroduced a measure he had sponsored in the 111th Congress (2009-10) to repeal the 1996 law.

Nadler's bill also would provide legal protection to all gay, bisexual and transgender Americans who are married under a state law, regardless of their state of residence. In the 111th Congress, the bill did not win the backing of Democratic leadership or key allies such as Barney Frank of Massachusetts, one of three openly gay members of Congress, who gave higher priority to other gay-rights bills deemed as having a better chance of passage.

When House GOP leaders decided in early 2011 to intervene in pending cases to defend the law, Nadler and a group of other Democrats called the move "partisanship at its worst."

While Nadler decries some forms of partisanship, he is a reliable practitioner. His party unity score — the percentage of votes on which he sided with a majority of Democrats against a majority of Republicans — has not fallen below 98 percent since 2002. It has never been lower than 95 percent.

As ranking Democrat on the Judiciary Committee's panel on the Constitution, Nadler seeks to constrain what he sees as undue growth of presidential power. He has been a vigorous opponent of the anti-terrorism law known as the Patriot Act, first passed in the wake of the Sept. 11, 2001, terrorist attacks on the Pentagon and the World Trade Center, located in the 8th District.

Nadler accused the George W. Bush administration of "making claims of power that nobody's ever made" about the extent of executive power. His criticisms of the Obama administration have been considerably more muted, but he has continued to seek to curb executive authority, introducing bills to circumscribe the government's use of the "state secrets" privilege to thwart lawsuits and to set procedural protections for the use of national security letters to obtain information.

Nadler contended that Bush committed potentially impeachable offenses with his Iraq and counterterrorism policies. When he was chairman of the Constitution Subcommittee, he held a series of hearings in 2008 to explore what he described as abuses of executive power. But Nadler eventually conceded that, as a practical matter, "you don't impeach somebody if you can't get a consensus in the nation."

Nadler supported Obama's decision to hold civilian trials for five individuals accused of conspiring in the Sept. 11 attacks. But, after the January 2010 announcement that the trials would be held in Lower Manhattan near Ground Zero, he and a handful of local politicians and advocates urged the Justice Department to select another location within the Southern District of New York, citing ongoing recovery efforts and financial burdens on the city. (Attorney General Eric H. Holder Jr. announced in April 2011 that all five would be prosecuted before military tribunals.) In 2008 he cosponsored legislation with other New York lawmakers to provide medical monitoring to people exposed to dust and debris after the attacks, and to reopen a federal victims' compensation fund to aid people sickened from exposure to toxic materials.

Nadler sits on the Transportation and Infrastructure Committee, where he hopes to secure funds in the next surface transportation bill for a freight rail tunnel under New York Harbor to connect Brooklyn with Bayonne, N.J. (The Brooklyn terminus of the proposed tunnel would be in the 8th District.) He said the tunnel would foster economic development, reduce air pollution and lower consumer costs in the city. He also wants to foster high-speed rail and find ways to fund highway and bridge improvements other than with the gasoline tax.

Nadler took on a more personal struggle in 2002 when he decided to undergo gastric bypass surgery to tackle obesity issues that had pushed the 5-foot-4-inch-tall lawmaker's weight to as high as 338 pounds. Years later, the weight loss is still "significant," as are the health benefits, according to his staff.

Born in Brooklyn, Nadler spent his early years on a New Jersey poultry farm. He said he was drawn to public service, in part, after watching his father rail against President Dwight D. Eisenhower and Agriculture Secretary Ezra Taft Benson, blaming them for policies that made it impossible for Nadler's family to keep the farm.

His family moved back to New York City after the farm failed. He stayed in the city to pursue an education, earning a degree in government from Columbia University and a law degree from Fordham University, which he attended at night while working at an off-track betting office during the day.

Nadler organized a group of Columbia students, dubbed the "West Side Kids," to advance a liberal agenda in New York politics. He was an aide to a New York state senator, and he campaigned for liberal Democrat Ted Weiss' election to Congress. In 1976, Nadler won a seat in the state Assembly.

When Weiss died on the eve of the 1992 Democratic primary, voters renominated him anyway, giving party officials the right to pick a successor. That set off a scramble among Democratic activists, with six candidates jumping into the frenetic nine-day race for the nomination. While other aspirants, such as former Rep. Bella S. Abzug, were better known to the public, Nadler had long-standing ties to party insiders who would cast the votes. He got the nomination and went on to win the special election, as well as the general election for a full term on the same day. He has since won re-election with ease.

Key Votes

2010

Overhaul the nation's health insurance system	YES
Allow for repeal of "don't ask, don't tell"	YES
Overhaul financial services industry regulation	YES
Limit use of new Afghanistan War funds to troop withdrawal activities	YES
Change oversight of offshore drilling and lift oil spill liability cap	YES
Provide a path to legal status for some children of illegal immigrants	YES
Extend Bush-era income tax cuts for two years	NO

2009

Expand the Children's Health Insurance Program	YES
Provide $787 billion in tax cuts and spending increases to stimulate the economy	YES
Allow bankruptcy judges to modify certain primary-residence mortgages	YES
Create a cap-and-trade system to limit greenhouse gas emissions	YES
Provide $2 billion for the "cash for clunkers" program	YES
Establish the government as the sole provider of student loans	YES
Restrict federally funded insurance coverage for abortions in health care overhaul	NO

CQ Vote Studies

	PARTY UNITY		PRESIDENTIAL SUPPORT	
	Support	Oppose	Support	Oppose
2010	98%	2%	86%	14%
2009	98%	2%	97%	3%
2008	99%	1%	14%	86%
2007	99%	1%	4%	96%
2006	99%	1%	15%	85%

Interest Groups

	AFL-CIO	ADA	CCUS	ACU
2010	100%	100%	14%	0%
2009	100%	95%	36%	0%
2008	100%	95%	53%	0%
2007	96%	95%	47%	0%
2006	100%	100%	27%	4%

New York 8

West Side of Manhattan; Borough Park; Coney Island

Starting west of Central Park, the 8th travels through Manhattan's West Side from 89th Street south to Wall Street and Battery Park, taking in part of the Theater District and Times Square, Chelsea, Greenwich Village, SoHo, and TriBeCa. At Manhattan's southern tip, it slips through the Brooklyn-Battery Tunnel to skim Brooklyn's western waterfront. It includes some working-class areas, much of Brighton Beach and some of Brooklyn's southern coastline, including Coney Island. The 8th had the state's fastest-growing population since 2000.

Manhattan's finance industry, at the center of the economic crisis, has shed tens of thousands of jobs and left millions of square feet of office space vacant but remains the district's economic touchstone. In lower Manhattan, reconstruction at the site of the Sept. 11 terrorist attacks on the World Trade Center is still under way. The new skyscrapers will offer office and retail space, and the complex will include a memorial and museum, residential property and an extensive transportation hub.

At the center of the 8th's portion of Brooklyn is Borough Park, with large, conservative and pro-Israel Hasidic and Orthodox Jewish populations. This area of Brooklyn is filed with quirky shops, eclectic restaurants and vibrant nightlife.

Manhattan's heavily Democratic West Side, with politically active gay, minority, artistic and academic communities, has sent liberal representatives to Congress for decades and overwhelmingly supported Democratic presidential candidates. There are GOP-leaning middle-class neighborhoods in Brooklyn, and John McCain won the 8th's portion of the borough with 55 percent of the 2008 presidential vote. But Brooklyn's conservative voters are outnumbered at the polls by the district's liberal bloc. In 2008, Barack Obama won 74 percent of the district's vote.

Major Industry
Finance, retail, tourism, small business

Cities
New York (pt.), 713,512

Notable
The 8th is home to the Statue of Liberty, Empire State Building, Governors Island, South Street Seaport, American Museum of Natural History, Penn Station, Madison Square Garden and City Hall.

Rep. Anthony Weiner (D)

Capitol Office
225-6616
www.house.gov/weiner
2104 Rayburn Bldg. 20515-3209; fax 226-7253

Committees
Energy & Commerce

Residence
Queens

Born
Sept. 4, 1964; Brooklyn, N.Y.

Religion
Jewish

Family
Wife, Huma Abedin

Education
State U. of New York, Plattsburgh, B.A. 1985 (political science)

Career
Congressional aide

Political Highlights
New York City Council, 1992-99; sought Democratic nomination for mayor of New York, 2005

ELECTION RESULTS

2010 GENERAL

Weiner (D)	67,011	60.8%
Bob Turner (R)	43,129	39.1%

2010 PRIMARY

Weiner (D, INDC, WFM)	unopposed

2008 GENERAL

Weiner (D, WFM)	112,205	93.0%
Alfred F. Donohue (C)	8,378	6.9%

Previous Winning Percentages
2006 (100%); 2004 (71%); 2002 (66%); 2000 (68%); 1998 (66%)

Elected 1998; 7th term

Weiner's political future is cloudy after revelations in spring 2011 that he had, on more than one occasion, sent lewd photographs of himself to young women via his Twitter account.

He compounded his problem by initially lying about the incident, claiming his Twitter account had been hacked and calling it a "prank." He denied having sent any photos, but refused to say whether the first photo made public was of him. He further aroused suspicion by saying he would hire a private investigator rather than filing a formal complaint with the FBI or Capitol Police. Days after the first instance came to light, conservative blogger Andrew Breitbart posted more photos that Weiner had apparently sent to other women, and Weiner called a news conference to acknowledge that he had lied.

Weiner, who at the time of the revelations had been married for less than a year to a longtime aide to Secretary of State Hillary Rodham Clinton, admitted to sending numerous sexually explicit messages and photographs to a half-dozen women he had met via Facebook over the past three years.

He refused to resign from Congress, but the controversy casts a shadow over his plans for the future, whether they include another run for the House or another try for the mayoralty of New York City.

The contrite husband the world watched at his June 2011 mea culpa news conference was a far cry from the brash and partisan Brooklyn-brawler image the liberal New York native typically presents.

At no time during the 111th Congress (2009-10) was Weiner's brand of doggedness — tabloids might call it hot doggedness — more on public display than when he gave an impassioned speech complete with theatrical gestures attacking Republicans in July 2010 for failing to do "the right thing on behalf of the heroes" of Sept. 11. He was defending legislation to provide $7.4 billion in medical care and compensation for first-responders and others who were exposed to toxic dust and debris from the World Trade Center.

Republicans argued that the bill would expand existing programs too much and objected to the measure's offset, arguing it would undermine the tax treaty system. They also didn't like that Democrats called up the measure under an expedited procedure that barred amendments and limited debate. After the bill fell short of the two-thirds necessary under the expedited procedure, leaders brought it back and passed it in September, but the Democratic Senate never took it up.

Even on national issues, Weiner's legislative focus has a local flavor.

He voted for the $700 billion financial rescue plan in the fall of 2008 because he said it was especially critical to the livelihoods of people who work on Wall Street. During debate over the measure, Weiner also appeared regularly on television — he's a frequent guest on MSNBC — to talk about the disproportionate impact the crisis had on his city: not just on bankers and traders, but also on the people working in the service industries that support Wall Street.

Since the Sept. 11 attacks, terrorism and security issues also have been a top priority for Weiner. The House passed his bill in 2008 to crack down on tobacco smugglers and illicit tobacco sales over the Internet, in part to reduce black-market money used to fund terrorist organizations such as Hezbollah; the Senate did not act on it.

Formerly a member of the Judiciary Committee, he is a strong proponent of the Community Oriented Policing Services, a federal program that helps states and localities hire more police officers. The program was designed to reduce street crime, but after Sept. 11 it became a tool to fund first-responder programs and emergency-response equipment. He helped secure $1 billion in the stimulus to hire more than 5,000 additional police officers.

The Sept. 11 attacks also deepened Weiner's activism on Middle East issues. Weiner, who is Jewish, serves a heavily Jewish constituency and is an unwavering advocate for Israel. When Hamas, a militant Islamic party that has called for the destruction of Israel, won a majority of seats in 2006 Palestinian parliamentary elections, Weiner called for a halt to U.S. aid. Weiner also opposed efforts by the Bush and Obama administrations to sell weapons guidance systems, F-15 strike jets and military helicopters to Saudi Arabia.

Weiner cosponsored a 2009 immigration overhaul that would have tightened border security and provided a path to citizenship for illegal immigrants. He also pushed a bill in 2008 to make it easier for international fashion models to get work visas. While the tabloids chided the then-unmarried Weiner for trying to "increase his dating pool," he said the bill promoted economic development. The Judiciary Committee approved the bill, but it was never taken up by the House.

From his seat on the Energy and Commerce Committee, he led an investigation showing that Brooklyn women had the longest wait time for mammography screenings — 7.4 weeks — in the New York City area. During the debate over the health care overhaul in the 111th Congress, Weiner fought hard for inclusion of a government-run public option for health insurance in the final bill. He didn't win that argument, but Weiner, who sits on the Health Subcommittee, was among the few Democrats who vigorously defended the bill on the campaign trail in 2010.

Weiner narrowly lost the 2005 New York City Democratic mayoral primary and briefly considered another challenge to incumbent Michael Bloomberg in 2009. An October 2010 poll showed Weiner leading a pack of six potential candidates for the 2013 Democratic primary, but the congressman's Twitter folly might have doomed his chances at Gracie Mansion.

New York tabloids delight in describing Weiner as a "political hot dog" and pronouncing, "Weiner on a roll!" He doesn't mind the wordplay and uses it himself, but that imagery came back to haunt him in the Twitter scandal.

The middle son of a lawyer father and schoolteacher mother, Weiner grew up in the Park Slope section of Brooklyn. He attended the State University of New York at Plattsburgh because of its prowess in his sport, ice hockey. After graduation, he spent six years as an aide to Democrat Charles E. Schumer, then representing New York in the House. In 1991, at age 27, Weiner became the youngest person at the time ever elected to the New York City Council. Seven years later, after Schumer left the House seat open for a successful Senate run, Weiner won a tight four-way primary by 489 votes. He coasted in the strongly Democratic district in November and in every election since.

Key Votes

2010

Overhaul the nation's health insurance system	YES
Allow for repeal of "don't ask, don't tell"	YES
Overhaul financial services industry regulation	YES
Limit use of new Afghanistan War funds to troop withdrawal activities	YES
Change oversight of offshore drilling and lift oil spill liability cap	YES
Provide a path to legal status for some children of illegal immigrants	YES
Extend Bush-era income tax cuts for two years	NO

2009

Expand the Children's Health Insurance Program	YES
Provide $787 billion in tax cuts and spending increases to stimulate the economy	YES
Allow bankruptcy judges to modify certain primary-residence mortgages	YES
Create a cap-and-trade system to limit greenhouse gas emissions	YES
Provide $2 billion for the "cash for clunkers" program	YES
Establish the government as the sole provider of student loans	YES
Restrict federally funded insurance coverage for abortions in health care overhaul	NO

CQ Vote Studies

	PARTY UNITY		PRESIDENTIAL SUPPORT	
	SUPPORT	OPPOSE	SUPPORT	OPPOSE
2010	96%	4%	86%	14%
2009	99%	1%	94%	6%
2008	99%	1%	15%	85%
2007	97%	3%	6%	94%
2006	96%	4%	23%	77%

Interest Groups

	AFL-CIO	ADA	CCUS	ACU
2010	100%	100%	13%	0%
2009	100%	100%	33%	0%
2008	100%	100%	59%	0%
2007	96%	90%	60%	0%
2006	100%	95%	40%	8%

New York 9

Parts of Brooklyn and Queens — Forest Hills, Rockaway, Sheepshead Bay

The Democratic-leaning, white-majority 9th takes in north-central and western Queens and slides along the Jamaica Bay coastline into southeastern Brooklyn. Almost 70 percent of residents live in Queens.

The district extends westward from near Nassau County at the edge of Oakland Gardens through Fresh Meadows and Hillcrest to Forest Hills. There are some wealthy communities in Queens in the northern arm of the district.

The 9th narrows and runs south from Forest Park — the third-largest park in Queens and home to free Queens Symphony Orchestra concerts each summer — to take in part of the Woodhaven, Ozone Park and Lindenwood neighborhoods. In these areas, Hispanics now outnumber whites, and the Asian population is rapidly expanding.

The district also takes in much of the Rockaway area in far southwestern Queens along the Atlantic Ocean. Breezy Point, a tight-knit private community at the tip of the Rockaways, is a traditionally Irish-American enclave.

In Brooklyn, the 9th includes Floyd Bennett Field, which was New York City's first municipal airport, and much of the Gateway National Recreation Area on Jamaica Bay. Farther west, Sheepshead Bay, a popular area fishing spot, has seen an influx of Russian immigrants.

Generally a Democratic stronghold, the 9th, particularly its Brooklyn portion, moved right in the aftermath of the Sept. 11 terrorist attacks. John McCain won the Brooklyn part with 57 percent of the 2008 presidential vote. The 9th was the only New York City district in which Barack Obama did not improve on John Kerry's 2004 presidential vote percentage. Obama was held to his second-lowest percentage (55 percent) of any New York City district here, but registered Democrats continue to outnumber Republicans by a more than 3-to-1 margin.

Major Industry
Service, finance, insurance

Cities
New York (pt.), 660,306

Notable
Howard Hughes' historic 1938 around-the-world flight started and ended at Floyd Bennett Field.

Rep. Edolphus Towns (D)

Capitol Office
225-5936
www.house.gov/towns
2232 Rayburn Bldg. 20515-3210; fax 225-1018

Committees
Energy & Commerce
Oversight & Government Reform

Residence
Brooklyn

Born
July 21, 1934; Chadbourn, N.C.

Religion
Baptist

Family
Wife, Gwendolyn Towns; two children

Education
North Carolina A&T State U., B.S. 1956; Adelphi U.,
M.S.W. 1973

Military
Army, 1956-58

Career
Professor; hospital administrator

Political Highlights
Brooklyn Borough deputy president, 1976-82

ELECTION RESULTS

2010 GENERAL

Towns (D)	95,485	91.1%
Diana Muniz (R)	7,419	7.1%
Ernest Johnson (C)	1,853	1.8%

2010 PRIMARY

Towns (D)	21,846	69.2%
Kevin Powell (D)	9,733	30.8%

2008 GENERAL

Towns (D)	155,090	94.2%
Salvatore Grupico (R, C)	9,565	5.8%

Previous Winning Percentages
2006 (92%); 2004 (92%); 2002 (98%); 2000 (90%);
1998 (92%); 1996 (91%); 1994 (89%); 1992 (96%);
1990 (93%); 1988 (89%); 1986 (89%); 1984 (85%);
1982 (84%)

Elected 1982; 15th term

Known throughout his career as a low-key liberal who prefers to work quietly, Towns moved into the spotlight when he served one term as chairman of the Oversight and Government Reform Committee. But he chose not to make a run at leading the panel's minority in the 112th Congress, saying he didn't have the backing of Minority Leader Nancy Pelosi of California.

"I decided to withdraw my candidacy following a conversation with you when you made it clear that I did not have your support," he wrote to his party leader in late 2010 after Democrats lost their majority. Aides to Pelosi, who was giving up the Speaker's office, denied the charge — but it wasn't the first time Towns and Pelosi failed to see eye to eye.

Towns has found himself at odds with Democratic leaders before, though in the past few years he had fallen more in line with his party's agenda.

Towns' 2005 vote in favor of the Central American Free Trade Agreement highlighted his willingness to stray from party orthodoxy, angered labor leaders in New York and led Pelosi to threaten to boot him off the Energy and Commerce Committee for not voting often enough with his party. His vote helped give the GOP a 217-215 win. Pelosi was also angry that Towns was one of two Democrats who missed a vote on a Republican budget that squeaked through the House during the 109th Congress (2005-06). and in 2007, he joined with a minority of House Democrats to vote for a free-trade accord with Peru that U.S. labor groups were cool toward.

Overall, his party unity scores — the percentage of votes on which he sided with a majority of Democrats against a majority of Republicans — were consistently in the low- to mid-90s for two decades. "I look at legislation and if I think it's good, I will go against the grain and support it," he said. In the years of Democratic ascendancy, though, Towns voted with Democrats about 98 percent of the time.

In the 112th Congress (2011-12), Towns returned to Energy and Commerce, while also keeping his membership on the Oversight panel.

Towns can look back on a career with some notable legislative successes — which often drew scant attention in a town full of more prominent and self-promoting lawmakers.

He helped bring considerable largesse to his Brooklyn district — including $153 million for a federal courthouse and a $150 million reconstruction bond for the borough's Interfaith Hospital — and built a political base that could someday be useful to his son, New York Assemblyman Darryl Towns, if he decides to run for Congress.

A champion of technology issues, he won inclusion of a provision in the 1996 Telecommunications Act that allowed small businesses and minority- and women-owned businesses to put money from a new Telecommunications Development Fund into interest-bearing accounts associated with the fund.

And in 1990 he achieved passage of the Student Right to Know Act, requiring colleges to report the graduation rates of their scholarship athletes.

Towns handled several high-profile hearings during his tenure as Oversight chairman, including an investigation in early 2010 into a string of car accidents involving the unintended acceleration of Toyota vehicles. The investigation severely damaged Toyota's image and culminated with Towns threatening to subpoena the company's chief executive, who eventually accepted an invitation to testify.

Towns didn't hold back in criticizing officials from his own party. Towns and the panel's top Republican at the time, Darrell Issa of California, who is now chairman, held multiple hearings to grill Obama administration officials about their enforcement of the $700 billion financial sector rescue law enacted in 2008 and their dealings with insurance conglomerate American International Group.

And he sponsored two House-passed bills aimed at strengthening oversight of the White House and making the records of former presidents more accessible.

But Towns received heavy criticism from his Republican counterparts in January 2010 for hesitating to call for an investigation into the Christmas Day bombing attempt aboard a commercial airliner after conducting a hearing to investigate Tareq and Michaele Salahi's breach of security at a White House state dinner. Towns shrugged off the criticism: "That's just the heat you take for being in a high-profile position."

Despite all of the attention, Towns never fully embraced the publicity associated with his role as Oversight chairman, preferring to stick to the work and keep his head down. "No fanfare," he said of the role in which the combative California Democrat Henry A. Waxman crusaded — with cameras often at the ready — against Bush administration policies and personnel.

Towns was born in southeastern North Carolina, the son of a sharecropper. He graduated from historically black North Carolina A&T State University in Greensboro. After a two-year stint in the Army, he worked as a teacher and hospital administrator and earned a master's degree in social work from Adelphi University in New York. In 1976, he was appointed deputy borough president of Brooklyn.

His chance to run for the House came in 1982 after redistricting gave the 11th District an almost even split of blacks and Hispanics. With support from party regulars, he fended off two Hispanic primary contenders to win the nomination with 50 percent of the vote, then won easily in November. Redistricting in 1992 put him in a newly drawn but just as Democratic 10th District, where he has faced tough primary battles several times. But he took 89 percent of the vote in the 1994 general election and has garnered at least 90 percent of the vote in every general election since.

In 2006, two Democratic contenders used his CAFTA vote against him; Towns won by a narrower margin than would be expected of a 12-term veteran from New York City. Two years later, he again faced a Democratic opponent, writer and activist Kevin Powell, who accused him of a lackluster legislative record and accepting excessive contributions from business interests overseen by Energy and Commerce. Towns won with ease, and beat Powell again in 2010.

Key Votes

2010

Overhaul the nation's health insurance system	YES
Allow for repeal of "don't ask, don't tell"	YES
Overhaul financial services industry regulation	YES
Limit use of new Afghanistan War funds to troop withdrawal activities	YES
Change oversight of offshore drilling and lift oil spill liability cap	YES
Provide a path to legal status for some children of illegal immigrants	YES
Extend Bush-era income tax cuts for two years	NO

2009

Expand the Children's Health Insurance Program	YES
Provide $787 billion in tax cuts and spending increases to stimulate the economy	YES
Allow bankruptcy judges to modify certain primary-residence mortgages	YES
Create a cap-and-trade system to limit greenhouse gas emissions	YES
Provide $2 billion for the "cash for clunkers" program	YES
Establish the government as the sole provider of student loans	YES
Restrict federally funded insurance coverage for abortions in health care overhaul	NO

CQ Vote Studies

	PARTY UNITY		PRESIDENTIAL SUPPORT	
	SUPPORT	OPPOSE	SUPPORT	OPPOSE
2010	97%	3%	83%	17%
2009	99%	1%	96%	4%
2008	99%	1%	13%	87%
2007	98%	2%	7%	93%
2006	94%	6%	30%	70%

Interest Groups

	AFL-CIO	ADA	CCUS	ACU
2010	93%	100%	13%	0%
2009	100%	100%	40%	0%
2008	100%	100%	56%	0%
2007	96%	90%	65%	0%
2006	100%	95%	53%	8%

New York 10

Part of Brooklyn — Bedford-Stuyvesant, Canarsie, Downtown Brooklyn, East New York

The boomerang-shaped 10th begins just inland of Brooklyn's industrial waterfront in Downtown Brooklyn and heads east, bounding back southwest after reaching the Queens border. The overwhelmingly Democratic district contains New York City's highest percentage of black residents. In south-central Brooklyn, the 10th scoops up a chunk west of Flatbush Avenue that includes part of Midwood. East of this area, the 10th takes in Georgetown and Canarsie, bordering Jamaica Bay. Canarsie's racial composition has changed dramatically, as neighborhoods that were once largely white now host many blacks of Caribbean descent and African-American families who moved in from other neighborhoods. Many families here are solidly middle-class, an exception for most of the 10th.

In the elbow of the boomerang is East New York, home to the Gateway Center, a large suburban-style retail project that spurred affordable housing in the area.

Farther north and west, the 10th includes Bedford-Stuyvesant. Once beset by crime and poverty, the neighborhood is experiencing ongoing revitalization as "Bed-Stuy" natives work to aid the rebirth while minimizing displacement of residents. In its northwestern corner, the district takes in Fort Greene and part of Williamsburg.

The 10th's declining manufacturing base has caused unemployment, and a landmark Pfizer plant closed in 2008. Government jobs in Downtown Brooklyn and education jobs at the 10th's colleges — such as Brooklyn College, Long Island University-Brooklyn and New York City College of Technology — aid the economy.

GOP candidates have found some pockets of support from Jewish voters in Williamsburg, but they pale in comparison with the overwhelming Democratic voting patterns of the rest of the 10th. Barack Obama was able to secure 91 percent of the district's presidential vote in 2008.

Major Industry
Government, higher education, small business, retail

Cities
New York (pt.), 677,721

Notable
The Spike Lee film "Do the Right Thing" was set in Bedford-Stuyvesant.

Rep. Yvette D. Clarke (D)

Capitol Office
225-6231
clarke.house.gov
1029 Longworth Bldg. 20515-3211; fax 226-0112

Committees
Homeland Security
Small Business

Residence
Brooklyn

Born
Nov. 21, 1964; Brooklyn, N.Y.

Religion
Christian

Family
Single

Education
Oberlin College, attended 1982-86 (Black studies)

Career
Local economic development director; state agency aide; state legislative aide; day care and youth program coordinator

Political Highlights
New York City Council, 2002-07; sought Democratic nomination for U.S. House, 2004

ELECTION RESULTS

2010 GENERAL

Clarke (D)	104,297	90.5%
Hugh C. Carr (R)	10,858	9.4%

2010 PRIMARY

Clarke (D, WFM)	unopposed

2008 GENERAL

Clarke (D, WFM)	168,562	92.8%
Hugh C. Carr (R)	11,644	6.4%

Previous Winning Percentages
2006 (90%)

Elected 2006; 3rd term

The daughter of Jamaican immigrants, Clarke is a bridge between her ethnically diverse constituency and the Democratic leadership in Congress. She legislates with a Brooklyn accent but identifies heavily with her Caribbean roots, keeping a sharp focus on homeland security and immigration issues.

"When people say immigration, they think Spanish-speaking Latinos," she said. "I'm an English-speaking 'sista' born in Brooklyn but, you know, I am a part of the immigrant experience."

That connection has made Clarke a vocal proponent for overhauling the U.S. immigration system to ease the process and provide illegal immigrants with opportunities to get "in the queue" to become legal residents and citizens. In representing a district that is almost 40 percent foreign born, Clarke also promotes measures to ensure better treatment of immigrants living in the United States. Her first bill, introduced just shy of a year after her election, aimed to reduce the backlog in processing requests made by immigration officials to the FBI. Another, which she introduced in April 2009, would make it a federal crime to exploit individuals seeking immigration assistance.

Clarke's Caribbean roots, coupled with the presence of a large Haitian immigrant community in her district, have also made her a tireless advocate for Haiti, even before the January 2010 earthquake. During her first term, she traveled to Haiti with the Congressional Black Caucus and backed efforts to cancel the country's debt. After the quake, she introduced a bill to allow Haitians with immigration petitions approved on or before the disaster to join their relatives in the United States, and authored another to create a fund for investing in businesses owned by Haitian citizens. As a member of the Homeland Security Committee, Clarke believes helping Haiti is both a moral obligation and in the strategic interest of the United States. "Those who wish to do harm to them and to our nation could certainly take root in that environment," she said.

On the Homeland Security panel, Clarke is the ranking Democrat on the Cybersecurity, Infrastructure Protection and Security Technologies panel. She has promoted efforts to protect chemical facilities and domestic supplies of radiological materials from terrorists.

In March 2010, she introduced a bill aimed at identifying and combating cybercrime abroad. She also pushed for a bill sponsored by Massachusetts Democrat Edward J. Markey that would authorize the Federal Energy Regulatory Commission to issue orders to protect the U.S. grid in the event of a presidential emergency declaration; the House passed the measure in June 2010 but it was not taken up by the full Senate.

At the same time, she has sought to ease the effects of some post-Sept. 11 terrorism laws on innocent citizens. In the 110th and 111th Congresses (2007-08; 2009-10), the House passed her bills to order the Homeland Security Department to create a comprehensive list of people cleared of alleged connections to terrorism. She said it would decrease the hassle for travelers subjected to repeat searches because they share a name or other identifying feature with someone on the terrorist watch list. The Senate did not take up either measure.

Clarke is a staunch liberal who supports abortion rights and voted to repeal the statutory ban on openly gay people serving in the military. A senior Democratic whip, she voted with her leadership 99 percent of the time on votes that split majorities of the two parties in the 111th Congress — including votes in favor of the $787 billion economic stimulus package, expansion of the Children's Health Insurance Program and creation of a cap-and-trade system to limit carbon emissions. She also backed the health care overhaul and was a strong proponent of establishing a government-run insurance program.

As secretary of the Congressional Black Caucus, however, she joined some of her colleagues in voting against a Democrat-backed business-tax exemption and transportation extension measure in March 2010 after a summer jobs program was dropped from the final language. Calling it a "protest vote," Clarke said the amended measure did "not go far enough" to create jobs for out-of-work constituents.

Clarke also looks out for her diverse constituency on the Small Business Committee, where she introduced a measure in 2009 to create grant and mentorship programs for small construction firms owned by women, veterans and minorities.

Born in Brooklyn, Clarke resides in the same Flatbush neighborhood where she grew up. Her father, Leslie L. Clarke Sr., was a civil engineer for the Port Authority of New York and New Jersey, while her mother, Una S.T. Clarke, worked as an accountant, early-childhood educator and education consultant before being elected to the New York City Council in 1991.

After attending New York City public schools, Clarke received a scholarship to Oberlin College, where she majored in black studies. She later served as business development director for the Bronx Empowerment Zone and the first director of the Bronx branch of the New York City Empowerment Zone.

Clarke took over her mother's seat on the city council when she stepped down because of term limits in 2001. She was re-elected twice. On the council, Clarke won adoption of an ordinance requiring city government buildings to have twice as many restroom stalls for women as for men. In 2007, once in Congress, she cosponsored a bill by her New York Democratic colleague Edolphus Towns that would apply the same requirement to federal buildings, and in the 111th Congress backed a pared version requiring at least a 1-to-1 ratio.

In 2000, Una Clarke lost a primary contest to incumbent House Democrat Major R. Owens. Four years later, the younger Clarke took her turn against Owens and lost, drawing 29 percent of the vote in a four-way primary won by Owens with a plurality.

When Owens announced that he would step down after the completion of his 12th term in January 2007, Clarke decided to try again. She bested a trio of other hopefuls, including the congressman's son, Chris Owens, to claim the nomination — tantamount to election in the heavily Democratic district. She sailed to re-election in 2008 and 2010.

Key Votes

2010
Overhaul the nation's health insurance system	YES
Allow for repeal of "don't ask, don't tell"	YES
Overhaul financial services industry regulation	YES
Limit use of new Afghanistan War funds to troop withdrawal activities	YES
Change oversight of offshore drilling and lift oil spill liability cap	YES
Provide a path to legal status for some children of illegal immigrants	YES
Extend Bush-era income tax cuts for two years	NO

2009
Expand the Children's Health Insurance Program	YES
Provide $787 billion in tax cuts and spending increases to stimulate the economy	YES
Allow bankruptcy judges to modify certain primary-residence mortgages	YES
Create a cap-and-trade system to limit greenhouse gas emissions	YES
Provide $2 billion for the "cash for clunkers" program	YES
Establish the government as the sole provider of student loans	YES
Restrict federally funded insurance coverage for abortions in health care overhaul	NO

CQ Vote Studies
	PARTY UNITY		PRESIDENTIAL SUPPORT	
	SUPPORT	OPPOSE	SUPPORT	OPPOSE
2010	98%	2%	76%	24%
2009	99%	1%	96%	4%
2008	99%	1%	16%	84%
2007	99%	1%	6%	94%

Interest Groups
	AFL-CIO	ADA	CCUS	ACU
2010	93%	95%	25%	4%
2009	100%	100%	33%	0%
2008	100%	100%	56%	0%
2007	100%	75%	64%	0%

New York 11
Part of Brooklyn — Flatbush, Crown Heights, Brownsville, Park Slope

The ethnically diverse 11th District, nestled in central Brooklyn, has remained majority-black despite changing demographics over the last decade; minorities overall make up almost three-fourths of the district's population.

At the heart of the 11th is Flatbush, a working-class neighborhood with a "country in the city" atmosphere that is still home to many black and Hispanic residents as well as Caribbean immigrants. In the district's far south, Midwood, traditionally an Orthodox Jewish center, has experienced an influx of diverse immigrant populations. Brownsville to the far east is heavily black, but white families have been moving in.

The 11th extends northwest through Crown Heights, home to the world headquarters of the Chabad-Lubavitch Hasidic Jews as well as a sizable black population. Like areas to the north (in the 10th), this area has seen recent gentrification, and some native residents have been priced out of their homes.

To the northwest, Prospect Park attracts more than 8 million visitors each year, and residents and visitors head to nearby Brooklyn Botanic Garden and the Brooklyn Museum of Art, which lures enthusiasts to its Egyptology collection. Further west, the 11th includes affluent pockets in Park Slope, Carroll Gardens, Cobble Hill and Brooklyn Heights.

Many residents work at the district's medical facilities, including Kings County Hospital Center and the State University of New York Downstate Medical Center. Dramatic increases in the number of eclectic small businesses and restaurants have helped support the local economy for much of the last decade.

The 11th's GOP pockets have a minimal effect on elections: Barack Obama won more than 90 percent of the district's 2008 presidential vote.

Major Industry
Health care, retail

Cities
New York (pt.), 632,408

Notable
Ebbets Field, where the Brooklyn Dodgers played from 1913 to 1957, was demolished in 1960 and replaced by a housing complex; the West Indian Day Carnival Parade attracts millions of visitors each year on Labor Day.

Rep. Nydia M. Velázquez (D)

Capitol Office
225-2361
www.house.gov/velazquez
2302 Rayburn Bldg. 20515-3212; fax 226-0327

Committees
Financial Services
Small Business - Ranking Member

Residence
Brooklyn

Born
March 28, 1953; Yabucoa, P.R.

Religion
Roman Catholic

Family
Divorced

Education
U. of Puerto Rico, B.A. 1974 (political science);
New York U., M.A. 1976 (political science)

Career
Puerto Rican Community Affairs Department
director; professor; congressional aide

Political Highlights
New York City Council, 1984-85; defeated for
election to New York City Council, 1984

ELECTION RESULTS

2010 GENERAL

Velázquez (D)	68,624	93.8%
Alice Gaffney (C)	4,482	6.1%

2010 PRIMARY

Velázquez (D, WFM)	unopposed

2008 GENERAL

Velázquez (D, WFM)	123,046	90.0%
Allan E. Romaguera (R, C)	13,747	10.0%

Previous Winning Percentages
2006 (90%); 2004 (86%); 2002 (96%); 2000 (86%);
1998 (84%); 1996 (85%); 1994 (92%); 1992 (77%)

Elected 1992; 10th term

Velázquez pairs liberal views on most foreign and social policy issues with support for the business community, especially the small-business sector she oversees as the ranking Democrat on the Small Business Committee.

Her views make for an unusual jumble that places her to the left of most members of her caucus and President Obama on the former set of issues, and to the right on the latter set.

Velázquez (full name: NID-ee-uh veh-LASS-kez) usually sticks to her guns, which meant — at least in 2010 — that she was not as reliable an ally for the president as one might have expected of a New York City Democrat.

On votes where Obama made his position clear, Velázquez gave her support 79 percent of the time in 2010, well below the Democratic Caucus average of 86 percent. She refused to go along with Obama's wishes in December, for example, after the president cut a deal with Republicans to extend tax cuts enacted under President George W. Bush. Earlier in the year, she voted twice to limit Obama's ability to continue the war in Afghanistan. In each case she was among a minority of Democrats defying the president, and in each case the president ultimately got his way.

Not so earlier in the year, though, when Obama asked the House to cut funding for an alternative engine for a fighter plane that the Pentagon said it didn't need. Velázquez helped hand Obama a loss, though the president got his revenge when the House voted to kill the engine in 2011.

Also in the 112th Congress (2011-12), Velázquez backed legislation to repeal a provision in the 2010 health care overhaul that small businesses had complained would subject them to burdensome new tax compliance rules. The provision was designed to capture more taxes that businesses owe, but sometimes don't pay, and to help pay for the health care law. But Velázquez said the costs outweighed the benefits. "Our tax code should reward growth, not serve as a roadblock to growth," she said.

Velázquez's liberal positions — she is critical of the 1996 welfare overhaul law for being too harsh on the poor, and she favors more liberal immigration policies — fit well with those of her constituents, a majority of whom are working-class minorities.

Her pro-business stances reflect her position of authority on the Small Business panel and with her donor base. Her biggest contributors are bankers and lawyers from New York's financial industry. In addition to her seat on Small Business, Velázquez holds a seat on the Financial Services Committee, which makes her especially important to that group.

Velázquez also takes plenty of money from unions, which can result in some tough decision-making, such as when public-sector unions pressure government agencies to contract out less work. Velázquez has been more willing than most Democrats to defend government contractors, particularly small companies and those owned by veterans and minorities.

Among Hispanic members of Congress, Velázquez is a pioneer. She was the first Puerto Rican woman elected to Congress and in 2007 became the first Hispanic woman to chair a full House committee. She also chaired the Congressional Hispanic Caucus in 2010 and took a lead role in pushing for legislation to allow the children of illegal immigrants who have gone on to U.S. colleges to have a chance at citizenship. The House passed the measure, but it stalled in the Senate.

She's sometimes played a prominent role in the politics of her ancestral home, opposing efforts by Congress to authorize a plebiscite that would have Puerto Ricans decide whether the island should become a state or remain a territory of the United States. Velázquez said she didn't mind a fair vote, but that the bill in question favored the statehood option. Her stance put her at odds with fellow New York Democrat Jose E. Serrano.

Velázquez was raised in Yabucoa, in the sugar cane region in southeastern Puerto Rico, with her twin sister and seven other siblings. Her father cut cane and her mother helped make ends meet by selling food to other cane workers. Her father also made cinder blocks and owned a cockfighting pit. He had only a third-grade education, but was a community leader and founded a political party in their hometown.

Velázquez was an eager student, skipping grades and entering the University of Puerto Rico at age 16. She was the first in her family to receive a college diploma, graduating with a degree in political science.

She went to New York City for graduate school and taught Puerto Rican Studies at Hunter College. She then became a special assistant to Democratic Rep. Edolphus Towns. In 1984, New York City council members appointed her to the council to replace one of their members who had been convicted of corruption. At 31, she was the first Hispanic woman to serve on the council, but served only two years before losing an election. She went back to Puerto Rico and worked in the territorial government, eventually returning to the mainland to oversee Puerto Rico's community relations office in New York City and, in 1992, to make another bid for public office.

Redistricting following the 1990 Census had required the New York State Assembly to eliminate three House seats. At the same time, Hispanic population growth had put pressure on the legislature to create a new seat where a Hispanic candidate would be favored. One result was elimination of nineterm Democrat Stephen J. Solarz's Brooklyn seat and the creation of a new, largely Hispanic district that would include parts of Brooklyn, Queens and lower Manhattan. That was Velázquez's opening. Solarz ran, too, but Velázquez won by 5 percentage points.

After the primary, medical records leaked to the New York Post revealed that less than a year earlier, Velázquez had tried to commit suicide by taking an overdose of sleeping pills. She held a press conference in which she acknowledged the attempt to take her own life, explaining that she was at the time dealing with depression stemming from her mother's health and a brother's addiction to drugs. Voters took the revelation in stride, and Velázquez won the general election with 77 percent of the vote. She has won re-election by solid margins in each election since.

Key Votes

2010

Overhaul the nation's health insurance system	YES
Allow for repeal of "don't ask, don't tell"	YES
Overhaul financial services industry regulation	YES
Limit use of new Afghanistan War funds to troop withdrawal activities	YES
Change oversight of offshore drilling and lift oil spill liability cap	YES
Provide a path to legal status for some children of illegal immigrants	YES
Extend Bush-era income tax cuts for two years	NO

2009

Expand the Children's Health Insurance Program	YES
Provide $787 billion in tax cuts and spending increases to stimulate the economy	YES
Allow bankruptcy judges to modify certain primary-residence mortgages	YES
Create a cap-and-trade system to limit greenhouse gas emissions	YES
Provide $2 billion for the "cash for clunkers" program	YES
Establish the government as the sole provider of student loans	YES
Restrict federally funded insurance coverage for abortions in health care overhaul	NO

CQ Vote Studies

	PARTY UNITY		PRESIDENTIAL SUPPORT	
	SUPPORT	OPPOSE	SUPPORT	OPPOSE
2010	96%	4%	79%	21%
2009	99%	1%	94%	6%
2008	100%	0%	14%	86%
2007	99%	1%	4%	96%
2006	99%	1%	10%	90%

Interest Groups

	AFL-CIO	ADA	CCUS	ACU
2010	100%	100%	13%	0%
2009	100%	100%	33%	0%
2008	100%	100%	50%	0%
2007	96%	95%	60%	0%
2006	93%	100%	27%	4%

New York 12

Lower East Side of Manhattan; parts of Brooklyn and Queens

The 12th combines part of Manhattan's Lower East Side with portions of Brooklyn and Queens. Minorities make up nearly three-fourths of the population of this working-class Democratic bastion, which still has a Hispanic plurality (45 percent) despite a decade of demographic shifts including an influx of white and Asian residents. The 12th's economy, anchored by the health care sector, also retains some of its blue-collar legacy affiliated with industries along the East River.

Two-thirds of the 12th's residents live in Brooklyn. In its southwestern corner, the district begins in Sunset Park, home to large Hispanic, Chinese and South Asian populations. The district takes in part of Park Slope and Red Hook and then narrows along Brooklyn's waterfront before enveloping the Brooklyn Navy Yard. It also includes part of Williamsburg and Greenpoint, which has a large Polish population. New high-rises in the Greenpoint and Williamsburg industrial waterfront areas may replace historic factories and port facilities, and local residents hope to keep vibrant commercial

corridors and residential areas from being dwarfed by new construction. The 12th also sends a sliver southeast, along the Brooklyn-Queens border, to the heavily Hispanic neighborhoods of Bushwick, Cypress Hills and City Line.

On the Queens side of the border, the district takes in parts of the Sunnyside and Woodside neighborhoods. Originally a heavily Irish area, the 12th's part of Queens now includes residents with a diverse mix of ethnic backgrounds, including a growing Hispanic population from many different countries. The district also includes the Brooklyn, Manhattan and Williamsburg bridges, and it crosses the East River into Manhattan to take in Chinatown, most of Little Italy, Alphabet City and the Lower East Side.

Major Industry
Health care, service

Cities
New York (pt.), 672,358

Notable
Brooklyn's Green-Wood Cemetery has more than 560,000 interred, including Leonard Bernstein, Horace Greeley and notorious 19th-century New York politician William M. "Boss" Tweed.

Rep. Michael G. Grimm (R)

Capitol Office
225-3371
grimm.house.gov
512 Cannon Bldg. 20515-3213; fax 226-1272

Committees
Financial Services

Residence
Staten Island

Born
Feb. 7, 1970; Brooklyn, N.Y.

Religion
Roman Catholic

Family
Divorced

Education
Baruch College, B.B.A. 1994; New York Law School, J.D. 2002

Military
Marine Corps, 1989-90; Marine Corps Reserve, 1990-97

Career
Health food store owner; FBI agent; stockbroker

Political Highlights
No previous office

ELECTION RESULTS

2010 GENERAL
Grimm (R)	65,024	51.3%
Michael E. McMahon (D)	60,773	47.9%

2010 PRIMARY
Grimm (R)	9,631	68.3%
Michael A. Allegretti (R)	4,476	31.7%

Elected 2010; 1st term

Grimm cites his days in the Marine Corps when he talks about the importance of teamwork in policymaking, and what he says is the lack of it in Congress. "It's stifled our ability to lead," he says. "In the military, there are arguments, there are fights. The Navy fights with the Marines. But when it's time to get back to work, we all have each other's hands and move forward."

"Congress needs to take a page out of the military's book," he continued. "At the end of the day, we're all Americans."

Grimm describes his politics as "just right of center" — he voted, along with every other Republican in the 112th Congress (2011-12), to repeal the 2010 health care overhaul law and opposes gay marriage. But he says he could side with Democrats if they introduce legislation he thinks would benefit his constituents. "If they put forth a bill that's good for my district and this country, I'm supporting it . . . regardless of who gets the credit."

He took on the conservative wing of his own party early when he criticized tea party activists and the "extreme wing of the Republican Party" for opposing a three-week stopgap spending bill for fiscal 2011.

"If we're going to do what we set out to do, we have to set realistic expectations, and cannot bow to the extreme right or left," he said.

His days as an undercover FBI agent on Wall Street, cracking down on white-collar crime, position him to back moves against corruption in big businesses. The only Republican House member from New York City, he will put those skills to use as a member of the Financial Services Committee.

As founder of a health-food restaurant and owner of a biofuels company, he supports policy initiatives that could help struggling and aspiring entrepreneurs alike. He advocates dispensing with capital gains taxes for the next two years and temporarily reducing the payroll tax by 30 percent to 40 percent.

Grimm defeated Michael Allegretti, a former aide to New York Mayor Michael Bloomberg, by almost 2-to-1 in the 2010 GOP primary, and took on one-term Democrat Michael E. McMahon in the general election. He rode the national Republican wave to a 3-percentage-point victory in the GOP-leaning district.

New York 13
Staten Island; part of southwest Brooklyn

The 13th District includes all of Staten Island (Richmond County) and a small portion of southwestern Brooklyn across the Verrazano-Narrows Bridge.

More than two-thirds of the district's mostly white and upper-middle-class population lives on Staten Island.

Staten Island is by far the least ethnically diverse of New York's five boroughs and is 64 percent white. Hispanic and black populations live mostly in the borough's northeast. There is an Asian presence in some mid-island neighborhoods, and the district has a significant Arab population, as well. Staten Island University Hospital is a key employer, and retail, finance and insurance jobs provide work.

The Brooklyn part of the 13th extends from the Verrazano into Bay Ridge, Dyker Heights and part of Bensonhurst, before buttonhooking south of Cropsey Avenue and moving east to take in part of Gravesend.

The 13th has a large Italian-American population on both sides of the Verrazano, and the predominately Catholic community gives the district a socially conservative edge. Although it has been a GOP stronghold for 30 years, the district sent a one-term Democrat to the U.S. House in 2008.

John McCain won a slim 51 percent of the 2008 presidential vote in the 13th, the only New York City district he carried.

Major Industry
Health care, retail, communications

Military Bases
Fort Hamilton (Army), 139 military, 399 civilian (2007)

Cities
New York (pt.), 686,525

Notable
The 1977 disco movie "Saturday Night Fever" was set in Bay Ridge.

Rep. Carolyn B. Maloney (D)

Capitol Office
225-7944
maloney.house.gov
2332 Rayburn Bldg. 20515-3214; fax 225-4709

Committees
Financial Services
Oversight & Government Reform
Joint Economic

Residence
Manhattan

Born
Feb. 19, 1946; Greensboro, N.C.

Religion
Presbyterian

Family
Widowed; two children

Education
Greensboro College, A.B. 1968

Career
State legislative aide; teacher

Political Highlights
New York City Council, 1982-93

ELECTION RESULTS

2010 GENERAL

Maloney (D)	107,327	75.0%
Ryan Brumberg (R)	32,065	22.4%
Tim Healy (C)	1,891	1.3%
Dino LaVerghetta (I)	1,617	1.1%

2010 PRIMARY

Maloney (D)	33,499	83.1%
Reshma Saujani (D)	6,799	16.9%

2008 GENERAL

Maloney (D, WFM)	183,190	79.9%
Robert G. Heim (R)	43,365	18.9%
Isiah Matos (LIBERT)	2,659	1.2%

Previous Winning Percentages
2006 (85%); 2004 (81%); 2002 (75%); 2000 (74%);
1998 (77%); 1996 (72%); 1994 (64%); 1992 (50%)

Elected 1992; 10th term

An unstinting advocate for women's rights, consumers, and the survivors and families of the Sept. 11 terrorist attacks, the liberal Maloney is a hard-charging advocate of government action across a broad range of issues.

She lost a bid for the ranking Democrat post on the Oversight and Government Reform Committee in the 112th Congress (2011-12) to the less senior Elijah E. Cummings of Maryland.

She also sits on the Financial Services and Joint Economic committees, where she had a hand in addressing the meltdown in the financial services industry in the waning days of George W. Bush's administration and the first years of President Obama's term. She helped hash out differences between the House and Senate versions of a financial regulatory overhaul enacted in 2010.

In fall 2008, she helped negotiate a $700 billion package to shore up the nation's financial system. Speaking on the House floor that September, Maloney said, "A wholesale failure of the banking system would be the financial equivalent of an economic heart attack." She joined other Democrats in early 2009 in seeking to recoup funds from the financial rescue law that were paid out in million-dollar bonuses to executives at American International Group Inc.

An equally important priority for her on Financial Services is addressing credit card billing practices, and she serves as ranking Democrat on the Financial Institutions and Consumer Credit Subcommittee. In 2009, Money magazine named her the "best friend a credit card user ever had."

In 2008, as the first woman to chair the Joint Economic Committee, she claimed a personal victory when the House passed her measure to curb practices such as retroactively increasing interest rates. The bill was vigorously opposed by the credit industry and many Republicans. The Senate did not take it up in the 110th Congress (2007-08). But she resumed her efforts in early 2009. The 111th Congress (2009-10) cleared the legislation and it was signed into law.

Maloney, who wears a silver bracelet with "9-11-01" engraved on it, has been tireless in her efforts on behalf of survivors of the 2001 terrorist attacks and the first-responders who worked to save them.

She was in her Capitol Hill office when a friend called to tell her a plane had crashed into the World Trade Center. After watching the news, she drove to New York and went straight to the site. Discovering that responders needed phones, she called Florida Republican C.W. Bill Young, then the chairman of the Appropriations Committee. Phones arrived the next morning.

To quantify New York City's economic losses and justify increased federal assistance, she commissioned studies from the Federal Reserve, the Government Accountability Office and the Congressional Research Service.

In the 111th Congress, Maloney spearheaded a bipartisan legislative effort to provide health care, monitoring and treatment for first-responders and community members exposed to deadly toxins in the aftermath of the World Trade Center collapse. "It's the least we can do as a grateful nation for the men and women who, as everyone was running away, ran in to save the lives of others," she said.

The measure was stalled for months by concerns about the cost, and the chambers didn't send the bill to the president until three days before Christmas 2010, when the House cleared it in its last roll call of the 111th Congress.

In 2005, she and New York Republican Peter T. King secured $75 million for the Centers for Disease Control and Prevention to screen, monitor and treat those injured or sickened in the attacks and their aftermath.

From her seat on Oversight and Government Reform, Maloney helped win enactment in 2004 of a reorganization of U.S. intelligence operations in response to the recommendations of the panel that investigated the attacks. She called it the "most important work I've done in Congress."

Maloney, a former co-chairwoman of the Caucus for Women's Issues, has long been concerned about the rights of women. She is the author of "Rumors of Our Progress Have Been Greatly Exaggerated: Why Women's Lives Aren't Getting Any Easier — And How We Can Make Real Progress For Ourselves and Our Daughters."

Maloney sought to demonstrate the plight of Afghan women under the Taliban by going to the House floor in October 2001 in a head-to-toe blue burqa. She repeatedly pushes without success an equal-rights constitutional amendment. She has had more success with narrower measures. In 1999, her legislation to permit breast-feeding on federal property became law. And in 2006, she and Republican Deborah Pryce of Ohio saw their bill to address sex trafficking enacted as part of a broader measure.

In 2010, Maloney pushed a requirement for private nursing areas for hourly employees and creation of an Office of Women's Health in the executive branch — both provisions were included in the health care overhaul enacted in March 2010.

Maloney hails from Greensboro, N.C. She visited New York City in her early 20s and decided to stay, eventually teaching adult education in East Harlem. She said she realized government had a greater impact than any teacher on the education of the city's youth, and she moved to Albany to work for the state legislature.

Five years later, she was elected to the New York City Council, where she served about 10 years.

In June 1992, Maloney stood in a scrum of New York's most powerful Democratic women, including former vice presidential candidate Geraldine Ferraro, waiting for the Supreme Court decision in *Planned Parenthood v. Casey*, an abortion case in which the court upheld Pennsylvania's parental consent and 24-hour waiting period while reaffirming the 1973 *Roe v. Wade* decision that legalized abortion.

Saying she was angry and frustrated by the decision, Maloney announced her intention to run against seven-term GOP Rep. Bill Green. Media hype about the "Year of the Woman" lent momentum to her underdog challenge. She also benefited from redistricting, which forced Green to campaign on some unfamiliar turf. She won narrowly, but her election victories since have been runaways in the overwhelmingly Democratic district.

Key Votes

2010

Overhaul the nation's health insurance system	YES
Allow for repeal of "don't ask, don't tell"	YES
Overhaul financial services industry regulation	YES
Limit use of new Afghanistan War funds to troop withdrawal activities	YES
Change oversight of offshore drilling and lift oil spill liability cap	YES
Provide a path to legal status for some children of illegal immigrants	YES
Extend Bush-era income tax cuts for two years	YES

2009

Expand the Children's Health Insurance Program	YES
Provide $787 billion in tax cuts and spending increases to stimulate the economy	YES
Allow bankruptcy judges to modify certain primary-residence mortgages	YES
Create a cap-and-trade system to limit greenhouse gas emissions	YES
Provide $2 billion for the "cash for clunkers" program	YES
Establish the government as the sole provider of student loans	YES
Restrict federally funded insurance coverage for abortions in health care overhaul	NO

CQ Vote Studies

	PARTY UNITY		PRESIDENTIAL SUPPORT	
	SUPPORT	OPPOSE	SUPPORT	OPPOSE
2010	98%	2%	87%	13%
2009	99%	1%	97%	3%
2008	99%	1%	17%	83%
2007	99%	1%	4%	96%
2006	94%	6%	33%	67%

Interest Groups

	AFL-CIO	ADA	CCUS	ACU
2010	100%	95%	25%	0%
2009	100%	95%	36%	0%
2008	100%	95%	65%	0%
2007	95%	90%	58%	0%
2006	93%	85%	43%	8%

New York 14

East Side of Manhattan; western Queens

Home to New York City's wealthy high society, the 14th's traditional old-money elite has been partially displaced by young, professional "limousine liberals," many of whom are in high-paying white-collar industries. The 14th has the nation's highest percentage of residents with at least a bachelor's degree (65 percent) and the country's highest percentage of people who walk to work (21 percent).

Taking in all of Central Park in the district's northwest corner, the 14th's western edge roughly follows Broadway south toward Union Square before narrowing to reach the Lower East Side. Landmarks include Carnegie Hall, Rockefeller Center, Grand Central Terminal, the United Nations, the Chrysler Building and Fifth Avenue's Museum Mile, which includes the Metropolitan Museum of Art.

But the tony neighborhoods of Manhattan's East Side do not tell the whole story of a district that crosses Roosevelt Island to pick up ethnic working-class sections of Queens, such as Astoria, which is still the city's traditional Greek hub despite an influx of other ethnic groups.

The 14th is both economically and geographically diverse — more than one-third of the district's population speaks a language other than English at home. Long Island City, once an industrial powerhouse, experienced decline but is seeing a resurgence through commercial development and the construction of waterfront luxury apartments. A burgeoning arts community has taken advantage of affordable housing in the area. Queens residents make up 29 percent of the district.

Republicans generally are unable to compete against the overwhelming Democratic presence in this district: Barack Obama won 78 percent of the 14th's presidential vote in 2008, and registered Democrats outnumber Republicans nearly 4 to 1. Extremely active politically, district residents are known for making some of the largest campaign contributions in the nation.

Major Industry

Finance, health care, tourism, communications, advertising, publishing

Cities

New York (pt.), 652,681

Notable

Gracie Mansion, in Carl Schurz Park, is the official residence of New York's mayor; the Museum of the Moving Image is in Astoria.

Rep. Charles B. Rangel (D)

Capitol Office
225-4365
www.house.gov/rangel
2354 Rayburn Bldg. 20515-3215; fax 225-0816

Committees
Ways & Means
Joint Taxation

Residence
Manhattan

Born
June 11, 1930; Manhattan, N.Y.

Religion
Roman Catholic

Family
Wife, Alma Rangel; two children

Education
New York U., B.S. 1957; St. John's U., LL.B. 1960

Military
Army, 1948-52

Career
Lawyer

Political Highlights
Assistant U.S. attorney, 1961-62; N.Y. Assembly,
1967-71; sought Democratic nomination for N.Y. City
Council president, 1969

ELECTION RESULTS

2010 GENERAL

Rangel (D)	91,225	80.2%
Michel Faulkner (R)	11,754	10.3%
Craig Schley (INDC)	7,803	6.9%
Roger Calero (SW)	2,647	2.3%

2010 PRIMARY

Rangel (D)	26,101	51.2%
Adam Clayton Powell IV (D)	11,834	23.2%
Joyce S. Johnson (D)	6,444	12.6%
Ruben D. Vargas (D)	2,703	5.3%
Jonathan Tasini (D)	2,634	5.2%
Vincent Scott Morgan (D)	1,210	2.4%

Previous Winning Percentages
2008 (89%); 2006 (94%); 2004 (91%); 2002 (88%);
2000 (92%); 1998 (93%); 1996 (91%); 1994 (97%);
1992 (95%); 1990 (97%); 1988 (97%); 1986 (96%);
1984 (97%); 1982 (97%); 1980 (96%); 1978 (96%);
1976 (97%); 1974 (97%); 1972 (96%); 1970 (87%)

Elected 1970; 21st term

Defiant and combative as ethics charges weigh on his political viability and reputation, Rangel occupies a precarious position as he enters his fifth decade in the House.

In a three-year span, he reached the pinnacle of his congressional career and then plummeted. After becoming the first black chairman of the Ways and Means Committee and serving as an influential voice on economic policy in 2007, Rangel descended rapidly in a swirl of ethics complaints and embarrassing revelations that cost him the gavel and led to his censure by the House in December 2010.

Five months earlier, the House Ethics Committee (then known as the Committee on Standards of Official Conduct) issued 13 charges against Rangel on a variety of matters, including use of a rent-stabilized Harlem apartment for a campaign office, failure to disclose personal assets and use of congressional letterhead as part of a fundraising campaign for a college center to be named for him. Most damaging to the leader of the tax-writing committee, Rangel was charged with under-reporting rental income from a villa in the Dominican Republic.

Rangel acknowledged mistakes, but said he was not corrupt and that he had not abused his office for personal gain. The ethics charges dogged him during an unusually competitive primary in September 2010, but he marshaled the campaign contributions and support he had built for years to win 51 percent of the vote and dispatch five challengers. He was then re-elected easily in the overwhelmingly Democratic district.

Although he remains a senior member of Ways and Means, Rangel's influence in the House has diminished considerably. Charming, funny and raspy-voiced, Rangel is still well-liked by his colleagues, but he can no longer collect campaign contributions as easily as he did while he was chairman.

And, even if he wanted to spread campaign cash around the Democratic Caucus, many of his colleagues wouldn't accept it. Some even called for his resignation.

But Rangel refused to go away quietly. In an August 2010 stemwinder on the House floor, he pleaded for a speedy, full ethics hearing. "I don't want anyone to feel embarrassed, awkward," he said. "Hey, if I was you, I may want me to go away, too. I am not going away. I am here."

Rangel had to relinquish the Ways and Means gavel even before the ethics panel issued its report. He stepped aside under pressure in March 2010 after a separate investigation led to the committee admonishing Rangel for accepting improper corporate sponsorship of conferences in the Caribbean.

But he retains seniority. On April 10, 2008, Rangel and Pete Stark of California, the No. 2 Democrat on Ways and Means, marked 12,500 days of service on the panel — the longest tenure in the committee's 220-year history.

On policy, Rangel defies easy classification. At first glance, he seems like an old-school liberal and can be unyielding in partisan fights. But business lobbyists and many Republicans know a different Rangel. When he took charge of Ways and Means in 2007, he tried to change the tone within the committee, which had soured under abrasive Republican Bill Thomas of California, who had just retired after six years as chairman. At the start of the 110th Congress (2007-08), he worked with the new top Republican, Jim McCrery of Louisiana, to advance legislation providing small-business tax breaks, relief for Hurricane Katrina victims, taxpayer identity protections and a ban on genetic discrimination by health insurers.

Rangel struck several other important agreements later in the 110th. He negotiated a trade framework with the Bush administration that strengthened labor and environmental standards, allowing a free-trade deal with Peru to become law. He paired a minimum wage increase with tax breaks, and pushed an economic stimulus package through Congress that provided tax rebates to individuals and investment incentives to businesses.

Even somewhat marginalized in the 111th Congress (2009-10), Rangel still helped shape the economic stimulus in early 2009 and the health care overhaul in 2010. He was on the outside looking in, though, as President Obama and Senate Republicans struck a deal to extend the Bush-era tax cuts for two years, a compromise Rangel voted against.

Over his long career, the Harlem-based Rangel has had his greatest legislative success with efforts to spur economic development in low-income neighborhoods. He wrote the 1993 "empowerment zones" law providing tax credits to businesses that move into blighted areas and the 1986 tax credit for developers of low-income housing. He is also one of the House's leading advocates of expanded trade with Caribbean countries, the ancestral home for many of his upper-Manhattan constituents.

Rangel was a passionate critic of the 1996 law ending welfare's status as an entitlement. After the U.S. invasion of Iraq in 2003, he spoke out against the military action and proposed legislation to reinstate the draft. He argued that the all-volunteer military relied too heavily on poor and working-class enlistees who needed jobs and education benefits.

His tenure had not been without setbacks even before his recent troubles. He was among the members swept up in the House bank scandal in the early 1990s, and in 1999 he was entangled in a financial scandal at Harlem's historic Apollo Theater. The state of New York later dropped a lawsuit against Rangel and others on the theater board, saying they acted in good faith.

Raised by his seamstress mother and her family in Harlem, Rangel dropped out of high school at 16, joined the Army and won a Purple Heart and Bronze Star in the Korean War, surviving firefights that claimed much of his unit. The harrowing experience provided the title of his autobiography: "And I Haven't Had a Bad Day Since." Once back home, he finished high school and college, then landed an internship in the local district attorney's office.

After four years in the New York Assembly, he set his sights on the U.S. House and ousted the incumbent, Adam Clayton Powell Jr., in the 1970 Democratic primary. He won his first general election with 87 percent of the vote and has amassed even larger wins ever since. Powell's namesake son was among those challenging Rangel in the 2010 primary.

Key Votes

2010

Overhaul the nation's health insurance system	YES
Allow for repeal of "don't ask, don't tell"	YES
Overhaul financial services industry regulation	YES
Limit use of new Afghanistan War funds to troop withdrawal activities	YES
Change oversight of offshore drilling and lift oil spill liability cap	YES
Provide a path to legal status for some children of illegal immigrants	YES
Extend Bush-era income tax cuts for two years	NO

2009

Expand the Children's Health Insurance Program	YES
Provide $787 billion in tax cuts and spending increases to stimulate the economy	YES
Allow bankruptcy judges to modify certain primary-residence mortgages	YES
Create a cap-and-trade system to limit greenhouse gas emissions	YES
Provide $2 billion for the "cash for clunkers" program	YES
Establish the government as the sole provider of student loans	YES
Restrict federally funded insurance coverage for abortions in health care overhaul	NO

CQ Vote Studies

	PARTY UNITY		PRESIDENTIAL SUPPORT	
	Support	Oppose	Support	Oppose
2010	98%	2%	85%	15%
2009	99%	1%	96%	4%
2008	100%	0%	16%	84%
2007	98%	2%	6%	94%
2006	96%	4%	27%	73%

Interest Groups

	AFL-CIO	ADA	CCUS	ACU
2010	100%	100%	13%	0%
2009	100%	95%	43%	0%
2008	100%	85%	61%	0%
2007	95%	95%	60%	0%
2006	100%	95%	40%	4%

New York 15

Northern Manhattan — Harlem, Washington Heights

The 15th takes in Upper Manhattan's Harlem and Washington Heights, stretching to Inwood at its tip, and picks up Marble Hill north of the Harlem River. East of Manhattan, it includes Randalls, Wards and Rikers islands, and a small industrial area of Queens. At only 10 square miles in size, the 15th is the nation's smallest district in area.

The past two decades have brought substantial change to the district, with Puerto Rican and Dominican immigrants — primarily in East Harlem and Washington Heights — supplanting an African-American majority. Hispanics now far outnumber non-Hispanic blacks, but low voter participation among Hispanics means the smaller black population (26 percent) continues to dominate the district's politics.

North Manhattan's 1994 federal empowerment zone designation resulted in an economic resurgence. Refurbished brownstones, new restaurants, national retail chains and prominent corporations have moved into the area. Washington Heights is experiencing similar revitalization.

The district's hospitals and colleges, along with its retail establishments and small businesses, provide much of the employment, although many jobs are out of reach to less-educated residents.

The 15th's universities include Columbia, and the area's health care industry hosts major research and teaching hospitals, including parts of New York Presbyterian Hospital. Many residents are employed on Rikers Island, the city's correctional facility in the East River that has roughly 13,000 inmates and is officially part of the Bronx, but is connected to Queens by a bridge.

Since its creation in 1944, the decidedly liberal 15th District seat has been held by two black Democrats: Adam Clayton Powell Jr. and Charles B. Rangel. In the 2008 presidential race, the district gave Barack Obama 93 percent, his second-highest percentage in the nation.

Major Industry
Health care, higher education, retail, city government

Cities
New York (pt.), 639,873

Notable
The 15th boasts legendary venues such as the Cotton Club and the Apollo Theater.

Rep. José E. Serrano (D)

Capitol Office
225-4361
serrano.house.gov
2227 Rayburn Bldg. 20515-3216; fax 225-6001

Committees
Appropriations

Residence
Bronx

Born
Oct. 24, 1943; Mayaguez, P.R.

Religion
Roman Catholic

Family
Divorced; five children

Education
Lehman College, attended 1979-80

Military
Army Medical Corps, 1964-66

Career
School district administrator; banker

Political Highlights
N.Y. Assembly, 1975-90; sought Democratic nomination for Bronx borough president, 1985

ELECTION RESULTS

2010 GENERAL

Serrano (D)	61,642	95.7%
Frank DellaValle (R)	2,758	4.3%

2010 PRIMARY

Serrano (D, WFP)	unopposed

2008 GENERAL

Serrano (D, WFM)	127,179	96.6%
Ali Mohamed (R, C)	4,488	3.4%

Previous Winning Percentages
2006 (95%); 2004 (95%); 2002 (92%); 2000 (96%);
1998 (95%); 1996 (96%); 1994 (96%); 1992 (91%);
1990 (93%); 1990 Special Election (92%)

Elected 1990; 11th full term

The gregarious Serrano moves easily through the halls of Congress, always ready with a quip or a joke. But his loquaciousness belies a serious-minded liberal ready to dig in his heels for a cause in which he believes.

Sporting a thick black mustache, Serrano is one of the most noticeable — and humorous — members of Congress. Frequently referencing his home in New York's South Bronx and his Puerto Rican roots, Serrano (full name: ho-ZAY sa-RAH-no, with a rolled 'R') keeps his colleagues and constituents laughing. Attending a tree-planting ceremony in New York in April 2009, he presented billionaire Mayor Michael Bloomberg with two new quarters honoring Puerto Rico and said: "I paid for these myself . . . I give you two so you can rub them together and see what you can make of it. This is the only country in the world where a guy who was born in a one-room flat with a latrine, grew up in public housing, is giving Michael Bloomberg two quarters."

But Serrano wasn't laughing in April 2010 when he asked Major League Baseball Commissioner Bud Selig to move the 2011 All-Star Game, slated to take place in Phoenix, to protest Arizona's law cracking down on illegal immigration. "With nearly one-third of all major leaguers coming from foreign countries, there is no way that a state with this discriminatory law should be the host," said Serrano, whose Bronx-based district is home to the Yankees.

A native of Puerto Rico, Serrano has been outspoken about the challenges facing Latinos and immigrant communities and is among the Hispanic lawmakers who have been frustrated that Democratic leaders did not tackle comprehensive immigration legislation in the 111th Congress (2009-10).

Serrano headed the Appropriations Subcommittee on Financial Services and General Government after Democrats took control of the House in 2007, and he remains as ranking Democrat with Republicans in charge of the 112th Congress (2011-12). His panel drafted a portion of the 2009 economic stimulus law that directed funds to the Small Business Administration and the General Services Administration. He called the final measure a "bold move" to help turn around the economy.

His panel has jurisdiction over the District of Columbia's budget, and Serrano has been an advocate of less federal interference in the city's affairs.

Serrano opposed the $700 billion package to shore up the financial services industry in fall 2008. "I was speaking for the people in the Bronx and people across the nation who are stuck without any help from our government," he said.

His role as an appropriator gives him ample opportunity to bring money home. He helped obtain federal money to clean up the Bronx River, plant trees in the borough and reduce air pollution from trucks, which is believed to be a contributing factor in the high incidence of asthma among his constituents. He proudly notes that a beaver was spotted in 2007 living in the Bronx River for the first time in two centuries. Biologists named it José, in Serrano's honor. In 2008, Serrano obtained $700,000 for the river.

Serrano has long been an advocate of easing restrictions on travel to Cuba. The 2009 catchall spending law included his provision to allow Americans with family members living in Cuba more expansive travel rights. The move garnered sharp protest from several members, including Democrat Debbie Wasserman Schultz, whose Florida district is home to a number of Cuban-Americans. "There is no reason to place harsh restrictions on those who simply wish to visit close family members," Serrano said. In the opening days of the 112th Congress he introduced a bill to lift the trade embargo on Cuba.

Serrano regularly weighs in on issues of importance to the island of his birth. Nearly 200,000 of Serrano's constituents are of Puerto Rican descent, and he believes citizens of the island should be allowed to decide whether it is granted statehood or independence. He was a strong supporter of a bill the House passed in April 2010 that aimed to give residents of the island a chance to vote on its political status. In 2000, Serrano was arrested outside the White House for protesting the Navy's continued use of the island of Vieques, off the coast of Puerto Rico, for training exercises using live bombs.

His voting record is solidly Democratic; during the party's four-year reign from 2007 to 2010, he sided with it almost 99 percent of the time on votes that saw a majority of Democrats oppose a majority of Republicans.

In 2007 he signed on to a bill to require the withdrawal of U.S. troops from Iraq within six months and cut off funding for the war thereafter. Citing "deep misgivings" about U.S. involvement in Afghanistan and Pakistan, Serrano in 2010 voted against a supplemental funding bill for the war in Afghanistan and backed the removal of U.S. forces from Pakistan unless Congress gives specific authority for them to be there.

The baseball-crazed nature of his native Puerto Rico has rubbed off on Serrano. The congressman has long offered legislation and ideas regarding the state of the game. He lobbied Selig on the draft status of Puerto Ricans and pushed for baseball to retire the No. 21 of Puerto Rican-born Pittsburgh Pirates great Roberto Clemente. He introduced a bill in early 2009 and again in 2011 to ease prohibitions on Cubans coming to the United States to play professional baseball.

Serrano grew up in the Millbrook Houses, a public housing project in the Bronx. His parents emigrated from Puerto Rico when he was 7, and Serrano said he learned English by listening to the Frank Sinatra records his father brought back from the Army. Serrano became a big fan, amassing a large collection of Chairman of the Board's records and sponsoring the 1997 measure that awarded Sinatra a Congressional Gold Medal. In 2008, he helped the U.S. Postal Service introduce a commemorative Sinatra stamp.

Serrano graduated from a vocational high school, served in the Army, took a job in a New York City bank and began making political contacts, which helped him win a state Assembly seat in 1974.

When Democratic Rep. Robert Garcia resigned his seat in 1990 after he was convicted of defense contract extortion, Serrano moved quickly to stake his claim. He breezed to victory with 92 percent of the vote in the special election and won a full term with 93 percent that November. He has won subsequent re-elections with at least 91 percent.

Key Votes

2010

Overhaul the nation's health insurance system	YES
Allow for repeal of "don't ask, don't tell"	YES
Overhaul financial services industry regulation	YES
Limit use of new Afghanistan War funds to troop withdrawal activities	YES
Change oversight of offshore drilling and lift oil spill liability cap	YES
Provide a path to legal status for some children of illegal immigrants	YES
Extend Bush-era income tax cuts for two years	NO

2009

Expand the Children's Health Insurance Program	YES
Provide $787 billion in tax cuts and spending increases to stimulate the economy	YES
Allow bankruptcy judges to modify certain primary-residence mortgages	YES
Create a cap-and-trade system to limit greenhouse gas emissions	YES
Provide $2 billion for the "cash for clunkers" program	YES
Establish the government as the sole provider of student loans	YES
Restrict federally funded insurance coverage for abortions in health care overhaul	NO

CQ Vote Studies

	PARTY UNITY		PRESIDENTIAL SUPPORT	
	SUPPORT	OPPOSE	SUPPORT	OPPOSE
2010	99%	1%	81%	19%
2009	99%	1%	94%	6%
2008	99%	1%	13%	87%
2007	98%	2%	5%	95%
2006	96%	4%	16%	84%

Interest Groups

	AFL-CIO	ADA	CCUS	ACU
2010	100%	100%	13%	0%
2009	100%	100%	33%	0%
2008	100%	100%	39%	8%
2007	91%	95%	55%	0%
2006	100%	90%	15%	4%

New York 16

South Bronx

The 16th, which covers the distressed neighborhoods of the South Bronx, is the nation's poorest district in terms of median household income and is one of the least educated.

More than one-third of families live on a household income of less than $15,000, and the area is plagued by urban ills and low rates of home ownership. Some South Bronx neighborhoods have begun to turn around, thanks to grass-roots community work, federal funding and commercial redevelopment efforts.

The South Bronx, inundated by a post-World War II influx of Hispanics to New York City, has elected men of Puerto Rican origin to the U.S. House since 1970. The 16th's strong Puerto Rican influence is complemented by African as well as South and Central American immigrant communities. The district's 2 percent non-Hispanic white population is the nation's lowest.

Subsidized economic development organizations have built several downtown developments of single-family and low-rise housing on vacant lots. Light manufacturing firms also have set up shop, replacing some of the heavy industry that moved out decades ago. The Fulton Fish Market, which moved from Lower Manhattan to Hunts Point, is the nation's largest grouping of seafood wholesalers.

The new, $1.5 billion Yankee Stadium opened in 2009 and replaced one of New York City's iconic landmarks. Local businesses rely on the economic benefit of catering to the droves who visit the "Bronx Bombers," but full redevelopment of community and park space promised as part of the stadium construction plan has been delayed. Fordham University also is in the 16th.

The 16th is one of the nation's most strongly Democratic districts — it gave Barack Obama his highest percentage in the 2008 presidential election (95 percent) — but like many districts with large minority and immigrant populations, voter turnout tends to be low.

Major Industry
Health care, light manufacturing, seafood distribution

Cities
New York (pt.), 693,819

Notable
The Edgar Allan Poe Cottage in the Bronx (the writer's last home) is owned by New York City.

Rep. Eliot L. Engel (D)

Capitol Office
225-2464
www.house.gov/engel
2161 Rayburn Bldg. 20515-3217; fax 225-5513

Committees
Energy & Commerce
Foreign Affairs

Residence
Bronx

Born
Feb. 18, 1947; Bronx, N.Y.

Religion
Jewish

Family
Wife, Patricia Ennis Engel; three children

Education
Hunter-Lehman College, B.A. 1969 (history); City U. of New York, Lehman College, M.A. 1973 (guidance & counseling); New York Law School, J.D. 1987

Career
Teacher; guidance counselor

Political Highlights
Bronx Democratic district leader, 1974-77;
N.Y. Assembly, 1977-88

ELECTION RESULTS

2010 GENERAL

Engel (D)	95,346	72.8%
Anthony Mele (R)	29,792	22.8%
York Kleinhandler (R)	5,661	4.3%

2010 PRIMARY

Engel (D, WFP)	unopposed

2008 GENERAL

Engel (D, INDC, WFM)	161,594	79.9%
Robert Goodman (R, C)	40,707	20.1%

Previous Winning Percentages
2006 (76%); 2004 (76%); 2002 (63%); 2000 (90%);
1998 (88%); 1996 (85%); 1994 (78%); 1992 (80%);
1990 (61%); 1988 (56%)

Elected 1988; 12th term

Engel, who has served in Congress for more than two decades, is known for being accessible to his constituents. Not only does he keep the majority of his staff in New York, but he also has an attitude that no complaint is too large or too small. From cable rate increases to broken traffic lights, Engel is a hands-on congressman. "Even if someone disagrees with how I vote, if they know I am hardworking and available to them, they're going to vote for me," he said.

Engel is among the few white lawmakers representing a majority-minority district, and its ethnic diversity has led him to be active on the Foreign Affairs Committee as well as on health and consumer issues. Engel is ranking Democrat on the Western Hemisphere Subcommittee and served as chairman from 2007 to 2010. He used the position to encourage assistance for Haiti to address food shortages and hurricane damage long before a devastating earthquake in January 2010 brought the nation to the forefront of legislators' minds.

In 2007, Engel supported a provision authorizing aid to Mexico and Latin America to fight illegal drugs. He applauded the Obama administration for its 2009 announcement that it would boost law enforcement along the border with Mexico to help stem drug-related violence. In 2010, he called on the administration to do more to block what he called "military-style" weapons from being imported into the United States, saying they were being trafficked illegally to Mexico.

Engel was an early proponent of U.S. intervention in Yugoslavia's civil war, and in 1993 he urged the Clinton administration to side against the Bosnian Serbs, who were accused of forcing the removal of Muslims. In early 2011 he backed limited U.S. involvement in Libya to assist rebels fighting Libyan leader Muammar el-Qaddafi.

Despite his visibility on Foreign Affairs, Engel's recent legislative victories came from his work on the Energy and Commerce Committee.

After the spring 2010 Gulf of Mexico oil spill involving a BP well, Engel introduced legislation that would prohibit oil polluters from receiving tax benefits for costs associated with the cleanup. "After being responsible for the worst environmental catastrophe in American history, they have used and abused the system, which has for too long permitted oil companies to degrade the environment," he said of BP. "Now they are looking to cut their losses at the expense of the American people. This is simply shameful."

Though a staunch Democrat — in the 111th Congress (2009-10) he supported his party 99 percent of the time on votes in which the majority of Democrats and Republicans divided — he steered several bills through the House with bipartisan support.

Among them were two pieces of health-related legislation. One provided for research on muscular dystrophy, and the other established a national registry to study data on amyotrophic lateral sclerosis (ALS), a disease that took his grandmother's life. Both bills sailed through Congress and were signed into law in October 2008.

Engel also has raised concerns about tuberculosis, calling it "the greatest curable infectious killer on this planet." In 2007, the House passed his bill to make fighting the disease globally a goal of the U.S. foreign assistance program, but the Senate did not act on it.

Engel's district includes significant foreign-born and lower-income populations, and he is quick to fight back when he feels his constituents are being mistreated. In 2007, he sponsored a House-passed bill to require calling-card companies to clearly disclose terms and fees. Engel said the cards, which are used by people making frequent overseas calls or those who cannot afford long-distance service, often fail to provide the services advertised.

He is fighting another local battle against a proposed airspace redesign that would dramatically increase traffic over Rockland County. Under such a plan, the noise would be "unbelievable" for the communities below, Engel said.

Engel has suggested that if he had known how "incompetent" the George W. Bush administration would be in executing the Iraq War, he would not have voted in 2002 to authorize it. In 2008, he voted in favor of an amendment that would require the withdrawal of U.S. troops from Iraq, though he voted for a war funding bill in 2010.

Engel was among the pro-Israel lawmakers who persuaded House Democratic leaders to drop a provision from a March 2007 war funding bill that would have barred the president from taking military action against Iran without congressional authorization. He argued Bush needed maximum flexibility to pressure Iran to end its nuclear program and its support of radical Islamic groups that foment violence against Israel.

He also sees Syria as a threat to Israel and the broader Middle East. During the 108th Congress (2003-04), he teamed up with Republican Ileana Ros-Lehtinen of Florida, who now chairs the committee, to win passage of a sanctions bill targeting Syria.

One of Engel's most noticeable quirks is that he always arrives early for the annual State of the Union address to grab an aisle seat in the House chamber, where he can greet the president and renew acquaintances with a number of ambassadors. "The constituents love it," he once explained. "And as long as they love it, I love it."

Engel grew up in the Democratic clubs of the Bronx and walked the picket lines with his father, a welder who was active in his union. He attended New York City public schools, where he later worked as a teacher and guidance counselor. He was elected in 1976 to the state Assembly, where he worked on housing and substance abuse issues. In 1988, he successfully challenged Democratic Rep. Mario Biaggi, who resigned after being convicted of bribery, conspiracy and extortion but remained on the ballot. He easily rebuffed a Biaggi comeback attempt in his 1992 election and has faced minimal opposition since.

In 2010, Engel and five others were the subject of an Office of Congressional Ethics review of lawmakers' use of excess per diem funds issued for official travel. At the beginning of 2011, the Ethics Committee said it would not pursue the allegations.

Key Votes

2010

Overhaul the nation's health insurance system	YES
Allow for repeal of "don't ask, don't tell"	YES
Overhaul financial services industry regulation	YES
Limit use of new Afghanistan War funds to troop withdrawal activities	NO
Change oversight of offshore drilling and lift oil spill liability cap	YES
Provide a path to legal status for some children of illegal immigrants	YES
Extend Bush-era income tax cuts for two years	NO

2009

Expand the Children's Health Insurance Program	YES
Provide $787 billion in tax cuts and spending increases to stimulate the economy	YES
Allow bankruptcy judges to modify certain primary-residence mortgages	YES
Create a cap-and-trade system to limit greenhouse gas emissions	YES
Provide $2 billion for the "cash for clunkers" program	YES
Establish the government as the sole provider of student loans	YES
Restrict federally funded insurance coverage for abortions in health care overhaul	NO

CQ Vote Studies

	PARTY UNITY		PRESIDENTIAL SUPPORT	
	SUPPORT	OPPOSE	SUPPORT	OPPOSE
2010	99%	1%	90%	10%
2009	99%	1%	97%	3%
2008	98%	2%	17%	83%
2007	98%	2%	6%	94%
2006	95%	5%	34%	66%

Interest Groups

	AFL-CIO	ADA	CCUS	ACU
2010	100%	100%	13%	0%
2009	100%	100%	40%	0%
2008	100%	95%	65%	0%
2007	95%	80%	53%	0%
2006	100%	95%	36%	4%

New York 17

North Bronx; part of Westchester and Rockland counties — Mount Vernon, part of Yonkers

The 17th takes in the northwestern part of the Bronx and parts of Westchester and Rockland counties just north of New York City. Blacks and Hispanics together constitute a majority of residents in the district, which is ethnically, racially and economically diverse.

Riverdale, a heavily Jewish neighborhood, sits at the western edge of the Bronx and is one of New York City's most affluent areas. It is home to numerous college preparatory schools, medical facilities and new apartment buildings. East of Riverdale, on the other side of Van Cortlandt Park and Woodlawn Cemetery, there is a large black population. The 17th reaches almost as far east as the huge Co-op City apartment complex (in the 7th). Nearly 45 percent of district residents live in the Bronx.

In Westchester County, home to almost one-fourth of the 17th's residents, the district takes in all of heavily black Mount Vernon, which hosts commercial industries and some notable health care facilities, including Mount

Vernon Hospital. Other black and Hispanic communities are found in southwestern Yonkers. There are predominantly white areas, many with residents of Italian and Irish descent, in the southeastern part of the city. Commuters lost one route to jobs in Manhattan when a ferry service across the Hudson River shut down in 2009.

The 17th narrows significantly in northern Yonkers, meandering north along Route 9 and the Hudson River to cross the Tappan Zee Bridge into Rockland County, where the rest of the district's population lives. The mostly suburban area is loaded with New York City commuters and also hosts a number of pharmaceutical manufacturing facilities as well as an Avon Products research and development site.

Barack Obama took 72 percent of the 17th's 2008 presidential vote — tallying 87 percent of the vote in the district's portion of the Bronx.

Major Industry

Health care, higher education, city government

Cities

New York (pt.), 294,919; Yonkers (pt.), 88,339; Mount Vernon, 67,292

Notable

Duke Ellington, Elizabeth Cady Stanton, F.W. Woolworth, Nellie Bly and "Bat" Masterson are among those buried in Woodlawn Cemetery.

Rep. Nita M. Lowey (D)

Capitol Office
225-6506
www.house.gov/lowey
2365 Rayburn Bldg. 20515-3218; fax 225-0546

Committees
Appropriations

Residence
Harrison

Born
July 5, 1937; Bronx, N.Y.

Religion
Jewish

Family
Husband, Stephen Lowey; three children

Education
Mount Holyoke College, B.A. 1959 (political science)

Career
Homemaker; state government aide

Political Highlights
N.Y. assistant secretary of state, 1985-87

ELECTION RESULTS

2010 GENERAL

Lowey (D)	104,836	63.4%
Jim Russell (R)	60,513	36.6%

2010 PRIMARY

Lowey (D, INDC, WFP)	unopposed

2008 GENERAL

Lowey (D, WFM)	174,791	68.5%
Jim Russell (R, C)	80,498	31.5%

Previous Winning Percentages
2006 (71%); 2004 (70%); 2002 (92%); 2000 (67%);
1998 (83%); 1996 (64%); 1994 (57%); 1992 (56%);
1990 (63%); 1988 (50%)

Elected 1988; 12th term

Lowey has been among the most ardent Democratic supporters of increasing spending on education, health care, the arts and foreign aid, and she is among the most vocal Democratic defenders of such funding as the new Republican majority looks for ways to trim federal deficits.

"We cannot let our current fiscal crisis create a future security crisis by cutting these invaluable programs," Lowey said at a hearing on the State Department budget in early 2011.

She opposed a catchall spending bill for fiscal 2011, saying it included "irresponsible cuts" in funding for the State Department and foreign assistance. "Despite broad agreement that U.S. national security is supported by a three-legged stool of defense, diplomacy and development, this bill dramatically weakens diplomacy and development," she said on the House floor.

Lowey chaired the State-Foreign Operations Appropriations Subcommittee in the 110th (2007-08) and 111th Congresses (2009-10), and also served as a senior member of the panel overseeing the budgets for the departments of Labor, Health and Human Services, and Education.

Lowey had a difficult choice of which Appropriations leadership spot to pick for the 112th Congress (2011-12). She could either continue as the top Democrat on the State-Foreign Operations Subcommittee or rise to the top of the Labor-Health and Human Services-Education panel. David R. Obey, the Wisconsin Democrat who led both the Appropriations Committee and its Labor-HHS panel, retired at the end of the 111th Congress.

Lowey stuck with her post as the top Democrat overseeing money spent on foreign aid, bypassing the chance to have more influence on a much larger budget. "I'll certainly be active on both committees," she said.

After the GOP reclaimed control of the House in the 2010 elections, Lowey lashed out at a key Republican for what she saw as a bid to undermine foreign aid funding. Majority Leader Eric Cantor of Virginia suggested separating money for Israel from the general foreign aid pool. Lowey argued that separating assistance for Israel would be a "counterproductive" ploy to "make it easier" for Republican members to reject the foreign aid bill while maintaining their pro-Israel bona fides.

"Too much is at stake to give Republicans in Congress a license to vote against the foreign aid budget," Lowey argued.

Lowey is one of the most formidable opponents of reinvigorated Republican attempts to cut funding for the Corporation for Public Broadcasting in the 112th Congress.

She has been down that road before, as one of the more prominent defenders of the program, which aids public television and radio stations, when the GOP previously took control of the House in 1995.

In making that argument, Lowey was taking on a powerful Republican who had just helped her keep her seat on the Appropriations Committee. Lowey had succeeded in first landing the seat in the 102nd Congress (1991-92) by aggressively lobbying the Democratic leadership. When the Republicans took over after the 1994 elections and vowed to cut committee rosters, Lowey's seat was considered lost. But rather than trust her own leaders to negotiate on her behalf, Lowey went directly to the decision-makers, pleading her case to incoming Speaker Newt Gingrich of Georgia and Appropriations Chairman Robert L. Livingston of Louisiana. She argued that by sparing only a few more Democratic seats, the incoming regime could maintain important diversity on the spending panel, and her seat was saved.

Lowey also sits on the panel that funds the Homeland Security Department. She has fought to ensure that New York gets money to prevent and respond to future terrorist attacks. At a 2008 hearing, she criticized the department's distribution of Urban Area Security Initiative money, which is meant for large cities with a significant risk of attacks, to places like Toledo and Omaha that "lucky for them, are neither high-threat nor high-risk."

She has not garnered less than 60 percent of the vote in a general election in her suburban district since 1994, allowing her to aid colleagues. She doled out more than $360,000 in contributions to fellow lawmakers and Democratic causes from her campaign fund during the 2007-08 election cycle, and more than $268,000 in the 2009-10 cycle. She helped raise $6 million for House Democrats' efforts to recruit and elect female candidates in 2000. Two years later, picked by party leaders to head the Democratic Congressional Campaign Committee, she set fundraising records. She then served as a "Hill-raiser" — a fundraiser who brings in more than $100,000 — for Hillary Rodham Clinton's 2008 presidential campaign. Lowey is one of the wealthiest members of Congress, with a minimum net worth of $14.9 million in 2009, according to Roll Call.

Lowey had hoped to advance to the Senate in 2000, but her dreams were dashed when Clinton moved to New York and made a successful run for the seat held by retiring Democrat Daniel Patrick Moynihan. Lowey, who bowed out gracefully, has since developed strong ties to the Clintons. When President Obama nominated Clinton for secretary of State, speculation arose that Lowey would be appointed to replace her, but Lowey again removed herself from consideration, saying she could do more as a senior member of the House.

Lowey was a homemaker in Queens when she volunteered in a neighbor's 1974 campaign for lieutenant governor. The neighbor was Mario Cuomo. Though Cuomo lost the primary race, new Democratic Gov. Hugh L. Carey appointed him secretary of state, and Cuomo hired Lowey to work in the anti-poverty division.

By the mid-1980s, Cuomo was governor and Lowey was the top aide to New York Secretary of State Gail Shaffer. Lowey made an impressive debut in electoral politics in 1988 to unseat two-term GOP Rep. Joseph J. DioGuardi in the then-20th District. She first survived a primary against Hamilton Fish V, publisher of The Nation magazine and scion of a famous Republican family in New York, and businessman Dennis Mehiel. For that cycle she raised $1.3 million, a huge sum for a challenger at the time, and won with 50 percent of the vote. Since then, she has outdistanced all competition.

Key Votes

2010

Overhaul the nation's health insurance system	YES
Allow for repeal of "don't ask, don't tell"	YES
Overhaul financial services industry regulation	YES
Limit use of new Afghanistan War funds to troop withdrawal activities	NO
Change oversight of offshore drilling and lift oil spill liability cap	YES
Provide a path to legal status for some children of illegal immigrants	YES
Extend Bush-era income tax cuts for two years	YES

2009

Expand the Children's Health Insurance Program	YES
Provide $787 billion in tax cuts and spending increases to stimulate the economy	YES
Allow bankruptcy judges to modify certain primary-residence mortgages	YES
Create a cap-and-trade system to limit greenhouse gas emissions	YES
Provide $2 billion for the "cash for clunkers" program	YES
Establish the government as the sole provider of student loans	YES
Restrict federally funded insurance coverage for abortions in health care overhaul	NO

CQ Vote Studies

	PARTY UNITY		PRESIDENTIAL SUPPORT	
	SUPPORT	OPPOSE	SUPPORT	OPPOSE
2010	98%	2%	95%	5%
2009	99%	1%	97%	3%
2008	99%	1%	14%	86%
2007	99%	1%	5%	95%
2006	98%	2%	23%	77%

Interest Groups

	AFL-CIO	ADA	CCUS	ACU
2010	100%	90%	25%	0%
2009	100%	100%	33%	0%
2008	100%	100%	67%	0%
2007	96%	95%	56%	0%
2006	100%	95%	40%	4%

New York 18

Most of Westchester County — New Rochelle, most of Yonkers

The 18th takes in large portions of southern and central Westchester County before hopping the Hudson River to pick up most of New City and Congers and all of Haverstraw in Rockland County. Mostly white-collar, the district is home to wealthy, educated suburbanites employed in health care, higher education and technology sectors, in Westchester County or via an easy commute into Manhattan or Connecticut.

The district includes a mix of residential and commercial territory in northern and central Yonkers, which has seen recent downtown revitalization. Much of the 18th's portion of Yonkers is middle class but it also includes a few wealthier neighborhoods such as Crestwood. The 18th also includes Ossining, site of Sing Sing prison — its location north of the city on the Hudson River led New Yorkers to refer to prison-bound criminals as being "sent up the river" — and many residents are advocating the transfer of prisoners upstate and redevelopment of the prime real estate into condominiums and shops.

The 18th also has working-class areas, such as parts of Sleepy Hollow, Port Chester and growing White Plains and New Rochelle. White Plains is home to Westchester County's largest retail hub and boasts the City Center complex and Renaissance Square hotel, shopping, and residential buildings. Both White Plains and New Rochelle are home to several colleges. The 18th hosts headquarters for PepsiCo in Purchase and defense contractor ITT in White Plains.

Some areas in Westchester County have been friendly to Republican candidates, but the working-class communities, coupled with some affluent Democratic areas, are more than enough to offset the GOP base. For many years, the district has had a sizable Jewish population, but the Hispanic population has boomed, mainly in Yonkers. Barack Obama carried the 18th overall with 62 percent of its vote in 2008.

Major Industry
Health care, higher education, retail

Cities
Yonkers (pt.), 107,637; New Rochelle, 77,062; White Plains, 56,853

Notable
North Tarrytown was renamed Sleepy Hollow in honor of the Washington Irving story set there.

Rep. Nan Hayworth (R)

Capitol Office
225-5441
hayworth.house.gov
1440 Longworth Bldg. 20515-3219; fax 225-3289

Committees
Financial Services

Residence
Mount Kisco

Born
Dec. 14, 1959; Chicago, Ill.

Religion
Lutheran

Family
Husband, Scott Hayworth; two children

Education
Princeton U., A.B. 1981 (biology); Cornell U., M.D. 1985

Career
Health care advertising firm executive; ophthalmologist

Political Highlights
No previous office

ELECTION RESULTS

2010 GENERAL

Hayworth (R)	109,956	52.6%
John Hall (D)	98,766	47.2%

2010 PRIMARY

Hayworth (R)	19,483	69.3%
Neil DiCarlo (R)	8,614	30.7%

Elected 2010; 1st term

Hayworth brings to the House Midwestern roots, an Ivy League education, and years of experience in medicine and health services.

She is a retired ophthalmologist who later became the vice president of a health care advertising agency, but had never held elected office prior to the 112th Congress (2011-12).

She wants to focus on "depowering" the 2010 health care overhaul — giving consumers more choices by facilitating the sale of insurance across state lines and ensuring that health savings accounts are not discouraged. Hayworth, whose husband is an ob-gyn, also wants to guarantee that doctors are adequately reimbursed by Medicare. "Right now, Medicare providers are headed for an enormous cut in reimbursements," Hayworth said. "That needs to be worked out, and that needs to be a pay-for."

One of two New York GOP freshmen appointed to the Financial Services Committee, Hayworth calls herself a fiscal conservative who wants to cut taxes and balance the budget by cutting non-defense spending.

"The Department of Education, unfortunately, however nobly intended, has not produced any benefit to our nation's students," Hayworth said. "We need to cut spending. We need to facilitate growth."

She takes a more moderate stance on social issues, supporting abortion-rights but opposing federal funding of abortions. She voted to block funding for Planned Parenthood in the catchall spending bill the House passed in February 2011.

Democrat John Hall, a former rock musician, ousted six-term Republican Sue W. Kelly in 2006 and was easily re-elected in 2008, both good years to be running as a Democrat. But 2010 proved to be a tougher year for Hall and his party in New York and across the nation.

Polls showed a close race from start to finish. The Democratic Congressional Campaign Committee spent $500,000 on television ads accusing Hayworth of wanting to privatize Medicare. Hayworth was able to distance herself from the unsuccessful statewide Republican candidates for governor and senator, and she won with almost 53 percent of the vote.

New York 19

Hudson Valley — Peekskill, West Point

Snug between Connecticut and New Jersey, the 19th links New York City suburbs to upstate New York. The Hudson River flows through the district's center, along which lie some of the state's richest communities. East and west of the river are rural towns and vegetable farms. The Westchester County portion of the district is known for elegant ex-urban homes inhabited by wealthy residents. Peekskill, with a working- and middle-class base, has a strong cultural and arts center, and a hospital in nearby Cortlandt Manor recently completed an expansion project.

Both sides of the river have steep embankments in the Hudson Highlands north of Peekskill. The U.S. Military Academy is here. Technology and research firms have moved into the mid-Hudson region south of Poughkeepsie, and there is a growing "green" job market. Rail commuter lots fill early each day as district residents commute to white-collar and public-sector jobs in New York City or southern Westchester County. Health care is a key industry in Orange County, which ranges from farms and small towns in the west to suburbia in the east.

The wealth in the 19th's south and the rural character of its western reaches, which extend to the foothills of the Catskill Mountains, make the district politically competitive.

Major Industry
Technology, agriculture

Military Bases
U.S. Military Academy, 1,165 military, 2,735 civilian (2009)

Cities
Peekskill, 23,583; Kiryas Joel, 20,175; Beacon, 15,541

Notable
The home and farm of John Jay, first chief justice of the United States, is in Katonah.

Rep. Chris Gibson (R)

Capitol Office
225-5614
gibson.house.gov
502 Cannon Bldg. 20515; fax 225-1168

Committees
Agriculture
Armed Services

Residence
Kinderhook

Born
May 13, 1964; Rockville Centre, N.Y.

Religion
Roman Catholic

Family
Wife, Mary Jo Gibson; three children

Education
Siena College, B.A. 1986 (history); Cornell U., M.P.A. 1995, Ph.D. 1998 (government)

Military
Army, 1986-2010

Career
Army officer; college instructor

Political Highlights
No previous office

ELECTION RESULTS

2010 GENERAL

Gibson (R)	130,178	54.8%
Scott Murphy (D)	107,075	45.1%

2010 PRIMARY

Gibson (R, C)	unopposed

Elected 2010; 1st term

Gibson spent nearly a quarter-century in the Army before retiring to pursue a political career. But the New York Republican doesn't want to be typecast in Congress as a military man.

That's not to say Gibson doesn't have some thoughts on military issues. A member of the Armed Services Committee, he's the author of a 2008 book, "Securing the State," which argues for a more cooperative relationship between civilian and military leaders. He praises Defense Secretary Robert M. Gates for doing a good job repairing that rift. And Gibson says he supports President Obama's approach to the wars in Afghanistan and Iraq.

Gibson, a member of the Agriculture Committee, says his first priority is the economy, particularly the hard-hit farm sector of his upstate district. That means cutting taxes and regulations while expanding free trade, said Gibson, who joined the Republican Study Committee, a group of the most conservative House members.

To that end, he voted in early 2011 to repeal the 2010 health care law and to block the EPA from instituting regulations aimed at combating climate change by capping emissions of greenhouse gases. He also would vote to make permanent the George W. Bush-era tax cuts that were extended for two years in 2010.

"There are three specific reasons small-business owners say they are not going to grow next year: taxes, regulation and health care costs," he said.

Gibson's predecessor, Democrat Scott Murphy, barely kept the seat in Democratic hands in a March 2009 special election to succeed Democrat Kirsten Gillibrand, who was appointed to fill the unexpired Senate term of Hillary Rodham Clinton when Clinton was named secretary of State.

Murphy's 700-vote margin of victory made the seat a prime target for Republicans in 2010.

Murphy won the endorsement of the National Rifle Association, but Gibson was able to tie him to the liberal Democratic House leadership and won going away in November, topping the incumbent by almost 10 percentage points.

New York 20

North Hudson Valley — Saratoga Springs, Glens Falls

Running along the state's eastern border, the 20th starts just outside Poughkeepsie and roughly follows Interstate 87 north into the scenic Adirondack Mountains and the resort areas of Lake George and Essex County. Lake Placid, in Essex County, is at the district's northern tip. The 20th covers much of the residential Hudson River Valley, where apple farms are the core of its agriculture industry. Although Albany, Schenectady and Troy are all in the 21st, the 20th claims most of their suburbs, helping fuel a population boom in southern Saratoga County. Saratoga Springs attracts tourists during the summer. Malta's Saratoga Technology + Energy Park and Saratoga Springs' Luther Forest Technology Campus add software, technology manufacturing and alternative energy jobs.

The 20th's western end is made up of mainly rural and rugged land and dairy farms from the Hudson River through Greene County, picking up parts of Delaware and Otsego counties. Much of this area hosts fishing, camping and other recreational sites. Saratoga County sets the tone politically for the district. The presence of unionized state workers outside Albany makes labor an important constituency, but farmers and small-town voters tend to favor the GOP. The 20th, which has the state's second-lowest minority percentage, gave Barack Obama 51 percent of its 2008 presidential vote, but John McCain did well in Greene County and eked out wins in the district's parts of Delaware, Otsego and Rensselaer counties.

Major Industry
Agriculture, tourism, manufacturing

Cities
Saratoga Springs, 26,586; Glens Falls, 14,700

Notable
The National Bottle Museum in Ballston Spa celebrates the history of glass bottle-making.

Rep. Paul Tonko (D)

Capitol Office
225-5076
tonko.house.gov
422 Cannon Bldg. 20515-3221; fax 225-5077

Committees
Budget
Science, Space & Technology

Residence
Amsterdam

Born
June 18, 1949; Amsterdam, N.Y.

Religion
Roman Catholic

Family
Single

Education
Clarkson U., B.S. 1971 (mechanical and industrial engineering)

Career
State public works engineer; state transportation agency employee

Political Highlights
Montgomery County Board of Supervisors, 1976-83 (chairman, 1981); N.Y. Assembly, 1983-2007; New York State Energy Research Development Authority president, 2007-08

ELECTION RESULTS

2010 GENERAL

Tonko (D)	124,889	59.2%
Theodore J. Danz Jr. (R)	85,752	40.7%

2010 PRIMARY

Tonko (D, INDC, WFP)	unopposed

2008 GENERAL

Tonko (D, WFM)	171,286	62.1%
James Buhrmaster (R, C)	96,599	35.0%
Phillip G. Steck (INDC)	7,965	2.9%

Elected 2008; 2nd term

Tonko is a conventional liberal with a focus on issues that affect energy and the environment. He applies his training as an engineer to the way he analyzes legislation, and colleagues turn to him on technical questions.

Engineers "take maybe five solutions that actually fit, and then from there determine which is the best solution," he said.

For Tonko, that's almost always his party's solution. On votes that split a majority of Democrats and Republicans in the 111th Congress (2009-10), Tonko sided with his party about 98 percent of the time.

Tonko accrued more than 30 years of policy experience at the state and local levels — particularly in energy-related issues — before arriving in Congress. He can be loquacious in trying to sway others; he regularly visits the House floor and has more than once invited like-minded colleagues to engage in hour-long colloquies.

He was especially vocal about the 2010 BP oil spill in the Gulf of Mexico. Tonko joined a group of Democrats lambasting the company and asking it to suspend its public relations efforts until the oil was cleaned up. He voted in favor of a measure that the House passed in September 2010 aimed at improving response times to oil pipeline disasters.

"This legislation will make sure incidents are reported swiftly so that the impacts of pipeline leaks and spills on people and the environment can be minimized," he said. "We also need to make sure that there is transparency in the process to hold companies accountable and ensure that public safety is the No. 1 priority."

Tonko was instrumental in helping the House Democratic leadership gain the support of upstate New York members for an energy bill that included a cap-and-trade system for carbon emissions. His colleagues were concerned, among other things, about how the program would distribute pollution allowances to coal-fired power plants.

They looked to Tonko as an expert; he chaired the Energy Committee in the New York Assembly for 15 years and later led a state agency focused on energy efficiency and affordability, working to establish a carbon cap-and-trade program. Tonko negotiated with a pair of senior Democrats, Henry A. Waxman of California and Edward J. Markey of Massachusetts, on behalf of the delegation to allow states to control their own compliance and to allow market transformation initiatives to count toward the energy efficiency standard.

Tonko focuses on his energy priorities as a member of the Science, Space and Technology Committee. He hopes to push development of a "green-collar" workforce that can form partnerships with local universities to promote conservation and environmental management. In the state Assembly, he sponsored a "Power for Jobs" program that provides low-cost power to employers throughout New York. He also sponsored one of the first laws in the country mandating a statewide target for the use of energy from renewable sources.

In September 2009, the House passed his bill to authorize $200 million annually, from 2010 through 2014, for a research and development program to try to improve production of wind turbines. General Electric's wind operations are located in Tonko's district. He successfully included in the House climate change bill a provision to authorize $65 million annually for fiscal years 2011 through 2014 for a research demonstration program on the efficiency of gas turbines, while also moving through the Science Committee a separate bill with the same language. Tonko also supports the production of hybrid-powered commercial vehicles and the expansion of high-speed rail.

A member of the revived Congressional Dairy Farmers Caucus, Tonko cosponsored with fellow New York Democratic freshman Scott Murphy a bill that would aim to reduce supply and help raise prices by providing financial incentives for dairy farmers to thin their herds or retire from the industry.

On the Budget Committee, Tonko is a defender of President Obama's spending priorities and a critic of Republican plans to bring the budget closer to balance. He called the House-passed catchall spending bill for fiscal 2011 "a step backward" and said it would hurt his region's job market.

He backed all of the Obama administration's economic initiatives, including the health care overhaul, even though it didn't include the government-run, single-payer option he advocated.

He pushed to include language in the measure to expand access to mental health and substance abuse services, similar to an effort he spearheaded in the state Assembly to require health insurers to cover mental health treatment. That law was named after Timothy O'Clair, a Schenectady 12 year old who hanged himself in 2001; Tonko said the boy was a constituent but also someone "who I knew, who I loved." He said the law is one of his proudest accomplishments.

Tonko was born in Amsterdam, N.Y., where he still lives. His grandparents were Eastern European immigrants who settled in the area. Tonko graduated from Amsterdam High School and trained as a mechanical and industrial engineer at Clarkson University in Potsdam.

He graduated in 1971 and entered politics a few years later — not with a career in mind, but to "feed a curiosity, to get it out of my system," he told the Albany Times-Union. He was elected to the Montgomery County Democratic Committee at age 22. Four years later, while working as an engineer with the state Department of Public Service, he became the youngest person elected to the county's board of supervisors.

In 1983, he was elected to the state Assembly, where he served for 24 years. He resigned in 2007 to become president and chief executive of the New York State Energy Research and Development Authority.

In 2008, he entered the race to replace retiring 10-term Democrat Michael R. McNulty. He defeated four other Democrats in the September primary, then breezed past GOP businessman James Buhrmaster in the general election with 62 percent of the vote. In 2010 he easily bested Republican Theodore Danz, owner of a heating and air conditioning company, taking 59 percent of the vote.

Key Votes

2010

Overhaul the nation's health insurance system	YES
Allow for repeal of "don't ask, don't tell"	YES
Overhaul financial services industry regulation	YES
Limit use of new Afghanistan War funds to troop withdrawal activities	YES
Change oversight of offshore drilling and lift oil spill liability cap	YES
Provide a path to legal status for some children of illegal immigrants	YES
Extend Bush-era income tax cuts for two years	NO

2009

Expand the Children's Health Insurance Program	YES
Provide $787 billion in tax cuts and spending increases to stimulate the economy	YES
Allow bankruptcy judges to modify certain primary-residence mortgages	YES
Create a cap-and-trade system to limit greenhouse gas emissions	YES
Provide $2 billion for the "cash for clunkers" program	YES
Establish the government as the sole provider of student loans	YES
Restrict federally funded insurance coverage for abortions in health care overhaul	NO

CQ Vote Studies

	PARTY UNITY		PRESIDENTIAL SUPPORT	
	Support	Oppose	Support	Oppose
2010	97%	3%	86%	14%
2009	99%	1%	97%	3%

Interest Groups

	AFL-CIO	ADA	CCUS	ACU
2010	100%	100%	0%	0%
2009	100%	100%	33%	0%

Capital District — Albany, Schenectady, Troy

As the terminus of the Erie Canal, which connects the Great Lakes to the Hudson River, New York's Capital District was one of the state's earliest industrial centers. Blue-collar workers and state employees give the Albany-Schenectady-Troy area a substantial union population and a solidly Democratic vote.

State budget shortfalls have led to layoffs in Albany, the capital. Nearly 13 percent of the district's workforce is employed by the state government, and the city government in Albany adds tens of thousands of jobs. The Egg performing arts complex located downtown at Empire State Plaza is a centerpiece of Albany's skyline.

Despite large-scale, decades-long industrial losses, manufacturing remains a force in the district. But the region has diversified with research and development, alternative energy and technology firms. Albany's College of Nanoscale Science and Engineering, which works on nanotech research and development, recently won a $57.5 million federal grant to develop new solar energy technology.

Rensselaer Polytechnic Institute and several liberal arts colleges also are in the 21st. Many members of the district's white-collar workforce are connected to the GE corporate and research facilities in Schenectady. The rest of the 21st includes rolling farm fields in the west and a gateway to the Adirondack Mountains in the north.

The 21st's Democrats are not self-described liberals but outnumber registered Republicans in the district's population centers in Albany and Rensselaer counties near the city of Albany and in Schenectady County. Barack Obama won here with 58 percent of the district's vote in the 2008 presidential election.

Major Industry
Government, technology, manufacturing

Military Bases
Watervliet Arsenal (Army), 1 military, 630 civilian (2011)

Cities
Albany, 97,856; Schenectady, 66,135; Troy, 50,129

Notable
Samuel Wilson, a meatpacker who provided the Army with much of its rations during the War of 1812, is believed to be the inspiration for "Uncle Sam" and is buried in Troy.

Rep. Maurice D. Hinchey (D)

Capitol Office
225-6335
www.house.gov/hinchey
2431 Rayburn Bldg. 20515-3222; fax 226-0774

Committees
Appropriations
Joint Economic

Residence
Hurley

Born
Oct. 27, 1938; Manhattan, N.Y.

Religion
Roman Catholic

Family
Wife, Allison Lee; three children

Education
State U. of New York, New Paltz, B.S. 1968 (political science & English), M.A. 1970 (English)

Military
Navy, 1956-59

Career
State education department aide; state highway toll collector; cement and paper mill equipment operator

Political Highlights
Democratic nominee for N.Y. Assembly, 1972; N.Y. Assembly, 1975-93

ELECTION RESULTS

2010 GENERAL

Hinchey (D)	98,661	52.6%
George K. Phillips (R)	88,687	47.3%

2010 PRIMARY

Hinchey (D, INDC, WFP)	unopposed

2008 GENERAL

Hinchey (D, INDC, WFM)	168,558	66.4%
George K. Phillips (R, C)	85,126	33.6%

Previous Winning Percentages
2006 (100%); 2004 (67%); 2002 (64%); 2000 (62%); 1998 (62%); 1996 (55%); 1994 (49%); 1992 (50%)

Elected 1992; 10th term

Hinchey earned a reputation in his younger days for standing up to bullies in New York City and throwing a few punches along the way. He also went to Catholic school and contemplated becoming a priest. The fighting and the praying stemmed from the same impulse.

"Looking out for other people, helping other people, has been the main objective of my life," Hinchey said.

Now, Hinchey prays and fights for liberal causes — raising taxes on the highest earners, extending unemployment benefits, subsidizing alternative energy sources, protecting wilderness areas and increasing federal regulation on behalf of food and drug safety.

Hinchey was one of the harshest critics of President George W. Bush, whom he called "the bully in the White House." And while Hinchey hailed President Obama in February 2009 as "the leader who can help guide us out of trouble," the Manhattan street fighter has pulled few punches with the current president. For instance, Hinchey opposed the president's 2010 year-end compromise to extend Bush-era tax cuts for two-years, assailing the measure, which became law, as a "very, very big mistake."

And from his seat on the Appropriations Committee, Hinchey indicated early on he wouldn't easily let Obama off the hook; he harshly criticized the administration when it proposed defense cuts that could cost jobs in his district, home to Lockheed Martin Corp. and Stewart Air National Guard Base.

As a member of the Defense Subcommittee, Hinchey pushed back hard when Obama looked to kill a program, contracted mainly to Lockheed in Hinchey's district, to replace a fleet of presidential helicopters. Obama said it exemplified "a procurement process gone amok."

But Hinchey said the helicopter program, initiated after the Sept. 11 terrorist attacks in order to provide the president safer and more-secure aircraft, "is too important to be derailed by politics." And he told local press of another imperative: his desire to save hundreds of jobs related to the program.

When the fiscal 2010 defense appropriations bill was cleared, it contained $129 million to sustain some of the technology work done in the district, while the Pentagon drew up new requirements for a revamped competition.

Environmental policies have long been another Hinchey passion, and he tends to them from his seat on the Interior-Environment spending panel.

A fight in the 1970s over the development of a power plant on the Hudson River was the primary reason for Hinchey's entry into electoral politics. Thirty-some years later, he sponsored an amendment to the fiscal 2008 Energy-Water spending bill that would have effectively barred the government from designating more National Interest Electric Transmission Corridors, which allow the construction of power lines in rural areas to serve urban centers.

Hinchey's district sits atop a rich supply of natural gas, and he has expressed concern about the potential environmental risks of hydraulic fracturing, or fracking, used to extract pockets of natural gas in shale deposits. He wants the EPA to examine the issue more closely.

He has long pushed a bill to designate millions of acres as wilderness. He took the issue over from former Utah Democrat Wayne Owens, who left the House in 1993. Former Utah Republican Christopher B. Cannon opposed it so strongly that he went to Hinchey's district in 1997 and held a news conference to push the New Yorker to delay the proposal. That only provoked Hinchey to introduce it, and he's done so in every Congress since, with Democratic Sen. Richard J. Durbin of Illinois.

Another Hinchey target has been management of the FDA, and he has attempted to overhaul the agency to end alleged inappropriate relationships with the drug industry. He won enactment of a law in 2005 requiring members of FDA advisory groups to disclose potential conflicts of interest. And he took aim at the agency in 2010 over its rules that allow nutrition labels to understate their calorie counts and other information by as much as 20 percent.

A typically reliable vote for party leaders, Hinchey can deviate on gun issues. In 1996, he was the only New York Democrat to vote to repeal a ban on certain semiautomatic weapons. Still, he supported the 1993 Brady bill, which calls for a five-day waiting period for handgun purchases. In 2004, he voted against repealing the District of Columbia's gun control law.

A handgun brought him unwelcome attention during his first term when he was charged with carrying a loaded one in his baggage at Reagan Washington National Airport. He pleaded no contest and was given a suspended sentence. He drew attention again in 2008 when he faced a second-degree harassment charge for allegedly swatting a National Rifle Association representative on the head at a street fair. A judge dismissed the charge.

Born in Manhattan, Hinchey spent most of his childhood in Greenwich Village until his family moved upstate, to Saugerties; when he was a teenager, he split his time between his new home and his old haunts in New York City.

His father, who served in the Army in World War II, worked at a cement plant while his mother raised their five children.

Hinchey joined the Navy after high school, serving aboard a destroyer in the Pacific. After his discharge, he returned home and worked in various jobs for five years, including at the local cement plant where his father had worked. He later enrolled at the State University of New York and paid his way by collecting tolls on the New York State Thruway.

Hinchey's parents had been active in local party politics, and after college he got involved in behind-the-scenes political activities while starting a career in education. He lost his first bid for the state Assembly in 1972, but won two years later to begin an 18-year tenure in Albany.

In 1992, when nine-term Democratic Rep. Matthew F. McHugh retired, Hinchey went after the seat. He started as the primary underdog, but prevailed against Binghamton Mayor Juanita M. Crabb. He then edged out Bob Moppert, a GOP county legislator, by 8,819 votes. He survived a 1994 rematch by an even closer margin. He won more easily until 2010, when he edged out teacher George K. Phillips, with 53 percent of the vote.

Hinchey announced in April 2011 that he was being treated for colon cancer, but said he would continue his congressional schedule.

Key Votes

2010

Overhaul the nation's health insurance system	YES
Allow for repeal of "don't ask, don't tell"	YES
Overhaul financial services industry regulation	YES
Limit use of new Afghanistan War funds to troop withdrawal activities	YES
Change oversight of offshore drilling and lift oil spill liability cap	YES
Provide a path to legal status for some children of illegal immigrants	YES
Extend Bush-era income tax cuts for two years	NO

2009

Expand the Children's Health Insurance Program	YES
Provide $787 billion in tax cuts and spending increases to stimulate the economy	YES
Allow bankruptcy judges to modify certain primary-residence mortgages	YES
Create a cap-and-trade system to limit greenhouse gas emissions	YES
Provide $2 billion for the "cash for clunkers" program	YES
Establish the government as the sole provider of student loans	YES
Restrict federally funded insurance coverage for abortions in health care overhaul	NO

CQ Vote Studies

	PARTY UNITY		PRESIDENTIAL SUPPORT	
	SUPPORT	OPPOSE	SUPPORT	OPPOSE
2010	99%	1%	90%	10%
2009	99%	1%	93%	7%
2008	98%	2%	15%	85%
2007	99%	1%	3%	97%
2006	98%	2%	7%	93%

Interest Groups

	AFL-CIO	ADA	CCUS	ACU
2010	100%	100%	13%	0%
2009	100%	100%	33%	0%
2008	100%	95%	50%	12%
2007	96%	100%	45%	0%
2006	100%	100%	27%	4%

New York 22

South central — Binghamton, Poughkeepsie, Ithaca

The scenic 22nd reaches from the hills above Cayuga Lake to the east bank of the Hudson River. Most residents are found at those extremes: Ithaca and Binghamton in the west and the Hudson Valley region, including Poughkeepsie, Newburgh and Kingston, in the east.

Ithaca, at the district's northwestern tip, is home to Cornell University, Ithaca College and a corps of liberal activists, and the city remains one of the few expanding economies in the 22nd. The district extends south from Ithaca to the Pennsylvania border, before turning east and stretching along the border from Tioga County to Sullivan County, taking in Broome County's Tri-Cities — Binghamton, Johnson City and Endicott. The 22nd then widens in Sullivan to head for Hudson River population centers in Orange, Ulster and Duchess counties.

Defense firms Lockheed Martin Corp. and BAE Systems are still key local employers in the district's western arm. The state university in Binghamton is an anchor for local economic development. And although traditional manufacturing jobs have declined in the district, high-tech manufacturing is important in the Hudson Valley region. There are thousands of jobs at a former IBM plant in Kingston that now hosts electronic and solar-energy manufacturing firms.

In general, the 22nd is rural, with a large portion of the Catskill Mountains in the center and many apple and dairy farms throughout. The Catskills' Borscht Belt, a prominent Jewish resort area, declined as tourists began vacationing in more exotic locales, but officials are hoping to reinvigorate the hospitality industry here.

The district's mixture of cities and farmland creates a politically diverse environment, although the region's blue-collar history and the liberal areas surrounding the 22nd's universities give Democrats an edge. Barack Obama took 59 percent of the district's 2008 presidential vote.

Major Industry
Higher education, agriculture, technology

Cities
Binghamton, 47,376; Poughkeepsie (pt.), 32,602; Ithaca, 30,014

Notable
Bethel was the site of the marathon Woodstock rock concert in 1969.

Rep. Bill Owens (D)

Capitol Office
225-4611
owens.house.gov
431 Cannon Bldg. 20515-3223; fax 226-0621

Committees
Agriculture
Armed Services
Small Business

Residence
Plattsburgh

Born
Jan. 20, 1949; Brooklyn, N.Y.

Religion
Roman Catholic

Family
Wife, Jane Owens; three children

Education
Manhattan College, B.S.B.A. 1971 (economics);
Fordham U., J.D. 1974

Military
Air Force Reserve, 1971-75; Air Force, 1975-79; Air
Force Reserve, 1979-82

Career
Lawyer; college instructor

Political Highlights
No previous office

ELECTION RESULTS

2010 GENERAL

Owens (D)	82,232	47.5%
Matt Doheny (R)	80,237	46.4%
Doug Hoffman (C)	10,507	6.1%

2010 PRIMARY

Owens (D, WFP)	unopposed

2009 SPECIAL

Owens (D, WFM)	73,137	48.3%
Doug Hoffman (C)	69,553	46.0%
Dierdre Scozzafava (R, I)	8,582	5.7%

Elected November 2009; 1st full term

After becoming the first Democrat to represent the 23rd District since the 19th century, Owens has been a fairly reliable — although by no means rock solid — vote for the party. He achieved his greatest legislative successes on the Homeland Security Committee, but had to surrender his seat on that panel following the Democratic losses in 2010.

Owens had a big target on his back going into his re-election race. His special-election win in 2009 had been something of a fluke. Republican county chairmen in the district had initially selected Dede Scozzafava, a moderate state assemblywoman, to run for the seat, which Republican John M. McHugh had given up to become secretary of the Army.

But grass-roots conservatives revolted, backing a rival challenge by accountant Doug Hoffman. In a remarkable turn of events, Scozzafava dropped out of the race less than a week before the November 2009 election and endorsed Owens, a little known Plattsburgh attorney who was not even a registered Democrat at the time party officials selected him for the race. But with Scozzafava's name still on the ballot, the Republican vote splintered. The result was a 2-percentage-point margin of victory for Owens.

Owens had been lucky and he knew it, so he set out immediately in 2010 to establish himself as an independent-minded representative attuned to the economic development needs of his upstate district. He encouraged fellow freshman representatives of both parties to get together to share ideas. And he took on big issues, like America's foreign debt with China, proposing to dig out of the hole by selling savings bonds to Americans. He didn't shy away from small-bore issues either, introducing a bill to provide government grants to encourage landowners to let syrup producers tap their maple trees. Neither bill moved, but Owens was undeterred, introducing a barrage of other measures aimed at creating upstate jobs.

He secured a slot on the Agriculture Committee and pledged to fight hard for the region's dairy farmers.

From his seat on the Armed Services panel, he stressed his own family's long history of military service and wooed military families and veterans, an important constituency in a district that's home to Fort Drum.

Owens' successes on homeland security matters included House passage of his amendment to computer security legislation in February 2010 to bolster research and development into cybersecurity strategies.

Later that summer, the House passed an Owens-authored bill to require the White House to develop a strategy to stem the smuggling of illegal drugs across the U.S.-Canadian border. Both pieces of legislation languished in the Senate, but Owens' activism was unusual for a freshman and got his party's attention.

On social issues, he straddled the fence, voting against an amendment to the health care overhaul to restrict federal funding of abortion. Later he voted to end the military's ban on openly gay servicemembers. At the same time, he reiterated his support for civil unions for same-sex couples, but not same-sex marriage, and cheered a Supreme Court decision that bolstered gun rights.

When the health care overhaul came up for a vote in 2009, Owens anguished over it, consulting experts on both sides. In the end, he fell in line, voting for final passage because he said it was the right thing to do for the economy. "I was presented with a simple choice: Do nothing and further burden our families and entrepreneurs, and allow our costs to spiral out of control, or take the first steps to reform our system in a way that will pay for itself," he said.

He also struggled with the year's other major legislation, revamping financial regulatory rules, first supporting a House version of the bill in December 2009 but opposing the final version six months later. Owens, who sits on the Small Business Committee, said he decided to vote "no" because the new regulatory regime was too burdensome for small-town banks. He nonetheless helped secure a change in the final law exempting lending by automobile dealers from the new rules.

Knowing tax cuts enacted during George W. Bush's presidency would expire at the end of 2010, Owens jumped ahead of his caucus in September, sending a letter to House leaders proposing a solution. The Owens plan would have granted a five-year extension of the tax cuts to middle-class taxpayers and a one-year extension for families with incomes up to $500,000. It was ignored, and Owens later fell in line behind a compromise plan endorsed by President Obama that extended all the rates for two years.

Meanwhile, upstate conservatives were licking their chops. Hoffman laid plans to run again but, as in 2009, Republicans weren't united. Party leaders again preferred another candidate, Matt Doheny, a Wall Street banker whose fortune would enable him to ensure his campaign had adequate funding.

Doheny edged Hoffman in a September primary and immediately set out to tie Owens to the liberal House Speaker from California, Nancy Pelosi. Owens worked hard to distance himself from Pelosi, running ads stressing how often he opposed the leadership, and the Democrats' House campaign committee poured money in to defend Owens.

Hoffman threw his support to Doheny, but his name remained on the ballot as the Conservative Party candidate. In the end, 6 percent of voters went for Hoffman and Owens squeaked by with a narrow win.

After the election, Owens told a local newspaper that he might vote for Ohio Republican John A. Boehner for Speaker, but later backtracked. He ended up voting for Pelosi.

Born in Brooklyn, N.Y., and raised on Long Island, Owens attended Manhattan College, where he obtained a degree in business administration in 1971. He earned a law degree three years later at Fordham University.

After graduating from law school, Owens enlisted in the Air Force and served as a captain at Plattsburgh Air Force Base. After completing his service, he decided to stay upstate, where he built a successful tax and business law practice before party officials selected him for the 2009 special-election race.

Key Votes

2010	
Overhaul the nation's health insurance system	YES
Allow for repeal of "don't ask, don't tell"	YES
Overhaul financial services industry regulation	NO
Limit use of new Afghanistan War funds to troop withdrawal activities	NO
Change oversight of offshore drilling and lift oil spill liability cap	YES
Provide a path to legal status for some children of illegal immigrants	NO
Extend Bush-era income tax cuts for two years	YES
2009	
Restrict federally funded insurance coverage for abortions in health care overhaul	NO

CQ Vote Studies

	PARTY UNITY		PRESIDENTIAL SUPPORT	
	SUPPORT	OPPOSE	SUPPORT	OPPOSE
2010	83%	17%	83%	17%
2009	87%	13%	86%	14%

Interest Groups

	AFL-CIO	ADA	CCUS	ACU
2010	79%	70%	50%	21%
2009	100%		43%	14%

New York 23

North — Watertown, Plattsburgh, Oswego

The vast 23rd covers more than one-fourth of the state, bordering Lake Champlain, the St. Lawrence Seaway and Lake Ontario. The waterways provide an inexpensive source of electricity, which has lured some heavy industry to the district. But most of the district is rural, full of small towns, dairy farms, maple syrup producers and colleges. It reaches south to Oneida Lake and Madison County.

Fort Drum (near Watertown, the district's largest city) is one of the largest and most modern Army facilities on the East Coast. It thus far has been safe from post-Cold War base closures, and consists of 107,000 acres and trains almost 80,000 troops annually.

Roughly 30 miles from Ontario, Watertown's economy relies on Canadian visitors. The proximity to waterways and forests made paper production a major industry in the district, but many mills have been forced to close their doors.

Unemployment remains a problem throughout the 23rd, as harsh winters and high transportation costs make attracting jobs difficult. A GM plant in Massena in St. Lawrence County closed in 2009, and the sprawling factory will be demolished. State correctional facilities are an economic driver in the 23rd, but ongoing state budget shortfalls will force closures. Bright spots include seasonal tourism — the 23rd covers much of the Adirondack Mountains, where winter weather caters to snowmobile riders and ice fishers, and long summers attract visitors to regional festivals and seasonal-use cottages.

The northeastern corner of the state had sent Republicans to the U.S. House since the 1872 election until 2009. Despite Republicans holding a voter registration edge in the district, Barack Obama won 52 percent of the 23rd's 2008 presidential vote. Opponent John McCain received his highest percentage in any county statewide in sparsely populated Hamilton (63 percent).

Major Industry
Agriculture, tourism, defense

Military Bases
Fort Drum, 18,023 military, 4,768 civilian (2011)

Cities
Watertown, 27,023; Plattsburgh, 19,989; Oswego, 18,142

Notable
Little Trees air fresheners were invented in Watertown, home to the headquarters and a manufacturing plant of Car-Freshner Corp.

Rep. Richard Hanna (R)

Capitol Office
225-3665
hanna.house.gov
319 Cannon Bldg. 20515-3224; fax 225-1891

Committees
Education & the Workforce
Small Business
Transportation & Infrastructure

Residence
Barneveld

Born
Jan. 25, 1951; Utica, N.Y.

Religion
Roman Catholic

Family
Wife Kim Hanna; two children

Education
Reed College, B.A. 1976 (economics and political science)

Career
Construction company owner; property development company manager

Political Highlights
Republican nominee for U.S. House, 2008

ELECTION RESULTS

2010 GENERAL

Hanna (R)	101,599	53.0%
Michael Arcuri (D)	89,809	46.8%

2010 PRIMARY

Hanna (R, INDC, C)	unopposed

Elected 2010; 1st term

Hanna leans toward the middle of the political spectrum, making him something of an outlier among his fellow Republican members of the freshman class of the 112th Congress. He says "neither party has it right" on everything, but Republicans have "a much better handle" on economic issues.

"I don't live in a world where ideology helps you," he said. "I live in a world of practical solutions."

A construction company owner and philanthropist, he sees rebuilding the economy as the core issue facing Congress.

Hanna's committee assignments lend themselves to a job-centric agenda: Transportation and Infrastructure, Education and the Workforce, and Small Business. The first bill he introduced would cut the top corporate tax rate from 35 percent to 25 percent over two years.

Hanna describes himself as a fiscal conservative and a social moderate; he favors civil unions for same-sex partners, backed repeal of the statutory ban on openly gay military servicemembers and supports abortion rights.

He was one of seven Republicans — and one of only two GOP freshmen — to oppose an amendment to block funding for Planned Parenthood that was added to the House version of a catchall spending bill for fiscal 2011.

He adds, though, that many "social issues are really a diversion from the desperate need we have to regrow our economy."

His father died when Hanna was 20, leaving Hanna and his sister to provide for the family. He put himself through college during the next several years and afterward founded Hanna Construction, which he still owns and manages. Since then, Hanna has played an active role in the community, serving on local boards and charities. He also is a "sustaining member" of the libertarian Cato Institute.

A native of the 24th District, Hanna first made a bid for office in 2008, losing to first-term Democrat Michael Arcuri by 4 percentage points.

Hanna challenged Arcuri again in 2010. In a much more favorable climate for Republicans, Hanna prevailed, winning 53 percent of the vote to Arcuri's 47 percent.

New York 24

Central — Utica, Rome, Auburn

The J-shaped 24th starts at the western edge of the Adirondack Mountains, sweeps through the central part of the state — south of Syracuse and north of Binghamton — and extends into the Finger Lakes region. In the heart of the Leatherstocking Region made famous by James Fenimore Cooper, the area is known for its rich history and depends on dairy farming and local colleges. Much of the 24th's central region is full of small-size towns that endure harsh winters and enjoy mild summers, and whose economies revolve around the farming seasons. These areas become crowded with visitors on fall foliage tours and trips to cider mills. The district hosts the Oneida Indian Nation's Turning Stone Casino in Verona and also boasts the National Baseball Hall of Fame in Cooperstown and the National Distance Running Hall of Fame in Utica.

In the west, the 24th is home to other historical gems, including the site of the 1848 Women's Rights Convention and the National Women's Hall of Fame in Seneca Falls. This area is the gateway to the Finger Lakes, which, among other things, attract wine connoisseurs to dozens of wineries. The 24th's main population center can be found in Oneida County. Oneida's Utica and Rome are aging industrial cities on the Mohawk River that suffered as manufacturing jobs left the state.

Environmental issues are important here, but voters are Yankee Republicans. Despite a GOP voter registration edge in the district, Democrat Barack Obama narrowly won the 24th's 2008 presidential vote (50 percent).

Major Industry
Agriculture, tourism, manufacturing, service

Cities
Utica, 62,235; Rome, 33,725; Auburn, 27,687

Notable
Francis Bellamy, author of the Pledge of Allegiance, is buried in Rome.

Rep. Ann Marie Buerkle (R)

Capitol Office
225-3701
buerkle.house.gov
1630 Longworth Bldg. 20515-3225; fax 225-4042

Committees
Foreign Affairs
Oversight & Government Reform
Veterans' Affairs
  (Health - Chairwoman)

Residence
Syracuse

Born
May 8, 1951; Auburn, N.Y.

Religion
Roman Catholic

Family
Divorced; six children

Education
Le Moyne College, B.S. 1977 (science); Syracuse U.,
J.D. 1993

Career
Assistant state attorney general; lawyer; homemaker;
nurse

Political Highlights
Republican nominee for Onondaga County
Legislature, 1987, 1989; Syracuse Common Council,
1994-95; defeated for election to Syracuse Common
Council, 1994

ELECTION RESULTS

2010 GENERAL

Buerkle (R)	104,602	50.1%
Dan Maffei (D)	103,954	49.8%

2010 PRIMARY

Buerkle (R, INDC, C)	unopposed

Elected 2010; 1st term

Buerkle is the first woman elected to Congress from the Syracuse area, and she will use her experience as a registered nurse and working mother of six to guide her while in Washington.

A conservative Republican and former anti-abortion activist, Buerkle is also an attorney who served briefly in the 1990s as a member of the Syracuse Common Council and as an assistant state attorney general.

She said her top priority would be health care. Buerkle voted early in the 112th Congress (2011-12) to repeal and block funding for the 2010 health care overhaul, and she chairs the Veterans' Affairs Subcommittee on Health. Buerkle also serves on the Oversight and Government Reform Committee.

Buerkle favors cutting taxes, controlling spending and reducing uncertainty about government tax and regulatory policies. "Businesses tell me all the time, 'I don't know what's going to happen next. I don't know what tax or regulation is coming down the pike,'" she says.

She supports making the George W. Bush-era tax cuts permanent and advocates eliminating the estate tax, which she calls "double taxation" and "a punishment for working hard and leaving your family some sort of legacy."

Seeing entitlement spending as the principal budgetary challenge, she says she's open to all ideas for bringing Social Security revenues in line with expenses. She would exempt older Americans from any changes to the program. But for those up to about age 40, "all of the options need to be looked at [to determine] what's going to make this work and what's going to be viable," she said.

Buerkle is vice chairwoman of the Foreign Affairs Subcommittee on Terrorism, Nonproliferation, and Trade. She backed the extension of expiring provisions of the anti-terrorism law known as the Patriot Act, saying "we have avoided another major terrorist attack on American soil since Sept. 11, 2001, because we have also been diligent in protecting our shores."

Buerkle upended one-term Democrat Dan Maffei in one of the year's closest elections. She won by less than 700 votes, and Maffei didn't concede until three weeks after Election Day.

New York 25

North central — Syracuse, most of Irondequoit

Syracuse, in the district's east, is the 25th's only major city and its economic hub. The district stretches west, roughly along Lake Ontario in the north and the Erie Canal in the south, from Onondaga County to reach most of Irondequoit in the Rochester suburbs. Syracuse and the Rochester area are home to diverse economies that rely on educational institutions to spur other industries. Small towns and farms fill much of the land between the two cities.

Seventy percent of the 25th's residents live in Onondaga County, which is home to Syracuse. Syracuse University and the State University of New York Upstate Medical University, both located in the city on University Hill, are the county's top two employers. Expansion at the Medical University is expected to be complete in 2013.

South of Syracuse, dairy and produce farms dot the landscape. The district also includes coastal and inland farming-based towns stretching from Moon Beach in the east to the banks of the Genesee River in the west. Many Rochester-area residents work in white-collar industries.

Minorities and blue-collar workers contribute to the Democratic vote in Syracuse, while GOP candidates get votes from conservatives scattered throughout the 25th, particularly in more lightly populated Wayne County, which voted for John McCain by a 10-percentage-point margin in the 2008 presidential election. The district as a whole gave 56 percent to Barack Obama.

Major Industry
Higher education, agriculture, health care

Cities
Syracuse, 145,170; Irondequoit (unincorporated) (pt.), 32,220

Notable
Syracuse University's Carrier Dome is the nation's largest on-campus domed stadium.

Rep. Kathy Hochul (D)

Capitol Office
225-5265
hochul.house.gov
1711 Longworth Bldg. 20515; fax 225-5910

Committees
Homeland Security

Residence
Hamburg

Born
Aug. 27, 1958; Buffalo, N.Y.

Religion
Roman Catholic

Family
Husband, William J. Hochul Jr.; two children

Education
Syracuse U., B.A. 1980 (political science);
Catholic U., J.D. 1983

Career
Deputy county clerk; homemaker; congressional
aide; lawyer

Political Highlights
Hamburg Town Board, 1996-2007; Erie County clerk,
2007-11

ELECTION RESULTS

2011 SPECIAL ELECTION*

Hochul (D)	48,530	47.2%
Jane L. Corwin (R)	43,836	42.6%
Jack Davis (TEA)	9,495	9.2%
Ian L. Murphy (GREEN)	1,130	1.1%

*Election results are unofficial

Elected May 2011; 1st term

Hochul won an unlikely victory in the Republican-leaning district by tarring her GOP opponent as an enemy of Medicare. She also benefited from the presence of a well-funded Tea Party candidate in the race.

Hochul (HO-kul), who served as Erie County clerk before her election to Congress, has Capitol Hill experience. In the 1980s she was an aide to Sen. Daniel Patrick Moynihan and to Rep. John J. LaFalce, who represented part of the current 26th for more than two decades.

She was highly critical of her Republican opponent, state Rep. Jane L. Corwin, for supporting the House GOP budget and its plans to overhaul Medicare. Hochul said she supports the current system and argues that measures aimed at cutting costs, such as bulk purchases of prescription drugs by the government, are enough to preserve the program as it now exists.

Hochul looks to be a dependable liberal vote on other issues as well. She is an abortion rights supporter who was endorsed by NARAL Pro-Choice New York. She opposes pending trade deals with Panama, Colombia and South Korea and won the backing of the state AFL-CIO. She also backs income tax increases on the highest earners. "Someone making half a million a year, I think they can contribute more," Hochul said during a debate in May. Her first committee assignment was to the Homeland Security panel.

The special election was necessitated by the abrupt resignation of Republican Christopher Lee following revelations of a flirtatious email exchange with a woman in which the married Lee included a shirtless image of himself.

Democratic county chairmen unanimously selected Hochul in March after Republican Party officials had quickly rallied around Corwin. The GOP move annoyed some tea partiers and eventually brought into the race businessman Jack Davis, who lost as the Democratic nominee in 2004 and 2006 and failed to win the GOP nomination for the special election.

National party organizations and independent expenditure groups poured hundreds of thousands of dollars into the race, and Corwin and Davis spent heavily from their personal fortunes. Based on election night results, Hochul won with 47 percent of the vote, to 43 percent for Corwin and 9 percent for Davis.

New York 26

Suburban Buffalo and Rochester; rural west

Stretching from suburban Buffalo to the Rochester suburbs, the Republican-leaning 26th scoops up miles of farmland between and to the south of the two cities. Slightly less than half the district's residents live in Niagara and Erie counties, and manufacturing still drives their local economies. Abundant dairy farms and apple orchards shape the rural regions.

The population is anchored in the district's portion of Erie County, particularly in Amherst. The north campus of the state university at Buffalo, which houses most of the university's programs, and corporate office parks are Amherst mainstays.

The 26th's share of Niagara County includes Lockport and North Tonawanda, which becomes a tourist hot spot each summer. Visitors are attracted to North Tonawanda's

Gateway Harbor Park, the last spot before the Erie Canal joins the Niagara River. Yahoo Inc. plans to expand its data center that opened in Lockport in 2010.

The 26th has had a noticeable GOP lean for decades, but voting habits differ across the district's seven counties and even registered Republicans will back some Democratic candidates. The district's portions of the population centers of Erie and Niagara counties vote Democratic, while Livingston to the south has a more Republican lean. Rural Wyoming, Genesee and Orleans counties are solidly Republican, but third-party candidates can do well in Monroe County outside of Rochester.

Major Industry
Manufacturing, agriculture, service

Cities
North Tonawanda, 31,568; Lockport, 21,165

Notable
The Herschell Carrousel Factory Museum is in North Tonawanda.

Rep. Brian Higgins (D)

Capitol Office
225-3306
www.house.gov/higgins
2459 Rayburn Bldg. 20515-3227; fax 226-0347

Committees
Foreign Affairs
Homeland Security

Residence
Buffalo

Born
Oct. 6, 1959; Buffalo, N.Y.

Religion
Roman Catholic

Family
Wife, Mary Jane Hannon; two children

Education
State U. of New York, Buffalo State, B.A. 1984 (political science), M.A. 1985 (history); Harvard U., M.P.A. 1996

Career
State and county legislative aide

Political Highlights
Buffalo Common Council, 1988-94; Democratic nominee for Erie County comptroller, 1993; N.Y. Assembly, 1999-2004

ELECTION RESULTS

2010 GENERAL

Higgins (D)	119,085	60.9%
Leonard A. Roberto (R)	76,320	39.1%

2010 PRIMARY

Higgins (D, WFP)	unopposed

2008 GENERAL

Higgins (D, WFM)	185,713	74.4%
Daniel Humiston (R, INDC)	56,354	22.6%
Harold Schroeder (C)	7,478	3.0%

Previous Winning Percentages
2006 (79%); 2004 (51%)

Elected 2004; 4th term

With an unassuming demeanor, Higgins tends to the many challenges facing his economically distressed Buffalo-based district, typically focusing on narrow issues away from Congress' high-profile debates. His time on the powerful Ways and Means Committee, to which he was selected in 2008, was short-lived: He lost the spot when Democrats lost their majority in the 2010 elections and saw their share of seats on the panel reduced.

Instead, he now looks to protect the region's interests from the Homeland Security Committee, where he led an effort to restore Urban Areas Security Initiative grant funding for midsize cities that was trimmed from the catchall spending bill the House passed in early 2011.

Higgins also has been a vocal critic of new flood maps from the Federal Emergency Management Agency, which he says do not accurately portray the flood risk in the area and have unfairly required some homeowners to purchase flood insurance.

"Again we see federal flood zone designations not based in science or reason placing unfair burdens on local homeowners and discouraging investment," he said.

As a member of the Foreign Affairs Committee and the Congressional Poland Caucus, Higgins backs changes to the Visa Waiver Program that would grant Poland eligibility to participate. The Buffalo region has a significant Polish-American population. He also opposes a requirement that travelers show passports for U.S.-Canada border crossings, saying it would have a negative economic impact on his area.

Higgins was on the Ways and Means panel when it considered health care overhaul legislation in the 111th Congress (2009-10). He supported inclusion of a government-run "public option," which he said would provide competition to private plans and drive down prices. That provision didn't make it into the final version of the bill, but Higgins voted for it anyway, as he did for virtually every leadership-backed measure that came to the floor while the Democrats' were in the majority from 2007 to 2010. During that period, on votes that split majorities of the two parties, Higgins sided with his fellow Democrats about 98 percent of the time.

Higgins was a strong supporter of the 2009 economic stimulus bill, and since its passage he has lauded projects in his district that have been the recipient of federal money. An ally of labor unions, Higgins is skeptical of free-trade deals. He voted against the Central America Free Trade Agreement in 2005 and two years later opposed a trade agreement with Peru.

To take a seat on Ways and Means, Higgins had to give up his seat on the Transportation and Infrastructure Committee, where he helped steer $42 million to his district in the 2005 surface transportation bill. In 2005, he took the lead in negotiations with the State Power Authority, demanding it help finance waterfront development in exchange for the right to operate the Niagara Power Project for a $391 million deal over the next 50 years. And at the behest of Democrat James L. Oberstar of Minnesota, who was then chairman of the committee, Higgins and Ohio Republican Michael R. Turner helped start a task force on revitalizing older cities.

Higgins is a reliable Democrat when it comes to social issues. He voted in 2010 to repeal the military's "don't ask, don't tell" policy and in 2008 to prohibit job discrimination based on sexual preference. In 2006, he voted against a bill that would make it a crime to transport a minor across state lines to obtain an abortion, and he voted to override President George W.

Bush's veto of a bill to expand federal funding for embryonic stem cell research, which uses surplus embryos from in vitro fertilization.

Higgins made local headlines in 2007 when, during a Sunday Mass in the church where he was baptized and married, a lay deacon rebuked him for supporting federal funding of embryonic stem cell research. Higgins walked out of the service and later got an apology from the pastor.

The Higgins family has been in Buffalo since his grandfather emigrated from Ireland as a 12-year-old orphan. His grandfather was a bricklayer, a trade he handed down to Higgins' father and uncles. Higgins and all four siblings helped lay bricks. His father served on the Buffalo Common Council, a job Higgins would hold as well, and later was a commissioner of the state workers' compensation board.

Higgins earned an undergraduate degree in political science from Buffalo State in 1984, followed by a master's degree in history a year later. He was elected to the Buffalo Common Council in 1987 at the age of 28.

After losing a 1993 bid for Erie County comptroller, he left upstate New York to get a master's degree at Harvard's Kennedy School of Government. He then returned home and worked as a legislative aide for the Erie County legislature and gave lectures at his alma mater, where he focused on the rise and fall of Buffalo as what he calls "one of the great industrial centers" of the United States. He was elected to the New York State Assembly in 1998, where he focused on local economic development.

When Republican Rep. Jack Quinn ended his 12-year run in Washington in 2004, Higgins jumped into the race and emerged the winner in a five-way Democratic primary. In the general election, he won by 3,774 votes, ending years of frustration for Democrats during the long tenure of Quinn, a moderate with a pro-labor voting record.

In late 2008, he was among the names considered to fill the Senate seat of New York Democrat Hillary Rodham Clinton, who became secretary of State. Leonard Lenihan, the Democratic chairman in Erie County, which includes Buffalo, backed Higgins, saying his appointment would blunt criticism that state Democrats are too New York City-centric. Ultimately, Democratic Gov. David A. Paterson went for an even newer face — Rep. Kirsten Gillibrand, who had just won her first re-election.

Higgins was re-elected easily that year, and again in 2010.

Higgins is a participant in the annual Congressional Hockey Challenge, which pits a team of lawmakers and staff against a team of lobbyists. Roll Call reported that Higgins' hockey claim to fame is having played with Patrick Kane Sr., father of the Chicago Blackhawks star.

Key Votes

2010

Overhaul the nation's health insurance system	YES
Allow for repeal of "don't ask, don't tell"	YES
Overhaul financial services industry regulation	YES
Limit use of new Afghanistan War funds to troop withdrawal activities	NO
Change oversight of offshore drilling and lift oil spill liability cap	YES
Provide a path to legal status for some children of illegal immigrants	NO
Extend Bush-era income tax cuts for two years	YES

2009

Expand the Children's Health Insurance Program	YES
Provide $787 billion in tax cuts and spending increases to stimulate the economy	YES
Allow bankruptcy judges to modify certain primary-residence mortgages	YES
Create a cap-and-trade system to limit greenhouse gas emissions	YES
Provide $2 billion for the "cash for clunkers" program	YES
Establish the government as the sole provider of student loans	YES
Restrict federally funded insurance coverage for abortions in health care overhaul	NO

CQ Vote Studies

	PARTY UNITY		PRESIDENTIAL SUPPORT	
	Support	Oppose	Support	Oppose
2010	98%	2%	90%	10%
2009	98%	2%	97%	3%
2008	99%	1%	20%	80%
2007	98%	2%	7%	93%
2006	89%	11%	33%	67%

Interest Groups

	AFL-CIO	ADA	CCUS	ACU
2010	93%	90%	25%	4%
2009	100%	100%	36%	0%
2008	100%	80%	65%	4%
2007	96%	95%	50%	0%
2006	100%	85%	43%	20%

New York 27

West — most of Buffalo; south and east suburbs

Tucked along the shores of Lake Erie in western New York, the 27th contains all of Erie County south of Buffalo and all but the northeastern corner of the city itself (which is in the 28th). Most of Buffalo's minority residents live in the 28th's portion of the city.

Nationwide economic downturns and a shrinking domestic auto market have hurt Buffalo's manufacturing base. The city's large blue-collar workforce used to rely on auto manufacturing, and shipping and cargo transportation were key to economic stability. Diversification into white-collar finance, insurance and real estate industries — growth driven mostly by two banks, HSBC and M&T, which provide thousands of area jobs and remained stable during the international financial crisis — bolstered the economy, but layoffs hit service and retail sectors. Health research facilities also are important in the Buffalo area.

Local leaders continue to see the waterfront as the core of Buffalo's renaissance effort. Development along the inner harbor is ongoing, and many officials believe the outer harbor presents a valuable opportunity to create both public space and commercial developments. The local professional sports teams, particularly football's Bills and hockey's Sabres, are a source of pride in the city.

The 27th follows the New York State Thruway southwest from Buffalo to take in all of Chautauqua County, which borders Lake Erie on the north and Pennsylvania on the south and west. This area is mainly made up of small communities that depend on agriculture and a robust grape-growing industry.

While some rural areas south of Buffalo in both Erie and Chautauqua counties can support Republicans, they cannot match the city's strong union ties: Barack Obama's 76 percent of the vote in Buffalo helped him win 54 percent of the 2008 presidential vote in the 27th.

Major Industry
Auto manufacturing, government, agriculture, tourism

Cities
Buffalo (pt.), 152,756; Cheektowaga (unincorporated), 75,178; West Seneca (unincorporated), 44,711; Jamestown, 31,146; Lackawanna, 18,141

Notable
Westfield, home to a Welch's plant, calls itself the "Grape Juice Capital of the World."

Rep. Louise M. Slaughter (D)

Capitol Office
225-3615
www.louise.house.gov
2469 Rayburn Bldg. 20515-3228; fax 225-7822

Committees
Rules - Ranking Member

Residence
Fairport

Born
Aug. 14, 1929; Harlan County, Ky.

Religion
Episcopalian

Family
Husband, Robert Slaughter; three children

Education
U. of Kentucky, B.S. 1951 (microbiology), M.P.H. 1953

Career
Market researcher; state government aide; microbiologist

Political Highlights
Monroe County Legislature, 1975-79; N.Y. Assembly, 1983-87

ELECTION RESULTS

2010 GENERAL

Slaughter (D)	102,514	64.9%
Jill A. Rowland (R)	55,392	35.1%

2010 PRIMARY

Slaughter (D, INDC, WFP)	unopposed

2008 GENERAL

Slaughter (D, INDC, WFM)	172,655	78.0%
David W. Crimmen (R, C)	48,690	22.0%

Previous Winning Percentages
2006 (73%); 2004 (73%); 2002 (62%); 2000 (66%);
1998 (65%); 1996 (57%); 1994 (57%); 1992 (55%);
1990 (59%); 1988 (57%); 1986 (51%)

Elected 1986; 13th term

Slaughter radiates the Southern-accented charm of her old Kentucky home. But when she's on a legislative campaign — especially about Medicare, genetic discrimination or other health issues — she can show the harder edge of her Rust Belt district in upstate New York.

She is an influential voice within her party and has served in the House longer than every Democratic woman but Marcy Kaptur of Ohio. She serves on the Democratic Steering and Policy Committee, which helps determine committee assignments, and in the 110th Congress (2007-08) became the first woman to chair the Rules Committee. She now is the ranking Democrat on the panel, making her the face of the party's efforts to stifle the GOP agenda through parliamentary process.

She had an early opportunity to poke the new majority on procedure after a pair of Republican lawmakers voted before being sworn into office in the opening days of the 112th Congress (2011-12).

Writing on her congressional blog, she said the "Republican majority threw their promises of transparency and accountability out the window and attempted to fix the Constitutional violation with a total of 4 minutes of debate."

Slaughter's background as a bacteriologist with a master's degree in public health makes her a player on health care issues. She was an enthusiastic supporter of the Democrats' health care overhaul law enacted in 2010 and had her name attached to a plan, deemed "the Slaughter solution" by its opponents, that would have allowed the House to clear the Senate version of the measure without voting on it. The idea was eventually scrapped.

She doesn't mince words when she thinks complex issues are being given short shrift. During consideration of the Medicare prescription drug bill in the 108th Congress (2003-04), Slaughter sarcastically noted that the House was to debate the issue for only three hours — compared with two weeks of Senate discussion. "We are not naming a post office here. We are considering . . . the most important change to Medicare since its creation," she said. On the other hand, when Democrats brought the health care overhaul bill to the floor for final consideration, the rule for the bill — written by Slaughter's committee — allowed no amendments to be offered.

Slaughter has fought a long battle against genetic discrimination. Early in the 109th Congress (2005-06), she was gearing up to do so again, after the Senate passed its version of a bill barring employers and insurers from discriminating against people based on their genetic profile. Opposition in the House had stalled the measure repeatedly in that chamber.

"For nearly a decade, I have championed this legislation because the American people have a right to expect that when they make the decision to undergo genetic testing, their private genetic information will be protected from abuse," Slaughter said. "Two presidents, two Senates, and legions of Americans have endorsed this bill. It's time for the House to act."

When President George W. Bush signed her measure into law in 2008, she called the legislation "the most important thing I have done in my life."

In addition to her interest in health care, Slaughter is a strong advocate of the arts and is the co-chairwoman of the Congressional Arts Caucus. In 2004, she won adoption of a House floor amendment boosting funds for the National Endowment for the Arts by $10 million and for the National Endowment for the Humanities by $3.5 million.

Slaughter lives in a suburb of Rochester where she has spent most of her adult life, but she was brought up in the mountains of Kentucky's Harlan County, a genuine coal miner's daughter. When she came to Congress in 1987, House Democratic leaders quickly took a liking to her warmth, grit and liberal views. They gave her a seat on the Rules Committee in 1989 and on the Budget Committee in 1991. But her rise through the party then slowed. She lost a bid to be vice chairwoman of the Democratic Caucus in the 104th Congress (1995-96). And she was edged out in the 105th Congress (1997-98) for the top Democratic slot on the Budget Committee. She left the panel after that defeat as her term expired.

In 2002, Democratic Whip Nancy Pelosi of California named Slaughter as her point person on "issues that concern women." In the 108th Congress, she was the Democratic co-chairwoman of the Congressional Caucus for Women's Issues. She once called a Republican plan to curtail family-planning aid to developing countries "inhumane," and she attacked as "shameful" the successful effort to ban a procedure opponents call "partial birth" abortion. In 2011, she said a GOP bill to bar federal funding for abortion "takes women back to the Dark Ages."

Her legislative successes include the establishment of a national task force to ensure that children get proper care in the event of a terrorist attack, and a bill to increase education about the anti-miscarriage drug DES, which studies have suggested causes an increased risk of cancer and abnormalities in the children of some women who take the drug.

Slaughter moved to New York in the 1950s, when her husband went to work as an executive with a local corporation. Her first brush with public policy came in 1971 when she joined with some neighbors to try to save a stand of trees from development. "I thought in my best Kentucky fashion that if I would put on my best dress and go and be very nice and polite and ask them to save this forest that they would say, 'Well, why not?' " she later told the Associated Press. "And they just handed me my hat."

The episode sparked an interest in politics. She served as a Monroe County legislator and as an assistant to Mario Cuomo, New York's secretary of state. In 1982, she ousted a Republican incumbent to move to the state Assembly, where she served four years before winning her seat in the House with 51 percent of the vote against first-term Republican Fred J. Eckert. Actor Richard Gere, with whom she shared an interest in Central American issues, campaigned door to door with her. He later headlined a 2002 fundraiser.

Not until 1998, in her seventh House election, did Slaughter begin to draw better than 60 percent. Reapportionment after the 2000 census cost New York two House seats, and the state legislature placed Slaughter in the same district as 14-term Democrat John J. LaFalce. When efforts to alter the map failed, LaFalce retired rather than face Slaughter in a primary. She won by 25 percentage points in 2002 and quickly began cultivating new parts of her district in Buffalo and Niagara Falls. She has not been seriously challenged since.

Key Votes

2010

Overhaul the nation's health insurance system	YES
Allow for repeal of "don't ask, don't tell"	YES
Overhaul financial services industry regulation	YES
Limit use of new Afghanistan War funds to troop withdrawal activities	YES
Change oversight of offshore drilling and lift oil spill liability cap	YES
Provide a path to legal status for some children of illegal immigrants	YES
Extend Bush-era income tax cuts for two years	NO

2009

Expand the Children's Health Insurance Program	YES
Provide $787 billion in tax cuts and spending increases to stimulate the economy	YES
Allow bankruptcy judges to modify certain primary-residence mortgages	YES
Create a cap-and-trade system to limit greenhouse gas emissions	YES
Provide $2 billion for the "cash for clunkers" program	YES
Establish the government as the sole provider of student loans	YES
Restrict federally funded insurance coverage for abortions in health care overhaul	NO

CQ Vote Studies

	PARTY UNITY		PRESIDENTIAL SUPPORT	
	SUPPORT	OPPOSE	SUPPORT	OPPOSE
2010	100%	0%	89%	11%
2009	99%	1%	95%	5%
2008	100%	0%	12%	88%
2007	99%	1%	4%	96%
2006	99%	1%	14%	86%

Interest Groups

	AFL-CIO	ADA	CCUS	ACU
2010	100%	100%	13%	0%
2009	100%	90%	45%	4%
2008	100%	95%	47%	0%
2007	100%	100%	47%	0%
2006	100%	85%	29%	9%

New York 28

Northwest — Rochester, part of Buffalo

A small strip of land along Lake Ontario connects the ends — Buffalo and Rochester — of the telephone-receiver-shaped 28th District. The district encompasses the northeastern portion of Buffalo, all of Niagara Falls and almost all of Rochester, giving the 28th most of the Democratic-rich voting areas in western New York. After a decade of significant population loss, particularly from Buffalo, the district is now one of the least populous in the nation ahead of decennial remapping.

Unemployment rates in Buffalo and Rochester have stayed low despite nationwide economic declines. Decades of job losses in the manufacturing sector have largely been offset by health care and service industry employment, but lower salaries have exacerbated the problems of Rochester's low-income residents.

The University of Rochester is the city's largest employer, and its optics institute is highly ranked, while the Rochester Institute of Technology has one of the nation's best imaging science departments. Despite layoffs at Eastman Kodak and Xerox, the two firms have helped drive Rochester's economy for years. Work at centers such as the Roswell Park Cancer Institute and the Hauptman-Woodward Medical Research Institute has helped transform the Buffalo region into a health care hub.

Niagara Falls attracts millions of tourists from around the world, but many of those visitors travel to the Canadian side of the border rather than the 28th's side. Local officials hope revitalization efforts and the Seneca Niagara Casino will continue to draw visitors to the U.S. shore.

Between Rochester and Buffalo, the 28th is home to rural communities that farm fruit and favor the GOP.

Minorities total 39 percent of the 28th's population, giving it a far higher proportion of minority residents than any other New York district north of Westchester County. Combined with the remnants of a blue-collar workforce, minorities helped Barack Obama win 68 percent of the district's 2008 presidential vote.

Major Industry

Service, tourism, higher education, research

Cities

Rochester (pt.), 210,541; Buffalo (pt.), 108,554; Tonawanda (unincorporated), 58,144; Niagara Falls, 50,193

Notable

Women's rights activist Susan B. Anthony and abolitionist Frederick Douglass are both buried in Rochester's Mount Hope Cemetery.

Rep. Tom Reed (R)

Capitol Office
225-3161
reed.house.gov
1037 Longworth Bldg. 20515-3229; fax 226-6599

Committees
Rules

Residence
Corning

Born
Nov. 18, 1971; Joliet, Ill.

Religion
Roman Catholic

Family
Wife, Jean Reed; two children

Education
Alfred U., B.A. 1993 (political science); Ohio Northern U., J.D. 1996

Career
Lawyer; real estate company owner

Political Highlights
Mayor of Corning, 2008-09

ELECTION RESULTS

2010 SPECIAL

Reed (R, C, I)	105,907	56.8%
Matthew Zeller (D, WFM)	80,480	43.2%

2010 GENERAL

Reed (R)	112,314	56.5%
Matthew Zeller (D)	86,099	43.3%

2010 PRIMARY

Reed (R, C)	unopposed

Elected 2010; 1st full term

Reed holds firm to his conservative views, while saying he is willing to work with Democrats and compromise to advance his ideas. In the spring of 2011, though, he joined the Rules Committee, which works with the GOP leadership to set the parameters of debate for legislation on the floor. His first priority on the committee is to serve his party's leaders by greasing the skids for Republican-backed legislation and deterring Democratic parliamentary tactics.

Although not technically a freshman because he took his seat in late 2010 as a result of a special-election victory that coincided with the general election, he also has been tasked with joining the four other GOP newcomers on the panel as conduits to the large freshman class. He says Speaker John A. Boehner of Ohio and other party leaders have done a good job of bringing the first-year members into the process.

"They actually take the effort to communicate with us and truly listen to us; that's powerful," Reed told Roll Call.

The Rules Committee is a partisan assignment, but Reed said he sees "self-righteous name-calling" as counterproductive. That didn't stop him from taking the lead in chastising Senate Democrats for what he saw as their lack of interest in cutting spending, which he considers his primary legislative focus.

"There has been no leadership coming out of the Senate," Reed said on Fox News in April 2011.

He supports a hard cap on non-defense discretionary appropriations to "force a national dialogue" on the deficit. He also backed the catchall appropriations bill the House passed in February 2011 that would cut $58 billion from fiscal 2011 spending. It included three Reed proposals: to cut $15 million for the Presidio Trust Fund; to remove an automatic pay increase for Foreign Service employees living outside the Washington, D.C. area; and to block funding for a sewage system in Tijuana, Mexico.

"At a time when we have to borrow 40 cents of every dollar we spend, every program has to be scrutinized to be sure U.S. taxpayers are getting a return on their investment," Reed said.

One area where he sees a role for government is on transportation spending. To join Rules in April 2011 he had to take a leave of absence from the Transportation and Infrastructure Committee. He says his experience as mayor of Corning made him aware of the importance of infrastructure to economic development.

"I am an outspoken advocate for limited government," he wrote in a Roll Call op-ed in early 2011. "Government should only do what individuals cannot. Making transportation and infrastructure investments is one of the legitimate roles of government."

During the campaign he vowed to fight to keep in place, for all income levels, the tax cuts enacted during the George W. Bush administration, and backed a two-year extension enacted in late 2010. But he had scathing words for the process that led to that vote. "Shame on the politicians whose inaction over a decade forced us onto this precarious ledge," he wrote in an op-ed following the vote.

Reed backed repeal of the health care overhaul enacted in 2010, calling the law a "monstrosity of new spending and government bureaucracy." He acknowledged that success is unlikely while Democrats control the Senate and President Obama is in the White House, but said it is important to keep debate going on the issue.

The son of a veteran of World War II and the Korean War, Reed voted in March 2011 against requiring U.S. troops to withdraw from Afghanistan within 30 days. "Until generals in the field tell us that al Qaeda and the Taliban are no longer a threat in Afghanistan, the mission is not complete," Reed said.

While saying that Libyan leader Muammar el-Qaddafi "needs to go," he was critical of Obama's handling of the turmoil in Libya in early 2011.

"We need clear leadership on this issue and I don't see it. . . . What is this 'no fly' zone and what role are American troops going to have?" he told the Hornell Evening Tribune. "The bottom line is I'm very concerned the president has not identified the mission to our troops and leaders."

He says he is "disturbed" at earmarks on defense spending bills, but would not vote against a broader defense bill or war funding legislation simply because they included earmarks. During the campaign, he backed "complete disclosure of earmarks from cradle to grave" and said the only requests he planned to make would be for "those directly related to national security, public safety, or infrastructure." House Republicans subsequently imposed a moratorium on earmarks for fiscal 2012.

One of 12 children, Reed lives with his wife and two children in the house his grandfather built in Corning. He served one term as mayor of his hometown before setting his sights on Congress.

Reed says he knew the country was headed down the wrong path when he saw President Obama's agenda, including the $787 billion stimulus law, which he calls a "horrible mistake."

"The moment rang in my head as, 'This is not sustainable,' " he said. He backed efforts early in the 112th Congress (2011-12) to end some of the programs funded by the legislation and return unspent stimulus money to the Treasury.

New York's 29th District, which takes in the southwestern portion of the state, had gone without a representative since March 2010, when Democrat Eric Massa resigned after being accused of sexually harassing male staff members.

Reed had declared his candidacy prior to Massa's announcement, and he defeated Democrat Matthew Zeller with 57 percent of the vote. He was elected to fill the remainder of Massa's term at the same time he was elected to the 112th Congress.

Just before he was to be sworn in, Reed was hospitalized in mid-November after he awoke feeling ill and suffering shortness of breath. He was diagnosed with a blood clot in his lungs and was released after four days.

Key Votes

2010

Provide a path to legal status for some children of illegal immigrants	NO
Extend Bush-era income tax cuts for two years	YES

CQ Vote Studies

	PARTY UNITY		PRESIDENTIAL SUPPORT	
	SUPPORT	OPPOSE	SUPPORT	OPPOSE
2010	92%	8%	29%	71%

Interest Groups

	AFL-CIO	ADA	CCUS	ACU
2010	0%		100%	100%

New York 29

Southern Tier — Elmira, Corning; Rochester suburbs

The 29th blankets much of the southwestern portion of New York known as the Southern Tier, encompassing a mix of forests, lakes, farms and small towns. It also reaches north to take in the western portion of the Finger Lakes region and some of Rochester's suburbs.

Agriculture helps drive the economy, mostly through farms and wineries. The Finger Lakes and surrounding parks draw thousands of visitors annually, and the Finger Lakes region is the nation's largest wine-producing area by volume outside of California.

In the north, the 29th takes in southern parts of Monroe County outside Rochester, where a plurality of the district's residents live. It wraps around the west, south and east sides of the city, taking in mostly GOP-leaning towns.

The 29th's westernmost point is Cattaraugus County, a rural area that includes Allegany State Park, St. Bonaventure University and the headquarters of kitchen cutlery maker CUTCO in Olean.

To the east, Republicans hold a roughly 2-to-1 registration advantage over Democrats in Allegany, Steuben and Yates counties.

Steuben County hosts a thriving tourism industry as well as Corning, one of the better-known U.S. company towns due to its glass products and costly crystal pieces.

Between Corning, which also is known for its optics industry, and Elmira, located in adjacent Chemung County, are several heavy manufacturing plants.

Republicans hold an edge over Democrats in voter registration in the district overall despite the legacy of a blue-collar workforce. Republican John McCain eked out a win here with a 50 percent majority in the 2008 presidential election. The 29th also has the lowest percentage of Hispanic residents (2 percent) in any New York district.

Major Industry
Agriculture, manufacturing, tourism

Cities
Elmira, 29,200; Brighton (unincorporated) (pt.), 26,836; Olean, 14,452

Notable
Watkins Glen International race track ("The Glen") is just south of Seneca Lake.

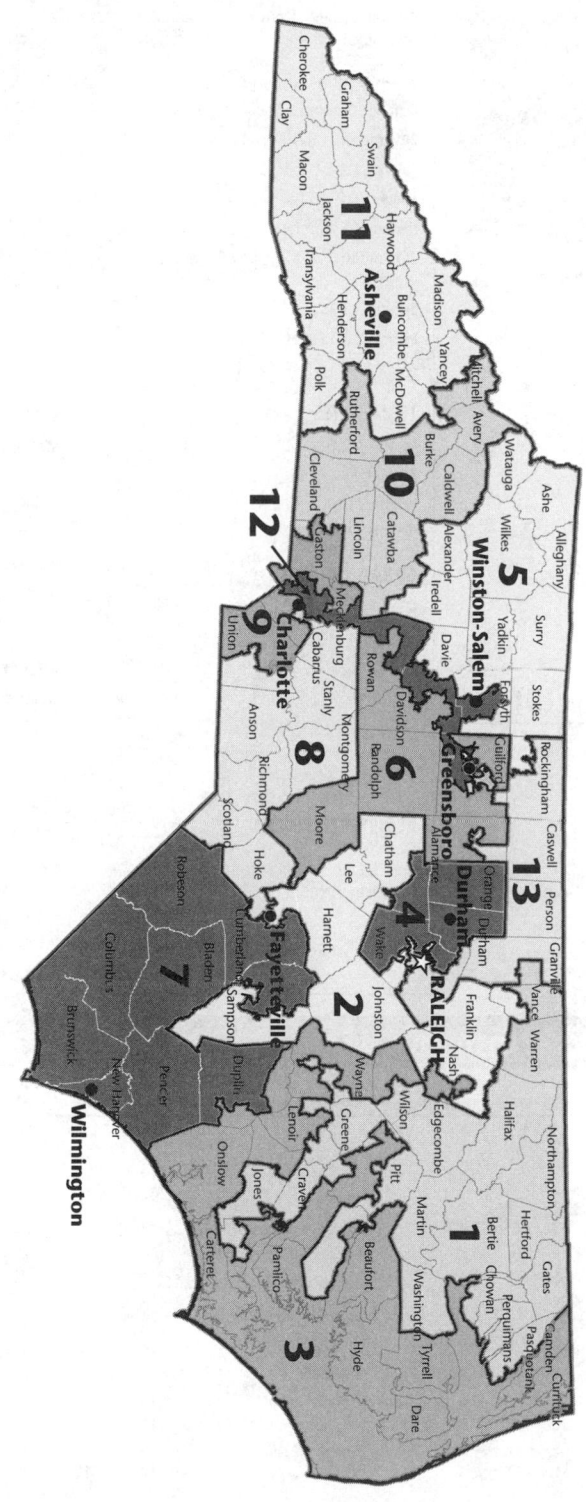

Gov. Bev Perdue (D)

First elected: 2008

Length of term: 4 years

Term expires: 1/13

Salary: $139,590

Phone: (919) 733-4240

Residence: New Bern

Born: January 14, 1947; Grundy, Va.

Religion: Episcopalian

Family: Husband, Bob Eaves; two children, two stepchildren

Education: U. of Kentucky, B.A. 1969 (history); U. of Florida, M.Ed. 1974 (educational administration), Ph.D. 1976 (educational administration)

Career: Geriatric health care specialist; teacher

Political highlights: N.C. House, 1987-90; N.C. Senate, 1991-2000; lieutenant governor, 2001-09

ELECTION RESULTS

2008 GENERAL

Bev Perdue (D)	2,146,189	50.3%
Pat McCrory (R)	2,001,168	46.9%
Michael C. Munger (LIBERT)	121,584	2.8%

Lt. Gov. Walter Dalton (D)

First elected: 2008

Length of term: 4 years

Term expires: 1/13

Salary: $123,198

Phone: (919) 733-7350

LEGISLATURE

General Assembly: Convenes in January in odd-numbered years. There is no statutory or constitutional requirement for when session must end.

Senate: 50 members, 2-year terms

2011 ratios: 31 R, 19 D; 44 men, 6 women

Salary: $13,951

Phone: (919) 733-4111

House: 120 members, 2-year terms

2011 ratios: 67 R, 52 D, 1 I; 88 men, 32 women

Salary: $13,951

Phone: (919) 733-4111

TERM LIMITS

Governor: 2 consecutive terms

Senate: No

House: No

URBAN STATISTICS

CITY	POPULATION
Charlotte	731,424
Raleigh	403,892
Greensboro	269,666
Winston-Salem	229,617
Durham	228,330

REGISTERED VOTERS

Democrat	44%
Republican	32%
Unaffiliated/other	24%

POPULATION

2010 population	9,535,483
2000 population	8,049,313
1990 population	6,628,637
Percent change (2000-2010)	+18.5%
Rank among states (2010)	10
Median age	36.6
Born in state	59.2%
Foreign born	6.5%
Violent crime rate	404/100,000
Poverty level	16.3%
Federal workers	86,244
Military	116,073

ELECTIONS

STATE ELECTION OFFICIAL

(919) 733-7173

DEMOCRATIC PARTY

(919) 821-2777

REPUBLICAN PARTY

(919) 828-6423

MISCELLANEOUS

Web: www.ncgov.com

Capital: Raleigh

U.S. CONGRESS

Senate: 1 Democrat, 1 Republican

House: 7 Democrats, 6 Republicans

2010 CENSUS STATISTICS BY DISTRICT

District	2008 Vote for President Obama	McCain	White	Black	Asian	Hispanic	Median Income	White Collar	Blue Collar	Service Industry	Over 64	Under 18	College Education	Rural	Sq. Miles
1	63%	37%	43%	49%	1%	5%	$31,890	48%	32%	21%	15%	24%	13%	52%	7,199
2	52	47	56	28	1	12	43,113	54	30	16	10	26	18	50	3,956
3	38	61	72	16	1	7	45,056	58	25	17	12	23	22	47	6,192
4	62	37	63	19	6	9	63,726	75	12	12	9	25	52	17	1,253
5	38	61	83	8	1	7	44,536	56	29	15	15	23	23	57	4,402
6	36	63	79	10	2	7	49,328	58	28	14	14	24	25	48	2,944
7	47	52	62	21	1	7	40,096	53	28	19	14	23	21	55	6,087
8	52	47	54	28	2	12	42,462	54	28	18	11	26	20	31	3,283
9	45	55	72	15	3	8	62,422	70	18	12	10	27	39	16	991
10	36	63	82	9	2	6	41,544	51	33	16	14	24	17	50	3,302
11	47	52	87	4	1	6	40,439	55	27	19	18	21	24	56	6,025
12	71	29	39	43	3	12	40,132	55	28	18	10	26	23	11	821
13	59	40	56	28	3	11	46,252	61	23	15	11	24	31	26	2,256
STATE	50	49	65	21	2	8	45,069	58	26	16	12	24	26	40	48,711
U.S.	53	46	64	12	5	16	51,425	60	23	17	13	25	28	21	3,537,438

Sen. Richard M. Burr (R)

Capitol Office
224-3154
burr.senate.gov
217 Russell Bldg. 20510-3306; fax 228-2981

Committees
Finance
Health, Education, Labor & Pensions
Veterans' Affairs - Ranking Member
Select Intelligence

Residence
Winston-Salem

Born
Nov. 30, 1955; Charlottesville, Va.

Religion
Methodist

Family
Wife, Brooke Burr; two children

Education
Wake Forest U., B.A. 1978 (communications)

Career
Marketing manager; kitchen appliance salesman

Political Highlights
Republican nominee for U.S. House, 1992; U.S. House, 1995-2005

ELECTION RESULTS

2010 GENERAL

Richard M. Burr (R)	1,458,046	54.8%
Elaine Marshall (D)	1,145,074	43.0%
Mike Beitler (LIBERT)	55,687	2.1%

2010 PRIMARY

Richard M. Burr (R)	297,993	80.1%
Brad Jones (R)	37,616	10.1%
Eddie Burks (R)	22,111	5.9%
Larry Linney (R)	14,248	3.8%

2004 GENERAL

Richard M. Burr (R)	1,791,450	51.6%
Erskine Bowles (D)	1,632,527	47.0%
Tom Bailey (LIBERT)	47,743	1.4%

Previous Winning Percentages
2002 House Election (70%); 2000 House Election (93%); 1998 House Election (68%); 1996 House Election (62%); 1994 House Election (57%)

Elected 2004; 2nd term

Burr is a serious-minded conservative who has won attention from his party's leaders for his diligent work on terrorism, health care and veterans' issues. His adherence to the Republican agenda helped him earn appointment as chief deputy whip in 2009, and he is considered a candidate to move up with the impending retirement of Minority Whip Jon Kyl of Arizona. He also won appointment to the powerful Finance Committee in 2011.

Burr's five terms in the House were marked by his reliability: on votes that split majorities of the two parties, he never sided with the GOP less than 92 percent of the time. In the Senate, he has been even more dependable.

As a North Carolina lawmaker, Burr is a champion for tobacco companies, including Reynolds American Inc., a big employer in his hometown of Winston-Salem. He opposed legislation directing the Food and Drug Administration to regulate tobacco, arguing in a 2008 opinion column in USA Today that giving the FDA control over tobacco would "severely impede the FDA's core mission" by taking the agency's focus away from existing problems such as drug and food safety. He joined his fellow North Carolina senator, Democrat Kay Hagan, in April 2009 on a less stringent alternative that would impose limits on marketing tobacco. He also helped win passage in 2004 of a popular tobacco buyout that steered $3.8 billion to his state's farmers. Personally, however, Burr is anti-tobacco. He quit smoking cigarettes in 1998 after making a televised vow to do so.

In September 2007, Burr took over as the top Republican on the Veterans' Affairs Committee. He worked closely with the George W. Bush administration to protect GOP priorities when Democrats moved in 2008 to expand education benefits for veterans under the GI Bill. He helped win inclusion of Bush's proposal to allow veterans to transfer unused benefits to family members.

But he doesn't always succeed. He sought to strip a provision from a 2008 veterans' bill that would make compensation payments to surviving Filipino soldiers who fought in World War II and replace them with housing and car grants for American veterans. "Is this the right priority at a time of war, when the needs of our men and women serving in Iraq and Afghanistan are so great?" he asked. But several senators who served in World War II objected to his attempt, and it was defeated.

In early 2011, he chided the Obama administration for being slow to implement a program enacted the previous year that provides key benefits to critically injured veterans.

A member of the Health, Education, Labor and Pensions Committee, Burr was chairman of its Bioterrorism and Public Health Preparedness Subcommittee in the 109th Congress (2005-06). He won enactment in late 2006 of his bill aimed at boosting the nation's preparedness for a bioterror attack or major disease outbreak. That was the culmination of Burr's two-year effort in the Senate to renew and update a 2002 law that strengthened defenses against biological or chemical attack in the aftermath of the Sept. 11 terrorist attacks. Burr had been a chief negotiator in drafting the original law.

He also sits on the Select Intelligence Committee. He and Democrat Bob Casey of Pennsylvania formed a caucus on terrorism and weapons of mass destruction in 2009.

Along with a pair of leading conservatives, Sen. Tom Coburn of Oklahoma and Rep. Paul D. Ryan of Wisconsin, Burr sponsored an alternative to the Democrats' health care overhaul in 2009, separately from the bill that Republican leaders endorsed. Their measure would have provided a tax credit to individuals to purchase insurance.

He joined an August 2010 letter to Health and Human Services Secretary Kathleen Sebelius demanding that her department stop running an ad campaign featuring actor Andy Griffith — something of a North Carolina icon from his days portraying the sheriff of fictional Mayberry — that touts the benefits of the health care overhaul.

"We can debate the merits of the new law, but co-opting public funds during a recession to make a political, poll-tested argument about the new law is wrong," read the letter, signed by Burr and four other Republican senators.

Demonstrating his flexibility and dealmaking bona fides, after initially blocking legislation to expand funding for the global fight against AIDS and other diseases, Burr helped hammer out a compromise enacted in 2008.

Burr supports increased domestic oil drilling along with expanding renewable energy. He also touts nuclear power, which provides almost one-third of his state's electricity. He was a likely candidate for the top GOP slot on the Energy and Natural Resources panel after ranking Republican Lisa Murkowski of Alaska lost her 2010 primary bid and launched a write-in campaign for re-election. But party leaders decided to leave her in the spot. Burr left the panel in May 2011 to join the Finance Committee.

Close ties to Republican Sen. John McCain of Arizona, his party's presidential nominee, led to Burr's inclusion on some early lists of potential vice presidential nominees in 2008. Burr played down such rumors, avowing no interest in following Aaron Burr, a distant relative who was a New York senator and vice president under Thomas Jefferson.

Burr made a bid for Republican Conference chairman when the No. 3 leadership post opened up in late 2007, but he lost to Lamar Alexander of Tennessee by a vote of 31-16. Burr said he thought the leadership could use a younger voice to "move forward with a new generation of voters."

Born in Virginia, Burr moved with his family to Winston-Salem when he was 6. His minister father, head of the city's 3,000-member First Presbyterian Church, was often gone, tending to his large flock. After college, Burr took a job with Carswell Distributing, selling appliances and teaching housewives how to cook with their newfangled microwave ovens. He rose to national sales manager. He also became active politically in the growing conservative anti-tax movement, co-chairing North Carolina Taxpayers United.

Burr came home from his job one day in 1991 and surprised his wife by announcing he wanted to run for Congress, even though he had no political experience and no clue what a congressman earned. He lost his first bid in 1992, got back in the fray two years later and won with 57 percent of the vote against state Sen. A.P. "Sandy" Sands. He arrived as part of the House GOP's historic Class of '94, but soon proved to be more pragmatic than many of his fellow newcomers. He played a large role in winning passage in 1997 of legislation to speed FDA approval of new drugs and medical devices.

Encouraged by state party officials to run for governor in 2000, Burr declined. He wanted to run for an open Senate seat in 2002, but deferred to Elizabeth Dole, the former Cabinet secretary who was the Bush administration's choice. He began preparing to run for the state's other Senate seat, held by Democrat John Edwards, more than a year in advance of the 2004 election, before Edwards announced he would not run again.

Burr weathered criticism for an initially lackluster campaign against Democrat Erskine Bowles, chief of staff to during Bill Clinton's administration. But aided by Bush's strong showing, Burr won with 52 percent of the vote to Bowles' 47 percent.

In 2010, he defeated the Democratic nominee, North Carolina Secretary of State Elaine Marshall, 55 percent to 43 percent.

Key Votes

2010

Pass budget reconciliation bill to modify overhauls of health care and federal student loan programs	NO
Proceed to disapproval resolution on EPA authority to regulate greenhouse gases	YES
Overhaul financial services industry regulation	NO
Limit debate to proceed to a bill to broaden campaign finance disclosure and reporting rules	NO
Limit debate on an extension of Bush-era income tax cuts for two years	YES
Limit debate on a bill to provide a path to legal status for some children of illegal immigrants	NO
Allow for a repeal of "don't ask, don't tell"	YES
Consent to ratification of a strategic arms reduction treaty with Russia	NO

2009

Prevent release of remaining financial industry bailout funds	YES
Make it easier for victims to sue for wage discrimination remedies	NO
Expand the Children's Health Insurance Program	NO
Limit debate on the economic stimulus measure	NO
Repeal District of Columbia firearms prohibitions and gun registration laws	YES
Limit debate on expansion of federal hate crimes law	NO
Strike funding for F-22 Raptor fighter jets	NO

CQ Vote Studies

	PARTY UNITY		PRESIDENTIAL SUPPORT	
	SUPPORT	OPPOSE	SUPPORT	OPPOSE
2010	96%	4%	43%	57%
2009	97%	3%	39%	61%
2008	99%	1%	81%	19%
2007	97%	3%	89%	11%
2006	94%	6%	88%	12%
2005	95%	5%	89%	11%
2004	92%	8%	79%	21%
2003	94%	6%	96%	4%
2002	95%	5%	92%	8%
2001	95%	5%	93%	7%

Interest Groups

	AFL-CIO	ADA	CCUS	ACU
2010	7%	5%	100%	92%
2009	6%	10%	71%	100%
2008	10%	5%	100%	79%
2007	5%	0%	73%	92%
2006	20%	10%	67%	92%
2005	29%	5%	94%	92%
2004	33%	10%	94%	87%
2003	27%	15%	93%	84%
2002	11%	0%	100%	96%
2001	17%	10%	96%	88%

Sen. Kay Hagan (D)

Capitol Office
224-6342
hagan.senate.gov
521 Dirksen Bldg. 20510; fax 224-1100

Committees
Armed Services
  (Emerging Threats & Capabilities - Chairwoman)
Banking, Housing & Urban Affairs
Health, Education, Labor & Pensions
Small Business & Entrepreneurship

Residence
Greensboro

Born
May 26, 1953; Shelby, N.C.

Religion
Presbyterian

Family
Husband, Chip Hagan; three children

Education
Florida State U., B.A. 1975 (American studies); Wake
Forest U., J.D. 1978

Career
Homemaker; bank executive

Political Highlights
N.C. Senate, 1999-2009

ELECTION RESULTS

2008 GENERAL

Kay Hagan (D)	2,249,311	52.6%
Elizabeth Dole (R)	1,887,510	44.2%
Christopher Cole (LIBERT)	133,430	3.1%

2008 PRIMARY

Kay Hagan (D)	801,920	60.1%
Jim Neal (D)	239,623	17.9%
Marcus W. Williams (D)	170,970	12.8%
Duskin C. Lassiter (D)	62,136	4.6%
Howard Staley (D)	60,403	4.5%

Elected 2008; 1st term

Hagan has shown herself to be a steadfast advocate for her state, and occasionally that puts her at odds with her party. But mostly she is a dependable Democratic vote, one who sided with the majority of her party 90 percent of the time in her first years in office.

Hagan said she learned early on — as the daughter of a Florida mayor and the niece of Democrat Lawton Chiles, a former Sunshine State governor and senator — that much of politics is local. With that experience helping to guide her, she distinguished herself from her party just months after arriving in the Senate.

In June 2009, Hagan was the only Democrat to vote against a bill to allow the Food and Drug Administration to regulate the manufacturing, sale and promotion of tobacco products — an industry linked to 255,000 North Carolina jobs, according to that state's Department of Agriculture and Consumer Services. Hagan backed an alternative proposal by her North Carolina colleague, Republican Richard M. Burr, to create a separate regulatory entity that could test only for nicotine levels and require that products be labeled accordingly. "I will not stand idly by while the FDA is put in charge of such a critical industry to North Carolina," said Hagan, who spent summers as a child helping harvest the crop on her grandparents' farm.

Like many of her Southern Democratic colleagues, Hagan is a passionate supporter of Second Amendment rights. Her Senate website describes gun ownership as "part of the fabric of North Carolina." In February 2009, she joined 40 Republicans and 21 other Democrats in voting to repeal the District of Columbia's firearms prohibitions and gun registration laws.

On most other issues, Hagan consistently sided with fellow Democrats. That included votes in favor of the $787 billion economic stimulus package, expansion of the Children's Health Insurance Program and the health care overhaul. She also voted to repeal the statutory ban on homosexuals serving openly in the military. "Anybody who's qualified should be able to serve," said Hagan, whose state is home to several large military posts.

A member of the Moderate Dems Working Group, Hagan backs balancing the federal budget with pay-as-you-go rules, which require new spending to be offset by cuts in other programs or tax increases. She also opposed a two-year extension of the Bush-era tax cuts that was enacted in late 2010 because it included the highest-income groups.

She expressed frustration with the use of short-term spending legislation to continue funding the government early in 2011. "We need to be sitting down," Hagan told Roll Call. "We need to have leadership from the president, but we also need to focus on the task at hand."

But Hagan has been an avid user of earmarks to fund local projects, claiming credit for $92.5 million for her state in the fiscal 2010 appropriations bills.

Hagan also supported allocating stimulus funds to North Carolina initiatives, including two $200 million grants for energy companies to develop smart energy grid technology, $49.2 million for a lithium-ion battery manufacturer and $39 million for an LED lighting company. A member of the Small Business and Entrepreneurship Committee, she cited the savings in energy costs as a way to boost small businesses. She introduced a bill in February 2011 to increase domestic production of lithium. Two of three companies capable of doing such work are located in North Carolina.

Her position on the Health, Education, Labor and Pensions Committee gave Hagan a front-row seat in the negotiations on the health care overhaul, as well as opportunities to forge relationships across party lines. She worked with Republicans Orrin G. Hatch of Utah and Michael B. Enzi of Wyoming to ensure that an amendment authorizing the FDA to approve generic versions of biologic drugs — substances generally derived from living cells, rather than chemicals — was retained through the many iterations of the legislation.

She also helped incorporate in the legislation a provision she cosponsored with Colorado Democrat Mark Udall to increase the number of primary care doctors in rural communities, and a measure to require national and state-by-state diabetes report cards and a review of diabetes medical education.

The author of North Carolina's financial literacy education law, Hagan hopes to incorporate a similar provision in the reauthorization of the Bush-era education law known as No Child Left Behind.

She also worked as a state senator to ban payday lending and introduced a bill in the U.S. Senate to restrict, although not end, the practice nationally.

On the Armed Services Committee, Hagan is an advocate for families previously afflicted by water contamination at North Carolina's Camp Lejeune, the largest Marine Corps base on the East Coast. She and Burr pushed the Navy to fund a mortality study on the contamination and included an amendment in the 2010 Defense spending bill to prevent the Navy from disposing of water contamination claims before certain studies are completed.

Though she never served herself, Hagan has several connections to the military; her father-in-law was a two-star Marine general, her brother and father both served in the Navy, and her husband is a Vietnam veteran who used the GI Bill to help pay for law school. She chairs the Emerging Threats and Capabilities Subcommittee.

A former bank official, Hagan added the Banking, Housing and Urban Affairs Committee to her portfolio in the 112th Congress (2011-12).

Hagan was born in Shelby, N.C., and her family later moved to Lakeland, Fla., where her father became the city's mayor. She attended college at Florida State University, then spent six months interning for her uncle in Washington, where she operated a senators-only elevator.

Afterward, she returned to North Carolina to attend Wake Forest University's law school, where she met her husband, Chip. The couple settled in Greensboro, where Hagan worked first as an attorney and then as a vice president in the estates and trust division for North Carolina National Bank (now Bank of America). She left after 10 years to raise her family.

She was recruited into politics by four-term Democratic Gov. James B. Hunt, who selected her to lead his Guilford County organization in his 1992 and 1996 campaigns. In 1998, Hunt and state Sen. Marc Basnight recruited Hagan to challenge a GOP state senator. She won and served five terms.

She was uncertain at first about the 2008 Senate race against Republican Elizabeth Dole, announcing in October 2007 that she would not be a candidate, then changing her mind a short time later.

Hagan won 60 percent of the vote in the Democratic primary and blanketed the state with campaign appearances as the national Democratic Party spent heavily in support of her. Emphasizing her North Carolina roots, she frequently jabbed Dole — wife of former Senate Majority Leader and 1996 GOP presidential nominee Bob Dole — for a life spent largely in Kansas and Washington. Hagan also benefited from a strong national Democratic tide that helped Barack Obama edge out the GOP nominee, Sen. John McCain of Arizona, to carry Republican-leaning North Carolina in the presidential race. President George W. Bush had easily won the state in 2000 and 2004. Late in the campaign, as polls began to indicate a Hagan victory, Dole ran television ads suggesting Hagan was an atheist. Hagan, a Sunday school teacher and elder at her church, fired back both in an ad, declaring "I believe in God," and a lawsuit, charging Dole with defamation. Hagan withdrew the lawsuit after winning by 8 percentage points.

Key Votes

2010

Pass budget reconciliation bill to modify overhauls of health care and federal student loan programs	YES
Proceed to disapproval resolution on EPA authority to regulate greenhouse gases	NO
Overhaul financial services industry regulation	YES
Limit debate to proceed to a bill to broaden campaign finance disclosure and reporting rules	YES
Limit debate on an extension of Bush-era income tax cuts for two years	NO
Limit debate on a bill to provide a path to legal status for some children of illegal immigrants	NO
Allow for a repeal of "don't ask, don't tell"	YES
Consent to ratification of a strategic arms reduction treaty with Russia	YES

2009

Prevent release of remaining financial industry bailout funds	NO
Make it easier for victims to sue for wage discrimination remedies	YES
Expand the Children's Health Insurance Program	YES
Limit debate on the economic stimulus measure	YES
Repeal District of Columbia firearms prohibitions and gun registration laws	YES
Limit debate on expansion of federal hate crimes law	YES
Strike funding for F-22 Raptor fighter jets	YES

CQ Vote Studies

	PARTY UNITY		PRESIDENTIAL SUPPORT	
	SUPPORT	OPPOSE	SUPPORT	OPPOSE
2010	88%	12%	95%	5%
2009	91%	9%	96%	4%

Interest Groups

	AFL-CIO	ADA	CCUS	ACU
2010	81%	85%	18%	4%
2009	94%	95%	43%	16%

Rep. G.K. Butterfield (D)

Capitol Office
225-3101
www.house.gov/butterfield
2305 Rayburn Bldg. 20515-3301; fax 225-3354

Committees
Energy & Commerce

Residence
Wilson

Born
April 27, 1947; Wilson, N.C.

Religion
Baptist

Family
Divorced; two children

Education
North Carolina Central U., B.A. 1971 (political science & sociology), J.D. 1974

Military
Army, 1968-70

Career
Child care center owner; lawyer

Political Highlights
Candidate for Wilson City Council, 1976; N.C. Superior Court judge, 1989-2001; N.C. Supreme Court, 2001-02; defeated for election to N.C. Supreme Court, 2002; N.C. Superior Court judge, 2003-04

ELECTION RESULTS

2010 GENERAL

G.K. Butterfield (D)	103,294	59.3%
Ashley Woolard (R)	70,867	40.7%

2010 PRIMARY

G.K. Butterfield (D)	46,509	72.9%
Chad Larkins (D)	17,262	27.1%

2008 GENERAL

G.K. Butterfield (D)	192,765	70.3%
Dean Stephens (R)	81,506	29.7%

Previous Winning Percentages
2006 (100%); 2004 (64%); 2004 Special Election (71%)

Elected 2004; 4th full term

Butterfield, who represents one of the nation's poorest districts, focuses on ways the government can help his constituents improve their lot in life. A descendant of slaves, he is a former state judge who maintains a relatively low profile on Capitol Hill. "I can say in two minutes what some people say in 20. And I say it just as well," he said.

Butterfield's party's leaders have recognized his behind-the-scenes contributions. He secured a coveted seat on the Energy and Commerce Committee in the 110th Congress (2007-08) and serves as ranking Democrat on its Subcommittee on Commerce, Manufacturing and Trade. He was helped by the fact he sits on the leadership-run Steering and Policy Committee, which makes committee assignments. In another measure of his standing in his party, in 2007 he was named one of nine chief deputy whips. He also serves as second vice chairman for the Congressional Black Caucus.

In 2009, then-Speaker Nancy Pelosi of California put him on the Committee on Standards of Official Conduct, where he served one term. In 2010, though, Butterfield became the subject of a committee investigation into allegations that he and five other lawmakers misused official travel funds. The renamed Ethics Committee announced in the first week of 2011 that it would not pursue the case.

Butterfield was the lone member of the committee to oppose the 2010 censure of New York Democrat Charles B. Rangel, accused of irregularities in his personal and campaign finances.

Butterfield was one of three Democrats on the panel who had received contributions from political action committees Rangel controlled. Though some watchdog groups called on the lawmakers to return the money or recuse themselves, Butterfield's spokesman said the most recent contribution of $1,000 came before his boss joined the panel and that it would have no effect on his decision-making.

When the censure motion came to the floor, Butterfield offered an amendment to lessen the penalty to a reprimand. "I urge my colleagues to vote to reprimand our colleague, let him know that he must be sanctioned for his carelessness, but let him know that this House understands fairness, justice and legal precedent." That failed on a 146-267 vote, and Rangel was censured by a vote of 333-79, with Butterfield voting "no."

His clout within the Democratic Caucus is considerable, and so is his loyalty to leadership. Butterfield strongly endorsed President Obama's $787 billion economic stimulus law, noting in January 2009 that five of his district's counties suffered from double-digit unemployment.

But the next month, he urged Obama — for whom he campaigned ardently in the presidential race — to protect working families from effects of legislation intended to curb greenhouse gas emissions. "When climate change legislation is enacted, poor people could be forced to bear a disproportionate share of the pain" through higher utility costs passed on to consumers, he said. He proposed that 35 percent of the money collected from credits or taxes on carbon dioxide be used to pay the electricity bills of the poorest customers.

Although his district has a heavy concentration of tobacco farmers, Butterfield backed legislation in 2008 and 2009 to authorize the Food and Drug Administration to regulate tobacco. He praised it for protecting tobacco farmers. Butterfield also supported Democratic legislation to expand the Children's Health Insurance Program — which covers children whose low-income families make too much money to qualify for Medicaid — even though its costs are covered by a big increase in the federal cigarette tax.

He is an advocate of efforts to bring high-tech training and equipment to poor rural areas like his district. In 2008, the House passed his bill to require donation of surplus federal electronic equipment, including computers, fax machines and printers, to schools in such areas. But the measure didn't advance in the Senate.

Butterfield grew up in Wilson. His great-grandfather was a white slave-holder who conceived a child with one of his slaves. The child, Butterfield's maternal grandfather, was born in the final days of slavery and became a minister. Butterfield's mother was a schoolteacher. His father, George Kenneth Butterfield, for whom Butterfield is named, was a native of Bermuda who came to the United States at age 16. A decade later, he opened a dental office and practiced for 50 years.

His father became a civic leader, and the all-white political establishment granted him the right to vote as a "favor," said Butterfield. The elder Butterfield began encouraging other blacks to register to vote but stopped under pressure from white leaders. He resumed the effort after the Great Depression. When literacy tests were introduced to discourage blacks from voting, Butterfield's father began teaching people to read. He then ran for the city council, winning narrowly in 1953.

In 1957, while the family was vacationing out of town, local officials substituted at-large elections for ward-by-ward elections, which had allowed the elder Butterfield to win among a black-majority constituency.

Those childhood events spurred Butterfield to study law. Ultimately, he got the last word in his father's long fight by handling several voting-rights lawsuits in eastern North Carolina counties, resulting in the court-ordered implementation of district elections for local officials.

On April 4, 1968, Butterfield was expecting to meet with the Rev. Martin Luther King Jr. at a voter registration rally in his hometown of Wilson. King was planning to visit North Carolina to help a friend's campaign. Instead, he went to Memphis to support striking sanitation workers and was assassinated.

Butterfield's first try for elected office was a losing city council bid in 1976. But he was elected a Superior Court judge in 1988 and held that job until Democratic Gov. Michael F. Easley elevated him to the state Supreme Court in 2001. After Butterfield lost a 2002 election for that seat in his own right, Easley reinstated him on the lower court.

In 2004, when Democratic Rep. Frank W. Ballance Jr. resigned, party officials tapped Butterfield to succeed him. He defeated Republican security consultant Greg Dority in the special election by 44 percentage points. His subsequent elections have been a breeze.

Key Votes

2010

Overhaul the nation's health insurance system	YES
Allow for repeal of "don't ask, don't tell"	YES
Overhaul financial services industry regulation	YES
Limit use of new Afghanistan War funds to troop withdrawal activities	NO
Change oversight of offshore drilling and lift oil spill liability cap	YES
Provide a path to legal status for some children of illegal immigrants	YES
Extend Bush-era income tax cuts for two years	NO

2009

Expand the Children's Health Insurance Program	YES
Provide $787 billion in tax cuts and spending increases to stimulate the economy	YES
Allow bankruptcy judges to modify certain primary-residence mortgages	YES
Create a cap-and-trade system to limit greenhouse gas emissions	YES
Provide $2 billion for the "cash for clunkers" program	YES
Establish the government as the sole provider of student loans	YES
Restrict federally funded insurance coverage for abortions in health care overhaul	NO

CQ Vote Studies

	PARTY UNITY		PRESIDENTIAL SUPPORT	
	Support	Oppose	Support	Oppose
2010	98%	2%	90%	10%
2009	99%	1%	97%	3%
2008	98%	2%	11%	89%
2007	97%	3%	5%	95%
2006	89%	11%	37%	63%

Interest Groups

	AFL-CIO	ADA	CCUS	ACU
2010	100%	90%	25%	5%
2009	100%	95%	40%	0%
2008	93%	100%	56%	12%
2007	100%	95%	58%	0%
2006	93%	95%	47%	16%

North Carolina 1

Northeast — part of Goldsboro, Rocky Mount and Greenville

Situated among eastern North Carolina tobacco fields and Baptist churches, the 1st is a poor, rural Democratic stronghold. It has the lowest education and income levels of any congressional district in the state. The 1st, which takes in all of 13 counties and parts of 10 others, has the highest percentage of black residents in the state, hosting a plurality of 49 percent.

The main body of the district sits along the Virginia border, with appendages winding south to take in parts of Rocky Mount, Wilson and Greenville, which shares East Carolina University with the adjacent 3rd District. Cotton fields prevail in the northern counties, while tobacco and poultry dominate farther south. There are still manufacturers scattered throughout the 1st, producing textiles, pharmaceuticals and machinery.

Unemployment rates have risen into double digits in the district's rural counties as widespread job losses continue. Health care and local government jobs prop up areas in Pitt and Greene counties, but areas such as Rocky Mount that have less-diversified economies have struggled as tobacco and cotton profits have fallen. Local officials in western counties hope to attract new jobs.

Registered Democrats outnumber Republicans by nearly 4-to-1 in the 1st, and Democrats generally dominate. However, unaffiliated white voters can support Republican candidates in coastal areas such as Perquimans and Chowan counties. Overall, the 1st gave Barack Obama his second-biggest win in the state with 63 percent of the vote.

Major Industry
Agriculture, health care, manufacturing

Military Bases
Marine Corps Air Station Cherry Point, 9,845 military, 4,780 civilian (2009); Seymour Johnson Air Force Base, 4,320 military, 938 civilian (2011)

Cities
Goldsboro (pt.), 32,827; Rocky Mount (pt.), 30,687; Greenville (pt.), 29,415; Wilson (pt.), 22,038

Notable
Caleb Bradham started selling "Brad's Drink" in 1898 at his New Bern drug store — the beverage is now known as Pepsi-Cola.

Rep. Renee Ellmers (R)

Capitol Office
225-4531
ellmers.house.gov
1533 Longworth Bldg. 20515-3302; fax 225-5662

Committees
Agriculture
Foreign Affairs
Small Business
   (Healthcare & Technology - Chairwoman)

Residence
Dunn

Born
Feb. 9, 1964; Ironwood, Mich.

Religion
Roman Catholic

Family
Husband, Brent Ellmers; one child

Education
Oakland U., B.S. 1990 (nursing)

Career
Hospital administrator; nurse

Political Highlights
Dunn Planning Board, 2006-11 (chairwoman, 2008-09)

ELECTION RESULTS

2010 GENERAL

Renee Ellmers (R)	93,876	49.5%
Bob Etheridge (D)	92,393	48.7%
Tom Rose (LIBERT)	3,505	1.8%

2010 PRIMARY

Renee Ellmers (R)	9,171	55.1%
Frank Deatrich (R)	4,280	25.7%
Todd Gailas (R)	3,190	19.2%

Elected 2010; 1st term

Ellmers is one of a number of health professionals among the large GOP freshman class in the 112th Congress, and she promises to try to undo much of the health care overhaul law enacted in 2010.

Touting herself as a fiscal and social conservative, the registered nurse — her husband is a doctor — is opposed to government-mandated insurance coverage. She voted to repeal and defund the 2010 law, but said "simply standing against Obamacare is not enough." Ellmers, who chairs the Small Business Subcommittee on Healthcare and Technology, would replace it with "free-market-based" changes aimed at increasing accessibility, lowering costs and improving technologies.

Ellmers said the key to creating jobs is removing the uncertainty facing businesses when it comes to health care costs and taxes.

Ellmers can look out for the district and state's tobacco growers from her seat on the Agriculture Committee and on the Small Business subcommittee responsible for agriculture issues.

On the Foreign Affairs panel, she has a hand in developing policy that has life-and-death implications for those stationed at the Army's Fort Bragg and Pope Air Force Base, both found in the 2nd District.

She backed reauthorization of expiring provisions of the anti-terrorist law known as the Patriot Act. And she offered qualified support for U.S. involvement in the fighting in Libya in 2011, while stressing that President Obama "needs to let us know what the mission in Libya is, what goals he has for the mission and what the plan is to achieve those goals."

Ellmers said her interest in politics was stirred while attending a town hall meeting her predecessor, Democrat Bob Etheridge, held on health care.

Ellmers' challenge to Etheridge was one of the tightest races in the country and garnered additional attention when Etheridge grabbed a young man trying to interview him, an incident caught on video.

Ellmers held a slim lead on election night, but Etheridge didn't concede until Nov. 19.

The final tally gave her a margin of just less than 1,500 votes.

North Carolina 2

Central — parts of Raleigh and Fayetteville

From the state capital of Raleigh, the 2nd pinwheels east, north and south to take in several fast-growing counties and part of Fayetteville. While the high-tech Research Triangle Park, the area's economic hub, lies in the neighboring 4th, its influence radiates through this eastern Piedmont district.

Research Triangle techies, university academics and government employees live in Raleigh (shared with the 4th and 13th districts). Sprawl is taking over in the growing and increasingly urban bedroom communities near Raleigh, but the surrounding counties retain a legacy of tobacco farming and blue-collar manufacturing jobs.

The district's strong military presence is centered around part of Fort Bragg (shared with the 7th and 8th) at its southwestern edge. The former Pope Air Force Base has been realigned into an Army airfield controlled by Fort Bragg, which has been reassigned thousands of new personnel since the 2005 round of base closings.

Its slight voter registration edge exaggerates the Democratic Party's ability to win across the 2nd. Federal and statewide Republican candidates run well here, especially in Johnston and Harnett counties. A black-majority section of Fayetteville and the mostly black southeastern part of Raleigh provide some Democratic votes.

Major Industry
Technology, military, agriculture

Military Bases
Fort Bragg (Army), 54,359 military, 7,022 civilian (2011) (shared with the 7th and 8th)

Cities
Fayetteville (pt.), 77,984; Raleigh (pt.), 69,914; Sanford, 28,094

Notable
A sign — made of brick — near Sanford names it the U.S. brick capital.

Rep. Walter B. Jones (R)

Capitol Office
225-3415
jones.house.gov
2333 Rayburn Bldg. 20515-3303; fax 225-3286

Committees
Armed Services
Financial Services

Residence
Farmville

Born
Feb. 10, 1943; Farmville, N.C.

Religion
Roman Catholic

Family
Wife, Joe Anne Jones; one child

Education
North Carolina State U., attended 1962-65 (history);
Atlantic Christian College, B.A. 1968 (history)

Military
N.C. National Guard, 1967-71

Career
Lighting company executive; insurance benefits
company executive; office supply company executive

Political Highlights
N.C. House, 1983-92 (served as a Democrat); sought
Democratic nomination for U.S. House, 1992

ELECTION RESULTS

2010 GENERAL

Walter B. Jones (R)	143,225	71.9%
Johnny Rouse (D)	51,317	25.7%
Darryl Holloman (LIBERT)	4,762	2.4%

2010 PRIMARY

Walter B. Jones (R)	21,551	76.9%
Bob Cavanaugh (R)	4,221	15.1%
Craig Weber (R)	2,261	8.1%

2008 GENERAL

Walter B. Jones (R)	201,686	65.9%
Craig Weber (D)	104,364	34.1%

Previous Winning Percentages
2006 (67%); 2004 (71%); 2002 (91%); 2000 (61%);
1998 (62%); 1996 (63%); 1994 (53%)

Elected 1994; 9th term

Jones is a Southern gentleman who says his decisions as a member of Congress are driven by his perception of God's will. His faith and strength of purpose often cause him to travel a separate, and sometimes lonely, road from the rest of his party. "My heart dictates my thinking many, many times," he said.

His voting record defies simple characterization. A former Democrat, he is fiercely conservative on social and fiscal matters and quit the Republican Study Committee — the caucus of the House's most conservative members — in 2006 after its leader at the time announced a compromise position on illegal immigration, an issue on which he takes an unyielding hard line. But he became one of the GOP's most passionate critics of the Iraq War after initially supporting it, and has called for an immediate withdrawal from Afghanistan.

In April 2010, Jones cosponsored a bill by Chris Van Hollen of Maryland — at the time chairman of the Democratic Congressional Campaign Committee — designed to roll back a Supreme Court decision that threw out many spending restrictions on third-party political groups. The legislation was seen by many Republicans as designed to hurt conservative-leaning organizations in the 2010 elections. Then-Minority Leader John A. Boehner of Ohio called the measure "a backroom deal to shred our Constitution for raw, ugly, partisan gain." In a twist, Jones ended up voting against the bill he cosponsored. It passed the House, but died in the Senate.

Jones also supports a voluntary public-financing system for political campaigns. He cosponsored Democratic legislation in 2009 to provide federal grants to candidates who agreed to accept no more than $100 per contributor for each election and meet certain fundraising targets.

He serves on the Financial Services Committee and was one of three House Republicans who supported a financial regulatory overhaul that became law in July 2010. Still, he was critical of government intervention to help the struggling banking and automobile industries earlier on in the financial crisis. He joined Republican Todd Tiahrt of Kansas in sponsoring a March 2009 resolution opposing any taxpayer-funded relief. "Instead of driving economic growth, these bailouts have done nothing but fuel public anger over how these institutions are spending the taxpayers' money," he said.

That month, he was among 10 Republicans who supported a Democratic bill to limit bonus payments to employees of companies receiving federal assistance.

As a member of the Armed Services Committee, Jones takes an avid interest in the Marine Corps. His district is home to Camp Lejeune, the Marines' East Coast headquarters, and he introduced a bill in 2009 to officially rename the Department of the Navy the Department of the Navy and Marine Corps in recognition of the two bureaus' longtime operation as a single entity.

Jones opposed the repeal of the "don't ask, don't tell" policy on gay servicemembers, saying "it is deeply troubling for this administration and the Democrat leadership to put their social and political agenda before our national security."

It is on Iraq that Jones most visibly separated himself from his party.

Jones voted in 2002 to authorize President George W. Bush to use force to topple Saddam Hussein. His support for the president's war policy was upended in 2005, however, when Jones said he had a spiritual awakening at the funeral of a Marine named Michael Bitz. After that, Jones decided the war was wrong.

His office writes every family that has lost someone in Iraq or Afghanistan, and he has photos, letters and military paraphernalia from the casualties' families. But he says he cannot read their letters because he becomes too emotional. He intends to write a book about the letters because, he says, "God wants me to."

When President Obama announced plans early in his administration to move troops out of Iraq and add forces in Afghanistan, Jones called for Obama to reconsider. "Let us know what we're going to do before we begin this escalation, because it will be too late if we're talking about this one year from now," he said in March 2009.

Two years after that, he backed a resolution by anti-war Democrat Dennis J. Kucinich of Ohio to require a U.S. withdrawal within six months. "I've seen enough broken bodies at Walter Reed and Bethesda," Jones said on Fox Business Network.

His opposition to the Iraq War met with hostility from Marines stationed at Camp Lejeune. When Bush made a public appearance in Fayetteville, not far from Jones' district, Jones was not invited to share the stage. Some local Republicans also disapproved: In 2006, Jones headed off the prospect of a primary challenge from some of them by holding town hall meetings where he explained his position. He won that election with nearly 70 percent of the vote. In 2008, however, he was challenged in the GOP primary for the first time since his 1994 election. But Jones fended off his challenger, Joe McLaughlin, by netting 59 percent of the vote. Jones got more than three-quarters of the vote in the 2010 primary and won re-election easily.

Jones grew up around politics and government. His father was Democratic Rep. Walter B. Jones Sr., a pragmatist who was a bit more liberal than his son. Jones attended Virginia's Hargrave Military Academy, which emphasized Christian values; he became a standout basketball player there. He graduated from Atlantic Christian College in 1968, did a stint in the National Guard, then took a job as a wine broker with a region covering North Carolina and Virginia. Raised a Baptist, he converted to Catholicism when he was 29.

Jones was almost 40 when he followed his father into politics. In 1982, the local Democratic Party asked him to finish the term of a state assemblyman who had died in office. Jones wound up staying for a decade.

In 1992, the senior Jones fell ill and retired from the House. Jones ran for his father's 1st District seat as a Democrat, but lost a primary runoff. The next year, he registered as a Republican, feeling he had more in common with the GOP. He ran in the 3rd District in 1994, and was swept into office by the strong GOP tide that year, winning with just under 53 percent of the vote.

Key Votes

2010

Overhaul the nation's health insurance system	NO
Allow for repeal of "don't ask, don't tell"	NO
Overhaul financial services industry regulation	YES
Limit use of new Afghanistan War funds to troop withdrawal activities	YES
Change oversight of offshore drilling and lift oil spill liability cap	NO
Provide a path to legal status for some children of illegal immigrants	NO
Extend Bush-era income tax cuts for two years	YES

2009

Expand the Children's Health Insurance Program	NO
Provide $787 billion in tax cuts and spending increases to stimulate the economy	NO
Allow bankruptcy judges to modify certain primary-residence mortgages	YES
Create a cap-and-trade system to limit greenhouse gas emissions	NO
Provide $2 billion for the "cash for clunkers" program	YES
Establish the government as the sole provider of student loans	NO
Restrict federally funded insurance coverage for abortions in health care overhaul	YES

CQ Vote Studies

	PARTY UNITY		PRESIDENTIAL SUPPORT	
	SUPPORT	OPPOSE	SUPPORT	OPPOSE
2010	72%	28%	51%	49%
2009	71%	29%	36%	64%
2008	77%	23%	37%	63%
2007	71%	29%	43%	57%
2006	64%	36%	53%	47%

Interest Groups

	AFL-CIO	ADA	CCUS	ACU
2010	50%	30%	71%	65%
2009	22%	15%	71%	83%
2008	53%	50%	59%	58%
2007	26%	50%	79%	71%
2006	62%	45%	50%	79%

North Carolina 3

East — Jacksonville, part of Greenville, Outer Banks

The 3rd runs along the eastern shore from the Virginia border to north of Wilmington, sweeping from the fragile barrier islands of the Outer Banks to the tobacco and peanut fields of the coastal plain. It is a large swath of rural land inlaid with waterways, affluent vacation towns and military facilities; the closest thing to skyscrapers here are the historic lighthouses that dot the shoreline.

Many residents' incomes rely on fishing, farming and tourism. The 3rd's military bases have a large impact on the economy, particularly the expansive Camp Lejeune, which contributes roughly $3 billion to the local economy annually. From the southernmost coast, two fingers of land reach northwest, taking in turkey, hog and wheat farms.

The western leg of the 3rd stretches from Onslow County in the south, where Jacksonville and Camp Lejeune are located, all the way north to Nash County, including western Rocky Mount. Another leg stretches northwest to Greenville in Pitt County. Prolonged economic downturns in manufacturing and agricultural production have hurt these areas. Greenville's East Carolina University (shared with the 1st) has helped prop up the local economy, but anticipated budget cuts will hit college-based employment.

Although there are significant numbers of registered Democrats here, the 3rd has a conservative bent and supports GOP candidates on the federal level. John McCain took 61 percent of the 2008 presidential vote.

Major Industry
Military, agriculture, tourism

Military Bases
Camp Lejeune Marine Corps Base, 47,200 military, 5,800 civilian (2011); New River Marine Corps Air Station, 5,814 military, 245 civilian (2009)

Cities
Jacksonville, 70,145; Greenville (pt.), 55,139; Wilson (pt.), 27,129

Notable
Dare County is named for Virginia Dare, the first child born of English parents in America (1587); Wilbur and Orville Wright made their first flight in Kitty Hawk; the infamous pirate Edward Teach, better known as Blackbeard, lived in Hammock House in Beaufort.

Rep. David E. Price (D)

Capitol Office
225-1784
price.house.gov
2162 Rayburn Bldg. 20515-3304; fax 225-2014

Committees
Appropriations

Residence
Chapel Hill

Born
Aug. 17, 1940; Erwin, Tenn.

Religion
Baptist

Family
Wife, Lisa Price; two children

Education
Mars Hill College, attended 1957-59; U. of North
Carolina, B.A. 1961 (American history & math); Yale U.,
B.D. 1964 (theology), Ph.D. 1969 (political science)

Career
Professor

Political Highlights
N.C. Democratic Party chairman, 1983-84; U.S. House,
1987-95; defeated for re-election to U.S. House, 1994

ELECTION RESULTS

2010 GENERAL

David E. Price (D)	155,384	57.2%
William "B.J." Lawson (R)	116,448	42.8%

2010 PRIMARY

David E. Price (D)	unopposed

2008 GENERAL

David E. Price (D)	265,751	63.3%
William "B.J." Lawson (R)	153,947	36.7%

Previous Winning Percentages
2006 (65%); 2004 (64%); 2002 (61%); 2000 (62%);
1998 (57%); 1996 (54%); 1992 (65%); 1990 (58%);
1988 (58%); 1986 (56%)

Elected 1986; 12th term

Did not serve 1995-97

Price's professorial demeanor comes naturally. A former political science professor who still lectures and publishes academic work, he uses his senior position on the Homeland Security Appropriations Subcommittee to steer funding to his research-heavy district, advance policies on border control and civil liberties, and oversee the relatively new bureaucracy of the department.

He pursues a centrist course on home-state issues such as tobacco regulation. But he generally votes with the majority of his party. He consistently backs abortion rights and environmental protection measures such as the cap-and-trade energy bill in the 111th Congress (2009-10), along with Obama administration priorities such as the financial regulation and health care overhauls.

Price, a former Duke University professor who continues to update his book, "The Congressional Experience," is co-chairman of the House Democracy Assistance Commission, which strengthens democratic institutions by assisting legislatures in emerging democracies through peer-to-peer relationships. The commission provides procedural and technical support for those institutions on issues such as budgetary analysis, executive oversight and institutional improvement. In 2010, the commission and its program, the House Democracy Partnership, partnered with the House parliamentarian and House clerk on a visit to the legislatures of Liberia, Kenya and Mali.

Price also keeps up his connections with academics. He gave the Pi Sigma Alpha address to the annual conference of the Southern Political Science Association in 2010. His appreciation for the complexities of the political and policy process earns respect from colleagues on both sides of the aisle.

Price said that overseeing homeland security funding was not what he envisioned when he first arrived in Congress more than two decades ago. He gained a seat on Appropriations during his third term and largely focused on education and science, two areas of importance to the Research Triangle constituents in his district. He landed a seat on the Homeland Security Subcommittee after the formation of the Homeland Security Department in 2003. The retirement of Minnesota Democrat Martin Olav Sabo and the Democratic takeover of Congress in 2006 propelled him to the chairmanship, and he stayed on as ranking Democrat after the Republicans took control in the 112th Congress (2011-12).

When he picked up the subcommittee gavel in 2007, Price immediately sought a broad assessment of the state of the 5-year-old department. He held two multiday hearings and brought in experts from the Sept. 11 commission, Rand Corp. and the Government Accountability Office, as well as the Homeland Security Department's inspector general. Price sought their guidance on how to think about the long term, rather than focus on one-year chunks of time.

Price shepherded through Congress in 2010 a law that provided $600 million to beef up patrol activity along the Mexican border with new personnel and equipment. The Senate had adjourned for a five-week recess but interrupted it briefly to complete work and send the legislation to President Obama.

Price had watched as drug-cartel-related violence raged along the border of Mexico in 2009 and 2010, leading Price to question how various agencies worked together on the gun-running issue when their jurisdictions cross. He requested that the Homeland Security Department provide data on the scope of gun smuggling, including the types of weapons being trafficked, along with lists of relevant agencies, laws and regulations involved with enforcement.

In the 2008 $41.1 billion spending bill, Price added a provision requiring enhanced privacy and civil liberties standards as a prerequisite for funding intelligence-gathering projects. The bill also aimed to promote accountability by freezing funding on numerous department programs until cost-benefit analyses have been conducted. Republicans objected, arguing it would hold up funding needed to build the 2,000-mile border fence between the United States and Mexico that was authorized in 2006. But Price prevailed.

For many years, Price has used his Appropriations seat to tend to the needs of his district, which has several private research and technology companies, as well as 11 colleges and universities. Through the 2009 economic stimulus bill and regular appropriations process, he has snagged tens of millions of dollars annually for many of the research centers.

Price, whose longtime involvement with campaign finance efforts continues in the 112th Congress, would prefer that taxpayers pay for campaigns. He opposed a bill the House passed in January 2011 that would end the Presidential Election Campaign Fund. Instead, he sponsored legislation intended to make the program more attractive to candidates by lifting spending limits, altering matching rates for small contributions, requiring increased disclosure, increasing the amount of the checkoff to $10 per individual and eliminating public funding for national party conventions.

Price was born and raised in the town of Erwin in eastern Tennessee. His father was the local high school principal, while his mother was an English teacher. He earned an undergraduate degree from the University of North Carolina, then went to Yale University for graduate study, earning political science and divinity degrees. As a political science professor in the 1970s, he became heavily involved in state Democratic politics. He served as chairman of the state party in 1983 and 1984, and in 1985 was a founding member of the national Democratic Leadership Council, a now-defunct group of moderates trying to steer the party toward the center of the political spectrum.

The contacts Price made helped him raise money and attract supporters for a successful House race in 1986. He beat out three opponents for the Democratic nomination, then ousted freshman Republican Bill Cobey Jr. by 12 percentage points. He won re-election three times by comfortable margins but lost to former Raleigh Police Chief Fred Heineman by 1,215 votes in the GOP landslide of 1994.

Price avenged that defeat in 1996, waging an aggressive campaign that emphasized door-to-door canvassing. He won by almost 11 percentage points and has prevailed easily in subsequent elections. In a district made more comfortably Democratic after the reapportionment following the 2000 census, Price had not dipped below 60 percent of the vote until 2010, when Republican William Lawson held him to 57 percent.

Key Votes

2010

Overhaul the nation's health insurance system	YES
Allow for repeal of "don't ask, don't tell"	YES
Overhaul financial services industry regulation	YES
Limit use of new Afghanistan War funds to troop withdrawal activities	NO
Change oversight of offshore drilling and lift oil spill liability cap	YES
Provide a path to legal status for some children of illegal immigrants	YES
Extend Bush-era income tax cuts for two years	YES

2009

Expand the Children's Health Insurance Program	YES
Provide $787 billion in tax cuts and spending increases to stimulate the economy	YES
Allow bankruptcy judges to modify certain primary-residence mortgages	YES
Create a cap-and-trade system to limit greenhouse gas emissions	YES
Provide $2 billion for the "cash for clunkers" program	YES
Establish the government as the sole provider of student loans	YES
Restrict federally funded insurance coverage for abortions in health care overhaul	NO

CQ Vote Studies

	PARTY UNITY		PRESIDENTIAL SUPPORT	
	SUPPORT	OPPOSE	SUPPORT	OPPOSE
2010	99%	1%	95%	5%
2009	100%	0%	97%	3%
2008	99%	1%	14%	86%
2007	99%	1%	4%	96%
2006	92%	8%	33%	67%

Interest Groups

	AFL-CIO	ADA	CCUS	ACU
2010	100%	95%	25%	0%
2009	100%	100%	33%	0%
2008	100%	100%	61%	0%
2007	100%	95%	55%	0%
2006	100%	95%	47%	4%

North Carolina 4

Central — Durham, Chapel Hill, part of Raleigh

The 4th revolves around Research Triangle Park and the three major universities at the vertices of the triangle. The medical and technological research park was created in the 1950s by a group of academics, politicians and businessmen who saw a need to diversify the state's economy beyond the traditional tobacco and textile industries. While based primarily in the Triangle, the 4th also passes through the rolling hills and evergreen forests of the Piedmont region.

Duke University in Durham represents the northern point of the triangle, while the University of North Carolina at Chapel Hill takes up the western point and North Carolina State University in Raleigh (shared with the 2nd and 13th districts) is the southeastern point. The extensive university and research presence gives the 4th the state's highest rate of college education for residents by a wide margin.

The Durham of James B. Duke's Lucky Strike cigarettes largely disappeared during decades of growth in the Research Triangle as developers began converting tobacco warehouses into apartment buildings. The region's educational and technological strengths have helped the Raleigh-Durham area land on the Forbes list of the 10 best places for business and careers for seven years in a row. While the 4th has not been immune to national economic downturns, its diversified economy and government workforce creates stability in the region.

The 4th is a Democratic stronghold, with the party drawing support not only from the large black population in Durham but also from the liberal atmosphere surrounding the university in Chapel Hill. A Democrat has held the district's U.S. House seat for all but four years since 1969, but the area's highly educated voters — one in five holds a postgraduate or professional degree — can be independent-minded. Durham County gave Democrat Barack Obama his highest percentage of any county statewide (76 percent), and he took the district with 62 percent overall.

Major Industry
Technology research, higher education

Cities
Durham, 228,330; Cary (pt.), 123,955; Raleigh (pt.), 67,043; Chapel Hill, 57,233

Notable
Universities in the 4th have won nine of the last 30 NCAA Division I men's basketball championships.

Rep. Virginia Foxx (R)

Capitol Office
225-2071
www.foxx.house.gov
1230 Longworth Bldg. 20515-3305; fax 225-2995

Committees
Education & the Workforce
(Higher Education & Workforce Training - Chairwoman)
Rules

Residence
Watauga County

Born
June 29, 1943; Bronx, N.Y.

Religion
Roman Catholic

Family
Husband, Tom Foxx; one child

Education
Lees-McRae College, attended 1961; Appalachian State Teachers' College, attended 1962-63; U. of North Carolina, B.A. 1968 (English), M.A.C.T. 1972 (sociology); U. of North Carolina, Greensboro, Ed.D. 1985 (curriculum and teaching/higher education)

Career
Community college president; state government official; nursery and landscaping company owner; professor; secretary

Political Highlights
Candidate for Watauga County Board of Education, 1974; Watauga County Board of Education, 1977-89; N.C. Senate, 1995-2004

ELECTION RESULTS

2010 GENERAL

Virginia Foxx (R)	140,525	65.9%
Billy Kennedy (D)	72,762	34.1%

2010 PRIMARY

Virginia Foxx (R)	38,174	79.8%
Keith Gardner (R)	9,639	20.2%

2008 GENERAL

Virginia Foxx (R)	190,820	58.4%
Roy Carter (D)	136,103	41.6%

Previous Winning Percentages
2006 (57%); 2004 (59%)

Elected 2004; 4th term

As a child growing up in the mountain hollows of western North Carolina, Foxx never imagined she would go into politics. She emerged from those humble beginnings to become a college administrator and state legislator with a can-do attitude and conservative world view.

"I grew up with no electricity and no running water. My parents had a sixth- and ninth-grade education. We were not people of means at all," she said. "But I tell people that this is the greatest country in the world . . . people who grew up in poverty can succeed if they work hard."

She has taken on leadership responsibilities in the House, as a member of the Rules Committee and as vice chairwoman of grass-roots development for the National Republican Congressional Committee. She also chairs the Education and the Workforce Subcommittee on Higher Education and Workforce Training.

While many politicians surround themselves with consultants and fundraisers, Foxx has a more hands-on approach. She writes her own mail, answers her own letters and makes her own phone calls.

She has compiled a dependably conservative record, boasting a 100 percent approval rating from the American Conservative Union for four consecutive years. Although typically a party loyalist, Foxx is perhaps best known for sticking to her guns — "Being true to my principles is most important to me," she said — even if it means going against her party or the grain.

In 2005, she was one of 11 House members to oppose the $59 billion emergency spending bill for the aid effort after Hurricane Katrina hit, explaining that she refused to support a bill that had "no plan for the spending of that money."

"I have to be a steward of the public's money and make sure it's being spent well," she said.

She was also one of 27 Republicans to vote against the Central America Free Trade Agreement (CAFTA), a major George W. Bush administration priority that passed the House by just two votes in 2005. Faced with pressure from Vice President Dick Cheney, Secretary of State Condoleezza Rice, U.S. Trade Representative Rob Portman and GOP Leader Tom Delay of Texas, Foxx stayed firm. She said that she gave her constituents her word to vote "no" because in 2007, Hanesbrands Inc. announced the closing of its fabrics plant in Winston-Salem as it pursued lower-cost production in the Caribbean and Central America. Foxx told constituents she voted against CAFTA because it would have repercussions like that.

House Republicans put Foxx on the Rules Committee in the 111th Congress (2009-10), a job that indulged her penchant for making caustic comments aimed at Democrats.

In a speech about the health care overhaul bill in November 2009, Foxx said the legislation was a greater threat than terrorism. "I believe we have more to fear from the potential of that bill passing than we do from any terrorist right now in any country," she said. The chattering class lambasted her, but she took nothing back.

In April 2009, she blasted Democrats for their plan to ban bonuses for executives of corporations that took financial rescue money. "I thought about just a common-sense way to describe this to people: The Democrats have a tar baby on their hands and they simply can't get away from it." Democrats called her comments racially insensitive. Foxx called them direct.

"I don't think anybody would say I'm too subtle," she said.

Foxx served on the Education and the Workforce Committee the last time the Republicans were in the majority, and she returns to the panel in the 112th Congress (2011-12).

She'll have a hand in reauthorizing the Bush-era No Child Left Behind law, and has criticized the Obama administration for proposing spending increases on programs she argues have not improved student achievement.

She served on the House-Senate conference committee in 2008 that drafted the final version of the first overhaul of the Higher Education Act in a decade. She was the only House member to vote against the bill in conference, and was one of 49 — all Republicans — to oppose the measure on the floor.

Foxx was first elected to the House at age 61 and was one of the oldest members of the freshman class of 2004. She was the first freshman to get a bill passed by the House in 2005, a measure allowing military personnel to put their combat pay into tax-deferred individual retirement accounts. Foxx introduced the bill after hearing from a constituent whose son, while serving in Iraq, tried to contribute combat pay to an IRA but was told he could not do so. Because combat pay is tax-exempt, many military personnel serving in Iraq and Afghanistan did not have any taxable earnings available for investment in IRAs. Bush signed the bill into law in 2006.

She grew up poor as the granddaughter of Italian immigrants. In her teens, she was the janitor at her high school as part of an after-school job. As she was sweeping floors one day, a teacher told her she was smart and needed to go to college, marry a college man and get out of town.

She did all three. She earned her bachelor's and advanced degrees from the University of North Carolina. She and her husband, Tom Foxx, started a successful nursery and landscaping business.

A former assistant dean of Appalachian State University and a president of Maryland Community College, she got her start in politics during a dozen years on the Watauga County Board of Education. She then served for a decade in the state Senate.

"Everywhere I have been, I have been able to help others. I was fulfilled in all of those jobs. I've always done the best job I could possibly do," she said.

When Republican Rep. Richard M. Burr decided to run for the Senate in 2004, Foxx prevailed over seven other Republicans in the primary and went on to beat Democrat Jim A. Harrell Jr. in November.

In 2006, she was unopposed in the primary and prevailed against Democrat Roger Sharpe, taking 57 percent of the vote. Two years later, she improved slightly on that showing, and she easily defeated local talk-radio host Billy Kennedy in 2010 with 66 percent of the vote.

Key Votes

2010

Overhaul the nation's health insurance system	NO
Allow for repeal of "don't ask, don't tell"	NO
Overhaul financial services industry regulation	NO
Limit use of new Afghanistan War funds to troop withdrawal activities	NO
Change oversight of offshore drilling and lift oil spill liability cap	NO
Provide a path to legal status for some children of illegal immigrants	NO
Extend Bush-era income tax cuts for two years	NO

2009

Expand the Children's Health Insurance Program	NO
Provide $787 billion in tax cuts and spending increases to stimulate the economy	NO
Allow bankruptcy judges to modify certain primary-residence mortgages	NO
Create a cap-and-trade system to limit greenhouse gas emissions	NO
Provide $2 billion for the "cash for clunkers" program	NO
Establish the government as the sole provider of student loans	NO
Restrict federally funded insurance coverage for abortions in health care overhaul	YES

CQ Vote Studies

	PARTY UNITY		PRESIDENTIAL SUPPORT	
	SUPPORT	OPPOSE	SUPPORT	OPPOSE
2010	99%	1%	26%	74%
2009	99%	1%	10%	90%
2008	97%	3%	84%	16%
2007	98%	2%	91%	9%
2006	97%	3%	83%	17%

Interest Groups

	AFL-CIO	ADA	CCUS	ACU
2010	7%	5%	75%	100%
2009	5%	0%	73%	100%
2008	7%	5%	78%	100%
2007	4%	0%	70%	100%
2006	14%	5%	93%	96%

North Carolina 5

Northwest — part of Winston-Salem

This northern Piedmont district stretches west from Winston-Salem through rolling hills and rural towns to the Tennessee border. Its northern counties, which run along the Virginia border, are filled with small rural towns such as Mount Airy, the childhood home of Andy Griffith and the inspiration for the fictional setting of his 1960s television series.

The district's major population center is in Winston-Salem and surrounding Forsyth County, home to R.J. Reynolds Tobacco. The company's corporate headquarters is in the 12th District (which has most of Winston-Salem), but its largest plant is in the 5th, in the aptly named town of Tobaccoville. Forsyth's economy has veered away from tobacco and textiles. Tobacco production is still important, but it now ranks second to health care, partly because of Wake Forest University's medical center.

With the decline of the tobacco industry, many tobacco producers have converted their farms into vineyards and wineries. The Yadkin Valley wine region, most of which is in the district, has become a tourist destination. The 5th also hosts the Krispy Kreme Doughnuts headquarters, a BB&T

division headquarters and a Tyson Foods division. Tyson, which is already Wilkes County's largest employer, is expanding. Despite a decade of job growth, the 5th shared in statewide economic downturns — Winston-Salem's unemployment rate hit double digits, and the closure of a Forsyth County Dell manufacturing site eliminated hundred of jobs here in 2009. Textile and blue-collar work still prevail in other counties, and grazing cattle wander over Surry County's low, rolling hills. The solidly GOP 5th is the state's most rural district, and the party dominates Davie and Yadkin counties, west of Winston-Salem. John McCain took his highest percentage statewide in Yadkin in the 2008 presidential election. The 5th's share of the largely Democratic Forsyth County leans Republican.

Major Industry
Health care, tobacco, agriculture, textiles

Cities
Winston-Salem (pt.), 96,279; Statesville (pt.), 24,505; Kernersville (pt.), 23,067

Notable
First organized in 1924, Union Grove's Old Time Fiddlers Convention (now called the Ole Time Fiddler's and Bluegrass Festival) is the nation's longest-running bluegrass festival.

Rep. Howard Coble (R)

Capitol Office
225-3065
coble.house.gov
2188 Rayburn Bldg. 20515-3306; fax 225-8611

Committees
Judiciary
(Courts, Commercial & Administrative Law - Chairman)
Transportation & Infrastructure

Residence
Greensboro

Born
March 18, 1931; Greensboro, N.C.

Religion
Presbyterian

Family
Single

Education
Appalachian State Teachers' College, attended 1949-50 (history); Guilford College, A.B. 1958 (history); U. of North Carolina, J.D. 1962

Military
Coast Guard, 1952-56, 1977-78; Coast Guard Reserve, 1960-82

Career
Lawyer; insurance claims supervisor

Political Highlights
N.C. House, 1969-70; assistant U.S. attorney, 1969-73; N.C. Department of Revenue secretary, 1973-77; Republican nominee for N.C. treasurer, 1976; N.C. House, 1979-84

ELECTION RESULTS

2010 GENERAL

Howard Coble (R)	156,252	75.2%
Sam Turner (D)	51,507	24.8%

2010 PRIMARY

Howard Coble (R)	31,663	63.5%
Billy Yow (R)	7,929	15.9%
Others	10,116	20.2%

2008 GENERAL

Howard Coble (R)	221,018	67.0%
Teresa Sue Bratton (D)	108,873	33.0%

Previous Winning Percentages
2006 (71%); 2004 (73%); 2002 (90%); 2000 (91%); 1998 (89%); 1996 (73%); 1994 (100%); 1992 (71%); 1990 (67%); 1988 (62%); 1986 (50%); 1984 (51%)

Elected 1984; 14th term

Coble is a plain-spoken former prosecutor whose independent streak sometimes puts him at odds with Republican leaders on economic policy and certain social policy issues.

His long history of keeping constituents satisfied and emphasizing fiscal responsibility wasn't enough to protect him from a GOP primary challenge in 2010, the first since he was first elected in 1984. Coble's five opponents argued it was time for new blood and questioned whether he was still up to the job. He admitted he wasn't necessarily comfortable "fighting your own family" in a primary but was relieved that the anti-incumbent wave "didn't hit us."

He won the primary and the general election handily, but his independence continued to cost him. At the start of the 112th Congress (2011-12), he lost a bid for chairman of the Judiciary Committee's newly reconstituted intellectual property panel he had hoped to lead, just as he'd earlier been bypassed for chairman of the full committee.

Coble proudly describes himself as "old school" but has adapted to the times. He joined the House Tea Party Caucus and allowed his campaign staff to launch a Facebook page in 2010 but drew the line at Twitter. "I'm too long in the tooth to tweet," Coble told the High Point Enterprise.

Coble generally tries to keep a low profile in Washington, even if he sometimes gets attention for his go-it-alone ways. But he is often seen back home in Greensboro.

Some of his views may be closer in line with President Obama than they were with Obama's predecessor — such as a willingness to more speedily bring troops home from Iraq and to allow expanded federal funding of stem cell research. But Coble has proved he is just as willing to go against the president and speak up when he disagrees. He voted against the 2009 economic stimulus bill, which he said few in Congress had read.

In fall 2008, he voted against a $700 billion measure to rescue the nation's ailing financial services sector, then supported a slightly altered version. "The political sky may fall on my head," he said as he announced his switch, "but I feel the limited access to credit or no access to capital may affect us all." But in early 2009 he voted against releasing the second half of that money. Looking back, Coble told the Greensboro News & Record in 2010 that he viewed the votes as "damned if you do, damned if you don't."

He was an early skeptic of President George W. Bush's policy in Iraq. He was among 17 Republicans who backed a Democratic resolution in early 2007 opposing Bush's call for more than 21,000 additional troops. He voted against the administration's requests to fund the war in 2005 and 2006. But in 2007 he voted for a $555 billion catchall spending bill that included $70 billion for military operations in Iraq and Afghanistan.

Coble also tangled with Republican leaders and the administration on the Central America Free Trade Agreement (CAFTA), which he considered a sensitive issue not just for his state, home to many of the nation's remaining textile factories, but personally. His mother sewed pockets onto overalls in a North Carolina textile factory in the days before air conditioning. Coble told Bush during a White House visit, "When I go into these plants and have employees plead with me to vote no, that's my mama talking to me." He was one of 27 Republicans to vote against CAFTA in 2005, although he did support the 2007 trade agreement with Peru.

And while Coble generally votes conservative on social matters, he has consistently supported federal funding for stem cell research, despite holding staunchly anti-abortion views. "Some of my Republican colleagues, and some Democrats, too, concluded that it was an abortion-rights issue, and I never did believe that," he explained.

Such votes help explain why he was denied the top Republican seat on the Judiciary Committee in favor of Lamar Smith of Texas at the start of the 110th Congress (2007-08). In the 112th Congress, Coble had hoped to lead the Intellectual Property, Competition and the Internet Subcommittee, but was denied again. Instead, he chairs the Subcommittee on Courts, Commercial and Administrative Law.

In 1998 he co-authored the Digital Millennium Copyright Act, which bans any computer program or device that circumvents the software that encrypts digital movies and music to prevent unauthorized reproduction.

Coble prides himself on returning leftover office funds to the federal coffers each year. He is one of the few lawmakers who declines to participate in the congressional pension program, calling it "a taxpayer rip-off." The idea — which he says has not been his "most brilliant financial decision" in terms of its impact on his own finances — has gained little traction, but Coble hoped some of the newcomers elected in 2010 might join him.

He has not been so frugal when it comes to steering money to the 6th District from his seat on the Transportation and Infrastructure Committee. In 2008 he helped tap $10 million to fund runway construction at his district's airport, and in 2005 he secured $50 million for the 6th in the surface transportation bill.

Coble was born in rural Guilford County to parents who had little formal education. His father spent 44 years working at the Belk department store chain, starting as a floor sweeper and working his way up to manager of the Greensboro store.

Coble built a career as a federal prosecutor before being appointed the state's chief tax collector in the mid-1970s. In 1984, after four years as a state representative, he earned a 164-vote GOP primary victory and the right to face freshman Democratic Rep. Robin Britt. Coble stressed his fiscal conservatism while painting Britt as an extravagant liberal who had voted against President Ronald Reagan on two of every three votes in 1983. Riding the coattails of Reagan's re-election landslide, Coble won by 2,662 votes.

Britt plotted a comeback, and in 1986 fell by only 79 votes. Britt challenged the election results but was unsuccessful.

Coble had little to worry about in subsequent elections until facing the six-way primary in 2010. He won handily with 64 percent of the vote and easily defeated Democratic challenger Sam Turner, a commercial airline pilot.

Key Votes

2010

Overhaul the nation's health insurance system	NO
Allow for repeal of "don't ask, don't tell"	NO
Overhaul financial services industry regulation	NO
Limit use of new Afghanistan War funds to troop withdrawal activities	NO
Change oversight of offshore drilling and lift oil spill liability cap	NO
Provide a path to legal status for some children of illegal immigrants	NO
Extend Bush-era income tax cuts for two years	YES

2009

Expand the Children's Health Insurance Program	NO
Provide $787 billion in tax cuts and spending increases to stimulate the economy	NO
Allow bankruptcy judges to modify certain primary-residence mortgages	NO
Create a cap-and-trade system to limit greenhouse gas emissions	NO
Provide $2 billion for the "cash for clunkers" program	YES
Establish the government as the sole provider of student loans	NO
Restrict federally funded insurance coverage for abortions in health care overhaul	YES

CQ Vote Studies

	PARTY UNITY		PRESIDENTIAL SUPPORT	
	SUPPORT	OPPOSE	SUPPORT	OPPOSE
2010	97%	3%	27%	73%
2009	95%	5%	23%	77%
2008	96%	4%	65%	35%
2007	94%	6%	80%	20%
2006	94%	6%	73%	27%

Interest Groups

	AFL-CIO	ADA	CCUS	ACU
2010	7%	5%	100%	96%
2009	10%	5%	80%	96%
2008	13%	20%	89%	88%
2007	4%	10%	88%	83%
2006	15%	10%	93%	92%

North Carolina 6

Central — parts of Greensboro and High Point

Located in the heart of the state, the 6th takes in part of the city of Greensboro and surrounding Guilford County, then spreads south to Moore County to pick up the upscale golf and retirement centers of Southern Pines and Pinehurst — host to two men's U.S. Open Championships in the last decade — near Fort Bragg. Solid GOP turf, the district gave John McCain 63 percent in the 2008 presidential race.

The 6th takes in two large chunks of Guilford County that are connected at a single point, on the Reedy Fork Creek in the northern part of the county. The Guilford portions surround Greensboro, although most of the city's more-diverse and Democratic-leaning population resides in the 12th and 13th districts. The rural part of the 6th is tobacco country: Roughly 1,800 residents are employed in factories for two brands owned by Lorillard Tobacco Company, which is based in the 13th.

Greensboro is home to a blend of manufacturing and service companies, particularly in the textile, furniture and insurance industries. It also hosts the North American headquarters of Volvo Trucks, the manufacturing and information technology operations of Volvo-affiliated Mack Trucks, and a major office of the VF Corp. (Wrangler Jeans). Elon University and the region's other colleges have helped diversify Greensboro's economy. FedEx operates out of a new regional hub at Greensboro's Piedmont-Triad International Airport, but an American Express credit card services center that employs nearly 2,000 people will close in 2011.

Like much of North Carolina, economic recession hit all business sectors in the district. Trade issues also loom large here, particularly in the textile and furniture industries. Nearby High Point is a national furniture manufacturing hub, and its market draws 85,000 people annually. But the rise of Las Vegas-based trade shows, falling occupancy at High Point's furniture showrooms, and foreign competition from Asia and elsewhere threaten the city's traditional dominance.

Major Industry
Tobacco, textiles, furniture manufacturing

Cities
Greensboro city (pt.), 82,793; High Point (pt.), 41,610; Burlington (pt.), 25,999; Asheboro, 25,012; Thomasville (pt.), 20,086

Notable
The Richard Petty Museum in Randleman honors the NASCAR legend.

Rep. Mike McIntyre (D)

Capitol Office
225-2731
www.house.gov/mcintyre
2133 Rayburn Bldg. 20515-3307; fax 225-5773

Committees
Agriculture
Armed Services

Residence
Lumberton

Born
Aug. 6, 1956; Lumberton, N.C.

Religion
Presbyterian

Family
Wife, Dee McIntyre; two children

Education
U. of North Carolina, B.A. 1978 (political science),
J.D. 1981

Career
Lawyer

Political Highlights
No previous office

ELECTION RESULTS

2010 GENERAL

Mike McIntyre (D)	113,957	53.7%
Ilario Pantano (R)	98,328	46.3%

2010 PRIMARY

Mike McIntyre (D)	unopposed

2008 GENERAL

Mike McIntyre (D)	215,383	68.8%
Will Breazeale (R)	97,472	31.2%

Previous Winning Percentages
2006 (73%); 2004 (73%); 2002 (71%); 2000 (70%);
1998 (91%); 1996 (53%)

Elected 1996; 8th term

McIntyre is part of the thinning ranks of moderate Democrats who hail from rural districts in the South. A member of the fiscally conservative Blue Dog Coalition, McIntyre sometimes splits with the majority of his party on economic and social issues. But he had grown increasingly loyal to the party over time — until 2010.

His voting record has a discernible path. In his first two terms, with Republicans in the majority and President Bill Clinton in the White House, McIntyre posted the lowest party unity scores — the percentage of votes on which he sided with a majority of Democrats against a majority of Republicans — of his career. Over his next three terms, with Republicans still in control of Congress and President George W. Bush in office, he became more of a Democratic partisan, with party unity scores 10 to 20 percentage points higher than in the Clinton years. After the Democrats took control of Congress following the 2006 election, his scores jumped higher still. He has made the journey from the mid-50s to the mid-80s in three distinct phases of his legislative career.

But in 2010, an election year, McIntyre's party loyalty score sank back to 70. Now, with the Republicans in charge again, he has continued to give signs of returning to his less partisan ways.

Even before Election Day 2010, he announced he would not support Nancy Pelosi of California for Speaker (he eventually voted for fellow North Carolinian Heath Shuler). He ran campaign ads distancing himself from Pelosi. McIntyre was one of three Democrats who joined every Republican in voting to repeal the health care overhaul enacted in 2010. And he was the first Democrat to sign on to a GOP balanced-budget constitutional amendment that includes a requirement for a three-fifths votes in each chamber to run a deficit, increase revenue or increase the debt limit, and two-thirds to breach the spending limit.

He stuck with Democrats, though, in voting against a House-passed appropriations bill that would cut $58 billion from fiscal 2011 spending.

On some of the highest-profile measures in the 111th Congress (2009-10), McIntyre departed from the party leadership. But he supported President Obama's $787 billion economic stimulus law in February 2009 after urging that more money be directed to rural areas for water, wastewater and community facilities projects. That was a common refrain when he chaired the Agriculture Committee's panel on specialty crops and rural development. Even while Vice President Joseph R. Biden Jr. visited eastern North Carolina to announce $1.2 billion in stimulus funds to help rural communities, McIntyre led his panel in hearings to further investigate the impact of the stimulus on such areas.

He used debate on a major rewrite of farm and nutrition programs in 2007 to enact a proposal that had been languishing for years: creating the Southeast Regional Crescent Commission to advance rural economic development and worker training in seven states, including North Carolina.

For years, McIntyre was a stout defender of the federal tobacco program. But in the early 2000s, he developed a plan to buy out tobacco growers. From 2003 through 2006, he was the top Democrat on the Agriculture panel with jurisdiction over tobacco programs, and he helped push a $10 billion tobacco buyout bill to passage in 2004. But he opposed a bill in spring 2009 to give the Food and Drug Administration power to regulate tobacco.

He also initially fought against the use of tobacco taxes to pay for an expansion of the Children's Health Insurance Program, which covers children whose low-income families make too much money to qualify for Medicaid. In 2007, he was one of eight Democrats who voted against such a bill. Less than a month later he reversed course and voted to override Bush's veto. McIntyre said he changed his mind because "there were amplifiers above our head" that made the politics around the bill solely about children. Those amplifiers, he said, were his own party's leaders. He supported a more expensive version of the bill in January 2009 that Obama signed into law.

McIntyre sits on the Armed Services Committee, where he is the ranking Democrat on the Seapower and Projection Forces Subcommittee. Fort Bragg employs many of his constituents, while Camp Lejeune is just over the 3rd District line to the east.

He was born and raised in Lumberton; his father was an optometrist and his mother was a bank branch manager. He was chairman of the Teen Democrats in high school and spent the summer after his junior year at a congressional seminar program in Washington. When he was 16, his father, a city council member, took him to a 1972 victory party for newly elected Rep. Charlie Rose. And he was standing at the back of the room when White House lawyer John Dean testified before the Senate Watergate Committee, which was chaired by North Carolina's legendary Democrat Sam J. Ervin Jr. The next summer, he worked as an intern in Rose's office.

At the University of North Carolina, he majored in political science and was vice president of the campus chapter of college Democrats. He later was an organizer of the Robeson County Young Democrats. After graduating from law school at the University of North Carolina, he was involved in community, church, civic and professional activities as he built a law practice in Lumberton.

When Rose announced his retirement in 1996, McIntyre was one of seven primary entrants. He took 23 percent of the vote, finishing second, then won the runoff against Rose Marie Lowry-Townsend. He then faced Bill Caster, a Republican New Hanover County commissioner and retired Coast Guard officer. McIntyre's lean-to-the-right stance on most issues helped blunt GOP attacks, and he won with 53 percent. He was not seriously challenged until 2010, when he faced Marine Corps veteran Ilario Pantano.

Republicans tried to tie McIntyre to the Democratic leadership. A National Republican Congressional Committee ad asked "who does Mike McIntyre work for?" and prominently featured Pelosi. Carolina native McIntyre labeled Pantano, who moved to the Tar Heel State from New York, a carpetbagger. McIntyre won with 54 percent of the vote.

Key Votes

2010

Overhaul the nation's health insurance system	NO
Allow for repeal of "don't ask, don't tell"	NO
Overhaul financial services industry regulation	NO
Limit use of new Afghanistan War funds to troop withdrawal activities	NO
Change oversight of offshore drilling and lift oil spill liability cap	YES
Provide a path to legal status for some children of illegal immigrants	NO
Extend Bush-era income tax cuts for two years	YES

2009

Expand the Children's Health Insurance Program	YES
Provide $787 billion in tax cuts and spending increases to stimulate the economy	YES
Allow bankruptcy judges to modify certain primary-residence mortgages	YES
Create a cap-and-trade system to limit greenhouse gas emissions	NO
Provide $2 billion for the "cash for clunkers" program	YES
Establish the government as the sole provider of student loans	YES
Restrict federally funded insurance coverage for abortions in health care overhaul	YES

CQ Vote Studies

	PARTY UNITY		PRESIDENTIAL SUPPORT	
	Support	Oppose	Support	Oppose
2010	70%	30%	64%	36%
2009	83%	17%	82%	18%
2008	89%	11%	17%	83%
2007	86%	14%	22%	78%
2006	74%	26%	63%	37%

Interest Groups

	AFL-CIO	ADA	CCUS	ACU
2010	57%	35%	75%	38%
2009	76%	50%	80%	38%
2008	93%	85%	61%	32%
2007	88%	85%	65%	44%
2006	79%	50%	73%	64%

North Carolina 7

Southeast — Wilmington, part of Fayetteville

The 7th stretches from the well-off historic port city of Wilmington in the southeast to the military-fueled commercial hub of Fayetteville in the north. In between lie tobacco fields, hog farms and manufacturing plants. A sliver of Fort Bragg, the huge military base that has added thousands of personnel as a result of 2005 base realignments, is on the edge of the 7th's portion of Fayetteville and is integral to the area.

Tobacco, textiles and agriculture also drive the local economy, although textile declines have led to high unemployment in some counties. Free-trade agreements are viewed with suspicion here. Like Fayetteville (shared with the 2nd and 8th), Wilmington's growth is reflected in its expanding medical center and emerging biotech industry. The city also has become a desirable retirement community, and the area's Atlantic beaches have made the district a tourist spot. Economic slowdowns, however, have hurt retail and tourism sectors.

The region's poor farmers, Lumbee Indians (mainly in Robeson County) and a cohesive black community in Fayetteville and rural Bladen County

provide a slight Democratic lean.

But wealthy condo-dwellers in Wilmington and surrounding New Hanover County, as well as voters in adjacent Brunswick County, exert a rightward influence in presidential elections. The 7th gave John McCain 52 percent in the 2008 presidential election.

Due in part to Robeson County, the 7th has the sixth-largest percentage of American Indians of any district in the nation, and the largest percentage of any district east of the Mississippi River. Almost 18 percent of Duplin County (shared with the 3rd) is Hispanic, and many residents there speak a language other than English at home.

Major Industry
Agriculture, military, manufacturing, tourism

Military Bases
Fort Bragg (Army), 54,359 military, 7,022 civilian (2011) (shared with the 2nd and 8th)

Cities
Wilmington, 106,476; Lumberton, 21,542; Fayetteville (pt.), 21,360

Notable
Wilmington has a strong film and television industry, with movies and shows such as "One Tree Hill" and "The Hunger Games" filmed there.

Rep. Larry Kissell (D)

Capitol Office
225-3715
kissell.house.gov
1632 Longworth Bldg. 20515-3308; fax 225-4036

Committees
Agriculture
Armed Services

Residence
Biscoe

Born
Jan. 31, 1951; Pinehurst, N.C.

Religion
Baptist

Family
Wife, Tina Kissell; two children

Education
Wake Forest U., B.A. 1973 (economics)

Career
Teacher; textile mill supervisor; chemical company foreman

Political Highlights
Democratic nominee for U.S. House, 2006

ELECTION RESULTS

2010 GENERAL

Larry Kissell (D)	88,776	53.0%
Harold Johnson (R)	73,129	43.7%
Thomas Hill (LIBERT)	5,098	3.0%

2010 PRIMARY

Larry Kissell (D)	24,541	62.7%
Nancy Shakir (D)	14,600	37.3%

2008 GENERAL

Larry Kissell (D)	157,185	55.4%
Robin Hayes (R)	126,634	44.6%

Elected 2008; 2nd term

Kissell survives as a moderate Democrat in a politically competitive district by opposing his liberal leadership on a handful of high-profile issues while generally lining up with his party.

His votes against Obama-administration-backed legislation during the 111th Congress (2009-10) — most notably the health care overhaul — helped insulate him against Republican attacks that fueled successful challenges to other Democrats in 2010. But he was enough of a party man to win late-in-the-campaign financial backing from the Democratic Congressional Campaign Committee (DCCC).

Despite the DCCC's support, after the election Kissell (KISS-ell) called for new leadership of the Democratic Caucus and voted to support fellow North Carolinian Heath Shuler for minority leader and Speaker in largely symbolic challenges to the outgoing Speaker, Nancy Pelosi of California.

"She should not be minority leader," Kissell told Politico. "We suffered a devastating defeat … in terms of the House of Representatives. In order to become a national party again, we should have new leadership in the next Congress."

But he was not among the three Democrats who voted to repeal 2010's health care overhaul law, and he was elected a regional whip for the 112th Congress (2011-12) while pledging to stay true to his middle-of-the-road compass, saying he was "honored to be able to bring a moderate approach to a leadership position within the caucus."

During the 111th Congress, Kissell sided with Democrats 93 percent of the time when majorities of the two parties voted differently.

But he opposed the health care law enacted in 2010, saying he could not break a promise to oppose any cuts in Medicare spending.

Kissell also was one of 44 Democrats in 2009 to oppose a bill to create a cap-and-trade system for curbing carbon emissions, saying it would put jobs at risk and increase energy costs. He was one of eight Democrats who voted against giving the Food and Drug Administration regulatory power over tobacco, a major crop in his state.

His independent streak notwithstanding, Kissell supported President Obama's $787 billion stimulus and financial regulatory overhaul legislation. Following the vote, he castigated financial firms, saying that "Wall Street has circumvented laws and oversight, putting the security and future of hard-working families at risk."

The day after Obama signed the Wall Street bill, Kissell voted with fellow Democrats to extend unemployment insurance benefits. He also endorsed the House Democrats' "Make It In America" agenda and sponsored legislation to require the Department of Homeland Security to buy U.S.-made goods.

Kissell's district includes diverse constituencies. Its swath of downtown Charlotte has a large black population that hews Democratic, but the district also includes heavily Republican Cabarrus County, Fort Bragg and rural areas (he serves on the Armed Services and Agriculture committees). The demographics are also changing. The Charlotte area has a fast-growing Hispanic population, creating tensions over immigration. He traveled to the U.S.-Mexico border in September, and afterward declared that "illegal immigration has had a devastating impact on the economy of our state and district."

Job losses have buffeted the textile-based industries in the district, which has made Kissell into an outspoken critic of free-trade deals such as the North American Free Trade Agreement, which he sponsored legislation to repeal. Kissell took flak from unions for his health care vote, but he considers himself an ally of organized labor and is a former textile worker himself. He blames trade policies for the job losses in the district, including the closure of the very plant where he worked.

In November 2010, he and other members of the House Trade Working Group met with Obama to discuss concerns about the U.S.-Korea Free Trade Agreement. He announced his opposition in early December.

Kissell grew up in Biscoe, a town of about 1,700 people in midstate Montgomery County. His mother was a schoolteacher and his father, a decorated World War II veteran, worked at the post office. Kissell earned an economics degree from Wake Forest University, and after graduation worked for a year at Union Carbide Corp. in Asheboro.

After moving back to Montgomery Country to work for Russell Hosiery, a family-owned textile company, he met his future wife, Tina.

Kissell worked at the company for 27 years, working his way up to manager. By 2001, he was ready for a change and applied for a job teaching social studies. He found teaching more rewarding than the business world but was frustrated by job losses in his hometown, including the closure of Kissell's former textile employer in 2003.

Inspired by a church sermon, he decided to run for Congress in 2006. Kissell nearly unseated Republican Robin Hayes, losing by 329 votes — one of the closest races that year. The result made him an early favorite for 2008.

In their second matchup, Hayes outraised Kissell by more than a 2-to-1 margin. But Kissell took advantage of the Democratic tide in the state and beat the five-term lawmaker with about 55 percent of the vote — running 3 percentage points ahead of the Democratic presidential nominee, Barack Obama, in the district. Kissell attributed his win to his next-door-neighbor background. He also demonstrated a fondness for headline-grabbing political stunts, such as when he campaigned with a goat named CAFTA (after the Central America Free Trade Agreement).

In 2010 Republicans tried to portray Kissell as having ridden into office on Obama's coattails, citing his support for administration-backed legislation as evidence of big-government leanings. The DCCC named him one of 40 lawmakers in its "Frontline Program," which provides extra resources to potentially vulnerable candidates. In the end, he had little trouble dispatching Republican Harold Johnson 53 percent to 44 percent.

Key Votes

2010

Overhaul the nation's health insurance system	NO
Allow for repeal of "don't ask, don't tell"	YES
Overhaul financial services industry regulation	YES
Limit use of new Afghanistan War funds to troop withdrawal activities	NO
Change oversight of offshore drilling and lift oil spill liability cap	YES
Provide a path to legal status for some children of illegal immigrants	NO
Extend Bush-era income tax cuts for two years	YES

2009

Expand the Children's Health Insurance Program	?
Provide $787 billion in tax cuts and spending increases to stimulate the economy	YES
Allow bankruptcy judges to modify certain primary-residence mortgages	NO
Create a cap-and-trade system to limit greenhouse gas emissions	NO
Provide $2 billion for the "cash for clunkers" program	YES
Establish the government as the sole provider of student loans	YES
Restrict federally funded insurance coverage for abortions in health care overhaul	NO

CQ Vote Studies

	PARTY UNITY		PRESIDENTIAL SUPPORT	
	SUPPORT	OPPOSE	SUPPORT	OPPOSE
2010	93%	7%	81%	19%
2009	93%	7%	89%	11%

Interest Groups

	AFL-CIO	ADA	CCUS	ACU
2010	79%	70%	50%	8%
2009	86%	75%	60%	20%

North Carolina 8

South central — parts of Charlotte, Fayetteville, Concord and Kannapolis

The 8th stretches from Charlotte in the west along part of the state's border with South Carolina all the way east to military-dominated Fayetteville. Charlotte adds an urban component to an otherwise suburban and rural district.

Cabarrus, a largely white and Republican county north of Charlotte, and Cumberland, which includes the 8th's share of Fayetteville, are the district's most populous counties. The population of Cabarrus has grown nearly 36 percent since 2000 as the district overall added more than 90,000 residents. In Mecklenburg County, the district almost reaches downtown Charlotte, heading as far west as Memorial Stadium. The 8th's share of the city has a sizable black population, giving the district's portion of Mecklenburg a decidedly Democratic lean.

Textile-based economies along Interstate 85, notably in Concord and Kannapolis, have suffered major losses as manufacturing jobs headed overseas. In the east, the 8th becomes poorer and more rural. Fort Bragg (shared with the 2nd and 7th) in Hoke and Cumberland counties in the Sandhills

part of the district lends the district a strong military flavor. Thousands of new residents have moved into this region in the last several years as Fort Bragg expanded to accommodate the 2005 round of base realignments and closures.

The 8th is politically competitive, although Democrats at the federal level have been gaining traction here. In 2010, Rep. Larry Kissell won in all but two of the counties wholly or partly in the 8th — Cabarrus and Stanly counties supported Republican challenger Harold Johnson — and Democrat Elaine Marshall took the border counties of Anson, Richmond and Scotland in her unsuccessful U.S. Senate run.

Major Industry
Military, manufacturing, agriculture, livestock

Military Bases
Fort Bragg (Army), 54,359 military, 7,022 civilian (2011) (shared with the 2nd and 7th)

Cities
Charlotte (pt.), 119,929; Fayetteville (pt.), 101,220; Concord (pt.), 69,301

Notable
The Charlotte Motor Speedway in Concord seats 140,000 people for its NASCAR races.

Rep. Sue Myrick (R)

Capitol Office
225-1976
myrick.house.gov
230 Cannon Bldg. 20515-3309; fax 225-3389

Committees
Energy & Commerce
Select Intelligence
(Terrorism, Human Intelligence, Analysis &
Counterintelligence - Chairwoman)

Residence
Charlotte

Born
Aug. 1, 1941; Tiffin, Ohio

Religion
Evangelical Methodist

Family
Husband, Ed Myrick; two children, three stepchildren

Education
Heidelberg College, attended 1959-60 (elementary education)

Career
Advertising executive; secretary

Political Highlights
Candidate for Charlotte City Council, 1981; Charlotte City Council, 1983-85; sought Republican nomination for mayor of Charlotte, 1985; mayor of Charlotte, 1987-91; sought Republican nomination for U.S. Senate, 1992

ELECTION RESULTS

2010 GENERAL

Sue Myrick (R)	158,790	69.0%
Jeff Doctor (D)	71,450	31.0%

2010 PRIMARY

Sue Myrick (R)	unopposed

2008 GENERAL

Sue Myrick (R)	241,053	62.4%
Harry Taylor (D)	138,719	35.9%
Andy Grum (LIBERT)	6,711	1.7%

Previous Winning Percentages
2006 (67%); 2004 (70%); 2002 (72%); 2000 (69%);
1998 (69%); 1996 (63%); 1994 (65%)

Elected 1994; 9th term

Myrick works on an unusual mix of issues — she wins kudos from the right for her high-energy opposition to radical Islamic terrorism while also working with Democrats to combat breast cancer.

A former chairwoman of the conservative Republican Study Committee, she is a reliable GOP vote and serves as a deputy whip. With Republicans back in the majority, Myrick's seniority and seats on the Select Intelligence and Energy and Commerce committees put her in position to shape policy on the issues she cares about most.

Myrick was one of the few conservatives who came out in support of Michigan's Fred Upton for the Energy and Commerce chairmanship rather than John Shimkus of Illinois or Joe L. Barton of Texas. She was rewarded with the title of vice chairwoman in the 112th Congress (2011-12).

Her biggest legislative victories were spurred by her personal battle with breast cancer. Myrick underwent surgery in late 1999 and received treatments for about six months. She kept up with floor votes by wearing a pink surgical mask to reduce the risk of infection. In 2000, she shepherded into law a measure that provides treatment for low-income women diagnosed with breast or cervical cancer. Six years later, she steered through the House a bill reauthorizing early-detection programs, although it stalled short of enactment. And in 2008, she and New York Democrat Nita M. Lowey wrote a law creating an interagency breast cancer research committee.

In 2009, she pushed back against a government-sponsored task force recommendation that called for fewer mammograms in part because of the risks of testing and false positives. During the health care debates in the 111th Congress (2009-10), she said that more government involvement in health care would likely increase waiting times for screening tests and procedures. She opposed the Democrats' overhaul, then voted to repeal it in 2011.

As a member of the Energy and Commerce Subcommittee on Health, she also advocates congressional action on mental health issues, in part because she has a granddaughter with bipolar disorder. But, Myrick said, she sometimes finds herself philosophically opposed to Democratic legislation on the issue, such as the initial version of a bill in the 110th Congress (2007-08) to require insurers to treat mental and physical illnesses equally. "I just hate mandates, which they had in there," she said.

Myrick is deeply troubled by Islamic terrorism, but her policy prescriptions made little headway while the Democrats were in charge. She can expect better results in the majority and as chairwoman of the Intelligence Subcommittee on Terrorism, Human Intelligence, Analysis and Counterintelligence.

In early 2011, she blasted Director of National Intelligence James R. Clapper Jr. for referring to the Muslim Brotherhood, poised at the time to claim a share of power in Egypt, as a "largely secular" organization.

"Either the administration doesn't know who the Muslim Brotherhood is, which shows incompetence, or they are apologizing for them, which is inappropriate for those in charge of protecting the American people," she said.

She introduced a "Wake Up, America" agenda in April 2008, calling for investigations of the nonprofit status of the Council on American-Islamic Relations and the process for selecting the government's Arabic translators, as well as the canceling of student scholarship visa programs with Saudi Arabia.

She breaks away from Republicans occasionally on issues that threaten the textile manufacturers in her district. She has been a skeptic of some trade deals that could threaten jobs in her state. But in 2002 she voted to grant President George W. Bush fast-track trade negotiating authority after Bush pledged to look out for the textile industry. She voted for the 2005 Central America Free Trade Agreement and the Peru Free Trade Agreement in 2007. In 2010, she voted for a bill — similar to one she had sponsored in past years — that would threaten China with tariffs if it did not allow its currency to appreciate.

In 2008, Myrick, whose hometown of Charlotte includes the headquarters of Bank of America Corp., was one of 25 Republicans who voted against the first version of a $700 billion rescue bill for the financial sector and switched their vote on the next version, which became law. She said she was swayed by conversations at home. "I talked to people I trust . . . good, solid businesses," she said. "They could not get credit."

Her conservatism and her status as the only Southern Republican woman in the GOP's class of 1994 helped win her a seat on the Budget Committee in her first term and a post on the Rules panel in her second. But in 1997 she joined a group who moved to depose Speaker Newt Gingrich of Georgia. The effort failed, and Myrick's influence in the House waned; she lost a race for secretary of the Republican Conference to Deborah Pryce of Ohio.

Born in Tiffin, Ohio, Myrick was reared on a farm. She attended Heidelberg College for a year before her parents decided their limited resources should be used for her three brothers' higher education. They figured "I'd just get married," Myrick said. She took a secretarial job at an Army depot.

Myrick entered the political arena in the early 1980s, when she and her husband sparred with the Charlotte City Council over the purchase of a property for use as a combination home and business. She ran for the council in 1981 and lost, but she was victorious two years later. She lost a bid to become mayor of Charlotte in 1985, but won the office in 1987 and was re-elected in 1989.

After five-term GOP Rep. Alex McMillan announced his retirement in 1994, Myrick's political experience gave her wide name recognition in a five-way Republican primary. Still, she struggled to win the nomination, prevailing only when news broke that her principal opponent, state House Minority Leader David Balmer, had falsified his résumé. That November, she met only modest Democratic resistance. She has easily won re-election since.

Myrick was among the first lawmakers to offer a smart phone application allowing constituents and others to follow their congressional activities. Myrick's app, available on iTunes, provides updates on legislation and upcoming events, as well as video.

Key Votes

2010

Overhaul the nation's health insurance system	NO
Allow for repeal of "don't ask, don't tell"	NO
Overhaul financial services industry regulation	NO
Limit use of new Afghanistan War funds to troop withdrawal activities	NO
Change oversight of offshore drilling and lift oil spill liability cap	NO
Provide a path to legal status for some children of illegal immigrants	NO
Extend Bush-era income tax cuts for two years	YES

2009

Expand the Children's Health Insurance Program	NO
Provide $787 billion in tax cuts and spending increases to stimulate the economy	NO
Allow bankruptcy judges to modify certain primary-residence mortgages	NO
Create a cap-and-trade system to limit greenhouse gas emissions	NO
Provide $2 billion for the "cash for clunkers" program	NO
Establish the government as the sole provider of student loans	NO
Restrict federally funded insurance coverage for abortions in health care overhaul	YES

CQ Vote Studies

	PARTY UNITY		PRESIDENTIAL SUPPORT	
	SUPPORT	OPPOSE	SUPPORT	OPPOSE
2010	98%	2%	27%	73%
2009	98%	2%	19%	81%
2008	99%	1%	79%	21%
2007	97%	3%	89%	11%
2006	96%	4%	92%	8%

Interest Groups

	AFL-CIO	ADA	CCUS	ACU
2010	7%	0%	88%	100%
2009	5%	0%	80%	96%
2008	14%	10%	94%	91%
2007	4%	10%	74%	96%
2006	14%	0%	100%	92%

North Carolina 9

South central — parts of Charlotte and Gastonia

The predominately Republican 9th centers around Charlotte, the largest metropolitan area in the state. Forty percent of district residents live within the city's limits, and 60 percent overall live in Mecklenburg County, which includes Charlotte. The 9th has been the fastest-growing district in the state since 2000 and is the most-populous heading into decennial remapping. The region's growth over the last two decades has brought the traffic congestion that usually accompanies sprawl.

The primarily white suburbs on the southern side of Charlotte provide the city with many of its bankers, brokers, accountants, health care professionals and other white-collar workers. Most of Charlotte's black residents live in the 8th or 12th districts. The 9th has the second-highest median household income in North Carolina, due to upper-middle-class areas such as Huntersville, in northern Mecklenburg County.

Charlotte, the nation's biggest banking center after New York, was hit hard by the nationwide credit and investment brokerage collapse. Job losses and instability at Bank of America and Wachovia, which was bought by San Francisco-based Wells Fargo, created uncertainty in the community. Energy sector jobs and defense contracting have helped diversify the economy recently, but several years of commercial real estate market declines, high home foreclosure and unemployment rates, and retail sector struggles concern residents.

To the west, Gastonia and surrounding towns have been hit by continuing declines in the textile industry. The 9th, however, lessened its dependence on manufacturing and textiles, and the population of Gastonia continues to grow. Union County, a suburban bedroom community located southeast of Charlotte, is the fastest-growing county in the state.

Republicans dominate elections in the 9th. Republican John McCain won 55 percent of the district's 2008 presidential vote. Since the 9th became a Charlotte-based district prior to the 1968 election, it has been represented in the U.S. House only by Republicans.

Major Industry
Finance, service, retail, manufacturing

Cities
Charlotte (pt.), 347,410; Gastonia (pt.), 65,497; Huntersville, 46,773

Notable
Pineville hosts the James K. Polk State Historic Site.

Rep. Patrick T. McHenry (R)

Capitol Office
225-2576
mchenry.house.gov
224 Cannon Bldg. 20515-3310; fax 225-0316

Committees
Financial Services
Oversight & Government Reform
(TARP, Financial Services & Bailouts of Public and
Private Programs - Chairman)

Residence
Cherryville

Born
Oct. 22, 1975; Charlotte, N.C.

Religion
Roman Catholic

Family
Wife, Giulia Cangiano

Education
North Carolina State U., attended 1994-97; Belmont
Abbey College, B.A. 2000 (history)

Career
Real estate broker; U.S. Labor Department special
assistant; campaign aide

Political Highlights
Republican nominee for N.C. House, 1998; N.C.
House, 2003-04

ELECTION RESULTS

2010 GENERAL

Patrick T. McHenry (R)	130,813	71.2%
Jeff Gregory (D)	52,972	28.8%

2010 PRIMARY

Patrick T. McHenry (R)	27,657	63.1%
Vance Patterson (R)	11,392	26.0%
Scott Keadle (R)	3,604	8.2%
David Michael Boldon (R)	1,181	2.7%

2008 GENERAL

Patrick T. McHenry (R)	171,774	57.6%
Daniel Johnson (D)	126,699	42.4%

Previous Winning Percentages
2006 (62%); 2004 (64%)

Elected 2004; 4th term

Once eager to engage in verbal sparring matches, McHenry is now trying to take a mellower, more measured approach to legislating. The new style, combined with a tighter focus on a handful of issues, is part of a calculated effort by the conservative to take a longer view of his congressional career.

But his more practiced skills will come in handy in the 112th Congress (2011-12) as chairman of the Oversight and Government Reform subcommittee keeping an eye on the Obama administration's handling of the various financial rescues enacted over the past few years.

McHenry opposed the $700 billion plan enacted in 2008 to rescue the ailing financial services industry. "I continue to believe that action is needed to stabilize our financial markets, but this is not the right approach," he said. "The U.S. Treasury has bailed out a number of financial institutions and yet the problem persists." One of his major tasks in the new Congress will be serving as a watchdog on the Troubled Asset Relief Program created by the law.

"We've got hundreds of billions of taxpayers' money in private institutions," McHenry told the Hickory Daily Record in late 2010. "We want to make sure where the funds are going and what they are being used for, and if taxpayers are going to be compensated for loaning this money."

McHenry came to the House in 2005 as the youngest member of Congress. At times he acted like it, hurling caustic comments and engaging regularly in procedural scraps on the House floor and partisan bickering on cable TV. He said a series of back injuries in 2007 prompted him to think critically about the way he was doing his job, and he started focusing on a narrower set of policies. "That was a wake-up call that I was doing too much and not doing any one component to the standard and the depth that I'd like to," he said in 2010.

In the 111th Congress (2009-10), McHenry pushed a limited-government agenda. "I realize that not every fight is my fight, and I've tried to focus on the key areas of concern for me, my state and my district," he said.

On the Financial Services Committee, he argued against the financial services regulatory overhaul that imposed new rules on the banking industry. "I think it restricts credit just at a time when our economy, especially small businesses, need access to credit," he said. In particular, he disagreed with the creation of a consumer protection bureau, contending that all regulators should have consumers' interests in mind. Going forward, McHenry wants to focus on the restructuring of Fannie Mae and Freddie Mac. He thinks a bipartisan agreement is possible, although he said he has no preconceived notion of what the right mortgage-finance policy should be.

On the Oversight and Government Reform panel, McHenry was the top Republican on the subcommittee that monitored the 2010 census. Despite his lack of formal power, he pushed back against an Obama administration idea of having the Census director report to the White House instead of the Commerce Department. He also complained loudly about the involvement of the community group ACORN. In both instances, the administration relented in the face of public pressure that McHenry helped generate. He also discouraged conservative citizens from avoiding the census by arguing that it was their patriotic duty to participate and that the census was not an intrusion that violated their privacy.

McHenry is not a prolific author of legislation, sponsoring just five measures in the 111th Congress. That doesn't mean he's inactive on the floor. He is a reliable vote and debater for Republican leaders, and as a deputy whip he helped orchestrate the steady GOP opposition to the Obama agenda in 2009 and 2010. McHenry was at the forefront of an effort in the 110th Congress (2007-08) to use a House procedure called the motion to recommit to win last-minute adoption of GOP-favored amendments to Democratic-written bills.

In an opinion piece posted on LincolnTribune.com in early February 2009, McHenry called the Democrats' economic stimulus plan a "massive spending bill" created in "a secretive, hasty and partisan process that clearly demonstrates the Democrat majority's disregard for America's desire for bipartisan cooperation in this time of crisis." He criticized Democrats for not offering enough tax relief for working families and small businesses.

McHenry rarely departs from the conservative line. He supports offshore drilling and gun owners' rights, opposes gay marriage and federal funding of embryonic stem cell research, and calls himself a "family values" man. A fiscal conservative, McHenry once said, "I have never voted for a tax increase on western North Carolina families and never will."

There are a couple of policy areas where the interests of his district cause McHenry to part ways with most Republicans. Western North Carolina was once heavily dependent on the textile and furniture industries, and residents blame trade liberalization policies for the loss of thousands of jobs. In 2005, McHenry was one of 27 Republicans to vote against the Central America Free Trade Agreement, and he voted in 2010 to authorize retaliatory tariffs on China for undervaluing its currency. He did, however, vote for a free-trade deal with Peru in 2007. He calls himself a "pragmatist" who supports government assistance to help retrain workers in trade-affected industries. Because of the high unemployment rate in his district, he has, on occasion, voted for extensions of unemployment benefits even without the budgetary offsets that he and other GOP members usually demand.

McHenry served as chairman of the state College Republicans and as treasurer for the national College Republicans organization in the late 1990s. He worked on several campaigns, including Robin Hayes' failed 1996 gubernatorial bid and George W. Bush's successful 2000 presidential race, in addition to his own contests for the state legislature.

When veteran GOP Rep. Cass Ballenger announced in 2004 that he would retire from the seat he had held since 1986, McHenry battled through a four-way Republican primary, combating criticism that he wasn't ready for the job. His second-place finish put him in a runoff against David Huffman, a well-known local sheriff. With a financial boost from the Club for Growth, a Washington-based group that supports fiscally conservative candidates, he won by 85 votes. That November, he defeated little-known Democratic Party activist Anne N. Fischer by more than 28 percentage points in the overwhelmingly Republican district. He has cruised to re-election since.

Key Votes

2010	
Overhaul the nation's health insurance system	NO
Allow for repeal of "don't ask, don't tell"	NO
Overhaul financial services industry regulation	NO
Limit use of new Afghanistan War funds to troop withdrawal activities	NO
Change oversight of offshore drilling and lift oil spill liability cap	NO
Provide a path to legal status for some children of illegal immigrants	NO
Extend Bush-era income tax cuts for two years	YES
2009	
Expand the Children's Health Insurance Program	NO
Provide $787 billion in tax cuts and spending increases to stimulate the economy	NO
Allow bankruptcy judges to modify certain primary-residence mortgages	NO
Create a cap-and-trade system to limit greenhouse gas emissions	NO
Provide $2 billion for the "cash for clunkers" program	NO
Establish the government as the sole provider of student loans	NO
Restrict federally funded insurance coverage for abortions in health care overhaul	YES

CQ Vote Studies

	PARTY UNITY		PRESIDENTIAL SUPPORT	
	SUPPORT	OPPOSE	SUPPORT	OPPOSE
2010	98%	2%	29%	71%
2009	99%	1%	11%	89%
2008	98%	2%	78%	22%
2007	99%	1%	92%	8%
2006	98%	2%	83%	17%

Interest Groups

	AFL-CIO	ADA	CCUS	ACU
2010	7%	0%	88%	96%
2009	5%	0%	73%	100%
2008	13%	10%	78%	100%
2007	8%	0%	75%	100%
2006	7%	10%	93%	92%

North Carolina 10

West — Hickory

Set among the small towns in the western part of the state, the 10th has a rustic, small-business and conservative flavor. A solidly Republican district, the 10th has sent GOP lawmakers to the U.S. House for 40 years, and many residents who consider themselves conservative Democrats will support Republicans in federal races.

While the 10th includes some suburban communities near Charlotte, it is mostly rural — only one town, Hickory, has a population of 40,000. Suburban sprawl has reached the eastern and southern edges of the 10th. In Hickory and other areas along U.S. Route 321, the furniture industry employs a large part of the workforce.

Historically, the economy of the southern counties was based largely on textile and furniture manufacturing, with cotton-growing areas in Cleveland County. In the north, there are Christmas tree growers, and tourists visit the mountains near the Tennessee border and ski in areas like Banner Elk.

The 10th has the state's highest percentage of blue-collar workers, and the district relies on factory jobs. Employment gaps in textile and furniture manufacturing have been compounded by job losses at key technology manufacturing employers.

Fiber-optic giant Corning Cable Systems closed its Hickory plant, but other businesses have moved in to the site. Local officials have marketed the region as a data center hub, welcoming Google, Apple and Facebook operations to the district's counties.

In the 2008 presidential election, Republican John McCain won the district with more than 63 percent of its vote — his highest percentage statewide. Every county wholly or partly in the 10th voted for McCain, and rural Avery (72 percent) and Mitchell (70 percent) counties along the Tennessee border gave McCain his second- and fourth-highest percentages in the state.

Major Industry
Manufacturing, agriculture

Cities
Hickory, 40,010; Mooresville (pt.), 32,646; Shelby, 20,323

Notable
Despite the 10th's longtime Republican slant, the longest-serving congressman from North Carolina, Democrat Bob Doughton, represented the 10th for 42 years.

Rep. Heath Shuler (D)

Capitol Office
225-6401
shuler.house.gov
229 Cannon Bldg. 20515; fax 226-6422

Committees
Budget
Transportation & Infrastructure

Residence
Waynesville

Born
Dec. 31, 1971; Bryson City, N.C.

Religion
Baptist

Family
Wife, Nikol Shuler; two children

Education
U. of Tennessee, B.A. 2001 (psychology)

Career
Real estate company owner; medical record smart card company president; professional football player

Political Highlights
No previous office

ELECTION RESULTS

2010 GENERAL
Heath Shuler (D)	131,225	54.3%
Jeff Miller (R)	110,246	45.7%

2010 PRIMARY
Heath Shuler (D)	26,223	61.4%
Aixa Wilson (D)	16,507	38.6%

2008 GENERAL
Heath Shuler (D)	211,112	62.0%
Carl Mumpower (R)	122,087	35.8%
Keith Smith (LIBERT)	7,517	2.2%

Previous Winning Percentages
2006 (54%)

Elected 2006; 3rd term

One of the most socially and fiscally conservative Democrats in the House, Shuler got a taste of national attention after the 2010 midterm elections when he challenged Nancy Pelosi of California for minority leader in the new Congress. He lost, but established himself as a leading voice for those seeking to bring the party closer to the center.

"It was never about winning; it was about giving the moderates a voice in this caucus," Shuler said. "We are strong because we are a big tent party, not in spite of it."

Instead, Shuler was elected co-chairman of the Blue Dog Coalition, a group of fiscally conservative Democrats. He also got a smattering of symbolic votes for Speaker from Democrats who wanted to cast a protest vote against Pelosi at the beginning of the 112th Congress (2011-12).

And Shuler got a seat on the Budget Committee, where he makes the case for bipartisan cooperation on spending cuts.

"If we lose our elections, if all of us lose our elections in 2012 because we made the right decision for the next generation, then that's good for us," he said at a March 2011 hearing. "And that's good for the American people. Because 10 years from now, they will say that will be the best Congress to have ever served."

Shuler started his congressional career by cutting one of his credit cards in half. "If you start overspending, one of the first things you need to do at home is cut your credit cards up. That is what we should do [in the government]," he said. "We can't live above our means."

In late 2008, Shuler voted twice against a $700 billion measure to shore up the nation's financial system. He continued to display his fiscal conservatism in the early months of President Obama's administration by being one of seven House Democrats to oppose Obama's $787 billion economic stimulus proposal. He said it didn't contain enough for infrastructure, pointing to its inclusion of $5.5 million for transportation in Buncombe County. "That won't quite build a bridge in Buncombe," he said.

A former pro football quarterback and a devout Christian, the congressman holds many positions that appear more in line with the GOP. He voted against the Democrats' top priority in the 111th Congress (2009-10), the health care overhaul, although he was not one of the three Democrats who joined Republicans in voting to repeal the law in early 2011. He also opposes abortion, gun control and same-sex marriage.

Shuler's independent streak began in his first term, when he departed from his party on 22 percent of votes pitting most Democrats against most Republicans, bucking party leaders more often than all but four Democrats. Only a half-dozen Democrats split with the party more often in 2010 — and every one of them lost their re-election races.

One of the first issues Shuler tended to in the 110th Congress (2007-08) was an effort to overhaul immigration policy.

He wants to beef up border security and opposes a path to citizenship for illegal immigrants. When debate on the issue stalled in 2007, he offered a bill that would have mandated employers participate in a government-sponsored employee verification system. The House Immigration Reform Caucus quickly rallied around the bill. But the chamber ultimately passed a five-year renewal of the program that calls for voluntary participation.

Despite various policy differences, Shuler said he joined the Democrats "because the party helps those who can't help themselves." From his seat on the Transportation and Infrastructure Committee, he tends to the concerns of a rural district struggling to protect its resources and renew its economy after the loss of manufacturing jobs.

Shuler achieved one of his biggest legislative goals for his district in 2010: He helped secure a $52 million settlement between Swain County and the Department of Interior over the "Road to Nowhere." It ended a controversy that began 67 years earlier, when the county gave the federal government its private land in what is now Great Smoky Mountains National Park, with the promise a major road would be built there. The road was never built, igniting a decades-long dispute.

Born Joseph Heath Shuler, he took up his middle name so he wouldn't be known as "Joe Junior." His father, Joseph Shuler, was a mail carrier in Bryson City, a gateway community to the Smokies. His mother helped run the town's youth baseball and football programs.

Shuler was in fifth grade when he fell in love with football. As starting quarterback, he led Swain County High School to back-to-back state championships before embarking on a standout career at the University of Tennessee; in 1993 he was the runner-up for the Heisman Trophy, awarded to college football's best player.

The Washington Redskins chose him third overall in the NFL draft in 1994. He never lived up to expectations, though, and retired after five years. In 1998, he returned to Knoxville, the site of his collegiate glory, and started a real estate company with his younger brother Benjie. Shuler later sold his share to his brother and moved to Waynesville, N.C.

In 2006, Rahm Emanuel of Illinois, chairman of the Democratic Congressional Campaign Committee, asked him to challenge GOP Rep. Charles H. Taylor. It was a tough battle, but Shuler received a boost in October of that year when the Wall Street Journal published a story questioning whether Taylor used his seat on the Appropriations Committee to benefit himself and business partners. Taylor spent more than twice Shuler's $1.8 million, but Shuler won by 8 percentage points.

In 2008 he faced Republican Carl Mumpower, a psychologist, conservative activist and Asheville city councilman. Shuler raised more than $1.6 million for the contest and was easily re-elected.

He faced a tougher challenge in 2010 against GOP opponent Jeff Miller, who tried to tie the congressman to the liberal Democratic leadership. But Shuler's pledge to challenge Pelosi helped remind voters of his distance from much of the rest of his party and he won, 54 percent to 46 percent.

Key Votes

2010

Overhaul the nation's health insurance system	NO
Allow for repeal of "don't ask, don't tell"	NO
Overhaul financial services industry regulation	YES
Limit use of new Afghanistan War funds to troop withdrawal activities	NO
Change oversight of offshore drilling and lift oil spill liability cap	YES
Provide a path to legal status for some children of illegal immigrants	NO
Extend Bush-era income tax cuts for two years	YES

2009

Expand the Children's Health Insurance Program	YES
Provide $787 billion in tax cuts and spending increases to stimulate the economy	NO
Allow bankruptcy judges to modify certain primary-residence mortgages	YES
Create a cap-and-trade system to limit greenhouse gas emissions	YES
Provide $2 billion for the "cash for clunkers" program	YES
Establish the government as the sole provider of student loans	YES
Restrict federally funded insurance coverage for abortions in health care overhaul	YES

CQ Vote Studies

	PARTY UNITY		PRESIDENTIAL SUPPORT	
	SUPPORT	OPPOSE	SUPPORT	OPPOSE
2010	60%	40%	71%	29%
2009	68%	32%	80%	20%
2008	83%	17%	18%	82%
2007	76%	24%	19%	81%

Interest Groups

	AFL-CIO	ADA	CCUS	ACU
2010	69%	50%	50%	22%
2009	86%	65%	53%	24%
2008	87%	75%	56%	24%
2007	88%	80%	55%	44%

North Carolina 11

West — Asheville

Based in the Great Smoky Mountains of Appalachia, the 11th is a largely rural district dotted with tree farms, wood mills and campgrounds. Agriculture and forestry long played a major role in the region's economy. Widespread layoffs have restricted economic opportunity in the westernmost counties of the 11th, some of which have the highest unemployment rates in the state. Metropolitan Asheville will depend on the growth of high-tech manufacturing to counter declines in traditional manufacturing, retail and construction sectors.

Asheville and surrounding Buncombe County take in one-third of the district's residents. The combination of small-town, mountain remoteness and the city's blend of urban amenities still draw young professionals and retirees to Asheville. Downtown condominiums and lofts have continued to sell, and several breweries anchor the local social scene.

People flock to the area's ski slopes, as well as to hiking trails in parks and forests and on Mount Mitchell (the highest peak east of the Mississippi River). More than 1 million tourists each year visit the Biltmore Estate, the nation's largest privately owned home.

The 11th has the highest median age and the smallest black population of any North Carolina district, and the Eastern Band of Cherokee Indians' reservation gives the district a larger-than-average American Indian population. Many of the state's Cherokee Indians are descendants of the Cherokees who hid in the western North Carolina mountains to avoid forced migration to Oklahoma.

Although there are areas of Democratic strength, the district traditionally leans Republican. Henderson County is solidly GOP territory, and the district overall gave Republican John McCain 52 percent in the 2008 presidential race. Democrat Barack Obama took a 14-percentage-point win in Buncombe County, and Jackson County — which George W. Bush won in 2004 — supported Obama with 52 percent.

Major Industry
Retail, forest products, health care, tourism

Cities
Asheville, 83,393; Hendersonville, 13,137

Notable
The National Climatic Data Center, the world's largest archive of weather data, is located in Asheville.

Rep. Melvin Watt (D)

Capitol Office
225-1510
www.house.gov/watt
2304 Rayburn Bldg. 20515-3312; fax 225-1512

Committees
Financial Services
Judiciary

Residence
Charlotte

Born
Aug. 26, 1945; Charlotte, N.C.

Religion
Presbyterian

Family
Wife, Eulada Watt; two children

Education
U. of North Carolina, B.S. 1967 (business administration); Yale U., J.D. 1970

Career
Nursing home owner; campaign aide; lawyer

Political Highlights
N.C. Senate, 1985-86

ELECTION RESULTS

2010 GENERAL

Melvin Watt (D)	103,495	63.9%
Greg Dority (R)	55,315	34.1%
Lon Cecil (LIBERT)	3,197	2.0%

2010 PRIMARY

Melvin Watt (D)	unopposed

2008 GENERAL

Melvin Watt (D)	215,908	71.6%
Ty Cobb Jr. (R)	85,814	28.4%

Previous Winning Percentages
2006 (67%); 2004 (67%); 2002 (65%); 2000 (65%);
1998 (56%); 1996 (71%); 1994 (66%); 1992 (70%)

Elected 1992; 10th term

An outspoken advocate for consumers whose district is home to the nation's second-largest banking center, Watt spent the past few years in the middle of most financial debates on Capitol Hill. He has learned to balance those two constituencies with skill, although he still finds himself courting trouble occasionally.

In June 2010, Watt was among eight Republican and Democratic lawmakers under investigation by the Office of Congressional Ethics for fundraising activities that coincided with key votes on the financial services overhaul.

He came under scrutiny after pulling an amendment, within two days of receiving multiple campaign contributions through a fundraiser with ties to companies that provide auto financing, that would have required auto dealers to be supervised by a new consumer protection regulator. Many colleagues, including members of the Congressional Black Caucus, rushed to his defense, and by the end of the summer he was cleared of wrongdoing.

Watt is a Yale-educated lawyer who emerged as a key ally of Massachusetts Democrat Barney Frank during Frank's four-year stint as chairman of the Financial Services Committee. Although he consistently votes with liberal members of his caucus, Watt said he is prepared to work closely with Republicans.

"I have as a high priority trying to not get adversarial with the people with whom I'm serving," Watt said a few weeks after the 2010 elections handed the House to Republicans. "I'm going to try to make as many accommodations as I can but I'm not going to change my opinions on substantive issues and I hope it doesn't become too personal."

When Democrats controlled the House, Watt chaired first the Financial Services Subcommittee on Oversight and Investigation, and then the subcommittee responsible for domestic monetary policy. When legislation to aid the housing industry became law in 2008, Watt joined Frank and several other panel Democrats in calling on mortgage holders to postpone foreclosing on any homes until the law went into effect. He urged colleagues to support a bill in early 2009 to permit bankruptcy judges to write down the principal and interest rate of loans for people whose mortgages are higher than the value of their homes.

Financial services companies credit Watt with giving their views a fair hearing, and he occasionally agrees with them. He opposed proposals to raise the $100,000 ceiling on federally insured deposits. But he has backed legislation to ban several credit card billing practices, siding with consumer groups over Wachovia and Bank of America, two of his district's largest employers.

Watt did not play much of a public role in late 2008 on the $700 billion effort to shore up the financial services industry. He supported the proposal despite objections from some of his constituents, saying he believed there was ample evidence it could avert greater crises.

As a member of the Judiciary Committee, Watt was the chief Democratic negotiator in 2006 on a measure to extend the 1965 Voting Rights Act. He produced a bipartisan bill that was praised by both the Republican chairman at the time, F. James Sensenbrenner Jr. of Wisconsin, and senior panel Democrat John Conyers Jr. of Michigan. Watt said he got heavily involved because the bill dealt with redistricting. "I've been the poster child of redistricting. My district was changed five times in a 10-year period, so people knew that I understood that issue," he said.

In the 112th Congress (2011-12), Watt is the top Democrat on Judiciary's

Intellectual Property, Competition and the Internet Subcommittee.

As Congressional Black Caucus (CBC) chairman in the 109th Congress (2005-06), Watt was embroiled in several high-profile issues. He objected to his party's treatment of Louisiana Democrat William J. Jefferson, who was the target of a federal corruption probe but had not yet been indicted. When the House voted in 2006 to remove Jefferson from the Ways and Means Committee, Watt argued that the Democratic Caucus used a double standard because Jefferson is black. There is no House rule calling for removal of a rank-and-file member not charged with a crime.

He took up the cause of Chaka Fattah of Pennsylvania, an appropriator and CBC member who unsuccessfully challenged Norm Dicks of Washington for the ranking Democrat spot on the spending committee in the 112th Congress. Watt tried and failed to have the Democratic Caucus bar Dicks, and most other committee chairmen and ranking members, from also serving as subcommittee chairmen.

Underpinning Watt's success is the determination he developed during a difficult early life. He grew up in rural Mecklenburg County in a tin-roofed shack that lacked running water and electricity. His mother raised him and his two brothers while working as a maid, and he earned money by shining shoes at a barbershop where he could not get his hair cut until night.

"People look at you in a suit as a member of Congress, and they think you've always been in a suit and always been a member of Congress," he once said. "I came out of a different kind of history."

After attending a segregated high school, he went on to graduate Phi Beta Kappa from the University of North Carolina, posting the highest academic average in the business school. He then earned his law degree from Yale.

Watt worked for several years as an attorney for a firm specializing in civil rights law. He interrupted his practice for a brief stint as an appointed state senator and to manage the 1990 Senate campaign of Democrat Harvey Gantt, who lost to GOP incumbent Jesse Helms that year.

In 1992, when a meandering majority-black district was created, Watt won it with relative ease. But the boundaries of Watt's district were challenged in court through the 1990s, and the 12th District's lines were redrawn twice during the decade in response to lawsuits alleging unconstitutional racial gerrymandering.

The state's map was redrawn again in 2001 when North Carolina received another House seat because of population gains. The Democrats in charge of the process made sure to give Watt safe territory. The changing shape of his district has proved more of a distraction than a political threat: He consistently wins with close to two-thirds or more of the vote.

Key Votes

2010

Overhaul the nation's health insurance system	YES
Allow for repeal of "don't ask, don't tell"	YES
Overhaul financial services industry regulation	YES
Limit use of new Afghanistan War funds to troop withdrawal activities	YES
Change oversight of offshore drilling and lift oil spill liability cap	YES
Provide a path to legal status for some children of illegal immigrants	YES
Extend Bush-era income tax cuts for two years	YES

2009

Expand the Children's Health Insurance Program	YES
Provide $787 billion in tax cuts and spending increases to stimulate the economy	YES
Allow bankruptcy judges to modify certain primary-residence mortgages	YES
Create a cap-and-trade system to limit greenhouse gas emissions	YES
Provide $2 billion for the "cash for clunkers" program	YES
Establish the government as the sole provider of student loans	YES
Restrict federally funded insurance coverage for abortions in health care overhaul	NO

CQ Vote Studies

	PARTY UNITY		PRESIDENTIAL SUPPORT	
	SUPPORT	OPPOSE	SUPPORT	OPPOSE
2010	95%	5%	90%	10%
2009	99%	1%	97%	3%
2008	99%	1%	15%	85%
2007	98%	2%	4%	96%
2006	97%	3%	17%	83%

Interest Groups

	AFL-CIO	ADA	CCUS	ACU
2010	92%	85%	38%	4%
2009	100%	95%	36%	0%
2008	100%	100%	61%	0%
2007	96%	90%	55%	0%
2006	100%	95%	47%	4%

North Carolina 12

Central — parts of Charlotte, Winston-Salem and Greensboro

The Democratic 12th winds north from Charlotte to the Triad area of Greensboro, Winston-Salem and High Point. The district became known as the mother of all racial gerrymanders when it was originally drawn for the 1992 elections. Struck down by the courts and widely ridiculed for a serpentine shape that aimed to maximize the black population, the 12th was redrawn twice in the 1990s. The current 12th is 43 percent black, 12 percent Hispanic and 39 percent white, and has a massive Democratic tilt. In the last three presidential elections, the district has given the Democratic nominee his best showing in the state.

While not as contorted as its 1990s predecessors, the current 12th zigzags from Charlotte along Interstate 85 north and east to take in part of Salisbury, and then scoops up large black populations in Winston-Salem, High Point and Greensboro. The district takes in 36 percent of Charlotte's population but 57 percent of its black residents, and 58 percent of Winston-Salem's population but nearly 80 percent of its black residents. Most of the 12th's black residents are lower- to middle-class.

Charlotte is home to the nation's biggest financial center outside of New York. Volatility in banking and investment had cast doubt over continued economic growth here, but energy and defense contracting sectors are replacing some financial services jobs.

The Biddleville neighborhood, west of the business district, hosts the predominately black Johnson C. Smith University and is a hub of the black community. But the city's downtown, known as "uptown," has its share of poverty and crime.

Highway infrastructure in the Triad area, including the junction of three interstates, couples with the Charlotte airport to create a stable base for trade. The vulnerable furniture manufacturing industry is vital to High Point's local economy.

Major Industry
Finance, transportation, health care

Cities
Charlotte (pt.), 264,085; Winston-Salem (pt.), 133,338; Greensboro (pt.), 70,408; High Point (pt.), 62,753; Salisbury (pt.), 29,476

Notable
A Woolworth's lunch counter in Greensboro was the site of the first major civil rights sit-in in 1960.

Rep. Brad Miller (D)

Capitol Office
225-3032
www.house.gov/bradmiller
1127 Longworth Bldg. 20515-3313; fax 225-0181

Committees
Financial Services
Science, Space & Technology

Residence
Raleigh

Born
May 19, 1953; Fayetteville, N.C.

Religion
Episcopalian

Family
Divorced

Education
U. of North Carolina, B.A. 1975 (political science);
London School of Economics, M.S.C. 1978 (comparative government); Columbia U., J.D. 1979

Career
Lawyer

Political Highlights
Wake County Democratic Party chairman, 1985-87;
sought Democratic nomination for N.C. secretary
of state, 1988; N.C. House, 1993-94; defeated for re-
election to N.C. House, 1994; N.C. Senate, 1997-2002

ELECTION RESULTS

2010 GENERAL

Brad Miller (D)	116,103	55.5%
William Randall (R)	93,099	44.5%

2010 PRIMARY

Brad Miller (D)	unopposed

2008 GENERAL

Brad Miller (D)	221,379	65.9%
Hugh Webster (R)	114,383	34.1%

Previous Winning Percentages
2006 (64%); 2004 (59%); 2002 (55%)

Elected 2002; 5th term

Ever since Miller visited Washington as a child, staying with his family at the home of an uncle stationed at the Pentagon, he was intrigued by the idea of working in the Capitol. Four decades later, Miller's election allowed him to begin building a reputation as a specialist on the U.S. banking and mortgage lending system.

"Since arriving in Congress, my No. 1 priority has been protecting homeowners and their ticket into the middle class," said Miller, the rare Southern Democrat who embraces the liberal label.

Responding to the financial crisis from his seat on the Financial Services Committee, Miller sponsored legislation targeting predatory lending practices in the mortgage industry and setting minimum requirements for home loans. Miller also pushed for the creation of an independent consumer financial protection regulator that will oversee Wall Street. Versions of both provisions were incorporated into a broader financial regulatory overhaul measure that became law in 2010.

In 2009, Miller succeeded in amending legislation that required credit card companies to give customers clearer disclosures and stable terms of agreement. Miller's provision required credit card bills to include more information, such as the total cost for someone making a minimum payment and assessments of how much customers would have to pay in order to pay off the balance in one, two or three years.

Miller also wrote a measure that would expand the definition of small-business lending and allow banks to extend credit for residential construction and land development to U.S. homebuilders. The House passed the bill overwhelmingly, but the Senate did not act on it. The work built on Miller's success in 2008 in enacting a law that eliminated some of the more exotic mortgage loans consumers had received.

His reliably Democratic voting record has won praise from labor unions and progressive organizations. His views reflect the political makeup of North Carolina's northern tier, which is more urban than many Southern districts. Thousands of transplants, particularly from the Northeast, have been attracted to the technology and biotechnology firms in the Research Triangle around Raleigh. The district also takes in sizable African-American neighborhoods, University of North Carolina at Greensboro students and faculty, and blue-collar textile workers, all Democratic-leaning constituencies.

Miller said he is looking out for his constituents as co-chairman of the Community College Caucus, particularly as North Carolinians who have been laid off from factory jobs search for training that can jump start a new career.

Miller also serves on the Science, Space and Technology Committee, where he is the ranking Democrat on the Energy and Environment Subcommittee.

He backed legislation in 2009 to create a cap-and-trade system to limit carbon emissions and opposed provisions added to a catchall spending bill in early 2011 that would bar the EPA from establishing a similar regime via regulation.

Formerly a member of the Foreign Affairs Committee, he has long called for an end to U.S. involvement in Iraq. Inspired by a trip to Kenya, Miller also said that U.S. citizens should help the impoverished of the world, particularly those who live in poor urban areas.

Miller started his foray into politics as an 11-year-old, when he handed out campaign brochures for a family friend running for local office. On election night, he went with his father to watch local officials at the Cumberland County Courthouse write results on a chalkboard as they came in. His father, manager of the post office in Fayetteville, died of a heart attack when Miller was 12. He and his siblings were raised by their mother, a school cafeteria bookkeeper.

Between undergraduate work at the University of North Carolina and Columbia University law school, Miller broadened his experience by getting a master's degree in comparative government at the London School of Economics. He clerked for a year for a federal appellate judge in Chapel Hill, then moved to Raleigh to work as a litigator at private firms. He became chairman of the Wake County Democratic Party and waited for an opportunity to run for office.

In 1988, he lost a Democratic primary for North Carolina secretary of state. He was primed to run for the state House in 1992 after redistricting created a new district that included his neighborhood. He won the seat but lost it in 1994.

He got even two years later by unseating a Republican in the state Senate, where he served three terms. While in the legislature, Miller wrote North Carolina's safe-gun-storage law, one of the first of its kind. He also cosponsored a law ending the state sales tax on food and pushed for higher teacher salaries and smaller class sizes.

When reapportionment after the 2000 census gave North Carolina a new House seat, Miller, as chairman of the state Senate redistricting committee, helped draw the new 13th District for himself, giving it a Democratic voter registration advantage and including much of his political base. In a fierce general-election race, Miller defeated Republican businesswoman Carolyn W. Grant by 12 percentage points.

In 2004, the Republican House Speaker, J. Dennis Hastert of Illinois, and Republican Sen. Elizabeth Dole of North Carolina campaigned for his opponent, lawyer and former Hill aide Virginia Johnson, but Miller won with 59 percent of the vote. Republican Vernon L. Robinson dubbed Miller a "San Francisco liberal" in 2006 — Miller once said "I went to college in the early '70s, so everyone was liberal. But I didn't get over it like some others did; I never grew out of it." Nevertheless, Miller won by a ratio of nearly 2-to-1 and duplicated that margin two years later in trouncing Republican Hugh Webster. The Republican wave held down his total in 2010, but he still defeated William Randall, 55 percent to 45 percent.

Key Votes

2010

Overhaul the nation's health insurance system	YES
Allow for repeal of "don't ask, don't tell"	YES
Overhaul financial services industry regulation	YES
Limit use of new Afghanistan War funds to troop withdrawal activities	NO
Change oversight of offshore drilling and lift oil spill liability cap	YES
Provide a path to legal status for some children of illegal immigrants	YES
Extend Bush-era income tax cuts for two years	NO

2009

Expand the Children's Health Insurance Program	YES
Provide $787 billion in tax cuts and spending increases to stimulate the economy	YES
Allow bankruptcy judges to modify certain primary-residence mortgages	YES
Create a cap-and-trade system to limit greenhouse gas emissions	YES
Provide $2 billion for the "cash for clunkers" program	YES
Establish the government as the sole provider of student loans	YES
Restrict federally funded insurance coverage for abortions in health care overhaul	NO

CQ Vote Studies

	PARTY UNITY		PRESIDENTIAL SUPPORT	
	SUPPORT	OPPOSE	SUPPORT	OPPOSE
2010	99%	1%	90%	10%
2009	99%	1%	97%	3%
2008	99%	1%	15%	85%
2007	97%	3%	6%	94%
2006	90%	10%	38%	62%

Interest Groups

	AFL-CIO	ADA	CCUS	ACU
2010	100%	100%	13%	0%
2009	100%	100%	33%	0%
2008	100%	100%	61%	0%
2007	96%	100%	47%	0%
2006	100%	90%	47%	17%

North Carolina 13

North central — parts of Raleigh and Greensboro

The 13th is defined by its urban anchors of Greensboro and Raleigh, which are connected by several rural counties along the Virginia border. More than half of the district's population lives in Wake County (Raleigh), including a large number of state government employees and recent arrivals to North Carolina.

The district encompasses northern and central Raleigh, an area that falls into the Research Triangle and is built around an economy of technology, biotech and financial services. The 13th takes in about two-thirds of Raleigh's residents (the city is shared with the 2nd and 4th), and its slice of the city includes most of downtown along the state Capitol. In Greensboro, the state's third-most-populous city, tobacco processing long was the city's economic backbone, and Lorillard Tobacco, the nation's third-largest tobacco company, is still important to the region. Tobacco's influence on the economy, however, has decreased.

Raleigh and Greensboro have grown rapidly and feature diverse economies, but there have been widespread layoffs in both cities. The northern,

rural areas of Rockingham, Caswell, Person and Granville counties, on the Virginia border, and Alamance County, south of Caswell and shared with the 6th, still rely heavily on farming and manufacturing, particularly tobacco and a waning textile sector. The 13th dips into Alamance to reach Burlington.

The 13th has an overall Democratic lean, in part because of a sizable black population and a number of white moderates and liberals in the urban areas. Despite high numbers of registered Democrats, the actual Democratic advantage at the polls tends to be narrow. The potential for swing voting exists in both the cities and suburbs, but the 13th moved to the left in the last presidential election, giving Barack Obama 59 percent in 2008. Obama won solidly in the district's portion of Guilford and Wake counties, but he lost in Person and Rockingham counties.

Major Industry

Technology, financial services, state government, agriculture

Cities

Raleigh (pt.), 266,935; Greensboro (pt.), 116,465; Wake Forest (pt.), 29,218

Notable

The University of North Carolina-Greensboro, Guilford College and Greensboro College are all in the district.

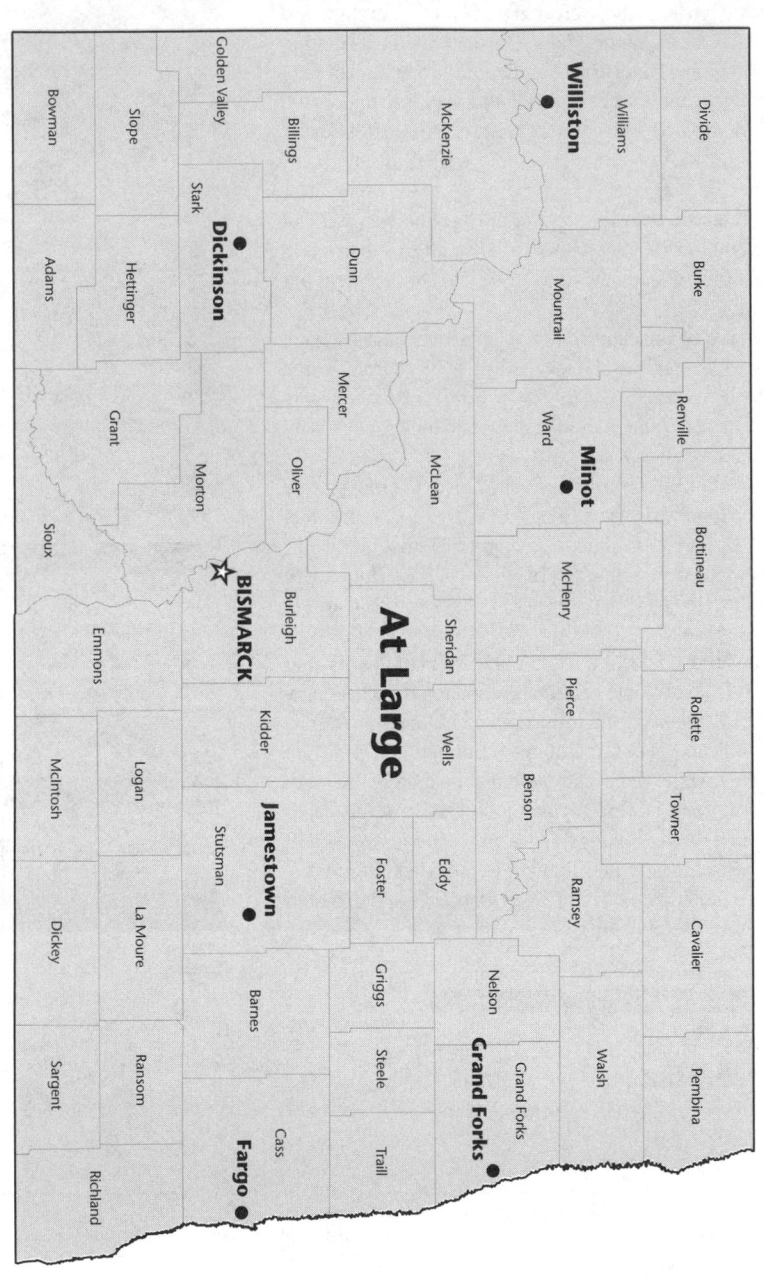

Gov. Jack Dalrymple (R)

Assumed office: Dec. 7, 2010, due to the election of John Hoeven to the U.S. Senate.

Length of term: 4 years

Term expires: 12/12

Salary: $105,036

Phone: (701) 328-2200

Residence: Casselton

Born: Oct. 16, 1948; Minneapolis, Minn.

Religion: Presbyterian

Family: Wife, Betsy Dalrymple; four children

Education: Yale U., B.A. 1970 (American studies)

Career: Farmer

Political highlights: N.D. House, 1985-2000; lieutenant governor, 2000-10

MOST RECENT ELECTION RESULTS

2008 General

John Hoeven (R)	235,009	74.4&
Tim Mathern (D)	74,279	23.5%
DeWayne Hendrickson (I)	6,404	2.0%

Lt. Gov. Drew Wrigley (R)

Appointed: Dec. 7, 2010

Length of term: 4 years

Term expires: 12/12

Salary: $85,614

Phone: (701) 328-2200

LEGISLATURE

Legislative Assembly: January-April in odd-numbered years

Senate: 47 members, 4-year terms

2011 ratios: 35 R, 12 D; 41 men, 6 women

Salary: $4,980; $148/day in session

Phone: (701) 328-2916

House: 94 members, 4-year terms

2011 ratios: 69 R, 25 D; 79 men, 15 women

Salary: $4,980; $148/day in session

Phone: (701) 328-2916

TERM LIMITS

Governor: No

Senate: No

House: No

URBAN STATISTICS

CITY	POPULATION
Fargo	105,549
Bismarck	61,272
Grand Forks	52,838
Minot	40,888
West Fargo	25,830

REGISTERED VOTERS

Voters do not register by party.

POPULATION

2010 population	672,591
2000 population	642,200
1990 population	638,800
Percent change (2000-2010)	+4.7%
Rank among states (2010)	48
Median age	36.6
Born in state	69.8%
Foreign born	2.1%
Violent crime rate	201/100,000
Poverty level	11.7%
Federal workers	11,919
Military	7,209

ELECTIONS

STATE ELECTION OFFICIAL
(701) 328-4146

DEMOCRATIC PARTY
(701) 255-0460

REPUBLICAN PARTY
(701) 255-0030

MISCELLANEOUS

Web: www.nd.gov

Capital: Bismarck

U.S. CONGRESS

Senate: 1 Democrat, 1 Republican

House: 1 Republican

2010 Census Statistics by District

District	2008 Vote for President Obama	McCain	White	Black	Asian	Hispanic	Median Income	White Collar	Blue Collar	Service Industry	Over 64	Under 18	College Education	Rural	Sq. Miles
AL	45%	53%	89%	1%	1%	2%	$45,140	58%	25%	17%	15%	22%	26%	44%	68,976
STATE	45	53	89	1	1	2	45,140	58	25	17	15	22	26	44	68,976
U.S.	53	46	64	12	5	16	51,425	60	23	17	13	25	28	21	3,537,438

Sen. Kent Conrad (D)

Capitol Office
224-2043
conrad.senate.gov
530 Hart Bldg. 20510-3403; fax 224-7776

Committees
Agriculture, Nutrition & Forestry
Budget - Chairman
Finance
   (Taxation & IRS Oversight - Chairman)
Indian Affairs
Select Intelligence
Joint Taxation

Residence
Bismarck

Born
March 12, 1948; Bismarck, N.D.

Religion
Unitarian

Family
Wife, Lucy Calautti; one child

Education
U. of Missouri, attended 1967; Stanford U., A.B. 1971
(government & political science); George
Washington U., M.B.A. 1975

Career
Management and personnel director

Political Highlights
Candidate for N.D. auditor, 1976; N.D. tax
commissioner, 1981-87

ELECTION RESULTS

2006 GENERAL
Kent Conrad (D)	150,146	68.8%
Dwight Grotberg (R)	64,417	29.5%
Roland Riemers (I)	2,194	1.0%

2006 PRIMARY
Kent Conrad (D)	unopposed

Previous Winning Percentages
2000 (62%); 1994 (58%); 1992 Special Election (63%);
1986 (50%)

Elected 1986; 4th full term

A prairie-state policy wonk, Conrad has long bemoaned Washington's failure to tackle soaring levels of government debt. He'll give it one more try, then ride off into retirement at the end of his current term in 2012.

In the letter announcing his plans to retire, Conrad cited the deficit as a motivating factor. "It is more important I spend my time and energy trying to solve these problems than to be distracted by a campaign for re-election," he wrote.

He was a member of the "Gang of Six" senators who pushed to get Congress to act on the budget-balancing proposals issued in December 2010 by the National Commission on Fiscal Responsibility and Reform, on which Conrad served. He also was among those saying President Obama needed to be more deeply involved in hashing out a resolution on fiscal 2011 spending.

"We really need a plan that goes way beyond five years. We're talking about making relatively modest changes now that will pay big dividends as time passes," he said in early 2011. "In that way, time is our friend. But for time to be our friend, we've got to use it. We've got to make decisions."

In many ways, Conrad embodies the tension apparent in Congress when members must decide between fiscal restraint and passing popular tax and spending measures.

As chairman of the Budget Committee, a senior member of the Finance panel and a member of the Joint Taxation Committee, Conrad has been a key player on major tax and spending issues. But while few doubt Conrad's concern about the state of the government's finances, his will to forcefully press the issue with colleagues has been a question throughout his career.

In the 111th Congress (2009-10), however, he began to shed his reputation for ambivalence by working to block policies favored by the Democratic leadership and the White House that would add to the deficit, such as a permanent increase in the amounts that Medicare pays to physicians, and by pressuring the administration and congressional leaders to create a commission charged with drawing up policy prescriptions for the growing debt. In January 2010, Conrad led a group of Senate moderates who refused to support must-pass legislation to raise the debt ceiling without assurances that such a commission would be established. Subsequent negotiations led to Obama creating the panel by executive order, with promises from House and Senate leaders to put its recommendations up for a vote.

Although the Budget Committee has limited legislative power, Conrad at times has used it as a megaphone while seeking leverage on priorities outside its jurisdiction.

During the early part of negotiations on the health care overhaul in July 2009, shortly before the Finance Committee was set to unveil a proposal to which Conrad was a key contributor, he called Congressional Budget Office Director Douglas Elmendorf before the committee and asked him whether he believed the health care legislation already produced by other committees would do enough to control costs: Elmendorf made it clear that he did not think so. Given the weight that CBO opinions carried during the debate, Finance was then in a position to present its proposal as the fiscally responsible alternative because it reflected more of what Elmendorf had cited as policies that could control costs.

Conrad's insistence that the health bill meet a certain fiscal standard rubbed some colleagues the wrong way, however, especially when they felt that he was not applying the same rigor to aspects that could negatively affect his home state. When there was discussion of allowing people under 65 to sign up for

Medicare, Conrad voiced his concern that physicians among his constituency might not receive high enough reimbursements. This drew an exasperated response from West Virginia Democrat John D. Rockefeller IV, who told reporters: "I'm really very tired of hearing about that from him. And it's always about North Dakota and it's never about any other part of the country."

Conrad has proved throughout his career that he can be relentless when dealing with issues important to his state, though he passed up a chance to chair the Agriculture, Nutrition and Forestry Committee in the 112th Congress (2011-12) to keep the gavel at Budget.

But he was a major player on the 2008 reauthorization of agriculture and nutrition programs, as he helped to secure a long-sought goal: a disaster relief fund for farmers and ranchers. His influence was felt as well in 2002, when he played a central role in rewriting a GOP-drafted 1996 farm law that sought to phase out traditional crop subsidies and replace them with fixed payments.

Conrad, who added a Select Intelligence Committee seat to his portfolio in the 112th Congress, also has pressed for millions of dollars in improvements to Air Force bases in Grand Forks and Minot, and is a staunch defender of funding for the 119th Fighter Wing unit of the Air National Guard, based in Hector.

Conrad's clean-cut image took a hit in 2008 in a controversy about whether he and Connecticut Democrat Christopher J. Dodd received favorable mortgages from Countrywide Financial. In Conrad's case, Portfolio magazine reported that Countrywide in 2004 had waived a 1-point fee on the refinancing of a Delaware beach house, saving him $10,700 on the loan. Both Conrad and Dodd denied any knowledge of special treatment and pointed out that the rates they received from Countrywide were market value at the time. Conrad also donated $10,700 to a Habitat for Humanity chapter in Bismarck.

Conrad also sits on the Indian Affairs Committee, where he worked on health issues with former home-state colleague Byron L. Dorgan, who chaired the committee and retired in 2010. On the wall in Conrad's office in Bismarck hangs a prized gift from the state's Standing Rock Sioux: a framed resolution bearing his honorary Sioux name, Namni Sni, or Never Turns Back.

Conrad's early years were marked by the death of his parents in an automobile accident when he was 5. He and his brothers were raised by his grandparents, who moved into the family home in Bismarck. However, he attended high school at a U.S. military base in Libya, where he lived with family friends. The experience clearly has shaped his views on Iraq and the broader Middle East. "Anybody who knows the history of that part of the world knows that whoever has gone in there, whatever their intentions, have quickly been seen as occupiers rather than liberators, and almost without exception it has ended badly," he said.

Upon returning to North Dakota, and while still a teenager, he headed a statewide campaign to lower the voting age from 21 to 19. The effort failed, but his engagement in politics continued. He was elected state tax commissioner in 1980 and gained popularity for his vigorous audits of out-of-state corporations. In 1986, the troubles besetting North Dakota's farms and small towns gave Conrad an opening against Republican Sen. Mark Andrews, whom Conrad defeated by 2,000 votes.

During that first campaign, Conrad pledged that he wouldn't seek reelection unless the trade and budget deficits were significantly reduced during his term. In April 1992, he kept his promise, and announced his retirement. But that September, North Dakota's senior senator, Democrat Quentin N. Burdick, died at age 84. Democrats persuaded Conrad to run in a December special election, and he defeated Republican state Rep. Jack Dalrymple. He has sailed to re-election each time since.

Conrad likes to make use of comprehensive visual aids. In 2001, the Rules and Administration Committee gave him his own printing equipment because he was running off more charts than all of his colleagues combined.

Key Votes

2010

Pass budget reconciliation bill to modify overhauls of health care and federal student loan programs	YES
Proceed to disapproval resolution on EPA authority to regulate greenhouse gases	NO
Overhaul financial services industry regulation	YES
Limit debate to proceed to a bill to broaden campaign finance disclosure and reporting rules	YES
Limit debate on an extension of Bush-era income tax cuts for two years	YES
Limit debate on a bill to provide a path to legal status for some children of illegal immigrants	YES
Allow for a repeal of "don't ask, don't tell"	YES
Consent to ratification of a strategic arms reduction treaty with Russia	YES

2009

Prevent release of remaining financial industry bailout funds	NO
Make it easier for victims to sue for wage discrimination remedies	YES
Expand the Children's Health Insurance Program	YES
Limit debate on the economic stimulus measure	YES
Repeal District of Columbia firearms prohibitions and gun registration laws	YES
Limit debate on expansion of federal hate crimes law	YES
Strike funding for F-22 Raptor fighter jets	YES

CQ Vote Studies

	PARTY UNITY		PRESIDENTIAL SUPPORT	
	SUPPORT	OPPOSE	SUPPORT	OPPOSE
2010	94%	6%	100%	0%
2009	89%	11%	95%	5%
2008	91%	9%	40%	60%
2007	87%	13%	44%	56%
2006	78%	22%	52%	48%
2005	76%	24%	48%	52%
2004	81%	19%	62%	38%
2003	85%	15%	58%	42%
2002	86%	14%	66%	34%
2001	90%	10%	66%	34%

Interest Groups

	AFL-CIO	ADA	CCUS	ACU
2010	94%	85%	36%	4%
2009	100%	95%	50%	13%
2008	100%	90%	57%	0%
2007	89%	80%	45%	12%
2006	93%	85%	45%	33%
2005	85%	85%	69%	21%
2004	100%	90%	53%	20%
2003	77%	80%	70%	15%
2002	100%	95%	45%	10%
2001	94%	85%	50%	36%

Sen. John Hoeven (R)

Capitol Office
224-2551
hoeven.senate.gov
120 Russell Bldg. 20510; fax 224-7999

Committees
Agriculture, Nutrition & Forestry
Appropriations
Energy & Natural Resources
Indian Affairs

Residence
Bismarck

Born
March 13, 1957; Bismarck, N.D.

Religion
Roman Catholic

Family
Wife, Mical Hoeven; two children

Education
Dartmouth College, B.A. 1979 (history & economics);
Northwestern U., M.B.A. 1981

Career
Bank CEO

Political Highlights
Governor, 2000-10

ELECTION RESULTS

2010 GENERAL

John Hoeven (R)	181,689	76.1%
Tracy Potter (D)	52,955	22.2%
Keith J. Hanson (LIBERT)	3,890	1.6%

2010 PRIMARY

John Hoeven (R)	65,075	99.8%

Elected 2010; 1st term

Hoeven was heavily recruited by Republican officials to run for the Senate. Minority Leader Mitch McConnell of Kentucky at one point during the campaign called Hoeven, the longest-serving and most popular governor in the country when he declared his candidacy, "the best recruit we've landed so far."

He received promises from McConnell that he would be given seats on the Appropriations and Energy and Natural Resources committees, and the leader more than kept his word. Hoeven (HO-ven) got not only those, but also others crucial to his home state. The assignments position Hoeven to bring funding and projects to his state, which has experienced a boom as a result of its growing energy industries.

"I want to be able to come down and have an immediate impact, work on issues important to our state and to our country," Hoeven said. "Appropriations touches just about everything that goes through Congress."

His Appropriations subcommittee assignments include Interior-Environment and Agriculture, and he also holds seats on the authorizing Agriculture, Nutrition and Forestry Committee and the Indian Affairs panel — all crucial to his home state.

As an appropriator, Hoeven's first duty is to fund the government. The former CEO and president of the Bank of North Dakota, he prefers to see the private sector take the lead in most cases.

"Government has got to create the kind of legal, tax and regulatory certainty that empowers the private sector, not continuing to grow government spending," he said on Fox Business Network in early 2011.

Hoeven opposed the one-year moratorium on earmarks put in place by Senate Republicans, preferring to keep the practice while making it more transparent.

As ranking Republican on the Legislative Branch spending panel, Hoeven proposed cutting the Senate's own budget by 7 percent, beyond the target set by the chamber. "I think we should look at making sure we do at least as much as the House did," he told Roll Call.

Hoeven joined a bipartisan group of 64 senators evenly split between the parties in urging President Obama to be more involved in reaching a deficit reduction deal using the report issued in December 2010 by the National Commission on Fiscal Responsibility and Reform as a basis for a broad agreement.

Hoeven sought the Energy and Natural Resources Committee slot to focus on shaping policy on energy, which has become the cornerstone of the state's economy. "In the energy world right now, they don't know what the rules of the road are going to be when it comes to carbon emissions," he said. "That holds them on the sidelines, so they don't invest. We have to make sure we can give them a favorable tax policy."

Hoeven opposes creation of a cap-and-trade system for carbon emissions. But he said there may be pieces of the energy bills that were in the works in the 111th Congress (2009-10) that he would support.

Development of energy resources such as oil from the Bakken shale formation has aided North Dakota's economy during Hoeven's tenure. While much of the rest of the country was mired in economic decline and busted state budgets, North Dakota's unemployment rate the month before the 2010 election was 3.7 percent, and the state enjoyed a $1 billion surplus.

"Gov. Hoeven has been a tremendous advocate for energy development in North Dakota, and it's exciting to have someone like him head to Washington," Ron Ness, president of the North Dakota Petroleum Council, told The New York Times. "He can bring the success from North Dakota's diverse energy development to Washington on a national scene."

As part of the state's energy development plan, called Empower North Dakota, Hoeven also backed development of wind power — plentiful on the Dakota plains — and other renewable-energy sources.

"Through Empower ND, we worked to create a business climate that incentivized energy companies across all industry sectors — including the oil industry — to invest in our state," he said on the Senate floor in March 2011. "We created the kind of legal, tax, and regulatory certainty that attracted capital, expertise — and jobs — to North Dakota.

Agriculture remains a major industry in North Dakota, and Hoeven expects to back legislation to support food production as well as biofuels.

As governor, Hoeven — a former Democrat — worked across party lines on health care and education issues. "I do think that's something that a governor brings to the mix," he said. "Governors have to work with people from both sides of the aisle."

Born in Bismarck, Hoeven went east for his education. He earned a bachelor's degree from Dartmouth College in New Hampshire and a master's degree in business administration from Northwestern University in Illinois.

He returned to North Dakota as executive vice president of First Western Bank in Minot and was active in civic affairs, but not electoral politics. In 1993 he moved up to become president and CEO of Bank of North Dakota, which almost doubled in size during his seven years at the helm.

He had never run for political office before seeking the governorship in 2000 — he had switched to the Republican Party only four years earlier.

He defeated Democratic state Attorney General Heidi Heitkamp, pulling away at the end to claim a 10-percentage-point win. He was easily re-elected in 2004 and 2008.

Heading into the 2010 Senate race, Hoeven was popular almost beyond belief. A December 2009 Rasmussen poll showed him with an 87 percent approval rating, a figure out of the ordinary for a newly elected official and all but unheard of for one who had been in office for almost a decade.

That popularity made him the obvious target for Republican recruiters, and in hypothetical matchups in late 2009 he led Democrat Byron L. Dorgan by more than 20 points. Soon after the first of the year, Dorgan announced he would not seek re-election.

Hoeven attended a February tea party rally in Bismarck featuring GOP Rep. Michele Bachmann of Minnesota, a conservative favorite. "We're a big-tent party and we need to include all kinds of people. This is us reaching out and getting people involved," Hoeven told the Bismarck Tribune.

His Democratic opponent, state Sen. Tracy Potter, was overmatched from the start. His charges that Hoeven was moving too far to the right largely fell on deaf ears.

Bismarck Tribune editor John Irby wrote in July: "In reality, Hoeven won the U.S. Senate race when Sen. Byron Dorgan retired." Polls all year reflected that reality, and Hoeven won 76 percent of the vote in November.

He didn't wait to be sworn in before beginning to weigh in on national issues. Hoeven was one of the 10 Republicans elected to the Senate in 2010 who called on Democrats to postpone a vote on a strategic arms reduction treaty with Russia until the 112th Congress (2011-12). But President Obama pushed hard for a vote, and Democratic leaders also wanted to vote before their majority shrank. So the request was denied and the Senate approved ratification of the treaty during the lame-duck session in December 2010.

Rep. Rick Berg (R)

Capitol Office
225-2611
berg.house.gov
323 Cannon Bldg. 20515-3401; fax 226-0893

Committees
Ways & Means

Residence
Fargo

Born
Aug. 16, 1959; Maddock, N.D.

Religion
Lutheran

Family
Wife, Tracy Berg; one child

Education
North Dakota State School of Science, attended
1977-78; North Dakota State U., B.A. 1981 (agricultural economics & communications)

Career
Property development company owner

Political Highlights
N.D. House, 1985-2010 (majority leader, 2003-09)

ELECTION RESULTS

2010 GENERAL

Rick Berg (R)	129,802	54.7%
Earl Pomeroy (D)	106,542	44.9%

2010 PRIMARY

Rick Berg (R)	54,662	89.3%
J.D. Donaghe (R)	6,441	10.5%

Elected 2010; 1st term

Berg ran for the House as a political outsider, despite having been part of North Dakota's political establishment as a member of the state House for more than two decades. Four months into his first term, he announced he would run for the Senate in 2012.

He's a fiscal and social conservative who favors minimizing the tax and regulatory burden on businesses and eliminating the federal estate tax. He is one of two freshman Republicans — the other is Diane Black of Tennessee — to win a seat on the tax-writing Ways and Means Committee.

Berg represents a state in the midst of an energy boom, and he wants to help move the country away from dependence on foreign sources of energy by developing more domestic sources, including the Bakken oil shale that has helped revitalize his state's economy. He also says the government needs to streamline the approval process for building nuclear power plants.

Berg has offered some outside-the-box ideas on entitlements, such as allowing oil and gas exploration in national parks — including North Dakota's Theodore Roosevelt National Park — and using the royalties to help fund Social Security.

Berg brings legislative experience from his time in the North Dakota House, as well as private sector experience as a partner in a property development company. He studied agriculture economics and communications while at North Dakota State University.

Berg was the favored candidate among influential national Republicans to challenge nine-term Democratic incumbent Earl Pomeroy.

Berg tied Pomeroy to some of the unpopular policies of President Obama and Speaker Nancy Pelosi of California, including the health care overhaul law enacted in 2010. In a race that ended up not being as close as many observers predicted, Berg won 55 percent of the vote to Pomeroy's 45 percent.

In May 2011, Berg declared his candidacy for the seat of retiring Democratic Sen. Kent Conrad.

North Dakota
At Large

North Dakota includes fertile eastern Red River farmlands, wheat-covered plains, arid grasslands and Teddy Roosevelt's beloved ranches near the western border.

The state's agriculture-based economy must withstand extreme weather conditions, including severe droughts to the west and flooding along the Red River. Wind energy, biofuel, coal, gas and oil are key in the western part of the state, and technology has emerged as a significant economic contributor in the eastern part of the state, with Fargo hosting a Microsoft campus.

Economic trends have intensified migration of the state's young people away from rural farming communities and into the cities of Fargo and Grand Forks, where a diversified economy, health care facilities and several universities provide greater job choice.

After two decades of sending an entirely Democratic delegation to Congress, the state elected Republican Gov. John Hoeven to the U.S. Senate and Republican Rick Berg to the U.S. House in 2010.

Eastern communities and American Indian reservations are more supportive of Democrats, but Republican roots are strong throughout the state — the state legislature and governorship are both GOP-controlled. John McCain carried the state with 53 percent of the vote in the 2008 presidential election.

Major Industry
Agriculture, energy, technology, health care, higher education

Military Bases
Minot Air Force Base, 5,386 military, 1,071 civilian; Grand Forks Air Force Base, 1,230 military, 338 civilian (2011)

Cities
Fargo, 105,549; Bismarck, 61,272; Grand Forks, 52,838; Minot, 40,888

Notable
The National Buffalo Museum is in Jamestown.

OHIO

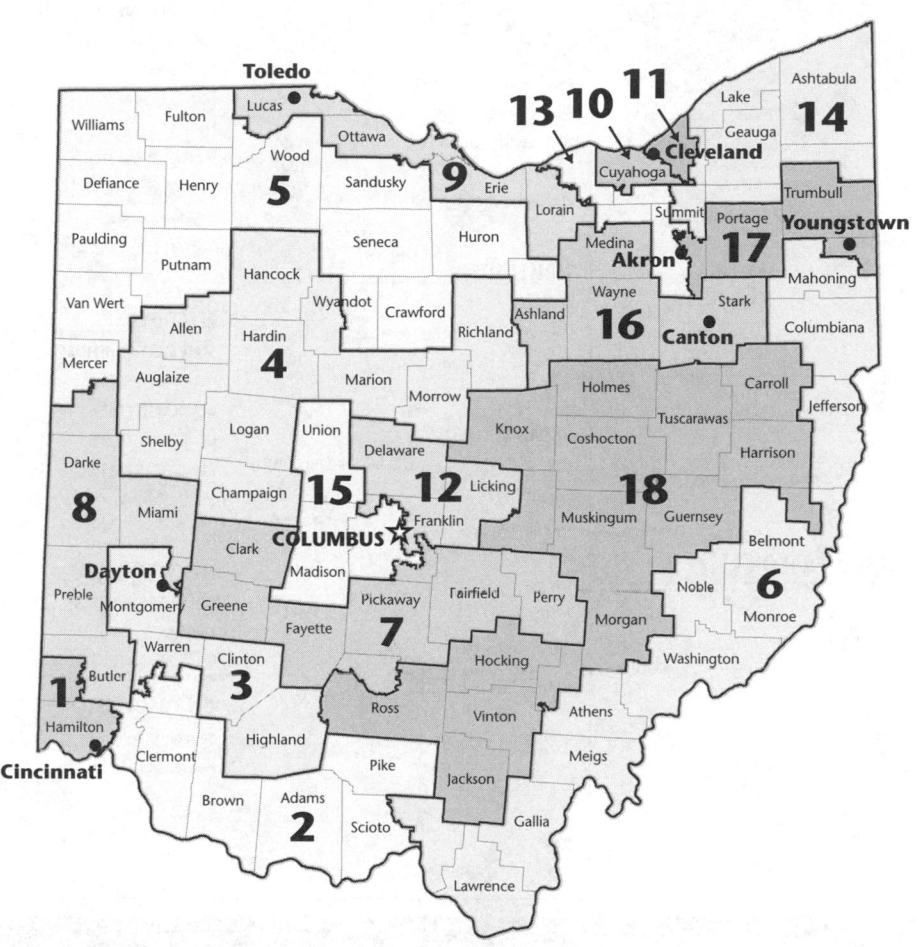

Gov. John R. Kasich (R)

First elected: 2010
Length of term: 4 years
Term expires: 1/15
Salary: $148,866
Phone: (614) 466-3555
Residence: Westerville
Born: May 13, 1952; McKees Rocks, Pa.
Religion: Christian
Family: Wife, Karen Kasich; two children
Education: Ohio State U., B.A. 1974 (political science)
Career: Television show host; investment banker; state legislative aide
Political highlights: Ohio Senate, 1979-83; U.S. House, 1983-2001

ELECTION RESULTS

2010 GENERAL

John R. Kasich (R)	1,889,186	49.0%
Ted Strickland (D)	1,812,059	47.0%
Ken Matesz (LIBERT)	92,116	2.4%
Dennis Spisak (GREEN)	58,475	1.5%

Lt. Gov. Mary Taylor (R)

First elected: 2010
Length of term: 4 years
Term expires: 1/15
Salary: $75,202
Phone: (614) 466-3555

LEGISLATURE

General Assembly: January-June in odd-numbered years; January-July in even-numbered years
Senate: 33 members, 4-year terms
2011 ratios: 23 R, 10 D; 25 men, 8 women
Salary: $60,584
Phone: (614) 466-4900
House: 99 members, 2-year terms
2011 ratios: 59 R, 40 D; 77 men, 22 women
Salary: $60,584
Phone: (614) 466-3357

TERM LIMITS

Governor: 2 terms
Senate: 2 consecutive terms
House: 4 consecutive terms

URBAN STATISTICS

CITY	POPULATION
Columbus	787,033
Cleveland	396,815
Cincinnati	296,943
Toledo	287,208
Akron	199,110

REGISTERED VOTERS

Voters do not register by party.

POPULATION

2010 population	11,536,504
2000 population	11,353,140
1990 population	10,847,115
Percent change (2000-2010)	+1.6%
Rank among states (2010)	7
Median age	37.9
Born in state	75.1%
Foreign born	3.6%
Violent crime rate	332/100,000
Poverty level	15.2%
Federal workers	93,577
Military	8,261

ELECTIONS

STATE ELECTION OFFICIAL
(614) 466-2585
DEMOCRATIC PARTY
(614) 221-6563
REPUBLICAN PARTY
(614) 228-2481

MISCELLANEOUS

Web: www.ohio.gov
Capital: Columbus

U.S. CONGRESS

Senate: 1 Democrat, 1 Republican
House: 13 Republicans, 5 Democrats

2010 CENSUS STATISTICS BY DISTRICT

District	2008 Vote for President Obama	McCain	White	Black	Asian	Hispanic	Median Income	White Collar	Blue Collar	Service Industry	Over 64	Under 18	College Education	Rural	Sq. Miles
1	55%	44%	63%	30%	1%	3%	$43,278	60%	22%	19%	13%	24%	24%	5%	416
2	40	59	90	4	2	2	56,136	65	21	15	13	25	32	27	2,612
3	47	51	78	17	2	2	47,736	60	23	17	14	24	25	15	1,595
4	38	60	90	5	1	2	45,647	50	34	16	14	24	15	41	4,620
5	45	53	92	1	1	5	48,056	49	36	16	14	24	16	51	6,128
6	48	50	94	3	1	1	39,243	52	29	19	16	21	16	50	5,198
7	45	54	84	10	1	2	49,659	58	25	17	13	24	21	29	2,848
8	38	61	87	6	2	3	49,722	55	28	16	13	25	20	22	2,014
9	62	36	76	15	1	5	45,073	55	26	18	14	24	21	14	1,102
10	59	39	80	8	2	7	46,106	60	22	18	15	23	25	1	195
11	85	14	34	59	2	3	34,710	61	18	21	15	24	26	0	135
12	54	44	68	22	4	3	57,106	70	15	15	10	26	37	12	1,016
13	57	42	80	12	2	5	50,853	61	23	16	14	24	26	7	531
14	49	49	91	4	2	2	58,442	63	23	14	15	24	30	26	1,797
15	54	45	80	9	4	5	50,675	66	19	15	10	23	35	9	1,178
16	48	50	91	5	1	2	48,424	56	27	17	15	24	21	26	1,732
17	62	36	82	12	1	3	40,640	53	28	19	15	22	18	16	1,006
18	45	53	95	2	<1	1	40,489	49	33	18	15	24	13	57	6,826
STATE	52	47	81	12	2	3	47,144	58	25	17	14	24	24	23	40,948
U.S.	53	46	64	12	5	16	51,425	60	23	17	13	25	28	21	3,537,438

Sen. Sherrod Brown (D)

Capitol Office
224-2315
brown.senate.gov
713 Hart Bldg. 20510-3503; fax 228-6321

Committees
Agriculture, Nutrition & Forestry
(Jobs, Rural Economic Growth & Energy
Innovation - Chairman)
Appropriations
Banking, Housing & Urban Affairs
(Financial Institutions & Consumer Protection -
Chairman)
Veterans' Affairs
Select Ethics

Residence
Avon

Born
Nov. 9, 1952; Mansfield, Ohio

Religion
Lutheran

Family
Wife, Connie Schultz; two children, two stepchildren

Education
Yale U., B.A. 1974 (Russian & East European studies);
Ohio State U., M.A. 1979 (education), M.A. 1981
(public administration)

Career
College instructor

Political Highlights
Ohio House, 1975-83; Ohio secretary of state, 1983-91; defeated for re-election as Ohio secretary of state, 1990; U.S. House, 1993-2007

ELECTION RESULTS

2006 GENERAL
Sherrod Brown (D)   2,257,369   56.2%
Mike DeWine (R)   1,761,037   43.8%

2006 PRIMARY
Sherrod Brown (D)   583,776   78.1%
Merrill Samuel Keiser (D) 163,628   21.9%

Previous Winning Percentages
2004 House Election (67%); 2002 House Election) (69%); 2000 House Election (65%); 1998 House Election (62%); 1996 House Election (60%); 1994 House Election (49%); 1992 House Election (53%)

Elected 2006; 1st term

The death of Edward M. Kennedy in 2009 left a void for liberal Democrats, and Brown is among those senators whom the left wing of the party expects to assume the Massachusetts senator's mantle on health care, labor issues and civil rights.

He joined the Appropriations Committee in the 112th Congress (2011-12), gaining a platform from which to be a strong defender of liberal spending priorities against the Republican majority in the House.

He was one of several Democrats to form a Social Security caucus in early 2011, and said proposals to cut the program should be taken off the table.

"Very few Democrats want to raise the retirement age. Very few Democrats want to cut a program that is the strongest pension program in America," he told Roll Call. "I just don't think there is any real split in the party."

Brown boasts a working-class persona that includes his occasionally unruly mop of hair, love of baseball and predilection for mentioning his state's localities in floor speeches. But Brown also holds two master's degrees and wrote a 2004 book on one of the topics about which he cares fervently: "Myths of Free Trade: Why American Trade Policy Has Failed."

Brown made his mark during his 14-year tenure in the House with vigorous opposition to the North American and Central America free-trade agreements, which he said have harmed the manufacturing industry in his state and across the nation and exacerbated the trade deficit. He said he would revamp trade pacts with incentives for corporations to create jobs in this country rather than outsource them.

"There's nothing I feel stronger about than how this country has sold out the middle class on trade issues," Brown said.

In 10 of his 14 years in the House and during his entire Senate tenure, Brown has received a 100 percent annual score from the AFL-CIO. Brown calls the inability of workers to receive a bigger share of the wealth they help to create "the most fundamental problem in our economy." He often says he wants to make Ohio the Silicon Valley of jobs in the alternative-energy sector to offset the heavy manufacturing losses.

His support for fighting global warming is often tempered by his concern for Ohio's industries. Brown was one of four Democrats to vote in June 2008 against proceeding to a vote on legislation to cap greenhouse gas emissions because, he said, it could hurt his state's economy.

Brown expressed concerns about the House's passage of clean-energy legislation in June 2009 and has not yet committed to voting for a Senate version. He is a member of the "Gang of 10," a group of senators who in April 2010 wrote to the Senate's chief authors of energy legislation outlining "provisions to address manufacturing competitiveness that must be included in any clean-energy legislation."

A member of the Banking, Housing and Urban Affairs Committee, Brown took a prominent role in trying to pass legislation in late 2008 to assist the Big Three U.S. automakers, which employ more than 30,000 workers in Ohio. The measure couldn't get through the Senate, but the outgoing George W. Bush administration subsequently agreed to provide some relief. When President Obama in March 2009 urged the United Auto Workers to make concessions, Brown called on General Motors' bondholders to "come to the table so debt can be restructured to manageable levels."

Brown chairs Banking's Financial Institutions and Consumer Protection Subcommittee, and he backed a successful $700 billion bill in fall 2008 to assist the ailing financial services industry. He said a failure to help the industry would greatly harm average Americans. But he said his support shouldn't be construed as being more supportive of giant banking and investment institutions. "I'm always skeptical of the upper-class accent that they use on Wall Street," he said.

The son of a doctor, Brown was a key player in enactment of the health care overhaul in 2010, and served as one of the chief spokesmen for the "public option," a government-run insurance plan that was ultimately jettisoned from the final package.

On the Agriculture, Nutrition and Forestry Committee, Brown has sought the input of his state's farmers in working on the reauthorization of farm programs in the 110th Congress (2007-08). One farmer's suggestion led Brown to propose a change — which made it into law — to replace subsidies based on declining crop prices with an alternative intended to protect against drops in either yield or prices. The law is due to be reauthorized in 2012.

He serves on the Veterans' Affairs Committee, and in 2010 introduced legislation that would expand collective bargaining rights for employees at the Department of Veterans Affairs.

He also has the responsibility of helping to police the conduct of his colleagues from his seat on the Select Ethics Committee.

Brown's liberalism extends to social issues and infuses both his public and private lives. Long divorced, he had become an enthusiastic reader of a local newspaper writer's columns about Cleveland's poor. Brown sent an admiring note to the writer, future Pulitzer Prize winner Connie Schultz. That led to a meeting and then to romance; less than a year after their first date in 2003, they were married.

To avoid a conflict of interest, Schultz gave up her column once Brown's Senate campaign got under way. She did, however, pen a 2007 book, ". . . and His Lovely Wife: A Memoir from the Woman Beside the Man," about her experience working for Brown's Senate campaign.

Raised in Mansfield, in the north-central part of the state, Brown's first taste of elected office came as student council president in high school. His interest in politics was sparked by the Vietnam War, the civil rights movement and the 1968 presidential candidacy of Robert F. Kennedy.

Brown was 21 when he was elected to the Ohio House in 1974 — the same year he earned a degree in Russian studies from Yale University. He served in the state legislature for eight years, followed by an eight-year stint as Ohio secretary of state. He was defeated for re-election in 1990 by Republican Bob Taft, who would later serve two terms as governor.

In 1992, Brown won in the open 13th District, which lies west of Cleveland, overcoming criticism that he moved into the district to run for Congress. He won a coveted seat on the Energy and Commerce Committee and focused on trade issues, particularly his strong opposition to the North American Free Trade Agreement, which President Bill Clinton supported. An avid, statistics-spouting baseball fan, Brown used his hobby to help win his committee assignment. He gave a favored baseball card — that of 1950s Boston Red Sox outfielder Jimmy Piersall, who suffered from mental illness — to influential California Democrat Vic Fazio, with the note: "Don't be crazy. Vote for Sherrod Brown for Energy and Commerce."

Brown narrowly won re-election in the Republican wave of 1994. But he won subsequent elections with ease and in the process amassed a huge campaign treasury in preparation for a bid for governor or senator.

Brown originally said he wouldn't challenge Republican Sen. Mike DeWine, but reversed himself in October 2005. DeWine hammered Brown's positions on tax policy and national security issues, but Brown won by 12 percentage points, racking up large percentages in the counties around Cleveland and Mahoning Valley — traditionally the most unionized part of Ohio.

Key Votes

2010

Pass budget reconciliation bill to modify overhauls of health care and federal student loan programs	YES
Proceed to disapproval resolution on EPA authority to regulate greenhouse gases	NO
Overhaul financial services industry regulation	YES
Limit debate to proceed to a bill to broaden campaign finance disclosure and reporting rules	YES
Limit debate on an extension of Bush-era income tax cuts for two years	NO
Limit debate on a bill to provide a path to legal status for some children of illegal immigrants	YES
Allow for a repeal of "don't ask, don't tell"	YES
Consent to ratification of a strategic arms reduction treaty with Russia	YES

2009

Prevent release of remaining financial industry bailout funds	X
Make it easier for victims to sue for wage discrimination remedies	YES
Expand the Children's Health Insurance Program	YES
Limit debate on the economic stimulus measure	YES
Repeal District of Columbia firearms prohibitions and gun registration laws	NO
Limit debate on expansion of federal hate crimes law	YES
Strike funding for F-22 Raptor fighter jets	YES

CQ Vote Studies

	PARTY UNITY		PRESIDENTIAL SUPPORT	
	SUPPORT	OPPOSE	SUPPORT	OPPOSE
2010	99%	1%	98%	2%
2009	99%	1%	96%	4%
2008	97%	3%	30%	70%
2007	97%	3%	35%	65%
2006	92%	8%	36%	64%
2005	97%	3%	7%	93%
2004	98%	2%	26%	74%
2003	99%	1%	11%	89%
2002	98%	2%	22%	78%
2001	98%	2%	12%	88%

Interest Groups

	AFL-CIO	ADA	CCUS	ACU
2010	100%	95%	9%	0%
2009	100%	100%	43%	0%
2008	100%	95%	63%	8%
2007	100%	95%	36%	0%
2006	93%	75%	40%	25%
2005	93%	100%	33%	4%
2004	100%	95%	24%	4%
2003	100%	100%	25%	16%
2002	100%	95%	25%	4%
2001	100%	95%	22%	4%

Sen. Rob Portman (R)

Capitol Office
224-3353
portman.senate.gov
338 Russell Bldg. 20510-3504

Committees
Armed Services
Budget
Energy & Natural Resources
Homeland Security & Governmental Affairs

Residence
Terrace Park

Born
Dec. 19, 1955; Cincinnati, Ohio

Religion
Methodist

Family
Wife, Jane Portman; three children

Education
Dartmouth College, B.A. 1978 (anthropology); U. of
Michigan, J.D. 1984

Career
Lawyer

Political Highlights
White House associate counsel, 1989; White House
Legislative Affairs director, 1989-91; U.S. House, 1993-
2005; U.S. trade representative, 2005-06; Office of
Management and Budget director, 2006-07

ELECTION RESULTS

2010 GENERAL

Rob Portman (R)	2,168,736	56.8%
Lee Fisher (D)	1,503,286	39.4%
Eric Deaton (CNSTP)	65,856	1.7%
Michael L. Pryce (I)	50,100	1.3%

2010 PRIMARY

Rob Portman (R)	unopposed

Previous Winning Percentages
2004 House Election (72%); 2002 House Election
(74%); 2000 House Election (74%); 1998 House Election (76%); 1996 House Election (72%); 1994 House
Election (77%); 1993 Special House Election (70%)

Elected 2010; 1st term

As a former House member, U.S. trade representative and director of the White House Office of Management and Budget, Portman brings plenty of experience and policy expertise to the Senate, as well as a decidedly more centrist approach to policy-making than some of his fellow GOP freshmen.

Portman is one of the few Republicans elected in 2010 who doesn't run from the appellation of "Washington insider." When he arrived in Congress in 1993, he had already been exposed to the institutional politics of Washington from vantage points both inside the White House and on K Street.

In endorsing him in the 2010 general election, the Cleveland Plain Dealer said he would "serve the state well" if he follows in the footsteps of his predecessor, Republican George V. Voinovich, and "resists . . . the siren call of blind party loyalty." The paper added: "The way he has run his campaign — in an old-school 'senatorial' fashion — offers hope that he would do just that."

Portman has vowed to "focus like a laser on jobs and Ohio's economy." As a budget director for President George W. Bush, he was a natural choice for the Budget Committee. He was highly critical of President Obama's fiscal 2012 budget, saying in a Republican response to the president's weekly radio address that Obama "rejected the dire warnings and recommendations of his own fiscal commission and not only kicked the can down the road but made the road more perilous by advocating deeper debt and ignoring bipartisan calls for entitlement reform and pro-growth policies, including tax reform and regulatory restraint."

He has a six-point job-creation plan that includes some state priorities, such as a national policy on manufacturing and enforcement of trade laws, and some themes common to nearly all GOP candidates, including a vow to repeal the health care overhaul enacted in 2010.

He also advocates reducing taxes and regulations on small businesses. With his brother and sister, he owns a small business himself — the historic Golden Lamb Inn in Lebanon, the oldest continuously operating hotel in Ohio.

Unlike several tea party-backed colleagues in the Senate, Portman has not disavowed earmarks, opting to sign onto a one-year moratorium rather than a complete ban and defending earmarks that can "withstand public scrutiny."

Besides taking a middle-of-the-road approach on earmarks, Portman also espouses some ideas that could garner Democratic support, though perhaps raise eyebrows among more conservative members of his own party.

"I've always been able to work across the aisle. I consider it sticking to principle — not compromises but finding common ground on a principled basis," he told Roll Call in early 2011.

Portman wants to see changes to the unemployment benefits system that would allow states with higher unemployment rates, such as Ohio, to access additional funding without congressional action.

Portman also supports increasing and expanding the federal Pell grants program to workers pursuing certifications and short-term training programs, and allowing people to use job-training funds for community or technical college tuition.

Before moving to the executive branch to serve as U.S. trade representative in 2005, Portman was the House Republican leadership's designated conduit to Bush.

But Portman was more than a messenger shuttling directives between the White House and the Capitol. He was handpicked for the job by Speaker J. Dennis Hastert of Illinois, who also gave Portman the additional responsibility of serving as the chairman of GOP leadership meetings.

The dual role allowed Portman to take advantage of his first career as a dealmaking lawyer for Patton, Boggs and Blow, the politically powerful Washington law firm, and to use some of the techniques he developed as the head of the White House Office of Legislative Affairs under President George Bush in the early 1990s.

His friendly style, command of substance, and reputation as a fair dealer have brought him praise from both sides of the political aisle. And his political parrying ability is so proficient that, during the 2000 presidential campaign, Portman was called on to play the part of the Democratic vice presidential nominee, Sen. Joseph I. Lieberman of Connecticut, in Dick Cheney's debate preparations. Lieberman chairs the Homeland Security and Governmental Affairs Committee, where Portman is the ranking Republican on the Contracting Oversight panel.

Portman also serves on Armed Services, as top GOP member on the Emerging Threats and Capabilities Subcommittee, and on Energy and Natural Resources.

A classic example of Portman's steady, persistent approach to building bipartisan consensus was his successful push to include tax incentives for retirement savings in the $1.35 trillion tax cut package enacted in 2001 — the only major component that was not proposed by Bush. Portman attributed the victory to "five years of blood, sweat and tears" with his Democratic ally, Benjamin L. Cardin of Maryland, now a Senate colleague.

Portman's clients at Patton, Boggs included Cincinnati-based banana producer Chiquita Brands International Inc. As a stalwart free-trader in Congress, he helped persuade fellow Republicans to support the law enacted in 2002 reviving fast-track procedures for congressional action on trade deals. In 2000 he was a main advocate of making permanent the normalized U.S.-China trade relationship.

The son of a lift truck dealer, Portman's family has deep roots in Ohio. His mother's parents bought and refurbished the Golden Lamb, a landmark that once hosted Mark Twain and Daniel Webster.

After volunteering on the 1988 Bush campaign and rising through the ranks in the White House lobbying shop, Portman returned to Cincinnati to work as a business lawyer.

He came to Congress in 1993 to replace Republican Bill Gradison, who resigned to become president of the Health Insurance Association of America. Portman, who had been an intern in Gradison's office in 1976, won a tight three-way primary against former Rep. Bob McEwen and homebuilder Jay Buchert. He then won the special election in the solidly conservative suburban district with 70 percent of the vote, and never fell below that number in winning subsequent races.

Bush nominated him for the trade post in March 2005, and he resigned from the House upon his confirmation in April. A year later, Bush tapped him to lead the Office of Management and Budget.

After Voinovich announced plans to retire, Portman quickly entered the race and ran unopposed for the Republican nomination.

On the Democratic side, Lt. Gov. Lee Fisher won a testy primary over Ohio Secretary of State Jennifer Brunner and started out the general-election campaign in good position in most polls. Fisher tried without much success to blame Portman for the failures of the Republican Congress and the Bush administration to control spending.

Portman pointed to Fisher's role as the state's "job czar" during a time when Ohio lost hundreds of thousands of jobs. Portman began pulling ahead by the end of June and led by double digits in most polls heading into October. He won by 18 percentage points.

CQ Vote Studies (while House member)				
	PARTY UNITY		PRESIDENTIAL SUPPORT	
	Support	Oppose	Support	Oppose
2005	99%	1%	100%	0%
2004	95%	5%	94%	6%
2003	95%	5%	98%	2%
2002	95%	5%	92%	8%
2001	98%	2%	93%	7%

Interest Groups (while House member)				
	AFL-CIO	ADA	CCUS	ACU
2005	0%	0%	100%	
2004	20%	10%	100%	88%
2003	13%	5%	97%	84%
2002	11%	0%	95%	92%
2001	8%	0%	100%	88%

Rep. Steve Chabot (R)

Capitol Office
225-2216
chabot.house.gov
2351 Rayburn Bldg. 20515-3501; fax 225-3012

Committees
Foreign Affairs
  (Middle East & South Asia - Chairman)
Judiciary
Small Business

Residence
Cincinnati

Born
Jan. 22, 1953; Cincinnati, Ohio

Religion
Roman Catholic

Family
Wife, Donna Chabot; two children

Education
College of William & Mary, A.B. 1975 (history); North
ern Kentucky U., J.D. 1978

Career
Lawyer; teacher

Political Highlights
Independent candidate for Cincinnati City Council,
1979; Republican candidate for Cincinnati City
Council, 1983; Cincinnati City Council, 1985-90;
Republican nominee for U.S. House, 1988; Hamilton
County Board of Commissioners, 1990-95; U.S.
House, 1995-2009; defeated for re-election to U.S.
House, 2008

ELECTION RESULTS

2010 GENERAL

Steve Chabot (R)	103,770	51.5%
Steve Driehaus (D)	92,672	46.0%
Jim Berns (LIBERT)	3,076	1.5%

2010 PRIMARY

Steve Chabot (R)	unopposed

Previous Winning Percentages
2006 (52%); 2004 (60%); 2002 (65%); 2000 (53%);
1998 (53%); 1996 (54%); 1994 (56%)

Elected 1994; 8th term

Did not serve 2009-11

Chabot is a diehard social and fiscal conservative who can count himself part of two historic freshman classes in the House: 1994 (the "Republican Revolution") and the even larger Class of 2010, which reclaimed the majority lost four years earlier.

Still a strong believer in the "Contract with America," which helped carry Republicans into their first majority in 40 years in 1994, he says his priorities are to "get control of the spending" and "restrain the growth of government."

Chabot (SHAB-it) says his seniority "will put me in a position to be able to immediately play a very active role in reversing the direction of this Congress from one of absolutely lack of restraint in spending to fiscal discipline and balanced budgets."

During his previous 14 years in the House, Chabot served on the Judiciary, Foreign Affairs and Small Business committees. Those stops included a stint as chairman of the Judiciary Subcommittee on the Constitution from 2001 to 2006 and as Small Business' ranking Republican in 2007 and 2008. He returned to all three panels in the 112th Congress (2011-12).

He had hoped to claim the Small Business gavel, but it went to Sam Graves of Missouri. Instead, Chabot is chairman of the Foreign Affairs Subcommittee on the Middle East and South Asia.

He called the Obama administration's early response to the unrest in Libya "tepid," and supported U.S. intervention when it came, but not without some reservations. "It's too unclear what the goals are and how we get out," Chabot told the Cincinnati Enquirer. "I also think that they should have gotten Congress' support before they acted."

In his first House tour, he was a founding member and co-chairman of the Congressional Taiwan Caucus and pushed for strengthening links with Taiwan and supporting democracy in the Asia-Pacific region.

Also during his previous 14-year tenure, he wouldn't let his party forget that the GOP came to power in 1994 by promising a balanced budget but then presided over several years of large deficits. He often voted against Republican-written spending bills when his party was in control.

He quickly proved just as insistent upon his return, voting for every additional spending cut offered on the floor when the House passed a catch-all spending bill that would trim fiscal 2011 spending by $58 billion. And when the House passed a compromise spending bill in April 2011, he voted against it, arguing that, among other things, the legislation did not cut deeply enough.

He has pushed to make permanent the 2001 and 2003 tax cuts, which were extended for two years in late 2010.

A fierce critic of President Obama's 2009 economic stimulus package and the 2010 health care overhaul law, Chabot backs allowing small businesses to band together to buy health insurance coverage for their workers. He introduced legislation in the 110th Congress (2007-08) that would have amended the Internal Revenue Code to allow a 100 percent deduction for health insurance costs of individuals.

When he previously served on the Judiciary Committee, Chabot had a forum for expressing his view that the nation is being brought low by "rogue" federal judges. As chairman of the Subcommittee on the Constitution from 2001 to 2006, he advocated numerous, ultimately unsuccessful, proposals to amend the Constitution to ban flag desecration, outlaw same-sex marriage, protect crime victims' rights and allow people to pray and display religious symbols on public property.

He was the principal House sponsor of a 2003 law outlawing the procedure known as "partial birth" abortion.

Though he isn't shy about voicing his conservative beliefs, Chabot often does so with a soft tone, rarely raising his voice or pounding the podium. But his rhetoric has a bite. In 1999, as one of the 13 impeachment managers who presented the House's case for removing President Bill Clinton from office, Chabot said of Clinton, "He raised his right hand and swore to tell the truth, the whole truth and nothing but the truth. Then he lied."

Chabot was born and raised in Cincinnati. His father was an optician, and Chabot lived in a trailer, working part-time jobs to help with tuition at his parochial high school.

In college, he majored in history, and then taught elementary school in Cincinnati while attending law school at night across the river at Northern Kentucky University. A few years after earning his law degree, he opened a neighborhood law practice.

Chabot's political career began on the Cincinnati City Council. After two failed bids, the first at age 26, Chabot finally won a seat in 1985. He lost a congressional bid against Democrat Thomas A. Luken in 1988, then won election in 1990 to Hamilton County's board of commissioners.

Chabot launched his second congressional campaign in 1994 against first-term Democrat David Mann. Emphasizing his blue-collar beginnings and Catholic roots, Chabot campaigned on a platform of lower taxes, less government and change in Washington. With national trends favoring the GOP, he won with 56 percent of the vote.

Redistricting after the 2000 census made the 1st District more Republican. But in 2006, Chabot drew a strong Democratic challenger, John Cranley, a Cincinnati city councilor. In response to Cranley's attacks that Washington had changed him, Chabot ran an ad saying he had lived in the same house for 21 years, been married to the same woman for 33 years, still cut his own grass and drove "the same old '93 Buick." He managed to hang on to the seat.

In 2008, Steve Driehaus, a member of a well-known Cincinnati political family, touted his experience as a grass-roots organizer and state legislator. Helped by Obama's coattails, Driehaus toppled Chabot by 5 percentage points.

Chabot got right back to work, announcing his candidacy in February 2009. With the political winds blowing from the other direction in 2010, Chabot upended the one-term Democrat, winning almost 52 percent of the vote to Driehaus' 46 percent.

CQ Vote Studies

	PARTY UNITY		PRESIDENTIAL SUPPORT	
	Support	Oppose	Support	Oppose
2008	94%	6%	64%	36%
2007	94%	6%	80%	20%
2006	89%	11%	95%	5%
2005	95%	5%	89%	11%
2004	95%	5%	79%	21%

Interest Groups

	AFL-CIO	ADA	CCUS	ACU
2008	13%	15%	83%	100%
2007	13%	10%	70%	100%
2006	21%	10%	93%	96%
2005	13%	0%	89%	96%
2004	20%	10%	95%	96%

Ohio 1

Western Cincinnati and suburbs

Nestled in Ohio's southwestern corner, the 1st takes in more than three-fourths of Cincinnati's residents. Traditional German Catholic conservatives in the city and a growing suburban base are crucial to Republicans, while the 1st's black-majority portion of Cincinnati is key to Democrats. A decade of population loss in Cincinnati has left the 1st, which has shed more than 14 percent of its populace since 2000, one of the least-populous districts in the nation ahead of decennial remapping. Hamilton County overall also lost population, although many suburban areas in the county have become more diverse as both black and white residents leave the city.

Research firms, corporate headquarters and a manufacturing base have fortified Cincinnati's economy. Corporate headquarters in the city, including Procter & Gamble, Macy's Inc. and Kroger, prop up the retail industry and have lured consumer market research and development firms. Despite a mostly white-collar workforce, manufacturing still provides blue-collar jobs, and General Electric's aircraft engine branch is headquartered in the city.

Access to the Ohio River to the south helped earn the city a reputation as a commercial hub. The new Horseshoe Casino Cincinnati downtown is expected to open in 2013, and construction and gaming operations will bring thousands of jobs to the area.

Cincinnati also is a cultural and entertainment hub. Among other locations, the 1st hosts the Museum Center at Union Terminal, Carew Tower (the city's tallest building) and Paul Brown Stadium — or "The Jungle," as the home field of football's Bengals is known locally.

Cincinnati's heavily black neighborhoods, including Over-the-Rhine, Avon-dale and Bond Hill, vote dependably Democratic. Outside of Cincinnati, Hamilton County is becoming slightly more Democratic as the county's GOP base moves farther north into growing Butler County. In 2008, Barack Obama carried the district with 55 percent of the presidential vote.

Major Industry
Consumer products, service

Cities
Cincinnati (pt.), 228,180; Norwood, 19,207

Notable
The National Underground Railroad Freedom Center is in Cincinnati.

Rep. Jean Schmidt (R)

Capitol Office
225-3164
www.house.gov/schmidt
2464 Rayburn Bldg. 20515-3502; fax 225-1992

Committees
Agriculture
   (Nutrition & Horticulture - Chairwoman)
Foreign Affairs
Transportation & Infrastructure

Residence
Miami Township

Born
Nov. 29, 1951; Cincinnati, Ohio

Religion
Roman Catholic

Family
Husband, Peter Schmidt; one child

Education
U. of Cincinnati, B.A. 1974 (political science)

Career
Teacher; homemaker

Political Highlights
Miami Township trustee, 1990-2000; Clermont County Republican Party chairwoman, 1996-98; Ohio House, 2001-04; sought Republican nomination for Ohio Senate, 2004

ELECTION RESULTS

2010 GENERAL

Jean Schmidt (R)	139,027	58.4%
Surya Yalamanchili (D)	82,431	34.7%
Marc Johnston (LIBERT)	16,259	6.8%

2010 PRIMARY

Jean Schmidt (R)	36,214	61.7%
Mike Kilburn (R)	13,007	22.2%
Debbi Alsfelder (R)	5,235	8.9%
Tim Martz (R)	4,225	7.2%

2008 GENERAL

Jean Schmidt (R)	148,671	44.8%
Victoria Wulsin (D)	124,213	37.5%
David Krikorian (I)	58,710	17.7%

Previous Winning Percentages
2006 (50%); 2005 Special Election (52%)

Elected 2005; 3rd full term

Schmidt rarely speaks on the House floor and calls herself a "quiet legislator." Her voting record is consistently conservative, reflecting the economic and social mores of her suburban and rural southern Ohio constituency.

A longtime anti-abortion activist who attends Mass each morning before going to work, Schmidt is a former president of the Cincinnati-area Right to Life organization. During debate on the Democrats' health care overhaul in March 2010, she noted that "perhaps worst of all, it allows federal funding for abortions for the first time in 34 years."

"I'd like to repeal it tomorrow . . . and start over," she told Cincinnati TV station WLWT in October. Three months later she cast that vote, backing House-passed repeal legislation.

Schmidt likes to point out that her interest in protecting life goes "beyond the child in the womb." She introduced legislation in 2009 to authorize post-placement counseling services to women who put their babies up for adoption. In 2010, she followed that up with a measure to provide a tax credit for women who choose adoption.

Unlike most conservatives, but consistent with Catholic teaching, she opposes the death penalty.

Generally, though, Schmidt matches her views on social issues with right-of-center economic policy positions. She supports making the 2001 and 2003 tax cuts permanent for all income groups and would prefer to replace the existing tax code with a flat tax. She initially voted against the $700 billion financial sector rescue plan in the fall of 2008, but she voted for the modified version when it came up for a vote less than a week later. "I could see that the financial markets were collapsing before us and felt that we needed to do something in order to stall this credit freeze," Schmidt said.

A member of the Transportation and Infrastructure Committee, she condemned President Obama's $787 billion economic stimulus package as "an excuse to spend taxpayer dollars on programs or projects that could not or have not been enacted in the normal course of business."

She joined the Foreign Affairs Committee in the 112th Congress (2011-12), where she sits on the Western Hemisphere Subcommittee and is an advocate of free trade agreements with Colombia and other Central and South American countries.

Now chairwoman of the Agriculture Subcommittee on Nutrition and Horticulture, she sponsored an amendment to the farm bill in 2008 that authorized states to provide nutrition education programs. She will play a role in rewriting the law in the 112th Congress.

Schmidt's congressional career got off to a rocky start in November 2005 when, less than three months after she had narrowly won a special election, she made a pointed reference to Pennsylvania Democrat — and decorated Marine veteran — John P. Murtha during a speech on the Iraq War: "cowards cut and run, Marines never do." When her comments sparked boos from other lawmakers in the chamber, Schmidt withdrew her words immediately. She later told reporters that she did not know Murtha was a veteran. She wrote him a note of apology, which he accepted.

Schmidt grew up in Clermont County, where her father, Gus Hoffman, owns Hoffman Auto Racing, a sprint car racing team started in 1929. She said the "best day of my life" was May 8, 1974, when her father's car qualified for the Indianapolis 500. By the late 1970s, she and her twin sister were working races for her dad's team. She still occasionally waves the green flag to start car races in her district. Raised on the family farm with two older brothers, Schmidt learned how to shoot a gun, and she regularly carries a Bersa semi-automatic handgun that her stockbroker husband gave her as a present.

She traces her interest in politics to the 1960 Kennedy-Nixon debates. "I liked the sound of Nixon, I liked the sound of Republican. I decided when I grew up, I wanted to be a Republican," said Schmidt, whose grandfather was vice chairman of the Hamilton County Democratic Party.

After graduating from the University of Cincinnati in 1974 with a degree in political science, Schmidt worked as a bank manager and fitness instructor and got involved in local party politics. In 1978, she took up running after giving birth to her daughter and suffering postpartum depression. Schmidt has since participated in dozens of marathons. In 2008 she was hit by a car while jogging. After initially shaking it off, she later had to scrap a trip to Afghanistan when the pain worsened and she realized she had broken ribs and vertebrae.

After a decade as township trustee, Schmidt went on to serve four years in the Ohio House. Following a loss in a campaign for the state Senate, she became president of the anti-abortion group. When Republican Rob Portman left Congress in early 2005 to become U.S. trade representative, Schmidt entered a crowded field of better-known Republicans, including former Rep. Bob McEwen and Pat DeWine, a county commissioner and son of then-Sen. Mike DeWine. She won, and then focused on social issues to beat Democrat and Iraq War veteran Paul Hackett by 3 percentage points.

In 2006, Schmidt staved off a primary challenge by McEwen before eking out a 2,517-vote victory over Democratic challenger Victoria Wulsin, a physician who ran a nonprofit AIDS prevention organization. The race was so close that Wulsin didn't concede until late November.

Schmidt faced a rematch with Wulsin in 2008, along with independent David Krikorian. Political analyst and Roll Call columnist Stuart Rothenberg said that, because of the weakness of the candidates, the contest may be the worst congressional race he has ever witnessed. Schmidt increased her victory total a bit, winning by 8 percentage points. She increased that to 23 points in 2010.

Following the 2008 election, Schmidt filed a $6.8 million defamation lawsuit against Krikorian over remarks he is alleged to have made accusing her of accepting contributions from groups linked to the Turkish government. The Office of Congressional Ethics announced in February 2011 that it was investigating Schmidt's alleged receipt of assistance in that case and others from a Turkish-American group.

Key Votes

2010	
Overhaul the nation's health insurance system	NO
Allow for repeal of "don't ask, don't tell"	NO
Overhaul financial services industry regulation	NO
Limit use of new Afghanistan War funds to troop withdrawal activities	NO
Change oversight of offshore drilling and lift oil spill liability cap	NO
Provide a path to legal status for some children of illegal immigrants	NO
Extend Bush-era income tax cuts for two years	NO
2009	
Expand the Children's Health Insurance Program	NO
Provide $787 billion in tax cuts and spending increases to stimulate the economy	NO
Allow bankruptcy judges to modify certain primary-residence mortgages	NO
Create a cap-and-trade system to limit greenhouse gas emissions	NO
Provide $2 billion for the "cash for clunkers" program	NO
Establish the government as the sole provider of student loans	NO
Restrict federally funded insurance coverage for abortions in health care overhaul	YES

CQ Vote Studies

	PARTY UNITY		PRESIDENTIAL SUPPORT	
	SUPPORT	OPPOSE	SUPPORT	OPPOSE
2010	98%	2%	24%	76%
2009	96%	4%	22%	78%
2008	95%	5%	72%	28%
2007	96%	4%	80%	20%
2006	96%	4%	97%	3%

Interest Groups

	AFL-CIO	ADA	CCUS	ACU
2010	0%	5%	75%	100%
2009	10%	0%	71%	100%
2008	21%	15%	94%	87%
2007	17%	15%	89%	92%
2006	14%	0%	100%	88%

Ohio 2

Eastern Cincinnati and suburbs; Portsmouth

The 2nd stretches from some wealthy areas in eastern Cincinnati and Hamilton County in southwestern Ohio to struggling rural communities in the southern portion of the state. A distinct split between its suburban and rural elements defines the district.

The district's economy had revolved around light manufacturing and the retail and service industries, but a home and commercial construction market collapse and job cuts at local manufacturing firms stalled the economy in the Cincinnati area.

The 2nd takes in less than one-fourth of Cincinnati's residents, including the upscale neighborhoods of Hyde Park and Mount Lookout. One-third of the population lives in Hamilton County, including the well-to-do areas of Madeira, Mariemont, Blue Ash and the Village of Indian Hill.

To the east, once-undeveloped Clermont County has attracted some business growth and residential development, in large part due to its low taxes. To the north, the population in Warren County has grown by 34 percent since 2000 as well-off families move in from Hamilton County. As more

suburban residents have moved in, Warren County has begun to shed its agricultural tradition.

In the district's east, Brown, Adams, Pike and Scioto counties are all struggling economically. Pike and Scioto depend mainly on soybeans, while tobacco is still big in Brown and Adams counties.

Unemployment rates in some of the district's rural Appalachian counties have hovered in double digits for years; local officials hope to spur growth here by investing in infrastructure projects and broadband Internet access. The 2nd is reliably Republican at the presidential level, and John McCain took the 2nd overall with 59 percent of its presidential vote in 2008.

The district's portion of Hamilton County gives broad support to GOP candidates, but sparsely populated Pike and Scioto backed incumbent Gov. Ted Strickland, a Democrat, in his unsuccessful 2010 re-election bid.

Major Industry

Manufacturing, service, retail, agriculture

Cities

Cincinnati (pt.), 68,763; Portsmouth, 20,226

Notable

Ulysses S. Grant's birthplace in Point Pleasant is a state historical site.

Rep. Michael R. Turner (R)

Capitol Office
225-6465
www.house.gov/miketurner
2454 Rayburn Bldg. 20515-3503; fax 225-6754

Committees
Armed Services
  (Strategic Forces - Chairman)
Oversight & Government Reform

Residence
Centerville

Born
Jan. 11, 1960; Dayton, Ohio

Religion
Protestant

Family
Wife, Lori Turner; two children

Education
Ohio Northern U., B.A. 1982 (political science); Case Western Reserve U., J.D. 1985; U. of Dayton, M.B.A. 1992

Career
Real estate developer; lawyer

Political Highlights
Mayor of Dayton, 1994-2002; defeated for re-election as mayor of Dayton, 2001

ELECTION RESULTS

2010 GENERAL

Michael R. Turner (R)	152,629	68.1%
Joe Roberts (D)	71,455	31.9%

2010 PRIMARY

Michael R. Turner (R)	50,317	85.9%
Rene L. Oberer (R)	8,267	14.1%

2008 GENERAL

Michael R. Turner (R)	200,204	63.3%
Jane Mitakides (D)	115,976	36.7%

Previous Winning Percentages
2006 (56%); 2004 (62%); 2002 (59%)

Elected 2002; 5th term

Turner is a reliable conservative on national security and social issues, but he has found common ground working with congressional Democrats on economic topics close to his blue-collar roots. He has increased his public profile by standing athwart President Obama's policies on nuclear weapons and missile defense.

As chairman of the Armed Forces Subcommittee on Strategic Forces, Turner said the Obama administration's decision not to fund two planned missile defense sites in Poland and the Czech Republic "has exposed the United States to gaps in protection."

He took to the pages of USA Today in April 2010 to lambast Obama's proposals for reducing U.S. nuclear arsenals. "Underpinning the president's drive for U.S. nuclear reductions appears to be an expectation that others will follow," Turner wrote. "There is no historical basis for this assumption."

He was encouraged, though, by proposals in Obama's fiscal 2012 budget that would boost funding for nuclear weapons modernization, calling it a "very positive" first step.

He opposed the Pentagon's decision to terminate the Marine Corps' Expeditionary Fighting Vehicle, which would have been built in Ohio.

"Now is not the time to leave our Marines dependent on a 40-year-old fleet of slow, lightly armored Amphibious Assault Vehicles that lack the firepower and mobility necessary to respond to the modern battlefield," Turner said.

One of his major parochial preoccupations is looking out for Wright-Patterson Air Force Base, a big winner in the most recent round of base realignments and closures (BRAC). Early in his congressional career, Turner was involved in efforts to secure almost $700 million for research and development at the base. More recently, he pointed to the "largest expansion since World War II" at the base, with preparations under way to receive 1,200 new jobs gained in the BRAC process.

Combining his duties on Armed Services and the Oversight and Government Reform Committee, he worked in 2009 with Jane Harman, a California Democrat, on legislation to develop a comprehensive system to prevent sexual assaults in the military, arising out of the sexual assault and murder of a Marine from his district.

Turner also has strong socially conservative views. He is outspoken in his opposition to same-sex marriage and abortion, opposed repeal of the statutory ban on military service by open homosexuals and was heavily involved in pushing a GOP bill recognizing a fetus as a legal victim when the fetus is injured or killed in an attack on the mother.

Turner earned a bit of national notoriety in 2007 after one of his constituents complained that the acting Architect of the Capitol had refused to include the word "God" in a certificate accompanying a flag flown over the Capitol in honor of the constituent's grandfather. Turner collected more than 160 signatures on a letter demanding a change in the policy, and the architect relented.

A former mayor of Dayton, Turner quickly emerged as a Republican authority on urban issues. In 2003, his first year in Congress, Turner was named chairman of a 24-member working group called Saving America's Cities, later subsumed into a broader House GOP task force. He is vice chairman of the Congressional Urban Caucus, he co-founded the Historic Preservation Caucus with North Carolina Democrat Brad Miller, and he is a co-founder of the Former Mayors Caucus.

His highest urban priority, he said, is legislation that would provide tax credits to companies that clean up polluted former industrial sites. Redevelopment of the sites, known as brownfields, was a priority during Turner's tenure as mayor from 1994 to 2002. He is credited with reversing Dayton's downtown decline with programs that built a new arts center and a minor league baseball stadium and restored the Great Miami riverfront. A project he dubbed "Rehabarama," a public-private partnership to restore historic houses, was recognized by the National Trust for Historic Preservation.

He supported a bill to expand a children's health insurance program — a measure that President George W. Bush vetoed twice but that Obama signed into law. In response to his state's foreclosure woes, Turner was one of seven House Republicans to back a bill allowing bankruptcy judges to modify mortgage terms for troubled homeowners, a proposal fellow Ohio Republican and then-Minority Leader John A. Boehner called "the worst idea in the world."

Turner was raised in Dayton and attended public schools. His father, Ray, worked for more than 40 years at a General Motors Corp. plant and was a member of the electrical workers union. His mother, Vivian, was an elementary school teacher. His father had dropped out of school at age 16 to work at the plant, but after putting his wife through school and pushing his son toward college, the elder Turner decided he did not want to be the only one in the family without a high school diploma, so he belatedly got one.

Turner practiced law and worked with nonprofit groups in Dayton dealing with low-income housing, homelessness and community development before winning his first term as mayor in 1993.

He lost his bid for a third term, but his bipartisan appeal caught the eye of GOP recruiters. When Bush tapped 12-term Democratic Rep. Tony P. Hall to serve as ambassador to three world hunger relief organizations, Turner became a favorite to run for the seat. He first defeated newspaper publisher Roy E. Brown, son and grandson of former members of Congress, in the primary, then took 59 percent of the vote to defeat Democrat Rick Carne, Hall's former chief of staff. Turner was easily re-elected in 2004 and 2006.

During the 2008 campaign, Turner faced questions related to his wife's work. The Dayton Development Coalition, a clearinghouse for federal earmarks and aid requests for Turner's district, hired his wife's public relations firm for a marketing campaign, netting her business more than $300,000 in profits. Turner said the council does not receive federal money and that he and his wife are careful to avoid questionable entanglements.

In the end, he won a fourth term with 63 percent of the vote. He won with 68 percent in 2010.

Key Votes

2010

Overhaul the nation's health insurance system	NO
Allow for repeal of "don't ask, don't tell"	NO
Overhaul financial services industry regulation	NO
Limit use of new Afghanistan War funds to troop withdrawal activities	NO
Change oversight of offshore drilling and lift oil spill liability cap	NO
Provide a path to legal status for some children of illegal immigrants	NO
Extend Bush-era income tax cuts for two years	YES

2009

Expand the Children's Health Insurance Program	YES
Provide $787 billion in tax cuts and spending increases to stimulate the economy	NO
Allow bankruptcy judges to modify certain primary-residence mortgages	YES
Create a cap-and-trade system to limit greenhouse gas emissions	NO
Provide $2 billion for the "cash for clunkers" program	YES
Establish the government as the sole provider of student loans	NO
Restrict federally funded insurance coverage for abortions in health care overhaul	YES

CQ Vote Studies

	PARTY UNITY		PRESIDENTIAL SUPPORT	
	SUPPORT	OPPOSE	SUPPORT	OPPOSE
2010	89%	11%	36%	64%
2009	71%	29%	61%	39%
2008	85%	15%	58%	42%
2007	82%	18%	62%	38%
2006	91%	9%	90%	10%

Interest Groups

	AFL-CIO	ADA	CCUS	ACU
2010	14%	10%	88%	82%
2009	33%	35%	80%	72%
2008	57%	55%	81%	63%
2007	54%	25%	100%	80%
2006	29%	5%	93%	80%

Ohio 3

Southwest — most of Dayton, Kettering, part of Warren County

Montgomery County and its largest city, Dayton, still dominate the 3rd despite a decade of population loss. Midway between Cincinnati and Dayton, fast-growing Warren County (shared with the 2nd) has bedroom communities for both cities. Clinton and Highland counties to the east are more rural but increasingly developed.

Dayton, tied to manufacturing for generations, has endured a torrent of departures that displaced its manufacturing base. In nearby Moraine, the closure of a General Motors SUV plant resulted in the loss of thousands of area jobs, at the plant and among suppliers, and reduced to a small fraction a GM-based workforce in the Dayton area that had still been as large as 19,000 employees a decade ago.

Despite general setbacks in traditional economic sectors, the area's aerospace and technology jobs draw white-collar workers, military operations provide a stable economic foundation and service-oriented sectors have expanded. The area's defense industry has had some success in attracting aerospace, medical research and information technology companies to

the area around Wright-Patterson Air Force Base (shared with the 7th). A new Caterpillar machinery distribution center, a GE research facility and firms in the "Tech Town" district in eastern Dayton (shared with the 7th) will bring new jobs.

The urban vote — driven by Dayton's black population and blue-collar workforce — gives Montgomery a very slight Democratic lean. The suburbs south of Dayton take in GOP-inclined, white-collar areas, and the counties outside of Montgomery give the 3rd its Republican flavor. John McCain won 51 percent of the district's vote in the 2008 presidential election.

Major Industry
Defense, service, manufacturing

Military Bases
Wright-Patterson Air Force Base, 6,611 military, 7,537 civilian (2009) (shared with the 7th District)

Cities
Dayton (pt.), 112,892; Kettering (pt.), 55,696; Trotwood, 24,431

Notable
The National Museum of the United States Air Force (at Wright-Patterson) is the world's largest and oldest military aviation museum.

Rep. Jim Jordan (R)

Capitol Office
225-2676
jordan.house.gov
1524 Longworth Bldg. 20515-3504; fax 226-0577

Committees
Judiciary
Oversight & Government Reform
  (Regulatory Affairs, Stimulus Oversight &
  Government Spending - Chairman)

Residence
Urbana

Born
Feb. 17, 1964; Troy, Ohio

Religion
Christian

Family
Wife, Polly Jordan; four children

Education
U. of Wisconsin, B.S. 1986 (economics); Ohio State U.,
M.A. 1991 (education); Capital U., J.D. 2001

Career
College wrestling coach

Political Highlights
Ohio House, 1995-2000; Ohio Senate, 2001-06

ELECTION RESULTS

2010 GENERAL

Jim Jordan (R)	146,029	71.5%
Doug Litt (D)	50,533	24.7%
Donald Kissick (LIBERT)	7,708	3.8%

2010 PRIMARY

Jim Jordan (R)	unopposed

2008 GENERAL

Jim Jordan (R)	186,154	65.2%
Mike Carroll (D)	99,499	34.8%

Previous Winning Percentages
2006 (60%)

Elected 2006; 3rd term

A champion high school and college wrestler, Jordan brings the same intensity to tackling federal spending that he used to take down competitors on the mat. In the new Congress, he leads the conservative Republican Study Committee and chairs the Oversight and Government Reform Committee's panel that oversees government spending.

He staked out a hard-line position on spending early in the 112th Congress (2011-12). After the House passed its version of a catchall spending bill for fiscal 2011 in February 2011, Jordan refused to back a short-term measure that gave lawmakers more time to work out a deal.

"With the federal government facing record deficits and a mammoth debt hanging over our economy and our future, we must do more than cut spending in bite-sized pieces," Jordan told Roll Call in March. He then voted against the spending bill that passed in April to fund the government through the rest of the fiscal year.

Before taking over as chairman of the RSC, he led the budget and spending task force for the group. He has consistently criticized Democrats' "fiscal irresponsibility" and offered spending-cut amendments to appropriations bills.

His proposal to cut an additional $22 billion beyond the $58 billion in cuts included in the February spending bill garnered only 147 votes — but it won a wide majority among freshman Republicans.

"These newly elected Republicans are the cavalry, sent by the American people to Washington to change things," said Jordan.

Concern about debt has led Jordan to fight fiscal policies that increase spending, no matter which party endorses them. Despite his district's dependence on automobile manufacturing, he strongly opposed President George W. Bush's proposed $14 billion in assistance for U.S. automakers in late 2008, a plan that did not become law. He voted against the $700 billion Troubled Asset Relief Program, which Bush signed into law in October 2008, and he condemned President Obama's $787 billion economic stimulus bill, which became law in February 2009.

Instead, Jordan supports efforts to revive the economy by cutting taxes. He backs making the Bush 2001 and 2003 tax cuts permanent and opposed the two-year extension enacted in late 2010, arguing it was "saddled with $95 billion in new federal spending that will increase the deficit, and also contains a massive increase in the estate tax that will hurt the families, farmers and small business owners in my district and across America."

Jordan also brought his concern about government intervention in the markets to the 2009 Bank of America hearings, where he accused the federal government of using "threats, intimidation and deception to impose growing command and control over our economy." Although his conservative views are diametrically opposite those of Democrat Dennis J. Kucinich — a fellow Ohioan who chaired the Oversight Subcommittee on Domestic Policy in the 111th Congress (2009-10) — Jordan says the two have enjoyed a "great working relationship." Kucinich even attended Jordan's oldest daughter's wedding in 2010 after she met her future husband when they both worked as pages in Washington, D.C., while Kucinich was sponsoring the groom's pageship.

Outside the fiscal arena, Jordan introduced a measure in the 110th Congress (2007-08) and again in the 111th that would require abortion providers to perform an ultrasound on a pregnant woman and show her the images before she consents to an abortion. In 2009, he led a bipartisan coalition of 180 lawmakers urging Obama to support longstanding anti-abortion policies in spending bills. Jordan launched himself into the Washington, D.C., gay marriage debate when he introduced a measure in 2009 to define marriage in the District as the union of one man and one woman.

From his seat on the Judiciary Committee, he has backed efforts to strengthen border security while opposing a path to citizenship for illegal immigrants. He also supports Republicans' "all of the above" energy plan that would permit new oil and gas drilling and expanded refinery capacity, as well as more incentives for renewable and alternative fuels.

Jordan grew up in the rural community of St. Paris, about an hour west of Columbus. His father worked at the local General Motors plant from his teens until he retired. His mother, who cared for Jordan and two younger siblings, supplemented the family income by running a cleaning business.

In junior high school, Jordan took a keen interest in wrestling, influenced by several relatives who were amateur wrestlers. After school, he could frequently be found behind the house in a wrestling room his father built for practicing. He went on to become a four-time state wrestling champion at Graham High School, where he lost only one match, and parlayed that success into a wrestling scholarship at the University of Wisconsin at Madison. He won two national championships there and was inducted into the University of Wisconsin Athletic Hall of Fame in 2005.

Between his junior and senior years, Jordan married his high school sweetheart. He returned to Ohio, where he went to graduate school at Ohio State University and began a career in coaching. His wife had just given birth to their fourth child in 1994 when Jordan decided to get into the contest to succeed a longtime GOP incumbent in the state House. "You get married, you have kids, you get tired of government taking your money and insulting your values, and you said, you know what, I'm going to run and see if I can make a difference," Jordan said.

During his six years in the Ohio House and six more in the state Senate, Jordan routinely bucked Republican leaders, often voting against proposals he said weren't conservative enough. He attended Capital University while serving in the state legislature and earned a law degree in 2001.

When Republican Rep. Michael G. Oxley retired in 2006, Jordan's time in the legislature served as his calling card in a six-candidate Republican field; he took more than 50 percent of the primary vote. In November, he cruised to victory over Democratic lawyer Richard E. Siferd. Despite the Democratic tide that helped Obama carry Ohio two years later, the strong GOP tilt of Jordan's district won him nearly two-thirds of the vote. He upped that to 72 percent in 2010.

Key Votes

2010

Overhaul the nation's health insurance system	NO
Allow for repeal of "don't ask, don't tell"	NO
Overhaul financial services industry regulation	NO
Limit use of new Afghanistan War funds to troop withdrawal activities	NO
Change oversight of offshore drilling and lift oil spill liability cap	NO
Provide a path to legal status for some children of illegal immigrants	NO
Extend Bush-era income tax cuts for two years	NO

2009

Expand the Children's Health Insurance Program	NO
Provide $787 billion in tax cuts and spending increases to stimulate the economy	NO
Allow bankruptcy judges to modify certain primary-residence mortgages	NO
Create a cap-and-trade system to limit greenhouse gas emissions	NO
Provide $2 billion for the "cash for clunkers" program	NO
Establish the government as the sole provider of student loans	NO
Restrict federally funded insurance coverage for abortions in health care overhaul	YES

CQ Vote Studies

	PARTY UNITY		PRESIDENTIAL SUPPORT	
	SUPPORT	OPPOSE	SUPPORT	OPPOSE
2010	99%	1%	22%	78%
2009	99%	1%	13%	87%
2008	95%	5%	85%	15%
2007	99%	1%	91%	9%

Interest Groups

	AFL-CIO	ADA	CCUS	ACU
2010	0%	5%	75%	100%
2009	5%	0%	73%	100%
2008	0%	0%	83%	100%
2007	4%	0%	70%	100%

Ohio 4

West central — Mansfield, Lima, Findlay

The 4th, a solid block of Corn Belt counties, also supports soybeans, livestock and Republicans. Not one of the 11 counties in the 4th has backed a Democratic presidential candidate since 1964, and John McCain swept the counties again in 2008. Two of the three most populous counties, Allen and Hancock, last voted Democratic in the Roosevelt-Landon contest of 1936.

Corn and soybeans are integral to the 4th's economy, and ethanol plants and a strong agricultural base have stabilized it during decades of decline in the auto manufacturing sector. A food processing plant has relocated to Lima — lured to the new Gateway Commerce Park at the junction of several highways and rail cargo transit lines — but the city relies on its health care sector.

Manufacturing remains important as the 4th tries to maintain its roots: Small industrial companies and large assembly plants continue to aid the economy. A plant in Lima that builds the Army's Abrams tank increased production after emerging safely from the 2005 round of military base closings and is a leading job provider in the area. A Ford engine plant in

Lima has rebounded after several years of job cuts, but unemployment remains a problem across the district.

Other manufacturing interests in the 4th include a large Whirlpool dishwasher plant in Findlay, as well as Cooper Tire & Rubber facilities in the city. Findlay also hosts a Marathon Petroleum production site and the company plans to base its new headquarters in the city. Budget shortfalls in several counties in the district endanger government jobs.

Democrats have very few pockets of support, but they can normally count on votes in Mansfield, which is more than one-fifth black. Those votes can help Democrats locally, but they barely make a dent in the 4th's overall Republican lean.

In the 2010 U.S. Senate race, Rob Portman won every county wholly or partly in the district by at least a 2-to-1 margin.

Major Industry
Agriculture, manufacturing, food processing, oil

Cities
Mansfield, 47,821; Findlay, 41,202; Lima, 38,771; Marion, 36,837

Notable
Astronaut Neil Armstrong's hometown of Wapakoneta has a museum in his honor.

Rep. Bob Latta (R)

Capitol Office
225-6405
latta.house.gov
1323 Longworth Bldg. 20515-3505; fax 225-1985

Committees
Energy & Commerce

Residence
Bowling Green

Born
April 18, 1956; Bluffton, Ohio

Religion
Roman Catholic

Family
Wife, Marcia Latta; two children

Education
Ohio Northern U., attended 1974-75; Bowling Green
State U., B.A. 1978 (history); Ohio Northern U.,
attended 1978-79; U. of Toledo, J.D. 1981

Career
Lawyer

Political Highlights
Ohio Republican Central Committee, 1986-88;
sought Republican nomination for U.S. House, 1988;
Ohio Republican Central Committee, 1990-92; Wood
County Commission, 1990-96; Ohio Senate, 1997-
2000; Ohio House, 2001-07

ELECTION RESULTS

2010 GENERAL

Bob Latta (R)	140,703	67.8%
Caleb Finkenbiner (D)	54,919	26.5%
Brian L. Smith (LIBERT)	11,831	5.7%

2010 PRIMARY

Bob Latta (R)	42,827	83.0%
Robert Wallis (R)	8,754	17.0%

2008 GENERAL

Bob Latta (R)	188,905	64.1%
George Mays (D)	105,840	35.9%

Previous Winning Percentages
2007 Special Election (57%)

Elected 2007; 2nd full term

Latta is a loyal conservative who rarely bends his pro-business and small-government principles. The exception is on matters that benefit the wheat, soybean and corn growers who populate the Maumee Valley. As someone who spends his weekends crisscrossing his district, the second largest in Ohio, Latta says constituent service is his top priority — a concept instilled while working for his father, Delbert L. Latta, a budget hawk who held the same seat for 30 years.

"My philosophy is that we're here to do one thing: No. 1 is constituent service," Latta said. "And the second is really on the legislative side. Because the folks back home didn't enact these laws. The folks back home didn't promulgate these rules. But boy, they are the ones that get hit with them."

Latta would like to see Congress spend less time in session and more on the road. He says committees — he is a member of the powerful Energy and Commerce panel — should hold more hearings across the country, and members should take more time to develop legislation. An assistant Republican whip, he is quick to criticize the speed at which legislation sometimes moves through Congress.

The soft-spoken Latta makes himself heard on electronic platforms — from Twitter to Facebook to Amplify. A founder of the Republican New Media Caucus, Latta says Republicans have been successful in getting information to constituents via multimedia. When the Republicans took over the majority in the 112th Congress (2011-12), he was named to the House Technology Operations Team, tasked with making the chamber a friendlier online environment, starting with the house.gov website.

"It's got a lot of information there, but the question is if you can find the information readily," Latta told Roll Call. "We can get more information out there so people don't have to read about it, they can see it right then."

Latta cited the health care overhaul debate in the 111th Congress (2009-10) as an example of effective use of multimedia, saying Republicans were able to get their message out in a number of different venues. He was a sharp critic of the package, lamenting its "devastating effects" on seniors and small businesses. At the start of the 111th, he voted against an expansion of the Children's Health Insurance Program, which covers children from lower-income families that make too much money to qualify for Medicaid.

He also opposed Democrats' energy legislation, arguing that their proposals for a cap-and-trade regime for greenhouse gas emissions would cost jobs. "Democrats claim that this plan will help the environment and create 'green jobs' that will benefit our nation," he wrote in an opinion piece in May 2009. "Any new jobs created will not even come close to compensating for jobs lost to this energy plan." A member of the Republicans' American Energy Solutions Group, he backs the GOP's "all-of-the-above strategy" involving more oil and gas exploration as well as increased use of alternative energy.

Latta supports a balanced-budget constitutional amendment and giving presidents a line-item veto. He joined his party in 2009 in opposing President Obama's $787 billion stimulus law, likening it to socialism. "If you want government to take everything, if you want government to take more and more over with the banks, more of the industries, all of a sudden you're going to have a government auto czar, right there, right down the line, that's socialism," he told the Toledo Blade in February 2009.

Latta backed the catchall spending bill the House passed in early 2011 that included $58 billion in cuts, and voted for almost all of the other proposed cuts offered on the floor. He also voted for the compromise spending bill passed in April funding the government through the remainder of fiscal 2011.

He opposed two versions of a bill — the second of which became law in autumn 2008 — to provide $700 billion in aid for the financial services industry, even after heavy lobbying from John A. Boehner, the fellow Ohio Republican who is now Speaker. After the second vote, he assured Boehner it wasn't personal: "I like John. This is not a referendum on John," he said, calling the package too expensive.

Latta chose constituents over party in supporting an override of Bush's veto of the Democrats' 2008 farm bill, saying the legislation would keep Ohio farmers employed. Latta, a former member of the Agriculture Committee, criticized Democratic proposals for the next rewrite, saying they focus too much on conservation and not enough on helping farmers.

Latta was 2 when his father won a seat in Congress in 1958. The family split time between residences in Bowling Green and Washington. By the time he entered fifth grade, he was enrolled in Virginia schools full time, though he returned to Ohio for high school.

He often spent days off from school with his father on Capitol Hill. When his father served on the Rules Committee, which governs floor debate on legislation, the younger Latta often sat behind Massachusetts Democrat Thomas P. "Tip" O'Neill Jr., who later became Speaker.

As a teenager, Latta helped his father by answering phone calls from local residents and taking shifts driving his father to and from local airports.

Latta worked for a Wood County judge while earning a history degree from Bowling Green State University. In 1981, he earned a law degree from the University of Toledo. He worked for a corporate law firm and in private practice before joining the Toledo Bank Trust Co.

Latta made a run for his father's seat in 1988 but lost to Paul E. Gillmor in the Republican primary by 27 votes. In 1990, he ran a successful race for commissioner in Wood County, defeating a Democratic incumbent. Six years later, he was elected to the Ohio legislature and served four years in the Senate and six in the House.

When Gillmor died in 2007, Latta made another run for the seat and took the primary after an often unruly campaign in which Latta and his chief primary opponent, state Sen. Steve Buehrer, accused each other of lying about their respective legislative records. He then defeated Democrat Robin Weirauch with 57 percent of the vote in the December 2007 special election. He was re-elected easily in 2008 and 2010.

Key Votes

2010

Overhaul the nation's health insurance system	NO
Allow for repeal of "don't ask, don't tell"	NO
Overhaul financial services industry regulation	NO
Limit use of new Afghanistan War funds to troop withdrawal activities	NO
Change oversight of offshore drilling and lift oil spill liability cap	NO
Provide a path to legal status for some children of illegal immigrants	NO
Extend Bush-era income tax cuts for two years	YES

2009

Expand the Children's Health Insurance Program	NO
Provide $787 billion in tax cuts and spending increases to stimulate the economy	NO
Allow bankruptcy judges to modify certain primary-residence mortgages	NO
Create a cap-and-trade system to limit greenhouse gas emissions	NO
Provide $2 billion for the "cash for clunkers" program	NO
Establish the government as the sole provider of student loans	NO
Restrict federally funded insurance coverage for abortions in health care overhaul	YES

CQ Vote Studies

	PARTY UNITY		PRESIDENTIAL SUPPORT	
	SUPPORT	OPPOSE	SUPPORT	OPPOSE
2010	99%	1%	25%	75%
2009	98%	2%	13%	87%
2008	99%	1%	73%	27%
2007	100%	0%	60%	40%

Interest Groups

	AFL-CIO	ADA	CCUS	ACU
2010	0%	0%	88%	100%
2009	5%	0%	80%	100%
2008	7%	15%	89%	96%

Northwest — Bowling Green, Tiffin, Fremont

Bordering Indiana and Michigan in the northwestern corner of the state, the 5th cuts south of Toledo into the north-central portion of Ohio. Flat farmland born from the once-impervious Great Black Swamp covers the middle of Ohio's second-largest district in land area. The 5th's largest jurisdiction is centrally located Wood County, with the rest of the population spread between counties east and west of Wood. North of Wood, across the Maumee River, the 5th picks up GOP-leaning southern suburbs in Toledo-dominated Lucas County (most of which is in the 9th).

The largest city in Wood County, and in the district, is Bowling Green. The city is heavily dependent on Bowling Green State University; officials hope the local Innovative Technology Park will help attract jobs to a region suffering from stagnation in its population and economy.

Wheat, tomatoes, soybeans and corn dominate most of the landscape in Wood. Many of the 5th's other counties form the heart of Ohio's wheat-growing country and depend on agriculture and food packaging. The 5th leads Ohio in wheat, soybean and corn production.

East and west of Wood, migrant-worker communities boost the district's Hispanic population to 5 percent. Manufacturing is important here, with a Heinz ketchup plant in Fremont, an Arm & Hammer Baking Soda site in Old Fort and a large Whirlpool washing machine production facility in Clyde. Unemployment remains high in some counties, but Van Wert, along the Indiana border, has made available a 1,600-acre state-funded industrial site in order to lure a major employer.

The 5th is strong GOP territory. Wood County, which backed Republican Rob Portman in the 2010 U.S. Senate race, gave a slight edge to Democratic Gov. Ted Strickland in his losing re-election effort as every other county wholly in the district backed Republican John Kasich. Mercer (shared with the 8th) and Van Wert were two of Kasich's best counties statewide.

Major Industry
Agriculture, manufacturing

Cities
Bowling Green, 30,028; Perrysburg, 20,623; Tiffin, 17,963

Notable
Perrysburg, named to honor Commodore Oliver Perry's victory over the British in the 1813 Battle of Lake Erie, is one of only two U.S. cities to have been planned by the federal government.

Rep. Bill Johnson (R)

Capitol Office
225-5705
billjohnson.house.gov
317 Cannon Bldg. 20515-3506; fax 225-5907

Committees
Foreign Affairs
Natural Resources
Veterans' Affairs
    (Oversight & Investigations - Chairman)

Residence
Marietta

Born
Nov. 10, 1954; Roseboro, N.C.

Religion
Protestant

Family
Wife, LeeAnn Johnson; four children

Education
Troy U., B.S. 1979 (computer science); Georgia Institute of Technology, M.S. 1984 (computer science)

Military
Air Force, 1973-78; Air Force, 1979-99

Career
Air Force officer; information technology executive

Political Highlights
No previous office

ELECTION RESULTS

2010 GENERAL

Bill Johnson (R)	103,170	50.2%
Charlie Wilson (D)	92,823	45.2%
Richard E. Cadle (CNSTP)	5,077	2.5%
Martin J. Elsass (LIBERT)	4,505	2.2%

2010 PRIMARY

Bill Johnson (R)	14,103	42.5%
Donald Allen (R)	12,406	37.4%
Richard Stobbs (R)	6,637	20.0%

Elected 2010; 1st term

Johnson represents a district that takes in part of the state's Appalachian areas, which have been particularly hard hit by the economic crisis, slumps in manufacturing and diminishing population.

Not surprisingly, he says the 112th Congress (2011-12) should make "fixing the economy and creating jobs" its top priority.

He backs a permanent extension of the George W. Bush-era tax cuts for all income levels and says reducing federal spending is the best way to protect Social Security. He opposes raising the retirement age.

"We need to get the federal government off the back of businesses. We have to grow the private sector," he told the Herald-Dispatch of Huntington, W.Va., just across the Ohio River from his district.

Johnson, a retired Air Force lieutenant colonel, serves on the Foreign Affairs Committee. He said fighting the war on terrorism "means treating our enemies as enemies — not as Americans with constitutional rights."

He said he opposed repeal of the "don't ask, don't tell" law that barred gays and lesbians from serving openly in the armed forces and that the controversy was a result not of problems arising in the military over the policy but from agitation by "the radical homosexual lobby."

He also won a spot on the Veterans' Affairs Committee, where he chairs the Oversight and Investigations Subcommittee.

Johnson's third committee assignment is Natural Resources. He backed an amendment to the catchall spending bill the House passed in early 2011 that would bar the EPA from putting in place any regulations pertaining to carbon emissions from stationary sources such as power plants.

Johnson initially considered running in the neighboring 17th District, but decided the more conservative 6th would be a better option.

He criticized his predecessor, two-term Democrat Charlie Wilson, for supporting the 2009 economic stimulus and the 2010 health care law. The contest was not originally on the party's radar, but Johnson got an October boost from a National Republican Congressional Committee ad campaign when polls tightened. He won with 50 percent of the vote, to Wilson's 45 percent.

Ohio 6

South and east — Boardman, Athens, Steubenville

The 6th parallels the Ohio River for nearly 300 miles, touching three states and taking in hardscrabble areas from Appalachia to the Mahoning Valley near Youngstown.

One-third of residents live in the district's north, in Mahoning and Columbiana counties, which still rely on waning steel, coal and manufacturing sectors. But the counties have been losing population steadily for decades. Jefferson County has lost population in each of the past five censuses and has Ohio's highest proportion of elderly residents. Several counties in the 6th's old coal mining areas have low household incomes, difficulty retaining younger residents and high unemployment rates. Athens (shared with the 18th), Scioto (shared with the 2nd), Meigs and Lawrence counties have some of the lowest incomes in the state.

The 6th leans conservative on social issues and now sends Republicans to the U.S. House and Senate, but it is highly competitive in presidential elections. Athens, in Athens County, is home to Ohio University and has a liberal slant — the county gave Democrat Ted Strickland his highest-percentage win statewide in his unsuccessful 2010 gubernatorial re-election race. Although Monroe, Belmont and Jefferson counties support some Democrats, Washington County has trended GOP. The 6th's share of Mahoning, which takes in Boardman and Poland, is more competitive than the solidly Democratic part of the county in the 17th. The southern counties blend populist fiscal policy with social conservatism and elect Republicans to the state legislature.

Major Industry
Service, manufacturing

Cities
Boardman (unincorp.), 35,376; Athens, 23,832

Notable
Gallipolis, in Gallia County, was founded in 1790 by a group of 500 French immigrants.

Rep. Steve Austria (R)

Capitol Office
225-4324
austria.house.gov
439 Cannon Bldg. 20515-3507; fax 225-1984

Committees
Appropriations

Residence
Beavercreek

Born
Oct. 12, 1958; Cincinnati, Ohio

Religion
Roman Catholic

Family
Wife, Eileen Austria; three children

Education
Marquette U., B.A. 1982 (political science)

Career
Financial services firm owner; state legislative aide

Political Highlights
Ohio House, 1999-2001; Ohio Senate, 2001-08
(majority whip, 2005-07)

ELECTION RESULTS

2010 GENERAL

Steve Austria (R)	135,721	62.2%
William R. Conner (D)	70,400	32.2%
John D. Anderson (LIBERT)	9,381	4.3%
David W. Easton (CNSTP)	2,811	1.3%

2010 PRIMARY

Steve Austria (R)	46,072	82.8%
John R. Mitchel (R)	9,535	17.1%

2008 GENERAL

Steve Austria (R)	174,915	58.2%
Sharen Neuhardt (D)	125,547	41.8%

Elected 2008; 2nd term

Austria is a former financial planner and state legislator who advocates smaller government and looks out for small business. He is a new member of the Appropriations Committee, where he takes a dim view of Democratic spending proposals he views as too costly.

Austria is no conservative firebrand, but he is a reliable Republican vote and a consistent critic of what he calls unsustainable budget deficits.

He sees his role on the Appropriations panel as serving his district while reining in spending and debt.

From his seat on the Military Construction-Veterans' Affairs Subcommittee, Austria can look out for Wright-Patterson Air Force Base, one of the district's largest employers, and the Springfield Air National Guard Base. He said he wants the Miami Valley to take the lead in developing the nation's strategy on tackling cybersecurity through a partnership among local universities, hospitals and the private sector.

He also backed federal loan guarantees to build a uranium enrichment plant in Piketon, in the neighboring 2nd District.

Austria also sits on the Appropriations subcommittee that funds the Justice Department. In 2009, he introduced a bill to bar the use of funds to transfer to Ohio enemy combatants detained at Guantánamo Bay, Cuba, or to build any facilities in the state to house them. Provisions included in several fiscal 2010 spending bills prohibited the use of funds to transfer detainees anywhere in the United States except for the purposes of prosecuting them or detaining them during legal proceedings.

His other Appropriations assignment is the State-Foreign Operations panel. He stirred a bit of controversy early in 2011 when he co-authored a letter with New Jersey Democrat Steven R. Rothman that was critical of Palestinian Authority President Mahmoud Abbas in the wake of the murder of an Israeli family by Palestinian attackers.

"Palestinian incitement continues and there is almost no effort by them to promote coexistence and peace," the letter read.

J Street, a liberal group that calls itself pro-Israel but is often critical of the Israeli government, said the letter was one-sided and painted an "inaccurate picture of the current status of the Israeli-Palestinian conflict."

On broader spending issues, Austria has proved to be just as dependable a conservative.

He opposed the $787 billion economic stimulus bill President Obama signed into law in 2009, saying it "contained too much wasteful borrowing and spending." Invoking his experience as a financial planner, he said, "I find the runaway spending and debt that has occurred over the past year to be deeply troubling,"

He made national headlines after giving an interview to the Columbus Dispatch, which quoted him comparing the stimulus plan to President Franklin D. Roosevelt's approach to spending. Roosevelt "tried to borrow and spend, he tried to use the Keynesian approach, and our country ended up in a Great Depression," Austria said. "That's just history." He later withdrew his statements, saying he never intended to blame Roosevelt for the Depression, which began before he was sworn in, but wanted to point out that the New Deal didn't cure the country's economic ills.

On the stimulus vote, he took a little heat from one constituency dear to his heart. Austria is the only first-generation Filipino-American in Congress, and his father fought with Filipino guerrillas against the Japanese during

World War II. The stimulus included money to make lump sum payments to Filipino veterans who fought alongside the United States in the war, an idea supported by Austria. But he wanted a vote on a separate bill, arguing that the money would not help stimulate the economy, a point conceded by the provision's sponsor, Senate Appropriations Chairman Daniel K. Inouye, a Hawaii Democrat.

In early 2009, Austria showed some willingness to cross party lines; he was one of 40 Republicans to back expansion of the Children's Health Insurance Program, which covers children whose lower-income families make too much money to qualify for Medicaid. But, like every other House Republican, he opposed the Democrats' health care overhaul, and he voted to repeal it in 2011. He introduced legislation incorporating a pair of ideas popular among conservatives and small-business owners: allowing a deduction for the health insurance costs of individuals and expanding health savings accounts.

He opposed the cap-and-trade bill designed to reduce carbon emissions. He endorsed the GOP's "all of the above" approach on energy, saying in an ad, "Where there's sun, put solar panels. Where there's corn, make ethanol. And where there's American oil, let's drill."

In addition to opposing the substance of the health care, cap-and-trade and stimulus bills, Austria objected to the process. "Having to deal with the size of these bills and the speed with which they pass has been a challenge," he told the Lancaster Eagle Gazette. He touts his cosponsorship, in some cases with many others, of measures to require that bills be posted online for at least 72 hours before a vote, that committees post bill text online within 24 hours of approval and that committee votes be posted within 48 hours.

Austria grew up in Xenia as the oldest of nine children. His mother was a nurse. His father, whom Austria calls his mentor, was a doctor who preceded him on the Greene County Republicans' central committee. Austria credits him with instilling a desire for public service. "My father was interested in politics, and in watching his involvement I realized that through public service I could have a positive impact on people's lives," he said.

He was elected to the Ohio House in 1998 and moved to the Senate two years later. As a state legislator, he backed laws to strengthen penalties against violent pedophiles, protect children from sex offenders on the Internet and make it a crime to drive while under the influence of illegal drugs.

In the campaign to replace retiring GOP Rep. David L. Hobson, for whom his wife once worked, Austria defeated three Republicans before facing attorney Sharen Neuhardt in the general election. He won with 58 percent of the vote. He was re-elected with 62 percent of the vote in 2010.

Key Votes

2010

Overhaul the nation's health insurance system	NO
Allow for repeal of "don't ask, don't tell"	NO
Overhaul financial services industry regulation	NO
Limit use of new Afghanistan War funds to troop withdrawal activities	NO
Change oversight of offshore drilling and lift oil spill liability cap	NO
Provide a path to legal status for some children of illegal immigrants	NO
Extend Bush-era income tax cuts for two years	YES

2009

Expand the Children's Health Insurance Program	YES
Provide $787 billion in tax cuts and spending increases to stimulate the economy	NO
Allow bankruptcy judges to modify certain primary-residence mortgages	NO
Create a cap-and-trade system to limit greenhouse gas emissions	NO
Provide $2 billion for the "cash for clunkers" program	YES
Establish the government as the sole provider of student loans	NO
Restrict federally funded insurance coverage for abortions in health care overhaul	YES

CQ Vote Studies

	PARTY UNITY		PRESIDENTIAL SUPPORT	
	SUPPORT	OPPOSE	SUPPORT	OPPOSE
2010	96%	4%	29%	71%
2009	93%	7%	35%	65%

Interest Groups

	AFL-CIO	ADA	CCUS	ACU
2010	7%	0%	88%	100%
2009	19%	15%	87%	88%

Central — Springfield, Lancaster, part of Columbus

The Republican-leaning 7th, based south of Columbus, is a diverse swath of land in south-central Ohio that includes urban, suburban and rural areas. Greene and Clark counties form the western arm of the 7th, but they are showing disparate trends — Greene experienced a more than 9 percent gain in population since 2000, but Clark shed residents. Wright-Patterson Air Force base, which anchors Greene, is Ohio's largest single-site employer. The county also has several colleges and universities. Clark and its county seat, Springfield, have hosted auto plants and technology companies. To the east, residents in Fayette, the least-populous county wholly in the 7th, breed horses.

Expansive residential growth near Columbus, a slice of which is in the 7th, has turned much of Fairfield County into white-collar bedroom communities. Pickaway County has suffered slower population growth and declines in manufacturing, as well as double-digit unemployment rates. Just north of Pickaway, Rickenbacker International Airport is a major cargo hub and key to Franklin County.

Perry County, in the district's eastern end, relies on manufacturing and agriculture but still struggles with high unemployment. Overall, the district's agricultural areas support corn, wheat and soybeans.

Republicans win at all levels here, although Clark and Perry counties have remained more competitive than other jurisdictions in the district. In his successful 2010 gubernatorial run, Republican John Kasich swept every county wholly within the district, racking up wide margins in Fairfield, Fayette and Greene.

Major Industry
Military, technology research, agriculture

Military Bases
Wright-Patterson Air Force Base, 6,611 military, 7,537 civilian (2009) (shared with the 3rd District)

Cities
Columbus (pt.), 68,222; Springfield, 60,608; Beavercreek, 45,193; Lancaster, 38,780; Fairborn, 32,352; Xenia, 25,719

Notable
The modern combine, invented in Springfield, helped revolutionize harvesting and the agriculture industry.

Rep. John A. Boehner (R)

Capitol Office
225-6205
johnboehner.house.gov
1011 Longworth Bldg. 20515-3508; fax 225-0704

Committees
No committee assignments

Residence
West Chester Township

Born
Nov. 17, 1949; Cincinnati, Ohio

Religion
Roman Catholic

Family
Wife, Debbie Boehner; two children

Education
Xavier U., B.S. 1977

Military
Navy, 1968

Career
Plastics and packaging executive

Political Highlights
Union Township Board of Trustees, 1982-84; Ohio
House, 1985-91

ELECTION RESULTS

2010 GENERAL

John A. Boehner (R)	142,731	65.6%
Justin A. Coussoule (D)	65,883	30.3%
David A. Harlow (LIBERT)	5,121	2.4%
James J. Condit Jr. (CNSTP)	3,701	1.7%

2010 PRIMARY

John A. Boehner (R)	50,555	84.7%
Thomas F. McMasters (R)	6,266	10.5%
Manfred R. Schreyer (R)	2,890	4.8%

2008 GENERAL

John A. Boehner (R)	202,063	67.9%
Nicholas von Stein (D)	95,510	32.1%

Previous Winning Percentages
2006 (64%); 2004 (69%); 2002 (71%); 2000 (71%);
1998 (71%); 1996 (70%); 1994 (100%); 1992 (74%);
1990 (61%)

Elected 1990; 11th term

Boehner's ascent to the speakership is a story of persistence and political redemption. Once cast out of the leadership ranks, he labored diligently as a committee chairman to win his way back into power.

Boehner (BAY-ner) took a different path to the top than his immediate predecessors, Republican J. Dennis Hastert of Illinois and Democrat Nancy Pelosi of California, both of whom were appropriators. Instead, after a stint in leadership, Boehner put in legislative spade work as chairman for five years of the Education and the Workforce Committee, where he displayed his skill as a bipartisan deal-cutter on President George W. Bush's 2001 No Child Left Behind education law and other measures.

Though he never served on the powerful spending panel, his management of the appropriations process is likely to mark Boehner's tenure as Speaker. He will also be judged by how he balances his raucous new majority's desire to shrink government with the reality of a Democratic Senate and president less inclined to cut spending.

Boehner arrived on Capitol Hill as a young Republican bent on changing the congressional culture at a time when his party was frozen out of power. But he has lately been seen as more of a creature of the institution than his younger lieutenants.

Still, he promised after Republicans regained control of the House in the 2010 elections that he would make changes, both symbolic and substantive, including cutting the size and budget of every House committee and trimming overall spending within the legislative branch.

"We should start with ourselves," Boehner said on CBS's "60 Minutes" in December 2010. "How about we start with cutting Congress?"

He backed longtime anti-earmark crusader Jeff Flake of Arizona for a place on the Appropriations Committee in the 112th Congress (2011-12) and encouraged other "reform-minded members" to follow Flake's example in seeking appointment to the panel.

Boehner has also backed a proposal to institute a new procedure referred to as "cut as you go," or "cut-go," that would bar bills creating new spending programs from coming to the floor under suspension of the rules unless the measures would eliminate other federal programs of equal or greater cost.

Outside the appropriations realm, Boehner threw his support behind several suggested changes to House proceedings, including eliminating floor votes on commemorative resolutions that celebrate sports teams, note civic achievements or name post offices.

The new strategies are an extension of the work Boehner began as minority leader in 2007 when he brought together a group of allies to work on revamping the Republican Party's image in hopes of better relaying its message to the public. But Boehner's desire to shake things up in the House goes all the way back to his first term, in the 102nd Congress (1991-92).

Then, he was one of the freshmen who railed against the excesses of incumbents and pushed for full disclosure during the 1992 scandal involving members who overdrew their House checking accounts. His zeal made him a favorite of the new breed of confrontational Republicans led by Newt Gingrich of Georgia, and four years later he became GOP Conference chairman, the No. 4 leader who handled message and communications. Boehner later lost his leadership post after being suspected of participating in a secret, failed effort among a handful of leaders to oust Gingrich.

After that, Boehner turned his attention to leading the Education Committee and to cultivating relationships with the next generation of Republicans who followed in the footsteps of the class of 1994.

His rehabilitation came full circle when he was elected majority leader in February 2006, after Tom DeLay of Texas resigned from the leadership. He got to enjoy that position for a little more than a year until the Republicans lost their majority in the 2006 elections.

Boehner served four years as minority leader, during which time he honed his laid-back leadership manner and encouraged input, both positive and negative, from colleagues. He made way for his ambitious No. 2, Virginia's Eric Cantor, to increasingly serve as a national face of the party. And ever attuned to the need to offer policy alternatives, he formed Republican task forces on earmarks, health care and other issues.

Boehner is no longer the young firebrand he once was, but he is still a reliable conservative, even though his devotion to the cause is sometimes questioned by conservative activists. He has proved to be an outspoken critic of the Obama administration, his rich baritone booming in futile opposition to virtually all of the economic initiatives offered during the first years of the Obama administration.

In November 2010, Boehner said he would seek to improve communication with the White House. "As I told the president," Boehner said, "I think that spending more time will help us find some common ground."

Boehner has an easy sense of humor, and is often the object of others' jokes about his tanned good looks, chain smoking and devotion to golf.

And he has a self-acknowledged tendency to cry in public, as he did on multiple occasions in the aftermath of the 2010 elections.

Boehner's back story is as good as any politician's rags-to-riches tale.

He spent his childhood in western Ohio's Rust Belt with 11 siblings, rising at 5 a.m. to help his father, Earl, sort bottles and mop floors at Andy's Cafe restaurant and bar. He worked his way through Xavier College as a janitor. After school, he and a partner bought a small plastics and packaging firm, Nucite Sales Inc., and built it into a multimillion-dollar business. His first political race brought him a seat on the local township board.

Boehner went on to serve six years in the Ohio House, then in 1990 joined the Republican primary field challenging Rep. Donald E. "Buz" Lukens, who had been convicted of having sex with a teenage girl. Boehner outspent the front-runner, former Rep. Thomas N. Kindness, and won with 49 percent of the vote. In November, he bested Democrat Gregory V. Jolivette, a former mayor of Hamilton, and has had easy re-elections since.

Key Votes

2010

Vote	
Overhaul the nation's health insurance system	NO
Allow for repeal of "don't ask, don't tell"	NO
Overhaul financial services industry regulation	NO
Limit use of new Afghanistan War funds to troop withdrawal activities	NO
Change oversight of offshore drilling and lift oil spill liability cap	NO
Provide a path to legal status for some children of illegal immigrants	NO
Extend Bush-era income tax cuts for two years	YES

2009

Vote	
Expand the Children's Health Insurance Program	NO
Provide $787 billion in tax cuts and spending increases to stimulate the economy	NO
Allow bankruptcy judges to modify certain primary-residence mortgages	NO
Create a cap-and-trade system to limit greenhouse gas emissions	NO
Provide $2 billion for the "cash for clunkers" program	NO
Establish the government as the sole provider of student loans	NO
Restrict federally funded insurance coverage for abortions in health care overhaul	YES

CQ Vote Studies

	PARTY UNITY		PRESIDENTIAL SUPPORT	
	SUPPORT	OPPOSE	SUPPORT	OPPOSE
2010	99%	1%	23%	77%
2009	98%	2%	12%	88%
2008	99%	1%	85%	15%
2007	99%	1%	93%	7%
2006	96%	4%	100%	0%

Interest Groups

	AFL-CIO	ADA	CCUS	ACU
2010	0%	0%	100%	100%
2009	5%	0%	80%	96%
2008	0%	0%	94%	92%
2007	4%	5%	79%	100%
2006	14%	5%	100%	88%

Ohio 8

Southwest — Hamilton, most of Middletown, part of Dayton

Hugging the state's western border, the 8th is fertile GOP ground that is steered economically and politically by Butler County, home to the district's two largest cities, Hamilton and Middletown. The district's solid Republican tilt is anchored in Butler, which has long been known for electing some of Ohio's more conservative state and congressional legislators. Butler and Miami counties propelled the district's growth through residential construction and commercial development. West Chester Township, in Butler, is one of the state's fastest-growing suburbs, and many residents commute to Cincinnati or Dayton. The 8th's manufacturing base, grounded in the steel industry, and a healthy agricultural sector have helped keep the district's economy relatively stable. The presence of Miami University in Oxford bolsters the local economy, and the university is investing in development of its regional campuses, all three of which are in the district. The 8th also encompasses a slice of Montgomery County, including parts of northeast Dayton near Wright-Patterson Air Force Base, which is in the 3rd and 7th districts.

About one-fifth of the 8th's residents live outside Butler in a string of fertile Corn Belt counties — Mercer (shared with the 5th), Darke and Preble. Corn and soybeans are the major cash crops here, and poultry and livestock also are moneymakers. Darke and Mercer are the two most productive agricultural counties in the state, and Mercer is the top county in agricultural sales.

Republican candidates win by wide margins across the district, especially in Darke and Preble counties. Exceptions to the GOP dominance in the district are the urban portion of Montgomery County and Oxford, although Republicans dominate the rest of Miami County, which is the 8th's second most-populous county. John McCain won his highest percentage statewide here in the 2008 presidential election.

Major Industry
Agriculture, manufacturing, higher education

Cities
Hamilton (pt.), 62,465; Middletown (pt.), 45,994; Fairfield, 42,510

Notable
The Voice of America Park is in West Chester Township.

Rep. Marcy Kaptur (D)

Capitol Office
225-4146
www.house.gov/kaptur
2186 Rayburn Bldg. 20515-3509; fax 225-7711

Committees
Appropriations
Budget

Residence
Toledo

Born
June 17, 1946; Toledo, Ohio

Religion
Roman Catholic

Family
Single

Education
U. of Wisconsin, B.A. 1968 (history); U. of Michigan, M.U.P. 1974 (urban planning); Massachusetts Institute of Technology, attended 1981 (urban planning)

Career
White House aide; urban planner

Political Highlights
No previous office

ELECTION RESULTS

2010 GENERAL

Marcy Kaptur (D)	121,819	59.4%
Rich Iott (R)	83,423	40.6%

2010 PRIMARY

Marcy Kaptur (D)	33,637	86.5%
Dale R. Terry (D)	5,256	13.5%

2008 GENERAL

Marcy Kaptur (D)	222,054	74.4%
Bradley Leavitt (R)	76,512	25.6%

Previous Winning Percentages
2006 (74%); 2004 (68%); 2002 (74%); 2000 (75%);
1998 (81%); 1996 (77%); 1994 (75%); 1992 (74%);
1990 (78%); 1988 (81%); 1986 (78%); 1984 (55%);
1982 (58%)

Elected 1982; 15th term

Kaptur has yet to hold a significant chairmanship or leadership post in nearly 30 years of House service, but she has made her mark as a passionate defender of blue-collar workers.

The most senior woman in the House, Kaptur has long challenged policies that she says benefit corporations and rich Americans at the expense of the middle class and poor. Her admirers include former independent presidential candidate Ross Perot, who unsuccessfully sought to have Kaptur, a fellow critic of the North American Free Trade Agreement, as his running mate in 1996. Michael Moore featured Kaptur in his 2009 film "Capitalism: A Love Story," which presented the leftist documentary filmmaker's take on the recent financial unrest.

A former urban planner, Kaptur said she was angered to hear of constituents who had been frightened by initial foreclosure notices and simply walked away from their homes without seeking help. She went on cable news shows and the House floor in 2009 to urge those facing foreclosure to get adequate legal representation and to make sure that the banks had the papers needed to prove their cases.

Kaptur was an outspoken critic of much of the federal response to the economic downturn, and her anger persisted even as her own party took the White House. While her key job in the House is serving as an appropriator, Kaptur also sits on the Budget Committee and formerly served on Oversight and Government Reform. From those seats, she grilled Obama administration officials on their handling of the financial rescue.

Kaptur questioned Treasury Secretary Timothy F. Geithner at a 2010 hearing about why he made more than 100 phone calls to a Goldman Sachs official around the time of the rescue of American International Group Inc., a move that benefited the firm's creditors, including Goldman. Kaptur also noted that day that Geithner's chief of staff had worked at Goldman, as had President George W. Bush's Treasury secretary, Henry M. Paulson Jr. At another 2010 hearing, Kaptur blamed the financial crisis on a "revolving door of influence-peddling of extraordinary proportions."

Congress also has been paying too much attention to corporate interests at the expense of the American public, in Kaptur's view. She blames this at least partly on the increased focused on raising money for re-election bids. To make that point, Kaptur in 2002 mounted a symbolic challenge to Californian Nancy Pelosi for the spot of Democratic leader. Once allowed to give a speech on the topic, she withdrew her name from the contest. In 2011, she got one vote for Speaker, from Illinois Democrat Daniel Lipinski.

She gave up her best chance for an important gavel to join the Defense Appropriations Subcommittee. She had been the top Democrat on the Agriculture Subcommittee from 1997 to 2005, but ceded that post shortly before her party regained control of Congress in the 2006 elections. That was the sacrifice she had to make to gain a seat on the Defense panel, a decision Kaptur says she has not regretted because it gave her the chance to direct Pentagon dollars to her district.

She secured $70 million to help one of her district's largest employers, Brush Wellman, build a plant for processing beryllium. Foreign companies have been trying to supplant U.S. businesses in the market for processing beryllium, which is used in telecommunications and optics devices.

She has found little to like in GOP spending plans in the 112th Congress (2011-12). A study, done by the conservative Heritage Action for America, of votes on the catchall spending bill the House passed in early 2011 showed that Kaptur voted for only one of the 21 unalloyed spending cuts considered on the House floor.

Since Kaptur arrived in Congress in 1983, the influence of the Midwest has ebbed. The Ohio delegation shrank from 21 to 18 members during those years, and will shrink by two more come 2012.

Kaptur noted the dominance of the delegations from the East and West coasts when she made a bid for Democratic Caucus vice chairwoman in November 2008.

"I felt we needed a voice from the heartland," she said of the race, which she lost to California's Xavier Becerra.

Kaptur remains grounded in her Ohio roots and has opted not to make the sacrifices usually required of those seeking to advance. Most weekends, she returns to the small house she grew up in and attends Mass at the same church where she was baptized.

She grows vegetables in her garden, paints watercolors and makes Polish coffee cakes and sausages at the holidays — activities she prefers to fundraising. Her views match those of her ethnic blue-collar constituents — Germans, Irish, Poles, Hungarians and Hispanics — who share the Catholic Church's opposition to abortion.

Kaptur is of the same stock; her father's parents were from western Poland and her mother's were from eastern Poland, in an area now part of Ukraine.

Her father, Stephen, ran a grocery store in Rossford, just south of Toledo, where he was known for giving credit to people who couldn't afford food for the week. After the 1997 death of her mother, Anastasia, Kaptur and her brother founded the nonprofit Anastasia Fund, which has helped support democracy movements in Ukraine, China and Mexico. Kaptur also has established the Kaptur Community Fund, which makes charitable donations in Toledo; she regularly contributes her congressional pay raise to the fund.

After graduating from college, she worked as a city planner, helping to create community development corporations to revitalize low-income areas of Toledo. That led to a job in the Carter administration as an adviser on urban policy.

Kaptur was studying for her doctorate in urban planning at the Massachusetts Institute of Technology when she was recruited to challenge first-term GOP Rep. Ed Weber in 1982. With northwestern Ohio in a deep recession, Weber's support for President Ronald Reagan's economic policies proved politically fatal; Kaptur won by 19 percentage points. She was held to 55 percent of the vote in 1984 but has won by wide margins since.

Key Votes

2010

Overhaul the nation's health insurance system	YES
Allow for repeal of "don't ask, don't tell"	YES
Overhaul financial services industry regulation	NO
Limit use of new Afghanistan War funds to troop withdrawal activities	NO
Change oversight of offshore drilling and lift oil spill liability cap	YES
Provide a path to legal status for some children of illegal immigrants	NO
Extend Bush-era income tax cuts for two years	NO

2009

Expand the Children's Health Insurance Program	YES
Provide $787 billion in tax cuts and spending increases to stimulate the economy	YES
Allow bankruptcy judges to modify certain primary-residence mortgages	YES
Create a cap-and-trade system to limit greenhouse gas emissions	YES
Provide $2 billion for the "cash for clunkers" program	YES
Establish the government as the sole provider of student loans	YES
Restrict federally funded insurance coverage for abortions in health care overhaul	YES

CQ Vote Studies

	PARTY UNITY		PRESIDENTIAL SUPPORT	
	Support	Oppose	Support	Oppose
2010	95%	5%	86%	14%
2009	94%	6%	90%	10%
2008	95%	5%	9%	91%
2007	96%	4%	8%	92%
2006	88%	12%	27%	73%

Interest Groups

	AFL-CIO	ADA	CCUS	ACU
2010	86%	85%	25%	8%
2009	95%	85%	40%	17%
2008	100%	100%	47%	13%
2007	100%	95%	47%	8%
2006	100%	85%	33%	21%

Ohio 9

North — Toledo, Sandusky

Along nearly 80 miles of Lake Erie's shoreline, the traditionally Democratic 9th moves east from Lucas County and Toledo into Cleveland's orbit in Lorain County. More than two-thirds of the district's population resides in Lucas. Outside of that county, farmland and vacation spots contribute to the local economy.

At the mouth of the Maumee River, the largest river flowing into the Great Lakes, Toledo still accounts for 46 percent of the 9th's residents despite a decade of population loss. Once nicknamed the "Glass City" because of its history in that industry, Toledo relied on auto manufacturing for decades. The city's blue-collar industries now struggle to provide enough jobs. Chrysler and General Motors once employed thousands of district residents, but production outlook for the local plants remains uncertain. The city's health care sector has grown due in part to the merger of the University of Toledo and the Medical University of Ohio.

Agriculture is important to the 9th, with greenhouse and fruit production leading the way, but tourism is a key secondary economy. Sandusky's Cedar Point Amusement Park attracts more than 3 million visitors annually to its 364-acre park and resort; it claims the most rides (75) and roller coasters (17) of any park in the world. In addition, millions of visitors travel to Lake Erie's Bass Islands each year, and Penn National Gaming plans to open a casino in Toledo in early 2012.

Toledo's large concentrations of ethnic blue-collar workers — Germans, Irish, Poles, Hungarians and Hispanics — make it a lonely Democratic outpost in rural, Republican northwestern Ohio. The 9th's easternmost county of Lorain (shared with the 13th) leans Democratic and takes in the strongly liberal area around Oberlin College. The district's Republicans tend to live in affluent suburbs on Toledo's west side, but are not enough to sway the district's vote at the federal level. Overall, the 9th gave Barack Obama 62 percent of its 2008 presidential vote.

Major Industry
Agriculture, health care, tourism

Cities
Toledo, 287,208; Sandusky, 25,793; Oregon, 20,291

Notable
Oberlin College, founded in 1833, was the first co-educational institution of higher learning in the United States.

Rep. Dennis J. Kucinich (D)

Capitol Office
225-5871
www.house.gov/kucinich
2445 Rayburn Bldg. 20515-3510; fax 225-5745

Committees
Education & the Workforce
Oversight & Government Reform

Residence
Cleveland

Born
Oct. 8, 1946; Cleveland, Ohio

Religion
Roman Catholic

Family
Wife, Elizabeth Kucinich; one child

Education
Case Western Reserve U., B.A., M.A. 1973 (speech communications)

Career
Video producer; public utility consultant; sportswriter

Political Highlights
Cleveland City Council, 1969-75; Democratic nominee for U.S. House, 1972; independent candidate for U.S. House, 1974; mayor of Cleveland, 1977-79; defeated for re-election as mayor of Cleveland, 1979; Cleveland City Council, 1983-85; sought Democratic nomination for U.S. House, 1988, 1992; Ohio Senate, 1995-97; sought Democratic nomination for president, 2004, 2008

ELECTION RESULTS

2010 GENERAL

Dennis J. Kucinich (D)	101,340	53.0%
Peter Corrigan (R)	83,807	43.9%
Jeff Goggins (LIBERT)	5,874	3.1%

2010 PRIMARY

Dennis J. Kucinich (D)	unopposed

2008 GENERAL

Dennis J. Kucinich (D)	157,268	57.0%
Jim Trakas (R)	107,918	39.1%
Paul Conroy (LIBERT)	10,623	3.8%

Previous Winning Percentages
2006 (66%); 2004 (60%); 2002 (74%); 2000 (75%); 1998 (67%); 1996 (49%)

Elected 1996; 8th term

Kucinich is the liberals' liberal. A scrappy, pro-labor and anti-war Midwestern populist, he doesn't let an absence of support from his party's leadership blunt his drive to push the Democratic Party, and the country at large, to the left. Among the mementos he keeps in his office is a script from the play "Man of La Mancha" — fitting for a lawmaker who engages in many quixotic quests.

Kucinich (ku-SIN-itch) is an occasional target of right-wing ridicule for his ideas, which include the creation of a Department of Peace, and for his lifestyle. He meditates, is a practicing vegan and enjoys a New Age crowd of admirers that includes actress Shirley MacLaine. But his stands on labor issues help keep him popular in his district, which includes the western part of Cleveland and some of its suburbs.

His abortive runs for president in 2004 and 2008, and a wedding in between to Elizabeth Harper, a British consultant for a monetary think tank who is three decades his junior, have broadened his fan base well beyond that of other lawmakers.

What remains to be seen is how successfully Kucinich sustains that base with the Democrats out of power in the House, and with a Democratic president who won strong support from liberals instead of a Republican president unpopular with them.

Also remaining to be seen is whether Kucinich decides to challenge President Obama in 2012 — many of the liberals who backed Obama in 2008 have grown restive about some of his actions, from increasing U.S. forces in Afghanistan to accepting an extension of the 2001 and 2003 tax cuts. Another unknown is whether Kucinich will be deprived of a district in the 2012 elections. The 2010 census will cost Ohio two congressional seats, and with state Republicans controlling the redistricting process, his may be targeted for elimination.

He backed most of Obama's early legislative initiatives, but he was critical of plans to withdraw combat forces from Iraq by 2010 while sending more to Afghanistan. "We're accelerating a war there instead of getting out," he told MSNBC in April 2009. "I think it's very dangerous." He was one of 17 Democrats to oppose the fiscal 2010 budget proposal, objecting to its funding for the wars.

Kucinich continued his crusade in 2010, dissenting from a war-funding bill and offering separate resolutions that year that would require the withdrawal of U.S. troops from Afghanistan and Pakistan.

In early 2011, he was critical of the U.S. military intervention in the fighting in Libya and suggested it might be an impeachable offense in the absence of congressional approval. He was not impressed by promises to turn the bulk of the fighting over to NATO.

"When you look at the Obama administration saying it is passing it off to NATO, it's still going to be run out of Washington," he said on Fox Business Network. "It will still be U.S. tax dollars that are helping to run the operation. And we need to find out if any of our pilots and our sailors are going to be involved in this. And finally, they're still going to have to come back to Congress to get authorization to participate with NATO."

He and Texas Republican Ron Paul, a frequent libertarian critic of U.S. foreign policy, backed a proposal to bar funding for the mission.

Kucinich serves on the Oversight and Government Reform Committee, where he chaired the Domestic Policy Subcommittee in the 111th Congress

(2009-10). His panel held hearings on topics as diverse as the possible links between cell phone use and tumors and the $700 billion financial services industry rescue — a measure he opposed in 2008. For a few weeks in late 2010, Kucinich campaigned to be the top Democrat on the committee in the 112th Congress (2011-12), but he ultimately withdrew the bid.

As a member of the Education and Labor Committee (renamed Education and the Workforce for the 112th), Kucinich has scored some legislative wins. In 2007, he won the inclusion of worker protection provisions in a NASA reauthorization bill. He wrote provisions in a 2008 energy bill aimed at establishing jobs and training programs for people to evaluate the energy efficiency of buildings.

On health care, Kucinich championed a single-payer system and came late to support of Obama's overhaul proposal in 2010. Health care and the withdrawal of American troops from Iraq were the most salient issues in each of his White House runs. After garnering little support in the early nominating contests in Iowa and New Hampshire, however, Kucinich dropped his second bid for the presidency in January 2008 in order to defend his House seat against four challengers in a Democratic primary.

Kucinich distinguishes himself not only by his perseverance but also by his rhetorical flourishes and self-deprecating wit. When he arrived in Congress, he handed out trading cards featuring himself as a 4-foot-9-inch, 97-pound backup high school quarterback in 1960.

The son of a truck driver who was often out of work, Kucinich and his six siblings moved frequently and sometimes slept in the family car. He worked two jobs to put himself through college, getting a master's degree in speech communications and launching a career as a copy editor, sportswriter and political commentator. Kucinich also has been a hospital orderly and a teacher.

Elected mayor of Cleveland at 31, he served a single term, during which the city fell into financial default after Kucinich refused to sell off the city's power company, Muny Light, as a condition of getting bank credit. In 1978 he barely survived a recall vote, and the next year lost to Republican George V. Voinovich. But later Kucinich won praise for not selling Muny Light and, bucking the GOP tide in 1994, he seized a state Senate seat from a Republican incumbent. Two years later, he toppled two-term Republican Rep. Martin R. Hoke. It was Kucinich's fifth try for Congress, a quest he began as an anti-Vietnam War candidate in 1972. He has won subsequent elections relatively easily. He faces the possibility of being a man without a district in 2012, and has suggested he might run for a House seat in Washington state if redistricting in Ohio eliminates his current base.

Key Votes

2010

Overhaul the nation's health insurance system	YES
Allow for repeal of "don't ask, don't tell"	YES
Overhaul financial services industry regulation	YES
Limit use of new Afghanistan War funds to troop withdrawal activities	YES
Change oversight of offshore drilling and lift oil spill liability cap	YES
Provide a path to legal status for some children of illegal immigrants	YES
Extend Bush-era income tax cuts for two years	YES

2009

Expand the Children's Health Insurance Program	YES
Provide $787 billion in tax cuts and spending increases to stimulate the economy	YES
Allow bankruptcy judges to modify certain primary-residence mortgages	YES
Create a cap-and-trade system to limit greenhouse gas emissions	NO
Provide $2 billion for the "cash for clunkers" program	YES
Establish the government as the sole provider of student loans	YES
Restrict federally funded insurance coverage for abortions in health care overhaul	NO

CQ Vote Studies

	PARTY UNITY		PRESIDENTIAL SUPPORT	
	SUPPORT	OPPOSE	SUPPORT	OPPOSE
2010	92%	8%	83%	17%
2009	90%	10%	82%	18%
2008	91%	9%	20%	80%
2007	94%	6%	14%	86%
2006	97%	3%	13%	87%

Interest Groups

	AFL-CIO	ADA	CCUS	ACU
2010	100%	90%	25%	0%
2009	81%	75%	60%	12%
2008	93%	95%	39%	8%
2007	89%	70%	35%	4%
2006	93%	100%	20%	4%

Ohio 10
Cleveland — West Side and suburbs

Taking in the western portion of Cleveland, the 10th follows the migration of its ethnic residents into the western and southern suburbs. The line between the 10th and 11th districts generally divides Cleveland's white and black neighborhoods. The 10th contains large concentrations of ethnic voters, including Poles and immigrants from a multitude of other Eastern European countries, as well as a growing Hispanic population. A decade of population loss in Cleveland has left the district one of the nation's least-populous ahead of decennial remapping.

Once solely dependent on manufacturing, this Democratic district has gradually made the transition to a service economy, with growth in the banking and financial services sectors as well. Although manufacturing is still the backbone of the city's economy, the 10th has attracted smaller technology companies, and Cleveland has undergone a decades-long downtown restoration. The 10th also is home to Cleveland Hopkins International Airport.

The immediate suburbs have a strong union presence and a Democratic tilt. Traditionally Democratic-leaning, middle-income communities that abut western Cleveland, such as Brooklyn and Lakewood, are losing population.

A blue-collar tradition in Brook Park makes that city decidedly Democratic. Brook Park's Ford auto plant has been repeatedly shut down and re-opened, but the plant now builds fuel-efficient engines and residents hope that the auto industry, once a regional economic driver, will continue to provide jobs. Farther west, incomes rise, as does the level of Republicanism: Bay Village, Westlake and Rocky River residents have above-average incomes.

The strong Democratic tendencies of Cleveland — matched up against the GOP lean of some of Cleveland's western and southern suburbs — give the 10th a decided but not overwhelming Democratic tilt. Barack Obama won 59 percent of the district's presidential vote in 2008.

Major Industry
Manufacturing, banking, technology

Cities
Cleveland (pt.), 169,820; Parma, 81,601; Lakewood, 52,131; Westlake, 32,729; North Olmsted, 32,718; Garfield Heights (pt.), 25,236

Notable
Cleveland is home to NASA's Glenn Research Center.

Rep. Marcia L. Fudge (D)

Capitol Office
225-7032
fudge.house.gov
1019 Longworth Bldg. 20515; fax 225-1339

Committees
Agriculture
Science, Space & Technology

Residence
Warrensville Heights

Born
Oct. 29, 1952; Cleveland, Ohio

Religion
Baptist

Family
Single

Education
Ohio State U., B.S. 1975 (business administration);
Cleveland State U., J.D. 1983

Career
Congressional aide; county government finance
administrator; sales and marketing representative;
law clerk

Political Highlights
Mayor of Warrensville Heights, 2000-08

ELECTION RESULTS

2010 GENERAL

Marcia L. Fudge (D)	139,684	82.9%
Thomas Pekarek (R)	28,752	17.1%

2010 PRIMARY

Marcia L. Fudge (D)	47,773	85.4%
Daniel W. Reilly (D)	5,385	9.6%
Isaac Powell (D)	2,783	5.0%

2008 SPECIAL

Marcia L. Fudge (D)	unopposed

2008 GENERAL

Marcia L. Fudge (D)	212,667	85.2%
Thomas Pekarek (R)	36,708	14.7%

Elected 2008; 2nd full term

Fudge has made a smooth transition from congressional aide — she served as chief of staff in the 1990s to her predecessor, the late Rep. Stephanie Tubbs Jones — to lawmaker. She combines problem-solving experience, honed as mayor of a Cleveland suburb, with a liberal world view.

Fudge has seats on the Agriculture and the Science, Space and Technology committees, but she has focused considerable attention on trying to alter the congressional ethics regime.

In 2010, she introduced legislation that would have set up new restrictions on when the Office of Congressional Ethics, established by the Democratic-led House in 2008, could open an investigation and would have required new standards for it to refer matters to the ethics committee.

"OCE is currently the accuser, judge and jury," Fudge said of the office, which pushed investigations of two high-profile black Democrats in 2010: Maxine Waters of California and former Ways and Means Chairman Charles B. Rangel of New York. "This isn't the case in the American justice system and it shouldn't be so in Congress."

Along with some other members of the Congressional Black Caucus, she said she would be open to shutting down the office in the 112th Congress (2011-12). "All options are on the table," she told Mother Jones magazine in December 2010. The new Republican leadership decided to keep the office.

On the legislative front, Fudge has worked to elevate Cleveland's public schools. She supported President Obama's $787 billion stimulus in 2009 in part because her district was expected to receive tens of millions of dollars for technology and updating infrastructure. As a former member of the Education and Labor (now Education and the Workforce) panel, Fudge looked for ways to aid research at Cleveland's Case Western Reserve University.

Fudge also is a strong backer of organized labor. Her mother, Marian Saffold, worked as a lab technician at a now-defunct Cleveland hospital and was one of the first black women to act as a union organizer for the American Federation of State, County and Municipal Employees. In early 2009, Fudge supported a Democratic bill, signed into law, that makes it easier for workers to bring wage discrimination lawsuits.

As mayor of Warrensville Heights, Fudge was credited with helping the city build 200 new homes and shore up a sagging retail base. Former Cleveland Mayor Jane Campbell described her to The Plain Dealer of Cleveland as "absolutely the hardest worker you have ever seen."

Like many Democrats in the Rust Belt manufacturing region, Fudge opposes free-trade deals. She joined other Ohio Democrats in early 2011 in opposition to a deal with South Korea that was backed by the Obama administration, arguing it would be bad for Ohio's auto industry.

She also aligned with the rest of her state's Democratic delegation in backing a 2008 bill to lend $14 billion to domestic automakers. Though the measure passed the House, it failed in the Senate.

Fudge's Science Committee assignment is important for an area with a robust aerospace industry, including the NASA Glenn Research Center in the nearby 10th District.

On the Agriculture Committee, a new assignment in the 112th Congress, Fudge is the ranking Democrat on the oversight subcommittee. Her urban/suburban district has virtually no farm interests, but she joins many in her party seeking to tackle global warming, a topic of interest for the panel. She supported legislation in 2009 to create a cap-and-trade system to limit carbon emissions. At the same time, she warns against requiring industry to do too much. "We must be aggressive enough to safeguard the environment, but not so overzealous that businesses cannot participate," Fudge told Investor's Business Daily in February 2009.

She credits her mother and maternal grandmother for getting her active in public service. When she was 10, Fudge went with a neighbor to see the Rev. Martin Luther King Jr. speak at the 1963 march on Washington. As a teenager she worked on the 1967 Cleveland mayoral bid of Carl Stokes, who became the first black mayor of a major U.S. city.

In high school she lettered in several sports and was named best female athlete in her class. She earned a business administration degree from Ohio State University in 1975 and eight years later earned a law degree from Cleveland State University.

In conversation, Fudge often talks about her allegiance to Delta Sigma Theta, a sorority of predominantly black college-educated women. It was through the Cleveland chapter that she met Tubbs Jones, who was known on Capitol Hill for wearing Delta Sigma Theta red. Fudge became a national president of the organization.

Her relationship with her predecessor blossomed in the early 1990s, when she worked under Tubbs Jones, who was then Cuyahoga County prosecutor. When Tubbs Jones was elected to Congress, Fudge became her chief of staff. She then won a 2000 mayoral race for Warrensville Heights.

When Tubbs Jones died in August 2008 after suffering an aneurysm, Fudge emerged as the front-runner to replace her. She won the backing of Cleveland Mayor Frank Jackson and former Ohio Democratic Rep. Louis Stokes as well as Tubbs Jones' sister, Barbara Tubbs Walker, who told The Plain Dealer she saw Fudge as "very talented and diverse and inclusive — she can bring the district together."

Tubbs Jones died after winning the Democratic nomination for the seat, so the Cuyahoga County Democratic Party's executive committee was charged with choosing her replacement for the November ballot. Fudge finished with 175 of the 280 committee members' votes in September, well ahead of runner-up C. J. Prentiss, a former Ohio Senate minority leader.

Fudge also won the special primary election to finish out the final weeks of Tubbs Jones' term, handily defeating nine other challengers with 74 percent of the vote, and was unopposed in the special's general election. In the November general election for her own two-year term, she trounced her GOP opponent, retired Naval reservist Thomas Pekarek, whom she defeated again in 2010.

Key Votes

2010

Overhaul the nation's health insurance system	YES
Allow for repeal of "don't ask, don't tell"	YES
Overhaul financial services industry regulation	YES
Limit use of new Afghanistan War funds to troop withdrawal activities	YES
Change oversight of offshore drilling and lift oil spill liability cap	YES
Provide a path to legal status for some children of illegal immigrants	YES
Extend Bush-era income tax cuts for two years	NO

2009

Expand the Children's Health Insurance Program	YES
Provide $787 billion in tax cuts and spending increases to stimulate the economy	YES
Allow bankruptcy judges to modify certain primary-residence mortgages	YES
Create a cap-and-trade system to limit greenhouse gas emissions	YES
Provide $2 billion for the "cash for clunkers" program	YES
Establish the government as the sole provider of student loans	YES
Restrict federally funded insurance coverage for abortions in health care overhaul	NO

CQ Vote Studies

	PARTY UNITY		PRESIDENTIAL SUPPORT	
	Support	Oppose	Support	Oppose
2010	98%	2%	83%	17%
2009	99%	1%	98%	2%
2008	100%	0%	100%	0%

Interest Groups

	AFL-CIO	ADA	CCUS	ACU
2010	93%	95%	25%	4%
2009	100%	100%	33%	0%
2008	100%			0%

Ohio 11

Cleveland — East Side and suburbs

The 11th is a diverse district economically and ethnically, although more than 90,000 residents have left since 2000. In addition to its African-American majority, the district also includes a substantial Jewish population. The district takes in poor, inner-city areas of Cleveland's East Side, as well as the city's downtown destinations, and extends eastward into various historic neighborhoods such as Little Italy and some upper-middle-class suburbs. The 11th takes in more than half of the residents of Cleveland — most of the district's black residents live in poverty-riddled inner-city neighborhoods, and the district overall has Ohio's lowest median household income. The district's black majority and liberal suburbanites combine to make it very Democratic.

University Circle is Cleveland's cultural center and home to Case Western Reserve University, the Cleveland Orchestra and the Cleveland Museum of Art. The Circle also is the heart of Cleveland's health care industry, taking in the University Hospitals of Cleveland, Cleveland Clinic and Louis Stokes Veterans Affairs Medical Center. Suburban growth west and south

of Cuyahoga County drew businesses and residents out of the city, and economic stability here will depend on medical and biotech firms based in the Cleveland Health-Tech Corridor. Driving west along historic Euclid Avenue, the city's geographic center includes the Rock and Roll Hall of Fame, the city's sports stadiums and Public Square.

The upper-middle-class suburbs of Cleveland Heights, Shaker Heights, University Heights and Beachwood are home to large communities of Jews and young professionals, forming some of Ohio's most liberal and racially integrated areas. Farther east, the 11th takes in areas such as Mayfield Heights, Richmond Heights, Lyndhurst and Pepper Pike, which has one of Ohio's highest income levels.

Major Industry
Health care, manufacturing, higher education

Cities
Cleveland (pt.), 226,995; Euclid (pt.), 48,920; Cleveland Heights, 46,121; Shaker Heights, 28,448; Maple Heights, 23,138

Notable
A landmark 1926 case brought by the city of Euclid was the first U.S. Supreme Court decision to uphold city zoning ordinances.

Rep. Pat Tiberi (R)

Capitol Office
225-5355
www.house.gov/tiberi
106 Cannon Bldg. 20515-3512; fax 226-4523

Committees
Ways & Means
   (Select Revenue Measures - Chairman)

Residence
Genoa Township

Born
Oct. 21, 1962; Columbus, Ohio

Religion
Roman Catholic

Family
Wife, Denice Tiberi; four children

Education
Ohio State U., B.A. 1985 (journalism)

Career
Congressional district aide; Realtor

Political Highlights
Ohio House, 1993-2001 (majority leader, 1999-2001)

ELECTION RESULTS

2010 GENERAL

Pat Tiberi (R)	150,163	55.8%
Paula Brooks (D)	110,307	41.0%
Travis M. Irvine (LIBERT)	8,710	3.2%

2010 PRIMARY

Pat Tiberi (R)	53,632	86.4%
Andrew G. Zukowski (R)	8,442	13.6%

2008 GENERAL

Pat Tiberi (R)	197,447	54.8%
David Robinson (D)	152,234	42.2%
Steven Linnabary (LIBERT)	10,707	3.0%

Previous Winning Percentages
2006 (57%); 2004 (62%); 2002 (64%); 2000 (53%)

Elected 2000; 6th term

With friends in high places, Tiberi won a seat on the Ways and Means Committee in 2007. A strong advocate of lower tax rates, he is eager to exercise his authority as chairman of its tax-writing Select Revenue Measures Subcommittee in the 112th Congress.

He said the GOP victory in the 2010 elections presented "a window of opportunity to enact comprehensive tax reform, and we must take advantage of it." Tiberi blasted President Obama's fiscal 2012 budget, saying it "spends too much, borrows too much and taxes too much."

After Republicans' electoral victory but before they settled into the House majority, Tiberi backed a two-year extension of the Bush-era tax cuts enacted in late 2010 while dismissing concerns that extending the cuts could add to the federal deficit. "Only in Washington, D.C., can it cost money to extend current law," Tiberi said.

Tiberi (TEA-berry) grew up in a Democratic household with an immigrant father who lost his blue-collar job, and works across the aisle on some matters. But he's a GOP loyalist with close ties to Speaker John A. Boehner. They not only hail from the same state, they also worked together on the Education and the Workforce Committee, which Boehner chaired during most of the George W. Bush administration.

Tiberi helped Boehner defeat Missouri Republican Roy Blunt in a tense intraparty fight for the No. 2 GOP leadership post in 2006 and backed Boehner again as he defeated conservative Mike Pence of Indiana to become minority leader in the 110th Congress (2007-08).

In his first two terms, Tiberi was a dependable supporter of Bush and the GOP leadership, but that changed as Bush's popularity dropped and Tiberi faced stiffer challenges at home. In the 109th Congress (2005-06), he expressed skepticism about Bush's proposal to create private investment accounts in Social Security and voted to prohibit cruel or degrading treatment of U.S. detainees.

During the 110th Congress, he voted for several major Democratic bills, including a measure to boost vehicle fuel-efficiency standards, one version of an expanded children's health insurance program, and legislation to combat foreclosures and stabilize Fannie Mae and Freddie Mac. He was one of 35 House Republicans to support a bill that sought to outlaw employment discrimination based on sexual orientation. He followed through in 2009, one of 40 House Republicans to support the children's health insurance expansion that President Obama signed early in his term.

Aside from those notable exceptions, though, Tiberi has been a loyal foot soldier. His annual party unity score — the percentage of votes on which he sided with a majority of Republicans against a majority of Democrats — has never fallen below 90. He opposed the Democrats' health care overhaul in the 111th Congress (2009-10). Tiberi criticized the Obama administration for arguing during legislative debate that the provision imposing an individual mandate for the purchase of health insurance was not a tax, then reversing position when defending the law in court and arguing that it is a tax.

He blasted the Democrats' cap-and-trade bill aimed at reducing carbon emissions. "Not only would this bill tax nearly every person who has the audacity to turn on a light switch and force the cost of American-made products and services to increase, this measure is simply a job-killer," he said in 2009.

Tiberi voted for the 2005 Central America Free Trade Agreement, which squeaked through, 217-215. He also was one of 25 Republicans who opposed the initial $700 billion bill to aid the ailing financial services sector in fall 2008, but he voted for the final version after fervent pleas from Boehner and the Bush administration.

One of Tiberi's main legislative accomplishments was a bipartisan effort in the 109th Congress that renewed the Older Americans Act, which governs social services for senior citizens.

Tiberi is the eldest of three children of Italian immigrants. His parents arrived in the United States three years before he was born. His mother was a seamstress; his father was a machinist who lost his job and his pension when his company restructured. Tiberi was the first in his family to go to college.

He met his wife at a Northland High School marching band alumni gathering: He played trumpet; she played flute. Tiberi, who was senior class president, says he had no interest in politics as a career until a political science class at Ohio State University led to an internship in the Columbus office of Republican Rep. John R. Kasich. At that point, he became a Republican.

He spent eight years handling constituent casework for Kasich. In 1992, state legislative district remapping created an open seat in his neighborhood. He won that election and spent four terms in the state House, rising to majority leader in 1999 and earning a reputation as a conservative willing to work with Democrats. He established a DNA database to track violent criminals and was a prime mover behind a state law that, for a time, limited large jury awards but later was ruled unconstitutional.

Barred by Ohio term limits from seeking re-election to the General Assembly in 2000, Tiberi was considering a career change when Kasich announced he was leaving the House. Kasich's support — and Boehner's backing — helped Tiberi cruise to an easy primary victory over three rivals. Democrats put up Columbus City Councilwoman Maryellen O'Shaughnessy, but Tiberi racked up big margins in the suburban GOP strongholds of Delaware and Licking counties and won by 9 percentage points.

In 2005, Tiberi helped Ohio Republicans defeat a ballot initiative that would have changed the redistricting process in a way that could have cost the GOP seats. As a token of gratitude, Thomas M. Reynolds of New York, then chairman of the National Republican Congressional Committee, gave Tiberi a framed map of the state signed by Ohio's GOP lawmakers. Every Ohio Republican incumbent on the November ballot won re-election in 2006.

Tiberi took 57 percent of the vote that year, defeating Bob Shamansky, a former one-term House member. He won again easily in 2008, despite Obama carrying his district by 10 percentage points, and breezed again in 2010.

Key Votes

2010

Overhaul the nation's health insurance system	NO
Allow for repeal of "don't ask, don't tell"	NO
Overhaul financial services industry regulation	NO
Limit use of new Afghanistan War funds to troop withdrawal activities	NO
Change oversight of offshore drilling and lift oil spill liability cap	NO
Provide a path to legal status for some children of illegal immigrants	NO
Extend Bush-era income tax cuts for two years	YES

2009

Expand the Children's Health Insurance Program	YES
Provide $787 billion in tax cuts and spending increases to stimulate the economy	NO
Allow bankruptcy judges to modify certain primary-residence mortgages	NO
Create a cap-and-trade system to limit greenhouse gas emissions	NO
Provide $2 billion for the "cash for clunkers" program	YES
Establish the government as the sole provider of student loans	NO
Restrict federally funded insurance coverage for abortions in health care overhaul	YES

CQ Vote Studies

	PARTY UNITY		PRESIDENTIAL SUPPORT	
	SUPPORT	OPPOSE	SUPPORT	OPPOSE
2010	91%	9%	33%	67%
2009	90%	10%	41%	59%
2008	92%	8%	60%	40%
2007	91%	9%	77%	23%
2006	92%	8%	87%	13%

Interest Groups

	AFL-CIO	ADA	CCUS	ACU
2010	7%	0%	88%	96%
2009	24%	15%	87%	83%
2008	40%	35%	94%	72%
2007	29%	20%	85%	88%
2006	36%	0%	100%	84%

Ohio 12

Central — Eastern Columbus and suburbs

The 12th includes the eastern half of Columbus in Franklin County and suburban counties to the north and east of the city. North of Franklin, Delaware is the state's fastest-growing county over the last decade, and the district overall added more than 125,000 residents. The district has a slight Republican lean, with a strong GOP influence in the suburbs balancing a Democratic tilt in Columbus.

The 12th's economy relies heavily on Columbus' business sector. The city hosts headquarters for several national chains, and the local economy has remained relatively stable. The service economy has led to significant growth in both the city and its adjacent areas over the past two decades. The district overall has the highest percentage of white-collar workers and college-educated residents in the state.

Democrats find support in the urban, largely black part of the district in Columbus. Within Franklin County, but outside Columbus, the 12th includes Dublin, an upscale, solidly GOP suburb in the northwest part of the county known to many as the headquarters of Wendy's. Dublin also is home to health care manufacturer Cardinal Health. Westerville, Gahanna

and Reynoldsburg — traditionally Republican areas outside Columbus — have shown some signs of Democratic support.

Delaware County, where the population has far more than doubled since 1990, has the state's lowest unemployment rate and its highest household income.

Republicans there and in western Licking County, whose numbers are swelling as a result of steady population growth, offset the Democrats in Franklin County.

John McCain took 59 percent of the 2008 presidential vote in Delaware County and 56 percent in Licking (shared with the 18th). But a strong showing in Franklin was enough for Democrat Barack Obama to win the district's overall vote with 54 percent.

Major Industry
Financial services, government, manufacturing, service

Cities
Columbus (pt.), 308,633; Dublin (pt.), 39,385; Westerville, 36,120; Reynoldsburg (pt.), 34,983; Delaware, 34,753; Gahanna, 33,248

Notable
The Anti-Saloon League, which lobbied successfully for Prohibition, was based in Westerville beginning in 1909.

Rep. Betty Sutton (D)

Capitol Office
225-3401
sutton.house.gov
1519 Longworth Bldg. 20515-3513; fax 225-2266

Committees
Armed Services
Natural Resources

Residence
Copley Township

Born
July 31, 1963; Barberton, Ohio

Religion
Methodist

Family
Husband, Doug Corwon; two stepchildren

Education
Kent State U., B.A. 1985 (political science); U. of Akron, J.D. 1990

Career
Lawyer; campaign aide; modeling school administrator

Political Highlights
Barberton City Council, 1990-91; Summit County Council, 1991-92 (vice president, 1992); Ohio House, 1993-2000

ELECTION RESULTS

2010 GENERAL

Betty Sutton (D)	118,806	55.7%
Tom Ganley (R)	94,367	44.3%

2010 PRIMARY

Betty Sutton (D)	37,460	79.4%
Justin P. Wooden (D)	9,706	20.6%

2008 GENERAL

Betty Sutton (D)	192,593	64.7%
David Potter (R)	105,050	35.3%

2008 PRIMARY

Betty Sutton (D)	unopposed

Previous Winning Percentages
2006 (61%)

Elected 2006; 3rd term

A former labor lawyer, Sutton speaks the populist language of the Democratic left, bemoaning conservative economic policies that she says benefit the few at the expense of the many.

Sutton rails against what she calls greedy insurance and oil companies, and she strongly advocates using the power of the federal government to intervene in markets in an effort to assist her middle-class constituents.

Sutton, a member of the Populist Caucus, represents a classic Rust Belt district that has been hit hard by the loss of manufacturing jobs. She opposes most free-trade agreements, including one struck by the Obama administration with South Korea.

She was an enthusiastic supporter of the "cash for clunkers" measure enacted in 2009 to give a boost to the auto industry. She also pushed Japan to include U.S. imports in its similar program.

Sutton had supported a bill in late 2008 to rescue the auto industry, and when that measure stalled in the Senate she backed President George W. Bush's move to use funds from a financial-industry rescue law signed earlier in the year. Sutton originally had opposed that bill, which provided $700 billion to shore up the nation's financial services sector, but supported it on a second vote.

From her former perch on the powerful Energy and Commerce Committee — she had to leave the panel in the wake of Democratic losses in the 2010 election — Sutton played a role in the contentious energy and health care debates of the past few years. A favorite cause has been holding down the price of gasoline. But, as a loyal Democrat, she also opposes expanded oil drilling on public lands and backed the party's energy legislation in 2009 that would have established a cap-and-trade system for carbon emissions, a bill that critics said would drive up energy prices.

A member of the Natural Resources Committee in the 112th Congress (2011-12), she also sponsored legislation that would charge oil companies a fee for unused offshore leases or revoke the lease if the company doesn't pay. Money raised by the fee would be used to subsidize production of energy from renewable fuels.

Sutton was a vocal proponent of including a government-run "public option" in the Democrats' health care overhaul legislation. She didn't succeed, but supported the final measure, saying "this is the moment when we will finally take the long-overdue step of ending the unconscionable practices of the insurance companies, who through their greed and disregard have enjoyed record profits even as American families have suffered, sometimes fatally because of their actions."

Sutton got her initiation into the House by sitting on the leadership-dominated Rules Committee during her first term, before moving to Energy and Commerce, and she almost always votes with her party's leadership — 99 percent of the time in 2008 and 2009, and only slightly less often in 2007 and 2010.

In the new Congress, she took a seat on the Armed Services Committee.

During the 110th Congress (2007-08) Sutton strongly pushed for setting a timeline for withdrawal of U.S. troops from Iraq. Then, concerned about soldiers kept on active duty after their enlistment period ended, she secured passage of a bill to ensure financial compensation for the soldiers. She said instead of forcing soldiers to serve, the military should improve its recruitment efforts. Her measure became law as part of a fiscal 2009 spending bill. Defense Secretary Robert M. Gates announced in March 2009 the department would end the practice of extending soldiers' duty.

The youngest in a family of six children, Sutton was reared in Barberton, a suburb of Akron. Her mother was clerk-treasurer for the city library, while her father worked in a boilermaker factory despite having a degree for teaching history.

Sutton's father died of lung cancer during her first year of law school. She said her father was concerned that his youngest child needed a stronger background than a political science degree. "I told him, 'It's OK, Dad, because I am going to run for office.' " The next year, she ran a door-to-door campaign and won a seat on the Barberton City Council. She then moved to the Summit County Council and later ran successfully for a seat in the Ohio House.

In Columbus, Sutton was known to alert the press of closed-door gatherings between lobbyists and legislators. When ethics became a campaign theme for Democrats in 2006, Sutton quickly touted her record. And while pushing two domestic violence bills in the 1990s, she testified before the state legislature about her own history of being in an abusive first marriage. "There were people who said, 'If you deal with domestic violence, they will pigeonhole you.' I said, 'The fact I know about this means I have to do it.' " Sutton has since married a retired firefighter, and her Capitol Hill office is adorned with firefighter memorabilia.

In the race to replace Democrat Sherrod Brown, now Ohio's senior senator, Sutton was one of 17 candidates, eight of them Democrats. She earned her party's nod by defeating former Rep. Tom Sawyer, shopping mall heiress Capri S. Cafaro and Gary J. Kucinich, a former Cleveland city councilman and brother of Democrat Dennis J. Kucinich, who represents the 10th District.

Throughout the campaign she criticized Sawyer's support for the 1993 North American Free Trade Agreement. Taking 31 percent of the vote, Sutton wound up winning the primary, which was a major victory for EMILY's List, a group that backs Democratic female candidates who support abortion rights.

In the 2006 general election, Sutton continued to campaign on a six-point anti-corruption platform against her GOP opponent, Lorain Mayor Craig Foltin, who had a record of winning on Democratic turf. Foltin could not overcome the poor environment for the GOP nationwide, and Sutton posted a 22-percentage-point victory over Foltin. Two years later, she easily defeated Republican David Potter, a medical-device salesman.

In 2010, while a slew of other Ohio and Midwestern liberals were going down to defeat in the Republican wave, Sutton won again — albeit by a much smaller margin. She took 56 percent of the vote against GOP car dealer Tom Ganley, who faced allegations by two women that he had sexually harassed them.

Key Votes

2010

Overhaul the nation's health insurance system	YES
Allow for repeal of "don't ask, don't tell"	YES
Overhaul financial services industry regulation	YES
Limit use of new Afghanistan War funds to troop withdrawal activities	NO
Change oversight of offshore drilling and lift oil spill liability cap	YES
Provide a path to legal status for some children of illegal immigrants	YES
Extend Bush-era income tax cuts for two years	YES

2009

Expand the Children's Health Insurance Program	YES
Provide $787 billion in tax cuts and spending increases to stimulate the economy	YES
Allow bankruptcy judges to modify certain primary-residence mortgages	YES
Create a cap-and-trade system to limit greenhouse gas emissions	YES
Provide $2 billion for the "cash for clunkers" program	YES
Establish the government as the sole provider of student loans	YES
Restrict federally funded insurance coverage for abortions in health care overhaul	NO

CQ Vote Studies

	PARTY UNITY		PRESIDENTIAL SUPPORT	
	SUPPORT	OPPOSE	SUPPORT	OPPOSE
2010	98%	2%	93%	7%
2009	99%	1%	97%	3%
2008	99%	1%	13%	87%
2007	98%	2%	4%	96%

Interest Groups

	AFL-CIO	ADA	CCUS	ACU
2010	100%	95%	14%	0%
2009	100%	100%	33%	0%
2008	100%	100%	61%	4%
2007	96%	100%	55%	0%

Ohio 13

Northeast — parts of Akron and suburbs, Cleveland suburbs

The lightning-bolt-shaped 13th runs southwest from the shores of Lake Erie west of Cleveland, through the city's mostly middle-class suburbs to Akron (shared with 17th). Summit is the most populous county in the 13th, making up 42 percent of the population.

Many tire factories have left Akron, once known as the world's rubber capital, but Goodyear is building a new headquarters complex at the edge of the district. Akron remains a scientific research hub, and the University of Akron's College of Polymer Science and Polymer Engineering is located here.

The National Inventors Hall of Fame in Akron has opened a specialized math, science and technology public middle school on its campus. The city also hosts some of Ohio's leading health care providers, such as the Akron Children's Hospital.

The 13th takes in nearly 60 percent of Akron's residents, including much of its black population. The city's black and ethnic white residents, the University of Akron community and its blue-collar workforce help it retain a Democratic character.

Bordering Lake Erie at the 13th's other end is Lorain County, which has relied on large steel and medical device plants. A U.S. Steel facility in Lorain is expected to expand, and both construction at the plant and permanent factory positions will bring jobs. The 13th's portions of Lorain County include staunchly Democratic Lorain and Sheffield Lake and Democratic-leaning Elyria. Both Avon and Avon Lake are upper-middle-class and GOP-friendly.

In the district's middle are some GOP-leaning communities in southern Cuyahoga County and northern Medina County. But Summit and Lorain's dominance gives the 13th a decided Democratic tilt. Barack Obama received 57 percent of the district's presidential vote in 2008.

Major Industry
Polymer research, steel, health care

Cities
Akron (pt.), 117,894; Lorain, 64,097; Elyria (pt.), 54,456; Cuyahoga Falls (pt.), 39,349; Brunswick, 34,255; Strongsville (pt.), 30,556

Notable
The American Toy Marble Museum is in Akron.

Rep. Steven C. LaTourette (R)

Capitol Office
225-5731
www.house.gov/latourette
2371 Rayburn Bldg. 20515-3514; fax 225-3307

Committees
Appropriations

Residence
Bainbridge Township

Born
July 22, 1954; Cleveland, Ohio

Religion
Methodist

Family
Wife, Jennifer LaTourette; six children

Education
U. of Michigan, B.A. 1976 (history); Cleveland State
U., J.D. 1979

Career
Lawyer

Political Highlights
Candidate for Lake County prosecutor, 1984; Lake
County prosecutor, 1989-94

ELECTION RESULTS

2010 GENERAL

Steven C. LaTourette (R)	149,878	64.9%
Bill O'Neill (D)	72,604	31.4%
John M. Jelenic (LIBERT)	8,383	3.6%

2010 PRIMARY

Steven C. LaTourette (R)	unopposed

2008 GENERAL

Steven C. LaTourette (R)	188,488	58.3%
Bill O'Neill (D)	125,214	38.7%
David Macko (LIBERT)	9,511	2.9%

Previous Winning Percentages
2006 (58%); 2004 (63%); 2002 (72%); 2000 (65%);
1998 (66%); 1996 (55%); 1994 (48%)

Elected 1994; 9th term

A former prosecutor and public defender, LaTourette is a longtime ally of Speaker John A. Boehner, a fellow Ohio Republican. Like Boehner, the genial LaTourette navigates easily on both sides of the aisle, a trait that could serve him well in the Republican-led 112th Congress, where he is expected to play an important role as a trusted lieutenant.

More Main Street Chamber of Commerce than tea party, he has an ability to get along with Democrats that has helped him in northeast Ohio, an area where union sentiment remains strong. LaTourette has sometimes taken moderate positions on labor, health care and other social services issues.

When Republicans pushed to House passage early in 2011 a measure that would shut down a program that provides emergency loans to unemployed homeowners facing foreclosure, LaTourette was one of just two Republicans to oppose it.

A longtime member of the Appropriations Committee, he was a strong proponent of earmarks before his party imposed a moratorium on the practice. And he frequently played up funding he brought home from the spending panel and his former seat on the Transportation and Infrastructure Committee, including grants for fire departments and funds for the Route 8 freeway project.

LaTourette was instrumental in saving a major Pentagon financial accounting office in Cleveland during the last base closure round, and unlike many of his Republican colleagues he favors a high-speed rail corridor connecting Cleveland and Chicago. He also played a major role in enacting the establishment of an arbitration process that helped save hundreds of auto dealers that were scheduled to close in the wake of the recent financial crisis.

With his beard and spectacles, LaTourette looks like a college professor and employs the smooth, persuasive style of a lawyer making his closing argument on the floor. Some say he would make an ideal federal judge. He has earned a reputation for leading after-hours member groups; he was a co-chairman, with former Democratic Rep. James L. Oberstar of Minnesota, of the Northeast-Midwest Coalition and was a co-founder in 2008 of the short-lived Caucus on the Middle Class.

He often emphasizes his dissents with GOP leadership. As a member of the Financial Services Committee during the 110th Congress (2007-08), he served as one of the leaders of the opposition in the fall of 2008 to the $700 billion financial rescue package that later became law. He called for a smaller package of $250 billion, criticized tax breaks for makers of rum and children's wooden arrows, and argued for tax incentives to encourage companies to buy troubled investments from banks. "I'd rather have rich guys in three-piece suits buy up this bad mortgage debt and get a tax break for doing so than have taxpayers foot the bill," he said.

In late 2008, he fought a proposed acquisition of Cleveland-based National City Corp. by a beneficiary of the financial rescue law, Pittsburgh-based PNC Financial Services Group Inc.

He tilts to the center on some Democratic initiatives on education and social programs and on union-backed priorities, such as a 2007 minimum wage hike and a House-passed proposal to permit unions to organize workplaces with petition drives instead of secret-ballot elections. He opposed a failed amendment to a catchall spending bill for fiscal 2011 that would have prohibited the application of the Davis-Bacon Law, which requires contractors to pay union-scale wages, to projects paid for by the bill.

In March 2011, he was one of seven Republicans to oppose a House-passed measure to cut off federal funding of NPR.

Yet such votes have failed to engender much opposition on the right, partly because LaTourette has been a loyal GOP vote on almost every major issue. He voted against the health care overhaul in 2010, opposed cap-and-trade legislation in 2009, and supports House Republicans in their refusal to accept earmarks while pushing for a clearer definition.

LaTourette opposes abortion and voted in 2004 and 2006 to amend the Constitution to outlaw same-sex marriage. In 2010, he opposed repeal of the statutory ban on homosexuals serving openly in the military.

He is an ally of Boehner, but his relationship with the GOP leadership has not always been so cozy. In early 2005, GOP leaders removed LaTourette and other Republican members from the ethics committee for being too quick to admonish former Republican leader Tom DeLay of Texas for ethical lapses.

LaTourette was raised in a politically active home. His mother and grandmother volunteered for the Cleveland area's longtime GOP congresswoman, Frances Payne Bolton. His grandmother inspired one of his legislative efforts, a bill requiring sweepstakes mailers to disclose the slim odds of winning. In her mid-80s, she had subscribed to Field and Stream magazine thinking it would boost her chances of winning.

In high school, he led a petition drive to permit students to wear jeans and grow facial hair — he has sported a beard since he was 18. Early in his House career, he allowed humor columnist Dave Barry to work as a volunteer press assistant and delivered a speech Barry wrote on tort overhaul: "As a lawyer, I am the last person to suggest that everybody in my profession is a money-grubbing, scum-sucking toad. The actual figure is only about 73 percent."

LaTourette was in his second term as Lake County prosecutor when he was asked by Republican leaders to run for Congress in 1994. Dubbing Democratic freshman Eric Fingerhut an out-of-touch liberal, LaTourette won by 5 percentage points.

LaTourette broke a term-limit pledge and continues to stress the importance of his seniority. In 2004, he survived a nasty re-election battle in which his personal life became an issue. After a messy divorce, LaTourette's ex-wife backed his Democratic opponent, shopping mall heiress Capri S. Cafaro. LaTourette later married his former chief of staff.

He has been re-elected by comfortable if not overwhelming margins. Even as Barack Obama carried Ohio in 2008, LaTourette easily beat former state appeals court judge Bill O'Neill. LaTourette repeated the feat against O'Neill in 2010, taking 65 percent of the vote.

Key Votes

2010

Vote	
Overhaul the nation's health insurance system	NO
Allow for repeal of "don't ask, don't tell"	NO
Overhaul financial services industry regulation	NO
Limit use of new Afghanistan War funds to troop withdrawal activities	NO
Change oversight of offshore drilling and lift oil spill liability cap	NO
Provide a path to legal status for some children of illegal immigrants	NO
Extend Bush-era income tax cuts for two years	YES

2009

Vote	
Expand the Children's Health Insurance Program	YES
Provide $787 billion in tax cuts and spending increases to stimulate the economy	NO
Allow bankruptcy judges to modify certain primary-residence mortgages	NO
Create a cap-and-trade system to limit greenhouse gas emissions	NO
Provide $2 billion for the "cash for clunkers" program	YES
Establish the government as the sole provider of student loans	NO
Restrict federally funded insurance coverage for abortions in health care overhaul	YES

CQ Vote Studies

	PARTY UNITY		PRESIDENTIAL SUPPORT	
	Support	Oppose	Support	Oppose
2010	80%	20%	44%	56%
2009	70%	30%	63%	37%
2008	82%	18%	46%	54%
2007	71%	29%	44%	56%
2006	82%	18%	73%	27%

Interest Groups

	AFL-CIO	ADA	CCUS	ACU
2010	23%	10%	88%	75%
2009	38%	25%	93%	68%
2008	73%	60%	76%	52%
2007	83%	55%	65%	52%
2006	50%	20%	93%	72%

Ohio 14

Northeast — Cleveland and Akron suburbs

The 14th District moves eastward along the Lake Erie shoreline from just outside Cleveland to the Pennsylvania border in the state's northeastern corner. The depressed far northeastern communities remain reliant on the ailing steel, chemical and auto manufacturing industries. Some former Cleveland residents have moved into Lake and Geauga counties from the city, and wealthy suburban residents help give the district the state's highest median household income.

The 14th's portion of Cuyahoga County includes the upscale villages of Bentleyville and Moreland Hills in the east, while Progressive Insurance is based in Mayfield Village. The district's lakeshore region in Lake and Ashtabula counties is home to fruit farms and much of Ohio's wine grape acreage. Despite being Ohio's smallest county in land area, Lake holds more than 35 percent of the district's residents. Chemical company Lubrizol has its headquarters in Wickliffe, which also is a manufacturing site for ABB, a power and automation technologies company.

South of Lake, the district takes in all of Geauga County — a Republican-leaning, affluent, well-educated area — and northern Portage County. Geauga lost the corporate headquarters and three factories for KraftMaid Cabinetry in 2010, but unemployment remains relatively low in the county. The 14th also includes northern Trumbull County and northeastern Summit County, taking in Stow and Twinsburg, where years of auto manufacturing job losses have rocked the local workforce.

In Lake, Republicans generally perform well in areas south of Mentor, such as Kirtland and Kirtland Hills, which are overwhelmingly wealthy and white. Democrats can do well in Painesville, where nearly half of Lake's blacks and Hispanics live. The 14th's Republican lean was just enough to give John McCain the district's presidential vote in the 2008 election — he won here by less than 1 percentage point.

Major Industry
Health care, chemicals, manufacturing

Cities
Mentor, 47,159; Stow, 34,837; Solon, 23,348; Willoughby, 22,268

Notable
Twinsburg calls its annual August gathering of twins the world's largest.

Rep. Steve Stivers (R)

Capitol Office
225-2015
stivers.house.gov
1007 Longworth Bldg. 20515-3515; fax 225-3529

Committees
Financial Services

Residence
Columbus

Born
March 24, 1965; Cincinnati, Ohio

Religion
United Methodist

Family
Wife, Karen Stivers; one child

Education
Ohio State U., B.A. 1989 (international studies), M.B.A. 1996

Military
Ohio Army National Guard, 1988-present

Career
Lobbyist; securities company executive; county party official; campaign aide

Political Highlights
Ohio Senate, 2003-08; Republican nominee for U.S. House, 2008

ELECTION RESULTS

2010 GENERAL

Steve Stivers (R)	119,471	54.2%
Mary Jo Kilroy (D)	91,077	41.3%
William Kammerer (LIBERT)	6,116	2.8%
David Ryon (CNSTP)	3,887	1.8%

2010 PRIMARY

Steve Stivers (R)	39,963	82.3%
John Adams (R)	5,894	12.1%
Ralph A. Applegate (R)	2,708	5.6%

2008 PRIMARY

Steve Stivers (R)	33,838	65.9%
Robert Wagner (R)	17,499	34.1%

Elected 2010; 1st term

Stivers promotes himself as a budget hawk who wants to cut federal spending and supports giving line-item veto authority to the president.

He backed the catchall spending bill the House passed in early 2011 that would have cut spending by $58 billion, but he opposed a number of amendments that would have cut even deeper. He then supported the April bill, which cut nearly $40 billion, that provided funding for the remainder of fiscal 2011.

And, while saying entitlement changes need to be on the table, he said during the campaign that he would oppose efforts to raise the retirement age for Social Security. "The promises made to our seniors must be promises kept," he said. He suggests costs can be cut by eliminating waste and fraud.

A member of the Financial Services Committee, he stresses the need "to give business more certainty so they will be willing to invest in their business and create jobs." To that end, he pushed legislation early in the 112th Congress (2011-12) to repeal a provision of the financial services overhaul enacted in 2010 that increased the legal liability of credit rating agencies and, Stivers said, hurt the asset-backed securities market, which is important to the auto industry.

A one-time supporter of a cap-and-trade system aimed at reducing carbon emissions, Stivers has abandoned that idea, the Columbus Dispatch reported. Instead he favors federal aid to boost nuclear power, clean coal and renewable fuels.

He has taken some other centrist stands. Stivers supports abortion rights, though he favors parental notification laws. He was one of 21 Republicans who opposed an amendment to a fiscal 2011 omnibus spending bill to bar funds for renovations at the U.N. headquarters in New York.

Stivers is a lieutenant colonel in the Ohio Army National Guard, where he has served for more than two decades. He also spent five years in the state Senate and worked as a banker in the private sector.

Stivers lost to Democrat Mary Jo Kilroy by about 2,300 votes in 2008. In their 2010 rematch, he was able to tie her to Obama administration policies unpopular in the GOP-leaning district and won by 13 percentage points.

Ohio 15
Western Columbus and suburbs

The 15th is centered in Franklin County and on Columbus, the state's centrally located capital. It takes in most of Columbus, including all of the city that lies west of High Street, a major north-south thoroughfare.

Ohio State University, one of the nation's largest universities and a key regional employer and research hub, is located in the 15th's part of Columbus, as are the Capitol, City Hall, and stadiums for soccer's Crew and hockey's Blue Jackets.

Columbus is not known as a tourist destination, but crowds descend for Ohio State home football games and a new casino will draw visitors. Franklin County's technology and research centers aid the 15th's economy, and there are state government jobs in Columbus. Despite layoffs at corporate headquarters, the workforce is still mostly white-collar.

West of Franklin County, Madison County is a major corn- and soybean-producing area. Marysville, in Union County, is home to soybean fields, livestock and Honda auto and motorcycle plants that keep the city's economy rolling.

The politically competitive 15th's portion of Franklin, where more than 85 percent of district residents live, leans left. Ohio State's academic community and areas in the west side of Columbus support Democrats, but Republicans are strong in the suburbs. In 2008, Barack Obama won the 15th, despite John McCain's strong showing in rural, and dependably Republican, Madison and Union counties. Union County last voted for a Democratic presidential candidate in 1932.

Major Industry
Government, health care, higher education

Cities
Columbus (pt.), 410,178; Grove City, 35,575

Notable
A full-scale replica of Christopher Columbus' ship the *Santa Maria* is in Columbus.

Rep. James B. Renacci (R)

Capitol Office
225-3876
renacci.house.gov
130 Cannon Bldg. 20515-3516; fax 225 3059

Committees
Financial Services

Residence
Wadsworth

Born
Dec. 3, 1958; Monongahela, Pa.

Religion
Roman Catholic

Family
Wife, Tina Renacci; three children

Education
Indiana U. of Pennsylvania, B.S. 1980 (accounting)

Career
Business management consultant; professional arena football team executive; nursing homes owner; accountant

Political Highlights
Wadsworth Board of Zoning Appeals, 1994-95; Wadsworth City Council president, 2000-03; mayor of Wadsworth, 2004-07

ELECTION RESULTS

2010 GENERAL

James B. Renacci (R)	114,652	52.1%
John Boccieri (D)	90,833	41.3%
Jeffrey J. Blevins (LIBERT)	14,585	6.6%

2010 PRIMARY

James B. Renacci (R)	30,358	49.2%
Matt Miller (R)	24,322	39.4%
Paul R. Schiffer (R)	5,048	8.2%
H. Doyle Smith (R)	1,919	3.1%

Elected 2010; 1st term

Renacci, a sports entrepreneur, car dealer and mayor, is a bottom-line kind of guy, an accountant who got into politics because he thought government budgets could be better drafted and executed.

He touts his conservative social values — for example he opposes abortion and federal funding of stem cell research — but fiscal responsibility was the main impetus of his campaign, and he will apply his accountant's trade as a member of the Financial Services Committee.

He backed repeal of the 2010 health care overhaul early in 2011. "It's a job-killing bill. And the problem we have today is, we have got to create jobs, not the government. Entrepreneurship has to create jobs," he said on PBS.

A 1980 graduate of the Indiana University of Pennsylvania, Renacci (reh-NAY-see) got his start in business as an accountant for a large firm in Pittsburgh, where he kept the books for nursing home companies. He left for Ohio in 1984 and started his own nursing home, which grew into a small group of nursing facilities. Fifteen years later he sold the nursing homes after his election to the city council in Wadsworth.

Renacci's various business investments have included minor league professional sports teams. From 2003 to 2009 he was co-owner of the Columbus Destroyers, an Arena Football League team. He is still a minority owner of a minor league baseball team in California called the Lancaster JetHawks.

In 2004 he was elected mayor of Wadsworth, and during his four years in office he claimed credit for balancing the city's budget without a tax increase by making across-the-board spending cuts. He also lured commercial development to the area and touted his pro-growth, limited spending, low-tax policies.

Traditionally a GOP district, the Canton-based 16th was carried by Republican John McCain in the 2008 presidential race while the House seat held for 36 years by Republican Ralph Regula, who retired, flipped to the Democrats when John Boccieri won the open-seat race.

During the 2010 campaign, Democrats highlighted the story of a woman who died in one of the nursing facilities Renacci owned. Renacci filed court papers against a labor union for defamation in an advertising campaign. He won the election by a relatively comfortable margin of 52 percent of the vote to 41 percent for Boccieri.

Ohio 16

Northeast — Canton

Settled in the northeast quadrant of Ohio, the 16th features a contrast between rural areas, which make up roughly one-quarter of the district's land, and urban Canton. Canton, with a manufacturing and steel-producing history, has retained a high-skill manufacturing base despite several factory closures.

To help offset manufacturing job losses, city officials have supported a transition to retail and service-based employment. Major employers include Aultman Hospital and Timken, a steel bearings manufacturer that has planned expansion of its production plant in the city. Outside Canton, the district hosts several colleges and universities.

As Canton's population continues its nearly 60-year decline — it now accounts for less than one-fifth of Stark County's population — the city's blue-collar Democratic base has become less important to the 16th's overall political picture. Massillon and Alliance, the county's next-most-populous cities, however, also lean Democratic.

As a whole, the 16th leans Republican primarily because of rural conservative areas west of Stark County, although northern Stark County is upper-middle-class and GOP-leaning as well.

Wayne County, a top state producer of oats, hay and dairy products, increasingly backs Republican candidates at all levels. The 16th also takes in most of Ashland County, which leans conservative. While Canton's political role has dimmed, the GOP margin in the 16th is not yet overwhelming.

Major Industry
Steel, health care, higher education

Cities
Canton, 73,007; Massillon, 32,149; Medina, 26,678; Wooster, 26,119; Alliance (pt.), 22,282

Notable
The Professional Football Hall of Fame and William McKinley's tomb are in Canton.

Rep. Tim Ryan (D)

Capitol Office
225-5261
timryan.house.gov
1421 Longworth Bldg. 20515-3517; fax 225-3719

Committees
Armed Services
Budget

Residence
Niles

Born
July 16, 1973; Niles, Ohio

Religion
Roman Catholic

Family
Divorced

Education
Youngstown State U., attended 1991-92; Bowling
Green State U., B.A. 1995 (political science); Franklin
Pierce Law Center, J.D. 2000

Career
Congressional aide

Political Highlights
Ohio Senate, 2001-02

ELECTION RESULTS

2010 GENERAL
Tim Ryan (D)	102,758	53.9%
Jim Graham (R)	57,352	30.1%
James A. Traficant Jr. (I)	30,556	16.0%

2010 PRIMARY
Tim Ryan (D)	48,750	78.7%
Dan Moadus (D)	7,520	12.1%
Robert Crow (D)	5,638	9.1%

2008 GENERAL
Tim Ryan (D)	218,896	78.1%
Duane Grassell (R)	61,216	21.8%

Previous Winning Percentages
2006 (80%); 2004 (77%); 2002 (51%)

Elected 2002; 5th term

Ryan lost his seat on the Appropriations Committee in the 112th Congress, but that has not deterred him from his efforts to use every available tool to try to revive the economy in the nation's Rust Belt.

Ryan had especially high hopes for the potential impact he could make after winning a seat on the Defense Appropriations Subcommittee in early 2010 after the death of the panel's chairman, John P. Murtha of Pennsylvania.

But Democratic losses in the 2010 elections forced him off the spending panel. He'll continue to have a say in military matters as a member of the Armed Services Committee, and on broader fiscal questions from his seat on the Budget Committee. He has criticized GOP proposals to cut spending and defended President Obama's fiscal 2012 blueprint as "the best budget you could put together given the circumstances."

A liberal friend of organized labor in the classic Midwestern mold, Ryan was a founding member of the Congressional Manufacturing Congress. He has said his aim is to help U.S. companies better compete with foreign rivals, particularly in fields involving clean-energy technologies.

In one of the highest-profile moments of his congressional career, Ryan in September 2010 saw the House pass his bill that would have made it more likely that the United States would impose duties on Chinese goods to aid U.S. manufacturers. Although 99 House Republicans supported the legislation, the measure did not move in the Senate. Even so, Ryan posted on Twitter that the vote was a major turning point for manufacturing and the middle class.

Ryan also keeps a close eye on trade and says agreements should "represent our values as a country." He helped lead opposition to a free trade deal with South Korea in early 2011 and voted against the Central America Free Trade Agreement in 2005 as well as deals with Peru and Panama in 2007.

While his politics are reminiscent of the age of Hubert H. Humphrey, his methods are entirely 21st century.

A fan of both Ohio's sports teams and its economy, Ryan used his active Twitter feed in the summer of 2010 to try to make a case for why basketball superstar LeBron James should stay with the Cleveland Cavaliers, arguing that his departure would cost the team "$100 million in value" and Northeast Ohio "hundreds of thousands in taxes." (Not swayed, James left to play for the Miami Heat.)

A pet cause he pushed as a member of the Labor-HHS-Education Appropriations Subcommittee was promoting training in meditation. He's an enthusiastic advocate, having described his own 45-minute daily routine in a USA Today article. A quote from Ryan appeared among the endorsements for a 2009 seminar led by author Jon Kabat-Zinn. Practices where people learn to simply follow their breath for a time may prevent or lessen the severity of illness and aid in concentration, Ryan said.

"We tell our kids in school, 'Pay attention, pay attention,'" Ryan said. "But no one has ever taught them how to pay attention."

Ryan is generally a reliable vote for his party, having sided with Democrats well over 90 percent of the time during the course of his career on votes that pit majorities of the two parties against each other. Like many colleagues from socially conservative, working-class districts, he supports gun ownership rights and opposes abortion — although he backed the Democrats' 2010 health care overhaul that critics said would allow federal dollars to be spent on abortion coverage.

After Democratic losses in 2004, he said the party suffered from unreasonable absolutism on social issues.

But Ryan bucked strong sentiment in his district when he voted in 2003 — and in 2005 — against a constitutional amendment to ban flag burning. He said he feared civil liberties were under assault. He has voted twice against amending the Constitution to ban same-sex marriage, and he backed the 2010 repeal of the statutory ban on homosexuals serving openly in the military.

Ryan has paid little mind to the growing wave of sentiment against earmarking — setting aside funding for projects of special interest to members. Instead, he promotes how directing spending home can help his district. "I'll be damned if I'm going to let somebody come in and tell us that somehow we're wasting money," he said.

Ryan's parents divorced when he was in grade school, and he and his older brother were raised by their mother and grandparents. His mother was a chief deputy clerk of Trumbull County. His grandmother worked for the county clerk of courts, his grandfather was a steelworker and both were union members. Ryan was a football player in high school and college until he ruined his knee. He studied political science at Ohio's Bowling Green State University and earned a law degree from New Hampshire's Franklin Pierce Law Center, where his studies included a stint in an international law program in Florence, Italy.

In the mid-1990s, he worked as an aide for the colorful Democratic Rep. James A. Traficant Jr. Ryan won election to the Ohio Senate in 2000, the year he completed law school. In 2002, with Traficant facing jail on bribery and racketeering charges (he was eventually expelled from the House), Ryan entered a competitive primary for the seat. He faced eight-term Democratic Rep. Tom Sawyer, who was thrown into the district by reapportionment. Sawyer outspent him 10-to-1, but Ryan prevailed and went on to easily defeat GOP state Sen. Ann Womer Benjamin.

He was re-elected with ease until 2010, when he was held to 54 percent against Republican Jim Graham and Traficant, who polled 16 percent running as an independent.

In early 2009 Ryan briefly considered a 2010 run for the Senate seat held by retiring Republican George V. Voinovich. He was later mentioned as a possible running mate for Gov. Ted Strickland in that year's gubernatorial race, but ultimately decided to run for re-election. He has been a very vocal critic of Republican Gov. John Kasich, the former House member who unseated Strickland, and is considered a possible candidate for governor in 2014.

Key Votes

2010

Overhaul the nation's health insurance system	YES
Allow for repeal of "don't ask, don't tell"	YES
Overhaul financial services industry regulation	YES
Limit use of new Afghanistan War funds to troop withdrawal activities	NO
Change oversight of offshore drilling and lift oil spill liability cap	YES
Provide a path to legal status for some children of illegal immigrants	YES
Extend Bush-era income tax cuts for two years	YES

2009

Expand the Children's Health Insurance Program	YES
Provide $787 billion in tax cuts and spending increases to stimulate the economy	YES
Allow bankruptcy judges to modify certain primary-residence mortgages	YES
Create a cap-and-trade system to limit greenhouse gas emissions	YES
Provide $2 billion for the "cash for clunkers" program	YES
Establish the government as the sole provider of student loans	YES
Restrict federally funded insurance coverage for abortions in health care overhaul	YES

CQ Vote Studies

	PARTY UNITY		PRESIDENTIAL SUPPORT	
	SUPPORT	OPPOSE	SUPPORT	OPPOSE
2010	98%	2%	93%	7%
2009	99%	1%	97%	3%
2008	98%	2%	20%	80%
2007	97%	3%	4%	96%
2006	90%	10%	37%	63%

Interest Groups

	AFL-CIO	ADA	CCUS	ACU
2010	93%	90%	38%	0%
2009	100%	95%	33%	4%
2008	100%	90%	61%	4%
2007	96%	95%	55%	0%
2006	92%	80%	47%	28%

Ohio 17

Northeast — Youngstown, Warren, part of Akron

Bordering Pennsylvania in part of northeastern Ohio's Mahoning Valley, including Youngstown, the 17th is a Democratic bastion. Once a leading steel producer, the valley now symbolizes industrial decline; most of the mills that have not been torn down are either silent or abandoned.

A plurality of district residents lives in Trumbull County (shared with the 14th). Sustained economic downturns hit the area hard. Manufacturing jobs recently employed as much as one-fourth of Trumbull's workforce, but unemployment here remains in double digits as auto assembly and parts manufacturing plants have shut down. Despite some economic diversification, young people searching for jobs look elsewhere and the district overall has lost 30,000 residents since 2000.

The population of Youngstown, in Mahoning County, hovered around 170,000 from the 1930s to the 1960s; the 2010 census found just 67,000 people living in the city. Youngstown's economic devastation and decades of population loss have forced local officials to plan for a smaller city,

converting vacant homes and commercial and industrial sites into open space, eventually abandoning some outer neighborhoods and demolishing some infrastructure.

The 17th's share of Mahoning County is solidly Democratic, and the county overall last voted for a GOP presidential candidate in 1972. Warren, Trumbull County's most populous city, propels the county's Democratic lean. Parts of Summit and Portage counties to the west are less solidly Democratic, although they still supported Barack Obama in the 2008 presidential election. The Summit portion includes the eastern half of Akron, a city that once produced 90 percent of the nation's tires and is still home to Goodyear Tire & Rubber. The Portage portion includes Kent, where Kent State University is located. Overall, Obama took 62 percent of the vote districtwide, which made the 17th his third-best district in Ohio.

Major Industry
Service, manufacturing

Cities
Akron (pt.), 81,216; Youngstown, 66,982; Warren, 41,557

Notable
The Butler Institute of American Art, dedicated in 1919, was one of the first museums to display only American art.

Rep. Bob Gibbs (R)

Capitol Office
225-6265
gibbs.house.gov
329 Cannon Bldg. 20515-3518; fax 225-3394

Committees
Agriculture
Transportation & Infrastructure
(Water Resources & Environment - Chairman)

Residence
Lakeville

Born
June 14, 1954; Peru, Ind.

Religion
Methodist

Family
Wife, Jody Gibbs; three children

Education
Ohio State U., A.A.S. 1974 (animal husbandry)

Career
Property management company owner; hog farmer

Political Highlights
Ohio House, 2003-09; Ohio Senate, 2009-10

ELECTION RESULTS

2010 GENERAL

Bob Gibbs (R)	107,426	53.9%
Zack Space (D)	80,756	40.5%
Lindsey Sutton (CNSTP)	11,246	5.6%

2010 PRIMARY

Bob Gibbs (R)	11,037	20.9%
Fred Dailey (R)	10,881	20.6%
Jeanette Moll (R)	10,013	19.0%
Ron Hood (R)	8,204	15.6%
Dave Daubenmire (R)	6,288	11.9%
Hombre M. Liggett (R)	4,065	7.7%
Michael D. Royer (R)	1,318	2.5%
Beau M. Bromberg (R)	894	1.7%

Elected 2010; 1st term

A farmer turned state legislator, Gibbs reflects the conservative outlook of his rural district, which sweeps across eastern and southern Ohio and includes rugged parts of Appalachia.

Gibbs says his top priorities are cutting the federal deficit, lowering the national debt and enacting small-business tax breaks to create jobs.

Many of his constituents work in the steel and coal industries or in agriculture — mostly dairy and beef cattle production — and he won a seat on the Agriculture Committee.

Gibbs chairs the Transportation and Infrastructure Subcommittee on Water Resources and Environment, where a favorite target is likely to be the EPA. "I am concerned that more regulations means more unfunded mandates to burden our cities and towns at a time when they need relief from those types of injustices," he said at a March 2011 hearing.

He voted for an amendment to a House-passed fiscal 2011 catchall spending bill that would bar the EPA from regulating carbon emissions from stationary sources, such as power plants. He backed the underlying bill, which would cut around $60 billion, and supported almost all of the spending reductions that were considered during floor debate. He also voted for the spending bill enacted in April 2011, which cut $40 billion dollars and funded the government though September.

Gibbs owns and operates a hog farm and is a former president of the Ohio Farm Bureau Federation. He served three terms in the Ohio House and won election to the state Senate in 2009. He won the 2010 Republican nomination for the U.S. House in an eight-candidate field with 21 percent of the vote, topping the runner-up by less than 200 votes.

Incumbent Democrat Zack Space won by comfortable margins in 2006 and 2008. He opposed the 2010 health care overhaul and won the endorsement of the National Rifle Association. But Gibbs was able to appeal to the district's conservative lean and take advantage of a bad year for Democrats nationally and a worse year for Democrats in Ohio to prevail, winning 54 percent of the vote to 41 percent for Space.

Ohio 18

East — Zanesville, Chillicothe

Ohio's most geographically vast district, the 18th envelops 12 whole counties and parts of four others in eastern and southern Ohio. Beginning in the north, the 18th takes in the rolling hills south of Canton and runs southwest to rugged areas of Appalachia. The socially conservative district depends on steel and coal jobs and includes a large Catholic population of ethnic Eastern Europeans and Greeks.

Tuscarawas is the 18th's most populous county. It relies on dairy and beef cattle production as well as a stalling manufacturing sector. Newark (shared with the 12th) in Licking County is slowly becoming a research and manufacturing center, and unemployment in the county remains below the state average.

South of Muskingum County (Zanesville), where unemployment rates remain high, the district narrows as it takes in struggling Morgan County and northwestern Athens County, although Ohio University and Athens are in the adjacent 6th District. Moving west, the 18th remains rural as it crosses forests to take in most of Ross County, including Chillicothe. The blue-collar 18th leans Republican at the federal level, but will send Democrats to state office.

Several counties here backed Democratic Gov. Ted Strickland in his unsuccessful 2010 re-election run. Republican John Kasich won eight of the counties wholly within the district — including Holmes, which gave him his largest winning margin statewide.

Major Industry
Steel, manufacturing, agriculture, coal

Cities
Zanesville, 25,487; Chillicothe, 21,901

Notable
Aviator Amelia Earhart called Zanesville "the most recognizable city in the country" from the air because of its Y-shaped bridge across the Muskingum and Licking rivers.

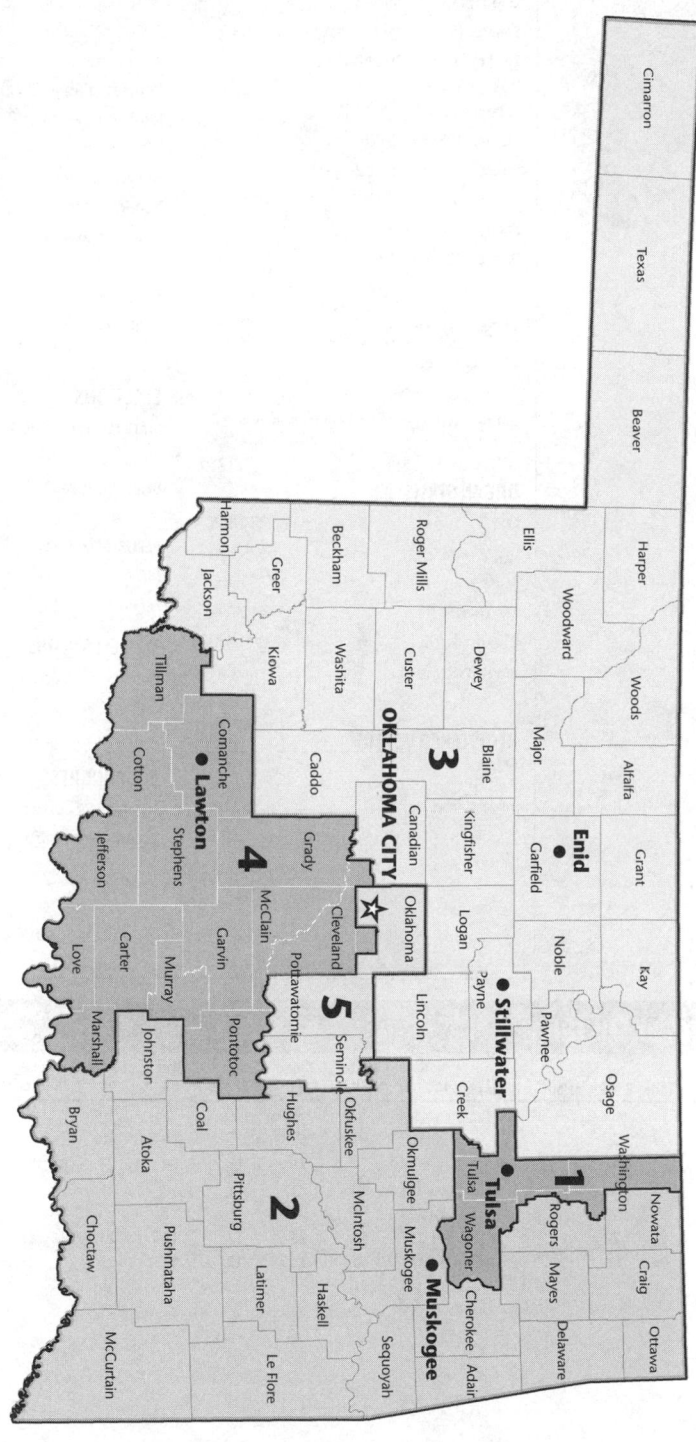

Gov. Mary Fallin (R)

First elected: 2010
Length of term: 4 years
Term expires: 1/15
Salary: $147,000
Phone: (405) 521-2342
Residence: Endmond
Born: December 9, 1954; Warrensburg, Mo.
Religion: Christian non-denominational
Family: Husband, Wade Christensen; two children, four stepchildren
Education: Oklahoma Baptist U., attended 1973-75; Oklahoma State U., B.S. 1977 (family relations and child development); U. of Central Oklahoma, attended 1979-81 (business administration)
Career: Real estate broker; hotel properties manager; state tourism agency official
Political highlights: Okla. House, 1990-94; lieutenant governor, 1995-2007; U.S. House, 2007-11

ELECTION RESULTS

2010 GENERAL

Mary Fallin (R)	625,506	60.4%
Jari Askins (D)	409,261	39.6%

Lt. Gov. Todd Lamb (R)

First elected: 2010
Length of term: 4 years
Term expires: 1/15
Salary: $114,713
Phone: (405) 521-2161

LEGISLATURE

Legislature: February-May
Senate: 48 members, 4-year terms
2011 ratios: 32 R, 16 D; 44 men, 4 women
Salary: $38,400
Phone: (405) 524-0126
House: 101 members, 2-year terms
2011 ratios: 70 R, 31 D; 86 men, 15 women
Salary: $38,400
Phone: (405) 521-2711

TERM LIMITS

Governor: 2 terms
Senate: No more than 12 years combined
House: No more than 12 years combined

URBAN STATISTICS

CITY	POPULATION
Oklahoma City	579,999
Tulsa	391,906
Norman	110,925
Broken Arrow	98,850
Lawton	96,867

REGISTERED VOTERS

Democrat	48%
Republican	41%
Unaffiliated	11%

POPULATION

2010 population	3,751,351
2000 population	3,450,654
1990 population	3,145,585
Percent change (2000-2010)	+8.7%
Rank among states (2010)	28
Median age	35.9
Born in state	61.4%
Foreign born	4.8%
Violent crime rate	501/100,000
Poverty level	16.2%
Federal workers	59,013
Military	21,673

ELECTIONS

STATE ELECTION OFFICIAL
(405) 521-2391
DEMOCRATIC PARTY
(405) 427-3366
REPUBLICAN PARTY
(405) 528-3501

MISCELLANEOUS

Web: www.ok.gov
Capital: Oklahoma City

U.S. CONGRESS

Senate: 2 Republicans
House: 4 Republicans, 1 Democrat

2010 Census Statistics by District

District	2008 Vote for President Obama	McCain	White	Black	Asian	Hispanic	Median Income	White Collar	Blue Collar	Service Industry	Over 64	Under 18	College Education	Rural	Sq. Miles
1	36%	64%	67%	9%	2%	10%	$46,465	61%	23%	16%	12%	26%	28%	10%	1,737
2	34	66	66	3	<1	4	35,407	50	32	18	15	25	15	64	20,563
3	27	73	77	4	1	8	41,554	54	29	17	14	24	20	49	34,089
4	34	66	73	6	2	7	45,399	59	24	17	12	25	22	37	10,212
5	41	59	60	14	3	14	40,815	61	22	18	13	25	28	12	2,067
STATE	34	66	69	7	2	9	41,861	57	26	17	13	25	22	35	68,667
U.S.	53	46	64	12	5	16	51,425	60	23	17	13	25	28	21	3,537,438

Sen. James M. Inhofe (R)

Capitol Office
224-4721
inhofe.senate.gov
205 Russell Bldg. 20510-3603; fax 228-0380

Committees
Armed Services
Environment & Public Works - Ranking Member
Foreign Relations

Residence
Tulsa

Born
Nov. 17, 1934; Des Moines, Iowa

Religion
Presbyterian

Family
Wife, Kay Inhofe; four children

Education
U. of Tulsa, B.A. 1973

Military Service
Army, 1957-58

Career
Real estate developer; insurance executive

Political Highlights
Okla. House, 1967-69; Okla. Senate, 1969-77;
Republican nominee for governor, 1974; Republican
nominee for U.S. House, 1976; mayor of Tulsa, 1978-
84; defeated for re-election as mayor of Tulsa, 1984;
U.S. House, 1987-94

ELECTION RESULTS

2008 GENERAL
James M. Inhofe (R)	763,375	56.7%
Andrew Rice (D)	527,736	39.2%
Stephen P. Wallace (I)	55,708	4.1%

2008 PRIMARY
James M. Inhofe (R)	116,371	84.2%
Evelyn L. Rogers (R)	10,770	7.8%
Ted Ryals (R)	7,306	5.3%
Dennis Lopez (R)	3,800	2.7%

2002 GENERAL
James M. Inhofe (R)	583,579	57.3%
David L. Walters (D)	369,789	36.3%
James Germalic (I)	65,056	6.4%

Previous Winning Percentages
1996 (57%); 1994 Special Election (55%); 1992 House
Election (53%); 1990 House Election (56%); 1988
House Election (53%); 1986 House Election (55%)

Elected 1994; 3rd full term

Inhofe has been the leading critic of climate change legislation in Congress since 2003, when he said on the Senate floor, "With all of the hysteria, all of the fear, all of the phony science, could it be that man-made global warming is the greatest hoax ever perpetrated on the American people?"

Now the top-ranking Republican on the Environment and Public Works Committee, Inhofe would be hard-pressed to offer more divergent views than those of the panel's chairwoman, Democrat Barbara Boxer of California. It makes for an interesting dynamic. When Boxer tried to move climate change legislation through the committee in 2009, Inhofe (IN-hoff) and most of his GOP colleagues walked out of the room, denying Boxer the quorum she needed to proceed.

The bill later foundered in the face of united GOP opposition. So even as Democrats will remain in charge of the Senate during the 112th Congress (2011-12), it's Inhofe who has won the battles on climate change, at least so far.

He is the author of legislation that would add a section to the Clean Air Act exempting greenhouse gases from Environmental Protection Agency jurisdiction and overturning several regulatory actions already taken by the agency related to emissions restrictions.

Indeed, because Senate rules make it possible for the minority party to require a 60-vote threshold for passage of most major bills, Inhofe has had virtual veto power over environmental legislation. When Democrat Benjamin L. Cardin of Maryland tried to move a bill aimed at cleaning up Chesapeake Bay in 2010, for example, he had to respond to Inhofe, who demanded that Cardin remove language opposed by industry groups that would set tough water pollution controls in the bay's watershed. An indication of Inhofe's power: Cardin agreed and the bill moved forward.

Inhofe also played a big role in forestalling legislation to increase the potential liability of offshore drillers in the aftermath of an oil spill in the Gulf of Mexico in the spring of 2010. Inhofe said the bill would have driven small companies out of the drilling business.

And while the threat of legislation addressing climate change has receded in the aftermath of Republican gains in the 2010 elections, Inhofe is still raring for a fight. The EPA declared in April 2009 that carbon dioxide posed a health hazard and has begun writing rules to limit emissions. Inhofe sees the effort as a backdoor campaign by global warming alarmists to achieve through regulation what they could not through legislation. The 2009 decision, he added, is "the beginning of a regulatory barrage that will destroy jobs, raise energy prices for consumers and undermine America's global competitiveness."

Brash and direct, Inhofe relishes playing the role of conservative contrarian and tweaking the mores of coastal liberals. For years, he has kept a framed document in his office, an interest group's assessment describing him as the Senate's most conservative member. He makes a point of ensuring visitors take note of it.

Inhofe has a lifetime "A+" grade from the National Rifle Association and has used his position on the Armed Services Committee to promote gun rights. In 2010, months after a terrorism-related shooting at Fort Hood in Texas, Inhofe introduced legislation barring the Defense Department from keeping records on guns owned privately by soldiers.

Inhofe shares many of the conservative views as his home-state GOP colleague, Tom Coburn, the Senate's most frequent blocker of Democratic legislation. Both adamantly opposed President Obama's health care overhaul and legislation to revamp banking regulations that were enacted in 2010, and have pledged to repeal the former. Meanwhile, they both support legislation rolling back all non-security discretionary spending to 2008 levels.

But one area on which the two Oklahomans disagree — and where Inhofe is a far more conventional Washington politician than Coburn — is the federal government's role in building infrastructure. While Coburn condemns the transportation funding process, Inhofe embraces it. Exploiting his seniority in the Senate, he has brought millions of dollars in earmarks back to Oklahoma for roads, bridges and military bases.

When another earmark critic in the Senate, Republican Jim DeMint of South Carolina, moved to ban the practice early in 2010, Inhofe challenged him on the Senate floor. "All you end up doing if you're successful is giving all this to Obama," Inhofe said, arguing that it was better for lawmakers to appropriate funds directly than allow Obama administration officials to divvy up the pie.

Inhofe won a temporary victory when 15 Republican colleagues joined him in voting against the ban. But later in the year, after Election Day, Senate Republicans imposed a prohibition on earmarks, and the majority Democrats eventually acquiesced.

Inhofe attends weekly prayer meetings held by the Fellowship Foundation, an evangelical Christian network that sponsors housing for members of Congress and the annual National Prayer Breakfast, and his religious views color his work on the Foreign Relations Committee. He's traveled regularly to Africa to do humanitarian work, calling it a "Jesus thing." He teamed with former Democratic Sen. Russ Feingold of Wisconsin on legislation, signed int law by Obama in 2010, that requires the president to develop a plan for providing support to regions affected by the Lord's Resistance Army, a notorious rebel group that has wreaked havoc in Uganda, Sudan and Congo.

Inhofe was born in Des Moines, Iowa, but his parents moved in 1942 to Tulsa in search of jobs in the insurance industry. Inhofe inherited their penchant for business; at 15, he worked as a door-to-door salesman. He lives just three houses away from the one in which he was raised.

Inhofe has about 50 years of experience as a pilot. He's never lost his love of flying, despite nearly losing his life on more than one occasion. In 2010, he landed his twin-engine Cessna 340 on a runway that was closed for repairs on a trip to his vacation home on South Padre Island in Texas. No one was hurt, but the airport manager was highly critical of Inhofe's actions. He had an even closer call in 2006 when his TV-8 single-engine stunt plane spun out of control upon landing in Tulsa, an incident he attributed to a malfunctioning rudder.

After two years as an Army private in the late 1950s, Inhofe followed his parents into insurance, then became a real estate developer. As a businessman, he became frustrated with an "over-regulated society," which launched him into a 10-year career in the Oklahoma Legislature.

While a state senator, Inhofe lost a 1974 campaign for governor to Democrat David L. Boren. Elected mayor of Tulsa in 1978, he was defeated for reelection in 1984. He bounced back two years later and picked up a House seat, taking 55 percent of the vote to succeed Democrat James R. Jones. He never cracked 56 percent in four elections, despite being in the state's most Republican district. In 1988, his campaign was complicated when he sued his brother over a stock sale involving the family insurance business.

In 1994, when Boren, who by then had moved to the Senate, decided to leave in the middle of his term, Inhofe made a run for the seat. He faced Rep. Dave McCurdy, a pro-business Democrat favored to win. McCurdy was closely associated with President Bill Clinton, whom he introduced at the 1992 Democratic National Convention, and Inhofe won by 15 percentage points. He hasn't had a tough race since.

Key Votes

2010

Pass budget reconciliation bill to modify overhauls of health care and federal student loan programs	NO
Proceed to disapproval resolution on EPA authority to regulate greenhouse gases	YES
Overhaul financial services industry regulation	NO
Limit debate to proceed to a bill to broaden campaign finance disclosure and reporting rules	NO
Limit debate on an extension of Bush-era income tax cuts for two years	YES
Limit debate on a bill to provide a path to legal status for some children of illegal immigrants	NO
Allow for a repeal of "don't ask, don't tell"	NO
Consent to ratification of a strategic arms reduction treaty with Russia	NO

2009

Prevent release of remaining financial industry bailout funds	YES
Make it easier for victims to sue for wage discrimination remedies	NO
Expand the Children's Health Insurance Program	NO
Limit debate on the economic stimulus measure	NO
Repeal District of Columbia firearms prohibitions and gun registration laws	YES
Limit debate on expansion of federal hate crimes law	NO
Strike funding for F-22 Raptor fighter jets	NO

CQ Vote Studies

	PARTY UNITY		PRESIDENTIAL SUPPORT	
	SUPPORT	OPPOSE	SUPPORT	OPPOSE
2010	96%	4%	39%	61%
2009	98%	2%	35%	65%
2008	99%	1%	75%	25%
2007	98%	2%	87%	13%
2006	94%	6%	88%	12%
2005	94%	6%	91%	9%
2004	98%	2%	92%	8%
2003	98%	2%	97%	3%
2002	96%	4%	96%	4%
2001	96%	4%	95%	5%

Interest Groups

	AFL-CIO	ADA	CCUS	ACU
2010	6%	0%	100%	96%
2009	11%	5%	71%	100%
2008	22%	5%	63%	96%
2007	5%	10%	80%	100%
2006	20%	0%	91%	100%
2005	21%	5%	83%	100%
2004	17%	10%	100%	100%
2003	0%	5%	100%	84%
2002	17%	10%	100%	100%
2001	25%	10%	93%	96%

Sen. Tom Coburn (R)

Capitol Office
224-5754
coburn.senate.gov
172 Russell Bldg. 20510-3602; fax 224-6008

Committees
Finance
Homeland Security & Governmental Affairs
Judiciary

Residence
Muskogee

Born
March 14, 1948; Casper, Wyo.

Religion
Baptist

Family
Wife, Carolyn Coburn; three children

Education
Oklahoma State U., B.S. 1970 (accounting); U. of
Oklahoma, M.D. 1983

Career
Physician; optical firm manager

Political Highlights
U.S. House, 1995-2001

ELECTION RESULTS

2010 GENERAL

Tom Coburn (R)	718,482	70.6%
Jim Rogers (D)	265,814	26.1%
Stephen P. Wallace (I)	25,048	2.5%

2010 PRIMARY

Tom Coburn (R)	223,997	90.4%
Evelyn L. Rogers (R)	15,093	6.1%
Lewis Kelly Spring (R)	8,812	3.6%

2004 GENERAL

Tom Coburn (R)	763,433	52.8%
Brad Carson (D)	596,750	41.2%
Sheila Bilyeu (I)	86,663	6.0%

Previous Winning Percentages
1998 House Election (58%); 1996 House Election
(55%); 1994 House Election (52%)

Elected 2004; 2nd term

Few senators have frustrated the current crop of Democratic leaders more than Coburn, who wears the epithet "obstructionist" like a badge of honor as he stands athwart the Senate yelling, "Stop!" In a body known for its chumminess, he doesn't mind offending his colleagues' sensibilities if it means standing by the small-government principles that have marked his congressional career.

Coburn's official website features a running ticker of the national debt — in excess of $14 trillion — an emblem of what has become his trademark issue.

He often stresses that he is not necessarily against the specific program being debated — but he wants Congress to figure out a way to pay for it. During a 2010 debate over a short-term extension of unemployment benefits and other programs, Coburn offered three unsuccessful amendments to offset the costs. He also demanded and got votes on amendments to offset the cost of a nearly $59 billion fiscal 2010 war supplemental spending bill by cutting other programs. The amendments lost, but not by a lot: One was tabled on a vote of 53-45, the other by 50-47. The proposals included freezing salaries of civilian federal employees and rescinding 5 percent of budget authority in certain fiscal 2010 appropriations bills.

Minority Leader Mitch McConnell of Kentucky appointed Coburn to serve on a 2010 fiscal commission that President Obama established by executive order. Coburn had voted against an amendment to a measure to raise the debt limit that would have established a statutory commission.

In the 112th Congress (2011-12), he was part of a "Gang of Six" senators pushing to turn the commission's recommendations into law, including changes to entitlement programs and a wide-ranging overhaul of the tax system. Both of those topics come under Coburn's purview as a member of the Finance Committee and as ranking Republican on the subcommittee with jurisdiction over Social Security. After months of fruitless talks, he left the group.

Coburn frequently places procedural holds on nominations and legislative business to address concerns or get answers from nominees. Unlike many senators, however, he has always disclosed his objections.

Coburn has waged an unwavering battle against earmarks, the funding for pet projects that lawmakers include in spending bills. One of his early victories on that front came in late 2006, when he teamed with Obama, then a Democratic senator from Illinois, on a bill establishing a searchable online database listing the recipients of all federal spending. He was an enthusiastic supporter of a ban on earmarks put in place by Senate Republicans for the 112th Congress.

Coburn prevented Senate consideration of a slew of lands bills in the 110th Congress (2007-08). So at the outset of the 111th Congress (2009-10) Majority Leader Harry Reid, a Nevada Democrat, quickly brought to the floor an omnibus lands measure that came to be known as the "Tomnibus." The Senate passed the bill in January 2009, but it took more than two months of procedural finagling by the majority before the measure was cleared by Congress and signed into law.

Coburn keeps a list of bills he's tracking on cards that he carries in the pocket of his suit jacket. "What I'm trying to do is create the expectation among my peers in the Senate that if you've got something that doesn't pass the smell test, I'm going to be challenging it, and if you really want it, then you got to come to the floor and debate me on it, on why we ought to do it," he told C-SPAN in 2007.

A practicing obstetrician, Coburn opposed the health care overhaul in the

111th Congress. He unsuccessfully pushed to eliminate the bill's employer mandate, which established monetary penalties for employers with more than 25 workers that do not provide health insurance coverage.

"If you have 27 workers, first thing you're going to do is lay off two people," Coburn said at the time. "We're going to see significant 10 to 15 percent lay-offs from small businesses."

While he was harshly critical of the bill, he offered suggestions to combat fraud, and could work to implement some of those in his new role as ranking member of the Homeland Security and Governmental Affairs panel's Permanent Subcommittee on Investigations. Obama wrote in a March 2010 letter that he might support a recommendation from Coburn to engage medical professionals in "random, undercover investigations of health care providers" receiving payments from federal programs.

Coburn also serves on the Judiciary Committee, one of few members bringing the perspective of a non-lawyer to the panel. He opposed the 2009 confirmation of Sonia Sotomayor to a seat on the Supreme Court and Elena Kagan's confirmation in 2010. He has expressed the view that testimony of judicial nominees should not be trusted. "Consideration of any judge in the future, in terms of this senator, is going to be borne out by what they've said before they got to the committee, not what they say to the committee, because we can no longer, as a body, trust what the nominees say in committee," he said as the Senate prepared to take up Kagan's nomination.

He is the ranking Republican on Judiciary's Subcommittee on Privacy, Technology and the Law.

Coburn has given an annual lecture to summer interns on the risks of sexually transmitted diseases, but his program faced an issue with the Senate Ethics Committee in 2009. "It's a collision of pizza, STDs and the Ethics Committee," Coburn spokesman John Hart told Roll Call in 2009. Outside groups had provided funding to purchase pizzas for the interns.

Coburn previously ran up against the Ethics Committee when he wanted to continue practicing medicine while the Senate is not in session.

In 2005, the panel refused to modify a long-standing ban on outside payment for professional services. Coburn wanted to keep collecting just enough fees from his obstetrics practice in Muskogee to cover his costs. The House had allowed him to do so; the Senate did not. He said he would keep on seeing patients anyway whenever he was home.

Coburn was born in Wyoming but grew up in Muskogee. He had a strained relationship with his father, an alcoholic who founded a successful optical business. (They reconciled six months before his father's death.) His father's company made equipment to process optical lenses and eventually became Muskogee's biggest employer.

After his junior year at Oklahoma State, Coburn married Carolyn Denton, a former Miss Oklahoma he'd had a crush on since elementary school. He went to work for his father at age 22 and for several years managed a Virginia branch of the business, Coburn Optical Products. He built it into a $40 million venture, which Revlon bought in 1975. Coburn moved back to Oklahoma and, at 31, decided to go to medical school.

He was a first-time candidate for public office when he ran for the House in the big Republican year of 1994. Incumbent Mike Synar, a Democrat, lost in the primary, and Coburn went on to beat Virgil R. Cooper, a 71-year-old retired middle school principal.

Coburn stuck to his term limits pledge, serving three terms in the House and then leaving. But he missed the fray, and in 2004 ran for the seat of retiring GOP Sen. Don Nickles. Coburn defeated moderate Democratic Rep. Brad Carson by more than 11 percentage points. He won re-election in 2010 by 44 points.

Key Votes

2010

Pass budget reconciliation bill to modify overhauls of health care and federal student loan programs	NO
Proceed to disapproval resolution on EPA authority to regulate greenhouse gases	YES
Overhaul financial services industry regulation	NO
Limit debate to proceed to a bill to broaden campaign finance disclosure and reporting rules	NO
Limit debate on an extension of Bush-era income tax cuts for two years	NO
Limit debate on a bill to provide a path to legal status for some children of illegal immigrants	NO
Allow for a repeal of "don't ask, don't tell"	NO
Consent to ratification of a strategic arms reduction treaty with Russia	NO

2009

Prevent release of remaining financial industry bailout funds	YES
Make it easier for victims to sue for wage discrimination remedies	NO
Expand the Children's Health Insurance Program	NO
Limit debate on the economic stimulus measure	NO
Repeal District of Columbia firearms prohibitions and gun registration laws	YES
Limit debate on expansion of federal hate crimes law	NO
Strike funding for F-22 Raptor fighter jets	YES

CQ Vote Studies

	PARTY UNITY		PRESIDENTIAL SUPPORT	
	SUPPORT	OPPOSE	SUPPORT	OPPOSE
2010	98%	2%	33%	67%
2009	99%	1%	27%	73%
2008	99%	1%	85%	15%
2007	96%	4%	89%	11%
2006	92%	8%	88%	12%
2005	93%	7%	91%	9%

Interest Groups

	AFL-CIO	ADA	CCUS	ACU
2010	13%	5%	82%	100%
2009	11%	5%	71%	100%
2008	0%	0%	75%	96%
2007	17%	5%	50%	100%
2006	27%	5%	64%	100%
2005	21%	5%	89%	100%

Rep. John Sullivan (R)

Capitol Office
225-2211
sullivan.house.gov
434 Cannon Bldg. 20515-3601; fax 225-9187

Committees
Energy & Commerce

Residence
Tulsa

Born
Jan. 1, 1965; Tulsa, Okla.

Religion
Roman Catholic

Family
Wife, Judy Sullivan; five children (one deceased)

Education
Northeastern State U., B.B.A 1992 (marketing)

Career
Petroleum marketing executive; real estate broker

Political Highlights
Okla. House, 1995-2002

ELECTION RESULTS

2010 GENERAL

John Sullivan (R)	151,173	76.8%
Angelia O'Dell (I)	45,656	23.2%

2010 PRIMARY

John Sullivan (R)	38,673	62.1%
Kenneth Rice (R)	10,394	16.7%
Nathan Dahm (R)	8,871	14.2%
Patrick Haworth (R)	1,737	2.8%
Craig Allen (R)	1,421	2.3%
Fran Moghaddam (R)	1,213	1.9%

2008 GENERAL

John Sullivan (R)	193,404	66.2%
Georgianna W. Oliver (D)	98,890	33.8%

Previous Winning Percentages
2006 (64%); 2004 (60%); 2002 (56%); 2002 Special
Election (54%)

Elected 2002; 5th full term

In describing his political philosophy, Sullivan relies on a conservative catchphrase: "If it's in the Yellow Pages, government shouldn't be doing it." Voters in his strongly Republican district appear to agree: His percentage of the vote has risen in each of his five re-election campaigns since he first won the seat in a 2002 special election.

Constituents have apparently forgiven his misspent youth in which drinking led to several arrests. His drinking continued during his time in public office, but in June 2009 Sullivan took a monthlong leave of absence from the House and checked himself into California's Betty Ford Center to combat his alcohol addiction. "I never was drunk on the House floor and I never was drunk at work. But I needed to get help to stop. I tried quitting on my own . . . but I failed every time," he said upon his return to Washington.

Now, much of his energy goes into energy. His seat on the Energy and Commerce Committee provides a platform for him to support his state's oil and gas industries and oppose efforts by the EPA to restrict carbon emissions using regulation.

"With fuel costs already on the rise, the last thing our country needs is for the EPA to implement regulations that will drive energy costs up and severely hamper small business' ability to grow and expand and create jobs," he said.

He criticized Obama's fiscal 2012 budget proposal for energy. "While gasoline prices continue to rise, and some experts are predicting $4 per gallon gas by this summer, the president wants to implement a massive tax increase on American energy production," he said.

He was named to a Republican energy task force in 2009 to help draft a legislative alternative to the Democrats' cap-and-trade bill, which passed the House but died in the Senate, setting the stage for the EPA's follow-up effort at a regulatory response.

He has been one of the GOP's strongest backers of increased domestic production of oil and natural gas and said he supports an "all of the above" energy strategy. Sullivan called natural gas — Oklahoma is the fourth-largest producer in the United States — "a bridge fuel until we can get to the place that everyone wants to get. We can't shoot the horse we're on until we can get on another one."

He helped lead an effort to protect the practice of hydraulic fracturing, a six-decade-old practice that involves injecting fluids into wells to help extract oil and gas, from expanded federal regulation.

On Energy and Commerce, Sullivan opposed the Democrats' health care overhaul in the 111th Congress (2009-10) and questioned the constitutionality of its mandate requiring individuals to purchase health insurance, a position at least two federal judges subsequently agreed with.

Sullivan vehemently opposed Republican President George W. Bush's effort to enact immigration legislation that would have provided a path to citizenship for millions of illegal immigrants already in the country. During a Bush visit to Capitol Hill in 2006, Sullivan urged action on measures to tighten border security before addressing Bush's proposal for a comprehensive immigration overhaul. Bush and Sullivan went back and forth, each trying to get the last word. "We have to have a comprehensive solution," Bush said. "But not now," Sullivan replied.

A member of the conservative Republican Study Committee, he opposed a $787 billion economic stimulus bill Obama signed into law in 2009 and voted against a bill that would allow bankruptcy judges to renegotiate mortgages, a task Sullivan argued should be outside the purview of government. He called it "another massive bailout that rewards irresponsible homebuyers."

In 2008, he voted against an effort to override President George W. Bush's veto of a farm bill that provides generous subsidies to Oklahoma farmers. Sullivan was among those urging spending cuts in other programs to offset the billions of dollars Congress appropriated in 2005 and 2006 to help the Gulf Coast recover from a devastating hurricane season.

But he supported in fall 2008 a $700 billion effort to stabilize the financial services industry. "This is for the well-being of our country, not for political popularity," Sullivan said.

Sullivan said his interest in politics was sparked when, as a child walking to kindergarten, he saw yard signs for presidential candidates Richard M. Nixon and George McGovern. Not knowing what they meant, he asked his parents if they could get one. That touched off an argument between his Democratic mother and Republican father that ended with his mom flinging a glass of orange juice at his dad. Ultimately, it was his father's political leanings that swayed the boy. He trailed along as his father worked to elect Henry Bellmon, Oklahoma's first Republican governor. In college, Sullivan initially majored in political science, then switched to marketing. He worked as a real estate broker and in petroleum marketing while running a political memorabilia business, and on several GOP campaigns. He ran for an open state House seat in 1994 and won. During seven years in the legislature, he battled to reduce sales taxes and estate taxes.

In 2001, he entered a five-way primary to succeed Republican Rep. Steve Largent, who was resigning to run for governor. Sullivan bested Cathy Keating, wife of GOP Gov. Frank Keating, in that race and then the Democratic nominee, former Tulsa School Board member Doug Dodd, in the special election. Sullivan's district had been redrawn to be more Republican for the 2002 general election, and he beat Dodd in a rematch.

His re-election in 2004 came after a tough campaign. Some past supporters — including a political consultant who once worked for Sullivan and accused his former boss of cheating him out of nearly $20,000 in fees — backed GOP businessman Bill Wortman in the primary. Sullivan's office later acknowledged that his aides used phony names to telephone call-in radio shows and pose easy questions to their boss. Wortman seized on that and two cases in which he said Sullivan lied about his police record. Sullivan beat Wortman and again prevailed over Dodd, this time with 60 percent of the vote. His winning margins have increased in each election since.

Key Votes

2010

Overhaul the nation's health insurance system	NO
Allow for repeal of "don't ask, don't tell"	NO
Overhaul financial services industry regulation	NO
Limit use of new Afghanistan War funds to troop withdrawal activities	NO
Change oversight of offshore drilling and lift oil spill liability cap	NO
Provide a path to legal status for some children of illegal immigrants	NO
Extend Bush-era income tax cuts for two years	NO

2009

Expand the Children's Health Insurance Program	NO
Provide $787 billion in tax cuts and spending increases to stimulate the economy	NO
Allow bankruptcy judges to modify certain primary-residence mortgages	NO
Create a cap-and-trade system to limit greenhouse gas emissions	-
Provide $2 billion for the "cash for clunkers" program	NO
Establish the government as the sole provider of student loans	NO
Restrict federally funded insurance coverage for abortions in health care overhaul	YES

CQ Vote Studies

	PARTY UNITY		PRESIDENTIAL SUPPORT	
	SUPPORT	OPPOSE	SUPPORT	OPPOSE
2010	98%	2%	26%	74%
2009	97%	3%	20%	80%
2008	97%	3%	69%	31%
2007	98%	2%	83%	17%
2006	97%	3%	95%	5%

Interest Groups

	AFL-CIO	ADA	CCUS	ACU
2010	0%	5%	75%	100%
2009	11%	0%	69%	100%
2008	13%	20%	100%	92%
2007	13%	5%	71%	100%
2006	15%	5%	100%	92%

Oklahoma 1

Tulsa; Wagoner and Washington counties

Wooden homes on small plots of land in the city's outskirts contrast with the skyscrapers of downtown Tulsa, the heart of the 1st. Tulsa and Oklahoma City, the two main metropolitan areas in the state, have a friendly rivalry. Tulsa is more insular and tied to old money than Oklahoma City and the rest of the state, and Tulsans like to distinguish themselves from the "dust-on-their-boots" stereotype of Oklahomans.

Once the "oil capital of the world," Tulsa thrived on drilling until the market dried up in the 1980s; after a recent revival Tulsa again relies on the energy sector. Dramatic fluctuations in the demand and price for oil in the last decade, however, have affected the downtown office real estate market. The city is still actively seeking to diversify its economic identity, and efforts that began two decades ago are now paying off. Tulsa has become a manufacturing hub for flight simulators, and while aviation and aerospace production remains profitable, financial services, telecommunications and small businesses have aided growth.

Real estate prices rose in many Tulsa neighborhoods even while falling elsewhere across the country, and young professionals are moving into midtown. Foreclosures hit some areas, but Tulsa and nearby cities seem to have avoided the homebuilding booms that eventually busted. South Tulsa is sprinkled with luxury homes, and subdivisions have sprung up in the fast-growing suburbs of Broken Arrow, Jenks and Owasso, which has nearly tripled in population since 1990.

Democrats can win local elections in the northern half of Tulsa, but Republicans dominate at the federal level. The region has voted for a Democratic presidential candidate only twice since 1920. Socially conservative issues play well in the district, which is the home of Oral Roberts University.

Major Industry

Oil, aerospace, telecommunications, financial services, defense manufacturing

Cities

Tulsa, 385,770; Broken Arrow, 98,850; Bartlesville, 35,747; Owasso (pt.), 28,891

Notable

Oral Roberts University is known for its 200-foot Prayer Tower and the "Praying Hands" sculpture at the campus' main entrance.

Rep. Dan Boren (D)

Capitol Office
225-2701
www.house.gov/boren
2447 Rayburn Bldg. 20515-3602; fax 225-3038

Committees
Natural Resources
Select Intelligence

Residence
Muskogee

Born
Aug. 2, 1973; Shawnee, Okla.

Religion
Methodist

Family
Wife, Andrea Boren; two children

Education
Texas Christian U., B.A. 1997 (economics); U. of
Oklahoma, M.B.A. 2001

Career
College fundraiser; bank teller; state utility regulation
commission aide; congressional district aide

Political Highlights
Okla. House, 2002-04

ELECTION RESULTS

2010 GENERAL

Dan Boren (D)	108,203	56.5%
Charles Thompson (R)	83,226	43.5%

2010 PRIMARY

Dan Boren (D)	66,439	75.6%
Jim Wilson (D)	21,496	24.4%

2008 GENERAL

Dan Boren (D)	173,757	70.5%
Raymond J. Wickson (R)	72,815	29.5%

Previous Winning Percentages
2006 (73%); 2004 (66%)

Elected 2004; 4th term

The third generation of his family to serve Oklahoma in Congress, Boren describes himself as a "pro-gun, pro-business" Democrat, although he sometimes seems like a man without a party. His ideological leanings are both a family tradition and a matter of survival in a district that backed Republican John McCain by a nearly 2-to-1 ratio in the 2008 presidential election.

In 2010, only 11 Democrats sided with their party less often than Boren on votes that split majorities of the two caucuses. Only two of them were re-elected. Boren announced in June 201 that he would not run again in 2012.

A member of the fiscally conservative Blue Dog Coalition, he has said he will never switch parties. But he is among the severest Democratic critics of party leader Nancy Pelosi of California, whom he refused to support for minority leader or Speaker in the 112th Congress (2011-12).

His disaffection is not just with the Democratic congressional leadership, but with President Obama as well. "If the next two years are like the last two years, he won't be successful," Boren told Roll Call. "If he moves to the middle, works with independents, works with moderates within our caucus, meets with Blue Dogs, he's got a real good chance of being successful."

Boren's differences with his party span a broad range of issues.

He was one of three Democrats to vote in early 2011 for repeal of the health care overhaul enacted less than a year earlier. And he introduced with Republican Mike Rogers of Michigan a measure that would allow individuals and small businesses to apply for waivers from the law, as many larger companies, some unions and even one state have done.

He was one of two Democrats to sign onto a "Dear Colleague" letter in support of legislation that would nullify the Federal Communications Commission's so-called net neutrality rules for broadband service providers.

As co-founder of the Natural Gas Caucus, Boren is working to block new EPA rules on hydraulic fracturing — a process known as fracking that involves injecting a mixture of water, sand and chemicals underground to release the gas in rock formations — until the EPA completes a congressionally mandated review of the technique in 2012. Environmentalists say the decades-old practice threatens the safety of drinking water.

He wrote a "Dear Colleague" letter in 2010 urging lawmakers to fund abstinence-only programs to combat teen pregnancy. He was the only Democrat to side with Republicans by voting in favor of giving the FBI access to records about books that people check out of libraries and buy in bookstores. He joined seven other Democrats in voting for a GOP-crafted lobbying and ethics bill in 2006, and was one of two Democrats in 2007 to vote against a bill to allow unions to organize workplaces without a secret ballot. In his first term, he supported the GOP's plan to crack down on illegal immigrants.

He is decidedly in favor of gun owners' rights, is on the National Rifle Association's board of directors and is a former co-chairman of the Congressional Sportsmen's Caucus. His office walls are covered with the fruits of his hunting trips: mounted deer heads, a wild turkey and a bearskin. After proposals to have the federal government increase its regulatory authority over waterways came to light in early 2010, Boren and three other members of the caucus wrote to the president demanding that sportsmen's interests be taken into consideration. He said he was inundated by input from constituents worried that recreational fishing would not receive "its fair share of consideration for use of our oceans."

But Boren drew the line against cooperating with Republicans on Social

Security, opposing President George W. Bush's plan to let individuals choose how to invest some of their own Social Security taxes. And he switched his position on the Children's Health Insurance Program, eventually supporting a bill to expand the program, which covers children from lower-income families that make too much money to qualify for Medicaid. He originally opposed it because a tobacco tax was to help pay for it.

Even as criticism of earmarks has increased, Boren continues to extol their virtues for his district, saying they usually divide spending that would likely take place anyway and rarely add on to the total.

Boren sits on the National Resources Committee, where as ranking Democrat on the Indian and Alaska Native Affairs Subcommittee he looks out for the nearly one-fifth of his constituents who are American Indians as ranking Democrat. He counts among his proudest accomplishments passage of a bill honoring "code talkers" who, by speaking in their native tongues on military radios during World Wars I and II, enabled U.S. forces to discuss operations confidentially. And he has sponsored a resolution to offer an official apology "to all native peoples on behalf of the United States."

Boren also sits on the Select Intelligence Committee, an assignment he described as "something that I've worked toward my entire career." His father, David L. Boren, a Democratic senator who resigned in 1994, chaired the Senate version of that panel.

Boren's grandfather Lyle Boren served in the House from 1937 to 1947. The 2nd District of today includes about half the area the elder Boren once represented. His father became governor of Oklahoma less than two years after Boren was born, but his parents later divorced, and he split his time between living in Oklahoma with his mother, the late Janna L. Robbins, and in Washington with his father, who was elected to the Senate in 1978. After college, he worked as an aide to Denise Bode, who headed the Oklahoma utility regulatory agency and once worked in his father's Senate office. In 2002, at 29, he beat an incumbent for an Oklahoma House seat. In the legislature, he was a proponent of tax cuts and efforts to make it more difficult for trial lawyers to press what he termed frivolous lawsuits. A year into his term, a U.S. House seat opened when Democrat Brad Carson left for an ultimately unsuccessful Senate bid. Boren didn't hesitate to go for it.

His name recognition helped him beat local District Attorney Kalyn Free, a member of the Cherokee Nation, in the primary. He sprinted past Republican Wayland Smalley, a horse breeder, in the general election. He won by more than 40 percentage points in 2006 and 2008, but was held to a 13-point margin of victory in 2010.

Key Votes

2010
Overhaul the nation's health insurance system	NO
Allow for repeal of "don't ask, don't tell"	-
Overhaul financial services industry regulation	NO
Limit use of new Afghanistan War funds to troop withdrawal activities	NO
Change oversight of offshore drilling and lift oil spill liability cap	NO
Provide a path to legal status for some children of illegal immigrants	NO
Extend Bush-era income tax cuts for two years	YES

2009
Expand the Children's Health Insurance Program	YES
Provide $787 billion in tax cuts and spending increases to stimulate the economy	YES
Allow bankruptcy judges to modify certain primary-residence mortgages	NO
Create a cap-and-trade system to limit greenhouse gas emissions	NO
Provide $2 billion for the "cash for clunkers" program	YES
Establish the government as the sole provider of student loans	YES
Restrict federally funded insurance coverage for abortions in health care overhaul	YES

CQ Vote Studies

	PARTY UNITY		PRESIDENTIAL SUPPORT	
	Support	Oppose	Support	Oppose
2010	69%	31%	68%	32%
2009	77%	23%	75%	25%
2008	91%	9%	36%	64%
2007	79%	21%	36%	64%
2006	54%	46%	85%	15%

Interest Groups

	AFL-CIO	ADA	CCUS	ACU
2010	58%	30%	100%	38%
2009	57%	40%	87%	44%
2008	73%	65%	78%	24%
2007	59%	50%	94%	57%
2006	57%	25%	100%	72%

Oklahoma 2
East — Muskogee, 'Little Dixie'

The 2nd's overall Democratic lean does not disguise a cultural split between the district's regions. Running from Kansas to Texas in eastern Oklahoma, the 2nd takes in outlying areas of Tulsa to the north and the "Little Dixie" region in the south. Farming and die-hard "Yellow Dog" Democrats typify southeastern Oklahoma, while northeastern residents are more liberal, at least by Oklahoma's standards. Still, both areas support Republicans in presidential races.

The district, especially Little Dixie, suffers from a high susceptibility to severe drought conditions. Southeast Oklahoma has been particularly hard-hit by long-term drought conditions that have escalated since 2005. Threats of fire, crop failures and reduced grazing options for livestock are concerns for farmers in a district that relies on ranching and agriculture. In addition to raising beef and poultry, farmers here cultivate peanuts and wheat. Non-farming unemployment rates remain high here, especially in McCurtain, Latimer and Huges counties.

Other natural resources bolster the region's economy. Small oil and natural gas wells dot the landscape. The timber industry in rocky southeastern

McCurtain County supports paper mills, saw mills and other secondary industries. Pittsburg County hosts McAlester Army Ammunition Plant, a high-capacity ordnance storage facility.

Farther north, the forested section in the foothills of the Ozark Mountains is a poor rural area with Democratic sympathies. Lakes and waterways — including Lake Eufaula, the state's largest lake — attract tourists. The remote locations here also appeal to the elderly: The 2nd has Oklahoma's largest proportion of people age 65 or older. The 2nd also has the nation's second-largest district share of American Indians (18 percent), and includes Tahlequah, the Cherokee Nation's capital.

Major Industry
Ranching, timber, oil and gas, agriculture

Military Bases
McAlester Army Ammunition Plant, 1 military, 1,517 civilian (2011)

Cities
Muskogee, 39,223; Claremore, 18,581; McAlester, 18,383

Notable
The American Indian "Trail of Tears" of 1838-39 ended in Tahlequah — about one-quarter of the Cherokee Nation died en route.

Rep. Frank D. Lucas (R)

Capitol Office
225-5565
www.house.gov/lucas
2311 Rayburn Bldg. 20515-3603; fax 225-8698

Committees
Agriculture - Chairman
Financial Services
Science, Space & Technology

Residence
Cheyenne

Born
Jan. 6, 1960; Cheyenne, Okla.

Religion
Baptist

Family
Wife, Lynda Lucas; three children

Education
Oklahoma State U., B.S. 1982 (agricultual economics)

Career
Farmer; rancher

Political Highlights
Republican nominee for Okla. House, 1984, 1986;
Okla. House, 1989-94

ELECTION RESULTS

2010 GENERAL

Frank D. Lucas (R)	161,927	78.0%
Frankie Robbins (D)	45,689	22.0%

2010 PRIMARY

Frank D. Lucas (R)	unopposed

2008 GENERAL

Frank D. Lucas (R)	184,306	69.7%
Frankie Robbins (D)	62,297	23.6%
Forrest Michael (I)	17,756	6.7%

Previous Winning Percentages
2006 (68%); 2004 (82%); 2002 (76%); 2000 (59%);
1998 (65%); 1996 (64%); 1994 (70%); 1994 Special
Election (54%)

Elected 1994; 9th full term

Lucas has deep roots in western Oklahoma, where a slice of the Santa Fe Trail once carried the commerce of the prairies and George Armstrong Custer fought the Southern Cheyenne. His "old-style conservative Republicanism" and chairmanship of the Agriculture Committee are good fits for the rural district, which covers almost half the state.

He was born and raised on a farm that his family has owned for more than a century, holding on to it even as many of his neighbors moved to towns and cities. That steady emptying of rural Oklahoma underlies much of Lucas' legislative agenda and his close attention to serving constituents. While he tends to such duties, his wife runs their beef cattle and wheat operation back home.

Lucas assumed the gavel of the Agriculture panel in the 112th Congress (2011-12), but he has already had a significant impact on farm policy. He had a hand in drafting the 2008 reauthorization of farm and nutrition programs, and he questions the direction of an Obama administration proposal that would shift focus away from support payments and export aid toward conservation and development of alternative-energy infrastructure in rural areas. "Are we going to have a farm bill that helps farmers produce food and fiber to meet the needs of this country and the world — or are we going to have a farm bill that focuses on making sure that people who live in the countryside can find jobs somewhere else, so they can drive to work every day and home at night and get our food from someone else on this planet?" Lucas told the North American Agricultural Journalists in April 2010.

He says the farm sector has already contributed its share of spending cuts in past years and should be spared sizable reductions as House Republicans look for ways to reduce the budget deficit. He successfully opposed an effort during debate on the catchall spending measure the House passed in early 2011 to cap commodity support payments at $250,000,

His environmental interests are sometimes in line with those of Democratic leaders. Lucas is an enthusiastic supporter of alternative fuels such as ethanol, and his state has plenty of the switch grass and corn used to make it. Lucas also is a promoter of wind and solar power, and during the 110th Congress (2007-08) he introduced legislation to provide tax breaks to farmers who install wind turbines on their land.

But he was concerned that farmers would be stuck with unnecessary fees and balked when the EPA, in late 2009, indicated it planned to establish a nationwide system for reporting greenhouse gas emissions, which would include animal-feed operations. He proposed legislation to bar the program from requiring livestock farmers to obtain an operating permit under the Clean Air Act. He called the EPA plan "an underhanded way of imposing cap and tax regulations on the American people."

In early 2011, Lucas told EPA Administrator Lisa P. Jackson that one of his priorities would be to rein in the agency, and he would work with other committees with broader jurisdiction over the EPA to do so.

On the Financial Services Committee, he opposed the panel's version of financial industry overhaul legislation in the 111th Congress (2011-12), saying the Agriculture Committee's bipartisan version was "carefully crafted and could sail through the House." In late 2008, he opposed both versions of a $700 billion measure — the second of which became law — aimed at rescuing the financial services sector.

Lucas also sits on the Science, Space and Technology Subcommittee on Space and Aeronautics, where he can keep an eye on the interests of the district's two Air Force bases, Altus and Vance. And he sponsored legislation in the mid-1990s that established the Washita Battlefield National Historic Site, where Custer and the 7th Cavalry attacked Black Kettle's Southern Cheyenne village in 1868. He also helped secure funding for a new visitors center.

Lucas is a social conservative and supports efforts to ban abortion and prohibit same-sex marriage. He helped pass a bill in 2006 that would keep the words "under God" in the Pledge of Allegiance. He voted against a renewal of the 2001 anti-terrorism law known as the Patriot Act, citing its lack of an expiration date. But he supported a short-term extension of expiring provisions in 2011.

When he was first elected, Lucas spent much of his time working on legislation stemming from the April 1995 bombing in downtown Oklahoma City that destroyed the Alfred P. Murrah Federal Building and killed 168 people. The federal building was in Lucas' original district, the now nonexistent 6th. In the years after the bombing, Lucas helped secure more than $100 million in federal funds for relief, recovery and rebuilding the area. He also won passage of a measure to establish a national memorial on the bombing site.

Lucas regularly introduces bills relating to his hobby of collecting coins. He has offered legislation to bar the government from claiming possession of coins minted before 1993 and to replace the nickel with a half-dime, which would be smaller and cheaper to produce and has some historic precedence: It was in use from 1792 to 1873 before nickel industry lobbyists persuaded Congress to make the nickel the only 5-cent piece. He said his favorite coin is a 1971 Eisenhower dollar. When he was 11 years old, he spent the year saving pennies to buy the coin, not knowing his grandmother was planning to give him one for Christmas. When she died shortly before the holiday, it was his grandfather who gave it to him.

As a child, Lucas accompanied his Republican father (his mother was a Texas Democrat) to local political events. At Oklahoma State University, he became a student senator and president of the College Republicans and volunteered in local campaigns. But he majored in agricultural economics and always came home to the family farm.

He eventually made two unsuccessful bids for a state House seat in what was then a mostly Democratic area, but he captured a seat in 1988.

Lucas made a bid for Congress when 10-term Democratic Rep. Glenn English resigned in early 1994. He won the nomination over four other Republicans. Stressing his work in agriculture and his lifelong residency in the district, he won 54 percent of the vote in the special election against Democrat Dan Webber Jr., a former aide to Oklahoma Democratic Sen. David L. Boren. That was Lucas' closest election. He has won handily since. In 2002, he ran in a newly redrawn 3rd District. Democrats did not field a candidate that year.

Key Votes

2010

Overhaul the nation's health insurance system	NO
Allow for repeal of "don't ask, don't tell"	NO
Overhaul financial services industry regulation	NO
Limit use of new Afghanistan War funds to troop withdrawal activities	NO
Change oversight of offshore drilling and lift oil spill liability cap	NO
Provide a path to legal status for some children of illegal immigrants	NO
Extend Bush-era income tax cuts for two years	YES

2009

Expand the Children's Health Insurance Program	NO
Provide $787 billion in tax cuts and spending increases to stimulate the economy	NO
Allow bankruptcy judges to modify certain primary-residence mortgages	NO
Create a cap-and-trade system to limit greenhouse gas emissions	NO
Provide $2 billion for the "cash for clunkers" program	NO
Establish the government as the sole provider of student loans	NO
Restrict federally funded insurance coverage for abortions in health care overhaul	YES

CQ Vote Studies

	PARTY UNITY		PRESIDENTIAL SUPPORT	
	SUPPORT	OPPOSE	SUPPORT	OPPOSE
2010	96%	4%	26%	74%
2009	89%	11%	17%	83%
2008	96%	4%	66%	34%
2007	91%	9%	80%	20%
2006	98%	2%	95%	5%

Interest Groups

	AFL-CIO	ADA	CCUS	ACU
2010	7%	0%	88%	100%
2009	5%	0%	80%	91%
2008	14%	15%	89%	96%
2007	4%	10%	85%	100%
2006	7%	5%	93%	88%

Oklahoma 3

Panhandle; west and north-central Oklahoma

Nothing stops the constant wind that forces its way across the 3rd's flat plains in western and north-central Oklahoma, an area that was devastated by the Dust Bowl in the 1930s. Few areas have suffered the vacillations of the oil industry more than the 3rd, and oil busts chased residents away over the years. Skyrocketing oil prices this decade made the small drilling operations across the district profitable.

Demand for domestic petroleum had revived oil exploration and industry demand for workers, but economic slowdowns have stalled growth recently. High-paying jobs and royalties for landowners who allow drilling have boosted the economy. Renewable-energy interests, such as grains for biofuel processing and wind farms, are also important.

The 3rd also depends on crops and livestock, and the district, the state's largest, leads Oklahoma in hogs, cattle, wheat, sorghum and sunflower seeds. Economic stability has kept unemployment rates low in the sparsely populated panhandle counties. In central Oklahoma, always thriving Stillwater, home to Oklahoma State University, brings droves to Boone Pickens Stadium to watch Big 12 football.

Bible Belt conservatism typifies the eastern plains areas north and west of Oklahoma City, while the southern part of the district is home to conservative Democrats who support Democrats for state office. Cimarron, Texas and Beaver counties on the panhandle are some of the most heavily Republican-voting counties in the state, and John McCain topped 85 percent in each of these counties in the 2008 presidential election. Overall, the 3rd gave McCain 73 percent of its vote, his highest percentage statewide, and the 16 counties that gave McCain his highest percentage margins in the state are wholly in the 3rd.

Major Industry
Oil, agriculture, military, higher education

Military Bases
Altus Air Force Base, 1,408 military, 1,267 civilian (2009); Vance Air Force Base, 1,233 military, 215 civilian (2011)

Cities
Enid, 49,379; Stillwater, 45,688; Ponca City, 25,387

Notable
Roger Mills County, on the western border, was named in 1892 by referendum in honor of then-U.S. Rep. Roger Q. Mills from Texas.

Rep. Tom Cole (R)

Capitol Office
225-6165
www.house.gov/cole
2458 Rayburn Bldg. 20515-3604; fax 225-3512

Committees
Appropriations
Budget

Residence
Moore

Born
April 28, 1949; Shreveport, La.

Religion
Methodist

Family
Wife, Ellen Cole; one child

Education
Grinnell College, B.A. 1971 (history); Yale U., M.A. 1974 (British history); U. of Oklahoma, Ph.D. 1984 (19th Century British history)

Career
Political consultant; party official; congressional district director; professor

Political Highlights
Okla. Republican Party chairman, 1985-89; Okla. Senate, 1989-91; Okla. secretary of state, 1995-99; U.S. House, 2009

ELECTION RESULTS

2010 GENERAL

Tom Cole (R)		unopposed

2010 PRIMARY

Tom Cole (R)	32,589	77.3%
R. J. Harris (R)	9,593	22.7%

2008 GENERAL

Tom Cole (R)	180,080	66.0%
Blake Cummings (D)	79,674	29.2%
David E. Joyce (I)	13,027	4.8%

Previous Winning Percentages
2006 (65%); 2004 (78%); 2002 (54%)

Elected 2002; 5th term

Cole, a stalwart conservative who sometimes creates unlikely alliances with Democrats, has positioned himself to shape both politics and policy, including pushing a Republican legislative agenda he helped develop. An appropriator and deputy GOP whip, Cole was part of the committee that helped draw up the "Pledge to America," a document of principles modeled on the "Contract With America" that Speaker Newt Gingrich of Georgia sought to pass after the 1994 GOP takeover of the House.

"It will give the American people a way to measure us," Cole said.

A longtime operative and fundraiser, Cole weathered a rocky period with the GOP leadership during his chairmanship of the National Republican Congressional Committee (NRCC). In early 2006, Cole chose the losing side in the contest for majority leader between Roy Blunt of Missouri and John A. Boehner of Ohio. He took over as NRCC chairman after that year's midterm election, then took heat for the committee's disarray and Democrats' gains in 2008. He was denied a return engagement as NRCC chairmanship and when Cole vied for an Appropriations Committee seat later that year, Boehner asked him to withdraw.

But "those days are over," Cole said. He remains a member of the NRCC's executive committee, co-chaired the 2010 summer dues drive and is a top fundraiser. He gained the coveted Appropriations seat in the 111th Congress (2009-10) and sits on three subcommittees: Interior-Environment, Defense and State-Foreign Operations. He also sits on the Budget committee.

He sees the Appropriations seat as a vehicle for rolling back Obama administration policies. He has been sharply critical of President Obama's economic agenda, and he voted against the $787 billion stimulus in 2009 and the health care overhaul in 2010.

"I think we're going to try to do a lot of things through the Appropriations Committee to try to get spending under control and 'defund' some of the initiatives that the president's pushed. Obamacare in particular will be a big target of ours," he said.

He won a legislative victory in early 2011 when the House passed his bill to terminate the Presidential Election Campaign Fund, which provides funding for presidential candidates who comply with certain spending and contribution limits and helps pay for national party conventions. Obama opted out of the system in the 2008 general election, the only major-party presidential candidate to do so in the program's 32-year history.

While Cole has made peace with the GOP House leadership, he remains prepared to criticize party members when he thinks it is merited. In mid-2010, he was among lawmakers who called for Republican National Committee Chairman Michael Steele's resignation after Steele criticized the war in Afghanistan, saying Steele's comments undercut forces in the field and undermined national interests.

Cole touts his designation as one of the most conservative House members, citing his "A" rating from the National Rifle Association and his anti-abortion views, but he freely admits that some positions put him at odds with some GOP colleagues. He supports charter schools and home-schooling, but he also supports two federal programs — known as TRIO and GEAR UP — that help disadvantaged students prepare for college. His district has three times as many students who use GEAR UP than the average congressional district, he said, making him a champion of the program in a way "consistent with being a conservative."

A fifth-generation Oklahoman, he is part Chickasaw Indian and the only Native American member of Congress. His district is home to 11 Indian tribes, and his advocacy for legislation benefiting American Indians sometimes draws him into alliances with Democrats. Not only did he vote in favor of legislation funding a legal settlement over unpaid royalties to American Indian landowners, he feels that the settlement was "not as generous as it should be."

In 2010, he amended an appropriations bill with language aimed at a Supreme Court ruling that prevented any Indian tribes from putting their land in trust — a move necessary for building a casino — if the tribe had been recognized after 1934, which Cole called "a huge deal" for many tribes. He also supports legislation that would give sovereignty to Native Hawaiians, which Democrats have largely backed.

"As long as I'm privileged to be in Congress, I'm going to be an advocate for Native Americans. Right now I'm the only one here. If don't speak up for 'em, who in the world is gonna?" he asks.

Cole represents two military bases, Fort Sill and Tinker Air Force Base, and he hopes to play a greater role in Defense appropriations. Because of the 2005 base realignment and closure process, some 10,000 soldiers and civilians are moving to the Fort Sill area, swelling the population of nearby Lawton by as much as 9 percent, which Cole said has been a boon to the area.

Cole is dry and plain-spoken, but his experience goes far beyond the district, which includes part of Oklahoma City, Norman and rural Western Oklahoma. He has a master's degree from Yale University, earned his doctorate in British history at the University of Oklahoma and studied as a Fulbright fellow at the University of London. Politics were part of the Cole household — his mother was a state legislator. His father was in the U.S. Air Force and later worked as a civilian employee at Tinker.

Cole served as state party chairman, state senator and Oklahoma secretary of state. He was a founding partner of Cole, Hargrave, Snodgrass & Associates, a political consulting firm. In 1994, he ran the successful House campaign of friend J.C. Watts.

When Watts decided to leave Congress in 2002, Cole ran for the open seat and defeated former Democratic state Sen. Darryl Roberts with 54 percent of the vote.

Cole had no Democratic opponent in 2004, won easy re-election in the next two races and faced no Democratic challenger again in 2010. He considered running for governor, but decided against it and supported the successful candidacy of fellow House member Mary Fallin.

Key Votes

2010

Overhaul the nation's health insurance system	NO
Allow for repeal of "don't ask, don't tell"	NO
Overhaul financial services industry regulation	NO
Limit use of new Afghanistan War funds to troop withdrawal activities	NO
Change oversight of offshore drilling and lift oil spill liability cap	NO
Provide a path to legal status for some children of illegal immigrants	NO
Extend Bush-era income tax cuts for two years	YES

2009

Expand the Children's Health Insurance Program	NO
Provide $787 billion in tax cuts and spending increases to stimulate the economy	NO
Allow bankruptcy judges to modify certain primary-residence mortgages	NO
Create a cap-and-trade system to limit greenhouse gas emissions	NO
Provide $2 billion for the "cash for clunkers" program	NO
Establish the government as the sole provider of student loans	NO
Restrict federally funded insurance coverage for abortions in health care overhaul	YES

CQ Vote Studies

	PARTY UNITY		PRESIDENTIAL SUPPORT	
	SUPPORT	OPPOSE	SUPPORT	OPPOSE
2010	89%	11%	29%	71%
2009	86%	14%	22%	78%
2008	95%	5%	73%	27%
2007	92%	8%	78%	22%
2006	96%	4%	95%	5%

Interest Groups

	AFL-CIO	ADA	CCUS	ACU
2010	7%	0%	88%	96%
2009	5%	0%	80%	92%
2008	7%	10%	94%	88%
2007	13%	10%	84%	100%
2006	21%	0%	100%	84%

Oklahoma 4

South central — Norman, Lawton, part of Oklahoma City

Home to the state's largest university and two military bases, the 4th covers part of Oklahoma City, its booming southern suburbs, and the western edges of "Little Dixie," so named for its Southern influence. McClain and Cleveland counties south of Oklahoma City each experienced more than 20 percent population growth between 2000 and 2010. On game days, Oklahomans flock to Norman in Cleveland County for Sooner football games at the University of Oklahoma.

Military jobs expanded during the 1990s, boosting the area's population and enhancing its defense presence. An artillery system cancellation in 2002 hurt Fort Sill and the city of Lawton, which is heavily dependent on the base, but the 2005 round of base realignments has brought roughly 10,000 new residents — as well as increased traffic — to the area.

The 4th's economy suffered from low oil prices a decade ago, and long-term drought conditions have decimated the region. Still, the oil industry and agriculture remain essential economic drivers. Farmers here grow soybeans, cotton, peanuts and wheat.

The 4th echoes the state's GOP preference in national elections. Although once confined to presidential races, the tendency now extends to congressional candidates and state legislators. Democrats remain competitive, especially in the district's rural, southern areas and around the university, although Republicans find strength in other parts of Norman. Overall, John McCain received 66 percent of the 4th's vote in the 2008 presidential election.

Major Industry
Military, higher education, oil, agriculture

Military Bases
Fort Sill (Army), 16,000 military, 4,500 civilian (2011); Tinker Air Force Base, 5,835 military, 14,105 civilian (2009)

Cities
Norman, 110,925; Oklahoma City (pt.), 97,716; Lawton, 96,867; Moore, 55,081; Midwest City (pt.), 46,045

Notable
The National Oceanic and Atmospheric Administration's National Weather Service Storm Prediction Center is located in Norman.

Rep. James Lankford (R)

Capitol Office
225-2132
lankford.house.gov
509 Cannon Bldg. 20515-3605; fax 226-1463

Committees
Budget
Oversight & Government Reform
 (Technology, Information Policy, Intergovernmental
 Relations & Procurement Reform - Chairman)
Transportation & Infrastructure

Residence
Oklahoma City

Born
March 4, 1968; Dallas, Texas

Religion
Baptist

Family
Wife, Cindy Lankford; two children

Education
U. of Texas, B.S.Ed. 1990 (secondary education-
history); Southwestern Theological Baptist Seminary,
M.Div. 1994 (biblical languages)

Career
Religious youth camp director

Political Highlights
No previous office

ELECTION RESULTS

2010 GENERAL

James Lankford (R)	123,236	62.5%
Billy Coyle (D)	68,074	34.5%
Clark Duffe (LIBERT)	3,067	1.6%
Dave White (I)	2,728	1.4%

2010 PRIMARY RUNOFF

James Lankford (R)	29,817	65.2%
Kevin Calvey (R)	15,902	34.8%

Elected 2010; 1st term

Lankford holds a master of divinity degree in biblical languages and spent years as a religious youth camp director, qualifications that distinguish him from the hordes of lawyers and career politicians that populate the House.

His 13 years as program director at a huge Baptist youth camp south of Oklahoma City helped him develop a network that proved invaluable to his grass-roots mobilization effort in the Republican primary and runoff.

He says the job also gave him leadership and business experience, as he applied the limited resources of a nonprofit corporation to the complexity of a large institution serving tens of thousands of people annually.

He has said he felt called to run for Congress because he believes the nation is "in great risk of losing our freedom to worship, live as traditional families, pass on a better life to our children, and speak out for the issues we hold dear. Our Constitution does not give us freedom; our Constitution recognizes the freedom given to us by God. Every generation must work to protect that freedom for the next generation."

Lankford's religious outlook informs his social conservatism. He opposes same-sex marriage and abortion.

But his legislative priorities are consistent with those of other freshman Republicans: stopping deficit spending, simplifying the tax code, shrinking the federal government, securing the border and increasing domestic energy production.

Oil and gas are crucial to his district's economy, and he supports expanded drilling for what he calls the pillars of the U.S. energy infrastructure. He also supports development of alternative energy resources.

He won assignments to the Budget, Transportation and Infrastructure, and Oversight and Government Reform committees.

Lankford's House predecessor, Republican Mary Fallin, left the seat open to make a successful run for governor. He finished first in a seven-candidate GOP primary, then won the runoff by an almost 2-to-1 margin. He had no trouble besting Democrat Billy Coyle in the strongly Republican district, winning 63 percent of the vote to 35 percent for Coyle.

Oklahoma 5

Most of Oklahoma City; Pottawatomie and Seminole counties

The 5th contains all of downtown Oklahoma City, including the governor's mansion and state Capitol, and is home to several colleges and universities. Oil and gas, along with some agriculture, make up a large chunk of the district's economy.

An oil price collapse roughly 20 years ago caused residents to leave the area and forced the city to diversify. Local manufacturing has taken hits, but job growth exists in the bioscience and technology fields. The 5th shares some of those jobs with the 3rd and 4th districts, as it does jobs linked to Tinker Air Force Base (in the 4th).

The Oklahoma City Arena, which hosts the NBA's Thunder, is part of long-term downtown revitalization efforts. Restaurants and apartments add to the vibrant feel of the city, and the Bricktown neighborhood, once filled with abandoned warehouses, is now a staple of the urban nightlife. Local officials hope that infrastructure redevelopment along Interstate 40 will promote commercial and residential growth between downtown areas and the Oklahoma River to the south. And waterfront redevelopment is expected to include condominiums, pedestrian-accessible retail and office space, and the American Indian Cultural Center & Museum.

Republicans dominate the 5th. The towns of Shawnee and Seminole, both home to large American Indian populations, and the largely black northeastern portion of Oklahoma City are not enough to threaten the GOP's hold.

Major Industry
Oil, technology, bioscience, government, higher education, agriculture

Cities
Oklahoma City (pt.), 457,679; Edmond, 81,405

Notable
Seminole County was accepted by the Seminole Nation tribes in exchange for their departure from the Florida Territory.

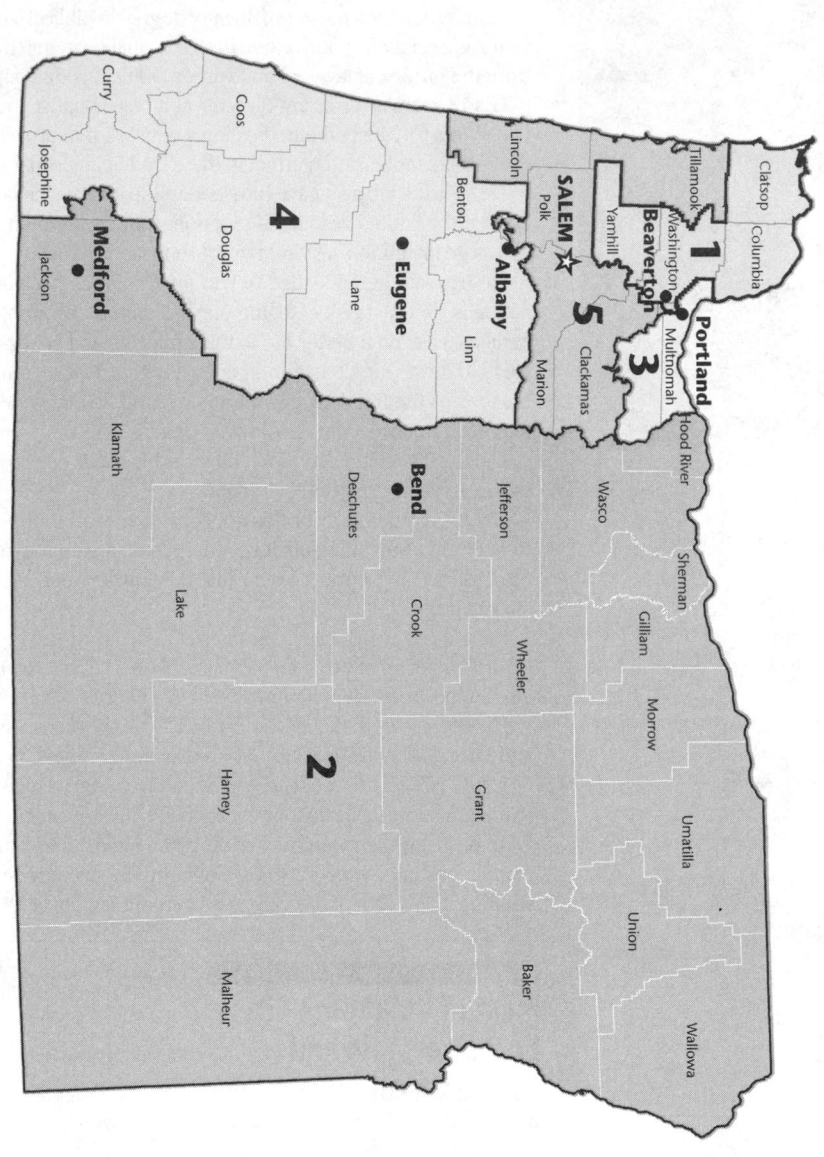

Gov. John Kitzhaber (D)

First elected: 2010
Length of term: 4 years
Term expires: 1/15
Salary: $93,600
Phone: (503) 378-3111
Residence: Portland
Born: March 5, 1947; Colfax, Wash.
Religion: Unspecified
Family: Divorced; one child
Education: Dartmouth College, A.B. 1969; U. of Oregon, M.D. 1973
Career: Physician
Political highlights: Ore. House, 1979-81; Ore. Senate, 1981-93 (president, 1985-93); governor, 1995-2003

ELECTION RESULTS

2010 GENERAL
John Kitzhaber (D)	716,525	49.3%
Chris Dudley (R)	694,287	47.8%
Greg Kord (CNSTP)	20,475	1.4%
Wes Wagner (LIBERT)	19,048	1.3%

Secretary of State
Kate Brown (D)

(no lieutenant governor)
Phone: (503) 986-1523

LEGISLATURE

Legislative Assembly: January-June in odd-numbered years, February-March in even-numbered years
Senate: 30 members, 4-year terms
2011 ratios: 16 D, 14 R; 21 men, 9 women
Salary: $21,612
Phone: (503) 986-1187
House: 60 members, 2-year terms
2011 ratios: 30 D, 30 R; 44 men, 16 women
Salary: $21,612
Phone: (503) 986-1187

TERM LIMITS

Governor: 2 terms
Senate: No
House: No

URBAN STATISTICS

CITY	POPULATION
Portland	583,776
Eugene	156,185
Salem	154,637
Gresham	105,594
Hillsboro	91,611

REGISTERED VOTERS

Democrat	54%
Republican	41%
Unaffiliated/others	5%

POPULATION

2010 population	3,831,074
2000 population	3,421,399
1990 population	2,842,321
Percent change (2000-2010)	+12.0%
Rank among states (2010)	27
Median age	37.7
Born in state	45.5%
Foreign born	9.2%
Violent crime rate	255/100,000
Poverty level	14.3%
Federal workers	34,234
Military	1,615

ELECTIONS

STATE ELECTION OFFICIAL
(503) 986-1518
DEMOCRATIC PARTY
(503) 224-8200
REPUBLICAN PARTY
(503) 595-8881

MISCELLANEOUS

Web: www.oregon.gov
Capital: Salem

U.S. CONGRESS

Senate: 2 Democrats
House: 4 Democrats, 1 Republican

2010 Census Statistics by District

District	2008 Vote for President Obama	McCain	White	Black	Asian	Hispanic	Median Income	White Collar	Blue Collar	Service Industry	Over 64	Under 18	College Education	Rural	Sq. Miles
1	61%	36%	74%	2%	7%	13%	$57,953	66%	19%	15%	10%	24%	37%	13%	2,941
2	43	54	82	<1	1	12	44,892	55	27	18	16	24	22	36	69,491
3	71	26	72	5	6	11	50,063	61	22	17	10	23	30	7	1,021
4	54	43	86	1	2	7	42,096	56	26	18	16	21	23	31	17,181
5	54	43	78	1	2	15	52,137	60	24	16	13	24	29	20	5,362
STATE	57	40	78	2	4	12	49,033	60	23	17	13	23	28	21	95,997
U.S.	53	46	64	12	5	16	51,425	60	23	17	13	25	28	21	3,537,438

Sen. Ron Wyden (D)

Capitol Office
224-5244
wyden.senate.gov
223 Dirksen Bldg. 20510-3703; fax 228-2717

Committees
Budget
Energy & Natural Resources
  (Public Lands & Forests - Chairman)
Finance
  (International Trade, Customs & Global
  Competitiveness - Chairman)
Select Intelligence
Special Aging

Residence
Portland

Born
May 3, 1949; Wichita, Kan.

Religion
Jewish

Family
Wife, Nancy Bass-Wyden; four children

Education
U. of California, Santa Barbara, attended 1967-69;
Stanford U., A.B. 1971 (political science); U. of Oregon,
J.D. 1974

Career
Senior citizen advocacy group state director; lawyer;
professor

Political Highlights
U.S. House, 1981-96

ELECTION RESULTS

2010 GENERAL

Ron Wyden (D)	825,507	57.2%
Jim Huffman (R)	566,199	39.2%
Others	49,434	3.4%

2010 PRIMARY

Ron Wyden (D)	333,652	89.6%
Loren Hooker (D)	25,152	6.8%
Pavel Goberman (D)	9,985	2.7%

Previous Winning Percentages
2004 (63%); 1998 (61%); 1996 Special Election (48%);
1994 House Election (73%); 1992 House Election
(77%); 1990 House Election (81%); 1988 House Election (99%); 1986 House Election (86%); 1984 House
Election (72%); 1982 House Election (78%); 1980
House Election (72%)

Elected 1996; 3rd full term

Wyden is a workhorse who often operates in a nonpartisan and collaborative fashion, and that style enabled him to settle into political security long before his party came to dominate Oregon politics. The son of a librarian and a writer, he studies the complexities of issues from health care to tax policy and can hold forth on almost any subject that stirs his interest, from global warming to the 1969 New York Knicks.

Wyden remains the eternal optimist, believing that ideas, relationships and good faith will ultimately triumph. "I simply don't accept the death of bipartisanship," he said.

When his friend and colleague Robert F. Bennett of Utah was defeated in a Republican nominating convention in 2010, Wyden made a plea for comity. "Bipartisanship shouldn't be a political death sentence," was the headline on a Washington Post opinion piece he wrote. "While it is certainly true that legislating can be (and is) turned into a zero-sum game . . . many issues present opportunities to build on the best ideas of both parties. No single party has a lock on all the good ideas."

Bennett was defeated, in part, because Republican activists in Utah objected to his cosponsorship of a health care overhaul bill that many on both sides of the aisle considered one of the most thoughtful plans presented. "Wyden-Bennett" was presented by its sponsors as the first truly bipartisan "universal coverage" measure in Senate history and as the product of collaboration between labor and business leaders. The bill would have overturned the existing system of employer-based health insurance, instead providing subsidies for Americans to buy coverage directly from private insurers.

The plan was never fully debated on the Senate floor during consideration of health care legislation in the 111th Congress (2009-10). Still, Wyden points out that some of his plan's provisions were incorporated into the final bill signed by the president, including pilot programs that could be established at the state level.

With that law in place, Wyden wants to speed up the process for allowing states to obtain waivers from some of its provisions. President Obama has called the idea "a reasonable proposal."

A member of the Special Aging Committee, he teamed with Wyoming Republican John Barrasso to introduce legislation that would ease restrictions on Medicare reimbursement for certain mental health services.

Wyden-Bennett was not the first time the Oregonian cultivated allies from both ends of the political spectrum. For years, he teamed with Republican Charles E. Grassley of Iowa to try to require senators who place secret holds on legislation to identify themselves. That effort bore fruit at the beginning of the 112th Congress (2011-12) with a change in Senate rules barring the practice.

Wyden is a foe of the tobacco industry, garnering wide TV coverage in 1994 when, as a House member, he asked a panel of tobacco executive witnesses whether they considered tobacco addictive. Under oath, they all denied that it is. He repeated the question in 1998 during Senate hearings, and four of the five CEOs recanted.

There is one health-related issue unique to Oregon: It is the only state in the country with a law permitting physician-assisted suicide. When Republicans were in the majority, Wyden devoted much time and energy to defending the law, scouring legislation to ensure no one slipped in provisions that would gut it.

Oregon is also the only state in the nation to conduct all of its elections by mail. Wyden successfully protected the mail-ballot system from changes when a federal law overhauling voting procedures was enacted at the end of 2002. He introduced an unsuccessful bill in 2007 to create an $18 million grant program to help other states transition to a vote-by-mail system.

Oregon's vast forests and many parks are also of high interest to Wyden as chairman of the Energy and Natural Resources Committee's Public Lands and Forests Subcommittee.

After a long battle with Republicans, he and the rest of his state's congressional delegation scored a significant victory in 2009 when their measure protecting wilderness around Mount Hood and other areas of the state was signed into law.

Logging's decline in the Pacific Northwest has damaged the economy of many of Oregon's rural communities, and Wyden has successfully sought more federal funding for them as compensation. In 2008, he proposed a compromise between environmentalists and timber companies to allow expanded logging of Oregon's overgrown forests. Wyden's plan would allow more trees to be cut, but it would preserve "old growth" trees and forbid clear-cutting.

Wyden chairs the Finance Subcommittee on International Trade, Customs and Global Competitiveness. He has been a strong advocate of using tax credit bonds — with which the federal government pays a tax credit to the bondholder in lieu of the issuer paying interest — to finance infrastructure spending. In February 2009, he worked with South Dakota Republican Sen. John Thune to include such "Build America Bonds" in the $787 billion economic stimulus bill.

He's a member of the Budget Committee and is a longtime backer of simplifying the tax code by lowering rates and eliminating deductions.

Wyden has worked for greater openness as a member of the Select Intelligence panel, pushing to declassify the amount of spending on spy programs. He also led the charge in 2003 against the George W. Bush administration's short-lived Total Information Awareness program, a domestic intelligence-gathering effort that he said would lead to spying on law-abiding citizens.

Wyden's parents were Jewish refugees from Nazi Germany. His mother spent part of her youth in Baghdad, where the family had fled. Wyden was born in Wichita, Kan., and steadily moved west as his father's journalism career advanced. He attended college on a basketball scholarship and retains his obsession with the game, including holding the unofficial congressional free-throw record (47 out of 50 in the House gym), and counting UCLA and Portland Trailblazer great Bill Walton as a good friend.

After abandoning his dream of playing professionally, he received his bachelor's degree from Stanford, then followed a girlfriend to Oregon, where he earned a law degree at the University of Oregon.

Wyden was Oregon executive director for the Gray Panthers, an organization promoting senior citizens' interests, when he first ran for the House in 1980. He ousted Democratic Rep. Robert B. Duncan in the primary and won with 72 percent of the vote in November in a Democratic, Portland-based district.

When Republican Sen. Bob Packwood resigned in disgrace in 1995 after a sexual-harassment controversy, Wyden jumped into the special-election race. He edged out fellow Democratic Rep. Peter A. DeFazio in the primary, then narrowly defeated Republican Gordon H. Smith (who subsequently won election to Oregon's other Senate seat and became a close ally of Wyden's before his 2008 defeat). Wyden has won his three re-elections with ease.

Wyden underwent surgery in December 2010 for early stage prostate cancer and was back at work when the Senate reconvened for votes in late January 2011.

Key Votes

2010

Pass budget reconciliation bill to modify overhauls of health care and federal student loan programs	YES
Proceed to disapproval resolution on EPA authority to regulate greenhouse gases	NO
Overhaul financial services industry regulation	YES
Limit debate to proceed to a bill to broaden campaign finance disclosure and reporting rules	YES
Limit debate on an extension of Bush-era income tax cuts for two years	?
Limit debate on a bill to provide a path to legal status for some children of illegal immigrants	YES
Allow for a repeal of "don't ask, don't tell"	YES
Consent to ratification of a strategic arms reduction treaty with Russia	YES

2009

Prevent release of remaining financial industry bailout funds	YES
Make it easier for victims to sue for wage discrimination remedies	YES
Expand the Children's Health Insurance Program	YES
Limit debate on the economic stimulus measure	YES
Repeal District of Columbia firearms prohibitions and gun registration laws	NO
Limit debate on expansion of federal hate crimes law	YES
Strike funding for F-22 Raptor fighter jets	YES

CQ Vote Studies

	PARTY UNITY		PRESIDENTIAL SUPPORT	
	SUPPORT	OPPOSE	SUPPORT	OPPOSE
2010	95%	5%	95%	5%
2009	98%	2%	97%	3%
2008	97%	3%	28%	72%
2007	95%	5%	39%	61%
2006	94%	6%	51%	49%
2005	94%	6%	26%	74%
2004	93%	7%	62%	38%
2003	93%	7%	47%	53%
2002	87%	13%	74%	26%
2001	90%	10%	64%	36%

Interest Groups

	AFL-CIO	ADA	CCUS	ACU
2010	100%	100%	0%	12%
2009	100%	100%	43%	4%
2008	100%	95%	50%	8%
2007	94%	95%	55%	4%
2006	100%	100%	42%	8%
2005	79%	95%	33%	4%
2004	100%	100%	59%	4%
2003	92%	90%	43%	15%
2002	85%	85%	60%	15%
2001	100%	95%	43%	8%

Sen. Jeff Merkley (D)

Capitol Office
224-3753
merkley.senate.gov
313 Hart Bldg. 20510; fax 228-3997

Committees
Banking, Housing & Urban Affairs
Budget
Environment & Public Works
Health, Education, Labor & Pensions

Residence
Portland

Born
Oct. 24, 1956; Eugene, Ore.

Religion
Lutheran

Family
Wife, Mary Sorteberg; two children

Education
Stanford U., B.A. 1979 (international relations);
Princeton U., M.P.A. 1982

Career
Nonprofit executive; computer repair company
owner; Congressional Budget Office analyst

Political Highlights
Ore. House, 1999-2009 (minority leader, 2003-07;
Speaker, 2007-09)

ELECTION RESULTS

2008 GENERAL

Jeff Merkley (D)	864,392	48.9%
Gordon H. Smith (R)	805,159	45.6%
David Brownlow (CNSTP)	92,565	5.2%

2008 PRIMARY

Jeff Merkley (D)	246,482	44.8%
Steve Novick (D)	230,889	42.0%
Candy Neville (D)	38,367	7.0%
Roger S. Obrist (D)	12,647	2.3%
Pavel Goberman (D)	12,056	2.2%
David Loera (D)	6,127	1.1%

Elected 2008; 1st term

Merkley came to the Senate in 2009 pushing fellow Democrats to leverage their newfound strength to enact liberal policies. Now he is entrenched as one of the chamber's leading voices for liberalism. But despite his efforts, he frequently comes up short.

He was a leader in Democratic efforts to change Senate rules at the beginning of the 112th Congress (2011-12), pushing to make it much more difficult to block legislation with a filibuster.

He had to settle for elimination of secret holds and the waiving of a requirement that amendments be read if they have been publicly available for at least three days.

Merkley was a key player during the financial services regulatory overhaul debate in 2010. He worked with Democrat Carl Levin of Michigan to develop a tough version of the so-called Volcker Rule banning banks from engaging in risky investment practices. But the provision was substantially weakened during the final hours of all-night conference committee negotiations in order to win enough votes to send the overhaul legislation to the White House.

Months into his first term, Merkley was also one of 16 Democratic senators to encourage the administration to support a government-run insurance plan in the health care overhaul. That idea was scrapped after outcry from Republicans and moderate Democrats.

He is known for his polite, personable demeanor. But the wrangling over the financial services and health care overhauls apparently did little to encourage him to be more conciliatory on the issues he considers important. "If you're completely satisfied, you're not reaching far enough," he once said.

Merkley is outspoken in his desire for tough clean-energy standards and did not budge on his position in September 2010 when environmental, labor and clean-energy groups encouraged lawmakers to approve legislation that attracted some GOP support. The bill would have required 15 percent of U.S. electricity to be generated from wind, solar energy or other renewable resources by 2021. But Merkley held out hope for his tougher position, which would institute a national renewables standard of 25 percent by 2025.

"When that moment comes, I'll see, but meanwhile I will keep fighting for a stronger standard," he said.

A member of the Budget and Environment and Public Works committees, he supported the 2009 economic stimulus law after pushing successfully for several energy-related provisions, including infrastructure improvements to modernize the nation's electricity grid and a program to upgrade schools and other public facilities to make them more energy efficient.

He also sits on the Health, Education, Labor and Pensions Committee, where he favored a bill in 2009 that aimed to make it easier for unions to organize workplaces without a secret ballot. "When workers are able to band together to improve their workplaces and wages, we strengthen the middle class," he said. The measure passed the House, but never got a vote in the Senate.

From his seat on the Banking, Housing and Urban Affairs Committee, he seeks ways to help families and workers during the economic downturn. He supported a bill in early 2009 to set new regulations on the credit card industry and rein in so-called predatory lending practices.

As a candidate in 2008, he spoke out against the $700 billion law aimed at rescuing the financial services industry, citing a lack of adequate oversight and accountability provisions. After taking office, he wrote Treasury

Secretary Timothy F. Geithner urging him to press other nations to contribute aid to the financial markets since foreign banks were receiving rescue funds, and to help recover bonuses paid to employees by companies that received rescue funds.

Despite his ideological bent, Merkley is open to making deals. He backed a bipartisan proposal by his state's senior senator, Democrat Ron Wyden, to convert employer-provided health benefits into higher wages to pay for regulated private health care plans.

Merkley won a victory in late 2010 when Obama signed into law his bill to criminalize the production and distribution of animal crush videos — sexual fetish videos of women mutilating small animals with their feet. A similar 1999 law was overturned earlier in the year by the Supreme Court on First Amendment grounds. "All Americans can understand that the deliberate and illegal torture of animals should not be turned into a video for sale and commercial production," Merkley told The Oregonian.

Merkley spent part of his youth in rural southwestern Oregon, where his father worked in a wood mill. But troubles in the timber industry prompted the family to move to Portland, where his father worked as an equipment mechanic and Merkley attended high school. He still lives in a three-bedroom ranch-style house in a working-class neighborhood in East Portland, near his boyhood home.

He cites his father's nightly dinner-table conversation as his inspiration to enter public service. "He would come home from work and watch the news and provide a commentary about what we could do to make things better," he said.

In the 1970s, Merkley was an intern for moderate GOP Sen. Mark O. Hatfield of Oregon; in the 1980s, he worked as a presidential fellow at the Pentagon. Then, as a CBO analyst, he wrote reports on weapons systems — including his 1988 opus, "The B-1B Bomber and Options for Enhancements."

While in Washington, Merkley met his future wife, Mary Sorteberg, who was working for the Lutheran Volunteer Corps at a homeless shelter. Merkley bought a house in the city, which he still owns and which serves as the Lutheran group's headquarters. After returning to Oregon, he served as director of Portland's Habitat for Humanity and became executive director of the World Affairs Council, an education group focused on international politics and culture.

Merkley began his five terms as a state legislator in 1999 and moved up the ladder rapidly. As Speaker from 2007 to 2009, he won enactment of a cap on consumer loan interest rates, a ban on junk food in schools, and recognition of domestic partnerships to lock in legal rights for same-sex couples.

In 2008, Merkley took on Republican Sen. Gordon H. Smith, while potential rivals such as Reps. Peter A. DeFazio and Earl Blumenauer took a pass. His campaign got off to a rough start — he survived an accident when a car he was riding in rolled over on an icy highway.

He took a $250,000 mortgage out on his Washington house (he owns four other properties in the Portland area) to finance his campaign and edged out Steve Novick, a Portland lawyer and political consultant, in the primary. In the general election, Merkley criticized the moderate Smith for neutralizing the liberal votes of Wyden. He also attacked Smith for supporting President George W. Bush's economic policies and for coming late to the campaign to end the Iraq War.

Smith raised $9.2 million for his campaign, about a third more than Merkley's $6.4 million, but the challenger got help from an ad blitz by the Democratic Senatorial Campaign Committee. Merkley won 49 percent of the vote, edging Smith by 3 percentage points.

Key Votes

2010

Pass budget reconciliation bill to modify overhauls of health care and federal student loan programs	YES
Proceed to disapproval resolution on EPA authority to regulate greenhouse gases	NO
Overhaul financial services industry regulation	YES
Limit debate to proceed to a bill to broaden campaign finance disclosure and reporting rules	YES
Limit debate on an extension of Bush-era income tax cuts for two years	?
Limit debate on a bill to provide a path to legal status for some children of illegal immigrants	YES
Allow for a repeal of "don't ask, don't tell"	YES
Consent to ratification of a strategic arms reduction treaty with Russia	YES

2009

Prevent release of remaining financial industry bailout funds	NO
Make it easier for victims to sue for wage discrimination remedies	YES
Expand the Children's Health Insurance Program	YES
Limit debate on the economic stimulus measure	YES
Repeal District of Columbia firearms prohibitions and gun registration laws	NO
Limit debate on expansion of federal hate crimes law	YES
Strike funding for F-22 Raptor fighter jets	YES

CQ Vote Studies

	PARTY UNITY		PRESIDENTIAL SUPPORT	
	SUPPORT	OPPOSE	SUPPORT	OPPOSE
2010	97%	3%	95%	5%
2009	98%	2%	96%	4%

Interest Groups

	AFL-CIO	ADA	CCUS	ACU
2010	100%	100%	0%	4%
2009	100%	100%	43%	4%

Rep. David Wu (D)

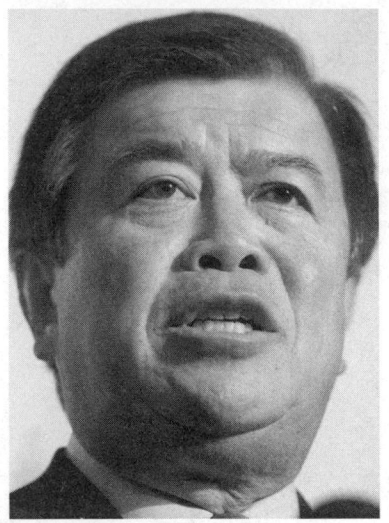

Capitol Office
225-0855
www.house.gov/wu
2338 Rayburn Bldg. 20515-3701; fax 225-9497

Committees
Education & the Workforce
Science, Space & Technology

Residence
Portland

Born
April 8, 1955; Hsinchu, Taiwan

Religion
Presbyterian

Family
Wife, Michelle Wu; two children

Education
Stanford U., B.S. 1977; Harvard Medical School, attended 1978; Yale U., J.D. 1982

Career
Lawyer

Political Highlights
No previous office

ELECTION RESULTS

2010 GENERAL

David Wu (D)	160,357	54.7%
Rob Cornilles (R)	122,858	41.9%
Donald LaMunyon (CNSTP)	3,855	1.3%
Chris Henry (PACGRN)	2,955	1.0%

2010 PRIMARY

David Wu (D)	61,439	80.9%
David Robinson (D)	14,102	18.6%

2008 GENERAL

David Wu (D)	237,567	71.5%
Joel Haugen (I)	58,279	17.5%
Scott Semrau (CNSTP)	14,172	4.3%
H. Joe Tabor (LIBERT)	10,992	3.3%
Chris Henry (PACGRN)	7,128	2.1%

Previous Winning Percentages
2006 (63%); 2004 (58%); 2002 (63%); 2000 (58%); 1998 (50%)

Elected 1998; 7th term

Wu's erratic behavior and self-professed mental health problems led to considerable consternation among his staff in late 2010, and raised the possibility that he might resign. But his colleagues and leadership stood by him and he was back performing his duties at the beginning of the 112th Congress.

Wu admitted behaving in an "unprofessional" way toward campaign and House staff in the weeks leading up to the 2010 elections, including the emailing of unusual pictures of himself. A half-dozen staff members quit, though none went public with their concerns until after Election Day.

"I sincerely regret some of the things I said and did, all of which you have been reading about in the papers," Wu wrote in a March 2011 letter to constituents. In February, he told ABC News that he was undergoing professional treatment and he was "in a good place now. I'm taking care of my two children. They're doing well. I'm taking care of my 88-year-old mother. I'm taking care of myself."

Wu's legislative priorities reflect the struggles and triumphs of his parents, Chinese scientists who immigrated to the United States. He backs a larger role for the federal government in scientific research and education funding and is a staunch defender of human rights and the free flow of information.

The first person of full Chinese ancestry to serve in Congress, Wu prefers to work behind the scenes to write legislation that meets his goals. He describes his politics as fiscally conservative and socially liberal, but he almost always sides with Democratic leaders on votes that split the parties.

Wu chaired the Science and Technology Subcommittee on Technology and Innovation in the 111th Congress (2009-10) and is the panel's top Democrat in the 112th Congress (2011-12). (The full committee has been renamed Science, Space and Technology.) He supported provisions in the 2009 economic stimulus law to provide money for health information technology and training. He also obtained funding in the catchall spending bill for fiscal 2009 for local projects, including millions for science research and education.

From his seat on the Education and Labor Committee (now known as Education and the Workforce), he sponsored bills to support the creation of "open textbooks" — openly licensed texts offered online for anyone to use — and to expand the deductibility of interest paid on student loans. During the 110th Congress (2007-08), he played a role in the reauthorization of a law funding higher education programs. The 2008 law includes a provision by Wu authorizing grants to institutions serving Asian-American populations.

Wu keeps an eye on U.S. relations with China, including its record on human rights. He supported a GOP-sponsored resolution during the 109th Congress (2005-06) sanctioning countries that sell arms or defense-related technology to China. In 2000, he voted against a law granting trade preferences to China, despite intense pressure from the Oregon business community to vote for it. Wu's decision so angered Nike Inc., which is based in his district, that the company's political action committee gave money to his opponent that year.

In the 111th Congress, Wu sponsored legislation that would repeal a provision in a 1992 law that tightened the limits on Chinese immigration to the United States following the Tiananmen Square crackdown.

Wu joined with human rights advocate Christopher H. Smith, a New Jersey Republican, in forming the House Global Internet Freedom Caucus in 2010. That followed a Treasury Department decision to revise economic sanctions to allow for the licensing of Web-based communications services — including instant messaging and e-mail — to people in Cuba, Iran and Sudan.

Wu's mental health problems were not his first brush with bad publicity. During the 109th Congress he intervened with the U.S. Bureau of Prisons in the case of an imprisoned Portland executive. Andrew Wiederhorn, whom he called a "friend and constituent," had pleaded guilty to taking part in a scheme to conceal massive investment losses from clients and to filing a false tax return. Wiederhorn, who now runs the California-based Fatburger chain, had donated thousands of dollars to Wu's campaign.

Wu's family history was shaped by war. His parents met after his father fled his home near Shanghai following the Japanese invasion prior to World War II. The couple moved to Taiwan to seek work — Wu was born there in Hsinchu — but the Chinese civil war that followed prevented them from returning to the mainland. His father left Taiwan to study in America, and Wu was 6 when he, his sisters and his mother finally followed. The family settled in Latham, N.Y., and two years later moved to southern California. His father is a metallurgist and his mother is a chemical engineer.

President John F. Kennedy's decision to allow more Chinese immigration to the United States allowed the family to reunite. "Because of one election, a very close election, the election of John Kennedy in 1960, we got our opportunity to come," Wu said, explaining that it was his inspiration for getting into public life.

He attended Stanford for his undergraduate studies and went to medical school at Harvard, where he roomed with future Senate Republican Leader Bill Frist of Tennessee. But Wu decided medicine wasn't for him, he left Harvard for Yale, where he earned a law degree.

After law school, he worked as a clerk for a federal judge in Portland, then briefly with a law firm in Palo Alto, Calif., before working on Gary Hart's 1984 presidential campaign. After Hart was defeated in the primaries, Wu worked on behalf of the Democratic nominee, Walter F. Mondale, in Portland and stayed there after the election, spending four years with a law firm before starting his own private practice specializing in intellectual property and technology law.

Wu made a run for the U.S. House when Democrat Elizabeth Furse announced her retirement in 1998. He edged past Washington County Commission Chairwoman Linda Peters in the primary and won a 3-percentage-point victory over public relations consultant Molly Bordonaro, a Republican, in the general. He hasn't had a close race since and won re-election in 2010 by 13 percentage points.

Key Votes

2010

Overhaul the nation's health insurance system	YES
Allow for repeal of "don't ask, don't tell"	YES
Overhaul financial services industry regulation	YES
Limit use of new Afghanistan War funds to troop withdrawal activities	NO
Change oversight of offshore drilling and lift oil spill liability cap	YES
Provide a path to legal status for some children of illegal immigrants	?
Extend Bush-era income tax cuts for two years	NO

2009

Expand the Children's Health Insurance Program	YES
Provide $787 billion in tax cuts and spending increases to stimulate the economy	YES
Allow bankruptcy judges to modify certain primary-residence mortgages	YES
Create a cap-and-trade system to limit greenhouse gas emissions	YES
Provide $2 billion for the "cash for clunkers" program	YES
Establish the government as the sole provider of student loans	YES
Restrict federally funded insurance coverage for abortions in health care overhaul	NO

CQ Vote Studies

	PARTY UNITY		PRESIDENTIAL SUPPORT	
	Support	Oppose	Support	Oppose
2010	91%	9%	87%	13%
2009	98%	2%	97%	3%
2008	97%	3%	13%	87%
2007	96%	4%	3%	97%
2006	92%	8%	23%	77%

Interest Groups

	AFL-CIO	ADA	CCUS	ACU
2010	100%	85%	13%	0%
2009	100%	100%	33%	0%
2008	100%	90%	50%	4%
2007	96%	100%	50%	0%
2006	100%	90%	33%	12%

Oregon 1

Western Portland and suburbs; Beaverton

Nestled on the western bank of the Willamette River, the 1st combines three distinct parts: western Portland suburbs; a northern section that follows the Columbia River to the Pacific Ocean and relies on traditional outdoor industries; and a southern branch that takes in all of Yamhill County and its part of the Willamette Valley wine region.

Washington County, which accounts for two-thirds of the district's population, has a highly educated workforce and has been the economic engine of the 1st for two decades. The area west of Portland that depends on a rebounding high-tech economy is still referred to as the "Silicon Forest." The populations of Hillsboro, Beaverton and the western suburbs exploded after 1990; aided by a light-rail line that reaches Hillsboro, which grew more than 30 percent between 2000 and 2010, towns that were once bedroom communities turned into satellite cities with their own commuter streams.

East of Washington County, the 1st's portion of Portland includes the Pearl District neighborhood, where old warehouses were turned into retail shops, art galleries, offices and condos, and new development has sprung up. The southern edge of the Pearl District is Burnside Street, home to the famous Powell's City of Books.

Outside the Portland metro area, the 1st struggles to keep traditional logging and fishing industries intact. Despite improved salmon and trout stocks, the region still faces declining profits. State officials hope to transition the workforce in both fields to emerging industries in electronics and agriculture. International trade is a hot issue for the number of large businesses.

Democrats do well in Multnomah and in the far northern counties of Clatsop and Columbia, while the GOP has a slight edge in Yamhill and elections in Washington County can be close. Democrat Barack Obama took the district with 61 percent of the 2008 presidential vote.

Major Industry
Electronics, computer manufacturing, wine production, nurseries

Cities
Hillsboro, 91,611; Beaverton, 89,803; Portland (pt.), 86,733; Aloha (unincorporated), 49,425; Tigard, 48,035

Notable
Nike's headquarters are in Beaverton.

Rep. Greg Walden (R)

Capitol Office
225-6730
www.walden.house.gov
2182 Rayburn Bldg. 20515-3702; fax 225-5774

Committees
Energy & Commerce
(Communications & Technology - Chairman)

Residence
Hood River

Born
Jan. 10, 1957; The Dalles, Ore.

Religion
Episcopalian

Family
Wife, Mylene Walden; two children (one deceased)

Education
U. of Oregon, B.S. 1981 (journalism); U. of Alaska,
attended 1974-75

Career
Radio station owner; congressional aide

Political Highlights
Ore. House, 1989-95 (majority leader, 1991-93); Ore.
Senate, 1995-97 (assistant majority leader, 1995-97)

ELECTION RESULTS

2010 GENERAL

Greg Walden (R)	206,245	73.9%
Joyce B. Segers (D)	72,173	25.9%

2010 PRIMARY

Greg Walden (R)	74,970	98.9%
write-ins (R)	818	1.1%

2008 GENERAL

Greg Walden (R)	236,560	69.5%
Noah Lemas (D)	87,649	25.8%
Tristin Mock (PACGRN)	9,668	2.8%
Richard D. Hake (CNSTP)	5,817	1.7%

Previous Winning Percentages
2006 (67%); 2004 (72%); 2002 (72%); 2000 (74%);
1998 (61%)

Elected 1998; 7th term

Walden's reputation as thoughtful and politically savvy has made him such a go-to guy for Republican leaders that in February 2010 they revived a spot for him at the leadership table that had been dormant since 2005.

When Republican Leader John A. Boehner of Ohio plucked the relatively obscure Walden from the backbenches and named him chairman of the Republican leadership, some outside the halls of Congress wondered why. But Walden was already operating on the fringes of the leadership circle, and his hidden portfolio shows that he was more than a bit player.

In addition to being a regular counsel for leaders on top issues, he may be the closest friend of National Republican Congressional Committee Chairman Pete Sessions of Texas, whom he serves as deputy chairman. And he was named chairman of the GOP transition team after the party's victory in the 2010 elections.

Walden is the fourth member of the House Republican Conference to hold the leadership chair post created in the mid-1990s for Pennsylvanian Robert S. Walker because then-Speaker Newt Gingrich of Georgia wanted to bring his close ally into the leadership circle. Where Walker served as liaison between Gingrich and committee chairmen, Walden's time is likely to be split between politics and policy.

While he's not well-known outside his district, Walden has built a reputation among members and staff as an able communicator who can help bridge differences among conference factions.

And he was willing to give up — at least temporarily — a seat on the powerful Energy and Commerce Committee to make room for party-switcher Parker Griffith of Alabama (who subsequently lost in the June 2010 GOP primary). Walden returned to the panel in the 112th Congress (2011-12) and assumed the chairmanship of the Subcommittee on Communications and Technology, which will deal with the thorny subject of so-called net neutrality. The full committee quickly moved his measure to nullify the Federal Communications Commission's rules governing how broadband service providers allow content to move through their networks. Walden contends the FCC lacks the authority to institute such rules.

The full chamber voted to bar funding to enforce the FCC rule during consideration of the House-passed catchall spending bill for fiscal 2011.

Walden, who also sits on the Energy and Power Subcommittee, opposed proposals for a cap on greenhouse gas emissions matched with a market-based industry-trading program. And like many in his party, he supported drilling for gas and oil off the nation's coasts.

He represents a district that includes all or part of 10 national forests and shares his constituents' dislike of federal intrusion into land use and environmental management. But he aims for bipartisan partnerships to seek solutions for limiting wildfires and helping rural counties hurt by cutbacks in logging.

Walden was one of 38 Republicans who joined the majority of Democrats to pass a land conservation bill in early 2009 designating millions of acres in nine states for preservation. Walden helped ensure the measure protects a vast swath in the Mount Hood National Forest.

At the ceremony when President Obama signed the bill into law, Walden handed the president a letter urging him to allow more timber to be cut in national forests to prevent future forest fires. Walden argues that speeding up forest management action in his district would curb high unemployment rates and help the health of the current forest. That issue was at the heart of why he favored a 2008 law to help the ailing financial services industry; the measure included an extension of the program that pays rural counties hurt by federally imposed logging restrictions.

Walden won enactment in 2003 of a Healthy Forests law that reversed decades of environmental policy and authorized logging and other steps to thin forests on public lands to reduce the threat of wildfires. The measure had been stymied for years by opposition from environmentalists and some Democrats. But Walden teamed up with Oregon's senior senator, Democrat Ron Wyden, and helped address insect infestations and other concerns.

He is an advocate for press freedoms. He earned a degree in journalism from the University of Oregon and worked at his father's radio station in Hood River as both a disc jockey and a talk show host. He and his wife later bought the business, and their company, Columbia Gorge Broadcasters Inc., operated five radio stations. In October 2007, he backed a bill to protect journalists from having to disclose their confidential sources. In 2009 he cosponsored a similar measure that the House passed by voice vote.

He has adopted a middle-ground position on abortion. He opposes federal funding for abortions and voted to outlaw a procedure its opponents call "partial birth" abortion. In November 2009, Walden joined the majority of House Republicans in voting for Michigan Democrat Bart Stupak's amendment to the health care overhaul bill that barred federal funding of abortion through a government plan. But he doesn't support a reversal of the Supreme Court's 1973 *Roe v. Wade* decision establishing a woman's right to an abortion. He said his views on the issue were shaped when he and his wife considered but rejected an abortion when the child she was carrying was diagnosed with a congenital heart defect. The baby boy was born prematurely and died.

Walden was raised on an 80-acre cherry orchard property in The Dalles, east of Portland. His father served in the Oregon legislature and his mother volunteered for the Red Cross.

Walden worked as an aide to Oregon GOP Rep. Denny Smith for about five years in the 1980s. He then served eight years in the state legislature, including three as House majority leader and two as assistant Senate majority leader.

When Republican Bob Smith decided to retire in 1998, Walden easily bested Democrat Kevin M. Campbell, a former county judge. His closest race since came in 2006, when he took 67 percent of the vote to defeat Democrat Carol Voisin, a Southern Oregon University instructor. In early 2009, Walden considered a 2010 run for governor but opted to pass on the race. He was re-elected to the House with 74 percent of the vote.

Key Votes

2010

Overhaul the nation's health insurance system	NO
Allow for repeal of "don't ask, don't tell"	NO
Overhaul financial services industry regulation	NO
Limit use of new Afghanistan War funds to troop withdrawal activities	NO
Change oversight of offshore drilling and lift oil spill liability cap	NO
Provide a path to legal status for some children of illegal immigrants	NO
Extend Bush-era income tax cuts for two years	YES

2009

Expand the Children's Health Insurance Program	NO
Provide $787 billion in tax cuts and spending increases to stimulate the economy	NO
Allow bankruptcy judges to modify certain primary-residence mortgages	NO
Create a cap-and-trade system to limit greenhouse gas emissions	NO
Provide $2 billion for the "cash for clunkers" program	YES
Establish the government as the sole provider of student loans	NO
Restrict federally funded insurance coverage for abortions in health care overhaul	YES

CQ Vote Studies

	PARTY UNITY		PRESIDENTIAL SUPPORT	
	SUPPORT	OPPOSE	SUPPORT	OPPOSE
2010	93%	7%	33%	67%
2009	83%	17%	44%	56%
2008	93%	7%	63%	37%
2007	82%	18%	62%	38%
2006	93%	7%	87%	13%

Interest Groups

	AFL-CIO	ADA	CCUS	ACU
2010	0%	0%	88%	96%
2009	25%	15%	86%	80%
2008	20%	30%	89%	75%
2007	42%	30%	90%	68%
2006	31%	15%	100%	80%

Oregon 2

East and southwest — Medford, Bend

The rural and sometimes rugged 2nd is Oregon's most reliably Republican district. It encompasses the eastern two-thirds of the state, taking in all of 19 counties and part of one other, and borders Washington, Idaho, Nevada and California. The federal government owns most of the land, which has fertile fields, towering mountains and protected forests.

Although downturns in the timber and fishing industries drove people away from Eastern Oregon in the 1980s and several of the vast, sparsely populated counties in the east continued to shed population after 2000, an influx of residents to areas west of Bend in Deschutes County has boosted the district's overall population.

The strength of the local agriculture industry lies in its diversity. Ranchers in the southeast raise livestock, while farmers in the north harvest more wheat than anywhere else in Oregon. From the district's northwest near Mount Hood south to the Rogue River Valley is a rich fruit belt: Almost all of the state's pears are grown in either Jackson County or Hood River County, which leads the nation in pear production. Cherries and apples are grown here as well, and Central Oregon hosts breweries. Construction of wind

farms in arid Harney County and along the Columbia River Gorge on the 2nd's northern border will bring jobs.

In Deschutes County in central Oregon, skyrocketing costs of living that paralleled Bend's population growth led to a housing market collapse. Adjacent to Deschutes, Crook County has continued to gain residents despite sustained unemployment rates above 15 percent. To the southwest, Medford, in Jackson County, relies on health care jobs. Southeast of Medford is Ashland, which has hosted the Oregon Shakespeare Festival since 1935. An independent streak, the legacy of a farming and ranching tradition, remains throughout the 2nd, and growing pockets of Democrats in Bend and Ashland are still too few to swing the district. John McCain took 54 percent of the 2008 presidential vote here, the only Oregon district he won.

Major Industry
Agriculture, forestry, tourism

Cities
Bend, 76,639; Medford, 74,907; Grants Pass, 34,533; Redmond, 26,215

Notable
Crater Lake is the deepest lake in the United States.

Rep. Earl Blumenauer (D)

Capitol Office
225-4811
blumenauer.house.gov
1502 Longworth Bldg. 20515; fax 225-8941

Committees
Budget
Ways & Means

Residence
Portland

Born
Aug. 16, 1948; Portland, Ore.

Religion
Unspecified

Family
Wife, Margaret Kirkpatrick; two children, two
stepchildren

Education
Lewis & Clark College, B.A. 1970 (political science),
J.D. 1976

Career
Public official

Political Highlights
Ore. House, 1973-77; Multnomah County Commission, 1978-86; candidate for Portland City Council,
1980; Portland City Council, 1986-96; candidate for
mayor of Portland, 1992

ELECTION RESULTS

2010 GENERAL

Earl Blumenauer (D)	193,104	70.0%
Delia Lopez (R)	67,714	24.6%
Jeffrey Lawrence (LIBERT)	8,380	3.0%
Michael Meo (PACGRN)	6,197	2.2%

2010 PRIMARY

Earl Blumenauer (D)	73,962	91.2%
John Sweeney (D)	6,774	8.4%

2008 GENERAL

Earl Blumenauer (D)	254,235	74.5%
Delia Lopez (R)	71,063	20.8%
Michael Meo (PACGRN)	15,063	4.4%

Previous Winning Percentages
2006 (74%); 2004 (71%); 2002 (67%); 2000 (67%);
1998 (84%); 1996 (67%); 1996 Special Election (70%)

Elected 1996; 8th full term

The bow-tie-wearing Blumenauer has a reputation for bipartisanship that is rarely reflected in his liberal voting record. His eccentric personal style helps bring awareness to his legislative priorities, such as boosting the use of bicycles and federal subsidies for renewable energy. It also helps that he sits on the Ways and Means Committee.

Blumenauer (BLUE-men-hour) has been in or running for public office virtually his entire adult life. He is well-practiced at political discourse and has a reputation for civility, in keeping with his home state's genteel politics.

But his devotion to environmental causes tested that civility when he was dismissive of a contrarian witness at a 2010 hearing of the now-defunct Select Committee on Energy Independence and Global Warming. "I find it a little embarrassing and sad that the minority witness is a journalist with no scientific training," Blumenauer said of Lord Christopher Monckton, a former adviser to British Prime Minster Margaret Thatcher.

Blumenauer told The New York Times in early 2009 that recovery from the economic downturn is "perhaps the best opportunity we will ever see" to spread his brand of environmental policy into U.S. infrastructure, with streetcar systems, bike and pedestrian paths, more-efficient energy transmission and alternative-fuel vehicle fleets for the federal government.

He introduced a bill in 2009 requiring 10 percent of revenue from a cap-and-trade program for trading greenhouse gas emissions credits to be spent on energy-efficient transportation projects.

When it comes to protecting the environment and addressing climate change, Blumenauer practices what he preaches. He commutes by bicycle between his Capitol Hill apartment and his office, and often rides to meetings at the White House. Blumenauer, a founder of the Congressional Bicycle Caucus, has long sought to increase the nation's use of two-wheelers. In the 110th Congress (2007-08), he proposed new tax benefits for commuters who ride bicycles to work. In 2007, he designed a "bike to work" program for congressional employees as part of a Democratic initiative to make the Capitol more environmentally friendly.

Blumenauer, who cycles everywhere when he is home in Portland, used the Bicycle Caucus and a seat on the Transportation and Infrastructure Committee that he occupied from 1997 to 2006 to help shepherd to his district millions of dollars for bike trails, pedestrian facilities and mass-transit systems. Blumenauer wants to include in the next surface transportation bill a provision requiring airport parking garages to provide spaces for bike storage.

Back in Washington, he joined a half-dozen Democratic colleagues in urging the new GOP leadership to dispense with Styrofoam in House cafeterias, claiming the cups are a health hazard and bad for the environment.

From his seat on the Budget Committee, Blumenauer advocates for mass transit, and he secured federal money for Portland to build a 5.8-mile Interstate Max light-rail line extension, which opened in 2004, between downtown and the Columbia River. He successfully pressed in 2007 to block federal rules that gave cities seeking funds for buses an advantage over those like Portland that have sought to expand the use of streetcars instead. Blumenauer also introduced legislation in June 2010 that would offer a tax credit to manufacturers to replace older railcars with more energy-efficient ones.

He worked for years to protect Mount Hood, 50 miles southeast of Portland. He got a provision into a public-lands bill that was signed into law in 2009 to designate almost 127,000 acres around it as federally protected wilderness.

Blumenauer's environmental agenda also extends to infrastructure issues. In August 2010, he introduced legislation that would tax bottled water and contaminants disposed of through water infrastructure, like toothpaste and toilet paper. The revenue from the tax would fund water and environmental infrastructure restoration.

In the 111th Congress (2009-10), Blumenauer backed all of President Obama's major initiatives, siding with his party almost 99 percent of the time on votes that divided a majority of Democrats from a majority of Republicans.

But Blumenauer finds common ground with Republicans on some trade issues, which are closely watched in his port-city district. In early 2006, Blumenauer was one of only eight House Democrats to vote against barring the sale of facilities at six major U.S. ports to a company owned by the United Arab Emirates. A year earlier, Blumenauer was one of 21 Democrats who voted against blocking the sale of U.S. oil giant Unocal to a company owned by the Chinese government. In both cases, the companies backed out of the transactions. He voted for the 2000 law making permanent normal U.S. trade relations with China, noting that one in five jobs in his district was tied to trade with the Pacific Rim.

On more-traditional trade deals, he goes back and forth.

In 2002 he opposed the revival of fast-track trade negotiating authority for the president. By 2003 and 2004, he was helping to round up House votes for a free-trade agreement with Chile and voting for trade pacts with Singapore, Australia and Morocco. Then in 2005 and 2006, he lined up with his fellow Democrats against the Central America Free Trade Agreement and a pact with Oman, but voted for an agreement with Bahrain.

An activist since his teens, Blumenauer was just one year out of college in 1971 when he testified before Congress in support of a constitutional amendment to lower the voting age to 18. Elected to the state House at 24, in four years he rose to chair the Revenue Committee, where he says he first developed an interest in tax policy. He then spent eight years on the Multnomah County Commission, followed by 10 years on the Portland City Council.

He ran unsuccessfully for mayor of Portland in 1992, but won a 1996 special election to the U.S. House. The 3rd District seat had become vacant after Democrat Ron Wyden won a special Senate election to replace Republican Bob Packwood, who had resigned the previous fall. Blumenauer easily took the primary and special election and has cruised to re-election since.

Key Votes

2010

Overhaul the nation's health insurance system	YES
Allow for repeal of "don't ask, don't tell"	YES
Overhaul financial services industry regulation	YES
Limit use of new Afghanistan War funds to troop withdrawal activities	YES
Change oversight of offshore drilling and lift oil spill liability cap	YES
Provide a path to legal status for some children of illegal immigrants	YES
Extend Bush-era income tax cuts for two years	NO

2009

Expand the Children's Health Insurance Program	YES
Provide $787 billion in tax cuts and spending increases to stimulate the economy	YES
Allow bankruptcy judges to modify certain primary-residence mortgages	YES
Create a cap-and-trade system to limit greenhouse gas emissions	YES
Provide $2 billion for the "cash for clunkers" program	NO
Establish the government as the sole provider of student loans	YES
Restrict federally funded insurance coverage for abortions in health care overhaul	NO

CQ Vote Studies

	PARTY UNITY		PRESIDENTIAL SUPPORT	
	Support	Oppose	Support	Oppose
2010	98%	2%	88%	12%
2009	99%	1%	93%	7%
2008	98%	2%	15%	85%
2007	97%	3%	6%	94%
2006	97%	3%	8%	92%

Interest Groups

	AFL-CIO	ADA	CCUS	ACU
2010	100%	100%	0%	5%
2009	95%	90%	40%	0%
2008	100%	95%	53%	12%
2007	96%	85%	50%	0%
2006	93%	90%	27%	8%

Oregon 3

North and east Portland; eastern suburbs

Split by the Willamette River, the city of Portland has two personalities. The eastern portion, covered by the 3rd, still depends on the blue-collar economy that has made the city a thriving international port for lumber and fruit. The Port of Portland and Portland International Airport make the city a center of trade and distribution. Computer chips and cappuccino drive the city's western side (in the 1st and 5th districts). Home foreclosures and a stalling construction sector, an economic staple here for decades, have hurt the Portland area.

Area sports fans watch basketball's Trailblazers at the Rose Garden arena on the eastern side of the Willamette, and Portland's many breweries are havens for beer enthusiasts. The 3rd's portion of Portland takes in the University of Portland, Reed College and several hospitals.

Compared with the rest of Portland, the 3rd is a multicultural haven. There is a large black population in precincts just east of the Willamette River, near Interstate 5 and Martin Luther King Jr. Blvd. A sizable Hispanic population resides in northeastern Portland and in Gresham and Wood Village

east of the city. Asians are numerous in east-central Portland, near 82nd Avenue and Interstate 205. Gresham, the district's second-largest city, was once a thriving farm community. It is now the easternmost stop on Portland's light-rail system and hopes to continue luring large-scale business investments to its growing downtown area.

Beyond the Portland metropolitan area, the district quickly turns rural. Its far eastern border reaches Mount Hood — Oregon's highest peak at 11,239 feet — and the Mount Hood National Forest in the western part of the Cascade Range.

Although there are politically competitive portions of rural Clackamas County, Portland's liberal leanings make the 3rd Oregon's strongest Democratic district. In the 2008 presidential election, Barack Obama won the 3rd with 71 percent of the vote, his highest percentage statewide.

Major Industry
Wholesale trade and distribution, health care, education

Cities
Portland (pt.), 471,692; Gresham, 105,594; Milwaukie, 20,291

Notable
"The Simpsons" creator Matt Groening grew up in Portland — perhaps coincidentally, many of his characters share the names of local streets.

Rep. Peter A. DeFazio (D)

Capitol Office
225-6416
www.house.gov/defazio
2134 Rayburn Bldg. 20515-3704; fax 225-0032

Committees
Natural Resources
Transportation & Infrastructure

Residence
Springfield

Born
May 27, 1947; Needham, Mass.

Religion
Roman Catholic

Family
Wife, Myrnie L. Daut

Education
Tufts U., B.A. 1969 (economics & political science); U. of Oregon, attended 1969-71 (international studies), M.S. 1977 (public administration & gerontology)

Military
Air Force, 1967-71

Career
Congressional aide

Political Highlights
Lane County Commission, 1982-86; sought Democratic nomination for U.S. Senate (special election), 1996

ELECTION RESULTS

2010 GENERAL

Peter A. DeFazio (D)	162,416	54.5%
Art Robinson (R)	129,877	43.6%
Mike Beilstein (PACGRN)	5,215	1.8%

2010 PRIMARY

Peter A. DeFazio (D)	74,568	97.8%
write-ins (D)	1,677	2.2%

2008 GENERAL

Peter A. DeFazio (D)	275,143	82.3%
Jaynee Germond (CNSTP)	43,133	12.9%
Mike Beilstein (PACGRN)	13,162	3.9%

Previous Winning Percentages
2006 (62%); 2004 (61%); 2002 (64%); 2000 (68%); 1998 (70%); 1996 (66%); 1994 (67%); 1992 (71%); 1990 (86%); 1988 (72%); 1986 (54%)

Elected 1986; 13th term

Since arriving in Congress more than two decades ago, DeFazio has rarely missed an opportunity to goad Republican opponents. But he doesn't shy from criticizing his own party either. He is a loud and persistent voice pushing a liberal, populist agenda, but he is also a savvy lawmaker adept at securing federal funds for his district.

Despite the partisanship of the health care debate during the 111th Congress (2009-10) — and DeFazio's own fondness for needling Republicans — he offered one of the few proposals that garnered widespread bipartisan support: a measure to end the health insurance industry's antitrust exemption, which DeFazio said could "result in a 10 to 12 percent reduction in insurance premiums." When the measure was not included in the Democrats' health care overhaul, DeFazio cosponsored a stand-alone bill to repeal the exemption that went to the House floor in February 2010, passing 406-19, with support from 153 Republicans. "This proves that health care solutions can be bipartisan," DeFazio said.

During negotiations on the final version of the health care bill, DeFazio vowed to oppose the legislation if a measure to increase the Medicare reimbursement rate for doctors in Oregon and other states was not included. At least one Democratic House colleague suggested the ultimatum was a bluff, but DeFazio stuck to his guns, saying he would need "ironclad assurances" that the reimbursement rate would be changed before supporting the bill. The effort worked. DeFazio helped strike a deal with the Obama administration, with a promise to take "specific steps" to address regional disparities by 2012. The deal cleared the way for DeFazio and several other Democrats in the Oregon delegation to support the overhaul.

It was not the first time DeFazio had taken issue with one of President Obama's major initiatives. He was one of seven House Democrats to oppose the $787 billion economic stimulus law in 2009. He said the plan's tax cuts were too large and it did not include enough infrastructure spending.

Obama noticed. During a subsequent meeting with House Democrats, DeFazio asked him about increasing infrastructure money in his fiscal 2010 budget. The president responded, "I know you think we need more for that because you voted against [the stimulus]. Don't think we're not keeping score, brother." A satisfied DeFazio — who supported the budget — said later, "At least I got his attention."

DeFazio has plenty to say on infrastructure spending. He is the ranking Democrat on the Transportation and Infrastructure Subcommittee on Highways and Transit, which has responsibility for drafting a bill reauthorizing highway and surface transportation programs. "We are dramatically underinvesting in our nation's surface transportation system. We aren't even keeping pace and maintaining the infrastructure built by the Eisenhower generation," he said.

The highway bill is also a chance for DeFazio to steer more federal dollars to his district. He secured $200 million to fix bridges along Interstate 5 in the last major highway bill, passed in 2005. "I got the single largest allocation for a Democrat," he says of his work at a time when the GOP was in control.

DeFazio has also been outspoken in his opposition to free-trade agreements. He opposed normalizing trade relations with China in 2000 and a free-trade pact in 2005 with five Central American countries. He contends that U.S. trade policy is "designed to export our manufacturing base and chase cheap labor around the world."

From his seat on the Natural Resources Committee, DeFazio often faces a juggling act on forest issues. His constituency includes two groups with conflicting interests: loggers, who oppose curbs on timber cutting, and environmentalists, who want restrictions. The competing pressures were evident in 2003, when DeFazio first opposed a sweeping forest-thinning bill championed by Oregon Republican Greg Walden, but then voted for a final version that included significant changes made by the Senate at Oregon Democrat Ron Wyden's insistence.

DeFazio, formerly a member of the Homeland Security Committee, has been active on security issues. After the Sept. 11 terrorist attacks, he led the House Democrats' campaign against GOP efforts to retain private contract workers as airport baggage screeners. The aviation security law that was ultimately enacted not only federalized the baggage screeners but also made a number of other security changes DeFazio had sought for years. He considers the implementation of these changes to be among his most important achievements in Congress.

DeFazio refuses to keep congressional pay raises beyond the rate of Social Security cost-of-living increases as long as government spending is in the red. Instead, he uses the money to fund two scholarships at each of five community colleges in his district. He established the scholarships for displaced timber workers and expanded them to include displaced workers in general, and then to include veterans of the wars in Iraq and Afghanistan. DeFazio establishes the criteria and a state agency administers the scholarships.

DeFazio grew up in Massachusetts. His first taste of politics came as a boy at the knee of his great-uncle, a classic Boston pol who followed the word Republican with the Boston-accented epithet "bastuhd" so often that young DeFazio thought it was one word — "Republicanbastuhd."

After graduating from Tufts University outside Boston, DeFazio attended graduate school at the University of Oregon. While a student there, he established an employment program for seniors that is still in existence. After earning a graduate degree in gerontology, he ran a senior citizens' program for a time, then landed a job as a specialist on elder issues with Oregon Democratic Rep. James Weaver, a hot-tempered populist.

In 1982, DeFazio struck out on his own, getting elected to the Lane County Commission. When Weaver announced he would not seek reelection in 1986, DeFazio stepped in. Casting himself as heir to Weaver's populist mantle, he squeaked by in the primary and then won the seat with 54 percent of the vote. He has held it safely since, though he was held to less than 55 percent of the vote by Republican Art Robinson in 2010.

Key Votes

2010

Overhaul the nation's health insurance system	YES
Allow for repeal of "don't ask, don't tell"	YES
Overhaul financial services industry regulation	YES
Limit use of new Afghanistan War funds to troop withdrawal activities	YES
Change oversight of offshore drilling and lift oil spill liability cap	YES
Provide a path to legal status for some children of illegal immigrants	YES
Extend Bush-era income tax cuts for two years	NO

2009

Expand the Children's Health Insurance Program	YES
Provide $787 billion in tax cuts and spending increases to stimulate the economy	NO
Allow bankruptcy judges to modify certain primary-residence mortgages	YES
Create a cap-and-trade system to limit greenhouse gas emissions	NO
Provide $2 billion for the "cash for clunkers" program	YES
Establish the government as the sole provider of student loans	YES
Restrict federally funded insurance coverage for abortions in health care overhaul	NO

CQ Vote Studies

	PARTY UNITY		PRESIDENTIAL SUPPORT	
	SUPPORT	OPPOSE	SUPPORT	OPPOSE
2010	95%	5%	85%	15%
2009	97%	3%	90%	10%
2008	93%	7%	13%	87%
2007	95%	5%	1%	99%
2006	91%	9%	17%	83%

Interest Groups

	AFL-CIO	ADA	CCUS	ACU
2010	93%	95%	13%	0%
2009	95%	95%	40%	12%
2008	100%	90%	50%	20%
2007	96%	90%	37%	4%
2006	93%	90%	47%	28%

Oregon 4

Southwest — Eugene, Springfield, part of Corvallis

Taking in the southern half of Oregon's Pacific coast and parts of the Cascade Mountains, the 4th's economy is dependent on the district's natural resources. Environmentalists, loggers and fishermen combine to give the 4th a potentially combustible political mix.

A steady decline in the forestry and fishing industries started a pattern of layoffs over the past several decades, keeping the 4th's population growth slower than the rest of the state. Agriculture in the 4th is based in the fertile valley between the Cascade and Coast mountain ranges. Although other areas now dominate Oregon's wine industry, the state's wine grape growing began in the Umpqua Valley in the early 1960s. The region continues to provide rich soil for that industry as well as for a variety of field crops.

Unemployment rates have remained high across the 4th, with rural southwestern Josephine County and more developed Douglas County hit particularly hard. Fishing towns in Coos and Curry counties still struggle. Lane County's Eugene and Springfield, the district's most populous cities,

have lost jobs in white-collar, construction and retail sectors.

Research at the University of Oregon in Eugene, still a hotbed of environmentalism, lured technology companies. Computer manufacturers and software developers still drive the area's economy despite some layoffs. Eugene, the self-proclaimed "Track Town U.S.A.," also is the center of the Oregon running culture.

The electoral success of liberal Rep. Peter A. DeFazio belies the 4th's political competitiveness. Eugene and Springfield make Lane County reliably Democratic. Linn and Douglas counties back Republicans, and Coos and Curry counties lean toward the GOP. Barack Obama won 54 percent of the 4th's 2008 presidential vote, but Democratic Gov. John Kitzhaber took only Lane and Benton (shared with the 5th) counties in 2010.

Major Industry
Forestry, agriculture, fishing, technology, tourism

Cities
Eugene, 156,185; Springfield, 59,403; Albany (pt.), 44,865; Corvallis (pt.), 34,514; Roseburg, 21,181

Notable
Much of the movie "Animal House" was filmed at the University of Oregon and in nearby Cottage Grove.

Rep. Kurt Schrader (D)

Capitol Office
225-5711
schrader.house.gov
314 Cannon Bldg. 20515-3705; fax 225-5699

Committees
Agriculture
Small Business

Residence
Canby

Born
Oct. 19, 1951; Bridgeport, Conn.

Religion
Episcopalian

Family
Separated; five children

Education
Cornell U., B.A. 1973 (government); U. of Illinois, B.S.
1975 (veterinary medicine), D.V.M. 1977

Career
Veterinarian; farmer

Political Highlights
Democratic nominee for Ore. House, 1994; Ore.
House, 1997-2003; Ore. Senate, 2003-08

ELECTION RESULTS

2010 GENERAL

Kurt Schrader (D)	145,319	51.2%
Scott Bruun (R)	130,313	46.0%
Chris Lugo (PACGRN)	7,557	2.7%

2010 PRIMARY

Kurt Schrader (D)	57,282	98.4%
write-ins (D)	945	1.6%

2008 GENERAL

Kurt Schrader (D)	181,577	54.2%
Mike Erickson (R)	128,297	38.3%
Sean Bates (I)	6,830	2.0%
Douglas Patterson (CNSTP)	6,558	2.0%
Alex Polikoff (PACGRN)	5,272	1.6%
Steve Milligan (LIBERT)	4,814	1.4%

Elected 2008; 2nd term

Schrader is a member of the fiscally conservative Blue Dog and moderate New Democrat coalitions. But on most issues, he sides with the Democratic leadership.

He's chairman of the Blue Dogs' Task Force on Fiscal Responsibility and previously served on the Budget Committee. He frequently makes rhetorical appeals to bipartisanship, but he opposed GOP-backed spending cuts passed by the House in early 2011, telling the Corvallis Gazette-Times that the extended debate on the legislation was "an orchestration of political theater that's never going to see the light of day. It made a bunch of new members feel good about themselves, but it added absolutely nothing to the discourse."

He suggested that the measure's $58 billion in cuts to a $3.7 trillion budget was akin to "going back to the Dark Ages."

Schrader argues that smaller cuts in discretionary spending and changes in entitlement programs in line with the recommendations of the president's fiscal commission are a better way to rein in the deficit. He also backs rules to require offsets for new spending or tax cuts.

He was one of more than 50 House Democrats endorsed by the National Rifle Association in 2010, a seal of approval he used to insulate himself from charges that he was too in tune with the party's liberal leadership.

"I think Nancy Pelosi did not get the National Rifle Association endorsement," Schrader said during an October debate, according to Salem's Statesman Journal. At the start of the 112th Congress (2011-12), he cast his vote in the Speaker's race for Minority Whip Steny H. Hoyer of Maryland.

But for the most part, Schrader votes with his Democratic colleagues — 94 percent of the time in the 111th Congress (2009-10) on votes that divided majorities of the two parties.

He said the $787 billion economic stimulus package was essential to reverse the nation's economic fortunes, and he successfully urged House and Senate negotiators to ensure that education funds were released immediately to prevent cuts in local school budgets.

He backed the Democrats' health care overhaul enacted in 2010, voted to establish the government as the sole provider of student loans, and supported creation of a cap-and-trade system to limit carbon emissions.

Schrader farms organic fruit and vegetables and still maintains his license from when he owned a veterinary clinic — a diverse background that he said benefits him as a member of the Agriculture and Small Business committees. In recognition of those jobs and his fiscal knowledge, House Democratic leaders named him chairman of Small Business' Finance and Tax Subcommittee shortly after his arrival on Capitol Hill. He's now the ranking Democrat on that panel's successor — the Economic Growth, Tax and Capital Access Subcommittee — and is the No. 2 Democrat on the full committee.

On Agriculture, Schrader advocates spending more to develop renewable-energy sources and has worked on forest-related issues with his Oregon Republican colleague, Greg Walden; the two men founded the Congressional Healthy Forests Caucus in July 2009.

Schrader was born in Bridgeport, Conn., and grew up in the suburbs outside Philadelphia. His father worked as an engineer at a chemical plant, and his mother stayed at home. The family eventually settled in Illinois, but Schrader said he always knew he would end up elsewhere. "I was never going to live east of the Mississippi River," he said. "I wanted to move out West, where the skies were big."

When he attended Cornell University, he initially intended to follow in his father's footsteps as an engineer. But in the summer before his senior year, he hitchhiked to Wyoming, where he decided to change paths and become a veterinarian. He met his future wife, Martha, at a Cornell zoology class in 1972, and they married in 1975, the year he obtained his bachelor's degree in veterinary medicine from the University of Illinois.

The Schraders moved to Oregon in 1978. They lived in the capital, Salem, then moved to Canby, south of Portland, where Schrader started his veterinary practice. In 1980, he became a member of the planning commission, where he stayed for 16 years and helped develop the city's land-use and parks plans.

Schrader tried for a seat in the Oregon House in 1994, losing narrowly, but two years later he won. He quickly rose through the ranks, becoming assistant House Democratic leader in his first term.

He moved to the state Senate in 2003. Schrader ran into a bit of trouble after it was discovered he had been delinquent in paying property taxes for years. He explained in 2008 that his family had experienced some financial turmoil and they had to decide which bills to pay first. (He subsequently inherited a small fortune after his grandfather died.)

When six-term Democratic Rep. Darlene Hooley announced she would retire at the end of the 110th Congress (2007-08), speculation arose as to which Schrader would run for the open seat — Kurt or Martha, who had been a Clackamas County commissioner since 2003. The couple decided that he had the best chance, even though he is a famously reticent campaigner. "He'd rather set his hair on fire than work a room," Jon Chandler, a lobbyist for the Oregon Home Builders Association, told The Oregonian in October 2008.

Nevertheless, Schrader easily won a five-person Democratic primary with nearly 54 percent of the vote.

In the general election, Republican businessman Mike Erickson sought to paint Schrader as a free-spending Democrat who would raise taxes. But Schrader won endorsements from some of the Republicans he had worked with in the state Senate and won with more than 54 percent, equaling Barack Obama's percentage of the district's presidential vote. Martha Schrader was appointed in January 2009 to fill her husband's state Senate seat.

Schrader faced another tough test in 2010 against state Rep. Scott Bruun. Late polls showed the race to be close, and the Republican outraised the incumbent in the quarter before Election Day. But Schrader won by 5 percentage points.

In May 2011, Schrader and his wife announced that they planned to divorce.

Key Votes

2010

Overhaul the nation's health insurance system	YES
Allow for repeal of "don't ask, don't tell"	YES
Overhaul financial services industry regulation	YES
Limit use of new Afghanistan War funds to troop withdrawal activities	YES
Change oversight of offshore drilling and lift oil spill liability cap	YES
Provide a path to legal status for some children of illegal immigrants	NO
Extend Bush-era income tax cuts for two years	NO

2009

Expand the Children's Health Insurance Program	YES
Provide $787 billion in tax cuts and spending increases to stimulate the economy	YES
Allow bankruptcy judges to modify certain primary-residence mortgages	YES
Create a cap-and-trade system to limit greenhouse gas emissions	YES
Provide $2 billion for the "cash for clunkers" program	NO
Establish the government as the sole provider of student loans	YES
Restrict federally funded insurance coverage for abortions in health care overhaul	NO

CQ Vote Studies

	PARTY UNITY		PRESIDENTIAL SUPPORT	
	SUPPORT	OPPOSE	SUPPORT	OPPOSE
2010	94%	6%	78%	22%
2009	95%	5%	92%	8%

Interest Groups

	AFL-CIO	ADA	CCUS	ACU
2010	86%	85%	13%	17%
2009	81%	80%	53%	8%

Oregon 5

Willamette Valley — Salem, parts of Portland and Corvallis

Oregon City, the western terminus of the 2,000-mile Oregon Trail, in 1844 became the first incorporated city west of the Mississippi River. The 5th District takes in the northern part of the Willamette Valley, the fertile region at the end of that arduous trek. It contains the state capital of Salem and then spills over the Coast Range to cover two Pacific counties, Tillamook and Lincoln. It also includes a small part of Portland (shared with the 1st and 3rd districts).

Clackamas, Marion and Polk counties are at the heart of the Willamette Valley, Oregon's most fertile farmland. The valley is the center of the state's trade in greenhouse crops, seeds and berries. Hops from Marion and Clackamas counties go into some of the nation's finest beers. Polk County grows cherries and wine grapes; wineries dot Polk and Marion counties. Once exclusively reliant on agriculture and timber, the 5th's economy has diversified and now supports environmental research and technology manufacturing. Salem and surrounding Marion County are home to

many government workers and host a food processing industry. Budget shortfalls have hurt Clackamas County's Portland suburbs such as Oregon City and Lake Oswego.

The 5th is highly competitive, thanks largely to independent voters in Marion and Clackamas counties and Republicans in Polk County. Registered Democrats outnumber Republicans in the district overall, but the margin is not overwhelming. Democratic Rep. Kurt Schrader won most of the counties in the 5th in 2010, but Polk backed GOP challenger Scott Bruun and Marion County gave Bruun a slight edge. Strong Democratic areas in the district include Corvallis (shared with the 4th), which is home to Oregon State University, and southwestern Multnomah County, which hosts some affluent liberals around Lewis & Clark College.

Major Industry
Agriculture, timber, food processing, manufacturing, state government

Cities
Salem, 154,637; Lake Oswego (pt.), 36,610; Keizer, 36,478; Oregon City (pt.), 31,673; Portland (pt.), 25,351; West Linn, 25,109

Notable
Salem's Willamette University, established in 1842, was the first university in the West.

PENNSYLVANIA

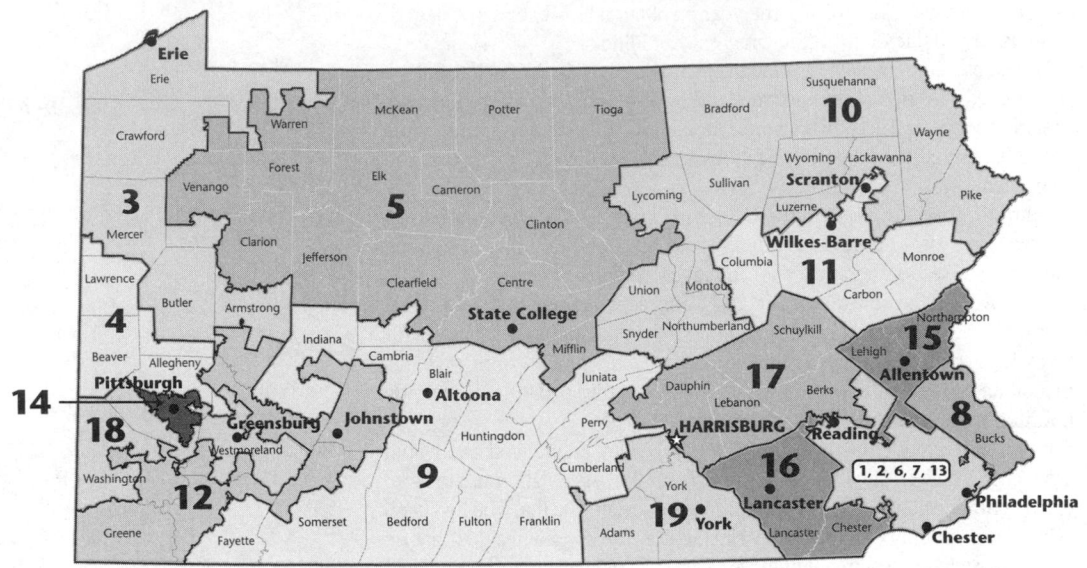

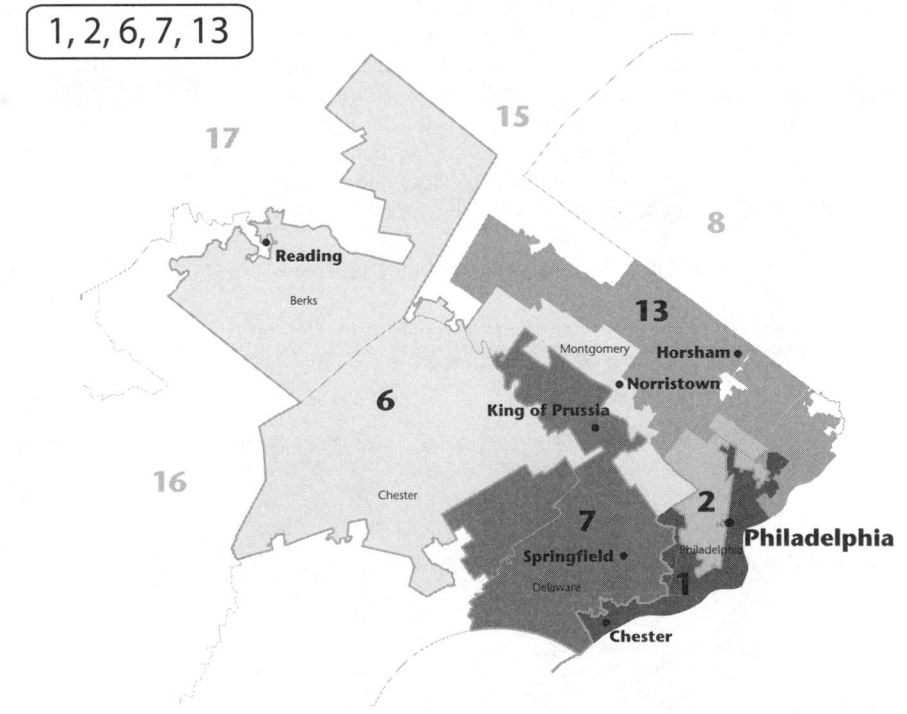

1, 2, 6, 7, 13

Gov. Tom Corbett (R)

First elected: 2010
Length of term: 4 years
Term expires: 1/15
Salary: $177,888
Phone: (717) 787-2500
Residence: Shaler Township
Born: June 17, 1949; Philadelphia, Pa.
Religion: Roman Catholic
Family: Wife, Susan Corbett; two children
Education: Lebanon Valley College, B.A. 1971 (political science); St. Mary's U. (Texas), J.D. 1975
Military Service: Pa. National Guard, 1971-84
Career: Lawyer; presidential and gubernatorial campaign aide; county prosecutor; teacher
Political highlights: Assistant U.S. attorney, 1980-83; Shaler Township Commission, 1988-89; U.S. attorney, 1989-93; Pa. attorney general, 1995-97, 2005-11

ELECTION RESULTS

2010 GENERAL

Tom Corbett (R)	2,172,763	54.5%
Dam Onorato (D)	1,814,788	45.5%

Lt. Gov. Jim Cawley (R)

First elected: 2010
Length of term: 4 years
Term expires: 1/15
Salary: $149,424
Phone: (717) 787-3300

LEGISLATURE

General Assembly: Year-round with recess
Senate: 50 members, 4-year terms
2011 ratios: 30 R, 20 D; 39 men, 11 women
Salary: $79,623
Phone: (717) 787-5920
House: 203 members, 2-year terms
2011 ratios: 112 R, 91 D; 170 men, 33 women
Salary: $79,623
Phone: (717) 787-5920

TERM LIMITS

Governor: 2 consecutive terms
Senate: No
House: No

URBAN STATISTICS

CITY	POPULATION
Philadelphia	1,526,006
Pittsburgh	305,704
Allentown	118,032
Erie	101,786
Reading	88,082

REGISTERED VOTERS

Democrat	51%
Republican	37%
Others	12%

POPULATION

2010 population	12,702,379
2000 population	12,281,054
1990 population	11,881,643
Percent change (2000-2010)	+3.4%
Rank among states (2010)	6
Median age	39.6
Born in state	75.2%
Foreign born	5.2%
Violent crime rate	381/100,000
Poverty level	12.5%
Federal workers	124,382
Military	5,215

ELECTIONS

STATE ELECTION OFFICIAL
(717) 787-5280
DEMOCRATIC PARTY
(717) 920-8470
REPUBLICAN PARTY
(717) 234-4901

MISCELLANEOUS

Web: www.pa.gov
Capital: Harrisburg

U.S. CONGRESS

Senate: 1 Democrat, 1 Republican
House: 12 Republicans, 7 Democrats

2010 Census Statistics by District

District	2008 Vote for President Obama	McCain	White	Black	Asian	Hispanic	Median Income	White Collar	Blue Collar	Service Industry	Over 64	Under 18	College Education	Rural	Sq. Miles
1	88%	12%	26%	46%	6%	19%	$32,909	56%	20%	24%	11%	27%	18%	0%	59
2	90	10	30	56	6	5	36,786	66	14	20	13	22	30	0	59
3	49	49	92	4	1	2	43,296	54	28	18	16	22	20	42	3,969
4	44	55	92	3	2	1	54,822	65	19	15	17	22	32	22	1,302
5	44	55	94	2	2	2	40,168	52	31	18	16	20	19	54	11,042
6	58	41	79	7	4	8	69,913	69	18	13	13	24	39	14	813
7	56	43	80	10	6	3	70,572	72	15	13	15	23	41	1	290
8	54	45	86	4	4	4	73,441	68	19	13	14	23	33	9	619
9	35	63	94	2	1	2	43,748	51	33	16	17	22	15	59	7,160
10	45	54	93	2	1	3	44,425	54	29	17	17	22	20	55	6,558
11	57	42	84	5	1	8	43,697	56	27	18	17	21	19	27	2,218
12	49	49	93	4	<1	1	38,520	53	28	19	18	20	16	38	2,752
13	59	41	75	10	7	7	59,897	67	18	15	16	23	32	2	255
14	70	29	68	24	3	2	36,122	63	16	21	16	19	27	0	162
15	56	43	77	5	3	14	57,340	61	24	15	15	23	26	13	845
16	48	51	79	4	2	13	56,050	57	28	15	14	26	26	24	1,290
17	48	51	83	8	2	6	50,261	57	27	16	16	22	20	31	2,335
18	44	55	93	3	2	1	55,339	67	19	15	17	21	33	16	1,432
19	43	56	87	4	2	5	57,139	59	27	15	14	23	24	29	1,658
STATE	55	44	79	10	3	6	49,737	61	23	16	15	22	26	23	44,817
U.S.	53	46	64	12	5	16	51,425	60	23	17	13	25	28	21	3,537,438

Sen. Bob Casey (D)

Capitol Office
224-6324
casey.senate.gov
393 Russell Bldg. 20510-3804; fax 228-0604

Committees
Agriculture, Nutrition & Forestry
    (Nutrition, Specialty Crops, Food & Agricultural
    Research - Chairman)
Foreign Relations
    (Near Eastern & South Central Asian Affairs
    - Chairman)
Health, Education, Labor & Pensions
Special Aging
Joint Economic - Chairman

Residence
Scranton

Born
April 13, 1960; Scranton, Pa.

Religion
Roman Catholic

Family
Wife, Terese Casey; four children

Education
College of the Holy Cross, A.B. 1982 (English);
Catholic U. of America, J.D. 1988

Career
Lawyer; campaign aide

Political Highlights
Pa. auditor general, 1997-2005; sought Democratic
nomination for governor, 2002; Pa. treasurer, 2005-07

ELECTION RESULTS

2006 GENERAL

Bob Casey (D)	2,392,984	58.7%
Rick Santorum (R)	1,684,778	41.3%

2006 PRIMARY

Bob Casey (D)	629,271	84.6%
Chuck Pennacchio (D)	66,364	8.9%
Alan Sandals (D)	48,113	6.5%

Elected 2006; 1st term

Casey's political pedigree and occasional departure from liberal orthodoxy — especially on abortion — put him in a position to bridge ideological divides within his party. Beyond performing that task, he is a dependable vote for the Democratic leadership.

The mild-mannered son of a politician flexed his negotiating muscles in December 2009 when lawmakers debated whether health care overhaul legislation would allow federal dollars to subsidize insurance plans that cover abortion. With the dispute threatening to take down the entire bill, Majority Leader Harry Reid, a Nevada Democrat, tasked Casey with crafting a compromise acceptable to enough senators on both sides of the debate.

The language Casey came up with was judged unacceptable by leading anti-abortion groups, including the U.S. Conference of Catholic Bishops and the National Right to Life Committee. But it satisfied the concerns of Democrat Ben Nelson of Nebraska, providing the crucial vote necessary to push the bill through the Senate and on toward enactment.

"I think we've moved forward with something that people have talked and talked and talked about for years.... That was a great achievement," said Casey, who sits on the Health, Education, Labor and Pensions (HELP) Committee.

Casey thinks he can play a similar role on climate change legislation. His status as a coal-state Democrat and a member of the Foreign Relations Committee helped earn him a position at the negotiating table.

"I think we can get there in a way that allows us to support a gradual transition that doesn't injure our ability to compete internationally," he said.

On many issues, Casey shares the same liberal views as his father, who served as governor of Pennsylvania from 1987 to 1995. But departing from the party line on abortion and gun rights has been central to the Casey's appeal to middle-of-the-road Keystone State voters. As leader of the anti-abortion wing of the Democratic Party, the elder Casey famously feuded with presidential nominee Bill Clinton in 1992 and was denied a speaking role at that year's convention.

Such intramural antagonism has not shaped the younger Casey's career nearly to the degree it did his father's. For one thing, Sen. Casey has received mixed ratings from abortion rights groups. NARAL Pro-Choice America gave him scores ranging from a 65 (out of 100) in 2007 to 0 in 2008 (Planned Parenthood scored him at 50 that year) to 25 in 2009. For another, he is a consistent Democratic vote — he sided with his party 97 percent of the time in the 111th Congress (2009-10) on votes that divided the two parties. But, perhaps most significantly, he endorsed Barack Obama for president in March 2008, weeks before the Illinois senator faced Sen. Hillary Rodham Clinton of New York in a fiercely fought primary in Pennsylvania. He became a key Obama surrogate in the general election campaign and says he has developed a friendship with the president.

Casey's position on the HELP Committee allows him to focus on some of his priorities, such as expanding access to child care and pre-kindergarten education. Casey reintroduced legislation in 2011 to award grants to states that establish or expand full-day pre-kindergarten programs.

Assuming a cause long championed by the defeated former Republican and Democratic Sen. Arlen Specter, Casey opposed proposed cuts in National Institutes of Health programs included in a catchall spending bill for fiscal 2011. He also sits on the Special Aging Committee.

In the 112th Congress (2011-12), Casey was named chairman of the Joint

Economic Committee, which holds hearings, conducts research and makes recommendations to the House and Senate on economic policy.

As a member of the Agriculture, Nutrition and Forestry Committee, Casey joined Richard G. Lugar, an Indiana Republican, to propose creating a "hunger czar" at the White House to pump up agriculture development aid and coordinate development policy across multiple agencies. "You want to be able to help in the short term but also to build the long-term facility that the developing world should have to feed their people with their own infrastructure," Casey said.

On the Foreign Relations Committee, where he chairs the Near Eastern and South Central Asian Affairs Subcommittee, Casey successfully pushed for passage of a bipartisan resolution that called on the U.N. Human Rights Council to review Iran's record, and he backs a bill by Republican Sen. John McCain of Arizona to sanction Iranian authorities responsible for human right violations.

Working with Republican Richard M. Burr of North Carolina, Casey helped form in 2009 a bipartisan caucus on weapons of mass destruction and terrorism to provide a forum for senators and staff members from committees with jurisdiction on the topic.

Despite acknowledging public criticism of earmarks, Casey defends seeking money for special projects in his state. "If there's a dollar that's available to the people of Pennsylvania, I don't want it to go to some other state, and I don't want some bureaucrat making that decision," he said.

Casey lives with his wife and children in working-class Scranton, where he grew up the fourth of eight children and the first son. His grandfather worked in the coal mines; his father became a lawyer before entering politics. The family's finances were sometimes volatile, given his father's numerous political campaigns and the vicissitudes of his employment, but Casey recalls a happy upbringing. All of the Casey children, except two brothers who practice law in Philadelphia, still live within 10 miles of one another.

Casey's father died in 2000, at age 68, of amyloidosis, a genetic condition in which proteins turn against the body and destroy internal organs. So far, Casey says, he has not felt tempted to undergo genetic testing to determine whether he is likely to be struck by the same illness.

Casey graduated from the College of the Holy Cross in 1982, then spent a year teaching fifth grade in Philadelphia with the Jesuits. Like his father, he got his law degree and practiced in Scranton until he won his first election, to be state auditor general, in 1996.

His hopes of following in his father's footsteps as governor were stymied in 2002, when then-Philadelphia Mayor Edward G. Rendell defeated him in a Democratic primary for the office. But Casey rebounded in 2004 by winning election as state treasurer, attracting the attention of Washington Democrats, who were gearing up for a challenge to Rick Santorum. The conservative senator, who at the time was the chamber's third-ranking GOP leader, was viewed as vulnerable in a state that had voted Democratic in the four previous presidential elections.

Casey easily defeated two lesser-known candidates to secure the Democratic nomination, then prepared for what was widely anticipated to be a close contest. But the perception of Casey as something of a social conservative helped disarm that potential GOP line of attack. With Santorum trailing in polls early in the race, Casey ran a low-key, careful campaign as if he were the incumbent, while Santorum ran like a challenger, bemoaning Casey's unwillingness to engage in a series of debates. The political wind was at the Democrats' backs, and Casey defeated Santorum by 17 percentage points, winning even outside the state's traditional Democratic bastions of Philadelphia and Pittsburgh.

Key Votes

2010

Pass budget reconciliation bill to modify overhauls of health care and federal student loan programs	YES
Proceed to disapproval resolution on EPA authority to regulate greenhouse gases	NO
Overhaul financial services industry regulation	YES
Limit debate to proceed to a bill to broaden campaign finance disclosure and reporting rules	YES
Limit debate on an extension of Bush-era income tax cuts for two years	YES
Limit debate on a bill to provide a path to legal status for some children of illegal immigrants	YES
Allow for a repeal of "don't ask, don't tell"	YES
Consent to ratification of a strategic arms reduction treaty with Russia	YES

2009

Prevent release of remaining financial industry bailout funds	NO
Make it easier for victims to sue for wage discrimination remedies	YES
Expand the Children's Health Insurance Program	YES
Limit debate on the economic stimulus measure	YES
Repeal District of Columbia firearms prohibitions and gun registration laws	YES
Limit debate on expansion of federal hate crimes law	YES
Strike funding for F-22 Raptor fighter jets	YES

CQ Vote Studies

	PARTY UNITY		PRESIDENTIAL SUPPORT	
	SUPPORT	OPPOSE	SUPPORT	OPPOSE
2010	99%	1%	98%	2%
2009	95%	5%	97%	3%
2008	93%	7%	35%	65%
2007	93%	7%	44%	56%

Interest Groups

	AFL-CIO	ADA	CCUS	ACU
2010	100%	90%	27%	0%
2009	94%	90%	43%	12%
2008	100%	90%	63%	8%
2007	100%	100%	36%	8%

Sen. Patrick J. Toomey (R)

Capitol Office
224-4254
toomey.senate.gov
B40B Dirksen Bldg. 20510-3802; fax 228-0284

Committees
Banking, Housing & Urban Affairs
Budget
Commerce, Science & Transportation
Joint Economic

Residence
Zionsville

Born
Nov. 17, 1961; Providence, R.I.

Religion
Roman Catholic

Family
Wife, Kris Toomey; three children

Education
Harvard U., A.B. 1984 (political philosophy)

Career
Restaurateur; investment banker; Club for Growth
president

Political Highlights
Allentown Government Study Commission, 1994-96;
U.S. House, 1999-2005; sought Republican nomina-
tion for U.S. Senate, 2004

ELECTION RESULTS

2010 GENERAL

Patrick J. Toomey (R)	2,028,945	51.0%
Joe Sestak (D)	1,948,716	49.0%

2010 PRIMARY

Patrick J. Toomey (R)	671,591	81.4%
Peg Luksik (R)	153,154	18.6%

Previous Winning Percentages
2002 House Election (57%); 2000 House Election
(53%); 1998 House Election (55%)

Elected 2010; 1st term

Toomey arrived in the Senate as a seasoned veteran of Congress and a move-ment conservative who puts his faith in free markets and limited government.

His economic agenda reflects the philosophy of the Club for Growth, the low-tax/free-market advocacy group he once led. Toomey supports cutting taxes and easing the regulatory burden on businesses. He said America is in danger of becoming a "bailout nation" and has argued that the Troubled Asset Relief Program created in 2008 to rescue the ailing financial services sector rewarded unnecessary risk-taking and defied sound principles of capitalism, in addition to being wasteful and lacking transparency.

"These guys in Washington are creating an environment that is having a chilling effect on small businesses, and medium and big businesses as well, and that's a big part of why we don't have the job growth that we badly need," Toomey said prior to his election.

After he won, he joined a group of nine GOP senators who threatened to block all legislation that is not related to the federal debt.

"It is always 'we will make the cuts in the future, but just let's agree to all the spending now.' That is what has happened. That's . . . exactly what has gotten us into this mess," he said on Fox News Channel in March 2011.

With Republican David Vitter of Louisiana, Toomey tried to move language that would keep the United States from avoiding default by prioritizing pay-ments to holders of government bonds in the event of the debt limit being reached. The provision failed on a party-line vote.

He also helped write a GOP-backed proposed constitutional amendment that would cap federal spending at 18 percent of gross domestic product and require a two-thirds vote of both chambers to raise taxes, with exceptions for wartime.

Toomey served on the Budget and Financial Services committees during his House tenure, which ran from 1999 to 2005, and won a seat on the Com-merce, Science and Transportation Committee, where he is ranking Repub-lican on the Consumer Protection, Product Safety and Insurance panel. He also serves on on the Budget, Banking, Housing and Urban Affairs and Joint Economic committees in the 112th Congress (2011-12).

He voted to repeal the Democrats' 2010 health care law, arguing that it costs too much and will kill jobs. He would prefer to overhaul the medical liability system and create market-based incentives to make it easier and less expensive for people to buy insurance.

"These reforms will neither bankrupt the country nor force people to lose their current, private coverage as the House bill would," he wrote in the Philadelphia Daily News in late 2009.

When he served in the House, Toomey was among the group of lawmakers who re-invigorated the Conservative Action Team and renamed it the Repub-lican Study Group, turning it into a highly influential segment of the GOP Conference.

While he made a name for himself on tax and budget issues, Toomey is also a reliable social conservative, opposing abortion and same-sex marriage and backing gun owners' rights.

He was one of the two GOP senators not hailing from so-called right-to-work states that backed legislation to bar establishment of union-only work-places (Kentucky's Rand Paul was the other).

He is a strong supporter of Israel. After terrorists murdered a Jewish fam-ily in Itamar and bombed a Jerusalem bus, Toomey signed onto a letter asking the Obama administration to get tougher on Palestinian incitement.

"The Itamar massacre was a sobering reminder that words matter, and that Palestinian incitement against Jews and Israel can lead to violence and terror," the senators wrote.

He also urged stronger sanctions on Chinese companies doing business with Iran in violation of a sanctions law enacted in 2010.

Toomey was born in Providence, R.I. His father laid cable for the Narragansett Electric Co.; his mother was a part-time secretary for their local Roman Catholic church.

After graduating from Harvard, Toomey spent seven years in the high-pressure world of international finance, trading futures contracts, swaps and other often-volatile financial instruments while living in New York, London and Hong Kong. In 1990, he switched his business focus, investing in a chain of sports-themed restaurants in Allentown and Lancaster called Rookies.

Toomey had little political experience prior to his first House bid other than a summer internship in the office of liberal Republican Sen. John H. Chafee of Rhode Island. But he said the 1994 elections convinced him that there was an "opportunity to change the direction of government" and make it more responsive to the citizenry. In 1994, he was elected to a two-year stint on the Allentown Government Study Commission, where he won enactment of a plan making it harder for the city council to raise taxes.

In 1998, Toomey jumped into the open-seat race created by the retirement of three-term moderate Democrat Paul McHale. In a six-candidate GOP primary, Toomey edged past the 1996 nominee, Bob Kilbanks, by less than 3 percentage points. He then faced veteran Democratic state Sen. Roy C. Afflerbach, who accused Toomey of having tenuous ties to the district. But the well-funded Toomey won comfortably.

In 2000, Toomey faced a well-financed challenge from former United Steelworkers local president Ed O'Brien, who depicted him as too conservative for the district. Toomey ran ads calling O'Brien an "old-fashioned liberal." In the end, Toomey captured 53 percent of the vote. In a rematch with O'Brien in 2002, Toomey had fundraising help from GOP heavyweights and won with more than 57 percent.

In 2004, Toomey challenged incumbent Republican Arlen Specter in the Senate primary. Making the case that Specter was too liberal, Toomey attracted support from many movement conservatives. But the state party apparatus — including conservative stalwart Sen. Rick Santorum — and national Republicans rallied around Specter, who held off Toomey's challenge by less than 2 percentage points and then won re-election.

Toomey went on to serve as president of the Club for Growth, enhancing his reputation among activists. He considered a campaign for governor, but decided to take one more shot at Specter. Again, the national Republican Party lined up behind the incumbent. But early polls showed Toomey running well ahead of Specter, and two weeks after Toomey formally entered the race, Specter announced he was switching parties.

The Democratic Senatorial Campaign Committee backed Specter — just as the National Republican Senatorial Committee had done six years earlier against Toomey — but two-term Rep. Joe Sestak, a former Navy admiral, had already entered the Democratic primary. Despite alleged importuning from the White House to make way for Specter, Sestak stayed in and topped Specter on primary day by 8 percentage points.

The general election was a bare-knuckle affair, with polls rarely separating the two candidates by more than a few points. Toomey benefited from tea party support, his long years toiling in the conservative vineyard and President Obama's unpopularity in the state. Sestak made the case that Republicans could not be trusted to clean up the economic mess they'd helped create — one vivid ad showed him cleaning up after his dog. On Election Day, Toomey prevailed with 51 percent of the vote.

CQ Vote Studies (while House member)				
	PARTY UNITY		PRESIDENTIAL SUPPORT	
	SUPPORT	OPPOSE	SUPPORT	OPPOSE
2004	98%	2%	94%	6%
2003	94%	6%	93%	7%
2002	96%	4%	88%	12%
2001	93%	7%	93%	7%

Interest Groups (while House member)				
	AFL-CIO	ADA	CCUS	ACU
2004	0%	0%	100%	100%
2003	13%	20%	90%	92%
2002	13%	0%	100%	100%
2001	8%	0%	95%	100%

Rep. Robert A. Brady (D)

Capitol Office
225-4731
www.house.gov/robertbrady
102 Cannon Bldg. 20515-3801; fax 225-0088

Committees
Armed Services
House Administration - Ranking Member
Joint Library
Joint Printing

Residence
Philadelphia

Born
April 7, 1945; Philadelphia, Pa.

Religion
Roman Catholic

Family
Wife, Debra Brady; two children

Education
St. Thomas More H.S., graduated 1963

Career
Union lobbyist; carpenter; local government official

Political Highlights
34th Ward Democratic Executive Committee, 1967-present (leader, 1980-present); candidate for Philadelphia City Council, 1983; Philadelphia Democratic Party chairman, 1986-present; sought Democratic nomination for mayor of Philadelphia, 2007

ELECTION RESULTS

2010 GENERAL

Robert A. Brady (D)		unopposed

2010 PRIMARY

Robert A. Brady (D)		unopposed

2008 GENERAL

Robert A. Brady (D)	242,799	90.8%
Mike Muhammed (R)	24,714	9.2%

Previous Winning Percentages
2006 (100%); 2004 (86%); 2002 (86%); 2000 (88%); 1998 (81%); 1998 Special Election (74%)

Elected 1998; 7th full term

As chairman of the House Administration Committee in the two previous Congresses, Brady wielded control over Capitol office space and parking spots. With House Democrats out of power in Washington, the best illustration of his clout now lies 150 miles north in Philadelphia, where he's one of the lucky few awarded his own free parking space right outside City Hall.

Brady, chairman of Philadelphia's Democratic City Committee for almost a quarter of a century, presides over machine politics in a city where ward bosses still boost voter turnout by paying "street money" to poll workers on Election Day. Democrats outnumber Republicans 3-to-1 there, making the city a crucial component of electoral strategy for any Democratic candidate seeking statewide office. As one of Brady's political lieutenants told The New York Times in 2010, "There's not a person running for statewide office that doesn't have to be extremely close to Bob Brady."

The machine sometimes fails, though, and it's unclear whether the operation will maintain its power in an era when many candidates are reaching voters through television and the Internet. Notably, Brady didn't deliver the city for Arlen Specter, the candidate backed by the Democratic establishment, in the 2010 U.S. Senate primary. Brady also failed in his own primary bid to become Philadelphia's mayor in 2007.

In Congress, Brady has built a relatively low-profile career, and he was largely content to follow the lead of another Pennsylvania power broker, Rep. John P. Murtha, who died in 2010. With Murtha's help, he secured the House Administration gavel in 2007, becoming the unofficial mayor of Capitol Hill with responsibility for overseeing nearly $1 billion in federal spending. He is now the ranking Democrat on the panel, which also has jurisdiction over election law. In the wake of the shooting of Democratic Rep. Gabrielle Giffords of Arizona in January 2011, Brady suggested making it a crime to "put a bulls eye" on a map of a member's district, a practice common to both parties for many years.

Brady's own legislative agenda tends to focus on home-state concerns. He sponsored a bill in 2010 that would compel the public authority in charge of the bridges between Pennsylvania and New Jersey to appoint an inspector general after the agency was found to be contributing money to charities with ties to its board members.

Brady, a former union carpenter, plays an informal role as a mediator in labor disputes back home. He has helped end walkouts by groups as varied as Teamsters, teachers and transportation workers. In 2010, he intervened in a dispute between nurses and Temple University Hospital. "I don't negotiate," he told the Philadelphia Inquirer. "I tell everybody the same thing: 'I don't want to know what you want. Tell me what you need to make a deal.'"

In perhaps his most notable mediation, Brady literally talked City Councilman Rick Mariano off the brink in 2005, after Mariano had gone to the top of City Hall in a highly publicized suicide scare just before he was to be indicted.

Brady's skill as a negotiator has come in handy in his role on the House Administration Committee. Soon after taking over as chairman in 2007, he settled a four-year-old debate by moving legislation to merge the previously separate Library of Congress and U.S. Capitol police forces. A member of the Armed Services Committee, Brady also pushes to employ more wounded veterans in administrative and support positions in the House complex.

Brady grew up in Philadelphia's Overbrook section and still lives there with his second wife, a former cheerleader for the Philadelphia Eagles. The neighborhood, which was Catholic and white when Brady was a child, is now mostly black.

Only by securing African-American support has Brady managed to survive. In Congress, he has cosponsored a resolution apologizing for slavery and published a book through the House Administration Committee about African-Americans who have served in Congress. He appeared with local NAACP leaders to push for creation of a federal commission to study ways to reduce incarceration rates. He calls Georgia Democratic Rep. John Lewis, a civil rights leader beaten during the 1965 march on Selma, Ala., his hero.

Brady's loyalty to organized labor reflects his working-class roots; he occasionally parts with Democratic colleagues on union matters. In 2001, Brady infuriated some longtime allies in the environmental lobby by supporting Bush's proposal to allow oil drilling in Alaska's Arctic National Wildlife Refuge, an idea backed by the Teamsters Union and the AFL-CIO's building trades division as part of a push for domestic energy jobs.

Brady once teamed up with Wilt Chamberlain in a neighborhood pickup basketball game and sparred with Muhammad Ali. The son of a policeman who died young and a supermarket checker, Brady had college scholarship offers but went to work as a carpenter instead to help support his family. After 12 years in the trade, he moved into a full-time post with the carpenters' union. Brady still carries a union card and has a lifetime score of 100 percent in the AFL-CIO's rating of congressional voting records.

He credits his decision to get into politics to a broken streetlight. Brady was worried about his mother walking home from her food market job at night, so he asked his local Democratic ward boss to fix it. When the committeeman failed to follow through, Brady ran for a local party post and won.

Once in the party organization, Brady hit it off with then-City Council President George X. Schwartz, securing his patronage by fixing up Schwartz's basement, gratis. When Schwartz was convicted in the 1980 Abscam scandal, in which undercover FBI agents offered money to members of Congress and some local and state officials for government contracts, Schwartz cleared the way for Brady to succeed him as the local Democratic ward leader. Brady made an unsuccessful bid for the city council in 1983 but continued to be a key player in city politics. He has been chairman of the city Democratic Party since 1986.

When Democratic Rep. Thomas M. Foglietta resigned to become ambassador to Italy, Brady won a 1998 special election to succeed him with 74 percent of the vote. He has rolled up bigger tallies since, even following his loss in the mayoral race; he was unopposed in 2010.

Key Votes

2010

Overhaul the nation's health insurance system	YES
Allow for repeal of "don't ask, don't tell"	YES
Overhaul financial services industry regulation	YES
Limit use of new Afghanistan War funds to troop withdrawal activities	NO
Change oversight of offshore drilling and lift oil spill liability cap	YES
Provide a path to legal status for some children of illegal immigrants	YES
Extend Bush-era income tax cuts for two years	YES

2009

Expand the Children's Health Insurance Program	YES
Provide $787 billion in tax cuts and spending increases to stimulate the economy	YES
Allow bankruptcy judges to modify certain primary-residence mortgages	YES
Create a cap-and-trade system to limit greenhouse gas emissions	YES
Provide $2 billion for the "cash for clunkers" program	YES
Establish the government as the sole provider of student loans	YES
Restrict federally funded insurance coverage for abortions in health care overhaul	NO

CQ Vote Studies

	PARTY UNITY		PRESIDENTIAL SUPPORT	
	SUPPORT	OPPOSE	SUPPORT	OPPOSE
2010	99%	1%	95%	5%
2009	99%	1%	96%	4%
2008	99%	1%	14%	86%
2007	99%	1%	5%	95%
2006	92%	8%	30%	70%

Interest Groups

	AFL-CIO	ADA	CCUS	ACU
2010	100%	95%	25%	0%
2009	100%	100%	33%	0%
2008	100%	100%	56%	0%
2007	100%	85%	44%	0%
2006	100%	95%	53%	16%

Pennsylvania 1

South and central Philadelphia; Chester

The birthplace of the Constitution, the 1st boasts many recognizable icons, such as the Liberty Bell and the Philly cheesesteak. With nearly 90 percent of its population in Philadelphia, the W-shaped 1st is the state's most racially and ethnically diverse district. The rest of the 1st falls in a working-class slice of Delaware County.

Beyond the historical streets, much of the 1st has a bleak economic landscape. The district has the state's lowest median household income — $33,000 puts the 1st in the bottom 10 districts nationally — and less than one-fifth of the population has a college education. Layoffs at key employer Aker Philadelphia Shipyard have hurt, and factory losses have been compounded by a construction sector downturn and cuts in the usually solid government, education and health care arenas. Philadelphia International Airport remains an important source of jobs.

Football's Eagles, baseball's Phillies, basketball's 76ers and hockey's Flyers play in arenas and stadiums on Broad Street in South Philadelphia, but plans for an entertainment venue near the sports complex have stalled.

In 2010, a new casino on the Delaware River opened in Philadelphia's Fishtown neighborhood, and soccer's Philadelphia Union began playing in a new stadium farther south in Chester. Other development along the Chester waterfront includes a Harrah's casino.

Blacks represent the largest population bloc in the 1st, at 46 percent, and the district has the state's highest percentage of Hispanic residents and lowest proportion of whites. The district also has a large Asian presence, concentrated in Philadelphia's Chinatown. The district's Italian-American population supports a famous food market, which is the oldest and largest outdoor market in the United States. The 1st's strong union presence and substantial minority population make it a slam-dunk for Democratic candidates. Barack Obama took 88 percent of the 2008 presidential vote here.

Major Industry
Government, health care, service, airport, shipbuilding

Cities
Philadelphia (pt.), 583,308; Chester, 33,972

Notable
Eastern State Penitentiary, now a museum, was the most expensive prison upon its opening in 1829 and held gangster Al Capone.

Rep. Chaka Fattah (D)

Capitol Office
225-4001
www.house.gov/fattah
2301 Rayburn Bldg. 20515-3802; fax 225-5392

Committees
Appropriations

Residence
Philadelphia

Born
Nov. 21, 1956; Philadelphia, Pa.

Religion
Baptist

Family
Wife, Renee Chenault-Fattah; four children

Education
Community College of Philadelphia, attended 1976
(political science); U. of Pennsylvania, M.A. 1986
(government administration)

Career
Public official

Political Highlights
Democratic candidate for Philadelphia City Commission, 1979; Pa. House, 1983-89; Pa. Senate, 1989-95; Consumer Party nominee for U.S. House (special election), 1991; sought Democratic nomination for mayor of Philadelphia, 2007

ELECTION RESULTS

2010 GENERAL

Chaka Fattah (D)	182,800	89.3%
Rick Hellberg (R)	21,907	10.7%

2010 PRIMARY

Chaka Fattah (D)	unopposed

2008 GENERAL

Chaka Fattah (D)	276,870	88.9%
Adam A. Lang (R)	34,466	11.1%

Previous Winning Percentages
2006 (89%); 2004 (88%); 2002 (88%); 2000 (98%);
1998 (87%); 1996 (88%); 1994 (86%)

Elected 1994; 9th term

Fattah is a savvy liberal with a policy agenda focused on education and urban issues. His long-shot bid for the top Democratic spot on the Appropriations Committee in the new Congress failed, but he remains in position to direct funding to his priorities.

He was 21st in seniority among Democrats on the spending panel when he announced he would challenge Washington's Norm Dicks for the role of ranking Democrat in the 112th Congress (2011-12). To support his cause, Fattah cited outgoing Appropriations Chairman David R. Obey of Wisconsin and California Democrat Henry A. Waxman, chairman of the Energy and Commerce Committee in the 111th Congress (2009-10), as examples of members who were chosen for gavels over more senior committee colleagues. "This is not an aberration, that a more junior member of a committee might become the chairman of the committee," Fattah said, to no avail. The job went to Dicks.

Fattah settled for ranking Democrat on the Commerce-Justice-Science Subcommittee.

He also pushed back against the GOP-imposed moratorium on earmarks for fiscal 2011 and fiscal 2012, expressing concern for national programs with local chapters such as Boys & Girls Clubs and the YMCA.

"This idea of defining what an earmark is is going to be an important issue. . . . But members will — under whatever the rules are — will try to get their priorities in these bills," he told Roll Call.

Fattah left the Education and the Workforce Committee in 2001 to have a greater hand in funding the education programs that have been his legislative priority for two decades.

In 2008, Congress cleared an overhaul of the Higher Education Act that included an update of GEAR UP, a program that aids low-income students in preparing for college. Fattah considers it his most significant legislative achievement.

Congress also included a tax credit backed by Fattah as part of the 2009 stimulus that allows students or their parents to claim a $2,500 credit for the cost of qualified tuition and related expenses — a provision President Obama has said he wants to make permanent.

In July 2010, Education Secretary Arne Duncan announced the creation of a commission to study school finance equity and how to close the funding gap between rich and poor public school districts — an initiative Fattah and California Democrat Michael M. Honda have strived to bring to fruition.

Fattah's top priority as chairman of the Congressional Urban Caucus has been the energy efficiency and conservation block grants program, which helps nearly 1,100 cities develop plans to implement energy efficiency projects. That work dovetails with his other spot on Appropriations: the Energy-Water Subcommittee. Though his voting record is staunchly liberal, Fattah credits a little-reported bipartisanship for helping push through his initiatives. He worked with Ohio Republican Michael R. Turner on the energy block grant program, and in 1998 seven Republicans on the Education Committee gave him the votes he needed to advance GEAR UP against the wishes of GOP Chairman Bill Goodling, a fellow Pennsylvanian.

"I think that the truth is that the press focuses a lot on the partisan bickering, but there is a lot of bipartisan cooperation," Fattah said.

His legislative responsibility is appropriating money, but he has introduced legislation — which has garnered no cosponsors — to raise some. His plan would abolish the individual income tax and replace it with a 1 percent fee on every transaction occurring in the United States, with the exception of stock sales. "In order to avoid a financial crisis of epic proportions," Fattah wrote in a February 2010 letter to colleagues, "Congress must take decisive action to implement a viable fiscal plan that will ensure long-term fiscal stability."

He backed the two-year extension of the Bush-era tax cuts enacted in late 2010. "I agree that the debt's a problem," he said on MSNBC. "But I do think that we also have an economic recovery that's critically important."

Fattah's academic career was atypical for a future member of Congress. He dropped out of high school in early 1974 and earned a General Equivalency Diploma later that year. He enrolled in undergraduate classes at a Philadelphia community college but never graduated. Later, while serving as a state lawmaker, he obtained a master's degree in 1986 from the University of Pennsylvania.

Born Arthur Davenport, one of several boys in a household headed by his widowed mother, his name changed when his mother married community activist David Fattah. He cites former Democratic Rep. William H. Gray III, a family friend, as one of his inspirations to become a lawmaker. Gray captured the Budget Committee chairmanship over a more senior member and later went on to become majority whip. "I had a real-life example of what the potential and power was of being a member of the United States Congress and what could be achieved," Fattah said.

After six years in the state House and in the midst of six in the state Senate, Fattah entered the 1991 special election to succeed Gray. But the Democratic Party backed longtime City Councilman Lucien E. Blackwell, so Fattah temporarily quit the party to run on the Consumer Party ticket. He lost.

When the state Senate — in which Fattah was still serving — handled redistricting following the 1990 census, the percentage of African-Americans in the 2nd District dropped from 80 percent to 62 percent. That undercut Blackwell, who had his base among West Philadelphia's poor and working-class blacks. Fattah challenged the incumbent in 1994, defeating him by 16 percentage points in the Democratic primary. In the overwhelmingly Democratic 2nd, Fattah has not been seriously challenged since.

Fattah ran unsuccessfully for mayor of Philadelphia in 2007, coming in fourth in the Democratic primary. He cited a Republican administration and uncertainty surrounding the Democrats' ability to win back congressional majorities as the impetus for the bid. He said that if he had known Democrats would win control of Congress and the White House, he "would never have thought then about running for mayor."

Key Votes

2010

Overhaul the nation's health insurance system	YES
Allow for repeal of "don't ask, don't tell"	YES
Overhaul financial services industry regulation	YES
Limit use of new Afghanistan War funds to troop withdrawal activities	NO
Change oversight of offshore drilling and lift oil spill liability cap	YES
Provide a path to legal status for some children of illegal immigrants	YES
Extend Bush-era income tax cuts for two years	YES

2009

Expand the Children's Health Insurance Program	YES
Provide $787 billion in tax cuts and spending increases to stimulate the economy	YES
Allow bankruptcy judges to modify certain primary-residence mortgages	YES
Create a cap-and-trade system to limit greenhouse gas emissions	YES
Provide $2 billion for the "cash for clunkers" program	YES
Establish the government as the sole provider of student loans	YES
Restrict federally funded insurance coverage for abortions in health care overhaul	NO

CQ Vote Studies

	PARTY UNITY		PRESIDENTIAL SUPPORT	
	Support	Oppose	Support	Oppose
2010	99%	1%	95%	5%
2009	99%	1%	97%	3%
2008	99%	1%	13%	87%
2007	99%	1%	6%	94%
2006	96%	4%	28%	72%

Interest Groups

	AFL-CIO	ADA	CCUS	ACU
2010	100%	95%	25%	0%
2009	100%	100%	33%	0%
2008	100%	95%	53%	0%
2007	96%	75%	55%	0%
2006	100%	100%	40%	8%

Pennsylvania 2

West Philadelphia; Chestnut Hill; Cheltenham

From the vantage point of the William Penn statue atop City Hall, one can see the 2nd stretching west and north over some of Philadelphia's long-established neighborhoods. The district encompasses Center City skyscrapers, then moves west across the Schuylkill River past the University of Pennsylvania and Drexel University. West Philadelphia, once Irish, Greek and Jewish, is now nearly all black and features pockets of middle-class and poor communities. Overall, a majority of the 2nd's residents are African-American and the district has experienced a decade of growth in its Hispanic population.

Except for the Montgomery County township of Cheltenham, the 2nd lies within Philadelphia. It includes the affluent city neighborhoods of Rittenhouse Square, one of five squares Penn designed in his original plan of the city, and Chestnut Hill, in the city's northwest corner. Fairmount Park, which flanks the river, houses the city's art museum, zoo and "Boathouse Row," and runs north along diverse, middle-class neighborhoods such as Brewerytown and Manayunk, ending in Chestnut Hill.

Areas just north of downtown and Temple University (shared with the 1st) have some of the city's lowest family incomes. Home values had plummeted in West Philadelphia and University City, Center City and Fairmount neighborhoods, but partnerships with local businesses provide some relief to poor areas. As part of the University of Pennsylvania's "Penn Compact," the school works with communities to improve education, public health, economic and job development, quality of life, and the landscape of West Philadelphia and nearby areas. And UPenn's medical school complements the 2nd's health care industry.

The 2nd's blue-collar workforce and large minority population give it an overwhelming Democratic majority. In the 2008 presidential election, Barack Obama had his best showing in the state here, taking 90 percent of the district's vote.

Major Industry
Higher education, health care, tourism

Cities
Philadelphia (pt.), 593,484; Glenside (unincorporated), 8,384

Notable
The steps of the Philadelphia Museum of Art were immortalized in the movie "Rocky;" the 30th Street Station is in West Philadelphia.

Rep. Mike Kelly (R)

Capitol Office
225-5406
kelly.house.gov
515 Cannon Bldg. 20515-3803; fax 225-3103

Committees
Education & the Workforce
Foreign Affairs
Oversight & Government Reform

Residence
Butler

Born
May 10, 1948; Pittsburgh, Pa.

Religion
Roman Catholic

Family
Wife, Victoria Kelly; four children

Education
U. of Notre Dame, B.A. 1970 (sociology)

Career
Car dealership owner

Political Highlights
Butler Area School Board, 1992-96; Butler City
Council, 2006-09

ELECTION RESULTS

2010 GENERAL

Mike Kelly (R)	111,909	55.7%
Kathy Dahlkemper (D)	88,924	44.3%

2010 PRIMARY

Mike Kelly (R)	15,428	28.1%
Paul L. Huber (R)	14,474	26.4%
Clayton W. Grabb (R)	7,486	13.6%
Steven M. Fisher (R)	6,499	11.8%
Ed Franz (R)	5,838	10.6%
Martha Moore (R)	5,151	9.4%

Elected 2010; 1st term

Kelly has described Democratic policies in Washington as roadblocks, a description that perhaps comes naturally to a man who has owned a car dealership in Pennsylvania.

"I think if there were more people in the legislature that had actually run a business, I think they'd have a better idea of what they're doing," he said.

He called the economic policies of the 111th Congress (2009-10) and the Obama administration "nothing short of generational theft," and he backed the catchall bill that would have cut $58 billion from fiscal 2011 spending as well as the April 2011 bill that provided funding for the government through September while cutting nearly $40 billion.

While Kelly attended numerous events for the tea party movement during his campaign, he did not join the Tea Party Caucus formed by Republican Michele Bachmann of Minnesota. "I'm not really painting myself in a corner right now," he said.

Kelly supports a legislative "sunset clause" that would mandate the expiration of federally funded programs unless Congress acts to renew them. He wants to work to create a friendlier environment for entrepreneurs and make the U.S. workforce more able to compete in the global market. He'll have a chance to work on those issues as a member of the Education and the Workforce Committee.

He was named vice chairman of the Foreign Affairs Subcommittee on Asia and the Pacific, as well as vice chairman of the Oversight and Government Reform panel that handles technology and procurement issues.

Kelly played football in high school and then at the University of Notre Dame, until he sustained a knee injury. He graduated with a degree in sociology and purchased an auto dealership from his father in 1995. He served on the Butler school board and then the Butler City Council.

The Erie-based 3rd District seat held by freshman Democrat Kathy Dahlkemper was an early target for the GOP in 2010. Kelly won a six-candidate GOP primary and defeated Dahlkemper by almost 12 percentage points.

Pennsylvania 3
Northwest — Erie

Nestled in the state's northwestern corner, the 3rd takes in all of Erie County — Pennsylvania's only Lake Erie coastline — and parts of six other counties. The economy of this Rust Belt, historically blue-collar area centers around the city of Erie's port.

Erie County, where more than two-fifths of the district's residents live, has retained an industrial feel despite decades of decline. Manufacturing still makes up a significant portion of the county's workforce, but residents increasingly rely on the service sector and health care industry. There are several high-tech companies here, and the city also lures visitors to public beaches and Presque Isle State Park during the warmer months. Outside of Erie, no city has more than 15,000 residents. These communities rely on small businesses and scores of tooling and machine shops, especially in Crawford County. Mercer County (a portion of which is in the 4th) still has some steel mills. Butler County in the south is dominated by manufacturing, but it also hosts Slippery Rock University.

The city of Erie's median household income is well below state and national averages, while surrounding areas are above the median. Pockets of black residents in northern and central Erie help give the county a Democratic lean. These Democratic tendencies are mostly offset by the GOP lean in Butler and Crawford counties. In 2010, Republican Mike Kelly captured the U.S. House, and GOP Sen. Patrick J. Toomey took wide margins across the district outside of Erie County, one of only six that Democrat Joe Sestak won statewide.

Major Industry
Manufacturing, service

Cities
Erie, 101,786; Sharon, 14,038

Notable
The rebuilt *U.S. Brig Niagara*, a fighting ship from the War of 1812, is docked in Erie.

Rep. Jason Altmire (D)

Capitol Office
225-2565
altmire.house.gov
332 Cannon Bldg. 20515-3804; fax 226-2274

Committees
Small Business
Transportation & Infrastructure

Residence
McCandless

Born
March 7, 1968; Kittanning, Pa.

Religion
Roman Catholic

Family
Wife, Kelly Altmire; two children

Education
Florida State U., B.S. 1990 (political science); George
Washington U., M.H.S.A. 1998 (health services
administration)

Career
Hospital association executive; lobbyist;
congressional aide

Political Highlights
No previous office

ELECTION RESULTS

2010 GENERAL

Jason Altmire (D)	120,827	50.8%
Keith Rothfus (R)	116,958	49.2%

2010 PRIMARY

Jason Altmire (D)	unopposed

2008 GENERAL

Jason Altmire (D)	186,536	55.9%
Melissa A. Hart (R)	147,411	44.1%

Previous Winning Percentages
2006 (52%)

Elected 2006; 3rd term

Altmire is a centrist both rhetorically and in his voting habits, reflecting the "down-the-middle" constituents of western Pennsylvania. He has opposed a majority of his party about 20 percent of the time during his first two terms, including some of the signature priorities of the Obama administration.

A member of the fiscally conservative Blue Dog Coalition, Altmire was among a group of Democrats who early on cautioned President Obama and Democratic leaders not to pursue an overambitious agenda that could result in favoring more-affluent areas over the heartland. "I'm not saying don't do big things. But maybe we should wait until we get the economy stabilized, in a year or so," he said.

They didn't take his advice, and Democrats lost their House majority in November 2010. When Nancy Pelosi of California announced that she would again seek to lead House Democrats as minority leader, Altmire took exception.

"I think it is inescapable that the message that was sent by the American people is they want a change in direction. And a change in direction means a change in leadership," he told Fox News six days after the election.

He did not support her for minority leader, and he backed North Carolina Democrat Heath Shuler for Speaker.

Altmire's most high-profile defection in the 111th Congress (2009-10) came with his vote against the health care overhaul enacted in 2010. He is a former hospital association executive and was part of a congressional task force on health care during President Bill Clinton's unsuccessful health care push in 1993, but he considered the overhaul a bridge too far.

"The cost of inaction on health care is great, but it would be an even bigger mistake to pass a bill that could compound the problem of skyrocketing health care costs," he said in March in explaining his vote. Ten months later, he voted against a GOP-backed measure to repeal the law.

He also opposed the GOP's catchall spending bill passed by the House early in 2011, but said Democrats were to blame for creating the necessity for writing the bill in the first place.

"We should have passed a budget," he said on Fox News. "We wouldn't be in this predicament unless we let ourselves get here. It is self-inflicted." But he voted for a subsequent spending bill that funded the government through September 2011 while cutting nearly $40 billion in spending.

Altmire's independent streak takes in energy policy, where he supports a comprehensive plan that includes nuclear power and increased domestic oil drilling. He also favors developing alternative resources such as coal-to-liquids — important issues for the former coal and steel towns of western Pennsylvania looking to spur economic growth. And he voted against Democratic energy legislation in 2009 that included a cap on greenhouse gas emissions coupled with a market-based emissions trading system.

Altmire also takes a more conservative stance on immigration than most members of his party. He wants to beef up border security and target employers who knowingly hire illegal immigrants. A member of the Republican-dominated House Immigration Reform Caucus, he opposes creating a path to citizenship for illegal immigrants.

The son of a former schoolteacher, Altmire favors revising the 2001 No Child Left Behind national education law, which he said has been drastically underfunded. In 2007, he supported the first reauthorization in almost a decade of Head Start, an early-childhood development program for low-income preschoolers. And despite being a social conservative, he voted against an amendment that would have allowed faith-based Head Start providers to take religion into account when hiring.

He refused to back two $700 billion proposals in fall 2008 — the second of which became law — to assist the ailing financial services sector, calling the legislation fundamentally flawed. But he supported a subsequent $14 billion bailout of U.S. automakers, which stalled in the Senate, as well as Obama's $787 billion stimulus package that became law, hailing the latter as a "targeted and transparent economic recovery plan."

Altmire sits on the Transportation and Infrastructure Committee. When the panel takes up a reauthorization of the 2005 surface transportation law, he hopes to secure funding for the future Allegheny Valley Commuter Rail and for completing the designation of the future I-376 corridor, which is expected to spur economic development in Allegheny County and points north.

Altmire's other committee assignment is Small Business, where he was chairman of the investigations and oversight subcommittee when the Democrats were in charge. He held hearings to review the effect of rising gas prices on small businesses and the impact of federal regulations on small home medical suppliers. He is now the subcommittee's ranking Democrat.

Altmire grew up as an only child in a working-class neighborhood of Lower Burrell. His mother taught special education to high school students; he never knew his father.

He lettered in two sports in high school and was a football player at Florida State. As a political science major, he helped Democratic Rep. Pete Peterson of Florida on his 1990 campaign. Altmire subsequently was offered a job on Capitol Hill, where he worked for several years as Peterson's congressional aide and went to school at night, earning a master's degree in health services administration from George Washington University. He ended up working for the Federation of American Hospitals and then the University of Pittsburgh Medical Center.

Altmire said he decided to run against GOP incumbent Melissa A. Hart because he couldn't understand how the district could be represented by someone with "such a right-of-center voting record." After besting businesswoman Georgia Berner in the primary, he linked Hart to President George W. Bush and the GOP congressional leadership and won with 52 percent of the vote. In a rematch two years later, Altmire defeated Hart with 56 percent. While four other Democratic House incumbents from Pennsylvania fell in 2010, Altmire held on by taking 51 percent against Republican Keith Rothfus.

State party leaders have suggested his moderate voting record could inspire a primary challenge from the left in 2012.

Key Votes

2010

Overhaul the nation's health insurance system	NO
Allow for repeal of "don't ask, don't tell"	YES
Overhaul financial services industry regulation	YES
Limit use of new Afghanistan War funds to troop withdrawal activities	NO
Change oversight of offshore drilling and lift oil spill liability cap	YES
Provide a path to legal status for some children of illegal immigrants	NO
Extend Bush-era income tax cuts for two years	YES

2009

Expand the Children's Health Insurance Program	YES
Provide $787 billion in tax cuts and spending increases to stimulate the economy	YES
Allow bankruptcy judges to modify certain primary-residence mortgages	YES
Create a cap-and-trade system to limit greenhouse gas emissions	NO
Provide $2 billion for the "cash for clunkers" program	YES
Establish the government as the sole provider of student loans	YES
Restrict federally funded insurance coverage for abortions in health care overhaul	YES

CQ Vote Studies

	PARTY UNITY		PRESIDENTIAL SUPPORT	
	Support	Oppose	Support	Oppose
2010	77%	23%	83%	17%
2009	78%	22%	75%	25%
2008	84%	16%	24%	76%
2007	77%	23%	15%	85%

Interest Groups

	AFL-CIO	ADA	CCUS	ACU
2010	79%	65%	50%	21%
2009	90%	70%	60%	20%
2008	100%	80%	61%	24%
2007	96%	95%	55%	28%

Pennsylvania 4

West — Pittsburgh suburbs

The 4th District begins in the southwestern corner of Mercer County and runs down the state's western border before heading east to wrap around the northern and eastern sides of Pittsburgh.

Historically a top steel producer, this one-time blue-collar district has yet to fully recover from economic hardships and has been battered by recent downturns.

The area's major highways and its proximity to Pittsburgh make the 4th attractive to commuters as well as to new and expanding companies. Although abandoned steel mills still line the rivers here, other job sectors are beginning to develop. The 4th's health care industry is a major employer, as are a growing number of computer firms. Larger companies, such as Philips Respironics in Murrysville and Alcoa-owned TRACO in Cranberry Township, bring jobs to the area. TRACO plans to expand, but a weak national homebuilding market has hurt Aliquippa-based wallboard manufacturer USG.

The district has yet to regain the population it had during its booming steel days, but some areas, including parts of southern Butler County, are experiencing residential growth and host a growing white-collar, well-educated workforce. Outside of Pittsburgh's exurbs, smaller communities produce numerous agricultural products, including corn, soybeans, dairy and winter wheat.

Although union tradition has kept the district Democratic at the local level, Republicans can break the Democratic grip. The 4th's GOP base is found mainly in small farming communities and wealthy Pittsburgh suburbs such as Franklin Park, Fox Chapel and Marshall Township. Democrat Jason Altmire has held on to his U.S. House seat even though Republican presidential candidate John McCain took 55 percent of the district's presidential vote in 2008 and a pair of Republicans, Sen. Patrick J. Toomey and Gov. Tom Corbett, found widespread support throughout the district in 2010.

Major industry
Health care, steel, manufacturing

Cities
Plum, 27,126; New Castle, 23,273

Notable
Oliver B. Shallenberger invented the electric meter, which indicated the amount of electrical energy dispensed or applied, in Rochester; New Castle calls itself the fireworks capital of the United States.

Rep. Glenn Thompson (R)

Capitol Office
225-5121
thompson.house.gov
124 Cannon Bldg. 20515-3805; fax 225-5796

Committees
Agriculture
   (Conservation, Energy & Forestry - Chairman)
Education & the Workforce
Natural Resources

Residence
Howard

Born
July 27, 1959; Bellefonte, Pa.

Religion
Protestant

Family
Wife, Penny Thompson; three children

Education
Pennsylvania State U., B.S. 1981 (recreation & parks);
Temple U., M.Ed. 1998 (sports management & leisure
studies)

Career
Rehabilitation therapist

Political Highlights
Bald Eagle Area School Board, 1990-95; Republican
nominee for Pa. House, 1998, 2000; Centre County
Republican Party chairman, 2002-08

ELECTION RESULTS

2010 GENERAL

Glenn Thompson (R)	127,427	68.7%
Michael Pipe (D)	52,375	28.2%
Vernon L. Etzel (LIBERT)	5,710	3.1%

2010 PRIMARY

Glenn Thompson (R)	unopposed

2008 GENERAL

Glenn Thompson (R)	155,513	56.7%
Mark B. McCracken (D)	112,509	41.0%
James Fryman (LIBERT)	6,155	2.2%

Elected 2008; 2nd term

Thompson provides a dependably conservative voice for Pennsylvania's largest district. His committee portfolio includes a pair of appointments that position him to wield considerable influence over energy policy, an issue of critical concern to the region. And he champions rural development, with the intention of improving the economy of the small towns throughout the district.

The largely untapped Marcellus Shale natural gas reserve lies underneath much of the district. With the proper exploration and drilling, Thompson says, the reserve could be "an incredibly important job creator" locally, as well as a boon for the nation as a whole. As chairman of the Agriculture Subcommittee on Conservation, Energy and Forestry and as a member of the Natural Resources Subcommittee on Energy and Mineral Resources, he promotes increasing domestic energy production.

He defends the use of high-pressure water and chemicals to extract gas and oil from rock — a practice known as hydraulic fracturing, or fracking — against critics who say it puts water supplies at risk of contamination.

"Plainly put, in a world where new access to productive energy fields is limited by the whims of dictators abroad and the laws of physics and the federal government here at home, hydraulic fracturing allows us to redefine what was previously impossible and capture what was previously unreachable," he wrote in a Washington Examiner opinion article in September 2009.

Thompson has overseen millions of dollars in federal grants brought to his district related to energy production. This included, in October 2010, a $10 million grant for transportation improvements needed to accommodate expanded Marcellus development.

He joined with all but two Republicans in adding an amendment to the House-passed catchall spending bill for fiscal 2011 that would bar the EPA from implementing any regulations related to the emission of greenhouse gases from stationary sources, such as power plants. In 2009, he vigorously opposed House energy legislation that would have created a cap-and-trade system for regulating carbon emissions, calling it "a $646 billion tax that will hit almost every American family, small business and family farm."

An Eagle Scout and former local Boy Scout Council president, Thompson continues to have an active role in scouting and has used those experiences to build his philosophy on government service. Though he outspokenly opposes the Democratic agenda, Thompson tries to uphold the Scouts' values in avoiding demonizing those with whom he disagrees. He invited the Democrat he defeated in 2008, Mark B. McCracken, to be his guest for President Obama's initial address to Congress.

He voted against the Democrats' health care overhaul during the 111th Congress (2009-10) and to repeal the law in early 2011. He fears the law will lead to millions of employers dropping their own insurance plans.

A former member of the Small Business Committee, Thompson spent 26 years in various positions in the regional Susquehanna Health System that serves his area, most recently as a rehabilitation services manager. He takes an avid interest in health care issues, and credits them for spurring his interest in running for Congress. "It was very obvious to me that these legislators were clueless about health care," he said.

Thompson, who is vice chairman of the Congressional Rural Caucus, said the current system does not fairly compensate rural hospitals and health providers for services. But Thompson thinks Democratic proposals focused too much on expanding insurance coverage and not enough on supporting community health centers and other low-cost providers. He also favors changing tort laws to reduce medical malpractice costs.

Thompson draws on his background as a former school board member in his duties on the Education and the Workforce Committee. He supports efforts to repeal the 2001 No Child Left Behind law, which relies on standardized testing. And he looks out for Pennsylvania State University, a major employer in his district; he and other members of the Pennsylvania delegation persuaded the Education Department in July 2009 to have state officials resubmit an application for economic stimulus funding to include Penn State and three other Keystone State colleges.

He pushed back against Obama administration efforts to tighten regulation of for-profit colleges, joining a bipartisan group of House members in early 2011 who challenged the impartiality of an investigation of the schools by the Government Accountability Office.

Thompson has lived in the district his entire life. He was born in Bellefonte and grew up in Howard, where he and his younger brother and sister all still live within walking distance of one another. Though his relatives had been dairy farmers in the area for generations, his father owned a sporting goods store. He and his wife, Penny, have been together since high school.

After graduating from Penn State in 1981, Thompson entered the health care field, working for a year at a group home for the disabled before joining Susquehanna Health. In 1998 he received his master's degree in education from Temple University.

He served five years as a member of the Bald Eagle Area School Board before mounting two unsuccessful challenges to Democratic state Rep. Mike Hanna in 1998 and 2000; he describes the two defeats as a good learning experience. He subsequently became chairman of Centre County's Republican Party, a post he held when Republican John E. Peterson announced his retirement from Congress. As he and his wife were about to become empty-nesters, with their three children leaving home, he decided it was worth entering the 2008 race.

Peterson's endorsement and the contacts Thompson had built as a local GOP chairman helped him prevail over eight primary challengers. He then faced McCracken, a Clearfield County commissioner and former school board official. McCracken campaigned as a supporter of gun rights interested in bringing fiscal responsibility to Washington, but he could not overcome the district's conservative lean — GOP presidential candidate John McCain took 55 percent of the vote there over Barack Obama — and Thompson's more than 4-to-1 advantage in fundraising. Thompson outdid McCain, winning nearly 57 percent of the vote. Thompson sailed to re-election over Democrat Michael Pipe in 2010, taking more than 68 percent of the vote.

Key Votes

2010

Overhaul the nation's health insurance system	NO
Allow for repeal of "don't ask, don't tell"	NO
Overhaul financial services industry regulation	NO
Limit use of new Afghanistan War funds to troop withdrawal activities	NO
Change oversight of offshore drilling and lift oil spill liability cap	NO
Provide a path to legal status for some children of illegal immigrants	NO
Extend Bush-era income tax cuts for two years	YES

2009

Expand the Children's Health Insurance Program	YES
Provide $787 billion in tax cuts and spending increases to stimulate the economy	NO
Allow bankruptcy judges to modify certain primary-residence mortgages	NO
Create a cap-and-trade system to limit greenhouse gas emissions	NO
Provide $2 billion for the "cash for clunkers" program	YES
Establish the government as the sole provider of student loans	NO
Restrict federally funded insurance coverage for abortions in health care overhaul	YES

CQ Vote Studies

	PARTY UNITY		PRESIDENTIAL SUPPORT	
	Support	Oppose	Support	Oppose
2010	93%	7%	31%	69%
2009	85%	15%	27%	73%

Interest Groups

	AFL-CIO	ADA	CCUS	ACU
2010	7%	0%	88%	100%
2009	19%	15%	87%	88%

Pennsylvania 5

North central — State College

The sprawling 5th covers one-fourth of the state's land area and takes in all or part of 17 counties in north-central Pennsylvania. Bordering New York to its north, the district extends as far south as Mifflin County and Centre County, which hosts Pennsylvania's largest university — Pennsylvania State University — in State College. The district's small towns are spread among state and national parks and forests.

State College, known by locals as "Happy Valley," is the 5th's most populated city. Despite some job cuts in traditional manufacturing sectors, Centre County has one of the state's lowest unemployment rates and has attracted electronics and computer firms. The global headquarters of AccuWeather is located just outside State College. The county also relies on small businesses.

The 5th's other counties remain tied to timber production, manufacturing, oil refining and tourism. Parts of the 5th's western region — most of which has experienced massive population loss in recent years — have been designated as the Oil Region National Heritage Area.

Still sparsely populated Forest County, though, has experienced the state's fastest rate of population growth since 2000, and more of the region's towns could welcome new residents and jobs as natural gas drilling increases across the Marcellus Shale.

Many tourists who visit the district travel through the Allegheny National Forest. In the east, the roughly 160,000 acres of the Tioga State Forest include the Grand Canyon of Pennsylvania. In southern Jefferson County, Punxsutawney, home of the famous groundhog Phil, draws national attention each February.

Much of the 5th — particularly the northern counties — votes Republican. Penn State keeps Centre County competitive for Democrats, but John McCain won 55 percent of the district's 2008 presidential vote.

Major Industry
Higher education, timber, tourism, manufacturing

Cities
State College, 42,034; St. Marys, 13,070

Notable
Drake's Well, the birthplace of the modern petroleum industry, is located on the banks of Oil Creek near Titusville; South Williamsport hosts the Little League World Series.

Rep. Jim Gerlach (R)

Capitol Office
225-4315
www.house.gov/gerlach
2442 Rayburn Bldg. 20515-3806; fax 225-8440

Committees
Ways & Means

Residence
West Pikeland Township

Born
Feb. 25, 1955; Ellwood City, Pa.

Religion
Protestant

Family
Wife, Karen Gerlach; three children,
three stepchildren

Education
Dickinson College, B.A. 1977 (political science);
Dickinson School of Law, J.D. 1980

Career
Lawyer

Political Highlights
Republican nominee for Pa. House, 1986; Pa. House,
1991-95; Pa. Senate, 1995-2003

ELECTION RESULTS

2010 GENERAL

Jim Gerlach (R)	133,770	57.1%
Manan Trivedi (D)	100,493	42.9%

2010 PRIMARY

Jim Gerlach (R)	35,575	79.8%
Pat Sellers (R)	8,998	20.2%

2008 GENERAL

Jim Gerlach (R)	179,423	52.1%
Bob Roggio (D)	164,952	47.9%

Previous Winning Percentages
2006 (51%); 2004 (51%); 2002 (51%)

Elected 2002; 5th term

Gerlach has defied the decline of Republican moderates from the Northeast. His politics of fostering compromise over confrontation has helped him fend off aggressive Democratic challengers in a district President Obama carried easily in 2008. After passing on the gubernatorial race in 2010, he won a coveted seat on the Ways and Means Committee in the 112th Congress.

Gerlach (GUR-lock) built his moderate voting record with several high-profile stands against President George W. Bush and the House GOP leadership on issues ranging from same-sex marriage to oil drilling on public lands. Only 11 House Republicans broke from their party on floor votes more often in 2010. His record practically mirrored the decline in Bush's approval ratings: In 2003, Gerlach backed the president's position 91 percent of the time; by 2008, that figure plummeted to 44 percent.

Because of the nature of his suburban swing district — Obama carried the 6th with 58 percent of the vote in 2008 — Republican leaders give Gerlach plenty of room to go his own way while looking for opportunities to help him out.

Adding him to the roster of the tax-writing Ways and Means Committee falls into that category, giving him a platform from which to weigh in on such meaty issues as health care, trade, entitlement spending and tax policy.

On a more parochial level, he has proposed cutting in half the federal excise tax on beer, which would aid Pennsylvania's more than 100 craft and micro-breweries.

In 2003, long before he joined Ways and Means, he was tapped as the lead sponsor of high-profile legislation eliminating the "marriage penalty" in the income tax code, even though he played hardly any role in the legislative deal-making.

When Obama took office, Gerlach stuck with his party on major economic initiatives — he called the $787 billion economic stimulus package a "spending orgy" and opposed the Democrats' health care overhaul — but found some issues to support in the Democratic president's early agenda.

In July 2010, Gerlach was one of 29 Republicans to vote to extend unemployment benefits without paying for the added cost. He said he was "fearful of cutting people off" who were out of work. He also sided with Democrats to expand the Children's Health Insurance Program, which covers children from lower-income families that make too much money to qualify for Medicaid, and overhaul food safety laws.

Despite working with Democrats on several occasions, Gerlach said the 111th Congress (2009-10) was not a positive place for bipartisanship. He said the high-profile fights over health care and financial regulation "highlighted what is wrong with the process."

Gerlach wants the House to change its rules to foster more bipartisanship. He said all proposed amendments that have both a Democratic and Republican sponsor should be debated and voted on. "What has been frustrating to me is the lack of efforts to bring together good ideas," Gerlach said, adding that although both parties have been heavy-handed in their rule of the House, "I think we've got to figure out, from an institutional standpoint, how to break through that partisanship."

Gerlach voted against the first version of a $700 billion bill to shore up the financial services sector in 2008, after concluding the bill's defeat would spur improvements to it. He voted for a revised version that included, among other provisions, a boost in the federal deposit insurance limit and language curtailing the reach of the alternative minimum tax, which was originally intended to target the highest-earning taxpayers but was not indexed for inflation. Later, he said he disapproved of the Obama administration's decision to use some of the money to purchase the stock of financial institutions.

Gerlach formerly served on the Transportation and Infrastructure Committee, where he was able to steer highway projects to his district. He is an ardent supporter of open-space preservation and co-founded the House Land Trust Caucus, now called the Land Conservation Caucus.

Gerlach was born and raised in Ellwood City, a small steel town north of Pittsburgh. His mother, who raised Gerlach and his two sisters on her own after his father was killed by a drunken driver when Gerlach was 5, "was just a terrific role model," he said. Before arriving in Congress, Gerlach spent 12 years as a state legislator. He was the prime sponsor of Pennsylvania's 1996 welfare overhaul.

When Pennsylvania lost two House seats in the reapportionment that followed the 2000 census, Gerlach's colleagues in the General Assembly redrew the congressional map with him in mind. No House incumbent chose to run in 2002 in the redrawn 6th District — which had a close partisan split, but overlapped with much of Gerlach's state Senate territory — and he was unopposed for the Republican nomination. That November, he won by 5,520 votes over Democratic lawyer Dan Wofford, the son of former U.S. Sen. Harris Wofford.

His three subsequent re-elections were also difficult; in 2008 he won by 4 percentage points, his largest margin to that point.

In the 110th Congress (2007-08), Gerlach was one of eight House Republicans from districts that Bush did not win in the 2004 election.

Early in 2007, the Federal Election Commission fined his campaign $120,000 — one of the largest fines ever — for inaccurate campaign finance reports in 2004 and 2005. Gerlach and the commission agreed a clerical error was to blame; his treasurer erroneously reported the entire amount of campaign funds raised in the cycle on a line calling for the amount of funds raised in just the last part of the year.

In February 2009, Gerlach filed paperwork to form an exploratory committee to seek Pennsylvania's governorship in 2010. But he dropped out of the Republican primary race in January, saying he "didn't think he could get the fundraising levels to be as competitive as he needed to be."

Gerlach turned his attention back to his re-election bid in 2010 and won with 57 percent of the vote over Democrat Manan Trivedi, a physician and Iraq War veteran.

Key Votes

2010

Overhaul the nation's health insurance system	NO
Allow for repeal of "don't ask, don't tell"	NO
Overhaul financial services industry regulation	NO
Limit use of new Afghanistan War funds to troop withdrawal activities	NO
Change oversight of offshore drilling and lift oil spill liability cap	NO
Provide a path to legal status for some children of illegal immigrants	NO
Extend Bush-era income tax cuts for two years	YES

2009

Expand the Children's Health Insurance Program	YES
Provide $787 billion in tax cuts and spending increases to stimulate the economy	NO
Allow bankruptcy judges to modify certain primary-residence mortgages	NO
Create a cap-and-trade system to limit greenhouse gas emissions	NO
Provide $2 billion for the "cash for clunkers" program	YES
Establish the government as the sole provider of student loans	NO
Restrict federally funded insurance coverage for abortions in health care overhaul	YES

CQ Vote Studies

	PARTY UNITY		PRESIDENTIAL SUPPORT	
	Support	Oppose	Support	Oppose
2010	83%	17%	43%	57%
2009	73%	27%	51%	49%
2008	75%	25%	44%	56%
2007	74%	26%	45%	55%
2006	70%	30%	69%	31%

Interest Groups

	AFL-CIO	ADA	CCUS	ACU
2010	14%	10%	100%	67%
2009	52%	20%	87%	76%
2008	64%	60%	81%	48%
2007	67%	40%	90%	52%
2006	57%	45%	79%	62%

Pennsylvania 6

Southeast — parts of Berks and Chester counties, Philadelphia suburbs

The 6th takes in urban, suburban and rural communities stretching from a slice of Montgomery County in the Philadelphia area, including the county seat of Norristown, through northern Chester County and southern and eastern portions of Berks County, including part of Reading and all of Kutztown. Most of the district's land is spread through sparsely populated towns.

Manufacturing remains important to the 6th, and factories are found throughout, especially in areas such as Coatesville, which, like other aging towns, hopes to revitalize its core downtown area. Vanguard, an investment management company, is based in the district, and a food processing sector should help stabilize the 6th's economy as it copes with high unemployment rates in Berks and Chester counties. Once known for its railroads and industrial prowess, the economy of Berks now includes service and retail jobs. Reading has moved away from its industrial image, becoming an entertainment and shopping hub outside of Philadelphia.

Much of the Berks County workforce depends on jobs at Reading Hospital and Medical Center.

With its share of historical sites and untouched land, the 6th enjoys a modest tourism industry. The district is home to covered bridges, old mill towns and Pennsylvania Dutch communities. It also is home to both the Hopewell Furnace National Historic Site in Elverson and Valley Forge National Historical Park (shared with the 7th), where George Washington trained Continental Army soldiers during the Revolutionary War. The generally competitive 6th backed Barack Obama by 17 percentage points in the 2008 presidential election despite continuing to support Republican Jim Gerlach for the U.S. House. Growth and water-use issues concern residents in the region, which is mostly situated in the area triangulated by Philadelphia, Reading and Lancaster.

Major Industry
Manufacturing, tourism, retail

Cities
Reading (pt.), 40,967; Norristown, 34,324; Pottstown, 22,377

Notable
The largest quilt sale in the United States takes places each year at the Kutztown Pennsylvania German Festival.

Rep. Patrick Meehan (R)

Capitol Office
225-2011
meehan.house.gov
513 Cannon Bldg. 20515-3807; fax 226-0280

Committees
Homeland Security
   (Counterterrorism & Intelligence - Chairman)
Oversight & Government Reform
Transportation & Infrastructure

Residence
Drexel Hill

Born
Oct. 20, 1955; Cheltenham, Pa.

Religion
Roman Catholic

Family
Wife, Carolyn Meehan; three children

Education
Bowdoin College, B.A. 1978 (classics & government);
Temple U., J.D. 1986

Career
Lawyer; congressional district and campaign aide;
professional hockey referee

Political Highlights
Delaware County district attorney, 1996-2001; U.S.
attorney, 2001-08

ELECTION RESULTS

2010 GENERAL

Patrick Meehan (R)	137,825	54.9%
Bryan Lentz (D)	110,314	44.0%
Jim Schneller (I)	2,708	1.1%

2010 PRIMARY

Patrick Meehan (R)	unopposed

Elected 2010; 1st term

Meehan quickly assumed a leading role in the sizable GOP Class of 2010. He captured one of three freshman seats on the Republican Steering Committee and was named chairman of a subcommittee with jurisdiction over counterterrorism and intelligence issues.

A member of the Transportation and Infrastructure Committee, he promises to push for federal spending on highways and mass transit while fighting tax increases on small businesses and individuals.

But Meehan, who was sworn in as U.S. attorney six days after the Sept. 11 terrorist attacks, will likely make terrorism issues his top priority. He won a rare plum for a freshman lawmaker — the gavel of the Homeland Security Subcommittee on Counterterrorism and Intelligence. Homeland Security Chairman Peter T. King, a New York Republican, called the former NHL referee "immensely qualified" for the post, pointing to his work in helping to establish an anti-terrorism advisory council in eastern Pennsylvania.

Meehan argued in a Roll Call op-ed that "law enforcement and intelligence officials cannot effectively combat the threat of terrorists without adequate tools to investigate suspects." He voted for a short-term extension of expiring provisions of the anti-terrorism law known as the Patriot Act, but says the provisions — to allow the government to seek court orders for "roving" wiretaps on suspects, to request access to "any tangible thing" deemed related to a terrorism investigation and to seek warrants to conduct surveillance of "lone wolf" foreign terrorist suspects who may not be connected to a group — should be made permanent.

He also serves on the Oversight and Government Reform Committee.

Meehan was considered a prize GOP recruit in the contest to succeed Democrat Joe Sestak, who ran unsuccessfully for the Senate. The Democrats put up state Rep. Bryan Lentz, an Iraq War veteran.

President Obama carried the district with 56 percent of the vote in 2008, and Sestak had won by double digits twice. But Meehan rode the national GOP wave and a strong Republican ticket above him to an 11-percentage-point victory.

Pennsylvania 7

Suburban Philadelphia — most of Delaware County

Anchored in the suburbs south and west of Philadelphia, the politically competitive 7th takes in heavily populated unincorporated townships in vast tracts of middle-class suburbia. It includes most of Delaware County, the district's population center, as well as southwestern Montgomery and eastern Chester counties.

Older suburbs in Delaware County are mostly white and working-class. Oil refineries and chemical facilities drive the economy around the Delaware River communities of Marcus Hook and Trainer, but several years of job cuts at these mainstays have hurt the workforce. Areas in Upper Merion Township in Montgomery County have grown since the 1990s opening of the Blue Route (Interstate 476), which links Interstate 95 along the Delaware River with the Schuylkill

Expressway near King of Prussia, home of a gigantic shopping mall complex.

A Boeing helicopter facility in Ridley Park and Lockheed Martin's plant in King of Prussia provide jobs, as do the district's pharmaceutical and technology sectors. The growth of white-collar jobs gave the 7th the state's most educated workforce, but layoffs have hurt some sectors. New residential developments, many of which have sprung up in less-populated areas of Chester County, are attracting city residents.

Either major party can win in federal elections here. Overall, Democrat Barack Obama took 56 percent of the district's vote in the 2008 presidential election.

Major Industry
Pharmaceuticals, defense, health care

Cities
Drexel Hill (unincorporated), 28,043; King of Prussia (unincorporated), 19,936

Notable
Villanova University hosts the largest student-organized Special Olympics festival.

Rep. Michael G. Fitzpatrick (R)

Capitol Office
225-4276
fitzpatrick.house.gov
1224 Longworth Bldg. 20515-3808; fax 225-9511

Committees
Financial Services

Residence
Levittown

Born
June 28, 1963; Philadelphia, Pa.

Religion
Roman Catholic

Family
Wife, Kathy Fitzpatrick; six children

Education
St. Thomas U. (Fla.), B.A. 1985 (political science);
Dickinson School of Law, J.D. 1988

Career
Lawyer

Political Highlights
Republican nominee for Pa. House, 1990, 1994;
Bucks County Board of Commissioners, 1995-2005;
U.S. House, 2005-07; defeated for re-election to U.S.
House, 2006

ELECTION RESULTS

2010 GENERAL

Michael G. Fitzpatrick (R)	130,759	53.5%
Patrick J. Murphy (D)	113,547	46.5%

2010 PRIMARY

Michael G. Fitzpatrick (R)	33,671	76.7%
Gloria Carlineo (R)	6,529	14.9%
Ira Hoffman (R)	2,424	5.5%
James Jones (R)	1,249	2.8%

Previous Winning Percentages
2004 (55%)

Elected 2010; 2nd term

Also served 2005-07

Fitzpatrick proved a fellow Irish American wrong in 2010, returning to Congress after a four-year hiatus and upending F. Scott Fitzgerald's adage that there are no second acts in American lives.

He was a one-term lawmaker representing a fiscally conservative, socially liberal swing district when he was swept out of office as Democrats captured the House in 2006. After sitting out the 2008 cycle, he returned in 2010 to reclaim the seat from Democrat Patrick J. Murphy.

He also earned a second chance on the Financial Services Committee, where he displayed something of an independent streak in his previous House tenure.

This time around, Fitzpatrick sounds less like the man who strayed from his party on about three of every 10 votes in the 109th Congress (2005-06) than like the mass of newly elected Republicans who are determined to shrink the size of government.

"I look back on the months I had there and I wish we had slowed the growth [of the deficit] a little quicker or cut a little deeper," he told the Allentown Morning Call in November 2010. "I wish we had been more aggressive in reducing government spending. I think that's what we were sent back here to do."

Fitzpatrick believes that government services work best at the local level and that Washington should allow more local flexibility in spending federal aid. His years as county official — Fitzpatrick was a Bucks County commissioner for a decade — might give him insight on how to improve the relationship between the federal government and local officials. When Hurricane Floyd ravaged the area in 1999, Fitzpatrick aggressively pursued the county's "fair share" of federal disaster funds and helped institute a program that included elevating houses above the flood plain of the Neshaminy Creek watershed.

He addressed the issue again in the House. After Hurricane Katrina hit the Gulf Coast, his bill to temporarily increase the borrowing authority of the Federal Emergency Management Agency for flood insurance claims was signed into law by President George W. Bush.

"The bill's important because what it's going to do is permit FEMA to make good on its obligations to pay out on these flood insurance contracts," Fitzpatrick said at the time. "Obviously, this is a set of unfortunate events in 2005 that this program was not set up to handle."

With FEMA redrawing flood zone maps in a way that affects whether homeowners need to buy flood insurance, the issue is certain to arise again in the 112th Congress (2011-12).

Fitzpatrick serves as vice chairman of the Financial Services Committee's Oversight and Investigations panel. He said his focus will be on closer scrutiny of government-backed lenders Fannie Mae and Freddie Mac, and examining the risks for taxpayers associated with "too big to fail" banks.

He also was named to the House Republican Policy Committee, which helps set legislative priorities for the party.

Although his voting record in his first term placed him among the most moderate Republicans, Fitzpatrick hews to the conservative line on a range of issues. He takes a tough stance on national security, backs stricter immigration enforcement, supports gun owners' rights and backed repeal of the Democrats' health care overhaul enacted in 2010 while promoting "free-market solutions" to boost insurance coverage.

He supports what he calls a "balanced" energy policy that includes nuclear power, development of clean-coal technology and "responsible" offshore drilling. He expects to be a champion for the development of natural gas from Pennsylvania's Marcellus Shale, which he says would provide both an increased supply of domestic energy and jobs for the state.

In line with most Republicans, he oppose creation of a cap-and-trade system to regulate carbon emissions, and voted in early 2011 to block the EPA from implementing such a program without the approval of Congress.

He wants to make the 2001 and 2003 tax cuts permanent for all income levels, arguing that allowing tax rates to rise would discourage job creation. "Government does not create jobs," he said. "Free enterprise, business, industry and entrepreneurs do."

Fitzpatrick was born in Philadelphia, and resides with his wife and six children in Levittown. He received his bachelor's degree in political science from St. Thomas University in Florida, then his law degree from Dickinson School of Law in 1988.

He made two unsuccessful bids for the Pennsylvania state House in the early 1990s, then won a seat on the Bucks County Board of Commissioners in 1995.

The surprise retirement decision by six-term Republican James C. Greenwood opened up an opportunity in the 8th District. Because Greenwood had already won the primary when he announced he was leaving Congress to take a lobbying job, party leaders were empowered to pick the new nominee. Fitzpatrick — the favorite of GOP leaders in Bucks County, the district's dominant jurisdiction — won the nod.

Democratic presidential candidate John Kerry carried the district by 3 percentage points, but Fitzpatrick won 55 percent of the vote.

In 2006, though, Fitzpatrick was weighed down by the unpopularity of President George W. Bush and the national Democratic trend. Murphy slipped by him by about 1,500 votes in one of the closest House races of the year.

Following that defeat, Fitzpatrick went back to practicing law and also dealt successfully with colon cancer.

Much as Murphy was able to tie Fitzpatrick to Bush in 2006, Fitzpatrick linked Murphy, who backed the health care overhaul and the cap-and-trade energy legislation, to President Obama and the Democratic leadership.

The strategy worked. Riding the national Republican wave and the district's discontent with Democratic policies, Fitzpatrick returned to Congress by a relatively comfortable 7-percentage-point margin.

CQ Vote Studies

	PARTY UNITY		PRESIDENTIAL SUPPORT	
	Support	Oppose	Support	Oppose
2006	66%	34%	65%	35%
2005	76%	24%	61%	39%

Interest Groups

	AFL-CIO	ADA	CCUS	ACU
2006	57%	40%	64%	46%
2005	47%	30%	74%	60%

Pennsylvania 8

Northern Philadelphia suburbs — Bucks County

North of Philadelphia, the 8th District takes in all of Bucks County, a small part of Montgomery County and a slice of Northeast Philadelphia. Founded in 1682 as one of the state's three original counties, Bucks' stately mansions, scenery and charm have attracted wealthy, white-collar residents. At more than $73,000, the 8th has the highest median household income in the state. Development here began in the 1950s with the opening of Levittown, one of the earliest planned U.S. suburbs.

Steel, once a major employer in Bucks, has suffered long-term decline and sustained loss of blue-collar jobs. A shuttered U.S. Steel plant in Fairless Hills, however, was redeveloped to lure varied heavy industry. The site now hosts a factory that manufactures parts for wind turbines and employs roughly 800 people. Local officials hope to bring new manufacturing jobs to industrial sites along the Delaware River.

Propping up the economy are small businesses and several hospitals. A deep-water port that was built during the district's steel-production heyday makes the 8th something of a distribution and warehouse center. One of the state's first racetrack and casino enterprises opened in the county in 2006, and Parx Racing and Casino draws visitors and revenue. But that economic diversity has not insulated the county from rising unemployment rates and cutbacks in social services.

Voters in the 8th tend to be fiscally conservative but support environmentalism and hold moderate stances on some social issues. In 2008, the district gave Democrat Barack Obama 54 percent of its presidential vote and backed Democratic Rep. Patrick J. Murphy for re-election to the U.S. House. But after several years of support for Democratic candidates at the federal level, the district reinstated former Republican Rep. Michael G. Fitzpatrick in 2010, and Republicans Patrick J. Toomey and Tom Corbett easily won Bucks County in their U.S. Senate and gubernatorial races. The area is represented by Republicans in the state legislature.

Major Industry
Health care, wholesale and retail trade

Cities
Levittown (unincorporated), 52,983; Philadelphia (pt.), 31,218

Notable
George Washington's Delaware River crossing is re-enacted at Washington Crossing each Christmas Day.

Rep. Bill Shuster (R)

Capitol Office
225-2431
www.house.gov/shuster
204 Cannon Bldg. 20515-3809; fax 225-2486

Committees
Armed Services
Transportation & Infrastructure
 (Railroads, Pipelines & Hazardous Materials -
 Chairman)

Residence
Hollidaysburg

Born
Jan. 10, 1961; McKeesport, Pa.

Religion
Lutheran

Family
Wife, Rebecca Shuster; two children

Education
Dickinson College, B.A. 1983 (political science
& history); American U., M.B.A. 1987

Career
Car dealer; tire company manager

Political Highlights
No previous office

ELECTION RESULTS

2010 GENERAL
Bill Shuster (R)	141,904	73.1%
Tom Conners (D)	52,322	26.9%

2010 PRIMARY
Bill Shuster (R)	unopposed

2008 GENERAL
Bill Shuster (R)	174,951	63.9%
Tony Barr (D)	98,735	36.1%

Previous Winning Percentages
2006 (60%); 2004 (70%); 2002 (71%); 2001 Special
Election (52%)

Elected 2001; 5th full term

Before he was elected to Congress, Shuster owned and managed his family's car dealership, a career he says shaped the lawmaker he was to become.

"You're dealing with customers," he told Roll Call. "You're convincing people to buy things; you're convincing people to vote for you."

Representing one of the Northeast's reddest districts, Shuster rarely strays from the party line, making him an easy sell to constituents. Since he was elected in 2001 to succeed his father, Bud, Shuster has sided with the Republicans on about 95 percent of the votes in which the majority of the two parties diverged.

That's a popular stance in a district where two-thirds of voters backed President George W. Bush in 2004 and 63 percent voted for Arizona Republican Sen. John McCain during the 2008 presidential election. Shuster's loyalty has won him praise among his colleagues and a post as deputy whip, which puts him on the front lines of shaping the GOP legislative agenda.

He also was named, for the 2010 election cycle, a regional chairman for the National Republican Congressional Committee, the House GOP's campaign arm. He is reprising that role for 2012.

Shuster is known for securing funds for his district to provide economic development and public works improvements. In this practice, he follows in the footsteps of his father. Bud Shuster was known as the "King of Asphalt" during his six-year reign as chairman of the Transportation and Infrastructure Committee, where he secured billions of dollars for highway construction.

Living up to his father's legacy has not been easy for Shuster, but he is accustomed to comparisons from constituents and colleagues.

"I'm a different person, but I think he has instilled in me the characteristics that make someone excel in life, and that's hard work and being honest and being committed to what you are doing," Shuster told the Pittsburgh Tribune-Review.

Bud Shuster was hired as a railroad lobbyist in 2007, the same year his son became ranking Republican on Transportation's Subcommittee on Railroads, Pipelines and Hazardous Materials — where he is now chairman. Government watchdog groups say such arrangements among relatives are troubling, but Bill Shuster said his father never lobbies him and doesn't need to — Bud Shuster has long had close relationships with more-senior committee members.

Shuster will play a key role in writing a new surface transportation bill, expected to happen in the 112th Congress (2011-12).

He also worked early in the 112th on a reauthorization of federal aviation programs, drawing some criticism for his provision that was added to the House-passed version of legislation to require the Federal Aviation Administration to consider how proposed regulations would affect individual segments of the aviation industry and tailor the rules to address those effects.

Relatives and friends of victims of a 2009 jet crash in New York say the amendment could stop a rule aimed at reducing pilot fatigue issues and increasing training requirements. Shuster said it was not his intent to affect current work by the FAA to address those issues.

The Senate-passed version of the FAA reauthorization did not include the Shuster language.

As a member of the Armed Services Committee, Shuster strongly backed President George W. Bush's Iraq policy while looking out for the Letterkenny Army Depot, a missile facility in Chambersburg in the southeast part of his district. He has joined other Republicans on the panel in arguing against cuts for missile defense in the face of threats from North Korea and other nations.

Shuster also supported President Obama's decision to increase troop levels in Afghanistan. In August 2010, he traveled with a congressional delegation to the war zone to assess the country's security situation.

Shuster's district includes Shanksville, where United Airlines Flight 93 crashed after passengers fought hijackers trying to fly the plane to Washington, D.C., on Sept. 11, 2001. In 2008, he secured $4.9 million to build a memorial at the crash site.

Shuster opposed Obama's early economic initiatives, including the $787 billion economic stimulus law. But he advocated use of stimulus money to fund education, sewer and water projects, and a Pittsburgh-to-Philadelphia high-speed rail line, among other ventures.

"I'm proud to be here to make these things happen," Shuster said, according to Public Opinion, a Chambersburg publication. "I'm doing what I was asked to do. If we're not fighting for the money, it's going to end up in Pittsburgh and Philadelphia."

In the fall of 2008, Shuster initially joined other conservatives in opposing the Bush administration's proposed $700 billion rescue package for the financial services sector. He voted for a reworked version a week later because, he said, it contained tougher oversight of the troubled industry.

But the former auto dealership owner refused to back a subsequent plan to assist domestic automakers. He said that to get his support, the proposal would have required more concessions from the United Auto Workers union.

Bud Shuster waited to resign until he was sworn in for a 15th term in January 2001, paving the way for his son to run for the seat in a special election. The younger Shuster won with 52 percent of the vote, narrowly defeating Democrat Scott Conklin, a Centre County commissioner. Bill Shuster followed his father onto Transportation and Infrastructure, where GOP leaders held a seat open for him.

Shuster was easily re-elected in 2002, but faced a tough campaign in 2004, after one of his congressional aides was accused of spying on his political opponent at home and at fundraising events. Shuster said the aide was acting independently, but the aide said Shuster had ordered the spying. The controversy almost cost him the GOP nomination; Michael DelGrosso, a financial consultant, lost the Republican primary by only about 2 percentage points to Shuster, who went on to win in November with 70 percent of the vote. He has won re-election without difficulty since.

Key Votes

2010	
Overhaul the nation's health insurance system	NO
Allow for repeal of "don't ask, don't tell"	NO
Overhaul financial services industry regulation	NO
Limit use of new Afghanistan War funds to troop withdrawal activities	NO
Change oversight of offshore drilling and lift oil spill liability cap	NO
Provide a path to legal status for some children of illegal immigrants	NO
Extend Bush-era income tax cuts for two years	YES
2009	
Expand the Children's Health Insurance Program	NO
Provide $787 billion in tax cuts and spending increases to stimulate the economy	NO
Allow bankruptcy judges to modify certain primary-residence mortgages	NO
Create a cap-and-trade system to limit greenhouse gas emissions	NO
Provide $2 billion for the "cash for clunkers" program	YES
Establish the government as the sole provider of student loans	NO
Restrict federally funded insurance coverage for abortions in health care overhaul	YES

CQ Vote Studies

	PARTY UNITY		PRESIDENTIAL SUPPORT	
	SUPPORT	OPPOSE	SUPPORT	OPPOSE
2010	98%	2%	27%	73%
2009	86%	14%	27%	73%
2008	94%	6%	67%	33%
2007	93%	7%	83%	17%
2006	97%	3%	93%	7%

Interest Groups

	AFL-CIO	ADA	CCUS	ACU
2010	7%	0%	88%	100%
2009	14%	5%	87%	88%
2008	13%	20%	94%	92%
2007	17%	10%	89%	96%
2006	14%	0%	100%	84%

Pennsylvania 9

South central — Altoona

Situated in the south-central part of Pennsylvania, the 9th District contains no booming metropolis — Altoona, the largest city, is tucked into the Allegheny Mountains and maintains a small-town feel. Most of the 9th's towns have populations numbering less than 5,000, making this one of the nation's 20 most rural districts.

Altoona's early growth was due to the Pennsylvania Railroad; its Horseshoe Curve permitted completion of a trans-Pennsylvania rail line. Dependent on transportation industries for centuries — first rail and later interstate highway — Altoona has focused economic development efforts on manufacturing interests and office parks. The city also has been working to repair neighborhoods, reduce blight and address municipal budget shortfalls. South of Altoona, Breezewood, the self-proclaimed "Traveler's Oasis," continues to lure road-weary travelers to hotels and fast-food restaurants with its garish display of signs at the Pennsylvania Turnpike interchange with southbound Interstate 70.

Still, the bulk of the district's land is rural and depends on agriculture. But that rural land is producing more than crops. Since 2001, there are more of the towering windmills that rise above farms in Somerset and Fayette counties (shared with 12th), and the output capacity of these utility- and small-scale windmills is increasing.

Most voters in the 9th oppose gun control and "big government" policies. Its small-business owners and farmers also tend to be fiscally conservative, and the district solidly backs Republicans at all levels. In the 2008 presidential election, John McCain won 63 percent of the district's vote overall — his best showing in the state. GOP Gov. Tom Corbett won easily across the district in 2010, and only Fayette County offered significant support for Democrat Joe Sestak in the U.S. Senate race.

Major Industry
Agriculture, manufacturing, service

Military Bases
Letterkenny Army Depot, 80 military, 1,716 civilian (2011)

Cities
Altoona, 46,320; Chambersburg, 20,268

Notable
A memorial to United Airlines Flight 93 is in Shanksville, where the hijacked airplane crashed in a field Sept. 11, 2001.

Rep. Tom Marino (R)

Capitol Office
225-3731
marino.house.gov
410 Cannon Bldg. 20515-3810; fax 225-9594

Committees
Foreign Affairs
Homeland Security
Judiciary

Residence
Lycoming Township

Born
Aug. 13, 1952; Williamsport, Pa.

Religion
Roman Catholic

Family
Wife, Edie Marino; two children

Education
Williamsport Area Community College, A.A. 1983;
Lycoming College, B.A. 1985 (political science &
secondary education); Dickenson School of Law,
J.D. 1988

Career
Lawyer; bakery worker

Political Highlights
Lycoming County district attorney, 1992-2002;
U.S. attorney, 2002-07

ELECTION RESULTS

2010 GENERAL
Tom Marino (R)	110,599	55.2%
Christopher Carney (D)	89,846	44.8%

2010 PRIMARY
Tom Marino (R)	24,435	41.0%
David Madeira (R)	18,524	31.1%
Malcolm L. Derk (R)	16,690	28.0%

Elected 2010; 1st term

Marino was the district attorney in his home county for a decade before serving as the George W. Bush administration's top federal prosecutor in a mostly rural region that stretches from Harrisburg to Scranton.

He has been given a committee portfolio heavy on national security and counterterrorism issues: Foreign Affairs, Judiciary and Homeland Security.

He brings a socially conservative outlook to Judiciary: He opposes abortion, gun control and creating a path to citizenship for illegal immigrants.

Marino — who describes himself as supportive of, but not part of, the tea party movement — expects to be a reliable vote for the GOP on all major areas but one: While most Republicans describe themselves as free-traders, he has expressed opposition to several pending trade liberalization agreements.

As Republicans push to reopen the debate on the health care law enacted in 2010, Marino can use his Judiciary assignment to advance his — and his party's — longstanding goal of limiting medical-malpractice litigation.

And Marino brings personal credentials to any health care debate: He has battled kidney cancer twice, and his daughter has cystic fibrosis. Marino voted in January 2011 to repeal the law, but emphasizes that certain changes are necessary, including coverage for those with pre-existing conditions — Marino said he could not find an insurance company to cover him.

Marino spent a decade as a Lycoming County district attorney before being named a U.S. attorney in 2002. While in that post, he appeared as a reference on a casino application of businessman Louis DeNaples, who had a decades-old felony conviction on his record and was investigated for alleged ties to organized crime. The reference allegations surfaced in August 2007 — Marino resigned in October, and then took a job with DeNaples.

Two-term Democrat Christopher Carney worked hard to make the DeNaples connection a campaign issue, and the Democratic Congressional Campaign Committee spent more than a half-million dollars helping him.

But Carney's support of unpopular Democratic policies, such as the health care overhaul, coupled with the national and statewide GOP waves aided Marino. He won with 55 percent of the vote, to 45 percent for Carney.

Pennsylvania 10

Northeast — Central Susquehanna Valley

Situated in the northeastern corner of Pennsylvania, the 10th is home to a portion of the Pocono Mountains region, a retreat known for its skiing, fishing and golfing. The district's southern arm dips into the Central Susquehanna Valley. The four Central Susquehanna Valley counties of Northumberland, Union, Snyder and Montour account for 30 percent of the population and contribute to the 10th's manufacturing, retail and service industries. Northumberland has many manufacturers, and a large solar energy field will go up next to the county's main industrial park. Montour is home to the Geisinger Health System and Danville State Hospital.

Some of the state's best areas for lumber, agriculture and natural gas drilling are here. Dairy farming is particularly prominent in Bradford County, although the industry has been hurt by falling prices. Tourism remains strong, especially during summer, when visitors come for the scenery in the district's east and for the Little League World Series, played annually in South Williamsport (in the adjacent 5th). Booming Pike County on the district's eastern border hosts residents who commute to New Jersey and New York City but prefer the small-town setting, cheaper land and access to main highways.

The 10th contains rural, socially conservative heartland, although Democrats crop up in Carbondale and Archbald in Lackawanna County and in parts of Luzerne County.

Major Industry
Agriculture, tourism, manufacturing, timber

Cities
Williamsport, 29,381; Kingston, 13,182

Notable
Thomas Edison first demonstrated his electrical lighting in 1883 by wiring the Sunbury Hotel (now named the Edison Hotel).

Rep. Lou Barletta (R)

Capitol Office
225-6511
barletta.house.gov
510 Cannon Bldg. 20515 3811; fax 225-6511

Committees
Education & the Workforce
Small Business
Transportation & Infrastructure

Residence
Hazleton

Born
Jan. 28, 1956; Hazleton, Pa.

Religion
Roman Catholic

Family
Wife, MaryGrace Barletta; four children

Education
Bloomsburg State College, attended 1973-76;
Luzerne County Community College, attended
1976-77

Career
Pavement marking company owner

Political Highlights
Republican nominee for Hazleton City Council,
1996; Hazleton City Council, 1998-2000; mayor of
Hazleton, 2000-10; Republican nominee for U.S.
House, 2002, 2008

ELECTION RESULTS

2010 GENERAL

Lou Barletta (R)	102,179	54.7%
Paul E. Kanjorski (D)	84,618	45.3%

2010 PRIMARY

Lou Barletta (R)	unopposed

Elected 2010; 1st term

Barletta made national news as mayor of Hazleton in 2006, when he vowed that his small city would be "the toughest place on illegal immigrants in America."

Lower courts struck down the ordinance cracking down on illegal immigrants that he pushed through the city council, but an Arizona law similar to Hazleton's was upheld by the U.S. Supreme Court in May 2011. Barletta did not win a seat on the Judiciary Committee, which handles most immigration legislation, but says illegal immigration will remain a signature issue for him.

On the economy, Barletta says there are many things that Congress can do to help create jobs, starting with a repeal of the health care overhaul enacted in 2010. He'll work on those issues as a member of the Education and the Workforce and Small Business committees.

He will get a chance to put his background in road construction to use on the Transportation and Infrastructure Committee. Barletta's father owned a road construction company, and Barletta co-founded his own construction firm, Interstate Road Marking Corp., before becoming mayor. He is expected to continue to promote a project to transform an abandoned coal-mining operation in Hazleton into a tourist destination with a 20,000-person amphitheater.

Born and raised in Hazleton, Barletta was elected to the city council in 1998, then served as mayor of his hometown from 2000 until his election to Congress. He first challenged longtime Democratic incumbent Paul E. Kanjorski in 2002, losing by about 13 percentage points. He tried again in 2008 and narrowed the gap to about 3 points.

The third time was the charm for Barletta. The political winds were blowing in his party's direction, and Kanjorski, chairman of a Financial Services subcommittee, was in the center of unpopular efforts to respond to the financial crisis.

"A wise man once said, 'If at first you don't succeed, try, try again,'" Barletta said. He took 55 percent of the vote, to 45 percent for Kanjorski.

Given the Democratic lean of the district, he is certain to be a prime target in 2012.

Pennsylvania 11

Northeast — Scranton, Wilkes-Barre

In the 20th century, the health of northeastern Pennsylvania's 11th was inextricably linked to the production, manufacturing and sale of coal. The industry virtually disappeared in the 1960s, and the loss significantly altered the economy of the Wyoming Valley.

Revitalization efforts are ongoing, including expansions to Wilkes-Barre/Scranton International Airport and the Wilkes-Barre VA Medical Center.

There also are long-term proposals to restore passenger and freight rail service from Scranton to New York City. To the southwest, the Wyoming Valley has received millions of dollars to repair levees originally damaged by Hurricane Agnes in 1972 and to prevent future damage. A portion of the funds was allocated for a riverfront project in Wilkes-Barre to create new landing areas and piers, a performance amphitheater, and walking trails.

Carbon County bridges the northern part of the Lehigh Valley and the Poconos region. Rural Monroe and Columbia counties in the Poconos are filled with residents who commute via Interstate 80 to their jobs in New Jersey and New York.

A legacy of union-oriented Democratic support remains, but the 11th has begun to favor the GOP: In 2010, Gov. Tom Corbett won every county in the 11th, and U.S. Rep. Lou Barletta lost only in Lackawanna County.

Major Industry
Manufacturing, retail trade, tourism

Military Bases
Tobyhanna Army Depot, 4 military, 4,184 civilian (2011)

Cities
Scranton, 76,089; Wilkes-Barre, 41,498

Notable
Scranton's Houdini Museum and Psychic Theater honors the magician's legacy.

Rep. Mark Critz (D)

Capitol Office
225-2065
critz.house.gov
1022 Longworth Bldg. 20515-3812; fax 225-5709

Committees
Armed Services
Small Business

Residence
Johnstown

Born
Jan. 5, 1962; Irwin, Pa.

Religion
Roman Catholic

Family
Wife, Nancy Critz; two children

Education
Indiana U. of Pennsylvania, B.S. 1987 (management information systems)

Career
Congressional district director and campaign aide; retail store systems manager

Political Highlights
Sought Democratic nomination for Johnstown City Council, 1997

ELECTION RESULTS

2010 GENERAL

Mark Critz (D)	94,056	50.8%
Tim Burns (R)	91,170	49.2%

2010 PRIMARY

Mark Critz (D)	58,817	71.5%
Ryan Bucchianeri (D)	16,965	20.6%
Ronald Mackell Jr. (D)	6,525	7.9%

2010 SPECIAL

Mark Critz (D)	72,218	52.6%
Tim Burns (R)	61,722	45.0%
Demo Agoris (LIBERT)	3,249	2.4%

Elected May 2010; 1st full term

Critz is emerging as an ideological departure from his former boss and predecessor, the late John P. Murtha, an 18-term, tough-talking Marine veteran who was an unapologetic supporter of liberal causes and a close ally of Democratic leader Nancy Pelosi of California.

During the 2010 campaign — Critz's first time through a regular campaign season — he went to great pains to distance himself from national party leaders. "I don't work for Nancy Pelosi and the leadership. I don't work for President Obama and the White House," he said in October.

Critz was also a vocal critic of the Democrats' health care overhaul and energy legislation that would create a cap-and-trade system aimed at reducing carbon emissions, two cornerstones of the Obama agenda that had earned Murtha's support.

"We need health insurance reform, but it must be done in a way that is consistent with our values," Critz said following the bill's final passage in March 2010. The legislation passed after Murtha's death in February but before voters chose Critz to replace him in a special election in May. "While this bill represents significant progress in reforming our broken health care system, there were flaws that would've kept me from supporting it."

He backed a resolution in early 2011 instructing four House committees to develop legislation to replace the overhaul. But he voted against the GOP-backed measure to repeal the law.

In endorsing Critz twice, Johnstown's Tribune-Democrat cited his decision to distance himself from Democratic leaders and their policies, as well as his established relationships with the local business community and his congressional colleagues.

Murtha's former district director, Critz once handled the distribution of hundreds of millions of dollars in federal funding that the chairman of the Defense Appropriations Subcommittee directed home.

Critz emphasizes the importance of transportation and defense projects — many of them funded by earmarks set aside by Murtha — as ways to attract new small and midsize businesses to a region where heavy industry is fading. He sits on the Armed Services Committee, and local defense contractors were generous donors to his campaign.

As a junior member, he does not exercise the same kind of clout as Murtha. But, like his predecessor, he considers such efforts to be an important component of his job. "I'm thrilled so far with the funds that I've been able to secure," Critz said. "One thing is for certain: Constituents want their representatives fighting to bring their fair share of federal funds back to our local communities."

Critz departed from Democratic orthodoxy when he opposed repeal of the statutory ban on gays and lesbians serving openly in the military. He was one of 15 Democrats to oppose the repeal enacted in late 2010.

A member of the Small Business Committee, he pledged to support incentives for companies that create local factory and mill jobs. Critz is a co-founder of the House Marcellus Shale Caucus, aimed at promoting development of the natural gas formation that sits below part of Pennsylvania and surrounding states.

International trade policy is also important to Critz's industrialized district. He has been a critic of Chinese trade practices and praised proposals that would eliminate tax policies that critics say encourage U.S. businesses to hire workers overseas.

Along with 64 of his Democratic colleagues, Critz signed onto symbolic legislation in September 2010 that opposed raising the Social Security retirement age. "After a lifetime of hard work, our seniors deserve a secure retirement that offers them peace of mind," Critz said. "That is why I promise to fight efforts to cut benefits, raise the retirement age, or allow Social Security to be privatized."

After Murtha died, the state Democratic Party Executive Committee selected Critz as its nominee in the special election, rather than former state Treasurer Barbara Hafer or two other candidates.

His GOP opponent, Tim Burns, tried to tie Critz, through the close relationship Murtha had with Pelosi, to the Democratic leadership in Congress. In one ad he said: "This election is very simple: If you think we need more bailouts, more government, higher taxes and that Nancy Pelosi's values are your values, then Mark Critz is your candidate."

Critz hit back, saying in an ad, "I'm pro-life and pro-gun. That's not liberal." Those declarations proved his social conservative bona fides in a district where registered Democrats outnumber Republicans 2-to-1 but Republican Sen. John McCain of Arizona won a slim victory in the 2008 presidential election against Barack Obama.

Attempts to implicate Critz in an ethics investigation of Murtha — Critz was interviewed by the Office of Congressional Ethics — also fell flat. "Burns has been running a television ad saying Democrat Mark Critz 'was investigated by the congressional ethics office.' That is simply not true," concluded FactCheck.org.

Critz emphasized his own southwestern Pennsylvania roots: Both of his parents are from the district, his wife works for the school district in Johnstown, where his twins attend school, and before taking his congressional staff position Critz worked as a manager of several local retail businesses.

Critz's campaign was aided by marquee names such as Vice President Joseph R. Biden Jr. and former President Bill Clinton, although Obama's unpopularity in the region kept the current president out of ads and off the stump.

In the May special election, he beat Burns by 8 percentage points.

A primary held the same day as the special election resulted in victories for Critz and Burns, who then faced each other again in the general election.

That contest was similar to the special election, with familiar charges slung and even more money spent by the parties and outside groups.

But the outcome was the same — although Burns closed the gap considerably — with Critz winning 51 percent to 49 percent.

Key Votes

2010

Allow for repeal of "don't ask, don't tell"	NO
Overhaul financial services industry regulation	NO
Limit use of new Afghanistan War funds to troop withdrawal activities	NO
Change oversight of offshore drilling and lift oil spill liability cap	YES
Provide a path to legal status for some children of illegal immigrants	NO
Extend Bush-era income tax cuts for two years	YES

CQ Vote Studies

	PARTY UNITY		PRESIDENTIAL SUPPORT	
	SUPPORT	OPPOSE	SUPPORT	OPPOSE
2010	88%	12%	69%	31%

Interest Groups

	AFL-CIO	ADA	CCUS	ACU
2010	70%	45%	67%	36%

Pennsylvania 12

Southwest — Johnstown

The oddly contorted 12th hopscotches across nine southwestern Pennsylvania counties, eight of which are shared with other districts. Once a booming center of coal, steel and iron production, this area is attempting to diversify in order to escape economic distress and industrial loss. Since 2000, the 12th has lost more than 5 percent of its population.

Johnstown, the district's most populous city, was once an industrial center, but floods, recession, the decline of the coal and steel industry, and scarce opportunities in manufacturing left the region with skyrocketing unemployment by the late 1980s.

The city and district have partly bounced back by attracting new biomedical research and health care companies, such as specialized care provider Conemaugh Health System, and a number of defense and research firms. Capitalizing on past hardships, the Johnstown Flood Museum also draws tourists to the area, and tourism now contributes more than $100 million to the region each year.

Despite these new industries, recent nationwide economic downturns have forced local businesses to cut jobs.

On the other side of the district in the state's southwestern corner, residents of rural Greene County — which borders West Virginia to its west and south and is the only county entirely within the 12th — continue to suffer.

Just north of Greene, Washington County's city of Washington has struggled with the departure of major employers, population loss and downtown blight. The district also includes Washington and Jefferson College and has a small agriculture industry, producing corn, wheat and cattle. The 12th has been a Democratic stronghold since the New Deal. Like other Pennsylvania towns with an industrial past and aging residents, Johnstown is more socially conservative than the national Democratic Party and wants federal help. At the presidential level, Republican candidates can compete, and John McCain won the district with 49 percent of its vote in 2008.

Major Industry
Manufacturing, service, health care, tourism

Cities
Johnstown, 20,978; Washington, 13,663

Notable
The National Drug Intelligence Center in Johnstown tracks illegal drugs.

Rep. Allyson Y. Schwartz (D)

Capitol Office
225-6111
schwartz.house.gov
1227 Longworth Bldg. 20515-3813; fax 226-0611

Committees
Budget
Foreign Affairs

Residence
Jenkintown

Born
Oct. 3, 1948; Queens, N.Y.

Religion
Jewish

Family
Husband, David Schwartz; two children

Education
Simmons College, B.A. 1970 (sociology); Bryn Mawr College, M.S.W. 1972

Career
Municipal child and elderly welfare official; women's health center founder; nonprofit health plan assistant director

Political Highlights
Pa. Senate, 1991-2004; sought Democratic nomination for U.S. Senate, 2000

ELECTION RESULTS

2010 GENERAL

Allyson Y. Schwartz (D)	118,710	56.3%
Dee Adcock (R)	91,987	43.7%

2010 PRIMARY

Allyson Y. Schwartz (D)	unopposed

2008 GENERAL

Allyson Y. Schwartz (D)	196,868	62.8%
Marina Kats (R)	108,271	34.5%
John McDermott (CNSTP)	8,374	2.7%

Previous Winning Percentages
2006 (66%); 2004 (56%)

Elected 2004; 4th term

Schwartz has established herself as one of the Democrats' leading health care experts and a formidable fundraiser. She authored several provisions of the 2010 health care overhaul, which she claims as her greatest legislative achievement.

She is also the lead recruiter for the Democratic Congressional Campaign Committee heading into the 2012 elections, in which the party hopes to regain the majority it lost in 2010.

Loss of that majority cost Schwartz some of her portfolio. Because of her party's depleted ranks, she had to surrender her seat on the Ways and Means Committee. She remains a member of the Budget Committee, where she is an avowed foe of GOP plans for reducing the deficit.

Schwartz is vice chairwoman of the moderate New Democrat Coalition and a self-described centrist, but her voting record is mostly liberal and partisan — on votes that divided a majority of Democrats and Republicans in the 111th Congress (2009-10), she sided with her party 98 percent of the time (and 99 percent of the time in 2008). That percentage has never fallen below 91.

But on select issues, she stakes out pro-business positions that don't always square with Democratic priorities.

During the debate on health care, Schwartz pushed for tax cuts for the biotechnology sector — not a frontline point of contention — and her work helped lead to the inclusion of a $1 billion tax credit for biotech investments.

Schwartz says she cherishes the subdued approach toward her work. "My name is not always on the front of the legislation, which is fine," she said.

That is not to say she always flies under the radar. Before Democrats took up the broader health care bill, Schwartz wrote two pieces of standalone legislation in 2009 that sought to increase the number of primary care physicians and to bar insurers from denying coverage to children with pre-existing conditions. Language from both was included in the overhaul.

Schwartz comes from a family steeped in the health industry. Her husband is a cardiologist and her brother is a physician. She said during the health care debate that she felt it was important to talk with her husband to get an inside view of the health care sector. "It was helpful to talk to him to see what it was really like," Schwartz said.

Schwartz also pushes for expansion of information technology throughout the health care sector, and she worked to ensure that $19 billion for health IT was included in Obama's $787 billion economic stimulus law in early 2009. More than $900,000 of stimulus money went to Schwartz's district to upgrade the Philadelphia Immunization Registry.

Before taking over the DCCC's recruiting effort, Schwartz headed up the group's Women LEAD program, an outreach effort aimed at involving women in politics and getting more of them elected to the House. She has been a contributor to her party's causes and colleagues, donating $425,000 to the DCCC during the 2009-10 election cycle. She is seen as a potential future leader of the committee due in large part to her fundraising prowess.

In the 112th Congress (2011-12), Schwartz took a seat on the Foreign Affairs Committee. As a freshman in 2005, she made her first House floor speech during a commemoration of the 60th anniversary of the liberation of the Auschwitz death camp in Poland. She described her mother's escape from Austria to America as a teenager in the early days of World War II. "Those who survived the Holocaust could not hide their gratitude and love for this country, relishing the opportunity and freedom granted to them as new Americans," Schwartz said. "My own love and respect for our country and my belief in our responsibility to each other stems in great part from this strong sense of patriotism."

Although Schwartz was born and raised in Queens, N.Y., her parents met in Philadelphia, where her father was a dental student and her mother had been sent by a group helping Jewish refugees. Her maternal grandmother committed suicide shortly before Schwartz's mother, as a teenager, escaped to the United States. "My mother was very clear that painful experiences in childhood don't necessarily make you stronger, which is maybe where my interest in children and family comes from," she said. Schwartz's mother could not overcome the pain; she committed suicide when Schwartz was 26. "These experiences stay with you. You just don't get past them by saying so," she said of her mother's traumas.

Schwartz moved to Philadelphia in the 1970s so her husband, David, could attend Jefferson Medical College. She earned her graduate degree in social work at Bryn Mawr.

Schwartz entered the public eye in 1975 as the co-founder and first director of a women's health clinic. She had spent a year at the Philadelphia Health Department as a graduate student, then worked for a fledgling HMO for three years before helping to start the Elizabeth Blackwell women's clinic, which offered a full range of health services, including abortions. She and her partners took out a bank loan to launch the clinic.

In 1983, Schwartz wrote health care position papers for Wilson Goode, who was running for mayor. He won, and during Goode's second term Schwartz became a deputy commissioner of Philadelphia's Department of Human Services, serving until her 1990 election to the state Senate. She defeated a 12-year incumbent to claim that seat, then stayed for 14 years.

Schwartz in 2000 entered the Democratic primary to run against GOP Sen. Rick Santorum. She finished second in a six-way primary, behind Rep. Ron Klink, who lost to Santorum that November.

A long-shot bid by 13th District Democrat Joseph M. Hoeffel to unseat then-Republican Sen. Arlen Specter in 2004 gave Schwartz an opening for a second try at Congress. She won a hard-fought primary. Then, calling on her solid political base and campaign bankroll, she won by more than 14 percentage points — trouncing ophthalmologist Melissa Brown, a three-time GOP candidate for the House. She was easily re-elected in 2006 and 2008. She demurred on the 2010 Senate race after Specter switched to the Democratic Party, and was re-elected over Republican Dee Adcock with 56 percent of the vote.

Key Votes

2010	
Overhaul the nation's health insurance system	YES
Allow for repeal of "don't ask, don't tell"	YES
Overhaul financial services industry regulation	YES
Limit use of new Afghanistan War funds to troop withdrawal activities	NO
Change oversight of offshore drilling and lift oil spill liability cap	YES
Provide a path to legal status for some children of illegal immigrants	YES
Extend Bush-era income tax cuts for two years	YES
2009	
Expand the Children's Health Insurance Program	YES
Provide $787 billion in tax cuts and spending increases to stimulate the economy	YES
Allow bankruptcy judges to modify certain primary-residence mortgages	YES
Create a cap-and-trade system to limit greenhouse gas emissions	YES
Provide $2 billion for the "cash for clunkers" program	YES
Establish the government as the sole provider of student loans	YES
Restrict federally funded insurance coverage for abortions in health care overhaul	NO

CQ Vote Studies

	PARTY UNITY		PRESIDENTIAL SUPPORT	
	SUPPORT	OPPOSE	SUPPORT	OPPOSE
2010	98%	2%	95%	5%
2009	98%	2%	96%	4%
2008	99%	1%	15%	85%
2007	96%	4%	8%	92%
2006	91%	9%	27%	73%

Interest Groups

	AFL-CIO	ADA	CCUS	ACU
2010	100%	90%	25%	0%
2009	100%	100%	40%	0%
2008	100%	90%	56%	0%
2007	96%	90%	55%	4%
2006	100%	85%	47%	16%

Pennsylvania 13

East — Northeast Philadelphia, part of Montgomery County

With its residents nearly evenly divided between Montgomery County and Northeast Philadelphia, the 13th combines white-collar suburbia with a portion of the city known for its blue-collar grit. The district extends northwest from the Delaware River in the city into northern Montgomery County suburbs and eventually out into more rural areas near the county's western border.

Prescription drugs and health care are big issues in the district, thanks to a large senior citizen population in Northeast Philadelphia. Education also draws attention, as Philadelphia public schools are in worse shape than Montgomery County schools. Public housing, home values and energy issues also are of concern to residents.

Many shopping centers, strip malls, health care and pharmaceutical firms, and small businesses are found throughout Northeast Philadelphia. But that diversification has not insulated the area from layoffs in the city and more affluent Montgomery County.

The 2005 round of military base realignments ordered Naval Air Station Willow Grove closed by 2011. The state plans to redevelop at least part of the base into a homeland security and emergency preparedness facility and maintain an operating airfield at the site. The district also includes Philadelphia Northeast Airport, a general aviation airport.

The 13th's portion of Philadelphia strongly favors Democratic candidates. The Montgomery County parts of the district are more competitive — Democrats have still enjoyed an advantage in recent statewide and federal races, but many areas are represented by Republicans at the local level. Overall, Democrat Barack Obama took 59 percent of the district's vote in the 2008 presidential election.

Major Industry
Health and business services, chemicals

Cities
Philadelphia (pt.), 317,996; Lansdale, 16,269

Notable
Pennypack Park, known as the green heart of Northeast Philadelphia, is home to the Pennypack Bridge — a stone bridge that has been in use since 1697.

Rep. Mike Doyle (D)

Capitol Office
225-2135
www.house.gov/doyle
401 Cannon Bldg. 20515-3814; fax 225-3084

Committees
Energy & Commerce

Residence
Forest Hills

Born
Aug. 5, 1953; Pittsburgh, Pa.

Religion
Roman Catholic

Family
Wife, Susan Doyle; four children

Education
Pennsylvania State U., B.S. 1975 (community development)

Career
Insurance company executive; state legislative aide

Political Highlights
Swissvale Borough Council, 1977-81 (served as a Republican)

ELECTION RESULTS

2010 GENERAL

Mike Doyle (D)	122,073	68.8%
Melissa Haluszczak (R)	49,997	28.2%
Ed Bortz (GREEN)	5,400	3.0%

2010 PRIMARY

Mike Doyle (D)	unopposed

2008 GENERAL

Mike Doyle (D)	242,326	91.3%
Titus North (GREEN)	23,214	8.7%

Previous Winning Percentages
2006 (90%); 2004 (100%); 2002 (100%); 2000 (69%); 1998 (68%); 1996 (56%); 1994 (55%)

Elected 1994; 9th term

The son and grandson of steelworkers, Doyle is a strong supporter of organized labor, opposed to free-trade deals and dedicated to preserving Pittsburgh's steel industry heritage. He has pushed to bring more high-tech employers to southwestern Pennsylvania in an effort to diversify the area's economy and expand the job market.

The Mon Valley's steel mills have long since stopped production, and Doyle wants to convert their remains into a national historic site. His legislation would include in the national park system the site of an infamous 1892 confrontation between striking steel workers and security agents hired by the Carnegie Steel Co., as well as other noteworthy locations associated with the nation's steel industry, a project he has worked on for several years.

"I want to make sure this nation and the world always remember the sacrifices made by the workers who labored in the mills in and around Pittsburgh," he said in introducing his latest version of the legislation in June 2010.

Over his decade and a half in Congress, Doyle has become more of a party loyalist. During the 1990s, his annual party unity scores — the percentage of votes on which he sided with a majority of Democrats against a majority of Republicans — were in the 60s and 70s. They ticked up into the low 90s for about five years, and have been in the high 90s since.

He backed all the early economic initiatives of President Obama's administration. During the George W. Bush years, he opposed the Central America and Peru free-trade agreements. One issue on which Doyle typically departs from Democratic orthodoxy is abortion. He supported the effort led by Michigan Democrat Bart Stupak to restrict federally funded insurance coverage for abortions in the Democrats' health care overhaul in 2009. But when the House voted in March 2010 on the final version of the legislation sans the Stupak language, he supported the bill. "It's not a perfect bill, and I'm sure we're going to be tweaking it along the way," he said.

Doyle sits on the Energy and Commerce Committee, giving him a powerful spot from which to seek federal aid for his district. "We're trying to make Pittsburgh an energy center for the country," he said.

During the 110th Congress (2007-2008), Doyle and California Republican Mary Bono Mack pushed legislation requiring improved energy conservation standards for federal buildings. Its provisions were expanded to include encouragement of conservation measures for construction in the private sector and became part of broader energy legislation enacted in December 2007.

In 2009 he voted for legislation that would create a cap-and-trade system for carbon emissions, which could be viewed as a risky vote for a western Pennsylvanian — except that he represents a district in which Obama took 70 percent of the vote in the 2008 presidential election.

Part of his effort to bring more industries to southwestern Pennsylvania was the establishment of the Doyle Center for Manufacturing Technology, a federally funded nonprofit group Doyle launched in 2003. The congressman secured several million dollars in government funds to create the center, which he said would provide "small local manufacturers with the tools they need to participate in the military contracts with big defense contractors like Boeing, Lockheed Martin and Raytheon." After receiving some criticism, Doyle removed his name from the center, changing it in 2008 to DSN Innovations.

Although Doyle is a mid-ranking member of the Energy and Commerce panel, holds no leadership post or subcommittee gavel and doesn't sit on Appropriations, he has still secured plenty of earmarks, the funding set-asides for projects in members' districts. In fiscal 2010, Doyle sponsored or cosponsored 28 earmarks totaling more than $23 million, according to figures compiled by the Center for Responsive Politics and Taxpayers for Common Sense.

Doyle has also championed a range of causes that could hardly be described as high-profile. From his seat on what is now the Communications and Technology Subcommittee, he won House passage of a measure he sponsored to allow for the creation of hundreds of new low-power FM radio stations.

In 2010, he introduced a measure that would require some federal agencies to provide online access to taxpayer-funded research within six months of its publication.

A founder and co-chairman of the Coalition for Autism Research and Education, Doyle pushed to include almost $30 million in spending bills for fiscal 2007-10 for continued autism research at the Defense Department. He is the sponsor of legislation that would boost federal support for treatment and research of the disorder.

Doyle is a fervent believer in animal rights, and his home state has long been notorious for its puppy mills. He introduced a bill in 2009 that would prevent research that uses dogs and cats obtained from USDA-licensed Class B animal dealers or brokers who acquire and sell animals.

As a young adult, Doyle never envisioned a future in government. "Growing up in Swissvale, when your dad's a steelworker, you don't think you're going to be a congressman," he said. His interest in politics was first piqued by the 1972 presidential race between GOP incumbent Richard Nixon and Democratic Sen. George McGovern. While studying community development at Penn State University, Doyle volunteered for the South Dakotan's losing campaign.

Doyle supported himself in college partly by working in the steel mills. After graduating from Penn State in 1975, he began work in a multi-line insurance agency before he was elected to the Swissvale Borough Council in 1977.

Shortly thereafter, Doyle began working for Republican state Sen. Frank A. Pecora and switched to the GOP out of deference to his boss. He switched back to the Democratic Party when Pecora changed parties in 1992 to mount an unsuccessful challenge against Republican Rep. Rick Santorum, who was seeking a second House term.

When Santorum ran successfully for the Senate in 1994, Doyle sought the open 18th District seat, winning a tightly contested seven-person primary with 20 percent of the vote. He won in November by 10 percentage points and took the next three elections with ease. From 2002 to 2008, Republicans did not contest Doyle's re-election. In 2010, GOP candidate Melissa Haluszczak won only 28 percent of the vote.

Key Votes

2010

Overhaul the nation's health insurance system	YES
Allow for repeal of "don't ask, don't tell"	YES
Overhaul financial services industry regulation	YES
Limit use of new Afghanistan War funds to troop withdrawal activities	YES
Change oversight of offshore drilling and lift oil spill liability cap	YES
Provide a path to legal status for some children of illegal immigrants	YES
Extend Bush-era income tax cuts for two years	YES

2009

Expand the Children's Health Insurance Program	YES
Provide $787 billion in tax cuts and spending increases to stimulate the economy	YES
Allow bankruptcy judges to modify certain primary-residence mortgages	YES
Create a cap-and-trade system to limit greenhouse gas emissions	YES
Provide $2 billion for the "cash for clunkers" program	YES
Establish the government as the sole provider of student loans	YES
Restrict federally funded insurance coverage for abortions in health care overhaul	YES

CQ Vote Studies

	PARTY UNITY		PRESIDENTIAL SUPPORT	
	Support	Oppose	Support	Oppose
2010	99%	1%	90%	10%
2009	99%	1%	97%	3%
2008	99%	1%	16%	84%
2007	98%	2%	5%	95%
2006	91%	9%	35%	65%

Interest Groups

	AFL-CIO	ADA	CCUS	ACU
2010	100%	90%	14%	0%
2009	100%	95%	33%	4%
2008	100%	95%	56%	0%
2007	96%	95%	53%	4%
2006	100%	85%	47%	12%

Pennsylvania 14

Pittsburgh and some close-in suburbs

The 14th encompasses all of Pittsburgh and some of the suburbs just outside the city's limits. An economic transformation from "steel capital" into the region's banking and health care hub made for a great success story in an otherwise suffering Rust Belt, but the 14th district has shed more than 60,000 residents since 2000.

Medical centers and universities, parks, skyscrapers, and technology firms have replaced the steel industry's smokestacks that once rose between and along the Allegheny, Monongahela and Ohio rivers. A thriving, corporate downtown has grown up in the "Golden Triangle," where the three rivers meet — four Fortune 500 companies maintain their corporate headquarters in downtown Pittsburgh.

Baseball's Pirates, at PNC Park, and football's Steelers, at Heinz Field, both play in modern stadiums just across the Allegheny from downtown, where hockey's Penguins play in the new Consol Energy Center.

Local officials have cleaned up, or "redd up" in Pittsburghese, the city, which for years had one of the lowest crime rates among the nation's largest metropolitan areas, but widespread layoffs concern officials and residents. Areas such as Monroeville and Penn Hills (both shared with the 18th) have attracted commercial development and some technology jobs, while other areas have languished. Many of Pittsburgh's neighborhoods, such as Bloomfield and Lawrenceville, retain their ethnic roots — mainly German, Italian, Irish and Polish. Squirrel Hill long has been the center of the city's Jewish population.

Even with the diversification of the 14th's economy, the district retains strong Democratic roots. Union strength translates into lopsided margins even for statewide candidates who lose, and Democrats far outnumber Republicans, whose regional outposts are in neighboring, suburban districts. Pittsburgh's staunch Democratic support helped Barack Obama take 70 percent of the 14th's vote in the 2008 presidential election.

Major Industry

Banking, government, health care, higher education

Cities

Pittsburgh, 305,704; West Mifflin, 20,313; McKeesport, 19,731

Notable

The Andy Warhol Museum celebrates Pittsburgh's native son.

Rep. Charlie Dent (R)

Capitol Office
225-6411
dent.house.gov
1009 Longworth Bldg. 20515-3815; fax 226-0778

Committees
Appropriations
Ethics

Residence
Allentown

Born
May 24, 1960; Allentown, Pa.

Religion
Presbyterian

Family
Wife, Pamela Dent; three children

Education
Pennsylvania State U., B.A. 1982 (foreign service & international politics); Lehigh U., M.P.A. 1993

Career
College fundraiser; electronics salesman; hotel clerk; congressional aide

Political Highlights
Pa. House, 1991-99; Pa. Senate, 1999-2005

ELECTION RESULTS

2010 GENERAL

Charlie Dent (R)	109,534	53.5%
John Callahan (D)	79,766	39.0%
Jake Towne (I)	15,248	7.4%

2010 PRIMARY

Charlie Dent (R)	31,618	82.9%
Mat Benol (R)	6,514	17.1%

2008 GENERAL

Charlie Dent (R)	181,433	58.6%
Sam Bennett (D)	128,333	41.4%

Previous Winning Percentages
2006 (54%); 2004 (59%)

Elected 2004; 4th term

The moderate Dent is a political survivor, often targeted but never taken down. He won a seat on the Appropriations Committee in the 112th Congress, giving him another weapon with which to fend off Democratic challengers.

Dent represents a district carried by both President Obama and the 2004 Democratic presidential nominee, Sen. John Kerry of Massachusetts, so he is attuned to the need to choose his positions with deliberation and seeks to build alliances with a wide range of colleagues. He co-chairs the Tuesday Group, an embattled band of House GOP centrists.

He stood against most of the major legislative initiatives of the Obama administration, opposing the $787 billion economic stimulus law, the health care overhaul — "a new trillion-dollar entitlement program that the bill does not realistically address how we will afford" — and House-passed legislation that would create a cap-and-trade system to regulate greenhouse gas emissions.

A former member of the Homeland Security Committee — he now sits on the Appropriations Subcommittee on Homeland Security — he favors tight restrictions on illegal immigration and a tough line on terrorism. In 2010, he sponsored legislation that would authorize the revocation of citizenship for Americans who engage in acts of terrorism against the United States.

But he's much more liberal than most Republicans when it comes to social issues such as abortion and gay rights. In late 2010, he was one of 15 Republicans to back a measure that repealed the statutory ban on gays and lesbians serving openly in the military. In early 2011, he was one of seven Republicans to oppose a provision added to a catchall spending bill that would block federal funding for Planned Parenthood.

In 2007, he was one of just 12 Republicans to reject an amendment to bar federal funding for international family planning groups that perform abortions. A liberal perspective on abortion runs in Dent's family: Mary Dent Crisp, his father's sister and a longtime GOP activist in Arizona, resigned her post as co-chairwoman of the Republican National Convention in 1980 to protest the party's anti-abortion platform plank. And he reacted favorably when Obama overturned President George W. Bush's restrictions on federally funded embryonic stem cell research.

On other issues, though, Dent is a more reliable Republican, and lines up with his party on about three of every four votes that separate majorities of the two parties. In late 2010, he voted for a two-year extension of the Bush-era income tax cuts and against a path to legal status for some children of illegal immigrants.

Dent originally opposed the George W. Bush administration's $700 billion financial rescue legislation in fall 2008, but switched his vote to enable a second version to become law. He said he wasn't enthusiastic about the amended version but that it was "vastly improved." He refused, however, to support a subsequent attempt to assist the domestic auto industry that passed the House but stalled in the Senate.

House Republican leaders in 2009 assigned Dent to what was then known as the Committee on Standards of Official Conduct, an assignment he readily acknowledged was "at times difficult and unpleasant."

He joined the panel's other Republicans in criticizing Chairwoman Zoe Lofgren, a California Democrat, for not scheduling public ethics trials of senior Democrats Charles B. Rangel of New York and Maxine Waters of California before the November 2010 elections.

Rangel was eventually censured by the House. Dent remains on the since-renamed Ethics Committee, which will have to address the Waters matter in the 112th Congress (2011-12).

Dent is a lifelong resident of Allentown, and his family has been in Pennsylvania since colonial times. His great-grandfather started a well-known hardware business in the district; his father worked at Bethlehem Steel in the human resources department and his mother was a high school teacher.

Dent says his political awakening came in high school, when he took a class on the Cold War. He majored in foreign service and international politics at Penn State, then interned with one of his predecessors in Congress, Republican Don Ritter. He went on to work as a salesman in the electronics industry and as a development officer for Lehigh University.

Dent says his experience at the university sparked his interest in running for office. In 1990, he ran for the Pennsylvania House, defeating a Democratic incumbent. He credits his upset win to knocking "on over 20,000 doors" and running a "door-to-door, grass-roots, shoe-leather campaign." Eight years later, he won an open state Senate seat, serving there for six years.

He decided to run for Congress in 2004 when conservative Republican Patrick J. Toomey gave up his House seat to launch an unsuccessful primary challenge to Arlen Specter, then a Republican. Dent won easily with 59 percent.

His bid for a second term in 2006 was expected to be a cakewalk. But Northampton County Councilman Charles Dertinger made a race of it despite a severe fundraising deficit — he raised $90,000 to Dent's $1.3 million — and little support from national Democrats. Playing off the party's national themes, Dertinger attempted to link Dent to Bush. Dent pulled out the victory, but his 54 percent share of the vote was a relatively close call.

Two years later, Allentown Democratic Party activist Sam Bennett challenged Dent. Bennett quickly took up the national Democratic Party themes, condemning the Iraq War and urging "change." But her slow fundraising gave Dent some reassurance, and he touted his "much stronger crossover appeal" among voters. He won with 59 percent of the vote in a district that gave Obama 56 percent.

In 2010, Dent was targeted early by the Democrats, but the national Republican sweep helped him claim 54 percent of the vote in a three-way race, besting Democrat John Callahan by 15 percentage points.

Dent has been mentioned as a potential challenger to Democratic Sen. Bob Casey in 2012, but he suggested early in the process that his new spot on Appropriations makes such a challenge less likely.

Key Votes

2010

Overhaul the nation's health insurance system	NO
Allow for repeal of "don't ask, don't tell"	NO
Overhaul financial services industry regulation	NO
Limit use of new Afghanistan War funds to troop withdrawal activities	NO
Change oversight of offshore drilling and lift oil spill liability cap	NO
Provide a path to legal status for some children of illegal immigrants	NO
Extend Bush-era income tax cuts for two years	YES

2009

Expand the Children's Health Insurance Program	YES
Provide $787 billion in tax cuts and spending increases to stimulate the economy	NO
Allow bankruptcy judges to modify certain primary-residence mortgages	NO
Create a cap-and-trade system to limit greenhouse gas emissions	NO
Provide $2 billion for the "cash for clunkers" program	NO
Establish the government as the sole provider of student loans	NO
Restrict federally funded insurance coverage for abortions in health care overhaul	YES

CQ Vote Studies

	PARTY UNITY		PRESIDENTIAL SUPPORT	
	SUPPORT	OPPOSE	SUPPORT	OPPOSE
2010	76%	24%	43%	57%
2009	73%	27%	46%	54%
2008	78%	22%	49%	51%
2007	75%	25%	49%	51%
2006	81%	19%	80%	20%

Interest Groups

	AFL-CIO	ADA	CCUS	ACU
2010	21%	25%	100%	61%
2009	43%	20%	87%	72%
2008	60%	55%	83%	56%
2007	42%	45%	100%	52%
2006	43%	30%	93%	72%

Pennsylvania 15
East — Allentown, Bethlehem

Centered in the Lehigh Valley about 60 miles north of Philadelphia and abutting the Delaware River, the 15th takes in Allentown, Bethlehem and Easton — historically known as steel and coal industry strongholds. The region once suffered from the Rust Belt blues that singer Billy Joel immortalized in his 1982 song "Allentown."

The area's economy has diversified over the past several decades: Health care employers and warehouse and distribution industries provide jobs, and small businesses now dot a landscape where factories and small farms once were mainstays. And despite the 2009 relocation of the corporate headquarters and some assembly jobs for Mack Trucks, the company has opened a customer call center and increased hiring at a local manufacturing plant.

Local leaders hope the transformation of the former Bethlehem Steel factory — once the Leigh Valley's largest employer and one of the world's largest steel manufacturers — into the Sands Casino Resort Bethlehem gaming, hotel, restaurant and retail venue will churn out revenue. Olympus America has its headquarters here, and other key employers include the

Lehigh Valley Hospital complex, electric utility PPL, technology company LSI Corp, and Emmaus-based Rodale Press.

Many of the district's towns, some with well-established Pennsylvania Dutch heritages, date to colonial times. But the 250-year-old German influence has been diluted by a century of immigration and steady migration from New Jersey and New York. White-collar commuters have brought higher incomes to the area, and there has been an influx of lower-income residents as well. Much of the growth in the Lehigh Valley has been in the Hispanic population. Blue-collar, ethnic workers provide a dwindling yet still-powerful base for Democrats, but an increasing white-collar core and a socially conservative streak among blue-collar voters have helped the GOP win House races here.

Major Industry
Technology, health care, warehousing, manufacturing

Cities
Allentown, 118,032; Bethlehem, 74,982; Easton, 26,800

Notable
The Valley Preferred Cycling Center, a premier site for track cycling, has hosted Olympic trial, Junior World Championship and World Cup races.

Rep. Joe Pitts (R)

Capitol Office
225-2411
www.house.gov/pitts
420 Cannon Bldg. 20515-3816; fax 225-2013

Committees
Energy & Commerce
(Health - Chairman)

Residence
Kennett Square

Born
Oct. 10, 1939; Lexington, Ky.

Religion
Protestant

Family
Wife, Virginia M. "Ginny" Pitts; three children

Education
Asbury College, A.B. 1961 (philosophy & religion);
West Chester State College, M.Ed. 1972
(comprehensive sciences)

Military
Air Force, 1963-69

Career
Nursery and landscaping business owner; teacher

Political Highlights
Pa. House, 1973-97

ELECTION RESULTS

2010 GENERAL

Joe Pitts (R)	134,113	65.4%
Lois K. Herr (D)	70,994	34.6%

2010 PRIMARY

Joe Pitts (R)	unopposed

2008 GENERAL

Joe Pitts (R)	170,329	55.8%
Bruce A. Slater (D)	120,193	39.4%
John A. Murphy (I)	11,768	3.9%

Previous Winning Percentages
2006 (57%); 2004 (64%); 2002 (88%); 2000 (67%);
1998 (71%); 1996 (59%)

Elected 1996; 8th term

Few congressional districts span a cultural gulf as wide as the one Pitts represents, from sprawling Philadelphia suburbs that help define the 21st century to pastoral farms of the Amish more evocative of the 19th. Pitts offers the diverse district a consistent conservatism, honed during a four-decade career in politics.

He is an advocate of cutting taxes and limiting the scope of the federal government. The son of missionaries, Pitts is also a clarion voice in opposition to abortion. While Michigan Democrat Bart Stupak was the focus of attention surrounding the battle over abortion during the health care overhaul debate in the 111th Congress (2009-10), the amendment at the center of the controversy was co-written by Pitts. When Stupak accepted a deal that weakened the prohibition on using federal funds to pay for abortions, Pitts said he was "disappointed."

Pitts, chairman of the Energy and Commerce Subcommittee on Health in the 112th Congress (2011-12), opposed the final version of the bill, calling it "shockingly irresponsible," and he backed its repeal in 2011.

Pitts also helped lead the way early in the 112th to dismantle the measure provision by provision. His panel and the full committee approved his legislation to block federal funding of abortion under the new law and five bills aimed at repealing its mandatory spending provisions.

Those moves were reflective of Pitts' conservative philosophy, which is consistent across a broad swath of issues.

Pitts, who paints and sculpts in his spare time, represents America's largest Amish community. He battled across multiple Congresses for a relaxation of child labor laws to ensure Amish teenagers could enter apprenticeships once their formal education was complete. It was finally included in a catchall spending law in 2004.

He also focuses on preserving farmland. He has favored capital gains tax breaks to provide an incentive for farmers to protect their land from development. He formed the Land Conservation Caucus with fellow Pennsylvania Republican Jim Gerlach and Democrat Christopher S. Murphy of Connecticut to promote and support land preservation measures.

Pitts chairs the House Values Action Team, a group of about 70 social conservatives who work with advocacy groups on the religious right. In July 2008 the group developed a "Values Agenda" that included proposals to ban abortion, outlaw same-sex marriage, allow prayer in public schools, ban flag burning and protect the Pledge of Allegiance from court challenges.

When Obama signed an executive order reinstating federal funding for embryonic stem cell research, Pitts said, "Obama has chosen to force American taxpayers to fund research that destroys human life against the objections of their conscience."

A former teacher, Pitts opposed the 2001 education overhaul known as No Child Left Behind, arguing that the law's stringent testing requirements force teachers to ignore materials that are not on standardized exams.

He has a strong interest in foreign policy and humanitarian work stemming from his childhood living in the back country in the Philippines as the son of missionaries. Pitts' Christian faith forms the nexus between his interest in foreign affairs and the domestic issues he strongly supports, and it is that faith which he says has driven him to reach out to distant peoples. Every year, he invites ambassadors from 195 countries to his district to tour businesses and cultural historic sites.

In the aftermath of the Sept. 11 terrorist attacks, Pitts and a handful of other lawmakers formed the Silk Road Caucus to promote greater contact between the United States and Central Asia. He has organized equipment drives for hospitals in Pakistan and is active in several human rights organizations.

Unlike many lawmakers with strong human rights agendas, he favored the 2000 law normalizing trade with China, arguing that increased engagement would spur the Communist government to improve its human rights record. Pitts consistently sides with the majority of his party on trade deals.

Pitts, a member of the Environment and the Economy Subcommittee, advocates a market-oriented and competition-based course when tackling climate change legislation, and he opposed the Democrats' cap-and-trade measure in the 111th Congress (2009-10). He supports boosting domestic production of coal and has pushed legislation to increase U.S. oil-refining capacity by building three new refineries on military bases that are slated for closure by the Base Realignment and Closure Commission. Pitts is also a supporter of increasing the use of nuclear energy, calling for a speedy regulatory process to approve new nuclear reactors.

After spending much of his youth in the Philippines, Pitts attended Asbury College in Kentucky, where he met his wife, Ginny. He earned a degree in philosophy and religion, and the two of them embarked on teaching careers. Pitts later joined the Air Force and served for five and a half years, including three tours of duty in Southeast Asia.

The family then moved to Pennsylvania, and Pitts returned to teaching high school math and science, and eventually started his own landscaping firm. In 1972, colleagues persuaded him to make a bid for an open state House seat. He served there for 24 years, including eight years as chairman of the Appropriations Committee.

When Republican Robert S. Walker decided to retire from the U.S. House in 1996, Pitts won a hard-fought five-way primary and won easily in November. Pitts pledged when he first ran for the House in 1996 to serve no more than 10 years, but he announced before the 2002 election that he had changed his mind, explaining that term limits diminish a "lame duck" lawmaker's effectiveness. He has been re-elected by wide margins.

Pitts once earned some notice for his participation in a men's singing quartet called the Capitol Four, which included GOP Reps. Kenny Hulshof of Missouri, Michael Pappas of New Jersey and John Thune of South Dakota. The group disbanded after the 105th Congress (1997-98) when Pappas was defeated.

Key Votes

2010

Vote	
Overhaul the nation's health insurance system	NO
Allow for repeal of "don't ask, don't tell"	NO
Overhaul financial services industry regulation	NO
Limit use of new Afghanistan War funds to troop withdrawal activities	NO
Change oversight of offshore drilling and lift oil spill liability cap	NO
Provide a path to legal status for some children of illegal immigrants	NO
Extend Bush-era income tax cuts for two years	YES

2009

Vote	
Expand the Children's Health Insurance Program	NO
Provide $787 billion in tax cuts and spending increases to stimulate the economy	NO
Allow bankruptcy judges to modify certain primary-residence mortgages	NO
Create a cap-and-trade system to limit greenhouse gas emissions	NO
Provide $2 billion for the "cash for clunkers" program	YES
Establish the government as the sole provider of student loans	NO
Restrict federally funded insurance coverage for abortions in health care overhaul	YES

CQ Vote Studies

	PARTY UNITY		PRESIDENTIAL SUPPORT	
	Support	Oppose	Support	Oppose
2010	98%	2%	25%	75%
2009	96%	4%	22%	78%
2008	98%	2%	76%	24%
2007	98%	2%	94%	6%
2006	95%	5%	84%	16%

Interest Groups

	AFL-CIO	ADA	CCUS	ACU
2010	7%	0%	88%	100%
2009	10%	5%	87%	96%
2008	0%	5%	88%	100%
2007	8%	0%	75%	100%
2006	8%	5%	92%	86%

Pennsylvania 16

Southeast — Lancaster, part of Reading

Located in southeastern Pennsylvania and bordering Delaware and Maryland, the 16th includes all of Lancaster County, the southern half of Chester County and portions of southwest Berks County, including part of Reading. The predominately white and mainly white-collar district also includes much of Pennsylvania Dutch Country.

The strong work ethic of the local labor force and the district's proximity to major roadways attract companies to the area, which is central to the mid-Atlantic's major markets. For several decades, economic expansion has attracted new residents both to populous Lancaster and still largely pastoral areas of Chester (shared with the 6th and 7th) counties. Some of the counties' farmland has been built over with tract housing to accommodate the population growth, and a significant proportion of the growth in Lancaster County has been among Hispanic residents.

Farm preservation remains a major concern, especially in Lancaster County, which has a diverse agricultural economy, produces more farm-based revenue than any other county in the state, and is a national leader in poultry and livestock raising. The Kennett Square area in Chester County still produces one of the nation's largest mushroom crops. Tourism also adds to the diversity of the 16th's economy. Millions of visitors annually flock to Dutch Country to gaze at Amish horse-drawn carriages, browse at quilt shops and dine in family-style restaurants.

Since the dawn of the Civil War, the areas of the 16th have favored the GOP at all levels, but Republican John McCain eked out only a slim, 51 percent majority in the 2008 presidential election. Lancaster County, which accounts for just more than 70 percent of the district population, has traditionally set the district's conservative political tone with its Amish heritage, and Republican Gov. Tom Corbett did 17 percentage points better in the county than he did statewide. But Democratic candidates can win votes in the more socially moderate Chester County.

Major Industry
Agriculture, tourism, manufacturing

Cities
Lancaster, 59,322; Reading (pt.), 47,115; West Chester, 18,461

Notable
The original five-and-dime store that started the Woolworth chain opened in Lancaster in 1879.

Rep. Tim Holden (D)

Capitol Office
225-5546
www.holden.house.gov
2417 Rayburn Bldg. 20515-3817; fax 226-0996

Committees
Agriculture
Transportation & Infrastructure

Residence
St. Clair

Born
March 5, 1957; St. Clair, Pa.

Religion
Roman Catholic

Family
Wife, Gwen Holden

Education
U. of Richmond, attended 1976-77; Bloomsburg U.,
B.A. 1980 (sociology)

Career
Probation officer; insurance broker; Realtor

Political Highlights
Schuylkill County sheriff, 1985-93

ELECTION RESULTS

2010 GENERAL

Tim Holden (D)	118,486	55.5%
Dave Argall (R)	95,000	44.5%

2010 PRIMARY

Tim Holden (D)	30,630	65.3%
Sheila Dow-Ford (D)	16,296	34.7%

2008 GENERAL

Tim Holden (D)	192,699	63.7%
Toni Gilhooley (R)	109,909	36.3%

Previous Winning Percentages
2006 (65%); 2004 (59%); 2002 (51%); 2000 (66%);
1998 (61%); 1996 (59%); 1994 (57%); 1992 (52%)

Elected 1992; 10th term

A former sheriff and a member of the fiscally conservative Blue Dog Coalition, Holden takes a centrist approach to serving his working-class district in central Pennsylvania — an approach that sometimes finds him straying from Democratic orthodoxy.

The Harrisburg Patriot News, in endorsing him in 2010, called the easy-going and affable Holden a "much-needed moderate voice in the Democratic caucus." Holden won that endorsement after abandoning his party leadership on a pair of signature issues in the 111th Congress (2009-10) — health care and energy.

He opposed the health care overhaul enacted in March 2010, citing the measure's cuts in Medicare and Medicaid and what he determined to be its insufficient restrictions on federal funding for abortions. But he was not one of the three Democrats who sided with Republicans on a vote to repeal the law in early 2011.

Holden also opposed legislation the House passed in 2009 that would have established a cap-and-trade system to limit greenhouse gas emissions.

When it came time to select leaders for the 112th Congress (2011-12) he opposed Californian Nancy Pelosi for both minority leader and Speaker. "She just drove the bus . . . off the Grand Canyon," Holden told The Pottsville Republican Herald. "I don't think she should be the leader of the Democratic Party."

Overall, though, Holden voted wit h a majority of his party against a majority of Republicans 91 percent of the time in the 111th Congress (2009-10), similar to his party unity scores in the 110th Congress (2007-08). His scores were typically 15 to 20 points lower when the Republicans held the majority.

He supported a GOP energy policy overhaul in 2005, as well as Republican bills to limit class action lawsuits and to cap damages in medical malpractice cases, and in 2006 he backed a tough border security bill that most House Democrats opposed. He once opposed funding for embryonic stem cell research, but later altered his position after talking with researchers and patients who might benefit. And he was among a group of lawmakers who urged Attorney General Eric H. Holder Jr. in 2009 not to reinstate the expired ban on certain semi-automatic weapons.

Holden typically sides with Democrats and organized labor on economic issues such as the minimum wage and extending unemployment benefits, and he opposes most trade agreements. In early 2009, he supported a pair of bills designed to strengthen the ability of workers to combat wage discrimination. He backed an expansion of the Children's Health Insurance Program, which covers children in lower-income families that make too much money to qualify for Medicaid.

A member of the Transportation and Infrastructure Committee, he supported President Obama's $787 billion economic stimulus law in 2009, saying it would bring $1.3 billion to his state for highways, bridges and mass transit.

He touts his successes in securing funding for local highway and transit projects in the 1998 and 2005 surface transportation laws, with another expected to be taken up during the 112th Congress. He has teamed with neighboring Republican Joe Pitts in pushing for a commuter rail link between Harrisburg and Carlisle. Another pet project is working to make the 17th District's coal reserves more marketable by spurring researchers to develop technology to burn the fuel more cleanly.

Holden aggressively seeks federal funding for a wide array of projects back home, a practice that has earned him some unwanted attention. Many of his earmarks over the years were obtained thanks to his allegiance to fellow Pennsylvania Democrat John P. Murtha, the late chairman of the Defense Appropriations Subcommittee. News media outlets reported in 2007 on a $3.2 million defense contract for Fidelity Technologies, a Pennsylvania firm that had at that point donated $10,550 to his re-election campaigns. Holden defended the earmark: "Who is going to contribute to your campaign, people you don't help?" he asked the Allentown Morning Call.

Holden is the No. 2 Democrat on the Agriculture Committee and is the ranking member of its Conservation, Energy and Forestry panel. He advocates creation of a second generation of alternative fuel sources, such as switch grass, and pushes to create such crops on the fertile ground of abandoned strip mines. As chairman during debate on the 2008 farm law, he had to rein in efforts by subcommittee members to tack on new programs that couldn't be financed under the bill's funding level. But his panel did include new incentives for alternative energy, as well as provisions that provide credit for conservation programs to benefit state farmers, authorize $440 million for water quality conservation in the Chesapeake Bay watershed and extend a program that compensates dairy farmers when milk prices fall.

Holden's great-grandfather John Siney founded the Miner's Benevolent Association, the forerunner of the United Mine Workers. His father, Joseph "Sox" Holden, was a Schuylkill County commissioner for almost two decades and a catcher for the Philadelphia Phillies from 1934 to 1936. Holden keeps his dad's No. 10 jersey framed in his office and played the same position at the annual Roll Call Congressional Baseball Game for charity.

Holden started college in Virginia on a football scholarship but returned home after a year to recuperate from a bout of tuberculosis, then stayed close by to finish school. He earned an insurance license and a real estate broker's license, and worked in both fields part time to make ends meet while he served as a probation officer, sergeant at arms in the Pennsylvania House and Schuylkill County sheriff. He won the sheriff's post at age 28.

When Democratic Rep. Gus Yatron retired in 1992, Holden won by 4 percentage points in what was then the 6th District. He won re-election with increasing margins until 2002, when he fought a closer contest against 20-year veteran GOP incumbent George W. Gekas in the newly drawn 17th District.

In 2004, Republican Scott Paterno, son of legendary Penn State football coach Joe Paterno, raised more than $1 million to try to unseat Holden. But Holden won by more than 20 percentage points. Two years later, Republican Matthew A. Wertz, citing health and personal reasons, suspended his campaign in September and Holden won by 29 percentage points. He took 64 percent in 2008. His victory margin narrowed to 11 percentage points in 2010 when he defeated GOP state Sen. Dave Argall.

Key Votes

2010	
Overhaul the nation's health insurance system	NO
Allow for repeal of "don't ask, don't tell"	YES
Overhaul financial services industry regulation	YES
Limit use of new Afghanistan War funds to troop withdrawal activities	NO
Change oversight of offshore drilling and lift oil spill liability cap	NO
Provide a path to legal status for some children of illegal immigrants	NO
Extend Bush-era income tax cuts for two years	YES

2009	
Expand the Children's Health Insurance Program	YES
Provide $787 billion in tax cuts and spending increases to stimulate the economy	YES
Allow bankruptcy judges to modify certain primary-residence mortgages	NO
Create a cap-and-trade system to limit greenhouse gas emissions	NO
Provide $2 billion for the "cash for clunkers" program	YES
Establish the government as the sole provider of student loans	YES
Restrict federally funded insurance coverage for abortions in health care overhaul	YES

CQ Vote Studies

	PARTY UNITY		PRESIDENTIAL SUPPORT	
	SUPPORT	OPPOSE	SUPPORT	OPPOSE
2010	86%	14%	81%	19%
2009	93%	7%	89%	11%
2008	95%	5%	20%	80%
2007	92%	8%	13%	87%
2006	79%	21%	56%	44%

Interest Groups

	AFL-CIO	ADA	CCUS	ACU
2010	71%	55%	88%	17%
2009	86%	75%	60%	16%
2008	100%	85%	61%	16%
2007	92%	80%	45%	16%
2006	100%	60%	53%	64%

Pennsylvania 17
East central — Harrisburg, Lebanon, Pottsville

Anchored in the eastern part of south-central Pennsylvania, the 17th is home to Harrisburg, the state capital, which sits 100 miles west of Philadelphia and 200 miles east of Pittsburgh. The 17th has two distinct zones: a stretch of agricultural land along the Susquehanna River in the west, and industrial areas in Schuylkill and Berks counties in the east. Here, in GOP-minded central Pennsylvania, state government and manufacturing remain key sources of employment.

Harrisburg's skyline is dominated by the Capitol, with a dome inspired by St. Peter's Basilica in Rome. With many government employees and a black plurality, the city typically votes Democratic. Visitors wanting a real taste of Dauphin County skip Harrisburg and go to Hershey, where even the streetlights are shaped like Hershey's Kisses. All of the company's chocolate production is expected to move to western Hershey in 2012, out of the center of town where the original chocolate factory stood emitting the most pleasant of industrial odors for a century.

The economy in Dauphin and Lebanon counties relies on health care, education and government jobs. Municipal and statewide budget shortfalls have caused concern. Harrisburg, in Dauphin, is a key distribution hub for metropolitan markets in the mid-Atlantic region, and it hosts the Penn State Milton S. Hershey Medical Center.

The 17th has a distinct Republican lean, but moderate Democrats can play here due to the district's mix of agrarian and industrial communities. The GOP is strong in Lebanon County and in the areas of Dauphin outside of Harrisburg, but the city's concentration of Democratic voters outweighs the county's conservative areas. Democrats are competitive in Schuylkill County, long a coal mining powerhouse, with comfortable margins at the state and U.S. House levels in Shenandoah, Pottsville and Mahanoy. Gov. Tom Corbett, a Republican, won every county wholly or partly in the district in 2010 even as Democratic Rep. Tim Holden held on in Schuylkill and Dauphin.

Major Industry
Government, service, manufacturing, tourism, agriculture, biotech

Cities
Harrisburg, 49,528; Lebanon, 25,477; Pottsville, 14,324

Notable
Pottsville is home to Yuengling, America's oldest active brewery.

Rep. Tim Murphy (R)

Capitol Office
225-2301
murphy.house.gov
322 Cannon Bldg. 20515-3818; fax 225-1844

Committees
Energy & Commerce

Residence
Upper St. Clair

Born
Sept. 11, 1952; Cleveland, Ohio

Religion
Roman Catholic

Family
Wife, Nan Missig Murphy; one child

Education
Wheeling College, B.S. 1974 (psychology); Cleveland
State U., M.A. 1976 (psychology); U. of Pittsburgh,
Ph.D. 1979 (psychology)

Military
Navy Reserve, 2009-present

Career
Psychologist; professor

Political Highlights
Pa. Senate, 1997-2003

ELECTION RESULTS

2010 GENERAL

Tim Murphy (R)	161,888	67.3%
Dan Connolly (D)	78,558	32.7%

2010 PRIMARY

Tim Murphy (R)	unopposed

2008 GENERAL

Tim Murphy (R)	213,349	64.1%
Steve O'Donnell (D)	119,661	35.9%

Previous Winning Percentages
2006 (58%); 2004 (63%); 2002 (60%)

Elected 2002; 5th term

Murphy shares many of the socially conservative views of his constituents in the Pittsburgh suburbs. But on his pet issue of health care, the child psychologist has found considerable common ground with Democrats — though not enough to back the overhaul legislation enacted in 2010.

"I had worked, in my teaching and practice, on a lot of health care issues," he said. "At that time, managed care was growing as a concern, and I wanted to make some changes on that. And while I thought elected officials were well-intended, they were not well-informed."

Murphy put his background in health care to use by taking a leadership role on the issue. In early 2009, he was named to a GOP group charged with coming up with a Republican alternative to the Democrats' plan. That effort bore no legislative fruit, however, and Murphy called the Democratic measure "a personal and professional disappointment," saying the law "is not the solution, and I know we can do better." In the 112th Congress (2011-12), he voted to both repeal and block funding for the law.

But before the debate on the centerpiece of the Democratic agenda began, Murphy often lined up with the opposition party on related legislation.

In early 2009, Murphy supported a bill to expand the Children Health's Insurance Program that Obama signed into law. It provides coverage to children of lower-income families that make too much money to qualify for Medicaid. He had supported similar legislation that President George W. Bush twice vetoed. And he engaged in a bipartisan effort, with Democrat Gene Green of Texas, when he introduced legislation in July 2010 to address the shortage of health care providers in community health centers across the country.

While he has used his seat on the Energy and Commerce Committee to influence health care issues, Murphy also has employed it as a platform for his views on energy policy. He supports increased use of nuclear power and more domestic oil drilling. In 2011, he introduced legislation to speed approval of offshore drilling permits. He introduced legislation in the 111th Congress (2009-10) that would expand oil and gas exploration on federal lands, with the revenue generated used to expand renewable-energy and conservation programs.

In keeping with the socially conservative outlook of his district, Murphy opposes abortion. When Energy and Commerce's Health Subcommittee approved legislation in early 2011 to bar federal funds from being used to cover the costs of any health insurance plan that includes coverage of abortion services, Murphy minced no words. "This is about killing babies and using federal money to do it," he said.

He voted against legislation to ban job discrimination based on sexual orientation and supported bills to allow faith-based Head Start providers to take religion into account when hiring.

When it comes to labor issues, though, Murphy tends to side with Democrats. In 2007, he voted to increase the federal minimum wage and opposed a free-trade deal with Peru that labor unions opposed. Murphy provided a crucial vote in favor of the Central America Free Trade Agreement in 2005, but labor unions forgave him that vote — until 2010, when the Pennsylvania AFL-CIO endorsed his opponent.

As vice chairman of the Congressional Steel Caucus, Murphy has taken strides to protect the productivity of the U.S. steel industry. In 2009, he introduced legislation that would require federally funded construction projects to use only American-made steel products.

He has testified before the International Trade Commission in an effort to combat allegedly unfair trade practices by China. Murphy also pleased populist constituents in the fall of 2008 when he opposed a law providing $700 billion to rescue ailing financial institutions.

In early 2009, Murphy opposed President Obama's $787 billion economic stimulus law. "I voted against the original Wall Street bailout bill and the so-called economic stimulus package knowing they would result in a breathtaking expansion of federal power, zero accountability, all paid for with taxpayer funds," he said.

Perhaps Murphy's most notable legislative success came in 2006, when the House passed his bill making it illegal for callers to "spoof" caller ID devices. The legislation was prompted by election-season phone calls critical of Murphy that had been rigged to appear as though they originated in his own offices. The bill died in the Senate; Murphy cosponsored a similar measure House Democrats passed early in the 110th Congress (2007-08) that also stalled.

Growing up as one of 11 children, Murphy paid his way through school by cleaning out horse stalls and digging graves. He supports vouchers and other programs that could allow low-income families to send their children to private or parochial schools.

Murphy, who taught himself to play guitar, performed in acoustic bands in high school, college and graduate school. The bands played in coffeehouses and once opened in Cleveland for banjo legend Earl Scruggs.

He earned a doctorate in psychology and worked in several hospitals in western Pennsylvania. He eventually opened his own practice, taught at the University of Pittsburgh and gave medical advice as "Dr. Tim" on Pittsburgh radio and television. In 2001, Murphy co-wrote a book, "The Angry Child: Regaining Control When Your Child Is Out of Control," which explored the sources of anger in children and recommended ways parents could respond.

Murphy entered elective politics as a state senator in 1996. Pennsylvania lost a pair of House seats in reapportionment after the 2000 census, but the Republican-controlled General Assembly drew an 18th District south of Pittsburgh configured to favor Murphy. He had become the presumptive heir to the seat when four-term Democrat Frank R. Mascara decided to mount what proved to be an unsuccessful primary challenge to Democrat John P. Murtha in the 12th District.

Murphy took 60 percent of the vote to defeat Democrat Jack M. Machek in 2002, and he hasn't had a close race in being re-elected four times.

Key Votes

2010

Overhaul the nation's health insurance system	NO
Allow for repeal of "don't ask, don't tell"	NO
Overhaul financial services industry regulation	NO
Limit use of new Afghanistan War funds to troop withdrawal activities	NO
Change oversight of offshore drilling and lift oil spill liability cap	NO
Provide a path to legal status for some children of illegal immigrants	NO
Extend Bush-era income tax cuts for two years	YES

2009

Expand the Children's Health Insurance Program	YES
Provide $787 billion in tax cuts and spending increases to stimulate the economy	NO
Allow bankruptcy judges to modify certain primary-residence mortgages	NO
Create a cap-and-trade system to limit greenhouse gas emissions	NO
Provide $2 billion for the "cash for clunkers" program	YES
Establish the government as the sole provider of student loans	NO
Restrict federally funded insurance coverage for abortions in health care overhaul	YES

CQ Vote Studies

	PARTY UNITY		PRESIDENTIAL SUPPORT	
	SUPPORT	OPPOSE	SUPPORT	OPPOSE
2010	81%	19%	52%	48%
2009	68%	32%	66%	34%
2008	76%	24%	45%	55%
2007	74%	26%	48%	52%
2006	91%	9%	87%	13%

Interest Groups

	AFL-CIO	ADA	CCUS	ACU
2010	43%	15%	88%	50%
2009	52%	15%	93%	68%
2008	73%	60%	81%	48%
2007	71%	40%	85%	68%
2006	43%	10%	93%	80%

Pennsylvania 18

West — Pittsburgh suburbs, part of Washington and Westmoreland counties

Taking in suburbs of Pittsburgh on three sides of the city, the socially conservative 18th moves east from Washington County through parts of southern Allegheny County into Westmoreland County.

Access to major waterways made the first half of the 20th century prosperous for parts of the district, which was once a prodigious steel producer. Now, many areas outside the Pittsburgh suburbs, especially in southwestern Washington and southeastern Westmoreland, are struggling economically.

More than half of the 18th's population lives in Allegheny County, which is dominated by Pittsburgh, located in the 14th District. The 18th's share of the suburbs includes well-off areas in southwestern Allegheny such as Upper St. Clair and Mount Lebanon, as well as middle- and working-class Democratic enclaves such as blue-collar Carnegie and Dormont, which are just southwest of Pittsburgh.

The district's universities and hospitals have lured some technology companies to the area, as has the 18th's high percentage of residents with a college degree (33 percent). In the district's northwest, thousands of area jobs are provided by Pittsburgh International Airport, and the new headquarters for Dick's Sporting Goods provides hundreds more. The airport has recovered from years of job cuts and flight volume decreases by US Airways; Southwest Airlines and AirTran also operated out of Pittsburgh. Economic downturns have forced layoffs in the region's health care sector.

The 18th includes most of Westmoreland County, which is a former Democratic bastion that has moved to the right, supporting Republican John McCain by nearly 17 percentage points in the 2008 presidential election. Overall, McCain captured 55 percent of the 18th's vote in 2008.

Major Industry
Health care, technology, manufacturing, steel

Cities
Bethel Park, 32,313; Monroeville (pt.), 23,710

Notable
Andy Warhol is buried in Bethel Park; the Meadowcroft Village at the Museum of Rural Life, near Avella in Washington County, preserves the history of mid-19th-century rural life in western Pennsylvania.

Rep. Todd R. Platts (R)

Capitol Office
225-5836
www.house.gov/platts
2455 Rayburn Bldg. 20515-3819; fax 226-1000

Committees
Armed Services
Education & the Workforce
Oversight & Government Reform
  (Government Organization, Efficiency & Financial
  Management - Chairman)

Residence
York

Born
March 5, 1962; York, Pa.

Religion
Episcopalian

Family
Wife, Leslie Platts; two children

Education
Shippensburg U., B.S. 1984 (public administration);
Pepperdine U., J.D. 1991

Career
Lawyer; gubernatorial and state legislative aide

Political Highlights
Sought Republican nomination for York County
Commission, 1995; Pa. House, 1993-2000

ELECTION RESULTS

2010 GENERAL

Todd R. Platts (R)	165,219	71.9%
Ryan S. Sanders (D)	53,549	23.3%
Joshua A. Monighan (I)	10,988	4.8%

2010 PRIMARY

Todd R. Platts (R)	51,792	70.0%
Mike Smeltzer (R)	22,210	30.0%

2008 GENERAL

Todd R. Platts (R)	218,862	66.6%
Philip J. Avillo Jr. (D)	109,533	33.4%

Previous Winning Percentages
2006 (64%); 2004 (92%); 2002 (91%); 2000 (73%)

Elected 2000; 6th term

A champion of oversight and government transparency, Platts holds himself to rigid personal standards. He takes no campaign contributions from political action committees or his own party's leaders and has never run a television campaign advertisement.

In the 112th Congress (2011-12), he brings his concerns about open government back to the chairmanship of the Oversight and Government Reform subcommittee with jurisdiction over financial management and efficiency of federal departments and agencies. He led the panel for two terms when Republicans were last in control of the House.

Platts said one of his priorities will be working with the Government Accountability Office and agency inspectors general to weed out systemic financial management problems. "Tax dollars should be treated in the same manner that families and small businesses treat their own funds — in the most efficient and responsible manner possible," he said.

Platts tends to take a conservative stance on most major fiscal measures. But he has opposed his leadership on a range of issues, and during the 110th Congress (2007-08) he was one of only three Republicans who voted for all six bills that Democrats brought to the House floor as part of their "first 100 hours" agenda. He said there have been no repercussions. "I've worked hard to have very good relations with my leadership," he said. Honesty helps a lot, he added. His positions are "never going to be a secret — they're going to know whether I'm voting against them or with them and why."

In March 2011, he sided with Democrats against a GOP-backed measure to revive a Washington, D.C., school voucher program opposed by city officials. Platts said he opposed the program because it was a local issue and because it was aimed at helping a small group of children rather than addressing larger problems plaguing the D.C. public school system.

His reputation for trying to keep government on the straight and narrow dates to his days as a member of the Pennsylvania House, where he aggravated colleagues with his unbending manner and by going after their perquisites of office.

He wonders why the government's books are not as tidy as his own. "If my checkbook is off by 10 cents, I'll stay up all night until I find that 10 cents," Platts once lectured a NASA official appearing before a subcommittee. "Your checkbook is off by $2 billion."

In 2009, Platts authored an amendment to the $787 billion stimulus bill with Maryland Democrat Chris Van Hollen to grant legal protections to federal employees that report fraud, waste or abuse during the allotment of funds. Though the amendment was eventually stripped out, Platts was able to include a smaller set of whistleblower rights for state and local employees who receive money from the federal government.

Platts teamed up with Democrats again in 2009 — this time as lead Republican cosponsor — to introduce stand-alone legislation to boost whistleblower protections for federal employees. An advocate of changing the earmarking process, Platts set up an advisory board made up of local community leaders to review all appropriations requests in his district.

His work toward transparency has not gone unnoticed. In 2010, he was one of four finalists for the top post at the Government Accountability Office.

In 2009, Platts joined the Armed Services Committee, saying he wanted to better serve military installations in his district, including Carlisle Barracks and the Defense Distribution Depot Susquehanna.

A member of the Education and the Workforce Committee, Platts supported a measure to expand the Children's Health Insurance Program, which provides coverage to children whose lower-income families make too much money to qualify for Medicaid, and was one of six Republicans to vote in favor of making the government the sole provider of student loans.

Platts also joined with Democrat Edward J. Markey of Massachusetts on a measure calling for 25 percent of the nation's electricity to be generated from renewable sources such as wind, solar and geothermal energy by 2025.

Overall in the 111th Congress (2009-10), Platts sided with Republicans on about four of every five votes that divided a majority of the two parties.

Platts' views on campaign finance qualify as eclectic. He argues that PAC contributions undermine the public's trust in government, but doesn't think the money compromises many of his colleagues. "If I took a PAC contribution, or even the individual contributions I get, it's not going to change my vote," he said. "But it will certainly change the perception of the public of what guides my votes and will diminish their trust."

He said he wouldn't take PAC contributions even if he faced a well-funded candidate; he has his staff write "void" on the PAC checks he sometimes receives unsolicited and returns them to their senders with a note of thanks.

Platts said he might have picked up his stubborn tendencies from his father, who with his mother bucked the local Little League establishment by insisting that every child who showed up at practice should play. His parents argued so vociferously to league officials that they implemented a rule requiring every child who practiced to receive playing time during games.

Being a member of Congress has been his ambition since he was a teenager. He worked for Republican Gov. Dick Thornburgh and served as a legislative committee staff member and assistant finance director for the state Republican Party. In 1992, he won election to the state legislature. He made an unsuccessful run for the York County Commission in 1995, then went on to win two more state House terms.

In early 1999, when Republican Rep. William F. Goodling announced his plan to retire, Platts was the first to jump into the race. Though greatly outspent in the GOP primary, he won with 33 percent of the vote. He defeated college professor Jeff Sanders in the general election and didn't face another Democratic opponent until 2006, when another professor, Phillip J. Avillo Jr., took barely 34 percent of the vote. Avillo tried again in 2008. Platts raised a mere $211,000 for his campaign, more than enough to swamp the underfunded Avillo, who spent $64,000. Platts took two-thirds of the vote.

He won 72 percent against Democrat Ryan Sanders in 2010.

Key Votes

2010

Overhaul the nation's health insurance system	NO
Allow for repeal of "don't ask, don't tell"	NO
Overhaul financial services industry regulation	NO
Limit use of new Afghanistan War funds to troop withdrawal activities	NO
Change oversight of offshore drilling and lift oil spill liability cap	NO
Provide a path to legal status for some children of illegal immigrants	NO
Extend Bush-era income tax cuts for two years	YES

2009

Expand the Children's Health Insurance Program	YES
Provide $787 billion in tax cuts and spending increases to stimulate the economy	NO
Allow bankruptcy judges to modify certain primary-residence mortgages	NO
Create a cap-and-trade system to limit greenhouse gas emissions	NO
Provide $2 billion for the "cash for clunkers" program	YES
Establish the government as the sole provider of student loans	YES
Restrict federally funded insurance coverage for abortions in health care overhaul	YES

CQ Vote Studies

	PARTY UNITY		PRESIDENTIAL SUPPORT	
	SUPPORT	OPPOSE	SUPPORT	OPPOSE
2010	85%	15%	43%	57%
2009	75%	25%	48%	52%
2008	80%	20%	49%	51%
2007	77%	23%	54%	46%
2006	72%	28%	80%	20%

Interest Groups

	AFL-CIO	ADA	CCUS	ACU
2010	21%	15%	88%	67%
2009	43%	30%	93%	76%
2008	47%	55%	78%	68%
2007	42%	45%	70%	64%
2006	50%	25%	93%	72%

Pennsylvania 19

South central — York, Gettysburg

Situated west of the Susquehanna River, mostly east of the South Mountain ridge and mostly south of Harrisburg (in the neighboring 17th District), the 19th's historic landscape has a Republican-leaning constituency and major agricultural and manufacturing industries.

Located along several major highways, the district is a prime location for manufacturing and distribution centers, including depots and logistical support facilities for the Defense Department, and York County serves as the 19th's industrial hub. Residential growth, a more recent trend, also can be attributed to the district's location — many Marylanders have moved here for lower taxes and affordable real estate. Adams, York and Cumberland counties have all grown rapidly for two decades.

Tourism also plays a major role in the district's economy. Nearly 2 million visitors each year come to see the site of the 1863 Battle of Gettysburg in Adams County, now a largely fruit-growing area. Many come for the annual re-enactment of one of the Civil War's most significant battles and to see monuments, military grave sites, historic markers and the site of Abraham Lincoln's Gettysburg Address.

The Gettysburg National Military Park Museum and Visitor Center opened in 2008, and the David Wills House, where Lincoln stayed while at Gettysburg, opened as a museum on the bicentennial of the president's birth in February 2009.

John McCain won 56 percent of the district's 2008 presidential vote. Adams County gave him 59 percent, while the more populated Cumberland (shared with the 9th) and York counties each gave him 56 percent. Democrats find more strength in the city of York, where blacks and Hispanics combined make up more than half of the population, and Gettysburg, which has a large college-age population.

Major Industry
Agriculture, manufacturing, distribution, defense, tourism

Military Bases
Carlisle Barracks, 434 military, 742 civilian (2009); Defense Distribution Depot Susquehanna, 296 military, 1,047 civilian (2004)

Cities
York, 43,718; Carlisle (pt.), 18,637

Notable
York served as the first U.S. capital in 1777-78 while the British occupied Philadelphia.

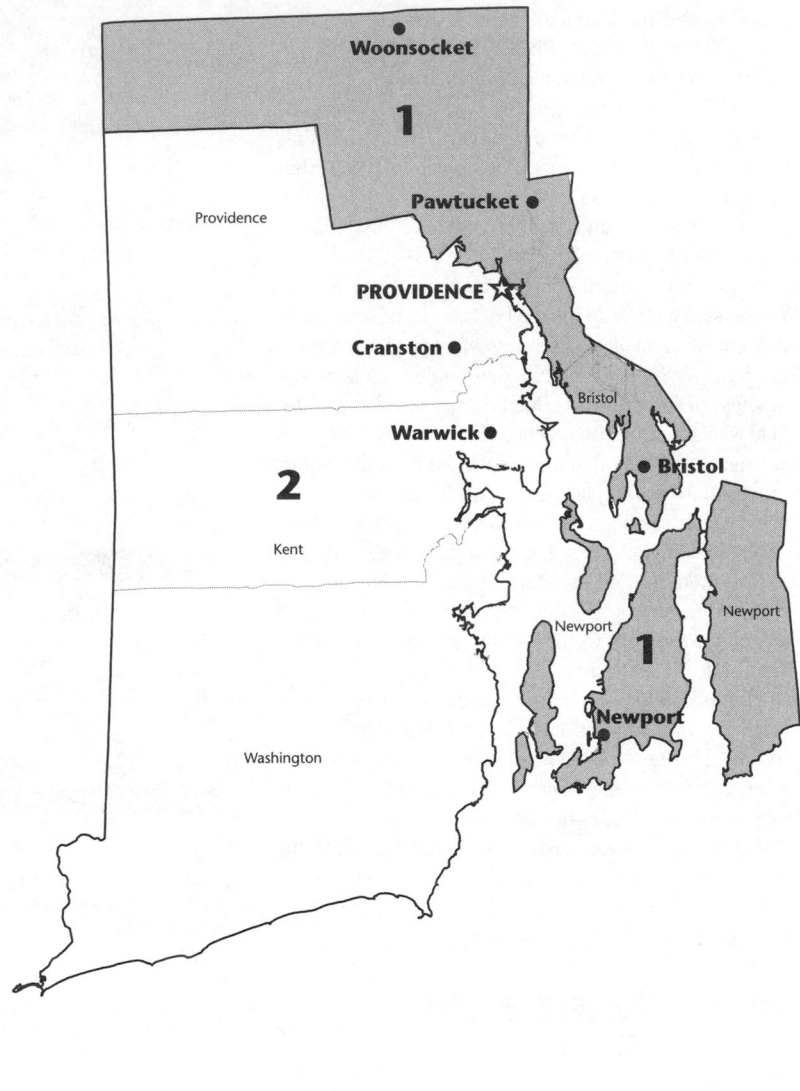

Woonsocket

1

Providence

Pawtucket ●

PROVIDENCE ☆

Cranston ●

Bristol

Warwick ●

2

Bristol

Kent

Newport

Newport

1

Washington

Newport

2

Gov. Lincoln Chafee (I)

First elected: 2010
Length of term: 4 years
Term expires: 1/15
Salary: $129,210
Phone: (410) 222-2080
Residence: Exeter
Born: March 26, 1953; Warwick, R.I.
Religion: Episcopalian
Family: Wife, Stephanie Chafee; three children
Education: Brown U., A.B. 1975 (classics)
Career: Defense company machine shop planner; blacksmith
Political highlights: Warwick City Council, 1986-91; Republican nominee for mayor of Warwick, 1990; mayor of Warwick, 1992-99; U.S. Senate, 1999-2007; defeated for re-election to U.S. Senate, 2006

ELECTION RESULTS

2010 GENERAL
Lincoln Chafee (I)	123,571	36.1%
John F. Robitaille (R)	114,911	33.6%
Frank T. Caprio (D)	78,896	23.0%
Kenneth J. Block (MDE)	22,146	6.5%

Lt. Gov. Elizabeth Roberts (D)

First elected: 2006
Length of term: 4 years
Term expires: 1/15
Salary: $104,011
Phone: (401) 222-2371

LEGISLATURE

General Assembly: January-June
Senate: 38 members, 2-year terms
2011 ratios: 29 D, 8 R, 1 I; 28 men, 10 women
Salary: $14,381
Phone: (401) 222-6655
House: 75 members, 2-year terms
2011 ratios: 65 D, 10 R; 56 men, 19 women
Salary: $14,381
Phone: (401) 222-2466

TERM LIMITS

Governor: 2 terms
Senate: No
House: No

URBAN STATISTICS

CITY	POPULATION
Providence	178,042
Warwick	82,672
Cranston	80,387
Pawtucket	71,148
East Providence	47,037

REGISTERED VOTERS

Unaffiliated	49%
Democrat	41%
Republican	10%

POPULATION

2010 population	1,052,567
2000 population	1,048,319
1990 population	1,003,464
Percent change (2000-2010)	+0.4%
Rank among states (2010)	43
Median age	38.6
Born in state	59.2%
Foreign born	12.6
Violent crime rate	253/100,000
Poverty level	11.5%
Federal workers	11,398
Military	1,490

ELECTIONS

STATE ELECTION OFFICIAL
(401) 222-2345
DEMOCRATIC PARTY
(401) 272-3367
REPUBLICAN PARTY
(401) 732-8282

MISCELLANEOUS

Web: www.ri.gov
Capital: Providence

U.S. CONGRESS

Senate: 2 Democrats
House: 2 Democrats

2010 Census Statistics by District

District	2008 Vote for President Obama	McCain	White	Black	Asian	Hispanic	Median Income	White Collar	Blue Collar	Service Industry	Over 64	Under 18	College Education	Rural	Sq. Miles
1	65%	34%	77%	5%	3%	11%	$53,585	62%	21%	17%	15%	21%	30%	4%	325
2	62	37	76	4	3	14	57,626	61	20	19	13	23	29	14	720
STATE	63	35	76	5	3	12	55,569	61	21	18	14	22	30	9	1,045
U.S.	53	46	64	12	5	16	51,425	60	23	17	13	25	28	21	3,537,438

Sen. Jack Reed (D)

Capitol Office
224-4642
reed.senate.gov
728 Hart Bldg. 20510-3903; fax 224-4680

Committees
Appropriations
(Interior-Environment - Chairman)
Armed Services
(Seapower - Chairman)
Banking, Housing & Urban Affairs
(Securities, Insurance & Investment - Chairman)

Residence
Jamestown

Born
Nov. 12, 1949; Providence, R.I.

Religion
Roman Catholic

Family
Wife, Julia Reed; one child

Education
U.S. Military Academy, B.S. 1971 (engineering);
Harvard U., M.P.P. 1973, J.D. 1982

Military Service
Army, 1971-79; Army Reserve, 1979-91

Career
Lawyer

Political Highlights
R.I. Senate, 1985-91; U.S. House, 1991-97

ELECTION RESULTS

2008 GENERAL

Jack Reed (D)	320,644	73.4%
Robert G. Tingle (R)	116,174	26.6%

2008 PRIMARY

Jack Reed (D)	48,038	86.8%
Christopher F. Young (D)	7,277	13.2%

2002 GENERAL

Jack Reed (D)	253,774	78.4%
Robert G. Tingle (R)	69,808	21.6%

Previous Winning Percentages
1996 (63%); 1994 House Election (68%); 1992 House
Election (71%); 1990 House Election (59%)

Elected 1996; 3rd term

Serious and hard-working, Reed has won bipartisan respect in the Senate and become a crucial ally of President Obama on two of the administration's most vexing policy issues: the war in Afghanistan and Wall Street regulation.

Reed is a wonkish Senate insider more likely to influence legislation in quiet negotiations or in committee hearings than on the floor or at news conferences. But he has increasingly become a more common guest on Sunday morning talk shows for his deep understanding of foreign policy and defense issues.

As a West Point graduate and former Army Ranger, Reed's military credentials made him a leader of the Democratic opposition to the Iraq War during the George W. Bush administration — he voted against the authorization to use military force in 2002 — and an advocate of shifting military resources to Afghanistan.

But with Obama in the White House, Reed initially opposed sending more combat forces to Afghanistan. He was one of a handful of senior Democratic senators who were consulted in 2009 during administration debates on a troop surge. When it came time for Obama to announce the buildup in a speech at West Point, though, the senator went with him to back the policy.

"The president probably came to the best decision," Reed said. "We have to increase forces, but we have to have a finite number of forces."

Reed also supported Obama's decision to intervene in the fighting in Libya in early 2011 and praised the president's handling of the situation.

Several of the top military leaders in Iraq and Afghanistan were his contemporaries at West Point, and Reed and Gen. John P. Abizaid, the former head of U.S. Central Command, were in the same parachute brigade in the 82nd Airborne Division. Though Reed never served in combat, he said his training and service give him an appreciation for the military's power — and its limits. "It's very impressive when you're lighting up the night sky pretty quickly," he once said. "But decisive action usually involves political, economic, social and cultural action as well."

Reed gets to the Middle East more often than most of his colleagues — he has been to Iraq and Afghanistan more than a dozen times. His lengthy trip reports, providing on-the-ground assessments of the wars, have become must-reads among Armed Services Committee members.

In July 2008, he joined Obama, then an Illinois senator and presidential contender, on a high-profile tour of the war zones. The trip fueled speculation about Reed's place in a possible Obama administration as a running mate or Defense secretary. Reed insisted he wasn't interested in being vice president and says he has no interest in moving to the Pentagon.

Reed has been a tough questioner of Defense Department witnesses. Serving as chairman of the panel's Seapower Subcommittee allows Reed to push for support for the Rhode Island-based Naval Undersea Warfare Center and Naval Education Training Center, and for funding that goes to Rhode Island contractors such as Textron Systems and Raytheon Co.

He also works to protect federal contracts for the building of attack submarines at the General Dynamics Electric Boat Corp., which employs roughly 10,000 workers in its Rhode Island and nearby Groton, Conn., facilities. He helped write provisions in the Senate version of the fiscal 2011 defense authorization bill that would call for the Pentagon to buy two fast-attack submarines annually, rather than the currently planned one, beginning in 2011.

But he has extended his influence beyond military matters into finance, health care and education — all while sending money back to his state as a member of the Appropriations Committee. In the 112th Congress (2011-12), he added the chairmanship of the Interior-Environment Subcommittee to his portfolio.

As a senior Democrat on the Banking, Housing and Urban Affairs Committee, Reed served on the conference committee negotiating financial regulatory overhaul legislation in 2010. He advocated strong consumer protection measures, more early-warning information for regulators about potential financial firm failures and more disclosures by hedge fund managers.

Reed championed a provision in the bill that would create an Office of Military Affairs within the measure's new Consumer Financial Protection Bureau to monitor and respond to complaints from military personnel about risky car loans. He said the idea for the provision drew directly from his experience as an Army officer, when he saw young soldiers taking on loans from car dealers that they could not afford.

Reed also was tapped to work on one of the bill's most complex and contentious provisions: derivatives regulation. Although several months of negotiations failed to yield a bipartisan compromise, new limits backed by Reed on the trading of the complex financial instruments were in the final bill.

He has devoted energy to affordable housing. Legislation, cosponsored with Missouri Republican Christopher S. Bond and aimed at consolidating federal homeless assistance programs and authorizing a new emergency grants program to serve people at risk of homelessness, was signed into law in 2009.

On major Democratic legislation, Reed has been a reliable supporter of his party's agenda. In 2010, he voted with a majority of Democrats against a majority of Republicans 98 percent of the time. His annual score has never fallen below 96 percent in his Senate career.

He's a liberal on social issues. In recent years he voted against banning a procedure opponents call "partial birth" abortion. He also opposed amending the Constitution to prohibit same-sex marriage and supported the late 2010 repeal of the statutory ban on openly gay individuals serving in the military.

Reed grew up in a working-class family in Cranston. His father, Joseph Reed, was a school custodian, and his mother, Mary Monahan, was a factory worker. His earliest political memory is of his mother watching the 1960 presidential election returns and reciting the rosary in hopes of a victory for fellow Catholic New Englander John F. Kennedy.

At age 12, Reed told his parents he wanted to go to a military service academy, spurred in part by Army football heroes of that era as well as seeing other family members serve in uniform. Reed was admitted, barely meeting the minimum height requirement. After graduation, the Army put him through a master's program at the John F. Kennedy School of Government at Harvard University. Reed then commanded a company of the 82nd Airborne and taught at West Point.

After attaining the rank of captain, he left the Army at age 29 to attend Harvard Law School. He returned home to a job in Rhode Island's biggest corporate law firm. In 1984, he won a seat in the state Senate. Six years later, Reed took 59 percent of the vote to win the U.S. House seat that Republican Claudine Schneider gave up to run for the Senate.

When Democratic Sen. Claiborne Pell decided to retire in 1996 after 36 years in office, Reed was ready. He captured the seat with 63 percent of the vote against Republican state Treasurer Nancy J. Mayer. He won re-election in 2002 with 78 percent, and six years later took 73 percent.

In 2005, at age 55, Reed married. He and Julia Hart, then 39, an employee of the Senate office that arranges international travel for senators, wed in West Point's Catholic chapel, a first marriage for both. Their daughter was born in January 2007.

Key Votes

2010

Pass budget reconciliation bill to modify overhauls of health care and federal student loan programs	YES
Proceed to disapproval resolution on EPA authority to regulate greenhouse gases	NO
Overhaul financial services industry regulation	YES
Limit debate to proceed to a bill to broaden campaign finance disclosure and reporting rules	YES
Limit debate on an extension of Bush-era income tax cuts for two years	YES
Limit debate on a bill to provide a path to legal status for some children of illegal immigrants	YES
Allow for a repeal of "don't ask, don't tell"	YES
Consent to ratification of a strategic arms reduction treaty with Russia	YES

2009

Prevent release of remaining financial industry bailout funds	NO
Make it easier for victims to sue for wage discrimination remedies	YES
Expand the Children's Health Insurance Program	YES
Limit debate on the economic stimulus measure	YES
Repeal District of Columbia firearms prohibitions and gun registration laws	NO
Limit debate on expansion of federal hate crimes law	YES
Strike funding for F-22 Raptor fighter jets	YES

CQ Vote Studies

	PARTY UNITY		PRESIDENTIAL SUPPORT	
	Support	Oppose	Support	Oppose
2010	98%	2%	98%	2%
2009	99%	1%	100%	0%
2008	99%	1%	35%	65%
2007	97%	3%	41%	59%
2006	96%	4%	53%	47%
2005	98%	2%	29%	71%
2004	98%	2%	60%	40%
2003	98%	2%	45%	55%
2002	98%	2%	66%	34%
2001	99%	1%	64%	36%

Interest Groups

	AFL-CIO	ADA	CCUS	ACU
2010	94%	90%	18%	0%
2009	94%	95%	43%	0%
2008	100%	95%	50%	4%
2007	100%	95%	40%	0%
2006	100%	100%	42%	4%
2005	93%	100%	33%	0%
2004	100%	100%	35%	0%
2003	100%	100%	26%	20%
2002	100%	100%	40%	0%
2001	100%	100%	36%	4%

Sen. Sheldon Whitehouse (D)

Capitol Office
224-2921
whitehouse.senate.gov
717 Hart Bldg. 20510-3904; fax 228-6362

Committees
Budget
Environment & Public Works
   (Oversight - Chairman)
Health, Education, Labor & Pensions
Judiciary
   (Crime & Terrorism - Chairman)
Special Aging

Residence
Newport

Born
Oct. 20, 1955; Manhattan, N.Y.

Religion
Episcopalian

Family
Wife, Sandra Whitehouse; two children

Education
Yale U., B.A. 1978 (architecture); U. of Virginia, J.D. 1982

Career
Lawyer; gubernatorial aide

Political Highlights
R.I. Department of Business Regulation director, 1992-94; U.S. attorney, 1994-98; R.I. attorney general, 1999-2003; sought Democratic nomination for governor, 2002

ELECTION RESULTS

2006 GENERAL

Sheldon Whitehouse (D)	206,043	53.5%
Lincoln Chafee (R)	178,950	46.5%

2006 PRIMARY

Sheldon Whitehouse (D)	69,290	81.5%
Christopher F. Young (D)	8,939	10.5%
Carl L. Sheeler (D)	6,755	7.9%

Elected 2006; 1st term

Even though Whitehouse ranks among the bottom third of Democrats in Senate seniority, he has worked his way into key roles on major legislative issues. In the George W. Bush years, the former prosecutor was a sharp critic of the administration's conduct of the war on terror.

Whitehouse played unexpected roles on two cornerstones of the Democratic agenda in the 111th Congress (2009-10): health care and climate change. In both instances, he pushed liberal proposals that didn't always make it into law but helped define the parameters of debate.

As Senate Democratic leaders awaited the end of post-election litigation in Minnesota in 2009, Whitehouse was given a temporary appointment to the Health, Education, Labor and Pensions Committee in time for that panel's consideration of health care overhaul legislation. In the 112th Congress (2011-12), he joined the panel full-time.

Whitehouse joined with Ohio Democrat Sherrod Brown in authoring the Senate version of a provision to create a government-run insurance program, the "public option." The proposal, which was not included in the Finance Committee's health care overhaul draft, was one of several provisions that fell by the wayside in the leadership's search for the 60 votes necessary to pass the bill. Whitehouse says he will try to resurrect the government-run program at some point.

As a member of the Environment and Public Works Committee he has been outspoken on climate change and the potential threat to coastal areas from rising sea levels.

He also sits on the Budget Committee. When the Senate adopted an amendment to the fiscal 2010 budget resolution prohibiting the use of a parliamentary procedure known as reconciliation to bar a filibuster of Democratic climate change legislation, Whitehouse tried and failed to gut the provision. He praised President Obama's fiscal 2012 budget, which included a deficit of $1.1 trillion, and said a House Republican plan "essentially relieves the richest Americans from any significant responsibilities to pay for the support of their country."

In addition, Whitehouse chairs the Judiciary Subcommittee on Crime and Terrorism and is a former member of the Select Intelligence panel, where he has played a high-profile role debating the implications of legal policy on national security matters.

He opposed the 2007 nomination of Michael B. Mukasey to be attorney general under President George W. Bush. During questioning at Mukasey's confirmation hearing, Whitehouse bore in on whether the nominee considered "waterboarding," a type of simulated drowning, to be torture. Mukasey did not answer to the satisfaction of Whitehouse, and days after the hearing he took to the floor to question whether the United States "will join that gloomy historical line leading from the Inquisition, through the prisons of tyrant regimes, through gulags and dark cells, and through Saddam Hussein's torture chambers?" He suggested that if the Senate confirmed Mukasey (as it did a week later), "we will have turned down that dark stairway."

Whitehouse was the sponsor of an amendment to the fiscal 2008 intelligence authorization bill that limited CIA and other executive branch interrogation tactics to those contained in the 2006 Army field manual, which banned waterboarding and other harsh tactics. A slightly modified version made it into the final bill, drawing a veto from Bush.

Whitehouse also was a vocal critic of the warrantless electronic surveillance program Bush launched after the Sept. 11 terrorist attacks. Whitehouse won the declassification of the legal opinions the administration had relied on in pursuing its surveillance activities. He helped draft an overhaul of the 1978 Foreign Intelligence Surveillance Act that tightened the rules for such spying, especially when the government intercepts the communications of U.S. citizens in contact with terrorist suspects abroad.

But Whitehouse parted company with many in his party to support the Bush administration's position in favor of retroactive legal immunity for telecommunications companies that had cooperated with the warrantless surveillance program.

"I've been a prosecutor. I've run wiretap investigations," he said. "I've come to recognize the importance of cooperation with the private sector. I've come to learn how valuable, in any investigation, that [surveillance] authority can be."

And he worked with Senate Minority Whip Jon Kyl, an Arizona Republican, and others to write compromise language for the reauthorization of expiring provisions of the 2001 anti-terrorism law known as the Patriot Act.

On the Intelligence panel, Whitehouse concentrated efforts on chairing a cybersecurity task force, saying cyberwarfare will be a major issue to address in the years ahead. He also serves on the Judiciary Subcommittee handling privacy and technology issues.

"We need to help people realize that, just as the driver who fails to replace faulty car brakes puts himself and other drivers at risk, so do individuals who fail to update their operating system or antivirus software," Whitehouse said in the April 2010 speech at the Center for Democracy and Technology.

Whitehouse lives in Newport, America's sailboat racing capital, and a sailing motif dominates his Senate office, from art on the walls to prints on some of the furniture. Newport and sailboats connote wealth and privilege, and Whitehouse has enjoyed and contended with both in his political career, being something of a patrician in a state with a blue-collar Democratic base.

Fellow Democrats often rib Whitehouse about his blueblood upbringing and his button-down ways. At a roast in 2002, Lt. Gov. Charles J. Fogarty offered Whitehouse a can of "Stiff Begone" as a cure for "the uptight WASP."

He also can make fun of himself. At a 1999 event, Whitehouse joked that "three times I tried to throw my hat into the ring before I ran. Each time the damn valet brought the hat back!"

Whitehouse's father, Charles S. Whitehouse, was a wealthy ambassador who worked for the CIA and State Department. Charles Whitehouse roomed at Yale with John H. Chafee, who later became a Republican senator and was the father of Lincoln Chafee, the Republican senator Whitehouse defeated in 2006.

Whitehouse was educated at St. Paul's, a boarding school in New Hampshire, and lived part of the time with his parents in Cambodia, France, Laos, South Africa and Vietnam. He majored in architecture as an undergraduate at Yale and earned his law degree from the University of Virginia. After law school, he clerked for the West Virginia Supreme Court, then worked in the Rhode Island attorney general's office which he would later run.

President Bill Clinton appointed him U.S. attorney in 1994. In that role, he launched an investigation into Vincent A. "Buddy" Cianci Jr., the Providence mayor. The corruption investigation came to be known in local media by its code name, "Operation Plunder Dome," and led to the eventual conviction of Cianci for racketeering and other charges.

Whitehouse was elected Rhode Island attorney general in 1998. In 2002 he made an unsuccessful bid for governor before unseating the younger Chafee in 2006.

Key Votes

2010

Pass budget reconciliation bill to modify overhauls of health care and federal student loan programs	YES
Proceed to disapproval resolution on EPA authority to regulate greenhouse gases	NO
Overhaul financial services industry regulation	YES
Limit debate to proceed to a bill to broaden campaign finance disclosure and reporting rules	YES
Limit debate on an extension of Bush-era income tax cuts for two years	YES
Limit debate on a bill to provide a path to legal status for some children of illegal immigrants	YES
Allow for a repeal of "don't ask, don't tell"	YES
Consent to ratification of a strategic arms reduction treaty with Russia	YES

2009

Prevent release of remaining financial industry bailout funds	NO
Make it easier for victims to sue for wage discrimination remedies	YES
Expand the Children's Health Insurance Program	YES
Limit debate on the economic stimulus measure	YES
Repeal District of Columbia firearms prohibitions and gun registration laws	NO
Limit debate on expansion of federal hate crimes law	YES
Strike funding for F-22 Raptor fighter jets	YES

CQ Vote Studies

	PARTY UNITY		PRESIDENTIAL SUPPORT	
	SUPPORT	OPPOSE	SUPPORT	OPPOSE
2010	99%	1%	97%	3%
2009	99%	1%	100%	0%
2008	95%	5%	41%	59%
2007	98%	2%	35%	65%

Interest Groups

	AFL-CIO	ADA	CCUS	ACU
2010	100%	90%	18%	0%
2009	94%	95%	43%	0%
2008	100%	90%	50%	8%
2007	100%	95%	36%	0%

Rep. David Cicilline (D)

Capitol Office
225-4911
cicilline.house.gov
128 Cannon Bldg. 20515-3901; fax 225-3290

Committees
Foreign Affairs
Small Business

Residence
Providence

Born
July 15, 1961; Providence, R.I.

Religion
Jewish

Family
Single

Education
Brown U., B.A. 1983 (political science); Georgetown U., J.D. 1986

Career
Lawyer; public defender

Political Highlights
Sought Democratic nomination for R.I. Senate, 1992; R.I. House, 1995-2003; mayor of Providence, 2003-11

ELECTION RESULTS

2010 GENERAL

David Cicilline (D)	81,269	50.6%
John Loughlin (R)	71,542	44.6%
Kenneth A. Capalbo (I)	6,424	4.0%

2010 PRIMARY

David Cicilline (D)	21,142	37.2%
Anthony Gemma (D)	13,112	23.1%
David A. Segal (D)	11,397	20.1%
Bill Lynch (D)	11,161	19.6%

Elected 2010; 1st term

After serving eight years as mayor of Providence, Cicilline arrived in the House with "a perspective and an understanding," he said, of the "urgency of what needs to be done" to get people back to work.

He has pushed for a Made in America block grant program to help manufacturers retrofit their businesses and retrain employees. A member of the Small Business Committee, he supports the creation of a National Infrastructure Bank to develop public-private partnerships for investment in infrastructure projects.

Cicilline argues that bringing troops home from Afghanistan as "expeditiously and responsibly as possible" is part of the solution, as well. "We spent $400 billion in Afghanistan, and we have bridges and water systems in our own country that need to be rebuilt."

Cicilline, who is openly gay, has said he will work for full equality for the lesbian, gay, bisexual and transgender community.

Cicilline also joined the Foreign Affairs Committee, where he spoke up for what he called the "very vibrant Cape Verdean community" in his district by defending funding for foreign aid provided to the Republic of Cape Verde, an island country off the west coast of Africa.

Although he is not a member of the Ethics Committee, Cicilline was chosen to serve on an investigative subcommittee for the panel as it resumes probes of cases that began in the 111th Congress (2009-10).

Cicilline won a rough-and-tumble four-way primary, winning 37 percent of the vote in the race to succeed Democrat Patrick J. Kennedy, who retired from Congress.

Promising poll numbers gave Republicans some hope that they might be able to win a second former Kennedy seat in 2010, following up on Scott P. Brown's victory in the Massachusetts Senate race to succeed the late Edward M. Kennedy, Patrick's father.

Republican state Rep. John Loughlin ran a respectable race, but could not overcome the district's Democratic lean. Cicilline won 51 percent of the vote, to 45 percent for Loughlin.

Rhode Island 1

East — Pawtucket, part of Providence, Newport

The 1st includes the state's entire border with Massachusetts and takes in industrial towns in the Blackstone Valley, before moving south to Pawtucket and the northeastern part of Providence, the state capital. It then runs south along the east bank of Narragansett Bay to pick up the scenic coastal town of Newport and the southeast island communities. Despite population loss overall, the district's Hispanic communities have boomed since 2000.

Eastern Rhode Island has not fully moved beyond its manufacturing past. The industrial workforce was hit hard by layoffs, and banking, biotech and health care jobs have not insulated the 1st's economy. A financial-sector collapse affected many area white-collar jobs, and economic declines created municipal budget shortfalls.

A maritime defense industry on the coast south of Providence provides some stability. Portsmouth-based defense contractors and a large naval base and training center in Newport fuel the industry. Visitors to Newport and Providence make tourism key.

The 1st's share of Providence includes the state Capitol, the affluent and picturesque East Side neighborhood, and Brown University and Providence College. While some small towns support the GOP, Democrats dominate the district, bolstered by students, government workers and minority voters.

Major Industry
Health care, government, education, tourism, defense, manufacturing

Military Bases
Naval Station Newport, 3,272 military, 4,363 civilian (2011)

Cities
Providence (pt.), 71,470; Pawtucket, 71,148

Notable
Touro Synagogue in Newport, dedicated in 1762, is the oldest synagogue in the nation.

Rep. Jim Langevin (D)

Capitol Office
225-2735
www.house.gov/langevin
109 Cannon Bldg. 20515; fax 225-5976

Committees
Armed Services
Select Intelligence

Residence
Warwick

Born
April 22, 1964; Warwick, R.I.

Religion
Roman Catholic

Family
Single

Education
Rhode Island College, B.A. 1990 (political science & public administration); Harvard U., M.P.A. 1994

Career
Public official

Political Highlights
R.I. House, 1989-95; R.I. secretary of state, 1995-2001

ELECTION RESULTS

2010 GENERAL

Jim Langevin (D)	104,442	59.9%
Mark Zaccaria (R)	55,409	31.8%
John O. Matson (I)	14,584	8.4%

2010 PRIMARY

Jim Langevin (D)	25,603	57.4%
Betsy Dennigan (D)	15,146	34.0%
Ernest Greco (D)	3,833	8.6%

2008 GENERAL

Jim Langevin (D)	158,416	70.1%
Mark Zaccaria (R)	67,433	29.9%

Previous Winning Percentages
2006 (73%); 2004 (75%); 2002 (76%); 2000 (62%)

Elected 2000; 6th term

Langevin may be best known as the first quadriplegic to serve in the House, but he has become an important voice on national security and defense issues. At the same time, he is a dependable liberal and a rock-solid vote for the Democratic leadership.

He serves on the Select Intelligence and Armed Services committees, and is the ranking Democrat on the latter's Subcommittee on Emerging Threats and Capabilities.

Langevin (LAN-juh-vin) held the gavel of the Strategic Forces panel in the 111th Congress (2009-10), after California Democrat Ellen O. Tauscher resigned to take a job at the State Department.

He has been an outspoken advocate for enhanced vigilance against cyber-attacks on American information technology infrastructure, and for investing in high-tech defenses against nuclear attack.

He played a major role in drafting the fiscal 2011 defense authorization bill. The original measure passed by the House included language by Langevin to create a National Office for Cyberspace in the White House to coordinate federal information security policies. The creation of such an office was one of the key recommendations of a blue-ribbon panel on cyber-security Langevin co-chaired in 2008.

"Cybersecurity is among the most serious economic and national security challenges we will face in the 21st century," Langevin said. "It is imperative that we stay ahead of the curve to ensure the security of our networks."

Langevin has also used his Armed Services post to bolster federal employees unions. The defense authorization bill included a Langevin amendment — aimed at turning back a contrary effort by Republicans — to ensure that the Pentagon could continue to replace private sector contractors with unionized federal workers, a battle likely to be revisited with Republicans back in control of the House.

At the same time, Langevin has worked to bring more Pentagon contracts to his district, particularly to Electric Boat's Quonset Point facility, which makes and assembles large sections of nuclear submarines.

Langevin has served since 2003 on the House Democrats' whip team and rarely votes against the wishes of party leaders. But as a Roman Catholic who opposes abortion in most cases, he backed language in the House's 2009 health care overhaul to bar the use of federal funding for abortion. When the language was later expunged from the final version, Langevin's support for the measure was in question. Ultimately he voted for it, saying that existing restrictions on abortion funding were adequate.

Langevin often finds himself at odds with leaders of the anti-abortion movement, despite his assurances that he opposes abortion except in the case of rape, incest or a threat to the life of the mother. In 2007, for example, Langevin angered abortion opponents by voting to allow federal funding of international family planning groups that provide abortions. In 2011, he opposed an amendment to a catchall spending bill that would bar federal funding for Planned Parenthood.

And he has long been an advocate of federal funding of embryonic stem cell research, in defiance of many abortion opponents who say the destruction of human embryos for research purposes is morally wrong. Langevin believes the research could hold promise for the treatment of spinal cord injuries like the one that, at age 16, left him paralyzed from the waist down. "Being pro-life isn't just about protecting life in the womb," Langevin said.

"It has to be about protecting and extending the quality of life for people who are living among us."

As a boy, Langevin dreamed of being a police officer or an FBI agent. He enrolled in a police department cadet program in his hometown of Warwick, riding along with officers and getting to know the police routine. On Aug. 22, 1980, he was in the police locker room with two members of the SWAT team. One of them inadvertently pulled the trigger of a loaded gun, discharging a bullet that ricocheted off a locker and hit Langevin in the neck. The bullet severed his spinal cord, leaving him unable to move his legs and with only minimal use of his arms and hands.

Langevin embraces his symbolic importance to people with disabilities. In July 2010, he became the first person in a wheelchair to preside over the House, marking the 20th anniversary of the passage of legislation aimed at making public facilities more accessible to people with disabilities. After the Capitol was evacuated after the Sept. 11 terrorist attacks, with no protocol for how to help people with disabilities get out, Langevin helped develop one.

He strongly believes that medical breakthroughs will eventually allow him to walk again. He backed 2009 legislation named for the late actor Christopher Reeve, who was paralyzed in an equestrian accident, to expand such research. In the 109th Congress (2005-06), he helped win enactment of a bill authorizing federal grants to agencies that recruit and train people to provide a respite to families caring for a disabled person at home. He continually pushes for increased funding for the program.

Langevin says it was the tremendous outpouring of support from the Warwick community after his injury that prompted him to go into politics. Four years after the accident, he volunteered in Frank Flaherty's campaign for mayor of Warwick. Flaherty recalls being amazed at Langevin's tenacity, making phone calls and stuffing envelopes despite his injury. Later, when Flaherty was still mayor and Langevin was in the state legislature, "he'd come in looking for something for his area of the city and he'd drive me crazy, chase me around. I used to threaten to unplug the battery on his wheelchair so I wouldn't have to listen," Flaherty told the Providence Journal.

While still in college, Langevin was elected as a delegate to the Rhode Island Constitutional Convention. In 1988, he won the first of three terms in the Rhode Island House. In 1994, he was elected secretary of state, and six years later, when Democratic Rep. Bob Weygand ran for the Senate, Langevin made a bid for his 2nd District seat and took 62 percent of the vote. He won at least 70 percent of the vote in each election until 2010, when he was held to 60 percent.

Key Votes

2010

Overhaul the nation's health insurance system	YES
Allow for repeal of "don't ask, don't tell	YES
Overhaul financial services industry regulation	YES
Limit use of new Afghanistan War funds to troop withdrawal activities	NO
Change oversight of offshore drilling and lift oil spill liability cap	YES
Provide a path to legal status for some children of illegal immigrants	YES
Extend Bush-era income tax cuts for two years	YES

2009

Expand the Children's Health Insurance Program	YES
Provide $787 billion in tax cuts and spending increases to stimulate the economy	YES
Allow bankruptcy judges to modify certain primary-residence mortgages	YES
Create a cap-and-trade system to limit greenhouse gas emissions	YES
Provide $2 billion for the "cash for clunkers" program	YES
Establish the government as the sole provider of student loans	YES
Restrict federally funded insurance coverage for abortions in health care overhaul	YES

CQ Vote Studies

	PARTY UNITY		PRESIDENTIAL SUPPORT	
	SUPPORT	OPPOSE	SUPPORT	OPPOSE
2010	97%	3%	93%	7%
2009	99%	1%	97%	3%
2008	99%	1%	15%	85%
2007	98%	2%	5%	95%
2006	94%	6%	30%	70%

Interest Groups

	AFL-CIO	ADA	CCUS	ACU
2010	100%	85%	25%	0%
2009	100%	95%	33%	4%
2008	100%	100%	61%	0%
2007	96%	100%	50%	0%
2006	93%	75%	33%	16%

Rhode Island 2

West — part of Providence, Warwick, Cranston

The 2nd takes in an eclectic mix of countryside, city life and shoreline that makes up the western two-thirds of the nation's smallest state. Bordering Connecticut on one side and the Narragansett Bay on the other, it covers rolling hills in the north, as well as most of the metropolitan area around Providence (shared with the 1st). In the south, Washington County's idyllic beaches and lakes attract tourists and residents alike.

As manufacturing continues a decades-long decline, the 2nd is attempting to transition from a blue-collar to a white-collar economy. A heavy statewide investment in developing the area's service economy had helped with stabilization, and the 2nd enjoyed some growth in the technology, financial services and health care industries. Maritime defense contractors here, including General Dynamics' Electric Boat submarine facility at Quonset Point, depend on major military manufacturing projects, some of which face funding obstacles. Aviation company Textron Systems has its corporate headquarters in the 2nd's part of Providence. Local officials hope to team firms in the emerging medical, life-science and alternative-energy sectors with the area's several major colleges, including Johnson & Wales University, Rhode Island College and the University of Rhode Island. Economic pressures here are causing population shifts. A decade of sluggish population growth coupled with demographic changes has led to a slightly more racially diverse 1st. As white residents have departed the Providence area, more blacks and Hispanics have moved in, increasing the city's already Democratic tendency.

The 2nd is home to many working- and middle-class towns that have a substantial and Democratic-leaning union presence, although the large Catholic population makes abortion a key issue that can affect electoral outcomes. No Republican presidential candidate has carried the district since 1984, and Barack Obama won with 62 percent in 2008.

Major Industry
Service, defense, higher education, banking, health care

Cities
Providence (pt.), 106,572; Warwick, 82,672; Cranston, 80,387

Notable
Block Island, 12 miles off the southern coast, is a scenic vacation spot that has 17 miles of beaches and 365 freshwater ponds.

Gov. Nikki R. Haley (R)

First elected: 2010
Length of term: 4 years
Term expires: 1/15
Salary: $106,078
Phone: (803) 734-2100
Residence: Lexington
Born: January 20, 1972; Bamberg, S.C.
Religion: Methodist
Family: Husband, Michael Haley; two children
Education: Clemson U., B.S. 1994 (accounting)
Career: Accountant
Political highlights: S.C. House, 2005-10 (majority whip, 2006-07)

ELECTION RESULTS

2010 GENERAL

Nikki R. Haley (R)	690,525	51.4%
Vincent A. Sheheen (D)	630,534	46.9%
Others	20,114	1.5%

Lt. Gov. Ken Ard (R)

First elected: 2010
Length of term: 4 years
Term expires: 1/15
Salary: $46,545
Phone: (803) 734-2080

LEGISLATURE

General Assembly: January-June
Senate: 46 members, 4-year terms
2011 ratios: 27 R, 19 D; 46 men
Salary: $10,400
Phone: (803) 212-6200
House: 124 members, 2-year terms
2011 ratios: 75 R, 48 D, 1 vacancy; 106 men, 17 women
Salary: $10,400
Phone: (803) 734-2010

TERM LIMITS

Governor: 2 consecutive terms
Senate: No
House: No

URBAN STATISTICS

CITY	POPULATION
Columbia	129,272
Charleston	120,083
North Charleston	97,471
Mount Pleasant	67,843
Rock Hill	66,154

REGISTERED VOTERS

Voters do not register by party.

POPULATION

2010 population	4,625,364
2000 population	4,012,012
1990 population	3,486,703
Percent change (2000-2010)	+15.3%
Rank among states (2010)	24
Median age	37.2
Born in state	60.1%
Foreign born	4.2%
Violent crime rate	671/100,000
Poverty level	17.1%
Federal workers	45,152
Military	32,518

ELECTIONS

STATE ELECTION OFFICIAL
(803) 734-9060

DEMOCRATIC PARTY
(803) 799-7798

REPUBLICAN PARTY
(803) 988-8440

MISCELLANEOUS

Web: www.sc.gov
Capital: Columbia

U.S. CONGRESS

Senate: 2 Republicans
House: 5 Republicans, 1 Democrat

2010 Census Statistics by District

District	2008 Vote for President Obama	McCain	White	Black	Asian	Hispanic	Median Income	White Collar	Blue Collar	Service Industry	Over 64	Under 18	College Education	Rural	Sq. Miles
1	42%	56%	71%	20%	2%	6%	$48,952	61%	21%	18%	13%	23%	28%	22%	2,645
2	45	54	63	27	2	7	51,334	63	21	16	13	25	32	34	4,767
3	35	64	74	19	1	4	41,543	53	31	16	15	23	20	50	5,392
4	38	60	70	19	2	7	44,442	58	27	15	13	25	25	26	2,151
5	46	53	63	30	1	4	40,419	53	32	16	13	25	18	53	7,035
6	64	35	41	54	1	3	33,184	50	30	20	13	24	16	52	8,120
STATE	45	54	64	28	1	5	43,572	57	27	17	13	24	23	40	30,109
U.S.	53	46	64	12	5	16	51,425	60	23	17	13	25	28	21	3,537,438

Sen. Lindsey Graham (R)

Capitol Office
224-5972
lgraham.senate.gov
290 Russell Bldg. 20510-4001; fax 224-3808

Committees
Appropriations
Armed Services
Budget
Judiciary
Special Aging

Residence
Seneca

Born
July 9, 1955; Seneca, S.C.

Religion
Southern Baptist

Family
Single

Education
U. of South Carolina, B.A. 1977 (psychology),
attended 1977-78 (public administration), J.D. 1981

Military Service
Air Force, 1982-88; Air Force Reserve, 1988-89; S.C.
Air National Guard, 1989-96; Air Force Reserve,
2003-present

Career
Lawyer; military prosecutor

Political Highlights
S.C. House, 1993-95; U.S. House, 1995-2003

ELECTION RESULTS

2008 GENERAL

Lindsey Graham (R)	1,076,534	57.5%
Bob Conley (D)	790,621	42.2%

2008 PRIMARY

Lindsey Graham (R)	187,736	66.8%
Buddy Witherspoon (R)	93,125	33.2%

2002 GENERAL

Lindsey Graham (R)	595,218	54.4%
Alex Sanders (D)	484,422	44.2%

Previous Winning Percentages
2000 House Election (68%); 1998 House Election
(100%); 1996 House Election (60%); 1994 House
Election (60%)

Elected 2002; 2nd term

A soft-spoken lawyer with a keen legal mind and solidly conservative instincts, Graham's willingness to work with Democrats makes him a closely watched lawmaker in the divided 112th Congress.

Graham is popular among Capitol Hill reporters because of his perpetual willingness to say what he really thinks — in a patient, Southern-accented voice — about even the most controversial issues. He has a tendency to buck his party leaders and go his own way, often staking out positions with widespread popular appeal.

Graham sometimes comes under fire in his solidly Republican state for his willingness to cross the aisle, but he downplays the criticism. "People at home expect me to be conservative, but they like the fact that I'm trying to solve problems," he said. Despite such nonchalance, Graham's well-earned reputation for independence will be put to the test in an environment where neither the Senate GOP caucus nor South Carolina Republicans have much appetite for mavericks.

During President George W. Bush's administration, Graham was a dealmaker on several major issues, including the battle over judicial nominations and the debate over the government's treatment of terrorist detainees. Graham kept that portfolio after President Obama took office in 2009. His background as a military prosecutor gives him credibility on the issue in the Senate and with the White House.

A member of the Judiciary and Armed Services committees, he said terrorists should be tried in the military justice system, either by military commission, court-martial or a hybrid of the two systems. The Obama White House courted Graham on the issue, and he supported Obama's decision to close the U.S. detention facility in Guantánamo Bay, Cuba, while sticking with his position on military tribunals. Graham worked closely with the administration on provisions in the fiscal 2010 defense authorization law to rewrite the rules for military commissions to try detainees. The administration came around to Graham's point of view, announcing in April 2011 that self-proclaimed Sept. 11 mastermind Khalid Sheikh Mohammed would be tried by a military tribunal at Guantánamo.

In 2009, when he was a member of the Homeland Security and Governmental Affairs Committee, Graham joined with Chairman Joseph I. Lieberman, a Connecticut independent, on including a provision in the fiscal 2010 Homeland Security spending bill to bar funds for the release of photos of terrorism detainees.

Graham showed his tendencies toward both combativeness and compromise in other ways.

He worked behind the scenes during the summer of 2009 to try to drum up GOP support for working with Democrats on an immigration policy overhaul. But in 2010, Graham hardened his position on the issue. He opposed a Justice Department lawsuit against an Arizona law that empowers local police to question and detain people suspected of being in the country illegally. Critics of the law said it is a legalized form of racial profiling. And he came out in support of amending the Constitution so that children born in the United States to illegal immigrant parents are not automatically U.S. citizens.

Graham voted in favor of the Supreme Court nominations Obama made in 2009 and 2010. Each time, he was the only GOP member of the Judiciary Committee to vote "aye."

"The Constitution puts a requirement on me, as a senator, to not replace my judgment for the president's," Graham said in announcing his support for Elena Kagan in 2010. During Sonia Sotomayor's confirmation hearing the previous year, Graham assured her at the outset that she would be confirmed, absent a "meltdown." But he didn't always treat Sotomayor gently. At one point, he read her a list of complaints that anonymous lawyers had made about her assertive style as a judge and suggested she might want to engage in some "self-reflection."

Graham took the lead in an effort to overhaul Social Security in the 109th Congress (2005-06), even though he did not hold any committee memberships or leadership positions that would have afforded him a natural power base. (He now serves on both Appropriations and Budget.) Instead, Graham held a series of bipartisan sessions for lawmakers in an effort to develop a proposal. He floated the idea of raising the payroll tax cap, as well as changing the formula for calculating benefits that was projected to halve the program's long-term deficit by giving smaller payouts to wealthier retirees. The effort collapsed under fierce Democratic opposition. But Graham vowed to keep working on the issue.

His search for the productive middle in politics marks an evolution from his early days on Capitol Hill. He arrived with the rambunctious House GOP Class of 1994 and was one of the leaders of a 1997 effort by conservatives to oust GOP Speaker Newt Gingrich of Georgia. Gingrich put down the insurrection, and Graham did not suffer any political consequences.

In 1998, Graham was one of the 13 House managers in the impeachment case against President Bill Clinton.

For all his headline-grabbing defections from the Republican fold, Graham is a conservative at heart. He stuck with his fellow Republicans in partisan Senate votes more than 92 percent of the time for all but one of his first eight years in the chamber. Graham backed an effort led by his fellow South Carolinian, Jim DeMint, to establish a moratorium on earmarks. He once joined an effort to shut down the National Endowment for the Arts and typically favors limiting the scope of the federal government. He is an opponent of gun control, and he has voted to amend the Constitution to outlaw flag desecration and ban same-sex marriage. Graham has backed legislation to make it a federal crime to harm a fetus in the course of committing any one of 68 federal offenses.

Graham is the son of a tavern owner and grew up racking billiard balls in his parents' bar in the textile town of Central. The death of both parents from illness when he was not yet out of college left him to care for his 13-year-old sister, Darline, whom he legally adopted. "It changes your world and you have to grow up a lot quicker," Graham said.

After law school, he joined the Air Force and later transferred to Germany as a prosecutor. Graham served on active duty in both the 1991 Persian Gulf War and, in 2007, the U.S. occupation of Iraq.

Graham won a state House seat in 1992 and saw an opportunity for advancement early in 1994, when 10-term Democratic Rep. Butler Derrick decided to retire from the U.S. House. Graham won easily that fall, beating Democratic state Sen. James Bryan with 60 percent of the vote to become the first Republican to represent his district since 1877.

He won three more terms with relative ease and began planning for a Senate run after Republican Strom Thurmond made it clear his seventh full term would be his last. By 2002, Graham was unopposed for his party's nomination. He easily beat Democrat Alex Sanders, a former president of the College of Charleston. In 2008, Graham bested orthodontist Buddy Witherspoon in the GOP primary by 34 percentage points and easily won re-election with nearly 58 percent over Democrat Bob Conley, a North Myrtle Beach engineer.

Key Votes

2010

Pass budget reconciliation bill to modify overhauls of health care and federal student loan programs	NO
Proceed to disapproval resolution on EPA authority to regulate greenhouse gases	YES
Overhaul financial services industry regulation	NO
Limit debate to proceed to a bill to broaden campaign finance disclosure and reporting rules	NO
Limit debate on an extension of Bush-era income tax cuts for two years	YES
Limit debate on a bill to provide a path to legal status for some children of illegal immigrants	NO
Allow for a repeal of "don't ask, don't tell"	NO
Consent to ratification of a strategic arms reduction treaty with Russia	NO

2009

Prevent release of remaining financial industry bailout funds	YES
Make it easier for victims to sue for wage discrimination remedies	NO
Expand the Children's Health Insurance Program	NO
Limit debate on the economic stimulus measure	NO
Repeal District of Columbia firearms prohibitions and gun registration laws	YES
Limit debate on expansion of federal hate crimes law	?
Strike funding for F-22 Raptor fighter jets	YES

CQ Vote Studies

	PARTY UNITY		PRESIDENTIAL SUPPORT	
	SUPPORT	OPPOSE	SUPPORT	OPPOSE
2010	95%	5%	47%	53%
2009	94%	6%	49%	51%
2008	97%	3%	72%	28%
2007	92%	8%	87%	13%
2006	82%	18%	91%	9%
2005	92%	8%	89%	11%
2004	92%	8%	92%	8%
2003	96%	3%	95%	5%
2002	89%	11%	82%	18%
2001	93%	7%	84%	16%

Interest Groups

	AFL-CIO	ADA	CCUS	ACU
2010	14%	5%	100%	92%
2009	28%	15%	86%	88%
2008	14%	15%	100%	82%
2007	0%	20%	100%	88%
2006	7%	0%	92%	83%
2005	29%	20%	83%	96%
2004	8%	25%	88%	92%
2003	17%	15%	83%	90%
2002	22%	15%	70%	83%
2001	17%	15%	78%	88%

Sen. Jim DeMint (R)

Capitol Office
224-6121
demint.senate.gov
167 Russell Bldg. 20510-4002; fax 228-5143

Committees
Banking, Housing & Urban Affairs
Commerce, Science & Transportation
Foreign Relations
Joint Economic

Residence
Greenville

Born
Sept. 2, 1951; Greenville, S.C.

Religion
Presbyterian

Family
Wife, Debbie DeMint; four children

Education
U. of Tennessee, B.S. 1973 (communications); Clemson U., M.B.A. 1981

Career
Market research company owner; advertising and sales representative

Political Highlights
U.S. House, 1999-2005

ELECTION RESULTS

2010 GENERAL

Jim DeMint (R)	810,771	61.5%
Alvin M. Greene (D)	364,598	27.6%
Tom Clements (GREEN)	121,472	9.2%
write-ins (WRI)	21,953	1.7%

2010 PRIMARY

Jim DeMint (R)	342,464	83.0%
Susan McDonald Gaddy (R)	70,194	17.0%

2004 GENERAL

Jim DeMint (R)	857,167	53.7%
Inez Tenenbaum (D)	704,384	44.1%

Previous Winning Percentages
2002 House Election (69%); 2000 House Election (80%); 1998 House Election (58%)

Elected 2004; 2nd term

DeMint's genial demeanor complements his growing role as a point man for his party's conservative wing. Capitalizing on momentum generated by the tea party movement, DeMint has prodded his party to embrace tougher curbs on earmarks, and candidates running against the establishment have sought his endorsement to confirm their bona fides.

With his book "Saving Freedom: We Can Stop America's Slide into Socialism," DeMint laid out a blueprint to curb spending and limit the scope of government. As chairman of the Senate Republican Steering Committee, DeMint has shown a mastery of parliamentary maneuvers to force tough votes on such themes. His proposal to ban earmarks — funding set-asides for special projects — was adopted by Senate Republicans in the 112th Congress (2011-12), and Appropriations Chairman Daniel K. Inouye, a Hawaii Democrat, acquiesced.

Although he invites all Republicans to the steering committee's weekly luncheon once they are elected, DeMint showed a preference for conservative upstarts against other candidates — including some incumbents. In a signature move, DeMint in 2009 backed former Rep. Patrick J. Toomey in the Senate race against Pennsylvania's moderate incumbent, Arlen Specter — five days before Specter switched parties. DeMint also gave early support to former state House Speaker Marco Rubio over his centrist rival in Florida, Gov. Charlie Crist, before Crist left the Republican Party in 2010. And he backed Rand Paul in Kentucky's Senate primary against the candidate favored by the state's senior senator, Minority Leader Mitch McConnell.

With bold moves and a leadership political action committee, DeMint collected chits for the 112th Congress and beyond while cementing his position as a leader of the most conservative wing of the GOP. He was a founder of the Senate Tea Party Caucus in early 2011, giving an institutional voice to the grass-roots movement that he helped promote.

DeMint's background in advertising and market research gives him the studied manner of a business executive in the Senate, but he voices anti-establishment themes on the stump. "Despite the clarion call for freedom from the American people, there is still a struggle within the Republican Party about who we are and what we stand for," he said at the 2010 Conservative Political Action Conference. "It's a fight between those who take their constitutional oath seriously and those who don't."

DeMint, a former House member, has close ties to Republicans elected in 1994 on the "Contract With America" platform. Some of DeMint's agenda echoes the old contract, including his proposed constitutional amendment to limit senators to two six-year terms. In 2010, he became an early supporter of a new manifesto dubbed the "Contract From America."

DeMint sends "Freedom Alerts" to voters and often takes the lead in high-profile fights. When Democrats deleted from a spending bill his proposal to build 300 miles of fencing along the U.S.-Mexico border in 2009, he looked for ways to force votes on similar proposals.

Some of his efforts have won him praise from his home state's media as well as the political right, but he hasn't always endeared himself to GOP colleagues. He has sometimes irritated fellow Republicans by pushing efforts to curb seniority as the basis for choosing committee chairmen and ranking members. He defends his efforts to shake up his party's status quo: "We don't have to be purists . . . but there have to be core principles, or there's no way for us to be a party," he said. "Maybe we could sign a pledge or something.

Limited government, free markets and personal freedom."

His conservative views on both social and fiscal issues pervade his work on his other committee assignments, which include Banking, Housing and Urban Affairs; Foreign Relations; and Joint Economic.

At a 2010 Foreign Relations hearing on a proposed nuclear arms reduction treaty, DeMint said, "it's unrealistic to believe that our treaty with Russia is going to reduce proliferation with countries like Iran and Syria and other rogue nations that are intent on developing nuclear weapons."

Of the Democrats' health care overhaul enacted in 2010, he told Fox News' Sean Hannity that "if this bill stands, it will bankrupt our country. It will destroy the health care system." He backed an attempt to repeal it in early 2011.

In many of DeMint's comments on President Obama's budgeting he asserted that the president showed a lack of commitment to his own pledge to overhaul earmarks. He called Obama's fiscal 2012 blueprint "an unserious budget that ignores the warnings of his own bipartisan deficit commission and chooses political expediency over real leadership."

A member of the aviation subcommittee of Commerce, Science and Transportation, DeMint blocked a quick confirmation of former FBI agent Erroll Southers to head the Transportation Security Administration, raising questions about his stance on collective bargaining rights for security employees. Southers eventually withdrew.

While in the House, DeMint was a leader among conservative lawmakers. But he also liked to emphasize his work on bipartisan legislation. In 2001, he gathered more than 280 cosponsorships on legislation to double the adoption tax credit to $10,000. The credit was included in the $1.35 trillion, 10-year tax cut enacted that year. DeMint is no fan of the federal income tax system and would like to see it replaced by a tax on the consumption of goods and services.

His loyalty to a pro-business agenda has gotten DeMint into trouble at home on occasion, especially for his pro-trade stances. In the House, he was derided in 2002 for joining the razor-thin majority that helped enact a law reviving the president's authority to negotiate treaties Congress must approve or reject without amendment. His vote infuriated the state's powerful textile interests, and it became the key issue when DeMint sought re-election to the House in 2002. He nevertheless won easily.

Raised by a single mother operating a dance school out of their home, DeMint and his three siblings grew up quickly, handling chores at a young age. Yet DeMint sparked controversy during his Senate campaign when he asserted during a debate that unwed mothers with live-in boyfriends should not teach in public schools. He also said a "practicing homosexual" should be barred. He later apologized, saying it was up to states to decide who is fit to teach.

DeMint entered politics in 1992 as an unpaid adviser to his predecessor in the House, Republican Bob Inglis. Six years later, when Inglis gave up the seat for an unsuccessful Senate bid, DeMint won the GOP nomination against state Sen. Mike Fair, who had the backing of the Christian Coalition. DeMint went on to win the general election by 18 percentage points.

Facing a self-imposed six-year term limit in the House in 2004, DeMint ran for the Senate. Veteran Sen. Ernest F. Hollings announced his retirement that year, and DeMint easily defeated former Gov. David Beasley in a GOP primary runoff before beating Inez Tenenbaum, the state education superintendent, that November. His victory gave South Carolina two Republican senators for the first time since Reconstruction. He won about 62 percent of the vote in 2010 against political unknown Alvin M. Greene, who came out of nowhere to win the Democratic nomination and barely campaigned in the general election.

Key Votes

2010

Pass budget reconciliation bill to modify overhauls of health care and federal student loan programs	NO
Proceed to disapproval resolution on EPA authority to regulate greenhouse gases	YES
Overhaul financial services industry regulation	NO
Limit debate to proceed to a bill to broaden campaign finance disclosure and reporting rules	NO
Limit debate on an extension of Bush-era income tax cuts for two years	NO
Limit debate on a bill to provide a path to legal status for some children of illegal immigrants	NO
Allow for a repeal of "don't ask, don't tell"	NO
Consent to ratification of a strategic arms reduction treaty with Russia	NO

2009

Prevent release of remaining financial industry bailout funds	YES
Make it easier for victims to sue for wage discrimination remedies	NO
Expand the Children's Health Insurance Program	NO
Limit debate on the economic stimulus measure	NO
Repeal District of Columbia firearms prohibitions and gun registration laws	YES
Limit debate on expansion of federal hate crimes law	NO
Strike funding for F-22 Raptor fighter jets	YES

CQ Vote Studies

	PARTY UNITY		PRESIDENTIAL SUPPORT	
	SUPPORT	OPPOSE	SUPPORT	OPPOSE
2010	99%	1%	29%	71%
2009	98%	2%	30%	70%
2008	100%	0%	84%	16%
2007	98%	2%	90%	10%
2006	97%	3%	90%	10%
2005	96%	4%	91%	9%
2004	98%	2%	92%	8%
2003	98%	2%	89%	11%
2002	97%	3%	85%	15%
2001	98%	2%	95%	5%

Interest Groups

	AFL-CIO	ADA	CCUS	ACU
2010	0%	5%	82%	100%
2009	12%	5%	71%	100%
2008	0%	0%	57%	100%
2007	5%	0%	55%	100%
2006	13%	0%	92%	100%
2005	21%	5%	89%	96%
2004	0%	0%	92%	100%
2003	7%	20%	93%	96%
2002	11%	0%	90%	100%
2001	0%	0%	96%	100%

Rep. Tim Scott (R)

Capitol Office
225-3176
timscott.house.gov
1117 Cannon Bldg. 20515-4001; fax 225-3407

Committees
Rules

Residence
Charleston

Born
Sept. 19, 1965; North Charleston, S.C.

Religion
Christian

Family
Single

Education
Presbyterian College, attended 1983-84; Charleston Southern U., B.S. 1988 (political science)

Career
Insurance agency owner; financial adviser

Political Highlights
Charleston County Council, 1995-2008 (chairman, 2002-03, 2007-08); Republican nominee for S.C. Senate, 1996; S.C. House, 2009-10

ELECTION RESULTS

2010 GENERAL

Tim Scott (R)	152,755	65.4%
Ben Frasier (D)	67,008	28.7%
Rob Groce (WFM)	4,148	1.8%
Robert Dobbs (GREEN)	3,369	1.4%
Keith Blandford (LIBERT)	2,750	1.2%
Jimmy Wood (INDC)	2,489	1.1%

2010 PRIMARY RUNOFF

Tim Scott (R)	46,989	68.3%
Paul Thurmond (R)	21,799	31.7%

Elected 2010; 1st term

Scott, one of two black Republicans in Congress, followed up on his historic election by quickly beginning his ascent up the GOP leadership ladder. He had a spot on the GOP transition team, serves as one of two freshman liaisons to the House leadership and landed a seat on the Rules Committee.

The symbolic value of Scott's victory in Charleston, the city where the Civil War began, has not been lost on him or the Republican Party. But he aims to be more than a symbol.

For starters, he chose not to join the Congressional Black Caucus, saying his campaign was never about race.

Supported during his campaign by prominent conservatives including 2008 GOP vice presidential nominee Sarah Palin and home-state Sen. Jim DeMint, Scott enthusiastically embraces conservative positions, including repealing the 2010 health care law and reducing federal spending.

Scott endorsed the Republican moratorium on earmarks for fiscal 2011 and fiscal 2012 and said he wants to end the practice altogether. "This has to stop if we are ever going to get our fiscal house in order," Scott said.

He stresses economic issues, but Scott is also a cultural conservative, opposing gun control, abortion and gay marriage.

Scott often talks about his life story, growing up in poverty and almost flunking out of school. He found a mentor in the proprietor of a local fast food restaurant, turned his life around and got a college degree.

He served 14 years on the Charleston County Council before becoming the first African-American Republican elected to the South Carolina House since Reconstruction.

He considered making a run for lieutenant governor in 2010 before joining a crowded Republican field — including the sons of the late Sen. Strom Thurmond and the late Gov. Carroll Campbell — to succeed retiring GOP Rep. Henry E. Brown Jr.

Scott finished first by a wide margin in the first round of voting and easily dispatched Paul Thurmond in the runoff. He then took almost two-thirds of the vote to win election in the solidly Republican district.

South Carolina 1

East — part of Charleston, Myrtle Beach

Taking in most of the state's coastline, the 1st is marked by two of South Carolina's landmark tourist destinations: Charleston and Myrtle Beach. Horry County, which includes Myrtle Beach, still has plenty of farmland but grew quickly in the last decade. The 1st tends to favor the GOP.

Nearly 80 percent of Charleston's residents live in the 1st, and the city is still one of the nation's busiest ports. There is a strong military presence here: Joint Base Charleston takes in the operations of an air force base and a naval weapons station. The city also is home to the Medical University of South Carolina. Although an icon of the New South, the city is surrounded by reminders of its antebellum history. The church steeples marking its skyline lend Charleston its nickname, the "Holy City."

Moving north, tobacco farming has long been prominent in inland areas, but rising cigarette taxes and a national decline in demand have cut into revenues. The Myrtle Beach area is as popular for its championship golf courses as for its beaches, and the housing market there has begun to rebound. Conservation efforts are directed at mitigating congestion, pollution, wetlands destruction and beach erosion following decades of residential and commercial growth.

Major Industry
Shipping, tourism, agriculture, military

Military Bases
Joint Base Charleston, 8,257 military, 3,948 civilian (2011)

Cities
Charleston (pt.), 94,695; Mount Pleasant, 67,843; North Charleston (pt.), 66,597; Summerville, 43,392; Goose Creek, 35,938

Notable
Charleston Harbor is home to Fort Sumter, where the first battle of the Civil War took place in 1861.

Rep. Joe Wilson (R)

Capitol Office
225-2452
www.joewilson.house.gov
2229 Rayburn Bldg. 20515-4002; fax 225-2455

Committees
Armed Services
    (Military Personnel - Chairman)
Education & the Workforce
Foreign Affairs

Residence
Springdale

Born
July 31, 1947; Charleston, S.C.

Religion
Presbyterian

Family
Wife, Roxanne Wilson; four children

Education
Washington and Lee U., B.A. 1969 (political science);
U. of South Carolina, J.D. 1972

Military
Army Reserve, 1972-75; S.C. National Guard, 1975-2003

Career
Lawyer; U.S. Energy Department official; campaign
aide

Political Highlights
Pine Ridge town judge, 1974-76; Republican nominee for S.C. Senate, 1976; Springdale town judge,
1977-80; S.C. Senate, 1985-2001

ELECTION RESULTS

2010 GENERAL

Joe Wilson (R)	138,861	53.5%
Rob Miller (D)	113,625	43.8%
Eddie McCain (LIBERT)	4,228	1.6%
Marc Beaman (CNSTP)	2,856	1.1%

2010 PRIMARY

Joe Wilson (R)	64,973	83.4%
Phil Black (R)	12,923	16.6%

2008 GENERAL

Joe Wilson (R)	184,583	53.7%
Rob Miller (D)	158,627	46.2%

Previous Winning Percentages
2006 (63%); 2004 (65%); 2002 (84%); 2001 Special
Election (73%)

Elected 2001; 5th full term

An energetic conservative long known for his pro-military stands, Wilson gained national notoriety with his "You lie!" outburst during President Obama's speech to a joint session of Congress on health care. Since that September 2009 incident, which drew a reprimand from the House, Wilson has kept a relatively low public profile while still continuing to promote his conservative agenda.

At the insistence of then-White House Chief of Staff Rahm Emanuel, a former House member who alleged that such behavior was unprecedented, Wilson eventually apologized to the administration, issuing a statement acknowledging his "inappropriate and regrettable" comment. The apology was accepted by Obama, but GOP leadership pleas with Wilson to publicly apologize on the House floor were unsuccessful. The House then passed — almost entirely along party lines — a resolution of disapproval of Wilson for violating congressional rules in a way that "degraded" the joint session. It was the mildest form of discipline a member can face.

Following Obama's next speech before Congress, the 2010 State of the Union address, Wilson posted a video message on Facebook in which he criticized the president's positions on health care, the economy and global warming. Wilson voted in early 2011 to repeal the health care law enacted in 2010.

Wilson's new fame benefited his fundraising. His reputation in state Republican circles may also have helped his son, Alan, in the race for attorney general of South Carolina. The younger Wilson won a tough GOP primary runoff and was elected in November 2010.

Even before his blast at Obama, Wilson was known for pushing his causes with boundless energy, rushing back and forth across Capitol Hill and delivering hundreds of one-minute speeches on the House floor. And incendiary remarks have embroiled him in controversy before.

In a 2002 C-SPAN discussion about Iraq's possible nuclear and biological weapon arsenal, liberal California Democratic Rep. Bob Filner suggested Iraq may have gotten some technologies from the United States, prompting Wilson to accuse Filner of "hatred of America." A year later, when Essie Mae Washington-Williams publicly identified herself as the biracial daughter of the late Strom Thurmond, Wilson accused her of trying to "smear" the Republican senator from South Carolina, for whom he had once worked as a college intern. When Thurmond's relatives said Washington-Williams was in fact part of their family, Wilson apologized but said that she should have remained silent.

Wilson sits on both the Armed Services and Foreign Affairs committees, where he presses his goals of fighting the war on terror and improving benefits for soldiers and reservists; he served in the South Carolina National Guard for nearly 30 years, retiring as a colonel, and in the Army Reserve for three years. In 2009 and again in 2011, Wilson has pushed legislation to enable National Guard members and reservists to obtain retirement pay earlier. In the 112th Congress (2011-12), he chairs the Armed Services Subcommittee on Military Personnel.

Wilson urged lawmakers in 2010 to avoid rushing into a repeal of the "don't ask, don't tell" statute that bars openly gay people from serving in the military, but the law was repealed late in the year. In March 2011, Wilson called the process to repeal the law "undemocratic" and promised close oversight of the new policy's implementation.

Wilson also sits on the Education and the Workforce Committee, where he tries to rein in federal involvement in local school decisions. In 2004, he saw enactment of his bill to expand a loan-forgiveness program for teachers in poverty-stricken public schools.

A member of both the conservative Republican Study Committee and the Tea Party Caucus, Wilson opposed all of Obama's economic initiatives and was an enthusiastic supporter of GOP spending proposals. He won praise from conservatives for backing all of the non-security spending cuts considered on the floor during debate on a catchall spending bill for fiscal 2011.

Wilson upset some of his constituents in 2008 when he announced he wouldn't seek earmarks — funding set-asides for projects in his district. He said that the importance of revamping the system justified his self-imposed abstinence. Although he kept to his pledge for the fiscal 2009 spending cycle, Wilson listed on his website nearly $118 million in earmarks for fiscal 2010. He then endorsed the GOP moratorium on the practice for 2011 and 2012.

Though he goes by "Joe," Wilson's full name is Addison Graves Wilson. His mother was a Democrat but her son always thought he might be a Republican and made the transition in the early 1960s while in high school.

He met the woman who would later become his wife at a camp for GOP teenagers where she was a camper and he was a counselor.

Wilson joined the staff of Rep. Floyd D. Spence, a South Carolina Republican, while in law school. He managed five of Spence's re-election campaigns and also was involved in several statewide GOP campaigns in the 1980s and 1990s while working as a real estate lawyer.

Wilson came up short in a contest for the state Senate in 1976, losing after a recount. After a two-year stint with the Department of Energy, he unseated a GOP state senator in 1984 and served four terms.

When Spence died in 2001, Wilson said he had received a deathbed endorsement. While Wilson's claim rankled some of his rivals, it was backed up by Spence's widow. He won the five-way GOP primary with nearly 76 percent of the vote and cruised to a 48-percentage-point win that November. Wilson immediately claimed a seat on Armed Services, which Spence had chaired from 1995 to 2001. Democrats didn't challenge Wilson in 2002. In 2004 and 2006, he beat Democratic attorney Michael Ray Ellisor with more than 60 percent of the vote. In 2008, Democrat Rob Miller, a retired Marine and Iraq War veteran, held Wilson to just under 54 percent of the vote.

Miller tried again in 2010 and, like Wilson, enjoyed a boost in fundraising after Wilson's outburst at Obama. But it wasn't enough, as Wilson won the rematch by about 10 percentage points.

Key Votes

2010

Overhaul the nation's health insurance system	NO
Allow for repeal of "don't ask, don't tell"	NO
Overhaul financial services industry regulation	NO
Limit use of new Afghanistan War funds to troop withdrawal activities	NO
Change oversight of offshore drilling and lift oil spill liability cap	NO
Provide a path to legal status for some children of illegal immigrants	NO
Extend Bush-era income tax cuts for two years	NO

2009

Expand the Children's Health Insurance Program	NO
Provide $787 billion in tax cuts and spending increases to stimulate the economy	NO
Allow bankruptcy judges to modify certain primary-residence mortgages	NO
Create a cap-and-trade system to limit greenhouse gas emissions	NO
Provide $2 billion for the "cash for clunkers" program	NO
Establish the government as the sole provider of student loans	NO
Restrict federally funded insurance coverage for abortions in health care overhaul	YES

CQ Vote Studies

	PARTY UNITY		PRESIDENTIAL SUPPORT	
	SUPPORT	OPPOSE	SUPPORT	OPPOSE
2010	97%	3%	24%	76%
2009	98%	2%	18%	82%
2008	98%	2%	82%	18%
2007	98%	2%	90%	10%
2006	97%	3%	92%	8%

Interest Groups

	AFL-CIO	ADA	CCUS	ACU
2010	7%	5%	75%	96%
2009	5%	0%	80%	96%
2008	7%	10%	100%	92%
2007	8%	10%	65%	96%
2006	7%	5%	91%	91%

South Carolina 2

Central and south — part of Columbia and suburbs, Hilton Head Island

The 2nd runs from the coast up the Georgia border and into central South Carolina, button-hooking north around Columbia to scoop up some of the capital city. The district's two ends take in wealthy areas — Columbia suburbs in Richland and Lexington counties, and Beaufort and Hilton Head Island in the south.

Government jobs remain the Columbia area's largest employment base, and ongoing private sector economic diversification has led to jobs in health care.

On the Georgia border, the Department of Energy's Savannah River Site nuclear complex (shared with the 3rd) still employs many district residents. Considerably poorer smaller towns and rural areas dot the land between Columbia and Hilton Head, a destination for retirees and tourists. Military issues are important here — recruits sweat at the Parris Island Marine Corps recruitment camp just up the shore from swank resorts. Fort Jackson in Richland County in the north and Beaufort Marine Corps Air Station add to the 2nd's heavy military presence.

Although the district overall is nearly two-thirds white, Allendale, Barnwell, Hampton and Jasper counties have high proportions of black residents. Many families in those counties live below the poverty line, relying on tenant farming and sharecropping. That area favored Barack Obama in the 2008 presidential election but makes up only a small portion of the 2nd's total vote. Overall, wealthy white-collar professionals in the north and along the coast push the 2nd into the Republican column.

Major Industry
Government, military, tourism, health care, agriculture

Military Bases
Fort Jackson (Army), 9,666 military, 2,654 civilian (2009); Beaufort Marine Corps Air Station, 4,700 military, 667 civilian; Marine Corps Recruit Depot (Parris Island), 1,961 military, 1,456 civilian (2011)

Cities
Columbia (pt.), 71,150; Hilton Head Island, 37,099

Notable
Mitchelville, established on Hilton Head Island during the Civil War, was the first U.S. town founded specifically for freed black slaves.

Rep. Jeff Duncan (R)

Capitol Office
225-5301
jeffduncan.house.gov
116 Cannon Bldg. 20515-4003; fax 225-3216

Committees
Foreign Affairs
Homeland Security
Natural Resources

Residence
Laurens

Born
Jan. 7, 1966; Greenville, S.C.

Religion
Baptist

Family
Wife, Melody Duncan; three children

Education
Clemson U., B.A. 1988 (political science)

Career
Real estate auction company owner; real estate broker; banker

Political Highlights
S.C. House, 2003-10

ELECTION RESULTS

2010 GENERAL

Jeff Duncan (R)	126,235	62.5%
Jane Dyer (D)	73,095	36.2%
John Dalen (CNSTP)	2,682	1.3%

2010 PRIMARY RUNOFF

Jeff Duncan (R)	37,352	51.5%
Richard Cash (R)	35,185	48.5%

Elected 2010; 1st term

Duncan plans to focus much of his legislative attention on cutting federal spending and promoting nuclear energy, specifically at the federal government's Savannah River site, a portion of which falls within his district.

He says energy independence is vital to national security and the health of the economy. He views nuclear power — and the Savannah River site, which has reactors as well as a national laboratory — as a key ingredient in that equation.

Two of his committee assignments will aid him in his quest: He serves on the Homeland Security and Natural Resources committees. He also serves on the Foreign Affairs panel.

Duncan, who developed solidly conservative credentials as a state legislator, is willing to work across the aisle on behalf of the nuclear facility. In particular, he wants to enlist the help of a fellow South Carolinian: James E. Clyburn, a member of the House Democratic leadership.

Duncan has taken an outside-the-box approach to cutting spending. His first bill would create a kind of anti-appropriations committee called the Committee on the Elimination of Nonessential Federal Programs, with the express purpose of reducing federal outlays.

In the state legislature in 2007, he sponsored a bill that would have allowed concealed-weapon permit holders to carry guns onto school properties. It was introduced following the shooting tragedy at Virginia Tech, when a student killed 33 people, including himself. Duncan argued that his bill would have allowed for self-defense and could have prevented or lessened the scope of the incident. The bill did not become law.

Duncan was a banker before being elected to the state House in 2002.

In 2010, he finished second in a six-candidate primary to succeed Republican J. Gresham Barrett, who ran unsuccessfully for governor. But he won the run-off, topping entrepreneur and anti-abortion activist Richard Cash by 3 percentage points.

He then won almost 63 percent of the vote in the general election, defeating Democrat Jane Dyer, a former Air Force pilot.

South Carolina 3

West — Anderson, Aiken, Greenwood

The largely rural, conservative 3rd District, on the eastern bank of the Savannah River, takes in South Carolina's hilly northwestern corner and the state's highest peaks.

To the south, an engineering base around the Energy Department's Savannah River Site nuclear complex (shared with the 2nd) keeps the regional economy relatively stable and lured Fortune 500 firms and several U.S. divisions of foreign companies to the area. Fujifilm's manufacturing and research facility in Greenwood employs more than 1,000 people in the area.

Agriculture is a key part of the economy, especially in southern areas: Aiken (shared with the 2nd), Edgefield and Saluda counties are among the state's top peach-producing counties. Cotton is another important crop. Farther north, Anderson's industrial economy relies on high-tech and automotive parts manufacturing, and many plants in a diminishing textile market have shifted to high-tech fiber manufacturing. The gem of Pickens County remains Clemson University, which is the economic and social nexus for the 3rd's northern tip.

The district votes solidly Republican in federal and statewide races. The less populous counties in the 3rd's midsection, including black-plurality McCormick County, are more rural and less GOP-leaning. The 3rd gave John McCain his highest percentage statewide in the 2008 presidential election.

Major Industry
Nuclear research, manufacturing, textiles, agriculture

Cities
Aiken (pt.), 26,744; Anderson, 26,686

Notable
Lake Thurmond, previously known as Clarks Hill Lake, was renamed for former GOP Sen. Strom Thurmond.

Rep. Trey Gowdy (R)

Capitol Office
225-6030
gowdy.house.gov
1237 Longworth Bldg. 20515-4004; fax 226-1177

Committees
Education & the Workforce
Judiciary
Oversight & Government Reform
   (Health Care, District of Columbia, Census & the
   National Archives - Chairman)

Residence
Spartanburg

Born
Aug. 22, 1964; Greenville, S.C.

Religion
Baptist

Family
Wife, Terri Gowdy; two children

Education
Baylor U., B.A. 1986 (history); U. of South Carolina,
J.D. 1989

Career
Lawyer

Political Highlights
Assistant U.S. attorney, 1994-2000; S.C. 7th Circuit
solicitor, 2001-10

ELECTION RESULTS

2010 GENERAL

Trey Gowdy (R)	137,586	63.4%
Paul Corden (D)	62,438	28.8%
Dave Edwards (CNSTP)	11,059	5.1%
Rick Mahler (LIBERT)	3,010	1.4%
C. Faye Walters (GREEN)	2,564	1.2%

2010 PRIMARY RUNOFF

Trey Gowdy (R)	54,412	70.7%
Bob Inglis (R)	22,590	29.3%

Elected 2010; 1st term

Gowdy has a clear test for evaluating whether to support a legislative proposal: Can the bill's sponsor point to the portion of the Constitution that empowers Congress to legislate in that area?

"I have to have a paradigm that you can consistently apply," the former federal prosecutor said. "My legislative paradigm would start with whether or not something is constitutional."

Gowdy, who also served as circuit solicitor (district attorney) for a decade, will be at home on the Judiciary Committee and among a crop of conservative, change-minded Republican freshmen.

Gowdy chairs the Oversight and Government Reform subcommittee with jurisdiction over the District of Columbia. The conservative Gowdy has little in common ideologically with Washington Mayor Vincent C. Gray, and the two are likely to clash on several issues, from abortion to gun control to school vouchers. But Gowdy holds out hope for a good working relationship.

"Our political philosophies are different. I'm not naive enough to think there's going to be a lot of political agreement between the mayor and I," Gowdy told Roll Call. "I'm hoping to find middle ground on the appropriateness of congressional oversight."

He also serves on the Education and the Workforce Committee.

Gowdy was born in Greenville as Harold W. Gowdy III. He earned a history degree from Baylor University, then a law degree from the University of South Carolina. His professional experience is rooted in the legal profession, and during his time as an assistant U.S. attorney, he prosecuted an "America's Most Wanted" suspect for robbery, carjacking and escaping authorities.

He challenged six-term Rep. Bob Inglis, who was something of a Republican maverick and had veered from his party on a few high-profile issues. Gowdy was able to paint Inglis as a Washington insider who became more moderate during his six terms in Congress.

Gowdy ran first in a five-candidate primary, then trounced Inglis in the runoff, winning more than 70 percent of the vote. He cruised to victory in November with almost 64 percent.

South Carolina 4

Northwest — Greenville, Spartanburg

Nestled in South Carolina's "upstate" region, the 4th is the state's most compact district and is centered on Greenville, the state's most-populous county. Greenville and Spartanburg counties together account for 95 percent of the district population. The 4th also takes in the northernmost tip of Laurens County and Union County, a heavily forested and lightly populated area.

Once known only for its textile mills, the area is now home to diversified manufacturing and warehousing industries. Michelin's North American base is in Greenville, and Spartanburg's BMW plant is the exclusive producer of several of the carmaker's sport utility models. Greenville has become a research hub, hosting the 250-acre International Center for Automotive Research — a public-private venture with Clemson University — and adjacent Millennium Campus office park. The area is no longer the textile capital of the world, but trade issues are still important here. Industry giant Milliken & Co. maintains its headquarters in Spartanburg. Agriculture also plays a role near Spartanburg, and the county's orchards yield large peach crops. The combination of business-oriented conservatives and social conservatives focused around Greenville's Bob Jones University keeps the 4th solidly Republican. John McCain won 60 percent of the 4th's 2008 presidential vote, and Republican Gov. Nikki Haley won both Greenville and Spartanburg counties easily in 2010.

Major Industry
Manufacturing, agriculture, textiles

Cities
Greenville, 58,409; Spartanburg, 37,013; Greer, 25,515; Mauldin, 22,889

Notable
Spartanburg was named for the local "Spartan Rifles" Revolutionary War militia.

Rep. Mick Mulvaney (R)

Capitol Office
225-5501
mulvaney.house.gov
1004 Longworth Bldg. 20515-4005; fax 225-0464

Committees
Budget
Small Business
  (Contracting & Workforce - Chairman)
Joint Economic

Residence
Indian Land

Born
July 21, 1967; Alexandria, Va.

Religion
Roman Catholic

Family
Wife, Pam Mulvaney; three children

Education
Georgetown U., B.S.F.S 1989 (international economics); U. of North Carolina, J.D. 1992

Career
Real estate developer; restaurateur; lawyer

Political Highlights
S.C. House, 2007-09; S.C. Senate, 2009-10

ELECTION RESULTS

2010 GENERAL

Mick Mulvaney (R)	125,834	55.1%
John M. Spratt Jr. (D)	102,296	44.8%

2010 PRIMARY

Mick Mulvaney (R)	unopposed

Elected 2010; 1st term

Mulvaney is part of a new generation of young fiscal conservatives in the Republican Party, but he doesn't lay all the blame for the government's money problems on Democrats.

"I got into politics in 2006 as a reaction to the Republican spending in the middle part of that decade," Mulvaney said. "I didn't like how my party was spending."

He defeated the man who served as chairman of the Budget Committee in the last two Congresses, Democrat John M. Spratt Jr., and he assumed a seat on the panel in the 112th Congress (2011-12).

After President Obama unveiled his fiscal 2012 budget, Mulvaney defended Republican budget priorities in Roll Call. "I don't know how a person can attack the notion of cutting $100 billion when there's a $1.65 trillion projected deficit," he said.

He praised the budget proposal put forth by Budget Chairman Paul D. Ryan, a Wisconsin Republican, as a "tremendous document."

A lawyer by training, Mulvaney has also worked in his family's home-building and real estate company. He landed a spot on the Small Business Committee, where he chairs the Contracting and Workforce Subcommittee. He also serves on the Joint Economic Committee.

He said he decided to run for Congress while watching Spratt get jeered at a November 2009 meeting on health care. Early in the new Congress, Mulvaney voted to repeal the health care overhaul law enacted in 2010. He hopes to follow that with "an alternative proposal that will bring some free-market reforms to health care," he said.

Mulvaney was elected to the state House in 2006 and the state Senate in 2008. When he decided to take on Spratt, he won the backing of both the tea party movement and the state's Republican establishment. He was unopposed for the GOP nomination.

Mulvaney won a relatively easy victory over Spratt, who had been in Congress since 1983, winning 55 percent of the vote to 45 percent for the incumbent.

South Carolina 5

North central — Rock Hill

The expansive 5th District covers all or part of 14 mostly rural counties in the north-central part of the state, stretching from near Charlotte, N.C., to the Columbia suburbs, while also spreading west to Newberry County and east to Dillon County. Tobacco farmers, white-collar Charlotte commuters and textile workers make this a conservative district, although it still clings to traditional Southern Democrat roots.

Lee, Darlington, Marlboro and Dillon counties grow wheat, as well as cotton for the textile mills that once dominated the economy here. Downsizing and closure of textile plants has led to high unemployment rates, and local officials struggle to keep existing textile jobs while expanding the local economy. Darlington and Dillon also depend heavily on tobacco farming.

Sumter, once the center of an agricultural landscape, also has manufacturing jobs. To the west, Shaw Air Force Base is a key employer. In York County to the north, Rock Hill hosts Winthrop University and white-collar commuters who work in Charlotte.

The 5th tends to favor Republicans in federal races, but conservative Democratic candidates who appeal to the district's numerous poor and rural residents can win in local races here. Democrats also are helped by the district's black residents, who make up 30 percent of the population — the largest of any South Carolina district except the black-majority 6th.

Major Industry
Agriculture, military, tobacco, textiles

Military Bases
Shaw Air Force Base, 6,000 military, 500 civilian (2011)

Cities
Rock Hill, 66,154; Sumter (pt.), 21,048

Notable
The annual Lee County Cotton Festival and Agricultural Fair celebrates the agricultural history of "King Cotton."

Rep. James E. Clyburn (D)

Capitol Office
225-3315
clyburn.house.gov
2135 Rayburn Bldg. 20515-4006; fax 225-2313

Committees
No committee assignments

Residence
Columbia

Born
July 21, 1940; Sumter, S.C.

Religion
African Methodist Episcopal

Family
Wife, Emily Clyburn; three children

Education
South Carolina State College, B.A. 1962 (social studies)

Career
State agency official, teacher

Political Highlights
Candidate for S.C. House, 1970; S.C. human affairs commissioner, 1974-92; sought Democratic nomination for S.C. secretary of state, 1978, 1986

ELECTION RESULTS

2010 GENERAL

James E. Clyburn (D)	125,459	62.9%
Jim Pratt (R)	72,661	36.4%

2010 PRIMARY

James E. Clyburn (D)	50,138	90.1%
Gregory Brown (D)	5,527	9.9%

2008 GENERAL

James E. Clyburn (D)	193,378	67.5%
Nancy Harrelson (R)	93,059	32.5%

Previous Winning Percentages
2006 (64%); 2004 (67%); 2002 (67%); 2000 (72%);
1998 (73%); 1996 (69%); 1994 (64%); 1992 (65%)

Elected 1992; 10th term

Clyburn, the third-ranking House Democrat, plays a multifaceted role in the leadership. He is a trusted peacemaking emissary to both urban liberals and the Blue Dog Coalition's rural moderates, and he also provides a back channel to the White House as a confidant of President Obama.

As majority whip in the 111th Congress (2009-10), Clyburn was the chief vote counter for his party and the highest ranking African-American in the House. With a comfortable Democratic margin, Clyburn usually could count on help from allies to move priorities such as the fiscal 2011 budget blueprint, Afghanistan War funding, the financial regulation law, the health care overhaul and the economic stimulus.

His title and his challenges are both different in the 112th Congress (2011-12).

With one less leadership position to go around in the minority, Clyburn chose not to force a confrontation with Minority Whip Steny H. Hoyer of Maryland. That avoided what might have been a bloody intramural battle, and Minority Leader Nancy Pelosi of California rewarded Clyburn by giving him a new title, assistant minority leader, and kept him in the third spot in the party's House hierarchy.

Whatever his title, Clyburn remains a highly visible member of the Democratic leadership team, making frequent appearances on television news shows.

He has said the party needs to do a better job getting out its message, and he will use his new post to help. "How do you expand the life of Medicare by 14 years and then lose the senior vote by 20 [percent]?" he said in a Roll Call interview two weeks after Election Day. "Seniors did not see in this health care vote all that we were doing."

Clyburn wasn't sitting on his hands before the election, waiting to see what happened in terms of the leadership as it appeared Democrats would lose their majority. In the 2009-10 election cycle, Clyburn's political action committee, Bridge PAC, doled out nearly $1 million to Democratic candidates and causes, according to CQ MoneyLine. "I'm trying to conduct myself in a way that people will think that I am a serious player for leadership, for no matter what the position might be," he said.

A glint of toughness sometimes cuts through Clyburn's folksy demeanor, as when he admonishes colleagues and the White House to avoid surprises. In July 2010, he rebuked the administration for suddenly firing — and later unsuccessfully trying to rehire — Shirley Sherrod, the Agriculture Department's Georgia director of rural development, after an edited video appeared showing her initial reluctance to help a white farmer 24 years ago. Clyburn told the New York Times that Obama "needs some black people around him" to prevent similar gaffes.

His own ties to Obama grew closer during the 2010 midterm campaign when he joined the president for a round of golf on Martha's Vineyard and in private chats. "I feel much more warmth to him than I used to," Clyburn said.

A 1960s civil rights activist, Clyburn leads his party's outreach to evangelical Christians. Clyburn says he stresses health care overhaul and environmental measures to religious groups, along with a gentle Biblical reminder that "faith without works is dead."

In South Carolina politics, Clyburn serves as the face of his party; he criticized the lack of political experience of Alvin Greene, the 2010 Democratic nominee against Republican Sen. Jim DeMint, and questioned whether he was a GOP "plant." Two years earlier, Clyburn urged former President Bill Clinton to tone down criticism of Obama. And when the 2008 primary season drew to a close, Clyburn was the first member of the House Democratic leadership team to endorse Obama. As Democrats gathered in Denver to make the nomination official, Clyburn was overcome by emotion. "I thought it would happen one day, but I never thought I would live to see it," he said.

Clyburn moved up rapidly in the leadership, becoming vice chairman of the House Democratic Caucus in 2003, then chairman in 2006. He was the first African-American elected to Congress from South Carolina since his great-uncle, George Washington Murray, served in the House during Reconstruction.

He was unopposed for the whip post at the start of the 110th Congress (2007-08) after a potential rival, Rahm Emanuel of Illinois, backed off, settling for Clyburn's old post as caucus chairman. Clyburn professes no interest in going elsewhere. "Any future I have will be in the House," he said in 2008.

A former appropriator, Clyburn calls earmarks for projects back home "an important part of my job" allowing him to serve poor families and rural communities. He stepped down as board chairman of a planned International African American Museum in Charleston after critics questioned several related earmarks. Clyburn said his resignation would avoid a potential conflict involving a nephew who worked as a project architect. He often emphasizes rural initiatives, such as his push in the 111th Congress for "rural star" energy conservation incentives and community health centers.

Clyburn attended Mather Academy, an all-black boarding school. He read books about his hero, Harry S. Truman, but his family belonged to the GOP — the party of Abraham Lincoln — until the mid-1960s, a time when most elected Southern Democrats were still clinging to segregation.

As a young man, Clyburn jumped into the civil rights movement, becoming an early member of the Student Nonviolent Coordinating Committee, affiliated with the Rev. Martin Luther King Jr.'s Southern Christian Leadership Conference. He was arrested several times.

After college, Clyburn became the state employment commission's lone black employee. In 1971, Democratic Gov. John West named him a special assistant for human resources, and in 1974 he became human affairs commissioner. In 1978 and 1986, he unsuccessfully sought the Democratic nomination for South Carolina secretary of state. When 1992 redistricting created the black-majority 6th District, he saw his opening. Robin Tallon, a white Democrat, chose not to seek re-election. Clyburn defeated four other black Democrats in the primary, won the general and has cruised to re-election since.

Key Votes

2010	
Overhaul the nation's health insurance system	YES
Allow for repeal of "don't ask, don't tell"	YES
Overhaul financial services industry regulation	YES
Limit use of new Afghanistan War funds to troop withdrawal activities	NO
Change oversight of offshore drilling and lift oil spill liability cap	YES
Provide a path to legal status for some children of illegal immigrants	YES
Extend Bush-era income tax cuts for two years	NO

2009	
Expand the Children's Health Insurance Program	YES
Provide $787 billion in tax cuts and spending increases to stimulate the economy	?
Allow bankruptcy judges to modify certain primary-residence mortgages	YES
Create a cap-and-trade system to limit greenhouse gas emissions	YES
Provide $2 billion for the "cash for clunkers" program	YES
Establish the government as the sole provider of student loans	YES
Restrict federally funded insurance coverage for abortions in health care overhaul	NO

CQ Vote Studies

	PARTY UNITY		PRESIDENTIAL SUPPORT	
	SUPPORT	OPPOSE	SUPPORT	OPPOSE
2010	99%	1%	93%	7%
2009	99%	1%	97%	3%
2008	99%	1%	18%	82%
2007	98%	2%	6%	94%
2006	94%	6%	35%	65%

Interest Groups

	AFL-CIO	ADA	CCUS	ACU
2010	100%	95%	13%	0%
2009	100%	100%	29%	0%
2008	100%	95%	56%	0%
2007	100%	95%	68%	0%
2006	100%	95%	50%	12%

South Carolina 6

Central and east — parts of Columbia, Florence and Charleston

A black-majority district designed to take in African-American areas in Columbia, Charleston and elsewhere in South Carolina, the 6th includes all or part of 15 counties in the eastern half of the state, starting near the North Carolina border and reaching the southeastern coast. Taking in some of South Carolina's poorest counties, the 6th has the state's lowest median household income, although it also includes historically black South Carolina State University and other institutions of higher learning.

In the rural portions of the district, many families depend on tobacco, corn, cotton and related agribusiness. These regions have low education levels and sustained high unemployment rates. Economic downturns have further hurt traditional mainstay employment sources, such as the textile industry.

Monster Worldwide, an online job recruitment and career resources firm, and H.J. Heinz have facilities in the mostly middle-class Florence (shared with the 5th District), and Calhoun County now hosts a Starbucks roasting plant. A new Boeing 787 assembly plant near the Charleston International Airport (in the adjacent 1st) is expected to begin production and bring thousands of manufacturing jobs to the Lowcountry.

The 6th's portion of Columbia includes the state Capitol complex, and the state's flagship university, the University of South Carolina. State and local government agencies provide area jobs, while private-sector employment in health care has expanded. In the coastal parts of the 6th, maritime industries and tourism support the economy.

The 6th supports Democratic candidates at all levels. Its black-majority areas — including its shares of Columbia and North Charleston, which are more than 60 percent black — make the 6th a Democratic lock.

Major Industry

Agriculture, government, higher education, tourism

Cities

Columbia (pt.), 58,122; Florence (pt.), 32,885; North Charleston (pt.), 30,874; Charleston (pt.), 25,388; Sumter (pt.), 19,476

Notable

Clarendon County (pop. 34,971) can claim five South Carolina governors, all related to each other.

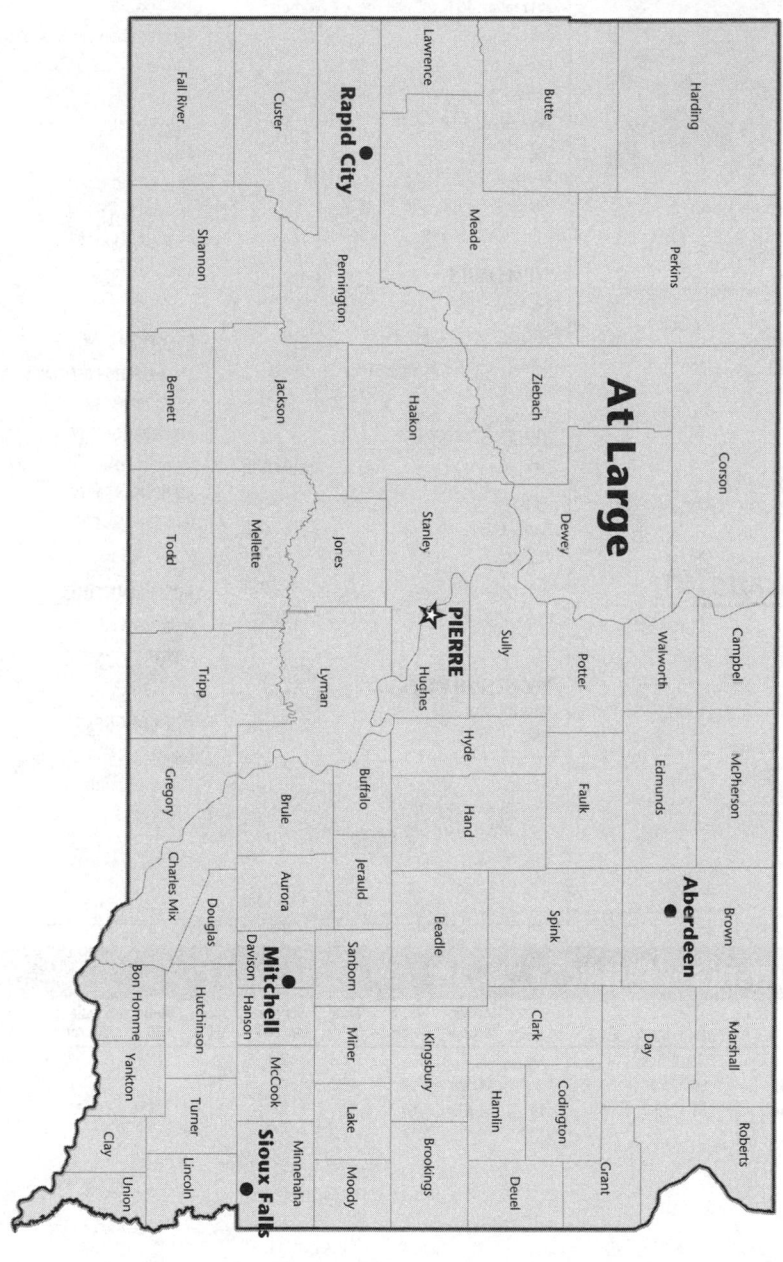

Gov. Dennis Daugaard (R)

First elected: 2010
Length of term: 4 years
Term expires: 1/15
Salary: $98,031
Phone: (605) 773-3212
Residence: Garretson
Born: June 11, 1953; Garretson, S.D.
Religion: Lutheran
Family: Wife, Linda Daugaard; three children
Education: U. of South Dakota, B.S. 1975 (government); Northwestern U., J.D. 1978
Career: Child welfare agency fundraiser and director; bank executive; lawyer
Political highlights: S.D. Senate, 1997-2003; lieutenant governor, 2003-11

ELECTION RESULTS

2010 GENERAL

Dennis Daugaard (R)	195,046	61.5%
Scott Heidepriem (D)	122,037	38.5%

Lt. Gov. Matt Michels (R)

First elected: 2010
Length of term: 4 years
Term expires: 1/15
Salary: $120,000
Phone: (605) 773-3661

LEGISLATURE

Legislature: January-March
Senate: 35 members, 2-year terms
2011 ratios: 30 R, 5 D; 28 men, 7 women
Salary: $6,000
Phone: (605) 773-3821
House: 70 members, 2-year terms
2011 ratios: 50 R , 19 D, 1 I; 56 men, 14 women
Salary: $6,000
Phone: (605) 773-3851

TERM LIMITS

Governor: 2 consecutive terms
Senate: 2 consecutive terms
House: 4 consecutive terms

URBAN STATISTICS

CITY	POPULATION
Sioux Falls	153,888
Rapid City	67,956
Aberdeen	26,091
Brookings	22,056
Watertown	21,482

REGISTERED VOTERS

Republican	46%
Democrat	37%
Others	17%

POPULATION

2010 population	814,180
2000 population	754,844
1990 population	696,004
Percent change (2000-2010)	+7.9%
Rank among states (2010)	46
Median age	37.0
Born in state	66.1%
Foreign born	2.2%
Violent crime rate	186/100,000
Poverty level	14.2%
Federal workers	14,026
Military	3,910

ELECTIONS

STATE ELECTION OFFICIAL
(605) 773-3537
DEMOCRATIC PARTY
(605) 271-5405
REPUBLICAN PARTY
(605) 224-7347

MISCELLANEOUS

Web: www.sd.gov
Capital: Pierre

U.S. CONGRESS

Senate: 1 Democrat, 1 Republican
House: 1 Republican

2010 Census Statistics by District

District	2008 Vote for President Obama	McCain	White	Black	Asian	Hispanic	Median Income	White Collar	Blue Collar	Service Industry	Over 64	Under 18	College Education	Rural	Sq. Miles
AL	45%	53%	85%	1%	1%	3%	$44,828	59%	25%	17%	14%	25%	25%	48%	75,885
STATE	45	53	85	1	1	3	44,828	59	25	17	14	25	25	48	75,885
U.S.	53	46	64	12	5	16	51,425	60	23	17	13	25	28	21	3,537,438

Sen. Tim Johnson (D)

Capitol Office
224-5842
johnson.senate.gov
136 Hart Bldg. 20510; fax 228-5765

Committees
Appropriations
    (Military Construction-VA - Chairman)
Banking, Housing & Urban Affairs - Chairman
Energy & Natural Resources
Indian Affairs

Residence
Sioux Falls

Born
Dec. 28, 1946; Canton, S.D.

Religion
Lutheran

Family
Wife, Barbara Johnson; three children

Education
U. of South Dakota, B.A. 1969 (government), M.A.
1970 (government); Michigan State U., attended
1970-71 (political science); U. of South Dakota, J.D.
1975

Career
Lawyer; county prosecutor; state legislative aide

Political Highlights
S.D. House, 1979-83; S.D. Senate, 1983-87; U.S. House,
1987-97

ELECTION RESULTS

2008 GENERAL

Tim Johnson (D)	237,889	62.5%
Joel Dykstra (R)	142,784	37.5%

2008 PRIMARY

Tim Johnson (D)		unopposed

2002 GENERAL

Tim Johnson (D)	167,481	49.6%
John Thune (R)	166,957	49.5%

Previous Winning Percentages
1996 (51%); 1994 House Election (60%); 1992 House
Election (69%); 1990 House Election (68%); 1988
House Election (72%); 1986 House Election (59%)

Elected 1996; 3rd term

Johnson has survived a major health crisis and a razor-thin electoral victory to find himself in charge of the Banking, Housing and Urban Affairs Committee in the 112th Congress. A prairie populist who looks out for his state's miners, ranchers and farmers, the fourth-generation South Dakotan is known for his deliberate approach and centrist views.

His legislative interests tend to center on farm policy, renewable energy, American Indian affairs and veterans' needs. But Johnson was deeply immersed in banking and financial industry issues as chairman of the Banking panel's Subcommittee on Financial Institutions in the 111th Congress (2009-10), and he played a large role in writing and passing the financial regulatory overhaul bill in 2010.

In the 112th Congress (2011-12), Johnson will play an even larger role, taking the full-committee gavel from retired Democrat Christopher J. Dodd of Connecticut. After a hectic two years consumed by an overhaul of the regulatory structure governing Wall Street, the panel is likely to moderate both its pace of activity and its approach to the financial services sector.

Johnson in the past has been more supportive of the credit card industry than Dodd. The industry is a major employer in his state, and Johnson was the only Senate Democrat to oppose the 2009 legislation that tightened credit card regulation.

The major issue facing the committee in 2011 will be the restructuring of Fannie Mae and Freddie Mac and overhauling the mortgage industry.

"While mortgage credit continues to be available, it is almost exclusively through Fannie Mae, Freddie Mac and the [Federal Housing Administration]. Maintaining the housing finance system in this way is not sustainable for the long term," Johnson said at a Banking Committee hearing in March 2011.

While Johnson is favored by many in the industry as more receptive to their interests, those ties have made him a target of consumer groups and more liberal Democrats, some of whom pushed to have committee chairmen elected rather than chosen by seniority. The move failed, but stood as a shot fired by liberals across Johnson's bow.

He has never completely fallen in line with his party, part of the balancing act required of a Democrat from a Republican-leaning state. In 2005, Johnson was one of two Democrats who voted to cut off a filibuster against renewing the anti-terrorism law known as the Patriot Act. Earlier that year, he helped Republicans to victories on laws to shield gun manufacturers, dealers and importers from lawsuits. The National Rifle Association endorsed him in 2008 for the first time in his Senate career.

More recently, Johnson was one of nine Senate Democrats to vote against the $700 billion rescue plan for the financial services industry. And in April 2009, he joined Republicans on the full Banking panel to oppose legislation aimed at barring what critics call predatory practices by the credit card industry. That bill passed in the Senate, 90-5; Johnson was the only Democrat voting "no."

He uses his seat on the Appropriations Committee — and his chairmanship of the panel on Military Construction and Veterans Affairs — to direct funds to an array of areas in his state, particularly those aimed at helping veterans and American Indians.

Johnson also is a member of the Indian Affairs Committee and cosponsored the Indian Veterans Housing Opportunity Act, a bill to keep American Indian veterans receiving disability compensation and survivor benefits from becoming ineligible for housing benefits under the Native American

Housing Assistance and Self-Determination Act.

On the Energy and Natural Resources Committee, Johnson has displayed a keen interest in expanding the use of ethanol and soy-based biodiesel as alternative fuels that can bolster his state's economy. He also seeks to expand the energy uses of wind, another resource South Dakota has in abundance.

He wrote a provision in the 2002 farm bill that required mandatory country-of-origin labels on fruit, vegetables and meat — helpful to the ranchers in his state — and then fought for years to get the provision implemented. He was repeatedly thwarted by congressional Republicans and the Bush administration, but the labeling requirement was part of a 2008 rewrite of the farm bill. The measure is expected to be reauthorized in 2012.

Johnson has developed a comfortable working relationship with Republican Sen. John Thune, who almost unseated Johnson in 2002. The two charter planes together for the long trips home and team up on issues important to their largely rural state.

Johnson and his family have dealt with more than their fair share of health problems. He and his wife are both cancer survivors; he had successful surgery for prostate cancer in 2004; Barbara Johnson has twice fought breast cancer. And he is deaf in his left ear as a result of surgery to remove a benign tumor discovered on his eardrum when he underwent a physical for and was refused admission to the U.S. military during the Vietnam War.

His biggest scare came at the start of the 110th Congress (2007-08), when he was recovering from emergency brain surgery. In December 2006, he suffered from a congenital arteriovenous malformation that caused bleeding in his brain and produced stroke-like symptoms. Before Congress convened in January 2007, the Senate held its collective breath; Democrats had just won a majority by the narrowest of margins, gaining control of 51 seats to 49 for Republicans.

Johnson was hospitalized for months and slowly regained strength, speech and mobility. He returned to work in September 2007.

Johnson won a seat in the state legislature in 1978, then ran for Congress in 1986 when Democrat Tom Daschle gave up the state's lone House seat for a Senate race. After a narrow primary win, Johnson easily won the general election.

When Johnson was elected to the House, Barbara gave up her tenured position as a University of South Dakota social work professor to move to Washington, where she became a public school social worker. All three Johnson children went to school in Virginia but returned to South Dakota for college. Their son Brooks served with the Army in Iraq and Afghanistan, making Johnson one of a handful of lawmakers to have a son or daughter see active duty in either war.

Family issues almost stopped Johnson from running for the Senate, even though he had a good shot at unseating GOP incumbent Larry Pressler in 1996. In the middle of the campaign, Johnson's wife first learned of her cancer. But she encouraged him to stay in, and he went on to win the race in another close call — by just 8,600 votes.

Six years later, his re-election bid sparked a titanic showdown between the two political parties. Thune was personally recruited by Bush to take on Johnson, while Daschle, by then the Senate's Democratic leader, jumped in full throttle to defend Johnson. Throughout the campaign, Johnson's quiet style was compared with that of the more gregarious and handsome Thune. Johnson prevailed by 524 votes. (Thune later unseated Daschle.)

Johnson ran for re-election in 2008 despite his health problems. His colleagues jumped in early to raise campaign funds while he was still hospitalized. Republicans, uncertain whether they would face Johnson or another Democratic candidate, struggled to recruit a high-profile challenger. Johnson handily defeated the eventual GOP nominee, state Rep. Joel Dykstra.

Key Votes

2010

Pass budget reconciliation bill to modify overhauls of health care and federal student loan programs	YES
Proceed to disapproval resolution on EPA authority to regulate greenhouse gases	NO
Overhaul financial services industry regulation	YES
Limit debate to proceed to a bill to broaden campaign finance disclosure and reporting rules	YES
Limit debate on an extension of Bush-era income tax cuts for two years	YES
Limit debate on a bill to provide a path to legal status for some children of illegal immigrants	YES
Allow for a repeal of "don't ask, don't tell"	YES
Consent to ratification of a strategic arms reduction treaty with Russia	YES

2009

Prevent release of remaining financial industry bailout funds	NO
Make it easier for victims to sue for wage discrimination remedies	YES
Expand the Children's Health Insurance Program	YES
Limit debate on the economic stimulus measure	YES
Repeal District of Columbia firearms prohibitions and gun registration laws	YES
Limit debate on expansion of federal hate crimes law	YES
Strike funding for F-22 Raptor fighter jets	YES

CQ Vote Studies

	PARTY UNITY		PRESIDENTIAL SUPPORT	
	SUPPORT	OPPOSE	SUPPORT	OPPOSE
2010	98%	2%	100%	0%
2009	95%	5%	96%	4%
2008	80%	20%	44%	56%
2007	88%	12%	29%	71%
2006	83%	17%	57%	43%
2005	83%	17%	45%	55%
2004	90%	10%	60%	40%
2003	93%	7%	50%	50%
2002	85%	15%	68%	32%
2001	87%	13%	71%	29%

Interest Groups

	AFL-CIO	ADA	CCUS	ACU
2010	94%	85%	27%	0%
2009	89%	95%	57%	8%
2008	100%	80%	75%	12%
2007	89%	40%	80%	0%
2006	87%	85%	50%	12%
2005	86%	95%	60%	13%
2004	100%	85%	59%	11%
2003	100%	80%	39%	15%
2002	100%	90%	53%	15%
2001	94%	85%	64%	32%

Sen. John Thune (R)

Capitol Office
224-2321
thune.senate.gov
511 Dirksen Bldg. 20510-4103; fax 228-5429

Committees
Agriculture, Nutrition & Forestry
Budget
Commerce, Science & Transportation
Finance

Residence
Sioux Falls

Born
Jan. 7, 1961; Pierre, S.D.

Religion
Protestant

Family
Wife, Kimberley Thune; two children

Education
Biola U., B.S. 1983 (business administration); U. of
South Dakota, M.B.A. 1984

Career
Lobbyist; local governments association executive;
U. S. Small Business Administration official; congres-
sional aide

Political Highlights
S.D. Republican Party executive director, 1989-91;
S.D. railroad director, 1991-93; U.S. House, 1997-2003;
Republican nominee for U.S. Senate, 2002

ELECTION RESULTS

2010 GENERAL

John Thune (R)		unopposed

2010 PRIMARY

John Thune (R)		unopposed

2004 GENERAL

John Thune (R)	197,848	50.6%
Tom Daschle (D)	193,340	49.4%

Previous Winning Percentages
2000 House Election (73%); 1998 House Election
(75%); 1996 House Election (58%)

Elected 2004; 2nd term

Thune's media skills, popularity among his colleagues and good looks have kept Republicans buzzing about just how high his political star might rise. But despite his heightened profile, Thune has been careful to stay rooted in South Dakota, a state that ousted his powerful predecessor, who was perceived as "going Washington."

After months of speculation, he announced in February 2011 that he would not be a candidate for president in 2012. Instead, he turned his attention to a potential move up the Senate leadership ladder and a new assignment on the Finance Committee in the 112th Congress (2011-12).

As the Republican Policy Committee chairman, No. 4 in the GOP leadership, Thune aims to craft his party's legislative stands. His colleagues unanimously elected him to the job in June 2009 after Nevada's John Ensign stepped down from the post following his public admission of an affair with his former campaign treasurer.

The announcement by Minority Whip Jon Kyl of Arizona that he would not run for re-election in 2012 set off a scramble as GOP senators began looking ahead to the 113th Congress (2013-14), with some quickly announcing their candidacies for various leadership posts. Thune moved more deliberately but is considered a potential candidate for the No. 2 Whip or No. 3 Conference chairman positions.

While Thune has taken himself out of the running for the White House for now, he has not removed himself from the debate about what his party should stand for. During the second term of the Bush administration, he said, "we did lose our way, and the American electorate took it out on us."

As Policy Committee chairman, Thune's go-to maneuver has been to try to attach unrelated amendments to high-profile Democratic bills, setting up politically uncomfortable votes for moderates in the opposing party.

In the summer of 2009, Thune nearly succeeded in adding to a hate crimes expansion measure an amendment that would have allowed licensed gun owners to carry concealed firearms across state lines in accordance with the laws in their home states. Thune managed to get 20 Democrats to vote for the amendment, which fell two votes short of adoption.

Another frequent target for Thune's amendments is the Troubled Asset Relief Program (TARP), a government initiative to pay billions to help keep failing banks afloat in the midst of the economic crisis.

Thune voted for the creation of TARP in 2008, but a year and a half later he offered an amendment to an unemployment insurance bill that would have effectively killed the program. A couple of months after that attempt failed, he offered a similar amendment to the debt ceiling legislation, again forcing Democrats to go on the record as voting in favor of keeping TARP alive.

Thune's policy positions are conservative across the board, although he tends to stay clear of the fray on explosive issues such as gay marriage and abortion. "Most social conservatives also tend to be fiscal conservatives," Thune said. "That is the thing that unites all wings of the Republican Party."

As a member of the Budget Committee, he called President Obama's budget plans "phantom leadership."

"The Democrats control the United States Senate. They have the majority. You have the president of the United States in the White House. Neither has put forward anything yet that is meaningful and serious when it comes to spending reduction and debt reduction," he said on MSNBC in March 2011.

Thune fought vehemently against the health care overhaul enacted in 2010, both as a frequent guest on news programs and as a behind-the-scenes agent of his party, attempting to persuade moderate Democrats that a vote for the bill would come back to haunt them come election time.

As a member of the Commerce, Science and Transportation Committee, he opposes efforts to cap greenhouse gas emissions and impose an emissions credit trading program. He backed a GOP proposal in early 2011 that would have barred the EPA from imposing such a system through regulatory means.

Thune's parochial concerns have made him some strange bedfellows. As a member of the Agriculture, Nutrition and Forestry Committee, he introduced a bill with New York Democrat Charles E. Schumer to stave off the possibility of the so-called "cow tax," which could charge farm states for the animals' methane emissions.

A former Armed Services Committee member, Thune has been a supporter of the wars in Iraq and Afghanistan. He has been critical of the withdrawal plans put forward by the administration, saying that Obama is trying to "have it both ways" by providing a timeline for Democrats skeptical of the additional troop deployment while saying transitions will be based on conditions on the ground to satisfy Republicans.

Thune showed his own party that he was no pushover just five months after he moved to the Senate, when Ellsworth Air Force Base was slated to be shut down by the Base Realignment and Closure Commission. He opposed the confirmation of Bush's embattled nominee for U.N. ambassador, John R. Bolton, and refused to budge for three months, holding up consideration of a defense authorization bill. Ultimately, Ellsworth was removed from the closure list. Since then, he said that he has worked to "BRAC-proof the base" by lobbying for earmarks and small legislative provisions that will keep Ellsworth central to the Air Force mission.

Thune grew up in the small town of Murdo, about 40 miles south of Pierre. He comes from a family of New Deal Democrats but was won over by Ronald Reagan's policies and world view.

He aspired to become a professional basketball player but said he was thwarted from reaching his NBA dreams by a "lack of leaping." But his aptitude on the court helped him break into politics. Impressed with Thune's performance in a game during his freshman year of high school, South Dakota GOP Rep. James Abdnor, who played high school basketball against Thune's father, a member of the South Dakota High School Basketball Hall of Fame, struck up a conversation with the young man and they stayed in touch over the years. After graduate school, Thune worked for then-Sen. Abdnor. After Abdnor was defeated for re-election in 1986 by Democratic Rep. Tom Daschle, Thune followed Abdnor to the Small Business Administration.

In 1989, Thune served a few months as deputy staff director of the Senate Small Business Committee and then returned to South Dakota, where he was executive director of the state Republican Party and then state railroad director. In 1993, he was named executive director of the South Dakota Municipal League, an association of local governments.

Three years later, Thune vied for the state's lone House seat, vacated by Democrat Tim Johnson, who ran successfully for the Senate. Thune defeated Lt. Gov. Carole Hillard in the GOP primary, then handily defeated Rick Weiland, a longtime aide to Daschle, by 21 percentage points in the general election. He was re-elected by impressive margins in 1998 and 2000.

In 2002, he challenged Johnson for his Senate seat, losing a squeaker by 524 votes. In 2004, avenging his patron Abdnor, Thune successfully turned the election into a referendum on Daschle's role as leader of his party and his posh lifestyle as a Washingtonian, eking out a victory over Daschle by just more than 1 percentage point.

Democrats didn't field a candidate against Thune in 2010.

Key Votes

2010

Pass budget reconciliation bill to modify overhauls of health care and federal student loan programs	NO
Proceed to disapproval resolution on EPA authority to regulate greenhouse gases	YES
Overhaul financial services industry regulation	NO
Limit debate to proceed to a bill to broaden campaign finance disclosure and reporting rules	NO
Limit debate on an extension of Bush-era income tax cuts for two years	YES
Limit debate on a bill to provide a path to legal status for some children of illegal immigrants	NO
Allow for a repeal of "don't ask, don't tell"	NO
Consent to ratification of a strategic arms reduction treaty with Russia	NO

2009

Prevent release of remaining financial industry bailout funds	YES
Make it easier for victims to sue for wage discrimination remedies	NO
Expand the Children's Health Insurance Program	NO
Limit debate on the economic stimulus measure	NO
Repeal District of Columbia firearms prohibitions and gun registration laws	YES
Limit debate on expansion of federal hate crimes law	NO
Strike funding for F-22 Raptor fighter jets	NO

CQ Vote Studies

	PARTY UNITY		PRESIDENTIAL SUPPORT	
	Support	Oppose	Support	Oppose
2010	99%	1%	33%	67%
2009	98%	2%	42%	58%
2008	95%	5%	76%	24%
2007	88%	12%	82%	18%
2006	95%	5%	87%	13%
2005	87%	13%	86%	14%
2002	83%	17%	82%	18%
2001	92%	8%	81%	19%

Interest Groups

	AFL-CIO	ADA	CCUS	ACU
2010	7%	0%	100%	100%
2009	6%	10%	86%	100%
2008	30%	10%	100%	84%
2007	16%	20%	55%	88%
2006	20%	0%	92%	100%
2005	21%	10%	93%	92%
2002	13%	10%	90%	88%
2001	33%	10%	91%	80%

Rep. Kristi Noem (R)

Capitol Office
225-2801
noem.house.gov
226 Cannon Bldg. 20515-4101; fax 225-5823

Committees
Education & the Workforce
Natural Resources

Residence
Castlewood

Born
Nov. 30, 1971; Watertown, S.D.

Religion
Evangelical Christian

Family
Husband, Bryon Noem; three children

Education
Northern State U., attended 1990-92; South Dakota
State U., attending (political science)

Career
Farmer; rancher; hunting lodge owner; restaurant
manager

Political Highlights
S.D. House, 2007-11 (assistant majority leader,
2009-11)

ELECTION RESULTS

2010 GENERAL

Kristi Noem (R)	153,703	48.1%
Stephanie Herseth Sandlin (D)	146,589	45.9%
B. Thomas Marking (I)	19,134	6.0%

2010 PRIMARY

Kristi Noem (R)	34,527	42.1%
Chris Nelson (R)	28,380	34.6%
Blake Curd (R)	19,134	23.3%

Elected 2010; 1st term

Noem made an immediate impact in Washington, claiming one of two freshman spots at the House GOP leadership table and quickly becoming a favorite on television news shows. She doesn't reject the "Palin of the Plains" appellation some have given her, but says she offers her own brand of solidly conservative politics.

Comparisons to the former Alaska governor aside, Noem was a favorite of tea party activists and party officials alike during the 2010 campaign, and her rapid rise through South Dakota politics has resulted in heightened expectations.

First elected to the state House in 2006, she became assistant majority leader in 2008. Two years later, she slipped past Democratic incumbent Stephanie Herseth Sandlin by just more than 2 percentage points to win election to the U.S. House.

While she has avoided being labeled a tea party candidate, Noem shares the movement's affinity for small government, free markets and transparency. "We need to get our economy back on track and get the excessive spending and government growth under control," said Noem, who joined the Republican Study Committee, the caucus of the most conservative House members.

Representing a state with a large agricultural sector, Noem hopes to play a role in developing a new farm bill — though she did not win a seat on the Agriculture Committee. (She serves on the Natural Resources and Education and the Workforce panels.) She says changes need to be made to federal crop subsidies, and while she is not opposed to continuing direct payments, Noem wants more focus on crop insurance and risk management.

In April 2011, she joined nine other lawmakers from Plains and Mountain states asking that the Agriculture Department redirect unspent Forest Service money to fighting the bark beetle infestation.

Noem was attending college when her father died in a farming accident. She left school to help run the family farm and ranch. She has raised cattle, showed quarter horses and enjoys pheasant and elk hunting.

South Dakota

At Large

A fertile agriculture-based economy keeps farmers and ranchers in business. But the lure of the state's cities — and their finance, technology and health care jobs — has driven steady migration away from the grasslands and cornfields.

Nearly two-thirds of all counties in the state have lost population since 2000, but Sioux Falls in the east and Rapid City in the west grew. Access to interstate highways and a concentration of jobs led to significant population growth in those areas, and new residents have settled in state capital Pierre, as well. The arid, hilly portion of the state around the Badlands, Mount Rushmore and other Black Hills attractions relies on ranching, mining and tourism.

South Dakota has one of the nation's highest percentages of American Indians, at nearly 9 percent of the population. But gaming revenue from Indian casinos has failed to eliminate the poverty conditions on reservations. Several of the nation's poorest counties are entirely within reservations here, including Ziebach County, which has the highest poverty rate in the country.

The Missouri River, which splits the state, used to be considered a political divide as well. Now, western ranching conservatives and increasing numbers of Republicans in the east edge out urban and farming Democrats at the polls. The GOP enjoys an 8-percentage-point voter registration advantage overall.

Major Industry
Agriculture, finance, tourism

Military Bases
Ellsworth Air Force Base, 3,589 military, 607 civilian (2011)

Cities
Sioux Falls, 153,888; Rapid City, 67,956

Notable
More than 200 Sioux were massacred in one day at Wounded Knee in 1890.

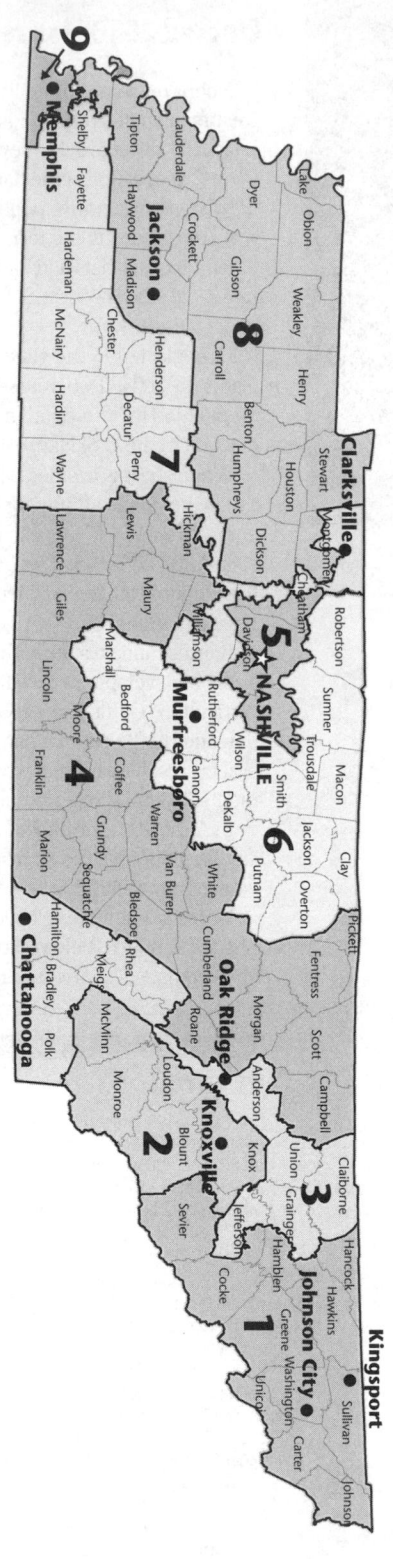

Gov. Bill Haslam (R)

First elected: 2010
Length of term: 4 years
Term expires: 1/15
Salary: $170,340
Phone: (615) 741-2001
Residence: Knoxville
Born: Aug. 23, 1958; Knoxville, Tenn.
Religion: Presbyterian
Family: Wife, Chrissy Haslam; three children
Education: Emory U., B.A. 1980 (history)
Career: Gas station and travel center company president; online and catalog sales CEO
Political highlights: Mayor of Knoxville, 2003-11

ELECTION RESULTS

2010 GENERAL

Bill Haslam (R)	1,041,545	65.9%
Mike McWherter (D)	529,851	33.5%

Lt. Gov. Ronald L. Ramsey (R)

First elected: 2007*
Length of term: 2 years
Term expires: 1/13
Salary: $57,027
Phone: (615) 741-2368

*Elected by the Senate

LEGISLATURE

General Assembly: 90 days over 2 years starting in January
Senate: 33 members, 4-year terms
2011 ratios: 20 R, 13 D; 26 men, 7 women
Salary: $19,009
Phone: (615) 741-2730
House: 99 members, 2-year terms
2011 ratios: 64 R, 34 D, 1 I; 82 men, 17 women
Salary: $19,009
Phone: (615) 741-2901

TERM LIMITS

Governor: 2 terms
Senate: No
House: No

URBAN STATISTICS

CITY	POPULATION
Memphis	646,889
Nashville-Davidson	626,681
Knoxville	178,874
Chattanooga	167,674
Clarksville	132,929

REGISTERED VOTERS

Voters do not register by party.

POPULATION

2010 population	6,346,105
2000 population	5,689,283
1990 population	4,877,185
Percent change (2000-2010)	+11.5%
Rank among states (2010)	17
Median age	37.3
Born in state	62.1%
Foreign born	4.0%
Violent crime rate	668/100,000
Poverty level	17.1%
Federal workers	67,862
Military	3,511

ELECTIONS

STATE ELECTION OFFICIAL
(615) 741-7956
DEMOCRATIC PARTY
(615) 327-9779
REPUBLICAN PARTY
(615) 269-4260

MISCELLANEOUS

Web: www.tn.gov
Capital: Nashville

U.S. CONGRESS

Senate: 2 Republicans
House: 7 Republicans, 2 Democrats

2010 Census Statistics by District

District	2008 Vote for President Obama	McCain	White	Black	Asian	Hispanic	Median Income	White Collar	Blue Collar	Service Industry	Over 64	Under 18	College Education	Rural	Sq. Miles
1	29%	70%	92%	2%	1%	3%	$37,054	52%	30%	18%	16%	21%	17%	45%	4,093
2	34	64	87	6	1	3	45,453	62	22	16	14	22	27	29	2,427
3	37	62	82	11	1	4	41,260	56	27	16	15	23	21	36	3,411
4	34	64	91	4	<1	3	37,410	49	35	16	16	23	14	68	10,038
5	56	43	62	25	3	9	46,519	64	20	17	11	23	31	11	894
6	37	62	84	7	1	5	46,576	55	31	14	11	25	20	47	5,480
7	34	65	77	14	3	4	61,387	66	20	14	11	26	33	39	6,292
8	43	56	72	23	1	3	37,644	51	33	17	13	25	15	53	8,262
9	77	23	27	63	2	7	36,958	57	24	19	10	27	23	0	321
STATE	42	57	76	17	1	5	42,943	57	26	16	13	24	22	36	41,217
U.S.	53	46	64	12	5	16	51,425	60	23	17	13	25	28	21	3,537,438

Sen. Lamar Alexander (R)

Capitol Office
224-4944
alexander.senate.gov
455 Dirksen Bldg. 20510-4204; fax 228-3398

Committees
Appropriations
Environment & Public Works
Health, Education, Labor & Pensions
Rules & Administration - Ranking Member
Joint Library
Joint Printing

Residence
Walland

Born
July 3, 1940; Maryville, Tenn.

Religion
Presbyterian

Family
Wife, Honey Alexander; four children

Education
Vanderbilt U., B.A. 1962 (Latin American history);
New York U., J.D. 1965

Career
Education consulting firm chairman; lobbyist;
university president; White House and congressional
aide; lawyer

Political Highlights
Republican nominee for governor, 1974; governor,
1979-87; Education secretary, 1991-93; sought
Republican nomination for president, 1996, 2000

ELECTION RESULTS

2008 GENERAL

Lamar Alexander (R)	1,579,477	65.1%
Robert D. Tuke (D)	767,236	31.6%
Edward L. Buck (I)	31,631	1.3%

2008 PRIMARY

Lamar Alexander (R)	unopposed

2002 GENERAL

Lamar Alexander (R)	891,420	54.3%
Bob Clement (D)	728,295	44.3%

Elected 2002; 2nd term

Alexander helps set the GOP's legislative agenda as Senate Republican Conference chairman, the No. 3 spot in the leadership, and he has set his sights on moving up. A former governor, he has become a spokesman for the interests of states as the federal government accrues more authority.

As chairman, he tries to develop consensus among his colleagues and then communicate their message. That approach sometimes leaves conservatives less than thrilled — they would rather highlight differences with Democrats. To mollify those lawmakers, Alexander gives them forums to let their voices be heard. North Carolina's Richard M. Burr, his former rival for the conference chairmanship, was assigned to manage promotion of the GOP health care alternative in the 111th Congress (2010-11). Oklahoma's James M. Inhofe was given time at a party caucus to explain his opposition to climate change legislation.

Alexander will need the support of conservatives to achieve his next leadership goal: succeeding the retiring Jon Kyl of Arizona as minority whip in the 113th Congress (2013-14).

Alexander says Republicans must cooperate with Democrats on areas of mutual agreement while outlining how they would do things differently. Nowhere is that more evident than in his role on the Environment and Public Works Committee, where the hard-line Inhofe is the top Republican.

On climate change, Alexander has urged President Obama to focus on areas where there is common ground between the two parties: doubling the number of electric vehicles (he recently leased a Nissan Leaf), increasing nuclear power, and boosting spending on energy research and development. He cosponsored legislation by North Dakota Democrat Byron L. Dorgan that would establish a nationwide electric-vehicle deployment program within the Energy Department to facilitate a national plug-in vehicle network. He also introduced a measure with Thomas R. Carper, a Delaware Democrat, to sharply reduce nitrogen oxide, sulfur dioxide and mercury emissions from power plants.

But Alexander sided with his party during negotiations on legislation to address the spring 2010 Gulf of Mexico oil spill, arguing against eliminating the cap on economic liability for damage from such spills. Alexander said removing the liability cap might drive oil drilling out of the gulf or turn over all offshore drilling to large companies that can afford such an open-ended risk.

The result, he warned, would be "more dependence on foreign oil, more dependence on tankers with a poor safety record, more dependence on Big Oil, and possibly higher prices."

He proved to be an ardent opponent of the Democrats' health care overhaul. Along with other Republican leaders, he urged Congress to push the reset button. "Our view, with all respect, is that this is a car that can't be recalled or fixed and that we ought to start over," he said at a White House health care summit.

Alexander, a former secretary of Education and Tennessee governor who made education the central focus of his administration, is likely to play a key role in writing an update of the George W. Bush-era No Child Left Behind law for elementary and secondary education.

Alexander also once served a stint as president of the University of Tennessee, making the Health, Education, Labor and Pensions Committee a natural fit. One of his proudest accomplishments is a bipartisan law aimed at maintaining U.S. leadership in science and technology by boosting funding for research and education in those fields. Although he called the measure "the most important piece of legislation in this session for our country's future," he lamented that it drew little attention when Bush signed it into law in 2007.

Alexander was elected to the conference chairmanship in December 2007, after the GOP whip, Trent Lott of Mississippi, announced his resignation from Congress and Kyl moved into the whip's job. To win the post, Alexander had to defeat the younger and more conservative Burr. Alexander trounced Burr by a vote of 31-16, drawing support from many of his older colleagues as well as younger moderates.

Alexander went after the whip post — the No. 2 leadership position — shortly after entering the Senate in 2003, campaigning as an optimistic, pragmatic conservative. But he couldn't fight off a last-minute challenge from Lott, a former majority leader who pulled off a one-vote victory in November 2006.

As a consolation prize of sorts, GOP leader Mitch McConnell of Kentucky named Alexander to a coveted seat on the Appropriations Committee. The assignment enables him to have a say in funding of the education, energy and environmental issues on which he spends most of his time.

As ranking Republican on the Energy-Water Subcommittee, Alexander carefully looks after the interests of the Tennessee Valley Authority, a power wholesaler, and his state's Oak Ridge National Laboratory, while pushing an agenda that would greatly boost the amount of money spent on physical sciences.

Alexander, who served two terms in the statehouse, has emerged as one of the most ardent advocates for state and local governments in Washington. During debate on the overhaul of the Higher Education Act in 2008, he joined state legislators who unsuccessfully tried to block a provision to penalize states that diminish their overall higher-education funding.

A seventh-generation Tennessean, Alexander was born and raised in the state's mountainous east. He worked his way through Vanderbilt University, where, as a student newspaper editor, he led a campaign to desegregate the school. After graduating with a degree in Latin American history, he earned a law degree at New York University. An accomplished musician, he played trombone, tuba and washboard at a Bourbon Street nightclub while clerking for a federal judge in New Orleans.

His first run for office, at age 34, was an unsuccessful 1974 bid for governor against Democrat Roy Blanton. Four years later, with the help and advice of a mentor and friend, Senate GOP leader Howard H. Baker Jr. of Tennessee, Alexander ran again. This time, he gained national attention by traversing the state on foot — he is a lifelong hiker — in what would become his trademark red-and-black plaid shirt. Voters liked it, electing him with 56 percent of the vote.

During eight years as governor, Alexander built a reputation as a pragmatist who brought businesses to Tennessee and pushed a major education package through a Democrat-controlled General Assembly. He then spent more than three years as the chief executive of Tennessee's state university system. He joined President George Bush's Cabinet in 1991, serving as secretary of Education for two years.

Alexander geared up for the 1996 presidential election, but his campaign foundered and he dropped out soon after finishing third in the New Hampshire primary. He set his sights on the 2000 nomination but stopped campaigning in the summer of 1999, when George W. Bush had become the front-runner.

Two years later, when Fred Thompson announced he was retiring after eight years in the Senate, Republicans looked to Alexander to take his place. In a bitter race against then-Rep. Bob Clement, Alexander won by 10 percentage points. He had an easier time in 2008, prevailing over Robert D. Tuke, a former state Democratic Party chairman, with 65 percent of the vote.

Key Votes

2010

Pass budget reconciliation bill to modify overhauls of health care and federal student loan programs	NO
Proceed to disapproval resolution on EPA authority to regulate greenhouse gases	YES
Overhaul financial services industry regulation	NO
Limit debate to proceed to a bill to broaden campaign finance disclosure and reporting rules	NO
Limit debate on an extension of Bush-era income tax cuts for two years	YES
Limit debate on a bill to provide a path to legal status for some children of illegal immigrants	NO
Allow for a repeal of "don't ask, don't tell"	NO
Consent to ratification of a strategic arms reduction treaty with Russia	YES

2009

Prevent release of remaining financial industry bailout funds	NO
Make it easier for victims to sue for wage discrimination remedies	NO
Expand the Children's Health Insurance Program	YES
Limit debate on the economic stimulus measure	NO
Repeal District of Columbia firearms prohibitions and gun registration laws	YES
Limit debate on expansion of federal hate crimes law	?
Strike funding for F-22 Raptor fighter jets	YES

CQ Vote Studies

	PARTY UNITY		PRESIDENTIAL SUPPORT	
	SUPPORT	OPPOSE	SUPPORT	OPPOSE
2010	87%	13%	52%	48%
2009	77%	23%	68%	32%
2008	92%	8%	77%	23%
2007	84%	16%	79%	21%
2006	94%	6%	93%	7%
2005	92%	8%	88%	12%
2004	95%	5%	98%	2%
2003	98%	2%	98%	2%

Interest Groups

	AFL-CIO	ADA	CCUS	ACU
2010	6%	10%	100%	80%
2009	39%	25%	86%	68%
2008	11%	25%	75%	72%
2007	21%	20%	82%	76%
2006	20%	5%	92%	72%
2005	21%	5%	100%	88%
2004	0%	15%	94%	92%
2003	0%	10%	100%	85%

Sen. Bob Corker (R)

Capitol Office
224-3344
corker.senate.gov
185 Dirksen Bldg. 20510-4205; fax 228-0566

Committees
Banking, Housing & Urban Affairs
Energy & Natural Resources
Foreign Relations
Special Aging - Ranking Member

Residence
Chattanooga

Born
Aug. 24, 1952; Orangeburg, S.C.

Religion
Protestant

Family
Wife, Elizabeth Corker; two children

Education
U. of Tennessee, B.S. 1974 (industrial management)

Career
Commercial real estate developer; construction
company owner

Political Highlights
Sought Republican nomination for U.S. Senate, 1994;
Tenn. Finance and Administration Department com-
missioner, 1995-96; mayor of Chattanooga, 2001-05

ELECTION RESULTS

2006 GENERAL

Bob Corker (R)	929,911	50.7%
Harold E. Ford Jr. (D)	879,976	48.0%

2006 PRIMARY

Bob Corker (R)	231,541	48.1%
Ed Bryant (R)	161,189	33.5%
Van Hilleary (R)	83,078	17.3%
Tate Harrison (R)	5,309	1.1%

Elected 2006; 1st term

Corker has established himself as a thoughtful, policy-oriented lawmaker willing to work with Democrats on the big issues. While he has sometimes struggled to turn bipartisan talk into tangible legislative accomplishment, he has scored the occasional victory.

A member of the Banking, Housing and Urban Affairs Committee, Corker led negotiations on the financial services overhaul in early 2010 for the GOP. When the talks appeared stalled, Corker continued to work on the measure for a month before Chairman Christopher J. Dodd, a Connecticut Democrat, cut the negotiations short and issued an overhaul bill of his own.

"I'd do it again," Corker said of his negotiations with Dodd. "The fact is, I was sent here by Tennesseans to try to solve problems. . . . I was glad to be involved even though we didn't get to a place I would have liked to have seen."

Though the negotiations failed, Dodd said he was "fortunate to have a strong partner in Sen. Corker."

As a junior member of the committee, Corker's talks with Dodd created tension within the GOP and hurt his relationship with the panel's ranking Republican, Richard C. Shelby of Alabama, for a time. "For a while, sure, it was strained," Corker said. "Is that all . . . bygones and by the wayside? Absolutely. If anything, during that time, we got to know each other in a different way than you normally would. I would say our relationship is probably better today than it was even before all this began."

Corker voted against the overhaul that the Senate passed in May 2010. Like many Republicans, he was critical of language allowing the government to dismantle large firms and expressed concern that the bill would create a new consumer protection regulator with too much unchecked authority.

Corker was also the main GOP negotiator on a bill to help ailing U.S. auto-makers in 2008. He offered a last-ditch proposal that would have required deep concessions from General Motors Corp. and Chrysler LLC bondholders and United Auto Workers. The legislation ultimately failed, but Corker's conditions were adopted by outgoing President George W. Bush when he provided $13.4 billion in emergency loans to GM and Chrysler.

Also in 2008, he helped write the $700 billion financial sector rescue package. Corker pressed for the $700 billion to be doled out in installments, an idea that became part of the law.

But when Congress voted in 2009 to release the second half, he voted no, saying the Obama administration had failed to provide specifics on how the money would be used. Corker and Democrat Mark Pryor of Arkansas introduced legislation to require the Treasury Department to provide greater detail about how banks were using the taxpayer dollars they received.

Corker, a member of the Energy and Natural Resources Committee, brought his bipartisan approach to energy policy within the "Gang of 10," a group of five Democrats and five Republicans who pushed unsuccessfully for an energy plan during the 110th Congress (2007-08) that included oil drilling, coal-to-liquid production and energy conservation. In the 112th Congress (2011-12), he could be a pivotal vote on climate change legislation. "We have to do something, when we do it, that drives our economy, that adds to our GDP, that makes us more energy secure and deals with climate at the same time," he said.

Corker is the ranking Republican on the Special Aging Committee and also sits on the Foreign Relations panel, where he has focused on the devastation left behind by the January 2010 earthquake in Haiti. Corker, who traveled there in July 2010, has used Foreign Relations hearings to express concern about the oversight of the reconstruction effort and the capacity of Haiti's government.

He is a workaholic; in the mid-1990s, he sometimes started his workdays as Tennessee's finance commissioner at 4 a.m. He admits his current job can be frustrating at times, especially after spending four years as mayor of Chattanooga. "Being mayor, you're able to create a vision and make it real," he said. "It's like being CEO of a company. Being in the Senate is like being on the board of directors. You don't see that immediate impact."

Corker, who was born in South Carolina, moved to Chattanooga when he was 11 after his father, a DuPont engineer, was transferred there. He adjusted quickly and was president of his senior class in high school. He worked a variety of jobs as a teenager, earned a college degree in industrial management, then took a job as a construction superintendent. College friends with coat-and-tie jobs were shocked when they would visit him on a job site. "I might not have shaved. I was drinking day-old coffee," he said. "I had mud all over me."

After four years, he started his own construction company with a pickup truck and $8,000 in savings. By the time he sold the company in 1990, it was operating in 18 states, with projects ranging from strip malls to apartments. He also owned Corker Group, a successful real estate development company, which he sold in 2006, retaining just two properties.

Corker's views on public policy were shaped by his work experience and his religion. In business, he felt a light hand from government was best. A church mission to Haiti in the 1980s opened his eyes to poverty and led him to an internal debate about whether he could make a bigger difference in public service or in the private sector. He began working weekends back home to revitalize inner-city neighborhoods and started a nonprofit group to help families secure affordable housing.

Corker first ran for the Senate in 1994, losing the primary to future Majority Leader Bill Frist. Corker had planned to run for governor that year but deferred to GOP Rep. Don Sundquist, who won and made Corker finance commissioner.

Elected mayor of Chattanooga in 2001, Corker launched a successful $120 million effort to transform the city's waterfront with a new park, a river walk, museum expansions and other features. Three years into his mayoral service, he was invited to join Frist and the senator's two young sons on their annual hike. Along the way, the GOP leader convinced Corker that he should consider running for the Senate seat from which Frist was retiring.

Corker entered the primary as an underdog against two former House members: Van Hilleary and Ed Bryant. They painted him as a moderate inconsistent on abortion. But Corker poured his own money into the race, and his branding as the only "non-career politician" in the field helped him win handily.

Democrats had cleared a path for Rep. Harold E. Ford Jr., a five-term centrist from Memphis who was seeking to become the first popularly elected African-American senator from the South. Corker emphasized his faith and his conservative values and made a pitch for votes by talking about his days "pouring concrete."

A late October television ad by the Republican National Committee satirized Ford's supposed attendance at a Super Bowl party sponsored by Playboy, closing with a white woman winking and saying, "Harold, call me." Democrats and civil rights groups erupted, calling the ad racist. Corker's campaign denounced the ad and asked the RNC to pull the commercial. Corker won by just less than 3 percentage points.

Corker has been mentioned as a possible chairman of the National Republican Senatorial Committee for the 2014 cycle, if he is re-elected in 2012.

Key Votes

2010

Pass budget reconciliation bill to modify overhauls of health care and federal student loan programs	NO
Proceed to disapproval resolution on EPA authority to regulate greenhouse gases	YES
Overhaul financial services industry regulation	NO
Limit debate to proceed to a bill to broaden campaign finance disclosure and reporting rules	NO
Limit debate on an extension of Bush-era income tax cuts for two years	YES
Limit debate on a bill to provide a path to legal status for some children of illegal immigrants	NO
Allow for a repeal of "don't ask, don't tell"	NO
Consent to ratification of a strategic arms reduction treaty with Russia	YES

2009

Prevent release of remaining financial industry bailout funds	YES
Make it easier for victims to sue for wage discrimination remedies	NO
Expand the Children's Health Insurance Program	YES
Limit debate on the economic stimulus measure	NO
Repeal District of Columbia firearms prohibitions and gun registration laws	YES
Limit debate on expansion of federal hate crimes law	?
Strike funding for F-22 Raptor fighter jets	YES

CQ Vote Studies

	PARTY UNITY		PRESIDENTIAL SUPPORT	
	SUPPORT	OPPOSE	SUPPORT	OPPOSE
2010	91%	9%	47%	53%
2009	87%	13%	54%	46%
2008	90%	10%	72%	28%
2007	87%	13%	83%	17%

Interest Groups

	AFL-CIO	ADA	CCUS	ACU
2010	6%	5%	100%	92%
2009	28%	10%	71%	84%
2008	10%	20%	75%	83%
2007	26%	20%	82%	83%

Rep. Phil Roe (R)

Capitol Office
225-6356
roe.house.gov
419 Cannon Bldg. 20515-4201; fax 225-5714

Committees
Education & the Workforce
  (Health, Employment, Labor & Pensions -
  Chairman)
Veterans' Affairs

Residence
Johnson City

Born
July 21, 1945; Clarksville, Tenn.

Religion
Methodist

Family
Wife, Pam Roe; three children

Education
Austin Peay State U., B.S. 1967 (biology); U. of
Tennessee, M.D. 1973

Military
Army Medical Corps, 1973-74

Career
Physician

Political Highlights
Johnson City Board of Commissioners, 2003-09
(mayor, 2007-09); sought Republian nomination for
U.S. House, 2006

ELECTION RESULTS

2010 GENERAL

Phil Roe (R)	123,006	80.8%
Michael Edward Clark (D)	26,045	17.1%
Kermit E. Steck (I)	3,110	2.0%

2010 PRIMARY

Phil Roe (R)	78,862	95.7%
Mahmood Sabri (R)	3,546	4.3%

2008 GENERAL

Phil Roe (R)	168,343	71.8%
Rob Russell (D)	57,525	24.5%
Joel Goodman (I)	3,988	1.7%
James W. Reeves (I)	2,544	1.1%

Elected 2008; 2nd term

Roe is a folksy-yet-firm conservative who has more faith in the private sector than in the federal government. His career as an obstetrician informs his skepticism about government intrusion into health care, while his stint as a budget-balancing city official gives him a disdain for Washington's spending habits.

Roe, the oldest Republican in the House freshman class of 2008, retired from medicine after a three-decade career in which he estimates he delivered more than 5,000 babies. He meets at least once a week to discuss health care with other physicians in Congress as part of the GOP Doctors' Caucus. Now chairman of the Education and the Workforce Subcommittee on Health, Employment, Labor and Pensions, he wants to draw attention to risks such as obesity and smoking and hopes to improve health care access without adding government paperwork or rules.

A frequent guest on news shows during the health care debate of 2009-10, he opposed the Democratic overhaul and proposed finding ways to reduce administrative costs that free up money to cover more individuals.

Aside from the policy differences, he also dissented from the process, complaining that neither he nor any of the dozen or so Republicans in the House with actual experience in practicing medicine were ever consulted by the majority. "Not one time," Roe told the Knoxville News Sentinel. "Not one of us was consulted about the health care bill."

After President Obama, in a rhetorical flourish, offered to go over the bill line by line with any lawmaker who asked, Roe accepted the offer, but said he never heard back from the White House.

Roe voted to repeal the law in January 2011. "If anybody believes this health care act is budget-neutral, I think you still believe in the Tooth Fairy," he said.

Roe is a member of the Republican Study Committee, the coalition of the most conservative House members, and he opposed most of Obama's economic initiatives during the 111th Congress (2009-10). Roe also was critical of the $700 billion financial rescue law passed in fall 2008, telling a local audience the following February that the federal government couldn't keep up with money being paid out. He called a House-passed bill in June 2009 aimed at curbing greenhouse gas emissions a "job-killer" and said lawmakers should offer businesses tax incentives to reduce emissions instead of applying a mandate.

Roe champions the "Fair Tax," which would replace all federal income taxes with a single national retail sales tax, or alternatively the flat tax espoused by Republican presidential hopeful Steve Forbes in the 1996 and 2000 GOP primaries.

On social issues, Roe is similarly conservative. He opposes abortion and favors cracking down on illegal immigration through tighter border security. He said he is "philosophically and morally opposed" to same-sex marriage and voted against the 2010 repeal of the statutory ban on gays and lesbians serving openly in the military.

Roe serves on the Veterans' Affairs Committee, where he sits on the Health Subcommittee and works to ensure generous treatment of those returning from war. Following reports about higher-than-usual levels of suicide among veterans returning from Iraq and Afghanistan, Roe said, "These service members are returning to their local communities and are not afforded the level of support that our active component soldiers receive when they return to their respective bases. This is a serious problem that must be addressed immediately."

Serving in the House indulges Roe's penchant for staying busy. An avid reader of fiction and biographies of historic figures such as Thomas Jefferson and John Adams, he also is a golfer, runner and outdoorsman. He has competed in Marine Corps marathons and climbed Mount Rainier four times, including ascending to the summit on his 60th birthday in 2005.

Roe grew up in Clarksville. His father worked in a factory and his mother was a bank teller. He graduated from high school in the final year in which its black and white students were segregated, something he said left an impression because it denied him a chance to make more friends. He recalled the experience in his first House floor speech, when he saluted Obama for becoming the nation's first African-American president.

Roe attended Austin Peay State University in his hometown and decided to become a doctor because he enjoyed science. He was so fond of his chemistry professor that he later endowed a scholarship in the educator's name at the school. He graduated from the University of Tennessee's medical school and was drafted into service in Vietnam, but said he received a one-year deferment because his services were needed at the local hospital. With the war in Vietnam winding down, he was sent to Korea for 13 months.

After setting up a successful practice in Johnson City in the northeast part of Tennessee, he became immersed in civic issues, serving six years on the city's planning commission. He also became a fundraiser for Austin Peay and the East Tennessee State University Foundation board.

In 2003, Roe was elected to the Johnson City Board of Commissioners, where after four years the commission elected him mayor. As both a commissioner and mayor, Roe boasts of passing six balanced budgets while cutting spending and not increasing taxes. "This [federal] government is huge, but it would not be that hard to balance the budget," he said. "There's just so many little programs that just keep on and on."

Roe first competed in the GOP primary in 2006, when Republican Bill Jenkins was retiring, but came in fourth behind David Davis, who won the seat. Roe ran again two years later, attacking Davis for earmarks — funding set-asides for members' districts — and ties to oil companies. He won by 482 votes, becoming the first Tennessee candidate in 42 years to defeat an incumbent congressman in a primary. He trounced Democrat Rob Russell in November in a district that gave John McCain 70 percent of its presidential vote, the Arizona GOP senator's highest percentage statewide. Roe won 81 percent of the vote in 2010.

Key Votes

2010

Overhaul the nation's health insurance system	NO
Allow for repeal of "don't ask, don't tell"	NO
Overhaul financial services industry regulation	NO
Limit use of new Afghanistan War funds to troop withdrawal activities	NO
Change oversight of offshore drilling and lift oil spill liability cap	NO
Provide a path to legal status for some children of illegal immigrants	NO
Extend Bush-era income tax cuts for two years	YES

2009

Expand the Children's Health Insurance Program	NO
Provide $787 billion in tax cuts and spending increases to stimulate the economy	NO
Allow bankruptcy judges to modify certain primary-residence mortgages	NO
Create a cap-and-trade system to limit greenhouse gas emissions	NO
Provide $2 billion for the "cash for clunkers" program	YES
Establish the government as the sole provider of student loans	NO
Restrict federally funded insurance coverage for abortions in health care overhaul	YES

CQ Vote Studies

	PARTY UNITY		PRESIDENTIAL SUPPORT	
	SUPPORT	OPPOSE	SUPPORT	OPPOSE
2010	97%	3%	31%	69%
2009	96%	4%	26%	74%

Interest Groups

	AFL-CIO	ADA	CCUS	ACU
2010	7%	0%	88%	96%
2009	14%	5%	87%	92%

Tennessee 1

Northeast — Tri-cities, Morristown

Rolling hills and mountains cover the 1st, which borders Virginia and North Carolina. The district combines a manufacturing sector to the east with smaller agricultural and tourism centers to the west and south. Some of the steady population growth throughout the district in the last decade has been driven by Hispanic residents settling in the 1st.

Near Virginia, the Tri-Cities of Kingsport, Johnson City and Bristol anchor the district's economy. They focus their energies on chemicals, auto parts and drug manufacturing, but the region frequently struggles with high unemployment rates.

Some growth in retail sales boosted the local economy but has not been completely able to offset several years of downturns. East Tennessee State University in Johnson City is a key employer and a medical hub for much of this part of Appalachia. To the northwest, Hancock County is severely impoverished. Farmers in Washington, Cocke and Greene counties raise livestock, tobacco and fruit, providing one of the only sources of economic stability here.

Hamblen County offers outdoor recreation, and Morristown, which is known for its Civil War heritage, boasts popular water sports sites. Farther south, tourists visit the Great Smoky Mountains National Park and the region's excursion circuit of outlet shopping malls and neon-lit amusement parks. Gatlinburg's Star Cars Museum houses famous cars from movies, and the Dollywood theme park in Pigeon Forge lures millions of tourists annually.

East Tennessee's strong Republican lean dates to the Civil War. In 2008, John McCain won the district with 70 percent of its presidential vote, his highest percentage statewide, and he did not take less than 65 percent of the vote in any of the 1st's dozen counties. Gov. Bill Haslam won every county wholly or partly in the district — some of them by considerably more than 3-to-1 margins — in the 2010 gubernatorial race.

Major Industry

Tourism, health care, manufacturing, farming

Cities

Johnson City, 63,152; Kingsport, 48,205; Morristown, 29,137; Bristol, 26,702; Greeneville, 15,062

Notable

Jonesborough, the state's oldest settlement, is home to the National Storytelling Festival.

Rep. John J. "Jimmy" Duncan Jr. (R)

Capitol Office
225-5435
www.house.gov/duncan
2207 Rayburn Bldg. 20515-4202; fax 225-6440

Committees
Natural Resources
Transportation & Infrastructure
 (Highways & Transit - Chairman)

Residence
Knoxville

Born
July 21, 1947; Lebanon, Tenn.

Religion
Presbyterian

Family
Wife, Lynn Duncan; four children

Education
U. of Tennessee, B.S. 1969 (journalism); George
Washington U., J.D. 1973

Military
Tenn. National Guard and Army Reserve, 1970-87

Career
Judge; lawyer

Political Highlights
Knox County Criminal Court judge, 1981-88

ELECTION RESULTS

2010 GENERAL

Jimmy Duncan (R)	141,796	81.8%
Dave Hancock (D)	25,400	14.6%
Joseph R. Leinweber Jr. (I)	2,497	1.4%
D. H. "Andy" Andrew (I)	1,993	1.1%

2010 PRIMARY

Jimmy Duncan (R)	unopposed

2008 GENERAL

Jimmy Duncan (R)	227,120	78.1%
Bob Scott (D)	63,639	21.9%

Previous Winning Percentages
2006 (78%); 2004 (79%); 2002 (79%); 2000 (89%);
1998 (89%); 1996 (71%); 1994 (90%); 1992 (72%);
1990 (81%); 1988 (56%); 1988 Special Election (56%)

Elected 1988; 12th full term

Duncan is an old-fashioned lawmaker. He eschews cell phones and email, while also paying little heed to the sort of party discipline that helps members move up the ranks. He has been passed over for senior positions in the past, but claimed the chairmanship of a key subcommittee in the 112th Congress that makes him a major player on highway funding.

"It's always easy to run as Santa Claus. It's always hard to run against Santa Claus. You just have people who won't say no to anybody. Both parties are at fault," he told a Blount County audience in August 2010.

Duncan's unwillingness to be a loyal Republican foot soldier lessened over the course of 2007, as he showed more loyalty to a Republican Party relegated to the minority.

Republican leaders that year passed over Duncan and three other senior members of the Transportation and Infrastructure Committee to award the party's top slot on the panel to John L. Mica of Florida. Duncan previously was bypassed for the chairmanship of the Resources Committee at the start of the 108th Congress (2003-04). In the 111th Congress (2009-10), he remained the fourth-ranking Republican on that panel, now called the Natural Resources Committee. Despite the removal of Alaska's Don Young from the top Republican spot, Duncan failed to move up the ladder — Young's slot went to Washington state's Doc Hastings, a more reliable party man and now chairman. Duncan ranks third on the committee in the 112th Congress (2011-12).

But Duncan, who had chaired subcommittees during the previous GOP reign, managed to snag a choice gavel with Republicans back in the majority. As chairman of the Transportation Subcommittee on Highways and Transit, he is positioned to play a major role in writing a new highway bill in the 112th. Duncan is a budget hawk, but has felt no compunction in the past about forwarding constituents' requests for projects to the committee, reasoning that they don't add to the bill's cost and if his district doesn't get the money, somebody else's will. But under the GOP earmark moratorium, he withdrew all requests.

Duncan has charted his path in Congress using the experience of his father, Republican John J. Duncan, who held the east Tennessee seat for more than 23 years. When Republicans took control of Congress in 1994, Duncan Jr. passed up a seat on the Ways and Means Committee, where his father served for two decades without ever being a chairman, because he thought he'd have a better shot at a top slot on Transportation and Infrastructure.

He was one of just six Republicans to vote in 2002 against authorizing President George W. Bush to go to war against Iraq and one of 17 in his party to vote in 2007 to oppose the president's decision to send more than 21,000 additional U.S. troops to the area. Ron Paul of Texas is the only other Republican still in the House who voted the same way on both occasions. In 2003, angry that the administration wasn't pushing Iraq to pick up some of the reconstruction tab, Duncan was one of five GOP House members to vote against a war funding bill.

In April 2009, he was one of 10 Republicans to vote in favor of the Democrats' bill to curb employee bonuses at companies receiving federal money from the 2008 law to rescue the financial services industry. In July, he was one of two to support expanded regulatory oversight of all executive compensation.

Duncan voted against both versions of a $700 billion measure to assist the financial services sector, the second of which became law. He also opposed a subsequent bill — which ultimately failed — to assist the auto industry. "We would come out of our economic problems much sooner if we let the free market work," he said.

He often votes against spending bills he regards as bloated — including President Obama's $787 billion economic stimulus law. In 1997, he voted to abolish crop insurance subsidies for tobacco, even though it was the largest cash crop grown by East Tennessee farmers.

There's something else Duncan doesn't spend much money on: communications technology. He doesn't carry a BlackBerry, rarely uses a cell phone and considers computers "the biggest time-wasters in the world."

As chairman of the Transportation Subcommittee on Water Resources and Environment during the 109th Congress (2005-06), he was unable to win enactment of a huge water resources bill. In April 2007, the committee's Democratic leaders pushed through the House a version that included $45 million in projects in Duncan's district that hadn't been in the previous measure. Duncan earlier chaired the Aviation Subcommittee and helped write the aviation security law enacted two months after the Sept. 11 terrorist attacks.

From his Natural Resources seat, Duncan backs increased domestic oil drilling, including the opening of Alaska's Arctic National Wildlife Refuge and ending a moratorium on most offshore oil and gas exploration. At a July 2010 Oversight and Government Reform Committee hearing on the Gulf of Mexico oil spill, Duncan pointed to such restrictions as one reason oil companies have to drill in the kind of deep water where the accident occurred.

"We simply cannot allow environmental radicals to drive the price of gas to $5 or higher," he said on the House floor in March 2011.

Previously a supporter of free-trade agreements, he said he has become increasingly concerned about domestic job losses to overseas manufacturers; he voted against the 2007 Peru agreement.

Duncan's father was part of a business group that brought minor league baseball to Knoxville in 1956. Young Duncan spent five and a half happy seasons as the Smokies' batboy and was the public address announcer during his first year in college. Then his father switched to politics, and Jimmy Duncan followed in his footsteps.

The younger Duncan served seven years as a criminal court judge in Knox County, building a reputation that would support his bid for office when his father, in failing health, announced that the 100th Congress (1987-88) would be his last. His father died in 1988, shortly after that announcement.

In his first House race, Duncan campaigned primarily as his father's successor, even appearing on the ballot as John J. Duncan, though he goes by Jimmy. He won 56 percent of the vote in both the special and general elections that year and has not been seriously challenged since.

Key Votes

2010

Overhaul the nation's health insurance system	NO
Allow for repeal of "don't ask, don't tell"	NO
Overhaul financial services industry regulation	NO
Limit use of new Afghanistan War funds to troop withdrawal activities	YES
Change oversight of offshore drilling and lift oil spill liability cap	NO
Provide a path to legal status for some children of illegal immigrants	NO
Extend Bush-era income tax cuts for two years	YES

2009

Expand the Children's Health Insurance Program	NO
Provide $787 billion in tax cuts and spending increases to stimulate the economy	NO
Allow bankruptcy judges to modify certain primary-residence mortgages	NO
Create a cap-and-trade system to limit greenhouse gas emissions	NO
Provide $2 billion for the "cash for clunkers" program	YES
Establish the government as the sole provider of student loans	NO
Restrict federally funded insurance coverage for abortions in health care overhaul	YES

CQ Vote Studies

	PARTY UNITY		PRESIDENTIAL SUPPORT	
	Support	Oppose	Support	Oppose
2010	96%	4%	22%	78%
2009	92%	8%	17%	83%
2008	94%	6%	67%	33%
2007	94%	6%	73%	27%
2006	89%	11%	74%	26%

Interest Groups

	AFL-CIO	ADA	CCUS	ACU
2010	14%	5%	88%	100%
2009	24%	10%	67%	92%
2008	0%	15%	72%	84%
2007	13%	20%	70%	84%
2006	14%	10%	87%	88%

Tennessee 2

East — Knoxville

Nestled in the valley of the Great Smoky Mountains at the mouth of the Tennessee River, the 2nd envelops Knoxville and stretches south and west to include several conservative, rural counties.

The district's economy is almost solely determined by the success of Knoxville, while surrounding areas are full of small towns and forests, lakes and parks. State budget shortfalls have threatened government- and state-funded higher education jobs, a sector that area residents have relied on for economic stability despite their criticisms of big government year after year.

Restaurants, hotels and other businesses in the district still depend on revenue from the influx of people who attend sporting events at the University of Tennessee, which is located in Knoxville. On football game days, the university's Neyland Stadium accommodates more than 102,000 orange-and-white clad Volunteer fans. The university's basketball arena and the Women's Basketball Hall of Fame also draw significant crowds. Knoxville had struggled for years to revitalize its downtown, but state and private medical facilities have spurred some economic growth, and rede-

velopment plans for East Knoxville continue. Rejuvenated areas of the city, such as historic Market Square, now attract many tourists. The district's less populous rural regions provide a tourist destination outside of Knoxville's orbit and continue to lure visitors to mountain locales.

Like all of East Tennessee, the 2nd has a long history of voting Republican, and the district has not sent a Democrat to the U.S. House since before the Civil War. Downtown Knoxville, which includes much of the city's black population and is the only real Democratic pocket, could not prevent Bill Haslam from taking more than 80 percent of the 2010 gubernatorial vote in surrounding Knox County. He won each of the 2nd's other counties by similarly wide margins.

Major Industry
Higher education, medical services, tourism, government

Cities
Knoxville, 178,874; Maryville, 27,465; Farragut, 20,676; Athens, 13,458

Notable
A statue in Haley Heritage Square honors "Roots" author Alex Haley; the town of Alcoa is named after the company whose plant there produces enough aluminum every minute to make 75,000 beverage cans.

Rep. Chuck Fleischmann (R)

Capitol Office
225-3271
fleischmann.house.gov
511 Cannon Bldg. 20515-4203; fax 225-3494

Committees
Natural Resources
Science, Space & Technology
Small Business

Residence
Ooltewah

Born
Oct. 11, 1962; Manhattan, N.Y.

Religion
Roman Catholic

Family
Wife, Brenda Fleischmann; three children

Education
U. of Illinois, B.A.L.A.S. 1983 (political science); U. of Tennessee, J.D. 1986

Career
Lawyer

Political Highlights
No previous office

ELECTION RESULTS

2010 GENERAL

Chuck Fleischmann (R)	92,032	56.8%
John Wolfe Jr. (D)	45,387	28.0%
Savas T. Kyriakidis (I)	17,077	10.5%
Mark DeVol (I)	5,773	3.6%

2010 PRIMARY

Chuck Fleischmann (R)	26,869	29.7%
Robin Smith (R)	25,454	28.1%
Tim Gobble (R)	14,274	15.8%
Van Irion (R)	10,492	11.6%
Tommy Crangle (R)	5,149	5.7%
Art Rhodes (R)	4,552	5.0%
Jean Howard-Hill (R)	1,259	1.4%

Elected 2010; 1st term

A longtime lawyer and occasional radio talk show host, Fleischmann is expected to be a solid Republican vote representing a solid Republican district. He won a seat on the Natural Resources Committee, where he supports expanded use of nuclear power, oil exploration in the Arctic National Wildlife Refuge and clean-coal development.

Fleischmann also has a spot on the Science, Space and Technology panel, giving him a post from which to look after the interests of the nuclear facility in Oak Ridge, located in the district.

Joining with every other Republican, he voted to repeal the health care law enacted in 2010, and he praised the fiscal 2012 spending plan produced by House Budget Chairman Paul D. Ryan of Wisconsin.

Testifying before the Budget Committee in March 2011, Fleischmann made clear his priorities.

"I am not here to ask for additional funding in certain areas or spending that might help with a pet project or campaign promise," he told the panel. "Rather, as a recently elected member of Congress, I want to stress the problems of our massive debt and uncontrollable spending and encourage you all to set us on a path of fiscal sustainability and stress my desire to help with this process."

Fleischmann earned a political science degree from the University of Illinois and a law degree from the University of Tennessee. He and his wife, Brenda, ran their own law firm for more than two decades — experience he says will help him on the Small Business Committee — before Fleischmann made his first bid for elected office, seeking to succeed GOP Rep. Zach Wamp, who ran for governor.

In a rough-and-tumble 11-candidate primary, Fleischmann edged out former state GOP Chairwoman Robin Smith, who was endorsed by a number of senior Republicans, including soon-to-be Majority Leader Eric Cantor of Virginia. Fleischmann had the backing of former Arkansas Gov. Mike Huckabee.

The primary victory all but assured his election in the strongly Republican Chattanooga-based district. He defeated Democrat John Wolfe in November by almost 30 percentage points.

Tennessee 3

East — Chattanooga, Oak Ridge

From the borders of Kentucky and Virginia to its north and Georgia and North Carolina to its south, the 3rd spans the height of Tennessee. Chattanooga, the district's largest city, has attracted technology and manufacturing jobs to the region.

The 3rd's geographic center falls near Oak Ridge, where multidisciplinary high-tech national research facilities sprawl over parts of Anderson and Roane counties. Once solely dependent on federal dollars, Oak Ridge, one site of the Manhattan Project, now promotes its "Secret City" history.

Nearly half of the 3rd's population resides in Hamilton County, which includes Chattanooga and abuts Georgia. Skilled technology manufacturing and auto assembly jobs boost the economy here. Renewal projects such as the Tennessee Aquarium, a rejuvenated waterfront and programs at a local University of Tennessee campus have revitalized downtown Chattanooga. To the east, Bradley — including the city of Cleveland — and Polk counties offer tours of the Cherokee National Forest and a rich history of the Cherokee Indians.

District residents support low-tax fiscal policies and hold conservative views on social issues, making the 3rd a Republican-leaning district. In 2008, John McCain took 74 percent of the presidential vote in Bradley County, his best county statewide.

Major Industry
Nuclear and high-tech research, technology, higher education

Cities
Chattanooga, 167,674; Cleveland, 41,285; Oak Ridge (pt.), 29,112; East Ridge, 20,979

Notable
The 1925 Scopes "Monkey" Trial in Dayton (Rhea County) upheld a law making it illegal to teach evolution.

Rep. Scott DesJarlais (R)

Capitol Office
225-6831
desjarlais.house.gov
413 Cannon Bldg. 20515-4204; fax 226-5172

Committees
Agriculture
Education & the Workforce
Oversight & Government Reform

Residence
South Pittsburg

Born
Feb. 21, 1964; Des Moines, Iowa

Religion
Episcopalian

Family
Wife, Amy DesJarlais; four children

Education
U. of South Dakota, B.S. 1987 (chemistry &
psychology), M.D. 1991

Career
Physician

Political Highlights
No previous office

ELECTION RESULTS

2010 GENERAL

Scott DesJarlais (R)	103,969	57.1%
Lincoln Davis (D)	70,254	38.6%
Paul H. Curtis (I)	3,178	1.7%
Gerald York (I)	2,159	1.2%

2010 PRIMARY

Scott DesJarlais (R)	27,812	37.1%
Jack Bailey (R)	20,420	27.3%
Kent Greenough (R)	11,413	15.2%
Ronald L. Harwell (R)	9,237	12.3%
Donald "Don" Strong (R)	5,992	8.0%

Elected 2010; 1st term

DesJarlais, a physician, says he was inspired to run by what patients were saying at his Jasper practice. People were talking less about hunting and fishing, he says, and more about their anger at the Obama administration.

He promised that he will be an "equal opportunity cutter" in Congress: "Every program in the government right now has waste and abuse in it," he said. "The Internal Revenue Service is a great example of a place to start, but there's so many departments that need to be pared down and cleaned up."

Bureaucracy limits all levels of the private sector, DesJarlais said. "Small businesses and corporations are being smothered by regulations that are keeping us from being competitive with foreign countries," he argued.

He said he will do "anything that reduces the size and scope of government and reduces taxes," and there are plenty of targets available to him from his seats on the Agriculture, Education and the Workforce, and Oversight and Government Reform panels.

DesJarlais identifies with the 1994 House GOP class and wants to revive one of its signature issues: term limits. They would help restore accountability and leadership in Congress, he said, moving it to an environment where a lawmaker can "say what you mean and mean what you say."

The 2010 health care law also is a target for DesJarlais, who worked in the family practice at a community hospital and said he can "lend a lot of expertise as a physician" on the issue. He voted to repeal the law early in the 112th Congress (2011-12).

Four-term Democratic incumbent Lincoln Davis, who has carefully cultivated a centrist image, was not originally thought to be in electoral peril in 2010. DesJarlais won a five-way primary but didn't raise a lot of money.

Democrats tried to make an issue of unsavory revelations from his divorce proceedings a decade ago, but Republicans tied Davis to the liberal Democratic leadership and criticized his support of President Obama's $787 billion economic stimulus.

The district's conservative lean came to the fore in the Republican wave, and DesJarlais outdistanced Davis by almost 20 percentage points.

Tennessee 4

Middle Tennessee — northeast and south

Stretching across more than 10,000 square miles from Kentucky in the north to Alabama and Georgia in the south, the 4th is Tennessee's most geographically vast district. Plains turn east into rolling hills that merge with the Cumberland Plateau and eventually the Appalachian Mountains.

The 4th falls in the orbits of Oak Ridge and Chattanooga in the east and Nashville in the west, but it is overwhelmingly rural.

No one major media market serves all of the 4th, forcing coverage to be shared among Oak Ridge, Chattanooga, Nashville and Huntsville, Ala. The district struggles with low median household incomes and education levels.

The 4th includes tobacco farms and light industry in the south. Spring Hill, in Maury County, hosts a General Motors engine plant. Proximity to Nashville has kept the populations of Maury and next-door Williamson County (shared with the 7th) growing. Tourism plays a small role in the district's economy, but the northern tier of the 4th does attract visitors to the Big South Fork National River and Recreation Area in Fentress, Pickett and Scott counties.

Although the 4th has an ancestrally Democratic lean, underlying social conservatism — manifested in opposition to abortion and gun control measures — gives the 4th a Republican edge in federal contests.

Major Industry
Agriculture, manufacturing, tobacco

Military Bases
Arnold Air Force Base, 218 military, 276 civilian (2009)

Cities
Columbia, 34,681; Tullahoma, 18,655

Notable
The Jack Daniel's sour mash whiskey distillery in Lynchburg is in dry Moore County.

Rep. Jim Cooper (D)

Capitol Office
225-4311
cooper.house.gov
1536 Longworth Bldg. 20515-4205; fax 226-1035

Committees
Armed Services
Oversight & Government Reform

Residence
Nashville

Born
June 19, 1954; Nashville, Tenn.

Religion
Episcopalian

Family
Wife, Martha Hayes Cooper; three children

Education
U. of North Carolina, B.A. 1975 (history & economics);
Oxford U., B.A., M.A. 1977 (Rhodes scholar); Harvard
U., J.D. 1980

Career
Investment firm owner; investment bank managing
director; lawyer

Political Highlights
U.S. House, 1983-95; Democratic nominee for U.S.
Senate, 1994

ELECTION RESULTS

2010 GENERAL
Jim Cooper (D)	99,162	56.2%
David Hall (R)	74,204	42.1%

2010 PRIMARY
Jim Cooper (D)	28,660	89.3%
Eric Pearson (D)	2,214	6.9%
Eric Schechter (D)	1,213	3.8%

2008 GENERAL
Jim Cooper (D)	181,467	65.8%
Gerard Donovan (R)	85,471	31.0%
Jon Jackson (I)	5,464	2.0%
John P. Miglietta (I)	3,196	1.2%

Previous Winning Percentages
2006 (69%); 2004 (69%); 2002 (64%); 1992 (66%);
1990 (69%); 1988 (100%); 1986 (100%); 1984 (75%);
1982 (66%)

Elected 2002; 11th term
Also served 1983-1985

A self-confessed "nerd," Cooper is a member of the Blue Dog Coalition of fiscally conservative House Democrats whose ranks were decimated in the 2010 elections. He digs into the policy details across a range of issues, including the budget deficit, health care and national security.

He is among his party's most experienced fiscal experts, having logged more than a decade in Congress and then eight years in the financial world before he returned to Capitol Hill in 2003 — "older, wiser and balder," in his words — for a second tour of duty. And he doesn't mind rankling his party's more liberal leaders with his tart and candid remarks.

Cooper says there are three languages Democrats aren't very good at speaking: business, military and faith. The Obama White House has not been very fluent in talking business, Cooper says, and making government more businesslike is one of Cooper's causes.

He cites the creation of the National Commission on Fiscal Responsibility and Reform as his greatest accomplishment in the 111th Congress (2009-10), even though the bill he sponsored with Virginia Republican Frank R. Wolf to create the commission never got out of committee. Instead, President Obama created the commission by executive order after the Senate did not pass its version of the legislation.

When the commission released its report in late 2010, Cooper challenged his colleagues who were critical of it.

"If you don't like the 'Moment of Truth' recommendations, then craft your own — and win majority votes of the House and Senate — while remembering that every day of delay costs us roughly $8 billion," he said.

Cooper has promoted other approaches, including a return to pay-as-you-go budget rules requiring both tax cuts and mandatory spending increases to be offset. The House voted to reinstate such rules in February 2010 — "a major legislative achievement that really belongs to all the Blue Dogs," according to Cooper. Republicans eased that requirement in the House rules package enacted at the start of the 112th Congress (2011-12).

One esoteric item on Cooper's agenda is to change the method of calculating the federal budget. He argues that, rather than the cash-accounting basis that reflects current expenditures and revenues only, accrual accounting, which recognizes statutory commitments to future spending, such as Social Security and Medicare obligations, would provide a more realistic picture of the condition of the federal budget.

Cooper is also well versed in health policy, a subject he has taught at Vanderbilt University for more than a decade. Despite his reputation as a budget hawk, Cooper voted for the Democrats' health care overhaul in the 111th Congress and said that, though it is still controversial, it is an "achievement of many lifetimes."

He likens the health care legislation to software development. "We were in health care 1.0 for many years. Now we've got to version 2.0," Cooper said. "So what we'll be talking about this first year is version 2.1," he added, predicting that there will be "a major health care bill every year now" making midcourse changes to the law as more information becomes available about what works and what doesn't.

Cooper cooperates with Republicans on many issues. As part of his leadership of an ad hoc Armed Services panel that examined the changing responsibilities of the military services, Cooper worked closely with the panel's top Republican at the time, Georgia's Phil Gingrey, to issue a report in 2008 that looked not only at the Pentagon but intelligence agencies and the State Department in highlighting such problems as interagency coordination. He was named to another panel to look at ways to improve the Pentagon's troubled procurement system, and legislation to address some of those problems was enacted in 2009.

Cooper is the top Democrat on the Armed Services Subcommittee on Oversight and Investigations and also serves on the Oversight and Government Reform Committee, where he has focused on the electric-cooperative industry. He said in a 2008 article published in the Harvard Journal on Legislation that too many co-ops have "taken on deeply troubling anti-consumer behaviors."

Cooper was among 19 Democrats to vote against the final version of the financial services regulatory overhaul in June 2010. He said that although he agreed with most of the regulatory changes in the legislation, he opposed it because he thought it was too hard on small banks.

Another of his eclectic causes is redistricting. He wants to require states to hold open hearings and use a website to increase public participation. He accuses both parties of conspiring to minimize the number of competitive districts.

Cooper has long had an affection for government. His father, Prentice, was Tennessee's governor in the 1960s. He made it through the University of North Carolina in just three years, attended Oxford as a Rhodes scholar, then earned a law degree from Harvard. After practicing law for two years, he ran for an open House seat in 1982 against Senate Majority Leader Howard H. Baker Jr.'s daughter, Cissy, and won easily, becoming at age 28 the youngest member of the House.

Despite his youthfulness, Cooper developed a reputation as a skilled dealmaker and was a key player on health care and telecommunications policy. But when he ran for the Senate in 1994, he was trounced by actor and lawyer Fred Thompson.

Cooper then took a break from politics. He entered the investment banking world and taught business at the Owen Graduate School of Management at Vanderbilt. He said those experiences helped him as a politician — and contends that all lawmakers ought to be more knowledgeable about financial issues, noting that even members of the Armed Services Committee need to understand the business world in looking at procurement.

When a House seat in Tennessee opened up in 2002 after Democrat Bob Clement decided to run for the Senate, Cooper jumped at the chance for a comeback. Despite surgery in June that year to remove a tumor from his colon — doctors said the cancer had not spread — Cooper won the August primary with 47 percent of the vote to 24 percent for his closest competitor. He captured 64 percent that November against businessman Robert Duvall and has had no trouble holding the seat since.

Key Votes

2010

Overhaul the nation's health insurance system	YES
Allow for repeal of "don't ask, don't tell"	YES
Overhaul financial services industry regulation	NO
Limit use of new Afghanistan War funds to troop withdrawal activities	NO
Change oversight of offshore drilling and lift oil spill liability cap	NO
Provide a path to legal status for some children of illegal immigrants	YES
Extend Bush-era income tax cuts for two years	NO

2009

Expand the Children's Health Insurance Program	YES
Provide $787 billion in tax cuts and spending increases to stimulate the economy	YES
Allow bankruptcy judges to modify certain primary-residence mortgages	YES
Create a cap-and-trade system to limit greenhouse gas emissions	YES
Provide $2 billion for the "cash for clunkers" program	YES
Establish the government as the sole provider of student loans	YES
Restrict federally funded insurance coverage for abortions in health care overhaul	YES

CQ Vote Studies

	PARTY UNITY		PRESIDENTIAL SUPPORT	
	SUPPORT	OPPOSE	SUPPORT	OPPOSE
2010	81%	19%	66%	34%
2009	83%	17%	85%	15%
2008	92%	8%	28%	72%
2007	88%	12%	16%	84%
2006	82%	18%	37%	63%

Interest Groups

	AFL-CIO	ADA	CCUS	ACU
2010	43%	55%	63%	35%
2009	90%	90%	40%	16%
2008	79%	60%	72%	20%
2007	88%	85%	75%	16%
2006	79%	70%	53%	40%

Tennessee 5

Nashville

Home of the Grand Ole Opry and the Country Music Hall of Fame and Museum, the 5th's Nashville long has been known for its place in country music history. The state capital, however, has left behind that one-dimensional image to become a cosmopolitan mecca for tourism, culture and higher education.

Despite the district's rich music tradition, declining record sales have led to years of widespread layoffs across Nashville-based record labels and left once-humming studios and corporate offices along Music Row vacant. But many residents here rely on state government jobs, and Nashville is a higher education hub for the Volunteer State.

Health care industries provide economic stability, and the city hosts several research facilities, including the Vanderbilt University Medical Center.

Recovery is ongoing from a major flood that destroyed billions of dollars in property in Nashville and forced record companies, retail shops, restaurants and businesses to close in 2010.

Nashville's Printers Alley is now an entertainment hotspot, but the name gives credence to the district's once-thriving publishing industry. Two large

sports arenas — the homes of football's Titans and hockey's Predators — enhance the district's entertainment sector. Meanwhile, area suburbs still rely on tourists and locals to support the retail and service economies based around bargain stores and other attractions.

The Nashville area's growth, which spread across most of the 5th, attracted young, Republican-leaning, upper-class couples to the neighborhoods of Bellevue and Hermitage and more than doubled the district's Hispanic population in the last decade.

The strongly Democratic urban core of minority residents, government employees, academics and unions, negates almost any chance that the district could fall into GOP hands. No Republican won Nashville's congressional seat during the 20th century, and Barack Obama took 60 percent of the Davidson County vote and 56 percent of the district's vote in the 2008 presidential race.

Major Industry
Music, health care, higher education, government, tourism

Cities
Nashville-Davidson (pt.), 574,761; Mount Juliet, 23,671

Notable
"The Hermitage" was the home of Andrew Jackson.

Rep. Diane Black (R)

Capitol Office
225-4231
black.house.gov
1531 Longworth Bldg. 20515-4206; fax 225-6887

Committees
Budget
Ways & Means

Residence
Gallatin

Born
Jan. 16, 1951; Baltimore, Md.

Religion
Christian

Family
Husband, David Black; three children

Education
Anne Arundel Community College, A.S.N. 1971;
Belmont U., B.S.N. 1992

Career
College instructor; nonprofit community and health
organization fundraiser; nurse

Political Highlights
Tenn. House, 1999-2005; Tenn. Senate, 2005-10

ELECTION RESULTS

2010 GENERAL

Diane Black (R)	128,517	67.3%
Brett Carter (D)	56,145	29.4%
Jim Boyd (I)	2,157	1.1%

2010 PRIMARY

Diane Black (R)	24,374	30.5%
Lou Ann Zelenik (R)	24,091	30.2%
Jim Tracy (R)	23,808	29.8%
Dave Evans (R)	3,974	5.0%
Kerry E. Roberts (R)	2,482	3.1%

Elected 2010; 1st term

Black occupies a seat that was long in the Democratic column, and she is one of two Republican freshmen to win a coveted spot on the tax-writing Ways and Means Committee to go with her assignment to the Budget Committee.

She says she wants to apply her conservative ideas to issues such as health care, the federal budget and immigration.

With a background as an emergency room nurse, Black has made her top priority repealing the 2010 health care overhaul.

"As a registered nurse, I believe patients, doctors and health care providers should be making health care decisions — not bureaucrats in Washington," Black said. Among her first votes in Congress was one to repeal the law.

Black, who was a leader in the state Senate's GOP caucus, is proposing an overhaul of Capitol Hill's budgeting process, advocating that lawmakers' paychecks be withheld for every day that Congress fails to meet its annual budget deadline. She also wants to end congressional pensions and adopt a constitutional amendment requiring a balanced federal budget.

She is an enthusiastic supporter of the spending blueprint produced by Budget Chairman Paul D. Ryan of Wisconsin.

"This Republican budget stands in sharp contrast to the one that the president released a few months ago, which would impose a $1.5 trillion tax hike on American families," she said.

Black is just as conservative on social issues, opposing gun control and supporting policies that limit abortion. She also wants to crack down on illegal immigration; she was endorsed by Jim Gilchrist, founder of the Minuteman Project, a citizens' group that patrols the U.S.-Mexico border.

Black won the GOP nomination by fewer than 300 votes in a seven-candidate primary, but defeated Democrat Brett Carter by almost 40 points in November to win a seat that had been held since 1985 by Democrat Bart Gordon, who retired.

Black felt safe enough in her race — and determined enough to be a force in Congress — that she donated $1,000 to more than a dozen Republican House candidates during the campaign.

Tennessee 6

Middle Tennessee — Murfreesboro

Nashville's population boom continues to spill into much of the 6th, which surrounds Tennessee's capital city (in the neighboring 5th) clockwise from the north to the south. The hilly countryside includes two notable college communities — Middle Tennessee State University in Murfreesboro, and Tennessee Tech University in Cookeville — establishing a top-tier industry for the district's economy.

Two decades of explosive population growth in Rutherford County (Murfreesboro) has led to commercial expansion. A well-developed highway system eases the commute from Murfreesboro into Nashville, but most residents have relied more on automobile manufacturing jobs in the 6th itself. Nissan's primary American plant in Smyrna is expanding production, and local auto parts manufacturers have supplied other plants located around the state.

Despite tobacco revenue losses in some of the 6th's farming communities, Robertson County is still a key tobacco producer. Book, video and music distribution also is big business in the district.

In recent elections, Republican candidates have benefited from the presence of newly arrived suburbanites in the historically Democratic 6th. Unionized conservative Democrats are losing their electoral clout as socially conservative tendencies launch Republicans into public office.

Major Industry
Distribution, higher education, tobacco, auto manufacturing

Cities
Murfreesboro, 108,755; Hendersonville, 51,372; Smyrna, 39,974; La Vergne, 32,588

Notable
Shelbyville is the heart of Tennessee Walking Horse country.

Rep. Marsha Blackburn (R)

Capitol Office
225-2811
www.house.gov/blackburn
217 Cannon Bldg. 20515-4207; fax 225-3004

Committees
Energy & Commerce

Residence
Brentwood

Born
June 6, 1952; Laurel, Miss.

Religion
Presbyterian

Family
Husband, Chuck Blackburn; two children

Education
Mississippi State U., B.S. 1973 (home economics)

Career
Retail marketing company owner; state economic development official; sales manager

Political Highlights
Williamson County Republican Party chairwoman, 1989-91; Republican nominee for U.S. House, 1992; Tenn. Senate, 1999-2002

ELECTION RESULTS

2010 GENERAL

Marsha Blackburn (R)	158,916	72.4%
Greg Rabidoux (D)	54,347	24.8%
J.W. "Bill" Stone (I)	6,320	2.9%

2010 PRIMARY

Marsha Blackburn (R)	unopposed

2008 GENERAL

Marsha Blackburn (R)	217,332	68.6%
Randy G. Morris (D)	99,549	31.4%

Previous Winning Percentages
2006 (66%); 2004 (100%); 2002 (71%)

Elected 2002; 5th term

Blackburn is a dedicated tax cutter and spending hawk who was well prepared for her party's newfound majority status — she began the 112th Congress with a stack of initiatives that had been waiting quite a while.

From her perch on the Energy and Commerce Committee, Blackburn can focus on limiting the reach of the EPA and optimizing what she call the "virtual marketplace matrix" — using technology to make the economy more efficient.

"That is going to be how we use the Internet, broadband, our electronic systems to deliver health care, education, commerce, entertainment, how those pipes are used and how we best use those in the future," she said.

Blackburn expects the Republican push to cut spending to give new life to a set of bills that she has backed since she was elected to the House in 2002 calling for across-the-board reductions.

"If we want to get spending under control, that's what we are going to have to do every year. My bills have called for 1, 2 or 5 [percent] across-the-board cuts," she said, adding that colleagues encouraged her to up the percentage given the current fiscal mood — her bills in the 112th Congress (2011-12) call for cuts of 5, 10 or 15 percent.

When House Administration Committee Chairman Dan Lungren of California called proposals for across-the-board cuts "a lazy member's way to achieve something" during debate on a catchall spending bill in early 2011, he drew Blackburn's ire.

"I take issue with saying any member of this House is lazy or this is a lazy process," said Blackburn, who led the debate in favor of a Republican Study Committee proposal to reduce funding for the legislative branch by 11 percent and most other funding by 5.5 percent. "I know not everyone is a fan of across-the-board cuts, but many of us are and so are our constituents."

Blackburn, who made an unsuccessful bid to join the leadership in a race for the GOP Conference chairmanship in the 110th Congress (2007-08), said she will focus solely on her legislation and her role on the Energy panel.

But in or out of the top ranks, her loyalty to leadership is rock solid.

She has always scored near the top in party loyalty, and Republican leaders in 2005 rewarded her with a coveted assignment to Energy and Commerce. She was bumped from the panel briefly when the GOP lost its majority, but regained the seat soon after the February 2007 death of panel member Charlie Norwood of Georgia.

She also was given a seat on the now-defunct Select Committee on Energy Independence and Global Warming, where she was wary of any proposals that could burden businesses.

At an April 2009 hearing on global warming, Blackburn grilled fellow Tennesseean and former Vice President Al Gore about "your motives" in pressing for climate change legislation, noting his partnership in a venture capital firm with investments in companies that might benefit from a cap-and-trade system to control carbon emissions. Gore claimed that "every penny that I have made I have put right into a nonprofit, the Alliance for Climate Protection, to spread awareness of why we have to take on this challenge."

Blackburn was known as a firebrand in the Tennessee Senate, particularly for her relentless and ultimately successful crusade against a state income tax. She displays a gold-plated ax with the words "Ax the Tax" in her House office as a reminder. In the House, she cosponsored legislation to allow residents of Tennessee and the eight other states without broadly based income taxes to deduct state sales taxes when calculating their federal tax liability, a provision that became law in 2004. Blackburn fights any proposed tax increases, instead urging cuts in domestic spending — including emergency spending for disaster relief following Hurricane Katrina in 2005.

Blackburn also looks out for the parochial interests of her region.

She helped steer to enactment a 2006 law gradually removing longstanding restrictions preventing Southwest Airlines from flying nonstop between Dallas' Love Field and most states. Southwest flies more than five times the passengers through Nashville than the next-busiest carrier.

Blackburn is a co-founder of the Congressional Songwriters Caucus and a strong advocate of copyright protections — an important issue in music cities Nashville and Memphis, located in neighboring districts. She plays guitar, piano and ukulele and loves listening to Bach.

Born in Mississippi, Blackburn learned civic involvement from her family. Her mother was active in the local 4-H clubs, and Blackburn went to college on a 4-H scholarship. She said her father instilled in her a sense of frugality.

Blackburn worked in a series of private-sector and government jobs before coming to Congress. She paid her way through college selling books door-to-door for the Nashville-based Southwestern Co. and worked there after college as well. She got her start in politics as Republican Party chairwoman in Williamson County. She first ran for Congress in 1992 against Democratic Rep. Bart Gordon, drawing 41 percent of the vote. In the mid-1990s, she served a stint as executive director of Tennessee's Film, Entertainment and Music Commission before winning a state Senate seat in 1998.

In 2002, she leveraged the income tax issue to prevail in a crowded 7th District primary field while four-term Republican Rep. Ed Bryant made an unsuccessful Senate bid. She was the first woman from Tennessee to be elected in her own right and remained the lone woman in the state's delegation until Republican Diane Black's election in 2010. She made explicit her avid support of gun owners' rights; in one of her campaign ads, she cited not just her support of the right to bear arms, but her perfect score on a marksmanship test with her Smith & Wesson .38.

She was unopposed in 2004. During her 2006 campaign, she was unscathed by a Memphis Commercial Appeal article reporting that her campaign committee and political action committee had given $123,000 to a company run by her lobbyist son-in-law.

Blackburn looked hard at the race to succeed Bill Frist, the Senate GOP leader who retired at the end of the 109th Congress (2005-06). But in early 2005, she decided against a bid. She has easily won re-election since.

Key Votes

2010

Overhaul the nation's health insurance system	NO
Allow for repeal of "don't ask, don't tell"	NO
Overhaul financial services industry regulation	NO
Limit use of new Afghanistan War funds to troop withdrawal activities	NO
Change oversight of offshore drilling and lift oil spill liability cap	NO
Provide a path to legal status for some children of illegal immigrants	NO
Extend Bush-era income tax cuts for two years	YES

2009

Expand the Children's Health Insurance Program	NO
Provide $787 billion in tax cuts and spending increases to stimulate the economy	NO
Allow bankruptcy judges to modify certain primary-residence mortgages	NO
Create a cap-and-trade system to limit greenhouse gas emissions	NO
Provide $2 billion for the "cash for clunkers" program	NO
Establish the government as the sole provider of student loans	NO
Restrict federally funded insurance coverage for abortions in health care overhaul	YES

CQ Vote Studies

	PARTY UNITY		PRESIDENTIAL SUPPORT	
	SUPPORT	OPPOSE	SUPPORT	OPPOSE
2010	98%	2%	32%	68%
2009	99%	1%	11%	89%
2008	99%	1%	78%	22%
2007	99%	1%	91%	9%
2006	98%	2%	89%	11%

Interest Groups

	AFL-CIO	ADA	CCUS	ACU
2010	0%	0%	88%	100%
2009	5%	0%	73%	100%
2008	0%	10%	83%	96%
2007	4%	5%	72%	100%
2006	14%	0%	100%	96%

Tennessee 7

Eastern Memphis suburbs; southern Nashville suburbs; most of Clarksville

A tailor-made, meandering district, the 7th touches five other Tennessee districts and borders Kentucky to the north and Mississippi and Alabama to the south. Its population centers fall near Memphis in the southwest and near Nashville in the east. The district has experienced the state's fastest population growth since 2000.

More than 30 percent of district residents live in Shelby County suburbs outside Memphis, giving the 7th a strongly anti-tax and socially conservative bent despite a Democratic past. Middle-class residents have migrated from downtown Memphis (in the 9th) to the outskirts of the county, a trend that helps explain the 7th's GOP shift.

Williamson County, outside Nashville, mirrors Shelby in its growth and Republican leanings. In 2010, Nissan opened its regional headquarters in Franklin, near what has been the company's primary North American manufacturing plant in Smyrna (in the 6th). Nissan plans to expand production of its electric vehicles at its plants in the area.

The bulk of the area between Shelby and Williamson sweeps over vast farming regions that produce corn, cotton and hogs. Northwest of Williamson, the district ambles northward along the Cumberland River to take in most of Clarksville. The Clarksville area has benefited from diverse manufacturing, a robust education sector around Austin Peay State University (nearby in the 8th) and expansions at Fort Campbell — which straddles the Tennessee-Kentucky line. John McCain won the district by 31 percentage points in the 2008 presidential election.

Major Industry
Agriculture, manufacturing

Military Bases
Fort Campbell, 30,438 military, 8,058 civilian (2011) (shared with Kentucky's 1st District)

Cities
Clarksville (pt.), 111,764; Bartlett (pt.), 54,493; Memphis (pt.), 51,153; Franklin (pt.), 48,549; Brentwood, 37,060; Germantown (pt.), 35,494

Notable
Shiloh National Military Park memorializes the soldiers who died in one of the bloodiest battles of the Civil War.

Rep. Stephen Fincher (R)

Capitol Office
225-4714
fincher.house.gov
1118 Longworth Bldg. 20515-4208; fax 225-1765

Committees
Agriculture
Transportation & Infrastructure

Residence
Frog Jump

Born
Feb. 7, 1973; Memphis, Tenn.

Religion
United Methodist

Family
Wife, Lynn Fincher; three children

Education
Crockett County H.S., graduated 1990

Career
Farmer

Political Highlights
No previous office

ELECTION RESULTS

2010 GENERAL

Stephen Fincher (R)	98,759	59.0%
Roy Herron (D)	64,960	38.8%
Donn Janes (I)	2,440	1.5%

2010 PRIMARY

Stephen Fincher (R)	35,024	48.5%
Ron Kirkland (R)	17,637	24.4%
George Flinn (R)	17,308	24.0%
Randy Smith (R)	1,546	2.1%
Bennie G. Watts (R)	720	1.0%

Elected 2010; 1st term

A political novice from a tiny town with the catchy name of Frog Jump, Fincher is a farmer and a gospel singer who headed to Washington with the goal of reining in spending and reducing the federal deficit.

Representing a district of rolling hills and farmland, Fincher hopes to play a role in writing a new farm bill, although he gave up his seat on the Agriculture Committee when he moved to the Financial Services panel in May 2011.

"The farm program, like many other government agencies, is full of abuse," Fincher, whose family farm has received subsidy payments, told a Memphis newspaper. "We need a better system than that but we don't have it and until we get it, we've got to deal with the one we've got now."

He was also among a group of lawmakers urging the EPA not to move ahead with tighter restrictions on dust, calling the agency "completely out of touch" with rural America.

Fincher sees extending tax cuts as more effective than stimulus spending at creating jobs in the private sector and speeding economic recovery.

But Fincher says he wants to become a "salesman" for his district by supporting projects that would benefit it.

He is a charter member of the Congressional Job Creators Caucus, a group open only to lawmakers with experience as small-business owners. He also joined the Republican Study Committee, the caucus of the most conservative members of the House.

Fincher joined the race for the 8th District seat early, before 11-term Democrat John Tanner announced in 2009 that he would retire at the end of the 111th Congress (2009-10). Fincher won an expensive five-candidate primary, doubling the vote total captured by the second-place finisher.

The Democratic nominee, state Sen. Roy Herron, came after Fincher using some of the same accusations his Republican primary opponents used — accusing Fincher of failing to fully disclose his assets and liabilities.

But Fincher was effective in calling Herron too liberal for the district, and won easily with 59 percent of the vote.

Tennessee 8

West — Jackson; parts of Memphis and Clarksville

The mighty Mississippi to the west and the Tennessee and Cumberland rivers to the east frame the rolling hills and flat farmland that make up the predominately rural 8th. As residents move in to Memphis' northern suburbs and Nashville's western outposts, this once Democratic-leaning district has increasingly strong Republican ties.

The 8th is poor, but stable manufacturing in the Jackson area protects the economy from further decline.

A Pringles potato chip facility in Jackson employs many district residents. Tire, auto parts and chicken processing plants dot less-populous areas. Mechanization hurt factory employment, but it improved productivity on the district's many small cotton and soybean farms.

Two state prisons provide much-needed government jobs, and a naval air station supports a significant portion of the workforce. In the north, Clarksville hosts Austin Peay State University and continues to experience population growth.

The Tennessee River feeds into Kentucky Lake in the northeast, where conservationists journey each summer. The waterways of the Tennessee Valley Authority dams and power plants attract many avid hunters and fishermen to the district. Thousands of birdwatchers flock to Reelfoot Lake in the northwest each winter to view bald eagle migration.

Major Industry
Manufacturing, agriculture, government

Military Bases
Naval Support Activity Mid-South, 929 military, 1,493 civilian (2009)

Cities
Jackson, 65,211; Memphis (pt.), 49,409; Clarksville (pt.), 21,165; Dyersburg, 17,145

Notable
Paris hosts a 60-foot-tall replica Eiffel Tower.

Rep. Steve Cohen (D)

Capitol Office
225-3265
cohen.house.gov
1005 Longworth Bldg. 20515-4209; fax 225-5663

Committees
Judiciary
Transportation & Infrastructure

Residence
Memphis

Born
May 24, 1949; Memphis, Tenn.

Religion
Jewish

Family
Single

Education
Vanderbilt U., B.A. 1971 (history); Memphis State U.,
J.D. 1973

Career
Lawyer

Political Highlights
Democratic nominee for Tenn. House, 1970; Tenn.
Constitutional Convention, 1977-78 (vice president,
1977-78); Shelby County Commission, 1978-80;
Shelby County General Sessions Court, 1980;
defeated for election to Shelby County General Ses-
sions Court, 1981; Tenn. Senate, 1983-2006; sought
Democratic nomination for governor, 1994; sought
Democratic nomination for U.S. House, 1996

ELECTION RESULTS

2010 GENERAL

Steve Cohen (D)	99,827	74.0%
Charlotte Bergmann (R)	33,879	25.1%

2010 PRIMARY

Steve Cohen (D)	63,402	78.7%
Willie W. Herenton (D)	17,153	21.3%

2008 GENERAL

Steve Cohen (D)	198,798	87.8%
Jake Ford (I)	11,003	4.9%
Dewey Clark (I)	10,047	4.4%
Mary Wright (I)	6,434	2.8%

Previous Winning Percentages
2006 (60%)

Elected 2006; 3rd term

Cohen is white and three-fifths of his constituents are black, an unusual circumstance for a House member and one reason he characterizes himself as a progressive Democrat whose first loyalty is not to his party but to the needs of his urban district.

It's territory he is quite familiar with. Cohen represented Memphis in the state Senate for about 24 years, and the 9th District includes most of the city. He works on legislation to help low-income residents and to promote the renewal of urban areas. Cohen said he is particularly proud of his vote in favor of the health care overhaul in the 111th Congress (2009-10) and work on health care issues in general, including increasing Tennessee's Medicaid Disproportionate Share Hospital payment and addressing high infant-mortality rates in his district.

As Republicans moved a repeal of the health care law through the House in early 2011, Cohen caused a stir when he compared GOP characteriza-tions of the law as a government takeover to the campaign of hatred against Jews by Nazi propagandist Joseph Goebbels.

"They say it's a government takeover of health care, a big lie, just like Goebbels," Cohen said on the House floor. "You say it enough, you repeat the lie, you repeat the lie, and eventually, people believe it. Like blood libel. That's the same kind of thing. The Germans said enough about the Jews and the people believed it and you had the Holocaust."

A week earlier, Cohen had decried "reckless and hateful speech" in a Roll Call op-ed.

He is a member of the Progressive Caucus and a firm liberal. On the rare occasions when Cohen strays from the party line, it's usually over an issue of economic importance to his district. For example, he opposed a provision of a Federal Aviation Administration reauthorization that would have required FedEx — a major Tennessee employer — to be governed under the same labor law as competitor UPS.

Cohen has fended off primary challenges from opponents who were seen as having more traditional ties to the district's black community. He won an August 2010 primary against former Memphis mayor Willie Herenton with 79 percent of the vote, and was easily re-elected in November. Shortly after his 2006 election, he sought but failed to be the first white member of the Congressional Black Caucus.

One of his biggest early successes came when the House approved his resolution offering a formal apology for slavery and for the segregationist policies of the Jim Crow era. Such an apology had long been discussed in Congress, but it was acted on only after Cohen, a member of the Judiciary Committee, began pushing the idea in early 2007. The House adopted the resolution just a few days before Cohen faced voters in a 2008 primary in which he faced two black challengers.

Cohen denied the primary race had anything to do with the timing of the floor vote on his resolution. But observers noted it was a bit strange that the resolution came up even though the Judiciary Committee had never con-sidered it.

He also supports studying the idea of making reparations to the millions of African-American descendants of slaves.

Cohen served one term as chairman of Judiciary's Subcommittee on Commercial and Administrative Law. He is now ranking Democrat on the successor Courts, Commercial and Administrative Law panel.

His measure prohibiting the recognition of foreign defamation judgments in U.S. courts was signed into law in August 2010. He has also sponsored bills to address racial disparities in the criminal justice system and to allow non-violent federal offenders who have served their sentences to have convictions expunged from their records.

A member of the Transportation and Infrastructure Committee, Cohen is in a position to help shape transportation issues that affect his district's status as a distribution hub, which in addition to FedEx includes barge traffic and major highways. He has cosponsored legislation to improve freight rail infrastructure and planning. A new surface-transportation law is at the top of the agenda for the 112th Congress (2011-12), and Cohen — in faithful liberal tradition — champions the measure as a job creator and a way to bring federal largesse to his district. He has brought home federal grants for institutions in his district, including Memphis International Airport, St. Jude Children's Research Hospital and the University of Tennessee's biocontainment laboratory.

Cohen is also passionate about issues surrounding how inner cities are designed and used. He introduced legislation in July 2010 to provide tax incentives for the establishment of supermarkets in certain areas, arguing that a large part of Memphis is a "food desert." He says the problem contributes to obesity by restricting the choices available to residents of those areas. Cohen has also focused his attention on parks, bike paths and inner-city rail.

He is a fourth-generation member of a Jewish family in Memphis. His father was a pediatrician and his mother was a housewife. He contracted polio when he was 5 years old and still walks with a noticeable limp.

Cohen graduated from Vanderbilt University, where he served as the school's "Mr. Commodore" mascot, then returned home from Nashville to get a law degree from Memphis State University. He first ran for office at 21, undertaking a losing bid for the Tennessee House.

Seven years later he was elected vice president of the Tennessee Constitutional Convention. A stint as a Shelby County commissioner followed, and in 1983 he was elected to the state Senate. Cohen became known as the "father of Tennessee's lottery" for his longtime advocacy of the idea. The winding road to enactment included a fight to amend the state Constitution, followed by a successful public referendum.

Cohen won his U.S. House seat in 2006 after Democrat Harold E. Ford Jr. announced he was giving up the district he had taken over from his father. Cohen survived a 15-candidate primary in which his race was a major issue, winning 31 percent of the vote. He coasted to victory that November.

Key Votes

2010

Overhaul the nation's health insurance system	YES
Allow for repeal of "don't ask, don't tell"	YES
Overhaul financial services industry regulation	YES
Limit use of new Afghanistan War funds to troop withdrawal activities	YES
Change oversight of offshore drilling and lift oil spill liability cap	YES
Provide a path to legal status for some children of illegal immigrants	+
Extend Bush-era income tax cuts for two years	NO

2009

Expand the Children's Health Insurance Program	YES
Provide $787 billion in tax cuts and spending increases to stimulate the economy	YES
Allow bankruptcy judges to modify certain primary-residence mortgages	YES
Create a cap-and-trade system to limit greenhouse gas emissions	YES
Provide $2 billion for the "cash for clunkers" program	YES
Establish the government as the sole provider of student loans	YES
Restrict federally funded insurance coverage for abortions in health care overhaul	NO

CQ Vote Studies

	PARTY UNITY		PRESIDENTIAL SUPPORT	
	Support	Oppose	Support	Oppose
2010	98%	2%	89%	11%
2009	98%	2%	96%	4%
2008	99%	1%	14%	86%
2007	97%	3%	4%	96%

Interest Groups

	AFL-CIO	ADA	CCUS	ACU
2010	100%	100%	14%	0%
2009	95%	100%	33%	0%
2008	100%	100%	61%	0%
2007	96%	100%	50%	0%

Tennessee 9

Memphis

The 9th takes in most of the state's largest city, Memphis, which sits atop the Mississippi River bluffs. Memphis is 63 percent African-American, and the 9th has by far the largest black population of any district statewide. Traditional GOP voters gravitated to the outskirts of Shelby County, making the 9th the most comfortably Democratic district in Tennessee and resulting in a decade of overall population loss from the district.

Memphis is the most populous city along the Mississippi and uses its central location between St. Louis and New Orleans, as well as Memphis International Airport, to thrive as a distribution center. The world's second-busiest cargo airport behind only Hong Kong International Airport, it hosts FedEx's global hub. FedEx and the presence of several passenger carriers based at the airport have boosted the region's economy, and local residents hope that Southwest Airlines' entrance into the market here will spur further growth. AutoZone, the nation's largest auto parts retailer, has headquarters in the 9th. The district also depends on St. Jude Children's Research Hospital and a local health care industry.

Renewal efforts have paved the way for some inner-city economic development and new residential communities downtown. Tourism is a mainstay for the 9th, and both the FedExForum and Liberty Bowl Memorial Stadium draw audiences. Music-minded Memphis visitors take in Beale Street, and tourists flock here to honor two icons — Elvis Presley and Martin Luther King Jr. In 1968, King was assassinated at the Lorraine Motel, which is now a civil rights museum.

The area first sent an African-American to Congress in 1974, initiating a reign of Democratic black political power in Memphis. Although local elections still tend to be decided along racial lines, residents historically vote for any Democrat in federal races. The 9th has favored Democratic candidates in U.S. House races with at least 60 percent of the vote for decades. In 2008, Barack Obama took 77 percent of the district's vote for president, by far his highest percentage in the state.

Major Industry
Distribution, health care, tourism

Cities
Memphis (pt.), 546,327; Collierville (pt.), 10,559

Notable
Graceland was the home of Elvis Presley.

TEXAS

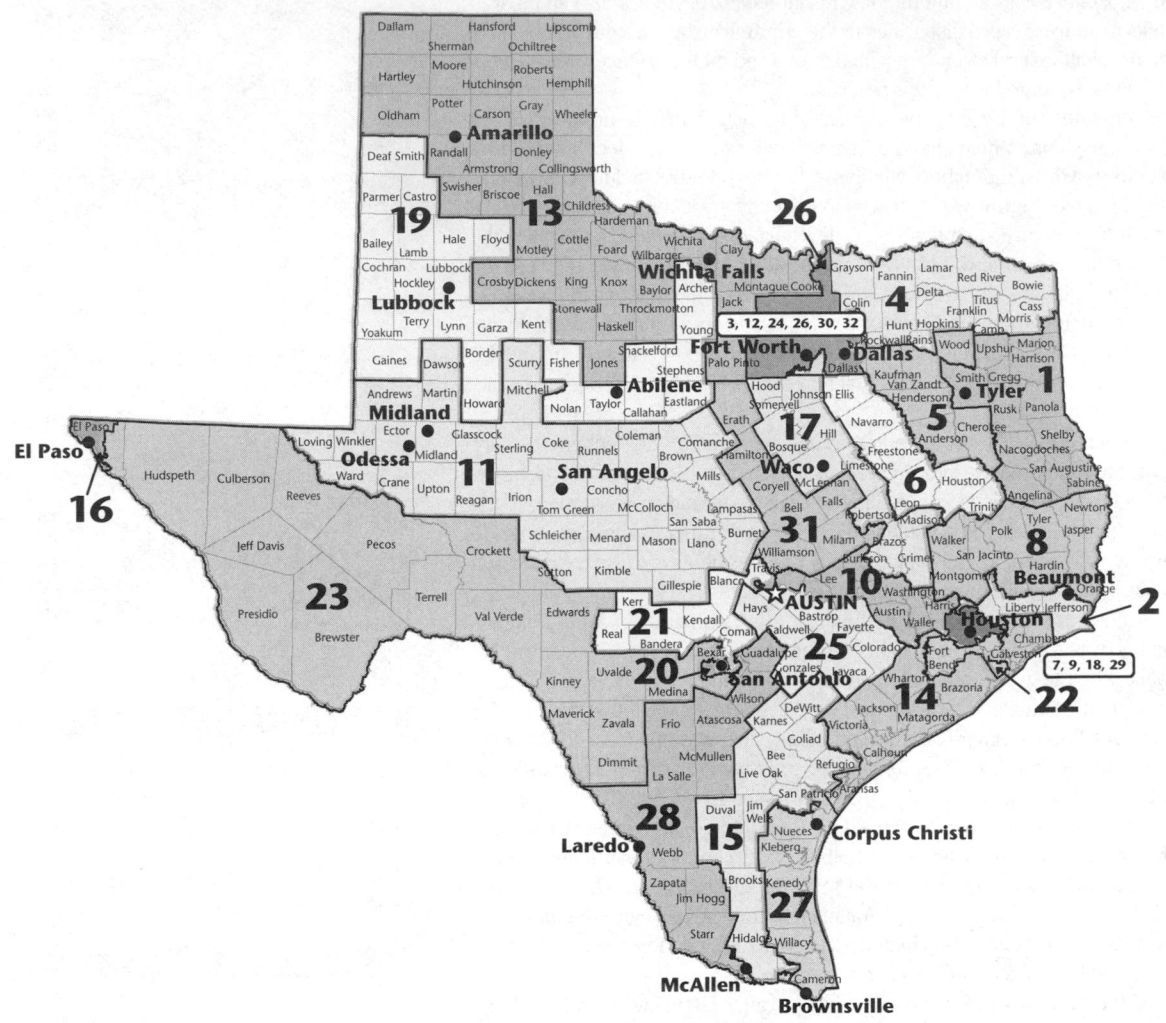

2010 CENSUS STATISTICS BY DISTRICT

District	2008 VOTE FOR PRESIDENT Obama	McCain	White	Black	Asian	Hispanic	Median Income	White Collar	Blue Collar	Service Industry	Over 64	Under 18	College Education	Rural	Sq. Miles
1	30%	69%	65%	17%	1%	15%	$40,904	53%	30%	17%	14%	26%	19%	49%	8,508
2	40	60	51	21	3	23	57,001	61	24	15	10	27	24	11	1,937
3	42	57	52	11	12	22	68,351	71	16	14	7	28	42	1	265
4	30	69	72	10	2	13	50,623	59	26	16	13	27	22	50	9,534
5	36	63	61	14	2	22	47,725	57	27	16	12	26	20	32	5,429
6	40	60	55	16	4	23	53,794	60	25	15	9	28	25	20	6,198
7	41	58	53	10	10	25	68,532	76	13	11	10	24	50	0	198
8	26	74	74	8	1	15	50,941	57	27	16	12	26	21	50	8,150
9	77	23	10	35	11	42	37,272	50	27	24	7	29	22	0	154
10	44	55	52	11	6	29	62,261	66	20	14	8	28	35	19	3,803
11	24	75	58	4	1	36	43,462	53	29	18	15	26	18	29	34,995
12	36	63	60	6	3	29	52,916	58	27	15	10	27	24	17	2,168
13	23	76	67	6	2	23	42,263	53	28	19	14	26	18	30	40,197
14	33	66	57	9	3	29	53,335	57	27	16	11	27	23	29	7,095
15	60	40	15	1	1	82	32,004	53	24	23	11	33	15	18	10,717

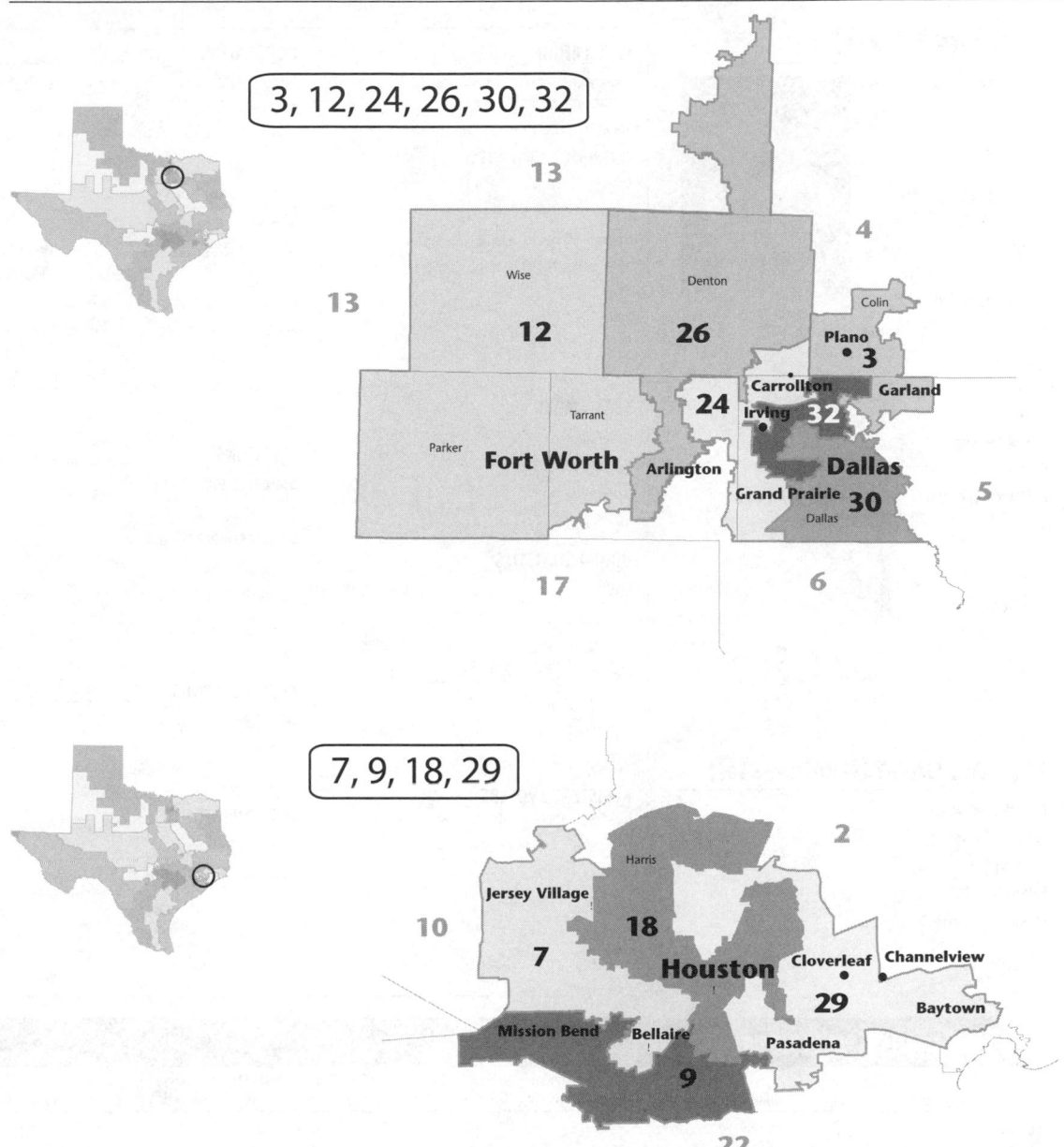

3, 12, 24, 26, 30, 32

7, 9, 18, 29

2010 CENSUS STATISTICS BY DISTRICT

District	2008 VOTE FOR PRESIDENT		White	Black	Asian	Hispanic	Median Income	White Collar	Blue Collar	Service Industry	Over 64	Under 18	College Education	Rural	Sq. Miles
	Obama	McCain													
16	66%	33%	14%	3%	1%	82%	$35,353	57%	23%	20%	11%	31%	19%	2%	581
17	32	67	66	10	2	21	42,130	56	27	17	12	25	21	36	7,691
18	77	22	16	36	3	43	36,949	49	31	20	8	29	18	0	227
19	27	72	58	5	1	34	39,644	55	26	19	13	26	20	26	25,268
20	64	36	18	7	2	72	36,651	54	24	22	10	28	16	0	184
21	41	58	60	6	4	28	60,896	71	15	14	12	25	40	19	5,130

Gov. Rick Perry (R)

First elected: 2002; assumed office Dec. 21, 2000, following the resignation of George W. Bush, R, to become president

Length of term: 4 years

Term expires: 1/15

Salary: $150,000

Phone: (512) 463-2000

Residence: Austin

Born: March 4, 1950; Paint Creek, Texas

Religion: Methodist

Family: Wife, Anita Perry; two children

Education: Texas A&M U., B.S. 1972 (animal science)

Military service: Air Force, 1972-77

Career: Farmer; rancher

Political highlights: Texas House, 1984-90; Texas department of Agriculture commissioner, 1990-98; lieutenant governor, 1999-2000

ELECTION RESULTS

2010 GENERAL

Rick Perry (R)	2,737,481	55.0%
Bill White (D)	2,106,395	42.3%
Kathie Glass (LIBERT)	109,211	2.2%

Lt. Gov. David Dewhurst (R)

First elected: 2002

Length of term: 4 years

Term expires: 1/15

Salary: $7,200

Phone: (512) 463-0001

LEGISLATURE

Legislature: January-May in odd-numbered years

Senate: 31 members, 4-year terms

2011 ratios: 19 R, 12 D; 25 men, 6 women

Salary: $7,200

Phone: (512) 463-0100

House: 150 members, 2-year terms

2011 ratios: 101 R, 49 D; 118 men, 32 women

Salary: $7,200

Phone: (512) 463-0845

TERM LIMITS

Governor: No

Senate: No

House: No

URBAN STATISTICS

CITY	POPULATION
Houston	2,099,451
San Antonio	1,327,407
Dallas	1,197,816
Austin	790,390
Fort Worth	741,206

REGISTERED VOTERS

Voters do not register by party.

POPULATION

2010 population	25,145,561
2000 population	20,851,820
1990 population	16,986,510
Percent change (2000-2010)	+20.6%
Rank among states (2010)	2
Median age	33.0
Born in state	60.9%
Foreign born	15.0%
Violent crime rate	491/100,000
Poverty level	17.2%
Federal workers	244,856
Military	131,548

ELECTIONS

STATE ELECTION OFFICIAL

(512) 463-5650

DEMOCRATIC PARTY

(512) 478-9800

REPUBLICAN PARTY

(512) 477-9821

MISCELLANEOUS

Web: www.texas.gov

Capital: Austin

U.S. CONGRESS

Senate: 2 Republicans

House: 23 Republicans, 9 Democrats

2010 CENSUS STATISTICS BY DISTRICT

District	2008 Vote for President Obama	McCain	White	Black	Asian	Hispanic	Median Income	White Collar	Blue Collar	Service Industry	Over 64	Under 18	College Education	Rural	Sq. Miles
22	41%	58%	45%	14%	13%	27%	$70,932	68%	20%	13%	8%	29%	34%	5%	971%
23	51	48	27	3	2	66	43,808	57	24	18	10	30	22	24	48,456
24	44	55	47	14	9	27	60,652	68	19	13	7	28	37	1	334
25	59	40	50	7	2	39	47,756	60	22	18	9	25	32	25	6,196
26	41	58	59	13	4	21	61,292	64	21	15	8	29	30	9	1,292
27	53	46	23	2	1	73	36,572	54	25	21	11	31	17	11	4,720
28	56	44	18	1	1	79	36,169	53	26	20	10	34	16	21	13,600
29	62	38	13	10	1	76	35,976	35	47	18	7	33	7	1	236
30	82	18	17	41	1	40	36,922	49	32	19	8	28	18	1	317
31	41	57	60	12	3	22	54,818	63	21	16	9	28	27	22	7,134
32	46	53	42	8	5	42	50,145	60	24	16	10	27	37	0	160
STATE	**44**	**56**	**45**	**11**	**4**	**38**	**48,199**	**59**	**24**	**17**	**10**	**28**	**25**	**17**	**261,797**
U.S.	**53**	**46**	**64**	**12**	**5**	**16**	**51,425**	**60**	**23**	**17**	**13**	**25**	**28**	**21**	**3,537,438**

Sen. Kay Bailey Hutchison (R)

Elected 1993; 3rd full term

Hutchison's high profile in Texas belies her status as a behind-the-scenes player in the Senate. She sits in Republican leadership meetings as a backroom counsel to Minority Leader Mitch McConnell of Kentucky and uses her committee seats to look out for the Lone Star State.

Coming off an unsuccessful run for the Republican nomination in the 2010 Texas gubernatorial race, Hutchison reversed her prior plans to resign and pledged to complete her third full term. She announced at the beginning of 2011 that she would not seek re-election in 2012.

Hutchison usually sticks with fellow Republicans — the annual percentage of votes in which she sided with a majority of her party against a majority of Democrats has fluctuated from the high 80s to the high 90s — but she is not entirely trusted by conservative activists because of her departures on sensitive issues.

In January 2009 she and the three other GOP women in the Senate joined all Democrats and then-Republican Arlen Specter of Pennsylvania in voting for a measure that would make it easier for women alleging wage discrimination to sue their employers. She also has supported legislation aimed at helping younger illegal immigrants stay in the country if they go to college or join the military, although she opposed a version of that legislation that fell five votes short of moving through the Senate in late 2010.

She has supported increased federal funding for embryonic stem cell research, which uses discarded embryos created for in vitro fertilization, and dodged questions on whether she would like to see the Supreme Court's 1973 *Roe v. Wade* decision legalizing abortion overturned. Hutchison also was an enthusiastic backer of President George W. Bush's doomed nomination of White House counsel Harriet Miers to the Supreme Court. Activists questioned Miers' credentials as well as her conservative bona fides, but Hutchison called her "totally qualified for the Supreme Court of the United States."

Hutchison's shaky standing with the conservative base manifested itself in her primary challenge to Gov. Rick Perry, whose campaign nicknamed the senator "Kay Bailout Hutchison" for her support of the $700 billion financial industry rescue program in 2008. Unable to shake Perry's portrait of her as a big-spending Washington insider, Hutchison lost by more than 20 points in the March primary.

Shortly after her gubernatorial primary loss, Hutchison announced that she would remain in the Senate, citing "intense concern" in Texas about the "direction of our federal government" under President Obama. "The stakes are so high," Hutchison said. "It's better that I stay and fill out my term."

Hutchison has not broken from her party on any significant issues since the primary, and even reversed her previous opposition to a ban on earmarks. Her support of the Senate Republican Conference's moratorium on earmarks in November 2010 came after her many years on the Appropriations Committee targeting billions of dollars for projects in her home state. But she still expressed reservations about giving up the power to direct money to specific needs in Texas. "If Congress does not direct any spending, the president will have 100 percent of the discretion in all federal programs," Hutchison warned.

First elected to the leadership team in 2000, Hutchison dropped a planned bid for the third-ranking post of Conference chairwoman in late 2007 because of opposition from conservatives in the caucus. For the 111th Congress (2009-10), she did not run for re-election as Republican Policy Committee chairwoman so she could concentrate on her gubernatorial bid. After her primary

Capitol Office
224-5922
hutchison.senate.gov
284 Russell Bldg. 20510-4304; fax 224-0776

Committees
Appropriations
Commerce, Science & Transportation
- Ranking Member
Rules & Administration

Residence
Dallas

Born
July 22, 1943; Galveston, Texas

Religion
Episcopalian

Family
Husband, Ray Hutchison; two children

Education
U. of Texas, J.D. 1967, B.A. 1992

Career
Broadcast journalist; lawyer; banking executive; candy company owner

Political Highlights
Texas House, 1973-76; National Transportation Safety Board, 1976-78; sought Republican nomination for U.S. House, 1982; Texas treasurer, 1991-93; sought Republican nomination for governor, 2010

ELECTION RESULTS

2006 GENERAL
Kay Bailey Hutchison (R)	2,661,789	61.7%
Barbara Ann Radnofsky (D)	1,555,202	36.0%
Scott Jameson (LIBERT)	97,672	2.3%

2006 PRIMARY
Kay Bailey Hutchison (R)	unopposed

Previous Winning Percentages
2000 (65%); 1994 (61%); 1993 Special Runoff Election (67%)

loss, McConnell announced in early 2010 that Hutchison would return to GOP leadership meetings as an unofficial adviser.

As a border-state senator, Hutchison is attentive to immigration matters. Given conservative opposition to legislation that would provide a path to citizenship for illegal immigrants, she has focused in recent years on border security by pressing for extra money for the Border Patrol and new technologies to be deployed by the Department of Homeland Security.

In addition to the largesse she has secured via appropriations, she has fought to ensure that Texans can continue to deduct the sales tax they pay from their federal taxes — Texas does not have a state income tax, which is a big federal deduction for taxpayers in states that do. She has also fought to keep tolls off the state's highways.

Hutchison is the top Republican on the Commerce, Science and Transportation Committee. From that post, she has been an ardent supporter of NASA, which employs thousands of people at the Lyndon B. Johnson Space Center in Houston. She helped fight an Obama administration proposal that targeted NASA for budget cuts and has pressed for quick movement on the development of a new launch vehicle to replace the space shuttle.

She also is the Senate sponsor of a measure that would block so-called net neutrality rules adopted by the Federal Communications Commission in December 2010 barring fixed broadband service providers from blocking content and unnecessarily discriminating in transmitting network traffic.

Her solid career and leadership experience have quieted critics who used to portray her as superficial. When she was Texas treasurer, the late liberal columnist Molly Ivins dubbed her "the Breck Girl," after an old shampoo commercial featuring a woman tossing her long tresses. But Hutchison is well aware of her role as a model for younger women, and in 2007 she published "Leading Ladies: American Trailblazers," featuring biographies of successful women across a range of fields. It was her third volume on accomplished American females.

She graduated in 1967 from the University of Texas School of Law, one of five women in a class of 500. She found law firms weren't willing to hire women, assuming they would get married and quit or move away. Instead, Hutchison took a job as a legal correspondent for a television station.

She grew up in La Marque, on the Gulf Coast. Her great-great-grandfather, Charles S. Taylor, was a signer of the Texas Declaration of Independence. In an elementary school diary, Hutchison once penciled, "I want to be president of the United States." But she says she never had any real political ambitions until a local GOP leader urged her to run for the state legislature. She did and was elected in 1972, a time when most women in Texas politics were Democrats.

In 1976, President Gerald R. Ford appointed her to the National Transportation Safety Board. Hutchison moved to Dallas in 1978 and married for a second time, to attorney Ray Hutchison, a former colleague in the state House. She unsuccessfully sought the GOP nomination for an open U.S. House seat in 1982. Hutchison spent a good chunk of the 1980s in the business world, as a banking executive and owner of a candy-manufacturing company.

Returning to politics in 1990, she was elected state treasurer. In 1993, she won a special election after President Bill Clinton chose longtime Democratic Sen. Lloyd Bentsen to be Treasury secretary and Democratic Gov. Ann W. Richards appointed Bob Krueger, a former House member, to the seat. Hutchison challenged him in the open election, also competing against Republican Reps. Joe L. Barton and Jack Fields. Krueger and Hutchison tied with 29 percent of the vote; she won the runoff with 67 percent. She has won easily ever since.

Key Votes

2010

Pass budget reconciliation bill to modify overhauls of health care and federal student loan programs	NO
Proceed to disapproval resolution on EPA authority to regulate greenhouse gases	YES
Overhaul financial services industry regulation	NO
Limit debate to proceed to a bill to broaden campaign finance disclosure and reporting rules	?
Limit debate on an extension of Bush-era income tax cuts for two years	YES
Limit debate on a bill to provide a path to legal status for some children of illegal immigrants	NO
Allow for a repeal of "don't ask, don't tell"	NO
Consent to ratification of a strategic arms reduction treaty with Russia	NO

2009

Prevent release of remaining financial industry bailout funds	YES
Make it easier for victims to sue for wage discrimination remedies	YES
Expand the Children's Health Insurance Program	YES
Limit debate on the economic stimulus measure	NO
Repeal District of Columbia firearms prohibitions and gun registration laws	YES
Limit debate on expansion of federal hate crimes law	NO
Strike funding for F-22 Raptor fighter jets	NO

CQ Vote Studies

	PARTY UNITY		PRESIDENTIAL SUPPORT	
	SUPPORT	OPPOSE	SUPPORT	OPPOSE
2010	99%	1%	30%	70%
2009	89%	11%	50%	50%
2008	94%	6%	67%	33%
2007	88%	12%	80%	20%
2006	91%	9%	84%	16%
2005	90%	10%	96%	4%
2004	89%	11%	94%	6%
2003	94%	6%	96%	4%
2002	92%	8%	96%	4%
2001	90%	10%	96%	4%

Interest Groups

	AFL-CIO	ADA	CCUS	ACU
2010	7%	0%	100%	96%
2009	33%	25%	57%	96%
2008	20%	20%	100%	76%
2007	26%	20%	90%	88%
2006	20%	5%	92%	84%
2005	14%	15%	94%	92%
2004	8%	25%	94%	84%
2003	0%	10%	100%	75%
2002	23%	5%	95%	100%
2001	19%	10%	85%	96%

Sen. John Cornyn (R)

Capitol Office
224-2934
cornyn.senate.gov
517 Hart Bldg. 20510-4302; fax 228-2856

Committees
Armed Services
Budget
Finance
Judiciary

Residence
Austin

Born
Feb. 2, 1952; Houston, Texas

Religion
Non-denominational Christian

Family
Wife, Sandy Cornyn; two children

Education
Trinity U., B.A. 1973 (journalism); St. Mary's U. (Texas),
J.D. 1977; U. of Virginia, LL.M. 1995

Career
Lawyer; real estate agent

Political Highlights
Texas District Court judge, 1985-91; Texas Supreme
Court, 1991-97; Texas attorney general, 1999-2002

ELECTION RESULTS

2008 GENERAL

John Cornyn (R)	4,337,469	54.8%
Richard J. Noriega (D)	3,389,365	42.8%
Yvonne Schick (LIBERT)	185,241	2.3%

2008 PRIMARY

John Cornyn (R)	997,216	81.5%
Larry Kilgore (R)	226,649	18.5%

2002 GENERAL

John Cornyn (R)	2,496,243	55.3%
Ron Kirk (D)	1,955,758	43.3%

Elected 2002; 2nd term

Cornyn has emerged as a respected conservative voice and is positioned to move up the Republican leadership ladder if he succeeds as the point man on GOP efforts to take control of the Senate in the 2012 elections.

Cornyn (CORE-nin), a good friend of former President George W. Bush, plays up his ties to the Lone Star State, often striding through the Senate wearing business suits and cowboy boots emblazoned with "United States Senate Texas."

But Cornyn comes across as more formal and less brash than Bush. His amiable approach to expressing disdain for Democratic ideas and promoting conservative positions has earned him plaudits within the GOP caucus and made him an increasingly frequent guest on cable talk shows.

Cornyn has also not been afraid to poke fun at himself. In his 2008 re-election campaign, he recorded a campaign video as cowboy-hatted, fringe-jacketed "Big Bad John," a takeoff on the 1960s hit song of the same name. The video became popular on YouTube; it included the lyrics "He rose to the top in just one term, kept Texas in power, made lesser states squirm."

While Cornyn did indeed rise quickly in his first term, he made a name for himself in his second as chairman of the National Republican Senatorial Committee, the Senate GOP's recruiting and fundraising arm. (He had previously served as vice chairman of the Senate Republican Conference.)

Cornyn took over the NRSC in 2009 and under his watch the GOP picked up seven seats in the Senate, despite having to defend several open Republican seats. Those gains have put Republicans within a handful of seats of controlling the chamber in the 113th Congress (2013-14). Cornyn, who volunteered for a second term at the NRSC without any opposition, told Roll Call that it would be a "disappointment" if Senate Republicans are still in the minority in 2013. "I think we have an opportunity to turn the corner and get in the majority," he said.

Cornyn took some heat for the party's early support of candidates who proved less than popular with the party's conservative base in states such as Florida, Nevada, Colorado, Kentucky and Delaware.

"It's not necessarily an advantage for a candidate, particularly in a contested primary, to be known as the person recruited by a national committee. I think we need to be conscious of that," he said.

Cornyn won't be back for a third term atop the NRSC. In February 2011, after Arizonan Jon Kyl announced he would not seek re-election, Cornyn announced he would seek to succeed Kyl as minority whip in the 113th Congress, kicking off a two-year race against Lamar Alexander of Tennessee.

Taking the NRSC post enabled Cornyn to give up a thankless job on the Select Ethics Committee, where he served as vice chairman in the 110th Congress (2007-08). The conclusion of his Ethics tenure also coincided with Cornyn acquiring a coveted slot on the Finance Committee, where he backed a compromise deal in 2010 to extend the Bush-era tax cuts for two years and opposed the Obama administration's health care overhaul.

While opposing the 2010 financial regulatory overhaul, Cornyn showed a willingness to work with Democrats on clarifying the intent of the law. On the Judiciary Committee, he teamed with Chairman Patrick J. Leahy of Vermont, whom he's repeatedly worked with on Freedom of Information Act issues, to win support for a bill that rescinded an exemption from public disclosure laws granted to the Securities and Exchange Commission under the original overhaul.

Cornyn retained his seat on the Budget Committee in the 112th Congress

(2011-12). He's been a lead backer of a balanced budget amendment and, with South Carolina Republican Jim DeMint, helped craft a GOP moratorium on earmarks.

As the top Republican on the Judiciary subcommittee that oversees immigration policy, Cornyn has taken a strong stance against immigration overhaul legislation that would provide a pathway to citizenship for illegal immigrants. Most recently, in December 2010, Cornyn helped defeat a measure that would have provided a path to legalization for hundreds of thousands of young adults brought illegally to the United States as children if they attended college or joined the U.S. military and met other requirements.

Cornyn signaled he will continue to seek broad immigration changes in the 112th Congress. "I believe that immigration is one of those issues that can't be addressed effectively on a piecemeal basis," he said in remarks to the Hispanic Leadership Network in January 2011. "Every component of our broken immigration system is connected to many other parts. Border security and interior enforcement go hand in hand, legal immigration directly impacts illegal immigration, and so on."

As chairman of the Judiciary Subcommittee on the Constitution in the 108th Congress (2003-04), Cornyn spearheaded efforts to pass proposed constitutional amendments banning same-sex marriage and flag burning. None of the proposals made it through the Senate.

A former Texas attorney general, district court judge and state Supreme Court judge, Cornyn opposed both of President Obama's Supreme Court nominees, Elena Kagan and Sonia Sotomayor.

Cornyn, who returned to the Armed Services Committee in the 112th Congress, backed going to war with Iraq and deploying a missile defense system. In 2005, he was one of just nine senators — all Republicans — to vote against an amendment banning cruel, inhumane or degrading treatment of prisoners captured in the fight against terrorism.

Cornyn also has been hawkish on the Pentagon budget, particularly regarding weapons spending. He's been a staunch backer of full funding the F-35 Joint Strike Fighter, an advanced warplane that would be built in Texas. And he opposed ratification the new strategic arms reduction treaty with Russia approved by the Senate in December 2010.

Cornyn is the son of a World War II B-17 pilot. His family eventually settled in San Antonio, where his father became an Air Force pathologist. A wrestler in high school and college, Cornyn majored in journalism at Texas' Trinity University. He waited tables while earning his real estate license. When that career faltered in a sagging economy, he went to law school. He later practiced in San Antonio, specializing in defending doctors against medical malpractice suits.

In 1984, some Republican friends — looking to crack the Democrats' longstanding hold on Texas' judicial elections — asked him to run for a state district court seat. He did, and he won. Six years later, he was elected to the state Supreme Court. In 1998, he won a bruising race to be attorney general race against Democrat Jim Mattox.

As attorney general, Cornyn chaired a commission tasked with proposing new political boundaries to the state legislature after the 2000 census. He presented a redistricting plan that could have resulted in major Republican gains. The courts eventually imposed a less partisan map.

When Republican Sen. Phil Gramm decided to retire in 2002, Cornyn ran for the seat and won a GOP primary against four little-known opponents. In the November race against former Dallas Mayor Ron Kirk, now the U.S. trade representative, Cornyn ran on his loyalty to Bush and won with 55 percent. Six years later, Cornyn's opponent was Richard J. "Rick" Noriega, a Democratic state representative from Houston. Cornyn swamped him in fundraising and won with 55 percent of the vote.

Key Votes

2010

Pass budget reconciliation bill to modify overhauls of health care and federal student loan programs	NO
Proceed to disapproval resolution on EPA authority to regulate greenhouse gases	YES
Overhaul financial services industry regulation	NO
Limit debate to proceed to a bill to broaden campaign finance disclosure and reporting rules	NO
Limit debate on an extension of Bush-era income tax cuts for two years	YES
Limit debate on a bill to provide a path to legal status for some children of illegal immigrants	NO
Allow for a repeal of "don't ask, don't tell"	NO
Consent to ratification of a strategic arms reduction treaty with Russia	NO

2009

Prevent release of remaining financial industry bailout funds	YES
Make it easier for victims to sue for wage discrimination remedies	NO
Expand the Children's Health Insurance Program	NO
Limit debate on the economic stimulus measure	-
Repeal District of Columbia firearms prohibitions and gun registration laws	YES
Limit debate on expansion of federal hate crimes law	NO
Strike funding for F-22 Raptor fighter jets	NO

CQ Vote Studies

	PARTY UNITY		PRESIDENTIAL SUPPORT	
	Support	Oppose	Support	Oppose
2010	99%	1%	38%	62%
2009	96%	4%	45%	55%
2008	97%	3%	73%	27%
2007	98%	2%	91%	9%
2006	97%	3%	91%	9%
2005	95%	5%	98%	2%
2004	97%	3%	96%	4%
2003	99%	1%	98%	2%

Interest Groups

	AFL-CIO	ADA	CCUS	ACU
2010	6%	0%	100%	100%
2009	17%	5%	71%	100%
2008	11%	20%	100%	79%
2007	0%	15%	80%	96%
2006	13%	0%	83%	96%
2005	14%	10%	89%	96%
2004	8%	5%	100%	100%
2003	0%	10%	100%	85%

Rep. Louie Gohmert (R)

Capitol Office
225-3035
www.house.gov/gohmert
2440 Rayburn Bldg. 20515-4301; fax 226-1230

Committees
Judiciary
Natural Resources

Residence
Tyler

Born
Aug. 18, 1953; Pittsburg, Texas

Religion
Baptist

Family
Wife, Kathy Gohmert; three children

Education
Texas A&M U., B.A. 1975 (history); Baylor U., J.D. 1977

Military
Army, 1978-82

Career
Lawyer; state prosecutor

Political Highlights
Smith County District Court judge, 1993 2002; Texas
Court of Appeals chief justice, 2002-03

ELECTION RESULTS

2010 GENERAL

Louie Gohmert (R)	129,398	89.7%
Charles Parkes (LIBERT)	14,811	10.3%

2010 PRIMARY

Louie Gohmert (R)	unopposed

2008 GENERAL

Louie Gohmert (R)	189,012	87.6%
Roger L. Owen (I)	26,814	12.4%

Previous Winning Percentages
2006 (68%); 2004 (61%)

Elected 2004; 4th term

Gohmert's conservative outrage often combines with his sense of humor to yield provocative, if sometimes impractical, policy proposals. He also has a knack for getting under the skin of some of his colleagues and shows no fear of giving offense.

After the FBI briefed lawmakers in the wake of the January 2011 shooting in Tucson that killed six and left Arizona Democratic Rep. Gabrielle Giffords seriously wounded, Gohmert complained that politics might have inhibited the bureau's representatives from providing the details he sought about the alleged shooter.

"It may be if the things he was reading, that he's a liberal, hates the flag, supports Marx, if those type of things turn out to be true, then it may be embarrassing to the current administration's constituents, and heaven help us we wouldn't want to embarrass the president's constituents," Gohmert told Roll Call.

In response to the shooting, he proposed allowing members of Congress to carry guns while in Washington — and in the Capitol and on the House floor — for self-protection.

Arguing in March 2010 that the Senate no longer serves its function as, in Thomas Jefferson's phrase, a "cooling saucer" for the passions of the House and the electorate, he advocated repeal of the 17th Amendment, which requires direct election of senators. That suggestion came in the wake of the health care debate, during which Gohmert suggested no one should vote for the bill who wasn't prepared to eat its almost 2,500 pages.

In the 110th Congress (2007-08), after the Supreme Court ruled that detainees had the right to challenge their detention in federal court, he introduced a bill to move detainees from the naval base at Guantánamo Bay, Cuba, to the grounds of the Supreme Court so the justices could "more effectively micromanage" them.

He was one of 34 House members who voted against a package of tax changes in early 2008, noting that some of the bill's benefits would go to people who paid no income taxes. "So," Gohmert said, "I asked the president there at the State of the Union, how do you give a rebate to people who didn't put any 'bate' in?"

Gohmert has been a dogged conservative voice on his committees, using his Natural Resources seat to push for more domestic energy production — oil and gas are among the major industries in his district — and using his Judiciary post to advance his socially conservative agenda. Gohmert's experience as a judge is reflected in the legislation he introduced in his first term to increase penalties against people who threaten or attack judges and prosecutors. He said it was prompted by the 2005 murder in Chicago of U.S. District Judge Joan Lefkow's husband and mother by a litigant she ruled against in a medical malpractice suit. Another incident occurred in Gohmert's hometown of Tyler: In February 2005, an armed man killed his ex-wife and wounded his son and several police officers outside the Smith County courthouse where Gohmert had presided. Gohmert, now vice chairman of the Judiciary Subcommittee on Crime, Terrorism and Homeland Security, said he has been threatened many times by defendants and people he put in jail.

Gohmert has strained the patience of his colleagues on multiple occasions. He incurred the wrath of Democrat Heath Shuler of North Carolina in 2007 when he borrowed a sign from outside Shuler's office to use in a floor presentation on the federal deficit. Roll Call reported that "Shuler, a former NFL quarterback, was spotted towering over a seated Gohmert, wagging a finger in his face."

During a Judiciary debate on a measure aimed at reducing recidivism rates of newly released prisoners, Gohmert tried nine times over three hours to add language expressly stating that faith-based organizations would be eligible for funds under the bill. All of his attempts were rejected.

He was similarly persistent during a 2007 debate on a bill to help former inmates adjust to life after imprisonment. He tried at two separate Judiciary meetings to strike the phrase "creed and religion" from an amendment designed to prohibit religious groups from taking an applicant's religious beliefs into consideration when hiring. Gohmert angered Jewish Democrats when he suggested that not allowing religious groups to hire only employees who accepted the tenets of their faith could force Jewish organizations to hire Nazis. "I said nothing inappropriate and nothing that should have been taken out of context. I meant what I said," he recalled. "You would be forced to hire people who wanted to work against what you wanted to do."

In 2009, he opposed expansion of federal hate crimes legislation. "Every human being in the world deserves to be equally protected, no matter who they are or who they go to bed with," he said in an impassioned speech during Judiciary Committee consideration of the measure.

Gohmert grew up in Mount Pleasant, an east Texas town of 8,000 where his father worked as an architect and his mother taught eighth-grade English. He hauled hay, pumped gas and worked at a construction site as a youth. He first won elected office as class president of his junior high school. He followed his father in attending Texas A&M University, where he was given an ROTC scholarship and rose to the rank of brigade commander in the school's Corps of Cadets.

Gohmert earned a degree from Baylor University's law school, then worked as a state assistant district attorney while waiting for his call to active military duty. He served four years as an Army lawyer at Fort Benning, Ga.

Returning to Texas in 1982, he worked as a civil litigator. His mother's death in 1991 prompted him to consider her advice to become a judge. He ran in 1992 after he was unable to find anyone willing to challenge the Smith County District Court incumbent. He served for the next 10 years, then was appointed by GOP Gov. Rick Perry to the Texas Court of Appeals.

After former House Majority Leader Tom DeLay succeeded in pushing through a Republican-dominated Texas redistricting plan, Gohmert unseated four-term Democratic Rep. Max Sandlin in 2004 by almost 24 percentage points. Gohmert easily won again in 2006. Democrats didn't field a candidate in 2008 or 2010.

Key Votes

2010
Overhaul the nation's health insurance system	NO
Allow for repeal of "don't ask, don't tell"	NO
Overhaul financial services industry regulation	NO
Limit use of new Afghanistan War funds to troop withdrawal activities	NO
Change oversight of offshore drilling and lift oil spill liability cap	NO
Provide a path to legal status for some children of illegal immigrants	NO
Extend Bush-era income tax cuts for two years	NO

2009
Expand the Children's Health Insurance Program	NO
Provide $787 billion in tax cuts and spending increases to stimulate the economy	NO
Allow bankruptcy judges to modify certain primary-residence mortgages	NO
Create a cap-and-trade system to limit greenhouse gas emissions	NO
Provide $2 billion for the "cash for clunkers" program	?
Establish the government as the sole provider of student loans	NO
Restrict federally funded insurance coverage for abortions in health care overhaul	YES

CQ Vote Studies

	PARTY UNITY		PRESIDENTIAL SUPPORT	
	Support	Oppose	Support	Oppose
2010	95%	5%	29%	71%
2009	95%	5%	15%	85%
2008	92%	8%	63%	37%
2007	97%	3%	82%	18%
2006	93%	7%	78%	22%

Interest Groups

	AFL-CIO	ADA	CCUS	ACU
2010	0%	5%	75%	96%
2009	5%	0%	79%	100%
2008	7%	10%	75%	96%
2007	9%	10%	80%	100%
2006	18%	5%	100%	96%

Texas 1

Northeast — Tyler, Longview

In this lush portion of East Texas, tree-covered hills and cypress swamps share space with what remains of the once-prominent oil centers in Longview and Tyler as well as Nacogdoches County.

More moderate population growth in comparison to some parts of the state and miles of forests and farmland are hallmarks of the 1st, which runs roughly 140 miles along the Louisiana border and takes in the Toledo Bend Reservoir. The district shares more traits with its traditionally laid-back Cajun neighbors than with the fast-paced urban life of nearby Dallas and its suburbs.

Timber is still central to the economy of the southern part of the 1st, complemented by poultry, dairy and beef cattle operations. Timber has faced stiff competition from foreign companies, but biomass energy production is an emerging industry here.

The district's timber crops required years to recover from wind damage and flooding after hurricanes Rita and Ike in 2005 and 2008. Although Sabine County has struggled with several years of unemployment rates higher than 15 percent, retirees moving in have kept the housing market relatively stable.

In Smith County, the 1st's western edge, Tyler's economy is growing. It has stable timber, natural gas and health care industries, with some hospital systems based in the city.

The area's workforce still relies on major manufacturing employers such as Eastman Chemical in Longview and Trane in Tyler. SYSCO has a regional distribution center in Longview, which is home to several large business and industrial parks.

Residents tend to be conservative, even among Democrats, and the region associates itself with the Bible Belt that stretches through much of the South. The 1st has one of the state's highest percentages of elderly residents, which makes health care access an important issue in rural areas. Many of the district's largest and most-populated counties — Nacogdoches, Rusk, Gregg and Smith — reliably favor Republicans. John McCain won 69 percent of the district's vote in the 2008 presidential election.

Major Industry
Timber, agriculture, manufacturing, steel, oil and gas

Cities
Tyler, 96,900; Longview, 80,455; Lufkin, 35,067; Nacogdoches, 32,996

Notable
Tyler boasts the nation's largest public rose garden, with 40,000 roses.

Rep. Ted Poe (R)

Capitol Office
225-6565
poe.house.gov
430 Cannon Bldg. 20515-4302; fax 225-5547

Committees
Foreign Affairs
Judiciary

Residence
Humble

Born
Sept. 10, 1948; Temple, Texas

Religion
Church of Christ

Family
Wife, Carol Poe; four children

Education
Abilene Christian College, B.A. 1970 (political science); U. of Houston, J.D. 1973

Military
Air Force Reserve, 1970-76

Career
County prosecutor; college instructor

Political Highlights
Harris County District Court judge, 1981-2003

ELECTION RESULTS

2010 GENERAL

Ted Poe (R)	130,020	88.6%
David W. Smith (LIBERT)	16,711	11.4%

2010 PRIMARY

Ted Poe (R)	unopposed

2008 GENERAL

Ted Poe (R)	175,101	88.9%
Craig Wolfe (LIBERT)	21,813	11.1%

Previous Winning Percentages
2006 (66%); 2004 (56%)

Elected 2004; 4th term

For someone who was shy as a child, Poe has certainly come out of his shell since entering Congress. According to C-SPAN, he is the most talkative member of the House, appearing on the chamber floor more often than any other member over the past four years to espouse his conservative viewpoint.

The issues vary, but the philosophical content is never in doubt. Poe likes to say he is a conservative first and a Republican second, and he signs off his deliveries with Walter Cronkite-like certainty: "And that's just the way it is."

Immigration is a frequent topic, and Poe is a member of Judiciary subcommittees handling immigration and homeland security, as well as the Foreign Affairs panel with jurisdiction on terrorism issues. He has referred to the U.S.-Mexico border as the "third front" in the war on terror.

He was among a bipartisan group of lawmakers who urged President Obama to deploy National Guard troops to address violence there.

"Border Patrol and local sheriffs on the border are out-manned, out-gunned and out-financed," Poe said.

After the Obama administration brought a lawsuit against Arizona's 2010 law targeting illegal immigrants, Poe was one of more than 80 GOP lawmakers who signed a friend of the court brief helping the defense. "We hear the rhetoric that illegals do jobs Americans won't do," he said in July 2010 on the House floor. "Now we have an actual situation where Arizona is getting sued for doing a job the American government won't do — protecting the security of the country and enforcing the law."

But Poe does vary the menu.

He became something of a sensation on YouTube with a May 2008 floor speech blasting provisions of a 2007 law that phases out use of incandescent bulbs in favor of more energy-efficient compact fluorescent lights. The video drew more than 5.7 million hits within 90 days of its posting. "You want to go down in history as giving a speech like the Gettysburg Address as a politician, and then you get known for light bulbs," Poe observed ruefully to his hometown newspaper, the Humble Observer.

A former county prosecutor who spent 22 years as a judge in Houston, he made it a point to publicly shame convicts in what became known as "Poe-etic justice." He now propounds his get-tough stance as a member of the Victims' Rights Caucus.

He was an outspoken supporter of legislation to require convicted sex offenders to report upcoming international travel in an effort to stifle the sex-tourism industry.

"It's important that we first take care and find out who those victims are. We should treat them as victims, those children that have been exploited," Poe said when the House passed the bill in July 2010. "The second thing we do, we find out who those slave traders are and we put them in jails throughout the world. . . . And the third thing is those consumers, those who pay to exploit children, some of those 25 percent from the United States, we not only lock them up, we let people know who they are. We publish their names, we put their photographs on the Internet, we let people know who these individuals are."

Poe also looks out for the economic interests of his suburban Houston district, such as energy production and Gulf Coast shipping. Topping his priorities is a project to widen and deepen the Sabine-Neches Waterway, where 20 percent to 30 percent of the nation's commercial jet fuel is produced and shipped. A 2007 water resources development law included Poe's language to fast track studies needed before the project can be built. Poe then joined other lawmakers of both parties in a successful override of President George W. Bush's veto of the bill.

The boot-wearing lawmaker is a proud Texan. Born in Temple and raised in Houston, Poe has filled his Capitol Hill office with photographs that he snapped of the Texas countryside. He said a major turning point in his life occurred when he was in ninth grade. "I was shy so my daddy made me take speech class so that I would talk more. I've been talking ever since, I guess," Poe said.

When C-SPAN tallied the number of days in the 110th (2007-08) and 111th (2009-10) Congresses that lawmakers appeared on the House floor to speak or insert comments into the Congressional Record, Poe outdistanced the competition.

Poe was deeply influenced by his grandmother, a "Yellow Dog Democrat," who died at the age of 99. "She never forgave me for being a Republican. She told me once, 'I'm not sure you can go to Heaven being a Republican.' She might have meant it too," Poe chuckled.

He said he was also affected by the story of William Barrett Travis, the Texas commander at the Battle of the Alamo. Posted at the door of Poe's personal office is a framed copy of Travis' Letter from the Alamo, which reads in part: "I am determined to sustain myself as long as possible and die like a soldier who never forgets what is due to his own honor and that of his country — Victory or Death."

He earned a political science degree from Abilene Christian College and a law degree from the University of Houston. Poe, who served in the Air Force Reserve, was an assistant district attorney and chief felony prosecutor for eight years and never lost a jury trial.

Poe said he became a Republican when Gov. William Clements named him to the bench. One of his more famous punishments required an auto thief to serve jail time — and to hand over the keys to his Trans Am to his victim, a 75-year-old grandmother, who drove the car until her stolen vehicle was recovered and repaired. He also once made a burglar stand on a sidewalk wearing a sign that read, "I stole from this store."

In 2004, Poe entered the race for the 2nd District, which had been redrawn under the direction of a fellow Texas Republican, House Majority Leader Tom DeLay, to favor the GOP. The district included almost half the former 9th District constituent base represented by four-term Democrat Nick Lampson. Poe ousted Lampson with 56 percent of the vote and has won easily since.

Key Votes

2010

Overhaul the nation's health insurance system	NO
Allow for repeal of "don't ask, don't tell"	NO
Overhaul financial services industry regulation	NO
Limit use of new Afghanistan War funds to troop withdrawal activities	NO
Change oversight of offshore drilling and lift oil spill liability cap	NO
Provide a path to legal status for some children of illegal immigrants	NO
Extend Bush-era income tax cuts for two years	NO

2009

Expand the Children's Health Insurance Program	?
Provide $787 billion in tax cuts and spending increases to stimulate the economy	NO
Allow bankruptcy judges to modify certain primary-residence mortgages	NO
Create a cap-and-trade system to limit greenhouse gas emissions	NO
Provide $2 billion for the "cash for clunkers" program	YES
Establish the government as the sole provider of student loans	NO
Restrict federally funded insurance coverage for abortions in health care overhaul	YES

CQ Vote Studies

	PARTY UNITY		PRESIDENTIAL SUPPORT	
	SUPPORT	OPPOSE	SUPPORT	OPPOSE
2010	99%	1%	24%	76%
2009	95%	5%	19%	81%
2008	94%	6%	68%	32%
2007	95%	5%	79%	21%
2006	90%	10%	85%	15%

Interest Groups

	AFL-CIO	ADA	CCUS	ACU
2010	0%	5%	75%	100%
2009	5%	5%	73%	92%
2008	7%	10%	56%	96%
2007	25%	5%	72%	96%
2006	21%	10%	87%	84%

Texas 2

East — Beaumont, Port Arthur, part of Houston and northern and eastern suburbs

The 2nd stretches 100 miles west from Louisiana and the Gulf of Mexico to some of Houston's more affluent northern suburbs. In the east are Beaumont, an oil city on the Neches River, and Port Arthur, 15 miles away on Sabine Lake, and the two cities anchor the 2nd's robust shipping-based economy. Areas along the Sabine River, the border between Texas and Louisiana, and the Bolivar Peninsula farther south, have been hit by several hurricanes in the last decade.

Petrochemical manufacturing dominates the area between Beaumont and Port Arthur. Major manufacturing sites here include an ExxonMobil Chemical plant in Beaumont and a Flint Hills Resources facility in Port Arthur. The 2nd has a large rural portion, with some less-populated areas in Jefferson and Liberty counties. Liberty County's population continues to grow, and many residents make the long commute into Houston.

A southern branch dips into Houston's eastern suburbs and takes in part of Baytown, a petrochemical city. The rest of the 2nd's portion of Harris

County, near Lake Houston and to its west, is suburban. Many residents work at George Bush Intercontinental Airport (in the adjacent 18th). The 2nd hosts several large companies in traditional blue-collar industries and a significant white-collar employment sector, but a lack of economic diversification has hurt the district, spurring high unemployment rates. Still majority-white with a fast-growing Hispanic population, the 2nd tends to vote like Texas overall — mostly conservative and Republican — but not overwhelmingly enough to shut out Democrats.

Harris County provides candidates with a solid Republican base, but the Beaumont area tends to favor moderate to conservative Democrats. Republican John McCain still won 60 percent of the district's 2008 presidential vote.

Major Industry
Petrochemicals, shipping, service

Cities
Beaumont, 118,296; Houston (pt.), 77,762; Atascocita (unincorporated), 65,844; Spring (unincorporated), 54,298; Port Arthur (pt.), 53,814

Notable
South of Beaumont, the Spindletop-Gladys City Boomtown Museum is located on the site of the 1901 gusher that began Texas' oil boom.

Rep. Sam Johnson (R)

Capitol Office
225-4201
samjohnson.house.gov
1211 Longworth Bldg. 20515-4303; fax 225-1485

Committees
Ways & Means
    (Social Security - Chairman)
Joint Taxation

Residence
Plano

Born
Oct. 11, 1930; San Antonio, Texas

Religion
Methodist

Family
Wife, Shirley Johnson; three children

Education
Southern Methodist U., B.B.A. 1951; George Washington U., M.S.I.A. 1974 (international affairs)

Military
Air Force, 1951-79

Career
Home builder; Air Force pilot; Top Gun flight school director

Political Highlights
Texas House, 1985-91

ELECTION RESULTS

2010 GENERAL

Sam Johnson (R)	101,180	66.3%
John Lingenfelder (D)	47,848	31.3%
Christopher Claytor (LIBERT)	3,602	2.4%

2010 PRIMARY

Sam Johnson (R)	unopposed

2008 GENERAL

Sam Johnson (R)	170,742	59.7%
Tom Daley (D)	108,693	38.0%
Christopher Claytor (LIBERT)	6,348	2.2%

Previous Winning Percentages
2006 (63%); 2004 (86%); 2002 (74%); 2000 (72%); 1998 (91%); 1996 (73%); 1994 (91%); 1992 (86%); 1991 Special Runoff Election (53%)

Elected 1991; 10th full term

Johnson, a prisoner at the infamous "Hanoi Hilton" for almost seven years during the Vietnam War, is best known for his spirited defense of U.S. involvement in Iraq and Afghanistan. But as a member of the Ways and Means Committee, he has increasingly focused his legislative energies on applying his convictions on limited government to taxes and health care.

Johnson has a prominent platform from which to champion those issues, as the third-ranking member on the panel and chairman of the Social Security Subcommittee. He abstained from bidding for the top GOP slot on the full committee in 2009, deferring to two senior Republicans. "I believe in seniority, and I didn't want to muddy the water," said Johnson, whose unassuming manner and easy Texas drawl usually keep him in good standing with colleagues of both parties.

Johnson opposed the Democrats' health care overhaul enacted in 2010 and voted to repeal it in 2011. He also questioned the constitutionality of the bill's mandate for people to buy health insurance, a position seconded by two federal judges as challenges to the law make their way through the courts.

Johnson supports health care changes that involve less intervention by the federal government. He has long been an advocate of legislation to make it easier for small businesses to band together to purchase health insurance through association health plans. Such plans would be exempt from state laws mandating coverage for specific conditions and treatments. The House passed his bill in July 2005, when Republicans controlled the chamber, but the measure died in the Senate.

Johnson shares his party's aversion to tax increases, and he backed the two-year extension of the George W. Bush-era tax cuts that was enacted in late 2010. But he can swallow his distaste on occasion if the increases are offset by other tax cuts — or the interests of his constituents are at stake. In 2008, Ways and Means considered Democratic-sponsored legislation to revive or renew a slew of tax breaks for individuals and businesses — including a sales tax deduction in states such as Texas that have no state income tax. Although the bill included other tax increases to offset the cost of the tax breaks, Johnson voted for the measure. He was one of just three Republicans to do so.

Johnson is a stalwart defender of the military and of U.S. involvement in Iraq and Afghanistan. A career Air Force pilot, he is a former director of the Air Force's "Top Gun" fighter pilot school. Johnson once roomed with Republican Sen. John McCain of Arizona during their time as prisoners of war, and he says he decided to become active in politics during those years, half of which were spent in solitary confinement.

After Obama announced a revised Afghanistan strategy that in addition to boosting troop levels also included a date to begin withdrawing forces, Johnson invoked his own history to make a point. "As a 29-year Air Force veteran and prisoner of war for nearly seven years, I know what happens when you try to run a war from the White House — you lose," he said on the House floor in December 2009. "We need to stop talking about exit strategies and troop withdrawal and focus on giving our troops the resources they want, need and deserve."

He had made a similar point when the House in 2007 narrowly passed a $124.2 billion war supplemental spending bill that aimed to set a timetable for the withdrawal of U.S. troops from Iraq. Johnson brought a hush to the chamber when he described the last days of the war in Vietnam. "Just think back to the dark day in history when we saw visions of American Marines airlifting Vietnamese out of the U.S. Embassy," he said. "Do you remember that? That's what happens when America makes a commitment, Congress cuts the funding, and we go home with our tails between our legs."

One of four founders of the Republican Study Committee, originally known as the Conservative Action Team, Johnson was named the most conservative member of the House in 2010 by National Journal, a designation he termed a "badge of honor." The last time his annual party unity score — the percentage of votes in which he sided with a majority of Republicans against a majority of Democrats — fell below 97 was 1998.

When he believed that fellow Texan George W. Bush strayed from conservative principles as president, Johnson opposed him. He voted against Bush's position on a 2006 measure to grant permanent normal trade relations to Vietnam. The bill, which failed in the House, later became law as part of a broader trade package.

Johnson also split with Bush over the president's efforts to combine tighter border controls with legalization options for illegal immigrants already living in the United States. Johnson has pushed for a crackdown at the border and introduced legislation to require employers to check the legal status of all their new workers. He also introduced legislation that would require those claiming a refundable child tax credit to supply their Social Security numbers, aimed at keeping illegal immigrants from claiming the credit.

Johnson did not plan on a military career. He said participation in the ROTC was mandatory when he went to high school. He was aiming for a career in business and law when the Korean War intervened and his entire ROTC class at Southern Methodist University was called to duty. Accepted into flight training school, he fell in love with flying and was sold on an Air Force career. He flew combat missions over Korea and Vietnam and was a member of the Thunderbirds precision flying team for two years.

Johnson does not talk much about his days as a prisoner of war, but he wrote a book about his experience, "Captive Warriors." He made an emotional return to Vietnam in 2006, accompanied by six other members of Congress and his wife, Shirley.

After retiring from the Air Force in 1979 as a colonel, Johnson went into the homebuilding business in Dallas. He got into local Republican Party affairs and won a seat in the Texas House in 1984. When GOP Rep. Steve Bartlett resigned in March 1991 to run for mayor of Dallas, Johnson overcame a tough scramble to win his party's nomination. He's had no trouble since then in the solidly Republican district.

Key Votes

2010

Overhaul the nation's health insurance system	NO
Allow for repeal of "don't ask, don't tell"	NO
Overhaul financial services industry regulation	NO
Limit use of new Afghanistan War funds to troop withdrawal activities	?
Change oversight of offshore drilling and lift oil spill liability cap	?
Provide a path to legal status for some children of illegal immigrants	NO
Extend Bush-era income tax cuts for two years	YES

2009

Expand the Children's Health Insurance Program	NO
Provide $787 billion in tax cuts and spending increases to stimulate the economy	NO
Allow bankruptcy judges to modify certain primary-residence mortgages	NO
Create a cap-and-trade system to limit greenhouse gas emissions	NO
Provide $2 billion for the "cash for clunkers" program	NO
Establish the government as the sole provider of student loans	NO
Restrict federally funded insurance coverage for abortions in health care overhaul	YES

CQ Vote Studies

	PARTY UNITY		PRESIDENTIAL SUPPORT	
	SUPPORT	OPPOSE	SUPPORT	OPPOSE
2010	99%	1%	25%	75%
2009	98%	2%	10%	90%
2008	99%	1%	81%	19%
2007	99%	1%	92%	8%
2006	98%	2%	82%	18%

Interest Groups

	AFL-CIO	ADA	CCUS	ACU
2010	0%	0%	100%	100%
2009	5%	0%	79%	100%
2008	0%	0%	83%	96%
2007	5%	0%	79%	100%
2006	17%	5%	91%	90%

Texas 3

Part of Dallas and northeast suburbs — Plano, part of Garland and McKinney

The rapidly expanding Dallas suburbs of Plano, McKinney, Frisco and Allen in Collin County form the heart of the 3rd, which also takes in part of Dallas itself and most of Garland and Rowlett in northeastern Dallas County. Following a decade of minority population growth, whites here now account only for a slim majority of residents. The district remains strongly Republican and has one of the state's highest median household incomes and rates of college education. Many residents rely on jobs in the vulnerable, but historically lucrative, banking, telecommunications and defense industries.

Many corporate headquarters have moved into the Plano area, and wealthy executives have been building expensive homes in Frisco and the surrounding areas for years. But the national housing crisis caused slowdowns in residential and commercial development, and municipal budget shortfalls in the region continue to worry local officials.

Major companies among the concentration of telecommunications and electronics firms along the U.S. Highway 75 "Telecom Corridor," including Electronic Data Systems and Texas Instruments, have shed thousands of jobs. Richardson benefited from technology firms and expanding banking and financial service industries in the past decade, but local schools may face teacher layoffs.

Although downtown Dallas is in the 30th, many white-collar workers commute to the city from residential areas in the 3rd.

Collin County, which has experienced two decades of explosive population growth, is filled with upwardly mobile professionals and is strongly Republican.

Thirty-three percent of the district's residents live in the northeastern corner of Dallas County. The district overall gave John McCain 57 percent of its vote in the 2008 presidential election.

Major Industry
Telecommunications, transportation, banking, defense

Cities
Plano (pt.), 254,525; Garland (pt.), 151,172; Dallas (pt.), 126,994; McKinney (pt.), 108,904; Frisco (pt.), 51,747; Allen (pt.), 45,269; Rowlett (pt.), 37,980

Notable
Parker's Southfork Ranch, which was the home of the fictional Ewing family of television's "Dallas," now offers tours and a glimpse of the gun that shot J.R.

Rep. Ralph M. Hall (R)

Capitol Office
225-6673
www.house.gov/ralphhall
2405 Rayburn Bldg. 20515-4304; fax 225-3332

Committees
Science, Space & Technology - Chairman

Residence
Rockwall

Born
May 3, 1923; Fate, Texas

Religion
Methodist

Family
Widowed; three children

Education
Texas Christian U., attended 1943 (pre-law); U. of
Texas, attended 1946-47 (pre-law); Southern
Methodist U., LL.B. 1951

Military
Navy, 1942-45

Career
Lawyer; aluminum company president

Political Highlights
Rockwall County judge, 1951-63; Texas Senate,
1963-73 (president pro tempore, 1968-69; served
as a Democrat); sought Democratic nomination for
lieutenant governor, 1972

ELECTION RESULTS

2010 GENERAL

Ralph M. Hall (R)	136,338	73.2%
VaLinda Hathcox (D)	40,975	22.0%
Jim Prindle (LIBERT)	4,729	2.5%
Shane Shepard (I)	4,244	2.3%

2010 PRIMARY

Ralph M. Hall (R)	39,579	57.4%
Steve Clark (R)	20,496	29.7%
John Cooper (R)	3,748	5.4%
Ray Hall (R)	3,190	4.6%
Lou Gigliotti (R)	1,044	1.5%
Joshua Kowert (R)	947	1.4%

Previous Winning Percentages
2008 (69%); 2006 (64%); 2004 (68%); 2002 (58%);
2000 (60%); 1998 (58%); 1996 (64%); 1994 (59%);
1992 (58%); 1990 (100%); 1988 (66%); 1986 (72%);
1984 (58%); 1982 (74%); 1980 (52%)

Elected 1980; 16th term

The oldest member of the House, the grandfatherly Hall backs domestic energy production and a leading U.S. role in space exploration as chairman of the Science, Space and Technology Committee.

A former renegade Democrat who switched to reliable Republican in 2004, Hall has since aligned himself with the tea party movement, joining the newly formed House Tea Party Caucus during the 111th Congress (2009-10).

His folksy humor — "there's nothing as bad as an unemployed son-in-law," he has said about job creation — and sharp political acumen help his reputation among lawmakers in both parties. While his party switch might have diminished his power when Democrats were in control of Congress, it helped prolong his career by allowing him to survive in a reconfigured district and set him up to lead the Science panel in the 112th Congress (2011-12).

With Republicans back in the majority, Hall takes the helm of a committee for the first time, positioning him to direct oversight of the Obama administration's science activities.

One of Hall's priorities for the 112th is NASA. Hall criticized the Obama administration's proposal in 2010 to restructure the agency, especially a plan to cancel the Constellation program, which is based at the Johnson Space Center in Houston. Hall argued that doing so would make the U.S. dependent on Russia for access to the International Space Station and that the agency is shifting away from what Hall thinks should be its priority: manned spaceflight.

"Ever since the president ran a line through Constellation, NASA's been in disarray," Hall said.

During the George W. Bush administration, Hall supported a proposal to send a man to Mars, a plan that held the potential to bring new missions to the Johnson Space Center. After the 2003 loss of the space shuttle Columbia, Hall pressed for a greater focus on safety, adding an amendment to the annual NASA funding bill directing the agency to conduct studies on improving space shuttle crew survivability.

Hall helped pass legislation to boost math and science education as well as funding for basic science research during the 110th Congress (2007-08), but opposed a broad science-program reauthorization bill during the 111th. He argued that the legislation had "good potential" but was too costly and included programs that were redundant.

Stylistically, Hall is anything but a firebrand. When he was a member of the Energy and Commerce Committee — a spot he gave up to become a committee chairman — he took a quiet approach to looking after Texas' oil and gas industry.

Hall opposes proposals to create a cap-and-trade system to limit carbon emissions and has contended that requirements for reductions could hurt the economy and U.S. competitiveness.

During the 111th Congress, Hall raised concerns about accusations of scientific misconduct at the University of East Anglia's Climatic Research Unit and questioned the science behind proposals to curb greenhouse gas emissions.

"Reasonable people have serious questions about our knowledge of the state of the science, the evidence and what constitutes a proportional response," Hall said at a Science Committee hearing in late 2010.

Hall strongly supports additional oil drilling on federal land and off U.S. coastlines, and especially in Alaska's Arctic National Wildlife Refuge. He said arguments that drilling in a portion of the area would harm the surrounding environment were "tantamount to saying dropping a silver dollar in the end zone of the New York Giants football team ruins the entire stadium."

After the 2010 oil spill in the Gulf of Mexico, he criticized the Obama administration's moratorium on deep-water drilling and backed a measure that would overhaul a federally funded ultra-deep-water drilling research program to focus on safer drilling technologies. The existing program, which Hall helped create, has been targeted for elimination by both the current and previous administration.

His flagging allegiance to Democrats was evident for years before he switched parties. In 1985, he voted "present" rather than support the re-election of liberal Democrat Thomas P. "Tip" O'Neill Jr. of Massachusetts as Speaker. In 2000, he publicly championed the presidential candidacy of Bush, then the Republican governor of Texas. After the 2002 election, Hall told GOP leaders he might back Republican J. Dennis Hastert of Illinois for Speaker if his vote were the deciding one.

He strayed from the party line more often than any other House member in the early 2000s. Some speculated he would leave the Democratic Party after the GOP took over Congress in 1994. Instead, he helped start the Blue Dog Coalition, a group of fiscally conservative House Democrats.

In 2003, the GOP-controlled Texas Legislature drew a new congressional map and established a Republican-leaning 4th District with only about a third of Hall's constituents. Facing a tough re-election, he registered as a Republican just before the state candidate filing deadline in January 2004.

Hall briefly made headlines in 2007, when the watchdog group Citizens for Responsibility and Ethics in Washington said in a report that he was among the 72 House members who used campaign funds to pay relatives or their relatives' employers. Hall told USA Today he hired his daughter-in-law because he trusts her: "I'm not sure that it's a good thing to do, but it's a safe thing to do."

A World War II veteran, Hall got an early start in politics, winning election as county judge, or chief executive, of Rockwall County in 1950 while still attending law school in nearby Dallas. Twelve years later, he moved to the state Senate and spent a decade there, rising to become president pro tempore.

After finishing fourth in the Democratic primary for lieutenant governor in 1972, he left public life for a time. But when 4th District Democrat Ray Roberts announced his retirement in 1980, Hall won the seat with 52 percent of the vote. He generally has won by comfortable margins since, although five candidates in the GOP primary in 2010 held him to 57 percent of the vote.

Key Votes

2010

Overhaul the nation's health insurance system	NO
Allow for repeal of "don't ask, don't tell"	NO
Overhaul financial services industry regulation	NO
Limit use of new Afghanistan War funds to troop withdrawal activities	NO
Change oversight of offshore drilling and lift oil spill liability cap	NO
Provide a path to legal status for some children of illegal immigrants	NO
Extend Bush-era income tax cuts for two years	YES

2009

Expand the Children's Health Insurance Program	NO
Provide $787 billion in tax cuts and spending increases to stimulate the economy	NO
Allow bankruptcy judges to modify certain primary-residence mortgages	NO
Create a cap-and-trade system to limit greenhouse gas emissions	NO
Provide $2 billion for the "cash for clunkers" program	YES
Establish the government as the sole provider of student loans	NO
Restrict federally funded insurance coverage for abortions in health care overhaul	YES

CQ Vote Studies

	PARTY UNITY		PRESIDENTIAL SUPPORT	
	SUPPORT	OPPOSE	SUPPORT	OPPOSE
2010	95%	5%	29%	71%
2009	92%	8%	31%	69%
2008	96%	4%	65%	35%
2007	92%	8%	80%	20%
2006	93%	7%	85%	15%

Interest Groups

	AFL-CIO	ADA	CCUS	ACU
2010	0%	0%	88%	96%
2009	14%	10%	93%	92%
2008	33%	30%	83%	84%
2007	8%	10%	90%	96%
2006	21%	5%	93%	84%

Texas 4

Northeast — Sherman, Texarkana, Paris

The 4th begins in Dallas' eastern and northern suburbs before moving east to less-populated and rural areas in the northeastern corner of the state. The district extends along the Oklahoma and Arkansas borders, taking in Texarkana, but its five western counties contain about two-thirds of the population.

It has Texas' second-highest percentage of white residents (72 percent) and lowest percentage of Hispanics (13 percent).

The district includes a mix of suburban and rural communities, with only one city having more than 40,000 residents. In the east, timber, oil and natural gas are big industries, while Dallas commuters and other white-collar workers populate the growing western counties, especially Collin. This area hosts soccer's FC Dallas at Pizza Hut Park, Frisco's regional sports complex that also is used as a retail center and entertainment venue. Manufacturing and small businesses drive much of the economy in the 4th. Food-processing plants are important, and there is a Tyson Foods meat production plant in Sherman, but industry giant Pilgrim's Pride left its one-time headquarters in Pittsburg in 2009.

The Texarkana area still depends on jobs at the Red River Army Depot. The

district struggles, as does the rest of the state, with finding adequate water supplies for its growing communities.

Transportation is also an issue for most of East Texas, and road and rail development will be key for the 4th, which is one of the nation's most-populous ahead of decennial remapping.

Associated with the Bible Belt that stretches through much of the South, the 4th is fertile territory for the GOP. Even Democrats, who can win local races in the east, tend to be conservative here. Every county in the 4th voted for the Republican presidential candidate in 2004 and 2008, and John McCain won 69 percent of the district's vote overall in 2008.

Major Industry

Manufacturing, agriculture, retail, health care

military bases

Red River Army Depot, 3 military, 3,300 civilian (2011)

Cities

Wylie (pt.), 41,012; Allen (pt.), 38,977; Sherman, 38,521; Rockwall, 37,490; Texarkana, 36,411; Greenville, 25,557; Paris, 25,171

Notable

Former House Speaker Sam Rayburn, a Democrat, hailed from Bonham, now home of the Sam Rayburn Library and Museum.

Rep. Jeb Hensarling (R)

Capitol Office
225-3484
www.house.gov/hensarling
129 Cannon Bldg. 20515-4305; fax 226-4888

Committees
Financial Services - Vice Chairman

Residence
Dallas

Born
May 29, 1957; Stephenville, Texas

Religion
Episcopalian

Family
Wife, Melissa Hensarling; two children

Education
Texas A&M U., B.A. 1979 (economics); U. of Texas, J.D. 1982

Career
Child support collection software firm owner; corporate communications executive; congressional district and campaign aide; lawyer; senatorial campaign committee executive director

Political Highlights
No previous office

ELECTION RESULTS

2010 GENERAL

Jeb Hensarling (R)	106,742	70.5%
Tom Berry (D)	41,649	27.5%
Ken Ashby (LIBERT)	2,958	2.0%

2010 PRIMARY

Jeb Hensarling (R)	unopposed

2008 GENERAL

Jeb Hensarling (R)	162,894	83.6%
Ken Ashby (LIBERT)	31,967	16.4%

Previous Winning Percentages
2006 (62%); 2004 (64%); 2002 (58%)

Elected 2002; 5th term

Hensarling is an unswerving conservative who prefers highlighting differences with Democrats to cutting deals. As chairman of the House Republican Conference, though, he has to find ways to deal with the Democratic Senate and White House while still maintaining his fiscal principles.

At first it appeared Hensarling (HENN-sur-ling) would have a contest on his hands for the conference chairmanship, the No. 4 leadership position. He had the backing of the GOP leadership team and a solid list of endorsements from the rank and file, but he faced a challenge from tea party champion Michele Bachmann of Minnesota. Bachmann dropped out before the vote and endorsed Hensarling.

He succeeded Mike Pence of Indiana in the job, just as he had previously succeeded Pence as chairman of the Republican Study Committee (RSC), the most conservative bloc of House Republicans.

Hensarling can be doctrinaire to the point of humorlessness in drawing lines between the two parties, and he doesn't seem to mind how others take it. "I didn't come to Washington to make friends, and I haven't been disappointed," he said.

As a member of the leadership, his freedom to criticize fellow Republicans for fiscal heresy is somewhat diminished, and he walked a fine line during debate early in the 112th Congress (2011-12) on a measure to fund the government for the rest of 2011. "On the one hand this is the single largest year-to-year cut in the federal budget. . . . Probably for that we all deserve medals, the entire Congress," he said on CNN in April. "Relative to the size of the problem, it is not even a rounding error. In that case we probably all deserve to be tarred and feathered."

The Texan, formerly the No. 2 Republican on the Budget Committee and a member of President Obama's National Commission on Fiscal Responsibility and Reform, was among the loudest critics of Obama's fiscal 2012 budget.

"The president is going to have to decide: Does he want to exploit the crisis or does he want to solve the crisis? And if we look at his budget that he's presented now, it appears he wants to exploit it," he said on CNN in February 2011.

Hensarling's devotion to free markets and small-government conservatism was also on display during the debate over a financial industry regulatory overhaul in 2010. Hensarling, now vice chairman of the Financial Services Committee, berated the legislation put forth by the panel's Democratic leadership. "It grants unparalleled discretionary powers to the federal government to pick winners and losers, ushering in a new era of crony capitalism," he said during the House and Senate conference on the legislation.

When Hensarling deviates from the party line, it is usually further to the right. In 2008, he split with President George W. Bush and Arizona Sen. John McCain, then on his way to winning the Republican presidential nomination, to oppose a bipartisan housing rescue proposal allowing the government to extend credit and buy stock in mortgage financiers Fannie Mae and Freddie Mac. "The bottom line: The taxpayer is about to be the big loser here. . . . I came here to protect free enterprise, not big banks," Hensarling said.

In the 111th Congress (2009-10) he sponsored legislation to cut off government financial support of Fannie and Freddie. His proposal was the third winner of the House Republicans' YouCut program, in which participants vote on proposals to cut federal spending with GOP lawmakers proposing each top vote-getter during legislative floor activity.

He served as one of five members of a congressionally established board that monitors the Troubled Asset Relief Program created in late 2008 to rescue the financial sector, but he resigned in December 2009, citing disappointment with the panel's work. Hensarling voted in 2008 against the $700 billion bailout plan, calling it a "step down the slippery slope to socialism."

Hensarling, who served as RSC chairman in the 110th Congress (2007-08), combines his conservative fiscal outlook with a dedicated social conservatism. He voted in both 2004 and 2006 for a constitutional amendment to ban same-sex marriage, and he opposes abortion, voting in 2006 to make it a felony to take a minor across state lines for the procedure. In 2009, he voted against legislation to expand federal hate-crime law to cover offenses based on sexual orientation. He opposed repeal of the statutory ban on gays and lesbians serving openly in the military — the so-called "Don't Ask, Don't Tell" policy — that was enacted in late 2010.

Hensarling is a political and ideological heir — part strategist, part policy wonk — to past GOP leaders from the Lone Star State such as former House Majority Leader Dick Armey, whom he counts as a mentor, and former Sen. Phil Gramm, for whom he once worked as an aide.

Born in Stephenville to a family of poultry farmers, Hensarling decided early that he wouldn't enter the family business. His first taste of politics came in 1964, when his Republican parents had him knocking on doors for presidential candidate Barry Goldwater. He started a Republican Club at his high school and acted as a GOP precinct captain at Texas A&M University, where he took a class on money and banking taught by Gramm.

After three years as a corporate lawyer, Hensarling was hired in 1985 to oversee Gramm's field offices in Texas. When Gramm became chairman of the National Republican Senatorial Committee in the run-up to the 1992 election, he made Hensarling its executive director.

He took a break from government to go home to Texas to start his own business, a firm that made computer software to help single parents collect child support payments. His varied business career also included a stint as vice president of Austin-based Green Mountain Energy Co., a provider of electricity from wind and solar power.

In 2002 the 5th District was reconfigured after Texas gained two seats in post-2000 census reapportionment. Republican Pete Sessions, who had represented the 5th for four terms, decided to run in the new 32nd District. Hensarling won a five-way primary for the nomination in the 5th and bested Democrat Ron Chapman, a Dallas-area judge, by 18 percentage points in the general election. He has coasted since.

Key Votes

2010

Overhaul the nation's health insurance system	NO
Allow for repeal of "don't ask, don't tell"	NO
Overhaul financial services industry regulation	NO
Limit use of new Afghanistan War funds to troop withdrawal activities	NO
Change oversight of offshore drilling and lift oil spill liability cap	NO
Provide a path to legal status for some children of illegal immigrants	NO
Extend Bush-era income tax cuts for two years	YES

2009

Expand the Children's Health Insurance Program	NO
Provide $787 billion in tax cuts and spending increases to stimulate the economy	NO
Allow bankruptcy judges to modify certain primary-residence mortgages	NO
Create a cap-and-trade system to limit greenhouse gas emissions	NO
Provide $2 billion for the "cash for clunkers" program	NO
Establish the government as the sole provider of student loans	NO
Restrict federally funded insurance coverage for abortions in health care overhaul	YES

CQ Vote Studies

	PARTY UNITY		PRESIDENTIAL SUPPORT	
	SUPPORT	OPPOSE	SUPPORT	OPPOSE
2010	99%	1%	29%	71%
2009	99%	1%	11%	89%
2008	99%	1%	87%	13%
2007	98%	2%	92%	8%
2006	96%	4%	85%	15%

Interest Groups

	AFL-CIO	ADA	CCUS	ACU
2010	0%	0%	88%	100%
2009	5%	0%	73%	100%
2008	0%	5%	78%	100%
2007	4%	0%	70%	100%
2006	7%	10%	93%	100%

Texas 5

Part of Dallas and east suburbs — Mesquite, part of Garland; Palestine

The 5th winds east and southeast from eastern Dallas through Dallas County suburbs and six other counties. Only 14 percent of Dallas County's population is here, but it is home to a plurality of the 5th's residents.

The 5th's part of Dallas differs from the glitz characterizing the portion in the neighboring 32nd.

The 5th takes in eastern and northeastern Dallas, which have more of a working-class flavor and are home to many small businesses. Areas near White Rock Lake, such as Old Lake Highlands, however, are upper-middle class. Mesquite, a suburb east of the city, is another population center. Located in far eastern Dallas County, its economic landscape continues to diversify, as manufacturing and business park development complement recreational and tourism projects. Union Pacific Railroad operates a distribution facility in the city's Skyline Industrial Park east of the Dallas-Fort Worth Metroplex.

Many of the district's suburbs have growing populations and provide easy access to a bustling metropolis while supplying the benefits of small-town life. Southeast of Dallas, the district moves from flat prairies into the forest region of East Texas.

Prisons are key employers in rural parts of the district, and cattle, natural gas and coal are important industries as well. Water resources for the growing population is a contentious issue here — an area of the Upper Neches River in Anderson and Cherokee counties long planned by local officials to be used as a reservoir will be instead designated a 25,000-acre wildlife refuge.

The 5th generally favors Republicans. GOP areas abound in northeastern Dallas and in Anderson and Henderson counties well southeast of the city. Some heavily Hispanic areas in Dallas County's southeastern precincts tend to vote more Democratic, and Mesquite often is politically competitive. Republican presidential candidate John McCain took 63 percent of the district's vote overall in 2008.

Major Industry
Small business, technology, prisons, ranching

Cities
Mesquite, 139,824; Dallas (pt.), 90,039; Garland (pt.), 75,702

Notable
Resistol Arena is home to the Mesquite Championship Rodeo.

Rep. Joe L. Barton (R)

Capitol Office
225-2002
joebarton.house.gov
2109 Rayburn Bldg. 20515-4306; fax 225-3052

Committees
Energy & Commerce

Residence
Ennis

Born
Sept. 15, 1949; Waco, Texas

Religion
Methodist

Family
Wife, Terri Barton; four children, two stepchildren

Education
Texas A&M U., B.S. 1972 (industrial engineering);
Purdue U., M.S. 1973 (industrial administration)

Career
Engineering consultant

Political Highlights
Sought Republican nomination for U.S. Senate
(special election), 1993

ELECTION RESULTS

2010 GENERAL

Joe L. Barton (R)	107,140	65.9%
David E. Cozad (D)	50,717	31.2%
Byron Severns (LIBERT)	4,700	2.9%

2010 PRIMARY

Joe L. Barton (R)	unopposed

2008 GENERAL

Joe L. Barton (R)	174,008	62.0%
Ludwig Otto (D)	99,919	35.6%
Max W. Koch III (LIBERT)	6,655	2.4%

Previous Winning Percentages
2006 (61%); 2004 (66%); 2002 (70%); 2000 (88%);
1998 (73%); 1996 (77%); 1994 (76%); 1992 (72%);
1990 (66%); 1988 (68%); 1986 (56%); 1984 (57%)

Elected 1984; 14th term

A conservative stalwart known for his skepticism of man-made global warming and his defense of an unregulated Internet, Barton saw his influence erode in 2011, even as his party reclaimed the House.

The reasons were, in part, of his own making: He infamously apologized to the chief executive of BP in the summer of 2010 after one of the company's rigs exploded in the Gulf of Mexico, causing a massive oil spill. Barton said he was ashamed of President Obama's effort — a "shakedown," he called it — to put pressure on the oil company to pay for the damages. Democrats lambasted him and Republican colleagues shuddered. And it nearly cost Barton his spot as the top Republican on the Energy and Commerce Committee, a fate he averted only by apologizing to the public and to his caucus.

But he lost out to Fred Upton of Michigan for the chairmanship in the 112th Congress (2011-12). The incident was not the explicit reason he lost the post: Republican Steering Committee members said he failed to present a compelling reason to ignore the caucus's rule limiting its members to three terms at the helm of important committees.

Upton graciously allowed Barton to continue on the committee as chairman emeritus, a title that Barton hopes will at least provide enough cachet for him to continue to win headlines for his signature issues.

Barton remains the House's leading skeptic of the science behind the proposition that increased levels of carbon dioxide and other greenhouse gases, due to human use of fossil fuels, are responsible for Earth's rising temperatures. A former oil company engineering consultant, Barton has long been the go-to guy in the House for the oil and gas industries, keystones of the Texas economy. They trust him to shield them from what they see as potentially drastic new rules aimed at combatting climate change.

He cosponsored an amendment to the House-passed version of a catchall 2011 spending bill that would block implementation by the EPA of a cap-and-trade program for controlling greenhouse gas emissions. The provision did not make it into the final measure, however.

Barton has also become a leading opponent of legislation to establish so-called net neutrality: the principle that Internet service providers such as AT&T and Verizon should not allow some Internet traffic to move more quickly across their networks than others. He helped squash legislation to implement that principle by Energy and Commerce's then-chairman, Democrat Henry A. Waxman of California, in 2010, and has criticized the Federal Communications Commission for moving forward on its own on the issue.

Barton has worked with Democratic colleagues, however, to ensure that big technology companies such as Apple, Google and Facebook respect the privacy of their users.

Barton is no pushover for GOP leaders. He voted against a bipartisan deal at the end of 2010 to extend Bush-era tax cuts on the grounds that the deal also included spending increases. "We simply can't keep spending money we don't have," he said. He was one of 36 Republicans to vote no. He also voted against a stopgap spending bill in early 2011 that gave GOP negotiators more time to work out a deal with Senate Democrats and the White House.

And he's serious enough about his principles to avoid populist appeals. He was among a minority of Republicans to stick to his free-trade bona fides in the fall of 2010 by voting against a bill that would've allowed the Commerce Department to launch a trade war with China if the department found that China had devalued its currency and put U.S. firms at an unfair disadvantage.

Those were conservative stances, but Barton is by no means doctrinaire. He picks and chooses his fights and sometimes favors government regulation and intervention in the economy. Like most of his GOP colleagues, he voted against providing government money to prop up ailing banks in 2008, for example, but broke with his caucus by supporting President George W. Bush's request for loan guarantees to help ailing automakers. The next year, he was among a minority of Republicans to support a program to provide cash incentives to car owners who traded in their old models for more fuel-efficient vehicles.

He also supported 2010 legislation to bolster regulation of the food industry after several food contamination scandals. And he's generated some enthusiasm on both sides of the aisle — particularly from Obama — for his 2009 bill to regulate how college football picks its best team. His measure would change out the computerized Bowl Championship Series in favor of a playoff system.

On social issues, Barton supports amending the Constitution to ban same-sex marriage and is a reliable anti-abortion vote. But he has backed federally supported stem cell research. He's hopeful that such work will help find cures to the ailments that felled his father, who died of complications from diabetes, and his brother, Texas District Judge Jon Barton, who succumbed to liver cancer in 2000 at age 44.

Born in Waco, Barton is the son of an agribusiness salesman and a schoolteacher. His father in his later years was a plant geneticist, breeding new strains of cotton. Barton studied industrial engineering at Texas A&M University, then earned a master's degree from Purdue University. He moved to Ennis and became an engineering consultant for Atlantic Richfield Co.

In 1981, Barton was a White House fellow at the Department of Energy when he got the government bug. He made a successful 1984 bid for the House seat of Republican Phil Gramm, who moved to the Senate.

Barton has won re-election easily since and often demonstrated an interest in higher office. He made an unsuccessful bid for the Senate when Democrat Lloyd Bentsen left in 1993 to be President Bill Clinton's Treasury secretary, then in 2006 briefly ran for minority leader before dropping out and endorsing the eventual winner, John A. Boehner of Ohio.

Barton mulled a second bid for the Senate when Gramm retired in 2002, but George W. Bush endorsed Republican John Cornyn, the former Texas attorney general and state Supreme Court justice. With the state's senior senator, Kay Bailey Hutchison not seeking re-election in 2012, Barton could make another run.

Key Votes

2010

Overhaul the nation's health insurance system	NO
Allow for repeal of "don't ask, don't tell"	NO
Overhaul financial services industry regulation	NO
Limit use of new Afghanistan war funds to troop withdrawal activities	NO
Change oversight of offshore drilling and lift oil spill liability cap	NO
Provide a path to legal status for some children of illegal immigrants	NO
Extend Bush-era income tax cuts for two years	NO

2009

Expand the Children's Health Insurance Program	NO
Provide $787 billion in tax cuts and spending increases to stimulate the economy	NO
Allow bankruptcy judges to modify certain primary-residence mortgages	NO
Create a cap-and-trade system to limit greenhouse gas emissions	NO
Provide $2 billion for the "cash for clunkers" program	YES
Establish the government as the sole provider of student loans	NO
Restrict federally funded insurance coverage for abortions in health care overhaul	YES

CQ Vote Studies

	PARTY UNITY		PRESIDENTIAL SUPPORT	
	SUPPORT	OPPOSE	SUPPORT	OPPOSE
2010	97%	3%	29%	71%
2009	91%	9%	21%	79%
2008	98%	2%	82%	18%
2007	95%	5%	88%	12%
2006	95%	5%	87%	13%

Interest Groups

	AFL-CIO	ADA	CCUS	ACU
2010	0%	5%	86%	96%
2009	14%	5%	92%	96%
2008	14%	10%	94%	96%
2007	4%	10%	85%	96%
2006	7%	15%	93%	88%

Texas 6

Suburban Dallas — Arlington; part of Fort Worth and Mansfield; Corsicana

The overwhelming majority of the 6th's land area is a boot-shaped band of counties that extends southeast from Ellis County, but nearly two-thirds of the district's population lives just north of Ellis in eastern or southern Tarrant County. This suburban-rural district takes in a sliver of Fort Worth and all of Arlington in the Dallas-Fort Worth Metroplex before stretching southeast along Interstate 45, where it becomes more rural and its economy more reliant on agriculture.

Arlington has mainly shed its blue-collar image, but the local General Motors assembly plant still employs thousands of workers. The University of Texas at Arlington is among the city's top employers, and the school has been an incubator for the city's growing technology sector. In addition, hundreds of thousands of people travel to Arlington each summer to visit the Six Flags Over Texas amusement park, while others head to the Rangers' ballpark for baseball. The new Cowboys Stadium opened here in September 2009.

South of Tarrant, most of the rest of the district's residents live in Ellis and Navarro counties. Ellis, which includes Waxahachie and Ennis, used to be dependent on cotton farming, but the cement industry has taken hold here.

Farther south, Freestone and Leon counties are rural, less populous and sustained by oil, ranching and farming. Houston County and northern Trinity County, east of Leon, have a fairly large timber industry.

Most of Tarrant is aligned with the GOP, although there is some Democratic strength in southern Fort Worth and eastern Arlington, where the population is more diverse. Ellis' overwhelming Republican support makes the 6th a safe haven for GOP candidates — John McCain took 60 percent of the district's vote in the 2008 presidential election.

Major Industry
Transportation, technology, agriculture

Cities
Arlington (pt.), 365,372; Fort Worth (pt.), 62,634; Mansfield (pt.), 54,716; Waxahachie, 29,621; Corsicana, 23,770

Notable
Squeeze-box melodies and traditional Czech culture on display at the National Polka Festival have drawn visitors to Ennis for more than 40 years.

Rep. John Culberson (R)

Capitol Office
225-2571
www.culberson.house.gov
2352 Rayburn Bldg. 20515-4307; fax 225-4381

Committees
Appropriations
(Military Construction-VA - Chairman)

Residence
Houston

Born
Aug. 24, 1956; Houston, Texas

Religion
Methodist

Family
Wife, Belinda Culberson; one child

Education
Southern Methodist U., B.A. 1981 (history); South
Texas College of Law, J.D. 1988

Career
Lawyer; political advertising agency employee; oil
rig mud logger

Political Highlights
Texas House, 1987-2001

ELECTION RESULTS

2010 GENERAL

John Culberson (R)	143,655	81.4%
Bob Townsend (LIBERT)	31,704	18.0%

2010 PRIMARY

John Culberson (R)	unopposed

2008 GENERAL

John Culberson (R)	162,635	55.9%
Michael Skelly (D)	123,242	42.4%
Drew Parks (LIBERT)	5,057	1.7%

Previous Winning Percentages
2006 (59%); 2004 (64%); 2002 (89%); 2000 (74%)

Elected 2000; 6th term

Culberson is an appropriator who calls himself "a very strict construction-ist of the Constitution." He is fond of invoking Thomas Jefferson, whose por-traits adorn his office walls, to make a point about where he thinks most governmental decisions should be made — at the state and local level. He is a charter member of the House Tea Party Caucus, and one of four members of the group who chairs an Appropriations subcommittee.

An assistant whip, the bespectacled Texan uses his Web savvy to help round up support for the party's initiatives and put out the GOP message calling for limited government and reduced spending. At the same time, he works to obtain federal funds to enable his district to pursue projects such as roads and medical and scientific research at local universities. And he takes a tough line on illegal immigration, a top concern of his Houston-based district.

Culberson chairs the Military Construction-Veterans' Affairs spending panel in the 112th Congress (2011-12). One of his priorities is ending the practice of requiring union-scale wages on building projects at military bases, which he says drives up the cost.

He told the Houston Chronicle that he hoped to create partnerships in the city between the Michael E. DeBakey VA Medical Center and the Texas Medical Center to provide better care for veterans.

Much of his previous focus as an appropriator had been on the subcommit-tee that handles NASA funding. He protects dollars for the Houston-based space program and has been critical of President Obama's plans to cut back on manned spaceflight.

Culberson endorsed the earmark moratorium put in place by House Republicans for the 112th Congress, but he has in the past sought the funding set-asides for projects in his district.

He had the biggest earmark in the fiscal 2010 spending bill for funding the Justice Department — $4.85 million for Operation Linebacker, an initiative developed by the Texas Border Sheriff's Coalition to deter illegal immigration and prevent border-related crime.

Culberson pushed hard through much of 2010 for a supplemental appro-priation for border security, saying at one hearing, "to a real extent, there's a war going on at the southern border." In August, the House passed a bill to provide $701 million.

Like many conservatives, Culberson believed former President George W. Bush's immigration policies were too lax, and he is no fan of the Obama administration's proposals either. He carries in his suit pocket a machine gun bullet he said he found on a tour at the International Bridge in Laredo. He uses it to illustrate his oft-repeated point: "We will either have law and order on the border or plata o plomo," which translates to "silver or lead," a threat referring to drug lords either bribing or killing people who stand in their way.

Culberson was one of more than 80 GOP lawmakers to sign a brief in defense of Arizona's 2010 law targeting illegal immigrants and against a law-suit brought by the Obama administration. And he cosponsored a bill to end birthright citizenship. "We're the only nation on earth that allows an illegal alien to give birth to an automatic citizen," he told KVUE.com in August 2010.

He championed the cause of two Border Patrol agents who were sentenced to prison in 2006 for shooting a fleeing Mexican drug trafficker and hiding evidence, saying it was an "unjust criminal prosecution of two officers who were protecting our borders from criminals and terrorists." Before leaving office in 2009, Bush commuted the officers' prison sentences.

Culberson has embraced new technology as a way to disseminate his message on immigration and other issues. "My ultimate goal is to become a real-time representative," he said. In August 2008 he joined fellow Republicans on the House floor during a congressional recess to protest the lack of a vote on expanding oil and gas drilling. While his fellow Republicans shouted their message from a lectern with the microphone off, Culberson posted messages on Twitter and uploaded video interviews with Republicans from his phone to Qik.com.

He was highly critical of the drilling moratorium put in place after the explosion and oil spill at an offshore rig in the Gulf of Mexico in spring 2010. "The administration's approach is ham-handed, poorly written and punitive to the honest, hardworking people who have been put in limbo by the prohibition on oil and gas exploration," he said.

Culberson is an amateur fossil collector and initially led opposition to an omnibus lands bill in early 2009 because it included a provision that would set heavy penalties for taking any paleontological resource from federal lands without a permit. Ultimately the language was modified to forestall criminal prosecution of visitors who remove a few stones containing fossils.

The third of four children, Culberson was born in Houston and is a lifelong resident of the district. His father was a political consultant and graphic designer who worked on GOP Sen. John Tower's re-election in 1966, when Culberson was 10. He recalls going with his father on campaign trips. He was campus chairman at Southern Methodist University for George Bush's 1980 presidential campaign. (Culberson represents Bush's old House district.) After college, Culberson worked with his father while getting his law degree.

At 30, he won a seat in the Texas House and stayed for 14 years while also practicing as a civil defense attorney. In the state House, Culberson waged an ultimately successful 11-year campaign to return control of the troubled Texas prison system to the state from the supervision of federal Judge William Wayne Justice. One of his goals is a constitutional amendment to give state legislatures the right to approve federal judges every 10 years.

When Rep. Bill Archer decided to retire in 2000, Culberson entered a crowded primary and won an expensive runoff, ensuring his election in the solidly Republican district. He was re-elected in 2008 with nearly 56 percent of the vote, his closest contest yet, after Democratic challenger Michael Skelly raised more than $3 million — including $1 million of his own money — to Culberson's $1.7 million. But in 2010, Democrats didn't field a candidate and Culberson took 82 percent of the vote.

Key Votes

2010

Overhaul the nation's health insurance system	NO
Allow for repeal of "don't ask, don't tell"	NO
Overhaul financial services industry regulation	NO
Limit use of new Afghanistan War funds to troop withdrawal activities	NO
Change oversight of offshore drilling and lift oil spill liability cap	NO
Provide a path to legal status for some children of illegal immigrants	NO
Extend Bush-era income tax cuts for two years	YES

2009

Expand the Children's Health Insurance Program	NO
Provide $787 billion in tax cuts and spending increases to stimulate the economy	NO
Allow bankruptcy judges to modify certain primary-residence mortgages	NO
Create a cap-and-trade system to limit greenhouse gas emissions	NO
Provide $2 billion for the "cash for clunkers" program	NO
Establish the government as the sole provider of student loans	NO
Restrict federally funded insurance coverage for abortions in health care overhaul	YES

CQ Vote Studies

	PARTY UNITY		PRESIDENTIAL SUPPORT	
	SUPPORT	OPPOSE	SUPPORT	OPPOSE
2010	97%	3%	26%	74%
2009	89%	11%	14%	86%
2008	97%	3%	77%	23%
2007	97%	3%	89%	11%
2006	97%	3%	95%	5%

Interest Groups

	AFL-CIO	ADA	CCUS	ACU
2010	0%	0%	100%	100%
2009	5%	0%	73%	100%
2008	7%	5%	88%	100%
2007	4%	0%	79%	100%
2006	14%	10%	93%	88%

Texas 7

Western Houston and suburbs — Bellaire, West University Place, Jersey Village

Situated in western Houston, the 7th starts inside the Interstate 610 loop at Main Street south of downtown before moving through the city's western outposts and into the suburbs. White-collar executives, good schools and religious conservatism characterize much of the 7th. Significant population growth in minority communities across the district has led to increasingly diverse neighborhoods. Two-thirds white in 2000, the district is now one-fourth Hispanic with 10 percent proportions for black and Asian residents. Much of Houston's gay and lesbian community is centered at the district's eastern point around the Montrose neighborhood.

The 7th includes some of Houston's oil and gas industry, as well as much of the Texas Medical Center, Houston's museum district (both of which are shared with the 9th and 18th districts), and the Galleria shopping and corporate complex.

The medical center collaborates with local universities and employs tens of thousands of area residents, but budget shortfalls are a concern. Rice University, which is adjacent to the medical center, focuses on nanotech and other applied sciences.

An emphasis on attracting technology firms and corporate headquarters has enabled the 7th to enjoy decades of economic growth despite periodic national downturns.

Close ties to the oil and gas and health care industries make the 7th one of the state's wealthiest districts.

Tony villages Piney Point, Bunker Hill and Hunters Creek, which are near Interstate 10 and surrounded on all sides by Houston, bring up the median household income, and the 7th's share of the city is largely middle class. The 7th also is one of the nation's 15 most-educated districts, with half of its residents age 25 years or older having earned at least a bachelor's degree.

Major Industry

Energy, health care, education and research, retail

Cities

Houston (pt.), 436,845; Bellaire (pt.), 16,855; West University Place, 14,787

Notable

On Sept. 12, 1962, during a speech at Rice University Stadium, President John F. Kennedy famously proclaimed that an American would reach the moon before the end of that decade.

Rep. Kevin Brady (R)

Capitol Office
225-4901
www.house.gov/brady
301 Cannon Bldg. 20515-4308; fax 225 5524

Committees
Ways & Means
(Trade - Chairman)
Joint Economic - Vice Chairman

Residence
The Woodlands

Born
April 11, 1955; Vermillion, S.D.

Religion
Roman Catholic

Family
Wife, Cathy Brady; two children

Education
U. of South Dakota, B.S. 1990 (mass communication)

Career
Chamber of commerce executive

Political Highlights
Texas House, 1991-96

ELECTION RESULTS

2010 GENERAL

Kevin Brady (R)	161,417	80.3%
Kent Hargett (D)	34,694	17.2%
Bruce West (LIBERT)	4,988	2.5%

2010 PRIMARY

Kevin Brady (R)	52,595	79.3%
Scott Baker (R)	8,614	13.0%
Tyler Russell (R)	3,542	5.3%
Melecio Franco (R)	1,565	2.4%

2008 GENERAL

Kevin Brady (R)	207,128	72.6%
Kent Hargett (D)	70,758	24.8%
Brian Stevens (LIBERT)	7,565	2.6%

Previous Winning Percentages
2006 (67%); 2004 (69%); 2002 (93%); 2000 (92%);
1998 (93%); 1996 General Election Runoff (59%)

Elected 1996; 8th term

Brady has a reputation as a reliable conservative who presses for free trade, spending restraint and lower taxes. A Ways and Means subcommittee chairman and a member of the GOP whip team, Brady is well positioned to advocate his pro-business and pro-trade agendas.

"I believe our goals as Republicans and the Congress should be to create the strongest economy of the 21st century," Brady said following Republican victories in the 2010 elections. "To do that we have to have a tax system that makes us much more competitive than the one we have . . . especially in international competition."

In September 2010, Brady voted against a measure that would have pressed China to raise the value of its currency, saying he was worried the measure could hurt U.S. efforts to compete in the Chinese market.

"We need a trade policy that opens markets, levels the playing field and finds innovative ways to move goods quicker and more affordably," Brady said.

As chairman of the Ways and Means Subcommittee on Trade in the 112th Congress (2011-12), he hopes to move forward on agreements with South Korea, Colombia and Panama.

"All three pending trade agreements are good agreements. The time to move forward with all three is now," he said at an April 2011 hearing.

Brady also serves as vice chairman of the Joint Economic Committee, which provides analysis and recommendations on economic and fiscal policy. In that role, he was not complimentary about President Obama's spending blueprint for 2012.

"I am disappointed that neither President Obama's budget nor the [president's] economic report really exhibited any urgency towards addressing our financial challenges in America," he told the House Budget Committee in March 2011. "In fact, it seemed to me the report laid out government spending as a path to economic growth in this country."

Although he is a stickler on policy, Brady's Southern geniality and calm manner make him approachable to members on both sides of the aisle. The Texan is known to crack jokes even during tough confrontations.

But his tenaciousness was on display in November 2009 when he had a heated exchange during a Ways and Means hearing with Treasury Secretary Timothy F. Geithner regarding the state of the U.S. economy and stimulus legislation. The exchange culminated in Brady asking Geithner if he would step down from his post.

Transforming government is a Brady theme. He routinely sponsors legislation to set expiration dates for each federal agency, department and program unless they are affirmatively renewed. The proposal is similar to a law he won in Texas that has eliminated 52 agencies. Just after taking office, Brady sponsored a measure designed to place such expiration limits on agencies. It ultimately failed as an amendment to other legislation.

Brady has worked for years to secure disaster relief and recovery funds for his district for the devastating 2005 Gulf Coast hurricanes. His district, close to the Louisiana border, was among the first to take in Katrina evacuees. Hurricane Rita later damaged 70,000 homes in the area and destroyed $1 billion in timber. He again helped push for federal assistance to respond to hurricanes in 2008 and led support for on extension of the National Flood Insurance Program in the 111th Congress (2009-10).

The Texan has also been a major proponent of ending the Obama administration's drilling moratoriums in the Gulf of Mexico that were put in place following the oil rig explosion there in April 2010. "We've been fighting to end the moratorium not just in name but in practice," Brady said. It's an "effort to create a stable regulatory environment that encourages investment and safe production."

He introduced legislation in the 111th Congress that would audit and investigate the BP fund to aid victims of the oil spill.

Concerned about stemming the flow of illegal immigrants, Brady worked on legislation with fellow Texas Republican Sam Johnson to require all employers to take part in an employee verification system.

Brady is a reliable Republican vote, but he split — for a while — with his party on the issue of gun rights. When he was 12 years old, his father, a lawyer, was shot and killed in a South Dakota courtroom by the deranged spouse of a client, and the incident helped shape his outlook on gun control. As a state representative in Texas — where he moved at age 26 to take a job with the Chamber of Commerce in Beaumont — Brady was one of two Republicans to oppose a bill allowing Texans to carry concealed weapons. But more recently he said the law has not been abused and has protected many individuals and small businesses "in tough areas." In April 2009, he warned against "potential overreaction to the Mexican drug violence" that could lead to curbing gun owners' rights.

He attended the University of South Dakota but left in 1978 without graduating because he had neglected to complete the paperwork for a work-study class. After an opponent in his first Texas House race in 1990 unearthed Brady's lack of a degree, Brady cleared up the incomplete grade. He went on to serve six years in the state legislature.

Brady decided to seek the U.S. House seat after Republican Jack Fields announced he wasn't running for re-election in the 8th district in 1996.

It took Brady four elections, but he eventually vanquished his chief rival for the seat. Republican physician Gene Fontenot emerged on top in the March primary for the GOP nomination, but he did not capture a majority of the vote. Brady had much stronger ties to the district and defeated Fontenot in the April runoff. But a three-judge federal panel redrew the 8th and 12 other Texas congressional districts in response to a Supreme Court ruling that found illegal racial gerrymandering at play in the Texas map. The federal court threw out the primary results from those districts and started the electoral process from scratch. In November, Fontenot forced Brady into a December runoff. Brady finally won the seat, taking 59 percent.

He has been safely ensconced since then and took 80 percent of the vote in 2010.

Key Votes

2010

Overhaul the nation's health insurance system	NO
Allow for repeal of "don't ask, don't tell"	NO
Overhaul financial services industry regulation	NO
Limit use of new Afghanistan War funds to troop withdrawal activities	NO
Change oversight of offshore drilling and lift oil spill liability cap	NO
Provide a path to legal status for some children of illegal immigrants	NO
Extend Bush-era income tax cuts for two years	YES

2009

Expand the Children's Health Insurance Program	NO
Provide $787 billion in tax cuts and spending increases to stimulate the economy	NO
Allow bankruptcy judges to modify certain primary-residence mortgages	NO
Create a cap-and-trade system to limit greenhouse gas emissions	NO
Provide $2 billion for the "cash for clunkers" program	NO
Establish the government as the sole provider of student loans	NO
Restrict federally funded insurance coverage for abortions in health care overhaul	YES

CQ Vote Studies

	PARTY UNITY		PRESIDENTIAL SUPPORT	
	SUPPORT	OPPOSE	SUPPORT	OPPOSE
2010	97%	3%	26%	74%
2009	97%	3%	11%	89%
2008	94%	6%	77%	23%
2007	95%	5%	86%	14%
2006	96%	4%	97%	3%

Interest Groups

	AFL-CIO	ADA	CCUS	ACU
2010	0%	0%	88%	100%
2009	5%	0%	73%	100%
2008	7%	10%	88%	86%
2007	4%	5%	75%	100%
2006	7%	5%	100%	88%

Texas 8

East central — The Woodlands, Conroe

A Republican stronghold, the 8th begins in Houston's rapidly growing Montgomery County suburbs north of the city and moves east through rural areas to the Louisiana border. Despite a decade of growth in the district's Hispanic population, the 8th still has the highest percentage of white residents in any Texas district (74 percent). The district gave John McCain 74 percent of its vote in the 2008 presidential election, and he won easily in each of its counties.

Located about 30 miles north of downtown Houston, The Woodlands — a large planned community that gets its name from its proximity to Sam Houston National Forest — is an exclusive area filled with large houses and some of the state's highest-rated schools. The area is a corporate and business center, and several petroleum and biotechnology companies have made their homes here.

The timber industry and some cattle ranches populate the northern part of Montgomery County, which suffered extensive damage during 2008's Hurricane Ike.

But much of the county is turning into suburbanized bedroom communi-

ties for Houston, and residents in the district have some of the longest commutes in the state.

Local officials in Montgomery County hope to develop regional commuter rail service for the growing workforce. Conroe has one of the largest lakes in the area and hosts wealthy owners of lakefront homes, retirees, golf courses, resorts and marinas. Some of the 8th's lakes provide drinking water to Houston. Farther north are Livingston and Huntsville, where the Texas State Penitentiary houses the state's death row and is a major employer.

In the southeastern part of the 8th, the economy relies on petrochemical production and on ship repair in Orange County and nearby Beaumont and Port Arthur (both in the 2nd District). Abundant pine forests in the district's east still support a vulnerable timber industry.

Major Industry
Petrochemicals, shipping, timber, education, prisons

Cities
The Woodlands (unincorporated) (pt.), 91,485; Conroe, 56,207; Huntsville, 38,548; Orange, 18,595

Notable
Texas' Lone Star flag was designed in Montgomery County in 1839.

Rep. Al Green (D)

Capitol Office
225-7508
www.house.gov/algreen
2201 Rayburn Bldg. 20515-4309; fax 225-2947

Committees
Financial Services

Residence
Houston

Born
Sept. 1, 1947; New Orleans, La.

Religion
Baptist

Family
Divorced

Education
Florida A&M U., attended 1966-71; Tuskegee
Institute of Technology, attended ; Texas Southern
U., J.D. 1973

Career
Lawyer; NAACP chapter president

Political Highlights
Harris County Justice of the Peace Court judge,
1977-2004; candidate for mayor of Houston, 1981

ELECTION RESULTS

2010 GENERAL
Al Green (D)	80,107	75.7%
Steve Mueller (R)	24,201	22.9%
Michael W. Hope (LIBERT)	1,459	1.4%

2010 PRIMARY
Al Green (D)	unopposed

2008 GENERAL
Al Green (D)	143,868	93.6%
Brad Walters (LIBERT)	9,760	6.4%

Previous Winning Percentages
2006 (100%); 2004 (72%)

Elected 2004; 4th term

A soft-spoken but resolute former civil rights leader, Green wants the federal government to do more to provide affordable housing, health care, higher wages and job security. Now an assistant Democratic whip, his agenda hasn't changed with Republicans in control of the House.

"I want to speak for the least, the last and the lost," Green said, meaning those in poverty, the last hired and first fired, and the lost due to mental or other challenges. "They too deserve representation. Part of my calling is helping all of my constituents."

He always wears a lapel pin that reads, "God is Good All the Time."

Green pointed to legislation the House passed in 2009 aimed at providing housing assistance and rental vouchers for homeless veterans as one of his proudest accomplishments, though the Senate never acted on the measure. Some of the provisions were included in other legislation.

"The good news is veterans are being taken care of," Green said.

From his seat on the Financial Services Committee, Green pays particular attention to housing, insurance and lender practices that critics say hurt low- to moderate-income neighborhoods.

He defended a pair of foreclosure mitigation programs the House voted to eliminate in March 2011. While acknowledging there were problems with the programs, which provide assistance to homeowners who owe more than their homes are worth and emergency loans to unemployed homeowners facing foreclosure, Green argued for their continued existence. "We can amend them; we need not end them," he said.

He successfully included in a 2009 national service law a provision encouraging volunteers to work on behalf of affordable housing for economically disadvantaged individuals.

Green initially opposed a $700 billion plan to aid the nation's troubled financial system in fall 2008. "We cannot give the perception that we're willing to help Wall Street but not take care of the people on Home Street," he told the Houston Chronicle. But he supported a slightly revised version that was signed into law.

Formerly a member of the Homeland Security Committee, Green has been an advocate of assistance for hurricane victims. During his first term in the House, his legislative priorities were largely put on hold as he tended to the thousands of evacuees who came to Houston in the aftermath of hurricanes Katrina and Rita — more than 20,000 victims came to his district alone. He spent much of his time dealing with the post-hurricane chaos, including meeting demands for increased police protection, education, housing and social services.

In 2007, he pushed through the House a proposal to extend a temporary housing voucher program run by the Federal Emergency Management Agency (FEMA) until the end of the year. During a hearing on FEMA's slow response to provide housing, Green noted the families of Sept. 11 victims received an average of $3.1 million in compensation. "We cannot treat the people of New York better than we treat people in New Orleans," said Green, who was born in the Crescent City.

After Hurricane Ike blew through Houston in September 2008, Green took to the streets of his district, speaking through a bullhorn and urging his constituents to remain calm. He backed inclusion of $22.9 billion in disaster relief as part of a catchall spending bill Congress cleared later that month.

In December 2010, Green introduced legislation to grant temporary protected status to Pakistanis affected by summer flooding in their home countries, allowing them to stay in the United States for a time.

Green's liberal instincts were also evident in his support during the health care overhaul debate of a "robust public option," a government-run insurance program that did not make it into the final version of the legislation, which he nevertheless supported.

"It has taken our nation many years to finally complete this much-needed reform of our health system," he said when the House passed the final version in March 2010. "However, this is not a final step, but rather a good next step that in the years to come we'll be proud we took."

And he pushes legislation that would index the minimum wage to ensure full-time workers remain above the federal poverty line.

Green often recites the eight-verse poem "The Cold Within" by James Patrick Kenny, which tells the story of six people who died in the cold because greed and spite kept each from contributing to a fire that would have kept them all warm. "The point is this," Green says. "If we don't learn to live together as brothers and sisters, we will perish as fools."

Green represents a racially diverse district, and he is a member of both the Congressional Black Caucus and the Asian Pacific American Caucus. Green said he feels comfortable moving in both circles, partially because he isn't entirely sure about his own ethnic background. "I don't know what I am," he said.

Green was born in New Orleans, the son of an auto mechanic and a maid. He grew up in Florida, where his maternal grandfather was a Methodist minister. He attended Florida A&M University and the Tuskegee Institute of Technology through work-study and grant programs. He didn't earn an undergraduate degree but eventually gained a law degree from the Thurgood Marshall School of Law at Texas Southern University. He then co-founded a law practice that included criminal defense. One of his adversaries in the courtroom, who became a good friend, was then-prosecutor Ted Poe — a Republican elected to represent Texas' 2nd District in 2004.

Green served 26 years as a justice of the peace. During the 1980s and early 1990s, he was president of the local chapter of the NAACP. He took advantage of the GOP-inspired remapping of Texas congressional districts prior to the 2004 election, which significantly altered the demographics of the 9th District and enabled him to score an easy primary victory over Democratic Rep. Chris Bell. He then won the general election with even greater ease. He faced no major party opposition in 2006 or 2008. In 2010, he defeated Republican Steve Mueller with 76 percent of the vote.

He shares the same name as the famous soul singer, which he said can be a disadvantage because "people often ask me to sing." Occasionally he obliges.

Key Votes

2010

Overhaul the nation's health insurance system	YES
Allow for repeal of "don't ask, don't tell"	YES
Overhaul financial services industry regulation	YES
Limit use of new Afghanistan War funds to troop withdrawal activities	NO
Change oversight of offshore drilling and lift oil spill liability cap	YES
Provide a path to legal status for some children of illegal immigrants	YES
Extend Bush-era income tax cuts for two years	YES

2009

Expand the Children's Health Insurance Program	YES
Provide $787 billion in tax cuts and spending increases to stimulate the economy	YES
Allow bankruptcy judges to modify certain primary-residence mortgages	YES
Create a cap-and-trade system to limit greenhouse gas emissions	YES
Provide $2 billion for the "cash for clunkers" program	YES
Establish the government as the sole provider of student loans	YES
Restrict federally funded insurance coverage for abortions in health care overhaul	NO

CQ Vote Studies

	PARTY UNITY		PRESIDENTIAL SUPPORT	
	SUPPORT	OPPOSE	SUPPORT	OPPOSE
2010	98%	2%	95%	5%
2009	99%	1%	97%	3%
2008	99%	1%	14%	86%
2007	98%	2%	3%	97%
2006	94%	6%	30%	70%

Interest Groups

	AFL-CIO	ADA	CCUS	ACU
2010	93%	90%	25%	0%
2009	100%	100%	33%	0%
2008	100%	100%	67%	4%
2007	100%	100%	50%	4%
2006	100%	95%	60%	20%

Texas 9

Southern Houston and suburbs — Mission Bend, part of Missouri City

The 9th, which takes in southern Houston and a few suburbs to the west, is Texas' smallest district in land area but is one of its most ethnically diverse — Hispanics make up 42 percent of residents, blacks 35 percent, Asians 11 percent and whites 10 percent.

The district's eastern edge takes in largely black communities such as Sunnyside, which is one of Houston's oldest black neighborhoods. The 9th stretches west to pick up the entertainment complex Reliant Park. Among other venues, the park hosts Reliant Stadium — the home field for football's Texans — and the historic Astrodome, which remains vacant as local officials debate how to repurpose the multi-use stadium.

The 9th's western portion takes in much of Houston's Asian community, with Chinese, Korean and Japanese enclaves as well as several South Asian immigrant communities. Almost one-third of district residents are foreign-born, the highest percentage in the state. Retail dominates here, and stores spring up with signs in both English and Asian languages. Lead-

ing the local health care sector, part of the Texas Medical Center falls in the 9th in the Hermann Park area (shared with the 7th and 18th districts). The district's portion of the medical center includes the Houston Academy of Medicine and the Michael E. Debakey VA Medical Center.

Job creation is a high priority among the area's many poor residents. Some of the area's "super neighborhoods," communities created by residents in order to better connect local needs to the city government, have focused on safety and housing issues.

The 9th strongly supports Democrats, and the district gave Barack Obama his third-highest percentage statewide (77 percent) in the 2008 presidential election.

Major Industry
Retail, health care, entertainment

Cities
Houston (pt.), 590,829; Mission Bend (unincorporated), 36,501; Missouri City (pt.), 21,709

Notable
The Chinatown area boasts the Hong Kong City Mall, one of the nation's largest Asian-themed malls.

Rep. Michael McCaul (R)

Capitol Office
225-2401
www.house.gov/mccaul
131 Cannon Bldg. 20515 4310; fax 225-5955

Committees
Ethics
Foreign Affairs
Homeland Security
   (Oversight, Investigations & Management - Chairman)
Science, Space & Technology

Residence
Austin

Born
Jan. 14, 1962; Dallas, Texas

Religion
Roman Catholic

Family
Wife, Linda McCaul; five children

Education
Trinity U., B.A. 1984 (business & history); St. Mary's U. (Texas), J.D. 1987

Career
Lawyer; federal prosecutor; U.S. Justice Department official; state deputy attorney general

Political Highlights
No previous office

ELECTION RESULTS

2010 GENERAL

Michael McCaul (R)	144,980	64.7%
Ted Ankrum (D)	74,086	33.0%
Jeremiah Perkins (LIBERT)	5,105	2.3%

2010 PRIMARY

Michael McCaul (R)	46,881	82.9%
Rick Martin (R)	5,038	8.9%
Joe Petronis (R)	4,656	8.2%

2008 GENERAL

Michael McCaul (R)	179,493	53.9%
Larry Joe Doherty (D)	143,719	43.1%
Matt Finkel (LIBERT)	9,871	3.0%

Previous Winning Percentages
2006 (55%); 2004 (79%)

Elected 2004; 4th term

The conservative McCaul has risen quickly in the Republican ranks. He was elected freshman class liaison and went on to become a member of the GOP vote-counting operation. He chairs a Homeland Security subcommittee and has been the ranking member on two others, and briefly considered a run for statewide office.

A member of the Republican Study Committee, a group of the most conservative House members, McCaul pushes fiscal restraint and opposed President Obama's major economic initiatives during the 111th Congress (2009-10), including the $787 billion stimulus and the health care overhaul.

But it is on issues of homeland and national security where he has rapidly ascended the committee ladder and carved out a policy niche.

His Homeland Security and Science, Space and Technology committee assignments allow him to be a major player on cybersecurity. In April 2010, he won adoption of an amendment to a Homeland Security Department research and development measure that would authorize the establishment of a Cybersecurity Preparedness Consortium, to train state and local officials to prepare and respond to a cyberattack. In the 110th Congress (2007-08) he served as the top Republican on the Homeland Security Subcommittee on Emerging Threats, Cybersecurity, and Science and Technology, where he was a vocal critic of Obama's delay in appointing a cybersecurity coordinator.

McCaul and the subcommittee chairman, Democrat Jim Langevin of Rhode Island, co-chaired the Center for Strategic and International Studies Commission on Cybersecurity for the 44th Presidency, which issued a post-election report containing cybersecurity recommendations for President Obama. They also co-chair the House Cybersecurity Caucus.

A former prosecutor and counterterrorism official, McCaul served as the top-ranking Republican on Homeland Security's Intelligence, Information Sharing and Terrorism Risk Assessment Subcommittee in the 111th Congress.

In the 112th Congress (2011-12), he chairs Homeland's oversight subcommittee, where he'll have a chance to grill Obama administration officials on issues ranging from border security to terrorism to disaster response.

Like most Texas Republicans, he sees illegal immigration as a major national security issue and has backed plans for tougher border security enforcement.

He applauded Obama's decision in May 2010 to send National Guard troops to the border, but said it wasn't enough. "I urge the Obama administration to show the same commitment to securing our borders as [Mexican] President [Felipe] Calderon has personally shown to tracking cartels, sharing intelligence and cooperating with the United States," McCaul said.

In April 2011, McCaul proposed designating violent Mexican drug cartels as terrorist organizations.

"When they're targeting our guys now as they are both in Mexico and in the United States, it seems to me we need to start taking this war, as President Calderon calls it, a lot more seriously," he said on Fox News.

During the 110th Congress, he hosted meetings in his district between local law enforcement authorities and representatives of the Immigration and Customs Enforcement agency in an effort to speed deportation of illegal immigrants arrested for alleged criminal activity.

In a Fox News interview in May 2010, McCaul pointed to the increased border crossing of so-called OTMs (other than Mexicans) as a "grave threat and a danger to our national security." At a Foreign Affairs Committee hearing in April 2010, he cited the growing links between Venezuela and Iran as creating the potential for nuclear weapons to be smuggled into the United States.

McCaul is a member of the Foreign Affairs panel, but one of his proudest accomplishments in the international arena came in an unofficial capacity. During a trip to Pakistan in summer 2008, he successfully urged then-President Pervez Musharraf to order the release of two American teenagers being held at a fundamentalist Islamic religious school in tribal areas. "Within days, the boys were coming home. That's a memory that will stay with me," he said.

In 2007 he accepted one of the most thankless jobs in Congress: an assignment to the Ethics Committee, then known as the Committee on Standards of Official Conduct, a role he has reprised in the 112th Congress. In 2008 he was named top Republican on a subcommittee to investigate Republican Rick Renzi of Arizona, who had been indicted on extortion, money-laundering and conspiracy charges in connection with a land-swap deal. The panel eventually suspended its probe at the request of the Justice Department to avoid interfering with the criminal case.

The role of ethics investigator is a familiar one for McCaul, who was a prosecutor in the Justice Department's public integrity section before becoming deputy to Texas Attorney General John Cornyn, who is now a Republican senator. McCaul later was chief of counterterrorism and national security in the U.S. attorney's office in Austin and led its Joint Terrorism Task Force.

McCaul attributes his career in public service to the example set by his father, a B-17 pilot during World War II, and his education at the Jesuit College Preparatory Academy of Dallas. Roll Call ranked him as the fifth wealthiest member of the House in 2009, with a minimum net worth of almost $74 million. His wife, Linda, is the daughter of Clear Channel Communications CEO Lowry Mays.

The 2004 GOP primary that marked McCaul's political debut was an eight-candidate free-for-all. He amassed support from Republican insiders and won the runoff with 63 percent of the vote. Democrats didn't field a candidate in November, and McCaul took nearly 79 percent of the vote in a newly drawn district.

In 2006, a bad year for Republicans, McCaul won with 55 percent of the vote and he took 54 percent two years later. In early 2009, he briefly contemplated a 2010 bid for state attorney general, but told the Austin American-Statesman in April that he had decided to run for re-election "because the challenges we face in Washington have never been greater." He won with almost 65 percent of the vote.

Key Votes

2010	
Overhaul the nation's health insurance system	NO
Allow for repeal of "don't ask, don't tell"	NO
Overhaul financial services industry regulation	NO
Limit use of new Afghanistan War funds to troop withdrawal activities	NO
Change oversight of offshore drilling and lift oil spill liability cap	NO
Provide a path to legal status for some children of illegal immigrants	NO
Extend Bush-era income tax cuts for two years	YES

2009	
Expand the Children's Health Insurance Program	NO
Provide $787 billion in tax cuts and spending increases to stimulate the economy	NO
Allow bankruptcy judges to modify certain primary-residence mortgages	NO
Create a cap-and-trade system to limit greenhouse gas emissions	NO
Provide $2 billion for the "cash for clunkers" program	?
Establish the government as the sole provider of student loans	NO
Restrict federally funded insurance coverage for abortions in health care overhaul	YES

CQ Vote Studies

	PARTY UNITY		PRESIDENTIAL SUPPORT	
	Support	Oppose	Support	Oppose
2010	95%	5%	26%	74%
2009	94%	6%	26%	74%
2008	95%	5%	68%	32%
2007	94%	6%	81%	19%
2006	94%	6%	90%	10%

Interest Groups

	AFL-CIO	ADA	CCUS	ACU
2010	0%	0%	100%	96%
2009	16%	0%	87%	96%
2008	13%	25%	89%	96%
2007	9%	15%	85%	96%
2006	21%	0%	100%	83%

Texas 10

East central — eastern Austin and western Houston suburbs, Brenham

The 10th stretches west from northern Houston suburbs, following U.S. Highway 290 to Austin, where it hugs downtown as it wraps around the city's northwestern edge. Along its 150-mile journey, the district picks up affluent suburbs, a technology belt and a chunk of farmland. The fastest rate of population growth in Texas, driven mostly by dramatic increases in Hispanic communities, added 50 percent more residents to the 10th between the 2000 and 2010 census counts and made it the nation's third-most populous district ahead of decennial remapping.

Narrowly missing the Democratic stronghold of Hyde Park and the University of Texas in Austin, the 10th instead takes in the more upscale areas of the Arboretum, Far West and the neighborhood of West Lake, part of Austin's hill country.

The district also reaches up to fast-growing Pflugerville and the northern suburbs, which host many of Austin's technology firms — IBM and Samsung have facilities in the city. Although most of the University of

Texas flagship campus is in the adjacent 21st, the 10th hosts its J.J. Pickle Research Campus.

As the district moves east from Austin, it becomes more rural, taking in the towns of Elgin, Giddings, Hempstead and Prairie View, as well as Brenham, home to ice cream maker Blue Bell Creameries.

The district then dips into suburbs in northwestern Harris County, including Tomball and part of Spring, which grew as people moved farther from downtown Houston. Most residents here commute, which makes transportation policy an important issue.

With a growing Hispanic presence, white residents account for a slim majority here, and the district takes in some areas, such as Prairie View, that are predominately black. The more rural areas of the district struggle with high levels of poverty. Although the 10th includes vastly different urban, suburban and rural areas, it is reliably Republican.

Major Industry
Software, technology, agriculture

Cities
Austin (pt.), 230,770; Pflugerville (pt.), 46,636; Brenham, 15,716

Notable
Serbin's annual "Wendish Fest" honors the area's link to Slavic culture.

Rep. K. Michael Conaway (R)

Capitol Office
225-3605
conaway.house.gov
2430 Rayburn Bldg. 20515-4311; fax 225-1783

Committees
Agriculture
   (General Farm Commodities & Risk Management
   - Chairman)
Armed Services
Ethics
Select Intelligence

Residence
Midland

Born
June 11, 1948; Borger, Texas

Religion
Baptist

Family
Wife, Suzanne Conaway; four children

Education
East Texas State U., B.B.A. 1970 (accounting)

Military
Army, 1970-72

Career
Accountant; bank chief financial officer; oil and gas
exploration company chief financial officer

Political Highlights
Midland school board, 1985-88; candidate for U.S.
House (special election), 2003

ELECTION RESULTS

2010 GENERAL

K. Michael Conaway (R)	125,581	80.8%
James Quillian (D)	23,989	15.4%
James A. Powell (LIBERT)	4,321	2.8%

2010 PRIMARY

K. Michael Conaway (R)	55,610	77.4%
Chris Younts (R)	9,586	13.3%
Al Cowan (R)	6,680	9.3%

2008 GENERAL

K. Michael Conaway (R)	189,625	88.3%
James R. Strohm (LIBERT)	25,051	11.7%

Previous Winning Percentages
2006 (100%); 2004 (77%)

Elected 2004; 4th term

Once an accountant, Conaway is a small-government conservative often enlisted by Republican leaders to lend his expertise in matters of federal spending practices. While he champions fiscal restraint, as long as the money is flowing he will work to steer dollars to his district's farmers.

He chairs the Agriculture Subcommittee on General Farm Commodities and Risk Management in the 112th Congress (2011-12), a panel with jurisdiction over programs for cotton, wheat, corn, soybeans and other crops.

But it was in response to a bipartisan effort in 2010 to end federal subsidies for the production of mohair, a fabric made from the coats of Angora goats, that Conaway vocally leapt to the defense of his constituents.

"[The mohair subsidy] fits in with the overall safety net for agriculture. We need to be able to feed ourselves and clothe ourselves," said Conaway, whose district is home to the Mohair Council of America.

He opposes attempts to impose a federal ban on the use of antibiotics in livestock feed. Conaway argues that no scientific evidence shows a clear link between such use of antibiotics and an increased resistance to antibiotics among humans.

Immigrant labor is important to his district's farmers, and Conaway in the past has backed a limited immigration policy overhaul that would have allowed illegal immigrants to register as temporary workers, but without the possibility of becoming citizens.

In 2007, he attached an amendment to an omnibus spending bill that provided $5 billion to eradicate weeds along the banks of the Rio Grande. Illegal immigrants used the weeds for cover, Conaway said — and besides, he added, the weeds suck up water from the dwindling river. "If the weeds were removed, the Rio Grande would be stronger and harder to cross," he said.

He applies a consistent standard of fiscal discipline as a member of the Armed Services Committee.

"We must not allow bureaucrats inside the Pentagon to continue to make critical financial decisions using outdated and cumbersome financial management systems," Conaway wrote in a Roll Call op-ed in March 2011.

He was tapped in 2009 as the top Republican on a panel charged with studying the Defense Department's problems in acquiring goods and services on time and on budget.

Conaway has been called on for other non-legislative tasks as well. He was named to a 22-member GOP transition team as the party prepared to take over the House in the 112th Congress. During the 110th Congress (2007-08), he headed an internal audit team for the National Republican Congressional Committee, the House GOP's campaign arm. After the committee's treasurer, Christopher J. Ward, repeatedly canceled meetings with him, Conaway investigated and found Ward had been preparing false financial statements for years. The embezzlement was estimated at $725,000.

Conaway is among the most loyal Republicans in the House. A member of the conservative Republican Study Committee, he voted with his party on 99 percent of the votes that pitted a majority of Republicans against a majority of Democrats in the 111th Congress (2009-10).

The former accountant opposed President Obama's economic initiatives, including a $787 billion economic stimulus law, an expansion of a children's health insurance program and the health care overhaul. He also opposed a fiscal 2009 omnibus spending bill while touting the more than $14.5 million in earmarks — special funding set-asides for projects in members' districts

— he helped obtain, including $1.7 million for the International Cotton Center to support research into "increasing the profitability and sustainability of cotton and other natural fiber production."

He pushes for expanded oil and gas production. Conaway was once a "roughneck" — a worker on a drilling rig — and from 1981 to 1986 was chief financial officer of and an investor in Arbusto Energy Inc. (later Bush Exploration), a Midland-based energy company owned by George W. Bush.

Conaway is a member of the Select Intelligence Committee, where he also practices his accounting trade: In July 2010 he asked the Office of Management and Budget (OMB) to ensure that the intelligence community receive a clean financial audit. "The intelligence community, which has grown substantially in size and budget since 9/11, is currently unable to satisfactorily account for the tax dollars, which it is given to protect the very individuals that provide that money," he wrote to OMB.

In 2009 he picked up a seat on the Committee on Standards of Official Conduct (now the Ethics Committee), where he was named to a special subcommittee to conduct a public trial of former Ways and Means Chairman Charles B. Rangel, a New York Democrat.

As a youth, Conaway played defensive end and offensive tackle on Odessa Permian High School's first state championship football team. (The school's football program was the basis for the book "Friday Night Lights," which later became a film and television series.) He won a football scholarship after graduating, but of his limited college football career, he said, "I didn't play a lot on Saturdays."

He was a pre-law major in college, but a professor persuaded him to switch to accounting. He received his degree from East Texas State University (now Texas A&M University-Commerce) in 1970. He was a military police officer at the Army's Fort Hood in Texas, then worked for Price Waterhouse & Co., settling in Midland. After working in the energy industry, he opened his own accounting firm in 1993.

When Bush was in his first year as governor of Texas, he appointed Conaway to the state Board of Public Accountancy, where Conaway served for seven years. He also is an ordained deacon in the Baptist Church.

His first elected office was a seat on the Midland school board. In 2003, he lost a House special election in the 19th District by 587 votes to fellow Republican Randy Neugebauer. A GOP-inspired congressional redistricting allowed Conaway to breeze to victory in 2004 in the new 11th while Neugebauer moved to the 19th District. He faced no major party opposition in 2006 or 2008 and took 81 percent of the vote in 2010.

Key Votes

2010

Overhaul the nation's health insurance system	NO
Allow for repeal of "don't ask, don't tell"	NO
Overhaul financial services industry regulation	NO
Limit use of new Afghanistan War funds to troop withdrawal activities	NO
Change oversight of offshore drilling and lift oil spill liability cap	NO
Provide a path to legal status for some children of illegal immigrants	NO
Extend Bush-era income tax cuts for two years	YES

2009

Expand the Children's Health Insurance Program	NO
Provide $787 billion in tax cuts and spending increases to stimulate the economy	NO
Allow bankruptcy judges to modify certain primary-residence mortgages	NO
Create a cap-and-trade system to limit greenhouse gas emissions	NO
Provide $2 billion for the "cash for clunkers" program	NO
Establish the government as the sole provider of student loans	NO
Restrict federally funded insurance coverage for abortions in health care overhaul	YES

CQ Vote Studies

	PARTY UNITY		PRESIDENTIAL SUPPORT	
	SUPPORT	OPPOSE	SUPPORT	OPPOSE
2010	99%	1%	26%	74%
2009	99%	1%	11%	89%
2008	97%	3%	76%	24%
2007	98%	2%	89%	11%
2006	98%	2%	93%	7%

Interest Groups

	AFL-CIO	ADA	CCUS	ACU
2010	0%	0%	88%	100%
2009	5%	0%	71%	100%
2008	0%	5%	89%	92%
2007	4%	5%	70%	96%
2006	7%	0%	100%	88%

Texas 11

West central — Midland, Odessa, San Angelo

Starting in Burnet County in the center of the state, the still mainly white and Republican 11th is characterized by stark plains, mesas and oil rigs. It slices from west of Austin to the New Mexico border, taking in San Angelo, Midland, Odessa and vast stretches of rural land.

In the west lies oil country and the Permian Basin, home to Midland and Odessa. Odessa's economy still relies heavily on petroleum, and the traditional oil and gas sector has rebounded after several years of job cuts. The city has become a regional telecommunications and distribution hub and also has seen growing interest in "green" development and alternative energy production.

While the western portion of the 11th is mostly high desert plains, the southeastern section moves into the highland lakes region, taking in part of the state's hill country. Here, agriculture dominates, with cotton, row crops, cattle, sheep, goats and small grains key to the economy. This region also is popular with hunters, and tourism has grown at the area's resorts and lakes.

A growing Hispanic population now makes up more than one-third of the district, and immigration continues to be an issue throughout the region as illegal workers still play a heavy role in the oil and agricultural industries. The 11th also has the state's highest percentage of residents over age 64 (15 percent) due to a relatively inexpensive cost of living and good area health care. Improving transportation routes is also a priority for the district, as it is for much of West Texas.

The immense 11th gave Republican John McCain 75 percent of its 2008 presidential vote, the second-highest percentage he received in any Texas congressional district.

Major Industry
Oil and gas, agriculture, cattle, tourism

Military Bases
Goodfellow Air Force Base, 2,271 military, 656 civilian (2009)

Cities
Midland, 111,147; Odessa, 99,940; San Angelo, 93,200; West Odessa (unincorporated), 22,707

Notable
The Globe of the Great Southwest in Odessa is a replica of the famous Elizabethan-era theater used by William Shakespeare.

Rep. Kay Granger (R)

Capitol Office
225-5071
kaygranger.house.gov
320 Cannon Bldg. 20515-4312; fax 225-5683

Committees
Appropriations
(State-Foreign Operations - Chairwoman)

Residence
Fort Worth

Born
Jan. 18, 1943; Greenville, Texas

Religion
Methodist

Family
Divorced; three children

Education
Texas Wesleyan U., B.S. 1965

Career
Insurance agency owner; teacher

Political Highlights
Fort Worth Zoning Commission, 1981-89; Fort Worth City Council, 1989-91; mayor of Fort Worth, 1991-95

ELECTION RESULTS

2010 GENERAL

Kay Granger (R)	109,882	71.9%
Tracey Smith (D)	38,434	25.1%
Matthew Solodow (LIBERT)	4,601	3.0%

2010 PRIMARY

Kay Granger (R)	40,325	70.0%
Mike Brasovan (R)	10,943	19.0%
Matthew E. Kelly (R)	6,361	11.0%

2008 GENERAL

Kay Granger (R)	181,662	67.6%
Tracey Smith (D)	82,250	30.6%
Shiloh Shambaugh (LIBERT)	4,842	1.8%

Previous Winning Percentages
2006 (67%); 2004 (72%); 2002 (92%); 2000 (63%); 1998 (62%); 1996 (58%)

Elected 1996; 8th term

Since leaving her position in the Republican leadership at the beginning of 2009, Granger has focused on the Appropriations subcommittee that handles State Department funding and foreign aid, a panel she now chairs.

Granger brings to the State-Foreign Operations Subcommittee an understanding of the issues involved in sending U.S. dollars overseas. She has served on Appropriations since 1999 and traveled heavily during her time on the Defense and Military Construction-VA subcommittees. She was part of the first congressional delegation to visit Iraq after the war began in 2003, and as co-chairwoman of the bipartisan Iraqi Women's Caucus she worked with female candidates seeking a role in that country's new government.

After serving as the ranking Republican on the State-Foreign Operations panel in the 111th Congress (2009-10), she is now chairwoman, working under tighter fiscal constraints and in a political atmosphere that is less than friendly to the notion of foreign aid.

"We looked at what we call the front-line states — Afghanistan, Iraq, Pakistan, Mexico and Israel — and said we'll fully fund those. But it does make for enormous cuts, primarily to our humanitarian efforts elsewhere," Granger said in April 2011.

Her involvement in international affairs has extended beyond the Capitol. She is a member of the Council on Foreign Relations, a board member of the International Republican Institute and served as a commissioner on the Center for Strategic and International Studies Smart Global Health Commission.

She has pushed successfully for the spending panel to hold hearings on the Merida Initiative, a $1.4 billion program to help the Mexican government fight drug trafficking, and noted in a May 2010 opinion piece in the Fort Worth Star-Telegram that "despite our location deep within Texas — hundreds of miles away from a deteriorating border — we are not immune from the violence that has accompanied an escalating drug war in Mexico."

Granger set her sights on leadership in her freshman term (1997-98), when she was named an assistant GOP whip. She made it to the elected leadership a decade later, becoming vice chairwoman of the Republican Conference for the 110th Congress (2007-08). But in late 2008, she declined to serve a second term.

Although she is no longer a part of the elected Republican leadership team, she had a hand in setting the agenda on the campaign side as the lone female vice chair of the National Republican Congressional Committee in the 2010 election cycle.

The former teacher, businesswoman and mayor, who touts herself as a "pro-choice Republican," tried to help Republicans reach out to moderate voters in 2008 by de-emphasizing hot-button issues such as abortion and same-sex marriage. She pushed to address family finances, advocating such ideas as full tax-deductibility for most medical expenses. Throughout President George W. Bush's tenure, however, she supported her party on about 96 percent of the votes that pitted majorities of the two parties against each other.

That included opposing a 2007 bill to expand the Children's Health Insurance Program. On that vote, she was one of 45 Republicans targeted by unions and political action groups to change her position. But she maintained her stance when Democrats moved similar legislation in 2009 that President Obama signed into law.

She expressed optimism in early 2009 regarding Obama's pledge of bipartisanship in addressing the economic crisis and tightening spending. But she raised a warning against potential tax hikes and cuts to the armed forces. And she voted against Obama's $787 billion stimulus plan, saying she believed the bill should have focused on tax relief and provided more for transportation and water infrastructure projects. She also blamed Democrats for a lack of transparency in moving the bill.

As one of his first acts as president, Obama overturned the "Mexico City" policy that prohibited federal funding of groups that perform or promote abortion overseas, a perennial point of contention during consideration of the foreign operations spending bill for which her subcommittee is responsible. But Granger criticized Obama's move and said it flouts a consensus that the United States should support family planning abroad, but nothing related to abortion.

Outside the appropriations sphere, Granger's background has shaped her legislative priorities.

She worked her way through school and watched a favorite niece struggle to save to pay for her daughter's education. She advocates tax-free education savings accounts and in 2008 supported a rewrite of the Higher Education Act that authorizes increases in federal financial aid programs and penalizes states that cut funding for institutions of higher education. Having raised three children alone, she has supported GOP efforts to allow compensatory time off in place of premium pay for overtime worked.

Granger was born in Greenville to two public school teachers who divorced when she was 13. After completing college, she became a teacher in the same Birdville school district that named an elementary school after her mother. She taught literature and journalism for 10 years. In 1978, she went into the insurance business, eventually founding her own agency. In 1981, she was appointed to the Fort Worth Zoning Commission, where she served until she won a seat on the city council in 1989. Two years later, she won a nonpartisan election to become mayor.

Both parties courted her when Democratic Rep. Pete Geren decided not to seek re-election in 1996. Granger chose to run as a Republican and resigned as mayor. She won the nomination handily, then defeated another former Fort Worth mayor, Hugh Parmer, by 17 percentage points. She was the first Republican woman elected to the House from Texas. Granger has not faced a close contest since.

In early 2009, she considered a run for the Senate seat that Kay Bailey Hutchison was expected to vacate (Hutchison ended up not resigning, but lost in the GOP primary for governor), but Granger reconsidered after getting her new Appropriations subcommittee assignment.

Key Votes

2010

Overhaul the nation's health insurance system	NO
Allow for repeal of "don't ask, don't tell"	NO
Overhaul financial services industry regulation	NO
Limit use of new Afghanistan War funds to troop withdrawal activities	NO
Change oversight of offshore drilling and lift oil spill liability cap	NO
Provide a path to legal status for some children of illegal immigrants	-
Extend Bush-era income tax cuts for two years	+

2009

Expand the Children's Health Insurance Program	NO
Provide $787 billion in tax cuts and spending increases to stimulate the economy	NO
Allow bankruptcy judges to modify certain primary-residence mortgages	NO
Create a cap-and-trade system to limit greenhouse gas emissions	NO
Provide $2 billion for the "cash for clunkers" program	NO
Establish the government as the sole provider of student loans	NO
Restrict federally funded insurance coverage for abortions in health care overhaul	YES

CQ Vote Studies

	PARTY UNITY		PRESIDENTIAL SUPPORT	
	SUPPORT	OPPOSE	SUPPORT	OPPOSE
2010	96%	4%	30%	70%
2009	88%	12%	21%	79%
2008	96%	4%	80%	20%
2007	94%	6%	81%	19%
2006	97%	3%	95%	5%

Interest Groups

	AFL-CIO	ADA	CCUS	ACU
2010	0%	0%	100%	100%
2009	6%	0%	77%	92%
2008	7%	5%	100%	92%
2007	4%	10%	79%	92%
2006	8%	5%	100%	76%

Texas 12

Part of Fort Worth and suburbs; Parker and Wise counties

The Republican-leaning 12th takes in most of western Tarrant County, including more than 60 percent of Fort Worth, and all of rural Parker and Wise counties. The mostly white, middle-class district grabs downtown Fort Worth but also has a mix of suburban and rural areas.

The 12th's economy is built around transportation. A major airport, a naval air base, several main railroad lines and interstate highways are in or adjacent to the district, supporting aerospace, distribution services and retail sectors. The Burlington Northern Santa Fe Railroad has its headquarters in the 12th, and Union Pacific is active here.

Fort Worth relies on a diversifying economy. The University of North Texas Health Science Center headlines the local medical-services industry near Fort Worth, defense contractor Lockheed Martin. creates jobs and fuels economic growth, and homebuilder D.R. Horton has begun to rebound after the national housing-market collapse.

The Stockyards district, once a stop on the cattle trails north into Okla-

homa, is now a national historic district celebrating Fort Worth's role in the American West.

The city's Sundance Square, named after the infamous outlaw, has become a downtown retail and entertainment destination.

There are still some Democratic areas in downtown Fort Worth, but areas in Tarrant County outside the city overwhelmingly favor the GOP, as do Parker and Wise counties.

Parker includes Weatherford, which has become more Republican as the Forth Worth suburbs have encroached. John McCain took 63 percent of the district's 2008 presidential vote.

Major Industry
Defense technology, transportation, health care

Military Bases
Naval Air Station Fort Worth, 2,574 military, 1,003 civilian (2011)

Cities
Fort Worth (pt.), 464,832; Haltom City (pt.), 42,392; Weatherford, 25,250

Notable
The National Cowgirl Museum and Billy Bob's Texas, a 127,000-square-foot honky-tonk and rodeo, are in Fort Worth.

Rep. William M. "Mac" Thornberry (R)

Capitol Office
225-3706
www.house.gov/thornberry
2209 Rayburn Bldg. 20515 4313; fax 225-3486

Committees
Armed Services
   (Emerging Threats & Capabilities - Chairman)
Select Intelligence

Residence
Clarendon

Born
July 15, 1958; Clarendon, Texas

Religion
Presbyterian

Family
Wife, Sally Thornberry; two children

Education
Texas Tech U., B.A. 1980 (history); U. of Texas, J.D. 1983

Career
Lawyer; cattleman; U.S. State Department official;
congressional aide

Political Highlights
No previous office

ELECTION RESULTS

2010 GENERAL

Thornberry (R)	113,201	87.0%
Keith Dyer (I)	11,192	8.6%
John T. Burwell (LIBERT)	5,650	4.3%

2010 PRIMARY

Thornberry (R)	unopposed

2008 GENERAL

Thornberry (R)	180,078	77.6%
Roger James Waun (D)	51,841	22.4%

Previous Winning Percentages
2006 (74%); 2004 (92%); 2002 (79%); 2000 (68%);
1998 (68%); 1996 (67%); 1994 (55%)

Elected 1994; 9th term

Thornberry is a thoughtful lawmaker with considerable experience in the legislative process. He put in years as a Capitol Hill aide and executive branch liaison to Congress before getting elected, and he is a respected voice on national security matters.

Despite that respect, he was denied the chairmanship of the Select Intelligence Committee in the 112th Congress (2011-12). The spot went to Mike Rogers of Michigan. And he twice lost bids to become ranking Republican on the Armed Services Committee. In December 2008, he lost to John M. McHugh of New York, who had more seniority. When McHugh left Congress to become President Obama's secretary of the Army in 2009, the Republican Steering Committee chose Howard P. "Buck" McKeon of California over Thornberry and Roscoe G. Bartlett of Maryland.

He did, however, win the gavel of the Armed Services Subcommittee on Emerging Threats and Capabilities in the 112th.

Thornberry has consistently advocated a strong defense while seeking to protect his district's military facilities. He secured authorization in the September 2006 defense policy bill for $2.3 billion for the V-22 Osprey tilt-rotor aircraft, $523 million to upgrade 18 Marine helicopters and $683 million for research and development of a new presidential helicopter. All of these provided jobs at the district's Bell-Boeing plant.

Thornberry's committee assignments have long provided him wide latitude to weigh in on national security issues.

Months before the Sept. 11 terrorist attacks, he drafted a bill to create a new department to oversee homeland security. In 2002, his measure served as the foundation for legislation that created the Department of Homeland Security. GOP leaders rewarded him in 2003 with a seat on the new Homeland Security Committee, giving him oversight as the department was built. Another of his ideas became reality in 2005 with the creation of an assistant secretary for cybersecurity.

By then, Thornberry had moved from Homeland Security to Intelligence and was chairman of that panel's new Oversight Subcommittee during the 109th Congress (2005-06). The subcommittee was established to monitor effectiveness of the law uniting U.S. intelligence functions under one director, and in 2006 it issued a report concluding the law's implementation had been a "mixed bag," in Thornberry's words. He found fault with the Office of the Director of National Intelligence's (DNI) approach to implementing the overhaul and concluded the DNI should be focusing on high priorities such as information-sharing.

He has focused on developing metrics to measure the improvement of intelligence capabilities. He points, for example, to the ability to quantify the increase of Arabic-language experts in the intelligence community.

During the 111th Congress (2009-10), Thornberry introduced legislation with Democrat Adam Smith of Washington to modernize the Smith-Mundt Act, which was written early in the Cold War to prevent the State Department from using its foreign propaganda to influence Americans at home.

"Whether it is the Internet, the most obvious example, or even satellite television broadcasts, it becomes extremely difficult to say this broadcast is not only intended for foreign audiences but will only go to foreign audiences," Thornberry said.

When the House adopted an amendment to the fiscal 2011 defense policy bill that would give the Government Accountability Office the authority to audit intelligence agencies, Thornberry sided with the Obama administration, which had earlier threatened a veto of another bill on the issue.

Early in the 112th, Speaker John A. Boehner of Ohio named Thornberry to lead an effort to coordinate the writing of cybersecurity legislation, a topic that falls under the jurisdiction of multiple committees.

For all his hawkishness, Thornberry looks beyond military power to combat America's enemies. He served on a bipartisan Smart Power Commission in 2007 that drew up recommendations for achieving U.S. national security goals with both lethal and non-lethal approaches. In 2008, he advocated adding a provision to the fiscal 2009 defense authorization bill that would improve coordination of the Defense Department's strategic communications.

Thornberry was a strong supporter of President George W. Bush's conduct of the Iraq War. His support didn't end with Bush leaving office; when Obama released memos in April 2009 detailing the harsh interrogation of terrorist detainees under the previous administration, Thornberry shied away from saying the detainees had been tortured.

"I think people are too free with the use" of that word, he said on MSNBC. "I recommend folks go on the Internet and read these memos because you will get a real feel for the carefully controlled, doctor-supervised circumstances under which these things were used."

Thornberry is in the ranching business with his brothers and owns one-third of the Thornberry Brothers Cattle Partnership. He traces his conservatism to his upbringing on the cattle ranch that has been in his family for more than 70 years.

"Someone in the federal government was telling us what to do on a farm seven miles down a dirt road outside a town of 2,000 people," he said.

But most of Thornberry's formative professional experiences were in Washington. He worked for five years as an aide in the House after graduating from the University of Texas law school in 1983. He was a legislative aide to Texas Republican Tom Loeffler, then was chief of staff for Larry Combest, another Texas Republican. In 1988, he was deputy assistant secretary of State for legislative affairs in the Reagan administration, where he was exposed to the inner workings of the House.

Thornberry took a break from politics in 1989 to work in an Amarillo law firm while helping run his family's cattle ranch, but he was soon back in it. In 1994, he sought the U.S. House seat held by Democrat Bill Sarpalius, who had become vulnerable after supporting tax increases as part of President Bill Clinton's 1993 budget plan. Thornberry beat Sarpalius with 55 percent of the vote. He has won re-election easily since.

Key Votes

2010

Overhaul the nation's health insurance system	NO
Allow for repeal of "don't ask, don't tell"	NO
Overhaul financial services industry regulation	NO
Limit use of new Afghanistan War funds to troop withdrawal activities	NO
Change oversight of offshore drilling and lift oil spill liability cap	NO
Provide a path to legal status for some children of illegal immigrants	NO
Extend Bush-era income tax cuts for two years	YES

2009

Expand the Children's Health Insurance Program	NO
Provide $787 billion in tax cuts and spending increases to stimulate the economy	NO
Allow bankruptcy judges to modify certain primary-residence mortgages	NO
Create a cap-and-trade system to limit greenhouse gas emissions	NO
Provide $2 billion for the "cash for clunkers" program	NO
Establish the government as the sole provider of student loans	NO
Restrict federally funded insurance coverage for abortions in health care overhaul	YES

CQ Vote Studies

	PARTY UNITY		PRESIDENTIAL SUPPORT	
	SUPPORT	OPPOSE	SUPPORT	OPPOSE
2010	99%	1%	26%	74%
2009	98%	2%	14%	86%
2008	98%	2%	82%	18%
2007	95%	5%	85%	15%
2006	97%	3%	95%	5%

Interest Groups

	AFL-CIO	ADA	CCUS	ACU
2010	0%	0%	88%	100%
2009	5%	0%	73%	100%
2008	0%	5%	89%	92%
2007	4%	5%	85%	100%
2006	7%	5%	100%	88%

Texas 13

Panhandle — Amarillo; Wichita Falls

The conservative and mostly white 13th covers much of the Texas Panhandle, including the city of Amarillo, then extends east along the Oklahoma border to take in the South Plains and much of the Red River Valley. It juts south twice to add more farmland as well as pick up Jones County's small part of Abilene. The district takes in Wichita Falls and reaches east to haul in the western half of Cooke County, about 50 miles north of Fort Worth. Massive and mainly rural, the 13th includes all or part of 44 counties, 40 of which have a population under 25,000.

Amarillo is still the Panhandle's economic hub despite declines in the once-dominant oil industry. Towers and pipes outside of the city produce a large supply of crude helium. Northeast of Amarillo, Pantex employs thousands at the nation's only nuclear weapons assembly and disassembly plant. The city also relies on military aircraft parts manufacturing for the V-22 Osprey and other Marine helicopters. A significant food processing sector includes key employer Tyson Foods.

Wichita Falls also was heavily dependent on the oil and gas industries, but today factories are numerous. Sheppard Air Force Base is a major employer despite losing thousands of jobs following the 2005 round of base closings. The city is a medical hub and a local prison provides jobs. The district's farmers, among the nation's top producers of cotton, sorghum, peanuts and wheat, rely on water from the Ogallala Aquifer.

The 13th is one of the state's most Republican districts, and the GOP excels in the rural towns that dot the area. In the 2008 presidential race, John McCain took 76 percent of the 13th's vote while winning eight of his 10 highest percentages statewide in the sparsely populated counties here, including his three highest in King, Roberts and Ochiltree. Blue-collar Wichita Falls also votes solidly GOP.

Major Industry
Agriculture, oil, manufacturing

Military Bases
Sheppard Air Force Base, 1,108 military, 1,179 civilian (2011)

Cities
Amarillo, 190,695; Wichita Falls, 104,553; Pampa, 17,994

Notable
Mineral Wells was a popular destination for people seeking to drink the water and soak themselves in specially constructed bathhouses.

Rep. Ron Paul (R)

Capitol Office
225-2831
www.house.gov/paul
203 Cannon Bldg. 20515-4314

Committees
Financial Services
(Domestic Monetary Policy & Technology - Chairman)
Foreign Affairs

Residence
Lake Jackson

Born
Aug. 20, 1935; Pittsburgh, Pa.

Religion
Protestant

Family
Wife, Carol Wells Paul; five children

Education
Gettysburg College, B.S. 1957 (pre-med); Duke U.,
M.D. 1961

Military
Air Force, 1963-65; Pa. Air National Guard, 1965-68

Career
Physician

Political Highlights
Republican nominee for U.S. House, 1974; U.S. House,
1976-77; defeated for re-election to U.S. House, 1976; U.S.
House, 1979-85; sought Republican nomination for U.S.
Senate, 1984; Libertarian nominee for president, 1988;
sought Republican nomination for president, 2008

ELECTION RESULTS

2010 GENERAL

Ron Paul (R)	140,623	76.0%
Robert Pruett (D)	44,431	24.0%

2010 PRIMARY

Ron Paul (R)	45,990	80.8%
Tim Graney (R)	5,499	9.7%
John Gay (R)	3,004	5.3%
Gerald D. Wall (R)	2,448	4.3%

2008 GENERAL

Ron Paul (R)	unopposed

Previous Winning Percentages
2006 (60%); 2004 (100%); 2002 (68%); 2000 (60%);
1998 (55%); 1996 (51%); 1982 (99%); 1980 (51%);
1978 (51%); 1976 Special Runoff Election (56%);

Elected 1996; 11th full term

Also served 1976-77, 1979-85

Long known as the House's "Dr. No" for his tendency to cast the lone vote against legislation, Paul is likely to find several similarly inclined allies in the 112th Congress, including his son Rand, a newly elected Republican senator from Kentucky. The large freshman class includes many tea party-backed Republicans who share his skepticism of government, although he notes that "it's easy to say one thing; to stick with your guns and vote that way is not always easy."

The Texas physician has a long history of sticking firmly to his guns, which has tended to limit his impact on Capitol Hill. But Paul was delighted to discover that his libertarian-leaning views struck a chord with GOP primary voters during his long-shot bid for the party's 2008 presidential nomination. Although he failed to win any primaries or caucuses, the run boosted his national profile and he has shown an inclination toward running again in 2012.

Paul has called for reductions in government that go well beyond those advocated by other conservatives. He wants to abolish most federal agencies, including the IRS and the Federal Reserve, and to return the monetary system to a gold standard. He's proposed a constitutional amendment that would abolish personal income, estate and gift taxes and prohibit the government from engaging in business in competition with the private sector.

While earnest and even-tempered, he can be passionate about his views. When asked during one presidential primary debate whether as president he would work to phase out the IRS, Paul responded with a smile, "immediately." He then added, "And you can only do that if you change our ideas about what the role of government ought to be."

He was among the six Republicans who voted in 2002 against giving President George W. Bush authority to use military force in Iraq. He says the resolution was unconstitutional because it transferred the right to declare war from Congress to the executive branch. Paul has remained a consistent critic of military interventions in foreign countries, and in 2010 he and Massachusetts Democrat Barney Frank campaigned for cuts in the defense budget to help trim the deficit.

A member of the Foreign Affairs Committee, Paul was the lone Republican dissenter — the only other "no" vote came from liberal Ohio Democrat Dennis J. Kucinich — on a 2007 resolution condemning the terrorist group Hezbollah and other pro-Syrian groups and backing the government of Lebanon. He takes a dim view of foreign aid, and he opposes U.S. support for the International Monetary Fund and the World Trade Organization. He also favors a U.S. withdrawal from the United Nations.

Paul's views found support on the campaign trail. Before the presidential primaries had even started, Paul raised $20 million during the last quarter of 2007, virtually all of it from individuals. It was twice as much as eventual nominee, Sen. John McCain of Arizona, collected from individuals in the same period. Paul's support in the primaries and caucuses never matched his fundraising — rarely breaching 10 percent — but he stayed in the race until June. He declined to endorse McCain in the general election, although he did campaign for GOP House candidates.

Paul's lowercase-l libertarian streak goes back decades, and he ran for the presidency in 1988 as the standard bearer of the Libertarian Party, receiving about 432,000 votes (0.5 percent of the total).

Now chairman of the Financial Services Subcommittee on Domestic Monetary Policy and Technology, Paul was a sharp critic of the $700 billion plan enacted in 2008 to shore up the financial services sector. He wrote legislation to require the Government Accountability Office to audit the Federal Reserve Board as it poured billions into the financial system — a proposal endorsed by Frank, then chairman of the full committee. Paul got 320 cosponsors and managed to insert the bill's basic language into the House version of the 2010 financial overhaul legislation, but the provision was not included in the final bill. He reintroduced the legislation in the new Congress.

Paul's libertarian beliefs make him an erratic ally of other GOP causes. He has said he believes marriage is the union of one man and one woman, yet voted in 2004 and 2006 against a proposed constitutional amendment to ban same-sex marriage, saying "everyone is an individual and ought to be treated equally." He also backed repeal in late 2010 of the statutory ban on gays and lesbians serving openly in the military. But Paul, an obstetrician, parts company with many libertarians to oppose abortion.

While Democrats ran the House in the 110th (2007-08) and 111th (2009-10) Congresses, Paul tended to side with his party more often than in previous years. During that four-year stretch, his annual party unity score — the percentage of votes in which he sided with a majority of Republicans against a majority of Democrats — climbed from 84 to 91. Previous years' scores tended to be in the 70s.

The son of dairy farmers, Paul grew up in a small town west of Pittsburgh. Like his four brothers, he began working at the family's dairy at age 5. Later, he delivered newspapers, worked in a pharmacy and drove a milk delivery truck. In high school, he was a track and field star, played football and baseball, and was on the wrestling team. He also was student body president.

In the early 1960s, he was a flight surgeon in the U.S. Air Force. He and his wife, Carol, moved to Texas in 1968, where he opened an obstetrical practice in Brazoria County.

Paul first won a seat in the House in an April 1976 special election to replace Democrat Bob Casey, defeating former Democratic state Rep. Bob Gammage. But in November's general election, Gammage felled Paul by 268 votes. In 1978, Paul won back the seat by 1,200 votes.

In 1984, Paul left his House seat for an unsuccessful Senate bid. He returned to the House 12 years later in the 14th District, which included areas he had represented before. In the primary, he ousted Greg Laughlin, who had held the seat since 1989 but had switched from the Democratic Party in 1995. He won the general election by just 3 percentage points, overcoming criticism that he supported the legalization of drugs. Since 2002 he has won re-election with at least 60 percent of the vote.

Key Votes

2010	
Overhaul the nation's health insurance system	NO
Allow for repeal of "don't ask, don't tell"	YES
Overhaul financial services industry regulation	NO
Limit use of new Afghanistan War funds to troop withdrawal activities	YES
Change oversight of offshore drilling and lift oil spill liability cap	NO
Provide a path to legal status for some children of illegal immigrants	NO
Extend Bush-era income tax cuts for two years	YES

2009	
Expand the Children's Health Insurance Program	NO
Provide $787 billion in tax cuts and spending increases to stimulate the economy	NO
Allow bankruptcy judges to modify certain primary-residence mortgages	NO
Create a cap-and-trade system to limit greenhouse gas emissions	NO
Provide $2 billion for the "cash for clunkers" program	NO
Establish the government as the sole provider of student loans	?
Restrict federally funded insurance coverage for abortions in health care overhaul	YES

CQ Vote Studies

	PARTY UNITY		PRESIDENTIAL SUPPORT	
	SUPPORT	OPPOSE	SUPPORT	OPPOSE
2010	91%	9%	24%	76%
2009	89%	11%	14%	86%
2008	89%	11%	70%	30%
2007	84%	16%	71%	29%
2006	68%	32%	36%	64%

Interest Groups

	AFL-CIO	ADA	CCUS	ACU
2010	0%	15%	88%	96%
2009	0%	5%	67%	91%
2008	8%	10%	47%	90%
2007	21%	15%	47%	77%
2006	31%	45%	60%	76%

Texas 14
Northern Gulf Coast — Victoria, Galveston

Taking in a 200-mile stretch of the Gulf Coast, the 14th extends from north of Galveston to Rockport, near Corpus Christi. Dominated by farms and petrochemical plants, the district leans Republican and is overwhelmingly dependent on its coastal and agricultural industries.

The district's population center is located in its northeast. More than half of its residents live in Galveston and Brazoria counties (both shared with the 22nd). Chemical companies, such as Dow and Sterling, have facilities in Texas City, Freeport and North Seadrift.

The Port of Galveston is a high-volume Gulf Coast cruise-ship port, and the University of Texas Medical Branch at Galveston is the city's largest employer. Recovery from billions of dollars in property damage from 2008's Hurricane Ike is ongoing. Plans include a $1 billion improvement to the Medical Branch campus, and officials hope tourism and the medical center will help stabilize the economy.

Victoria, an oil and chemical center where Exelon Corp. plans to build a nuclear power plant, is the district's only city outside of Galveston County that has more than 30,000 residents.

Farther south, the 14th lures nature lovers to Goose Island State Park and the Aransas National Wildlife Refuge. Inland farming — rice, sorghum, corn and cattle — and commercial shrimping along the coast provide employment for many district residents, although imports threaten the local industry.

Now mostly Republican and socially conservative, the 14th has Democratic roots and a sizable minority population (43 percent) that is mostly Hispanic (29 percent overall).

But every county here backed John McCain in the 2008 presidential race, with Chambers County giving him 75 percent. Locally, Republicans tend to do very well in rural counties, but factory jobs in the Galveston area allow unions to wield some political power.

Major Industry
Petrochemicals, agriculture, shrimping

Cities
League City (pt.), 81,926; Victoria, 62,592; Galveston, 47,743; Texas City (pt.), 33,864; Lake Jackson, 26,849

Notable
Galveston claims to be the site of many Texas firsts, including the first telephone (1878), medical college (1886) and golf course (1898).

Rep. Rubén Hinojosa (D)

Capitol Office
225-2531
hinojosa.house.gov
2262 Rayburn Bldg. 20515-4315; fax 225-5688

Committees
Education & the Workforce
Financial Services

Residence
Mercedes

Born
Aug. 20, 1940; Edcouch, Texas

Religion
Roman Catholic

Family
Wife, Martha Hinojosa; five children

Education
U. of Texas, B.B.A. 1962; U. of Texas, Pan American, M.B.A. 1980

Career
Food processing executive

Political Highlights
Mercedes school board, 1972-74; Texas State Board of Education, 1974-84 (chairman of special populations)

ELECTION RESULTS

2010 GENERAL
Rubén Hinojosa (D)	53,546	55.7%
Eddie Zamora (R)	39,964	41.6%
Aaron I. Cohn (LIBERT)	2,570	2.7%

2010 PRIMARY
Rubén Hinojosa (D)	37,430	83.7%
Doug "La Perla" Purl (D)	7,282	16.3%

2008 GENERAL
Rubén Hinojosa (D)	107,578	65.7%
Eddie Zamora (R)	52,303	31.9%
Gricha Raether (LIBERT)	3,827	2.3%

Previous Winning Percentages
2006 (62%); 2004 (58%); 2002 (100%); 2000 (88%); 1998 (58%); 1996 (62%)

Elected 1996; 8th term

Hinojosa, a mild-mannered Texan, focuses his energy on a handful of issues that dominate the political discussion in his heavily Hispanic district— bilingual education, immigration and the sluggish economy. He is a formidable opponent of those who do not share his views.

Hinojosa (full name: ru-BEN ee-na-HO-suh) attended a school where he and other Mexican-American children were segregated from white students. His parents, who had fled Mexico during the 1910 revolution, spoke only Spanish, as did Hinojosa and his 10 siblings. But his parents "understood intuitively that education was the path to a better life," he said.

He served as chairman of the Education and Labor Subcommittee on Higher Education, Lifelong Learning and Competitiveness during the recent four years of Democratic hegemony. In the 112th Congress (2011-12), he is the ranking Democrat on the Higher Education and Workforce Training panel of the rechristened Education and the Workforce Committee.

Hinojosa sees education, trade and transportation as the most powerful ways to improve life in his border district.

Hinojosa is a staunch advocate of the Education Department's TRIO programs, which provide outreach to and support for disadvantaged students. When the committee approved legislation in July 2009 making the federal government the sole provider of student loans, it included a proposal by Hinojosa that extended special funding for historically black colleges.

He supported education bills in 2007 and 2008 that authorized $200 million in grants over five years to help increase the number of Latino graduates in science, technology, engineering and mathematics.

During a debate to reauthorize the Higher Education Act in 1997 — his first year in Congress — Hinojosa was the driving force behind an effort to redirect existing programs to help the neediest students, including Hispanics and American Indians.

Since then, he has helped win increases in aid to colleges that serve large numbers of Hispanic students, with funding ballooning from $12 million in 1998 to $95 million in 2006. The authorization level jumped to $175 million in fiscal 2009 through a higher education bill he helped write. He also strengthened Head Start early-childhood development programs under a renewal of that law cleared in 2007.

On immigration, Hinojosa backs a path to citizenship for the millions of illegal immigrants in the United States, as well as proposals that would allow children in the country illegally to have access to college and financial aid.

"I say we should not turn away these children who offer so much promise," he wrote in The Hill newspaper.

Hinojosa has opposed GOP efforts at tightening border security, voting against legislation in 2006 that authorized the construction of 700 miles of fencing along the U.S.-Mexico border. "While a physical fence may work for certain parts of the border, at others it would choke off economic prosperity," Hinojosa said. He joined other South Texas lawmakers in urging President Obama in early 2009 to temporarily suspend construction of the fence.

After initial efforts at immigration overhaul collapsed in 2007, a piecemeal approach was considered, including an enforcement-heavy bill by North Carolina Democrat Heath Shuler that drew the support of some conservative Democrats. Hinojosa and fellow Hispanic Caucus members fought that bill and others, which Hinojosa told the Houston Chronicle were based on "pointless political stunts and fear-mongering." He and other Hispanic leaders went public with their anger toward the Democratic leadership on the issue in 2008, threatening to entangle other measures and raising the specter of damaging Hispanic turnout for Obama's presidential candidacy. In the new Congress, he serves as first vice chairman of the Hispanic Caucus.

A member of the Financial Services Committee, Hinojosa was a strong supporter in fall 2008 of the $700 billion plan to aid the nation's financial services sector. He praised Obama's $787 billion economic stimulus law for its provisions aimed at helping small businesses.

Hinojosa voted with a majority of his party against a majority of Republicans about 98 percent of the time in the 111th Congress (2009-10), the highest party unity score of his career. But he has not always been that dependable a Democratic vote. As recently as 2006, under a GOP majority, his score hit a low of 78 and his numbers have fluctuated considerably through the years. In the 108th Congress (2003-04), he backed President George W. Bush on about 37 percent of the House votes on which the president took a position, almost 10 points higher than that of the average House Democrat.

Hinojosa sees increased trade as offering the hope of improved highways, commerce and jobs for his constituents, and he was one of four Texas Democrats who broke ranks with their party in 2002 to authorize the Bush administration to negotiate trade agreements that Congress can approve or reject but cannot amend. He was one of 15 Democrats who supported the Central America Free Trade Agreement in 2005.

He also broke with fellow Democrats in backing a 2003 law banning a procedure opponents call "partial birth" abortion, supporting a 2005 GOP effort to limit the scope of the Endangered Species Act and voting for a 2006 bill to lift a moratorium on most offshore oil leasing nationwide.

After getting an undergraduate degree at the University of Texas, Hinojosa joined the family business, H&H Foods, serving 20 years as its president and chief financial officer. He was elected to the local school board in the early 1970s and later served a decade on the Texas Board of Education before making a successful bid for the U.S. House in 1996. He won a hotly contested five-way battle in the primary, then beat Republican minister Tom Haughey by 26 percentage points in November. He won a rematch with Haughey in 1998 by 17 points and has won comfortably since, although Republican Eddie Zamora, a Navy veteran, held him to just less than 56 percent in 2010.

Capitol Annex, a Texas political newsletter, quoted unnamed sources in February 2009 as saying that Obama was considering appointing Hinojosa as ambassador to Mexico. Hispanic Caucus members earlier had touted him as a potential secretary of Education.

Key Votes

2010

Overhaul the nation's health insurance system	YES
Allow for repeal of "don't ask, don't tell"	YES
Overhaul financial services industry regulation	YES
Limit use of new Afghanistan War funds to troop withdrawal activities	YES
Change oversight of offshore drilling and lift oil spill liability cap	NO
Provide a path to legal status for some children of illegal immigrants	YES
Extend Bush-era income tax cuts for two years	YES

2009

Expand the Children's Health Insurance Program	YES
Provide $787 billion in tax cuts and spending increases to stimulate the economy	YES
Allow bankruptcy judges to modify certain primary-residence mortgages	YES
Create a cap-and-trade system to limit greenhouse gas emissions	YES
Provide $2 billion for the "cash for clunkers" program	YES
Establish the government as the sole provider of student loans	YES
Restrict federally funded insurance coverage for abortions in health care overhaul	NO

CQ Vote Studies

	PARTY UNITY		PRESIDENTIAL SUPPORT	
	SUPPORT	OPPOSE	SUPPORT	OPPOSE
2010	97%	3%	90%	10%
2009	99%	1%	97%	3%
2008	97%	3%	22%	78%
2007	97%	3%	8%	92%
2006	78%	22%	49%	51%

Interest Groups

	AFL-CIO	ADA	CCUS	ACU
2010	100%	75%	38%	0%
2009	100%	90%	31%	0%
2008	100%	80%	59%	9%
2007	100%	90%	63%	4%
2006	93%	60%	87%	36%

Texas 15

South central — Harlingen, Edinburg, part of McAllen

Based in southern Texas, the 15th takes in agricultural and cattle areas southeast of San Antonio and then dips down to the state's border with Mexico. Consecutive years of intense drought have threatened the production from ranchers and farmers in the district.

Drawn as a Hispanic-majority district, the 15th currently has, at 82 percent, the highest percentage of Hispanic residents of any congressional district. The minority population drives the district's Democratic lean. The less-populous northern counties back Republicans, and the southern counties vote strongly Democratic. Overall, the 15th gave Barack Obama 60 percent of its 2008 presidential vote.

While the district reaches more than 225 miles north to south, its population is skewed to the south. Nearly two-thirds of the 15th's residents live in Hidalgo County (shared with the 28th), and nine in 10 of Hidalgo's residents are Hispanic.

This is one of the nation's poorest areas, and community leaders struggle to establish jobs and provide job training. Along the Mexico side of the border, maquiladoras — plants that use low-cost labor and import many parts from the United States and export products back to the U.S. — are still economic mainstays. Retail and trade with Mexican border cities add jobs.

In 2009, UnitedHealth Group opened a service center in Harlingen, at the southernmost tip of the district, that employs hundreds of workers. Federal funding for energy projects could generate more jobs in Hidalgo.

International trade has prompted local leaders in South Texas to push for improvements in transportation infrastructure — the region is one of the largest populated areas without easy access to an interstate highway, and many traffic problem spots are in the 15th's counties.

Major Industry

Trade, manufacturing, agriculture, health care

Cities

McAllen (pt.), 78,027; Edinburg, 77,100; Harlingen (pt.), 64,459; Pharr (pt.), 38,815; Weslaco, 35,670; San Juan, 33,856; Alice, 19,104

Notable

Caro Brown, the first woman to win a Pulitzer Prize for journalism, worked at the Alice Daily News during the 1940s and 1950s.

Rep. Silvestre Reyes (D)

Capitol Office
225-4831
www.house.gov/reyes
2210 Rayburn Bldg. 20515-4316; fax 225-2016

Committees
Armed Services
Veterans' Affairs

Residence
El Paso

Born
Nov. 10, 1944; Canutillo, Texas

Religion
Roman Catholic

Family
Wife, Carolina Reyes; three children

Education
U. of Texas, attended 1964-65; Texas Western College, attended 1965-66 (criminal justice); El Paso Community College, A.A. 1977 (criminal justice)

Military
Army, 1966-68

Career
U.S. Border Patrol assistant regional official and agent

Political Highlights
Canutillo School Board, 1968-70

ELECTION RESULTS

2010 GENERAL

Silvestre Reyes (D)	49,301	58.1%
Tim Besco (R)	31,051	36.6%
Bill Collins (LIBERT)	4,319	5.1%

2010 PRIMARY

Silvestre Reyes (D)	unopposed

2008 GENERAL

Silvestre Reyes (D)	130,375	82.1%
Benjamin Eloy Mendoza (I)	16,348	10.3%
Mette A. Baker (LIBERT)	12,000	7.6%

Previous Winning Percentages
2006 (79%); 2004 (68%); 2002 (100%); 2000 (68%); 1998 (88%); 1996 (71%)

Elected 1996; 8th term

Reyes has made national security the thrust of his congressional career. He came by it naturally: A former Army helicopter gunner and Border Patrol agent, he represents a district that is home to the Army's Fort Bliss and sits just across the Rio Grande from Juarez, Mexico.

After two terms as chairman of the Select Intelligence Committee, Reyes relinquished his seat on the panel, but he remains on Armed Services and rejoined Veterans' Affairs in the 112th Congress (2011-12).

On national security issues, as with most things, Reyes (full name: sil-VES-treh RAY-ess, with rolled R) has moderate tendencies, although he does not buck his party leadership in any way that risks gravely offending them. Friendly and easygoing, his sharpest edge may be his affection for pulling pranks on colleagues.

During his tenure as Intelligence chairman, Reyes made it a priority to enact for the first time since 2004 a reauthorization of spy agency programs. The bill was central to his efforts to re-establish congressional oversight of intelligence agencies. Working with Senate counterparts in protracted negotiations on how far to expand congressional notification of intelligence activities, the House cleared legislation days before fiscal 2010 concluded and President Obama signed it into law.

Along the way, he had to fend off liberal members of his committee who wanted any bill to include strict prohibitions against the use of harsh interrogation tactics on terror suspects. The stance was pragmatic, since he shared their revulsion at the use of such techniques, but he knew the inclusion of those restrictions would make House passage more difficult.

Likewise, in 2007, although he opposed granting retroactive legal immunity to telecommunications companies that assisted the George W. Bush administration's warrantless surveillance program, he accepted it as part of a compromise bill after it became clear the Senate and Bush were more closely aligned on the immunity issue.

Internal House politics played a factor in the decision by then-Speaker Nancy Pelosi of California to tap Reyes as chairman. In 2007, she passed over Jane Harman of California, the panel's senior Democrat and a political rival of hers, and rejected Florida's Alcee L. Hastings, whose federal judgeship in Florida had ended in scandal when Congress impeached and removed him in 1989. Reyes was third in line for the job.

But controversy dogged his selection. He told Newsweek that "20,000 to 30,000" more troops were needed in Iraq to "dismantle the militias," a view opposite that of Pelosi. Then, in an interview with Congressional Quarterly that received worldwide attention, Reyes failed a pop quiz. Asked whether al Qaeda was Sunni or Shiite, Reyes replied, "al Qaeda, they have both." He added, "Predominately — probably Shiite." (The terrorist organization's Sunni roots are key to its founding.)

Reyes was one of two Hispanic chairmen in the House in the 111th Congress (2009-10), and he had already surpassed his time on the term-limited panel, where he served at Pelosi's pleasure.

Reyes spent 26 years in the Border Patrol and has walked a careful line on immigration issues in Congress. He twice joined California Republican David Dreier on a bill to stiffen penalties for employers who hire illegal immigrants and to create a new worker identification system. But he opposed a 2006 law authorizing a 700-mile fence along the Mexican border and continues to press for more Border Patrol personnel and a guest worker program.

Following an increase in drug-related violence in Mexico in 2009, Reyes assured the Senate Foreign Relations Committee that violence hadn't spilled across the border. But it had touched him personally. In June 2008, a relative of his by marriage was seized by gunmen in Ciudad Juarez. Notified by Reyes' staff, U.S. Immigration and Customs Enforcement agents helped arrange the relative's return after her family paid a $32,000 ransom.

Now the No. 2 Democrat on the Armed Services panel and the ranking member on the Tactical Air and Land Forces Subcommittee, Reyes has been critical of the Pentagon's slow response to hardware requests from commanders in the field. "The system for responding to urgent needs has become overly onerous, complex, bureaucratic and slow," Reyes said at a hearing of his subcommittee in March 2011.

Reyes was a prime mover of legislation signed into law in 2006 that prohibits protests near national cemeteries during the funerals of soldiers killed in action. The law was aimed primarily at the members of the Topeka, Kan.-based Westboro Baptist Church, who frequently conduct anti-gay demonstrations outside the funerals of fallen servicemembers — and whose right to do so was upheld by the Supreme Court in early 2011.

Reyes leans rightward on some of the same topics as other Southern Democrats. He voted for an amendment offered to the Democrats' health care overhaul that would prohibit the use of federal funds to cover abortions. Ultimately, though, Reyes stood with party leadership on health care and the other major initiatives of the 111th Congress.

The oldest of 10 children, Reyes was born and raised on a farm in Canutillo, Texas, five miles outside El Paso. His father, grandfather and uncle grew cotton and alfalfa on two farms totaling 2,000 acres.

He briefly attended the University of Texas at Austin on a debate scholarship. Working while attending classes proved difficult, and after a year he returned home and enrolled in what was then Texas Western College (now the University of Texas at El Paso). When he took a break from the spring semester in 1966, he was drafted into the Army, serving two and a half years, including 13 months in Vietnam as a helicopter crew chief and gunner. In 1969, he joined the Border Patrol, eventually becoming sector chief in McAllen and El Paso.

Community leaders in El Paso persuaded Reyes to run for Congress when Democrat Ronald D. Coleman announced his retirement. Reyes became the district's first Hispanic representative after defeating a former Coleman aide in the primary and runoff, and then winning the general election in 1996. Since then, he has easily won re-election.

Key Votes

2010

Vote	
Overhaul the nation's health insurance system	YES
Allow for repeal of "don't ask, don't tell"	YES
Overhaul financial services industry regulation	YES
Limit use of new Afghanistan War funds to troop withdrawal activities	NO
Change oversight of offshore drilling and lift oil spill liability cap	?
Provide a path to legal status for some children of illegal immigrants	YES
Extend Bush-era income tax cuts for two years	NO

2009

Vote	
Expand the Children's Health Insurance Program	YES
Provide $787 billion in tax cuts and spending increases to stimulate the economy	YES
Allow bankruptcy judges to modify certain primary-residence mortgages	YES
Create a cap-and-trade system to limit greenhouse gas emissions	YES
Provide $2 billion for the "cash for clunkers" program	YES
Establish the government as the sole provider of student loans	YES
Restrict federally funded insurance coverage for abortions in health care overhaul	YES

CQ Vote Studies

	PARTY UNITY		PRESIDENTIAL SUPPORT	
	SUPPORT	OPPOSE	SUPPORT	OPPOSE
2010	98%	2%	93%	7%
2009	99%	1%	99%	1%
2008	97%	3%	24%	76%
2007	96%	4%	9%	91%
2006	85%	15%	47%	53%

Interest Groups

	AFL-CIO	ADA	CCUS	ACU
2010	100%	75%	0%	0%
2009	100%	95%	40%	4%
2008	100%	70%	67%	8%
2007	96%	95%	63%	4%
2006	100%	80%	57%	36%

Texas 16

West — El Paso and suburbs

Situated along the Rio Grande in the desert landscape that characterizes the western reaches of Texas, the 16th takes in El Paso and some of its suburbs. Joined to Mexico and El Paso's sister city, Ciudad Juarez, by the Bridge of the Americas, the 16th is 81.5 percent Hispanic, the second-highest proportion of any district nationwide.

Mexico has had a deep effect on the area's economy, culture and demographics, and growth in El Paso was fueled by trade with Mexico long before free-trade zones and global markets flourished.

Companies on the U.S. side of the border provide supplies and services to plants in Mexico, and residents from Ciudad Juarez cross the border to shop in El Paso.

NAFTA aided an explosion of maquiladoras, plants that use low-cost labor and import many parts from the United States and export products back; expansion at Fort Bliss underpins non-manufacturing economic growth. Fort Bliss was already key to the 16th's economy before the base was assigned thousands of new jobs as a result of the 2005 round of base realignments.

The area's growing population threatened to overwhelm its water supply, but conservation efforts largely have succeeded, and a new desalination plant, which may eventually run on solar power, serves the Fort Bliss community.

El Paso remains one of the safest large cities in the nation, but residents and officials worry about increasing drug cartel violence in Ciudad Juarez. There have been dips in recreational travel across the border as well as increased federal border enforcement efforts.

Democrats held the 16th's U.S. House seat for all but two years in the 20th century. In 2008, Barack Obama took 66 percent of the presidential vote here, his fourth-highest percentage in the state.

Major Industry
Trade, defense, manufacturing

Military Bases
Fort Bliss (Army), 20,065 military, 2,203 civilian (2009)

Cities
El Paso, 649,121; Socorro (pt.), 31,968

Notable
The National Border Patrol Museum boasts aircraft, vehicles and boats.

Rep. Bill Flores (R)

Capitol Office
225-6105
flores.house.gov
1505 Longworth Bldg. 20515-4317; fax 225-0350

Committees
Budget
Natural Resources
Veterans' Affairs

Residence
Bryan

Born
Feb. 25, 1954; Warren Air Force Base, Wyo.

Religion
Baptist

Family
Wife, Gina Flores; two children

Education
Texas A&M U., B.B.A. 1976 (accounting); Houston
Baptist U., M.B.A. 1985

Career
Energy company executive; oil drilling company
financial manager; accountant

Political Highlights
No previous office

ELECTION RESULTS

2010 GENERAL

Bill Flores (R)	106,696	61.8%
Chet Edwards (D)	63,138	36.6%
Richard B. Kelly (LIBERT)	2,808	1.6%

2010 PRIMARY RUNOFF

Bill Flores (R)	21,913	65.1%
Rob Curnock (R)	11,730	34.9%

Elected 2010; 1st term

Flores arrived in Washington with no previous political experience, but says his business success prepared him for service in Congress. He worked his way up from modest means to become chief executive of Phoenix Exploration Co., an oil and natural gas firm.

"I know what it means to sign a paycheck, make a payroll, balance a budget, repay debt, acquire health care coverage," he said. "That's what sets me apart."

A member of the Budget Committee, he called problems facing Medicare funding "the biggest gaping wound that we have in our future financial security" at a hearing in March 2011.

Flores supports permanently extending the 2001 and 2003 tax cuts, freezing any unspent funds from the $787 billion economic stimulus, creating a federal payroll-tax holiday, repealing the 2010 health care overhaul and blocking creation of a cap-and-trade system for greenhouse gas emissions.

Flores' experience in the energy field will serve him well on the Natural Resources Committee, where he sits on the Energy and Mineral Resources panel. He has introduced legislation aimed at boosting offshore oil and gas development.

He also sits on the Veterans' Affairs Committee.

Like most Texas Republicans, Flores is interested in promoting tighter border security. On social issues, he opposes same-sex marriage and is anti-abortion. He also calls himself an advocate of congressional term limits.

Flores finished first in a five-way GOP primary and easily claimed the nomination in a runoff. He faced 10-term Democrat Chet Edwards, chairman of an Appropriations subcommittee who had the endorsement of the National Rifle Association.

Edwards had won a number of close races in his congressional career, but the district is overwhelmingly Republican — GOP presidential candidate John McCain won two-thirds of the vote there in 2008.

Flores rode the district's conservative lean and the Republican wave to an easy 25-percentage-point victory.

Texas 17

East central — Waco, College Station, Bryan

The conservative 17th begins south of Fort Worth and moves southeast through farmland to reach Bryan and College Station in Brazos County. On the way, it picks up Waco and Crawford, both in centrally located McLennan County.

Thirty percent of district residents live in Waco or surrounding McLennan County. Waco, the 17th's largest city and the largest population center between Austin and Dallas, hosts Baylor University and a strong education sector. Defense-related firms offer additional jobs in the county.

The district jogs east and then southeast from Waco, meandering through increasingly populated counties and into Brazos. College Station is home to Texas A&M University, which includes the George Bush Presidential Library and Museum.

Unlike the more liberal University of Texas at Austin, Texas A&M has a conservative agricultural and military tradition.

Johnson County, in the 17th's northeastern corner, has become a bedroom community for Fort Worth and is home to some of the city's southern suburbs. The county's most populous city, Cleburne, and nearby communities rely on light manufacturing. Along the Squaw Creek Reservoir west of Johnson, a nuclear plant in Somervell County employs many district residents. Energy concerns also are important to northern counties that cover parts of the Barnett Shale natural gas reservoir.

Major Industry
Agriculture, education, manufacturing

Cities
Waco, 124,805; College Station, 93,857; Bryan, 76,201; Cleburne, 29,337

Notable
Waco hosts a Dr Pepper museum celebrating the soft drink invented there in 1885.

Rep. Sheila Jackson Lee (D)

Capitol Office
225-3816
www.jacksonlee.house.gov
2160 Rayburn Bldg. 20515-4318; fax 225-3317

Committees
Homeland Security
Judiciary

Residence
Houston

Born
Jan. 12, 1950; Queens, N.Y.

Religion
Seventh-day Adventist

Family
Husband, Elwyn Lee; two children

Education
Yale U., B.A. 1972 (political science); U. of Virginia, J.D. 1975

Career
Lawyer; congressional aide

Political Highlights
Democratic nominee for Texas District Court judge, 1984; Democratic nominee for Harris County Probate Court judge, 1986; Houston municipal judge, 1987-89; Democratic nominee for Texas District Court judge, 1988; Houston City Council, 1990-95

ELECTION RESULTS

2010 GENERAL

Sheila Jackson Lee (D)	85,108	70.2%
John Faulk (R)	33,067	27.3%
Mike Taylor (LIBERT)	3,118	2.6%

2010 PRIMARY

Sheila Jackson Lee (D)	21,570	67.0%
Jarvis Johnson (D)	9,133	28.4%
Sean Roberts (D)	1,508	4.7%

2008 GENERAL

Sheila Jackson Lee (D)	148,617	77.3%
John Faulk (R)	39,095	20.3%
Mike Taylor (LIBERT)	4,486	2.3%

Previous Winning Percentages
2006 (77%); 2004 (89%); 2002 (77%); 2000 (76%); 1998 (90%); 1996 (77%); 1994 (73%)

Elected 1994; 9th term

Jackson Lee has made a name for herself as an outspoken lawmaker with strong opinions. She rarely misses an opportunity to appear on camera, whether it's a policy interview on C-SPAN or grabbing a spot on the center aisle for the State of the Union address so she can be seen shaking the president's hand. A Houston Chronicle reporter called her "ubiquitous."

But her ability to get things done can be impeded by her abrasive personality. Multiple Washingtonian magazine surveys of Capitol Hill aides called her the "meanest" member of the House (she also received high rankings in the "most talkative" and "show horse" categories). Former aides have told publications that she berates staffers for minor failures and would call them at all hours to drive her the short distance between her residence and the Capitol. Jackson Lee has dismissed such complaints as unwarranted.

She made a splash in August 2009 during a health care town hall meeting in Houston when she appeared to be making a phone call while a constituent was asking her a question. The audience was outraged and began heckling Jackson Lee, who said that she was merely calling the House's information hotline in order to better answer the question.

Jackson Lee's legislative responsibilities include her role as ranking Democrat on the Homeland Security Subcommittee on Transportation Security.

She introduced legislation in the 112th Congress (2011-12) that would make it a crime to distribute images recorded by screening technology at airports used by the Transportation Security Administration (TSA). Privacy groups have called use of the technology an invasion of privacy.

Jackson Lee also wants Congress to move away from the focus on aviation security and do more to shore up rail and bus systems. In 2007, she helped shepherd through legislation intended to improve security for rail and mass transit. It was signed into law as part of a broader measure to implement the recommendations of the Sept. 11 commission, and Jackson Lee ensured that the bill would benefit her district by including a provision to establish a transportation security center at Texas Southern University.

She introduced legislation in 2009 to overhaul and reauthorize TSA and is a champion of legislation to grant agency employees, including airport baggage screeners, the same personnel and collective bargaining rights as other government employees.

Jackson Lee backed legislation following the BP oil spill off the Gulf Coast that would compensate victims for their losses. The legislation also would eliminate the cap on economic liability for companies with more than $1 billion in profits.

After Hurricane Ike raged through the Houston region in the fall of 2008, causing widespread damage and leaving millions without power, Jackson Lee helped coordinate disaster relief and emergency aid, and she worked with the governor to extend unemployment benefits. She also introduced legislation to help electric utilities be better prepared for disasters.

She is a strong advocate for the space program — including the Johnson Space Center in Houston — and has suggested that NASA should consider using the space shuttle past its scheduled 2011 retirement. As President George W. Bush walked down the aisle for his 2008 State of the Union address, she whispered to him, "Remember NASA."

Jackson Lee is a loyal Democrat. She backed all the major legislative initiatives of the Obama administration during the 111th Congress (2009-10). In the fall of 2008, as the Bush administration neared its conclusion, she broke with the House leadership on the $700 billion financial rescue package. Joining 33 other Democrats who voted against the initial version of the bill, she said she wanted to be sure that it included rigorous oversight and would benefit ordinary Americans. But she backed a second version, which was signed into law, telling the Houston Chronicle she did so only reluctantly, but that it was "the first step to putting our country on the right track economically."

As a member of the Judiciary Committee, Jackson Lee seeks to change laws that impose stiffer sentences for crack-cocaine offenses than for powder-cocaine usage. Critics say the disparity has a disproportionate impact on minorities.

Jackson Lee used to serve on the Foreign Affairs Committee. Her district contains a substantial number of immigrants from Pakistan, and she is co-chairwoman of the Congressional Pakistan Caucus. The killing in Sudan that many have termed a genocide has also drawn her attention. In April 2006, she was among five members of Congress arrested for disorderly conduct at a protest at the Sudanese Embassy in Washington. They were released after each paid a $50 fine. She traveled to the country in 2007.

Among Jackson Lee's role models was Democratic Rep. Barbara Jordan, the eloquent liberal from Houston who served from 1973 to 1979. "I had the privilege of being part of the generation of people who were moved by movements and moved by the voices and messages of Medgar Evers, Martin Luther King and Fannie Lou Hamer," Jackson Lee once said. "I always viewed my charge from their history and stories to be a change-maker."

She was born in Queens, N.Y., and educated at Yale and the University of Virginia law school, where she was one of three African-Americans in her class. She moved to Texas when her husband took a job with the University of Houston. After two unsuccessful bids for local judgeships, she was appointed a municipal judge in 1987.

Three years later, after another failed election campaign for a judgeship, she won an at-large seat on the city council, where her initiatives included a law imposing penalties on gun owners who fail to keep weapons away from children. She also pushed for expanded summer hours at city parks and recreation centers as a way to reduce gang activity.

She came to Congress after beating incumbent Democrat Craig Washington in the 1994 primary election. Washington had lost the support of the Houston business establishment and several other important constituencies, and Jackson Lee garnered 63 percent of the vote in the primary. In the heavily Democratic district, that win was tantamount to election. She has cruised to re-election since.

Key Votes

2010

Overhaul the nation's health insurance system	YES
Allow for repeal of "don't ask, don't tell"	YES
Overhaul financial services industry regulation	YES
Limit use of new Afghanistan War funds to troop withdrawal activities	YES
Change oversight of offshore drilling and lift oil spill liability cap	NO
Provide a path to legal status for some children of illegal immigrants	YES
Extend Bush-era income tax cuts for two years	NO

2009

Expand the Children's Health Insurance Program	YES
Provide $787 billion in tax cuts and spending increases to stimulate the economy	YES
Allow bankruptcy judges to modify certain primary-residence mortgages	YES
Create a cap-and-trade system to limit greenhouse gas emissions	YES
Provide $2 billion for the "cash for clunkers" program	YES
Establish the government as the sole provider of student loans	YES
Restrict federally funded insurance coverage for abortions in health care overhaul	NO

CQ Vote Studies

	PARTY UNITY		PRESIDENTIAL SUPPORT	
	Support	Oppose	Support	Oppose
2010	99%	1%	84%	16%
2009	99%	1%	96%	4%
2008	98%	2%	14%	86%
2007	98%	2%	4%	96%
2006	93%	7%	34%	66%

Interest Groups

	AFL-CIO	ADA	CCUS	ACU
2010	93%	95%	25%	0%
2009	100%	95%	33%	0%
2008	100%	100%	59%	4%
2007	100%	100%	55%	0%
2006	100%	100%	53%	16%

Texas 18

Downtown Houston

The 18th takes in the central part of downtown Houston, with appendages spreading south and northeast, as well as a C-shaped swath out to the northwest and north. The 18th, which includes some of the city's poorest areas, is filled with downtown's older black neighborhoods, growing Hispanic areas and progressive residents. Downtown Houston has seen revitalization, with ongoing efforts in residential, retail and corporate construction.

The district is diverse and increasingly Hispanic: In a reversal of proportions over the past decade, 36 percent of residents are black and 43 percent are Hispanic. Some of the district's most heavily black areas are just south of downtown, and Hispanic communities have expanded beyond longtime neighborhoods between Interstate 45 and the Eastex Freeway just north of downtown.

While the 18th is mainly inner-city urban, it also includes the Heights, a trendier area populated by some young professionals. The northern arm of the 18th picks up George Bush Intercontinental Airport.

Downtown office buildings are filled with oil and gas employees and other white-collar and service workers, but most of the workforce commutes here from outside the district. Downtown hosts corporate giants, such as CenterPoint Energy, whose headquarters are housed in its iconic — and well-lit — skyscraper.

Workers can avoid high daytime temperatures by using the miles of underground tunnels that connect many of the city's buildings. The 18th also takes in the Theater District, with the Hobby Center for the Performing Arts, and is home to baseball's Astros, basketball's Rockets and Comets, and soccer's Dynamo.

The 18th's large minority populations make it one of the most strongly Democratic districts in Texas, and Texas Southern University and the University of Houston add to the area's liberal bent. Barack Obama won 77 percent of the 18th's 2008 presidential vote, his second-highest percentage statewide.

Major Industry
Energy, government, business services, entertainment

Cities
Houston (pt.), 518,131

Notable
Houston's KUHT became the nation's first public TV station in May 1953.

Rep. Randy Neugebauer (R)

Capitol Office
225-4005
www.randy.house.gov
1424 Longworth Bldg. 20515-4319; fax 225-9615

Committees
Agriculture
Financial Services
　(Oversight & Investigations - Chairman)
Science, Space & Technology

Residence
Lubbock

Born
Dec. 24, 1949; St. Louis, Mo.

Religion
Baptist

Family
Wife, Dana Neugebauer; two children

Education
Texas Tech U., B.B.A. 1972 (accounting)

Career
Land developer; homebuilding company executive; bank executive

Political Highlights
Lubbock City Council, 1992-98

ELECTION RESULTS

2010 GENERAL

Randy Neugebauer (R)	106,059	77.8%
Andy Wilson (D)	25,984	19.1%
Richard Peterson (LIBERT)	4,315	3.2%

2010 PRIMARY

Randy Neugebauer (R)	unopposed

2008 GENERAL

Randy Neugebauer (R)	168,501	72.4%
Dwight Fullingim (D)	58,030	24.9%
Richard Peterson (LIBERT)	6,080	2.6%

Previous Winning Percentages
2006 (68%); 2004 (58%); 2003 Special Runoff Election (51%)

Elected 2003; 4th full term

Neugebauer is a self-described "less government, less taxes kind of person" and a leading opponent of Democratic proposals to increase regulation of the financial sector. But he gained the most notoriety for a single outburst on the House floor unrelated to his usual role as a conservative voice on the Financial Services Committee.

In March 2010, in the last days of the stormy health care debate in the House, Democrat Bart Stupak of Michigan was speaking on the floor about a deal he had struck on the overhaul legislation's abortion language. As he spoke, someone from the Republican side shouted "baby killer." Two days later, Neugebauer (NAW-geh-bow-er) said it was him.

"In the heat and emotion of the debate, I exclaimed the phrase 'it's a baby killer' in reference to the agreement reached by the Democratic leadership," he said. "While I remain heartbroken over the passage of this bill and the tragic consequences it will have for the unborn, I deeply regret that my actions were mistakenly interpreted as a direct reference to Congressman Stupak himself."

Neugebauer is a member of the Republican Study Committee, a group of the House's most conservative members, and a charter member of the Tea Party Caucus. He chairs the Financial Services Oversight and Investigations Subcommittee, and has been a stout foe of President Obama's agenda.

He opposed the overhaul of financial sector regulations, saying the measure will "make bailouts and government protection for failure permanent while reducing choices and increasing the cost of credit, ultimately leading to fewer jobs at a time when new jobs are needed most."

In June 2010 he opposed legislation to create a $30 billion lending fund to invest in financial institutions such as community banks that could expand the availability of credit to small businesses. Republicans called the measure a miniature version of the Troubled Asset Relief Program (TARP), which aimed to stabilize the financial sector in 2008.

Neugebauer also strongly opposed the $700 billion TARP law. "I do not believe that the people of the 19th District, who made conservative lending and investment decisions, should have to pay for the mistakes made on Wall Street, nor do I believe that ultimately our children and grandchildren should have to pay for these mistakes either," he said.

Neugebauer also opposed an expansive housing package earlier in the year, even though he had managed to win a few changes during committee consideration. He said he opposed the final version because it created an affordable-housing trust fund to be financed through future revenues of mortgage giants Fannie Mae and Freddie Mac, which are government-sponsored enterprises (GSEs). The House defeated his efforts to amend what he called a "Robin Hood" provision.

But he has won some Democratic support — including from the Obama administration — for a measure that is part of a GOP package of bills aimed at dismantling operations at Fannie and Freddie. The bill would gradually raise the GSEs' guarantee fees in an effort to bring private capital back into the mortgage market.

One of his pet peeves is the frequent use of "emergency" spending, which does not count against the annual caps, to get around limits on discretionary spending. "We need to stop spending money we don't have, and the emergency spending process needs to cease," he said in 2008. When the House passed an emergency spending bill in 2006 to fund the Iraq War that also provided $19.2

billion in hurricane relief on top of the $51.8 billion in emergency spending appropriated soon after Hurricane Katrina hit in 2005, Neugebauer tried but failed to split off the hurricane money and require that it be offset.

On the Agriculture Committee, he spent much of the 110th Congress (2007-08) working to protect his district's many cotton, wheat and peanut producers, along with its cattle ranchers, as the panel put together a five-year reauthorization of agriculture and nutrition programs. In one of his rare splits with the George W. Bush administration, he supported a successful override of the president's veto of the final legislation. The law is set to be reauthorized in 2012.

A member of the Science, Space and Technology Committee, he backs development of alternative energy sources. His district is home to the Horse Hollow Wind Energy Center, the nation's largest wind farm. In the 110th Congress, he cosponsored legislation to expedite judicial reviews of legal challenges to drilling for oil and natural gas on public lands.

Neugebauer was born in St. Louis, where his parents met in college, but he was raised in his mother's hometown of Lubbock. His father sold insurance, and his mother worked as a real estate agent and interior designer. They divorced when Neugebauer was 9, and his father died soon after.

At Texas Tech University he became so skilled at back flips, twists and other moves that he joined a touring trampoline group called The Flying Matadors. He graduated with a degree in accounting and became a commercial real estate developer and homebuilder. He was elected to the Lubbock City Council in 1992, serving until 1998, and is a deacon in his Baptist church.

Neugebauer, who married his high school sweetheart, arrived in the House in June 2003 after winning a special election to replace Republican Larry Combest, who resigned that year. He faced 13 Republicans and two Democrats in the special election. In an initial round of balloting, he and accountant K. Michael Conaway, who had close ties to Bush, finished first and second, respectively. He won the runoff by just 587 votes. (Conaway was elected in 2004 in the neighboring 11th District.)

When Neugebauer ran for re-election in 2004, he benefited from a Texas redistricting engineered by former House Majority Leader Tom DeLay and other state Republicans that matched him against 26-year Democratic Rep. Charles W. Stenholm, the most conservative of congressional Democrats. He defeated Stenholm by 18 percentage points after spending $3 million. He has won by wide margins since.

In March 2011, Neugebauer was named a regional chairman of the National Republican Congressional Committee for the 2012 election cycle.

Key Votes

2010

Overhaul the nation's health insurance system	NO
Allow for repeal of "don't ask, don't tell"	NO
Overhaul financial services industry regulation	NO
Limit use of new Afghanistan War funds to troop withdrawal activities	NO
Change oversight of offshore drilling and lift oil spill liability cap	NO
Provide a path to legal status for some children of illegal immigrants	NO
Extend Bush-era income tax cuts for two years	YES

2009

Expand the Children's Health Insurance Program	NO
Provide $787 billion in tax cuts and spending increases to stimulate the economy	NO
Allow bankruptcy judges to modify certain primary-residence mortgages	NO
Create a cap-and-trade system to limit greenhouse gas emissions	NO
Provide $2 billion for the "cash for clunkers" program	NO
Establish the government as the sole provider of student loans	NO
Restrict federally funded insurance coverage for abortions in health care overhaul	YES

CQ Vote Studies

	PARTY UNITY		PRESIDENTIAL SUPPORT	
	SUPPORT	OPPOSE	SUPPORT	OPPOSE
2010	99%	1%	30%	70%
2009	99%	1%	10%	90%
2008	98%	2%	80%	20%
2007	99%	1%	88%	12%
2006	97%	3%	87%	13%

Interest Groups

	AFL-CIO	ADA	CCUS	ACU
2010	0%	0%	88%	100%
2009	5%	0%	79%	100%
2008	0%	5%	82%	96%
2007	4%	0%	70%	100%
2006	7%	5%	100%	100%

Texas 19

West central — Lubbock, Abilene, Big Spring

The conservative 19th starts in the Panhandle and heads south and east through cattle and cotton country around Lubbock to Abilene. It swings north, almost to Wichita Falls. With ranches, cattle and remnants of the cowboy lifestyle, the 19th offers a taste of the Wild West.

The western part of the district, which includes Lubbock, is heavily agricultural, although that industry extends east through most of the district. Lubbock, the district's largest city, thrives on the surrounding acres of cotton, calling itself the world's largest cottonseed-processing center. Home to Texas Tech University, the city has become an educational and medical hub for the southwest Panhandle. Lubbock's Depot District has brought development and revenue to its downtown, and a wine industry outside the city provides a little economic boost. Lubbock County accounts for 40 percent of the district's population, which is majority white with growing numbers of Hispanic residents.

Abilene also has made an effort to revitalize its downtown, and local offi-

cials are seeing results as a telecommunications sector develops. A nearby Air Force base is a stable part of the economy, and the prison industry has done well, with several facilities around the district.

Peanut farms are found throughout the 19th, especially in Gaines County, but famine and drought have hurt cattle and cotton over the past decade. In areas such as Shackelford County, wind power is a developing industry. As in much of the South, conservative Democrats used to dominate the area: In 1978, George W. Bush lost a race for the Lubbock-area House seat to a Democrat. But the 19th has become a Republican stronghold at all levels. John McCain took 72 percent of the district's presidential vote in 2008.

Major Industry
Cattle, agriculture, oil and gas, defense

Military Bases
Dyess Air Force Base, 4,760 military, 379 civilian (2011)

Cities
Lubbock, 229,573; Abilene (pt.), 111,918; Big Spring, 27,282

Notable
Lubbock's Buddy Holly Center honors the local-native musician, who died in a February 1959 plane crash in Iowa.

Rep. Charlie Gonzalez (D)

Capitol Office
225-3236
www.house.gov/gonzalez
1436 Longworth Bldg. 20515-4320; fax 225-1915

Committees
Energy & Commerce
House Administration
Joint Printing

Residence
San Antonio

Born
May 5, 1945; San Antonio, Texas

Religion
Roman Catholic

Family
Wife, Belinda Trevino; one child

Education
U. of Texas, B.A. 1969 (government); St. Mary's U.
(Texas), J.D. 1972

Military
Texas Air National Guard, 1969-75

Career
Lawyer; teacher

Political Highlights
Bexar County judge, 1982-87; Texas District Court
judge, 1988-97

ELECTION RESULTS

2010 GENERAL

Charlie Gonzalez (D)	58,645	63.6%
Clayton Trotter (R)	31,757	34.4%
Michael Idrogo (LIBERT)	1,783	1.9%

2010 PRIMARY

Charlie Gonzalez (D)	unopposed

2008 GENERAL

Charlie Gonzalez (D)	127,298	71.9%
Robert Litoff (R)	44,585	25.2%
Michael Idrogo (LIBERT)	5,172	2.9%

Previous Winning Percentages
2006 (87%); 2004 (65%); 2002 (100%); 2000 (88%);
1998 (63%)

Elected 1998; 7th term

Gonzalez, chairman of the Congressional Hispanic Caucus, prides himself on being an independent-minded moderate who seeks bipartisan solutions on immigration, health care and other divisive issues. The last time Republicans were in the majority, he was not a sure thing to support the Democratic leadership. Under Democratic rule, he was virtually a lock.

The son of a famously iconoclastic member of Congress — Henry B. Gonzalez, who served in the House for 37 years — and a member of the moderate New Democrat Coalition, he said he shares some of his father's individualistic spirit but is more of a believer in working within the party structure. Between them, the Gonzalez family has represented the San Antonio-based district for nearly 50 years.

Gonzalez was chosen, with no opposition, to lead the Hispanic Caucus in the 112th Congress (2011-12) after serving one term as the group's first vice chairman.

He has served since 2004 on the Energy and Commerce Committee. A member of the Subcommittee on Energy and Power, Gonzalez supports exploring a wide range of energy resources, including clean coal, nuclear, solar and wind. But as lawmakers in 2009 weighed a way to reduce carbon emissions, Gonzalez questioned just how quickly the country could transition to battery-powered cars and trucks. "It does trouble me that we're not dealing with realistic expectations," he told the Dallas Morning News. "Let's be realistic about the need for domestic production and refining capacity in the United States."

Gonzalez also sits on the Health Subcommittee. He backed a 2009 law to expand the Children's Health Insurance Program, which provides coverage to children whose families make too much money to qualify for Medicaid.

He joined Republican Phil Gingrey of Georgia on legislation to boost the use of information technology in doctors' offices; aspects of it were included in a separate measure that Energy and Commerce approved in July 2008, but then languished in the Ways and Means Committee.

Gonzalez is the No. 2 Democrat on the subcommittee handling trade, an issue on which he has a mixed voting record. He enthusiastically touted the benefits of the 1993 North American Free Trade Agreement, which his father had virulently opposed. But in siding with labor unions, which had promoted his first congressional bid, he reversed course to vote against the 2002 fast-track law giving the president authority to negotiate trade deals that cannot be amended by Congress. He again joined the majority of his party in 2005 to vote against implementing a free-trade agreement with most Central American countries. Two years later, however, he supported a free-trade agreement with Peru, saying the strengthened economic ties "will truly improve the standard of living for Americans and Peruvians alike." And in 2008, he voted with nearly all House Democrats for a resolution to postpone fast-track action on a free-trade accord with Colombia.

Gonzalez's other primary committee assignment is House Administration, where he chaired a task force established to investigate allegations that voting machine errors contributed to the razor-thin 2006 victory by Republican Vern Buchanan in Florida's 13th District. The task force voted in 2008 to dismiss Democrat Christine Jennings' challenge based on a Government Accountability Office report.

His House Administration duties also include an assignment to the Joint Printing Committee.

In the 111th Congress (2009-10) he served on the Judiciary Committee, where his background as a state district court judge in San Antonio served him well on the panels overseeing the courts, border security and international law. Like the rest of the Hispanic caucus, in 2009 he enthusiastically supported the first Hispanic nominee to the Supreme Court, Sonia Sotomayor.

He supported an expansion of federal hate crime law to cover offenses based on a victim's sexual orientation or gender identity. He also voted for 2007 legislation to ban job discrimination based on sexual orientation, and in 2006 voted to override a Bush veto of an expansion of federal funding for embryonic stem cell research. He led the Hispanic Caucus' successful campaigns in 2002 and 2003 against confirming Miguel A. Estrada as the first Latino on the U.S. Court of Appeals for the District of Columbia Circuit.

Gonzales has been a passionate advocate of a broad immigration overhaul that includes a path to citizenship for the millions of illegal immigrants already in the country.

"Our current broken system that posts 'Keep Out' signs along our borders while allowing U.S. employers to hold 'Help Wanted' signs creates an imbalance in the way we deal with immigration policy," he wrote for The Hill in October 2010.

He supported stand-alone legislation in late 2010 that would have granted conditional non-immigrant status to certain children of illegal immigrants. The bill was passed by the House but died in the Senate.

The Texan voted with his party on virtually every issue in the 111th Congress, siding with a majority of Democrats against a majority of Republicans 99 percent of the time. When Republicans were in the majority earlier in his career, his party unity scores typically ran 5 to 10 percentage points lower.

Gonzalez is the third of eight children and the only one who followed his father into public life. He was a teenager when his father was first elected to Congress. Gonzalez earned a bachelor's degree in government from the University of Texas at Austin and a law degree from St. Mary's School of Law in San Antonio. After spending time in private practice, he was elected to the county bench in 1982 and spent 15 years as a local and state trial judge.

When his father announced his retirement, Gonzalez jumped into a seven-way Democratic primary to succeed him in 1998. Gonzalez won the nomination with 62 percent of the vote in a runoff. In the general election, he won with 63 percent. In 2000 and 2002 Gonzalez faced no major-party opposition, and he has cruised to victory since. Gonzalez topped his 2010 opponent, tea party-backed Clayton Trotter, with 64 percent of the vote.

Key Votes

2010

Overhaul the nation's health insurance system	YES
Allow for repeal of "don't ask, don't tell"	YES
Overhaul financial services industry regulation	YES
Limit use of new Afghanistan War funds to troop withdrawal activities	NO
Change oversight of offshore drilling and lift oil spill liability cap	NO
Provide a path to legal status for some children of illegal immigrants	YES
Extend Bush-era income tax cuts for two years	YES

2009

Expand the Children's Health Insurance Program	YES
Provide $787 billion in tax cuts and spending increases to stimulate the economy	YES
Allow bankruptcy judges to modify certain primary-residence mortgages	YES
Create a cap-and-trade system to limit greenhouse gas emissions	YES
Provide $2 billion for the "cash for clunkers" program	YES
Establish the government as the sole provider of student loans	YES
Restrict federally funded insurance coverage for abortions in health care overhaul	NO

CQ Vote Studies

	PARTY UNITY		PRESIDENTIAL SUPPORT	
	SUPPORT	OPPOSE	SUPPORT	OPPOSE
2010	98%	2%	95%	5%
2009	99%	1%	97%	3%
2008	98%	2%	23%	77%
2007	97%	3%	7%	93%
2006	89%	11%	33%	67%

Interest Groups

	AFL-CIO	ADA	CCUS	ACU
2010	100%	90%	38%	0%
2009	100%	100%	36%	0%
2008	100%	90%	61%	8%
2007	96%	95%	60%	4%
2006	100%	95%	57%	16%

Texas 20

Downtown San Antonio

While maintaining ties to its history, San Antonio — the heart of the 20th District — has grown into one of the nation's largest cities. The strongly Democratic 20th, which is located entirely in Bexar (pronounced BEAR) County, takes in a majority of the city, including the heavily Hispanic and largely poor West Side, downtown San Antonio and some close-in communities.

A huge military presence in San Antonio long fueled the economy. A "mega-base" created after the 2005 round of base closings linked the 20th's Lackland Air Force Base with other local installations. The former Kelly Air Force Base, closed in the mid-1990s, was redeveloped into a high-tech, aeronautics and manufacturing business park supervised by Port San Antonio. Telecommunications and solar energy employers in the district also provide jobs.

Beyond the military and technology sectors, the Baptist Medical Center and several Christus Santa Rosa facilities make the district a regional health care hub. Tourism and convention business have boosted the city's economy: The Alamo, site of the famous 1836 battle, is in the heart of downtown; the scenic Paseo del Rio that winds along the San Antonio River draws visitors; and crowds fill the nearby Alamodome arena.

Most of the recent population growth here has taken place outside the urban center and among Hispanic residents. There are still several mostly black neighborhoods along the 20th's southeastern edge near downtown, adding Democratic strength in this Hispanic-majority district. The only significant GOP presence is in the largely white, higher-income areas northwest and northeast of downtown San Antonio.

Major Industry
Health care, tourism, military, telecommunications, trade

Military Bases
Joint Base San Antonio (shared with the 21st and 28th), 36,184 military, 15,945 civilian (2011)

Cities
San Antonio (pt.), 640,009; Leon Valley (pt.), 10,141

Notable
Theodore Roosevelt recruited his "Rough Riders," the 1st U.S. Volunteer Cavalry in the Spanish-American War, at the bar in the Menger Hotel (built 1859), which is adjacent to the Alamo and still open.

Rep. Lamar Smith (R)

Capitol Office
225-4236
lamarsmith.house.gov
2409 Rayburn Bldg. 20515-4321; fax 225-8628

Committees
Homeland Security
Judiciary - Chairman
Science, Space & Technology

Residence
San Antonio

Born
Nov. 19, 1947; San Antonio, Texas

Religion
Christian Scientist

Family
Wife, Beth Smith; two children

Education
Yale U., B.A. 1969 (American studies); Southern
Methodist U., J.D. 1975

Career
Lawyer; rancher; reporter

Political Highlights
Texas House, 1981-82; Bexar County Commissioners
Court, 1983-85

ELECTION RESULTS

2010 GENERAL

Lamar Smith (R)	162,924	68.9%
Lainey Melnick (D)	65,927	27.9%
James Strohm (LIBERT)	7,694	3.2%

2010 PRIMARY

Lamar Smith (R)	61,923	81.4%
Stephen Schoppe (R)	14,166	18.6%

2008 GENERAL

Lamar Smith (R)	243,471	80.0%
James Stohm (LIBERT)	60,879	20.0%

Previous Winning Percentages
2006 (60%); 2004 (62%); 2002 (73%); 2000 (76%);
1998 (91%); 1996 (76%); 1994 (90%); 1992 (72%);
1990 (75%); 1988 (93%); 1986 (61%)

Elected 1986; 13th term

Smith, the mild-mannered chairman of the Judiciary Committee, relies on a mix of pointed argument and sly sarcasm to confront President Obama and congressional Democrats while advancing his conservative priorities.

From his perch atop Judiciary and his seat on Homeland Security, Smith has played a leading role in the continuing debate on immigration.

When the Obama administration filed a lawsuit in 2010 challenging an Arizona law cracking down on illegal immigrants, Smith charged it was "the height of irresponsibility and arrogance." And when a Muslim-American was arrested for a foiled attempt to detonate a bomb in Times Square in 2010, Smith wrote, "Our national security policy should consist of more than relying on dumb bombers and smart citizens."

Smith also pressed the Obama administration to investigate two causes taken up by conservative media outlets: allegations of voter intimidation by the New Black Panther Party and voter registration fraud by the community-organizing group ACORN.

A reliable party supporter, Smith is a member of the conservative Republican Study Committee and in the 111th Congress (2009-10) helped found the Media Fairness Caucus, which is aimed at correcting what he perceives as liberal media bias. He also sits on the House Republican Steering Committee, which makes committee assignments.

One topic on which he has found common ground with Democrats is overhauling the nation's patent laws. Smith has continued to work closely with Judiciary Committee Democrats, including ranking member John Conyers Jr. of Michigan and Howard L. Berman of California, who shared a common frustration about the direction patent overhaul took in the Senate in the 111th Congress. "When inventors and businesses invest in research and development that result in patents, they have the right to benefit from their efforts. The American economy also benefits by the jobs these patents create," he wrote in a November 2010 Roll Call op-ed.

But it is on terrorism and immigration where Smith has taken a particularly high-profile role in the GOP caucus.

Smith said he's been frustrated by a lack of action on improving intelligence gathering and interrogation tactics in order to thwart future terrorist attacks, strengthening immigration enforcement.

Meeting the terrorist threat, which he says "has changed, but it has not diminished," is a top priority for the Judiciary Committee.

When Obama announced he would close the U.S. military detention facilities at Guantánamo Bay, Cuba, Smith introduced a bill to bar the release of any of the detainees within the territorial United States.

"We should not close the terrorist detention center," he wrote in Roll Call. "The Pentagon has reported that 20 percent of released Gitmo terrorists have returned to planning attacks against Americans."

After the Obama administration announced in April 2011 that it would try five alleged conspirators implicated in the Sept. 11 attacks in military tribunals, Smith claimed some of the credit.

"If Congress tied his hands, we tied his hands in the right way and helped him reach the right conclusion," Smith said in response to complaints from Attorney General Eric H. Holder Jr. about restrictions Congress imposed on the administration.

Smith also spearheads GOP efforts to renew provisions of the antiterrorism law known as the Patriot Act. And he led the fight during the 110th

Congress (2007-08) to retain provisions in a foreign surveillance bill granting immunity protections for telecommunications companies.

Smith constantly pushes for stronger border security. He believes lax enforcement of immigration laws contributed to the 2001 terrorist attacks, and he opposed President George W. Bush's 2007 proposal to create a path to citizenship for illegal immigrants. Smith joined with New York Republican Peter T. King to write the House Republicans' alternative, which would have barred illegal immigrants from obtaining legal status, made English the official language of the United States and required tamper-proof birth certificates for all Americans. He authored a 1996 law that increased penalties for document fraud and the smuggling of illegal immigrants and made it easier for illegal immigrants to be detained at the border or deported.

In 2007, he delayed passage of a bill to give the District of Columbia full voting rights in the House. Near the end of the debate, Smith offered a motion that called for adding language to repeal the District's ban on handguns and other local gun control laws. His motion caused the sponsors to pull the bill from the floor, but it later passed in the House without the gun control language. Efforts to repeal the gun ban stalled a similar District voting bill in early 2009.

In the 110th, Smith was the Republican point man during consideration of a Democratic proposal to put a layer of outside review atop the internal House ethics process. Smith countered the Democratic plan by proposing an expansion of the existing ethics committee to include four former House members, two from each party, and to rotate the chairmanship between the two parties.

Smith's family arrived in Texas around 1850, just five years after it was admitted as a state, and the family's political involvement stretches back almost that long. His grandfather was district attorney in San Antonio and an unsuccessful House candidate. His great-grandfather was a San Antonio judge, and his great-great-grandfather was mayor of Galveston.

After graduating from Yale, Smith worked as a business reporter for the Christian Science Monitor in Boston. He then got a law degree and returned to San Antonio. He was elected to a seat in the state legislature in Austin, then served on the Bexar County Commission.

Republican Tom Loeffler gave up his House seat in 1986 to run, unsuccessfully, for governor. After Bush — then a Midland oilman with one losing congressional race under his belt — decided not to seek the seat, Smith won a six-way primary. He then defeated former Democratic state Sen. Pete Snelson. Smith garnered at least 70 percent of the vote in subsequent elections until 2004 and 2006, when he won with just more than 60 percent. He had no Democratic opposition in 2008, and won by more than 40 points in 2010.

Key Votes

2010

Vote	
Overhaul the nation's health insurance system	NO
Allow for repeal of "don't ask, don't tell"	NO
Overhaul financial services industry regulation	NO
Limit use of new Afghanistan War funds to troop withdrawal activities	NO
Change oversight of offshore drilling and lift oil spill liability cap	NO
Provide a path to legal status for some children of illegal immigrants	NO
Extend Bush-era income tax cuts for two years	YES

2009

Vote	
Expand the Children's Health Insurance Program	NO
Provide $787 billion in tax cuts and spending increases to stimulate the economy	NO
Allow bankruptcy judges to modify certain primary-residence mortgages	NO
Create a cap-and-trade system to limit greenhouse gas emissions	NO
Provide $2 billion for the "cash for clunkers" program	NO
Establish the government as the sole provider of student loans	NO
Restrict federally funded insurance coverage for abortions in health care overhaul	YES

CQ Vote Studies

	PARTY UNITY		PRESIDENTIAL SUPPORT	
	SUPPORT	OPPOSE	SUPPORT	OPPOSE
2010	96%	4%	26%	74%
2009	86%	14%	22%	78%
2008	95%	5%	70%	30%
2007	96%	4%	84%	16%
2006	97%	3%	97%	3%

Interest Groups

	AFL-CIO	ADA	CCUS	ACU
2010	0%	0%	88%	100%
2009	10%	5%	87%	96%
2008	20%	15%	100%	88%
2007	13%	15%	84%	88%
2006	7%	0%	100%	84%

Texas 21

Central — northeast San Antonio and suburbs, part of Austin and suburbs

The 21st is a Republican, mainly urban and suburban district that takes in most of San Antonio and part of Austin and also extends westward to scoop up some of Texas' rugged Hill Country. Overall, the fast-growing district, which is among the nation's most-populous ahead of decennial remapping, is almost 60 percent white with an increasingly Hispanic population.

A slight majority of district residents live in Bexar (pronounced BEAR) County in the GOP-leaning north and northeast parts of San Antonio and its suburbs. The district also includes employment anchors San Antonio International Airport and Fort Sam Houston, which is part of the newly realigned Joint Base San Antonio. Canyon Lake is a popular recreation spot in the eastern portion of the 21st.

Roughly one-fifth of district residents live in Austin's burgeoning Travis County. The 21st's share of the county encompasses the main University of Texas campus and parts of downtown Austin, including the Capitol and

governor's mansion as well as the Bob Bullock Texas State History Museum. The 21st also takes in some wealthy suburbs and rural areas in western Travis County, including Lake Travis and surrounding attractions. Comal County, located northeast of San Antonio, makes up only one-eighth of the district's population, but it adds to the district's GOP tilt. The 21st's share of the Texas Hill Country includes Bandera, Kerr and Real counties.

The district favored Republican presidential candidate John McCain in 2008, giving him 58 percent of its vote.

Major Industry
Technology, government, higher education, defense

Military Bases
Joint Base San Antonio (shared with the 20th and 28th), 36,184 military, 15,945 civilian (2011)

Cities
San Antonio (pt.), 309,139; Austin (pt.), 100,663; New Braunfels (pt.), 47,586

Notable
Bandera bills itself the cowboy capital of the world; Austin is home to North America's largest urban colony of Mexican free-tailed bats.

Rep. Pete Olson (R)

Capitol Office
225-5951
olson.house.gov
312 Cannon Bldg. 20515-4322; fax 225-5241

Committees
Energy & Commerce

Residence
Sugar Land

Born
Dec. 9, 1962; Fort Lewis, Wash.

Religion
United Methodist

Family
Wife, Nancy Olson; two children

Education
Rice U., B.A. 1985 (computer science); U. of Texas,
J.D. 1988

Military
Navy, 1988-98

Career
Congressional aide; Navy Senate liaison

Political Highlights
No previous office

ELECTION RESULTS

2010 GENERAL

Pete Olson (R)	140,537	67.5%
Kesha Rogers (D)	62,082	29.8%
Steven Susman (LIBERT)	5,538	2.7%

2010 PRIMARY

Pete Olson (R)	unopposed

2008 GENERAL

Pete Olson (R)	161,996	52.4%
Nick Lampson (D)	140,160	45.4%
John Wieder (LIBERT)	6,839	2.2%

Elected 2008; 2nd term

A newcomer to electoral politics when he won his first House race, Olson nevertheless arrived in Congress with something of a head start. He had served as the Navy's Senate liaison and as a top staff member for two Republican senators from Texas, John Cornyn and Phil Gramm. Olson matches the fiscal and social conservatism of those lawmakers, and also that of his House predecessor, former Republican Leader Tom DeLay.

Olson claimed a seat on the Energy and Commerce Committee in the 112th Congress (2011-12), where he will continue to try to protect his district's petrochemical jobs in the wake of the massive spring 2010 oil spill in the Gulf of Mexico.

He introduced legislation in the previous Congress to lift the Obama administration's offshore drilling moratorium, saying the ban "turns an economic challenge into an economic disaster." And he opposed lifting the $75 million liability cap for oil spill damage, arguing it would drive smaller companies out of business.

"They cannot afford and they cannot purchase a $10 billion or an indefinite cover, indefinite liability for some sort of spill," he said at a June 2010 Transportation and Infrastructure Committee hearing.

Olson served on a House Republican energy task force that promoted increased domestic drilling and nuclear power. He was a fierce critic of a bill the House passed in June 2009 to address global warming.

In April 2011, he backed legislation that would prohibit the EPA from regulating greenhouse gases in any effort to address climate change.

"The Clean Air Act did not include greenhouse gases and Congress, not EPA, is the one with the authority to amend that law," Olson said.

Those views are in line with Olson's overall conservative outlook.

The first bill he introduced sought to require state health departments to disclose whether any federal Medicaid funds they receive go to groups that perform or grant referrals for abortions. He reintroduced the measure in the 112th Congress.

He also espoused his limited-government views while blasting President Obama's and House Democrats' approach to health care. "Raising taxes, eliminating choices for Americans and placing the government in charge of health care is not reform at all," he said in late 2009.

Olson, formerly a member of the Homeland Security Committee, also espouses get-tough views on illegal immigration. He advocates "fences, increased surveillance, increased manpower [and] detention facilities" to strengthen borders while giving law enforcement officials more funding and training to fight crime among those living in the United States illegally. On behalf of the ports in the Houston and Galveston areas, he calls for greater port security to deter potential terrorists.

Olson's district is home to many employees of NASA's Johnson Space Center and he once aspired to become an astronaut himself. He takes a dim view of Obama administration proposals to cancel the Constellation program, NASA's next-generation system to replace the space shuttle, and scale back human space flight. "Japan, India and China have set their sights on the moon. Why are we pulling back America's dominance in human space flight? It is deplorable that the president would willingly accept second-tier status for the U.S. on an issue of this magnitude," he wrote in The Hill newspaper in February 2010.

He also joined other Texas lawmakers in protesting the administration's decision not to name Houston as a permanent home for any of the retired space shuttles and suggested Congress might act to override the decision legislatively.

Olson was born at an Army medical center in Fort Lewis, Wash.; his father had enrolled in ROTC in college and spent two years on active duty. The family eventually settled in Seabrook, Texas, where his father worked in paper manufacturing and his mother stayed at home. At 6-foot-3, Olson was a member of his high school's top-ranked basketball team. He graduated from Rice University with a degree in computer science and went to law school at the University of Texas.

After passing the Texas bar exam in 1988, Olson joined the Navy, hoping the service would provide flight experience useful to joining NASA. He failed to win acceptance to test pilot school but did become a decorated aviator, flying missions over the Persian Gulf after Operation Desert Storm. In 1994 his air crew was named the Pacific Fleet's best in anti-submarine warfare.

He eventually received an assignment in Washington, where he served with the Joint Chiefs of Staff, then became Senate liaison for the Navy and got to know Gramm, who hired him in 1998. When Gramm retired and Cornyn won his seat in 2002, Olson began a five-year stint as Cornyn's chief of staff.

After DeLay's resignation following a 2006 indictment in a campaign finance case, Houston GOP City Councilwoman Shelley Sekula Gibbs won a special election to serve the few remaining weeks of DeLay's unexpired term. But she lost a general-election race to Democrat Nick Lampson, who had served four terms in the House before his district was redrawn. Meanwhile, Olson — with encouragement from his Texas connections — moved to the district to run for the seat in 2008. Despite carpetbagger charges, Olson had little trouble defeating Sekula Gibbs in a primary runoff, getting more than two-thirds of the vote.

In November, Olson won more than 52 percent of the vote — 6 percentage points less than the Republican presidential candidate, Arizona Sen. John McCain, received in the district, but enough to win. Olson won with 68 percent in 2010.

Not long after taking office, he suffered a health scare. While exercising at the House gym in March 2009, he fainted and was rushed to George Washington University Hospital. Doctors determined he suffered from a slow heartbeat, or bradycardia, and inserted a pacemaker in his chest to regulate his heart; Olson ended up missing one week's worth of House votes. He said several months afterward that he had fully recovered.

Key Votes

2010

Overhaul the nation's health insurance system	NO
Allow for repeal of "don't ask, don't tell"	NO
Overhaul financial services industry regulation	NO
Limit use of new Afghanistan War funds to troop withdrawal activities	NO
Change oversight of offshore drilling and lift oil spill liability cap	NO
Provide a path to legal status for some children of illegal immigrants	NO
Extend Bush-era income tax cuts for two years	YES

2009

Expand the Children's Health Insurance Program	NO
Provide $787 billion in tax cuts and spending increases to stimulate the economy	NO
Allow bankruptcy judges to modify certain primary-residence mortgages	NO
Create a cap-and-trade system to limit greenhouse gas emissions	NO
Provide $2 billion for the "cash for clunkers" program	NO
Establish the government as the sole provider of student loans	NO
Restrict federally funded insurance coverage for abortions in health care overhaul	YES

CQ Vote Studies

	PARTY UNITY		PRESIDENTIAL SUPPORT	
	SUPPORT	OPPOSE	SUPPORT	OPPOSE
2010	98%	2%	26%	74%
2009	97%	3%	13%	87%

Interest Groups

	AFL-CIO	ADA	CCUS	ACU
2010	0%	0%	88%	100%
2009	5%	0%	80%	100%

Texas 22

Southeast Houston and southern suburbs — Sugar Land, Pearland, part of Pasadena

The 22nd includes most of Fort Bend County, a chunk of northern Brazoria County, a piece of Galveston County south of Houston and a slice of the city itself. The 22nd has the highest median household income of any district in the state, and wealthy, white-collar residents have kept a Republican hold on the district.

One of the state's, and nation's, most populous districts ahead of decennial remapping, the 22nd hosts several cities that have boomed over the past decade. Pearland, in Brazoria County, led the population growth, and Fort Bend County no longer accounts for a majority of district residents. A solidly white-majority district when it was drawn, white residents now make up just less than 45 percent of the population.

In Fort Bend, the 22nd takes in Sugar Land, which has transformed from a sugar-growing hub into booming suburbia since the 1960s. The district also includes affluent areas surrounding the Lyndon B. Johnson Space Center in Galveston County. Wealthy NASA scientists and astronauts live nearby in Clear Lake.

On its northeastern edge, the 22nd takes in part of upscale southeastern Harris County, where almost 40 percent of district residents live. Some of the county's wealthiest areas are in southeastern Houston, near Ellington Airport, a former Air Force base that now hosts space center aircraft operations and a few commercial sites. The district sneaks north to grab Houston's Hobby Airport.

Although a Democrat briefly took the U.S. House seat here against a Republican write-in opponent in 2006, the district's recent congressional and presidential votes have swung back to strong GOP support.

Major Industry
Aerospace, transportation, agriculture

Cities
Houston (pt.), 134,734; Pearland (pt.), 91,113; Sugar Land, 78,817; Pasadena (pt.), 64,394; Missouri City (pt.), 45,649; Deer Park (pt.), 32,010

Notable
The annual "Texian Market Days" in Fort Bend County include re-enactments of 1830s pioneer life.

Rep. Francisco "Quico" Canseco (R)

Capitol Office
225-4511
canseco.house.gov
1339 Longworth Bldg. 20515-4323; fax 225-2237

Committees
Financial Services

Residence
San Antonio

Born
July 30, 1949; Laredo, Texas

Religion
Roman Catholic

Family
Wife, Gloria Canseco; three children

Education
Saint Louis U., B.A. 1972 (history), J.D. 1975

Career
Lawyer; banker; real estate developer

Political Highlights
Sought Republican nomination for U.S. House, 2004, 2008

ELECTION RESULTS

2010 GENERAL

Canseco (R)	74,853	49.4%
Ciro D. Rodriguez (D)	67,348	44.4%
Craig T. Stephens (I)	5,432	3.6%
Martin Nitschke (LIBERT)	2,482	1.6%

2010 PRIMARY RUNOFF

Canseco (R)	7,210	52.6%
Will Hurd (R)	6,488	47.4%

Elected 2010; 1st term

Canseco won the only 2010 congressional race that featured Hispanic nominees from both major parties. He said his priorities will be to reduce taxes for small businesses as a way to create jobs and to replace the 2010 health care overhaul.

Canseco, who won a seat on the Financial Services Committee, pointed to his experience developing shopping centers and investing in a community bank as evidence that he can be a strong advocate for small businesses. In particular, he said, businesses should be allowed to expand their tax exemptions for net operating losses as a way to "weather the tough economic times, make needed purchases and prevent further layoffs."

He also says Congress should cut taxes for people in the 10 percent and 15 percent income-tax brackets and prevent unemployment benefits from being taxed, because it "only adds insult to injury."

The 23rd District is 65 percent Hispanic and shares a long border with Mexico. Canseco's stance on immigration generally follows the GOP line: He opposes a path to citizenship for illegal immigrants already in the United States and supports deporting those who commit crimes. In June 2010 he told the San Antonio Express-News that he backs Arizona's law aimed at cracking down on illegal immigration, saying it "parallels the federal government and in many ways is more benign."

Born in Laredo, Canseco earned a degree in history and then a law degree from St. Louis University. He practiced law throughout Texas before moving into real estate development. He also has served as a bank legal counsel and on the board of directors of two banks.

Canseco unsuccessfully sought the GOP nomination in the neighboring 28th District in 2004 and the 23rd District — larger than most states east of the Mississippi River — in 2008.

In 2010, he finished second by half a percentage point in a five-man GOP primary, then won the runoff with about 53 percent of the vote.

He defeated five-term Democrat Ciro D. Rodriguez, winning 49 percent of the vote to the incumbent's 44 percent.

Texas 23

Southwest — south and northwest San Antonio and suburbs, Del Rio

Larger than most states east of the Mississippi River, the 23rd has more than 700 miles of border with Mexico along the Rio Grande River, skimming El Paso in the west and reaching as far east as San Antonio, the district's population center. More than 60 percent of residents live in the city or surrounding Bexar (pronounced BEAR) County; most of the 23rd's population growth since 2000 has been in San Antonio.

Counties along the border include some of the nation's poorest areas and are overwhelmingly Hispanic. Seasonal employment, an influx of immigrants and access to Mexican labor are hallmarks of the economy, which also relies on trade and manufacturing. In San Antonio, the Air Force's Brooks

City-Base was ordered closed as part of the 2005 round of base realignments and was redeveloped into a technology and research business park. Historically lower home prices shielded much of San Antonio from the national housing market crisis.

South San Antonio's Democratic and Hispanic lean contrasts with the Republican, mostly white areas in the city's north and in its suburbs that generally provide a GOP tilt here in federal races. But in 2008, Barack Obama narrowly won the district with 51 percent of its presidential vote.

Major Industry
Agriculture, trade, tourism

Military Bases
Laughlin Air Force Base, 1,506 military, 825 civilian (2011)

Cities
San Antonio (pt.), 378,190; Del Rio, 35,591

Notable
Texas' largest county, Brewster, is roughly 6,200 square miles.

Rep. Kenny Marchant (R)

Capitol Office
225-6605
www.marchant.house.gov
1110 Longworth Bldg. 20515-4324; fax 225-0074

Committees
Ways & Means

Residence
Coppell

Born
Feb. 23, 1951; Bonham, Texas

Religion
Nazarene

Family
Wife, Donna Marchant; four children

Education
Southern Nazarene U., B.A. 1974 (religion); Nazarene
Theological Seminary, attended 1975-76

Career
Real estate developer; homebuilding company
owner

Political Highlights
Carrollton City Council, 1980-84 (mayor pro tem-
pore, 1983-84); mayor of Carrollton, 1984-86; Texas
House, 1987-2005

ELECTION RESULTS

2010 GENERAL

Kenny Marchant (R)	100,078	81.6%
David Sparks (LIBERT)	22,609	18.4%

2010 PRIMARY

Kenny Marchant (R)	33,283	84.1%
Frank Roszell (R)	6,298	15.9%

2008 GENERAL

Kenny Marchant (R)	151,434	56.0%
Tom Love (D)	111,089	41.1%
David A. Casey (LIBERT)	7,972	2.9%

Previous Winning Percentages
2006 (60%); 2004 (64%)

Elected 2004; 4th term

Marchant is a workhorse. He's a dedicated advocate of smaller government who has been described as "about as fiscally conservative as a congressman can get."

During his lengthy career in Texas government, he was the state House
Republican chairman in 2002 when his party won control of the chamber for
the first time since Reconstruction. He effectively was the caucus chairman,
whip and policy chairman all in one, preferring to work behind the scenes and
in committees. "I've never been much of an orator," Marchant (MARCH-unt)
said. "Probably, in 18 years in the Texas House, I gave eight speeches."

Marchant is a member of the Republican Study Committee, the coalition
of conservative House Republicans. In 2009 he also joined a new Property
Rights Action Caucus, an informal group he said he hoped could "develop a
groundswell of public sentiment for sensible legislation protecting private
property from unnecessary and unconstitutional intrusion." And he joined
the newly formed House Tea Party Caucus in 2010.

Marchant won a seat on the Ways and Means Committee in the 112th
Congress (2011-12), giving him a prominent platform from which he can
champion lower taxes and reduced regulation.

He said President Obama's fiscal 2012 budget "continues the nation on the
path of irresponsible spending and all but ignores calls by the American
people to meaningfully rein in government."

He backed the final version of the catchall spending bill, which became law
in April 2011, that cut federal spending by $38 billion.

Before joining Ways and Means, Marchant brought a state-level perspective to his work on the Financial Services Committee, having chaired the
Financial Institutions panel, among others, in the Texas House. He called the
Democrats' overhaul of the financial regulatory system in 2010 "an empty,
politically motivated effort at 'reform' that will continue to thwart our economic recovery."

Marchant opposed both versions of a $700 billion bill to aid the nation's
ailing financial sector, the second of which became law. He also opposed the
2008 law to rescue troubled mortgage giants Fannie Mae and Freddie Mac
and assist struggling homeowners.

Combining his Financial Services experience with his strong views on
illegal immigration, he has sponsored bills that would require anyone buying
a home or modifying a home loan held by Fannie Mae or Freddie Mac to have
their immigration status confirmed by the E-Verify program used by employers to check whether employees can work legally in the United States.

Marchant was a strong critic of President Obama's $787 billion econom-
ic stimulus law in early 2009. He denounced it as "payback to [Democrats']
special interests at the expense of the American people, who continue to
suffer while Congress writes checks for programs we do not need with
money we do not have." He compared the interest groups eagerly seeking
provisions inserted in the measure to "people impatiently clamoring for
beads at Mardi Gras."

He also opposed the Democrats' health care overhaul enacted in 2010 and
voted to repeal it in 2011.

Overall, during his first three terms in Washington, Marchant proved
himself to be a reliable Republican vote, siding with the GOP almost 98
percent of the time on votes where a majority of Republicans opposed a
majority of Democrats.

An exception was his 2007 vote in favor of raising the minimum wage. He said an increase was long overdue, though he complained that Democrats rebuffed Republican attempts to link the hike to helping small businesses.

Marchant's bona fides within the party were apparent even before his 2005 arrival on Capitol Hill. He helped draw the redistricting map that was planned by former House Majority Leader Tom DeLay of Texas to create more GOP seats, including the one Marchant now holds.

In line with his penchant for avoiding the limelight, when Congress debated a 2007 resolution in opposition to President George W. Bush's plan to send thousands more U.S. troops to Iraq, Marchant went to the House floor a couple of times with speech in hand, but arrived too late and missed his chance. He had his remarks in support of Bush's strategy entered into the Congressional Record.

Marchant, a homebuilder and developer, is one of the wealthiest members of the House, with assets worth at least $18.4 million in 2009, according to Roll Call. He assists area churches through the Marchant Family Foundation, which also contributes funds for educational scholarships and aids local charities.

He grew up near Farmers Branch, where his father and two uncles owned a four-chair barbershop. "We went to church three or four times a week, and I went to church camps," Marchant recalled. "All of my activities basically revolved around the church." He received a degree in religion from Southern Nazarene University in Bethany, Okla., and attended the Nazarene Theological Seminary in Kansas City, Mo. But after a year of study, as he and his wife, Donna, were expecting their first child, Marchant said he found that "I was not very happy, and began to doubt that was really, really what I should plan to do."

Returning to Texas, Marchant became a roofing contractor, resuming work he had done to pay his way through college. From there, he began importing and installing wooden shingles, then building new homes and developing lots to sell to builders. He chaired the local homebuilders association, which suspected city inspectors of soliciting bribes. That spurred him to run for and win a seat on the Carrollton City Council in 1980. Four years later, he was elected mayor.

In 1987, he moved to the state House, where he served until he won his first congressional race in 2004 with 64 percent of the vote. He has had a relatively easy time with re-election.

Three weeks after Election Day 2010, Marchant underwent double bypass heart surgery. He was back at work when Congress reconvened in January.

Key Votes

2010

Overhaul the nation's health insurance system	NO
Allow for repeal of "don't ask, don't tell"	NO
Overhaul financial services industry regulation	NO
Limit use of new Afghanistan War funds to troop withdrawal activities	NO
Change oversight of offshore drilling and lift oil spill liability cap	NO
Provide a path to legal status for some children of illegal immigrants	-
Extend Bush-era income tax cuts for two years	-

2009

Expand the Children's Health Insurance Program	NO
Provide $787 billion in tax cuts and spending increases to stimulate the economy	NO
Allow bankruptcy judges to modify certain primary-residence mortgages	NO
Create a cap-and-trade system to limit greenhouse gas emissions	NO
Provide $2 billion for the "cash for clunkers" program	YES
Establish the government as the sole provider of student loans	NO
Restrict federally funded insurance coverage for abortions in health care overhaul	YES

CQ Vote Studies

	PARTY UNITY		PRESIDENTIAL SUPPORT	
	Support	Oppose	Support	Oppose
2010	99%	1%	26%	74%
2009	98%	2%	15%	85%
2008	98%	2%	82%	18%
2007	97%	3%	89%	11%
2006	98%	2%	97%	3%

Interest Groups

	AFL-CIO	ADA	CCUS	ACU
2010	0%	5%	100%	95%
2009	11%	5%	73%	100%
2008	0%	0%	83%	100%
2007	9%	10%	78%	96%
2006	7%	0%	100%	92%

Texas 24
Part of Dallas and western suburbs — Grand Prairie, Carrollton, part of Irving

Taking in most of the more-affluent suburbs sandwiched between Dallas and Fort Worth, the 24th was designed to be a Republican stronghold, but the district gave John McCain only 55 percent of its 2008 presidential vote, 10 percentage points less than George W. Bush won here in 2004. A decade of demographic shifts has transformed this once predominantly white district — the Hispanic population here grew by 84 percent in the past decade, and white residents now account for only 47 percent of the population.

The district's economy revolves around Dallas-Fort Worth International Airport and the businesses the airport has attracted to the area. The airport, located in the middle of the 24th and a small part of which is in the neighboring 26th, is the largest employer in the district. East of the airport, a corporate hub in Irving's Las Colinas financial district, which is shared with the 32nd, also fuels the district's economy. The area combines financial stability with low tax rates, high quality of life and good transportation — all

of which contribute to its reputation as a prime destination for domestic and international corporate relocation.

The 12,000-acre business and residential planned community boasts thousands of companies. Many residents from the wealthy suburbs commute into either Fort Worth or Dallas, making transportation policy, particularly plans for highway upgrades and commuter rail expansions, a major issue here.

Although most of the area's attractions and entertainment venues are in neighboring districts, the 24th hosts the Lone Star Park and the Verizon Theatre, both of which are in Grand Prairie, and the Gaylord Texan resort and convention center in Grapevine. The southern part of the district takes in almost all of Joe Pool Lake and its surrounding parks, an area with camping, marinas and expanding home development.

Major Industry
Transportation, manufacturing, corporate headquarters

Cities
Grand Prairie (pt.), 170,039; Carrollton (pt.), 119,095; Irving (pt.), 74,956; Dallas (pt.), 55,319; Euless (pt.), 51,277; Bedford (pt.), 46,979

Notable
Grand Prairie is home to the National Championship Indian Pow Wow.

Rep. Lloyd Doggett (D)

Capitol Office
225-4865
www.house.gov/doggett
201 Cannon Bldg. 20515-4325; fax 225-3073

Committees
Budget
Ways & Means

Residence
Austin

Born
Oct. 6, 1946; Austin, Texas

Religion
Methodist

Family
Wife, Libby Belk Doggett; two children

Education
U. of Texas, B.B.A. 1967, J.D. 1970

Career
Lawyer

Political Highlights
Texas Senate, 1973-85; Democratic nominee for U.S.
Senate, 1984; Texas Supreme Court, 1989-94

ELECTION RESULTS

2010 GENERAL

Lloyd Doggett (D)	99,967	52.8%
Donna Campbell (R)	84,849	44.8%
Jim Stutsman (LIBERT)	4,431	2.3%

2010 PRIMARY

Lloyd Doggett (D)	unopposed

2008 GENERAL

Lloyd Doggett (D)	191,755	65.8%
George L. Morovich (R)	88,693	30.4%
Jim Stutsman (LIBERT)	10,848	3.7%

Previous Winning Percentages
2006 (67%); 2004 (68%); 2002 (84%); 2000 (85%);
1998 (85%); 1996 (56%); 1994 (56%)

Elected 1994; 9th term

Representing a district President Obama carried by almost 20 percentage points in 2008, Doggett is a reliably liberal vote within the Democratic Caucus. He is a firm supporter of party leadership and is also influential with other Democrats who respect his knowledge of tax and fiscal policy.

His annual party unity score — the percentage of votes on which he sided with a majority of Democrats against a majority of Republicans — has never fallen below 90, and has consistently been higher in the 2000s than it was in the 1990s.

From his position on the powerful Ways and Means Committee, Doggett has sought to require lobbyists seeking tax benefits to reveal their employers and to block the "international shenanigans" that allow some multinational corporations to avoid U.S. taxes. When Obama unveiled his plan in May 2009 to significantly change how U.S.-based multinationals are taxed, it included aspects of Doggett's proposal.

When Congress aimed to provide $26 billion to fill gaps in state budgets in the summer of 2010, Doggett included a provision in the legislation requiring Texas Republican Gov. Rick Perry to certify that the state would maintain its current level of education funding for the next three years, even though no other state had to meet a similar standard. Doggett, now the ranking Democrat on the Ways and Means subcommittee with jurisdiction over welfare programs, said the provision was necessary because the state used money from the 2009 economic stimulus in ways the federal government did not like.

The spending deal signed into law in April 2011 repealed the provision. Doggett called that move "one of many unwise concessions made to Republicans to avoid their threatened government shutdown."

"We gave [Perry] an opportunity to do right by Texas schoolchildren instead of repeating the wrongs from last year," Doggett told the Austin American-Statesman. Perry said the provision was unworkable — claiming he could not bind future legislatures — and possibly unconstitutional.

Doggett says the House should lead by example on environmental issues by being more energy efficient. He is diligent about recycling in his Capitol Hill office and is an avid bicyclist; a wreck in 2008 left him with three broken bones in his leg. Early in the 112th Congress (2011-12), he introduced legislation offering a tax credit for investment in systems that convert waste product into energy sources.

He authored climate change legislation that would have gone further to reduce greenhouse gases than bills supported by his party's leaders. His bill, introduced in the 110th Congress (2007-08), aimed to reduce the nation's carbon emissions by 80 percent over the next 42 years, compared with 1990 levels, by creating a cap-and-trade system to control carbon dioxide emissions. As lawmakers took up the issue in the 111th Congress (2009-10), Doggett continued to propose a cap-and-trade plan that added "training wheels" for the early years of the program. It called for an oversight board to forecast and select emission allowance prices through 2019, with the market setting prices after that.

He was one of three Texans — all Democrats — to support a measure to repeal the $75 million cap on liability for offshore oil spills and increase regulation of leases for offshore development.

Doggett also serves on the Budget Committee. He opposed the budget agreement reached in April 2011 that trimmed about $40 billion from fiscal 2011 spending, saying it was "not my cup of tea."

He backed Obama's $787 billion economic stimulus law in 2009, calling it an "imperfect but responsible response" to the nation's economic woes.

The technology industry has expanded Austin's economy, and Doggett pays attention to its needs. He founded and co-chairs the bipartisan House Information Technology Roundtable, a group that promotes dialogue among businesses, policymakers and the public on technology issues.

Doggett spent his first 12 years in Congress in the minority, where he seldom missed an opportunity to upbraid conservatives, particularly fellow Texan and former House Majority Leader Tom DeLay.

He also has devoted much of his time to opposing the Iraq War. During House consideration in late 2002 of a resolution authorizing the president to take military action against Iraq, he led an ad hoc whip organization to round up votes in opposition.

Doggett's antipathy toward Republicans made him a top target when DeLay led a drive to redraw Texas' congressional districts in 2003 in a successful bid to enlarge the GOP majority in the House. The Republican redistricting plan dismantled Doggett's 10th District, but he quickly decided to run in the new 25th, which stretched 350 miles from Austin to the Texas-Mexico border and was drawn to elect a Hispanic candidate. He gave up his hillside West Austin home and moved to the heavily Hispanic east side.

In June 2006, the Supreme Court ruled the GOP-drawn map unconstitutional because it diluted the political influence of Hispanic voters in the 23rd District. Subsequently, a three-judge panel redrew the 23rd and four nearby districts, including the 25th. The new map made Doggett's district more compact and less Hispanic, and added rural farming counties to his constituency.

Born and raised in Austin, Doggett attended the University of Texas, where he was elected student body president. Within two years of earning his law degree in 1970, he won election to the state Senate and stayed until 1985.

In 1984, he ran for the U.S. Senate, winning the Democratic primary but getting crushed in the general by GOP Rep. Phil Gramm. Four years later, Doggett won a seat on the Texas Supreme Court, which handles only civil cases. He was on the bench when 81-year-old Democratic Rep. J.J. Pickle announced his retirement in 1994.

Doggett was the first Democrat to announce his candidacy, and his quick start spared him a tough primary. Raising $1.2 million, he surmounted that year's GOP tide and won by 16 percentage points over real estate consultant A. Jo Baylor. He consistently won re-election by significant margins until 2010, when Republican Donna Campbell, an emergency room physician, held him to 53 percent of the vote.

Key Votes

2010

Overhaul the nation's health insurance system	YES
Allow for repeal of "don't ask, don't tell"	YES
Overhaul financial services industry regulation	YES
Limit use of new Afghanistan War funds to troop withdrawal activities	NO
Change oversight of offshore drilling and lift oil spill liability cap	YES
Provide a path to legal status for some children of illegal immigrants	YES
Extend Bush-era income tax cuts for two years	NO

2009

Expand the Children's Health Insurance Program	YES
Provide $787 billion in tax cuts and spending increases to stimulate the economy	YES
Allow bankruptcy judges to modify certain primary-residence mortgages	YES
Create a cap-and-trade system to limit greenhouse gas emissions	YES
Provide $2 billion for the "cash for clunkers" program	NO
Establish the government as the sole provider of student loans	YES
Restrict federally funded insurance coverage for abortions in health care overhaul	NO

CQ Vote Studies

	PARTY UNITY		PRESIDENTIAL SUPPORT	
	SUPPORT	OPPOSE	SUPPORT	OPPOSE
2010	95%	5%	86%	14%
2009	95%	5%	89%	11%
2008	97%	3%	11%	89%
2007	98%	2%	3%	97%
2006	97%	3%	21%	79%

Interest Groups

	AFL-CIO	ADA	CCUS	ACU
2010	86%	95%	13%	4%
2009	95%	95%	33%	12%
2008	100%	90%	50%	8%
2007	96%	95%	53%	4%
2006	92%	90%	23%	8%

Texas 25

South central — most of Austin

The 25th is a compact, Austin-dominated district. The district takes in the southern portion of Travis County (Austin), including Austin-Bergstrom International Airport. Nearly 60 percent of district residents live in Travis, nearly all of whom live within the city limits. The economy here revolves around the University of Texas (located in the 21st), state government and the technology industry.

Austin's ties to the academic community and the public sector, coupled with its racial and ethnic diversity, give Travis, and thus the 25th District, a decidedly liberal tilt.

Travis was the only one of Texas' 254 counties that voted against a state constitutional amendment banning same-sex marriage in November 2005. The "Keep Austin Weird" movement, driven by the small-business community, is taken very seriously by the city's residents, as is playing host to the SXSW music, film and interactive media festival each March and the ACL music festival every fall.

Southwest of Travis lies Hays County, where the population has increased by more than 60 percent since 2000. Most of that growth has been in the

county's Hispanic and Asian communities, and many of the new residents moved in from Travis County.

From Travis and Hays, the 25th fans southeast to scoop up less populous areas. Bastrop County, located east of Austin, has experienced robust population growth.

Fayette, Gonzales, Lavaca and Colorado counties, which form the eastern half of the 25th, consistently vote Republican — each gave John McCain at least a 30-percentage-point margin of victory over Barack Obama in the 2008 presidential election and supported the Republican challenger in the 2010 U.S. House race.

But these conservative-leaning areas do not have the population to dislodge the 25th from its Democratic moorings — the district overall gave Obama 59 percent of its vote in the 2008 presidential race.

Major Industry
Higher education, state government, technology, ranching, agriculture

Cities
Austin (pt.), 423,260; San Marcos (pt.), 44,894; Kyle, 28,016

Notable
The Texas House named Lockhart the barbecue capital of Texas in 1999.

Rep. Michael C. Burgess (R)

Capitol Office
225-7772
burgess.house.gov
2241 Rayburn Bldg. 20515-4326; fax 225-2919

Committees
Energy & Commerce
Joint Economic

Residence
Lewisville

Born
Dec. 23, 1950; Rochester, Minn.

Religion
Episcopalian

Family
Wife, Laura Burgess; three children

Education
North Texas State U., B.S. 1972 (biology), M.S. 1976
(physiology); U. of Texas Health Science Center,
Houston, M.D. 1977; U. of Texas Southwestern Medical Center, Dallas, M.S. 2000 (medical management)

Career
Physician

Political Highlights
No previous office

ELECTION RESULTS

2010 GENERAL

Michael C. Burgess (R)	120,984	67.0%
Neil L. Durrance (D)	55,385	30.7%
Mark Boler (LIBERT)	4,062	2.2%

2010 PRIMARY

Michael C. Burgess (R)	44,047	85.8%
James Herford (R)	7,284	14.2%

2008 GENERAL

Michael C. Burgess (R)	195,181	60.2%
Ken Leach (D)	118,167	36.4%
Stephanie Weiss (LIBERT)	11,028	3.4%

Previous Winning Percentages
2006 (60%); 2004 (66%); 2002 (75%)

Elected 2002; 5th term

Burgess is a physician, like his forebears, and his background informs his views on health care. An obstetrician-gynecologist from the Republican Party's conservative wing, he is a relentless advocate of market-based proposals to improve the nation's health system.

He used his seat on the Energy and Commerce Committee to become a key player in the health care overhaul debate during the 111th Congress (2009-10), while serving as a reliably conservative vote on other issues. He pushes for a flat tax, generally supports free-trade agreements, and opposes abortion and federal funding of embryonic stem cell research.

His adherence to conservative principles and desire for a leadership shake-up led him to mount an unsuccessful challenge to Michigan's Thaddeus McCotter for the Republican Policy Committee chairmanship in November 2008 following his party's weak showing at the polls.

Since that failed bid, he has been gaining clout in other ways. In the 112th Congress (2011-12) he is the No. 2 Republican on the Health Subcommittee of Energy and Commerce. He founded the Congressional Health Care Caucus at the start of the 111th, providing a platform from which he could oppose Democratic efforts to overhaul the system and also invite experts to discuss and debate policies to educate members and staff.

Burgess was appointed to a GOP group charged with devising an alternative health care overhaul in 2009, although he agreed with some of the law's provisions, such as stopping insurance companies from denying coverage to patients on the basis of pre-existing conditions.

"Democrats were so eager to pass health care legislation — any health care legislation — that they settled for a rushed and ineffective law," he wrote in Roll Call a year after the law was enacted.

Early in the 112th Congress he voted to repeal the measure, and says the key now is to focus on overseeing its implementation.

"I wish it could be ripped out tomorrow, but until it is we need to do our due diligence at the agency level," he said.

Burgess promotes GOP mainstays such as curbing medical-malpractice lawsuits, expanding the private sector's role in Medicare and tightening income eligibility for families covered by the Children's Health Insurance Program (CHIP), which covers children from low-income families that make too much money to qualify for Medicaid.

Burgess fought Democrats' efforts to expand CHIP, though they ultimately prevailed in early 2009 on a bill similar to two measures President George W. Bush vetoed. He was particularly upset Democrats didn't restrict illegal immigrants' access to the program and loosened identity check and enrollment requirements. "You have to show your ID before you cash a check at the grocery store," Burgess said. "Why should we not require someone to show identification before they sign up for this benefit?"

On another health care issue — Medicare payments for physicians — Burgess has supported successful attempts at reversing scheduled cuts and providing slight increases in Medicare payments to doctors, while introducing legislation that would implement a permanent change to the formula Medicare uses to determine those payments. He also joined in the successful override of Bush's veto of legislation in 2008 that blocked a cut in physician payments. Burgess said a continuation of the current formula will lead to physicians dropping out of the Medicare program altogether, leaving seniors with fewer providers.

But he didn't go for a 2009 Democratic bill to give the Food and Drug Administration (FDA) broader powers to regulate nicotine, saying the agency was already spread too thin. He lamented that the House rejected his alternative to give the FDA power to ban nicotine entirely. "Giving the FDA the power to reduce nicotine levels to zero would be the single-most important tool we could provide the agency to control this dangerous product," he said.

Another of his priorities is reining in medical malpractice suits, which to him is "an issue of fundamental fairness." Burgess, who estimates he has delivered more than 3,000 babies, was sued in the late 1980s by a family whose baby died during a difficult cesarean section. He was not in charge of the delivery, he said, but was called in to assist another obstetrician. He said the incident helped convince him that the medical liability system needed to be overhauled.

Burgess holds a pilot's license and is also a biker, something his aides didn't know until Burgess told them he wanted to do an event promoting motorcycle safety. "As a doctor, I've been in plenty of emergency rooms and trauma centers. Take it from me: You don't want to be involved in a crash of any kind, especially one involving a motorcycle," Burgess said at the May 2008 event.

He also holds a seat on the Energy and Power Subcommittee. He supports conservation and the promotion of alternative energy sources, while also backing drilling for oil in Alaska's Arctic National Wildlife Refuge "or any other federal lands where geologic data supports exploration." He criticized the Obama administration's moratorium on deep-water offshore drilling following the April 2010 oil spill in the Gulf of Mexico.

Burgess' grandfather was an obstetrician who worked at the Royal Victoria Hospital in Montreal. His father, a general surgeon, moved to the United States to get away from Canada's government-run health care system. His sister is a nurse; his brother is a pathologist. "It's in my DNA," he said of medicine.

He had no prior political experience when he ran for the seat previously held by Republican Dick Armey, a former majority leader. To take Armey's place, Burgess had to defeat the nine-term lawmaker's son, Scott Armey, in the 2002 primary. The 26th District had just been redrawn to favor the younger Armey, who finished first in the six-way primary but faced a runoff. Burgess campaigned against him by handing out literature declaring, "My dad is not Dick Armey," and prevailed in the runoff with 55 percent of the vote. He won easily that November in the solidly Republican district and has won re-election with little problem since.

Key Votes

2010

Overhaul the nation's health insurance system	NO
Allow for repeal of "don't ask, don't tell"	NO
Overhaul financial services industry regulation	NO
Limit use of new Afghanistan War funds to troop withdrawal activities	NO
Change oversight of offshore drilling and lift oil spill liability cap	NO
Provide a path to legal status for some children of illegal immigrants	NO
Extend Bush-era income tax cuts for two years	NO

2009

Expand the Children's Health Insurance Program	NO
Provide $787 billion in tax cuts and spending increases to stimulate the economy	NO
Allow bankruptcy judges to modify certain primary-residence mortgages	NO
Create a cap-and-trade system to limit greenhouse gas emissions	NO
Provide $2 billion for the "cash for clunkers" program	NO
Establish the government as the sole provider of student loans	NO
Restrict federally funded insurance coverage for abortions in health care overhaul	YES

CQ Vote Studies

	PARTY UNITY		PRESIDENTIAL SUPPORT	
	SUPPORT	OPPOSE	SUPPORT	OPPOSE
2010	96%	4%	31%	69%
2009	96%	4%	17%	83%
2008	94%	6%	73%	27%
2007	94%	6%	82%	18%
2006	93%	7%	87%	13%

Interest Groups

	AFL-CIO	ADA	CCUS	ACU
2010	7%	5%	75%	96%
2009	0%	0%	71%	100%
2008	14%	10%	76%	96%
2007	8%	10%	74%	100%
2006	21%	5%	92%	83%

Texas 26

Eastern Fort Worth and suburbs; most of Denton County

The 26th stretches north from southeastern Fort Worth and its surrounding suburbs to take in almost all of Denton County and the eastern part of rural Cooke County. The district's economy depends mainly on transportation, with many white-collar industries providing jobs.

The heart of the district is fast-growing Denton County, the southern part of which is filled with burgeoning upper-middle-class Dallas-Fort Worth suburbs. Time Warner Cable has large facilities here, and education and technology are important.

The University of North Texas engineering program emphasizes nanotech research and applications. Parts of the expansive Barnett Shale natural gas reservoir are located in Denton, and drilling provides thousands of jobs in the region.

Forty percent of residents live in Fort Worth and its Tarrant County suburbs, mainly in middle-class areas such as North Richland Hills.

The 26th also grabs Forest Hill and Everman, areas south of downtown

with relatively large black populations. Much of Cooke is agricultural, relying on cattle and dairy farms, with oat and wheat farms as well.

The interstates and highways here carry the district's commuters to jobs elsewhere in the region.

The 26th snags a small part of Dallas-Fort Worth International Airport. Fort Worth Alliance Airport (shared with the 12th) was the nation's first airport to be built specifically to serve business needs. The area around Alliance will host a Deloitte training campus. Bell Helicopter Textron's headquarters is in Hurst.

Voters here support Republicans, giving presidential candidate John McCain 58 percent of the district's vote in 2008.

Major Industry
Transportation, telecommunications

Cities
Fort Worth (pt.), 208,310; Denton, 113,383; Lewisville (pt.), 67,480; Flower Mound (pt.), 64,457; North Richland Hills (pt.), 63,215; Frisco (pt.), 44,500

Notable
The Texas Motor Speedway is in Denton County; the town council in Clark changed the town's name to DISH in 2005 to win 10 years of free basic satellite television from DISH Network for all 125 residents.

Rep. Blake Farenthold (R)

Capitol Office
225-7742
www.house.gov/ortiz
2110 Rayburn Bldg. 20515-4327; fax 226-1134

Committees
Homeland Security
Oversight & Government Reform
Transportation & Infrastructure

Residence
Corpus Christi

Born
Dec. 12, 1961; Corpus Christi, Texas

Religion
Episcopalian

Family
Wife, Debbie Farenthold; two children

Education
U. of Texas, B.S.R.T.F. 1985 (radio-televisio-film); St. Mary's U. (Texas), J.D. 1989

Career
Web services consulting company owner; lawyer

Political Highlights
No previous office

ELECTION RESULTS

2010 GENERAL

Blake Farenthold (R)	51,001	47.8%
Solomon P. Ortiz (D)	50,226	47.1%
Edward Mishou (LIBERT)	5,372	5.0%

2010 PRIMARY RUNOFF

Blake Farenthold (R)	4,742	51.3%
James Duerr (R)	4,496	48.7%

Elected 2010; 1st term

Farenthold, a lawyer and radio talk show host, says government is "too big and too expensive," and he offers conservative solutions to what he says ails the country. But he says the most pressing issue for his district, which runs from Brownsville to Corpus Christi, is immigration.

He backs tougher employer sanctions and tighter border security. He also supports a guest worker program that would bring more people into the country if they have jobs waiting and says that such a program could include a path to citizenship.

But he argues that those who arrived in the United States illegally must go to the "back of the line" in terms of seeking permanent residency. A member of the Homeland Security Committee, he also said more funding is required for the border patrol and advocates a closer working relationship with Mexican authorities.

Farenthold also serves on the Oversight and Government Reform Committee. The first bill he introduced would require federal agencies to post their receipts and expenditures on their official websites.

On the Transportation and Infrastructure panel, a priority will be upgrading U.S. 77 to an interstate, and he offered legislation to that effect in April 2011. Farenthold calls the Rio Grande Valley the biggest metropolitan area in the country not served by the Interstate Highway System.

Farenthold finished second in the four-candidate GOP primary, 2 percentage points behind moderate James Duerr. He reversed that in the runoff, winning by 2 points.

His contest with 14-term Democrat Solomon P. Ortiz was one of the closest of 2010. After the original unofficial count showed Farenthold leading by 799 votes, Ortiz asked for a recount. The final tally gave Farenthold a 775-vote margin and Ortiz conceded about three weeks after Election Day.

Farenthold bears a name famous in Texas politics, although he has a different ideological outlook than his step-grandmother, Frances Tarleton "Sissy" Farenthold, a pioneering political woman and longtime liberal Democratic activist.

Texas 27

Southern Gulf Coast — Corpus Christi, Brownsville

Anchored by Corpus Christi in the north, the 27th runs south to the Rio Grande River, with the Gulf of Mexico on its eastern coast. Ranches and industries tied to the coast are the mainstays between the two largest cities, Corpus Christi and Brownsville. North of Corpus Christi, it also takes in more than half of San Patricio County's population.

Corpus Christi relies on tourism, oil and gas. Petrochemical refining, also found up and down the coast, is more common here, as is the storing and shipping of wind turbines out of the port. The area's military bases are key to the region's economic health.

In the Rio Grande Valley, the port city of Brownsville struggles with illegal immigration, drug smuggling and poverty. Manufacturing plants and maquiladoras — sites in Mexico that use low-cost labor and import parts from the United States — help the economy. Wetland ecotourism and visitors from Mexico boost Brownsville's economy. The Hispanic-majority district (73 percent) had elected the same Democrat to the U.S. House since its creation prior to the 1982 election. But GOP support in Neuces and San Patricio counties was just enough to give the seat to Republican Blake Farenthold in 2010.

Major Industry
Manufacturing, trade, tourism, military, petrochemicals

Military Bases
Naval Air Station Corpus Christi, 1,542 military, 2,700 civilian; Corpus Christi Army Depot, 5 military, 3,760 civilian (2009); Naval Air Station Kingsville, 586 military, 204 civilian (2011)

Cities
Corpus Christi (pt.), 305,215; Brownsville, 175,023; Kingsville, 26,213

Notable
Padre Island National Seashore runs most of the district's length.

Rep. Henry Cuellar (D)

Capitol Office
225-1640
www.house.gov/cuellar
2463 Rayburn Bldg. 20515-4328; fax 225-1641

Committees
Agriculture
Homeland Security

Residence
Laredo

Born
Sept. 19, 1955; Laredo, Texas

Religion
Roman Catholic

Family
Wife, Imelda Cuellar; two children

Education
Laredo Community College, A.A. 1976 (political science); Georgetown U., B.S.F.S. 1978; U. of Texas, J.D. 1981; Laredo State U., M.B.A. 1982 (international trade); U. of Texas, Ph.D. 1998 (government)

Career
Lawyer; international trade firm owner

Political Highlights
Texas House, 1987-2001; Texas secretary of state, 2001; Democratic nominee for U.S. House, 2002

ELECTION RESULTS

2010 GENERAL

Henry Cuellar (D)	62,773	56.3%
Bryan Underwood (R)	46,740	42.0%
Stephen Kaat (LIBERT)	1,889	1.7%

2010 PRIMARY

Henry Cuellar (D)	unopposed

2008 GENERAL

Henry Cuellar (D)	123,494	68.7%
Jim Fish (R)	52,524	29.2%
Ross Lynn Leone (LIBERT)	3,722	2.1%

Previous Winning Percentages
2006 (68%); 2004 (59%)

Elected 2004; 4th term

When he first arrived in Congress in 2005, Cuellar was one of the most conservative members of the Democratic Caucus, siding with Republicans about one-third of the time in his first term. But when Democrats took over the House following the 2006 election, his voting record took a turn leftward.

The numbers paint the picture. That first year in office, Cuellar (KWAY-are) sided with a majority of his party against a majority of Republicans 70 percent of the time. His party unity score was even lower — 63 — the next year. The following three years, under a Democratic majority, Cuellar found the party positions to his liking 88, 94 and 91 percent of the time.

And on all of the Obama administration's major economic initiatives during the 111th Congress (2009-10) — the health care overhaul, creation of a cap-and-trade system to limit carbon emissions, the $787 billion stimulus — Cuellar lined up with his Democratic colleagues.

In the 112th Congress (2011-12), he was named a vice chairman of the Democratic Steering and Policy Committee, giving him a role in coordinating the party's message.

That's quite a turnaround for a man who endorsed George W. Bush for president in 2000 and served as Texas secretary of state under Bush's successor as governor, Republican Rick Perry.

A member of the fiscally conservative Blue Dog Coalition, in most cases Cuellar made a pragmatic choice on the Democratic legislation, winning changes he favored before voting for the bills.

As an abortion foe, Cuellar was one of the last Democratic holdouts on the health care overhaul over concerns about language that critics said would allow for government funding of the procedure. But he announced in March 2010 that he would vote for the bill after President Obama agreed to sign an executive order restating that the law does not allow federal funding for abortions — critics called it a fig leaf — and after securing a provision that is intended to protect state medical malpractice laws.

Cuellar, a member of the Agriculture Committee, was skeptical of the energy legislation designed to limit greenhouse gas emissions because of Texas farm groups' concerns, but voted for the bill after securing an amendment to bolster natural gas use, a win for a district that sits atop a natural gas basin.

Cuellar also looks out for his border district from the Homeland Security Committee, where he is ranking Democrat on the Subcommittee on Border and Maritime Security. He has opposed construction of a border fence aimed at reducing illegal immigration, a measure he calls a "12th-century solution to a 21st-century problem."

Instead, Cuellar argues for more federal troops and funding. He joined fellow Hispanic Caucus members in unsuccessfully pushing for a broad immigration overhaul in the 111th Congress.

Cuellar, who grew up speaking Spanish at home, is a former member of the Oversight and Government Reform Committee. He won approval of an amendment to a Head Start bill requiring program administrators to provide more understandable assessments of their progress in teaching English as a second language.

Other efforts at government accountability include a measure to streamline the Federal Emergency Management Agency preparedness funding program that was signed into law in October 2010. Cuellar also won passage of a bill to require the government to develop performance measures and standards to determine whether agencies are providing high-quality customer service, and he was able to amend another measure to require a report to Congress on the effectiveness of a hotline that receives reports of child abuse.

Lack of accountability was one reason he cited for voting against the initial financial industry rescue bill in fall 2008. But a few days later, he voted for the second iteration of the package. Later, he was one of 27 Democrats to vote against the House version of legislation to strengthen regulation of the financial industry, after voting for a failed amendment by Idaho Democrat Walt Minnick to weaken a new consumer protection agency.

Cuellar was the eldest of eight children born to migrant workers with an elementary school education. But they insisted their children obtain an education, and he earned law and business degrees in addition to a doctorate in government.

He was elected to the Texas House in 1986 and served 14 years. He was appointed Texas secretary of state in early 2001, but resigned later that year to prepare for a 2002 campaign against Republican incumbent Henry Bonilla in the 23rd District. He lost by just a little more than 4 percentage points.

In 2004, a new GOP-drawn congressional map moved part of Webb County, Cuellar's base, to the 28th District, a heavily Hispanic and primarily San Antonio-based district that had been represented since 1997 by Democrat Ciro D. Rodriguez. Cuellar challenged Rodriguez in the primary, even though Rodriguez had backed Cuellar's 2002 campaign against Bonilla. Cuellar eked out a 58-vote win that was certified only after a series of recounts, lawsuits and accusations of fraud.

Rodriguez was back to challenge Cuellar in 2006. Liberal activists and labor unions sided with Rodriguez and circulated a photograph of Bush affectionately taking Cuellar's face in his hands after the 2006 State of the Union address. But Cuellar, touting his accessibility and ability to bring federal funds to the district, won the primary by almost 13 percentage points.

No Republican opposed Cuellar in the 2006 general election, but he had to wage another campaign after a federal court redrew his district and four others to comply with a Supreme Court decision partially invalidating the Texas map. The new map strengthened Cuellar by including all of Webb County in the 28th District. He won 68 percent in a special November election. (Rodriguez, meanwhile, took advantage of the second chance and unseated Bonilla in the adjacent 23rd District.)

Cuellar slightly bettered his total in 2008. He did not fare as well in the Republican wave of 2010, but still handily defeated Republican Bryan Underwood with 56 percent of the vote.

Key Votes

2010

Overhaul the nation's health insurance system	YES
Allow for repeal of "don't ask, don't tell"	YES
Overhaul financial services industry regulation	NO
Limit use of new Afghanistan War funds to troop withdrawal activities	NO
Change oversight of offshore drilling and lift oil spill liability cap	NO
Provide a path to legal status for some children of illegal immigrants	YES
Extend Bush-era income tax cuts for two years	YES

2009

Expand the Children's Health Insurance Program	YES
Provide $787 billion in tax cuts and spending increases to stimulate the economy	YES
Allow bankruptcy judges to modify certain primary-residence mortgages	YES
Create a cap-and-trade system to limit greenhouse gas emissions	YES
Provide $2 billion for the "cash for clunkers" program	YES
Establish the government as the sole provider of student loans	YES
Restrict federally funded insurance coverage for abortions in health care overhaul	YES

CQ Vote Studies

	PARTY UNITY		PRESIDENTIAL SUPPORT	
	SUPPORT	OPPOSE	SUPPORT	OPPOSE
2010	93%	7%	90%	10%
2009	91%	9%	92%	8%
2008	94%	6%	30%	70%
2007	88%	12%	16%	84%
2006	63%	37%	85%	15%

Interest Groups

	AFL-CIO	ADA	CCUS	ACU
2010	79%	75%	63%	13%
2009	90%	85%	60%	12%
2008	87%	80%	72%	12%
2007	92%	90%	70%	20%
2006	64%	35%	100%	68%

Texas 28

South central — Laredo; part of McAllen

Webb and Hidalgo counties on the Mexican border are the two major population hubs for the heavily Hispanic, Democratic-leaning and fast-growing 28th, which also skims north along Interstate 35 to take in a sliver of Bexar County northeast of San Antonio, including Randolph Air Force Base. At 78.9 percent, the 28th is the third-most-heavily Hispanic district in the nation, just behind Texas' 16th and 15th districts.

About 30 percent of district residents live in Webb, where international trade is crucial for Laredo, the nation's largest inland port of entry, where the population has grown 25 percent since 2000.

Webb has the highest percentage of Hispanic residents of any county in the nation, slightly edging out Starr County near the district's southern tip. Trucking is key to Laredo's economy, and peanuts, cotton, sorghum, carrots and beef dominate the agricultural market. Federal efforts to stem drug-related border violence have put a spotlight on Laredo.

A second 30 percent of the 28th's population lives in Hidalgo County, another expanding area where the district takes 40 percent of McAllen's residents and almost all of Mission.

Like Webb and Starr, the 28th's share of Hidalgo (the county is shared with the 15th) is overwhelmingly Hispanic.

Starr and adjacent Zapata County also are among the most economically depressed counties in the nation, and the 28th overall has a greater share of residents below the poverty line than any other Texas district. Republican votes in Guadalupe, McMullen and Wilson counties to the north cannot counter the strongly Democratic southern counties. In the 2008 presidential race, Starr gave Barack Obama 85 percent, his highest percentage statewide, and the district overall gave Obama 56 percent of its vote.

Major Industry
Agriculture, international trade, defense

Military Bases
Joint Base San Antonio (shared with the 20th and 21st), 36,184 military, 15,945 civilian (2011)

Cities
Laredo, 236,091; Mission (pt.), 72,182; McAllen (pt.), 51,850

Notable
The "streets of Laredo" inspired titles for a cowboy ballad and a novel.

Rep. Gene Green (D)

Capitol Office
225-1688
www.house.gov/green
2470 Rayburn Bldg. 20515-4329; fax 225-9903

Committees
Energy & Commerce

Residence
Houston

Born
Oct. 17, 1947; Houston, Texas

Religion
Methodist

Family
Wife, Helen Albers Green; two children

Education
U. of Houston, B.B.A. 1971; Bates College of Law, attended 1971-77

Career
Lawyer

Political Highlights
Texas House, 1973-85; Texas Senate, 1985-92

ELECTION RESULTS

2010 GENERAL
Gene Green (D)	43,257	64.6%
Roy Morales (R)	22,825	34.1%
Brad Walters (LIBERT)	866	1.3%

2010 PRIMARY
Gene Green (D)	unopposed

2008 GENERAL
Gene Green (D)	79,718	74.6%
Eric Story (R)	25,512	23.9%
Joel Grace (LIBERT)	1,564	1.5%

Previous Winning Percentages
2006 (74%); 2004 (94%); 2002 (95%); 2000 (73%); 1998 (93%); 1996 (68%); 1994 (73%); 1992 (65%)

Elected 1992; 10th term

The business of Green's district is oil, and the 10-term representative has proved it's possible to balance liberal Democratic values with staunchly defending the interests of oil companies.

Much of his efforts in 2010, for example, were spent trying to persuade the Obama administration to again allow offshore drilling in the Gulf of Mexico following a catastrophic oil spill in April caused by the explosion of a BP rig.

Green's efforts helped persuade President Obama to lift a temporary moratorium put in place after the spill, but a permitting slowdown by the Interior Department kept Green in high dudgeon. "Thousands of families depend on this industry and continue to suffer," he said.

The oil spill was a big blow to Green, who for several years had pushed Congress to open all U.S. offshore areas to drilling. Obama had seemed to be moving his way until the spill. In its aftermath, restarting that debate could take years.

Green also saw his hopes for a compromise on climate change derailed when Republicans captured the House in the November 2010 elections. He would like to see legislation both to preclude a regulatory approach to the problem now in the works at the EPA and to bring certainty to the refiners in his district.

In 2009, Green backed a House climate change bill, which would have set a cap on emissions of greenhouse gases and required companies to buy allowances in order to pollute, after working out a deal to protect refiners' bottom lines by providing them free emissions allowances. Divisions among Democrats in the Senate prevented any further action.

Green is worried that any EPA-backed strategy would hurt refiners worse than the House bill would have. He has pushed legislation that would require the EPA to delay its plans in order for Congress to work out a deal. "The U.S. Congress, not EPA, should develop energy policies that have far-reaching implications," he said. But he voted against a measure in April 2011 that would overturn the EPA's 2009 finding that carbon dioxide is a pollutant under the Clean Air Act.

As ranking Democrat on the Energy and Commerce Subcommittee on Environment and the Economy, Green is in a good spot to weigh in on energy policy, even though he doesn't see eye to eye on the issue with the committee's top Democrat, Henry A. Waxman of California. In mid-2008, Democratic leaders tapped Green to chair the Subcommittee on Environment and Hazardous Materials to replace a colleague who had resigned. But Green's stint as chairman was short-lived. When Waxman challenged the committee's then-chairman, John D. Dingell of Michigan, later that year, Green sided with Dingell. Waxman won the chairmanship, and after Green's panel was merged with another subcommittee, Green was the odd man out.

But the committee has a new chairman in the 112th Congress (2011-12) — Republican Fred Upton of Michigan — with whom Green has cooperated in the past. The two joined together in 2010 in urging the Federal Communications Commission to stay out of the business of regulating the Internet, arguing that Congress is better suited to write the rules.

Apart from oil-related issues, Green tends to vote in lock step with his caucus. In 2010, he backed bills to overhaul health care — his district has the highest percentage of working-age uninsured people in the country, at 52 percent — and to revamp regulation of the banking industry. He sided with Obama and the majority of the Democratic Caucus in the House — and not party liberals — later in the year in voting to extend the Bush-era tax cuts. Republicans insisted on the tax cuts as a condition for extending unemployment benefits, and Green said his vote was an exercise in realpolitik. "I have a lot of hard-working, blue-collar people in my district who are at the end of their unemployment benefits," he told the Houston Chronicle.

Green has also fought hard to keep federal dollars flowing to Houston's Johnson Space Center and has pushed legislation to provide help to any Space Center employees who lose their jobs as a result of budget cuts.

Green's vote on the health care bill was no surprise. In 2007, his bill to upgrade states' trauma care systems was signed into law. It was a victory Green had sought since hearing about a man who was seriously injured in a car accident and could not get treatment at a crowded Houston trauma center. The man had to be taken to Austin, where he died the next day. In 2008, Green won enactment of legislation to expand community clinics and to attack the spread of tuberculosis, which remains a problem in border communities.

Green also tends to constituent needs through his annual Immunization Day, which provides free vaccinations to children, and Citizenship Day, which helps legal immigrants obtain citizenship. More than two out of three residents of Green's district are Hispanic.

Green completed his three-term limit on the ethics panel in the 110th Congress (2008-09), but over the next two years retained his role as chairman of an investigative panel looking into the financial dealings of former Ways and Means Chairman Charles B. Rangel, a veteran New York Democrat. The panel ultimately recommended that Rangel be reprimanded for, among other things, soliciting donations from people with business before his committee for a program named after him at the City College of New York.

Born, raised and educated in Houston, Green grew up in an area called "Redneck Alley," home to mostly working-class whites. He attended the University of Houston, where he obtained a degree in business administration. While attending law school, he won a seat in the Texas Legislature, where he served for nearly two decades before he made a bid for Congress in 1992.

He won a hard-fought five-way primary in a district that was drawn after the 1990 Census to enhance the political power of Houston's growing Hispanic population. He bested Houston City Council member Ben Reyes in two runoffs; the first was voided after election officials found some Republicans had illegally crossed over and cast ballots. Green won the general election with 65 percent of the vote, defeated Reyes in a 1994 primary rematch and has won easily since.

Key Votes

2010

Overhaul the nation's health insurance system	YES
Allow for repeal of "don't ask, don't tell"	NO
Overhaul financial services industry regulation	YES
Limit use of new Afghanistan War funds to troop withdrawal activities	NO
Change oversight of offshore drilling and lift oil spill liability cap	NO
Provide a path to legal status for some children of illegal immigrants	YES
Extend Bush-era income tax cuts for two years	NO

2009

Expand the Children's Health Insurance Program	YES
Provide $787 billion in tax cuts and spending increases to stimulate the economy	YES
Allow bankruptcy judges to modify certain primary-residence mortgages	YES
Create a cap-and-trade system to limit greenhouse gas emissions	YES
Provide $2 billion for the "cash for clunkers" program	YES
Establish the government as the sole provider of student loans	YES
Restrict federally funded insurance coverage for abortions in health care overhaul	NO

CQ Vote Studies

	PARTY UNITY		PRESIDENTIAL SUPPORT	
	SUPPORT	OPPOSE	SUPPORT	OPPOSE
2010	97%	3%	88%	12%
2009	98%	2%	96%	4%
2008	94%	6%	26%	74%
2007	94%	6%	7%	93%
2006	84%	16%	43%	57%

Interest Groups

	AFL-CIO	ADA	CCUS	ACU
2010	100%	80%	25%	4%
2009	100%	100%	40%	0%
2008	100%	80%	59%	26%
2007	100%	95%	63%	12%
2006	100%	85%	50%	33%

Texas 29

Part of Houston and eastern suburbs — most of Pasadena and Baytown

The blue-collar, overwhelmingly Hispanic 29th arcs from northern to southeastern Houston, with an eastern tail that extends out of the city to Baytown.

The district is full of refineries and factories that employ union workers who help provide a solid Democratic lean, despite traditionally poor voter turnout in the Hispanic community. The 29th includes working-class areas outside of the Interstate 610 loop such as Jacinto City, Galena Park, South Houston and much of Pasadena (shared with the 22nd) and Baytown (shared with the 2nd).

Hispanics make up more than three-fourths of the district's population. The heaviest concentrations of Hispanics are in South Houston, Jacinto City, Houston and Pasadena. More than one-fourth of district residents are not U.S. citizens, and 60 percent speak a language other than English at home.

The 29th's portion of Houston has lost residents since 2000, and now slightly less than half of the district's residents live in the city. The district picks up the Houston Ship Channel, which handles high levels of foreign and domestic traffic, and most of middle-class Channelview.

The heart of Houston's petrochemical complex is along the channel, which has caused concern among residents about possible health effects of living so close to an industrial corridor.

International competition and natural disasters are perennial concerns for the local petrochemical industry.

The 29th has the state's largest blue-collar workforce and the lowest high school graduation rate (46 percent of residents who are 25 or older) in the nation. One-third of district residents are age 17 or under, the second-highest percentage in the state. The district gave Barack Obama 62 percent of its 2008 presidential vote.

Major Industry
Petrochemicals, energy, shipping, construction

Cities
Houston (pt.), 328,303; Pasadena (pt.), 84,649; Baytown (pt.), 32,104

Notable
The Battleship Texas, docked at the San Jacinto Battleground state park, became the nation's first battleship memorial museum in 1948.

Rep. Eddie Bernice Johnson (D)

Capitol Office
225-8885
www.house.gov/ebjohnson
2468 Rayburn Bldg. 20515-4330; fax 226-1477

Committees
Science, Space & Technology - Ranking Member
Transportation & Infrastructure

Residence
Dallas

Born
Dec. 3, 1935; Waco, Texas

Religion
Baptist

Family
Divorced; one child

Education
Texas Christian U., B.S. 1967 (nursing); Southern
Methodist U., M.P.A. 1976

Career
Business relocation company owner; nurse; U.S.
Health, Education & Welfare Department official

Political Highlights
Texas House, 1973-77; Texas Senate, 1987-93

ELECTION RESULTS

2010 GENERAL

Eddie Bernice Johnson (D)	86,322	75.7%
Stephen E. Broden (R)	24,668	21.6%
J.B. Oswalt (LIBERT)	2,988	2.6%

2010 PRIMARY

Eddie Bernice Johnson (D)	unopposed

2008 GENERAL

Eddie Bernice Johnson (D)	168,249	82.5%
Fred Wood (R)	32,361	15.9%
Jarrett Woods (LIBERT)	3,366	1.6%

Previous Winning Percentages
2006 (80%); 2004 (93%); 2002 (74%); 2000 (92%);
1998 (72%); 1996 (55%); 1994 (73%); 1992 (72%)

Elected 1992; 10th term

Johnson's Dallas district is one of the safest Democratic seats in Texas. And that's a good thing for Johnson, who was embroiled in scandal in 2010 after the Dallas Morning News reported that she'd given thousands of dollars in college scholarships to her relatives as well as children of a top aide, in violation of anti-nepotism rules.

Johnson initially said the recipients of the Congressional Black Caucus Foundation awards — two grandsons, two great-nephews and two children of a top aide — were worthy of the money, then said she'd been unaware of caucus rules that barred relatives from applying for the scholarships. Finally, she blamed her chief of staff.

Johnson repaid the foundation the $31,000 cost of the scholarships and named a third party to oversee her future scholarship picks. "I have acknowledged I made a mistake," she said during an appearance on CNN. "I have tried to make everything whole. I have paid all the money out of my personal funds, and I'm ready to move on."

The foundation's chairman, Democratic Rep. Donald M. Payne of New Jersey, criticized the "self-dealing" and "unethical behavior" and pledged to investigate. But Johnson's constituents were more forgiving. Two weeks after the story broke, in mid-September, local ministers rallied behind her at Dallas City Hall. "We still believe in our congresswoman. She still has our support," Baptist minister Denny Davis told the Morning News. A community activist said she was presenting Johnson with hundreds of "notes of love."

The outcry was a testament to Johnson's legacy as the first African-American politician to represent Dallas in Congress, and her success in bringing home federal dollars.

Johnson is a former chairwoman of the Transportation and Infrastructure Subcommittee on Water Resources and Environment and still serves on the panel, a prime spot from which to win federal funds such as the $298 million authorization she secured in 2007 for a flood-control project in her district. In 2009, Johnson pushed through the House a wastewater bill that included the first reauthorization of the Clean Water State Revolving Fund in 15 years, as well as legislation to boost security around wastewater plants. As the senior Texan on the full committee, she'll play a key role in writing a new surface transportation bill in the 112th Congress (2011-12).

During the 110th Congress (2007-08), she joined a Congressional Black Caucus committee established to help secure more earmarked funding for projects in black members' districts after a report in Congressional Quarterly revealed that they were getting less than white-majority districts. Johnson frequently looks for opportunities to encourage federal agencies to steer more of their grant money to minorities.

At the same time, Johnson hopes her legacy in Congress will include pushing the Black Caucus toward effective coalitions with business groups rather than relying exclusively on its traditional allies in labor, the clergy and civil rights. She bucked fellow Democrat and Black Caucus member John Lewis of Georgia, for example, after Lewis proposed legislation requiring buses to have seatbelts, and instead cosponsored legislation by Pennsylvania Republican Bill Shuster that would have mandated a study of the issue before any requirements could take effect.

Johnson is the ranking Democrat on the Science, Space and Technology Committee, where she has pushed legislation aimed at improving the number of women and minorities in math, science and engineering in universities and colleges at both the student and staff level. She also has lobbied for the expansion of minority participation in science research. During the 111th Congress (2009-10), she secured language in bills aimed at funding research into improving cybersecurity and reducing computer waste to encourage federal agencies to look to minority grant applicants.

And as the Black Caucus' chairwoman in 2001 and 2002, she hosted the caucus' first technology and energy summits to bridge the digital divide in poor communities and to encourage minority students to study science.

As a young girl attending segregated schools in Waco, Johnson's goal was to go to medical school and become a doctor. But her high school counselor encouraged her to become a nurse because "nurses were more feminine." Johnson earned an undergraduate degree in nursing and a master's in public administration from Southern Methodist University. She rose to be chief psychiatric nurse at the veterans' hospital in Dallas.

Johnson won election to the state House in 1972 — the first black woman from Dallas to achieve the distinction. In the late 1970s, she turned to private business, setting up Eddie Bernice Johnson and Associates, which helped businesses expand or relocate in the Dallas-Fort Worth area. She continued to run the business after her 1986 election to the state Senate and expanded the company's reach in 1988 to include airport concessions management.

Wielding her power in the state legislature, Johnson drew a U.S. House district preordained to elect her in 1992. Initially, her electoral fate was caught up in the judicial and legislative wrangling over minority-majority House districts, including the 30th. After the U.S. Supreme Court in 1996 threw out some House districts in Texas as "racial gerrymanders," Johnson landed in a redrawn district that was 42 percent new to her. But she captured a 55 percent majority in an eight-person contest and has won by wide margins ever since.

The scholarship imbroglio isn't Johnson's first brush with scandal and, like the others, seems to have had little effect on her electoral prospects. During the 108th Congress (2003-04), a former aide accused her of discrimination. Johnson invoked Congress' constitutional protection from being questioned about "speech or debate" and asserted the former aide's duties were "directly related to the due functioning of the legislative process." An appeals court ruled that lawmakers can mount a defense by claiming employment decisions were based on legislative concerns, and a federal district court judge threw out the case for lack of evidence in October 2007. All the controversy didn't hurt Johnson at the ballot box, as she cruised to another easy victory in 2008 and repeated the feat in 2010.

Key Votes

2010

Overhaul the nation's health insurance system	YES
Allow for repeal of "don't ask, don't tell"	YES
Overhaul financial services industry regulation	YES
Limit use of new Afghanistan War funds to troop withdrawal activities	NO
Change oversight of offshore drilling and lift oil spill liability cap	YES
Provide a path to legal status for some children of illegal immigrants	YES
Extend Bush-era income tax cuts for two years	?

2009

Expand the Children's Health Insurance Program	YES
Provide $787 billion in tax cuts and spending increases to stimulate the economy	YES
Allow bankruptcy judges to modify certain primary-residence mortgages	YES
Create a cap-and-trade system to limit greenhouse gas emissions	YES
Provide $2 billion for the "cash for clunkers" program	YES
Establish the government as the sole provider of student loans	YES
Restrict federally funded insurance coverage for abortions in health care overhaul	NO

CQ Vote Studies

	PARTY UNITY		PRESIDENTIAL SUPPORT	
	SUPPORT	OPPOSE	SUPPORT	OPPOSE
2010	99%	1%	90%	10%
2009	99%	1%	97%	3%
2008	99%	1%	14%	86%
2007	97%	3%	4%	96%
2006	94%	6%	35%	65%

Interest Groups

	AFL-CIO	ADA	CCUS	ACU
2010	93%	85%	14%	0%
2009	100%	95%	29%	0%
2008	100%	100%	56%	0%
2007	100%	80%	60%	0%
2006	100%	95%	60%	16%

Texas 30

Downtown Dallas and southern suburbs

Confined to Dallas County, the 30th stretches from Dallas Love Field southeast into downtown Dallas. It then dips south to take in some suburbs, such as Lancaster, where many black families have relocated after leaving the city. Black residents account for 41 percent of the population — the highest percentage in any Texas district — and 40 percent of residents are Hispanic.

Love Field is a hub for Southwest Airlines, whose headquarters are in the 30th. Federal restrictions on Dallas-area flight patterns and regional-only service are expected to completely phase out by 2014, and American Airlines, based out of the expansive Dallas-Fort Worth International Airport (in the 24th and 26th), will start flying out of Love Field again in 2013. A $500 million capital improvement project at Love is expected to double passenger traffic. Expansion at the airport, combined with a growing population, has heightened concerns regarding road congestion and air pollution in the area.

Although less than half of district residents hold white-collar jobs, the Dallas-Fort Worth Metroplex is a banking, high-tech and transportation center and the district is home to several Fortune 500 firms.

Economic downturns, however, have hurt municipal budgets. Downtown Dallas attracts visitors to the American Airlines Center, home to basketball's Mavericks and hockey's Stars, although the historic Cotton Bowl hosted its last namesake college football game in 2009. Dallas is developing a five-acre urban park and pedestrian paths connecting Uptown and Downtown Dallas.

Democrats run particularly well in the heavily black precincts just south of Illinois Avenue, and in largely Hispanic precincts near Love Field. In 2008, the 30th — the only Democratic district in the Dallas-Fort Worth area — gave Barack Obama 82 percent of its presidential vote, his highest percentage statewide.

Major Industry
Transportation, banking, technology

Cities
Dallas (pt.), 551,858; DeSoto, 49,047; Lancaster, 36,361

Notable
Dealey Plaza and the Texas School Book Depository, where John F. Kennedy was assassinated in 1963, are in downtown Dallas.

Rep. John Carter (R)

Capitol Office
225-3864
www.house.gov/carter
409 Cannon Bldg. 20515-4331; fax 225-5886

Committees
Appropriations

Residence
Round Rock

Born
Nov. 6, 1941; Houston, Texas

Religion
Lutheran

Family
Wife, Erika Carter; four children

Education
Texas Technological College, B.A. 1964 (history); U. of Texas, J.D. 1969

Career
Lawyer; state legislative aide

Political Highlights
Candidate for Texas House, 1980; Texas District Court judge, 1981-2001

ELECTION RESULTS

2010 GENERAL

John Carter (R)	126,384	82.5%
Bill Oliver (LIBERT)	26,735	17.5%

2010 PRIMARY

John Carter (R)	52,321	89.8%
Raymond Yamka (R)	5,910	10.1%

2008 GENERAL

John Carter (R)	175,563	60.3%
Brian P. Ruiz (D)	106,559	36.6%
Barry N. Cooper (LIBERT)	9,182	3.2%

Previous Winning Percentages
2006 (59%); 2004 (65%); 2002 (69%)

Elected 2002; 5th term

A conservative former judge who has allied himself with tea party activists, Carter has been a major critic of President Obama's policies, and has served as a GOP point man on ethics problems confronting Democrats — though he is not on the Ethics Committee and has faced some ethical questions of his own over the years.

Re-elected to his third term as GOP Conference secretary in 2010, Carter has focused considerable attention on former Ways and Means Chairman Charles B. Rangel, a New York Democrat, who was censured by the House for a number of financial and fundraising violations. Carter accused Democratic House leadership of stalling congressional punishment, putting it off until after the 2010 elections, which he said prevented voters in Rangel's district from being able to give him appropriate consideration for office.

Carter has also criticized a host of Obama's initiatives, including the health care overhaul signed into law in 2010, and the $787 billion economic stimulus enacted in 2009. He accused the administration of being "more focused on groping grandma at the airport" — a reference to new Transportation Security Administration guidelines — than on stopping drug smugglers and al Qaeda terrorist network supporters from moving across the border with Mexico.

He was one of a dozen Republican House members to sponsor a bill that would have required future presidential candidates to supply a copy of their birth certificate — a measure arising out of questions raised by some Obama critics about where he was born.

Carter's district is home to Fort Hood, the largest army post in the United States, and he is co-chairman of the House Army Caucus. He took a high-profile role after the shooting on the base in 2009 in which the gunman, Nidal Malik Hasan, an Army major of Palestinian descent, killed 13 people and wounded 32 others. Carter has introduced legislation authorizing the same status for Fort Hood victims as that awarded casualties of the Sept. 11 attack on the Pentagon, and granting whistleblower protections to military and civilian personnel who report potential threats from radical Islamic sympathizers.

A member of the Appropriations Committee, Carter was a proponent of earmarks, which secured millions of dollars for his district in 2009, including $10.8 million for a Family Life Center at Fort Hood. But he changed course in 2010, voting with others in the Republican Conference to stop requesting earmarks, saying the process "has been so abused that it must be brought to an absolute halt until this madness is stopped and a better process can be found."

Carter also aligned himself with the growing grass-roots movement of fiscal conservatives, joining the newly formed House Tea Party Caucus in July 2010. At the time, he issued a statement saying that key GOP leaders were sending a message that they were working "hand-in-hand with tea party activists to restore conservative principles in Washington."

Carter also voted against a 2007 measure to ban job discrimination based on sexual orientation; he supported a ban on late-term abortions; and he has been part of pushes for strong border security against illegal immigration.

Carter refused to back the $700 billion financial sector rescue law in fall 2008, telling Fox News that "overwhelmingly, the taxpayers back home think this is insane." After the House adjourned for the August recess in 2008, Carter helped then-Minority Leader John A. Boehner of Ohio lead a small group of Republicans in protest against the Democrats' refusal to vote on a GOP energy plan to end a moratorium on oil and gas drilling along the outer continental shelf. He accused the Democratic Party of being "an ostrich with its head in the sand."

Carter has been in the midst of ethical debates since he came to the House in 2003 as an ally of House Majority Leader Tom DeLay, who, like him, is originally from the Houston area. When DeLay ran into trouble with a campaign fundraising investigation in 2005, Carter was one of 20 Republicans who voted to retain Republican-written rules allowing leaders to keep their jobs if indicted. The rules were later withdrawn.

Carter also drew some negative press when it was revealed he was among eight lawmakers, including DeLay (who resigned from the House in September 2005), who had accepted trips to South Korea from a registered foreign agent. The lawmakers said they were unaware that the organization paying for the trip was an agent of the South Korean government.

Carter acknowledged that he failed to disclose nearly $300,000 in profits from the sale of Exxon stock in 2006 and 2007. He later amended his financial disclosure forms to include the amount of capital gains from past stock sales.

A former state district judge, Carter left the bench after 20 years to run for Congress, he said, because of the Sept. 11 terrorist attacks. He successfully lobbied for an amendment to apply the death penalty for an act of terrorism that results in deaths. It was passed as part of the 2005 reauthorization of the anti-terrorism law known as the Patriot Act.

The son of the general manager of Humble Oil and Refining Co., the precursor to Exxon, Carter had a comfortable upbringing. During high school, he worked summers on oil and gas pipelines, and later on, during a summer in Holland, he worked on a pipeline project for Bechtel Corp.

As a law student at the University of Texas at Austin, Carter said, he was one of a handful of conservatives. "I think I had the only Goldwater button in law school. I got criticized by several professors," he said.

His interest in politics was sparked when he worked as a counsel for the Texas legislature. He moved his family to the small town of Round Rock, set up a law practice, and in 1980 ran unsuccessfully for a seat in the state House. Carter then briefly resumed his practice until he was appointed district court judge of Williamson County in 1981. The following year he won election to the position. In his first U.S. House race in 2002, Carter won a GOP primary runoff with 57 percent of the vote. He then received 69 percent of the vote in a defeat of Democrat David Bagley.

He has been held under 60 percent only once since then, in 2006. Democrats didn't field a candidate against him in 2010, but Libertarian candidate Bill Oliver drew almost 18 percent of the vote in an unsuccessful run.

Key Votes

2010

Overhaul the nation's health insurance system	NO
Allow for repeal of "don't ask, don't tell"	NO
Overhaul financial services industry regulation	NO
Limit use of new Afghanistan War funds to troop withdrawal activities	NO
Change oversight of offshore drilling and lift oil spill liability cap	NO
Provide a path to legal status for some children of illegal immigrants	NO
Extend Bush-era income tax cuts for two years	YES

2009

Expand the Children's Health Insurance Program	NO
Provide $787 billion in tax cuts and spending increases to stimulate the economy	NO
Allow bankruptcy judges to modify certain primary-residence mortgages	NO
Create a cap-and-trade system to limit greenhouse gas emissions	NO
Provide $2 billion for the "cash for clunkers" program	NO
Establish the government as the sole provider of student loans	NO
Restrict federally funded insurance coverage for abortions in health care overhaul	YES

CQ Vote Studies

	PARTY UNITY		PRESIDENTIAL SUPPORT	
	SUPPORT	OPPOSE	SUPPORT	OPPOSE
2010	98%	2%	26%	74%
2009	89%	11%	16%	84%
2008	99%	1%	80%	20%
2007	95%	5%	86%	14%
2006	97%	3%	95%	5%

Interest Groups

	AFL-CIO	ADA	CCUS	ACU
2010	0%	0%	88%	100%
2009	10%	0%	79%	96%
2008	0%	5%	94%	96%
2007	4%	0%	80%	100%
2006	15%	0%	100%	88%

Texas 31

East central — north Austin suburbs, Killeen

The Republican 31st is made up of suburbs and rural areas extending from the northern Austin suburbs through fertile farmland in central Texas to Erath County, located about 60 miles southwest of Fort Worth.

In the south, the 31st's largest population base is in Williamson County, one of Texas' fastest-growing since 2000. A suburban enclave north of Austin, the county enjoyed economic growth that lured new residents to jobs with high-tech employers such as Dell. TECO-Westinghouse Motor Company also is based in Round Rock.

The 31st's other fast-growing population center is Bell County, located just north of Williamson. Fort Hood, a huge Army base near Killeen that is split with Coryell County, is a crucial part of the area's economy, contributing about $7 billion annually. Six state correctional facilities in Coryell County also provide jobs.

Agriculture, especially dairy and grains, is a staple in rural Erath and Hamilton counties in the northern 31st. Cattle and poultry ranches and farms growing corn and sorghum dot the landscape of eastern counties.

Plummeting aluminum prices and declining demand for aluminum products forced the closure of the Aluminum Company of America (ALCOA) smelting plant near Rockdale as well as businesses that worked with the industry giant.

The plant had been Rockdale's primary employer since the discovery of lignite deposits in the 1950s.

The 31st favors the GOP in both its rural and suburban areas. Erath, the district's northernmost county, gave John McCain 77 percent of its 2008 presidential vote. Williamson County, in the southern portion, gave McCain 56 percent. He won the 31st with 57 percent.

Major Industry
Military, technology, agriculture

Military Bases
Fort Hood (Army), 46,500 military, 6,000 civilian (2011)

Cities
Killeen, 127,921; Round Rock (pt.), 98,525; Temple, 66,102; Cedar Park city (pt.), 48,448; Georgetown, 47,400; Austin (pt.), 35,697

Notable
Nolan Ryan owns the Round Rock Express, a minor-league affiliate of the Texas Rangers, the major league team he pitched for and now owns.

Rep. Pete Sessions (R)

Capitol Office
225-2231
sessions.house.gov
2233 Rayburn Bldg. 20515-4332; fax 225-5878

Committees
Rules

Residence
Dallas

Born
March 22, 1955; Waco, Texas

Religion
United Methodist

Family
Wife, Nete Sessions; two children

Education
Southwest Texas State U., attended 1973-74; Southwestern U., B.S. 1978 (political science)

Career
Public policy analyst; telephone company executive

Political Highlights
Sought Republican nomination for U.S. House (special election), 1991; Republican nominee for U.S. House, 1994

ELECTION RESULTS

2010 GENERAL

Pete Sessions (R)	79,433	62.6%
Grier Raggio (D)	44,258	34.9%
John Jay Myers (LIBERT)	3,178	2.5%

2010 PRIMARY

Pete Sessions (R)	30,509	83.7%
David Smith (R)	5,937	16.3%

2008 GENERAL

Pete Sessions (R)	116,283	57.2%
Eric Roberson (D)	82,406	40.6%
Alex Bischoff (LIBERT)	4,421	2.2%

Previous Winning Percentages
2006 (56%); 2004 (54%); 2002 (68%); 2000 (54%); 1998 (56%); 1996 (53%)

Elected 1996; 8th term

Few people gave Sessions much of a chance when he took over the chairmanship of the National Republican Congressional Committee at the beginning of the 2010 election cycle. The committee is the House Republicans' political arm, playing a lead role in recruiting new candidates, raising money and running advertisements, and its chairman is usually judged by November's election results.

By that gauge, Sessions should overcome his doubters. The 2010 elections saw the House GOP pick up 63 seats and reclaim the majority. But despite his big victory, Sessions still has something to prove. His victory, his detractors say, was more a product of the prevailing political winds than of Sessions' electoral genius. Sessions, they add, is too much of an ideologue to represent the GOP and too prone to overheated rhetoric to become a more important figure in the party. Democrats, meanwhile, openly deride him for alleged ethical failings — principally his friendship with financier Allen Stanford, who has been accused by the government of operating a Ponzi scheme, and for once hosting a fundraiser at a Las Vegas burlesque club.

Sessions, a devout conservative and loyal ally of the man he helped make House Speaker, John A. Boehner of Ohio, could have used his success as a launching pad to a higher post in leadership. Instead, he decided to stay on for another term as the NRCC chairman. And Sessions intends to prove his critics wrong by expanding the Republican majority further in the 2012 election. It'll be a tall task given the large number of swing districts now in GOP hands and the relative paucity of winnable seats held by Democrats.

Boehner believes Sessions is the man for the job, calling him the "architect" of the GOP's 2010 win. Whatever his political skills, Sessions is undoubtedly an accomplished fundraiser. Between his own political action committee and his campaign funds, he was able to dole out more than $1 million to fellow Republicans during the 2010 cycle. And while the NRCC still trails the Democrats' campaign committee, Sessions narrowed the gap from $60 million in 2008 to $30 million in 2010, in terms of cash raised and spent. He's hoping to pass on some of that know-how in a new role he's taken on in 2011, mentoring the huge, 87-person class of House Republican freshmen.

A member of the conservative Republican Study Committee, Sessions opposed the Democrats' signature legislative victories of 2010, including legislation overhauling financial regulations and the health insurance system, the latter even though census figures revealed that his district has the highest rate of uninsured people of any GOP-controlled district in the country.

But he broke ranks with other conservatives to back a $700 billion rescue package for the nation's financial services sector in fall 2008. And as NRCC chairman, he pragmatically backed moderate candidates over conservative primary challengers when he thought they had the best chance of winning.

Sessions is a member of the Rules Committee, which sets the parameters for floor debate on bills and is an important lever of the House leadership. He's the vice chairman of the panel during the 112th Congress (2011-12), second in command to chairman David Dreier of California.

He caused a bit of embarrassment for Dreier and the leadership at the beginning of the new Congress. He and GOP Rep. Mike Fitzpatrick of Pennsylvania were not on the House floor with other members to be sworn in, but Sessions voted eight times before taking the oath a day later. Those votes were later nullified because, under the Constitution, only sworn members can vote and conduct other official congressional business.

There is one issue on which Sessions regularly reaches across the aisle.

The father of a son who has Down syndrome, Sessions worked with Democrat Henry A. Waxman of California on a bill that was enacted in 2006 to help families with incomes above the poverty line buy into Medicaid coverage for children with special needs. He co-chairs the bipartisan Congressional Down Syndrome Caucus.

Texas Republicans hope to gain more power in their state as the decennial redistricting process creates four new districts prior to the 2012 election, the most new seats for any state in the country. Sessions hopes his colleagues in the state legislature will redraw his district lines to make it safer. The 32nd was the only district in Texas not to grow in the last 10 years and though Sessions has won by comfortable margins, the demographics are trending Democratic. Hispanics and blacks now make up a majority of district residents.

Sessions pulls out a photo of his wife, Nete, who is Mexican, when asked about his political appeal to his Hispanic constituents. "I am very aware of Hispanic needs and am in tune with their needs as parents on the issues of jobs, health care and education," he said. Like most Texas Republicans, though, he wants a crackdown on illegal immigration and says the high number of uninsured people in his district is explained in large part by Hispanics living there illegally.

Sessions is the son of William S. Sessions, a former federal judge who served as FBI director from 1987 to 1993. He was born in Waco and educated at Southwestern University in Georgetown, Texas. After college, he went to work at Southwestern Bell Telephone Co. and Bell Communications Research.

He ran for Congress in 1991, finishing sixth in a special election to succeed 3rd District GOP Rep. Steve Bartlett, who left to run for mayor of Dallas. In 1994, Sessions quit his job to make an unsuccessful bid against incumbent Democrat John Bryant of the 5th District. After that, he worked as vice president for public policy at the National Center for Policy Analysis, a conservative think tank in Dallas.

When Bryant left his seat in 1996 to run for the Senate, Sessions took 53 percent of the vote against John Pouland, a former Dallas County Democratic chairman. Following the 2000 census and the subsequent redistricting, Sessions ran in the newly created 32nd District, which had more Republican voters. His house was still in the 5th, but a mere two blocks from the boundary. Sessions cruised to victory with 68 percent of the vote. In 2003, state Republicans, led by former House Majority Leader Tom DeLay of Texas, redrew the map again. The new 32nd, which includes his home, pitted Sessions against 13-term Democrat Martin Frost. Sessions prevailed with 54 percent in the costliest election of 2004 and has won comfortably since.

Key Votes

2010

Overhaul the nation's health insurance system	NO
Allow for repeal of "don't ask, don't tell"	NO
Overhaul financial services industry regulation	NO
Limit use of new Afghanistan War funds to troop withdrawal activities	NO
Change oversight of offshore drilling and lift oil spill liability cap	NO
Provide a path to legal status for some children of illegal immigrants	NO
Extend Bush-era income tax cuts for two years	YES

2009

Expand the Children's Health Insurance Program	NO
Provide $787 billion in tax cuts and spending increases to stimulate the economy	NO
Allow bankruptcy judges to modify certain primary-residence mortgages	NO
Create a cap-and-trade system to limit greenhouse gas emissions	NO
Provide $2 billion for the "cash for clunkers" program	NO
Establish the government as the sole provider of student loans	NO
Restrict federally funded insurance coverage for abortions in health care overhaul	YES

CQ Vote Studies

	PARTY UNITY		PRESIDENTIAL SUPPORT	
	SUPPORT	OPPOSE	SUPPORT	OPPOSE
2010	99%	1%	26%	74%
2009	99%	1%	12%	88%
2008	99%	1%	85%	15%
2007	98%	2%	91%	9%
2006	98%	2%	100%	0%

Interest Groups

	AFL-CIO	ADA	CCUS	ACU
2010	0%	0%	88%	100%
2009	0%	0%	75%	100%
2008	0%	5%	100%	92%
2007	4%	10%	94%	96%
2006	10%	0%	100%	96%

Texas 32

Northern Dallas; most of Irving and Richardson

The hook-shaped 32nd is located in northern and western Dallas County and essentially encircles downtown Dallas. It includes a chunk of the city and part of Dallas' northern and western suburbs. Although it does not include downtown, the 32nd is home to much of the Dallas business community. Many district residents work downtown, and several Fortune 500 companies are located off the Lyndon B. Johnson Freeway, which runs as the northwestern border of the district.

Beginning southwest of downtown, in the Hispanic area of Oak Cliff, the district moves west through heavily Hispanic areas in Cockrell Hill and a section of Grand Prairie into the southern part of Irving (shared with the 24th). Irving has a vibrant and growing Hispanic population, although there are still white, blue-collar, middle-class areas. North Irving is home to high-income, technology-oriented professionals in Las Colinas, where many large companies are based. Texas Stadium, the former home of the Dallas Cowboys, was demolished in 2010.

The district then curves east to re-enter Dallas and also take in the exclusive "Park Cities," made up of Highland Park and University Park. This area, almost entirely white, has its own school system and local government and is home to Southern Methodist University (SMU).

The 32nd continues north to the county line, through less-exclusive neighborhoods. The metropolitan area's "telecom corridor" also is in northern Dallas, although standard-bearer Texas Instruments is based just outside the district in the 3rd.

Other technology and finance firms in Richardson (shared with the 3rd) provide jobs for the white-collar workforce. Many residents work at Dallas-Forth Worth International Airport or Dallas Love Field airport, both of which border the 32nd.

The 32nd is Republican — the GOP is particularly strong in the wealthy communities near SMU — and John McCain took 53 percent of the vote here in the 2008 presidential race.

Major Industry
Telecommunications, oil, retail, higher education

Cities
Dallas (pt.), 373,548; Irving (pt.), 141,334; Richardson (pt.), 70,612

Notable
The George W. Bush presidential library at SMU will open in 2013.

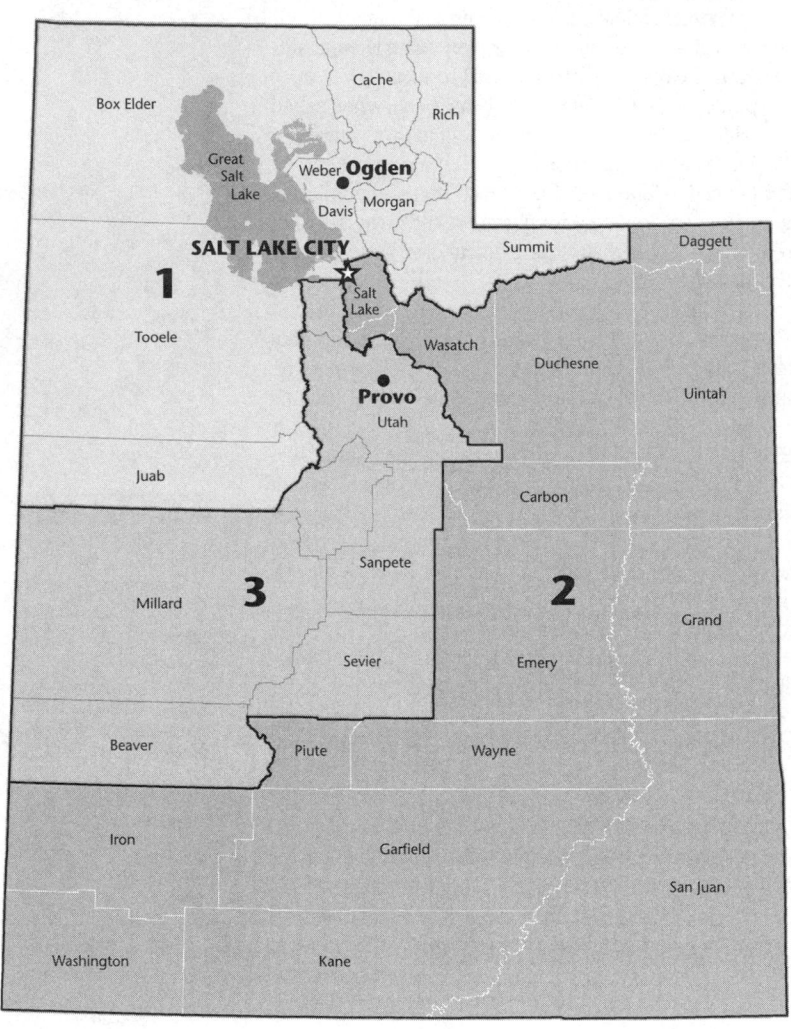

Gov. Gary R. Herbert (R)

First elected: 2010; assumed office Aug. 11, 2009, following the resignation of Jon Huntsman Jr., R, to become ambassador to China.

Length of term: 4 years

Term expires: 1/13

Salary: $109,900

Phone: (801) 538-1000

Residence: Orem

Born: May 7, 1947; American Fork, Utah

Religion: Mormon

Family: Wife, Jeanette Herbert; six children

Education: Brigham Young U., attended 1965-70

Military Service: Utah National Guard 1970-76

Career: Realtor; child care center owner

Political highlights: Utah County Commission, 1990-2004; lieutenant governor, 2005-09

ELECTION RESULTS

2010 GENERAL

Gary R. Herbert (R)	412,151	64.1%
Peter Corroon (D)	205,246	31.9%
Farley Anderson (I)	13,038	2.0%
Andrew McCullough (LIBERT)	12,871	2.0%

Lt. Gov. Gregory S. Bell (R)

First elected: 2010; assumed office Sept. 1, 2009, following the elevation of Herbert to governor.

Length of term: 4 years

Term expires: 1/13

Salary: $104,405

Phone: (801) 538-1000

LEGISLATURE

Legislature: 45 days yearly January-March

Senate: 29 members, 4-year terms

2011 ratios: 22 R, 7 D; 25 men, 4 women

Salary: $117/day

Phone: (801) 538-1035

House: 75 members, 2-year terms

2011 ratios: 58 R, 17 D; 60 men, 15 women

Salary: $117/day

Phone: (801) 538-1029

TERM LIMITS

Governor: 3 terms

Senate: No

House: No

URBAN STATISTICS

CITY	POPULATION
Salt Lake City	186,440
West Valley City	129,480
Provo	112,488
West Jordan	103,712
Orem	88,328

REGISTERED VOTERS

Registration by party began in May 1999, however, not all voters have declared an affiliation and the numbers are kept on a county basis.

POPULATION

2010 population	2,763,885
2000 population	2,233,169
1990 population	1,722,850
Percent change (2000-2010)	+23.8%
Rank among states (2010)	34
Median age	28.5
Born in state	62.5%
Foreign born	7.6%
Violent crime rate	213/100,000
Poverty level	11.5%
Federal workers	41,880
Military	6,237

ELECTIONS

STATE ELECTION OFFICIAL
(801) 538-1041

DEMOCRATIC PARTY
(801) 328-1212

REPUBLICAN PARTY
(801) 533-9777

MISCELLANEOUS

Web: www.utah.gov

Capital: Salt Lake City

U.S. CONGRESS

Senate: 2 Republicans

House: 2 Republicans, 1 Democrat

2010 Census Statistics by District

District	2008 Vote for President Obama	McCain	White	Black	Asian	Hispanic	Median Income	White Collar	Blue Collar	Service Industry	Over 64	Under 18	College Education	Rural	Sq. Miles
1	33%	64%	80%	1%	2%	14%	$55,184	60%	25%	16%	9%	31%	28%	11%	20,768
2	40	58	84	1	2	9	55,256	66	19	15	11	29	33	15	45,624
3	29	67	77	1	2	16	56,497	60	25	15	7	33	25	9	15,751
STATE	34	63	80	1	2	13	55,642	62	23	15	9	31	29	12	82,144
U.S.	53	46	64	12	5	16	51,425	60	23	17	13	25	28	21	3,537,438

Sen. Orrin G. Hatch (R)

Capitol Office
224-5251
hatch.senate.gov
104 Hart Bldg. 20510-4402; fax 224-6331

Committees
Finance - Ranking Member
Health, Education, Labor & Pensions
Judiciary
Special Aging
Joint Taxation

Residence
Salt Lake City

Born
March 22, 1934; Pittsburgh, Pa.

Religion
Mormon

Family
Wife, Elaine Hatch; six children

Education
Brigham Young U., B.S. 1959 (history);
U. of Pittsburgh, J.D. 1962

Career
Lawyer; songwriter

Political Highlights
Sought Republican nomination for president, 2000

ELECTION RESULTS

2006 GENERAL

Orrin G. Hatch (R)	356,238	62.4%
Pete Ashdown (D)	177,459	31.1%
Scott N. Bradley (CNSTP)	21,526	3.8%
Roger I. Price (PC)	9,089	1.6%

Previous Winning Percentages
2000 (66%); 1994 (69%); 1988 (67%); 1982 (58%);
1976 (54%)

Elected 1976; 6th term

Among his colleagues, Hatch is revered in the Senate for his willingness to reach across the aisle and cut deals on major legislation. He's a conservative but not uncompromisingly so, working with Democrats over the years on the health care, financial and judicial issues on which he specializes.

For more than 30 years, over the course of six election campaigns, Hatch has turned that into a winning formula. He's never faced a tough race, but he might in 2012.

In 2010, the conservative tea party movement felled Hatch's longtime GOP colleague from Utah, Robert F. Bennett, who strayed from conservative orthodoxy on immigration, health care and the 2008 law that provided $700 billion to rescue the ailing financial sector.

The last is a vote that Hatch had in common with Bennett. And with the increasing electoral influence of the tea party, Hatch is worried about keeping his job for the first time in his career.

Most worrisome to Hatch are polls in his home state showing Utah Rep. Jason Chaffetz running neck and neck with him in a potential 2012 Republican nominating contest. Since the Utah GOP uses a party convention system as a first step in nominating candidates, Hatch has to persuade the state's most conservative and activist Republicans that they should give him, the longest serving senator in the state's history, another term.

In response, Hatch has shifted his rhetorical focus.

Instead of being seen working with Democrats, he is visibly trying to stymie them. As the top Republican on the Finance Committee, he's pushing for a broad overhaul of the tax code, a balanced budget amendment to the Constitution, repeal of the health care law enacted in 2010, a crackdown on illegal immigration and a downsizing of the federal workforce.

He's also making a public effort to meet with tea party activists and sell his conservative record. The results have been mixed. At the 2011 Conservative Political Action Committee conference — a major annual confab for activists — Hatch apologized for his vote on the Wall Street bailout.

"All I can say is there aren't many people who will say, 'I'm sorry,'" he said. "I'm one who will." The crowd was unconvinced, repeatedly booing, until Hatch pleaded: "You may disagree but you're not there having to make these decisions." An attendee heckled back: "You won't be soon."

But Hatch's efforts have not all been for naught. He won over one of the major tea party groups, Tea Party Express, which has pledged not to oppose him in 2012, and he remains comfortably ahead of Chaffetz when it comes to raising funds for the looming election.

Hatch is a GOP loyalist on many issues, but not usually quite as much as he was in 2010, when he sided with his party on 97 percent of the votes that split majorities of the parties. Only twice in his long career — 2003 and 2004 —has he sided with his party more often.

During the 111th Congress (2009-10), he opposed the health care overhaul and Wall Street regulatory measures, arguing they would hurt the economy. He was equally dismissive of Obama's early economic initiatives, including a $787 billion economic stimulus law. But he supported compromise legislation at the end of 2010 extending the Bush-era tax cuts while also continuing unemployment benefits as a means of jump-starting the economy.

In addition to his seat on Finance, Hatch is active on the Health, Education, Labor and Pensions panel and is a former chairman of the Judiciary Committee, where he still serves. On Judiciary, Hatch has been in the middle of some of the Senate's most explosive fights, such as those over Supreme Court nominations.

Still, until 2009, Hatch had never opposed a nominee to the Supreme Court. But Hatch deviated from his long history and voted against both of Obama's picks, Sonia Sotomayor and Elena Kagan. In each case, he said he feared the new justices would legislate from the bench. Both won confirmation.

Hatch, who also serves on the Special Aging Committee, has also alienated some social conservatives by supporting embryonic stem cell research, which some liken to abortion. In 2010, Congress enacted Hatch's bill reauthorizing research into stem cells from cord blood, which can be used to treat leukemia and certain lymphomas. Because the stem cells are retrieved from the umbilical cord and placenta after childbirth, and not from embryos, they are not controversial.

Hatch has also raised concerns on the right because he maintained a long and fruitful relationship with liberal icon Edward M. Kennedy of Massachusetts; he and Kennedy had advanced a number of bills before Kennedy passed away in August 2009. "We're like two brothers who fight each other all the time, but deep down care about each other," Hatch told The Salt Lake Tribune.

A frugal workaholic, Hatch is also an urbane clotheshorse, art lover and successful songwriter whose work has been performed by the Osmonds and Gladys Knight. Hatch is friendly with U2 lead singer Bono. After Kennedy was diagnosed with brain cancer, Hatch wrote a song in his friend's honor called "Headed Home," aimed at paying tribute to Kennedy's eventual return to work; among the lyrics were, "Just honor him / honor him / and every fear will be a thing of the past.'"

Hooked on music since he started taking piano lessons at age 6, Hatch started writing poetry in college. In 1996, singer-songwriter Janice Kapp Perry asked him to write some hymns with her. He wrote 10 songs in a weekend, the core of the "My God Is Love" album. Since then, he's produced several discs of religious, romantic and patriotic songs.

Born in Pittsburgh, Hatch grew up in poverty. The family lost their home during the Great Depression, so Hatch's father, a lathe operator, borrowed $100 to buy an acre of land in the hills above Pittsburgh, where he built a home of blackened lumber salvaged from a fire. The family grew their own food; Hatch tended the chickens and sold their eggs.

During World War II, when Hatch was 11, his beloved older brother, Jesse, a B-24 nose gunner, died in a bombing raid over Italy. Just weeks afterward, a lock of hair over Hatch's forehead turned white. When it came time for Hatch to serve his mission as a young Mormon, he chose to serve two, one for himself and one for Jesse.

He worked his way through Brigham Young University in Utah and law school at the University of Pittsburgh as a janitor, an all-night desk clerk in a girls' dormitory and a lathe operator. To house a growing family that included three of his six children by the time he finished law school, he plastered the inside of his family's old chicken coop.

He returned to Utah in 1969 and was an attorney with a thriving private practice when he decided in 1976 to run for the Senate seat then held by Democrat Frank Moss. In his 2002 autobiography "Square Peg," Hatch said he ran because the country was grappling with inflation, deficit spending, high unemployment and a weakened military. He won the GOP nomination over Jack W. Carlson, a former assistant secretary of Interior, then defeated Moss with 54 percent of the vote.

He's won handily since, his only electoral defeat coming in 1999 when he launched a quixotic bid for the GOP presidential nomination. Lacking money and broad political support, he finished last in Iowa's GOP caucuses and dropped out the next week, endorsing George W. Bush.

Key Votes

2010

Pass budget reconciliation bill to modify overhauls of health care and federal student loan programs	NO
Proceed to disapproval resolution on EPA authority to regulate greenhouse gases	YES
Overhaul financial services industry regulation	NO
Limit debate to proceed to a bill to broaden campaign finance disclosure and reporting rules	NO
Limit debate on an extension of Bush-era income tax cuts for two years	YES
Limit debate on a bill to provide a path to legal status for some children of illegal immigrants	-
Allow for a repeal of "don't ask, don't tell"	-
Consent to ratification of a strategic arms reduction treaty with Russia	NO

2009

Prevent release of remaining financial industry bailout funds	#
Make it easier for victims to sue for wage discrimination remedies	NO
Expand the Children's Health Insurance Program	NO
Limit debate on the economic stimulus measure	NO
Repeal District of Columbia firearms prohibitions and gun registration laws	YES
Limit debate on expansion of federal hate crimes law	NO
Strike funding for F-22 Raptor fighter jets	NO

CQ Vote Studies

	PARTY UNITY		PRESIDENTIAL SUPPORT	
	SUPPORT	OPPOSE	SUPPORT	OPPOSE
2010	97%	3%	46%	54%
2009	85%	15%	58%	42%
2008	93%	7%	80%	20%
2007	82%	18%	76%	24%
2006	93%	7%	88%	12%
2005	96%	4%	93%	7%
2004	98%	2%	94%	6%
2003	98%	2%	99%	1%
2002	93%	7%	98%	2%
2001	95%	5%	97%	3%

Interest Groups

	AFL-CIO	ADA	CCUS	ACU
2010	8%	0%	100%	100%
2009	22%	20%	86%	88%
2008	20%	10%	100%	80%
2007	29%	30%	91%	76%
2006	20%	5%	92%	84%
2005	14%	5%	100%	92%
2004	8%	10%	100%	96%
2003	0%	10%	100%	80%
2002	23%	5%	100%	95%
2001	6%	5%	86%	96%

Sen. Mike Lee (R)

Capitol Office
224-5444
lee.senate.gov
316 Hart Bldg. 20510-4403; fax 228-1168

Committees
Energy & Natural Resources
Foreign Relations
Judiciary
Joint Economic

Residence
Alpine

Born
June 4, 1971; Mesa, Ariz.

Religion
Mormon

Family
Wife, Sharon Lee; three children

Education
Brigham Young U., B.A. 1994 (political science), J.D. 1997

Career
Lawyer; gubernatorial aide

Political Highlights
Assistant U.S. attorney, 2002-05

ELECTION RESULTS

2010 GENERAL

Mike Lee (R)	390,179	61.6%
Sam F. Granato (D)	207,685	32.8%
Scott N. Bradley (CNSTP)	35,937	5.7%

2010 PRIMARY

Mike Lee (R)	98,512	51.2%
Tim Bridgewater (R)	93,905	48.8%

Elected 2010; 1st term

Lee sat in on most of his father's arguments before the U.S. Supreme Court when Rex Lee served as solicitor general in the 1980s. The younger Lee clerked for Supreme Court Justice Samuel A. Alito Jr. and was an assistant U.S. attorney under President George W. Bush. But he sees his transition from the judicial branch and legal work to the legislative branch as a "continuum" rather than a career change.

As a lawyer, Lee says, he often came across statutes riddled with loopholes and complicated wording. One way to "clean up the mess," he decided, was to help write the legislation himself.

"There are limits on what the court can do," said Lee, who won a seat on the Judiciary Committee. "The courts aren't there to be the first and last interpreter of the Constitution. They are prohibited from acting unless there are two or more parties to a dispute. That is the only time, but there are a lot of questions that never result in this kind of dispute."

Like most Republicans, Lee also wants to tackle the federal deficit. "I've been worrying about the deficit for a long time, since the 1980s," he said. "We had a $3 trillion deficit back then. Now that's multiplied, and soon it will be five times more than when I first started worrying."

His first piece of legislation, offered in February 2011, was a balanced-budget amendment to the Constitution that would limit federal spending to 18 percent of gross domestic product, unless two-thirds of the House and Senate override the restriction. Lee would like to see Congress follow the example set by state legislatures that have imposed balanced-budget requirements, and he suggested that doing so might require cutting federal spending by somewhat less than half.

"One methodology to get there would be to ask each federal agency, each federal department, to propose a budget that would be slashed by a certain amount, maybe as high as 40 percent, and then examine that and figure out what impact it would have," Lee said in an October debate. "There is no single formula that could carry the magic bullet, but we do know . . . if we don't try anything, we're never going to get there."

Lee believes that lowering the deficit will lead to jobs. "In order to create jobs, Congress has to control what it spends so it's not stuck with so much debt that it has to inflate the dollar to pay it off," he said. "Any time you require Congress to discipline itself to spend less, it increases confidence in investments and people investing, and when they invest more, they create more jobs."

The issue is also a matter of principle for Lee, who says that the deficit increases corruption by allowing members to avoid accountability for spending taxpayer money on unnecessary programs.

"Every war we fought, starting with the Revolution, required the country to incur debt, but it has become so easy that it's gotten out of control," he said. "It allows Congress to overspend and create new programs and benefits for constituents without having any new money to pay for it."

On the Energy and Natural Resources Committee, Lee supports opening up the nation's natural energy resources, including a proposal to drill for oil and gas in the Arctic National Wildlife Refuge in Alaska, and to extract shale oil from rock in Utah, Colorado and Wyoming.

He testified in February 2010 before a Utah House committee in favor of legislation to allow Utah to assert eminent-domain rights against the federal government on public lands in the state.

"We are in fact being compelled into an undue obedience to the general government by virtue of the fact that they control 70 percent of our land, and on top of that tell us that we don't exercise the bundle of rights accompanied with state sovereignty," he told the lawmakers. "They're wrong."

The bill was signed into law a month later.

Lee supports a repeal of the health care overhaul enacted in March 2010 and turning much of the responsibility for the issue over to the states. "States are in charge of regulating almost every aspect of the medical profession. It ought to be the states that cover the social welfare net, including that portion of that net that deals with providing health insurance to the poor," he said in the October debate.

Lee calls the Constitution "the instruction manual for Congress," and he has several ideas for improving the document, beyond the balanced-budget amendment.

In what he calls a clarification of the original intent of the 14th Amendment, he wants to end automatic citizenship for children born to illegal immigrants by legislative means, rather than by a constitutional amendment.

He also backs a 12-year term limit for members of the House and Senate, although he says he would not term-limit himself in the absence of a requirement for everybody.

Perhaps most quixotically, he has voiced support for repealing the 17th Amendment and returning the election of senators to state legislators, as a way to empower states.

Lee also sits on the Foreign Relations Committee. After President Obama committed U.S. forces to aid rebels fighting the government of Muammar el-Qaddafi in Libya, he cosponsored a measure that called for Obama to submit to Congress a description of U.S. policy objectives, a plan to achieve those objectives, an estimate of the costs of the operation and a description of limitations placed on military operations.

Lee grew up in Utah and Washington, D.C., and the law was a frequent dinner table topic. After his service as solicitor general under President Ronald Reagan, Rex Lee became president of Brigham Young University, where Mike Lee earned his undergraduate and law degrees.

After graduating from law school, he served as a law clerk for a district court judge in Utah, then for Alito, who at the time was on the U.S. Court of Appeals for the 3rd Circuit. He practiced appellate and Supreme Court litigation in D.C. before moving back to Utah to serve as an assistant U.S. attorney.

He was general counsel to Republican Gov. Jon Huntsman before returning to Washington for a one-year clerkship with Alito, who had joined the Supreme Court. It was then back to Utah again to work in private practice.

Conservative activists were looking for a candidate to take on incumbent Republican Robert F. Bennett, who had supported the $700 billion financial industry rescue in 2008 and had chafed those to his right in the party with his stances on health care and immigration.

The early front-runner was state Attorney General Mark Shurtleff. But citing family concerns, he withdrew a year before the election.

That left Bennett to contend with Lee and businessman Tim Bridgewater. Both topped Bennett at the state GOP convention in May 2010, leaving him no spot on the primary ballot. Bennett endorsed Bridgewater, but Lee nipped him 51 percent to 49 percent in the primary a month later.

That was tantamount to election in heavily Republican Utah, and Lee cruised past Democrat Sam Granato, a Salt Lake City restaurateur, with 62 percent of the vote.

"I'm about as tea party as they come," Lee said on election night.

In April 2011, Lee started his own leadership political action committee, to help fund conservative candidates. He quickly endorsed Rep. Jeff Flake, who is running for Senate in Arizona, and Texas Solicitor General Ted Cruz.

Rep. Rob Bishop (R)

Capitol Office
225-0453
www.house.gov/robbishop
123 Cannon Bldg. 20515-4401; fax 225-5857

Committees
Natural Resources
    (National Parks, Forests & Public Lands - Chairman)
Rules

Residence
Brigham City

Born
July 13, 1951; Salt Lake City, Utah

Religion
Mormon

Family
Wife, Jeralynn Bishop; five children

Education
U. of Utah, B.A. 1974 (political science)

Career
Teacher; lobbyist

Political Highlights
Utah House, 1979-95 (Speaker, 1993-95); Utah
Republican Party chairman, 1997-2001

ELECTION RESULTS

2010 GENERAL
Rob Bishop (R)	135,247	69.2%
Morgan E. Bowen (D)	46,765	23.9%
Kirk D. Pearson (CNSTP)	9,143	4.7%
Jared Paul Stratton (LIBERT)	4,307	2.2%

2010 PRIMARY
Rob Bishop (R)	unopposed

2008 GENERAL
Rob Bishop (R)	196,799	64.8%
Morgan E. Bowen (D)	92,469	30.5%
Kirk D. Pearson (CNSTP)	7,397	2.4%
Joseph G. Buchman (LIBERT)	6,780	2.2%

Previous Winning Percentages
2006 (63%); 2004 (68%); 2002 (61%)

Elected 2002; 5th term

Bishop has woven a consistent narrative thread through more than two decades in elected office: an aversion to big government. Democrats and liberal policies are a frequent target of his dry and irreverent humor, but he has turned his wit on fellow Republicans as well.

"I want to leave this office with less power to do things than when I came here," he is fond of saying.

Bishop, who served on the GOP transition committee planning for the 112th Congress (2011-12) and then joined the Rules Committee, helped develop the new House rule requiring every bill to include a provision explaining what part of the Constitution authorizes it.

From his seat on the Natural Resources Committee, where he chairs the National Parks, Forests and Public Lands Subcommittee, Bishop cites the 1972 Clean Water Act as emblematic of the tendency to put too much power in the hands of Washington.

"Most Westerners are extremely concerned about the massive accumulation of federal power," said Bishop, former chairman of the Congressional Western Caucus. "In the past year, the federal government has taken control over our banks, cars and health care. Now they are seeking to gain control over every drop of water, from backyard puddles to the arid playas of the West."

Bishop led the charge in 2009 against Democrats' climate change legislation aimed at reducing carbon emissions. Referring to Democratic claims that the measure would create "green" jobs, Bishop told The Salt Lake Tribune that "some of those jobs are as real as the Jolly Green Giant: It is a great ad concept, but it doesn't exist."

When Republicans unveiled their energy proposal in May 2009, Bishop invoked two other Roberts: Frost, the poet, and Zemeckis, the film director. "There's two roads in the woods that merge. Each one will take you to an extremely different conclusion, and we have to decide which one we wish to go down," he said. "Remember those sequels to 'Back to the Future' where there were the two worlds? Our world is the one where the McFly family is happy. The Democrat version is the one where Biff runs everything."

Bishop also can be scathing about fellow Republicans whom he feels too often used their previous time in the majority to expand the reach of government. "I have had a problem with some conservatives in the last few years," he said. "We have tended to be kinder and gentler in the way we want to control people's lives. But we are still trying to control them. It would be simpler if we just don't get involved."

Bishop argues that environmental concerns have overtaken good sense at the border. He introduced legislation in 2010 and again in 2011 that would bar the Interior and Agriculture secretaries from doing anything to interfere with border security on public land under their jurisdiction.

He chastises those who want to turn large swaths of public land into conservation areas. In 2007, he questioned Massachusetts Democrat Barney Frank's bill to designate parts of a Bay State river as scenic or recreational, giving it special protections. "In fact, the only part of this river that's scenic is the graffiti that's found on the bridges and the human embankments that are part of this river system," he said. "The only thing that's wild about this river are the gangs that wrote this graffiti in the first place."

In 2006, he won enactment of a measure establishing a wilderness area in Utah's western desert near the Air Force's Utah Test and Training Range, blocking a proposed nuclear waste dump on the Skull Valley Goshute Indian Reservation. And in a catchall public-lands bill enacted in early 2009, he successfully included two bills allowing for a swap of about 1,600 acres between the U.S. Forest Service and Bountiful City, giving the city control over land where the Bountiful Lions Club gun range and the Davis Aqueduct are situated.

A former part-time lobbyist for the Utah Shooting Sports Council, Bishop has sought to protect gun and hunting laws in land transactions. He applauded enactment of a measure in May 2009 that allows people to carry concealed firearms into some national parks. "This legislation ensures that unelected bureaucrats and judges cannot override the Second Amendment rights of law-abiding citizens on National Park System and Fish and Wildlife land in states permitting concealed firearms," Bishop said.

Bishop has been critical of President Obama's plans to cancel the next-generation NASA rocket program; the primary contractor employs thousands of Utahns. Bishop wants to protect those jobs, and also argues that ending the program is bad not just for the space program but for national security.

His district is home to Hill Air Force Base, which he helped save from the 2005 round of base closures. He promotes the F-35A stealth fighter plane, known as the joint strike fighter, that is intended to replace the F-16 and A-10. Some of the planes would be stationed at Hill.

Bishop, a member of the conservative Republican Study Committee, is typically loyal to his leadership. But he was one of 26 Republicans to vote in early 2011 against a three-month extension of expiring provisions of the anti-terrorism law known as the Patriot Act. He was one of 13 Republicans to vote in 2006 against a reauthorization of the law, arguing the measure didn't provide sufficient protection for civil liberties.

When Bishop was a boy, his father, an accountant, served as mayor of his hometown of Kaysville, as a GOP delegate and as a campaign volunteer. "I remember him vividly, sitting at the telephone at the kitchen table, calling delegates. I thought that everybody did that," he said.

After college, Bishop taught high school English, debate and history, later adding German and Advanced Placement government courses. He spent two years in Germany as part of his Mormon mission experience.

He continued teaching after he won election to the Utah House, where he served 16 years, the last two as Speaker. After a stint as state Republican Party chairman, Bishop jumped into the 2002 race to succeed retiring Republican James V. Hansen in the U.S. House. He defeated state House Majority Leader Kevin Garn for the GOP nomination, then won the general election with 61 percent of the vote. He has easily won his subsequent re-elections.

Key Votes

2010	
Overhaul the nation's health insurance system	NO
Allow for repeal of "don't ask, don't tell"	NO
Overhaul financial services industry regulation	NO
Limit use of new Afghanistan War funds to troop withdrawal activities	NO
Change oversight of offshore drilling and lift oil spill liability cap	NO
Provide a path to legal status for some children of illegal immigrants	NO
Extend Bush-era income tax cuts for two years	YES
2009	
Expand the Children's Health Insurance Program	NO
Provide $787 billion in tax cuts and spending increases to stimulate the economy	NO
Allow bankruptcy judges to modify certain primary-residence mortgages	NO
Create a cap-and-trade system to limit greenhouse gas emissions	NO
Provide $2 billion for the "cash for clunkers" program	NO
Establish the government as the sole provider of student loans	NO
Restrict federally funded insurance coverage for abortions in health care overhaul	YES

CQ Vote Studies

	PARTY UNITY		PRESIDENTIAL SUPPORT	
	SUPPORT	OPPOSE	SUPPORT	OPPOSE
2010	97%	3%	26%	74%
2009	96%	4%	11%	89%
2008	96%	4%	78%	22%
2007	97%	3%	80%	20%
2006	97%	3%	89%	11%

Interest Groups

	AFL-CIO	ADA	CCUS	ACU
2010	8%	0%	88%	100%
2009	5%	0%	79%	100%
2008	8%	0%	81%	100%
2007	10%	10%	88%	100%
2006	15%	10%	93%	87%

Utah 1

North — part of Salt Lake City, Ogden

In the late 1840s, Mormon pioneers led by Brigham Young journeyed into the mountainous terrain of northern Utah. Today, the 1st — covering the northernmost part of the state — remains the center of the Mormon world. The district contains more than half of Salt Lake City, bringing in most of downtown and Temple Square, which includes the Tabernacle and the headquarters of the Church of Jesus Christ of Latter-day Saints. Salt Lake City International Airport also is in the 1st.

Ogden, the district's second-largest city, was once a lively railroad town but today includes facilities for such major employers as Autoliv, a car safety systems manufacturer, and the IRS, which operates a call center downtown. Defense is important to the 1st. The 2005 round of base realignments saved Hill Air Force Base, one of the state's largest employers, but closed the Deseret Chemical Depot.

The 1st contains much of Utah's ski country in the north-central part of the state, including Park City, a wealthy resort town and winter sports destination.

In rural areas, especially in Box Elder and Cache counties along the Idaho

border, agriculture is king. Utah State University is in Logan in Cache County.

Many areas of Salt Lake City lean Democratic at the state and federal levels, but wealthy suburbs in heavily populated Salt Lake and Davis counties give the district its solid Republican lean.

Most of the rural areas favor Republicans, although Democrats pick up some votes in Park City. Overall, John McCain took 64 percent of the district's 2008 presidential vote.

Major Industry
Manufacturing, defense, technology, tourism, agriculture

Military Bases
Hill Air Force Base, 4,255 military, 11,701 civilian (2009); Dugway Proving Ground, 586 military, 742 civilian; Tooele Army Depot, 2 military, 524 civilian (2011)

Cities
Salt Lake City (pt.), 99,079; Ogden, 82,825; Layton, 67,311; Logan, 48,174; Bountiful, 42,552; Roy, 36,884; Tooele, 31,605; Clearfield, 30,112

Notable
Great Salt Lake is the largest saltwater lake in the Western Hemisphere; Park City is the home of the U.S. Ski and Snowboard Team.

Rep. Jim Matheson (D)

Capitol Office
225-3011
www.house.gov/matheson
2434 Rayburn Bldg. 20515-4402; fax 225-5638

Committees
Energy & Commerce

Residence
Salt Lake City

Born
March 21, 1960; Salt Lake City, Utah

Religion
Mormon

Family
Wife, Amy Matheson; two children

Education
Harvard U., A.B. 1982 (government); U. of California,
Los Angeles, M.B.A. 1987

Career
Energy company project manager; environmental
policy think tank advocate; energy consulting firm
owner

Political Highlights
No previous office

ELECTION RESULTS

2010 GENERAL

Jim Matheson (D)	127,151	50.5%
Morgan Philpot (R)	116,001	46.1%
Randall Hinton (CNSTP)	4,578	1.8%

2010 PRIMARY

Jim Matheson (D)	23,067	67.3%
Claudia Wright (D)	11,227	32.7%

2008 GENERAL

Jim Matheson (D)	220,666	63.4%
Bill Dew (R)	120,083	34.5%
Matthew Arndt (LIBERT)	4,576	1.3%

Previous Winning Percentages
2006 (59%); 2004 (55%); 2002 (49%); 2000 (56%)

Elected 2000; 6th term

The only Democrat in Utah's five-seat congressional delegation, Matheson walks a fine line between his party and the voters back home.

He generally sides with his party on education, labor and environmental issues, but as a member of the fiscally conservative Blue Dog Coalition, he tends to vote with Republicans on national security and tax matters.

Matheson regularly plays down his party affiliation, preferring to call attention to his swing voting and focus on issues that matter to his constituents.

He was with his party in backing President Obama's $787 billion economic stimulus law in 2009, saying he believed it would boost job creation. But Matheson opposed the Democratic health care overhaul, the signature issue of 2010. It was that vote, above all others, that inspired a primary challenge from the left. Matheson stuck with all but three fellow Democrats in opposing the GOP effort to repeal the measure at the beginning of the 112th Congress (2011-12).

In the 111th Congress (2009-10), Matheson was among the House Democrats who split with their party most often on votes that pitted majorities of the two parties against each other — about 17 percent of the time in his case.

During the administration of George W. Bush, he was among those Democrats who most frequently supported the president. Matheson backed Bush's tax cuts of 2001 and 2003, as well as a 2004 corporate tax cut. He also joined Republicans to back a 2005 bill to repeal the federal estate tax. And he voted in late 2010 to extend the Bush-era cuts for two years.

A member of the Energy and Commerce Committee, Matheson sided with Michigan Democrat John D. Dingell in his ultimately unsuccessful bid to retain the panel's chairmanship against a vigorous challenge by the more liberal Henry A. Waxman, a California Democrat, in late 2008. Matheson worked the phones for Dingell and suggested that efforts to reach consensus on upcoming climate change legislation would be lost if there was a change in committee leadership.

As efforts on that legislation got under way in 2009, Matheson — who leads the Blue Dogs' energy task force — gave Waxman credit for seeking consensus and including him in some early talks. But he also warned that Democrats might be moving too fast and not taking into consideration concerns of industry and regional differences. He opposed the measure in committee and was one of 44 Democrats to vote against it on the House floor.

In April 2011, he was one of 19 Democrats to vote for a House-passed bill to bar the Environmental Protection Agency from regulating greenhouse gases in any effort to address climate change.

Matheson sticks with the Utah delegation on environmental issues. He and former Utah Republican Sen. Robert F. Bennett won enactment of their bill to set 256,000 acres off-limits to energy exploration as part of an omnibus lands bill that President Obama signed into law in March 2009. He criticized discussions at the Bureau of Land Management about creating more national monuments in the West without local input.

Party leaders give Matheson leeway to vote how he needs, and he was named a chief deputy whip and joined the Democratic Steering and Policy Committee in the new Congress.

In 2007, when the House passed a bill to grant voting rights to the Democratic delegate from the District of Columbia and to add a House seat for Republican-dominated Utah, Democratic leaders held up the bill until they were reassured that it wouldn't jeopardize Matheson's seat. The legislation ultimately was blocked in the Senate. They did the same in 2010 — House language would have created an at-large seat rather than carve out a fourth district, a proposal that drew a filibuster threat from home-state Republican Sen. Orrin G. Hatch.

When legislation to advance construction of a nuclear waste dump at Nevada's Yucca Mountain came before the 107th Congress (2001-02), Matheson voted against it, saying Westerners had been exposed to enough nuclear dangers. In 2009, he supported the idea of creating a blue-ribbon panel to discuss alternatives for nuclear waste disposal.

Matheson joined with Utah Republicans in an effort to win resumption of federal compensation to people who became ill as a result of exposure to radiation from atomic bomb testing in Nevada. Compensation for those "downwinders" was authorized in 1990, but funding was halted in 2000. The issue resonates with Matheson, whose father died in 1990 of bone marrow cancer, a disease linked to radiation exposure. Scott Matheson, a two-term governor, had lived in an area of southern Utah affected by the nuclear tests.

Although his father was the governor, Matheson said his mother, Norma, was more responsible for his interest in public service because she was involved in many civic projects. He said his Mormon upbringing infused him with a sense of moral purpose.

While majoring in government at Harvard, he served a summer internship in the office of House Speaker Thomas P. "Tip" O'Neill Jr., a Massachusetts Democrat. After college, he worked at an environmental policy think tank in Washington for three years. He returned to Utah after graduate school, worked in private-sector energy jobs and started an energy consulting firm.

In 2000, Matheson ran for the House seat held by Republican Merrill Cook, who lost the primary to Internet executive Derek W. Smith. Smith received a dose of bad press over his past business practices, and Matheson sailed to victory by 15 percentage points. In post-2000-census redistricting, Republicans redrew the 2nd District to make it more GOP-friendly. But Matheson eked out a victory in 2002 by 1,641 votes. He has solidified his grip since and was elected in 2008 to a fifth term with 63 percent.

In 2010, he was forced into a primary when Democrats dissatisfied with his centrism — particularly his vote against the health care law — gave Claudia Wright, a retired high school teacher and college gender studies instructor, 45 percent of the vote at the Democratic state convention in May. In the June primary Matheson defeated Wright, a self-described progressive lesbian, by a better than 2-to-1 margin. In November he beat former GOP state Rep. Morgan Philpot by about 4 percentage points.

Key Votes

2010

Overhaul the nation's health insurance system	NO
Allow for repeal of "don't ask, don't tell"	YES
Overhaul financial services industry regulation	YES
Limit use of new Afghanistan War funds to troop withdrawal activities	NO
Change oversight of offshore drilling and lift oil spill liability cap	NO
Provide a path to legal status for some children of illegal immigrants	NO
Extend Bush-era income tax cuts for two years	YES

2009

Expand the Children's Health Insurance Program	YES
Provide $787 billion in tax cuts and spending increases to stimulate the economy	YES
Allow bankruptcy judges to modify certain primary-residence mortgages	NO
Create a cap-and-trade system to limit greenhouse gas emissions	NO
Provide $2 billion for the "cash for clunkers" program	YES
Establish the government as the sole provider of student loans	YES
Restrict federally funded insurance coverage for abortions in health care overhaul	YES

CQ Vote Studies

	PARTY UNITY		PRESIDENTIAL SUPPORT	
	SUPPORT	OPPOSE	SUPPORT	OPPOSE
2010	82%	18%	74%	26%
2009	84%	16%	75%	25%
2008	86%	14%	32%	68%
2007	79%	21%	20%	80%
2006	66%	34%	67%	33%

Interest Groups

	AFL-CIO	ADA	CCUS	ACU
2010	71%	60%	75%	17%
2009	67%	55%	80%	24%
2008	67%	55%	78%	36%
2007	83%	75%	80%	36%
2006	57%	45%	87%	64%

Utah 2

South and east — part of Salt Lake City, rural Utah

Taking in plateaus, towering cliffs, forests and mountain trails, the 2nd cuts a reverse L-shaped swath across eastern and southern Utah from eastern Salt Lake City in the north to Four Corners in the southeastern corner of the state and then west across Utah's southern tier. Much of eastern Salt Lake County consists of bedroom communities such as Murray. The area also is home to health care firms, a stadium for soccer's Real Salt Lake in Sandy and the University of Utah.

In the southwestern portion of the 2nd, St. George in Washington County has attracted retirees for decades. But large portions of the 2nd struggle. Nearly 30 percent of residents in San Juan County, home to part of the Navajo Nation, live in poverty, by far the highest percentage in the state. Garfield and San Juan counties have the state's highest unemployment rates. In Grand, artists and residents who rely on seasonal tourism-based jobs populate Moab, a haven for outdoor enthusiasts.

Land-use issues are important in the 2nd, which includes all five of the state's national parks — Arches, Bryce Canyon, Canyonlands, Capitol Reef and Zion. Much of the district is federal land. San Juan County contains Utah's quadrant of Four Corners, the only point in the United States where four states meet. Carbon County in the middle of the state hosts a dwindling mining sector.

The district's portion of Salt Lake County, where just more than half of the 2nd's residents live, provides some Democratic votes. In the 2008 presidential election, Grand County gave Democrat Barack Obama a slim majority of 51 percent, his second-highest percentage in the state and one of only three counties that he won in Utah.

John McCain, who took 58 percent of the 2nd's presidential vote overall, won his highest percentage statewide (82 percent) in Uintah County in the east.

Major Industry
Manufacturing, tourism, ranching

Cities
Sandy, 87,461; Salt Lake City (pt.), 87,361; St. George, 72,897; Millcreek (unincorporated), 62,139; Murray (pt.), 46,551; Lehi (pt.), 44,175

Notable
San Juan County includes Utah's portion of Monument Valley.

Rep. Jason Chaffetz (R)

Capitol Office
225-7751
chaffetz.house.gov
1032 Longworth Bldg. 20515-4403; fax 225-5629

Committees
Budget
Judiciary
Oversight & Government Reform
  (National Security, Homeland Defense & Foreign
  Operations - Chairman)

Residence
Alpine

Born
March 26, 1967; Los Gatos, Calif.

Religion
Mormon

Family
Wife, Julie Chaffetz; three children

Education
Brigham Young U., B.A. 1989 (communications)

Career
Public relations firm owner; gubernatorial and campaign aide; pharmaceutical company marketing executive; alternative fuel company marketing executive; personal care products company executive

Political Highlights
Utah Valley University Board of Trustees, 2007-08

ELECTION RESULTS

2010 GENERAL

Jason Chaffetz (R)	139,721	72.3%
Karen Hyer (D)	44,320	22.9%
Douglas Sligting (CNSTP)	4,596	2.4%
Jake Shannon (LIBERT)	2,945	1.5%

2010 PRIMARY

Jason Chaffetz (R)	unopposed

2008 GENERAL

Jason Chaffetz (R)	187,035	65.6%
Bennion L. Spencer (D)	80,626	28.3%
Jim Noorlander (CNSTP)	17,408	6.1%

Elected 2008; 2nd term

Chaffetz is a fiscal conservative who wants a smaller government that plays less of a role in the lives of "over-regulated and overtaxed" Americans. Energetic and ambitious, he has evinced an interest in a potential Senate candidacy.

Chaffetz (CHAY-fits) addresses his concerns not only from the Budget Committee but also from the Oversight and Government Reform panel, a post he sought so he could stress accountability for government spending. "Washington is not known for shrinking," he said.

As top Republican on Oversight's Federal Workforce, Postal Service and the District of Columbia Subcommittee in the 111th Congress (2009-10), Chaffetz took a keen interest in the 2010 census. In April 2010, he derided claims by Commerce Department officials that the latest census, which cost $14.7 billion, was saving money compared with the 2000 count, which cost $6.5 billion to count 10 percent fewer people. "If you look at 2000 and 2010, based on what was initially mailed back in, we got exactly the same result," he said.

A member of the conservative Republican Study Committee, Chaffetz wants to abolish the Education Department and says the Medicare prescription drug benefit and No Child Left Behind education law were "bad ideas." He opposed President Obama's $787 billion economic stimulus law and the health care overhaul enacted in March 2010.

In June 2009, he and Texas Republican Kevin Brady formed a Sunset Caucus of 46 Republicans seeking to identify and cut "wasteful government programs" during the annual appropriations process.

He opposed the compromise spending measure for the second half of fiscal 2011, arguing that the bill's cuts didn't go far enough.

"We're $1.6 trillion in deficit this year. We went from an $8.67 trillion debt to over $14 trillion in the last 48 months, a 60 percent rise in our debt," he said on CNN. "To me, that means you have to cut spending. And the $38 billion, $39 billion just wasn't enough.

He praised the House Republican spending outline for fiscal 2012 produced by Budget Chairman Paul D. Ryan of Wisconsin that proposed $4 trillion in cuts over 10 years.

"The cuts are important because we need to be on a trajectory to actually maintain the fiscal sanity that is in this country," Chaffetz said.

Now chairman of the Oversight and Government Reform Subcommittee on National Security, Homeland Defense and Foreign Operations, Chaffetz has an ambition to serve on the Intelligence Committee. He has sought opportunities to increase his knowledge of foreign policy by traveling abroad. In his first six months in office, according to The Salt Lake Tribune, he test-drove an armored vehicle in Iraq, played ping-pong with airmen in Afghanistan, toured the prison at Guantánamo Bay, Cuba, and met with the chancellor of Germany.

In November 2009, as Obama was preparing to unveil a troop increase and new strategy for Afghanistan, Chaffetz said it was time to end U.S. involvement. Breaking with his party on the war, he said, was "one of the most difficult decisions I made during my freshman year."

In 2011, he expressed reservations about the United States intervening in the violence in Libya, particularly without a vote by Congress.

Chaffetz sparked a bit of controversy with comments he made in February 2010 that seemed to suggest some sympathy for the idea that the Sept. 11 terrorist attacks on the World Trade Center were an inside job. "I know there's still a lot to learn about what happened and what didn't happen," he said. But he quickly backed away, issuing a statement saying, "I am not sympathetic to claims that 9/11 was a government conspiracy. I have never believed the government was in any way complicit or responsible for those attacks."

Chaffetz is one of the few members of the Judiciary Committee who is not a lawyer. But one of the issues that propelled him to victory in his 2008 primary win over incumbent Chris Cannon was his more conservative stance on illegal immigration. Chaffetz opposes any legislation that would offer a path toward citizenship for illegal immigrants.

Born in Los Gatos, Calif., Chaffetz grew up in California, Arizona and Colorado. He went to Utah in the mid-1980s to play football at Brigham Young University, where he was a placekicker. Chaffetz's father's first wife was Kitty Dickson, who later married Massachusetts Gov. Michael S. Dukakis. While in college, Chaffetz — then a Democrat — was a Utah co-chairman of Dukakis' 1988 presidential campaign.

After college, he worked 11 years for Nu Skin Enterprises, most of that time as a spokesman. He also worked part-time for a few years as a sports reporter, producer, editor and anchor for KUTV. He and his brother then formed a corporate communications and marketing firm, Maxtera Inc., before Chaffetz went into politics full time.

Inspired by President Ronald Reagan, Chaffetz became a Republican after college and continued to dabble in politics, including a stint as a volunteer in Chris Cannon's 1996 House bid. He worked on Jon Huntsman Jr.'s gubernatorial campaign in 2003 — first as communications director, then as campaign manager. When Huntsman won in 2004, he named Chaffetz as his chief of staff. Chaffetz stepped down after less than a year, citing desires to make more money and spend more time with his family. Rumors circulated that state legislators had complained that he barred access to the governor and was too inexperienced for the job.

Chaffetz considered a run for Congress in 2004 against 2nd District Democrat Jim Matheson but decided against it. Instead, he took on Cannon in 2008, and easily defeated him in the GOP primary before trouncing Democratic journalist and professor Bennion L. Spencer in November. He was easily re-elected in 2010.

After three-term GOP Sen. Robert F. Bennett failed to win renomination at Utah Republicans' state convention in May 2010, Chaffetz said he might consider challenging six-term Republican Sen. Orrin G. Hatch in 2012. "I respect everything that Sen. Hatch has done, but the question is whether 36 years in the U.S. Senate might be enough," he told the Salt Lake Tribune in May 2010.

Key Votes

2010

Overhaul the nation's health insurance system	NO
Allow for repeal of "don't ask, don't tell"	NO
Overhaul financial services industry regulation	NO
Limit use of new Afghanistan War funds to troop withdrawal activities	YES
Change oversight of offshore drilling and lift oil spill liability cap	NO
Provide a path to legal status for some children of illegal immigrants	NO
Extend Bush-era income tax cuts for two years	NO

2009

Expand the Children's Health Insurance Program	NO
Provide $787 billion in tax cuts and spending increases to stimulate the economy	NO
Allow bankruptcy judges to modify certain primary-residence mortgages	NO
Create a cap-and-trade system to limit greenhouse gas emissions	NO
Provide $2 billion for the "cash for clunkers" program	NO
Establish the government as the sole provider of student loans	NO
Restrict federally funded insurance coverage for abortions in health care overhaul	YES

CQ Vote Studies

	PARTY UNITY		PRESIDENTIAL SUPPORT	
	Support	Oppose	Support	Oppose
2010	93%	7%	21%	79%
2009	96%	4%	11%	89%

Interest Groups

	AFL-CIO	ADA	CCUS	ACU
2010	0%	10%	75%	100%
2009	5%	0%	80%	100%

Utah 3

Central — part of Salt Lake County, Provo

Utah's centrally located 3rd District takes in some Salt Lake City suburbs and then follows Interstate 15 south to Provo and Orem, the district's economic hubs. It stretches west to pick up rural Millard and Beaver counties on the state's western border. A heavily Mormon-influenced district, the 3rd has the nation's lowest median age (25.4).

Salt Lake County's residents, in the northernmost tip of the district, make up slightly less than half of the 3rd's population. West Valley City, in Salt Lake County, hosts most of the district's Asian residents, and the county's Hispanic population has skyrocketed. After a decade of population growth, mainly in Utah County around the Orem and Provo nexus, the 3rd ranks as one of the nation's fastest-growing districts and is the sixth most-populous district ahead of decennial remapping.

Provo's predominately Mormon Brigham Young University, founded by its namesake in 1875, is one of the state's largest employers. Students and graduates from BYU and other district colleges continue to lure businesses to the Provo-Orem area. Some big-name software firms maintain key facilities here, and companies in the dietary supplement industry have headquarters in the 3rd.

Outside Utah and Salt Lake counties, cattle ranching, farming, mining and tourism sustain small-town life. Ranchers in Millard County and hog farmers in Beaver County tend to vote Republican, but some former mining communities like Magna, which now hosts aerospace manufacturers, will support Democratic candidates.

Overall, the district has a heavy GOP tilt, and John McCain received 67 percent of the 3rd's vote in the 2008 presidential election, his best showing in the state.

Major Industry
Technology, mining, higher education, ranching

Cities
West Valley City, 129,480; Provo, 112,488; West Jordan, 103,712; Orem, 88,328; Taylorsville, 58,652; South Jordan (pt.), 50,418

Notable
Philo T. Farnsworth, credited with inventing television, lived in Provo; Millard County, and its county seat Fillmore, are named after the 13th president.

Grand Isle

Franklin

Orleans

Essex

Lamoille

● **Burlington**

Caledonia

Chittenden

MONTPELIER
☆

Washington

● **Barre**

Addison

Orange

At Large

Rutland
●

Windsor

Rutland

Bennington

Windham

● **Bennington**

● **Brattleboro**

Gov. Peter Shumlin (D)

First elected: 2010
Length of term: 2 years
Term expires: 1/13
Salary: $142,542
Phone: (802) 828-3333
Residence: Putney
Born: March 24, 1956; Brattleboro, Vt.
Religion: Unspecified
Family: Separated; two children
Education: Wesleyan U., B.A. 1979 (government)
Career: Travel organization director; dairy farm owner
Political highlights: Putney Board of Selectmen, 1983-90 (chairman, 1983-90); Vt. House, 1989-93; Vt. Senate, 1993-2003 (minority leader, 1995-96; president pro tempore, 1997-2003); Democratic nominee for lieutenant governor, 2002; Vt. Senate, 2007-11 (president pro tempore, 2007-11)

ELECTION RESULTS

2010 GENERAL
Peter Shumlin (D)	119,543	49.5%
Brian E. Dubie (R)	115,212	47.7%
Others	6,850	2.8%

Lt. Gov. Phil Scott (R)

First elected: 2010
Length of term: 2 years
Term expires: 1/13
Salary: $60,507
Phone: (802) 828-2226

LEGISLATURE

General Assembly: January-April
Senate: 30 members, 2-year terms
2011 ratios: 22 D, 8 R; 19 men, 11 women
Salary: $605/week
Phone: (802) 828-2241
House: 150 members, 2-year terms
2011 ratios: 94 D, 48 R, 5 PRO, 3 I; 93 men, 57 women
Salary: $605/week
Phone: (802) 828-2247

TERM LIMITS

Governor: No
Senate: No
House: No

URBAN STATISTICS

CITY	POPULATION
Burlington	42,417
Essex	19,587
South Burlington	17,904
Colchester	17,067
Rutland	16,495

REGISTERED VOTERS

Voters do not register by party.

POPULATION

2010 population	625,741
2000 population	608,827
1990 population	562,758
Percent change (2000-2010)	+2.8%
Rank among states (2010)	49
Median age	40.6
Born in state	52.2%
Foreign born	3.7%
Violent crime rate	131/100,000
Poverty level	11.4%
Federal workers	6,917
Military	565

ELECTIONS

STATE ELECTION OFFICIAL
(802) 828-2464
DEMOCRATIC PARTY
(802) 229-1783
REPUBLICAN PARTY
(802) 223-3411

MISCELLANEOUS

Web: www.vermont.gov
Capital: Montpelier

U.S. CONGRESS

Senate: 1 Democrat, 1 independent
House: 1 Democrat

2010 Census Statistics by District

District	2008 Vote for President Obama	McCain	White	Black	Asian	Hispanic	Median Income	White Collar	Blue Collar	Service Industry	Over 64	Under 18	College Education	Rural	Sq. Miles
AL	67%	30%	94%	1%	1%	1%	$51,284	62%	22%	17%	14%	21%	33%	62%	9,250
STATE	67	30	94	1	1	1	51,284	62	22	17	14	21	33	62	9,250
U.S.	53	46	64	12	5	16	51,425	60	23	17	13	25	28	21	3,537,438

Sen. Patrick J. Leahy (D)

Capitol Office
224-4242
leahy.senate.gov
437 Russell Bldg. 20510-4502; fax 224-3479

Committees
Agriculture, Nutrition & Forestry
Appropriations
(State-Foreign Operations - Chairman)
Judiciary - Chairman
Rules & Administration
Joint Library

Residence
Middlesex

Born
March 31, 1940; Montpelier, Vt.

Religion
Roman Catholic

Family
Wife, Marcelle Leahy; three children

Education
St. Michael's College, B.A. 1961 (political science);
Georgetown U., J.D. 1964

Career
Lawyer

Political Highlights
Chittenden County state's attorney, 1966-75

ELECTION RESULTS

2010 GENERAL

Patrick J. Leahy (D)	151,281	64.3%
Len Britton (R)	72,699	30.9%
Daniel Freilich (I)	3,544	1.5%
Cris Ericson (USM)	2,731	1.2%
Stephen J. Cain (I)	2,356	1.0%

2010 PRIMARY

Patrick J. Leahy (D)	64,515	89.1%
Daniel Freilich (D)	7,892	10.9%

2004 GENERAL

Patrick J. Leahy (D)	216,972	70.6%
John "Jack" McMullen (R)	75,398	24.5%
Cris Ericson (M)	6,486	2.1%
Craig Barclay Hill (GREEN)	3,999	1.3%
Keith Stern (I)	3,300	1.1%

Previous Winning Percentages
1998 (72%); 1992 (54%); 1986 (63%); 1980 (50%);
1974 (50%)

Elected 1974; 7th term

Leahy's wry humor and partisan stubbornness help him survive and prosper as chairman of the Judiciary Committee, home to some of the most ferocious ideological battles in Congress. He is a staunch defender of civil liberties and helped win the confirmations of President Obama's first two picks for the Supreme Court.

Leahy is second in seniority among Senate Democrats. His political longevity allows him to pursue multiple policy interests — including overhauling federal patent law, promoting his version of balancing security and liberty, and boosting foreign aid.

In the 111th Congress (2009-10), he spent much of his time working to get Sonia Sotomayor and Elena Kagan confirmed as justices on the U.S. Supreme Court. Now in his seventh term, Leahy has been on the Judiciary panel since 1979 and has participated in confirmation hearings for every sitting justice.

He tried to deflect criticism of Sotomayor's statement that because of her experiences, she felt that a "wise Latina" could reach better conclusions than a white man. At the hearings, Leahy sought to direct attention instead toward her judicial record, praising her as a "restrained, experienced and thoughtful judge." Sotomayor was confirmed easily in August 2009.

Nearly a year later, Leahy ushered Kagan — a former Harvard Law School dean — through the confirmation process. A longtime proponent of looking beyond federal appellate courts for Supreme Court nominees, Leahy defended Kagan against critics who questioned her qualifications. Confirmed in August 2010, Kagan had not previously served as a judge of any kind.

Leahy occasionally draws criticism from Democratic allies who say he is too accommodating, particularly on GOP judicial nominations. He caught a lot of flak from liberal groups in 2005 for his support of John G. Roberts Jr., President George W. Bush's nominee for chief justice. But Leahy later opposed conservative Supreme Court nominee Samuel A. Alito Jr., and was part of a quixotic filibuster attempt by Massachusetts Democrats John Kerry and Edward M. Kennedy.

As one of the most partisan places on Capitol Hill, the Judiciary Committee routinely features quarrels over lower-court nominees as well as Supreme Court picks. As has been the case for more than a decade, during the 111th Congress the panel saw numerous lower court nominees it had approved in partisan votes blocked from consideration on the floor — the minority refuses to let the nominees be quickly confirmed, and the majority leadership refuses to devote precious floor time to fighting through procedural thickets.

An ardent defender of Obama's nominees, Leahy has accused Republicans of engaging in a "pattern of obstruction and delay" — the same charge that he and fellow Democrats faced when blocking Bush's judicial nominees. In April 2010, Leahy threatened to keep the Senate in session overnight and through weekends if necessary to clear a backlog. "Republicans used to contend that any nomination reported by the committee was entitled to an up-or-down vote [on the floor]," said Leahy, who consistently rejected that argument when he was in the minority. "That was then, I guess, and this is now."

Legislatively, an overhaul of federal patent law has been at the top of Leahy's agenda, and in March 2011 he won Senate passage of his measure, which would implement a system to grant patents to inventors who are "first to file" rather than to those who are "first to invent," which is the current criterion.

Proponents of Leahy's legislation argue that it will simplify the process and reduce the number of legal challenges. The measure also would allow the

Patent and Trademark Office to set fees for applicants, and to keep all the revenue it generates.

Leahy was Judiciary chairman during the Sept. 11 terrorist attacks, and he had a hand in writing the first major legislation enacted in response, the 2001 anti-terrorism law known as the Patriot Act, which expanded law enforcement powers to investigate suspected terrorists. Leahy worked to modify the measure, warning that it infringed on civil liberties. "As draconian as it was, the terrorism bill was far more constitutional than it would have been had I not been chairman," he said.

He backs an extension of the law that would, in his view, provide more safeguards for civil liberties by imposing a stricter standard for seeking information in an investigation, setting a tougher standard for access to library and bookseller records, and putting further restrictions on the government's use of national security letters — secret demands for information or data — in counterterrorism investigations.

Leahy opposed the U.S. invasion of Iraq and was a frequent critic of Bush's conduct of the war and of related policies in the war on terror. He didn't relent after Bush's departure: In February 2009, he proposed a "truth commission" to investigate topics such as detainee and interrogation policies, the war in Iraq, and the hiring and firing of U.S. attorneys.

As chairman of the Appropriations subcommittee in charge of the State Department's budget, he has sought to increase spending for humanitarian efforts overseas and was highly critical of the plan developed by House Budget Chairman Paul D. Ryan of Wisconsin to trim foreign assistance.

"It's a reckless proposal that would endanger Americans here and abroad, and severely weaken U.S. global leadership," Leahy told Foreign Policy's The Cable blog in April 2011.

Leahy also looks out for the interests of his rural state. A member of the Agriculture, Nutrition and Forestry Committee, he is a defender of Northeastern dairy farmers during conflicts with other dairy-producing regions. In 2008, he engineered the renewal of the Milk Income Loss Contract Program, a price-support subsidy for dairy farmers. He also works on internal Senate issues as a member of the Rules and Administration Committee.

In his 70s, Leahy remains plugged into pop culture and technology. He is a devotee of the bands the Grateful Dead and Phish, as well as a fan of Batman. He and his son had cameos in the 1997 film "Batman and Robin," and Leahy had another Batman movie cameo in "The Dark Knight" in 2008. An avid photographer, he has taken his camera all over the world and had his work published in newspapers and magazines.

Leahy's father was an Irish-American who ran a printing business in Montpelier out of the same building that housed the family. When he walked to school, Leahy went by — and sometimes through — the state Capitol, and his mother rented rooms to state lawmakers when the legislature was in session. His mother's family — Italian immigrants — worked in Vermont's granite quarries.

Leahy's first exposure to the Senate was in the early 1960s when he was a student at Georgetown Law School. Aiming to be a prosecutor or a U.S. senator, he ended up doing both, serving as a local prosecutor for eight years before being elected to the Senate in 1974 when a Watergate-fueled voter backlash helped him beat a favored Republican. At 34, he was the youngest elected senator in state history. He withstood the GOP landslide of 1980 to win his first re-election by just 2,500 votes. That close call lured former GOP Gov. Richard A. Snelling out of retirement to challenge him six years later. But by then Leahy was well-financed and comfortably entrenched, and Vermont's electorate was increasingly Democratic. He won with 63 percent of the vote and has coasted to re-election each time since.

Key Votes

2010

Pass budget reconciliation bill to modify overhauls of health care and federal student loan programs	YES
Proceed to disapproval resolution on EPA authority to regulate greenhouse gases	NO
Overhaul financial services industry regulation	YES
Limit debate to proceed to a bill to broaden campaign finance disclosure and reporting rules	YES
Limit debate on an extension of Bush-era income tax cuts for two years	NO
Limit debate on a bill to provide a path to legal status for some children of illegal immigrants	YES
Allow for a repeal of "don't ask, don't tell"	YES
Consent to ratification of a strategic arms reduction treaty with Russia	YES

2009

Prevent release of remaining financial industry bailout funds	NO
Make it easier for victims to sue for wage discrimination remedies	YES
Expand the Children's Health Insurance Program	YES
Limit debate on the economic stimulus measure	YES
Repeal District of Columbia firearms prohibitions and gun registration laws	NO
Limit debate on expansion of federal hate crimes law	YES
Strike funding for F-22 Raptor fighter jets	YES

CQ Vote Studies

	PARTY UNITY		PRESIDENTIAL SUPPORT	
	SUPPORT	OPPOSE	SUPPORT	OPPOSE
2010	100%	0%	98%	2%
2009	98%	2%	96%	4%
2008	98%	2%	30%	70%
2007	95%	5%	35%	65%
2006	97%	3%	46%	54%
2005	97%	3%	36%	64%
2004	94%	6%	58%	42%
2003	97%	3%	51%	49%
2002	98%	2%	67%	33%
2001	98%	2%	62%	38%

Interest Groups

	AFL-CIO	ADA	CCUS	ACU
2010	100%	100%	0%	0%
2009	100%	95%	43%	8%
2008	100%	100%	50%	4%
2007	100%	95%	36%	0%
2006	93%	95%	33%	0%
2005	86%	100%	28%	0%
2004	100%	100%	50%	8%
2003	85%	85%	35%	16%
2002	100%	95%	55%	0%
2001	100%	100%	38%	8%

Sen. Bernard Sanders (I)

Capitol Office
224-5141
sanders.senate.gov
332 Dirksen Bldg. 20510-4503; fax 228-0776

Committees
Budget
Energy & Natural Resources
Environment & Public Works
(Green Jobs & the New Economy - Chairman)
Health, Education, Labor & Pensions
(Primary Health & Aging - Chairman)
Veterans' Affairs
Joint Economic

Residence
Burlington

Born
Sept. 8, 1941; Brooklyn, N.Y.

Religion
Jewish

Family
Wife, Jane O'Meara Sanders; four children

Education
Brooklyn College, attended 1959-60; U. of Chicago,
B.A. 1964 (political science)

Career
College instructor; freelance writer; documentary
filmmaker; carpenter

Political Highlights
Liberty Union candidate for U.S. Senate, 1972; Liberty
Union candidate for governor, 1972; Liberty Union candidate for U.S. Senate, 1974; Liberty Union candidate
for governor, 1976; mayor of Burlington, 1981-89; independent candidate for governor, 1986; independent
candidate for U.S. House, 1988; U.S. House, 1991-2007

ELECTION RESULTS

2006 GENERAL

Bernard Sanders (I)	171,638	65.4%
Rich Tarrant (R)	84,924	32.4%

2006 PRIMARY

Bernard Sanders (D)	35,954	94.2%
others	2,232	5.8%

Previous Winning Percentages
2004 House Election (68%); 2002 House Election (64%);
2000 House Election (69%); 1998 House Election (63%);
1996 House Election (55%); 1994 House Election (50%);
1992 House Election (58%); 1990 House Election (56%)

Elected 2006; 1st term

After 16 years as a self-described "outsider in the House," Sanders is enjoy-ing his newfound clout as a first-term senator. The Vermont independent, who caucuses with the Democrats but identifies himself as a socialist, might have tempered his behavior to the Senate's more collegial atmosphere, but he remains a passionate and provocative defender of liberal causes.

On two of the major Democratic initiatives in the 111th Congress (2009-10) — the health care overhaul and financial services regulation — Sanders worked to push the debate to the left. But, on both occasions, he supported the final bills, calling each of them an important "step forward."

During the health care debate, Sanders offered an amendment that would have established a "single-payer, Medicare-for-all health care system," some-thing he had advocated for years. Sanders acknowledged that his proposal would "not pass or even get very many votes," but he regarded the debate as a historic milestone. He was infuriated, however, when his amendment became a tool for stalling the debate rather than moving it forward. When the measure went to the Senate floor in December 2009, Oklahoma Republican Tom Coburn objected to a routine motion to waive a reading of the amend-ment. By forcing the entire 767-page amendment to be read aloud, Coburn used precious floor time as Democrats rushed to pass legislation before the holiday recess. After three hours, Sanders withdrew his amendment and put an end to the read-a-thon. In a fiery floor speech he said, "Everybody in this country understands that our nation faces a significant number of major crises . . . and the best the Republicans can do is try to bring the United States gov-ernment to a halt by forcing a reading of a 700-page amendment."

Sanders, who often rails against Wall Street and decries the gap between rich and poor, won inclusion of an amendment in the 2010 financial services regulatory overhaul that requires the Federal Reserve to release information about the loans it made during the financial crisis that unfolded in 2008. The same amendment also charges the Government Accountability Office with conducting an audit of the Federal Reserve. Though Sanders adamantly defended the public's "right to know where their hard-earned taxpayer dollars are going," he did agree to soften his amendment's provisions at the urging of Federal Reserve Chairman Ben S. Bernanke.

As the only member of the Democratic Caucus to serve on both the Ener-gy and Natural Resources Committee and the Environment and Public Works Committee, Sanders is a major player on environmental issues. He was a voice of outrage following the April 2010 explosion of an offshore oil rig that result-ed in a massive spill in the Gulf of Mexico. He cosponsored legislation that would retroactively eliminate a liability cap for such spills. He introduced another bill that would ban all future offshore drilling. Echoing President Obama, Sanders also tried to tie the spill to a need for broader changes in energy policy, saying on MSNBC: "If there's any silver lining to this absolute, horrendous environmental disaster, I hope it is that the American people . . . understand not only that we've got to terminate offshore oil drilling, but that we have to transform our energy system away from fossil fuel into energy efficiency and sustainable energy."

In 2009 he was named chairman of the Environment and Public Works panel on Green Jobs and the New Economy and said he would continue working to boost renewable energy sources and new job opportunities, including Vermont-based weatherization and solar projects. Sanders and then-Democratic Sen. Hillary Rodham Clinton of New York successfully included in a 2007 energy bill a $125 million authorization to train workers in "green-collar jobs."

Sanders also sits on the Veterans' Affairs and Health, Education, Labor and Pensions committees, where he has promoted increased federal spending on higher education. During the 110th Congress (2007-08), he cosponsored with Virginia Democrat Jim Webb a new GI Bill to provide up to $90,000 to cover tuition at colleges in a veteran's home state.

And he helped obtain funding for a Vermont program that attempts to send a specialist to the home of every veteran returning from Iraq or Afghanistan, offering treatment for post-traumatic stress disorder, traumatic brain injuries and other mental health issues.

Sanders, a member of the Budget Committee, was one of four members of the Senate Democratic Caucus to oppose the final version of the catchall bill passed halfway through fiscal 2011 that trimmed $40 billion from the year's spending. "This budget is Robin Hood in reverse," he said. "It takes from struggling working families and gives to multimillionaires."

Sanders has long described himself as a socialist and defends against any negative connotation of the term. When Alabama GOP Rep. Spencer Bachus said in April 2009 that he could count 17 socialists in Congress, Sanders responded with an opinion column in The Boston Globe: "Spencer Bachus is one of the few people I know from Alabama. I bet I'm the only socialist he knows, although he darkly claims there are 17 socialists lurking in the House of Representatives. I doubt there are any other socialists, let alone 17 more, in all of Congress. I also doubt that Bachus understands much about democratic socialism." Sanders, the first self-identified socialist in the House since Wisconsin's Victor L. Berger served four terms early in the 20th century, keeps a plaque on his office wall honoring Eugene V. Debs, the founder of the American Socialist Party.

Sanders was born and raised in the New York City borough of Brooklyn. His mother died at 46 when he was 19. His father, a Jewish immigrant from Poland whose family was killed in the Holocaust, was a paint salesman.

After college, Sanders lived on a kibbutz in Israel. He returned briefly to New York, then in 1968 joined the wave of liberals abandoning urban life for pastoral Vermont. Sanders held a variety of jobs in the Green Mountain State, from freelance writer to carpenter, and built a foundation in left-wing politics.

While other transplants flocked to the Democratic Party, Sanders helped found the Liberty Union Party. He ran unsuccessfully for statewide office four times in the early 1970s. He then focused on local office and in 1981 unseated the Democratic mayor of Burlington by 10 votes. He became the city's first socialist mayor and won three more two-year terms by pursuing populist goals while presiding over the revitalization of the city's downtown.

Sanders was seen as a spoiler when he ran in 1988 for Vermont's lone House seat, vacated when Republican James M. Jeffords ran for the Senate. But Sanders lost to Republican Peter Smith by only 4 percentage points. In a 1990 rematch, Sanders won with 56 percent of the vote.

Sanders barely held on during the national Republican wave of 1994. In 2000, he captured the highest total of his House career with 69 percent of the vote.

When Jeffords announced plans to retire from the Senate, Sanders jumped in to the race. Campaigning as a Democrat, he had no trouble beating four political unknowns in the primary, then ran as an independent in the general election. His Republican rival, software magnate Rich Tarrant, spent $7 million of his own money and tried to paint Sanders as a radical, but Sanders won with 65 percent of the vote. He enjoyed the financial backing of the Democratic Senatorial Campaign Committee headed by New York Sen. Charles E. Schumer, who had attended the same schools as Sanders in Brooklyn.

Key Votes

2010

Pass budget reconciliation bill to modify overhauls of health care and federal student loan programs	YES
Proceed to disapproval resolution on EPA authority to regulate greenhouse gases	NO
Overhaul financial services industry regulation	YES
Limit debate to proceed to a bill to broaden campaign finance disclosure and reporting rules	YES
Limit debate on an extension of Bush-era income tax cuts for two years	NO
Limit debate on a bill to provide a path to legal status for some children of illegal immigrants	YES
Allow for a repeal of "don't ask, don't tell"	YES
Consent to ratification of a strategic arms reduction treaty with Russia	YES

2009

Prevent release of remaining financial industry bailout funds	YES
Make it easier for victims to sue for wage discrimination remedies	YES
Expand the Children's Health Insurance Program	YES
Limit debate on the economic stimulus measure	YES
Repeal District of Columbia firearms prohibitions and gun registration laws	NO
Limit debate on expansion of federal hate crimes law	YES
Strike funding for F-22 Raptor fighter jets	YES

CQ Vote Studies

	PARTY UNITY		PRESIDENTIAL SUPPORT	
	SUPPORT	OPPOSE	SUPPORT	OPPOSE
2010	99%	1%	95%	5%
2009	97%	3%	86%	14%
2008	98%	2%	30%	70%
2007	97%	3%	33%	67%
2006	98%	2%	15%	85%
2005	97%	3%	15%	85%
2004	98%	2%	29%	71%
2003	95%	5%	15%	85%
2002	98%	2%	18%	82%
2001	97%	3%	16%	84%

Interest Groups

	AFL-CIO	ADA	CCUS	ACU
2010	100%	95%	0%	4%
2009	100%	100%	29%	12%
2008	100%	100%	38%	8%
2007	100%	95%	27%	4%
2006	100%	100%	27%	8%
2005	93%	100%	33%	8%
2004	100%	95%	30%	4%
2003	100%	100%	14%	20%
2002	100%	95%	16%	0%
2001	100%	100%	22%	8%

Rep. Peter Welch (D)

Capitol Office
225-4115
welch.house.gov
1404 Longworth Bldg. 20515-4501; fax 225-6790

Committees
Agriculture
Oversight & Government Reform

Residence
Hartland

Born
May 2, 1947; Springfield, Mass.

Religion
Roman Catholic

Family
Wife, Margaret Cheney; eight children

Education
College of the Holy Cross, A.B. 1969 (history); U. of
California, Berkeley, J.D. 1973

Career
Lawyer; county public defender

Political Highlights
Vt. Senate, 1981-89 (minority leader, 1983-85;
president pro tempore, 1985-89); sought Democratic nomination for U.S. House, 1988; Democratic
nominee for governor, 1990; Vt. Senate, 2002-06
(president pro tempore, 2003-06)

ELECTION RESULTS

2010 GENERAL

Peter Welch (D)	154,006	64.6%
Paul D. Beaudry (R)	76,403	32.0%
Gus Jaccaci (I)	4,704	2.0%
Jane Newton (S)	3,222	1.4%

2010 PRIMARY

Peter Welch (D)	unopposed

2008 GENERAL

Peter Welch (D)	248,203	83.2%
Mike Bethel (I)	14,349	4.8%
Jerry Trudell (EINDC)	10,818	3.6%
Thomas Hermann (PRO)	9,081	3.0%
Cris Ericson (I)	7,841	2.6%
Jane Newton (LU)	5,307	1.8%

Previous Winning Percentages
2006 (53%)

Elected 2006; 3rd term

Welch personifies the widely held perception of the modern Vermonter: liberal in outlook, a transplant to the state, possessed of an activist past, and holding an abiding love for nature.

Beyond the stereotype of the anti-establishment 1960s-style community organizer that Welch once was, he's a loyal Democrat who almost always votes the party line and was named a chief deputy whip in the 112th Congress (2011-12).

But he lost his seat on the Energy and Commerce Committee, a victim of the 2010 elections that trimmed the Democrats' numbers on the powerful panel from 36 to 23.

During his one term on the panel, Welch was a voice of outrage in hearings on the April 20, 2010, oil spill in the Gulf of Mexico. "We were told that what could never happen did happen. We were told that, if the unimaginable happened, we had a fail-safe mechanism that would make certain there would be no harm. And of course, the tragedy is that these assurances prove wrong," he said at a hearing shortly after the BP oil disaster.

In June 2010, Welch and about four dozen other lawmakers signed a letter to the chief executive officer of BP demanding that the oil company suspend payment of its dividend until it had paid for the cleanup.

In 2009, Welch pushed a bill to encourage the retrofitting of homes and government buildings to boost energy efficiency by 20 percent or more. The initiative was partly inspired by Efficiency Vermont, the nation's first statewide provider of energy efficiency services. Welch also sponsored legislation that would give thousands of dollars in rebates to people who renovate their homes with energy-saving windows and doors.

Welch serves on the Oversight and Government Reform Committee, and in 2010 his office became the first in the Longworth House Office Building to undergo House-wide energy efficiency upgrades, which included the installation of special toilets and lights. After he discovered that every year his two offices produce 56 tons of carbon dioxide, he began spending personal money to make them carbon neutral. (Congressional rules prohibit members from spending office funds for such purposes.) Welch offsets the greenhouse gas emissions related to his office activities by paying a carbon-offset provider in Vermont.

As the state's lone voice in the House, Welch addresses a broad swath of local issues. He joined the Agriculture Committee in the 112th Congress, finding a spot from which he can serve the interests of the dairy farmers and other agriculture concerns important to the Green Mountain State's economy. During debate on the 2008 reauthorization of farm programs, Welch pushed proposals to help small family farms compete against larger corporate operations. The measure is due to be reauthorized in the new Congress.

Welch has also worked to expand broadband access to rural areas, which he likens in its significance to rural electrification during President Franklin D. Roosevelt's administration.

Welch served on the House ethics panel in the 111th Congress (2009-10), where he became involved in a high-profile investigation of Ways and Means Chairman Charles B. Rangel's financial dealings. In early 2009, Welch returned political contributions he had received from the New York Democrat and his political action committee.

Welch grew up in Springfield, Mass., the third of six children in an Irish Catholic family. His father was a dentist and his mother a homemaker. He attended Cathedral Catholic High School, where he received the school's scholar athlete award after helping his team win the 1964 and 1965 city championships in basketball — a significant event in the city where the game was invented.

In 1965, Welch enrolled at the nearby College of the Holy Cross, which his father and three other siblings also attended. But after getting caught up in the political and social turmoil of the time, he moved to Chicago, where he worked on housing discrimination.

Welch went home briefly, then back to Chicago at the height of the Vietnam War and civil rights protests throughout the country. He continued his community work while taking a few classes at Loyola University.

Welch eventually returned to Holy Cross, graduating magna cum laude in 1969 with a degree in history. He then returned to Chicago, this time as an inaugural Robert F. Kennedy Fellow, and spent 1970 resuming his work for the Contract Buyers' League, which fought against discriminatory housing policies.

After earning a law degree at the University of California at Berkeley in 1973, Welch spent six months backpacking the Pan-American Highway from Berkeley to Santiago, Chile. Back in the United States, Welch went to work in private practice in White River Junction, Vt. His future wife, Joan Smith, was a sociology professor at Dartmouth College, just across the Connecticut River. They married in 1976.

He entered politics in 1981, becoming the second Democrat ever elected to represent Windsor County in the state Senate. In 1982, he was elected minority leader, and in 1984 led his party as it took over the majority for the first time in history. He was elected president pro tempore for two terms before making a failed bid for Congress in 1988.

After running unsuccessfully for governor in 1990, Welch went behind the scenes in politics while working in a law firm and caring for his wife, who was diagnosed with cancer in the mid-1990s. She died in 2004. (Welch remarried in January 2009, to Margaret Cheney, a state representative.)

Welch supported Democrat Howard Dean's gubernatorial re-election bid in 2000 and was awarded with an appointment to the state Senate, where he again became president pro tempore in 2003. Welch then served as an adviser to Dean's unsuccessful presidential campaign in 2004.

When independent Rep. Bernard Sanders left open his seat in 2006 for what would prove to be a successful Senate bid, Welch was the choice to face GOP nominee Martha Rainville, the state's adjutant general. Welch won with 53 percent of the vote. He's been re-elected by wide margins twice.

Key Votes

2010

Overhaul the nation's health insurance system	YES
Allow for repeal of "don't ask, don't tell"	YES
Overhaul financial services industry regulation	YES
Limit use of new Afghanistan War funds to troop withdrawal activities	YES
Change oversight of offshore drilling and lift oil spill liability cap	YES
Provide a path to legal status for some children of illegal immigrants	YES
Extend Bush-era income tax cuts for two years	NO

2009

Expand the Children's Health Insurance Program	YES
Provide $787 billion in tax cuts and spending increases to stimulate the economy	YES
Allow bankruptcy judges to modify certain primary-residence mortgages	YES
Create a cap-and-trade system to limit greenhouse gas emissions	YES
Provide $2 billion for the "cash for clunkers" program	YES
Establish the government as the sole provider of student loans	YES
Restrict federally funded insurance coverage for abortions in health care overhaul	NO

CQ Vote Studies

	PARTY UNITY		PRESIDENTIAL SUPPORT	
	SUPPORT	OPPOSE	SUPPORT	OPPOSE
2010	96%	4%	83%	17%
2009	98%	2%	92%	8%
2008	98%	2%	15%	85%
2007	98%	2%	5%	95%

Interest Groups

	AFL-CIO	ADA	CCUS	ACU
2010	93%	95%	13%	4%
2009	100%	90%	33%	0%
2008	100%	90%	56%	8%
2007	96%	95%	55%	0%

Vermont

At Large

Resting on the shores of Lake Champlain and rolling through the rustic Green Mountains, the nation's second-least-populous state feels like a good, small-town neighbor.

Small businesses and family farms make up the majority of Vermont's workforce. The once-prosperous dairy industry, which still comprises a significant portion of the state's agricultural output, has been hit hard by increased production in the West and volatile demand and pricing trends. The manufacturing sector depends on a few key employers, such as IBM, as well as the arrival of new manufacturers drawn by state incentives. Municipal and statewide budget shortfalls have cast doubt on the stability of government jobs.

Officials also hope to lure tourists, so prevalent on the ski slopes in the winter, to the state year-round. In addition, they continue to attempt to persuade urban dwellers from other states — flatlanders, as they are called here — to buy summer homes, especially in the scenic northeast.

Once a remote rural bastion of Yankee Republicanism, Vermont moved solidly to the left 20 years ago as young liberal urbanites joined the remnants of the late-1960s counterculture settlers. In state and federal races, the strongly progressive voters in Burlington and surrounding Chittenden County — the state's most populous — outvote libertarian conservatives. In some years, the state's liberal Progressive Party and other left-leaning independents have split Democratic voters, occasionally aiding GOP victories.

The state's rural areas, including the Northeast Kingdom, still hold small pockets of GOP votes, but Democrats dominate central Vermont and the southeastern corner.

Many small urban centers, such as Montpelier and Rutland, support Democratic candidates. Republican Gov. Jim Douglas held office for eight years, but Democrat Peter Shumlin narrowly defeated Republican Brian Dubie in 2010.

Major Industry
Manufacturing, dairy farming, tourism

Cities
Burlington, 42,417; South Burlington, 17,904; Rutland, 16,495

Notable
Ben & Jerry's ice cream began in a renovated Burlington gas station.

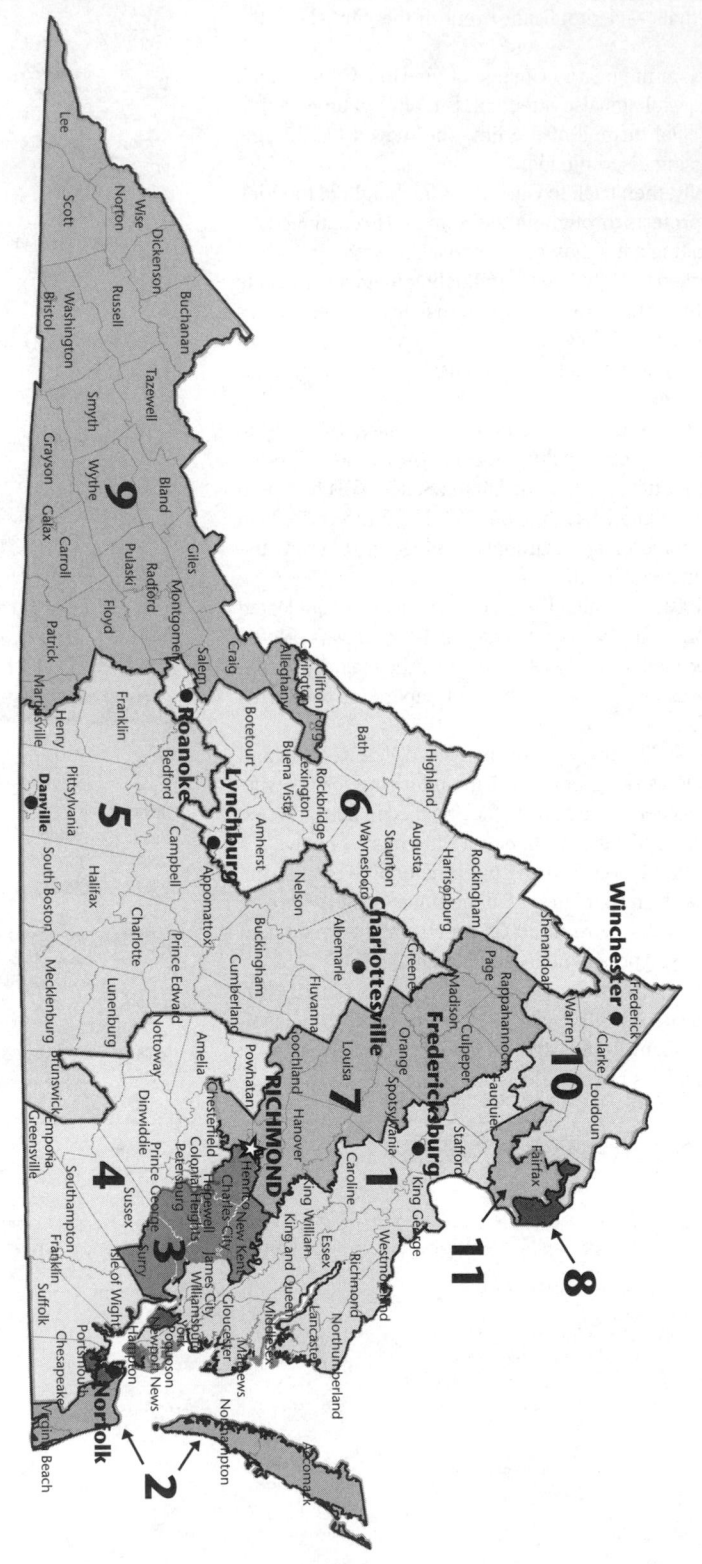

Gov. Bob McDonnell (R)

First elected: 2009
Length of term: 4 years
Term expires: 1/14
Salary: $175,000
Phone: (804) 786-2211
Residence: Glen Allen
Born: June 15, 1954; Philadelphia, Pa.
Religion: Roman Catholic
Family: Wife, Maureen McDonnell; five children
Education: U. of Notre Dame, B.B.A. 1976 (management); Boston U., M.S. 1980 (business administration and management); CBN U., M.A. 1989 (public policy), J.D. 1989
Career: Lawyer; city prosecutor; newspaper sales manager; hospital supply company manager
Political highlights: Va. House, 1991-2005; Va. attorney general, 2006-09

ELECTION RESULTS

2009 GENERAL
Bob McDonnell (R)   1,163,651   58.6%
Creigh Deeds (D)   818,950   41.3%

Lt. Gov. Bill Bolling (R)

First elected: 2005
Length of term: 4 years
Term expires: 1/14
Salary: $36,321
Phone: (804) 786-2078

LEGISLATURE

General Assembly: 60 days January-March in even-numbered years; 40 days January-February in odd-numbered years
Senate: 40 members, 4-year terms
2011 ratios: 22 D, 18 R; 32 men, 8 women
Salary: $17,640
Phone: (804) 698-7410
House: 100 members, 2-year terms
2011 ratios: 59 R, 39 D, 2 I; 81 men, 19 women
Salary: $17,640
Phone: (804) 698-1500

TERM LIMITS

Governor: No consecutive terms
Senate: No
House: No

URBAN STATISTICS

CITY	POPULATION
Virginia Beach	437,994
Norfolk	242,803
Chesapeake	222,209
Richmond	204,214
Newport News	180,719

REGISTERED VOTERS

Voters do not register by party.

POPULATION

2010 population	8,001,024
2000 population	7,078,515
1990 population	6,187,358
Percent change (2000-2010)	+13.0%
Rank among states (2010)	12
Median age	36.7
Born in state	50.5%
Foreign born	9.8%
Violent crime rate	227/100,000
Poverty level	10.5%
Federal workers	289,166
Military	63,160

ELECTIONS

STATE ELECTION OFFICIAL
(804) 864-8901
DEMOCRATIC PARTY
(804) 644-1966
REPUBLICAN PARTY
(804) 780-0111

MISCELLANEOUS

Web: www.virginia.gov
Capital: Richmond

U.S. CONGRESS

Senate: 2 Democrats
House: 8 Republicans, 3 Democrats

2010 Census Statistics by District

District	2008 Vote Obama	McCain	White	Black	Asian	Hispanic	Median Income	White Collar	Blue Collar	Service Industry	Over 64	Under 18	College Education	Rural	Sq. Miles
1	48%	51%	68%	19%	3%	7%	$66,535	64%	20%	16%	12%	25%	31%	36%	3,773
2	50	48	63	21	5	7	58,188	63	20	16	11	24	29	8	961
3	76	24	35	55	2	5	41,493	56	25	20	11	24	20	8	1,118
4	50	49	58	33	2	5	59,137	60	25	15	11	25	23	29	4,489
5	48	51	72	22	2	3	42,522	56	27	17	16	21	21	64	8,922
6	42	57	81	11	1	4	45,913	57	26	16	16	21	24	35	5,647
7	46	53	72	17	4	5	64,474	68	18	14	12	24	37	30	3,514
8	69	30	55	13	11	18	88,124	76	10	13	10	20	60	0	123
9	40	59	92	4	1	2	36,125	52	31	17	16	20	17	66	8,803
10	53	46	64	7	12	13	95,048	72	15	13	8	28	48	17	1,856
11	57	42	55	11	15	16	103,808	74	12	13	9	27	52	4	388
STATE	53	46	65	19	5	8	60,316	64	20	15	12	24	33	27	39,594
U.S.	53	46	64	12	5	16	51,425	60	23	17	13	25	28	21	3,537,438

Sen. Jim Webb (D)

Capitol Office
224-4024
webb.senate.gov
248 Russell Bldg. 20510-4604; fax 228-6363

Committees
Armed Services
(Personnel - Chairman)
Foreign Relations
(East Asian & Pacific Affairs - Chairman)
Veterans' Affairs
Joint Economic

Residence
Falls Church

Born
Feb. 9, 1946; St. Joseph, Mo.

Religion
Protestant

Family
Wife, Hong Le Webb; five children, one stepchild

Education
U. of Southern California, attended 1963-64; U.S.
Naval Academy, B.S. 1968; Georgetown U., J.D. 1975

Military Service
Marine Corps, 1968-72

Career
Screenwriter; author; journalist; U.S. Defense
Department official; congressional aide; lawyer

Political Highlights
Secretary of the Navy, 1987-88

ELECTION RESULTS

2006 GENERAL

Jim Webb (D)	1,175,606	49.6%
George Allen (R)	1,166,277	49.2%
G. Gail Parker (IGREEN)	26,102	1.1%

2006 PRIMARY

Jim Webb (D)	83,298	53.5%
Harris Miller (D)	72,486	46.5%

Elected 2006; 1st term

Webb's directness, military bearing and literary achievements make him something of an odd fit for the chummy and practical Senate. Novelist, lawyer and former Republican, he is first and last a Marine. Uncomfortable with the small talk and glad-handing of politics, he nevertheless managed to defeat a popular incumbent and was the unrivaled star of the Senate Democratic freshman class of 2006.

After one term, though, he decided to bow out, announcing early in 2011 that he would not seek a second term in 2012.

The decision to not seek re-election fit with Webb's eclectic political record and persona.

Webb joined with Republicans in January 2010 in rejecting Democratic plans to force a final Senate vote on health care legislation before newly elected Republican Scott P. Brown of Massachusetts had been seated, although Webb backed the legislation when it came to a vote.

Likewise, Webb was a vocal critic of congressional efforts to repeal the military's "don't ask, don't tell" policy before the Pentagon had completed a review. He then praised the report that the military issued when the review was complete, calling it "an incredible piece of work."

He joined a handful of other moderate Democrats as early critics of the administration's plan, since abandoned, to hold civilian trials of suspected terrorists in New York City.

When President Obama's Defense Department recommended the elimination of the Joint Forces Command based in Norfolk, Webb, a member of the Armed Services Committee, questioned the legal basis for the decision and said that he was "deeply troubled" by Defense Secretary Robert M. Gates' lack of consultation with Congress.

Despite his occasional maverick excursions, Webb remains a fairly reliable Democratic vote, siding with his party about 86 percent of the time on votes in which a majority of Democrats split from a majority of Republicans.

Webb, the author of a 2008 political manifesto titled "A Time to Fight," has also been involved with a group of first-term Democrats in pushing leadership to take a more confrontational position when it comes to battling Republicans. Although he is not a public face of the group like Sheldon Whitehouse of Rhode Island, colleagues have said that Webb plays a key behind-the-scenes role.

The decorated Vietnam veteran and Navy secretary under President Ronald Reagan has made his name as an expert on national security. He solidified that reputation during his first two years in the Senate. As a member of the Veterans' Affairs Committee, he won enactment of enhanced education benefits for veterans and challenged President George W. Bush on the Iraq War.

Webb, who also sits on the Foreign Relations Committee, worked with Democrat Claire McCaskill of Missouri to shepherd into law a Wartime Contracting Commission with a broad mandate to investigate allegations of waste and fraud in Iraq and Afghanistan.

He served notice early in the 111th Congress (2009-10) that he wouldn't defer to Obama on military matters. When the administration proposed cuts to Navy ships, many of which berth in Newport News, Webb pushed back. "I have a very strong view — one developed over many years — that we must grow the Navy's force structure in order for us to meet our strategic and security interests around the world now, and those we are likely to face in the future," he said.

He has been generally supportive of Obama's Afghanistan policy while expressing certain reservations about the clarity of the mission, saying in July 2010 that the strategy is "becoming more and more opaque."

As Iraq has faded from the headlines, Webb has devoted more of his attention to domestic matters. A member of the Joint Economic Committee, he espouses a populist economic platform that highlights what he views as the perils of globalization and corporate excess.

But his support for nuclear power and more development of domestic sources of oil means that he presses for a more comprehensive approach to energy independence than many Democrats are comfortable with.

Judging by Webb's pre-Senate career, retirement will not find him idle. In addition to his military and political lives, he is a law school graduate, served as a congressional committee counsel and is an award-winning writer. He is the author of eight books, perhaps the best-known of which are his 1978 Vietnam novel "Fields of Fire" and the highly praised "Born Fighting," a history of the Scots-Irish in America, which was turned into a Smithsonian Channel documentary hosted by Webb. He did some screenwriting and was an executive producer of the 2000 movie "Rules of Engagement," which was based on a story by Webb and starred Tommy Lee Jones and Samuel L. Jackson.

But Webb comes off as more warrior than scholar. His frankness — some call it rudeness — earned him attention even before he was sworn in. At a post-election reception at the White House, Bush asked Webb about the senator-elect's son Jimmy, a Marine who was serving in Iraq. Webb tersely responded, "That's between me and my boy, Mr. President."

In March 2007, Webb was again in the news after an aide was arrested for carrying a loaded handgun into a Senate office building. The gun belonged to Webb, who described the incident as a mix-up. But he also used it to highlight his support for gun owners' rights and Virginia's concealed-carry law.

Webb's father was an Air Force pilot who fought in World War II, and the family hopped around the country during his youth. The Webbs were by and large Democratic, but he became a Republican because he agreed with the GOP's national security positions.

After attending the University of Southern California for one year, Webb transferred to the Naval Academy. In 1967, he lost an Academy boxing championship to Oliver L. North, who would later become a household name for his role in the Iran-Contra affair. "Both were popular and disliked each other," a Navy boxing coach told The Associated Press in 1991.

Webb graduated from Annapolis and from the Marine officers' school in Quantico, where he finished first in his class of 243. As an infantryman during the Vietnam War, he was awarded the Navy Cross, the Silver Star, two Bronze Stars and two Purple Hearts. Webb's third wife, whom he met long after his service, is Vietnamese, and he speaks the language fluently.

He emerged on the national political scene because of his concerns about the war in Iraq, writing in a newspaper column shortly before the Senate voted to authorize the war in 2002: "Those who are pushing for a unilateral war in Iraq know full well that there is no exit strategy if we invade and stay."

Less than a year before the November 2006 election, it seemed unlikely Democrats could unseat George Allen, viewed as a potential GOP presidential candidate. Webb didn't join the race until February 2006 and began the fall campaign against Allen as a distinct underdog. The race shifted sharply in August when Allen used the word "macaca" to mock an Indian-American volunteer for Webb who had been videotaping him at a campaign appearance. Critics skewered Allen for using an epithet that refers to a monkey, though Allen denied knowing it was a racial slur. Once the video streaked across the Internet and media outlets gave it massive coverage, the incident doomed Allen's re-election campaign and his presidential ambitions. Webb pulled out a 9,329-vote victory.

Key Votes

2010

Pass budget reconciliation bill to modify overhauls of health care and federal student loan programs	YES
Proceed to disapproval resolution on EPA authority to regulate greenhouse gases	NO
Overhaul financial services industry regulation	YES
Limit debate to proceed to a bill to broaden campaign finance disclosure and reporting rules	YES
Limit debate on an extension of Bush-era income tax cuts for two years	YES
Limit debate on a bill to provide a path to legal status for some children of illegal immigrants	YES
Allow for a repeal of "don't ask, don't tell"	YES
Consent to ratification of a strategic arms reduction treaty with Russia	YES

2009

Prevent release of remaining financial industry bailout funds	NO
Make it easier for victims to sue for wage discrimination remedies	YES
Expand the Children's Health Insurance Program	YES
Limit debate on the economic stimulus measure	YES
Repeal District of Columbia firearms prohibitions and gun registration laws	YES
Limit debate on expansion of federal hate crimes law	YES
Strike funding for F-22 Raptor fighter jets	YES

CQ Vote Studies

	PARTY UNITY		PRESIDENTIAL SUPPORT	
	SUPPORT	OPPOSE	SUPPORT	OPPOSE
2010	85%	15%	95%	5%
2009	84%	16%	94%	6%
2008	89%	11%	42%	58%
2007	87%	13%	41%	59%

Interest Groups

	AFL-CIO	ADA	CCUS	ACU
2010	100%	85%	36%	13%
2009	94%	100%	43%	20%
2008	100%	95%	63%	8%
2007	100%	85%	45%	16%

Sen. Mark Warner (D)

Capitol Office
224-2023
warner.senate.gov
459A Russell Bldg. 20510; fax 224-6295

Committees
Banking, Housing & Urban Affairs
  (Security & International Trade - Chairman)
Budget
  (Government Performance - Chairman)
Commerce, Science & Transportation
Rules & Administration
Select Intelligence
Joint Economic

Residence
Alexandria

Born
Dec. 15, 1954; Indianapolis, Ind.

Religion
Presbyterian

Family
Wife, Lisa Collis; three children

Education
George Washington U., B.A. 1977 (political science);
Harvard U., J.D. 1980

Career
Campaign aide and party fundraiser; technology
venture capitalist

Political Highlights
Commonwealth Transportation Board, 1990-94; Va.
Democratic Party chairman, 1993-95; Democratic
nominee for U.S. Senate, 1996; governor, 2002-06

ELECTION RESULTS

2008 GENERAL

Mark Warner (D)	2,369,327	65.0%
James S. Gilmore III (R)	1,228,830	33.7%

2008 PRIMARY

Mark Warner (D)	unopposed

Elected 2008; 1st term

A successful entrepreneur and former state party chairman, Warner works behind the scenes as a self-described "radical centrist" trying to build coalitions on economic issues. Once an activist state governor, he is still figuring out how to balance the expectation that first-term senators don't drive policy with his desire to play a bigger role.

"I have this problem, probably not unlike many other governors who've made this transition: 'OK, you know you've got to pick one or two areas and stick to them.' I'm still struggling with that," he said.

He has had some success striking bipartisan deals on health care and financial regulation. "There's nothing intellectually better about a bipartisan solution," Warner said, "other than the fact that for most Americans, who generally don't trust either party enough to give them a blank check, seeing that there's a bipartisan solution I think is very reassuring."

Warner is a member of the Budget Committee and one of the "Gang of Six" senators who worked to develop a deficit reduction plan in the 112th Congress (2011-12) based on the 2010 proposals of President Obama's fiscal commission.

"I think we've got the makings of a grand bargain. And if we can start with that bipartisan basis, I actually believe we'll get it done and surprise a lot of the pundits," he said on CNN in April 2011.

Warner leads a bipartisan Task Force on Governmental Performance to look at how the government measures the cost effectiveness of federal agencies and programs. He said the group has made "some incremental progress." He wants clearer metrics for government performance and says there is truth in the Republican argument that regulations burden businesses. He's thinking about a pay-as-you-go approach to regulation where whenever a new regulation is added, you have to take one away.

Warner leads the Senate Democrats' business outreach. "Even when we're doing substantively right things, we don't always do a great job of communicating that and engaging with the business community," he said. Policies that encourage companies to move money off their balance sheets back into the economy require repairing relations among the business community, congressional Democrats and the White House, Warner said. He helped pass small-business lending legislation in 2010. In 2009, he urged the Obama administration to use a portion of money from the financial industry bailout legislation to ease the flow of credit to small businesses.

Warner, who voted for the health care overhaul that became law in 2010, wants to follow up on the law's implementation. "I still think the health care bill was too much coverage and not near enough cost containment," he says. In late 2009, Warner and 10 other Democratic freshman senators fashioned a package of cost-containment amendments to the overhaul to encourage innovation and accountability in the health care system. The provisions received some bipartisan support in the Senate and were incorporated into the final measure. Warner wants to work with Republicans on slowing the growth of Medicare costs and promoting a transition from volume-based health care to one that focuses on outcomes.

Based on the number of hours invested, Warner's biggest legislative effort so far has been financial regulation, which he is involved with as a member of the Banking, Housing and Urban Affairs Committee. He partnered with Bob Corker, a Tennessee Republican and fellow Banking Committee member, in writing many of the provisions of the financial regulatory overhaul bill dealing with preventing systemic risk and developing a process for dealing with firms considered "too big to fail."

A proponent of greater government transparency and accountability, Warner has pushed for changes to economic initiatives enacted in 2008 and 2009. Warner pressed Treasury Secretary Timothy F. Geithner in early 2009 to make public more details about what has happened to the $700 billion in financial sector bailout funds Congress approved in 2008. To drive home his demands, Warner introduced legislation to require Treasury to use a single database, in a standardized format, to detail the actions of fund recipients and contractors. Along with other moderates from both parties, he helped pare Obama's economic stimulus package in 2009 — ultimately enacted as a $787 billion law — and he later pressed Cabinet officers to ensure the money was spent efficiently and monitored carefully.

Also a member of the Commerce, Science and Transportation Committee, Warner often talks about improving the nation's competitiveness to keep up with the rising economies of India and China. He calls for increased spending on infrastructure, including on transportation and broadband Internet access, and wants to help drive a global innovation plan for the country.

On energy issues, Warner supports an all-of-the-above approach that embraces clean-coal technology, nuclear power and expanded domestic oil drilling — including off Virginia's coastline — as well as alternative energy sources. "If you're ever going to get a grand bargain on energy, both sides are going to have to come in with less," he says. "As long as oil is part of that transition, there ought to be American oil."

He also serves on the Select Intelligence Committee and the Rules and Administration panel.

Warner grew up in Indiana and Connecticut, then attended college in Washington. After law school at Harvard, he took a job as a fundraiser for the Democratic National Committee. Warner persuaded investors to purchase cellular telephone licenses the government was selling in the 1980s and was an early investor in the cellular company Nextel. As he made money, he stayed active in the Democratic political scene, managing L. Douglas Wilder's successful 1989 campaign in Virginia to become the nation's first elected black governor. He also served as state party chairman from 1993 to 1995.

Warner first ran for the Senate in 1996, spending $10 million of his fortune in an unsuccessful campaign against Republican incumbent John W. Warner (no relation). His close loss enhanced his standing in Virginia Democratic circles and helped lay the groundwork for his successful statehouse run in 2001.

As governor, Warner eliminated a budget deficit in part by raising taxes. But he worked with GOP leaders in Richmond to produce a package that also included spending cuts. He implemented businesslike changes to state government, especially at Virginia's transportation department. As chairman of the National Governors Association in 2004 and 2005, he led a national education initiative.

His efforts helped propel his approval ratings to the mid-70s, unheard-of heights for a Democrat in a state that until 2008 had not supported a Democratic presidential nominee since 1964. When Warner left office in January 2006, speculation immediately arose that he would run for president. But after initial steps such as visiting key primary states, he demurred. "While politically this appears to be the right time for me to take the plunge, at this point, I want to have a real life," he said in October 2006.

Almost a year later, John W. Warner's retirement announcement led him to try for the Senate again. He faced Republican James S. Gilmore III, his predecessor as Virginia governor. Warner coasted to victory with 65 percent of the vote.

Key Votes

2010

Pass budget reconciliation bill to modify overhauls of health care and federal student loan programs	YES
Proceed to disapproval resolution on EPA authority to regulate greenhouse gases	NO
Overhaul financial services industry regulation	YES
Limit debate to proceed to a bill to broaden campaign finance disclosure and reporting rules	YES
Limit debate on an extension of Bush-era income tax cuts for two years	YES
Limit debate on a bill to provide a path to legal status for some children of illegal immigrants	YES
Allow for a repeal of "don't ask, don't tell"	YES
Consent to ratification of a strategic arms reduction treaty with Russia	YES

2009

Prevent release of remaining financial industry bailout funds	NO
Make it easier for victims to sue for wage discrimination remedies	YES
Expand the Children's Health Insurance Program	YES
Limit debate on the economic stimulus measure	YES
Repeal District of Columbia firearms prohibitions and gun registration laws	YES
Limit debate on expansion of federal hate crimes law	YES
Strike funding for F-22 Raptor fighter jets	YES

CQ Vote Studies

	PARTY UNITY		PRESIDENTIAL SUPPORT	
	Support	Oppose	Support	Oppose
2010	90%	10%	97%	3%
2009	92%	8%	96%	4%

Interest Groups

	AFL-CIO	ADA	CCUS	ACU
2010	81%	80%	36%	8%
2009	89%	95%	43%	24%

Rep. Rob Wittman (R)

Capitol Office
225-4261
wittman.house.gov
1317 Longworth Bldg. 20515-4601; fax 225-4382

Committees
Armed Services
(Oversight & Investigations - Chairman)
Natural Resources

Residence
Montross

Born
Feb. 3, 1959; Washington, D.C.

Religion
Episcopalian

Family
Wife, Kathryn Wittman; two children

Education
Virginia Polytechnic Institute and State U., B.S. 1981
(biology); U. of North Carolina, M.P.H. 1990 (health
policy and administration); Virginia Commonwealth
U., Ph.D. 2002 (public policy and administration)

Career
State health agency official; environmental health
inspector

Political Highlights
Montross Town Council, 1986-96 (mayor 1992-96);
Westmoreland County Board of Supervisors, 1996-
2005 (chairman 2004-05); Va. House, 2006-07

ELECTION RESULTS

2010 GENERAL

Rob Wittman (R)	135,564	63.9%
Krystal M. Ball (D)	73,824	34.8%
G. Gail Parker (IGREEN)	2,544	1.2%

2010 PRIMARY

Rob Wittman (R)	28,956	88.0%
Catherine T. Crabill (R)	3,963	12.0%

2008 GENERAL

Rob Wittman (R)	203,839	56.6%
Bill S. Day Jr. (D)	150,432	41.8%
Nathan D. Larson (LIBERT)	5,265	1.5%

Previous Winning Percentages
2007 Special Election (61%)

Elected 2007; 2nd full term

Wittman's eager, soft-spoken nature and down-to-earth demeanor are a good fit for the district, where he has been a fixture in local and state politics for more than two decades. His committee assignments — Armed Services and Natural Resources — fit squarely with his constituents' interests in supporting the Marine Corps base at Quantico and a shipbuilding facility in Newport News, as well as preserving Chesapeake Bay.

He is a fiscal and social conservative in a district that has absorbed an influx of Washington commuters over the past several years; the 1st supported Arizona Republican Sen. John McCain's 2008 presidential bid with only 51 percent of the vote. The preponderance of government workers in the region has spurred Wittman to champion teleworking.

As chairman of Armed Services' Oversight and Investigations Subcommittee, Wittman has pushed for a re-evaluation of the Navy's 30-year shipbuilding plan. According to Wittman and reports from the Congressional Research Service, the plan, released February 2010, does not properly prepare the department for the desired 313-ship fleet. Wittman says the plan would get the Navy to 288. "We have to come up with a plan that's realistic, that's properly resourced to get us to 313 ships," he said. "My concern is that we're retiring ships faster than we're building them."

He also joined with other Virginia lawmakers in questioning the Navy's decision-making process in plans referenced in the 2010 Quadrennial Defense Review to refurbish the Mayport Naval Station in Jacksonville, Fla., to handle a nuclear-powered aircraft carrier. And Wittman worked with his Virginia colleagues in sounding the alarm about reports in early 2009 that Navy inspectors found six ships unfit for their missions.

From his subcommittee, where he was the ranking Republican in the 111th Congress (2009-10), he released an assessment of the professional military education program in May 2010.

A biologist, former environmental health official and avid sport fisherman, Wittman sits on the Natural Resources Subcommittee on Fisheries, Wildlife, Oceans and Insular Affairs. His bill to allow non-U.S. funds to be used to satisfy non-federal matching requirements for conservation projects implemented in Canada became law in 2010.

He seeks to expedite the process for wind energy development off Virginia's coast, saying his district is poised to begin work. "Virginia could be the central point for building windmills to put all up and down the East Coast," he said.

But Wittman's main environmental focus is the Chesapeake Bay. He seeks a reorganization and reauthorization of the funding for the bay's restoration process. The Chesapeake Bay Accountability and Recovery Act, which he sponsored, would require a multi-agency budget for restoration activities. He applauded the George W. Bush administration's designation in late 2008 of blue crab in the Chesapeake Bay as a "resource disaster," and a subsequent $20 million in funding to help address the situation. Six months later, he announced reports indicating signs of a recovery. Also in 2008, he pushed legislation to better oversee the bay's oyster restoration project.

Although he applauds such spending initiatives to help local projects, he believes Washington needs to "get back to the conservative principles of controlling spending, particularly when it comes to federal earmarks." Prior to abstaining from submitting earmarks with the rest of House Republicans, Wittman requested only military construction and certain other defense-related earmarks, listing all on his website and stating in the Congressional Record when they were allocated.

Wittman is a dependable GOP vote on most issues. He sided with his party on nine of every 10 votes in 2010 in which a majority of Republicans voted differently than a majority of Democrats.

Wittman, like many of his constituents, commutes to Washington each day. He introduced legislation in 2009 and again in 2011 that would allow an income tax credit for expenses incurred in teleworking, and he supported a measure that would require the creation of federal telework policies in each agency.

He was born in the District of Columbia in 1959, and eight months later was adopted and moved to Richmond. His mother was a homemaker before earning a teaching degree. His father, an auditor, often worked in the Northern Neck, a picturesque peninsula nestled between the Potomac and the Rappahannock rivers. Wittman now represents that area, where he spent summers working on fishing boats and tomato farms.

The congressman fishes and hunts in his spare time and has a fiberglass replica of a 308-pound tuna that he caught off the coast of Mexico hanging in his D.C. office.

Wittman attended Benedictine Military Institute, an all-boys military school in Richmond. He was active in student government and the school newspaper. He then earned a bachelor's degree in biology in 1981 from Virginia Tech. After college, he worked as a fisherman in the Northern Neck before becoming an environmental specialist for Virginia's health department. He worked his way up from district supervisor to field director of the shellfish sanitation division.

He served on the Montross Town Council for a decade, the last four years as the town's mayor. In 1995 he was elected to the Westmoreland County Board of Supervisors and then won an election to the Virginia legislature in 2005.

Wittman won a special election in December 2007 to replace Republican Rep. Jo Ann Davis, who had died of breast cancer just two months before. At the nominating convention he was one of 11 Republicans — and the only sitting elected official — vying for the seat. Wittman won in the fifth round of balloting, after two close contenders withdrew and threw their support behind him. He then defeated Democrat Philip Forgit, an Iraq War veteran and former teacher, with 61 percent of the vote.

In 2008, he won by 57 percent of the vote, while McCain was squeaking past Obama in the district, and won 64 percent in 2010.

Key Votes

2010

Overhaul the nation's health insurance system	NO
Allow for repeal of "don't ask, don't tell"	NO
Overhaul financial services industry regulation	NO
Limit use of new Afghanistan War funds to troop withdrawal activities	NO
Change oversight of offshore drilling and lift oil spill liability cap	NO
Provide a path to legal status for some children of illegal immigrants	NO
Extend Bush-era income tax cuts for two years	YES

2009

Expand the Children's Health Insurance Program	NO
Provide $787 billion in tax cuts and spending increases to stimulate the economy	NO
Allow bankruptcy judges to modify certain primary-residence mortgages	NO
Create a cap-and-trade system to limit greenhouse gas emissions	NO
Provide $2 billion for the "cash for clunkers" program	NO
Establish the government as the sole provider of student loans	NO
Restrict federally funded insurance coverage for abortions in health care overhaul	YES

CQ Vote Studies

	PARTY UNITY		PRESIDENTIAL SUPPORT	
	SUPPORT	OPPOSE	SUPPORT	OPPOSE
2010	90%	10%	31%	69%
2009	88%	12%	31%	69%
2008	93%	7%	63%	37%
2007	100%	0%	75%	25%

Interest Groups

	AFL-CIO	ADA	CCUS	ACU
2010	7%	5%	88%	92%
2009	19%	5%	87%	92%
2008	20%	35%	83%	92%
2007	0%			100%

East — parts of Newport News and Hampton, Fredericksburg

The GOP-friendly 1st lies along the Potomac River and Chesapeake Bay, stretching from Northern Virginia suburbs and exurbs of Washington all the way south to the shipbuilding cities of Hampton and Newport News. Along the way, popular tourist destinations, such as Williamsburg, Jamestown and Yorktown, recall Virginia's colonial past.

Industry here revolves around military facilities and NASA sites, which have attracted private-sector technology firms. Nearly one-fourth of workers in the 1st are employed by the government, which helps insulate the area from widespread layoffs. Colleges and universities also stabilize the district's economic base, as do shipbuilding and tourism. Inland counties, such as Stafford, Spotsylvania and Caroline, are driven by education, health care and agriculture sectors.

The 1st's northern counties have absorbed Washington commuters who continue to move down the Interstate 95 corridor farther from the city. Spotsylvania County, midway between Richmond and Washington and

one-fifth of which is in the 7th, and Stafford County, north of Fredericksburg, have grown quickly since 2000, particularly within the Hispanic population.

The 1st is solidly Republican, and the party controls local offices and the U.S. House seat here, but John McCain won only 51 percent of the 1st's 2008 presidential vote.

Major Industry
Defense, technology, agriculture, tourism, higher education

Military Bases
Marine Corps Base Quantico, 7,489 military, 9,621 civilian; Naval Surface Warfare Center, Dahlgren Division, 340 military, 4,482 civilian; Naval Weapons Station Yorktown, 1,315 military, 751 civilian (2011); Fort A.P. Hill (Army), 2 military, 250 civilian (2009)

Cities
Newport News (pt.), 75,176; Hampton (pt.), 31,712

Notable
George Washington and Robert E. Lee both were born in Westmoreland County, and their birth sites attract visitors; Jamestown, settled in 1607, was the first permanent English settlement in North America.

Rep. Scott Rigell (R)

Capitol Office
225-4215
rigell.house.gov
327 Cannon Bldg. 20515-4602; fax 225-4218

Committees
Armed Services
Homeland Security
Science, Space & Technology

Residence
Virginia Beach

Born
May 28, 1960; Titusville, Fla.

Religion
Protestant

Family
Wife, Teri Rigell; four children

Education
Brevard Community College, A.A. 1981; Mercer U., B.B.A 1983 (management); Regent U., M.B.A. 1990

Military
Marine Corps Reserve, 1978-84

Career
Car dealership owner

Political Highlights
Va. Motor Vehicle Dealer Board, 1995-99

ELECTION RESULTS

2010 GENERAL

Scott Rigell (R)	88,340	53.1%
Glenn Nye (D)	70,591	42.4%
Kenny E. Golden (I)	7,194	4.3%

2010 PRIMARY

Scott Rigell (R)	14,396	39.5%
Ben Loyola Jr. (R)	9,762	26.8%
Bert K. Mizusawa (R)	6,342	17.4%
Scott W. Taylor (R)	2,950	8.1%
Jessica D. Sandlin (R)	1,620	4.4%
Ed C. Maulbeck (R)	1,372	3.8%

Elected 2010; 1st term

Rigell represents one of the nation's most dense populations of current or former servicemembers, and he has vowed to improve the quality of life for military personnel and veterans.

He serves on the Armed Services, Homeland Security, and Science, Space and Technology committees, giving him a broad portfolio on national security matters.

"If we're going to put them in harm's way, we owe them the very best — that would mean focusing in on the benefits awarded [to personnel], the quality of the training and accessibility of health care," said Rigell, a second-generation Marine. His coastal district includes Naval Station Norfolk and Langley Air Force Base.

Rigell (RIDGE-uhl), who founded an automotive company in 1991, has promised to attack the deficit by rooting out "terrible inefficiencies" in government. "I've been creating jobs for 20-plus years," he said. "I've borrowed money; I've paid it back. I have firsthand knowledge of the kind of lending environment we need for business to grow."

"Americans instinctively know that no family, no business, no country, not even America, can stay on this path of borrowing more than 40 cents out of every dollar that we are spending," he told the Budget Committee in March 2011. "That is truly going to lead, in my view, to catastrophic consequences."

He opposed the final version of the catchall funding bill for fiscal 2011, joining 58 other Republicans who felt the measure's $40 billion in spending cuts did not do enough to address the deficit.

Rigell won a six-way GOP primary with about 40 percent of the vote in 2010, then faced first-term Democrat Glenn Nye.

Nye took some hits for supporting the $787 billion economic stimulus package in 2009. Democrats struck back on his behalf by pointing out that Rigell's auto dealership sold more than 100 cars under the "cash for clunkers" program that was partially funded by the legislation.

Rigell won 53 percent of the vote, enough for a nearly 11-percentage-point margin of victory.

Virginia 2

Southeast — Virginia Beach, parts of Norfolk and Hampton, Eastern Shore

Taking in the state's Atlantic coastline, the 2nd is dominated by Virginia Beach, a center for white-collar military families and retirees. The district takes in parts of Norfolk and Hampton and crosses the Chesapeake Bay inlet to Virginia's Eastern Shore.

Growth in Virginia Beach slowed amid military base closings and a national recession. The 2005 BRAC round ordered the 2011 closure of Fort Monroe, in Hampton, but increases at the 2nd's other bases and development of the fort's land may mean the 2nd will avoid job losses. The 2nd also includes nearly half of largely blue-collar and Democratic-leaning Norfolk (shared with the 3rd). Its naval base, shipbuilding and shipping drive the economy.

Conservatism in the district is rooted in military and economic issues rather than social questions. Barack Obama won 50 percent of the district's vote in the 2008 presidential election, but the GOP took back the U.S. House seat from a one-term Democrat in 2010.

Major Industry
Military, tourism, shipbuilding

Military Bases
Naval Station Norfolk, 50,035 military, 13,952 civilian; Joint Base Langley-Eustis (shared with the 3rd), 13,000 military, 6,650 civilian; Joint Expeditionary Base Little Creek-Fort Story, 14,300 military, 5,845 civilian; Naval Air Station Oceana, 10,473 military, 2,042 civilian; Naval Air Station Oceana Dam Neck Annex, 2,937 military, 1,592 civilian (2011)

Cities
Virginia Beach, 437,994; Norfolk (pt.), 116,839; Hampton (pt.), 45,798

Notable
The Norfolk Botanical Garden has more than 30 themed gardens.

Rep. Robert C. Scott (D)

Capitol Office
225-8351
www.house.gov/scott
1201 Longworth Bldg. 20515-4603; fax 225-8354

Committees
Education & the Workforce
Judiciary

Residence
Newport News

Born
April 30, 1947; Washington, D.C.

Religion
Episcopalian

Family
Divorced

Education
Harvard U., A.B. 1969; Boston College, J.D. 1973

Military
Mass. National Guard, 1970-74; Army Reserve, 1974-76

Career
Lawyer

Political Highlights
Va. House, 1978-83; Va. Senate, 1983-93; Democratic nominee for U.S. House, 1986

ELECTION RESULTS

2010 GENERAL

Robert C. Scott (D)	114,754	70.0%
C.L. "Chuck" Smith Jr. (R)	44,553	27.2%
James J. Quigley (LIBERT)	2,383	1.4%
John D. Kelly (I)	2,039	1.2%

2010 PRIMARY

Robert C. Scott (D)	unopposed

2008 GENERAL

Robert C. Scott (D)	239,911	97.0%
write-ins	7,377	3.0%

Previous Winning Percentages
2006 (96%); 2004 (69%); 2002 (96%); 2000 (98%);
1998 (76%); 1996 (82%); 1994 (79%); 1992 (79%)

Elected 1992; 10th term

Scott likes to call his approach to governing "evidence-based," a phrase he uses to differentiate his efforts from what he considers "sound bite legislation." He is a stalwart liberal on the Judiciary Committee who has long espoused civil libertarian views. A member of the Congressional Black Caucus, he pushes for increased federal intervention on education, jobs and health care, and he is active on defense issues, reflecting the priorities of his coastal Virginia district.

As ranking Democrat and former chairman of Judiciary's panel on Crime, Terrorism and Homeland Security, Scott argues that programs to educate and provide jobs and family support for people in the criminal justice system are more influential and cost-effective than punitive efforts.

"If you put money into prevention and early intervention, getting young people onto the right track and keep them on the right track, they wouldn't get into trouble to begin with," he said. "You wouldn't need to wait for them to drop out of school, join a gang and then get locked up."

One of his top judicial priorities became law in August 2010, with a bill that reduced the disparity in crack and powder cocaine sentences by changing the comparison ratio for quantities from 100-to-1 to 18-to-1. Since crack is more prevalent in cities, and a much smaller amount of it draws a minimum five years of jail time, he and other critics said the law disproportionately affected poor blacks. He called the bill "good progress," although it did not completely reach his goal of equality.

Scott also boasts he has greatly cut the number of bills with mandatory minimum sentences that leave the Judiciary Committee.

He won House passage in December 2009 of his bill that would create penalties for malicious misuse of caller ID, and then, in the following month, House passage of his bill that would create a center for college campus safety in the Justice Department. In February 2009, the House passed a bill that would require states receiving federal grants for law enforcement to report prisoner deaths to the attorney general.

"We made, I think, significant progress on focusing criminal law on more evidence and substantive based, rather than slogans and sound bites — which traditionally is how you pass legislation," he said. "I think when the Youth Promise Act was introduced, it made a significant change in attitude. You don't have to pass foolishness in order to get intelligent, evidence-based legislation enacted."

During the George W. Bush administration, Scott was a persistent foe of proposals to expand law enforcement authority. He was a vocal opponent of the 2001 anti-terrorism law known as the Patriot Act, enacted with overwhelming support by Congress six weeks after the Sept. 11 terrorist attacks. He said the new intelligence-gathering provisions in the statute trampled on individual liberties. He voted against a short-term extension of expiring provisions early in the 112th Congress (2011-12).

He also is a continual critic of Republican attempts to aid faith-based organizations. In 2007, Scott helped remove a provision from the Head Start reauthorization bill that would have allowed faith-based providers to take applicants' adherence to the groups' beliefs into consideration when hiring. "If you allow discrimination in federally funded programs, you essentially lose your moral authority to enforce civil rights laws," Scott said.

From his seat on the Education and the Workforce Committee, Scott argues that standardized test scores place low-income school districts and their students at a disadvantage, and he hopes to address the issue in a reauthorization of the 2001 No Child Left Behind Act expected in the new Congress. "No Child Left Behind exposed shortcomings, but it didn't have the mechanism to improve education," he said.

A former member of the Army Reserve and National Guard, Scott is one of the stronger pro-Pentagon voices in the Congressional Black Caucus. He promotes the interests of his district's shipbuilders and military bases; Northrop Grumman, Newport News and the Army's Fort Eustis are major employers. He joined other Virginia lawmakers in late 2008 in urging President-elect Obama to block the proposed move of a Norfolk-based aircraft carrier to Florida. He also joined the delegation in August 2010 in urging reversal of a Defense Department recommendation to close the Joint Forces Command in the Hampton Roads area, calling the reasoning and process for closure "just bizarre."

His district also is home to one of the nation's largest cigarette plants, a south Richmond facility operated by Philip Morris USA. But he backed an April 2009 House-passed bill allowing the Food and Drug Administration to regulate the manufacturing, sale and promotion of tobacco products.

Scott expresses hesitation at allowing drilling or wind development off the Virginia coast, saying that the same environmental standards should apply to East Coast drilling as are in place on the West Coast.

Scott is the son of a surgeon and a teacher. When local white officials resisted court-ordered integration of the public school system, the Scotts, like other well-to-do black families, sent their son to Groton, the prestigious Massachusetts preparatory school, on a voucher. He graduated from Harvard University and Boston College's law school. He then returned to Newport News and became active in local civic groups, which eventually led him into politics.

Scott won a seat in the state House in 1977 and in five years moved to the state Senate. He was unsuccessful in his first run for Congress in 1986, but made another run six years later after redistricting resulted in a 3rd District that was 64 percent black. With no incumbent running, he took two-thirds of the vote in a three-way Democratic primary and breezed to victory in November.

He won by lopsided margins again in 1994 and 1996, but a federal panel struck down the 3rd District's boundaries in 1997. The new lines drawn by the General Assembly set the black population at 54 percent, and Scott won handily in 1998, with 76 percent of the vote. He has easily won re-election since.

Key Votes

2010

Overhaul the nation's health insurance system	YES
Allow for repeal of "don't ask, don't tell"	YES
Overhaul financial services industry regulation	YES
Limit use of new Afghanistan War funds to troop withdrawal activities	YES
Change oversight of offshore drilling and lift oil spill liability cap	YES
Provide a path to legal status for some children of illegal immigrants	YES
Extend Bush-era income tax cuts for two years	NO

2009

Expand the Children's Health Insurance Program	YES
Provide $787 billion in tax cuts and spending increases to stimulate the economy	YES
Allow bankruptcy judges to modify certain primary-residence mortgages	YES
Create a cap-and-trade system to limit greenhouse gas emissions	YES
Provide $2 billion for the "cash for clunkers" program	YES
Establish the government as the sole provider of student loans	YES
Restrict federally funded insurance coverage for abortions in health care overhaul	NO

CQ Vote Studies

	PARTY UNITY		PRESIDENTIAL SUPPORT	
	Support	Oppose	Support	Oppose
2010	97%	3%	86%	14%
2009	98%	2%	96%	4%
2008	99%	1%	11%	89%
2007	98%	2%	3%	97%
2006	95%	5%	27%	73%

Interest Groups

	AFL-CIO	ADA	CCUS	ACU
2010	100%	100%	13%	0%
2009	100%	95%	33%	4%
2008	100%	100%	53%	8%
2007	100%	100%	50%	4%
2006	100%	100%	27%	4%

Virginia 3
Southeast — parts of Richmond, Norfolk and Newport News, Portsmouth

The black-majority 3rd moves from the state capital of Richmond southeast to military and shipbuilding territory, taking in parts of Newport News, Hampton and Norfolk, and the entire city of Portsmouth.

The 3rd has long benefited from hosting one of the nation's largest ports, at Hampton Roads, and from Richmond's financial sector. Although now owned by Wells Fargo, Wachovia is still a key employer. While the 3rd has not been immune to layoffs, state government jobs around Richmond and port-related jobs to the south have mitigated the impact of economic downturns. Richmond also is home to one of the largest cigarette plants in the nation, a Philip Morris USA facility.

The Hampton Roads area has a heavy concentration of naval installations as well as associated shipbuilding and ship repair firms. Among these is the nation's largest privately owned shipyard — Huntington Ingalls Industries — which builds aircraft carriers and submarines. All three of the 3rd's military bases were affected by personnel changes from the 2005 round of

base realignments, but none were slated for closure.

Richmond, Portsmouth and Norfolk, which have substantial black populations, all gave Barack Obama at least 70 percent of their 2008 presidential vote. Overall, Obama took 76 percent of the 3rd's vote, his best showing statewide. Despite Democrats' dominance of the 3rd, Republicans are strong in some areas, particularly in New Kent County and Prince George County, which is shared with the 4th District.

Major Industry
Defense, shipbuilding and repair, shipping, government, tobacco

Military Bases
Joint Base Langley-Eustis (shared with the 2nd), 13,000 military, 6,650 civilian; Norfolk Naval Shipyard at Portsmouth, 8,650 military, 1,200 civilian (2011); Naval Medical Center Portsmouth, 2,793 military, 1,291 civilian (2009)

Cities
Richmond (pt.), 150,010; Norfolk (pt.), 125,964; Newport News (pt.), 105,543; Portsmouth, 95,535; Hampton (pt.), 59,926

Notable
The Edgar Allan Poe Museum is in Richmond, where Poe lived.

Rep. J. Randy Forbes (R)

Capitol Office
225-6365
www.house.gov/forbes
2438 Rayburn Bldg. 20515-4604; fax 226-1170

Committees
Armed Services
   (Readiness - Chairman)
Judiciary

Residence
Chesapeake

Born
Feb. 17, 1952; Chesapeake, Va.

Religion
Baptist

Family
Wife, Shirley Forbes; four children

Education
Randolph-Macon College, B.A. 1974 (political science); U. of Virginia, J.D. 1977

Career
Lawyer; state legislative aide

Political Highlights
Va. House, 1990-97 (Republican floor leader, 1994-97); Va. Republican Party chairman, 1996-2000; Va. Senate, 1997-2001 (Republican floor leader, 1998-2000)

ELECTION RESULTS

2010 GENERAL

J. Randy Forbes (R)	123,659	62.3%
Wynne V.E. LeGrow (D)	74,298	37.4%

2010 PRIMARY

J. Randy Forbes (R)	unopposed

2008 GENERAL

J. Randy Forbes (R)	199,075	59.5%
Andrea Miller (D)	135,041	40.4%

Previous Winning Percentages
2006 (76%); 2004 (64%); 2002 (98%); 2001 Special Election (52%)

Elected 2001; 5th full term

Forbes is a defense hawk and a budget hawk, and he sees no contradiction between the two. Tidewater Virginia has one of the largest concentrations of military bases in the nation, giving the lawmaker both a parochial and a policy interest in Pentagon spending.

As chairman of the Armed Services Subcommittee on Readiness, he argues against what he calls "budget-driven" defense proposals. "For the first time in years, we are seeing an administration that is content with our federal budget driving our defense and national security strategy, rather than our defense and national security strategy driving our budget priorities," he wrote in a May 2010 opinion piece.

While he expressed general satisfaction with the defense authorization bill for fiscal 2011, he nonetheless voted against it because it included a provision that would end the military's "don't ask, don't tell" policy barring service by openly gay individuals. "I simply cannot support a bill that places a social agenda above our first priority to defend America," he said. He also opposed a stand-alone measure that repealed the statutory ban in late 2010.

Forbes has also been critical of Defense Secretary Robert M. Gates and the Obama administration for secrecy in the budget process. He has blasted Gates, who also served under President George W. Bush and is due to retire in 2011, for instituting a "gag order" by requiring Pentagon officials to sign a non-disclosure agreement. And when the Pentagon did not submit a shipbuilding plan as required by law, Forbes asked from the House floor, "How can the secretary of Defense look at our men and women in uniform and say, 'We expect you to follow the law, to follow the statutes that Congress has passed and the president has signed, but they apply to you and not me?'"

Forbes looks out for the region's military bases, including Fort Lee, which he helped spare from the 2005 round of base closings. The base was instead chosen for expansion. His latest battle is an attempt to overturn a Navy decision to move one of two aircraft carriers stationed at Norfolk to Naval Station Mayport in Florida; he argues that such a move would not make budget or strategic sense.

For several years Forbes has expressed growing concern for the military threat posed by China, and he now contends that the threat goes beyond conventional weapons to the realm of cyberspace. He wants to investigate cyber-attacks by China and other nations on the U.S. military. He has pressed for legislation to discourage foreign companies from selling sensitive military technology to China. He also has demanded that the Navy take more seriously the threat of new Chinese missile technology and has encouraged the Pentagon to use modeling and simulation technology to prepare for potential threats.

Forbes is a fan of computer modeling and simulation in other contexts as well. He helped win inclusion of a provision in the 2008 overhaul of the Higher Education Act to provide grants to enhance universities' modeling and simulation study programs. In 2009, he and former Democratic Rep. Patrick J. Kennedy of Rhode Island pushed legislation to spur the increased use of such technology to allow doctors to practice difficult medical procedures in lifelike situations.

Forbes takes a dim view of what he and fellow members of the conservative Republican Study Committee consider excessive federal spending. He voted against a $700 billion law to aid the nation's financial services sector in fall 2008. He also opposed President Obama's $787 billion economic stimulus law in February 2009 and blasted the Democrats' health care overhaul, enacted in 2010, as "reckless spending."

He also opposed the final version of the catchall spending bill for fiscal 2011, saying the measure's $40 billion in spending cuts did not go far enough in reducing the deficit.

From the Judiciary Committee, Forbes takes a tough-on-crime approach, backing mandatory prison sentences. He won House passage in 2006 of a bill targeting illegal immigrants who belong to criminal gangs, and, as a state legislator in the 1990s, Forbes helped shepherd a proposal to abolish parole for convicted felons. But he also supports prisoner rehabilitation and re-entry programs.

Forbes pushes a "Manhattan Project" to end U.S. dependence on foreign energy sources. His bill went nowhere during the 110th Congress (2007-08), but its free-market incentives — big prize money for renewable-energy innovations — earned him plaudits in his district and in national publications such as The Wall Street Journal.

A Sunday school teacher for more than 20 years, Forbes is co-founder of the Congressional Prayer Caucus and leads weekly prayer meetings just off the House floor. He is the sponsor of legislation that would reaffirm "In God We Trust" as the official motto of the United States and encourage display of the motto in government buildings.

Forbes grew up in what was then rural Chesapeake, where his grandparents farmed. He returned to the area after law school and worked in private practice for several years. Inspired by his father, who sold life insurance and was active in the community, he won a seat in the Virginia House of Delegates in 1989, rising to become Republican floor leader, and later served in the state Senate.

When a former law school classmate, George Allen, became governor, he made Forbes chairman of the state Republican Party. Under Forbes' watch from 1996 to 2000, the party became the dominant power in Virginia politics. In 2001, he geared up to run for lieutenant governor, but when conservative Democrat Norman Sisisky died that March, Forbes ran for the House instead. He won the nomination at a contentious convention, then faced state Sen. Louise Lucas, a black Democrat and former shipyard worker. Both parties poured money into the race, but Forbes won in balloting that broke along racial lines.

Redistricting after the 2000 census moved several African-American neighborhoods into the neighboring 3rd District. Democrats sued, but a federal appeals court upheld the plan in September 2004. Forbes faced no competition in 2002, and he has not been seriously challenged since. He won almost 60 percent of the vote in 2008 even as Obama was carrying the district by a percentage point in the presidential race, and won 62 percent in 2010.

Key Votes

2010

Overhaul the nation's health insurance system	NO
Allow for repeal of "don't ask, don't tell"	NO
Overhaul financial services industry regulation	NO
Limit use of new Afghanistan War funds to troop withdrawal activities	NO
Change oversight of offshore drilling and lift oil spill liability cap	NO
Provide a path to legal status for some children of illegal immigrants	NO
Extend Bush-era income tax cuts for two years	NO

2009

Expand the Children's Health Insurance Program	NO
Provide $787 billion in tax cuts and spending increases to stimulate the economy	NO
Allow bankruptcy judges to modify certain primary-residence mortgages	NO
Create a cap-and-trade system to limit greenhouse gas emissions	NO
Provide $2 billion for the "cash for clunkers" program	NO
Establish the government as the sole provider of student loans	NO
Restrict federally funded insurance coverage for abortions in health care overhaul	YES

CQ Vote Studies

	PARTY UNITY		PRESIDENTIAL SUPPORT	
	SUPPORT	OPPOSE	SUPPORT	OPPOSE
2010	94%	6%	26%	74%
2009	90%	10%	25%	75%
2008	95%	5%	60%	40%
2007	94%	6%	77%	23%
2006	93%	7%	93%	7%

Interest Groups

	AFL-CIO	ADA	CCUS	ACU
2010	7%	5%	75%	100%
2009	10%	0%	86%	96%
2008	25%	25%	78%	91%
2007	13%	20%	79%	92%
2006	29%	10%	100%	92%

Virginia 4
Southeast — Chesapeake, Petersburg

Located among the rivers and swamps of southeastern and south-central Virginia, the 4th begins in Hampton Roads in the growing city of Chesapeake before heading west into rural tobacco- and peanut-producing areas. It then bends north to reach the Tri-Cities area — Petersburg, Hopewell and Colonial Heights — south of Richmond.

Hampton Roads depends on the military, and a 2011 Defense Department decision to reorganize the U.S. Joint Forces Command may cost the district jobs.

The population of Chesapeake, by far the 4th's most populous city, has grown for decades as manufacturing and other industries moved in alongside residents who commute to nearby Norfolk or Virginia Beach. Farther north, the Tri-Cities area hosts Fort Lee, which gained thousands of new positions on base and residents in the community following the 2005 round of base realignments.

Outside the 4th's population centers, tobacco and peanut farming play a central role in the economy. There also are pork-producing facilities here in sparsely populated counties such as Isle of Wight, home to Smithfield

Hams, and Sussex.

The 4th traditionally votes Republican at the national and statewide levels, but Democrats fare better in areas with sizable black voting blocs — the district has the state's second-largest black population (33 percent) — and can win local elections across the 4th.

Petersburg, which is nearly four-fifths black, gave Democrat Barack Obama 88 percent of its presidential vote in 2008, his best showing in the state. Overall, Obama won the district by just more than 1 percentage point.

Major Industry
Military, agriculture, tobacco, health care, manufacturing

Military Bases
Fort Lee (Army), 6,254 military, 2,985 civilian (2009); Naval Support Activity Norfolk, Northwest Annex, 1,326 military, 1,458 civilian; Defense Supply Center, Richmond, 42 military, 2,850 civilian (2011)

Cities
Chesapeake, 222,209; Suffolk, 84,585; Petersburg, 32,420

Notable
Suffolk, which calls itself the peanut capital of the world, is the birthplace of Planters' Mr. Peanut and hosts an annual Suffolk Peanut Festival.

Rep. Robert Hurt (R)

Capitol Office
225-4711
hurt.house.gov
1516 Longworth Bldg. 20515-4605; fax 225-5681

Committees
Financial Services

Residence
Chatham

Born
June 16, 1969; Manhattan, N.Y.

Religion
Presbyterian

Family
Wife, Kathy Hurt; three children

Education
Hampden-Sydney College, B.A. 1991 (English); Mississippi College, J.D. 1995

Career
Lawyer; county prosecutor

Political Highlights
Chatham Town Council, 2000-01; Va. House, 2002-08; Va. Senate, 2008-11

ELECTION RESULTS

2010 GENERAL

Robert Hurt (R)	119,560	50.8%
Tom Perriello (D)	110,562	47.0%
Jeffrey A. Clark (I)	4,992	2.1%

2010 PRIMARY

Robert Hurt (R)	17,120	48.4%
James K. McKelvey (R)	9,153	25.9%
Mike G. McPadden (R)	3,460	9.8%
Kenneth C. Boyd (R)	2,608	7.4%
Feda Morton (R)	1,626	4.6%
Laurence Verga (R)	802	2.3%
Ron L. Ferrin (R)	583	1.6%

Elected 2010; 1st term

Hurt is a conservative who says his first task is to reduce the size of government.

To that end, he joined 58 other Republicans in opposing the final version of a catchall spending bill for fiscal 2011 that would have trimmed spending by $40 billion, arguing that it didn't do enough.

He called a proposal by Budget Chairman Paul D. Ryan of Wisconsin that would cut spending by $4 trillion over a decade "an honest, straightforward, and responsible approach."

Hurt sits on the Financial Services Committee, where he serves as vice chairman of the Insurance, Housing and Community Opportunity panel. He backed measures early in the 112th Congress (2011-12) to terminate several foreclosure aid programs championed by the Obama administration. In each case, he won adoption of his amendments to direct any savings to deficit reduction.

He allies himself with social as well as fiscal conservatives and counts himself among those opposed to same-sex marriage and abortion.

Hurt was born and spent his early childhood years in New York, but grew to adulthood in Chatham, in the western portion of the district. He received an undergraduate degree in English from Hampden-Sydney College and a law degree from the Mississippi College School of Law. He served as a county prosecutor and on the Chatham Town Council prior to being elected to the Virginia House in 2001. He moved to the state Senate in 2008.

One-term Democrat Tom Perriello was viewed as vulnerable because of his support of key items in the party's agenda, including the $787 billion economic stimulus, the cap-and-trade energy bill and the health care overhaul.

Hurt was viewed with suspicion at first by some tea party activists because of his support for a 2004 state tax increase. But he won a seven-way primary by a wide margin.

He got plenty of help from the National Republican Congressional Committee and beat Perriello by about 4 percentage points, winning almost 51 percent of the vote.

Virginia 5

South central — Danville, Charlottesville

Rich in Civil War landmarks, the 5th extends from the central part of Virginia just north of Charlottesville to Southside on the south-central border with North Carolina.

The mostly rural 5th is relatively poor and relies on agriculture and textiles. Once the heart of tobacco country, the industry has suffered a decline, which has led to high unemployment in the district's southwestern corner. Manufacturing has taken a more prominent role, although jobs have dwindled in some areas. Danville is a tobacco and textile center on the North Carolina border, and to the west, Martinsville struggles with unemployment. Charlottesville, in the northern part of the 5th, has a growing public sector. The 5th's northern tip also has several wineries.

While the 5th is reliably conservative, party labels hold little meaning here: Rep. Virgil H. Goode Jr. switched parties in 2002 and kept his U.S. House seat for six terms until losing to Democrat Tom Perriello in 2008, the same year 13 of the 18 counties wholly or partially in the district backed GOP presidential candidate John McCain. In 2010, Republican Robert Hurt took the seat from Perriello. One notable exception to the 5th's conservative posture is Charlottesville, home to the University of Virginia.

Charlottesville gave Barack Obama 78 percent of its vote in the 2008 presidential election — his third-best showing statewide. Overall, McCain took 51 percent of the district's vote.

Major Industry
Agriculture, manufacturing, textiles, service

Cities
Charlottesville, 43,475; Danville, 43,055

Notable
Confederate Gen. Robert E. Lee surrendered at Appomattox Court House, ending the Civil War.

Rep. Robert W. Goodlatte (R)

Capitol Office
225-5431
www.house.gov/goodlatte
2240 Rayburn Bldg. 20515-4606; fax 225-9681

Committees
Agriculture
Judiciary
 (Intellectual Property, Competition & the Internet
 - Chairman)
Education & the Workforce

Residence
Roanoke

Born
Sept. 22, 1952; Holyoke, Mass.

Religion
Christian Scientist

Family
Wife, Maryellen Goodlatte; two children

Education
Bates College, B.A. 1974 (government); Washington
and Lee U., J.D. 1977

Career
Lawyer; congressional aide

Political Highlights
Roanoke City Republican Committee chairman,
1980-83; 6th Congressional District Republican Party
chairman, 1983-88

ELECTION RESULTS

2010 GENERAL

Robert W. Goodlatte (R)	127,487	76.3%
Jeffrey W. Vanke (I)	21,649	13.0%
Stuart M. Bain (LIBERT)	15,309	9.2%
write-ins (WRI)	2,709	1.6%

2010 PRIMARY

Robert W. Goodlatte (R)	unopposed

2008 GENERAL

Robert W. Goodlatte (R)	192,350	61.6%
S. "Sam" Rasoul (D)	114,367	36.6%
Janice Lee Allen (I)	5,413	1.7%

Previous Winning Percentages
2006 (75%); 2004 (97%); 2002 (97%); 2000 (99%);
1998 (69%); 1996 (67%); 1994 (100%); 1992 (60%)

Elected 1992; 10th term

The unassuming Goodlatte labors over the details of legislation and tends to leave the partisan jousting to others. His voting record is solidly conservative, but his willingness to reach across the aisle has made him a player on almost every major computer- and Internet-related bill Congress considers. He also teams with Democrats on agricultural issues.

Goodlatte (GOOD-lat) sees keeping budget deficits under control as his top priority. He has long advocated a balanced-budget constitutional amendment — he introduced legislation proposing one in the opening days of the 112th Congress (2011-12) —and adamantly opposed President Obama's economic initiatives, arguing that they cost too much and yielded too few results for the money spent.

During the past four Congresses, overhauling the tax code has also been a top priority for Goodlatte. He wants to see a three-year sunset put on the current federal income tax code, during which time a replacement system would be debated and enacted. "It could be a flat tax, fair tax, any of a whole host of other taxes," Goodlatte says. "But while most members of Congress believe there should be tax reform, there is a lack of consensus about what it should be. This calls their bluff by putting the first priority on agreeing to get rid of the current tax code." He reintroduced legislation abolishing the tax code in January 2011.

Chairman of the Judiciary Subcommittee on Intellectual Property, Competition and the Internet and co-chairman of the Congressional Internet Caucus, Goodlatte has a special interest in technology policy as it affects rural areas. As a lawyer in Roanoke, he took advantage of the latest communications and information technology to build a competitive practice that included a specialty in immigration law. He sees communications technology today as comparable to the railroad in the 19th century. "If the railroad came through your town and connected you with the rest of the country, you'd boom. If it didn't, you'd go bust," he said.

He has worked on legislation to protect users' privacy, preserving intellectual copyright protections for artists and creators of software, shielding children from indecent material and safeguarding consumers from fraud. In 2004, the House overwhelmingly passed his measure setting criminal penalties for using privacy-invading "spyware" to tap into personal computers to steal information or damage hardware.

Two years later, he steered into law a bill to curb Internet gambling by prohibiting gambling businesses from accepting credit cards and electronic transfers for online betting. The measure also modified the 1961 Wire Act to clarify that its prohibitions also apply to Internet gambling, not just sports bets placed over telephone wires.

Goodlatte's positions on technology are driven by the philosophy that government generally should stay out of the way of innovators and entrepreneurs. That is a conservative's perspective, but Goodlatte notes that many Internet-related issues lend themselves to bipartisanship. In 2007, he backed a bill sponsored by Democrat Anna G. Eshoo of California to permanently ban Internet access taxes, but the two wound up reluctantly endorsing a compromise seven-year extension of the existing moratorium.

As leader of a House Republican working group on technology issues, he says the GOP majority will consider research and development tax breaks and more H-1B visas for skilled foreign workers as ways to boost the technology industry. A member of the Education and Workforce Committee,

Goodlatte has also said he would like to grant permanent resident status to foreign students who earn graduate degrees in the sciences, technology, engineering and mathematics.

But Goodlatte takes a hard line against illegal immigration. He voted in 2006 to authorize construction of a 700-mile fence along the border with Mexico, and in 2007 he joined North Carolina Democrat Heath Shuler in sponsoring legislation to require employers to verify the legal status of all of their workers. He wants to eliminate the annual visa lottery program that grants permanent resident status based on what Goodlatte calls "pure luck."

"I wouldn't be in favor of the comprehensive reform that President Obama talks about," Goodlatte says. "I think there are lots of immigration bills that merit individual consideration, and that's how they ought to be approached — take each one at a time, not roll them all into one big mass and then try to pass it all including a massive amnesty program."

When he served as the top Republican on the Agriculture Committee, Goodlatte helped write the five-year reauthorization of agriculture and nutrition programs enacted in 2008 over Bush's veto. Now the No. 2 Republican on the panel, he'll play a central role in writing a new farm law in the in 112th Congress.

Goodlatte chaired the Agriculture Committee for four years before the Democrats won the majority in the House in the 2006 elections. During that period, he helped pass Bush's Healthy Forests Initiative, expediting the cutting of timber in areas prone to wildfires, and a long-sought buyout program for tobacco farmers.

Goodlatte grew up in western Massachusetts. His father managed a Friendly's ice cream store, and his mother worked part time in a department store. His parents liked to visit places of historical significance, feeding Goodlatte's lifelong interest in presidential history. Vacations for the lawmaker often include a stop at the home of a U.S. president. His favorite stop was President Ronald Reagan's California ranch. In 2006, the House passed Goodlatte's bill providing funds for a Woodrow Wilson presidential library in his district. (The 28th president was born in Staunton.)

Goodlatte was president of the College Republicans at Bates College in Maine. After getting a law degree at Washington and Lee University in Lexington, Va., he entered private practice and also worked for the area's Republican congressman, M. Caldwell Butler. He considered running for Congress in 1986, but the birth of his second child at the start of the campaign season kept him out of the race. In 1992, however, when Democratic Rep. Jim Olin retired after five terms, Goodlatte decided the time was right. He won easily and has done so ever since.

Key Votes

2010

Overhaul the nation's health insurance system	NO
Allow for repeal of "don't ask, don't tell"	NO
Overhaul financial services industry regulation	NO
Limit use of new Afghanistan War funds to troop withdrawal activities	NO
Change oversight of offshore drilling and lift oil spill liability cap	NO
Provide a path to legal status for some children of illegal immigrants	NO
Extend Bush-era income tax cuts for two years	YES

2009

Expand the Children's Health Insurance Program	NO
Provide $787 billion in tax cuts and spending increases to stimulate the economy	NO
Allow bankruptcy judges to modify certain primary-residence mortgages	NO
Create a cap-and-trade system to limit greenhouse gas emissions	NO
Provide $2 billion for the "cash for clunkers" program	NO
Establish the government as the sole provider of student loans	NO
Restrict federally funded insurance coverage for abortions in health care overhaul	YES

CQ Vote Studies

	PARTY UNITY		PRESIDENTIAL SUPPORT	
	SUPPORT	OPPOSE	SUPPORT	OPPOSE
2010	95%	5%	26%	74%
2009	96%	4%	14%	86%
2008	94%	6%	64%	36%
2007	95%	5%	78%	22%
2006	99%	1%	95%	5%

Interest Groups

	AFL-CIO	ADA	CCUS	ACU
2010	7%	0%	88%	100%
2009	5%	0%	73%	100%
2008	14%	15%	83%	96%
2007	17%	15%	75%	92%
2006	14%	0%	100%	92%

Virginia 6

Northwest — Roanoke, Lynchburg

Running along the Shenandoah Valley, the conservative 6th slides down much of Virginia's western border with West Virginia, combining mountainous terrain, small towns, midsize cities and natural beauty.

Roanoke, the 6th's most populous city, hosts several industries, including furniture and electrical products manufacturing. Roanoke has attracted some biomedical and biotech companies to business parks in redeveloped areas of the city, but nationwide economic downturns and population loss in some parts of the city have stalled economic growth. Several years of high bankruptcy and foreclosure rates hit Lynchburg hard, but the housing market is beginning to rebound.

The area north of the district's metropolitan areas of Roanoke and Lynchburg has experienced significant population growth since 2000: Harrisonburg now is the state's 12th-most populous city. Harrisonburg, which has benefitted from service sector job growth, also has seen a marked increase in Hispanic residents.

Rural areas of the 6th still depend mainly on dairy farming, livestock and poultry. The district has a sizable Mennonite population and attracts tourists to see the scenic Blue Ridge Mountains and their natural caverns. The 6th also hosts colleges and universities, including James Madison University in Harrisonburg.

The 6th has a large population of senior citizens, a mostly white-collar workforce and a generous dose of Republicans, although the rural valley's brand of Republicanism has traditionally been a moderate one, and Democrats and independents can win some local elections.

Roanoke has a strong Democratic base with union ties, but Republicans have done well in Roanoke's suburbs, in Lynchburg and in most rural areas. Overall, John McCain took 57 percent of the 6th's vote in the 2008 presidential election, his second-best tally in the state.

Major Industry
Agriculture, livestock, manufacturing, tourism, higher education

Cities
Roanoke, 97,032; Lynchburg, 75,568; Harrisonburg, 48,914

Notable
Thomas Jefferson's Poplar Forest in Bedford County features tours of Jefferson's octagonal "other" home.

Rep. Eric Cantor (R)

Capitol Office
225-2815
cantor.house.gov
303 Cannon Bldg. 20515-4607; fax 225-0011

Committees
No committee assignments

Residence
Glen Allen

Born
June 6, 1963; Richmond, Va.

Religion
Jewish

Family
Wife, Diana Fine Cantor; three children

Education
George Washington U., B.A. 1985 (political science);
College of William & Mary, J.D. 1988; Columbia U.,
M.S. 1989 (real estate development)

Career
Lawyer; real estate developer; campaign aide

Political Highlights
Va. House, 1992-2001

ELECTION RESULTS

2010 GENERAL

Eric Cantor (R)	138,209	59.2%
Rick E. Waugh Jr. (D)	79,616	34.1%
Floyd C. Bayne (IGREEN)	15,164	6.5%

2010 PRIMARY

Eric Cantor (R)	unopposed

2008 GENERAL

Eric Cantor (R)	233,531	62.7%
Anita Hartke (D)	138,123	37.1%

Previous Winning Percentages
2006 (64%); 2004 (76%); 2002 (69%); 2000 (67%)

Elected 2000; 6th term

As majority leader, Cantor has emerged as a powerful partner for his boss, Speaker John A. Boehner of Ohio, and remains a key driver in the GOP's push to recruit new candidates and appeal to independent voters.

Youthful, articulate and relentlessly on message, the House Republicans' No. 2 leader has served as a champion for the party's right wing and has encouraged the GOP to develop a stronger message aimed at small businesses and suburban families.

Cantor won election to his leadership position in November 2010 without opposition after sending colleagues a 22-page manifesto envisioning a streamlined floor calendar, an end to measures honoring "individuals, groups, events and institutions," and a "methodical march" on GOP priorities. After winning his caucus post, Cantor said, "Job one is for us is to cut federal spending and to remove the uncertainty that has been hampering job creation."

Cantor, who was Boehner's choice to represent House Republicans in deficit reduction talks with the Obama administration in April 2011, has a penchant for getting out front on bold initiatives that offers a contrast to Boehner's somewhat more deliberate approach. For example, Cantor called in the final weeks of the 2010 campaign for extending the GOP's voluntary one-year earmark moratorium, while Boehner waited until after the election to cement approval by his caucus of the extension.

Although he was widely viewed as a leader-in-waiting, Cantor made clear during the 2010 campaign that he aimed to be second in command and would not challenge Boehner in a race for the top Republican post, regardless of the election's outcome. And despite occasional differences, the two men have forged a complementary partnership. "We have a very productive relationship. We talk frequently. We meet regularly," Cantor said.

In his lone term as whip in the 111th Congress (2009-10), Cantor honed a smooth style as the chief GOP vote counter. He also worked with his top lieutenant and successor, Kevin McCarthy of California, to link their caucus to constituents via the Internet and social media.

But, unlike Boehner and McCarthy, Cantor retains a formal membership in the Republican Study Committee, the party's conservative wing.

After the health care fight, which culminated in enactment of an overhaul in 2010, Cantor played a dual role by denouncing vandalism aimed at Democrats while defending the GOP against partisan attacks. He also revealed that a gunshot had struck a window in one of his district offices. Days later, in a separate probe, authorities charged a Philadelphia man with threatening Cantor.

A former tax writer and a lawyer with a master's degree in real estate development from Columbia University, Cantor often takes a lead role in developing business-related themes and promotes GOP alternatives on major legislation. He helped produce an alternative stimulus plan featuring small-business tax breaks, which aided in solidifying unified GOP opposition to Obama's $787 billion economic stimulus law.

As a leader of the party's "Young Guns" recruitment program, he has helped promote GOP efforts to appeal to younger voters and business groups without alienating social conservatives. Cantor and two co-authors — McCarthy and Budget Committee Chairman Paul D. Ryan of Wisconsin — wrote a book, "Young Guns," about their vision for the party. And armed with $3.7 million in receipts for his leadership political action committee in the 2010 cycle, Cantor served as a generous benefactor to colleagues.

But some efforts to raise his profile have hit snags. A Cantor-backed leadership caucus that sponsored a series of town halls in 2009 for party leaders to vet policy ideas was shut down after Democrats and an ethics watchdog group attacked the use of congressional staff for such activities.

In 2003, Cantor hopped over more senior colleagues to snag a plum job as chief deputy to GOP whip Roy Blunt of Missouri. Three years later Cantor was poised to take a step up, but Blunt held on as whip after losing to Boehner in a race for leader.

As the only Jewish Republican in the House, Cantor is a nexus between the party's pro-Israel Christian conservatives and traditionally Democratic Jewish campaign donors. Just after the 2010 election, he met with Israeli Prime Minister Benjamin Netanyahu in New York. In 2008, he helped his party's presidential nominee, Arizona Sen. John McCain, raise money from the Jewish community and was mentioned as a possible McCain running mate.

The low point for Cantor over the past few years was getting wrapped up in the Jack Abramoff influence-peddling scandal. Cantor was among the leaders who in 2003 signed a letter that helped an American Indian tribe represented by lobbyist Abramoff. Cantor received $12,000 in campaign donations through him, and later gave $10,000 of the money to a Richmond-area charity.

Cantor grew up in a well-to-do, politically active Richmond family. His father, Eddie, was on the board of the Virginia Housing Development Authority, and his mother, Mary Lee, was a board member of the Family and Children's Trust Fund and the Science Museum of Virginia.

While in college, Cantor interned for Rep. Thomas J. Bliley Jr. of Virginia, driving the Republican's campaign car around the district he would one day represent. He also worked as an aide to Walter A. Stosch, a member of the Virginia House of Delegates.

Cantor worked in the family real estate business before he was elected to Congress. His wife, Diana, was the founding executive director of the Virginia College Savings Plan and serves on the board of directors of Media General Inc. and Domino's Pizza.

When Stosch ran for the state Senate in 1991, Cantor made a bid for the open seat. The 28-year-old out-organized and outspent two rivals with more experience and won, becoming the youngest member of the House of Delegates. Bliley's campaign machinery stood behind Cantor when needed, and Cantor frequently served as Bliley's campaign chairman. When Bliley announced his retirement in 2000, Cantor joined the race to replace him. He won the primary by a scant 263 votes. But in November he sailed to victory, and his re-elections have been routine.

Key Votes

2010	
Overhaul the nation's health insurance system	NO
Allow for repeal of "don't ask, don't tell"	NO
Overhaul financial services industry regulation	NO
Limit use of new Afghanistan War funds to troop withdrawal activities	NO
Change oversight of offshore drilling and lift oil spill liability cap	NO
Provide a path to legal status for some children of illegal immigrants	NO
Extend Bush-era income tax cuts for two years	YES
2009	
Expand the Children's Health Insurance Program	NO
Provide $787 billion in tax cuts and spending increases to stimulate the economy	NO
Allow bankruptcy judges to modify certain primary-residence mortgages	NO
Create a cap-and-trade system to limit greenhouse gas emissions	NO
Provide $2 billion for the "cash for clunkers" program	NO
Establish the government as the sole provider of student loans	NO
Restrict federally funded insurance coverage for abortions in health care overhaul	YES

CQ Vote Studies

	PARTY UNITY		PRESIDENTIAL SUPPORT	
	SUPPORT	OPPOSE	SUPPORT	OPPOSE
2010	98%	2%	27%	73%
2009	97%	3%	21%	79%
2008	98%	2%	79%	21%
2007	98%	2%	89%	11%
2006	98%	2%	95%	5%

Interest Groups

	AFL-CIO	ADA	CCUS	ACU
2010	0%	0%	88%	100%
2009	5%	0%	71%	100%
2008	7%	5%	94%	92%
2007	4%	0%	80%	100%
2006	7%	5%	100%	92%

Virginia 7

Central — part of Richmond and suburbs

The solidly Republican 7th begins in part of Richmond and its affluent old-money suburbs, then reaches northwest to the Shenandoah Valley through farmland and new Washington exurbs.

Many of the 7th's residents work in Richmond, a longtime center of state government and commerce. Richmond also was one of the South's early manufacturing centers, concentrating on tobacco processing. Richmond-based Philip Morris USA continues to employ thousands of district residents.

The northeastern stretch of the 7th is changing, as declining traditional farming communities transform into exurban areas filled with new residents with long commutes to Washington or its close-in suburbs. The population in Culpeper County has grown by more than one-third since 2000, and the district as a whole added more than 100,000 residents. The northern 7th also boasts a local wine industry.

A plurality of district residents lives in Henrico County (shared with the 3rd), which cups Richmond in a backward C-shape.

Henrico traditionally has voted Republican, although it backed Democrats in the 2008 U.S. Senate and presidential elections. Chesterfield County (shared with the 4th) borders Richmond to the south and west and has a stronger GOP lean.

The 7th's portion of Democratic-leaning Richmond includes some Republican voters who live in the city's western end.

As a whole, the 7th is reliably Republican, and it is difficult for Democratic candidates to stitch together victories here.

All the counties that are located entirely in the district voted for Republican John McCain in the 2008 presidential election — only Caroline and Henrico counties, which are split with the 1st and 3rd districts, respectively, backed Barack Obama. McCain won 53 percent of the 7th's presidential vote.

Major Industry

Agriculture, government, manufacturing

Cities

Richmond (pt.), 54,204; Tuckahoe (unincorporated), 44,990; Mechanicsville (unincorporated), 36,348

Notable

Luray Caverns, in Page County, features a pipe organ made of stalactites; James Madison's Montpelier estate is in Orange County.

Rep. James P. Moran (D)

Capitol Office
225-4376
moran.house.gov
2239 Rayburn Bldg. 20515-4608; fax 225-0017

Committees
Appropriations

Residence
Arlington

Born
May 16, 1945; Buffalo, N.Y.

Religion
Roman Catholic

Family
Separated; four children

Education
College of the Holy Cross, B.A. 1967 (economics); City
U. of New York, Bernard M. Baruch School of Finance,
attended 1967-68; U. of Pittsburgh, M.P.A. 1970

Career
Investment broker; congressional aide; U.S. Health,
Education and Welfare Department analyst

Political Highlights
Alexandria City Council, 1979-84 (vice mayor, 1982-
84); mayor of Alexandria, 1985-90 (served as an
independent 1985-88)

ELECTION RESULTS

2010 GENERAL

James P. Moran (D)	116,404	61.0%
J. Patrick Murray (R)	71,145	37.3%
J. Ron Fisher (IGREEN)	2,707	1.4%

2010 PRIMARY

James P. Moran (D)	unopposed

2008 GENERAL

James P. Moran (D)	222,986	67.9%
Mark W. Ellmore (R)	97,425	29.7%
J. Ron Fisher (IGREEN)	6,829	2.1%

Previous Winning Percentages
2006 (66%); 2004 (60%); 2002 (60%); 2000 (63%);
1998 (67%); 1996 (66%); 1994 (59%); 1992 (56%);
1990 (52%)

Elected 1990; 11th term

Moran's pugnacious temperament, inflammatory remarks and sometimes spotty personal finances have been known to cause him trouble and
embarrass his allies. Still, he was given a plum legislative assignment in the
111th Congress — head of an Appropriations subcommittee — although it
turned out not to be quite so plum.

With Republicans back in charge in the 112th Congress (2011-12), Moran
surrendered the gavel of the Interior-Environment panel. And, in his less
than one term at the top, he was unable to push a stand-alone spending bill
through the House.

He will still wield power as the top Democrat on the panel, leaving him in
position to take care of constituent needs such as the recreational areas
along the George Washington Memorial Parkway, which shadows the
Potomac River in his district.

And, despite his penchant for combativeness, Moran has a reputation as
an able negotiator. A co-founder of the moderate New Democrat Coalition,
he has cut deals across party lines to bring in millions of dollars for local
roads, education programs, law enforcement and low-income housing.

Moran also sits on the Defense Appropriations panel, where he has been
a critic of U.S. policy in Iraq and Afghanistan.

In December 2010, he said the Afghan conflict was not winnable. "I don't
see us prevailing over any period of time, even if we extend this to 2014. We've
lost 1,400 troops. We've spent $345 billion. And we really are not prevailing in
this conflict because I don't think we can win militarily," he said on MSNBC.

Moran also strongly opposed the Iraq War, voting in 2002 against authorizing the use of force, and often supporting calls for withdrawal. Based on
his feelings about the war, he found himself on the wrong side of the contest
for majority leader in 2006. He sided with Pennsylvania Democrat John P.
Murtha, a decorated Marine veteran who led Democratic opposition to the
war, in his challenge to Steny H. Hoyer of Maryland. If Murtha had won,
Moran would have had a shot at the chairmanship of the Interior-Environment Subcommittee in the 110th Congress (2007-08). Instead, Moran held
his party's No. 2 slot on that panel, for the time being, behind Norm Dicks
of Washington.

When Murtha died in February 2010, Dicks took the late lawmaker's place
as head of the Defense Subcommittee, clearing the way for Moran to replace
Dicks as cardinal of the Interior panel.

Moran, whose district includes the Pentagon, also tends to constituent
needs as a member of the Military Construction-Veterans' Affairs spending panel. He is an energetic advocate for more pay and better health and
retirement benefits for federal workers, including, of course, those in the
Defense Department. He criticized President Obama's December 2010
proposal for a freeze on the pay of federal workers.

He has been vocal about the impact that the Pentagon's Base Realignment and Closure program will have on traffic around Fort Belvoir's office
sites in Northern Virginia. He and a pair of fellow Virginia Democrats,
Rep. Gerald E. Connolly and Sen. Mark Warner, sent a letter to Defense
Secretary Robert M. Gates in July 2010 calling for off-site transportation
improvements to help accommodate the influx of more than 27,000
employees to three area military facilities in 2011.

And he is working to see the State Department and related agencies
receive more resources — even if they must come from the Defense budget

he oversees — to conduct development, diplomacy and nation-building. "Many conflicts are not going to lend themselves to military solutions," he said.

Moran's position on the Defense subcommittee opened him and six of his colleagues up to an ethics investigation into their relationship with the PMA Group, a now-defunct lobbying firm that shut down in February 2009 following an FBI raid spurred by allegations of improper campaign contributions. PMA was Moran's top donor in the 2008 election cycle, giving him $37,500. The lawmakers were ultimately cleared of any wrongdoing by the House ethics committee, and federal prosecutors did not press charges against any of them.

Moran has made headlines in the past for other questionable decisions and for arguably offensive remarks. In 2002, the Washington Post reported that Moran borrowed $50,000 from an America Online executive and used the money to trade in stocks, before repaying it months later. He has commented on at least two occasions that the Jewish community pushed for the Iraq War. In an incident just before the March 2003 invasion of Iraq, his remarks prompted Democratic leader Nancy Pelosi of California to strip him of his post in the whip organization, despite his apology. More recently, he decried his GOP opponent in the 2010 election, retired Army Col. Patrick Murray, for not performing "any kind of public service." He later said he was referring to Murray's lack of civic involvement.

Moran grew up in a Boston suburb, one of seven siblings, all of whom have been involved in politics. First elected to the Alexandria City Council in 1979, Moran saw his career derailed briefly five years later when, after pleading no contest to a misdemeanor conflict-of-interest charge, he resigned as vice mayor. He ran as an independent the next year and unseated the incumbent mayor. He was serving as mayor in 1990 when he ran for Congress, upsetting six-term Republican Stan Parris in taking 52 percent of the vote.

Republicans tested Moran in 1992 and 1994 with a quality challenger in Kyle E. McSlarrow, but Moran prevailed by wide margins. In 2002 and 2004, he slipped to about 60 percent, a sign that voters were tiring of his family problems and financial dealings. Moran's wife of 11 years, Mary, filed for divorce in 1999, a day after calling police during a domestic argument. In court filings, she blamed the couple's poor finances on $120,000 in bad stock trades that Moran had made. He married for a third time in 2004 to LuAnn Bennett, a commercial real estate developer.

In the 2006 and 2008 elections, Moran bounced back, capturing 66 percent and 68 percent of the vote. His share was somewhat smaller, 61 percent, in 2010.

Key Votes

2010

Overhaul the nation's health insurance system	YES
Allow for repeal of "don't ask, don't tell"	YES
Overhaul financial services industry regulation	YES
Limit use of new Afghanistan War funds to troop withdrawal activities	NO
Change oversight of offshore drilling and lift oil spill liability cap	YES
Provide a path to legal status for some children of illegal immigrants	YES
Extend Bush-era income tax cuts for two years	NO

2009

Expand the Children's Health Insurance Program	YES
Provide $787 billion in tax cuts and spending increases to stimulate the economy	YES
Allow bankruptcy judges to modify certain primary-residence mortgages	YES
Create a cap-and-trade system to limit greenhouse gas emissions	YES
Provide $2 billion for the "cash for clunkers" program	YES
Establish the government as the sole provider of student loans	YES
Restrict federally funded insurance coverage for abortions in health care overhaul	NO

CQ Vote Studies

	PARTY UNITY		PRESIDENTIAL SUPPORT	
	SUPPORT	OPPOSE	SUPPORT	OPPOSE
2010	97%	3%	85%	15%
2009	98%	2%	97%	3%
2008	98%	2%	15%	85%
2007	98%	2%	5%	95%
2006	90%	10%	33%	67%

Interest Groups

	AFL-CIO	ADA	CCUS	ACU
2010	93%	100%	13%	8%
2009	100%	85%	50%	0%
2008	100%	95%	61%	0%
2007	96%	95%	55%	0%
2006	93%	95%	53%	16%

Virginia 8

Washington suburbs — Arlington, Alexandria, part of Fairfax County

Taking in the close-in Northern Virginia suburbs of Washington, the 8th is mostly upper-income and strongly Democratic — in no small part because of a racially and ethnically diverse population of blacks, Asians and Hispanics, who together total more than 40 percent of residents, as well as one of the nation's largest number of residents of Arab ancestry.

The 8th bustles with high-tech firms and defense contractors drawn to the district's substantial military presence, including the Pentagon and Fort Belvoir, which received nearly 20,000 new military, civilian and contractor jobs following the 2005 round of base realignments. Employers in the government, defense and technology fields rely on a well-educated workforce, and 60 percent of residents here have a college degree, the second-highest mark in the nation.

Nearly half of the district's residents live in an elongated swath of growing Fairfax County that reaches from the Potomac River, near Mount Vernon (shared with the 11th), past Falls Church and Tysons Corner to Reston.

Gridlock plagues the commute into Washington, and local officials are looking to develop areas in the northern arm of the district into more self-contained urban areas.

Alexandria and Arlington tend to give Democratic statewide candidates some of their highest vote percentages. A GOP presidential candidate has not won a majority in either jurisdiction since 1972, and the 8th gave Barack Obama 69 percent of its 2008 presidential vote.

Major Industry
Government, technology, defense, service

Military Bases
Pentagon, 11,000 military, 13,000 civilian (2005); Fort Belvoir (Army), 6,691 military, 14,424 civilian; Joint Base Myer-Henderson Hall, 7,920 military, 1,374 civilian (2011)

Cities
Arlington (unincorporated), 207,627; Alexandria, 139,966; Reston (unincorporated) (pt.), 57,533

Notable
The Torpedo Factory Art Center in Alexandria was a World War II munitions factory that has been converted into an art school and gallery.

Rep. Morgan Griffith (R)

Capitol Office
225-3861
morgangriffith.house.gov
1108 Longworth Bldg. 20515-4609; fax 225-0076

Committees
Energy & Commerce

Residence
Salem

Born
March 15, 1958; Philadelphia, Pa.

Religion
Protestant

Family
Wife, Hilary Griffith; three children

Education
Emory & Henry College, B.A. 1980 (history);
Washington and Lee U., J.D. 1983

Career
Lawyer

Political Highlights
Salem Republican Committee chairman, 1986-88,
1991-94; Va. House, 1994-2011 (majority leader,
2000-11)

ELECTION RESULTS

2010 GENERAL

Morgan Griffith (R)	95,726	51.2%
Rick Boucher (D)	86,743	46.4%
Jeremiah D. Heaton (I)	4,282	2.3%

Elected 2010; 1st term

Griffith brings a conservative record and extensive experience in state government to Congress, where he won a prized seat on the Energy and Commerce Committee.

That affords him a front-row seat for debates on energy legislation, which is so important to the coal mining interests in his region.

He is a virulent foe of proposals to create a cap-and-trade system to limit carbon emissions, and he backed legislation to bar the EPA from implementing such a program via regulation.

Griffith shares the small-government outlook held by much of the outsized Republican class of 2010. He voted against the final version of a catch-all spending bill for fiscal 2011, saying it was a step in the right direction, but that the $40 billion in spending cuts did not do enough to address the deficit.

Griffith said he plans to continue the socially conservative path he blazed in Richmond. He plans to support legislation to curb abortion and to protect gun owners' rights, and he intends to oppose same-sex marriage.

Griffith served 16 years in the Virginia House, including a decade as majority leader, the first Republican ever to hold that office.

He was the consensus party choice to challenge 14-term Democrat Rick Boucher, who hadn't even drawn a Republican opponent in 2008 and hadn't been seriously challenged since 1984.

As a senior member of Energy and Commerce, Boucher had backed the Democrats' cap-and-trade bill in 2009. His argument that he helped include coal industry protections in the measure failed to insulate him.

The National Republican Congressional Committee and independent expenditure groups spent more than $500,000 to aid Griffith.

Democrats tried to paint the Republican as a carpetbagger who did not live in the 9th District. Griffith responded with an ad in which he used a tape measure to show how far outside the district his home is — "about a foot," he said. Griffith won 51 percent of the vote to Boucher's 46 percent.

Redistricting is likely to bring Griffith's home within the boundaries of his new district.

Virginia 9

Southwest — Blacksburg, Bristol

Encompassing the mountains and forests of Virginia's southwestern corner, the rural 9th District hosts the college towns of Blacksburg and Radford, as well as the smaller coal and factory towns nestled close to neighboring West Virginia, North Carolina, Tennessee and Kentucky.

The district has struggled with a weak economic base and stagnant population. The 9th is Virginia's poorest district, with a median household income of $36,000. It has the state's highest percentage of blue-collar workers, who hold coal mining and manufacturing jobs. Despite the presence of one of the state's largest universities — Virginia Tech in Blacksburg — the 9th has Virginia's lowest percentage of college-educated residents (17 percent).

Jobs and construction at the new headquarters of a digital advertising firm in Blacksburg will boost the local economy. And state and local leaders have worked to improve district residents' quality of life by promoting the scenic Blue Ridge Parkway to attract tourism revenue.

Known for its competitive elections, the 9th is characterized by its ornery isolation from the political establishment in Richmond. The district supports Republicans in presidential elections but had elected a Democrat to Congress for more than two decades until 2010. Democrats can win in local races.

Major Industry
Manufacturing, coal mining, agriculture

Cities
Blacksburg, 42,620; Christiansburg, 21,041; Bristol, 17,835

Notable
Abingdon's still-thriving Barter Theatre allowed local residents to exchange excess produce and livestock for admission during the Depression.

Rep. Frank R. Wolf (R)

Capitol Office
225-5136
house.gov/wolf
241 Cannon Bldg. 20515-4610; fax 225-0437

Committees
Appropriations
(Commerce-Justice-Science - Chairman)

Residence
Vienna

Born
Jan. 30, 1939; Philadelphia, Pa.

Religion
Presbyterian

Family
Wife, Carolyn Wolf; five children

Education
Pennsylvania State U., B.A. 1961 (political science);
Georgetown U., LL.B. 1965

Military
Army Reserve, 1962-63

Career
Lawyer; congressional aide; lobbyist; U.S. Interior
Department official

Political Highlights
Sought Republican nomination for U.S. House, 1976;
Republican nominee for U.S. House, 1978

ELECTION RESULTS

2010 GENERAL

Frank R. Wolf (R)	131,116	62.9%
Jeffrey R. Barnett (D)	72,604	34.8%
William B. Redpath (LIBERT)	4,607	2.2%

2010 PRIMARY

Frank R. Wolf (R)	unopposed

2008 GENERAL

Frank R. Wolf (R)	223,140	58.8%
Judy M. Feder (D)	147,357	38.8%
Neeraj C. Nigam (I)	8,457	2.2%

Previous Winning Percentages
2006 (57%); 2004 (64%); 2002 (72%); 2000 (84%);
1998 (72%); 1996 (72%); 1994 (87%); 1992 (64%);
1990 (61%); 1988 (68%); 1986 (60%); 1984 (63%);
1982 (53%); 1980 (51%)

Elected 1980; 16th term

Wolf is an energetic and passionate advocate on a host of issues ranging from international human rights to the national debt, and he prides himself on being a thorn in the side of high-ranking officials of all political stripes — be they Barack Obama, George W. Bush or the king of Morocco.

With the United States suffering a sluggish economy and soaring federal debt, fiscal responsibility has been one of Wolf's major focuses, but he has not supported the larger cuts proposed by some conservatives. Wolf, a senior appropriator, supported the final version of a catchall bill for fiscal 2011 that trimmed spending by $40 billion, after opposing an earlier effort to return spending to 2006 levels.

But he backed the House GOP budget for fiscal 2012, which called for about $4 trillion in cuts over 10 years.

In the 111th Congress (2009-10), he joined with Democrat Jim Cooper of Tennessee to push bipartisan legislation creating a commission to study ways to cut the federal budget deficit. That effort was superseded by President Obama's creation of a deficit commission by executive order.

Wolf has a forum for his interest in human rights and religious freedom as chairman of the Appropriations Committee's panel with jurisdiction over the Justice Department, and as co-chairman of the Tom Lantos Human Rights Commission. In June 2010, he held hearings on the deportations of Christians from Morocco, expressing disappointment in the Moroccan government — and in the Obama administration — for what he perceived as its silence on the issue. He also serves on the panel handling spending for the State Department.

One of his proudest accomplishments in his long career — he's the 10th most senior Republican in the House — is a 1998 law that established a new government body to monitor religious freedom abroad. He said the International Religious Freedom Commission has given victims of persecution "a forum to speak truth" and to put pressure on U.S. policymakers to act on their behalf.

Wolf criticized Bush for attending the 2008 Olympics in China, citing its government's support for the regime in Sudan — widely believed to be responsible for genocide in its Darfur region — and Beijing's domestic human rights record. The first member of the House to travel to Darfur, he has said the Obama administration is "setting us back on human rights" and should be doing more to address the situation there.

He was a force behind the creation of the Iraq Study Group, a panel composed of policy experts that recommended a new course in Iraq in late 2006, although not the one eventually taken. Since the attempted Christmas Day 2009 bombing of a Northwest Airlines flight bound for Detroit, Wolf has been pressing the Obama administration to create an outside panel much like the Iraq Study Group to evaluate U.S. counterterrorism strategy.

Wolf holds deep Christian beliefs and often displays a socially conservative side, as in his vote to restrict abortion funding in the health care overhaul that was signed into law in 2010. He joined the rest of his Republican colleagues in voting against the overhaul measure and supporting its repeal in 2011, but he has crossed party lines on other issues.

In the 111th Congress, he split with Republicans on 18 percent of the votes that pitted the two parties against each other. Two years earlier, he joined Democrats in an unsuccessful bid to override Bush's veto of a bill expanding the Children's Health Insurance Program, which covers children whose low-income families make too much money to qualify for Medicaid; he was one of 40 House Republicans supporting the 2009 version that was signed into law.

Wolf's district is home to thousands of federal employees, and in 2009 he was one of three original GOP cosponsors of legislation to grant them up to four weeks of paid parental leave. A leading proponent of telecommuting and its potential to relieve the region's clogged roads, Wolf has used his seat on the Appropriations panel handling transportation spending to send home millions of dollars for related projects. Earlier in his career, he fought for federal funds to complete the Washington area's subway system, and he was a staunch advocate of extending Metrorail service to Washington Dulles International Airport, a project now under construction.

A history buff, Wolf is often involved in efforts to preserve historic sites in his district. Despite opposition from some conservatives who said it could impede local development decisions, he won enactment in 2008 of a law designating a 175-mile corridor from Gettysburg, Pa., to Charlottesville, Va., as a National Heritage Area. It is modeled after the Shenandoah Valley Battlefields National Historic District, which Wolf helped create in the late 1990s.

Wolf was born and raised in Philadelphia, the son of a police officer and a cafeteria worker. His interest in politics grew out of a boyhood fascination with history and a desire to find a way to overcome a stutter. In college, Wolf majored in political science, then earned his law degree from Georgetown University in Washington. He became an aide to Pennsylvania GOP Rep. Edward G. Biester, then a deputy assistant in the Interior Department during the Nixon and Ford administrations. Later, he worked as a lobbyist for baby food and farm-implement manufacturers.

Most members of his family were Democrats, but Wolf said he became a Republican because of his beliefs in lower taxes, a strong national defense and a tough approach to fighting communism during the Cold War.

He credits President Ronald Reagan with getting him into office. After being unsuccessful in his first two attempts to win a House seat, Wolf in a 1980 rematch with Rep. Joseph L. Fisher — the Democrat who had defeated him in 1978 — rode the Reagan surge to a narrow victory.

Wolf had a tough re-election race in 1982, then enjoyed smooth rides until his 2006 battle with former Georgetown University Public Policy Institute Dean Judy M. Feder. With the 10th District becoming incrementally more Democratic, Wolf had more of a struggle than he was accustomed to. He still won 57 percent to 41 percent, but that was a deviation from his previous 30-point margins. He widened his margin against Feder in 2008, taking nearly 59 percent. He won 63 percent of the vote in 2010.

Key Votes

2010

Overhaul the nation's health insurance system	NO
Allow for repeal of "don't ask, don't tell"	NO
Overhaul financial services industry regulation	NO
Limit use of new Afghanistan War funds to troop withdrawal activities	NO
Change oversight of offshore drilling and lift oil spill liability cap	NO
Provide a path to legal status for some children of illegal immigrants	NO
Extend Bush-era income tax cuts for two years	NO

2009

Expand the Children's Health Insurance Program	YES
Provide $787 billion in tax cuts and spending increases to stimulate the economy	NO
Allow bankruptcy judges to modify certain primary-residence mortgages	NO
Create a cap-and-trade system to limit greenhouse gas emissions	NO
Provide $2 billion for the "cash for clunkers" program	NO
Establish the government as the sole provider of student loans	NO
Restrict federally funded insurance coverage for abortions in health care overhaul	YES

CQ Vote Studies

	PARTY UNITY		PRESIDENTIAL SUPPORT	
	Support	Oppose	Support	Oppose
2010	89%	11%	29%	71%
2009	79%	21%	43%	57%
2008	87%	13%	66%	34%
2007	79%	21%	58%	42%
2006	85%	15%	80%	20%

Interest Groups

	AFL-CIO	ADA	CCUS	ACU
2010	7%	10%	88%	92%
2009	29%	10%	93%	80%
2008	21%	30%	94%	79%
2007	38%	40%	80%	68%
2006	50%	10%	67%	64%

Virginia 10

North — part of Fairfax County, Loudoun County

Located in the northern tip of Virginia, the 10th bridges a dizzying range of economies and lifestyles, with mountains and farmland at one end and congested Washington suburbs at the other. A hotbed of economic activity, the 10th is a predominately white-collar area that includes some of the nation's wealthiest counties — Loudoun and parts of Fairfax and Fauquier — that are home to young professionals and their families.

Most of the district's population resides in the Northern Virginia region — the densely populated suburbs west and south of Washington that are split among several districts — and many residents commute to jobs in Washington or the urbanized area inside the Capital Beltway. About 30 percent of district residents live in Fairfax County, which is shared with the 8th and 11th districts. Explosive population growth in technology-magnet Loudoun County, which includes Leesburg and Washington Dulles International Airport, accounts for the 10th's place as one of the fastest-growing districts in the nation since 2000.

Agriculture and manufacturing fuel the economy in the rest of the 10th, which is solidly Republican and less densely populated. Clarke and Frederick counties produce about half of Virginia's apples and peaches. Winchester, within fast-growing Frederick County, is the center of the state's apple-growing industry.

The 10th swung left in the 2008 presidential race, giving Democrat Barack Obama 53 percent of its vote, with parts of Fairfax and Frederick counties carrying the most Democratic weight. Loudoun County also backed Obama in 2008, but the district as a whole still tends to vote Republican in federal and state legislative races. Slow-growth advocates play a role in local politics as the region grapples with its rapid expansion. The 10th also struggles with violent gang activity.

Major Industry

Technology, government, manufacturing, agriculture

Cities

McLean (unincorporated) (pt.), 46,331; Ashburn (unincorporated), 43,511; Leesburg, 42,616; Centreville (unincorporated)(pt.), 39,345

Notable

The Enola Gay, which dropped an atomic bomb in World War II, is at the National Air and Space Museum's Udvar-Hazy Center near Dulles.

Rep. Gerald E. Connolly (D)

Capitol Office
225-1492
connolly.house.gov
424 Cannon Bldg. 20515; fax 225-3071

Committees
Foreign Affairs
Oversight & Government Reform

Residence
Fairfax

Born
March 30, 1950; Boston, Mass.

Religion
Roman Catholic

Family
Wife, Catherine Connolly; one child

Education
Maryknoll College, B.A. 1971 (literature); Harvard U.,
M.P.A. 1979

Career
Government relations executive; congressional aide;
nonprofit international aid organization director

Political Highlights
Fairfax County Board of Supervisors, 1995-2003; Fairfax County Board of Supervisors chairman, 2004-09

ELECTION RESULTS

2010 GENERAL

Gerald E. Connolly (D)	111,720	49.2%
Keith Fimian (R)	110,739	48.8%

2010 PRIMARY

Gerald E. Connolly (D)	unopposed

2008 GENERAL

Gerald E. Connolly (D)	196,598	54.7%
Keith Fimian (R)	154,758	43.0%
Joseph P. Oddo (IGREEN)	7,271	2.0%

Elected 2008; 2nd term

Connolly is a dependable Democratic vote and guardian of the interests of the tens of thousands of government employees — current and retired — who populate his Northern Virginia district.

He quickly moved onto the Oversight and Government Reform Committee, where his predecessor — Thomas M. Davis III — was once ranking Republican. Drawing from his work as a member of the Fairfax County Board of Supervisors, he pushes to institute successful local government practices at the federal level. He supported passage of a bill by New York Democrat Edolphus Towns aimed at ensuring oversight of the expenditure of money provided by the 2009 economic stimulus, which he also supported. Connolly had introduced a similar measure.

He questioned Defense Secretary Robert M. Gates' proposal to cut defense contracting costs by 10 percent, citing both substantive national security concerns and "the obvious impact on the economy and workforce in Northern Virginia."

To assist commuters in the densely populated, traffic-congested region, Connolly helped persuade the Transportation Department and the Federal Highway Administration to allow all drivers access to a pair of HOV ramps on Interstate 66 during off-peak hours.

He echoed GOP complaints that President Obama's plan to extend the Bush-era income tax cuts only to married couples with income of less than $250,000 would unfairly hit small-business owners and hurt a lot of families in his affluent district. "We are managing a very fragile recovery, and now is not the time to raise taxes on anyone," said Connolly, who backed a two-year extension of the cuts that was enacted in late 2010.

Generally, though, Connolly backs Obama and the Democratic leadership. On votes that divided a majority of Democrats from a majority of Republicans, Connolly sided with his party on more than nine of every 10 votes in the 111th Congress (2009-10).

And he was an enthusiastic supporter of the Democrats' health care overhaul enacted in March 2010.

"Forty-five years ago, when I was a young debater, the national debate topic was, 'Would the adoption of Medicare lead to socialized medicine in America?' The same distortions used then are being used by the same opposition forces now," he said on the House floor.

He campaigned vigorously in 2008 on the need for energy conservation and a reduction in greenhouse gas emissions, then helped secure votes for House passage of a Democratic bill in June 2009 that included a cap on carbon emissions and would have created a system for companies to buy and sell pollution allowances. He opposed GOP efforts early in the 112th Congress (2011-12) to block the EPA from creating such a system through its regulatory authority.

Connolly also sits on the Foreign Affairs Committee, where he is the No. 2 Democrat on the Middle East and South Asia Subcommittee, and he also serves on the Terrorism, Nonproliferation and Trade Subcommittee. As an aide for the Senate Foreign Relations Committee from 1979 to 1989, he specialized in foreign development aid and helped manage committee oversight of international narcotics control and United Nations and Middle East policies.

During his tenure on the Board of Supervisors, Connolly was a supporter of the Islamic Saudi Academy, a Saudi Embassy-funded school that critics — including the congressionally created U.S. Commission on International Religious Freedom — said were using textbooks that promoted violence. He came under fire for accepting Saudi-connected campaign contributions while backing a renewal of the school's lease.

Connolly, a former seminary student, calls politics a "logical extension" of his earlier study of religion. He turned away from his pursuit of the priesthood, he said, in part because of his frustration with the church's reluctance to speak out against the Vietnam War.

Connolly grew up in Boston, where his grandmother settled after leaving Northern Ireland at 17. His father helped spark his passion for politics, bringing 8-year-old Connolly along to erect placards for John F. Kennedy's Senate campaign in Boston. Connolly's mother was a nurse, and his father worked in life insurance and served as a ward committee member, which brought the family close to Democrat Thomas P. "Tip" O'Neill Jr., Speaker of the House from 1977 to 1987. Connolly used O'Neill's gavel, a gift from a constituent, when he first presided over the House in 2009.

He studied at Maryknoll Fathers Junior Seminary in Pennsylvania in the mid-1960s. In addition to his disillusionment over Vietnam, doubts about a life of celibacy led him away from the priesthood.

After graduating with a degree in literature from Maryknoll College in 1971, he worked for nonprofit organizations, including the American Freedom From Hunger Foundation, where he met his future wife, Catherine Smith, a former nun.

After earning a master's degree in public administration at Harvard, Connolly worked for the Senate Foreign Relations Committee. He then returned to the private sector, serving as vice president for the Washington office of SRI International, formerly the Stanford Research Institute. He also helped found the Washington International Corporate Circle program, which provides analysis for international businesses.

Connolly was elected to the Fairfax County Board of Supervisors in 1995 and became chairman in 2004.

To succeed the retiring Davis in 2008, Connolly won a heated Democratic primary, then had little trouble defeating Republican Keith Fimian in November, winning by 12 percentage points. The 2010 rematch against Fimian was a different story, with Connolly prevailing by fewer than 1,000 votes in a race that wasn't certified until a week after Election Day.

Before former Gov. Tim Kaine announced he would seek the Democratic nomination, Connolly briefly considered a 2012 run for the Senate seat held by retiring Democrat Jim Webb.

Key Votes

2010

Overhaul the nation's health insurance system	YES
Allow for repeal of "don't ask, don't tell"	YES
Overhaul financial services industry regulation	YES
Limit use of new Afghanistan War funds to troop withdrawal activities	NO
Change oversight of offshore drilling and lift oil spill liability cap	YES
Provide a path to legal status for some children of illegal immigrants	YES
Extend Bush-era income tax cuts for two years	YES

2009

Expand the Children's Health Insurance Program	YES
Provide $787 billion in tax cuts and spending increases to stimulate the economy	YES
Allow bankruptcy judges to modify certain primary-residence mortgages	YES
Create a cap-and-trade system to limit greenhouse gas emissions	YES
Provide $2 billion for the "cash for clunkers" program	YES
Establish the government as the sole provider of student loans	YES
Restrict federally funded insurance coverage for abortions in health care overhaul	NO

CQ Vote Studies

	PARTY UNITY		PRESIDENTIAL SUPPORT	
	SUPPORT	OPPOSE	SUPPORT	OPPOSE
2010	90%	10%	93%	7%
2009	97%	3%	96%	4%

Interest Groups

	AFL-CIO	ADA	CCUS	ACU
2010	86%	85%	25%	4%
2009	95%	95%	47%	0%

Washington suburbs — parts of Fairfax and Prince William counties

Anchored in the suburbs of Washington, the 11th is home to a well-educated, professional and upper-income workforce that boasts the nation's highest median household income (nearly $104,000). Like other nearby suburban areas, the 11th has become more racially and ethnically diverse — it has the state's largest Asian population (15 percent) and second-highest Hispanic population (16 percent).

Sixty percent of the population lives in Fairfax County (shared with the 8th and 10th districts). The balance lives in Prince William County, a fast-growing area south and west of Fairfax, or in Fairfax city, a separate jurisdiction within Fairfax County. Many residents work in Washington, either for the federal government or for private companies linked to the government. Technology contributes to local economic growth, and Fairfax County's office parks are home to dozens of companies, including energy consulting firm ICF International's headquarters and major facilities for Verizon and Boeing.

Gridlock and the state's longest commute times place traffic congestion at the top of local priorities. Although the 11th tends to lean left on social issues and right on fiscal issues, some residents here are willing to accept tax increases to pay for transportation improvements. Decades of economic growth and the related traffic woes have made telecommuting an increasingly attractive option for area workers. Local officials in Fairfax County suburbs such as Annandale hope to implement smart-growth plans for redesigned surface roads and commercial centers.

The 11th's population and economic growth has made it politically competitive. Barack Obama won 57 percent of the 11th's 2008 presidential vote, but the district only narrowly re-elected Democrat Gerald E. Connolly to the U.S. House in 2010.

Major Industry
Government, technology, service

Cities
Dale City (unincorporated), 65,969; Lake Ridge (unincorporated), 41,058; Burke (unincorporated), 41,055; Annandale (unincorporated) (pt.), 39,362

Notable
George Washington's estate, Mount Vernon, is on the Potomac River in Fairfax County.

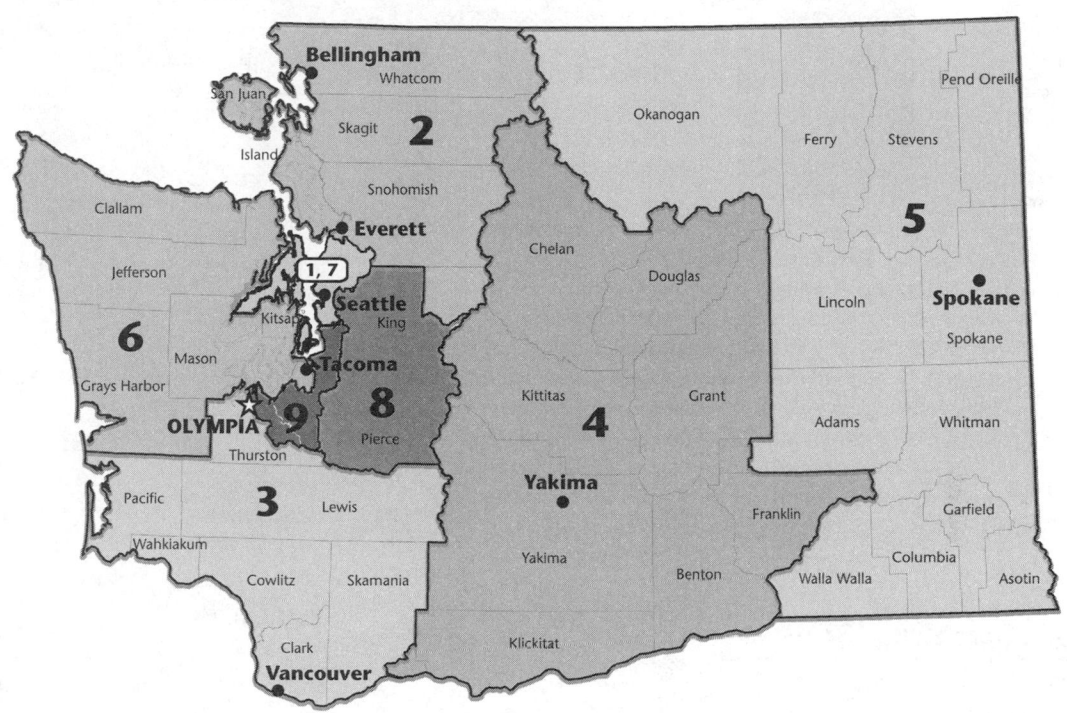

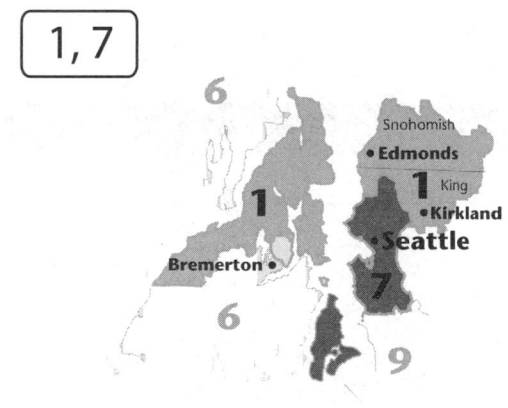

1, 7

Gov. Christine Gregoire (D)

Pronounced: GREG-wahr
First elected: 2004
Length of term: 4 years
Term expires: 1/13
Salary: $166,891
Phone: (360) 902-4111
Residence: Olympia
Born: March 24, 1947; Adrian, Mich.
Religion: Roman Catholic
Family: Husband, Mike Gregoire; two children
Education: U. of Washington, B.A. 1969 (speech & sociology); Gonzaga U., J.D. 1977
Career: Lawyer; state social services department caseworker; clerk typist
Political highlights: Wash. Department of Ecology director, 1988-92; Wash. attorney general, 1993-2004

ELECTION RESULTS

2008 GENERAL
Christine Gregoire (D)	1,598,738	53.2%
Dino Rossi (R)	1,404,124	46.8%

Lt. Gov. Brad Owen (D)

First elected: 1996
Length of term: 4 years
Term expires: 1/13
Salary: $93,948
Phone: (360) 786-7700

LEGISLATURE

Legislature: 105 days January-May in odd-numbered years; 60 days in January-March in even-numbered years
Senate: 49 members, 4-year terms
2011 ratios: 27 D, 22 R; 32 men, 17 women
Salary: $42,106
Phone: (360) 786-7550
House: 98 members, 2-year terms
2011 ratios: 56 D, 42 R; 67 men, 31 women
Salary: $42,106
Phone: (360) 786-7750

TERM LIMITS

Governor: No
Senate: No
House: No

URBAN STATISTICS

CITY	POPULATION
Seattle	608,660
Spokane	208,916
Tacoma	198,397
Vancouver	161,791
Bellevue	122,363

REGISTERED VOTERS

Voters do not register by party.

POPULATION

2010 population	6,724,540
2000 population	5,894,121
1990 population	4,866,692
Percent change (2000-2010)	+14.1%
Rank among states (2010)	13
Median age	36.8
Born in state	47.2%
Foreign born	11.7%
Violent crime rate	331/100,000
Poverty level	12.3%
Federal workers	92,594
Military	46,161

ELECTIONS

STATE ELECTION OFFICIAL
(360) 902-4180
DEMOCRATIC PARTY
(206) 583-0664
REPUBLICAN PARTY
(206) 575-2900

MISCELLANEOUS

Web: www.access.wa.gov
Capital: Olympia

U.S. CONGRESS

Senate: 2 Democrats
House: 5 Democrats, 4 Republicans

2010 Census Statistics by District

District	2008 Vote for President Obama	McCain	White	Black	Asian	Hispanic	Median Income	White Collar	Blue Collar	Service Industry	Over 64	Under 18	College Education	Rural	Sq. Miles
1	62%	36%	73%	3%	12%	8%	$72,352	70%	16%	13%	10%	24%	40%	5%	439
2	56	42	80	1	3	10	55,125	56	26	18	12	24	25	31	6,564
3	53	45	83	1	3	7	54,240	59	25	16	12	25	24	29	7,515
4	40	58	60	1	1	34	45,476	51	32	17	12	29	20	29	19,051
5	46	52	85	1	2	6	44,071	61	21	19	14	23	26	28	22,864
6	57	40	73	5	5	8	47,967	56	24	20	15	22	23	21	6,781
7	83	15	64	8	14	8	58,547	71	13	16	11	16	51	2	141
8	56	42	71	3	13	7	81,585	70	18	13	9	27	41	12	2,579
9	58	40	63	7	9	12	56,225	58	24	18	11	25	23	5	608
STATE	58	41	73	3	7	11	56,384	62	22	16	12	24	31	18	66,544
U.S.	53	46	64	12	5	16	51,425	60	23	17	13	25	28	21	3,537,438

Sen. Patty Murray (D)

Capitol Office
224-2621
murray.senate.gov
448 Russell Bldg. 20510-4704; fax 224-0238

Committees
Appropriations
(Transportation-HUD - Chairwoman)
Budget
Health, Education, Labor & Pensions
(Employment & Workplace Safety - Chairwoman)
Rules & Administration
Veterans' Affairs - Chairwoman
Joint Printing

Residence
Seattle

Born
Oct. 11, 1950; Bothell, Wash.

Religion
Roman Catholic

Family
Husband, Rob Murray; two children

Education
Washington State U., B.A. 1972

Career
Parenting class instructor

Political Highlights
Candidate for Shoreline School Board, 1983; Shoreline School Board, 1983-89; Wash. Senate, 1989-93

ELECTION RESULTS

2010 GENERAL

Patty Murray (D)	1,314,930	52.4%
Dino Rossi (R)	1,196,164	47.6%

2010 PRIMARY (Open)

Patty Murray (D)	670,284	46.2%

2004 GENERAL

Patty Murray (D)	1,549,708	55.0%
George Nethercutt (R)	1,204,584	42.7%
J. Mills (LIBERT)	34,055	1.2%
Mark B. Wilson (GREEN)	30,304	1.1%

Previous Winning Percentages
1998 (58%); 1992 (54%)

Elected 1992; 4th term

The one-time "mom in tennis shoes" now inhabits the powerful inner circle of the Senate Democratic leadership, where she is a devoted liberal proponent of government intervention in the economy and a fierce defender of her state's economic interests.

When Murray was first elected in 1992, it was dismissed as a fluke; she also was rated by congressional staffers in 2002 and 2004 as one of the least intelligent senators in Washingtonian magazine's "Best and Worst of Congress" list.

But she is now poised to ascend even higher than her current postings as Democratic Conference secretary — the party's No. 4 spot in the leadership — and chairwoman of the Democratic Senatorial Campaign Committee. She has also become a seasoned insider on the Appropriations Committee, where she leads the Transportation-Housing and Urban Development Subcommittee, and she's next in line to chair the Budget Committee.

On a leadership team that includes media-savvy Majority Whip Richard J. Durbin of Illinois and voluble Democratic Caucus Vice Chairman Charles E. Schumer of New York, Murray is decidedly lower-key. However, for many Senate Democrats, Murray is the person to approach for resolution to internal problems. She also has been described as the glue that keeps the leadership team cohesive, often acting as the voice of reason when its discussions stray off-course.

Murray brings another asset to the leadership: She remains relentlessly on message, unlike the unpredictable quips that tend to emerge from Schumer and Majority Leader Harry Reid of Nevada.

Murray is methodical and has a hand in national issues ranging from Amtrak policy to education. But she says Congress must stay focused on things affecting everyday Americans, and her speeches typically refer to a constituent or quote one. A prominent instance came at the president's health care summit in February 2010 when Murray — a member of the Health, Education, Labor and Pensions Committee — told the story of a woman who died after losing her job and health care coverage.

From her Appropriations post, she makes sure her state gets a healthy share of federal funding. She has been compared favorably to Washington's legendary Democratic Sen. Warren Magnuson, who was famed for securing billions of federal dollars for the state. She also once drew criticism from Arizona Republican John McCain, an opponent of the funding set-asides known as earmarks, for attaching $3 million for a maritime museum to the transportation spending bill in 2001. Murray sat stone-faced in the Senate chamber as McCain blasted the project as "pork-barrel spending."

During the 110th Congress (2007-08), she emerged as a trusted lieutenant to ailing Appropriations Chairman Robert C. Byrd of West Virginia. Byrd and Reid tapped her, rather than more-senior panel members, to serve as floor manager for key spending bills. In 2007, she steered through both a supplemental spending measure and the annual Homeland Security bill, but such opportunities dried up in 2008 because of a standoff between President George W. Bush and congressional Democrats. When Byrd gave up the gavel in 2009, the task returned to the new chairman, Hawaii Democrat Daniel K. Inouye.

In the aftermath of the 2008 economic meltdown, Murray has also been a prominent proponent of stimulating the economy by funding transportation and infrastructure projects. During debate on President Obama's economic stimulus package in early 2009, she proposed an additional $25 billion for infrastructure projects. Prior to that, Murray successfully fought for $8 billion in general revenues to shore up a faltering Highway Trust Fund in the fiscal 2009 transportation bill, which was part of an omnibus spending measure.

Newly installed as chairwoman of the Veterans' Affairs Committee in the 112th Congress (2011-12), Murray said she will monitor proposed GOP spending cuts "like a hawk" for their impact on veterans.

She has pushed for more funding for health care, particularly for veterans with traumatic brain injuries. When Obama proposed to collect money from private insurance companies for treating veterans with service-connected disabilities at VA hospitals, she said any budget request with the provision would be "dead on arrival," and the president eventually backed off.

Murray may not be as vocal as some senators, but she will go after what she wants in other ways. She was one of a few Democrats who threatened to block funding for some of Bush's pet projects until he agreed to include a full year's Iraq War funding estimate in his fiscal 2009 budget.

And though she eschews labels such as "feminist," Murray is concerned with women's issues. She once vowed to hold up the nomination of the head of the Food and Drug Administration until the agency made a decision on approving over-the-counter sales of morning-after birth control pills.

She is a fierce promoter of her state's two mega-employers, Microsoft Corp. and Boeing Co. She repeatedly denounced the long-running federal antitrust case against Microsoft. And she flew into action when the Air Force in 2008 decided to award a $35 billion contract for a fleet of new aerial tankers to a consortium made up of Northrop Grumman Corp. and the North American arm of the European Aeronautic Defence and Space Co., or EADS, which owns the airplane manufacturer Airbus. Murray said U.S. tax dollars should not go to boost a foreign company and she threatened to withhold funds for the tankers or impose other penalties on the Air Force. The original deal was scrapped after the Government Accountability Office concluded the Air Force had violated its own contracting rules. Boeing won the contract on the second go-round.

Murray's backing of government social programs and her work ethic stem from her childhood. She and her six siblings put in long hours at their father's dime store. They often they made their own clothes and went without health care. When Murray was a teenager, her father was diagnosed with multiple sclerosis and stopped working. The family briefly went on welfare until her mother completed a government-funded program that enabled her to work as a bookkeeper.

When Murray went to college, she worked to help pay for it. Her jobs included working in a glass shop, as a secretary and, one summer, cleaning bathrooms in a state park.

In the early 1980s, angered when the state legislature planned to eliminate a preschool program in which her children were enrolled, Murray packed the kids into the car and drove to the capital to complain. She was dismissed by a legislator who told her, "You can't make a difference. You're just a mom in tennis shoes." Murray said of the incident, "I drove home as angry as I could be, saying he has no right to tell me I can't make a difference." She organized a successful statewide campaign to revive the program. That led Murray to six years on a school board and four years in the state Senate.

In her 1992 U.S. Senate quest, she bested better-known moderates with years of congressional experience in the primary and general elections. She was re-elected in 1998 with 58 percent of the vote. In 2004 she faced George Nethercutt, a Republican House member who had beaten Democratic Speaker Thomas S. Foley in 1994. Murray won by 12 percentage points. Her 2010 race against Republican Dino Rossi was her closest re-election contest. She bested Rossi by less than 5 percentage points.

Key Votes

2010

Pass budget reconciliation bill to modify overhauls of health care and federal student loan programs	YES
Proceed to disapproval resolution on EPA authority to regulate greenhouse gases	NO
Overhaul financial services industry regulation	YES
Limit debate to proceed to a bill to broaden campaign finance disclosure and reporting rules	YES
Limit debate on an extension of Bush-era income tax cuts for two years	YES
Limit debate on a bill to provide a path to legal status for some children of illegal immigrants	YES
Allow for a repeal of "don't ask, don't tell"	YES
Consent to ratification of a strategic arms reduction treaty with Russia	YES

2009

Prevent release of remaining financial industry bailout funds	NO
Make it easier for victims to sue for wage discrimination remedies	YES
Expand the Children's Health Insurance Program	YES
Limit debate on the economic stimulus measure	YES
Repeal District of Columbia firearms prohibitions and gun registration laws	NO
Limit debate on expansion of federal hate crimes law	YES
Strike funding for F-22 Raptor fighter jets	NO

CQ Vote Studies

	PARTY UNITY		PRESIDENTIAL SUPPORT	
	SUPPORT	OPPOSE	SUPPORT	OPPOSE
2010	97%	3%	98%	2%
2009	97%	3%	95%	5%
2008	99%	1%	28%	72%
2007	97%	3%	38%	62%
2006	92%	8%	59%	41%
2005	95%	5%	33%	67%
2004	91%	9%	63%	37%
2003	97%	3%	49%	51%
2002	86%	14%	75%	25%
2001	96%	4%	65%	35%

Interest Groups

	AFL-CIO	ADA	CCUS	ACU
2010	100%	95%	27%	0%
2009	94%	95%	43%	0%
2008	100%	95%	63%	0%
2007	100%	90%	64%	0%
2006	93%	95%	50%	4%
2005	79%	95%	44%	0%
2004	92%	90%	75%	8%
2003	85%	90%	43%	10%
2002	92%	90%	55%	10%
2001	100%	85%	64%	4%

Sen. Maria Cantwell (D)

Capitol Office
224-3441
cantwell.senate.gov
511 Dirksen Bldg. 20510-4705; fax 228-0514

Committees
Commerce, Science & Transportation
(Aviation Operations, Safety & Security - Chairwoman)
Energy & Natural Resources
(Energy - Chairwoman)
Finance
Indian Affairs
Small Business & Entrepreneurship

Residence
Edmonds

Born
Oct. 13, 1958; Indianapolis, Ind.

Religion
Roman Catholic

Family
Single

Education
Miami U. (Ohio), B.A. 1980 (public policy)

Career
Public relations consultant; Internet audio company
executive

Political Highlights
Wash. House, 1987-92; U.S. House, 1993-95; defeated
for re-election to U.S. House, 1994

ELECTION RESULTS

2006 GENERAL

Maria Cantwell (D)	1,184,659	56.8%
Mike McGavick (R)	832,106	39.9%
Bruce Guthrie (LIBERT)	29,331	1.4%
Aaron Dixon (GREEN)	21,254	1.0%

2006 PRIMARY

Maria Cantwell (D)	570,677	90.8%
Hong Tran (D)	33,124	5.3%
Mike the Mover (D)	11,274	1.8%
Goodspaceguy Nelson (D)	9,454	1.5%

Previous Winning Percentages
2000 (49%); 1992 House Election (55%)

Elected 2000; 2nd term

Cantwell uses her business acumen and propensity for dealmaking to champion the interests of her home state and to stake out policy turf on energy, the environment and financial regulation. She has positioned herself as an emerging player in the Democratic ranks who isn't afraid to make her opinions known.

Those opinions are generally in line with her party — in the 111th Congress (2009-10), she voted with a majority of Democrats against a majority of Republicans 93 percent of the time. When she diverges, it is usually to the left.

Her smarts and television-ready looks would seem to combine to make her ready for political stardom. But she has been criticized for a sense of aloofness that can make her seem more the dot-com executive she once was than the public figure she now is. Sometimes she doesn't even make an opening statement at hearings, forgoing the free time to opine that few senators can resist.

But there have been signs that Cantwell is coming out of her shell — sometimes to her Democratic colleagues' dismay.

She was one of two Democrats to vote against initial Senate passage of the financial industry regulation overhaul measure in 2010, arguing that it would not do enough to rein in banks and others, although she did vote in favor of the conference report that finalized the legislation.

And she has used the gavel of the Energy and Natural Resources Subcommittee on Energy to score both policy and public relations points. As oil spewed into the Gulf of Mexico in spring 2010 following an explosion on the Deepwater Horizon drilling rig, Cantwell proposed a permanent ban on offshore drilling on the West Coast.

She also was an outspoken opponent of the leadership's plan for a cap-and-trade system for greenhouse gas emissions. Such a program, she says, could create a market vulnerable to collapse. In 2009 she and Maine Republican Susan Collins introduced a "cap and dividend" alternative, limiting the trade of carbon credits to those producing the emissions.

Through her position on the Energy panel, Cantwell worked to get $11 billion for "smart grid" technologies, designed to control electricity flow to consumers while reducing costs, included in the 2009 economic stimulus law.

She also worked earlier to include tax provisions on renewables in the $700 billion financial services bailout that became law in fall 2008 — but she was one of nine Democrats to vote against the bill.

In 2008, Cantwell decided the Commodity Futures Trading Commission wasn't doing enough to control speculation in energy futures markets, so she blocked nominations to the agency. Similarly, she cheered when the Federal Trade Commission (FTC) took steps in 2008 to go after players in the petroleum futures market suspected of deceptive practices. The previous year, Cantwell played a role in the legislation that gave the FTC that authority.

In 2005, she led opposition to a plan to open a sliver of the Arctic National Wildlife Refuge to energy exploration. The crusade earned her the enmity of a powerful fellow senator at the time, Republican Ted Stevens of Alaska, though his vow of electoral retaliation was unsuccessful.

Cantwell also sits on the Commerce, Science and Transportation Committee, a post important for her state's economy, which depends on international trade and technology. She serves on — and formerly chaired — its subcommittee on fisheries and the Coast Guard, where she looked into a $24 billion,

25-year plan to upgrade the Coast Guard's fleet that was plagued by errors, delays and cost overruns. The Senate passed her bill to overhaul the program and mandate stricter oversight in 2007. Following the 2010 Gulf Coast oil spill, she pushed to fast-track a reauthorization bill for the Coast Guard, which was expected to play a central role in containing and cleaning up the disaster.

In the 112th Congress (2011-12), she claimed the gavel of Commerce's aviation panel, giving her a platform to protect Washington's aerospace industry.

On the Finance Committee, Cantwell won adoption of an amendment to the financial regulation bill that would make manipulation in derivatives swaps markets illegal. In 2009, she introduced a bill with Arizona Republican John McCain to separate commercial and investment banks by reviving the Glass-Steagall Act, which was repealed more than a decade ago. They proposed the idea as an amendment to the financial regulation overhaul but later withdrew it.

A senior member of the Budget Committee, she joined with other Senate Democratic women to defend funding for Planned Parenthood, which was a target of House GOP budget cutters early in 2011.

On local matters, Cantwell has backed benefits for former workers at the Hanford Nuclear Reservation, some of whom fell ill when they worked with plutonium used in the production of nuclear weapons. A member of the Small Business and Entrepreneurship Committee, she has traveled to Cuba, Mexico and China to drum up interest for Washington's apple, potato and lentil growers. Her work on the Indian Affairs Committee has included winning approval in 2010 of a measure to allow tribes in her state to lease land for much longer periods, increasing the opportunities for development.

Cantwell, a native of Indiana, was exposed early to politics by her father, Paul Cantwell, who brought the family to the nation's capital in 1965 when he took a job working for home-state Democratic Rep. Andrew Jacobs Jr. He later moved back to Indiana and took a seat as a county commissioner.

After earning a degree in public policy at Miami University in Ohio, Cantwell worked on the unsuccessful gubernatorial campaign of Jerry Springer, who went on to talk-show fame. In 1983, she moved to the Seattle area to be a political organizer for Democratic presidential candidate Alan Cranston, a U.S. senator from California. She worked in public relations, then was elected to the state legislature, serving from 1987 to 1992. She was elected to the U.S. House in 1992, the same year her father was elected to the Indiana House. She served only one term before getting knocked out in the Republican tide of 1994.

Cantwell put politics aside for a few years, joining Seattle Internet startup RealNetworks, the software company that invented RealPlayer and other online audio and video products. She rose to be senior vice president of consumer products and made a small fortune before the stock's value plummeted in 2000.

She tapped into that wealth for a 2000 Senate run. She blew past the favored Democratic opponent, state Insurance Commissioner Deborah Senn, in Washington's open primary. She then spent $10 million to unseat incumbent Republican Slade Gorton. Cantwell carried only five of the state's 39 counties, all around Puget Sound, in her narrow general-election victory. With just more than 2,000 votes separating the candidates, the results were so close that her victory was not declared official until nearly a month after the election.

In 2006, Stevens made good on his threat to campaign against her. But the Alaskan's support for Republican Mike McGavick backfired when the candidate had to return $14,000 Stevens helped him raise from an Alaska oil company that figured in an FBI criminal investigation. Cantwell won the race by 17 percentage points.

Key Votes

2010

Pass budget reconciliation bill to modify overhauls of health care and federal student loan programs	YES
Proceed to disapproval resolution on EPA authority to regulate greenhouse gases	NO
Overhaul financial services industry regulation	YES
Limit debate to proceed to a bill to broaden campaign finance disclosure and reporting rules	YES
Limit debate on an extension of Bush-era income tax cuts for two years	YES
Limit debate on a bill to provide a path to legal status for some children of illegal immigrants	YES
Allow for a repeal of "don't ask, don't tell"	YES
Consent to ratification of a strategic arms reduction treaty with Russia	YES

2009

Prevent release of remaining financial industry bailout funds	YES
Make it easier for victims to sue for wage discrimination remedies	YES
Expand the Children's Health Insurance Program	YES
Limit debate on the economic stimulus measure	YES
Repeal District of Columbia firearms prohibitions and gun registration laws	NO
Limit debate on expansion of federal hate crimes law	YES
Strike funding for F-22 Raptor fighter jets	NO

CQ Vote Studies

	PARTY UNITY		PRESIDENTIAL SUPPORT	
	Support	Oppose	Support	Oppose
2010	92%	8%	95%	5%
2009	94%	6%	95%	5%
2008	97%	3%	28%	72%
2007	94%	6%	39%	61%
2006	92%	8%	54%	46%
2005	92%	8%	36%	64%
2004	90%	10%	66%	34%
2003	96%	4%	52%	48%
2002	82%	18%	81%	19%
2001	98%	2%	64%	36%

Interest Groups

	AFL-CIO	ADA	CCUS	ACU
2010	94%	90%	45%	12%
2009	94%	95%	43%	8%
2008	100%	100%	50%	12%
2007	95%	95%	64%	4%
2006	87%	95%	58%	12%
2005	86%	95%	56%	8%
2004	83%	95%	65%	8%
2003	85%	90%	39%	15%
2002	85%	80%	55%	25%
2001	100%	100%	50%	12%

Rep. Jay Inslee (D)

Capitol Office
225-6311
www.house.gov/inslee
2329 Rayburn Bldg. 20515-4701; fax 226-1606

Committees
Energy & Commerce

Residence
Bainbridge Island

Born
Feb. 9, 1951; Seattle, Wash.

Religion
Protestant

Family
Wife, Trudi Inslee; three children

Education
Stanford U., attended 1969-70; U. of Washington, B.A. 1973 (economics); Willamette U., J.D. 1976

Career
Lawyer

Political Highlights
Wash. House, 1989-93; U.S. House, 1993-95; defeated for re-election to U.S. House, 1994; sought Democratic nomination for governor, 1996

ELECTION RESULTS

2010 GENERAL

Jay Inslee (D)	172,642	57.7%
James Watkins (R)	126,737	42.3%

2010 PRIMARY (Open)

Jay Inslee (D)	90,208	55.8%

2008 GENERAL

Jay Inslee (D)	233,780	67.8%
Larry Ishmael (R)	111,240	32.2%

Previous Winning Percentages
2006 (68%); 2004 (62%); 2002 (56%); 2000 (55%); 1998 (50%); 1992 (51%)

Elected 1998; 8th term

Also served 1993-95

Inslee's legislative portfolio is focused on energy and the environment, and he approaches those issues from the left end of the political spectrum.

He sits on the Energy and Commerce Committee, where he is a vocal proponent of Democratic proposals to reduce greenhouse gas emissions and increase the use of renewable energy sources.

Inslee opposed GOP efforts in early 2011 to block the EPA from implementing a regulatory regime to cut carbon emissions similar to the one Democrats failed to enact legislatively in the 111th Congress (2009-10).

He says new technologies can keep global temperatures in check, but government must provide a boost. In 2009, Inslee co-founded the Sustainable Energy and Environmental Caucus.

"When it comes to technology, what seems impossible looking forward often looks inevitable looking backward," he said.

Inslee is generally civil, though he took some heat for a May 2010 confrontation at a hearing of the now-defunct Select Committee on Energy Independence and Global Warming in which he was discourteous and condescending toward climate-change skeptic Lord Christopher Monckton.

Inslee displays a detailed understanding of energy technology, something that was rumored to have put him on the short list of candidates for Interior secretary in the Obama administration. It is an important quality given that his district gets its electricity from the Energy Department's giant Bonneville Power Administration.

After the 2010 Gulf of Mexico oil rig explosion and spill, he introduced legislation to ensure that offshore facilities have the latest technology for blowout preventers and emergency shutoff equipment.

He has fought to bar oil and gas drilling in the salmon-rich area of Bristol Bay off Alaska. Energy exploration had been banned following the Exxon Valdez spill in 1989. The George W. Bush administration repeatedly tried to lift that moratorium, which was eventually allowed to lapse in 2008.

But Inslee offered some kind words for petroleum in a February 2011 Roll Call op-ed.

"We waste oil in prodigious amounts, burning it in wildly inefficient vehicles and ignoring its future value as a feedstock for millions of products from pharmaceuticals to advanced electronics," he wrote. "If you love oil, why not help figure out a way not to waste its black beauty?"

Inslee's district is home to Microsoft and numerous biotechnology firms, and he is a proponent of "net neutrality," which would bar content restrictions by Internet service providers. He ran into a bit of controversy in May 2010 when he circulated a letter backing a proposal by Federal Communications Commission Chairman Julius Genachowski to stiffen broadband regulation. Digital fingerprints seemed to show the letter was written not by Inslee but by the policy director of a media watchdog group; Inslee's office said they merely borrowed some ideas.

In September 2010, the FCC approved rules for the use of unused television spectrum, known as "white space," for high-speed wireless broadband service. He had sponsored legislation in 2007 that directed the FCC to resolve the issue.

Inslee also looks out for the thousands of Boeing Co. employees in his district. He authored an amendment to the fiscal 2011 defense policy bill that would require the Pentagon to consider the use of illegal subsidies by companies in awarding a contract for a new air refueling tanker. Boeing alleged its competitor for the contract, Airbus, gets such subsidies from European governments.

He is an occasional supporter of free trade, defying the majority of his caucus in 2007 to support a trade deal with Peru. He was one of 14 Democrats to vote in 2008 to sustain President George W. Bush's veto of the reauthorization of farm programs, agreeing with Bush that the bill's subsidies for growers were in need of an overhaul.

Inslee is more comfortable representing the Seattle suburbs than he was in his first House term, a 1993-95 stint representing a rural and more conservative stretch across the center of the state. He is more partisan now than when he first came to Congress — he voted with his party 98 percent of the time when majorities of the two parties split in the 111th Congress (his score was in the mid-80s in his first term) — but he says that working across the aisle on the House floor, or even on the baseball field, improves things.

"I like having a good relationship with them," said Inslee, a regular participant in the annual congressional baseball game for charity, sponsored by CQ Roll Call. "Life is better when you have more friends and less arguing."

Inslee grew up in Seattle, where his father was a high school biology teacher and a coach. Inslee was a star football and basketball player. He was accepted to Stanford University but left after a year for the University of Washington because his savings from summer jobs during high school ran out. He then earned a law degree, married his high school sweetheart and settled in tiny Selah in south-central Washington, where he practiced law for 18 years. He won a seat in the state legislature in 1988, serving two terms.

When Republican Rep. Sid Morrison announced he would vacate the 4th District seat to run for governor in 1992, Inslee won a narrow primary victory and an equally narrow victory that November over Republican Doc Hastings.

Inslee bucked his party on some high-visibility votes. He opposed a five-day waiting period for handgun purchases. But he also voted to ban some types of semi-automatic weapons, which provoked the National Rifle Association to pour resources into defeating him. In a rematch, Inslee lost to Hastings. Following his loss, he settled on Bainbridge Island and resumed legal work. He then waged an unsuccessful primary bid for governor in 1996.

He ran another campaign in 1998, unseating two-term Republican Rep. Rick White in the suburban Seattle 1st District. Inslee steadily increased his victory margins, to a high of nearly 36 percentage points in 2008, before slipping back to a 16-point spread in 2010. He is considered a likely candidate for governor in 2012 if two-term Democratic Gov. Christine Gregoire does not seek a third term.

Key Votes

2010

Overhaul the nation's health insurance system	YES
Allow for repeal of "don't ask, don't tell"	YES
Overhaul financial services industry regulation	YES
Limit use of new Afghanistan War funds to troop withdrawal activities	YES
Change oversight of offshore drilling and lift oil spill liability cap	YES
Provide a path to legal status for some children of illegal immigrants	YES
Extend Bush-era income tax cuts for two years	NO

2009

Expand the Children's Health Insurance Program	YES
Provide $787 billion in tax cuts and spending increases to stimulate the economy	YES
Allow bankruptcy judges to modify certain primary-residence mortgages	YES
Create a cap-and-trade system to limit greenhouse gas emissions	YES
Provide $2 billion for the "cash for clunkers" program	YES
Establish the government as the sole provider of student loans	YES
Restrict federally funded insurance coverage for abortions in health care overhaul	NO

CQ Vote Studies

	PARTY UNITY		PRESIDENTIAL SUPPORT	
	SUPPORT	OPPOSE	SUPPORT	OPPOSE
2010	99%	1%	88%	12%
2009	98%	2%	94%	6%
2008	99%	1%	15%	85%
2007	98%	2%	5%	95%
2006	93%	7%	28%	72%

Interest Groups

	AFL-CIO	ADA	CCUS	ACU
2010	93%	95%	13%	4%
2009	100%	100%	36%	0%
2008	100%	90%	61%	12%
2007	100%	80%	63%	4%
2006	93%	90%	47%	12%

Washington 1

Puget Sound (west and east) — North Seattle suburbs

Nestled on Washington's Puget Sound between mountain ranges to the east and west, the 1st District has become a suburban haven for employees of technology giants and biotech companies located throughout the greater Seattle area.

The eastern portion of the 1st, which includes the northern borders of Lake Washington and runs along the eastern coast of the sound, accounts for more than 80 percent of the district's population. Naval bases spur the economy on the west side of the sound.

Layoffs at aviation, computer software and manufacturing companies hurt the local economy in the last decade, but the district's median household income remains high ($72,000) and residents hold white-collar, high-tech jobs. Bothell, in southern Snohomish County, has a strong biotech and biomedical equipment sector.

Tourism is important to the 1st. Travelers can take a 35-minute ferry ride from downtown Seattle to Bainbridge Island or drive north on Interstate 5

to one of the casinos in the 2nd District. The Sammamish River Valley is home to leading Washington wineries and outdoor recreation sites, while the Future of Flight Aviation Center and Boeing Tour attracts visitors to Mukilteo.

Democrats have the edge in the district, with its well-educated, socially liberal professionals. The King and Snohomish portions of the district have stronger Democratic leans, but Patty Murray also won the 1st's chunk of Kitsap in the 2010 U.S. Senate election.

Major Industry
Software, military, tourism

Military Bases
Naval Base Kitsap, 15,600 military, 13,700 civilian (shared with the 6th); Naval Undersea Warfare Center Keyport, 25 military, 1,500 civilian (2011)

Cities
Kirkland (pt.), 48,126; Redmond (pt.), 40,336; Edmonds, 39,709; Lynnwood, 35,836; Shoreline (pt.), 35,802; Bothell, 33,505

Notable
Poulsbo is home to the annual Scandinavian celebration Viking Fest; the Junior Softball World Series is played each summer in Kirkland.

Rep. Rick Larsen (D)

Capitol Office
225-2605
www.house.gov/larsen
108 Cannon Bldg. 20515-4702; fax 225-4420

Committees
Armed Services
Transportation & Infrastructure

Residence
Everett

Born
June 15, 1965; Arlington, Wash.

Religion
Methodist

Family
Wife, Tiia Karlen; two children

Education
Pacific Lutheran U., B.A. 1987 (political science);
U. of Minnesota, M.P.A. 1990

Career
Dental association lobbyist; port economic
development official

Political Highlights
Snohomish County Council, 1998-2000 (chairman,
1999)

ELECTION RESULTS

2010 GENERAL

Rick Larsen (D)	155,241	51.1%
John Koster (R)	148,722	48.9%

2010 PRIMARY (Open)

Rick Larsen (D)	73,734	42.0%
Diana McGinness (D)	10,548	6.0%
Larry Kalb (D)	7,627	4.4%

2008 GENERAL

Rick Larsen (D)	217,416	62.4%
Rick Bart (R)	131,051	37.6%

Previous Winning Percentages
2006 (64%); 2004 (64%); 2002 (50%); 2000 (50%)

Elected 2000; 6th term

Larsen is a moderate — though loyal — Democrat who works at not drawing much attention to himself. His world view is communitarian and his political philosophy is firmly rooted in the social democratic ethos his Scandinavian forebears brought to the American Northwest. "I grew up believing that one's obligation to the community is equal to one's obligation to oneself," he said.

A vice chairman of the centrist New Democrat Coalition, Larsen has occasionally sided with Republicans over the years, but became a more dependable party man in the four years Democrats had the majority from 2007 to 2010. In his first year in Congress, he sided with a majority of Democrats against a majority of Republicans 80 percent of the time. In the 111th Congress (2009-10), his party unity score was 98.

As the 112th Congress (2011-12) began, he opposed GOP budget and spending proposals, but he voted for the compromise measure that trimmed $40 billion from fiscal 2011 spending.

When Republicans were previously in charge of the House, Larsen was among the minority of House Democrats who supported a 2005 bankruptcy overhaul making it harder for consumers to erase their debts. He has backed a permanent repeal of the estate tax. He voted for President George W. Bush's 2001 tax cut package, although not for the 2003 follow-up. And he opposed extending the cuts beyond their 2010 expiration.

Larsen is a supporter of international trade, which benefits his export-oriented state and district. In 2002, he was one of only 25 Democrats who voted to give the president fast-track authority to negotiate trade agreements that Congress cannot amend. But he joined most of his party in opposing the 2005 Central America Free Trade Agreement, and has voted for only a couple of bilateral trade deals since then (with Oman and Peru) that were opposed by a majority of House Democrats.

He was a co-founder of the U.S.-China Working Group and of the Congressional Asia-Pacific Economic Cooperation Caucus. "Washington state has always maintained a good relationship with China," he said. "The first engineer hired by Boeing was a Chinese national."

But he has been critical of China's refusal to overhaul its currency. "China's currency policy is not only hurting U.S.-China trade because it is making products manufactured in the U.S. more expensive to export, but it is also hurting their own economic interest," he said in September 2010.

A member of the Armed Services Committee, Larsen can watch out for Boeing Co., which houses a large aerospace facility in Everett. He was a vocal supporter of Boeing's efforts to land the contract for a new air refueling tanker, which the company finally did in early 2011, a potential employment boon for the 2nd District.

He also supported a 2009 bill to transform the Defense Department's weapons acquisitions programs. The bill aims to add oversight to the procurement process and prevent conflicts of interest for the military's major acquisitions programs. Efforts to change the procurement practices were sparked after the Government Accountability Office reported that 96 of the largest acquisition programs had run $296 billion over budget since they began.

He voted in 2002 against authorizing the United States to use force against Iraq, and he supported Obama's plan to draw down U.S. troops in that country and shift the focus to Afghanistan.

He backed the late 2010 repeal of the statutory "don't ask, don't tell" policy that barred openly gay servicemembers.

In the 110th Congress (2007-08), Larsen won enactment of his signature bill to designate more than 106,000 acres of land about 60 miles northeast of Seattle as a protected wilderness area. Larsen had sponsored the bill in four straight Congresses, and though it had bipartisan support in the state's congressional delegation and passed the Senate, former Resources Committee Chairman Richard W. Pombo — a conservative California Republican often at odds with the environmental lobby — had refused to move it. When Democrats took the majority in the 2006 elections, Larsen's bill won swift passage.

Larsen is the ranking Democrat on the Transportation and Infrastructure Subcommittee on Coast Guard and Maritime Transportation. He counts among his legislative successes a law he helped pass in his freshman term to improve pipeline safety after a 1999 explosion in Bellingham killed three people.

In 2005, he won enactment of provisions designed to provide safeguards to mail-order brides from abroad.

Larsen, whose family is originally from Norway, was born and raised in Snohomish County, just north of Seattle. He was one of eight children of a utility company power-line worker. Both of his parents were involved in community activities, and his father was a city councilman.

After earning a bachelor's degree in political science and a master's in public affairs, Larsen worked for the Port of Everett, helping businesses comply with clean-water requirements. He then became the director of public affairs for the Washington Dental Association.

His first foray into electoral politics came in 1997, when he waged a successful door-to-door campaign for the Snohomish County Council. He chaired the council in 1999.

When three-term Republican Rep. Jack Metcalf retired in 2000, local Democratic Party strategists got behind Larsen, who also received campaign help from organized labor and other traditionally Democratic organizations, such as abortion rights and environmental groups. He prevailed by 12,000 votes against GOP state Rep. John Koster.

Redistricting following the 2000 census did little to change the competitive nature of the 2nd District, and the 2002 race between Larsen and Norma Smith, a former aide to Metcalf, was hard-fought. Larsen squeaked through by fewer than 9,000 votes.

He won re-election fairly easily until 2010, when he edged Republican John Koster, 51 percent to 49 percent.

Key Votes

2010	
Overhaul the nation's health insurance system	YES
Allow for repeal of "don't ask, don't tell"	YES
Overhaul financial services industry regulation	YES
Limit use of new Afghanistan War funds to troop withdrawal activities	NO
Change oversight of offshore drilling and lift oil spill liability cap	YES
Provide a path to legal status for some children of illegal immigrants	YES
Extend Bush-era income tax cuts for two years	YES
2009	
Expand the Children's Health Insurance Program	YES
Provide $787 billion in tax cuts and spending increases to stimulate the economy	YES
Allow bankruptcy judges to modify certain primary-residence mortgages	YES
Create a cap-and-trade system to limit greenhouse gas emissions	YES
Provide $2 billion for the "cash for clunkers" program	YES
Establish the government as the sole provider of student loans	YES
Restrict federally funded insurance coverage for abortions in health care overhaul	NO

CQ Vote Studies

	PARTY UNITY		PRESIDENTIAL SUPPORT	
	SUPPORT	OPPOSE	SUPPORT	OPPOSE
2010	98%	2%	95%	5%
2009	98%	2%	97%	3%
2008	98%	2%	16%	84%
2007	96%	4%	6%	94%
2006	89%	11%	35%	65%

Interest Groups

	AFL-CIO	ADA	CCUS	ACU
2010	93%	90%	25%	0%
2009	100%	100%	43%	0%
2008	100%	90%	56%	0%
2007	96%	95%	65%	0%
2006	86%	85%	67%	20%

Washington 2

Puget Sound — Bellingham, most of Everett

Extending from the Cascade Mountains to San Juan Island in the northwestern corner of the state, the 2nd covers an area that is mostly rural in its topography and moderate in its politics. Most residents live near Interstate 5, a densely populated technology corridor that runs alongside the Puget Sound, while rural areas just west of the mountains provide open expanses of land, much of it national forest. In between lies a fertile agricultural plain.

Everett, the 2nd's most populous city, is home to Boeing's largest aerospace facility, which employs thousands of district residents. Firms linked to Seattle's technology industries are located in the district, and these white-collar jobs are integral to the local economy. The district is home to several ports, including those in Everett and Bellingham.

Although no longer dominant, natural resources industries continue to provide some jobs in the rural east, and agriculture workers produce everything from raspberries to dairy products. Tourism also is a significant part of the economy, with visitors drawn to the state and national forests that line the western slope of the Cascade Range in eastern Whatcom, Skagit and Snohomish counties. Slow-paced San Juan County, a collection of islands southwest of Bellingham, also lures tourists and has attracted retirees — it has the highest median age in the state (52 years). West of the mountains and north of Mount Vernon, residents are closer to Vancouver, British Columbia, than to Seattle.

The 2nd tends to be politically competitive and represented by centrists. The urban centers of Everett in the south and Bellingham in the north are liberal, while rural areas lean conservative. Overall, Republican candidate Dino Rossi won the 2nd's portions of Island, Skagit and Snohomish counties in the 2010 U.S. Senate race.

Major Industry
Aviation, technology, shipping, agriculture, tourism

Military Bases
Naval Air Station Whidbey Island, 7,650 military, 1,200 civilian; Naval Station Everett, 5,403 military, 464 civilian (2011)

Cities
Everett (pt.), 93,232; Bellingham, 80,885; Marysville, 60,020

Notable
There are no stoplights on the San Juan Islands.

Rep. Jaime Herrera Beutler (R)

Capitol Office
225-3536
herrerabeutler.house.gov
1130 Longworth Bldg. 20515-4703; fax 225-3478

Committees
Small Business
Transportation & Infrastructure

Residence
Camas

Born
Nov. 3, 1978; Glendale, Calif.

Religion
Christian

Family
Husband, Daniel Beutler

Education
Seattle Pacific U., attended 1996-98; Bellevue
Community College, A.A. 2003; U. of Washington, B.A.
2004 (communications)

Career
Congressional aide

Political Highlights
Wash. House, 2007-11

ELECTION RESULTS

2010 GENERAL

Jaime Herrera Beutler (R)	152,799	53.0%
Denny Heck (D)	135,654	47.0%

2010 PRIMARY (Open)

Jaime Herrera Beutler (R)	46,001	27.8%
David W. Hedrick (R)	22,621	13.7%
David B. Castillo (R)	19,995	12.1%

Elected 2010; 1st term

Herrera Beutler is no stranger to Capitol Hill: As a former aide to fellow Washington Republican Cathy McMorris Rodgers and an intern in the George W. Bush White House, she is familiar with the workings of the nation's capital.

At 32, she is one of the youngest members of Congress and the youngest woman.

Unlike many of her freshman GOP colleagues, Herrera Beutler is seen as more of an "establishment" Republican (she bested two more-conservative candidates in the primary, including one backed by the tea party movement), a good fit given her district's swing status. She has criticized fellow Republicans for not reining in deficit spending or passing their own health care legislation while in the majority.

When Republicans pushed legislation through the House in March 2011 to shut down a program that provides emergency loans to unemployed homeowners facing foreclosure, Herrera Beutler was one of two Republicans to vote against the bill.

Her agenda in Congress is expected to focus on job creation, a direction dictated by her district's economic woes. The 3rd District's unemployment rate is higher than the national average, and its counties' rates are among the highest in the state.

Herrera Beutler has a good spot from which to address those concerns, serving as vice chairwoman of the Transportation and Infrastructure Subcommittee on Water Resources and Environment. She also sits on the Small Business Committee.

The seat opened when six-term Democrat Brian Baird announced he was retiring. Herrera Beutler ran first among Republicans in Washington's open primary, doubling the second-place finisher, and faced Democrat Denny Heck, a communications entrepreneur, in November. She won 53 percent of the vote to Heck's 47 percent.

She ran under the name Jaime Herrera, but announced just before Christmas that she was adding the last name of her husband, Daniel Beutler.

Washington 3

Southwest — Vancouver, most of Olympia

Located in Washington's southwestern corner, the politically competitive 3rd District is home to two enclaves of liberal Democratic voters — the state capital of Olympia and the city of Vancouver — and to Republican communities in the suburbs and countryside.

The two cities are connected by Interstate 5, west and east of which lies considerable open rural territory.

The district's population center is Clark County (Vancouver), where more than half of the 3rd's residents live. Tens of thousands of county residents cross the Columbia River each day to jobs in Oregon, many of them in Portland. Clark's population growth over the last two decades made the home construction industry a cornerstone of the local economy, but a housing market crisis put the brakes on development.

The distressed economy and high foreclosure rates in the district affected the 3rd's extensive timber industry — the vast stretches of woodlands east in the Cascade Mountains and west in Wahkiakum and Pacific counties supply the lumber for homes and commercial construction. Fishing and oyster harvesting are prominent on Pacific County's coast.

The district's other population pocket and cultural hub is Olympia in Thurston County at the 3rd's northern tip. Olympia's workforce relies on government and service-industry jobs.

Major Industry
Timber, computer hardware, manufacturing

Cities
Vancouver, 161,791; Olympia (pt.), 38,907

Notable
Mount St. Helens erupted May 18, 1980, killing 57 people and destroying enough timber for 300,000 two-bedroom homes.

Rep. Doc Hastings (R)

Capitol Office
225-5816
www.house.gov/hastings
1203 Longworth Bldg. 20515-4704; fax 225-3251

Committees
Natural Resources - Chairman

Residence
Pasco

Born
Feb. 7, 1941; Spokane, Wash.

Religion
Protestant

Family
Wife, Claire Hastings; three children

Education
Columbia Basin College, attended 1959-61; Central
Washington U., attended 1964

Military
Army Reserve, 1964-69

Career
Paper supply business owner

Political Highlights
Wash. House, 1979-87; Republican nominee for U.S.
House, 1992

ELECTION RESULTS

2010 GENERAL

Doc Hastings (R)	156,726	67.6%
Jay Clough (D)	74,973	32.4%

2010 PRIMARY (Open)

Doc Hastings (R)	82,909	58.7%
Shane Fast (R)	9,214	5.5%

2008 GENERAL

Doc Hastings (R)	169,940	63.1%
George Fearing (D)	99,430	36.9%

Previous Winning Percentages
2006 (60%); 2004 (63%); 2002 (67%); 2000 (61%);
1998 (69%); 1996 (53%); 1994 (53%)

Elected 1994; 9th term

Hastings claimed the top Republican spot on the Natural Resources Committee in 2009, after eight years of toil on the ethics committee, and moved up to chairman after Republicans won the House in 2010. He is a supporter of drilling for oil in coastal waters and Alaska's Arctic National Wildlife Refuge, and he advocates an expansion of nuclear power and renewable energy sources, particularly hydroelectric, both important to his state.

A parliamentary tactician, the former Rules Committee member played a leading role in mobilizing opposition to the Democrats' legislative response to the Gulf of Mexico oil spill through the spring and summer of 2010, and that work continued into the 112th Congress (2011-12).

Hastings said in early 2011 that the condition for Republican support for tougher drilling safety laws would be "that we have a viable offshore oil and gas industry and that we can create jobs and do it in the safest way we possibly can."

In late 2010, Hastings led an abortive attempt to shift primary jurisdiction over energy issues to his panel from the Energy and Commerce Committee. It didn't work, but Natural Resources will weigh in nonetheless. His committee approved bills in April 2011 to require regulators to offer lease sales in the Gulf of Mexico and off Virginia's coast and to speed up approval of drilling permits.

The year before, when the Obama administration and Democratic leaders pushed a measure that would lift the $75 million cap on liability for offshore oil spills and revamp federal oversight of the oil industry, Hastings pushed back. He blasted deletion of a provision, added by the Natural Resources Committee, to create an independent commission to study the cause of the spill. He backed creation of the panel because, he said, the one appointed by Obama was loaded with foes of drilling and lacked technical expertise.

Hastings also was a leading voice when Republicans attempted, unsuccessfully, to require the administration to release documents related to plans to designate as national monuments more than 10 million acres in nine Western states.

In early 2009, Hastings and other Republicans objected to the process of bringing a series of public-lands bills to the floor in a single piece of legislation. The bill, which he complained included 100 measures that had never passed in the House, was rejected on an initial vote to reach a full two-thirds majority needed to pass under expedited procedures. But it passed on a second vote and was subsequently signed into law. He had an exchange with Rules Chairwoman Louise M. Slaughter, a New York Democrat, during debate on the bill. She had barred from consideration his amendment to ensure wheelchair access to recreational areas. Her move spurred a shouting match with Republican David Dreier of California in Hastings' absence, with Slaughter contending Hastings' proposal was a ruse to stall the bill. Hastings subsequently wrote Slaughter a letter stating "deep personal regret" that she had made comments "about my truthfulness."

Hastings hadn't served on Natural Resources since the 104th Congress (1995-96), but in the 111th (2009-10) he beat out Utah Republican Rob Bishop for the top GOP post, which came open after embattled Alaska Republican Don Young pulled his name from consideration.

As founder and chairman of the House Nuclear Cleanup Caucus, he seeks to expedite environmental restoration of radioactive waste sites. His district is home to the Hanford Nuclear Reservation, once a major employer as the leading producer of nuclear material for weapons. It now stands idle as the nation's most toxic relic of the Cold War, and Hastings has secured hundreds of millions of dollars to clean it up.

In 2004, he backed a law calling for a federal study of the potential for adding historic Manhattan Project sites, including the Hanford reactor, to the National Park System. He played an important role in the August 2008 designation of Hanford's B Reactor as a National Historic Landmark.

In mid-2008, as top-ranking Republican on the ethics panel, then known as the Committee on Standards of Official Conduct, he led the call for an investigation of Ways and Means Chairman Charles B. Rangel for alleged financial and fundraising improprieties. Although no longer on the panel, he continued to serve on the investigative subcommittee reviewing the conduct of the New York Democrat, who was censured by the House in late 2010. Hastings had served on the ethics panel since 2001 and held its gavel in 2005 and 2006 at the behest of then-Speaker J. Dennis Hastert, an Illinois Republican who reportedly included Hastings on a list of potential successors as Speaker in the event of a disaster.

Hastings is a loyal Republican and conservative who opposed all the major economic initiatives of the Obama administration. But he funnels federal dollars to support farmers in his district and protests what he sees as unfair foreign competition to Washington state's lucrative apple industry. He wrote to Agriculture Secretary Tom Vilsack in May 2009 requesting the department purchase 1 million boxes of apples to support growers across the country. He also favors a proposed free-trade agreement with Colombia as a means to promote his state's agriculture products abroad. But in 2007, he was one of just 16 Republicans to vote against the U.S.-Peru free-trade agreement, which he called unfair to the state's asparagus growers.

Born Richard Norman Hastings, he has been known as "Doc" since childhood. Before coming to Congress, Hastings ran his family's paper supply business in Pasco and was active in local GOP politics. He was elected to the Washington House in 1978 and served eight years, including stints as assistant majority leader and chairman of the GOP caucus.

In 1992, he had support from GOP religious activists and was considered the most conservative of the four Republicans running to succeed GOP Rep. Sid Morrison, who ran unsuccessfully for governor that year. Hastings won the primary handily, but narrowly lost the election to Democrat Jay Inslee. In a 1994 rematch, Hastings cast the campaign as a referendum on Inslee's support for President Bill Clinton. Hastings ousted Inslee (who now represents the 1st District) and has won handily since.

Key Votes

2010

Overhaul the nation's health insurance system	NO
Allow for repeal of "don't ask, don't tell"	NO
Overhaul financial services industry regulation	NO
Limit use of new Afghanistan War funds to troop withdrawal activities	NO
Change oversight of offshore drilling and lift oil spill liability cap	NO
Provide a path to legal status for some children of illegal immigrants	NO
Extend Bush-era income tax cuts for two years	YES

2009

Expand the Children's Health Insurance Program	NO
Provide $787 billion in tax cuts and spending increases to stimulate the economy	NO
Allow bankruptcy judges to modify certain primary-residence mortgages	NO
Create a cap-and-trade system to limit greenhouse gas emissions	NO
Provide $2 billion for the "cash for clunkers" program	NO
Establish the government as the sole provider of student loans	NO
Restrict federally funded insurance coverage for abortions in health care overhaul	YES

CQ Vote Studies

	PARTY UNITY		PRESIDENTIAL SUPPORT	
	SUPPORT	OPPOSE	SUPPORT	OPPOSE
2010	98%	2%	27%	73%
2009	89%	11%	19%	81%
2008	98%	2%	70%	30%
2007	95%	5%	81%	19%
2006	97%	3%	95%	5%

Interest Groups

	AFL-CIO	ADA	CCUS	ACU
2010	0%	0%	88%	100%
2009	5%	0%	80%	96%
2008	13%	15%	88%	96%
2007	9%	10%	74%	100%
2006	7%	0%	100%	88%

Washington 4

Central — Yakima and Tri-Cities

Lying just east of the Cascade Mountains, the 4th District includes some of the state's most fertile land as well as large stretches of the Columbia River (shared with the 3rd and 5th), which works its way down the middle of the district before turning west to form most of the state's border with Oregon.

Yakima County is the 4th's largest, both in land area and population, and is home to the Yakima Valley, known as the fruit bowl of the Northwest. It includes Yakama Indian Reservation and part of the U.S. Army's Yakima Training Center, which spreads into Kittitas County.

Heavily irrigated agriculture drives the valley, which is full of apple orchards and fields of hops. In fact, the valley accounts for 75 percent of the total U.S. hops acreage and hosts the Hop Growers of America.

Benton County to the east takes in the 4th's other population center. The Tri-Cities of Kennewick, Pasco and Richland on the Columbia River are a hotbed for scientific research.

This area also is home to the Energy Department's Hanford nuclear site and Pacific Northwest National Laboratory, which is the district's largest employer. Hanford is the nation's most contaminated nuclear site and has been targeted for accelerated cleanup. Projects to demolish parts of the site and construct new facilities to protect groundwater have begun.

The Wenatchee National Forest still provides some timber jobs. The Columbia Basin Project delivers water to the area's wineries and potato, corn and fruit farms. Many of these agrarian areas have attracted populations that are majority Hispanic.

The 4th is the state's most conservative district: It gave John McCain his highest percentage statewide (58 percent) in the 2008 presidential race and did the same for GOP candidate Dino Rossi in the 2010 U.S. Senate election (60 percent).

Major Industry
Scientific research, fruit orchards and other agriculture, timber

Cities
Yakima, 91,067; Kennewick, 73,917; Pasco, 59,781; Richland, 48,058

Notable
The oldest skeleton ever found in North America was discovered on the banks of the Columbia River near Kennewick in 1996.

Rep. Cathy McMorris Rodgers (R)

Capitol Office
225-2006
www.mcmorris.house.gov
2421 Rayburn Bldg. 20515-4705; fax 225-3392

Committees
Energy & Commerce

Residence
Spokane

Born
May 22, 1969; Salem, Ore.

Religion
Christian non-denominational

Family
Husband, Brian Rodgers; two children

Education
Pensacola Christian College, B.A. 1990 (pre-law); U. of Washington, M.B.A. 2002

Career
State legislative aide; fruit orchard worker

Political Highlights
Wash. House, 1994-2004 (minority leader, 2002-03)

ELECTION RESULTS

2010 GENERAL

Cathy McMorris Rodgers (R)	177,235	63.7%
Daryl Romeyn (D)	101,146	36.3%

2010 PRIMARY (Open)

Cathy McMorris Rodgers (R)	106,191	62.5%

2008 GENERAL

Cathy McMorris Rodgers (R)	211,305	65.3%
Mark Mays (D)	112,382	34.7%

Previous Winning Percentages
2006 (56%); 2004 (60%)

Elected 2004; 4th term

McMorris Rodgers is a trusted ally of Speaker John A. Boehner of Ohio and a member of both the GOP leadership team and the Energy and Commerce Committee. She works to protect her district's military and agricultural assets, while offering a family-friendly face for the GOP through her work on health issues, as well as her role as the mother of a child with Down syndrome.

McMorris Rodgers embraces limited government. "I want to protect as much freedom as possible for the individual," she said. She praises tea party activists and touts her endorsement as one of Sarah Palin's "mama grizzlies" — Palin views her "as part of the solution, as working to represent conservative values from a woman's perspective," McMorris Rodgers said.

She opposed the $700 billion Wall Street rescue package in late 2008 and, fearing a "Euro-TARP," proposed legislation to prohibit U.S. loans to the International Monetary Fund to shore up European Union states. "Americans are suffering from bailout fatigue," she said. "We all need to get focused on getting our fiscal houses in order."

She parts with conservatives on some issues and split with President George W. Bush on some high-profile bills. In 2007, she voted to override the president's veto of legislation to expand the Children's Health Insurance Program — which covers children from low-income families that make too much money to qualify for Medicaid — although the attempt failed. But she opposed a more expensive version in 2009 that President Obama signed into law, and she voted to repeal the health care overhaul law enacted in 2010.

Formerly a subcommittee chairwoman on the Education and the Workforce panel, McMorris Rodgers has hosted hearings on promoting family-friendly workplaces. She was unpleasantly surprised in June 2010 when a bill to establish a Labor Department award to recognize employers for developing work-life balance policies was rejected in the face of opposition from the conservative Republican Study Committee, of which she is a member. "It just highlighted that I have some work to do," she said.

In the 2008 overhaul of the Higher Education Act, she won inclusion of provisions promoting scholarships for students pursuing studies in math, science, engineering and computer science and allowing school districts to enlist mid-career professionals as adjunct teachers.

In the 110th Congress (2007-08), she co-chaired the bipartisan Congressional Caucus for Women's Issues, where she and other members supported legislation enacted in 2008 to ban discrimination by insurers or employers based on the results of genetic testing.

In 2008, McMorris Rodgers launched the Congressional Down Syndrome Caucus to promote research and raise educational expectations and outcomes for children with Down syndrome, and to help provide family and community support. "I feel like in many ways, I've had my eyes opened," she said of her son, Cole, "and he's given me a whole new purpose for being in Congress."

As GOP conference vice chairwoman, a job she won after running unopposed at Boehner's behest, McMorris Rodgers regularly uses and promotes social networking tools such as Twitter, Facebook and YouTube to communicate with voters (she announced her second pregnancy in August 2010 on Facebook and Twitter). Boehner tapped her in 2009 to head a Republican task force to come up with a policy on earmarks, which led her to create an online database tracking all earmark requests. The highest-ranking woman in the GOP Conference, she helped recruit a record number of women to run for Congress as Republicans.

Locally, she looks out for Fairchild Air Force Base, home to much of the Air Force's West Coast tanker fleet. She co-chairs the Congressional Military Families Caucus, which she helped found in 2009 to address the needs of military spouses and children. Her husband is a retired Navy officer.

She promotes hydropower — plentiful in her district and, she says, overlooked elsewhere — as clean, renewable energy. She launched the Congressional Hydropower Caucus in 2008 to advocate its expansion to boost domestic energy supplies.

McMorris Rodgers is a descendant of pioneers who traveled the Oregon Trail to the Pacific Northwest in the 1850s. Her family lived in British Columbia for years, moving to Kettle Falls on the Columbia River 30 miles south of the Canadian border as she and her brother, Jeff, were preparing to enter high school. Her father, Wayne, bought an orchard and opened a fruit stand, where she and her brother pruned, thinned, picked and sold produce. Her father also chaired the Stevens County Republican Party and was president of the local Chamber of Commerce. She was the first in her family to attend college, working her way through with jobs that ranged from McDonald's to housekeeping.

When she graduated, family friend Bob Morton asked her to manage his campaign for the state House. He won, and she became a legislative assistant in his office. When Morton was appointed to the state Senate in 1993, his young protégé — 24 at the time — was appointed to replace him in the state House. She won the seat in her own right the next year and was elected minority leader in 2002.

Two years later, while Republican George Nethercutt was unsuccessfully attempting to unseat Democratic Sen. Patty Murray, McMorris Rodgers won a three-way Republican primary for Nethercutt's House seat. She trounced the Democratic candidate, Spokane businessman Don Barbieri, by 19 percentage points.

In 2005, while she was home over the August recess, a campaign volunteer brought her brother to the congresswoman's "pink flamingo" summer fundraiser. The two talked only briefly, but Brian Rodgers followed up with a letter. They married a year later, in the midst of her first re-election campaign. She won that race with 56 percent of the vote in a climate that had turned hostile to the GOP. In 2008 and 2010, she won with almost two-thirds of the vote.

In December 2010 she became the first congresswoman to give birth to two children while in office.

Key Votes

2010

Overhaul the nation's health insurance system	NO
Allow for repeal of "don't ask, don't tell"	NO
Overhaul financial services industry regulation	NO
Limit use of new Afghanistan War funds to troop withdrawal activities	NO
Change oversight of offshore drilling and lift oil spill liability cap	NO
Provide a path to legal status for some children of illegal immigrants	-
Extend Bush-era income tax cuts for two years	YES

2009

Expand the Children's Health Insurance Program	NO
Provide $787 billion in tax cuts and spending increases to stimulate the economy	NO
Allow bankruptcy judges to modify certain primary-residence mortgages	NO
Create a cap-and-trade system to limit greenhouse gas emissions	NO
Provide $2 billion for the "cash for clunkers" program	NO
Establish the government as the sole provider of student loans	NO
Restrict federally funded insurance coverage for abortions in health care overhaul	YES

CQ Vote Studies

	PARTY UNITY		PRESIDENTIAL SUPPORT	
	SUPPORT	OPPOSE	SUPPORT	OPPOSE
2010	97%	3%	28%	72%
2009	95%	5%	23%	77%
2008	95%	5%	64%	36%
2007	92%	8%	71%	29%
2006	98%	2%	92%	8%

Interest Groups

	AFL-CIO	ADA	CCUS	ACU
2010	0%	0%	100%	96%
2009	5%	0%	80%	96%
2008	20%	20%	89%	92%
2007	9%	15%	75%	85%
2006	15%	5%	100%	96%

Washington 5

East — Spokane

With beautiful forests and lush fields, the 5th is anchored by the greater Spokane region, which takes in nearly two-thirds of the district's population and is an economic hub for the Inland Northwest.

Once dependent on manufacturing, Spokane's economy now relies on health care, finance and service jobs.

The largest city between Seattle and Minneapolis, it also serves as a nexus for retail, trade and telecommunications companies. Fairchild Air Force Base, 10 miles west of downtown, is one of the metropolitan area's key employers.

North of Spokane, among mountains and national and state forests, no city surpasses the 5,000-resident mark. Although logging and mining used to drive the economy, both industries have declined in recent decades. Okanogan County is known for ranches and orchards.

The Colville Indian Reservation, one of three reservations in the district, takes up large portions of Okanogan and Ferry counties.

At the corner of Okanogan and Lincoln counties, the Grand Coulee Dam — the nation's largest hydropower producer — crosses the Columbia River into the 4th.

The southern 5th's fertile soil produces some of the world's most sought-after wheat and the Walla Walla sweet onion. At the foot of the Blue Mountains near Oregon, Walla Walla hosts a thriving arts community and two colleges.

Area wineries lure tourists, but economic slowdowns in the Northwest may hurt the city.

The 5th tends to strongly favor the GOP. In the 2008 presidential race, John McCain won 11 of the district's 12 counties. Republican Dino Rossi won 59 percent of the district's 2010 U.S. Senate vote.

Major Industry
Agriculture, health care, service, finance

Military Bases
Fairchild Air Force Base, 4,678 military, 516 civilian (2011)

Cities
Spokane, 208,916; Spokane Valley, 89,755; Walla Walla, 31,731

Notable
The Fort Walla Walla Museum's "Living History" performances celebrate the city's heritage and the lives of 19th-century residents.

Rep. Norm Dicks (D)

Capitol Office
225-5916
www.house.gov/dicks
2467 Rayburn Bldg. 20515-4706; fax 226-1176

Committees
Appropriations - Ranking Member

Residence
Belfair

Born
Dec. 16, 1940; Bremerton, Wash.

Religion
Lutheran

Family
Wife, Suzanne Dicks; two children

Education
U. of Washington, B.A. 1963 (political science), J.D.
1968

Career
Congressional aide

Political Highlights
No previous office

ELECTION RESULTS

2010 GENERAL

Norm Dicks (D)	151,873	58.0%
Doug Cloud (R)	109,800	42.0%

2010 PRIMARY (Open)

Norm Dicks (D)	90,596	56.6%

2008 GENERAL

Norm Dicks (D)	205,991	66.9%
Doug Cloud (R)	102,081	33.1%

Previous Winning Percentages
2006 (71%); 2004 (69%); 2002 (64%); 2000 (65%);
1998 (68%); 1996 (66%); 1994 (58%); 1992 (64%);
1990 (61%); 1988 (68%); 1986 (71%); 1984 (66%);
1982 (63%); 1980 (54%); 1978 (61%); 1976 (74%)

Elected 1976; 18th term

Dicks has served on the Appropriations Committee since he was first elected to the House more than three decades ago. But his hand really has been near the purse strings for closer to four decades, counting his stint as an aide to Washington Democrat Warren G. Magnuson, who served on the Senate Appropriations Committee.

When Dicks moved from an aide to Magnuson to junior member of the House spending panel in 1976, he told a reporter at the time, "I never thought I'd give up that much power voluntarily."

Despite his lengthy seasoning, Dicks did not gain the helm of an Appropriations subcommittee until 2007, when he took over as chairman of the Interior-Environment panel. But after the 2010 death of Pennsylvania's John P. Murtha, who was the longtime top Democrat on the Defense panel, Dicks became the first new member in that slot in 21 years.

A beefy and ruddy former college linebacker with a booming voice, Dicks now serves as ranking Democrat on the full committee, as well as on the Defense Subcommittee.

Dicks is like Murtha in some ways — physically impressive, sometimes gruff and blunt. The first thing people who know Dicks say about him is that he is smart and hardworking. And he requires his staff to work hard, preparing thick binders of materials for many meetings.

But he has shown signs he will make his own distinctive mark. One difference is Dicks' emphasis on intelligence matters, such as procurements of reconnaissance aircraft and satellites. Dicks served on the Select Intelligence Oversight Panel, a special Appropriations subcommittee set up to enhance oversight of U.S. spy agencies that was discontinued in the 112th Congress (2011-12), and was the top Democrat on the Select Intelligence Committee for most of the 1990s. In 1998 he and California Republican Christopher Cox led a bipartisan investigation of China's efforts to obtain U.S. technology. At Dicks' insistence, the panel examined security lapses at nuclear weapons laboratories that allegedly enabled China to obtain highly classified data.

A self-described fan of military hardware, his office sports models of planes and a submarine. Dicks has earned a reputation as the "representative from Boeing." The company, now based in Chicago, was for years headquartered in Seattle and still maintains facilities in Washington, including one that will build the new KC-X refueling plane. Dicks championed that initiative even when it was plagued by scandal. The program was derailed in 2004 when an Air Force official who oversaw the acquisition took steps to favor Boeing as she sought a job with the company. The program was relaunched after that and, in 2008, Northrop Grumman and EADS North America upset Boeing in the competition only to see Boeing win a protest, forcing the Pentagon to start over. Boeing finally won the contract in spring 2011. But Dicks has worked against some Boeing programs, including missile-defense initiatives.

Beyond his devotion to his state's defense industries, Dicks is predictably Democratic. He sided with his party almost 99 percent of the time in the 111th Congress (2009-10) on votes that divided majorities of the two parties.

He has long been a champion of earmarks, once calling them "an important legislative tool that separates us from the executive branch." But in 2010, he backed the Democratic plan to bar earmarks for for-profit entities, saying the issue had become too "sensitive." Dicks says Congress needs to develop a new definition of earmark, and he argues that the committee should be able to add funds where it deems they are needed. That kind of spending is not an earmark, he maintains, even if it benefits some lawmakers or regions, but rather is known as a "committee add" or "programmatic add."

Earmarks have developed a bad reputation in part because of the perception — in some cases the reality — of quid pro quo transactions. Dicks himself was dogged by allegations that he was involved in less-than-kosher dealings with a lobbying firm. The Committee on Standards of Official Conduct (as the Ethics Committee was then known) eventually dismissed charges that Dicks and six other members of the Defense spending panel traded earmarks for campaign contributions from the PMA Group.

Dicks underwent a transformation on the war in Iraq. He backed the invasion in 2002 and was among a bipartisan group of nine House members picked by the Bush administration to help secure votes on the resolution authorizing the president to use force against Iraq. But by 2006, Dicks' views on the war had changed. He supported several attempts to set a target for withdrawing U.S. troops and voted in 2007 for a resolution opposing President George W. Bush's plan to send more than 21,000 additional U.S. combat troops into Iraq. He has remained supportive of the U.S. effort in Afghanistan, while questioning how long the commitment should last.

Dicks' district encompasses such scenic areas as Olympic National Park, Puget Sound and mountain-rimmed coastlines along the Pacific. It also has a large American Indian constituency. As chairman of the Interior-Environment panel for nearly three years, he focused on boosting maintenance and staffing at national parks and increasing spending on health care for American Indians. He also secured millions for salmon protection and for the rehabilitation of the city of Tacoma. In early 2009, he joined a debate as old as the Forest Service by proposing that it move from the Agriculture Department to the Interior Department. The idea gained little traction.

Dicks grew up in Bremerton, the son of an electrician at Puget Sound Naval Shipyard. He excelled at sports and played football at the University of Washington. After graduating with a degree in political science, he went to law school with an eye on a career in politics.

He got his first taste of campaigning by pouring drinks aboard the campaign plane for the Democratic candidate for governor in 1968. In need of a job when his candidate lost, Dicks was hired by Magnuson. When 6th District Democratic incumbent Floyd V. Hicks was named to the state Supreme Court in 1976, Dicks went home to run for the seat. He easily won that November and has carried his district with at least 60 percent of the vote in all but three elections, including 2010, when he was held to 58 percent.

Key Votes

2010

Overhaul the nation's health insurance system	YES
Allow for repeal of "don't ask, don't tell"	YES
Overhaul financial services industry regulation	YES
Limit use of new Afghanistan War funds to troop withdrawal activities	NO
Change oversight of offshore drilling and lift oil spill liability cap	YES
Provide a path to legal status for some children of illegal immigrants	YES
Extend Bush-era income tax cuts for two years	YES

2009

Expand the Children's Health Insurance Program	YES
Provide $787 billion in tax cuts and spending increases to stimulate the economy	YES
Allow bankruptcy judges to modify certain primary-residence mortgages	YES
Create a cap-and-trade system to limit greenhouse gas emissions	YES
Provide $2 billion for the "cash for clunkers" program	YES
Establish the government as the sole provider of student loans	YES
Restrict federally funded insurance coverage for abortions in health care overhaul	NO

CQ Vote Studies

	PARTY UNITY		PRESIDENTIAL SUPPORT	
	SUPPORT	OPPOSE	SUPPORT	OPPOSE
2010	98%	2%	98%	2%
2009	99%	1%	97%	3%
2008	98%	2%	19%	81%
2007	97%	3%	7%	93%
2006	86%	14%	33%	67%

Interest Groups

	AFL-CIO	ADA	CCUS	ACU
2010	100%	90%	25%	0%
2009	100%	100%	40%	0%
2008	100%	90%	67%	0%
2007	96%	95%	50%	0%
2006	93%	85%	50%	8%

Washington 6

West — Bremerton, Tacoma, Olympic Peninsula

The 6th includes the Olympic Mountains, which drop to the coast of the Pacific Ocean in the district's west. The lush Olympic National Park and Olympic National Forest constitute more than one-third of the 6th's land and make the area a very popular tourist destination. Surrounding the mountainous region, communities are striving to move beyond the timber and fishing industries.

To the southwest, the Port of Grays Harbor is a shipping center. Port Angeles and Port Townsend along the Olympic Peninsula's northern and eastern shores rely on the ferries, airports and bridges that deliver tourists and connect residents to the central Puget Sound area.

More than half of the 6th's residents live near Tacoma and its suburbs in the south Puget Sound region. Revitalization efforts near the waterfront and the University of Washington-Tacoma lured some people back to downtown, but many areas of the city have shed residents since 2000. Once a key railroad terminus, the city's economy still relies on manufacturing and shipping jobs. Cargo shipping revenue losses have hurt the 6th,

but a military presence in the eastern portion of the district stabilizes the economy. Bremerton, located north of Tacoma, is home to naval facilities, and the 6th has a large Coast Guard presence.

Tacoma's blue-collar, heavily unionized electorate gives Democrats the edge in the district's portion of Pierce County. But independent voters, who can be socially moderate, have prevented the 6th from moving out of the reach of the GOP. Barack Obama took 57 percent of the district's 2008 presidential vote, but Patty Murray won only 53 percent here in the 2010 U.S. Senate race.

Major Industry
Shipping, timber, fishing, health care, tourism

Military Bases
Naval Base Kitsap, 15,600 military, 13,700 civilian (shared with the 1st) (2011); Puget Sound Naval Shipyard and Intermediate Maintenance Facility, 560 military, 9,900 civilian (2009)

Cities
Tacoma (pt.), 179,868; Bremerton, 37,729; University Place, 31,144; Lakewood (pt.), 27,277; Parkland (unincorporated) (pt.), 26,657

Notable
Port Townsend celebrates the rhododendron bloom with "Rhody Fest."

Rep. Jim McDermott (D)

Capitol Office
225-3106
www.house.gov/mcdermott
1035 Longworth Bldg. 20515-4707; fax 225-6197

Committees
Ways & Means

Residence
Seattle

Born
Dec. 28, 1936; Chicago, Ill.

Religion
Episcopalian

Family
Wife, Therese Hansen; two children

Education
Wheaton College (Ill.), B.S. 1958; U. of Illinois, M.D. 1963

Military
Navy Medical Service Corps, 1968-70

Career
Psychiatrist; Foreign Service officer

Political Highlights
Wash. House, 1971-73; sought Democratic nomination for governor, 1972; Wash. Senate, 1975-87; Democratic nominee for governor, 1980; sought Democratic nomination for governor, 1984

ELECTION RESULTS

2010 GENERAL

Jim McDermott (D)	232,649	83.0%
Bob Jeffers-Schroder (I)	47,741	17.0%

2010 PRIMARY (Open)

Jim McDermott (D)	110,914	79.8%
Bill Hoffman (D)	6,135	4.4%
S. Sutherland (D)	4,999	3.6%
Donovan Rivers (D)	4,781	3.4%
Scott Sizemore (D)	3,220	2.3%

2008 GENERAL

Jim McDermott (D)	291,963	83.6%
Steve Beren (R)	57,054	16.3%

Previous Winning Percentages
2006 (79%); 2004 (81%); 2002 (74%); 2000 (73%); 1998 (88%); 1996 (81%); 1994 (75%); 1992 (78%); 1990 (72%); 1988 (76%)

Elected 1988; 12th term

McDermott's interest in helping the poor has guided his actions in the House. On the rare occasion when the staunch liberal disagrees with Democratic leaders, it is because they don't go as far as he would like in tackling what he considers economic and social disparities.

Whatever maturity McDermott has achieved as a legislator, he still shows some of the bombastic tendencies that have marked much of his House career. And often his outlandish remarks make bigger headlines than his legislative accomplishments.

In the 112th Congress (2011-12), McDermott — who has said that he represents the most trade-dependent city in America — is the top Democrat on the Ways and Means Subcommittee on Trade. He backs the U.S.-South Korea free trade agreement finalized by the Obama administration but has raised questions about deals with Colombia and Panama.

As chairman of the committee's Income Security and Family Support panel in the 111th Congress (2009-10), he shepherded several bills and amendments aimed at helping people down on their luck. In September 2010, the House passed his bill to allow the Health and Human Services Department to continue approving new programs that test new strategies in state child welfare programs.

Earlier in the year, he led an effort to increase regulation on companies that use "conflict minerals" originating from the Democratic Republic of Congo in their manufacturing. The House passed the bill as part of financial regulatory overhaul legislation in July.

That same month, McDermott chided his colleagues for failing to extend unemployment benefits for people who had lost their jobs during the economic downturn. "Last night millions of families in every corner of America had trouble putting dinner on the table because of this foolishness," he said. "And I don't know how anyone is going to go to a Fourth of July parade or picnic after voting 'no' on this."

McDermott has found little traction for some of his other anti-poverty bills, including one to provide gasoline stamps to help low-income workers pay for commuting costs. He also pushed a bill that would have required the Census Bureau to produce poverty statistics that are more up-to-date.

He is more often in the news — and in trouble — for rash statements and questionable behavior than for his left-wing agenda, although the two often coincide. He was formally admonished after he mocked President George W. Bush in a floor speech for saying the United States was "kicking ass" in Iraq. In December 2007, he voted against a House resolution honoring Christmas — an action he said he took to stick a finger in the eye of its sponsor, Iowa Republican Steve King, for voting against expanding a health care program for children.

In perhaps the most notorious incident of his career, McDermott was ordered to pay Republican John A. Boehner of Ohio, now the Speaker of the House, nearly $1.1 million in 2008. McDermott received a copy of a recording of an intercepted 1996 cell phone call between Boehner and then-Speaker Newt Gingrich of Georgia and revealed it to the media. In May 2007, a federal appeals court ruled McDermott had violated House rules by leaking the call. McDermott insisted it was worth the fight — and the huge settlement — to protect what he contends was his First Amendment right to release the taped conversation.

During his years in the minority, where he now finds himself again, McDermott relished throwing verbal bombshells at the GOP. During a floor speech in

December 2005, he waved two red Christmas stockings to illustrate what he considered the impact of Republican fiscal policies. From the "poor" stocking, he transferred small presents representing benefits for the elderly and disabled, loans for college students, food stamp funds, and so on. "What's left for poor people?" McDermott asked with a flourish. "Look at that! A lump of coal!"

He termed the fiscal 2012 House Republican budget "nonsense" and "a fraud."

He almost always sides with his party on votes that divide majorities of Democrats and Republicans — 99 percent of the time in the 111th Congress (2009-10) — and he supported President Obama's early economic initiatives. The only psychiatrist in Congress, McDermott backed his party's health care overhaul, which was enacted in 2010, though he favors a single-payer system.

McDermott protested U.S. involvement in Vietnam in the 1960s, and he voted against the 2002 resolution authorizing Bush to use force in Iraq. He was featured as a critic of the war in Michael Moore's 2004 film "Fahrenheit 9/11." He opposed Obama's troop surge in Afghanistan and joined 55 lawmakers in sending a letter to the president in September 2009 warning of a "military quagmire" in a time of economic turmoil.

Born and raised in Illinois, McDermott came from a poor, conservative and deeply religious family. His father, a bond underwriter, and his mother, a telephone operator and homemaker, started a church in the garage of their two-bedroom home. His three siblings slept in one bedroom; his parents in the other. McDermott, the oldest child, had the couch.

McDermott attended the conservative evangelical Wheaton College in Illinois. His bend toward liberalism began afterward, during medical school at the University of Illinois, when he voted for John F. Kennedy in the 1960 presidential election.

McDermott's residency training ultimately took him to Seattle. After a two-year stint in the Navy Medical Service Corps, he launched a career in medicine in Seattle. He won a seat in the state House in 1970 running on an abortion rights platform. After two years in the state House and a two-year break, he won four state Senate elections. He also lost three bids for governor.

McDermott left the state Senate in 1987 to go to Africa as a Foreign Service medical officer. Less than a year later, when Democratic Rep. Mike Lowry announced his plans to run for the Senate, McDermott announced — in Kinshasa, Zaire — his intention to run for Lowry's seat in 1988. He won the primary with 38 percent of the vote and easily topped Republican Robert Edwards, winning 76 percent. He has not been seriously challenged in the overwhelmingly Democratic district, and won 83 percent of the vote in 2010.

Key Votes

2010

Overhaul the nation's health insurance system	YES
Allow for repeal of "don't ask, don't tell"	YES
Overhaul financial services industry regulation	YES
Limit use of new Afghanistan War funds to troop withdrawal activities	YES
Change oversight of offshore drilling and lift oil spill liability cap	YES
Provide a path to legal status for some children of illegal immigrants	YES
Extend Bush-era income tax cuts for two years	NO

2009

Expand the Children's Health Insurance Program	YES
Provide $787 billion in tax cuts and spending increases to stimulate the economy	YES
Allow bankruptcy judges to modify certain primary-residence mortgages	YES
Create a cap-and-trade system to limit greenhouse gas emissions	YES
Provide $2 billion for the "cash for clunkers" program	YES
Establish the government as the sole provider of student loans	YES
Restrict federally funded insurance coverage for abortions in health care overhaul	NO

CQ Vote Studies

	PARTY UNITY		PRESIDENTIAL SUPPORT	
	SUPPORT	OPPOSE	SUPPORT	OPPOSE
2010	99%	1%	88%	12%
2009	99%	1%	93%	7%
2008	98%	2%	17%	83%
2007	98%	2%	7%	93%
2006	97%	3%	15%	85%

Interest Groups

	AFL-CIO	ADA	CCUS	ACU
2010	100%	100%	13%	0%
2009	100%	95%	36%	4%
2008	100%	95%	50%	8%
2007	96%	85%	50%	4%
2006	93%	95%	20%	4%

Washington 7

Seattle and suburbs

The most populous city in the Pacific Northwest, Seattle is nicknamed the "Emerald City," and it remains the gem of the Evergreen State. The city anchors the 7th, which is diverse, liberal and well-educated. From the top of the iconic Space Needle, tourists can see the Seattle skyline and both the Cascade and Olympic mountain ranges.

The 7th is home to technology industry leaders such as Amazon.com and other large corporations such as coffee giant Starbucks.

Amazon opened a new campus in the South Lake Union neighborhood in 2010, and The Bill and Melinda Gates Foundation, which donates billions of dollars annually to global health and development projects and to national education and technology projects, has built new headquarters by the Space Needle. Seattle also has emphasized the development of biotech businesses.

The maritime industry — centered around the bustling Port of Seattle — remains a major employer. The University of Washington also is in the 7th. Despite economic diversity here, budget shortfalls and city government layoffs concern residents.

Seattle has some of the nation's worst traffic congestion, but local officials hope multi-use development downtown and a multibillion-dollar expansion of the region's light-rail network will alleviate some of the pressure.

The percentage of Seattle residents who describe themselves as members of two races is nearly double the national average.

At 14 percent, Asians make up Seattle's largest minority population and have influenced the International District. The Capitol Hill and University District neighborhoods are destinations for both residents and tourists. The 7th's urban setting and large population of minorities and singles make it a liberal bastion.

Democratic candidates regularly dominate the district in all races. In the 2010 U.S. Senate election, Democratic incumbent Patty Murray won 81 percent of the district's vote.

Major Industry
Internet technology, computer software, trade, health care, aviation

Cities
Seattle (pt.), 597,095; Shoreline (pt.), 17,205

Notable
The Fraternal Order of Eagles was founded in 1898 at a Seattle shipyard.

Rep. Dave Reichert (R)

Capitol Office
225-7761
www.house.gov/reichert
1730 Longworth Bldg. 20515-4708; fax 225-4282

Committees
Ways & Means

Residence
Auburn

Born
Aug. 29, 1950; Detroit Lakes, Minn.

Religion
Lutheran - Missouri Synod

Family
Wife, Julie Reichert; three children

Education
Concordia College (Ore.), A.A. 1970

Military
Air Force Reserve, 1971-76; Air Force, 1976

Career
Police officer; grocery warehouse worker

Political Highlights
King County sheriff, 1997-2005

ELECTION RESULTS

2010 GENERAL

Dave Reichert (R)	161,296	52.0%
Suzan DelBene (D)	148,581	48.0%

2010 PRIMARY (Open)

Dave Reichert (R)	76,118	47.2%
Ernest Huber (R)	9,376	5.8%
Tim Dillon (R)	8,291	5.1%

2008 GENERAL

Dave Reichert (R)	191,568	52.8%
Darcy Burner (D)	171,358	47.2%

Previous Winning Percentages
2006 (52%); 2004 (52%)

Elected 2004; 4th term

A former sheriff who gained fame for his pursuit of the Green River serial killer, Reichert wants to be known as a "thinker" in Congress. That desire comes from his law enforcement background, carefully analyzing evidence and assembling the pieces of a puzzle. "Rather than just follow some ideology, I think about each vote and analyze the vote based upon the facts," he said.

His blend of fiscal conservatism and moderate views on the environment and social policy have proved to be an electoral winner in his affluent, Democratic-leaning district.

That approach has allowed him to work with Democrats on a range of issues, including ones relating to the environment, a personal focus for him. "It's about solving problems," Reichert (RIKE-ert) told The Seattle Times in 2008. "This bickering back and forth is a waste of time. It's tiresome. I just think sometimes it gets childish."

Reichert was among the Republicans President Obama wooed aggressively as he tried to win bipartisan backing for his economic stimulus package in early 2009. But not a single House Republican supported the final $787 billion bill. "It should be a trusting relationship, kind of like a marriage," Reichert, whose party was then in the minority, said of the majority's responsibility to communicate. "If I look at my wife and listen, and then go and do whatever I want to do, it's not a partnership."

In 2008 he voted against the $700 billion plan to shore up the financial services sector, asserting, "This proposed remedy could be more harmful than the illness."

Reichert was in tune with his party on those votes, but he aligns with Democrats on other matters. In 2009, he joined with a majority of his fellow House Republicans on just 68 percent of all floor votes pitting the majorities of the two parties against one another — down from 75 percent the year before. That figure climbed to 80 percent in 2010.

One of the issues on which he sided with Democrats was the cap-and-trade legislation in 2009. He voted for the measure, saying he liked the support for nuclear, wind and solar technologies — though he disliked the tax portions of the legislation.

In an opinion piece in 2007, Reichert wrote that the GOP needs to "embrace" the environmental movement. "Too many Republicans have forgotten that conservation is conservative," he wrote.

In the 112th Congress (2011-12), he reintroduced a bill that would add more than 20,000 acres to the Alpine Lakes Wilderness in his home state — it passed in the House in the 111th (2009-10), but not in the Senate.

Republican leaders haven't scorned him because of his departures from the party line. In January 2009, they awarded him a prized slot on the Ways and Means Committee, which handles tax, trade and health care legislation. Since the trade-dependent 8th District's inception in 1980, its representatives have always eventually earned a seat on the panel. Reichert, a member of the Trade Subcommittee, is a strong supporter of free trade.

He also sits on the Health Subcommittee, where he advocates expanding access, improving quality of care, and using advances in science to improve health care and prevention. He has particularly focused on children's health care. In 2009, he was one of 40 Republicans voting for a bill, which Obama signed into law, expanding the Children's Health Insurance Program, which covers children from low-income families that make too much money to qualify for Medicaid. But Reichert did not support the 2010 health care overhaul — believing it failed to address crucial issues, including cost containment — and voted to repeal and defund it in early 2011.

In his first term, when the GOP controlled the House, Reichert got his top-choice committee assignment — Homeland Security — and parlayed his law enforcement background into the chairmanship of the Emergency Communications, Preparedness and Response Subcommittee. He drafted high-profile bills to improve communication between first-responders and to restructure the Federal Emergency Management Agency within the Department of Homeland Security.

The oldest of seven children of an abusive father, Reichert grew up in conditions that were far from ideal. The family lived in a two-bedroom duplex in a rough neighborhood; the boys slept in the garage. Reichert took on the role of protector. It stuck, and he began thinking about a career in police work.

A tuition waiver at a two-year college in Oregon got him on track, and spots as a pitcher on the baseball team and quarterback on the football team brought out his leadership skills.

Reichert tried six times before he passed the test required to get hired by the King County sheriff's office, but once there he thrived. He started as a patrol officer in 1972, later became an undercover agent and made sergeant in 1990. Seven years later, he was elected sheriff.

In a twist of fate, Reichert became sheriff just before the 2001 capture of Green River serial killer Gary Ridgway, a case Reichert had supervised earlier in his career. Ridgway confessed to killing at least 48 women in the early 1980s in the Seattle area. Reichert published a book in 2004, "Chasing the Devil: My Twenty Year Quest to Capture the Green River Killer," and donated his $150,000 in royalties to a clinic that cares for drug-addicted babies.

The story made Reichert a media star, but he decided to see the case to its conclusion rather than run for governor, as he was being urged to do. Instead, when six-term Republican Rep. Jennifer Dunn decided not to run for re-election in 2004, Reichert went for her 8th District seat. His name recognition gave him a huge advantage in the GOP primary. In the general election, he faced another local celebrity, radio commentator Dave Ross. The national parties' campaign committees spent more on the contest than on any other House race in 2004, and Reichert prevailed by 5 percentage points.

For the 2006 and 2008 elections, Reichert beat Microsoft executive Darcy Burner in close contests. In 2010, Reichert underwent brain surgery for an injury sustained when a tree branch hit his head while chopping wood. He recovered, and went on to beat another Microsoft executive, Democrat Suzan DelBene, with 52 percent of the vote.

Key Votes

2010

Overhaul the nation's health insurance system	NO
Allow for repeal of "don't ask, don't tell"	NO
Overhaul financial services industry regulation	NO
Limit use of new Afghanistan War funds to troop withdrawal activities	NO
Change oversight of offshore drilling and lift oil spill liability cap	NO
Provide a path to legal status for some children of illegal immigrants	NO
Extend Bush-era income tax cuts for two years	YES

2009

Expand the Children's Health Insurance Program	YES
Provide $787 billion in tax cuts and spending increases to stimulate the economy	NO
Allow bankruptcy judges to modify certain primary-residence mortgages	NO
Create a cap-and-trade system to limit greenhouse gas emissions	YES
Provide $2 billion for the "cash for clunkers" program	YES
Establish the government as the sole provider of student loans	NO
Restrict federally funded insurance coverage for abortions in health care overhaul	YES

CQ Vote Studies

	PARTY UNITY		PRESIDENTIAL SUPPORT	
	SUPPORT	OPPOSE	SUPPORT	OPPOSE
2010	80%	20%	38%	62%
2009	68%	32%	56%	44%
2008	75%	25%	53%	47%
2007	73%	27%	46%	54%
2006	80%	20%	82%	18%

Interest Groups

	AFL-CIO	ADA	CCUS	ACU
2010	7%	20%	100%	67%
2009	62%	45%	80%	60%
2008	60%	60%	78%	56%
2007	54%	40%	85%	48%
2006	23%	25%	73%	56%

Washington 8

Eastside Seattle suburbs; Bellevue; eastern Pierce County

The 8th is Washington's wealthiest district, and it takes in the prosperous King County suburbs outside Seattle in its west as well as large rural areas in its east and south. Seattle's Eastside suburbs have been fertile ground for technology businesses, and the area's development caused traffic congestion and fueled debates over infrastructure upgrades and "smart" growth. The 8th's population center is Bellevue, which is a retail and financial services hub and one of the state's most diverse areas; nearly one-fourth of the city's population is Asian and more than 30 percent is foreign-born. Microsoft has a key presence in Bellevue, and its headquarters are in the 8th's portion of Redmond.

Boeing Co. is a major employer, and its local facilities will build a new Air Force tanker. Bellevue's corporate residents also include the travel website Expedia and truck manufacturer PACCAR.

The 8th takes in most of the rest of King County to the east and a large portion of Pierce County, including the fringes of Tacoma's suburbs. The less populous portions of King and Pierce are home to wide-ranging farm production, including berries, vegetables, livestock and nursery plants. The eastern halves of King and Pierce rise into the Cascade Range.

Most of Mount Rainier National Park — including the peak itself, which is the highest point in Washington and in the Cascades — is within the 8th. The 8th's population boom has added some urban and Democratic votes. Beyond the suburbs, the electorate tends to be fiscally conservative and socially moderate.

Barack Obama took 56 percent of the vote in the 2008 presidential election, but GOP candidate Dino Rossi narrowly won the district in the 2010 U.S. Senate race. The area's growing number of minority voters will continue to influence elections.

Major Industry
Aviation, manufacturing, computer software

Cities
Bellevue, 122,363; South Hill (unincorporated) (pt.), 49,250; Renton (pt.), 48,206; Sammamish, 45,780; Kent (pt.), 41,946; Auburn (pt.), 41,711

Notable
Mount Rainier, an active volcano, is the most heavily glaciated peak in the lower 48 states.

Rep. Adam Smith (D)

Capitol Office
225-8901
www.house.gov/adamsmith
2402 Rayburn Bldg. 20515-4709; fax 225-5893

Committees
Armed Services - Ranking Member

Residence
Tacoma

Born
June 15, 1965; Washington, D.C.

Religion
Episcopalian

Family
Wife, Sara Smith; two children

Education
Fordham U., B.A. 1987 (political science); U. of Washington, J.D. 1990

Career
City prosecutor; lawyer

Political Highlights
Wash. Senate, 1991-97

ELECTION RESULTS

2010 GENERAL

Adam Smith (D)	123,743	54.8%
Richard "Dick" Muri (R)	101,851	45.1%

2010 PRIMARY (Open)

Adam Smith (D)	63,866	51.2%

2008 GENERAL

Adam Smith (D)	176,295	65.4%
James Postma (R)	93,080	34.6%

Previous Winning Percentages
2006 (66%); 2004 (63%); 2002 (59%); 2000 (62%);
1998 (65%); 1996 (50%)

Elected 1996; 8th term

When Republicans last ruled the House, Smith voted like a centrist, opposing the Democratic leadership with regularity. But he moved leftward after Democrats took control in 2007. While he still deviates occasionally on trade and certain national security issues, gone are the days when he would line up with the GOP on one of every four or five votes.

He became a loyal enough party man to win the top Democratic spot on the Armed Services Committee in the 112th Congress (2011-12) in a tough three-way race over Loretta Sanchez of California and Silvestre Reyes of Texas.

He praised President Obama's April 2011 proposals for trimming the budget deficit and criticized the House-passed GOP plan, while saying that Pentagon spending needs to be part of the equation.

Once a strong supporter of President George W. Bush's policy in Iraq — he sided with Republicans in 2006 against setting a troop withdrawal deadline — Smith became one of Bush's toughest critics after Democrats took the majority. He joined the chorus demanding a deadline, even offering his own resolution to terminate the congressional authorization for the war, and opposed the troop surge. But when U.S. combat operations officially ended in August 2010, he acknowledged that "a brighter future for Iraqis also means greater security for America."

He praised Obama's plan to boost forces in Afghanistan and Pakistan. "President Obama's strategy puts America's focus back where it should be: on the threat from al Qaeda," Smith said in March 2009.

After Obama committed U.S. forces to help stem the violence in Libya in early 2011, Smith was somewhat supportive of the policy while suggesting that the president should have sought congressional involvement before the decision to involve Americans was made.

As chairman of the Armed Services Subcommittee on Terrorism and Unconventional Threats and Capabilities in the 111th Congress (2009-10), he held hearings on ways to disrupt terrorist financing networks.

His concerns about national security have occasionally led him astray from his party. A member of the Select Committee on Intelligence in the 110th Congress (2007-08), he was among the minority of Democrats to vote for a measure to reauthorize the Foreign Intelligence Surveillance Act, enhancing the administration's spying authority and essentially guaranteeing immunity for telecommunications companies that assisted in a warrantless surveillance program.

Smith looks out for Boeing Co. and his district's two military installations: Fort Lewis, the Army's largest training base on the West Coast, and McChord Air Force Base. He vigorously protested the Air Force's 2008 decision to award a new multibillion-dollar air tanker contract to a consortium of Northrop Grumman Corp. and the North American division of the European Aeronautic Defence & Space Co., the parent company of Airbus, and applauded when Boeing won the contract in a reopened competition in 2011.

Though he no longer serves on the Foreign Affairs Committee, he still takes a strong interest in U.S. relations with other countries. He led an early-2009 delegation on a trip to Africa and the Middle East, where he said several countries present "growing national security concerns and troubling humanitarian crises." He said upon his return: "From Kenya to Yemen, poverty and governance problems fuel instability, violence and extremism. This is a region that the United States cannot afford to neglect, both for national security and humanitarian reasons."

A leader of the business-friendly New Democrats, he is an advocate of intellectual property protections. In 2008, Smith and Democrat Ron Kind of Wisconsin led a group of lawmakers urging the U.S. trade representative to take a tougher line against Thailand, which had been granting exceptions to patent rights of U.S. pharmaceutical companies for cancer and cardiovascular drugs. Other Democrats disagreed, urging U.S. officials to support steps that make low-cost medicines available to citizens of poor, developing nations.

Although timber giant Weyerhaeuser Co. is headquartered in the 9th District, Smith usually sides with urban Democrats against more logging on public lands. But in 2003 he voted for the final version of the GOP's Healthy Forests Restoration Act, which allows the thinning of many forest areas for wildfire prevention. He opposed a more sweeping version of the bill.

Smith is a free-trade advocate. In 2002 he split with his party leaders and backed legislation giving the president fast-track authority to negotiate trade agreements that Congress cannot amend. In the 108th Congress (2003-04), he voted for trade accords with Australia, Chile, Morocco and Singapore. In 2005, however, he voted against the Central America Free Trade Agreement, pleasing unions that had criticized his earlier pro-trade votes but antagonizing many businesses in his trade-friendly district. By 2007 he returned to the pro-trade side, backing a Peru trade deal that a majority of House Democrats opposed. In the new Congress, he has expressed support for deals with Colombia and Panama.

Over the first decade of his congressional tenure — all in the minority — Smith sided with his party on 83 percent of the votes in which a majority of Democrats differed from a majority of Republicans, with a career-low annual party unity score of 75 in 1999. In the four years of the Democratic majority, from 2007 to 2010, his annual party unity score average ranged from 93 to 97.

Smith's father, who worked as a baggage handler at Seattle-Tacoma International Airport, died of a heart attack when Smith was 19. The family went on welfare, and Smith worked his way through college loading trucks for UPS. He was a Teamsters union member and still supports organized labor on most issues other than trade.

The fall after he earned his law degree in 1990, he won a state Senate seat in an upset and, at 25, became the youngest state senator in the country. The victory was bittersweet, however. Just days before his election, his mother suffered a stroke and died. A few weeks later, he received a letter from his father's sister revealing she was actually his birth mother and that he was adopted.

In 1996 he challenged Republican incumbent Randy Tate, a favorite of social conservatives, who had ridden into office on the GOP wave of 1994. Smith won by 3 percentage points and has been re-elected fairly comfortably since. In 2010 he topped Republican Dick Muri, a Pierce County councilman, 55 percent to 45 percent.

Key Votes

2010

Overhaul the nation's health insurance system	YES
Allow for repeal of "don't ask, don't tell"	YES
Overhaul financial services industry regulation	YES
Limit use of new Afghanistan War funds to troop withdrawal activities	NO
Change oversight of offshore drilling and lift oil spill liability cap	YES
Provide a path to legal status for some children of illegal immigrants	YES
Extend Bush-era income tax cuts for two years	NO

2009

Expand the Children's Health Insurance Program	YES
Provide $787 billion in tax cuts and spending increases to stimulate the economy	YES
Allow bankruptcy judges to modify certain primary-residence mortgages	YES
Create a cap-and-trade system to limit greenhouse gas emissions	YES
Provide $2 billion for the "cash for clunkers" program	YES
Establish the government as the sole provider of student loans	YES
Restrict federally funded insurance coverage for abortions in health care overhaul	NO

CQ Vote Studies

	PARTY UNITY		PRESIDENTIAL SUPPORT	
	SUPPORT	OPPOSE	SUPPORT	OPPOSE
2010	96%	4%	90%	10%
2009	93%	7%	94%	6%
2008	97%	3%	20%	80%
2007	95%	5%	7%	93%
2006	88%	12%	45%	55%

Interest Groups

	AFL-CIO	ADA	CCUS	ACU
2010	86%	90%	0%	8%
2009	95%	95%	47%	0%
2008	100%	85%	67%	4%
2007	100%	95%	65%	0%
2006	85%	75%	57%	21%

Washington 9

South Seattle suburbs; small part of Tacoma

Taking in numerous cities in the south Puget Sound region, the 9th runs south of Seattle along Interstate 5 before picking up small parts of Tacoma and Olympia, the state capital, en route to rural areas that offer spectacular views of Mount Rainier's 14,410-foot peak (in the 8th).

Just south of the Seattle city line, the 9th's northern end takes in predominately middle-class King County suburbs, where just less than half of the population lives.

This area includes most of Burien, SeaTac and Tukwila (both shared with the 7th), and Renton (shared with the 8th).

SeaTac, named after the area's main cities, includes the region's major airport and is home to the corporate headquarters for Alaska Air Group. Key employers here include Boeing and timber giant Weyerhaeuser, which has headquarters in Federal Way. A newly realigned "mega-base" linked the 9th's Army and Air Force sites, and construction to accommodate expansion at the base has boosted the economy.

South of King, Pierce County's suburbs account for nearly 40 percent of the 9th's population. Pierce also includes the deep-water Port of Tacoma, which helped diversify the area's economy and attract companies looking for fast distribution opportunities. The portion of Thurston County in the 9th includes part of Olympia (shared with the 3rd) as well as the most rural portion of the district.

Overall, Democrats have gained an edge in the 9th — Barack Obama won 58 percent of the 9th's 2008 presidential vote, 5 percentage points more than John Kerry took in 2004. Blue-collar aviation and port workers give the party a base throughout the district, but Democrats fare better in the 9th's portions of King and Thurston than in Pierce.

Major Industry
Aviation manufacturing, trade, technology

Military Bases
Joint Base Lewis-McChord, 43,375 military, 10,852 civilian (2011)

Cities
Federal Way, 89,306; Kent (pt.), 50,465; Renton (pt.), 41,763; Puyallup (pt.), 36,943; Lacey (pt.), 34,475; Lakewood (pt.), 30,886

Notable
The 17-day Western Washington Fair in Puyallup is the largest annual event in the state.

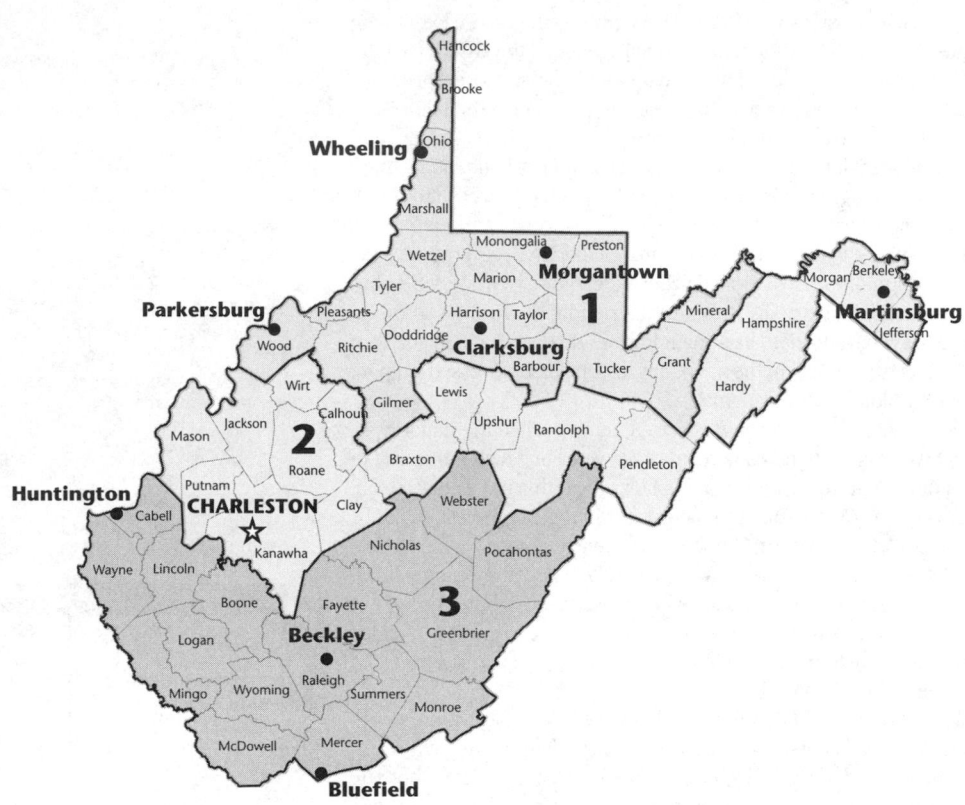

Gov. Earl Ray Tomblin (D)

Assumed office: Took office Nov. 15, 2010, due to the resignation of Joe Manchin III, D, who was elected to the U.S. Senate.

Length of term: 4 years

Term expires: 1/13

Salary: $95,000

Phone: (304) 558-2000

Residence: Chapmanville

Born: March 15, 1952; Logan County, W.Va.

Religion: Presbyterian

Family: Wife, Joanne Jaeger Tomblin; one child

Education: West Virginia U., B.S. 1974; Marshall U., 1975 M.B.A

Career: Property manager; teacher

Political highlights: W.Va. House, 1975-81; W.Va. Senate, 1981-present (president, 1995-present)

RECENT ELECTION RESULTS

2008 GENERAL

Joe Manchin III (D)	492,697	69.8%
Russ Weeks (R)	181,612	25.7%
Jesse Johnson (MOUNT)	31,486	4.5%

Acting Senate President Jeffrey V. Kessler (D)

(no lieutenant governor)

Phone: (304) 845-2580

LEGISLATURE

Legislature: January-March, limit of 60 days

Senate: 34 members, 4-year terms

2011 ratios: 28 D, 6 R; 32 men, 2 women

Salary: $20,000

Phone: (304) 340-7800

House: 100 members, 2-year terms

2011 ratios: 71 D, 29 R; 76 men, 24 women

Salary: $20,000

Phone: (304) 340-3200

TERM LIMITS

Governor: 2 consecutive terms

Senate: No

House: No

URBAN STATISTICS

CITY	POPULATION
Charleston	51,400
Huntington	49,138
Parkersburg	31,492
Morgantown	29,660
Wheeling	28,486

REGISTERED VOTERS

Democrat	54%
Republican	29%
Unaffiliated	16%
Other	1%

POPULATION

2010 population	1,852,994
2000 population	1,808,344
1990 population	1,793,477
Percent change (2000-2010)	+2.5%
Rank among states (2010)	37
Median age	40.4
Born in state	71.5%
Foreign born	1.3%
Violent crime rate	267/100,000
Poverty level	17.7
Federal workers	26,740
Military	1,199

ELECTIONS

STATE ELECTION OFFICIAL
(304) 558-6000

DEMOCRATIC PARTY
(304) 342-8121

REPUBLICAN PARTY
(304) 768-0493

MISCELLANEOUS

Web: www.wv.gov

Capital: Charleston

U.S. CONGRESS

Senate: 2 Democrats

House: 2 Republicans, 1 Democrat

2010 Census Statistics by District

District	2008 Vote for President Obama	McCain	White	Black	Asian	Hispanic	Median Income	White Collar	Blue Collar	Service Industry	Over 64	Under 18	College Education	Rural	Sq. Miles
1	42%	57%	95%	2%	1%	1%	$37,212	54%	27%	19%	16%	21%	19%	46%	6,286
2	44	55	92	4	1	2	41,960	56	27	17	15	22	19	54	8,459
3	42	56	93	4	<1	1	32,730	53	29	19	16	21	14	62	9,332
STATE	43	56	93	3	1	1	37,356	54	28	18	16	21	17	54	24,078
U.S.	53	46	64	12	5	16	51,425	60	23	17	13	25	28	21	3,537,438

Sen. John D. Rockefeller IV (D)

Capitol Office
224-6472
rockefeller.senate.gov
531 Hart Bldg. 20510-4802; fax 224-7665

Committees
Commerce, Science & Transportation - Chairman
Finance
    (Health Care - Chairman)
Veterans' Affairs
Select Intelligence
Joint Taxation

Residence
Charleston

Born
June 18, 1937; Manhattan, N.Y.

Religion
Presbyterian

Family
Wife, Sharon Percy; four children

Education
International Christian U. (Tokyo), attended 1957-60;
Harvard U., A.B. 1961 (Asian languages & history)

Career
VISTA volunteer; college president

Political Highlights
W.Va. House, 1967-69; W.Va. secretary of state,
1969-73; Democratic nominee for governor, 1972;
governor, 1977-85

ELECTION RESULTS

2008 GENERAL

John D. Rockefeller IV (D)	447,560	63.7%
Jay Wolfe (R)	254,629	36.3%

2008 PRIMARY

John D. Rockefeller IV (D)	271,425	77.1%
Sheirl L. Fletcher (D)	51,073	14.5%
Billy Hendricks Jr. (D)	29,707	8.4%

2002 GENERAL

John D. Rockefeller IV (D)	275,281	63.1%
Jay Wolfe (R)	160,902	36.9%

Previous Winning Percentages
1996 (77%); 1990 (68%); 1984 (52%)

Elected 1984; 5th term

A quest that began almost two decades ago came to fruition for Rockefeller in 2010 when Congress passed and President Obama signed into law a measure that greatly expanded the role of government in the nation's health care system. He played a central role in shaping the legislation as chairman of one powerful committee and a senior member on another.

On issues as diverse as health care, national security and the Internet, Rockefeller can dispense partisan rhetoric with the best of them — but he also relies on a sharp intellect, unpretentiousness and self-deprecating humor to achieve his goals.

At the outset of the 111th Congress (2009-10), the lanky and bookish Rockefeller wielded his seniority to take the gavel of the Commerce, Science and Transportation Committee. The panel's jurisdiction cuts a broad swath across the economy, driving Rockefeller's attention toward the domestic policy arena and away from sparring with Republicans over national security.

From his perch atop the Select Committee on Intelligence during the presidency of George W. Bush, Rockefeller clashed frequently with Republicans over the war in Iraq, the treatment of detainees and other intelligence-related issues. He still serves on that panel.

As chairman of the Commerce Committee, he's displayed a mastery of detail for complex policy disputes — the result of the many years he's spent toiling on the panel.

In a testament to his reputation as a pragmatic consensus builder, he has developed a friendly working relationship with ranking Republican Kay Bailey Hutchison of Texas, and much — though hardly all — of the legislation that has advanced through the panel has done so with bipartisan support. Rockefeller helped broker agreement on long-stalled bills to reauthorize and overhaul the Federal Aviation Administration and the Surface Transportation Board. Work continues on cybersecurity legislation and an auto safety bill sparked by the high-profile recall of millions of Toyotas.

He differs from Hutchison and most Republicans, though, in defending the Federal Communications Commission's regulatory approach to barring broadband service providers from blocking content and unnecessarily discriminating in transmitting network traffic, so-called net neutrality. Hutchison has sponsored a measure to nullify the FCC rules.

As a senior member of the Finance Committee, where he chairs the Health Care Subcommittee, Rockefeller played a central role in shaping the health care overhaul. In the Senate, he led the ultimately unsuccessful push to include a government-run public option in the legislation but ultimately voted for the final bill. "Today, we walked on the right side of history," he said the day the measure was signed into law.

With enactment of the legislation in March 2010, Rockefeller put to rest a key piece of unfinished business dating from the early years of the Clinton administration.

His introduction to what would become a personal cause came after George J. Mitchell, a Maine Democrat, vacated the chairmanship of what was then known as the Health Subcommittee when he became majority leader following the 1988 elections. Then-Finance Chairman Lloyd Bentsen, a Texas Democrat, handed Rockefeller the Medicare portfolio, and Mitchell subsequently gave him his seat on the Pepper Commission, a bipartisan, bicameral body charged with finding ways to provide the uninsured with coverage and to pay for long-term care for the elderly.

With the 1992 election of Bill Clinton as president, Rockefeller found an ally who shared his belief that government should expand its role in providing health coverage. He soon found himself as chief congressional surrogate for Clinton's doomed health care plan.

After Republicans took control of the House and the Senate in the 1994 elections, Rockefeller conceded that the health care proposal was part of the reason.

"Maybe it was too much to expect that in two years you could have changed so much of the health care system," he said at the time. "But we didn't know that when we started, and there wasn't any reason for us to know that."

Rockefeller is a committed liberal on social issues and a reliable vote for the administration and his party's leadership. But on one high-profile matter — controlling greenhouse gases — Rockefeller's loyalties to his state override those to his party and president. Citing the economic impact on West Virginia's coal industry, Rockefeller has resisted efforts to advance legislation that would place limits on emissions, insisting that any proposal must also provide generous federal assistance to clean-coal technology. "I believe that climate change and the science of it is for real, there's no question," he said in June 2010. "I also think that very carbon-rich states like West Virginia should have a chance."

Some moderate Democrats from coal-producing regions have rallied behind Rockefeller's go-slow stance, posing a challenge to White House efforts to unify the party behind one of the president's key legislative priorities. In June 2010, Rockefeller was one of six Senate Democrats to vote in favor of an unsuccessful resolution of disapproval by Alaska Republican Lisa Murkowski that would have blocked the EPA from regulating greenhouse gases. He was not one of the four to back a similar provision in 2011, however. In the 112th Congress (2011-12), his proposal for a two-year delay, which he calls a "time-out on EPA regulations," garnered only 12 votes.

His stand on climate legislation reflects Rockefeller's devotion to his adopted home state, where he has established deep roots since arriving in 1964 as a 27-year-old VISTA volunteer in possession of youthful idealism and one of the most famous names in American history. The path to the Mountain State was perhaps an unlikely one for Rockefeller, the great-grandson of Standard Oil Co. founder John D. Rockefeller, who at one point was considered the world's richest man. "Jay," as he prefers to be known, grew up on Manhattan's Upper East Side — far from the coal mines and poverty of West Virginia. He studied at Exeter Prep and Harvard University, and he spent three years studying in Japan.

The time he spent as a volunteer in Emmons, a small town on the Big Coal River in West Virginia, would forever change his life, and he can still get misty when recalling his VISTA days. During a late-night markup of the health care overhaul in 2009, Rockefeller described the experience as being "reborn," becoming emotional as he described the poverty he encountered in the hardscrabble town. "I could not leave. And it was because I [had] become so devoted to those people and the unfairness," he said.

Although he had planned to stay only one year, he became active in politics, later winning a seat in the state legislature and serving as secretary of state. Rockefeller lost a bid for governor in 1972, but he used the opportunity to boost his connections to the state by becoming president of West Virginia Wesleyan College. He won his second attempt at the governor's office in 1976, serving two terms before winning the seat of retiring Democratic Sen. Jennings Randolph in 1984. In that contest, he barely squeaked out a win, securing just 52 percent of the vote despite spending $12 million of his vast personal fortune. He has since been re-elected four times by more comfortable margins.

Key Votes

2010

Pass budget reconciliation bill to modify overhauls of health care and federal student loan programs	YES
Proceed to disapproval resolution on EPA authority to regulate greenhouse gases	YES
Overhaul financial services industry regulation	YES
Limit debate to proceed to a bill to broaden campaign finance disclosure and reporting rules	YES
Limit debate on an extension of Bush-era income tax cuts for two years	YES
Limit debate on a bill to provide a path to legal status for some children of illegal immigrants	YES
Allow for a repeal of "don't ask, don't tell"	YES
Consent to ratification of a strategic arms reduction treaty with Russia	YES

2009

Prevent release of remaining financial industry bailout funds	NO
Make it easier for victims to sue for wage discrimination remedies	YES
Expand the Children's Health Insurance Program	YES
Limit debate on the economic stimulus measure	YES
Repeal District of Columbia firearms prohibitions and gun registration laws	NO
Limit debate on expansion of federal hate crimes law	YES
Strike funding for F-22 Raptor fighter jets	YES

CQ Vote Studies

	PARTY UNITY		PRESIDENTIAL SUPPORT	
	SUPPORT	OPPOSE	SUPPORT	OPPOSE
2010	97%	3%	97%	3%
2009	98%	2%	100%	0%
2008	84%	16%	45%	55%
2007	91%	9%	35%	65%
2006	84%	16%	55%	45%
2005	93%	7%	40%	60%
2004	88%	12%	64%	36%
2003	96%	4%	50%	50%
2002	90%	10%	71%	29%
2001	97%	3%	66%	34%

Interest Groups

	AFL-CIO	ADA	CCUS	ACU
2010	100%	85%	27%	8%
2009	93%	85%	40%	0%
2008	100%	85%	63%	0%
2007	100%	85%	45%	8%
2006	100%	60%	83%	10%
2005	86%	100%	50%	4%
2004	100%	90%	41%	12%
2003	92%	100%	30%	15%
2002	100%	90%	45%	15%
2001	100%	100%	43%	12%

Sen. Joe Manchin III (D)

Capitol Office
224-3954
manchin.senate.gov/
303 Hart Bldg. 20510-4801; fax 228-0002

Committees
Armed Services
Energy & Natural Resources
Special Aging

Residence
Fairmont

Born
Aug. 24, 1947; Fairmont, W.Va.

Religion
Roman Catholic

Family
Wife, Gayle Manchin; three children

Education
West Virginia U., B.A. 1970 (business administration)

Career
Carpet store owner; coal brokerage company owner

Political Highlights
W.Va. House, 1983-85; W.Va. Senate, 1987-97; sought
Democratic nomination for governor, 1996; W.Va.
secretary of state, 2001-05; governor, 2005-10

ELECTION RESULTS

2010 SPECIAL

Joe Manchin III (D)	283,358	53.5%
John Raese (R)	230,013	43.4%
Jesse Johnson (MOUNT)	10,152	1.9%
Jeff Becker (CNSTP)	6,425	1.2%

2010 PRIMARY

Joe Manchin III (D)	68,827	73.1%
Ken Hechler (D)	16,267	17.3%
Sheirl L. Fletcher (D)	9,108	9.7%

Elected 2010; 1st term

Manchin's victory in the special election to fill the seat once held by the late Democrat Robert C. Byrd promises a continuation of the legendary senator's practice of using the federal government to benefit the Mountain State. But on a host of other issues, Manchin will walk a fine line between his liberal party and his state's more moderate political inclinations.

The former governor didn't get the seat he had hoped for on the Appropriations Committee, which Byrd chaired for years and used to steer millions of federal dollars to West Virginia. But he did win a spot on the Energy and Natural Resources Committee and its Subcommittee on Energy, making him a central player on an issue crucial to his coal-producing state's economy.

Manchin was one of four Democrats to join with all but one Republican in voting in April 2011 to block the EPA from regulating stationary sources of carbon dioxide and other greenhouse gases to address climate change.

He criticized President Obama's speech in March 2011 on energy policy, saying it "did not go far enough to address the brutal truth that this nation will never become energy secure or independent unless we utilize all of our resources, including coal, natural gas, wind, solar, hydro and biofuels."

In January 2011, Manchin criticized the EPA for retroactively vetoing an already-approved coal-mining permit for the Spruce No. 1 Mine in Logan County. He called the move "fundamentally wrong" and "a shocking display of overreach" by the agency.

"According to the EPA, it doesn't matter if you did everything right, if you followed all of the rules. Why? They just change the rules," said Manchin, who in February introduced legislation to prevent the agency from altering the rules after permits have been granted.

He made the jump to Washington — cutting short his second term as governor — with a long list of legislative priorities, including a proposal for a balanced-budget amendment to the Constitution. He suggested he might vote against an increase in the debt limit unless any increase came with a proposal for reducing the federal deficit over the long term.

"I have never put together a budget — be it my family's or as governor — that was based on how much we wanted to spend, but on what we had," Manchin told Roll Call in March 2011.

When Obama released his fiscal 2012 spending blueprint in February 2011, Manchin said that "given our fiscal challenges, it does not go far enough. This is not what the country needs or expects." He had slightly kinder words for a follow-up proposal from the White House, although he took issue with its reliance on tax increases and said spending cuts had to come first.

He endorsed a long-term proposal that would cut much deeper than Obama suggested, imposing spending caps in 2013 that would shrink spending to 20.6 percent of gross domestic product by fiscal 2022. That is much closer to the 20 percent figure put forth by House Budget Chairman Paul D. Ryan of Wisconsin than to Obama's budget, which calls for spending about 24 percent of GDP.

He won't always be a reliable vote for his own party on social issues either. Manchin is a foe of abortion and same-sex marriage and opposed the late 2010 repeal of the statutory "don't ask, don't tell" policy barring openly gay people from serving in the military, although he then sent out a statement saying he thought the policy "probably should be repealed in the near future." Manchin missed the vote on the repeal measure, causing a small controversy when he opted to attend a previously planned family Christmas party.

He also missed a vote on legislation, which passed the House at the end of the 111th Congress (2009-10) but did not make it in the Senate, that would have provided a path to legal status for certain illegal-immigrant children who attend college or join the military. Manchin had announced his opposition to both bills but said he might be able to support an immigration measure if it included a graduation requirement.

An avid hunter, he also opposes most gun control measures — an iconic moment from the 2010 campaign came when Manchin literally fired a rifle shot through a copy of the Democrats' cap-and-trade bill, affording him a chance to tell voters about his opposition to his party's energy legislation and boast of his endorsement by the National Rifle Association.

He'll be on firmer Democratic ground in pushing legislation aimed at encouraging U.S. companies to move overseas jobs to the United States and tightening mine safety regulations.

A member of the Armed Services Committee, he also voted in favor of the strategic arms reduction treaty with Russia that the Senate approved in December 2010.

Representing a state that has one of the highest per capita populations of seniors, Manchin also serves on the Special Aging Committee.

As governor, Manchin enjoyed approval ratings consistently around 70 percent. Before being elected governor, he served as secretary of state and in both houses of the West Virginia legislature. He worked in several family-owned businesses before entering politics.

Manchin hails from the small coal mining town of Farmington. He attended West Virginia University on a football scholarship, then went into business, owning a carpet store and a coal brokerage company. He got his start in politics in the state House, winning election in 1982 and serving one term, then moving to the state Senate, where he served until 1997. He ran for the Democratic nomination for governor in 1996, losing to Charlotte Pritt, but came back to win election as secretary of state four years later. He was elected governor in 2004 and was re-elected in 2008.

After Byrd died in June 2010, Manchin appointed Democrat Carte P. Goodwin, his former general counsel, to fill the spot. The state legislature then passed, and Manchin signed into law, a measure clarifying that the seat would be filled by a special election in November.

Manchin quickly entered the race and took 73 percent of the vote in an August primary. The GOP's potentially strongest option, Rep. Shelley Moore Capito, opted not to enter the race. Instead, businessman John Raese won the nomination.

Considered a moderate, Manchin campaigned at a distance from the White House, promising not to "rubber stamp" Obama's policies.

Early on he had kind words for the Democrats' health care overhaul enacted in March 2010. He later tried to distance himself from the law, although he stopped short of calling for its repeal (and he opposed a GOP effort at repeal early in 2011).

Polls showed a close contest for most of the campaign, with the popular Manchin being dragged down by Obama's unpopularity in the state. In the end, though, Manchin topped Raese by 10 percentage points.

Because he won a special election, Manchin was seated shortly after Election Day and participated in the lame-duck session at the end of the 111th Congress.

He will have to defend the seat again in 2012.

Manchin was considered a potential party switcher, but he insists he will remain a Democrat.

Republicans suggested the party-switching rumors originated from Manchin's own camp with an eye on the 2012 campaign.

Key Votes

2010

Limit debate on an extension of Bush-era income tax cuts for two years	YES
Limit debate on a bill to provide a path to legal status for some children of illegal immigrants	-
Allow for a repeal of "don't ask, don't tell"	?
Consent to ratification of a strategic arms reduction treaty with Russia	YES

CQ Vote Studies

	PARTY UNITY		PRESIDENTIAL SUPPORT	
	SUPPORT	OPPOSE	SUPPORT	OPPOSE
2010	88%	12%	90%	10%

Interest Groups

	AFL-CIO	ADA	CCUS	ACU
2010	100%		75%	33%

Rep. David B. McKinley (R)

Capitol Office
225-4172
mckinley.house.gov
313 Cannon Bldg. 20515-4801; fax 225-7564

Committees
Energy & Commerce

Residence
Wheeling

Born
March 28, 1947; Wheeling, W.Va.

Religion
Episcopalian

Family
Wife, Mary McKinley; four children

Education
Purdue U., B.S.C.E. 1969

Career
Civil engineer; architectural engineering company owner

Political Highlights
W.Va. House, 1980-95; W.Va. Republican Party chairman, 1990-94; sought Republican nomination for governor, 1996

ELECTION RESULTS

2010 GENERAL

David B. McKinley (R)	90,660	50.4%
Mike Oliverio (D)	89,220	49.6%

2010 PRIMARY

David B. McKinley (R)	14,783	34.9%
Mac Warner (R)	11,353	26.8%
Sarah Minear (R)	8,994	21.2%
Thomas Stark (R)	3,636	8.6%
Patricia Levenson (R)	2,110	5.0%
Cindy Hall (R)	1,533	3.6%

Elected 2010; 1st term

After a 15-year hiatus from public office, McKinley returned as a pro-business conservative who ran a campaign that was as much about his experience as a small-business owner as it was about his seven terms in the state legislature.

He was one of five Republican freshmen to win a coveted seat on the Energy and Commerce Committee, where he endorses his party's efforts to block the EPA from regulating greenhouse gases.

McKinley views himself as a loyal conservative, but he diverges from the path from time to time. He has disagreed with national GOP leaders on trade policy (he says West Virginia needs a more level playing field to be competitive) and opposes raising the Social Security retirement age.

He backed the House-passed version of a catchall spending bill for fiscal 2011 that would have cut $61 billion, while opposing an alternative by the conservative Republican Study Committee — of which he is a member — that would have rolled spending back to 2006 levels. He backed the final, compromise version of the bill that trimmed spending by $40 billion.

McKinley was among a group of freshman Republicans whose personal cell phone numbers and e-mail addresses were released by one of the largest coalitions of tea party advocates, which claimed he and the others were in danger of being "co-opted" by Washington insiders.

The owner of an architectural and engineering firm, in many ways McKinley is an engineer first and a politician second. In Charleston, he opposed a bill to increase the weight limit of trucks on state highways that was backed by the coal industry. Although he considers himself a friend of coal, the civil engineer in him was certain that raising the weight limit would be too destructive to West Virginia's roads.

State Sen. Mike Oliverio defeated scandal-plagued 14-term incumbent Alan B. Mollohan in the Democratic primary, making McKinley's task more difficult than it might have been. Oliverio ran as a conservative Democrat, but McKinley prevailed by 1,440 votes in the ninth closest House race of 2010.

West Virginia 1
North — Parkersburg, Wheeling, Morgantown

Located in the northernmost part of the state, the 1st is the most urban of West Virginia's districts but still has a large rural component. It contains six of the state's 10 largest cities and West Virginia University. Wheeling is an industrial commercial center in the northern panhandle, and Parkersburg is a regional trade hub in the west. Wheeling, Parkersburg and other areas along the Ohio border depend on health care jobs as well as chemicals and plastics manufacturing.

Years of population loss in Wheeling and Weirton have hurt the economic base. To the east, West Virginia University drives Morgantown in Monongalia County, which boasts the state's lowest unemployment rate, a diverse economy with high-tech jobs and major interstate routes.

Coal and struggling steel companies are still among the 1st's biggest employers, but a technology sector has developed. The FBI, Energy Department and NASA have facilities in the district.

The 1st elected Democrats to Congress for decades, but the GOP fares well in statewide and local elections, particularly in Doddridge County and areas to the southwest. Wheeling, in the Northern Panhandle, is often a target of national political campaigns because its media market reaches into neighboring Ohio and Pennsylvania. The 1st gave Republican John McCain 57 percent of the vote in the 2008 presidential election.

Major Industry
Technology, coal, steel, chemicals

Cities
Parkersburg, 31,492; Morgantown, 29,660; Wheeling, 28,486; Weirton, 19,746

Notable
Confederate Gen. Thomas "Stonewall" Jackson was born in Clarksburg.

Rep. Shelley Moore Capito (R)

Capitol Office
225-2711
capito.house.gov
2443 Rayburn Bldg. 20515-4802; fax 225-7856

Committees
Financial Services
    (Financial Institutions & Consumer Credit -
    Chairwoman)
Transportation & Infrastructure

Residence
Charleston

Born
Nov. 26, 1953; Glen Dale, W.Va.

Religion
Presbyterian

Family
Husband, Charles L. Capito Jr.; three children

Education
Duke U., B.S. 1975 (zoology); U. of Virginia, M.Ed. 1976
(counselor education)

Career
University system information center director;
college career counselor

Political Highlights
W.Va. House, 1997-2001

ELECTION RESULTS

2010 GENERAL

Shelley Moore Capito (R)	126,814	68.5%
Virginia Lynch Graf (D)	55,001	29.7%
Phil Hudok (CNSTP)	3,431	1.8%

2010 PRIMARY

Shelley Moore Capito (R)	unopposed

2008 GENERAL

Shelley Moore Capito (R)	147,334	57.1%
Anne Barth (D)	110,819	42.9%

Previous Winning Percentages
2006 (57%); 2004 (57%); 2002 (60%); 2000 (48%)

Elected 2000; 6th term

The long-anticipated political reshuffling in West Virginia's statewide offices has begun, and Capito — a moderate Republican in a state with a mixed political identity — is likely to be a player.

Her role was not, however, to pursue the seat once held by the late Democratic Sen. Robert C. Byrd. Although she was widely viewed as the strongest potential GOP contender after Byrd died in June 2010, Capito took a pass on the special election eventually won by the Democratic governor, Joe Manchin III. She could be a Senate candidate in the future or make a run for the governorship, once held by her father, Arch A. Moore Jr.

"I'm not one to really plan very far ahead, but I do have my eye on a bigger race, maybe a statewide race," she said. "I have to search my own heart and say where I can feel like I can do the most good or would want to contribute the most."

Meanwhile, Capito spent much of her time during the 111th Congress (2009-10) focusing on energy issues. She helped lead the Republican opposition to the Democratic cap-and-trade legislation designed to reduce greenhouse gas emissions. Capito said the bill would be a job killer in her state, where the coal industry is one of the main economic engines. In the 112th Congress (2011-12), she backed legislation to prohibit the EPA from regulating greenhouse gases.

She vigorously supports increased domestic energy production, especially from coal. "If it's good for coal mining, it's good for West Virginia," she said.

After a fire at the Sago Mine in Capito's district killed 12 miners in January 2006, she joined with Democrats to push stricter mine safety rules into law. She was one of just seven House Republicans to vote for a follow-up bill in 2008. Following the April 2010 explosion in the Upper Branch Mine that killed 29 workers, Capito cosponsored legislation that granted subpoena authority to the committee investigating the explosion.

As a member of the Financial Services Committee, she had a hand in the sweeping overhaul of the nation's financial regulatory structure. While she supported a housing overhaul that became law in 2008, she opposed the subsequent $700 billion rescue package for the financial services industry, saying it lacked adequate protection for taxpayers. She now serves as chairwoman of the Financial Institutions and Consumer Credit Subcommittee, where she is a leading GOP voice in pushing changes to the regulatory overhaul enacted in 2010. She sponsored legislation that won the support of top Democrat Barney Frank of Massachusetts to delay a provision in the law that limits the fees banks can charge retailers for debit card transactions.

Of more direct interest to West Virginia, Capito also serves on the Transportation and Infrastructure Committee. She has worked to bring road and other projects to the state, in the grand tradition of Byrd, but says the Republicans' earmark moratorium will benefit the process in the long run.

"Taking a pause and, in some ways, not pursuing earmarks has freed up time and energies to pursue other things like the bigger policies of cap-and-trade and health care and job creation and those kind of things," she said.

West Virginia has a mixed political personality — sending Democrats Byrd and John D. Rockefeller IV to the Senate in election after election, but trending Republican in presidential elections. Capito rides that divide, siding with a majority of House Republicans on most tax, defense, regulatory and energy issues, while often joining Democrats on labor, trade and health care. She is a member of the moderate Republican Main Street Partnership.

Capito was one of 17 Republicans to vote for five of the six bills in the Democrats' "first 100 hours" agenda at the beginning of the 110th Congress (2007-08), including a measure to raise the minimum wage.

She split with President George W. Bush more often than the typical House Republican, backing him less than half the time on votes on which he staked out a position in the 110th.

Earlier in her House career, when Bush sought to overhaul Medicare by creating a prescription drug benefit for seniors, Capito was a close ally. Appointed vice chairwoman of a GOP prescription drug task force, Capito campaigned for the plan before its enactment in 2003.

But when Bush sought to overhaul Social Security in 2005, Capito balked. She called the administration's proposal to create individual investment accounts a "tough sell."

Capito was 2 when her father won his first House election, and he was governor when she went to college. He served 12 years before his career ended when he pleaded guilty to federal charges that included taking illegal campaign contributions for his gubernatorial campaign. He served three years in prison and paid $750,000 to settle a lawsuit.

In 1972 Capito was a Cherry Blossom Princess for the annual festival in Washington, D.C. She missed being chosen queen by one notch on a spinning wheel. She said the experience "gave me nice exposure to Washington at that time." She was the first princess ever elected to Congress; Republican Sen. Lisa Murkowski of Alaska was the second.

Capito went to college planning to become a doctor, but she decided it would be tougher to balance motherhood with a career in medicine than with one in politics. She waited until her youngest child was 11 to enter politics, winning a seat in the state House of Delegates in 1996.

Four years later, she ran for the 2nd District seat, which opened up when Democrat Bob Wise ran successfully for governor. She narrowly beat wealthy class action attorney Jim Humphreys, a Democrat who plowed almost $7 million into the race. In their 2002 rematch, the most expensive House campaign that year, Capito prevailed by 20 percentage points. She has kept on winning, and took almost 69 percent of the vote in 2010. When she's not legislating or politicking, she remains an avid tennis player, a sport she pursued in college. She also runs and she plays in the annual congressional softball game pitting female lawmakers against female members of the press corps.

Key Votes

2010

Overhaul the nation's health insurance system	NO
Allow for repeal of "don't ask, don't tell"	NO
Overhaul financial services industry regulation	NO
Limit use of new Afghanistan War funds to troop withdrawal activities	?
Change oversight of offshore drilling and lift oil spill liability cap	NO
Provide a path to legal status for some children of illegal immigrants	NO
Extend Bush-era income tax cuts for two years	YES

2009

Expand the Children's Health Insurance Program	YES
Provide $787 billion in tax cuts and spending increases to stimulate the economy	NO
Allow bankruptcy judges to modify certain primary-residence mortgages	NO
Create a cap-and-trade system to limit greenhouse gas emissions	NO
Provide $2 billion for the "cash for clunkers" program	YES
Establish the government as the sole provider of student loans	NO
Restrict federally funded insurance coverage for abortions in health care overhaul	YES

CQ Vote Studies

	PARTY UNITY		PRESIDENTIAL SUPPORT	
	SUPPORT	OPPOSE	SUPPORT	OPPOSE
2010	86%	14%	36%	64%
2009	76%	24%	44%	56%
2008	82%	18%	46%	54%
2007	79%	21%	49%	51%
2006	88%	12%	87%	13%

Interest Groups

	AFL-CIO	ADA	CCUS	ACU
2010	8%	10%	100%	82%
2009	40%	30%	93%	75%
2008	73%	60%	78%	48%
2007	67%	35%	90%	56%
2006	43%	15%	100%	80%

West Virginia 2

Central — Charleston, Eastern Panhandle

The economically diverse 2nd spans the mountainous state from the Ohio border to the Eastern Panhandle at Harpers Ferry.

It is home to poor coal mining areas and isolated towns, as well as the more prosperous capital city of Charleston and bedroom communities in the east.

Beginning in the 1990s, the district's easternmost counties began filling with Washington commuters, launching sustained expansion — the 2nd has grown by nearly 8 percent since 2000 — and the district has the highest median household income in the state, at nearly $42,000.

Charleston, the district's pre-eminent city, is a center for chemical plants, state employees and retail shopping.

Chemical producers are key employers here, and new natural gas drilling in the Marcellus Shale may bring ethane conversion jobs here. Telemarketing firms flocked to the state in the last decade, and call centers around the district still provide jobs. State government offices offer stability in Kanawha County.

The mountainous regions north and east of Kanawha County remain dependent on coal, although production has dropped, particularly in Clay County.

Federal rules and enforcement may continue to affect coal production. Putnam County takes in Buffalo, which is home to a Toyota plant that has rebounded following precipitous declines in the domestic auto industry. Local sawmills shut down as the home construction sector waned and raw lumber exports dropped, but timber industry employers hope to diversify by marketing lumber byproducts and luring biomass production companies to the region.

The 2nd was loyal to Democrats in U.S. House elections for 18 years before electing a Republican in 2000. Expanding GOP territories dot the district, and the 2nd now supports Republican presidential candidates. John McCain won 55 percent of the district's 2008 presidential vote.

Major Industry

Chemicals, manufacturing, coal, lumber, telemarketing centers

Cities

Charleston, 51,400; Martinsburg, 17,227; South Charleston, 13,450

Notable

The Buffalo plant was Toyota's first automatic transmission production facility outside of Japan.

Rep. Nick J. Rahall II (D)

Capitol Office
225-3452
www.rahall.house.gov
2307 Rayburn Bldg. 20515-4803; fax 225-9061

Committees
Transportation & Infrastructure - Ranking Member

Residence
Beckley

Born
May 20, 1949; Beckley, W.Va.

Religion
Presbyterian

Family
Wife, Melinda Rahall; three children

Education
Duke U., B.A. 1971 (political science); George Washington U., attended 1972 (graduate studies)

Career
Broadcasting executive; travel agent; congressional aide

Political Highlights
No previous office

ELECTION RESULTS

2010 GENERAL

Nick J. Rahall II (D)	83,636	56.0%
Elliott E. Maynard (R)	65,611	44.0%

2010 PRIMARY

Nick J. Rahall II (D)	44,929	67.5%
Bruce Barilla (D)	21,620	32.5%

2008 GENERAL

Nick J. Rahall II (D)	133,522	66.9%
Marty Gearheart (R)	66,005	33.1%

Previous Winning Percentages
2006 (69%); 2004 (65%); 2002 (70%); 2000 (91%);
1998 (87%); 1996 (100%); 1994 (64%); 1992 (66%);
1990 (52%); 1988 (61%); 1986 (71%); 1984 (67%);
1982 (81%); 1980 (77%); 1978 (100%); 1976 (46%)

Elected 1976; 18th term

Out of the majority, Rahall has transitioned from chairman of the Natural Resources Committee to top Democrat on the Transportation and Infrastructure Committee. He's lost some control over resource policies that are important to his coal-dependent state, but he'll be in a better position to direct infrastructure spending back home.

And back home, where he is known as "Nicky Joe," Rahall made his reputation in the manner of his former boss and mentor, the late Democratic Sen. Robert C. Byrd: He brings home federal dollars and fiercely protects the interests of his rural district.

Rahall has long been a senior member of the Transportation panel, but has kept a low public profile on that committee in recent years in order to focus on resource issues. Still, analysts who have been around for the past few surface transportation bills say he was heavily involved in shaping them and has a deep knowledge of transportation issues.

He worked as an aide to Byrd in the 1970s, and his office is filled with coal industry paraphernalia and pictures of the two men together. Rahall has said he was closer to Byrd than any man other than his father.

Rahall's sanguine, good-old-boy style serves him well, especially in his relationship with Minority Leader Nancy Pelosi of California. When rising oil and gas prices drove energy to the top of the political agenda in the summer of 2008, while Democrats controlled the House, Rahall helped Pelosi move legislation by acting as a go-between for the liberal Speaker and more moderate members of the caucus, especially those in coal, oil and industrial states. His collegial style and reputation for protecting both the coal industry and the environment helped build support, and Democrats passed Rahall's bill to open new areas to drilling.

Nevertheless, Rahall has largely maintained support from environmentalists by pushing for conservation and trying to reduce subsidies for oil drilling. He opposed a 2007 energy bill that increased fuel economy standards for new automobiles — one of just four House Democrats to do so — partly because the bill didn't include provisions to curtail the subsidies (or contain provisions promoting experimental clean-coal technology).

As a Democrat from a region of West Virginia particularly dependent on mining, he is in a more difficult position as the Obama administration and Democratic leaders push a climate change policy focused on capping carbon emissions and creating a market-based trading program for emissions credits. He opposed the legislative effort to do so in the 111th Congress (2009-10).

And he was one of 19 Democrats to back House-passed legislation in the 112th Congress (2011-12) that would prohibit the EPA from regulating greenhouse gases in any effort to address climate change.

Though he was reluctant to impose new burdens on the coal industry when it came to climate change legislation, Rahall threw his support behind legislation in 2010 and 2011 that would create sweeping new regulations to help shore up safety at coal mines, following a 2010 explosion in the Upper Big Branch mine that killed 29 people. In 2006, after accidents in the Sago and Aracoma mines killed 14 workers, Rahall supported passage of a mine safety law that raised fines for safety violations, required wireless communications equipment and tracking devices in all underground mines and established grants for new mine safety technology.

Rahall's ties to Byrd and close adherence to the mores of his district have helped him survive politically as a Democrat in an increasingly conservative part of the country. Though he has become more loyal to his party in recent years — he voted in favor of the health care overhaul in 2010 and is considered a reliable union supporter — he continues to deviate sharply from his fellow Democrats on many social issues. In 2007, he voted to maintain a ban on federal funding for international organizations that perform abortions, and he opposed a ban on job discrimination based on sexual preference. A member of the National Rifle Association, he voted in 2008 to eliminate a restrictive District of Columbia handgun law. In 2010 he opposed legislation that would create a path to citizenship for children of illegal immigrants who serve in the military or attend college.

The grandson of Lebanese immigrants, Rahall is among the few outspoken House critics of U.S. policy toward Israel. He encourages closer ties with Arab countries and was one of eight lawmakers who opposed a resolution expressing unconditional support for Israel in its 2006 conflict with the Lebanese Hezbollah terrorist group. He was one of five House members to vote against a January 2009 resolution supporting Israel's retaliation for attacks by Palestinians in Gaza.

Rahall grew up affluent. His paternal grandfather peddled goods in coal camps. Rahall's father ran a five-and-dime store and later a women's clothing shop, which eventually enabled him to invest in a chain of radio and television stations.

Rahall graduated from Duke University and, after working for Byrd, returned to his family's broadcasting business. In 1976 at age 27, he ran for the House, taking advantage of Democratic Rep. Ken Hechler's decision to run for governor. Rahall spent family money on a media campaign none of his foes could match and won the nomination with 37 percent of the vote. Hechler, who lost the gubernatorial primary, then mounted a write-in drive to keep his seat, but Rahall prevailed.

Rahall had some fits and starts — gambling debts in the mid-1980s, a guilty plea to an alcohol-related reckless driving charge in 1988, and bad publicity surrounding trips taken at lobbyists' expense in the 1990s. But he is the 10th-most-senior Democrat in the chamber in the 112th Congress and hadn't had anything approaching a tough re-election race until 2010, when he defeated Republican Elliott Maynard with 56 percent of the vote.

During Rahall's 2010 campaign, it came to light that Tanya Rahall, his sister who is a lobbyist, was in the midst of a lawsuit brought by her former employer for allegedly threatening to use her influence with her brother to blackball the company from doing business on Capitol Hill after their business dealings went sour. Rahall denied any wrongdoing.

Key Votes

2010

Overhaul the nation's health insurance system	YES
Allow for repeal of "don't ask, don't tell"	NO
Overhaul financial services industry regulation	YES
Limit use of new Afghanistan War funds to troop withdrawal activities	NO
Change oversight of offshore drilling and lift oil spill liability cap	YES
Provide a path to legal status for some children of illegal immigrants	NO
Extend Bush-era income tax cuts for two years	YES

2009

Expand the Children's Health Insurance Program	YES
Provide $787 billion in tax cuts and spending increases to stimulate the economy	YES
Allow bankruptcy judges to modify certain primary-residence mortgages	YES
Create a cap-and-trade system to limit greenhouse gas emissions	NO
Provide $2 billion for the "cash for clunkers" program	YES
Establish the government as the sole provider of student loans	YES
Restrict federally funded insurance coverage for abortions in health care overhaul	YES

CQ Vote Studies

	PARTY UNITY		PRESIDENTIAL SUPPORT	
	Support	Oppose	Support	Oppose
2010	94%	6%	88%	12%
2009	97%	3%	94%	6%
2008	97%	3%	18%	82%
2007	94%	6%	9%	91%
2006	82%	18%	47%	53%

Interest Groups

	AFL-CIO	ADA	CCUS	ACU
2010	93%	60%	25%	8%
2009	95%	85%	53%	12%
2008	93%	85%	67%	8%
2007	96%	85%	60%	16%
2006	93%	65%	47%	48%

West Virginia 3

South — Huntington, Beckley

The largely rural 3rd takes in the state's southern counties and borders Virginia, Kentucky and Ohio. Continuing layoffs and declining production have hurt the region still known as the "coal district," home to many of the state's leading coal-producing counties.

The last 30 years have been hard on the 3rd. As the coal industry mechanized production, the need for manpower was sharply reduced. Unemployment rates in counties along much of the Virginia border are higher than the national average.

These struggles, combined with persistent pockets of Appalachian poverty, give the district the eighth-lowest median household income in the nation, at slightly less than $33,000.

The 3rd was the only West Virginia district to lose population between 2000 and 2010, and the local job market has not fully recovered from several years of high unemployment rates.

Huntington, which rests along the Ohio River, is by far the district's largest city and home to Marshall University. The 3rd attracts visitors with its ski resorts, whitewater rafting and The Greenbrier, a luxury resort in White Sulphur Springs that hosts golf tournaments, conferences and congressional party retreats. Raleigh County is home to Tamarack, a state and private cultural center featuring in-house artisans, live music, regional cuisine and retail shopping.

Despite a continued Democratic lead in party registration in every county and an overall districtwide preference for Democrats elsewhere on the ballot, the 3rd has trended Republican at the presidential level.

George W. Bush lost the 3rd by just 4 percentage points in 2000, but won the district in 2004 with 53 percent of the vote. In the 2008 presidential election, although Democrat Barack Obama's two highest percentages statewide were in Boone (54 percent) and McDowell (53 percent) counties, John McCain took 56 percent of the district's vote.

Major Industry
Coal, wood products, tourism

Cities
Huntington, 49,138; Beckley, 17,614; Bluefield, 10,447

Notable
The New River Gorge Bridge, in Fayette County, is the second-longest steel-arch bridge in the world and the nation's second-highest bridge; the Port of Huntington Tri-State is the nation's largest inland shipping port.

Gov. Scott Walker (R)

First elected: 2010

Length of term: 4 years

Term expires: 1/15

Salary: $137,092

Phone: (608) 266-1212

Residence: Wauwatosa

Born: Nov. 2, 1967; Colorado Springs, Colo.

Religion: Non-denominational Christian

Family: Wife, Tonette Walker; two children

Education: Marquette U., attended 1986-90

Career: Humanitarian relief nonprofit fundraiser

Political highlights: Wis. House, 1993-2002; Milwaukee County executive, 2002-10

ELECTION RESULTS

2010 GENERAL

Scott Walker (R)	1,128,941	52.3%
Tom Barrett (D)	1,004,303	46.5%

Lt. Gov. Rebecca Kleefisch (R)

First elected: 2010

Length of term: 4 years

Term expires: 1/15

Salary: $76,262

Phone: (608) 266-3516

LEGISLATURE

Legislature: 10 floor periods of varying lengths over a 2-year session

Senate: 33 members, 4-year terms

2011 ratios: 19 R, 14 D; 25 men, 8 women

Salary: $49,943

Phone: (608) 266-2517

Assembly: 99 members, 2-year terms

2011 ratios: 59 R, 38 D, 1 I, 1 vacancy; 75 men, 23 women

Salary: $49,943

Phone: (608) 266-1501

TERM LIMITS

Governor: No

Senate: No

House: No

URBAN STATISTICS

CITY	POPULATION
Milwaukee	594,833
Madison	233,209
Green Bay	104,057
Kenosha	99,218
Racine	78,860

REGISTERED VOTERS

Voters do not register by party.

POPULATION

2010 population	5,686,986
2000 population	5,363,675
1990 population	4,891,769
Percent change (2000-2010)	+6.0%
Rank among states (2010)	20
Median age	37.8
Born in state	71.9%
Foreign born	4.3
Violent crime rate	257/100,000
Poverty level	12.4%
Federal workers	37,022
Military	2,046

ELECTIONS

STATE ELECTION OFFICIAL

(608) 266-8005

DEMOCRATIC PARTY

(608) 255-5172

REPUBLICAN PARTY

(608) 257-4765

MISCELLANEOUS

Web: www.wisconsin.gov

Capital: Madison

U.S. CONGRESS

Senate: 1 Democrat, 1 Republican

House: 5 Republicans, 3 Democrats

2010 Census Statistics by District

District	2008 Vote for President Obama	McCain	White	Black	Asian	Hispanic	Median Income	White Collar	Blue Collar	Service Industry	Over 64	Under 18	College Education	Rural	Sq. Miles
1	51%	47%	82%	5%	2%	9%	$57,790	59%	27%	15%	13%	25%	25%	16%	1,680
2	69	30	84	4	3	6	56,075	65	20	15	11	22	35	24	3,511
3	58	41	94	1	2	2	49,251	54	29	17	13	23	23	57	13,565
4	75	24	42	35	3	17	38,085	54	25	20	10	27	21	0	112
5	41	58	90	2	3	4	68,490	68	20	12	14	24	39	15	1,273
6	50	49	91	1	2	4	50,869	51	33	16	14	23	19	39	5,641
7	56	42	93	1	2	2	46,118	52	32	16	16	23	19	58	18,787
8	53	45	88	1	2	4	50,210	54	30	16	14	24	22	44	9,740
STATE	56	42	83	6	2	6	51,569	57	27	16	13	24	25	32	54,310
U.S.	53	46	64	12	5	16	51,425	60	23	17	13	25	28	21	3,537,438

Sen. Herb Kohl (D)

Capitol Office
224-5653
kohl.senate.gov
330 Hart Bldg. 20510-4903; fax 224-9787

Committees
Appropriations
   (Agriculture - Chairman)
Banking, Housing & Urban Affairs
Judiciary
   (Antitrust, Competition Policy & Consumer Rights
   - Chairman)
Special Aging - Chairman

Residence
Milwaukee

Born
Feb. 7, 1935; Milwaukee, Wis.

Religion
Jewish

Family
Single

Education
U. of Wisconsin, B.A. 1956; Harvard U., M.B.A. 1958

Military Service
Army Reserve, 1958-64

Career
Department and grocery store owner; professional
basketball team owner

Political Highlights
Wis. Democratic Party chairman, 1975-77

ELECTION RESULTS

2006 GENERAL
Herb Kohl (D)	1,439,214	67.3%
Robert Gerald Lorge (R)	630,299	29.5%
Rae Vogeler (WG)	42,434	2.0%
Ben J. Glatzel (I)	25,096	1.2%

2006 PRIMARY
Herb Kohl (D)	308,178	85.7%
Ben Masel (D)	51,245	14.2%

Previous Winning Percentages
2000 (62%); 1994 (58%); 1988 (52%)

Elected 1988; 4th term

A multimillionaire who finances his own campaigns, Kohl shuns publicity while quietly working to protect the dairy industry, the elderly and farm programs. In May 2011, he announced he would not seek a fifth term.

Perhaps the most introverted member of the Senate, Kohl is known for thoughtful gestures, such as sending out boxes of Wisconsin chocolates, and providing breakfast in his office on Wednesdays for visiting constituents. But he's not afraid to take a tough stance.

Late in 2010, Kohl said he would place a hold on Michele Leonhart, the White House's nominee to lead the Drug Enforcement Agency, because Kohl feels that DEA rules cause health care workers to needlessly deny painkillers to people living in nursing homes. Heightened scrutiny of prescribing practices has resulted in elderly people suffering in pain as nurses and doctors strive to adhere to the Controlled Substances Act, he said. He grilled Leonhart about this at a November hearing of the Judiciary Committee.

"When I met with you in early May, you assured me that this was a priority, and that you also would address the problem swiftly," said Kohl, who is the No. 2 Democrat on Judiciary and chairman of the Special Committee on Aging. "It appears that DEA is putting paperwork before pain relief. I would like to see much more progress made on this issue before you are confirmed."

After getting assurances from the Justice Department that the medication would be delivered to patients, Kohl released his hold.

As chairman of Judiciary's Antitrust, Competition Policy and Consumer Rights Subcommittee, he has pushed legislation to stop makers of brand-name drugs from paying would-be competitors to delay the market entry of cheaper generic versions of their products. The bill might save the federal government as much as $2.6 billion over 10 years by reducing its drug costs.

"At this time of spiraling health care costs, we cannot turn a blind eye to these anti-competitive backroom deals that deny consumers access to affordable generic drugs," Kohl said.

Kohl has worked with Republican Charles E. Grassley of Iowa on that effort, and also on nursing home legislation. Grassley told Milwaukee magazine that he's accomplished more with Kohl while talking less to him than any other senator. "I'll bet he never has done anything to harm or hurt anybody behind their back," Grassley said in the magazine's 2010 profile of Kohl.

As chairman of the Appropriations Subcommittee on Agriculture, Kohl has pressed for accountability while looking out for Wisconsin's economic mainstay — farming. In the 110th Congress (2007-08), he included in the law to reauthorize farm programs a provision to permit interstate sales of state-inspected meat products, which he says will help smaller entrepreneurs expand their markets.

Kohl joined the Banking, Housing and Urban Affairs Committee in the 110th Congress. The financial services overhaul enacted in 2010 makes regulators responsible for decisions on issues ranging from determining fair charges on debit card swipe fees to deciding when a risky firm should be taken over, and Kohl pledged to make sure the American public gets the intended benefits. "I am going to keep a watchful eye on the regulators to make sure they are given adequate resources and oversight to do the job that they have been charged with," Kohl said on the Senate floor in 2010.

Kohl is typically a loyal party vote. Yet he considers himself a moderate who sees partisanship as the biggest obstacle to legislating, so at times he steps across the aisle to further his goals. He joined in 2007 with New Mexico Republican Pete V. Domenici on a bill calling for a nationwide system of background checks to identify job applicants who have criminal pasts.

In 2001, he was one of a dozen Democrats to vote for President George W. Bush's $1.35 trillion tax cut, and one of 15 Democrats to back the initial version of the GOP's spending blueprint for the year. However, he opposed Bush's 2003 plan for $350 billion in tax cuts over 11 years. He voted for a two-year extension in late 2010.

With Republicans narrowing the gap in the Senate and taking control of the House in the 112th Congress (2011-12), Kohl's interest in reining in the federal deficit might be revived, though he expressed no support for the spending proposal put forth by fellow Wisconsinite Paul D. Ryan, the Republican chairman of the House Budget Committee. His preoccupation with the deficit echoed that of his predecessor in the Senate, Democrat William Proxmire, renowned for his sermons against government excess.

Kohl was among the 53 senators who voted in January 2010 in support of a bid by Senate Budget Chairman Kent Conrad, a North Dakota Democrat, and Judd Gregg of New Hampshire, the committee's ranking Republican, to establish a powerful commission to tackle the federal debt. The effort failed — 60 votes were needed — but it paved the way for President Obama's fiscal commission, which in December made a set of sweeping recommendations on the budget.

Even though Kohl said he would not endorse the commission's entire plan, particularly changes to Social Security, he praised the effort and called it "an important step to getting our fiscal house in order."

Kohl, one of the wealthiest members of Congress, considers himself something of a bargain for the taxpayer. Though he has to receive the pay increases given to members of Congress, at the end of each year he writes a check to the Bureau of Public Debt for the difference between his salary (currently $174,000) and the $89,500 he earned upon joining the Senate. He also has returned more than $5 million in unspent office allocations.

Kohl's parents immigrated to the United States in the 1920s — his mother from Russia, his father from Poland. They opened a small food store on Milwaukee's south side, where Kohl worked after school and on weekends. One of his childhood friends (and later his college roommate) was Bud Selig, who went on to become a successful car dealer, owner of the Milwaukee Brewers baseball team and commissioner of Major League Baseball.

After earning a master's degree in business from Harvard, Kohl returned home and, with his two brothers, set about expanding the family grocery business into a department store chain in 1962 — the same year that Sam Walton opened the first Wal-Mart Discount City store in Arkansas. The Kohls eventually owned hundreds of stores before selling the chain in 1979.

In 1985, Kohl bought the Milwaukee Bucks NBA franchise, primarily to keep the team from relocating. He was a fan, and he saw the deal as "a combination of my own personal interest and public need."

Kohl's first public involvement in politics came in 1975 when Democratic Gov. Patrick Lucey asked him to chair the state Democratic Party. He did the job for two years, despite his discomfort with some of its public aspects. In 1988, when Proxmire stepped down after 31 years in the Senate, Democrats pressed an initially ambivalent Kohl to run. He had plenty of name recognition, and spent nearly $7.5 million (most of it his own money) on the campaign. Kohl's total outlay was double the previous state record.

He won a three-way Democratic primary with 47 percent of the vote, and defeated GOP state Sen. Susan Engeleiter by 4 percentage points in the fall. Kohl has won with comfortable margins each time since, and his slogan in each campaign is the same: "Nobody's senator but yours." (This was also a theme used by Massachusetts Republican Scott P. Brown during his successful 2010 Senate bid.)

Key Votes

2010

Pass budget reconciliation bill to modify overhauls of health care and federal student loan programs	YES
Proceed to disapproval resolution on EPA authority to regulate greenhouse gases	NO
Overhaul financial services industry regulation	YES
Limit debate to proceed to a bill to broaden campaign finance disclosure and reporting rules	YES
Limit debate on an extension of Bush-era income tax cuts for two years	YES
Limit debate on a bill to provide a path to legal status for some children of illegal immigrants	YES
Allow for a repeal of "don't ask, don't tell"	YES
Consent to ratification of a strategic arms reduction treaty with Russia	YES

2009

Prevent release of remaining financial industry bailout funds	NO
Make it easier for victims to sue for wage discrimination remedies	YES
Expand the Children's Health Insurance Program	YES
Limit debate on the economic stimulus measure	YES
Repeal District of Columbia firearms prohibitions and gun registration laws	NO
Limit debate on expansion of federal hate crimes law	YES
Strike funding for F-22 Raptor fighter jets	YES

CQ Vote Studies

	PARTY UNITY		PRESIDENTIAL SUPPORT	
	SUPPORT	OPPOSE	SUPPORT	OPPOSE
2010	94%	6%	100%	0%
2009	95%	5%	97%	3%
2008	94%	6%	37%	63%
2007	96%	4%	38%	62%
2006	91%	9%	57%	43%
2005	89%	11%	45%	55%
2004	95%	5%	66%	34%
2003	94%	6%	50%	50%
2002	84%	16%	79%	21%
2001	89%	11%	69%	31%

Interest Groups

	AFL-CIO	ADA	CCUS	ACU
2010	94%	90%	36%	8%
2009	100%	100%	43%	8%
2008	100%	95%	63%	4%
2007	95%	95%	45%	0%
2006	87%	90%	50%	16%
2005	86%	100%	67%	13%
2004	92%	100%	44%	4%
2003	100%	95%	35%	25%
2002	92%	85%	60%	15%
2001	88%	90%	54%	16%

Sen. Ron Johnson (R)

Capitol Office
224-5323
ronjohnson.senate.gov
386 Russell Bldg. 20510-4904; fax 224-2725

Committees
Appropriations
Budget
Homeland Security & Governmental Affairs
Special Aging

Residence
Oshkosh

Born
April 8, 1955; Mankato, Minn.

Religion
Lutheran

Family
Wife, Jane Johnson; three children

Education
U. of Minnesota, B.S. 1977 (accounting), attended
1977-79 (business administration)

Career
Plastics manufacturing company owner; shipping
supply company machine operator; accountant

Political Highlights
No previous office

ELECTION RESULTS

2010 GENERAL

Ron Johnson (R)	1,125,999	51.9%
Russ Feingold (D)	1,020,958	47.0%
Rob Taylor (CNSTP)	23,473	1.1%

2010 PRIMARY

Ron Johnson (R)	504,644	84.8%
Dave Bond Westlake IV (R)	61,633	10.4%
Stephen M. Finn (R)	28,929	4.9%

Elected 2010; 1st term

Johnson, a business owner and accountant who had never served in public office before winning election to the Senate, has little good to say about the business practices of the federal government or the way it accounts for its money.

Dubbed an "Ayn Rand-loving, pro-life Lutheran" by the conservative Weekly Standard magazine, Johnson was criticized during his victorious campaign against 18-year incumbent Democrat Russ Feingold for being vague on how he would reduce spending and spur job creation. "I don't think this election is about details," he responded at one point, according to the St. Paul Pioneer Press.

Once in the Senate — and as a member of both the Appropriations and Budget committees — he signed on as a cosponsor of legislation by Tennessee Republican Bob Corker and Missouri Democrat Claire McCaskill that would limit all discretionary and mandatory spending to a declining percentage of the gross domestic product.

He praised the proposal written by fellow Wisconsin Republican Paul D. Ryan, chairman of the House Budget Committee, calling it "a serious proposal that takes the discussion from talking about billions of dollars of deficit spending to the trillions of dollars that is really the issue."

Johnson, who also sits on the Special Aging Committee, voted to repeal the health care overhaul law enacted in 2010. And he urges reduced regulation and lower taxes.

"The Small Business Administration estimates that government regulations cost our economy $1.7 trillion annually," he said in the Republican response to the president's weekly radio address in late January 2011. "According to the IRS's own figures, it cost taxpayers 6.1 billion hours to comply with tax code just last year."

He was among a number of conservative GOP candidates who signed the "Contract From America," the platform inspired by the 1994 "Contract With America." The new contract calls for a moratorium on earmarks until Congress balances the budget; a two-thirds majority in Congress to pass earmarks and tax increases; a flat-tax system; and limits on federal spending.

Johnson was named ranking Republican on the Homeland Security and Governmental Affairs Subcommittee on Oversight of Government Management, the Federal Workforce and the District of Columbia — a position he says gives him another spot from which to keep close watch on federal spending.

He is a social conservative, opposing abortion rights and federal funding of embryonic stem cell research. "My basic belief is you don't want to get in a situation where you're creating life though destroying it," Johnson told The Associated Press in October 2010. He also supports gun owners' rights, winning the endorsement of the National Rifle Association.

Johnson is a skeptic on man-made climate change, saying "it's not settled science" and speculating that sunspots create natural changes in Earth's temperature, a position backed by some scientists. "We certainly should not penalize our economy to the tune of a trillion dollars when we have this weakened economy," he told Fox News.

Johnson was born and raised in neighboring Minnesota. To earn money as a kid, he mowed lawns, shoveled snow from driveways, delivered newspapers, baled hay and worked as a golf caddie. In his teen years, he was a dishwasher and night manager at a Walgreen's Grill.

To earn extra money, his family worked in its basement to produce soap balls to sell to a local bath factory, according to a profile in the Milwaukee Journal Sentinel.

Johnson lived at home and worked full time while attending the University of Minnesota. He says he was able to graduate from college debt free, with $7,000 in the bank. "The greatest compliment my parents would ever give somebody is, 'That person is a really hard worker.' It's a part of who you are," Johnson told the Journal Sentinel.

He began working as an accountant for Josten's, which sells school rings and yearbooks, then moved to Oshkosh, Wis., in 1979 to help launch a plastics manufacturing firm with his brother-in-law. The company, Pacur, produces a specialty plastic used in medical device packaging and high-tech printing applications.

In a rare venture into the political world before the Senate race, Johnson testified before the Wisconsin legislature in opposition to a bill that would have extended the statute of limitations for civil liability in child sexual abuse cases. The law was aimed primarily at the Roman Catholic Church. Johnson, a Lutheran, was active in the Green Bay Diocese Finance Council and in financially supporting Catholic schools in the region. He feared the law would bankrupt the diocese and possibly force the closure of area schools.

"I think its a valid question to ask if the employer of the perpetrator should also be severely damaged, possibly destroyed, in a legitimate desire for justice?" he told the lawmakers. At the same time, he called for the diocese to cooperate fully in any investigations. The bill was not approved by either chamber.

In the autumn of 2009, Johnson was invited to speak to a group of tea party activists in Oshkosh. His scathing dissertation on the health care overhaul inspired some of the participants to urge him to get into the Senate race.

By spring 2010 he was seriously considering it. In April, the leading potential Republican candidate, former Gov. Tommy G. Thompson, announced he would not enter the race. A month later, Johnson got in.

He swept to the GOP nomination, winning both the state party endorsement at a May convention and the support of tea party activists like those he had impressed the previous fall. He easily captured the nomination in the September primary, winning 85 percent of the vote over small-business owner Dave Westlake.

A poll conducted the day after the primary showed Johnson running ahead of Feingold, 51 percent to 44 percent.

Having never run for office before, though, he stumbled out of the gate, making a number of verbal gaffes — at one point he said he was running because he heard Dick Morris say on Fox News that "some rich guy" was what Wisconsin Republicans needed to beat Feingold.

But Feingold also made a few unforced errors. Known throughout his career as an advocate for tighter regulation of campaigns, he had to pull an ad that included a clip from an NFL game without permission.

Feingold also accused Johnson of supporting drilling for oil in the Great Lakes — he doesn't — and of backing the licensing of handguns; Johnson used that term, but actually meant permits for carrying concealed weapons. He ran a radio ad to clarify that point and to distinguish himself in another way from his opponent: "I'm not a slick politician, and I made a mistake. It wasn't the first time, and it probably won't be the last."

And, despite Johnson's "rich guy" tag and Feingold's career-long reputation as an advocate for stricter campaign regulations, the incumbent outraised and outspent Johnson about 3-to-2, according to the Center for Responsive Politics. About two-thirds of Johnson's money was his own.

On election night, Johnson topped Feingold by more than 100,000 votes, winning 52 percent of the vote to Feingold's 47 percent.

Rep. Paul D. Ryan (R)

Capitol Office
225-3031
paulryan.house.gov
1233 Longworth Bldg. 20515-4901; fax 225-3393

Committees
Budget - Chairman
Ways & Means

Residence
Janesville

Born
Jan. 29, 1970; Janesville, Wis.

Religion
Roman Catholic

Family
Wife, Janna Ryan; three children

Education
Miami U. (Ohio), B.A. 1992 (political science & economics)

Career
Congressional aide; economic policy analyst

Political Highlights
No previous office

ELECTION RESULTS

2010 GENERAL

Paul D. Ryan (R)	179,819	68.2%
John Heckenlively (D)	79,363	30.1%
Joseph Kexel (LIBERT)	4,311	1.6%

2010 PRIMARY

Paul D. Ryan (R)	unopposed

2008 GENERAL

Paul D. Ryan (R)	231,009	64.0%
Marge Krupp (D)	125,268	34.7%
Joseph Kexel (LIBERT)	4,606	1.3%

Previous Winning Percentages
2006 (63%); 2004 (65%); 2002 (67%); 2000 (67%); 1998 (57%)

Elected 1998; 7th term

Ryan's skills as a telegenic policy wonk have helped him emerge as a prominent spokesman for congressional Republicans. As chairman of the Budget Committee and author of a plan to cut federal spending by $4 trillion over 10 years, he is the party's point man in the debate likely to dominate the 112th Congress.

Ryan is now routinely mentioned as one of the GOP's brightest stars and a future presidential or vice presidential candidate. Though he has been working on his ideas since he first came to Congress, until now they have gained little currency.

Bolstered by the election of 87 House GOP freshmen in 2010, most of whom are alight with the idea of reducing the scope of government, Ryan has at last found a ready audience — and foot soldiers ready to enlist in his crusade.

For most people, the federal budget is just numbers in a ledger. For Ryan, it's a cause. His plan aims at nothing less than amending the social contract between government and the governed. That change, he says, is not a choice, but a necessity.

"Washington has not been telling you the truth about the magnitude of the problems we are facing," he said in the Republican response to President Obama's weekly radio address in April 2011. "Unless we act soon, government spending on health and retirement programs will crowd out spending on everything else, including national security. It will literally take every cent of every federal tax dollar just to pay for these programs."

In January 2010, Ryan gained considerable attention when he unveiled the second edition of his "Roadmap for America's Future," an ambitious proposal to eliminate projected future federal deficits by overhauling the tax code — he also serves on the tax-writing Ways and Means Committee — along with Social Security and the health care system. The "Roadmap" served as a precursor to the fiscal 2012 budget he wrote, which the House passed in April 2011.

Obama mentioned Ryan's plan while addressing House Republicans at their annual retreat, calling it a "serious proposal" while noting areas of disagreement. Other administration officials and Democratic congressional leaders sought to draw attention to Ryan's proposed changes to Medicare, which they argued would reduce benefits and transfer more costs onto recipients.

Ryan was highly visible during debate on health care overhaul legislation in the 111th Congress (2009-10). He and California Republican Devin Nunes joined a pair of Republican senators, Tom Coburn of Oklahoma and Richard M. Burr of North Carolina, in introducing an alternative that would have authorized state health insurance exchanges and provided tax credits to families for insurance purchases while repealing the tax deduction for employer-provided health insurance. Ryan strongly opposed the final health care overhaul legislation, calling it "paternalistic" and "arrogant," and voted to repeal it in early 2011.

Ryan says his philosophy of individualism and entrepreneurial capitalism was influenced most deeply by novelist Ayn Rand. He lists the late New York Rep. Jack F. Kemp, his former boss and the 1996 GOP vice presidential nominee, as his political role model. "Jack had a huge influence on me, his brand of inclusive conservatism, his pro-growth, happy-warrior style. That was infectious to me," Ryan told the Milwaukee Journal Sentinel in 2009.

Even though he is a member of the conservative Republican Study Committee, Ryan sometimes splits with party activists, especially on regional issues. In 2008 he voted in favor of the creation of the Troubled Asset Relief Program, arguing that the $700 billion program was needed to avoid economic collapse. He also supported aid to the domestic auto industry, which historically has had a major presence in Ryan's hometown of Janesville. A June 2010 profile in the libertarian magazine Reason noted this dual persona, calling Ryan "one of the staunchest and most serious small-government advocates in Congress today" who is also "a savvy Washington politician who defends parochial, home-state interests when necessary."

The youngest of four children, Ryan was 16 when his father died. His mother used Social Security survivor's benefits to help pay for his college education. He said that helped shape his personal and political beliefs. "It made me more of a self-starter and scrapper," Ryan said. He "wasn't one of these guys who thought from second grade on that he wanted to run for Congress." But after college, he took a job as an aide to Wisconsin GOP Sen. Bob Kasten. His direct speaking style mirrors that of his two mentors, Kemp and William J. Bennett, former Republican Cabinet secretaries and co-founders of Empower America, a conservative think tank where Ryan worked. He also worked for Kansas Republican Sam Brownback in the House and Senate.

After five years in Washington, he returned to Wisconsin to join his family's earth-moving and construction business. When GOP Rep. Mark W. Neumann ran for the Senate in 1998, Ryan sought the open seat. His opponent in November was Democrat Lydia Spottswood, a former Kenosha City Council president who nearly beat Neumann in 1996. Ryan proved a superior campaigner — he earned the nickname "Robocandidate" — and won by more than 27,000 votes, a surprisingly large margin given that the previous three races in the district had been decided by no more than 4,000 votes. He entered Congress in January 1999 as the youngest member of that year's freshman class — 28 years old.

He has since won each re-election with more than 62 percent of the vote. George W. Bush offered to make him his budget director during his second term, an offer Ryan turned down.

He hasn't ruled out a future Senate bid, but has said he will not be a presidential candidate in 2012, despite the importuning of many conservatives. "My head is not that big and my kids are too small," he told The New York Times in 2010. However, in the same interview, he left open the possibility of accepting the vice presidential nomination if offered. "I'd cross that bridge if we ever come to it," he said.

Key Votes

2010

Overhaul the nation's health insurance system	NO
Allow for repeal of "don't ask, don't tell"	-
Overhaul financial services industry regulation	NO
Limit use of new Afghanistan War funds to troop withdrawal activities	NO
Change oversight of offshore drilling and lift oil spill liability cap	NO
Provide a path to legal status for some children of illegal immigrants	NO
Extend Bush-era income tax cuts for two years	YES

2009

Expand the Children's Health Insurance Program	NO
Provide $787 billion in tax cuts and spending increases to stimulate the economy	NO
Allow bankruptcy judges to modify certain primary-residence mortgages	NO
Create a cap-and-trade system to limit greenhouse gas emissions	NO
Provide $2 billion for the "cash for clunkers" program	NO
Establish the government as the sole provider of student loans	NO
Restrict federally funded insurance coverage for abortions in health care overhaul	YES

CQ Vote Studies

	PARTY UNITY		PRESIDENTIAL SUPPORT	
	SUPPORT	OPPOSE	SUPPORT	OPPOSE
2010	98%	2%	24%	76%
2009	97%	3%	17%	83%
2008	97%	3%	86%	14%
2007	96%	4%	80%	20%
2006	94%	6%	93%	7%

Interest Groups

	AFL-CIO	ADA	CCUS	ACU
2010	0%	0%	88%	96%
2009	10%	0%	73%	96%
2008	20%	15%	83%	84%
2007	26%	15%	75%	96%
2006	14%	0%	100%	92%

Wisconsin 1

Southeast — Kenosha, Racine

From the wealthy Milwaukee suburbs on the coast of Lake Michigan to the center of Rock County in central Wisconsin, the 1st blends rural communities with some of the state's largest industrial areas. The district's two largest cities, Racine and Kenosha, are sandwiched between Milwaukee and Chicago along the lake and Interstate 94.

Kenosha and Walworth counties, two major manufacturing areas, have experienced faster population growth than the state's average. Much of this expansion is due to new residents attracted by lower housing prices and cheaper living and who commute to Milwaukee or Chicago, both less than an hour's drive away.

Manufacturing losses and several years of extensive layoffs at major regional employers such as Abbott Laboratories, an Illinois-based pharmaceutical company, hurt the local economies in Kenosha, Racine and Rock counties.

But SC Johnson and Son, the consumer products manufacturer, continues to have a major presence in the area. On the other side of the district, Janesville lost a primary source of jobs when the General Motors plant there closed in 2008, but union workers hope the automaker will reopen the plant. Resorts catering to wealthy vacationers from nearby Chicago ring Lake Geneva and Lake Delavan in Walworth County and have given the area a bit of an economic boost.

The 1st consistently backs conservative Rep. Paul D. Ryan but is split rather evenly between the parties. Its GOP lean isn't assured in presidential elections: George W. Bush won here in 2004 by 7 percentage points, but Barack Obama took 51 percent in 2008.

Republican Ron Johnson beat Democrat Russ Feingold in each of the three counties entirely within the district in 2010, but won only 52 percent in once strongly Democratic Kenosha County while taking the U.S. Senate seat.

Major Industry
Agriculture, manufacturing

Cities
Kenosha, 99,218; Racine, 78,860; Janesville (pt.), 63,122; Greenfield (pt.), 36,705; Franklin, 35,451; Oak Creek, 34,451

Notable
Racine hosts the annual Salmon-A-Rama fishing contest; C. Latham Sholes invented the typewriter in Kenosha.

Rep. Tammy Baldwin (D)

Capitol Office
225-2906
tammybaldwin.house.gov
2446 Rayburn Bldg. 20515-4902; fax 225-6942

Committees
Energy & Commerce

Residence
Madison

Born
Feb. 11, 1962; Madison, Wis.

Religion
Unspecified

Family
Dissolved partnership

Education
Smith College, A.B. 1984 (math & government); U. of
Wisconsin, J.D. 1989

Career
Lawyer

Political Highlights
Madison City Council, 1986; Dane County Board of
Supervisors, 1986-94; Wis. Assembly, 1993-99

ELECTION RESULTS

2010 GENERAL

Tammy Baldwin (D)	191,164	61.8%
Chad Lee (R)	118,099	38.2%

2010 PRIMARY

Tammy Baldwin (D)	unopposed

2008 GENERAL

Tammy Baldwin (D)	277,914	69.3%
Peter Theron (R)	122,513	30.6%

Previous Winning Percentages
2006 (63%); 2004 (63%); 2002 (66%); 2000 (51%);
1998 (52%)

Elected 1998; 7th term

Baldwin is one of the most liberal members of Congress, and her seat on the Energy and Commerce Committee positions her well to promote her interests in health care. A persistent critic of President George W. Bush, she now has a president in Barack Obama whose politics are more to her liking, but finds herself with less clout in a Republican-led House.

Baldwin came to Congress with the overriding objective of providing universal health coverage, and saw her quest fulfilled — somewhat — with enactment in 2010 of the Democrats' health care overhaul. But that law does not include either the government-run insurance option preferred by many liberals or the Canadian-style single-payer system backed by Baldwin. When the House passed the final version, Baldwin called it "the first of many improvements" and said, "Our work is not done."

She is the first woman elected to Congress from Wisconsin and the first openly gay woman to win a seat in either chamber. She exchanged marriage vows in 1998 with Lauren Azar, a lawyer, though same-sex unions are not legal in Wisconsin (their partnership was later dissolved). With Democrat Barney Frank of Massachusetts, she founded the Lesbian, Gay, Bisexual, and Transgender Equality Caucus in 2008.

She backs legislation — bound to go nowhere in the GOP-led House — to repeal the 1996 law known as the Defense of Marriage Act, and applauded when Obama's Justice Department said it would not defend the law in court.

As a Judiciary Committee member in the 110th Congress (2007-08), Baldwin was a cosponsor and vocal advocate of legislation expanding hate crime laws to cover crimes motivated by the victim's sexual orientation. The House passed the bill in 2007, but it failed to win enactment. Baldwin and other supporters were back again in the 111th Congress (2009-10), winning swift House passage of their legislation. "Americans across the country, young and old alike, must hear Congress clearly affirm that hate-based violence targeting gays, lesbians, transgender individuals, women, and people with disabilities will not be tolerated," she said.

She no longer serves on the Judiciary panel.

In 2007, she joined Frank and Republicans Deborah Pryce of Ohio and Christopher Shays of Connecticut in sponsoring legislation to outlaw employment discrimination based on sexual orientation or gender identity. The House passed the bill after removing workplace protections for transgender individuals. The Senate did not call up the measure. Baldwin said she was pleased the House had passed the bill for the first time but unhappy transgender individuals were "carved out."

In September 2010 the Energy and Commerce Health Subcommittee approved her bill to require the Department of Health and Human Services to ask about an individual's sexual orientation if they participate in HHS programs or surveys. Baldwin said the information was "vitally needed to protect the health of all Americans — including LGBT Americans," but the measure never moved any further.

In the 110th, Bush signed into law two health bills she had sponsored. The first, which she considers one of her most significant achievements in Congress, reauthorized and expanded a screening program for breast and cervical cancer. The second expanded benefits for veterans with impaired vision.

Baldwin also takes pride in several provisions she helped draft during committee action on a 2007 energy law that raised vehicle fuel efficiency standards and promoted energy-efficient appliances. One required consumer appliances to have a standby mode using no more than one watt of electricity, while another promoted new technology to use excess steam from industrial processes for energy purposes.

A member of the Progressive Caucus, Baldwin was one of six House members who cosponsored a 2008 resolution calling for an impeachment inquiry of Bush. She said Bush should be held accountable for alleged abuses of power by members of his administration.

But she also seeks common ground with Republicans when it will help her achieve her goals. She has worked with Georgia Republican Tom Price — former chairman of the Republican Study Committee, the House's most conservative faction — on legislation to allow states to use federal grants in a variety of ways to help provide health insurance. She and Iowa Republican Tom Latham also teamed up on a measure aimed at reducing a nationwide nursing shortage.

Baldwin was a bipartisan hit in 1999, her first year in office, with a speech at the annual Congressional Dinner of the Washington Press Club Foundation. "I'm one of the first elected officials who represents a group historically discriminated against," Baldwin said. "A group that has been kept out of jobs, harassed at the workplace. A group that's been unfairly stereotyped and made the object of rude and base humor. Of course, I'm talking about blondes . . . especially blondes named Tammy."

Born and raised in Madison, home to the University of Wisconsin and a hotbed of liberalism, Baldwin reflects the views of her constituency and the passion for politics of her upbringing. Her maternal grandparents raised her while her mother attended the university and participated in civil rights and anti-war demonstrations. Her grandfather was a biochemist, and her grandmother worked at the costume lab at the university theater.

Baldwin got into politics while she was still in law school. In 1986, at age 24, she won election as a Dane County supervisor. She says she was inspired in part by the Democrats' nomination two years earlier of Geraldine A. Ferraro for vice president. After four terms as a county supervisor, in 1992 she was elected to the Wisconsin Assembly, where she served six years.

With her own impressive fundraising and help from EMILY's List, a political action committee that supports Democratic female candidates who back abortion rights, Baldwin edged out two well-known opponents in the 1998 primary for the House. She then beat former state Insurance Commissioner Josephine Musser by 6 percentage points. In 2000, she eked out a 3-percentage-point victory over Republican John Sharpless, a history professor. She has prevailed handily since, winning with 62 percent of the vote in 2010.

Key Votes

2010

Overhaul the nation's health insurance system	YES
Allow for repeal of "don't ask, don't tell"	YES
Overhaul financial services industry regulation	YES
Limit use of new Afghanistan War funds to troop withdrawal activities	YES
Change oversight of offshore drilling and lift oil spill liability cap	YES
Provide a path to legal status for some children of illegal immigrants	YES
Extend Bush-era income tax cuts for two years	NO

2009

Expand the Children's Health Insurance Program	YES
Provide $787 billion in tax cuts and spending increases to stimulate the economy	YES
Allow bankruptcy judges to modify certain primary-residence mortgages	YES
Create a cap-and-trade system to limit greenhouse gas emissions	YES
Provide $2 billion for the "cash for clunkers" program	YES
Establish the government as the sole provider of student loans	YES
Restrict federally funded insurance coverage for abortions in health care overhaul	NO

CQ Vote Studies

	PARTY UNITY		PRESIDENTIAL SUPPORT	
	SUPPORT	OPPOSE	SUPPORT	OPPOSE
2010	99%	1%	85%	15%
2009	99%	1%	96%	4%
2008	99%	1%	14%	86%
2007	99%	1%	3%	97%
2006	99%	1%	13%	87%

Interest Groups

	AFL-CIO	ADA	CCUS	ACU
2010	100%	100%	13%	0%
2009	100%	95%	45%	0%
2008	100%	100%	56%	0%
2007	96%	100%	45%	0%
2006	100%	95%	20%	0%

Wisconsin 2

South — Madison

Once described by former GOP Gov. Lee Dreyfus as "78 square miles surrounded by reality," Madison has long been Wisconsin's liberal centerpiece. The capital city is the 2nd's political heart, although growing numbers of socially liberal, fiscally conservative young professionals in the suburbs may have a future impact.

Located on an isthmus between two lakes — Mendota and Menona — Madison's high quality of life is diminished only by its biting winters. The state university system's flagship campus has a major influence on the city, and an educated, white-collar population fuels the local economy. University graduates, resources and expertise have boosted associated industries, such as biotech. The Madison area's relatively stable economy based around the university and government jobs have largely insulated the district's housing and job markets. Other large employment bases include light manufacturing firms.

Outside of Madison, the 2nd resembles most of the rest of Wisconsin. Strong milk and grain production make the 2nd the state's top agricultural region. Tourists are lured to the district by New Glarus, touted as America's "Little Switzerland," in Green County in the district's southwest. The Wisconsin Dells — ancient natural limestone formations along the Wisconsin River — attract visitors to the district's north, which also features many commercial waterparks.

The 2nd generally is divided politically into Madison vs. everywhere else, with residents of the university- and government-dominated capital standing in contrast to social conservatives and residents of area farming communities.

Dane County — which gave Barack Obama his second-highest percentage statewide (73 percent) as he took 69 percent of the district's 2008 presidential vote overall — gave incumbent Democratic Sen. Russ Feingold his highest percentage (70 percent) in his unsuccessful 2010 re-election race.

Major Industry
Higher education, agriculture, government

Cities
Madison, 233,209; Beloit (pt.), 36,942; Sun Prairie, 29,364; Fitchburg, 25,260

Notable
The Ringling Brothers started their circus — which later merged with Barnum and Bailey's "Greatest Show on Earth" — in Baraboo in 1884.

Rep. Ron Kind (D)

Capitol Office
225-5506
www.house.gov/kind
1406 Longworth Bldg. 20515-4903; fax 225-5739

Committees
Ways & Means

Residence
La Crosse

Born
March 16, 1963; La Crosse, Wis.

Religion
Lutheran

Family
Wife, Tawni Kind; two children

Education
Harvard U., A.B. 1985; London School of Economics,
M.A. 1986; U. of Minnesota, J.D. 1990

Career
Lawyer; county prosecutor

Political Highlights
No previous office

ELECTION RESULTS

2010 GENERAL

Ron Kind (D)	126,380	50.3%
Dan Kapanke (R)	116,838	46.5%
Michael Krsiean (I)	8,001	3.2%

2010 PRIMARY

Ron Kind (D)	unopposed

2008 GENERAL

Ron Kind (D)	225,208	63.2%
Paul Stark (R)	122,760	34.4%
Kevin Barrett (LIBERT)	8,236	2.3%

Previous Winning Percentages
2006 (65%); 2004 (56%); 2002 (63%); 2000 (64%);
1998 (71%); 1996 (52%)

Elected 1996; 8th term

Kind tries to emulate the fiscally frugal tradition of former Sen. William Proxmire, the Wisconsin Democrat for whom he once interned. As a member of the Ways and Means Committee, Kind had a hand in many of the major initiatives of the 111th Congress, some of them considered anything but frugal by critics.

In the 112th Congress (2011-12), he has continued that trend, opposing the GOP version of a catchall bill that would have cut $61 billion from fiscal 2011 spending, but then backed a compromise version trimming $40 billion that became law.

On the tax writing panel, he has taken a leading role in pushing to use the tax code to boost the health of Americans, although he once said that he was "not a big subscriber to social engineering through the tax code."

He backed the Democrats' health care overhaul in 2010 — a vote that contributed to the closest re-election contest of his career — and he has weighed in on the issue in other ways.

The overhaul measure included a national exchange — intended to boost competition and make shopping for coverage easier — that is similar to one in legislation that Kind sponsored. "It's exactly the type of plan I've been promoting for the past few years," he said on WISN-TV in 2009.

He also backs tax breaks for "wellness activities" that are designed to encourage people "to increase their physical activity."

Even as he became a more dependable vote for the Democratic leadership's agenda, Kind continued to preach and practice a sort of personal austerity. He donates his congressional pay raises to charity and returns about 10 percent of his office allotment to the federal Treasury each year. In 2008, he swore off earmarks, the funding set-asides for special projects in members' districts or states.

And, like Proxmire, Kind isn't afraid to embrace unpopular causes. During consideration of the reauthorization of agriculture and nutrition programs in the 110th Congress (2007-08), Kind joined forces with Wisconsin Republican Paul D. Ryan to try to cut farm subsidies and redirect the savings toward conservation, nutrition, rural development and deficit reduction. The effort failed, but Kind praised President Obama for proposing to go after the same subsidies that he had tried to curtail.

But federal protection for the dairy industry is the top parochial issue for a district that includes Eau Claire, the historic center of the U.S. dairy industry. In 2004, Kind successfully proposed several provisions aimed at encouraging increased milk consumption in public schools.

Kind also would like to see more federal spending on public education. But he lost some of his ability to influence education policy when he gave up his seat on the Education and the Workforce Committee for the Ways and Means spot. Earlier in his Capitol Hill career, his amendments to boost professional development for teachers and to help recruit teachers and principals were included in the 2001 No Child Left Behind Act. He continues to push for schools to provide more physical fitness instruction as part of his wellness agenda.

Representing western Wisconsin's dairy country and raised in La Crosse on the banks of the Mississippi River, Kind enjoys hunting and calls himself a river rat. He is a co-chairman of the Congressional Sportsmen's Caucus and the Upper Mississippi Caucus. He grew up hunting, fishing, camping and biking and says his outdoor life fostered "a greater appreciation of the importance of preserving and protecting our resources."

He is one of four vice chairmen of the moderate New Democrat Coalition, and during his first decade in Congress his voting record had a distinct centrist tone. But when Democrats took over the House following the 2006 elections, Kind began siding with his party more often than in the past — almost 97 percent of the time on votes pitting the parties against each other in the 110th Congress. He typically had scored below 90 percent under Republican majorities. In 2009, he returned to that range, voting with his party 86 percent of the time — though he was there for his party on the most contentious and expensive measures, including the health care overhaul, the $787 billion economic stimulus and legislation to create a cap-and-trade system to limit greenhouse gas emissions. His voting record bounced back up to 95 percent in 2010.

Perhaps Kind's most lasting legislative legacy so far is the Veterans History Project at the Library of Congress. The operation has collected more than 60,000 video and audio tapes, letters and cards, photographs, drawings, and other mementos from soldiers in the wars of the 20th and 21st centuries. Kind introduced the bill creating the project in September 2000, and it sped through Congress in less than a month. The idea for the project came to him on a Father's Day weekend as Kind was sitting in the yard with his father and uncle — veterans of the Korean conflict and of World War II, respectively. He had never heard them tell war stories before, and he grabbed a video camera to capture them for his children.

Kind was raised in a blue-collar neighborhood, the son of a union leader. He was a high school football and basketball star, and won an academic scholarship to Harvard University, where he played quarterback before suffering a career-ending shoulder injury. As a summer intern for Proxmire in 1984, he did research for the senator's annual "Golden Fleece" awards, which showcased what Proxmire considered to be wasteful federal spending.

After graduate school and law school, Kind worked two years at a Milwaukee law firm, then returned home to La Crosse to become a county prosecutor. When GOP Rep. Steve Gunderson announced his retirement, Kind entered the 1996 race. With little money, he waged a grass-roots campaign and beat Jim Harsdorf with 52 percent of the vote. He had no trouble getting re-elected — never taking less than 54 percent of the vote — until 2010. Independent groups criticized Kind for his health care vote, and two doctors alleged that he demanded campaign contributions in return for a meeting — a charge Kind denied. Republican state Sen. Dan Kapanke gave Kind the closest race of his career, but the Democrat prevailed by almost 4 percentage points.

Key Votes

2010

Overhaul the nation's health insurance system	YES
Allow for repeal of "don't ask, don't tell"	YES
Overhaul financial services industry regulation	YES
Limit use of new Afghanistan War funds to troop withdrawal activities	NO
Change oversight of offshore drilling and lift oil spill liability cap	YES
Provide a path to legal status for some children of illegal immigrants	YES
Extend Bush-era income tax cuts for two years	NO

2009

Expand the Children's Health Insurance Program	YES
Provide $787 billion in tax cuts and spending increases to stimulate the economy	YES
Allow bankruptcy judges to modify certain primary-residence mortgages	NO
Create a cap-and-trade system to limit greenhouse gas emissions	YES
Provide $2 billion for the "cash for clunkers" program	YES
Establish the government as the sole provider of student loans	YES
Restrict federally funded insurance coverage for abortions in health care overhaul	NO

CQ Vote Studies

	PARTY UNITY		PRESIDENTIAL SUPPORT	
	SUPPORT	OPPOSE	SUPPORT	OPPOSE
2010	95%	5%	87%	13%
2009	86%	14%	83%	17%
2008	95%	5%	28%	72%
2007	96%	4%	7%	93%
2006	88%	12%	34%	66%

Interest Groups

	AFL-CIO	ADA	CCUS	ACU
2010	100%	95%	13%	4%
2009	86%	90%	47%	8%
2008	100%	80%	72%	8%
2007	96%	90%	60%	12%
2006	100%	85%	53%	25%

Wisconsin 3

West — Eau Claire, La Crosse

Comprising most of western Wisconsin, the 3rd District is an agricultural and dairy powerhouse, home to hundreds of thousands of cows. The district still leads the state in dairy production even as corporate farming takes over, milk prices drop and fewer family farms thrive.

Following declines in manufacturing, Eau Claire and La Crosse both now rely on their large hospital systems, which are among the biggest employers in the district. The five four-year college branches of Wisconsin's state university system that are located in the district have placed an emphasis on computer and technology education.

Meanwhile, St. Croix County — filled with bedroom communities inhabited by commuters to Minneapolis-St. Paul just across the Mississippi River, which forms the Minnesota state line — is experiencing the fastest population growth in the state.

Recreational tourism also contributes to the 3rd's economy. The Mississippi River provides a 250-mile natural western border to the district, snaking from near Minnesota's Twin Cities to the Illinois border along rolling prairies and rich soil. Birdwatchers flock to the river to spot bald eagles perched on the steep bluffs, and lakes in the north attract sportsmen and retirees.

Made up of traditionally competitive counties, the 3rd has a slight Democratic lean overall and voted solidly for Barack Obama in the 2008 presidential election. In taking 58 percent of the vote here, he won every county wholly or partly in the 3rd except for St. Croix in the northwest, which backed John McCain with 51 percent of its vote.

Major Industry
Dairy farming, tourism, technology, health care, manufacturing

military bases
Fort McCoy (Army), 1,687 military, 1,250 civilian (2011)

Cities
Eau Claire (pt.), 63,902; La Crosse, 51,320; Onalaska, 17,736

Notable
Taliesin, Frank Lloyd Wright's estate, is in Spring Green; Pepin hosts the annual "Laura Ingalls Wilder Days," honoring the native-born author of the "Little House" books and holding demonstrations of the crafts, music and daily life of 1870s Wisconsin.

Rep. Gwen Moore (D)

Capitol Office
225-4572
www.house.gov/gwenmoore
2245 Rayburn Bldg. 20515-4904; fax 225-8135

Committees
Budget
Financial Services

Residence
Milwaukee

Born
April 18, 1951; Racine, Wis.

Religion
Baptist

Family
Single; three children

Education
Marquette U., B.A. 1978 (political science)

Career
State agency legislative analyst; city development specialist; VISTA volunteer

Political Highlights
Wis. Assembly, 1989-92; Wis. Senate, 1993-2004 (president pro tempore, 1997-98)

ELECTION RESULTS

2010 GENERAL

Gwen Moore (D)	143,559	69.0%
Dan Sebring (R)	61,543	29.6%
Eddie Ahmad Ayyash (I)	2,802	1.3%

2010 PRIMARY

Gwen Moore (D)	33,107	83.7%
Paul Morel (D)	6,430	16.3%

2008 GENERAL

Gwen Moore (D)	222,728	87.6%
Michael D. LaForest (I)	29,282	11.5%

Previous Winning Percentages
2006 (71%); 2004 (70%)

Elected 2004; 4th term

A one-time teenage single mother on welfare, Moore is a steadfast liberal and strong believer in the efficacy of government programs designed to address social ills such as poverty, hunger and domestic violence.

Moore's view of the role of government is not likely to carry the day in the Republican-led House in the 112th Congress (2011-12), but she does not intend to go along quietly. "There's a role for the minority," she said. "There are so many ideological members in the majority party who believe that we should reduce the deficit on the backs of poor people. I anticipate being a lot more vocal and articulate than I've been in the past."

A member of the Budget Committee, she is a critic of the spending proposals put forth by one of her Wisconsin colleagues, Republican Paul D. Ryan, the committee's chairman. "Budgets aren't just about numbers," she said. "They're about priorities, and it's extremely important to be there to be a voice for the priorities that a budget construct can bring about."

Moore also sits on the Financial Services Committee. In fall 2008, she supported the $700 billion rescue of the financial services sector, saying a credit crisis would hurt the poor. During the 2010 debate over the financial regulatory overhaul, she sought to strengthen Wall Street's regulators and establish a $1 billion loan program to assist unemployed individuals at risk of home foreclosure.

Moore is proudest of her work with former Democratic Rep. Paul W. Hodes of New Hampshire on a 2008 law that aims to ensure dependent students who take a medically necessary leave of absence don't lose their health insurance. She also cheered the expansion of the Children's Health Insurance Program, which President George W. Bush twice vetoed, and the health care overhaul, both signed into law by President Obama.

During the 109th Congress (2005-06), she won approval of legislation to protect the identity of domestic violence victims who receive homeless assistance. And she successfully pressed for an amendment to help public housing assistance recipients become homeowners by allowing them to improve their creditworthiness with prompt rent payments.

In May 2009 she successfully shepherded into law the first reauthorization of the McKinney-Vento Homeless Assistance Act in two decades. The law expanded the definition of "homeless," and thus eligible for aid, to include those fleeing from domestic violence with no place to go and individuals and families who are within 14 days of losing their housing.

"The face of homelessness has changed," she said. "It's the people who are going to be homeless within a couple weeks. I think it recognized the importance of intervening before people are actually on the street."

Moore also boasts of having steered millions of dollars in transportation improvements and funds for a new medical center to Milwaukee, along with more than $1 million for Milwaukee Public Schools programs. She won inclusion of a provision to study the effects of climate change on the Great Lakes in a 2010 House-passed bill aimed at boosting U.S. competitiveness.

A member of the Democratic Steering and Policy Committee, which makes committee assignments, she sided with New York Democrat Carolyn B. Maloney against fellow Congressional Black Caucus member Elijah E. Cummings of Maryland in the contest for ranking member of the Oversight and Government Reform Committee in the 112th Congress.

Vice chairwoman of the bipartisan Congressional Caucus for Women's Issues during the 111th Congress (2009-10), Moore applauded House passage in January 2009 of two bills aimed at strengthening the ability of workers to sue for alleged wage discrimination. She introduced legislation to expand services for domestic violence victims and lobbied for passage on the Dr. Phil show. A version of her bill became law.

Moore was born in Racine, the eighth of nine children of a factory worker father and a teacher. She said her father taught her self-reliance, a trait that propelled her through school and her career.

She got into politics as a student in Milwaukee's public schools in the late 1960s, inspired by the Rev. Martin Luther King Jr. and the civil rights movement. She served as student council president of North Division High School, where she pushed city officials to replace an aging building that lacked science labs and showers for athletes. Moore also organized a school walkout over a lack of textbooks describing the post-slavery history of African-Americans. A picture of a young Moore leading the protest is on display today inside America's Black Holocaust Museum in Milwaukee.

At age 18, Moore got pregnant during her freshman year at Marquette University. She went on government assistance but continued her studies in political science, taking eight years to earn her bachelor's degree. She then went to work as an AmericaCorps VISTA volunteer and organized a community credit union in her North Milwaukee neighborhood.

She later worked in a variety of government jobs, including as a neighborhood development specialist for Milwaukee's city government. In 1988 she was elected to the Wisconsin Assembly and later captured a seat in the state Senate. In 2004, when Democrat Gerald D. Kleczka decided to retire, Moore entered a competitive primary for the 4th District seat. She was aided by a racially divided vote in that year's mayoral race in which Tom Barrett, who is white, narrowly defeated acting Mayor Marvin Pratt, who is black. That November, she prevailed over Republican Gerald H. Boyle, an Iraq War veteran, and became the first African-American member of Congress from Wisconsin.

Moore's victory was marred by the arrest in January 2005 of her 25-year-old son, Sowande Omokunde, one of five workers for the Kerry-Edwards presidential campaign charged with slashing the tires of GOP get-out-the-vote vehicles on Election Day. The judge sentenced Omokunde and three co-defendants to several months in jail. Moore got more unwanted press later in the year when a local newspaper reported that her sister had been paid $44,000 for work on her campaign, though she lives in Georgia. Voters in her heavily Democratic district didn't seem to mind; Moore has easily won re-election since.

Key Votes

2010

Overhaul the nation's health insurance system	YES
Allow for repeal of "don't ask, don't tell"	YES
Overhaul financial services industry regulation	YES
Limit use of new Afghanistan War funds to troop withdrawal activities	YES
Change oversight of offshore drilling and lift oil spill liability cap	YES
Provide a path to legal status for some children of illegal immigrants	YES
Extend Bush-era income tax cuts for two years	NO

2009

Expand the Children's Health Insurance Program	YES
Provide $787 billion in tax cuts and spending increases to stimulate the economy	YES
Allow bankruptcy judges to modify certain primary-residence mortgages	YES
Create a cap-and-trade system to limit greenhouse gas emissions	YES
Provide $2 billion for the "cash for clunkers" program	YES
Establish the government as the sole provider of student loans	YES
Restrict federally funded insurance coverage for abortions in health care overhaul	NO

CQ Vote Studies

	PARTY UNITY		PRESIDENTIAL SUPPORT	
	SUPPORT	OPPOSE	SUPPORT	OPPOSE
2010	96%	4%	87%	13%
2009	99%	1%	99%	1%
2008	99%	1%	19%	81%
2007	99%	1%	4%	96%
2006	98%	2%	13%	87%

Interest Groups

	AFL-CIO	ADA	CCUS	ACU
2010	93%	100%	13%	0%
2009	100%	100%	33%	0%
2008	100%	95%	50%	4%
2007	96%	95%	53%	0%
2006	93%	100%	20%	4%

Wisconsin 4

Milwaukee

On the shores of Lake Michigan, the 4th takes in all but a handful of Milwaukee's residents. Wisconsin's largest city, once rooted in manufacturing, has become more cosmopolitan. It has a major art museum, the world's largest summer music festival, and professional sports teams: basketball's Bucks, baseball's Brewers and minor league hockey's Admirals. It is home to the original tap of Miller Brewing, now part of the MillerCoors conglomerate, and Harley-Davidson.

Milwaukee has lost population since the 1960s, mainly due to a shrinking blue-collar manufacturing base. Areas that grew in the last decade include neighborhoods in the city's south side that are home to much of Milwaukee's Hispanic population. The Milwaukee area hosts the headquarters for Fortune 500 firms — auto parts manufacturer Johnson Controls and global staffing company ManpowerGroup both boast "green" headquarters in the area. A large student population is spread among the city's colleges, including the local University of Wisconsin campus and Marquette University.

Milwaukee, once known for the stark racial, cultural and economic differences in formerly segregated parts of the city, is minority-majority: blacks (35 percent) and Hispanics (17 percent) together outnumber whites. The largely black neighborhoods in the north-central part of the city have shed population since 2000, and many of the city's white residents from areas in the south, where Polish and German immigrants once settled, have left as more Hispanic residents have moved in.

Milwaukee once was the socialist hub of the country, even going so far as to elect the nation's first Socialist mayor.

This history, combined with the city's remaining blue-collar enclaves, large minority population and strong union presence, makes the 4th the state's most Democratic district.

Milwaukee overwhelmingly supported Barack Obama in the 2008 presidential election, giving him 75 percent of its vote.

Major Industry
Machinery manufacturing, service

Cities
Milwaukee (pt.), 594,770; West Allis (pt.), 21,236; South Milwaukee, 21,156

Notable
The world's largest four-sided clock is on the Allen-Bradley building.

Rep. F. James Sensenbrenner Jr. (R)

Elected 1978; 17th term

The prickly, no-nonsense Sensenbrenner does not suffer fools gladly. He has twice been a committee chairman, wielding the gavel with iron efficiency. A solid conservative vote on most issues, he continues to be a forceful voice on issues related to terrorism and the criminal justice system.

He now serves as the No. 2 Republican on both the Judiciary and Science, Space and Technology committees, while chairing the former's Subcommittee on Crime, Terrorism and Homeland Security.

Sensenbrenner bristles when confronted by a journalist asking an uninformed question or a witness giving an uninformed answer. Colleagues are granted no immunity, either.

A June 2005 Judiciary Committee hearing on the anti-terrorism law known as the Patriot Act, which he helped write, is a classic of the genre. As was usually the case, the chairman kept a close eye on the clock and quickly gaveled down anyone violating the committee's rule allotting five minutes per member for questions. After a closing monologue in which he derided the questioning as off-topic, he ended the meeting while Democrats were talking and walked out of the room, gavel in hand.

A GOP colleague told The New York Times in 2006 that Sensenbrenner treats everyone equally — "like dogs." The following day, he circulated a basket of dog biscuits at a committee meeting.

When he moved into the minority for four years, Sensenbrenner took on a different role, if not a different persona.

Sensenbrenner was the ranking Republican on the Select Committee on Energy Independence and Global Warming, where he often sparred with Democrats over the science and economic implications of climate change. After a May 2010 hearing in which Democrats belittled a witness called by the minority, Sensenbrenner compared their actions to the scandal surrounding a 2009 leak of controversial e-mails written by climate researchers.

"[The] hearing echoed the shameful culture exposed by the Climategate e-mails," Sensenbrenner said at a later hearing. "Climategate revealed a scientific culture that is more interested in defending its findings than in finding truth. It showed some of the most prominent scientists in the world actively working to sabotage legitimate scientists who dared to challenge their work."

When it appeared that leaders of the new Republican majority elected to the 112th Congress (2011-12) would eliminate the Global Warming panel, Sensenbrenner argued they should instead "rebrand" it as a vigorous overseer "to ensure the administration doesn't bend to unrealistic international demands — and that the EPA doesn't attempt to do what Congress wouldn't," he wrote in Roll Call days after the election. He also tried to enlist the help of some K Street lobbyists in his quest to keep the panel in operation. But his advice went unheeded and the committee was dissolved.

On the Science Committee, which he once chaired, Sensenbrenner advocates alternative-fuel vehicles. He has pushed to House passage, in both the 110th (2007-08) and 111th (2009-10) Congresses, legislation to encourage research and production of hybrid-powered commercial trucks.

On most social issues, he is an ardent conservative, opposing abortion, gun control and same-sex marriage. He backed the decision by Speaker John A. Boehner of Ohio to defend the 1996 Defense of Marriage Act in court after the Justice Department said it would no longer defend the law's constitutionality.

In his final months as Judiciary chairman in 2006, Sensenbrenner defied President George W. Bush on immigration policy, leading a group that favored

Capitol Office
225-5101
sensenbrenner.house.gov
2449 Rayburn Bldg. 20515-4905; fax 225-3190

Committees
Judiciary
 (Crime, Terrorism & Homeland Security - Chairman)
Science, Space & Technology

Residence
Menomonee Falls

Born
June 14, 1943; Chicago, Ill.

Religion
Anglican Catholic

Family
Wife, Cheryl Sensenbrenner; two children

Education
Stanford U., A.B. 1965 (political science);
U. of Wisconsin, J.D. 1968

Career
Lawyer

Political Highlights
Wis. Assembly, 1969-75; Wis. Senate, 1975-79

ELECTION RESULTS

2010 GENERAL

Sensenbrenner (R)	229,642	69.3%
Todd P. Kolosso (D)	90,634	27.4%
Robert R. Raymond (I)	10,813	3.3%

2010 PRIMARY

Sensenbrenner (R)	unopposed

2008 GENERAL

Sensenbrenner (R)	275,271	79.6%
Robert R. Raymond (I)	69,715	20.2%

Previous Winning Percentages
2006 (62%); 2004 (67%); 2002 (86%); 2000 (74%); 1998 (91%); 1996 (74%); 1994 (100%); 1992 (70%); 1990 (100%); 1988 (75%); 1986 (78%); 1984 (73%); 1982 (100%); 1980 (78%); 1978 (61%)

a bill emphasizing border security over Bush's proposal, which included a path to citizenship for millions of illegal immigrants already in the country. Some of Sensenbrenner's ideas made it into law, including a plan to build a 700-mile fence on the U.S.-Mexico border. The year before, Congress cleared his bill compelling states to demand proof of legal U.S. residency when issuing driver's licenses, the so-called Real ID — a requirement that has been delayed multiple times.

Also in his final year as Judiciary chairman, he won an extension of the 1965 Voting Rights Act and was riled that some Republicans threw up roadblocks by trying to eliminate requirements for bilingual assistance at polling places.

He worked with Democrat Steny H. Hoyer of Maryland to push through Congress in 2008 a bill to expand the category of people classified as disabled and ensure that protections under the 1990 Americans with Disabilities Act aren't withheld from anyone meeting those standards. Lawmakers said Supreme Court rulings had imposed unwarranted limits on the law's reach. Sensenbrenner's wife, Cheryl, is disabled and previously served as board chairwoman for the American Association of People with Disabilities.

Heir to the Kimberly-Clark paper and cellulose manufacturing fortune and one of the wealthiest members of Congress, Sensenbrenner has spent his entire career in politics and government since graduating from law school in 1968. Unlike virtually all of his colleagues, who annually disclose the value of their assets in broad ranges, Sensenbrenner for years went beyond the letter of the law by disclosing the exact value of his assets and liabilities in the Congressional Record. He switched to the standard disclosure form in 2010, however, which had the effect of knocking him off the list of the 50 richest members of Congress compiled by Roll Call.

As a teenager, Sensenbrenner helped his math teacher win a race for county surveyor. He studied political science at Stanford University, earned a law degree from the University of Wisconsin, then was elected to the state Assembly. He spent a decade in the legislature, part of it as assistant Senate minority leader.

When U.S. Rep. Bob Kasten, a Republican, ran unsuccessfully for governor in 1978, Sensenbrenner, with a solid political base in Milwaukee's affluent suburbs bordering Lake Michigan, was the obvious successor. He dipped into family wealth to overcome primary opponent Susan Engeleiter, a state legislator, by fewer than 1,000 votes, then won the general election with 61 percent of the vote. He has not been seriously challenged since.

Sensenbrenner announced in August 2009 he had been diagnosed with early-stage prostate cancer. He completed treatment in June 2010.

Key Votes

2010

Overhaul the nation's health insurance system	NO
Allow for repeal of "don't ask, don't tell"	NO
Overhaul financial services industry regulation	NO
Limit use of new Afghanistan War funds to troop withdrawal activities	NO
Change oversight of offshore drilling and lift oil spill liability cap	NO
Provide a path to legal status for some children of illegal immigrants	NO
Extend Bush-era income tax cuts for two years	YES

2009

Expand the Children's Health Insurance Program	NO
Provide $787 billion in tax cuts and spending increases to stimulate the economy	NO
Allow bankruptcy judges to modify certain primary-residence mortgages	NO
Create a cap-and-trade system to limit greenhouse gas emissions	NO
Provide $2 billion for the "cash for clunkers" program	NO
Establish the government as the sole provider of student loans	NO
Restrict federally funded insurance coverage for abortions in health care overhaul	YES

CQ Vote Studies

	PARTY UNITY		PRESIDENTIAL SUPPORT	
	SUPPORT	OPPOSE	SUPPORT	OPPOSE
2010	98%	2%	24%	76%
2009	98%	2%	15%	85%
2008	98%	2%	82%	18%
2007	96%	4%	91%	9%
2006	92%	8%	84%	16%

Interest Groups

	AFL-CIO	ADA	CCUS	ACU
2010	7%	0%	88%	100%
2009	5%	0%	73%	100%
2008	0%	10%	67%	96%
2007	4%	0%	75%	96%
2006	21%	10%	87%	83%

Wisconsin 5

Southeast — Milwaukee suburbs

A mix of suburbs, glacier-carved landscape and Lake Michigan shoreline, Wisconsin's 5th District experienced a decade of rapid job and population growth. Washington and Waukesha counties became destinations for Milwaukee-area white-collar workers leaving the city and settling their families in the affluent suburbs.

These communities offer employment in all sectors and do not rely on Milwaukee's economy for jobs, although some residents still make the daily trip into the city along Interstate 94. Waukesha County's population has grown by more than 25 percent since 1990, although that growth slowed recently. Washington County grew by nearly 40 percent over the same period. Most residents in Ozaukee County, north of Milwaukee, commute out of the county to service or office jobs.

Despite the nationwide decline in the manufacturing sector and some production cuts at district plants, the industry is still represented in Waukesha County, home to most of the 5th's factory jobs.

Briggs and Stratton, located in Wauwatosa, manufactures engines for outdoor equipment. Other key employers in the county are Kohl's Department Store, which has its headquarters in Menomonee Falls, and Quad/Graphics, a printing company based in Sussex. The northern and western outskirts of the 5th are still mostly rural and populated with dairy farms and cattle ranches.

Many residents of the 5th still proudly celebrate their diverse European heritages — German, Belgian, Dutch and Eastern European folk festivals attract tourists almost every weekend of the summer. Vacationers travel to the Port Washington area in Ozaukee County for the recreational fishing and boating opportunities along Lake Michigan.

The 5th is the most heavily Republican district in Wisconsin and the only one in the state that supported John McCain in the 2008 presidential election, in which he won 58 percent of the district's vote.

Major Industry
Manufacturing, retail, health care

Cities
Waukesha, 70,718; Wauwatosa, 46,396; West Allis (pt.), 39,175

Notable
Watertown's Schurz Family started the nation's first kindergarten in 1856.

Rep. Tom Petri (R)

Capitol Office
225-2476
www.house.gov/petri
2462 Rayburn Bldg. 20515-4906; fax 225-2356

Committees
Education & the Workforce
Transportation & Infrastructure
 (Aviation - Chairman)

Residence
Fond du Lac

Born
May 28, 1940; Marinette, Wis.

Religion
Lutheran

Family
Wife, Anne Neal Petri; one child

Education
Harvard U., A.B. 1962 (government), J.D. 1965

Career
Lawyer; Peace Corps volunteer; White House aide

Political Highlights
Wis. Senate, 1973-79; Republican nominee for U.S. Senate, 1974

ELECTION RESULTS

2010 GENERAL
Tom Petri (R)   183,271   70.7%
Joseph C. Kallas (D)   75,926   29.3%

2010 PRIMARY
Tom Petri (R)   unopposed

2008 GENERAL
Tom Petri (R)   221,875   63.7%
Roger A. Kittelson (D) 126,090   36.2%

Previous Winning Percentages
2006 (99%); 2004 (67%); 2002 (99%); 2000 (65%);
1998 (93%); 1996 (73%); 1994 (99%); 1992 (53%);
1990 (100%); 1988 (74%); 1986 (97%); 1984 (76%);
1982 (65%); 1980 (59%); 1979 Special Election (50%)

Elected 1979; 16th full term

Petri's middle-of-the-road Republicanism is popular at home, where he has been re-elected for three decades, and he has had success working with Democrats on education and transportation issues. But within his own party, he has paid a price for his moderate ways.

Now the fifth-most-senior House Republican, Petri (PEA-try) was passed over for the Education and the Workforce Committee gavel in 2001 despite his seniority on the panel. He had hoped to become the ranking GOP member on the Transportation and Infrastructure Committee in 2007, when term limits forced Don Young of Alaska to step aside. Petri had the support of Minority Leader John A. Boehner of Ohio, but the GOP Steering Committee passed him over once again, reaching several rungs down the seniority ladder to elevate Florida's John L. Mica. In June 2009, when California Republican Howard P. "Buck" McKeon traded the ranking member spot on the renamed Education and Labor panel for the top GOP spot on Armed Services, a similar scenario ensued, with conservative John Kline of Minnesota, 10th in committee seniority, winning out over Petri.

The next month, he supported a White House-backed bill to make the federal government the sole provider of student loans. When the Education panel voted in July 2009, he was one of two Republicans in favor. The provision became law as part of the 2010 health care overhaul, which Petri voted against; he also backed repeal early in the 112th Congress (2011-12).

Petri didn't bother to contest the chairmanship when Republicans reclaimed the majority in 2010. Instead, he sits as the No. 2 Republican on the once-again renamed Education and the Workforce panel and as No. 3 on Transportation, where he chairs the Aviation Subcommittee, which is a boon for his district.

The 6th is home to a division of Oshkosh Corp. that manufactures aircraft rescue and fire-fighting vehicles, aircraft manufacturer Basler Turbo Conversions, and the Experimental Aircraft Association, which attracts 750,000 aviation enthusiasts to Oshkosh for its festival every summer.

In April 2011, he helped guide through the House a long-delayed reauthorization of the Federal Aviation Administration that would set funding for the FAA at 2008 levels. The agency's last full reauthorization was enacted in 2003; it expired in 2007.

Petri has been an advocate of less intrusive airport security procedures, urging the Transportation Security Administration to focus more on combining intelligence data with tools such as fingerprints and other biometric data to identify likely threats, and to be less reliant on checkpoint screening that includes whole-body scanners and pat-downs.

A typical example of his split-the-difference philosophy was seen in his backing of expanded powers for the National Transportation Safety Board while he was questioning the need for a bigger budget for the agency.

"Given the size of the federal deficit, and the improvement in aviation safety resulting in fewer aviation accidents requiring NTSB's attention, we are concerned with the level of funding authorized in this bill," Petri said when the Transportation panel approved a reauthorization of the NTSB in March 2010.

During President George W. Bush's administration, Petri's departures from the party line included votes to increase the minimum wage and to allow the federal government to negotiate prescription drug prices on behalf of Medicare recipients.

And despite pressure from Bush, in fall 2008 he opposed both versions of a $700 billion bill — the second of which was signed into law — to aid the troubled financial services industry. "The plan, as it was presented to Congress, was a breathtaking grasp for power which should have alarmed everyone," he said. "The plan which was ultimately passed was a bit better, but still a cause for great concern."

Shortly after President Obama took office, Petri came close to being the Republican vote Obama was looking for to demonstrate bipartisanship on his economic stimulus plan. Yet Petri's complaint wasn't that the bill spent too much — the standard line of his GOP colleagues — but that not enough of the bill's $787 billion went for infrastructure. "It seems to me that we ought to spend more on crumbling infrastructure and actually get something lasting for the spending."

But Petri was one of 40 Republicans early in the new administration to back expansion of the Children's Health Insurance Program, which covers children from families that make too much money to qualify for Medicaid.

Born Thomas Rudolph Everett Jr. in northern Wisconsin, Petri spent his early childhood in San Juan, Puerto Rico, where his Navy pilot father was stationed. After his father was killed in World War II, his mother remarried, and although Petri eventually took the name of his stepfather, he continued to be known to family and friends as "Tim," a nickname his paternal grandmother gave him at age 2 to distinguish him from his biological father.

As a teenager, Petri got his first job as a disc jockey at the local radio station. He soon became the host of "Teen Time," a weekly show that made him the Badger State's youngest on-air personality. He worked his way through Harvard as a teller at a local bank, earning a law degree. He clerked for Judge James E. Doyle Sr. — whose son would become a Democratic governor of Wisconsin — before joining the Peace Corps for a stint in Somalia. Once home, Petri started a law practice in Fond du Lac. In 1972, at age 32, he won a state Senate seat.

Petri was the GOP Senate nominee against Democrat Gaylord Nelson in 1974, but lost in the aftermath of the Watergate scandal. The exposure from that race, however, helped him win a 1979 special election to replace Republican William A. Steiger, who had died of a heart attack one month after winning his seventh House term. Petri easily won election to a full term in 1980. He coasted until his 1992 campaign, when he was hit by negative publicity about 77 overdrafts at the private bank for House members. He pulled through with 53 percent of the vote, his worst re-election total ever. He has won easily each time since then.

Key Votes

2010

Overhaul the nation's health insurance system	NO
Allow for repeal of "don't ask, don't tell"	NO
Overhaul financial services industry regulation	NO
Limit use of new Afghanistan War funds to troop withdrawal activities	NO
Change oversight of offshore drilling and lift oil spill liability cap	NO
Provide a path to legal status for some children of illegal immigrants	NO
Extend Bush-era income tax cuts for two years	YES

2009

Expand the Children's Health Insurance Program	YES
Provide $787 billion in tax cuts and spending increases to stimulate the economy	NO
Allow bankruptcy judges to modify certain primary-residence mortgages	NO
Create a cap-and-trade system to limit greenhouse gas emissions	NO
Provide $2 billion for the "cash for clunkers" program	YES
Establish the government as the sole provider of student loans	YES
Restrict federally funded insurance coverage for abortions in health care overhaul	YES

CQ Vote Studies

	PARTY UNITY		PRESIDENTIAL SUPPORT	
	Support	Oppose	Support	Oppose
2010	94%	6%	38%	62%
2009	89%	11%	26%	74%
2008	91%	9%	62%	38%
2007	88%	12%	68%	32%
2006	90%	10%	85%	15%

Interest Groups

	AFL-CIO	ADA	CCUS	ACU
2010	14%	10%	88%	88%
2009	24%	10%	80%	92%
2008	33%	40%	72%	80%
2007	38%	30%	85%	72%
2006	14%	5%	87%	76%

Wisconsin 6

East central — Oshkosh, Sheboygan, Fond du Lac

In 1854, a group of dissatisfied Whigs, Free Soilers and Democrats met in a Ripon schoolhouse in Fond du Lac County to dream up the Republican Party. Today, the 6th District's farms and small towns still hold primarily socially conservative Lutherans and Catholics, but the district also hosts the state's largest population of blue-collar workers. In the 2008 presidential election, Democrat Barack Obama edged out John McCain here, but with only 49.7 percent of the vote.

Manitowoc County, on Lake Michigan, has a longstanding reputation as a shipbuilding center. South along the lake, Sheboygan County is famed for its meat processing, calling itself the "bratwurst capital of the world." The county once relied on manufacturing jobs; it is home to plumbing company Kohler, which has cut hundreds of jobs recently. Near the inland Lake Winnebago, Oshkosh — where the OshKosh B'Gosh overalls originated more than a century ago — is a major producer of specialty trucks but relies on military contracts. The district's struggling paper industry is based mainly in Neenah and Menasha.

Areas in the district's western reaches remain farming territory. The district's agriculture sector, which remains one of the strongest in the nation, produces dairy and grains. Large corporate farms have acquired some small farms, making them more profitable, and others have turned away from dairy to new crops such as beans, peas and corn. Fruits and vegetables thrive in Adams County, and Marquette and Waushara counties grow Christmas trees.

Many of the 6th's residents are descendants of German immigrants who settled the area in the 1850s, and the district still claims more people of German ancestry (49 percent) than any other in the nation. In recent waves of immigration, the Hmong population continues to grow in Sheboygan, Manitowoc and Winnebago counties.

Major Industry
Agriculture, tourism, manufacturing, paper

Cities
Oshkosh, 66,083; Sheboygan, 49,288; Fond du Lac, 43,021; Manitowoc, 33,736; Neenah, 25,501

Notable
The Wisconsin Maritime Museum is in Manitowoc and offers tours of the World War II-era USS Cobia submarine.

Rep. Sean P. Duffy (R)

Capitol Office
225-3365
duffy.house.gov
1208 Longworth Bldg. 20515-4907; fax 225-3240

Committees
Financial Services
Joint Economic

Residence
Ashland

Born
Oct. 3, 1971; Hayward, Wis.

Religion
Roman Catholic

Family
Wife, Rachel Campos-Duffy; six children

Education
St. Mary's College (Minn.), B.A. 1994 (marketing);
William Mitchell College of Law, J.D. 1999

Career
County prosecutor; lawyer; bus driver; professional
timber sports competitor; reality show personality

Political Highlights
Ashland County district attorney, 2002-10

ELECTION RESULTS

2010 GENERAL

Sean P. Duffy (R)	132,551	52.1%
Julie Lassa (D)	113,018	44.4%
Gary Kauther (I)	8,397	3.3%

2010 PRIMARY

Sean P. Duffy (R)	41,032	66.1%
Daniel E. Mielke (R)	21,075	33.9%

Elected 2010; 1st term

Duffy's résumé includes roles as a bus driver, lawyer, lumberjack and reality television personality. To the role of congressman, he promises to bring a vastly more conservative outlook than his predecessor, 20-term Democrat David R. Obey.

Duffy — previously best known for appearing on the TV show "The Real World" in 1997 — has said he ran for Congress in response to the 2009 economic stimulus package, shepherded in part by Obey, then chairman of the Appropriations Committee.

Indeed, like many in the GOP freshman class, Duffy saw much of the work of the 111th Congress (2009-10) as doing more harm than good.

"We're at a point where we have to get serious about the fiscal problems that we face," Duffy said on CNN in April 2011.

A member of the Financial Services and Joint Economic committees, he backed the catchall bill trimming $40 billion from fiscal 2011 spending that became law, as well as an earlier GOP-backed version that would have cut $61 billion.

Duffy has spent much of his life in heavily wooded northern Wisconsin, where he grew up the 10th of 11 children. Lumber is a big part of his family's history, going back to his great-great grandfather, who worked for the Northwestern Lumber Company. Duffy has followed in that tradition by competing in — and winning — numerous lumberjack competitions. The money he earned from such events helped pay his way through college and law school.

While in law school, Duffy appeared on MTV's "The Real World." He says that the best part of the experience was that he met his future wife, Rachel Campos, who had appeared on an earlier season of the program.

After a stint in his father's legal practice, he became a special prosecutor and later a district attorney.

Duffy was initially seen as facing a steep climb in his bid to oust Obey, but the veteran announced in May 2010 that he would retire after 40 years in the House. That left Duffy to face state Sen. Julie Lassa, whom he defeated by about 8 percentage points.

Wisconsin 7

Northwest — Wausau, Superior, Stevens Point

Wisconsin's 7th, the state's largest and most rural district, stretches north and west from the central counties to the Apostle Islands in the waters of southern Lake Superior. Small towns checker the district.

Farming sustains the economy, although cold weather in the north shaves a full month off the growing season.

Dairy farms are the agricultural heart of the district. Centrally located Marathon County leads Wisconsin in dairy production. The nutrient-rich soil in the Central Sands country in the state's midsection produces seed potatoes, cranberries, vegetables and ginseng.

Some metalworking and paper factories still produce their goods, although the district has lost blue-collar jobs. Stevens Point and Wausau are local insurance hubs.

The tranquil lifestyle in the small towns appeals to senior citizens, and the 7th's hundreds of lakes in the north are a natural draw for tourists. The University of Wisconsin campuses at Stevens Point and Superior attract young people to Marathon and Douglas counties, while Polk County capitalizes on its proximity to the Minneapolis-St. Paul metropolitan area. Many Hmong immigrants have settled in Marathon County.

Blue-collar regions around Stevens Point and along Lake Superior in the north still back Democrats, but descendants of Scandinavian immigrants and a Christian Right contingent form the Republican base.

Major Industry
Agriculture, paper, manufacturing

Cities
Wausau, 39,106; Superior, 27,244

Notable
The American Birkebeiner, from Cable to Hayward, is North America's largest cross-country ski marathon.

Rep. Reid Ribble (R)

Capitol Office
225-5665
ribble.house.gov
1513 Longworth Bldg. 20515-4908; fax 225-5729

Committees
Agriculture
Budget
Transportation & Infrastructure

Residence
De Pere

Born
April 5, 1956; Neenah, Wis.

Religion
Baptist

Family
Wife, DeaNa Ribble; two children

Education
Appleton East H.S., graduated 1974

Career
Roofing construction company president

Political Highlights
No previous office

ELECTION RESULTS

2010 GENERAL

Reid Ribble (R)	143,998	54.8%
Steve Kagen (D)	118,646	45.1%

2010 PRIMARY

Reid Ribble (R)	38,521	48.0%
Roger Roth (R)	25,704	32.0%
Terri McCormick (R)	14,107	17.6%
Marc Savard (R)	1,968	2.4%

Elected 2010; 1st term

Ribble presents himself as a cautious lawmaker wary of federal actions that stifle job growth. During three decades running a roofing company, he says, he learned valuable skills that can be repurposed for legislative work — such as knowing how to balance a budget and complete projects on time and in order.

The federal government needs to give businesses a breather after all the uncertainty stemming from legislation such as the 2010 health care overhaul, he said.

"The business community has no idea what the impact will be," Ribble said about the law. "The regulations haven't been spelled out.... Government does one thing, and then there's 15 unintended consequences."

Ribble says he has talked to business owners who told him that in the current environment, they would rather pay more overtime than hire more workers. "There's a cumulative effect of every piece of legislation that American businesses have to respond to," he said. "That's really strangling job creation right now."

A member of the Budget Committee, Ribble argues that Congress must make a legitimate effort to balance the books. "Every single American understands that there's waste in government right now," he said, and government officials "talk about it, but they still do it."

Ribble is a member of the Republican Study Committee, a group of the most conservative members of the House, and he backed the RSC proposal to cut fiscal 2011 spending to 2006 levels. That plan won 93 votes, and he eventually backed the compromise plan that trimmed spending by $40 billion.

Ribble hoped for and got a seat on the Agriculture Committee. The region he represents has extensive forests, which fall under the panel's jurisdiction, as well as apple and cherry orchards and vineyards.

Two-term Democrat Steve Kagen was something of an anomaly in the historically Republican 8th, having won 51 and 54 percent of the vote in strong Democratic years. In 2010 the district's voters returned to form, giving Ribble a nearly 10-percentage-point victory margin.

Wisconsin 8

Northeast — Green Bay, Appleton

On autumn Sundays, all eyes in Wisconsin turn to the 8th to watch football's Green Bay Packers. Regardless of the team's fortunes, the Packers represent the emotional heart of the state, and they pull in millions of dollars. But the 8th's traditionally blue-collar economy depends on natural resources.

The district's northern reaches have shed residents but host the state's largest tracts of forests, historically supplying paper mills in the Fox River Valley stretching southwest from Green Bay.

Paper manufacturers here spent a decade modernizing their equipment but now are shutting down plants and cutting jobs. Fertile soil in the district's south supports grain, and the open land hosts ranches. Appleton still has some high-skill manufacturing plants, as do Green Bay and other towns in Brown County.

Forests and lakes in Vilas County, near the Michigan border, attract outdoorsmen and nature lovers. Economic downturns affected the market for upscale second homes for vacationers from Milwaukee and Chicago, but the Door County peninsula jutting into Lake Michigan has 250 miles of shore that lure tourists to vineyards, apple and cherry orchards, and artists' colonies. The 8th also is home to six American Indian tribes and their reservation-based casinos.

A significant and politically active Catholic community has contributed to a long history of social conservatism in the 8th, but Brown County has some competitive areas and Democrats dominate Menominee County.

Major Industry
Agriculture, casinos, paper, tourism

Cities
Green Bay, 104,057; Appleton (pt.), 70,944

Notable
The snowmobile was invented in Sayner.

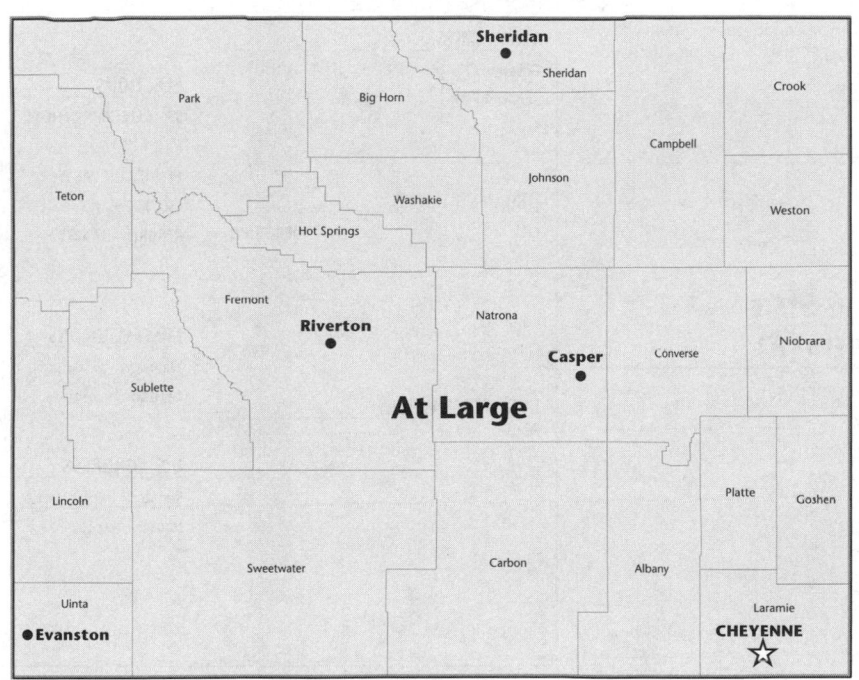

Gov. Matt Mead (R)

First elected: 2010
Length of term: 4 years
Term expires: 1/15
Salary: $105,000
Phone: (307) 777-17434
Residence: Cheyenne
Born: March 11, 1962; Jackson, Wyo.
Religion: Episcopalian
Family: Wife, Carol Mead; two children
Education: U. of Texas, B.A. 1984 (communications); U. of Wyoming, J.D. 1987
Career: Rancher; lawyer; deputy county attorney; federal prosecutor; special assistant state attorney general
Political highlights: U.S. attorney, 2001-07

ELECTION RESULTS

2010 GENERAL

Matt Mead (R)	123,780	71.8%
Leslie Petersen (D)	43,240	25.1%
Mike Wheeler (LIBERT)	5,362	3.1%

Secretary of State Max Maxfield (R)

(no lieutenant governor)
First elected: 2006
Length of term: 4 years
Term expires: 1/15
Salary: $92,000
Phone: (307) 777-5333

LEGISLATURE

Legislature: 40 days January-March in odd-numbered years; 20 days February-March in even-numbered years
Senate: 30 members, 4-year terms
2011 ratios: 26 R, 4 D; 29 men, 1 woman
Salary: $150/day in session
Phone: (307) 777-7881
House: 60 members, 2-year terms
2011 ratios: 50 R, 10 D; 47 men, 13 women
Salary: $150/day in session
Phone: (307) 777-7881

TERM LIMITS

Governor: 2 terms
Senate: No
House: No

URBAN STATISTICS

CITY	POPULATION
Cheyenne	59,466
Casper	55,316
Laramie	30,816
Gillette	29,087

REGISTERED VOTERS

Republican	68%
Democrat	22%
Unaffiliated/others	10%

POPULATION

2010 population	563,626
2000 population	493,782
1990 population	453,588
Percent change (2000-2010)	+14.1%
Rank among states (2010)	50
Median age	36.7
Born in state	42.0%
Foreign born	2.6%
Violent crime rate	228/100,000
Poverty level	9.8%
Federal workers	8,121
Military	3,407

ELECTIONS

STATE ELECTION OFFICIAL
(307) 777-7186
DEMOCRATIC PARTY
(307) 473-1457
REPUBLICAN PARTY
(307) 234-9166

MISCELLANEOUS

Web: www.wyoming.gov
Capital: Cheyenne

U.S. CONGRESS

Senate: 2 Republicans
House: 1 Republican

2010 Census Statistics by District

District	2008 Vote for President Obama	McCain	White	Black	Asian	Hispanic	Median Income	White Collar	Blue Collar	Service Industry	Over 64	Under 18	College Education	Rural	Sq. Miles
AL	33%	65%	86%	1%	1%	9%	$51,990	53%	30%	17%	12%	24%	23%	35%	97,100
STATE	33	65	86	1	1	9	51,990	53	30	17	12	24	23	35	97,100
U.S.	53	46	64	12	5	16	51,425	60	23	17	13	25	28	21	3,537,438

Sen. Michael B. Enzi (R)

Capitol Office
224-3424
enzi.senate.gov
379A Russell Bldg. 20510-5004; fax 228-0359

Committees
Budget
Finance
Health, Education, Labor & Pensions
  - Ranking Member
Small Business & Entrepreneurship

Residence
Gillette

Born
Feb. 1, 1944; Bremerton, Wash.

Religion
Presbyterian

Family
Wife, Diana Enzi; three children

Education
George Washington U., B.A. 1966 (accounting);
U. of Denver, M.S. 1968 (retail marketing)

Military Service
Wyoming Air National Guard, 1967-73

Career
Accountant; computer programmer; shoe store
owner

Political Highlights
Mayor of Gillette, 1975-83; Wyo. House, 1987-91;
Wyo. Senate, 1991-96

ELECTION RESULTS

2008 GENERAL

Michael B. Enzi (R)	189,046	75.6%
Chris Rothfuss (D)	60,631	24.3%

2008 PRIMARY

Michael B. Enzi (R)	unopposed

2002 GENERAL

Michael B. Enzi (R)	133,710	73.0%
Joyce Jansa Corcoran (D)	49,570	27.0%

Previous Winning Percentages
1996 (54%)

Elected 1996; 3rd term

Enzi is one of the Senate's most conservative members, as measured by his voting record. But his ability to find common ground on some of the most divisive issues of the day casts him more as dealmaker than ideologue.

The former accountant and shoe store owner shuns divisive rhetoric in applying what he calls the "80 percent rule" of legislating. "I truly believe that if senators choose to focus on the 80 percent of things we can all agree on instead of the 20 percent we are never going to agree on, we'll be able to achieve more for the American people and the people of Wyoming. . . . It also works in many aspects of life beyond politics," he said.

That approach enabled Enzi — top Republican on the Health, Education, Labor and Pensions (HELP) Committee — to be one of three Senate GOP negotiators during the early debate on health care overhaul legislation in the 111th Congress (2009-10). It didn't hurt that he sits on the Finance and Budget committees, which also handled the bill. He is known to employ a folksy Wyoming proverb: "If you're not at the table, you're on the menu."

Along with Charles E. Grassley of Iowa and Olympia J. Snowe of Maine, Enzi represented the GOP in the so-called Gang of Six, a bipartisan collection of senators seeking to forge a compromise on the health care bill during the summer of 2009. The group came up empty after three months, a portent of the partisan nature of the debate that would follow.

The search for common ground on health care was no fool's errand for Enzi. He and the late HELP Chairman Edward M. Kennedy, a Massachusetts Democrat, joined forces to enact several major pieces of legislation, including measures to expand mental health insurance coverage and the first overhaul in a decade of the law governing aid to higher education.

When Enzi chaired the committee in the 109th Congress (2005-06), having an accountant's knack for numbers came in handy as he led negotiations with Kennedy on an overhaul of the law governing the pension system.

During the 112th Congress (2011-12), he is part of a senior group of lawmakers working on a reauthorization of the No Child Left Behind education law.

He had long sought a seat on Finance, which has jurisdiction over tax and trade matters in addition to health care. He acknowledged in April 2008 that he considered not seeking a third term because GOP leaders had twice denied him a spot. When the leadership passed him over in January 2008 in favor of the less senior but politically endangered New Hampshire Republican John E. Sununu, Enzi told The Associated Press it was "a down time" in his life. Sununu lost his re-election bid, making room for Enzi. Sitting on both Finance and HELP positions him to be at the heart of Republican attempts to amend, "de-fund" and repeal the health care law.

It also gives him a dual platform from which to criticize President Obama's selection of Donald M. Berwick to lead the Centers for Medicare and Medicaid Services. In March 2011, he and Orrin G. Hatch of Utah, the ranking Republican on Finance, got 42 GOP senators to sign a letter asking Obama to withdraw Berwick's nomination. The Democrat-controlled Senate has never voted on Berwick, who has stirred opposition for his positive views of the government-run Canadian health system; Obama gave him a recess appointment to lead the agency in 2010.

From his seat on the Budget Committee, Enzi joined the panel's other Republicans in asking Obama to submit a revised fiscal 2012 budget after he gave an April 2011 speech in which he laid out spending plans that were significantly different than those included in his original 2012 budget submitted two months earlier.

He was one of 15 Senate Republicans to oppose President George W. Bush's $700 billion package of assistance for the banking industry in October 2008, saying the plan lacked "a guarantee of proper oversight and accountability for the taxpayer."

A member of the Small Business and Entrepreneurship Committee, Enzi says many lawmakers have no notion of the problems faced by such businesses. While some lawmakers refer to companies with 100 to 500 workers as small businesses, he says, "To me, a small business is when the person who writes the checks also sweeps the front walk, cleans the toilets and waits on the customers."

Before taking the HELP gavel in 2005, Enzi had served four years as chairman of the Banking, Housing and Urban Affairs Committee's Securities and Investment Subcommittee. From that perch, he worked in 2002 with Maryland Democrat Paul S. Sarbanes, then chairman of the full Banking panel, to pass new federal standards for accounting and corporate governance of public companies.

He opposed the Democrats' financial regulatory overhaul measure and heaped his own brand of folksy scorn on the provision that would create a new federal consumer protection agency. "The dadgum government's going to be in everybody's pocket," he said on the Senate floor in May 2010.

Enzi generally favors liberalized foreign trade, including agricultural trade with Cuba and expanded ties with China, something that could help his state's farmers and ranchers. In 2007 he supported the trade agreement between the United States and Peru and cast the only dissenting vote on extending a ban on U.S. imports from Myanmar; he said unilateral sanctions often hurt U.S. businesses. But he voted against the 2005 Central America Free Trade Agreement, which was opposed by the Wyoming Stock Growers Association because it did not include a provision requiring country-of-origin labeling for beef.

In general, he displays the prototypical Western conservative's skepticism about an overweening federal government and is a solid social conservative, opposing abortion rights and gay marriage.

Enzi was born in Bremerton, Wash., where his father had worked in the naval shipyards during World War II. The family moved to Wyoming soon after his birth. After graduating from high school in Sheridan, Enzi headed east to George Washington University in Washington, D.C., where he earned an accounting degree. He returned west to the University of Denver, where he collected a master's in retail marketing in 1968. The following year, he married and moved back to Wyoming with his wife, Diana, settling in Gillette, where they started their own small business, NZ Shoes. They later added stores in Sheridan and Miles City, Mont.

Enzi began his political career by winning the 1974 mayoral election in Gillette when he was 30. In 1986, he won a seat in the state House and by 1991 was serving in the state Senate.

When Republican Sen. Alan K. Simpson retired after 18 years, Enzi sought the seat. He narrowly won the 1996 primary by building a network of supporters drawn in part from the Wyoming Christian Coalition. He took the general election by 12 percentage points over Democrat Kathy Karpan, a former two-term Wyoming secretary of state.

In 2002, he won re-election with 73 percent of the vote over Democrat Joyce Jansa Corcoran, the former mayor of Lander. Six years later, he took almost 76 percent against University of Wyoming professor Chris Rothfuss. Enzi's re-election was never in doubt, but he refused to have his campaign take any polls. "I don't do polls because, on a weekend, I talk to more people than a pollster does," he told The Associated Press.

Key Votes

2010

Pass budget reconciliation bill to modify overhauls of health care and federal student loan programs	NO
Proceed to disapproval resolution on EPA authority to regulate greenhouse gases	YES
Overhaul financial services industry regulation	NO
Limit debate to proceed to a bill to broaden campaign finance disclosure and reporting rules	NO
Limit debate on an extension of Bush-era income tax cuts for two years	YES
Limit debate on a bill to provide a path to legal status for some children of illegal immigrants	NO
Allow for a repeal of "don't ask, don't tell"	NO
Consent to ratification of a strategic arms reduction treaty with Russia	NO

2009

Prevent release of remaining financial industry bailout funds	YES
Make it easier for victims to sue for wage discrimination remedies	NO
Expand the Children's Health Insurance Program	NO
Limit debate on the economic stimulus measure	NO
Repeal District of Columbia firearms prohibitions and gun registration laws	YES
Limit debate on expansion of federal hate crimes law	NO
Strike funding for F-22 Raptor fighter jets	YES

CQ Vote Studies

	PARTY UNITY		PRESIDENTIAL SUPPORT	
	Support	Oppose	Support	Oppose
2010	97%	3%	42%	58%
2009	98%	2%	43%	57%
2008	99%	1%	78%	22%
2007	96%	4%	89%	11%
2006	98%	2%	91%	9%
2005	94%	6%	84%	16%
2004	97%	3%	98%	2%
2003	99%	1%	97%	3%
2002	95%	5%	93%	7%
2001	95%	5%	99%	1%

Interest Groups

	AFL-CIO	ADA	CCUS	ACU
2010	7%	5%	100%	96%
2009	11%	10%	86%	100%
2008	10%	5%	75%	96%
2007	5%	10%	55%	96%
2006	8%	5%	91%	96%
2005	21%	10%	78%	96%
2004	9%	5%	100%	96%
2003	0%	5%	100%	80%
2002	17%	10%	89%	100%
2001	20%	10%	100%	92%

Sen. John Barrasso (R)

Capitol Office
224-6441
barrasso.senate.gov
307 Dirksen Bldg. 20510-5003; fax 224-1724

Committees
Energy & Natural Resources
Environment & Public Works
Foreign Relations
Indian Affairs - Vice Chairman

Residence
Casper

Born
July 21, 1952; Reading, Pa.

Religion
Presbyterian

Family
Wife Bobbi Barrasso; three children

Education
Georgetown U., B.S. 1974 (biology), M.D. 1978

Career
Surgeon

Political Highlights
Sought Republican nomination for U.S. Senate, 1996;
Wyo. Senate, 2003-07

ELECTION RESULTS

2008 GENERAL

John Barrasso (R)	183,063	73.4%
Nick Carter (D)	66,202	26.5%

2008 PRIMARY

John Barrasso (R)	unopposed

Appointed June 2007; 1st term

Barrasso, a transplanted Westerner and orthopedic surgeon, reflects the prevailing wisdom among conservatives in his region and profession. He speaks forcefully about using Wyoming's vast natural resources and with the air of an expert when dissecting Democratic proposals on health care.

He joined the party leadership team in September 2010, winning the election as conference vice chairman after Alaska Republican Lisa Murkowski, who lost the GOP primary, resigned the spot following her decision to seek re-election as a write-in candidate. Barrasso says he is interested in moving up the ladder in the 113th Congress (2013-14), as either chairman of the National Republican Senatorial Committee — the Senate GOP's campaign arm — or as head of the Republican Policy Committee — the No. 4 leadership position.

He sits on both the Environment and Public Works and Energy and Natural Resources panels, where he looks out for his state's coal industry amid the Obama administration's push for climate change legislation. He opposes a proposal to cap greenhouse gas emissions and set up a market-based trading system for emissions credits.

Barrasso (buh-RASS-o) has been a vocal critic of the Intergovernmental Panel on Climate Change, the U.N. body that was accused of using manipulated research to support its conclusions about climate change. He used a February 2010 Senate floor speech to call for "President Obama to direct his Cabinet to stop supporting any policies that relied in whole and in part on the fraudulent United Nations reports."

In spring 2009, Barrasso slowed, but did not prevent, the confirmation of Regina McCarthy to be assistant administrator for air and radiation at the EPA. He said McCarthy, commissioner of the Connecticut Department of Environmental Protection, hadn't fully answered his questions about the impact of the administration's proposal to label carbon dioxide and five other gases as threats to public health because of their supposed role in contributing to climate change. That proposal would open the door to regulating such gases under the Clean Air Act. Barrasso has been a strong supporter of proposals to block the EPA from exercising that authority.

On resources policy, Barrasso continues a Wyoming legacy: The state has had a senator on the committee overseeing the issue since 1899, less than a decade after it became a state.

The first bill Barrasso introduced was a measure to protect 1.2 million acres in the Wyoming Range of west-central Wyoming's Bridger-Teton National Forest from oil and gas development. The measure was signed into law as part of an omnibus lands measure in 2009. That same catchall measure also included Barrasso's bill to create a five-year grant program to provide compensation for ranchers who lose livestock to wolves.

But it is on health care where Barrasso has been most visible. An experienced television personality, less than a month after the overhaul became law in 2010 he began delivering a series of "doctor's second opinion" floor speeches critiquing the legislation.

"We know that the cost of health care is going up. The president said that health care premiums would lower for families by $2,500. No family has seen that," he said in a floor speech almost a year after the law was enacted.

He also co-hosted the "Senate Doctors Show," a series of Web video clips in which Barrasso and Oklahoma Republican Tom Coburn, an obstetrician, discussed health care issues.

Barrasso had influence on health care issues even before he arrived in the Senate as the 2007 appointee to succeed the late Republican Craig Thomas. But he opposed expanding federal funding for stem cell research, which uses surplus embryos from in vitro fertilization procedures, striking a blow against proponents who had hoped their new colleague would support the measure. Majority Leader Harry Reid, a Nevada Democrat, had postponed a vote on the issue until after Thomas' vacancy was filled, hoping his successor would help Democrats override President George W. Bush's veto of expanded funding.

In a 1996 GOP primary race for the Senate — won by Michael B. Enzi — Barrasso took a more moderate position on abortion than he does today. He opposed federal funding for abortions through Medicaid but said a decision on the procedure should be between a woman and her doctor. Subsequently, during four years in the state Senate, he took increasingly conservative positions and sponsored a bill to increase the penalty for killing a pregnant woman. He said most forms of abortion should be banned.

Barrasso also serves on the Foreign Relations Committee, where he opposed the nomination of Mari Carmen Aponte to be ambassador to El Salvador, expressing concerns about a 12-year relationship she had with Roberto Tamayo, whom the FBI suspected had ties to Cuban intelligence operatives. She has never been confirmed but serves under a 2010 recess appointment.

On Indian Affairs, where he is vice chairman, Barrasso has pushed for more energy development on tribal lands. "Some tribes . . . have been blessed with mineral and energy resources, which, if developed with care and with planning, could play a major role in turning around the local economies and reservation communities," he said at a February 2009 hearing.

Barrasso grew up in Reading, Pa., part of a blue-collar Republican family. His paternal grandfather worked as a cement finisher after emigrating from Italy in the early 1900s. His father, also named John, joined the industry after quitting school in ninth grade to supplement the family's income during the Great Depression, and he enlisted in the Army during World War II.

After the war, his father returned to cement finishing, and his mother stayed home with the three children. At age 8, Barrasso made his first trip to Washington, for the 1961 inauguration of Democrat John F. Kennedy as president, though, as Barrasso recalls, his father had voted for Vice President Richard Nixon, the Republican candidate. Barrasso later returned to study at Georgetown University, where he majored in biology and went on to earn a medical degree.

He spent summers in Reading, laying cement during the week and working at a racetrack on weekends. As a college student, he visited Wyoming and fell in love with the western landscape. After finishing his postgraduate medical residency in New Haven, Conn., he and his now-ex-wife moved to Casper, where they raised two children.

Barrasso wrote a newspaper column called "Keeping Wyoming Healthy" and gave health and fitness commentaries on television. For two decades, he hosted state broadcasts of the annual Jerry Lewis Telethon, which raises money for the Muscular Dystrophy Association.

Barrasso's 1996 bid to replace retiring Republican Sen. Alan K. Simpson was his first campaign for public office; after losing by less than 3 percentage points in the primary, he signed on as Enzi's finance chairman. Barrasso was elected to the Wyoming Senate in 2002 and re-elected in 2006. He was appointed to the U.S. Senate in 2007, after Thomas died of leukemia. Wyoming had a Democratic governor, but state law required he select from among a slate of candidates chosen by the incumbent senator's party. He easily won a special election in 2008 to fill out the remainder of the term, taking 73 percent of the vote. He will be up for re-election in 2012.

Key Votes

2010

Pass budget reconciliation bill to modify overhauls of health care and federal student loan programs	NO
Proceed to disapproval resolution on EPA authority to regulate greenhouse gases	YES
Overhaul financial services industry regulation	NO
Limit debate to proceed to a bill to broaden campaign finance disclosure and reporting rules	NO
Limit debate on an extension of Bush-era income tax cuts for two years	YES
Limit debate on a bill to provide a path to legal status for some children of illegal immigrants	NO
Allow for a repeal of "don't ask, don't tell"	NO
Consent to ratification of a strategic arms reduction treaty with Russia	NO

2009

Prevent release of remaining financial industry bailout funds	YES
Make it easier for victims to sue for wage discrimination remedies	NO
Expand the Children's Health Insurance Program	NO
Limit debate on the economic stimulus measure	NO
Repeal District of Columbia firearms prohibitions and gun registration laws	YES
Limit debate on expansion of federal hate crimes law	NO
Strike funding for F-22 Raptor fighter jets	YES

CQ Vote Studies

	PARTY UNITY		PRESIDENTIAL SUPPORT	
	SUPPORT	OPPOSE	SUPPORT	OPPOSE
2010	98%	2%	37%	63%
2009	98%	2%	44%	56%
2008	99%	1%	76%	24%
2007	96%	4%	84%	16%

Interest Groups

	AFL-CIO	ADA	CCUS	ACU
2010	6%	0%	100%	100%
2009	11%	5%	86%	100%
2008	10%	5%	75%	96%
2007	0%	10%	75%	100%

Rep. Cynthia M. Lummis (R)

Capitol Office
225-2311
lummis.house.gov
113 Cannon Bldg. 20515-5001; fax 225-3057

Committees
Appropriations

Residence
Cheyenne

Born
Sept. 10, 1954; Cheyenne, Wyo.

Religion
Lutheran - Missouri Synod

Family
Husband, Al Wiederspahn; one child

Education
U. of Wyoming, B.S. 1976 (animal science), B.S. 1978 (biology), J.D. 1985

Career
Rancher; lawyer; gubernatorial aide

Political Highlights
Wyo. House, 1979-83, 1985-93; Wyo. Senate, 1993-95; Wyo. State Lands and Investment acting director, 1997-98; Wyo. treasurer, 1999-2007

ELECTION RESULTS

2010 GENERAL

Cynthia M. Lummis (R)	131,661	70.4%
David Wendt (D)	45,768	24.5%
John V. Love (LIBERT)	9,253	4.9%

2010 PRIMARY

Cynthia M. Lummis (R)	84,063	82.8%
Evan Liam Slafter (R)	17,148	16.9%

2008 GENERAL

Cynthia M. Lummis (R)	131,244	52.6%
Gary Trauner (D)	106,758	42.8%
W. David Herbert (LIBERT)	11,030	4.4%

Elected 2008; 2nd term

Three decades of experience in Wyoming politics helped cement for Lummis the notion that state and local governments — and citizens themselves — are in a better position than the federal government to guide decisions affecting their regions. Being elected to Congress and joining the Appropriations Committee has not demonstrably altered her views on that subject.

Lummis won a coveted seat on the spending panel in the 112th Congress (2011-12), just her second term. Her assignment includes spots on the Agriculture and Interior-Environment Subcommittees, both crucial to her state's ranching and resource-based economy.

In 2010, she helped launch the 10th Amendment Task Force, aimed at promoting the dispersal of decision-making and funding away from Washington and back to states, local governments and individuals. She hailed inclusion of a provision in the final version of a catchall spending for fiscal 2011 that returned management of the gray wolf population to the state.

Lummis, a strong advocate of views prevalent among Western conservatives — including resource development, gun owners' rights, and fiscal and social conservatism — was raised with three siblings on her family's Laramie County cattle ranch, now in its fourth generation of family ownership. It's a valuable spread, and she was ranked as the 50th richest member of Congress in 2009 by Roll Call, with a minimum net worth of $5.4 million.

She backs revision of the Endangered Species Act to bring what she calls a more balanced approach to protecting wildlife. She cites as an example the need to manage cattle differently at her family ranch in Laramie County than at the ranch in Platte County that she owns with her husband, Al Wiederspahn, a former Democratic colleague in the Wyoming House and a Cheyenne attorney. "Unique ecosystems require a unique set of solutions," she said. "The one-size-fits-all, dictated-from-Washington solution doesn't work for Wyoming."

In 2010, she introduced a bill to require public disclosure of payments to environmental groups and others who have won lawsuits against the government. The payments are provided for under a 1980 law that allows plaintiffs who sue the federal government and win to collect payment for attorney's fees and court costs. Lummis wrote in a February 2010 opinion piece that the "environmental litigation industry" is the main beneficiary of the law and "there has been no congressional oversight of the program for 15 years."

She opposed a 2009 omnibus public lands bill, which became law, that designated more than 2 million acres of new wilderness areas in several states and put portions of the Wyoming Range off-limits to drilling. Lummis said she would have preferred to make the drilling ban temporary. She also spoke out against a bill by New York Democrat Carolyn B. Maloney to protect millions of acres in the Northern Rockies as wilderness because the legislation was drafted without the input of area lawmakers. But she has backed protecting sites when there is local input. She introduced a bill in November 2009 to authorize the secretary of the Interior to determine the suitability of adding Wyoming's Heart Mountain Relocation Center, where more than 10,000 Japanese-Americans were held during World War II, as a unit of the National Park Service.

"I understand the reticence some have toward acquiring new federal land, particularly out West, where so much of our land is already federally owned," Lummis said at an April 2010 hearing of the Natural Resources Subcommittee on National Parks, Forests and Public Lands Subcommittee

— she served on the panel in the 111th Congress (2009-10). "I want to assure my colleagues that this study has been done the right way, from the bottom up. The bill is broadly supported at the local level."

Lummis said she supports an "all of the above" energy policy that includes incentives for new technology as well as further development of alternative energy. "Wyoming has what America needs," Lummis said. "We have oil, gas, coal, uranium, solar, biomass, and the technology is being developed in Wyoming to recover these resources, renewable and non-renewable."

She opposed the House Democrats' 2009 energy bill that included a system for capping emissions and allowing businesses to buy and trade allowances. She voted for a measure in early 2011 that would prohibit the EPA from regulating greenhouse gases in any effort to address climate change.

Lummis served on a House GOP task force looking at ways to help rural areas, which make up much of Wyoming, the least populated state. In July 2009 she introduced a measure to allow satellite TV providers to broadcast in-state educational stations outside their local markets, which would be beneficial to viewers living far from population centers.

She credits her daughter with introducing her to social media networks as a way of keeping in touch with constituents. During budget negotiations in early 2009, she said, she "Twittered for the entire 14 hours," alerting constituents about attempts to change the legislation.

Lummis is a social conservative who opposes abortion and gay marriage. She hailed a provision signed into law in May 2009 that allows visitors to national parks and wildlife refuges to carry loaded firearms.

Her experience as a college intern for Wyoming's Senate Agriculture Committee prompted her entry into politics. At 24, she became the youngest woman elected to the state legislature, where an early assignment to the House Judiciary Committee convinced her to attend law school. She later returned to the legislature, ultimately serving 12 years in the state House and two years in the state Senate before twice being elected state treasurer.

After failing to win appointment to the Senate following the 2007 death of GOP Sen. Craig Thomas, Lummis announced her candidacy for the House seat being vacated by Republican Barbara Cubin. She won a four-way GOP primary, then faced Democrat Gary Trauner, a businessman who had lost to Cubin in 2006 by less than 1 percentage point. Lummis won that November with 53 percent of the vote, boosted by turnout in the heavily Republican state that enabled GOP Sen. John McCain of Arizona to carry it in the presidential election with nearly two-thirds of the vote. She easily won re-election in 2010, taking 70 percent of the vote.

Key Votes

2010	
Overhaul the nation's health insurance system	NO
Allow for repeal of "don't ask, don't tell"	NO
Overhaul financial services industry regulation	NO
Limit use of new Afghanistan War funds to troop withdrawal activities	NO
Change oversight of offshore drilling and lift oil spill liability cap	NO
Provide a path to legal status for some children of illegal immigrants	NO
Extend Bush-era income tax cuts for two years	YES
2009	
Expand the Children's Health Insurance Program	NO
Provide $787 billion in tax cuts and spending increases to stimulate the economy	NO
Allow bankruptcy judges to modify certain primary-residence mortgages	NO
Create a cap-and-trade system to limit greenhouse gas emissions	NO
Provide $2 billion for the "cash for clunkers" program	NO
Establish the government as the sole provider of student loans	NO
Restrict federally funded insurance coverage for abortions in health care overhaul	YES

CQ Vote Studies

	PARTY UNITY		PRESIDENTIAL SUPPORT	
	SUPPORT	OPPOSE	SUPPORT	OPPOSE
2010	95%	5%	26%	74%
2009	98%	2%	10%	90%

Interest Groups

	AFL-CIO	ADA	CCUS	ACU
2010	0%	0%	88%	100%
2009	5%	0%	80%	100%

Wyoming

At Large

Wyoming, the least populated state in the nation, basks in its wide-open spaces, which define its libertarian politics and natural-resources-based economy. The Grand Tetons' jagged peaks rise from the floor of the Jackson Hole Valley to their nearly 14,000-foot apex, less than 10 miles from the nation's steepest ski slopes at Jackson Hole Mountain.

Tourist attractions such as Yellowstone National Park, the first national park, are economic staples.

The state relies on ranching and mining, but wind turbines have been popping up along the landscape. Although the state lacks a highly diversified economy, stability in retail and government jobs attracted some out-of-state workers from areas hit hard by the nationwide recession. Consistent population growth in the state has added almost 70,000 residents since 2000, and only two of the state's counties — Hot Springs and Platte — shed residents.

Most residents are happy with relative seclusion, a tranquil lifestyle and moderate population growth. Residents savor their land and resources and reject government intrusion, especially regarding land use. State lawmakers are loath to raise taxes. Wyoming, with a statewide 4 percent sales tax, has no corporate or personal income taxes.

Voters here favor the GOP but sometimes allow personality to triumph over party if a Democrat is moderate and unaffiliated with the national party. John McCain won 65 percent of Wyoming's 2008 presidential vote, his second-best statewide showing in the nation.

Wyoming, which has not elected a Democrat to the U.S. House since 1976, chose a Democratic governor in seven of the last 10 elections. But Republican Matt Mead easily won the 2010 gubernatorial race, taking every county in the state.

Major Industry
Mining, tourism, agriculture

Military Bases
Francis E. Warren Air Force Base, 2,719 military, 587 civilian (2010)

Cities
Cheyenne, 59,316; Laramie, 30,816; Gillette, 29,087

Notable
In 1920, Jackson became the first U.S. town ever to elect an all-female slate — mayor, council and marshal.

Del. Eni F.H. Faleomavaega (D)

Capitol Office
225-8577
www.house.gov/faleomavaega
2422 Rayburn Bldg. 20515-5201; fax 225-8757

Committees
Foreign Affairs
Natural Resources

Residence
Pago Pago

Born
Aug. 15, 1943; Vailoatai, A.S.

Religion
Mormon

Family
Wife, Hinanui Bambridge Hunkin; five children

Education
Brigham Young U., A.A. 1964, B.A. 1966 (political science); Texas Southern U., attended 1969 (law); U. of Houston, J.D. 1972; U. of California, Berkeley, LL.M. 1973

Military
Army, 1966-69; Army Reserve, 1983-2001

Career
Lawyer; territorial prosecutor; congressional aide

Political Highlights
Democratic candidate for U.S. House, 1984; lieutenant governor, 1985-89

ELECTION RESULTS

2010 GENERAL

Eni F.H. Faleomavaega (D)	6,176	56.3%
Aumua Amata (D)	4,438	40.4%
Tuika Tuika (NPA)	357	3.2%

2008 GENERAL

Eni F.H. Faleomavaega (D)	7,498	60.4%
Aumua Amata (R)	4,349	35.0%
Rosie F. Tago Lancaster (I)	570	4.6%

Previous Winning Percentages
2006 (47%); 2004 (65%); 2002 (41%); 2000 (46%);1998 (86%); 1994 (64%); 1992 (65%); 1990 (55%); 1988 (51%)

Elected 1988; 12th term

Faleomavaega has become a key voice on U.S. relations with Asian and Pacific nations during his more than two decades in the House. He is a senior member of the Foreign Affairs Committee and is ranking Democrat on its panel on Asia and the Pacific.

He has expressed displeasure about the lack of attention the United States pays to the Pacific region and blasted Republican efforts to cut State Department and foreign assistance funding in a catchall spending bill for fiscal 2011. He accused the Republican majority of taking "a machete and a sledgehammer" to the foreign operations budget.

Faleomavaega (full name: EN-ee FOL-ee-oh-mav-ah-ENG-uh) evinces a calm demeanor but is dogged in his determination to improve the economic lot of the island territory. His seat on the Natural Resources Committee gives him a voice on oceans policy, central to his constituency's existence. In early 2009, Faleomavaega appealed for a delay in a 2007 minimum wage hike — which he had reluctantly supported — contending worsening economic conditions would hamper companies' ability to comply.

He has pushed for assistance for the countries he believes are most vulnerable to dangers posed by global climate change. "Examples of the impact of developed countries' emissions on poorer countries can be found around the world, including the South Pacific, where my own home lies," Faleomavaega said at a 2010 hearing of the Asia and the Pacific Subcommittee, which he chaired at the time.

Faleomavaega attended high school in Hawaii, where his father was stationed in the Navy. After college, he joined the Army and served in Vietnam before heading to the mainland for law school. After working for eight years in Washington, he returned to Pago Pago in 1981, serving as a deputy attorney general, then as lieutenant governor. He was elected delegate in 1988 and has had a few tough re-election battles, but in 2008 he took 60 percent of the vote and in 2010 he won a three-way race with 56 percent.

He is a "matai" — a Samoan chief. Faleomavaega is actually his title; his family name is Hunkin.

American Samoa

At Large

In the heart of Polynesia, American Samoa is the nation's southernmost territory. Located about 2,500 miles southwest of Hawaii, it is composed of five volcanic islands and two outlying coral atolls. Its total land area is 77 square miles, slightly more than the District of Columbia. Tourists venture here for snorkeling, fishing, hiking and the islands' secluded beaches.

An 1899 treaty gave the United States control over the islands in the eastern portion of the Samoan archipelago. During World War II, the U.S. Marine Corps, attracted by the deep-water harbor at Pago Pago, made the island an advanced training and staging center. Today it is an unincorporated territory of the United States, administered by the Interior Department.

Residents are U.S. nationals, not citizens, and the territory has had a non-voting delegate since 1981.

Most land here is communally owned. Per capita income is very low ($8,000), and federal aid, including welfare and food stamps, is vital. Economic growth, even in the promising tourism sector, is hindered by American Samoa's isolation, limited transportation and susceptibility to hurricanes and tsunamis. In recent years, there has been a concerted government effort to cope with the islands' limited resources of fresh water.

Tuna fishing is key to the private-sector economy, and one of the islands' two canneries expects major renovations to be complete in 2012. Widespread unemployment across the territory concerns officials and residents.

Major Industry
Government, fishing, handicrafts, tourism

Villages (2000)
Tafuna, 8,409; Nu'uuli, 5,154; Pago Pago, 4,278

Notable
Anthropologist Margaret Mead studied on Ta'u and wrote "Coming of Age in Samoa."

Del. Eleanor Holmes Norton (D)

Capitol Office
225-8050
www.norton.house.gov
2136 Rayburn Bldg. 20515-5101; fax 225-3002

Committees
Oversight & Government Reform
Transportation & Infrastructure

Residence
Washington

Born
June 13, 1937; Washington, D.C.

Religion
Episcopalian

Family
Divorced; two children

Education
Antioch College, B.A. 1960 (history); Yale U., M.A. 1963 (American studies); Yale U., LL.B. 1964

Career
Professor; lawyer

Political Highlights
New York City Human Rights Commission, 1971-77; Equal Employment Opportunity Commission chairwoman, 1977-81

ELECTION RESULTS

2010 GENERAL

Eleanor Holmes Norton (D)	117,990	88.9%
Missy Reilly Smith (R)	8,109	6.1%
Rick Tingling-Clemmons (GREEN)	4,413	3.3%
write-ins (WRI)	1,359	1.0%

2010 PRIMARY

Eleanor Holmes Norton (D)	116,277	90.2%
Douglass Sloan (D)	11,857	9.2%

2008 GENERAL

Eleanor Holmes Norton (D)	228,376	92.3%
Maude Louise Hills (GREEN)	16,693	6.7%

Previous Winning Percentages
2006 (97%); 2004 (91%); 2002 (93%); 2000 (90%); 1998 (90%); 1996 (90%); 1994 (89%); 1992 (85%); 1990 (62%)

Elected 1990; 11th term

Norton doesn't have a vote on the House floor, but that has never stopped her from being a vocal participant in the chamber's business. She is an outspoken advocate for D.C. voting rights and guards the District's home rule authority.

Her longtime goal has been full D.C. representation in the House.

A 2007 D.C. voting bill passed the House but collapsed in the Senate. In 2009, the Senate passed a bill that included an amendment to nullify most of the city's gun control laws. More than a year later, the House appeared set to consider its version, but the bill was removed from the legislative calendar because some Democrats — including Norton — objected to the gun provision.

Early in the 112th Congress (2011-12) Norton was particularly vociferous about efforts to restrict the District of Columbia's use of local funds to pay for abortions. She also opposed inclusion of funding for a D.C. school voucher program in the catchall spending bill for fiscal 2011. Her effort to boost funding for the District's public schools instead failed on a largely party-line vote.

From her seat on the Oversight and Government Reform Committee, Norton is a watchdog of the Smithsonian: She has introduced legislation to change the way the institution's board is selected, to apply the Freedom of Information Act and other open government laws to the institution and to guarantee free admission to exhibits from the permanent collection.

Norton, who also sits on the Transportation and Infrastructure Committee, has worked to rejuvenate southeast D.C.'s economy by relocating the Department of Homeland Security headquarters there (she previously served on the Homeland Security Committee).

A native Washingtonian, Norton graduated in the last segregated class at Dunbar High School. Her father was a city employee, her mother a teacher. After earning a law degree at Yale and working in Mississippi with civil rights groups, she took a job with the American Civil Liberties Union.

She was teaching law at Georgetown University in 1990 when Democrat Walter E. Fauntroy gave up his delegate post to run for mayor. She won that year with 62 percent of the vote and has routinely won with more than 90 percent since.

District of Columbia

At Large

"Taxation Without Representation." That slogan on the District's license plates sums up residents' displeasure at not being able to participate fully in a democracy they host. The city's budget and laws are subject to review and veto by Congress, a body in which residents have no vote. Although residents do vote for president, a non-voting delegate in the House (continuously since 1971) and an elected mayor (since 1974), efforts to gain full participation in the U.S. government — including bids for statehood — have not yet succeeded.

It is no surprise that the main business of the nation's capital is government. Hundreds of thousands work for the federal or local governments or in related private-sector work, such as lobbying, law and journalism. It also is no surprise that the District draws hordes of tourists who come to see the Smithsonian museums and national monuments.

The city's wealth is concentrated in its north-west quadrant, but some revitalized areas, such as those just east of the U.S. Capitol, attract national chains and young professionals. Development along the Anacostia River and in the northeast quadrant may spur economic growth. The District's population has grown since 2000, but its longtime black majority has dwindled to just 50 percent.

Major Industry
Government, professional services

Military Bases
Joint Base Anacostia-Bolling, 13,054 military, 2,977 civilian; Joint Base Myer-Henderson Hall (shared with Virginia's 8th District), 7,920 military, 1,374 civilian; Naval Support Activity Washington, 3,147 military, 14,015 civilian (2011)

Population
Washington, 601,723

Notable
Since residents began casting votes for president in 1964, the Republican candidate's share has ranged from a high of 22 percent in 1972 to a low of 7 percent in 2008.

Del. Madeleine Z. Bordallo (D)

Capitol Office
225-1188
www.house.gov/bordallo
2441 Rayburn Bldg. 20515-5301; fax 226-0341

Committees
Armed Services
Natural Resources

Residence
Tumuning

Born
May 31, 1933; Graceville, Minn.

Religion
Roman Catholic

Family
Widowed; one child

Education
Saint Mary's College (Ind.), attended 1952-53; The
College of St. Catherine, attended 1953

Career
Guam first lady; shoe company founder; radio show
host

Political Highlights
Guam Senate, 1981-83, 1987-95; Democratic
nominee for governor, 1990; lieutenant governor,
1995-2003

ELECTION RESULTS

2010 GENERAL

Madeleine Z. Bordallo (D)		unopposed

2008 GENERAL

Madeleine Z. Bordallo (D)	28,247	94.6%
write-ins	1,617	5.4%

Previous Winning Percentages
2006 (97%); 2004 (97%); 2002 (65%)

Elected 2002; 5th term

A Minnesota native who has lived most of her life in Guam, Bordallo protects the Pacific island's interests as a member of the Natural Resources Committee and serves as point person for a multibillion-dollar military expansion that feeds the island's economy.

On the Armed Services Committee, Bordallo (bore-DAA-yo) watches over the $15 billion buildup, which includes the transfer of thousands of troops from Japan. The fiscal 2011 defense policy bill passed by the House included more than $560 million in construction funding for Guam.

The measure also included a provision authorizing reparations to victims of atrocities committed by the Japanese forces that occupied Guam during World War II, long a priority for Bordallo. The reparations language was stripped from the final version of the legislation, and Bordallo introduced a stand-alone bill early in 2011.

As chairwoman of the Natural Resources Subcommittee on Insular Affairs, Oceans and Wildlife during the 111th Congress (2009-10), Bordallo pushed legislation to boost fish and wildlife research and marine and coastal resource management.

Her family moved to the 212-square-mile island from Minnesota when she was 15 so her father could take a job as the principal of the island's only high school. She returned after attending college in the Midwest to study music.

She married Ricardo J. Bordallo, the scion of a wealthy and politically connected island family. He served as the island's governor, and she won a seat in the legislature. In 1990, caught up in a corruption case, Ricardo Bordallo wrapped himself in the Guam flag, chained himself to a statue of Chief Kepuha on the island's main thoroughfare and shot himself in the head.

That year she lost the gubernatorial race to Republican Joseph F. Ada. She remained in the legislature and later served as lieutenant governor.

In 2002, when five-term Democratic Del. Robert A. Underwood ran unsuccessfully for governor, Bordallo defeated Ada in the U.S. House race with 64 percent of the vote. The first woman to seek the island's delegate post, she has run unopposed in every election since.

Guam
At Large

"Where America's day begins," Guam is the largest and most southerly island in the Marianas archipelago. At 212 square miles, it is about three times the size of the District of Columbia. More than 3,800 miles west of Hawaii and across the International Date Line from the U.S. mainland, Guam is closer to Tokyo than to Honolulu.

The indigenous people, the Chamorros, first had contact with Europeans in 1521 with the visit of Ferdinand Magellan. Spain ceded Guam to the United States in 1898, and the U.S. Navy administered Guam until 1950, when residents were granted U.S. citizenship and elected a local government. Guam has had a non-voting delegate in the House since 1973. Although residents are citizens, they may not vote in presidential elections. Guam's economy is heavily dependent on a U.S. military presence, which is expected to increase here by 2014, when thousands of U.S. Marines will begin relocation to Guam

from bases in Japan. A tropical climate, pristine beaches and a picturesque countryside make the island an ideal vacation spot, and tourism is vital to the local economy. Per capita income in 2008 was $13,089. Most food and other consumer goods are imported. In recent years, Guam has had to cope with large influxes of illegal immigrants, who pay smugglers to sneak them onto the island to seek asylum in the United States.

Major Industry
Military, tourism, construction, shipping

Military Bases
Naval Base Guam, 2,905 military, 1,519 civilian (2011); Andersen Air Force Base, 2,170 military, 400 civilian (2004)

Districts (2000)
Dededo, 42,980; Yigo, 19,474; Tamuning, 18,012

Notable
If measured from its base at the bottom of the undersea Marianas Trench, Mount Humuyong Manglo would be the highest mountain in the world.

Del. Gregorio Kilili Camacho Sablan (D)

Capitol Office
225-2646
sablan.house.gov
423 Cannon Bldg. 20515; fax 226-4249

Committees
Agriculture
Natural Resources

Residence
Saipan

Born
Jan. 19, 1955; Saipan, N. Marianas

Religion
Roman Catholic

Family
Wife, Andrea C. Sablan; six children

Education
U. of Hawaii, Manoa, attended 1989-90

Military
Army, 1981-86

Career
Election commission director; gubernatorial aide

Political Highlights
N. Marianas Democratic Party chairman, 1982-83; N.
Marianas House, 1982-86

ELECTION RESULTS

2010 GENERAL

Sablan (D)	4,896	43.2%
Joseph Camacho (COV)	2,744	24.2%
Juan N. Babauta (R)	1,978	17.5%
Jesus Borja (D)	1,707	15.1%

2008 GENERAL

Sablan (D)	2,474	24.3%
Pete A. Tenorio (R)	2,117	20.8%
John Gonzalez (I)	1,855	18.3%
Juan Tudela Lizama (I)	1,819	17.9%
Luis Palacios Crisostimo (I)	946	9.3%
David Mendiola Cing (D)	307	3.0%
Felipe Quitugua Atalig (I)	249	2.4%
Chong Man Won (I)	230	2.3%
John Henry Davis Jr. (I)	164	1.6%

Elected 2008; 2nd term

Sablan achieved a quick success in Congress on a tourism issue critical to his constituents. He also has looked for innovative ways to serve his constituents and worked out a system that allows them to testify before Congress by video.

Sablan worked with fellow lawmakers and officials from the Northern Marianas and Guam to persuade the Department of Homeland Security to delay the application of federal immigration law to the commonwealth. The law would effectively restrict travel to the Northern Marianas from Russia and China — both valuable tourist markets — and would institute a visa waiver program to allow Hong Kong tourists and other eligible visitors longer visits there. Sablan said the commonwealth needed more time to make preparations. In October 2009, DHS said it would permit visitors from China and Russia to enter the islands visa-free. Two months later the State Department said it would begin offering expedited visas to Chinese flight crews.

A member of the Agriculture and Natural Resources panels, Sablan backs a measure to study the establishment of a national park on the island of Rota.

Sablan was born on Saipan. At age 11 he moved with his family to Micronesia. He is employed in what could be considered the family business: His father was a Saipan representative, and both his uncle and grandfather had been mayor. He finished high school in Saipan before moving to the mainland United States. He was named deputy chief administrative officer to Northern Marianas Gov. Carlos S. Camacho in 1981 before being elected to the commonwealth House in 1982. After a year working for Hawaii Democratic Sen. Daniel K. Inouye, Sablan attended the University of Hawaii at Manoa before he returned to Saipan, where he served as special assistant for management and budget under Gov. Froilan C. Tenorio. In 1999, he was named executive director of the Commonwealth Election Commission.

President George W. Bush signed legislation creating the Northern Marianas delegate position in 2008. Sablan won a nine-way race for the U.S. House seat that year and was easily re-elected in 2010.

Northern Mariana Islands

At Large

A string of more than a dozen mostly volcanic islands forming the eastern boundary of the Philippine Sea in the tropical Pacific Ocean, the Northern Mariana Islands rely on the federal government and tourism. Saipan, the commonwealth's largest island and capital, supports more than 90 percent of the population and most of the local economy. Tinian and Rota are the commonwealth's other inhabited islands.

After three centuries of colonization by Spain, decades of control by Germany and then Japan, and participation in a territorial structure with other Micronesian islands, the Northern Marianas in 1976 became a commonwealth of the United States. Residents are U.S. citizens but cannot vote in presidential elections. Formerly represented in Washington by a resident representative, the Northern Marianas gained a delegate to the U.S. House with a two-year term in 2009.

Tourists and prospective members of the workforce arrive in large numbers from Asia, and Asians make up a significant portion of the population.

Filipinos and Chamorros, a native island population, make up the largest individual ethnic groups, and many residents here are of multiple ethnicities.

The federal government is a stable source of jobs, as well as a source of economic subsidies. Hotels are among the largest employers on the islands, but employment rates, family incomes and population have decreased over the past decade. The median household income in the Northern Marianas was roughly $17,000 in 2004.

Major industry
Government, tourism

Islands (2000)
Saipan, 62,382; Tinian, 3,540; Rota, 3,283

Notable
More than 85 percent of the population speaks a language other than English at home.

Res. Cmmsr. Pedro R. Pierluisi (D)

Capitol Office
225-2615
pierluisi.house.gov
1213 Longworth Bldg. 20515-5401; fax 225-2154

Committees
Ethics
Judiciary
Natural Resources

Residence
San Juan

Born
April 26, 1959; San Juan, P.R.

Religion
Roman Catholic

Family
Wife, Maria Elena Carrion; four children

Education
Tulane U., B.A. 1981 (American history); George
Washington U., J.D. 1984

Career
Lawyer

Political Highlights
P.R. secretary of Justice, 1993-96

ELECTION RESULTS

2008 GENERAL

Pedro R. Pierluisi (NP)	1,010,285	53.0%
Alfredo Salazar (POPDEM)	810,093	42.5%
Carlos Lopez (PR)	46,123	2.4%
Jessica Birriel (PRI)	37,865	2.0%

Elected 2008; 1st term

The only House member with a four-year term, Pierluisi has been a leader in pursuing statehood for Puerto Rico while looking after the island's parochial interests.

Pierluisi (pea-air-loo-EE-see) drafted a bill to provide for a two-step process for Puerto Ricans to choose statehood, independence or to retain the island's status as a U.S. commonwealth. The House passed the bill in April 2010 after amending it to require the commonwealth option be included in the second stage of voting. Critics said the original version was tilted to favor statehood. The Senate never considered the measure.

His work on the Natural Resources Committee has included backing legislation by Democratic Del. Madeleine Z. Bordallo of Guam that would authorize increased funding for programs and research aimed at protecting coral reefs.

Pierluisi also sits on the Judiciary Committee. He served as Puerto Rico's attorney general for four years during the 1990s and was recruited by White House officials to lobby key members of Congress on President Bill Clinton's 1994 crime bill.

He took on some new party tasks in the 112th Congress (2011-12), joining the Ethics Committee and serving as a national chairman of the Democratic Congressional Campaign Committee. Pierluisi is a member of the pro-business New Democrat Coalition, but he almost always sides with his party. On votes in which a majority of Republicans and Democrats split, he voted with his party 99 percent of the time in 2009 and 100 percent in 2010. Delegates cannot vote on the passage of bills, but prior to the 112th Congress they could cast recorded votes on the House floor on amendments when the chamber was acting as the Committee of the Whole.

Pierluisi said his interest in public service stems from his father, Jorge, a former secretary of housing for Puerto Rico. He served as a part-time aide to Baltasar Corrada, former resident commissioner, during the 1980s. In November 2008, he defeated Alfredo Salazar to succeed Republican Luis Fortuño, who ran a successful campaign for governor.

Puerto Rico

At Large

Puerto Rico, the largest and most populated (3.7 million) of the territories, has been a self-governing commonwealth of the United States since 1952. Median household income here in 2009 was about $18,000 — high by Caribbean standards, but still less than half that of the poorest state — and the island has lost population since 2000.

Christopher Columbus arrived in Puerto Rico in 1493, and the Spanish arrived 15 years later. The Spanish brought slaves to work in the sugar cane fields, and slavery was not abolished on the island until 1873. Spain ceded the territory to the United States in 1898 following the Spanish-American War. Its residents became U.S. citizens in 1917, but they cannot vote for president. Since 1901, Puerto Ricans have been represented in the House by a resident commissioner.

The island's political status has been a longstanding issue, with various factions favoring continued commonwealth status, statehood or independence. In 2008, Puerto Ricans elected a pro-statehood ticket as Luis Fortuño, a former resident commissioner who caucused with the GOP, was elected governor and Pedro R. Pierluisi won the U.S. House seat.

Puerto Rico's economy, one of the most stable in the Caribbean, relies on its tourism industry and industrial sector. Millions of tourists visit Puerto Rico each year, although some only stop for a day; El Yunque tropical forest and local beaches are popular destinations. Mainland U.S. firms also invest heavily here, encouraged by tax incentives and by duty-free access to the United States.

Major industry
Manufacturing, service, tourism

Military Bases
Fort Buchanan, 190 military, 699 civilian (2004)

Cities
San Juan (unincorporated), 381,931; Bayamón (unincorporated), 185,996

Notable
Coliseo Roberto Clemente was named after the baseball star and Puerto Rico native.

Del. Donna M.C. Christensen (D)

Capitol Office
225-1790
www.house.gov/christian-christensen
1510 Longworth Bldg. 20515-5501; fax 225-5517

Committees
Energy & Commerce

Residence
St. Croix

Born
Sept. 19, 1945; Teaneck, N.J.

Religion
Moravian

Family
Separated; two children

Education
Saint Mary's College (Ind.), B.S. 1966 (biology);
George Washington U., M.D. 1970

Career
Physician; health official

Political Highlights
Virgin Is. Democratic Territorial Committee, 1980-97
(chairwoman, 1980-82); Virgin Is. Board of Education,
1984-86; Virgin Is. acting commissioner of health,
1993-94; sought Democratic nomination for U.S.
House, 1994

ELECTION RESULTS

2010 GENERAL

Donna M.C. Christensen (D)	19,844	71.7%
Jeffrey Moorhead (None)	5,063	18.3%
Vincent Emile Danet (R)	2,329	8.4%
Guillaume Mimoun (None)	419	1.5%

2008 GENERAL

Donna M.C. Christensen (D)	18,237	99.6%

Previous Winning Percentages
2006 (63%); 2004 (66%); 2002 (68%); 2000 (78%);
1998 (80%); 1996 General Runoff Election (52%)

Elected 1996; 8th term

A physician and former public health official, Christensen parlayed her seat on the Energy and Commerce Committee into a role helping push the Democrats' health care overhaul into law in 2010. She is a staunch defender of the law against GOP attempts to repeal and block funding for it.

She had to surrender her Energy and Commerce seat after the 2010 elections decimated Democratic ranks, but she reclaimed it when Jane Harman of California resigned early in the 112th Congress (2011-12).

The former acting health commissioner of the Virgin Islands, Christensen did not win the elimination of the cap on federal Medicaid funding for U.S. territories she sought in the health care overhaul, but it did include increased funding for the territories.

Among her other priorities is a constitutional amendment to grant U.S. territories the right to vote in presidential elections.

During the 110th Congress (2007-08), President George W. Bush signed into law her measure creating a new House delegate for the Northern Mariana Islands — a seat filled by Gregorio Kilili Camacho Sablan, who ran as an independent but later joined the Democratic Caucus.

The daughter of a St. Croix judge, Christensen was inspired by a booklet encouraging African-American students to consider careers in medicine. She attended medical school at George Washington University and did postgraduate training in San Francisco and Washington, D.C., before returning to the Virgin Islands.

Over her 20-year medical career she worked in clinics and hospitals on St. Croix and later became acting commissioner of health.

She lost her first race for delegate in 1994. But in 1996 she edged out incumbent Victor O. Frazer, who ran as an independent, and Republican Kenneth Mapp in a three-way battle. She has won easily since, and in 2010 bested the second-place finisher by more than a 3-1 ratio.

In 2010, the Ethics Committee exonerated Christensen for accepting Caribbean trips from corporations in 2007 and 2008, ruling that she was unaware of the corporate funding.

Virgin Islands
At Large

The Virgin Islands, just east of Puerto Rico, are known for their subtropical climate, beautiful beaches, duty-free shopping and — far too often — being in the path of tropical storms. The first three attributes have helped build a tourism industry, while the storms — and, more recently, budget shortfalls — have made economic development an uneven and difficult process.

Spain asserted its authority over the islands after Christopher Columbus arrived in 1493, and over the next century Spanish settlers killed or drove out the native Indians. But Spain showed no real interest in setting up a colony on the Virgin Islands. Denmark established a colony on St. Thomas in the mid-17th century, and sugar plantations drove the islands' economy until slavery was abolished in 1848. The U.S. government bought the islands from Denmark for $25 million in 1917.

The Virgin Islands form an unincorporated territory under the jurisdiction of the Interior Department. The territory is composed of 68 islands and cays, but only four are inhabited. Its population is roughly 110,000. Residents are U.S. citizens but may not vote for president. The Virgin Islands has had a non-voting House delegate since 1973.

Cruise ships make regular stops at the islands, principally at the capital of Charlotte Amalie on St. Thomas but also in neighboring St. Croix. Passengers stream ashore to take advantage of duty-free shopping, and most tourists leave without spending a night. A large petroleum refinery and a rum distillery on St. Croix, as well as light industry on other islands, are the primary sources of private-sector jobs.

Major Industry
Tourism, petroleum refining, rum distilling

Cities (2000)
Charlotte Amalie, 11,004; Christiansted, 2,637

Notable
The Virgin Islands is the only U.S. territory where traffic travels on the left.

Member Statistics

The sweeping Republican victories in the 2010 House elections returned the party to the majority after only four years — one-tenth the amount of time the party waited between its last two majorities.

Nearly one-fifth of the members of the 112th Congress are in their first full term.

That has skewed the average age — the 112th is younger than the 111th by nearly one year. The average tenure has also dipped — 9.8 years in the House and 11.4 years in the Senate, down from 10.3 and 13.4 in the 111th Congress.

The 112th Congress includes 15 Mormons, three Buddhists, two Muslims and one atheist. Catholics continue to be the single largest denomination, with 157 members.

112th Congress by the Numbers

2,041 The approximate number of miles between the hometowns of House Speaker John A. Boehner (West Chester Township, Ohio) and Senate Majority Leader Harry Reid (Searchlight, Nev.).

101 The number of members who joined the House or the Senate at the start of the 112th, the largest crop of congressional newcomers since the 103rd Congress, elected in 1992: 89 members new to the House, all but nine of whom are Republicans; 12 new to the Senate (11 Republicans and one Democrat).

72 The percentage of white constituents in Florida Republican Rep. Allen B. West's 22nd District. It's the highest share of white residents represented by a black House member.

63 The percentage of black constituents in Tennessee's 9th District, represented by Democrat Steve Cohen. The district has the highest percentage of black residents represented by a white House member.

58 The difference in age between the oldest member of Congress, Rep. Ralph M. Hall, R-Texas, and the youngest, Rep. Aaron Schock, R-Ill.

56.7 The highest percentage of population gain for a congressional district between the 2000 census and the 2010 census. Nevada's 3rd District, represented by Republican Joe Heck, went from 666,082 residents to 1,043,855 residents.

22.7 The highest percentage of a population loss for a congressional district between the 2000 census and the 2010 census. Louisiana's 2nd District lost 145,210 residents in 10 years.

19 The number of House freshmen serving as subcommittee chairmen.

13 The number of congressional districts that are 70 percent or more Hispanic, according to the 2010 census.

5 The number of former members who returned to the House in 2011: Charles Bass, R-N.H., Steve Chabot, R-Ohio, Michael G. Fitzpatrick, R-Pa., Steve Pearce, R-N.M., and Tim Walberg, R-Mich.

0 The number of children or grandchildren of Joseph P. and Rose Kennedy in the 112th Congress.

Get to know the 112th Congress by perusing these fact files, charts and statistics. They provide a handy reference guide to the demographic characteristics of members, as well as details on who belongs to which committees and caucuses. And you can test your congressional IQ with "Did You Know?"

House Seniority

REPUBLICANS

House Republicans determine seniority by length of service. Members who previously served in the House are usually given credit for most of that service.

For members who joined at the beginning of a Congress, service is credited from the first day of the session. Seniority for members who won special elections is credited from the date of the election.

Reps. Rodney Alexander and Ralph M. Hall began their tenure as Democrats. The GOP Conference credited their service as Democrats toward their seniority. No credit is given for other prior service, such as serving as a governor.

1.	C.W. Bill Young, Fla.	Jan. 21, 1971
2.	Don Young, Alaska	March 6, 1973
3.	Jerry Lewis, Calif.	Jan. 15, 1979
4.	F. James Sensenbrenner Jr., Wis.	Jan. 15, 1979
5.	Tom Petri, Wis.	April 3, 1979
6.	David Dreier, Calif.	Jan. 5, 1981
7.	Ralph M. Hall, Texas	Jan. 5, 1981
8.	Harold Rogers, Ky.	Jan. 5, 1981
9.	Christopher H. Smith, N.J.	Jan. 5, 1981
10.	Frank R. Wolf, Va.	Jan. 5, 1981
11.	Dan Burton, Ind.	Jan. 3, 1983
12.	Joe L. Barton, Texas	Jan. 3, 1985
13.	Howard Coble, N.C.	Jan. 3, 1985
14.	Elton Gallegly, Calif.	Jan. 6, 1987
15.	Wally Herger, Calif.	Jan. 6, 1987
16.	Lamar Smith, Texas	Jan. 6, 1987
17.	Fred Upton, Mich.	Jan. 6, 1987
18.	John J. "Jimmy" Duncan Jr., Tenn.	Nov. 8, 1988
19.	Dana Rohrabacher, Calif.	Jan. 3, 1989
20.	Cliff Stearns, Fla.	Jan. 3, 1989
21.	Ileana Ros-Lehtinen, Fla.	Aug. 29, 1989
22.	Ron Paul, Texas	Jan. 7, 1997
	Also served 1976-77, 1979-85	
23.	John A. Boehner, Ohio	Jan. 3, 1991
24.	Dave Camp, Mich.	Jan. 3, 1991
25.	Sam Johnson, Texas	May 18, 1991
26.	Spencer Bachus, Ala.	Jan. 5, 1993
27.	Roscoe G. Bartlett, Md.	Jan. 5, 1993
28.	Ken Calvert, Calif.	Jan. 5, 1993
29.	Robert W. Goodlatte, Va.	Jan. 5, 1993
30.	Peter T. King, N.Y.	Jan. 5, 1993
31.	Jack Kingston, Ga.	Jan. 5, 1993
32.	Donald Manzullo, Ill.	Jan. 5, 1993
33.	Howard P. "Buck" McKeon, Calif.	Jan. 5, 1993
34.	John L. Mica, Fla.	Jan. 5, 1993
35.	Ed Royce, Calif.	Jan. 5, 1993
36.	Frank D. Lucas, Okla.	May 10, 1994
37.	Rodney Frelinghuysen, N.J.	Jan. 4, 1995
38.	Doc Hastings, Wash.	Jan. 4, 1995
39.	Walter B. Jones, N.C.	Jan. 4, 1995
40.	Tom Latham, Iowa	Jan. 4, 1995
41.	Steven C. LaTourette, Ohio	Jan. 4, 1995
42.	Frank A. LoBiondo, N.J.	Jan. 4, 1995
43.	Sue Myrick, N.C.	Jan. 4, 1995
44.	William M. "Mac" Thornberry, Texas	Jan. 4, 1995
45.	Edward Whitfield, Ky.	Jan. 4, 1995
46.	Jo Ann Emerson, Mo.	Nov. 5, 1996
47.	Dan Lungren, Calif.	Jan. 4, 2005
	Also served 1979-89	
48.	Robert B. Aderholt, Ala.	Jan. 7, 1997
49.	Kevin Brady, Texas	Jan. 7, 1997
50.	Kay Granger, Texas	Jan. 7, 1997
51.	Joe Pitts, Pa.	Jan. 7, 1997
52.	Pete Sessions, Texas	Jan. 7, 1997
53.	John Shimkus, Ill.	Jan. 7, 1997
54.	Mary Bono Mack, Calif.	April 7, 1998
55.	Steve Chabot, Ohio	Jan. 5, 2011
	Also served 1995-2009	
56.	Judy Biggert, Ill.	Jan. 6, 1999
57.	Gary G. Miller, Calif.	Jan. 6, 1999
58.	Paul D. Ryan, Wis.	Jan. 6, 1999
59.	Mike Simpson, Idaho	Jan. 6, 1999
60.	Lee Terry, Neb.	Jan. 6, 1999
61.	Greg Walden, Ore.	Jan. 6, 1999
62.	Charles Bass, N.H.	Jan. 5, 2011
	Also served 1995-2007	
63.	Brian P. Bilbray, Calif.	June 13, 2006
	Also served 1995-2001	
64.	Todd Akin, Mo.	Jan. 3, 2001
65.	Eric Cantor, Va.	Jan. 3, 2001
66.	Shelley Moore Capito, W.Va.	Jan. 3, 2001
67.	Ander Crenshaw, Fla.	Jan. 3, 2001
68.	John Culberson, Texas	Jan. 3, 2001
69.	Jeff Flake, Ariz.	Jan. 3, 2001
70.	Sam Graves, Mo.	Jan. 3, 2001
71.	Darrell Issa, Calif.	Jan. 3, 2001
72.	Timothy V. Johnson, Ill.	Jan. 3, 2001
73.	Mike Pence, Ind.	Jan. 3, 2001
74.	Todd R. Platts, Pa.	Jan. 3, 2001
75.	Denny Rehberg, Mont.	Jan. 3, 2001
76.	Mike Rogers, Mich.	Jan. 3, 2001
77.	Pat Tiberi, Ohio	Jan. 3, 2001
78.	Bill Shuster, Pa.	May 15, 2001
79.	J. Randy Forbes, Va.	June 19, 2001
80.	Jeff Miller, Fla.	Oct. 16, 2001
81.	Joe Wilson, S.C.	Dec. 18, 2001
82.	John Sullivan, Okla.	Feb. 15, 2002
83.	Rodney Alexander, La.	Jan. 7, 2003
84.	Rob Bishop, Utah	Jan. 7, 2003
85.	Marsha Blackburn, Tenn.	Jan. 7, 2003
86.	Jo Bonner, Ala.	Jan. 7, 2003
87.	Michael C. Burgess, Texas	Jan. 7, 2003
88.	John Carter, Texas	Jan. 7, 2003
89.	Tom Cole, Okla.	Jan. 7, 2003
90.	Mario Diaz-Balart, Fla.	Jan. 7, 2003
91.	Trent Franks, Ariz.	Jan. 7, 2003
92.	Scott Garrett, N.J.	Jan. 7, 2003
93.	Jim Gerlach, Pa.	Jan. 7, 2003
94.	Phil Gingrey, Ga.	Jan. 7, 2003
95.	Jeb Hensarling, Texas	Jan. 7, 2003
96.	Steve King, Iowa	Jan. 7, 2003
97.	John Kline, Minn.	Jan. 7, 2003
98.	Thaddeus McCotter, Mich.	Jan. 7, 2003
99.	Candice S. Miller, Mich.	Jan. 7, 2003
100.	Tim Murphy, Pa.	Jan. 7, 2003
101.	Devin Nunes, Calif.	Jan. 7, 2003
102.	Mike D. Rogers, Ala.	Jan. 7, 2003
103.	Michael R. Turner, Ohio	Jan. 7, 2003

104. Randy Neugebauer, Texas	June 3, 2003
105. Charles Boustany Jr., La.	Jan. 4, 2005
106. K. Michael Conaway, Texas	Jan. 4, 2005
107. Geoff Davis, Ky.	Jan. 4, 2005
108. Charlie Dent, Pa.	Jan. 4, 2005
109. Jeff Fortenberry, Neb.	Jan. 4, 2005
110. Virginia Foxx, N.C.	Jan. 4, 2005
111. Louie Gohmert, Texas	Jan. 4, 2005
112. Connie Mack, Fla.	Jan. 4, 2005
113. Kenny Marchant, Texas	Jan. 4, 2005
114. Michael McCaul, Texas	Jan. 4, 2005
115. Patrick T. McHenry, N.C.	Jan. 4, 2005
116. Cathy McMorris Rodgers, Wash.	Jan. 4, 2005
117. Ted Poe, Texas	Jan. 4, 2005
118. Tom Price, Ga.	Jan. 4, 2005
119. Dave Reichert, Wash.	Jan. 4, 2005
120. Lynn Westmoreland, Ga.	Jan. 4, 2005
121. Jean Schmidt, Ohio	Aug. 3, 2005
122. John Campbell, Calif.	Dec. 7, 2005
123. Steve Pearce, N.M.	Jan. 5, 2011
	Also served 2003-09
124. Michele Bachmann, Minn.	Jan. 4, 2007
125. Gus Bilirakis, Fla.	Jan. 4, 2007
126. Vern Buchanan, Fla.	Jan. 4, 2007
127. Jim Jordan, Ohio	Jan. 4, 2007
128. Doug Lamborn, Colo.	Jan. 4, 2007
129. Kevin McCarthy, Calif.	Jan. 4, 2007
130. Peter Roskam, Ill.	Jan. 4, 2007
131. Adrian Smith, Neb.	Jan. 4, 2007
132. Paul Broun, Ga.	July 17, 2007
133. Bob Latta, Ohio	Dec. 11, 2007
134. Rob Wittman, Va.	Dec. 11, 2007
135. Steve Scalise, La.	May 3, 2008
136. Steve Austria, Ohio	Jan. 6, 2009
137. Bill Cassidy, La.	Jan. 6, 2009
138. Jason Chaffetz, Utah	Jan. 6, 2009
139. Mike Coffman, Colo.	Jan. 6, 2009
140. John Fleming, La.	Jan. 6, 2009
141. Brett Guthrie, Ky.	Jan. 6, 2009
142. Gregg Harper, Miss.	Jan. 6, 2009
143. Duncan Hunter, Calif.	Jan. 6, 2009
144. Lynn Jenkins, Kan.	Jan. 6, 2009
145. Leonard Lance, N.J.	Jan. 6, 2009
146. Blaine Luetkemeyer, Mo.	Jan. 6, 2009
147. Cynthia M. Lummis, Wyo.	Jan. 6, 2009
148. Tom McClintock, Calif.	Jan. 6, 2009
149. Pete Olson, Texas	Jan. 6, 2009
150. Erik Paulsen, Minn.	Jan. 6, 2009
151. Bill Posey, Fla.	Jan. 6, 2009
152. Phil Roe, Tenn.	Jan. 6, 2009
153. Tom Rooney, Fla.	Jan. 6, 2009
154. Aaron Schock, Ill.	Jan. 6, 2009
155. Glenn Thompson, Pa.	Jan. 6, 2009
156. Tom Graves, Ga.	June 8, 2010
157. Tom Reed, N.Y.	Nov. 2, 2010
158. Marlin Stutzman, Ind.	Nov. 2, 2010
159. Michael G. Fitzpatrick, Pa.	Jan. 5, 2011
	Also served 2005-07
160. Tim Walberg, Mich.	Jan. 5, 2011
	Also served 2007-09
161. Sandy Adams, Fla.	Jan. 5, 2011
162. Justin Amash, Mich.	Jan. 5, 2011
163. Lou Barletta, Pa.	Jan. 5, 2011

164. Dan Benishek, Mich.	Jan. 5, 2011
165. Rick Berg, N.D.	Jan. 5, 2011
166. Diane Black, Tenn.	Jan. 5, 2011
167. Mo Brooks, Ala.	Jan. 5, 2011
168. Larry Bucshon, Ind.	Jan. 5, 2011
169. Ann Marie Buerkle, N.Y.	Jan. 5, 2011
170. Francisco "Quico" Canseco, Texas	Jan. 5, 2011
171. Chip Cravaack, Minn.	Jan. 5, 2011
172. Rick Crawford, Ark.	Jan. 5, 2011
173. Jeff Denham, Calif.	Jan. 5, 2011
174. Scott DesJarlais, Tenn.	Jan. 5, 2011
175. Robert Dold, Ill.	Jan. 5, 2011
176. Sean P. Duffy, Wis.	Jan. 5, 2011
177. Jeff Duncan, S.C.	Jan. 5, 2011
178. Renee Ellmers, N.C.	Jan. 5, 2011
179. Blake Farenthold, Texas	Jan. 5, 2011
180. Stephen Fincher, Tenn.	Jan. 5, 2011
181. Chuck Fleischmann, Tenn.	Jan. 5, 2011
182. Bill Flores, Texas	Jan. 5, 2011
183. Cory Gardner, Colo.	Jan. 5, 2011
184. Bob Gibbs, Ohio	Jan. 5, 2011
185. Chris Gibson, N.Y.	Jan. 5, 2011
186. Paul Gosar, Ariz.	Jan. 5, 2011
187. Trey Gowdy, S.C.	Jan. 5, 2011
188. Tim Griffin, Ark.	Jan. 5, 2011
189. Morgan Griffith, Va.	Jan. 5, 2011
190. Michael G. Grimm, N.Y.	Jan. 5, 2011
191. Frank Guinta, N.H.	Jan. 5, 2011
192. Richard Hanna, N.Y.	Jan. 5, 2011
193. Andy Harris, Md.	Jan. 5, 2011
194. Vicky Hartzler, Mo.	Jan. 5, 2011
195. Nan Hayworth, N.Y.	Jan. 5, 2011
196. Joe Heck, Nev.	Jan. 5, 2011
197. Jaime Herrera Beutler, Wash.	Jan. 5, 2011
198. Tim Huelskamp, Kan.	Jan. 5, 2011
199. Bill Huizenga, Mich.	Jan. 5, 2011
200. Randy Hultgren, Ill.	Jan. 5, 2011
201. Robert Hurt, Va.	Jan. 5, 2011
202. Bill Johnson, Ohio	Jan. 5, 2011
203. Mike Kelly, Pa.	Jan. 5, 2011
204. Adam Kinzinger, Ill.	Jan. 5, 2011
205. Raúl R. Labrador, Idaho	Jan. 5, 2011
206. Jeff Landry, La.	Jan. 5, 2011
207. James Lankford, Okla.	Jan. 5, 2011
208. Billy Long, Mo.	Jan. 5, 2011
209. Tom Marino, Pa.	Jan. 5, 2011
210. David B. McKinley, W.Va.	Jan. 5, 2011
211. Patrick Meehan, Pa.	Jan. 5, 2011
212. Mick Mulvaney, S.C.	Jan. 5, 2011
213. Kristi Noem, S.D.	Jan. 5, 2011
214. Rich Nugent, Fla.	Jan. 5, 2011
215. Alan Nunnelee, Miss.	Jan. 5, 2011
216. Steven M. Palazzo, Miss.	Jan. 5, 2011
217. Mike Pompeo, Kan.	Jan. 5, 2011
218. Ben Quayle, Ariz.	Jan. 5, 2011
219. James B. Renacci, Ohio	Jan. 5, 2011
220. Reid Ribble, Wis.	Jan. 5, 2011
221. Scott Rigell, Va.	Jan. 5, 2011
222. David Rivera, Fla.	Jan. 5, 2011
223. Martha Roby, Ala.	Jan. 5, 2011
224. Todd Rokita, Ind.	Jan. 5, 2011
225. Dennis A. Ross, Fla.	Jan. 5, 2011
226. Jon Runyan, N.J.	Jan. 5, 2011

227. Bobby Schilling, Ill.	Jan. 5, 2011	
228. David Schweikert, Ariz.	Jan. 5, 2011	
229. Austin Scott, Ga.	Jan. 5, 2011	
230. Tim Scott, S.C.	Jan. 5, 2011	
231. Steve Southerland II, Fla.	Jan. 5, 2011	
232. Steve Stivers, Ohio	Jan. 5, 2011	
233. Scott Tipton, Colo.	Jan. 5, 2011	

234. Joe Walsh, Ill.	Jan. 5, 2011
235. Daniel Webster, Fla.	Jan. 5, 2011
236. Allen B. West, Fla.	Jan. 5, 2011
237. Steve Womack, Ark.	Jan. 5, 2011
238. Rob Woodall, Ga.	Jan. 5, 2011
239. Kevin Yoder, Kan.	Jan. 5, 2011
240. Todd Young, Ind.	Jan. 5, 2011

DEMOCRATS

House Democrats determine seniority by length of service. Members who previously served in the House are given some credit for that service — when they return they are ranked above other members of that entering class.

For members who join at the start of a Congress, service is credited from the session's first day. Seniority for members who won special elections is credited from the election's date. No credit is given for other prior service, such as serving as a senator or governor.

1.	John D. Dingell, Mich.	Dec. 13, 1955
2.	John Conyers Jr., Mich.	Jan. 4, 1965
3.	Charles B. Rangel, N.Y.	Jan. 21, 1971
4.	Pete Stark, Calif.	Jan. 3, 1973
5.	George Miller, Calif.	Jan. 14, 1975
6.	Henry A. Waxman, Calif.	Jan. 14, 1975
7.	Edward J. Markey, Mass.	Nov. 2, 1976
8.	Norm Dicks, Wash.	Jan. 4, 1977
9.	Dale E. Kildee, Mich.	Jan. 4, 1977
10.	Nick J. Rahall II, W.Va.	Jan. 4, 1977
11.	Barney Frank, Mass.	Jan. 5, 1981
12.	Steny H. Hoyer, Md.	May 19, 1981
13.	Howard L. Berman, Calif.	Jan. 3, 1983
14.	Marcy Kaptur, Ohio	Jan. 3, 1983
15.	Sander M. Levin, Mich.	Jan. 3, 1983
16.	Edolphus Towns, N.Y.	Jan. 3, 1983
17.	Gary L. Ackerman, N.Y.	March 1, 1983
18.	Peter J. Visclosky, Ind.	Jan. 3, 1985
19.	Peter A. DeFazio, Ore.	Jan. 6, 1987
20.	John Lewis, Ga.	Jan. 6, 1987
21.	Louise M. Slaughter, N.Y.	Jan. 6, 1987
22.	Nancy Pelosi, Calif.	June 2, 1987
23.	Jerry F. Costello, Ill.	Aug. 9, 1988
24.	Frank Pallone Jr., N.J.	Nov. 8, 1988
25.	Eliot L. Engel, N.Y.	Jan. 3, 1989
26.	Nita M. Lowey, N.Y.	Jan. 3, 1989
27.	Jim McDermott, Wash.	Jan. 3, 1989
28.	Richard E. Neal, Mass.	Jan. 3, 1989
29.	Donald M. Payne, N.J.	Jan. 3, 1989
30.	José E. Serrano, N.Y.	March 20, 1990
31.	Robert E. Andrews, N.J.	Nov. 6, 1990
32.	David E. Price, N.C.	Jan. 7, 1997
	Also served 1987-95	
33.	Rosa DeLauro, Conn.	Jan. 3, 1991
34.	James P. Moran, Va.	Jan. 3, 1991
35.	Collin C. Peterson, Minn.	Jan. 3, 1991
36.	Maxine Waters, Calif.	Jan. 3, 1991
37.	John W. Olver, Mass.	June 4, 1991
38.	Ed Pastor, Ariz.	Sept. 24, 1991
39.	Jerrold Nadler, N.Y.	Nov. 3, 1992
40.	Jim Cooper, Tenn.	Jan. 7, 2003
	Also served 1983-95	
41.	Xavier Becerra, Calif.	Jan. 5, 1993
42.	Sanford D. Bishop Jr., Ga.	Jan. 5, 1993
43.	Corrine Brown, Fla.	Jan. 5, 1993
44.	James E. Clyburn, S.C.	Jan. 5, 1993

45.	Anna G. Eshoo, Calif.	Jan. 5, 1993
46.	Bob Filner, Calif.	Jan. 5, 1993
47.	Gene Green, Texas	Jan. 5, 1993
48.	Luis V. Gutierrez, Ill.	Jan. 5, 1993
49.	Alcee L. Hastings, Fla.	Jan. 5, 1993
50.	Maurice D. Hinchey, N.Y.	Jan. 5, 1993
51.	Tim Holden, Pa.	Jan. 5, 1993
52.	Eddie Bernice Johnson, Texas	Jan. 5, 1993
53.	Carolyn B. Maloney, N.Y.	Jan. 5, 1993
54.	Lucille Roybal-Allard, Calif.	Jan. 5, 1993
55.	Bobby L. Rush, Ill.	Jan. 5, 1993
56.	Robert C. Scott, Va.	Jan. 5, 1993
57.	Nydia M. Velázquez, N.Y.	Jan. 5, 1993
58.	Melvin Watt, N.C.	Jan. 5, 1993
59.	Lynn Woolsey, Calif.	Jan. 5, 1993
60.	Bennie Thompson, Miss.	April 13, 1993
61.	Sam Farr, Calif.	June 8, 1993
62.	Lloyd Doggett, Texas	Jan. 4, 1995
63.	Mike Doyle, Pa.	Jan. 4, 1995
64.	Chaka Fattah, Pa.	Jan. 4, 1995
65.	Sheila Jackson Lee, Texas	Jan. 4, 1995
66.	Zoe Lofgren, Calif.	Jan. 4, 1995
67.	Jesse L. Jackson Jr., Ill.	Dec. 12, 1995
68.	Elijah E. Cummings, Md.	April 16, 1996
69.	Earl Blumenauer, Ore.	May 21, 1996
70.	Leonard L. Boswell, Iowa	Jan. 7, 1997
71.	Danny K. Davis, Ill.	Jan. 7, 1997
72.	Diana DeGette, Colo.	Jan. 7, 1997
73.	Rubén Hinojosa, Texas	Jan. 7, 1997
74.	Ron Kind, Wis.	Jan. 7, 1997
75.	Dennis J. Kucinich, Ohio	Jan. 7, 1997
76.	Carolyn McCarthy, N.Y.	Jan. 7, 1997
77.	Jim McGovern, Mass.	Jan. 7, 1997
78.	Mike McIntyre, N.C.	Jan. 7, 1997
79.	Bill Pascrell Jr., N.J.	Jan. 7, 1997
80.	Silvestre Reyes, Texas	Jan. 7, 1997
81.	Steven R. Rothman, N.J.	Jan. 7, 1997
82.	Loretta Sanchez, Calif.	Jan. 7, 1997
83.	Brad Sherman, Calif.	Jan. 7, 1997
84.	Adam Smith, Wash.	Jan. 7, 1997
85.	John F. Tierney, Mass.	Jan. 7, 1997
86.	Gregory W. Meeks, N.Y.	Feb. 3, 1998
87.	Lois Capps, Calif.	March 10, 1998
88.	Barbara Lee, Calif.	April 7, 1998
89.	Robert A. Brady, Pa.	May 19, 1998
90.	Jay Inslee, Wash.	Jan. 6, 1999

		Also served 1993-95
91.	Tammy Baldwin, Wis.	Jan. 6, 1999
92.	Shelley Berkley, Nev.	Jan. 6, 1999
93.	Michael E. Capuano, Mass.	Jan. 6, 1999
94.	Joseph Crowley, N.Y.	Jan. 6, 1999
95.	Charlie Gonzalez, Texas	Jan. 6, 1999
96.	Rush D. Holt, N.J.	Jan. 6, 1999
97.	John B. Larson, Conn.	Jan. 6, 1999
98.	Grace F. Napolitano, Calif.	Jan. 6, 1999
99.	Jan Schakowsky, Ill.	Jan. 6, 1999
100.	Mike Thompson, Calif.	Jan. 6, 1999
101.	Anthony Weiner, N.Y.	Jan. 6, 1999
102.	David Wu, Ore.	Jan. 6, 1999
103.	Joe Baca, Calif.	Nov. 16, 1999
104.	William Lacy Clay, Mo.	Jan. 3, 2001
105.	Susan A. Davis, Calif.	Jan. 3, 2001
106.	Michael M. Honda, Calif.	Jan. 3, 2001
107.	Steve Israel, N.Y.	Jan. 3, 2001
108.	Jim Langevin, R.I.	Jan. 3, 2001
109.	Rick Larsen, Wash.	Jan. 3, 2001
110.	Jim Matheson, Utah	Jan. 3, 2001
111.	Betty McCollum, Minn.	Jan. 3, 2001
112.	Mike Ross, Ark.	Jan. 3, 2001
113.	Adam B. Schiff, Calif.	Jan. 3, 2001
114.	Stephen F. Lynch, Mass.	Oct. 16, 2001
115.	Timothy H. Bishop, N.Y.	Jan. 7, 2003
116.	Dennis Cardoza, Calif.	Jan. 7, 2003
117.	Raúl M. Grijalva, Ariz.	Jan. 7, 2003
118.	Michael H. Michaud, Maine	Jan. 7, 2003
119.	Brad Miller, N.C.	Jan. 7, 2003
120.	C.A. Dutch Ruppersberger, Md.	Jan. 7, 2003
121.	Tim Ryan, Ohio	Jan. 7, 2003
122.	Linda T. Sánchez, Calif.	Jan. 7, 2003
123.	David Scott, Ga.	Jan. 7, 2003
124.	Chris Van Hollen, Md.	Jan. 7, 2003
125.	Ben Chandler, Ky.	Feb. 17, 2004
126.	G.K. Butterfield, N.C.	July 20, 2004
127.	John Barrow, Ga.	Jan. 4, 2005
128.	Dan Boren, Okla.	Jan. 4, 2005
129.	Russ Carnahan, Mo.	Jan. 4, 2005
130.	Emanuel Cleaver II, Mo.	Jan. 4, 2005
131.	Jim Costa, Calif.	Jan. 4, 2005
132.	Henry Cuellar, Texas	Jan. 4, 2005
133.	Al Green, Texas	Jan. 4, 2005
134.	Brian Higgins, N.Y.	Jan. 4, 2005
135.	Daniel Lipinski, Ill.	Jan. 4, 2005
136.	Gwen Moore, Wis.	Jan. 4, 2005
137.	Allyson Y. Schwartz, Pa.	Jan. 4, 2005
138.	Debbie Wasserman Schultz, Fla.	Jan. 4, 2005
139.	Doris Matsui, Calif.	March 8, 2005
140.	Albio Sires, N.J.	Nov. 13, 2006
141.	Jason Altmire, Pa.	Jan. 4, 2007
142.	Bruce Braley, Iowa	Jan. 4, 2007
143.	Kathy Castor, Fla.	Jan. 4, 2007
144.	Yvette D. Clarke, N.Y.	Jan. 4, 2007
145.	Steve Cohen, Tenn.	Jan. 4, 2007
146.	Joe Courtney, Conn.	Jan. 4, 2007
147.	Joe Donnelly, Ind.	Jan. 4, 2007
148.	Keith Ellison, Minn.	Jan. 4, 2007
149.	Gabrielle Giffords, Ariz.	Jan. 4, 2007
150.	Mazie K. Hirono, Hawaii	Jan. 4, 2007
151.	Hank Johnson, Fla.	Jan. 4, 2007
152.	Dave Loebsack, Iowa	Jan. 4, 2007
153.	Jerry McNerney, Calif.	Jan. 4, 2007
154.	Christopher S. Murphy, Conn.	Jan. 4, 2007
155.	Ed Perlmutter, Colo.	Jan. 4, 2007
156.	John Sarbanes, Md.	Jan. 4, 2007
157.	Heath Shuler, N.C.	Jan. 4, 2007
158.	Betty Sutton, Ohio	Jan. 4, 2007
159.	Tim Walz, Minn.	Jan. 4, 2007
160.	Peter Welch, Vt.	Jan. 4, 2007
161.	John Yarmuth, Ky.	Jan. 4, 2007
162.	Laura Richardson, Calif.	Aug. 21, 2007
163.	Niki Tsongas, Mass.	Oct. 16, 2007
164.	André Carson, Ind.	March 11, 2008
165.	Jackie Speier, Calif.	April 8, 2008
166.	Donna Edwards, Md.	June 17, 2008
167.	Marcia L. Fudge, Ohio	Nov. 18, 2008
168.	Gerald E. Connolly, Va.	Jan. 6, 2009
169.	Martin Heinrich, N.M.	Jan. 6, 2009
170.	Jim Himes, Conn.	Jan. 6, 2009
171.	Larry Kissell, N.C.	Jan. 6, 2009
172.	Ben Ray Luján, N.M.	Jan. 6, 2009
173.	Gary Peters, Mich.	Jan. 6, 2009
174.	Chellie Pingree, Maine	Jan. 6, 2009
175.	Jared Polis, Colo.	Jan. 6, 2009
176.	Kurt Schrader, Ore.	Jan. 6, 2009
177.	Paul Tonko, N.Y.	Jan. 6, 2009
178.	Mike Quigley, Ill.	April 7, 2009
179.	Judy Chu, Calif.	July 14, 2009
180.	John Garamendi, Calif.	Nov. 3, 2009
181.	Bill Owens, N.Y.	Nov. 3, 2009
182.	Ted Deutch, Fla.	April 13, 2010
183.	Mark Critz, Pa.	May 18, 2010
184.	Karen Bass, Calif.	Jan. 5, 2011
185.	John Carney, Del.	Jan. 5, 2011
186.	David Cicilline, R.I.	Jan. 5, 2011
187.	Hansen Clarke, Mich.	Jan. 5, 2011
188.	Colleen Hanabusa, Hawaii	Jan. 5, 2011
189.	William Keating, Mass.	Jan. 5, 2011
190.	Cedric L. Richmond, La.	Jan. 5, 2011
191.	Terri A. Sewell, Ala.	Jan. 5, 2011
192.	Frederica S. Wilson, Fla.	Jan. 5, 2011
193.	Kathy Hochul, N.Y.	May 24, 2011

Party Switchers

Four current members changed their party affiliation after they were elected to Congress. Several other members switched before coming to Congress; they are not listed below.

House

Rodney Alexander, La.
Democrat to Republican on Sept. 7, 2004

Ralph M. Hall, Texas
Democrat to Republican on Jan. 5, 2004

Senate

Joseph I. Lieberman, Conn.
Democrat to independent on Jan. 4, 2007

Richard C. Shelby, Ala.
Democrat to Republican on Nov. 9, 1994

Senate Seniority

Seniority is determined by the length of consecutive Senate service from the date of swearing-in. Tie-breakers for those who join the Senate on the same day, in order of precedence, are: previous Senate service, service as the vice president, previous House service, service in the Cabinet, service as a state governor. If a tie still exists, they are ranked according to their state's population at the time of swearing in.

Independents Joseph I. Lieberman and Bernard Sanders caucus with the Democrats. Richard C. Shelby was a Democrat and the GOP Conference credited that service toward his seniority ranking.

DEMOCRATS

1.	Daniel K. Inouye, Hawaii	Jan. 9, 1963
2.	Patrick J. Leahy, Vt.	Jan. 14, 1975
3.	Max Baucus, Mont.	Dec. 15, 1978
4.	Carl Levin, Mich.	Jan. 15, 1979
5.	Jeff Bingaman, N.M.	Jan. 3, 1983
6.	John Kerry, Mass.	Jan. 2, 1985
7.	Tom Harkin, Iowa	Jan. 3, 1985
8.	John D. Rockefeller IV, W.Va.	Jan. 15, 1985
9.	Barbara A. Mikulski, Md.	Jan. 6, 1987
10.	Harry Reid, Nev.	Jan. 6, 1987
11.	Kent Conrad, N.D.	Jan. 6, 1987
12.	Herb Kohl, Wis.	Jan. 3, 1989
13.	Daniel K. Akaka, Hawaii	April 28, 1990
14.	Dianne Feinstein, Calif.	Nov. 4, 1992
15.	Barbara Boxer, Calif.	Jan. 5, 1993
16.	Patty Murray, Wash.	Jan. 5, 1993
17.	Ron Wyden, Ore.	Feb. 6, 1996
18.	Richard J. Durbin, Ill.	Jan. 7, 1997
19.	Tim Johnson, S.D.	Jan. 7, 1997
20.	Jack Reed, R.I.	Jan. 7, 1997
21.	Mary L. Landrieu, La.	Jan. 7, 1997
22.	Charles E. Schumer, N.Y.	Jan. 6, 1999
23.	Bill Nelson, Fla.	Jan. 3, 2001
24.	Thomas R. Carper, Del.	Jan. 3, 2001
25.	Debbie Stabenow, Mich.	Jan. 3, 2001
26.	Maria Cantwell, Wash.	Jan. 3, 2001
27.	Ben Nelson, Neb.	Jan. 3, 2001
28.	Frank R. Lautenberg, N.J.	Jan. 7, 2003
	Also served 1983-2001	
29.	Mark Pryor, Ark.	Jan. 7, 2003
30.	Robert Menendez, N.J.	Jan. 18, 2006
31.	Benjamin L. Cardin, Md.	Jan. 4, 2007
32.	Sherrod Brown, Ohio	Jan. 4, 2007
33.	Bob Casey, Pa.	Jan. 4, 2007
34.	Jim Webb, Va.	Jan. 4, 2007
35.	Claire McCaskill, Mo.	Jan. 4, 2007
36.	Amy Klobuchar, Minn.	Jan. 4, 2007
37.	Sheldon Whitehouse, R.I.	Jan. 4, 2007
38.	Jon Tester, Mont.	Jan. 4, 2007
39.	Mark Udall, Colo.	Jan. 6, 2009
40.	Tom Udall, N.M.	Jan. 6, 2009
41.	Jeanne Shaheen, N.H.	Jan. 6, 2009
42.	Mark Warner, Va.	Jan. 6, 2009
43.	Kay Hagan, N.C.	Jan. 6, 2009
44.	Jeff Merkley, Ore.	Jan. 6, 2009
45.	Mark Begich, Alaska	Jan. 6, 2009
46.	Michael Bennet, Colo.	Jan. 22, 2009
47.	Kirsten Gillibrand, N.Y.	Jan. 27, 2009
48.	Al Franken, Minn.	July 7, 2009
49.	Joe Manchin III, W.Va.	Nov. 15, 2010
50.	Chris Coons, Del.	Nov. 15, 2010
51.	Richard Blumenthal, Conn.	Jan. 5, 2011

REPUBLICANS

1.	Richard G. Lugar, Ind.	Jan. 4, 1977
2.	Orrin G. Hatch, Utah	Jan. 4, 1977
3.	Thad Cochran, Miss.	Dec. 27, 1978
4.	Charles E. Grassley, Iowa	Jan. 5, 1981
5.	Mitch McConnell, Ky.	Jan. 3, 1985
6.	Richard C. Shelby, Ala.	Jan. 6, 1987
7.	John McCain, Ariz.	Jan. 6, 1987
8.	Kay Bailey Hutchison, Texas	June 14, 1993
9.	James M. Inhofe, Okla.	Nov. 30, 1994
10.	Olympia J. Snowe, Maine	Jan. 4, 1995
11.	Jon Kyl, Ariz.	Jan. 4, 1995
12.	Pat Roberts, Kan.	Jan. 7, 1997
13.	Jeff Sessions, Ala.	Jan. 7, 1997
14.	Susan Collins, Maine	Jan. 7, 1997
15.	Michael B. Enzi, Wyo.	Jan. 7, 1997
16.	Michael D. Crapo, Idaho	Jan. 6, 1999
17.	Lisa Murkowski, Alaska	Dec. 20, 2002
18.	Saxby Chambliss, Ga.	Jan. 7, 2003
19.	Lindsey Graham, S.C.	Jan. 7, 2003
20.	Lamar Alexander, Tenn.	Jan. 7, 2003
21.	John Cornyn, Texas	Jan. 7, 2003
22.	Richard M. Burr, N.C.	Jan. 3, 2005
23.	Jim DeMint, S.C.	Jan. 3, 2005
24.	Tom Coburn, Okla.	Jan. 3, 2005
25.	John Thune, S.D.	Jan. 3, 2005
26.	Johnny Isakson, Ga.	Jan. 3, 2005
27.	David Vitter, La.	Jan. 3, 2005
28.	Bob Corker, Tenn.	Jan. 4, 2007
29.	John Barrasso, Wyo.	June 25, 2007
30.	Roger Wicker, Miss.	Dec. 31, 2007
31.	Mike Johanns, Neb.	Jan. 6, 2009
32.	Jim Risch, Idaho	Jan. 6, 2009
33.	Scott P. Brown, Mass.	Feb. 4, 2010
34.	Mark Steven Kirk, Ill.	Nov. 29, 2010
35.	Dan Coats, Ind.	Jan. 5, 2011
36.	Roy Blunt, Mo.	Jan. 5, 2011
37.	Jerry Moran, Kan.	Jan. 5, 2011
38.	Rob Portman, Ohio.	Jan. 5, 2011
39.	John Boozman, Ark.	Jan. 5, 2011
40.	John Hoeven, N.D.	Jan. 5, 2011
41.	Marco Rubio, Fla.	Jan. 5, 2011
42.	Patrick J. Toomey, Pa.	Jan. 5, 2011
43.	Ron Johnson, Wis.	Jan. 5, 2011
44.	Rand Paul, Ky.	Jan. 5, 2011
45.	Mike Lee, Utah	Jan. 5, 2011
46.	Kelly Ayotte, N.H.	Jan. 5, 2011
47.	Dean Heller, Nev.	May 9, 2011

INDEPENDENTS

1.	Joseph I. Lieberman, Conn.	Jan. 3, 1989	2.	Bernard Sanders, Vt.	Jan. 4, 2007

Former Governors

Ten senators have served as governor.

Member	Years	Member	Years
Sen. Lamar Alexander, R-Tenn.	1979-87	Sen. Ben Nelson, D-Neb.	1991-99
Sen. Thomas R. Carper, D-Del.	1993-2001	Sen. Jim Risch, R-Idaho	2006
Sen. John Hoeven, R-N.D. *	2000-10	Sen. John D. Rockefeller IV, D-W.Va.	1977-85
Sen. Mike Johanns, R-Neb.	1999-2005	Sen. Jeanne Shaheen, D-N.H.	1997-2003
Sen. Joe Manchin III, D-W.Va.	2005-10	Sen. Mark Warner, D-Va.	2002-06

Former Lieutenant Governors

Four House members, three senators and two delegates have served as lieutenant governor.

Member	Years	Member	Years
Del. Madeleine Z. Bordallo, D-Guam	1995-2003	Sen. John Kerry, D-Mass.	1983-85
Rep. John Carney, D-Del.*	2001-09	Rep. Denny Rehberg, R-Mont.	1991-97
Del. Eni F.H. Faleomavaega, D-Am. Samoa	1985-89	Sen. Harry Reid, D-Nev.	1971-75
Rep. John Garamendi, D-Calif.	2007-09	Sen. Jim Risch, R-Idaho	2003-06, 2007-09
Rep. Mazie K. Hirono, D-Hawaii	1994-2002		

Former Representatives in the Senate

25 Republicans, 22 Democrats, 1 independent

Member	House Service	Member	House Service
Daniel K. Akaka, D-Hawaii	1977-90	Tim Johnson, D-S.D.	1987-97
Max Baucus, D-Mont.	1975-78	Mark Steven Kirk, R-Ill.	2001-10
Roy Blunt, R-Mo.†	1997-2011	Jon Kyl, R-Ariz.	1987-95
John Boozman, R-Ark. †	2001-11	John McCain, R-Ariz.	1983-87
Barbara Boxer, D-Calif.	1983-93	Robert Menendez, D-N.J.	1993-2006
Sherrod Brown, D-Ohio	1993-2007	Barbara A. Mikulski, D-Md.	1977-87
Richard M. Burr, R-N.C.	1995-2005	Jerry Moran, R-Kan. †	1997-2011
Maria Cantwell, D-Wash.	1993-95	Bill Nelson, D-Fla.	1979-91
Benjamin L. Cardin, D-Md.	1987-2007	Rob Portman, R-Ohio †	1993-2005
Thomas R. Carper, D-Del.	1983-93	Jack Reed, D-R.I.	1991-97
Saxby Chambliss, R-Ga.	1995-2003	Harry Reid, D-Nev.	1983-87
Dan Coats, R-Ind.	1981-89	Pat Roberts, R-Kan.	1981-97
Tom Coburn, R-Okla.	1995-2001	Bernard Sanders, I-Vt.	1991-2007
Thad Cochran, R-Miss.	1973-78	Charles E. Schumer, D-N.Y.	1981-99
Michael D. Crapo, R-Idaho	1993-99	Richard C. Shelby, R-Ala.	1979-87
Jim DeMint, R-S.C.	1999-2005	Olympia J. Snowe, R-Maine	1979-95
Richard J. Durbin, D-Ill.	1983-97	Debbie Stabenow, D-Mich.	1997-2001
Kirsten Gillibrand, D-N.Y.	2007-09	John Thune, R-S.D.	1997-2003
Lindsey Graham, R-S.C.	1995-2003	Patrick J. Toomey, R-Pa. †	1999-2005
Charles E. Grassley, R-Iowa	1975-81	Mark Udall, D-Colo.	1999-2009
Tom Harkin, D-Iowa	1975-85	Tom Udall, D-N.M.	1999-2009
James M. Inhofe, R-Okla.	1987-94	David Vitter, R-La.	1999-2005
Daniel K. Inouye, D-Hawaii	1959-63	Roger Wicker, R-Miss.	1995-2007
Johnny Isakson, R-Ga.	1999-2005	Ron Wyden, D-Ore.	1981-96

*New to Congress
† New to the Senate

Women in Congress

Senate (12 D, 5 R)
Kelly Ayotte, R-N.H.*
Barbara Boxer, D-Calif.
Maria Cantwell, D-Wash.
Susan Collins, R-Maine
Dianne Feinstein, D-Calif.
Kirsten Gillibrand, D-N.Y.
Kay Hagan, D-N.C.
Kay Bailey Hutchison, R-Texas
Amy Klobuchar, D-Minn.
Mary L. Landrieu, D-La.
Claire McCaskill, D-Mo.
Barbara A. Mikulski, D-Md.
Lisa Murkowski, R-Alaska
Patty Murray, D-Wash.
Jeanne Shaheen, D-N.H.
Olympia J. Snowe, R-Maine
Debbie Stabenow, D-Mich.

House (51 D, 24 R)
Sandy Adams, R-Fla.*
Michele Bachmann, R-Minn.
Tammy Baldwin, D-Wis.
Karen Bass, D-Calif.*
Shelley Berkley, D-Nev.
Judy Biggert, R-Ill.
Diane Black, R-Tenn.*
Marsha Blackburn, R-Tenn.
Mary Bono Mack, R-Calif.
Del. Madeleine Z. Bordallo, D-Guam
Corrine Brown, D-Fla.
Ann Marie Buerkle, R-N.Y.*

Shelley Moore Capito, R-W.Va.
Lois Capps, D-Calif.
Kathy Castor, D-Fla.
Del. Donna M.C. Christensen, D-V.I.
Judy Chu, D-Calif.
Yvette D. Clarke, D-N.Y.
Susan A. Davis, D-Calif.
Diana DeGette, D-Colo.
Rosa DeLauro, D-Conn.
Donna Edwards, D-Md.
Renee Ellmers, R-N.C.*
Jo Ann Emerson, R-Mo.
Anna G. Eshoo, D-Calif.
Virginia Foxx, R-N.C.
Marcia L. Fudge, D-Ohio
Gabrielle Giffords, D-Ariz.
Kay Granger, R-Texas
Colleen Hanabusa, D-Hawaii*
Vicky Hartzler, R-Mo.*
Nan Hayworth, R-N.Y.*
Jaime Herrera Beutler, R-Wash.*
Mazie K. Hirono, D-Hawaii
Kathy Hochul, D-N.Y.*
Sheila Jackson Lee, D-Texas
Lynn Jenkins, R-Kan.
Eddie Bernice Johnson, D-Texas
Marcy Kaptur, D-Ohio
Barbara Lee, D-Calif.
Zoe Lofgren, D-Calif.
Nita M. Lowey, D-N.Y.
Cynthia M. Lummis, R-Wyo.
Carolyn B. Maloney, D-N.Y.

Doris Matsui, D-Calif.
Carolyn McCarthy, D-N.Y.
Betty McCollum, D-Minn.
Cathy McMorris Rodgers, R-Wash.
Candice S. Miller, R-Mich.
Gwen Moore, D-Wis.
Sue Myrick, R-N.C.
Grace F. Napolitano, D-Calif.
Kristi Noem, R-S.D.*
Del. Eleanor Holmes Norton, D-D.C.
Nancy Pelosi, D-Calif.
Chellie Pingree, D-Maine
Laura Richardson, D-Calif.
Martha Roby, R-Ala.*
Ileana Ros-Lehtinen, R-Fla.
Lucille Roybal-Allard, D-Calif.
Linda T. Sánchez, D-Calif.
Loretta Sanchez, D-Calif.
Jan Schakowsky, D-Ill.
Jean Schmidt, R-Ohio
Allyson Y. Schwartz, D-Pa.
Terri A. Sewell, D-Ala.*
Louise M. Slaughter, D-N.Y.
Jackie Speier, D-Calif.
Betty Sutton, D-Ohio
Niki Tsongas, D-Mass.
Nydia M. Velázquez, D-N.Y.
Debbie Wasserman Schultz, D-Fla.
Maxine Waters, D-Calif.
Frederica S. Wilson, D-Fla.*
Lynn Woolsey, D-Calif.

Oldest Members of Congress

Member	Birth date
Rep. Ralph M. Hall, R-Texas	5/3/1923
Sen. Frank R. Lautenberg, D-N.J.	1/23/1924
Sen. Daniel K. Inouye, D-Hawaii	9/7/1924
Sen. Daniel K. Akaka, D-Hawaii	9/11/1924
Rep. Roscoe G. Bartlett, R-Md.	6/3/1926
Rep. John D. Dingell, D-Mich.	7/8/1926
Rep. John Conyers Jr., D-Mich.	5/16/1929
Rep. Louise M. Slaughter, D-N.Y.	8/14/1929
Rep. Dale E. Kildee, D-Mich.	9/16/1929
Rep. Charles B. Rangel, D-N.Y.	6/11/1930
Rep. Sam Johnson, R-Texas	10/11/1930
Rep. C.W. Bill Young, R-Fla.	12/16/1930
Rep. Howard Coble, R-N.C.	3/18/1931
Rep. Sander M. Levin, D-Mich.	9/6/1931
Rep. Pete Stark, D-Calif.	11/11/1931

Youngest Members of Congress

Member	Birth date
Rep. Aaron Schock, R-Ill.	5/28/1981
Rep. Justin Amash, R-Mich.*	4/18/1980
Rep. Jaime Herrera Beutler, R-Wash.*	11/3/1978
Rep. Adam Kinzinger, R-Ill.*	2/27/1978
Rep. Duncan Hunter, R-Calif.	12/7/1976
Rep. Ben Quayle, R-Ariz.*	11/5/1976
Rep. Marlin Stutzman, R-Ind.	8/31/1976
Rep. Martha Roby, R-Ala.*	7/26/1976
Rep. Kevin Yoder, R-Kan.*	1/8/1976
Rep. Patrick T. McHenry, R-N.C.	10/22/1975
Rep. Jared Polis, D-Colo.	5/12/1975
Rep. André Carson, D-Ind.	10/16/1974
Rep. Cory Gardner, R-Colo.*	8/22/1974
Rep. Jon Runyan, R-N.J.*	11/27/1973
Rep. Devin Nunes, R-Calif.	10/1/1973

* New to Congress

Minorities in Congress

American Indian

House (1 R)
Tom Cole, R-Okla.

Asian

Senate (2 D)
Daniel K. Akaka, D-Hawaii
Daniel K. Inouye, D-Hawaii

House (8 D, 1 R)
Steve Austria, R-Ohio
Judy Chu, D-Calif.
Del. Eni F.H. Faleomavaega, D-Am. Samoa
Colleen Hanabusa, D-Hawaii*
Mazie K. Hirono, D-Hawaii
Michael M. Honda, D-Calif.
Doris Matsui, D-Calif.
Del. Gregorio Kilili Camacho Sablan, D-N. Marianas
David Wu, D-Ore.

Hispanic

Senate (1 D, 1 R)
Robert Menendez, D-N.J.
Marco Rubio, R-Fla.*

House (18 D, 7 R)
Joe Baca, D-Calif.
Xavier Becerra, D-Calif.
Francisco "Quico" Canseco, R-Texas*
Henry Cuellar, D-Texas
Mario Diaz-Balart, R-Fla.
Bill Flores, R-Texas*
Charlie Gonzalez, D-Texas
Raúl M. Grijalva, D-Ariz.
Luis V. Gutierrez, D-Ill.
Jaime Herrera Beutler, R-Wash.*
Rubén Hinojosa, D-Texas
Raúl R. Labrador, R-Idaho*
Ben Ray Luján, D-N.M.
Grace F. Napolitano, D-Calif.
Ed Pastor, D-Ariz.
Res. Cmmsr. Pedro R. Pierluisi, D-P.R.
Silvestre Reyes, D-Texas
David Rivera, R-Fla.*
Ileana Ros-Lehtinen, R-Fla.
Lucille Roybal-Allard, D-Calif.
Linda T. Sánchez, D-Calif.
Loretta Sanchez, D-Calif.
José E. Serrano, D-N.Y.
Albio Sires, D-N.J.
Nydia M. Velázquez, D-N.Y.

Black

House (42 D, 2R)
Karen Bass, D-Calif.*
Sanford D. Bishop Jr., D-Ga.
Corrine Brown, D-Fla.
G.K. Butterfield, D-N.C.
André Carson, D-Ind.
Del. Donna M.C. Christensen, D-V.I.
Hansen Clarke, D-Mich.*
Yvette D. Clarke, D-N.Y.
William Lacy Clay, D-Mo.
Emanuel Cleaver II, D-Mo.
James E. Clyburn, D-S.C.
John Conyers Jr., D-Mich.
Elijah E. Cummings, D-Md.
Danny K. Davis, D-Ill.
Donna Edwards, D-Md.
Keith Ellison, D-Minn.
Chaka Fattah, D-Pa.
Marcia L. Fudge, D-Ohio
Al Green, D-Texas
Alcee L. Hastings, D-Fla.
Jesse L. Jackson Jr., D-Ill.
Sheila Jackson Lee, D-Texas
Eddie Bernice Johnson, D-Texas
Hank Johnson, D-Ga.
Barbara Lee, D-Calif.
John Lewis, D-Ga.
Gregory W. Meeks, D-N.Y.
Gwen Moore, D-Wis.
Del. Eleanor Holmes Norton, D-D.C.
Donald M. Payne, D-N.J.
Charles B. Rangel, D-N.Y.
Laura Richardson, D-Calif.
Cedric I. Richmond, D-La.*
Bobby L. Rush, D-Ill.
David Scott, D-Ga.
Robert C. Scott, D-Va.
Tim Scott, R-S.C.*
Terri A. Sewell, D-Ala.*
Bennie Thompson, D-Miss.
Edolphus Towns, D-N.Y.
Maxine Waters, D-Calif.
Melvin Watt, D-N.C.
Allen B. West, R-Fla.*
Frederica S. Wilson, D-Fla.*

Born Abroad

There are 13 lawmakers and three delegates who were born outside the 50 states and Washington, D.C.

Member	Country
Del. Eni F.H. Faleomavaega, D-Am. Samoa	Am. Samoa
Rep. Geoff Davis, R-Ky.	Canada
Rep. Ileana Ros-Lehtinen, R-Fla.	Cuba
Rep. Albio Sires, D-N.J.	Cuba
Sen. Michael Bennet, D-Colo.	India
Rep. Diana DeGette, D-Colo.	Japan
Rep. Mazie K. Hirono, D-Hawaii	Japan
Del. Gregorio Kilili Camacho Sablan, D-N. Marianas	N. Marianas
Rep. Chris Van Hollen, D-Md.	Pakistan
Sen. John McCain, R-Ariz.	Panama Canal Zone
Rep. Jim Himes, D-Conn.	Peru
Rep. Raúl R. Labrador, R-Idaho*	Puerto Rico
Res. Cmmsr. Pedro R. Pierluisi, D-P.R.	Puerto Rico
Rep. José E. Serrano, D-N.Y.	Puerto Rico
Rep. Nydia M. Velázquez, D-N.Y.	Puerto Rico
Rep. David Wu, D-Ore.	Taiwan

* New to Congress

Former Congressional Staffers

Below are the 82 members who previously worked as paid, full-time congressional aides. Internships, fellowships and campaign work are not included.

Member	Congressional Office	Years
Sen. Lamar Alexander, R-Tenn.	Sen. Howard H. Baker Jr., R-Tenn.	1967-68
Rep. Jason Altmire, D-Pa.	Rep. Pete Peterson, D-Fla.	1991-96
Rep. Charles Bass, R-N.H.	Sen. William S. Cohen, R-Maine	1974
	Rep. David F. Emery	1975-79
Sen. Richard Blumenthal, D-Conn.	Sen. Abraham A. Ribicoff, D-Conn.	1975-76
Rep. Jo Bonner, R-Ala.	Rep. Sonny Callahan, R-Ala.	1985-2002
Rep. Dan Boren, D-Okla.	Rep. Wes Watkins, R-Okla.	2000-01
Sen. Barbara Boxer, D-Calif.	Rep. John L. Burton, D-Calif.	1974-76
Rep. Dave Camp, R-Mich.	Rep. Bill Schuette, R-Mich.	1984-87
Rep. Dennis Cardoza, D-Calif.	Rep. Gary A. Condit, D-Calif.	1989
Rep. John Carney, D-Del.	Sen. Joseph R. Biden Jr.	1987-89
Rep. Hansen Clarke, D-Mich.	Rep. John Conyers Jr., D-Mich.	1989-90
Rep. William Lacy Clay, D-Mo.	House Clerk	1977-83
Sen. Dan Coats, R-Ind.	Rep. Dan Quayle, R-Ind.	1976-80
Rep. Tom Cole, R-Okla.	Rep. Mickey Edwards, R-Okla.	1982-84
Sen. Susan Collins, R-Maine	Rep./Sen. William S. Cohen, R-Maine	1975-87
Rep. Gerald E. Connolly, D-Va.	Senate Foreign Relations Committee	1979-89
Rep. John Conyers Jr., D-Mich.	Rep. John D. Dingell, D-Mich.	1958-61
Rep. Jim Costa, D-Calif.	Rep. John Krebs, D-Calif.	1975-76
Rep. Mark Critz, D-Pa.	Rep. John P. Murtha, D-Pa.	2001-10
Rep. Peter A. DeFazio, D-Ore.	Rep. James Weaver, D-Ore.	1977-82
Rep. Rosa DeLauro, D-Conn.	Sen. Christopher J. Dodd, D-Conn.	1981-87
Rep. Charlie Dent, R-Pa.	Rep. Don Ritter, R-Pa.	1982
Rep. Norm Dicks, D-Wash.	Sen. Warren G. Magnuson, D-Wash.	1968-76
Rep. Robert Dold, R-Ill.	House Government Reform and Oversight Committee	1996-98
Del. Eni F.H. Faleomavaega, D-Am. Samoa	Del. A.U. Fuimaono, D-Am. Samoa	1973-75
	House Interior and Insular Affairs Committee	1975-81
Rep. Bob Filner, D-Calif.	Sen. Hubert H. Humphrey, D-Minn.	1975
	Rep. Donald M. Fraser, D-Minn.	1976
	Rep. Jim Bates, D-Calif.	1984
Rep. Jeff Fortenberry, R-Neb.	Senate Governmental Affairs subcommittee	1985-86
Rep. Barney Frank, D-Mass.	Rep. Michael Harrington, D-Mass.	1971-72
Rep. Marcia L. Fudge, D-Ohio	Rep. Stephanie Tubbs Jones, D-Ohio	1999
Rep. Cory Gardner, R-Colo.	Sen. Wayne Allard, R-Colo.	2002-05
Rep. Robert W. Goodlatte, R-Va.	Rep. M. Caldwell Butler, R-Va.	1977-79
Rep. Tim Griffin, R-Ark.	House Government Reform Committee	1997-99
Rep. Frank Guinta, R-N.H.	Rep. Jeb Bradley, R-N.H.	2003-05
Sen. Tom Harkin, D-Iowa	Rep. Neal Smith, D-Iowa	1969-70
Rep. Jeb Hensarling, R-Texas	Sen. Phil Gramm, R-Texas	1985-89
Rep. Jaime Herrera Beutler, R-Wash.	Rep. Cathy McMorris Rodgers, R-Wash.	2005-07
Rep. Kathy Hochul, D-N.Y.	Rep. John J. LaFalce, D-N.Y.	1984-86
	Sen. Daniel Patrick Moynihan, D-N.Y.	1986-88
Rep. Bill Huizenga, R-Mich.	Rep. Peter Hoekstra, R-Mich.	1997-2003
Rep. Randy Hultgren, R-Ill.	Rep. J. Dennis Hastert, R-Ill.	1988-90
Rep. Steve Israel, D-N.Y.	Rep. Richard L. Ottinger, D-N.Y.	1980-83
Rep. Sheila Jackson Lee, D-Texas	House Select Committee on Assassinations	1977-78
Sen. Mark Steven Kirk, R-Ill.	Rep. John Edward Porter, R-Ill.	1984-89
	House International Relations Committee	1995-2000
Rep. Barbara Lee, D-Calif.	Rep. Ronald V. Dellums, D-Calif.	1975-86
Rep. Jerry Lewis, R-Calif.	Rep. Jerry L. Pettis, R-Calif.	1967
Rep. Daniel Lipinski, D-Ill.	Rep. Rod R. Blagojevich, D-Ill.	1999-2000
Rep. Zoe Lofgren, D-Calif.	Rep. Don Edwards, D-Calif.	1970-79
Rep. Kevin McCarthy, R-Calif.	Rep. Bill Thomas, R-Calif.	1987-2002
Sen. Mitch McConnell, R-Ky.	Sen. Marlow W. Cook, R-Ky.	1969-70
Rep. Jim McGovern, D-Mass.	Rep. Joe Moakley, D-Mass.	1981-93
Rep. Patrick Meehan, R-Pa.	Sen. Arlen Specter, R-Pa.	1990, 1992-94
Sen. Jeff Merkley, D-Ore.	Congressional Budget Office	1985-89

Rep. John L. Mica, R-Fla.	
Rep. James P. Moran, D-Va.	
Rep. Pete Olson, R-Texas	
Rep. Erik Paulsen, R-Minn.	
Rep. Nick J. Rahall II, D-W.Va.	
Rep. Denny Rehberg, R-Mont.	
Rep. Laura Richardson, D-Calif.	
Rep. David Rivera, R-Fla.	
Sen. Pat Roberts, R-Kan.	
Rep. Tom Rooney, R-Fla.	
Rep. Peter Roskam, R-Ill.	
Rep. Paul D. Ryan, R-Wis.	
Rep. Tim Ryan, D-Ohio	
Sen. Olympia J. Snowe, R-Maine	
Rep. Jackie Speier	
Rep. William M. "Mac" Thornberry, R-Texas	
Sen. John Thune, R-S.D.	
Rep. Pat Tiberi, R-Ohio	
Sen. Tom Udall, D-N.M.	
Rep. Fred Upton, R-Mich.	
Rep. Chris Van Hollen, D-Md.	
Rep. Nydia M. Velázquez, D-N.Y.	
Rep. Peter J. Visclosky, D-Ind.	
Rep. Greg Walden, R-Ore.	
Sen. Jim Webb, D-Va.	
Rep. Anthony Weiner, D-N.Y.	
Sen. Roger Wicker, R-Miss.	
Rep. Frank R. Wolf, R-Va.	
Rep. Rob Woodall, R-Ga.	
Rep. John Yarmuth, D-Ky.	
Rep. Todd Young, R-Ind.	

Sen. Paula Hawkins, R-Fla.	1981-85
Senate Appropriations Committee	1976-79
Sen. Phil Gramm, R-Texas	1998-2002
Sen. John Cornyn, R-Texas	2002-07
Rep. Jim Ramstad, R-Minn.	1990-94
Sen. Robert C. Byrd, D-W.Va.	1971-74
Rep. Ron Marlenee, R-Mont.	1979-82
Sen. Conrad Burns, R-Mont.	1989-91
Rep. Juanita Millender-McDonald, D-Calif.	1996-98
Sen. Connie Mack, R-Fla.	1989
Sen. Frank Carlson, R-Kan.	1967-68
Rep. Keith G. Sebelius, R-Kan.	1968-80
Sen. Connie Mack, R-Fla.	1993
Rep. Tom DeLay, R-Texas	1985-86
Rep. Henry J. Hyde, R-Ill.	1986-87
Sen. Bob Kasten, R-Wis.	1992
Rep./Sen. Sam Brownback, R-Kan.	1995-97
Rep. James A. Traficant Jr., D-Ohio	1995-97
Rep. William S. Cohen, R-Maine	1973
Rep. Leo Ryan, D-Calif.	1976-78
Rep. Tom Loeffler, R-Texas	1983-85
Rep. Larry Combest, R-Texas	1985-88
Sen. James Abdnor, R-S.D.	1985-86
Senate Small Business Committee	1989
Rep. John R. Kasich, R-Ohio	1983-91
Sen. Joseph R. Biden Jr., D-Del.	1973
Rep. David A. Stockman, R-Mich.	1977-81
Sen. Charles McC. Mathias Jr., R-Md.	1985-87
Senate Foreign Relations Committee	1987-89
Rep. Edolphus Towns, D-N.Y.	1983
Rep. Adam Benjamin Jr., D-Ind.	1977-82
Rep. Denny Smith, R-Ore.	1981-86
House Veterans' Affairs Committee	1977-81
Rep. Charles E. Schumer, D-N.Y.	1985-91
Rep. Trent Lott, R-Miss.	1980-82
Rep. Edward G. Biester, R-Pa.	1968-71
Rep. John Linder, R-Ga.	1994-2010
Sen. Marlow W. Cook, R-Ky.	1971-74
Sen. Richard G. Lugar, R-Ind.	2001-03

Born in D.C.

Member
Rep. Jo Ann Emerson, R-Mo.
Rep. Hank Johnson, D-Ga.
Del. Eleanor Holmes Norton, D-D.C.
Rep. Bill Posey, R-Fla.
Rep. Robert C. Scott, D-Va.
Rep. Adam Smith, D-Wash.
Rep. Cliff Stearns, R-Fla.
Rep. Rob Wittman, R-Va.

Former Pages

There are 10 members of Congress who once served as congressional pages:

Member	Years
Sen. Michael Bennet, D-Colo.	—
Rep. Dan Boren, D-Okla.	1989
Rep. Jim Cooper, D-Tenn.	1970
Rep. Ander Crenshaw, R-Fla.	1961
Rep. John D. Dingell, D-Mich.	1938-42
Rep. Rush D. Holt, D-N.J.	1963-64
Sen. Mike Lee, R-Utah	1987
Sen. Mark Pryor, D-Ark.	1982
Rep. Ben Quayle, R-Ariz.	1991-92
Sen. Roger Wicker, R-Miss.	1967

Members Who Served in the Military

There are 115 members with military service, including in the National Guard and reserves. The years of service includes both active and inactive duty, and an asterisk denotes a combat veteran.

Senate (13 R, 12 D)	Years
Daniel K. Akaka, D-Hawaii *	1945-47
Jeff Bingaman, D-N.M.	1968-74
Richard Blumenthal, D-Conn.	1970-75
Scott P. Brown, R-Mass.	1979-present
Thomas R. Carper, D-Del. *	1968-91
Dan Coats, R-Ind.	1966-68
Thad Cochran, R-Miss.	1959-61
Michael B. Enzi, R-Wyo.	1967-73
Lindsey Graham, R-S.C.	1982-1996, 2003-present
Tom Harkin, D-Iowa	1962-74
James M. Inhofe, R-Okla.	1957-58
Daniel K. Inouye, D-Hawaii *	1943-47
Johnny Isakson, R-Ga.	1966-72
John Kerry, D-Mass. *	1966-70
Mark Steven Kirk, R-Ill.	1989-present
Herb Kohl, D-Wis.	1958-64
Frank R. Lautenberg, D-N.J.	1942-46
Richard G. Lugar, R-Ind.	1957-60
John McCain, R-Ariz. *	1958-81
Bill Nelson, D-Fla.	1965-71
Jack Reed, D-R.I.	1971-91
Pat Roberts, R-Kan.	1958-62
Jeff Sessions, R-Ala.	1973-86
Jim Webb, D-Va. *	1968-72
Roger Wicker, R-Miss.	1976-2004

House (64 R, 26 D)	Years
Sandy Adams, R-Fla.	1974-75
Todd Akin, R-Mo.	1972-80
Rodney Alexander, R-La.	1965-71
Joe Baca, D-Calif.	1966-68
Spencer Bachus, R-Ala.	1969-71
Sanford D. Bishop Jr., D-Ga.	1971
John A. Boehner, R-Ohio	1968
Leonard L. Boswell, D-Iowa *	1956-76
Paul Broun, R-Ga.	1964-73
Vern Buchanan, R-Fla.	1970-76
Larry Bucshon, R-Ind.	1989-98
Dan Burton, R-Ind.	1956-62
G.K. Butterfield, D-N.C.	1968-70
Howard Coble, R-N.C. *	1952-56, 1960-82
Mike Coffman, R-Colo. *	1972-94, 2005-06
K. Michael Conaway, R-Texas	1970-72
John Conyers Jr., D-Mich. *	1948-57
Chip Cravaack, R-Minn.	1981-2005
Rick Crawford, R-Ark.*	1985-89
Geoff Davis, R-Ky.	1976-87
Peter A. DeFazio, D-Ore.	1967-71
Jeff Denham, R-Calif.	1984-2000
John D. Dingell, D-Mich. *	1944-46
John J."Jimmy" Duncan Jr., R-Tenn.	1970-87

	Years
Eni F.H. Faleomavaega, D-Am. Samoa	1966-69, 1983-2001
John Fleming, R-La.	1976-82
Rodney Frelinghuysen, R-N.J. *	1969-71
Chris Gibson, R-N.Y. *	1986-2010
Louie Gohmert, R-Texas	1978-82
Charlie Gonzalez, D-Texas	1969-75
Tim Griffin, R-Ark. *	1996-present
Michael G. Grimm, R-N.Y. *	1989-97
Brett Guthrie, R-Ky.	1987-2002
Ralph M. Hall, R-Texas *	1942-45
Andy Harris, R-Md.	1988-2005
Doc Hastings, R-Wash.	1964-69
Joe Heck, R-Nev. *	1991-present
Maurice D. Hinchey, D-N.Y.	1956-59
Duncan Hunter, R-Calif. *	2002-08
Darrell Issa, R-Calif.	1970-72, 1976-88
Bill Johnson, R-Ohio	1973-99
Sam Johnson, R-Texas *	1951-79
Walter B. Jones, R-N.C.	1967-71
Peter T. King, R-N.Y.	1968-73
Adam Kinzinger, R-Ill. *	2001-present
John Kline, R-Minn. *	1969-94
Jeff Landry, R-La.	1987-98
Edward J. Markey, D-Mass.	1968-73
Jim McDermott, D-Wash.	1968-70
Gary G. Miller, R-Calif.	1967
Tim Murphy, R-Pa.	2009-present
Rich Nugent, R-Fla.	1969-75
Pete Olson, R-Texas	1988-98
Bill Owens, D-N.Y.	1971-82
Steven M. Palazzo, R-Miss. *	1988-present
Bill Pascrell Jr., D-N.J.	1961-67
Ron Paul, R-Texas	1963-68
Steve Pearce, R-N.M. *	1970-76
Gary Peters, D-Mich.	1993-2000, 2001-05
Collin C. Peterson, D-Minn.	1963-69
Joe Pitts, R-Pa. *	1963-69
Ted Poe, R-Texas	1970-76
Mike Pompeo, R-Kan.	1986-91
Charles B. Rangel, D-N.Y. *	1948-52
Dave Reichert, R-Wash.	1971-76
Silvestre Reyes, D-Texas *	1966-68
Scott Rigell, R-Va.	1978-84
Phil Roe, R-Tenn.	1973-74
Harold Rogers, R-Ky.	1956-63
Mike Rogers, R-Mich.	1985-88
Tom Rooney, R-Fla.	2000-04
Bobby L. Rush, D-Ill.	1963-68
Gregorio Kilili Camacho Sablan, D-M.P.	1981-86
Robert C. Scott, D-Va.	1970-76
José E. Serrano, D-N.Y.	1964-66

John Shimkus, R-Ill.	1980-2008	Steve Womack, R-Ark.	1979-2009
Pete Stark, D-Calif.	1955-57	C.W. Bill Young, R-Fla.	1948-57
Cliff Stearns, R-Fla.	1963-67	Don Young, R-Alaska	1955-57
Steve Stivers, R-Ohio *	1988-present	Todd Young, R-Ind.	1995-2000
Mike Thompson, D-Calif. *	1969-73		
Edolphus Towns, D-N.Y.	1956-58		
Tim Walz, D-Minn.	1981-2005		
Allen B. West, R-Fla. *	1983-2004		
Edward Whitfield, R-Ky.	1967-73		
Joe Wilson, R-S.C.	1972-2003		
Frank R. Wolf, R-Va.	1962-63		

Members Whose Children Served in Iraq or Afghanistan

Member	Child's Name	Relationship	Branch
Rep. Todd Akin, R-Mo.	Perry Akin	son	Marines
Rep. Jo Ann Emerson, R-Mo.	Jessica Gladney	stepdaughter	Army
Sen. Tim Johnson, D-S.D.	Brooks Johnson	son	Army
Rep. John Kline, R-Minn.	John Daniel Kline	son	Army
Rep. Rich Nugent, R-Fla.	Ryan Nugent	son	Army
	Casey Nugent	son	Army
Rep. Ileana Ros-Lehtinen, R-Fla.	Douglas Lehtinen	stepson	Marines
	Lindsey Nelson Lehtinen	daughter-in-law	Marines
Rep. Lucille Roybal-Allard, D-Calif.	Guy Mark Allard	stepson	Army
Rep. Glenn Thompson, R-Pa.	Logan Thompson	son	Army
Sen. Jim Webb, D-Va.	Jimmy Webb	son	Marines
Rep. Joe Wilson, R-S.C.	Alan Wilson	son	S.C. National Guard

Eagle Scouts

Rep. Gary L. Ackerman, D-N.Y.
Sen. Lamar Alexander, R-Tenn.
Rep. Sanford D. Bishop Jr., D-Ga.
Sen. Jeff Bingaman, D-N.M.
Sen. Sherrod Brown, D-Ohio
Rep. Russ Carnahan, D-Mo.
Sen. Thad Cochran, R-Miss.
Rep. Jim Cooper, D-Tenn.
Sen. Michael D. Crapo, R-Idaho
Rep. Robert Dold, R-Ill.

Sen. Michael B. Enzi, R-Wyo.
Rep. Michael G. Fitzpatrick, R-Pa.
Rep. Louie Gohmert, R-Texas
Rep. Sam Graves, R-Mo.
Rep. Jeb Hensarling, R-Texas
Sen. Mike Lee, R-Utah
Sen. Richard G. Lugar, R-Ind.
Sen. Jeff Merkley, D-Ore.
Sen. Ben Nelson, D-Neb.
Rep. Phil Roe, R-Tenn.

Rep. Dana Rohrabacher, R-Calif.
Sen. Jeff Sessions, R-Ala.
Rep. Pete Sessions, R-Texas
Rep. Christopher H. Smith, R-N.J.
Rep. Steve Stivers, R-Ohio
Rep. Glenn Thompson, R-Pa.
Sen. Patrick J. Toomey, R-Pa.
Rep. Greg Walden, R-Ore.
Rep. Joe Wilson, R-S.C.

Peace Corps Volunteers

Member	Country	Years
Rep. Sam Farr, D-Calif.	Colombia	1964-66
Rep. John Garamendi, D-Calif.	Ethiopia	1966-68
Rep. Michael M. Honda, D-Calif.	El Salvador	1965-67
Rep. Tom Petri, R-Wis.	Somalia	1966-67

Fastest Members of Congress

Some members participate in an annual 3-mile footrace in Washington, D.C. Here are the times posted by the 18 who ran in the May 2011 race. Sen. John Thune was the only member to run the course in less than 20 minutes.

Member	Time	Member	Time
Sen. John Thune, R-S.D.	18:54	Rep. Earl Blumenauer, D-Ore.	28:11
Rep. Aaron Schock, R-Ill.	20:12	Rep. José E. Serrano, D-N.Y.	29:42
Rep. Russ Carnahan, D-Mo.	24:29	Sen. Jack Reed, D-R.I.	30:13
Rep. Jean Schmidt, R-Ohio	24:49	Sen. Charles E. Grassley, R-Iowa	31:40
Rep. John Sullivan, R-Okla.	25:09	Rep. Mark Critz, D-Pa.	31:53
Rep. Todd R. Platts, R-Pa.	25:49	Sen. Jeff Bingaman, D-N.M.	33:35
Rep. Charlie Dent, R-Pa.	25:50	Sen. Kay Hagan, D-N.C.	35:05
Sen. Kelly Ayotte, R-N.H.	26:40	Sen. Kay Bailey Hutchison, R-Texas	43:05
Rep. Rob Wittman, R-Va.	26:40	Sen. Richard G. Lugar, R-Ind.	44:40

Most and Least Legislation

These members served in the entire 111th Congress (2009-10) and introduced the most and least legislation. Members whose names are in italics are no longer in Congress.

Most — Senate

Charles E. Schumer, D-N.Y.*	155
Arlen Specter, D-Pa.	134
Dianne Feinstein, D-Calif.*	125
Bob Casey, D-Pa.	124
John Kerry, D-Mass.*	120
Sherrod Brown, D-Ohio	117
Robert Menendez, D-N.J.	116
Harry Reid, D-Nev.*	113
David Vitter, R-La.	100
Russ Feingold, D-Wis. *	91
Blanche Lincoln, D-Ark.	91

Most — House

Alcee L. Hastings, D-Fla.*	83
Ileana Ros-Lehtinen, R-Fla.	78
Carolyn B. Maloney, D-N.Y.*	74
Joe Sestak, D-Pa.	71
Sheila Jackson Lee, D-Texas*	69
John Conyers Jr., D-Mich.	67
Bob Filner, D-Calif.*	64
Ron Paul, R-Texas*	64
Barbara Lee, D-Calif.*	62
Jim McDermott, D-Wash.	57
Jim McGovern, D-Mass.	57

Least — Senate

Jim Risch, R-Idaho	5
Richard C. Shelby, R-Ala. †	7
Bob Corker, R-Tenn. †	8
Michael B. Enzi, R-Wyo.	10
Thad Cochran, R-Miss. †	11
Jon Kyl, R-Ariz.	11
Tom Coburn, R-Okla. †	13
Judd Gregg, R-N.H.	13
Mike Johanns, R-Neb.	15
John Barrasso, R-Wyo.	16
Jeff Sessions, R-Ala.	16
Mark Warner, D-Va.	16

Least — House

Lynn Westmoreland, R-Ga. †	0
Gregg Harper, R-Miss.	1
Ander Crenshaw, R-Fla. †	2
Frank D. Lucas, R-Okla. †	2
Harold Rogers, R-Ky. †	2
David Scott, D-Ga.	2
C.W. Bill Young, R-Fla. †	2
Steve Austria, R-Ohio	3
Sanford D. Bishop Jr., D-Ga.	3
Jo Bonner, R-Ala.	3
James E. Clyburn, D-S.C.	3
John W. Olver, D-Mass.	3
Lincoln Diaz-Balart, R-Fla. †	3

* Also in the top 10 in the 110th Congress

† Also in the bottom 10 in the 110th Congress

Members Whose Parent Served in Congress

There are 27 members with a parent who served in Congress. Walter B. Jones is the only one listed who belongs to a different political party than his parent.

Member	Parent	Years Parent Served
Sen. Mark Begich, D-Alaska	Rep. Nick Begich, D-Alaska	1971-72
Rep. Gus Bilirakis, R-Fla.*	Rep. Michael Bilirakis, R-Fla	1983-2007
Rep. Dan Boren, D-Okla.	Sen. David L. Boren, D-Okla.	1979-94
Rep. Shelley Moore Capito, R-W.Va.	Rep. Arch A. Moore Jr., R-W.Va.	1957-69
Rep. Russ Carnahan, D-Mo.	Sen. Jean Carnahan, D-Mo.	2001-02
Rep. William Lacy Clay, D-Mo.*	Rep. William L. Clay, D-Mo.	1969-2001
Rep. John D. Dingell, D-Mich.*	Rep. John D. Dingell Sr., D-Mich.	1933-55
Rep. John J. "Jimmy" Duncan Jr., R-Tenn.*	Rep. John J. Duncan, R-Tenn.	1965-88
Rep. Rodney Frelinghuysen, R-N.J.	Rep. Peter H. Frelinghuysen, R-N.J.	1953-75
Rep. Charlie Gonzalez, D-Texas*	Rep. Henry B. Gonzalez, D-Texas	1961-99
Rep. Rush D. Holt, D-N.J.	Sen. Rush Dew Holt, D-W.Va.	1935-41
Rep. Duncan Hunter, R-Calif.*	Rep. Duncan Hunter, R-Calif.	1981-2009
Rep. Walter B. Jones, R-N.C.	Rep. Walter B. Jones Sr., D-N.C.	1966-92
Sen. Jon Kyl, R-Ariz.	Rep. John H. Kyl, R-Iowa	1959-65, 1967-73
Rep. Bob Latta, R-Ohio	Rep. Delbert L. Latta, R-Ohio	1959-89
Rep. Daniel Lipinski, D-Ill.*	Rep. William O. Lipinski, D-Ill.	1983-2005
Rep. Connie Mack, R-Fla.	Rep./Sen. Connie Mack, R-Fla.	1983-2001
Sen. Lisa Murkowski, R-Alaska*	Sen. Frank H. Murkowski, R-Alaska	1981-2002
Rep. Nancy Pelosi, D-Calif.	Rep. Thomas D'Alesandro Jr., D-Md.	1939-47
Sen. Mark Pryor, D-Ark.	Rep./Sen. David Pryor, D-Ark.	1966-73, 1979-97
Rep. Ben Quayle, R-Ariz.	Rep./Sen. Dan Quayle, R-Ind.	1977-89
Rep. Lucille Roybal-Allard, D-Calif.	Rep. Edward R. Roybal, D-Calif.	1963-93
Rep. John Sarbanes, D-Md.	Rep./Sen. Paul S. Sarbanes, D-Md.	1971-2007
Rep. Bill Shuster, R-Pa.*	Rep. Bud Shuster, R-Pa.	1973-2001
Sen. Mark Udall, D-Colo.	Rep. Morris K. Udall, D-Ariz.	1961-91
Sen. Tom Udall, D-N.M.	Rep. Stewart L. Udall, D-Ariz.	1955-61

* Directly succeeded his or her parent in the same seat

Relatives Serving Together in Congress

Siblings	Years Serving	Siblings	Years Serving
Sen. Carl Levin, D-Mich.	1979-present	Rep. Linda T. Sánchez, D-Calif.	2003-present
Rep. Sander M. Levin, D-Mich.	1983-present	Rep. Loretta Sanchez, D-Calif.	1997-present

Cousins	Years Serving	Father and Son	
Sen. Mark Udall, D-Colo.*	1999-present	Rep. Ron Paul, R-Texas	1976-77, 1979-85, 1997-present
Sen. Tom Udall, D-N.M.*	1999-present	Sen. Rand Paul, R-Ky.	2011-present

* First elected to the House

Members Whose Spouse Served in Congress

Spouses	Spouse	Spouse's Service
Rep. Mary Bono Mack, R-Calif.*	Rep. Sonny Bono, R-Calif.	1995-98
Rep. Lois Capps, D-Calif.	Rep. Walter Capps, D-Calif.	1997
Rep. Jo Ann Emerson, R-Mo.	Rep. Bill Emerson, R-Mo.	1981-96
Rep. Doris Matsui, D-Calif.	Rep. Robert T. Matsui, D-Calif.	1979-2005
Sen. Olympia J. Snowe, R-Maine	Rep. John R. McKernan Jr., R-Maine	1983-87
Rep. Niki Tsongas, D-Mass.	Rep./Sen. Paul E. Tsongas, D-Mass.	1975-85

* Current Republican Reps. Mary Bono Mack, Calif., and Connie Mack, Fla., are married to each other

Pronunciation Guide for Congress

Some members of Congress whose names are frequently mispronounced:

Rep. Robert B. Aderholt, R-Ala. – ADD-er-holt
Sen. Daniel K. Akaka, D-Hawaii – uh-KAH-kuh
Rep. Justin Amash, R-Mich. – ah-MAHSH
Sen. Kelly Ayotte, R-N.H. – EYH-ott
Rep. Michele Bachmann, R-Minn. – BOCK-man
Rep. Spencer Bachus, R-Ala. – BACK-us
Sen. John Barrasso, R-Wyo. – buh-RASS-o
Rep. John Barrow, D-Ga. – BEAR-oh
Rep. Xavier Becerra, D-Calif. – HAH-vee-air beh-SEH-ra
Rep. Gus Bilirakis, R-Fla. – bil-uh-RACK-iss
Rep. Earl Blumenauer, D-Ore. – BLUE-men-hour
Rep. John A. Boehner, R-Ohio – BAY-ner
Sen. John Boozman, R-Ark. – BOZE-man
Del. Madeleine Z. Bordallo, D-Guam – bore-DAA-yo
Rep. Charles Boustany Jr., R-La. – boo-STAN-knee
Rep. Paul Broun, R-Ga. – BROWN
Rep. Larry Bucshon, R-Ind. – boo-SHON
Rep. Ann Marie Buerkle, R-N.Y. – BUR-kul
Rep. Francisco "Quico" Canseco, R-Texas – KEY-koh
Rep. Shelley Moore Capito, R-W.Va. – CAP-ih-toe
Rep. Michael E. Capuano, D-Mass. – KAP-you-AH-no
Rep. Steve Chabot, R-Ohio – SHAB-it
Rep. Jason Chaffetz, R-Utah – CHAY-fits
Sen. Saxby Chambliss, R-Ga. – SAX-bee CHAM-bliss
Rep. David Cicilline, D-R.I. – sis-uh-LEE-nee
Sen. John Cornyn, R-Texas – CORE-nin
Sen. Michael D. Crapo, R-Idaho – CRAY-poe
Rep. Chip Cravaack, R-Minn. – kruh-VACK
Rep. Joseph Crowley, D-N.Y. – KRAU-lee
Rep. Henry Cuellar, D-Texas – KWAY-are
Rep. Peter A. DeFazio, D-Ore. – da-FAH-zee-o
Rep. Diana DeGette, D-Colo. – de-GET
Rep. Rosa DeLauro, D-Conn. – da-LAUR-o
Rep. Scott DesJarlais, R-Tenn. – DAY-zhur-lay
Rep. Ted Deutch, D-Fla. – DOYTCH
Rep. Mario Diaz-Balart, R-Fla. – DEE-az ba-LART
Sen. Michael B. Enzi, R-Wyo. – EN-zee
Rep. Anna G. Eshoo, D-Calif. – EH-shoo
Del. Eni F.H. Faleomavaega, D-A.S. – EN-ee FOL-ee-oh-mav-ah-ENG-uh
Rep. Blake Farenthold, R-Texas – FAIR-enth-old
Rep. Chaka Fattah, D-Pa. – SHOCK-ah fa-TAH
Sen. Dianne Feinstein, D-Calif. – FINE-stine
Rep. Rodney Frelinghuysen, R-N.J. – FREE-ling-high-zen
Rep. Elton Gallegly, R-Calif. – GAL-uh-glee
Rep. John Garamendi, D-Calif. – gare-uh-MEN-dee
Rep. Jim Gerlach, R-Pa. – GUR-lock
Sen. Kirsten Gillibrand, D-N.Y. – KEER-sten JILL-uh-brand
Rep. Robert W. Goodlatte, R-Va. – GOOD-lat
Rep. Paul Gosar, R-Ariz. – go-SAR
Rep. Raúl M. Grijalva, D-Ariz. – gree-HAHL-va
Rep. Frank Guinta, R-N.H. – GIN (sounds like "grin")-ta
Rep. Luis V. Gutierrez, D-Ill. – loo-EES goo-tee-AIR-ez

Rep. Martin Heinrich, D-N.M. – HINE-rick
Rep. Jeb Hensarling, R-Texas – HENN-sur-ling
Rep. Jaime Herrera Beutler, R-Wash. – JAY-me HER-air-ah BUT-ler
Rep. Rubén Hinojosa, D-Texas – ru-BEN ee-na-HO-suh
Rep. Mazie K. Hirono, D-Hawaii – may-ZEE hee-RO-no
Rep. Kathy Hochul, D-N.Y. – HO-kul
Sen. John Hoeven, R-N.D. – HO-ven
Rep. Tim Huelskamp, R-Kan. – HYOOLS-camp
Rep. Bill Huizenga, R-Mich. – HI-zing-uh
Sen. James M. Inhofe, R-Okla. – IN-hoff
Sen. Daniel K. Inouye, D-Hawaii – in-NO-ay
Rep. Darrell Issa, R-Calif. – EYE-sah
Sen. Mike Johanns, R-Neb. – JOE-hanns (rhymes with cans)
Rep. Larry Kissell, D-N.C. – KISS-ell
Sen. Amy Klobuchar, D-Minn. – KLO-buh-shar
Rep. Dennis J. Kucinich, D-Ohio – ku-SIN-itch
Sen. Jon Kyl, R-Ariz. – KILE
Rep. Doug Lamborn, R-Colo. – LAMB-born
Sen. Mary L. Landrieu, D-La. – LAN-drew
Rep. Jim Langevin, D-R.I. – LAN-juh-vin
Rep. Steven C. LaTourette, R-Ohio – la-tuh-RETT
Rep. Frank A. LoBiondo, R-N.J. – lo-bee-ON-dough
Rep. Dave Loebsack, D-Iowa – LOBE-sack
Rep. Zoe Lofgren, D-Calif. – ZO LOFF-gren
Rep. Nita M. Lowey, D-N.Y. – LO-ee
Rep. Blaine Luetkemeyer, R-Mo. – LUTE-ka-myer
Rep. Ben Ray Luján, D-N.M. – loo-HAHN
Rep. Donald Manzullo, R-Ill. – man-ZOO-low
Rep. Kenny Marchant, R-Texas – MARCH-unt
Rep. John L. Mica, R-Fla. – MY-cah
Rep. Michael H. Michaud, D-Maine – ME-shoo
Rep. Jerrold Nadler, D-N.Y. – NAD-ler
Rep. Randy Neugebauer, R-Texas – NAW-geh-bow-er
Rep. Kristi Noem, R-S.D. – NOHM
Rep. Devin Nunes, R-Calif. – NEW-ness
Rep. Steven M. Palazzo, R-Miss. – puh-LAZZ-oh
Rep. Frank Pallone Jr., D-N.J. – puh-LOAN
Rep. Bill Pascrell Jr., D-N.J. – pass-KRELL
Rep. Ed Pastor, D-Ariz. – pas-TORE
Rep. Nancy Pelosi, D-Calif. – pa-LO-see
Rep. Tom Petri, R-Wis. – PEA-try
Res. Cmmsr. Pedro R. Pierluisi, D-P.R. – pea-air-loo-EE-see
Rep. Chellie Pingree, D-Maine – Like "Shelley"
Rep. Jared Polis, D-Colo. – POE-liss
Rep. Mike Pompeo, R-Kan. – pom-PAY-oh
Rep. Nick J. Rahall II, D-W.Va. – RAY-haul
Rep. Denny Rehberg, R-Mont. – REE-berg
Rep. Dave Reichert, R-Wash. – RIKE-ert
Rep. James B. Renacci, R-Ohio – reh-NAY-see
Rep. Silvestre Reyes, D-Texas – sil-VES-treh RAY-ess (rolled 'R')

(continued on p. 1109)

Pronunciation Guide (continued)

Rep. Scott Rigell, R-Va. – RIDGE-uhl
Sen. Jim Risch, R-Idaho – Rhymes with "wish"
Rep. Dana Rohrabacher, R-Calif. – ROAR-ah-BAH-ker
Rep. Todd Rokita, R-Ind. – ro-KEE-ta
Rep. Ileana Ros-Lehtinen, R-Fla. – il-ee-AH-na ross-LAY-tin-nen
Del. Gregorio Kilili Camacho Sablan, D-N. Marianas – greg-OREO key-LEE-lee ka-MAH-cho sab-LAHN
Rep. Steve Scalise, R-La. – skuh-LEASE
Rep. Jan Schakowsky, D-Ill. – shuh-KOW-ski
Rep. José E. Serrano, D-N.Y. – ho-ZAY sa-RAH-no (rolled 'R')
Rep. Terri A. Sewell, D-Ala. – SUE-ell
Rep. John Shimkus, R-Ill. – SHIM-kus

Rep. Heath Shuler, D-N.C. – SHOO-lur
Rep. Albio Sires, D-N.J. – SEAR-eez (like "series")
Rep. Jackie Speier, D-Calif. – SPEAR
Sen. Debbie Stabenow, D-Mich. – STAB-uh-now
Sen. John Thune, R-S.D. – THOON
Rep. Pat Tiberi, R-Ohio – TEA-berry
Rep. Niki Tsongas, D-Mass. – SONG-gus
Rep. Nydia M. Velázquez, D-N.Y. – NID-ee-uh veh-LASS-kez
Rep. Peter J. Visclosky, D-Ind. – vis-KLOSS-key
Rep. Tim Walz, D-Minn. – WALLS
Rep. Anthony Weiner, D-N.Y. – WEE-ner
Rep. Lynn Woolsey, D-Calif. – WOOL-zee

Congressional Half-Life

Members who have served more than half of their life in Congress. Length of service and percentage figures are as of the start of the 112th Congress.

Member	Age at Swearing-In	Length of Service	Percent of Life in Congress
Rep. John D. Dingell, D-Mich.	29 years, 158 days	55 years, 22 days	65
Sen. Daniel K. Inouye, D-Hawaii	34 years, 348 days	51 years, 136 days	60
Rep. John Conyers Jr., D-Mich.	35 years, 233 days	46 years	56
Rep. Nick J. Rahall II, D-W.Va.	27 years, 229 days	34 years	55
Rep. George Miller, D-Calif.	29 years, 242 days	36 years	55
Rep. Edward J. Markey, D-Mass.	30 years, 114 days	34 years, 63 days	53
Sen. Max Baucus, D-Mont.	33 years, 34 days	36 years	52
Sen. Thad Cochran, R-Miss.	35 years, 27 days	38 years	52
Rep. Christopher H. Smith, R-N.J.	27 years, 307 days	30 years	52
Rep. David Dreier, D-Calif.	28 years, 184 days	30 years	51
Sen. Patrick J. Leahy, D-Vt.	34 years, 289 days	36 years	51
Sen. Tom Harkin, D-Iowa	35 years, 56 days	36 years	51
Rep. Henry A. Waxman, D-Calif.	35 years, 124 days	36 years	50
Sen. Olympia J. Snowe, R-Maine	31 years, 328 days	32 years	50

Note: Sen. Charles E. Schumer, D-N.Y., achieved the half-life mark on Feb. 18, 2011, and Rep. C.W. Bill Young, R-Fla., reached it on Feb. 26, 2011. Other lawmakers who will join the list during the 112th Congress include Rep. Charles B. Rangel, D-N.Y. (Sept. 2, 2011), Sen. Ron Wyden, D-Ore. (Sept. 9, 2012) and Rep. Don Young, R-Alaska (Dec. 1, 2012).

Dean of the Delegation

These are the longest-serving members of Congress from each state.

State	Member	First Elected	State	Member	First Elected
Alabama	Sen. Richard C. Shelby, R	*1978	Montana	Sen. Max Baucus, D	*1974
Alaska	Rep. Don Young, R	1973	Nebraska	Rep. Lee Terry, R	1998
Arizona	Sen. John McCain, R	1982	Nevada	Sen. Harry Reid, D	*1982
Arkansas	Rep. Mike Ross, D	2000	New Hampshire	Rep. Charles Bass, N.H.	**1994
California	Rep. Pete Stark, D	1972	New Jersey	Rep. Christopher H. Smith, R	1980
Colorado	Rep. Diana DeGette, D	1996	New Mexico	Sen. Jeff Bingaman, D	1982
Connecticut	Sen. Joseph I. Lieberman, I	1988	New York	Rep. Charles B. Rangel, D	1970
Delaware	Sen. Thomas R. Carper, D	*1982	North Carolina	Rep. Howard Coble, R	1984
Florida	Rep. C.W. Bill Young, R	1970	North Dakota	Sen. Kent Conrad, D	1986
Georgia	Rep. John Lewis, D	1986	Ohio	Rep. Marcy Kaptur, D	1982
Hawaii	Sen. Daniel K. Inouye, D	*1959	Oklahoma	Sen. James M. Inhofe, R	*1986
Idaho	Sen. Michael D. Crapo, D	*1992	Oregon	Sen. Ron Wyden, D	*1980
Illinois	Sen. Richard J. Durbin, D	*1982	Pennsylvania	Rep. Tim Holden, D	1992
Indiana	Sen. Richard G. Lugar, R	1976	Rhode Island	Sen. Jack Reed, D	*1990
Iowa	Sen. Charles E. Grassley, R	†*1974	South Carolina	Rep. James E. Clyburn, D	1992
Kansas	Sen. Pat Roberts, R	*1980	South Dakota	Sen. Tim Johnson, D	*1986
Kentucky	Rep. Harold Rogers, R	1980	Tennessee	Rep. John J. "Jimmy" Duncan Jr., R	1988
Louisiana	Sen. Mary L. Landrieu, D	1996	Texas	Rep. Ralph M. Hall, R	1980
Maine	Sen. Olympia J. Snowe, R	*1978	Utah	Sen. Orrin G. Hatch, R	1976
Maryland	Sen. Barbara A. Mikulski, D	*1976	Vermont	Sen. Patrick J. Leahy, D	1974
Massachusetts	Rep. Edward J. Markey, D	1976	Virginia	Rep. Frank R. Wolf, R	1980
Michigan	Rep. John D. Dingell, D	1955	Washington	Rep. Norm Dicks, D	1976
Minnesota	Rep. Collin C. Peterson, D	1990	West Virginia	Rep. Nick J. Rahall II, D	1976
Mississippi	Sen. Thad Cochran, R	*1972	Wisconsin	Rep. F. James Sensenbrenner Jr., R	1978
Missouri	Sen. Roy Blunt, R	††1996	Wyoming	Sen. Michael B. Enzi, R	1996

*First elected to the House
**Did not serve 2007-10
† Sen. Tom Harkin, D, also was elected to the House in 1974, but Grassley reached the Senate four years before Harkin
†† Rep. Jo Ann Emerson, R, was also elected to the House in 1996, but Blunt reached the Senate first

Law Enforcement Officers

Member	Job
Sandy Adams, R-Fla.	Deputy county sheriff
Jerry F. Costello, D-Ill.	Law enforcement official
Michael G. Grimm, R-N.Y.	FBI agent
Tim Holden, D-Pa.	County sheriff, probation officer
Jeff Miller, R-Fla.	Deputy county sheriff

Member	Job
Rich Nugent, R-Fla.	County sheriff
Dave Reichert, R-Wash.	County sheriff, police officer
Silvestre Reyes, D-Texas	U.S. Border Patrol official
Mike Rogers, R-Mich.	FBI agent

Restaurateurs

Member	Job
Rep. Mary Bono Mack, R-Calif.	Restaurateur
Rep. Ken Calvert, R-Calif.	Restaurant executive
Rep. Mick Mulvaney, R-S.C.	Restaurateur
Rep. Kristi Noem, R-S.D.	Restaurant manager
Rep. Bobby Schilling, R-Ill.	Restaurateur
Rep. Cliff Stearns, R-Fla	Hotel and restaurant executive
Sen. Patrick J. Toomey, R-Pa.	Restaurateur

Professional Athletes

Member	Sport
Rep. Sean P. Duffy, R-Wis.	Timber sports competition
Rep. Jon Runyan, R-N.J.	Football
Rep. Heath Shuler, D-N.C.	Football

*Rep. Patrick Meehan, R-Pa., was a professional hockey referee

Member Occupations

	HOUSE			SENATE			112th
	Democrat	Republican	Total	Democrat	Republican	Total	CONGRESS
Public Service/Politics	141	97	238	27	22	49	287
Business	80	150	230	15	23	38	268
Law	88	82	170	33*	30	63	233
Education	47	31	78	10*	7	17	95
Real Estate	4	37	41	2	5	7	48
Agriculture	6	19	25	1	4	5	30
Medicine/Doctor	2	17	19	4		4	23
Labor/Blue Collar	7	7	14	1*	2	3	17
Journalism	4	6	10	4*	2	6	16
Homemaker/Domestic	8	6	14	1		1	15
Health Care	4	6	10			0	10
Military	1	8	9		1	1	10
Secretarial/Clerical	5	5	10			0	10
Law Enforcement	3	6	9			0	9
Engineering	4	3	7			0	7
Entertainment/Actor	1	1	2	2	1	3	5
Professional Sports	1	3	4			0	4
Science	2	2	4			0	4
Technical	2	2	4			0	4
Artistic/Creative				3*		3	3
Clergy	1	2	3			0	3
Aeronautics		2	2			0	2
Miscellaneous	1		1	1		1	2

Notes: Some members have had more than one occupation, and some members have had more than one separate occupation within a category. Delegates are not included.
* Total includes independents Joseph I. Lieberman, Conn., and Bernard Sanders, Vt.

M.D.s

Member	Field
Sen. John Barrasso, R-Wyo.	Orthopedic surgeon
Rep. Dan Benishek, R-Mich.	Surgeon
Rep. Charles Boustany Jr., R-La.	Heart surgeon
Rep. Paul Broun, R-Ga.	Physician
Rep. Larry Bucshon, R-Ind.	Heart surgeon
Rep. Michael C. Burgess, R-Texas	Obstetrician
Rep. Bill Cassidy, R-La.	Gastroenterologist
Del. Donna M.C. Christensen, D-Virgin Is.	Physician
Sen. Tom Coburn, R-Okla.	Obstetrician
Rep. Scott DesJarlais, R-Tenn.	Physician
Rep. John Fleming, R-La.	Physician
Rep. Phil Gingrey, R-Ga.	Obstetrician
Rep. Andy Harris, R-Md.	Physician
Rep. Nan Hayworth, R-N.Y.	Ophthalmologist
Rep. Jim McDermott, D- Wash.	Psychiatrist
Sen. Rand Paul, R-Ky.	Ophthalmologist
Rep. Ron Paul, R-Texas	Obstetrician
Rep. Tom Price, R-Ga.	Orthopedic surgeon
Rep. Phil Roe, R-Tenn.	Physician

Nurses

Rep. Karen Bass, D-Calif.
Rep. Diane Black, D-Tenn.
Rep. Ann Marie Buerkle, R-N.Y.
Rep. Lois Capps, D-Calif.
Rep. Renee Ellmers, R-N.C.
Rep. Eddie Bernice Johnson, D-Texas
Rep. Carolyn McCarthy, D-N.Y.

Engineers and Physicists

Member	Job
Rep. Roscoe G. Bartlett, R-Md.	Biomedical engineer
Rep. Joe L. Barton, R-Texas	Engineering consultant
Rep. Martin Heinrich, D-N.M.	Mechanical draftsman
Rep. Rush D. Holt, N.J.	Physicist
Rep. David B. McKinley, R-W.Va.	Civil engineer
Rep. Jerry McNerney, D-Calif.	Wind engineer
Rep. Bill Posey, R-Fla.	Space program inspector
Rep. Steve Scalise, R-La.	Software engineer
Rep. Paul Tonko, D-N.Y.	State public works engineer

Member Religious Affiliations

	HOUSE			SENATE			112th
	Democrat	Republican	Total	Democrat	Republican	Total	CONGRESS
Roman Catholic	70	63	133	15	9	24	157
Baptist	25	36	61		8	8	69
Protestant - Unspecified	10	44	54	6	4	10	64
Methodist	12	25	37	4	7	11	48
Presbyterian	11	21	32	6	9	15	47
Jewish	25	1	26	12*		12	38
Episcopalian	13	20	33	1	3	4	37
Lutheran	8	13	21	3	1	4	25
Mormon	1	7	8	2	4	6	14
Unspecified	5		5	1		1	6
Eastern Orthodox	1	3	4		1	1	5
United Church of Christ/ Congregationalist		2	2	2	1	3	5
African Methodist Episcopal	3		3			0	3
Buddhist	3		3			0	3
Christian Scientist		3	3			0	3
Muslim	2		2			0	2
Seventh-day Adventist	1	1	2			0	2
Atheist	1		1			0	1
Community of Christ	1		1			0	1
Christian Reformed Church		1	1			0	1
Quaker	1		1			0	1
Unitarian				1		1	1

Delegates are not included
* Includes independents Joseph I. Lieberman, Conn., and Bernard Sanders, Vt.

New to Congress

Senate (1 D, 6 R)
Kelly Ayotte, R-N.H.
Richard Blumenthal, D-Conn.
John Hoeven, R-N.D.
Ron Johnson, R-Wis.
Mike Lee, R-Utah
Rand Paul, R-Ky.
Marco Rubio, R-Fla.

House (10 D, 80 R)
Sandy Adams, R-Fla.
Justin Amash, R-Mich.
Lou Barletta, R-Pa.
Karen Bass, D-Calif.
Dan Benishek, R-Mich.
Rick Berg, R-N.D.
Diane Black, R-Tenn.
Mo Brooks, R-Ala.
Larry Bucshon, R-Ind.
Ann Marie Buerkle, R-N.Y.
Francisco "Quico" Canseco, R-Texas
John Carney, D-Del.
David Cicilline, D-R.I.
Hansen Clarke, D-Mich.
Chip Cravaack, R-Minn.
Rick Crawford, R-Ark.
Jeff Denham, R-Calif.
Scott DesJarlais, R-Tenn.
Robert Dold, R-Ill.
Sean P. Duffy, R-Wis.
Jeff Duncan, R-S.C.
Renee Ellmers, R-N.C.
Blake Farenthold, R-Texas
Stephen Fincher, R-Tenn.
Chuck Fleischmann, R-Tenn.

Bill Flores, R-Texas
Cory Gardner, R-Colo.
Bob Gibbs, R-Ohio
Chris Gibson, R-N.Y.
Paul Gosar, R-Ariz.
Trey Gowdy, R-S.C.
Tim Griffin, R-Ark.
Morgan Griffith, R-Va.
Michael G. Grimm, R-N.Y.
Frank Guinta, R-N.H.
Colleen Hanabusa, D-Hawaii
Richard Hanna, R-N.Y.
Andy Harris, R-Md.
Vicky Hartzler, R-Mo.
Nan Hayworth, R-N.Y.
Joe Heck, R-Nev.
Jaime Herrera Beutler, R-Wash.
Kathy Hochul, D-N.Y.
Tim Huelskamp, R-Kan.
Bill Huizenga, R-Mich.
Randy Hultgren, R-Ill.
Robert Hurt, R-Va.
Bill Johnson, R-Ohio
William Keating, D-Mass.
Mike Kelly, R-Pa.
Adam Kinzinger, R-Ill.
Raúl R. Labrador, R-Idaho
Jeff Landry, R-La.
James Lankford, R-Okla.
Billy Long, R-Mo.
Tom Marino, R-Pa.
David B. McKinley, R-W.Va.
Patrick Meehan, R-Pa.
Mick Mulvaney, R-S.C.
Kristi Noem, R-S.D.

Rich Nugent, R-Fla.
Alan Nunnelee, R-Miss.
Steven M. Palazzo, R-Miss.
Mike Pompeo, R-Kan.
Ben Quayle, R-Ariz.
James B. Renacci, R-Ohio
Reid Ribble, R-Wis.
Cedric L. Richmond, D-La.
Scott Rigell, R-Va.
David Rivera, R-Fla.
Martha Roby, R-Ala.
Todd Rokita, R-Ind.
Dennis A. Ross, R-Fla.
Jon Runyan, R-N.J.
Bobby Schilling, R-Ill.
David Schweikert, R-Ariz.
Austin Scott, R-Ga.
Tim Scott, R-S.C.
Terri A. Sewell, D-Ala.
Steve Southerland II, R-Fla.
Steve Stivers, R-Ohio
Scott Tipton, R-Colo.
Joe Walsh, R-Ill.
Daniel Webster, R-Fla.
Allen B. West, R-Fla.
Frederica S. Wilson, D-Fla.
Steve Womack, R-Ark.
Rob Woodall, R-Ga.
Kevin Yoder, R-Kan.
Todd Young, R-Ind.

Senators Up for Election in 2012

21 Democrats, 10 Republicans, 2 independents

Daniel K. Akaka, D-Hawaii*
John Barrasso, R-Wyo.
Jeff Bingaman, D-N.M.*
Scott P. Brown, R-Mass.
Sherrod Brown, D-Ohio
Maria Cantwell, D-Wash.
Benjamin L. Cardin, D-Md.
Thomas R. Carper, D-Del.
Bob Casey, D-Pa.
Kent Conrad, D-N.D.*
Bob Corker, R-Tenn.

Dianne Feinstein, D-Calif.
Kirsten Gillibrand, D-N.Y.
Orrin G. Hatch, R-Utah
Dean Heller, R-Nev. **
Kay Bailey Hutchison, R-Texas*
Amy Klobuchar, D-Minn.
Herb Kohl, D-Wis.*
Jon Kyl, R-Ariz.*
Joseph I. Lieberman, I-Conn.*
Richard G. Lugar, R-Ind.
Joe Manchin III, D-W.Va.

Claire McCaskill, D-Mo.
Robert Menendez, D-N.J.
Ben Nelson, D-Neb.
Bill Nelson, D-Fla.
Bernard Sanders, I-Vt.
Olympia J. Snowe, R-Maine
Debbie Stabenow, D-Mich.
Jon Tester, D-Mont.
Jim Webb, D-Va.*
Sheldon Whitehouse, D-R.I.
Roger Wicker, R-Miss.

* Not running for re-election
** Appointed and expected to stand for election in 2012

Senate Presidential Support and Opposition

Support scores represent how often a senator sided with President Obama on roll call votes on which the president took a clear position beforehand. Opposition scores represent how often a senator voted against the president's position. During the 111th Congress (2009-10), there were 143 Senate votes on which the president took a position. Only members who voted on more than half of those are listed.

111TH CONGRESS: TOP SCORERS

Support — Democrats
Richard J. Durbin, Ill.	100.0
Charles E. Schumer, N.Y.	99.3
Jack Reed, R.I.	99.3
Robert Menendez, N.J.	99.3
Benjamin L. Cardin, Md.	98.6
Carl Levin, Mich.	98.6
Sheldon Whitehouse, R.I.	98.6
Herb Kohl, Wis.	98.6
Thomas R. Carper, Del.	98.6
Amy Klobuchar, Minn.	98.6
John Kerry, Mass.	98.5
Barbara A. Mikulski, Md.	98.5
Ted Kaufman, Del. *	98.4
John D. Rockefeller IV, W.Va.	98.4
Al Franken, Minn.	98.1
Daniel K. Akaka, Hawaii	97.9
Harry Reid, Nev.	97.9
Bob Casey, Pa.	97.9
Christopher J. Dodd, Conn. *	97.8
Kirsten Gillibrand, N.Y.	97.8
Tim Johnson, S.D.	97.8
Bill Nelson, Fla.	97.8
Mary L. Landrieu, La.	97.8

Support — Republicans
Susan Collins, Maine	77.6
Olympia J. Snowe, Maine	74.1
George V. Voinovich, Ohio *	70.6
Lisa Murkowski, Alaska	63.4
Richard G. Lugar, Ind.	62.2
Lamar Alexander, Tenn.	61.0
Judd Gregg, N.H. *	59.8
Christopher S. Bond, Mo.	59.5
Thad Cochran, Miss.	55.1
Orrin G. Hatch, Utah	52.6
Robert F. Bennett, Utah *	52.0
Bob Corker, Tenn.	51.1
Richard C. Shelby, Ala.	50.7
Mike Johanns, Neb.	50.4
Sam Brownback, Kan. *	48.9
Lindsey Graham, S.C.	48.2
Roger Wicker, Miss.	45.1
Charles E. Grassley, Iowa	44.8
Mitch McConnell, Ky.	43.4
Johnny Isakson, Ga.	43.3

Opposition — Democrats
Ben Nelson, Neb.	16.8
Evan Bayh, Ind. *	15.0
Russ Feingold, Wis. *	14.1
Claire McCaskill, Mo.	12.3
Bernard Sanders, Vt. †	10.1
Blanche Lincoln, Ark. *	7.1
Arlen Specter, Pa. *	7.1
Robert C. Byrd, W.Va.*	6.7
Mark Pryor, Ark.	6.4
Jim Webb, Va.	5.6
Mark Begich, Alaska	5.1
Maria Cantwell, Wash.	4.9
Kay Hagan, N.C.	4.4
Byron L. Dorgan, N.D.*	4.3
Jeff Merkley, Ore.	4.3
Ron Wyden, Ore.	3.8
Joseph I. Lieberman, Conn. †	3.6
Patty Murray, Wash.	3.6
Mark Udall, Colo.	3.6
Max Baucus, Mont.	3.5
Tom Harkin, Iowa	3.5
Mark Warner, Va.	3.5
Tom Udall, N.M.	3.5

Opposition — Republicans
Jim DeMint, S.C.	70.4
Tom Coburn, Okla.	70.0
Jim Bunning, Ky. *	66.4
John Ensign, Nev. *	63.6
James M. Inhofe, Okla.	63.0
John Thune, S.D.	61.9
David Vitter, La.	59.7
Jeff Sessions, Ala.	59.1
Richard M. Burr, N.C.	59.1
Pat Roberts, Kan.	58.8
John Barrasso, Wyo.	58.7
John McCain, Ariz.	58.6
Saxby Chambliss, Ga.	58.1
John Cornyn, Texas	58.0
Kay Bailey Hutchison, Texas	57.9
Jon Kyl, Ariz.	57.6
Michael B. Enzi, Wyo.	57.6
Jim Risch, Idaho	57.5
Michael D. Crapo, Idaho	57.1

* No longer in Congress
† Independents in the 112th Congress, Lieberman and Sanders, caucus with the Democrats

Senate Party Unity and Opposition

Support scores represent how often a senator voted with his or her party's majority against a majority of the other party. Opposition scores represent how often a senator voted against his or her party's majority. In the 111th Congress (2009-10), there were 521 such "party unity" votes in the Senate. Only members who voted on more than half of those are listed.

111TH CONGRESS: TOP SCORERS

Support — Democrats
Roland W. Burris, Ill. *	99.8
Richard J. Durbin, Ill.	99.6
Sherrod Brown, Ohio	99.4
Benjamin L. Cardin, Md.	99.2
Barbara A. Mikulski, Md.	99.2
Charles E. Schumer, N.Y.	99.2
Sheldon Whitehouse, R.I.	99.2
Frank R. Lautenberg, N.J.	99.0
Carl Levin, Mich.	99.0
Jack Reed, R.I.	99.0
Kirsten Gillibrand, N.Y.	99.0
Patrick J. Leahy, Vt.	98.8
Al Franken, Minn.	98.6
Daniel K. Inouye, Hawaii	98.5
Tom Harkin, Iowa	98.4
John Kerry, Mass.	98.4
Daniel K. Akaka, Hawaii	97.9
Debbie Stabenow, Mich.	97.9
Ted Kaufman, Del. *	97.9
Bernard Sanders, Vt. †	97.9
Christopher J. Dodd, Conn. *	97.7
Robert Menendez, N.J.	97.7
John D. Rockefeller IV, W.Va.	97.7

Support — Republicans
Tom Coburn, Okla.	98.6
John Thune, S.D.	98.5
Jim DeMint, S.C.	98.0
John Barrasso, Wyo.	97.9
John Cornyn, Texas	97.7
Saxby Chambliss, Ga.	97.6
Michael B. Enzi, Wyo.	97.5
John McCain, Ariz.	97.3
James M. Inhofe, Okla.	97.2
Jim Bunning, Ky. *	97.1
Jeff Sessions, Ala.	97.0
Richard M. Burr, N.C.	96.7
Jim Risch, Idaho	96.3
Mitch McConnell, Ky.	96.2
Johnny Isakson, Ga.	95.9
Jon Kyl, Ariz.	95.9
Michael D. Crapo, Idaho	95.5
David Vitter, La.	95.2
John Ensign, Nev. *	95.1
Lindsey Graham, S.C.	94.1

Opposition — Democrats
Ben Nelson, Neb.	41.3
Evan Bayh, Ind. *	34.5
Claire McCaskill, Mo.	22.4
Russ Feingold, Wis. *	21.9
Blanche Lincoln, Ark. *	21.4
Arlen Specter, Pa. *	18.0
Jim Webb, Va.	15.7
Mark Pryor, Ark.	11.6
Joseph I. Lieberman, Conn. †	11.6
Amy Klobuchar, Minn.	10.6
Kay Hagan, N.C.	10.5
Michael Bennet, Colo.	10.5
Jon Tester, Mont.	9.1
Mark Warner, Va.	8.9
Kent Conrad, N.D.	8.5
Bill Nelson, Fla.	8.4
Mary L. Landrieu, La.	8.3
Mark Udall, Colo.	8.3
Max Baucus, Mont.	7.7
Byron L. Dorgan, N.D. *	7.4
Mark Begich, Alaska	7.2
Maria Cantwell, Wash.	6.6

Opposition — Republicans
Susan Collins, Maine	42.6
Olympia J. Snowe, Maine	40.3
George V. Voinovich, Ohio *	37.6
Lisa Murkowski, Alaska	24.5
Christopher S. Bond, Mo. *	22.1
Richard G. Lugar, Ind.	21.9
Lamar Alexander, Tenn.	18.4
Thad Cochran, Miss.	18.3
Judd Gregg, N.H. *	18.0
Robert F. Bennett, Utah *	14.1
Richard C. Shelby, Ala.	11.6
Bob Corker, Tenn.	11.2
Orrin G. Hatch, Utah	9.6
Roger Wicker, Miss.	8.2
Charles E. Grassley, Iowa	7.5
Kay Bailey Hutchison, Texas	7.1
Sam Brownback, Kan. *	6.7
Mike Johanns, Neb.	6.5
Pat Roberts, Kan.	6.2

* No longer in Congress
† Independents in the 112th Congress, Lieberman and Sanders, caucus with the Democrats

House Presidential Support and Opposition

Support scores represent how often a House member sided with President Obama on roll call votes on which the president took a clear position beforehand. Opposition scores represent how often a member voted against the president's position. During the 111th Congress (2009-10), there were 114 House votes on which the president took a position. Only members who voted on more than half of those are listed.

111TH CONGRESS: TOP SCORERS

Support — Democrats

John Sarbanes, Md.	97.3
Steny H. Hoyer, Md.	97.3
Norm Dicks, Wash.	97.3
Lois Capps, Calif.	97.3
Adam B. Schiff, Calif.	97.3
Howard L. Berman, Calif.	97.3
Henry A. Waxman, Calif.	97.3
Timothy H. Bishop, N.Y.	96.5
David E. Price, N.C.	96.5
Al Green, Texas	96.5
Nita M. Lowey, N.Y.	96.5
Brad Sherman, Calif.	96.5
Susan A. Davis, Calif.	96.5
Rick Larsen, Wash.	96.5
Dave Loebsack, Iowa	96.5
Vic Snyder, Ark. *	96.5
Russ Carnahan, Mo.	96.5
Joe Sestak, Pa. *	96.5
Chris Van Hollen, Md.	96.5
Silvestre Reyes, Texas	96.5
Phil Hare, Ill. *	96.5

Support — Republicans

Anh "Joseph" Cao, La. *	68.5
Tim Murphy, Pa.	60.7
Frank A. LoBiondo, N.J.	57.9
Michael N. Castle, Del. *	57.9
Christopher H. Smith, N.J.	56.1
Steven C. LaTourette, Ohio	55.8
Vernon J. Ehlers, Mich. *	52.7
Michael R. Turner, Ohio	51.8
Ileana Ros-Lehtinen, Fla.	50.4
Dave Reichert, Wash.	49.5
Jim Gerlach, Pa.	47.8
Mark Steven Kirk, Ill. **	47.1
Fred Upton, Mich.	46.5
Candice S. Miller, Mich.	46.5
Peter T. King, N.Y.	46.4
Todd R. Platts, Pa.	46.0
Charlie Dent, Pa.	44.7
Lincoln Diaz-Balart, Fla. *	44.5
Judy Biggert, Ill.	42.5
Mario Diaz-Balart, Fla.	42.5
Ginny Brown-Waite, Fla.*	41.9

Opposition — Democrats

Gene Taylor, Miss. *	52.3
Bobby Bright, Ala. *	46.9
Walt Minnick, Idaho *	34.2
Travis W. Childers, Miss. *	31.5
Glenn Nye, Va. *	30.7
Harry E. Mitchell, Ariz. *	29.8
Betty Sutton, Ohio	29.2
Ann Kirkpatrick, Ariz. *	28.6
Jim Marshall, Ga. *	27.9
Dan Boren, Okla.	27.5
Frank Kratovil Jr., Md. *	27.2
Jim Matheson, Utah	25.7
Mike McIntyre, N.C.	24.6
Stephanie Herseth Sandlin, S.D.*	24.6
John Adler, N.J. *	23.4
Heath Shuler, N.C.	23.1
Jim Cooper, Tenn.	22.3
Jason Altmire, Pa.	21.9
Collin C. Peterson, Minn.	21.9
Harry Teague, N.M. *	21.2
Parker Griffith, Ala. * †	20.8
Lincoln Davis, Tenn. *	19.8
Joe Donnelly, Ind.	18.4

Opposition — Republicans

Jeff Flake, Ariz.	87.7
Nathan Deal, Ga. *	87.5
Trent Franks, Ariz.	86.0
Paul Broun, Ga.	85.7
John Linder, Ga. *	85.3
Jason Chaffetz, Utah	85.1
Sam Johnson, Texas	84.5
John Shadegg, Ariz. *	84.3
Virginia Foxx, N.C.	84.2
Doug Lamborn, Colo.	84.2
John A. Boehner, Ohio	84.1
John Campbell, Calif.	84.1
Jim Jordan, Ohio	84.1
Steve King, Iowa	84.1
Cynthia M. Lummis, Wyo.	83.9
J. Gresham Barrett, S.C. *	83.3
K. Michael Conaway, Texas	83.3
Ed Royce, Calif.	83.3
Bob Latta, Ohio	83.0
Tom Price, Ga.	83.0
Kevin Brady, Texas	83.0
Rob Bishop, Utah	82.9
Mike Pence, Ind.	82.9

* No longer in Congress
** Elected to the Senate in 2010
† Only includes votes cast as a Democrat prior to switching parties in December 2009

House Party Unity and Opposition

Support scores represent how often a House member voted with his or her party's majority against a majority of the other party. Opposition scores represent how often a member voted against his or her party's majority. In the 111th Congress (2009-10) there were 766 such "party unity" votes in the House. Only members who voted on more than half of those are listed.

111TH CONGRESS: TOP SCORERS

Support — Democrats

Doris Matsui, Calif.	100
Lois Capps, Calif.	99.9
David E. Price, N.C.	99.9
Mazie K. Hirono, Hawaii	99.7
John B. Larson, Conn.	99.7
Jim McGovern, Mass.	99.7
John W. Olver, Mass.	99.7
Louise M. Slaughter, N.Y.	99.7
Chris Van Hollen, Md.	99.7
Tammy Baldwin, Wis.	99.6
James E. Clyburn, S.C.	99.6
Mike Doyle, Pa.	99.6
Anna G. Eshoo, Calif.	99.6
Henry A. Waxman, Calif.	99.6
Howard L. Berman, Calif.	99.5
Robert A. Brady, Pa.	99.5
André Carson, Ind.	99.5
Kathy Castor, Fla.	99.5
Diana DeGette, Colo.	99.5
Patrick J. Kennedy, R.I. *	99.5
Sander M. Levin, Mich.	99.5
John Lewis, Ga.	99.5
George Miller, Calif.	99.5
Steven R. Rothman, N.J.	99.5
Linda T. Sánchez, Calif.	99.5

Support — Republicans

Jeb Hensarling, Texas	99.6
Virginia Foxx, N.C.	99.3
Trent Franks, Ariz.	99.3
Doug Lamborn, Colo.	99.3
Mike Pence, Ind.	99.3
Randy Neugebauer, Texas	99.2
Pete Sessions, Texas	99.2
Jim Jordan, Ohio	99.1
Lynn Westmoreland, Ga.	99.0
K. Michael Conaway, Texas	98.9
Steve King, Iowa	98.9
J. Gresham Barrett, S.C. *	98.8
Bob Latta, Ohio	98.8
Marsha Blackburn, Tenn.	98.7
John A. Boehner, Ohio	98.7
John Shadegg, Ariz. *	98.7
William M. "Mac" Thornberry, Texas	98.6
Patrick T. McHenry, N.C.	98.5
Tom Price, Ga.	98.5
Todd Akin, Mo.	98.4
Paul Broun, Ga.	98.4
Wally Herger, Calif.	98.4
Kenny Marchant, Texas	98.4
Ed Royce, Calif.	98.4
Sam Johnson, Texas	98.3

Opposition — Democrats

Bobby Bright, Ala. *	59.1
Walt Minnick, Idaho *	57.8
Gene Taylor, Miss. *	46.7
Harry E. Mitchell, Ariz. *	42.6
Travis W. Childers, Miss. *	40.5
Glenn Nye, Va. *	35.4
Heath Shuler, N.C.	34.6
Frank Kratovil Jr., Md. *	33.2
Parker Griffith, Ala. * †	30.0
Ann Kirkpatrick, Ariz. *	28.4
Baron P. Hill, Ind. *	26.5
Gabrielle Giffords, Ariz.	25.3
Dan Boren, Okla.	25.2
Joe Donnelly, Ind.	24.4
Scott Murphy, N.Y. *	23.2
Jim Marshall, Ga. *	23.1
Brad Ellsworth, Ind. *	22.7
Jason Altmire, Pa.	22.5
Mike McIntyre, N.C.	21.4

Opposition — Republicans

Anh "Joseph" Cao, La. *	36.2
Walter B. Jones, N.C.	29.0
Dave Reichert, Wash.	28.2
Christopher H. Smith, N.J.	28.2
Tim Murphy, Pa.	27.8
Frank A. LoBiondo, N.J.	26.9
Steven C. LaTourette, Ohio	26.7
Vernon J. Ehlers, Mich. *	26.2
Michael N. Castle, Del. *	25.9
Charlie Dent, Pa. *	25.9
Don Young, Alaska	25.4
Ileana Ros-Lehtinen, Fla.	25.3
Jim Gerlach, Pa.	23.7
Lincoln Diaz-Balart, Fla. *	23.5
Michael R. Turner, Ohio	23.2
Mark Steven Kirk, Ill. **	21.9
Todd R. Platts, Pa.	21.9
Mario Diaz-Balart, Fla.	21.5
Peter T. King, N.Y.	20.9

* No longer in Congress
** Elected to the Senate in 2010
† Only includes votes cast as a Democrat prior to switching parties in December 2009

House Democrats Who Voted Against Pelosi

On Jan. 5, 2011, every House Republican voted for Ohio's John A. Boehner as Speaker for the 112th Congress; 173 Democrats voted for Nancy Pelosi of California. These Democrats cast ballots for other members.

Voted for Heath Shuler, N.C.
Jason Altmire, Pa.
Dan Boren, Okla.
Jim Cooper, Tenn.
Joe Donnelly, Ind.
Tim Holden, Pa.
Larry Kissell, N.C.
Jim Matheson, Utah
Mike McIntyre, N.C.
Michael H. Michaud, Maine
Mike Ross, Ark.
Heath Shuler, N.C.

Voted for John Lewis, Ga.
John Barrow, Ga.
Gabrielle Giffords, Ariz.

Voted for Dennis Cardoza, Calif.
Jim Costa, Calif.

Voted for Jim Costa, Calif.
Dennis Cardoza, Calif.

Voted for Jim Cooper, Tenn.
Ron Kind, Calif.

Voted for Marcy Kaptur, Ohio.
Dennis Lipinski, Ill.

Voted for Steny H. Hoyer, Md.
Kurt Schrader, Ore.

Note: Sanford D. Bishop Jr. of Georgia voted present and Peter A. DeFazio of Oregon did not vote

New Democrat Coalition

The New Democrats are a group of pro-business Democratic House moderates.

Chairman: Joseph Crowley, N.Y.

Jason Altmire, Pa.
John Barrow, Ga.
Shelley Berkley, Nev.
Lois Capps, Calif.
Russ Carnahan, Mo.
John Carney, Del.
André Carson, Ind.
Gerald E. Connolly, Va.
Jim Cooper, Tenn.
Joe Courtney, Conn.
Susan A. Davis, Calif.
Eliot L. Engel, N.Y.
Gabrielle Giffords, Ariz.
Charlie Gonzalez, Texas
Martin Heinrich, N.M.
Brian Higgins, N.Y.
Jim Himes, Conn.
Rush D. Holt, N.J.
Jay Inslee, Wash.
Ron Kind, Wis.
Rick Larsen, Wash.

Carolyn McCarthy, N.Y.
Mike McIntyre, N.C.
Gregory W. Meeks, N.Y.
James P. Moran, Va.
Christopher S. Murphy, Conn.
Bill Owens, N.Y.
Ed Perlmutter, Colo.
Gary Peters, Mich.
Pedro R. Pierluisi, P.R.
Jared Polis, Colo.
Laura Richardson, Calif.
Cedric L. Richmond, La.
Loretta Sanchez, Calif.
Adam B. Schiff, Calif.
Kurt Schrader, Ore.
Allyson Y. Schwartz, Pa.
David Scott, Ga.
Terri A. Sewell, Ala.
Adam Smith, Wash.
Debbie Wasserman Schultz, Fla.
David Wu, Ore.

Blue Dog Coalition

The Blue Dogs are a group of the House's most fiscally conservative Democrats.

Co-Chairmen: John Barrow, Ga.; Mike Ross, Ark.; Heath Shuler, N.C.

Jason Altmire, Pa.
Joe Baca, Calif.
Sanford D. Bishop Jr., Ga.
Dan Boren, Okla.
Leonard L. Boswell, Iowa
Dennis Cardoza, Calif.
Ben Chandler, Ky.
Jim Cooper, Tenn.

Jim Costa, Calif.
Henry Cuellar, Texas
Joe Donnelly, Ind.
Gabrielle Giffords, Ariz.
Tim Holden, Pa.
Jim Matheson, Utah
Mike McIntyre, N.C.
Michael H. Michaud, Maine

Collin C. Peterson, Minn.
Loretta Sanchez, Calif.
Adam B. Schiff, Calif.
Kurt Schrader, Ore.
David Scott, Ga.
Mike Thompson, Calif.

Progressive Caucus

The Progressive Caucus is a group of the most liberal lawmakers. All members are House Democrats, except independent Sen. Bernard Sanders.

Co-Chairmen: Keith Ellison, Minn., and Raúl M. Grijalva, Ariz.

Tammy Baldwin, Wis.
Karen Bass, Calif.
Xavier Becerra, Calif.
Earl Blumenauer, Ore.
Robert A. Brady, Pa.
Corrine Brown, Fla.
Michael E. Capuano, Mass.
André Carson, Ind.
Donna M.C. Christensen, V.I.
Judy Chu, Calif.
David Cicilline, R.I.
Yvette D. Clarke, N.Y.
William Lacy Clay, Mo.
Emanuel Cleaver II, Mo.
Steve Cohen, Tenn.
John Conyers Jr., Mich.
Elijah E. Cummings, Md.
Danny K. Davis, Ill.
Peter A. DeFazio, Ore.
Rosa DeLauro, Conn.
Donna Edwards, Md.
Sam Farr, Calif.
Chaka Fattah, Pa.
Bob Filner, Calif.
Barney Frank, Mass.
Marcia L. Fudge, Ohio

Luis V. Gutierrez, Ill.
Maurice D. Hinchey, N.Y.
Mazie K. Hirono, Hawaii
Michael M. Honda, Calif.
Jesse L. Jackson Jr., Ill.
Sheila Jackson Lee, Texas
Eddie Bernice Johnson, Texas
Hank Johnson, Ga.
Marcy Kaptur, Ohio
Dennis J. Kucinich, Ohio
Barbara Lee, Calif.
John Lewis, Ga.
Dave Loebsack, Iowa
Ben Ray Luján, N.M.
Carolyn B. Maloney, N.Y.
Edward J. Markey, Mass.
Jim McDermott, Wash.
Jim McGovern, Mass.
George Miller, Calif.
Gwen Moore, Wis.
James P. Moran, Va.
Jerrold Nadler, N.Y.
Eleanor Holmes Norton, D.C.
John W. Olver, Mass.
Frank Pallone Jr., N.J.
Ed Pastor, Ariz.

Donald M. Payne, N.J.
Chellie Pingree, Maine
Jared Polis, Colo.
Charles B. Rangel, N.Y.
Laura Richardson, Calif.
Lucille Roybal-Allard, Calif.
Bobby L. Rush, Ill.
Linda T. Sánchez, Calif.
Bernard Sanders, Vt.
Jan Schakowsky, Ill.
José E. Serrano, N.Y.
Louise M. Slaughter, N.Y.
Pete Stark, Calif.
Bennie Thompson, Miss.
John F. Tierney, Mass.
Nydia M. Velázquez, N.Y.
Maxine Waters, Calif.
Melvin Watt, N.C.
Henry A. Waxman, Calif.
Peter Welch, Vt.
Frederica S. Wilson, Fla.
Lynn Woolsey, Calif.

Republican Study Committee

The RSC is the most conservative bloc and dominant force within the House Republican caucus. The list below is not comprehensive, as the caucus permits individual members to decide whether to publicize their membership.

Chairman: Jim Jordan, Ohio

Sandy Adams, Fla.
Robert B. Aderholt, Ala.
Todd Akin, Mo.
Justin Amash, Mich.
Steve Austria, Ohio
Michele Bachmann, Minn.
Spencer Bachus, Ala.
Roscoe G. Bartlett, Md.
Joe L. Barton, Texas
Dan Benishek, Mich.
Rick Berg, N.D.
Brian P. Bilbray, Calif.
Gus Bilirakis, Fla.
Rob Bishop, Utah
Diane Black, Tenn.
Marsha Blackburn, Tenn.
Jo Bonner, Ala.
Kevin Brady, Texas
Mo Brooks, Ala.
Paul Broun, Ga.
Vern Buchanan, Fla.
Larry Bucshon, Ind.
Ann Marie Buerkle, N.Y.
Michael C. Burgess, Texas
Dan Burton, Ind.
Dave Camp, Mich.
John Campbell, Calif.
Francisco "Quico" Canseco, Texas
Eric Cantor, Va.
John Carter, Texas
Bill Cassidy, La.
Steve Chabot, Ohio
Jason Chaffetz, Utah
Howard Coble, N.C.
Mike Coffman, Colo.
Tom Cole, Okla.
K. Michael Conaway, Texas
Rick Crawford, Ark.
John Culberson, Texas
Geoff Davis, Ky.
Jeff Denham, Calif.
Scott DesJarlais, Tenn.
Sean P. Duffy, Wis.
Jeff Duncan, S.C.

Renee Ellmers, N.C.
Blake Farenthold, Texas
Stephen Fincher, Tenn.
Jeff Flake, Ariz.
Chuck Fleischmann, Tenn.
John Fleming, La.
Bill Flores, Texas
J. Randy Forbes, Va.
Jeff Fortenberry, Neb.
Virginia Foxx, N.C.
Trent Franks, Ariz.
Cory Gardner, Colo.
Scott Garrett, N.J.
Bob Gibbs, Ohio
Chris Gibson, N.Y.
Phil Gingrey, Ga.
Louie Gohmert, Texas
Robert W. Goodlatte, Va.
Paul Gosar, Ariz.
Trey Gowdy, S.C.
Kay Granger, Texas
Sam Graves, Mo.
Tom Graves, Ga.
Tim Griffin, Ark.
Morgan Griffith, Va.
Michael G. Grimm, N.Y.
Frank Guinta, N.H.
Brett Guthrie, Ky.
Ralph M. Hall, Texas
Richard Hanna, N.Y.
Gregg Harper, Miss.
Andy Harris, Md.
Vicky Hartzler, Mo.
Nan Hayworth, N.Y.
Jeb Hensarling, Texas
Wally Herger, Calif.
Jaime Herrera Beutler, Wash.
Tim Huelskamp, Kan.
Bill Huizenga, Mich.
Randy Hultgren, Ill.
Duncan Hunter, Calif.
Robert Hurt, Va.
Darrell Issa, Calif.
Lynn Jenkins, Kan.
Bill Johnson, Ohio

Sam Johnson, Texas
Mike Kelly, Pa.
Steve King, Iowa
Jack Kingston, Ga.
Adam Kinzinger, Ill.
John Kline, Minn.
Raúl R. Labrador, Idaho
Doug Lamborn, Colo.
Jeff Landry, La.
James Lankford, Okla.
Bob Latta, Ohio
Billy Long, Mo.
Frank D. Lucas, Okla.
Blaine Luetkemeyer, Mo.
Cynthia M. Lummis, Wyo.
Dan Lungren, Calif.
Connie Mack, Fla.
Donald Manzullo, Ill.
Kenny Marchant, Texas
Michael McCaul, Texas
Tom McClintock, Calif.
Patrick T. McHenry, N.C.
Howard P. "Buck" McKeon, Calif.
David B. McKinley, W.Va.
Cathy McMorris Rodgers, Wash.
Gary G. Miller, Calif.
Jeff Miller, Fla.
Mick Mulvaney, S.C.
Sue Myrick, N.C.
Randy Neugebauer, Texas
Kristi Noem, S.D.
Rich Nugent, Fla.
Alan Nunnelee, Miss.
Pete Olson, Texas
Steven M. Palazzo, Miss.
Steve Pearce, N.M.
Mike Pence, Ind.
Joe Pitts, Pa.
Ted Poe, Texas
Mike Pompeo, Kan.
Bill Posey, Fla.
Tom Price, Ga.
Ben Quayle, Ariz.

Tom Reed, N.Y.
James B. Renacci, Ohio
Reid Ribble, Wis.
Scott Rigell, Va.
Martha Roby, Ala.
Phil Roe, Tenn.
Mike D. Rogers, Ala.
Todd Rokita, Ind.
Tom Rooney, Fla.
Peter Roskam, Ill.
Dennis A. Ross, Fla.
Ed Royce, Calif.
Paul D. Ryan, Wis.
Steve Scalise, La.
Bobby Schilling, Ill.
Jean Schmidt, Ohio
Aaron Schock, Ill.
David Schweikert, Ariz.
Austin Scott, Ga.
Tim Scott, S.C.
Pete Sessions, Texas
John Shimkus, Ill.
Lamar Smith, Texas
Steve Southerland II, Fla.
Cliff Stearns, Fla.
Steve Stivers, Ohio
Marlin Stutzman, Ind.
John Sullivan, Okla.
Glenn Thompson, Pa.
William M. "Mac" Thornberry, Texas
Scott Tipton, Colo.
Michael R. Turner, Ohio
Tim Walberg, Mich.
Joe Walsh, Ill.
Daniel Webster, Fla.
Allen B. West, Fla.
Lynn Westmoreland, Ga.
Joe Wilson, S.C.
Rob Wittman, Va.
Steve Womack, Ark.
Rob Woodall, Ga.
Kevin Yoder, Kan.
Todd Young, Ind.

Tea Party Caucus

The Tea Party Caucus is a group of House Republicans who promote limited government, reduced federal spending and strict adherence to the Constitution.

Chairwoman: Michele Bachmann, Minn.

Sandy Adams, Fla.
Robert B. Aderholt, Ala.
Todd Akin, Mo.
Rodney Alexander, La.
Roscoe G. Bartlett, Md.
Joe L. Barton, Texas
Gus Bilirakis, Fla.
Rob Bishop, Utah
Diane Black, Tenn.
Paul Broun, Ga.
Michael C. Burgess, Texas
Dan Burton, Ind.
John Carter, Texas
Bill Cassidy, La.
Howard Coble, N.C.
Mike Coffman, Colo.
Ander Crenshaw, Fla.
John Culberson, Texas
Jeff Duncan, S.C.
Blake Farenthold, Texas
Stephen Fincher, Tenn.
John Fleming, La.
Trent Franks, Ariz.
Phil Gingrey, Ga.
Louie Gohmert, Texas
Vicky Hartzler, Mo.
Wally Herger, Calif.
Tim Huelskamp, Kan.
Lynn Jenkins, Kan.

Steve King, Iowa
Doug Lamborn, Colo.
Jeff Landry, La.
Blaine Luetkemeyer, Mo.
Kenny Marchant, Texas
Tom McClintock, Calif.
David B. McKinley, W.Va.
Gary G. Miller, Calif.
Mick Mulvaney, S.C.
Randy Neugebauer, Texas
Rich Nugent, Fla.
Steve Pearce, N.M.
Mike Pence, Ind.
Ted Poe, Texas
Tom Price, Ga.
Denny Rehberg, Mont.
Phil Roe, Tenn.
Dennis A. Ross, Fla.
Ed Royce, Calif.
Steve Scalise, La.
Pete Sessions, Texas
Adrian Smith, Neb.
Lamar Smith, Texas
Cliff Stearns, Fla.
Tim Walberg, Mich.
Joe Walsh, Ill.
Allen B. West, Fla.
Lynn Westmoreland, Ga.
Joe Wilson, S.C.

Other Caucus Leadership

Moderate Dems Working Group
Sen. Thomas R. Carper, Del., co-chairman
Sen. Kay Hagan, N.C., co-chairwoman
Sen. Mark Udall, Colo., co-chairman

Congressional Asian Pacific American Caucus
Rep. Judy Chu, D-Calif., chairwoman

Congressional Black Caucus
Rep. Emanuel Cleaver II, D-Mo., chairman

Congressional Caucus for Women's Issues
Rep. Cynthia M. Lummis, R-Wyo., co-chairwoman
Rep. Gwen Moore, D-Wis., co-chairwoman

Congressional Hispanic Caucus
Rep. Charlie Gonzalez, D-Texas, chairman

Winners Outspent by Opponents

General-election winners in 2010 who spent less than their opponents. Totals cover the period of Jan. 1, 2009, through Dec. 31, 2010. Losing incumbents are in *italics*.

(in order of spending margin)

Senate

Member	Expenditures	Opponent	Expenditures
Richard Blumenthal, D-Conn.	$8,718,286	Linda McMahon, R	$50,181,464
John Boozman, R-Ark.	3,165,777	*Blanche Lincoln, D*	11,545,776
Harry Reid, D-Nev.	22,548,567	Sharron Angle, R	28,262,487
Chris Coons, D-Del.	3,869,062	Christine O'Donnell, R	6,676,655
Kelly Ayotte, R-N.H.	3,540,079	Paul W. Hodes, D	4,893,222
Ron Johnson, R-Wis.	15,316,651	*Russ Feingold, D*	15,544,093

House

Member	Expenditures	Opponent	Expenditures
Betty Sutton, D-Ohio (13)	$1,781,137	Tom Ganley, R	$8,317,960
Chris Gibson, R-N.Y. (20)	1,734,219	*Scott Murphy, D**	5,571,745
Daniel Webster, R-Fla. (8)	1,756,775	*Alan Grayson, D*	5,573,272
Timothy H. Bishop, D-N.Y. (1)	3,097,008	Randy Altschuler, R	5,713,405
Steve Southerland II, R-Fla. (2)	1,290,929	*Allen Boyd, D*	3,814,064
Ann Marie Buerkle, R-N.Y. (25)	759,777	*Dan Maffei, D*	3,114,128
Morgan Griffith, R-Va. (9)	1,029,522	*Rick Boucher, D*	3,325,898
Randy Hultgren, R-Ill. (14)	1,572,578	*Bill Foster, D*	3,843,739
Michael G. Fitzpatrick, R-Pa. (8)	2,062,733	*Patrick J. Murphy, D*	4,287,244
Bob Gibbs, R-Ohio (18)	1,090,872	*Zack Space, D*	2,931,978
Joe Walsh, R-Ill. (8)	624,903	*Melissa Bean, D*	2,451,348
Raúl R. Labrador, R-Idaho (1)	771,293	*Walt Minnick, D*	2,534,139
Jon Runyan, R-N.J. (3)	1,618,073	*John Adler, D*	3,285,638
Michael G. Grimm, R-N.Y. (13)	1,249,139	*Michael E. McMahon, D*	2,910,115
Vicky Hartzler, R-Mo. (4)	1,456,176	*Ike Skelton, D*	3,107,552
Tim Walberg, R-Mich. (7)	1,647,379	*Mark Schauer, D*	3,278,131
Rick Berg, R-N.D. (AL)	2,094,847	*Earl Pomeroy, D*	3,690,646
Chip Cravaack, R-Minn. (8)	630,728	*James L. Oberstar, D*	2,223,357
Sandy Adams, R-Fla. (24)	1,266,664	*Suzanne M. Kosmas, D*	2,561,831
Scott Tipton, R-Colo. (3)	1,207,832	*John Salazar, D*	2,474,562
Robert Hurt, R-Va. (5)	2,542,276	*Tom Perriello, D*	3,782,680
Charles Bass, R-N.H. (2)	1,249,005	Ann McLane Kuster, D	2,486,894
Joe Heck, R-Nev. (3)	1,409,242	*Dina Titus, D*	2,624,598
Cory Gardner, R-Colo., 4	2,407,602	*Betsy Markey, D*	3,612,696
Dave Reichert, R-Wash. (8)	2,770,293	Suzan DelBene, D	3,942,493
Laura Richardson, D-Calif. (37)	663,731	Star Parker, R	1,826,846
Rene Ellmers, R-N.C. (2)	908,108	*Bob Etheridge, D*	1,904,688
Mick Mulvaney, R-S.C. (5)	1,510,414	*John M. Spratt Jr., D*	2,497,633
Cedric L. Richmond, D-La. (2)	1,134,506	*Anh "Joseph" Cao, R*	2,106,025
Dan Lungren, R-Calif. (3)	1,974,501	Ami Bera, D	2,935,828
Tom Marino, R-Pa. (10)	705,071	*Christopher Carney, D*	1,657,586
Marcy Kaptur, D-Ohio (9)	1,041,035	Rich Iott, R	1,976,613
Paul Gosar, R-Ariz. (1)	1,172,287	*Ann Kirkpatrick, D*	1,998,802
Austin Scott, R-Ga. (8)	1,024,631	*Jim Marshall, D*	1,820,049
Reid Ribble, R-Wis. (8)	1,307,557	*Steve Kagen, D*	2,100,786
Lou Barletta, R-Pa. (11)	1,291,165	*Paul E. Kanjorski, D*	2,083,660
Mike Kelly, R-Pa. (3)	1,306,960	*Kathy Dahlkemper, D*	2,024,801
Adam Kinzinger, R-Ill. (11)	1,827,192	*Debbie Halvorson, D*	2,509,211
Blake Farenthold, R-Texas (27)	568,298	*Solomon P. Ortiz, D*	1,244,876
Bobby Schilling, R-Ill. (17)	1,117,731	*Phil Hare, D*	1,759,078
Richard Hanna, R-N.Y. (24)	1,260,258	*Michael Arcuri, D*	1,886,555
David Schweikert, R-Ariz. (5)	1,721,364	*Harry E. Mitchell, D*	2,308,400
Bill Johnson, R-Ohio (6)	668,670	*Charlie Wilson, D*	1,236,213
Bill Owens, D-N.Y. (23)*	2,973,345	Matt Doheny, R	3,440,808

(continued on page 1123)

(continued from page 1122)

Scott DesJarlais, R-Tenn. (4)	$957,680	*Lincoln Davis*, D	1,411,746
Bill Flores, R-Texas (17)	3,389,497	*Chet Edwards*, D	3,841,632
Jaime Herrera Beutler, R-Wash. (3)	1,534,650	Denny Heck, D	1,965,997
Gerald E. Connolly, D-Va. (11)	2,466,046	Keith Fimian, R	2,870,147
Rick Crawford, R-Ark. (1)	1,249,963	Chad Causey, D	1,613,863
Andy Harris, R-Md. (1)	2,383,184	*Frank Kratovil Jr.*, D	2,622,108
Todd Young, R-Ind. (9)	1,950,159	*Baron P. Hill*, D	2,172,570
Marlin Stutzman, R-Ind. (3)*	596,783	Thomas Hayhurst, D	794,802
Marthy Roby, R-Ala. (2)	1,240,276	*Bobby Bright*, D	1,435,626
Nan Hayworth, R-N.Y. (19)	2,129,637	*John Hall*, D	2,292,623
Frank Guinta, R-N.H. (1)	1,558,063	*Carol Shea-Porter*, D	1,682,124
Rob Wittman, R-Va. (1)	971,827	Krystal M. Ball, D	1,086,494
Eddie Bernice Johnson, D-Texas (30)	572,968	Stephen E. Broden, R	662,764
Robert Dold, R-Ill. (10)	2,903,831	Dan Seals, D	2,941,994

* Includes special-election expenditures

Closest Elections of 2010

Race	Winner	Votes	Loser	Votes	Margin
Illinois 8	Joe Walsh, R	98,115	Rep. Melissa Bean, D	97,825	290
New York 1	Rep. Timothy H. Bishop, D	98,316	Randy Altschuler, R	97,723	593
Kentucky 6	Rep. Ben Chandler, D	119,812	Andy Barr, R	119,165	647
New York 25	Ann Marie Buerkle, R	104,602	Rep. Dan Maffei, D	103,954	648
Texas 27	Blake Farenthold, R	51,001	Rep. Solomon P. Ortiz, D	50,226	775
Virginia 11	Rep. Gerald E. Connolly, D	111,720	Keith Fimian, R	110,739	981
West Virginia 1	David B. McKinley, R	90,660	Mike Oliverio, D	89,220	1,440
North Carolina 2	Renee Ellmers, R	93,876	Rep. Bob Etheridge, D	92,393	1,483
Nevada 3	Joe Heck, R	128,916	Rep. Dina Titus, D	127,168	1,748
New York 23	Rep. Bill Owens, D	82,232	Matt Doheny, R	80,237	1,995

Fewest Votes Received

Winning House candidates in contested elections who received the fewest votes in 2010:

Member	Votes Received
Gene Green, D-Texas (29)*	43,257
Jim Costa, D-Calif. (20)*	46,247
Silvestre Reyes, D-Texas (16)	49,301
Loretta Sanchez, D-Calif. (47)*	50,832
Blake Farenthold, R-Texas (27)	51,001
Rubén Hinojosa, D-Texas (15)*	53,546
Charlie Gonzalez, D-Texas (20)	58,645
Ed Pastor, D-Ariz. (4)*	61,524
José E. Serrano, D-N.Y., (16)	61,642
Henry Cuellar, D-Texas (28)	62,773

*Also finished in the top 10 in the 2008 election

Most Votes Received

Winning House candidates who received the most votes in 2010:

Member	Votes Received
Jim McDermott, D-Wash. (7)*	232,649
F. James Sensenbrenner Jr., R-Wis. (5)*	229,642
Denny Rehberg, R-Mont. (AL)*	217,696
Mike Coffman, R-Colo. (6)	217,368
Rich Nugent, R-Fla. (5)	208,815
Greg Walden, R-Ore. (2)	206,245
Spencer Bachus, R-Ala. (6)*	205,288
Tom Price, R-Ga. (6)	198,100
Earl Blumenauer, D-Ore. (3)	193,104
Tammy Baldwin, D-Wis. (2)*	191,164

*Also finished in the top 10 in the 2008 election

Top 10 Senate Spenders in 2010

Based on FEC reports of expenditures from Jan. 1, 2009, through Dec. 31, 2010, the first column lists the top spenders who were elected or re-elected in the 2010 election. Losing incumbents are in italics.

Member	Expenditures	Opponent	Expenditures
Barbara Boxer, D-Calif.	$26,959,369	Carly Fiorina, R	$22,794,349
Harry Reid, D-Nev.	22,548,567	Sharron Angle, R	28,262,487
Marco Rubio, R-Fla.	21,638,315	Charlie Crist, I*	13,608,676
John McCain, R-Ariz.	20,490,726	Rodney Glassman, D	1,401,586
Charles E. Schumer, D-N.Y.	18,143,841	Jay Townsend, R	217,593
Patrick J. Toomey, R-Pa.	16,998,137	Joe Sestak, D	7,524,257
Ron Johnson, R-Wis.	15,316,651	*Russ Feingold*, D	15,544,093
Rob Portman, R-Ohio	15,054,910	Lee Fisher, D	6,383,162
Patty Murray, D-Wash.	14,873,696	Dino Rossi, R	9,421,111
Mark Steven Kirk, R-Ill.	14,146,756	Alexi Giannoulias, D	9,926,766

*Democrat Kendrick B. Meek spent 8,849,701.

Top 10 House Spenders in 2010

Based on FEC reports of expenditures from Jan. 1, 2009, through Dec. 31, 2010, the first column lists the top spenders who were elected or re-elected in the 2010 election. Losing incumbents are in italics.

Member	Expenditures	Opponent	Expenditures
Michele Bachmann, R-Minn. (6)	$11,652,656	Tarryl Clark, D	$4,692,865
John A. Boehner, R-Ohio (8)	9,876,911	Justin A. Coussoule, D	247,030
Allen B. West, R-Fla. (22)	6,519,713	*Ron Klein*, D	5,319,671
Eric Cantor, R-Va. (7)	5,407,656	Rick E. Waugh, D	148,349
Joe Wilson, R-S.C. (2)	4,765,083	Rob Miller, D	3,134,569
Steny H. Hoyer, D-Md. (5)	4,687,713	Charles J. Lollar, R	575,231
Scott Rigell, R-Va. (2)	4,599,653	*Glenn Nye*, D	2,274,753
Barney Frank, D-Mass. (4)	4,305,447	Sean Bielat, R	2,436,274
Charles B. Rangel, D-N.Y. (15)	4,139,258	Michel Faulkner, R	220,389
Steve Israel, D-N.Y. (2)	3,941,248	John Gomez, R	404,111

10 Least Expensive Winning 2010 House Campaigns

The chart is based on expenditures from Jan. 1, 2009, through Dec. 31, 2010, for contested elections.

Member	Expenditures	Member	Expenditures
Doug Lamborn, R-Colo. (5)	$230,383	Phil Roe, R-Tenn. (1)	$346,589
Todd R. Platts, R-Pa. (19)	250,797	Grace F. Napolitano, D-Calif. (38)	350,881
Timothy V. Johnson, R-Ill. (15)	270,407	Al Green, D-Texas (9)	357,611
Rob Bishop, R-Utah (1)	302,771	Roscoe G. Bartlett, R-Md. (6)	367,098
Rob Woodall, R-Ga. (7)	323,801	Pete Stark, D-Calif. (13)	371,119

Republican Wins in Obama Districts

In 2010, 61 Republicans won in districts whose voters preferred Democrat Barack Obama for president in 2008. The second column of numbers shows the percentage with which Obama won in the district, and the last column shows how far the House Republican ran ahead or behind Obama in the district.

	Member's Win	Obama	+/-		Member's Win	Obama	+/-
Tom Petri, Wis. (6)	71%	50%	+21%	Dan Benishek, Mich. (1)	52%	50%	+2%
Ileana Ros-Lehtinen, Fla. (18)	69	51	+18	Pat Tiberi, Ohio (12)	56	54	+2
Paul D. Ryan, Wis. (1)	68	51	+17	Reid Ribble, Wis. (8)	55	53	+2
Dave Camp, Mich. (4)	66	50	+16	Nan Hayworth, N.Y. (19)	53	51	+2
C.W. Bill Young, Fla. (10)	66	52	+14	Frank Guinta, N.H. (1)	54	53	+1
Tom Latham, Iowa (4)	66	53	+13	Dan Lungren, Calif. (3)	50	49	+1
Howard P. "Buck" McKeon, Calif. (25)	62	49	+12	Steve Stivers, Ohio (15)	54	54	-
J. Randy Forbes, Va. (4)	62	50	+12	Mary Bono Mack, Calif. (45)	51	52	-
Donald Manzullo, Ill. (16)	65	53	+12	Jaime Herrera Beutler, Wash. (3)	53	53	-
Frank A. LoBiondo, N.J. (2)	66	54	+12	Michael G. Fitzpatrick, Pa. (8)	54	54	-
Mike Rogers, Mich. (8)	64	53	+11	Jim Gerlach, Pa. (6)	57	58	-1
Lee Terry, Neb. (2)	61	50	+11	Patrick Meehan, Pa. (7)	55	56	-1
John Campbell, Calif. (48)	60	49	+11	Francisco "Quico" Canseco, Texas (23)	49	51	-2
Frank R. Wolf, Va. (10)	63	53	+10	Tim Walberg, Mich. (7)	50	52	-2
Judy Biggert, Ill. (13)	64	54	+10	Jon Runyan, N.J. (3)	50	52	-2
Elton Gallegly, Calif. (24)	60	51	+9	Lou Barletta, Pa. (11)	55	57	-2
Leonard Lance, N.J. (7)	59	50	+9	Charlie Dent, Pa. (15)	54	56	-2
Fred Upton, Mich. (6)	62	54	+8	Renee Ellmers, N.C. (2)	49	52	-3
Peter Roskam, Ill. (6)	64	56	+8	Bobby Schilling, Ill. (17)	53	56	-3
Kevin Yoder, Kan. (3)	58	51	+7	Steve Chabot, Ohio (1)	51	55	-4
Erik Paulsen, Minn. (3)	59	52	+7	Randy Hultgren, Ill. (14)	51	55	-4
Ken Calvert, Calif. (44)	56	50	+6	Sean P. Duffy, Wis. (7)	52	56	-4
Brian P. Bilbray, Calif. (50)	57	51	+5	Dave Reichert, Wash. (8)	52	56	-4
Thaddeus McCotter, Mich. (11)	59	54	+5	Chip Cravaack, Minn. (8)	48	53	-5
Adam Kinzinger, Ill. (11)	57	53	+4	Blake Farenthold, Texas (27)	48	53	-5
Daniel Webster, Fla. (8)	56	52	+4	Ann Marie Buerkle, N.Y. (25)	50	56	-6
Chris Gibson, N.Y. (20)	55	51	+4	Joe Heck, Nev. (3)	48	55	-7
David Dreier, Calif. (26)	54	51	+3	Joe Walsh, Ill. (8)	48	56	-8
Scott Rigell, Va. (2)	53	50	+3	Charles Bass, N.H. (2)	48	56	-8
Richard Hanna, N.Y. (24)	53	50	+3	Robert Dold, Ill. (10)	51	61	-10
Allen B. West, Fla. (22)	54	52	+2				

Democratic Wins in McCain Districts

In 2010, 12 Democrats won in districts whose voters preferred Republican John McCain for president in 2008. The second column of numbers shows the percentage with which McCain won in the district, and the last column shows how far the House Democrat ran ahead or behind McCain in the district.

	Member's Win	McCain	+/-		Member's Win	McCain	+/-
Collin C. Peterson, Minn. (7)	55%	50%	+5%	Mike Ross, Ark. (4)	58%	58%	-
Tim Holden, Pa. (17)	56	51	+5	Gabrielle Giffords, Ariz. (8)	49	52	-3%
Heath Shuler, N.C. (11)	54	52	+2	Jason Altmire, Pa. (4)	51	55	-4
Mark Critz, Pa. (12)	51	49	+2	Ben Chandler, Ky. (6)	50	55	-5
Mike McIntyre, N.C. (7)	54	52	+2	Jim Matheson, Utah (2)	50	58	-8
Nick J. Rahall II, W.Va. (3)	56	56	-	Dan Boren, Okla. (2)	57	66	-9

Hispanic Districts

Congressional districts with the largest percentage of Hispanics (Hispanics may be of any race):

District	Percent	Member
Texas 15	82.5	Hinojosa, D
Texas 16	81.5	Reyes, D
Texas 28	78.9	Cuellar, D
California 34	78.7	Roybal-Allard, D
Texas 29	76.0	Green, D
Florida 21	75.6	Diaz-Balart, R
California 38	75.4	Napolitano, D
Illinois 4	73.5	Gutierrez, D
Texas 27	73.2	Farenthold, R
Florida 25	71.6	Rivera, R

Black Districts

Congressional districts with the largest percentage of African-Americans:

District	Percent	Member
Illinois 2	68.8	Jackson, D
Mississippi 2	66.2	Thompson, D
Tennessee 9	63.2	Cohen, D
Alabama 7	62.6	Sewell, D
Illinois 1	62.2	Rush, D
Ohio 11	59.3	Fudge, D
Michigan 14	58.9	Conyers, D
Michigan 13	58.5	Clarke, D
New York 10	58.4	Towns, D
Louisiana 2	58.2	Richmond, D

Asian Districts

Congressional districts with the largest percentage of Asians:

District	Percent	Member
Hawaii 1	51.4	Hanabusa, D
California 15	36.4	Honda, D
California 13	36.0	Stark, D
California 12	33.4	Speier, D
New York 5	32.6	Ackerman, D
California 8	31.1	Pelosi, D
California 16	28.3	Lofgren, D
California 29	27.7	Schiff, D
Hawaii 2	24.9	Hirono, D
California 32	22.1	Chu, D

American Indian Districts

Congressional districts with the largest percentage of American Indians:

District	Percent	Member
Arizona 1	19.1	Gosar, R
Oklahoma 2	18.4	Boren, D
New Mexico 3	17.3	Luján, D
Alaska AL	14.4	Young, R
South Dakota AL	8.5	Noem, R
North Carolina 7	7.8	McIntyre, D
Oklahoma 1	6.6	Sullivan, R
Oklahoma 3	6.2	Lucas, R
Montana AL	6.1	Rehberg, R
Oklahoma 4	5.8	Cole, R

Oldest Districts

Congressional districts with the highest median age:

District	Median Age	Member
Florida 13	47.7	Buchanan, R
Florida 14	46.3	Mack, R
Florida 10	45.4	Young, R
Florida 5	45.2	Nugent, R
Florida 19	45.0	Deutch, D
Florida 16	44.8	Rooney, R
Florida 22	44.4	West, R
Michigan 1	43.9	Benishek, R
Massachusetts 10	43.3	Keating, D
Pennsylvania 18	43.0	Murphy, R

Youngest Districts

Congressional districts with the lowest median age:

District	Median Age	Member
Utah 3	25.4	Chaffetz, R
California 20	27.7	Costa, D
California 43	27.7	Baca, D
Arizona 4	27.9	Pastor, D
Texas 29	28.4	Green, D
New York 16	28.9	Serrano, D
Utah 1	29.1	Bishop, R
California 47	29.2	Sanchez, D
Illinois 4	29.3	Gutierrez, D
Texas 28	29.4	Cuellar, D

Statistics in the boxes appearing on pp. 1126-1127 are from the U.S. Census Bureau

Richest Districts

Congressional districts with the highest median household income in 2009:

District	Income	Member
Virginia 11	103,808	Connolly, D
New Jersey 11	98,279	Frelinghuysen, R
Virginia 10	95,048	Wolf, R
New Jersey 7	93,875	Lance, R
California 14	93,328	Eshoo, D
New York 3	91,382	King, R
New Jersey 5	91,029	Garrett, R
New York 2	89,883	Israel, D
California 42	88,450	Miller, R
New Jersey 12	88,383	Holt, D

Poorest Districts

Congressional districts with the lowest median household income in 2009:

District	Income	Member
New York 16	23,073	Serrano, D
Kentucky 5	27,884	Rogers, R
Mississippi 2	30,107	Thompson, D
Alabama 7	31,021	Sewell, D
Michigan 13	31,489	Clarke, D
North Carolina 1	31,890	Butterfield, D
Texas 15	32,004	Hinojosa, D
West Virginia 3	32,730	Rahall, D
Pennsylvania 1	32,909	Brady, D
South Carolina 6	33,184	Clyburn, D

Districts With Most Government Workers

Congressional districts with the largest percentage of workers employed by local, state or federal government organizations:

District	Percent	Member
Maryland 5	29.4	Hoyer, D
Maryland 4	26.5	Edwards, D
Florida 2	25.8	Southerland, R
Alaska AL	24.8	Young, R
Virginia 1	24.2	Wittman, R
New York 21	24.2	Tonko, D
Virginia 11	23.9	Connolly, D
Virginia 8	23.7	Moran, D
New Mexico 2	23.5	Pearce, R
New York 10	23.4	Towns, D

Most Educated Districts

Congressional districts with the largest percentage of people 25 and older with at least a bachelor's degree:

District	Percent	Member
New York 14	64.9	Maloney, D
Virginia 8	59.8	Moran, D
California 30	58.4	Waxman, D
California 14	56.1	Eshoo, D
Maryland 8	55.4	Van Hollen, D
New York 8	54.8	Nadler, D
Virginia 11	52.4	Connolly, D
California 48	52.0	Campbell, R
North Carolina 4	51.9	Price, D
Georgia 6	51.4	Price, R

Least Educated Districts

Congressional districts with the largest percentage of people 25 and older without a high school diploma:

District	Percent	Member
Texas 29	45.8	Green, D
California 34	45.2	Roybal-Allard, D
California 20	44.8	Costa, D
California 47	43.1	Sanchez, D
New York 16	41.2	Serrano, D
California 31	40.5	Becerra, D
Illinois 4	36.8	Gutierrez, D
Arizona 4	36.3	Pastor, D
Texas 28	35.4	Cuellar, D
Texas 15	35.4	Hinojosa, D

Districts With Most Foreign Born

Congressional districts with the largest percentage of residents born outside the United States (Americans born abroad are not included):

District	Percent	Member
Florida 21	55.5	Diaz-Balart, R
Florida 18	51.9	Ros-Lehtinen, R
California 31	51.4	Becerra, D
California 47	48.1	Sanchez, D
New York 5	47.1	Ackerman, D
Florida 25	45.3	Rivera, R
California 34	44.5	Roybal-Allard, D
New York 6	43.3	Meeks, D
California 29	43.2	Schiff, D
California 28	42.3	Berman, D

House Committees

House standing and select committees are listed by their full names. Membership is in order of seniority on the panel. Leadership committees are on page 1140.

In the full-committee rosters, Republicans are in roman type and Democrats are in *italics*. A vacancy indi-cates that a committee or subcommittee seat had not been filled at press time, May 2011. Subcommittee vacancies do not necessarily indicate vacancies on full committees or vice versa.

AGRICULTURE

- Phone: (202) 225-2171 - Office: 1301 Longworth

REPUBLICANS (26)	DEMOCRATS (20)
Frank D. Lucas, Okla., Chairman	*Collin C. Peterson, Minn., Ranking Member*
Robert W. Goodlatte, Va.	*Tim Holden, Pa.*
Timothy V. Johnson, Ill.	*Mike McIntyre, N.C.*
Steve King, Iowa	*Leonard L. Boswell, Iowa*
Randy Neugebauer, Texas	*Joe Baca, Calif.*
K. Michael Conaway, Texas	*Dennis Cardoza, Calif.*
Jeff Fortenberry, Neb.	*David Scott, Ga.*
Jean Schmidt, Ohio	*Henry Cuellar, Texas*
Glenn Thompson, Pa.	*Jim Costa, Calif.*
Tom Rooney, Fla.	*Tim Walz, Minn.*
Marlin Stutzman, Ind.	*Kurt Schrader, Ore.*
Bob Gibbs, Ohio	*Larry Kissell, N.C.*
Austin Scott, Ga.	*Bill Owens, N.Y.*
Scott Tipton, Colo.	*Chellie Pingree, Maine*
Steve Southerland II, Fla.	*Joe Courtney, Conn.*
Rick Crawford, Ark.	*Peter Welch, Vt.*
Martha Roby, Ala.	*Marcia L. Fudge, Ohio*
Tim Huelskamp, Kan.	*Gregorio Kilili Camacho Sablan, N. Marianas*
Scott DesJarlais, Tenn.	*Terri A. Sewell, Ala.*
Renee Ellmers, N.C.	*Jim McGovern, Mass.*
Chris Gibson, N.Y.	
Randy Hultgren, Ill.	
Vicky Hartzler, Mo.	
Bobby Schilling, Ill.	
Reid Ribble, Wis.	
Vacancy	

Conservation, Energy & Forestry
Thompson, Pa. (chairman), Goodlatte, Stutzman, Gibbs, Tipton, Southerland, Roby, Huelskamp, Hultgren, Ribble
Holden, Schrader, Owens, McIntyre, Costa, Walz, Pingree, Maine, Fudge, Sablan

Department Operations, Oversight & Credit
Fortenberry (chairman), Johnson, King, Crawford
Fudge, McGovern, Baca

General Farm Commodities & Risk Management
Conaway (chairman), King, Neugebauer, Schmidt, Gibbs, Scott, Crawford, Roby, Huelskamp, Ellmers, Gibson, Hultgren, Hartzler, Schilling
Boswell, McIntyre, Walz, Kissell, McGovern, Cardoza, Scott, Courtney, Welch, Sewell

Livestock, Dairy & Poultry
Rooney (chairman), Goodlatte, King, Neugebauer, Conaway, Huelskamp, DesJarlais, Gibson, Ribble, Vacancy
Cardoza, Scott, Courtney, Holden, Boswell, Baca, Schrader, Owens

Nutrition & Horticulture
Schmidt (chairwoman), King, Rooney, Southerland, Crawford
Baca, Pingree, Sablan

Rural Development, Research, Biotechnology & Foreign Agriculture
Johnson (chairman), Thompson, Stutzman, Scott, Hultgren, Hartzler, Schilling
Costa, Cuellar, Welch, Sewell, Kissell

APPROPRIATIONS
• Phone: (202) 225-2771   • Office: H-307 Capitol

REPUBLICANS (29)	DEMOCRATS (21)
Harold Rogers, Ky., Chairman	*Norm Dicks, Wash.,*
C.W. Bill Young, Fla.	*Ranking Member*
Jerry Lewis, Calif.	*Marcy Kaptur, Ohio*
Frank R. Wolf, Va.	*Peter J. Visclosky, Ind.*
Jack Kingston, Ga.	*Nita M. Lowey, N.Y.*
Rodney Frelinghuysen, N.J.	*José E. Serrano, N.Y.*
Tom Latham, Iowa	*Rosa DeLauro, Conn.*
Robert B. Aderholt, Ala.	*James P. Moran, Va.*
Jo Ann Emerson, Mo.	*John W. Olver, Mass.*
Kay Granger, Texas	*Ed Pastor, Ariz.*
Mike Simpson, Idaho	*David E. Price, N.C.*
John Culberson, Texas	*Maurice D. Hinchey, N.Y.*
Ander Crenshaw, Fla.	*Lucille Roybal-Allard, Calif.*
Denny Rehberg, Mont.	*Sam Farr, Calif.*
John Carter, Texas	*Jesse L. Jackson Jr., Ill.*
Rodney Alexander, La.	*Chaka Fattah, Pa.*
Ken Calvert, Calif.	*Steven R. Rothman, N.J.*
Jo Bonner, Ala.	*Sanford D. Bishop Jr., Ga.*
Steven C. LaTourette, Ohio	*Barbara Lee, Calif.*
Tom Cole, Okla.	*Adam B. Schiff, Calif.*
Jeff Flake, Ariz.	*Michael M. Honda, Calif.*
Mario Diaz-Balart, Fla.	*Betty McCollum, Minn.*
Charlie Dent, Pa.	
Steve Austria, Ohio	
Cynthia M. Lummis, Wyo.	
Tom Graves, Ga.	
Kevin Yoder, Kan.	
Steve Womack, Ark.	
Alan Nunnelee, Miss.	

Agriculture
Kingston (chairman), Latham, Emerson, Aderholt, Lummis, Nunnelee, Graves
Farr, DeLauro, Bishop, Kaptur

Commerce-Justice-Science
Wolf (chairman), Culberson, Aderholt, Bonner, Austria, Graves, Yoder
Fattah, Schiff, Honda, Serrano

Defense
Young (chairman), Lewis, Frelinghuysen, Kingston, Granger, Crenshaw, Calvert, Bonner, Cole
Dicks, Visclosky, Moran, Kaptur, Rothman, Hinchey

Energy-Water
Frelinghuysen (chairman), Lewis, Simpson, Rehberg, Alexander, Womack, Nunnelee
Visclosky, Pastor, Fattah, Olver

Financial Services
Emerson (chairwoman), Alexander, Bonner, Diaz-Balart, Graves, Yoder, Womack
Serrano, Lee, Visclosky, Pastor

Homeland Security
Aderholt (chairman), Carter, Culberson, Frelinghuysen, Latham, Crenshaw, Dent
Price, Roybal-Allard, Lowey, Olver

Interior-Environment
Simpson (chairman), Lewis, Calvert, LaTourette, Cole, Flake, Lummis
Moran, McCollum, Hinchey, Serrano

Labor-HHS-Education
Rehberg (chairman), Lewis, Alexander, Kingston, Granger, Simpson, Flake, Lummis
DeLauro, Lowey, Jackson, Roybal-Allard, Lee

Legislative Branch
Crenshaw (chairman), LaTourette, Emerson, Rehberg, Calvert
Honda, Price, Bishop

Military Construction-VA
Culberson (chairman), Young, Carter, Flake, Austria, Yoder, Nunnelee
Bishop, Farr, McCollum, Moran

State-Foreign Operations
Granger (chairwoman), Lewis, Wolf, Cole, Diaz-Balart, Dent, Austria
Lowey, Jackson, Schiff, Rothman

Transportation-HUD
Latham (chairman), Wolf, Carter, LaTourette, Diaz-Balart, Dent, Womack
Olver, Pastor, Kaptur, Price

ARMED SERVICES
• Phone: (202) 225-4151   • Office: 2120 Rayburn

REPUBLICANS (35)	DEMOCRATS (27)
Howard P. "Buck" McKeon, Calif., Chairman	Adam Smith, Wash., Ranking Member
Roscoe G. Bartlett, Md.	Silvestre Reyes, Texas
William M. "Mac" Thornberry, Texas	Loretta Sanchez, Calif.
	Mike McIntyre, N.C.
Walter B. Jones, N.C.	Robert A. Brady, Pa.
Todd Akin, Mo.	Robert E. Andrews, N.J.
J. Randy Forbes, Va.	Susan A. Davis, Calif.
Jeff Miller, Fla.	Jim Langevin, R.I.
Joe Wilson, S.C.	Rick Larsen, Wash.
Frank A. LoBiondo, N.J.	Jim Cooper, Tenn.
Michael R. Turner, Ohio	Madeleine Z. Bordallo, Guam
John Kline, Minn.	Joe Courtney, Conn.
Mike D. Rogers, Ala.	Dave Loebsack, Iowa
Trent Franks, Ariz.	Gabrielle Giffords, Ariz.
Bill Shuster, Pa.	Niki Tsongas, Mass.
K. Michael Conaway, Texas	Chellie Pingree, Maine
Doug Lamborn, Colo.	Larry Kissell, N.C.
Rob Wittman, Va.	Martin Heinrich, N.M.
Duncan Hunter, Calif.	Bill Owens, N.Y.
John Fleming, La.	John Garamendi, Calif.
Mike Coffman, Colo.	Mark Critz, Pa.
Tom Rooney, Fla.	Tim Ryan, Ohio
Todd R. Platts, Pa.	C.A. Dutch Ruppersberger, Md.
Scott Rigell, Va.	
Chris Gibson, N.Y.	Hank Johnson, Ga.
Vicky Hartzler, Mo.	Kathy Castor, Fla.
Joe Heck, Nev.	Betty Sutton, Ohio
Bobby Schilling, Ill.	Colleen Hanabusa, Hawaii
Jon Runyan, N.J.	
Austin Scott, Ga.	
Tim Griffin, Ark.	
Steven M. Palazzo, Miss.	
Allen B. West, Fla.	
Martha Roby, Ala.	
Mo Brooks, Ala.	
Todd Young, Ind.	

Emerging Threats & Capabilities
Thornberry (chairman), Miller, Kline, Shuster, Conaway, Gibson, Schilling, West, Franks, Hunter
Langevin, Sanchez, Andrews, Davis, Ryan, Ruppersberger, Johnson, Castor

Military Personnel
Wilson (chairman), Jones, Coffman, Rooney, Heck, West, Scott, Hartzler
Davis, Brady, Bordallo, Loebsack, Tsongas, Pingree

Oversight & Investigations
Wittman (chairman), Conaway, Brooks, Young, Rooney, Coffman
Cooper, Andrews, Sanchez, Hanabusa

Readiness
Forbes (chairman), Rogers, Heck, Scott, LoBiondo, Gibson, Hartzler, Schilling, Runyan, Griffin, Palazzo, Roby
Bordallo, Reyes, Courtney, Loebsack, Giffords, Kissell, Owens, Ryan, Hanabusa

Seapower & Projection Forces
Akin (chairman), Hunter, Coffman, Rigell, Griffin, Palazzo, Young, Bartlett, Forbes, Wittman, Platts
McIntyre, Davis, Langevin, Larsen, Courtney, Pingree, Critz, Johnson, Sutton

Strategic Forces
Turner (chairman), Franks, Lamborn, Brooks, Thornberry, Rogers, Fleming, Rigell, Scott
Sanchez, Langevin, Larsen, Heinrich, Garamendi, Ruppersberger, Sutton

Tactical Air & Land Forces
Bartlett (chairman), LoBiondo, Fleming, Rooney, Platts, Hartzler, Runyan, Roby, Jones, Akin, Wilson, Turner, Shuster, Lamborn
Reyes, McIntyre, Cooper, Giffords, Tsongas, Kissell, Heinrich, Owens, Garamendi, Critz, Castor

BUDGET
• Phone: (202) 226-7270   • Office: 207 Cannon

REPUBLICANS (22)	DEMOCRATS (16)
Paul D. Ryan, Wis., Chairman	Chris Van Hollen, Md., Ranking Member
Scott Garrett, N.J.	Allyson Y. Schwartz, Pa.
Mike Simpson, Idaho	Marcy Kaptur, Ohio
John Campbell, Calif.	Lloyd Doggett, Texas
Ken Calvert, Calif.	Earl Blumenauer, Ore.
Todd Akin, Mo.	Betty McCollum, Minn.
Tom Cole, Okla.	John Yarmuth, Ky.
Tom Price, Ga.	Bill Pascrell Jr., N.J.
Tom McClintock, Calif.	Michael M. Honda, Calif.
Jason Chaffetz, Utah	Tim Ryan, Ohio
Marlin Stutzman, Ind.	Debbie Wasserman Schultz, Fla.
James Lankford, Okla.	Gwen Moore, Wis.
Diane Black, Tenn.	Kathy Castor, Fla.
Reid Ribble, Wis.	Heath Shuler, N.C.
Bill Flores, Texas	Paul Tonko, N.Y.
Mick Mulvaney, S.C.	Karen Bass, Calif.
Tim Huelskamp, Kan.	
Todd Young, Ind.	
Justin Amash, Mich.	
Todd Rokita, Ind.	
Frank Guinta, N.H.	
Rob Woodall, Ga.	

EDUCATION & THE WORKFORCE
• Phone: (202) 225-4527   • Office: 2181 Rayburn

REPUBLICANS (23)
John Kline, Minn., Chairman
Tom Petri, Wis.
Howard P. "Buck" McKeon, Calif.
Judy Biggert, Ill.
Todd R. Platts, Pa.
Joe Wilson, S.C.
Virginia Foxx, N.C.
Robert W. Goodlatte, Va.
Duncan Hunter, Calif.
Phil Roe, Tenn.
Glenn Thompson, Pa.
Tim Walberg, Mich.
Scott DesJarlais, Tenn.
Richard Hanna, N.Y.
Todd Rokita, Ind.
Larry Bucshon, Ind.
Trey Gowdy, S.C.
Lou Barletta, Pa.
Kristi Noem, S.D.
Martha Roby, Ala.
Joe Heck, Nev.
Dennis A. Ross, Fla.
Mike Kelly, Pa.

DEMOCRATS (17)
George Miller, Calif., Ranking Member
Dale E. Kildee, Mich.
Donald M. Payne, N.J.
Robert E. Andrews, N.J.
Robert C. Scott, Va.
Lynn Woolsey, Calif.
Rubén Hinojosa, Texas
Carolyn McCarthy, N.Y.
John F. Tierney, Mass.
Dennis J. Kucinich, Ohio
David Wu, Ore.
Rush D. Holt, N.J.
Susan A. Davis, Calif.
Raúl M. Grijalva, Ariz.
Timothy H. Bishop, N.Y.
Dave Loebsack, Iowa
Mazie K. Hirono, Hawaii

Early Childhood, Elementary & Secondary Education
Hunter (chairman), Kline, Petri, Biggert, Platts, Foxx, Goodlatte, Hanna, Barletta, Noem, Roby, Kelly
Kildee, Payne, Scott, McCarthy, Holt, Davis, Grijalva, Hirono, Woolsey

Health, Employment, Labor & Pensions
Roe (chairman), Wilson, Thompson, Walberg, DesJarlais, Hanna, Rokita, Bucshon, Barletta, Noem, Roby, Heck, Ross
Andrews, Kucinich, Loebsack, Kildee, Hinojosa, McCarthy, Tierney, Wu, Holt, Scott

Higher Education & Workforce Training
Foxx (chairwoman), Kline, Petri, McKeon, Biggert, Platts, Roe, Thompson, Hanna, Bucshon, Barletta, Heck
Hinojosa, Tierney, Wu, Bishop, Andrews, Davis, Grijalva, Loebsack, Miller

Workforce Protections
Walberg (chairman), Kline, Goodlatte, Rokita, Bucshon, Gowdy, Noem, Ross, Kelly
Woolsey, Payne, Kucinich, Bishop, Hirono, Miller

ENERGY & COMMERCE
• Phone: (202) 225-2927   • Office: 2125 Rayburn

REPUBLICANS (31)
Fred Upton, Mich., Chairman
Joe L. Barton, Texas
Cliff Stearns, Fla.
Edward Whitfield, Ky.
John Shimkus, Ill.
Joe Pitts, Pa.
Mary Bono Mack, Calif.
Greg Walden, Ore.
Lee Terry, Neb.
Mike Rogers, Mich.
Sue Myrick, N.C.
John Sullivan, Okla.
Tim Murphy, Pa.
Michael C. Burgess, Texas
Marsha Blackburn, Tenn.
Brian P. Bilbray, Calif.
Charles Bass, N.H.
Phil Gingrey, Ga.
Steve Scalise, La.
Bob Latta, Ohio
Cathy McMorris Rodgers, Wash.
Gregg Harper, Miss.
Leonard Lance, N.J.
Bill Cassidy, La.
Brett Guthrie, Ky.
Pete Olson, Texas
David B. McKinley, W.Va.
Cory Gardner, Colo.
Mike Pompeo, Kan.
Adam Kinzinger, Ill.
Morgan Griffith, Va.

DEMOCRATS (23)
Henry A. Waxman, Calif., Ranking Member
John D. Dingell, Mich.
Edward J. Markey, Mass.
Edolphus Towns, N.Y.
Frank Pallone Jr., N.J.
Bobby L. Rush, Ill.
Anna G. Eshoo, Calif.
Eliot L. Engel, N.Y.
Gene Green, Texas
Diana DeGette, Colo.
Lois Capps, Calif.
Mike Doyle, Pa.
Jan Schakowsky, Ill.
Charlie Gonzalez, Texas
Jay Inslee, Wash.
Tammy Baldwin, Wis.
Mike Ross, Ark.
Anthony Weiner, N.Y.
Jim Matheson, Utah
G.K. Butterfield, N.C.
John Barrow, Ga.
Doris Matsui, Calif.
Donna M.C. Christensen, V.I.

Commerce, Manufacturing & Trade
Bono Mack (chairwoman), Blackburn, Stearns, Bass, Harper, Lance, Cassidy, Guthrie, Olson, McKinley, Pompeo, Kinzinger, Barton, Upton
Butterfield, Gonzalez, Matheson, Dingell, Towns, Rush, Schakowsky, Ross, Waxman

Communications & Technology
Walden (chairman), Terry, Stearns, Shimkus, Bono Mack, Rogers, Bilbray, Bass, Blackburn, Gingrey, Scalise, Latta, Guthrie, Kinzinger, Barton, Upton
Eshoo, Markey, Doyle, Matsui, Barrow, Christensen, Towns, Pallone, Rush, DeGette, Waxman

Energy & Power
Whitfield (chairman), Sullivan, Shimkus, Walden, Terry, Burgess, Bilbray, Scalise, McMorris Rodgers, Olson, McKinley, Gardner, Pompeo, Griffith, Barton, Upton
Rush, Inslee, Matheson, Dingell, Markey, Engel, Green, Capps, Doyle, Gonzalez, Waxman

Environment & the Economy

Shimkus (chairman), Murphy, Whitfield, Pitts, Bono Mack, Sullivan, Bass, Latta, McMorris Rodgers, Harper, Cassidy, Gardner, Barton, Upton
Green, Baldwin, Butterfield, Barrow, Matsui, Pallone, DeGette, Capps, Waxman

Health

Pitts (chairman), Burgess, Whitfield, Shimkus, Rogers, Myrick, Murphy, Blackburn, Gingrey, Latta, McMorris Rodgers, Lance, Cassidy, Guthrie, Barton, Upton
Pallone, Dingell, Towns, Engel, Capps, Schakowsky, Gonzalez, Baldwin, Ross, Weiner, Waxman

Oversight & Investigations

Stearns (chairman), Terry, Sullivan, Murphy, Burgess, Blackburn, Myrick, Bilbray, Gingrey, Scalise, Gardner, Griffith, Barton, Upton
DeGette, Schakowsky, Ross, Weiner, Markey, Green, Christensen, Dingell, Waxman

FINANCIAL SERVICES

• Phone: (202) 225-7502   • Office: 2129 Rayburn

REPUBLICANS (34)

Spencer Bachus, Ala., Chairman
Peter T. King, N.Y.
Ed Royce, Calif.
Frank D. Lucas, Okla.
Ron Paul, Texas
Donald Manzullo, Ill.
Walter B. Jones, N.C.
Judy Biggert, Ill.
Gary G. Miller, Calif.
Shelley Moore Capito, W.Va.
Jeb Hensarling, Texas
Scott Garrett, N.J.
Randy Neugebauer, Texas
Patrick T. McHenry, N.C.
John Campbell, Calif.
Michele Bachmann, Minn.
Thaddeus McCotter, Mich.
Kevin McCarthy, Calif.
Steve Pearce, N.M.
Bill Posey, Fla.
Michael G. Fitzpatrick, Pa.
Lynn Westmoreland, Ga.
Blaine Luetkemeyer, Mo.
Bill Huizenga, Mich.
Sean P. Duffy, Wis.
Nan Hayworth, N.Y.
James B. Renacci, Ohio
Robert Hurt, Va.
Robert Dold, Ill.
David Schweikert, Ariz.
Michael G. Grimm, N.Y.
Francisco "Quico" Canseco, Texas
Steve Stivers, Ohio
Stephen Fincher, Tenn.

DEMOCRATS (27)

Barney Frank, Mass., Ranking Member
Maxine Waters, Calif.
Carolyn B. Maloney, N.Y.
Luis V. Gutierrez, Ill.
Nydia M. Velázquez, N.Y.
Melvin Watt, N.C.
Gary L. Ackerman, N.Y.
Brad Sherman, Calif.
Gregory W. Meeks, N.Y.
Michael E. Capuano, Mass.
Rubén Hinojosa, Texas
William Lacy Clay, Mo.
Carolyn McCarthy, N.Y.
Joe Baca, Calif.
Stephen F. Lynch, Mass.
Brad Miller, N.C.
David Scott, Ga.
Al Green, Texas
Emanuel Cleaver II, Mo.
Gwen Moore, Wis.
Keith Ellison, Minn.
Ed Perlmutter, Colo.
Joe Donnelly, Ind.
André Carson, Ind.
Jim Himes, Conn.
Gary Peters, Mich.
John Carney, Del.

Capital Markets & Government Sponsored Enterprises

Garrett (chairman), Schweikert, King, Royce, Lucas, Manzullo, Biggert, Hensarling, Neugebauer, Campbell, McCotter, McCarthy, Pearce, Posey, Fitzpatrick, Hayworth, Hurt, Grimm, Stivers, Dold
Waters, Ackerman, Sherman, Hinojosa, Lynch, Miller, Maloney, Moore, Perlmutter, Donnelly, Carson, Himes, Peters, Green, Ellison

Domestic Monetary Policy & Technology

Paul (chairman), Jones, Lucas, McHenry, Luetkemeyer, Huizenga, Hayworth, Schweikert
Clay, Maloney, Meeks, Green, Cleaver, Peters

Financial Institutions & Consumer Credit

Capito (chairwoman), Royce, Manzullo, Jones, Hensarling, McHenry, McCotter, McCarthy, Pearce, Westmoreland, Luetkemeyer, Huizenga, Duffy, Dold, Canseco, Grimm, Fincher
Maloney, Gutierrez, Watt, Ackerman, Hinojosa, McCarthy, Baca, Miller, Scott, Velázquez, Meeks, Lynch, Carney

Insurance, Housing & Community Opportunity

Biggert (chairwoman), Hurt, Miller, Capito, Garrett, McHenry, Westmoreland, Duffy, Dold, Stivers
Gutierrez, Waters, Velázquez, Cleaver, Clay, Watt, Sherman, Capuano

Oversight & Investigations

Neugebauer (chairman), Fitzpatrick, King, Bachmann, Pearce, Posey, Hayworth, Renacci, Canseco, Fincher
Capuano, Lynch, Waters, Baca, Miller, Ellison, Himes, Carney

International Monetary Policy & Trade

Miller (chairman), Dold, Paul, Manzullo, Campbell, Bachmann, McCotter, Huizenga
McCarthy, Moore, Carson, Scott , Perlmutter, Donnelly

ETHICS

• Phone: (202) 225-7103 • Office: 1015 Longworth

REPUBLICANS (5)

Jo Bonner, Ala., Chairman
Michael McCaul, Texas
K. Michael Conaway, Texas
Charlie Dent, Pa.
Gregg Harper, Miss.

DEMOCRATS (5)

Linda T. Sánchez, Calif., Ranking Member
Mazie K. Hirono, Hawaii
John Yarmuth, Ky.
Donna Edwards, Md.
Pedro R. Pierluisi, P.R.

FOREIGN AFFAIRS
- Phone: (202) 225-5021   • Office: 2170 Rayburn

REPUBLICANS (26)

Ileana Ros-Lehtinen, Fla., Chairwoman
Christopher H. Smith, N.J.
Dan Burton, Ind.
Elton Gallegly, Calif.
Dana Rohrabacher, Calif.
Donald Manzullo, Ill.
Ed Royce, Calif.
Steve Chabot, Ohio
Ron Paul, Texas
Mike Pence, Ind.
Joe Wilson, S.C.
Connie Mack, Fla.
Jeff Fortenberry, Neb.
Michael McCaul, Texas
Ted Poe, Texas
Gus Bilirakis, Fla.
Jean Schmidt, Ohio
Bill Johnson, Ohio
David Rivera, Fla.
Mike Kelly, Pa.
Tim Griffin, Ark.
Tom Marino, Pa.
Jeff Duncan, S.C.
Ann Marie Buerkle, N.Y.
Renee Ellmers, N.C.
Vacancy

DEMOCRATS (20)

Howard L. Berman, Calif., Ranking Member
Gary L. Ackerman, N.Y.
Eni F.H. Faleomavaega, A.S.
Donald M. Payne, N.J.
Brad Sherman, Calif.
Eliot L. Engel, N.Y.
Gregory W. Meeks, N.Y.
Russ Carnahan, Mo.
Albio Sires, N.J.
Gerald E. Connolly, Va.
Ted Deutch, Fla.
Dennis Cardoza, Calif.
Ben Chandler, Ky.
Brian Higgins, N.Y.
Allyson Y. Schwartz, Pa.
Christopher S. Murphy, Conn.
Frederica S. Wilson, Fla.
Karen Bass, Calif.
William Keating, Mass.
David Cicilline, R.I.

Africa, Global Health & Human Rights
Smith (chairman), Fortenberry, Griffin, Marino, Buerkle
Payne, Bass, Carnahan

Asia & the Pacific
Manzullo (chairman), Paul, Johnson, Burton, Royce, Chabot, Kelly, Duncan
Faleomavaega, Wilson, Ackerman, Sherman, Meeks, Cardoza

Europe & Eurasia
Burton (chairman), Gallegly, Bilirakis, Griffin, Marino, Schmidt, Poe
Meeks, Engel, Sires, Deutch

Middle East & South Asia
Chabot (chairman), Pence, Wilson, Fortenberry, Buerkle, Ellmers, Rohrabacher, Manzullo, Mack, McCaul, Bilirakis, Marino
Ackerman, Connolly, Deutch, Cardoza, Chandler, Higgins, Schwartz, Murphy, Keating

Oversight & Investigations
Rohrabacher (chairman), Kelly, Paul, Poe, Rivera
Carnahan, Cicilline, Bass

Terrorism, Nonproliferation & Trade
Royce (chairman), Poe, Duncan, Johnson, Griffin, Buerkle, Ellmers
Sherman, Cicilline, Connolly, Higgins, Schwartz

Western Hemisphere
Mack (chairman), McCaul, Schmidt, Rivera, Smith, Gallegly
Engel, Sires, Faleomavaega, Payne

HOMELAND SECURITY
- Phone: (202) 226-8417   • Office: H2-176 Ford

REPUBLICANS (19)

Peter T. King, N.Y., Chairman
Lamar Smith, Texas
Dan Lungren, Calif.
Mike D. Rogers, Ala.
Michael McCaul, Texas
Gus Bilirakis, Fla.
Paul Broun, Ga.
Candice S. Miller, Mich.
Tim Walberg, Mich.
Chip Cravaack, Minn.
Joe Walsh, Ill.
Patrick Meehan, Pa.
Ben Quayle, Ariz.
Scott Rigell, Va.
Billy Long, Mo.
Jeff Duncan, S.C.
Tom Marino, Pa.
Blake Farenthold, Texas
Mo Brooks, Ala.

DEMOCRATS (14)

Bennie Thompson, Miss., Ranking Member
Loretta Sanchez, Calif.
Sheila Jackson Lee, Texas
Henry Cuellar, Texas
Yvette D. Clarke, N.Y.
Laura Richardson, Calif.
Danny K. Davis, Ill.
Brian Higgins, N.Y.
Jackie Speier, Calif.
Cedric L. Richmond, La.
Hansen Clarke, Mich.
William Keating, Mass.
Kathy Hochul, N.Y.
Vacancy

Border & Maritime Security
Miller (chairwoman), Rogers, McCaul, Broun, Quayle, Rigell, Duncan
Cuellar, Sanchez, Jackson Lee, Higgins, Clarke

Counterterrorism & Intelligence
Meehan (chairman), Broun, Cravaack, Walsh, Quayle, Rigell, Long
Speier, Sanchez, Cuellar, Higgins, Vacancy

Cybersecurity, Infrastructure Protection & Security Technologies
Lungren (chairman), McCaul, Walberg, Meehan, Long, Marino
Clarke, Richardson, Richmond, Keating

Emergency Preparedness, Response & Communications
Bilirakis (chairman), Walsh, Rigell, Marino, Farenthold
Richardson, Clarke, Vacancy

Oversight, Investigations & Management
McCaul (chairman), Bilirakis, Long, Duncan, Marino
Keating, Clarke, Davis

Transportation Security
Rogers (chairman), Lungren, Walberg, Cravaack, Walsh, Brooks
Jackson Lee, Davis, Speier, Richmond

HOUSE ADMINISTRATION
• Phone: (202) 225-8281 • Office: 1309 Longworth

REPUBLICANS (6)	DEMOCRATS (3)
Dan Lungren, Calif., Chairman	*Robert A. Brady, Pa.,*
Gregg Harper, Miss.	*Ranking Member*
Phil Gingrey, Ga.	*Zoe Lofgren, Calif.*
Aaron Schock, Ill.	*Charlie Gonzalez, Texas*
Todd Rokita, Ind.	
Rich Nugent, Fla.	

Elections
Harper (chairman), Schock, Nugent, Rokita
Gonzalez, Brady

Oversight
Gingrey (chairman), Schock, Nugent, Rokita
Lofgren, Gonzalez

JUDICIARY
• Phone: (202) 225-3951 • Office: 2138 Rayburn

REPUBLICANS (23)	DEMOCRATS (16)
Lamar Smith, Texas, Chairman	*John Conyers Jr., Mich., Ranking Member*
F. James Sensenbrenner Jr., Wis.	*Howard L. Berman, Calif.*
Howard Coble, N.C.	*Jerrold Nadler, N.Y.*
Elton Gallegly, Calif.	*Robert C. Scott, Va.*
Robert W. Goodlatte, Va.	*Melvin Watt, N.C.*
Dan Lungren, Calif.	*Zoe Lofgren, Calif.*
Steve Chabot, Ohio	*Sheila Jackson Lee, Texas*
Darrell Issa, Calif.	*Maxine Waters, Calif.*
Mike Pence, Ind.	*Steve Cohen, Tenn.*
J. Randy Forbes, Va.	*Hank Johnson, Ga.*
Steve King, Iowa	*Pedro R. Pierluisi, P.R.*
Trent Franks, Ariz.	*Mike Quigley, Ill.*
Louie Gohmert, Texas	*Judy Chu, Calif.*
Jim Jordan, Ohio	*Ted Deutch, Fla.*
Ted Poe, Texas	*Linda T. Sánchez, Calif.*
Jason Chaffetz, Utah	*Debbie Wasserman Schultz, Fla.*
Tim Griffin, Ark.	
Tom Marino, Pa.	
Trey Gowdy, S.C.	
Dennis A. Ross, Fla.	
Sandy Adams, Fla.	
Ben Quayle, Ariz.	
Vacancy	

Constitution
Franks (chairman), Pence, Chabot, Forbes, King, Jordan
Nadler, Quigley, Conyers, Scott

Courts, Commercial & Administrative Law
Coble (chairman), Gowdy, Gallegly, Franks, Ross, Vacancy
Cohen, Johnson, Watt, Quigley

Crime, Terrorism & Homeland Security
Sensenbrenner (chairman), Gohmert, Goodlatte, Lungren, Forbes, Poe, Chaffetz, Griffin, Marino, Gowdy, Adams, Quayle
Scott, Cohen, Johnson, Pierluisi, Chu, Deutch, Wasserman Schultz, Jackson Lee, Quigley

Immigration Policy & Enforcement
Gallegly (chairman), King, Lungren, Gohmert, Poe, Gowdy, Ross
Lofgren, Jackson Lee, Waters, Pierluisi

Intellectual Property, Competition & the Internet
Goodlatte (chairman), Coble, Sensenbrenner, Chabot, Issa, Pence, Jordan, Poe, Chaffetz, Griffin, Marino, Adams, Quayle, Vacancy
Watt, Conyers, Berman, Chu, Deutch, Sánchez, Wasserman Schultz, Nadler, Lofgren, Jackson Lee, Waters

NATURAL RESOURCES
• Phone: (202) 225-2761 • Office: 1324 Longworth

REPUBLICANS (27)	DEMOCRATS (21)
Doc Hastings, Wash., Chairman	*Edward J. Markey, Mass., Ranking Member*
Don Young, Alaska	*Dale E. Kildee, Mich.*
John J. "Jimmy" Duncan Jr., Tenn.	*Peter A. DeFazio, Ore.*
Louie Gohmert, Texas	*Eni F.H. Faleomavaega, A.S.*
Rob Bishop, Utah	*Frank Pallone Jr., N.J.*
Doug Lamborn, Colo.	*Grace F. Napolitano, Calif.*
Rob Wittman, Va.	*Rush D. Holt, N.J.*
Paul Broun, Ga.	*Raúl M. Grijalva, Ariz.*
John Fleming, La.	*Madeleine Z. Bordallo, Guam*
Mike Coffman, Colo.	*Jim Costa, Calif.*
Tom McClintock, Calif.	*Dan Boren, Okla.*
Glenn Thompson, Pa.	*Gregorio Kilili Camacho Sablan, N. Marianas*
Jeff Denham, Calif.	*Martin Heinrich, N.M.*
Dan Benishek, Mich.	*Ben Ray Luján, N.M.*
David Rivera, Fla.	*John Sarbanes, Md.*
Jeff Duncan, S.C.	*Betty Sutton, Ohio*
Scott Tipton, Colo.	*Niki Tsongas, Mass.*
Paul Gosar, Ariz.	*Pedro R. Pierluisi, P.R.*
Raúl R. Labrador, Idaho	*John Garamendi, Calif.*
Kristi Noem, S.D.	*Colleen Hanabusa, Hawaii*
Steve Southerland II, Fla.	*Vacancy*
Bill Flores, Texas	
Andy Harris, Md.	
Jeff Landry, La.	
Chuck Fleischmann, Tenn.	
Jon Runyan, N.J.	
Bill Johnson, Ohio	

Energy & Mineral Resources
Lamborn (chairman), Gohmert, Broun, Fleming, Coffman, Thompson, Benishek, Rivera, Duncan, Gosar, Flores, Landry, Fleischmann, Johnson
Holt, DeFazio, Bordallo, Costa, Boren, Sablan, Heinrich, Sarbanes, Sutton, Tsongas, Vacancy

Fisheries, Wildlife, Oceans & Insular Affairs
Fleming (chairman), Young, Wittman, Duncan, Southerland, Flores, Harris, Landry, Runyan
Sablan, Faleomavaega, Pallone, Bordallo, Pierluisi, Hanabusa, Vacancy

Indian & Alaska Native Affairs
Young (chairman), McClintock, Denham, Benishek, Gosar, Labrador, Noem
Boren, Kildee, Faleomavaega, Luján, Hanabusa

National Parks, Forests & Public Lands
Bishop (chairman), Young, Duncan, Lamborn, Broun, Coffman, McClintock, Rivera, Tipton, Labrador, Noem, Johnson
Grijalva, Kildee, DeFazio, Holt, Heinrich, Sarbanes, Sutton, Tsongas, Garamendi

Water & Power
McClintock (chairman), Gohmert, Denham, Tipton, Gosar, Labrador, Noem
Napolitano, Grijalva, Costa, Luján, Garamendi

OVERSIGHT & GOVERNMENT REFORM
• Phone: (202) 225-5074   • Office: 2157 Rayburn

REPUBLICANS (23)
Darrell Issa, Calif., Chairman
Dan Burton, Ind.
John L. Mica, Fla.
Todd R. Platts, Pa.
Michael R. Turner, Ohio
Patrick T. McHenry, N.C.
Jim Jordan, Ohio
Jason Chaffetz, Utah
Connie Mack, Fla.
Tim Walberg, Mich.
James Lankford, Okla.
Justin Amash, Mich.
Ann Marie Buerkle, N.Y.
Paul Gosar, Ariz.
Raúl R. Labrador, Idaho
Patrick Meehan, Pa.
Scott DesJarlais, Tenn.
Joe Walsh, Ill.
Trey Gowdy, S.C.
Dennis A. Ross, Fla.
Frank Guinta, N.H.
Blake Farenthold, Texas
Mike Kelly, Pa.

DEMOCRATS (17)
Elijah E. Cummings, Md., Ranking Member
Edolphus Towns, N.Y.
Carolyn B. Maloney, N.Y.
Eleanor Holmes Norton, D.C.
Dennis J. Kucinich, Ohio
John F. Tierney, Mass.
William Lacy Clay, Mo.
Stephen F. Lynch, Mass.
Jim Cooper, Tenn.
Gerald E. Connolly, Va.
Mike Quigley, Ill.
Danny K. Davis, Ill.
Bruce Braley, Iowa
Peter Welch, Vt.
John Yarmuth, Ky.
Christopher S. Murphy, Conn.
Jackie Speier, Calif.

Federal Workforce, U.S. Postal Service & Labor Policy
Ross (chairman), Amash, Jordan, Chaffetz, Mack, Walberg, Gowdy
Lynch, Norton, Connolly, Davis

Government Organization, Efficiency & Financial Management
Platts (chairman), Mack, Lankford, Amash, Gosar, Guinta, Farenthold
Towns, Cooper, Connolly, Norton

Health Care, District of Columbia, Census & the National Archives
Gowdy (chairman), Gosar, Burton, Mica, McHenry, DesJarlais, Walsh
Davis, Norton, Clay, Murphy

National Security, Homeland Defense & Foreign Operations
Chaffetz (chairman), Labrador, Burton, Mica, Platts, Turner, Gosar, Farenthold
Tierney, Braley, Welch, Yarmuth, Lynch, Quigley

Regulatory Affairs, Stimulus Oversight & Government Spending
Jordan (chairman), Buerkle, Mack, Labrador, DesJarlais, Guinta, Kelly
Kucinich, Cooper, Speier, Braley

TARP, Financial Services & Bailouts of Public and Private Programs
McHenry (chairman), Guinta, Buerkle, Amash, Meehan, Walsh, Gowdy, Ross
Quigley, Maloney, Welch, Yarmuth, Speier, Cooper

Technology, Information Policy, Intergovernmental Relations & Procurement Reform
Lankford (chairman), Kelly, Chaffetz, Walberg, Labrador, Meehan, Farenthold
Connolly, Murphy, Lynch, Speier

RULES
• Phone: (202) 225-9191   • Office: H-312 Capitol

REPUBLICANS (9)
David Dreier, Calif., Chairman
Pete Sessions, Texas
Virginia Foxx, N.C.
Rob Bishop, Utah
Rob Woodall, Ga.
Rich Nugent, Fla.
Tim Scott, S.C.
Daniel Webster, Fla.
Tom Reed, N.Y.

DEMOCRATS (4)
Louise M. Slaughter, N.Y., Ranking Member
Jim McGovern, Mass.
Alcee L. Hastings, Fla.
Jared Polis, Colo.

SCIENCE, SPACE & TECHNOLOGY
• Phone: (202) 225-6371   • Office: 2321 Rayburn

REPUBLICANS (23)
Ralph M. Hall, Texas, Chairman
F. James Sensenbrenner Jr., Wis.
Lamar Smith, Texas
Dana Rohrabacher, Calif.
Roscoe G. Bartlett, Md.
Frank D. Lucas, Okla.
Judy Biggert, Ill.
Todd Akin, Mo.
Randy Neugebauer, Texas
Michael McCaul, Texas
Paul Broun, Ga.
Sandy Adams, Fla.
Ben Quayle, Ariz.
Chuck Fleischmann, Tenn.
Scott Rigell, Va.
Steven M. Palazzo, Miss.
Mo Brooks, Ala.
Andy Harris, Md.
Randy Hultgren, Ill.
Chip Cravaack, Minn.
Larry Bucshon, Ind.
Dan Benishek, Mich.
Vacancy

DEMOCRATS (17)
Eddie Bernice Johnson, Texas, Ranking Member
Jerry F. Costello, Ill.
Lynn Woolsey, Calif.
Zoe Lofgren, Calif.
David Wu, Ore.
Brad Miller, N.C.
Daniel Lipinski, Ill.
Gabrielle Giffords, Ariz.
Donna Edwards, Md.
Marcia L. Fudge, Ohio
Ben Ray Luján, N.M.
Paul Tonko, N.Y.
Jerry McNerney, Calif.
John Sarbanes, Md.
Terri A. Sewell, Ala.
Frederica S. Wilson, Fla.
Hansen Clarke, Mich.

Energy & Environment
Harris (chairman), Rohrabacher, Bartlett, Lucas, Biggert, Akin, Neugebauer, Broun, Fleischmann
Miller, Woolsey, Luján, Tonko, Lofgren, McNerney

Investigations & Oversight
Broun (chairman), Sensenbrenner, Adams, Hultgren, Bucshon, Benishek, Vacancy
Edwards, Lofgren, Miller, McNerney

Research & Science Education
Brooks (chairman), Bartlett, Quayle, Palazzo, Harris, Hultgren, Bucshon, Benishek
Lipinski, Clarke, Tonko, Sarbanes, Sewell

Space & Aeronautics
Palazzo (chairman), Sensenbrenner, Smith, Rohrabacher, Lucas, Akin, McCaul, Adams, Rigell, Brooks
Giffords, Fudge, Costello, Sewell, Wu, Edwards, Wilson

Technology & Innovation
Quayle (chairman), Smith, Biggert, Neugebauer, McCaul, Fleischmann, Rigell, Hultgren, Cravaack
Wu, Sarbanes, Wilson, Lipinski, Giffords, Luján

SELECT INTELLIGENCE
• Phone: (202) 225-4121   • Office: HVC-304 Capitol

REPUBLICANS (12)
Mike Rogers, Mich., Chairman
William M. "Mac" Thornberry, Texas
Sue Myrick, N.C.
Jeff Miller, Fla.
K. Michael Conaway, Texas
Peter T. King, N.Y.
Frank A. LoBiondo, N.J.
Devin Nunes, Calif.
Lynn Westmoreland, Ga.
Michele Bachmann, Minn.
Tom Rooney, Fla.
Joe Heck, Nev.

DEMOCRATS (8)
C.A. Dutch Ruppersberger, Md., Ranking Member
Mike Thompson, Calif.
Jan Schakowsky, Ill.
Jim Langevin, R.I.
Adam B. Schiff, Calif.
Dan Boren, Okla.
Luis V. Gutierrez, Ill.
Ben Chandler, Ky.

Oversight & Investigations
Westmoreland (chairman), Miller, Nunes, Bachmann, Rooney
Schakowsky, Thompson, Boren

Technical & Tactical Intelligence
Heck (chairman), Thornberry, LoBiondo, Nunes, Bachmann
Schiff, Langevin, Chandler

Terrorism, Human Intelligence, Analysis & Counterintelligence
Myrick (chairwoman), Conaway, King, LoBiondo, Rooney
Thompson, Boren, Gutierrez

SMALL BUSINESS

- Phone: (202) 225-5821   • Office: 2361 Rayburn

REPUBLICANS (15)
Sam Graves, Mo., Chairman
Roscoe G. Bartlett, Md.
Steve Chabot, Ohio
Steve King, Iowa
Mike Coffman, Colo.
Mick Mulvaney, S.C.
Scott Tipton, Colo.
Chuck Fleischmann, Tenn.
Jaime Herrera Beutler, Wash.
Allen B. West, Fla.
Renee Ellmers, N.C.
Joe Walsh, Ill.
Jeff Landry, La.
Lou Barletta, Pa.
Richard Hanna, N.Y.

DEMOCRATS (11)
Nydia M. Velázquez, N.Y.,
  Ranking Member
Kurt Schrader, Ore.
Mark Critz, Pa.
Jason Altmire, Pa.
Yvette D. Clarke, N.Y.
Judy Chu, Calif.
David Cicilline, R.I.
Cedric L. Richmond, La.
Gary Peters, Mich.
Bill Owens, N.Y.
William Keating, Mass.

Agriculture, Energy & Trade
Tipton (chairman), Bartlett, King, Fleischmann, Ellmers, Landry, Vacancy
Critz, Cicilline, Keating, Chu

Economic Growth, Tax & Capital Access
Walsh (chairman), Chabot, King, Coffman, Mulvaney, Fleischmann, Vacancy
Schrader, Clarke, Cicilline, Chu, Peters

Healthcare & Technology
Ellmers (chairwoman), King, Mulvaney, Tipton, Fleischmann, Herrera Beutler, Walsh
Richmond, Altmire, Peters

Investigations, Oversight & Regulations
Coffman (chairman), Tipton, Herrera Beutler, West, Walsh, Landry
Altmire, Schrader

Contracting & Workforce
Mulvaney (chairman), King, Coffman, West, Landry, Ellmers, Vacancy
Chu, Schrader, Critz, Clarke, Richmond

TRANSPORTATION & INFRASTRUCTURE

- Phone: (202) 225-9446   • Office: 2165 Rayburn

REPUBLICANS (33)
John L. Mica, Fla., Chairman
Don Young, Alaska
Tom Petri, Wis.
Howard Coble, N.C.
John J. "Jimmy" Duncan Jr., Tenn.
Frank A. LoBiondo, N.J.
Gary G. Miller, Calif.
Timothy V. Johnson, Ill.
Sam Graves, Mo.
Bill Shuster, Pa.
Shelley Moore Capito, W.Va.
Jean Schmidt, Ohio
Candice S. Miller, Mich.
Duncan Hunter, Calif.
Andy Harris, Md.
Rick Crawford, Ark.
Jaime Herrera Beutler, Wash.
Frank Guinta, N.H.
Randy Hultgren, Ill.
Lou Barletta, Pa.
Chip Cravaack, Minn.
Blake Farenthold, Texas
Larry Bucshon, Ind.
Billy Long, Mo.
Bob Gibbs, Ohio
Patrick Meehan, Pa.
Richard Hanna, N.Y.
Jeff Landry, La.
Steve Southerland II, Fla.
Jeff Denham, Calif.
James Lankford, Okla.
Reid Ribble, Wis.
Vacancy

DEMOCRATS (26)
Nick J. Rahall II, W.Va.,
  Ranking Member
Peter A. DeFazio, Ore.
Jerry F. Costello, Ill.
Eleanor Holmes Norton, D.C.
Jerrold Nadler, N.Y.
Corrine Brown, Fla.
Bob Filner, Calif.
Eddie Bernice Johnson, Texas
Elijah E. Cummings, Md.
Leonard L. Boswell, Iowa
Tim Holden, Pa.
Rick Larsen, Wash.
Michael E. Capuano, Mass.
Timothy H. Bishop, N.Y.
Michael H. Michaud, Maine
Russ Carnahan, Mo.
Grace F. Napolitano, Calif.
Daniel Lipinski, Ill.
Mazie K. Hirono, Hawaii
Jason Altmire, Pa.
Tim Walz, Minn.
Heath Shuler, N.C.
Steve Cohen, Tenn.
Laura Richardson, Calif.
Albio Sires, N.J.
Donna Edwards, Md.

Aviation
Petri (chairman), Cravaack, Coble, Duncan, LoBiondo, Graves (Mo.), Schmidt, Guinta, Hultgren, Farenthold, Long, Meehan, Southerland, Lankford, Vacancy, Vacancy
Costello, Carnahan, Lipinski, DeFazio, Filner, Johnson, Boswell, Holden, Capuano, Hirono, Cohen, Norton

Coast Guard & Maritime Transportation
LoBiondo (chairman), Landry, Young, Coble, Harris, Guinta, Cravaack, Farenthold
Larsen, Cummings, Brown, Bishop, Hirono, Michaud

Economic Development, Public Buildings & Emergency Management

Denham (chairman), Crawford, Johnson, Hultgren, Barletta, Gibbs, Meehan, Hanna, Vacancy
Norton, Shuler, Michaud, Carnahan, Walz, Edwards, Filner

Highways & Transit

Duncan (chairman), Hanna, Young (Alaska), Petri, Coble, LoBiondo, Miller (Calif.), Johnson, Graves, Shuster, Capito, Schmidt, Miller (Mich.), Harris, Crawford, Herrera Beutler, Guinta, Barletta, Farenthold, Bucshon, Long, Gibbs, Southerland
DeFazio, Nadler, Filner, Boswell, Holden, Capuano, Michaud, Napolitano, Hirono, Altmire, Walz, Shuler, Cohen, Richardson, Sires, Edwards, Johnson, Cummings

Railroads, Pipelines & Hazardous Materials

Shuster (chairman), Miller (Calif.), Graves, Capito, Schmidt, Miller (Mich.), Herrera Beutler, Hultgren, Barletta, Bucshon, Long, Meehan, Hanna, Landry, Denham, Vacancy, Vacancy
Brown, Nadler, Larsen, Bishop, Michaud, Napolitano, Lipinski, Altmire, Walz, Richardson, Sires, DeFazio, Costello

Water Resources & Environment

Gibbs (chairman), Herrera Beutler, Young, Duncan, Miller (Calif.), Johnson, Shuster, Capito, Miller (Mich.), . Hunter, Harris, Crawford, Cravaack, Bucshon, Landry, Denham, Lankford, Vacancy
Bishop, Costello, Norton, Carnahan, Edwards, Brown, Filner, Johnson, Capuano, Napolitano, Altmire, Cohen, Richardson, Hirono

VETERANS' AFFAIRS

• Phone: (202) 225-3527   • Office: 335 Cannon

REPUBLICANS (15)	DEMOCRATS (11)
Jeff Miller, Fla., Chairman	*Bob Filner, Calif.,*
Cliff Stearns, Fla.	*Ranking Member*
Doug Lamborn, Colo.	*Corrine Brown, Fla.*
Gus Bilirakis, Fla.	*Silvestre Reyes, Texas*
Phil Roe, Tenn.	*Michael H. Michaud, Maine*
Marlin Stutzman, Ind.	*Linda T. Sánchez, Calif.*
Bill Flores, Texas	*Bruce Braley, Iowa*
Bill Johnson, Ohio	*Jerry McNerney, Calif.*
Jeff Denham, Calif.	*Joe Donnelly, Ind.*
Jon Runyan, N.J.	*Tim Walz, Minn.*
Dan Benishek, Mich.	*John Barrow, Ga.*
Ann Marie Buerkle, N.Y.	*Russ Carnahan, Mo.*
Tim Huelskamp, Kan.	
Vacancy	
Vacancy	

Disability Assistance & Memorial Affairs

Runyan (chairman), Lamborn, Buerkle, Stutzman, Vacancy
McNerney, Barrow, Michaud, Walz

Economic Opportunity

Stutzman (chairman), Bilirakis, Johnson, Huelskamp, Denham
Braley, Sánchez, Walz

Health

Buerkle (chairwoman), Stearns, Bilirakis, Roe, Benishek, Denham, Runyan
Michaud, Brown, Reyes, Carnahan, Donnelly

Oversight & Investigations

Johnson (chairman), Stearns, Lamborn, Roe, Benishek, Flores
Donnelly, McNerney, Barrow, Filner

WAYS & MEANS
• Phone: (202) 225-3625 • Office: 1102 Longworth

REPUBLICANS (22)

Dave Camp, Mich.,
  Chairman
Wally Herger, Calif.
Sam Johnson, Texas
Kevin Brady, Texas
Paul D. Ryan, Wis.
Devin Nunes, Calif.
Pat Tiberi, Ohio
Geoff Davis, Ky.
Dave Reichert, Wash.
Charles Boustany Jr., La.
Peter Roskam, Ill.
Jim Gerlach, Pa.
Tom Price, Ga.
Vern Buchanan, Fla.
Adrian Smith, Neb.
Aaron Schock, Ill.
Lynn Jenkins, Kan.
Erik Paulsen, Minn.
Kenny Marchant, Texas
Rick Berg, N.D.
Diane Black, Tenn.
Vacancy

DEMOCRATS (15)

Sander M. Levin, Mich.,
  Ranking Member
Charles B. Rangel, N.Y.
Pete Stark, Calif.
Jim McDermott, Wash.
John Lewis, Ga.
Richard E. Neal, Mass.
Xavier Becerra, Calif.
Lloyd Doggett, Texas
Mike Thompson, Calif.
John B. Larson, Conn.
Earl Blumenauer, Ore.
Ron Kind, Wis.
Bill Pascrell Jr., N.J.
Shelley Berkley, Nev.
Joseph Crowley, N.Y.

Health
Herger (chairman), Johnson, Ryan, Nunes, Reichert,
  Roskam, Gerlach, Price, Vacancy
Stark, Thompson, Kind, Blumenauer, Pascrell

Human Resources
Davis (chairman), Smith, Paulsen, Berg, Price, Black,
  Boustany
Doggett, McDermott, Lewis, Crowley

Oversight
Boustany (chairman), Black, Gerlach, Buchanan, Schock,
  Jenkins, Marchant
Lewis, Becerra, Kind, McDermott

Select Revenue Measures
Tiberi (chairman), Roskam, Paulsen, Berg, Boustany,
  Marchant, Vacancy
Neal, Thompson, Larson, Berkley

Social Security
Johnson (chairman), Brady, Tiberi, Schock, Paulsen, Berg,
  Smith
Becerra, Doggett, Berkley, Stark

Trade
Brady (chairman), Davis, Reichert, Herger, Nunes,
  Buchanan, Smith, Schock, Jenkins
McDermott, Neal, Doggett, Crowley, Larson

House Leadership

DEMOCRATIC LEADERS

Minority Leader... Nancy Pelosi
Minority Whip... Steny H. Hoyer
Assistant Leader... James E. Clyburn
Caucus Chairman... John B. Larson
Caucus Vice Chairman....................................... Xavier Beccera

Chief Deputy Whips: John Lewis (senior),
G.K. Butterfield, Joseph Crowley, Diana DeGette,
Jim Matheson, Ed Pastor, Jan Schakowsky,
Debbie Wasserman Schultz, Maxine Waters, Peter Welch

DEMOCRATIC CONGRESSIONAL CAMPAIGN COMMITTEE

863-1500   430 S. CAPITOL ST. SE 20003
Chairman ....Steve Israel
Chairman of Finance ....Joseph Crowley
Chairwoman of Recruiting
and Candidate Services...........................Allyson Y. Schwartz
Chairman of Community Outreach..................Keith Elllison
Chairman of Community Mobilization ....Pedro R. Pierluisi
Frontline Program Chairman.................................Jim Himes

Business Council Co-Chairmen: John Carney,
Richard E. Neal

Red to Blue Program Co-Chairs: Donna Edwards,
Jared Polis

HOUSE DEMOCRATIC STEERING & POLICY COMMITTEE

225-0100   235 CANNON
Chairwoman... Nancy Pelosi
Steering Co-Chairwoman....................................Rosa DeLauro
Policy Co-Chairman... George Miller
Vice Chairwoman ....Debbie Wasserman Schultz
Vice Chairman ....Henry Cuellar
Freshman Class Representative ....Karen Bass

Members: Robert E. Andrews, John Barrow,
Xavier Becerra, Bruce Braley, G.K. Butterfield, Michael E.
Capuano, Kathy Castor, David Cicilline, James E. Clyburn,
Joseph Crowley, Diana DeGette, Norm Dicks, Mike Doyle,
Keith Ellison, Barney Frank, Gabrielle Giffords,
Mazie K. Hirono, Steny H. Hoyer, Steve Israel,
Sheila Jackson Lee, Marcy Kaptur, Rick Larsen,
John B. Larson, Sander M. Levin, John Lewis, Zoe Lofgren,
Jim Matheson, Betty McCollum, Gwen Moore,
James P. Moran, Jerrold Nadler, Ed Pastor,
Collin C. Peterson, Jared Polis, Bobby L. Rush,
Linda T. Sánchez, Jan Schakowsky, Allyson Y. Schwartz,
Heath Shuler, Louise M. Slaughter, Jackie Speier,
Niki Tsongas, Chris Van Hollen, Tim Walz, Maxine Waters,
Henry A. Waxman

REPUBLICAN LEADERS

Speaker ....John A. Boehner
Majority Leader..Eric Cantor
Majority Whip.. Kevin McCarthy
Conference Chairman...Jeb Hensarling
Conference Vice Chairwoman... Cathy McMorris Rodgers
Conference Secretary..John Carter
Chief Deputy Whip... Peter Roskam
Chairman of the Leadership ....Greg Walden

NATIONAL REPUBLICAN CONGRESSIONAL COMMITTEE

479-7070   320 FIRST ST. SE 20003
Chairman ....Pete Sessions
Deputy Chairman...Greg Walden
Communications Vice Chairwoman...................Diane Black
Finance Vice Chairman..Vern Buchanan
Grassroots Vice Chairwoman ....Virginia Foxx
Coalitions Vice Chairman.....................................Devin Nunes
Regional Chairs Vice Chairman.................................Ed Royce
Recruitment Vice Chairman................................. Steve Scalise
Mentoring Vice Chairman....................................John Shimkus
Redistricting Vice Chairman...................Lynn Westmoreland

Regional Chairmen: Mike Coffman, Geoff Davis,
Jeff Denham, John Fleming, Tom Graves,
Michael G. Grimm, Steven C. LaTourette, Candice S. Miller,
Randy Neugebauer, Kristi Noem, Mike Pompeo,
Bill Shuster

Ex Officio Members: John A. Boehner, Eric Cantor,
John Carter, David Dreier, Jeb Hensarling,
Kevin McCarthy, Cathy McMorris Rodgers, Tom Price,
Tim Scott

POLICY COMMITTEE

225-4501   403 CANNON
Chairman ....Tom Price

HOUSE REPUBLICAN STEERING COMMITTEE

225-0600 H-232 CAPITOL
Chairman .... John A. Boehner

Members: Spencer Bachus, Ken Calvert, Dave Camp,
Eric Cantor, John Carter, Tom Cole, David Dreier,
Robert W. Goodlatte, Gregg Harper, Doc Hastings,
Joe Heck, Jeb Hensarling, Tom Latham,
Steven C. LaTourette, Cynthia M. Lummis,
Kevin McCarthy, Cathy McMorris Rodgers,
Patrick Meehan, Jeff Miller, Tom Price, Harold Rogers,
Mike Rogers, Todd Rokita, Peter Roskam, Paul D. Ryan,
Steve Scalise, Pete Sessions, John Shimkus, Bill Shuster,
Lamar Smith, Fred Upton, Greg Walden,
Lynn Westmoreland

Senate Committees

The standing and select committees of the Senate are listed by their full names. Membership is given in order of seniority on the panel.

On full-committee rosters, Democrats are shown in roman type; members of the minority party, Republicans, are shown in *italic* type; independents are labeled.

The word "vacancy" indicates that a committee or subcommittee seat had not been filled at press time, May 2011. Subcommittee vacancies do not necessarily indicate vacancies on full committees or vice versa.

Leadership committees are listed on page 1148.

AGRICULTURE, NUTRITION & FORESTRY
• Phone: (202) 224-2035   • Office: 328A Russell

DEMOCRATS (11)
Debbie Stabenow, Mich., Chairwoman
Patrick J. Leahy, Vt.
Tom Harkin, Iowa
Kent Conrad, N.D.
Max Baucus, Mont.
Ben Nelson, Neb.
Sherrod Brown, Ohio
Bob Casey, Pa.
Amy Klobuchar, Minn.
Michael Bennet, Colo.
Kirsten Gillibrand, N.Y.

REPUBLICANS (10)
Pat Roberts, Kan., Ranking Member
Richard G. Lugar, Ind.
Thad Cochran, Miss.
Mitch McConnell, Ky.
Saxby Chambliss, Ga.
Mike Johanns, Neb.
John Boozman, Ark.
Charles E. Grassley, Iowa
John Thune, S.D.
John Hoeven, N.D.

Commodities & Markets
Nelson (chairman), Conrad, Baucus, Brown, Bennet, Gillibrand
Chambliss, Cochran, Johanns, Boozman, Grassley

Conservation, Forestry & Natural Resources
Bennet (chairman), Leahy, Harkin, Conrad, Baucus, Klobuchar
Boozman, Lugar, Cochran, McConnell, Chambliss

Jobs, Rural Economic Growth & Energy Innovation
Brown (chairman), Harkin, Conrad, Nelson, Casey, Klobuchar
Thune, Lugar, Chambliss, Grassley, Hoeven

Livestock and Dairy
Gillibrand (chairwoman), Leahy, Baucus, Nelson, Casey, Klobuchar
Johanns, McConnell, Boozman, Grassley, Thune

Nutrition, Specialty Crops, Food & Agricultural Research
Casey (chairman), Leahy, Harkin, Brown, Bennet, Gillibrand
Lugar, Cochran, McConnell, Johanns, Hoeven

ARMED SERVICES
• Phone: (202) 224-3871   • Office: 228 Russell

DEMOCRATS (14)
Carl Levin, Mich., Chairman
Joseph I. Lieberman, Conn. (I)
Jack Reed, R.I.
Daniel K. Akaka, Hawaii
Ben Nelson, Neb.
Jim Webb, Va.
Claire McCaskill, Mo.
Mark Udall, Colo.
Kay Hagan, N.C.
Mark Begich, Alaska
Joe Manchin III, W.Va.
Jeanne Shaheen, N.H.
Kirsten Gillibrand, N.Y.
Richard Blumenthal, Conn.

REPUBLICANS (12)
John McCain, Ariz., Ranking Member
James M. Inhofe, Okla.
Jeff Sessions, Ala.
Saxby Chambliss, Ga.
Roger Wicker, Miss.
Scott P. Brown, Mass.
Rob Portman, Ohio
Kelly Ayotte, N.H.
Susan Collins, Maine
Lindsey Graham, S.C.
John Cornyn, Texas
David Vitter, La.

Airland
Lieberman (I) (chairman), Nelson, McCaskill, Manchin, Gillibrand, Blumenthal
Brown, Inhofe, Sessions, Wicker, Vitter

Emerging Threats & Capabilities
Hagan (chairwoman), Reed, Udall, Manchin, Shaheen, Gillibrand
Portman, Chambliss, Brown, Graham, Cornyn

Personnel
Webb (chairman), Lieberman (I), Akaka, McCaskill, Hagan, Begich, Blumenthal
Graham, Chambliss, Brown, Ayotte, Collins, Vitter

Readiness & Management Support
McCaskill (chairwoman), Akaka, Nelson, Webb, Udall, Begich, Manchin, Shaheen
Ayotte, Inhofe, Chambliss, Portman, Collins, Graham, Cornyn

Seapower
Reed (chairman), Akaka, Webb, Hagan, Blumenthal
Wicker, Sessions, Ayotte, Collins

Strategic Forces
Nelson (chairman), Lieberman (I), Reed, Udall, Begich, Shaheen, Gillibrand
Sessions, Inhofe, Wicker, Portman, Cornyn, Vitter

APPROPRIATIONS
• Phone: (202) 224-7363   • Office: S-128 Capitol

DEMOCRATS (16)	REPUBLICANS (14)
Daniel K. Inouye, Hawaii, Chairman	*Thad Cochran, Miss., Ranking Member*
Patrick J. Leahy, Vt.	*Mitch McConnell, Ky.*
Tom Harkin, Iowa	*Richard C. Shelby, Ala.*
Barbara A. Mikulski, Md.	*Kay Bailey Hutchison, Texas*
Herb Kohl, Wis.	*Lamar Alexander, Tenn.*
Patty Murray, Wash.	*Susan Collins, Maine*
Dianne Feinstein, Calif.	*Lisa Murkowski, Alaska*
Richard J. Durbin, Ill.	*Lindsey Graham, S.C.*
Tim Johnson, S.D.	*Mark Steven Kirk, Ill.*
Mary L. Landrieu, La.	*Dan Coats, Ind.*
Jack Reed, R.I.	*Roy Blunt, Mo.*
Frank R. Lautenberg, N.J.	*Jerry Moran, Kan.*
Ben Nelson, Neb.	*John Hoeven, N.D.*
Mark Pryor, Ark.	*Ron Johnson, Wis.*
Jon Tester, Mont.	
Sherrod Brown, Ohio	

Agriculture
Kohl (chairman), Harkin, Feinstein, Johnson, Nelson, Pryor, Brown
Blunt, Cochran, McConnell, Collins, Moran, Hoeven

Commerce-Justice-Science
Mikulski (chairwoman), Inouye, Leahy, Kohl, Feinstein, Reed, Lautenberg, Nelson, Pryor, Brown
Hutchison, Shelby, McConnell, Alexander, Murkowski, Johnson, Collins, Graham

Defense
Inouye (chairman), Leahy, Harkin, Durbin, Feinstein, Mikulski, Kohl, Murray, Johnson, Reed
Cochran, McConnell, Shelby, Hutchison, Alexander, Collins, Murkowski, Graham, Coats

Energy-Water
Feinstein (chairwoman), Murray, Johnson, Landrieu, Reed, Lautenberg, Harkin, Tester, Durbin
Alexander, Cochran, McConnell, Hutchison, Shelby, Collins, Murkowski, Graham

Financial Services
Durbin (chairman), Lautenberg, Nelson
Moran, Kirk

Homeland Security
Landrieu (chairwoman), Lautenberg, Inouye, Leahy, Murray, Tester
Coats, Cochran, Shelby, Murkowski, Moran

Interior-Environment
Reed (chairman), Feinstein, Leahy, Mikulski, Kohl, Johnson, Nelson, Tester, Landrieu
Murkowski, Alexander, Cochran, Collins, Johnson, Blunt, Hoeven

Labor-HHS-Education
Harkin (chairman), Inouye, Kohl, Murray, Landrieu, Durbin, Reed, Pryor, Mikulski, Brown
Shelby, Cochran, Hutchison, Alexander, Johnson, Kirk, Graham, Moran

Legislative Branch
Nelson (chairman), Tester, Brown (Ohio)
Hoeven, Graham

Military Construction-VA
Johnson (chairman), Inouye, Landrieu, Murray, Reed, Nelson, Pryor, Tester
Kirk, Hutchison, McConnell, Murkowski, Blunt, Hoeven, Coats

State-Foreign Operations
Leahy (chairman), Inouye, Harkin, Mikulski, Durbin, Landrieu, Lautenberg, Brown
Graham, McConnell, Kirk, Blunt, Coats, Johnson, Hoeven

Transportation-HUD
Murray (chairwoman), Mikulski, Kohl, Durbin, Leahy, Harkin, Feinstein, Johnson, Lautenberg, Pryor
Collins, Shelby, Hutchison, Alexander, Kirk, Coats, Moran, Blunt, Johnson

BANKING, HOUSING & URBAN AFFAIRS
• Phone: (202) 224-7391   • Office: 534 Dirksen

DEMOCRATS (12)	REPUBLICANS (10)
Tim Johnson, S.D., Chairman	*Richard C. Shelby, Ala., Ranking Member*
Jack Reed, R.I.	*Michael D. Crapo, Idaho*
Charles E. Schumer, N.Y.	*Bob Corker, Tenn.*
Robert Menendez, N.J.	*Jim DeMint, S.C.*
Daniel K. Akaka, Hawaii	*David Vitter, La.*
Sherrod Brown, Ohio	*Mike Johanns, Neb.*
Jon Tester, Mont.	*Patrick J. Toomey, Pa.*
Herb Kohl, Wis.	*Mark Steven Kirk, Ill.*
Mark Warner, Va.	*Jerry Moran, Kan.*
Jeff Merkley, Ore.	*Roger Wicker, Miss.*
Michael Bennet, Colo.	
Kay Hagan, N.C.	

Economic Policy
Tester (chairman), Warner, Hagan, Johnson
Vitter, Wicker, Johanns

Financial Institutions & Consumer Protection
Brown (chairman), Reed, Schumer, Menendez, Akaka, Tester, Kohl, Merkley, Hagan
Corker, Moran, Crapo, Johanns, Toomey, DeMint, Vitter

Housing, Transportation & Community Development
Menendez (chairman), Reed, Schumer, Akaka, Brown, Tester, Kohl, Merkley, Bennet
DeMint, Crapo, Corker, Toomey, Kirk, Moran, Wicker

Securities, Insurance & Investment
Reed (chairman), Schumer, Menendez, Akaka, Kohl, Warner, Merkley, Bennet, Hagan, Johnson
Crapo, Toomey, Kirk, Corker, DeMint, Vitter, Moran, Wicker

Security & International Trade
Warner (chairman), Bennet, Brown, Johnson
Johanns, Kirk

BUDGET
• Phone: (202) 224-0642   • Office: 624 Dirksen

DEMOCRATS (12)	REPUBLICANS (11)
Kent Conrad, N.D., Chairman	*Jeff Sessions, Ala., Ranking Member*
Patty Murray, Wash.	*Charles E. Grassley, Iowa*
Ron Wyden, Ore.	*Michael B. Enzi, Wyo.*
Bill Nelson, Fla.	*Michael D. Crapo, Idaho*
Debbie Stabenow, Mich.	*John Cornyn, Texas*
Benjamin L. Cardin, Md.	*Lindsey Graham, S.C.*
Bernard Sanders, Vt. (I)	*John Thune, S.D.*
Sheldon Whitehouse, R.I.	*Rob Portman, Ohio*
Mark Warner, Va.	*Patrick J. Toomey, Pa.*
Jeff Merkley, Ore.	*Ron Johnson, Wis.*
Mark Begich, Alaska	*Kelly Ayotte, N.H.*
Chris Coons, Del.	

Government Performance
Warner (chairman), Whitehouse, Cardin
Crapo, Thune

COMMERCE, SCIENCE & TRANSPORTATION
• Phone: (202) 224-0411   • Office: 254 Russell

DEMOCRATS (13)	REPUBLICANS (12)
John D. Rockefeller IV, W.Va., Chairman	*Kay Bailey Hutchison, Texas, Ranking Member*
Daniel K. Inouye, Hawaii	*Olympia J. Snowe, Maine*
John Kerry, Mass.	*Jim DeMint, S.C.*
Barbara Boxer, Calif.	*John Thune, S.D.*
Bill Nelson, Fla.	*Roger Wicker, Miss.*
Maria Cantwell, Wash.	*Johnny Isakson, Ga.*
Frank R. Lautenberg, N.J.	*Roy Blunt, Mo.*
Mark Pryor, Ark.	*John Boozman, Ark.*
Claire McCaskill, Mo.	*Patrick J. Toomey, Pa.*
Amy Klobuchar, Minn.	*Marco Rubio, Fla.*
Tom Udall, N.M.	*Kelly Ayotte, N.H.*
Mark Warner, Va.	*Dean Heller, Nev.*
Mark Begich, Alaska	

Aviation Operations, Safety & Security
Cantwell (chairwoman), Inouye, Boxer, Nelson, Lautenberg, Klobuchar, Udall, Warner, Begich
Thune, DeMint, Wicker, Isakson, Blunt, Boozman, Toomey, Heller

Communications, Technology & the Internet
Kerry (chairman), Inouye, Boxer, Nelson, Cantwell, Lautenberg, Pryor, McCaskill, Klobuchar, Udall, Warner, Begich
DeMint, Snowe, Thune, Wicker, Isakson, Blunt, Boozman, Toomey, Rubio, Ayotte, Heller

Competitiveness, Innovation & Export Promotion
Klobuchar (chairwoman), Kerry, Cantwell, Pryor, Udall, Warner, Begich
Blunt, DeMint, Thune, Boozman, Ayotte, Heller

Consumer Protection, Product Safety & Insurance
Pryor (chairman), Kerry, Boxer, McCaskill, Klobuchar, Udall
Toomey, Wicker, Thune, Boozman, Heller

Oceans, Atmosphere, Fisheries & Coast Guard
Begich (chairman), Inouye, Kerry, Nelson, Cantwell, Lautenberg, Klobuchar, Warner
Snowe, Wicker, Isakson, Boozman, Rubio, Ayotte, Heller

Science & Space
Nelson (chairman), Inouye, Kerry, Cantwell, Pryor, Warner
Boozman, Wicker, Rubio, Ayotte, Heller

Surface Transportation and Merchant Marine
Lautenberg (chairman), Inouye, Kerry, Boxer, Cantwell, Pryor, McCaskill, Klobuchar, Udall, Warner, Begich
Wicker, Thune, DeMint, Isakson, Blunt, Boozman, Toomey, Rubio, Ayotte, Heller

ENERGY & NATURAL RESOURCES

• Phone: (202) 224-4971   • Office: 304 Dirksen

DEMOCRATS (12)
Jeff Bingaman, N.M.,
   Chairman
Ron Wyden, Ore.
Tim Johnson, S.D.
Mary L. Landrieu, La.
Maria Cantwell, Wash.
Bernard Sanders, Vt. (I)
Debbie Stabenow, Mich.
Mark Udall, Colo.
Jeanne Shaheen, N.H.
Al Franken, Minn.
Joe Manchin III, W.Va.
Chris Coons, Del.

REPUBLICANS (10)
Lisa Murkowski, Alaska,
   Ranking Member
John Barrasso, Wyo.
Jim Risch, Idaho
Mike Lee, Utah
Rand Paul, Ky.
Dan Coats, Ind.
Rob Portman, Ohio
John Hoeven, N.D.
Dean Heller, Nev.
Bob Corker, Tenn.

Energy

Cantwell (chairwoman), Wyden, Johnson, Landrieu,
   Sanders (I), Udall, Shaheen, Franken, Manchin, Coons
Risch, Barrasso, Lee, Paul, Coats, Portman, Hoeven, Corker

National Parks

Udall (chairman), Landrieu, Sanders (I), Stabenow,
   Franken, Manchin, Coons
Barrasso, Paul, Coats, Portman, Corker

Public Lands & Forests

Wyden (chairman), Johnson, Landrieu, Cantwell,
   Udall, Shaheen, Franken, Coons
Barrasso, Risch, Lee, Paul, Portman, Hoeven

Water & Power

Shaheen (chairwoman), Wyden, Johnson, Cantwell,
   Sanders (I), Stabenow, Manchin
Lee, Risch, Coats, Hoeven, Corker

ENVIRONMENT & PUBLIC WORKS

• Phone: (202) 224-8832   • Office: 410 Dirksen

DEMOCRATS (10)
Barbara Boxer, Calif.,
   Chairwoman
Max Baucus, Mont.
Thomas R. Carper, Del.
Frank R. Lautenberg, N.J.
Benjamin L. Cardin, Md.
Bernard Sanders, Vt. (I)
Sheldon Whitehouse, R.I.
Tom Udall, N.M.
Jeff Merkley, Ore.
Kirsten Gillibrand, N.Y.

REPUBLICANS (8)
James M. Inhofe, Okla.,
   Ranking Member
David Vitter, La.
John Barrasso, Wyo.
Jeff Sessions, Ala.
Michael D. Crapo, Idaho
Lamar Alexander, Tenn.
Mike Johanns, Neb.
John Boozman, Ark.

Children's Health & Environmental Responsibility

Udall (chairman), Whitehouse, Gillibrand
Alexander, Vitter

Clean Air & Nuclear Safety

Carper (chairman), Baucus, Lautenberg, Cardin,
   Sanders (I), Merkley
Barrasso, Vitter, Sessions, Alexander, Johanns

Green Jobs & the New Economy

Sanders (I) (chairman), Carper, Merkley
Boozman, Sessions

Oversight

Whitehouse (chairman), Cardin, Sanders (I)
Johanns, Boozman

Superfund, Toxics & Environmental Health

Lautenberg (chairman), Baucus, Carper, Merkley,
   Gillibrand
Crapo, Alexander, Johanns, Boozman

Transportation & Infrastructure

Baucus (chairman), Carper, Lautenberg, Cardin,
   Sanders (I), Whitehouse, Udall
Vitter, Barrasso, Sessions, Crapo, Johanns, Boozman

Water & Wildlife

Cardin (chairman), Baucus, Lautenberg, Whitehouse,
   Udall, Gillibrand
Sessions, Barrasso, Vitter, Crapo, Alexander

FINANCE

- Phone: (202) 224-4515   • Office: 219 Dirksen

DEMOCRATS (13)
Max Baucus, Mont.,
    Chairman
John D. Rockefeller IV, W.Va.
Kent Conrad, N.D.
Jeff Bingaman, N.M.
John Kerry, Mass.
Ron Wyden, Ore.
Charles E. Schumer, N.Y.
Debbie Stabenow, Mich.
Maria Cantwell, Wash.
Bill Nelson, Fla.
Robert Menendez, N.J.
Thomas R. Carper, Del.
Benjamin L. Cardin, Md.

REPUBLICANS (11)
*Orrin G. Hatch, Utah,
    Ranking Member
Charles E. Grassley, Iowa
Olympia J. Snowe, Maine
Jon Kyl, Ariz.
Michael D. Crapo, Idaho
Pat Roberts, Kan.
Michael B. Enzi, Wyo.
John Cornyn, Texas
Tom Coburn, Okla.
John Thune, S.D.
Richard M. Burr, N.C.*

Energy, Natural Resources & Infrastructure
Bingaman (chairman), Rockefeller, Conrad, Kerry,
    Cantwell, Nelson, Carper
Cornyn, Grassley, Roberts, Enzi, Thune

Fiscal Responsibility & Economic Growth
Nelson (chairman), Baucus, Conrad, Bingaman
Crapo, Coburn, Vacancy

Health Care
Rockefeller (chairman), Bingaman, Kerry, Wyden,
    Stabenow, Cantwell, Menendez, Carper, Cardin
Vacancy, Grassley, Kyl, Roberts, Enzi, Cornyn, Coburn

International Trade, Customs & Global Competitiveness
Wyden (chairman), Rockefeller, Kerry, Schumer,
    Stabenow, Nelson, Menendez
Thune, Hatch, Grassley, Crapo, Roberts

Social Security, Pensions & Family Policy
Stabenow (chairwoman), Rockefeller, Schumer, Cardin
Coburn, Hatch, Kyl

Taxation & IRS Oversight
Conrad (chairman), Baucus, Kerry, Schumer, Wyden,
    Cantwell, Nelson, Menendez, Carper, Cardin
Kyl, Snowe, Crapo, Roberts, Enzi, Cornyn, Thune, Vacancy

FOREIGN RELATIONS

- Phone: (202) 224-4651   • Office: 446 Dirksen

DEMOCRATS (10)
John Kerry, Mass., Chairman
Barbara Boxer, Calif.
Robert Menendez, N.J.
Benjamin L. Cardin, Md.
Bob Casey, Pa.
Jim Webb, Va.
Jeanne Shaheen, N.H.
Chris Coons, Del.
Richard J. Durbin, Ill.
Tom Udall, N.M.

REPUBLICANS (9)
*Richard G. Lugar, Ind.,
    Ranking Member
Bob Corker, Tenn.
Jim Risch, Idaho
Marco Rubio, Fla.
James M. Inhofe, Okla.
Jim DeMint, S.C.
Johnny Isakson, Ga.
John Barrasso, Wyo.
Mike Lee, Utah*

African Affairs
Coons (chairman), Cardin, Webb, Durbin, Udall
Isakson, Inhofe, Lee, Corker

East Asian & Pacific Affairs
Webb (chairman), Boxer, Casey, Shaheen, Coons
Inhofe, Risch, Barrasso, Rubio

European Affairs
Shaheen (chairwoman), Cardin, Casey, Webb, Durbin
Barrasso, Risch, Corker, DeMint

International Development
Cardin (chairman), Menendez, Coons, Durbin, Udall
Corker, Rubio, Risch, Inhofe

International Operations & Organizations
Boxer (chairwoman), Menendez, Casey, Shaheen, Durbin
DeMint, Inhofe, Isakson, Barrasso

Near Eastern & South Central Asian Affairs
Casey (chairman), Boxer, Menendez, Cardin, Coons,
    Udall
Risch, Corker, Lee, Rubio, Isakson

Western Hemisphere, Peace Corps & Global Narcotics Affairs
Menendez (chairman), Boxer, Webb, Shaheen, Udall
Rubio, Lee, DeMint, Isakson, Barrasso

HEALTH, EDUCATION, LABOR & PENSIONS
• Phone: (202) 224-5375   • Office: 428 Dirksen

DEMOCRATS (12)
Tom Harkin, Iowa, Chairman
Barbara A. Mikulski, Md.
Jeff Bingaman, N.M.
Patty Murray, Wash.
Bernard Sanders, Vt. (I)
Bob Casey, Pa.
Kay Hagan, N.C.
Jeff Merkley, Ore.
Al Franken, Minn.
Michael Bennet, Colo.
Sheldon Whitehouse, R.I.
Richard Blumenthal, Conn.

REPUBLICANS (10)
Michael B. Enzi, Wyo.,
  Ranking Member
Lamar Alexander, Tenn.
Richard M. Burr, N.C.
Johnny Isakson, Ga.
Rand Paul, Ky.
Orrin G. Hatch, Utah
John McCain, Ariz.
Pat Roberts, Kan.
Lisa Murkowski, Alaska
Mark Steven Kirk, Ill.

Children & Families
Mikulski (chairwoman), Murray, Sanders (I), Casey, Hagan, Merkley, Franken, Bennet, Blumenthal
Burr, Alexander, Isakson, Paul, McCain, Roberts, Kirk

Employment & Workplace Safety
Murray (chairwoman), Bingaman, Franken, Bennet, Whitehouse, Blumenthal
Isakson, Alexander, Hatch, Kirk

Primary Health & Aging
Sanders (I) (chairman), Mikulski, Bingaman, Casey, Hagan, Merkley, Whitehouse
Paul, Burr, Isakson, Hatch, Murkowski

HOMELAND SECURITY & GOVERNMENTAL AFFAIRS
• Phone: (202) 224-2627   • Office: 340 Dirksen

DEMOCRATS (9)
Joseph I. Lieberman, Conn. (I), Chairman
Carl Levin, Mich.
Daniel K. Akaka, Hawaii
Thomas R. Carper, Del.
Mark Pryor, Ark.
Mary L. Landrieu, La.
Claire McCaskill, Mo.
Jon Tester, Mont.
Mark Begich, Alaska

REPUBLICANS (8)
Susan Collins, Maine,
  Ranking Member
Tom Coburn, Okla.
Scott P. Brown, Mass.
John McCain, Ariz.
Ron Johnson, Wis.
Rob Portman, Ohio
Rand Paul, Ky.
Jerry Moran, Kan.

Contracting Oversight
McCaskill (chairwoman), Carper, Pryor, Tester, Begich
Portman, Collins, McCain, Paul, Moran

Disaster Recovery & Intergovernmental Affairs
Pryor (chairman), Akaka, Landrieu, Tester
Paul, Brown, Johnson

Federal Financial Management
Carper (chairman), Levin, Akaka, Pryor, McCaskill, Begich
Brown, Coburn, McCain, Johnson, Portman

Oversight of Government Management
Akaka (chairman), Levin, Landrieu, Begich
Johnson, Coburn, Moran

Permanent Investigations
Levin (chairman), Carper, Landrieu, McCaskill, Tester, Begich
Coburn, Collins, Brown, McCain, Paul

INDIAN AFFAIRS
• Phone: (202) 224-2251   • Office: 838 Hart

DEMOCRATS (8)
Daniel K. Akaka, Hawaii, Chairman
Daniel K. Inouye, Hawaii
Kent Conrad, N.D.
Tim Johnson, S.D.
Maria Cantwell, Wash.
Jon Tester, Mont.
Tom Udall, N.M.
Al Franken, Minn.

REPUBLICANS (6)
John Barrasso, Wyo.,
  Vice Chairman
John McCain, Ariz.
Lisa Murkowski, Alaska
John Hoeven, N.D.
Michael D. Crapo, Idaho
Mike Johanns, Neb.

JUDICIARY
• Phone: (202) 224-7703   • Office: 224 Dirksen

DEMOCRATS (10)
Patrick J. Leahy, Vt., Chairman
Herb Kohl, Wis.
Dianne Feinstein, Calif.
Charles E. Schumer, N.Y.
Richard J. Durbin, Ill.
Sheldon Whitehouse, R.I.
Amy Klobuchar, Minn.
Al Franken, Minn.
Chris Coons, Del.
Richard Blumenthal, Conn.

REPUBLICANS (8)
Charles E. Grassley, Iowa,
  Ranking Member
Orrin G. Hatch, Utah
Jon Kyl, Ariz.
Jeff Sessions, Ala.
Lindsey Graham, S.C.
John Cornyn, Texas
Mike Lee, Utah
Tom Coburn, Okla.

Administrative Oversight & the Courts
Klobuchar (chairwoman), Leahy, Kohl, Whitehouse, Coons
Sessions, Grassley, Lee, Coburn

Antitrust, Competition Policy & Consumer Rights
Kohl (chairman), Schumer, Klobuchar, Franken, Blumenthal
Lee, Grassley, Cornyn

Constitution, Civil Rights & Human Rights
Durbin (chairman), Leahy, Whitehouse, Franken, Coons, Blumenthal
Graham, Kyl, Cornyn, Lee, Coburn

Crime & Terrorism
Whitehouse (chairman), Kohl, Feinstein, Durbin, Klobuchar, Coons
Kyl, Hatch, Sessions, Graham

Immigration, Refugees & Border Security
Schumer (chairman), Leahy, Feinstein, Durbin, Franken, Blumenthal
Cornyn, Grassley, Hatch, Kyl, Sessions

Privacy, Technology & the Law
Franken (chairman), Schumer, Whitehouse, Blumenthal
Coburn, Hatch, Graham

RULES & ADMINISTRATION
• **Phone:** (202) 224-6352   • **Office:** 305 Russell

DEMOCRATS (10)	REPUBLICANS (8)
Charles E. Schumer, N.Y., Chairman	*Lamar Alexander, Tenn., Ranking Member*
Daniel K. Inouye, Hawaii	*Mitch McConnell, Ky.*
Dianne Feinstein, Calif.	*Thad Cochran, Miss.*
Richard J. Durbin, Ill.	*Saxby Chambliss, Ga.*
Ben Nelson, Neb.	*Kay Bailey Hutchison, Texas*
Patty Murray, Wash.	*Pat Roberts, Kan.*
Mark Pryor, Ark.	*Richard C. Shelby, Ala.*
Tom Udall, N.M.	*Roy Blunt, Mo.*
Mark Warner, Va.	
Patrick J. Leahy, Vt.	

SELECT ETHICS
• **Phone:** (202) 224-2981   • **Office:** 220 Hart

DEMOCRATS (3)	REPUBLICANS (3)
Barbara Boxer, Calif., Chairwoman	*Johnny Isakson, Ga., Vice Chairman*
Mark Pryor, Ark.	*Pat Roberts, Kan.*
Sherrod Brown, Ohio	*Jim Risch, Idaho*

SELECT INTELLIGENCE
• **Phone:** (202) 224-1700   • **Office:** 211 Hart

DEMOCRATS (8)	REPUBLICANS (7)
Dianne Feinstein, Calif., Chairwoman	*Saxby Chambliss, Ga., Ranking Member*
John D. Rockefeller IV, W.Va.	*Olympia J. Snowe, Maine*
Ron Wyden, Ore.	*Richard M. Burr, N.C.*
Barbara A. Mikulski, Md.	*Jim Risch, Idaho*
Bill Nelson, Fla.	*Dan Coats, Ind.*
Kent Conrad, N.D.	*Roy Blunt, Mo.*
Mark Udall, Colo.	*Marco Rubio, Fla.*
Mark Warner, Va.	

SMALL BUSINESS & ENTREPRENEURSHIP
• **Phone:** (202) 224-5175   • **Office:** 428A Russell

DEMOCRATS (10)	REPUBLICANS (9)
Mary L. Landrieu, La., Chairwoman	*Olympia J. Snowe, Maine, Ranking Member*
Carl Levin, Mich.	*David Vitter, La.*
Tom Harkin, Iowa	*Jim Risch, Idaho*
John Kerry, Mass.	*Marco Rubio, Fla.*
Joseph I. Lieberman, Conn. (I)	*Rand Paul, Ky.*
Maria Cantwell, Wash.	*Kelly Ayotte, N.H.*
Mark Pryor, Ark.	*Michael B. Enzi, Wyo.*
Benjamin L. Cardin, Md.	*Scott P. Brown, Mass.*
Jeanne Shaheen, N.H.	*Jerry Moran, Kan.*
Kay Hagan, N.C.	

SPECIAL AGING

• Phone: (202) 224-5364   • Office: G31 Dirksen

DEMOCRATS (11)	REPUBLICANS (10)
Herb Kohl, Wis., Chairman	*Bob Corker, Tenn.,*
Ron Wyden, Ore.	*Ranking Member*
Bill Nelson, Fla.	*Susan Collins, Maine*
Bob Casey, Pa.	*Orrin G. Hatch, Utah*
Claire McCaskill, Mo.	*Mark Steven Kirk, Ill.*
Sheldon Whitehouse, R.I.	*Dean Heller, Nev.*
Mark Udall, Colo.	*Jerry Moran, Kan.*
Michael Bennet, Colo.	*Ron Johnson, Wis.*
Kirsten Gillibrand, N.Y.	*Richard C. Shelby, Ala.*
Joe Manchin III, W.Va.	*Lindsey Graham, S.C.*
Richard Blumenthal, Conn.	*Saxby Chambliss, Ga.*

VETERANS' AFFAIRS

• Phone: (202) 224-9126   • Office: 412 Russell

DEMOCRATS (8)	REPUBLICANS (7)
Patty Murray, Wash.,	*Richard M. Burr, N.C.,*
Chairwoman	*Ranking Member*
John D. Rockefeller IV, W.Va.	*Johnny Isakson, Ga.*
Daniel K. Akaka, Hawaii	*Roger Wicker, Miss.*
Bernard Sanders, Vt. (I)	*Mike Johanns, Neb.*
Sherrod Brown, Ohio	*Scott P. Brown, Mass.*
Jim Webb, Va.	*Jerry Moran, Kan.*
Jon Tester, Mont.	*John Boozman, Ark.*
Mark Begich, Alaska	

Senate Leadership

DEMOCRATIC LEADERS

President ....Vice President Joseph R. Biden Jr.
President Pro Tempore.....................................Daniel K. Inouye
Majority Leader..Harry Reid
Majority Whip...Richard J. Durbin
Conference Vice Chairman......................Charles E. Schumer
Conference Secretary..Patty Murray
Chief Deputy Whip..Barbara Boxer

Deputy Whips: Thomas R. Carper, Mark Pryor

DEMOCRATIC SENATORIAL CAMPAIGN COMMITTEE

224-2447   120 MARYLAND AVE. NE 20002
Chairwoman..Patty Murray

POLICY COMMITTEE

224-3232   419 HART
Chairman.. Charles E. Schumer
Vice Chairwoman...Debbie Stabenow

Regional Chairwomen: Amy Klobuchar, Mary L. Landrieu, Patty Murray

Members: Sherrod Brown, Thomas R. Carper, Dianne Feinstein, Tim Johnson, Frank R. Lautenberg, Joseph I. Lieberman, Barbara A. Mikulski, Bill Nelson, Harry Reid, Ron Wyden
Ex-Officio Members: Richard J. Durbin, Patty Murray

STEERING AND OUTREACH COMMITTEE

224-9048   712 HART
Chairman ....Mark Begich
Vice Chairman ....Daniel K. Akaka

Members: Max Baucus, Jeff Bingaman, Barbara Boxer, Kent Conrad, Richard J. Durbin, Kirsten Gillibrand, Tom Harkin, Daniel K. Inouye, John Kerry, Herb Kohl, Carl Levin, Patrick J. Leahy, Mark Pryor, Harry Reid, John D. Rockefeller IV

REPUBLICAN LEADERS

Minority Leader..Mitch McConnell
Minority Whip ....Jon Kyl
Conference Chairman.....................................Lamar Alexander
Conference Vice Chairman................................John Barrasso
Chief Deputy Whip..Richard M. Burr

Deputy Whips: Roy Blunt, Michael D. Crapo, Saxby Chambliss, Rob Portman, Olympia J. Snowe, David Vitter, Roger Wicker

NATIONAL REPUBLICAN SENATORIAL COMMITTEE

675-6000   425 SECOND ST. NE 20002
Chairman ....John Cornyn

POLICY COMMITTEE

224-2946   347 RUSSELL
Chairman ....John Thune

COMMITTEE ON COMMITTEES

224-6142   239 DIRKSEN
Chairman ....Michael D. Crapo

Joint Committees

JOINT ECONOMIC
• Phone: (202) 224-5171 • Office: G-01 Dirksen

SENATE MEMBERS

DEMOCRATS (6)
Bob Casey, Pa., Chairman
Jeff Bingaman, N.M.
Amy Klobuchar, Minn.
Jim Webb, Va.
Mark Warner, Va.
Bernard Sanders, Vt. (I)

REPUBLICANS (4)
Jim DeMint, S.C.
Dan Coats, Ind.
Mike Lee, Utah
Patrick J. Toomey, Pa.

HOUSE MEMBERS

REPUBLICANS (6)
Kevin Brady, Texas, Vice Chairman
Michael C. Burgess, Texas
John Campbell, Calif.
Sean P. Duffy, Wis.
Justin Amash, Mich.
Mick Mulvaney, S.C.

DEMOCRATS (4)
Maurice D. Hinchey, N.Y.
Carolyn B. Maloney, N.Y.
Loretta Sanchez, Calif.
Elijah E. Cummings, Md.

JOINT LIBRARY
• Phone: (202) 225-2061 • Office: 1309 Longworth

SENATE MEMBERS

DEMOCRATS (3)
Charles E. Schumer, N.Y., Vice Chairman
Richard J. Durbin, Ill.
Patrick J. Leahy, Vt.

REPUBLICANS (2)
Lamar Alexander, Tenn.
Thad Cochran, Miss.

HOUSE MEMBERS

REPUBLICANS (3)
Dan Lungren, Calif.
Gregg Harper, Miss.
Ander Crenshaw, Fla.

DEMOCRATS (2)
Robert A. Brady, Pa.
Zoe Lofgren, Calif.

JOINT PRINTING
• Phone: (202) 224-6352 • Office: 305 Russell

SENATE MEMBERS

DEMOCRATS (3)
Charles E. Schumer, N.Y., Chairman
Patty Murray, Wash.
Tom Udall, N.M.

REPUBLICANS (2)
Lamar Alexander, Tenn.
Saxby Chambliss, Ga.

HOUSE MEMBERS

REPUBLICANS (3)
Dan Lungren, Calif.
Gregg Harper, Miss.
Aaron Schock, Ill.

DEMOCRATS (2)
Robert A. Brady, Pa.
Charlie Gonzalez, Texas

JOINT TAXATION
• Phone: (202) 225-3621 • Office: 1625 Longworth

SENATE MEMBERS

DEMOCRATS (3)
Max Baucus, Mont., Vice Chairman
John D. Rockefeller IV, W.Va.
Kent Conrad, N.D.

REPUBLICANS (2)
Orrin G. Hatch, Utah
Charles E. Grassley, Iowa

HOUSE MEMBERS

REPUBLICANS (3)
Dave Camp, Mich., Chairman
Wally Herger, Calif.
Sam Johnson, Texas

DEMOCRATS (2)
Sander M. Levin, Mich.
Charles B. Rangel, N.Y.

Did You Know?

Most people know that Illinois Democratic Rep. Jesse L. Jackson Jr. is the son of a famous civil rights activist.

Fewer are aware that Jackson vacuums his office carpet for relaxation, holds a black belt in tae kwon do and gets around Capitol Hill on his own Segway.

Like Jackson, every member brings a touch of individuality to the job of lawmaker.

Rep. **Gary L. Ackerman**, D-N.Y., has as a Washington residence a houseboat on the Potomac River called the Unsinkable II. The original Unsinkable turned out not to be, he says.

Michigan Republican Rep. **Justin Amash**'s father lived in a Palestinian refugee camp as a child before his family immigrated to the United States in the 1950s.

Rep. **Robert E. Andrews**, D-N.J., used Rahm Emanuel — later his House colleague, then White House chief of staff and now mayor of Chicago — as an opposition researcher in his first campaign in 1990.

Ohio GOP Rep. **Steve Austria** is the only first-generation Filipino-American in Congress; his father fought with Filipino guerrillas against the Japanese during World War II.

New Hampshire Republican Sen. **Kelly Ayotte** is attached to a famous Supreme Court case: *Ayotte v. Planned Parenthood of Northern New England*, which involved a challenge to the state's parental notification abortion law.

Rep. **Roscoe G. Bartlett**, R-Md., holds 20 patents, including ones for components in breathing equipment used by pilots, astronauts and rescue workers.

Rep. **Karen Bass**, D-Calif., has brown belts in tae kwon do and hapkido martial arts.

As a young man, Sen. **Max Baucus**, D-Mont., hitchhiked around Europe with gypsies and says he had an epiphany to enter public service while traveling in the Belgian Congo.

Nevada Democratic Rep. **Shelley Berkley** was married in 1999 at Bally's casino in Las Vegas with 19 bridesmaids to attend to her — among them Dina Titus, who later served one term as her Democratic House colleague.

Sen. **Richard Blumenthal**, D-Conn., was once a tennis partner of Donald H. Rumsfeld, when the George W. Bush-era Defense secretary was head of the Office of Economic Opportunity in the Nixon administration.

Sen. **Barbara Boxer**, D-Calif., is the author of two political thrillers featuring a heroic liberal Democratic senator from California.

The son of a longtime Georgia state senator, Georgia Republican Rep. **Paul Broun** used to give up his bedroom when his father's colleague from Plains, Jimmy Carter, would visit Athens.

North Carolina Republican Sen. **Richard M. Burr** is a descendant of Aaron Burr, the New York senator and vice president who killed Alexander Hamilton in a famous duel.

A fourth-generation Californian, Republican Rep. **John Campbell** is a member of the Sons of Union Veterans and has occasionally participated in Civil War re-enactments. His great-grandfather on his father's side, Alexander, was elected to the California Assembly in 1860 on the same GOP ticket as Abraham Lincoln.

Rep. **Shelley Moore Capito**, R-W.Va., was the first Cherry Blossom Princess elected to Congress; Republican Sen. **Lisa Murkowski** of Alaska was the second.

California Democrats **Dennis Cardoza** and **Jim Costa**, who voted for each other for Speaker in 2011, both have forebears who immigrated from the Azores. California Republican Rep. **Devin Nunes** also is descended from the Azores.

Delaware is the only state represented by lawmakers whose last names begin with the same letter: Sens. **Thomas R. Carper** and **Chris Coons** and Rep. **John Carney**, all Democrats.

Rep. **André Carson**, D-Ind., was an aspiring rapper during high school, performing at local variety shows under the stage name "Juggernaut."

Georgia Republican Sens. **Saxby Chambliss** and **Johnny Isakson** met in college. When their stay-at-home wives (who were in the same sorority) are in Washington, the couples frequently dine together. When they're not, Chambliss and Isakson are part of a group of Republican men who eat out together and gather at one another's homes. The pack has included Sens. **Lindsey Graham** of South Carolina, **Tom Coburn** of Oklahoma, **John Thune** of South Dakota and **Richard M. Burr** of North Carolina, and occasionally House Speaker **John A. Boehner** of Ohio.

To pay for his education at the University of Maryland, Rep. **William Lacy Clay**, D-Mo., was a U.S. House of Representatives doorman for seven years.

To prove his environmental bona fides, Democratic Missouri Rep. **Emanuel Cleaver II** uses a 1998 Ford Econoline van, converted to run on vegetable oil as an office-on-wheels in his district.

Rep. **James E. Clyburn**, D-S.C., is the first African-American elected to Congress from South Carolina since 1896, when his great-uncle, George Washington Murray, was in the House.

Rep. **Steve Cohen**, D-Tenn., was diagnosed with polio as a child, but he was too young to take the vaccine that his father, a doctor, was helping Jonas Salk test.

When Rep. **Anna G. Eshoo**, D-Calif., was in high school in Connecticut, President Harry S. Truman once gave her a ride home from school.

Del. **Eni F.H. Faleomavaega**, D-A.S., is a "matai," or chief. Faleomavaega is actually his title; his family name is Hunkin.

Rep. **Blake Farenthold**, a conservative Texas Republican, is the step-grandson of longtime liberal Democratic activist Frances Tarleton "Sissy" Farenthold.

Rep. **Chaka Fattah**, D-Pa., was born Arthur Davenport. Fattah's mother changed his name when she married community activist David Fattah. She called him "Chaka" in honor of a Zulu warrior.

Rep. **John Fleming**, R-La., owns 30 Subway restaurant franchises.

Rep. **Rodney Frelinghuysen**, R-N.J., is the sixth member of his family to serve in Congress.

Sen. **Charles E. Grassley**, R-Iowa, works on the family farm on weekends and tucks a cell phone inside his cap while driving the tractor so he will feel the vibrations of an incoming call.

As a young Hill aide on a 1969 trip to Vietnam, Sen. **Tom Harkin,** D-Iowa, discovered the "tiger cages," squalid underground cells where the South Vietnamese government secretly kept prisoners of war. Harkin's revelation got worldwide attention.

Sen. **Orrin G. Hatch**, R-Utah, has written songs and movie soundtracks performed by the Osmonds and Gladys Knight. He often scribbles lyrics between votes and has produced several discs of religious, romantic and patriotic songs.

Rep. **Rush D. Holt**, D-N.J., a physicist, is a former champion on the TV quiz show "Jeopardy." Sen. **Charles E. Schumer** appeared on the high school quiz program "It's Academic" in 1967 and was captain of his team.

In 1993, Oklahoma Republican Sen. **James M. Inhofe** became the only member of Congress to fly an airplane around the world. He retraced Wiley Post's journey, the first solo flight to circle the globe.

Sen. **Daniel K. Inouye**, D-Hawaii, was awarded a Medal of Honor in 2000 for heroism in World War II. A member of the famed all-Nisei "Go for Broke" 442nd Regimental Combat Team, he lost his right arm when he advanced alone to take out a machine gunner who had pinned down his men.

There are more Buddhists in Congress (**Hank Johnson** of Georgia and Hawaii's **Mazie K. Hirono** and **Colleen Hanabusa**) than Muslims (**Keith Ellison** of Minnesota and **André Carson** of Indiana). All are Democrats.

Rep. **Sam Johnson**, R-Texas, spent almost seven years in a North Vietnamese prison camp. For a brief stretch, he shared a cell with fellow prisoner of war Sen. **John McCain**, R-Ariz.

Illinois GOP Rep. **Timothy V. Johnson** struck up a friendship with Boston Celtics basketball star Ray Allen when the Celtics visited the White House in September 2008. Allen said his son acquired Type 1 juvenile diabetes along with a cluster of other youths in Boston's affluent suburbs; Johnson's father is a diabetic. According to Boston magazine, Johnson promised to help in getting the Centers for Disease Control and Prevention look into the matter.

Massachusetts Democratic Sen. **John Kerry** is the richest member of Congress, with an estimated minimum net worth of 188.37 million, according to a Roll Call survey of members'

2009 financial disclosure forms. California Republican Rep. **Darrell Issa** is the richest House member, with an estimated minimum net worth of 160.05 million.

Rep. **Adam Kinzinger**, R-Ill., served in both Illinois and Wisconsin Air National Guard units, and he conducted five tours in Iraq and Afghanistan as a pilot.

During his service in the Marine Corps, Minnesota Republican Rep. **John Kline** carried the "football" — the briefcase with nuclear war codes — for Presidents Jimmy Carter and Ronald Reagan and flew the presidential helicopter, Marine One.

Ohio Democratic Rep. **Dennis J. Kucinich** was so unpopular as mayor of Cleveland that he wore a bulletproof vest to throw out the first pitch at an Indians game.

Rep. James Lankford, R-Okla., has a master's of divinity degree with a focus on biblical languages.

Utah Republican Sen. **Mike Lee** clerked for Supreme Court Justice Samuel A. Alito Jr.; his father, Rex Lee, argued cases before the high court when he served as solicitor general under President Ronald Reagan.

Connecticut independent Sen. **Joseph I. Lieberman** taught Democratic Sens. **Sherrod Brown** of Ohio and **Amy Klobuchar** of Minnesota in separate seminar classes at Yale University. Klobuchar's program was about the Democratic Party.

At Duke University, the judge of Illinois Democrat **Daniel Lipinski**'s doctoral thesis was Democratic Rep. **David E. Price** of North Carolina, who was between congressional stints.

Rep. **Billy Long**, R-Mo., was voted best auctioneer in the Ozarks seven years in a row.

Rep. **Stephen F. Lynch**, D-Mass., donated more than half his liver to his brother-in-law.

Rep. **Patrick Meehan**, R-Pa., is a former National Hockey League referee.

Rep. **Candice S. Miller**, R-Mich., earned the honorary title "Old Goat" in 2001 when she competed in her 25th Port Huron to Mackinac Island sailboat race.

Rep. **George Miller**, D-Calif., and Sens. **Charles E. Schumer,** D-N.Y., and **Richard J. Durbin**, D-Ill., have shared a Capitol Hill rowhouse of such notorious disarray that it merited a New York Times write-up and a visit from an ABC News television crew in early 2007.

Republican Sen. **Lisa Murkowski** is the first woman to represent Alaska, the first person ever appointed to the Senate by her father and the first person to win election as a write-in candidate since Strom Thurmond in 1954.

Pennsylvania GOP **Rep. Tim Murphy** taught himself to play guitar and once opened for banjo legend Earl Scruggs. Michigan Republican Rep. **Thaddeus McCotter** once played in a band called Sir Funk-a-Lot. Murphy also dug graves to earn money for college.

Democratic Sen. **Ben Nelson** of Nebraska once threw a party for other Ben Nelsons. Twelve people from Nebraska, 10 from other states and one dog attended.

Rep. **Randy Neugebauer**, R-Texas, was so skilled at back flips, twists and other moves that while at Texas Tech he joined the Flying Matadors trampoline troupe.

Republican Rep. **Kristi Noem** won the South Dakota Snow Queen contest, a title that sent her around the state giving speeches.

Rep. **John W. Olver**, D-Mass., attended a three-room schoolhouse, graduating at age 15. He finished college when he was 18 and earned a doctorate from the Massachusetts Institute of Technology at age 24.

As a girl, Speaker **Nancy Pelosi**, D-Calif., slept above stacks of the Congressional Record. Her father, Thomas D'Alesandro Jr., was a Maryland congressman and stored them under her bed in their Baltimore rowhouse.

Wisconsin Republican Rep. **Tom Petri**'s first job was hosting a radio show called "Teen Time," a weekly program that made him the state's youngest on-air personality.

Democrat **Pedro R. Pierluisi**, the resident commissioner from Puerto Rico, is the only member of Congress with a four-year term.

Rep. **Mike Pompeo** of Kansas is the only member of Congress who is also a member of the Republican National Committee.

Rep. **Bill Posey**, R-Fla., is an accomplished stock-car racer and won an award for short-track driver achievement.

Rep. **Dave Reichert**, R-Wash., was the original lead detective in the Green River serial killer task force. Almost 20 years later, as the King County sheriff, he announced the arrest of Gary Ridgway in 2001.

Sen. **Harry Reid**, D-Nev., took on organized crime as chairman of the Nevada Gaming Commission. A bomb was once found under the hood of his car.

Rep. **James B. Renacci**, R-Ohio, has been an owner of an Arena Football League team, the Columbus Destroyers, and a minor league baseball team, the Lancaster JetHawks of the California League.

Kansas Republican **Pat Roberts** is the first person ever to have served as chairman and ranking member of the House Agriculture Committee and ranking member of the Senate Agriculture panel.

Rep. **Dana Rohrabacher**, R-Calif., says John Wayne taught him how to drink tequila.

Idaho Republican Sen. **Jim Risch** thrived in the courtroom as the prosecutor for Ada County, but his efforts to crack down on narcotics almost cost him his life when leaders of a drug ring made a failed attempt to plant a bomb in his car. Risch became Idaho's shortest-tenured governor when he filled out the seven-month term of Gov. Dirk Kempthorne, who had left the state in 2006 to be President George W. Bush's Interior secretary.

Florida Republican Rep. **Tom Rooney** may be best known as the grandson of Pittsburgh Steelers founder Art Rooney. As a youth, he spent summers working as a ball boy. He went on to play football at Washington and Jefferson College and Syracuse University.

Illinois Republican Rep. **Peter Roskam** is the only member of Congress to have served with President Obama when Obama served in the Illinois Senate. GOP Rep. **Randy Hultgren** served in the Illinois House at the same time.

Illinois Democratic Rep. **Bobby L. Rush** is a former Black Panther who served six months in prison on a weapons charge. Rush also is the only politician to ever defeat Barack Obama in an election — a 2000 Democratic primary for the House.

House Budget Chairman **Paul D. Ryan**, R-Wis., says his philosophy of individualism and entrepreneurial capitalism was influenced most deeply by novelist and objectivist philosopher Ayn Rand.

Illinois Republican Rep. **Aaron Schock**, the youngest member of Congress, posed bare-chested for the cover of Men's Health magazine.

Reps. **F. James Sensenbrenner Jr.**, R-Wis., and **Kevin McCarthy**, R-Calif., are both lottery winners. Sensenbrenner put his 250,000 toward charities and investments; McCarthy invested the 5,000 from his scratch-off ticket to open "Kevin O's Deli."

Rep. **José E. Serrano**, D-N.Y., learned to speak English by listening to Frank Sinatra records.

Democratic Rep. **Terri A. Sewell** is the first African-American woman to serve in Congress from Alabama.

Republican Sen. **Olympia J. Snowe** is so popular in her home state of Maine that in 2008 the town of Bethel, hoping for a record, built a 122-foot snow woman and named it "Olympia."

Rep. **Pete Stark,** D-Calif., is recognized by the American Humanist Association as the highest-ranking U.S. official and the first member of Congress to proclaim that he is an atheist.

Rep. **Mike Thompson**, D-Calif., a wine enthusiast, grows organic sauvignon grapes. House Minority Leader **Nancy Pelosi** owns a vineyard in Thompson's hometown and California Republican Rep. **Devin Nunes** is part owner of the Alpha Omega winery.

Colorado Democrats **Mark Udall** and **Michael Bennet** are the first pair to represent their state in the Senate as freshmen since 1995, when Republicans Bill Frist and Fred Thompson represented Tennessee.

In 1983, while working as a White House aide, Rep. **Fred Upton**, R-Mich., proposed to his wife during a Baltimore Orioles baseball game, hiring an airplane to fly overhead with a banner reading, "Amey this is the inning to say yes."

Michigan Republican **Tim Walberg** holds a House seat that changed hands four times in four elections — Democrat Joe Schwarz won the seat in 2004 after Republican Nick Smith retired; Walberg won in 2006; Democrat Mark Schauer unseated Walberg in 2008; and Walberg recaptured the seat in 2010.

Rep. **Tim Walz**, D-Minn., earned the rank of command sergeant major in the Army National Guard, making him the highest-ranking enlisted soldier ever to serve in Congress.

In 1967, Virginia Democratic Sen. **Jim Webb**, as a student at the U.S. Naval Academy, lost a boxing championship to Oliver L. North, who would later become a household name for his role in the Iran-Contra affair.

Rep. **David Wu**, D-Ore., went to medical school at Harvard, where he roomed with future Senate Republican Leader Bill Frist of Tennessee.

Glossary of Congressional Terms

Congress has a language all its own. Below are some terms often heard during legislative debate on the floor and in committee, and sprinkled throughout the profiles of lawmakers found in the 2012 edition of CQ Roll Call's Politics in America.

Act: Legislation that has passed both houses of Congress and been signed into law by the president.

Adjourn: To close a legislative day.

Amendment: A change in a bill or document by adding, substituting or deleting portions.

Appropriations Bill: Legislation that provides funding for government agencies and programs.

Authorization Bill: Legislation establishing or extending a program and setting funding limits and policy.

Bill: Legislation introduced in either the House or Senate that, if enacted, has the force of law.

Budget Resolution: Concurrent resolution that establishes spending and revenue targets for the upcoming fiscal year. It does not become law but provides a framework for Congress as it considers other measures.

By Request: Phrase used when a member introduces a bill at the request of an executive agency or private organization but does not necessarily endorse the legislation.

Calendar: List and schedule of bills to be considered by a committee or chamber.

Caucus: Collection of members of Congress, usually organized by party or shared interest. In the House, the party caucuses are known as the Republican Conference and Democratic Caucus. In the Senate, both are formally known as conferences.

Chairman/Chairwoman: Presiding officer of a committee or the Committee of the Whole.

Chamber: Place where the entire House or Senate meets to conduct business; also can refer to the House of Representatives or the Senate itself.

Clean Bill: A new bill, reflecting revisions made by a committee to an earlier version of the legislation.

Cloakrooms: Small rooms off the House and Senate floor where members can rest and hold informal conferences.

Closed Hearings: Hearings closed to all but members, staff and witnesses testifying; also called executive hearings.

Closed Rule: In the House, a rule that prohibits floor amendments.

Cloture: Method of limiting debate or ending a filibuster in the Senate. At least 60 senators must vote in favor before cloture can be invoked. Once cloture is invoked, there can be 30 more hours of debate.

Cosponsor: Member who joins in sponsoring legislation but who is not the principal sponsor or the one who introduced the legislation.

Committee: A group of members assigned to give special consideration to certain bills that fall into subject areas within the committee's jurisdiction.

Committee of the Whole: A mechanism to expedite business in the House whereby the House itself meets as a committee, allowing for less rigid rules and a quorum of 100 instead of 218.

Companion Bills: Identical, or nearly identical, bills introduced separately in both the Senate and the House.

Concurrent Resolution: Legislation used to express the position of the House and Senate. Does not have the force of law, if enacted.

Conference Committee: Meeting between representatives and senators to resolve differences when two versions of a bill have been passed by the House and Senate. It can produce a conference report that is sent to both chambers for approval.

Congressional Record: Official transcript of the proceedings in Congress.

Continuing Resolution: A joint resolution to appropriate funds, usually for a short period of time and often in the absence of a regular appropriations bill. It is frequently used at the beginning of a fiscal year if work on appropriations measures has not been completed.

Discharge Petition: In the House, a petition for the purpose of removing a bill from the control of a committee. A discharge petition must be signed by a majority of members.

Discretionary Spending: Funding for programs or agencies determined by Congress through the appropriations process.

Earmark: There is considerable debate about what qualifies as an earmark, but generally it is congressionally directed funding, issued through an appropriations or authorization bill, for a project in a member's district or state.

Engrossed Bill: Final copy of a bill passed by either the House or Senate with amendments. The bill is then delivered to the other chamber.

Enrolled Bill: Final copy of a bill that has passed both the House and Senate in identical form.

Extension of Remarks: When a member of Congress inserts material in the Congressional Record that is not directly related to the debate under way.

Filibuster: Tactic used in the Senate whereby a minority intentionally delays a vote by extending proceedings such as using unlimited debate. The cloture process can overcome a filibuster.

Final Passage: Approval of a bill after all amendments have been voted on.

Fiscal Year: Accounting year. For the federal government, the fiscal year begins Oct. 1.

Five-Minute Rule: Rule that allows any House member to propose an amendment and debate it for five minutes. Opponents and supporters of the amendment have five minutes to debate it.

Floor Manager: A member who attempts to direct a bill through the debate and amendment process to a final vote.

Germane: Amendments that are relevant to the underlying bill. All amendments in the House must be germane. A non-germane amendment would add new and different subject matter, or its subject matter may be irrelevant to the bill or other measure it seeks to amend. Senate rules permit non-germane amendments in all but a few specific circumstances — most often, after cloture is invoked.

Hearing: Committee sessions for receiving testimony from witnesses.

Holds: A courtesy afforded senators that allows them to delay legislation. The senator placing the hold must do so in writing, and the notice is published in the Congressional Record.

Hopper: Box on the desk of the clerk of the House where sponsors submit their bills.

Hour Rule: When the House is sitting as the full House, each member has one hour to debate amendments. In the Committee of the Whole, the five-minute rule is in effect.

Jefferson's Manual: Basic rules of parliamentary procedure drafted by Thomas Jefferson that guide both chambers.

Joint Committee: Committee composed of members of both the House and Senate.

Joint Resolution: Legislation similar to a bill that has the force of law if passed by both houses and signed by the president, generally used for special circumstances and to propose constitutional amendments.

Lame Duck: Member of Congress (or the president) who was defeated for, or did not seek, re-election but whose term has not yet expired.

Leader Time: In the Senate, 10 minutes given to the majority and minority leaders at the beginning of each day Congress is in session.

Legislative Day: In the Senate, the period of time between convening until the Senate adjourns, not necessarily a calendar day.

Lobbying: The process of attempting to influence the passage, defeat or content of legislation by individuals or a group other than members of Congress.

Logrolling: Quid pro quo process whereby members help each other get particular measures passed. One member will help another on one piece of legislation in return for similar help.

Mandatory Spending: Funding for programs or agencies provided directly through authorization bills, such as entitlement programs.

Majority Leader: Chief spokesman and strategist for the majority party, elected by members of the majority party. In the House, the majority leader is the second-ranking lawmaker, behind the Speaker.

Marking Up a Bill: Process, usually in committee, of analyzing a piece of legislation section by section and making changes.

Member: A U.S. senator or U.S. representative.

Minority Leader: Chief spokesman and strategist for the minority party, elected by members of the minority party.

Modified Open Rule: In the House, permission to offer amendments to a particular bill during floor debate under certain restrictions set by the Rules Committee, such as a time limit or a requirement that the amendments be printed ahead of time in the Congressional Record.

Motion: Proposal presented to a legislative body for consideration.

Motion to Concur: Proposal to agree to the other chamber's altered version of a measure passed by both the House and the Senate. The chamber can also vote on a motion to concur with further amendments to the measure.

Motion to Recommit: Proposal to send a bill or resolution back to a committee. The motion to recommit can contain instructions for the committee, such as amending the legislation. The minority party in the House may use the motion to recommit to propose changes immediately prior to a vote on final passage.

Motion to Table: Proposal to kill a bill or amendment by cutting off consideration of it. Such motions are not debatable.

Omnibus Bill: Legislation that combines different bills regarding a single broader subject into one measure, such as appropriations bills.

One-Day Rule: In the Senate, a requirement that measures reported from committee be held for at least one legislative day before being brought to the floor.

Open Rule: In the House, permission to offer any amendments to a particular bill during floor debate.

Override a Veto: When both the House and Senate vote by a two-thirds majority to enact a bill over a presidential veto of the legislation.

Pairing: System whereby two members jointly agree not to vote on a particular matter.

Party Unity Score: CQ's measure of the percentage of votes in which a member sides with his or her party when a majority of one party votes against a majority of the other party.

Petition: Plea by an individual or organization for a chamber to consider particular legislation.

Pocket Veto: When the president kills a bill by withholding his signature when Congress has recessed or adjourned, preventing him from returning the measure. A true pocket veto denies Congress the opportunity to override the veto, but presidents and Congresses have disagreed about when pocket vetoes may occur.

Point of Order: An objection that language, an amendment or bill is in violation of a rule.

President of the Senate: The vice president of the United States is designated by the Constitution as the president of the Senate. That individual casts a vote only in cases of a tie.

Previous Question: In the House, a request to end all debate and force a vote on the motion, bill or other measure under consideration.

Private Bill: Bill designed to benefit a certain individual or business.

President Pro Tempore: Senator who presides over the Senate in the absence of the vice president of the United States. The president pro tem is usually the longest-serving member of the majority party.

Public Law: Designation used for legislation that has been passed by both chambers and signed by the president or enacted over a presidential veto. Private bills become private laws.

Quorum: The number of senators or representatives who must be present

before a legislative body can conduct official business.

Quorum Call: In the Senate, a method of determining whether there is a quorum. Often used to suspend debate without adjourning.

Ranking Member: The leading member of the minority party on a committee. The ranking member may be referred to as the ranking Democrat or ranking Republican, depending on which party is in the minority of the relevant chamber.

Recess: Temporary halt to proceedings, with a time set for proceedings to resume. It also describes periods when the House or Senate is not in session.

Reconciliation: Process in which the budget resolution includes instructions to committees to report legislation that changes laws dealing with mandatory spending or taxes. The resulting measures are not subject to filibusters in the Senate.

Recorded Vote: Vote in which members of Congress indicate their vote for listing in the Congressional Record.

Rescission Bill: Legislation that revokes spending authority previously granted by Congress.

Resolution: A measure adopted only in one house to express the sentiment of that chamber. A simple resolution does not have the force of law.

Rider: A measure added to another, often unrelated, bill with the purpose of one piece of legislation passing on the strength of another.

Roll Call Vote: A vote in which a record is kept. The House uses electronic vote recording; the Senate uses oral voting.

Seniority: A member's rank in a chamber based on length of congressional service and other factors, including tenure in certain other elected offices. Often used to determine rank on committees.

Seriatim Consideration: Consideration of a motion line by line.

Sine Die: Final adjournment at the end of a session, of which there are two in each Congress. Bills under consideration but not enacted by the end of the Congress must be reintroduced in the next session.

Speaker: The presiding officer of the House, elected by members of that chamber.

Sponsor: The representative or senator who introduces a measure.

Suspend the Rules: Procedural action to expedite debate in the House. A motion to suspend the rules requires the votes of two-thirds of those present and is debatable for 40 minutes. Members cannot offer amendments.

Teller Vote: A vote in the House in which members file past tellers who count the votes. The total vote is recorded, but no record is kept on how each member voted. A teller vote is rarely used.

Three-Day Rule: In the House, a requirement that legislation be held for at least three calendar days (not counting weekends and holidays) before being brought to the floor. Similar to the One-Day Rule in the Senate.

Unanimous Consent: A procedure whereby a matter is considered agreed to if no member on the floor objects. It can be used to pass legislation or set the terms for floor debate. Unanimous consent motions save time by eliminating the need for a vote.

Unlimited Debate: In the Senate, the right of any senator to talk as long as desired during floor debates on a bill.

Whip: Assistant leader for each party in each chamber who keeps other members of the party informed of the legislative agenda of the leader. Also tracks sentiment among party members for certain legislation and tries to persuade members to be present and vote for measures important to the leadership.

Yield: Permission granted by the member who has the floor to another member who wishes to make a comment or ask a question.

Index

C

I

S

T

Y